THE STATESMAN'S YEARBOOK

1998–99

Until nations are generous they never will be wise.
True policy is generous policy. All selfishness may
gain small ends but lose great ones. Expedients may
answer for the moment; they gain a point but do not
establish a principle.

Washington Irving, *Journals and Notebooks*.
March 1824

Credits

Publisher	Ian Jacobs (London)
	Garrett Kiely (New York)
Editor	Dr Barry Turner
Editorial Assistant	Jill Fenner
Research	Nicholas Heath-Brown
	Dione Daffin
	Michèle Roche
	S. Mukherjee
	Rowland Stone
	Linus Nordquist
	Sally Page
	Jana Hermon
	Caroline Ball
	Lorraine Brunning
	Thea Bennett
	Elestr Lee
	Gayle Chong-Kwan
	Brenda Weller
Index	Gary Hall
Marketing	Emma Hardcastle
	Catherine Jones
Production	Jeremy Macdonald

THE
STATESMAN'S
YEAR-BOOK

THE ESSENTIAL POLITICAL AND ECONOMIC GUIDE
TO ALL THE COUNTRIES OF THE WORLD

1998–1999

EDITED BY

BARRY TURNER

ST.MARTIN'S
PRESS

First published in 1864
135th edition 1998

For information, write:
ST. MARTIN'S PRESS, INC.
175 Fifth Avenue, New York, N.Y. 10010

Library of Congress Catalog Card No. 4-3776

ISBN 0-312-21588-6

Typeset in Great Britain by
A.J. Latham Ltd,
Bedfordshire

Printed in England by
BPC Wheatons, Exeter

PREFACE

Readers who are familiar with *The Statesman's Yearbook* will observe some changes in this edition. The appearance of a world map and the visual representation of national flags is immediately noticeable. But more significantly, we have given a stronger political context to the purely statistical information by a series of articles on world affairs and by extending the Key Historical Events section at the head of every entry to produce a succinct but reasonably comprehensive overview of each country's history.

Ideas for long-term improvements include the steady expansion of information on social, economic and political matters and a new Culture section which will cover major libraries, museums, galleries, festivals and heritage sites. Another possibility is to establish a *Statesman's Yearbook* presence on the Internet for readers who need an immediate update on events at home and abroad.

Ideas and suggestions for further improvements are welcome. Simply write to The Editor, The Statesman's Yearbook, Macmillan Reference, 25 Eccleston Place, London SW1W 9NF or fax on 0171-881 8001.

B.T.

CONTENTS

The State: Yesterday and Today by Robert Cooper xv
CHRONOLOGY xxi
ADDENDA xxxi

Part I: International Organizations

Americas

Asia/Pacific

Middle East

CONTENTS

THE STATE: YESTERDAY AND TODAY

by Robert Cooper

The world today is organized into states, 185 of them if we take the membership of the United Nations. Max Weber defined the state as the body which had a monopoly on the legitimate use of force, implying a state monopoly not just on force but also on law. The state system thus divides the world into separate exclusive territorial jurisdiction.

It was not always so. In mediaeval Europe jurisdictions of kings, local landowners, free cities, occasionally the professional groups competed with each other and with the much more important jurisdiction of the church. In those times there was no state in any modern sense. Kings conducted state business as an extension of their private lives. Wars were often about inheritance—national territory was a kind of family property—and ambassadors were sent abroad to secure the right marriage for the king, with the objective of extending the family property/national territory.

The modern state began as power—both legal authority and military or civil force—was concentrated at one point. Force could be used to give authority to the state's own laws at home and to protect it against attempts by other states to impose their jurisdiction from outside.

The crucial figure in the philosophy of the modern state is Machiavelli. He argued that the moral concepts which applied to individuals and to families did not apply to states—that behaviour, such as lying, cheating and violence, which was not permissible among individuals, was both necessary and acceptable among states. This escape from the universal moral doctrine of the church was an essential element in the creation of a modern state. So was the separation of state power from the interests of individuals or families. No developing country today can consider itself modern if its state or government is too much in the hands of one family or one group of families.

The state came into existence as an island of law and order in an increasingly chaotic sea, as the authority of the church broke down. But the price of establishing law and order within the state was the creation of an anarchy outside. Legitimacy was exclusive to states and force was controlled by states. Among states there was neither law nor order.

On the domestic side, the creation of territorial states with exclusive jurisdictions was a success. It brought first order, then prosperity. More slowly came the growth of political rights and democracy. Hegel's insight that history should be seen as the growth of the idea of liberty, and that this idea should be associated with the growth of the state, is at bottom right. The problem, however, has been to deal with the international anarchy created by exclusive domestic jurisdictions.

Attempts to solve this problem have usually rested on the creation of something like the state at a higher level: a supra-national authority which would have an international monopoly over law and over the use of force. None of these efforts has been very promising since states have, on the whole, not been willing to submit themselves entirely to outside authority. The League of Nations and the UN have disappointed those who hoped for a world authority with the same power internationally as the modern state enjoys domestically.

The other approach to international order is the system known as the balance of power. This was often more a hope than a method. It did, nevertheless, run with the grain of national independence and state sovereignty. To defend their jurisdiction states would operate in temporary alliances to prevent any single state from dominating them. (Alliances were essentially temporary since anything else would compromise independence.) The difficulty with this system was that it entailed periodic wars.

In the last hundred years there have been three major changes in the state system. First, there are many more states. Second, democracy has become the norm. (Even where it is not observed it is usually an aspiration.) Third, the state system is largely organized on a multilateral basis. Something of this revolution can be seen in the changing pattern of Britain's Diplomatic Service. In 1914 Britain had nine ambassadors. Today there are roughly 140 ambassadors or high commissioners accredited to roughly 180 countries, plus nine ambassadors to multilateral organizations.

Democratization and the increase in the number of states are two sides of the same coin. The bulk of the new states has emerged as western colonial empires broke up under pressure for self-determination. A world of empires has become a world of nation states. This has not lead in every case to democracy but the wish for an indigenous rather than a foreign government is one step in this direction.

In other cases such as that of the former Soviet Union and Yugoslavia the process has happened the other way round. The collapse of an authoritarian regime and the coming of democracy have lead to break up. A democracy requires a strong sense of identity and a willingness to sacrifice individual interests for the good of the community. Why else should anyone accept being overruled in a majority vote? The question of when a community with a strong sense of identity has the right to secede and become a state in its own right remains one of the most intractable problems in international relations.

This world of multiple states has proceeded neither in the direction of supranational organisation nor along the lines of balance of power theory, with the emphasis on the independence of individual states. Instead a third way has been taken, through multilateralism and international law.

The striking feature of international relations today is how much business is done in multilateral fora. Trade relations are handled in the WTO or the OECD, international finance in the IMF or the World Bank, health in the WHO. Some groupings are informal (the G8); some are based on treaties; some like NATO take the form of alliances. Almost every region has its own organization: the OAU, the OAS, the Arab League, ASEAN. Europe has several: the OSCE, the Council of Europe, NATO, the WEU and the EU itself.

Both the quantity and the quality of multilateral institutions are new. There has never before, for example, been an alliance like NATO, a multimember peace-time alliance operating a single system of command. The EU is no less historically unique. It has created a common body of law. All of the states concerned accept the jurisdiction of the EU court for matters over which the EU has competence.

What has happened to state sovereignty in this new arrangement of the world? If the essence of the state—and so of sovereignty—is its monopoly over law and over force then we must note that in today's world these are by no means so absolute as they once were. A state which signs a treaty or joins an international institution is often accepting some limits on its freedom of action. This is true of the European Convention on Human Rights, the UN, the WTO and above all the EU.

The state's monopoly on law can thus be compromised by international agreements. Even the monopoly on force can be overridden by the UN—eg the no-fly zones over Iraq. Or states may conclude arrangements—such as exist within Europe—that allow their police to operate (within certain limits) in neighbouring countries.

And yet it would be foolish to conclude that sovereignty was no longer a meaningful term. There is still, after all, a difference between Luxembourg and Bavaria. In today's world sovereignty is best viewed in two ways. First the monopoly of force and law still exists potentially: states can still withdraw from treaty obligations and from institutions.

Second, sovereignty means a seat at the table. Sovereignty used to be defined primarily in terms of independence. Today it should be thought of as the ability to cooperate in international institutions. We know that Luxembourg is a sovereign state (and Bavaria is not) because Luxembourg sits at the EU Council table. This is one reason why the question of recognition of states matters so much.

The philosophy of the modern state was outlined by Machiavelli: an amoral philosophy appropriate to states governed by princes, often at war with each other. In the 400 years since Machiavelli the pattern has been the pursuit of interest, secret treaties, breaches of faith, shifting alliances according to interest and advantage. The world today is no longer like this. It is too complicated—the game of nations is possible among a small number of states but not among 180. It is too dangerous—the technology of the 20th century including nuclear weapons means that the price of war is now very high. Common interest in trade, cross-border investment, and the environment, require a more orderly world. Out of this has come multilateralism and, at least among advanced states, a recognition that they have an interest in a functioning system of international law.

To Churchill's alternatives: Jaw jaw and war war we are adding a third: law law. In international relations history—Hegel might say today—is the growing idea of international law.

Robert Cooper is Minister at the British Embassy, Bonn. Before his present posting he was Head of Policy Planning Staff at the Foreign and Commonwealth Office. He has published a number of articles and essays on international relations including, through Demos, THE POST-MODERN STATE AND THE WORLD ORDER. He holds the Deutsche Tanz Verein bronze medal for ballroom dancing.

The opinions expressed in this article are the author's own and should not be taken as an expression of government policy.

CHRONOLOGY

CHRONOLOGY
March 1997 – March 1998

Week beginning 30 March, 1997

Helmut Kohl declared his candidacy for re-election as Chancellor in 1998.

India's Congress Party withdrew support for coalition government.

USA enforced new immigration laws.

6 April, 1997

Rebels in Zaïre (now Democratic Republic of the Congo) scored significant victories including the capture of Mbuyi-Mayi, a leading diamond town and Lubumbashi, the country's second city.

Elections in Haiti attracted less than 15% of those eligible to vote.

The restriction of civil freedoms in Hong Kong was foretold by the Chinese administration in waiting.

13 April, 1997

Angola achieved a government of national unity after 30 years of war.

China and Taiwan agreed direct shipping links.

20 April, 1997

A French general election was announced for 25 May and 1 June.

The siege at the Japanese ambassador's residence in Peru ended with a rescue assault by crack troops. 14 left-wing guerrillas and one hostage died.

Bulgaria's election was won by the United Democrats who promised a drive against corruption.

The Indian Congress Party rejoined the coalition government under a new prime minister, Inder Kumar Gujral.

27 April, 1997

Labour won the British general election by a landslide. Tony Blair became prime minister.

Privatization was extended in Russia to include telecommunications.

4 May, 1997

The US Congress and the White House agreed to balance the national budget within five years.

The world's biggest goldfield in Indonesia was found to be nothing of the sort. Shares plummeted.

São Tomé recognized Taiwan.

11 May, 1997

Agreement between Russia and NATO prepared the way for countries in Central and Eastern Europe to join the alliance.

A general election in Ireland was announced for 6 June.

18 May, 1997

Rebel forces led by Laurent Kabila were victorious in Zaïre, now renamed the Democratic Republic of the Congo.

Economic reform stalled in Mongolia after former communist Natsagiin Bagabandi was elected president.

Central India was hit by an earthquake while Bangladesh suffered a cyclone.

25 May, 1997

In the French general election, the Socialist Communist Alliance inflicted heavy defeat on the ruling centre right coalition. Alain Juppé resigned the premiership.

In Iran, the presidential election was won by the moderate Muhammad Khatami.

A military coup in Sierra Leone forced out the elected government.

Poland approved a new constitution which gives more power to parliament.

Financial scandal hit the government of Macedonia leading to the resignation of three senior ministers.

1 June, 1997

Lionel Jospin became prime minister of France at the head of a Socialist Communist coalition.

The ruling Golkar party in Indonesia won the general election.

A friendship treaty between Russia and Ukraine gave four-fifths of the Black Sea fleet to Russia.

The Liberals were returned in Canada's general election.

Algeria's general election was marred by accusations of ballot rigging in favour of the ruling parties.

8 June, 1997

The general election in Ireland led to victory for Fianna Fáil at the expense of the ruling Fine Gael. Bertie Ahern became prime minister.

Taiwan announced military exercises to be held when Hong Kong is handed over to the Chinese.

15 June, 1997

The European Union held a summit in Amsterdam to agree a formula for accepting countries in Eastern Europe.

The Islamist-led Turkish government resigned.

William Hague was elected leader of Britain's Conservative Party.

22 June, 1997

Iraq put restrictions on UN arms inspectors.

Sinn Fein was told that it can join Northern Ireland peace talks without the IRA having to disarm.

29 June, 1997

Britain handed back Hong Kong to China.

Violence resumed in Colombia where guerrilla forces rejected peace talks.

In Albania, the general election was won by the Socialists.

6 July, 1997

Poland, the Czech Republic and Hungary were invited to join NATO.

Estonia, Slovenia, Poland, the Czech Republic and Hungary were invited to negotiate to join the EU.

The ruling Institutional Revolutionary Party was overthrown in Mexico's general election.

The Communists took control of Cambodia.

13 July, 1997

The economic crisis in south-east Asia began to look desperate as Malaysian and Thai currencies went into free fall.

Plans were announced to streamline the UN and to speed up decision making.

20 July, 1997

Swiss banks published the names of 2,000 account holders who have not been heard of since the end of the second world war.

Sali Berisha resigned as Albanian president following his party's defeat in national elections.

Charles Taylor was elected President of Liberia.

India's vice president, Kocheril Raman Narayanan, moved up to the presidency, the first 'untouchable' to do so.

Cuts in Russian armed forces were announced.

Laos and Myanmar joined ASEAN.

27 July, 1997

Floods in eastern Germany, Poland and the Czech Republic were estimated to have cost over US$5bn.

3 August, 1997

Famine was threatened in Ethiopia.

Israeli forces attacked Hizbollah strongholds in southern Lebanon.

General Hugo Banzer was sworn in as Bolivia's president.

Franjo Tudjman was sworn in as Croatia's president.

10 August, 1997

India and Pakistan celebrated the 50th anniversary of independence from Britain.

The IMF agreed a US$16bn. loan to Thailand to rescue its economy from financial collapse.

Russia's privatization minister Alfred Kokh resigned to be replaced by Maxim Boyko.

17 loss-making state owned companies were closed in Romania.

17 August, 1997

The French government announced plans to reduce unemployment by creating 350,000 public sector jobs.

Vincent Siew became prime minister of Taiwan.

A Canadian-led initiative to ban anti-personnel landmines was supported reluctantly by the USA.

24 August, 1997

Violence in Algeria headed international news with the slaughter of 64 residents of a mountain village.

A row broke out between Britain and Montserrat over the help given, or lack of it, after the island was devastated by a volcanic eruption.

The former president of South Africa, F. W. de Klerk, announced his retirement from politics.

31 August, 1997

Diana, Princess of Wales and her companion Dodi Al Fayed died in a car crash in Paris.

Suicide bombers killed six people in central Jerusalem.

Negotiations between Kenya and the IMF collapsed on President Moi's failure to combat corruption.

Malaysia's prime minister, Mahathir Mohamad, launched an attack on foreign speculators, blaming them for the collapse of the Malaysian currency.

Arkady Gukasyan was elected president of Nagorno-Karabakh, the region of Armenia disputed by Azerbaijan.

7 September, 1997

One of the largest ever world-wide television audiences witnessed the funeral service of Diana, Princess of Wales at Westminster Abbey.

Sinn Fein, the political wing of the IRA, repudiated violence and joined all party talks on the future of Northern Ireland.

The 2004 Olympic Games went to Athens.

14 September, 1997

The UN claimed that the difference in income per head between the seven richest and seven poorest nations has doubled in 30 years.

President Clinton asked Congress for fast track authority to negotiate free trade deals.

The IMF forecast an annual 4·5% growth for the world economy over the next 5 years.

Morocco and the nationalist Polisaro Front reached agreement over the disputed territory of Western Sahara.

21 September, 1997

Poland's general election marked a revival of Solidarity, the anti-communist trade union which was set to form the next government in alliance with the Freedom Union.

Smog caused by forest fires blanketed south-east Asia.

28 September, 1997

The USA considered sanctions against the French oil company Total and its Russian and Malaysian partners for investing in Iranian natural gas.

The Catholic Church in France accepted part responsibility for the deportation of Jews in the second world war.

The Pope visited Brazil.

5 October, 1997

The UN imposed sanctions on Sierra Leone after a military coup in May.

Terrorist violence in Algeria led to the death of 180 civilians including children.

12 October, 1997

Italy's prime minister Romano Prodi was confirmed in office after a split with his Communist allies which threatened to bring down his government.

France's Socialist government pledged to reduce the working week to 36 hours.

Tony Blair, Britain's prime minister, met Gerry Adams, leader of Sinn Fein, the first such encounter in nearly 80 years.

Jerzy Buzek was made prime minister of Poland.

19 October, 1997

Iraq's obstruction of UN weapon inspectors led the USA and Britain to propose new sanctions.

Forces loyal to President Pascal Lissouba accepted defeat in the Republic of the Congo.

Norway's election produced a centre right government, the first in 25 years.

Montenegro elected Milo Djukanović, a moderate president in defiance of Yugoslavia's federal president, Slobodan Milošević.

26 October, 1997

American nationals working with the UN weapons inspection team in Iraq were told to leave the country within the week.

Commonwealth countries threatened to expel Nigeria if elections were not held within the year.

Indonesia's troubled economy was bailed out by an IMF loan backed by Singapore and Malaysia.

A Chinese-American summit led to mutual trade concessions.

2 November, 1997

Jim Bolger, New Zealand's prime minister, was voted out of office by his own party.

Chavalit Yongchaiyudh, Thailand's prime minister, resigned in the wake of financial crisis.

Mary McAleese from Northern Ireland was elected president of the Irish Republic.

Main roads in France were barricaded by striking lorry drivers.

9 November, 1997

Chuan Leekpai became Thailand's prime minister.

Peace talks to end Sudan's 14-year civil war were adjourned until April.

A general election in Kenya was announced for 29 Dec.

Turkish forces entered northern Iraq in pursuit of Kurdish rebels.

16 November, 1997

Russia's finance minister Anatoly Chubais lost his job over a favourable publishing deal for a book on privatization.

Islamic terrorists gunned down 62 tourists at the Temple of Hatshepsut at Luxor in Upper Egypt.

Hungarians voted in favour of joining NATO.

23 November, 1997

Winnie Madikizela-Mandela, former wife of the South African president, appeared before the Truth and Reconciliation Commission to face accusations of murder and assault.

A general election in Jamaica was announced for 18 Dec.

30 November, 1997

President Yeltsin visited Sweden and announced that Russia's nuclear stockpile will be reduced by a third.

In the Czech Republic, prime minister Václav Klaus resigned in the wake of a financial scandal.

Carlos Flores was elected president of Honduras.

7 December, 1997

A UN international conference in Kyoto recommended that industrial countries clean up the air with a 5·2% cut in gas emissions by 2012.

The financial crisis in south-east Asia claimed five merchant banks in South Korea while the government took control of two more banks.

14 December, 1997

NATO foreign ministers decided to keep troops in Bosnia after the original June 1998 deadline.

The continuing row in Iraq over inspection of presidential sites by UN officials brought a threat of US retaliatory action.

Kim Dae-Jung, one-time dissident, was elected president of South Korea.

Janet Jagan was elected president of Guyana.

Josef Tošovský, governor of the Czech Republic's central bank, headed a caretaker government in the run up to an election.

21 December, 1997

A report from the US Centre on Budget and Policy Priorities showed that while the income of the richest families had grown by 30% since the late '70s, the income of the poorest had fallen by 21%.

Former president Kaunda of Zambia was arrested in the wake of an abortive army *coup* in Oct.

28 December, 1997

In Vietnam, the Communist leadership passed from Do Muoi to hardliner Le Kha Phien.

4 January, 1998

Valdas Adamkus, who has lived most of his life in America, was elected president of Lithuania.

Daniel arap Moi was re-elected president of Kenya.

Israel's foreign minister resigned.

Unrest in Indonesia following the financial crisis threatened the Suharto regime.

An influx of Kurdish refugees into Italy set up fears of a cross border spread into the rest of Europe.

Russia introduced a new rouble worth a thousand old ones.

US forces departed Panama.

11 January, 1998

The USA moved closer to war with Iraq where there were objections to Americans among the UN arms inspectors.

Some shape was given to the peace talks in Northern Ireland with British and Irish proposals for political and administrative links between Ulster and the Republic.

Indonesia promised economic reforms in return for IMF aid.

18 January, 1998

Václav Havel was re-elected president of the Czech Republic.

The Islamist Welfare Party was banned in Turkey.

President Clinton defended himself against charges of sexual harassment.

The Pope visited Cuba.

A EU delegation to Algeria came to no conclusion at all as to how religious/political violence can be ended.

25 January, 1998

Corruption in Japan's finance ministry led to the resignation of the finance minister.

Gro Harlem Brundtland, a former Norwegian prime minister, was made director general of the World Health Organization.

1 February, 1998

French negotiators tried to find a peaceful settlement to the arms inspection issue in Iraq.

Speculative attacks on the rouble put up Russian interest rates to 42%.

8 February, 1998

The pressure on Iraq built up with the gathering of American forces in the Gulf backed by Britain, Australia and Canada.

The French parliament approved a law to reduce the working week to 35 hours by 2000.

Georgia's president, Eduard Shevardnadze, narrowly escaped an assassination attempt.

15 February, 1998

The military junta in Sierra Leone was quashed by a Nigerian-led intervention force.

Oil prices fell to a four year low.

An election in Denmark was announced for March 11.

22 February, 1998

Kofi Annan, the UN Secretary General, pulled off a diplomatic coup by persuading Saddam Hussein to cooperate with weapons inspectors and to allow unrestricted access.

Mossad, the Israeli secret service, faced a shakeup after the arrest of one of its agents in Switzerland.

The Northern Ireland peace initiative lost one of its major components when Sinn Fein was expelled for 16 days following the IRA murder of two Protestants.

1 March, 1998

The Indian general election gave the Bharatiya Janata Party the biggest number of seats but not enough to form a majority government.

Gerhard Schröder, premier of Lower Saxony, was chosen as Social Democrat candidate to run against Helmut Kohl in Sept.

8 March, 1998

Denmark's Social Democrat led coalition was returned to power with a one-seat majority.

Violence accelerated in Kosovo, the Albanian populated province of Serbia.

General Augusto Pinochet, Chile's former dictator, resigned as army chief of staff to become a life senator.

President Suharto of Indonesia was re-elected to serve his seventh term.

15 March, 1998

Zhu Rongji took over as prime minister of China.

The National Front made sufficient advances in French regional elections to hold the balance of power in several areas previously governed by the moderate right.

22 March, 1998

President Yeltsin fired his cabinet and made Sergei Kiriyenko, formerly energy minister, acting prime minister.

Eleven countries were judged to be eligible to join the single European currency.

Japan attempted to revive its economy with a massive financial injection.

The Pope visited Nigeria and called for the release of political prisoners.

29 March, 1998

Radu Vasili became prime minister of Romania.

Ukraine's Communist Party triumphed in the general election.

Robert Kocharian was elected president of Armenia.

ADDENDA

ADDENDA

All dates are 1998 unless stated otherwise

ARMENIA. Following Prime Minister Robert Kocharian's victory in the presidential election held on 16 and 30 March, Armen Darbinian, the *Finance and Economy Minister*, succeeded him as Prime Minister in April. Eduard Sandoyan became the new *Finance and Economy Minister*.

AUSTRIA. In the presidential election held on 19 April Thomas Klestil was elected to another six-year term, obtaining 63·5% of the votes cast, with his nearest rival, Gertraud Knoll, polling 13·5% of votes cast. There were 5 candidates in total.

BELGIUM. On 23 April the *Interior Minister* Johan Vande Lanotte and the *Justice Minister* Stefaan de Clerck resigned as a consequence of the escape of the convicted sex offender, Marc Dutroux. Dutroux was later recaptured.

BRAZIL. In April, the government was reduced by the death of two senior ministers, Sergio Vieira da Motta, *Communications Minister* and Luis Eduardo Magalhaes, government leader in the lower house of Congress. In a cabinet reshuffle, Antonio Kandir at *Planning*, Francisco Neves Dornelles at *Industry, Trade and Tourism* and Iris Rezende Machado at *Justice* lost their jobs. José Serra replaced Carlos César Silva de Albuquerque as *Health Minister*. José Botafogo Goncalves was appointed *Trade and Industry Minister* while Paulo Paiva moved from *Labour* to *Planning and Budget*.

DENMARK. Parliamentary elections were held on 11 March. The Social Democratic Party won 65 seats, with 36% of the votes cast; the Liberal Party 43 with 24%; the Conservative Party 17 with 8·9%; the Danish People's Party and the Socialist People's Party both with 13, with 7·4% and 7·5% respectively; and the 28 remaining seats went to 5 other parties. The coalition government led by Poul Nyrup Rasmussen of the Social Democratic Party remained in office.

In the cabinet reshuffle which followed, Jan Trøjborg moved from *Business and Industry* to *Research*, being replaced by Pia Gjellerup; Margrethe Vestager replaced Ole Vig Jensen at *Education and Ecclesiastical Affairs*; Carsten Koch moved from *Taxation* to *Health*, being replaced by Ole Stavad; Jytte Andersen moved from *Labour* to *Housing and Building*, being replaced by Ove Hygum; Elsebeth Gerner Nielsen replaced Ebbe Lundgaard at *Culture*; and Sonja Mikkelsen replaced Bjorn Westh at *Transport*.

THE FAROE ISLANDS. In parliamentary elections on 30 April the People's Party (FF) and the Party for People's Government (TF) each won 8 seats, the Equality Party (JF) 7 seats, the Union Party (SF) 6 seats, the Self-Government Party (SSF) 2 seats and the Centre Party (MF) 1 seat. Anfinn Kallsberg (FF) became Prime Minister, with a government formed by the FF, TF and SSF.

FRANCE. Elections for the country's 22 regional councils were held on 15 March and over the next two weeks. The vote for the main parties in government (Socialists, Communists and Greens) was 38% and for the moderate right-wing parties (RPR and UDF) 36%. The National Front won 15%. In order to deprive the Left of an overall victory, the Right forged local alliances with the National Front in 5 regions.

GERMANY. In state parliament elections in Lower Saxony on 1 March the Social Democratic Party received 47·9% of the votes cast to secure an absolute majority, gaining 83 seats, the Christian Democratic Union 35·9% and the Greens 7·0%.

On 26 April in Saxony-Anhalt's state election the SPD received 35·9% of votes cast giving them 47 seats, the CDU 22·0%, the PDS (former Communists) 19·6% and the DVU (extreme right) 12·9%.

HAITI. On 7 April the lower house of Parliament approved President René Préval's nominee for Prime Minister, Hervé Denis. The vote by the Chamber of Deputies was 41 to 23, with 3 abstentions. Approval must be given by the Senate and both houses must support his government plan.

HONG KONG. Pro-democracy candidates won 63% of the popular vote in the Legislative Council election held on 25 May. This compares to the 51% won in the 1995 election. But under an electoral system which allows only a third of the seats to be chosen by the entire electorate, the pro-democracy members will remain a minority political force.

HUNGARY. The general election held on 24 May gave victory to the centre right opposition led by Fidesz Hungarian Civic Party, ending four years of socialist-led government. Fidesz captured 148 seats compared with only 20 in the 1994 election. The Socialists dropped from 209 seats to 134. Viktor Orban, a 34-year-old former student activist and Fidesz leader, became Prime Minister.

INDIA. In the parliamentary elections held between 16 Feb. and 7 March the Bharatiya Janata Party (Hindu Nationalists) won 178 seats, the Indian National Congress 145, the Communist Party of India (Marxist) 32 and Samajwadi Party 21. Other parties won fewer than 20 seats each.

Atal Behari Vajpayee, leader of the BJP, was sworn in as Prime Minister on 18 March and formed a multi-party coalition government which comprised: *Home Affairs:* Lal Krishna Advani. *Civil Aviation:* Anant Kumar. *Industry:* Sikander Bakht. *Chemicals and Fertilizers, also in charge of Food:* Surjit Singh Barnala. *Labour:* Satyanarain Jatiya. *Human Resources Development, also in charge of Science and Technology:* Murli Manohar Joshi. *Parliamentary Affairs, also in charge of Tourism:* Madan Lal Khurana. *Power:* P. Rangarajan Kumaramangalam. *Textiles:* Kashi Ram Rana. *Finance:* Yashwant Sinha. *Information and Broadcasting:* Sushma Swaraj. *Defence:* George Fernandes. *Railways:* Nitish Kumar. *Law, Justice and Company Affairs:* M. Thambi Durai. *Surface Transport:* R. Muthiah. *Urban Development:* Ram Jethmalani. *Communications:* Buta Singh. *Commerce:* R. K. Hegde. *Environment and Forests:* Suresh Prabhakar Prabhu. *Steel and Mines:* Naveen Patnaik. *Petroleum and Natural Gas:* V. K. Ramamurthy.

Five underground nuclear detonations in northwest India (mid-May) were described as a 'terrible mistake' by President Bill Clinton but were welcomed enthusiastically by the Indian public.

INDONESIA. After several days of rioting and looting had left large areas of the capital, Jakarta, in ruins, President Suharto resigned (21 May) and was succeeded by his Vice President Bacharuddin Jusuf Habibie.

SOUTH KOREA. Although Kim Jong-pil's nomination as Prime Minister was still to be accepted by the National Assembly, a new cabinet was announced at the end of March which comprised: *Minister of Agriculture and Forestry:* Kim Song-hun. *Commerce, Industry and Energy:* Pak Tae-yong. *Construction and Transportation:* Yi Chong-mu. *Culture and Tourism:* Sin Nak-kyun. *Education:* Yi Hae-chan. *Environment:* Choe Chae-uk. *Finance and Economy:* Yi Kyu-song. *Foreign Affairs and Trade:* Pak Chong-su. *Government Administration and Local Autonomy:* Kim Chong-kil. *Health and Welfare:* Chu Yang-cha. *Information and Communication:* Pae Sun-hun. *Justice:* Pak Sang-chon. *Labour Affairs:* Yi Ki-ho. *Maritime Affairs and Fisheries:* Kim Son-kil. *National Defence:* Chon Yong-taek. *Science and Technology:* Kang Chang-hui. *Unification:* Kang In-tok.

KUWAIT. On 15 March the cabinet resigned to avoid a showdown in parliament in a no-confidence vote against Shaikh Soud Nasser al-Sabah, the *Information and Health Minister* and a member of the ruling family. On 16 March the Amir accepted the resignation but reappointed the Prime Minister and asked him to form a new cabinet.

In the resulting reshuffle Shaikh Soud Nasser al-Sabah moved to *Oil*; Nassar

Abdullah al-Roudhan, who had been a *Deputy Prime Minister* and *Finance Minister*, retained his position as a *Deputy Prime Minister* but became *State Minister for Cabinet Affairs* instead of *Finance Minister*; Abdul Aziz Dakhil al-Dakhil moved from *State Minister for Cabinet Affairs* to *Commerce and Industry*; Ali Salim al-Sabah became *Finance and Communications Minister*; Jasim Mohammed al-Aoun moved from *Communications, Electricity and Water* to *Social Affairs, Labour and Housing*; Hamud Abdallah al-Ruqba became *Minister for Public Works, Electricity and Water*; Ahmed Khalid al-Kulaib moved from *Social Affairs and Labour* to *Justice, Religious Endowments (Awqaf) and Islamic Affairs*, instead of Mohammed Dhaifallah Sharar, who moved to the newly created post of *Minister of National Assembly Affairs*; Dr Adil Khalid al-Sabih became *Minister of Public Health* and *acting Minister of Education and Higher Education*; Yusif Mohammed Sumait became *Minister of Information*; Ali Musa Musa became *Minister of Planning*.

MOLDOVA. In parliamentary elections held on 22 March the PCM (Communists) won 40 seats with 30·1% of the votes and the CDM (nationalists) 26 with 19·2%. 24 seats went to the PMDP and 11 to the PFD.

MOROCCO. Following the election in Nov. 1997 Prime Minister Abderrahmane Youssoufi formed a new cabinet in March, comprising: *Minister of State for Foreign Affairs and Co-operation:* Abdellatif Filali. *Minister of State for the Interior:* Driss Basri. *Minister of Agriculture, Rural Development and Fisheries:* Habib Maliki. *Civil Service and Administrative Reform:* Aziz Houcine. *Communication:* Mohamed Larbi Messari. *Cultural Affairs:* Mohamed Achari. *Development Planning, Environment, Urban Development and Housing:* Mohamed Yazghi. *Economy and Finance:* Fathallah Oualalou. *Endowment and Religious Affairs:* Abdelkebir Alaoui M'Daghri. *Energy and Mines:* Youssef Tahiri. *Equipment:* Bouamour Taghouane. *Health:* Abdelouhad Fassi. *Higher Education, Executive Training and Scientific Research:* Najib Zerouali. *Human Rights:* Mohamed Oujar. *Industry, Commerce and Handicrafts:* Alami Tazi. *Justice:* Omar Azziman. *National Education:* Ismail Alaoui. *Public Sector and Privatization:* Rachid Filali. *Parliamentary Relations:* Mohamed Bouzouba. *Social Development, Solidarity, Employment, Vocational Training and Government Spokesman:* Khalid Alioua. *Tourism:* Hassan Sabbar. *Transport and Merchant Marine:* Mustapha Mansouri. *Youth and Sports:* Ahmed Moussaoui. *Minister Delegate to the Prime Minister for Administration of National Defence:* Abderrahmane Sbai.

NETHERLANDS. In parliamentary elections held on 6 May the ruling coalition gained a substantial victory. The PVDA, party of Prime Minister Wim Kok, won 45 seats with 29% of the votes cast, the VVD 38 with 24·7%, the CDA 29 with 18·4%, D66 14 with 9% and Green Left 11 with 7·2%. The remaining 13 seats were won by 4 other parties.

ROMANIA. On 2 April Radu Vasile became Prime Minister and on 15 April a new cabinet was validated by Parliament, comprising: *Minister of State and Minister of Defence:* Victor Babiuc. *Minister of State and Minister of Justice:* Valeriu Stoica. *Minister of Domestic Affairs:* Gavril Dejeu. *Foreign Affairs:* Andrei Gabriel Plesu. *Finance:* Daniel Daianu. *Industry and Trade:* Radu Mircea Berceanu. *Labour and Social Protection:* Alexandru Athanasiu. *Privatization:* Sorin Petre Dimitriu. *Agriculture and Food:* Dinu Gavrilescu. *Transport:* Traian Basescu. *Public Works and Land Planning:* Nicolae Stefan Noica. *Communications:* Sorin Pantis. *Water, Forests and Environment Protection:* Romica Tomescu. *National Education:* Andrei Marga. *Health:* Baranyi Francisc. *Reform:* Ioan Avram Muresan. *Tourism:* Sorin Frunzaverde. *Science and Technology:* Horia Ene. *Culture:* Ion Caramitru. *Youth and Sports:* George Crin Antonescu.

SEYCHELLES. Both presidential and parliamentary elections were held on 22 March. In the presidential election France Albert René was re-elected for a 5th term, obtaining 66·7% of the votes, with his nearest rival, Wavel Ramkalawan of the

United Opposition, polling 19·5%. In the parliamentary elections the ruling SPPF gained 30 seats, the UO gained 3 and the Democratic party gained 1.

SIERRA LEONE. Following the President's return from exile on 10 March, he named a new cabinet, with himself as *Minister of Defence*. Other Ministers were: *Agriculture and Environment:* Dr Harry Will. *Education:* Dr Alpha Wurie. *Energy and Power:* Thaimu Bangura. *Finance and Economic Planning:* Dr James Jonah. *Fisheries:* Lawrence Kamara. *Foreign Affairs:* Dr Sama Banya. *Health and Sanitation:* Sulaiman Tejan Jalloh. *Information, Broadcasting and Tourism:* Dr Julius Spencer. *Internal Affairs and Local Government:* Charles Margai. *Justice and Attorney General:* Solomon Berewa. *Labour, Social Welfare and Sports:* Abass Collier. *Lands, Housing and Gender Affairs:* Shirley Gbujama. *Mineral Resources:* Mohammed Deen. *Presidential Affairs:* Momodu Koroma.

TUVALU. Elections were held on 26 March. Only non-partisans were elected as there are no political parties.

UK—NORTHERN IRELAND. The referendum on the future of Northern Ireland (23 May) produced a 71% vote in favour of the Good Friday peace agreement. A corresponding referendum in the Irish Republic led to an overwhelming 94·4% in support. As a consequence, in June, Ulster's 1·2m. voters elect the first power-sharing administration since the collapse of the Sunningdale Agreement in 1974.

UKRAINE. Parliamentary elections were held on 29 March. The Communist Party of Ukraine emerged as by far the largest single party, winning more seats than the next 2 most successful parties combined, although around 1 in 4 of the 450 seats went to candidates with no party affiliation.

In the cabinet reshuffle which followed the election Borys Supikhanov became *Minister of Agriculture*, Vasyl Rohovyy *Minister of Economy*, Borys Tarasyuk *Minister of Foreign Affairs*, and Leonid Derkach *Chief of the Security Service*. No Ministers were appointed for *Fisheries, Forestry, Science and Technology, Statistics* or *Transport*.

PART I

INTERNATIONAL ORGANIZATIONS

TAKING THE UNITED NATIONS INTO THE TWENTY-FIRST CENTURY

William J Durch

Two years past its fiftieth birthday, the United Nations remained in mid-life crisis, short of funds and long on critics, especially in the US Congress. But the international organization also showed new signs of vigour under a new Secretary-General. Kofi Annan assumed office determined to make the UN serve not just governments but their peoples, and to make it both relevant and visible on issues that matter to both. A remarkably candid report commissioned by Mr Annan early in his tenure noted that 'lasting damage is being inflicted worldwide by the perception of the Organization as a distant, global bureaucracy with little direct relevance to the lives of ordinary people.' Although the UN is involved day-to-day in issues that polls show matter to people—like narcotics control, disease prevention, the environment, development, and human rights—it gets little credit, especially among people in wealthier countries whose governments pay 90 per cent of the UN's bills. They associate the organization with good deeds and peaceful interventions but see few direct benefits from its actions, so their support for the UN, while broad, is nowhere very deep. In an age of competition for scarce public funds, this is not good news for the organization, which until quite recently was exceptionally bad at both marketing and defending itself. Staff viewed their task as serving the member states, like retainers to an especially large and feuding family, and so churned out tons of meeting reports in six languages and ran overlapping programmes voted by the General Assembly's rampant majority.

Ironically, however, as its 'talk shop' image grew, the UN was also becoming more field-operation oriented. Burgeoning internal conflict in the developing world gave the UN High Commissioner for Refugees millions of stateless people to care for each year. UNICEF, the children's programme, mounted major immunization campaigns around the world and, as the Cold War ended, UN peacekeepers fanned out to help more than a dozen countries make the difficult transition from civil war to something more like peace.

Kofi Annan's reform programme took aim at both the image problem and the substance behind it—a combination of bureaucratic inertia and member state micro management. To improve its public image, the UN finally moved onto the Internet and its World Wide Web. The Web in particular offers a way to reach a rapidly-growing global audience, *especially* in the crucial wealthy countries, but not only there. As of mid-1997, 171 countries, rich and poor, had Internet access and the number of computers hooked up globally was growing at a rate of several hundred thousand per month. Via this new electronic UN (http://www.un.org.), national delegations can find electronic meeting agendas and proceedings that used to fell trees by the hundreds when published on paper. Anyone who is interested can download treaties, documents, data, and press releases, find out what any arm of the UN does, and log into unofficial websites that analyze its activities and its spending. In short, the Web has opened up a whole new way in which the UN can communicate directly with its far-flung constituencies.

To address issues of inefficiency and waste, Mr Annan undertook to revamp the UN Secretariat from top to bottom. Restructuring proposals were unveiled on schedule in July 1997 and by the end of the year had been endorsed by the General Assembly. Included in the package was a new post of Deputy Secretary-General—a change long sought by reformers—to serve as the Secretary-General's alter-ego, assume some of the growing management burden, and take charge of implementing reform. In January 1998, Mr Annan announced the appointment of veteran Canadian diplomat Louise Fréchette to fill that post.

Also included was a concept called 'results based budgeting', essentially an appeal to member states to leave programme details to UN staff and focus oversight solely on whether jobs got done on time and within budget. Once implemented, it promises to make the UN a much more efficient place.

Largely impervious to reform edicts from New York are the UN's 'specialized agencies' like the International Monetary Fund (IMF), International Telecommunications Union (ITU) or World Health Organization (WHO). Each is the collective international persona of the specialized government ministries (finance, telecommunications, health, and the like) that populate the agencies' governing councils. These separately funded and chartered institutions operate largely out of the limelight. Several predate the UN Charter and have direct, if unsung, impact on many peoples' lives: WHO helped to eliminate smallpox worldwide and is closing in on measles and polio. ITU sets the rules for commercial, governmental and other use of radio, television and microwave frequencies, without which there would be daily electronic chaos. The IMF steadies shaky economics and squeezes the inflationary excess out of swollen government budgets. A dozen other agencies work in similarly specialized fields; some work very well while others could be shut down without being missed.

The United Nations was originally conceived primarily to deter and resist aggression through collective action. This function was frustrated at an early date but, over the years, peacekeeping and mediation of smaller conflicts and negotiation of arms control agreements evolved in its stead. The Security Council has the authority under the Charter to intervene in any situation that may threaten international peace and security, including intervention into a state's internal affairs. Such interventions in the 1990s enjoyed only mixed success and were almost entirely unsuccessful in the case of ongoing civil wars. Americans remember Somalia, Europeans Bosnia, and Africans Rwanda. Until the major powers of the world find reason and will to endow the UN with ability to call up and command combat forces, future such encounters are likely to be left to state-led military coalitions or to regional institutions like the North Atlantic Treaty Organization (as is the case in Bosnia). Implementing Security Council sanctions, as the UN Special Commission on Iraq (UNSCOM) has been attempting to do since mid-1991, also requires forceful backing. Equipped with moral authority alone, UNSCOM could not function.

Although the UN does not handle combat well, an ability to rapidly organize and deploy post-conflict peacekeepers, as proposed by the government of Canada and others, would be a distinct and valuable capacity. Key setbacks suffered by several UN peace operations are traceable to long delays in force deployment and the resulting loss of momentum for the local peace process.

The Secretary-General would like the UN to increase its involvement in conflict-prevention action. Beyond preventive diplomacy, it seeks to relieve the pressures that lead to conflict, for example, grinding poverty or ethnic or religious intolerance. Linking the UN's many development assistance programmes to the overarching goal of conflict prevention is one way of making them seem more relevant to the member states who pay the UN's bills, but it also provides a rationale for refocusing that assistance from governments to the people who need help the most.

The UN's principal arms negotiating forum, now known as the Conference on Disarmament (CD), generated the Nuclear Non-Proliferation Treaty (NPT) in 1968, the Chemical Weapons Convention in 1993 and the Comprehensive (Nuclear) Test Ban Treaty in 1996. Compliance with the NPT is monitored by the International Atomic Energy Agency (IAEA), which also helped UNSCOM dig out Iraq's covert nuclear weapons programme, a programme that would have been discovered sooner if the IAEA had more teeth. The two newer treaties have such teeth, in the form of tough onsite inspection provisions and the ability to refer treaty violations to the UN Security Council for further action.

In addition to safeguarding international security, the Charter committed the organization to advance the cause of 'human rights and fundamental freedoms'. The Universal Declaration of Human Rights passed the General Assembly in 1948 with no dissenting votes and just a handful of abstentions (6 East European states, Saudi Arabia, and South Africa). Binding covenants on civil and political rights, and economic and social rights, followed in the 1960s. These agreements, while not universally ratified, nonetheless set basic norms by which government performance has come to be judged, not only by other governments but by their own peoples. Human rights monitoring also has been an integral part of some recent UN peacekeeping work, starting with El Salvador in 1991. A newly consolidated Office of the High

Commissioner for Human Rights with a new commissioner, former president of Ireland Mary Robinson, indicate commitment to strengthen the UN's role in promoting human rights.

The third major purpose of the UN as defined by the Charter is 'solving international problems of an economic, social, cultural or humanitarian character'. The organization's involvement in these issues has followed global trends and the distribution of power in the General Assembly. As poor states gained a majority there, the UN became more heavily involved in economic development. As the environmental movement took hold, the UN established an environmental programme. In 1985, UN members signed the Vienna Convention to restore the atmosphere's ozone layer and subsequently set deadlines for taking ozone-depleting chemicals off the market. In 1992, the Conference on Environment and Development adopted the Framework Convention on Climate Change. In December 1997, 160 signatories of that Convention met in Kyoto, Japan, where industrialized countries accepted the principle of binding commitments to cut their emissions of greenhouse gases below those prevailing in 1990, and to do so by 2012.

In the process of dealing with these social, environmental and humanitarian issues, the UN is slowly learning a new role as promoter of civil society independent of government, and is beginning to see international non-governmental organizations as potential allies. Humanitarian organizations use the UN's Relief Web information clearinghouse to find out what's happening in crises around the globe and who's doing what to help. Eight in 10 people who went to Kyoto for the 1997 climate change meeting were unofficial 'delegates', not government representatives. Every UN conference in recent years has had a similar private, non-profit corona that influenced its ultimate outcome. Civil society's growing importance is reflected in Kofi Annan's call for the General Assembly in the year 2000 to be accompanied by a People's Millennium Assembly that directly represents, in some fashion, the budding civil societies of the globe.

There is irony that, in a period of rapid technological, economic and political change, the UN Charter still enshrines the power relations of the 1940s. The permanent members of the Security Council are the winners of World War Two, yet the losers (Germany, Italy and Japan) now fund one-third of the UN's budget, almost twice the total contributed by permanent members France, Britain, Russia and China. All three 'losers' would like a permanent seat at the table, as would populous states like India. A seat without a veto is unlikely to be acceptable to them, but the current permanent members are unlikely either to share their veto power or let it be constricted or watered down.

Reforms that pass the Council and the General Assembly must be ratified by two-thirds of the UN's membership, including all five permanent Council members. In other words, any change in the Charter requires the support of 67 United States Senators. In all likelihood, therefore, the Security Council is likely to remain a monument to international relations circa 1945.

While its formal security structures may be frozen in time, the rest of the UN system, veto-free, is capable of adaptation given the leadership and the latitude. In the future, for example, governments may well find that key tasks (fighting organized crime or excesses in currency and securities trading) require global institutions with significant, if narrowly defined, enforcement powers. They may finally concede that the need for global governance grows in proportion to the power of markets, as it did within all modern industrial states. The voting publics of those states demanded it. As the power of global civil society grows with the help of information technologies, some of which have yet to be invented, such demands will likely arise again.

William J. Durch is Senior Associate of The Henry L. Stimson Center, Washington, D.C.

THE UNITED NATIONS (UN)

Origin and Aims. The United Nations is an association of states which have pledged themselves to maintain international peace and security and co-operate in solving international political, economic, social, cultural and humanitarian problems towards achieving this end. The name 'United Nations' was devised by United States President Franklin D. Roosevelt and was first used in the Declaration by United Nations of 1 Jan. 1942, during the Second World War, when representatives of 26 nations pledged their Governments to continue fighting together against the Axis Powers.

The United Nations Charter, the constituting instrument of the UN, was drawn up by the representatives of 50 countries at the United Nations Conference on International Organization, which met in San Francisco from 25 April to 26 June 1945. Those delegates deliberated on the basis of proposals worked out by the representatives of China, the Soviet Union, the United Kingdom and the United States at Dumbarton Oaks (Washington, DC) from 21 Aug. to 28 Sept. 1944. The Charter was signed on 26 June 1945 by the representatives of the 50 countries. Poland, which was not represented at the Conference, signed it later and became one of the original 51 Member States. Nothing contained in the Charter authorizes the organization to intervene in matters which are essentially within the domestic jurisdiction of any state.

The United Nations officially came into existence on 24 Oct. 1945, with the deposit of the requisite number of ratifications of the Charter with the US Department of State. United Nations Day is celebrated on 24 Oct. each year.

Over the past five decades, international co-operation has brought advances in every area of the United Nations Charter but the post-cold war era brings new challenges to the UN. Peacekeeping operations, for which demand has increased sharply, now operate under greatly expanded mandates in response to the bitter conflicts which menace societies from within. Today, 80% of the UN's work is devoted to helping developing countries build the capacity to help themselves. This includes promoting the creation of independent and democratic societies, which it is hoped will offer vital support for the Charter's goals in the 21st century; the protection of human rights; saving children from starvation and disease; providing relief assistance to refugees and disaster victims; countering global crime, drugs and disease; and assisting countries devastated by war and the long-term threat of landmines.

Members. Membership is open to all peace-loving nations which accept the obligations of the Charter and, in the judgement of the Organization, are willing and able to carry them out. New Member States are admitted by the General Assembly on the recommendation of the Security Council. The Charter provides for the suspension or expulsion of a Member for violation of its principles, but no such action has ever been taken. At the start of 1998, there were 185 member states. (For a list of these, see below.)

Finance. Assessments on member states constitute the main source of funds. These are in accordance with a scale specified by the Assembly, and determined primarily by the country's share of the world economy and ability to pay, in the range 25%–0·01%. The Organization is prohibited by law from borrowing from commercial institutions. A Working Group on the Financial Situation of the United Nations was established in 1994 to address the long-standing financial crisis which has come about because of the non-payment of assessed dues by many Member States, severely threatening the Organization's ability to fulfil its mandates. As of mid-July 1997, Member States owed the UN a total of US$2,300m.

Official languages. Arabic, Chinese, English, French, Russian and Spanish.

Structure. The UN has six principal organs established by the founding Charter. All have their headquarters in New York except the International Court of Justice, which has its seat in The Hague. These core bodies work through dozens of related agencies, operational programmes and funds, and through special agreements with separate, autonomous, intergovernmental agencies, known as Specialized Agencies, in order to provide an increasingly cohesive programme of action in the fields of peace

and security, justice and human rights, humanitarian assistance, and social and economic development. The six principal UN organs are as follows:

1. **The General Assembly,** composed of all members, is the main deliberative body; each member has 1 vote. It meets once a year, commencing on the third Tuesday in Sept., and normally runs until mid-Dec. At the start of each session, the Assembly elects a new President, 21 vice-presidents and the chairmen of its seven main committees, listed below. To ensure equitable geographical representation, the presidency of the Assembly rotates each year among the five geographical groups of states: African, Asian, Eastern European, Latin American, and Western European and other States. Special sessions may be convoked by the Secretary-General if requested by the Security Council, by a majority of members, or by 1 member if the majority of the members concur. Emergency sessions may be called within 24 hours at the request of the Security Council on the vote of any 9 Council members, or a majority of United Nations members, or 1 member if the majority of members concur. Decisions on important questions, such as peace and security, new membership and budgetary matters, require a two-thirds majority; other questions require a simple majority of members present and voting.

The work of the General Assembly is divided between 6 Main Committees, on which every member state is represented. These are: Disarmament and International Security Committee (First Committee); Economic and Financial Committee (Second Committee); Social, Humanitarian and Cultural Committee (Third Committee); Special Political and Decolonization Committee (Fourth Committee); Administrative and Budgetary Committee (Fifth Committee); Legal Committee (Sixth Committee).

There is also a General Committee charged with the task of co-ordinating the proceedings of the Assembly and its Committees; and a Credentials Committee. The General Committee consists of 29 members: the president and 21 vice-presidents of the General Assembly and the chairmen of the 6 main committees. The Credentials Committee consists of 9 members appointed by the Assembly on the proposal of the President at each session. In addition, the Assembly has 2 standing committees—an Advisory Committee on Administrative and Budgetary Questions, and a Committee on Contributions; and may establish subsidiary and *ad hoc* bodies when necessary to deal with specific matters. These include: Special Committee on Peacekeeping Operations (34 members), Human Rights Committee (18 members), Committee on the Peaceful Uses of Outer Space (61 members), Conciliation Commission for Palestine (3 members), Conference on Disarmament (38 members), International Law Commission (34 members), Scientific Committee on the Effects of Atomic Radiation (21 members), Special Committee on the Implementation of the Declaration on the Granting of Independence to Colonial Countries and Peoples (25 members), and Commission on International Trade Law (36 members).

The General Assembly has the right to discuss any matters within the scope of the Charter and, with the exception of any situation or dispute on the agenda of the Security Council, may make recommendations on any such questions or matters. While it has no power to compel action by any Government, its recommendations are seen to carry the weight of world opinion. Occupying a central position in the UN, the Assembly receives reports from other organs, admits new members, directs activities for development, sets policies and determines programmes for the Secretariat, appoints the Secretary-General, who reports annually to it on the work of the Organization, and approves the UN budget.

Under the "Uniting For Peace" resolution adopted by the General Assembly in Nov. 1950, the Assembly is also empowered to take action if the Security Council, because of a lack of unanimity of its permanent members, fails to exercise its primary responsibility for the maintenance of international peace and security in any case where there appears to be a threat to the peace, breach of the peace or act of aggression. In this event, the General Assembly may consider the matter immediately with a view to making appropriate recommendations to members for collective measures, including, in the case of a breach of the peace or act of aggression, the use of armed force when necessary, to maintain or restore international peace and security.

2. **The Security Council** has primary responsibility, under the Charter, for the main-

tenance of international peace and security. It is so organised as to be able to function continuously. A representative of each of its members must be present at all times at UN Headquarters, but it may meet elsewhere as best facilitates its work.

The Presidency of the Council rotates monthly, according to the English alphabetical order of members' names. The Council consists of 15 members: 5 permanent and 10 non-permanent elected for a 2-year term by a two-thirds majority of the General Assembly. Each member has 1 vote. Retiring members are not eligible for immediate re-election. Any other member of the United Nations may participate without a vote in the discussion of questions specially affecting its interests. Decisions on procedural questions are made by an affirmative vote of at least 9 members. On all other matters, the affirmative vote of 9 members must include the concurring votes of all permanent members (subject to the provision that when the Council is considering methods for the peaceful settlement of a dispute, parties to the dispute abstain from voting). Consequently, a negative vote from a permanent member has the power of veto, and all five permanent members have exercised this right at one time or other. If a permanent member does not support a decision but does not wish to veto it, it may abstain. Under the Charter, the Security Council alone has the power to take decisions which member states are obligated to carry out.

The Council has 2 standing committees at present—the Committee of Experts on Rules of Procedure and the Committee on the Admission of New Members. In addition, as needed, it may establish *ad hoc* committees and commissions, such as the Committee on Council Meetings away from Headquarters.

When a threat to peace is brought before the Council, its first action is usually to recommend to the parties agreement by peaceful means. It may undertake mediation and set forth principles for a settlement, and may take measures to enforce its decisions by ceasefire directives, economic sanctions, peacekeeping missions, or in some cases, by collective military action. For the maintenance of international peace and security, the Council can, in accordance with special agreements to be concluded, call on the armed forces, assistance and facilities of the member states. It is assisted by a Military Staff Committee consisting of the Chiefs of Staff of the permanent members of the Council or their representatives.

The Council also makes recommendations to the Assembly on the appointment of the Secretary-General and, with the Assembly, elects the judges of the International Court.

Permanent Members. China, France, Russia, UK, USA (Russia took over the seat of the former USSR in Dec. 1991).

Non-Permanent Members. Costa Rica, Japan, Kenya, Portugal, Sweden (until 31 Dec. 1998), Bahrain, Brazil, Gabon, Gambia, Slovenia (until 31 Dec. 1999)

Finance. The total cost of all UN peacekeeping operations in 1996 was US$1,400m. Assessments for 1997 were expected to total US$1,300m.

3. **The Economic and Social Council (ECOSOC)** is responsible under the General Assembly for co-ordinating the functions of the UN with regard to international economic, social, cultural, educational, health and related matters. The year-round work of the Council is carried out by related organizations, specialized agencies, and subsidiary bodies, commissions and committees, which meet regularly and report back to it.

It consists of 54 member states elected by a two-thirds majority of the General Assembly for a 3-year term. Members are elected according to the following geographic distribution: Africa, 14 members; Asia, 11; Eastern Europe, 6; Latin America and Caribbean, 10; Western Europe and other States, 13. A third of the members retire each year. Retiring members are eligible for immediate re-election. Each member has 1 vote. Decisions are made by a majority of the members present and voting. The Council holds one 5-week substantive session a year, alternating between New York and Geneva, and one organizational session in New York. The substantive session includes a high-level special meeting attended by Ministers, to discuss major economic and social issues. Special sessions may be held if required. The President is elected for 1 year and is eligible for immediate re-election.

The subsidiary machinery of ECOSOC is as follows.

Nine Functional Commissions. Statistical Commission; Commission on Population and Development; Commission for Social Development; Commission on Human Rights (and Subcommission on Prevention of Discrimination and Protection of Minorities); Commission on the Status of Women; Commission on Narcotic Drugs (and Subcommission on Illicit Drug Traffic and Related Matters in the Near and Middle East); Commission on Science and Technology for Development; Commission on Crime Prevention and Criminal Justice; Commission on Sustainable Development.

Five Regional Economic Commissions. ECA (Economic Commission for Africa, Addis Ababa, Ethiopia); ESCAP (Economic and Social Commission for Asia and the Pacific, Bangkok); ECE (Economic Commission for Europe, Geneva); ECLAC (Economic Commission for Latin America and the Caribbean, Santiago, Chile); ESCWA (Economic Commission for Western Asia, Amman, Jordan).

Nine Standing Committees and Subsidiary Expert Bodies. Committee for Programme and Co-ordination; Commission on Human Settlements; Committee on Non-Governmental Organizations; Committee on Natural Resources; Committee for Development Planning; Committee on Negotiations with Intergovernmental Agencies; Commission on Transnational Corporations; Committee on Economic, Social and Cultural Rights; Committee on New and Renewable Sources of Energy and on Energy for Development.

Other related operational programmes, funds and special bodies, which report to ECOSOC (and/or the General Assembly), include: The United Nations Children's Fund (UNICEF); Office of the United Nations High Commissioner for Refugees (UNHCR); United Nations Conference on Trade and Development (UNCTAD); United Nations Development Programme (UNDP) and Population Fund (UNFPA); United Nations Environment Programme (UNEP); World Food Programme (WFP) and World Food Council (WFC); International Research and Training Institute for the Advancement of Women (INSTRAW); United Nations International Drug Control Programme (UNDCP).

In addition, the Council may make arrangements for consultation with international non-governmental organizations (NGOs) and, after consultation with the member concerned, with national organizations. There are over 1,500 NGOs which have consultative status with the Council. NGOs may send observers to the Council's public meetings and those of its subsidiary bodies, and may submit written statements relevant to its work. They may also consult with the UN Secretariat on matters of mutual concern.

Members. (1998): Algeria, Argentina, Bangladesh, Belarus, Belgium, Brazil, Canada, Cape Verde, Central African Republic, Chile, China, Colombia, Comoros, Cuba, Czech Republic, Djibouti, El Salvador, Finland, France, Gabon, Gambia, Germany, Guyana, Iceland, India, Italy, Japan, Jordan, Korea (Republic of), Latvia, Lebanon, Lesotho, Mauritius, Mexico, Mozambique, New Zealand, Nicaragua, Oman, Pakistan, Poland, Romania, Russia, St Lucia, Sierra Leone, Spain, Sri Lanka, Sweden, Togo, Tunisia, Turkey, United Kingdom, United States, Vietnam, Zambia.

Finance. The UN has US$4,600m. a year to spend on economic and social development.

4. **The Trusteeship Council** was established to ensure that Governments responsible for administering Trust Territories take adequate steps to prepare them for self-government or independence. It consists of five permanent members of the Security Council. The task of decolonization was completed in 1994, when the Security Council terminated the Trusteeship Agreement for the last of the original UN Trusteeships (Palau), administered by the US. All Trust Territories attained self-government or independence either as separate States or by joining neighbouring independent countries. Since 1994 the Council's role has been under review. The proposal from UN Secretary-General Kofi Annan, in the second part of his reform programme, in July 1997, is that it should be reborn as an environmental body.

Members. China, France, Russia, UK, USA.

5. **The International Court of Justice** is the principal judicial organ of the UN. It operates under a Statute, which is an integral part of the United Nations Charter. All UN members are *ipso facto* parties to the Statute of the Court. The Court is composed of 15 judges, each of a different nationality elected with an absolute majority to 9-year terms of office by both the General Assembly and the Security Council. The composition of the Court must also reflect the main forms of civilization and principal legal systems of the world. Elections are held every 3 years for one-third of the seats, and retiring judges may be re-elected. Members do not represent their respective governments but sit as independent magistrates in the Court, and must possess the qualifications required in their respective countries for appointment to the highest judicial offices, or be jurists of recognized competence in international law. Candidates are nominated by the national panels of jurists in the Permanent Court of Arbitration established by the Hague Conventions of 1899 and 1907. The Court elects its own President and Vice-President for a 3-year term, and is permanently in session.

Decisions are taken by a majority of judges present, subject to a quorum of 9 members, with the President having a casting vote. Judgement is final and without appeal, but a revision may be applied for within 10 years from the date of the judgement on the ground of a new decisive factor. When the Court does not include a judge possessing the nationality of a State party to a case, that State has the right to appoint a person to sit as judge *ad hoc* for that case, on equal terms with Members. Disputes concerning the jurisdiction of the Court are settled by the Court's own decision.

Since 1946, the Court has delivered 61 judgements on disputes concerning *inter alia* land frontiers and maritime boundaries, territorial sovereignty, the non-use of force, non interference in the internal affairs of States, diplomatic relations, hostage-taking, the right of asylum, nationality, guardianship, rights of passage and economic rights.

While the Court normally sits in plenary session, it can form chambers of 3 or more judges to deal with specific matters. Judgements by chambers are considered as rendered by the full Court. In 1993, in view of the global expansion of environmental law and protection, the Court formed a 7-member Chamber for Environmental Matters.

Competence and Jurisdiction. Only States may apply to or appear before the Court, which is open only to parties to its Statute, which automatically includes all Members of the UN. The conditions under which the Court will be open to other states are laid down by the Security Council. Nauru and Switzerland are the only non-UN members to have become parties to the Statute. The jurisdiction of the Court covers all matters which parties refer to it, and all matters provided for in the Charter or in treaties and conventions in force. The Court may apply in its decision: *(a)* international conventions; *(b)* international custom; *(c)* the general principles of law recognized by civilized nations; and *(d)* as subsidiary means for the determination of the rules of law, judicial decisions and the teachings of highly qualified publicists. If the parties agree, the Court may decide a case *ex aequo et bono.* The Court may also give advisory opinions on legal questions to the General Assembly, the Security Council, certain other organs of the UN and a number of international organizations.

Judges. The present composition of the Court, which holds office until 5 Feb. 2000, is as follows: Rosalyn Higgins (UK), Gilbert Guillaume (France), Gonzalo Parra-Aranguren (Venezuela), Christopher G. Weeramantry, Vice-President (Sri Lanka), Raymond Ranjeva (Madagascar), Shigeru Oda (Japan), Géza Herczegh (Hungary), Shi Jiuyong (China), Carl-August Fleischhauer (Germany), Abdul G. Koroma (Sierra Leone), Mohammed Bedjaoui (Algeria), Pieter H. Kooijmans (Netherlands), José F. Rezek (Brazil), Stephen M. Schwebel, President (USA), Vladlen S. Vereshchetin (Russia).

Finance. The expenses of the Court are borne by the UN. No court fees are paid by parties to the Statute.

Official languages. English, French.

Headquarters: The Peace Palace, 2517 KJ The Hague, Netherlands. The Court may sit elsewhere if it chooses to.

Website: http://www.icj-cij.org.

Registrar: Eduardo Valencia-Ospina (Colombia).

6. **The Secretariat** services the other 5 organs of the UN, administering their programmes and carrying out the Organization's day-to-day work with its increasingly streamlined staff of some 8,900 at the UN Headquarters in New York and all over the world. At its head is the Secretary-General, appointed by the General Assembly on the recommendation of the Security Council for a 5-year, renewable term. The Secretary-General acts as chief administrative officer in all meetings of the General Assembly, Security Council, Economic and Social Council and Trusteeship Council. An Office of Internal Oversight, established in 1994 under the tenure of former Secretary-General Boutros Boutros-Ghali (Egypt), pursues a cost-saving mandate to investigate and eliminate waste, fraud and mismanagement within the system. The Secretary-General is assisted by Under-Secretaries-General and Assistant Secretaries-General. A new appointment of Deputy Secretary-General was agreed in principle by the General Assembly in 1997 and was announced in Jan. 1998.

A Quiet Revolution. The agenda of the UN's 52nd General Assembly (1997) was dominated by the Secretary-General's reform plans to make the UN leaner, more efficient and more effective, cutting administrative costs by as much as a third by the year 2000. Initiatives included the rationalization and consolidation of the UN's bureaucratic machinery by merging overlapping programmes and departments, and streamlining management, in an attempt to shift resources from administration to development work for the poorest nations.

The proposals included the establishment of a new, less-personal, cabinet-style administration; the appointment of a Deputy Secretary-General; and a Millennium Assembly in 2000 with a companion People's Assembly to focus on defining the UN's role for the 21st century.

Finance. The Secretariat had a zero-growth budget of US$2,600m. for the 2-year period 1996–97. This represented over US$250m. in savings achieved through efficiency gains and a 25 per cent cut in staff (from a 1984 high of more than 12,000 to 8,900 by 1998). The budget proposed for 1998–99 cuts a further US$120m., bringing it to US$2,480m.

Headquarters: United Nations Plaza, New York, NY 10017, USA.

Website: http://www.un.org.

Secretary-General: Kofi Annan (app. 1 Jan. 1997, Ghana). *Deputy Secretary-General:* Louise Fréchette (app. 12 Jan. 1998, Canada).

MEMBER STATES OF THE UN

The 185 member states at Jan. 1998, with percentage scale of contributions to the Regular Budget and Peacekeeping Operations Budget (PKO), and year of admission:

	% contributions		Year of		% contributions		Year of
	Reg.	PKO	admission		Reg.	PKO	admission
Afghanistan	0·01	0.001	1946	Bahrain	0·02	0.004	1971
Albania	0·01	0.002	1955	Bangladesh	0·01	0.001	1974
Algeria	0·16	0.032	1962	Barbados	0·01	0.002	1966
Andorra	0·01	0.010	1993	Belarus[1], [2]	0·28	0.140	1945
Angola	0·01	0.001	1976	Belgium[1]	1·09	1.011	1945
Antigua and Barbuda	0·01	0.001	1981	Belize	0·01	0.001	1981
Argentina[1]	0·48	0.096	1945	Benin	0·01	0.001	1960
Armenia	0·05	0.010	1992	Bhutan	0·01	0.001	1971
Australia[1]	1·47	1.481	1945	Bolivia[1]	0·01	0.002	1945
Austria	0·87	0.871	1955	Bosnia-Herzegovina	0·01	0.002	1992
Azerbaijan	0·11	0.022	1992	Botswana	0·01	0.001	1966
Bahamas	0·02	0.004	1973	Brazil[1]	1·51	0.325	1945

	% contributions Reg.	PKO	Year of admission		% contributions Reg.	PKO	Year of admission
Brunei	0·02	0.004	1984	Kuwait	0·19	0.038	1963
Bulgaria	0·08	0.016	1955	Kyrgyzstan	0·03	0.006	1992
Burkina Faso	0·01	0.001	1960	Laos	0·01	0.001	1955
Burundi	0·01	0.001	1962	Latvia	0·08	0.016	1991
Cambodia	0·01	0.002	1955	Lebanon[1]	0·01	0.002	1945
Cameroon	0·01	0.002	1960	Lesotho	0·01	0.001	1966
Canada[1]	2.82	3.112	1945	Liberia[1]	0·01	0.002	1945
Cape Verde	0·01	0.001	1975	Libya	0·20	0.040	1955
Central African Rep.	0·01	0.001	1960	Liechtenstein	0·01	0.010	1990
Chad	0·01	0.001	1960	Lithuania	0·08	0.016	1991
Chile[1]	0·08	0.016	1945	Luxembourg[1]	0·07	0.070	1945
China[1]	0·90	0.914	1945	Macedonia[8]	0·01	0.002	1993
Colombia[1]	0·10	0.020	1945	Madagascar	0·01	0.001	1960
Comoros	0·01	0.001	1975	Malawi	0·01	0.001	1964
Congo, Rep. of the	0·01	0.002	1960	Malaysia[9]	0·14	0.028	1957
Congo,				Maldives	0·01	0.001	1965
Dem. Rep. of the[3]	0.01	0.002	1960	Mali	0·01	0.001	1960
Costa Rica[1]	0·01	0.002	1945	Malta	0·01	0.002	1964
Côte d'Ivoire	0·01	0.002	1960	Marshall Islands	0·01	0.002	1991
Croatia	0·09	0.018	1992	Mauritania	0·01	0.000	1961
Cuba[1]	0·05	0.010	1945	Mauritius	0·01	0.002	1968
Cyprus	0·03	0.006	1960	Mexico[1]	0·94	0.158	1945
Czech Republic[4]	0·25	0.250	1993	Micronesia	0·01	0.002	1991
Denmark[1]	0·72	0.721	1945	Moldova	0·08	0.016	1992
Djibouti	0·01	0.001	1977	Monaco	0·01	0.010	1993
Dominica	0·01	0.001	1978	Mongolia	0·01	0.002	1961
Dominican Republic[1]	0·01	0.002	1945	Morocco	0·03	0.006	1956
Ecuador[1]	0·02	0.004	1945	Mozambique	0·01	0.000	1975
Egypt[1, 5]	0·08	0.016	1945	Myanmar[10]	0·01	0.000	1948
El Salvador[1]	0·01	0.002	1945	Namibia	0·01	0.000	1990
Equatorial Guinea	0·01	0.001	1968	Nepal	0·01	0.000	1955
Eritrea	0·01	0.001	1993	Netherlands[1]	1·59	1.591	1945
Estonia	0·04	0.008	1991	New Zealand[1]	0·24	0.246	1945
Ethiopia[1]	0·01	0.001	1945	Nicaragua[1]	0·01	0.002	1945
Fiji	0·01	0.002	1970	Niger	0·01	0.000	1960
Finland	0·62	0.621	1955	Nigeria	0·11	0.022	1960
France[1]	6·49	7.925	1945	Norway[1]	0·56	0.560	1945
Gabon	0·01	0.002	1960	Oman	0·04	0.008	1971
Gambia	0·01	0.001	1965	Pakistan	0·06	0.012	1947
Georgia	0·11	0.022	1992	Palau	0·01	0.000	1994
Germany[6]	9·63	9.066	1973	Panama[1]	0·01	0.002	1945
Ghana	0·01	0.002	1957	Papua New Guinea	0·01	0.000	1975
Greece[1]	0·38	0.209	1945	Paraguay[1]	0·01	0.002	1945
Grenada	0·01	0.001	1974	Peru[1]	0·06	0.012	1945
Guatemala[1]	0·02	0.004	1945	Philippines[1]	0·06	0.012	1945
Guinea	0·01	0.001	1958	Poland[1]	0·33	0.066	1945
Guinea-Bissau	0·01	0.001	1974	Portugal	0·28	0.196	1955
Guyana	0·01	0.002	1966	Qatar	0·04	0.008	1971
Haiti[1]	0·01	0.001	1945	Romania	0·15	0.030	1955
Honduras[1]	0·01	0.002	1945	Russia[1, 11]	2.87	5.271	1945
Hungary	0·14	0.028	1955	Rwanda	0·01	0.000	1962
Iceland	0·03	0.030	1946	St Kitts and Nevis	0·01	0.000	1983
India[1]	0·17	0.062	1945	St Lucia	0·01	0.000	1979
Indonesia[7]	0·14	0.028	1950	St Vincent			
Iran[1]	0·45	0.090	1945	and Grenadines	0·01	0.000	1980
Iraq[1]	0·14	0.028	1945	Samoa	0·01	0.000	1976
Ireland, Rep. of	0·21	0.210	1955	San Marino	0·01	0.010	1992
Israel	0·27	0.054	1949	São Tomé			
Italy	5·39	5.254	1955	e Príncipe	0·01	0.000	1975
Jamaica	0·01	0.002	1962	Saudi Arabia[1]	0·71	0.142	1945
Japan	17.98	15.661	1956	Senegal	0·01	0.000	1960
Jordan	0·01	0.002	1955	Seychelles	0·01	0.000	1976
Kazakhstan	0·19	0.038	1992	Sierra Leone	0·01	0.000	1961
Kenya	0·01	0.002	1963	Singapore[12]	0·14	0.028	1965
Korea (North)	0·05	0.010	1991	Slovakia[4]	0·08	0.000	1993
Korea (South)	0·82	0.164	1991	Slovenia	0·07	0.014	1992

	% contributions		Year of		% contributions		Year of
	Reg.	PKO	admission		Reg.	PKO	admission
Solomon Islands	0·01	0.000	1978	Turkmenistan	0·03	0.006	1992
Somalia	0·01	0.000	1960	Uganda	0·01	0.000	1962
South Africa[1]	0·32	0.320	1945	Ukraine[1]	1·09	0.958	1945
Spain	2·38	2.382	1955	United Arab			
Sri Lanka	0·01	0.002	1955	Emirates	0·19	0.038	1971
Sudan	0·01	0.000	1956	UK[1]	5·07	6.568	1945
Suriname	0·01	0.000	1975	USA[1]	25·00	30.862	1945
Swaziland	0·01	0.002	1968	Uruguay[1]	0·04	0.008	1945
Sweden	1·09	1.231	1946	Uzbekistan	0·13	0.026	1992
Syria[1, 13]	0·05	0.010	1945	Vanuatu	0·01	0.000	1981
Tajikistan	0·02	0.004	1992	Venezuela[1]	0·33	0.066	1945
Tanzania[14]	0·01	0.000	1961	Vietnam	0·01	0.002	1977
Thailand	0·13	0.026	1946	Yemen[15]	0·01	0.000	1947
Togo	0·01	0.000	1960	Yugoslavia[1, 16]	0·10	0.020	1945
Trinidad and Tobago	0·03	0.006	1962	Zambia	0·01	0.000	1964
Tunisia	0·03	0.006	1956	Zimbabwe	0·01	0.000	1980
Turkey[1]	0·38	0.076	1945				

[1] Original member. [2] As Byelorussia, 1945-91. [3] As Zaire, 1960-97.
[4] Pre-partition Czechoslovakia (1945-92) was an original member.
[5] As United Arab Republic, 1958-71, following union with Syria (1958-61).
[6] Pre-unification (1990) as two states: The Federal Republic of Germany and the German Democratic Republic.
[7] Withdrew temporarily, 1965-66.
[8] Pre-independence (1992), as part of Yugoslavia, which was an original member.
[9] As the Federation of Malaya till 1963, when the new federation of Malaysia (including Singapore, Sarawak and Sabah) was formed.
[10] As Burma, 1948-89. [11] As USSR, 1945-91. [12] As part of Malaysia, 1963-65.
[13] As United Arab Republic, by union with Egypt, 1958-61.
[14] As two states: Tanganyika, 1961-64, and Zanzibar, 1963-64, prior to union as one republic under new name.
[15] As Yemen, 1947-90, and Democratic Yemen, 1967-90, prior to merger of the two.
[16] Excluded from the General Assembly 1992.

Publications. Yearbook of the United Nations. New York, 1947 ff.—United Nations Chronicle. Quarterly.—Monthly Bulletin of Statistics.—General Assembly: Official-Records: Resolutions.—Reports of the Secretary-General of the United Nations on the Work of the Organization. 1946 ff.—Charter of the United Nations and Statute of the International Court of Justice.—Official Records of the Security Council, the Economic and Social Council, Trusteeship Council and the Disarmament Commission.—Demographic Yearbook. New York.— Basic Facts about the United Nations. New York, 1995.—Statistical Yearbook. New York, 1947 ff.—Yearbook of International Statistics. New York, 1950 ff.—World Economic Survey. New York, 1947 ff.—Economic Survey of Asia and the Far East. New York, 1946 ff.—Economic Survey of Latin America. New York, 1948 ff.—Economic Survey of Europe. New York, 1948 ff.—Economic Survey of Africa. New York, 1960 ff.—United Nations Reference Guide in the Field of Human Rights. UN Centre for Human Rights, 1993.

Further Reading

Arnold, G., World Government by Stealth: The Future of the United Nations. Macmillan, 1998
Baehr, P. R. and Gordenker, L., The United Nations in the 1990s. 2nd ed. London, 1994
Bailey, S. D. and Daws, S., The United Nations: a Concise Political Guide. 3rd ed. London, 1994
Baratta, J. P., United Nations System [Bibliography]. Oxford and New Brunswick (NJ), 1994
Beigbeder, Y., The Internal Management of United Nations Organizations: the Long Quest for Reform. London, 1997
Durch, W. J., The Evolution of UN Peacekeeping: Case Studies and Comparative Analysis. New York, 1993
Ginifer, J. (ed), Development Within UN Peace Missions. London, 1997
Luard, E., The United Nations: How It Works and What It Does. 2nd ed. London, 1994
New Zealand Ministry of Foreign Affairs, UN Handbook. 1997
Osmanczyk, E., Encyclopaedia of the United Nations. London, 1985
Parsons, A., From Cold War to Hot Peace: UN Interventions, 1947–94. London, 1995
Pugh, M., The UN, Peace and Force. London, 1997
Ratner, S. R., The New UN Peacekeeping: Building Peace in Lands of Conflict after the Cold War. London, 1995

Righter, R., *Utopia Lost: the United Nations and World Order.* New York, 1995
Roberts, A. and Kingsbury, B. (eds.) *United Nations, Divided World: the UN's Roles in International Relations.* 2nd ed. Oxford, 1994.
Simma, B. (ed.) *The Charter of the United Nations: a Commentary.* OUP, 1995
Williams, D., *The Specialised Agencies of the United Nations.* London, 1987

UNITED NATIONS SYSTEM

Operational Programmes and Funds. The total operating expenses for the entire UN system, including the World Bank, IMF and all the UN funds, programmes and specialized agencies come to US$18,200m. a year. Some 53,300 people work in the UN system, which includes the Secretariat and 28 other organizations.

Social and economic development, aimed at achieving a better life for people everywhere, is a major part of the UN system of organizations. In the forefront of efforts to bring about such progress is the United Nations Development Programme (UNDP), the world's largest agency for multilateral technical and pre-investment co-operation. It is the funding source for most of the technical assistance provided for sustainable human development by the UN system, and helps people in 174 countries and territories, supporting some 6,000 projects, which focus on poverty elimination, environmental regeneration, job creation and the advancement of women.

UNDP assistance is provided only at the request of governments and in response to their priority needs, integrated into over-all national and regional plans. Its activities are funded mainly by voluntary contributions outside the regular UN budget. 87% of the UNDP's core programme funds go to countries with an annual *per capita* GNP of US$750 or less, which are home to 90% of the world's poorest peoples. Headquartered in New York, the UNDP is governed by a 36-member Executive Board, representing both developing and developed countries.

Administrator: James Gustave Speth (USA).

UN development programmes include the *United Nations Children's Fund (UNICEF).* Established in 1946 to deliver post-war relief to children, UNICEF now concentrates its assistance on development activities aimed at improving the quality of life for children and mothers in developing countries. Working in some 150 countries, its programmes focus on immunization, primary healthcare, nutrition and basic education. *The State of the World's Children Report*, published annually by UNICEF, has helped to spread acceptance by local and national leaders of a strategy for child health and nutrition which UNICEF estimates could save the lives of 7m. children. UNICEF has focused on popularising 4 primary healthcare techniques which are low in cost and produce results in a relatively short time. These include: oral rehydration therapy to fight the effects of diarrhoeal infections, which kill some 4m. children each year; expanded immunization against the 6 most common childhood diseases; child growth monitoring; and promotion of breastfeeding. UNICEF works closely with the World Health Organization (WHO), providing training, equipment and the services of healthcare professionals. It is the world's largest supplier of oral rehydration salts and vaccines, and of the 'cold chain' equipment needed to deliver them.

Executive Director: Carol Bellamy (USA).

The *UN Population Fund (UNFPA)*, established in 1969, carries out development programmes in over 130 countries and territories, and is the largest international provider of population assistance to developing countries. In 1996, it provided support to 168 countries. The Fund's aims are to build up capacity to respond to needs in population and family planning; to promote awareness of population problems in both developed and developing countries and possible strategies to deal with them; to assist developing countries at their request in dealing with population problems.

The Fund provides assistance for sustainable reproductive healthcare and family planning; for population data collection, analysis and demographic research; and for population policy formulation, as well as for special programme interests, such as gender issues, ageing and HIV/AIDS. In addition, it provides most of the funding for the *United Nations Population Information Network (POPIN)*, a decentralized

community of population institutions, whose objectives are to identify, establish, strengthen and co-ordinate information activities at international, national and regional levels; and to facilitate the availability and exchange of population information and related issues. UNFPA's *State of the World Population Report* is published annually.

Executive Director: Dr Nafis Sadik (Pakistan).

The *UN Environment Programme (UNEP)*, established in 1972, works to encourage sustainable development through sound environmental practices everywhere. Its activities cover a wide range of issues, from atmosphere and terrestrial ecosystems to the promotion of environmental science and information which is central to its role. Information networks and monitoring systems established by the UNEP include: the Global Environment Monitoring System (GEMS); Global Resource Information Database (GRID); INFOTERRA, with focal points in 170 countries; and the International Register of Potentially Toxic Chemicals (IRPTC). Its research and synthesis of environmental information has generated a number of *State-of-the-Environment Reports*, and its 1992 Conference (the Earth Summit) in Rio de Janeiro broke new ground in reversing environmental deterioration, with a comprehensive blueprint for action on global sustainable development in the adoption of Agenda 21 by the then largest-ever gathering of world leaders, with more than 100 Heads of State or Government in attendance. At the request of the Earth Summit, a Commission on Sustainable Development was established by the General Assembly to oversee activities to combat problems such as desertification, the global depletion of fish, and issues affecting small islands. The most important funding mechanism towards this end is the Global Environment Facility (GEF) which is managed jointly by UNDP, UNEP and the World Bank.

Executive Director: Elizabeth Dowdeswell (Canada).

Other UN programmes working for development include: the *UN Conference on Trade and Development (UNCTAD)*, which promotes international trade, particularly by developing countries, in an attempt to increase their participation in the global economy; and the *World Food Programme (WFP)*, the world's largest international food aid organization, which is dedicated to both emergency relief and development programmes.

The *UN Centre for Human Settlements (Habitat)*, which assists over 600m. people living in health-threatening housing conditions, was established in 1978. The 58-member UN Commission on Human Settlements (UNCHS), Habitat's governing body, meets every 2 years. The Centre serves as the focal point for human settlements action and the co-ordination of activities within the UN system.

In addition to its regular programmes, the UNDP administers various special-purpose funds, such as the *UN Capital Development Fund (UNCDP)*, a multilateral donor agency working to develop new solutions for poverty reduction in the least developed countries; the *United Nations Volunteers (UNV)* and the *UN Development Fund for Women (UNIFEM)*, whose mission is the empowerment of women and gender equality in all levels of development planning and practice. Its 3 areas of immediate concern are: strengthening women's economic capacity; engendering governance and leadership; and promoting women's rights. Together with the World Bank and UNEP, the UNDP is one of the managing partners of the Global Environment Facility (GEF), a US$2,000m. fund to help countries translate global concerns into national action so as to help fight ozone depletion, global warming, loss of biodiversity and pollution of international waters. The UNDP is also one of six UN sponsors of a global programme on HIV/AIDS.

The United Nations Development Programme has a unique network of 134 country offices. At country level, it is responsible for all UN development activity. The head of each country office acts as Resident Co-ordinator for UNDP.

The *United Nations Drug Control Programme (UDCP)*, established 1991 and headquartered in Vienna, has 22 field offices around the world. UNDCP spearheads international efforts at fighting drug abuse and trafficking. Its annual budget is in the

region of US$70m. At the core of its activities are 3 internationally agreed conventions (treaties) on policy. The Commission on Narcotic Drugs, the body which oversees UNDCP, meets once a year.

Executive Director: Pino Arlacchi (Italy).

The UN work in crime prevention and criminal justice aims to lessen the human and material costs of crime and its impact on socio-economic development. The UN Congress on the Prevention of Crime and Treatment of Offenders has convened every 5 years since 1950 and provides a forum for the presentation of policies and progress. The Ninth Congress (Cairo, 1995) also reviewed practical measures aimed at combating corruption among public officials. The *Commission on Crime Prevention and Criminal Justice*, a functional body of ECOSOC, established 1992, seeks to strengthen UN activities in the field, and meets annually in Vienna. The interregional research and training arm of the UN crime and criminal justice programme is the *United Nations Interregional Crime and Justice Research Institute (UNICRI)* in Rome. An autonomous body, it seeks through action-oriented research to contribute to the formulation of improved policies in crime prevention and control.

Humanitarian assistance to refugees and victims of natural and man-made disasters is also an important function of the UN system. The main refugee organizations within the system are the *Office of the United Nations High Commissioner for Refugees (UNHCR) and the United Nations Relief and Works Agency for Palestine Refugees in the Near East (UNRWA)*.

UNHCR, created in 1951, was charged primarily with resettling 1·2m. European refugees left homeless in the aftermath of the Second World War, and was envisioned as a temporary office with a projected lifespan of 3 years. Today, with more than 27m. people in over 140 countries under its concern, it has become one of the world's principal humanitarian agencies. Headquartered in Geneva, its Executive Committee comprises 53 member states. It has offices in 115 countries, with a 5,000 member staff, and has twice been awarded the Nobel Peace Prize. The High Commissioner is elected by and reports annually to the UN General Assembly through ECOSOC.

The work of UNHCR is humanitarian and non-political. International protection is its primary function. Its main objective is to promote and safeguard the rights and interests of refugees. In so doing UNHCR devotes special attention to promoting a generous policy of asylum on the part of Governments and seeks to improve the legal status of refugees in their country of residence. Crucial to this status is the principle of *non-refoulement*, which prohibits the expulsion from or forcible return of refugees to a country where they may have reason to fear persecution. UNHCR pursues its objectives in the field of protection by encouraging the conclusion of intergovernmental legal instruments in favour of refugees, by supervising the implementation of their provisions and by encouraging Governments to adopt legislation and administrative procedures for the benefit of refugees. UNHCR is often called upon to provide material assistance (i.e. the provision of food, shelter, medical care and essential supplies) while durable solutions are being sought. Durable solutions generally take one of 3 forms: voluntary repatriation, local integration or resettlement in another country.

UNHCR works in tandem with governmental and non-governmental organizations, and within the UN framework its closest partnership is with the World Food Programme. Other partners include UNICEF, WHO, UNDP and the Department of Humanitarian Affairs. The Red Cross (ICRC and IFRC) and the International Organization for Migration are also close allies. Financial institutions such as the World Bank are also likely to increase their involvement with UNHCR in addressing the social and economic conditions underlying many refugee movements. At present, UNHCR is funded almost entirely by voluntary contributions. UNHCR expenditure in 1997 amounted to over US$1,000m.

High Commissioner: Sadako Ogata (Japan).

UNRWA was created by the General Assembly in 1949 as a temporary, non-political agency to provide relief to the nearly 750,000 people who became refugees as a result of the disturbances during and after the creation of the State of Israel in the

former British Mandate territory of Palestine. 'Palestine refugees', as defined by UNRWA's mandate, are persons or descendants of persons whose normal residence was Palestine for at least 2 years prior to the 1948 conflict and who, as a result of the conflict, lost their homes and means of livelihood. UNRWA has also been called upon to help persons displaced by renewed hostilities in the Middle East in 1967. The situation of Palestine refugees in south Lebanon, affected in the aftermath of the 1982 Israeli invasion of Lebanon, was of special concern to the Agency in 1984. Over 2m. refugees are registered with UNRWA. Education and basic healthcare account for over 80% of the Agency's budget, financed by voluntary contributions from Governments. Its mandate is renewed at intervals by the UN General Assembly.

The UN's activities in the field of human rights are the primary responsibility of the *High Commissioner for Human Rights*, a post established in 1993 under the direction and authority of the Secretary-General. The High Commissioner is nominated by the Secretary-General for a 4-year term, renewable once. The principal co-ordinating human rights organ of the UN is the *Commission on Human Rights*, set up by ECOSOC in 1946. It has 53 members elected for 3-year terms, meets for 6 weeks in Geneva each year, and is aided in its task by a Subcommission on Prevention of Discrimination and Protection of Minorities, composed of 26 experts from all over the world. The implementation of international human rights treaties is monitored by 6 committees (also called treaty bodies): the Human Rights Committee; the Committee against Torture; Committee on the Rights of the Child; Committee on Economic, Cultural and Social Rights; Committee on the Elimination of Racial Discrimination; Committee on Elimination of Discrimination against Women.

Training and Research Institutes. There are 6 training and research institutes within the UN, all of them autonomous.

United Nations Institute for Training and Research (UNITAR). Established in 1963 to enhance the effectiveness of the UN in achieving its major objectives. Recently, its focus has shifted to training, with basic research being conducted only if extra-budgetary funds can be made available. Training is provided at various levels for personnel on assignments under the UN, its specialized agencies or related organizations. By 1996, more than 24,000 participants from 180 countries had attended UNITAR courses, seminars or workshops.

Address: Palais des Nations, 1211 Geneva 10, Switzerland.

United Nations Institute for Disarmament Research (UNIDIR). Established by the General Assembly in 1980 to undertake research on disarmament and related problems, particularly international security issues, its programme is reviewed annually subject to approval by its Board of Trustees, and its Director reports to the General Assembly.

Address: Palais des Nations, 1211 Geneva 10, Switzerland.

United Nations Research Institute for Social Development (UNRISD). Established in 1963 to conduct multidisciplinary research into the social dimensions of contemporary problems affecting development, it aims to provide governments, development agencies, grassroots organizations and scholars with a better understanding of how development policies and processes of economic, social and environmental change affect different social groups.

Address: Palais des Nations, 1211 Geneva 10, Switzerland.

United Nations International Research and Training Institute for the Advancement of Women (INSTRAW). Established by ECOSOC and endorsed by the General Assembly in 1976, INSTRAW provides training, conducts research, and collects and disseminates information to stimulate and assist women's advancement and integration into the development progress. Its 11-member Board of Trustees, which reports to ECOSOC, meets annually to review its programme and to formulate the principles and guidelines for INSTRAW's activities.

Address: POB 21747, Santo Domingo, Dominican Republic.

United Nations University (UNU). Sponsored jointly by the UN and UNESCO, UNU is guaranteed academic freedom by a charter approved by the General Assembly in 1973. It is governed by a 28-member Council of scholars and scientists, of whom 24 are appointed by the Secretary-General of the UN and the Director-General of UNESCO. Not traditional in the sense of having students and awarding degrees, it works through networks of collaborating institutions and individuals to undertake multidisciplinary research on problems of human survival, development and welfare; and to strengthen research and training capabilities in developing countries. It also provides postgraduate fellowships to scholars and scientists from developing countries.

Address: 53-70 Jingumae 5-chome, Shibuya-ku, Tokyo 150, Japan.

University for Peace. Founded in 1980 to conduct research on, *inter alia*, disarmament, mediation, the resolution of conflicts, preservation of the environment, international relations, peace education and human rights. The University has a European centre in Belgrade.

Address: POB 138, Ciudad Colon, Costa Rica.

Information. *The UN Statistics Division* in New York provides a wide range of statistical outputs and services for producers and users of statistics worldwide, facilitating national and international policy formulation, implementation and monitoring. It produces printed publications of statistics and statistical methods in the fields of international merchandise trade, national accounts, demography and population, gender, industry, energy, environment, human settlements and disability, as well as general statistics compendiums including the *Statistical Yearbook* and *World Statistics Pocketbook.* Many of its databases are available on CD-ROM, diskette, magnetic tape and the Internet.

Website: http://www.un.org/Depts/unsd.

UN Information Centres. Millbank Tower, 21st Floor, London SW1P 4QH; Public Inquiries Unit, Department of Public Information, Room GA-57, United Nations Plaza, New York, NY 10017.

Website: http://www.un.org.

SPECIALIZED AGENCIES
OF THE UN

The intergovernmental agencies related to the UN by special agreements are separate autonomous organizations which work with the UN and each other through the co-ordinating machinery of the Economic and Social Council. 14 of them are 'Specialized Agencies' within the terms of the UN Charter, and report annually to ECOSOC.

FOOD AND AGRICULTURE ORGANIZATION OF THE UNITED NATIONS (FAO)

Origin. In 1943, the International Conference on Food and Agriculture, at Hot Springs, Virginia, set up an Interim Commission, based in Washington, with a remit to establish an organization. Its Constitution was signed on 16 Oct. 1945 in Quebec City. Today, membership totals 175 countries. The European Union was made a member as a 'regional economic integration organization' in 1991.

Aims and Activities. The aims of FAO are to raise levels of nutrition and standards of living; to improve the production and distribution of all food and agricultural products from farms, forests and fisheries; to improve the living conditions of rural populations; and, by these means, to eliminate hunger. Its priority objectives are to encourage sustainable agriculture and rural development as part of a long-term

strategy for the conservation and management of natural resources; and to ensure the availability of adequate food supplies, by maximizing stability in the flow of supplies and securing access to food by the poor.

In carrying out these aims, FAO promotes investment in agriculture, better soil and water management, improved yields of crops and livestock, agricultural research and the transfer of technology to developing countries; and encourages the conservation of natural resources and rational use of fertilizers and pesticides; the development and sustainable utilization of marine and inland fisheries; the sustainable management of forest resources and the combating of animal disease. Technical assistance is provided in all of these fields, and in nutrition, agricultural engineering, agrarian reform, development communications, remote sensing for climate and vegetation, and the prevention of post-harvest food losses. In addition, FAO works to maintain global biodiversity with the emphasis on the genetic diversity of crop plants and domesticated animals; and plays a major role in the collection, analysis and dissemination of information on agricultural production and commodities. Finally, FAO acts as a neutral forum for the discussion of issues, and advises governments on policy, through the convention of international conferences like the 1996 World Food Summit in Rome.

Special FAO programmes help countries prepare for, and provide relief in the event of, emergency food situations, in particular through the setting up of food reserves. The *Special Programme for Food Security through Food Production in Low-Income Food-Deficit Countries*, launched in 1994, is designed to assist target countries to increase food production and productivity as rapidly as possible, primarily through the widespread adoption by farmers of available improved production technologies, with the emphasis on high-potential areas. FAO provides support for the global co-ordination of the programme and helps attract funds. The *Emergency Prevention System for Transboundary Animal and Plant Pests and Diseases (EMPRES),* established in 1994, strengthens FAO's existing contribution to the prevention, control and eradication of diseases and pests, with locusts and rinderpest among its priorities. *The Global Information and Early Warning System* provides current information on the world food situation and identifies countries threatened by shortages to guide potential donors. The *People's Participation Programme* promotes the involvement of rural people in decision-making, and the policy-making and activities affecting their lives. Together with the UN, FAO sponsors *the World Food Programme (WFP).*

Finance. The budget for the 1998–99 biennium is US$650m. FAO's Regular Programme budget, financed by contributions from member governments, covers the cost of its secretariat and Technical Co-operation Programme (TCP), and part of the costs of several special programmes.

The technical assistance programme is funded by extra-budgetary sources. Its single largest contributor is the UN Development Programme (UNDP), which in 1996 accounted for US$47m., or 19% of field project expenditures. Increasingly important are the trust funds that come from donor countries and international financing institutions, totalling some US$158m., or 65% of technical assistance funds. FAO's contribution under its TCP and Special Programme for Food Security was US$39m., or 16%. Its total field programme expenditure for 1996 was an estimated US$244·1m. In 1996, there were 1,906 field projects in operation: 32% in Africa, 23% in Asia and the Pacific, 11% in Latin America and the Caribbean, 11% in the Near East, 4% in Europe, and 19% interregional or global.

Organization. The FAO Conference, composed of all members, meets every other year to determine policy and approve the FAO's budget and programme. The 49-member Council, elected by the Conference, serves as FAO's governing body between conference sessions. Much of its work is carried out by dozens of regional or specialist commissions, such as the Asia-Pacific Fishery Commission, the European Commission on Agriculture and the Commission on Plant Genetic Resources. The Director-General is elected for a renewable 6-year term.

Headquarters: Viale delle Terme di Caracalla, 00100 Rome, Italy.

Website: http://www.fao.org.
Director-General: Jacques Diouf (Senegal).

Publications. Ceres (bi-monthly) 1968 ff; *Unasylva* (quarterly) 1947 ff; *The State of Food and Agriculture* (annual), 1947 ff.; *Animal Health Yearbook* (annual), 1957 ff.; *Production Yearbook* (annual), 1947 ff.; *Trade Yearbook* (annual), 1947 ff.; *FAO Commodity Review* (annual), 1961 ff.; *Yearbook of Forest Products* (annual), 1947 ff.; *Yearbook of Fishery Statistics* (in two volumes); *FAO Fertilizer Yearbook; FAO Plant Protection Bulletin* (quarterly); *Environment and Energy Bulletin; Food Outlook* (monthly); *The State of World Fisheries and Aquaculture* (annual); *The State of the World's Forests; World Watch List for Domestic Animal Diversity.*

INTERNATIONAL BANK FOR RECONSTRUCTION AND DEVELOPMENT (IBRD) — THE WORLD BANK

Origin. Conceived at the UN Monetary and Financial Conference at Bretton Woods (New Hampshire, USA) in July 1944, the IBRD, frequently called the World Bank, began operations in June 1946, its purpose being to provide funds, policy guidance and technical assistance to facilitate economic development in its poorer member countries. The Group comprises 4 other organizations (see below).

Activities. The Bank obtains its funds from the following sources: capital paid in by member countries; sales of its own securities; sales of parts of its loans; repayments; and net earnings. A resolution of the Board of Governors of 27 April 1988 provides that the paid-in portion of the shares authorized to be subscribed under it will be 3%. The Bank is self-supporting, raising most of its money on the world's financial markets. In the fiscal year ending 30 June 1997, it achieved a net income of US$1,285m ; medium- and long-term borrowing equivalent of US$15,100m. in 18 currencies; average medium to long-term borrowing costs, after swaps, of 5.01%; financial returns on its investment folio of 5%; a reserves-to-loan ratio of 14%; and decline in its net administrative expenditure in real terms to a figure set at $1,177m.

The Bank lends in the region of US$22,000m a year. As of 30 June 1997, it had lent a total of US$106,000m. to member countries. 89% of borrowers took advantage of the new single-currency loans which became available in June 1996 to provide borrowers with the flexibility to select IBRD loan terms that are consistent with their debt-managing strategy and suited to their debt servicing capacity. In order to eliminate wasteful overlapping of development assistance and to ensure that the funds available are used to the best possible effect, the Bank has organized consortia or consultative groups of aid-giving nations for many countries. These include Bangladesh, Belarus, Bolivia, Bulgaria, Egypt, Ethiopia, Jordan, Kazakhstan, Kenya, Kyrgyzstan, Macedonia, Malawi, Mauritania, Moldova, Mozambique, Nicaragua, Pakistan, Peru, Romania, Sierra Leone, Tanzania, the [Palestinian] West Bank and Gaza Strip, Zambia, Zimbabwe and the Caribbean Group for Co-operation in Economic Development.

For the purposes of its analytical and operational work, in 1996 the IBRD characterized economies as follows: low-income (average annual *per capita* GNP of $785 or less); middle-income ($786–9,635); and high-income ($9,636 or more).

A wide variety of technical assistance is at the core of IBRD's activities. It acts as executing agency for a number of pre-investment surveys financed by the UN Development Programme. Resident missions have been established in 64 developing member countries and there are regional offices for East and West Africa, the Baltic States and South-East Asia which assist in the preparation and implementation of projects. The Bank maintains a staff college, the *Economic Development Institute* in Washington, DC, for senior officials of member countries. In 1997, the institute held training workshops on anti-corruption strategies and public integrity in more than 10 countries as part of IBRD's initiative to combat corruption.

The Strategic Compact. Unanimously approved by the Executive Board in March 1997, the Strategic Compact set out a plan for fundamental reform to make the Bank more effective in delivering its regional programme and in achieving its basic mission of reducing poverty. Decentralizing the Bank's relationships with borrower countries is central to the reforms. The effectiveness of devolved country manage-

ment and the bank's promotion of good governance and anti-corruption measures to developing countries are likely to be key policies of the new strategy.

Organization. As of July 1997, the Bank had 180 members, each with voting power in the institution, based on shareholding which in turn is based on a country's economic growth. The president is selected by the Bank's Board of Executive Directors. The Articles of Agreement do not specify the nationality of the president but by custom the US Executive Director makes a nomination, and by a long-standing, informal agreement, the president is a US national (while the managing director of the IMF is European). The initial term is 5 years, with a second of 5 years or less.

European office: 66 avenue d'Iéna, 75116 Paris, France. *London office:* New Zealand House, Haymarket, London SW1Y 4TE, England. *Tokyo office:* Kokusai Building, 1-1, Marunouchi 3-chome, Chiyoda-ku, Tokyo 100, Japan.
Headquarters: 1818 H St., NW, Washington, DC, 20433, USA.
Website: http://www.worldbank.org.
President: James D. Wolfensohn (USA).

Publications. World Bank Annual Report; Summary Proceedings of Annual Meetings; The World Bank and International Finance Company, 1986; *The World Bank Atlas* (annual); *Catalog of Publications,* 1986 ff; *World Development Report* (annual); *World Bank Economic Review* (thrice yearly); *World Bank and the Environment* (annual); *World Bank News* (weekly); *World Bank Research Observer; World Tables* (annual*); Social Indicators of Development* (annual); *ICSID Annual Report; ICSID Review: Foreign Investment Law Journal* (twice yearly); *Research News* (quarterly).

INTERNATIONAL DEVELOPMENT ASSOCIATION (IDA) A lending
agency established in 1960 and administered by the IBRD to provide assistance on concessional terms to the poorest developing countries. Its resources consist of subscriptions and general replenishments from its more industrialized and developed members, special contributions, and transfers from the net earnings of IBRD.

As of 30 June 1997, the IDA had lent a total of US $101,600m. for 2,780 development projects in around 100 countries. 1997, however, saw overall loan commitments for the poorest countries fall by almost a third, to $4,600m., with commitments 15% down on the lower end of its US$5,300-6,600m. planning range for that year. The biggest shortfall has been in lending to Africa.

Officers and staff of the IBRD serve concurrently as officers and staff of the IDA at the World Bank headquarters.

INTERNATIONAL FINANCE CORPORATION (IFC) Established in
July 1956 to help strengthen the private sector in developing countries, through the provision of long-term loans, equity investments, guarantees, standby financing, risk management and quasi-equity instruments such as subordinated loans, preferred stock and income notes. It helps to finance new ventures and assist established enterprises to expand, improve or diversify, and provides a variety of advisory services to public and private sector clients. To be eligible for financing, projects must be profitable for investors, must benefit the economy of the country concerned, and must comply with IFC's environmental guidelines.

About 80% of its funds are borrowed from the international financial markets through public bond issues or private placements, 20% from the IBRD. Its authorized capital is US$2,450m.; paid-in capital at 30 June 1996 was $2,076m. The IFC invested US$6,700m. in project financing in 1997 and approved 276 private-sector projects in around 80 countries. It has 172 members.

Headquarters: 1850 I St., NW, Washington, DC, 20433, USA.
Website: http://www.ifc.org.

Publications. Annual Reports; What IFC Does, 1988; *How to Work with IFC,* 1988; *Emerging Stock Markets Factbook* (annual); *Global Agribusiness Series; Lessons of Experience* (series).

MULTILATERAL INVESTMENT GUARANTEE AGENCY (MIGA)
Established in 1988 to encourage the flow of foreign direct investment to, and among, developing member countries, MIGA is the insurance arm of the World

Bank. It provides investors with investment guarantees against non-commercial risk, such as expropriation and war, and gives advice to governments on improving climate for foreign investment. It may insure up to 90% of an investment, with a current limit of US$50m. per project. As of June 1997, it had issued 293 guarantees for US$3,400m. in coverage. In Jan. 1998, it had 141 member countries. Located at the World Bank headquarters (see above).

INTERNATIONAL CENTRE FOR SETTLEMENT OF INVEST-MENT DISPUTES (ICSID) Founded in 1966 to promote increased flows of international investment by providing facilities for the conciliation and arbitration of disputes between governments and foreign investors. It does not engage in such conciliation or arbitration. This is the task of conciliators and arbitrators appointed by the contracting parties, or as otherwise provided for in the Convention. Recourse to conciliation and arbitration by members is entirely voluntary.

As of 31 Oct. 1997, its Convention had been signed by 143 countries, and 47 cases had been registered by it (3, conciliation; 44, arbitration). 12 arbitrations were pending before the Centre in Jan. 1998. Disputes have involved a variety of investment sectors: agriculture, banking, construction, energy, health, industrial, mining and tourism.

ICSID also undertakes research, publishing and advisory activities in the field of foreign investment law. Like the IDA and MIGA, it is located at the World Bank headquarters in Washington (see above).

Secretary-General: Ibrahim F. I Shihata (Egypt).

Publications. ICSID Annual Report; News from ICSID; ICSID Review: Foreign Investment Law Journal; Investment Laws of the World; Investment Treaties.

Further Reading

Caufield, C., *Masters of Illusion: The World Bank and the Poverty of Nations.* London, 1997
Nelson, P. J., *The World Bank and Non-Government Organizations: The Limits of Apolitical Development.* London, 1995
Salda, A. C. M., *World Bank:* [Bibliography]. Oxford and New Brunswick (NJ), 1993
Wilson, C. R., *The World Bank Group: A Guide to Information Sources.* New York, 1991

INTERNATIONAL CIVIL AVIATION ORGANIZATION (ICAO)

Origin. The Convention providing for the establishment of the ICAO was drawn up by the International Civil Aviation Conference held in Chicago in 1944. A Provisional International Civil Aviation Organization (PICAO) operated for 20 months until the formal establishment of ICAO on 4 April 1947. The Convention on International Civil Aviation superseded the provisions of the Paris Convention of 1919 and the Pan American Convention on Air Navigation of 1928.

Functions. It assists international civil aviation by establishing technical standards for safety and efficiency of air navigation and promoting simpler procedures at borders; develops regional plans for ground facilities and services needed for international flying; disseminates air-transport statistics and prepares studies on aviation economics; fosters the development of air law conventions. As an administrative arm of the UN Development Programme, it provides technical assistance to states in developing civil aviation programmes.

Organization. The principal organs of ICAO are an Assembly, consisting of all members of the Organization, and a Council, which is composed of 33 states elected by the Assembly for 3 years, which meets in virtually continuous session. In electing these states, the Assembly must give adequate representation to: (1) states of major importance in air transport; (2) states which make the largest contribution to the provision of facilities for the international civil air navigation; and (3) those states not otherwise included whose election would ensure that all major geographical areas of the world were represented. The ICAO's main subsidiary bodies are: 15-member Air Navigation Commission appointed by the Council; Committee on Joint Support of

Air Navigation Services; Personnel Committee; the Finance Committee; Committee on Unlawful Interference; Technical Co-operation Committee; Air Transport Committee (all open to Council members); and the Legal Committee, on which all 185 of the Organization's members may be represented. The budget approved for 1998 was US$54·6m.

Headquarters: 999 University St., Montreal, PQ, Canada H3C 5H7.
Secretary-General: Renato Claudio Costa Pereira (Brazil).

Publications. Annual Report of the Council; ICAO Journal (10 yearly; quarterly in Russian); *ICAO Training Manual; Aircraft Accident Digest; Procedures for Air Navigation Services.*

INTERNATIONAL FUND FOR AGRICULTURAL DEVELOPMENT (IFAD)

The idea for an International Fund for Agricultural Development arose at the 1974 World Food Conference. An agreement to establish IFAD entered into force on 30 Nov. 1977, and the agency began its operations the following month. IFAD's purpose is to mobilize additional funds for improved food production and better nutrition among low-income groups in developing countries through projects and programmes directly benefiting the poorest rural populations while preserving their natural resource base. In line with the Fund's focus on the rural poor, its resources are made available in highly concessional loans and grants. By Oct. 1996, the Fund had invested US$4,870m. in financing 461 projects in 110 developing countries.

Organization. The highest body is the Governing Council, on which all 160 member countries are represented. Operations are overseen by an 18-member Executive Board (with 17 alternate members), which is responsible to the Governing Council. The Fund works with many co-operating institutions, including the World Bank, regional development banks and financial agencies, and other UN agencies; many of these co-finance IFAD projects.

Headquarters: 107 Via del Serafico, Rome, 00142, Italy.
President: Fawzi H. Al-Sultan (Kuwait).

Publications. Annual Report; IFAD Update (thrice yearly); *Staff Working Papers* (series); *The State of World Rural Poverty.*

INTERNATIONAL LABOUR ORGANIZATION (ILO)

Origin. The ILO was established in 1919 under the Treaty of Versailles as an autonomous institution associated with the League of Nations. An agreement establishing its relationship with the UN was approved in 1946, making the ILO the first Specialized Agency to be associated with the UN. An intergovernmental agency with a tripartite structure, in which representatives of governments, employers and workers participate, it seeks through international action to improve labour and living conditions, to promote productive employment and social justice for working people everywhere. In 1946 the ILO was recognized by the United Nations as a specialized agency. On its fiftieth anniversary in 1969, it was awarded the Nobel Peace Prize. In 1997, it numbered 174 members.

Functions. One of the ILO's principal functions is the formulation of international standards in the form of International Labour Conventions and Recommendations. Member countries are required to submit Conventions to their competent national authorities with a view to ratification. If a country ratifies a Convention it agrees to bring its laws into line with its terms and to report periodically how these regulations are being applied. More than 6,451 ratifications of 181 Conventions had been deposited by 7 Oct. 1997. Procedures are in place to ascertain whether Conventions thus ratified are effectively applied. Recommendations do not require ratification, but Member States are obliged to consider them with a view to giving effect to their provisions by legislation or other action. By 7 Oct. 1997, the International Labour Conference had adopted 188 Recommendations.

Activities. In addition to its research and advisory activities, the ILO extends technical co-operation to governments under its regular budget and under the UN
Development Programme and Funds-in-Trust in the fields of employment promotion,
human resources development (including vocational and management training),
development of social institutions, small-scale industries, rural development, social
security, industrial safety and hygiene, productivity, etc. Technical co-operation also
includes expert missions and a fellowship programme.

In 1994 the technical services offered by the ILO to its tripartite constituents came
under scrutiny leading to a re-affirmation of technical co-operation as one of the principal means of ILO action. In 1994 the process of implementing the new Active
Partnership Policy made significant progress and the 14 multidisciplinary advisory
teams began to engage ILO constituents in a dialogue centred on the identification of
Country Objectives to form the basis of the ILO's contribution.

The 85th Session of the *International Labour Conference* (Geneva, 2–19 June
1997) was marked by extensive discussions on a set of proposals submitted by the
Director-General, the most far-reaching of which aims to ensure 'universal respect
for fundamental workers' rights in the global economy' through the adoption of a
solemn "Declaration" on the subject. In June, the Governing Body agreed to consider the possibility of including an additional item relating to such a Declaration on the
agenda of its 1998 Conference.

The 1997 ILC also adopted a new Convention on private employment agencies,
with the aim of increasing the efficiency of labour markets and protecting job seekers using their services. This is a revision of the Fee Changing Employment Agencies
Convention of 1949 (No. 96). In addition, a discussion on contract labour opened the
way towards the possible adoption of a Convention and Recommendation on the matter, and the Conference called for the adoption in 1998 of an instrument on general
conditions to stimulate job creation in small and medium-sized enterprises. It noted
that such enterprises generate more than 80% of new jobs in the world today. The delegates also amended Article 19 of the ILO Constitution to facilitate the updating of
international labour standards.

Finance. In 1996, expenditure on operational activities, under all sources of funding,
totalled US$98·2m. The three leading programmes (representing 66% of total expen-
diture) were in employment and training (US$18·6m.), enterprise and co-operative
development (US$23·3m.) and development policies (US$22·8m.). Other programmes dealt with working conditions and environment (US$11·6m.), including an
International Programme for the Elimination of Child Labour (US$8·4m.).

Interregional and global activities accounted for some US$17·8m. In terms of
regional distribution, Africa accounted for over 37% of total expenditure
(US$36·7m.), Asia and the Pacific for 25% (nearly US$25m.), and Latin America and
the Caribbean for 10% (more than US$10m.). Expenditure in Europe decreased from
US$8·8m. in 1995 to US$6m. in 1996; in the Arab States programmes remained
stable at US$2·6m.

The ILO's *International Institute for Labour Studies* promotes the study and discussion of policy issues. The core theme of its activities is the interaction between
labour institutions, development and civil society in a global economy. It identifies
emerging social and labour issues by opening up new areas for research and action;
and encourages systematic dialogue on social policy between the tripartite constituency of the ILO and the international academic community, and other public
opinion-makers. It achieves its mandate through research networks; courses and seminars; social policy forums; internships; visiting scholar and internship programmes;
and publications.

The *International Training Centre* of the ILO, in Turin, was set up in 1965 to lead the
training programmes implemented by the ILO as part of its technical co-operation
activities. Member States and the UN system also call on its resources and experience, and a UN Staff College was established on the Turin Campus in 1996.

Organization. The International Labour Conference is the supreme deliberative organ
of the ILO; it meets annually in Geneva. National delegations are composed of 2 government delegates, 1 employers' delegate and 1 workers' delegate. The Governing

Body, elected by the Conference, is the Executive Council. It is composed of 28 government members, 14 workers' members and 14 employers' members. 10 governments of countries of industrial importance hold permanent seats on the Governing Body. These are: Brazil, China, Germany, France, India, Italy, Japan, Russia, UK and USA. The remaining 18 government members are elected every 3 years. Workers' and employers' representatives are elected as individuals, not as national candidates. The International Labour Office serves as secretariat, operational headquarters, research centre and publishing house. The ILO has regional offices in London (for UK and Republic of Ireland), Abidjan (for Africa), Bangkok (for Asia and the Pacific), Lima (for Latin America and the Caribbean) and Beirut (for Arab States). The ILO budget for 1998–99 is US$481m.

Headquarters: International Labour Office, CH-1211 Geneva 22, Switzerland.
London Office: Vincent House, Vincent Square, London, SW1P 2NB.
Website: http://www.ilo.org.
Director-General: Michel Hansenne (Belgium).
Chairman: Ahmed Ahmed El Amawy (Egypt).

Publications. Regular periodicals in English, French and Spanish include: *International Labour Review; Labour Law Documents; Bulletin of Labour Statistics; Year Book of Labour Statistics; International Labour Documentation; Official Bulletin* and *Labour Education; World of Work Magazine; Yearbook of Labour Statistics* (annual); *World Labour Report* (annual); *World Employment* (annual).

INTERNATIONAL MARITIME ORGANIZATION (IMO)

Origin. The International Maritime Organization (formerly the InterGovernmental Maritime Consultative Organization) was established as a specialized agency of the UN by a convention drafted in 1948 at a UN maritime conference in Geneva. The Convention became effective on 17 March 1958 when it had been ratified by 21 countries, including 7 with at least 1m. gross tons of shipping each. The IMCO started operations in 1959 and changed its name to the IMO in 1982.

Functions. To facilitate co-operation among governments on technical matters affecting merchant shipping, especially concerning safety at sea; to prevent and control marine pollution caused by ships; to facilitate international maritime traffic. The IMO is responsible for convening international maritime conferences and for drafting international maritime conventions. It also provides technical assistance to countries wishing to develop their maritime activities, and acts as a depositary authority for international conventions regulating maritime affairs. *The World Maritime University (WMU)*, at Malmö, Sweden, was established in 1983.

Organization. The IMO had 155 members (and 2 associate members) in 1997. The Assembly, composed of all member states, normally meets every 2 years. The 32-member Council acts as governing body between sessions. There are 4 principal committees (on maritime safety, legal matters, marine environment protection and technical co-operation), which submit reports or recommendations to the Assembly through the Council, and a Secretariat. The budget for 1996–97 amounted to £36·6m.

Headquarters: 4 Albert Embankment, London SE1 7SR, UK.
Secretary-General: William A. O'Neil (Canada).

Publications. IMO News.

INTERNATIONAL MONETARY FUND (IMF)

The International Monetary Fund was established on 27 Dec. 1945 as an independent international organization and began financial operations on 1 March 1947; its relationship with the UN is defined in an agreement of mutual co-operation which came into force on 15 Nov. 1947. The first amendment to the IMF's articles creating the special drawing right (SDR) took effect on 28 July 1969. The second amendment took effect on 1 April 1978. The third amendment came into force on 11 Nov. 1992; it allows for the suspension of voting and related rights of a member which persists in its failure to settle its outstanding obligations to the IMF.

Aims. To promote international monetary co-operation, the expansion of international trade and exchange rate stability; to assist in the removal of exchange restrictions and the establishment of a multilateral system of payments; and to alleviate any serious disequilibrium in members' international balance of payments by making the financial resources of the IMF available to them, usually subject to economic policy conditions to ensure the revolving nature of IMF resources.

Activities. Each member of the IMF undertakes a broad obligation to collaborate with the IMF and other members to ensure orderly exchange arrangements and to promote a system of stable exchange rates. In addition, members are subject to certain obligations relating to domestic and external policies that can affect the balance of payments and the exchange rate. The IMF makes its resources available, under proper safeguards, to its members to meet short-term or medium-term payment difficulties. The first allocation of SDRs was made on 1 Jan. 1970 with five SDR allocations since then. SDRs in existence now total SDR 21,400m.

To enhance its balance of payments assistance to its members, the IMF established a compensatory financing facility on 27 Feb. 1963; temporary oil facilities in 1974 and 1975; a trust fund in 1976; and an extended facility for medium-term assistance to members with special balance of payments problems on 13 Sept. 1974. In Mar. 1986, it established the structural adjustment facility (SAF) to provide assistance to low-income countries. In Dec. 1987, it established the enhanced structural adjustment facility (ESAF) to provide further assistance to low-income countries facing high levels of indebtedness. In Aug. 1988, the compensatory and contingency financing facility was established, succeeding the compensatory financing facility. The new facility provides broader protection to members pursuing IMF-supported adjustment programmes. Because of the importance of continuing concessional ESAF support, the IMF in 1996 endorsed proposals for a continuation of ESAF operations beyond the year 2000, when current ESAF resources are expected to be fully committed. There is to be an interim period of operations from 2001–2004 for which new financing would be mobilized. This would be followed in 2005, or earlier, by a self-sustained ESAF.

Capital Resources. In April 1997, the Interim Committee of the Fund's Board of Governors endorsed the concept of an amendment that would make the promotion of capital account liberalization one of the Fund's purposes and would give the Fund the appropriate jurisdiction over capital movements. The capital resources of the IMF comprise SDRs and currencies that the members pay under quotas calculated for them when they join the IMF. Members' quotas are linked to their drawing rights on the IMF under both regular and special facilities, their voting power, and their share of SDR allocations. Every IMF member is required to subscribe to the IMF an amount equal to its quota. An amount not exceeding 25% of the quota has to be paid in reserve assets, the balance in the member's own currency. The members with the largest quotas are: 1st, the USA; joint 2nd, Germany and Japan; joint 4th, France and the UK.

An increase of almost 60% in IMF quotas became effective in Nov. 1992 as a result of the 9th General Review of Quotas. Quotas were not increased under the 10th General Review. The total of members' quotas in Sept. 1997 was SDR 145,300m. In the 11th General Review, the IMF's Executive Board adopted a resolution at its 1997 annual meeting, approving a one-time equity allocation of SDRs of SDR 21,400m., which would equalize all members' ratio of SDRs to quota at 29·3%. The Board also agreed to recommend a 45% increase in IMF quotas, which would raise total quotas to SDR 209,500m.

Borrowing Resources. The IMF is authorized under its Articles of Agreement to supplement its resources by borrowing. In Jan. 1962, a 4-year agreement was concluded with 10 industrial members (Belgium, Canada, France, Germany, Italy, Japan, Netherlands, Sweden, UK, USA) who undertook to lend the IMF up to US$6,000m. in their own currencies, if this should be needed to forestall or cope with an impairment of the international monetary system. Switzerland subsequently joined the group. These arrangements, known as the General Arrangements to Borrow (GAB), have been extended several times. In early 1983, agreement was reached to increase

the credit arrangements under the GAB to SDR 17,000m.; to permit use of GAB resources in transactions with IMF members that are not GAB participants; to authorize Swiss participation; and to permit borrowing arrangements with non-participating members to be associated with the GAB. Saudi Arabia and the IMF have entered into such an arrangement under which the IMF will be able to borrow up to SDR 1,500m. to assist in financing purchases by any member for the same purpose and under the same circumstances as in the GAB. The changes became effective by 26 Dec. 1983. In view of the expected continuing high demand for IMF's resources, a doubling of borrowed resources under the GAB to SDR 34,000m. was endorsed through the development of New Arrangements to Borrow in 1996.

In order to oversee the compliance of members with their obligations under the Articles of Agreement, the IMF is required to exercise firm surveillance over their exchange rate policies. In conjunction with the need for up-to-date reliable data to support its surveillance activities, it encourages member countries to make available to the public and to financial markets core financial and economic data.

The IMF works with the IBRD (World Bank) to address the problems of the 41 most heavily indebted poor countries (33 in Sub-Saharan Africa) through their Initiative for the Heavily Indebted Poor Countries (HIPCs). It is designed to ensure that HIPCs with a sound track record of economic adjustment can attain a sustainable debt situation over the medium term.

Organization. The highest authority is the Board of Governors on which each member government is represented. Normally the Governors meet once a year, and may take votes by mail or other means between meetings. The Board of Governors has delegated many of its powers to the 24 executive directors in Washington, who are appointed or elected by individual member countries or groups of countries. Each appointed director has voting power proportionate to the quota of the government he or she represents, while each elected director casts all the votes of the countries represented. The managing director is selected by the executive directors and serves as chairman of the Executive Board, but may not vote except in case of a tie. The term of office is for 5 years, but may be extended or terminated at the discretion of the executive directors. The managing director is responsible for the ordinary business of the IMF, under the direction of the executive directors, and supervises a staff of about 2,200. Under a long-standing, informal agreement, the managing director is European (while the President of the World Bank is a US national). There are 3 deputy managing directors. In Jan. 1998, the IMF had 181 members.

The *IMF Institute* is a specialized department of the IMF providing training in macroeconomic analysis and policy, and related subjects for officials of member countries, at the Fund's headquarters in Washington and at the Joint Vienna Institute (JVI). Since its establishment in 1964, the Institute has trained more than 10,900 officials from 181 countries. Courses in Washington are in Arabic, English, French and Spanish; at the JVI, in English, with Russian interpretation.

Headquarters: 700 19th St. NW, Washington, D.C., 20431. Offices in Paris and Geneva.

*Website:*http://www.imf.org.

Managing Director: Michel Camdessus (France).

Publications. Annual Report; International Financial Statistics (monthly); *IMF Survey* (2 a month); *Balance of Payments Statistics Yearbook*; *Staff Papers* (4 a year); *IMF Economic Reviews* [of the economies of member countries]; *Direction of Trade Statistics* (quarterly); *Government Finance Statistics Yearbook; World Economic Outlook* (2 a year); *The International Monetary Fund, 1945-65: Twenty Years of International Monetary Co-operation*, 3 vols. Washington, 1969; de Vries, M. G., *The International Monetary Fund, 1966–1971: The System Under Stress*, 2 vols. Washington, 1976; *The International Monetary Fund 1972–1978: Co-operation on Trial*. 3 vols. Washington, 1985.

Further Reading

Humphreys, N. K., *Historical Dictionary of the International Monetary Fund*. Metuchen (NJ), 1994

James, H., *International Monetary Cooperation since Bretton Woods*. OUP, 1996

Salda, A. C. M., *The International Monetary Fund*. [Bibliography) Oxford and New Brunswick (NJ), 1993

INTERNATIONAL TELECOMMUNICATION UNION (ITU)

Origin. Formed from the merger, in 1932, of the Telegraph Convention (1865) and the Radiotelegraph Convention (1906) under the new name of the International Telecommunication Union, the ITU became a Specialized Agency of the UN in 1947 and is governed by a new Constitution and Convention which came into force on 1 July 1994.

Functions. To maintain and extend international co-operation for the improvement and rational use of telecommunications of all kinds, and promote and offer technical assistance to developing countries in the field of telecommunications; to promote the development of technical facilities and their most efficient operation to improve the efficiency of telecommunication services, increasing their usefulness and making them, so far as possible, generally available to the public; to harmonize the actions of nations in the attainment of these ends.

Organization. The supreme organ of the ITU is the Plenipotentiary Conference, which normally meets every 4 years. A 46-member Council, elected by the Conference, meets annually in Geneva and is responsible for ensuring the co-ordination of the 4 permanent organs at ITU headquarters: the General Secretariat; Radiocommunication Sector; Telecommunication Standardization Sector; and Telecommunication Development Sector. The Secretary-General is also elected by the Conference. ITU has 187 member countries; a further 363 scientific and technical companies, public and private operators, broadcasters and other organizations are also ITU members.

Headquarters: Place des Nations, CH-1211 Geneva 20, Switzerland.
*Website:*http://www.itu.ch
Secretary-General: Dr Pekka Tarjanne (Finland).

UNITED NATIONS EDUCATIONAL, SCIENTIFIC AND CULTURAL ORGANIZATION (UNESCO)

Origin. UNESCO's Constitution was signed in London on 16 Nov. 1945 by 37 countries and the Organization came into being in Nov. 1946 on the premise that: "Since wars begin in the minds of men, it is in the minds of men that the defences of peace must be constructed". In Jan. 1998, UNESCO had 187 members including the UK, which rejoined in 1997. They include 4 Associate Members with no single member status in the UN (Aruba; British Virgin Islands; Macau; Netherlands Antilles). The USA is not a member.

Aims and Activities. UNESCO's primary objective is to contribute to peace and security in the world by promoting collaboration among the nations through education, science, communication and culture in order to further universal respect for justice, the rule of the law, human rights and fundamental freedoms, affirmed for all peoples of the world by the UN Charter.

Education. Various activities support and foster national projects to renovate education systems and develop alternative educational strategies towards a goal of lifelong education for all. The 4 main areas of focus, today, are: to provide basic education for all; expand access to basic education; improve the quality of basic education; and education for the 21st century. There are regional and sub-regional offices for education in 53 countries.

Science. UNESCO seeks to promote international scientific co-operation and encourages scientific research designed to improve living conditions. Science co-operation offices have been set up in Cairo, Jakarta, Nairobi, New Delhi, Montevideo and Venice. A *Sciences in the Service of Development* programme aims to provide support to member states in the fields of higher education, advanced training and

research in natural and social sciences, and in the application of these sciences to development. It focuses on questions concerning issues such as peace, human rights, youth, the management of social transformations, the human genome, and man and the biosphere.

Communication. Here, activities are geared to promoting the free flow of information, freedom of expression, press freedom, media independence and pluralism. In this way, UNESCO endeavours, by disseminating information, carrying out research and providing advice to increase the scope and quality of press, film and radio services throughout the world.

Culture. In the cultural field, UNESCO's focus areas are research on the link between culture and development, and action to conserve and protect the world's cultural inheritance, by assisting member states in studying and preserving both the physical and the non-physical heritage of their societies.

Organization. The General Conference, composed of representatives from each member state, meets biennially to decide policy, programme and budget. A 58-member Executive Board elected by the Conference meets twice a year and there is a Secretariat. In addition, national commissions act as liaison groups between UNESCO and the educational, scientific and cultural life of their own countries. The budget for 1996–97 was over US$455m.

Headquarters: UNESCO House, 7 Place de Fontenoy, 75352 Paris, France.
Website: http://www. unesco.org.
Director-General: Federico Mayor (Spain).

Periodicals. Museum International (quarterly); *International Social Science Journal* (quarterly); *Impact of Science on Society* (quarterly); *Unesco Courier* (monthly); *Prospects* (quarterly); *Copyright Bulletin* (twice-yearly,); *Nature and Resources* (quarterly); *Unesco Sources* (monthly); *World Education Report* (biennial); *World Science Report* (biennial).

UNITED NATIONS INDUSTRIAL DEVELOPMENT ORGANIZATION (UNIDO)

Origin. UNIDO became an autonomous organization within the UN Secretariat in 1966, superseding the Centre for Industrial Development which had been operating since 1961. Its General Conference in 1975 recommended its conversion to a UN Specialized Agency, and this was achieved in 1986.

Aims. UNIDO is dedicated to promoting sustainable industrial development in countries with developing and transition economies. It harnesses the joint forces of government and the private sector to foster competitive industrial production and raise capacity; to develop international industrial partnerships and provide technical cooperation services; and to promote socially equitable and environmentally friendly industrial development. UNIDO's ultimate goal is to create a better life for people by laying the industrial foundations for long-term prosperity and economic strength.

Activities. The 1993 General Conference approved a recommendation for the reform and revitalization of the Organization. The reform process concentrated on the re-orientation of UNIDO's activities to adjust to the economic environment of the 1990s, and was completed in Dec. 1995.

In June 1997, reform was back on the agenda when the Industrial Development Board met in Vienna to consider ways of reforming the Organization.

In Dec. 1997, the 7th session of the General Conference adopted the *Business Plan for the Future Role and Functions of UNIDO*, which defines future programmes and activities of the Organization. The Conference also approved the regular budget for the biennium 1998–99, reflecting the new programme priorities.

Organization. The General Conference meets every 2 years to determine policy and approve the budget. It consists of representatives of all member states. The 53-member governing body (33 members from developing countries) is the Industrial Development Board, elected for 4 years by the General Conference. The General

Conference also elects a 27-member Programme and Budget Committee for 2-year terms of office, and appoints a Director-General for 4 years.

In early 1998, a restructuring of the Organization, and precise definition of its products, services and programmes, will come into place under the new Director-General.

In March 1998, UNIDO had 168 members. The USA withdrew from the Organization at the end of 1996. Australia gave notice of its intent to withdraw at the end of 1997.

The budget for 1996-97 was US$210m. ($181m. from members' contributions, $29m. from reimbursement of technical co-operation support costs).

In 1997 the total value of technical co-operation activities was US$97·3m. The value of contracts awarded was US$37·5m.; orders for equipment came to US$19·7m., and training and other costs amounted to US$10·3m. IN 1997 new projects worth a total of almost US$93m. were approved.

Headquarters: POB 300, A-1400 Vienna, Austria.
Website: http://www.unido.org.
Director-General: Carlos Alfredo Magarinos.

Publications. Annual Report; Environmental Technology Monitor (quarterly), *Industrial Development Global Report* (annual); *International Yearbook of Industrial Statistics; UNIDO Links* (monthly); *UNIDO Matters* (bi-monthly).

UNIVERSAL POSTAL UNION (UPU)

Origin. The UPU was established in 1875, when the Universal Postal Convention adopted by the Postal Congress of Berne on 9 Oct. 1874 came into force. It has 189 member countries.

Functions. The aim of the UPU is to assure the organization and perfection of the various postal services, and to promote the development of international collaboration in the field. To this end, UPU members are united in a single postal territory for the reciprocal exchange of correspondence. A Specialized Agency of the UN since 1948, the UPU is governed by its Constitution, adopted in 1964 (Vienna), and subsequent protocol amendments: (1969, Tokyo; 1974, Lausanne; 1984, Hamburg; 1989, Washington; 1994, Seoul).

Organization. It is composed of a Universal Postal Congress which meets every 5 years; a 41-member Council of Administration, which meets annually and is responsible for supervising the affairs of the UPU between Congresses; a 40-member Postal Operations Council; and an International Bureau which functions as the permanent secretariat, responsible for strategic planning and programme budgeting. The budget for 1998 is 35·7m. Swiss francs.

Headquarters: Weltpoststrasse 4, 3000 Berne 15, Switzerland.
Website: http://ibis.ib.upu.org.
Director-General: Thomas E. Leavey (USA).

Publications. The UPU Looks to the Future: Seoul Postal Strategy, 1994; *Postal Statistics* (annual*); *UPU Annual Report; Union Postale* (quarterly); *Universal Postal List of Localities,* 1997 (also on CD-ROM); *Post 2005: Core Business Scenarios,* 1997.

WORLD HEALTH ORGANIZATION (WHO)

Origin. An International Conference convened by the UN Economic and Social Council to consider a single health organization resulted in the adoption on 22 July 1946 of the Constitution of the World Health Organization, which came into force on 7 April 1948.

Functions. WHO's objective, as stated in the first article of the Constitution, is 'the attainment by all peoples of the highest possible level of health'. As the directing and co-ordinating authority on international health, it establishes and maintains collaboration with the UN, specialized agencies, government health administrations, professional and other groups concerned with health. The Constitution also directs WHO to assist governments to strengthen their health services; to stimulate and advance work to eradicate diseases; to promote maternal and child health, mental health, medical research and the prevention of accidents; to improve standards of teaching and training in the health professions, and of nutrition, housing, sanitation, working conditions and other aspects of environmental health. The Organization is also empowered to propose conventions, agreements and regulations, and make recommendations about international health matters; to revise the international nomenclature of diseases, causes of death and public health practices; to develop, establish and promote international standards concerning foods, biological, pharmaceutical and similar substances.

Methods of work. Co-operation in country projects is undertaken only on the request of the government concerned, through the 6 regional offices of the Organization. Worldwide technical services are made available by headquarters. Expert committees, chosen from the 55 advisory panels of experts, meet to advise the Director-General on a given subject. Scientific groups and consultative meetings are called for similar purposes. To further the education of health personnel of all categories, seminars, technical conferences and training courses are organized, and advisors, consultants and lecturers are provided. WHO awards fellowships for study to nationals of member countries.

Activities. The main thrust of WHO's activities in recent years has been towards promoting national, regional and global strategies for the attainment of the main social target of the Member States for the coming years: 'Health for All by the Year 2000', or the attainment by all citizens of the world of a level of health that will permit them to lead a socially and economically productive life. Almost all countries indicated a high level of political commitment to this goal; and guiding principles for formulating corresponding strategies and plans of action were subsequently prepared.

The 50th World Health Assembly which met in 1997 adopted numerous resolutions on public health issues. *The World Health Report, 1997: Conquering suffering, enriching humanity* focused on 'non-communicable diseases'. It warned that the human and social costs of cancer, heart disease and other chronic diseases will rise unless confronted now.

The number of cancer cases is expected to double in most countries over the next 25 years. There will be a 33% increase in lung cancers in women and a 40% increase in prostate cancers in men in European Union countries alone by 2005. The incidence of other cancers is also rising rapidly, especially in developing countries. Heart disease and stroke, the leading causes of death in richer nations, will become more common in poorer countries. Globally, diabetes will more than double by 2025, with the number of people affected rising from about 135m. to 300m, and there is likely to be a huge rise in some mental disorders, especially dementias and particularly Alzheimer's disease. Already an estimated 29m. people suffer from dementia, and at least 400m. suffer from other mental disorders ranging from mood and personality disorders to neurological conditions like epilepsy, which affects some 40m. worldwide.

These projected increases are reported to be due to a combination of factors, not least population ageing and the rising prevalence of unhealthy lifestyles. Average life expectancy at birth globally reached 65 years in 1996. It is now well over 70 years in many countries and is approaching 80 years in some. There are today an estimated 380m. people over 65 years or more. By 2020 that number is expected to rise to more than 690m.

The report warns that many countries will increasingly come under the double burden of both infectious (the focus of the 1996 World Health Report) and non-communicable diseases, and recommends that the 2 should be fought simultaneously on a global scale.

The 10 leading killer diseases in the world today are: coronary heart disease, 7·2m. deaths; cancer (all sites), 6·3m; cerebrovascular disease, 4·6m; acute lower respiratory infection, 3·9m; tuberculosis, 3m; chronic obstructive pulmonary disease, 2·9m; diarrhoea and dysentery, 2·5m; malaria, 2·1m; HIV/AIDS, 1·5m; hepatitis B, 1·2m. Tobacco-related deaths, primarily from lung cancer and circulatory disease, amount to 3m. a year, 6% of total deaths. Smoking accounts for 1 in 7 cancer cases worldwide, and if the trend of increasing consumption in many countries continues, the epidemic has many more decades to run.

In response, WHO has called for an intensified and sustained global campaign to encourage healthy lifestyles and attack the main risk factors responsible for many of these diseases: unhealthy diet, inadequate physical activity, smoking and obesity.

Priorities for Action. These were summarized by the Report as follows:
1. Integration of disease-specific interventions in both physical and mental health into a comprehensive chronic disease control package that incorporates prevention, diagnosis, treatment and rehabilitation, and improved training of health professionals.
2. Fuller application of existing cost-effective methods of disease detection and management, including improved screening, taking into account the genetic diversity of individuals.
3. A major intensified but sustained global campaign to encourage healthy lifestyles, with an emphasis on the health development of children and adolescents in relation to risk factors such as diet, exercise and smoking.
4. Healthy public policies, including sustainable funding, and legislation on pricing and taxation, in support of disease prevention programmes.
5. Acceleration of research into new drugs and vaccines, and into the genetic determinants of chronic diseases.
6. Alleviation of pain, reduction of suffering and provision of palliative care for those who cannot be cured.

Other issues reported on to the Assembly included tropical diseases, violence, the sale of medical products through the Internet, persistent organic pollutants and cloning in human reproduction.

Cloning in human reproduction. The 1997 Assembly adopted a resolution affirming that the use of cloning for the replication of human individuals is ethically unacceptable and contrary to human integrity and morality. In accepting the resolution delegates recognized the need to respect the freedom of ethically acceptable scientific activity and to ensure access to the benefits of its applications.

Joint UN Programme on HIV/AIDS (UNAIDS). In 1996 the Assembly reviewed implementation of the global strategy for the prevention and control of AIDS, and progress of the Joint UN Programme on HIV/AIDS (UNAIDS), which became operational in 1996. The impact of the HIV/AIDS epidemic is seen to be expanding and intensifying, particularly in developing countries, and new resource mobilization mechanisms were called for to support countries in combating HIV/AIDS. The Assembly requested WHO to facilitate the incorporation of UNAIDS-specific policies, norms and strategies into the activities of WHO at global, regional and country levels, and to collaborate in all aspects of resource mobilization for HIV/AIDS activities.

World Health Day is observed on 7 April every year. The theme chosen for 1997 World Health Day was Emerging Infectious Diseases. The theme for 1998 is Safe Motherhood. World No-Tobacco Day is held on 31 May each year; International Day Against Drug Abuse on 26 June; World AIDS Day on 1 Dec.

Organization. The principal organs of WHO are the World Health Assembly, the Executive Board and the Secretariat. Each of the 192 member states has the right to be represented at the Assembly, which meets annually in Geneva. The 32-member Executive Board is composed of technically qualified health experts designated by as many member states as elected by the Assembly. The Secretariat consists of technical and administrative staff headed by a Director-General, who is appointed for not more than two 5-year terms. Health activities in member countries are carried out through regional organizations which have been established in Africa (Brazzaville), South-East Asia (New Delhi), Europe (Copenhagen), Eastern Mediterranean (Alexandria) and Western Pacific (Manila). The Pan American Sanitary Bureau in Washington serves as the regional office of WHO for the Americas.

Finance. The global programme budget for 1998-99 adopted by the World Health Assembly in May 1997 was US$842·7m.

Headquarters: Avenue Appia, CH-1211 Geneva 27, Switzerland.
Website: http://www.who.ch.
Director-General: Dr Hiroshi Nakajima (Japan).

Publications. Annual Report on World Health; World Health Forum (quarterly); *Bulletin of WHO* (6 issues a year); *International Digest of Health Legislation* (quarterly); *World Health.* (6 issues a year); *Health and Safety Guides; International Statistical Classification of Diseases and Related Health Problems; WHO Technical Report Series; WHO AIDS Series; Public Health Papers; World Health Statistics Annual; World Health Statistics Quarterly* (monthly); *Weekly Epidemiological Record; WHO Drug Information* (quarterly).

WORLD INTELLECTUAL PROPERTY ORGANIZATION (WIPO)

Origin. The Convention establishing WIPO was signed at Stockholm in 1967 by 51 countries, and entered into force in April 1970. In 1974, WIPO became a specialized agency of the UN. WIPO took over the functions of the United International Bureaux for the Protection of Intellectual Property (BIRPI), established in 1893 to administer the affairs of the 2 principal international intellectual property treaties then in existence: the Paris Convention for the Protection of Industrial Property (1883) and the Berne Convention for the Protection of Literary and Artistic Works (1886).

Functions. WIPO is responsible for the promotion of the protection of intellectual property throughout the world through co-operation among states. Intellectual property comprises two main branches: industrial property (inventions, trademarks and industrial designs) and copyright and neighbouring rights (literary, musical, artistic, photographic and audiovisual works).

Activities. WIPO administers various international treaties or unions, of which the most important are the Paris (for industrial property) and Berne (for the protection of literary and artistic works) unions. In 1996, 2 new international treaties were concluded in Geneva. These were the WIPO Copyright Treaty (WCT) and the WIPO Performances and Phonograms Treaty (WPPT). WIPO's work to promote the protection of intellectual property includes a substantial programme of development co-operation for the benefit of developing countries.

As regards standard-setting, WIPO prepares new treaties concerning the protection of intellectual property and undertakes the revision of existing ones. It carries out studies on issues in the field of intellectual property that could be the subject of model laws or guidelines for implementation at the national or international levels, and maintains international registration services (patents, trademarks, industrial designs, appellations of origin and audiovisual works).

Organization. WIPO has 3 governing bodies: the General Assembly, the Conference and the Co-ordination Committee. Each treaty administered by WIPO has one or more Governing Bodies of its own, composed of representatives of the respective member states. In addition, the Paris and Berne Unions have Assemblies and Executive Committees. There are also a number of Permanent Committees, such as the Permanent Committee on Industrial Property Information. The executive head of WIPO is the Director-General, who is elected by the General Assembly. As at 10 Dec. 1997, WIPO had 166 member states, with an international staff of around 650. The budget for 1996–97 was Sw. Fr. 300m, 85% of which is covered by revenue earned by the Organization's international registration and publication activities, with the other 15% coming primarily from contributions made by member states.

Official languages. Arabic, Chinese, English, French, Russian and Spanish.
Headquarters: 34, chemin des Colombettes, 1211 Geneva 20, Switzerland.
Website: http://www.wipo.int.
Director-General: Dr Kamil Idris (Sudan).

Periodicals. Industrial Property and Copyright (monthly, bi-monthly, in Spanish); *PCT Gazette* (weekly); *PCT Newsletter* (monthly); *International Designs Bulletin* (monthly); *WIPO Gazette of International Marks* (fortnightly); *Intellectual Property in Asia and the Pacific* (quarterly).

WORLD METEOROLOGICAL ORGANIZATION (WMO)

Origin. A 1947 (Washington) Conference of Directors of the International Meteorological Organization (est. 1873) adopted a Convention creating the World Meteorological Organization. The WMO Convention became effective on 23 March 1950 and WMO was formally established on 19 March 1951, when the first session of its Congress was convened in Paris. It was recognized as a Specialized Agency of the UN in 1951.

Functions. (1) To facilitate worldwide co-operation in the establishment of networks of stations for the making of meteorological observations as well as hydrological or other geophysical observations related to meteorology, and to promote the establishment and maintenance of meteorological centres charged with the provision of meteorological and related services; (2) to promote the establishment and maintenance of systems for the rapid exchange of meteorological and related information; (3) to promote standardization of meteorological and related observations and ensure the uniform publication of observations and statistics; (4) to further the application of meteorology to aviation, shipping, water problems, agriculture and other human activities; (5) to promote activities in operational hydrology and to further close co-operation between meteorological and hydrological services; and (6) to encourage research and training in meteorology and, as appropriate, to assist in co-ordinating the international aspects of such research and training.

Organization. WMO has 179 member states and 6 member territories responsible for the operation of their own meteorological services. Congress, which is its supreme body, meets every 4 years to approve policy, programme and budget, and adopt regulations. The Executive Council meets at least once a year to prepare studies and recommendations for Congress, and supervises the implementation of Congress resolutions and regulations. It has 36 members, comprising the President and 3 Vice-Presidents, as well as the Presidents of the 6 Regional Associations (Africa, Asia, South America, North and Central America, South-West Pacific, Europe), whose task is to co-ordinate meteorological activity within their regions, and 26 members elected in their personal capacity. There are 8 Technical Commissions composed of experts nominated by members of WMO, whose remit includes the following areas: basic systems, climatology, instruments and methods of observation, atmospheric sciences, aeronautical meteorology, agricultural meteorology, hydrology, marine meteorology. A permanent Secretariat is maintained in Geneva, and there are 3 regional offices for Africa, Asia and the Pacific, and the Americas. The budget for 1996–99 is 255m. Swiss francs.

Headquarters: Casa Postale 2300, CH-1211, Geneva 2, Switzerland.
Secretary-General: Prof. G. O. P. Obasi (Nigeria).

Publications. WMO Bulletin. (quarterly); *WMO Annual Report.*

OTHER ORGANS RELATED TO THE UN

INTERNATIONAL ATOMIC ENERGY AGENCY (IAEA)

Origin. An intergovernmental agency, the IAEA was established in 1957 under the aegis of the UN and reports annually to the General Assembly. Its Statute was approved on 26 Oct. 1956 at a conference at UN Headquarters.

Functions. To accelerate and enlarge the contribution of atomic energy to peace, health and prosperity throughout the world; and to ensure that assistance provided by it or at its request or under its supervision or control is not used in such a way as to further any military purpose. In addition, under the terms of the Non-Proliferation Treaty, the Treaty of Tlatelolco, the Treaty of Rarotonga, the Pelindaba Treaty and the

Bangkok Treaty, to verify states' obligation to prevent diversion of nuclear fissionable material from peaceful uses to nuclear weapons or other nuclear explosive devices.

Activities. The IAEA gives advice and technical assistance to developing countries on nuclear power development, nuclear safety, radioactive waste management, legal aspects of atomic energy use, and prospecting for and exploiting nuclear raw materials. In addition, it promotes the use of radiation and isotopes in agriculture, industry, medicine and hydrology through expert services, training courses and fellowships, grants of equipment and supplies, research contracts, scientific meetings and publications. During 1997 there were over 1,000 operational projects for technical co-operation. These activities involved 3,610 expert assignments while 1,718 persons received training abroad.

Safeguards are the technical means applied by the IAEA to verify that nuclear equipment or materials are used exclusively for peaceful purposes. IAEA safeguards cover more than 95% of civilian nuclear installations outside the 5 nuclear-weapon states (China, France, Russia, UK and USA). These 5 nuclear-weapon states have concluded agreements with the Agency which permit the application of IAEA safeguards to all their nuclear activities. Installations in non-nuclear-weapon states under safeguards or containing safeguarded material at 1 Jan. 1997 were 229 power reactors, 176 research reactors and critical assemblies, 13 conversion plants, 42 fuel fabrication plants, 6 reprocessing plants, 11 enrichment plants, and 461 other installations. In 1995, 2,285 inspections were conducted under the safeguard agreements at 884 nuclear installations in 63 non-nuclear-weapon states, and 3,805 samples of uranium and plutonium were analysed. By Jan. 1997 a total of 214 safeguard agreements were in force with 131 states. A programme designed to prevent and combat illicit trafficking of nuclear weapons came into force in April 1996.

Organization. The Statute provides for an annual General Conference, a 35-member Board of Governors and a Secretariat headed by a Director-General. The IAEA had 127 member states in Jan. 1998.

There are also research laboratories in Austria and Monaco. *The International Centre for Theoretical Physics* was established in Trieste, in 1964, and is operated jointly by UNESCO and the IAEA.

Headquarters: Vienna International Centre, PO Box 100, A-1400 Vienna, Austria.
Website: http://www.iaea.or.at/worldatom.
Director-General: Mohamed El Baradei (Egypt).

Publications. Annual Report; IAEA Bulletin (quarterly); *IAEA Newsbriefs* (bi-monthly); *IAEA Yearbook; INIS Atomindex* (twice monthly); *INIS Reference Series; Legal Series; Nuclear Fusion* (monthly); *Nuclear Safety Review* (annual); *Technical Directories; Technical Reports Series.*

INTERNATIONAL SEABED AUTHORITY (ISA)

The Authority was to be established one year after the UN Convention on the Law of the Sea (UNCLOS), adopted in 1982, had been ratified by 60 countries. The final ratification was received on 16 Nov. 1993. On 16 Nov. 1994, the Convention came into force; and the ISA was established in Kingston, Jamaica, to function as an autonomous international organization in relationship with the UN. Following its initial financing from the UN budget, its administrative expenses were to be met by assessed contributions from its members.

The Convention on the Law of the Sea covers almost all ocean space and its uses: navigation and overflight, resource exploration and exploitation, conservation and pollution, fishing and shipping. It entitles coastal states and inhabited islands to proclaim a 200-mile exclusive economic zone or continental shelf (which may be larger). Its 320 Articles and 9 Annexes constitute a guide for behaviour by states in the world's oceans, defining maritime zones, laying down rules for drawing sea boundaries, assigning legal rights, duties and responsibilities to States, and providing machinery for the settlement of disputes.

The *International Tribunal for the Law of the Sea (ITLOS)*, founded in Oct. 1996 and based in Hamburg, adjudicates on disputes with respect to ISA's activities. It comprises 21 judges elected by signatories from 5 world regional blocs: 5 each from Africa and Asia; 4 from Western Europe and North America; 4 from Latin America; and 3 from Eastern Europe. Judges serve for 9 years, but 7 of the inaugural judges will serve for 3 years only and another 7 will serve for 6. Disputing parties may also take their case to the International Court of Justice in The Hague, or to a temporary arbitration tribunal.

Organization. The Assembly, consisting of representatives of all parties (over 160) to the Convention on the Law of the Sea, is the supreme organ. The 36-member Council, elected by the Assembly, includes 18 members elected from 4 of the Authority's major-interest groups: 4 largest investors in seabed minerals; 4 major importers of seabed minerals; 4 major land-based exporters of the same; 6 developing countries representing special interests. The Secretariat serves all the bodies of the Authority.

Headquarters: 14-20 Port Royal St., Kingston, Jamaica.
Secretary-General: Satya N. Nandan (Fiji).

Publications. UN Law of the Sea Bulletin (3 a year).

WORLD TRADE ORGANIZATION (WTO)

Origin. The WTO is founded on the General Agreement on Tariffs and Trade (GATT), which entered into force on 1 Jan. 1948. Its 23 original signatories were members of a Preparatory Committee appointed by the UN Economic and Social Council to draft the charter for a proposed International Trade Organization. Since this charter was never ratified, the General Agreement remained the only international instrument laying down trade rules. In Dec. 1993, there were 111 contracting parties, and a further 22 countries applying GATT rules on a *de facto* basis. On 15 April 1994, trade ministers of 125 countries signed the Final Act of the GATT Uruguay Round of negotiations at Marrakesh, bringing the WTO into being on 1 Jan. 1995. As of Sept. 1997, the WTO had 132 members.

The object of the Act is the liberalization of world trade. By it, member countries undertake to apply fair trade rules covering commodities, services and intellectual property. It provides for the lowering of tariffs on industrial goods and tropical products; the abolition of import duties on a variety of items; the progressive abolition of quotas on garments and textiles; the gradual reduction of trade-distorting subsidies and import barriers; and agreements on intellectual property and trade in services. Members are required to accept the results of the Uruguay Round talks in their entirety, and subscribe to all the WTO's agreements and disciplines. There are no enforcement procedures, however; decisions are ultimately reached by consensus.

Functions. The WTO is the legal and institutional foundation of the multilateral trading system. Surveillance of national trade policies is an important part of its work. At the centre of this is the *Trade Policy Review Mechanism (TPRM)*, agreed by Ministers in 1994 (Article III of the Marrakesh Agreement). The TPRM was broadened in 1995 when the WTO came into being, to cover services trade and intellectual property. Its principal objective is to facilitate the smooth functioning of the multilateral trading system by enhancing the transparency of members' trade policies. All members are subject to review under the TPRM, which mandates that 4 members with the largest share of world trade (European Union, USA, Japan, Canada) be reviewed every 2 years; the next 16, every 4 years; and others every 6, with a longer period able to be fixed for the least-developed members. Also, in 1994, flexibility of up to 6 months was introduced into the review cycles, and in 1996, it was agreed that every second review of each of the first 4 trading entities should be an interim review. Reviews are conducted by the Trade Policy Review Body (TPRB) on the basis of a policy statement by the member under review and a report by economists in the Secretariat's Trade Policy Review Division.

The *International Trade Centre* (since 1968 operated jointly with the United

Nations through UNCTAD) was established by GATT in 1964 to provide information and training on export markets and marketing techniques, and thereby to assist the trade of developing countries. In 1984 the Centre became an executing agency of the UN Development Programme, responsible for carrying out UNDP-financed projects related to trade promotion.

Organization. A 2-yearly ministerial meeting is the ultimate policy-making body. The 132-member General Council has some 30 subordinate councils and committees. The *Dispute Settlement Body* was set up to deal with disputes between countries. Appeals against its verdicts are heard by a 7-member *Appellate Body.* In 1997, it was composed of representatives of Egypt, European Union, Japan, New Zealand, Philippines, USA and Uruguay. Dispute panels may be set up *ad hoc,* and objectors to their ruling may appeal to the Appellate Body whose decision is virtually binding. Refusal to comply at this stage results in the application of trade sanctions. Each appeal is heard by 3 of the Appellate Body members. Before cases are heard by dispute panels, there is a 60-day consultation period. The previous GATT Secretariat now serves the WTO, which has no resources of its own other than its operating budget. The budget for 1997 was 116m. Swiss francs.

Headquarters: Centre William Rappard, 154 rue de Lausanne, CH-1211 Geneva 21, Switzerland.

Website: http://www.wto.org.

Director-General: Renato Ruggiero (Italy).

Publications. Annual Report; International Trade Trends and Statistics (annual); *WTO Focus* (10 a year).

Further Reading

Croome, J., *Reshaping the World Trading System.* WTO, 1996
Preeg, E., *Traders in a Brave New World.* Chicago Univ. Press, 1996

NORTH ATLANTIC TREATY ORGANIZATION (NATO)

Origin and History. On 4 April 1949 the foreign ministers of Belgium, Canada, Denmark, France, Iceland, Italy, Luxembourg, the Netherlands, Norway, Portugal, the UK and the USA signed the North Atlantic Treaty, establishing the *Atlantic Alliance.* In 1952, Greece and Turkey acceded to the Treaty; in 1955, came the Federal Republic of Germany, and in 1982 Spain, bringing the total to 16 member nations in Jan. 1998.

Functions. The Atlantic Alliance was established as a defensive political and military alliance of independent countries in accordance with the terms of the UN Charter. It provides common security for its members through co-operation and consultation in political, military and economic as well as scientific and other non-military fields. The Alliance also links the security of North America to that of Europe. NATO is the organization which enables the goals of the Alliance to be implemented.

Reform and Transformation of the Alliance. Following the demise of the Warsaw Pact in 1991, and the improved relations with Russia, NATO has undertaken a fundamental transformation of structures and policies to meet the new security challenges in Europe. Attention has focused in particular on the need to reinforce the political role of the Alliance.

An essential component of this transformation has been the establishment of close security links with the states of Central and Eastern Europe and those of the former USSR through the North Atlantic Co-operation Council (NACC), established in Dec. 1991 as an integral part of NATO's new Strategic Concept, which was adopted by heads of state and government at a summit in Rome earlier that year. In addition, on 30 May 1997 following the ministerial meeting of the NACC in Sintra, Portugal, the the *Euro-Atlantic Partnership (EACP)* was inaugurated. This is a new co-operative mechanism, replacing the NACC, involving 44 member countries and building upon the political and military co-operation already established under the NACC and, later, the *Partnership for Peace (PFP)* programme.

The Partnership for Peace Programme. The PFP builds on the momentum of co-operation created by the North Atlantic Co-operation Council. It was launched at the 1994 Brussels Summit and is expanding and intensifying political and military co-operation throughout Europe. Its core objectives are: the facilitation of transparency in national defence planning and budgeting processes; democratic control of defence forces; members' maintenance of capability and readiness to contribute to operations under the authority of the UN; development of co-operative military relations with NATO (joint planning, training and exercises) in order to strengthen participants' ability to undertake missions in the fields of peacekeeping, search and rescue, and humanitarian operations; development, over the longer term, of forces better able to operate with those of NATO member forces. NATO will consult with any active Partner which perceives a direct threat to its territorial integrity, political independence or security; and active participation in the Partnership is to play an important role in the process of NATO's expansion.

PFP has been a key factor in promoting the spirit of practical co-operation and commitment to the democratic principles which underpin the Atlantic Alliance. One of the most tangible aspects of the PFP has been the holding of joint peacekeeping exercises. PFP exercises take place on a regular basis in both NATO and Partner countries. A large number of nationally sponsored exercises in the spirit of PFP have also been set up. There are now 27 PFP partners: Albania, Armenia, Austria, Azerbaijan, Belarus, Bulgaria, Czech Republic, Estonia, Finland, Georgia, Hungary, Kazakhstan, Kyrgyzstan, Latvia, Lithuania, Macedonia, Malta, Moldova, Poland, Romania, Russia, Slovakia, Slovenia, Sweden, Turkmenistan, Ukraine and Uzbekistan. Many of these countries have accepted the Alliance's invitation to send liaison officers to permanent facilities at NATO Headquarters in Brussels and to the Partnership Co-ordination Cell in Mons, Belgium, where the Supreme Headquarters Allied Powers Europe (SHAPE) is located.

Other key reforms undertaken include a reduced and more flexible force structure, development of increased co-ordination and co-operation with other international institutions (EU, UN, WEU), implementation of the concept of Combined Joint Task Forces (CJTFs), development of the European Security and Defence Identity (ESDI), and the agreement to make NATO's assets and experience available to support international peace enforcement operations.

In Jan. 1994, NATO heads of state and government welcomed the entry into force of the Maastricht Treaty, establishing the European Union. The Treaty included an arrangement on the development of a common foreign policy, which was intended to be a mechanism to strengthen the European pillar of Combined Joint Task Forces (CJTFs), and the separable capabilities of NATO and the WEU. At the meeting of NATO Foreign Ministers in Berlin in June 1996, agreement was reached on the implementation of CJTF policy. The agreement will facilitate NATO's new missions in crisis management and peace support operations by providing the flexibility needed to deploy at short notice forces specifically tailored to a particular contingency. The agreement also enables CJTFs to be made available for operations undertaken by the WEU, and represents a decisive and effective step towards the emergence of the new European Security and Defence Identity (ESDI) within the Alliance.

NATO's military capabilities and its adaptability to include forces of non-NATO countries were decisive factors in the Alliance's role in implementing the Bosnian Peace Agreement. Following the signing of the Agreement in Paris on 14 Dec. 1995, and on the basis of the UN Security Council's Resolution 1031, NATO commenced implementation of the military aspects of the accord through the NATO-led multinational force, the Implementation Force (IFOR), under an operation code-named Joint Endeavour. Its task was to help the parties implement the peace accord to which they had freely agreed and create a secure environment for civil and economic reconstruction. IFOR in Bosnia was the largest ever military operation undertaken by the Alliance.

Enlargement. In Dec. 1994, NATO foreign ministers initiated a study on

Enlargement, which was followed by intensified individual dialogues with interested partner countries and by an analysis of the relevant factors associated with the admission of new members. The conclusion was that, subject to agreed criteria, the accession of new members would enhance security and extend stability throughout the Euro-Atlantic area.

On 27 May 1997, in Paris, NATO and Russia signed the Founding Act on Mutual Relations, Co-operation and Security, committing them to build together a lasting peace in the Euro-Atlantic area, and establishing a new forum for consultations and co-operation called the NATO-Russia Permanent Joint Council.

Two days later, in Sintra, Portugal, a NATO-Ukraine charter was drawn up and initialled, to be signed in Madrid the following July. At the same time, Foreign Ministers agreed to enhance their dialogue, begun in 1995, with 6 countries of the Mediterranean (Egypt, Israel, Jordan, Mauritania, Morocco, Tunisia), and a new committee, the Mediterranean Co-operation Group was established to take the Mediterranean Dialogue forward.

The subsequent July meeting of Heads of State and Government in Madrid decided to invite 3 countries (Czech Republic, Hungary and Poland) to begin accession negotiations. On 16 Nov. 1997, 85.6% of Hungarians endorsed that initiative and voted in favour of joining NATO. By Dec. 1997, the 3 had signed accession agreements, and provided the parliaments of all current members approve and ratify the revision to the North Atlantic Treaty, they will join NATO in 1999.

Organization. The North Atlantic Council (NAC) is the highest decision-making body and forum for consultation within the Atlantic Alliance. It is composed of Permanent Representatives of all 16 member countries meeting together at least once a week. The NAC also meets at higher levels involving foreign ministers or heads of state or government, but it has the same authority and powers of decision-making, and its decisions have the same status and validity at whatever level it meets. All decisions are taken on the basis of consensus, reflecting the collective will of all member governments. The NAC is the only body within the Atlantic Alliance which derives its authority explicitly from the North Atlantic Treaty. The NAC has responsibility under the Treaty for setting up subsidiary bodies. Committees and planning groups have since been created to support the work of the NAC or to assume responsibility in specific fields such as defence planning, nuclear planning and military matters.

The *Military Committee* is responsible for making recommendations to the Council and the Defence Planning Committee on military matters and for supplying guidance to the Allied Commanders. Composed of the Chiefs-of-Staff of member countries (Iceland, which has no military forces, may be represented by a civilian), the Committee is assisted by an International Military Staff. It meets at Chiefs-of-Staff level at least twice a year but remains in permanent session at the level of national military representatives. The area covered by the North Atlantic Treaty is divided into 2 commands: European and the Atlantic.

Finance. The co-ordination of military plans and defence expenditures rests on detailed and comparative analysis of the capabilities of member countries. In 1997, the cost of enlargement sparked a potentially damaging dispute between the USA and European members of the Alliance following Pentagon estimates that the cost would be in the region of US$27,000m. to US$35,000m. over a 12-year period. Later assessments, taking into account the fact that Britain, France and Germany are already engaged in improving and increasing the mobility of their rapid-reaction or crisis forces, reduced the estimate to current members to US$1,300m. over 10 years, with the cost of improved military capability in line with NATO standards in new member countries being the responsibility of new members.

Under the terms of the Partnership for Peace strategy, partner countries undertake to make available the necessary personnel, assets, facilities and capabilities to participate in the programme, and share the financial cost of any military exercises in which they participate.

Headquarters: NATO, 1110 Brussels, Belgium.
*Website:*http://www.nato.int.

Secretary-General: Javier Solana Madariaga (Spain).

Publications. NATO Basic Fact Sheets; NATO Facts and Figures; NATO Handbook; NATO Review (6 a year).

Further Reading

Carr, F. and Ifantis, K., *NATO in the New European Order.* London, 1996
Cook, D., *The Forging of an Alliance.* London, 1989
Heller, F. H. and Gillingham, J. R. (eds.) *NATO: the Founding of the Atlantic Alliance and the Integration of Europe.* London, 1992
Smith, J. (ed.) *The Origins of NATO.* Exeter Univ. Press, 1990
Williams, P., *North Atlantic Treaty Organization.* [Bibliography]. Oxford and New Brunswick (NJ), 1994

BANK FOR INTERNATIONAL SETTLEMENTS (BIS)

Origin. Founded in 1930 to settle the question of German First World War reparations, the BIS now functions as the central banks' bank. Its assets are owned by 41 central banks.

Aims. To promote co-operation between central banks; provide facilities for international financial operations, monetary and economic research; and act as agent or trustee in international financial settlements.

Finance. The authorized share capital of the Bank is 1,500m. gold francs, divided into 600,000 shares of equal nominal value (2,500 gold francs per share), and at the close of the financial year, in 1997, 517,125 shares were in issue. In 1997, it held US$113,100m. (about 7% of world foreign exchange reserves) on behalf of some 120 central banks and international financial institutions.

Organization and Membership. The 11-member Board of Directors consists of the governors of the central banks of the following member countries: Belgium, Canada, France, Germany, Italy, Japan, the Netherlands, Sweden, Switzerland, the UK and the USA. The Chairman of the Board may act as President.

3 Standing Committees operate within the BIS: Basle Committee on Banking Supervision; Euro-Currency Standing Committee; and Committee on Payment and Settlement Systems; and a number of specialized Groups have been set up such as the Group of Experts on Monetary and Economic Databank Questions, and the Co-ordinating Service for Central Banks and International Organizations.

The admission to membership in 1996-97 of an additional 9 central banks in Asia, Latin America, the Middle East and Europe ended the previously heavy concentration of BIS shareholding central banks in the industrialized world. As at 31 Mar. 1997, the Bank's balance sheet stood at 66·8 billion gold francs (US$135,600m.), with funds (capital and reserves) at 2·4 billion (US$5,500m.).

The BIS has had a long and close association with the Group of Ten (G10) and participates at G10 meetings.

Headquarters: Centralbahnplatz 2, 4002 Basle, Switzerland.
Website: http://www.bis.org.
Chairman: Alfons Verplaetse (Belgium).

Further Reading

Deane, M. and Pringe, R., *The Central Banks.* London and New York, 1995
Fleming, *Who's Who in Central* Banking. London, 1997
Goodhart, C. A. E., *The Central Bank and the Financial System.* London, 1995

ORGANISATION FOR ECONOMIC CO-OPERATION AND DEVELOPMENT (OECD)

Origin. Founded in 1961 to replace the Organisation for European Economic Co-operation (OEEC). The change of title marks the Organisation's altered status and functions: with the accession of Canada and USA as full members it ceased to be a purely European body, and at the same time added development aid to the list of its priorities. The OECD provides a forum where the representatives of the governments of industrialized democracies can discuss and attempt to co-ordinate their economic and social policies.

Members. Australia, Austria, Belgium, Canada, Czech Republic, Denmark, Finland, France, Germany, Greece, Hungary, Iceland, Ireland, Italy, Japan, Korea (Republic of), Luxembourg, Mexico, Netherlands, New Zealand, Norway, Poland, Portugal, Spain, Sweden, Switzerland, Turkey, UK and USA.

Activities. The main fields of programming are: economy; energy; development co-operation; international trade; finance, fiscal and enterprise affairs; food, agriculture and fisheries; environment; science, technology and industry; education, employment, labour and social affairs.

Relations with non-member countries. In 1990, the *Centre for Co-operation with Economies in Transition (CCET)* was established to act as OECD's point of contact for Central and East European countries seeking guidance in moving towards a market economy. Relations in Asia, Africa and Latin America are co-ordinated by the *Liaison and Co-ordination Unit;* and with developing countries, through 1) its aid monitoring group, the *Development Assistance Committee,* 2) the *Development Centre,* which researches social and economic issues in the developing world, and 3) the *Club du Sahel,* which acts as a forum between the countries of west Africa and OECD assistance agencies.

Relations with other international organizations. The EU Commission generally takes part in the work of OECD under a protocol signed at the same time as the OECD Convention. EFTA may also send representatives to attend OECD meetings, and there are official or working relations with a number of other international governmental organizations including the ILO, FAO, IMF, IBRD, UNCTAD and the IAEA. Special arrangements establishing close links with the Council of Europe were concluded in 1962.

NGOs deemed to be widely representative in general economic matters or in a specific economy sector can be granted a consultative status enabling them to discuss subjects of common interest with a Liaison Committee chaired by the Secretary-General, and be consulted in a particular field by the relevant OECD Committee or its officers.

Organization. The supreme body is the Council, composed of 1 representative from each member country. It meets either at Heads of Permanent Delegations level (about twice a month) under the chairmanship of the Secretary-General, or at ministerial level (usually once a year) under the chairmanship of a minister of a country elected annually to this function. Decisions and recommendations are adopted by mutual agreement of all members of the Council.

The Council is assisted by a 14-member Executive Committee. The major part of the Organisation's work is prepared and carried out in specialized committees, working parties and sub-groups, of which there exist over 200. Committees and other bodies are, as a rule, composed of civil servants coming either from capitals or from the Permanent Delegations to the OECD which are established as normal diplomatic missions and headed by ambassadors. They are serviced by an International Secretariat headed by the OECD Secretary-General. Funding is by contributions from member states, based on a formula related to their size and economy.

3 other bodies are part of the OECD system: the *International Energy Agency (IEA),* the *Nuclear Energy Agency (NEA)* and the *Centre for Educational Research and Innovation (CERI).*

Headquarters: 2, rue André Pascal, 75775 Paris Cedex 16, France.
Website: http://www.oecd.org.
Secretary-General: Donald J. Johnston (Canada).

Publications. *Activities of OECD* (annual); *The Agricultural Outlook 1997-2001* (annual); *Energy Balances* (quarterly); *Energy Technologies for the 21st Century; Ethics in the Public Sector; Financial Market Trends* (3 a year); *Foreign Trade Statistics* (monthly); *Globalisation of Industry; Higher Education Management* (3 a year); *Main Developments in Trade* (annual); *Main Economic Indicators* (monthly); *Microfinance for the Poor?; OECD Observer* (bi-monthly); *OECD Economic Outlook* (2 a year); *OECD Economic Surveys of Member Countries* (annual); *OECD Employment Outlook* (annual); *Oil, Gas, Coal and Electricity Statistics* (quarterly statistics); *Quarterly Labour Force Statistics; Science, Technology, Industry Review* (2 a year); *Short-term Economic Indicators: Transition Economies* (quarterly).

Further Reading

Blair, D. J., *Trade Negotiations in the OECD: Structures, Institutions and States.* London, 1993

EUROPEAN UNION (EU)

Origin. The Union is founded on the existing European communities set up by the Treaties of Paris (1951) and Rome (1957), supplemented by revisions, the Single European Act in 1986, the Maastricht Treaty on European Union in 1992, and the draft Treaty of Amsterdam in 1997.

History. On 19 Sept. 1946, in Zurich, Winston Churchill called for a 'united states of Europe'. Two years later, the Congress of Europe (the meeting in The Hague of nearly 1,000 Europeans from 26 countries calling for a united Europe) resulted in the birth in 1949 of the Council of Europe, a European assembly of nations whose aim (Art. 1 of the Statute) was: 'to achieve a greater unity between its members for the purpose of safeguarding and realising the ideals and principles which are their common heritage'.

On 18 Apr. 1951, subsequent to a proposal by the French foreign minister Robert Schuman (Schuman Declaration), Belgium, France, the Federal Republic of Germany, Italy, Luxembourg and the Netherlands signed the Treaty of Paris establishing the *European Coal and Steel Community (ECSC)*. The treaty provided for the pooling of coal and steel production and was regarded as a first step towards a united Europe. Encouraged by the success of the ECSC, plans were laid down for the establishment of 2 more communities. *The European Economic Community (EEC)* and *the European Atomic Energy Community (EAEC or Euratom)* were subsequently created under separate treaties signed in Rome on 25 March 1957. The treaties provided for the establishment by stages of a common market with a customs union at its core, the approximation of economic policies, and the promotion of growth in the nuclear industries for peaceful purposes.

To this end, Euratom was awarded monopoly powers of acquisition of fissile materials for civil purposes (it is not concerned with the military uses of nuclear power). Subsequently, the various powers of the 3 communities (ECSC, EAEC, EEC, sometimes referred to collectively as the European Community or EC) were transferred by a treaty signed in Brussels in 1965 to a single Council and single Commission of the European Communities, today the core of the EU. The Commission is advised on matters relating to EAEC by a Scientific and Technical Committee.

Enlargement. On 30 June 1970, membership negotiations began between the European Community and the UK, Denmark, Ireland and Norway. On 22 Jan. 1972, all 4 countries signed a Treaty of Accession, and with the exception of Norway which later rejected membership in a referendum in Nov. that year, the UK, Denmark and Ireland became full members on 1 Jan. 1973 (though Greenland exercised its autonomy under the Danish Crown to secede in 1985). Greece joined on 1 Jan. 1981; Spain and Portugal on 1 Jan. 1986. The former German Democratic Republic entered into full membership on reunification with Federal Germany in Oct. 1990, and following referendums in favour, Austria, Finland and Sweden became members on 1 Jan. 1995. In a referendum in Nov. 1994, Norway again rejected membership.

Single European Act. The enlarging of the Community resulted in renewed efforts to promote European integration, culminating in the signing in Dec. 1985 of the Single European Act. The SEA represented the first major revision of the Treaties of Rome and provided for greater involvement of the European Parliament in the decision-making process.

Maastricht Treaty on European Union. Further amendments were agreed at the Maastricht Summit of Dec. 1991 in the draft Treaty on European Union whereby moves to a common currency were agreed subject to specific conditions (including an opt-out clause for the UK) and the social dimension was recognized in a protocol (not applicable to the UK) allowing member states to use EC institutions for this purpose. Ratification by member states of the Maastricht Treaty proved unexpectedly controversial. In June 1992, the Danish electorate in a referendum voted against it, then reversed the decision in a second referendum in May 1993. Ratification was finally completed during 1993, with the UK ratifying on 2 Aug., and the European Union (EU) officially came into being on 1 Nov. that year.

Further Enlargement. On 16 July 1997, Jacques Santer presented *Agenda 2000*, the European Commission's detailed strategy for consolidating the Union through enlargement as far eastwards as the Ukraine, Belarus and Moldova. It recommended the early start of accession negotiations with Hungary, Poland, Estonia, the Czech Republic and Slovenia under the provision of Article 0 of the Maastricht Treaty whereby 'any European State may apply to become a member of the Union' (subject to the Copenhagen Criteria set by the European Council at its summit in 1993). The first accession could be as early as 2001 though Agenda 2000 assumes 2003 to be more likely.

Meanwhile, other central and eastern European applicants (Bulgaria, Latvia, Lithuania, Romania and Slovakia) enjoy associate agreements to help speed up their preparations for membership. Applications to join the EU have been received by Cyprus (already favourably received), Turkey, Malta and Switzerland, and the Prince of Liechtenstein has made it known that he wishes his government to apply.

Objectives. The ultimate goal of the EU is 'an ever closer union among the peoples of Europe, in which decisions are taken as closely as possible to the citizen'. Priorities include the implementation of the Treaty of Amsterdam (new rights for citizens, freedom of movement, strengthening the institutions of the EU, employment); economic and monetary union; further expansion of the scope of the Communities; implementation of a common foreign and security policy; and development in the fields of justice and home affairs.

Members. As at Jan. 1998: Austria, Belgium, Denmark, Finland, France, Germany, Greece, Republic of Ireland, Italy, Luxembourg, the Netherlands, Portugal, Spain, Sweden and the UK.

Structure. The institutional arrangements of the EU provide for an independent policy-making executive with powers of proposal (European Commission), various consultative and advisory bodies, and a decision-making body drawn from the Governments (Council of Ministers).

Website: http://www.europa.eu.int.

1. **European Commission** consists of 20 members appointed by the member states to serve for 5 years. The President of the Commission is selected by a consensus of prime ministers and serves a 5-year term. In addition to its power of proposal, the Commission acts as the EU executive body and as guardian of the Treaties. In this it has the right of initiative (putting proposals to the Council of Ministers for action) and of execution (once the Council has decided); and it can take the other institutions or individual countries before the European Court of Justice should any of these renege upon its responsibilities. Decisions on legislative proposals made by the Commission are taken in the Council of the European Union. Members of the Commission swear an oath of independence, distancing themselves from partisan

influence from any source. The Commission operates through 23 Directorates-General.

Official languages. Danish, Dutch, English, Finnish, French, German, Greek, Italian, Portuguese, Spanish and Swedish.

Headquarters: 200 rue de la Loi, B-1049 Brussels, Belgium.
Secretary-General: David Williamson.

The present Commission took office on 23 Jan. 1995. Members, their nationality and political affiliation (CD, Christian-Democrat; Cons, Conservative; Ind Lab, Independent Labour; Lab, Labour; Lib, Liberal; R, Radical; Ri, Rightist; S, Socialist; SD, Social-Democrat) are as follows:

President: Jacques Santer (Luxembourg, CD; app. 1994) Responsible for monetary and institutional affairs, foreign policy and common security.

Vice-president: Sir Leon Brittan (UK, Cons) Trade policy and relations with industrialized countries of America and the Pacific Zone.

Vice-president: Manuel Marin (Spain, S) Relations with the Southern Mediterranean, Near East, Latin America and part of Asia.

Agriculture and rural development: Franz Fischler (Austria, Cons).

Budget, personnel and administration: Erkki Liikanen (Finland, S).

Competition: Karel van Miert (Belgium, S).

Consumers, fisheries and humanitarian aid: Emma Bonino (Italy, R).

Environment and nuclear safety, and Cohesion Fund: Ritt Bjerregaard (Denmark, S).

Domestic market, financial services and taxation: Mario Monti (Italy, Ind Lib).

Economic, financial and monetary affairs: Yves Thibault de Silguy (France, Ri).

Energy and primary materials: Christos Papoutsis (Greece, S).

External relations with central and eastern Europe, the CIS and other European countries; common foreign security policy and human rights (with the President): Hans van den Broek (Netherlands, CD).

Immigration, internal and judicial affairs: Anita Gradin (Sweden, S).

Industrial affairs, information and telecommunications: Martin Bangemann (Germany, Lib).

Institutional questions and relations with the European Parliament: Marcelino Oreja (Spain, CD).

Regional policies and funding: Monika Wulf-Mathies (Germany, SD).

Relations with South Africa and ACP Countries: João de Deus Pinheiro (Portugal, Lib).

Science, research and development, education and training: Edith Cresson (France, S).

Social affairs and employment: Pádraig Flynn (Ireland, Cons).

Transport and the Cohesion Fund: Neil Kinnock (UK, Lab).

2. **The European Council.** Since 1974, Heads of State or Government meet at least twice a year (in the capital of the member state currently exercising the presidency of the Council of European Union) in the form of the European Council or European Summit as it is commonly known. Its membership includes the President of the European Commission, and the President of the European Parliament is invited to make a presentation at the opening session.

The European Council has become an increasingly important element of the Union, setting priorities, giving political direction, providing the impetus for its development and resolving contentious issues that prove too difficult for the Council of the European Union. It has become directly responsible for common policies within the fields of foreign and security policy, justice and home affairs. Though there was no provision made for its existence in the original Treaty of Rome, its position was later acknowledged and formalized in the Single European Act.

3. **Council of the European Union (Council of Ministers)** Consists of foreign ministers from the 15 national governments and is the only institution which directly represents the member states' national interests. It is the Union's principal decision-making body. Here, members legislate for the Union, set its political objectives, co-ordinate their national policies and resolve differences between themselves

and other institutions. The presidency rotates every 6 months. Meetings are held in Brussels, except in April, June and Oct. when all meetings are in Luxembourg. In 1994, the Council held around 100 formal ministerial sessions during which it adopted some 300 regulations, 50 directives and 160 decisions.

Decisions are taken either by qualified majority vote or by unanimity. Since the adoption of the Single European Act, an increasing number of decisions are by majority vote, though some areas such as taxation are reserved to unanimity. 27 votes are needed to veto a decision, and member states carry the following vote weightings: France, Germany, Italy and the UK, 10; Spain, 8; Belgium, Greece, the Netherlands and Portugal, 5; Austria and Sweden, 4; Denmark, Finland and the Republic of Ireland, 3; Luxembourg, 2.

Each member state has a national delegation in Brussels known as the Permanent Representation, headed by Permanent Representatives, senior diplomats whose committee (Coreper) prepares ministerial sessions. Coreper meets weekly and its main task is to ensure that only the most difficult and sensitive issues are dealt with at ministerial level. Coreper is also the point of reference for many of the Council's working groups of national experts. Specialist Councils such as the Agriculture Council meet to discuss matters related to individual policies.

The Secretariat provides the practical infrastructure of the Council at all levels.

Legislation. The Community's legislative process starts with a proposal from the Commission (either at the suggestion of its services or in pursuit of its declared political aims) to the Council. The Council generally seeks the views of the European Parliament on the proposal, and the Parliament adopts a formal Opinion after consideration of the matter by its specialist Committees. The Council may also (and in some cases is obliged to) consult the Economic and Social Committee which similarly delivers an opinion. When these opinions have been received, the Council will decide. Most decisions are taken on a majority basis, but will take account of reservations expressed by individual member states. The text eventually approved may differ substantially from the original Commission proposal.

Provisions of the Treaties and secondary legislation may be either directly applicable in Member States or only applicable after Member States have enacted their own implementing legislation. Community law, adopted by the Council (or by Parliament and the Council in the framework of the co-decision procedure) may take the following forms: (1) *Regulations*, which are of general application and binding in their entirety and directly applicable in all member states; (2) *Directives*, which are binding upon each Member State as to the result to be achieved within a given time, but leave the national authority the choice of form and method of achieving this result; and (3) *Decisions*, which are binding in their entirety on their addressees. In addition the Council and Commission can issue recommendations and opinions which have no binding force.

Transparency. The Council is making strong efforts to make more of its work accessible to its citizens. Votes on legislative matters, as well as the explanations of these votes, are now automatically made public. Other attempts to improve transparency include briefings for journalists and the provision of background notes on subjects under discussion.

Europe Day is celebrated on 9 May each year.

Headquarters: 170 rue de la Loi, B-1048 Brussels, Belgium.
Secretary-General: Jürgen Trumpf.

4. **European Parliament** Consists of 626 members, 567 elected for 5-year terms from 12 member states on 9 and 12 June 1994. All EU citizens may stand or vote in their adoptive country of residence. Germany returned 99 members, France, Italy and the UK 87 each, Spain 64, the Netherlands 31, Belgium, Greece and Portugal 25 each, Denmark 16, Ireland 15 and Luxembourg 6. Seats allocated to countries which joined in Jan. 1995, and where elections were subsequently held, were: Sweden 22, Austria 21 and Finland 16.

Political groupings. European Socialist Party (PES) 215 seats; European People's Party (EPP) 182; Union for Europe (UFE) 57; Liberal Democratic and Reformist

Party (ELDR) 43; European United Left (EUL) 33; Greens 27; European Radical Alliance (ERA) 20; Independents for a Europe of Nations (I-EdN) 18; non-attached 31.

The Parliament has a right to be consulted on a wide range of legislative proposals and forms one arm of the Community's Budgetary Authority. Under the Single European Act, it gained greater authority in legislation through the 'concertation' procedure under which it can reject certain Council drafts in a second reading procedure. Under the Maastricht Treaty, it gained the right of 'co-decision' on legislation with the Council of Ministers on a restricted range of domestic matters.

It also plays an important role in appointing the President and members of the Commission. If the worst comes to the worst, it can pass a motion of censure on the Commission and force it to resign. In addition, the President of the European Council must report to the Parliament on progress in the development of foreign and security policy.

Parliament's seat is in Strasbourg where the 1-week plenary sessions are held each month. In the Chamber, members sit in political groups, not as national delegations. All the activities of the Parliament and its bodies are the responsibility of the Bureau, consisting of the President and 14 Vice-Presidents elected for a two-and-a-half year period. The Conference of Presidents is responsible for organizing Parliament's work and drawing up the agenda for plenary sessions.

Parliamentary committees generally meet for 2 weeks a month in Brussels for ease of contact with the the Commission and Council of Ministers.

Location: Brussels, but meets at least once a month in Strasbourg.
President: José Gil-Robles Gil-Delgado (Spain; EPP).

5. The **Court of Justice of the European Communities** composed of 13 judges and 6 advocates-general is responsible for the adjudication of disputes arising out of the application of the treaties, and its findings are enforceable in all member countries. A Court of First Instance (est. 1989) handles certain categories of cases, including cases arising under the competition rules of the EC and cases brought by Community officials.

Address: Palais de la Cour de Justice, Kirchberg, Luxembourg.
President: Gil Carlos Rodríguez Iglesias (Spain).

6. The **Court of Auditors of the European Communities** was established by a treaty of 22 July 1975 which took effect on 1 June 1977. It consists of 12 members and was raised to the status of a full EU institution by the 1993 Maastricht Treaty. It audits all income and current and past expenditure of the EU.

Address: 12, rue Alcide de Gasperi, L-1615 Luxembourg.
President: Bernhard Friedmann (Germany).

Major Policy Areas. The major policy areas of the EU were laid down in the Treaty of Rome of 25 Mar. 1957 which guaranteed certain rights to the citizens of all member states, including the outlawing of economic discrimination by nationality, and equal pay for equal work as between men and women.

The single internal market. The single internal market represents the core of the process of economic integration and is characterized by the removal of obstacles to the 4 fundamental *freedoms of movement for persons, goods and capital.* Under the Treaty, individuals or companies from 1 Member State may establish themselves in another country (for the purposes of economic activity) or sell goods or services there on the same basis as nationals of that country. With a few exceptions, restrictions on the movement of capital have also been ended. Under the Single European Act the member states bound themselves to achieve the suppression of all barriers to free movement of persons, goods and services by 31 Dec. 1992.

The *Schengen Accord* abolished border controls on persons and goods between those EU and non-EU states which have signed it. It came into effect on 26 March 1995 and was signed by Austria, Belgium, Denmark, Finland, France, Germany, Greece, Iceland, Italy, Luxembourg, Netherlands, Norway, Portugal, Spain and Sweden.

Economic and Monetary Union. The establishment of the single market provided for the next phase of integration: economic and monetary union. The *European Monetary System (EMS)* was founded in March 1979 to control inflation, protect European trade from international disturbances and ultimately promote convergence between the European economies. At its heart was the *Exchange Rate Mechanism (ERM).* The ERM is run by the finance ministries and central banks of the EU countries on a day-to-day basis; monthly reviews are carried out by the EU Monetary Committee (finance ministries) and the EU Committee of Central Bankers. Greece and Sweden are not in the ERM; the UK suspended its membership on 17 Sept. 1992. In Jan. 1995, Austria joined the ERM. Finland followed in 1996, and in Nov. that year the Italian lira, which had been temporarily suspended, was re-admitted.

Members are obliged to restrict the fluctuations in the value of their currencies to a variation 'band', of 15% (2·25% for Germany and the Netherlands) higher or lower than a central rate established by comparing all the currencies in the ERM and the European Currency Unit, the ecu. If a currency reaches its top or bottom limits, central banks are obliged to buy or sell currency on the foreign exchanges. Further stabilization measures would involve adjustment of national interest rates, central bank borrowing from other central banks or withdrawal of reserves from the European Monetary Co-operation Fund. The adjustment of last resort is re- or devaluation. In July 1993, following intensive currency speculation on European financial markets, forcing the weaker currencies to the edge of their permitted bands, the ERM almost collapsed. In response the fluctuation margins were widened.

The ecu's value in national currencies is calculated and published daily.

Under the Maastricht Treaty the second stage in economic and monetary union began with the establishment of the European Monetary Institute (see below) in order to prepare for the implementation of a single monetary policy and single currency. A future European Central Bank (ECB) will take over the tasks of the EMI once a single policy and currency are in place.

European Monetary Union (EMU). EMU currency is scheduled to come into use on 1 Jan. 2002 and will consist of the euro of 100 cents, with coins of 1, 2, 5, 10, 20 and 50 cents and 1 euro and notes of 5, 10, 20, 50, 100, 200 and 500 euros. From 1 July 2002 it will be the only legal currency in EMU countries. EU member countries not in EMU will select a central rate for their currency in consultation with members of the euro bloc and the European Central Bank. The rate is set according to an assessment of each country's chances of joining the euro zone.

An agreement on the legal status of the euro and currency discipline, the Stability and Growth Pact, was reached by all member states at the Dublin summit on 13 Dec. 1996. Financial penalties will be applied to member states running a GDP deficit (negative growth) of up to 0·75%. If GDP falls between 0·75% and 2%, EU finance ministers will have discretion as to whether to apply penalties. Members running an excessive deficit will be automatically exempt from penalties in the event of a natural disaster or if the fall in GDP is at least 2% over 1 year.

Environment. The Single European Act gave environmental policy its place with the view of making the protection of the environment an integral part of economic and social policies. Community policy aims at preventing pollution (the Prevention Principle), rectifying pollution at source, and imposing the costs of prevention or rectification upon the polluters themselves (the Polluter Pays Principle). The European Environment Agency (see below) was established to ensure that policy was based on reliable scientific data.

The Common Agricultural Policy (CAP). The objectives set out in the Treaty are to increase agricultural productivity, to ensure a fair standard of living for the agricultural community, to stabilize markets, to assure supplies, and to ensure reasonable consumer prices. In Dec. 1960 the Council laid down the fundamental principles on which the CAP is based: a single market, which calls for common prices, stable currency parities and the harmonizing of health and veterinary legislation; Community preference, which protects the single Community market from imports; common financing, through the European Agricultural Guidance and Guarantee Fund (EAGGF), which seeks to improve agriculture through its Guidance section, and to stabilize markets against world price fluctuations through market intervention, with levies and refunds on exports. At present, common market organizations cover over 95% of EU agricultural production.

Following the disappearance of stable currency parities, artificial currency levels have been applied in the CAP. This factor, together with over-production due to high producer prices, meant that the CAP consumed about two-thirds of the Communities' budget. It was finally agreed in May 1992 to reform CAP and lessen over-production by reducing the price supports to farmers by 29% for cereals, 15% for beef and 5% for dairy products. In June 1995, the guaranteed intervention price for beef was decreased by 5%. In July 1996, agriculture ministers agreed a reduction in the set-aside rate for cereals from 10% to 5%. Fruit and vegetable production subsidies were fixed at no more than 4% of the value of total marketed production, rising to 4·5% in 1999. Compensatory grants are made available to farmers who remove land from production or take early retirement. The CAP reform aims in the long term to make the agricultural sector more responsive to the level of supply and demand.

The Beef Crisis. In July 1994 Community ministers adopted measures to prevent the spread of bovine spongiform encephalopathy (BSE) by imposing strict controls on carcass beef trade. In March 1996, owing to increased fears about possible links between BSE and Creutzfeldt-Jakob Disease (CJD) and a collapse in consumer confidence in the beef market, the Commission accepted that member countries could unilaterally stop imports of beef on health grounds.

By 22 March, 12 EU countries had taken the step of banning UK beef, and on 27 March the Commission agreed a ban on exports from the UK of live cattle, beef and beef products. The UK responded to the crisis with a programme of selective slaughter to eradicate BSE from the national herd, then later repudiated the agreement and applied for the ban to be suspended. This was duly rejected by the European Court of Justice in July 1996 and an additional cull on the UK herd was requested. Removal of the embargo is now expected to be made in phases.

Customs Union and External Trade Relations. Goods or Services originating in one Member State have free circulation within the EU, which implies common arrangements for trade with the rest of the world. Member States can no longer make bilateral trade agreements with third countries; this power has been ceded to the EU. The Customs Union was achieved in July 1968.

In Oct. 1991 a treaty forming the *European Economic Area (EEA)* was approved by the member states of the then EC and European Free Trade Association (EFTA). Association agreements which could lead to accession or customs union have been made with Cyprus, Estonia, Latvia, Lithuania, Israel, Malta, Morocco and Turkey. The customs union with Turkey came into force on 1 Jan. 1996. Commercial, industrial, technical and financial aid agreements have been made with Algeria, Egypt, Jordan, Lebanon, Morocco, Russia, Syria, Tunisia and the former Yugoslavia. In 1976 Canada signed a framework agreement for co-operation in industrial trade, science and natural resources, and a transatlantic pact was signed with the USA in Dec. 1995. Co-operation agreements also exist with a number of Latin American countries and groupings, and with Arab and Asian countries, and an economic and commercial agreement has been signed with the Association of South East Asian Nations (ASEAN). Partnership and co-operation agreements were signed with Ukraine in June 1994, Kazakhstan in Jan. 1995, Kyrgyzstan in Feb. 1995 and with Uzbekistan in June 1996. In the Development Aid sector, the EU has an agreement (the Lomé Convention, originally signed in 1975 but renewed and enlarged in 1979 and 1984) with some 60 African, Caribbean and Pacific (ACP) countries which removes customs duties without reciprocal arrangements for most of their imports to the Community.

The application of common duties has been conducted mainly within the framework of the *General Agreement on Tariffs and Trade (GATT),* which was succeeded in 1995 by the establishment of the World Trade Organization.

Fisheries. The Common Fisheries Policy (CFP) came into effect in Jan. 1983, according to which all EU fishermen have equal access to the waters of member countries (a zone extending up to 200 nautical miles from the shore around all its coastlines), with the total allowable catch for each species being set and shared out between member countries according to pre-established quotas, with in some cases 'historic rights' applying, as well as special rules to conserve stock, preserve marine biodiversity, and the sustainable pursuit of fishing.

A number of agreements are in place with other countries (Canada, Norway, USA and some African countries) allowing reciprocal fishing rights. When Greenland withdrew from the Community in 1985 EU boats retained their fishing rights subject to quotas and limits, which were revised in 1995 owing to concern about overfishing of Greenland halibut. Agreements were initialled with Estonia, Latvia, Lithuania and Argentina in 1992.

Transport. Under the Maastricht Treaty, the Community must contribute to the establishment and development of trans-European networks in the areas of transport, telecommunications and energy infrastructures.

Competition. The Competition (anti-trust) law of the EU is based on 2 principles: that businesses should not seek to nullify the creation of the common market by the erection of artificial national (or other) barriers to the free movement of goods; and against the abuse of dominant positions in any market. These two principles have led among other things to the outlawing of prohibitions on exports to other Member States, of price-fixing agreements and of refusal to supply; and to the refusal by the Commission to allow mergers or takeovers by dominant undertakings in specific cases. Increasingly heavy fines are imposed on offenders.

A number of structural funds have been established in an attempt to counter specific problems within and across the Community. These include:

European Social Fund. Provides resources with the aim of combating long-term unemployment and facilitating integration into the labour market of young people and the socially disadvantaged. The 1996 budget included an allocation of almost ecu 7,146m. for the Fund's commitments.

European Regional Development Fund. Intended to compensate for the unequal rate of development among different regions of the EU by encouraging investment and improving infrastructure in 'problem regions'.

Finances. The general budget of the EU covers all EEC and Euratom expenditure, and the administrative expenditure of the ECSC.

EU revenue in ecu 1m.:

	1997
Own resources	81,754
Miscellaneous Community taxes, levies and dues	476
Administrative operation of the institutions	97
Contributions to EU programmes	16
Borrowing and lending	18
Miscellaneous	5
Total	82,366

Expenditure for 1996 was ecu 85,094m.

The resources of the Community (the levies and duties mentioned above, and up to a 1·4% VAT charge) have been surrendered to it by Treaty. The Budget is made by the Council and the Parliament acting jointly as the Budgetary Authority. The Parliament has control, within a certain margin, of non-obligatory expenditure (where the amount to be spent is not set out in the legislation concerned), and can also reject the Budget. Otherwise, the Council decides. An agreement of 1992 fixed the permissible ceiling of expenditure at 1·2% of EC GDP in 1993 and 1994, rising to 1·27% in 1999. In Dec. 1994, taking into account the enlargement of the EU to 15 countries (from 1 Jan. 1995), it was agreed to set a level of maximum expenditure at ecu 75,500m., in 1995, increasing to ecu 87,000m., in 1999.

The Consultative Bodies There are 3 main consultative committees whose members are appointed in a personal capacity and are not bound by any mandatory instruction.

1. *Economic and Social Committee.* The 222-member committee is consulted by the Council of Ministers or by the European Commission, particularly with regard to

agriculture, free movement of workers, harmonization of laws and transport. It is served by a permanent and independent General Secretariat, headed by a Secretary-General.

Secretary-General: Adriano Graziosi.

2. *ECSC (European Coal and Steel Community) Consultative Committee.* A 108-member committee representing producers, workers, consumers and traders in the coal and steel industry. Appointed by the Council for a 2-year term and attached to the Commission, it plays an advisory role on the coal and steel sectors.

3. *Committee of the Regions.* A new advisory body established by the Maastricht Treaty and consisting of 222 full members and an equal number of alternate members appointed by the Council for a 4-year term. The Committee must be consulted on matters regarding education, culture, public health, trans-European networks, economic and social cohesion, and on any issue with regional implications.

President: Pasqual Maragall I. Mara (Spain).

In addition to these, there are many advisory committees dealing with all aspects of EU policy and several hundred special interest groups, which may hold unofficial talks with the Commission.

EU General information. Available as free-of-charge publications. The Official Journal, other official documents, specialized publications and databases addressing professional needs can be ordered from the EUR-OP network.

Address: Jean Monnet Building, rue Alcide de Gasperi, L-2920 Luxembourg.

The **EU Ombudsman** was inaugurated in 1995. The present incumbent is Jacob Söderman (Finland).

EUROPEAN INVESTMENT BANK (EIB) Created in 1958 by the 6 founder member states of the EEC under the Treaty of Rome to which its statute is annexed, its role was reaffirmed in a protocol to the Maastricht Treaty. Its governing body is the Board of Governors, consisting of ministers designated by member states. Its main task is to further regional development within the Community by financing capital projects; modernizing or converting undertakings; or developing new activities. To this end, it raises on the markets substantial volumes of funds which it directs on favourable terms.

Address: 100 bd Konrad Adenauer, L-2950 Luxembourg.
President: Sir Brian Unwin.

EUROPEAN MONETARY INSTITUTE Established by the Maastricht Treaty on 1 Jan. 1994 as the precursor of a European Central Bank (ECB). Its purpose is to strengthen the co-ordination of monetary policies of member states with a view to ensuring price stability, and to make the necessary preparations required for the establishment of the European System of Central Banks (ESCB), for the conduct of a single monetary policy and creation of a single European currency, the Euro. The EMI is scheduled to be replaced by the ESCB at the start of Stage II of the process of economic and monetary union in 1999, when the changeover to euro is due to start.

Address: 29 Kaiserstrasse, 60311 Frankfurt-am-Main, Germany.
President: Willem Duisenberg (Netherlands).

EUROPEAN ENVIRONMENT AGENCY Launched by the EU in 1993 with a mandate to orchestrate, cross-check and put to strategic use information of relevance to the protection and improvement of Europe's environment. Based in Copenhagen, it has a mandate to ensure objective, reliable and comprehensive information on the environment at European level to enable its members to take the requisite measures to protect it. The Agency carries out its tasks through the European Information and Observation Network (EIONET). Membership is open to countries outside the EU that share the Agency's concerns. Current membership includes all EU countries, Iceland, Liechtenstein and Norway.

EUROPOL Founded in 1994 to exchange criminal intelligence between EU countries. Its precursor was the European Drug Unit whose field of operations was extended in 1994 to include traffic in nuclear and radioactive substances, illegal immigration and stolen vehicles. All EU states are represented by liaison officers (ELOs) working for their national police, gendarme or customs services. The 1995 budget was ecu 4·5m. Member countries subscribe in proportion to their GNP.

Co-ordinator: Jürgen Storbeck (Germany).

STATISTICAL OFFICE OF THE EUROPEAN COMMUNITIES (EUROSTAT) Eurostat's mission is to provide the EU with a high-quality statistical service. It receives statistical data collected according to uniform rules from the national statistical institutes of member states, then consolidates and harmonizes the data, before making them available to the public as printed or electronic publications. The data are directly available from the Data Shop network and from EUR-OP distribution networks.

Address: Jean Monnet Building, L-2920 Luxembourg.
*Data Shop:*Rue de la Loi 120, B-1049 Brussels, Belgium.

Further Reading

Official Journal of the European Communities.—General Report on the Activities of the European Communities (annual, from 1967).*—The Agricultural Situation in the Community.* (annual).*—The Social Situation in the Community.* (annual).*—Report on Competition Policy in the European Community.* (annual).*—Basic Statistics of the Community* (annual).*— Bulletin of the European Community* (monthly).*—Register of Current Community Legal Instruments.* 1983
Europe (monthly), obtainable from the Information Office of the European Commission, 8 Storey's Gate, London, SW1P 3AT; European Parliament. *Members of the European Parliament, 4th Electoral Period, 1994–99.* 1995
Brittan, L., *The Europe We Need.* London, 1994
Cox, A. and Furlong, P., *A Modern Companion to the European Community: a Guide to Key Facts, Institutions and Terms.* Aldershot, 1992
Crawford, M., *One Money for Europe: the Economics and Politics of EMU.* 2nd ed. London, 1996
Delors, J., *Our Europe: the Community and National Development.* London, 1993
Dinan, D., *Ever Closer Union? An Introduction to the European Community.* London, 1994.
Dod's European Companion. Hurst Green, East Sussex. Occasional
Hitiris, T., *European Community Economics: a Modern Introduction.* London, 1991
Hurwitz, L. and Lequesne, C. (eds.) *The State of the European Community: Policies, Institutions and Debates in the Transition Years.* Harlow, 1992
Kirschner, E. J., *Decision-Making in the European Community: the Council Presidency and European Integration.* Manchester Univ. Press, 1992
Leonardi, R., *Convergence, Cohesion and Integration in the European Union.* London, 1995
Lewis, D. W. P., *The Road to Europe: History, Institutions and Prospects of European Integration, 1945–1993.* Berne, 1994
Newman, M., *Democracy, Sovereignty and the European Union.* Farnborough, 1996
Nugent, N., *The Government and Politics of the European Union.* 3rd ed. London, 1994
Nuttall, S. J., *European Political Co-operation.* Oxford, 1993
Paxton, J., *European Communities.* [Bibliography]. Oxford and New Brunswick (NJ), 1992
Weigall, D. and Stirk, P., *The Origins and Development of the European Community.* Leicester Univ. Press, 1992
Westlake, M., *Modern Guide to the European Parliament.* London, 1994
Williams, A. M., *The European Community: the Contradictions of Integration.* 2nd ed. Oxford, 1994
Winters, L. and Venables, A. (eds.) *European Integration: Trade and Industry.* CUP, 1993

COUNCIL OF EUROPE

Origin and Membership. In 1948, the Congress of Europe, bringing together at The Hague nearly 1,000 influential Europeans from 26 countries, called for the creation of a united Europe, including a European Assembly. This proposal, examined first by the Ministerial Council of the Brussels Treaty Organization, then by a conference of ambassadors, was at the origin of the Council of Europe, which is, with its 40 member States, the widest organization bringing together all European democracies. The Statute of the Council was signed at London on 5 May 1949 and came into force 2 months later.

The founder members were Belgium, Denmark, France, Ireland, Italy, Luxembourg, the Netherlands, Norway, Sweden and the UK. Turkey and Greece joined in 1949, Iceland in 1950, the Federal Republic of Germany in 1951 (having been an associate since 1950), Austria in 1956, Cyprus in 1961, Switzerland in 1963, Malta in 1965, Portugal in 1976, Spain in 1977, Liechtenstein in 1978, San Marino in 1988, Finland in 1989, Hungary in 1990, Czechoslovakia (after partitioning, the Czech Republic and Slovakia rejoined in 1993) and Poland in 1991, Bulgaria in 1992, Estonia, Lithuania, Romania and Slovenia in 1993, Andorra in 1994, Albania, Latvia, Macedonia, Moldova and Ukraine in 1995, Croatia and Russia in 1996.

Membership is limited to European states which 'accept the principles of the rule of law and of the enjoyment by all persons within [their] jurisdiction of human rights and fundamental freedoms'. The Statute provides for both withdrawal (Article 7) and suspension (Articles 8 and 9). Greece withdrew during 1969–74.

Aims and Achievements. Article 1 of the Statute states that the Council's aim is 'to achieve a greater unity between its members for the purpose of safeguarding and realising the ideals and principles which are their common heritage and facilitating their economic and social progress'; 'this aim shall be pursued... by discussion of questions of common concern and by agreements and common action'. The only limitation is provided by Article 1 (d), which excludes 'matters relating to national defence'.

The main areas of the Council's activity are: human rights, the media, social and socio-economic questions, education, culture and sport, youth, public health, heritage and environment, local and regional government, and legal co-operation. 163 Conventions and Agreements have been concluded covering such matters as social security, cultural affairs, conservation of European wildlife and natural habitats, protection of archaeological heritage, extradition, medical treatment, equivalence of degrees and diplomas, the protection of television broadcasts, adoption of children and transportation of animals.

Treaties in the legal field include the adoption of the European Convention on the Suppression of Terrorism, the European Convention on the Legal Status of Migrant Workers and the Transfer of Sentenced Persons. The Committee of Ministers adopted a European Convention for the protection of individuals with regard to the automatic processing of personal data (1981), a Convention on the compensation of victims of violent crimes (1983), a Convention on spectator violence and misbehaviour at sport events and in particular at football matches (1985), the European Charter of Local Government (1985), and a Convention for the Prevention of Torture and Inhuman or Degrading Treatment or Punishment (1987). The European Social Charter of 1961 sets out the social and economic rights which all member governments agree to guarantee to their citizens.

European Social Charter. The Charter defines the rights and principles which are the basis of the Council's social policy, and guarantees a number of social and economic rights to the citizen, including the right to work, the right to form workers' organizations, the right to social security and assistance, the right of the family to protection and the right of migrant workers to protection and assistance. Two committees, comprising independent and government experts, supervise the parties' compliance with their obligations under the Charter. A revised charter, incorporating new rights such as protection for those without jobs and opportunities for workers with family responsibilities, was opened for signature on 3 May 1996 and signed by 9 members.

Human rights. The promotion and development of human rights is one of the major tasks of the Council of Europe. The European Convention on Human Rights, signed in 1950, set up special machinery to guarantee internationally fundamental rights and freedoms. The 31-member *European Commission of Human Rights* investigates alleged violations of the Convention submitted to it either by States or, in most cases, by individuals. Its findings can then be examined by the *European Court on Human Rights* (est. 1959), whose obligatory jurisdiction has been recognized by 38 States, or by the Committee of Ministers empowered to take binding decisions by two-thirds majority vote.

In Oct. 1997, leaders of the 40 members of the Council of Europe met in Strasbourg to reinforce and extend the organization's watchdog role on human rights in Europe, turning its human rights court into a full-time body and appointing a human rights mediator, and to encourage more members, particularly in Eastern Europe, to sign the Council's social charter. The summit, only the second in the Council's 48-year history, also endorsed the idea of a continent-wide ban on human cloning, and closer co-operation to combat corruption, organized crime and money laundering.

President of the European Commission of Human Rights: Stefan Trechsel (Switzerland).

President of the European Court on Human Rights: Rolv Ryssdal (Norway).

The Social Development Fund, formerly the Resettlement Fund, was created in 1956. The main purpose of the Fund is to give financial aid in the spheres of housing, vocational training, regional planning and development. Since 1956 the Fund has granted loans totalling ecu 10,000m.

The *European Youth Foundation* provides money to subsidize activities by European youth organizations in their own countries.

Structure. Under the Statute, two organs were set up: an inter-governmental *Committee of [Foreign] Ministers* with powers of decision and recommendation to governments, and an inter-parliamentary deliberative body, the *Parliamentary Assembly* (referred to in the Statute as the Consultative Assembly) —both served by the Secretariat. A Joint Committee acts as an organ of co-ordination and liaison between the two and gives members an opportunity to exchange views on matters of important European interest. In addition, a number of committees of experts have been established. On municipal matters the Committee of Ministers receives recommendations from the Congress of Local and Regional Authorities of Europe. The Committee usually meets twice a year and has a rotatory chair; their deputies meet for several days each month.

The *Parliamentary Assembly* consists of 286 parliamentarians elected or appointed by their national parliaments (Albania 4, Andorra 2, Austria 6, Belgium 7, Bulgaria 6, Croatia 5, Cyprus 3, the Czech Republic 7, Denmark 5, Estonia 3, Finland 5, France 18, Germany 18, Greece 7, Hungary 7, Iceland 3, Ireland 4, Italy 18, Latvia 3, Liechtenstein 2, Lithuania 4, Luxembourg 3, Macedonia 3, Malta 3, Moldova 5, Netherlands 7, Norway 5, Poland 12, Portugal 7, Romania 10, Russia 18, San Marino 2, Slovakia 5, Slovenia 3, Spain 12, Sweden 6, Switzerland 6, Turkey 12, Ukraine 12, UK 18). It meets 3 times a year for approximately a week. The work of the Assembly is prepared by parliamentary committees. Since June 1989 representatives of a number of central and East European countries have been permitted to attend as non-voting members ('special guests'), namely Armenia, Azerbaijan, Bosnia-Hercegovina and Georgia.

Although without legislative powers, the Assembly acts as the powerhouse of the Council, initiating European action in key areas by making recommendations to the Committee of Ministers. As the widest parliamentary forum in Western Europe, the Assembly also acts as the conscience of the area by voicing its opinions on important current issues. These are embodied in Resolutions. The Ministers' role is to translate the Assembly's recommendations into action, particularly as regards lowering the barriers between the European countries, harmonizing their legislation or introducing, where possible, common European laws, abolishing discrimination on grounds of nationality, and undertaking certain tasks on a joint European basis.

Official languages. English and French.
Headquarters: Council of Europe, F-67075, Strasbourg, Cedex, France.
Secretary-General: Daniel Tarschys (Sweden).

Publications. European Yearbook, The Hague; *Yearbook on the Convention on Human Rights,* Strasbourg; *Catalogue of Publications* (annual); *Forum* (quarterly); *A Future for Our Past* (2 a year); *Naturopa Newsletter* (monthly); *Sports Information Bulletin* (quarterly).

Further Reading

Cook, C. and Paxton, J., *European Political Facts, 1900–96.* London, 1997

WESTERN EUROPEAN UNION (WEU)

Origin. The WEU has its origins in the 1948 Brussels Treaty of Economic, Social and Cultural Collaboration and Collective Self-Defence signed by the foreign ministers of the UK, France, Netherlands, Belgium and Luxembourg, establishing the Western Union. With the subsequent signature of the North Atlantic Treaty, the functions of the Western Union defence organization were transferred to the North Atlantic Treaty command on 20 Dec. 1950 and it was decided that the reorganization should not affect the right of Western Union defence ministers and chiefs of staff to meet to consider matters of mutual concern to the Brussels Treaty powers.

At a Conference of Ministers held in Paris from 20–23 Oct. 1954, these decisions were embodied in 4 Protocols modifying the Brussels Treaty: the Federal Republic of Germany and Italy were to accede to the Western Union; the occupation of West Germany was to end; West Germany was to be invited to accede to the North Atlantic Treaty; and provisions were made concerning armaments control and the UK's military presence in Europe. These came into force on 6 May 1955. Under the Paris Agreement, the Western Union was renamed the Western European Union.

Members. In Jan. 1998: Belgium, France, Germany, Greece, Italy, Luxembourg, Netherlands, Portugal, Spain and the UK. Spain and Portugal became members in 1990; Greece in 1995. In 1991 at Maastricht, the WEU decided to extend invitations to other members of the EU to accede to the WEU or seek observer status, and to European members of NATO to become associate members. In Jan. 1998, Austria, Denmark, the Republic of Ireland, Finland and Sweden had observer status; Iceland, Norway and Turkey are associated members; Bulgaria, Czech Republic, Estonia, Hungary, Latvia, Lithuania, Poland, Romania, Slovakia and Slovenia are associate partners.

Reform. At a meeting of the foreign and defence ministers of WEU members held in Rome on 26–27 Oct. 1984, the Council adopted the *Rome Declaration* and a document on institutional reform. Member Governments supported the reactivation of the Organization as a means of strengthening the European contribution to the North Atlantic Alliance and improving defence co-operation among the countries of Western Europe.

In 1987, WEU foreign and defence ministers adopted the *Hague Platform on European Security Interests,* defining the conditions and criteria for European security, and the responsibilities of WEU members to provide an integrated Europe with a security and defence dimension. During the Gulf War, at the end of 1990 and early 1991, co-ordinated action took place among WEU nations contributing forces and other forms of support to the coalition forces involved in the liberation of Kuwait.

In Maastricht, on 10 Dec. 1991, WEU ministers stated that: 'WEU will be developed as the defence component of the European Union and as the means to strengthen the European pillar of the Atlantic Alliance. To this end, it will formulate common European defence policy and carry forward its concrete implementation through the further development of its own operational role.' The Declaration then proposed ways of strengthening WEU's relations with the European Union and NATO, as well as measures to develop its operational role. A number of practical decisions were taken, including the transfer of the seat of the WEU Council and Secretariat-General from London to Brussels, which was completed in Jan. 1993.

At a meeting in Bonn in June 1992, they went on to adopt the *Petersberg Declaration,* agreeing that the WEU should have a military capability in order to conduct humanitarian and rescue tasks, peacekeeping tasks and tasks of combat forces in crisis management, including peacemaking (the so-called 'Petersberg tasks') at the initiative of the WEU Council or following a request by the European Union, the OSCE or the UN.

At the Alliance Summit of Jan. 1994, NATO leaders gave their full support to the development of a European Security and Defence Identity (ESDI) and to the strengthening of the WEU. They declared their readiness to make collective assets of the Alliance available for WEU operations. The Alliance leaders also endorsed the concept of Combined Joint Task Forces (CJTFs) with the objective not only of adapting Alliance structures to NATO's new missions but also of improving co-operation with the WEU, and in order to reflect the emerging ESDI. They also approved WEU's proposal to hold joint WEU-NATO Council meetings to discuss how to address future contingencies.

The Declaration adopted by the WEU Council of Ministers on 22 July 1997, on the 'role of WEU and its relations with the European Union and with the Atlantic Alliance', recalls that WEU is an integral part of the development of the European Union, giving the Union access to an operational capability, in particular in the context of the Petersberg missions, and that it is an essential element in the European Security and Defence Identity within the Atlantic Alliance.

In the context of the Yugoslav conflict, WEU has undertaken 3 operations, 2 of them to help in the enforcement of sanctions imposed by the UN Security Council (the WEU/NATO operation SHARP GUARD in the Adriatic and the WEU Danube operation) and one to assist in the European Union administration of the town of Mostar. In recent years, WEU has assisted in the Albanian police reorganization.

Organization. Since the 1984 reforms, the Council, supreme authority of the WEU, meets twice a year at ministerial level (foreign and defence) in the capital of the presiding country. The presidency rotates biannually. The Permanent Council, chaired by the Secretary-General, meets weekly at ambassadorial level, at the seat of the Secretariat-General in Brussels. The WEU Assembly comprises 115 parliamentarians of member states, and meets twice a year, usually in Paris. There are Permanent Committees on: defence questions and armaments; general affairs; scientific questions; budgetary affairs and administration; rules of procedure and privileges; and parliamentary and public relations.

A *WEU Institute for Security Studies* was set up in Paris in 1990, and the WEU has a satellite centre at Torrejon de Ardoz in Spain.

Headquarters: WEU, B-1000 Brussels, Belgium.
Secretary-General: José Cutileiro (Portugal).

ORGANIZATION FOR SECURITY AND CO-OPERATION IN EUROPE (OSCE)

Origin. Initiatives from both NATO and the Warsaw Pact culminated in the first summit Conference on Security and Co-operation in Europe (CSCE) attended by heads of state and government in Helsinki on 30 July–1 Aug. 1975, which adopted the Helsinki Final Act laying down 10 principles concerning human rights, self-determination and the inter-relations of the participant states. To this end, Review Conferences have been held in Belgrade (1977–78), Madrid (1980–83), Vienna (1986–89), Helsinki (1992) and Budapest (1994).

The Helsinki Final Act comprises 4 main sections: 1) security in Europe, including commitments to non-aggression and respect for human rights; 2) co-operation in the fields of economics, science, technology and the environment; 3) co-operation in humanitarian and related fields, including promotion of cultural exchange and free movement of peoples; 4) a commitment to the process of consultation and increased co-operation.

Activities. At the Paris summit of 19–21 Nov. 1990, the members of NATO and the Warsaw Pact signed a Treaty on the Reduction of Conventional Forces in Europe (CFE) and a declaration that they were 'no longer adversaries' and did not intend to 'use force against the territorial integrity or political independence of any state'. All the 34 participants adopted the Confidence and Security-Building Measures (CSBMs), which pertained to the exchange of military information, verification of military installations, objection to unusual military activities etc., and signed the *Charter of Paris*. The Charter sets out principles of human rights, democracy and the rule of law to which all the signatories undertake to adhere, lays down the bases for east-west co-operation and other future action, and institutionalizes the OSCE.

In July 1992, member nations unanimously agreed to set up an armed peace-keeping force. In 1994, at the Budapest review conference, the Forum for Security Co-operation (FSC) adopted the Vienna Document 1994, paving the way for co-operation on defence planning, and establishing a programme for military con-tacts and co-operation. At the same time, the Forum adopted documents addressing global exchange of military information, principles governing conventional arms transfers, and stabilizing measures for localized crisis situations.

On 1 Jan. 1995, the CSCE changed its name to the Organization for Security and Co-operation in Europe (OSCE).

Members. By 1998, the founder members, Austria, Belgium, Bulgaria, Canada, Cyprus, the Czech Republic (formerly as Czechoslovakia), Denmark, Finland, France, Germany, Greece, Holy See, Hungary, Iceland, Ireland, Italy, Liechtenstein, Luxembourg, Malta, Monaco, Netherlands, Norway, Poland, Portugal, Romania, Russia (succeeding USSR), San Marino, Slovakia (formerly as Czechoslovakia), Spain, Sweden, Switzerland, Turkey, UK, USA and Yugoslavia (currently suspen-ded), had been joined by Albania, Armenia, Azerbaijan, Belarus, Bosnia-Hercegovina, Croatia, Estonia, Georgia, Kazakhstan, Kyrgyzstan, Latvia, Lithuania, Macedonia, Moldova, Slovenia, Tajikistan, Turkmenistan, Ukraine and Uzbekistan.

Organization. Summit conferences of heads of state or government take place every 2 years to set the priorities and political orientation of the Organization. The Ministerial Council (formerly the Council of Foreign Ministers) is the central deci-sion-making and governing body, and meets at least once a year. The Council's agent, co-ordinating OSCE activities, is the Senior Council (formerly the Committee of Senior Officials). It meets at least twice a year in Prague, and once as the Economic Forum. The Permanent Council in Vienna is responsible for day-to-day operational tasks and comprises permanent representatives of members states. The Forum for Security Co-operation (FSC) meets weekly in Vienna.

The Secretariat includes a *Conflict Prevention Centre* which provides operational support for OSCE missions.

The OSCE Parliamentary Assembly is formally independent, but maintains close links with the OSCE process. Meetings take place annually in rotation. It is sup-ported by a secretariat in Copenhagen.

The *High Commissioner on National Minorities* has the duty of early and impar-tial evaluation of ethnic conflicts and recommendation of action, and has an office in The Hague. There is also an *Office for Democratic Institutions and Human Rights* in Warsaw and a *Court of Conciliation and Arbitration* in Geneva.

The budget for 1996 was US$55m. of which 46% was allocated to OSCE activi-ties in Bosnia-Hercegovina.

Headquarters: Kärntner Ring 507, 1010 Vienna, Austria.
Secretary–General: Giancarlo Aragona (Italy).

Further Reading

Freeman, J., *Security and the CSCE Process: the Stockholm Conference and Beyond.* London, 1991

EUROPEAN BANK FOR RECONSTRUCTION AND DEVELOPMENT (EBRD)

History and Membership. A treaty to establish the EBRD was signed in May 1990; it was inaugurated on 15 April 1991. It had 41 original members: the European Commission, the European Investment Bank, all the EEC countries and all the countries of eastern Europe except Albania. Albania became a member in Oct. 1991, all the republics of the former USSR in March 1992, and Bosnia-Hercegovina in April 1996, bringing the total membership to 60 in 1998.

Capital. Its founding capital is ecu 10,000m., of which the USA contributed 10%, the UK, France, Germany, Italy, Japan 8·5% each, and the USSR 6%. In 1996, the Board of Governors agreed to increase the Bank's capital base to ecu 20,000m. The Bank borrows in various currencies on world capital markets.

Objectives. It was set up to foster the transition towards market-oriented economies in central and eastern Europe, to lend funds at market rates to companies and countries 'committed to, and applying, the fundamental principles of multiparty democracy, pluralism and market economics'. Facilities were extended to the countries of the former USSR in 1992.

A policy statement of May 1991 placed initial emphasis on programmes: to support the creation and strengthening of infrastructures; privatization and reform of the financial sector, including development of capital markets and privatization of commercial banks; development of productive competitive private sectors of small and medium-sized enterprises in industry, agriculture and services; restructuring industrial sectors to put them on a competitive basis; encouraging foreign investment; and the promotion of sustainable and environmentally sound development.

Activities. Under a phased programme, countries which fulfil certain development criteria graduate out of the Bank's sphere of operations. By 1997, the Bank had approved 450 projects, involving ecu 9,960m. of EBRD's own funds, which were expected to mobilize an additional ecu 20,100m. Of the approved projects, 370 had been signed, committing ecu 7,700m. of EBRD funds. 70% of total approved funding was for private sector projects. In 1996, operating profit before provisions was ecu 97·3m.

Project-related technical co-operation is a major part of EBRD's activities. By 1997, 47 co-operation fund agreements with bilateral donors, totalling ecu 424m. had been made with the Bank for this purpose; 1,471 projects, with a total estimated cost of ecu 398m. had been committed.

Organization. There is a Board of Governors with full management powers, and a 23-member Board of Directors elected for a 3-year term, which is involved in day-to-day operations. The President is elected by the Board of Governors for a 4-year term. There are 24 regional offices in 22 of its countries of operations.

Headquarters: 1 Exchange Square, London EC2A 2EH.
Website: http://www.ebrd.com
Secretary-General: Antonio Maria Costa.

EUROPEAN FREE TRADE ASSOCIATION (EFTA)

History and Membership. The Stockholm Convention establishing the Association entered into force on 3 May 1960. Founder members were Austria, Denmark, Norway, Portugal, Sweden, Switzerland and the UK. With the accession of Austria, Denmark, Finland, Portugal, Sweden and the UK to the EU, EFTA was reduced to 4 member countries: Iceland, Liechtenstein, Norway and Switzerland.

Activities. Free trade in industrial goods among members was achieved by 1966. Co-operation with the EU began in 1972 with the signing of free trade agreements and culminated in the establishment of a *European Economic Area (EEA),* encompassing the free movement of goods, services, capital and labour throughout EFTA and the EU countries. The Agreement was signed by all members of the EU and EFTA on 2 May 1992, but was rejected by Switzerland in a referendum on 6 Dec. 1992. Entry into force took place on 1 Jan. 1994.

The main provisions of the EEA Agreement are: free movement of products within the EEA from 1993 (with special arrangements to cover food, energy, coal and steel); EFTA to assume EU rules on company law, consumer protection, education, the environment, research and development and social policy; EFTA to adopt EU competition rules on anti-trust matters, abuse of a dominant position, public procurement, mergers and state aid; EFTA to create an EFTA Surveillance Authority and an EFTA Court; individuals to be free to live, work and offer services throughout the EEA, with mutual recognition of professional qualifications; capital movements to be free with some restrictions on investments; EFTA countries not to be bound by the Common Agricultural Policy (CAP) or Common Fisheries Policy (CFP).

The EEA-EFTA states have established a Surveillance Authority and a Court to ensure implementation of the Agreement among the EFTA-EEA states. Political direction is given by the EEA Council which meets twice a year at ministerial level, while ongoing operation of the Agreement is overseen by the EEA Joint Committee. Legislative power remains with national governments and parliaments.

EFTA has formal relations with several other states. Declarations on co-operation were signed with Hungary, former Czechoslovakia and Poland (1990), Bulgaria, Estonia, Latvia, Lithuania and Romania (1991), Slovenia and Albania (1992), Egypt, Morocco and Tunisia (1995), the former Yugoslav Republic of Macedonia and the Palestine Liberation Organization (1996), Jordan and Lebanon (1997). Co-operation with Yugoslavia was suspended in Nov. 1991. Free trade agreements have been signed with Turkey (1991), Israel and Czechoslovakia (1992, with protocols on succession with the Czech Republic and Slovakia in 1993), Poland and Romania (1992), Bulgaria and Hungary (1993), Estonia, Latvia, Lithuania and Slovenia (1995), Morocco (1997). Contacts with the Gulf Co-operation Council have also been established.

A Central European Free Trade Area (CEFTA) has also now been established between the Czech Republic, Hungary, Poland, Slovakia and Slovenia.

Organization. The operation of the free trade area among the EFTA states is the responsibility of the EFTA Council which meets regularly at ambassadorial level in Geneva. The Council is assisted by a Secretariat and standing committees. Each EFTA country holds the chairmanship of the Council for 6 months. For EEA matters there is a separate committee structure.

Brussels Office (EEA matters, press and information): 74 rue de Trèves, B-1040 Brussels.

Deputy Secretary-General, Brussels: Guttorm Vik (Norway).

Headquarters: 9–11 rue de Varembé, 1211 Geneva 20, Switzerland.

Website: http://www.efta.int.

Secretary-General: Kjartan Jóhansson (Iceland).

Publications. Convention Establishing the European Free Trade Association; EFTA Annual Report; EFTA Fact Sheets: Information Papers on Aspects of the EEA.

CENTRAL EUROPEAN INITIATIVE (CEI)

In July 1990, Austria, Czechoslovakia, Hungary, Italy and Yugoslavia met on Italy's initiative to form an economic and political co-operation group in the region between the Adriatic and the Baltic Sea.

Members. (1998) Austria, Bosnia-Hercegovina, Croatia, Czech Republic, Hungary, Italy, Macedonia, Poland, Slovakia, Slovenia.

Associate Members. Belarus, Bulgaria, Romania, Ukraine.

Headquarters: Ministry of Foreign Affairs, Bem Rakpart 47, Budapest II, Hungary.

COUNCIL OF BALTIC SEA STATES

Founded in 1992 in Copenhagen following a meeting of the European Commission there.

Members. Germany, Denmark, Iceland, Norway, Sweden, Finland, Estonia, Latvia, Lithuania, Russia, Poland.

Aims. To help transform the former Communist countries into free-market economies to prepare them for closer relations with the EU, without duplicating the work of existing international organizations; to promote co-operation in areas of aid to new democratic institutions, economic development, humanitarian aid, energy and the environment, cultural programmes and education, transport and communication.

The Council meets at ministerial level once a year, chaired by rotating foreign ministers (by the Environment Minister in the case of Finland). This session is the supreme decision-making body. Between annual meetings the Committee of Senior Officials meets once a month. A number of action programmes have already been adopted.

Headquarters: S-103 33 Stockholm, Sweden.
Website: http://www.baltinfo.org.
Director: Ewa Persson Goransson.

BLACK SEA ECONOMIC CO-OPERATION GROUP (BSEC)

Founded 1992 to promote economic co-operation in the region. Priority areas of interest include: transport and communications, energy, environmental protection, tourism, trade and industrial co-operation, agriculture and agro-industry, healthcare and pharmaceutics, science and technology, finance administration.

Members. Albania, Armenia, Azerbaijan, Bulgaria, Georgia, Greece, Moldova, Romania, Russia, Turkey, Ukraine.

Observers. Austria, Egypt, Israel, Italy, Poland, Slovakia, Tunisia.

There is a *BSEC Business Council*, and a *Black Sea Trade and Development Bank* was established in Thessalonika, Greece, in 1993, with a founding capital of US$300m.

In May 1994, members met to try and create a mechanism for the solution of conflicts in the region, under the auspices of the Group's Interparliamentary Legal and Political Affairs Committee.

Headquarters: Istinye Cad. Musir Fuad Pasa Yalisi, Eski Tersane 80860, Istinye, Istanbul, Turkey.
Secretary-General: Evgeni Kotovoy (Russia).

DANUBE COMMISSION

History and Membership. The Danube Commission was constituted in 1949 according to the Convention on the regulation of shipping on the Danube signed in Belgrade on 18 Aug. 1948. The Belgrade Convention declared that navigation on the Danube from Ulm to the Black Sea (with access to the sea through the Sulina arm and the Sulina Canal) is equally free and open to the nationals, merchant shipping and merchandise of all states as to harbour and navigation fees as well as conditions of merchant navigation. The Commission holds annual sessions and is composed of 1 representative from each of its members countries: Austria, Bulgaria, Hungary, Romania, Russia, Slovakia, Ukraine and the Federal Republic of Yugoslavia. Croatia, Germany and Moldova have observer status.

Functions. To ensure that the provisions of the Belgrade Convention are carried out; to establish a uniform buoying system on all navigable waterways; to establish the basic regulations for navigation on the river and ensure facilities for shipping; to co-ordinate the regulations for river, customs and sanitation control as well as the hydrometeorological service; to collect relevant statistical data concerning navigation on the Danube.

Recent events, including the emergence of newly independent states with justified interests in the region, will require a new multilateral agreement on management of the river. The scope of the original Convention may also be broadened to include new areas such as energy production and environmental protection.

Official languages. French, Russian.

Headquarters: Benczúr utca 25, H-1068 Budapest, Hungary.
Director-General: Hellmuth Strasser (Austria).

THE COMMONWEALTH

The Commonwealth is a free association of sovereign independent states, numbering 54 at the beginning of 1998, representing over a quarter of the world's population. There is no charter, treaty or constitution; the association is expressed in co-operation, consultation and mutual assistance for which the Commonwealth Secretariat is the central co-ordinating body.

Origin. The Commonwealth was first defined by the Imperial Conference of 1926 as a group of 'autonomous Communities within the British Empire, equal in status, in no way subordinate one to another in any aspect of their domestic or external affairs, though united by a common allegiance to the Crown, and freely associated as members of the British Commonwealth of Nations'. The basis of the association changed from one owing allegiance to a common Crown, and the modern Commonwealth was born in 1949 when the member countries accepted India's intention of becoming a republic at the same time as continuing 'her full membership of the Commonwealth of Nations and her acceptance of the King as the symbol of the free association of its independent member nations and as such the Head of the Commonwealth'. In 1997, the Commonwealth consisted of 33 republics and 21 monarchies, of which 16 are Queen's realms. All acknowledge the Queen symbolically as Head of the Commonwealth. The Queen's legal title rests on the statute of 12 and 13 Will. III, c. 3, by which the succession to the Crown of Great Britain and Ireland was settled on the Princess Sophia of Hanover and the 'heirs of her body being Protestants'.

A number of territories, formerly under British jurisdiction or mandate, did not join the Commonwealth: Egypt, Iraq, Transjordan, Burma (now Myanmar), Palestine, Sudan, British Somaliland, South Cameroons and Aden. 4 countries, Ireland in 1948, South Africa in 1961, Pakistan in 1972, and Fiji in 1987 have left the Commonwealth. Pakistan was re-admitted to the Commonwealth in 1989, South Africa in 1994, Fiji in 1997. Nigeria was suspended in 1995 for violation of human rights. Mozambique, admitted in Nov. 1995, is the first member state not to have been a member of the former British Commonwealth or Empire. Nauru and Tuvalu are special members, with the right to participate in all functional Commonwealth meetings and activities but not to attend meetings of Commonwealth Heads of Government.

MEMBER STATES OF THE COMMONWEALTH

The 54 member states at Jan. 1998, with year of admission:

	Year of admission		Year of admission
Antigua and Barbuda	1981	Dominica	1978
Australia[1]	1931	Fiji[3]	1997
Bahamas	1973	Gambia	1965
Bangladesh	1972	Ghana	1957
Barbados	1966	Grenada	1974
Belize	1981	Guyana	1966
Botswana	1966	India	1947
Brunei[2]	1984	Jamaica	1962
Cameroon	1995	Kenya	1963
Canada[1]	1931	Kiribati	1979
Cyprus	1961	Lesotho	1966

	Year of admission		Year of admission
Malawi	1964	Seychelles	1976
Malaysia	1957	Sierra Leone	1961
Maldives	1982	Singapore	1965
Malta	1964	Solomon Islands	1978
Mauritius	1968	South Africa[7]	1994
Mozambique	1995	Sri Lanka	1948
Namibia	1990	Swaziland	1968
Nauru[4]	1968	Tanzania	1961
New Zealand[1]	1931	Tonga[2]	1970
Nigeria[5]	1960	Trinidad and Tobago	1962
Pakistan[6]	1989	Tuvalu	1978
Papua New Guinea	1975	Uganda	1982
St Kitts and Nevis	1983	United Kingdom	1931
St Lucia	1979	Vanuatu	1980
St Vincent and Grenadines	1979	Zambia	1964
Samoa	1970	Zimbabwe	1980

[1] Independence given legal effect by the Statute of Westminster 1931.
[2] Brunei and Tonga had been sovereign states in treaty relationship with the UK.
[3] Left 1987; rejoined 1997. [4] Nauru was first a Mandate, then a Trust territory.
[5] Membership suspended 1995. [6] Left 1972, rejoined 1989. [7] Left 1961, rejoined 1994.

Dependent Territories and Associated States. There are 13 British dependent territories, 6 Australian external territories, 2 New Zealand dependent territories and 2 New Zealand associated states. A dependent territory is a territory belonging by settlement, conquest or annexation to the British, Australian or New Zealand Crown.

UK dependent territories administered through the Foreign and Commonwealth Office comprise, in the Indian Ocean. British Indian Ocean Territory; in the Mediterranean: Gibraltar; in the Atlantic Ocean: Bermuda, Falkland Islands, South Georgia and South Sandwich Islands, British Antarctic Territory, St Helena and Dependencies (Ascension and Tristan da Cunha); in the Caribbean: Montserrat, British Virgin Islands, Cayman Islands, Turks and Caicos Islands, Anguilla; in the Western Pacific: Pitcairn Group of Islands.

The Australian external territories are: Coral Sea Islands, Cocos (Keeling) Islands, Christmas Island, Heard and McDonald Islands, Australian Antarctic and Ashmore and Cartier Islands. The New Zealand dependent territories are: Tokelau Islands and the Ross Dependency. The New Zealand associated states are: Cook Islands and Niue.

British Government Department. With effect from 17 Oct. 1968, the Secretary of State for Foreign and Commonwealth Affairs is responsible for the conduct of relations with members of the Commonwealth as well as with foreign countries. While constitutional responsibility to Parliament for the government of the British dependent territories rests with the Secretary of State for Foreign and Commonwealth Affairs, the administration of the territories is carried out by the Governments of the territories themselves.

Aims and Conditions of Membership. Membership involves acceptance of certain core principles, as set out in the Harare Declaration of 1991, and is subject to the approval of other member states. The Harare Declaration charts a course to take the Commonwealth into the 21st century and affirms members' continued commitment to the Singapore Declarations of 1971, by which members committed themselves to the pursuit of world peace and support of the UN.

The core principles defined by the Harare Declaration are: political democracy, human rights, good governance and the rule of law, and the protection of the environment through sustainable development. Commitment to these principles was made binding as a condition of membership at the 1993 Heads of Government meeting in Cyprus.

The Millbrook Action Programme of 1995 aims to support countries in implementing the Harare Declaration, providing assistance in constitutional and judicial matters, running elections, training and technical advice. Violations of the Harare Declaration will provoke a series of measures by the Commonwealth Secretariat, including: expression of disapproval, encouragement of bilateral actions by member states, appointment of fact-finders and mediators, stipulation of a period for the restoration of democracy, exclusion from ministerial meetings, suspension of all participation and aid and finally punitive measures including trade sanctions. An 8-member *Ministerial Action Group* may be convened by the Secretary-General as and when necessary to deal with violations. The Group held its first meeting in Dec. 1995. Its terms of reference are as set out in the Millbrook Action Programme.

The *Commonwealth Parliamentary Assembly* was founded in 1911. As defined by its constitution, its objectives are to 'promote knowledge of the constitutional, legislative, economic, social and cultural aspects of parliamentary democracy'. It meets these objectives by organizing conferences, meetings and seminars for members, arranging exchange visits between members, publishing books, newsletters, reports, studies and a quarterly journal and providing an information service. Its principal governing body is the General Assembly, which meets annually during the Commonwealth Parliamentary Conference and is composed of members attending that Conference as delegates. The Assembly elects an Executive Committee comprising a Chair, President, Vice-President, Treasurer and 27 regional representatives, which meets twice a year. The Chair is elected for 3-year terms. The Assembly is financed by membership fees levied on each branch and based on the number of delegates entitled to attend the Commonwealth Parliamentary Conference. The Secretariat is headed by the Secretary-General, with access to Heads of Government; the Secretariat is staffed by officers from member countries and is financed by contributions from member governments.

Commonwealth Secretariat. The Commonwealth Secretariat is an international body at the service of all 54 member countries. It provides the central organization for joint consultation and co-operation in many fields. It was established in 1965 by Commonwealth Heads of Government as a 'visible symbol of the spirit of co-operation which animates the Commonwealth', and has observer status at the UN General Assembly.

The Secretariat disseminates information on matters of common concern, organizes and services meetings and conferences, co-ordinates many Commonwealth activities, and provides expert technical assistance for economic and social development through the multilateral Commonwealth Fund for Technical Co-operation. The Secretariat is organized in divisions and sections which correspond to its main areas of operation: international affairs, economic affairs, food production and rural development, youth, education, information, applied studies in government, science and technology, law and health. Within this structure the Secretariat organizes the biennial meetings of Commonwealth Heads of Government (CHOGMs), annual meetings of Finance Ministers of member countries, and regular meetings of Ministers of Education, Law, Health, and others as appropriate. To emphasize the multilateral nature of the association, meetings are held in different cities and regions within the Commonwealth. Heads of Government decided that the Secretariat should work from London as it has the widest range of communications of any Commonwealth city, as well as the largest assembly of diplomatic missions.

Commonwealth Heads of Government Meetings (CHOGMs). Outside the UN, the CHOGM remains the largest inter-governmental conference in the world. Meetings are held every 2 years. The theme for the 1997 CHOGM in Edinburgh was the promotion of inter-Commonwealth trade, investment and development. At the Commonwealth Business Forum 2 days before the CHOGM, Tony Blair announced the British Government's decision to sell its majority holding in the Commonwealth Development Corporation and introduce private capital to the Corporation, which would effectively become a public-private partnership. The CDC invests £300m. a year in 54 of the poorest parts of the world, and manages 34 businesses worldwide. The hope is that this will allow the CDC to raise money in financial markets which it is banned from doing under Treasury rules as a state-owned company. The proceeds from the sale will go back into development aid.

A host of Commonwealth organizations and agencies are dedicated to enhancing inter-Commonwealth relations and the development of the potential of

Commonwealth citizens. A list of these can be obtained from the *Commonwealth Institute* in London.

Commonwealth Day is celebrated on the second Monday in March each year. The theme for 1998 is sport.

Headquarters: Marlborough House, Pall Mall, London, SW1Y 5HX, UK.
*Website:*http://www.commonwealth.org.uk
Secretary-General: Emeka Anyaoku (Nigeria).

Selected publications. Commonwealth Yearbook; The Commonwealth Today; Commonwealth Currents (quarterly); *Directory of Commonwealth Organizations.*

Further Reading

The Cambridge History of the British Empire. 8 vols. CUP, 1929 ff.
Austin, D., *The Commonwealth and Britain.* London, 1988
Chan, S., *Twelve Years of Commonwealth Diplomatic History: Summit Meetings, 1979-1991.* Lampeter, 1992
Hall, H. D., *Commonwealth: A History of the British Commonwealth.* London and New York, 1971
Judd, D. and Slinn, P., *The Evolution of the Modern Commonwealth.* London, 1982
Keeton, G. W. (ed.) *The British Commonwealth: Its Laws and Constitutions.* 9 vols. London, 1951 ff.
Larby, P. and Hannam, H., *The Commonwealth.* [Bibliography]. Oxford and New Brunswick (NJ), 1993
McIntyre, W. D., *The Significance of the Commonwealth, 1965-90.* London, 1991
Moore, R. J., *Making the New Commonwealth.* Oxford, 1987

COMMONWEALTH OF INDEPENDENT STATES (CIS)

The Commonwealth of Independent States is a community of independent states which proclaimed itself the successor to the Union of Soviet Socialist Republics in some aspects of international law and affairs. The member states are the founders, Russia, Belarus and Ukraine, and 9 subsequent adherents: Armenia, Azerbaijan, Georgia, Kazakhstan, Kyrgyzstan, Moldova, Tajikistan, Turkmenistan and Uzbekistan. The common affairs of the CIS are conducted on a multilateral, inter-state basis rather than by central institutions. It provides a framework for military, foreign policy and economic co-ordination.

History. Extended negotiations in the Union of Soviet Socialist Republics (USSR) in 1990 and 1991, under the direction of President Gorbachev, sought to establish a 'renewed federation' or, subsequently, to conclude a new union treaty that would embrace all the 15 constituent republics of the USSR at that date. According to a referendum conducted in Mar. 1991, 76% of the population (on an 80% turnout) wished to maintain the USSR as a 'renewed federation of equal sovereign republics in which the human rights and freedoms of any nationality would be fully guaranteed'. In Sept. 1991, the 3 Baltic republics—Estonia, Latvia and Lithuania—were nonetheless recognized as independent states by the USSR State Council, and subsequently by the international community. Most of the remaining republics reached agreement on the broad outlines of a new 'union of sovereign states' in Nov. 1991, which would have retained a directly elected President and an all-union legislature, but which would have limited central authority to those powers specifically delegated to it by the members of the union.

A referendum in Ukraine in Dec. 1991, however, showed overwhelming support for full independence, and following this the 3 Slav republics (Russia, Belarus and Ukraine) concluded the Minsk Agreement on 8 Dec. 1991, establishing a Commonwealth of Independent States (CIS), headquartered in Minsk. The USSR, as a subject of international law and a geopolitical reality, was declared no longer in existence, and each of the 3 republics individually renounced the 1922 treaty through which the USSR had been established.

The CIS declared itself open to other former Soviet republics, and to states elsewhere that shared its objectives, and on 21 Dec. 1991 in Alma-Ata, a further declaration was signed with 8 other republics: Armenia, Azerbaijan, Kazakhstan, Kyrgyzstan, Moldova, Tajikistan, Turkmenistan and Uzbekistan. The declaration committed signatories to recognize the independence and sovereignty of other members, to respect human rights including those of national minorities, and to the observance of existing boundaries. Relations among the members of the CIS were to be conducted on an equal, multilateral basis, but it was agreed to endorse the principle of unitary control of strategic nuclear arms and the concept of a 'single economic space'. In addition, members pledged themselves to discharge the obligations that arose from the international treaties and agreements to which the USSR had been a party. In a separate agreement the heads of member states agreed that Russia should take up the seat at the United Nations formerly occupied by the USSR, and a framework of inter-state and intergovernment consultation was established. Following these developments Mikhail Gorbachev resigned as USSR President on 25 Dec. 1991, and on 26 Dec., the USSR Supreme Soviet voted a formal end to the 1922 Treaty of Union, and dissolved itself.

Institutions. The principal organs of the CIS, according to the agreement concluded in Alma-Ata on 21 Dec. 1991, are the Council of Heads of States, which meets twice a year, and the Council of Heads of Government, which meets every 3 months. Both councils may convene extraordinary sessions, and may hold joint sittings. A Council of CIS Foreign Ministers was also established in Dec. 1993.

At a summit meeting of heads of states (with the exception of Azerbaijan) in July 1992, agreements were reached on the formation of a CIS peacekeeping force; the establishment of an economic arbitration court and a way to divide former Soviet assets abroad; and some progress was made towards the creation of economic co-ordinating structures. At a subsequent meeting in Jan. 1993, Russia, Belarus, Armenia, Kazakhstan, Kyrgyzstan, Turkmenistan and Uzbekistan agreed on a charter to these ends, to establish a defence alliance, economic co-ordination committee and inter-state court. Three participants (Ukraine, Moldova and Tajikistan) agreed only to a declaration that any state would be free to sign the charter in future, and that an inter-state bank should be set up.

The *CIS Inter-State Bank* was set up in Dec. 1993, with a starting capital of 5,000m. roubles, to facilitate multilateral clearing of CIS inter-state transactions. Members' contributions (by %), based on their share of foreign trade turnover in 1990, were as follows: Russia, 50%; Ukraine, 20·7%; Belarus, 8·4%; Kazakhstan, 6·1%; Uzbekistan, 5·5%; Moldova, 2·9%; Armenia, 1·8%; Tajikistan, 1·6%; Kyrgyzstan, 1·5%; Turkmenistan, 1·5%.

In accordance with the Agreement on Armed Forces and Border Troops, concluded on 30 Dec. 1991, a peacekeeping force ('white helmets') to be deployed in intra-CIS conflicts at the request of member states, and with the consent of the parties to the conflict, was duly established. CIS members contribute to this force in proportion to the size of their armed forces; the commander is appointed on each occasion by the CIS heads of state. In 1993, the office of Commander-in-Chief of CIS Joint Armed Forces was replaced by that of Chief of Joint Staff for Co-ordinating Military Co-operation.

On 24 Sept. 1993, Russia, Armenia, Azerbaijan, Belarus, Kazakhstan, Kyrgyzstan, Moldova, Tajikistan and Uzbekistan signed an agreement to form an economic union, with Ukraine and Turkmenistan as associated members. Georgia, which was admitted to the CIS in Dec. 1993, signed some of the provisions. In Oct. 1994, a summit meeting established the *Inter-Government Economic Committee* to be based in Moscow. Members include all CIS states except Turkmenistan. The Committee's decisions are binding if voted by 80% of the membership. Russia commands 50% of the voting power. The Committee's remit is to co-ordinate energy, transport and communications policies. A *Payments Union* was also agreed, to regulate payments between member states with non-convertible independent currencies.

On 29 March 1996, Belarus, Kazakhstan, Kyrgyzstan and Russia signed an agreement increasing their mutual economic and social integration by creating a

Community of Integrated States. The agreement established a Supreme Inter-Governmental Council comprising heads of state and government and foreign ministers, with a rotatory Chair, an integration committee of Ministers and an Inter-Parliamentary Committee.

On 2 April 1996, the Presidents of Belarus and Russia signed a treaty providing for political, economic and military integration, creating the nucleus of a *Commonwealth of Sovereign Republics.* The agreement establishes a Supreme Council comprising the Presidents, Prime Ministers and Speakers of both countries. A further treaty was signed on 22 May 1997, instituting common citizenship, common deployment of military forces and the harmonization of the 2 economies with a view to the creation of a common currency.

In March 1994, the CIS was accorded observer status in the UN.

Headquarters: 220000 Minsk, Kirava 17, Belarus.
Executive Secretary: Ivan M. Korotchenya.

Further Reading

Brzezinski, Z. and Sullivan, P. (eds.) *Russia and the Commonwealth of Independent States: Documents, Data and Analysis.* Armonk (NY), 1996

ORGANIZATION OF AMERICAN STATES (OAS)

Origin. On 14 April 1890, representatives of the American republics, meeting in Washington at the First International Conference of American States, established an International Union of American Republics and, as its central office, a Commercial Bureau of American Republics, which later became the Pan-American Union. This international organization's object was to foster mutual understanding and co-operation among the nations of the western hemisphere. This led to the adoption on 30 April 1948 by the Ninth International Conference of American States, at Bogotá, Colombia, of the Charter of the Organization of American States. This co-ordinated the work of all the former independent official entities in the inter-American system and defined their mutual relationships. The Charter of 1948 subsequently was amended by the Protocol of Buenos Aires (1967) and the Protocol of Cartagena de Indias (1985).

Members. This is on a basis of absolute equality, with each country having 1 vote and there being no veto power. Members (1998): Antigua and Barbuda, Argentina, Bahamas, Barbados, Belize, Bolivia, Brazil, Canada, Chile, Colombia, Costa Rica, Cuba (suspended 1962), Dominica, Dominican Republic, Ecuador, El Salvador, Grenada, Guatemala, Guyana, Haiti, Honduras, Jamaica, Mexico, Nicaragua, Panama, Paraguay, Peru, St Kitts and Nevis, St Lucia, St Vincent and the Grenadines, Suriname, Trinidad and Tobago, USA, Uruguay, Venezuela.

Permanent Observers. Algeria, Angola, Austria, Belgium, Bosnia-Hercegovina, Croatia, Cyprus, Czech Republic, Egypt, Equatorial Guinea, EU, Finland, France, Germany, Ghana, Greece, Holy See, Hungary, India, Israel, Italy, Japan, Kazakhstan, Republic of Korea, Latvia, Lebanon, Morocco, the Netherlands, Pakistan, Poland, Portugal, Romania, Russia, Saudi Arabia, Spain, Sri Lanka, Sweden, Switzerland, Tunisia, UK, Ukraine.

Purpose and Activities. To strengthen the peace and security of the continent; promote and consolidate representative democracy, with due respect for the principle of non-intervention; prevent possible causes of difficulties and ensure the peaceful settlement of disputes among member states; provide for common action in the event of aggression; seek the solution of political, juridical and economic problems; promote by co-operative action economic, social and cultural development; and achieve an effective limitation of conventional weapons in order to devote maximum resources to economic and social development.

The Santiago Commitment to Democracy and the Renewal of the Inter-American

System. With the emergence of democratically elected governments throughout the continent, the OAS has been increasingly concerned with the preservation, protection and promotion of democracy. At its 21st Regular Session (Santiago, Chile, 1991) the OAS General Assembly adopted the Santiago Commitment to Democracy and the Renewal of the Inter-American System as well as the Protocol of Washington (1992) to amend the Charter by provisions of the resolution 1080 on representative democracy. The latter calls for collective action in the event of a 'sudden or irregular interruption of the democratic political institutional process or of the legitimate exercise of power by the democratically elected government in any of the Organization's member states'. Specifically, the Assembly approved an Article which provides that a member of OAS whose democratically constituted government has been overthrown by force may be suspended from the exercise of the right to participate in the sessions of OAS organs, and spells out the way such suspension shall be applied.

The Protocol of Washington also incorporates among the essential purposes of the OAS the eradication of extreme poverty which constitutes an obstacle to the full democratic development of the peoples of the hemisphere. This commitment was further strengthened by amendments under the Protocol of Managua the following year, with measures designed to improve the delivery of technical co-operation to such member states. At its 20th Special Session (Feb. 1994, Mexico City), the OAS General Assembly approved a resolution on a commitment to a partnership for development and struggle to overcome extreme poverty.

Declaration of Belém do Pará. At its 24th Regular Session (June 1994, Belém do Pará), the General Assembly adopted the Declaration of Belém do Pará, in which the Ministers of Foreign Affairs and Heads of Delegation of Member States declared their commitment to strengthening the OAS as the main hemispheric forum of political consensus, so that it may support: the realization of the aspirations of member states in promoting and consolidating peace, democracy, social justice, and development, in accordance with the purposes and principles of the Charter; their decision to promote and deepen co-operative relations in the economic, social, educational, cultural, scientific, technological and political fields; their commitment to continue and further the dialogue on hemispheric security in order to consolidate and strengthen mutual confidence; their determination to continue to contribute to the objective of general and complete disarmament, under effective international control; their determination to strengthen regional co-operation to increase the effectiveness of efforts to combat the illicit use of narcotic drugs and traffic therein; their decision to co-operate in a reciprocal effort towards preventing and punishing terrorist acts, methods and practices, and the development of international law in this matter; and their commitment to promote economic and social development for the indigenous populations of their countries.

The OAS also carries out programmes to promote the economic and social development of its member states. Specialized training is provided for Latin American and Caribbean citizens each year in development-related fields; and development projects are executed each year in response to requests from member governments.

Organization. Under its Charter the OAS accomplishes its purposes by means of:
(a) The General Assembly, which meets annually.
(b) The Meeting of Consultation of Ministers of Foreign Affairs, held to consider problems of an urgent nature and of common interest.
(c) The Councils: The Permanent Council, which meets on a permanent basis at OAS headquarters and carries out decisions of the General Assembly, assists the member states in the peaceful settlement of disputes, acts as the Preparatory Committee of that Assembly, submits recommendations with regard to the functioning of the Organization, and considers the reports to the Assembly of the other organs. The Inter-American Council for Integral Development (CIDI) (formed from the merger of two previous councils, the Inter-American Economic and Social Council and the Inter-American Council for Education, Science and Culture) directs and monitors OAS technical co-operation programmes.
(d) The Inter-American Juridical Committee which acts as an advisory body to the OAS on juridical matters and promotes the development and codification of interna-

tional law. 11 jurists, elected for 4-year terms by the General Assembly, represent all the American States.

(e) The Inter-American Commission on Human Rights which oversees the observance and protection of human rights. 7 members elected for 4-year terms by the General Assembly represent all the OAS member states.

(f) The General Secretariat, which is the central and permanent organ of the OAS.

(g) The Specialized Conferences, meeting to deal with special technical matters or to develop specific aspects of inter-American co-operation.

(h) The Specialized Organizations, intergovernmental organizations established by multilateral agreements to discharge specific functions in their respective fields of action, such as women's affairs, agriculture, child welfare, Indian affairs, geography and history, and health.

The Secretary-General is elected by the General Assembly for 5-year terms. The General Assembly approves the annual budget which is financed by quotas contributed by the member governments. The budget for 1996 amounted to US$100·6m.

Headquarters: 17th Street and Constitution Avenue, NW, Washington, DC, 20006, USA.

Secretary-General: César Gaviria Trujillo (Colombia).

Publications. Charter of the Organization of American States. 1948.—As Amended by the Protocol of Buenos Aires in 1967 and the Protocol of Cartagena de Indias in 1985; The OAS and the Evolution of the Inter-American System; Annual Report of the Secretary-General; Status of Inter-American Treaties and Conventions (annual).

Further Reading

Sheinin, D., *The Organization of American States* [Bibliography]. Oxford and Metuchen (NJ), 1995

INTER-AMERICAN DEVELOPMENT BANK (IDB)

The IDB, the oldest and largest regional multilateral development institution, was established in 1959 to help accelerate economic and social development in Latin America and the Caribbean. The Bank's original membership included 19 Latin American and Caribbean countries and the USA. Today, membership totals 46 nations, including non-regional members.

Members. Argentina, Austria, Bahamas, Barbados, Belgium, Belize, Bolivia, Brazil, Canada, Chile, Colombia, Costa Rica, Croatia, Denmark, Dominican Republic, Ecuador, El Salvador, Finland, France, Germany, Guatemala, Guyana, Haiti, Honduras, Israel, Italy, Jamaica, Japan, Mexico, Netherlands, Nicaragua, Norway, Panama, Paraguay, Peru, Portugal, Slovenia, Spain, Suriname, Sweden, Switzerland, Trinidad and Tobago, UK, USA, Uruguay, Venezuela.

In carrying out its mission, the Bank has mobilized some US$206,000m. for project financing, and its lending has increased dramatically from the US$294m. approved in 1961 to US$6,700m. in 1996.

Current lending priorities include poverty reduction and social equity, modernization and integration, and the environment. The Bank has a Fund for Special Operations for lending on concessional terms for projects in countries classified as economically less developed. An additional facility, the Multilateral Investment Fund (MIF), was created in 1992 to help promote and accelerate investment reforms and private-sector development throughout the region.

The Board of Governors is the Bank's highest authority. Governors are usually Ministers of Finance, Presidents of Central Banks or officers of comparable rank. The Board of Directors is the Bank's executive body. The IDB has country offices in each of its borrowing countries, and in Paris and Tokyo.

Headquarters: 1300 New York Avenue, NW, Washington, DC 20577, USA
Website: http://www.iadb.org.
President: Enrique V. Iglesias (Uruguay).

CENTRAL AMERICAN COMMON MARKET (CACM)

In Dec. 1960, El Salvador, Guatemala, Honduras and Nicaragua concluded the General Treaty of Central American Economic Integration under the auspices of the Organization of Central American States (ODECA) in Managua. Long-standing political and social conflicts in the area have repeatedly dogged efforts to establish integration towards the establishment of a common market. *Members.* Costa Rica, El Salvador, Guatemala, Honduras, Nicaragua and Panama.

A protocol to the 1960 General Treaty signed by all 6 members in Oct. 1993 reaffirmed an eventual commitment to full economic integration with a common external tariff of 20% to be introduced only voluntarily and gradually.

A Treaty on Democratic Security in Central America was signed by all 6 members at San Pedro Sula, Honduras in Dec. 1995, with a view to achieving a proper 'balance of forces' in the region, intensifying the fight against trafficking of drugs and arms, and reintegrating refugees and displaced persons.

In addition, the CACM countries signed a new framework co-operation agreement with the EC in Feb. 1993, revising the previous (1985) failing agreement between them, to provide support to CACM's integration plans.

Headquarters: 4a Avda 10–25, Zona 14, Apdo 1237, Guatemala City, Guatemala.
Secretary-General: Haroldo Rodas Melgar.

LATIN AMERICAN INTEGRATION ASSOCIATION (LAIA)

The LAIA was established to promote freer trade among member countries in the region.

Members. (11) Argentina, Bolivia, Brazil, Chile, Colombia, Ecuador, Mexico, Paraguay, Peru, Uruguay, Venezuela.

Observers. (17) China, Commission of the European Communities, Costa Rica, Cuba, Dominican Republic, El Salvador, Guatemala, Honduras, Inter-American Development Bank, Italy, Nicaragua, Organization of American States, Panama, Portugal, Spain, UN Development Programme, UN Economic Commission for Latin America and the Caribbean.

Headquarters: calle Cebollati 1461, Casilla de Correo 577, 11000 Montevideo, Uruguay.

THE ANDEAN COMMUNITY

On 26 May 1969, an agreement was signed by Bolivia, Chile, Colombia, Ecuador and Peru establishing the Cartagena Agreement (also referred to as the Andean Pact or the Andean Group). Chile withdrew from the Group in 1976. Venezuela, which was initially actively involved, did not sign the agreement until 1973. In 1997, Peru announced its withdrawal for 5 years; and Panama joined.

The Act of Caracas signed at the Group's 5th meeting in May 1991 established a free trade zone between member states to come into effect on 1 Jan. 1992 as the first step towards the creation of a common market. There is a common external tariff in 4 bands from 5% to 20%. Tariffs between Bolivia, Colombia and Ecuador were abolished in Oct. 1992.

In Mar. 1996 at the Group's 8th summit in Trujillo in Peru, member countries (Bolivia, Colombia, Ecuador, Peru, Venezuela) signed a reform protocol to the Agreement, according to which the Group would be superseded by the Andean Community, in order to promote greater economic, commercial and political integration between member countries under a new Andean Integration System (SAI).

Organization. The Group's Presidential Council, composed of the presidents of the member states, provides the political leadership of the Community. The Commission, consisting of a plenipotentiary representative from each member country, is assisted by 2 Consultative Councils. The Council of Foreign Ministers meets annually to formulate common external policy. The Secretary-General is elected by the Council of Foreign Ministers. There is also a Parliament, (Parlamento Andino) which sits in Bogota, Colombia, and comprises 5 members from each country; it makes recommendations on regional policy. The Court of Justice, which began operating in 1984, resolves disputes between members and interprets legislation. It comprises 5 judges, one from each country, appointed for a renewable period of 6 years.

Headquarters: Avda Paseo de la Republica 3895, San Isidro, Lima 27, Peru.
Website: http://www.rcb.net.pe/junac.
Secretary-General: Dr Jose Antonio Garcia Belaunde.

SOUTHERN COMMON MARKET (MERCOSUR)

Founded in March 1991 by the Treaty of Asunción between Argentina, Brazil, Paraguay and Uruguay, the treaty committed the signatories to the progressive reduction of tariffs culminating in the formation of a common market on 1 Jan. 1995. This duly came into effect as a free trade zone affecting 90% of commodities. A common external tariff averaging 14% applies to 80% of trade with countries outside Mercosur. Details were agreed at foreign minister level by the Protocol of Ouro Preto signed on 17 Dec. 1994.

In 1996, Chile negotiated a free-trade agreement with Mercosur which came into effect on 1 Oct. Two weeks later, Bolivia signed the same. In Dec. that year, an agreement conferring associate membership on Bolivia was also endorsed.

Organization. The member states' foreign ministers form a Council responsible for leading the integration process, the chairmanship of which rotates every 6 months. The permanent executive body is the Common Market Group of member states, which takes decisions by consensus. There is a Trade Commission and Joint Parliamentary Commission, an arbitration tribunal whose decisions are binding on member countries, and a secretariat in Montevideo.

Headquarters: Rincon 575 P12, 11000 Montevideo, Uruguay.
Administrative Secretary: Manuel Olarreaga.

ASSOCIATION OF CARIBBEAN STATES (ACS)

The Convention establishing the ACS was signed on 24 July 1994 in Cartagena de Indias, Colombia, with the aim of promoting integration among all the countries of the Caribbean, comprising 25 full Member States and a number of potential Associate Members.

Members. Antigua and Barbuda, Bahamas, Barbados, Belize, Colombia, Costa Rica, Cuba, Dominica, Dominican Republic, El Salvador, Grenada, Guatemala, Guyana, Haiti, Honduras, Jamaica, Mexico, Nicaragua, Panama, St Lucia, St Kitts and Nevis, St Vincent and the Grenadines, Suriname, Trinidad and Tobago, Venezuela.
The CARICOM Secretariat, the Latin American Economic System (SELA), the Central American Integration System (SICA) and the Permanent Secretariat of the General Agreement on Central American Economic Integration (SIECA) were declared Founding Observers of the ACS.

Functions. The ACS is an organization for consultation, co-operation and concerted action in the context of economic integration and functional co-operation. Its objectives are enshrined in the Convention and are focused around the following: the strengthening of the regional co-operation and integration process, with a view to creating an enhanced economic space in the region; preserving the environmental integrity of the Caribbean Sea which is regarded as the common patrimony of the peoples of the region; and promoting the sustainable development of the Great Caribbean.

Organization. The main organs of the Association are the Ministerial Council and the Secretariat. There are also Special Committees on: Trade Development and External

Economic Relations; Protection and Conservation of the Environment and the Caribbean Sea; Natural Resources; Tourism; Budget and Administration; Science and Technology; Health; and Education and Culture.

Headquarters: ACS Secretariat, 11-13 Victoria Ave., POB 660, Port of Spain, Trinidad and Tobago.

Website: http://www.acs-aec.org.

Secretary-General: Dr Simón Molina Duarte (Venezuela).

CARIBBEAN COMMUNITY (CARICOM)

Origin. The Treaty of Chaguaramas establishing the Caribbean Community and Common Market was signed by the Prime Ministers of Barbados, Guyana, Jamaica and Trinidad and Tobago at Chaguaramas, Trinidad, on 4 July 1973, and entered into force on 1 Aug. 1973.

6 further countries (Belize, Dominica, Grenada, St Lucia, St Vincent and the Grenadines, Montserrat) signed the Treaty on 17 April 1974, and the Treaty came into effect for those countries on 1 May 1974. Antigua acceded to membership on 4 July that year, St Kitts and Nevis on 26 July; the Bahamas on 4 July 1983 (not Common Market), Suriname on 4 July 1995, Haiti (not Common Market) on 4 July 1997.

Members. Antigua and Barbuda, Bahamas, Barbados, Belize, Dominica, Grenada, Guyana, Haiti, Jamaica, Montserrat, St Kitts and Nevis, St Lucia, St Vincent and the Grenadines, Suriname and Trinidad and Tobago. The British Virgin Islands and Turks and Caicos Islands are associate members. The Dominican Republic and Haiti have observer status.

The Caribbean Community has 3 areas of activity: (i) economic co-operation through the Caribbean Common Market; (ii) co-ordination of foreign policy; (iii) functional co-operation in areas such as health, education and culture, labour and manpower development, and women's affairs.

The Caribbean Common Market provides for the establishment of a Common External Tariff (CET); a common protective policy and the progressive co-ordination of external trade policies; the adoption of a scheme for the harmonization of fiscal incentives to industry; double taxation arrangements among member countries; the co-ordination of economic policies and development planning; and a special regime for the less developed countries of the community.

In 1997, efforts continued to accelerate the development and operation of the CARICOM Single Market and Economy (CS&ME). Protocol 1, amending the Treaty of Chaguaramas, which provides for the restructuring of the organs and institutions of the Community, was signed and is being applied provisionally pending its ratification and entry into force. Protocol II has been signed by 11 member states. It provides for the right of establishment, provision of services and movement of capital which constitute the control elements of the CS&ME. On ratification of this protocol, the foundation will be laid for the free movement of factors of production, giving CARICOM nations the right to establish business for the production of goods and services throughout participating countries.

The Community also established the *Regional Negotiating Machinery (RNM)* to co-ordinate the region's external negotiations. Priority areas are the Free Trade Association Agreement, post-Lomé IV Convention EU-ACP (African Caribbean Pacific) relations, the non-economic initiatives of the Miami summit and World Trade Organization negotiations.

Structure. The Conference of Heads of Government is the principal organ of the Community, and its primary responsibility is to determine the policy of the Community. It is the final authority of the Community and the Common Market, and for the conclusion of treaties and relationships between the Community and international organizations and States. It is responsible for financial arrangements to meet the expenses of the Community.

The Community Council of Ministers is the second highest organ of the Community and consists of Ministers of Government responsible for Community Affairs. The Community Council has primary responsibility for the development of

OECS   71

Community strategic planning and co-ordination in the areas of economic integration, functional co-operation and external relations.

The Bureau of Heads of Government was established on 1 Jan. 1993 with competence to initiate proposals, update consensus, mobilize action and secure the implementation of Community decisions. It comprises the current chairperson of the Conference of Heads of Government, rotating on a 6-monthly basis, and the outgoing and incoming chairpersons, as well as the Secretary-General who acts as chief executive officer.

The Secretariat, successor to the Commonwealth Caribbean Regional Secretariat, is the principal administrative organ of the Community and Common Market. The Secretary-General is appointed by the Conference on the recommendation of the Council for a term not exceeding 5 years and may be reappointed. The Secretary-General shall act in that capacity in all meetings of the Conference, Council, and of institutions of the Community.

Institutions of *the Community*. Ministerial Councils established by the Conference of Heads of Government to assist the principal organs are: Council for Trade and Economic Development (COTED); the Council for Foreign and Community Relations (COFCOR); the Council for Human and Social Development (COHSOD); and the Council for Finance and Planning (COFAP).

The inaugural meeting of the *Association of Caribbean Community Parliamentarians* (ACCP) took place in Barbados in May 1996. The ACCP arose out of a concept presented by the Prime Minister of Barbados at the 8th Conference of Heads of Government Meeting in 1987. It is a representative and deliberative institution which associates the people of the region through their chosen representatives with the promotion of regional development.

Associate Institutions. Caribbean Disaster Emergency Response Agency (for hurricanes); Caribbean Development Bank; Caribbean Examinations Council; Council of Legal Education; University of the West Indies; University of Guyana; Caribbean Meteorological Organization; Eastern Caribbean Central Bank; Organization of Eastern Caribbean States (OECS).

Headquarters: Bank of Guyana Building, PO Box 10827, Georgetown, Guyana.

Secretary-General: Edwin W. Carrington (Trinidad and Tobago).

Publications. CARICOM Perspective. (2 a year); *Annual Report; Treaty Establishing the Caribbean Community.*

Further Reading

Parry, J. H., *et. al. A Short History of the West Indies*. Rev. ed. London, 1987

ORGANIZATION OF EASTERN CARIBBEAN STATES (OECS)

Founded 1981 when 7 eastern Caribbean states signed the Treaty of Basseterre agreeing to co-operate with each other to promote unity and solidarity among the members.

Members. (1998) Antigua and Barbuda, Dominica, Grenada, Montserrat, St Kitts and Nevis, St Lucia, and St Vincent and the Grenadines. The British Virgin Islands and Anguilla have associate membership.

Functions. As set out in the Treaty of Basseterre: to promote co-operation among members and to defend their sovereignty, territorial integrity and independence; to assist member states in the realization of their obligations and responsibilities to the international community with due regard to the role of international law as a standard of conduct in their relationships; to assist member states in the realization of their obligations and responsibilities to the international community with due regard to the role of international issues and to establish and maintain, where possible, arrangements for joint overseas representation and common services; to promote economic integration among members; to pursue these through its respective institutions by discussion of questions of common concern and by agreement on common action.

OECS's work is carried out through a number of specialized institutions, work units or projects in 7 countries. Main areas of interest include: natural resources and solid waste management; education reform, technical and vocational education; pharmaceuticals; trade and agricultural diversification; investment promotion; and civil aviation.

Headquarters: Morne Fortune, PO Box 179, Castries, St Lucia.
Director-General: Swinburne Lestrade.

ASIAN DEVELOPMENT BANK

A multilateral development finance institution established in 1966 to promote economic and social progress in the Asian and Pacific region, the Bank's strategic objectives in the medium term are to foster economic growth, reduce poverty, improve the status of women, support human development (including population planning) and protect the environment.

The bank's capital stock is owned by 56 member countries, 40 regional, 16 non-regional. The bank makes loans and equity investments, and provides technical assistance grants for the preparation and execution of development projects and programmes; promotes investment of public and private capital for development purposes; and assists in co-ordinating development policies and plans in its developing member countries (DMCs).

The bank gives special attention to the needs of smaller or less developed countries, giving priority to regional, subregional and national projects which contribute to the economic growth of the region and promote regional co-operation. Loans from ordinary capital resources on non-concessional terms account for about 70% of cumulative lending. Loans from the bank's principal special fund, the Asian Development Fund, are made on highly concessional terms almost exclusively to the poorest borrowing countries.

Regional members. Afghanistan, Australia, Bangladesh, Bhutan, Cambodia, China, Cook Islands, Fiji, Hong Kong, India, Indonesia, Japan, Kazakhstan, Kiribati, Republic of Korea, Kyrgyzstan, Laos, Malaysia, Maldives, Marshall Islands, Micronesia, Mongolia, Myanmar, Nauru, Nepal, New Zealand, Pakistan, Papua New Guinea, Philippines, Samoa, Singapore, Solomon Islands, Sri Lanka, Taiwan, Thailand, Tonga, Tuvalu, Uzbekistan, Vanuatu, Vietnam.

Non-regional members. Austria, Belgium, Canada, Denmark, Finland, France, Germany, Italy, Netherlands, Norway, Spain, Sweden, Switzerland, Turkey, UK, USA.

Organization. The bank's highest policy-making body is its Board of Governors, which meets annually. Its executive body is the 12-member Board of Directors (each with an alternate), 8 from the regional members, 4 non-regional.

The ADB also has seven resident missions: in Dhaka, Bangladesh; Phnom Penh, Cambodia; New Delhi, India; Jakarta, Indonesia; Kathmandu, Nepal; Islamabad, Pakistan; Hanoi, Vietnam; and a regional mission in Port Vila, Vanuatu. There are also 3 representative offices: in Tokyo, Frankfurt and Washington; and resident missions are being set up in Kazakhstan, Uzbekistan and Sri Lanka.

Headquarters: 6 ADB Avenue, Mandaluyong, Metro Manila, Philippines.

ECONOMIC CO-OPERATION ORGANIZATION (ECO)

An intergovernmental organization established in 1985 by Iran, Pakistan and Turkey for the purpose of promoting regional economic co-operation among member states. Afghanistan, Azerbaijan, Kazakhstan, Kyrgyzstan, Tajikistan, Turkmenistan and Uzbekistan joined in 1992, bringing the total of member states to 10.

The aim of the Organization is to establish a common market of Moslem states. At a conference in Tehran in Feb. 1992, it was agreed to introduce preferential tariffs between member states, set up a development bank in Istanbul, and co-operate in the modernization of transport, communications, industry and agriculture. In 1993, a protocol on Preferential Tariff Arrangements was signed between Turkey, Iran and Pakistan.

At the 1995 summit of heads of state, it was agreed to set up 4 regional institutions: a trade and development bank, a shipping line, an airline and a reinsurance company.

The long-term perspectives and priorities of ECO are defined in the form of 2 Action Plans: the Quetta Plan of Action, and the Istanbul Declaration and Economic Co-operation Strategy, which was adopted in 1996.

The highest policy and decision-making body is the Council of Ministers which meets annually. Also, the heads of state or government meet annually to review the progress and implementation of projects and programmes as well as to serve as the highest-level forum for exchange of views on regional and global issues of common interest to ECO members. ECO has observer status at the UN General Assembly.

Headquarters: 1 Golbou Alley, Kamraniyeh, Tehran, Iran.
Secretary-General: H. E. Mr. Onder Ozar (Turkey).

COLOMBO PLAN

History. Founded in 1950 to promote the development of newly independent Asian member countries, the Colombo Plan has grown from a group of 7 Commonwealth nations into an organization of 24 countries. Originally the Plan was conceived for a period of 6 years. This was renewed from time to time until the Consultative Committee gave the Plan an indefinite lifespan in 1980.

The Plan is multilateral in approach, bilateral in operation: multilateral in that it takes cognizance of the problems of development of member countries in the Asia and Pacific region and endeavours to deal with them in a co-ordinated way; bilateral because negotiations for assistance are made direct between a donor and a recipient country.

Members. Afghanistan, Australia, Bangladesh, Bhutan, Cambodia, Fiji, India, Indonesia, Iran, Japan, South Korea, Laos, Malaysia, Maldives, Myanmar, Nepal, New Zealand, Pakistan, Papua New Guinea, Philippines, Singapore, Sri Lanka, Thailand and USA.

Aims. The aims of the Colombo Plan are: (1) to provide a forum for discussion, at local level, of development needs; (2) to facilitate development assistance by encouraging members to participate as donors and recipients of technical co-operation; and (3) to execute programmes to advance development within member countries. The Plan currently has 4 programmes:

Public administration. Provides training in all sectors of public administration in the context of market-oriented economies.

South-South Co-operation. Utilizes the technological successes of one developing country to help another, through training and transferral of skills. With the focus on the private sector, training is provided in: fisheries management, productivity improvement, small enterprises, poverty alleviation, human resource development in industry and agriculture, investment and trade promotion and technology, environmental issues in agriculture and tourism.

Drug Advisory Programme. Initiated 1972, works with governments, international bodies and NGOs in the region to deliver more effective anti-narcotics programmes. It works both in supply (controlling availability of drugs) and demand (helping counter the culture and providing assistance to addicts).

Colombo Plan Staff College for Technician Education. Established 1973, trains management and technical staff from member countries. It is separately financed by most member countries and functions under the guidance of its own Governing Board, consisting of the heads of member countries' permanent diplomatic missions in the Philippines.

Structure. A Council representing each member government meets several times a year to identify development issues, recommend measures to be taken and ensure implementation.

Headquarters: 12 Melbourne Avenue, PO Box 596, Colombo 4, Sri Lanka.
Director: Dr Hak-Su Kim.

ASIA-PACIFIC ECONOMIC CO-OPERATION (APEC)

Origin and Aims. APEC was founded in Nov. 1989 to devise programmes of co-operation between member nations, through the establishment of meetings of economic leaders, trade and foreign ministers. It was institutionalized in June 1992 after a meeting in Bangkok, at which it was agreed to set up a secretariat in Singapore. APEC is now the primary vehicle for promoting open trade and practical economic co-operation in the region. Its goal is to advance Asia-Pacific economic dynamism and a sustained sense of common purpose and community. Its member economies had a combined GDP of over US$13 trillion in 1995. Following Peru's 1997 entry into the Group, it had 19 member countries in Jan. 1998.

Members. Australia, Brunei, Canada, Chile, China, Hong Kong, Indonesia, Japan, Korea (Republic of), Malaysia, Mexico, New Zealand, Papua New Guinea, Peru, Philippines, Singapore, Taiwan, Thailand and the USA.

Activities. In the Seoul Declaration of 1991, APEC recognized 'the important contribution of the private sector to the dynamism of APEC economies', and ministers set forth a commitment to realize the goals of free and open trade and investment in the region. This was further strengthened by the first meeting of APEC economic leaders in 1993, and by the second meeting, in 1994, with the Declaration of Common Resolve, whereby it was agreed to achieve the goal of free and open trade and investment in the region no later than 2010 for the industrialized economies, 2020 for the developing economies. The Osaka Action Agenda, adopted by leaders in Osaka, Japan, in 1995, draws up a blueprint for implementing the commitment to this goal. The *Manila Action Plan for APEC (MAPA)* is the culmination of these efforts. It was adopted at the Manila summit of Nov. 1996 and came into operation on 1 Jan. 1997.

Headquarters: 438 Alexandra Road, Alexandra Point, Singapore 119958.
Website: http://www.apec.org.
Executive Director: Jack Whittleton (Canada).

PACIFIC COMMUNITY

Until Feb. 1998 known as the South Pacific Commission, this is a regional inter-governmental organization founded in 1947 under an Agreement commonly referred to as the Canberra Agreement. It is funded by assessed contributions from its 27 members and by voluntary contributions from member and non-member countries, international organizations and other sources.

Members. American Samoa, Australia, Cook Islands, Fiji, France, French Polynesia, Guam, Kiribati, Marshall Islands, Micronesia, Nauru, New Caledonia, New Zealand, Niue, Northern Mariana Islands, Palau, Papua New Guinea, Pitcairn Islands, Samoa, Solomon Islands, Tokelau, Tonga, Tuvalu, UK, USA, Vanuatu and Wallis and Futuna.

Functions. The Commission has 3 main areas of work: land resources, marine resources and social resources. It conducts research and provides technical assistance and training in these areas to its 22-member Pacific Island countries and territories of the Pacific.

Organization. The South Pacific Conference is the governing body of the Community. Its key focus is to appoint the Director-General, to consider major national or regional policy issues and to note changes to the Financial and Staff Regulations approved by the CRGA, the Committee of Representatives of Governments and Administrations. It meets every 2 years. The CRGA meets once a year and is the principal decision-making organ of the Community. There is also a regional office in Fiji.

Headquarters: BP D5, 98848 Nouméa Cedex, New Caledonia
Website: http://www.spc.org.nc.
Director-General: Robert Dun (Australia).

SOUTH PACIFIC FORUM (SPF)

The South Pacific Forum held its first meeting of Heads of Government in New Zealand in 1971. The SPF provides an opportunity for informal discussions to be held on a wide range of issues. It meets annually or as necessary. The Forum has no written constitution or international agreement governing its activities nor any formal rules relating to its purpose, membership or conduct of meeting. Decisions are reached by consensus. In Oct. 1994, the Forum was granted observer status to the UN.

Members. (1998) Australia, Cook Islands, Fiji, Kiribati, Marshall Islands, Micronesia, Nauru, New Zealand, Niue, Palau, Papua New Guinea, Samoa, Solomon Islands, Tonga, Tuvalu, and Vanuatu .

The South Pacific Bureau for Economic Co-operation (SPEC*)* was established by the Agreement of 17 April 1973 at the 4th meeting of the SPF, and in 1988 at the 19th meeting SPEC was reorganized and renamed as the *South Pacific Forum Secretariat.*

Functions. The Secretariat's mission is to enhance the economic and social well-being of the South Pacific peoples, in support of the efforts of the national governments. Its particular responsibility is to facilitate, develop and maintain co-operation and consultation between and among its 16 member countries. Its mandate includes the identification of opportunities for the modification of trade patterns; investigation of development methods which are in keeping with the concept of regional enterprise and free and open trade; establishment of an advisory service on technical assistance, aid and investment finance; provision of economic expertise and assistance.

Activities. The Secretariat has 4 core divisions: Trade and Investment; Political and International Affairs; Development and Economic Policy; Corporate Services. Its focus is on providing a policy advisory role on issues which cannot be fully assessed on a national basis, and on providing high-level policy advice on trade and investment to members.

The *South Pacific Nuclear-Free Zone Treaty* (of Rarotonga) was signed in 1985, prohibiting the acquisition, stationing or testing of nuclear weapons in the region. The major nuclear powers were to sign a protocol to the treaty. Russia and China signed in 1987; France, the UK and USA did not. In July 1995, when the French government decided to resume testing in French Polynesia, pressure was brought to bear on the 3 governments to sign. All 3 announced their intention to accede by mid-1996. In Jan. 1996 France announced its intention to cut short its programme, and all 3 countries signed up to the Treaty in March that year.

Organization. The Secretariat is headed (since 1977) by a Secretary-General and a Deputy Secretary-General. They form the Executive. It is governed by an executive committee, the Forum Officials Committee, which acts as intermediary between it and the Forum.

Headquarters: Ratu Sukuna Road, Suva, Fiji.
Secretary-General: Ieremia Tabai.

ASSOCIATION OF SOUTH EAST ASIAN NATIONS (ASEAN)

History and Membership. ASEAN is a regional intergovernmental organization formed by the governments of Indonesia, Malaysia, the Philippines, Singapore and Thailand through the Bangkok Declaration which was signed by their foreign ministers on 8 Aug. 1967. Brunei joined in 1984, Vietnam in 1995, Laos and Myanmar in 1997. The decision on whether to admit Cambodia, which has for some time enjoyed observer status in ASEAN, was deferred in July 1997 due to civil unrest there. Papua New Guinea also has observer status. In 1998, the combined GDP of member countries was estimated to be US$500,000m.

Objectives. The main objectives are to accelerate economic growth, social progress and cultural development, to promote active collaboration and mutual assistance in matters of common interest, to ensure the political and economic stability of the South East Asian region, and to maintain close co-operation with existing international and regional organizations with similar aims.

Activities. Principal projects concern economic co-operation and development, with the intensification of intra-ASEAN trade, and trade between the region and the rest of the world; joint research and technological programmes; co-operation in transportation and communications; promotion of tourism, South East Asian studies, cultural, scientific, educational and administrative exchanges.

The decision to set up an *ASEAN Free Trade Area (AFTA)* was taken at the Fourth Summit meeting in Singapore in 1992, with the aim of creating a common market in 15 years. The first step towards this was the Common Effective Preferential Tariff (CEPT) Scheme Agreement, setting a common tariff regime for manufactured and processed agricultural goods.

In Dec. 1995, heads of government meeting in Bangkok signed a treaty establishing a South-East Asia Nuclear-Free Zone, which was extended to cover offshore economic exclusion zones. Individual signatories were to decide whether to allow port visits or transportation of nuclear weapons by foreign powers through territorial waters.

The *ASEAN Regional Forum (ARF)* was proposed at a meeting of foreign ministers in July 1993 to discuss security issues in the region. Its first formal meeting took place in July 1994 attended by all 7 members and its Dialogue Partners (Australia, Canada, the EU, Japan, Republic of Korea, New Zealand and the USA) and observers (People's Republic of China, Laos, Papua New Guinea, Russia and Vietnam).

Organization. The highest authority is the meeting of Heads of Government, which takes place on a formal basis every 3 years, with informal meetings each year in between. The highest policy-making body is the annual Meeting of Foreign Ministers, commonly known as AMM, the ASEAN Ministerial Meeting, which convenes in each of the member countries on a rotational basis in alphabetical order. The AEM (ASEAN Economic Meeting) meets formally or informally each year to direct ASEAN economic co-operation. The AEM and AMM report jointly to the heads of government at summit meetings.

The ASEAN Standing Committee (ASC) is the policy arm and organ of co-ordination between the AMMs. An advisory body to the permanent committees, the ASC reviews the work of committees with a view to implementing policy guidelines set by the AMM. There are 5 economic committees under the AEM, and 5 non-economic committees that recommend and draw up programmes for co-operation. These committees are responsible for the operation and implementation of projects in their respective fields.

Each capital has its own national secretariat. The central secretariat in Jakarta is headed by the Secretary-General, a post that revolves among the member states in alphabetical order every 3 years.

Headquarters: POB 2072, Jakarta 12110, Indonesia.
Website: http://www.asean.or.id.
Secretary-General: Ajit Singh (Malaysia).

ASEAN MEKONG BASIN DEVELOPMENT CO-OPERATION (MEKONG GROUP)
The ministers and representatives of Brunei, Cambodia, China, Indonesia, Laos, Malaysia, Myanmar, Philippines, Singapore, Thailand and Vietnam met in Kuala Lumpur on 17 June 1996 and agreed the following basic objectives for the Group. Its principal objectives are to co-operate in the economic and social development of the Mekong Basin area and strengthen the link between it and ASEAN member countries, through a process of dialogue and common project identification.

Priorities include: development of infrastructure capacities in the fields of transport, telecommunications, irrigation and energy; development of trade and investment-generating activities; development of the agricultural sector to enhance production for domestic consumption and export; sustainable development of forestry resources and development of mineral resources; development of the industrial sector especially small to medium enterprises; development of tourism; human resource development and support for training; co-operation in the fields of science and technology.

Further Reading

Broinowski, A., *Understanding ASEAN.* London, 1982;–(ed.) *ASEAN into the 1990s.* London, 1990
Tran Van Hoa (ed), *Economic Developments and Prospects in the ASEAN.* London, 1997
Wawn, B., *The Economies of the ASEAN Countries.* London, 1982

SOUTH ASIAN ASSOCIATION FOR REGIONAL CO-OPERATION (SAARC)

SAARC was established to accelerate the process of economic and social development in member states through joint action in agreed areas of co-operation. The Foreign Ministers of the 7 member countries met for the first time in New Delhi in Aug. 1983 and adopted the Declaration on South Asian Regional Co-operation whereby an Integrated Programme of Action (IPA) was launched. The charter establishing SAARC was adopted at the first summit meeting in Dhaka in Dec. 1985.

Members. Bangladesh, Bhutan, India, Maldives, Nepal, Pakistan, Sri Lanka.

Objectives. To promote the welfare of the peoples of South Asia; to accelerate economic growth, social progress and cultural development; to promote and strengthen collective self-reliance among members; to promote active collaboration and mutual assistance in the economic, social, cultural, technical and scientific fields; to strengthen co-operation with other developing countries, and among themselves through international forums on matters of common interest.

Co-operation within the framework is based on respect for the principles of sovereign equality, territorial integrity, political independence, non-interference in the internal affairs of other states; and mutual benefit. Agreed areas of co-operation include the eradication of poverty by the year 2002 through an Agenda of Action plan. A 3-tier mechanism has been put in place towards the implementation of this goal.

Members signed a Preferential Trading Agreement (SAPTA) on 7 Dec. 1995 and are working towards the realization of a South Asian Free Trade Area by 2000, and no later than 2005.

Organization. The highest authority of the Association rests with the heads of state or government. The Council of Foreign Ministers, which meets twice a year, is responsible for formulating policy, reviewing progress and deciding on new areas of co-operation and the mechanisms deemed necessary for that. The Council is supported by a Standing Committee of Foreign Secretaries, and by 2 other committees, the Programming Committee and the Technical Committee. There is a secretariat in Kathmandu, headed by a Secretary-General, who is assisted in his work by 7 Directors, 1 from each member state.

Decisions at all levels are taken on the basis of unanimity. Bilateral and contentious issues are excluded from deliberations.

Headquarters: PO Box 4222, Kathmandu, Nepal.

THE LEAGUE OF ARAB STATES

Origin. The League of Arab States is a voluntary association of sovereign Arab states, established by a Pact signed in Cairo on 22 March 1945 by the representatives of Egypt, Iraq, Saudi Arabia, Syria, Lebanon, Jordan and Yemen. It seeks to promote closer ties among member states and to co-ordinate their economic, cultural and security policies with a view to developing collective co-operation, protecting national security and maintaining the independence and sovereignty of member states, in order to enhance the potential for joint Arab action across all fields.

Members. (1998) Algeria, Bahrain, Comoros, Djibouti, Egypt, Iraq, Jordan, Kuwait, Lebanon, Libya, Mauritania, Morocco, Oman, Palestine, Qatar, Saudi Arabia, Somalia, Sudan, Syria, Tunisia, United Arab Emirates and Republic of Yemen.

Joint Action. In the political field, the League is entrusted with defending the supreme interests and national causes of the Arab world through the implementation of joint action plans at regional and international levels, and with examining any disputes that may arise between member states with a view to settling them by peaceful means. The Joint Defence and Economic Co-operation Treaty signed in 1950 provided for the establishment of a Joint Defence Council as well as an Economic Council (renamed the Economic and Social Council in 1977). Economic, social and cultural activities constitute principal and vital elements of the joint action initiative.

Arab Common Market. The Arab Common Market came into operation on 1 Jan. 1965. The agreement, reached on 13 Aug. 1964 and open to all the Arab League states, has been signed by Iraq, Jordan, Syria and Egypt. The agreement provides for the abolition of customs duties on agricultural products and natural resources within 5 years, by reducing tariffs at an annual rate of 20%. Customs duties on industrial products are to be reduced by 10% annually. The agreement also provides for the free movement of capital and labour between member countries, the establishment of common external tariffs, the co-ordination of economic development and the framing of a common foreign economic policy.

In May 1997, in a move to finance economic reforms, 2 funds totalling US$900m. were set up.

Organization. The machinery of the League consists of a Council, 11 specialized ministerial committees entrusted with drawing up common policies for the regulation and advancement of co-operation in their fields (information, internal affairs, justice, housing, transport, social affairs, youth and sports, health, environment, telecommunications and electricity), and a permanent secretariat. On the Council each state has 1 vote. Councils may meet in any of the Arab capitals. Its functions include mediation in disputes between members or a member and a country outside the League. The Secretariat is the executive organ of the Council and ministerial councils. There are also 22 specialized agencies.

The League is considered to be a regional organization within the framework of the United Nations at which its Secretary-General is an observer. It has permanent delegations in New York and Geneva for the UN, in Addis Ababa for the Organization of African Unity (OAU), as well as offices in Bonn, Vienna, Brussels, Athens, Madrid, Washington DC, New Delhi, Beijing, Moscow, Rome, London and Paris.

Headquarters: Al Tahrir Square, Cairo, Egypt.
Secretary-General: Ahmed Esmat Abdel-Meguid (Egypt).

Further Reading

Clements, F. A., *Arab Regional Organizations.* [Bibliography]. Oxford and New Brunswick (NJ), 1992
Gomaa, A. M., *The Foundation of the League of Arab States.* London, 1977

CO-OPERATION COUNCIL FOR THE ARAB STATES OF THE GULF

Origin. Generally known as the Gulf Co-operation Council (GCC), the Council was established in 1982 by Bahrain, Kuwait, Oman, Qatar, Saudi Arabia and the United Arab Emirates, to promote solidarity and political, economic and social co-operation between the Arab oil-producing states on the west coast of the Persian Gulf.

Activities. Co-operation on military and security issues, not expressly mentioned in the founding agreement of the GCC, was formally introduced by a Supreme Council decision in 1991. In a declaration adopted by the heads of state meeting at Abu Dhabi in May 1982, emphasis was placed on the commitment of members to combine efforts to protect their mutual sovereignty, independence and territorial integrity, and ensure stability in the region which should 'remain outside the sphere of international conflicts'.

In Nov. 1984, the Peninsula Shield Force, a rapid deployment force against external aggression, was established. The PSF subsequently took part in the US-led anti-Iraq alliance, which also led to closer links being formed between GCC member states and Egypt and Syria. This resulted in the Declaration of Damascus, signed by all 8 states, establishing a regional peacekeeping force. In 1995 a security pact was signed between Bahrain, Oman, Saudi Arabia and UAE to counter regional terrorism and crime.

In April 1991, in the wake of the Gulf War, the GCC announced its decision to finance a multimillion-dollar Development Fund to assist 'friendly' countries, namely Egypt and Syria, with the intention of creating greater political and economic stability in the region.

In June 1997 the 6 member states, together with Egypt and Syria, agreed to set up a common market.

Organization. Policy is decided by a Supreme Council of heads of state who meet annually. The Ministerial Council of foreign ministers ordinarily meets quarterly. The Secretary-General is appointed by the Supreme Council for a 3-year term.

Headquarters. POB 1153, Riyadh 11462, Saudi Arabia.
Secretary-General: Jamil Ibrahim al Hujaylan (Saudi Arabia).

Further Reading

Twinam, J.W., *The Gulf, Co-operation and the Council: an American Perspective.* Washington, 1992

ORGANIZATION OF THE PETROLEUM EXPORTING COUNTRIES (OPEC)

Origin and Aims. Founded in Baghdad in 1960 by Iran, Iraq, Kuwait, Saudi Arabia and Venezuela. The principal aims are: to unify the petroleum policies of member countries and determine the best means for safeguarding their interests, individually and collectively; to devise ways and means of ensuring the stabilization of prices in international oil markets with a view to eliminating harmful and unnecessary fluctuations; and to secure a steady income for the producing countries, an efficient, economic and regular supply of petroleum to consuming nations, and a fair return on their capital to those investing in the petroleum industry.

Members. (1998) Algeria, Indonesia, Iran, Iraq, Kuwait, Libya, Nigeria, Qatar, Saudi Arabia, United Arab Emirates and Venezuela. Membership applications may be made by any other country having substantial net exports of crude petroleum, which has fundamentally similar interests to those of member countries. Gabon became an associated member in 1973 and a full member in 1975, but in 1996 withdrew owing to difficulty in meeting its percentage contribution.

It is estimated that OPEC members possess 75% of the world's known reserves of crude petroleum, of which about two-thirds are in the Middle East.

Organization. The main organs are the Conference, the Board of Governors and the Secretariat. The Conference, which is the supreme authority meeting at least twice a year, consists of delegations from each member country, normally headed by the respective minister of oil, mines or energy. All decisions, other than those concerning procedural matters, must be adopted unanimously.

Headquarters: Obere Donaustrasse 93, A–1020 Vienna, Austria.
Website: http://www.opec.org.
Secretary-General: Dr Rilwanu Lukman (Nigeria).

Publications. Annual Statistical Bulletin; Annual Report; OPEC Bulletin (monthly); *OPEC Review* (quarterly); *Facts and Figures* (occasional); *OPEC General Information and Chronology.*

Further Reading

Al-Chalabi, F., *OPEC at the Crossroads.* Oxford, 1989
Skeet, *OPEC: 25 Years of Prices and Policies.* CUP, 1988

OPEC FUND FOR INTERNATIONAL DEVELOPMENT The OPEC Special Fund was established in 1976 to provide financial aid on advantageous terms to developing countries (other than OPEC members) and international development agencies whose beneficiaries are developing countries. In 1980 the fund was transformed into a permanent autonomous international agency and renamed the OPEC Fund for International Development. It is administered by a Ministerial Council and a Governing Board. Each member country is represented on the Council by its finance minister.

The initial endowment of the fund amounted to US$800m. At the start of 1996, pledged contributions totalled US$3,435m., and the fund had extended 659 loans totalling US$3,272·6m. of which US$2,295·9m. or 70·2% was for project financing, US$724·2m. (22·1%) for balance-of-payments support and US$252·5 (7·7%) for programme funding.

Headquarters: POB 995, A–1011 Vienna, Austria.
Website: http://www.opec.org.
Director-General: Dr Yesufu Seyyid Abdulai (Nigeria).

ARAB MAGHREB UNION

Founded in 1989 to promote political co-ordination, co-operation and 'complementarity' across various fields, with integration wherever and whenever possible.

Members. Algeria, Libya, Mauritania, Morocco, Tunisia.

By late 1996, joint policies and projects under way or under consideration included: the establishment of the Maghreb Investment and Foreign Trade Bank to fund joint agricultural and industrial projects; free movement of citizens within the region; joint transport undertakings, including railway improvements and a Maghreb highway; creation of a customs union; and establishment of a common market.

A Declaration committing members to the establishment of a free trade zone was adopted at the AMU's last summit in Tunis. In Nov. 1992, members adopted a charter on protection of the environment.

Headquarters: 27 rue Okba, Agdal, Rabat, Morocco.
Secretary-General: Mohammed Amamou (Tunisia).

ORGANIZATION OF AFRICAN UNITY (OAU)

History. On 25 May 1963, the heads of state or government of 32 African countries, at a conference in Addis Ababa, signed a charter establishing an Organization of African Unity. Membership comprises 53 of the 54 African countries. The only state that is not a member is Morocco, which withdrew in 1985 following admittance of the disputed state of Western Sahara as a member in 1982. In Nov. 1995, the following countries were suspended from voice and vote for failure to pay their dues: Central African Republic, Chad, Comoros, Equatorial Guinea, Guinea-Bissau, Niger, Sao Tome e Principe, Seychelles and Sierra Leone.

Aims. OAU's chief objectives are the furtherance of African unity and solidarity; the co-ordination of political, economic, cultural, health, scientific and defence policies; the elimination of colonialism in Africa; and the defence of sovereignty, territorial integrity and independence.

Activities. In June 1991, the heads of state of member countries signed a treaty to create an Africa-wide economic community by 2000, and in 1993, a mechanism was adopted for conflict prevention, management and resolution by the OAU.

Organization. The Assembly of the Heads of State and Government is the principal policy-making organ, and meets annually. The Council of Ministers meets twice a year, with each session electing its own chairperson. There is also a permanent secretariat headed by the Secretary-General elected for a 4-year term by the Assembly.

The Commission of Mediation, Conciliation and Arbitration is a 21-member body (no state may have more than 1 member) elected by the Assembly for a 5-year term, to hear and settle disputes between member states by peaceful means. There are also specialized commissions for economic, social, transport and communication, education, science, culture and health, defence, human rights and labour affairs. The biennial budget for 1996-98 was US$61.45m.

Official languages. Arabic, French, Portuguese and English.
Headquarters: POB 3243, Addis Ababa, Ethiopia.
Secretary-General: Dr Salim Ahmed Salim (Tanzania).

Further Reading

El-Ayouty, Y. (ed.) *The Organization of African Unity after Thirty Years.* New York, 1994
Harris, G., *The Organization of African Unity.* [Bibliography]. Oxford and New Brunswick (NJ), 1994

AFRICAN DEVELOPMENT BANK

Established to promote economic and social development in the region.

Regional Members. (52) Algeria, Angola, Benin, Botswana, Burkina Faso, Burundi, Cameroon, Cape Verde, Central African Republic, Chad, Comoros, Congo (Rep. of), Congo (Dem. Rep. of), Côte d'Ivoire, Djibouti, Egypt, Equatorial Guinea, Eritrea, Ethiopia, Gabon, Gambia, Ghana, Guinea, Guinea-Bissau, Kenya, Lesotho, Liberia, Libya, Madagascar, Malawi, Mali, Mauritania, Mauritius, Morocco, Mozambique, Namibia, Niger, Nigeria, Rwanda, São Tomé e Príncipe, Senegal, Seychelles, Sierra Leone, Somalia, Sudan, Swaziland, Tanzania, Togo, Tunisia, Uganda, Zambia, Zimbabwe.

Non-regional Members. (25) Argentina, Austria, Belgium, Brazil, Canada, China, Denmark, Finland, France, Germany, India, Italy, Japan, Republic of Korea, Kuwait, Netherlands, Norway, Portugal, Saudi Arabia, Spain, Sweden, Switzerland, United Arab Emirates, UK, USA.

Headquarters: 01 BP 1387, Abidjan 01, Côte d'Ivoire.

ECONOMIC COMMUNITY OF WEST AFRICAN STATES (ECOWAS)

Founded 1975 as a regional common market, it has now become involved in political disputes, and in 1993 amended its charter to assume responsibility for the regulation of regional armed conflicts. Its military arm is Ecomog.

Members. (1998) Benin, Burkina Faso, Cape Verde, Côte d'Ivoire, Gambia, Ghana, Guinea, Guinea-Bissau, Liberia, Mali, Mauritania, Niger, Nigeria, Senegal, Sierra Leone, Togo.

Organization. It meets at yearly summits which rotate in the different capitals of member states. There is a secretariat in Abuja.

Headquarters: 60 Yakubu Gowon Crescent, Asokoro, Abuja, Nigeria.

SOUTHERN AFRICAN DEVELOPMENT COMMUNITY (SADC)

History and Membership. The Declaration and Treaty establishing the SADC (replacing the South African Development Co-ordination Conference, SADCC, established in 1980 on the adoption of the Lusaka Declaration to reduce the region's economic dependence on South Africa and combat the effects of sanctions) was signed at the summit of heads of state or government on 17 July 1992 in Windhoek, Namibia.

Members. The 10 founder member countries (Angola, Botswana, Lesotho, Malawi, Mozambique, Namibia, Swaziland, Tanzania, Zambia, Zimbabwe) have been joined by South Africa (1994) and Mauritius (1995). Each member state has responsibility to co-ordinate a sector or sectors on behalf of all other members.

Aims and Activities. The core aims of the SADC are to promote economic integration and strengthen regional solidarity, peace and security. The founding treaty imposes binding obligations on members, and provides for the establishment of an arbitration tribunal.

At the Johannesburg summit in Aug. 1995, an agreement was reached committing members to the sharing of water resources. A treaty to eliminate internal trade barriers by 2000 is also being drawn up; and in 1994, SADC ministers of defence meeting in Arusha, Tanzania, approved the establishment of a regional rapid deployment peacekeeping force to contain regional conflicts or civil unrest in member states.

Official languages. English, Portuguese.
Headquarters: Private Bag 0095, Gaborone, Botswana.
Executive Secretary: Kaire Mbuende (Namibia).

LAKE CHAD BASIN COMMISSION

Established by a Convention and Statute signed on 22 May 1964 by Cameroon, Chad, Niger and Nigeria, and later by the Central African Republic, to regulate and control utilization of the water and other natural resources in the Basin; to initiate, promote and co-ordinate natural resources development projects and research within the Basin area; and to examine complaints and promote settlement of disputes, with a view to promoting regional co-operation.

In Dec. 1977, at Enugu in Nigeria, the 3rd summit of heads of state of the commission signed the protocol for the Harmonization of the Regulations Relating to Fauna and Flora in member countries, and adopted plans for the multidonor approach towards major integrated development for the conventional basin. An international campaign to save Lake Chad following a report on the environmental degradation of the conventional basin was launched by heads of state at the 8th summit of the Commission in Abuja in March 1994.

The Commission operates an annual budget of CFA 400m., and receives assistance from various international and donor agencies including the FAO, and UN Development and Environment Programmes.

Headquarters: BP 727, N'Djamena, Chad.
Executive Secretary: Bobboi Jauro.

WORLD COUNCIL OF CHURCHES

The World Council of Churches was formally constituted on 23 Aug. 1948 in Amsterdam. Today, member churches number over 330 from more than 100 countries.

Origin. The World Council was founded by the coming together of diverse Christian movements, including the overseas mission groups gathered from 1921 in the International Missionary Council, the Faith and Order Movement founded by American Episcopal Bishop Charles Brent, and the Life and Work Movement led by Swedish Lutheran Archbishop Nathan Söderblom. On 13 May 1938, at Utrecht, a provisional committee was appointed to prepare for the formation of a World Council of Churches, under the chairmanship of William Temple, then Archbishop of York.

Membership. The basis of membership (1975) states: 'The World Council of Churches is a fellowship of Churches which confess the Lord Jesus Christ as God and Saviour according to the Scriptures and therefore seek to fulfil together their common calling to the glory of the one God, Father, Son and Holy Spirit.' Membership is open to Churches which express their agreement with this basis and satisfy such criteria as the Assembly or Central Committee may prescribe. Today, more than 330 Churches of Protestant, Anglican, Orthodox, Old Catholic and Pentecostal confessions belong to this fellowship.

Activities. WCC programmes are organized by a range of supervisory committees drawn from member churches. The 4 programme units are: Unity and Renewal; Churches in Mission: Health, Education Witness; Justice, Peace and Creation; and Sharing and Service.

In August 1997, the WCC launched a Peace to the City campaign, as the initial focus of a programme to overcome violence in troubled cities.

Organization. The governing body of the World Council, consisting of delegates specially appointed by the member Churches, is the Assemby, which meets every 7 or 8 years to frame policy. It has no legislative powers and depends for the implementation of its decisions upon the action of member Churches. The 8th Assembly in Harare, in 1998, has as its theme, 'Turn to God, Rejoice in Hope'. A 150-member Central Committee meets annually to carry out the Assembly mandate, with a smaller 28-member Executive Committee meeting twice a year. The General Secretariat includes Offices for Church and Ecumenical Relations, Inter-religious Relations, Programme Co-ordination, Department of Communication, Office of Management and Finance, and the *Ecumenical Institute* at Bossey.

The total WCC budget for 1996 amounted to 103m. Swiss francs, funded by the churches and their agencies, and other project-related organizations.

Headquarters: PO Box 2100, 150 route de Ferney, 1211 Geneva 2, Switzerland. *Website:* http://www.wcc-coe.org. *General Secretary:* Rev. Dr Konrad Raiser

Publications. Annual Reports; Dictionary of the Ecumenical Movement, Geneva, 1991; *Directory of Christian Councils,* 1985; *A History of the Ecumenical Movement.* Geneva, 1993; *Ecumenical Review* (quarterly); *Ecumenical News International* (weekly); *International Review of Mission* (quarterly).

Further Reading

Castro, E., *A Passion for Unity.* Geneva, 1992
Potter, P., *Life in all its Fullness.* Geneva, 1981
Raiser, K., *Ecumenism in Transition.* Geneva, 1994
Van Elderen, M., *Introducing the World Council of Churches.* Geneva, 1990
Vermaat, J. A. A., *The World Council of Churches and Politics.* New York, 1989
Visser 't Hooft, W. A., *The Genesis and Formation of the World Council of Churches.* Geneva, 1982; *Memoirs.* Geneva, 1987

UNREPRESENTED NATIONS AND PEOPLES ORGANIZATION (UNPO)

UNPO is an international organization created by nations and peoples around the world who are not represented as such in the world's principal international organizations, such as the UN. Founded in 1991, UNPO has over 50 members representing over 100m. people.

Membership. Open to all nations and peoples unrepresented, subject to adherence to the 5 principles which form the basis of UNPO's charter: equal right to self-determination of all nations and peoples; adherence to internationally accepted human rights standards; to the principles of democracy; promotion of non-violence; and protection of the environment. Applicants must show that they constitute a 'nation or people' as defined in the Covenant.

Functions and Activities. UNPO offers an international forum for occupied nations, indigenous peoples, minorities, and oppressed majorities who struggle to regain their lost countries, preserve their cultural identities, protect their basic human and economic rights, and safeguard their environment.

It does not represent those peoples; rather it assists and empowers them to represent themselves more effectively. To this end, it provides professional services and facilities as well as education and training in the fields of diplomacy, international and human rights law, democratic processes and institution building, conflict management and resolution, and environmental protection. The Organization is funded by members, private foundations and voluntary contributions.

By Jan. 1998, 5 former members of UNPO (Armenia, Belau, Estonia, Georgia and Latvia) subsequently achieved full independence and gained representation in the UN.

Headquarters: 40A Javastraat, NL-2585 AP The Hague, Netherlands.
Website: http://www.unpo.ee.
General Secretary: Michael van Walt.

INTERNATIONAL ORGANIZATION FOR MIGRATION (IOM)

Established in Brussels in 1951 to help solve European population and refugee problems though migration, and to stimulate the creation of new economic opportunities in countries lacking certain manpower. IOM is committed to the principle that humane and orderly migration benefits migrants and society.

Members. Albania, Angola, Argentina, Armenia, Australia, Austria, Bangladesh, Belgium, Bolivia, Bulgaria, Canada, Chile, Colombia, Costa Rica, Croatia, Cyprus, Czech Republic, Denmark, Dominican Republic, Ecuador, Egypt, El Salvador, Finland, France, Germany, Greece, Guatemala, Haiti, Honduras, Hungary, Israel, Italy, Japan, Kenya, Liberia, Luxembourg, Netherlands, Nicaragua, Norway, Pakistan, Panama, Paraguay, Peru, Philippines, Poland, Portugal, Republic of Korea, Senegal, Slovak Republic, Sri Lanka, Sweden, Switzerland, Tajikistan, Thailand, Uganda, USA, Uruguay, Venezuela and Zambia. A further 48 governments and a large number of government agencies and NGOs have observer status.

Activities. As an intergovernmental body, IOM acts with its partners in the international community to: assist in meeting the operational challenges of migration; advance understanding of migration issues; encourage social and economic development through migration; work towards effective respect of human dignity and the wellbeing of migrants. Since 1952 the IOM has assisted over 10m. refugees and migrants. The operational budget for 1997 was US$238·1m.

Headquarters: Route des Morillons 17, POB 71, 1211 Geneva 19, Switzerland.
Website: http://www.iom.ch.
Director-General: James N. Purcell Jr (USA).

WORLD CUSTOMS ORGANIZATION

Established in 1952 as the Customs Co-operation Council, the World Customs Organization is an intergovernmental body with worldwide membership, whose mission it is to enhance the effectiveness and efficiency of customs administrations throughout the world. In Jan. 1998 it had 145 member countries or territories.

Headquarters: Rue de l'Industrie 26-38, B-1040 Brussels, Belgium.
Secretary-General: J. W. Shaver (US).

INTERNATIONAL MOBILE SATELLITE ORGANIZATION (INMARSAT)

Founded in 1979 to provide worldwide communication for commercial, distress and safety applications at sea, in 1985 its operating agreement was amended to include aeronautical communications, and in 1988 this was further extended to allow for the provision of global land-mobile communications. In Jan. 1998 it had 79 member countries.

Organization. The Assembly of all Parties to the Convention meets every 2 years. There is also a 22-member Council of representatives of national telecommunications administrations as well as an executive Directorate.

Headquarters: 99 City Road, London EC1Y 1AX, UK.
Director-General: Warren Grace.

INTERNATIONAL TELECOMMUNICATIONS SATELLITE ORGANIZATION (INTELSAT)

Intelsat was founded in 1964 to own and operate the worldwide commercial satellite communications system. In 1997, there were 139 member states. Costs are borne by members in proportion to their usage of the system. 24 Intelsat satellites in geosynchronous orbit provide a global communications service, including most of the world's overseas traffic.

Objectives. To provide international telephone and TV services, a digital data transmission service (Intelnet), a business service (IBS) and domestic telecommunications services.

Organization. The Assembly of Parties attended by representatives of member governments meets every 2 years to consider policy and long-term aims, and matters of interest to members. Practical aspects of the system are dealt with at the annual Meeting of Signatories. There is a 27-member Board of Governors.

Headquarters: 3400 International Drive, NW, Washington, DC, 20008-3098, USA.
Director-General: Irving Goldstein (USA).

INTERNATIONAL CONFEDERATION OF FREE TRADE UNIONS (ICFTU)

Origin. The founding congress of the ICFTU was held in London in Dec. 1949 following the withdrawal of some Western trade unions from the World Federation of Trade Unions (WFTU), which had come under Communist control. The constitution, as amended, provides for co-operation with the UN and the ILO, and for regional organizations to promote free trade unionism, especially in developing countries. The ICFTU represents some 124m. workers across 196 affiliated organizations in 136 countries.

Aims. The ICFTU aims to promote the interests of working people and to secure recognition of workers' organizations as free bargaining agents; to reduce the gap between rich and poor; and to defend fundamental human and trade union rights. In 1996, it campaigned for the adoption by the WTO of a social clause, with legally binding minimum labour standards.

Organization. The Congress meets every 4 years. It elects the Executive Board of 50 members nominated on an area basis for a 4-year period; 5 seats are reserved for women, nominated by the Women's Committee; and the Board meets at least once a year. Various committees cover economic and social policy, violation of trade union and other human rights, trade union co-operation projects and also the administration of the International Solidarity Fund. There are joint ICFTU–International Trade Secretariat committees for co-ordinating activities.

The ICFTU has branch offices in Geneva and New York, and regional organizations in America (Caracas), Asia (Singapore) and Africa (Nairobi).

Headquarters: Bd. Emile Jacqmain 155, Brussels 1210, Belgium.
Website: http://www.icftu.org.
General Secretary: Bill Jordan (UK).

Publications. Free Labour World (monthly); *Occupational Health and Safety Bulletin; Survey of Violations of Trade Union Rights* (annual); *World Economic Review* (annual).

WORLD FEDERATION OF TRADE UNIONS (WFTU)

Origin and History. The WFTU was founded in 1945 on a worldwide basis, representing trade union organizations in more than 50 Communist and non-Communist countries. From the outset the American Federation of Labor declined to participate. In Jan. 1949, with the WFTU under Communist control, British, US and Netherlands trade union organizations withdrew and went on to found the ICFTU (see above); by June 1951 all non-Communist trade unions and the Yugoslav federation had withdrawn.

By the 1990s, after the collapse of the European Communist regimes, membership became uncertain; unions broke their links with the Communist parties and most were later accepted into the ICFTU. Most of the national trade union centres in Africa and Latin America moved to the ICFTU after 1989, and the French Confédération Générale du Travail has proposed withdrawal to its members.

At the Nov. 1994 congress in Damascus, most WFTU delegates came from the developing countries (Cuba, India, South Korea, Vietnam).

In a move towards decentralization, regional offices have been set up in New Delhi (India), Havana (Cuba), Dakar (Senegal), Damascus (Syria), and Moscow (Russia).

Headquarters: Branicka 112, 14700 Prague 4, Czech Republic.
Website: http://www.wftu.org.
General Secretary: Aleksandr Zharikov (Russia).

WORLD CONFEDERATION OF LABOUR (WCL)

Founded in 1920 as the International Federation of Christian Trade Unions, it went out of existence in 1940 as a large proportion of its 3·4m. members were in Italy and Germany, where affiliated unions were suppressed by the Fascist and Nazi regimes. Reconstituted in 1945 and declining to merge with the WFTU or ICFTU, its policy was based on the papal encyclicals *Rerum novarum* (1891) and *Quadragesimo anno* (1931), and in 1968 it became the WCL and dropped its openly confessional approach.

Today, it has Protestant, Buddhist and Moslem member confederations, as well as a mainly Roman Catholic membership. In its concern to defend trade union freedoms and assist trade union development, the WCL differs little in policy from the ICFTU above. A membership of 11m. in about 90 countries is claimed. The biggest group is the Confederation of Christian Trade Unions (CSC) of Belgium (1·2m.).

Organization. The WCL is organized on a federative basis which leaves wide discretion to its autonomous constituent unions. Its governing body is the Congress, which meets every 4 years. The Congress appoints (or re-appoints) the Secretary-General at each 4-yearly meeting. The General Council which meets at least once a year, is composed of the members of the Confederal Board (at least 22 members, elected by the Congress) and representatives of national confederations, international trade federations, and trade union organizations where there is no confederation affiliated to the WCL. The Confederal Board is responsible for the general leadership of the WCL, in accordance with the decisions and directives of the Council and Congress. There are regional organizations in Latin America (Caracas), Africa (Banjul, Gambia) and Asia (Manila), and a liaison centre in Montreal.

Headquarters: 33 rue de Trèves, Brussels 1040, Belgium.
Secretary-General: Carlos Luís Custer (Argentina).

Publications. Annual Report; Labour Press and Information Bulletin (6 a year).

PART II

COUNTRIES OF THE WORLD

A—Z

AFGHANISTAN

Jamhuria Afghanistan

(Republic of Afghanistan)

Capital: Kabul
Population: 20·5m.

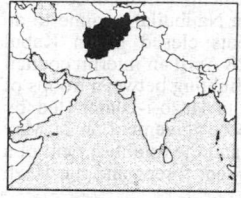

KEY HISTORICAL EVENTS. Ahmad Sháh Durráni consolidated Afghanistan as a kingdom, ruling with an advisory council of tribal chiefs from 1747 until his death in 1773. His frontiers extended into modern Kashmir and Pakistan, although by 1770 he had suffered reversals at the hands of the Sikhs in the Punjab. After 1773 the unity of Afghanistan was threatened by internal quarrels. In 1816-24 there was civil war, ending in victory for the Barakzay clan whose leader Dost Mohammed became Amir in 1826. His capital was Kabul.

By then the Punjab and Kashmir had been lost, the British had become dominant in India and the Russian empire was ambitious to expand southwards. The British, believing that Dost Mohammed was unwilling or unable to resist Russia, invaded Afghanistan in 1839 in an attempt to replace him with their own protégé, Shah Shoja. An apparent British victory in 1840 was followed by actual defeat when the Afghans murdered Shah Shoja and British forces were forced to retreat from Kabul with heavy losses.

Dost Mohammed was restored in 1843 and made friendship treaties with Britain in 1855 and 1857; he died in 1863 and was succeeded by his third son Shir 'Ali Khan. There was then civil war between two branches of the family and once more the Russians and the British tried to exploit internal instability. There was a second war with Britain (1878-79. In 1879 Shir 'Ali Khan fled leaving his son Ya'qúb Khan on the throne. In 1880 the British recognized the rival, 'Abdor Rahmán Khan, in return for his undertaking to accept British control of his foreign policy. He defeated internal uprisings and in 1893 he accepted the Durand Line as his frontier with Russia.

Habíbolláh Khan (1901-19) continued the relationship with Britain in return for a subsidy. During the First World War he succeeded in remaining neutral. However, there was popular support in Afghanistan for the Ottoman Turks, and Habíbolláh's refusal to ally himself with them against Britain led to his assassination in 1919. His son and successor Amánolláh declared total independence from Britain at his coronation. Fighting broke out, but Britain then recognized the independence of Afghanistan at the Treaty of Rawalpindi, 1919.

Amánolláh was a reforming Khan who antagonized the conservatives of traditional society. Tribal revolt and banditry reached a climax in 1928 and the Khan abdicated in 1929 to be replaced first by Habíbolláh (soon murdered) and then by Mohammed Nadir (1929-33). The latter signed a friendship treaty with Russia. He was murdered in 1933 and succeeded by Mohammed Záhir who (like Nadir towards the end of his reign) took the title of Shah. Záhir Shah ruled with the advice, and under the influence, of his family for 40 years. In 1964 he was able to overcome opposition and put through a constitution establishing parliamentary democracy (effective 1965). In 1973 there was a military *coup* led by his cousin and brother-in-law Mohammed Daoud who abolished the 1964 constitution and declared a republic. Záhir Shah abdicated on 24 Aug. 1973.

The republic inherited pressure for tribal autonomy and economic crises mainly brought about by drought and famine. In April 1978 President Daoud was overthrown and killed in a further *coup* which installed a pro-Soviet government led by the People's Democratic Party. The new president was Noor Mohammad Taraki who signed a new treaty of friendship with the Soviet Union. In Sept. 1979 Taraki was overthrown, whereupon the Soviet Union invaded Afghanistan in Dec., deposed his successor and placed Babrak Karmal at the head of government.

In Dec. 1986 Sayid Mohammed Najibullah became president amid continuing civil war between government and rebel Moslem forces. Whereas in the 1960s both the USSR and the USA had financed government projects, in 1987 the USSR pro-

vided considerable military support and development aid to the pro-Soviet administration while the USA extended more limited support to the rebels. In the mid-1980s
the UN began negotiations on the withdrawal of Soviet troops and the establishment
of a government of national unity. Soviet troops began withdrawing from
Afghanistan in early 1988.

After talks in Nov. 1991 with Afghan opposition movements ('mujahideen') the
Soviet government agreed to transfer its support from the Najibullah regime to an
'Islamic Interim Government'. As mujahideen insurgents closed in on Kabul
President Najibullah stepped down on 16 April 1992. On 28 April an interim council
received power from the outgoing government. Factional fighting between troops of
the Minister of Defence, Ahmed Shah Massoud, and the Hezb-i-Islami, led by
Gulbuddin Hekmatyar, continued until the signing of a peace agreement on 21 May
providing for the withdrawal of armed forces from Kabul and the establishment of a
neutral zone. On 11 Aug. 1992 fighting between government forces and the Hezb
broke out again.

Late in 1994 a newly-formed militant Islamic movement, 'Taliban' (i.e. 'students
of religion'), took possession of Kandahar and routed Hekmatyar's Hezb-i-Islami at
Kabul in Feb. 1995. They were in turn defeated by the troops of President Rabbani,
who regained possession of Kabul by 11 March 1995, but had rallied by Sept. 1995
and captured Herat, carrying out air and rocket raids on Kabul in Nov. 1995. On 13
May 1996 Hekmatyar and President Rabbani formed an alliance against the Taliban.

On 26 Sept. 1996 Taliban forces captured Kabul and set up an interim government
under Mohamed Rabbani. Former President Najibullah and his brother were hanged,
and Afghanistan was declared a complete Islamic state under Sharia law.

Government forces which had retreated to the north of Kabul, in alliance with an
Uzbek warlord, Abdul Rashid Dostam, and a pro-Iranian Sh'ite faction, Hezb-i-
Wahdat, then counter-attacked.

A new Taliban offensive was launched on 27 Dec. 1996 which established a battle
line some 50 km north of Kabul.

Peace talks held under UN auspices in Islamabad on 13-15 Jan. 1997 between the
Taliban and their opponents broke down on the issue of demilitarizing Kabul. Only
three countries, Pakistan, Saudi Arabia and the United Arab Emirates, recognize
Taliban as the legal government.

TERRITORY AND POPULATION. Afghanistan is bounded in the north by
Turkmenistan, Uzbekistan and Tajikistan, east by China, east and south by Pakistan
and west by Iran.

The area is 251,773 sq. miles (652,090 sq. km). Population according to the last
(1979) census was 15,551,358, of which some 2·5m. were nomadic tribes. Estimate
(1994, excluding nomads) 20·5m. (21% urban). Population density, 25 per sq. km. In
1995 there remained 3·5m. refugees in Pakistan and Iran. Infant mortality, 1991, 296
per 1,000 live births; annual growth rate, 2·6%; expectation of life, 42·5 years in
1990.

The capital, Kabul, had an estimated population of 0·7m. in 1993. Other towns
(with UN population estimates, 1988): Kandahar (225,500), Herat (177,300), Mazar
i Sharif, (130,600), Jalalabad (55,000).

Main ethnic groups: Pashtuns, 35-38%; Tajiks, 25-30%; Hazaras, 10-15%;
Uzbeks, 10%; Turkman, 5%; Others, 2%. The official languages are Pashto and Dari.

CLIMATE. The climate is arid, with a big annual range of temperature and very
little rain, apart from the period Jan. to April. Winters are very cold, with considerable snowfall, which may last the year round on mountain summits. Kabul. Jan. 27°F
(−2·8°C), July 76°F (24·4°C). Annual rainfall 13" (338 mm).

CONSTITUTION AND GOVERNMENT. After the removal of President
Najibullah power was exercised by a 10-member Ruling Council chaired by
Burhanuddin Rabbani who became interim President of the Republic on 28 June
1992. In Dec. 1992 a Grand Council of 1,335 national delegates convened and
re-elected Burhanuddin Rabbani President. The Grand Council was wound up after

205 of its members had been designated a constituent assembly. President Rabbani's mandate expired in June 1994 but he remained in office.

President: Burhanuddin Rabbani (b. 1942; Jamiat Party; sworn in 2 Jan. 1993).

In March 1998 the government comprised: *Prime Minister:* Abdul Rahim Ghafoorzai. *Vice Presidents:* Ahmad Shah Massoud, Abdul Ghaffar (Jumbish Milli Party), Sadiq Parwani (Hezbi Wahdat Party). *Defence:* Ahmad Shah Massoud. *Foreign Affairs (acting):* Dr Abd'allah. *Interior:* Jaji Mohaqiq.

Local Government: There are 32 provinces each administered in theory by an appointed governor.

DEFENCE

Army. Army organization disintegrated into factional groups after the deposition of President Najibullah in April 1992. Equipment included 700 T-54/-55/-62 main battle tanks. Strength was (1993) about 40,000, mainly conscripts, but most units of the Army are well below strength, largely as a result of desertions.

Air Force. Prior to the overthrow of the regime of President Najibullah in 1992 the Air Force had about 180 combat aircraft and 5,000 officers and men. Since then, the service has also been broken into various factions and few combat aircraft remain airworthy; the helicopters and transport aircraft fleet are also largely grounded.

INTERNATIONAL RELATIONS

Membership. Afghanistan is a member of the UN and Colombo Plan.

ECONOMY

Currency. The unit of currency is the *afghani* (AFA) of 100 *puls*. Notes are in denominations of 1, 2, 5, 10, 100, 500 and 1,000 afghanis.

Banking and Finance. The Afghan State Bank is the largest of the 3 main banks and also undertakes the functions of a central bank, holding the exclusive right of note issue. Foreign banks have been permitted to operate since 1990.

Weights and Measures. The metric system is in increasingly common use. Local units include: 1 *khurd* = 0·244 lb.; 1 *pao* = 0·974 lb.; 1 *charak* = 3·896 lb.; 1 *sere* = 16 lb.; 1 *kharwar* = 1,280 lb. or 16 maunds of 80 lb. each; 1 *gaz* = 40 inches; 1 *jarib* = 60 x 60 kabuli yd or $^1/_2$ acre; 1 *kulha* = 40 jaribs (area in which $2^1/_2$ kharwars of seed can be sown); 1 jarib yd = 29 inches.

ENERGY AND NATURAL RESOURCES

Electricity. Most generating plant is hydro-electric. Installed capacity was estimated at 408 MW in 1993.

Oil and Gas. Oil reserves are estimated at 100m. tonnes; gas at 100,000m. cu. metres. A consortium of oil and gas companies led by Unocal plans a $2bn. natural gas pipeline from Turkmenistan through Afghanistan to Pakistan.

Minerals. Mineral resources are scattered and little developed: Coal, iron ore, beryllium, gold, silver, lapis lazuli, asbestos, mica, sulphur, chrome and copper.

Agriculture. The greater part of Afghanistan is mountainous but there are many fertile plains and valleys. In 1991 there were 7·91m. ha of arable land, 0·14m. ha of permanent cropland and 30m. ha of pasture. 9·07m. persons depended on agriculture in 1990. 2·76m. ha were irrigated in 1991.

Production, 1992, in 1,000 tonnes: Wheat, 1,650; barley, 150; maize, 300; rice, 300. Livestock (1992): Cattle, 1·65m.; horses, 0·4m.; camels, 265,000; sheep, 13·5m.; goats, 2·15m.; chickens, 7m.

INDUSTRY.
Industry is small-scale and largely based on the processing of local agricultural produce. Manufactures include cement, coalmining, cotton textiles,

small vehicle assembly plants, fruit canning, carpet making, leather tanning, foot-wear manufacture, sugar manufacture, preparation of hides and skins, and building.

Labour. The economically active population was 4·91m. in 1990, of whom 54·8% worked in agriculture.

FOREIGN ECONOMIC RELATIONS

Commerce. In 1991 imports totalled US$411m. and exports US$140m. Main export commodities in 1990 were karakul skins (US$3m.), raw cotton (US$3m.), dried fruit and nuts (US$93m.), carpets (US$44m.) and wool (US$10m.).

COMMUNICATIONS

Roads. There are some 18,000 km of roads, of which 2,800 km are surfaced. All roads, particularly outside the towns, are in a very poor state of repair as a result of military action.

Railways. There are no railways in the country, but the Oxus bridge opened in 1982, brought a short-section of 1,524mm gauge track into the country from Uzbekistan. A Trans-Afghan Railway is proposed in an Afghan-Pakistan-Turkmen agreement of 1994.

Civil Aviation. There are international airports at Kabul (Khwaja Rawash Airport) and Kandahar, and 18 domestic airports. The national carrier is Ariana Afghan Airlines. In 1995 it had 2 B-727-100s, 3 B-727-200 Advs and 8 ex-Soviet aircraft. Air India and Aeroflot Russian International Airlines also operate services. There are direct flights from Kabul to Amritsar, Bandar Abbas (Iran), Delhi, Dubai, Moscow, Prague and Tashkent.

Shipping. There are practically no navigable rivers. A port has been built at Qizil Qala on the Oxus and there are 3 river ports on the Amu Darya, linked by road to Kabul.

Telecommunications. Telephones, installed in most of the large towns, numbered 31,200 in 1978. There is telegraphic communication between all the larger towns and with other parts of the world. Radio and TV Afghanistan is government-controlled. In 1993 there were 1·5m. radio receivers and about 100,000 television receivers (colour by PAL and SECAM).

SOCIAL INSTITUTIONS

Justice. A Supreme Court was established in June 1978. If no provision exists in the Constitution or in the general laws of the State, the courts follow the Hanafi juris-prudence of Islamic law.

Religion. The predominant religion is Islam. 84% of the population are Sunni Moslems and 15% Shi'ites.

Education. Some 25% of the population were estimated to be literate in 1990. There are elementary schools throughout the country, but secondary schools exist only in Kabul and provincial capitals. Both elementary and secondary education are free. In 1985 there were 580,000 pupils (16,000 teachers) in primary education and 105,000 pupils (5,700 teachers) in secondary education. In 1995-96 there were 5 universities, 1 university of Islamic studies, 1 state medical institute and 1 polytechnic. Kabul University had 9,500 students and 500 academic staff.

Health. In 1990 there were 2,233 doctors, 267 dentists, 1,451 nurses, 510 pharma-cists and 338 midwives.

DIPLOMATIC REPRESENTATIVES

Of Afghanistan in Great Britain (31 Prince's Gate, London, SW7 1QQ)
Chargé d'Affaires: Ahmad Wali Masud.

Of Great Britain in Afghanistan (Karte Parwan, Kabul)
Ambassador: Vacant.

Of Afghanistan in the USA (2341 Wyoming Ave., NW, Washington, D.C., 20008)
Chargé d'Affaires: Yar Mohammad Mohabbat.

Of the USA in Afghanistan (Wazir Akbar Khan Mina, Kabul)
Ambassador: Vacant.

Of Afghanistan to the United Nations
Ambassador: Dr Ravan A. G. Farhadi.

Further Reading

Amin, S. H., *Law, Reform and Revolution in Afghanistan.* London, 1991
Arney, G., *Afghanistan.* London, 1990
Hyman, A., *Afghanistan under Soviet Domination, 1964–1991.* 3rd ed. London, 1992
Jones, S., *Afghanistan.* [Bibliography]. Oxford and Santa Barbara (CA), 1991
Roy, O., *Islam and Resistance in Afghanistan.* 2nd ed. CUP, 1990
Rubin, B.R., *The Fragmentation of Afghanistan: State Formation and Collapse in the International System.* Yale Univ. Press, 1995.—*The Search for Peace in Afghanistan: from Buffer State to Failed State.* Yale Univ. Press, 1996
Sykes, P. M., *A History of Afghanistan.* 2 vols. New York, 1975

ALBANIA

Republika e Shqipërisë

Capital: Tirana
Population: 3·5m.
GDP per head: (PPP$) 2,788
HDI/world rank: 0·655/102

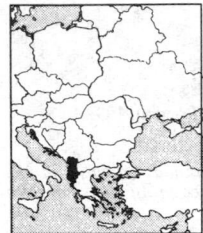

KEY HISTORICAL EVENTS. Of Illyrian origin, the Albanian clans were compelled to recognize the suzerainty of the expanding Ottoman empire in 1385. Split since 1054 between Rome (Catholics) and Constantinople (Orthodox), many Albanians converted to Islam and were able to rise high in the Ottoman administration. One such was Gjergj Kastrioti (1405-68), surnamed Skanderbeg, who defected from his Turkish commandership in 1443, reconverted to Christianity and maintained, with help from Naples, Venice and the Papal States, a guerrilla resistance to the Turks. In 1431 the Turks introduced a fiefdom system, whereby land was held in return for military or civil service. These fiefdoms became hereditary estates, and a class of large landowners developed. With the decline of central power, some lords acquired a wide measure of local autonomy.

After the Russo-Turkish war of 1877-78, an Albanian League was set up at Prizren to resist the cession of Albanian territory ordered by the Treaty of San Stefano and the Congress of Berlin. Demands grew for autonomy from the Turkish government, and although the League was suppressed by force in 1881, revolts continued. Expectations of reform from the Young Turk government of 1909 were disappointed. After the defeat of Turkey in the Balkan war of 1912, Albanian nationalists under the leadership of Ismail Kemal, a liberal opposition deputy in the Turkish parliament, proclaimed Albania's independence at Vlorë on 28 Nov. 1912 and set up a provisional government with Kemal at its head.

The London conference of 1912-13 recognized Albania's independence and chose the German, Prince William of Wied, as ruler, aided by a government of landowners and an international control commission. Weid's 6 month reign was bedevilled by subversion. During the First World War Albania became a battlefield for warring occupation forces. By the secret Treaty of London (26 April 1915) Britain, France and Russia offered Italy large tracts of Albania as an inducement to enter the war; and on 3 June 1917 the Italian commander in Albania declared Albania's independence under Italian protection. Such clandestine arrangements, however, were in conflict with the US President Woodrow Wilson's 'Fourteen Points' which emphasized self-determination and open treaties. In Jan. 1920, 50 Albanian regional delegates met at Lushnjë to protest to the peace conference against partitioning. They set up a regency council of 4 (representing the religious denominations) and formed a government under Sulejman Delvina. Irregular forces ejected the Italians who, however, retained the island of Sazan. Albania was admitted to the League of Nations on 20 Dec. 1920. In Nov. 1921 the conference of ambassadors confirmed her 1913 frontiers with minor alterations.

A parliament was elected in April 1921 in which 2 factions emerged led respectively by Ahmet Zogu, representing conservative landowners, and the Orthodox Bishop Fan Noli, representing the intelligentsia and urbanized middle class. Zogu became prime minister in 1922 and secured 40 out of 95 seats in the elections of Dec. 1923, but his government's harshness and corruption provoked a military *coup* on 10 June 1924. Zogu fled to Yugoslavia and Fan Noli set up a government which was idealistic but ineffective and made the fatal step of recognizing the Soviet Union. In Dec. 1924, with Yugoslav help Zogu drove Noli into exile and set up a personal authoritarian régime. On 1 Sept. 1928 he proclaimed himself King Zog I.

Italian influence grew from the mid-1920s. A friendship pact was signed with Italy in 1926 and a defence treaty in 1927. In April 1939 Mussolini invaded Albania outright and set up a puppet state, uniting the Italian and Albanian crowns. Zog went into exile.

During the Second World War Albania suffered first Italian and then German occupation. Resistance was carried on by royalist, nationalist republican and communist movements, often at odds with each other. The latter enjoyed the support of Tito's partisans, who were instrumental in forming the Albanian Communist Party on 8 Nov. 1941. Communists dominated the Anti-Fascist National Liberation Committee which became the Provisional Democratic Government on 22 Oct. 1944 after the German withdrawal, with Enver Hoxha, a French-educated school teacher and member of the Communist Party Central Committee, at its head. Large estates were broken up and the land distributed, though full collectivization was not brought in until 1955-59. Britain, the USA and the USSR recognized the provisional government on condition that free elections were held, but at the elections of 2 Dec. 1945 only communists and their sympathizers were allowed to stand. The new national assembly met in Jan 1946, proclaimed a people's republic and promulgated a Soviet-type constitution.

In 1946 Yugoslav plans to incorporate Albania were set in motion with a customs union and Treaty of Mutual Aid. Hoxha emerged as an opponent, and managed to delay the tactics of the pro-Yugoslav faction until the Stalin-Tito rift of 1948 gave him a chance to espouse the Moscow line. Close ties were forged with the USSR, but following Khrushchev's reconciliation with Tito in 1956 China replaced the Soviet Union as Albania's powerful patron from 1961 until the end of the Maoist phase in 1977. The régime then adopted a policy of 'revolutionary self-sufficiency'. In Dec. 1981 Mehmet Shehu, then prime minister, allegedly committed suicide. Hoxha died on 11 April 1985.

Following the collapse of the Soviet empire there were demonstrations against the government often led by students. In Dec 1990 the People's Assembly adopted a decree legalizing opposition parties. A Communist government was elected in March 1991, but following a general strike resigned in June. A successor government was itself replaced by a non-party interim government in Dec. 1991. A non-Communist government was elected in March 1992.

In 1997 Albania was disrupted by financial crises caused by the collapse of fraudulent pyramid finance schemes. A period of violent anarchy, with many fatalities, led to the fall of the administration led by President Berisha and to fresh elections which returned a Socialist-led government. A UN peacekeeping force withdrew in Aug. 1997 but sporadic violence continued with the opposition calling for new elections.

TERRITORY AND POPULATION. Albania is bounded in the north by Yugoslavia, east by Macedonia, south by Greece and west by the Adriatic. The area is 28,748 sq. km (11,101 sq. miles). At the census of 1989 the population was 3,184,417. Estimate, 1997, 3·5m. The capital is Tirana (population in 1,000 in 1991, 251); other large towns are Durrës (86·9), Shkodër (83·7), Elbasan (83·2), Vlorë (76), Korçë (67·1), (populations in 1990) Fier (37), Berat (37), Lushnjë (24), Kavajë (23) and Gjirokastër (Argyrocastro) (21).

Vital statistics, 1988: Marriages, 28,174; births, 80,241; deaths, 17,027; divorces, 2,597. Rates (per 1,000, 1996, est.): Births, 22·21; deaths, 7·64. Infant mortality was 27 per 1,000 live births in 1993. Life expectancy in 1994, 70·5 years. Growth rate, 1991, 1·8% per annum. Abortion was legalized in 1991.

The country is administratively divided into 26 districts, 66 towns, 306 town boroughs, 537 village unions and 2,844 villages.

Districts	Area (sq. km)	Population (1990)	Districts	Area (sq. km)	Population (1990)
Berat	1,027	180,489	Lushnjë	712	137,830
Dibrë	1,568	153,775	Mat	1,028	78,754
Durrës	848	251,029	Mirditë	867	51,701
Elbasan	1,481	248,676	Permet	929	40,419
Fier	1,175	251,115	Pogradec	725	73,333
Gjirokastër	1,137	67,392	Pukë	1,034	50,286
Gramsh	695	44,791	Sarandë	1,097	89,456
Kolonjë	805	25,291	Shkodër	2,528	241,549
Korçë	2,181	218,219	Skrapar	775	47,605
Krujë	607	109,876	Tepelenë	817	51,022
Kukës	1,330	104,731	Tirana	1,238	374,483
Lezhë	479	63,505	Tropojë	1,043	45,965
Librazhd	1,013	73,871	Vlorë	1,609	180,725

Districts are named after their capitals; exceptions: Tropojë, capital—Bajram Curri; Mat—Burrel; Mirditë—Rrëshen; Skrapar—Çorovodë; Dibrë—Peshkopi; Kolonjë—Ersekë.

At the 1989 census, members of ethnic minorities totalled 64,816, including 58,758 Greeks and 4,697 Macedonians. 2m. ethnic Albanians live in Yugoslavia, mainly in Kosovo.

The official language is Albanian.

CLIMATE. Mediterranean-type, with rainfall mainly in winter, but thunderstorms are frequent and severe in the great heat of the plains in summer. Winters in the highlands can be severe, with much snow. Tirana. Jan. 44°F (6·8°C), July 75°F (23·9°C). Annual rainfall 54" (1,353 mm). Shkodër. Jan. 39°F (3·9°C), July 77°F (25°C). Annual rainfall 57" (1,425 mm).

CONSTITUTION AND GOVERNMENT. A new constitution was promulgated on 26 April 1991. The supreme legislative body is the single-chamber *National Assembly* of 155 deputies, 115 directly elected and 40 elected by proportional representation, for 4-year terms. Where no candidate wins an absolute majority, a run-off election is held. Senior members of the former Communist Party, or members of parliament before May 1991, are not permitted to stand in national or local elections until 2002.

A draft new constitution, submitted to a referendum in Nov. 1994, was rejected by 53·8% of votes cast; turn-out was 75%.

Parliamentary elections were held in 2 rounds on 29 June and 6 July 1997. A new socialist-led government took power in the summer of 1997.

Prime Minister: Fatos Nano (Socialist Party).

Deputy Prime Minister: Bashkim Fino (SP). *Foreign:* Paskal Milo (Social Democratic Party). *Defence:* Sabit Brokaj (SP). *Interior:* Neritan Ceka (Democratic Alliance). *Public Economy and Privatization:* Ulli Bufi (SP). *Labour, Social Affairs and Women:* Elinaz Sherifi (SP). *Food and Agriculture:* Lufter Xhuveli (Agrarian Party). *Finance:* Arben Malaj (SP). *Trade and Tourism:* Shaqir Vukaj (SP). *Public Affairs and Transport:* Gaqo Apostoli (SDP). *Culture, Youth and Sport:* Arta Dade (SP). *Health and Environment:* Leonard Solis (Human Rights Union). *Legislative Reform and Relations with People's Assembly:* Arben Imami (Democratic Alliance). *Cooperation and Economic Development:* Ennelinda Meksi (SP). *Justice:* Thimio Kondi (Independent). *State Secretary for Euro-Atlantic Integration:* Maqo Lakrori (SP). *State Secretary for Policy of Defence:* Perikli Teta (Democratic Allance). *State Secretary in the Interior Ministry:* Ndre Legisi (SP). *State Secretary for Local Government:* Lush Perpali (SP).

Local government. There are 12 prefectures each under a prefect nominated by the Prime Minister, subdivided into 36 districts. Elected councils function at district, municipal and commune level. There are 64 city and 310 commune mayoralties. Elections were held on 20 and 26 Oct. 1996; turn-out was 72%. The DP gained 58 city and 267 commune mayoralties. The OSCE refused to monitor the elections because it was not permitted sufficient observers.

National anthem: 'Rreth Flamurit të për bashkuar' ('The flag that united us in the struggle'); words by A. S. Drenova, music by C. Porumbescu.

DEFENCE. Conscription is for 15 months.

Army. The Army consists of 9 infantry divisions. Equipment includes 138 T-34 and 721 T-59 main battle tanks. Strength (1996) 60,000 (including 20,000 conscripts). There is an internal security force of 5,000; frontier guards number 5,000. There is a People's Militia of 3,500.

Navy. The combatant navy includes 2 submarines, 2 offshore patrol craft, 24 hydrofoil torpedo boats, 11 inshore patrol craft and 4 inshore minesweepers. Auxiliaries include 2 tankers and about 10 service craft. Navy personnel in 1996 totalled 2,500 officers and ratings, including 350 coastal defence guards. There are naval bases at Durrës and Vlorë.

Air Force. The Air Force, controlled by the Army, had (1997) about 7,000 personnel (1,400 conscripts), and operated 70 combat aircraft, mostly Chinese. There are 5 aviation regiments, 3 with fighters, 1 with transport aircraft and 1 with helicopters. In 1997 the USA agreed to supply Cessna T-37 trainers.

INTERNATIONAL RELATIONS

Membership. Albania is a member of the UN, the Council of Europe, the Central European Initiative and the NATO Partnership for Peace.

ECONOMY

Policy. Priority is given to the development of agriculture and the exploitation of tourism and natural resources. Privatization of land, small businesses and housing was effected in 1991–93. A privatization programme for large enterprises was initiated in 1995 under the aegis of the National Privatization Agency. Sales are at auction or through vouchers.

Performance. GDP fell by 6% in 1997 after the collapse of pyramid finance schemes. Unemployment was 15·8% in 1997.

Budget. The fiscal year is the calendar year.

Budgets (in 1m. leks):

	1991	1992	1993	1994
Revenue	5,168	12,500	32,164	46,049
Of which:				
Income tax	608	1,586	4,660	4,140
Turnover tax	2,259	2,365	4,991	4,959
Non-tax	774	3,756	9,349	10,084
Current expenditure	9,195	21,426	38,582	52,125
Of which:				
Personnel	1,854	5,380	10,120	15,442
Subsidies	3,345	4,045	2,443	2,225
Social security	1,982	3,341	7,302	10,821
Capital expenditure	1,007	2,154	8,229	11,736

Currency. The monetary unit is the *lek* (ALL) notionally of 100 *qindars*. In Aug. 1965 a new *lek* was introduced: 10 old *leks* = 1 new *lek*. There are 5, 10, 20 and 50 *qindar* coins and a 1 lek coin; notes are for 1, 3, 5, 10, 50, 100, 500 and 1,000 leks. In Sept. 1991 the lek was pegged to the ecu at a rate of 30 leks = 1 ecu. In June 1992 it was devalued from 50 to 110 to US$1. Annualized inflation was 14·5% in 1995 (85% in 1993), but in Feb. 1998 was reported to be nearing 50%. In Feb. 1996 the UK restored 1,574 kg of gold which had been held in compensation under a French-UK-US trusteeship for the mining of 2 British warships in the 'Corfu incident' of 1946.

Banking and Finance. The central bank and bank of issue is the formally independent Bank of Albania, founded in 1925 with Italian aid as the Albanian State Bank and renamed in 1993. Its *governor* is Qarmil Tusha. In 1996 there were 3 state-owned commercial banks, 1 foreign bank and 2 joint ventures.

A stock exchange opened in Tirana in 1996.

Weights and Measures. The metric system is in force.

ENERGY AND NATURAL RESOURCES

Electricity. Albania is rich in hydro-electric potential. Electric power production in 1994 was 3,904m. kWh.

Oil and Gas. Offshore exploration began in 1991. Oil has been produced onshore since 1920. Oil reserves are some 540m. tonnes. Output of crude in 1992, 0·99m.

tonnes. Natural gas is extracted. Reserves, 8,000m. cu. metres. Output, 1993, 100m. cu. metres. Oil investment includes the building of a 40 km pipeline to the Adriatic coast. A consortium led by Premier Oil, an independent UK company, signed an agreement in Dec. 1997 to develop Albania's biggest onshore oil field, Patos Merinze, by investing US$250m. Production is to increase from 6,000 bbls. a day to more than 25,000 within 4 years.

Minerals. Mineral wealth is considerable and includes lignite, chromium, copper and nickel. Production, 1994 (in 1,000 tonnes): Lignite, 169; chromium ore, 223; copper ore, 178; iron-nickel ore (1991), 931. Nickel reserves are 60m. tonnes of iron containing 1m. tonnes of nickel, but extraction had virtually ceased by 1996. A consortium of British and Italian companies is modernizing the chrome industry with the aim of making Albania the leading supplier of ferrochrome to European stainless steel producers.

Agriculture. In 1996, 60% of the population depended upon agriculture, which contributed 56% of GDP. The country is mountainous, except the Adriatic littoral and the Korçë Basin, which are fertile. Only 25% of the land area is suitable for cultivation. In 1992 there were 0·57m. ha of arable land, 0·13m. ha of permanent cropland and 0·4m. ha of pasture. 0·43m. ha were irrigated.

A law of Aug. 1991 privatized co-operatives' land. Families received allocations according to their size made by village committees. In 1994 there were 0·42m. private farms; holdings averaged 1·4 ha. Since 1995 owners have been permitted to buy and sell agricultural land. In 1988 there were 21,033 tractors (in 15HP units).

Production (in 1,000 tonnes), 1994: Total grains, 508 (including maize, 151); sugar-beet, 60; potatoes, 86; barley, 33; sunflower seeds, 2; tobacco, 13; dried beans, 16; soya beans, 1; fodder, 20; vegetables (including water melons), 585.

Livestock, 1994: Cattle, 0·67m.; sheep, 1·48m.; goats, 1·02m.; pigs, 1m.; horses (1993), 0·11m.; chickens, 3·6m. Livestock products, 1994 (in 1,000 tonnes): Beef and veal, 50; pork, 20; mutton and goat, 33; chicken, 4; wool, 3; milk, 764,000 litres; 285m. eggs.

Forestry. Forests covered 1,046,150 ha in 1988, mainly oak, elm, pine and birch. In 1991 382,000 cu. metres of sawn timber were produced.

Fisheries. The catch in 1993 was 3,500 tonnes.

INDUSTRY. Output is small, and the principal industries are agricultural product processing, textiles, oil products and cement. Closures of loss-making plants in the chemical and engineering industries built up in the Communist era led to a 60% decline in production by 1993. Output, 1994 (in 1,000 tonnes): Rolled steel, 17; phosphate fertilizer, 11; ammonium nitrate, 6; sulphuric acid, 4; cement, 240; cigarettes, 1; soap, 3; vegetable oil, 6; 40m. bricks; 3m. articles of knitwear; beer, 7·2m. litres; wine, 0·5m. litres.

Labour. In 1994 the workforce was 1·54m., including 0·6m. in the private sector. Estimated unemployed in June 1993, 0·44m. (0·24m. females). Registered unemployment rate, 1996, 17·6%.

Minimum wages may not fall below one-third of maximum. Hours of labour: 8-hour day, 6-day week and 12 days yearly paid holiday. Retirement age is 60 for men and 55 for women. Average monthly wage, 1990: 570 leks.

Trade Unions. Independent trade unions became legal in Feb. 1991.

FOREIGN ECONOMIC RELATIONS. Foreign investment was legalized in Nov. 1990. Foreign debt was some US$1,118m. in 1994. Remittances from Albanians working abroad totalled US$334m. in 1993.

In June 1992 the USA granted most-favoured-nation status.

Commerce. Exports in 1994 totalled US$187m.; imports, US$603m. In 1994 exports included 45·3% manufactures, 26·7% fuels and lubricants, 14·3% foodstuffs, tobacco and live animals, 4·6% raw materials, 3·4% machinery and transport equipment; imports: 31·8% machinery and transport equipment, 25·5% foodstuffs, tobacco and live animals, 18·9% manufactures, 10·9% fuels and lubricants, 6·5% chemical products.

Main export markets, 1995 (% of total trade): Italy, 51·1%; Greece, 9·7%; Germany, 6·1%; Turkey, 6%. Main import suppliers: Italy, 36·8%; Greece, 26·1%; Germany, 4·8%; Turkey, 3·9%.

Tourism. In 1994 there were some 60,000 foreign visitors, 63% on business trips. In 1995 there were 3,000 hotel beds.

COMMUNICATIONS

Roads. In 1995 there were 2,900 km of paved main roads, 5,000 km of unpaved secondary roads and 9,500 km of rural tracks. 0·16m. vehicles were registered in 1996.

Railways. Total length in 1996 was 742 km. 4m. passengers and 0·6m. tonnes of freight were carried in 1995.

Civil Aviation. The national carrier is Albanian Airlines, a joint venture with a Kuwaiti firm. It began operations in Oct. 1995 with 1 Airbus 320. In 1996 it flew services to Athens, Bologna, Brussels, Istanbul, London, Munich, Paris, Rome and Skopje. Tirana (Rinas Airport) is also served by Adria Airways, Alitalia, Austrian Airlines, Balkan Bulgarian, Croatia Airlines, Lufthansa, Malév, Olympic, Swissair and Tarom. 0·2m. passengers used Rinas in 1995 (30,000 in 1990).

Shipping. In 1995 merchant shipping totalled 80,954 GRT. The main ports are Durrës, Vlorë, Sarandë and Shëngjln. 1·1m. tonnes of freight were carried in 1988 (769,000 tonnes overseas).

Telecommunications. Number of post and telegraph offices (1988), 635; telephones (1996), 52,000. A state-owned mobile telephone network was set up in 1996, initially serving 8,000 subscribers. Broadcasting is regulated by the National Council for Radio-Television, 1 member of which is appointed by the president, and the other 6 by the permanent Commission on the Media, which is composed equally of representatives of government and opposition parties. The National Council broadcasts a national radio programme and a second radio programme from 14 stations. There are also regional programmes and an external service. In 1993 there were 210,000 radio and 0·3m. TV receivers (colour by PAL).

Cinemas. In 1990 there were 108 cinemas with an attendance of 3·3m.

Press. In 1995 there were 4 national dailies, 2 owned by political parties, and 45 other newspapers.

SOCIAL INSTITUTIONS

Justice. A new criminal code was introduced in June 1995. The administration of justice is presided over by the *Council of Justice*, chaired by the President of the Republic, which appoints judges to courts. A Ministry of Justice was re-established in 1990 and a Bar Council set up. In Nov. 1993 the number of capital offences was reduced from 13 to 6 and the death penalty abolished for women.

Religion. The population is 70% of Moslem origin, mainly Sunni with some Belaktashi, 20% Orthodox and 10% Roman Catholic. The Albanian Orthodox Church is autocephalous; it is headed by an Exarch and 3 metropolitans. In 1993 there were 47 priests. The Roman Catholic cathedral in Shkodër has been restored. In 1993 there were 4 Roman Catholic bishops. Percentages of the population actively practising were estimated in 1996 as Moslems, 20%; Orthodox, 6%; Roman Catholics, 3%.

Education. Primary education is free and compulsory in 8-year schools from 7 to 15 years. Secondary education is also free and lasts 4 years. Secondary education is divided into 3 categories: General; technical and professional; vocational. There were, in 1988, 3,251 nursery schools with 121,000 pupils and 5,299 teachers, 1,691 primary schools with 547,000 pupils (5,000 part-time) and 27,862 teachers, 485 secondary schools with 194,000 pupils (63,000 part-time) and 9,004 teachers (including 442 vocational secondary schools with 135,000 pupils and 7,221 teachers), and 8 tertiary institutions, with 25,000 students (5,000 part-time) and 1,659 lecturers. In 1991–92 there were some 2,500 schools with 0·8m. pupils and 50,000 teachers. In 1995–96 there were 4 universities, 1 agricultural university, 1 technological university, 1 polytechnic, 1 academy of fine arts and 1 higher institute of physical education. There were 14,699 university students and 1,138 academic staff in 1994–95. Adult literacy is 85%.

Health. Medical services are free, though medicines are charged for. In 1993 there were 40 hospitals, 6,308 doctors and 6,801 nurses. In 1995 there were about 10,000 hospital beds.

DIPLOMATIC REPRESENTATIVES

Of Albania in Great Britain (38 Grosvenor Gdns., London SW1W 0EB)
Ambassador: Agim Besim Fagu.

Of Great Britain in Albania (Rruga Skenderberg 12, Tirana)
Ambassador: Andrew Tesoriere.

Of Albania in the USA (1150 18th St., NW, Washington DC 20036)
Ambassador: Lublin Dilja.

Of the USA in Albania
Ambassador: Marisa R. Lino.

Of Albania to the United Nations
Ambassador: Agim Nesho.

Of Albania to the European Union
Ambassador: Artur Kuko.

Further Reading

Bland, W. B., *Albania.* [Bibliography] Oxford and Santa Barbara, 1988
Hutchings, R., *Historical Dictionary of Albania.* Lanham (MD), 1996
Sjoberg, O., *Rural Change and Development in Albania.* Boulder (CO.), 1992
Vickers, M., *The Albanians: a Modern History.* London, 1995
Vickers, M. and Pettifer, J., *Albania: from anarchy to a Balkan Identity.* Farnborough, 1997
Winnifrith, T. (ed.) *Perspectives on Albania.* London, 1992

National statistical office: Statistical Institute of Albania, Tirana.

ALGERIA

Jumhuriya al-Jazairiya
ad-Dimuqratiya ash-Shabiya

(People's Democratic Republic
of Algeria)

Capital: Algiers
Population: 28·58m.
GNP: US$46·1bn.
HDI/world rank: 0·737/82

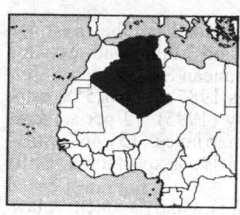

KEY HISTORICAL EVENTS. The first Algerian kingdom emerged from the Punic Wars. Massinissa reigned over his kingdom of Numidia from 202-148BC and his dynasty lasted until 106BC when his grandson Jugurtha became a Roman client. As part of the Roman Empire, Numidia flourished, becoming known as the 'granary of Rome'.

With the decline of the Roman Empire, Algeria became part of the powerful Berber empires of the Almoravids and Almohads. Tlemcen became the eastern capital of the Almohads and flourished as a centre of Islam. During this period Algerian seaports like Algiers, Annaba and Bijaya thrived on trade with European markets. The demise of the Almohad empire created a power vacuum which led to the rise of piracy along what became known as the Barbary Coast. Coastal cities hired corsairs to seize merchant vessels and gain an advantage in the fierce competition for trade on the high seas. It was not until late in the 18th century that Europeans were able to challenge the Barbary pirates of Algeria with superior naval power and artillery. In 1815 a US naval squadron under Captain Stephen Decatur attacked Algiers and forced its governor to sign a treaty banning piracy against US ships.

Persistent attacks on European shipping caused the British and Dutch to combine their forces against the Algerians and almost totally destroyed their fleet in 1816. The French took Algiers in 1830 and, despite formidable resistance, by 1857 the whole country was in French control. The French settlers who subsequently arrived developed political and economic power at the expense of the indigenous Moslem population. In Nov. 1954 the *Front de Libération Nationale* (FLN), representing the Moslem majority, sought national independence by open warfare against the French administration and armed forces. There was extensive loss of life and property during the fighting which continued unabated until in March 1962 a cease-fire was agreed between the French government and the nationalists. The conflict marked the only successful challenge to colonialism by a Middle Eastern country. Against the wishes of the French in Algeria, Gen. De Gaulle conceded Algerian independence on 3 July 1962.

The Political Bureau of the FLN took over the functions of government, a National Constituent Assembly was elected and the Republic was declared on 25 Sept. 1962. The founder of the FLN, Ahmed Ben Bella, became prime minister, becoming president the following year. On 15 June 1965 the government was overthrown by a junta of army officers, who established a Revolutionary Council under Col. Houari Boumédienne. After 10 years of rule, Boumédienne proposed that elections should be held for a president and a National Assembly. The proposed new constitution was accepted in a referendum in Nov. 1976 and Boumédienne was elected president (unopposed), securing more than 99% of the votes cast. A National Assembly was elected in Feb. 1977, only FLN members being allowed as candidates.

On the death of the president in Dec. 1978 the Revolutionary Council again took over the government. Col. Bendjedid Chadli was proposed president, and a referendum accepted him. When he stood for re-election in 1984, as the sole candidate, he was chosen for a further 5 years. But in Dec. 1991, when the Islamic Salvation Front (FIS) won the first round, the President resigned and his functions were assumed by a High Committee of State. The second round of elections was cancelled. In March 1992 the FIS was dissolved by court order. The head of state, Mohamed Boudiaf, was assassinated on 29 July 1992, and a campaign of terrorism was launched by Moslem fundamentalists which has continued to the present day. It is estimated that over

100,000 lives have been lost since the war between the Government and the Islamists began in 1992. Additionally, more than 1,000 Algerians have 'disappeared' after being arrested by government forces.

Liamine Zeroual was appointed State President in Jan. 1994 and elected President on 16 Nov. 1995. Hopes that violence would be brought to an end by the parliamentary poll of June 1997 were disappointed and local elections in Oct. 1997 brought opposition accusations of ballot rigging. 1998 began with reports of over 1,000 civilians being slaughtered in the previous 2 weeks.

TERRITORY AND POPULATION. Algeria is bounded in the west by Morocco and Western Sahara, south-west by Mauritania and Mali, south-east by Niger, east by Libya and Tunisia, and north by the Mediterranean Sea. It has an area of 2,381,741 sq. km (919,595 sq. miles). Population (census 1987) 22,971,558; estimate (1995) 28,575,000. (44·3% urban). Population density (1995), 12 per sq. km. Vital statistics, 1991: Births, 755,459; deaths, 116,120; marriages, 151,467; stillbirths, 17,520. Rates: Births, 30·1%; deaths, 6%; growth, 2·41%. Expectation of life (1992), 65·6 years. 2·5m. Algerians live in France.

83% of the population speak Arabic, 17% Berber; French is widely spoken. A law of Dec. 1996 made Arabic the sole official language.

The populations (1987 Census) of the 48 *wilayat* were as follows:

Adrar	216,931	Mila	511,047
Ain Defla	536,205	Mostaganem	504,124
Ain Témouchent	271,454	M'Sila	605,578
Annaba (Bône)	453,951	Naâma	112,858
Batna	757,059	Ouahran (Oran)	916,578
al-Bayadh	155,494	Ouargla	286,696
Béchar	183,896	al-Oued	379,512
Béjaia (Bougie)	697,669	Oum al-Bouaghi	402,683
Biskra	429,217	Qacentina (Constantine)	662,330
Bordj Bou Arreridj	429,009	Relizane	545,061
Bouira	525,460	Saida	235,240
al-Boulaida (Blida)	704,462	Sétif	997,482
Boumerdes	646,870	Sidi-bel-Abbès	444,047
Cheliff (Orléansville)	679,717	Skikda	619,094
Djelfa	490,240	Souk Ahras	298,236
Guelma	353,329	Tamanrasset	94,219
Ghardaia	215,955	at-Tarf	276,836
Illizi	19,698	Tébessa	409,317
al-Jaza'ir (Algiers)	1,687,579	Tiaret	574,786
Jijel	471,319	Tindouf	16,339[1]
Khenchela	243,733	Tipaza	615,140
Laghouat	215,183	Tissemsilt	227,542
Mascara	562,806	Tizi-Ouzou	931,501
Médéa	650,623	Tlemcen	707,453

[1] Excluding Saharawi refugees (170,000 in 1988) in camps.

The capital is Algiers (1995 population, 2,168,000). Other major towns (with 1987 census populations): Oran, 609,823; Constantine, 440,842; Annaba, 222,518; Batna, 181,601; Sétif, 170,182; Sidi-bel-Abbès, 152,778; Skikda, 128,747; Biskra, 128,280; Blida, 127,284; Béjaia, 114,534; Mostaganem, 114,037; Tlemcen, 107,632; Tébassa, 107,559; Béchar, 107,311.

CLIMATE. Coastal areas have a warm temperate climate, with most rain in winter, which is mild, while summers are hot and dry. Inland, conditions become more arid beyond the Atlas Mountains. Algiers. Jan. 54°F (12·2°C), July 76°F (24·4°C). Annual rainfall 30" (762 mm). Biskra. Jan. 52°F (11·1°C), July 93°F (33·9°C). Annual rainfall 6" (158 mm). Oran. Jan. 54°F (12·2°C), July 76°F (24·4°C). Annual rainfall 15" (376 mm).

CONSTITUTION AND GOVERNMENT. A referendum was held on 28 Nov. 1996. The electorate was 16,434,527; turn-out was 79·6%. The electorate approved by 85·81% of votes cast a new Constitution which defines the fundamental components of the Algerian people as Islam, Arab identity and Berber identity. It was signed into law on 7 Dec. 1996. Political parties are permitted, but not if based on a separatist feature such as race, religion, sex, language or region. The terms of office of the President are limited to 2, but the President's powers of nomination are widened (General-Secretary of the Government, governor of the national bank, judges, chiefs of security organs and prefects). Parliament is bicameral: A 380-member *National Assembly* elected by direct universal suffrage using proportional representation, and a 144-member *Council of the Nation*, one third nominated by the President and two-thirds indirectly elected by the 48 local authorities. The Council of the Nation debates bills passed by the National Assembly which become law if a three-quarters majority is in favour. At the presidential elections on 16 Nov. 1995 the electorate was 15,969,904; turn-out was 74·92%. Gen. Lamine Zeroual (National Democratic Rally) was elected for a second term with 61·34% of votes cast against 3 opponents. Elections for the National Assembly were held on 5 June 1997. There were 7,486 candidates from 39 parties. The electorate was 16·8m. Turn-out was officially put at 65·4%. The National Democratic Rally (RND) gained 155 seats, the Society for Peace Movement (MSP) 69 and the National Liberation Front (FLN) 64. Other parties won the remaining 92 seats.

President and Minister for National Defence: Gen. Lamine Zeroual (b. 1941; sworn in 27 Nov. 1995).

In March 1998 the government comprised:

Prime Minister: Ahmed Ouyahia.

Agriculture and Fisheries: Boulahouadjeb Benalia. *Commerce:* Belaid Bakhti. *Communication, Culture and Government Spokesman:* Habib Chaouki Hamraoui. *Energy and Mines:* Youcef Yousfi. *Equipment, Urban and Rural Development:* Abderrahmane Belayat. *Finance:* Abdelkrim Harchaoui. *Foreign Affairs:* Ahmed Attaf. *Health and Population:* Yahia Guidoum. *Higher Education and Scientific Research:* Amar Tou. *Housing:* Abdelkader Bounekraf. *Industry and Restructuring:* Abdelmajid Menasra. *Interior, Local Communities and Environment:* Mustapha Benmansour. *Justice:* Mohamed Adami. *Labour, Social Protection and Vocational Training:* Hacene Laskri. *National Education:* Boubakeur Benbouzid. *National Solidarity and Family:* Rabea Mechernene. *Posts and Telecommunications:* Mohamed Salah Youyou. *Religious Affairs:* Bouabdallah Ghoulemallah. *Small and Medium-sized Enterprises:* Bougerra Soltani. *Tourism and Handicrafts:* Abdelkader Bengrina. *Transportation:* Sid Ahmed Boulil. *Veterans Affairs:* Mohamed Said Abadou. *Youth and Sports:* Mohamed Aziz Derouaz.

National anthem: 'Qassaman bin nazilat Il-mahiqat' ('We swear by the lightning that destroys'); words by M. Zakaria, tune by Mohamed Fawzi.

Local government. There are 48 provincial (*wilayat*) councils, headed by prefects (*walis*) appointed by the President, and 1,539 local authorities.

DEFENCE. Conscription is for 18 months (6 months basic training and 12 months civilian tasks) at the age of 19.

Army. There are 6 military regions. The Army had a strength of 107,000 (75,000 conscripts) in 1996, organized in 2 armoured and 2 mechanized divisons, 5 motorized infantry brigades, 1 airborne division, and 7 artillery and 5 air defence battalions. Equipment includes 330 T-54/-55, 330 T-62 and 300 T-72 main battle tanks. The Ministry of the Interior maintain a Gendarmerie of 25,000 personnel and National Security Forces of 20,000. The Republican Guard numbers 1,200.

Navy. The Naval combatant force consists of 2 modern Russian-built diesel-powered patrol submarines, 3 frigates, 3 missile-armed corvettes, 11 fast missile craft, 8 other patrol craft, 1 ocean minesweeper, 2 tank landing ships, and 1 tank landing craft. There are some 10 auxiliaries. An associated coastguard 500 strong operates 28 fast cutters. Naval personnel in 1997 totalled 7,000. There are naval bases at Algiers, Annaba, Mers el Kebir, and Jijel.

Air Force. The Air Force in 1997 had about 200 combat aircraft and 10,000 person-nel. There are 8 squadrons of MiG-21s, 5 squadrons of MiG-23 variable-geometry interceptors and fighter-bombers, 3 squadrons of Su-20 variable-geometry attack air-craft, more than 30 Mi-24 assault helicopters and gunships, 17 C-130H Hercules, 3 F.27, 4 Il-76 and 5 An-12 transports and a variety of smaller transports, a wing of helicopters mainly operating Mi-8/17s and training units equipped with CM.170 Magister and L-39 Albatros armed jet counter-insurgency/trainers, and two-seat versions of operational types. Surface-to-air missile units have Soviet-built 'Guidelines', 'Goas', 'Gainfuls' and 'Gaskins'.

INTERNATIONAL RELATIONS

Membership. Algeria is a member of UN, OAU, the Arab League and OPEC.

ECONOMY

Policy. A law on privatization of July 1995 envisages the creation of small and medium size businesses in commerce, tourism and transport. Strategic industries (gas and oil) and large industrial complexes are to remain state-owned. Some 1,200 small and 50 large businesses were offered for sale to Algerian citizens; 30% of the shares are reserved for employees (5% free of charge).

Performance. GDP growth was 4% in 1995 (0·6% in 1994; –1·2% in 1993).

Budget. The fiscal year starts on 1 Jan. In 1994 budget revenue was (in DA 1m.): 474,100 (including 221,800 from oil and 184,300 from direct taxation); expenditure: 613,700 (including 74,100 on education; 46,800 on defence; 23,900 on home affairs; 19,800 on public health; 12,400 on veterans' affairs).

Currency. The unit of currency is the *Algerian dinar* (DZD) of 100 *centimes*. There are banknotes of DA 10, 20, 50, 100, 200, 500 and 1,000 and coins of 1, 2, 5, 20 and 50 centimes and DA 1, 5 and 10. DA 211,410m. were in circulation in 1993. Foreign exchange reserves were US$2,296m. in May 1996; gold reserves were US$1,565m. in Sept. 1993. Inflation was 15·1% in 1996. The dinar was devalued by 28·6% in April 1994.

Banking and Finance. The central bank and bank of issue is the Banque d'Algérie. The *Governor* is Abdelwahab Keramane. In 1996 there were 5 state-owned commer-cial banks. Private banking recommenced in Sept. 1995.

Weights and Measures. The metric system is in use.

ENERGY AND NATURAL RESOURCES

Electricity. Production (1992) 17,636m. kWh. 7% is hydro-electric.

Oil and Gas. A law of Nov. 1991 permits foreign companies to acquire up to 49% of known oil and gas reserves. Oil and gas production accounted for 23·2% of GDP in 1994. Oil production in 1995 was 1·21m. bbls. a day. Production of natural gas in 1995 was 150,000m. cu. metres. Proven reserves are 3,700,000m. cu. metres.

Minerals. Output in 1992 (in tonnes): Iron ore 2,565,300; lead, 1,507; phosphates, 1,173; zinc, 7,488. There are also deposits of mercury, silver, copper, antimony, kaolin, marble, onyx, salt and coal.

Agriculture. In 1994, agriculture accounted for 9·6% of GDP. Much of the land is unsuitable for agriculture. The northern mountains provide grazing. There were an estimated 7·09m. ha of arable land in 1991, 0·57m. ha of permanent crops and 31m. ha of permanent pasture. 0·43m. ha were irrigated in 1992. In 1987 the government sold back to the private sector land which had been nationalized on the declaration of independence in 1962; a further 0·5m. ha, expropriated in 1973, were returned to some 30,000 small landowners in 1990. In 1992 6m. persons were dependent upon agriculture, the agricultural workforce being 1·44m. There were 91,500 tractors and 9,500 combine harvesters in 1991.

The chief crops in 1993 were (in 1,000 tonnes): Wheat, 1,350; barley, 800; dates, 265; potatoes, 1,200; oranges, 270; mandarins and tangerines, 96; watermelons, 395; wine, 65; tomatoes, 515; olives, 130; onions, 232; oats, 40.

Livestock (in 1,000), 1993: Horses, 84; mules, 107; asses, 340; cattle, 1,460; camels, 130; sheep, 18,800; goats, 2,500.

Forestry. Forests cover 4·7m. ha. The greater part of the state forests are brushwood, but there are large areas with cork-oak trees, Aleppo pine, evergreen oak and cedar. The dwarf-palm is grown on the plains, alfa on the table-land. Timber is cut for firewood and for industrial purposes and for bark for tanning.

Fisheries. There are extensive fisheries for sardines, anchovies, sprats, tunny fish, and shellfish.

INDUSTRY. 1992 output of state enterprises (in 1,000 tonnes): Pig iron, 930; crude steel, 768; rolled steel, 439; steel tubes, 106; concrete bars, 134; cement, 7,093; bricks, 1,776; ammonitrates, 193; phosphate fertilizers, 154; tobacco, 24; (in units) tractors, 3,009; lorries, 2,434; TV sets, 218,000.

Labour. In 1994 the economically active population was estimated at 6,814,000. In 1996 the workforce numbered about 5·4m. of whom 1m. were engaged in agriculture. Some 1·2m. non-agricultural workers were employed in the private sector; 2m. workers were unemployed.

FOREIGN ECONOMIC RELATIONS. Foreign debt was US$32,940m in May 1996. Foreign investors are permitted to hold 100% of the equity of companies, and to repatriate all profits.

Commerce. In 1995 exports were valued at US$10,260m. and imports at US$10,200m.

Main trade partners in 1994, with percentages of total trade: USA (exports, 16·4%; imports, 14·2%); Italy (15·9%; 11·1%); France (14·2%; 28·8%); Germany (10·2%; 5·5%).

1994 exports included (in US$1m.): Crude oil, 1,980; gas, 2,270; condensates, 2,190; refined products, 1,670.

Tourism. In 1995, there were 97,650 foreign visitors.

COMMUNICATIONS

Roads. There were in 1991, 26,179 km of national highways and 22,132 km of local roads. There were 1,104,000 vehicles registered in 1990. In 1991 55m. passengers were conveyed by public transport and 6·2m. tonnes of freight.

Railways. In 1995 there were 3,210 km of 1,432 mm route (301 km electrified) and 1,156 km of 1,055 mm gauge. In 1995 the railways carried 8·6m. tonnes of freight and 44·2m. passengers.

Civil Aviation. There is an international airport at Algiers (Houari Boumediene). The national carrier is the state-owned Air Algérie, which had 3 A310-200s, 2 B-767-200s, 9 B-727-200 Advs, 13 B-737-200 Advs, 2 B-737-200C Advs, 3 B-767-300s, 7 F-27-400Ms and 2 other aircraft in 1995. Algeria is also served by Air France, Alitalia, Balkan, Egyptair, Libyan Arab Airlines, Royal Air Maroc, Saudia and Tunis Air. In 1993 the airports handled 6m. passengers and 27,851 tonnes of freight.

Shipping. In 1991, 17·2m. tonnes of cargo were unloaded and 64·9m. tonnes loaded, and 382,880 passengers embarked or disembarked. The state shipping line, Compagnie Nationale Algérienne de Navigation, owned 70 vessels in 1994. The shipping fleet totalled 1·09m. GRT in 1994, including oil tankers, 52,547 GRT.

Telecommunications. There were, in 1991, 2,877 post offices; number of telephones (1991), 862,000; telex subscribers, 10,487. The state-controlled Radiodiffusion Algérienne and Entreprise Nationale de Télévision broadcast home services in Arabic, Kabyle (Berber) and French and an external service. There are 18 TV transmitting stations (colour by PAL). In 1993 there were 6·0m. radio and 2m. TV receivers.

Press (1995). There were 5 daily newspapers, with a combined circulation of 1m.

SOCIAL INSTITUTIONS

Justice. The judiciary is constitutionally independent. Judges are appointed by the Supreme Council of Magistrature chaired by the President of the Republic. Criminal justice is organized as in France. The Supreme Court is at the same time Council of State and High Court of Appeal. The death penalty is in force for terrorism.

Religion. The 1996 Constitution made Islam the state religion, established a consultative *High Islamic Council*, and forbids practices 'contrary to Islamic morality'. Virtually the whole population are Sunni Moslems. There are about 150,000 Christians, mainly Roman Catholic. In 1995, the latter had an archbishop, 130 priests and 250 nuns.

Education. Adult literacy was 60·6% in 1992. In 1995 there were 17,186 state primary schools with 169,010 teachers and 4,617,000 pupils, 3,934 middle and secondary schools with 150,397 teachers and 2,844,864 pupils, of whom 43·9% were female.

In 1995-96, there were 6 universities, 2 universities of science and technology, 5 university centres, 1 agronomic institute, 1 telecommunications institute, 1 veterinary institute, 1 school of architecture and town planning and 1 *école normale supérieure*. In 1996 there were 160,000 university students and 7,947 academic staff.

Health. In 1991 there were 24,719 doctors, 7,563 dental surgeons and 2,575 pharmacists. In 1990 there were 284 hospitals (with 60,124 beds), 1,309 health centres, 510 poly clinics, 475 maternity clinics and 3,344 care centres.

Welfare. Welfare payments to 7·4m. beneficiaries on low incomes were introduced in March 1992.

DIPLOMATIC REPRESENTATIVES

Of Algeria in Great Britain (54 Holland Park, London, W11 3RS)
Ambassador: Ahmed Benyamina.

Of Great Britain in Algeria (Résidence Cassiopée, 7 Chemin des Glycines, Algiers)
Ambassador: J. Francois Gordon.

Of Algeria in the USA (2118 Kalorama Rd., NW, Washington, D.C., 20008)
Ambassador: Ramtane Lamamra.

Of the USA in Algeria (4 Chemin Cheich Bachir Ibrahimi, Algiers)
Ambassador: Ronald E. Neumann.

Of Algeria to the United Nations
Ambassador: Abdallah Baali.

Of Algeria to the European Union
Ambassador: Missoum Sbih.

Further Reading

Ageron, C.-R., *Modern Algeria: a History from 1830 to the Present*. London, 1991
Bennoune, M., *The Making of Contempory Algeria, 1830–1987*. CUP, 1988
Eveno, P., *L'Algérie*. Paris, 1994
Heggoy, A. A. and Crout, R. R. *Historical Dictionary of Algeria*. Metuchen (NJ), 1995
Horne, A., *A Savage War of Peace: Algeria 1954-1962*. London 1977
Lawless, R. I., *Algeria*. [Bibliography]. 2nd ed. Oxford and Santa Barbara, 1995
Ruedy, J., *Modern Algeria: the Origins and Development of a Nation*. Indiana Univ. Press, 1992
Stone, M., *The Agony of Algeria*. Columbia University Press, 1997
Stora, B., *Histoire de l'Algérie depuis l'Indépendance*. Paris, 1994

National statistical office: Office National des Statistiques, 8 rue des Moussebiline, Algiers.

ANDORRA

Principat d'Andorra

Capital: Andorra-la-Vella
Population: 72,766
GDP per head: US$16,200

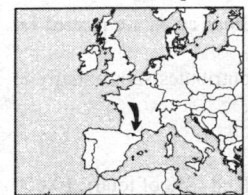

KEY HISTORICAL EVENTS. The political status of Andorra was regulated by the *Paréage* of 1278 which placed Andorra under the joint suzerainty of the Comte de Foix and of the Bishop of Urgel. The rights vested in the house of Foix passed by marriage to that of Bearn and, on the accession of Henri IV, to the French crown. A new democratic constitution was adopted in 1993.

TERRITORY AND POPULATION. The co-principality of Andorra is situated in the eastern Pyrenees on the French–Spanish border. The country is mountainous. Area, 450 sq. km. In lieu of a census, a register of population is kept. The registered population in 1 July 1996 was 72,766; 0-14 years, 16%; 15-64 years, 73%; 65 and over, 11%. Births (per 1,000 inhabitants), 10·2; deaths, 2·9. Life expectancy: male, 86·47 years; female, 95·2.

The chief towns are Andorra-la-Vella, the capital (population, 22,387) and its suburb Escaldes-Engordany (13,177). 30% of the residential population are Andorran, 61% Spanish and 6% French. Catalan is the official language; Spanish is widely spoken.

CLIMATE. Escaldes Engordany. Jan. 36°F (2·3°C), July 67°F (19·3°C). Annual rainfall 32" (808 mm).

CONSTITUTION AND GOVERNMENT. The joint heads of state are the President of the French Republic and the Bishop of Urgel, the co-princes.

A new democratic constitution was approved by 74·2% of votes cast at a referendum on 14 March 1993. The electorate was 9,123; turn-out was 75·7%. The new Constitution, which came into force on 4 May 1993, makes the co-princes a single constitutional monarch and provides for a parliament, the *General Council of the Andorran Valleys*, elected by universal suffrage. The General Council has 28 members elected, 2 from each of the 7 parishes and 14 elected from the single national constituency, for 4 years. In 1982 an *Executive Council* was appointed and legislative and executive powers were separated. The General Council elects the President of the Executive Council, who is the head of the government

There is a *Constitutional Court* of 4 members who hold office for 8-year terms, renewable once.

Elections to the General Council were held on 15 Feb. 1997. Electorate, 10,837. The Liberal Union gained 18 seats.

President, Executive Council: Marc Forné Molne (Liberal Union).

Agriculture, Commerce and Industry: Joan Tomas. *Culture and Social Welfare:* Pere Canturri Montanya. *Economy:* Joan Tomas Roca. *Education Youth and Sports:* Carme Sala Sausa. *Finance:* Susagna Arasanz Serra. *Foreign Affairs:* Manuel Mas Ribo. *Health:* Josep Gojcoechea Utrillo. *Tourism:* Enric Pujal Areny.

National anthem. 'El Gran Carlemany, mon pare' ('Great Charlemagne, my father'); words by Enric Marfany, tune by D.J. Benlloch i Vivò).

Local Government. Andorra is divided into 7 parishes, each of which is administered by a Communal Council. Councillors are elected for 4-year terms by universal suffrage.

INTERNATIONAL RELATIONS. The 1993 Constitution empowers Andorra to conduct its own foreign affairs, with consultation on matters affecting France or Spain.

Membership. Andorra is a member of the UN, UNESCO, WIPO and the Council of Europe.

ECONOMY

Budget. 1993: Revenue, US$138m. Expenditure, US$177m.

Currency. French and Spanish currency are both in use. *Diner* coins are minted for collectors.

Banking. The banking sector, with its tax haven status, contributes substantially to the economy.

ENERGY AND NATURAL RESOURCES

Agriculture. In 1992 there were some 1,000 ha of arable land (2% of total), 10,000 ha of forests (22%) and 25,000 ha of pasture (56%). Tobacco and potatoes are principal crops. The principal livestock activity is sheep raising.

INDUSTRY

Labour. Only 1% of the workforce is employed in agriculture, the rest in tourism, commerce, services and light industry. Manufacturing consists mainly of cigarettes, cigars and furniture.

FOREIGN ECONOMIC RELATIONS. Andorra is a member of the EU Customs Union for industrial goods, and a third country for agricultural produce. There is a free economic zone.

1997 exports, US$46·2m.; imports, US$920·2m.

Tourism. Tourism is the main industry, averaging 13m. visitors a year and accounting for 80% of GDP.

COMMUNICATIONS

Roads. There are 269 km of roads (198 km paved). Motor vehicles (1993): motor cars, 36,660; lorries and vans, 4,343.

Civil Aviation. There is an airport for Andorran traffic at Seo de Urgel.

Telecommunications. Servei de Telecomunicacions d'Andorra relays French and Spanish programmes. Radio Andorra is a commercial public station; Radio Valira is commercial. Number of receivers (1993), radio, 10,000; TV, 70,000; telephones, 21,258.

SOCIAL INSTITUTIONS

Justice. Justice is administered by the High Council of Justice, comprising 5 members appointed for single 6-year terms. The independence of judges is constitutionally guaranteed. Judicial power is exercised in civil matters in the first instance by Magistrates' Courts and a Judge's Court. Criminal justice is administered by the Corts consisting of the judge of appeal, 2 *rahonadors* elected by the General Council of the Valleys, a general attorney and an attorney nominated for 5 years alternately by each of the co-princes.

Religion. The Roman Catholic is the established church, but the 1993 Constitution guarantees religious liberty.

Education. Free education in French- or Spanish-language schools is compulsory: 6 years primary starting at 6 years, followed by 4 years secondary. A Roman Catholic school provides education in Catalan. In 1993–94 there were 18 schools altogether with 9,163 pupils.

Health. In 1993 there were 2 hospitals and 118 doctors.

DIPLOMATIC REPRESENTATIVES

Of Great Britain in Andorra
Ambassador: C. D. Brighty, CMG, CVO (resides in Madrid).

Of Andorra in the USA and to the United Nations
Deputy Permanent Representative: Juli Minoves Triquell.

US interests in Andorra are represented by the Consultate General's office in Barcelona.

Of Andorra to the European Union
Ambassador: Meritxell Mateu i Pi.

Further Reading

Taylor, B., *Andorra.* [Bibliography]. Oxford and Santa Barbara (CA), 1993

ANGOLA

República de Angola

Capital: Luanda
Population: 11·5m.
GDP per head: (PPP$) 1,600
HDI/world rank: 0·335/157

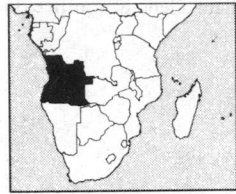

KEY HISTORICAL EVENTS. The earliest people in Angola, as in most of sub-Saharan Africa, were hunter-gatherers. They were displaced by Bantu-speaking farmers who by the 14th century were organized in several powerful states such as the kingdoms of Kongo and Mbundu. The rulers of Mbundu were called *ngola*, from which the Portuguese derived the name Angola. The Portuguese first made contact with Kongo in 1491, and for some time thereafter its kings were Catholic and their capital was renamed São Salvador.

Only brief Dutch occupation in the 1640s interrupted 4 centuries of Portuguese rule along the coast, from which hundreds of thousands of slaves were shipped and where, by the 19th century, a small Portuguese-speaking African and *mestiço* (half-European) élite had emerged. Inland, African states remained independent until the 19th century.

The Portuguese founded Luanda in 1875, and from the 1870s gradually occupied the interior of Angola, often called Portuguese West Africa. The occupation was slow in the face of strong African resistance (such as the Bailundo rising of 1902), and Portuguese rule was only fully established about 1920. Angola remained a Portuguese colony until 11 June 1951, when it became an Overseas Province of Portugal.

After the coup d'état in Portugal in April 1974, negotiations between Portugal, the MPLA (People's Movement for the Liberation of Angola), the FNLA (National Front for the Liberation of Angola) and UNITA (National Union for the Total Liberation of Angola) resulted in the signing of the Alvor Agreement in January 1975, under which a quadripartite transitional government was formed, with a view to elections in October and independence on 11 November. The FNLA tried to seize power by force, but was driven out of the capital. As independence approached, the invasion from the north was combined with a South African invasion in support of UNITA. The MPLA declared independence and, subsequently, with the help of Cuban troops, defeated the FNLA in the north and drove the invading South African army out of the country. South African invasions and the occupation of large areas of Angola continued until the signing of the New York Agreement in December 1988, under which South Africa agreed to withdraw its forces from Angola and Namibia (and grant independence to Namibia), while Angola and Cuba agreed to the phased withdrawal of Cuban troops.

After many abortive attempts to end the internal conflict with UNITA, a peace agreement was signed on 31 May 1991, to be monitored by the UN, and with US, Portuguese and Soviet observers, under which the government and UNITA armies were to be disbanded, a single national army formed and multi-party elections held. In Sept. 1992 the MPLA won the elections and José Eduardo dos Santos was re-elected President, against UNITA leader Jonas Savimbi, but the latter rejected the election results, withdrew his generals from the unified army and went back to war, seizing an estimated 70% of the country

On 15 Sept. 1993 the UN Security Council unanimously adopted an embargo on arms and fuel supplies to UNITA. On 20 Nov. 1994 an agreement was signed in Lusaka, but not at presidential level (by Venâncio de Moura, Minister of External Relations, and Eugênio Manuvacola, then UNITA secretary-general) because Jonas Savimbi failed to turn up. The Lusaka Protocol provided for the quartering and disarming of UNITA troops, the integration of 26,300 of them in the single national army, and the demobilization of the remainder. The government also agreed to offer UNITA a substantial number of posts in central and local government, as well as ambassadorial posts. It also required the extension of central administration to all UNITA-held areas, and free movement of people and goods throughout the country.

New elections would be held when the UN deemed that conditions permitted. Despite the fact that the military aspects of the Protocol were not completed, the government went ahead with the political ones, and in April 1997 the 70 elected UNITA deputies took their seats in the National Assembly, and a Government of Unity and National Reconciliation was sworn in, including officials from UNITA and all other parties with seats in the National Assembly. There were continued delays in the completion of the registration and demobilization of UNITA troops, and on 29 Oct. 1997 the UN Security Council imposed a further package of sanctions on UNITA, including the closure of its offices abroad and restrictions on travel abroad by its officials.

On 9 Jan. 1998 it was announced that a breakthrough in negotiations between the government and UNITA rebels had been reached, and that Jonas Savimbi, UNITA's leader, would soon be going to the capital, Luanda, to meet with President dos Santos.

TERRITORY AND POPULATION. Angola is bounded in the north by the Republic of the Congo, north and north-east by the Democratic Republic of the Congo, east by Zambia, south by Namibia and west by the Atlantic Ocean. The area is 1,246,700 sq. km (481,354 sq. miles) including the province of Cabinda, an exclave of territory separated by 30 sq. km of territory of the Democratic Republic of the Congo. The population at census, 1970, was 5,646,166, of whom 14% were urban. Official estimate, 1995, 11·5m. (50% urban); density, 9 per sq. km. Expectation of life was 47·2 years in 1994. Birth rate was 50·7; death rate 18·5. Population figures are rough estmates because the civil war has led to huge movements of population.

There were 0·3m. Angolan refugees in the Democratic Republic of the Congo, Zambia and the Republic of the Congo in 1995.

Area, population and chief towns of the provinces:

Province	Area (in sq km)	Population estimate, 1992 (in 1,000)	Chief town
Bengo	31,371	196·1	Caxito
Benguela	31,788	656·6	Benguela
Bié	70,314	1,119·8	Kuito
Cabinda	7,270	152·1	Cabinda
Cuando-Cubango	199,049	139·6	Menongue
Cuanza Norte	24,190	385·2	Ndalatando
Cuanza Sul	55,660	694·5	Sumbe
Cunene	89,342	241·2	Ondjiva
Huambo	34,274	1,521·0	Huambo
Huíla	75,002	885·1	Lubango
Luanda	2,418	1,588·6	Luanda
Lunda Norte	102,783	305·9	Lucapa
Lunda Sul	45,649	169·1	Saurimo
Malanje	97,602	906·0	Malanje
Moxico	223,023	319·3	Luena
Namibe	58,137	107·3	Namibe
Uíge	58,698	802·7	Uíge
Zaire	40,130	237·5	Mbanza Congo

The most important towns (populations) are Luanda, the capital (1995, 2·25m.), Huambo (1995, 0·4m.), Lobito (1970, 59,258), Benguela (1970, 40,996), Lubango (1984, 105,000), Malanje (1970, 31,559) and Namibe (formerly Moçâmedes, 1981, 0·1m.).

The main ethnic groups are Umbundo (Ovimbundo), Kimbundo, Bakongo, Chokwe, Ganguela, Luvale and Kwanyama.

CLIMATE. The climate is tropical, with low rainfall in the west but increasing inland. Temperatures are constant over the year and most rain falls in March and April. Luanda. Jan. 78°F (25·6°C), July 69°F (20·6°C). Annual rainfall 13" (323 mm). Lobito. Jan. 77°F (25°C), July 68°F (20°C). Annual rainfall 14" (353 mm).

CONSTITUTION AND GOVERNMENT. Under the Constitution adopted at independence, the sole legal party was the MPLA. In Dec. 1990, however, the MPLA announced that the Constitution would be revised to permit opposition parties. The supreme organ of state is the 220-member *National Assembly.* There is an executive *President* elected for renewable terms of 5 years, who appoints a *Council of Ministers.*

At the presidential and parliamentary elections of 29–30 Sept. 1992 the electorate was 4,862,748. Turn-out was about 90%. Eduardo Dos Santos (MPLA) was re-elected as President with 49·5% of votes cast as against 40·7% for his single opponent, Jonas Savimbi (UNITA). The latter refused to accept the result.

The MPLA gained 129 seats in the National Assembly with 53·74% of votes cast, UNITA 70 with 34%.

On 11 April 1997 a Government of National Unity was installed, with 3 ministerial posts going to UNITA.

President: José Eduardo dos Santos (b. 1943; re-elected 9 Dec. 1985 and 29–30 Sept. 1992).

In March 1998 the Government comprised:
Prime Minister: Fernando de Franca Dias Van-Dunem.
Agriculture and Rural Development: Carlos Antonio Fernandes. *Assistance and Social Reintegration:* Albino Malungo. *Commerce:* Victorino Domingos Hossi. *Culture:* Ana Maria do Oliveira. *Education:* Antonio Burity da Silva Neto. *Energy and Water:* Joao Moreira Pinto Saraiva. *External Relations:* Venâncio de Moura. *Finance:* Mario de Alcantara Monteiro. *Fisheries:* Maria de Fatima Monteiro Jardim. *Geology and Mines:* Marcos Samondo. *Health:* Anastacio Ruben Sikata. *Hotels and Tourism:* Jorge Alicerces Valentim. *Industry:* Manuel Diamantino Borges Duque. *Interior:* Santana Andre Pitra 'Petroff'. *Justice:* Paulo Tjipilica. *National Defence:* Gen. Pedro Sebastiao. *News Media:* Pedro Hendrick Vaal Neto. *Petroleum:* Albina Faria de Assis 'Africano'. *Planning:* Emmanuel Moreira Carneiro. *Posts and Telecommunications:* Licinio Tavares Ribeiro. *Public Administration, Employment and Social Welfare:* Antonio Domingos Pitra Costa Neto. *Science and Technology:* Francisco Mubengai. *Social Communication:* Pedro Hendrick Vaal Neto. *Territorial Administration:* Fernando Faustino Muteka. *Transport:* Andre Luis Brandao. *War Veterans:* Pedro Jose Van Dunem. *Women's Affairs:* Joana Lina Ramos Baptista Christiano. *Youth and Sports:* Jose da Rocha Sardinha de Castro.

National anthem: 'O Pátria, nunca mais esqueceremos' ('Oh Fatherland, never shall we forget'); words by M. R. Alves Monteiro, tune by R. A. Dias Mingas.

Local government: The 18 provinces, each under a Governor appointed by the President and an elected legislative of from 55 to 85 members, are subdivided into 139 districts.

DEFENCE. Conscription is for 2 years.

Army. In 1997 the Army had 25 regiments. Total strength 98,000. Equipment includes Soviet 100 T-34, 100 T-54/55 and some T-62 and T-72 main battle tanks.

Navy. The Navy, almost all Soviet-built, includes 5 inshore patrol craft, 1 mine-hunter, 1 landing ship and 6 landing craft, together with 10 auxiliary vessels. Naval personnel in 1997 totalled about 1,500. Naval bases are at Luanda, Lobito and Namibe.

Air Force. The Angolan People's Air Force (FAPA) was formed in 1976 and had (1996) about 5,000 personnel. Since the elections in 1992 and the relative calm, the Air Force has been run down and serviceability of combat aircraft is low. There are 5 combat squadrons, 2 with MiG-23s and 1 each with Mig-21s, Su-22s and Su-25s. The transport force, including An-26s, An-32s and Aviocars, is still active, as are the helicopter formations, mainly equipped with Mi-8/17s and Mi-25s. Pilatus PC-7 and PC-9 trainers are equipped for counter-insurgency operations.

INTERNATIONAL RELATIONS

Membership. Angola is a member of the UN, OAU, SADC and is an ACP state of the EU.

ECONOMY

Policy. Reforms are under way to introduce a market economy and restore private property. An Economic and Social Programme covered 1995–96.

Performance. GDP growth was 5% in 1995 (8·6% in 1994).

Budget. The 1995 budget envisaged recurrent revenue (in 1,000m. former kwanzas) of 3,765·3 (of which taxes, 2,257·6; royalties, 1,159); capital revenue of 15·8 (mainly from privatization); recurrent expenditure of 2,515·6 and capital expenditure of 2,177·2.

Currency. The unit of currency is the *readjusted kwanza* (AOK) of 100 *lwei*, which replaced the former new kwanza at Kzr1 = Nkz1,000 in July 1995. There were notes of 100, 500, 1,000, 5,000, 10,000, 50,000 and 100,000 former kwanzas, which remained legal tender until 1996. In Jan. 1994 a 2-tier system was replaced by a single floating exchange rate. Foreign exchange reserves were US$163m. in 1995; gold reserves, 46,500 troy oz. in 1990. Inflation was an annualized 7,500% in 1996.

Banking and Finance. Banking was re-opened to commercial competition in 1991. The Banco Nacional de Angola is the central bank and bank of issue (*Governor*, António Furtado) All banks remain state-owned, though the government is progressively reducing its stake in them. An agricultural bank and a commercial and industrial bank were founded in 1991. 5 Portuguese banks have branches, as well as the French Banque Paribas, the Equator Bank, and the African Development Bank.

Weights and Measures. The metric system is in force.

ENERGY AND NATURAL RESOURCES

Electricity. Production (1994) totalled 1,027·8m. kWh (772m. kWh hydro-electric in 1991).

Oil. Oil is produced mainly in the Cabinda exclave and contributed 49·9% of Angolan GDP in 1994. Total production (1992) 25·57m. tonnes.

Minerals. Production of diamonds in 1992 totalled 1,235,000 carats); the illegal export of diamonds is the chief source of income for UNITA. Other minerals produced include (1991) granite, 635,000 cu. metres; marble, 244,000 cu. metres; salt, 6,600 tonnes. Iron ore, phosphate, manganese and copper deposits exist.

Agriculture. Agriculture contributed 12% of GDP in 1994. In 1992 there were 3m. ha of arable land, 0·5m. ha of permanent crops and 29m. ha of permanent pasture. In 1993 7m. persons depended upon agriculture, of whom 2·69m. were economically active. The principal cash crops (with 1993 production, in 1,000 tonnes): Sugar-cane (290), coffee (5), bananas (280), palm oil (40), palm kernels (12), seed cotton (12); others include tobacco, citrus fruit and sisal. Food crops comprise cassava (1,870), maize (274), sweet potatoes (170) and dry beans (36).

Livestock (1993): 3·2m. cattle, 250,000 sheep, 1,550,000 goats, 810,000 pigs.

Forestry. In 1990 there were 52·95m. ha of forests, including mahogany and other hardwoods. Production (1991) 25·6m. cu. metres (7·9m. cu. metres sawn wood).

Fisheries. In 1993 the fishing fleet had 73 vessels over 100 GRT totalling 17,332 GRT. Total catch (1993) was 122,000 tonnes.

INDUSTRY. The principal manufacturing branches are foodstuffs, textiles and oil refining. Output, 1991 (in tonnes): Maize flour, 21,200; wheat flour, 18,900; bread, 25,100; soap, 4,700; plate glass, 6,900; plastic bags, 1,600; pesticides, 46; zinc sheets, 6,012; cable, 112; 52,000 radio sets; 15,600 TV sets.

Labour. The economically active population was 4·08m. in 1990 (1·57m. females, 0·29m. aged 10–15), of whom 69·8% worked in agriculture.

FOREIGN ECONOMIC RELATIONS. In 1995 total foreign debt was US$11,880m.

Commerce. Imports and exports for calendar years in US$1m.:

	1991	1992	1993	1994	1995
Imports	1,347	1,988	1,463	1,633	1,700
Exports	3,449	3,833	2,900	3,002	3,880

Main exports, 1994 (in US$1m.): Crude oil, 2,821; diamonds, 96; refined oil, 61; gas, 14. Chief import suppliers (1991 trade in US$1m.): Portugal, 587; USA, 207; France, 194; Japan, 153; Brazil, 144. Chief export markets: USA, 1,751; France, 328; Germany, 174; Brazil, 152; Netherlands, 131.

COMMUNICATIONS

Roads. There were, in 1994, about 75,000 km of roads (7,955 km asphalted and 7,870 km gravelled), and in 1989, 125,000 passenger cars and 42,000 commercial vehicles. Many roads remain mined as a result of the civil war; a programme of de-mining and rehabilitation is under way.

Railways. The length of railways open for traffic in 1987 was 2,952 km comprising 2,798 km of 1,067 mm gauge and 154 km of 600 mm gauge. The Benguela Railway runs from Lobito to the Democratic Republic of the Congo border at Dilolo where it connects with the National Railways of the Democratic Republic of the Congo. Other lines link Luanda with Malanje; Gunza with Gabela; and Namibe with Menongue. In 1993 railways carried 4m. passengers and 2·8m. tonnes of freight.

Civil Aviation. There is an international airport at Luanda (Fourth of February). The national carrier is Linhas Aéreas de Angola (TAAG). In 1995 it operated 1 B-707-320B, 3 B-737-200 Advs, 1 B-737-200C, 1 F-27-200, 1 F-200-400M, 2 F-27-600s and 3 ex-Soviet aircraft. There are also services by Aeroflot, Air France, Air Gabon, Air Namibia, Ethiopian Airlines, Lina Congo, SABENA, SAA and TAP. 0·46m. passengers were carried in 1991 (0·11m. international).

Shipping. There are ports at Luanda, Lobito and Namibe, and oil terminals at Malongo, Lobito and Soyo. 1·24m. tonnes of cargo were discharged in 1994. There are 3 state shipping companies. In 1995 the merchant fleet totalled 0·12m. GRT, including oil tankers, 2,665 GRT.

Telecommunications. There were 78,000 telephones in 1991.

The government-controlled Rádio Nacional de Angola broadcasts 3 programmes and an international service. There are also regional stations. Televisão Popular de Angola transmits from 7 stations (colour by PAL). In 1993 there were 0·45m. radio and 50,000 TV receivers.

Press. The government daily is the *Jornal de Angola*. (The *Diário da República* is the official gazette.) There is a weekly called the *Correio da Semana*, and there are around 100 specialized and independent publications.

SOCIAL INSTITUTIONS

Justice. The Supreme Court and Court of Appeal are in Luanda. The death penalty was abolished in 1992.

Religion. In 1992 there were 9·39m. Christians, the remainder following traditional animist religion.

Education. The education system provides 3 levels of general education totalling 8 years, followed by schools for technical training, teacher training or pre-university studies. Enrolment (in 1,000) in 1991-92: Pre-school, 188. General education first level, 923; second level, 141; third level, 42. Technical training, 12·7; teacher training, 109; pre-university studies (1990-91), 6·1. There is 1 university. Private schools have been permitted since 1991. The University of Luanda has campuses at Luanda, Huambo and Lubango. It had 8,954 students in 1991-92. The adult literacy rate is 42·5%.

Health. In 1990 there were 662 doctors, 10 dentists, 9,334 nurses, 4,165 medical auxiliaries and 266 hospitals and health centres with 11,857 beds. There were 1,339 medical posts.

DIPLOMATIC REPRESENTATIVES

Of Angola in Great Britain (98 Park Lane, London, W1)
Ambassador: António da Costa Fernandes.

Of Great Britain in Angola (Rua Diogo Cão, 4, Luanda)
Ambassador: R. D. Hart.

Of Angola in the USA
Ambassador: António Franca.

Of the USA in Angola (32 rua Houari Boumedienne, Miramar, Luanda)
Ambassador: Donald K. Steinberg.

Of Angola to the United Nations
Ambassador: Afonso Van Dunem 'Mbinda'.

Of Angola to the European Union
Ambassador: José Guerreiro Alves Primo.

Further Reading

Anstee, M. J., *Orphan of the Cold War: the Inside Story of the Collapse of the Angolan Peace Process, 1992–93.* London, 1996
James, W. M., *Political History of the War in Angola.* New York, 1991
Roque, F., *Económia de Angola.* Lisbon, 1991
Somerville, K., *Angola: Politics, Economics and Society.* London and Boulder, 1986

National statistical office: Instituto Nacional de Estatística, Luanda.

ANTIGUA AND BARBUDA

Capital: St John's
Population: 100,000
GNP: US$0·5bn.
HDI/world rank: 0·892/29

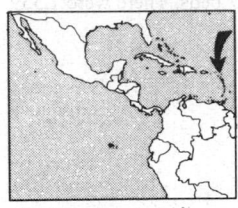

KEY HISTORICAL EVENTS. Antigua and Barbuda make up the island nation of the lesser Antilles in the Eastern Caribbean. Most of the population is descended from African slaves brought in during colonial times to work on sugar plantations.

The country was sighted by Christopher Columbus on his second voyage to the West Indies in 1493. The Spaniards attempted to settle on the island in 1520 as did the French in 1629. Antigua was eventually colonized in the year 1632 and in 1667, under the Treaty of Breda, it became a British Colony. Barbuda was colonized in 1628 and granted to the Cordrington Family in 1680. By the late 19th century, however, it had reverted to the British Crown.

Although planned as a slave-breeding colony, it never became one; the slaves became self-reliant sailors, hunters, fishermen and skilled workers, coming to regard the land as communally owned.

Antigua and Barbuda formed part of the Leeward Islands Federation from 1871 until 30 June 1956 when Antigua and Barbuda became a separate Crown Colony. It was part of the West Indies Federation from 3 Jan. 1958 until 31 May 1962 and became an Associated State of the UK on 27 Feb. 1967. Antigua and Barbuda gained independence on 1 Nov. 1981.

TERRITORY AND POPULATION. Antigua and Barbuda comprises 3 islands of the Lesser Antilles situated in the Eastern Caribbean with a total land area of 442 sq. km (171 sq. miles); it consists of Antigua (280 sq. km), Barbuda, 40 km to the north (161 sq. km) and uninhabited Redonda, 40 km to the south-west (1 sq. km). The population at the census of 1991 was 65,962 (1,400 on Barbuda). Estimate, 1995, 63,900 (1,500 on Barbuda); urban 36·2%. Expectation of life, 1993: Males, 71·1 years, females, 75·3. The chief towns are St John's, the capital on Antigua (30,000 inhabitants in 1995) and Codrington (1,200), the only settlement on Barbuda.

CLIMATE. A tropical climate, but drier than most West Indies islands. The hot season is from May to Nov., when rainfall is greater. Mean annual rainfall is 40" (1,000 mm).

CONSTITUTION AND GOVERNMENT. H.M. Queen Elizabeth, as Head of State, is represented by a Governor-General appointed by her on the advice of the Prime Minister. There is a bicameral legislature, comprising a 17-member Senate appointed by the Governor-General and a 17-member House of Representatives elected by universal suffrage for a 5-year term. The Governor-General appoints a Prime Minister and, on the latter's advice, other members of the Cabinet.

Barbuda is administered by a 9-member directly-elected council.

At the elections of March 1994 the Antigua Labour Party (ALP) gained 11 seats, the United Progressive Party, 5 and the Barbuda People's Movement, 1.

Governor-General: Sir James Carlisle, GCMG.

In March 1998 the government comprised:
Prime Minister, Minister of Defence, External Affairs, Information, Telecommunications, Civil Aviation, Internatinal Transportation, and Gaming: Lester Bird (ALP). *Finance and Social Security, Agriculture, Lands and Fisheries:* John E. St. Luce. *Justice, Legal Affairs and Attorney-General:* Radford Hill. *Public Utilities, Public Works, Local Transportation and Energy:* Robin Yearwood. *Trade, Industry, Commerce and Consumer Affairs:* Hilroy Humphries. *Education, Youth, Sports and Community Development:* Bernard Percival. *Labour and Home Affairs:* Adolphus

Eleazer Freeland. *Tourism, Culture and Environment:* Dr Rodney Williams. *Health and Civil Service Affairs:* Samuel Aymer. *Planning and Implementation:* Molwyn Joseph. *Prime Minister's Office:* Henderson Simon.

National anthem: 'Fair Antigua and Barbuda, we thy sons and daughters stand'; words by N. H. Richards, tune by W. G. Chambers.

DEFENCE. The Antigua and Barbuda Defence Force numbers 150. A coastguard service has been formed.

INTERNATIONAL RELATIONS

Membership. Antigua and Barbuda is a member of the UN, the Commonwealth, CARICOM, ACS, OAS, OECS and is an ACP state of the EU.

ECONOMY

Budget. The budget for 1996 envisaged recurrent revenue of EC$284·8m. and recurrent expenditure of EC$305·9m.

Currency. The unit of currency is the *Eastern Caribbean dollar* (XCD), issued by the Eastern Caribbean Central Bank. There are coins of 1, 2, 5, 10, 25 and 50 cents and EC$1, and notes of EC$5, 10, 20, 50 and 100. Foreign exchange reserves in Sept. 1993 were US$38·7m.

Banking and Finance. In 1993, 9 commercial banks were operating (6 foreign). There is also the Antigua Co-operative Bank and a government savings bank.

In 1981 Antigua established an offshore banking sector which in 1997 had 52 banks registered and operating.

ENERGY AND NATURAL RESOURCES

Water. Water shortages are frequent. There is a desalination plant with a capacity of 0·6m. gallons per day.

Agriculture. Cotton and fruits are the main crops. Production (1993) of fruits, 9,000 tonnes.

Livestock (1993): Cattle, 16,000; pigs, 4,000; sheep, 13,000; goats, 12,000.

INDUSTRY. Manufactures include toilet tissue, stoves, refrigerators, blenders, fans, garments and rum (molasses imported from Guyana).

Labour. In 1991 the economically active population was 26,753.

FOREIGN ECONOMIC RELATIONS. Foreign debt was US$260m. in 1994.

Commerce. Imports in 1992 amounted to US$261m. and exports to US$55m. The main trading partners were the USA, the UK and Canada.

Tourism. Tourism is the main industry, contributing about 70% of GDP and 80% of foreign exchange earnings and related activities. In 1995 there were 191,401 staying visitors and 227,443 cruise ship arrivals.

COMMUNICATIONS

Roads. In 1995 there were 384 km of main roads, 164 km of secondary roads, 320 km of rural roads and 293 km of other roads.

Civil Aviation. V. C. Bird International Airport is near St John's. Antigua is served by Air Canada, Air France, Air Jamaica, American Airlines, British Airways, BWIA, Caledonian Airlines, Condor Flugdienst and LIAT. There are flights to Barbados, Dominica, Frankfurt, Grenada, Guadeloupe, Jamaica, Martinique, Miami, the Netherlands Antilles, New York, Orlando, Puerto Rico, St Kitts-Nevis, St Lucia, St Vincent, Toronto, Trinidad, the UK, the British and US Virgin Islands and Washington DC. A domestic flight links Antigua and Barbuda Airport.

Shipping. The main port is the St John's deep water harbour.

Telecommunications. Telephone supply, 1995: 40 lines per 100 inhabitants. There is a mobile phone system. The government-owned Antigua and Barbuda Broadcasting Service broadcasts a radio and TV programme (colour by NTSC). There are 2 commercial radio and a commercial TV station, a religious radio station and relay stations. In 1993 there were estimated to be 75,000 radio and 28,000 TV receivers.

Press. In 1997 there were 3 opposition political newspapers, 1 pro-government privately-owned newspaper and 1 independent newspaper as well as a weekly trade-union-owned publication. The Chamber of Commerce has a monthly publication.

SOCIAL INSTITUTIONS

Justice. Law is based on UK common law as exercised by the Eastern Caribbean Supreme Court (ECSC) on St Lucia. There are Magistrates' Courts and a Court of Summary Jurisdiction. Appeals lie to the Court of Appeal of ECSC, or ultimately to the UK Privy Council.

Religion. The majority of the population are Anglican.

Education. Adult literacy was 90% in 1995. There were 72 government primary and secondary schools in 1992–93. Other schools were run by religious organizations.

Health. In 1997 there were 3 hospitals.

Welfare. The state operates a Medical Benefits Scheme providing free medical attention, and a Social Security Scheme, providing age and disability pensions and sickness benefits.

DIPLOMATIC REPRESENTATIVES

Of Antigua and Barbuda in Great Britain (15 Thayer St., London, W1M 5LD)
High Commissioner: Ronald M. Sanders, CMG.

Of Great Britain in Antigua and Barbuda (11, Old Parham Rd., St John's)
High Commissioner: R. Thomas, CMG (resides in Bridgetown).

Of Antigua and Barbuda in the USA (3400 International Dr., NW, Washington, D.C., 20008)
Ambassador: Lionel Alexander Hurst.

The US Embassy is based in Barbados.

Of Antigua and Barbuda to the United Nations
Ambassador: Dr Patrick A. Lewis.

Further Reading

Berleant-Schiller, R., *et al.*, *Antigua and Barbuda.* [Bibliography] Oxford and Santa Barbara (CA), 1995

ARGENTINA

República Argentina

Capital: Buenos Aires
Population: 34·6m.
GDP per head: (PPP$) 8,937
GNP: US$275·7bn.
HDI/world rank: 0·884/36

KEY HISTORICAL EVENTS. In 1515 Juan Diaz de Solis discovered the Rio de le Planta. In 1534 Pedro de Mondoza was sent by the King of Spain to take charge of the 'Gobernación y Capitania de las tierras del Rio de la Plata', and in Feb. 1536 he founded the city of the 'Puerto de Santa María del Buen Aire'. In 1810 the population rose against Spanish rule, and in 1816 Argentina proclaimed its independence. Civil wars and anarchy followed until, in 1853, stable government was established.

In this century there have been a succession of military *coups*. The first took place in 1930, the second in 1943 when Gen. Juan Domingo Peron won control. His regime was autocratic but popularist and nationalistic and propagated some social reforms. His wife Eva (Evita), played a major role, giving the regime an almost cult-like following. She died in 1955 and a civilian administration followed until 1966 when the next military *coup* led to seven years of government by the military. However, a political party had established itself around the Perons, and when elections were held in 1973 the Peronists were the victors; Gen. Peron was elected president. When he died in 1974, his widow Isobel succeeded him as president. She was deposed in 1976 following another military *coup*, which established a three-man junta with Gen. Jorge Videla, C.-in-C. of the army, as president. The new government instituted a savagely repressive attitude towards any opposition.

Videla was succeeded as president first by Gen. Viola and then by Gen. Leopoldo Galtieri, the army C.-in-C. In April 1982 Galtieri, in an effort to distract attention from domestic failings, invaded the Falkland Islands (Islas Malvinas). The subsequent military defeat helped to precipitate the fall of Galtieri and the junta in July 1982. Return to civilian rule took place on 10 Dec. 1983. A new Constitution was adopted in Aug. 1994.

TERRITORY AND POPULATION. The second largest country in South America, the Argentine Republic is bounded in the north by Bolivia, in the north-east by Paraguay, in the east by Brazil, Uruguay and the Atlantic Ocean and the west by Chile. The republic consists of 23 provinces and 1 federal district with the following areas and populations at the 1991 census:

Provinces	Area Sq. km.	Population (1991 census)	Capital	Population (1991 census)
Federal Capital	200	2,965,403	Buenos Aires	–
Buenos Aires	307,571	12,594,974	La Plata	542,567
Corrientes	88,199	795,594	Corrientes	258,103
Entre Ríos	78,781	1,020,257	Paraná	277,338
Chaco	99,633	839,677	Resistencia	292,350
Santa Fé	133,007	2,798,422	Santa Fé	406,388
Formosa	72,066	398,413	Formosa	148,074
Misiones	29,801	788,915	Posadas	210,755
Jujuy	53,219	512,329	San Salvador de Jujuy	180,102
Salta	155,488	866,153	Salta	370,904
Santiago del Estero	136,351	671,988	Santiago del Estero	263,471
Tucumán	22,524	1,142,105	San Miguel de Tucumán	622,324
Córdoba	165,321	2,766,683	Córdoba	1,208,713
La Pampa	143,440	259,996	Santa Rosa	80,592
San Luis	76,748	286,458	San Luis	110,136
Catamarca	102,602	264,234	Catamarca	132,626
La Rioja	89,680	220,729	La Rioja	103,727
Mendoza	148,827	1,412,481	Mendoza	121,696

Provinces	Area Sq. km.	Population (1991 census)	Capital	Population (1991 census)
San Juan	89,651	528,715	San Juan	352,691
Neuquén	94,078	388,833	Neuquén	243,803
Chubut	224,686	357,189	Rawson	19,161
Rio Negro	203,013	506,772	Viedma	57,473
Santa Cruz	243,943	159,839	Rio Gallegos	64,640
Tierra del Fuego	21,571	69,369	Ushuaia	29,166

Argentina also claims territory in Antarctica.

The area is 2,780,400 sq. km excluding the claimed Antarctic territory and the population at the 1991 census was 32,615,528 (16,677,548 females); 1996 estimate, 34·6m. In 1993, 86·6% lived in urban areas. Vital statistics rates, 1994 (per 1,000 population): Birth, 19·7; death, 7·5; infant mortality, 22·0 per 1,000 live births. Expectation of life in 1995 was 68·6 years for men and 75·7 for women.

The official census included the 'sovereign territories of Argentina in the Antarctic': Population 3,300.

In April 1990 the National Congress declared that the Falklands and other British-held islands in the South Atlantic were part of the new province of Tierra del Fuego formed from the former National Territory of the same name. 1991 census data for Tierra del Fuego above do not include these territories. The 1994 Constitution reaffirms Argentine sovereignty over the Falkland Islands.

The population of the principal metropolitan areas in 1992 (provisional) was: Buenos Aires, 11,662,050; Córdoba, 1,179,420; Rosario, 1,157,372; Mendoza, 801,920; La Plata, 676,128; Tucumán, 642,473.

95% speak the national language, Spanish, while 3% speak Italian, 1% Guaraní and 1% other languages.

CLIMATE. The climate is warm temperate over the pampas, where rainfall occurs at all seasons, but diminishes towards the west. In the north and west, the climate is more arid, with high summer temperatures, while in the extreme south conditions are also dry, but much cooler. Buenos Aires. Jan. 74°F (23·3°C), July 50°F (10°C). Annual rainfall 37" (950 mm). Bahía Blanca. Jan. 74°F (23·3°C), July 48°F (8·9°C). Annual rainfall 21" (523 mm). Mendoza. Jan. 75°F (23·9°C), July 47°F (8·3°C). Annual rainfall 8" (190 mm). Rosario. Jan. 76°F (24·4°C), July 51°F (10·6°C). Annual rainfall 35" (869 mm). San Juan. Jan. 78°F (25·6°C), July 50°F (10°C). Annual rainfall 4" (89 mm). San Miguel de Tucumán. Jan. 79°F (26·1°C), July 56°F (13·3°C). Annual rainfall 38" (970 mm). Ushuaia. Jan. 50°F (10°C), July 34°F (1·1°C). Annual rainfall 19" (475 mm).

CONSTITUTION AND GOVERNMENT. On 10 April 1994 elections were held for a 230-member constituent assembly to reform the 1853 constitution. The Justicialist National Movement (Peronist) gained 38·8% of votes cast and the Radical Union, 20%. On 22 Aug. 1994 this assembly unanimously adopted a new Constitution. This reduces the presidential term of office from 6 to 4 years, but permits the President to stand for 2 terms. The President is no longer elected by an electoral college, but directly by universal suffrage. A presidential candidate is elected who gains more than 45% of votes cast, or 40% if at least 10% ahead of an opponent; otherwise there is a second round. The Constitution attenuates the President's powers by instituting a *Chief of Cabinet*. The *National Congress* consists of a Senate and a Chamber of Deputies: The Senate comprises 72 members, 3 nominated by each provincial legislature and 3 from the Federal District for 9 years (one-third retiring every 3 years). The Chamber of Deputies comprises 259 members directly elected by universal suffrage (at age 18). Elections for half the seats were held on 3 Oct. 1993. The ruling Justicialist Party (JP; Peronist) gained 42% of votes cast, the Radical Civil Union 31%. Representation in the Chamber of Deputies following the 1993 elections was: JP, 126 seats; Radicals, 83; others, 50. Elections for the remaining seats were held on 14 May 1995. The JP gained 132 seats (and 38 in the Senate). In the presidential elections held on 14 May 1995 Carlos Saúl Menem was re-elected in the first round by 49% of votes cast.

On 6 August 1997 the Radical Union and centre-left Frepaso parties joined together to form the Alliance to fight against the Peronists in the forthcoming lower house of Congress elections in Oct. 1997. 127 of the 257 seats were up for election. On 26 Oct. 1997 the JP suffered its first legislative defeat since 1983. The Alliance received 36·5% of votes cast and in the 10 provinces where no coalition existed the two parties separately collected an additional 9·6%, bringing the opposition tally to 46·1%. The JP received nearly 36% of votes cast, losing 12 seats and its absolute majority in Congress (it remains the largest single political bloc). The Alliance has no agreed candidate or method of choosing one for the 1999 Presidential elections. Menem's main Justicialist rival and leading hopeful for the presidential candidacy, Eduardo Duhalde, suffered a set back when his wife, Hilde Duhalde, was defeated in the 1997 Congress elections in the province of Buenos Aires, a previous Peronist bastion of power. In Dec. 1997 the growing crisis of confidence in the police led Eduardo Duhalde to embark on a 90-day crisis programme to reform the discredited force.

President: Carlos Saúl Menem (b. 1930; JP; sworn in 8 July 1995).
Vice-President: Dr Carlos Ruckauf.
The Cabinet comprised in March 1998:
Economy and Public Works: Roque Fernández. *Education and Culture:* Susana Decibe. *Foreign Relations:* Dr Guido José Maria di Tella. *Interior:* Dr Carlos Corach. *Labour and Social Security:* Antonio Erman González. *Health and Social Welfare:* Dr Alberto Mazza. *Justice:* Raúl Granillo Ocampo. *Defence:* Jorge Dominguez

National anthem: Oid, mortales, el grito sagrado Libertad ('Hear, mortals, the sacred cry of Liberty'; words by V. López y Planes, 1813; tune by J. Blas Parera).

Provincial and Local Government: 23 provincial gubernatorial elections were held Aug.–Dec. 1991. Peronists won 14 governorships.

DEFENCE. Conscription was abolished in 1995.

Army. There are 5 military regions. The Army is organized in 3 corps, 1 with 1 armoured, 1 mechanized and 1 training brigade; 1 with 1 infantry and 1 mountain brigade, and 1 with 1 armoured, 1 mountain and 2 mechanized brigades. Equipment in 1996 included 96 M-4 Sherman and 200 TAM main battle tanks and about 100 aircraft, including 23 Mohawks for reconnaissance and 35 UH-1H Iroquois transport helicopters. In 1996 the Army was 41,000 strong, of whom 13,400 were conscripts. The trained reserve numbers about 250,000, of whom 200,000 belong to the National Guard and 50,000 to the Territorial Guard.

There is a paramilitary gendarmerie of 18,000 run by the Ministry of Defence.

Navy. The light aircraft carrier *Veinticinco de Mayo* remains in reserve. Combatant forces include 3 German-built diesel submarines with 1 more in major refit, 4 modern German-built destroyers, 2 British-built guided missile destroyers (Type 42), 4 German-designed and 3 French-built frigates, 2 old training frigates, 2 fast torpedo craft, 5 patrol ships, 4 coastal minesweepers, 2 minehunters and 1 tank landing ship. Auxiliaries include 1 survey ship, 2 training ships, 3 transports, 1 icebreaker and numerous harbour and service craft. Serviceability is reported as very poor.

The new construction programme includes 2 diesel submarines (both building—but slowly) and 2 small frigates nearing completion but being offered for sale.

The Naval Aviation Service has some 32 combat aircraft and 15 helicopters with (1996) 3,500 personnel, in 5 wings. Aircraft include 8 Super-Etendard strike aircraft, 7 EMB-326 and 5 EMB-339A light jet armed trainers, 2 Lockheed Electra maritime surveillance aircraft and 6 S-2E carrier-adapted Tracker anti-submarine aircraft, as well as varied training, transport and general purpose aircraft. There is a squadron of 7 SH-3 anti-submarine helicopters, 4 Alouettes and 4 S-61 transport helicopters. The remaining Super-Etendards and Trackers as well as Sea King and Alouette helicopters could operate from the aircraft carrier if she is re-activated.

Personnel 1997, 20,000 including 3,500 marines, 4 reinforced battalions equipped with armoured personnel carriers and about 40 artillery pieces.

Main bases are at Buenos Aires, Puerto Belgrano (HQ and Dockyard), Mar del Plata, Ushuaia and Puerto Deseado.

The Prefectura Naval Argentina (PNA) for Coast Guard and rescue duties was 13,000 strong in 1996 and operates 5 910-tonne corvettes with helicopter and hangar, an ex-whaler of 700 tonnes, and 23 patrol vessels.

Air Force. The Air Force is organized into Air Operations, Air Regions, Materiel and Personnel Commands. Air Operations Command, responsible for all operational flying, is made up of air brigades, each with 1 to 4 squadrons, usually operating from a single base. No. I Air Brigade is a military air transport service, with responsibility also for LADE (state airline) operations into areas of Argentina not served by civilian companies. Its equipment includes 9 C-130 Hercules and 10 F.27 Friendship/Troopship turboprop transports, 2 KC-130H Hercules tanker/transports, 3 twin-turbofan F.28 Fellowship freighters, 15 Guarani IIs, the Presidential Boeing 757, 4 707s, 2 VIP Fellowships, and many older or smaller types. No. II Air Brigade comprises a photographic squadron with Guarani IIs and Learjets. No. III Air Brigade has 2 squadrons of IA 58 Pucara twin-turboprop COIN aircraft. No. IV Air Brigade comprises 2 ground attack squadrons, one equipped with about 20 Paris light jet combat and liaison aircraft, and the other with 15 IA 63 Pampas. No. V Air Brigade comprises 2 squadrons with a total of about 18 A-4 Skyhawk strike aircraft. No. VI Air Brigade has 30 Dagger (Israeli-built Mirage III) fighters, equipping 2 squadrons, 1 squadron of Mirage 5 fighter-bombers, and 1 squadron with 15 Mirage IIIE fighter-bombers and 4 Mirage IIID trainers. No. VII Air Brigade has 2 helicopter squadrons with 12 armed Hughes 500M, 6 Bell 212, 4 Bell UH-1 and 2 Chinook helicopters. There is a flying school at Córdoba, equipped with turboprop-powered Embraer Tucanos and Paris jets. There were (1997) 12,000 personnel (1,200 conscripts) and 220 combat aircraft.

INTERNATIONAL RELATIONS

Membership. Argentina is a member of the UN, OAS and Mercosur and is set to apply for membership of the OECD. Diplomatic relations with Britain broken since the 1982 Falklands War were reopened in 1990. Praising Argentina's 'call to peace' US President Clinton plans to give the country 'major non-NATO ally' status (Nov. 1997). The alignment with US foreign policy comes after years of anti-American sentiment and a policy of neutrality.

ECONOMY

Policy. In 1990, the government introduced a programme privatizing some 40 public enterprises. An economic plan entering into force on 1 April 1991 guaranteed the convertibility of the currency, lowered interest rates and opened the economy to foreign imports. Agricultural export taxes were abolished in March 1991. Argentina suffered a severe recession in 1995 but since then privatization and deregulation have improved the economy's prospects into the medium term. Tax evasion and fraud remain a major occurrence but tighter controls are being instituted. In February 1998 the IMF approved a 3 year US$2·8bn. extended fund facility for Argentina. The accord sets a target for this year's fiscal deficit of US$3·5bn., just over 1% of GDP, against the 1996 US$4·5bn. target.

Performance. The economy grew by 4·4% in 1996, after falling 4·6% in 1995. Consumer spending is recovering gradually from the 1995 recession. GDP growth in 1997 totalled 8·4%.

Budget. The financial year commences on 1 Jan. Estimated revenue in 1996 (in US$1m.) was 53,323·2 and expenditure, also 53,323·2.

Currency. The monetary unit is the *peso* (ARP) which replaced the austral on 1 Jan. 1992 at a rate of 1 peso = 10,000 australs. There are notes of 1, 2, 5, 10, 20, 50 and 100 pesos. In 1994, 12,346m. pesos were in circulation. Inflation was 0·2% in 1996.

Banking and Finance. In 1996 there were 20 government banks, 100 private banks, 28 foreign banks and 27 other financial institutions. Bank and non-bank total

monetary resources totalled US$67,449m. as at Dec. 1996. The *Governor* of the
Central Bank is Pedro Pou. Convertibility regulations of April 1991 require the
Central Bank to back the entire currency in circulation with its foreign currency
reserves.

There is a stock exchange at Buenos Aires.

Weights and Measures. The metric system is legal.

ENERGY AND NATURAL RESOURCES

Electricity. Electric power production (1995) was 62,478m. kWh (7,066m. kWh
nuclear). In 1995 there were 2 nuclear plants.

Oil and Gas. Crude oil production (1996) 46m. cu. metres. Reserves were estimated
at some 411m. cu. metres in 1996. The oil industry was privatized in 1993. Natural
gas production (1996) 34,650m. cu. metres. Reserves were about 688,333m. cu.
metres in 1996.

Minerals. An estimated 215,000 tonnes of washed coal were produced in 1996.
Other minerals (with estimated production in 1996) include iron ore (3,388 tonnes of
metal), gold (837 kg in 1995), silver (47,787 kg), tungsten, beryllium, clays (3·3m.
tonnes), marble, lead (10,521 tonnes of metal), zinc (36,697 tonnes of metal), borates
(244,933 tonnes), bentonite (0·11m. tonnes) and granite. Production from the $1·1bn.
Alumbrera copper and gold mine, the country's biggest mining project, in Catamarca
province in the north-west started in late 1997. In 1993 the mining laws were
reformed and state regulation was swept away creating a more stable tax regime for
investors. In December 1997 Argentina and Chile signed a treaty laying the legal and
tax framework for mining operations straddling the 5,000 km border allowing
mining products to be transported out through both countries.

Agriculture. In 1996 there were 23·5m. ha of arable land, 2·1m. ha of permanent
crops and 142m. ha of permanent pasture. 3·24m. persons depended on agriculture in
1993, of whom 1,166,000 were economically active. 1·7m. ha were irrigated in 1992.

Livestock (1996): Cattle, 50,861,000; sheep, 523,953; pigs, 1,414,350; horses
(1994), 3·3m. Wool production, 1996, was 43,069 tonnes; butter (1994), 42,000
tonnes; beef (1994), 2·56m. tonnes.

Crop production (in 1,000 tonnes) in 1995–96: Wheat, 9,200; sugar-cane, 11,814;
rice, 974; maize, 10,465; potatoes, (1994–95) 1,914; tobacco, 98·2; sunflower seed,
5,557. Cotton, vine, citrus fruit, olives, soya, and yerba maté (Paraguayan tea) are
also cultivated.

Forestry. The woodland area was 44,975,115 ha in 1994. Production in 1995
included 1·51m. cu. metres of sawn wood, 56,468,340 tonnes of logs and 76,000
tonnes of tannin.

Fisheries. Fish landings in 1996 amounted to 1,225,958 tonnes.

INDUSTRY. Production (1996 in tonnes): Paper, 1,123,000; primary iron,
3,388,000; crude steel, 4,065,000; primary aluminium, 184,533; sulfuric acid,
219,562; cement, 5,117,000; synthetic rubber, 57,994; polyethylene, 180,849; sugar,
1,290,000; vegetable oils, 4,044,000. Motor vehicles produced totalled 313,150;
tractors, 5,589; tyres, 7,593,000. In Aug. 1997 the government forecast industrial
production would grow by 8% over the year.

Labour. The economically active population was 13·2m. in 1991, of whom 10·4%
worked in agriculture. 2·12m. persons were registered unemployed at July 1996. In
May 1997 the 6 monthly unemployment figures showed a 1·3 point fall to 16·1%,
down from a peak of more than 18%.

FOREIGN ECONOMIC RELATIONS. External debt was US$99,708m. in
1996.

Commerce. Foreign trade (in US$1m.):

	1991	1992	1993	1994	1995	1996
Imports	8,275	14,872	16,784	21,590	20,122	23,762
Exports	11,978	12,235	13,118	15,839	20,963	23,811

Principal exports in 1996 (in US$1m.) were cereals (2,560), residues and waste from the food industry (2,367), oils and fats (1,890), fuels, mineral oils and distillates (3,089), oilseeds and fruits (964) and fish, shellfish and molluscs (945).

Principal imports in 1996 (in US$1m.) were boilers, machines and mechanical equipment (4,576), electrical machinery and equipment (2,976), land vehicles (3,095), organic chemical products (1,387), plastic materials (1,106) and cast iron and steel (424).

In 1996 imports (in US$1m.) were mainly from Brazil (5,326), USA (4,749), Germany (1,427), Italy (1,503), Japan (725), Chile (559) and France (1,181); exports went mainly to Brazil (6,615), USA (1,973), Netherlands (1,225), Germany (565), Chile (1,766), Italy (721) and Spain (724).

The trade balance deteriorated to a deficit of almost US$4·9bn. in 1997.

In Jan. 1998 Canadian and Argentine business leaders signed 70 contracts worth $200m. in mining, atomic energy and finance sectors.

Tourism. In 1996, an estimated 4,285,648 tourists visited Argentina.

COMMUNICATIONS

Roads. In 1994 there were 36,837 km of national and provincial highways. The 4 main roads constituting Argentina's portion of the Pan-American Highway were opened in 1942.

Railways. Much of the 33,000 km state-owned network (on 1,000 mm, 1,435 mm and 1,676 mm gauges; 210 km electrified) was privatized in 1993–94. 30-year concessions were awarded to 5 freight operators; long-distance passenger services are run by contractors to the requirements of local authorities. Metro, light rail and suburban railway services are also operated by concessionaires.

In 1996 railways carried 16,980,000 tonnes of freight and 419,455,000 passengers.

The metro and light rail network in Buenos Aires extends to 46 km.

Civil Aviation. There is an international airport at Buenos Aires (Ministro Pistarini). In 1995 the national carrier, Aerolíneas Argentinas, 15% state-owned, operated 3 A310-300s, 1 B-707-320B, 8 B-727-200 Advs, 4 B-737-200s, 6 B-737-200 Advs, 1 B-737-200C, 6 B-747-200Bs and 6 other aircraft. Services are also operated by Aeroflot Russian Airlines, Aeroperú, Air France, Alitalia, American Airlines, Avianca, British Airways, BWIA, Canadian Airlines, Cubana, Iberia, KLM, Ladeco, Lan-Chile, Lapsa, Lloyd Aéreo Boliviano, Lufthansa, Malaysia Airlines, Pluna, SAA, Swissair, United Airlines, VASP and Varig.

In 1996 5,559,000 passengers and 139,467 tonnes of freight were carried on international flights and 5,904,000 passengers and 16,447 tonnes of freight on internal flights.

Shipping. The merchant fleet, 1993, consisted of 1,413 vessels totalling 1,799,633 GRT, of which 176 were tankers totalling 586,744 GRT.

Telecommunications. The telephone service Entel was privatized in 1990. There are state-owned, provincial, municipal and private radio stations overseen by the Secretaria de Comunicaciones, the Comité Federal de Radiodifusión, the Servicio Oficial de Radiodifusión (which also operates an external service and a station in Antarctica) and the Asociación de Teleradiodifusoras Argentinas. In 1991 there were 21,582,456 radio and 7,165,000 TV (colour by PAL) receivers.

Cinemas. In 1993 there were 260 cinemas.

SOCIAL INSTITUTIONS

Justice. Justice is administered by federal and provincial courts. The former deal only with cases of a national character, or those in which different provinces or inhabitants of different provinces are parties. The chief federal court is the Supreme Court, with 5 judges whose appointment is approved by the Senate. Other federal courts are the appeal courts, at Buenos Aires, Bahía Blanca, La Plata, Córdoba, Mendoza, Tucumán and Resistencia. Each province has its own judicial system, with a Supreme Court (generally so designated) and several minor chambers. The death penalty was re-introduced in 1976 for the killing of government, military police and judicial officials, and for participation in terrorist activities.

The police force is centralized under the Federal Security Council.

Religion. The Roman Catholic religion is supported by the State and membership was 30·08m. in 1992. There are several Protestant denominations. The Jewish congregation numbered 0·35m. in 1992.

Education. Adult literacy was 96% in 1996. In 1996, 1,116,951 children attended pre-school institutions, 5,250,329 primary schools, 2,594,329 secondary schools and 391,778 tertiary colleges. Numbers of teachers in 1994-95: Pre-school, 63,751; primary, 277,064; secondary, 228,289; tertiary, 40,160.

In 1996, in the public sector, there were 33 universities; 1 technical university; and university institutes of aeronautics, military studies, naval and maritime studies and police studies. In the private sector, there were 15 universities; 7 Roman Catholic universities; 1 Adventist university; universities of business administration, business and social science, the cinema, notarial studies, social studies, and theology; and university institutes of biomedical science, health and the merchant navy. In 1996, there were 790,775 university students and 128,478 academic staff.

Health. Free medical attention is obtainable from public hospitals. In 1996 there were 7,243 beds available in public health care institutions.

Welfare. Until the end of 1996 trade unions had a monopoly in the handling of the compulsory social security contributions of employees, but private insurance agencies are now permitted to function alongside them.

DIPLOMATIC REPRESENTATIVES

Of Argentina in Great Britain (65 Brook Str., London, W1Y 1YE)
Ambassador: Rogelio Pfirter.

Of Great Britain in Argentina (Dr Luis Agote 2141/52, 1425 Buenos Aires)
Ambassador: William Marsden, CMG.

Of Argentina in the USA (1600 New Hampshire Ave., NW, Washington, D.C., 20009)
Ambassador: Diego Guelar.

Of the USA in Argentina (4300 Colombia, 1425, Buenos Aires)
Ambassador: James R. Cheek.

Of Argentina to the United Nations
Ambassador: Fernando Petrella.

Of Argentina to the European Union
Ambassador: Juan Uranga.

Further Reading

INDEC. *Statistical Yearbook of Argentina*
Bethell, I. (ed.) *Argentina since Independence.* CUP, 1994
Biggins, A., *Argentina.* [Bibliography]. Oxford and Santa Barbara, 1990
Lewis, P., *The Crisis of Argentine Capitalism.* North Carolina Univ. Press, 1990
Manzetti, L., *Institutions, Parties and Coalitions in Argentine Politics.* Univ. of Pittsburgh Press, 1994
Rock, D., *Argentina 1516–1982.* London, 1986
Shumway, N., *The Invention of Argentina.* California Univ. Press, 1991
Wynia, G. W., *Argentina: Illusions and Realities.* 2nd ed. Hoddesdon, 1993

National statistical office: Instituto Nacional de Estadística y Censos (INDEC). Av. Presidente Julio A. Roca 609, 1067 Buenos Aires. *Director:* Dr Hector E. Montero.
Website: http://www.indec.mecon.ar/default.htm

ARMENIA

Hayastani Hanrapetoutiun

(Republic of Armenia)

Capital: Yerevan
Population: 3·7m.
GDP per head: (PPP$) 1,737
HDI/world rank: 0·651/103

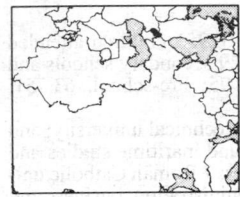

KEY HISTORICAL EVENTS. The early history of Armenia was one of foreign domination with, at various times, the Turkish, Persian and Russian empires claiming control. In the early part of this century the Armenians under Turkish rule suffered brutal persecution. Armenia enjoyed a brief period of independence after World War One but in 1920 the country was proclaimed a Soviet Socialist Republic. The Soviet-Turkish Treaty of Kars (March 1921), confirmed the Turkish possession of the former Government of Kars and of the Surmali District of the Government of Yerevan. From 1922 to 1936, Armenia formed part of the Transcaucasian Soviet Federal Socialist Republic. In 1936 it was proclaimed a constituent republic of the USSR.

With the dramatic changes in Soviet politics initiated by Mikhail Gorbachev after 1985, Armenia began to assert its cultural and political identity though a territorial dispute with Azerbaijan over Nagorno-Karabakh was the big issue until the 1991 referendum on independence when 99% of voters supported a breakaway from the Soviet Union. A declaration of independence in Sept. 1991 was followed by presidential elections after which President Ter-Petrosyan came to an agreement on economic cooperation with the other Soviet republics and joined the CIS. A new constitution adopted in July 1995 led to National Assembly elections. 1,369 candidates representing 13 parties stood; turn-out was 54·9%. The Republican Bloc, in which the Pan-Armenian National Movement (PANM) was the major element, won 119 seats with 42·66% of votes cast; the Shamiram Women's Party, 8 with 16·88%; the Communist Party, 7 with 12·1%; the National Democratic Union, 5 with 7·51%; the National Self-Determination Union, 3 with 5·57%; the Armenian Liberal Democratic Party, 1 with 2·52%; the Armenian Revolutionary Federation Dashnaktsoutioun, 1 with 2%. 45 ind. were also elected.

A presidential election followed in Sept. 1996. There were 4 candidates. President Ter-Petrosyan was re-elected by 51·75% of the 2,210,189 votes cast. OSCE observers noted 'very serious irregularities' in the conduct of the elections.

Hostilities with Azerbaijan were brought to an end with a 1994 cease-fire but negotiations on a territorial settlement continue.

TERRITORY AND POPULATION. Armenia covers an area of 29,800 sq. km (11,490 sq. miles). It is bounded in the north by Georgia, in the east by Azerbaijan and in the south and west by Turkey and Iran. The 1989 census population was 3,304,776, of whom Armenians accounted for 96·0% (1996), Azerbaijanis 2·6%, Kurds 1·7% and Russians 1·6%. Estimate, Jan. 1995, 3,742,000 (1·8m. male; 2·5m. urban). Vital statistics rates, 1994 (per 1,000 population): Births, 15·8; deaths, 7·4; growth, 8·4; infant mortality (per 1,000 live births), 17·1.

The capital is Yerevan (1·2m. population in 1994). Other large towns are Kumairi (formerly Leninakan) (120,000) and Kirovakan (159,000).

CONSTITUTION AND GOVERNMENT. The head of state is the *President*, directly elected for 5-year terms. Parliament is a 190-member *National Assembly*, of which 150 members are directly elected on a first-past-the-post system, and 40 by proportional representation, distributed among those parties gaining more than 5% of votes cast. The government is nominated by the President.

President Ter-Petrosyan resigned in Feb. 1998 in a row over the disputed enclave of Nagorno-Karabakh. In the election which resulted, Robert Kocharian, the Prime Minister, won, obtaining 59·7% of the votes in the second round on 30 March 1998, having previously obtained 38·8% in the first round of voting on 16 March.

President: Robert Kocharian, formerly President of Nagorno-Karabakh, the Armenian-inhabited enclave in Azerbaijan.

In March 1998 the government comprised:

Prime Minister: Robert Kocharian.
Minister of Foreign Affairs (Acting): Vartan Oskanian. *Defence:* Vazgen Sarkissian. *Justice:* Marat Alexanian. *Education and Science:* Artashes Petrossian. *Health:* Dr. Gagik Stamboltsian. *Culture, Youth and Sport:* Armen Smbatian. *Ecology and Natural Resources:* Sargis Shahazizian. *Trade, Services, Tourism and Industry:* Garnik Nanagoulian. *Communications:* Grigor Poghpatian. *Agriculture and Food Supplies:* Vladimir Movsisian. *Transport:* Henrik Kochinian. *Finance and Economy:* Armen Darbinian. *Energy:* Gagik Martirossian. *Internal Affairs and National Security:* Serge Sarkissian. *Social Security:* Mrs Hranoush Hakobian. *Urban Planning and Construction:* Felix Pirumian. *Privatization:* Pavel Ghaltakhchain. *Operational Issues:* Shahen Karamanukian.

The *Speaker* is Babken Ararktsyan.

National anthem: 'Mer Hayrenik azat, ankakh' ('Land of our fathers, free and independent'); words by M. Nalbandyan, tune by B. Kanachyan.

DEFENCE. There is conscription for 18 months.

Army. Current troop levels are at 32,682 troops. There are approximately 300,000 Armenians who have received some kind of military service experience within the last 15 years. The Defence Ministry is aiming for a standing army of 70,000.

Army organization: 4 Motorized Rifle Brigades, 1 Special Forces Regiment, 1 Artillery Brigade, 1 Artillery Regiment, 1 Anti-tank Regiment, 2 Surface-to-Air Missile (SAM) Brigades, 1 Independent Helicopter Squadron.

Paramilitary Forces. Personnel at the disposal of the Ministry of the Interior are estimated at 30,000. Most personnel are from local militia or police forces.

INTERNATIONAL RELATIONS. There is a dispute over the mainly Armenian-populated enclave of Nagorno-Karabakh, which lies within Azerbaijan's borders.

Membership. Armenia is a member of the UN, CIS and the NATO Partnership for Peace.

ECONOMY

Policy. A privatization scheme was launched on 1 March 1995 under the auspices of a Privatization Commission.

Performance. Real GDP growth was 3·3% in 1997. The conflict with Azerbaijan is a serious brake on economic development.

Budget. Budgetary revenue in 1995 was US$237m.; expenditure in 1995 was US$318m.

Currency. In Nov. 1993 a new currency unit, the *dram* (AMD) of 100 *lumma*, was introduced to replace the rouble. There are coins of 1, 2, 3, 5, 10, 20 and 50 lumma, notes of 1, 2, 5, 10, 25, 50, 100, 200 and 500 drams. Inflation was 17·4% in 1997. Foreign exchange reserves (including gold) were US$127·5m. in June 1996.

Banking and Finance. The President of the Central Bank (founded in 1993) is Bagrat Asatryan. In 1997 there were 33 commercial banks (1 state-owned).

ENERGY AND NATURAL RESOURCES

Electricity. Output of electricity in 1996 was 6,300m. kWh. A nuclear plant closed in 1989 was re-opened in 1995 because of the blockade of the electricity supply by Azerbaijan; it was anticipated that domestic supply would be raised from 4 to 12 hours daily.

Minerals. There are deposits of copper, zinc, aluminium, molybdenum, marble and granite.

Agriculture. The chief agricultural area is the valley of the Arax and the area round Yerevan. Here there are cotton plantations, orchards and vineyards. Almonds, olives and figs are also grown. In the mountainous areas the chief pursuit is livestock raising. Land under cultivation in 1993, 1·3m. ha, of which 0·4m. ha were accounted for by commercial farming, in 298,100 farms. Private and commercial agriculture accounted for 96% of the value of agricultural output.

INDUSTRY. Among the chief industries are the chemical, producing chiefly synthetic rubber and fertilizers, and the extraction and processing of building materials, ginning- and textile-mills, carpet weaving, and food processing, including wine-making.

Labour. In 1997 the population of working age was 1·98m., of whom 1·5m. were employed; 36% in agriculture, 22% in industry. The registered unemployment rate was 9% of the workforce in Oct. 1996. The average monthly income in 1996 was 6,000 drams.

FOREIGN ECONOMIC RELATIONS

Commerce. In 1995 imports were valued at US$673m. and exports at US$270m. The main trading partners are Russia, Turkmenistan and Iran.

COMMUNICATIONS

Roads. There were 11,300 km (10,500 km with hard surface) of motor roads in 1996.

Railways. Total length in 1996 was 840 km of 1,000 mm gauge (590 km electrified). There is a tramway in Yerevan.

Civil Aviation. There is an international airport at Yerevan (Zvartnots). The state-owned Armenian Airlines is operational since 1995.

Telecommunications. The state-owned Armenian Radio broadcasts 2 national programmes and relays of Radio Moscow and Voice of America, and a foreign service, Radio Yerevan (Armenian, English, French, Spanish, Arabic, Kurdish, Russian). Television broadcasting is by the state-controlled Armenian Television (colour by SECAM).

Press. In 1997 there were 80 daily publications.

SOCIAL INSTITUTIONS

Justice. In 1994, 9,923 crimes were reported, including 201 murders or attempted murders.

Religion. Armenia adopted Christianity in 301AD, thus becoming the first Christian nation in the world. The Armenian Apostolic Church is headed by its Catholicos (Karekin II, b. 1932) whose seat is at Etchmiadzin, and who is head of all the Armenian (Gregorian) communities throughout the world. In 1995 it numbered 7m. adherents (4m. in diaspora). The Catholicos is elected by representatives of parishes. The Catholicos of the diaspora is Kachechyan of Cilicia, with seat at Antelias.

Education. In Jan. 1994, 0·1m. children, 23% of those eligible. attended pre-school institutions. In 1994-95 there were 590,000 pupils in 1,400 primary and secondary schools; 69 technical colleges with 25,200 students; 14 higher educational institutions with 46,500 students. Yerevan houses the Armenian Academy of Sciences, 43 scientific institutes, a medical institute and other technical colleges, and a state university. In Jan. 1989, 33 institutions with 3,330 scientific staff were under the Academy of Sciences; scientific workers in 101 institutions totalled 21,800.

  In 1995-96 there were 2 universities (including the American University), an engineering university, 10 other institutes of higher education and a conservatory.

Health. In Jan. 1994 there were some 14,000 doctors, 36,200 junior medical personnel and 183 hospitals with 31,000 beds.

Welfare. In Jan. 1995 there were 437,000 age, and 202,000 other pensioners.

DIPLOMATIC REPRESENTATIVES

Of Armenia in Great Britain (25A Cheniston Gdns, London W8 6TG)
Ambassador: Vacant.

Of Great Britain in Armenia (28 Charents St., Yerevan 375010)
Ambassador: Dr John Mitchiner.

Of Armenia in the USA (122 C St., NW, Washington DC 20001)
Ambassador: Rouben Shugarian.

Of the USA in Armenia (18 Gen. Bagramian, Yerevan)
Ambassador: Peter Tomsen.

Of Armenia to the United Nations
Ambassador: Dr Movses Abelian.

Of Armenia to the European Union
Ambassador: Gagit Shahbazian.

Further Reading

Brook, S., *Claws of the Crab: Georgia and Armenia in Crisis.* London, 1992
Hovannisian, R. G., *The Republic of Armenia.* 4 vols. Univ. of California Press, 1996
Lang, D.M., *Armenia: Cradle of Civilization.* London, 1978. *The Armenians: a People in Exile.* London, 1981
Malkasian, M., *Ga-Ra-Bagh: the Emergence of the National Democratic Movement in Armenia.* Wayne State Univ. Press, 1997
Nersessian, V. N., *Armenia.* [Bibliography]. Oxford and Santa Barbara (CA), 1993
Walker, C. J., *Armenia.* 2nd ed. London, 1990

AUSTRALIA

Commonwealth
of Australia

Capital: Canberra
Population: 17·89m.
GDP per head: (PPP$) 19,285
HDI/world rank: 0·931/14

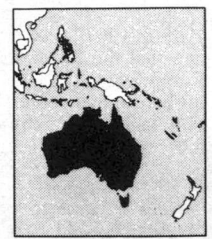

KEY HISTORICAL EVENTS. Various dates are given for the discovery of Australia, including 1522 in which year it was sighted by Magellan's followers. Capt. Cook discovered the east coast in 1770 and initially the British planned to establish a colony there; instead, however, the government decided to set up a penal settlement. In 1801 Matthew Flinders, a British naval officer, completed the charting of Australia. He suggested that the name Australia replace New Holland, and this took place in 1817.

The appointment of Lachlan Macquarie as Governor in 1809 began a period of development in which Australia ceased primarily to be a penal settlement. The crossing of the Blue Mountains in 1813 was the first of many expeditions which led to discovery and use of vast areas of good grazing land.

On 1 Jan. 1901 the 6 separately constituted colonies of New South Wales, Victoria, Queensland, South Australia, Western Australia and Tasmania were federated under the name of the Commonwealth of Australia, the designation of 'colonies' being at the same time changed into that of 'states'—except in the case of Northern Territory which was transferred from South Australia to the Commonwealth as a 'territory' on 1 Jan. 1911.

In 1911 the Commonwealth acquired from the State of New South Wales the Canberra site for the Australian capital. Building operations were begun in 1923 and a Federal Parliament was opened at Canberra in 1927. A further area at Jervis Bay was acquired in 1915.

Territories under the administration of Australia in Jan. 1998, but not included in it, are Norfolk Island, the territory of Ashmore and Cartier Islands, and the Australian Antarctic Territory (acquired on 24 Aug. 1936), the latter comprising all the islands and territory, other than Adélie Land, situated south of 60° S. lat. and between 160° and 45° E. long. The Coral Sea Islands became an External Territory in 1969.

The British Government transferred sovereignty in the Heard and McDonald Islands to the Australian Government on 26 Dec. 1947. Cocos (Keeling) Islands on 23 Nov. 1955 and Christmas Island on 1 Oct. 1958 were also transferred to Australian jurisdiction.

Since the Second World War, Australia has played an increasingly important role in Asia and the Pacific. For most of this period central government has been in the hands of the Australian Labor Party (ALP) which, in the last decade, has shifted its stance on state control and economic planning to allow for an ambitious programme of privatization. In March 1986, the Australia Act abolished the remaining legislative, executive and judicial controls of the British Parliament.

TERRITORY AND POPULATION. Australia, excluding external territories, covers a land area of 7,682,300 sq. km, extending from Cape York (10° 41' S) in the north some 3,680 km to Tasmania (43° 39' S), and from Cape Byron (153° 39' E) in the east some 4,000 km west to Western Australia (113° 9' E). External territories under the administration of Australia comprise the Ashmore and Cartier Islands, Australian Antarctic Territory, Christmas Island, the Cocos (Keeling) Islands, the Coral Sea Islands, the Heard and McDonald Islands and Norfolk Island. For these *see below.*

Growth in Census population has been:

1901	3,774,310	1961	10,508,186	1981	15,053,600
1911	4,455,005	1966	11,599,498	1986	15,763,000
1921	5,435,734	1971	12,755,638	1991	16,852,258
1947	7,579,358	1976	13,915,500	1996	17,892,423

Of the 1996 census population, 9,043,199 were females.
Areas and populations of the States and Territories at the 1996 census:

States and Territories	Area (sq. km)	Population	Per sq. km
New South Wales (NSW)	801,600	6,038,696	7·5
Victoria (Vic.)	227,600	4,373,520	19·2
Queensland (Qld.)	1,727,200	3,368,850	2·0
South Australia (SA)	984,000	1,427,936	1·5
Western Australia (WA)	2,525,500	1,726,095	0·7
Tasmania (Tas.)	67,800	459,659	6·8
Northern Territory (NT)	1,346,200	195,101	0·1
Australian Capital Territory (ACT)	2,400	299,243	124·7

Rate of population increase (per 1,000) in 1995: 7·3 (natural), 11·3 (with migration).

85·3% of the population was urban at the 1991 census. Resident population (estimate) in capitals and other statistical districts with more than 150,000 population, 30 June 1995:

Capital	State	Population	Capital	State	Population
Canberra[1]	ACT	332,100	Darwin	NT	79,200
Sydney	NSW	3,770,100	Statistical district		
Melbourne	Vic.	3,217,400	Newcastle	NSW	465,900
Brisbane	Qld.	1,488,900	Wollongong	NSW	253,600
Adelaide	SA	1,080,700	Gold Coast[2]	Qld.	319,100
Perth	WA	1,262,200	Geelong	Vic.	152,700
Hobart	Tas.	194,800	Sunshine Coast	Qld.	124,900

[1] Includes Queanbeyan.   [2] Includes part of Tweed Shire (in NSW).

At 30 June 1995 the age-group distribution was: Under 15, 3,867,600; 15–64, 12,032,100; 65 and over, 2,154,300. The median age of the 1996 census population was 34 years. Life expectancy in 1994 was 75 (males), 80·9 (females).

Australians born overseas (census 1996), 3,908,213, of whom 36·2% were from the UK, Ireland or New Zealand.

Aboriginals have been included in population statistics only since 1967. At the 1996 census 352,970 people identified themselves as being of indigenous origin. A 1992 High Court ruling that the Meriam people of the Murray Islands had land rights before the European settlement reversed the previous assumption that Australia was terra nullius before that settlement. The Native Title Act setting up a system for deciding land claims by Aborigines came into effect on 1 Jan. 1994.

Vital statistics for 1994:

States and Territories	Marriages	Divorces	Births	Deaths	Infant deaths
New South Wales	38,814	13,999	87,557	44,476	530
Victoria	26,972	11,320	64,422	32,313	338
Queensland	20,797	9,762	46,481	21,830	290
South Australia	8,909	4,192	19,475	11,725	96
Western Australia	10,366	5,024	25,114	10,297	138
Tasmania	2,889	1,544	6,781	3,950	37
Northern Territory	766	344	3,610	772	48
ACT	1,661	2,071	4,807	1,346	27
Total	111,174	48,256	258,247	126,709	1,504
Rate[1]	6·4	2·7	14·5	7·1	5·8[2]

[1]Resident (estimate).   [2] Per 1,000 live births registered.

Suicide rates (per 100,000 population, 1994): 12·7 (men, 20·6; women, 4·8).

Overseas arrivals and departures:

	1993	1994	1995
Arrivals	5,409,300	5,886,200	6,450,600
of whom long-term	197,930	221,910	253,930
(including settlers)	(65,680)	(77,940)	(96,970)
Departures	5,338,500	5,810,200	6,344,600
of whom long-term	140,430	114,660	121,490
(including former settlers and other residents)	(28,080)	(27,020)	(27,870)

The 1994–95 quota for settlers was 86,000. The Migration Act of Dec. 1989 sought to curb illegal entry and ensure that annual immigrant intakes were met but not exceeded. Provisions for temporary visitors to become permanent were restricted.

CLIMATE. Over most of the continent, four seasons may be recognised. Spring is from Sept. to Nov., Summer from Dec. to Feb., Autumn from March to May and Winter from June to Aug., but because of its great size there are climates that range from tropical monsoon to cool temperate, with large areas of desert as well. In Northern Australia there are only two seasons, the wet one lasting from Nov. to March, but rainfall amounts diminish markedly from the coast to the interior. Central and southern Queensland are subtropical, north and central New South Wales are warm temperate, as are parts of Victoria, Western Australia and Tasmania, where most rain falls in winter. Canberra. Jan. 68°F (20°C), July 42°F (5·6°C). Annual rainfall 25" (635 mm). Adelaide. Jan. 73°F (22·8°C), July 52°F (11·1°C). Annual rainfall 21" (528 mm). Brisbane. Jan. 77°F (25°C), July 58°F (14·4°C). Annual rainfall 45" (1,153 mm). Darwin. Jan. 83°F (28·3°C), July 77°F (25°C). Annual rainfall 59" (1,536 mm). Hobart. Jan. 62°F (16·7°C), July 46°F (7·8°C). Annual rainfall 23" (585 mm). Melbourne. Jan. 67°F (19·4°C), July 49°F (9·4°C). Annual rainfall 26" (659 mm). Perth. Jan. 74°F (23·3°C), July 55°F (12·8°C). Annual rainfall 35" (873 mm). Sydney. Jan. 71°F (21·7°C), July 53°F (11·7°C). Annual rainfall 47" (1,215 mm).

CONSTITUTION AND GOVERNMENT. *Federal Government:* Under the Constitution legislative power is vested in a Federal Parliament, consisting of the Queen, represented by a Governor-General, a Senate and a House of Representatives. Under the terms of the constitution there must be a session of parliament at least once a year.

The *Senate* comprises 76 Senators (12 for each State voting as one electorate and as from Aug. 1974, 2 Senators respectively for the Australian Capital Territory and the Northern Territory). Senators representing the States are chosen for 6 years. The terms of Senators representing the Territories expire at the close of the day next preceding the polling day for the general elections of the House of Representatives. In general, the Senate is renewed to the extent of one-half every 3 years, but in case of disagreement with the House of Representatives, it, together with the House of Representatives, may be dissolved, and an entirely new Senate elected. The *House of Representatives* consists, as nearly as practicable, of twice as many Members as there are Senators, the numbers chosen in the several States being in proportion to population as shown by the latest statistics, but not less than 5 for any original State. Elections to the Senate are on the single transferable vote system; voters list candidates in order of preference. A candidate must reach a quota to be elected, otherwise the lowest-placed candidate drops out and his or her votes are transferred to other candidates. Elections to the House of Representatives are on the alternative vote system; voters list candidates in order of preference, and if no one candidate wins an overall majority, the lowest-placed drops out and his or her votes are transferred. The Northern Territory has been represented by 1 Member in the House of Representatives since 1922, and the Australian Capital Territory by 1 Member since 1949 and 2 Members since May 1974. The Member for the Australian Capital Territory was given full voting rights as from the Parliament elected in Nov. 1966. The Member for the Northern Territory was given full voting rights in 1968. The House of Representatives continues for 3 years from the date of its first meeting, unless sooner dissolved.

Every Senator or Member of the House of Representatives must be a subject of the

Queen, be of full age, possess electoral qualifications and have resided for 3 years within Australia. The franchise for both Houses is the same and is based on universal (males and females aged 18 years) suffrage. Compulsory voting was introduced in 1925. If a Member of a State Parliament wishes to be a candidate in a federal election, he must first resign his State seat.

Executive power is vested in the *Governor-General* advised by an Executive Council. The Governor-General presides over the Council, and its members hold office at his pleasure. All Ministers of State, who are members of the party or parties commanding a majority in the lower House, are members of the Executive Council under summons. A record of proceedings of meetings is kept by the Secretary to the Council. At Executive Council meetings the decisions of the Cabinet are (where necessary) given legal form, appointments made, resignations accepted, proclamations, regulations and the like made.

The policy of a ministry is, in practice, determined by the Ministers of State meeting without the Governor-General under the chairmanship of the Prime Minister. This group is known as the *Cabinet.* There are 11 Standing Committees of the Cabinet comprising varying numbers of Cabinet and non-Cabinet Ministers. In Labour Governments all Ministers have been members of Cabinet. In Liberal and National Country Party Governments, only the senior ministers. Cabinet meetings are private and deliberative and records of meetings are not made public. The Cabinet does not form part of the legal mechanisms of Government; the decisions it takes have, in themselves, no legal effect. The Cabinet substantially controls, in ordinary circumstances, not only the general legislative programme of Parliament but the whole course of Parliamentary proceedings. In effect, though not in form, the Cabinet, by reason of the fact that all Ministers are members of the Executive Council, is also the dominant element in the executive government of the country.

The legislative powers of the Federal Parliament embrace trade and commerce, shipping, etc., taxation, finance, banking, currency, bills of exchange, bankruptcy, insurance; defence; external affairs, naturalization and aliens, quarantine, immigration and emigration; the people of any race for whom it is deemed necessary to make special laws; postal, telegraph and like services; census and statistics; weights and measures; astronomical and meteorological observations; copyrights; railways; conciliation and arbitration in disputes extending beyond the limits of any one State; social services; marriage, divorce etc.; service and execution of the civil and criminal process; recognition of the laws, Acts and records, and judicial proceedings of the States. The Senate may not originate or amend money bills; and disagreement with the House of Representatives may result in dissolution and, in the last resort, a joint sitting of the two Houses. No religion may be established by the Commonwealth. The Federal Parliament has limited and enumerated powers, the several State parliaments retaining the residuary power of government over their respective territories. If a State law is inconsistent with a Commonwealth law, the latter prevails.

The Constitution also provides for the admission or creation of new States. Proposed laws for the alteration of the Constitution must be submitted to the electors, and they can be enacted only if approved by a majority of the States and by a majority of all the electors voting.

The Australia Acts 1986 removed residual powers of the British government to intervene in the government of Australia or the individual states.

In Feb. 1998 an Australian Constitutional Convention voted for Australia to become a republic. A national referendum is to be held in 1999.

The 38th Parliament was elected on 21 March 1996.

House of Representatives (1996): Liberal Party (LP), 75 seats; Australian Labor Party (ALP), 49; National Party, 19; independents, 5.

Senate (1996): Australian Labor Party, 30; Liberal Party, 30; Australian Democratic Party, 7; National Party, 6; Greens, 2; Country Liberal Party, 1.

The *President* of the Senate is Kerry Sibraa.

Governor-General: Sir William Deane, AC, KBE (assumed office 16 Feb. 1996).

National anthem: Advance Australia Fair (adopted 19 April 1984; words and tune by P. D. McCormick). The 'Royal Anthem' (i.e. 'God Save the Queen') is used in the presence of the British Royal Family.

An LP-NP coalition government was formed in March 1996 which in March 1998 comprised:
Prime Minister: John Howard (LP).
Cabinet: Deputy Prime Minister and Minister for Trade: Tim Fischer (NP). *Treasurer:* Peter Costello. *Primary Industries and Energy:* John Anderson. *Environment, Leader of the Government in the Senate:* Robert Hill. *Communications, the Information Economy and the Arts:* Richard Alston. *Workplace Relations and Small Business, Leader of the House:* Peter Reith. *Social Security:* Jocelyn Newman. *Foreign Affairs:* Alexander Downer. *Industry, Science and Technology:* John Moore. *Defence:* Ian McLachlan. *Health and Family Services:* Dr Michael Wooldridge. *Finance and Administration:* John Fahey. *Employment, Education, Training and Youth Affairs, Minister assisting the Prime Minister for the Public Service:* Dr David Kemp. *Attorney-General:* Daryl Williams, AM, QC. *Transport and Regional Development:* Mark Vaile.
Outer Ministry: Immigration and Multicultural Affairs: Philip Ruddock. *Schools, Vocational Education and Training:* Christopher Ellison. *Assistant Treasurer:* Rod Kemp. *Resources and Energy:* Warwick Parer. *Customs and Consumer Affairs:* Warren Truss. *Status of Women:* Judi Moylan. *Defence Industry, Science and Personnel:* Bronwyn Bishop. *Justice:* Amanda Vanstone. *Family Services:* Warwick Smith. *Veterans' Affairs:* Bruce Scott. *Aboriginal and Torres Strait Islander Affairs:* John Herron. *Sport and Tourism, Minister assisting the Prime Minister for the Sydney 2000 Games:* Andrew Thomson. *Special Minister of State, Minister assisting the Prime Minister:* Nick Minchin. *Regional Development, Territories and Local Government:* Alex Somlyay.
The *Speaker* is Robert George Halverson, OBE.
The leader of the Opposition is Kim Beazley (ALP).

State Government: In each of the 6 States (New South Wales, Victoria, Queensland, South Australia, Western Australia, Tasmania) there is a State government whose constitution, powers and laws continue, subject to changes embodied in the Australian Constitution and subsequent alterations and agreements, as they were before federation. The system of government is basically the same as that described above for the Commonwealth—*i.e.*, the Sovereign, her representative (in this case a Governor), an upper and lower house of Parliament (except in Queensland, where the upper house was abolished in 1922), a cabinet led by the Premier and an Executive Council. Among the more important functions of the State governments are those relating to education, health, hospitals and charities, law, order and public safety, business undertakings such as railways and tramways, and public utilities such as water supply and sewerage. In the domains of education, hospitals, justice, the police, penal establishments, and railway and tramway operation, State government activity predominates. Care of the public health and recreative activities are shared with local government authorities and the Federal Government, social services other than those referred to above are now primarily the concern of the Federal Government, and the operation of public utilities is shared with local and semi-government authorities.

Administration of Territories. Since 1911, responsibility for administration and development of the Australian Capital Territory (ACT) has been vested in Federal Ministers and Departments. The ACT became self-governing on 11 May 1989.
The ACT House of Assembly has been accorded the forms of a legislature, but continues to perform an advisory function for the Minister for the Capital Territory.
On 1 July 1978 the Northern Territory of Australia became a self-governing Territory with expenditure responsibilities and revenue-raising powers broadly approximating those of a State.

Local Government. The system of municipal government is broadly the same throughout Australia, although local government legislation is a State matter.
Each State is sub-divided into areas known variously as municipalities, cities, boroughs, towns, shires or district councils, totalling about 900. Within these areas

the management of road, street and bridge construction, health, sanitary and garbage services, water supply and sewerage, and electric light and gas undertakings, hospitals, fire brigades, tramways and omnibus services and harbours is generally part of the functions of elected aldermen and councillors. State governments may also be responsible for some services.

In some instances, *e.g.*, in New South Wales, a number of local government authorities combine to conduct a public undertaking such as the supply of water or electricity. State taxation revenue was $A26,757m. in 1993–94; local, $A5,266m.

Howard, C., *Australia's Constitution*. Melbourne, 1985
Lucy, R., *The Australian Form of Government*. Melbourne, 1985

DEFENCE. The Minister for Defence has responsibility under legislation for the control and administration of the Defence Force. The Chief of Defence Force Staff is vested with command of the Defence Force. He is the principal military adviser to the Minister. The Secretary, Department of Defence is the Permanent Head of the Department. He is the principal civilian adviser to the Minister and has statutory responsibility for financial administration of the Defence outlay. The Chief of Defence Force Staff and the Secretary are jointly responsible for the administration of the Defence Force except with respect to matters falling within the command of the Defence Force or any other matter specified by the Minister.

The Chief of Naval Staff, the Chief of the General Staff and the Chief of the Air Staff command the Navy, Army and Air Force respectively. They have delegated authority from the Chief of Defence Force Staff and the Secretary to administer matters relating to their particular Service.

The structure of Defence is characterized by 3 organizational types: *(i)* A Central Office comprising 5 groups of functional orientated Divisions: Strategic Policy and Force Development; Supply and Support; Manpower and Financial Services; Management and Infrastructure Services; and, Defence Science and Technology; *(ii)* the 3 Armed Services of the Defence Force, each having a Service Office element in addition to the command structure; and *(iii)* a small number of outrider organizations concerned with such specialist fields as intelligence and natural disasters.

Defence Support. The Department of Defence Support purchases goods and services for defence purposes; provides technical expertise and other assistance to the defence industry; involves Australian industry in defence equipment to the maximum practical extent; administers the Australian Offsets Program so as to stimulate technological advancement and broaden the capabilities of strategic industries; within overall defence policies helps the capacity, efficiency and capability of Australian industry to design and export defence materiel; manages the Government's munitions and aircraft factories, and dockyards; markets defence and allied products and services to help maintain strategic industries.

Army. Overall organization and financial control of the Army is vested in the Chief of General Staff. The Army is organized in a Land Headquarters and a Northern Command.

The strength of the Army was 25,400, including 2,600 women, in 1997. There was 1 infantry division, 1 armoured regiment, 1 armoured reconnaissance regiment, 1 armoured personnel carrier squadron, 4 infantry battalions, 2 artillery regiments, 1 air defence regiment, 2 combat engineer regiments, 1 special forces regiment and 2 aviation regiments. Equipment included 90 Leopard 1A3 main battle tanks. The Army Aviation Corps has 4 fixed-wing transports, and 120 helicopters.

The effective strength of the Army Reserve in 1997 was 25,100.

Women have been eligible for combat duties since 1993.

Navy. The Chief of Naval Staff is assisted by the Deputy Chief of Naval Staff and Assistant Chiefs for Personnel and for Materiel. The command, operation and administration of the Fleet is vested in the Maritime Commander, Australia headquartered at Sydney.

The fleet includes 1 new Swedish-designed Collins class and 3 UK-built Oxley class diesel submarines, 3 US-built guided missile destroyers, 1 new ANZAC class German-designed frigate, 4 US- and 2 Australian-built guided missile frigates and

1 older frigate, 6 mine countermeasure vessels, 2 ex-US landing ships being converted for helicopter operations, 5 tank landing craft and 16 inshore patrol craft. Major auxiliaries include 2 fleet replenishment tankers and 2 survey ships, and there are some 80 minor auxiliaries and service craft.

A further 5 Collins class submarines and 5 ANZAC class frigates are under construction.

The Fleet Air Arm operates a shore-based anti-submarine helicopter squadron of 7 Sea Kings and 16 S-70B Seahawk helicopters for the guided missile frigates. There are additionally 2 transport and 1 survey aircraft and 9 transport and utility helicopters.

The fleet main base is at Sydney, with subsidiary bases at Cockburn Sound (Western Australia), Cairns and Darwin.

The all-volunteer Navy was (1997) 14,300 strong including 990 Fleet Air Arm.

Air Force. Command of the Royal Australian Air Force (RAAF) is vested in the Chief of the Air Staff (CAS) assisted by the Deputy Chief of the Air Staff, Chief of Air Force Operations and Plans, Chief of Air Force Materiel, Chief of Air Force Personnel, Chief of Air Force Technical Services, Director-General Supply—Air Force and Assistant Secretary Resources Planning.

The CAS administers and controls RAAF units through two commands: Operational Command and Support Command. Operational Command is responsible to the CAS for the command of operational units and the conduct of their operations within Australia and overseas. Support Command is responsible to the CAS for training of personnel, and the supply and maintenance of service equipment.

Flying establishment comprises 16 squadrons, of which 2 are equipped with 22 F-111 strike/reconnaissance aircraft. Of the others, 3 are equipped with missile-armed F-18 Hornet interceptors and 3 with Orion maritime reconnaissance aircraft. There are 5 transport squadrons, 2 with Hercules turboprop transports, 1 with Caribou STOL transports, 1 with Boeing 707 tanker and transport aircraft, and 1 with Falcon 900 VIP transports. Primary training has been transferred to a civilian school. Training aircraft include Pilatus PC-9 turboprop-powered basic trainers, Aermacchi MB 326H jets for pilot training, and HS 748 aircraft for navigator training. A training unit has F-18 Hornets for crew conversion.

Training for commissioned rank is carried out at the RAAF Academy and Officers' Training School, both located at Point Cook, Victoria. Other major training activities which lead to commissioned rank include basic aircrew training and technical and commercial cadet schemes. Basic ground training to tradesman level is conducted at RAAF technical training schools. Higher command and staff training is, in the main, carried out at the RAAF Staff College, Fairbairn, ACT.

Personnel (1997) 17,700, including 2,700 women. There is also an Australian Air Force Reserve, 4,400 strong. There were 125 combat aircraft.

INTERNATIONAL RELATIONS

Membership. Australia is a member of the UN, the Commonwealth, OECD, Colombo Plan, the South Pacific Forum and the Pacific Community.

ECONOMY

Policy. Since 1942 the Federal Government alone has levied taxes on incomes. In return for vacating this field of taxation, the State Governments are reimbursed by grants from the Federal Government out of revenue received. Payments to the States represent about one-third of Federal Government outlays, and in turn the payments State Governments receive from the Federal Government account for nearly half of their revenues.

The Financial Agreement of 1927 established the Australian Loan Council which represents the Federal and six State Governments, and co-ordinates domestic and overseas borrowings by these governments, including annual borrowing programmes. The Federal Government acts as a central borrowing agency in raising loans to finance the major part of those programmes. The Loan Council in 1984 agreed upon arrangements for the co-ordination of borrowings by semi-government and local authorities and government-owned companies.

Reforms were initiated at a special Premiers' Conference in Oct. 1990 to form a partnership between the Commonwealth, States, Territories and local government with a view to improving national efficiency, international competitiveness and enhancing delivery and quality of government services. In July 1991 the premiers agreed a programme of inter-state standardization and integration in such areas as the railway system, electricity grid, product control and professional qualifications.

Performance. GDP at factor cost (at current prices) was $A412,314m. in 1995 ($A389,371m. in 1994). Real GDP growth year-on-year was 3·8% in Sept. 1996.

Budget. In 1929, under a financial agreement between the Federal Government and States, approved by a referendum, the Federal Government took over all State debts existing on 30 June 1927 and agreed to pay $A15·17m. a year for 58 years towards the interest charges thereon, and to make substantial contributions towards a sinking fund on State debt. The Sinking Fund arrangements were revised under an amendment to the agreement in 1976.

Outlays and revenues of the Commonwealth Government for years ending 30 June (in $A1m.):

	1994–95	1995–96	1996–97[1]
Total outlays	121,877	126,694	129,686
including			
Defence	9,795	10,011	10,027
Education	10,093	10,590	11,064
Health	17,134	18,583	19,408
Social security and welfare	43,302	46,744	48,897
Housing	1,116	1,201	1,122
Culture and recreation	1,263	1,425	1,390
Economic services	8,505	8,661	7,767
Public services	7,713	7,796	8,689
Payments to States, NT and local government	15,074	13,798	16,797
Public debt interest	8,005	9,135	9,781
Total revenue	110,247	121,649	130,160
including			
Customs duty	3,474	3,124	3,010
Excise duty	12,001	12,849	13,360
Sales tax	11,624	12,955	13,890
PAYE income tax	50,928	56,442	61,470
Other individual tax	9,178	10,078	10,930
Prescribed payments	2,169	2,179	2,340
Company tax	15,588	18,252	19,700
Superannuation	1,913	1,634	1,800
Withholding tax	903	1,349	1,170
Fringe benefits tax	2,740	3,031	3,180
Interest, rent and dividends	· · ·	5,254	5,132

[1] Estimate.

Currency. On 14 Feb. 1966 Australia adopted a system of decimal currency. The currency unit, the *Australian dollar* (AUD), is divided into 100 *cents*. Notes are issued in denominations of $A5, 10, 20, 50 and 100. Coins are issued in denominations of 5, 10, 20 and 50 cents and $A1. Gold bullion legal tender coins weighing 1 kg (the 'Australian Nugget'), 10 oz. and 2 oz. with respective face values of $A10,000, $A2,500 and $A500 were introduced in March 1991, and a 1 kg platinum coin with a face value of $A3,000 was issued in Oct. 1992.

Foreign currency reserves were $A20,184m. in 1995.

The estimated inflation rate for the year ending June 1996 was 3·1%.

Money in circulation in June 1995, $A18,233m.

Banking and Finance. The banking system comprises:

(a) The Reserve Bank of Australia is the central bank and bank of issue. Its *Governor* is appointed for 7-year terms (present incumbent, Ian Macfarlane, appointed 1996). Its Rural Credits Department provides short-term credit for the marketing of primary produce. Its assets were $A45,217m. in Nov. 1996 and its liabilities $A45,217m., of which notes on issue, $A19,457m.; deposits by trading banks, $A4,072m.; deposits by Commonwealth Government, $A1,781m.; of the assets are: Gold and foreign exchange (including IMF Special Drawing Rights), $A20,748m., treasury notes $A7,533m., other Commonwealth Government securities $A16,370m. Its functions and responsibilities derive from the Reserve Bank Act 1959, the Banking Act 1959, and the Financial Corporations Act 1974.

(b) 4 major banks: (i) The Commonwealth Bank of Australia; (ii) The Australia and New Zealand Banking Group Ltd; (iii) Westpac Banking Corporation and (iv) National Australia Bank.

(c) Other banks: (i) 3 State Government banks—The State Bank of New South Wales, The State Bank of South Australia, and the Rural and Industries Bank of Western Australia; (ii) one joint stock bank—The Bank of Queensland Ltd, formerly The Brisbane Permanent Building and Banking Co. Ltd, which has specialized business in one district only; (iii) The Australian Bank Ltd; (iv) branches of 17 overseas banks—the restrictions on foreign banks operating in Australia, and on foreign investment in the merchant banks, were lifted in 1984-85.

(d) The Commonwealth Development Bank of Australia commenced operations on 14 Jan. 1960. Its function is to provide finance for primary production and small business.

(e) The Australian Resources Development Bank Ltd opened on 29 March 1968, to assist Australian enterprises in developing Australia's natural resources, through direct loans and equity investment or by re-financing loans made by trading banks. The bank is jointly owned by the 4 major Australian trading banks.

(f) The Primary Industry Bank of Australia Ltd commenced operations on 22 Sept. 1978. The equity capital of the bank consists of eight shares. Seven shares are held by the Australian Government and the major trading banks while the eighth share is held equally by the 4 State banks. The main objective of the bank is to facilitate the provision of loans to primary producers on longer terms than are otherwise generally available. The role of the bank is restricted to re-financing loans made by banks and other financial institutions.

(g) The Banking Legislation Amendment Act of 1989 removed the legislative differences between savings and trading banks. In June 1995 there were 49 authorized banks under 44 banking groups. In June 1995 there were 6,655 branches and 5,897 agencies.

Total deposits in Oct. 1996 were $A295,940m. (including $A8,380m. of non-residents' deposits).

(h) In March 1992 there were 45 building societies. Assets were $A13,701m. in Oct. 1996. Building societies are permitted to have up to 50% of their assets in non-home loans.

There is an Australian Stock Exchange (ASX).

Weights and Measures. The metric system is in use.

ENERGY AND NATURAL RESOURCES

Electricity. Electricity supply is the responsibility of the State governments. At 30 June 1994 total installed capacity was 37·3m. kW. Production 1995–96, 167,510m. kWh (11% hydro-electric).

Oil and gas. The main fields are Gippsland (Vic.) and Carnarvon (WA). Crude oil production was 33,910m. litres in 1995-96; natural gas, 31,000m. cu. metres.

Minerals. Australia is a leading producer of bauxite and diamonds. Coal is Australia's major source of energy. Reserves are large (1995 estimate: 69,000m. tonnes) and easily worked. The main fields are in New South Wales and Queensland. Production in 1995-96 was 243·02m. tonnes. Brown coal (lignite) reserves are mainly in Victoria and were estimated at 41,700m. tonnes in 1990. Production, 1994-95 was 48·3m. tonnes.

Production of other major minerals in 1995-96 (1,000 tonnes): Bauxite, 42,655; copper, 365; iron ore and concentrate, 142,936; manganese ore, 2,177; nickel, 104; tin, 8·66; uranium, 5·11; gold, 253 tonnes.

Agriculture. In 1995 there were 116,193 farms. Farms in 1994 covered 463·3m. ha. 414m. ha were grazing or fallow, 16·9m. ha sown to crops. The most important are (1995–96) wheat (16·98m. tonnes from 9·72m. ha); sugar-cane (37·37m. tonnes from 0·38m. ha); barley (5·5m. tonnes from 3·2m. ha); oats (1·94m. tonnes from 1·18m. ha); rice (0·95m. tonnes from 0·15m. ha). Vineyards (62,048 ha) produced 531m. litres of wine from 777,373 tonnes of grapes in 1993–94. In 1994-95, 766,917 tonnes of grapes were harvested from 62,291 ha of vines.

Gross value of agricultural production in 1995-96, $A27,169m., including (in $A1m.): Crops, 15,257; livestock slaughtering, 5,976; wool, 3,264; other livestock products, 5,936.

In 1993, 71,803 farms had cattle and 56,026 had sheep.

Livestock (in 1,000) at 31 March 1996:

	NSW	Vic.	Qld	SA	WA	Tas.	NT	ACT	Australia
Cattle	6,661	4,579	10,483	1,206	1,817	733	1,525 [1]	13 [2]	27,012
Sheep	42,720	22,069	9,924	12,996	29,806	4,016	...	0·08	126,320
Pigs	724	467	633	420	323	35	7	...	2,609
Poultry[3]	27,377	14,728	10,055	5,094	6,025	...	225	217	70,608 [2]

[1] 31 March 1995.   [2] 31 March 1994.   [3] 31 March 1993.

Livestock products (in 1,000 tonnes) for the year ending 30 June 1995: Beef, 1,742; veal, 38; lamb and mutton, 589; pigmeat, 349; poultry meat, 462; wool (1994), 865; milk, 8,206m. litres.

Williams, D. B. (ed.), *Agriculture in the Australian Economy*. 3rd ed Sydney Univ. Press and OUP, 1991

Forestry. The Federal Government is responsible for forestry at the national level. Each State is responsible for the management of publicly-owned forests. Total forest cover was 105·26m. ha at 30 June 1995, made up of (in 1,000 ha): Native forest, 40,719 (privately owned, 11,273); woodland, 63,426; plantations, 1,119 (privately owned, 359). The major part of wood supplies derives from coniferous plantations, of which there were 964,000 ha in 1995. Production was 3·43m. cu. metres of sawn timber and 954,000 tonnes of wood pulp in 1995–96.

Fisheries. The Australian Fishing Zone covers an area 16% larger than the Australian land mass and is the third largest fishing zone in the world, but fish production is insignificant by world standards due to low productivity of the oceans. The major commercially exploited species are prawns, rock lobster, abalone, tuna, other fin fish, scallops, oysters and pearls. In 1993-94, 209,263 tonnes of fish, crustaceans and molluscs valued at $A1,607m. were produced.

INDUSTRY. Statistics of manufacturing industries, June 1994: Number of firms, 44,921; persons employed (1995), 1,111,000; salaries paid, $A28,309m.; turnover, $A185,115m. (excludes small single-establishment enterprises employing fewer than 4 persons)

Manufacturing by sector as at June 1994:

	No. of firms	Persons Employed	Salaries in $A1m.	Turnover in $A1m.
Food, beverages and tobacco	3,590	168,100	5,034	40,936
Textiles, clothing, footwear and leather products	4,503	77,000	1,825	9,602
Wood and paper products	3,985	62,000	1,790	10,740
Printing, publishing and recording media	5,274	89,600	2,831	11,920
Chemical, petroleum, coal and associated products	3,026	89,400	3,270	29,060
Non-metallic mineral products	1,936	39,400	1,315	8,909
Metal products	7,576	146,100	4,842	33,669
Machinery and equipment	9,011	196,000	6,181	34,661
Other manufacturing	6,020	55,000	1,220	5,617

Manufactured products in 1994–95 included: Bricks, 1,863m.; cement, 7·1m. tonnes; carpets, 47·3m. sq. metres; confectionery (1993-94), 180,210 tonnes; electric motors, 3·1m.; washing machines, 305,100; refrigerators, 408,000; TV sets

(1993-94), 163,000; pig iron, 7·4m. tonnes; crude steel, 7·8m. tonnes; tobacco, 23,083 tonnes; woollen wove, 8·6m. sq. metres; woollen yarn, 23,083 tonnes; scoured wool (1993-94), 154,242 tonnes; motor cars, 301,100; caravans, 9,394; beer, 1,789m. litres; sulphuric acid (1993-94), 62,231 tonnes; superphosphates, 1·36m. tonnes.

Labour. In June 1996 the total workforce (persons aged 15 and over) numbered 9,063,000, of whom 8·3m. (3,578,000 female) were employed. In Sept. 1997 there were 8,415,400 employed persons and the unemployment rate was 86%. In 1994 the labour force included 354,100 employers, 6,647,400 wage and salary earners and 802,200 self-employed. The majority of wage and salary earners have had their minimum wages and conditions of work prescribed in awards by the Industrial Relations Commission, which in April 1991 awarded a 2·5% rise, making the minimum weekly wage about $A442, but in Oct. 1991 the Commission decided to allow direct employer-employee wage bargaining, provided agreements reached are endorsed by the Commission. In some States, some conditions of work (e.g., weekly hours of work, leave) are set down in State legislation. Average weekly wage, Aug. 1996, $A566·60 (men, $A673·50; women, $A445·10). Average working week, 1994: 35·9 hours (males 40·9; females 29·3). 4 weeks annual leave is standard.

Employees in all States are covered by workers' compensation legislation and by certain industrial award provisions relating to work injuries.

During 1995 there were 643 industrial disputes in progress which accounted for 547,600 working days lost. In these disputes 344,300 workers were involved.

The following table shows the distribution of employed persons by industry in 1994, by sex and average weekly hours worked:

Industry	Numbers (in 1,000)		Hours worked	
	Persons	(Females)	Per person	(Females)
Agriculture, forestry, fishing and hunting	395·8	(126·5)	42·9	(29·9)
Mining	88·9	(10·6)	41·8	(38·2)
Manufacturing	1,107·3	(295·6)	38·3	(32·9)
Electricity, Gas and Water	83·9	(12·3)	37·1	(28·5)
Construction	605·8	(89·0)	37·5	(21·1)
Wholesale trade	518·1	(162·1)	39·5	(32·2)
Retail trade	1,199·5	(610·9)	32·2	(25·6)
Transport and storage	385·5	(82·4)	40·1	(33·0)
Property and business services	791·9	(363·6)	37·1	(30·9)
Education	578·6	(382·2)	34·4	(31·4)
Cultural and recreation services	193·7	(95·0)	32·4	(28·1)
Accommodation, cafés and restaurants	393·9	(217·0)	32·8	(28·5)
Communication	153·0	(44·7)	36·9	(30·0)
Finance and insurance	320·9	(187·0)	36·3	(32·6)
Government administration and defence	370·4	(156·4)	34·4	(31·4)
Health and community services	746·6	(569·1)	32·4	(28·1)
Personal and other services	297·0	(153·0)	33·3	(29·3)
Totals	8,230·8	(3,557·7)	35·9	(29·5)

In May 1994, 1,588,300 wage and salary earners worked in the public sector and 4,156,900 in the private sector.

The following table shows the distribution of employed persons in 1994 according to the *Australian Standard Classification of Occupations*:

Occupation	Employed persons (in 1,000)	
	Persons	(Females)
Managers and administrators	881·3	(216·7)
Professionals	1,149·1	(506·6)
Para-professionals	466·8	(223·1)
Tradespersons	1,192·4	(129·0)
Clerks	1,347·9	(1,062·9)
Salespersons and personnel service	1,389·2	(898·8)
Plant and machine operators, and drivers	581·7	(81·4)
Labourers and related workers	1,222·5	(439·2)
	8,230·8	(3,557·7)

In June 1996, 766,700 persons (8·5% of the labour force) were unemployed, (including 311,400 females) of whom 380,300 persons were seeking full-time work. In June 1995, 243,100 persons had been unemployed for more than one year. In Aug. 1997 there were 63,900 job vacancies.

Trade Unions. In June 1994 there were 157 trade unions with 2,890,200 members (1,135,600 females). About 44% of wage and salary earners (36% females) were estimated to be members of unions. In 1994 there were 26 unions with fewer than 100 members and 13 unions with 80,000 or more members. Many of the larger trade unions are affiliated with central labour organizations, the oldest and by far the largest being the Australian Council of Trade Unions formed in 1927. In July 1992 the Industrial Relations Legislation Amendment Act freed the way for employers and employees to negotiate enterprise-based awards and agreements. In a 1995 wage accord trade unions committed themselves to the objective of keeping inflation at 2-3%, and the government agreed to create 0·6m. jobs by 1999 and raised the 'safety net' wage rates to a weekly $A12-14.

FOREIGN ECONOMIC RELATIONS. In 1990 Australia and New Zealand completed a Closer Economic Relations agreement (initiated in 1983) which establishes free trade in goods. Gross foreign debt was $A235,482m. as at 30 June 1996.

Commerce. Merchandise imports and exports for years ending 30 June, in $A1m.:

	Imports	Exports
1993–94	64,470	64,574
1994–95	74,634	67,063
1995–96	71,792	76,043

The Australian customs tariff provides for preferences to goods produced in and shipped from certain countries as a result of reciprocal trade agreements. These include the UK, New Zealand, Canada and Ireland.

Merchandise exports and imports, 1994-95 (in $A1m.):

	Exports	Imports
Live animals	452	101
Meat and preparations	3,653	47
Dairy goods and eggs	1,413	173
Fish, shellfish and their preparations	1,143	609
Cereals and preparations	2,521	207
Vegetables and fruit	872	534
Sugar and honey	1,729	86
Coffee, tea, cocoa, spices and their manufactures	173	505
Animal feed (excl. unmilled cereal)	387	109
Miscellaneous edible products	207	451
Beverages	506	336
Tobacco and manufactures	43	186
Raw hides and skins	486	4
Oil seeds and fruit	110	133
Crude rubber (incl. synthetic and reclaimed)	12	153
Cork and wood	633	613
Pulp and waste paper	44	160
Textile fibres (not wool tops)	4,589	188
Crude fertilizers, minerals (not coal, petroleum, gems)	367	182
Metal ores and scrap	7,600	169
Crude animal and vegetable materials	226	193
Coal, coke and briquettes	6,939	22
Petroleum and products	2,951	3,608
Gas, natural and manufactured	1,355	38
Animal oils and fats	220	3
Fixed vegetable oils and fats	4	208
Processed oils and fats, waxes thereof	38	20
Organic chemicals	85	1,795
Inorganic chemicals	309	639
Dyeing, colouring and tanning materials	401	372
Medicinal and pharmaceutical products	768	1,562

	Exports	Imports
Essential oils, perfume and cleansing preparations	257	568
Manufactured fertilizers	24	535
Plastics in primary forms	282	923
Plastics in non-primary forms	143	719
Chemical materials and products	401	897
Leather and manufactures, dressed furskins	515	166
Rubber manufactures	145	1,045
Cork and wood manufactures (not furniture)	98	329
Paper, board and pulp	267	1,859
Textile yarn, fabrics and products	464	2,455
Non-metallic mineral goods	737	1,214
Iron and steel	1,579	1,287
Non-ferrous metals	4,509	679
Metal manufactures	693	1,876
Power generators	724	1,769
Special machinery, industrial	919	3,790
Metalworking machinery	140	573
General machinery and parts, industrial	940	4,301
Office machines and data-processing equipment	1,587	5,728
Telecommunications and sound equipment	540	3,362
Electrical machinery and parts	1,220	4,909
Road vehicles (inc. air-cushion vehicles)	1,080	8,677
Other transport equipment	926	2,050
Sanitary, plumbing, heating and lighting fittings, pre-fabricated buildings	52	218
Furniture and parts	76	444
Travel goods, handbags etc.	15	338
Clothing and accessories	302	1,637
Footwear	58	570
Professional, scientific and controlling instruments	442	1,834
Photographic and optical goods, watches and clocks	509	1,207
Miscellaneous manufactured articles	852	4,462
Other commodities and transactions	412	25
Gold and other coin	206	2
Non-monetary gold	4,820	710
Confidential items	896	59
Total trade	67,063	74,634

Trade by bloc or country in 1995–96 (in $A1m.):

	Exports	Imports
APEC	57,676	52,009
ASEAN	11,760	7,365
EU	8,457	19,387
OPEC	4,566	3,259
China	3,780	4,010
Japan	16,428	10,816
South Korea	6,613	2,293
New Zealand	5,600	3,591
Singapore	3,553	2,613
Taiwan	3,449	2,585
UK	2,827	4,882
USA	4,608	17,545
Other countries	29,184	29,456
	76,043	77,792

Tourism. During 1995, 3,725,800 overseas visitors arrived in Australia intending to stay for less than 12 months; tourists spent $A13,105m. in 1995.

COMMUNICATIONS

Roads. There are 810,000 km of roads (16,000 km of National Highways). At 30 June 1995, 8,391,500 cars, 2,246,700 vans, trucks and buses and 297,200 motor cycles were registered. New registrations, 1995–96, included 531,785 cars, 104,757 vans, trucks and buses and 22,345 motor cycles. In 1995, 2,014 persons were killed in road accidents (1,959 in 1994).

Railways. There are 7 government-owned railway systems. In 1991 the National Rail Corporation was set up to market inter-state freight service. Statistics for the year ended 30 June 1994:

System	Route length in km[4]	Passenger journeys, 1,000	Goods carried, (1,000 tonnes)	Freight earnings, ($A1,000)
State:				
New South Wales	9,810	236,900	65,500	836,186
Victoria	5,107	105,542	12,017	158,747
Queensland	9,357	39,339	92,092	1,101,688
South Australia[3]	120	8,720	. . .	. . .
Western Australia	5,583	16,446	27,726	269,494
Australian National [1,2]	6,235	223	14,942	276,324
	36,212	407,170	212,277	2,642,439

[1] The Australian National Railways operates services of the former Commonwealth Railways, the non-metropolitan South Australian Railways and the Tasmanian Railways.
[2] Excludes Adelaide metropolitan rail passenger services and the Tasmanian Region.
[3] The South Australian State Transport Authority operates services in the Adelaide metropolitan area.
[4] Inter-system traffic is included in the total for each system over which it passes.

The State railway gauges are: New South Wales, 1,435 mm; Victoria, 1,600 mm (325 km, 1,435 mm); Queensland, 1,067 mm (111 km, 1,435 mm); South Australia, 1,600mm for 2,533km plus 1,824km, 1,435 mm and the rest 1,067 mm; West Australia, 137 km, 1,435 mm and the rest 1,067 mm, and Tasmania, 1,067 mm. Australian National Railways comprises 3,530 km of 1,435 mm ('standard') gauge, 1,173 km of 1,600 mm ('broad') gauge and 1,532 km of 1,067 mm ('narrow') gauge routes. Under various Commonwealth–State standardization agreements, all the State capitals are now linked by standard gauge track (except Darwin; the Central Australia railway extends only as far north as Alice Springs).

The National Rail Corporation operating as 'National Rail' was incorporated in Sept. 1991; terminal operations commenced in 1993. It is scheduled to take over inter-state rail freight operations and the ownership of rail assets.

There are also private industrial and tourist railways, and tramways in Adelaide, Melbourne and Sydney.

Civil Aviation. Qantas Airways, Australia's international airline, in 1995 operated 4 A300B4-200s, 16 B-737-300s, 17 B-737-400s, 3 B-747-200Bs, 2 B-747-200B Combis, 6 B-747-300s, 18 B-747-400s, 7 B-767-200ERs and 14 B-767-300ERs. In 1992 Qantas merged with Australian Airlines and in 1993 25% of the company was purchased by British Airways. The remainder is government-owned. In 1993–94, 10·6m. passengers and 475,962 tonnes of freight were flown on international flights. There are 12 international airports, the main ones being Adelaide, Brisbane, Darwin, Melbourne, Perth, Sydney and Townsville. Services are also provided by Aeroflot, Aerolíneas Argentinas, Air Calédonie, Air China, Air France, Air India, Air Mauritius, Air Nauru, Air New Zealand, Air Niugini, Air Pacific, Air Vanuatu, Air Zimbabwe, Alitalia, All Nippon, American Airlines, Ansett, AOM, Biritsh Airways, Canadian Airlines, Cathay Pacific, Continental Airlines and Air Micronesia, Egyptair, Garuda Indonesia, Gulf Air, Japan Airlines, JAT, KLM, Korean Air, Lauda Air, Lufthansa, Malaysia Airlines, Middle East Airlines, Olympic Airlines, Philippine Airlines, Polynesian Airlines, Royal Brunei Airlines, Royal Tongan Airlines, SAA, Singapore Airlines, Solomon Airlines, Thai Airways, United Airways, United Airlines, Vietnam Airlines, Virgin Atlantic, Western Airlines.

Internal airlines carried 21,465,300 passengers in 1993–94 and 217,900 tonnes of freight. Domestic airlines were deregulated in Oct. 1990.

At 30 June 1994 there were 400 Commonwealth or licensed aerodromes in Australia and its Territories. At 14 Dec. 1995, 9,633 aircraft were registered in Australia.

Shipping. The chief ports are Sydney, Newcastle, Port Kembla; Melbourne, Geelong, Westernport; Hay Point, Gladstone, Brisbane; Port Hedland, Dampier, Port Walcott, Fremantle. In 1995 the merchant fleet comprised 104 vessels totalling 3·45m. DWT. 21 vessels (7·99% of tonnage) were registered under foreign flags. Total tonnage registered, 3·04m. GRT, including tankers, 0·8m. GRT and container ships, 0·12m. GRT.

Coastal cargo handled at Australian ports in 1993–94 (in gross weight tonnes): Loaded, 45,274,000; unloaded, 45,976,000.

Telecommunications. Postal services are operated by Australia Post, operating under the Australian Postal Corporation Act, 1989 as a government business enterprise. Revenue was $A2,568·4m. in 1993–94, expenditure $A2,284·5m. There were 3,992 post offices and other agencies in 1994. 4,325m. postal items were handled.

Internal telecommunications were operated by Telecom Australia, while services to other countries were operated by the Overseas Telecommunications Corporation. In 1991 these merged to form Telstra, a general carrier providing both domestic and international services in competition with other licensed general carriers. Telstra was scheduled for privatization in 1997. In 1997 commercial providers comprised a general carrier, a fibre-optic local telephone network and a mobile telephone network.

Three telecommunications satellites are in orbit covering the entire continent.

Broadcasting is regulated by the Australian Broadcasting Authority, established in 1992 under the Broadcasting Services Act 1992. Foreign ownership of commercial radio and TV companies is restricted to 20%. The national broadcasting service is provided by the Australian Broadcasting Corporation (ABC), an independent statutory corporation receiving 85% of its funding from sales and other revenues, and the Special Broadcasting Service. The latter's function is to provide multilingual radio and TV services for all Australians, reflecting a multicultural society. There are also commercial radio and TV services operated by companies under licence, subscription TV services, public radio services operated on a non-profit basis and a parliamentary radio service to state capitals, Canberra and Newcastle. The short-wave international service Radio Australia broadcasts in English, Bahasa Malay, Cantonese, Chinese, French, Khmer, Thai, Tok Pisin and Vietnamese. Radio Australia had an audience of 10m. in 1997.

In 1995 there were estimated to be 23·3m. radios and in 1992 9·2m. TV sets in use.

Cinemas. In 1995 there were 1,137 cinemas with an annual attendance of 69m. 18 movies were produced and 1 co-production.

Press (1995). There were 69 daily newspapers with a weekly combined circulation of some 4·6m.

SOCIAL INSTITUTIONS

Justice. The judicial power of the Commonwealth of Australia is vested in the High Court of Australia (the Federal Supreme Court), in the Federal courts created by the Federal Parliament (the Federal Court of Australia and the Family Court of Australia) and in the State courts invested by Parliament with Federal jurisdiction.

High Court. The High Court consists of a Chief Justice and 6 other Justices, appointed by the Governor-General in Council. The Constitution confers on the High Court original jurisdiction, *inter alia*, in all matters arising under treaties or affecting consuls or other foreign representatives, matters between the States of the Commonwealth, matters to which the Commonwealth is a party and matters between residents of different States. Federal Parliament may make laws conferring original jurisdiction on the High Court, *inter alia*, in matters arising under the Constitution or under any laws made by the Parliament. It has in fact conferred jurisdiction on the High Court in matters arising under the Constitution and in matters arising under certain laws made by Parliament.

The High Court may hear and determine appeals from its own Justices exercising original jurisdiction, from any other Federal Court, from a Court exercising Federal jurisdiction and from the Supreme Courts of the States. It also has jurisdiction to hear and determine appeals from the Supreme Courts of the Territories. The right of appeal from the High Court to the Privy Council in London was abolished in 1986.

Other Federal Courts. Since 1924, 4 other Federal courts have been created to exercise special Federal jurisdiction, i.e. the Federal Court of Australia, the Family Court of Australia, the Australian Industrial Court and the Federal Court of Bankruptcy. The Federal Court of Australia was created by the Federal Court of Australia Act 1976 and began to exercise jurisdiction on 1 Feb. 1977. It exercises such original jurisdiction as is invested in it by laws made by the Federal Parliament including jurisdiction formerly exercised by the Australian Industrial Court and the Federal Court of Bankruptcy, and in some matters previously invested in either the High Court or State and Territory Supreme Courts. The Federal Court also acts as a court of appeal from State and Territory courts in relation to Federal matters. Appeal from the Federal Court to the High Court will be by way of special leave only. The State Supreme Courts have also been invested with Federal jurisdiction in bankruptcy.

State Courts. The general Federal jurisdiction of the State courts extends, subject to certain restrictions and exceptions, to all matters in which the High Court has jurisdiction or in which jurisdiction may be conferred upon it.

Industrial Tribunals. The chief federal industrial tribunal is the Australian Conciliation and Arbitration Commission, constituted by presidential members (with the status of judges) and commissioners. The Commission's functions include settling industrial disputes, making awards, determining the standard hours of work and wage fixation. Questions of law, the judicial interpretation of awards and imposition of penalties in relation to industrial matters, are dealt with by the Industrial Division of the Federal Court.

Religion. Under the Constitution the Commonwealth cannot make any law to establish any religion, to impose any religious observance or to prohibit the free exercise of any religion. The following percentages refer to those religions with the largest number of adherents at the census of 1991. The census question on religious adherence was not obligatory, however.

Christian, 74% of population: Catholic, 27·3%; Anglican, 23·8%; Uniting Church, 8·2%; Presbyterian and Reformed, 4·3%; Orthodox, 2·8%; Baptist, 1·7%; Lutheran, 1·5%; Pentecostal, 0·9%; Churches of Christ, 0·5%; Jehovah's Witnesses, 0·4%; Salvation Army, 0·4%. Religion other than Christian 2·6%; no religion, 12·9%; no statement, 10·5%.

The Anglican Synod voted for the ordination of 10 women in Nov. 1992.

Thompson, R. C., *Religion in Australia, a History.* OUP, 1995

Education. The Governments of the Australian States and the Northern Territory have the major responsibility for education, including the administration and substantial funding of primary, secondary, and technical and further education. In most States, a single Education Department is responsible for these three levels, but in New South Wales and South Australia there is a separate department responsible solely for technical and further education and in Victoria, a Technical and Further Education Board. Furthermore, in New South Wales an Education Commission advises the Minister on primary, secondary and post-secondary education.

The Australian Government is responsible for education in Norfolk Island, Christmas Island and the Cocos (Keeling) Islands. It also provides supplementary finance to the States and is responsible for the total funding of universities and colleges of advanced education. It has special responsibilities for student assistance, education programmes for Aboriginal people and children from non-English-speaking backgrounds, and for international relations in education.

The Australian Constitution empowers the Federal Government to make grants to the States and to place conditions upon such grants. The National Board of Employment, Education and Training was established in 1988 to advise the Federal Government on the financial needs of educational institutions. It is assisted by 4 councils: The Schools Council, the Higher Education Council, the Employment and Skills Formation Council and the Australian Research Council.

The Commonwealth has been working with the states to develop a national perspective for schools and a common curriculum. The Curriculum Corporation has been established under the auspices of the Australian Education Council.

School attendance is compulsory between the ages of 6 and 15 years (16 years in Tasmania), at either a government school or a recognized non-government educational institution. Many children attend pre-schools for a year before entering school (usually in sessions of 2-3 hours, for 2-5 days per week). Government schools are usually co-educational and comprehensive. Non-government schools have been traditionally single-sex, particularly in secondary schools, but there is a trend towards co-education. Tuition is free at government schools, but fees are normally charged at non-government schools.

Primary and secondary schools at July 1994:

	Schools		Teachers[1]		Pupils[2]	
States and Territories	Govern- ment	Non- govern- ment	Govern- ment schools	Non- govern- ment schools	Govern- ment schools	Non- govern- ment schools
New South Wales	2,187	862	47,371	19,142	755,771	296,078
Victoria	1,731	679	34,635	16,661	520,328	252,866
Queensland	1,323	406	25,718	8,933	403,234	145,297
South Australia	674	189	12,665	4,057	181,640	64,371
Western Australia	767	251	14,055	5,048	223,105	76,307
Tasmania	233	68	4,207	1,372	64,061	21,298
Northern Territory	147	26	1,991	471	26,934	7,212
ACT	97	39	2,738	1,281	39,865	21,013
Australia	7,159	2,520	143,379	56,965	2,214,938	884,442

[1] Full-time teachers plus the full-time equivalent of part-time teaching.
[2] Full-time pupils only.

In post-secondary education, tuition fees were abolished in 1974 and student allowances are provided for full-time students subject to a means test. Universities are autonomous institutions. From 1 Jan. 1989 the university and college of advanced education sectors were merged by the Federal Government. The resulting institutions are self-governing, though funded by the Federal Government. A private university sector is developing. The major part of technical and further education is provided in government-administered technical and further education institutions (TAFE). These had 1,782,225 students in 1993.

In 1996 there were 36 universities in the Unified National System which receive Commonwealth funding. These operate under state legislation. Outside this system, the Australian National University, Canberra University and the Australian Maritime College receive Commonwealth funding on a contract basis. There were 585,396 university students in 1994. Academic staff (and students) by university: NSW: Sydney, 2,500 (30,995); New South Wales, 1,823 (26,295); New England, 544 (13,638); Newcastle, 858 (14,721); Macquarie, 754 (15,526); Wollongong, 833 (11,266); Southern Cross, 283 (6,374); Sydney University of Technology, 1,011 (20,986); Western Sydney, 1,073 (21,207); Charles Sturt, 572 (16,369); Vic.: Melbourne, 2,576 (29,930); Monash, 2,391 (37,316); La Trobe, 1,380 (21,180); Deakin, 1,039 (24,538); Ballarat, 256 (3,911); Victoria University of Technology, 630 (13,693); Swinburne University of Technology, 420 (8,831); Royal Melbourne Institute of Technology, 1,244 (24,343); Qld.: Queensland, 1,884 (24,590); James Cook, 598 (7,847); Griffith, 1,004 (17,415); Queensland University of Technology, 1,252 (25,874); Central Queensland, 347 (8,383); Southern Queensland, 386 (12,957); Bond (1993), 310 (1,643); SA: Adelaide, 1,041 (12,899); Flinders, 777 (10,243); South Australia, 1,209 (21,817); WA: Western Australia, 958 (12,370); Curtin

University of Technology, 1,052 (19,326); Edith Cowan, 830 (16,845); Murdoch, 461 (7,860); Notre Dame (1993), 33 (200); Tas.: Tasmania, 877 (11,618); NT: Northern Territory, 275 (3,779); ACT: Canberra, 416 (8,553); Australian National, 1,494 (10,290); Australian Catholic University, 520 (8,439).

Teacher education usually takes place in colleges of advanced education, though a substantial number of secondary teachers and a few primary teachers receive their pre-service education in a university.

The Australian Government provides assistance for students. The Assistance for Isolated Children Scheme provides special support to families whose children are isolated from schooling or are handicapped. AUSTUDY is a means-tested scheme to assist students aged 16 years and over enrolled for full-time study in approved courses at secondary and post-secondary institutions. Allowances are also available for post-graduate study and overseas study. Aboriginal students are eligible for assistance under the ABSTUDY scheme. Federal government expenditure on these schemes was $A1,602m. in 1994. In addition, under the Higher Education Contribution Scheme students may be funded by a government loan repaid interest-free later through the tax system. The Federal Government introduced a supplementary loans scheme for eligible students in 1993. The States also offer various schemes of assistance, principally at the primary and secondary levels.

National bodies with a co-ordinating, planning or funding role include: the Australian Education Council, comprising the Federal and State Ministers of Education, the Conference of Directors-General of Education, the Australian Council for Educational Research and advisory bodies, the National Aboriginal Education Committee, and the Vocational Education Employment and Training Advisory Committee.

Commonwealth government expenditure on education (public and private sectors) in 1994–95 was estimated at $A10,056m.

Health. In 1992 there were 1,079 acute hospitals; there were an average 4·5 hospital beds per 1,000 population. There were 1,104 hospitals (general). The Royal Flying Doctor Service serves remote areas. Commonwealth government expenditure on health (1994–95) was estimated at $A17,276m.

Welfare. All Commonwealth Government social security pensions, benefits and allowances are financed from the Commonwealth Government's general revenue. In addition, assistance is provided for welfare services.

Expenditure on main programmes, 1994–95, $A43,449m.

The following summarizes the conditions of the major benefits.

Age and disability pensions—age pensions are payable to men 65 years of age or more and women 60 years and 6 months of age or more who have lived in Australia for a specified period and, unless permanently blind, also satisfy an income test. Persons over 16 years of age who are permanently blind or permanently incapacitated for work to the extent of at least 85% may receive an invalid pension. Invalid pension is paid subject to a residence qualification, income and assets test, unless the person is permanently blind. Additional amounts are paid to pensioners with dependent children. Supplementary assistance may be paid to a pensioner paying rent or private lodging subject to an income test. Remote area allowance is payable to pensioners living in certain remote areas, except for those aged 70 or more receiving the special rate of age pension. Supplementary assistance, additional pension for children, mother's/guardian's allowance and remote area allowance are not taxable.

In 1994–95, age pensioners received a total of $A11,884m., and disability support pensioners received $A4,525m.

Wife pension—payable to the wife of an age or invalid pensioner if she is not eligible for a pension in her own right. The maximum rate and the income test are identical to those for age and invalid pensioners. The amount paid out in 1994–95 was $A161·4m. Wife Pension is being phased out; new grants have ceased since 1 July 1995.

Carer pension—payable to a person who is providing constant care and attention at home for a severely disabled age or invalid pensioner living in the same house, where the carer is not eligible for pension in his own right. Since March 1996 Carer Pension has been extended to carers of non-pensioners meeting the Basic Family Payment assets and income criteria. The maximum rate and the income test are identical to those for age and invalid pensions. The amount paid out in 1992–93 was $A100·8m.

Sole parent pensions—sole parents who have custody, care and control of any dependent children may, if they satisfy a residence requirement and an income test, receive sole parent pensions. Mother's/guardian's allowance, additional pension for each dependent child, supplementary assistance and remote area allowance are also payable.

In 1994–95, 324,941 beneficiaries received a total of $A2,552·3m.

Rehabilitation allowance—persons undertaking a rehabilitation programme with the Commonwealth Rehabilitation Service who are eligible for a social security pension or benefit are eligible to receive a non taxable rehabilitation allowance during treatment or training and for up to 6 months thereafter. The allowance is equivalent to the invalid pension and is subject to the same income test. The amount paid out in 1992–93 was $A14m.

Maternity Allowance—was introduced from 1 Feb. 1996 to assist families with the costs associated with a new baby (including forgone income). It is paid as a lump sum for each new child to families meeting the Family Payment residence, income and assets criteria.

Basic Family Payment—is paid subject to an income and assets test to assist families with children under 16 years or dependent full-time students aged 16 years to 18 years. Since July 1996 payments to students age 16 and over are paid by the Department of Employment, Education and Training through the AUSTUDY system. It is not subject to income tax.

In 1994–95, 1,804,118 families comprising 3,486,316 children received a total of $A2,016·8m.

Additional Family Payment—payable subject to an income test to families with one or more children eligible for family allowances so long as they are not in receipt of any Commonwealth pension, benefit or allowance which provides additional payment for dependent children; this is not taxable.

In 1991–92, 241,241 families received a total $A723·9m.; in 1994–95 payments totalled $A3,535m.

From 1 Jan. 1996 Additional Family Payment was amalgamated with Basic Family Payment.

Child disability allowance—payable to parents or guardians of severely physically or mentally handicapped children in the family home and needing constant care and attention. The allowance is free of an income test but is subject to a residence qualification similar to that for family allowance.

In 1994–95 allowances totalling $A185·1m. were paid on behalf of 87,123 children.

Double orphan's pension—the guardian of a child under 16 years of age or of a full-time student under 25, both of whose parents are dead, or one of whose parents is dead and the whereabouts of the other parent unknown, and for refugee children where both parents are outside Australia or in prison, may receive double orphan's pension. The payment is not subject to an income test nor is it taxable. The amount paid out in 1994–95 was $A1·6m. to 1,314 recipients.

Unemployment and sickness benefits—are paid, subject to an income test, to persons between the ages of 18 and 16 respectively and age pensioners who are unemployed, able and willing to work and making efforts to obtain work, or temporarily unable to work because of sickness or injury. Unemployment benefit was replaced in July 1991 by a two-payment structure under the 'Newstart Strategy'. A 'Jobsearch Allowance' is payable to persons aged 18 and over who have been unemployed for less than 12 months, and to unemployed 16 and 17-year olds. A 'Newstart Allowance' is payable to those who have been unemployed for more than 1 year and are aged 18 and over. Income support under this structure is means-tested and linked to active labour market programmes. To be granted benefit a person must have resided in Australia for at least 12 months preceding his or her claim or intend to remain in Australia permanently. For unemployment benefit purposes unemployment must not be due to industrial action by that person or by members of a union to which that person is a member. Special benefits may be granted to persons not qualified above. 773,659 unemployment beneficiaries received a total of $A7,061m. in the year to June 1996; 46,050 sickness beneficiaries received a total of $A413·2m. in the year to June 1996 and 39,026 mature age allowance beneficiaries received a total of $A356·6m. in the year ended June 1995.

Service Pensions are paid by the Department of Veterans' Affairs, similar to the age and invalid pensions provided by the Department of Social Security. Male Veterans who have reached the age of 60 years or are permanently unemployable, and who served in a theatre of war, are eligible subject to an income test. Female Veterans who served abroad and who have reached the age of 55 or are permanently unemployable, are also eligible. Wives of service pensioners are also eligible provided that they do not receive a pension from the Department of Social Security. *Disability pension* is a compensatory payment in respect of incapacity attributable to war service. It is paid at a rate commensurate with the degree of incapacity and is free of any income test. A separate allowance may be paid to dependants. In 1993–94 $A2,382m. of service pensions and $A1,507m. of disability and dependants' pensions were paid out; in 1994 there were 325,800 eligible veterans.

In addition to cash benefits, welfare services are provided either directly or through State and Local government authorities and voluntary agencies, for people with special needs.

Medicare. On 1 Feb. 1984 the Commonwealth Government introduced a universal health scheme known as Medicare. This covers: Automatic entitlement under a single public health fund to medical and optometrical benefits of 85% of the Medical Benefits Schedule fee, with a maximum patient payment for any service where the Schedule fee is charged; access without direct charge to public hospital accommodation and to inpatient and outpatient treatment by doctors appointed by the hospital; the restoration of funds for community health to approximately the same real level as 1975; a reduction in charges for private treatment in shared wards of public hospitals, and increases in the daily bed subsidy payable to private hospitals.

The Medicare programme is financed in part by a 1·5% levy on taxable incomes, with low income cut-off points, which were $A12,689 p.a. for a single person in 1995 and $A22,975 p.a. for a family with an extra allowance of $A2,258 for each child. The Commonwealth Government subsidises registered health insurance organizations by contributing to the Health Benefits, and makes an annual contribution to the Reinsurance Trust Fund of $A20m. for payments of benefits to patients with hospital treatment in excess of 35 days.

Medicare benefits are available to all persons ordinarily resident in Australia. Visitors from the UK, New Zealand, Italy, Sweden, the Netherlands and Malta have immediate access to necessary medical treatment, as do all visitors staying more than 6 months.

Medical Benefits. The Health Insurance Act provides for a Medical Benefits Schedule which lists medical services and the Schedule (standard) fee applicable in each State in respect of each medical service. Schedule fees are set and updated by an independent fees tribunal appointed by the Government. The fees so determined are to apply for Medicare benefits purposes.

Home and Community Care Program was introduced in 1985 to provide support services to enable aged and disabled persons to live at home. It is jointly funded by the Commonwealth and State or Territory Governments. Commonwealth funding was $A399m. in 1994–95.

Culture. In 1993 there were over 1,700 museums and art museums operating in Australia. 39m. people aged 15 years and over visited a museum at least once in the year ending March 1995, while 313m. visited an art museum.

At March 1995, 2,722,100 people aged 15 years and over had attended at least one performance of musical theatre in the past year; 2,336,300 people, other theatre; 2,634,400 people, other performing arts; 1,407,500 people, dance performances. Popular music concerts were attended by 3,790,700 people and classical music concerts by 2,634,400.

In 1993 there were 515 cinemas (940 screens). In the year ending March 1995, attendance at cinemas by people aged 15 years and over was 8,734,000.

In the year ending March 1995, 5,403,100 people visited a national, State or local library at least once.

DIPLOMATIC REPRESENTATIVES

Of Australia in Great Britain (Australia House, Strand, London, WC2B 4LA)
High Commissioner: Neal Blewett.

Of Great Britain in Australia (Commonwealth Ave., Canberra)
High Commissioner: A. C. S. Allan.

Of Australia in the USA (1601 Massachusetts Ave., NW, Washington, D.C., 20036)
Ambassador: John McCarthy.

Of the USA in Australia (Moonah Pl., Canberra)
Ambassador: Vacant.

Of Australia to the United Nations
Ambassador: Penelope Wensley.

Of Australia to the European Union
Ambassador: Donald Kenyon.

Further Reading

Australian Bureau of Statistics (ABS). *Year Book Australia.—Pocket Year Book Australia.—Monthly Summary of Statistics.* ABS also publish numerous specialized statistical digests.
Australian Encyclopædia. 12 vols. Sydney, 1983
Blainey, G., *A Short History of Australia.* Melbourne, 1996
The Cambridge Encyclopedia of Australia. CUP, 1994
Clark, M., *Manning Clark's History of Australia;* abridged by M. Cathcart. London, 1994
Concise Oxford Dictionary of Australian History. 2nd ed. OUP, 1995
Docherty, J. D., *Historical Dictionary of Australia.* Metuchen (NJ), 1993
Emy, H. and Hughes, O., *Australian Politics: Realities in Conflict.* Sydney, 1991
Gilbert, A. D. and Inglis, K. S. (eds.) *Australians: a Historical Library.* 5 vols. CUP, 1988
Hancock, K. (ed.) *Australian Society.* Cambridge Univ. Press, 1990
Hocking, B. (ed.) *Australia towards 2000.* London, 1990
Kepars, I., *Australia.* [Bibliography] 2nd ed. Oxford and Santa Barbara, 1994
Oxford History of Australia. vol 2: 1770–1860. OUP, 1992. vol 5: 1942–88. OUP, 1990
The Oxford Illustrated Dictionary of Australian History. OUP, 1993
Serle, P., *Dictionary of Australian Biography.* 2 vols. Sydney, 1949
Turnbull, M., *The Reluctant Republic.* London, 1994
Who's Who in Australia. Melbourne, 1906 to date

For other more specialized titles see under CONSTITUTION AND GOVERNMENT *and* AGRICULTURE, *above*

National library: The National Library, Canberra, ACT.
National statistical office: Australian Bureau of Statistics (ABS), Belconnen, ACT. The statistical services of the states are integrated with the Bureau.
ABS Website: http://www.statistics.gov.au/

AUSTRALIAN TERRITORIES

AUSTRALIAN CAPITAL TERRITORY

KEY HISTORICAL EVENTS. The area, now the Australian Capital Territory (ACT), was explored in 1820 by Charles Throsby, who named it Limestone Plains, and settlement commenced in 1824. Until its selection as the seat of government it was a quiet pastoral and agricultural community with a few large holdings and a sprinkling of smaller settlers.

In 1901 the Commonwealth constitution stipulated that a land tract of at least 260 sq. km in area and not less than 160 km from Sydney be set aside from New South Wales and reserved as a capital district. The Canberra, formerly called Yass-Canberra, site was adopted by the Seat of Government Act 1908. The present site, together with an area for a port at Jervis Bay, was surrendered by New South Wales and accepted by the Commonwealth in 1909, and by subsequential proclamation the Territory became vested in the Commonwealth from 1 Jan. 1911. In 1911 an international competition was held for the city plan. The plan chosen was that of W. Burley Griffin, of Chicago. Construction was delayed by the First World War and it was not until 1927 that, with the transfer of parliament and certain departments, Canberra became in fact the seat of government.

TERRITORY AND POPULATION. The area is 2,432 sq. km (including Jervis Bay area). Population (1996 census), 299,243. Vital statistics for 1995: Births, 4,415; deaths, 1,114; marriages, 1,753; divorces, 1,787. Infant mortality (per 1,000 live births), 4·8.

CONSTITUTION AND GOVERNMENT. The ACT became self-governing on 11 May 1989. It is represented by 3 members in the Commonwealth House of Representatives and 2 senators.

The parliament of the ACT, the *Legislative Assembly*, consists of 17 members elected for a 3-year term. Its responsibilities are at state and local government level. The Legislative Assembly elects a Chief Minister and a 3-member cabinet. At the elections of 19 Feb. 1995 the Liberal Party won 7 seats, Labor 6, Greens 2 and ind 2. The Liberals formed a coalition government with the minority parties.

Chief Minister: Kate Carnell.

FINANCE. In 1987–88 the ACT was given its own budget. It is treated equitably with the States regarding local revenue raising, expenditure and assistance by the Commonwealth government. In 1995–96 current outlays were $A1,131m., capital outlays $A189m. and revenue $A1,210m.

PRODUCTION. Outside Canberra the Territory is mainly reserved for forestry and nature conservation (Namadgi National Park is 105,000 ha). A considerable amount of reafforestation (mostly pine) has been undertaken, the total area of coniferous plantations at 30 June 1993 being 17,000 ha. Farming is mainly in grazing: Livestock (1995 estimate), 12,780 cattle, 77,741 sheep, and 269,875 poultry. In 1994-95, 1,052 tonnes of beef and veal and 440 tonnes of greasy wool were produced.

EDUCATION. In Feb. 1997 there were 185 government schools comprising 82 pre-schools, 98 primary and secondary schools (including colleges) and 5 special schools. There were 44,066 students in government schools; 4,035 in pre-schools, 21,762 in primary schools, 11,058 in high schools, 6,815 in colleges and 396 in special schools. Non-government schools numbered 46 comprising 4 pre-schools and 42 primary and secondary schools (including colleges). There were 21,795 students in non-government schools: 87 in pre-schools, 10,637 in primary schools, 8,229 in high schools and 2,842 in colleges. Vocational education and training is provided by the Canberra Institute of Technology and the ACT Schools Authority, which had an estimated total of 18,809 students in 1995. There are 4 higher education institutions: The Australian National University (9,925 students in 1996); the University of Canberra (8,541); the Australian Defence Force Academy (1,527); the Australian Catholic University (566).

Further Reading

Australian Capital Territory in Focus (formerly *Statistical Summary*). Australian Bureau of Statistics. Annual.
Wigmore, L., *Canberra: A History of Australia's National Capital.* 2nd ed. Canberra, 1971

NORTHERN TERRITORY

KEY HISTORICAL EVENTS. The Northern Territory, after forming part of New South Wales, was annexed on 6 July 1863 to South Australia and in 1901 entered the Commonwealth as a corporate part of South Australia. The Commonwealth Constitution Act of 1900 made provision for the surrender to the Commonwealth of any territory by any state, and under this provision an agreement was entered into on 7 Dec. 1907 for the transfer of the Northern Territory to the Commonwealth, and it formally passed under the control of the Commonwealth Government on 1 Jan. 1911.

On 1 Feb. 1927, the Northern Territory was divided for administrative purposes into two territories but in 1931 it was again administered as a single territory under the control of an Administrator in Darwin.

The Legislative Council for the Northern Territory, constituted in 1947, was reconstituted in 1959. On 1 July 1978, self-government was granted to the Northern Territory.

TERRITORY AND POPULATION. The Northern Territory is bounded by the 26th parallel of S. lat. and 129° and 138° E. long. Its total area is 1,346,200 sq. km and includes adjacent islands. The greater part of the interior consists of a tableland rising gradually from the coast to a height of about 700 metres. On this tableland there are large areas of excellent pasturage. The southern part of the Territory is generally sandy and has a small rainfall, but water may be obtained by means of sub-artesian bores.

The population of the Territory at the 1996 Census was 195,101. The capital, seat of Government and principal port is Darwin, on the north coast; population 66,800 in June 1995. Other main centres include Katherine (10,809), 330 km south of Darwin; Alice Springs (27,902), in Central Australia; Tennant Creek (3,856), a rich mining centre 500 km north of Alice Springs; Nhulunbuy (3,920), a bauxite mining centre in the Gove Peninsula Province in eastern Arnhem Land; and Jabiru, a model town built to serve the rich Uranium Province in eastern Arnhem Land. Palmerston is a Darwin satellite town (13,121); Yulara (2,217) is a resort village serving Uluru National Park and Ayers Rock. There also are a number of large self-contained Aboriginal communities. People identifying themselves as Aboriginal numbered 44,486 and Torres Strait Islanders 714 at the 1996 Census.

Vital statistics for 1995: Births, 3,766; deaths, 813; marriages, 797; divorces, 432. Infant mortality per 1,000 live births, 14.

CONSTITUTION AND GOVERNMENT. The Northern Territory (Self-Government) Act 1978 established the Northern Territory as a body politic as from 1 July 1978, with Ministers having control over and responsibility for Territory finances and the administration of the functions of government as specified by the Federal Government. Regulations have been made conferring executive authority for the bulk of administrative functions. At 31 Dec. 1979 the only important powers retained by the Commonwealth related to rights in respect of Aboriginal land, some significant National Parks and the mining of uranium and other substances prescribed in the Atomic Energy Act. Proposed laws passed by the Legislative Assembly require the assent of the Administrator. The Governor-General may disallow any law assented to by the Administrator within 6 months of the Administrator's assent.

The Northern Territory has federal representation, electing 1 member to the House of Representatives and 2 members to the Senate.

The Legislative Assembly has 25 members, directly elected for a period of 4 years. The Chief Minister, Deputy Chief Minister and Speaker are elected by, and from, the members. The *Administrator* (Dr Neil Conn) appoints Ministers on the advice of the Leader of the majority party.

The Legislative Assembly elected in 1994 comprised in 1997: Country Liberal Party, 18; Australian Labor Party, 7.

The Country Liberal Party Cabinet was as follows in March. 1998:
Chief Minister, Attorney-General, Minister for Young Territorians, Women's Policy, Statehood, Defence Support: Shane Stone.

*Deputy Chief Minister, Treasurer, Police, Fire and Emergency Services, Tourism,
Public Employment, Industrial Relations:* Mike Reed. *Leader of Government
Business, Transport and Infrastructure Development, Territory Ports, the Austral
Asia Railway:* Barry Coulter. *Vice President Executive Council, Health, Family and
Children's Services, Senior Territorians, Work Health, Minister responsible for the
Menzies School of Health Research and for the Liquor Commission:* Denis Burke.
Resource Development, Correctional Services, Essential Services: Eric Poole. *Asian
Relations, Trade and Industry, Regional Development, the Arts and Museums,
Minister responsible for the Territory Insurance Office:* Daryl Manzie. *Lands,
Planning and Environment, Primary Industry and Fisheries, Ethnic Affairs:* Nick
Palmer. *Education and Training, Communications and Advanced Technology, Racing
and Gaming, Sport and Recreation:* Peter Adamson. *Parks and Wildlife, Aboriginal
Development, Local Government, Housing:* Tim Baldwin.

Local Government. Local government was established in Darwin in 1957 and later in
3 regional centres. These are each managed by a mayor and a municipal council
elected at intervals of not more than 4 years by universal adult franchise. Provision
has been made for a limited form of local government for smaller communities. In
1996 there were 6 municipal and 32 community government councils and 29 other
incorporated community associations responsible for local government.

FINANCE. Budgets in $A1m.:

	1992–93	1993–94	1994–95	1995–96	1996–97
Revenue	1,400	1,451	1,512	1,645	1,720
Expenditure	1,502	1,844	1,584	1,601	1,702

Using uniform presentation standards, total revenue in 1996–97 was $A1,720m. of
which $A1,237m. were grants to the Northern Territory from the Commonwealth,
and $A348m. was raised by the Northern Territory Government which included
$A309m. through state-like taxes.

Expenditure during 1996–97 included $A348m. for education; $A47m. for housing and community amenities; $A306m. for health; $A165m. for public order and
safety and $A129m. for transport and communication.

$A81m. of Territory borrowings were repaid in 1996–97, while other financing
transactions of $A9m. (consisting mainly of cash balances) were used. Net debt
declined by $A42m. to $A1,311m.

ENERGY AND NATURAL RESOURCES

Oil and Gas. Significant oil and gas reserves have been discovered and developed
offshore in the Joseph Bonaparte Gulf and Timor Sea areas and onshore in the
Amadeus Basin. In 1995, 1,718 megalitres of oil (97% from offshore fields in the
Timor Sea) and 383,746 megalitres of natural gas were produced. Total value of oil
and gas production in 1994–95 was $A281·25m. and in 1996–97 about $A229m.
Natural gas is piped from the Amadeus Basin to Darwin. In 1998, 15 offshore oil and
gas fields had been discovered in the past 4 years (7 of them in 1997), with a success
rate of about 30%, and development and exploration programmes were under way.

Minerals. The most important natural resources are minerals, and mining is one of
the largest industries. Value of production (including uranium) in 1996–97 was estimated at $A1,438m., including (in $A1m.): Gold bullion, 347; manganese ore, 226;
bauxite, 131; alumina, 356; base metals, 221; uranium oxide, 110. In 1994–95 the
Territory produced 90% of Australia's manganese, 14·5% of its bauxite and 6·5% of
gold bullion. In terms of value it produced 29% of its uranium. In the financial year
1995–96 mining contributed 11·7% ($A530m.) of Gross State Product.

Agriculture. Cattle production constitutes the largest farming industry. Livestock,
1995–96: Cattle, 1,501,587; domesticated buffalo, 8,850; pigs, 2,500; horses, 6,977.
In 1996 the total value of the cattle industry was $A133·7m., from which 199,044
head were exported live at a value of $A848m. The value of other animal industries
including buffalo, pigs, poultry, eggs, milk and crocodiles was estimated at $A154m.
in 1996. In 1997 there were 8 crocodile farms: Production at 2 with abattoir facilities

comprised 4,595 animals slaughtered and 15,689 kg of meat sold in the period 1 Jan.–30 June 1997.
Horticultural production was valued at $A414m. in 1996 for fruit and vegetables. The main crops were mangoes, bananas, melons and grapes.
In 1995–96, 3,894 ha were used for grain crops, seed and hay production with an industry value of $A24m.

Fisheries. The total value of the fishing industry in 1996 was $A107·1m. Of this, prawns contributed $A30·8m.; aquaculture, $A55m.; barramundi, $A2·8m.; mud crab, $A7·4m.; all snapper species, $A3·5m.; shark, $A1·8m. The expanding aquaculture industry produces crayfish, prawns, giant clams and beta carotene extracts.

Environment. There are 93 parks and reserves covering 43,709 sq. km. Twelve of the parks are classified as national parks, including the Kakadu and Uluru-Kata Tjuta National Park.

INDUSTRY. In 1994 there were 255 manufacturing establishments (with 4 or more persons employed). Turnover was $A673m. in 1991–92. 2,700 persons were employed in manufacturing in 1994. In the financial year 1995–96 manufacturing contributed 5% ($A277m.) of Gross State Product.

Labour. The labour force totalled 94,100 in Nov. 1997, of whom 90,500 were employed. The unemployment rate was 3·9%.

Trade Unions. At June 1995, 27 trade unions had 19,000 members.

Tourism. In 1995–96, nearly 13m. people visited the Territory, with tourist expenditure totalling $A715·9m.

COMMUNICATIONS

Roads. There were (in 1997) 6,269 km of sealed road. They include three major interstate links: The Stuart Highway from Darwin to the South Australian border (1,787 km), the Barkley Highway, Three Ways to the Queensland border (434 km), and the Victoria Highway, Katherine to the Western Australian border (470 km). In addition to this there were 6,550 km of gravel roads and 4,795 km of formed roads. Total roads, excluding township and municipal, 20,926 km. Registered motor vehicles (excluding tractors and trailers) at 31 Oct. 1997 numbered 97,366, including 87,593 passenger vehicles and 3,798 motorcycles. There were 61 fatalities in road accidents in 1995.

Railways. In 1980 Alice Springs was linked to the Trans-continental network by a standard (1,435 mm) gauge railway to Tarcoola in South Australia (831 km). In 1998 the governments of the Northern Territory and South Australia were seeking the participation of the private sector to complete the construction of the Austral Asia Railway. The completion of the railway between Darwin and Alice Springs (1,410 km) will be a strategic link in the seamless Austral Asia Trade Route.

Civil Aviation. Darwin and most regional centres in the Territory are serviced by daily flights to all State capitals and major cities. There are direct international services connecting Darwin to Singapore, Kuala Lumpur, Bali, Brunei, Kupang and Tokyo. In 1996–97 Darwin airport handled 0·84m. domestic and 165,000 international passengers, Alice Springs 864,000 domestic passengers and Ayers Rock 265,000.

Shipping. Regular freight shipping services connect Darwin with both the east and west coasts of Australia, South East Asia and the rest of the world. In 1998 there were 10 shipping lines making regular calls, and cruise ships and naval vessels also include Darwin as a port of call.
The Port of Darwin is equipped to handle bulk, container and roll-on-roll-off traffic. 3,654 vessels visited the port and it handled 1,289,849 tonnes of cargo in 1996–97. There is a sheltered morning basin which provides 85 non-tidal berths.

Commercial and pleasure vessels also call at the ports of Melville Bay (Gove) and Milner Bay (Groote Eylandt) and at Seven Spirit Bay on a regular basis.

Telecommunications. Darwin's radio services include 4 ABC stations, 1 SBS station, 2 commercial stations and a community station.

Darwin has 2 commercial, 1 ABC and 1 SBS TV service.

Alice Springs radio services include 4 ABC stations, 2 commercial and 2 community stations. It has 2 commercial, 1 ABC and 1 SBS TV service.

Most other Northern Territory centres have 1 commercial and 1 national radio service, with 1 each of ABC, SBS and commercial television, many of these being provided by self-help projects.

SOCIAL INSTITUTIONS

Justice. Voluntary euthanasia for the terminally ill was legalized in 1995. However, the federal Prime Minister stated that the High Court of Australia would consider cases of euthanasia as murder, and the law was overturned by the federal Senate on 24 March 1997. The first person to have recourse to legalized euthanasia died on 22 Sept. 1996.

Education. In 1995 there were 2,966 children and 82 teachers in 56 government and private pre-schools. Education is compulsory from the age of 6 to 15 years. There were (1995) 27,280 full-time students enrolled in 148 government primary, secondary and special schools with 2,028 full-time equivalent teaching staff, and 7,562 full-time students enrolled in 26 private primary and secondary schools with 514 full-time equivalent teaching staff. The proportion of migrant and of Aboriginal and Torres Strait Islander students in the Territory is high, with the 2 latter comprising 34·7% of all full-time enrolments in 1995 (9,169 primary and 2,905 secondary students). Schools range from single classrooms and transportable units catering for the needs of small Aboriginal communities and pastoral properties to urban high schools and secondary colleges (years 11–12) catering for about 7,500 students. Bilingual programmes operate in some Aboriginal communities where traditional Aboriginal culture prevails. Secondary education extends from school years 8 to 12 (7 to 12 in Alice Springs). The Northern Territory University (NTU) was founded in 1989 by amalgamating the existing University College of the Northern Territory and the Darwin Institute of Technology, with the technical and further education courses hitherto offered by the latter to be conducted by an Institute of Technical and Further Education within the new University. At 31 March 1995, 4,350 students were enrolled in a total of 4,398 higher education courses at the NTU. Batchelor College, a multi-purpose institution of Aboriginal tertiary education, had 1,315 students enrolled in higher education or TAFE courses in 1995. There are 5 colleges of higher education, with a total of 3,943 full- and part-time students enrolled in 1993. The TAFE sector had 4,174 students enrolled in tertiary courses in 1992.

Health. In 1997 there were 6 hospitals (5 public and 1 private) with 711 beds. Community health services are provided from urban and rural Health Centres including mobile units. Remote communities are served by the Aerial Medical Service and by resident Aboriginal health workers.

Further Reading

Profile of Australia's Northern Territory—1997/98. Protocol and Public Affairs Branch, Dept. of the Chief Minister, GPO Box 4396, Darwin

The Northern Territory: Annual Report. Dept. of Territories, Canberra, from 1911. Dept. of the Interior, Canberra, from 1966–67. Dept. of Northern Territory, from 1972

Australian Territories, Dept. of Territories, Canberra, 1960 to 1973. Dept. of Special Minister of State, Canberra, 1973–75. Department of Administrative Services, 1976

Northern Territory in Focus (formerly *Statistical Summary*). Australian Bureau of Statistics, Canberra, from 1960

Donovan, P. F., *A Land Full of Possibilities: A History of South Australia's Northern Territory 1863–1911.* 1981.—*At the Other End of Australia: The Commonwealth and the Northern Territory 1911–1978.* Univ. of Queensland Press, 1984

Heatley, A., *The Government of the Northern Territory*. Univ. of Queensland Press, 1979.—
Almost Australians: the Politics of Northern Territory Self-Government. Australian National
Univ. Press, 1990
Mills, C. M., *A Bibliography of the Northern Territory*. Canberra, 1977
Powell, A., *Far Country: A Short History of the Northern Territory*. Melbourne Univ. Press,
1982

AUSTRALIAN EXTERNAL TERRITORIES

AUSTRALIAN ANTARCTIC TERRITORY. An Imperial Order in Council
of 7 Feb. 1933 placed under Australian authority all the islands and territories other
than Adélie Land situated south of 60° S. lat. and lying between 160° E. long. and
45° E. long. The Order came into force with a Proclamation issued by the Governor-
General on 24 Aug. 1936 after the passage of the Australian Antarctic Territory
Acceptance Act 1933. The boundaries of Adélie Land were definitively fixed by a
French Decree of 1 April 1938 as the islands and territories south of 60° S. lat. lying
between 136° E. long. and 142° E. long. The Australian Antarctic Territory Act 1954
declared that the laws in force in the Australian Capital Territory are, so far as they
are applicable and are not inconsistent with any ordinance made under the Act, in
force in the Australian Antarctic Territory.

The area of the territory is estimated at 6,119,818 sq. km (2,362,875 sq. miles).

There is a research station on MacRobertson Land at lat. 67° 37' S. and long. 62°
52' E. (Mawson), one on the coast of Princess Elizabeth Land at lat. 68° 34' S. and
long. 77° 58' E. (Davis) and one at lat. 66° 17' S. and long. 110° 32' E. (Casey). The
Antarctic Division also operates a station on Macquarie Island.

COCOS (KEELING) ISLANDS. The Cocos (Keeling) Islands are 2 separate
atolls comprising some 27 small coral islands with a total area of about 14·2 sq. km,
and are situated in the Indian Ocean at 12° 05' S. lat. and 96° 53' E. long. They lie
2,768 km north-west of Perth and 3,685 km west of Darwin.

The main islands are West Island (the largest, about 10 km from north to south) on
which is an airport and an animal quarantine station, and most of the European community; Home Island, occupied by the Cocos Malay community; Direction, South
and Horsburgh Islands, and North Keeling Island, 24 km to the north of the group.

The islands were discovered in 1609 by Capt. William Keeling but remained uninhabited until 1826. In 1857 the islands were annexed to the Crown; in 1878 responsibility was transferred from the Colonial Office to the Government of Ceylon, and
in 1886 to the Government of the Straits Settlement. By indenture in 1886 Queen
Victoria granted all land in the islands to George Clunies-Ross and his heirs in
perpetuity (with certain rights reserved to the Crown). In 1903 the islands were incorporated in the Settlement of Singapore and in 1942–46 temporarily placed under the
Governor of Ceylon. In 1946 a Resident Administrator, responsible to the Governor
of Singapore, was appointed.

On 23 Nov. 1955 the Cocos Islands were placed under the authority of the
Australian Government as the Territory of Cocos (Keeling) Islands. An
Administrator, appointed by the Governor-General, is the Government's representative in the Territory and is responsible to the Minister for Territories and Local
Government. The Cocos (Keeling) Islands Council, established as the elected body
of the Cocos Malay community in July 1979, advises the Administrator on all issues
affecting the Territory.

In 1978 the Australian Government purchased the Clunies-Ross family's entire
interests in the islands, except for the family residence. A Cocos Malay co-operative
was established to take over the running of the Clunies-Ross copra plantation and to
engage in other business with the Commonwealth in the Territory, including construction projects. In 1993 the Australian Government took control of the Clunies-
Ross family residence also.

The population of the Territory (1993) was 593, distributed between Home Island
(75%) and West Island (25%).

The islands are low-lying, flat and thickly covered by coconut palms, and surround a lagoon in which ships drawing up to 7 metres may be anchored, but which is extremely difficult for navigation.

An equable and pleasant climate, affected for much of the year by the south-east trade winds. Temperatures range over the year from 68° F (20° C) to 88° F (31·1° C) and rainfall averages 80" (2,000 mm) a year.

The Cocos (Keeling) Islands Act 1955 is the basis of the Territory's administrative, legislative and judicial systems. Under section 8 of this Act, those laws which were in force in the Territory immediately before the transfer continued in force there.

Roads. There are 15 km of roads.

Civil Aviation. There are 5 flights a fortnight to Perth (Western Australia), 1 weekly to Singapore and 1 daily to Jakarta (Indonesia).

Telecommunications. In 1992 there were 190 radio receivers and 287 telephones.

Religion. About 85% are Moslems and 15% Christians.

Education. In 1992 there were 2 primary schools (on Home Island and West Island) with 98 pupils and 7 teachers and 1 teaching assistant, 2 secondary schools with 70 pupils and 9 teachers and 1 teaching assistant, and 29 students in a technical school.

Health. In 1992 there was 1 doctor and 7 nursing personnel, with 5 beds in clinics.

Administrator: Barry Cunningham.

CHRISTMAS ISLAND is an isolated peak in the Indian Ocean, lat. 10° 25' 22" S., long. 105° 39' 59" E. It lies 360 km S. 8° E. of Java Head, and 417 km N. 79° E. from Cocos Islands, 1,310 km from Singapore and 2,623 km from Fremantle. Area about 135 sq. km. The climate is tropical with temperatures varying little over the year at 27° C. The wet season lasts from Nov. to April with an annual total of about 2,673 mm. The island was formally annexed by the UK on 6 June 1888, placed under the administration of the Governor of the Straits Settlements in 1889, and incorporated with the Settlement of Singapore in 1900. Sovereignty was transferred to the Australian Government on 1 Oct. 1958. The population at the 1991 census was 1,275; 1994 estimate, 2,500 of whom 1,300 were of Chinese, 400 of Malay and 800 of Australian/European origin.

The legislative, judicial and administrative systems are regulated by the Christmas Island Act, 1958–73. They are the responsibility of the Commonwealth Government and operated by an Administrator. The Territory underwent major changes to its legal system when the Federal Parliament passed the Territories Law Reform Bill of 1992; Commonwealth and State laws applying in the state of Western Australia now apply in the Territory as a result, although some laws have been repealed to take into account the unique status of the Territory. The first Island Assembly was elected in Sept. 1985, and is now replaced by the elected members of the Christmas Island Shire Council.

Extraction and export of rock phosphate dust is the main industry. The Government is also encouraging the private sector development of tourism.

Electricity. Production (1994–95) 20m. kWh.

Roads. In 1993 there were 205 km of roads, 917 passenger cars and 362 commercial vehicles.

Civil Aviation. There are twice-weekly flights to Perth (Western Australia), fortnightly to Singapore, and weekly to Jakarta (Indonesia).

Shipping. In 1991, 40,000 tonnes of cargo were loaded and 45,600 tonnes discharged at the port. 2,000 cu. metres of general cargo were also discharged.

Telecommunications (1992). There is one post office and 1,500 radio receivers. A local radio and television station operate 24 hours per day.

Religion. About 50% are Buddhists or Taoists, 16% Moslems and 30% Christians.

Education. In 1995 there was a district high school with 50 pre-primary, 369 primary and 73 secondary level pupils.

Health. In 1994 there were 2 doctors, a visiting dentist, a pharmacist, and 1 hospital with 10 beds.

Administrator: M. J. Grimes.

NORFOLK ISLAND. 29° 02' S. lat. 167° 57' E. long., area 3,455 ha, population, (June 1993), 1,896. The island was formerly part of the colony of New South Wales and then of Van Diemen's Land. It was a penal colony 1788–1814 and 1825–55. In 1856 it received all 194 descendants of the *Bounty* mutineers from Pitcairn Island. It has been a distinct settlement since 1856, under the jurisdiction of the state of New South Wales; and finally by the passage of the Norfolk Island Act 1913, it was accepted as a Territory of the Australian Government. The Norfolk Island Act 1957 is the basis of the Territory's legislative, administrative and judicial systems. An Administrator, appointed by the Governor-General and responsible to the Minister for Territories and Local Government, is the senior government representative in the Territory.

The Norfolk Island Act 1979 gives Norfolk Island responsible legislative and executive government to enable it to run its own affairs to the greatest practicable extent. Wide powers are exercised by the Norfolk Island Legislative Assembly of 9 elected members, and by an Executive Council, comprising the executive members of the Legislative Assembly who have ministerial-type responsibilities. The seat of administration is Kingston, the only major settlement. The Act preserves the Commonwealth's responsibility for Norfolk Island as a Territory under its authority, indicating Parliament's intention that consideration would be given to an extension of the powers of the Legislative Assembly and the political and administrative institutions of Norfolk Island within 5 years. Some powers were transferred in 1985 and further transfers are being considered.

The office of the Administrator's financed from Commonwealth expenditure which in 1991–92 was approximately $A493,000; local revenue for 1990–91 totalled $A6,411,000; expenditure, $A6,222,000.

Public revenue is derived mainly from tourism, the sale of postage stamps, customs duties, liquor sales and company registration and licence fees. Residents are not liable for income tax on earnings within the Territory, nor are death and personal stamp duties levied.

In 1991–92, 27,351 visitors travelled to Norfolk Island. Descendants of the *Bounty* mutineer families constitute the 'original' settlers and are known locally as 'Islanders', while later settlers, mostly from Australia, New Zealand and the UK, are identified as 'mainlanders'. Over the years the Islanders have preserved their own lifestyle and customs, and their language remains a mixture of West Country English, Gaelic and Tahitian.

Roads. There are 80 km of roads (53 km paved), 1,802 passenger cars and 90 commercial vehicles.

Telecommunications. There is one post office and (1984) 1,090 telephones, 400 television and (1987) 1,500 radio receivers.

Press. There is one weekly with a circulation of 1,200.

SOCIAL INSTITUTIONS

Justice. The island's Supreme Court sits as required and a Court of Petty Sessions exercises both civil and criminal jurisdiction.

Religion. 40% of the population are Anglicans.

Education. A school is run by the New South Wales Department of Education covering pre-school to 10th year. It had 322 pupils at 30 June 1990.

Health. In 1985 there were 2 doctors, a pharmacist and a hospital with 20 beds.

Administrator: Alan Gardner Kerr.

HEARD AND McDONALD ISLANDS. These islands, about 2,500 miles south-west of Fremantle, were transferred from UK to Australian control as from 26 Dec. 1947. Heard Island is about 43 km long and 21 km wide; Shag Island is about 8 km north of Heard. The total area is 412 sq. km (159 sq. miles). The McDonald Islands are 42 km to the west of Heard. In 1985–88 a major research programme was set up by the Australian National Antarctic Research Expeditions to investigate the wildlife as part of international studies of the Southern Ocean ecosystem. Subsequent expeditions followed from June 1990 throughout 1992.

TERRITORY OF ASHMORE AND CARTIER ISLANDS. By Imperial Order in Council of 23 July 1931, Ashmore Islands (known as Middle, East and West Islands) and Cartier Island, situated in the Indian Ocean, some 320 km off the north-west coast of Australia (area, 5 sq. km), were placed under the authority of the Commonwealth.

Under the Ashmore and Cartier Islands Acceptance Act, 1933, the islands were accepted by the Commonwealth under the name of the Territory of Ashmore and Cartier Islands, and the effective date was proclaimed by the Governor-General to be 10 May 1934. It was the intention that the Territory should be administered by the State of Western Australia, but owing to administrative difficulties the Territory was annexed to and deemed to form part of the Northern Territory of Australia (by amendment to the Act in 1938) with relevant laws of the Northern Territory, applying to the Territory of Ashmore and Cartier Islands. Responsibility for the administration of Ashmore and Cartier Islands rests with the Minister for the Arts, Sport, the Environment, Tourism and Territories.

On 16 Aug. 1983 a national nature reserve was declared over Ashmore Reef and the area so declared is now known as Ashmore Reef National Nature Reserve.

The islands are uninhabited but Indonesian fishing boats, which have traditionally plied the area, fish within the Territory and land to collect water in accordance with an agreement between the governments of Australia and Indonesia.

TERRITORY OF CORAL SEA ISLANDS. The Coral Sea Islands became a Territory of the Commonwealth of Australia under the Coral Sea Islands Act 1969. It comprises scattered reefs and islands over a sea area of about 1m. sq. km. The Territory is uninhabited apart from a meteorological station on Willis Island.

Further Reading

Australian Department of Arts, Sport, the Environment, Tourism and Territories. *Christmas Island: Annual Report.—Cocos (Keeling) Islands: Annual Report.—Norfolk Island: Annual Report.*

NEW SOUTH WALES

KEY HISTORICAL EVENTS. Originally, the name New South Wales was applied to the entire east coast of Australia when Capt. James Cook claimed the land for the British Crown on 23 Aug. 1770. The separate colonies of Tasmania, South Australia, Victoria and Queensland were proclaimed in the 19th century, and in 1911 and 1915 the Australian Capital Territory around Canberra and Jervis Bay was ceded to the Commonwealth. New South Wales was thus gradually reduced to its present area. The first settlement was made at Port Jackson in 1788 as a penal settlement; a partially elective council was established in 1843, and responsible government in 1856.

Gold discoveries from 1851 had brought a large influx of immigrants and responsible government was at first unstable, 7 ministries holding office in the 5 years after 1856. The times were somewhat lawless and bitter conflict arose from loose land laws enacted in 1861. Lack of transport hampered agricultural expansion.

New South Wales federated with the other Australian states to form the Commonwealth of Australia in 1901.

TERRITORY AND POPULATION. New South Wales is situated between the 29th and 38th parallels of S. lat. and 141st and 154th meridians of E. long., and comprises 309,433 sq. miles (801,600 sq. km), inclusive of Lord Howe Island, 6 sq. miles (17 sq. km), but exclusive of the Australian Capital Territory (911 sq. miles, 2,359 sq. km) and 28 sq. miles (73 sq. km) at Jervis Bay.

Lord Howe Island, 31° 33' 4" S., 159° 4' 26" E., which is part of New South Wales, is situated about 702 km north-east of Sydney; area, 1,654 ha, of which only about 120 ha are arable; resident population, estimate (30 June 1989), 320. The Island, which was discovered in 1788, is of volcanic origin. Mount Gower, the highest point, reaches a height of 866 metres.

The Lord Howe Island Board manages the affairs of the Island and supervises the Kentia palm-seed industry.

Census population of New South Wales (including full-blood Aboriginals from 1966):

	Males	Females	Persons	Population per sq. km	Average annual increase % since previous census
1901	710,264	645,091	1,355,355	2	1·86
1911	857,698	789,036	1,646,734	2	1·97
1921	1,071,501	1,028,870	2,100,371	3	2·46
1933	1,318,471	1,282,376	2,600,847	3	1·76
1947	1,492,211	1,492,627	2,984,838	4	0·99
1954	1,720,860	1,702,669	3,423,529	4	1·98
1961	1,972,909	1,944,104	3,917,013	5	1·94
1971	2,307,210	2,293,970	4,601,180	6	1·66
1981	2,548,984	2,577,233	5,126,217	6	1·42
1986	2,684,570	2,717,311	5,401,881	7	1·05
1991	2,844,532	2,886,415	5,730,947	7	6·10

The 1996 census population was 6,038,696. At 30 June 1995 the estimated resident population was 6,115,100 (3,076,400 females); population density, 7·6 per sq. km.

The state is divided into 12 *Statistical Divisions*. The population of these (in 1,000) in 1995 was: Sydney, 3,772·7; Hunter, 559; Illawarra, 369·2; Richmond-Tweed, 200·1; Mid-North Coast, 261·7; Northern, 187·6; North Western, 119·4; Central West, 174·7; South Eastern, 180·6; Murrumbidgee, 151·3; Murray, 111·4; Far West, 27·5. Population of the Statistical Subdivisions Newcastle (within Hunter) and Wollongong (within Illawarra) was 466 and 253·6 respectively.

Vital statistics for calendar years:

	Live births	Marriages	Divorces	Deaths
1993	89,354	39,993	14,753	43,069
1994	87,977	38,814	13,999	44,763
1995	87,849	37,828	14,945	44,773

The annual rates per 1,000 of mean estimated resident population in 1995 were: Births, 14·4; deaths, 7·3; marriages, 6·2; infant mortality, 5·7 per 1,000 live births. Expectation of life in 1995: Males, 74·95 years, females, 80·84.

CONSTITUTION AND GOVERNMENT. Within the State there are three levels of government: The Commonwealth Government, with authority derived from a written constitution; the State Government with residual powers; the local government authorities with powers based upon a State Act of Parliament, operating within incorporated areas extending over almost 90% of the State.

The Constitution of New South Wales is drawn from several diverse sources; certain Imperial statutes such as the Commonwealth of Australia Constitution Act (1900); the Australian States Constitution Act (1907); an element of inherited English law; amendments to the Commonwealth of Australia Constitution Act; the (State) Constitution Act; the Australia Acts of 1986; the Constitution (Amendment) Act 1987 and certain other State Statutes; numerous legal decisions; and a large amount of English and local convention.

The Parliament of New South Wales may legislate for the peace, welfare and good government of the State in all matters not specifically reserved to the Commonwealth Government.

The State Legislature consists of the Sovereign, represented by the Governor, and two Houses of Parliament, the Legislative Council (upper house) and the Legislative Assembly (lower house).

Australian citizens aged 18 and over, and other British subjects who were enrolled prior to 26 Jan. 1984, men and women aged 18 years and over, are entitled to the franchise. Voting is compulsory. The optional preferential method of voting is used for both houses.

The Legislative Council has 42 members elected for a term of office equivalent to three terms of the Legislative Assembly, with 21 members retiring at the same time as the Legislative Assembly elections. The whole State constitutes a single electoral district. In 1995, the Council consisted of the following parties: Australian Labor Party (ALP), 17; Liberal Party of Australia (Lib), 12; National Party (NP), 6; Call to Australia Group (CTA), 2; Australian Democrats (AD), 2; A Better Future for Our Children, 1; Shooters' Party, 1; The Greens, 1.

The Legislative Assembly has 99 members elected in single seat electoral districts for a maximum period of 4 years. The Legislative Assembly elected in 1995 consisted of the following parties: ALP, 50; Lib, 29; NP, 17; ind, 3.

Governor: Gordon J. Samuels, AC, QC, MA.

The New South Wales ALP Ministry, in March. 1998, was as follows:
Premier, Minister for Arts and Ethnic Affairs: Robert Carr (b. 1948).

Deputy Premier, Minister for Health and Aboriginal Affairs: Andrew Refshauge. *Treasury, State Development, Energy:* Michael Egan. *Police:* Paul Whelan. *Olympic Games:* Michael Knight, *Fair Trading and Emergency Services:* Brian Langton. *Transport and Roads:* Patrick Scully. *Education and Training:* John Aquilina. *Environment:* Pam Allan. *Public Works and Services:* Ronald Dyer. *Community Services, Ageing, Disability Services and Women:* Faye Lo Po'. *Attorney-General, Industrial Relations:* Jeffrey Shaw. *Agriculture, Land and Water Conservation:* Richard Amery. *Urban Affairs, Planning and Housing:* Craig Knowles. *Regional Development and Rural Affairs:* Harry Woods. *Energy, Tourism, Corrective Services:* Robert Debus. *Gaming and Racing:* Richard Face. *Mineral Resources and Fisheries:* Robert Martin. *Sport and Recreation:* Gabrielle Harrison. *Local Government:* Ernest Page. *Information Technology, Forestry and Ports:* Kimberley Yeadon.

The *Speaker* is John Murray.

Local Government. A system of local government extends over most of the State, including the whole of the Eastern and Central land divisions and almost three-quarters of the sparsely populated Western division. Since 1 July 1993, an area established for local government purposes is known as a council or city council, and the terms municipality or shire have been abandoned (except for Sutherland Shire). At 1 July 1993 there were 39 city councils and 138 councils. In addition there is one unincorporated area in the far west of the State. Local government councils most importantly provide the general services of administration, health, community amenities, recreation and culture, roads and debt servicing. County councils administer electricity or water supply or render other local services of common benefit in districts which comprise a number of councils.

ECONOMY

Budget. State Government outlays (in $A1m.) for financial years ending 30 June:

	1992–93	1993–94	1994–95
General public services	1,081	1,281	799
Public order and safety	1,695	1,737	1,892
Education	6,188	6,461	6,847
Health	3,883	4,098	4,408
Social security and welfare	1,234	1,389	1,442
Housing and community amenities	1,342	1,063	1,630
Recreation and culture	569	619	229

	1992–93	1993–94	1994–95
Fuel and energy	590	734	783
Agriculture, forestry and fishing	517	497	484
Mining, manufacturing and construction	16	23	25
Transport and communications	2,861	3,116	2,905
Other economic affairs	740	822	864
Other purposes	2,774	3,570	3,429
Total	*23,468*	*25,411*	*25,736*

State Government receipts for 1994–95 included taxes, fees and fines, $A10,561m. and Commonwealth Government grant, $A10,209m.

State Government taxes, fees and fines, by type:

	1992–93	1993–94	1994–95
Employers' payroll taxes	2,326	2,424	2,661
Taxes on property—			
Taxes on immovable property	671	596	537
Taxes on financial and capital transactions	1,941	2,479	2,395
Taxes on provision of goods and services—			
Excises and levies	30	31	30
Taxes on gambling	909	988	1,071
Taxes on insurance	722	753	784
Taxes on goods and performance of activities—			
Motor vehicle taxes	1,002	1,113	1,241
Franchise taxes	1,294	1,397	1,437
Other taxes on use of goods etc.	32	34	35
Fees and fines—			
Compulsory fees	193	206	200
Fines	191	182	170

Banking and Finance. Banking business is transacted chiefly by the Commonwealth Bank of Australia, the State Bank of New South Wales (government banks) and 3 private banks. In June 1996, 42 banking groups (15 domestic and 27 foreign) operated 2,245 branches and 3,463 agencies in New South Wales.

Lending activity of financial institutions in New South Wales in 1995–96 comprised (in $A1m.): Business loans, 61,435·2; personal, 11,000·1; house purchase, 17,118·9; lease financing, 3,260·8.

ENERGY AND NATURAL RESOURCES

Electricity. In 1994 the total nominal capacity of the Electricity Commission of New South Wales system was 11,520 MW. 57,700m. kWh were produced in 1994–95.

Minerals. New South Wales contains extensive mineral deposits. For the year ended 30 June 1995, turnover from 111 mining establishments in the coal and metal ore mining industries employing 14,869 people was $A4,618m. The value of selected metallic minerals produced in 1994–95 was $A578·5m.; industrial minerals, $A181·1m.; construction materials, $A475·7m. Output of principal products:

	1992–93	1993–94	1994–95
Antimony concentrates (tonnes)	2,114	812	1,129
Brick clay and shale (1,000 tonnes)	2,729	2,307	2,882
Coal (1,000 tonnes)	84,211	84,014	88,588
Copper concentrates (tonnes)	174,703	157,584	155,714
Gold (kg)	10,309	10,049	30,128
Lead concentrates (tonnes)	315,997	319,697	320,469
Limestone (1,000 tonnes)	3,554	3,809	4,004
Magnesite (tonne)	26,159	15,737	14,368
Magnetite (tonne)	45,670	43,808	39,920
Rutile concentrates (tonnes)	50,386	39,543	36,424
Construction sand (1,000 tonnes)	10,647	11,030	10,645
Zinc concentrates (tonnes)	586,300	599,258	604,879
Zircon concentrates (tonnes)	44,510	34,803	31,329

Agriculture. In 1994–95 GDP at factor cost for agriculture, forestry, hunting and fishing was $A2,809m. Farm income (including Australian Capital Territory) was $A116m. At 31 March 1995 there were 42,288 establishments with agricultural activity. These had an area of 603m. ha, of which 34m. ha were used for cropping.

Principal crops in the years ended 31 March 1994 (and 1995) with production in tonnes: Wheat for grain, 5,086 (875); barley for grain, 1,357 (291); oats for grain, 618 (197); rice, 1,042 (1,016); cotton (raw and seed), 766 (756); oilseeds, 298 (147); sugar-cane, 1,674 (1,825); hay, 1,259 (799). (Data relates to farms whose estimated value of agricultural operations was $A5,000 or more at the census.)

The total area under grapes at 31 March 1995 was 14,437 ha (including 1,811 ha not bearing); the production of table grapes was 8,439 tonnes; of wine grapes, 104,687 tonnes; for drying, 25,823 tonnes (fresh weight).

In 1994–95, there were 3,225 ha of banana plantations; production, 41,900 tonnes. There were 4·16m. citrus fruit trees; production (1994), 260,491 tonnes.

At 31 March 1995 there were 42·87m. sheep and lambs, 5·87m. beef cattle, 0·37m. dairy cattle and 0·79m. pigs. The production of shorn and crutched wool in 1993–94 was 222,640 tonnes (greasy). In 1995–96 production (in tonnes) of butter was 5,195; cheese, 18,287; beef and veal, 479,000; mutton, 120,848 and lamb, 63,436; pig meat, 96,272.

INDUSTRY AND TRADE

Industry. A wide range of manufacturing is undertaken in the Sydney area, and there are large iron and steel works near the coalfields at Newcastle and Port Kembla.

Manufacturing establishments' operations, 1993–94:

Industry	No. of establishments[1]	No. of persons employed[2]	Wages and salaries[3] ($A1m.)	Turnover ($A1m.)
Food, beverages and tobacco	1,000	50,402	1,629·2	12,413·8
Textiles, clothing, footwear and leather	1,531	23,212	540·2	2,955·5
Wood and paper products	1,401	19,197	542·2	3,370·6
Printing, publishing and recorded media	2,039	35,179	1,182·4	5,423·9
Petroleum, coal, chemical and associated products	1,052	33,051	1,222·9	11,266·0
Non-metallic mineral products	574	11,620	402·6	2,747·9
Metal products	2,747	55,924	2,012·5	13,199·0
Machinery and equipment	3,049	62,046	2,034·3	9,578·7
Other manufacturing	1,788	16,169	384·0	1,752·1
Total manufacturing	15,181	306,799	9,950·2	62,707·6

[1] Operating at 30 June 1994.
[2] Persons employed at 30 June 1994, including working proprietors.
[3] Excludes drawings of working proprietors.

Some of the principal articles manufactured in 1995–96 were: 757,000 tonnes of plain wheat flour; 635m. clay bricks; 68·54m. sq. metres of man-made fibre woven fabric; 1,821,000 sq. metres of textile floor coverings; 3,925,000 pairs of footwear; 4·68m. men's and boys' shirts; 798,000 tonnes of hardwood chips; 361,000 tonnes of plastics in primary forms.

Labour. In May 1996 the labour force was estimated to number 3,017,400 persons, of whom 2,785,600 were employed: 488,800 as salespersons and personal service workers; 466,800 as clerks; 436,800 as professionals; 388,900 as labourers and related workers; 379,100 as tradepersons; 288,800 as managers and administrators; 179,100 as plant and machine operators and drivers, and 157,200 as para-professionals. There were 231,900 unemployed.

Industrial tribunals are authorized to fix minimum rates of wages and other conditions of employment. Their awards may be enforced by law, as may be industrial agreements between employers and organizations of employees, when registered.

The principal State arbitration and conciliation tribunal is the Industrial Commission of New South Wales. The Commission is empowered to exercise all the powers conferred on subsidiary tribunals, and has in addition authority to determine any widely defined 'industrial matter', to adjudicate in case of illegal strikes and lockouts, to investigate union ballots when irregularities are alleged and to hear appeals from subsidiary tribunals. Subsidiary tribunals are Conciliation Committees for various industries, each having an equal number representing employers and employees and a Conciliation Commissioner as chairman.

Trade Unions. Registration of trade unions is effected under the New South Wales Trade Union Act 1881, which follows substantially the Trade Union Acts of 1871 and 1876 of England. Registration confers a quasi-corporate existence with power to hold property, to sue and be sued, etc., and the various classes of employees covered by the union are required to be prescribed by the constitution of the union. For the purpose of bringing an industry under the review of the State industrial tribunals, or participating in proceedings relating to disputes before Commonwealth tribunals, employees and employers must be registered as industrial unions, under State or Commonwealth industrial legislation respectively. At 30 June 1995 there were 73 trade unions with a total membership of 1,001,600.

Commerce. External commerce, exclusive of inter-state trade, is included in the statement of the commerce of Australia. Overseas commerce of New South Wales in $A1m. for years ending 30 June:

	Imports	Exports		Imports	Exports
1990-91	22,383	11,992	1993-94	28,491	14,651
1991-92	23,296	11,700	1994-95	33,280	15,199
1992-93	26,418	13,156	1995-96	34,927	16,592

The major commodities exported in 1995–96 (in $A1m.) were coal, not agglomerated (3,289·9), aluminium (1,106·1), wool and other animal hair (716·3), meat (542·6) and parts and accessories for office machines and computers (503·1). Principal imports were computers (2,898·6), parts and accessories for computers (1,694·4), telecommunications equipment, parts and accessories of radio, TV, video, etc. (1,603) and medical and private motor vehicles (1,464·1).

Principal destinations of exports in 1995–96 (in $A1m.) were Japan (4,051·2), New Zealand (1,592·3), South Korea (1,199·2), Hong Kong (1,018·2), USA (918·3) and Taiwan (913·8). Major sources of supply were USA (8,431), Japan (4,251·3), UK (2,408·8), Germany (2,075·3), China (1,759·5), Taiwan (1,414·1) and New Zealand (1,409·9).

Tourism. In the year ended 30 June 1996, 1,719,900 overseas visitors arrived for short term visits. At 30 June 1996 there were 1,743 hotels and motels providing 57,920 rooms, and 791 caravan parks.

COMMUNICATIONS

Roads. In 1996 there were 179,960 km of public roads of all sorts. The Roads and Traffic Authority of New South Wales is responsible for the administration and upkeep of major roads. In 1996 there were 20,350 km of roads under its control, comprising 3,010 km of national highways, 14,370 km of state roads and 2,970 km of regional and local roads.

The number of registered motor vehicles (excluding tractors and trailers) at 31 May 1995 was 3,332,500, including 2,684,800 passenger vehicles, 430,800 light commercial vehicles, 127,600 trucks, 13,500 buses and 75,800 motor cycles. There were 617 fatalities in road accidents in 1995–96.

Railways. In 1996 the Rail Access Corporation was formed to own and maintain the railway infrastructure. It leases trackage rights to the State Rail Authority, which operates passenger trains, and to the Freight Rail Corporation. At 30 June 1996, 8,851 km of government railway were open (618 km electrified). In 1995–96, 258·8m. passengers were carried and 63·84m. tonnes of freight. Also open for traffic are 325 km of Victorian Government railways which extend over the border; 68 km of private railways (mainly in mining districts) and 53 km of Commonwealth Government-owned track.

A tramway opened in Sydney in 1996. There is also a small overhead railway in the city centre.

Civil Aviation. Sydney is the major airport in New South Wales and Australia's principal international air terminal.

Shipping. The main ports are at Sydney, Newcastle, Port Kembla and Botany Bay. Visits by vessels to the ports of New South Wales in 1992–93 totalled 4,245 (97·43m. GRT). The number of overseas vessels which entered in 1992–93 was 3,091.

SOCIAL INSTITUTIONS

Justice. Legal processes may be conducted in Local Courts presided over by magistrates or in higher courts (District Court or Supreme Court) presided over by judges. There is also an appellate jurisdiction. Persons charged with the more serious crimes must be tried before a higher court.

Children's Courts have been established with the object of removing children as far as possible from the atmosphere of a public court. There are also a number of tribunals exercising special jurisdiction, *e.g.*, the Industrial Commission and the Compensation Court.

At 4 June 1995 there were 6,414 persons in prison.

Religion. At the 1991 census of those who stated a religion, 29·5% were Roman Catholic and 27·3% Anglican. Non-Christian religions accounted for 3·5%.

Education. The State Government maintains a system of free primary and secondary education, and attendance at school is compulsory from 6 to 15 years of age. Nongovernment schools are subject to government inspection.

In 1995 there were 2,190 government schools with 755,252 pupils (448,325 primary and 306,927 secondary) and 48,839 teachers, and 865 non-government schools with 300,614 pupils (157,734 primary and 142,880 secondary) and 19,627 teachers.

There were 185,995 students in higher education in 1995. The largest number of students (23%) were enrolled in arts, humanities and social sciences.

The University of Sydney, founded in 1850, had 29,600 students in 1995. There are 7 colleges providing residential facilities at the university. The University of New England at Armidale, previously affiliated with the University of Sydney, was incorporated in 1954, and in 1995 had 13,815 students.

The University of New South Wales was established in 1949. Enrolments in 1995 numbered 26,534. There are 7 colleges providing residential facilities at the university. The University of Newcastle, previously affiliated with the University of New South Wales, was granted autonomy from 1965, and in 1995 had 17,047 students. The University of Wollongong, also previously associated with the University of New South Wales, became autonomous in 1975, and in 1995 had 11,641 students. Macquarie University in Sydney, established in 1964, had 17,370 students in 1995. In 1995 the University of Technology, Sydney, had 20,706 students, the University of Western Sydney, 22,803, and Charles Sturt University, 18,483.

Colleges of advanced education were merged with universities in 1990.

Post-school technical and further education is provided at State TAFE colleges. Enrolments in 1995 totalled 411,643 (87% being part-time).

Social Welfare. The Commonwealth Government makes provision for social benefits, such as age and disability pensions, widows' pensions, supporting parents' benefits, family allowances, and unemployment, sickness and special benefits.

The number of age and disability pensions (including wives' and carers' pensions) current in New South Wales on 30 June 1995 was: Age, 555,786 (carers, 15,649); disability, 205,054 (carers, 45,133). Expenditure for the year ended 30 June 1995 was $A4,174m. for age pensions and $A1,577m. for disability pensions.

In addition there were 21,084 widows' pensions current at 30 June 1995. Expenditure on widows' pensions totalled $A193m. Sole parent pensions, 109,804; expenditure was $A893m.

Under the Basic Family Payment scheme, which commenced in 1993, at 30 June 1995, 1,134,757 children and students in 586,158 families were receiving payments totalling $A684m.

254,222 unemployment, 16,102 sickness and 9,512 special benefits were payable in June 1995 totalling $A2,607m. (monthly average).

Direct State Government social welfare services are limited, for the most part, to the assistance of persons not eligible for Commonwealth Government pensions or benefits and the provision of certain forms of assistance not available from the Commonwealth Government. The State also subsidizes many approved services for needy persons.

Health. At 30 June 1995 there were 21,624 medical practitioners, 3,822 dentists and 73,178 nurses. In 1994 there were 210 public hospitals with 19,190 beds and 88 private hospitals with 5,855 beds.

Further Reading

Statistical Information: The NSW Government Statistician's Office was established in 1886, and in 1957 was integrated with the Commonwealth Bureau of Census and Statistics (now called the Australian Bureau of Statistics). *Deputy Commonwealth Statistician:* Denis Farrell. Its principal publications are:
New South Wales Year Book (1886/87–1900/01 under the title *Wealth and Progress of New South Wales*). Annual.—*Regional Statistics.—New South Wales Pocket Year Book.—Monthly Summary of Statistics.—New South Wales in Brief.*

State Library: The State Library of NSW, Macquarie St., Sydney.

QUEENSLAND

KEY HISTORICAL EVENTS. Queensland was first visited by Capt. Cook in 1770. From 1778 it was part of New South Wales and was formed into a separate colony, with the name of Queensland, by letters patent of 8 June 1859, and responsible government was conferred.

Although by 1868 gold had been discovered, wool was the colony's principal product. The first railway line was opened in 1865.

Queensland federated with the other Australian states to form the Commonwealth of Australia in 1901.

TERRITORY AND POPULATION. Queensland comprises the whole north-eastern portion of the Australian continent, including the adjacent islands in the Pacific Ocean and in the Gulf of Carpentaria. Estimated area 1,727,200 sq. km.

The increase in the population as shown by the censuses since 1901 has been as follows (including Aboriginals from 1966):

Year	Census counts Males	Females	Total	Intercensal increase Numerical	Rate per annum %
1901	277,003	221,126	498,129	—	—
1911	329,506	276,307	605,813	107,684	1·98
1921	398,969	357,003	755,972	150,159	2·24
1933	497,217	450,317	947,534	191,562	1·86
1947	567,471	538,944	1,106,415	158,881	1·11
1954	676,252	642,007	1,318,259	211,844	2·53
1961	774,579	744,249	1,518,828	200,569	2·04
1966	849,390	824,934	1,674,324	144,857	1·84
1971	921,665	905,400	1,827,065	152,741	1·76
1976	1,024,611	1,012,586	2,037,197	210,132	2·20
1981	1,153,404	1,141,719	2,295,123	257,926	2·41
1986	1,295,630	1,291,685	2,587,315	292,192	2·43
1991	1,482,406	1,495,404	2,977,810	390,495	2·60

The 1996 census population was 3,368,850. At the 1991 census there were 70,070 Aboriginals and Torres Strait Islanders.

Since the 1981 census, official population estimates are according to place of usual residence and are referred to as estimated resident population. Estimated resident population at 30 June 1995, 3,277,373.

Statistics on birthplaces from the 1991 census are as follows: Australia, 80·7% (83·6% in 1986); UK and Ireland, 6·2% (6·1%); other countries, 17·1% (14·4%); at sea and not stated, 2·3% (1·4%).

Vital statistics (including Aboriginals) for calendar years:

	Total births	Marriages	Divorces	Deaths
1992	46,240	20,316	8,984	20,496
1993	46,778	20,704	9,935	19,972
1994	46,578	20,798	9,762	21,655

The annual rates per 1,000 population in 1994 were: Marriages, 6·5; births, 14·6; deaths, 6·8. The infant death rate was 6·2 per 1,000 live births.

Brisbane, the capital, had at 30 June 1991 (estimate) a resident population of 1,358,000 (Statistical Division). The estimated resident populations of the other major centres (Statistical Districts) at 30 June 1995 (preliminary) were: Gold Coast-Tweed, (including that part in New South Wales) 326,859; Townsville, 124,925; Sunshine Coast, 150,187; Cairns, 100,891; Rockhampton, 67,764; Mackay, 58,641; Bundaberg, 54,821 and Gladstone, 36,885.

CONSTITUTION AND GOVERNMENT. Queensland, formerly a portion of New South Wales, was formed into a separate colony in 1859, and responsible government was conferred. The power of making laws and imposing taxes is vested in a parliament of one house—the *Legislative Assembly*, which comprises 89 members, returned from 4 electoral zones for 3 years, elected from single-member constituencies at compulsory ballot.

Queensland elects 26 members to the Commonwealth House of Representatives.

The Elections Act, 1983, provides franchise for all males and females, 18 years of age and over, qualified by 6 months' residence in Australia and 3 months in the electoral district.

Following a by-election to the Legislative Assembly in Feb. 1996 the Australian Labor Party held 44 seats, the National Party (NP), 29, the Liberal Party (LP), 15 and ind 1.

Governor of Queensland: Maj. Gen. Peter Arnison.

An NP-LP coalition government was formed in Feb 1996, comprising:
Premier: Robert Edward Borbridge.

Deputy Premier, Treasurer, Minister for the Arts: Joan Mary Sheldon. *Attorney-General and Justice:* Denver Edward Beanland. *Education:* Robert Joseph Quinn. *Public Works, Housing:* David J. H. Watson. *Economic Development and Trade, Minister assisting the Premier:* Douglas John Slack. *Transport and Main Roads:* Vaughan Gregory Johnson. *Police and Corrective Services, Racing:* Theo Russell Cooper. *Environment:* Brian George Littleproud. *Local Government and Planning:* Diane Elizabeth McCauley. *Health:* Michael James Horan. *Training and Industrial Relations:* Santo Santoro. *Natural Resources:* Lawrence James Springborg. *Mines and Energy:* Thomas John Gilmore. *Emergency Services, Sport:* Michael Desmond Veivers. *Tourism, Small Business and Industry:* Bruce William Davidson. *Families, Youth and Community Care:* Naomi K. W. Wilson. *Primary Industries, Fisheries and Forestry:* Marcus Hosking Rowell.

Leader of the House: Anthony Fitzgerald.

Local Government. At 1 July 1994, following a reorganization of local government boundaries, the state was subdivided into 18 cities, 3 towns and 107 shires. These are under the management of aldermen or councillors, who are elected by all persons 18 years and over. Elections were held on 25 June 1994. With effect from 22 March 1995, the number of shires was reduced to 104 by the mergers of 3 with cities. By-elections for the 3 newly formed city councils took place on 11 March 1995.

In addition to government grants and subsidies, local authority revenue is derived from general rates, paid by landowners on the unimproved capital value of land, and by charging for some specific services. For the year ended 30 June 1994, the receipts and expenditure (including loans) for the 128 local authorities balanced at $A1,778m.

ECONOMY

Budget. In 1994–95 current outlays by the state totalled $A9,482m., of which $A6,646m. were general government final consumption expenditure, and capital outlays totalled $A2,741m. Revenue and grants received totalled $A13,148m.

Commonwealth payments for current purposes totalled $A5,421m. and for capital purposes, $A517m.

Banking and Finance. In June 1995 deposits at all banks in Queensland totalled $A33,577m., of which $A8,770m. were current, $A17,364m. were term deposits and $A3,946m. were investment savings. Other lending totalled $A42,941m. In 1994–95 permanent building societies had total assets of $A5,929·5m.

ENERGY AND NATURAL RESOURCES

Electricity. Installed capacity in 1991–92 was 5,285 MW. Output 1993–94, 31,831m. kWh, of which 24,001m. kWh was consumed by 1,355,793 customers. Some 0·9% of production is hydro-electric; most power stations are coal-fired.

Water. In the western portion of the State water is comparatively easily found by sinking artesian bores. At 30 June 1988, 3,700 such bores had been drilled, of which 2,595 were flowing.

Minerals. Principal minerals produced during 1994–95 (in tonnes): Copper, 189,854; coal, 94,496,000; lead, 166,584; zinc, 236,059; bauxite, 9,335,000; mineral sands concentrates, 313,177; silver, 428,245 (kg); gold, 27,888 (kg); crude oil, 910·3m. litres. Total value of output, at the mine, was $A5,430·4m.

Agriculture. In 1994–95 there were 32,849 agricultural establishments farming 149,688,000 ha. Livestock on farms and stations at 31 March 1995 numbered 9,974,000 cattle, 11,577,000 sheep and lambs and 644,000 pigs. Total wool production in the year ended 31 March 1995, 51,935 tonnes. The total area under crops during 1993–94 was 2,394,000 ha.

	Area (1,000 ha)		Production (tonnes)	
Crop	1993–94	1994–95	1993–94	1994–95
Sugar-cane, crushed	323	347	29,638,000	31,145,000
Wheat	556	401	555,000	225,000
Maize	28	27	87,000	80,000
Sorghum	399	519	852,000	917,000
Barley	232	94	261,000	73,000
Potatoes	5	5	118,002	109,000
Pumpkins	3	3	32,882	33,000
Tomatoes	4	3	102,124	101,000
Peanuts	21	13	43,639	23,000
Tobacco	1	1	3,930	4,000
Apples[1]	. . .	492	26,305	27,873
Grapes[2]	1	1	4,049	3,903
Citrus[1]	. . .	620	62,823	49,086
Bananas[2]	5	5	153,256	150,345
Pineapples[2]	4	3	157,395	138,465
Green forage and hay	441	440	290,000[3]	. . .
Cotton (raw)	84	88	81,249	110,945

[1] Number of trees 6 years and over (in 1,000). [2] Bearing area only. [3] Hay only.

The gross value of agricultural commodity production in 1994–95 amounted to $A5,466m., which comprised crops, $A2,970m.; livestock disposals, $A1,916m., and livestock products, $A580m.

Forestry. A considerable area consists of natural forest, eucalyptus, pine and cabinet woods being the timbers mostly in evidence; a large quantity of ornamental woods is utilized by cabinet makers. The amount of sawn timber processed in 1994–95 was 651,979 cu. metres of pine and 238,310 cu. metres of other wood.

INDUSTRY AND TRADE

Industry. In 1994–95, manufacturing establishments recorded $A27,982m. in turnover, paid $A4,017m. in wages and salaries and (at 30 June 1995) employed 139,300 persons. The largest manufacturing sector was food, beverages and tobacco with 30·8% of turnover, 25·7% of wages and salaries paid and 24·6% of employment.

Labour. In May 1996 the labour force numbered 1,680,900, of whom 1,524,200 (646,200 females) were employed. Unemployment was 9·3%.

Trade Unions. There were 51 trade unions in 1995 with 451,500 members.

Commerce. Total value of direct overseas imports and exports (in $A1,000) f.o.b. port of shipment for both imports and exports:

	1990-91	1991-92	1992-93	1993-94	1994-95
Imports	4,903,467	5,626,715	6,334,175	6,869,158	7,771,035
Exports	10,727,490	10,865,144	11,798,170	11,984,172	12,510,814

In 1994–95 interstate exports totalled $A5,326,975 and imports $A12,496,497. Chief sources of imports in 1994–95 (in $A1m.): Japan, 1,636·6; USA 1,327·7; EU, 1,298·6; Papua New Guinea, 757·5 New Zealand, 571·2. Exports went chiefly to: Japan, 3,956·1; EU, 1,606·8; South Korea, 1,105·6; USA, 694·2; Taiwan, 556·4.

The chief exports overseas in 1994–95 (in $A1m.) were: Coal, 4,124·5; sugar, 1,661·7; meat and meat preparations, 1,594·9; non-ferrous metals, 836·3; metalliferous ores and metal scrap, 627·3; machinery and transport equipment, 545·3. Principal overseas imports were: Road vehicles, 1,689·3; petroleum and petroleum products, 792·4; machinery, specialized for particular industries, 526·7; nonmonetary gold, 401·3.

Tourism. Overseas visitors to Australia who specified Queensland as their primary destination numbered 1,110,500 in 1995.

COMMUNICATIONS

Roads. At 30 June 1995 there were 175,650 km of roads open to the public. Of these, 64,279 km were surfaced with sealed pavement.

At 30 June 1995 motor vehicles registered (in 1,000) totalled 2,038·9, comprising 1,504·2 passenger vehicles, 372 light commercial vehicles, 79·7 trucks, 12·8 buses and 70·2 motor cycles. There were 456 fatalities in road accidents in 1995.

Railways. Queensland Rail is owned by the State government. Total length of line at 30 June 1996 was 9,452 km, of which 1,783 km were electrified. In 1994–95, 37·9m. passengers and 96·8m. tonnes of freight were carried.

Civil Aviation. Queensland is well served with a network of air services, with overseas and interstate connexions. Subsidiary companies provide planes for taxi and charter work, and the Flying Doctor Service operates throughout western Queensland. In 1993 there were 134 licensed airports. In 1994–95 Brisbane handled 1,838,023 international passengers with 53,593 tonnes of freight; Cairns, 641,377 with 12,779 tonnes and Townsville, 1,611 with 95 tonnes. The number of aircraft registered at 30 June 1995 was 2,186.

Shipping. Queensland has 14 modern trading ports, 2 community ports and a number of non-trading ports. In 1994–95, cargo discharged was 26,483,000 mass tonnes and cargo loaded was 106,081,000 mass tonnes.

Telecommunications. There were 1·45m. telephones in 1993. At 30 June 1995 there were 440 post offices and postal agencies. In addition to the national networks Queensland is served by 13 public radio stations (non-profit-making), 44 commercial radio stations and 3 commercial TV channels.

SOCIAL INSTITUTIONS

Justice. Justice is administered by Higher Courts (Supreme and District), Magistrates' Courts and Children's Courts. The Supreme Court comprises the Chief Justice, and 19 judges; the District Courts, 30 district court judges of whom 1 is chairman. Stipendiary magistrates preside over the Magistrates' and Children's Courts, except in the smaller centres, where justices of the peace officiate. A parole board may recommend prisoners for release.

The total number of appearances in the Higher Courts resulting in convictions in 1993–94 was 3,703; appearances resulting in convictions in Magistrates' Courts totalled 96,398, and proven offences in Children's Courts totalled 4,422. At 30 June 1995 there were 12 correctional centres with 2,870 prisoners (104 females). The total police force was 6,486 at 30 June 1995.

Religion. Religious affiliation at the 1991 census: Roman Catholic, 25·4%; Anglican, 25·2%; Uniting Church, 10·4%; Presbyterian, 5·4%; Lutheran, 2·3%; Baptist, 1·9%; other Christian, 6·4%; non-Christian, 1%; no religion, 11·6%; not stated, 10%.

Education. Education is compulsory between the ages of 6 and 15 years and is provided free in government schools.

In July 1992, pre-school education and child care was provided at 742 government and 800 non-government centres with 6,448 teaching and other staff and 92,874 children.

Primary and secondary education comprises 12 years of full-time formal schooling and is provided by both the government and non-government sectors. In 1995, the State administered 1,317 schools with 264,567 primary students and 140,983 secondary students. In 1995 there were 25,805 teachers in government schools. There were 408 private schools in 1995 with 77,377 primary students and 73,185 secondary students. Educational programmes at private schools were provided by 9,429 teachers in 1995.

In 1995 there were 21,509 full-time students at TAFE institutes. The 6 publicly funded universities had 100,031 full-time students in 1995. Teaching staff totalled 12,153.

Health. In 1994-95 there were 194 hospitals (146 public with over 9,900 beds), 7 psychiatric institutions and 200 nursing care homes. At 30 June 1996 there were 6,834 doctors, 3,150 specialists, 1,994 dentists and 34,889 registered nurses.

Social Welfare. Welfare institutions providing shelter and social care for the aged, the handicapped, and children, are maintained or assisted by the State. A child health service is provided throughout the State. Age, invalid, widows', disability and war service pensions, family allowances, and unemployment and sickness benefits are paid by the Federal Government. At 30 June 1995, age pensioners in the State numbered 270,710 and invalid/disability support pensioners, 104,115 (including wife and carer pensioners); disability pensioners, 67,219; and service pensioners, 70,006 (including dependants).

There were 8,350 widows' and 64,283 sole parent pensions current at 30 June 1995, and at the same date basic family payment was being paid for 670,345 children under 16 years and eligible students aged 16 to 24 years in 345,484 families.

Further Reading

Statistical Information: The Statistical Office (313 Adelaide St., Brisbane) was set up in 1859. *Deputy Commonwealth Statistician:* R. A. Crockett. *A Queensland Official Year Book* was issued in 1901, the annual *ABC of Queensland Statistics* from 1905 to 1936 with exception of 1918 and 1922. Present publications include: *Queensland Year Book.* Annual, from 1937 (omitting 1942, 1943, 1944, 1987, 1991). —*Queensland Pocket Year Book.* Annual from 1950.— *Monthly Summary of Statistics, Queensland.* From Jan. 1961

Australian Sugar Year Book. Brisbane, from 1941
Johnston, W. R., *A Bibliography of Queensland History.* Brisbane, 1981.—*The Call of the Land: A History of Queensland to the Present Day.* Brisbane, 1982
Johnston, W. R. and Zerner, M., *Guide to the History of Queensland.* Brisbane, 1985

State Library: The State Library of Queensland, Queensland Cultural Centre, South Bank, South Brisbane.

SOUTH AUSTRALIA

KEY HISTORICAL EVENTS. South Australia was surveyed by Tasman in 1644 and charted by Flinders in 1802. It was formed into a British province by letters of patent of Feb. 1836, and a partially elective legislative council was established in 1851.

From 6 July 1863, the Northern Territory was placed under the jurisdiction of South Australia until the establishment of the Commonwealth of Australia in 1901.

TERRITORY AND POPULATION. The total area of South Australia is 380,070 sq. miles (984,377 sq. km). The settled part is divided into counties and hundreds. There are 49 counties proclaimed, covering 23m. ha, of which 19m. ha are occupied. Outside this area there are extensive pastoral districts, covering 76m. ha, 49m. of which are under pastoral leases.

At the 1991 census the population was 1,446,299 (728,677 females; 16,249 Aboriginal and Torres Strait Islander people, of whom 8,323 were female). Estimated mean resident population at 31 Dec. 1993 was 1,463,200. The 1996 census population was 1,427,936.

Vital statistics:

	Live Births	Marriages	Divorces	Deaths
1991	19,640	9,392	4,215	11,176
1992	19,311	9,423	4,074	10,925
1993	20,078	. . .	4,063	11,528

The infant mortality rate in 1992 was 6·1 per 1,000 live births.

The Adelaide Statistical Division had 1,023,617 persons at the 1991 census in 22 cities and 8 municipalities and other districts. Cities outside this area (with 1991 census populations) are Whyalla (25,526), Mount Gambier (21,153), Port Augusta (14,595), Port Pirie (14,110) and Port Lincoln (11,345).

CONSTITUTION AND GOVERNMENT. South Australia was formed into a British province by letters patent of Feb. 1836, and a partially elective Legislative Council was established in 1851. The present Constitution dates from 24 Oct. 1856. It vests the legislative power in an elected Parliament, consisting of a Legislative Council and a House of Assembly. The former is composed of 22 members. Every 4 years half the members retire, and the resulting vacancies are filled at a general election on the basis of proportional representation with the State as one multi-member electorate. The qualifications of an elector are, to be an Australian citizen, or a British subject who on 25 Jan. 1984 was enrolled on a Commonwealth electoral roll and/or at some time between 26 Oct. 1983 and 25 Jan. 1984 inclusive was enrolled on an electoral roll for a South Australian Assembly district or a Commonwealth electoral roll in any State. The person must be of at least 18 years of age and have lived continuously in Australia for at least 6 months, in South Australia for at least 3 months and in the sub-division for which he is enrolled at least 1 month. War service may substitute for residential qualifications in some cases. By the Constitution Act Amendment Act, 1894, the franchise was extended to women, who voted for the first time at the general election of 25 April 1896. The qualifications for election as a member of both Houses are the same as for an elector. Certain persons are ineligible for election to either House.

The House of Assembly consists of 47 members elected for 4 years, representing single electorates. Election of members of both Houses takes place by preferential secret ballot. Voting is compulsory for those on the Electoral Roll.

The House of Assembly, elected on 11 Dec. 1993, consists of the following members: Liberal Party of Australia (LP), 36; Australian Labor Party (ALP), 11. The Legislative Council consists of 11 LP, 9 ALP and 2 Australian Democrat members.

Electors enrolled (11 Dec. 1993) numbered 1,006,035.

The executive power is vested in a Governor appointed by the Crown and an Executive Council, consisting of the Governor and the Ministers of the Crown. The Governor has the power to dissolve the House of Assembly but not the Legislative Council unless that Chamber has twice consecutively with an election intervening defeated the same or substantially the same Bill passed in the House of Assembly by an absolute majority.

Governor: Sir Eric James Neal, AC.

In Feb. 1998 the Liberal Ministry was as follows:
Premier, Minister for Multicultural Affairs: John Wayne Olsen.
Deputy Premier, Minister for Industry: Graham Alexander Ingerson. *Treasurer:* Robert Ivan Lucas. *Justice, Attorney-General, Consumer Affairs, Police, Correctional Services and Emergency Services:* Kenneth Trevor Griffin. *Human Services:* Dean Craig Brown. *Transport and Urban Planning, the Arts, Status of Women:* Diana Vivienne Laidlaw. *Government Enterprises:* Michael Harry Armitage. *Education, Children's Services and Training, Youth and Employment:* Malcolm Robert Buckby. *Environment and Heritage, Aboriginal Affairs:* Dorothy Christine

Kotz. *Primary Industries, Natural Resources and Regional Development:* Robert Gerard Kerin.

Ministers are jointly and individually responsible to the legislature for all their official acts.

Local Government. The closely settled part of the State (mainly near the sea-coast and the River Murray) is incorporated into local government areas, and sub-divided into district councils (rural areas only), municipal corporations (mainly metropolitan, but including larger country towns) and cities (more densely populated areas with a qualification of 15,000 residents in the Adelaide metropolitan area, and 10,000 in the country). At 1 Jan. 1994 there were 118 local government authorities. The main functions of councils are the construction and maintenance of roads and bridges, sport and recreational facilities and garbage collection and disposal.

The number and area of the sub-divisions, together with expenditure (in $A1,000) for the year ended 30 June 1992, were:

	No.	Area (1,000 ha)	Roads and bridges	Recreation and culture	All other	Total expenditure
Adelaide statistical division	30	189·3	74,033	87,935	71,252	452,224
Other municipal corporations and district councils	89	15,225·9	58,093	25,756	26,702	213,158
Total	119	15,415·3	132,126	113,691	97,956	665,382

ECONOMY

Budget. Public sector revenue and outlays (in $A1m.) for years ended 30 June:

	1990	1991	1992	1993	1994
Revenue	4,787	5,154	5,324	6,139	6,433
Outlays	5,516	6,172	8,134	6,995	6,555

Banking and Finance. In March 1993 the average weekly balance of deposits held by all banks was $A14,651m. The average weekly balance of loans, advances and bills discounted was $A17,240m.

NATURAL RESOURCES

Minerals. The value of minerals produced in 1992–93 was $A1,312·2m. (metallic minerals, $A288·1m.; opals, $A39·2m.; natural gas, $A371m.; crude oil, $A175·7m.; condensates, $A135·1m.; liquefied petroleum gas, $A113·2m.; coal, $A54·7m.; construction materials, $A82·1m.). The principal metallic minerals produced are iron ore, copper, uranium oxide, gold and silver.

Agriculture. Total area of agricultural establishments, at 31 March 1993, was 56,554,511 ha.

Soil Conservation. A Department of Agriculture programme to deal with the problems of erosion and soil conservation includes the planting of cereal rye, perennial rye and other grasses to check sand drifts; contour furrowing and contour banking; contour planting with vines and fruit trees; and several water-diversion schemes.

Gross value of agricultural production (in $A1,000), 1992–93: Crops, 1,355,133; livestock slaughtering, 387,657; livestock products, 474,649. Total gross value, 2,217,439.

Sown area (in ha) and output (in tonnes) of the chief crops in 1992–93: Wheat, 1,419,451 and 2,421,214; barley, 1,023,310 and 1,855,320; oats, 191,929 and 164,500; hay, 121,419 and 419,545; vines, 26,134 and 286,138.

Fruit culture is extensive, and in 1992–93, 253,522 tonnes of citrus and 62,092 tonnes of other orchard fruit were produced. Other products, in addition to root crops and vegetables, are grass seeds and oil seeds.

Livestock, 31 March 1993: 1,104,179 cattle, 15,701,756 sheep and 434,665 pigs. In 1993, 102,333 tonnes of wool clip and (1992–93) 436m. litres of milk were produced.

Irrigation. For the year ended 31 March 1993, 117,117 ha were under irrigated culture, being used as follows: Vineyards, 20,564; fruit (excluding grapes), 15,604; vegetables, 9,164; other crops, 9,904 and pasture, 61,881.

INDUSTRY AND TRADE

Industry. The turnover for manufacturing industries for 1991–92 was $A15,443m.

Industry sub-division	Establish-ments (No.)	Persons employed (1,000)	Wages and salaries ($A1m.)	Turnover ($A1m.)
Food, beverages and tobacco	441	15·0	378	2,705
Textiles	69	2·2	70	436
Clothing and footwear	122	3·4	76	319
Wood, wood products and furniture	505	6·8	155	678
Paper, paper products, printing and publishing	321	6·8	213	930
Chemical, petroleum and coal products	83	2·6	93	1,260
Non-metallic mineral products	161	2·9	88	508
Basic metal products	62	6·1	248	1,486
Fabricated metal products	512	6·8	173	831
Transport equipment	179	14·4	444	3,918
Other machinery and equipment	482	12·9	360	1,578
Miscellaneous manufacturing	312	6·5	171	794
Total	3,249	86·2	2,410	15,443

Practically all forms of secondary industry are to be found, the most important being motor vehicle manufacture, saw-milling and the manufacture of household appliances, basic iron and steel, meat and meat products, and wine and brandy.

Labour. Two systems of industrial arbitration and conciliation for the adjustment of industrial relations between employers and employees are in operation—the State system, which operates when industrial disputes are confined to the territorial limits of the State, and the Federal system, which applies when disputes involve other parts of Australia as well as South Australia.

The industrial tribunals are authorized to fix minimum rates of wages and other conditions of employment, and their awards may be enforced by law. Industrial agreements between employers and organizations of employees, when registered, may be enforced in the same manner as awards.

Commerce. Overseas imports and exports in $A1m. (year ending 30 June):

	1989–90	1990–91	1991–92	1992–93	1993–94
Imports	2,050·0	2,193·7	2,396·9	3,068·1	2,803·4
Exports	2,841·3	3,005·4	3,505·1	3,756·3	3,873·1

Principal exports in 1993–94 were (in $A1m.): Cereals and cereal preparations, 435·2; road vehicles, parts and accessories, 350·8; meat and meat preparations, 323·9; textile fibres and their wastes, 280·6; non-ferrous metals, 279·6; petroleum and petroleum products, 273·5; beverages, 239·1; fish, seafood and their preparations, 186·6.

Principal imports in 1993–94 were (in $A1m.): Road vehicles, parts and accessories, 663·6; machinery, 505·6; petroleum and petroleum products, 404·6.

In 1993–94 the leading suppliers of imports were (in $A1m.): Japan (845·1), USA (362·2), UK (146·3), New Zealand (104·4). Main export markets were Japan (622·6), USA (392·3), New Zealand (312·4), UK (259·5), China (219·9), Hong Kong (165).

Tourism. In June 1993 there were 360 hotels and motels with 10,632 rooms; 211 caravan parks had a total of 24,434 sites.

COMMUNICATIONS

Roads. At 30 June 1994, of the roads customarily used by the public, there were 2,749 km of national highways, 9,557 km of arterial roads and 82,919 km of local roads, totalling 95,225 km. Lengths of road classified by surface were as follows: Sealed, 25,319 km; unsealed, 69,906 km. Costs of construction and maintenance are shared by the State and Commonwealth governments and by the councils of the local areas. Motor vehicles registered at 30 June 1994: Passenger and other motor vehicles, 893,200; motorcycles, 27,000. In 1993 there were 218 fatalities in road accidents.

Railways. At 30 June 1993, Australian National Railways operated 4,415 km of railway in country areas. TransAdelaide operated 120 km of railway in the metropolitan area of Adelaide, which carried 8·4m. passengers in 1994–95.

There is a tramway in Adelaide.

Civil Aviation. There is an international airport at Adelaide. During 1992–93, 56,872 aircraft movements, 3,022,204 passengers and 24,781 tonnes of freight were handled on domestic and international services. In July 1994 there were 27 licensed aerodromes.

Shipping. There are 7 state and 4 private deep sea ports. In 1993, 741 vessels conducting overseas trade entered South Australia with 3·62m. import tonnes of cargo and left with 6·51m. export tonnes. In 1993–94 the state-owned ports handled 13·6m. tonnes of cargo out of a total of 21·02m. tonnes.

Telecommunications. At 30 June 1991, there were 510 post offices. Telephone services in operation totalled 805,478 at 30 June 1994. Apart from the national services, there were in 1993, 13 commercial and 13 public radio stations and 4 commercial TV stations. There were 64 radio and 34 television stations at 30 June 1992.

SOCIAL INSTITUTIONS

Justice. There is a Supreme Court, which incorporates admiralty, civil, criminal, land and valuation, and testamentary jurisdiction; district criminal courts, which have jurisdiction in many indictable offences, and magistrates courts, which include the Youth Court. Circuit courts are held at several places. In the year ended 31 Dec. 1991, there were 1,943 appearances in the higher criminal courts. In 1,164 of those cases, the defendant was found guilty of the major charge. In 1994 the police force numbered 3,813. There were 5,685 prisoners received under sentence in 1992–93.

Religion. Religious affiliation at the 1991 census: Catholic, 236,252; Anglican, 191,060; Uniting Church, 123,864; Lutheran, 34,395; Orthodox, 36,599; Baptist, 22,151; Presbyterian, 17,275; other Christians, 19,923. Non-Christians, 16,464; indefinite, 2,734; no religion, 182,101; not stated, 108,620.

Education. Education is secular and is compulsory for children 6–15 years of age. Primary and secondary education at government schools is free. In 1993 there were 19,430 children in 321 pre-school centres. In 1993 there were 861 schools operating, of which 184 were non-government and 675 government schools, the latter comprising 473 primary, 2 primary-secondary, 88 secondary, 53 area, 22 special, 21 rural and 16 Aboriginal schools. There were 124,802 children in government and 36,481 in non-government primary schools, and 59,818 children in government and 26,126 in non-government secondary schools. 10 Institutes of Vocational Education were formed in 1993 by a merger of the former 19 TAFE colleges. There were 44,471 students at the 3 universities in 1993.

Social Welfare. The number of pensioners at 30 June 1993 was: Age, 150,583; disability support, 38,592; wife's/carer's pension, 15,434; widow's, 5,189; sole parent, 26,011; rehabilitation, 33.

Further Reading

Statistical Information: The State branch of the Australian Bureau of Statistics is at 55 Currie St., Adelaide (GPO Box 2272). *Deputy Commonwealth and Government Statistician:* P. M. Gardner. Although the first printed statistical publication was the *Statistics of South Australia, 1854* with the title altered to *Statistical Register* in 1859, there is a written volume for each year back to 1838. These contain simple records of trade, demography, production, etc. and were prepared only for the use of the Colonial Office; one copy was retained in the State.

The publications of the State branch include the *South Australian Year Book*, the *Pocket Year Book of South Australia* and a *Monthly Summary of Statistics, South Australia*, a quarterly bulletin of building activity, a quarterly bulletin of tourist accommodation and approximately

40 special bulletins issued each year as particulars of various sections of statistics become available.

Gibbs, R. M., *A History of South Australia: From Colonial Days to the Present*. Adelaide, 1984
Whitelock,D., *Adelaide, 1836–1976: A History of Difference*. Univ.of Queensland Press, 1977

State Library: The State Library of S.A., North Terrace, Adelaide. *State Librarian:* Frances H. Awcock.

TASMANIA

KEY HISTORICAL EVENTS. Abel Janszoon Tasman discovered Van Diemen's Land (Tasmania) on 24 Nov. 1642. The island became a British settlement in 1803 as a dependency of New South Wales; in 1825 its connection with New South Wales was terminated; in 1851 a partially elected Legislative Council was established, and in 1856 responsible government came into operation. On 1 Jan. 1901 Tasmania was federated with the other Australian states into the Commonwealth of Australia.

TERRITORY AND POPULATION. Tasmania is a group of islands separated from the mainland by Bass Strait with an area (including islands) of 68,049 sq. km, or 6·8m. ha, of which 6,408,600 ha form the area of the main island. The population at 10 consecutive censuses (including full-blood Aboriginals from 1966) was:

	Population		Population
1947	257,078	1976	402,868
1954	308,752	1981	418,957
1961	350,340	1986	436,353
1966	371,435	1991	452,837
1971	390,413	1996	459,659

At the census of 6 Aug. 1996, 23,103 were born in the UK or Ireland, 11,120 in other European countries and 394,774 in Australia. Estimated resident population at 31 Dec. 1996, 474,200 (240,100 females).

Vital statistics for calendar years:

	Marriages	Divorces	Births	Deaths
1994	2,887	1,544	6,844	3,911
1995	2,840	1,279	6,558	3,739
1996	2,654	1,582	6,419	3,884

The largest cities and towns (with populations at the 1996 Census) are Hobart (189,944), Launceston (95,982), Devonport (23,814) and Burnie (19,283).

CONSTITUTION AND GOVERNMENT. Parliament consists of the Governor, the Legislative Council and the House of Assembly. The Council has 19 members, elected by adults with 6 months' residence. Members sit for 6 years, 3 retiring annually and 4 every sixth year. There is no power to dissolve the Council. Vacancies are filled by by-elections. The House of Assembly has 35 members; the maximum term for the House of Assembly is 4 years. Women received the right to vote in 1903. Proportional representation was adopted in 1907, the method now being the single transferable vote in 7-member constituencies. Casual vacancies in the House of Assembly are determined by a transfer of the preference of the vacating member's ballot papers to consenting candidates who were unsuccessful at the last general election.

A Minister must have a seat in one of the two Houses.

At the elections of Feb. 1996 the Liberal Party won 16 seats in the House of Assembly, the Australian Labor Party 14, the Tasmanian Greens 4, ind 1.

The Legislative Council is predominantly independent without formal party allegiance; 4 members are Labor-endorsed and 1 Liberal.

Governor: Sir Guy Green, AC, KBE.

A minority Liberal government was formed on 15 March 1996, which in Jan. 1998 comprised:

Premier, Treasurer, Minister for State Development: Tony Rundle.
Deputy Premier, Minister for Education and Vocational Training, Arts, Sports and Recreation: Sue Napier. *Police and Public Safety, Forests, Mines:* John Beswick. *Transport, Energy, Inland Fisheries:* Thomas Cleary. *Finance, Public Sector Administration, Industrial Relations, Leader of the Government in the House:* Ron Cornish. *Attorney General, Justice, Tourism, Workplace Standards:* Ray Groom. *Environment, Land Management:* Peter Hodgman. *Status of Women, Community Development, Local Government, Multicultural and Ethnic Affairs, Aboriginal Affairs:* Denise Swan. *Community and Health Services:* Peter McKay. *Primary Industries and Fisheries, Racing:* Bill Bonde.

Local Government. The State is divided into 29 municipal areas comprising the cities of Hobart, Launceston, Glenorchy, Clarence, Burnie and Devonport and 23 municipalities. The number of municipalities was reduced from 46 in 1993 because of the amalgamation of smaller into larger municipalities. The cities and municipalities are managed by elected aldermen and councillors, respectively, with reference to local matters such as sanitation and health services, domestic water supplies and roads and bridges within each particular area. The chief sources of revenue are rates (based on assessed annual value) levied on owners of property and government grants.

Tasmanian Islands. Two inhabited Tasmanian islands (King and Flinders) are organized as municipalities. Nearly 1,360 km south-east lies Macquarie Island (123 sq. km), part of the State, and used only as a research base and meteorological station.

ECONOMY

Budget. The revenue is derived chiefly from taxation (pay-roll, motor, lottery and land tax, business franchises and stamp duties), and from grants and reimbursements from the Commonwealth Government. Customs, excise, sales and income tax are levied by the Commonwealth Government, which makes grants to Tasmania for both revenue and capital purposes.

Specific Purpose Grants are mainly used to provide essential services such as hospitals, housing, roads and educational services, while General Purpose Revenue Funds have been paid since 1942 to compensate the State for the loss of income tax to the federal government.

Consolidated Revenue Fund receipts and expenditure, in $A1m., for financial years ending 30 June:

	1993–94	1994–95	1995–96
Revenue	1,728·6	1,770·9	1,851·5
Expenditure	1,789·0	1,820·1	1,885·7

Net State and local government debt, 1995–96, $A3,308m.

In 1995–96 State Government revenue from taxes, fees and fines amounted to $A657m., of which pay-roll tax provided $A142m.; motor tax, $A83m.; taxes on property, $A287m.; taxes on gambling and insurance, $A84m. and franchise taxes, $A148m.

Banking and Finance. Trading bank activity in Tasmania is divided between 3 private banks and the Commonwealth Trading Bank. The 6 savings banks operating in Tasmania are the Commonwealth Savings Bank, 2 trustee savings banks and 3 private savings banks operated by trading banks.

ENERGY AND NATURAL RESOURCES

Electricity. Installed capacity was 2,505 MW in 1995–96. Energy generated in 1995–96, 9,096 GWh. Tasmania has good supplies of hydro-electric power because of assured rainfall and high level water storages (natural and artificial). The Hydro-Electric Commission is the sole commercial supplier of electricity.

Minerals. Output of principal metallic minerals in 1995–96 was (in tonnes): Zinc, 198,376; iron ore pellets, 1,681,332; copper, 11,481; lead, 38,565; tin, 8,647; tungsten, 77; gold, 1·02; silver, 144. Coal production, 559,300 tonnes. Value of output,

1995–96 (in $A1,000): Metallic minerals, 338,056; non-metallic and fuel minerals, 44,596; construction materials, 28,933.

Agriculture. The estimated gross value of recorded production from agriculture in 1995–96 was (in $A1m.): Livestock products, 229·1; livestock slaughterings and other disposals, 118; crops, 301·7; total gross value, 648·8. There were 4,640 agricultural establishments in 1995–96, occupying a total area of 1,948,800 ha. Area (in 1,000 ha) and production (in 1,000 tonnes) of the principal crops:

| | 1993–94 | | 1994–95 | | 1995–96 | |
	Area	Production	Area	Production	Area	Production
Wheat	1·6	5·3	1·3	2·8	1·1	4·1
Barley	15·2	40·8	14·0	27·1	14·0	38·5
Oats	6·7	12·7	8·3	11·3	10·1	18·4
Green peas	7·3	35·1	6·0	37·9	6·1	30·0
Potatoes	6·9	291·4	6·1	255·7	7·6	302·0
Hay	50·4	229·3	48·9	183·4	63·5	277·9
Hops (bearing) (dry)	0·8	2·1	0·8	1·8	0·7	1·9

Livestock at 31 March 1996: Sheep, 3,862,300; cattle, 717,600; pigs, 26,400.

Wool produced during 1995–96 was 15,997 tonnes, valued at $A69·1m. Butter production in 1995–96 was 9,589 tonnes; cheese, 25,371 tonnes. In 1995–96, 52,400 tonnes of apples and 1,989 tonnes of grapes were produced.

Forestry. Indigenous forests cover a considerable part of the State, and the sawmilling and woodchipping industries are very important. Production of sawn timber in 1995–96 was 349,300 cu. metres. 4,470,900 cu. metres of logs were used for milling and chipping in 1995–96. Newsprint and paper are produced from native hardwoods, principally eucalypts.

Fisheries. Estimated gross value of fisheries production was $A196m. in 1995–96.

INDUSTRY AND TRADE

Industry. The most important manufactures for export are refined metals, newsprint and other paper manufactures, pigments, woollen goods, fruit pulp, confectionery, butter, cheese, preserved and dried vegetables, sawn timber, and processed fish products. The electrolytic-zinc works at Risdon near Hobart treat large quantities of local and imported ore, and produce zinc, sulphuric acid, superphosphate, sulphate of ammonia, cadmium and other by-products. At George Town, large-scale plants produce refined aluminium and manganese alloys. During 1995–96, 3,820,100 tonnes (green weight) of woodchips were produced. In 1994–95 employment in manufacturing establishments was 22,100; wages and salaries totalled $A668m.; turnover, $A4,354m.

Labour. In Oct. 1996, 224,000 persons (60·7% of the civilian population aged 15 and over) were in the workforce, of whom 200,100 were employed.

Trade Unions. In 1996, Tasmania had the highest rate of trade union membership of any Australian State, 39·3%. This compared with 42·9% in Aug. 1994 and 50·5% in Aug. 1992.

Commerce. In 1995–96 exports totalled $A1,619·7m. to overseas countries. The principal countries of destination in 1995–96 (with values in $A1m.) for overseas exports were: Japan, 494·3; Hong Kong,122·3; USA, 115·5; UK, 114·5; Taiwan, 105·5; Indonesia, 93·9; Malaysia, 93·5; Republic of Korea, 90·5. In 1995–96 direct imports into Tasmania totalled $A351·4m. from overseas countries. The principal countries of origin in 1995–96 (with values in $A1m.) for overseas imports were: USA, 67·3; New Zealand, 39; Japan, 37·2; UK, 32.

The main commodities by value (in $A1m.) exported to overseas countries in 1995–96 were: Non-ferrous metals, 406·8; cork and wood, 240; metalliferous ores and metal scrap, 190·2; transport equipment (except road vehicles), 123·1; dairy products, 110·2; iron and steel, 105·9; fish, crustaceans and molluscs, 103·9; meat and meat preparations, 63·9; vegetables and fruit, 58·3. The main imports from overseas countries in 1995–96 (in $A1m.) were: Pulp and waste paper, 466; machinery specialized for particular industries, 322; road vehicles, 313; power generating machinery and equipment, 253; general industrial machinery and parts, 216.

Tourism. In 1996, 949,525 passengers arrived (834,039 by air from other Australian states or New Zealand and 115,486 by sea).

COMMUNICATIONS

Roads. In 1998 there were approximately 24,000 km of roads open to general traffic, of which 370 km were National Highway and 3,350 km were arterial State roads. Motor vehicles registered at 30 June 1995 comprised 237,100 cars and station wagons, 75,500 commercial vehicles and 7,200 motor cycles.

Railways. A 733 km freight-only rail network services many of the State's principal industries via links with all major ports and cities. 1,942,700 tonnes of freight were carried in 1993–94.

Civil Aviation. Regular passenger and freight services connect the south, north and north-west of the State with the mainland. Air New Zealand provides a direct international service to Christchurch between Oct. and March. For the year ended 30 June 1996 the 6 main airports handled 1,725,000 passengers and 9,004 tonnes of freight.

Shipping. In 1995–96, 10,783,576 mass tonnes of cargo were carried through the 4 major ports. Passenger ferry services connect Tasmania with the mainland and offshore islands.

Telecommunications. At 30 June 1997 there were 34 post offices and 152 licensees. There were 4 TV broadcasters and 27 radio stations.

SOCIAL INSTITUTIONS

Justice. The Supreme Court of Tasmania, with civil, criminal, ecclesiastical, admiralty and matrimonial jurisdiction, established by Royal Charter on 13 Oct. 1823, is a superior court of record, with both original and appellate jurisdiction, and consists of a Chief Justice and 6 puisne judges. There are also inferior civil courts with limited jurisdiction, licensing courts, mining courts, courts of petty sessions and coroners' courts.

In 1995–96 there were 52,330 recorded offences, of which 47,737 were against property, 2,661 against the person and 1,791 fraud and similar offences. The total police force at June 1995 was 1,049. There is one prison, with 1,138 imprisonments in 1995–96.

Religion. At the census of 1996 the following numbers of adherents of the principal religions were recorded:

Anglican Church	156,192	Other Christian	28,515
Roman Catholic	89,156	Indefinite and not stated	45,606
Uniting Church	34,901	No religion	76,859
Presbyterian	13,977	Non Christian	3,661
Baptist	9,727		
		Total	458,594

Education. Education is controlled by the State and is free, secular and compulsory between the ages of 6 and 16. In 1996, government schools had a total enrolment of 62,776 pupils, including 26,679 at secondary level; 69 private schools had a total enrolment of 21,406 pupils, including 10,296 at secondary level.

Technical and further education is conducted at technical and community colleges in the major centres throughout the state. In 1996 there were 26,588 students enrolled in the Division of Technical and Further Education and almost 30,000 students in the Division of Adult Education.

Tertiary education is offered at the University of Tasmania in Hobart and Launceston and the Australian Maritime College in Launceston. The University (established 1890) had (1996) 12,611 students (68% full-time) and 1,653 academic staff. The Maritime College had 904 student enrolments in June 1995.

Social Welfare. The number of pensioners in Tasmania on 30 June 1996 was: Age (including wife and carer pensioners), 43,483; disability support, 16,993; war (service), 14,852; widows, 1,061.

Further Reading

Statistical Information: The State Government Statistical Office (200 Collins St., Hobart), established in 1877, became in 1924 the Tasmanian Office of the Australian Bureau of Statistics, but continues to serve State statistical needs as required.
Deputy Commonwealth Statistician and Government Statistician of Tasmania: Denis W. Rogers.
Main publications: *Annual Statistical Bulletins (e.g., Demography, Courts, Agricultural Industry, Finance, Manufacturing Establishments* etc.).—*Tasmanian Pocket Year Book.* Annual (from 1913).—*Tasmanian Year Book.* Annual (from 1967).—*Monthly Summary of Statistics* (from July 1945).

Kepars, I., *Tasmania* [Bibliography]. Oxford and Santa Barbara (CA), 1997
Robson, L., *A History of Tasmania. Vol. 1: Van Diemen's Land from the Earliest Times to 1855.* Melbourne, 1983

State Library: The State Library of Tasmania, 91 Murray St., Hobart. *State Librarian:* Robyn Collins, BA, MLibSc.

VICTORIA

KEY HISTORICAL FACTS. The first permanent settlement in the area was formed at Portland Bay in 1834. Regular government was first established in 1839. Victoria, formerly a portion of New South Wales, was, in 1851, at much the same time as gold was discovered, proclaimed a separate colony, with a partially elective legislative council. A new constitution giving responsible government to the colony was proclaimed on 23 Nov. 1855. This event had far-reaching effects, as the population increased from 76,162 in 1850 to 589,160 in 1864. By this time the main impetus behind the search for gold had waned and the new arrivals availed themselves of the opening of the pastoral and agricultural lands to smaller holders and the gradual development of manufacturing industries.

Victoria federated with the other Australian states to form the Commonwealth of Australia in 1901.

TERRITORY AND POPULATION. The State has an area of 227,600 sq. km, and a resident population (estimate) of 4,501,100 at 30 June 1995; density, 19·8 per sq. km. The 1996 census population was 4,373,520.

Estimated population at 30 June 1995, within 11 'Statistical Divisions': Melbourne, 3,218,051; Barwon, 238,767; Western District, 101,550; Central Highlands, 133,969; Wimmera, 52,840; Mallee, 88,932; Loddon, 156,081; Goulburn, 184,731; Ovens-Murray, 88,696; East Gippsland, 82,254; Gippsland, 155,812.

Population of urban centres with over 10,000 inhabitants at the 1991 census: Melbourne, 2,761,995; Geelong, 126,306; Ballarat, 64,980; Bendigo, 57,427; Shepparton-Mooroopna, 30,511; Melton, 29,039; Warrnambool, 23,946; Albury-Wodonga (Wodonga Part), 23,639; Mildura, 23,176; Traralgon, 19,699; Cranbourne, 18,886; Sunbury, 18,533; Moe-Yallourn, 17,990; Wangaratta, 15,984; Morwell, 15,423; Sale, 13,858; Horsham, 12,552; Bairnsdale, 10,770; Colac, 10,241; Portland, 10,115; Craigieburn, 10,098; Ocean Grove-Barwon Heads, 10,069.

Vital statistics for calendar years:

	Births	Marriages	Divorces	Deaths
1993	64,049	27,418	10,935	31,197
1994	63,974	26,974	11,228	32,353
1995	62,591	26,607	11,838	32,425

The annual rates per 1,000 of the mean resident population (estimate) in 1995 were: Marriages, 5·9; births, 13·9; deaths, 7·2; divorces, 2·6. Infant mortality rate, 1995, 4·9 per 1,000 live births. Expectation of life, 1995: Males, 75·6 years; females, 81·2 years.

CONSTITUTION AND GOVERNMENT. Victoria, formerly a portion of New South Wales, was, in 1851, proclaimed a separate colony, with a partially elective Legislative Council. In 1856 responsible government was conferred, the legislative power being vested in a parliament of two Houses, the Legislative Council and the Legislative Assembly. At present the Council consists of 44 members who are elected for 2 terms of the Assembly, one-half retiring at each election. The Assembly consists of 88 members, elected for 4 years from the date of its first meeting unless sooner dissolved by the Governor. Members and electors of both Houses must be aged 18 years and Australian citizens or those British subjects previously enrolled as electors, according to the Constitution Act 1975. No property qualification is required, but judges, members of the Commonwealth Parliament, undischarged bankrupts and persons convicted of an offence which is punishable by life imprisonment, may not be members of either House. Single voting (one elector one vote) and compulsory preferential voting apply to Council and Assembly elections. Enrolment for Council and Assembly electors is compulsory. The Council may not initiate or amend money bills, but may suggest amendments in such bills other than amendments which would increase any charge. A bill shall not become law unless passed by both Houses.

Governor: Sir James Gobbo.

In the exercise of the executive power the Governor is advised by a Cabinet of responsible Ministers. Section 50 of the Constitution Act 1975 provides that the number of Ministers shall not at any one time exceed 22, of whom not more than 6 may sit in the Legislative Council and not more than 17 may sit in the Legislative Assembly.

At the elections of 23 March 1996 the Liberal and National Party coalition was re-elected, with 34 seats in the Legislative Council and 58 in the Legislative Assembly.

The Liberal-National coalition Cabinet was as follows in March 1998:
Premier, Minister for Multicultural Affairs and for the Arts: Jeffrey Gibb Kennett. *Deputy Premier, Minister for Agriculture and Resources:* Pat McNamara. *Transport:* Robin Cooper. *Education:* Phil Gude. *Housing, Minister responsible for Aboriginal Affairs:* Ann Henderson. *Tertiary Education, Minister assisting the Premier on Multicultural Affairs:* Phil Honeywood. *Police and Emergency Services, Corrections:* Bill McGrath. *Planning and Local Government:* Rob Maclellan. *Youth, Community Services:* Dr Denis Napthine. *Sport, Rural Development:* Tom Reynolds. *Treasurer, Minister for Multi-Media:* Alan Stockdale. *Conservation and Land Management:* Marie Tehan. *Attorney-General, Fair Trading, Women's Affairs:* Jan Wade. *Small Business, Tourism:* Louise Asher. *Industry, Science and Technology:* Mark Birrell. *Roads and Ports:* Geoff Craige. *Finance, Gaming:* Roger Hallam. *Health and the Aged:* Rob Knowles.

Local Government. At 30 June 1996 the state was divided into 78 municipal districts, comprising 31 cities (including 4 greater cities), 6 rural cities, 40 shires and 1 borough. The only unincorporated areas are the Yallourn Works Area, French Island (154 sq. km), Lady Julia Percy Island (1·3 sq. km), Bass Strait Islands (3·8 sq. km) and part of the Gippsland Lakes (309 sq. km). The constitution of cities, towns, boroughs and shires is based on statutory requirements concerning population, rate revenue and net annual value of rateable property.

ECONOMY

Budget. State and local government outlays and receipts (excluding financial enterprises e.g. government savings banks, insurance offices, etc.) in $A1m.:
State 1994–95: Current outlays, 16,419; capital outlays, 2,134. Revenue, 18,299. State expenditure included: Education, 4,557; health, 3,064; general public services, 1,767; transport and communications, 1,511; public order and safety, 1,129. Revenue included: Property taxes, 2,155; payroll taxes, 1,841; taxes on uses of goods and performance of activities, 1,884; taxes on provision of goods and services, 1,681.
Local 1994–95: Outlays, 2,055, including transport and communications, 504; recreation and culture, 407; general public services, 364; housing and community

amenities, 283; social security and welfare, 244. Revenue, 2,101, including taxes, fees and fines, 1,420; Commonwealth and State grants, 576.

Banking and Finance. The State Bank of Victoria, the largest bank in the State, provides domestic and international services for business and personal customers and is the largest supplier of housing finance in Victoria. In 1990 it ran into debt and was acquired by the Commonwealth from the Victorian government in Sept. 1990.

The 11 major trading banks in Victoria are the Commonwealth Bank of Australia, the Australia and New Zealand Banking Group, the Westpac Banking Corporation, the National Australia Bank, the Bank of Melbourne, the St George Bank, the Challenge Bank, the Metway Bank, the State Bank of New South Wales, Bendigo Bank and Citibank. Banks had a total of 1,679 branches and 3,040 agencies between them at 30 June 1996.

In June 1996 bank deposits repayable in Australia totalled $A71,285m.; other lending, $A73,304m.

There were 6 permanent building societies in 1994-95.

ENERGY AND NATURAL RESOURCES

Electricity. Electricity production in 1993-94 was 35,442m. kWh.

In 1993 the State Government began a major restructure of the government-owned electricity industry along competitive lines. The distribution sector was privatized in 1995 and 3 generator companies in 1996.

About 90% of power generated is supplied by 4 brown-coal fired generating stations. There are 2 other thermal stations and 3 hydro-electric stations in north-east Victoria. Victoria is also entitled to approximately 30% of the output of the Snowy Mountains hydro-electric scheme and half the output of the Hume hydro-electric station, both of which are in New South Wales.

Oil and Natural Gas. Crude oil in commercially recoverable quantities was first discovered in 1967 in 2 large fields offshore in East Gippsland in Bass Strait between 65 and 80 km from land. These fields, with 10 other fields since discovered, have been assessed as containing initial recoverable reserves of more than 2,930m. bbls of treated crude oil. Estimated reserves of crude oil (1994) 113,000m. litres; gas, 139,000m. cu. metres.

In 1994-95 Victoria produced 46·6% of Australia's crude oil and 313% of its natural gas. Production of crude oil (1994-95), 14,598m. litres.

Natural gas was discovered offshore in East Gippsland in 1965. The initial recoverable reserves of treated gas are 220,400m. cu. metres. Natural gas is distributed to residential and industrial consumers through a network of 23,400 km of mains.

Liquefied petroleum gas is produced after extraction of the propane and butane fractions from the untreated oil and gas.

Brown Coal. Major deposits of brown coal are located in the Central Gippsland region and comprise approximately 94% of the total resources in Victoria. In 1993 the resource was estimated to be 0·2m. megatonnes, of which about 52,000 megatonnes was economically recoverable. It is young and soft with a water content of 60% to 70%. In the La Trobe Valley section of the region, the thick brown coal seams underlie an area from 10 to 30 km wide extending over approximately 70 km from Yallourn in the west to the south of Sale in the east. It can be won continuously in large quantities and at low cost by specialized mechanical plant.

The primary use of these reserves is to fuel electricity generating stations. Production of brown coal in 1994-95 was 50,679,000 tonnes, value $A414m.

Minerals. Production, 1994-95: Gold, 4,370 kg; (in 1,000 tonnes): Copper concentrate, 58; zinc concentrate, 13; bauxite, 2.

Land Settlement. Of the total area of Victoria (22·76m. ha), 13,973,915 ha on 30 June 1984 were either alienated or in process of alienation. The remainder (8,786,085) constituted Crown land as follows: Perpetual leases, grazing and other leases and licences, 2,160,352; reservations including forest and timber reserves, water, catchment and drainage purposes, national parks, wildlife reserves, water frontages and other reserves, plus unoccupied and unreserved including areas set aside for roads, 6,625,733.

Agriculture. In 1994-95 there were 37,070 agricultural establishments with a total area of 12,719,000 ha; the gross value of agricultural commodities produced was $A5,147,387,000. The following table shows the area under the principal crops and the produce of each for 2 seasons (in 1,000 units)[1]:

Season	Total crop area Ha	Wheat Ha	Tonnes	Oats Ha	Tonnes	Barley Ha	Tonnes	Potatoes Ha	Tonnes	Hay Ha	Tonnes
1993–94	2,317	780	2,022	186	362	639	1,386	12	322	492	1,991
1994–95	2,163	822	944	148	201	492	448	10	280	419	1,605

[1] Excluding establishments with an estimated value of agricultural operations less than $A5,000.

In 1994-95 there were 21,592 ha of vineyards with 18,989 ha of bearing vines, yielding 137,613 tonnes of grapes for wine-making and 139,822 tonnes for drying or table use. Other produce (in tonnes), 1994-95: Almonds, 2,805; pears, 138,696; apples, 98,971; oranges, 84,253; kiwi fruit, 2,731; strawberries, 2,921; tobacco (dry), 2,893; tomatoes, 139,541.

Livestock (in 1,000), 1994-95: Beef cattle, 2,663; dairy cattle, 1,622; sheep, 21,361; pigs, 439.

Animal products (in tonnes), 1994-95: Wool clip, 123,303; poultry, 116,383; mutton, 64,000; lamb, 111,000; milk, 5,113m. litres; 40·1m. dozen eggs; honey, 3,302.

INDUSTRY AND TRADE

Industry. At 30 June 1993 there were 11,692 manufacturing establishments. In 1994-95 there were 295,800 persons employed in the manufacturing sector. Selected articles manufactured (in tonnes), 1995–96: Butter and butteroil, 118,830; cheese, 168,365; wheat flour, 182,517; wool yarn, 17,198; wool cloth, 3,006 sq. metres; 11,000 vehicles for goods and materials; plastics in primary forms, 788,000; 260m. clay bricks; ready mixed concrete, 3,023,000 cu. metres.

Labour. In May 1996 there were 2,283,800 persons in the labour force (63·7% of the civilian population aged 15 years and over) of whom 2,092,300 were employed: Agriculture, forestry and fishing, 98,000; mining, 4,300; manufacturing, 360,200; electricity, gas and water, 15,800; construction, 138,200; wholesale and retail trade, 440,300; transport and storage, 97,900; accommodation, cafes and restaurants, 91,500; communication, 52,000; finance, insurance, property and business services, 288,500; public administration and defence, 71,400; education, 134,800; health and community services, 183,600; culture, recreation, personal and other services, 115,700. There were 191,500 unemployed persons in May 1996 (8·4% of the labour force).

Trade Unions. There were 61 trade unions with a total membership of 669,700 at 30 June 1995.

Commerce. The total value of the overseas imports and exports of Victoria, including bullion and specie, was as follows (in $A1m.):

	1990–91	1991–92	1992–93	1993–94	1994–95	1995–96
Imports	14,902	15,353	18,147	20,770	23,967	24,666
Exports[1]	8,803	9,545	11,044	12,349	13,006	15,392

[1] Includes re-exports.

The chief exports in 1995–96 (in $A1m.) were: Dairy products and birds' eggs, 1,364; textile fibres and their wastes, 1,083; non-ferrous metals, 1,025; meat and meat preparations, 656; petroleum, petroleum products and related materials, 592; road vehicles, 569; cereals and cereal preparations, 527. Exports in 1995–96 (in $A1m.) went mainly to Japan, 1,954; Republic of Korea, 1,922; New Zealand, 1,594; Singapore, 1,162; Hong Kong, 821; USA, 785; Malaysia, 737.

The chief imports in 1995–96 (in $A1m.) were: Road vehicles, 2,629; general industrial machinery and equipment and machine parts, 1,718; electrical machinery, apparatus and appliances and parts, 1,633; miscellaneous manufactured articles, 1,395; machinery for particular industries, 1,340; telecommunications and sound recording and reproducing apparatus and equipment, 1,146; textile yarns, fabrics, made-up articles and related products, 1,131. Imports in 1995–96 (in $A1m.) came mainly from the USA, 5,838; Japan, 3,429; Germany, 1,996; China, 1,675; the UK, 1,502; New Zealand, 1,207; Italy, 807.

COMMUNICATIONS

Roads. In 1996 there were 151,681 km of roads open for general traffic, consisting of 1,005 km of National Highways, 6,742 km of state highways and freeways, 14,179 km of main and tourist roads, 232 km of forest roads and 129,523 km of other roads and streets. The number of registered motor vehicles (other than tractors) at 30 June 1995 was 2,868,900. There were 418 fatalities in road accidents in 1995.

Railways. All the railways are the property of the State and are under the management of the Public Transport Corporation, responsible to the Victorian Government.

At 30 June 1995, 4,917 km of government railway were open, comprising 3,716 km of 1,600 mm gauge (385 km electrified) and 1,201 km of 1,435 mm gauge. In 1995–96, 6·88m. tonnes of freight and 7m. passengers (non-urban) were carried. Metropolitan services carried 229·5m. passengers. Melbourne's tramway and light rail network extends to 240 km.

Civil Aviation. In 1995–96, at Melbourne (Tullamarine) airport there were 10,829,000 domestic and regional passenger movements and 2,095,000 international passenger movements. Total freight and mail handled was 233,284 tonnes.

Shipping. The 4 major commercial ports are at Melbourne, Geelong, Portland and Hastings. Together, these ports serviced 3,479 ships with a total trade of 32,655,000 mass tonnes in 1994–95.

Telecommunications. In 1991 there were 3·1m. telephones. In 1993–94 there were 63 businesses providing television services and 14 providing radio services. There were 3 public broadcasters in radio and 2 in television.

SOCIAL INSTITUTIONS

Justice. There is a Supreme Court with a Chief Justice and 21 puisne judges. There are a county court, magistrates' courts, a court of licensing, and a bankruptcy court, etc.

Major crime during 1991–92: 306,190 offences were reported to the police; 89,252 offences were cleared and 79,888 people were proceeded against.

At 30 June 1995 there were 15 prisons and 2,828 prisoners in custody.

Religion. There is no State Church, and no State assistance has been given to religion since 1875. At the 1991 census the following were the enumerated numbers of the principal religions: Catholic, 1,237,399; Anglican, 772,632; Uniting, 342,493 (including Methodist); Orthodox, 199,063; Presbyterian, 193,300; other Christian, 255,375; Moslem, 49,617; Jewish, 33,882; Buddhist, 42,350; no religion, 612,074; not stated, 474,921.

Education. In 1995 there were 1,711 government schools with 514,805 pupils and 34,106 full-time teaching staff plus full-time equivalents of part-time teaching staff: 301,515 pupils were in primary schools and 213,290 in secondary schools. As from 1990 students attending special schools have not been identified separately and have been allocated to either primary or secondary level of education. They are integrated where possible into mainstream education. There were in 1995, 675 non-government schools, excluding commercial colleges, with 16,959 teaching staff and 255,472 pupils: 130,096 pupils at primary schools and 125,376 pupils at secondary schools.

All higher education institutions, excluding continuing education and technical and further education (TAFE), now fall under the Unified National System, and can no longer be split into universities and colleges of advanced education. In addition, a number of institutional amalgamations and name changes occurred in the 12 months prior to the commencement of the 1992 academic year. In 1995 there were 9 higher education institutions with 167,528 students. There had been 4 universities: Deakin (founded 1974), La Trobe (1964), Melbourne (1853) and Monash (1958).

Health. In 1994–95 there were 125 public hospitals with 12,153 beds and (1993–94) 113 private hospitals; 4,007 general practitioners and 2,537 specialists.

Social Services. Victoria was the first State of Australia to make a statutory provision for the payment of Age Pensions. The Act providing for the payment of such pensions came into operation on 18 Jan. 1901, and continued until 1 July 1909, when the Australian Invalid and Old Age Pension Act came into force. The Social Services Consolidation Act, which came into operation on 1 July 1947, repealed the various legislative enactments relating to age (previously old-age) and invalid pensions, maternity allowances, child endowment, and unemployment, and sickness benefits and while following in general the Acts repealed, considerably liberalized many of their provisions: It has since been amended. On 30 June 1996 there were 410,122 age and 115,580 invalid pensioners. In 1994–95, the amounts paid in age and invalid pensions (including payments to 12,177 wives and spouse carers of age pensioners and 31,394 of invalid pensioners) were \$A3,035,432,000 and \$A1,056,769,000 respectively.

Under the Australian Unemployment and Sickness Benefit Act 1944, amounts paid and beneficiaries, 1994–95: \$A1,864,749,000 to 208,010 unemployment, \$A96,523,000 to 10,856 sickness, \$A561,245,000 to 71,417 supporting parents and \$A67,675,000 to 6,142 special benefits.

At 30 June 1995, there were 14,122 widow pensioners receiving \$A125,411,000.

In 1994–95 the total amount paid in family allowances was \$A495,167,000 to 440,179 families with 848,657 children and students, and institutions; \$A44,814,000 was paid to 21,586 recipients of child disability allowance and (1991–92) \$A163,541,000 in family allowance supplement to 56,071 families with 131,404 children.

Further Reading

Australian Bureau of Statistics Victorian Office. *Victorian Year Book.—Summary of Statistics (annual).*

State library: The State Library of Victoria, 328 Swanston St., Melbourne, 3000. *State statistical office:* Victorian Office, Australian Bureau of Statistics, 525 Collins Street, Melbourne 3000. *Deputy Commonwealth Statistician:* Stuart Jackson.

WESTERN AUSTRALIA

KEY HISTORICAL EVENTS. In 1791, the British navigator George Vancouver, in the *Discovery*, took formal possession of the country around King George Sound. In 1826 the Government of New South Wales sent 20 convicts and a detachment of soldiers to King George Sound and formed a settlement then called Frederickstown. The following year, Capt. James Stirling surveyed the coast from King George Sound to the Swan River, and in May 1829 Capt. Charles Fremantle took possession of the territory. In June 1829, Capt. Stirling founded the Swan River Settlement, now the Commonwealth State of Western Australia, and the towns of Perth and Freemantle, and was appointed Lieut.-Governor.

Large grants of land were made to the early settlers, and agricultural and pastoral occupations were pursued by a small population with varying success until, in 1850, with the colony in a languishing condition, the inhabitants' petition that it might be made a penal settlement was acceded to. Between 1850 and 1868 (in which year transportation ceased), 9,668 convicts were sent out.

In 1870, partially representative government was instituted, and in 1890 the administration was vested in the Governor, a legislative council and a legislative assembly. The legislative council was, in the first instance, nominated by the Governor, but in 1893 it became elective.

Western Australia federated with the other Australian states to form the Commonwealth of Australia in 1901.

TERRITORY AND POPULATION. Western Australia lies between 113° 09' and 129° E. long. and 13° 44' and 35° 08' S. lat.; its area is 2,525,500 sq. km.

The population at each census from 1947 was as follows[1]:

	Males	Females	Total		Males	Females	Total
1947	258,076	244,404	502,480	1976	599,959	578,383	1,178,342
1954	330,358	309,413	639,771	1981	659,249	642,807	1,300,056
1961	375,452	361,177	736,629	1986	736,131	722,888	1,459,019
1966	432,569	415,531	848,100	1991	793,626	792,767	1,586,393
1971	539,332	514,502	1,053,834				

[1] 1961 and earlier exclude persons of predominantly Aboriginal descent; from 1966 figures refer to total population (*i.e.*, including Aborigines). Figures from 1971 are based on estimated resident population.

The population at the 1996 census was 1,726,095. Of the total 1991 census population, 1,097,500 were born in Australia. Married persons numbered 683,554 (340,607 males and 342,947 females); widowers, 12,967; widows, 53,892; divorced, 29,854 males and 36,247 females; never married, 199,261 males and 156,450 females. Estimated resident population at 31 Dec. 1994 was 1,715,300 (853,900 females).

Perth, the capital, had an estimated resident population of 1,239,400 at June 1994. Of this, the area administered by the City of Perth had a population of 80,517 while the population in the area for which the City of Fremantle is responsible (which includes the chief port of the State) was 23,834.

Principal local government areas outside the metropolitan area, with population at 30 June 1991 (estimate): Bunbury, 25,657; Geraldton, 20,587; Mandurah, 26,838; Roebourne, 17,291; Port Hedland, 12,599; Albany, 11,186; Busselton, 13,528; Kalgoorlie-Boulder, 26,079.

Vital statistics for calendar years[1]:

	Births	Marriages	Divorces	Deaths
1992	25,052	10,118	4,540	9,902
1993	25,081	10,382	4,654	10,318
1994	25,114	10,366	5,024	10,297

[1] Figures are on state of usual residence basis.

CONSTITUTION AND GOVERNMENT. In 1870 partially representative government was instituted, and in 1890 the administration was vested in the Governor, a Legislative Council and a Legislative Assembly. The Legislative Council was, in the first instance, nominated by the Governor, but it was provided that in the event of the population of the colony reaching 60,000, it should be elective. In 1893 this limit of population being reached, the Colonial Parliament amended the Constitution accordingly.

The *Legislative Council* consists of 34 members elected for a term of 4 years. There are 6 electoral regions for Legislative Council elections. 4 return 5 members and 2, 7 members. Each member represents the entire region.

There are 57 members of the *Legislative Assembly*, each member representing one of the 57 electoral districts of the State. Members are elected for the duration of the Assembly which may be for a period of up to 4 years. The qualifications applying to candidates and electors are identical for the Legislative Council and the Legislative Assembly. A candidate must be at least 18 years of age and free from legal incapacity, be an Australian citizen, and be enrolled, or qualified for enrolment, as an elector. A member of the Commonwealth Parliament or of the legislature of a territory or another state, an undischarged bankrupt or a debtor against whose estate there is a subsisting receiving order in bankruptcy, or a person who has been attainted or convicted of treason or felony is disqualified from membership of the legislature. No person may hold office as a member of the Legislative Assembly and the Legislative Council at the same time. An elector must be at least 18 years of age, be an Australian citizen (or a British subject who was at some time within the 3 months preceding 26 Jan. 1984 an elector of the Assembly or the Commonwealth parliament), be free from legal incapacity, and must have resided in Western Australia for 3 months continuously and in the electoral district for which he or she claims enrolment for a continuous period of 1 month immediately preceding the date of his or her claim.

Enrolment is compulsory for all qualified persons. Voting at elections is on the preferential system and is compulsory for all enrolled persons. A system of proportional representation is used to elect members of the Legislative Council.

Ordinary members of the legislature were paid (1996) a salary of $A81,042 a year with an additional electorate allowance, ranging from $A19,512 to $A36,099 a year according to location of the electorate. All members of Parliament also receive a basic postage and lettergram allowance of $A5,400.

In addition to the basic member's salary, electorate and postage allowances, the Premier receives (1997) a salary and expense of office allowances of $A106,975. On the same basis the Deputy Premier receives $A78,611; the Leader of the Government in the Legislative Council $A72,938; and other ministers $A64,834.

Legislative Assembly representation after the Dec. 1996 election: Liberal Party, 29; Australian Labor Party, 19; National Party of Australia, 6; Independent, 3. Legislative Council: Liberal Party, 14; Australian Labor Party, 12; National Party of Australia, 3; Greens (Western Australia), 3; Australian Democrats, 2.

Governor: Maj.-Gen. Michael Jeffery, AC, MC.
Lieut-Governor: David Kingsley Malcolm, AC.

In Feb. 1998 the Cabinet comprised:
Premier, Treasurer, Minister for Public Sector Management, and for Federal Affairs: Richard F. Court.
Deputy Premier, Minister for Commerce and Trade, Regional Development and Small Business: Hendy Cowan. *Resources Development and Energy, Education, Leader of the House in the Legislative Assembly:* Colin James Barnett. *Primary Industry and Fisheries:* Monty House. *Environment, Employment and Training:* Cheryl Edwardes. *Transport:* Eric Charlton. *Family and Children's Services, Seniors' and Women's Interests:* Rhonda K. Parker. *Finance, Racing and Gaming:* Max Evans. *Attorney-General, Justice, the Arts:* Peter Foss. *Labour Relations, Planning, Heritage:* Graham Kierath. *Housing, Aboriginal Affairs, Water Resources:* Kim D. Hames. *Mines, Tourism, Sport and Recreation:* Norman Moore. *Police and Emergency Services:* J. H. Day. *Local Government, Disability Services:* Paul Omodei. *Health:* Kevin Prince. *Works, Services, Multicultural and Ethnic Affairs, Youth:* Mike F. Board. *Lands, Fair Trading, Parliamentary and Electoral Affairs:* Doug J. Shave.

Local Government. The only unincorporated area in mainland Western Australia is King's Park, a public reserve of about 403 ha. in Perth. Including the lord-mayoralty of Perth there were 18 cities, 11 towns and 110 shires at 30 June 1993. The executive body in each of these districts is normally an elected council, presided over by a mayor (city and town) or a president (shire), but in certain circumstances it may be a commissioner appointed by the Governor. Their functions include road construction and repair, the provision of parks and recreation grounds, the administration of building controls and health and library services. Finance is derived largely from rates levied on property owners as well as charges for services and government grants.

ECONOMY

Budget. Revenue and expenditure (in $A), as reported in the Consolidated Revenue Fund, in years ended 30 June:

	1992	1993	1994	1995
Revenue	5,134,520,520	5,061,500,000	6,028,000,000	6,020,600,000
Expenditure	5,123,222,596	5,061,500,000	6,113,300,000	5,998,100,000

Main items of revenue in 1994–95: Departmental ($A590,410,983), taxation ($A2,340,253,929), timber and mining ($A426,731,764), from Federal funds ($A2,421,787,099). Western Australia had a gross debt of $A24,399m. on 30 June 1994 ($A6,707m. from Public Trading Enterprises, $A6,104m. General Government debt and $A11,588m. State Public sector debt).

Banking and Finance. There are 28 banks including the Commonwealth Trading Bank and the Rural and Industries Bank of Western Australia.

ENERGY AND NATURAL RESOURCES

Minerals. Mining is important. Until the mid-1960s the major mineral produced was gold. It was then replaced by iron ore in terms of value, and has at various times fallen behind nickel concentrates, bauxite, oil, mineral sands and salt. In the latter half of the 1980s gold enjoyed a resurgence and in 1987–88 exceeded iron ore in value terms.

The total ex-mine value of minerals from mining and quarrying in 1993–94 was $A12,924m. Principal minerals produced in 1993–94 were: Iron ore, 124·3m. tonnes, value $A2,630·6m.; gold bullion, 193 kg, value $A3,256·8m.; crude oil, 8,752·6 kilolitres, value $A1,299·8m.; natural gas, 4,915,300m. kilolitres, value $A441·9m.; salt, 6·8m. tonnes, value $A152·3m.; diamonds, 27·7m. carats, value $A470·2m.; heavy mineral sands concentrates valued at $A416·3m.; alumina, 7,933·3 tonnes, value $A1,702·1m.; nickel concentrates, 678,667 tonnes, value $A637m.; tin concentrates, 209 tonnes, value $A1·4m.; black coal, 5m. tonnes, value $A235·1m.

Agriculture.

| | 1993–94 | | 1994–95 | |
Crop	Area 1,000 ha	Production 1,000 tonnes	Area 1,000 ha	Production 1,000 tonnes
Wheat	3,859	6,702	3,974	5,652
Oats	275	514	261	435
Barley	776	1,356	590	945
Lupins	929	1,177	1,200	989

Production, 1992–93 (in tonnes), of apples, 36,551; pears, 8,311, and oranges, 6,000.

Irrigation has been established by the government along the south-western coastal plain and in the north Reservoirs with an aggregate capacity of 6,207m. cu. metres provided irrigation water for 88,408 ha in 4 districts during 1991–92.

Livestock at 31 March 1994 (in 1,000): Cattle, 1,713; sheep, 32,693; pigs, 288. The wool clip in 1993–94 was 179,606 tonnes.

Forestry. The area of State forests and timber reserves at 30 June 1990 was 1,894,756 ha; production of sawn timber was 781,440 cu. metres in 1993, principally Jarrah and Karri hardwoods.

Fisheries. The catch of fish, crustaceans and molluscs in 1991–92 totalled 55,484 tonnes for a gross value of $A374·2m. Of this, rock lobsters, with a total catch of 12,202 tonnes accounted for $A252·1m.

INDUSTRY AND TRADE

Industry. Heavy industry is concentrated in the south-west, and is largely tied to export-orientated mineral processing, especially alumina and nickel. Other significant manufacturing industries include meat and seafood processing, production of timber and wood products, metal fabrication and production of industrial and mining machinery. The North West Shelf development has stimulated recent growth in industries involved in providing materials and equipment during the construction phase, as well as in new and existing industries using gas in processing.

The following table shows manufacturing industry statistics for 1993–94[1]:

Industry sub-division	Number of establishments operating at 30 June	Persons employed[2] 1,000	Wages and salaries $A1m.	Turnover $A1m.
Food, beverages and tobacco	355	11·1	314	2,680
Textiles, clothing, footwear and leather products	232	3·7	83	318
Wood and paper products	319	4·6	128	695
Printing and publishing and recorded media	405	6·1	171	649
Chemical, petroleum, coal and associated products	243	5·4	190	2,717
Non-metallic mineral products	216	4·9	158	1,017

Industry sub-division	Number of establishments operating at 30 June	Persons employed[2] 1,000	Wages and salaries $A1m.	Turnover $A1m.
Metal products	686	14·0	484	3,841
Machinery and equipment	878	10·5	286	1,474
Other manufacturing	627	5·8	125	564
Total	3,960	66·2	1,940	13,957

[1] Excludes single establishment enterprises with fewer than 4 persons employed.
[2] At 30 June. Includes working proprietors.

Labour. The labour force was 829,000 employed and 65,300 unemployed in June 1995. The average weekly wage in May 1995 was $A539·90 (males $A656·60, females $A403·90).

The Western Australian Industrial Appeal Court consists of 3 Judges, one of whom is the Presiding Judge. The members are nominated by the Chief Justice of Western Australia. An appeal lies to the Court from decisions of the President of the Western Australian Industrial Commission, the Full Bench or the Commission in Court Session. The Western Australian Industrial Commission consists of a President (who must be a judge), a Chief Industrial Commissioner, a Senior Commissioner, and 'such number of other Commissioners as may, from time to time, be necessary'. The President or a Commissioner sitting or acting alone constitutes the Commission and may exercise the appropriate powers of the Commission. The Commission can inquire into any industrial matter and make an award, order or declaration relating to such matter. The Commission may also make inquiries where industrial action has occurred or is likely to occur. The Commission in Court Session is constituted by not less than 3 Commissioners sitting or acting together, and may make General Orders, hear matters referred by the Commission, and hear appeals from decisions of Boards of Reference.

The Full Bench is constituted by not less than 3 members of the Commission, 1 of whom is the President, and may hear matters referred by the Commission on questions of law, and appeals from decisions of the Commission and Industrial Magistrates.

The following table shows details of the number of industrial awards, unions and members registered with the Western Australian Industrial Commission.

At 30 June	1990	1991	1992	1993	1994
Awards in force	610	587	447	431	376
Employee organizations:					
Number	72	83	62	64	65
Membership	174,312	231,569	212,061	216,524	205,650
Employer organizations:					
Number	15	21	18	17	. . .
Membership	2,180	3,132	3,188	3,065	. . .

[1] Excluding the Builders' Union.

During 1994 there were 82 industrial disputes involving 15,700 workers. A total of 27,400 working days were lost.

Commerce. Foreign commerce is comprised in the statement of the commerce of the Commonwealth of Australia.

Value of foreign imports and exports (i.e. excluding inter-state trade) for years ending 30 June (in $A1m.):

	1991–92	1992–93	1993–94
Imports	3,548·2	4,966·0	4,793·0
Exports[1]	14,039·5	14,993·0	15,690·0

[1] Including ships' stores.

Total value of trade (including inter-state trade), 1992–93: Imports, $A11,160·6m.; exports, $A18,117·1m.

Selected overseas exports (in $A1m.) for 1993–94: Iron ore and concentrates, 2,765·1; petroleum and products, 929·9; gold bullion, 3,285·7; meat and meat products, 163·2; fish, crustaceans, molluscs, etc., 413·3; cereals and other cereal preparations, 656·8; metalliferous ores and metal scrap, 2,999·4; textile fibres and other work, 656·8; salt (1992–93), 179.

Selected overseas imports (in $A1m.) for 1993–94: Petroleum and products, 678·4; machinery, 875·9; road vehicles, 690; miscellaneous manufactured articles, 33·5 (1992–93).

The chief countries exporting to Western Australia in 1993–94 were (in $A1m.): USA, 934; Japan, 828·6; UAE, 388·4; South Korea, 255·7; Main export markets in 1993–94 (in $A1m.): Japan, 3,999; South Korea, 1,204; UK, 1,180; Singapore, 1,009; Hong Kong, 698; China, 665.

Tourism. In 1993–94 there were 447,000 overseas, and 366,000 interstate visitors.

COMMUNICATIONS

Roads. At 30 June 1992 there were 140,976 km of prepared and formed roads comprising 8,232 km of highways, 7,493 km of main roads, 8,397 km of secondary roads and 116,854 km unclassified. Of these, 43,031 km are sealed. In addition, there are 29,222 km of roads unprepared except for clearing which are used for forestry traffic.

New motor vehicles registered during the year ended 30 June 1994 were 63,178.

In 1995 there were 208 fatalities in road accidents.

Railways. At 30 June 1994 the State had 5,411 km of State government railway and 731 km of Federal line, the latter being the western portion of the Trans Australian line (Kalgoorlie–Port Pirie), which links the State railway system to those of the other States of the Commonwealth. At 30 June 1989, mining companies operated 1,198 km of private railways for the transport of ore to ports on the north-west coast. In 1994–95 state railways carried 29·3m. tonnes and 247,000 passengers. Perth suburban lines (91·5 km electrified), controlled by a separate authority, carried 16·2m. passengers in 1993–94.

Civil Aviation. An extensive system of regular air services operates for passengers, freight and mail. During 1992–93, Perth Airport handled 32,346 aircraft movements and 2,036,461 passengers on domestic and international services.

Shipping. In 1990–91, the number of overseas direct vessels through the major ports was: Port of Fremantle, 1,231 entered, 1,035 cleared; Port Hedland, 327 entered, 418 cleared; other ports, 218 entered, 1,316 cleared. The gross weight (in tonnes) of overseas cargo through those ports was: Port of Fremantle, 29,140,000 discharged, 26,885,000 loaded; Port Hedland, 543,000 discharged, 37,980,000 loaded; other ports, 85,520,000 discharged, 95,665,000 loaded.

Telecommunications. Postal, telephone and telegraph facilities are afforded at 393 offices. Telephone services connected totalled 728,734 at 30 June 1990.There were 186 radio broadcasting and 226 television stations, including translator stations, in operation at 30 June 1991.

SOCIAL INSTITUTIONS

Justice. Justice is administered by a Supreme Court, consisting of a Chief Justice, 12 other judges and 3 masters; a District Court comprising a chief judge and 14 other judges; a Magistrates Court, a Chief Stipendiary Magistrate, 36 Stipendiary Magistrates and Justices of the Peace, as at 30 June 1990. All courts exercise both civil and criminal jurisdiction except Justices of the Peace who deal with summary criminal matters only. Juvenile offenders are dealt with by the Children's Court. Overall responsibility for the Children's Court is vested in a President, who has the status of a District Court Judge. A children's court may be constituted by a judge, a magistrate or 2 lay members. Each has different sentencing powers. For certain offences involving first offenders under the age of 16 years who have pleaded guilty, such cases may be dealt with by the Children's (suspended Proceedings) Panel which comprises a representative from the Department for Community Services and one from the Police Department. The Family Court also forms part of the justice system and comprises a Chief Judge, 4 other judges, 7 magistrates/registrars and exercises both State and Federal jurisdictions.

In 1993–94, 209,907 crimes were reported (57,638 cleared). 111,580 charges were laid in the courts (including children) in 1992–93; 35,581 persons were convicted. Persons in prison at 31 Dec. 1994 numbered 2,078.

Religion. At the census, 30 June 1991, the principal denominations were: Anglican, 418,800; Catholic, 408,600; Uniting, 93,200; Presbyterian, 48,300; Baptist, 25,900; other Christian, 112,100; all other, including not stated and no religion, 480,200.

Education. School attendance is compulsory from the age of 6 until the end of the year in which the child attains 15 years. A non-compulsory year of education is available to children from the beginning of the year in which they reach 5 years of age, at pre-primary centres attached to most government primary schools or at community-based and privately owned pre-school centres, and at some non-government schools. Children may be enrolled during their fourth year where vacancies exist. In 1994 there were 705 government primary and secondary schools providing free education to 223,105 students and 249 non-government primary and secondary schools providing education, for which fees are charged, to 76,307 students.

Technical and Further Education (TAFE) is offered by the Department of TAFE, a sub-department of the Ministry of Education, and by three independent regional colleges. The latter also provide higher education facilities. Additionally, higher education is available through 5 universities.

Tertiary education (1994):

	Academic Staff [1]	Students Enrolled
University of Western Australia	958	12,370
Murdoch University	461	7,060
Curtin University of Technology	1,052	19,326
Edith Cowan University	830	16,845
University of Notre Dame, Australia	33 [2]	200 [2]

[1] Teaching and research.   [2] 1993.

State government expenditure from consolidated revenue on education during the year ended 30 June 1995 amounted to $A1,060,707,156.

Health. At 30 June 1992 there were 88 acute public hospitals, 22 acute private hospitals, and 4 day hospitals.

Social Welfare. The Department for Community Development is responsible for the provision of welfare and community services throughout the State. Operations and planning are managed through a decentralized structure of 5 regions and 21 districts. There are 8 directorates (2 support, 1 special services and 5 regional).

Direct services provided to the community include emergency financial assistance, family and substitute care, and counselling and psychological services. The Department supervises children's Day Care Centres. There is a 24-hour emergency welfare service provided through the Crisis Care Unit. Specialist units work in the areas of child abuse, adoptions, youth activities and Family Court counselling.

The Department provides residential facilities for the temporary accommodation, care and training of children, is responsible for young offenders recommended for detention or remand by a Court and also supervises young offenders subject to non-custodial court orders.

Age, invalid, widows', disability and service pensions, and unemployment benefits are paid by the Federal Government. The number of pensioners in Western Australia at 30 June 1993 was: Age, 121,387; invalid, 36,817; widows, 5,545; disability, 36,817; service, 35,003 (1991); and sole parents, 24,558 (1990). There were 79,903 recipients of unemployment benefits at 30 June 1993, comprising 46,610 job-search allowance recipients and 33,294 newstart allowance recipients.

During 1992–93 the department provided emergency assistance in 59,345 cases. This assistance, valued at $A4,745,388, was in the form of cash, vouchers to purchase goods and services, and payment on behalf of individuals.

Further Reading

Statistical Information: The State Government Statistician's Office was established in 1897 and now functions as the Western Australian Office of the Australian Bureau of Statistics (Level 16

Exchange Plaza, 2 The Esplanade, Perth). *Deputy Commonwealth Statistician and Government Statistician:* Ian Castles. Its principal publications are: *Western Australian Year Book* (new series, from 1957). *Western Australia: Facts and Figures* (from 1989). *Monthly Summary of Statistics* (from 1958)

Broeze, F. J. A. (ed.) *Private Enterprise, Government and Society.* Univ. of Western Australia, 1993

Crowley, F. K., *Australia's Western Third: A History of Western Australia from the First Settlements to Modern Times.* (Rev. ed.). Melbourne, 1970

Stannage, C. T. (ed.) *A New History of Western Australia.* Perth, 1980

State Library: Alexander Library Building, Perth.

AUSTRIA

Republik Österreich

Capital: Vienna
Population: 8·05m.
GDP per head: (PPP$) 28,667
HDI/world rank: 0·932/12

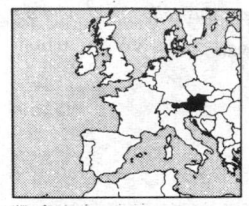

KEY HISTORICAL EVENTS. Governed by the Hapsburgs from 1282, Austria served thereafter as the centre of their expanding power and empire; an empire which lasted until 1918. At their greatest extent under Charles V (1519-55) the Hapsburg dominions included part of Hungary (wholly conquered from the Turks in 1688), Belgium, Italian territories, Spain and its vast empire. Spain was soon separated, and the Hapsburgs struggled to gain international recognition of their dynastic holdings. The Pragmatic Sanction of 1713 was only partially successful in this, but the Empire survived the War of the Austrian Succession (1740-63). Polish territory was annexed in 1772 and 1795. The Empire, represented by Prince Metternich at the Congress of Vienna, in 1815, recovered the influence in Germany and Italy it had lost during the French Revolutionary and Napoleonic Wars. It remained the major power in Central Europe till defeated in 1866 by Prussia and her German allies, a position confirmed by the unification of Germany in 1870-71 under Prussian leadership. Hungarian nationalism, the main obstacle to the integration of the Empire, was in 1867 appeased by the *Ausgleich* or Compromise: the state became known as the Dual Monarchy of Austria-Hungary.

As national feeling spread to the other peoples in the Empire, politics turned increasingly on national rivalries and aspirations. Tension was particularly high among the Serbs of Bosnia (annexed 1908) who looked to the independent state of Serbia. It was at Sarajevo in Bosnia on 28 June 1914 that the heir to the throne, Archduke Franz Ferdinand, was assassinated by Serbian nationalists, an event that triggered the First World War. The Empire, allied with Germany, suffered severely in the war with 1·2m. dead out of a population of 52m. In 1918 the Empire disintegrated into its national units.

The Treaty of St Germain (1919) left substantial populations of German speakers in Italy and Czechoslovakia. The federal constitution of 5 Oct 1920 introduced proportional representation; Christian Socialists dominated the governments (except for 1929-30) until 1938. But the Socialists were strong, and the general strike of July 1927 and the rising of Feb. 1934 induced Chancellor Dolfuss to end parliamentary democracy and introduce Fatherland Front backed by the paramilitary Heimwehr. The Nazis who assassinated Dolfuss on 25 July 1934 helped to bring about the *Anschluss* or Union with Germany which was achieved by a German invasion on 12 March 1938. Until 1945 Austria was Ostmark, a province of the Third Reich.

Although the 1943 Moscow Conference of Allied Foreign Ministers regarded Austria as the first victim of German aggression, Austria was occupied by Britain, France, USA and USSR (and paid reparations over a ten-year period). Independence came with the Austrian State Treaty of 15 May 1955.

TERRITORY AND POPULATION. Austria is bounded in the north by Germany and the Czech Republic, east by Slovakia and Hungary, south by Slovenia and Italy, and west by Switzerland and Liechtenstein. It has an area of 83,858 sq. km (32,378 sq. miles). Population (1995) 8·05m. Previous population censuses: (1923) 6·53m., (1934) 6·76m., (1951) 6·93m., (1971) 7·49m., (1981) 7·56m., (1991) 7·80m.

In 1991, 93·4% of residents were of Austrian nationality and 94% were German-speaking, with linguistic minorities of Slovenes (29,000), Croats (60,000), Hungarians (33,000) and Czechs (19,000). 65% were urban. Population estimate, 1996, 8,059,385. The areas, populations and capitals of the 9 federal states:

Federal States	Area sq. km	(1995)	Population (1996)	State capitals
Vienna (Wien)	415	1,592,596	1,595,000	Vienna
Lower Austria (Niederösterreich)	19,174	1,518,254	1,524,000	St Pölten

Federal States	Area sq. km	(1995)	Population (1996)	State capitals
Burgenland	3,965	274,334	275,000	Eisenstadt
Upper Austria (Oberösterreich)	11,980	1,385,769	1,381,00	Linz
Salzburg	7,154	506,850	509,000	Salzburg
Styria (Steiermark)	16,388	1,206,317	1,207,00	Graz
Carinthia (Kärnten)	9,533	560,994	563,000	Klagenfurt
Tyrol	12,648	658,312	660,000	Innsbruck
Vorarlberg	2,601	343,109	344,000	Bregenz

Vital statistics, 1996: Live births, 88,800; stillbirths, 389; deaths, 80,800; marriages, 42,300; divorces, 18,100. Suicide rates over 1990–95 (per 100,000 population): All, 22·6; men, 34·6; women, 11·6.

The populations of the principal towns at the census of 1991: Vienna, 1,539,848; Graz, 237,810; Linz, 203,044; Salzburg, 143,978; Innsbruck, 118,112; Klagenfurt, 89,415; Villach, 54,640; Wels, 52,594; St Pölten, 50,026.

The official language is German. For orthographical changes agreed in 1996 see GERMANY: Territory and Population.

CLIMATE. The climate is alpine. According to the elevation winters are cold with snowfall. In the eastern parts summers are warm and dry.

Vienna, Jan. –0·6°C, July 20·1°C. Annual rainfall 607 mm. Graz, Jan. –1·5°C, July 19·3°C. Annual rainfall 838 mm. Innsbruck, Jan. –1·1°C, July 18·7°C. Annual rainfall 864 mm. Salzburg, Jan. –1·3°C, July 18·3°C. Annual rainfall 1,169 mm.

CONSTITUTION AND GOVERNMENT. The Constitution of 1 Oct. 1920 was restored on 27 April 1945. Austria is a democratic federal republic comprising 9 states *(Länder)*, with a federal *President (Bundespräsident)* directly elected for not more than 2 successive 6-year terms, and a bicameral National Assembly which comprises a National Council and a Federal Council.

In the second round of the presidential elections on 24 May 1992 Thomas Klestil was elected against a single opponent by 56·85% of votes cast.

The National Council *(Nationalrat)* comprises 183 members directly elected for a 4-year term by proportional representation in a 3-tier system by which seats are allocated at the level of 43 regional and 9 state constituencies, and 1 federal constituency. Any party gaining 4% of votes cast nationally is represented in the National Council. Elections were held on 17 Dec. 1995; in 4 constituencies they had to be repeated on 13 Oct. 1996 which led to the re-allocation of 1 seat. The electorate was 5·8m; turn-out was 86%. The Social Democratic Party (SPÖ) won 71 seats with 31% of votes cast (65 with 34·9% in 1994); the People's Party (ÖVP), 52 with 28·2% (52 with 27·7%); the Freedoms (formerly FPÖ), 41 with 16·8% (42 with 22·5%); the Liberal Forum (LIF), 10 with 11·4% (11 with 6%); the Greens, 9 with 11·4% (13 with 7·3%).

In Oct. 1997 the party composition of the National Council was: SPÖ, 71; ÖVP, 52; FPÖ, 42; Greens, 9; LIF, 9.

The Federal Council *(Bundesrat)* has 64 members appointed by the 9 states for the duration of the individual State Assemblies' terms; the number of deputies for each state is proportional to that state's population. In Oct. 1997 the ÖVP held 26 seats, the SPÖ, 24 and the FPÖ, 14.

The head of government is a *Federal Chancellor*, who is appointed by the President (usually the head of the party winning the most seats in National Council elections). The *Vice-Chancellor* and *Council of Ministers* are appointed by the President at the Chancellor's recommendation..

Federal President: Dr Thomas Klestil (b. 1933; ÖVP) (elected 24 May 1992; sworn in 8 July).

Following the Dec. 1995 elections, the SPÖ and ÖVP agreed in March 1996 to form a coalition government, which in March 1998 consisted of the following members:

Chancellor: Dr Viktor Klima (b. 1947; SPÖ).

Vice-Chancellor, Minister of Foreign Affairs: Dr Wolfgang Schüssel (ÖVP).

Minister of the Environment, Youth and Family: Martin Bartenstein (ÖVP).
Economic Affairs: Johann Farnleitner (ÖVP). *Interior:* Karl Schlögl (SPÖ). *Defence:*
Werner Fasslabend (ÖVP). *Labour, Health and Social Affairs:* Lore Hostasch (SPÖ).
Education and Culture: Elisabeth Gehrer (ÖVP). *Science and Transport:* Caspar
Einem (SPÖ). *Women's Affairs and Consumer Protection:* Barbara Prammer (SPÖ).
Justice: Nikolaus Michalek (ind). *Agriculture and Forestry:* Wilhelm Molterer
(ÖVP). *Finance:* Rudolf Edlinger (SPÖ).
   The *President of the Nationalrat* (Speaker) is Heinz Fischer (SPÖ).

   National anthem: 'Land der Berge, Land am Strome' ('Land of mountains, land on
the river'; words by Paula Preradovic; tune attributed to Mozart).

European Parliament. Austria has 21 representatives. At the Oct. 1996 elections turn-
out was 67·21%. The ÖVP won 7 seats with 29·7% of votes cast; the SPÖ, 6 with
29·2%; the FPÖ, 6 with 27·5%; the Greens, 1 with 6·8%; the LIF, 1 with 4·3%.

State and local government. Each state (*Land*) has its assembly. Seats gained by
parties at the latest state elections:
   Burgenland (June 1996): SPÖ, 17; ÖVP, 14; FPÖ, 5.
   Carinthia (March 1994): SPÖ, 14; FPÖ, 13; ÖVP, 9.
   Lower Austria (May 1993): ÖVP, 26; SPÖ, 20; FPÖ, 7; Left Bloc, 3.
   Salzburg (March 1994): ÖVP, 14; SPÖ, 11; FPÖ, 8; Greens, 3.
   Styria (Dec. 1995): ÖVP, 21; SPÖ, 21; FPÖ, 10; Greens, 2; LIF, 2.
   Tyrol (March 1994): ÖVP, 19; SPÖ, 7; FPÖ, 6; Greens, 4.
   Upper Austria (Oct. 1991): ÖVP, 26; SPÖ, 19; FPÖ, 11.
   Vienna (Oct. 1996): SPÖ, 43; FPÖ, 29; ÖVP, 15; Greens, 7; LIF, 6.
   Vorarlberg (Sept. 1994): ÖVP, 20; FPÖ, 7; SPÖ, 6; Greens, 3.

   Every community has a Council, which chooses one of its members to be head of
the Community (burgomaster) and a committee for the administration and execution
of its resolutions. The provincial assemblies of the former Tyrol meet as the Regional
Provincial Parliament of North Tyrol, South Tyrol and Trentino.

DEFENCE. The Federal President is C.-in-C. of the armed forces. Conscription is
for a 7-month period, with liability for 30 days reservist refresher training spread
over 10 years.

Army. There are 3 corps. 1 comprises 3 mechanized infantry brigades, 1 engineer
battalion, 1 reconnaissance battalion, 1 artillery regiment, 2 provincial military commands and a number of infantry regiments. The other 2 each comprise: 1 engineer
battalion, 1 reconnaissance regiment, 1 artillery regiment, 3 provincial military commands and between 4 and 6 infantry regiments. Equipment includes 169 M-60A3
main battle tanks. Personnel, 1996, 51,500 (34,000 conscripts). The army aviation
division comprises 3 aviation and 3 air-defence regiments with about 6,000 personnel, more than 160 aircraft and a number of fixed and mobile radar stations. Some 24
Draken interceptors equip a surveillance wing responsible for the defence of Austrian
air space and a fighter-bomber squadron operates SAAB 105s. Helicopters equip
7 squadrons for transport/support, communication, observation, search and rescue
duties. Fixed-wing aircraft such as PC-6s, PC-7s and Skyvans are operated as
trainers and for transport. The procurement of a fourth generation fighter, armed helicopters and medium range air-defence missiles is planned for the end of the decade.
   After a major reorganization of the armed forces conducted during the first half of
the 1990s, a slimming process will continue. Until the end of 1999, the peacetime
organization of the forces will be further reduced to two corps comprising three
infantry brigades and a number of territorial units. On mobilization, the total force
will then amount to 110,000 personnel.

INTERNATIONAL RELATIONS

Membership. Austria is a member of the UN, EU, Council of Europe, the Central
European Initiative, OECD and NATO Partnership for Peace. Austria is a signatory
to the Schengen Accord abolishing border controls between Belgium, Denmark,
Finland, France, Germany, Greece, Iceland, Italy, Luxembourg, Netherlands,
Norway, Portugal, Spain and Sweden.

ECONOMY

Policy. In 1991 some 50% of production derived from the state-owned or state-protected sector, but a privatization programme in accordance with EU directives had largely been completed by 1995.

Performance. Real GDP growth was 1· 6% in 1996 (1·8% in 1995) and estimated 1·8% in 1997. It is estimated that the economy will expand by an average of 2·5% between 1998 and 2002, essentially due to foreign trade.

Budget. The federal budget for calendar years provided revenue and expenditure (ordinary and extraordinary) as follows (in 1m. schilling):

	1993	1994	1995	1996
Revenue	601,445	626,629	646,689	665,097
Expenditure	699,685	731,447	764,593	754,463

VAT is 20% (10% reduced rate).

Currency. The unit of currency is the *schilling* (ATS) of 100 *groschen*. There are notes of 20, 50, 100, 500, 1,000 and 5,000 schillings. The schilling is linked to the German Mark at DM1 = 7 schillings. Inflation was estimated at 1·3% in 1997, compared to 1·9% in 1996 and 4·1% in 1992. In 1997 foreign exchange amounted to 196,816m. and note circulation to 167,580m schilling.

Banking and Finance. The National Bank of Austria, opened on 2 Jan. 1923, was taken over by the German Reichsbank on 17 March 1938. It was re-established on 3 July 1945. Its *President* is Klaus Liebscher. Bank accounts up to 0·2m. schilling are anonymous for Austrians, but foreign depositors must declare their identity.

There were 1,042 banks in June 1996. The 10 principal banks with total assets (in 1m schilling, June 1996): Bank Austria, 700,052 (merger of Zentralsparkasse and Länderbank in Oct. 1991; the state retains a 21·7% stake); Creditanstalt-Bankverein, 653,714 (the state has a 49·4% stake in it); Girocredit Bank AG der Sparkassen, 321,662; Österreichische Kontrollbank AG, 257,480; Bank für Arbeit und Wirtschaft AG, 237,944; Bank der Österreichischen Postsparkasse, 227,016; Raiffeisen Zentralbank Österreich AG, 230,623; Die Erste Österreichische Spar-Casse-Bank, 223,042; Bank für Oberösterreich und Salzburg (Oberbank), 81,298; Österreichische Volksbanken AG, 72,583.

There is a stock exchange in Vienna (Börse).

Weights and Measures. The metric system is in force.

ENERGY AND NATURAL RESOURCES

Electricity. Electricity is supplied by the United Enterprise (Verbundkonzern) and a regional company for each of the 9 states, 4 of which are partly privatized. There are also some 270 municipal and private electricity companies. Electric energy produced (1m. kWh): 1996, 54,837.

Oil. The commercial production of petroleum began in the early 1930s. Production of crude oil (in tonnes): 1996, 965,398.

Gas. Production of natural gas (in 1,000 cu. metres): 1996, 1,491,706.

Minerals. The mineral production (in tonnes) was as follows:

	1994	1995		1994	1995
Lignite	1,368,317	1,262,967	Talcum	135,371	140,162
Iron ore	1,644,000	2,107,000	Kaolin	467,320	478,929
Raw magnesite[1]	654,127	784,523	Gypsum	1,011,807	974,827
Graphite	12,162	11,877			

[1] Including recovery from slag.

Agriculture. 165,700 persons were employed full-time in agriculture in 1995. In 1995 the total area cultivated amounted to 3,429,659 ha (estimate).

The chief products (area in 1,000 ha, yield in tonnes) were as follows:

| | 1994 | | 1995 | | 1996 | |
	Area	Yield	Area	Yield	Area	Yield
Wheat	241·0	1,255,122	255·9	1,301,310	247·6	1,239,723
Rye	77·0	318,790	76·8	313,835	51·2	156,227
Barley	252·7	1,184,350	229·1	1,065,188	259·6	1,082,789
Oats	49·4	171,716	40·8	161,645	41·6	152,705
Potatoes	29·7	593,720	27·0	724,426	26·3	768,973

Livestock (1996): Cattle, 2,271,969; pigs, 3,663,747; sheep, 380,861; goats, 54,471; horses, 73,234; poultry, 12,979,954.

Forestry. Forested area in 1992, 3·9m. ha (46% of the land area) of which 78% coniferous. Felled timber, in 1,000 cu. metres: 1994, 14,359·6; 1995, 13,805·8; 1996, 15,010,2.

INDUSTRY. Output (in tonnes if not stated otherwise):

	1994	1995		1994	1995
Raw steel	4,398,887	4,989,701	Glass (flat)		
Rolled steel	3,820,353	3,968,039	(1,000 sq. metres)	5,995	6,464
Cellulose	1,197,451	1,231,291	Cement	4,828,460	3,843,652
Cardboard	413,345	386,325	Salt (unrefined)	785,835	833,516
Paper	3,190,069	3,212,945	Sugar (refined)	458,262	442,539
Sawnwood			Margarine	47,195	48,536
(1,000 cu. metres)	7,538	7,696	Milk	597,000	582,256
Viscose staple yarn	36,479	34,383	Fertilizers	1,222,578	1,135,105

In 1995, 8,487 industrial establishments employed 467,271 persons, producing a value of 840,183·7m. schillings (excluding VAT).

Labour. In 1996 there were 3,709,800 employed persons. There were 19,000 job vacancies. In June 1997 there were 193,800 registered unemployed, a rate of 5·9%.

The number of foreigners who may be employed in Austria is limited to 9% of the potential workforce.

There were no strikes in 1996.

FOREIGN ECONOMIC RELATIONS. The budgetary external debt was 296,474m. schillings in 1996.

Commerce. Imports and exports are as follows (excluding coined gold):

| | Imports | | Exports | |
	1995	1996	1995	1996
Quantity (1,000 tonnes)	52,614	55,390	28,108	28,745
Value (1m. sch.)	668,031	712,760	580,014	612,190

Main export markets (% of total exports) in 1996: Germany, 43·6%; Italy, 8·8%; Switzerland, 3·8%; France, 4·9%. Main import suppliers: Germany, 38·4%; Italy, 8·9%; France, 5·4%; Switzerland, 4·4%.

Tourism. Tourism is an important industry. In 1997, 18,000 hotels and boarding-houses had a total of 640,200 beds available; 17,090,000 foreigners visited Austria; of these 452,833 came from the UK and 533,057 from the USA. Tourist receipts were 148,251m. schillings in 1995.

COMMUNICATIONS

Roads. On 31 Dec. 1995 federal roads had a total length of 10,269 km, 1,607 km autobahn; provincial roads, 23,472 km. On 31 Dec. 1996 there were registered 5,038,207 motor vehicles, including 3,690,692 passenger cars, 293,614 lorries, 9,740 buses, 411,771 tractors and 560,191 motorcycles.

Railways. The major railways are nationalized. Length of route in 1996, 5,849 km, of which 3,418 km were electrified. There are also 19 private railways with a total length of 605 km. In 1995, 193m. passengers and 70m. tonnes of freight were carried by Federal Railways.

There is a metro and tramway in Vienna, and tramways in Gmunden, Graz, Innsbruck and Linz.

Civil Aviation. Austrian Airlines is 51·9% state-owned. In 1996 it operated 4 A310-300s, 2 A340-200s, 1 A321-111, 7 MD-81s, 6 MD-82s, 2 MD-83s, 5 MD-87s. There are international airports at Vienna (Schwechat), Linz, Salzburg, Graz, Klagenfurt and Innsbruck. In 1996, 229,235 commercial aircraft and 12,175,557 passengers arrived and departed; 114,940 tonnes of freight, 12,225 tonnes of transit freight and 7,758 tonnes of mail were handled.

Shipping. The Danube is an important waterway. Goods traffic (in 1,000 tonnes): 6,542 in 1993; 7,706 in 1994; 8,791 in 1995; 9,303 in 1996 (including the Rhine-Main-Danube Canal).

Telecommunications. Postal, telegraph and telephone services are mainly state owned. In 1996 there were 3,779,000 telephone main connections.

The 'Österreichische Rundfunk' (Austrian Broadcasting Corporation) is state-controlled. Private TV broadcasting is not permitted. It transmits 4 national and 9 regional radio programmes. An additional programme in English and French can be received all over the country; there is also a 24 hour foreign service (short wave). Broadcasting is financed by licence payments and advertisements. There were 2·79m. registered listeners in Dec. 1996. 2 TV programmes are transmitted (colour by PAL), with 2·64m. licences in 1996.

Cinemas (1996). There were 401 cinemas.

Press. There were 12 daily newspapers (6 of them in Vienna) in 1995. For 1996 it was estimated that 76·8% of the population over 14 years read daily newspapers.

SOCIAL INSTITUTIONS

Justice. The Supreme Court of Justice (*Oberster Gerichtshof*) in Vienna is the highest court in the land. In addition, there were in 1995 4 higher state courts (*Oberlandesgerichte*), 16 state courts (*Landesgerichte*) and 187 local courts (*Bezirksgerichte*).

Religion. In 1991 there were 6,081,454 Roman Catholics (78%), 388,709 Protestants (5%), 158,776 (2%) Moslems, 223,631 others (2·9%), 672,251 without religious allegiance (8·6%) and 270,965 (3·5%) unknown. The Roman Catholic Church has 2 archbishoprics and 7 bishoprics.

Education (1995–96). There were 5,081 general compulsory schools (including special education) with 73,868 teachers and 689,127 pupils. Of all kinds of secondary schools there were 1,180 with 500,000 pupils.

There were also 122 commercial academies with 39,218 pupils and 5,205 teachers; 312 schools of technical and industrial training (including schools of hotel management and catering) with 6,902 teachers and 65,777 pupils; 61 higher schools of women's professions (secondary level) with 19,342 pupils; 8 training colleges of social workers with 1,276 pupils; 129 trade schools with 15,016 pupils.

The dominant institutions of higher education are the 12 universities and 6 colleges of arts, which are publicly financed. In 1994 Higher Technical Study Centres (*Fachhochschul-Studiengänge*, FHS) were established, which are private, but government-dependent, institutions. In the winter term 1996–97 there were 213,510 students enrolled at the universities, 6,835 at the colleges of arts and 3,756 at 33 FHS. About 15,000 teachers (full-time equivalent) provide tertiary level education.

Health. In 1996 there were 31,945 doctors, 328 hospitals and 76,252 hospital beds.

Welfare. Maternity/paternity leave is for 18 months.

DIPLOMATIC REPRESENTATIVES

Of Austria in Great Britain (18 Belgrave Mews West, London, SW1X 8HU)
Ambassador: Eva Novotny.

Of Great Britain in Austria (Jaurèsgasse 12, 1030 Vienna)
Ambassador: Anthony Figgis, CMG.

Of Austria in the USA (3524 International Court, NW, Washington, D.C., 20008)
Ambassador: Dr Helmut Türk.

Of the USA in Austria (Boltzmanngasse 14/3 and 16, A-1091 Vienna)
Ambassador: Swanee Hunt.

Of Austria to the United Nations
Ambassador: Dr Ernst Sucharipa.

Further Reading

Austrian Central Statistical Office. *Main publications: Statistisches Jahrbuch für die Republik Österreich.* New Series from 1950. Annual.—*Statistische Nachrichten.* Monthly.—*Beiträge zur österreichischen Statistik* (1,104 vols.).—*Statistik in Österreich 1918–1938.* [Bibliography] 1985.—*Veröffentlichungen des Österreichischen Statistischen Zentralamtes 1945–1985.* [Bibliography], 1990.—*Republik Österreich, 1945–1995.*

Brook-Shepherd, G., *The Austrians: a Thousand-Year Odyssey.* London, 1996
Peniston-Bird, C. M., *Vienna,* Oxford 1997
Salt, D., *Austria* [Bibliography]. Oxford and Santa Barbara (CA), 1986
Sully, M. A., *A Contemporary History of Austria.* London, 1990
Wolfram, H. (ed.) *Österreichische Geschichte.* 10 vols. Vienna, 1994

National statistical office: Austrian Central Statistical Office, POB 9000, A-1033 Vienna.
   Website: http://www.oestat.gv.at/index.htm
National library: Österreichische Nationalbibliothek, Josefsplatz, 1015 Vienna.

AZERBAIJAN

Azarbaijchan Respublikasy

Capital: Baku
Population: 7·43m.
GDP per head: (PPP$) 1,670
HDI/world rank: 0·636/106

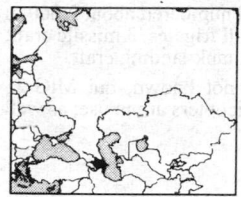

KEY HISTORICAL EVENTS. The 'Mussavat' (Nationalist) party, which dominated the National Council or Constituent Assembly of the Tatars, declared the independence of Azerbaijan on 28 May 1918, with a capital, first at Ganja (Elizavetpol) and later at Baku. On 28 April 1920 Azerbaijan was proclaimed a Soviet Socialist Republic. From 1922, with Georgia and Armenia it formed the Transcaucasian Soviet Federal Socialist Republic. In 1936 it assumed the status of one of the Union Republics of the USSR. In 1990 it adopted a declaration of republican sovereignty, and in Aug. 1991 declared itself formally independent; this was approved by 99·6% of votes at a referendum in Jan. 1992. Under the presidency of Gaidar Aliev, parliament ratified its adhesion to the CIS on 20 Sept. 1993.

A treaty of friendship and co-operation was signed with Russia on 3 July 1997.

TERRITORY AND POPULATION. Azerbaijan is bounded in the west by Armenia, in the north by Georgia and the Russian Federation (Dagestan), in the east by the Caspian sea and in the south by Iran. Its area is 86,600 sq. km (33,430 sq. miles), and it includes the Nakhichevan Autonomous Republic and the largely Armenian-inhabited Nagorno-Karabakh.

The 1989 census population was 7,021,178, of whom 82·7% were Azerbaijanis, 5·6% Russians, 5·6% Armenians and 2·4% Lezgins. Estimate, Jan. 1995, 7,431,000 (3·6m. males; 4m. urban). Chief cities: Baku (estimated 1997 population, 1·72m.), Gyanda (295,000) and Sumgait (271,000).

Vital statistics rates, 1994 (per 1,000 population): Births, 24·2; deaths, 7·3; growth, 16·9; infant mortality (per 1,000 live births), 28·2. Life expectancy is 71·0 years.

The official language is Azeri.

CONSTITUTION AND GOVERNMENT. At elections on 3 Oct. 1993 Heydar Aliyev was elected President against 2 opponents with 98·8% of votes cast.

Parliament is the 125-member *Melli-Majlis.* 100 seats are contested on a majority basis, and 25 distributed proportionally among political parties. For the majority seats there is a minimum 50% turn-out requirement. There is an 8% threshold. A constitutional referendum and parliamentary elections were held on 12 Nov. 1995. Turnout for the referendum was 86%. The new Constitution was approved by 91·9% of votes cast. At the parliamentary elections, 386 candidates from 8 parties and independents stood; turn-out was 79·5%. Run-off elections were held on 26 Nov. The New Azerbaijan Party (NAP) gained 70% of votes cast. (The OSCE declared these elections 'not in accordance with international standards.')

President: Heydar Aliyev (b. 1924; NAP; sworn in 10 Oct. 1993).

In March 1998 the government comprised:

Prime Minister: Artur Rasizade.

Foreign Affairs: Tofiq Zulfiqarov. *Interior:* Ramil Usubov. *Culture:* Polad Byulbyulogly. *Education:* Misir Mardanov. *National Security:* Namig Abbasov. *Defence:* Safar Abiev. *Media and Information:* Siruz Tebrizli. *Communications:* Nadir Ahmedov. *Agriculture:* Ershad Aliev. *The Economy:* Namik Nasrullaev. *Justice:* Sudaba Hasanova. *Health:* Ali Insanov. *Finance:* Fikret Usifov. *Labour and Social Protection (Acting):* Ilgar Ragimov. *Social Security:* Ali Nagiev. *Youth and Sport:* Abulfaz Karaev.

National anthem: 'Azerbaijan! Azerbaijan!'; words by A. Javady, tune by U. Hajebaev.

DEFENCE. Conscription is for 17 months.

Army. The Army is organized in 1 tank, 12 motor rifle, 1 air assault, 2 motor rifle training and 2 artillery brigades; and 2 motor rifle, 2 mountain infantry and 1 anti-tank regiment. Equipment includes 325 T-55 and T-72 main battle tanks. Personnel, 1997, 53,300. There is also a paramilitary Ministry of the Interior militia of about 20,000.

Navy. The flotilla is based at Baku on the Caspian Sea and numbered about 2,200 in 1997. It operates 34 miscellaneous vessels, including 2 small frigates, 3 missile craft, 18 fast patrol craft, 14 mine-countermeasure vessels and 1 tank landing craft.

Air Force. How many ex-Soviet aircraft are usable is not known, but MiG-21 fighters, Su-25 close support aircraft and Mi-24 armed helicopters are in use, as well as L-29 Delfin armed trainers. Personnel, 11,200 in 1997.

INTERNATIONAL RELATIONS

Membership. Azerbaijan is a member of the UN, CIS, the NATO Partnership for Peace, OSCE, OIC, IMO, WB, IMF, EBRD, BSEC and OEC. There is a dispute with Armenia over the status of the chiefly Armenian populated enclave of Nagorno-Karabakh.

ECONOMY

Performance. Real GDP growth was 5·8% in 1997. This was largely thanks to foreign investment into the country in anticipation of the forthcoming oil boom.

Budget. The 1998 budget envisaged revenue of 3,071,729·8m. manats, (of which profits tax accounted for 498,000m. manats and VAT 800,000m. manats) and expenditure of 3,796,847·3m. manats, (of which social welfare accounted for 88,275·4m. manats, education 825,842·9m. manats, health 290,143m. manats and social protection 340,000m. manats). In 1993, revenue was 53,600m. manats, of which profits tax accounted for 13,000m. manats, and VAT 12,500m. manats. Expenditure was 64,800m. manats and welfare 24,000m. manats.

Currency. The *manat* (AZM), of 100 *gyapiks* replaced the rouble in Jan. 1994. There are coins of 5, 10 and 50 gyapiks, notes of 1, 2, 5, 10, 50, 100, 250, 500, 1,000, 10,000 and 50,000 manats. Inflation was an 4·0% in 1997 (19·0% in 1996). Foreign exchange reserves were US$457m. in 1997.

Banking and Finance. The central bank and bank of issue is the National Bank (*Chairman*, Elman Rustamov). In 1996 there were 112 commercial and 4 state-owned banks. With capital requirements increasing, number of commercial banks are rapidly decreasing.

ENERGY AND NATURAL RESOURCES

Electricity. Output was 17,005m. kWh in 1996.

Oil and Gas. The most important industry is crude oil extraction; production (including gas concentrate) was 11·1m. tonnes in 1996. Natural gas, 6,500m. cu. metres. Baku is at the centre of oil exploration in the Caspian.

Minerals. The republic is rich in natural resources: Iron, aluminium, copper, lead, zinc, precious metals, sulphur pyrites, limestone and salt. In 1991, 1·6m. tonnes of iron ore were produced.

Agriculture. The chief agricultural products are grain, cotton, rice, grapes, fruit, vegetables, tobacco and silk. The Mexican rubber plant *grayule* has been acclimatized. A new kind of high-yielding winter wheat has been produced for use in mountainous parts of the republic.

Livestock on 1 Jan. 1994: Cattle, 1·6m.; pigs, 0·05m.; sheep and goats, 4·5m.

Output of main agricultural products (in 1m. tonnes) in 1993: Grain, 1·1; cotton, 0·3; potatoes, 0·2; vegetables, 0·5; fruit and berries, 0·3; meat, 0·09; milk, 0·8; and 660m. eggs.

Fisheries. About 10 tonnes of caviar are produced annually.

INDUSTRY. There are iron and steel, aluminium, copper, chemical, cement, machinery and oil related equipment, building materials, food, timber, synthetic rubber, salt, textiles and fishing industries. Output was valued at 123,000m. manats in current prices in 1993, 93·2% of the 1992 figure. Output, 1993 (in tonnes): Rolled ferrous metals, 0·2m.; mineral fertilizers, 30,000; cement, 0·6m.; processed meat, 16,500; milk products, 48,000; fabrics, 116m. sq. metres; footwear, 4·1m. pairs; 200 lathes; 90 lorries; 8,700 TV sets; 229,000 refrigerators, freezers and air conditioners.

Labour. In 1996 the population of working age was 4·5m. of whom 2·9m. were employed, 67·5% in the state sector and 17·2% in co-operatives (in 1991). There were 31,900 registered unemployed in 1996 (0·7% of the labour force), of whom 4,400 were receiving benefits. The average monthly salary in 1997 was 125,500 manats.

FOREIGN ECONOMIC RELATIONS. Foreign debt was US$567m. in 1997.

Commerce. In 1996 imports were valued at US$961·0m. (1995—667·6m.) and exports at US$631·0m. (1995—547·4m.).

COMMUNICATIONS

Roads. There were 30,400 km of motor roads (28,600 km hard-surfaced) in 1990. 533m. passengers and 21·9m. tonnes of freight were carried in 1993.

Railways. Total length was 2,118 km in 1994 of 1,520 mm gauge (1,310 km electrified). In 1994, 10·6m. passengers and 12·9m. tonnes of freight were carried.
There is a metro and tramway in Baku and a tramway in Sumgait.

Shipping. In 1995, merchant shipping totalled 0·48m. GRT, including oil tankers, 0·23m. GRT.

Civil Aviation. There is an international airport at Baku. The national carrier is the state-owned Azerbaijan Airlines, which has routes to Istanbul and other Turkish cities and in 1995 operated 2 B-707-320Cs, 2 B-727-200s and 38 ex-Soviet aircraft. In 1993, 1·5m. passengers and 14,400 tonnes of freight were carried.

Telecommunications. The government-controlled Azerbaijan Radio broadcasts 2 national and 1 regional programme, a relay of Radio Moscow and a foreign service, Radio Baku (Azeri, Arabic, Iranian and Turkish).

Press. In 1995, 422 newspapers were registered with the Ministry of Justice, but only about 50 were actually appearing. There is 1 daily, published by parliament, with a circulation of 5,000, and 2 independent thrice-weeklies with a combined circulation of 30,000. 73 journals were registered in 1995, but only 12 were appearing. 80% of all newspapers circulate in the Baku area.

SOCIAL INSTITUTIONS

Justice. In 1994, 18,533 crimes were reported, including 605 murders or attempted murders.

Religion. In 1993 the population was 62% Shia Moslem and 26% Sunni Moslem, the balance being mainly Orthodox Christian.

Education. In 1993–94 there were 1·4m. pupils in 4,332 primary and secondary schools and 2,200 children (16% of those eligible) attended pre-school institutions. There were 78 technical colleges with 33,900 students, and 23 higher educational institutions, including a state university at Baku, with 94,300 students (including correspondence students). The Azerbaijan Academy of Sciences, founded in 1945, has 30 research institutions. Adult literacy 96·3%.

Health. In 1994 there were 28,800 doctors, 70,100 junior medical personnel and 787 hospitals with 76,900 beds.

Welfare. In Jan. 1994 there were 797,000 age pensioners and 454,000 other pensioners.

NAKHICHEVAN

Area, 5,500 sq. km (2,120 sq. miles), population (Jan. 1994), 315,000. Capital, Nakhichevan (66,800). This territory, on the borders of Turkey and Iran, forms part of Azerbaijan although separated from it by the territory of Armenia. Its population in 1989 was 95·9% Azerbaijani. It was annexed by Russia in 1828. In June 1923 it was constituted as an Autonomous Region within Azerbaijan. On 9 Feb. 1924 it was elevated to the status of Autonomous Republic. The 1996 Azerbaijani Constitution defines it as an Autonomous State within Azerbaijan.

70% of the people are engaged in agriculture, of which the main branches are cotton and grapes growing. Fruit and grapes are also produced.

In 1989–90 there were 219 primary and secondary schools with 60,200 pupils, and 2,200 students in higher educational institutions.

In Jan. 1990 there were 381 doctors and 2,445 junior medical personnel.

NAGORNO-KARABAKH

Area, 4,400 sq. km (1,700 sq. miles); population (Jan. 1990), 192,400. Capital, Khankendi (33,000). Populated by Armenians (76·9% at the 1989 census) and Azerbaijanis (21·5%) and a separate khanate in the 18th century, it was established on 7 July 1923 as an Autonomous Region within Azerbaijan.

Main industries are silk, wine, dairying and building materials. Crop area is 67,200 ha; cotton, grapes and winter wheat are grown. There are 33 collective and 38 state farms.

In 1989–90 34,200 pupils were studying in primary and secondary schools, 2,400 in colleges and 2,100 in higher educational institutions. In Feb. 1988 the Supreme Soviet voted to assume Armenian rather than Azerbaijani sovereignty, and the area was placed under a 'special form of administration' subordinate to the USSR government in 1989. In Sept. 1991 the regional Soviet and the Shaumyan district Soviet jointly declared a Nagorno-Karabakh republic, which declared itself independent with a 99·9% popular vote (only the Armenian community took part in this vote as the Azeri population had already been expelled from Nagorno-Karabakh) in Dec. 1991. The autonomous status of the region was meanwhile abolished by the Azerbaijan Supreme Soviet in Nov. 1991, and the capital renamed Khankendi. A presidential decree of Jan. 1992 placed the region under direct rule. Azeri-Armenian fighting for possession of the region culminated in its occupation by Armenia in 1993, despite attempts at international mediation. Negotiations on settlements are conducted within the OSCE Minsk Group.

DIPLOMATIC REPRESENTATIVES

Of Azerbaijan in Great Britain (4 Kensington Court, London, W8 5DL)
Ambassador: Mahmud Mamed-Kuliyev.

Of Great Britain in Azerbaijan (2 Izmir St., Baku 370065)
Ambassador: Roger Thomas.

Of Azerbaijan in the USA
Chargé d'Affaires: Hafiz Pashayev.

Of the USA in Azerbaijan (83 Azadliq Prospekt, Baku)
Ambassador: Stanley Escudero.

Of Azerbaijan to the United Nations
Ambassador: Eldar Koulev.

Of Azerbaijan to the European Union
Ambassador: Mir-Gamza Efendiev.

BAHAMAS

Commonwealth of
The Bahamas

Capital: Nassau
Population: 284,000
GNP: US$3·2bn.
GDP per head (PPP$) 15,875
HDI/world rank: 0·894/28

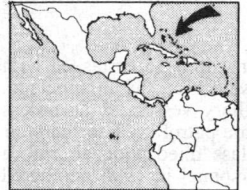

KEY HISTORICAL EVENTS. The Bahamas were discovered by Columbus in 1492 but the Spanish did not make a permanent settlement. British settlers arrived in the 17th century and it was occupied by Britain, except for a short period in the 18th century, until it gained independence. Internal self-government with cabinet responsibility was introduced on 7 Jan. 1964 and full independence achieved on 10 July 1973.

TERRITORY AND POPULATION. The Commonwealth of The Bahamas consists of 700 islands and more than 1,000 cays off the south-east coast of Florida extending for about 260,000 sq. miles. Only 22 islands are inhabited. Land area, 5,382 sq. miles (13,939 sq. km).

The areas and populations of the major islands in 1990 were as follows:

	Area (in sq. km)	Population		Area (in sq. km)	Population
Grand Bahama	1,373	40,898	Exuma Islands	290	3,556
Abaco	1,681	10,003	San Salvador	163	465
Bimini Islands	23	1,639	Rum Cay	78	53
Berry Islands	31	628	Long Island	448	2,949
New Providence	207	172,196	Ragged Island	23	89
Andros	5,957	8,177	Crooked Island	238	412
Eleuthera, Harbour Island			Acklins Island	389	405
and Spanish Wells	518	10,584	Mayaguana	285	312
Cat Island	388	1,698	Inagua Islands	1,671	985

1990 census population, 255,049 (130,091 females). 1996 estimate, 284,000; density, 20 per sq. km. The capital is Nassau on New Providence Island (178,000 in 1996); the other large town is Freeport (45,000) on Grand Bahama. Vital statistics rates, 1994 (per 1,000 population): Birth, 22·3; death, 5·6; marriage, 9·3; infant mortality (per 1,000 live births), 19·7. Expectation of life was 69 years for males and 76 for females in 1990–95.

CLIMATE. Winters are mild and summers pleasantly warm. Most rain falls in May, June, Sept. and Oct., and thunderstorms are frequent in summer. Rainfall amounts vary over the islands from 30" (750 mm) to 60" (1,500 mm). Nassau. Jan. 71°F (21·7°C), July 81°F (27·2°C). Annual rainfall 47" (1,179 mm).

CONSTITUTION AND GOVERNMENT. The Commonwealth of The Bahamas is a free and democratic sovereign state. Executive power rests with Her Majesty the Queen, who appoints a Governor-General to represent her, advised by a Cabinet whom he appoints. There is a bicameral legislature. The *Senate* comprises 16 members all appointed by the Governor-General, 9 on the advice of the Prime Minister, 4 on the advice of the Leader of the Opposition, and 3 after consultation with both of them. The *House of Assembly* consists of 40 members elected from single-member constituencies for a maximum term of 5 years. At the election of 14 March 1997, the Free National Movement gained 34 seats and the Progressive Liberal Party, 6.

Governor-General: Sir Orville Turnquest, GCMG, QC.

The Cabinet in March 1998 was composed as follows:
Prime Minister: Hubert Alexander Ingraham.
Deputy Prime Minister and Minister of National Security with responsibility for the Public Service and Public Utilities: Frank H. Watson. *Agriculture and Fisheries:* Earl Deveaux. *Attorney General and Justice:* Tennyson R. G. Wells. *Consumer*

Welfare and Aviation: Pierre V. Dupuch. *Foreign Affairs:* Janet Gwenneth Bostwick. *Education:* Dame Ivy Leona Dumont. *Finance and Planning:* William C. Allen. *Health and Environment:* Ronald Knowles. *Labour, Immigration and Training:* Theresa Moxey-Ingraham. *Public Works:* O. A. Tommy Turnquest. *Social Development and Housing:* Algernon S. P. B. Allen. *Transport:* James F. Knowles.

National anthem: 'Lift up your head to the rising sun, Bahamaland'; words and tune by T. Gibson.

DEFENCE. The Royal Defence Force is a primarily maritime force tasked with naval patrols and protection duties in the extensive waters of the archipelago. Equipment comprises 4 coastal defence vessels, 2 auxiliary vessels, 2 Dauntless search and rescue craft and 10 assorted coastal and inshore patrol craft for harbour and shallow water operations. There are also 2 cabin-class fixed wing aircraft, a Cessna Golden Eagle 421C and a Cessna Titan 404. Personnel in 1996 numbered 850, and the base is at Coral Harbour on New Providence Island.

INTERNATIONAL RELATIONS

Membership. The Commonwealth of The Bahamas is a member of the UN, OAS, the Commonwealth, CARICOM and is an ACP state of the EU.

ECONOMY

Budget (in B$1m.):

	1995-96	1996-97
Revenue	663·0	714·9
Expenditure	677·7	667·0

The main sources of revenue are customs duties and receipts from fees, post office and public utilities. There is no direct taxation.

Currency. The unit of currency is the *Bahamian dollar* (BSD) of 100 *cents.* Notes: B$0·50, 1, 3, 5, 10, 20, 50, 100; coins: 1, 5, 10, 15, 25, 50 cents, $1, 2, 5. American currency is generally accepted. Annual inflation was 1·4% in December 1996. Foreign exchange reserves were US$163·0m. in 1996.

Banking and Finance. The Central Bank of The Bahamas was established in 1974. Its Governor is Julian Francis. The Bahamas is an important centre for offshore banking. Financial business produces about 20% of GDP. In December 1996, 425 banks and trust companies were licensed, about half being branches of foreign companies.

Weights and Measures. The UK (Imperial) system is in force.

ENERGY AND NATURAL RESOURCES

Electricity. In 1996, installed capacity was 424 MW, all thermal. Output, 1996, 1,290 MWh.

Minerals. Aragonite is extracted from the seabed.

Agriculture. In 1996 there were some 8,444 ha of arable land, 3,921 ha of permanent crops and 2,230 ha of pasture. Production (in 1,000 tonnes), 1993: Sugar-cane, 200; vegetables and melons, 28; fruit, 12.

Livestock (1994): Cattle, 769; sheep, 6,292; goats, 13,580; pigs, 4,777; poultry, 1m.

Fisheries. In 1995 the total catch was valued at B$59·7m., mainly lobsters.

INDUSTRY. 2 industrial sites, one in New Providence and the other in Grand Bahama, have been developed as part of an industrialization programme. The main products are pharmaceutical chemicals, salt and rum.

Labour. The workforce was estimated at 146,635 in 1996. Unemployment was 11·5%.

Trade Unions. In 1996 there were 43 unions, the largest being The Bahamas Hotel Catering and Allied Workers' Union (5,000 members).

FOREIGN ECONOMIC RELATIONS. Public-sector foreign debt was US$410·5m. in 1994. There is a freeport zone of Grand Bahama. Although a member of CARICOM, the Bahamas is not a signatory to its trade protocols.

Commerce. In 1993 imports (excluding bullion and specie) were valued at US$223·9m., and exports at US$1,149·9m.

The principal exports are oil products and transshipments, chemicals, fish, rum and salt.

In 1996, the main export markets were: USA, 81%; Canada, 1·9%; Sweden, 7%; Singapore, 7%. The main import suppliers were: USA, 90·3%; Japan, 0·3%; France, 1·1%.

Tourism. Tourism is the most important industry, accounting for about 50% of GDP. In 1996 there were 1,633,105 stop-over and 1,685,668 cruise-ship visitors. Tourist expenditure was US$1,450m. in 1996.

COMMUNICATIONS

Roads. There are about 1,636 km of paved roads and 2,000 km of gravel roads. In 1996, 84,234 motor vehicles were registered on New Providence.

Civil Aviation. There are international airports at Nassau, Freeport (Grand Bahama Island), Moss Town (Andros) and Paradise Island (New Providence). The national carrier is the state-owned Bahamasair, which operated 6 aircraft in 1995, and flew to Miami, Newark, Orlando and Tampa. Scheduled flights are also operated by Air Canada; Air Jamaica; American Airlines; American TransAir; AOM; British Airways; Caledonian Airways; Canadian Airlines; Carnival Airlines; Condor Flugdienst; Delta Airlines; Gulfstream International Airlines; Turks and Caicos Airways; United Airlines; USAir.

Shipping. The Bahamas has an open shipping register. In 1996, registered shipping totalled 38·4m DWT, of which 8% was Bahamian-owned.

Telecommunications. In 1985 there were 127 post offices. New Providence and most of the other major islands have automatic telephone systems in operation, interconnected by a radio network, while local distribution within the islands is by overhead and underground cables. In 1996 there were 132,267 telephones in use. International telecommunications service is provided by a submarine cable system to Florida, USA, and an INTELSAT Standard 'A' Earth Station and a Standard 'F2' Earth Station. International operator assisted and direct dialling telephone services are available to all major countries. There is an automatic Telex system and a packet switching system for data transmission, and land mobile and marine telephone services. The Broadcasting Corporation of The Bahamas is a government-owned company which operates 5 radio broadcasting stations and a TV service with 3 channels. In 1997, 3 independent radio stations were operating. In 1996 there were 58,000 television and 0·2m. radio receivers. TV colour is by NTSC. There is cable TV on Grand Bahama and New Providence.

Cinemas (1996). There are 3 cinemas.

Press (1995). There were 2 national dailies and 2 weeklies.

SOCIAL INSTITUTIONS

Justice (1986). 32,878 cases (traffic, 11,334; criminal, 17,970; civil, 2,178; domestic, 1,396) were dealt with in the magistrates' court, and civil, 1,561; divorce, 516; criminal, 200 in the Supreme Court. The strength of the police force (1995) was 2,223 officers.

Religion. Religious adherents as at the 1996 census: Baptist, 32%; Anglican/Episcopalian, 20%; Roman Catholic, 19%; Protestant, 12%; Church of God, 6%; Methodist, 6%.

Education. Education is compulsory between 5 and 14 years. Adult literacy was 98% in 1996. In 1996 there were 210 schools (49 independent). Total school enrolment, Sept. 1996, 61,118. Courses lead to The Bahamas General Certificate of Secondary Education (BGCSE). Independent schools provide education at primary, secondary and high school levels.

The 4 institutions offering higher education are: The Government-sponsored College of The Bahamas, established in 1974; the University of the West Indies (regional), affiliated with The Bahamas since 1960; the Bahamas Hotel Training College, sponsored by the Ministry of Education and the hotel industry; and The Bahamas Technical and Vocational Institute, established to provide basic skills. Several schools of continuing education offer secretarial and academic courses.

Health. In 1996 there was a government general hospital (436 beds) and a psychiatric/geriatric care centre (502 beds) in Nassau, and a hospital in Freeport (82 beds). The Family Islands, comprising 20 health districts, had 13 health centres and 107 main clinics in 1996. There were 2 private hospitals (86 beds) in New Providence in 1993.

DIPLOMATIC REPRESENTATIVES

Of The Bahamas in Great Britain (10 Chesterfield St., London, W1X 8AH)
High Commissioner: Arthur Foulkes.

Of Great Britain in The Bahamas (Bitco Bldg., East St., Nassau)
High Commissioner: Peter M. Young.

Of The Bahamas in the USA (2220 Massachusetts Ave., NW, Washington, D.C., 20008)
Ambassador: Sir Arlington Butler.

Of the USA in The Bahamas (Mosmar Bldg., Queen St., Nassau)
Ambassador: Sidney Williams.

Of The Bahamas to the United Nations
Ambassador: Maurice Moore.

Of The Bahamas to the European Union
Ambassador: Arthur Foulkes.

Further Reading
Albury, P., *The Story of The Bahamas.* London, 1975.—*Paradise Island Story.* London, 1984
Boultbee, P. G., *Bahamas.* [Bibliography] Oxford and Santa Barbara, 1989
Cash, P., *et al., Sources of Bahamian History.* London, 1991
Craton, M. and Saunders, G., *Islanders in the Stream: a History of the Bahamian People.* vol. 1. Univ. of Georgia Press, 1992
Hughes, C. A., *Race and Politics in The Bahamas.* Univ. of Queensland Press, 1981
Hunte, G., *The Bahamas.* London, 1975

BAHRAIN

Dawlat al Bahrayn

(State of Bahrain)

Capital: Manama
Population: 586,109
GNP: US$4·1bn.
HDI/world rank: 0·870/43

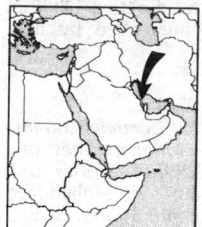

KEY HISTORICAL EVENTS. Bahrain was controlled by the Portuguese from 1521 until 1602. The Khalifa family gained control in 1783 and has ruled since that date, rejecting claims of suzerainty from Persia (Iran) and the Ottoman Empire. British assistance was sought to retain independence and in 1861 Bahrain and Britain signed a treaty of peace and friendship, and from 1861 until 1971 Bahrain was in all but name a British protectorate. Treaties signed in 1882 and in 1892 gave Britain responsibility for defence and foreign policy.

In 1970 a Council of State was established, so that the ruling family was no longer the sole executive power.

On 15 Aug. 1971 a new treaty of friendship was signed with Britain. This replaced all earlier treaties, and at the same time Bahrain declared its independence. Shaikh Isa bin Salman Al-Khalifa became the Amir with the Council of State as a cabinet. A constitution was ratified in June 1973 providing for a National Assembly of 30 members, popularly elected for a 4-year term, together with all members of the cabinet (appointed by the Amir). Elections took place in Dec. 1973. However, the relationship between the National Assembly and the Khalifa family was not successful and in 1975 the National Assembly was dissolved and the Amir has since ruled solely through the cabinet. In 1987 the main island was joined to the Saudi mainland by a causeway.

TERRITORY AND POPULATION. The State of Bahrain forms an archipelago of 36 low-lying islands in the Arabian (Persian) Gulf, between the Qatar peninsula and the mainland of Saudi Arabia. The total area is 706·6 sq. km. The island Bahrain (578 sq. km) is connected by a 1·5-mile causeway to the second largest island, Muharraq to the north-east, and by a causeway with the island of Sitra to the east. A causeway links Bahrain with Saudi Arabia. From Sitra oil pipelines and a causeway carrying a road extend out to sea for 3 miles to a deep-water anchorage.

Population (1995 est.) 586,109 (247,380 females; 362,181 Bahraini; 83% urban); density, 829·5 per sq. km. Vital statistics, 1994: Births, 13,766 (Bahraini, 10,394); deaths, 1,695 (Bahraini, 322); infant deaths, 267 (Bahraini, 212). Rates (per 1,000) for Bahrainis: Birth, 29·2; death, 3·4; natural increase, 3·9; infant mortality (per 1,000 live births), 20·4. For non-Bahrainis: Birth, 15·9; death, 1·5; natural increase, 14·4; infant mortality, 16·3. In 1994 there were 2,973 marriages (2,416 Bahraini) and 663 divorces (518 Bahraini).

There are 12 regions: Central, Eastern, Hamad Town, Hidd Town, Isa Town, Jidhafs, Manama, Muharraq, Northern, Rifa'a, Sitra, Western. Manama, the capital and commercial centre, had a 1991 census population of 136,999. Other towns are Muharraq (74,254), Rifa'a (45,596), Jidhafs (44,769), Sitra (36,755) and Isa Town (34,509).

Arabic is the official language. English is widely used in business.

CLIMATE. The climate is pleasantly warm between Dec. and March but from June to Sept. the conditions are very hot and humid. The period June to Nov. is virtually rainless. Bahrain. Jan. 66°F (19°C), July 97°F (36°C). Annual rainfall 5·2" (130 mm).

RULING HOUSE: The ruling family is the Al-Khalifa who have been in power since 1782. The present Amir, HH Shaikh Isa bin Sulman Al-Khalifa, GCMG (born 1933) succeeded on 2 Nov. 1961. *Crown Prince:* Shaikh Hamad bin Isa Al-Khalifa, KCMG.

CONSTITUTION AND GOVERNMENT. A Constitution was ratified in June 1973 providing for a National Assembly of 30 members, popularly elected for a 4-year term, together with a Cabinet, appointed by the Amir. Elections took place in Dec. 1973, but in Aug. 1975 the Amir dissolved the Assembly and has since ruled through the Cabinet alone.

By decree of the Amir on 20 Dec. 1992 a *Consultative Council* was set up. It consists of 30 members nominated by the Amir for 4-year terms. Friction between Bahrain's Shia Muslims and their Sunni rulers has been intensified by high unemployment.

In March 1998 the cabinet was composed as follows:

Prime Minister: Shaikh Khalifa bin Sulman Al-Khalifa (b. 1935).

Defence: Shaikh Khalifa bin Ahmed Al-Khalifa. *Transport and Communications:* Shaikh Ali bin Khalifa bin Sulman Al-Khalifa. *Housing, Municipalities and Environment:* Shaikh Khalid bin Abdulla Al-Khalifa. *Cabinet Affairs and Information:* Mohammed Ibrahim Al-Mutawa. *Education:* Abdul-Aziz Mohammed Al-Fadhil. *Health:* Dr Faisal Radhi Al-Musawi. *Justice and Islamic Affairs:* Shaikh Abdullah bin Khalid Al-Khalifa. *Labour and Social Affairs:* Abdul-Nabi al-Shoala. *Power and Water:* Abdullah Mohammed Jumaa. *Interior:* Shaikh Mohammed bin Khalifa bin Hamad Al-Khalifa. *Foreign Affairs:* Shaikh Mohammed bin Mubarak Al-Khalifa. *Finance and National Economy:* Ibrahim Abdul Karim Mohammed. *Oil and Industry:* Shaikh Isa bin Ali Hamad Al-Khalifa. *Commerce:* Ali Saleh Abdullah Al-Saleh. *Works and Agriculture:* Majid Al-Jishi. *Chairman of the Consultative Council:* Ibrahim Mohammed Humaidan.

National anthem: 'Bahrain ona, baladolaman' ('Our Bahrain, secure as a country'); words by M. S. Ayyash, tune anonymous.

DEFENCE. The Crown Prince is C.-in-C. of the armed forces. An agreement with the USA of Oct. 1991 gives port facilities to the US Navy and provides for mutual manoeuvres.

Army. The Army consists of 1 infantry brigade, 1 artillery brigade and 1 air defence battalion. Equipment includes 106 M-60A3 main battle tanks. Personnel, 1996, 8,500. There is a paramilitary police force of 9,000 with 5 helicopters.

Navy. The Naval force based at Mina Sulman consists of 2 West German-built missile corvettes with helicopter facilities, 4 fast missile craft, 6 fast patrol craft and 4 small amphibious transports. Personnel in 1996 numbered 1,000. There is also a Coast Guard of 250 with 20 coastal patrol craft, 4 other vessels and 1 hovercraft.

Air Force. 1 fighter squadron operates 12 F-5E/F Tiger IIs, while a second unit has 12 F-16s. 6 AH-64 Apache and 3 MBB BO 105 helicopters are also in use as well as an S-70 VIP helicopter. Personnel (1995), 1,500.

INTERNATIONAL RELATIONS

Membership. Bahrain is a member of UN, the Arab League, the Gulf Co-operation Council and OAPEC.

ECONOMY

Budget. The 1996 budget envisaged revenue of BD530m. (of which BD285m. from oil) and expenditure of BD644m.

Currency. The unit of currency is the *Bahraini dinar* (BHD), divided into 1,000 *fils*. There are notes of 500 fils and 1, 5, 10, 20 dinars and coins of 100, 50, 25, 10, 5 and 1 fils. Annualized inflation was 0·9% in 1994. Foreign exchange reserves were US$1,279·9m. in 1995. BD103·8m. were in circulation in March 1996. Gold reserves were US$43·4m. in 1995.

Banking and Finance. The Bahrain Monetary Agency (*Governor*, Abdullah Hassam Saif) has central banking powers. In 1994 there were 17 commercial banks, 2 Islamic banks, 2 specialized banks, 22 investment banks and 47 offshore banking units. 38 foreign banks had representative offices. Offshore banking units may not engage in local business; their assets totalled US$62,503m. in March 1996.

There is a stock exchange linked with those of Kuwait and Oman.

Weights and Measures. The metric system is in use.

ENERGY AND NATURAL RESOURCES

Electricity. In 1995, generating capacity was 1,100 MW. 4,550m. kWh were produced in 1994.

Oil and Gas. In 1931 oil was discovered. Operations were at first conducted by the Bahrain Petroleum Co. (BAPCO) under concession. In 1975 the government assumed a 60% interest in the oilfield and related crude oil facilities of BAPCO. Production of crude oil in 1992 was 1·9m. tonnes. Oil reserves in 1988 were 150m. bbls. Current production is around 50,000 barrels a day.

There were known natural gas reserves of 7·1m. cu. ft. in 1987. Production, 1993, 7,670m. cu. metres. Gas reserves are government-owned.

Water. Water is obtained from artesian wells and desalination plants and there is a piped supply to Manama, Muharraq, Isa Town, Rifa'a and most villages. In 1994 total water production was 24,364m. gallons; daily consumption 66·75m.

Agriculture. There are about 900 farms and small holdings (average 2·5 ha) operated by about 2,500 farmers who produce a wide variety of fruits (23,000 tonnes in 1993) and vegetables (10,000 tonnes). The major crop is alfalfa for animal fodder. 19,000 tonnes of dates were produced in 1993.

Livestock (1993): Cattle, 16,000; camels, 1,000; sheep, 9,000; goats, 17,000; poultry 1m.

Fisheries. In 1990 the government operated a fleet of 2 large and 5 smaller trawlers totalling 1,004 GRT. In 1994 total landings weighed 7,630 tonnes of which 2,256 tonnes were shellfish.

INDUSTRY. Industry is being developed with foreign participation: Aluminium smelting (and ancillary industries), ship-building and repair, petrochemicals, electronics assembly and light industry. Aluminium production was 450,749 tonnes in 1995.

Traditional crafts include boat-building, weaving and pottery.

Labour. The workforce (estimate 1995) was 0·26m. of which 50% were Bahraini. There were 3,383 persons registered unemployed in 1989.

FOREIGN ECONOMIC RELATIONS. Totally foreign-owned companies have been permitted to register since 1991. Foreign debt was US$3,106m. in 1993.

Commerce. In 1995 imports totalled BD1,362·9m. and exports, BD1,384·5m., of which oil accounted for BD922·9m. In 1994, the principal exports were (in US$1m.): Petroleum products, 2,225; manufactures, 885. Principal imports: Mineral fuels, 1,248; machinery and transport equipment, 807; manufactures, 587; chemicals, 321.

In 1994 the main export markets were: India, 21·5%; Japan, 12·2%; Saudi Arabia, 5·8%; USA, 5·6%; UAE, 4·8%. Main import suppliers: Saudi Arabia, 40%; USA, 13·1%; UK, 6·8%; Japan, 5·2%; Switzerland, 4·6%.

Tourism. In 1994 there were 44 hotels with 5,175 beds. 1,105,927 tourist nights were spent in 1994.

COMMUNICATIONS

Roads. A 25-km causeway links Bahrain with Saudi Arabia. In 1995 there were 2,816 km of roads (2,101 km hard-surfaced), including 321 km of main roads and 430 km of secondary roads. In 1994 there were 161,865 registered vehicles. There were 63 deaths in road accidents in 1994.

Civil Aviation. Bahrain International Airport is at Muharraq. Bahrain has a 25% share (with Oman, Qatar and UAE) in Gulf Air, which in 1995 operated 12 A320-200s, 3 A340-300s, 1 B-757-200PF, 18 B-767-300ERs and 5 other aircraft. Services are also operated by Aeroflot Russian Airlines, Air India, Air Lanka, Air Malta, Alitalia, American Airlines, Balkan Bulgarian, Biman Bangladesh, British Airways, Cathay Pacific Airways, Cyprus Airways, CSA, Egyptair, Finnair, Gulf Air, Iran Air, KLM, Korean Air, Kuwait Airways, Lufthansa, Middle East Airlines, Northwest Airlines, Pakistan International Airlines, Royal Brunei Airlines, Royal Jordanian, Saudia, Syrian Arab Airlines, Turkish Airlines, Yemenia and Zas. In 1994, 727,951 passengers arrived and 727,498 departed by air.

Shipping. In 1995, the merchant fleet totalled 0·24m. GRT, including oil tankers, 98,297 GRT. The port of Mina Sulman is a free transit and industrial area; about 800 vessels are handled annually. In 1994, 3,864 passengers arrived and 3,963 departed by sea.

Telecommunications. The government has a 37% stake in Bahrain Telecommunications (BATELCO). There were 0·12m. telephone lines in 1995 and 5,057 fax machines in 1994. Radio Bahrain is government-controlled, Bahrain Television part-commercial. In 1993 there were 0·32m. radio and 0·27m. TV receivers (colour by PAL).

Cinemas. There were 3 cinemas in 1995. Attendance was 656,989 in 1994.

Press. In 1996 there were 2 official daily newspapers.

SOCIAL INSTITUTIONS

Justice. Criminal law is codified, based on English jurisprudence. The death penalty is authorized. In 1994, 189 cases were dealt with by summary and cassation courts, 820 by sharia courts, 8,051 by civil courts, 3,616 by executive courts, 2,967 by appeal courts and 8,061 by criminal courts (including 5,315 traffic offences). 2,965 crimes (5 murders) were registered and 4,015 sentences passed (excluding traffic offences).

Religion. Islam is the State religion. In 1996 85% of the population were Moslem (60% Shi'ite in 1990) and 7·3% Christian. There are also Jewish, Bahai, Hindu and Parsee minorities.

Education. Literacy was 83·5% of the population over 15 in 1992. Government schools provide free education from primary to technical college level. Schooling is in 3 stages: Primary (6 years), intermediate (3 years) and secondary (3 years). Secondary education may be general or specialized.

Government school statistics for 1993–94:

	Pupils		Schools		Teachers	
	Boys	Girls	Boys	Girls	Male	Female
Primary	29,533	29,148	50	47	1,203	1,343
Intermediate	13,380	13,143	22	25	944	1,143
Secondary	10,413	10,982	12	11	1,120	799

In 1993–94 there were also in the private sector 86 nurseries; and 33 schools with 4,046 Bahraini and 19,554 non-Bahraini pupils, and 144 Bahraini and 1,435 non-Bahraini teachers. There are 2 universities with, in 1993–94, 7,006 students (4,059 female) and 473 teachers and colleges of health science and catering. In 1993 there were 57 adult education centres with 5,175 students (3,341 female) and 420 teachers.

Health. There is a free medical service for all residents. In 1994 there were 278 doctors in government service and 96 in private practice, and 49 dentists. In 1994, there were 7 general hospitals, 5 maternity hospitals and 19 health centres.

Social Security. In 1976 a pensions, sickness benefits and unemployment, maternity and family allowances scheme was established. Employers contribute 7% of salaries and Bahraini employees, 11%. In 1994, 36,612 persons received state benefit payments totalling BD3,715,158. BD5,975,700 was paid out to pensioners, and BD306,600 to recipients of social insurance.

DIPLOMATIC REPRESENTATIVES

Of Bahrain in Great Britain (98 Gloucester Rd., London, SW7 4AU)
Ambassador: Shaikh Abdul Aziz bin Mubarak Al-Khalifa.

Of Great Britain in Bahrain (21 Government Ave., P.O. Box 114, Manama, 306)
Ambassador: Ian Lewty.

Of Bahrain in the USA (3502 International Dr., NW, Washington D.C., 20008)
Ambassador: Muhammad Abdul Ghaffar.

Of the USA in Bahrain (Road No. 3119, P.O. Box 26431, Manama)
Ambassador: David M. Ransom.

Of Bahrain to the United Nations
Ambassador: Jassim Buallay.

Further Reading

Bahrain Monetary Authority. *Quarterly Statistical Bulletin.*
Central Statistics Organization. *Statistical Abstract.* Annual.

Al-Khalifa, A. and Rice, M. (eds.) *Bahrain through the Ages.* London, 1993
Al-Khalifa, H. bin I., *First Light: Modern Bahrain and its Heritage.* London, 1995
Lawson, F. H., *Bahrain: The Modernization of Autocracy.* Boulder, 1989
Rumaihi, M. G., *Bahrain: Social and Political Change since the First World War.* New York and London, 1976
Unwin, P. T. H., *Bahrain.* [Bibliography]. London and Santa Barbara, 1984

National statistical office: Central Statistics Organisation, Council of Ministers, Manama.

BANGLADESH

Gana Prajatantri Bangladesh

(People's Republic of Bangladesh)

Capital: Dhaka
Population: 125·34m.
GDP per head: (PPP$) 1,331
GNP: US$26·6bn.
HDI/world rank: 0·368/144

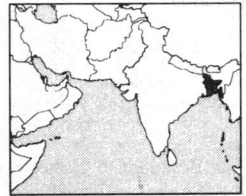

KEY HISTORICAL EVENTS. In the first half of the 18th century, the eastern territory of the Bengali people was ruled by the Nawab of Bengal. His defeat by the British East India Company in 1757 and the company's assumption of control of the area marked the beginning of the British Empire in India.

The first formal partition of Bengal was made by the Government of India in 1905. East Bengal, which was predominantly Moslem and also rural and poor, was united with Assam to form a new province. The partition was extremely unpopular with Bengali Hindus who claimed that their Bengali nationality was more important than their religious diversity. In 1912 East and West Bengal were reunited—a move unpopular with the Moslems.

Independent India was partitioned according to religion in 1947. West Bengal became part of India while East Bengal elected to join Pakistan as East Pakistan. The province, however, was separated from West Pakistan physically and ethnically, it was still poor and it continued to be neglected. Differences became unmanageable when East Pakistan's Awami League, campaigning for greater autonomy, won the majority of seats in the federal parliament in Dec. 1970. There was civil war from March to Dec. 1971. With the help of Indian troops, the Pakistani forces were defeated and the East broke away as an independent state to become the Republic of Bangladesh. The Awami League leader, Sheikh Mujibur Rahman was its first president. The constitution of 1972 provided parliamentary democracy, but in Jan. 1975 the president banned political parties and began to rule with an advisory parliament. In Aug. 1975, he was murdered and martial law was introduced. His successor as head of state, Maj.-Gen. Ziaur Rahman, was murdered by a group of army officers in May 1981. In March 1982, there was a further army *coup* after a short period of ineffective civilian government. Lieut.-Gen. Ershad was installed at the head of a military government and assumed the presidency in Dec. 1983. He was re-elected on 15 Oct. 1986. Following popular unrest President Ershad declared a state of emergency on 27 Nov. 1990, but was forced to resign on 4 Dec. and arrested on 12 Dec. He was later sentenced to 20 years imprisonment.

Democratic parliamentary elections were held in Feb. 1991 and a new President, Abdur Rahman Biswas, was elected on 8 Oct. Continuing unrest reflected the increasing strength of Islamic fundamentalism. Sheikh Hasina Wajed was sworn in as Prime Minister in June 1996 (one of her first acts was the release of former President Ershad) and in July, a former Chief Justice, Shahabuddin Ahmed, was elected president.

TERRITORY AND POPULATION. Bangladesh is bounded in the west and north by India, east by India and Myanmar and south by the Bay of Bengal. The area is 57,295 sq. miles (148,393 sq. km). In 1992 India granted a 999-year lease of the Tin Bigha corridor linking Bangladesh with its enclaves of Angarpota and Dahagram. At the 1991 census the population was 111,455,000 (54,141,000 females). Estimate, July 1997: 125,430,000. Population density, 1991, 740 per sq. km. In 1994 the birth-rate was 23·7 per 1,000 population; death-rate, 10·2; marriage rate, 10·7; infant mortality, 77 per 1,000 live births. Growth rate was 2·4% in 1992. Life expectancy, 1994: Males, 58·2 years, females, 57·9. The country is administratively divided into 5 divisions, subdivided into 64 *zila*. Area (in sq. km) and population (in 1,000) in 1994 of the 5 divisions:

	Area	Population
Barisal division	13,297	7,757
Chittagong division	46,367	29,015
Dhaka division	31,119	33,940
Khulna division	22,274	13,243
Rajshahi division	34,513	27,500

The populations of the chief cities (1991 Census) were as follows:

Dhaka[1]	3,397,187	Mymensingh	185,517	Nawabganj	121,205
Chittagong[2]	1,363,998	Barisal	163,481	Pabna	104,479
Khulna[3]	545,849	Jessore	160,198	Tangail	104,387
Rajshahi[4]	299,671	Tongi	154,175	Saidpur	102,030
Narayanganj	268,952	Comilla	143,282	Jamalpur	101,242
Rangpur	203,931	Dinajpur	126,189	Naogaon	100,794

[1] Metropolitan area 6,105,160.   [2] Metropolitan area 2,040,663.   [3] Metropolitan area 877,388.
[4] Metropolitan area 517,136.

The official language is Bengali. English is also in use for official, legal and commercial purposes.

CLIMATE. A tropical monsoon climate with heat, extreme humidity and heavy rainfall in the monsoon season, from June to Oct. The short winter season (Nov. Feb.) is mild and dry. Rainfall varies between 50" (1,250 mm) in the west to 100" (2,500 mm) in the south-east and up to 200" (5,000 mm) in the north-east. Dhaka, Jan. 66°F (19°C), July 84°F (28·9°C). Annual rainfall 81" (2,025 mm). Chittagong, Jan. 66°F (19°C), July 81°F (27·2°C). Annual rainfall 108" (2,831 mm).

CONSTITUTION AND GOVERNMENT. Bangladesh is a unitary republic. The Constitution came into force on 16 Dec. 1972 and provides for a parliamentary democracy. The head of state is the *President*, elected by parliament every 5 years, who appoints a *Vice-President*. A referendum of Sept. 1991 was in favour of abandoning the executive presidential system and opted for a parliamentary system. Turnout was low. There is a *Council of Ministers* to assist and advise the President. The President appoints the government ministers. Presidential elections were held on 23 July 1996; Shahabuddin Ahmed was elected unopposed.

Parliament has one chamber of 300 members directly elected every 5 years by citizens over 18. There are additionally 30 seats reserved for women members elected by Parliament. At the elections of 12 June 1996 the electorate was 57m.; turnout was 70%. The Awami League gained 146 seats, the Bangladesh National Party (BNP) 116, the Jatiya Party, 32. A coalition was formed between the Awami League and the Jatiya Party, but in March 1998 the Jatiya Party quit the 'national consensus' government.

President: Shahabuddin Ahmed (b. 1930; Awami League; elected 23 July 1996, sworn in 8 Oct. 1996).

In Feb. 1998 the government included:
Prime Minister with responsibility for Defence, Establishment and Health, Environment and Forests, Information, Shipping and Planning, Special Affairs, Textiles and Cabinet Division: Sheikh Hasina Wajed (b. 1947; Awami League; sworn in 23 June 1996).

Minister of Law, Justice and Parliamentary Affairs: Syed Ishtiaq Ahmed. *Water Resources:* Abdur Razzak. *Foreign Affairs:* Abdus Samad Azad. *Finance:* Shah Kibria. *Local Government, Rural Development and Co-operatives:* Zillur Rahman. *Communications:* Anwar Hossain Manju. *Health and Family Welfare:* Salahuddin Yusuf. *Posts and Telecommunications:* Mohammad Nasim. *Commerce and Industries:* Tofail Ahmed. *Food:* A. Z. Naziruddin. *Agriculture:* Matia Chowdhury. *Home Affairs:* Maj. Rafiqul Islam Islam. *Energy and Mineral Resources:* Lieut.-Gen. Nooruddin Khan. *Education:* A. S. Sadeque.. *Shipping:* A. Abdur Rob.

National anthem: 'Amar Sonar Bangla, ami tomay bhalobashi' ('My golden Bengal, I love you'); words and tune by Rabindranath Tagore.

Local Government. The country is divided into 5 divisions, each headed by a Divisional Commissioner, and subdivided into 64 districts administered by Deputy Commissioners and elected District Council. The districts are divided into 490 *thana,* of which 30 are urban.

DEFENCE. The supreme command of defence services is vested in the President.

Army. There are 7 infantry divisional headquarters, with 16 infantry brigades, 1 armoured brigade, 2 artillery brigades, 1 engineer brigade and 2 armoured regiments. Strength (1996) 101,000. There are also an armed police reserve, 5,000 strong, 20,000 security guards (Ansars) and the Bangladesh Rifles (border guard) numbering 30,000. Equipment includes 60 Soviet T-54 and 80 Chinese Type-59 main battle tanks.

Navy. Naval bases are at Chittagong, Kaptai, Khulna and Dhaka. The fleet comprises 1 new Chinese-built missile-armed frigate, 3 old ex-British frigates, 8 Chinese-built fast missile craft, 8 Chinese-built fast torpedo boats, 1 ex-British offshore patrol vessel, 15 other patrol craft, 5 inshore minesweepers, 5 locally-built 70-tonne river gunboats, 1 oiler, 1 repair vessel and 12 auxiliaries. Personnel, 1996, 9,000.

Air Force. There are 11 squadrons, 2 with F-7M interceptors, 2 with A-5 fighter-bombers, 1 with F-6 fighter-bombers, 3 with JetRanger Bell 212 and Mi8/17 helicopters, 1 with AN-26 transports, 1 with BT-6 basic trainers and 1 with Magister jet trainers. The US Government is supplying T-37s to replace the Magisters, while the Czech Republic has delivered L-39 trainers. Personnel strength, (1996) 6,500. There were 70 combat aircraft in 1995.

INTERNATIONAL RELATIONS

Membership. Bangladesh is a member of the UN, the Commonwealth and the Colombo Plan.

ECONOMY

Policy. The National Economic Council is responsible for policy. The prospective development of large natural gas reserves is expected to push up annual growth to 7·8%. Alongside the 5-year plan are 3-year rolling plans and annual development plans.

Performance. In 1996 economic growth was 5·7% with industrial growth at 3·6%. Corporate earnings grew by 9% in 1997. Trade liberalization measures were introduced 1994–96.

Budget. The fiscal year ends on 30 June. Budget, 1994–95: Revenue, Tk.137,300m. Expenditure, Tk.99,200m.

Currency. The unit of currency is the *taka* (BDT) of 100 *paisas,* which was floated in 1976. There are 1, 5, 10, 25 and 50 paisa and 1 taka coins and 1, 2, 5, 10, 20, 50, 100 and 500 taka notes. Money supply, 1992: Tk.82,572m. (of which Tk.45,344m. were in circulation). Foreign exchange reserves, 1994: US$2,800m. Inflation was 5% in 1992.

Banking and Finance. Bangladesh Bank is the central bank. There are 3 nationalized commercial banks, 11 private commercial banks, 4 specialized banks and 7 foreign commercial banks. In May 1992 the Bangladesh Bank had Tk.22,402m. deposits; Tk.33,612m. foreign liabilities, Tk.57,619m. assets. The scheduled banks had Tk.244,533m. deposits, Tk.53,442m. assets and Tk.36,289m. borrowings from the Bangladesh Bank. Post office savings deposits were Tk.6,265·7m. in 1994.

There is a stock exchange in Dhaka.

Weights and Measures. The metric system was introduced from July 1982, but some imperial and traditional measures are still in use. 1 *maund* = 37·32 kg = 40 *seers*; 1 *seer* = 0·93 kg.

ENERGY AND NATURAL RESOURCES

Electricity. Installed capacity, June 1994, 2,608 MW.; electricity generated, 1993–94, 9,784m. kWh.; consumption, 7,448m. kWh.

Gas. There are 17 natural gas fields with recoverable reserves of 10,438,700m. cu. ft. Production, 1993–94, 6,338m. cu. metres; consumption, 5,964m. cu. metres.

Water. India and Bangladesh are working towards agreement on sharing the water of the river Ganges.

Minerals. The principal minerals are lignite, limestone, china clay and glass sand. There are reserves of good-quality coal of 300m. tonnes. Production, 1992–93: Limestone, 23,209m. tonnes (value Tk.13·93m.); china clay, 1,637m. tonnes (Tk.12·48m.).

Agriculture. In 1993 81·29m. persons depended upon agriculture, of whom 25·94m. were economically active. Agriculture contributes over 30% of GDP. There are 8·8m. ha of arable and 0·6m. ha of pasture. About 3·25m. ha is irrigated.

Bangladesh is a major producer of jute: Production, 1994, 806,000 tonnes.

Rice is the most important food crop; production in 1995 (in million metric tonnes), 16·83. Other crops (1,000 tonnes): Sugar-cane, 7·45; wheat, 1·24; tobacco, 3·7; pulses, 0·53; tea, 4·7; potatoes, 1·95.

Livestock in 1994 (in 1,000): Cattle, 24,130; goats, 28,050; sheep, 1,070; buffalo, 870. Livestock products in 1994 (tonnes): Beef and veal, 145,000; cow milk, 774,000; buffalo milk, 24,000; goats' milk, 1,048,000; eggs, 102,000.

Forestry. The area under forests is 4·72m. acres. Output of timber, 1993–94, was 6·77m. cu. ft.

Fisheries. Bangladesh is a major producer of fish and products. There are 500,000 sea- and 800,000 inland-fishermen, with 1,249 mechanized boats, including 52 trawlers, and 3,317 motor boats. Inland catch, 1993–94, was 838,000 tonnes; sea, 253,000 tonnes.

INDUSTRY. Industry contributed 9·4% of GDP in 1992–93. The principal industries are jute and cotton textiles, tea, paper, newsprint, cement, chemical fertilizers and light engineering.

Production, 1994–95 (in 1,000 tonnes unless otherwise stated): Jute goods, 550,000; cotton yarn, 57·59m. kg.; cotton cloth, 31·73m. metres; cement, 316; sugar, 270; vegetable oil, 13; fertilizer, 1,981; paper, 83; bicycles (1992–93) 12,965; motor vehicles, 610; television sets, 22,916.

Labour. In 1990-91, the labour force was 51·2m. (20·1m. female), of whom 50·2m. (19·7m.) were employed (5·7m. children between 10 and 14 years were also employed). Employment (in 1,000) by industry: Agriculture, forestry and fishing, 33,303; manufacturing, 5,925; trade and catering, 4,285; services, 1,909; transport and communications, 1,611. Average daily industrial wages, 1992–93, by division: Dhaka, skilled Tk.80·61, unskilled Tk.51·68; Rajshani, skilled Tk.61·88, unskilled Tk.47·60; Khulna, skilled 80·61; unskilled 59·10; Chittagong, skilled 61·79, unskilled 49·95. On average, wage rates (US$0·23 an hour, 1997) are among the lowest of developing countries. Labour unrest was widespread in 1996.

FOREIGN ECONOMIC RELATIONS. Foreign companies are permitted wholly to own local subsidiaries. Tax concessions are available to foreign firms in the export zones of Dhaka and Chittagong. Foreign debt was US$17·1m. in 1996.

Commerce. The main exports are jute and jute goods, tea, hides and skins, newsprint, fish and garments, and the main imports are machinery, transport equipment, manufactured goods, minerals, fuels and lubricants. In 1994 exports were valued at US$2,534m., and imports at US$4,098m.

Main trading partners are USA, Hong Kong and Singapore.

Principal exports (in US$m.), Raw jute, 52; jute goods, 272; tea, 38; leather, 168; frozen shrimps and prawns, 198; clothing, 1,292.

Tourism. In 1995 there were 156,231 foreign visitors. Receipts, 24 (US$m.).

COMMUNICATIONS

Roads. There are 8,862 km of main roads and 6,742 km of paved secondary roads. In 1995 there were 27,243 buses, 34,936 lorries, 2,235 taxis, 46,561 motorized rickshaws and 39,454 private cars. There are 411,000 rickshaws and 727,000 bullock carts.

Railways. In 1993 there were 2,706 km of railways, comprising 884 km of 1,676 mm gauge and 1,822 km of metre gauge. In 1993-94 they carried 2·5m. tonnes of freight and 45m. passengers.

Civil Aviation. There are international airports at Dhaka (Zia), Chittagong and Sylhet, and 7 domestic airports. Bangladesh Biman Airlines is state-owned. In 1995 it operated 2 BAe ATPs, 5 DC-10-30s and 2 F-28-4000s and has domestic flights from Zia International Airport and services to Calcutta, Kathmandu, Bombay, Dubai, Abu Dhabi, Jeddah, Bangkok, Singapore, London, New York, Doha, Kuwait, Amsterdam, Rome, Karachi, Kuala Lumpur, Bahrain, Tripoli, Athens and Muscat. Services are also operated by Aeroflot, British Airways, Dragonair, Druk-Air, Emirates, Gulf Air, Indian Airlines, KLM, Kuwait Airways, Malaysia Airlines, Myanma Airways, Northwest Airlines, Pakistan International Airlines, Saudia, Singapore Airlines and Thai Airways. 2,127,000 passengers and 49,746 tonnes of freight passed through all airports in 1993.

Shipping. There are sea ports at Chittagong and Mongla, and inland ports at Dhaka, Chandpur, Barisal, Khulna and 5 other towns. There are 5,000 miles of navigable inland waterways. The Bangladesh Shipping Corporation owned 18 ships in 1994. Total tonnage registered, 1995, 0·53m. GRT, including oil tankers, 86,388 GRT. In 1993–94 the 2 sea ports handled 8·20m. tonnes of imports and 1·66m. tonnes of exports. Vessels entered (1992–93) 1,460 and cleared, 1,467. The Bangladesh Inland Water Transport Corporation had 288 vessels in 1994. 70·29m. passengers were carried in 1992–93.

Telecommunications. There were 8,312 post offices and 249,800 telephones in 1994. International communications are by the Indian Ocean Intelsat IV satellite.
   The government-controlled Radio Bangladesh and part-commercial Bangladesh Television transmit a home service and an external service radio programmes and a TV programme (colour by PAL). In 1995 there were 3·2m. radio and 6·1m. TV receivers.

Cinemas. In 1994 there were 946 cinemas with 420,000 seats. 130 full-length films were made.

Press. In 1994 there were 179 daily newspapers in Bengali with a circulation of 1·86m. and 13 in English with a circulation of 0·18m. There were 235 other periodicals (18 in English) with a circulation of 1·26m. In 1994, 1,258 book titles were published (122 in English).

SOCIAL INSTITUTIONS

Justice. The Supreme Court comprises an Appellate and a High Court Division, the latter having control over all subordinate courts. Judges are appointed by the President and retire at 65. There are benches at Comilla, Rangpur, Jessore, Barisal, Chittagong and Sylhet, and courts at District level.

Religion. Islam is the state religion. In 1992 the population was 86·7% Moslem and 12·1% Hindu.

Education. In 1993–94 there were 95,886 primary schools, with 16·7m. pupils and 312,186 teachers. In 1992–93 there were 11,382 secondary schools, with 4·7m. pupils and 129,655 teachers; 1,031 colleges of further education (797 private), with 912,895 students and 26,263 teachers. In 1993–94 there were 80 professional colleges with 43,503 students and 2,752 teachers.

In 1995–96, there were 5 universities, an Islamic university, an open university and universities of agriculture, engineering and technology, and science and technology; there were 5 teacher training colleges, 5 medical, 3 law and 2 fine arts colleges, an institute of ophthalmology and a rehabilitation institute. In 1994–95, there were 92,654 university students and 2,217 academic staff. Adult literacy rate, 37·3%.

Health. In 1994 there were 639 state and 280 private hospitals with a total of 35,795 beds. There were 24,911 doctors, 9,630 nurses, 7,713 midwives and 75,567 other medical personnel.

DIPLOMATIC REPRESENTATIVES

Of Bangladesh in Great Britain (28 Queen's Gate, London, SW7 5JA)
High Commissioner: A. H. Mahmood Ali.
(There are also Assistant High Commissioners in Birmingham and Manchester)

Of Great Britain in Bangladesh (United Nations Rd., Baridhara, Dhaka 12)
High Commissioner: David C. Walker, CMG., CVO.

Of Bangladesh in the USA (2201 Wisconsin Ave., NW, Washington, D.C., 20007)
Ambassador: Hamayun Kabir.

Of the USA in Bangladesh (Madani Ave., Baridhara, Dhaka 1212)
Ambassador: David N. Merrill.

Of Bangladesh to the United Nations
Ambassador: Anwarul Karim Chowdhury.

Of Bangladesh to the European Union
Ambassador: Asm Khairul Anam.

Further Reading

Bangladesh Bureau of Statistics. *Statistical Yearbook of Bangladesh.—Statistical Pocket Book of Bangladesh.*

Baxter, C., *Bangladesh: a New Nation in an Old Setting.* Boulder (CO), 1986
Chowdhury, R., *The Genesis of Bangladesh.* London, 1972
Hajnoczy, R., *Fire of Bengal.* Bangladesh Univ. Press, 1993
O'Donnell, C. P., *Bangladesh: Biography of a Muslim Nation.* Boulder (CO), 1986
Ziring, L., *Bangladesh from Mujib to Ershad: an Interpretive Study.* OUP, 1993

National statistical office: Bangladesh Bureau of Statistics, Ministry of Planning, Dhaka

BARBADOS

Capital: Bridgetown
Population: 300,000
GNP: US$1·7bn.
HDI/world rank: 0·907/25

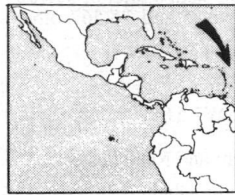

KEY HISTORICAL EVENTS. Barbados was settled by the British during the 1620s. In 1627 a Governor was appointed with a legislative council. In 1639 a House of Assembly was created. The sovereignty of Barbados never changed hands as the constitution gradually developed. Barbados was developed as a sugar plantation economy, initially on the basis of slavery until its abolition in the 1840s.

In the 19th century an executive council with ministerial powers was established. In 1951 universal suffrage was introduced, followed in 1954 by a complete ministerial system with cabinet government. Full internal self-government was attained in Oct. 1961.

From 1958–62 Barbados was a member of the short-lived Federation of the West Indies. On 30 Nov. 1966 Barbados became an independent sovereign state within the Commonwealth.

TERRITORY AND POPULATION. Barbados lies to the east of the Windward Islands. Area 166 sq. miles (430 sq. km). In 1990 the census population was 260,491; 1994 estimate, 300,000. Bridgetown is the principal city: Population, 6,720 in 1990.

Growth rate (1994), 2 per 1,000 population; birth rate, 13·4; death rate, 8·7; infant mortality, 9·8 per 1,000 live births; expectation of life, 1991: Males, 72·9 years; females, 77·4.

CLIMATE. An equable climate in winter, but the wet season, from June to Nov., is more humid. Rainfall varies from 50" (1,250 mm) on the coast to 75" (1,875 mm) in the higher interior. Bridgetown. Jan. 76°F (24·4°C), July 80°F (26·7°C). Annual rainfall 51" (1,275 mm).

CONSTITUTION AND GOVERNMENT. The Governor-General is the head of state. Parliament consists of a Senate and a House of Assembly. The *Senate* comprises 21 members appointed by the Governor-General, 12 being appointed on the advice of the Prime Minister, 2 on the advice of the Leader of the Opposition and 7 in the Governor-General's discretion. The *House of Assembly* comprises 28 members elected every 5 years. In 1963 the voting age was reduced to 18.

The *Privy Council* is appointed by the Governor-General after consultation with the Prime Minister. It consists of 12 members and the Governor-General as chairman. It advises the Governor-General in the exercise of the royal prerogative of mercy and in the exercise of his disciplinary powers over members of the public and police services.

In the general election of Sept. 1994 turn-out was 60%; the Barbados Labour Party (BLP) gained 19 seats, the Democratic Labour Party, 8 and the National Democratic Party, 1.

Governor-General: Sir Clifford Husbands, GCMG, KA.

In March 1998, the government comprised:
Prime Minister, Minister of Finance and Economic Affairs, Civil Service: Owen Arthur (b. 1950; BLP).
Deputy Prime Minister, Minister of Foreign Affairs, Tourism and International Transport: Billie Miller. *Attorney-General, Minister of Home Affairs:* David Simmons, QC. *Agriculture and Rural Development:* Rawle Eastmond. *Education, Youth Affairs and Culture:* Mia Mottley. *Health and Environment:* Elizabeth Thompson. *Labour, Community Development and Sport:* Rudolph Greenidge. *Public Works, Transport and Housing:* George Payne. *Industry, Commerce and Business*

Development: Sen. Reginald Farley. *International Trade:* Sen. Phillip Goddard. *State:* Ronald Toppin.

National anthem. 'In plenty and in time of need'; words by Irvine Burgie, tune by V. R. Edwards.

DEFENCE. The Barbados Defence Force has a strength of about 1,000. A small maritime unit numbering 110 (1996) operates 5 lightly-armed coastal patrol vessels.

INTERNATIONAL RELATIONS

Membership. Barbados is a member of UN, OAS, CARICOM, the Commonwealth and is an ACP state of the EU.

ECONOMY

Budget. The financial year runs from April. The budget for 1995–96 put total revenue at 1,150 (BDS$ m.) and recurrent expenditure at 1,264 (BDS$ m.).
VAT at 15% was introduced in Jan. 1997.

Currency. The unit of currency is the *Barbados dollar* (BDS$) of 100 *cents.* There are coins of 1, 5, 10 and 25 cents and BDS$1, and notes of BDS$2, 5, 10, 20, 50 and 100. Inflation was 3·7% in 1993. In Dec. 1993 BDS$176,987,000 were in circulation. Foreign exchange reserves were BDS$286·5m. in Dec. 1993.

Banking and Finance. The central bank and bank of issue is the Central Bank of Barbados, which had total assets of BDS$753·74m. in Dec. 1994. The total assets of commercial banks were BDS$2,650·06m.; savings banks' deposits, BDS$1,231·57m. Barbados is of growing importance as an offshore banking centre. In 1993 there were 1,171 international business companies, 926 foreign sales corporations, 190 exempt insurance companies and 23 offshore banks.
There is a stock exchange which participates in the regional Caribbean exchange.

NATURAL RESOURCES

Electricity. Production (1994) 571m. kWh.

Oil and Gas. There is 1 oilfield. Crude oil production (1994) 453,427 bbls and reserves (1994), 3·2m. bbls. Output of gas (1994) 28·9m. cu. metres and reserves 200m. cu. metres.

Agriculture. The agricultural sector accounted for 5·1% (provisional) of GDP in 1994 (24% in 1967). In 1994, 5·1% of the total labour force were employed in agriculture. Of the total area of 42,995 ha, about 18,211 ha are arable land, which is intensively cultivated. In 1994, 7,800 ha were under sugar-cane cultivation and 1,280 ha were planted with vegetables and root crops, of which 34·9% were sweet potatoes, yams and carrots. Cotton was successfully replanted in 1983. Production, 1994 (in tonnes): Sugar-cane, 0.5m.; sweet potatoes, 1,254; yams, 1,173; carrots, 1,047; onions, 726; tomatoes, 565; cucumbers, 367; cabbages, 514; beets, 699; cotton 49·9. Meat and dairy products, 1994 (in tonnes): Pork, 1,688; mutton, 55; beef, 866; veal, 13; poultry, 10,152; milk, 7,297; eggs, 1,322.
Livestock (1994): Cattle, 33,000; sheep, 66,000; goats, 38,000; pigs, 45,000; poultry, 2m.

Fisheries. In 1994 there were 740 fishing vessels employed during the flying-fish season. Large numbers of these boats are laid up from July to Oct. The catch in 1994 was 4,338 tonnes.

INDUSTRY. Industrial establishments in 1994 numbered 442 and ranged from the manufacture of processed food to small specialized products such as garment manufacturing, furniture and household appliances, electrical components, plastic products and electronic parts. In 1994, 51,396 tonnes of sugar were produced.

Labour. In 1994 the workforce was 128,800 (60,800 females), of whom 96,900 were employed (46,500 females). Unemployment was 22% of the workforce in 1994.

Trade Unions. About one-third of employees are unionized. The Barbados Workers' Union was founded in 1938 and has the majority of members. There are also a National Union of Public Workers and 2 teachers' unions.

FOREIGN ECONOMIC RELATIONS

Commerce. Total trade for calendar years in BDS$1,000:

	1990	1991	1992	1993
Domestic Imports	1,407,918	1,397,719	1,048,457	1,153,881
Domestic Exports	253,916	241,420	269,139	272,242

In 1993 the main exports (in BDS$1,000) were: Electrical components, 50,329; sugar, 47,678; chemicals, 42,177; foodstuffs, 32,284; clothing, 9,293; other manufactures, 69,360. Imports: Foodstuffs, 189,130; motor cars, 27,893; other durables, 37,055; other manufactures, 81,782.

Tourism. In 1994, tourism contributed 15·51% of GDP. In 1995 there were 442,632 stop-over arrivals (425,632 in 1994) and 484,670 cruise ship arrivals (459,502 in 1994). Tourists spent BDS$1,195·1m. in 1994.

COMMUNICATIONS

Roads. There are 2,333 km of paved roads. In 1994 there were 40,120 private cars, 2,442 hired cars and taxis, 865 buses including minibuses and 10,797 other vehicles including motorcycles.

Civil Aviation. The Grantley Adams International Airport is 11 km from Bridgetown, served in 1995 by Air Canada, Air Jamaica, Air Martinique, American Airlines, BWIA, British Airways, Canadian Airlines, Cardinal Airlines, Condor, Helenair, LIAT, LTU, Martinair Holland and Surinam Airways.

Shipping. There is a deep-water harbour at Bridgetown. 665,595 tonnes of cargo were handled in 1994. Shipping registered in 1995 totalled 0·11m. GRT, including oil-tankers, 76,219 GRT. The number of merchant vessels entering in 1994 was 1,956, of 17·3m. net tons.

Telecommunications. There is a general post office in Bridgetown and 16 branches on the island. In 1991 there were 87,343 telephones in service. The Caribbean Broadcasting Corporation is a government-owned commercial TV and radio service. There are 2 other commercial services. In 1993 there were 200,000 radios and 69,350 television sets (colour by NTSC).

Cinemas. There were (1992) 2 cinemas and 1 drive-in cinema for 600 cars.

Press. In 1995, there were 2 daily newspapers, 5 weeklies and a monthly.

SOCIAL INSTITUTIONS

Justice. Justice is administered by the Supreme Court and Justices' Appeal Court; and by magistrates' courts. All have both civil and criminal jurisdiction. There is a Chief Justice, 3 judges of appeal, 5 puisne judges of the Supreme Court and 9 magistrates. The death penalty is authorized. Final appeal lies to the Privy Council in London.

In 1995, the police force numbered 1,200.

Religion. At the 1990 census count, 32·9% of the population were Anglicans, 12·6% Pentecostalists, 5·9% Methodists, 4·4% Roman Catholics, 4·5% Seventh Day Adventists, 16·8% other religions and 22·9% no stated religion.

Education. Adult literacy is 99%. In 1991-92 there were 26,921 primary, 21,261 secondary and 202 vocational pupils in government schools and 2,573 pre-primary/primary and 3,818 secondary pupils in private schools. There were 22 secondary schools altogether in 1994-95. Education is free in all government-owned and maintained institutions from primary to university level.

In 1994-95 the University of the West Indies in Barbados (founded 1963) had 2,883 students and the Samuel Jackman Prescod Polytechnic 1,311.

Health. In 1995 there was 1 general hospital, 1 geriatric hospital, 1 psychiatric hospital, 1 leprosy hospital, 5 district hospitals and 8 health centres. In 1992 there were 1,966 hospital beds and 312 doctors.

Welfare. The National Insurance and Social Security Scheme provides contributory sickness, age, maternity, disability and survivors benefits. Sugar workers have their own scheme.

DIPLOMATIC REPRESENTATIVES

Of Barbados in Great Britain (1 Great Russell St., London, WC1B 3JY)
High Commissioner: Peter Simmons.

Of Great Britain in Barbados (Lower Collymore Rock, Bridgetown)
High Commissioner: Richard Thomas, CMG.

Of Barbados in the USA (2144 Wyoming Ave., NW, Washington, D.C. 20008)
Ambassador: Courtney Blackman.

Of the USA in Barbados (PO Box 302, Bridgetown)
Ambassador: Jeanette Hyde.

Of Barbados to the United Nations
Ambassador: Carlston Boucher.

Of Barbados to the European Union
Ambassador: Michael King.

Further Reading

Beckles, H., *A History of Barbados: from Amerindian Settlement to Nation-State.* Cambridge Univ. Press, 1990
Hoyos, F. A., *Barbados: A History from the Amerindians to Independence.* 2nd ed. London, 1992.—*Tom Adams: a Biography.* London, 1988
Potter, R. B. and Dann, G. M. S., *Barbados* [Bibliography]. Oxford and Santa Barbara (CA), 1987

National statistical office: Barbados Statistical Service, Fairchild Street, Bridgetown.

BELARUS

Respublika Belarus

Capital: Minsk
Population: 10·3m.
GNP per head: (PPP$) 4,713
HDI/world rank: 0·806/62

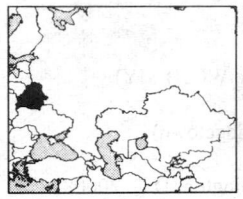

KEY HISTORICAL EVENTS. Though part of the Russian Empire since the late 18th century, national sentiment remained strong. War with Germany and revolution in Russia provided the opportunity for a declaration of independence (25 March 1918) but with the defeat of Germany, Soviet forces reasserted control. The Belorussian Soviet Socialist Republic was set up on 1 Jan. 1919. Under the Treaty of Riga (18 March 1921), Western Belarus became part of Poland. Integration with Russia was close until the Gorbachev reforms of the mid-1980s encouraged demands for greater freedom. On 25 Aug. 1991, Belarus declared its independence and in December it became a founder member of the CIS. The failure to win compensation for the Chernobyl nuclear disaster on the Ukrainian border caused friction with Moscow. The Communists retained power in Belarus despite formidable opposition and it was not until a new constitution was adopted in March 1994 and the following presidential election which brought Alyaksandr Lukashenka to power that the economic reformers began to influence events. Even so, by 1996 only 11% of state enterprises had been privatized and the government remains pro-Russian.

A referendum held over 9–24 Nov. 1996 extended the President's term of office from 3 to 5 years; increased the President's powers to rule by decree; and created a parliamentary upper house.

TERRITORY AND POPULATION. Belarus is situated along the Western Dvina and Dnieper. It is bounded in the west by Poland, north by Latvia and Lithuania, east by Russia and south by Ukraine. The area is 207,600 sq. km (80,134 sq. miles). The capital is Minsk (1·7m. population in 1994). Other important towns are Homel, Vitebsk, Mahilyou, Bobruisk, Hrodno and Brest. On 2 Nov. 1939 western Belorussia was incorporated with an area of over 108,000 sq. km and a population of 4·8m. The total population in 1995 was estimated at 10·3m. Major ethnic groups: 78% Belarussians, 13% Russians, 4% Poles, 3% Ukrainians, 1% Jews, 1% others.

Belarus comprises 6 provinces. Areas and populations, Jan. 1991:

Province	Area sq. km	Population 1991	Capital	Population 1991
Brest	32,300	1,483,700	Brest	277,000
Homel	40,400	1,628,400	Homel	503,300
Hrodno	25,000	1,188,700	Hrodno	284,800
Minsk	40,800	3,256,000	Minsk	1,633,600
Mahilyou	29,000	1,269,400	Mahilyou	363,000
Vitebsk	40,100	1,434,200	Vitebsk	369,200

CLIMATE. Moderately continental and humid with temperatures averaging 20°F (6°C) in January and 64°F (18°C) in July. Annual precipitation is 22-28" (550-700mm.).

CONSTITUTION AND GOVERNMENT. A new Constitution was adopted on 15 March 1994. It provides for a *President* who must be a citizen of at least 35 years of age, have resided for 10 years in Belarus and whose candidacy must be supported by the signatures of 70 deputies or 100,000 electors. The parliament is the Supreme Soviet of 260 members, which is directly elected. The first 2 rounds of parliamentary elections were held on 14 and 28 May 1995, as a result of which 120 deputies were elected. At the third round on 29 Nov. 1995 for 141 constituencies not elected in May, turnout was 61·8%; 20 candidates were elected. A fourth round was held on 10 Dec. 1995 when enough deputies were elected to form a quorum. Presidential elections were held on 23 June 1994. The electorate was 7·2m.; turn-out was 79%. Alyaksandr Lukashenka gained 45% of votes cast against 5 opponents, and was elected President at a run-off on 11 July 1994 by 80·1% of votes cast against 1 opponent. Turn-out was 69·9%.

There is an 11-member *Constitutional Court*. The chief justice and 5 other judges are appointed by the President.

4 referendums held on 14 May 1995 gave the President powers to dissolve parliament, work for closer economic integration with Russia, establish Russian as an official language of equal status with Belorussian and introduce a new flag.

At the referendum of 9–24 Nov. 1996 turn-out was 84·05%. 79% of votes cast were in favour of the creation of an upper house of parliament nominated by provincial governors and 70% in favour of extending the presidential term of office by 2 years to 5 years. The Supreme Soviet was dissolved and a 110-member lower *House of Representatives* established.

President: Alyaksandr Lukashenka (b. 1955; sworn in 20 July 1994).

In March 1998 the government comprised:

Prime Minister: Syarhei Linh (b. 1949).

First Deputy Prime Minister: Petr Prakapovich. *Deputy Prime Minister:* Uladzimir Harkun, Vasily Dolgolev, Valery Kokorev, Leonid Kozik, Uladzimir Zamyatalin. *Minister of Defence:* Alyaksandr Chumakau. *Foreign Affairs:* Ivan Antanovich. *Interior:* Valentsic Agolets. *Justice:* Gennady Vorontsov. *Commerce:* Petr Kozlov. *Economy:* Uladzimir Shimov. *Finance:* Nikolai Korbut. *Health:* Inessa Drobyshevskaya. *Education:* Vasil Strazher. *Culture:* Alexander Sosnovsky. *Agriculture:* Ivan Shakolo.. *Social Security:* Volga Dargel. *Business and Investment:* Alexander Sazonov. *Architecture and Construction:* Viktor Vetrov. *CIS Affairs:* Valentin Velichko. *Communications:* Vladimir Goncharenko. *Emergency Situations:* Ivan Kenik. *Foreign Economic Relations:* Mikhail Marinich. *Forestry:* Valentin Zorin. *Fuel and Energy:* Valentin Gerasimov. *Housing and Municipal Services:* Boris Batura. *Industry:* Anatoliy Kharlap. *Labour:* Ivan Lyakh. *Natural Resources and Environmental Protection:* Mikhail Rusaga. *Sports and Tourism:* Vladimir Makeychik. *State Property and Privatization:* Vasiliy Novak. *Statistics and Analysis:* Vladimir Nichiporovich.

National anthem: The music is that of the former Soviet anthem. 2 competitions for a new anthem have been held without a result.

Local Government. Elections were held in 1995.

DEFENCE. Conscription is for 18 months. A treaty with Russia of April 1993 co-ordinates their military activities. All nuclear weapons had been transferred to Russia by Dec. 1996.

Army. In 1996 ground forces numbered 50,500 and were organized in Ministry of Defence troops comprising 2 motor rifle, 1 airborne, 1 artillery and 1 rear defence division, 1 independent airborne brigade and 2 artillery and 2 multiple rocket launcher regiments; 1 surface-to-surface missile, 1 anti-tank, 1 special forces and 2 surface-to-air missile brigades; and 3 corps (1 with 3 mechanized, 1 surface-to-surface missile and 1 surface-to-air missile brigade and 1 artillery and 1 multiple rocket launcher regiment; 1 with 1 mechanized, 1 surface-to-surface missile and 1 surface-to-air missile brigade and 1 artillery and 1 multiple rocket launcher regiment; and 1 non-combatant). Equipment includes 2,348 main battle tanks (381 T-55, 170 T-62 and 1,797 T-72), 419 medium-range launchers, 60 surface-to-surface and 350 surface-to-air missiles.

Air Force. The Air Force operates 3 fighter regiments with MiG-23s, MiG-29s and Su-27s, 2 ground attack regiments equipped with Su-25 aircraft and 1 bomber regiment with Su-24s. Helicopter assets are divided among 4 regiments with 300 machines, and 1 transport regiment has over 40 aircraft. Personnel, 1996, 25,700 with about 200 combat aircraft.

INTERNATIONAL RELATIONS. A treaty of friendship with Russia was signed on 21 Feb. 1995. A further treaty signed by the respective presidents on 2 April 1997 provides for even closer integration.

Membership. Belarus is a member of the UN, CIS, IMF, World Bank, European Bank, the Central European Initiative and the NATO Partnership for Peace.

ECONOMY

Policy. Subsidies were removed in Jan. 1992 but under a reform programme of Jan. 1993 53% of retail prices were state-controlled. An economic programme for 1994 limited credit, linked the National Bank's base rate to inflation and abolished subsidies on dairy products and bread. Some 50% of state enterprises were scheduled for privatization under a scheme initiated in April 1994. GDP was valued at 12,619,000m. roubles in 1993, 91% of the 1992 figure.

Budget. The 1996 budget envisaged revenue of 56,950,000m. roubles, and expenditure of 62,940,000m. roubles. Budget income in 1993 (in 1,000m. roubles), 3,624·9, including profits tax, 1,065·4; VAT, 998·3; excise duty, 437·7; income tax, 258·3. Expenditure in 1992 was 314·1, including subsidies to state enterprises, 131·5; welfare, 96·2.

Currency. The rouble was retained under an agreement of Sept. 1993 and a treaty with Russia on monetary union of April 1994. Foreign currencies ceased to be legal tender in Oct. 1994.

Banking and Finance. The central bank is the National Bank (*Chair*, Tamara Vinnikova). In 1996 there were 36 commercial banks (3 specialized), 1 development bank and 1 commercial savings bank (The State Savings Bank merged with a commercial bank in 1995).

ENERGY AND NATURAL RESOURCES

Electricity. Output was 33,400m. kWh in 1993.

Oil and Gas. In 1993, 2m. tonnes of crude oil (including gas concentrate) and 300m. cu. metres of natural gas were produced.

Minerals. Particular attention has been paid to the development of the peat industry with a view to making Belarus as far as possible self-supporting in fuel. There are over 6,500 peat deposits. There are rich deposits of rock salt and of iron ore.

Agriculture. Belarus is hilly, with a general slope towards the south. It contains large tracts of marsh land, particularly to the south-west.

Agriculturally, it may be divided into 3 main sections—Northern: Growing flax, fodder, grasses and breeding cattle for meat and dairy produce; Central: Potato growing and pig breeding; Southern: Good natural pasture land, hemp cultivation and cattle breeding for meat and dairy produce. Agricultural output was valued at 10,500m. roubles (in constant 1983 prices) in 1993. 19·6% of the workforce is employed in agriculture.

Output of main agricultural products (in 1m. tonnes) in 1993: Grain, 7·5; meat and fats, 0·8; milk, 5·6; potatoes, 11·6; vegetables, 1; sugar-beet, 1·6; and 3,505m. eggs. In 1994, there were 5·8m. cattle, 4·2m. pigs and 0·3m. sheep and goats.

Since 1991 individuals may own land and pass it to their heirs, but not sell it. The area under cultivation was 11·9m. ha in 1993, of which the private subsidiary sector accounted for 1·4m. ha. There were 2,700 farms. The private and commercial sectors accounted for 38% of the value of agricultural output in 1993 (particularly potatoes and vegetables).

Forestry. Forests occupy around 35·5% of the country. There are valuable reserves of oak, elm, maple and white beech. 5·8m. cu. metres of timber were produced in 1991. Total stock is over 1,000m. cu. metres.

INDUSTRY. Industrial production was valued at 16,868,000m. roubles in current prices in 1993, or 90% of the 1992 figure. There are food-processing, chemical, textile, artificial silk, flax-spinning, motor vehicle, leather, machine-tool and agricultural machinery industries. Output in 1993 (in tonnes): Rolled ferrous metals, 0·7m.; mineral fertilizers, 2·5m.; paper, 58,800; cement, 1·9m.; milk products, 1·4m.; artificial fabrics, 293,000; fabrics, 372m. cu. metres; footwear, 33·4m. pairs; 10,000 lathes; 30,800 lorries; 82,400 tractors; 609,000 TV sets; 738,000 refrigerators and freezers.

Labour. In 1993 the population of working age was 6m., of whom 4·76m. were employed, 69·2% in the state sector and 17·2% in co-operatives.

Trade Unions. Trade unions are grouped in the Federation of Trade Unions of Belarus.

FOREIGN ECONOMIC RELATIONS

Commerce. In 1993 imports were valued at US$747·2m. and exports at US$715·2m.

COMMUNICATIONS

Roads. In 1996 there were 51,000 km of motor roads (50,100 km hard-surfaced). In 1993, 1,702m. passengers and 209m. tonnes of freight were carried.

Railways. In 1995 there were 5,523 km of 1,520 mm gauge railways (889 km electrified). In 1995, 125m. passengers and 73·4m. tonnes of freight were carried.

Civil Aviation. The national carrier is Belavia, which flew 73 ex-Soviet aircraft in 1995. In 1993, 0·5m. passengers and 3,000 tonnes of freight were carried. There are 7 airports serving 56 airlines.

Inland Waterways. In 1993, 0·3m. passengers and 8·9m. tonnes of freight were carried.

Telecommunications. The government-controlled Belarus Radio broadcasts 2 national programmes and various regional programmes, a foreign service (Belorussian, German) and a shared relay with Radio Moscow. Belarus Television broadcasts on 1 channel (colour by SECAM).

Press (1989). Of 220 newspapers published 131 were in Belorussian. Daily circulation of Belorussian-language newspapers, 1·8m., other languages, 3·6m.

SOCIAL INSTITUTIONS

Justice. The death penalty is retained following the constitutional referendum of Nov. 1996.
120,254 crimes were reported in 1994.

Religion. The Orthodox is the largest church. There is a Roman Catholic archdiocese of Minsk and Mahilyou, and 5 dioceses embracing 455 parishes.

Education. The number of children in 5,187 primary and secondary schools was 1·5m. in 1993-94. 0·5m. children attended 4,693 pre-school institutions in 1994.
In 1995-96, there were 4 universities; specialized universities of agriculture, culture, economics, informatics and radio-electronics, linguistics, teacher training and transport; academies of agriculture, arts, music, physical culture and sport and a polytechnical academy; 4 medical, 3 polytechnical and 3 teacher training institutes, and institutes of agriculture, co-operation, light industry technology, machine-building and veterinary science. In 1993-94, there were 304,600 students in higher education.

Health. In 1994 there were 43,900 doctors, 116,000 junior medical staff and 878 hospitals with 129,000 beds.

Welfare. In Jan. 1994 there were 1,987,000 age, and 0·6m. other pensioners.

DIPLOMATIC REPRESENTATIVES

Of Belarus in Great Britain (6 Kensington Court, London W8 5DL)
Ambassador: Uladzimir Shchasny.

Of Great Britain in Belarus (37 Karl Marx St., Minsk 220030)
Ambassador: Jessica Pearce.
Of Belarus in the USA (1511 K Street NW, Washington, D.C., 20005)
Chargé d'Affaires: Valery Tsapcala.

Of the USA in Belarus (46 Starovilenskaya, Minsk)
Ambassador: D. Spekhard.

Of Belarus to the United Nations
Ambassador: Alyaksandr Sychou.

Of Belarus to the European Union
Ambassador: Vladimir Labunov.

Further Reading

Marples, D. R. *Belarus: from Soviet Rule to Nuclear Catastrophe.* London, 1996
Zaprudnik, J., *Belarus at the Crossroads in History.* Boulder (CO), 1993

BELGIUM

Royaume de Belgique
Koninkrijk België

(Kingdom of Belgium)

Capital: Brussels
Population: 10·2m.
GDP per head: (PPP$) 20,985
HDI/world rank: 0·932/13

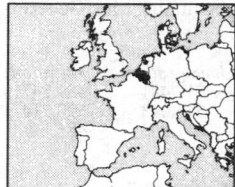

KEY HISTORICAL EVENTS. The Netherlands became part of the duchy of Burgundy in the late 14th century and through dynastic marriage came under the control of the Spanish Hapsburgs in 1504. When the northern provinces rebelled against Spanish rule in the 1570s, the southern provinces pledged their allegiance to Catholicism and the Spanish crown. The War of the Spanish Succession (1701–14) ended with the cession of Belgium to the Austrian Hapsburgs. Briefly annexed to France during the Napoleonic war, Belgium and Holland were reunited by the Treaty of Paris (1815) to form one state. The Belgians rose in revolt against this arrangement, and the kingdom of Belgium was formed as an independent state in 1830. A National Congress elected Prince Leopold of Saxe-Coburg as King of the Belgians, and he ascended the throne as Leopold I on 21 July 1831. By the Treaty of London, 15 Nov. 1831, the neutrality of Belgium was guaranteed by Austria, Russia, Great Britain and Prussia. It was not until after the signing of the Treaty of London, 19 April 1839, which established peace between Leopold I and the King of the Netherlands, that all the states of Europe recognized the kingdom of Belgium.

In 1914 Belgian neutrality was violated by the German invasion. As a consequence Britain declared war on Germany.

In the Second World War Belgium was again invaded by Germany. On this occasion the king, Leopold III, immediately surrendered, although an exiled Belgian Government operated from Britain during the war. In 1950 Leopold III abdicated in favour of his son, Baudouin.

In the post-war years linguistic problems have caused persistent quarrelling between the Flemish (Dutch)-speaking north of the country and the French-speaking Walloons of the south. This animosity has been accentuated by increasing industrialization and consequent population movements.

Following constitutional reforms voted by parliament in May 1993, Belgium became a federal state.

TERRITORY AND POPULATION. Belgium is bounded in the north by the Netherlands, north-west by the North Sea, west and south by France, east by Germany and Luxembourg. Its area is 30,528 sq. km. The Belgian exclave of Baarle-Hertog in the Netherlands has an area of 7 sq. km, and a population (1996) of 2,702. Population 10·2m. (1997 estimate); (5,198,446 females); density, 333 per sq. km. There were 911,921 resident foreign nationals in 1997.

Dutch (Flemish) is spoken by the Flemish section of the population in the north, French by the Walloon south. The linguistic frontier passes south of the capital, Brussels, which is bilingual. Some German is spoken in the east. Each language has official status in its own community. (Bracketed names below contain French or Dutch alternatives.)

Area, population and chief towns of the 10 provinces on 1 Jan. 1997:

Province	Area (sq. km)	Population	Chief Town
Flemish Region			
Antwerp	2,867	1,635,640	Antwerp (Anvers)
Flemish Brabant	2,106	1,004,692	Leuven (Louvain)
East Flanders	2,982	1,354,737	Ghent (Gand)
West Flanders	3,144	1,123,786	Bruges (Brugge)
Limburg	2,422	779,969	Hasselt

Province	Area (sq. km)	Population	Chief Town
Walloon Region			
Walloon Brabant	1,091	341,565	Wavre
Hainaut (Henegouwen)	3,786	1,284,347	Mons (Bergen)
Liège (Luik)	3,862	1,014,941	Liège (Luik)
Luxembourg	4,440	242,526	Arlon (Aarlen)
Namur (Namen)	3,666	437,426	Namur (Namen)

Population of the regions on 1 Jan. 1997: Brussels Capital Region, 950,597; Flemish Region, 5,898,824; Walloon Region, 3,320,805 (including the German-speaking Region, 69,703).

Vital statistics:

	Births	Deaths	Marriages	Divorces	Immigration[1]	Emigration[1]
1994	115,361	103,566	51,962	22,041	517,481	499,847
1995	114,226	104,590	51,402	34,983	514,093	500,714
1996	115,214	104,140	50,598	28,384	511,095	486,247

[1] Including internal.

The most populous towns, with estimated population on 1 Jan. 1997:

Brussels	950,597	St Niklaas (St Nicolas)	68,049
Antwerp (Anvers)	453,030	Tournai (Doornik)	67,891
Ghent (Gand)	225,469	Hasselt	67,552
Charleroi	204,899	Genk	62,336
Liège (Luik)	189,510	Seraing	61,077
Brugge (Bruges)	115,500	Verviers	53,620
Namur (Namen)	105,243	Roeselare (Roulers)	53,611
Mons (Bergen)	91,997	Mouscron (Moeskroen)	52,764
Leuven (Louvain)	87,789	Turnhout	36,626
La Louvière	76,809	Herstal	36,565
Aalst (Alost)	76,197	Lokeren	36,123
Kortrijk (Courtrai)	75,639	Vilvoorde (Vilvorde)	33,806
Mechelen (Malines)	75,255	Lier (Lierre)	31,705
Ostend	68,049		

CLIMATE. Cool temperate climate, influenced by the sea, giving mild winters and cool summers. Brussels. Jan. 36°F (2·2°C), July 64°F (17·8°C). Annual rainfall 33" (825 mm). Ostend. Jan. 38°F (3·3°C), July 62°F (16·7°C). Annual rainfall 31" (775 mm).

ROYAL HOUSE. The reigning King is **Albert II,** born 6 June 1934, who succeeded his brother, Baudouin, on 9 Aug. 1993. Married on 2 July 1959 to Paola Ruffo di Calabria, daughter of Don Fuleo and Donna Luisa Gazelli de Rossena. *Offspring:* Prince Philippe, Duke of Brabant, b. 15 April 1960; Princess Astrid, b. 5 June 1962; Prince Laurent, b. 19 Oct. 1963. Princess Astrid married Archduke Lorenz of Austria, 22 Sept. 1984. *Offspring:* Prince Amedeo, b. 21 Feb. 1986; Princess Maria Laura, b. 26 Aug. 1988; Prince Joachim, b. 9 Dec. 1991; Princess Luisa Maria, b. 11 Oct. 1995.

The Dowager Queen. Queen Fabiola de Mora y Aragón, daughter of the Conde de Mora y Aragón and Marqués de Casa Riera; married to King Baudouin on 15 Dec. 1960. *Sister of the King.* Josephine Charlotte, Princess of Belgium, b. 11 Oct. 1927; married to Prince Jean of Luxembourg, 9 April 1953. *Half-brother and half-sisters of the King.* Prince Alexandre, b. 18 July 1942; Princess Marie Christine, b. 6 Feb. 1951; Princess Maria-Esmeralda, b. 30 Sept. 1956. *Aunt of the King.* Princess Marie-José, b. 4 Aug. 1906, married to Prince Umberto (King Umberto II of Italy in 1946) on 8 Jan. 1930.

A constitutional amendment of June 1991 permits women to accede to the throne.

The King receives an annual tax-free sum from the civil list of 244m. francs for the duration of his reign; Prince Philippe receives 13·5m. francs; Queen Fabiola, 45m. francs.

CONSTITUTION AND GOVERNMENT. According to the constitution of 1831, Belgium is a constitutional, representative and hereditary monarchy. The legislative power is vested in the King, the federal parliament and the community and regional councils. The King convokes parliament after an election or the resignation of a government, and has the power to dissolve it in accordance with Article 46 of the Constitution.

Constitutional reforms begun in Dec. 1970 culminated in May 1993 in the transformation of Belgium from a unitary into a 'federal state, composed of communities and regions'. The communities are 3 in number and based on language: Flemish, French and German. The regions also number 3, and are based territorially: Flemish, Walloon and the Capital Brussels.

Since 1995 the federal parliament has consisted of a 150-member *Chamber of Representatives*, directly elected by obligatory universal suffrage from 20 constituencies on a proportional representation system for 4-year terms; and a *Senate* of 71 members (excluding senators by right, i.e. certain members of the Royal Family). 25 senators are elected by a Flemish, and 15 by a French, electoral college; 21 are designated by community councils (10 Flemish, 10 French and 1 German). These senators co-opt a further 10 senators (6 Flemish and 4 French).

The federal parliament's powers relate to constitutional reform, federal finance, foreign affairs, defence, justice, internal security, social security and some areas of public health. The Senate is essentially a revising chamber, though it may initiate certain legislation, and is equally competent with the Chamber of Representatives in matters concerning constitutional reform and the assent to international treaties.

The number of ministers in the federal government is limited to 15. The Council of Ministers, apart from the Prime Minister, must comprise an equal number of Dutch- and French-speakers. Members of parliament, if appointed ministers, are replaced in parliament by the runner-up on the electoral list for the minister's period of office. Community and regional councillors may not be members of the Chamber of Representatives or Senate.

Elections were held on 21 May 1995. The electorate was 7,199,440; turn-out was 6,562,149. Flemish Christian Social Party (CVP) won 29 seats with 17·18% of votes cast, Flemish Liberal and Democratic Party (VLD) 21 with 13·15%, Francophone Socialist Party (PS) 21 with 11·87%, Flemish Socialist Party (SP) 20 with 12·56%, Francophone Liberal Reform Party-Democratic Front of Francophones (PRL-FDF) 18 with 10·26%, Francophone Christian Social Party 12 with 7·73%, Vlaams Blok (VB) 11 with 7·83%, Francophone Ecology Party (ECOLO) 6 with 4·01%, Volksunie (VU) 5 with 4·67%, Flemish Ecology Party (AGALEV) 5 with 4·43%, National Front (FN) 2 with 2·28%.

A 4-party coalition government was formed in June 1995 which in March 1998 comprised:

Prime Minister: Jean-Luc Dehaene (CVP).

4 Deputy Prime Ministers: Elio di Rupo (PS) *(Communications and Economic Affairs)*; Johan Vande Lanotte (SP) *(Interior)*; Philippe Maystadt (PSC) *(Finance and Foreign Trade)*; Herman Van Rompuy (CVP) *(Budget)*. *Cabinet Ministers. Science Policy:* Yvan Ylieff (PS). *Health and Pensions:* Marcel Colla (SP). *Foreign Affairs:* Eric Derycke (SP). *Employment and Work, with responsibility for Equality of the Sexes:* Miet Smet (CVP). *Social Affairs:* Magda De Galan (PS). *Agriculture and Small Business:* Karel Pinxten (CVP). *Transport:* Michel Daerden (PS). *Justice:* Stefaan De Clerck (CVP). *Civil Service:* André Flahaut (PS). *Defence:* Jean-Paul Poncelet (PSC).

There are 2 *Secretaries of State* who are not members of the Council of Ministers: Reginald Moreels (CVP) *(Foreign Aid)*; Jan Peeters (SP) *(Security, Social Integration and Environment)*.

National anthem: La Brabançonne; words by C. Rogier, tune by F. van Campenhout). The Flemish version is 'O Vaderland, o edel land der Belgen' (Oh Fatherland, noble land of the Belgians).

European Parliament. Belgium has 25 representatives. At the June 1994 elections turn-out was 90·7%. The CVP won 4 seats with 17% of votes cast (group in European Parliament: Popular European Party); the Flemish Liberal and Democratic Party, 3 with 11·4% (Liberal, Democratic and Reformist Group); the PS, 3 with 11·4% (European Socialist Party); the SP, 3 with 11% (European Socialist Party); the PRL,

3 with 9% (Liberal, Democratic and Reformist Group); the Vlaams Blok, 2 with
7·8% (Radical European Alliance); the PSC, 2 with 7% (Popular European Party);
Agalev, 1 with 6·7% (Greens); the Ecology Party, 1 with 4·8% (Greens); Volksunie,
1 with 4·4% (Europe of Nations); the National Front, 1 with 2·9% (Radical European
Alliance); PSC, 1 with 0·2% (Popular European Party).

Community, Regional and Local Government. Communities and Regions elect parliaments ('councils') which in turn form governments. The Flemish Community and
the Flemish Region are represented by a single council, whereas the French
Community and the Walloon Region have a council each. There are also councils for
the Brussels Capital Region and the German-speaking Region.

The areas of competence of Community Councils are culture, education, the
media, medicine, protection of young people, the use of languages, some branches of
scientific research and international relations affecting any of these areas.

Regional Councils have responsibility for land use, town-planning, the environment, conservation and rural renewal, housing, water resources, overseeing provincial and local authorities, labour, public works, transport, the economy, credit, foreign trade, agriculture, energy, some branches of scientific research and international relations affecting any of these areas. Regions raise their own revenues and also
have a right to draw upon central government funds in some cases. Grants are available from the federal budget when the regional average product is lower than the
national level.

Community and Regional Councils and Governments in 1995:

Community/Region	Seat	No. of Council members	No. of Government members	Chief Minister
Flemish Council	Brussels	124[1]	11[3]	Luc van den Brande
French Community	Brussels	94[2]	4	Laurette Onkelinx
Walloon Region	Namur	75	7	Robert Collignon
Brussels Capital Region	Brussels	75	5	Charles Picqué
German-speaking Community	Eupen	25	3	Joseph Maraite

[1] Including 6 representatives of Flemings in Brussels.
[2] Includes 19 representatives of French-speakers in Brussels.
[3] 11 is the maximum number; the actual number in 1996 was 9.

There are 10[1] provinces and 589 communes with elected councils under a governor and burgomaster respectively. Governors and burgomasters are appointed by the
King. Elections were held on 9 Oct. 1994.

[1] The 19 communes of the Brussels Capital Region stand outside the provincial administrative
structure. They are administered by a governor appointed by the King.

DEFENCE. Conscription was abolished in 1995 and the Armed Forces were
restructured. It is aimed progressively to reduce the size of the armed forces in 1997,
making more use of civilian personnel. In 1995, after the dissolution of the Interior
Forces Command of the Ground Forces, the Interforces Territorial Command was
created. It is responsible for assignments to assure the safety of the National Territory
and for logistic support in those fields which are mutual for the different forces. In
1997 the unit totalled 3,870 personnel, comprising a Staff and three Groups: General
Support (including engineers), Infrastructure and Signals.

Army. The Army was restructured in 1995 into 3 divisions. The first, the Intervention
Force, comprises 3 mechanized brigades, 1 paracommando brigade, 1 light aviation
group (helicopter battalions) and support troops. The second, the Combat Support
Division, comprises 5 branch training schools and 10 schools. The third, the
Logistical Support Division, comprises 1 supply group, 1 maintenance group, and 1
logistical battalion. Total strength (1997) 28,200, reducing to 27,500. The
Gendarmerie ceased to be part of the Army in Jan. 1992.

Equipment includes 132 Leopard main battle tanks, 211 combat reconnaissance
tracked vehicles, 122 howitzers, 1,039 armoured personnel carriers and 28 Epervier
remotely-piloted vehicles. Aircraft operated: 10 Islander aircraft, 32 Alouette II helicopters and 46 Agusta A109 helicopters.

Navy. The naval forces, based at Ostend and Zeebrugge, include 3 frigates including 1 in reserve, 2 ocean minehunters, 7 coastal tripartite minehunters, 1 research ship and 1 training sailing vessel. Naval personnel in 1997 totalled 2,600.

The naval air arm comprises 3 Alouette SA-318 general utility helicopters.

Air Force. The Belgian Royal Air Force has a strength of (1997) 11,300 personnel and comprises a Tactical Air Force and a Training and Support Command (schools and logistical units). The Tactical Air Force includes 2 tactical wings (each has 36 F-16s), an operational reserve of 18 F-16s, 1 transport wing (equipped with 11 C-130s, 2 Boeing 727s and 11 smaller passenger aircraft) and 1 wing of SF.260 and Alpha Jet trainers (in process of being replaced by 2 A310-200s) and 5 Sea King helicopters for search and rescue missions.

INTERNATIONAL RELATIONS

Membership. Belgium is a member of the UN, EU, Council of Europe, NATO, OECD and WEU. Belgium is a signatory to the Schengen Accord abolishing border controls between Austria, Belgium, Denmark, Finland, France, Germany, Greece, Iceland, Italy, Luxembourg, the Netherlands, Norway, Portugal, Spain and Sweden.

ECONOMY

Budget. In 1995, federal revenue (in 1,000m. BEF) was 2,589·8 and expenditure, 2,100; regional and community revenue was 928·3 and expenditure, 985·3.

VAT is 21% (reduced rate, 6%).

In 1997 Government debt as a percentage of GDP was 123·6% (after 125·1% forecast). Inflation in 1997 was 1·8% (1998 forecast, 2·1%).

Currency. The unit of currency is the *Belgian franc* (BEF) of 100 *centimes.* There are coins of 50 centimes and 1, 5, 20 and 50 francs and notes of 100, 200, 500, 1,000, 2,000 and 10,000 francs. On 30 June 1997 the notes in circulation totalled BEF482bn.

Banking and Finance. The National Bank of Belgium was established in 1850. The governor—in 1997 Alfons Verplaetse—is appointed for a 5-year period. The Bank's independence is guaranteed by the law of 22 March 1993 regarding the status and the supervision of credit institutions. The national Bank of Belgium is in charge of the issue of bank notes, the execution of exchange rate policy and the conduct of monetary policy. Furthermore, it is the Bank of banks and cashier of the federal state.

The law of 22 March 1993 regarding the status and the supervision of *credit institutions* define the legal provisions governing banking activity. It transposes into Belgian legislation the European Directive of 15 December 1989 on the co-ordination of laws, regulations and administrative provisions relating to the taking up and pursuit of the business of credit institutions and the Directive of 6 April 1992 on the supervision of credit institutions on a consolidated basis.

The term 'credit institutions' covers Belgian credit institutions and those which come under the law of another country, be it a member of the European Union or not, with a registered office in Belgium. The activity of credit institutions must consist of receiving deposits and other repayable funds from the public and granting credit on their own account.

The law of 22 March 1993 applies to all credit institutions: banks, savings banks and public credit institutions. Consequently, these three major groups of credit institutions whose activity has been largely despecialized have been subject since 1993 to the same rules regarding status and supervision by the Banking and Finance Commision. Moreover, by the law of 6 April 1995 relating to secondary markets, status and supervision of investment firms, intermediaries and investment consultants, credit institutions have also direct access to securities stock exchanges.

On 30 June 1997, 135 credit institutions, with a balance sheet total of BEF29,971bn, were established in Belgium: 96 credit institutions governed by Belgian law and 39 by foreign law.

The law of 4 December 1990 on financial transactions and financial markets defines the legal frame for collective investment institutions, the sole object of which is the collective investment of capital raised from the public. It transposes into Belgian legislation the European Directive of 20 December 1985 on the co-ordination of laws, regulations and administrative provisions relating to undertakings for collective investment in transferable securities.

On 30 June 1997, 323 collective investment institutions (99 Belgian and 224 foreign) were marketed in Belgium and supervised by the Banking and Finance Commission.

Stock exchange legislation was subject to an important reform with the law of 6 April 1995 relating to secondary markets, status and supervision of investment firms, intermediaries and investment consultants. This law fundamentally modified the competitive environment and strengthened conditions for securities dealers. On 30 June 1997, 61 securities dealers were operating in Belgium with the approval of the Banking and Finance Commission.

Weights and Measures. The metric system is in force.

ENERGY AND NATURAL RESOURCES

Electricity. The production of electricity amounted to 72,359m. kWh. in 1996. 59% was nuclear-produced in 1995.

Gas. Production of gas, 1996, 422,412m. cu. metres.

Minerals. Output (in tonnes) for 4 calendar years:

	1993	1994	1995	1996
Coke	3,909,280	3,735,744	3,696,076	3,549,789
Cast iron	8,178,891	8,979,387	9,198,831	8,626,651
Wrought steel	10,118,116	11,265,234	11,539,883	10,751,711
Finished steel	9,750,433	10,979,804	11,035,293	10,962,985

Agriculture. There were, in 1996, 1,375,284 ha under cultivation, of which 294,823 ha were under cereals, 30,692 ha vegetables, 127,647 ha industrial plants, 181,991 ha root crops and 619,115 ha pastures and meadows.

Chief crops	Area in ha		Produce in tonnes		
	1995	1996	1993	1994	1995
Wheat	196,828	196,393	1,427,672	1,385,098	1,453,213
Barley	53,684	50,468	390,569	346,239	356,600
Oats	6,293	5,387	54,167	42,442	28,300
Rye	2,677	1,844	10,350	11,737	9,126
Potatoes	55,846	61,043	2,175,189	1,661,592	2,307,946
Beet (sugar)	98,810	97,990	6,264,267	5,393,732	6,080,570
Beet (fodder)	9,094	9,333	995,072	855,766	851,680
Tobacco	373	384	1,563	1,459	1,008

In 1996 there were 26,762 horses, 3,242,600 cattle, 155,391 sheep, 11,197 goats and 7,225,352 pigs.

Forestry. In 1996 forest covered 608,151 ha.

Fisheries. In 1995 the fishing fleet had a total tonnage of 23,031 GRT. Total catch, 1995, 20,519 tonnes.

INDUSTRY. Output (1996) of sugar factories and refineries, 979,169 tonnes; 10 distilleries, 37,066 hectolitres of alcohol; breweries, 17,407,700 hectolitres of beer; margarine factories, 351,309 tonnes.

Labour. Retirement age is flexible for men and 60–65 for women. In 1997 (Labour Force Survey), 1,057,000 persons worked in industry and 2,782,000 in other sectors. There were 457,000 registered unemployed in June 1997 (9·7%; 9·1% forecast in 1998).

FOREIGN ECONOMIC RELATIONS. In 1922 the customs frontier between

Belgium and Luxembourg was abolished; their foreign trade figures are amalgamated.

Commerce. Trade by selected countries (in BEF1m.):

	Imports from			Exports to		
	1994	1995	1996[1]	1994	1995	1996[1]
Argentina	9,570	7,415	10,886	5,556	6,458	7,305
Australia	11,000	10,292	14,027	14,537	17,548	17,230
Brazil	20,952	22,443	23,650	10,880	28,542	18,049
Canada	24,865	30,349	26,315	17,092	14,220	14,568
Congo (Dem. Rep)	21,708	20,384	21,873	4,599	5,609	6,430
Denmark	26,538	29,364	29,032	40,471	45,199	44,892
France	663,112	691,754	722,543	825,719	860,889	887,385
Germany	837,225	942,388	963,347	923,499	1,022,159	1,019,888
India	31,590	32,895	37,238	60,867	75,977	76,216
Italy	179,202	192,536	204,218	218,304	241,124	262,894
Netherlands	741,971	799,812	901,565	584,377	632,989	674,127
Russia	45,744	39,654	39,066	24,789	30,673	39,369
South Africa	21,483	22,427	22,060	15,083	15,746	16,527
Switzerland	67,402	65,573	61,656	91,038	88,189	88,728
UK	394,468	398,740	442,531	373,791	388,045	459,021
USA	227,695	252,651	292,450	216,850	184,798	216,769

[1] Provisional.

Imports and exports for 6 calendar years (in BEF1m.):

	Imports	Exports		Imports	Exports
1991	4,116,262	4,023,361	1994	4,220,568	4,603,024
1992	4,023,293	3,969,811	1995	4,517,417	4,952,738
1993	3,842,506	4,175,428	1996[1]	4,850,482	5,201,412

[1] Provisional.

Tourism. In 1996, 28,729,420 tourist nights were spent in 3,648 establishments in accommodation for 628,477 persons. The number of overnight stays accounted for by leisure, holiday and recreation was 22,637,036, with 1,687,543 for congresses and conferences and 3,804,003 for other business purposes. Total number of tourists reached 9,702,695 (6,717,425 leisure, 793,024 conference and 1,822,019 other business purposes). Receipts totalled 201·1m. francs.

COMMUNICATIONS

Roads. Length of roads, 1996: Motorways, 1,674 km; other state roads, 12,600 km; provincial roads, 1,326 km; local roads, about 128,200 km. The number of motor vehicles registered on 1 Aug. 1997 was 5,513,146, including 4,563,039 passenger cars, 15,878 buses, 455,556 lorries, 43,797 non-agricultural tractors, 158,928 agricultural tractors, 225,696 motor cycles and 50,252 special vehicles. In 1995 there were 50,744 road accidents, with 1,337 fatalities.

Railways. The main Belgian lines were a State enterprise from their inception in 1834. In 1926 the *Société Nationale des Chemins de Fer Belges (SNCB)* was formed to take over the railways. The State is sole holder of the ordinary shares of SNCB, which carry the majority vote at General Meetings. The length of railway operated in 1996 was 3,380 km, (electrified, 2,460 km). Revenue in 1996 was 73,537m. francs; expenditure, 72,334m. francs. In 1996, 57·1m. tonnes of freight and 142m. passengers were carried.

The regional transport undertakings Vlaamse Vervoermaatschappij and Société Régionale Wallonne de Transport operate electrified light railways around Charleroi (19 km) and from De Panne to Knokke (68 km). There is also a metro and tramway in Brussels (165 km), and tramways in Antwerp (180 km) and Ghent (29 km).

Civil Aviation. There are international airports at Brussels and Antwerp (Deurne). In 1994, 5·73m. passengers departed and 5·61m. arrived. The national airline Sabena (*Société anonyme belge d'exploitation de la navigation aérienne*) was set up in 1923. It was announced in Nov. 1990 that it was to be partially privatized, the state retaining a 25% stake. Sabena operates routes to Europe, North and South America, North,

Central and South Africa and to the Near, Middle and Far East. In 1995 its fleet comprised 32 aircraft. In 1995 Sabena flew 90m. km, carrying 4,665,122 passengers and 415 tonne/km of freight. 61 other airlines operate services.

Shipping. On 1 Jan. 1997 the merchant fleet was composed of 30 vessels of 609,372 tonnes. There were 8 shipping companies. In 1994, 33·8m. tonnes of cargo were loaded and 65·5m. tonnes discharged at Belgian ports. In 1995, 14,326 vessels entered, and 14,506 cleared, the port of Antwerp.

The length of navigable inland waterways was 1,493·3 km in 1995. 103·1m. tonnes of freight were carried on inland waterways in 1994.

Telecommunications. In 1995 there were 1,635 post offices, with a gross revenue totalling 50,540m. francs.

In 1994 there were 4,526,309 telephone subscribers, 126,944 mobile telephone subscribers and 7,351 telex subscribers.

Broadcasting is organized according to the language communities. VRT, RTBF and BRF fulfil the public service of broadcasting in Flemish, French and German respectively.

VRT (Vlaamse Radio en Televisie-omroep) is organized by decree as a public sector public limited company, which has concluded a management contract with the Flemish Government. It has 6 radio and 3 TV services: Radio 1 (news), Radio 2 (regional stations), Radio 3 (cultural), Studio Brussels (youth emphasis), Radio Donna (entertainment) and RVI (world service), TV 1 Canvas and KetNet (youth programmes). It transmits from 10 radio and 5 TV stations.

RTBF has 5 radio and 3 TV services: La Première (news. mudic, general), FW (news and entertainment), Musique 3 (classical music and culture), Bruxelles Capitale (news and entertainment), Radio 21 (youth emphasis); La Une (general), La Deux (culture and documentaries), Eurosport 21. It transmits from 12 radio and 7 TV stations.

BRF transmits a radio programme from 3 stations.

TV colour is by PAL. There are also 4 commercial networks: VTM (Dutch; cable only), RTL-TVi (French; 1 station), Canal Plus (French; 3 stations) and Filmnet (Dutch pay-TV; 2 channels).

Number of receivers (1996): car radios, 2,830,980; TVs, 3,417,424 (3,356,671 colour).

Cinemas (1996). There were 454 cinemas, with a seating capacity of 105,639.

Press. In 1993 there were 33 dailies in 94 regional editions (18 in French, 14 in Dutch and 1 in German). Total circulation in 1992, 2,057,169.

SOCIAL INSTITUTIONS

Justice. Judges are appointed for life. There is a court of cassation, 5 courts of appeal, and assize courts for political and criminal cases. There are 27 judicial districts, each with a court of first instance. In each of the 222 cantons is a justice and judge of the peace. There are, besides, various special tribunals. There is trial by jury in assize courts. The death penalty, which had been in abeyance for 45 years, was formally abolished in 1991.

The Gendarmerie ceased to be part of the army in Jan. 1992.

Religion. There is full religious liberty, and part of the income of the ministers of all denominations is paid by the State. In 1993 there were 9·06m. Roman Catholics. Numbers of clergy, 1996: Roman Catholic, 3,899; Protestant, 84; Anglican, 9; Jews, 26; Greek Orthodox, 39. There are 8 Roman Catholic dioceses subdivided into 260 deaneries. The Protestant (Evangelical) Church is under a synod. There is also a Central Jewish Consistory, a Central Committee of the Anglican Church and a Free Protestant Church.

Education. Following the constitutional reform of 1988, education is the responsibility of the Flemish and Wallon communities. There were 4,399 (1994–95) primary schools, with 743,361 pupils and 4,094 infant schools, with 426,439 pupils. 1,845

(1994–95) middle schools had a total of 3,285 pupils in the general classes and 41,616 in the technical classes in the traditional system and 751,273 in the new system.

Under the French and German linguistic systems there were 22 (1994–95) schools for training secondary teachers (4,578 students); 23 for training elementary teachers (5,233 students); 13 technical normal schools with 498 students and 16 normal infant schools with 3,864 pupils.

Higher Education (1994–95). Higher education is given in state universities: Ghent (17,484 students), Liège (13,442), Mons (2,590), the Polytechnic Faculty in Mons (1,069), the Antwerp State University Centre (2,031), the Gembloux Faculty of Agronomical Sciences (956), the Royal Military School in Brussels (456) and in the private universities: Catholic University of Louvain (45,443), the Free University of Brussels (24,888), University Institution Antwerp (2,515), St Ignatius Antwerp (3,341), Our Lady of Peace in Namur (4,545), Catholic University Faculty in Mons (1,463), St Louis in Brussels (1,229), St Aloysius in Brussels (726), the Limburg University Centre (2,378) and the Protestant Faculty of Theology in Brussels (119). The total number of students in university colleges, faculties and institutes was 124,945.

There are 5 royal academies of fine arts and 5 royal conservatoires at Brussels, Liège, Ghent, Antwerp and Mons.

Health. On 1 Jan. 1997 there were 38,690 physicians, 7,152 dentists and 14,238 pharmacists. Hospital beds numbered 77,181 in 1994.

Social Security. Expenditure in 1994 (in 1m. francs): Sickness and injury benefit (wage-earners), 511,259; (self-employed), 38,792; unemployment benefit, 247,623; retirement and survivors' (wage-earners), 437,819; (self-employed), 67,206; family allowances, 163,712.

DIPLOMATIC REPRESENTATIVES

Of Belgium in Great Britain (103 Eaton Sq., London, SW1W 9AB)
Ambassador: Lode Willems.

Of Great Britain in Belgium (Britannia Hse., rue Joseph II 28, 1040 Brussels)
Ambassador: David H. Colvin, CMG.

Of Belgium in the USA (3330 Garfield St., NW, Washington, D.C., 20008)
Ambassador: André Adam.

Of the USA in Belgium (Blvd. du Régent 27, 1000 Brussels)
Ambassador: Alan J. Blinken.

Of Belgium to the United Nations
Ambassador: Alex Reyn.

Further Reading

The Institut National de Statistique. *Statistiques du commerce extérieur* (monthly). *Bulletin de Statistique.* Bi-monthly. *Annuaire Statistique de la Belgique* (from 1870).—*Annuaire statistique de poche* (from 1965).

Service Fédéral d'Information. *Guide de l'Administration Fédérale.* Occasional
Deprez, K., and Vos, L., *Nationalism in Belgium – Shifting Identities, 1780-1995*, London 1998
Fitzmaurice, J., *The Politics of Belgium: a Unique Federalism.* Farnborough, 1996
Hermans, T. J. *et al.* (eds.) *The Flemish Movement: a Documentary History.* London, 1992
Riley, R. C., *Belgium.* [Bibliography] Oxford and Santa Barbara (CA), 1989

National statistical office: Institut National de Statistique, Rue de Louvain 44, 1000 Brussels.
Service Fédérale d'Information: POB 3000, 1040 Brussels 4.

BELIZE

Capital: Belmopan
Population: 219,296
GNP: US$0·5bn.
HDI/world rank: 0·806/63

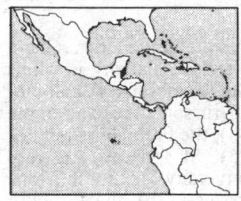

KEY HISTORICAL EVENTS. A low-lying country on the Central American mainland, Belize was the home of the Mayan civilization, which flourished from about 300 BC to 900 AD. In 1502 Columbus sailed into and named the Bay of Honduras, although he did not actually visit the area later known as British Honduras. European settlement was established in 1638 by shipwrecked British sailors. These were later joined by British soldiers and sailors disbanded after the capture of Jamaica from Spain in 1655. Spain claimed sovereignty over the entire New World except for certain Portuguese possessions and so there were numerous attacks from nearby Spanish settlements during the next century. Victory was won by the settlers in the Battle of St George's Caye in 1798. In 1862 British Honduras was formally declared a British colony, subordinate to Jamaica.

From an early date the settlers had governed themselves under a system of democracy by public meeting. A constitution was granted in 1765 and, with some modification, continued until 1840 when an executive council was created.

In 1853 the public meeting was replaced by a legislative assembly, with the British Superintendent, an office created in 1786 at the settlers' request, as chairman. British settlers began to penetrate the interior as coastal timber became exhausted. The Indians resisted this penetration and the 19th century was punctuated by clashes between the two. When the settlement became a colony in 1862, the Superintendent was replaced by a Lieut.-Governor under the Governor of Jamaica. The frontier with Guatemala was agreed by Convention in 1859 but was declared invalid by Guatemala in 1940.

The Crown Colony system of government was introduced in 1871, and the legislative assembly by its own vote was replaced by a nominated legislative council with an official majority, presided over by the Lieut.-Governor.

The administrative connection with Jamaica was severed in 1884 when the title of Lieut.-Governor was changed to that of Governor.

Universal suffrage was introduced in 1964 and thereafter the majority of the legislature were elected rather than appointed, and the ministerial system was adopted in 1971. In June 1974 British Honduras became Belize.

Independence was achieved on 21 Sept. 1981 and a new constitution introduced.

TERRITORY AND POPULATION. Belize is bounded in the north by Mexico, west and south by Guatemala and east by the Caribbean. Fringing the coast there are 3 atolls and some 400 islets (cays) in the world's second longest barrier reef (140 miles) which was declared a world heritage in 1997. Area, 22,963 sq. km.

There are 6 districts as follows, with area, population at the 1991 census and chief city:

District	Area (in sq. km)	Population	Chief City	Population
Corozal	1,860	28,217	Corozal	7,062
Belize	4,307	56,131	Belize City	44,087
Orange Walk	4,636	29,462	Orange Walk	10,966
Cayo	5,196	35,194	San Ignacio	8,962
Stann Creek	2,554	18,061	Dangriga	6,435
Toledo	4,413	17,275	Punta Gorda	3,458

Population (1996 census, est.), 219,296. In 1996 (est.) the birth rate per 1,000 was 32·8 and the death rate 5·73; infant mortality in 1996 (est.) was 33·9 per 1,000 births and there were 1,138 marriages. Life expectancy was 68·53 years in 1996. In 1995, some 45,000 Belizeans were working abroad.

The capital Belmopan had a population of 3,852 in 1993. Other towns (with 1993 population) are: Belize City (47,724), Orange Walk Town (11,922), San Ignacio (9,701), Corozal Town (7,645), Dangriga (6,966).

English is the official language. Spanish is widely spoken. At the 1996 census (est.) the main ethnic groups were Mestizo (Spanish-Maya), 44%, Creole (African descent), 30%, Mayans, 11% and Garifuna (Caribs), 7%.

CLIMATE. A tropical climate with high rainfall and small annual range of temperature. The driest months are Feb. and March. Belize. Jan. 74°F (23·3°C), July 81°F (27·2°C). Annual rainfall 76" (1,890 mm).

CONSTITUTION AND GOVERNMENT. The Constitution, which came into force on 21 Sept. 1981, provided for a National Assembly, with a 5-year term, comprising a 29-member *House of Representatives* elected by universal suffrage, and a *Senate* consisting of 8 members, 5 appointed by the Governor-General on the advice of the Prime Minister, 2 on the advice of the Leader of the Opposition and 1 on the advice of the Belize Advisory Council.

At the general election of 30 June 1993 the United Democratic Party (UDP) won 16 seats and the People's United Party 13.

Governor-General: Sir Colville Young, GCMG.

The cabinet in March 1998 was composed as follows:

Prime Minister and Minister of Finance and Economic Development: The Rt Hon. Manuel Esquivel (b. 1940; UDP).

Deputy Prime Minister, Attorney-General, Minister of Foreign Affairs and National Security: Dean Barrow. *Natural Resources:* Eduardo Juan. *Trade and Industry:* Alfredo Martinez. *Works:* Melvin Hulse. *Health and Sports:* Salvador Fernandez. *Tourism and the Environment:* Henry Young. *Agriculture and Fisheries:* Russell García. *Energy, Science, Technology and Transport:* Joseph Cayetano. *Education and Public Service:* Elodio Aragón. *Housing, Urban Development and Co-operatives, Home Affairs and Labour:* Hubert Elrington. *Youth Development, Women's Affairs and Human Resources:* Philip Goldson. *National Co-ordination and Mobilization:* Ruben Campos.

The *Speaker* is B. Q. Pitts.

National anthem: 'O, Land of the Free'; words by S. A. Haynes, tune by S. W. Young.

Local Government. At elections to 7 municipalities in March 1991 the electorate was 23,215 and 19,527 votes were cast. The PUP gained control of 5 town boards and the UDP of 2.

DEFENCE. The Belize Defence Force consists of 1 infantry battalion, with 5 active and 3 reserve companies. The Air Wing operates 2 Islander patrol aircraft and a T.67 Firefly trainer. There is also a Maritime wing. In 1996 it numbered 50 and operated 1 fast patrol craft and 10 boats and support craft. Total personnel (1996) 1,050, with a reserve militia of 700.

INTERNATIONAL RELATIONS. While asserting a longstanding territorial claim on Belize, Guatemala recognized Belize's independence in Sept. 1991. In return Belize reduced its maritime zones to 3 miles in the south, subject to final agreement on a maritime boundary.

Membership. Belize is a member of the UN, the Commonwealth, OAS, CARICOM and is an ACP state of the EU.

ECONOMY

Policy. The National Social and Economic Council was set up in 1993 to provide a forum for discussion between the public and private sectors. There are national economic plans.

Budget. The 1995-96 budget envisaged total revenue, $B255·4m. and recurring expenditure of $B267·4m.

Currency. The unit of currency is the *Belize dollar* (BZD) of 100 *cents*. There are coins of 1-, 5-, 10-, 25- and 50-cent and $B1, and notes of $B 2, 5, 10, 20, 50 and 100. Money supply was $B380·2m. in 1991. Since 1976 $B2 has been fixed at US$1.

Banking and Finance. A Central Bank was established in 1981 (*governor*, Keith Arnold). There were (1993) 4 commercial banks of which 2 are locally-owned, and a Government Savings Bank. The Development Finance Corporation provides long-term credit for development of agriculture and industry. Amendments to the Banking Ordinance permit offshore banking.

ENERGY AND NATURAL RESOURCES

Electricity. Production (1988) 90·5m. kWh. Supply 110 and 220 volts; 60 Hz. A rural electrification unit was set up in 1991.

Agriculture. 0·8m. ha are suitable for agriculture, but in 1994 only 121,400 ha were in use. In 1992 agriculture and produce-processing provided 25% of GDP and 40% of employment. The main crops are sugar-cane, citrus fruits and bananas. Maize, rice and kidney beans are grown for domestic consumption.

Forestry. 1m. ha were under forests in 1988, which include mahogany, cedar, Santa Maria, pine and rosewood and many secondary hardwoods, as well as woods suitable for pulp.

Fisheries. There were (1995) 13 registered fishing co-operatives.

INDUSTRY. Manufacturing is mainly confined to processing agricultural products and timber. There is also a clothing industry. Sugar production was 105,397 tonnes in 1993-94 (100,200 tonnes in 1992-93).

Labour. The labour market alternates between full employment, often accompanied by local shortages in the citrus and sugar-cane harvesting (Jan.–July), and under-employment during the wet season (Aug.–Dec.), aggravated by the seasonal nature of the major industries.

Trade Unions. There are 14 accredited unions with an estimated membership of 8,200 (about 55% of the labour force).

FOREIGN ECONOMIC RELATIONS

Commerce. In 1993 imports amounted to $B562m., exports, $B263m. Main exports in 1993 were sugar ($B82·9m.); clothes, ($B40·6m.); citrus products, ($B27·9m.); fish products, ($B26·4m.); bananas, ($B24·2m.).

Main export markets in 1995: USA, UK, Canada, Mexico, Jamaica. Main import suppliers: USA, UK, Canada, Mexico.

Tourism. Tourists totalled 107,641 in 1993 spending US$72·5m.

COMMUNICATIONS

Roads. In 1995 there were 416 km of main roads and 1,834 km of other roads.

Civil Aviation. There is an international airport (Philip S. W. Goldson) at Belize City. The national carrier is Maya Airways, which operated 1 aircraft in 1995. American Airlines, Continental Airlines and Air Micronesia, Island Air and Taca International Airlines also operate services. Domestic air services provide connections to all main towns and 3 of the main offshore islands.

Shipping. The main port is Belize City, with a modern deep-water port able to handle containerized shipping. There are also ports at Commerce Bight and Big Creek. In 1995, the merchant marine totalled 0·43m. GRT, including oil tankers, 0·11m. GRT and container vessels, 17,641 GRT. 9 cargo shipping lines serve Belize, and there are coastal passenger services to the offshore islands and Guatemala.

Telecommunications. Number of telephones (1995), 28,250 (about half in Belize City). Belize Telecommunications Ltd has instituted a country-wide fully automatic telephone dialling facility. There were 1,200 mobile telephones in 1995, 1,000 paging users, 300 voice mail users and 200 Internet customers. There are 7 main post offices and 61 sub-post offices.

The Broadcasting Corporation of Belize operates a national broadcasting service. Proportion of programmes, 60% in English, the remainder in Spanish and the Amerindian languages. There is also a commercial radio station. There are 2 commercial TV channels (colour by NTSC). There are satellite links with Bermuda, the USA and the UK, and radio links with Central America. In 1993 there were some 100,000 radio and 27,048 TV sets in use.

Press. There were 4 weekly newspapers and several monthly magazines in 1995.

SOCIAL INSTITUTIONS

Justice. Each of the 6 judicial districts has summary jurisdiction courts (criminal) and district courts (civil), both of which are presided over by magistrates. There is a Supreme Court, a Court of Appeal and a Family Court. There is a Director of Public Prosecutions, a Chief Justice and 2 Puisne Judges.

In 1995, the police force was 450 strong.

Religion. In 1995 58% of the population was Roman Catholic and 34% Protestant, including Anglican, Methodist, Seventh Day Adventist, Mennonite, Nazarene, Jehovah's Witness, Pentecostal and Baptist. There was a small group of Bahai.

Education. 93% literacy was claimed in 1991. Education is in English. State education is managed jointly by the government and the Roman Catholic and Anglican Churches. It is compulsory for children between 6–14 years and primary education is free. In 1992, 241 primary schools had 48,612 pupils with 1,861 teachers (1989); 31 secondary schools, 9,457 pupils with, in 1988, 576 teachers; 8 other post secondary schools, with in 1987, 932 students and 69 teachers. There is a Technical College offering craft and technical courses, a vocational Training Centre providing courses for primary school leavers, a Youth Development Centre and a College of Agriculture. There is a teachers' training college. The University College of Belize opened in 1986. There are 2 government-maintained special schools for disabled children. The University of the West Indies maintains an extra-mural department in Belize City.

Health. In 1994 there were 7 government hospitals (1 in Belmopan, 1 in Belize City and 1 in each of the other 5 districts) and an infirmary for geriatric and chronically ill patients, with in 1990, 94 doctors and 525 hospital beds. Medical services in rural areas are provided by health care centres and mobile clinics.

DIPLOMATIC REPRESENTATIVES

Of Belize in Great Britain (22 Harcourt House, 19 Cavendish Sq., London, W1M 9AD)
High Commissioner: Dr Ursula H. Barrow.

Of Great Britain in Belize (P.O. Box 91, Belmopan)
High Commissioner: Gordon Baker.

Of Belize in the USA (3400 International Dr., NW, Washington, D.C., 20008)
Ambassador: James S. Murphy.

Of the USA in Belize (Gabourel Lane and Hutson St., Belize City)
Ambassador: George C. Bruno.

Of Belize to the United Nations
Ambassador: Vacant.

Further Reading

Dobson, D., *A History of Belize.* Belize, 1973
Fernandez, J., *Belize: Case Study for Democracy in Central America.* Aldershot, 1989
Grant, C. H., *The Making of Modern Belize.* CUP, 1976
Wright, P. and Coutts, B. E., *Belize.* [Bibliography] 2nd ed. Oxford and Santa Barbara, 1993

National statistical office: Central Statistical Office, Belmopan.

BENIN

République du Bénin

Capital: Porto-Novo
Population: 5·71m.
GDP per head: (PPP$) 1,696
HDI/world rank: 0·368/146

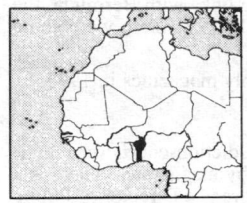

KEY HISTORICAL EVENTS. The People's Republic of Benin is the former Republic of Dahomey. Dahomey was called after the historic kingdom of Dahomey or Abomey, conquered by the French in 1892–94. The new name given to the country on 30 Nov. 1975 came from the Bight of Benin and the former 'French Bight of Benin Settlements', themselves called after the ancient kingdom of Benin in modern Nigeria. The kingdom of Dahomey was a powerful, well-organized state from the 17th century, trading extensively in slaves through the port of Whydah with the Portuguese, British and French. On the coast an educated African elite grew up in the 19th century.

After the defeat of Dahomey, whose monarchy was abolished, the French occupied territory inland up to the River Niger, and created the colony of Dahomey as part of French West Africa. Subsequently, there were several African revolts, a number occurring during the First World War. The African elite protested frequently at French rule and, as African nationalism blossomed after the Second World War, Dahomey saw lively political activity and the formation of several parties.

Dahomey became independent on 1 Aug. 1960 with a coalition of 3 parties in power and Hubert Maga as president. Opposition to his rule led to a military coup by Gen. Christophe Soglo in Oct. 1963. Soglo handed over power to another political leader, Sourou-Migan Apithy, but returned to power in late 1965. Two years later he was deposed and replaced by another military regime, led by Col. Alphonse Alley. Alley handed over in 1968 to a civilian president, Émile Derlin-Zinsou. In Dec. 1969 a 3-man military junta took control; elections were held in early 1970, after which a Presidential Council was installed in power, consisting of Maga, Apithy and Justin Ahomadegbe. Maga chaired the Council until May 1972 when he handed over to Ahomadegbe.

In Oct. 1972 Gen. Mathieu Kérékou seized power and installed a new left-wing regime committed to socialist policies. A constitution was adopted in 1977, based on a single Marxist-Leninist party, the *Parti de la Révolution Populaire du Bénin* (PRPB). Despite persistent economic problems, factional fighting within its ranks and frequent plots and attempts at its overthrow, the regime has retained power.

TERRITORY AND POPULATION. Benin is bounded in the east by Nigeria, north by Niger and Burkina Faso, west by Togo and south by the Gulf of Guinea. The area is 112,622 sq. km, and the population, census 1992, 4,855,349. Estimate (1996) 5·71m.; density, 50·7 per sq. km.

Vital statistics rates, 1996 estimates (per 1,000 population). Births, 46·8; deaths, 13·5. Infant mortality (per 1,000 live births), 105·1. Expectation of life in 1996 was 52·7 years (50·7 for males and 54·7 for females). Growth rate, 3·3%.

The areas, populations and capitals of the 6 provinces are as follows:

Province	Sq. km	Census 1992	Capital	Census 1992
Atakora	31,200	648,330	Natitingou	57,535
Borgou	51,000	816,278	Parakou	106,708
Zou	18,700	813,985	Abomey	65,725
Mono	3,800	646,954	Lokossa	52,909
Atlantique	3,200	1,060,310	Cotonou	533,212
Ouéme	4,700	869,492	Porto-Novo	177,660

Other large towns (with 1992 census population): Djougou (132,192), Bohicon (81,121), Kandi (74,169), Ouidah (64,068).

In 1992 the main ethnic groups numbered (in 1,000): Fon, 1,930; Yoruba, 590; Adja, 540; Bariba, 420; Aizo, 420; Somba, 320; Fulani, 270. The official language is French. Over half the people speak Fon.

CLIMATE. In coastal parts there is an equatorial climate, with a long rainy season from March to July and a short rainy season in Oct. and Nov. The dry season increases in length from the coast, with inland areas having rain only between May and Sept. Porto-Novo. Jan. 82°F (27·8°C), July 78°F (25·6°C). Annual rainfall 52" (1,300 mm). Cotonou. Jan. 81°F (27·2°C), July 77°F (25°C). Annual rainfall 53" (1,325 mm).

CONSTITUTION AND GOVERNMENT. The Benin Party of Popular Revolution (PRPB) held a monopoly of power from 1977 to 1989.

In Feb. 1990 a 'National Conference of the Vital Elements (*'Vives forces'*) of the Nation' proclaimed its sovereignty and appointed Nicéphore Soglo *Prime Minister* of a provisional government. At a referendum in Dec. 1990, 93·2% of votes cast were in favour of the new constitution, which has introduced a presidential regime. The *President* is directly elected for renewable 5-year terms. Parliament is the 83-member *National Assembly*, elected by proportional representation for 4-year terms.

A 30-member advisory *Social and Economic Council* was set up in 1994. There is a *Constitutional Court*.

Presidential elections were held in 2 rounds on 3 and 18 March 1996. The electorate was 2,524,262; turn-out was 77·6%. There were 7 candidates for the first round, won by President Nicéphore Soglo with 35·69% of votes cast. At the run-off on 18 March Mathieu Kérékou was elected with 52·49% of votes cast. Parliamentary elections were held on 28 March and 28 May 1995. Some 2,600 candidates, representing 50 parties, stood. The electorate was 2,531,122. Benin Renaissance (BR) gained 21 seats; the Democratic Renewal Party, 18; Action Front for Renewal and Development, 14; the Social Democratic Party, 8; Our Common Cause, 4; Rally of Liberal Democrats, 4; Alliance for Democracy and Progress, 3; Impulse to Progress and Democracy, 2; others, 1 each.

President: Mathieu Kérékou (b. 1934; elected 18 March 1996; sworn in 4 April 1996).

In March 1998 the government comprised:
Prime Minister: Adrien Houngbedji.
Minister of Defence: Sévérin Adjovi. *Justice:* Ismaël Tidjani Serpos. *Culture and Communication:* Thimothée Zannou. *National Education and Scientific Research:* Djidjoho Léonard Padonou. *Mines, Energy and Hydraulics:* Emmanuel Golou. *Environment, Housing and Urbanism*: Sahidou Dango-Nadey. *Finance:* Moïse Mensah. *Foreign Affairs and Co-operation:* Pierre Osho. *Health, Social Protection and Women's Affairs:* Marina d'Almeida-Massougbodji. *Industry, Small and Medium Enterprises:* Félix Adimi. *Interior, Security and Territorial Administration:* Théophile N'da. *Planning, Economic Restructuring and Promotion of Employment:* Albert Tevoedjre. *Public Works and Transport:* Kamarou Fassassi. *Rural Development:* Jérôme Sacca Kina. *Youth, Sports and Leisure:* Damien Alahassa. *Civil Service, Labour and Administrative Reform:* Assouma Yakoubou. *Commerce, Handicrafts and Tourism:* Gatien Houngbedji.

The *Speaker* of the National Assembly is Bruno Amoussou (Social Democratic Party).

National anthem: 'L'Aube Nouvelle' ('New Dawn'); words and tune by Gilbert Dagnon.

Local Government. The 6 provinces are divided into 84 districts. In Nov. 1990 elections were held for mayors and district chiefs.

DEFENCE. There is selective conscription for 18 months.

Army. The Army consists of 3 infantry, 1 para-commando and 1 engineer battalions, 1 armoured squadron and 1 artillery battery. Equipment includes 20 PT-76 light tanks. Strength (1996) 4,500, with an additional 2,500-strong paramilitary gendarmerie.

Navy. The flotilla comprises 1 French-built inshore craft and 4 Soviet-built inshore patrol craft reported in reserve. There is 1 tug. Personnel in 1996 numbered 150, and the force is based at Cotonou.

Air Force. The Air Force has suffered a shortage of funds and in 1995 operated only 1 Twin Otter and 2 Ecureuil helicopters. Personnel, 1996, 100.

INTERNATIONAL RELATIONS

Membership. Benin is a member of the UN, OAU and is an ACP state of the EU.

ECONOMY

Policy. The Second Structural Adjustment Programme began in 1991, which seeks to provide resources for priority social and economic goals by economies, reforms and rationalization. An action plan envisages some privatization. Price controls were imposed in 1994.

Performance. In 1995 real GDP growth was 6·3%.

Budget. The fiscal year is the calendar year. In 1994 revenue was 127,100m. francs CFA and expenditure, 161,800m. francs CFA, of which 108,400m. francs CFA were current expenditure. The 1995 budget balanced at 204,000m. francs CFA.

Currency. The monetary unit is the *franc CFA* (XOF), with a parity value of 100 francs CFA to 1 French franc. There are coins of 5, 10, 25, 50 and 100 francs CFA, and banknotes of 500, 1,000, 5,000 and 10,000 francs CFA. 45,580m. francs CFA were in circulation in 1993. Foreign exchange reserves were US$197·9m. in 1995. Gold reserves were US$2·8m in 1993. Annualized inflation was 25% in 1995 (54% in 1994).

Banking and Finance. The bank of issue and the central bank is the regional West African Central Bank (BCEAO). There are 5 private commercial banks. Total deposits were 182,000m. francs CFA in May 1995.

ENERGY AND NATURAL RESOURCES

Electricity. In 1993, 236·1m. kWh were produced or imported. A solar energy programme was initiated in 1993.

Oil. The Semé oilfield, located 10 miles offshore, was discovered in 1968. Production commenced in 1982 and was 195,000 tonnes in 1992.

Agriculture. Benin's economy is underdeveloped, and is dependent on subsistence agriculture. In 1992, 2·93m. persons depended on agriculture, of whom 1·35m. were economically active. 36·8% of GDP was furnished by agriculture in 1993. Small independent farms produce about 90% of output. In 1991 1·42m. ha were arable, 0·45m. ha permanent crops and 0·44m. ha permanent pasture. The chief food products, 1994–95 (in 1,000 tonnes) were: Cassava, 1,145·8; yams, 1,250·5; maize, 491·5; sorghum and millet, 137·6; beans, 64; rice, 13·7, while cash crops were: Groundnuts, 77·6; cotton, 251·2; sugar-cane, 34·6.

Livestock 1992, (in 1,000): Cattle, 1,000; sheep, 920; goats, 1,120; pigs, 750; poultry, 25,000.

Forestry. There were (1989) 3·52m. ha of forest, mainly in the north. Timber production in 1991 was 5·2m. cu. metres, of which 4·9m. cu. metres were for fuel.

Fisheries. In 1991 there were 8 fishing boats totalling 1,078 GRT. Total catch, 41,000 tonnes, of which fresh fish, 21,076 tonnes, marine fish, 11,310 tonnes and shellfish, 7,704 tonnes.

INDUSTRY. Only about 2% of the workforce is employed in industry. The main activities include palm-oil processing, brewing and the manufacture of cement, sugar and textiles. Also important are cigarettes, food, construction materials and petroleum. Firms by product in 1994: Printing, paper, publishing, 33; chemicals, 22; wood, 16; foodstuffs, 11.

Labour. The economically active population numbered 1·34m. in 1990.

Trade Unions. In 1973 all trade unions were amalgamated to form a single body, the *Union Nationale des Syndicats des Travailleurs du Bénin*. In 1990 some unions declared their independence from this Union, which itself broke its links with the PRPB. In 1992 there were 3 trade union federations.

FOREIGN ECONOMIC RELATIONS. Commercial and transport activities, which make up 36% of GDP, are extremely vulnerable to developments in neighbouring Nigeria, with which there is a significant amount of illegal trade. Foreign debt was US$1,619m. in 1994.

Commerce. Imports in 1995, US$380m.; exports, US$300m. The main exports in 1994 were cotton (US$132m.) and crude oil (US$12m.). Other exports include cocoa, palm oil, palm kernel cake and oil and cotton cake.

Principal export markets, 1994: Morocco, 37·6%; Portugal, 13·8%; Libya, 7·9%; Italy, 5·8%; USA, 5·3%. Principal import suppliers: France, 24·3%; Thailand, 11·9%; Netherlands, 7%; China, 6·4%; Hong Kong, 6%; USA, 5·6%.

Main imports include foodstuffs, beverages, tobacco, petroleum products, intermediate goods, capital goods and light consumer goods.

Tourism. In 1990 some 50,000 foreign visitors brought in US$47m. in revenue.

COMMUNICATIONS

Roads. There were 7,500 km of classified roads in 1994. In 1992 there were 2,212 road accidents with 349 fatalities.

Railways. There are 578 km of metre-gauge railway. In 1994, 0·6m. passengers and 250m. tonne-km of freight were carried.

Civil Aviation. The international airport is at Cotonou. It handled 244,217 passengers in 1992. There are other airports at Abomey, Natitingou, Kandi and Parakou. Benin is a member of Air Afrique. Benin Interregional flies to Burkina Faso, Niger and Togo as well as domestic destinations. Services are also provided by Aeroflot, Air Burkina, Air France, Air Gabon, Cameroon Airlines, Ghana Airways, Nigeria Airways and Sabena.

Shipping. There is a port at Cotonou. In 1992 the merchant fleet numbered 12 ships totalling 1,666 GRT. 1·36m. tonnes of cargo were unloaded and 0·22m. tonnes loaded in 1992.

Telecommunications. There were, in 1994, about 10,000 telephones. The media are overseen by the 9-member Haute Autorité de l'Audiovisuel et de la Communication. The government-controlled Office de Radiodiffusion et Télévision du Bénin broadcasts a radio programme from Cotonou and a regional programme from Parakou, and a TV service (colour by SECAM) from Cotonou. In 1993 there were 0·35m. radio and some 20,000 TV sets.

Press. In 1995 there were 2 daily newspapers.

SOCIAL INSTITUTIONS

Justice. The Supreme Court is at Cotonou. There are Magistrates Courts, and a *tribunal de conciliation* in each district. The legal system based on French civil law and customary law.

Religion. Some 70% of the population follow traditional animist beliefs. In 1994 there were 1·1m. Roman Catholics and 0·8m. Moslems.

Education. Adult literacy rate was 37% in 1995 (48·7% among males and 25·8% among females). There were, in 1990–91, 457,100 pupils in 2,808 primary schools with 13,200 teachers and 72,256 pupils in secondary and high schools with 2,493 teachers. The University of Benin (Cotonou) had 9,000 students and 240 academic staff in 1994–95.

DIPLOMATIC REPRESENTATIVES

Of Benin in Great Britain
Ambassador: Vacant (resides in Paris).

Of Great Britain in Benin
Ambassador: G. S. Burton, CMG (resides in Abuja).

Of Benin in the USA (2737 Cathedral Ave., NW, Washington, D.C., 20008)
Ambassador: Lucien Tonoukouin.

Of the USA in Benin (Rue Caporal Anani Bernard, Cotonou)
Ambassador: John A. Yates.

Of Benin to the United Nations
Ambassador: Fassassi Yacoubou.

Of Benin to the European Union
Ambassador: Saliou Aboudou.

Further Reading

Eades, J. S. and Allen, C. *Benin* [Bibliography]. Oxford and Santa Barbara (CA), 1997

BHUTAN

Druk-yul

(Kingdom of Bhutan)

Capital: Thimphu
Population: 0·6m.
GDP per head: (PPP$) 1,289
GNP: US$0·3bn.
HDI/world rank: 0·338/155

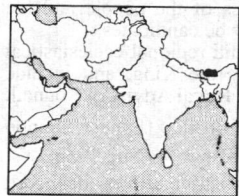

KEY HISTORICAL EVENTS. A sovereign kingdom in the Himalayas, Bhutan was governed by a spiritual ruler and a temporal ruler—the Dharma and Deb Raja—from the 17th century. The capital was Funakha. The interior was organized into districts for defence. Districts were controlled by governors and each district's central fort (*dzhong*) by a fort commander. These officials formed the electoral council appointing the Deb Raja.

The British East India Company made a treaty with Bhutan in 1774, but relations were uneasy and there were violent incidents. The British annexed a number of borderland areas in an attempt to contain Bhutanese raiders.

During the 19th century civil wars were fought between district governors for the office of the Deb Raja. The election became a formality, and the governors of Tongsa and Paro were the most frequently chosen, because they were the strongest. The appointment of new governors was likewise settled by force.

By 1860, the British in India were disturbed by the instability of Bhutan. An attempt to interfere in 1863 resulted in a short frontier war, ending with a treaty in 1865. The British annexed part of Dewangiri and agreed to pay the rulers of Bhutan an annual subsidy.

In 1907, the office of Dharma Raja came to an end. The governor of Tongsa, Ugyen Wangchuk, was then chosen Maharajah of Bhutan, the throne becoming hereditary in his family (the title is now King of Bhutan). He concluded a further treaty with the British in 1910 allowing internal autonomy but British control of foreign policy. The treaty was renewed with the Government of India in 1949; the subsidy was further increased and the annexed area of Dewangiri returned to Bhutan.

India concluded a fresh treaty with Bhutan on 8 Aug. 1949 under which Bhutan continues to be guided by India in its external relations, and India undertakes not to interfere in the internal administration of Bhutan. The subsidy paid to Bhutan was increased to Rs 0·5m. In the early 1990s, tens of thousands of 'illegal immigrants', mostly Nepali-speaking Hindus, were forcibly expelled. Eight years on, there are still nearly 90,000 people claiming to be Bhutánese refugees in camps set up by UNHCR in eastern Nepal.

TERRITORY AND POPULATION. Bhutan is situated in the eastern Himalayas, bounded in the north by Tibet and on all other sides by India. In 1949 India retroceded 32 sq. miles of Dewangiri, annexed in 1865. Area about 18,000 sq. miles (46,500 sq. km); Official population estimate, 1996, 0·6m. A Nepalese minority makes up 30–35% of the population, mainly in the south. Life expectancy: 66. The capital is Thimphu (1993, 30,340 population).

The official language is Dzongkha.

CLIMATE. The climate is largely controlled by altitude. The mountainous north is cold, with perpetual snow on the summits, but the centre has a more moderate climate, though winters are cold, with rainfall under 40" (1,000 mm). In the south, the climate is humid sub-tropical and rainfall approaches 200" (5,000 mm).

ROYAL HOUSE. The reigning King is **Jigme Singye Wangchuck**, who succeeded his father Jigme Dorji Wangchuck (died 21 July 1972).

In 1907 the Trongsa Penlop (the governor of the province of Trongsa in central Bhutan), Sir Ugyen Wangchuk, GCIE, KCSI, was elected as the first hereditary Maharaja of Bhutan. The Bhutanese title is Druk Gyalpo, and his successor is now addressed as King of Bhutan. Educated in Britain, King Wangchuk is opposed to certain Western influences such as television and jeans.

CONSTITUTION AND GOVERNMENT. There is no formal constitution. There is an absolute monarchy which in practice acts in consultation with a National Assembly (*Tshogdu*), which was reinstituted in 1953. This has 150 members and meets at least once a year. Two-thirds are representatives of the people and are elected for a 3-year term. All Bhutanese over 30 years may be candidates.

12 monastic representatives are elected by the central and regional ecclesiastical bodies, while the remaining members are nominated by the King, and include members of the Council of Ministers (the Cabinet) and the Royal Advisory Council.

National anthem: 'Druk tsendhen koipi gyelknap na' ('In the Thunder Dragon Kingdom'); words by Dasho Shinkar Lam, tune by A. Tongmi.

Local government: There are 20 districts, each under a district officer *(dzongda)* responsible to the Royal Civil Service Commission through the Home Ministry.

DEFENCE

Army. There was (1996) an Army of 6,000 men. 3 to 5 weeks militia training was introduced in 1989 for senior students and government officials, and 3 months training for some 10,000 volunteers from the general population in 1990 and 1991. Since 1992 only refresher training has been implemented.

INTERNATIONAL RELATIONS

Membership. Bhutan is a member of the UN.

ECONOMY

Policy. The 8th development plan (1997–2002) allows for expenditure of Nu35,169m. Hydro-electric power and industries are stressed. The 7th plan (1992–97) emphasized forest and mineral exploitations, education and medical facilities.

Budget. The budget for 1996–97 envisaged current expenditure of Nu2,198m. and internal domestic revenue of Nu1,950m.

Currency. The unit of currency is the *ngultrum* (BTN) of 100 *chetrum*, at parity with the Indian rupee. There are coins of 1, 5, 10, 25 and 50 chetrum and 1 ngultrum, and notes of 1, 2, 5, 10, 20, 50, 100 and 500 ngultrum. Indian currency is also legal tender.

Banking and Finance. The Bank of Bhutan was established in 1968. The headquarters are at Phuentsholing with 26 branches throughout the country. The Royal Monetary Authority (founded 1982) acts as the central bank. Deposits (Dec. 1995) Nu2,816·3m. Foreign Exchange reserves: US$120m. International debt: US$80m.

ENERGY AND NATURAL RESOURCES

Electricity. Installed capacity at June 1995 was 342 mWh (of which 336 mWh were hydro-electric). Production (1994) was 1,685m. kWh. In 1995, 38 towns and 297 villages had electricity.

Minerals. Large deposits of limestone, marble, dolomite, slate, graphite, lead, copper, coal, talc, gypsum, beryl, mica, pyrites and tufa have been found. Most mining activity (principally limestone, coal, slate and dolomite) is small-scale.

Agriculture. The area under cultivation in 1996 was 0·36m. ha. The chief products (1990 production in 1,000 tonnes) are rice (43), millet (7), wheat (5), barley (4), maize (40), potatoes (31), oranges (58), apples (5), handloom cloth, timber and cardamom.

Livestock (1994, in 1,000): Cattle, 308; pigs, 46; sheep, 32; goats, 27; horses, 23; yaks, 37; poultry, 158.

Forestry. In 1996, 2·98m. ha were forested.

INDUSTRY. In 1995 there were 3,206 licensed industrial establishments, of which 1,785 were service, 1,085 construction and 336 manufacturing industries. Of the latter, 167 were forest-based, 81 agriculture-based and 35 mineral-based.

FOREIGN ECONOMIC RELATIONS. The cumulative outstanding convertible currency debt at 30 June 1996 was US$81m. To the same date, cumulative debt service payments totalled US$7m.

Financial support is received from India, the UN and other international aid organizations.

Commerce. Trade with India dominates but oranges and apples, timber, cardamom and liquor are also exported to the Middle East, Singapore and Europe.

Tourism. Tourism is the largest source of foreign exchange (1994, US$1·91m. gross). In 1996, 5,150 tourists visited Bhutan (4,765 in 1995).

COMMUNICATIONS

Roads. In 1995 there were about 3,216 km of roads and in 1994, 6,154 registered vehicles, including 5,419 private cars, jeeps or scooters, and 655 heavy vehicles. In the entire kingdom there is only one set of traffic lights.

Civil Aviation. In 1997 Druk-Air made 2 weekly flights to Delhi via Kathmandu and 3 weekly services to Bangkok alternately via Rangoon (Yangon), Dhaka and Calcutta using 2 71-seater BAe-146s.

Telecommunications. In 1994 there were 2 general post offices, 56 post offices and 23 branch post offices. In 1994 there were 45 km of telephone lines, 22 automatic exchanges and 4,609 telephones.

An international microwave link connects Thimphu to the Calcutta and Delhi satellite connections. A telecommunications link between Thimphu and London by Intelsat-satellite was inaugurated in 1990. Thimphu and Phuentsholing are connected by telex to Delhi.

In 1994 there were 52 radio stations for internal administrative communications, and 13 hydro-met stations, with an estimated 15,000 radio receivers. Bhutan Broadcasting Service (autonomous since 1992) broadcasts a daily programme in English, Sharchopkha, Dzongkha and Nepali. There is no local television station. Satellite and cable television are illegal.

Cinemas. There are 2 in Thimphu and 4 others.

Press. There is 1 weekly newspaper, published in English, Dzongkha and Nepali. Total circulation (1996) about 12,000.

SOCIAL INSTITUTIONS

Justice. The High Court consists of 8 judges appointed by the King. There is a Magistrate's Court in each district, under a *Thrimpon*, from which appeal is to the High Court at Thimphu.

Religion. Government estimates, 1995: 70% of the population are Mahayana Buddhists, 25% Hindu and 5% Moslem.

Education. In April 1996 there were 9,257 pupils and 225 teachers in community schools, 53,097 pupils and 1,374 teachers in primary schools, 18,762 pupils and 650 teachers in 20 junior high and 10 high schools and 1,795 pupils and 203 teachers in technical, vocational and tertiary-level schools. There were 1,248 students and 61 teachers in 7 private schools. Many students receive higher technical training in India, as well as under the UN Development Programme and the Colombo Plan, in Australia, Germany, New Zealand, Japan, Singapore, the USA and the UK. In Oct. 1990, 140 students were receiving university education in India. Adult literacy rate: 41·1%.

Health. There were (1996) 27 hospitals, 32 dispensaries, 97 basic health units, 10 indigenous dispensaries, 454 outreach clinics, 19 malaria centres and 3 training institutes. In 1994 beds totalled 970; there were 100 doctors and 578 paramedics in 1994. Free health facilities are available to 90% of the population.

DIPLOMATIC REPRESENTATIVE

Of Bhutan to the United Nations
Ambassador: Ugyen Tshering.

Of Bhutan to the European Union
Ambassador: Jigmi Thinley.

Further Reading

Bhutan, Himalayan Kingdom. Bhutan Government, Thimphu, 1979

Aris, M., *Bhutan: The Early History of an Himalayan Kingdom.* Warminster, 1979.— *The Raven Crown: the Origins of Buddhist Monarchy in Bhutan.* London, 1994
Chakravarti, B., *A Cultural History of Bhutan.* 2nd rev. ed., 2 vols. Chitteranjan, 1981
Collister, P., *Bhutan and the British.* London, 1987
Das, B. N., *Mission to Bhutan: a Nation in Transition.* New Delhi, 1995
Dogra, R. C., *Bhutan:* [Bibliography]. Oxford and Santa Barbara, 1991
Edmunds, T. O., *Bhutan: Land of the Thunder Dragon.* London, 1988
Hickman, K., *Dreams of the Peaceful Dragon: a Journey through Bhutan.* London, 1987
Hutt, M., *Bhutan: Perspectives on Conflict and Dissent.* London, 1994
Mehra, G. N., *Bhutan: Land of the Peaceful Dragon.* Rev. ed. New Delhi, 1985
Misra, H. N., *Bhutan: Problems and Policies.* New Delhi, 1988
Parmanand, *The Politics of Bhutan: Retrospect and Prospect.* Delhi, 1992
Rahul, R., *Royal Bhutan.* New Delhi, 1983
Rose, L. E., *The Politics of Bhutan.* Cornell Univ. Press, 1977
Rustomji, N., *Bhutan: The Dragon Kingdom in Crisis.* OUP, 1978
Savada, A. M. (ed.) *Nepal and Bhutan: Country Studies.* Washington, DC, 1993
Sinha, A. C., *Bhutan: Ethnic Identity and National Dilemma.* Delhi, 1991
Strydonck, G. van, *et al.*, *Bhutan: a Kingdom of the Eastern Himalayas.* Geneva and London, 1984
Verma, R., *India's Role in the Emergence of Contemporary Bhutan.* Delhi, 1988

National statistical office: Central Statistical Organization, Thimphu

BOLIVIA

República de Bolivia

Capital: Sucre
Seat of Government: La Paz
Population: 7·6m.
GDP per head: (PPP$) 2,598
GNP: US$5·6bn.
HDI/world rank: 0·589 /113

KEY HISTORICAL EVENTS. Bolivia was part of the Inca Empire until conquered by the Spanish in the 16th century. In 1776 it became part of the viceroyalty of Buenos Aires. Independence was won and the Republic of Bolivia was proclaimed on 6 Aug. 1825. During the first 154 years of its independence, Bolivia had 189 governments, many of them installed by coups. Largely civilian governments from 1880 gave way to mainly military ones after 1936. In 1952 a revolution led by the MNR (National Revolutionary Movement) brought about agrarian reform and nationalization of the tin mines, Bolivia's chief source of wealth. In the 1960s the Argentinian revolu-tionary and former minister of the Cuban government, Ernesto 'Che' Guevara, was killed in Bolivia while fighting with a left-wing guerrilla group. In 1971, Bolivian instability reached a peak with the brief establishment of a revolutionary Popular Assembly during the regime of Gen. Torres. Later repression under Gen. Hugo Banzer took a heavy toll of the left-wing parties. An attempt to hold elections in July 1978 led to Gen. Juan Pereda Asbún (supported by the army) carrying out a military coup. In Nov. he was in turn overthrown by Gen. David Padilla Arancibia, the army commander. Elections in July 1979 proved indecisive, and an interim government was formed until it was overthrown in Nov. by yet another army coup, which won power for a mere two weeks.

The 1980 elections were as inconclusive as those of the previous year and a coup followed, led by the army C.-in-C. Gen. Luis Garcia Meza. However in 1981 he was forced to resign in favour of Gen. Celso Torrelio Villa. When the new president tried introducing civilians to the Cabinet and adopting a liberal attitude to trade unions, he was superseded by Gen. Guido Vildoso Calderón. Civilian rule was restored in Oct. 1982 when Dr Siles Zuazo (who had won a small majority in the two previous elections) became president. There followed a period of economic reform embracing free markets and open trade. The minister responsible for economic changes, Gonzalo Sanchez de Lozada, was elected president in 1993. In 1997 he was succeeded by Gen. Hugo Banzer Suarez.

TERRITORY AND POPULATION. Bolivia is a landlocked state bounded in the north and east by Brazil, south by Paraguay and Argentina and west by Chile and Peru, with an area of some 424,165 sq. miles (1,098,581 sq. km). A coastal strip of land on the Pacific passed to Chile after a war in 1884. In 1953 Chile declared Arica a free port and Bolivia has certain privileges there.

Population estimate, 1996: 7,588,392 (60·3% urban); density, 6·9 per sq. km. The population growth rate has been estimated at 2·3% for the years 1995-2000; in 1996 the birth rate was estimated at 33·97 per 1,000 population; death rate, 9·41 per 1,000; infant mortality, 68·36 per 1,000 live births. Expectation of life was 60·8 years in 1996. Area and population of the departments (capitals in brackets) at the 1992 census and as estimated in 1996:

Departments	Area (sq. km)	Census 1992	Estimate 1996
La Paz (La Paz)	133,98	1,900,786	2,224,552
Cochabamba (Cochabamba)	55,631	1,110,205	1,371,087
Potosí (Potosí)	118,218	645,889	737,424
Santa Cruz (Santa Cruz)	370,621	1,364,389	1,601,516
Chuquisaca (Sucre)	51,524	453,756	537,033
Tarija (Tarija)	37,623	291,407	357,623
Oruro (Oruro)	53,588	340,114	380,030
	Area	*Census*	*Estimate*

Departments	(sq. km)	1992	1996
Beni (Trinidad)	213,564	276,174	327,336
Pando (Cobija)	63,827	38,072	51,791
Total	1,098,581	6,420,792	7,588,392

Population (1992 census) of the principal towns: La Paz, 711,036; Santa Cruz, 694,616; Cochabamba, 404,102; El Alto, 404,367; Oruro, 183,194; Sucre, 130,952; Potosí, 112,291; Tarija, 90,000.

Spanish is the official and commercial language. The Amerindian languages Aymará and Quechua are spoken exclusively by 22% and 5·2% of the population respectively; Tupi Guaraní is also spoken.

CLIMATE. The varied geography produces different climates. The low-lying areas in the Amazon Basin are warm and damp throughout the year, with heavy rainfall from Nov. to March; the Altiplano is generally dry between May and Nov. with sunshine but cold nights in June and July, while the months from Dec. to March are the wettest. La Paz. Jan. 53°F (11·7°C), July 47°F (8·3°C). Annual rainfall 23" (574 mm). Sucre. Jan. 55°F (13°C), July 49°F (9·4°C). Annual rainfall 27" (675 mm).

CONSTITUTION AND GOVERNMENT. Bolivia's first constitution was adopted on 19 Nov. 1826. The *President* is elected by universal suffrage for a 5-year term. If 50% of the vote is not obtained, the result is determined by a secret ballot in Congress amongst the leading 2 candidates. The President appoints the members of his Cabinet. There is a bicameral legislature; the *Senate* comprises 27 members, 3 from each department, and the *Chamber of Deputies* 130 members, all serving terms of 5 years. A constitutional amendment of 1996 introduced direct elections for 65 deputies; the remainder are nominated by party leaders. Voting is compulsory.

Presidential and parliamentary elections were held on 1 June 1997. The electorate was 3·2m. Gen. Hugo Banzer Suarez gained 22·3% of the votes cast and Juan Carlos Durán 17·7%. As no candidate gained an absolute majority, Congress elected Gen. Hugo Banzer Suarez President on 4 Aug. 1997.

Presidential and parliamentary elections were scheduled for June 2002.

President: Gen. Hugo Banzer Suarez (ADN; sworn in Aug.1997).

Vice-President: Jorge Quiroga (ADN).

The Cabinet was composed as follows in March 1998:

Foreign Affairs: Dr Javier Murillo (ADN). *Finance:* Edgar Millares (ADN). *Economic Development:* Ivo Kuljis (UCS). *Sustainable Development and Environment:* Erick Reyes Villa (NFR). *Presidency:* Carlos Iturralde (ADN). *Health:* Dr Tonchi Marinkovic (MIR). *Defence:* Fernando Kieffer (ADN). *Home Office:* Guido Nayar (ADN). *Labour:* Leopoldo López (MIR). *Justice:* Dr Ana Maria Cortez (ADN). *Education:* Tito Hoz de Vila (ADN). *Housing:* Javier Escobar (CONDEPA). *International Trade and Investment:* Dr Jorge Crespo (MIR). *Agriculture:* Luís Freddy Conde (CONDEPA). Parties represented: Acción Democrática Nacionalista (ADN). Movimiento de Izquierda Revolucionaria (MIR). Unidad Cívica Solidaridad (UCS). Conciencia de Patria (CONDEPA). Nueva Fuerza Republicana (NFR).

National anthem: 'Bolivianos, el hado propicio' ('Bolivians, the propitious fate'); words by I. de Sanjinés; tune by B. Vincenti.

Local Government: The republic is divided into 9 departments, with 94 provinces administered by sub-prefects, and 1,713 cantons administered by corregidores. Each department has a prefect appointed by the President and a legislature elected by municipal councillors. There are 312 municipalities. Elections are held every 5 years.

DEFENCE. There is selective conscription for 12 months at the age of 18 years.

Army. There are 6 military regions. The Army consists of 2 armoured battalions, 1 mechanized cavalry regiment and a Presidential Guard infantry regiment under direct Headquarters command, and 10 divisions comprising altogether 8 cavalry groups, 1 motorized infantry regiment, 22 infantry, 1 artillery, 1 armoured, 1 airborne and 6 engineer battalions. Equipment includes 36 Kuerassier SK-105 light tanks. There are 1 King Air 90, 1 Super King Air 200 and 2 C-212 Aviocar transports. Strength (1997) 25,000 (18,000 conscripts).

Navy. A small force exists for river and lake patrol duties, comprising 9 small patrol craft operating on Lake Titicaca and in the 6,000-mile Beni and Bolivia-Paraguay river systems, and also 1 Cessna 402 transport and 1 Cessna 206 for patrol duties. 1 ocean-going transport for use to and from Bolivian free zones in Argentina and Uruguay and 2 17-tonne hospital craft on Lake Titicaca complete the inventory.

Personnel in 1996 totalled 4,500, including 2,000 marines.

Air Force. The Air Force, established in 1923, has 6 combat-capable Groups, 4 equipped with T-33 armed jet trainers, 1 with armed PC-7s and 1 with Hughes 500 helicopters, for counter-insurgency operations. A search and rescue helicopter Group has 6 Brazilian-assembled Lamas and 20 UH-1 Iroquois. Other types in service include Brazilian T-23 Uirapuru and American T-41 primary trainers and Italian SF-260 basic trainers, 1 Electra transport, 6 Fokker F.27 and 2 Israeli-built Arava twin-turboprop light transports, 5 Convair transports, 2 Learjet VIP aircraft, 11 C-130/L-100 Hercules, 3 C-47s, 15 Turbo-Porters and some single- and twin-engined light aircraft, some confiscated from drug smugglers. Personnel strength (1996) about 4,000 (2,000 conscripts).

INTERNATIONAL RELATIONS

Membership. Bolivia is a member of the UN, OAS, LAIA, the Andean Group and the Amazon Pact, and is an associate member of Mercosur.

ECONOMY

Policy. Following the collapse of the international tin market in 1985 and severe inflation, a New Economic Policy was introduced derestricting foreign trade, ending price controls and subsidies and freezing public-sector wages. A privatization programme affecting some 60 state-owned enterprises was instituted in June 1992. A programme of capitalization aims to attract foreign investment into state enterprises in oil, telephones, electricity supply, railways, airlines and smelters, while distributing 50% of the shares to adult citizens to be held in retirement accounts.

Performance. Real GDP growth was estimated at 4·0% in 1996.

Currency. The unit of currency is the *boliviano* (BOB) of 100 *centavos*, which replaced the *peso* on 1 Jan. 1987 at a rate of 1 boliviano = 1m. pesos. There are coins of 5, 10, 20 and 50 centavos and notes of 2, 5, 10, 20, 50, 100 and 200 bolivianos. Inflation was an annualized 8·7% in 1996. Foreign exchange reserves were US$851m. in 1996.

Banking and Finance. The Central Bank (*governor*, Juan Antonio Morales) is the bank of issue. In 1996 there were 20 commercial banks operating, including 5 foreign. There is also a State Bank and 8 specialized development banks.

There are stock exchanges in La Paz and Santa Cruz.

Weights and Measures. The metric system is legal, but the old Spanish system is also employed.

ENERGY AND NATURAL RESOURCES

Electricity. Installed capacity was estimated at 804,300 kW. in 1995. Estimated production from all sources (1995), 3·02bn. kWh.

Oil and Gas. There are petroleum and natural gas deposits in the Santa Cruz-Camiri areas. Production of crude oil in 1996 was 10,682,314 barrels. Work has begun on a US$1·9 bn. pipeline from eastern Bolivia to São Paulo in Brazil. National gas output was 117,573 cu. ft in 1996.

Minerals. Mining accounts for 5·76% of GDP (1996 estimate). Tin-mining had been the mainstay of the economy until the collapse of the international tin market in 1985. Production, 1996 (in tonnes): Zinc, 144,763·62; lead, 16,537·75; tin, 14,777·08; antimony, 6,487·40; wolfram, 733·46; silver, 384·29; gold, 14,942·13 fine kg.

Agriculture. In 1996 agriculture contributed 14·95% of GDP (estimate). The rural population was estimated at 3,012,260 in 1996, 39·70% of total population. Output in 1,000 tonnes in 1996 (estimate) was: Sugar-cane, 4,120; rice, 343; coffee, 22; maize, 613 ; potatoes, 715; wheat, 98. In 1992, 77,000 tonnes of coca (the source of cocaine) were grown. Since 1987 Bolivia has received international (mainly US) aid to reduce the amount of coca grown, with compensation for farmers who co-operate. Livestock, 1993 (in 1,000): Cattle, 5,800; horses, 322; asses and mules, 710; pigs, 2,273; sheep, 7,512; goats, 1,450; poultry, 33m.

Forestry. Forests cover 55·8m. ha. Tropical forests with woods ranging from the 'iron tree' to the light balsa are exploited. Roundwood production was 1·63m. cu. metres in 1991; wood cut for fuel totalled 1·13m. cu. metres.

INDUSTRY. At the 1992 census there were 14,389 factories employing a total of 76,718 persons. The principal manufactures are foodstuffs and tobacco, and textiles.

Labour. In 1994 the minimum wage was fixed at 160 bolivianos a month.

Trade Unions. Unions are grouped in the Confederación de Obreros Bolivianos.

FOREIGN ECONOMIC RELATIONS. An agreement of Jan. 1992 with Peru gives Bolivia duty-free transit for imports and exports through a corridor leading to the Peruvian Pacific port of Ilo from the Bolivian frontier town of Desaguadero, in return for Peruvian access to the Atlantic via Bolivia's roads and railways. The mining code of 1991 gives tax incentives to foreign investors. Foreign debt was US$4,355·6m. in 1996 (estimate).

Commerce. The value of imports and exports in US$1m.

	1990	1991	1992	1993	1994	1995
Imports	715	970	1,090	1,206	1,122	1,308
Exports	900	849	710	728	985	1,041

Exports of timber were worth US$82,579,000 in 1992. Main exports, 1995 (in US$1,000): Zinc, 151; gold, 119; tin, 83; natural gas, 94; jewellery, 88.

Main export markets, 1996: USA, 26·1%; EU (especially UK, Germany and Belgium), 22·3%; Argentina, Peru and Colombia, 39·3%. Main import suppliers: Brazil, Argentina and Chile, 36·8%; EU (Germany, Belgium and Italy), 36·8%; Japan, 12%.

Imports and exports pass chiefly through the ports of Arica and Antofagasta in Chile, Mollendo-Matarani in Peru, through La Quiaca on the Bolivian-Argentine border and through river-ports on the rivers flowing into the Amazon.

Tourism. Revenue from tourism was estimated at US$168m. in 1992.

COMMUNICATIONS

Roads. The total length of the road system was 52,328 km in 1996 (estimate), of which 3,045 km were hard-surfaced. Motor cars in use in 1996, 90,699 (estimate); total vehicles, 429,554.

Railways. In 1994, the state railway ENFE network totalled 3,697 km of metre gauge, comprising unconnected Eastern (1,423 km) and Andina (2,274 km) systems, and carried 0·8m. passengers and 1·4m. tonnes of freight.

Civil Aviation. The 2 international airports are La Paz (El Alto) and Santa Cruz (Viru Viru). The national airlines are the state-owned Aerosur, which operated 8 aircraft in 1995, and Lloyd Aéreo Boliviano (97·5% state-owned), which in 1995 operated 2 A310-300s, 1 B-707-320C, 1 B-727, 1 B-727-100, 1 B-727-100C, 3 B-727-200 Advs and 1 F-27-200. The airline runs regular services between La Paz and Lima, São Paulo, Buenos Aires, Miami, Caracas, Salta and Arica as well as many internal services. Other airlines serving Bolivia are Aerolíneas Argentinas, Aeroperú, American Airlines, Lan Chile, Lufthansa and Varig.

Shipping. Lake Titicaca and about 12,000 miles of rivers are open to navigation.

Telecommunications. There were 191,000 telephones in 1988. The broadcasting authority is the Dirección General de Telecomunicaciones. There were (1987) about 85 radio stations, the majority of which are local and commercial. There is a commercial government television service. There are 4 private television stations and 1 University station (educational channel) in La Paz. In 1993 there were 4m. radio and 0·5m. TV (colour by NTSC) receivers.

Cinemas. In 1989 there were 30 cinemas in La Paz and 50 in other cities.

SOCIAL INSTITUTIONS

Justice. Justice is administered by the Supreme Court, superior department courts (of 5 or 7 judges) and courts of local justice. The Supreme Court, with headquarters at Sucre, is divided into two sections, civil and criminal, of 5 justices each, with the Chief Justice presiding over both. Members of the Supreme Court are chosen on a two-thirds vote of Congress.

Religion. The Roman Catholic church was disestablished in 1961. It is under a cardinal (in Sucre), an archbishop (in La Paz), 6 bishops and vicars apostolic. It had 7·16m. adherents in 1992.

Education. Literacy was 63% in 1994. Primary instruction is free and obligatory between the ages of 6 and 14 years. In 1993 there were 11,878 schooling facilities; 10,485 public and 1,393 private. The national rate of school attendance (6–19-year-olds) reaches 74·3%.

In 1994-95 there were 7 universities, 2 technical universities, 1 Roman Catholic university, 1 musical conservatory, and colleges in the following fields: Business, 6; teacher training, 4; industry, 1; nursing, 1; technical teacher training, 1; fine arts, 1, rural education, 1; physical education, 1. There were 103,900 university students in 1995-96 and 4,920 academic staff.

Welfare. Retirement pensions are funded by the state out of its share of the capitalization of enterprises. Previously established funds covered only some 10% of the workforce, and are being allowed to run down. A second compulsory contributory pension fund was started in 1997 for all workers aged 21 or over.

DIPLOMATIC REPRESENTATIVES

Of Bolivia in Great Britain (106 Eaton Sq., London, SW1W 9AD)
Ambassador: Vacant.

Of Great Britain in Bolivia (Avenida Arce 2732, La Paz)
Ambassador: David F. C. Ridgeway, OBE.

Of Bolivia in the USA (3014 Massachusetts Ave, NW, Washington, D.C., 20008)
Ambassador: Fernando Cossio.

Of the USA in Bolivia (Banco Popular Del Peru Bldg, La Paz)
Ambassador: Curt W. Kamman.

Of Bolivia to the United Nations
Ambassador: Vacant.

Of Bolivia to the European Union
Ambassador: Vacant.

Further Reading

Fifer, J. V., *Bolivia: Land, Location and Politics Since 1825.* CUP, 1972
Klein, H., *Bolivia: The Evolution of a Multi-Ethnic Society.* OUP, 1982
Yeager, G. M., *Bolivia.* [Bibliography] Oxford and Santa Barbara, 1988

National statistical office: Instituto Nacional de Estadistica, Casilla Postal 6129, La Paz.
  Website: http://www.ine.gov.bov/

BOSNIA-HERCEGOVINA

Capital: Sarajevo
Population: 4·37m.

Republika Bosna i
Hercegovina

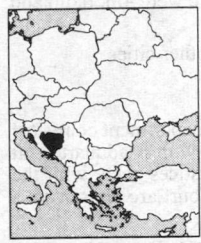

KEY HISTORICAL EVENTS. Settled by Slavs in the 7th century, Bosnia was conquered by the Turks in 1463 when much of the population was gradually converted to Islam. At the Congress of Berlin (1878) the territory was assigned to Austro-Hungarian administration under nominal Turkish suzerainty. Austria-Hungary's outright annexation in 1908 generated international tensions which contributed to the outbreak of the First World War.

After 1918, Bosnia Hercegovina became part of a new kingdom of Serbs, Croats and Slovenes under the Serbian monarchy. Its name was changed to Yugoslavia in 1929.
(See YUGOSLAVIA for developments up to and beyond the second world war.)

On 15 Oct. 1991 the National Assembly adopted a 'Memorandum on Sovereignty', the Serbian deputies abstaining. This envisaged Bosnian autonomy within a Yugoslav federation. A referendum on independence was held on 29 Feb.–1 March 1992. Turn-out was 63·04%, the Serbian population largely boycotting it; 99·78% of votes cast were in favour. In March 1992 an agreement was reached under EC auspices by Moslems, Serbs and Croats to set up 3 autonomous ethnic communities under a central Bosnian authority.

Bosnia-Hercegovina declared itself independent on 5 April 1992, and was recognized by the EC and USA on 7 April. The 2 Serbian members of the Bosnian collective presidency resigned. Fighting broke out between the Serb, Croat and Moslem communities, with particularly heavy casualties and destruction in Sarajevo, leading to extensive Moslem territorial losses and an exodus of refugees. UN-sponsored ceasefires from June on were repeatedly violated. On 29 June the UN Security Council unanimously voted for the deployment of UN forces to secure the functioning of Sarajevo Airport and protect humanitarian aid missions.

On 13 Aug. 1992 the UN Security Council voted by 12 to nil with 3 abstentions (China, India and Zimbabwe) to authorize the use of force if necessary to ensure the delivery of humanitarian aid to besieged civilians. Internationally-sponsored peace talks were held in Geneva in Jan. and at the UN in Feb. 1993, but Serb-Moslem-Croat fighting continued.

A NATO ultimatum of 10 Feb. 1994 gave Bosnian Serbs 10 days to withdraw their artillery from around Sarajevo. NATO forces used air strikes for the first time against Serb forces at Gorazde on 10 April. In Aug. Yugoslavia ceased supplying Bosnian Serbs and sealed the frontier.

An upsurge in fighting began in Oct. with Moslem-Croat attacks in the Bihać area. The Moslem advance was beaten back by Serb forces which bombed Bihać with napalm on 18 Nov. NATO air forces retaliated with a raid on the Serbian airfield, but Serb forces occupied Bihać. On 12 Nov. 1994 the USA ended its embargo on the supply of arms to Bosnian forces.

On 23 Dec. Bosnian Serbs and Moslems signed a country-wide interim ceasefire. Bosnian Croats also signed on 2 Jan. 1995. However, Croatian Serbs and the Moslem secessionist forces under Fikret Abdić did not sign the agreement, and fighting continued.

On 28 May 1995 Bosnian Serb forces took some 400 UN peacekeeping troops hostage. Under pressure from Serbian President Milošević all had been released by 18 June.

On 16 June 1995 Bosnian government forces launched an attack to break the Bosnian Serb siege of Sarajevo. On 11 July Bosnian Serb forces began to occupy UN security zones despite retaliatory NATO air strikes, and on 28 Aug. shelled Sarajevo.

To stop the shelling of UN safe areas, more than 60 NATO aircraft attacked Bosnian Serb military installations on 30-31 Aug. Further air strikes on military targets began on 5 Sept. after Bosnian Serbs failed to comply with demands that they withdraw heavy weapons from around Sarajevo.

On 26 Sept. in Washington the foreign ministers of Bosnia, Croatia and Yugoslavia (the latter negotiating for the Bosnian Serbs) agreed a draft Bosnian constitution under which a central government would handle foreign affairs and commerce and a Serb Zone and a Moslem-Croat Federation would run their internal affairs. The Bosnian Presidency and Parliament would be elected, one third from the Serb Republic (i.e. the Serb zones of Bosnia) and two thirds from the Moslem-Croat Federation. A ceasefire came into force on 12 Oct. 1995.

In Dayton (Ohio) on 21 Nov. 1995 the prime ministers of Bosnia, Croatia and Yugoslavia initialled a US-brokered agreement to end hostilities in Bosnia, and this was signed by the respective presidents on 14 Dec. in Paris. The Bosnian state was divided into a Serb Republic containing 49% of Bosnian territory and a Croat-Moslem Federation. A central government authority representing all ethnic groups with responsibility for foreign and monetary policy and citizenship issues was established and free elections held. On 20 Dec. 1995 a 63,000-strong NATO contingent (IFOR) took over from UN peacekeeping forces to enforce the Paris peace agreements and set up a 4-km separation zone between the Serb and Moslem-Croat territories. Some 1,500 advisers were sent by the UN to help in the formation and training of local civil police units.

Following the expiry of the mandate of IFOR on 20 Dec. 1996 a new NATO 30,000-strong Stabilization Force (SFOR) took over peacekeeping duties until mid-1998. Czech, Polish and Russian troops were also attached to SFOR. But in Dec. 1997, NATO defence ministers decided that troops would stay on after the 1998 deadline.

TERRITORY AND POPULATION. The republic is bounded in the north and west by Croatia and in the east and south-east by Yugoslavia. It has a coastline of only 20 km with no harbours. Its area is 51,129 sq. km. The capital is Sarajevo.

Population at the 1991 census: 4,377,033 (34·2% urban), of which the predominating ethnic groups were Moslems (1,905,829), Serbs (1,369,258) and Croats (755,892). Population density per sq. km, (mid-1995): 87·7. By 1996, 1,319,250 Bosnians had taken refuge abroad, including 0·45m. in Yugoslavia, 0·32m. in Germany, 0·17m. in Croatia and 0·12m. in Sweden. Vital statistics rates, 1990 (per 1,000 population): Birth, 13·8; death, 6·4; growth, 8·4; infant mortality (per 1,000 live births), 15·3. 1990-95 UN estimates: Birth 13·4; death, 7·0.

Population (1991 census) of the principal cities: Sarajevo, 415,631 (est. 1993, 383,00); Banja Luka, 142,644; Zenica, 96,238.

The official language is Serbo-Croat.

CONSTITUTION AND GOVERNMENT. On 18 March 1994 in Washington Bosnian Moslems and Croats reached an agreement for the creation of a federation of cantons with a central government responsible for foreign affairs, defence and commerce. It is envisaged that there will be a president elected by a 2-house legislature alternating annually between the nationalities.

On 30 March 1994 a 123-member constituent assembly adopted the constitution by 112 votes in favour. On 31 May 1994 the National Assembly approved the creation of the Moslem Croat federation. Alija Izetbegović remained the unitary states' President. An interim government with Hasan Muratović as *Prime Minister* was formed on 30 Jan. 1996.

Following the Dayton agreement the following government structure was established in 1996:

Heading the state is a 3-member *Presidency* (1 Croat, 1 Moslem, 1 Serb) with a rotating president. The Presidency is elected by direct universal suffrage, and is responsible for foreign affairs and the nomination of the prime minister. There is a 2-chamber parliament: The *Chamber of Representatives* (which meets in Sarajevo) comprises 42 directly elected deputies, two-thirds Croat and Moslem and one-third

Serb; and the *Chamber of Peoples* (which meets in Lukavica) comprises 5 Croat, 5 Moslem and 5 Serb delegates.

Below the national level the country is divided into 2 self-governing entities along ethnic lines.

The **Croat-Moslem Federation** is headed by a President and Vice-President, alternately Croat and Moslem, a 140-member Chamber of Representatives and a 74-member Chamber of Peoples. The **Serb Republic** is also headed by an elected President and Vice-President, and there is a National Assembly of 140 members, elected by proportional representation.

Elections were held on 14 Sept. 1996 for all these institutions for a 2-year term of office. The electorate was 2·34m. Representatives of 49 parties and 33 independent candidates in all stood for the elections, which were monitored by the OSCE and 1,200 international observers. OSCE estimated that turn-out was 82%.

Elected to the national *Presidency* were Alija Izetbegović (b. 1925; Moslem; Party of Democratic Action, SDA; *President*); Momćilo Krajišnik (Serb; Serb Democratic Party, SDS; *Vice-President*); Kresimir Zubak (Croat; Croat Democratic Union, HDZ; *Vice-President*). The *President of the Serb Republic* is Biljana Plavšić (SDS). Party composition of the ethnic parliaments: Croat-Moslem, 54% SDA, 24·5% HDZ; Serb, 52% SDS, 16% SDA.

Central government is conducted by a *Council of Ministers*, which comprises Moslem and Serb Co-Prime Ministers and a Croat Deputy Prime Minister. The Co-Prime Ministers alternate in office every week.

Co-Prime Ministers: Haris Silajdžić (Moslem); Boro Bosić (Serb).

Deputy Prime Minister: Neven Tomić (Croat). *Minister of Foreign Affairs:* Jadranko Prlić (Croat). *Foreign Trade and Economic Relations:* Mirsad Kurtović. *Civil Affairs:* Spasoje Albijanić (Croat). These 3 ministries are also jointly controlled by 2 deputy ministers from each community.

A further round of elections in the Serb Republic in Nov. 1997 brought a swing against hardline nationalists in favour of the moderates. A new party led by Biljana Plavšić, President of the Serb Republic, who wants cooperation with the West, secured nearly a fifth of the vote. Her prime minister Milorad Dodik has distanced himself from supporters of the former president Radovan Karadžić who faces war-crime charges.

Local Government. In the Croat-Moslem Federation there are 10 cantons with elected local assemblies.

DEFENCE

Army. In 1998 the Army numbered some 40,000 and was organized in 5 corps headquarters. There were 40 infantry, 1 reconnaissance, 1 special forces brigades and 19 artillery regiments. Equipment included 80 T-34 and T-35 main battle tanks. The Croatian Defence Council also had personnel of some 16,000 active in the country, with 50 main battle tanks, while the forces of the Serb Republic were estimated at up to 30,000, with 500 main battle tanks. The USA supplied 16 UH1 Iroquois helicopters in 1996 to join 3 Mi-8s and is assisting in training and equipping the armed forces.

INTERNATIONAL RELATIONS. The Serb Republic and Yugoslavia signed an agreement on 28 Feb. 1997 establishing 'special parallel relations' between them. The agreement envisages co-operation in cultural, commercial, security and foreign policy matter, allows visa-free transit of borders and includes a non-aggression pact. A customs agreement followed on 31 March.

ECONOMY

Budget.

(million Deutsche Marks)	1994	1995
Revenue	535·7	874·3
Expenditure	668·4	1,051·4

Currency. Dinars are issued by the National Bank of Bosnia-Hercegovina in Sarajevo in denominations up to 100,000. The new dinar, introduced in Aug. 1994, has an official value fixed at 100 BHD = 1 Deutsche Mark.

Banking and Finance. The Dayton agreement stipulated that the governor of the Central Bank must not be a Bosnian citizen. The present governor is Serge Robert (France).

ENERGY AND NATURAL RESOURCES

Electricity. 1990 output, 14,632m. kWh.

Agriculture. The cultivated area is 1·58m. ha. 1993 yields[1] (in 1,000 tonnes): Wheat, 350; maize, 750; potatoes, 230; cabbages, 36; sugar beets, 55; plums, 50. Livestock in 1994[1] (1,000 head): Cattle, 390; sheep, 600; pigs, 223; poultry (million), 7.

Fisheries. Total catch of freshwater fish in 1993 (in 1,000 tonnes), 2·5[1].

[1] FAO estimates.

INDUSTRY. In 1991 there were 7,823 enterprises (4,563 private, 1,882 social, 655 limited companies, 322 co-operatives and 157 public). Production (in 1,000 tonnes) 1994: Lignite, 1,400; 1990: crude steel, 1,421; aluminium, 89; cement, 797. Cars (1990), 38,000; tractors, 34,000; lorries, 16,000; TV receivers, 21,000.

Labour. Population of working age, 1990, 3m. Non-agricultural workforce, 1·05m. (379,000 women). There were 283,000 unemployed in 1990

FOREIGN ECONOMIC RELATIONS

Commerce. 1990 external trade (in US$1m.): Exports, 2,876; imports, 2,548.

COMMUNICATIONS

Roads. In 1990 there were 21,168 km of roads, 11,436 km classified as modern. In 1990 there were 437,000 passenger cars and 59,000 lorries.

Railways. There were 1,021 km of railways in 1991 (795 km electrified); they carried 554m. passenger-km and 1,946m. tonne-km of freight.

Telecommunications. In 1995 there were 840,000 radio receivers.

Press. In 1995 there were 2 daily newspapers with a combined circulation of 520,000.

SOCIAL INSTITUTIONS

Religion. At the 1991 census 40% of the population were Moslem, 31% Orthodox and 15% Roman Catholic.

Education. In 1990–91 there were 543,500 pupils in primary schools, 173,100 in secondary schools and 2,400 in tertiary schools. In 1995 there were 4 universities.

Social Security. In 1990 there were 380,000 pensions (including 140,000 old age).

DIPLOMATIC REPRESENTATIVES

Of Bosnia-Hercegovina in Great Britain (320 Regent St., London, W1R 5AB)
Ambassador: Vacant.

Of Great Britain in Bosnia-Hercegovina (8 Tina Ujevića, Sarajevo)
Ambassador: Charles G. Crawford.

Of Bosnia-Hercegovina in the USA
Ambassador: Sven Alkalaj.

Of the USA in Bosnia-Hercegovina
Ambassador: John K. Menzies.

Of Bosnia-Hercegovina to the United Nations
Ambassador: Muhamad Sačirbej.

Of Bosnia-Hercegovina to the European Union
Ambassador: Vacant.

Further Reading

Bert, Wayne, *The Reluctant Superpower: United States Policy in Bosnia, 1991-1995*. New York,
    1997
Cigar, N., *Genocide in Bosnia: the Policy of Ethnic Cleansing*. Texas Univ. Press, 1995
Fine, J. V. A. and Donia, R. J., *Bosnia-Hercegovina: a Tradition Betrayed*. Farnborough, 1994
Friedman, F., *The Bosnian Muslims: Denial of a Nation*. Boulder (CO), 1996
Garde, P., *Journal de Voyage en Bosnie-Herzégovine*. Paris, 1995
Malcolm, N., *Bosnia: a Short History*. 2nd ed. London, 1996
O'Ballance, E., *Civil War in Bosnia, 1992-94*. London, 1995
Rieff, David, *Slaughterhouse: Bosnia and the Failure of the West*. New York, 1997
Sells, M. A., *The Bridge Betrayed: Religion and Genocide in Bosnia*. California Univ. Press,
    1996

BOTSWANA

Republic of Botswana

Capital: Gaborone
Population: 1·48m.
GDP per head: (PPP$) 5,367
GNP: US$4·0bn.
HDI/world rank: 0·673/97

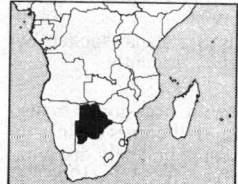

KEY HISTORICAL EVENTS. The Tswana or Batswana people are the principal inhabitants of the country formerly known as Bechuanaland and now called Botswana. The 8 main communities of the Batswana are the Bakgatla, Bakwena, Bangwaketse, Bamalete, Bamangwato, Barolong, Batawana and Batlokwa.

Dominant in the area from the 17th century, the Batswana were disturbed in the early 19th century by invasions of Nguni peoples fleeing from Shaka in the mass immigration called the *Mfecane*, and by Boers moving east in the Great Trek. They clashed with the Boers, but obtained the support of British missionaries (including David Livingstone). King Khama III, a Christian who became ruler of the Bamangwato in 1872, appealed with other chiefs to Britain because of the Boer danger. In 1885 Britain took control and the territory was formally declared a protectorate in 1895. Britain ruled through her High Commissioner in South Africa and a Resident Commissioner whose office was at Mafeking. When the post of South African High Commissioner was abolished in 1964, the British representative restyled Commissioner and placed directly under the Colonial Secretary in London. The seat of government was moved to Gaborone in 1965. Frequent suggestions for the addition of Bechuanaland and the other two High Commission Territories to South Africa were rejected, the Africans being strongly against the idea. Economically, however, the country was very closely tied to that of South Africa and has remained so.

The British left much day-to-day administration in the hands of the Tswana chiefs. They set up an African Advisory Council in 1920 and a European Advisory Council for the (never very numerous) white residents in 1921; a Joint Advisory Council was created in 1950.

Seretse Khama, ruler of the Bamangwato since 1923 when he was 4 years old, was deposed in 1950 because of South African opposition to his marriage to a white woman. He returned in 1956 and joined the African Advisory Council in 1957. In Dec. 1960 Bechuanaland received its first constitution. Elections followed in 1961 for African members of the Legislative Council, of whom Seretse was one. In 1962 he formed the Bechuanaland Democratic Party, now the Botswana Democratic party (BDP). Further constitutional change brought full self government in 1965 and full independence on 30 Sept. 1966. Sir Seretse Khama became president.

The BDP easily won elections in 1969, 1974 and 1979. President Khama died on 13 July 1980 and was succeeded by Dr Quett Masire, without any change of policy. For years Botswana had great difficulties with the neighbouring settler regime in Rhodesia, until that country became Zimbabwe in 1980. Such difficulties continued with South Africa; Botswana supported African resistance to the Pretoria regime but at the same time it was economically dependent on South Africa. Many border clashes and other incidents between Botswana and South Africa culminated in South African raids on African National Congress offices in Gaborone. Improved relations between the two countries had to wait on the ending of apartheid.

TERRITORY AND POPULATION. Botswana is bounded in the west and north by Namibia, north-east by Zambia and Zimbabwe and east and south by South Africa. The area is 581,730 sq. km. Population (1991 census), 1,326,796 (45·7% urban). Estimate, 1996, 1,478,000.

Vital statistics rates, 1996 estimates (per 1,000 population). Births, 33·3; deaths, 17·0. Infant mortality (per 1,000 live births), 54·2. Expectation of life in 1996 was 46·0 years (44·9 for males and 47·1 for females). The impact of AIDS has caused life expectancy to sink back to levels last seen in the mid 1960s. Growth rate, 1·63% per annum.

The country is divided into 10 districts (Central, Chobe, Ghanzi, Kgalagadi, Kgatleng, Kweneng, Ngamiland, Ngwaketse, North East and South East).

The main towns (with population, 1991 census) are Gaborone (133,468), Francistown (65,244), Selebi-Phikwe (39,772), Molepolole (36,931), Kanye (31,354), Serowe (30,260), Mahalapye (28,079), Maun (26,769), Lobatse (26,052) and Mochudi (25,542).

The official language is English; the national language is Setswana, spoken by 75% of the population. 12% speak Sishona, 3·4% San and 2·5% Hottentot.

CLIMATE. In winter, days are warm and nights cold, with occasional frosts. Summer heat is tempered by prevailing north-east winds. Rainfall comes mainly in summer, from Oct. to April, while the rest of the year is almost completely dry with very high sunshine amounts. Gaborone. Jan. 79°F (26·1°C), July 55°F (12·8°C). Annual rainfall varies from 650 mm in the north to 250 mm in the south-east. The country is prone to droughts.

CONSTITUTION AND GOVERNMENT. The Constitution adopted on 30 Sept. 1966 provides for a republican form of government headed by the President with 3 main organs: The Legislature, the Executive and the Judiciary. The executive rests with the President who is responsible to the National Assembly. The President is elected for 5-year terms by the National Assembly.

The *National Assembly* consists of 47 members, 40 elected by universal suffrage, and 7 elected by itself. Elections are held every 5 years. Voting is on the first-past-the-post system.

The President is an *ex-officio* member of the Assembly.

There is also a *House of Chiefs* to advise the Government. It consists of the Chiefs of the 8 tribes who were autonomous during the days of the British protectorate, plus 4 members elected by and from among the sub-chiefs in 4 districts; these 12 members elect a further 3 politically independent members.

At the elections of 15 Oct. 1994 the Botswana Democratic Party gained 27 seats and the Botswana National Front 13.

President: Festus Mogae (sworn in on 1 April 1998).

In March 1998 the Cabinet was as follows:

Vice-President and Minister of Finance and Development Planning: Festus Mogae. *Presidential Affairs and Public Affairs:* Ponatshego Kedikilwe. *Foreign Affairs:* Lieut.-Gen. Mompati Merafhe. *Health:* Chapson Butale. *Works, Transport and Communications:* Daniel Kwelagobe. *Commerce and Industry:* George Kgoroba. *Mineral Resources and Water Affairs:* David N. Magang. *Education:* Dr Gaositwe Chiepe. *Labour and Home Affairs:* Bahiti Temane. *Agriculture:* Ronald Sebego. *Local Government, Lands and Housing:* Margaret Nasha.

National anthem: 'Fatshe leno la rona' ('Blessed be this noble land'); words and tune by K. T. Motsete.

Local Government. Local government is carried out by 10 district, 1 city (Gaborone), 3 town, and 3 township councils. Revenue is obtained mainly from sales taxes, from rates in the towns and from central government subventions in the districts.

DEFENCE

Army. The Army is organized in 2 brigades comprising 4 infantry, 2 field artillery and 2 air defence battalions, 1 engineer regiment and 1 commando unit. Personnel (1997), 7,000.

Air Force. Equipment includes 5 BAC Strikemaster light strike aircraft, 5 Britten-Norman Defender armed light transports for border patrol, counter-insurgency and casualty evacuation duties, 7 PC-7 basic trainers, 2 CN-235 turboprop-powered medium transports, 2 C-212 turboprop passenger/cargo transports, 4 Islander,

5 Ecureuil and 6 Bell 412 helicopters and 2 Cessna 152 light aircraft. 13 second-hand CF-5 fighters were being delivered in 1997. Personnel (1997), 500.

INTERNATIONAL RELATIONS

Membership. Botswana is a member of the UN, the Commonwealth, OAU, SADC and is an ACP state of the EU.

ECONOMY

Policy. The Eighth National Development Plan is running from 1997 to 2003. It is intended to stimulate industries and economic activities that can take over from mines and create jobs.

Performance. In 1997 the economy grew by 7%, compared with a projected 5·7%.

Budget. The fiscal year begins in April. Budgets for recent years (in P1m.):

	1991–92	1992–93	1993–94	1994–95	1995–96
Revenue	3,969·0	4,503·6	5,103·0	4,352·9	5,377·7
Expenditure	2,691·3	3,209·3	3,924·5	4,017·8	4,760·8

Items of 1993–94 revenue (in P1m.) included: Mineral taxes, 2,456; customs pool, 830; other revenue, 1,858.

Expenditure: Recurrent, 3,470; development and capital transfer, 1,735.

Currency. The unit of currency is the *pula* (BWP) of 100 *thebe*. There are coins of 1, 5, 10, 25, and 50 thebe and 1 and 2 pula, and notes of 5, 10, 20, 50 and 100 pula. Inflation was 9·8% in Oct. 1996. Foreign exchange reserves were P13,263m. in Aug. 1995.

Banking and Finance. There were 4 commercial banks at 1 Jan. 1996 with 46 branches. Total assets were P3,729m. at 30 Nov. 1995. The Bank of Botswana (*Governor*, H. C. L. Hermans), established in 1976, is the central bank. The National Development Bank, founded in 1964, has 6 regional offices and agricultural, industrial and commercial development divisions. The Botswana Co-operative Bank is banker to co-operatives and thrift and loan societies. The government-owned Post Office Savings Bank operates throughout the country.

There is a stock exchange.

Weights and Measures. The metric system is in use.

ENERGY AND NATURAL RESOURCES

Electricity. The coal-fired power station at Morupule supplies cities and major towns. Production (1994–95) 916·6m. kWh.

Water. Surface water resources are about 18,000m. cu. metres a year. Nearly all flows into northern districts from Angola through the Okavango and Kwando river systems. The Zambezi, also in the north, provides irrigation in the Chobe District. In the south-east, there are dams to exploit the ephemeral flow of the tributaries of the Limpopo. 80% of the land has no surface water, and must be served by some 6,000 boreholes.

Minerals. Botswana is the world's biggest diamond producer. Debswana, a partnership between the government and De Beers, runs 3 mines producing around 17·5m. carats a year, with plans to double the capacity of the largest mine from 6m. to 12m. carats a year. Coal reserves are estimated at 17,000m. tonnes. There is also salt and soda ash. Mineral production, 1994: Diamonds, 15,547,178 carats (value P1,807m.); copper–nickel ore, 3,462,823 tonnes; coal, approximately 0·94m. tonnes.

Agriculture. 70–80% of the total land area is desert. 80% of the population is rural, 71% of all land is 'tribal', protected and allocated to prevent over-grazing, maintain small farmers and foster commercial ranching. Agriculture provides a livelihood for over 80% of the population, but accounts for only 5% of GDP. Cattle-rearing is the chief industry after diamond-mining, and the country is more a pastoral than an agricultural one, crops depending entirely upon the rainfall. 100,446 persons worked in agriculture in 1991. In 1990, 128,000 ha were sown to sorghum. In 1993 the number of cattle was 1,821,000. 80% were owned by traditional farmers, about half owning fewer than 20 head. In 1990 there were: Goats, 2·09m.; sheep, 301,000; poultry, 2m.; pigs, 16,000. A serious outbreak of cattle lung disease in 1995–96 led to the slaughter of around 300,00 animals, more than a tenth of the total national herd.

Production (1993, in 1,000 tonnes): Maize, 4·3; sorghum, 16·5; (1992) millet, 1; roots and tubers, 8; pulses, 12; seed cotton, 3; vegetables, 16; fruit, 11.

17% of the land is set aside for wildlife conservation and 20% for wildlife management areas, with 4 national parks and game reserves.

Forestry. There are forest nurseries and plantations. Concessions have been granted to harvest 7,500 cu. metres in Kasane and Chobe Forestry Reserves and up to 2,500 cu. metres in the Masame area. In 1994, 1·5m. cu. metres of roundwood were cut.

INDUSTRY. Meat is processed and textiles, foodstuffs and soap manufactured. 565 companies were registered at the end of 1992. Rural technology is being developed and traditional crafts encouraged.

Labour. In March 1994, 321,200 persons were in formal employment. At the 1991 census there were 276,950 paid employees (including informal employment) and 28,764 self-employed. A further 76,101 persons worked on a non-cash basis, e.g. as family helpers. 60,757 were seeking work. In March 1994 there were 12,342 Botswana nationals employed in the mines of South Africa. In 1991 there were 57,001 building workers, 34,322 in trade and 29,325 in domestic service. Average earnings in 1994 in the formal sector were P807 per month. Botswana's biggest individual employer is Debswana Diamond Company, with a workforce (1997) of nearly 6,000.

FOREIGN ECONOMIC RELATIONS. Botswana is a member of the Southern African Customs Union (SACU) with Lesotho, Namibia, South Africa and Swaziland. There are no foreign exchange restrictions.

Commerce. In 1994 imports totalled P4,392m. More than three-quarters of all imports are from the SACU countries, the main commodities being machinery and electrical equipment, foodstuffs, vehicles and transport equipment, textiles, and petroleum products.

In 1994 export earnings totalled P4,962m., including diamonds (P3,727m.), copper and nickel (P266m.) and beef (P215m.).

In addition to the SACU countries, other significant trading partners are Switzerland and the UK, and for imports, the USA.

Tourism. There were 770,000 foreign visitors in 1997.

COMMUNICATIONS

Roads. In 1996 some 4,600 km of road were bitumen-surfaced out of a total of 18,327 km. In 1994 there were 101,454 registered motor vehicles including 27,058 cars and 42,696 light duty vehicles.

Railways. The main line from Mafikeng in South Africa to Bulawayo in Zimbabwe traverses Botswana. With 3 branches the total was (1994) 971 km. In 1993–94 railways carried 0·3m. passengers and 1·7m. tonnes of freight.

Civil Aviation. There is an international airport at Gaborone (Sir Seretse Khama) and 6 domestic airports. The national carrier is the state-owned Air Botswana, which had 3 aircraft in 1995. Services are also operated by Air Zimbabwe, British Airways, Commercial Airways and, Kalahari Air Services. Direct services are operated to the UK, Namibia, Tanzania, Zambia and Zimbabwe.

Telecommunications. There are 109 post offices and 65 agencies. There were some 50,000 working telephone lines by 1995. The government-controlled Radio Botswana broadcasts daily on 2 channels in English and Setswana. A commercial television company transmits on a 50 km-radius from Gaborone (colour by SECAM). There were 1·9m. radio and 27,000 TV sets in 1995.

Press. In 1995 there was 1 government newspaper (distributed free) and 5 independent newspapers, with a total circulation of about 100,500, and 6 other periodicals.

SOCIAL INSTITUTIONS

Justice. Law is based on the Roman-Dutch law of the former Cape Colony, but judges and magistrates are also qualified in English common law. The Court of Appeal has jurisdiction in respect of criminal and civil appeals emanating from the High Court and in all criminal and civil cases and proceedings. Magistrates' courts and traditional courts are in each administrative district. As well as a national police force there are local customary law enforcement officers.

Religion. Freedom of worship is guaranteed under the Constitution. About 50% of the population is Christian. Non-Christian religions include Bahais, Moslems and Hindus.

Education. Adult literacy rate (1995) 69·8% (male, 80·5%; female, 59·9%). Basic free education, introduced in 1986, consists of 7 years of primary and 3 years of junior secondary schooling. In 1994 enrolment in 670 primary schools was 310,128, and 93,250 pupils at secondary level. In 1993 there were 67 primary, 163 community junior and 23 senior secondary schools. In 1993 there were 1,261 students in teacher training colleges. 'Brigades' (community-managed private bodies) provide lower level vocational training. The Department of Non-Formal Education offers secondary level correspondence courses and is the executing agency for the National Literacy Programme. There is 1 university (6,673 students in 1995–96).

Health (1994). There were 16 general hospitals, a mental hospital, 13 health centres, 200 clinics and 310 health posts. There were also 701 stops for mobile health teams. In 1994 there were 339 doctors and 3,329 nurses. The health facilities are the concern of central and local government, medical missions, mining companies and voluntary organizations.

DIPLOMATIC REPRESENTATIVES

Of Botswana in Great Britain (6 Stratford Pl., London, W1N 9AE)
High Commissioner: Tuelonyana Ditlhabi-Olipant.

Of Great Britain in Botswana (Private Bag 0023, Gaborone)
High Commissioner: David C. B. Beaumont.

Of Botswana in the USA (4301 Connecticut Ave., NW, Washington, D.C., 20008)
Ambassador: Archie Mogwe.

Of the USA in Botswana (PO Box 90, Gaborone)
Ambassador: Robert C. Krueger.

Of Botswana to the United Nations
Ambassador: Legwaila Joseph Legwaila.

Of Botswana to the European Union
Ambassador: Sasara George.

Further Reading

Central Statistics Office. *Statistical Bulletin* (Quarterly).
Ministry of Information and Broadcasting. *Botswana Handbook.* — *Kutlwano* (monthly).
Colclough, C. and McCarthy, S., *The Political Economy of Botswana.* OUP, 1980
Harvey, C., (ed.) *Papers on the Economy of Botswana.* London and Nairobi, 1981
Molomo, M. G. and Mokopakgosi, B. (eds.) *Multi-Party Democracy in Botswana.* Harare, 1991
Parson, J., *Botswana: Liberal Democracy and Labour Reserve in Southern Africa.* Aldershot, 1984
Perrings, C., *Sustainable Development and Poverty Alleviation in Sub-Saharan Africa: the Case of Botswana.* London, 1995

National statistical office: Central Statistics Office, Private Bag 0024, Gaborone.

BRAZIL

República Federativa do
Brasil

Capital: Brasília (Federal District)
Population: 157·1m.
GDP per head: (PPP$) 5,362
GNP: US$536·3bn.
HDI/world rank: 0·783/68

KEY HISTORICAL EVENTS. Brazil, South America's largest country, was colonized by the Portuguese following the arrival of Admiral Pedro Alvares Cabral on 22 April 1500. In 1815 the colony was declared 'a kingdom'. When, in 1822, the Portuguese king, João VI, returned home after using Rio de Janeiro as his capital during the French occupation of Portugal, his eldest surviving son, Dom Pedro, was chosen 'Perpetual Defender' of Brazil by a National Congress. He proclaimed the independence of the country on 7 Sept. 1822, and was chosen 'Constitutional Emperor and Perpetual Defender' on 12 Oct. 1822, with the title Emperor Pedro I. He abdicated in 1831 and was succeeded in 1840 by his son, Pedro II. Pedro ruled for nearly 50 years. His policies were liberal and included the gradual abolition of slavery.

Under the dictatorship of President Vargas from 1930 to 1945, some areas (such as São Paulo) saw considerable economic development. Vargas was succeeded by Presidents Kubitschek and Quadros.

Juscelino Kubitschek, popularly known as JK, was elected president in 1956. Promising '50 years progress in five' he brought 40 years inflation in four. A big spender, he created roads and hydroelectric plants. Brasilia, supposed to be the catalyst for development of Brazil's huge interior, was built.

Janio Quadros became the next president in 1961 on a wave of public euphoria. But when he decorated Che Guevara in a public ceremony he upset the rightwing military. A few days later Quadros resigned after only six months in office. João Goulart, his vice-president, took over. His leftist policies led to his overthrow by the military in 1964. This was followed by 20 years of single party rule and censored press.

Brazil's military regime was not as brutal as those of Chile or Argentina, but at its height, around 1968 and 1969, the use of torture was widespread. The generals benefited from the Brazilian economic miracle in the late '60s and '70s when the economy was growing more than 10% every year. Brazil became one of the biggest industrial nations in the world, but unco-ordinated growth made bureaucracy, corruption and inflation explode.

In 1980 a militant working-class movement sprung up under the charismatic leadership of a worker called Lula. The popular opposition together with economic problems forced the military slowly to announce the so-called 'abertura' (opening): A slow process of returning the government to democracy.

Tancredo Neves surprised his military opponents by winning the 1985 elections, but tragically died shortly before assuming power. José Sarney, his vice-president, took over. With a new finance minister every three months, the country drifted into economic chaos and foreign debt reached Cr$115,000m.

In 1989, Fernando Collor de Mello, governor of a forgotten state in the north-east, won a hard-fought victory over the Labour Party candidate, Lula. One of the main promises of the incoming government was to cut inflation and attack corruption. When he assumed control in March 1990, Collor took drastic measures: In an attempt to reduce inflation caused by excess liquidity in the market, he confiscated 80% of every bank account worth more than US$1,200, promising to release it 18 months later with interest. He announced the privatization of state-owned companies and the opening of Brazilian markets to foreign competition and capital.

By 1992 few promises had been met, most of the popular goodwill was gone and Collor found his government shaken by scandals and corruption linked directly to his family, and inflation was heading again into astronomical figures. The parliament, under public pressure, forced an impeachment. Itamar Franco, Collor's vice-president, took office for three years.

Fernando Henrique Cardoso, former finance minister responsible for the 'plano Real', the economic plan to end inflation, was elected president at the end of 1994.

TERRITORY AND POPULATION. Brazil is bounded in the east by the Atlantic and on its northern, western and southern borders by all the Latin American countries except Chile and Ecuador. The area is 8,547,395 sq. km including 55,457 sq. km of inland water. Population as at censuses 1 Sept. 1980 and 1 Sept. 1991:

Federal Unit and Capital	Area (sq. km)	Census 1991	Census 1996
North	3,869,639		
Rondônia (Porto Velho)	238,513	1,132,692	1,231,007
Acre (Rio Branco)	153,150	417,718	483,726
Amazonas (Manaus)	1,577,820	2,103,243	2,389,279
Roraima (Boa Vista)	225,116	217,583	247,131
Pará (Belém)	1,253,165	4,950,060	5,510,849
Amapá (Macapá)	143,454	289,397	379,459
Tocantins (Palmas)	278,421	919,863	1,048,642
North-East	1,561,177[1]		
Maranhão (São Luís)	333,366	4,930,253	5,222,565
Piauí (Teresina)	252,378	2,582,137	2,673,176
Ceará (Fortaleza)	146,348	6,366,647	6,809,794
Rio Grande do Norte (Natal)	53,307	2,415,567	2,558,660
Paraíba (João Pessoa)	56,585	3,201,114	3,305,616
Pernambuco (Recife)	98,938	7,127,855	7,399,131
Alagoas (Maceió)	27,933	2,514,100	2,633,339
Sergipe (Aracajú)	22,050	1,491,876	1,624,175
Bahia (Salvador)	567,295	11,867,991	12,541,745
South-East:	927,287		
Minas Gerais (Belo Horizonte)	588,384	15,743,152	16,673,097
Espírito Santo (Vitória)	46,184	2,600,618	2,802,707
Rio de Janeiro (Rio de Janeiro)	43,910	12,807,706	13,406,379
São Paulo (São Paulo)	248,809	31,588,925	34,120,886
South	577,214		
Parana (Curitiba)	199,709	8,448,713	9,003,804
Santa Catarina (Florianópolis)	95,443	4,541,994	4,875,244
Rio Grande do Sul (Porto Alegre)	282,062	9,138,670	9,637,682
Central West	1,612,078		
Mato Grosso (Cuiabá)	906,807	2,027,231	2,235,832
Mato Grosso do Sul (Campo Grande)	358,159	1,780,373	1,927,834
Goiás (Goiânia)	341,290	4,018,903	4,315,868
Distrito Federal (Brasília)	5,822	1,601,094	1,821,946
Total	8,547,395	146,825,475	157,079,573

[1] Including disputed areas between states of Piauí and Ceará (2,977 sq. km).

Density, 17 per sq. km. The 1991 census showed 72,485,122 males and 74,340,353 females. The urban population comprised 75·6% in 1989. Life expectancy was 66 years in 1996.

The official language is Portuguese.

Population of principal cities (1996 census):

São Paulo	9,839,436	Porto Alegre	1,288,879	São Luis	780,833
Rio de Janeiro	5,551,538	Manaus	1,157,357	Duque de Caxias	715,089
Salvador	2,211,539	Belém	1,144,312	Maceió	723,230
Belo Horizonte	2,091,448	Goiânia	1,004,098	São Bernardo do	
Fortaleza	1,965,513	Guarulhos	972,384	Campo	660,396
Brasília	1,821,946	Campinas	908,906	Natal	656,037
Curitiba	1,476,253	São Gonçalo	833,379	Teresina	655,473
Recife	1,346,045	Nova Iguaçu	826,188	Santo André	625,564

Osasco	622,912	Feira de Santana	450,487	Londrina	421,343
Campo Grande	600,069	Niterói	450,364	Santos	412,243
João Pessoa	549,363	Uberlândia	438,986	Joynville	397,951
Jaboatão	529,966	São João de Meriti	434,323	Campos dos	
Contagem	492,350	Cuiabá	433,355	Goytacazes	389,547
São José dos		Sorocaba	431,561	Olinda	349,380
Campos	486,467	Aracaju	428,194	Diadema	323,116
Ribeirão Preto	456,252	Juiz de Fora	424,479	Jundiaí	293,373

The principal metropolitan areas (census, 1996) were São Paulo (16,583,234), Rio de Janeiro (10,192,097), Belo Horizonte (3,803,249), Porto Alegre (3,246,869), Salvador (2,709,084), Recife (3,087,967), Fortaleza (2,582,820), Curitiba (2,425,361), Belém (1,485,569) and Vitória (1,182,354).

CLIMATE. Because of its latitude, the climate is predominantly tropical, but factors such as altitude, prevailing winds and distance from the sea cause certain variations, though temperatures are not notably extreme. In tropical parts, winters are dry and summers wet, while in Amazonia conditions are constantly warm and humid. The N.E. sertão is hot and arid, with frequent droughts. In the south and east, spring and autumn are sunny and warm, summers are hot, but winters can be cold when polar air-masses impinge. Brasilia. Jan. 72°F (22·3°C), July 68°F (19·8°C). Annual rainfall 63" (1,603 mm). Belém. Jan. 78°F (25·8°C), July 80°F (26·4°C). Annual rainfall 102" (2,315 mm). Manaus. Jan. 79°F (26·1°C), July 80°F (26·7°C). Annual rainfall 110" (2,842 mm). Recife. Jan. 80°F (26·6°C), July 77°F (24·8°C). Annual rainfall 94" (2,474 mm). Rio de Janeiro. Jan. 83°F (28·5°C), July 67°F (19·6°C). Annual rainfall 67" (1,758 mm). São Paulo. Jan. 75°F (24°C), July 57°F (13·7°C). Annual rainfall 71" (1,800 mm). Salvador. Jan. 80°F (26·5°C), July 74°F (23·5°C). Annual rainfall 90" (2,315 mm). Porto Alegre. Jan. 75°F (23·9°C), July 62°F (16·7°C). Annual rainfall 67" (1,775 mm).

CONSTITUTION AND GOVERNMENT. The present Constitution came into force on 5 Oct. 1988, the eighth since independence. The *President* and *Vice-President* are elected for a 4-year term and are not immediately re-eligible. To be elected candidates must secure 51% of the votes, otherwise a second round of voting is held to elect the President between the two most voted candidates. Voting is compulsory for men and women between the ages of 18 and 70 and optional for illiterates, persons from 16 to 18 years old and persons over 70. A referendum on constitutional change was held on 21 April 1993. Turn-out was 80%. 66·1% of votes cast were in favour of retaining a republican form of government, and 10·2% for re-establishing a monarchy. 56·4% favoured an executive presidency, 24·7% parliamentary supremacy.

At the elections of 3 Oct. 1994 Fernando Henrique Cardoso was elected President by 54·3% of votes cast against 6 opponents.

A constitutional amendment of June 1997 authorizes the re-election of the President, state governors and mayors for a second term.

Congress consists of an 81-member *Senate* (3 Senators per federal unit) and a 513-member *Chamber of Deputies*. The Senate is two-thirds directly elected (50% of these elected for 8 years in rotation) and one-third indirectly elected. The Chamber of Deputies is elected by universal franchise for 4 years. There is a *Council of the Republic* which is convened only in national emergencies. Elections were held in Oct. 1990 for the governors of the 26 states and 1 federal district, 27 senators (one-third of the Senate), 503 federal deputies and 1,049 state deputies. Some 70,000 candidates from 22 parties stood. The electorate was 84m.

In Feb. 1995 the composition of Congress was:

Senate: Cardoso coalition, 33 seats; Democratic Movement, 23; right-wing parties, 7; Workers' Party and allies, 7; others, 11.

Chamber of Deputies: Cardoso coalition, 182 seats; Democratic Movement, 107; right-wing parties, 100; Workers' Party and allies, 80; others, 44.

President: Fernando Henrique Cardoso (b. 1931; Social Democrat; sworn in 1 Jan. 1995).

In March 1998 the government comprised:
Justice: Iris Rezende Machado. *Navy:* Mauro Cesar Rodrigues Pereira. *Army:* Zenildo Zoroastro de Lucena. *External Relations:* Luiz Felipe Lampreia. *Finance:* Pedro Sampaio Malan. *Transport:* Eliseu Padilha. *Agriculture:* Arlindo Porto Neto. *Education:* Paulo Renato de Souza. *Culture:* Francisco Correa Weffort. *Labour:* Paulo Paiva. *Social Security:* Reinhold Stephanes. *Air Force:* Lélio Viana Lobo. *Health:* Carlos César Silva de Albuquerque. *Industry, Trade and Tourism:* Francisco Neves Dornelles. *Mining and Energy:* Raimundo Brito. *Communications:* Sergio Vieira da Motta. *Science and Technology:* José Israel Vargas. *Environment:* Gustavo Krause. *Planning and Budget:* Antonio Kandir. *Sports:* Edson Arantes do Nascimento ('Pele'). Presidential, congressional and state elections are due in Oct./Nov. 1998.

National anthem: 'Ouviram do Ipiranga. . .' ('They hear the river Ipiranga'); words by J. O. Duque Estrada; tune by F. M. da Silva.

Local Government. Brazil consists of 27 federal units (26 states and 1 federal district). Each has its distinct administrative, legislative and judicial authorities and its own constitution and laws, which must, however, agree with federal constitutional principles. The governors and members of the legislatures are elected for 4-year terms. The country is sub-divided into 5,507 municipalities, each under an elected mayor and municipal council, and then further sub-divided into districts. The Federal District is the national capital, inaugurated in 1960; it is divided into 12 administrative Regions, the first Region being Brasília. Gubernatorial elections were held for all 27 federal units etc. in Oct.–Nov. 1994. Municipal elections were held on 30 Oct. 1996 and, for municipalities with at least 0·2m. electors, on 15 Nov. 1996.

Constituição da Republica Federativa do Brasil. Brasília, 1988
Baaklini, A. I., *The Brazilian Legislature and Political System.* London, 1992
Martinez-Lara, J., *Building Democracy in Brazil: the Politics of Constitutional Change.* London, 1996

DEFENCE. Conscription is for 12 months, extendable by 6 months.

Army. There are 7 military commands and 11 military regions. The Army consists of 8 divisions, 1 armoured cavalry, 3 armoured infantry, 4 mechanized cavalry, 13 motor infantry, 1 mountain, 4 jungle, 1 frontier, 1 airborne and 2 coast and air defence brigades, 3 cavalry guard regiments, 28 artillery and 2 engineer groups. Equipment includes 61 Leopard I main battle tanks and 333 light tanks. Strength 200,000 (125,000 conscripts). A helicopter brigade has 50 Dauphin and Ecureuil helicopters and 3 Bandeirante transports.

There are para-military state militias under Army control and considered an Army reserve, totalling about 385,000 personnel.

Navy. The principal ship of the Navy is the 20,200-tonne Light Aircraft Carrier *Minas Gerais,* formerly the British *Vengeance,* completed in 1945, purchased in 1956, which normally operates an air group of 8 S-2E Tracker anti-submarine aircraft, and 8 ASH-3H anti-submarine Sea King helicopters.

There are also 5 diesel submarines (1 built in Germany, 1 in Brazil and 3 British Oberon-class) and 16 frigates including 4 Type 22 Batch 1 (Broadwood class) bought from the UK in 1995 and 1996. The fleet still includes 1 old ex-US Gearing class destroyer and 2 Sumner class, but these are decommissioning. There are 3 offshore and 6 inshore minesweepers and a patrol force numbering about 30 including 9 tug/trawler types, 6 ex-US inshore craft, 2 locally-built and a number for work on the rivers. Major auxiliaries include 2 oilers, 1 repair ship, 4 transports, 4 survey and rescue, 1 training frigate and 5 tugs. There are some 70 minor auxiliaries. Amphibious forces consist of 2 ex-US landing ships (dock) and 1 tank landing ship. A further diesel submarine is being built.

Fleet Air Arm personnel only fly helicopters, the 6 S-2E Tracker anti-submarine aircraft held for carrier operations and the 20 shore-based maritime patrol EMB-111 being operated by the Air Force. Naval aircraft include 7 ASH-3 Sea King for carrier service, 5 Lynx, and 17 Esquilo for embarkation in the smaller ships. Utility and search-and-rescue duties are performed by 16 Bell 206B Sea Ranger, and 6 Super

Puma helicopters. Naval bases are at Rio de Janeiro, Aratu (Bahia), Belém, Natal, Rio Grande do Sul and Salvador, with river bases at Ladario and Manaus.

Active personnel, 1997, totalled 64,700, including 14,600 well-equipped Marines and 1,200 in Naval Aviation.

The Brazil navy is preparing to buy 20 McDonnell Douglas A-4 Skyhawk fighter bombers from Kuwait for US$70m. (£43m.) as part of a long-term project to increase its ability to protect military and civilian shipping. The jets will be the Brazilian navy's first fixed-wing aircraft and will be operated from its single aircraft carrier, the Minas Gerais.

Air Force. The Air Force is organized in 6 zones, centred on Belém, Recife, Rio de Janeiro, São Paulo, Porto Alegre and Brasília. The 1a GDA (Air Defence Group) has 12 Mirage IIIE fighters and 4 Mirage IIID trainers, integrated with Roland mobile short-range surface-to-air missile systems deployed by the Army, and a radar/communications/computer network. Two fighter groups have 3 squadrons of F-5E Tiger II supersonic fighter-bombers and two-seat F-5B/Fs; 3 others operate AT-26 (Aermacchi MB 326G) Xavante light jet attack/trainers, licence-built by Embraer in Brazil and 2 squadrons operate the AM-X fighter-bomber, jointly developed by Italy and Brazil; 79 AM-Xs are being delivered. Counter-insurgency squadrons are equipped with armed Ecureuil helicopters for liaison and observation. 2 air-sea rescue units are equipped with Bandeirantes. Equipment of transport units includes 1 squadron of C-130E/H Hercules transports; 1 squadron of Boeing 707 tanker/transports; 1 group made up of a squadron of HS 748 and a second squadron of Bandeirante turboprop transports; 2 troop-carrier groups with DHC-5 Buffaloes; 1 group with Bandeirantes; 1 group with UH-1 Iroquois and Super Puma helicopters; and 7 independent squadrons with Bandeirantes. Light aircraft for liaison duties include 30 Embraer U-7s (licence-built Piper Senecas), 30 Neiva Regente lightplanes and 7 Cessna Caravans. The VIP transport group has 2 Boeing 737s, 11 HS 125 twin-jet light transports, 4 Embraer Brasilias, 6 Embraer Xingu (VU-9) twin-turboprop pressurized transports and Ecureuil and JetRanger helicopters. Training is performed primarily on locally-built T-25 Universal and turboprop T-27 Tucano (EMB-312) basic trainers, and AT-26 Xavante armed jet basic trainers. Personnel strength (1997) 50,000 (5,000 conscripts).

INTERNATIONAL RELATIONS

Membership. Brazil is a member of the UN, OAS and Mercosul.

ECONOMY

Policy. In 1991 a National Reconstruction Plan was introduced to promote growth and investment and reduce the role of the state. State monopolies in ports, communications and fuels were reduced and agricultural and industrial subsidies ended. A sixth economic plan was introduced in 1993 to cut spending and accelerate privatization. Since Oct. 1994 the government has authorized privatization of the energy, electricity, petrochemicals and telecommunications sectors. After an initial stage in which steel, petrochemical, fertilizers and mining industries were privatized, the programme was headed by roads, railways, sea ports, electricity and telecommunications in 1997. During 1990–95, 22 state-owned and 19 partly state-owned companies were privatized. The Real Plan, a monetary and economic stability programme, was launched in July 1994. In Nov. 1997 the government announced a package of proposed spending cuts and tax rises worth R$20,000m. to reduce the long-standing fiscal and balance-of-payments deficits.

Revenue from privatization (US$m.): 1991, 1·99; 1992, 3·38; 1993, 4·19; 1994, 2·32; 1995, 1·63; 1996, 4·75.

The Brazilian Congress has approved a controversial tax-raising decree which forms a central part of the government's R$20bn. (£11bn.) fiscal package designed to head off further financial market turbulence. Brazilians who earn more than R$1,800 a month will pay 10 per cent more income tax, the tax on income from fixed income investments has increased from 15 per cent to 20 per cent and fiscal incentives to companies investing in the north and north-east of the country have been reduced by 25 per cent.

Performance. Inflation fell from 2,500% in 1993 to 22% in 1995 and 11·1% in 1996, and was forecast to be from 4-6% in 1997. Real GDP growth was 2·9% in 1996 (4·2% in 1995).

Budget. 1995/96 (in R$1,000) revenue was 229,722,437 and expenditure 173,992,572.

Internal federal debt, July 1996 was R$176,478m. Internal states and municipalities (main securities outstanding), R$49,672m.

Currency. The unit of currency is the *real* (equal to 100 centavos) which was introduced on 1 July 1994 to replace the former cruzeiro real at a rate of 1 real (R$1) = 2,750 cruzeiros reais (CR$2,750). The real was devalued 6·54% in June 1995. There are coins of 1, 5, 10, 25 and 50 centavos and R$1, and notes of R$1, 5, 10, 50 and 100. The real was devalued in Sept. 1994 and March 1995. Foreign exchange reserves were US$51,840m. in Dec. 1995.

Banking and Finance. On 31 Dec. 1964 the Banco Central do Brasil (*President*, Gustavo Loyola) was founded as the national bank of issue.

The Bank of Brazil (founded in 1853 and reorganized in 1906) is a state-owned commercial bank; it had 3,125 branches in 1995 throughout the republic. On 31 Dec. 1995 deposits were R$40,137m. In 1994 there were 6 public-sector banks and 24 banks controlled by state governments.

There are 9 stock exchanges of which Rio de Janeiro and São Paulo are the most important. All except São Paulo are linked in the National Electronic Trading System (Senn).

Lees, F. A. et al. (eds.), *Banking and Financial Deepening in Brazil*. London, 1990

Weights and Measures. The metric system has been compulsory since 1872.

ENERGY AND NATURAL RESOURCES

Electricity. Hydro-electric potential capacity was estimated at 255,000 MW per year in Dec. 1990, of which 41% belonged to the Amazon hydro-electric basin. Installed capacity (1995) 55,512 MW of which 50,687 MW were hydro-electric. There is 1 nuclear power plant, supplying some 0·2% of total output. Production (1995) 260,678m. kWh (231,389m. kWh hydro-electric in 1993).

Oil. There are 13 oil refineries, of which 11 are state-owned. Crude oil production (1995), 40,018,481 cu. metres (745,000 bbls. a day). In 1997, domestic production of 1m. bbls a day met 55% of demand. The state petroleum company Petrobrás was negotiating joint ventures with up to 70 interested foreign companies to develop some of its oil fields, many off-shore. Crude oil reserves were estimated at 11,600m. bbls in 1997.

Gas. Production (1995) 8,043,869,000 cu. metres. The World Bank has approved the financing for the construction of the 3,150 km Bolivia-Brazil gas pipeline, one of Latin America's biggest infrastructure projects. The cost of the project is put at around US$2bn. (£1·2bn.). The pipeline runs from the Bolivian interior across the Brazilian border at Puerto Suarez-Corumbá to the far southern port city of Porto Alegre.

Minerals. The chief minerals are bauxite, gold, iron ore, manganese, nickel, phosphates, platinum, tin and uranium. Brazil is the only source of high-grade quartz crystal in commercial quantities; output, 1992, 38,148 tonnes raw, 27,275 tonnes processed. It is a major producer of chrome ore: Output, 1992, 948,788 tonnes; reserves, 1992, 14·2m. tonnes. Other minerals, with 1992 output in tonnes, are mica, 14; zirconium, 15,017; beryllium 1,412; graphite, 685,850; and magnesite, 1,161,200. Along the coasts of the states of Rio de Janeiro, Espírito Santo and Bahia are found monazite sands containing thorium: Output, 1991, 560 tonnes; estimated reserves, 1991, 772,000 tonnes. Manganese ores of high content are important: Output, 1995, 3,395,078 tonnes; estimated reserves, 1992, 81·2m. tonnes. Output, 1992 (in tonnes) of bauxite, 12,763,150; mineral salt, 1,230,608; tungsten ore, 28,767, unrough, 205; lead, 334,426; asbestos, 3,895,805; coal, 9,241,099. Primary aluminium production in 1989 was 888,000 tonnes. Deposits of coal exist in Rio Grande do Sul, Santa Catarina and Paraná. Total reserves were estimated at 5,190·2m. tonnes in 1988.

Iron is found chiefly in Minas Gerais, notably the Cauê Peak at Itabira. The Government is opening up iron-ore deposits in Carajás, in the northern state of Pará, with estimated reserves of 35,000m. tonnes, representing a 66% concentration of high-grade iron ore. Total output of iron ore, 1992, mainly from the Cia. Vale do Rio Doce mine at Itabira, was 205,346,525 tonnes.

Production of tin ore (cassiterite, processed) was 33,749 tonnes in 1992; output of barytes, 72,171 tonnes, and of phosphate rock, 15·5m. tonnes.

Gold is chiefly from Pará (18,837 kg in 1992), Mato Grosso (18,009 kg) and Minas Gerais (23,120 kg); total production (1992), 80,543 kg processed. Silver output (processed in 1992) 20,042 tonnes. Diamond output in 1992 was 1,285,402 carats (157,805 carats from Minas Gerais, 1m. carats from Mato Grosso).

Agriculture. In 1992, 35·67m. people depended on agriculture, of whom 13·25m. were economically active. There were 5·83m. farms in 1985. Arable land covers 7% of the total area of the country, permanent crops 1% and meadows and pastures 19%. Production (in tonnes):

	1994	1995		1994	1995
Bananas			Grapes	806,609	825,359
(1,000 bunches)	572,165	568,086	Coconut		
Beans	3,368,430	2,946,267	(1,000 fruits)	902,217	949,399
Cassava	24,452,358	25,315,620	Coffee	2,612,538	1,856,889
Castor-beans	53,497	32,474	Cotton	1,367,183	1,451,061
Oranges			Maize	32,487,400	36,273,306
(1,000 fruits)	87,091,089	98,065,502	Soya	24,912,345	25,651,272
Potatoes	2,480,162	2,676,926	Sugar-cane	292,070,449	303,557,343
Rice	10,499,455	11,220,994	Wheat	2,092,424	1,534,148
Sisal	131,421	118,066	Cocoa	330,398	296,493
Tomatoes	2,678,147	2,698,252			

Harvested coffee area, 1995, 1,867,071 ha, principally in the states of Minas Gerais, Espírito Santo, São Paulo and Paraná. Harvested cocoa area, 1995, 737,698 ha. Bahia furnished 82% of the output in 1994. 2 crops a year are grown. Harvested castor-bean area, 1995, 75,479 ha. Tobacco output was 455,277 tonnes in 1994, grown chiefly in Rio Grande do Sul and Santa Catarina.

Rubber is produced chiefly in the states of Acre, Amazonas, Rondônia and Pará. Output, 1995, 44,268 tonnes (natural). Brazilian consumption of rubber in 1995 was 155,229 tonnes. Plantations of tung trees were established in 1930; output, 1992, 1,536 tonnes.

2·8m. ha were irrigated in 1992.

Livestock (in 1,000) 1994: Cattle, 158,243; pigs, 35,142; sheep, 18,436; goats, 10,879; horses, 6,356; asses, 1,313 and mules, 1,987. Livestock slaughtered for meat in 1994 (in 1,000): Cattle, 15,512; pigs, 14,575; sheep and lambs, 763; goats, 729; poultry, 1,447,525. Livestock products, 1994: Milk, 15,784m. litres; wool, 25,993 tonnes; honey, 17,514 tonnes; hen's eggs, 23,077m.

Fisheries. The fishing industry had a 1993 catch of 780,000 tonnes.

Environment. Brazil has the world's biggest river system and about a quarter of the world's primary rainforest. Current environmental issues are deforestation in the Amazon Basin, air and water pollution in Rio de Janeiro and São Paulo (the world's third-largest city), and land degradation and water pollution caused by improper mining activities. Contaminated drinking water causes 70% of child deaths.

An independent study commissioned by NASA found that the rate of deforestation was on the decline (to 11,000 sq. km in 1992-93, close to half the annual deforestation rate in the decade from 1978-88) and stated that the government had been extremely active since 1990 in reducing the rate of illegal deforestation. In 1996 the government ruled that Amazonian landowners could log only 20% of their holdings, instead of 50%, as had previously been permitted. In 1997 the government's environmental agency, Ibama, levied fines of nearly US$11m. on illicit loggers.

INDUSTRY. The main industries are textiles, shoes, chemicals, cement, lumber, iron ore, tin, steel, aircraft, motor vehicles and parts and other machinery and equipment. The National Iron and Steel Co. at Volta Redonda, State of Rio de Janeiro, furnishes a substantial part of Brazil's steel. Total output, 1995: crude steel, 25,076,000 tonnes.

Cement output, 1995, was 28,261,000 tonnes. Output of paper, 1994, was 5,653,517 tonnes. Production of rubber tyres for motor vehicles (1992), 30,306,000 units; motor vehicles (1994), 1,581,389.

Labour. The work force in 1996 numbered 68,040,206, of whom 14,180,519 were in agriculture and 13,233,866 (including the construction industry) worked in industry. A constitutional amendment of Oct. 1996 prohibits the employment of children under 14 years. In 1996, there was a minimum monthly wage of R$112. Unemployment was 5·7% in 1997, against 5·4% in 1996.

Trade Unions. The main union is the United Workers' Centre (CUT).

FOREIGN ECONOMIC RELATIONS. In 1990 Brazil repealed most of its protectionist legislation. Import tariffs on some 13,000 items were reduced in 1995. Since 1991 direct foreign investment on equal terms with domestic has been permitted. Foreign investment nearly tripled in 1996, reaching US$9,900m., much of it as a result of the privatization programme. In 1991 the government permitted an annual US$100m. of foreign debt to be converted into funds for environmental protection. Foreign debt (including states and municipalities) on 31 Dec. 1996 amounted to US$144,092m. Total foreign debt, 1996, US$173,900m.

Commerce. Imports and exports for calendar years in US$1,000.:

	1993	1994	1995	1996
Imports	25,256,001	33,078,710	49,857,613	53,286,251
Exports	38,596,848	43,545,163	46,506,287	47,747,000

Estimate for 1997 trade deficit: US$783m.

Principal imports in 1996 were (in US$1m.): Machinery and electrical equipment, 15,671; chemical products, 6,840; transport equipment, 5,512; crude oil, 2,576; food-stuffs, 3,459; coal and coke, 755; fertilizers, 860; cast iron and steel, 792.

Principal exports in 1996 were (in 1,000 tonnes): Soya, 3,646; iron, manganese and other ores, 987; coffee, 833; orange juice, 1,180; sugar, 5,989; tobacco, 282; cocoa beans, 33; (in US$1m.) transport equipment, 3,720; machine tools, 187.

Main export markets, 1995 (in US$1m.): USA, 8,798; Argentina, 4,041; Japan, 3,102; Netherlands, 2,918; Germany, 2,158. Main import suppliers: USA, 11,873; Argentina, 5,446; Germany, 5,139; Italy, 2,725; Japan, 2,543.

Tourism. In 1996, 1,991,416 tourists visited Brazil. 657,942 were Argentinean, 224,577 US citizens, 200,423 Uruguayan, 102,106 German, 90,716 Paraguayan, 84,001 Italian, 63,900 Chilean, 59,502 Spanish, 55,257 French, 52,183 Portuguese, 38,520 UK citizens, 33,505 Swiss, 30,219 Japanese.

COMMUNICATIONS

Roads. There were (1994) 1,824,363 km of highways of which 1,660,352 km were in operation. Less than 10% of roads are paved. In 1997 there were 15m. cars and 1·1m. active trucks. Some 56% of freight is carried by truck.

Railways. Public railways are operated by two administrations, the Federal Railways (RFFSA) formed in 1957 and São Paulo Railways (Fepasa) formed in 1971, which is confined to the state of São Paulo. They are in process of privatization; all 6 branches of the RFFSA network were under private management by the end of Aug. 1997. RFFSA had a route-length of 22,069 km (65 km electrified) in 1994 and Fepasa 4,344 km (1,044 km electrified). An RFFSA subsidiary, CBTU (the Brazilian Urban Train Company), runs passenger services in some cities, while others are in the hands of the local authorities. Principal gauges are metre (24,720 km) and 1,600 mm (5,419 km). Traffic moved by RFFSA in 1994 amounted to 86m. tonnes of freight and

(1993) 1,713m. passengers. Fepasa carried 19·1m. tonnes and 104·9m. passengers in 1993.

There are several important independent freight railways, including the Vitoria à Minas (898 km in 1993), the Ferroeste (238 km), the Carajas (opened 1985, 1,076 km in 1991) and the Amapa (194 km). There are metros in São Paulo (44 km), Rio de Janeiro (23 km), Belo Horizonte (14 km), Porto Alegre (28 km) and Brasília (38·5 km).

Civil Aviation. There are international airports at Rio de Janeiro and São Paulo (Guarulhos). The 4 national airlines are Viação Aérea Rio Grande do Sul (Varig), with 49% of the domestic market, Cruzeiro do Sul, Transbrasil and Viação Aérea São Paulo (Vasp; 38% state-owned). Brazilian airlines carried 19,456,882 passengers (11,431,556 domestic) in 1994. Brazil is also served by Aeroflot, Aerolíneas Argentinas, Aeroperú, Air Aruba, Air France, Alitalia, American Airlines, Avianca, British Airways, Canadian Airlines, Cubana, Delta, Iberia, JAL, KLM, Korean Air, Lacsa, Ladeco, Lan-Chile, Lapsa, Lloyd Aéreo Boliviano, Lufthansa, Pluna, SAA, SAS, Swissair, TAAG, TAP, Tower Airlines and United Airlines.

Shipping. Inland waterways, mostly rivers, are open to navigation over some 43,000 km. Santos and Rio de Janeiro are the 2 leading ports; there are 19 other large ports. During 1994, 34,015 vessels entered and cleared the Brazilian ports; 360m. tonnes of cargo were loaded and unloaded. In 1997, Santos handled 0·85m. container units. In 1995 the merchant fleet comprised 249 vessels totalling 10·22m. DWT, representing 1·55% of the world's total fleet tonnage. 16 vessels (14·67% of tonnage) were registered under foreign flags. Total tonnage registered, 5·3m. GRT, including oil tankers, 2·12m. GRT, and container ships, 192,777 GRT.

Telecommunications. There were 10,989 post and telegraph offices in 1994. Telephone services are provided by a state-owned company and 27 federally-controlled companies operating in individual states. Mobile phone services were opened to the private sector in 1996. There were 16,883,601 telephones in 1995. In 1995 there were 2,033 radio and 119 television stations (colour by PAL). In 1993 there were 60m. radio and 30m. television receivers.

Cinemas There are 3,737 cinemas.

Press Daily sale of newspapers in 1996 was 6·5m.

SOCIAL INSTITUTIONS

Justice. There is a Supreme Federal Court of Justice at Brasília composed of 11 judges, and a Supreme Court of Justice; all judges are appointed by the President with the approval of the Senate. There are also Regional Federal Courts, Labour Courts, Electoral Courts and Military Courts. Each state organizes its own courts and judicial system in accordance with the federal Constitution.

The prison population was 0·13m. in 1996. In 1995 there were 511 prisons. In 1997 a further 55 were under construction.

Religion. At the 1980 census Roman Catholics numbered 105,861,113 (89% of the total), Protestants, 7,885,846 (6·6%) and Spiritualists, 1,538,230. Roman Catholic estimates in 1991 suggest that 90% were baptized Roman Catholic but only 35% were regular attenders. In 1991 there were 338 bishops and some 14,000 priests.

In 1992 there were 0·2m. Jews. There are numerous sects, some evangelical and some African-derived (e.g. *Candomble*).

Education. Elementary education is compulsory. Adult literacy was 80% in 1997. There were 50,646 literacy classes in 1993 with 1,584,147 students and 75,413 teachers. In 1996 there were 77,740 pre-primary schools with 4,270,376 pupils and 219,517 teachers; 195,544 primary schools, with 30,520,748 pupils and 1,346,285 teachers; 12,603 secondary schools, with 4,208,766 pupils and 275,845 teachers; and 873 higher education institutions, with 1,594,668 students and 150,823 teachers.

The tertiary education sector includes 114 universities (53 private, 37 federal, 20 state and 4 municipal), 85 private and 3 municipal college-faculty federations and

671 other higher education institutions (514 private, 80 municipal, 57 state and 20 federal).

Extensive education reforms are under way to increase the average length of schooling, currently (1997) 5 and a half years.

Health. In 1992 there were 49,676 hospitals and clinics (22,584 private) of which 7,430 were for in-patients (5,316 private). In 1987 there were 206,382 doctors, 28,772 dentists, 6,094 pharmacists and 29,082 nurses.

DIPLOMATIC REPRESENTATIVES

Of Brazil in Great Britain (32 Green St., London, W1Y 4AT)
Ambassador: Rubens Antonio Barbosa.

Of Great Britain in Brazil (Av. das Nações, CP 07-0586, 70.359, Brasília, D.F.)
Ambassador: Donald Keith Haskell, CMG, CVO.

Of Brazil in the USA (3006 Massachusetts Ave., NW, Washington, D.C., 20008)
Ambassador: Paulo Tarso Flecha de Lima.

Of the USA in Brazil (Av. das Nações, Lote 03, Quadra 801, CEP: 70403-900, Brasília, D.F.)
Ambassador: Melvyn Levitsky.

Of Brazil to the United Nations
Ambassador: Celso Luiz Nunes Amorim.

Of Brazil to the European Union
Ambassador: Jório Dauster Magalhães e Silva.

Further Reading

Instituto Brasileiro de Geografia e Estatística. *Anuário Estatístico do Brasil.—Censo Demográfico de 1991.—Indicadores IBGE.* Monthly
Boletim do Banco Central do Brasil. Banco Central do Brasil. Brasília. Monthly
Baer, W., *The Brazilian Economy: Growth and Development.* 4th ed. New York, 1995
Burns, E. B., *A History of Brazil.* 2nd ed. Columbia Univ. Press, 1980
Dickenson, John, *Brazil* [Bibliography] Oxford and Santa Barbara, 1997
Eakin, Marshall C., *Brazil: The Once and Future Country.* New York, 1997
Falk, P. S. and Fleischer, D. V., *Brazil's Economic and Political Future.* Boulder (CO), 1988
Font, M. A., *Coffee, Contention and Change in the Making of Modern Brazil.* Oxford, 1990
Guirmaraes, R. P., *Politics and Environment in Brazil: Ecopolitics of Development in the Third World.* New York, 1991
Mainwaring, S., *The Catholic Church and Politics in Brazil, 1916–86.* Stanford Univ. Press, 1986
Stepan, A. (ed.) *Democratizing Brazil: Problems of Transition and Consolidation.* OUP, 1993
Welch, J. H., *Capital Markets in the Development Process: the Case of Brazil.* London, 1992

For other more specialized titles see under CONSTITUTION AND GOVERNMENT *and* BANKING AND FINANCE, *above.*

National library: Biblioteca Nacional Avenida Rio Branco 219 39, Rio de Janeiro, RJ.
National statistical office: Instituto Brasileiro de Geografia e Estatística (IBGE), Rua General Canabarro 666, 20.271-201 Maracanã, Rio de Janeiro, RJ. *Website:* http:/www.ibge.gov.br/

BRUNEI

Negara Brunei Darussalam—
State of Brunei Darussalam

Capital: Bandar Seri Begawan
Population: 299,939
GDP per head: (PPP$) 30,447
GNP: US$4bn.
HDI/world rank: 0·882/38

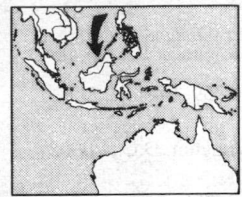

KEY HISTORICAL EVENTS. Situated on the northern coast of Borneo, Brunei was trading with China during the 6th century, and through allegiance to the Javanese Majapahit Kingdom in the 13th-15th centuries, it came under Hindu influence. In the early 15th century, with the decline of the Majapahit Kingdom and widespread conversion to Islam, Brunei became an independent Sultanate.

When Magellan anchored his ships off Brunei in 1521, Bolkiah (the fifth Sultan) controlled most of Borneo, its neighbouring islands and the Suhi Archipelago. By the end of the 16th century, however, the power of Brunei was on the wane. Cessions were made to Great Britain, the Rajah of Sarawak and the British North Borneo Company until by the middle of the 19th century the State had been reduced to its present limits.

Brunei became a British protectorate in 1888 and in 1906 accepted a British Resident who exercised control over all matters except the Islamic faith and Malay custom. The discovery of major oil fields in the western end of the State in the 1920s brought economic stability to Brunei and created a new style of life for the population. Brunei was occupied by the Japanese in 1941 and liberated by the Australians in 1945.

Self-government was introduced in 1959 but Britain retained responsibility for foreign affairs. In 1962 an attempt was made by a section of the community to overthrow the Sultan, Sir Omar Ali Saifuddin. In 1965 constitutional changes were made which led to direct elections for a new Legislative Council. In 1967 Sultan Sir Omar Ali Saifuddin abdicated in favour of his eldest son, Sultan Sir Muda Hassanal Bolkiah, who was crowned in 1968.

The sultan negotiated a new treaty with the British in 1979 and full independence and sovereignty was gained on 1 Jan. 1984.

TERRITORY AND POPULATION. Brunei, on the coast of Borneo, is bounded in the north-west by the South China Sea and on all other sides by Sarawak (Malaysia), which splits it into two parts, the smaller portion forming Temburong district. Area, 2,226 sq. miles (5,765 sq. km). Population (1991 census) 260,482; (1996 estimate) 299,939. The 4 districts are Brunei/Muara (1993: 181,600), Belait (56,000), Tutong (30,700), Temburong (about 8,000). The capital is Bandar Seri Begawan (census 1991: 45,867); other large towns are Seria (1991: 21,082) and Kuala Belait (21,163). Ethnic groups include Malays, 64% and Chinese, 20%.

Vital statistics rates, 1996: Birth per 1,000 population, 25·5; death, 5·1; infant mortality per 1,000 live births, 24·2; population growth, 256%. There were 1,874 marriages in 1993. Life expectancy in 1996: Males, 69·82 years; females, 73·04.

The official language is Malay but English is in use.

CLIMATE. The climate is tropical marine, hot and moist, but nights are cool. Humidity is high and rainfall heavy, varying from 100" (2,500 mm) on the coast to 200" (5,000 mm) inland. There is no dry season. Bandar Seri Begawan. Jan. 80°F (26·7°C), July 82°F (27·8°C). Annual rainfall 131" (3,275 mm).

RULER. The Sultan and Yang Di Pertuan of Brunei Darussalam is HM Paduka Seri Baginda Sultan Haji Hassanal Bolkiah Mu'izzidin Waddaulah. He succeeded on 5 Oct. 1967 at his father's abdication and was crowned on 1 Aug. 1968.

274

CONSTITUTION AND GOVERNMENT. On 29 Sept. 1959 the Sultan promulgated a Constitution, but parts of it have been in abeyance since Dec. 1962. There is no legislature and supreme power is vested in the Sultan.

The Council of Ministers was composed as follows in March 1998:
Prime Minister, Minister of Defence and of Finance: The Sultan.
Foreign Affairs: Prince Haji Mohammad Bolkiah. *Home Affairs:* Pehin Dato Haji Isa bin Ibrahim. *Education:* Pehin Dato Haji Abdul Aziz bin Umar. *Law:* Pengiran Haji Bahrin bin Abbas. *Industry and Primary Resources:* Pehin Dato Haji Abdul Rahman bin Mohammad Taib. *Religious Affairs:* Pehin Dato Dr Haji Mohammad Zain bin Serudin. *Development:* Pengiran Dato Dr Haji Ismail bin Damit. *Culture, Youth and Sports:* Pehin Dato Haji Hussain bin Mohammad Yusof. *Health:* Dato Dr Haji Johar bin Noordin. *Communications:* Dato Haji Zakaria bin Sulaiman.

National anthem: 'Ya Allah, lanjutkan lah usia' ('O God, long live His Majesty'); words by P. Rahim, tune by I. Sagap.

DEFENCE

Army. The armed forces are known as the Task Force and contain the naval and air elements. Only Malays are eligible for service. Strength (1997) 3,900. Military units include 3 infantry battalions, 1 armoured reconnaissance squadron, 1 engineer squadron, 1 special forces squadron and 1 surface-to-air missile battalion. Equipment includes 16 Scorpion light tanks.

There is a paramilitary Gurkha reserve unit 2,300 strong.

Navy. The Royal Brunei Armed Forces Flotilla comprises 3 fast missile-armed attack craft of 200 tonnes and 3 coastal patrol boats. There are also 2 landing craft, 2 utility craft and 3 small patrol boats. The River Division operates 24 fast assault boats. Personnel in 1996 numbered 700.

3 coastal patrol craft operate with 7 smaller boats for the Marine Police.

Air Wing. The Air Wing of the Royal Brunei Armed Forces was formed in 1965. Current equipment includes 6 MBB BO 105, 2 Bell 206B JetRanger, 1 Bell 214, 1 S-70 Black Hawk and 11 Bell 212 helicopters, and 2 SF.260M piston-engined trainers. Personnel (1996), 400.

Police. The Royal Brunei Police numbers 1,750 officers and men (1997). In addition, there are 500 additional police officers mostly employed on static guard duties.

INTERNATIONAL RELATIONS

Membership. Brunei is a member of the UN, the Commonwealth and ASEAN.

ECONOMY

Budget. The budget for 1993 envisaged expenditure of B$3,397m. and revenue of B$3,416m.

Currency. The unit of currency is the *Brunei dollar* or *ringgit* (BND) of 100 *cents*, which is at parity with the Singapore dollar (also legal tender). There are coins of 1, 5, 10, 20 and 50 cents and notes of B$1, 5, 10, 25, 50, 100, 1,000 and 10,000. B$459·7m. were in circulation in 1992.

Banking and Finance. The Brunei Currency Board is the note-issuing monetary authority. In 1993 there were 7 banks (1 incorporated in Brunei) with a total of 33 branches. Savings deposits totalled B$999·3m. in 1993, fixed time deposits B$1,935·4m. Total assets of banks in 1993 were B$6,567·7m.

ENERGY AND NATURAL RESOURCES

Electricity. Electric power production (1993) was 1,449m. kWh. Installed capacity was 402,500 kW, consumption, 1,250m. kWh.

Oil. The Seria oilfield, discovered in 1929, has passed its peak production. The high level of crude oil production is maintained through the increase of offshore oilfields production. There were 735 producing wells at 31 Dec. 1993. Production was 8·85m. tonnes in 1992. The crude oil is exported directly, and only a small amount is refined at Seria for domestic uses.

Gas. Natural gas is produced (9,789m. cu. metres in 1993) at one of the largest liquefied natural gas plants in the world and is exported to Japan.

Agriculture. The main crops produced in 1993 were, rice (1,000 tonnes), vegetables (4,500 tonnes), cereals (1,000 tonnes) and fruits (1,000 tonnes).

Livestock in 1993: Cattle,1,450; buffaloes,3,500; pigs (1992),4,400; chickens,4m.

Forestry. Most of the interior is under forest, containing large potential supplies of serviceable timber. In 1993 production of round timber was 119,200 cu. metres; sawn timber, 63,000 cu. metres.

Fisheries. The 1993 catch totalled 1,727 tonnes, including 1,340 tonnes of marine fish.

INDUSTRY. Brunei depends primarily on its oil industry. Other minor products are rubber, pepper, sawn timber, gravel and animal hides. Local industries include boat-building, cloth weaving and the manufacture of brass- and silver-ware.

FOREIGN ECONOMIC RELATIONS

Commerce. In 1993 (and 1994) imports c.i.f. totalled B$2,012·6m. (US$1,800m.); exports f.o.b. B$3,684·5m. (US$2,400m.). In 1993 crude oil exports totalled B$1,785·6m., liquefied natural gas, B$1,591·4m. In 1994 Singapore supplied 29% of imports, the UK 19% and the USA 13%. Japan took 50% of all exports.

Tourism. There were 411,876 visitor arrivals in 1992 (38,035 tourists). 1,353 males and 1,371 females made the pilgrimage to Mecca in 1993.

COMMUNICATIONS

Roads. There were (1993) 2,443 km of road, of which 1,296 km have a permanent surface. The main road connects Bandar Seri Begawan with Kuala Belait and Seria. In 1993 there were 129,772 private cars, 13,320 goods vehicles and 4,702 motor cycles. There were 79 fatalities in 3,864 road accidents in 1993.

Civil Aviation. Brunei International Airport serves 0·8m. passengers annually. The national carrier is the state-owned Royal Brunei Airlines (RBA), which in 1995 operated 3 B-757-200ERs, 7 B-767-300ERs and 2 other aircraft. RBA and Singapore Airlines provide daily services linking Brunei and Singapore. RBA also operates services to Bangkok, Manila, Kuala Lumpur, Kuching, Kota Kinabalu, Hong Kong, Darwin, Jakarta, Taipei, Bali, Perth, London, Frankfurt, Jeddah, Bahrain and Dubai (via Singapore). Cathay Pacific Airways also operates to Brunei and on to Western Australia from Hong Kong. British Airways provides a weekly service between Brunei and UK. Malaysian Airlines System has air connections from neighbouring regions. In 1993, 790,000 passengers and 24,425 tonnes of freight were carried.

Shipping. Regular shipping services operate from Singapore, Hong Kong, Sarawak and Sabah to Bandar Seri Begawan, and there is a daily passenger ferry between Bandar Seri Begawan and Labuan. 97 sea-going vessels were licensed in 1993.

Telecommunications. There were 17 post offices (1993) and a telephone network (76,900 telephones in 1993) linking the main centres. Radio Television Brunei operates on medium- and shortwaves in Malay, English, Chinese and Nepali. Number of receivers (1993): Radio 0·1m. and television 85,000 (colour by PAL).

Press. In 1993 there was a local newspaper with a circulation of 76,200.

SOCIAL INSTITUTIONS

Justice. The Supreme Court comprises a High Court and a Court of Appeal and the

Magistrates' Courts. The High Court receives appeals from subordinate courts in the districts and is itself a court of first instance for criminal and civil cases. The Judicial Committee of the Privy Council in London is the final court of appeal. Shariah Courts deal with Islamic law. 25,310 crimes were reported in 1993.

Religion. The official religion is Islam. In 1991, 67% of the population were Moslem (mostly Malays), 13% Buddhists and 10% Christian.

Education. The government provides free education to all citizens from pre-school up to the highest level at local and overseas universities and institutions. In 1994 there were 165 kindergartens and schools, with 10,717 children and 506 teachers in kindergartens. In 1994 there were 158 primary schools with 42,270 pupils and 2,772 teachers. There were 2,413 teachers in secondary schools for 28,851 pupils. In 1993 there were 7 technical and vocational colleges with 1,593 students and 371 teachers and a teacher training college with 418 students and 28 teachers.

In 1993 the University of Brunei Darussalam (founded 1985) had 1,138 students and 207 teachers, and an institute of advanced education 310 students and 71 teachers.

Adult literacy rate, 1995, 88·2% (male, 92·6%, female 83·4%).

Health. Medical and health services are free to citizens and those in government service and their dependants. Citizens are sent overseas at government expense for medical care not available in Brunei. Flying medical services are provided to remote areas. In 1993 there were 10 hospitals with 967 beds; there were 197 doctors, 27 dentists, 10 pharmacists, 254 midwives and 1,228 nursing personnel.

DIPLOMATIC REPRESENTATIVES

Of Brunei in Great Britain (19/20 Belgrave Sq., London, SW1X 8PG)
High Commissioner: Pehin Dato Jaya Abdul Latif.

Of Great Britain in Brunei (2/01 2nd Flr. Block D, Kompleks Bangunan Yayasan, Sultan Haji Hassanal Bolkiah, Jalan Pretty, Bandar Seri Begawan 1921)
High Commissioner: I. R. Callan, CMG.

Of Brunei in the USA (2600 Virginia Ave., NW, Washington, D.C., 20037)
Ambassador: Puteh ibni Mohammad Alam.

Of the USA in Brunei (Teck Guan Plaza, Bandar Seri Begawan 2085)
Ambassador: Glen R. Rase.

Of Brunei to the United Nations
Ambassador: Pengiran Maidin Pengiran Mashim.

Of Brunei to the European Union
Ambassador: Dato Seri Laita Jasa Awang Mohd Daud.

Further Reading

Ministry of Finance Statistics Department. *Brunei Darussalam Statistical Yearbook.*
Cleary, M. and Wong, S. Y., *Oil, Economic Development and Diversification in Brunei.* London, 1994
Krausse, S. C. E. and G. H., *Brunei.* [Bibliography] Oxford and Santa Barbara (CA), 1988
Saunders, G., *History of Brunei.* OUP, 1996

National statistical office: Ministry of Finance Statistics Department.

BULGARIA

Republika Bulgaria

Capital: Sofia
Population: 8·34m.
GDP per head: (PPP$) 4,533
HDI/world rank: 0·780/69

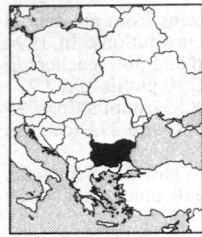

KEY HISTORICAL EVENTS. The Bulgarians take their name from an invading Asiatic horde (Bulgars) and their language from the Slav population with whom they merged after 680. From 681 to 1018 and 1185 to 1389 the Bulgarians carved out empires against a background of conflict with Byzantium and Serbia, and established a civilization of which the Orthodox missionaries Cyril and Methodius, credited with the invention of the Slavonic alphabet, are noteworthy exemplars.

After the Serb-Bulgarian defeat at Kosovo in 1389 Bulgaria finally succumbed to Ottoman encroachment. The Bulgar landowners were replaced by military and civil officials who held land in return for state service. The Ottoman empire's decline, however, engendered corruption and exactions, uprisings and reprisals.

The 1876 rebellion met with brutal repression which provoked great power intervention. Russia invaded Turkey in 1877 and imposed upon her the Treaty of San Stefano (March 1878) which established a 'big Bulgaria' extending into Macedonia and Thrace. Conceiving this as a threat to the balance of power, Britain and Austria-Hungary pressurized Russia into revising these boundaries by the Treaty of Berlin (July 1878): Macedonia and Thrace reverted to Turkey, Eastern Rumelia became semi-autonomous and Bulgaria proper a principality under Turkish suzerainty.

Under the Treaty a constituent assembly at Tôrnovo voted a liberal constitution which provided for a single-chamber parliament elected by male suffrage. The throne was offered to the German Prince Alexander of Battenberg. In 1885 Eastern Rumelia was united to Bulgaria by a *coup d'état*. Alexander accepted the unification against the wishes of Russia, who forced his abdication in 1886. He was replaced by Ferdinand of Saxe-Coburg-Gotha, who did not gain Russian recognition until 1896. Prime Minister Stefan Stambolov achieved a period of prosperity, but Ferdinand engineered his resignation in 1894 and henceforth ruled personally through manipulation of the political parties.

After Austria annexed Bosnia in 1908, Bulgaria declared itself independent. To block Austrian expansion into the Balkans Russia encouraged Greece, Serbia, Montenegro and Bulgaria to form a Balkan League in 1912. The League successfully attacked Turkey (first Balkan War, 1912), but in the dispute which followed over the territorial spoils (principally in Macedonia) Bulgaria failed to secure her claims against her formal allies by force (second Balkan War, 1913). Territorial aspirations led Bulgaria to join the First World War on the German side in Oct. 1915 and the peace settlement (Neuilly, 1919) left her with little gained.

Economic decline caused by the war produced social unrest, Ferdinand was forced to abdicate in favour of his son, Boris III, in Oct. 1918, and the radical Agrarian Party took office, headed by Alexander Stamboliiski. The latter's reformism, friendship with Yugoslavia (a contender for Macedonia) and high-handed behaviour generated various currents of opposition, and he was assassinated after a *coup* in June 1923. The Communist Party held its hand during this, but launched an abortive rising in Sept. 1923, and bombed Sofia cathedral in April 1925, killing 120 people. This led to a reign of government terror against all radicals. Bedevilled by Macedonian terrorism and the effects of the world economic depression, parliamentary government was ended by a military *coup* in May 1934. In 1935 Boris established a royal dictatorship under which political parties were banned. Boris died in 1943 and was succeeded by a regency.

Increasingly drawn into the German economic orbit, and in pursuit of the San Stefano territories, Bulgaria joined the Nazis against Britain in March 1941, but retained diplomatic relations with the Soviet Union. On Sept. 1944 the Soviet Union

278

declared war and sent its troops across the frontiers. Wartime opposition to the government had centred round the Communist-dominated Fatherland Front, which formed a government on 9 Sept. A referendum on 8 Sept. 1946 abolished the monarchy, and a people's republic was proclaimed. In 1947 the Soviet-type 'Dimitrov' constitution replaced the Tôrnovo constitution of 1879. Georgi Dimitrov, a veteran Communist leader who had secured acquittal from a Nazi court after charges of complicity in the arson of the Reichstag, was Prime Minister until his death in 1949. The 'Titoist' purges of late Stalinism were presided over by Vulko Chervenkov, but he was soon eclipsed by Todor Zhivkov who became leader of the BCP in 1954 and Prime Minister in 1962.

In May 1971 a new constitution led to Zhivkov's election as first President of the newly formed State Council. He was re-elected in 1976, 1981 and 1986. When demonstrations in Sofia in Nov. 1989 occasioned by the Helsinki Agreement ecological conference, broadened into demands for political reform, Todor Zhivkov was replaced as Communist Party leader and head of state by the foreign minister Petur Mladenov. In Dec. the National Assembly approved 21 measures of constitutional reform, including the abolition of the Communist Party's sole right to govern. The government was succeeded in Feb. 1990 by the Communist government of Andrei Lukanov. Attempts at economic reform led to demonstrations and a general strike. Lukanov's government was replaced by a caretaker government in Nov. 1990. A new constitution and fresh elections produced a non-Communist government in Oct. 1991 but strikes and unrest continued while political divisions virtually paralyzed government. Elections in Dec. 1994 were won by an alliance led by Zhan Videnov, a former Communist turned Socialist who failed to deliver on his promise of painless reform. In 1996 Peter Stoyanov was elected as an anti-Communist pro reform President. In the election the following April the anti-Communist Union of Democratic Forces (UDF) coalition led by Ivan Kostov and Alexander Bozhkov swept back to power.

TERRITORY AND POPULATION. The area of Bulgaria is 110,994 sq. km (42,855 sq. miles). It is bounded in the north by Romania, east by the Black Sea, south by Turkey and Greece and west by the United Republic of Yugoslavia and the Republic of Macedonia. The country is divided into 9 regions.

Area and population in 1996:

Region	Area (sq. km)	Pop. (1,000)	Region	Area (sq. km)	Pop. (1,000)
Bourgas	14,724	847	Rousse	10,843	760
Haskovo	13,824	889	Sofia (city)	1,311	1,192
Lovech	15,150	990	Sofia (region)	19,021	967
Montana	10,607	616	Varna	11,929	901
Plovdiv	13,585	1,214			

The capital, Sofia, has regional status. The population at the census of 1992 was 8,472,724 (females, 4,515,936). Population on 31 Dec. 1996 was 8,339,847 (females, 4,263,000; urban, 68·1%). Population density 75·1 per sq. km.

Population of principal towns (1996): Sofia, 1,141,712; Plovdiv, 344,326; Varna, 301,421; Bourgas, 199,470; Rousse, 168,051; Stara Zagora, 151,218; Pleven, 127,945; Sliven, 107,267; Dobrich, 104,074; Shumen, 97,126; Pernik, 90,460; Yambol, 90,239; Pazardzhik, 82,295; Khaskovo, 80,972; Vratsa, 77,069; Gabrovo, 75,220.

Vital statistics, 1996: Live births, 72,743; deaths, 117,056. Rates per 1,000 population, 1996: Birth, 8·6; death, 14·0; marriage, 4·3; infant deaths, 15·6; growth per 1,000 live births, −5·4. Abortions, 1996, 93,540, of which 9,389 were spontaneous. Expectation of life in 1996 was 70·6 years (males, 67·1; females, 74·9).

Ethnic groups at the 1992 census: Bulgarians, 7,271,185; Turks, 800,052; Gypsies, 313,396.

CLIMATE. The southern parts have a Mediterranean climate, with winters mild and moist and summers hot and dry, but further north the conditions become more continental, with a larger range of temperature and greater amounts of rainfall in summer and early autumn. Sofia. Jan. 28°F (−2·2°C), July 69°F (20·6°C). Annual rainfall 25·4" (635 mm).

CONSTITUTION AND GOVERNMENT. A new constitution was adopted at Turnovo in July 1991. The *President* is directly elected for not more than 2 5-year terms. Candidates for the presidency must be at least 40 years old and have lived for the last 5 years in Bulgaria. American-style primary elections were introduced in 1996; voting is open to all the electorate. A primary was held on 11 June 1996 for the opposition presidential candidate; turn-out was 12%. There were 2 candidates. Presidential elections were held in 2 rounds on 27 Oct. and 3 Nov. 1996. Petur Stoyanov won the first round against 12 opponents with 44·1% of votes cast; turn-out was 62·7%. He also won the run-off round with 59·7% of votes cast; turn-out was 61·5%.

The 240-member *National Assembly* is directly elected by proportional representation. The President nominates a candidate from the largest parliamentary party as *Prime Minister*. At the elections of 19 April 1997, a United Democratic Forces coalition was elected, obtaining 137 seats with 52·26% of the votes cast, and on 14 May 1997 Ivan Kostov (UDF) became Prime Minister.

President: Petar Stoyanov (b. 1948; Union of Democratic Forces; sworn in 19 Jan. 1997). *Vice-President:* Todor Kavaldjiev.

In March 1998 the government comprised:

Prime Minister: Ivan Kostov.

Deputy Prime Ministers: Aleksandur Bozhkov, Evgeniy Bakurdzhiev, Veselin Metodiev.

Agriculture, Forests and Agrarian Reform: Ventsislav Vurbanov. *Culture:* Ema Moskova. *Defence:* Georgi Ananiev. *Education and Science:* Veselin Metodiev. *Environment and Water:* Evdokiya Maneva. *Finance:* Muravey Radev. *Foreign Affairs:* Nadezhda Mikhaylova. *Health:* Petur Boyadzhiev. *Industry:* Aleksandur Bozhkov. *Interior:* Bogomil Bonev. *Justice and Legal Euro-Integration:* Vasil Gotsev. *Labour and Social Policy:* Ivan Neykov. *Regional Development and Urbanization:* Evgeniy Bakurdzhiev. *State Administration:* Mario Tagarinski. *Trade and Toursim:* Valentin Vasilev. *Transportation:* Wilhelm Kraus.

The *Speaker* is Blagovest Sendov (BSP).

National anthem: 'Gorda stara planina' ('Proud and ancient mountains'); words and tune by T. Radoslavov.

Local Government. Local authorities for the 9 regions and 278 districts within them are elected for 30 months. Elections were held for mayors and councillors on 29 Oct. and 12 Nov. 1995. Turn-out was 54·7% for the former and 53·1% for the latter. A large majority of mayorships were won by the BSP and its allies. In the elections for councillors the BSP and its allies won 41% of votes cast, the UDF 24·1%, the PU 12·3%, the Movement for Rights and Freedom 8·2% and the Bulgarian Business Bloc 5%.

DEFENCE. Conscription was reduced from 18 to 12 months in 1992.

Army. There are 3 military districts based on Sofia, Plovdiv and Sliven. In 1997 the Army had a strength of 51,600, including 33,300 conscripts, and is organized in 4 tank, 1 mechanized, 1 surface-to-air missile and 1 airborne brigade, 3 motor rifle divisions and 3 artillery, 3 anti-tank, 1 surface-to-air missile and 3 air defence brigades. Equipment includes 177 T-34, 1,276 T-55 and 333 T-72 main battle tanks. There are 12 regiments of border guards numbering 12,000.

Navy. The Navy, all ex-Soviet or Soviet-built, comprises 2 'Romeo' class old diesel submarines, 1 Koni class small frigate, 4 'Poti', 1 'Tarantul' and 2 'Pauk' class corvettes, 6 'Osa' class missile craft, 10 patrol vessels, 4 coastal and 16 inshore minesweepers. There are 2 medium landing ships and 20 craft. Major auxiliaries include 2 oilers, 2 research ships, 1 electronic intelligence gatherer, 2 training ships and 1 tug. There are some 20 minor auxiliaries and service craft. There are 2 regiments of coastal artillery including some missile-armed, and some 10 shore-based Ka-25 and Mi-14 helicopters. The naval headquarters is at Varna, and there are bases at Atiya and at Vidin on the Danube. Personnel in 1996 totalled 6,000.

Air Force. The Air Force had (1996) 20,100 personnel (16,000 conscripts). There are

3 wings of MiG-21/23/29 interceptors; 3 wings of fighter/ground attack MiG-23s and Su-20/25s; 1 regiment of Mi-24 helicopter gunships; a total of about 20 Tu-134, L-410, An-2 and An-24/26 transport aircraft; some 45 Mi-2 and Mi-8/17 helicopters; and Yak-18T, L-29 Delfin and L-39 Albatros trainers. Soviet-built 'Guideline', 'Goa' and 'Ganef' surface-to-air missiles have also been supplied to Bulgaria.

INTERNATIONAL RELATIONS

Membership. Bulgaria is a member of the UN, the Council of Europe, the Central European Initiative and the NATO Partnership for Peace, and is an Associate Member of the EU and an Associate Partner of the WEU.

ECONOMY

Policy. At the beginning of 1992, 95% of enterprises were still in state ownership. A plan to privatize a further 500 large and medium-sized firms was introduced in 1993. Mining, energy, oil processing, railways and munitions production remain in state hands. A law of April 1992 allocates 10% of the proceeds of privatization to agricultural development, 20% to the compensation of former owners, 30% to social funds and 40% to local management councils to cover irrecoverable debts. A Centre for Mass Privatization was set up in 1994 to supervise a new stage of privatization.

Privatized firms enjoy a 5-year tax exemption. 67 loss-making public enterprises were wound up in 1996.

Performance. In 1996 GDP was 1,660,237m. leva. GDP growth was negative in 1996, at –4%.

Budget. The fiscal year is the calendar year. In 1998 budget revenue was envisaged at 4,416,000m. leva and expenditure, 5,411,000m. leva. VAT was first set in operation in 1995. In 1996 there was an increase in VAT from 18% to 22%.

Currency. The unit of currency is the *lev* (BGL) of 100 *stotinki*. Notes are issued for 1, 2, 5, 10, 20, 50, 100, 200, 500 and 1,000 leva and coins for 1, 2, 5, 10, 20, 50 stotinki and 1, 2, 5, 10, 20 and 50 leva. Foreign exchange reserves were US$1·3bn. in Dec. 1997. Gold reserves were 36·5m. tonnes. Runaway inflation (566·0% in 1997 but set to 27·0% in 1998) forced the closure of 14 banks in 1996. In June 1997 the new government introduced a currency board financial system which stablized the lev and renewed economic growth. Under it the lev is pegged to the German mark at DM1 = 1,000 leva. Privatization is to be speeded up. In May 1996 the lev was devalued by 68%.

Banking and Finance. The National Bank (*Governor*, Svetoslav Gavriiski b. 1948) is the central bank and bank of issue. There is a Foreign Trade Bank (founded 1964) and a State Savings Bank, the latter serving local enterprises as well as the public. In 1996, there were savings accounts totalling 81,606m. leva. There were 41 commercial banks in 1996.

There is a stock exchange in Sofia.

Weights and Measures. The metric system is in general use. On 1 April 1916 the Gregorian calendar came into force.

ENERGY AND NATURAL RESOURCES

Electricity. Bulgaria has little oil, gas or high-grade coal and energy policy is based on the exploitation of its low-grade coal and hydro-electric resources. But the country is a major distribution centre for energy in the Black Sea region, a fact underlined by the 1997 deal with Russia which guarantees gas supplies to Bulgaria while clearing the way to the construction of a transit gas pipeline between Russia and western Turkey. There is 1 nuclear power station. Output, 1996, 42,710m. kWh (thermal, 21,714m. kWh; nuclear, 18,082m. kWh; hydro-electric, 2,914m. kWh).

Oil. Oil is extracted in the Balchik district on the Black Sea, in an area 100 km north of Varna and at Dolni Dubnik near Pleven. There are refineries at Bourgas (annual capacity 5m. tonnes) and Dolni Dubnik (7m. tonnes). Crude oil production (1996) was 32,000 tonnes; gas, 18·75m. cu. metres.

Minerals. Production in 1996: Manganese ore, 13,100 tonnes; iron ore, 282,000 tonnes; lignite, 28·10m. tonnes; brown coal, 3·06m. tonnes; hard coal, 31·30m. tonnes.

Agriculture. In 1996 agricultural land covered 6,164,000 ha, of which 4,693,000 ha were arable. In 1996 sown area was 2,902,000 ha; there were 277,000 ha of meadows and 1,471,000 ha of commons and pastures.

Legislation of 1991 and 1992 provided for the redistribution of collectivized land to its former owners up to 30 ha. Landless peasants received state land or compensation in lieu. Bulgarians resident abroad may acquire such land, as may also legal bodies with up to 50% foreign ownership. It may be rented out, but not sold for 3 years. There were 2,073 agricultural collectives and firms in 1992. There were 2,435 private farms in 1996.

Production in 1996 (in 1,000 tonnes, with percentage from private holdings): Wheat, 1,786 (27·2%); maize, 1,089 (67·3%); barley, 456 (27·6%); sugar beet, 87 (35·6%); sunflower seed, 530 (15·5%); seed cotton, 11 (4·5%); tobacco, 31 (96·8%); tomatoes, 325 (90·2%); potatoes, 320 (96·6%); grapes, 660 (63·9%). Bulgaria is a leading producer of attar of roses. In 1993 an estimated 3,000 ha were under rose cultivation, with an annual output of over 1,500 kg. Other products (in 1,000 tonnes) in 1996: Meat, 578 (86·8%); wool, 9 (92·1%); honey, 4·60 (98·0%); eggs, 1,734m. (74·8%); litres of milk 1,387m. (88·0%)

Livestock (1996, in 1,000): Cattle, 582 (milch cows, 358) (in private holdings, 473 and 309); sheep, 3,020 (2,843); pigs, 1,500 (1,173); poultry, 16,227 (13,478).

There were 24,293 tractors in use in 1995.

Forestry. Forest area, 1996, was 3,878,000 ha (1·29m. ha coniferous, 2·58m. ha broad-leaved). 16,000 ha were afforested in 1996 and 1·931m. cu. metres of building timber were cut.

Fisheries. Catch, 1996: 15,300 tonnes.

INDUSTRY. In 1996 there were 342,261 registered economic units. Units by ownership: State, 9,682; municipal, 9,820; joint-stock companies, 3,588; co-operative; 5,410; social organizations, 6,306; associations, 2,483; foreign ventures, 9,005; resident, 307,448. In 1996 the private sector accounted for 45·9% of production.

In 1996 there were produced (in 1,000 tonnes): Pig iron and ferro-alloys, 1,513; steel, 2,457; rolled steel, 1,898; artificial fertilizers, 559; sulphuric acid, 518; cement, 2,132; paper, 174; cotton fabric, 69·2m. metres; woollen fabric, 12m. metres. 10,000 TV sets (5,900 colour) and 36,200 refrigerators were made.

Labour. In Nov. 1996, 646,600 employees worked in the private sector. There is a 42½-hour 5-day working week. Retirement is at 55 for women and 60 for men, or 52 and 57 after 25 years in the last employment. The average wage (excluding peasantry) was 13,269 leva per month in 1996; minimum wage was 1,200 leva per month. Population of working age (males 16–59; females 16–54), 1996, 4,746,790 (47·6% females). At the end of 1996 the economically-active population was 3,576,200 (1,681,000 females), of whom 3,085,400 were employed. Unemployment was 12·5% in 1996.

Trade Unions. An independent white-collar trade union movement, Podkrepa, was formed in 1989. It claimed 100,000 members in July 1990. The former official Central Council of Trade Unions reconstituted itself in 1990 as the Confederation of Independent Trade Unions.

FOREIGN ECONOMIC RELATIONS. Legislation in force as of Feb. 1992 abolished restrictions imposed in 1990 on the repatriation of profits and allows foreign nationals to own and set up companies in Bulgaria. Western share participation in joint ventures may exceed 50%. Talks began with international financial institutions in Feb. 1998 on the question of a 3-year recovery and restructuring programme. Total foreign debt was US$10,500m. in Jan. 1996.

Commerce. In 1996, exports totalled US$4·6m. and imports, US$4·3m.

Principal exports in 1996 (in tonnes): meat, (pork and poultry), 6,700; livestock, tomatoes, 22,500; cheese, 5,700; wine, 214,500; tobacco, 21,200; soda ash, 631,200; carbamide, 733,000; ammonium nitrate, 746,800; polyethylene, 49,800; footwear, 5·51m. pairs; rolled iron and steel products, 819,600 (1994); zinc, 57,800 (1994); electric motors, 486,800 items. Principal imports: Pepper, 397,000; newsprint, 32,600; cotton, 18,500; wool, 4,700,000; iron and steel tubes, 22,800; buses, 743 items; motor cars, 35,100 items; lorries, 3,000 items; sugar, 312,700; coal, 231,300; anthracite, 2,006,100; crude oil, 5·9m. (1994); petrol, 107,100 (1992); natural gas, 5,261·5m. cu. metres (1994).

Main export markets in 1996 (trade in 1m. leva): Russian Federation, 76,938; Germany, 74,722; Greece, 61,384; Italy, 78,951. Main import suppliers: Russian Federation, 337,121; Germany, 98,418; Italy, 53,352; Greece, 30,793.

Tourism. There were 6,810,688 foreign visitors in 1996, of whom 2,191,911 were tourists. 3,006,292 Bulgarians made visits abroad.

COMMUNICATIONS

Roads. In 1996 there were 37,300 km of hard-surfaced roads, including 277 km (1994) of motorways and 2,935 km (1994) of main roads. 817m. passengers and 40·669m. tonnes of freight were carried in 1996. There were 4,875 road accidents in 1991 with 1,114 fatalities.

Railways. In 1996 there were 4,293 km of 1,435 mm gauge railway (2,655 km electrified). 66·1m. passengers and 30·1m. tonnes of freight were carried.

There is a tramway in Sofia.

Civil Aviation. There is an international airport at Sofia (Vrazhdebna). The state-owned Balkan Airlines is the national carrier. In 1995 it had 4 A320-200s, 3 B-737-500s, 2 B-767-200ERs and 41 ex-Soviet aircraft. In 1996 it carried 1·22m. passengers and 10,000 tonnes of freight. Services are also operated by Aeroflot, Air France, Air Koryo, Air Malta, Air Moldova, Air Ukraine, Alitalia, Armenian Airlines, Austrian Airlines, British Airways, CSA, El Al, Hemus Air, Libyan Airlines, LOT, Lufthansa, Malév, Olympic, Swissair, Syrian Arab Airlines and Tarom.

Shipping. In 1995, the merchant fleet totalled 1·84m. GRT, including oil tankers, 0·42m. GRT and container ships, 63,305 GRT. Bourgas is a fishing and oil-port. Varna is the other important port. There is a rail ferry between Varna and Ilitchovsk (Ukraine). In 1996 20,000 passengers and 17·07m. tonnes of cargo were carried. There were 74,000 km of inland waterways in 1996. 11,000 passengers and 1·00m. tonnes of freight were carried.

Telecommunications. In 1996 there were 3,502 post and telecommunications offices and 3,107,400 telephones (2,231,900 private). Broadcasting is under the aegis of the state-controlled Bulgarian National Radio and Bulgarian Television. There are 4 national and 6 regional radio programmes. A service for tourists is broadcast from Varna. There are 2 TV programmes; Bulgaria also receives transmissions from the French satellite channel TV5. An independent TV channel started broadcasting in 1994. Colour programmes by SECAM system. Radio receiving sets in 1996, 1,389,800; television, 1,470,700.

Cinemas (1996). There were 219 cinemas (attendance, 3·69m.).

Press. In 1996 there were 1,053 newspapers with an annual circulation of 454m. and 635 other periodicals. 5,100 book titles were published in 22·9m. copies in 1996.

SOCIAL INSTITUTIONS

Justice. A law of Nov. 1982 provides for the election (and recall) of all judges by the National Assembly. There are a Supreme Court, 28 provincial courts (including Sofia) and regional courts. Jurors are elected at the local government elections.

The maximum term of imprisonment is 20 years. 'Exceptionally dangerous crimes' carry the death penalty.

The Prosecutor General and judges are elected by the Supreme Judicial Council established in 1992.

In 1996 there were 13,097 crimes reported (227 murders) and 16,376 convicted persons (1,076 females, 1,188 juveniles under 17).

Religion. 'The traditional church of the Bulgarian people' (as it is officially described), is that of the Eastern Orthodox Church. It was disestablished under the 1947 Constitution. In 1953 the Bulgarian Patriarchate was revived. The Patriarch is Maksim (enthroned 1971). The seat of the Patriarch is at Sofia. There are 11 dioceses, each under a Metropolitan, 10 bishops, 2,600 parishes, 1,700 priests, 400 monks and nuns, 3,700 churches and chapels, one seminary and one theological college.

Anti-Maksim schismatics set up a rival synod in 1992 and elected Pimen patriarch in 1996.

In 1992 there were some 70,000 Roman Catholics with 53 priests, in 3 bishoprics. In 1987 there were 10,000 Uniates with 20 priests. At the 1992 census 7,349,544 Christians were recorded and 1,110,295 Moslems (Pomaks). There is a Chief Mufti elected by regional muftis.

Education. Education is free, and compulsory for children between the ages of 7 and 16. Complete literacy is claimed.

In 1996 there were 3,713 kindergartens (247,000 children, 23,353 teachers); 3,286 primary schools with 71,431 teachers and 944,733 pupils; 129 special needs schools with 2,336 teachers and 13,849 pupils; 7 vocational technical schools with 125 teachers and 3,384 pupils; 203 secondary vocational technical schools with 5,113 teachers and 77,299 pupils; 337 technical colleges and schools of art with 13,943 teachers and 125,887 students; 46 post-secondary institutions with 3,018 teachers and 24,981 students; 42 institutes of higher education, with 23,285 teachers and 235,701 students. There are 4 state universities, an American university, and universities of mining and geology, and architecture, civil engineering and geodesy.

There were 62 private schools with 5,874 pupils in 1996–97.

The Academy of Sciences was founded in 1869.

Health. All medical services are free. Private medical services were authorized in Jan. 1991. In 1996 there were 289 hospitals and clinics with 86,160 beds. There were 29,529 doctors, 5,467 dentists, 1,736 pharmacists, 6,576 midwives, 6,910 medical auxiliaries and 51,269 nurses.

Welfare. Retirement and disablement pensions and temporary sick pay are calculated as a percentage of previous wages (respectively 55–80%, 35–100%, 69–90%) and according to the nature of the employment. Free medical treatment is available to all, but private practice also exists. Medicines are free to people with chronic conditions or on low incomes.

In 1996 there were 2,381,128 recipients of pensions; disbursements were 121,191m. leva. The average annual pension was 49,681 leva.

DIPLOMATIC REPRESENTATIVES

Of Bulgaria in Great Britain (186-188 Queen's Gate, London, SW7 5HL)
Ambassador: Vacant.

Of Great Britain in Bulgaria (Blvd. Vassil Levski 38, Sofia)
Ambassador: R. G. Short, MVO.

Of Bulgaria in the USA (1621 22nd St., NW, Washington, D.C., 20008)
Ambassador: Snejana Botoucharova.

Of the USA in Bulgaria (1 Saborna St., Sofia)
Ambassador: Avis Bohlen.

Of Bulgaria to the United Nations
Ambassador: Philip Dimitrov.

Of Bulgaria to the European Union
Ambassador: Evgeni Ivanov.

Further Reading

Central Statistical Office. *Statisticheski Godishnik.—Statisticheski Spravochnik* (annual).— *Statistical Reference Book of Republic of Bulgaria* (annual).
Kratka Bulgarska Entsiklopediia (Short Bulgarian Encyclopaedia), 5 vols. Sofia, 1963–69

Crampton, R. J., *A Short History of Modern Bulgaria.* CUP, 1987.—*Bulgaria.* [Bibliography] Oxford and Santa Barbara (CA), 1989.—*A Concise History of Bulgaria.* CUP, 1997

National statistical office: Natsionalen Statisticheski Institut/Central Statistical Office, Sofia. *Chairman:* Zakhari Karamfilov.

BURKINA FASO

République Démocratique
du Burkina Faso

Capital: Ouagadougou
Population: 10·62m.
GDP per head: (PPP$) 796
GNP: US$3bn.
HDI/world rank: 0·221/172

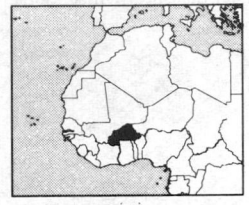

KEY HISTORICAL EVENTS. Formerly known as Upper Volta, the country's name was changed in 1984 to Burkina Faso, meaning 'the land of honest men'. The area it covers was settled by farming communities until their invasion by the Mossi people in the 11th century, who set up several powerful kingdoms—Ouagadougou, Yatenga and Tenkogodo. These successfully resisted Islamic crusades and attacks by neighbouring empires for seven centuries until conquered by the French between 1895 and 1903.

France made Upper Volta a separate colony in 1919, only to abolish it as such in 1932, dividing its territory between the Ivory Coast (now Côte d'Ivoire), French Sudan (now Mali) and Niger. In 1947 the territory of Upper Volta was reconstituted. For much of the colonial era the people of Upper Volta suffered from military and labour conscription, forced labourers being often sent to the Ivory Coast. After the abolition of forced labour in 1946 Voltaic men continued to emigrate to the Ivory Coast and Ghana, this time voluntarily. Upper Volta remained a desperately poor country often hit by drought, particularly in 1972-74 and again in 1982-84.

After independence, President Maurice Hameogo and his *Union Démocratique Voltaique* (UDV) ruled until 3 Jan. 1966, when the army took power under Gen. Sangoule Lamizana. His régime surrendered some power to civilians in 1971, under a new constitution allowing for an elected assembly and with a government consisting of two-thirds civilians and one-third military officers. But after three years Lamizana, who had remained president, and his military colleagues again took power.

Their régime created a new governmental political party in 1975. A new constitution was drawn up and approved by referendum in 1977, and elections were held to a new national assembly in 1978. Joseph Conombo, as prime minister, formed a coalition government. Gen. Lamizana was elected president.

In 1980 a *coup d'état* overthrew this new régime and Col. Saye Zerbo, at the head of a *Comité Militaire de Redressement pour le Progrés National* (CMRPN), held power for two years. Then, on 7 Nov. 1982, the CMRPN was overthrown in another *coup* and replaced by the *Conseil du Salut de Peuple* (CSP), headed by Jean-Baptiste Ouedraogo. Younger, more radical officers now came to the fore, but there was serious tension within the CSP, leading to the arrest of the leading radical, Capt. Thomas Sankara, on 17 May 1983 and then, on 4 Aug. 1983, to a new *coup d'état* which put him in power.

Sankara and his radical military colleagues formed a *Conseil National de la Révolution* (CNR) and installed a left-wing régime, with Revolutionary Defence Committees (*Comités de Défense de la Révolution*, CDR) operating at local level. The régime aimed at ending exploitation, and sought to curb food traders. Although it established close relations with the similar régime in Ghana, and with Libya, it also maintained fairly normal relations with France and remains in the franc zone.

A border dispute between Burkina Faso and Mali led to fighting in 1974 and again in Dec. 1985. A year later, on 22 Dec. 1986, the International Court of Justice ruled on the dispute, dividing the contested area into roughly equal shares for each; both countries accepted the judgement. Sankara was overthrown and killed in a *coup* on 15 Oct. 1987, the fifth since 1960, led by his friend Capt. Blaise Compaoré.

TERRITORY AND POPULATION. Burkina Faso is bounded in the north and west by Mali, east by Niger and south by Benin, Togo, Ghana and the Côte d'Ivoire. Area: 274,122 sq. km; population (census, 1985) 7,967,019 (3,846,518 males).

Estimate (1996), 10,623,323; density, 38·8 per sq. km. Vital statistics (1996): Birth rate per 1,000 population, 47·02; death, 19·99; infant mortality, 117·8 per 1,000 live births; expectation of life, 43·21 years; growth rate, 2·53%. The largest cities (1985 census) are Ouagadougou, the capital (442,223), Bobo-Dioulasso (231,162), Koudougou (51,670), Ouahigouya (38,604), Banfora (35,204), Kaya (25,799), Fada N'Gourma and Tenkodogo.

Areas and populations of the 30 provinces:

Province	Sq. km	Estimate 1991	Province	Sq. km	Estimate 1991
Bam	4,017	173,516	Nahouri	3,843	119,114
Bazéga	5,313	352,104	Namentenga	7,755	214,564
Bougouriba	7,087	242,986	Oubritenga	4,693	328,682
Boulgou	9,033	465,845	Oudalan	10,046	123,495
Boulkiemdé	4,138	393,900	Passoré	4,078	232,278
Comoé	18,393	296,083	Poni	10,361	258,647
Ganzourgou	4,087	223,555	Sanguié	5,165	234,079
Gnagnan	8,600	272,203	Sanmatenga	9,213	404,563
Gourma	26,613	350,336	Séno	13,473	269,892
Houet	16,672	724,803	Sissili	13,736	297,598
Kadiogo	1,169	652,377	Soum	13,350	217,972
Kénédougou	8,307	162,010	Sourou	9,487	313,355
Kossi	13,177	389,360	Tapoa	14,780	187,785
Kouritenga	1,627	227,060	Yatenga	12,292	558,318
Mouhoun	10,442	329,115	Zoundwéogo	3,453	175,166

The principal ethnic groups are the Mossi (49%), Fulani (8%), Mandé (7%), Bobo (7%), Gourounsi (7%), Gourmantché (7%), Bissa (4%), Lobi-Dagari (4%), Sénoufo (2%). French is the official language.

CLIMATE. A tropical climate with a wet season from May to Nov. and a dry season from Dec. to April. Rainfall decreases from south to north. Ouagadougou. Jan. 76°F (24·4°C), July 83°F (28·3°C). Annual rainfall 36" (894 mm).

CONSTITUTION AND GOVERNMENT. At a referendum in June 1991 a new constitution was approved; there is an executive presidency. At the presidential elections of 1 Dec. 1991 Blaise Compaoré was the sole candidate, and was elected by 86·4% of votes cast. The electorate was 3·5m.; turn-out was 27·3%.

Parliament consists of the 111-member *Assembly of People's Deputies*, elected by universal suffrage, and the 178-member *Chamber of Representatives*, a consultative body representing social, religious, professional and political organizations. There is also a 90-member *Economic and Social Council. National Assizes* of about 2,000 representatives of a broad spectrum of government, public, social and professional bodies may be convened by the President ad hoc to discuss public issues. a constitutional amendment of 1997 permits the President an indefinite number of terms of office.

At the elections of 11 May 1997 the Congress for Democracy and Progress (CDP) won 101 seats; the Party for Democracy and Progress (PDP), 6; the African Democratic Rally (UDV/RDA), 2, and the Alliance for Democracy and Federation, 2. The electorate was 5m. and turn-out was 50%

In March. 1998 the government comprised:

President, Head of Government: Capt. Blaise Compaoré

Agriculture: Michel Koutaba. *Animal Resources:* Alassane Sere. *Civil Service and Institutional Development:* Juliette Bonkoungou. *Culture and Communications:* Mahamoudou Ouédraogo. *Defence:* Albert D. Millogo. *Economy and Finance:* Tertius Zongo. *Employment, Labour and Social Security:* Elie Sarre. *Energy and Mines:* Elie Ouédraogo. *Foreign Affairs:* Ablassé Ouédraogo. *Health:* Ludovic Alain Tou. *Industry, Trade and Crafts:* Idrissa Zampalegre. *Justice:* Yarga Larba. *Basic Education and Literacy:* Baworo Seydou Sanou. *Infrastructure, Housing and Town Planning:* Joseph Kaboré. *Relations with Parliament:* Cyril Goungounga. *Higher Education and Scientific Research:* Christophe Dabiré. *Social Affairs and the Family:* Bana Ouandaogo. *Territorial Administration and Security:* Yero Boly. *Transport and Tourism:* Bedouma Alain Yoda. *Youth and Sport:* Joseph

Tiendrébéogo. *Regional Integration:* Viviane Yolande Compaoré. *Promotion of Women:* Alice Tiendrébéogo.

National anthem: 'Contre la férule humiliante' ('Against the shameful fetters'); words by T. Sankara, tune anonymous.

Local government. The country is divided into 30 provinces and 250 districts.

DEFENCE. There are 6 military regions. All forces form part of the Army.

Army. The Army consists of 8 infantry companies, 1 airborne company and tank, artillery and engineer support units. Equipment includes 83 armoured cars. Strength (1997), 5,600 with a paramilitary Gendarmerie of 4,200.

Air Force. Equipment comprises 1 Super King Air 200, 1 Aero Commander 500 and 1 Reims/Cessna Super Skymaster for transport and liaison duties, 1 Cessna 172 trainer, and 1 Dauphin and 2 Alouette III helicopters. Personnel total (1997) 200.

INTERNATIONAL RELATIONS

Membership. Burkina Faso is a member of the UN, OAU and is an ACP state of the EU.

ECONOMY

Policy. A development programme for 1994–96, based mainly on agriculture and costing 62,000m. francs CFA, is being financed largely by foreign aid. It is proposed to privatize and restructure the banking and industrial sectors. 11 enterprises had been privatized by Nov. 1994. A second phase of privatization was then initiated.

Price controls were imposed on basic items following the devaluation of the franc CFA in Jan. 1994.

Budget. The 1994 budget envisaged expenditure of 373,000m. francs CFA and domestic revenue of 296,000m. francs CFA.

Currency. The unit of currency is the *franc CFA* (XOF) with a parity rate of 100 francs CFA to 1 French franc. In Sept. 1994, 91,030m. francs CFA were in circulation. In 1994 foreign exchange reserves were US$237·2m.; gold reserves were 11,000 troy oz in 1993.

Banking and Finance. The bank of issue which functions as the central bank is the regional West African Central Bank (BCEAO; *Governor*, Boukary Ouédraogo). There are 3 commercial banks, 4 specialized development institutions, a savings bank, 5 non-bank credit institutions and an investment company.

Weights and Measures. The metric system is in use.

ENERGY AND NATURAL RESOURCES

Electricity. Production of electricity (1993) was 190m. kWh. There are 5 thermal power stations with a total capacity in 1995 of 38·9MW. Hydro-electric capacity in 1994 was 15 MW.

Minerals. There are deposits of manganese, zinc, limestone, phosphate and diamonds. Gold production was 1·8 tonnes in 1992.

Agriculture. In 1991 there were 3·55m. ha of arable land and 10m. ha of permanent pasture. 20,000 ha were irrigated. 7·98m. persons depended on agriculture, of whom 4·12m. were economically active. Production (1992, in 1,000 tonnes): Sorghum, 1,292; millet, 784; sugar-cane, 340; maize, 341; groundnuts, 143; rice, 47; cotton, 172; sesame, 8. Rice and groundnuts are of increasing importance.

Livestock (1992, in 1,000): Cattle, 4,096; sheep, 5,350; goats, 6,860; pigs, 530; asses, 427; horses, 22.

Forestry. In 1994, 6·66m. ha were forested and 9·7m. cu. metres of roundwood were cut.

Fisheries. River fishing produces about 5,500 tonnes annually. There is some fish farming.

INDUSTRY. In 1994 manufacturing contributed 14% of GDP, mainly food-processing and textiles. Plant is primitive, and employs only about 1% of the workforce. There are about 100 firms, most publicly-owned.

Labour. In 1990 the labour force was 4,744,000.

Trade Unions. There are 4 federations: the CGTB, USTB, CNTB and ONSL.

FOREIGN ECONOMIC RELATIONS. Foreign debt was US$1,311m. in 1994.

Commerce. In 1994 imports totalled US$361·5m. and exports US$225·9m. Value of main exports (in US$1m.), 1994: Cotton, 59; gold, 22. Principal export markets, 1994: France, 13·2%; Côte d'Ivoire, 10·8%; Thailand, 10·2%; Italy, 7·8%; Taiwan, 7·2%. Principal import suppliers: Côte d'Ivoire, 25·6%; France, 15·6%; Niger, 3·5%; Nigeria, 3%; Japan, 2·3%.

COMMUNICATIONS

Roads. The road system comprises 13,134 km, of which 4,396 km are national, 1,744 km departmental, 2,364 km regional and 1,940 km unclassified roads. Only 1,500 km are asphalted.

Railways. The railway from Abidjan in Côte d'Ivoire to Kaya (622 km of metre-gauge within Burkina Faso) is operated by the mixed public-private company Sitarail, a concessionaire to both governments. The railways carried 0·6m. passengers and 0·2m. tonnes of freight in 1993.

Civil Aviation. The international airports are Ouagadougou and Bobo-Dioulasso. The national carrier is Air Burkina (66% state-owned) which had 2 aircraft in 1995, and operates flights to Abidjan, Brussels, Niamey and Paris.

Telecommunications. There were, in 1993, about 21,000 telephones. Radio and television services (colour by SECAM) are provided by the state-controlled Radiodiffusion-Télévision Burkina. Radio Bobo is a regional service and there is a commercial radio station. In 1995 there were estimated to be 0·29m. radio and 60,000 television receivers.

Press. There were 3 dailies (1 government-owned) with a combined circulation of 15,000 and 2 weeklies in 1995.

SOCIAL INSTITUTIONS

Justice. Civilian courts replaced revolutionary tribunals in 1993. There is a Supreme Court in Ouagadougou and Courts of Appeal at Ouagadougou and Bobo-Dioulasso.

Religion. In 1991 there were 4·81m. Moslems and 1·9m. Christians (mainly Roman Catholic). Many of the remaining population follow traditional animist religions.

Education. In 1995 adult literacy was 19·2% (male, 29·5%; female, 9·2%). The 1994–96 development programme has established an adult literacy campaign and centres for the education of 10–15-year-old non-school-attenders. In 1995 there were 3,233 primary schools with 12,354 teachers and 650,195 pupils. In 1992 there were 115,753 pupils in secondary schools and 9,452 students in higher education.

DIPLOMATIC REPRESENTATIVES

Of Burkina Faso in Great Britain
Ambassador: Youssouf Ouédraogo (resides in Brussels).

Of Great Britain in Burkina Faso
Ambassador: Margaret I. Rothwell, CMG (resides in Abidjan).

Of Burkina Faso in the USA (2340 Massachusetts Ave., NW, Washington, D.C., 20008)
Ambassador: Gaëten Rimwanguiya Ouédraogo.

Of the USA in Burkina Faso (PO Box 35, Ouagadougou)
Ambassador: Sharon P. Wilkinson.

Of Burkina Faso to the United Nations
Ambassador: Gaëtan Rimwanguiya Ouédraogo.

Of Burkina Faso to the European Union
Ambassador: Youssouf Ouédraogo.

Further Reading

Decalo, S., *Burkina Faso* [Bibliography]. Oxford and Santa Barbara (CA), 1994
Nnaji, B. O., *Blaise Compaoré: Architect of the Burkina Faso Revolution.* Lagos, 1991

BURUNDI

Republika y'Uburundi

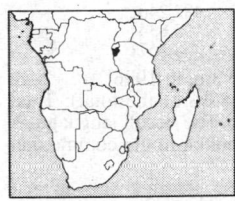

Capital: Bujumbura
Population: 5·36m.
GDP per head: (PPP$) 698
HDI/world rank: 0·247/169

KEY HISTORICAL EVENTS. Tradition recounts the establishment of a Tutsi kingdom in the 16th cen-tury. German military occupation in 1890 incor-porated the territory into German East Africa. From 1919 Burundi formed part of Ruanda-Urundi administered by the Belgians, first as a League of Nations mandate and then as a UN trust territory. Internal self-government was granted on 1 Jan. 1962, followed by independence on 1 July 1962.

On 8 July 1966 Prince Charles Ndizeye deposed his father Mwami Mwambutsa IV, suspended the constitution and made Capt. Michel Micombero Prime Minister. On 1 Sept. Prince Charles was enthroned as Mwami Ntare V. On 28 Nov., while the Mwami was attending a Head of States Conference in incorporated Kinshasa (Congo), Micombero declared Burundi a republic with himself as president.

On 31 March 1972 Prince Charles returned to Burundi from Uganda and was placed under house arrest. On 29 April 1972 President Micombero dissolved the Council of Ministers and took full power; that night heavy fighting broke out between rebels from both Burundi and neighbouring countries, and the ruling Tutsi, apparently with the intention of destroying the Tutsi hegemony. Prince Charles was killed during the fighting and it was estimated that up to 120,000 were killed. On 14 July 1972 President Micombero reinstated a Government with a Prime Minister. On 1 Nov. 1976 President Micombero was deposed by the Army, as was President Bagaza on 3 Sept. 1987. Pierre Buyoya assumed the presidency on 1 Oct. 1987.

On 1 June 1993 President Buyoya was defeated in elections by Melchior Ndadaye, who thus became the country's first Hutu president, but on 21 Oct. President Ndadaye and 6 ministers were killed in an attempted military coup. A wave of Tutsi-Hutu massacres broke out, and it is generally accepted that over 100,000 people have been killed since then. On 6 April 1994 the new president, Cyprien Ntaryamira, was also killed, possibly assassinated, together with the President of Rwanda.

On 25 July 1996 the army seized power, installing Maj. Pierre Buyoya as president for the second time after deposing President Sylvestre Ntibantunganya, dissolving parliament and prohibiting political parties. Parties were permitted to function again in Sept. 1996, but the rebel movement has grown in strength and the civil war between Tutsi and Hutu groups shows no sign of ending. A single attack in Jan. 1998 by a group of rebels left more than 280 Hutus dead.

TERRITORY AND POPULATION. Burundi is bounded in the north by Rwanda, east and south by Tanzania and west by the Democratic Republic of the Congo, and has an area of 27,834 sq. km (10,759 sq. miles). The population at the 1990 census was 5,292,793; estimate (1996) 5,356,000; population density, 208·5 per sq. km. Since 1994 there have also been some 0·3m. Rwandan refugees, mainly Hutu. 7·5% of the population was urban in 1996. Vital statistics rates, 1994 (per 1,000 pop-ulation): Birth, 45·6; death, 20·3. Life expectancy in 1994, 43·5.

There are 15 regions, all named after their chief towns. Area and population:

Region	Area (in sq. km.)	Population (1990 census)
Bubanza	1,093	222,953
Bujumbura	1,334	608,931
Bururi	2,515	385,490
Cankuzo	1,940	142,707
Cibitoke	1,639	279,843
Karuzi	1,459	287,905
Kayanza	1,229	443,116
Kirundo	1,711	401,103
Kitega	1,989	596,174

Region	Area (in sq. km.)	Population (1990 census)
Makamba	1,972	223,799
Muhinga	1,825	373,382
Muramuya	1,530	441,653
Ngozi	1,468	482,246
Rutana	1,898	195,834
Ruyigi	2,365	238,567

The capital, Bujumbura, had an estimated population of 0·3m. in 1996.

There are 3 ethnic groups—Hutu (Bantu, forming over 83% of the total): Tutsi (Nilotic, less than 15%); Twa (pygmoids, less than 1%). The local language is Kirundi. French is also an official language. Kiswahili is spoken in the commercial centres.

CLIMATE. An equatorial climate, modified by altitude. The eastern plateau is generally cool, the easternmost savanna several degrees hotter. The wet seasons are from March to May and Sept. to Dec. Bujumbura. Jan. 73°F (22·8°C), July 73°F (22·8°C). Annual rainfall 33" (825 mm).

CONSTITUTION AND GOVERNMENT. The Constitution of 1981 provided for a one-party state. In Jan. 1991 the government of President Buyoya, leader of the sole party, the Party of Unity and National Progress (Uprona), proposed a new constitution which was approved by a referendum in March 1992 (with 89% of votes cast in favour) legalizing parties not based on ethnic group, region or religion, and providing for presidential elections by direct universal suffrage.

There is a *National Assembly* with 81 members elected from 16 constituencies by proportional representation. There is a 5% threshold. Government activities are overseen by a 10-member *National Security Council*, of which the President and Prime Minister are members.

At the presidential elections of 1 June 1993 the electorate was 2·36m.; turn-out was 97·18%. Melchior Ndadaye was elected against former President Buyoya and one other opponent with 64·79% of votes cast, and sworn in on 10 July 1993. Following his assassination Cyprien Ntaryamira was elected President by the National Assembly on 13 Jan. 1994 to serve out President Ndadaye's 5-year term of office. After the latter's death and possible assassination Sylvestre Ntibantunganya (b. 1956; Frodebu) was elected *President* by the National Assembly on 5 Sept. 1994 against 5 opponents.

At the parliamentary elections of 29 June 1993, 740 candidates stood representing 6 parties. The Front for Democracy in Burundi (Frodebu) gained 65 seats with 71·4% of votes cast and Uprona, 16 with 21·4%.

On 25 July 1996 Maj. Pierre Buyoya (b. 1950; Uprona) was installed as *Interim President* after a military coup, and sworn in as *President* on 27 Sept.

Pascal-Firmin Ndimira became *Prime Minister* and formed a 'transitional government of national unity'.

Most countries do not recognize either Maj. Pierre Buyoya as President or the government which has been formed. A number of Frodebu MPs elected in June 1993 have been killed in the meantime.

National anthem: 'Uburundi Bwacu' ('Dear Burundi'); words by a committee, tune by M. Barengayabo.

Local Government: The 15 regions are each under a military governor, and are subdivided into 114 districts and then into communes.

DEFENCE. The Army had a strength (1997) of 18,500, plus some 3,500 in paramilitary units. Equipment includes a small naval flotilla and air force flight of 6 SF 260, 3 Cessna 150 and 1 DO27 liaison aircraft, 3 Alouette III and 1 armed Gazelle helicopter. The Army comprises 5 infantry and 2 light-armed battalions. There were 100 air force personnel in 1997.

INTERNATIONAL RELATIONS

Membership. Burundi is a member of the UN and OAU and is an ACP state of the EU.

ECONOMY

Budget. In 1996 total revenue (in 1m. Burundi francs) was 46,601; expenditure was 75,405.

Currency. The unit of currency is the *Burundi franc* (BIF) of 100 *centimes*. There are coins of 1, 5 and 10 francs and notes of 10, 20, 50, 100, 500, 1,000 and 5,000 francs. 10,766m. francs were in circulation in 1990. Inflation was 14·9% in 1994. Gold reserves were valued at US$4·3m. in 1992; foreign exchange reserves, US$169·2m.

Banking and Finance. The Bank of the Republic of Burundi is the central bank and bank of issue and there are 3 commercial banks; a state development bank, a savings bank and a property investment bank. Bank deposits totalled 10,680m. francs in 1989; savings banks deposits, 9,474 francs.

Weights and Measures. The metric system operates.

ENERGY AND NATURAL RESOURCES

Electricity. Electricity production was (1991) 99·5m. kWh.

Minerals. Gold is mined on a small scale. Deposits of nickel (280m. tonnes) and vanadium remain to be exploited. There are proven reserves of phosphates of 17·6m. tonnes.

Agriculture. The main economic activity and 85% of employment is subsistence agriculture, which contributed 54% of GDP in 1994. Beans, cassava, maize, sweet potatoes, groundnuts, peas, sorghum and bananas are grown according to the climate and the region.

The main cash crop is coffee, of which about 95% is arabica. It accounts for 90% of exports and taxes and levies on coffee constitute a major source of revenue. A coffee board (OCIBU) manages the grading and export of the crop. Production (1992) 34,000 tonnes. The main food crops (production 1992, in 1,000 tonnes) are cassava (597), yams (8), bananas (1,645), dry beans (346), maize (178), sorghum (67), groundnuts (99) and peas (37). Other cash crops are cotton (8) and tea (6).

Cattle play an important traditional role, and there were about 440,000 head in 1992. There were (1992) some 932,000 goats, 370,000 sheep and 105,000 pigs.

Forestry. Forests cover an estimated 66,000 ha. Production (1994) was 4·8m. cu. metres, the majority of it for fuel.

Fisheries. There is a small commercial fishing industry on Lake Tanganyika.

INDUSTRY. In 1994 manufacturing contributed 20% of GDP. Textile and leather industries constituted 20% of production, foodstuffs 13% and agricultural industries 9%. In 1992 production of sugar totalled 17,302 tonnes.

FOREIGN ECONOMIC RELATIONS. With Rwanda and the Democratic Republic of the Congo, Burundi forms part of the Economic Community of the Great Lakes. Foreign debt was 353,095m. francs in 1996.

Commerce. The total value of exports in 1992 was (in 1m. Burundi francs) 15,361; imports, 46,106. Main exports,: Coffee, 10,033; manufactures, 2,009; tea, 1,899. Main imports: Producer goods, 16,933; equipment, 16,217; consumer goods, 12,937. Main export markets, 1992: Belgium, 33·7%; Germany, 27·4%; USA, 7·8%; France, 4·9%. Main import suppliers: Belgium, 14·9%; France, 11·1%; Tanzania, 8·9%; Japan, 8·1%.

Tourism. In 1987 there were 79,745 foreign visitors of whom 19,380 were tourists.

COMMUNICATIONS

Roads. In 1993 there were 5,162 km of roads of which 310 km were paved. In 1987 there were 12,260 passenger cars and 7,672 commercial vehicles.

Civil Aviation. The national carrier is the state-owned Air Burundi, which had 2 aircraft in 1995. In 1988, about 9,000 international and 2,000 domestic passengers were carried by Air Burundi and 43,755 passengers and 4,868 tonnes of freight passed through Bujumbura International airport. There are local airports at Kitega, Nyanza-Lac, Kiofi and Nyakagunda. International services are also provided by Air France, Air Rwanda, Air Tanzania, Cameroon Airlines, Ethiopian Airlines, Kenya Airways and Sabena.

Shipping. There are lake services from Bujumbura to Kigoma (Tanzania) and Kalémie (Zaïre). The main route for exports and imports is via Kigoma, and thence by rail to Dar es Salaam.

Telecommunications. There were 38 post offices in 1983 and 7,200 telephones in 1987. Broadcasting is provided by the state-controlled Radiodiffusion et Télévision du Burundi. In 1993 there were estimated to be 0·05m. radio and 4,500 TV (colour by SECAM) receivers.

Press. There was (1995) one daily newspaper *(Le Renouveau)* with a circulation of 20,000.

SOCIAL INSTITUTIONS

Justice. There is a Supreme Court, an appeal court and a court of first instance at Bujumbura and provincial courts in each provincial capital.

Religion. In 1993 there were 3·69m. Roman Catholics with an archbishop and 3 bishops. About 3% of the population are Pentecostal, 1% Anglican and 1% Moslem, while the balance follow traditional tribal beliefs.

Education. Adult literacy rate was 35·3% in 1995 (49·3% among males and 22·5% among females). In 1993 there were 651,086 pupils in 1,418 primary schools with 10,400 teachers, 55,713 pupils in 97 secondary schools with 2,652 teachers and 4,256 students in 8 higher education institutes with 556 teachers. In 1995–96 there were 3,750 students and 170 academic staff at the university.

Health. In 1987 there were 32 hospitals with 3,239 beds and 209 treatment centres. In 1987 there were 272 doctors, 10 dentists, 29 pharmacists, 1,060 nursing personnel and 80 midwives.

DIPLOMATIC REPRESENTATIVES

Of Burundi in Great Britain
Ambassador: Leonidas Ndoricimpa (resides in Brussels).

Of Great Britain in Burundi
Ambassador: K. Oliver, OBE (resides in Kigali).

Of Burundi in the USA (2233 Wisconsin Ave., NW, Washington, D.C., 20007)
Ambassador: Severin Ntahomvukiye.

Of the USA in Burundi (PO Box 1720, Ave. du Zaïre, Bujumbura)
Ambassador: Morris N. Hughes.

Of Burundi to the United Nations
Ambassador: M. Gamaliel Ndaruzaniye.

Of Burundi to the European Union
Ambassador: Vacant.

Further Reading

Daniels, M., *Burundi:* [Bibliography]. Oxford and Santa Barbara (CA), 1992
Lemarchand, R., *Burundi: Ethnic Conflict and Genocide.* CUP, 1996
Weinstein, W., *Historical Dictionary of Burundi.* Metuchen (NJ), 1976

National statistical office: Service des Etudes et Statistiques, Ministère du Plan, Bujumbura.

CAMBODIA

Preah Reach Ana Pak Kampuchea

(Kingdom of Cambodia)

Capital: Phnom Penh
Population: 9·86m.
GDP per head: (PPP$) 1,084
HDI/world rank: 0·348/153

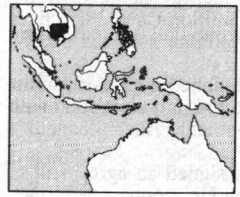

KEY HISTORICAL EVENTS. The recorded history of Cambodia starts at the beginning of the Christian era with the Kingdom of Fou-Nan, whose territories at one time included parts of Thailand, Malaya, Cochin-China and Laos. The kingdom was absorbed at the end of the 6th century by the Khmers. Attacked on either side by the Vietnamese and the Thai from the 15th century onwards, Cambodia was saved from annihilation by the establishment of a French protectorate in 1863. Thailand eventually recognized the protectorate and renounced all claims to suzerainty in exchange for Cambodia's north-western provinces of Battambang and Siem Reap, which were, however, returned under a Franco–Thai convention of 1907, confirmed in the Franco–Thai treaty of 1937. In 1904 the province of Stung Treng, formerly administered as part of Laos, was attached to Cambodia.

A nationalist movement began in the 1930s, and anti-French feeling strengthened in 1940–41 when the French submitted to Japanese demands for bases in Cambodia and allowed Thailand to annex Cambodian territory. On 9 March 1945 the Japanese suppressed the French administration and King Norodom Sihanouk proclaimed Cambodia's independence. British troops occupied Phnom Penh in Oct. 1945, and the re-establishment of French authority was followed by a Franco–Cambodian *modus vivendi* of 7 Jan. 1946, which promised a constitution embodying a constitutional monarchy. Elections for a National Consultative Assembly were held on 1 Sept. 1946 and a Franco–Thai agreement of 17 Nov. 1946 ensured the return to Cambodia of provinces annexed by Thailand in 1941.

In 1949 Cambodia was granted independence as an Associate State of the French Union. The transfer of the French military powers to the Cambodian government on 9 Nov. 1953 is considered in Cambodia as the attainment of sovereign independence. In Jan. 1955 Cambodia became financially and economically independent, both of France and the other two former Associate States of French Indo-China, Vietnam and Laos.

Anti-French guerrilla bands had operated in the jungle from 1945, the most important being a nationalist group known as the Khmer Issarak led by Son Ngoc Thanh. By 1953 Communist bands drawn from the Vietnamese minority and controlled by the Vietminh were active, and in 1954 regular Vietminh forces invaded Cambodia.

Fighting came to an end on 21 July 1954, with the Geneva Agreement. This led to the withdrawal of French and Vietminh troops. Most of the Khmer Issarak bands then surrendered. The International Control Commission responsible for the implementation of the Geneva Agreements was withdrawn in Dec. 1969 at the request of Prince Sihanouk.

Following a period of increasing economic difficulties and growing indirect involvement in the Vietnamese war, Prince Sihanouk was deposed in March 1970 and on 9 Oct. 1970 the Kingdom of Cambodia became the Khmer Republic. From 1970 hostilities extended throughout most of the country involving North and South Vietnamese and US forces as well as republican and anti-republican Khmer troops. During 1973 direct US and North Vietnamese participation in the fighting came to an end, leaving a civil war situation which continued during 1974 with large-scale fighting between the Khmer Republic supported by US arms and economic aid and the United National Cambodian Front including 'Khmer Rouge' communists supported by North Vietnam and China.

After unsuccessful attempts to capture Phnom Penh in 1973 and 1974, the Khmer Rouge ended the five-year war in April 1975, when the remnants of the republican forces surrendered the city.

From April 1975 the Khmer Rouge instituted a harsh and highly centralized regime. They cut the country off from normal contact with the world and expelled all foreigners. All cities and towns were forcibly evacuated and the population were set to work in the fields.

The regime had difficulties with the Vietnamese from 1975 and this escalated into full-scale fighting in 1977–78. On 7 Jan. 1979 Phnom Penh was captured by the Vietnamese, and the Prime Minister, Pol Pot, fled. Over 2 million Cambodian lives were lost from 1975 to 1979. In Dec. 1985 the Khmer Rouge still had 30,000 guerrillas fighting the Vietnamese in Cambodia.

In June 1982 the Khmer Rouge (who claim to have abandoned their Communist ideology and to have disbanded their Communist party) entered into a coalition with Son Sann's Kampuchean People's National Liberation Front and Prince Sihanouk's group.

On 23 Oct. 1991 the warring factions and 19 countries signed an agreement in Paris instituting a ceasefire in Cambodia to be monitored by UN troops. On 31 Oct. the UN Security Council unanimously agreed to establish a UN Transitional Authority in Cambodia (UNTAC), and on 28 Feb. 1992 the Security Council voted to send a force of 22,000 soldiers, police and officials to disarm the factions and organize elections.

Following the election of a constituent assembly in May 1993, a new constitution was promulgated on 23 Sept. 1993 restoring parliamentary monarchy.

During 1993–94 the Khmer Rouge continued hostilities against the government in disregard of the 1991 Paris Agreement, refusing to take part in the 1993 elections. They were formally banned by the National Assembly in June 1994. By 1996 the Khmer Rouge had split into two warring factions. The leader of one, Ieng Sary, who had been sentenced to death in his absence for genocide, was pardoned by the King in Sept. 1996. In early Nov. 1996 Ieng Sary and some 4,000 of his forces threw in their lot with government forces.

In July 1997 Hun Sen, the second prime minister, engineered a coup which led to the ousting of first prime minister, Prince Norodom Ranariddh. Prince Ranariddh went into exile but returned in March 1998 as guest of a Japanese-brokered plan to ensure 'fair and free' elections.

TERRITORY AND POPULATION. Cambodia is bounded in the north by Laos and Thailand, west by Thailand, east by Vietnam and south by the Gulf of Thailand. It has an area of about 181,035 sq. km (69,898 sq. miles).

Population, 5,756,141 (census, 1981) of whom 93% were Khmer, 4% Vietnamese and 3% Chinese. Estimate, based on the UN's electoral roll (1996), 9,857,000 (12% urban); density, 54 per sq. km.

Vital statistics rates, 1996 estimates (per 1,000 population). Births, 43·5; deaths, 15·8. Infant mortality (per 1,000 live births), 107·8. Expectation of life in 1996 was 49·9 years (48·4 for males and 51·4 for females). Growth rate, 2·77% per annum.

The capital, Phnom Penh, had an estimated population of 0·92m. in 1994. Other cities are Kompong Cham and Battambang. Ethnic composition, 1994: Khmer, 89%; Vietnamese, 6%; Chinese, 3%; Cham, 2%; Lao-Thai, 1%. Khmer is the official language.

CLIMATE. A tropical climate, with high temperatures all the year. Phnom Penh. Jan. 78°F (25·6°C), July 84°F (28·9°C). Annual rainfall 52" (1,308 mm).

MONARCHY. A parliamentary monarchy was re-established by the 1993 constitution. Prince Norodom Sihanouk (b. 31 Oct. 1922) regained the throne (which had been abolished in 1955) as King on 23 Sept. 1993. He had previously reigned from 1941 to 1955. The protocol of succession is to be determined by a Throne Council consisting of the Speaker and 2 Deputy Speakers, the First and Second Prime Ministers and 2 Buddhist patriarchs. In Jan. 1996 King Sihanouk's wife, Queen Monineath, was dubbed 'First Lady'.

CONSTITUTION AND GOVERNMENT. Elections for a 120-member constituent assembly were held under UN auspices in May 1993. The electorate was

4·7m. 20 parties presented candidates (the Khmer Rouge did not take part). Turn-out was 90%. The royalist FUNCINPEC gained 58 seats with 45·47% of votes cast, the Cambodian People's Party (CPP) 51 with 38·22%, the Buddhist Democratic Liberal Party (BDLP) 10 and Molinaka 1.

On 14 June 1993 the constituent assembly elected Prince Sihanouk head of state, and on 21 Sept. adopted a constitution (promulgated on 23 Sept.) by 113 votes to 5 with 2 abstentions making him monarch of a parliamentary democracy. The constitution converted the constituent assembly into a legislature sitting for a 5-year term.

An 18-member government was formed in Oct. 1993 led by Prince Ranariddh (b. 1944, son of King Sihanouk; FUNCINPEC), with Hun Sen (CPP) as Second Prime Minister. In July 1997 Hun Sen mounted a successful coup, and Ung Huot, the former Minister for Foreign Affairs, subsequently became First Prime Minister. Elections were scheduled for July 1998.

National anthem: 'Jham kraham cral' ('Bright red blood was spilt'); words and tune anonymous.

Local Government. There are 21 provinces administered by governors.

DEFENCE. The King is C.-in-C. of the armed forces.

Army. Conscription is for 5 years. Strength (1997) 36,000 including 7 infantry divisions, 3 independent infantry brigades and 9 independent infantry and 3 armoured regiments. Equipment includes 250 T-54/-55/-59 main battle tanks. There are also provincial (50,000) forces, and paramilitary local forces.

Navy. The navy is believed to include 2 ex-Soviet hydrofoil patrol craft, 10 inshore patrol craft and a miscellany of riverine and support craft. Naval personnel in 1996 totalled about 1,200.

Air Force. Aviation operations were resumed in 1988 under the aegis of the Army, equipment includes a squadron of 10 MiG-21 fighters being refurbished with Israeli help, 15 Mil Mi-8/17 transport helicopters, and 2 Ecureuil helicopters. At least 4 An-24 and 2 Yak-40 transports are in use as well as 6 L-39 trainers. Personnel (1996), 500.

INTERNATIONAL RELATIONS. In Jan. 1998 the European Union agreed to provide the Cambodian government with over US$11m., primarily to fund voter registration for the election due to be held in July 1998.

Membership. Cambodia has failed to secure a seat at the UN or membership of ASEAN.

ECONOMY

Budget. In 1994 revenues were estimated to be $210m. and expenditures $346m.

Currency. The unit of currency is the *riel* (KHR) of 100 *sen.* There are banknotes of 5, 50, 100, 200, 500 and 1,000 riels. Inflation was 6% in 1995.

Banking and Finance. In 1964 all bank functions were taken over by the National Bank of Cambodia, which is the bank of issue.

ENERGY AND NATURAL RESOURCES

Electricity. Production (1993) 160m. kWh.

Minerals. There are phosphates and high-grade iron-ore deposits. Some small-scale gold panning and gem (mainly zircon) mining is carried out.

Agriculture. The majority of the population is engaged in agriculture, fishing or forestry. Some 8m. ha of the total land area are cultivable. Before the spread of war the high productivity provided for a low, but well-fed standard of living for the peasant farmers, the majority of whom owned the land they worked before agriculture was collectivized. A relatively small proportion of the food production entered the cash economy. The war and unwise pricing policies led to a disastrous reduction in production to a stage in which the country became a net importer of rice. Private ownership of land was restored by the 1989 Constitution.

A crop of 1·8m. tonnes of rice was produced in 1994. Rubber production in 1992 amounted to 35,000 tonnes. Production of other crops, 1994 (in tonnes): Maize, 64,000; dry beans, 14,000; soybeans, 40,000.

Livestock (1994): Cattle, 2·58m.; buffaloes, 829,000; pigs, 2·15m.; horses, 21,000; poultry, 8m.

Forestry. Some 8m. ha of the land area are covered by forests, 3·8m. ha of which are reserved by the Government to be awarded to concessionaires, and are not at present worked to any extent. The remainder is available for exploitation by the local residents, and as a result some areas are over-exploited and conservation is not practised. There are substantial reserves of pitch pine.

Fisheries. There are large freshwater fish resources. 1993 catch, 108,900 tonnes.

INDUSTRY. Some development of industry had taken place before the spread of open warfare in 1970, but little was in operation by the 1990s except rubber processing, sea-food processing, jute sack making and cigarette manufacture. In the private sector small family concerns produce a wide range of goods. Apart from rice-mills, about 70 factories were functioning in 1994.

FOREIGN ECONOMIC RELATIONS. Foreign investment has been encouraged since 1989. Legislation of 1994 exempts profits from taxation for 8 years, removes duties from various raw and semi-finished materials and offers tax incentives to investors in tourism, energy, the infrastructure and labour-intensive industries.

Commerce. Imports in 1995, $630·5m.; exports, $240·7m. The main exports are timber, rubber, soybeans and sesame. Main imports include cigarettes, construction materials, petroleum products, machinery and motor vehicles. The principal partners for exports are Singapore, Japan, Thailand, China (in particular Hong Kong), Indonesia and Malaysia, and for imports, Singapore, Vietnam, Japan, Australia, China (again, in particular Hong Kong) and Indonesia.

COMMUNICATIONS

Roads. There were an estimated 34,100 km of roads in 1994, of which 3,000 km were paved and 31,100 km unpaved.

Railways. Main lines link Phnom Penh with Sisophon near the Thai border and the port of Kompong Som (total 603 km, metre-gauge). After a long period of disruption due to political unrest, limited services were restored on both lines in 1992, when 1·2m. passengers and 0·1m. tonnes of freight were carried.

Civil Aviation. Pochentong airport is 10 km from Phnom Penh. Royal Air Cambodia was reconstituted in Jan. 1995 with 60% of the equity government-owned. It had 1 B-737-400 in 1995. There are regular domestic services, and services to Bangkok, Ho Chi Minh-ville, Hong Kong, Kuala Lumpur and Singapore. There are also services by Aeroflot, Air Lao and Air Vietnam.

Shipping. There is an ocean port at Kompong Som; the port of Phnom Penh can be reached by the Mekong (through Vietnam) by ships of between 3,000 and 4,000 tonnes.

Telecommunications. There are telephone exchanges in all the main towns. Number of telephones in 1993, 6,000. Broadcasting is provided by the state-owned Voice of the People of Cambodia and Cambodian Television (colour by PAL). In 1995 there were an estimated 85,000 TV and 1·1m. radio sets.

Press. There are 21 newspapers, 2 of which are in English.

SOCIAL INSTITUTIONS

Religion. The Constitution of 1989 reinstated Buddhism as the state religion; it had 8·2m. adherents in 1994. About 2,800 monasteries were active in 1994. There are small Roman Catholic and Moslem minorities.

Education. In 1994–95 there were 1,703,716 pupils in primary schools, 297,555 in secondary schools and in 1990–91, 8,095 in vocational establishments. There is a university (with 8,400 students and 350 academic staff in 1995–96) and a fine arts university. Adult literacy rate was 35% in 1994 (48% among males and 22% among females).

Health. In 1984 there were 200 doctors, 130 pharmacists and 146 hospitals and clinics with 16,200 beds.

DIPLOMATIC REPRESENTATIVES

Of Great Britain in Cambodia (29, St. 75, Phnom Penh)
Ambassador: C. G. Edgar.

Of Cambodia in the USA
Ambassador: Var Huoth.

Of the USA in Cambodia (27, EO St. 240, Phnom Penh)
Ambassador: Kenneth M. Quinn.

Of Cambodia to the United Nations
Ambassador: Vacant.

Of Cambodia to the European Union
Ambassador: Namhong Hor.

Further Reading

Ablin, D. A. and Hood, M., (eds.) *The Cambodian Agony.* London and New York, 1987
Barron, J. and Paul, A., *Murder of a Gentle Land.* New York, 1977
Chandler, D. P., *A History of Cambodia.* 2nd ed. Boulder (CO), 1996
Jarvis, Helen, *Cambodia* [Bibliography]. Oxford and Santa Barbara (CA), 1997
Martin, M. A, *Cambodia: A Shattered Society.* California Univ. Press, 1994
Peschoux, C., *Le Cambodge dans la Tourmente: le Troisième Conflit Indochinois, 1978–1991.* Paris, 1992.—*Les 'Nouveaux' Khmers Rouges.* Paris, 1992

CAMEROON

République du Cameroun—
Republic of Cameroon

Capital: Yaoundé
Population: 14·3m.
GDP per head: (PPP$) 2,120
GNP: US$8·7bn.
HDI/world rank: 0·468/133

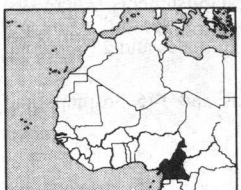

KEY HISTORICAL EVENTS. The name Cameroon is derived from the Portuguese *camaráes* (prawns), applied by the Portuguese navigators who from 1472 came for the crayfish in the Wouri river estuary. Called Kamerun in German and Cameroun in French, the estuary was later called the Cameroons River by British navigators. The Duala people living there were important traders, selling slaves and later palm oil to Europeans. They signed on 12 July 1884 a treaty establishing German rule over Kamerun. Originally covering the Duala's territory on the Wouri, this German colony later expanded to cover a large area inland, to which the name Kamerun was also applied.

The area occupied was home to a large number of African peoples; Betis, Bassas, Bamilekes, Bamouns, Tikars, Fulanis and many others. Some, like the Betis and Bassas, had only small traditional states; others had larger ones, notably in the 19th century, the kingdom of Bamoun and the Moslem Fulani state of Adamawa, whose territory was largely incorporated in German Kamerun although its capital, Yola, was included in Nigeria. Resistance to German colonization was strong, and it was about 20 years before German rule was established over the whole territory. In 1911, France ceded large adjoining areas of its neighbouring colonies (Chad, Ubangi-Shari, Middle-Congo and Gabon) to the Germans, who called this new territory Neu-Kamerun.

The Duala people, advanced in education and important traders, planters and junior government officials, became increasingly critical of German rule, especially when many were evicted from their homes in Douala City in 1914 and one Duala paramount chief, Rudolf Duala Manga Bell, was executed.

In the First World War Allied forces rapidly occupied Douala and then fought the Germans over a wide area, until the last Germans left in early 1916. The occupied territory was provisionally partitioned between France and Britain in 1916, a division confirmed in 1919 when each obtained a League of Nations mandate over its section. British Cameroons consisted of 2 areas, British Southern Cameroons and British Northern Cameroons, adjoining Nigeria. France's mandated territory of Cameroun occupied most of the former German colony. Its capital was at first at Douala, and then, from 1921, at Yaoundé. The Dualas continued to take the lead in anti-colonial protest, and in 1929 their paramount chiefs signed a petition calling for self-government.

In the Second World War French Cameroun was occupied at an early stage by the Free French. From 1944, reforms in the French colonial empire allowed African trade unions and parties, and nationalism spread rapidly. In 1946, the French and British territories became Trust Territories of the UN. Africans in British Southern Cameroons joined in the nationalist politics of Nigeria, and for some years British Southern Cameroons was represented in the parliament and government of Nigeria's Eastern Region. In French Cameroun the *Union des Populations du Cameroun* (UPC), founded in 1948, became the major nationalist party, calling for independence and 'reunification' with British Cameroons and appealing for UN support.

In the 1950s other parties emerged, encouraged by the French to rival the radical UPC, notably the *Bloc des Democrates Camerounais* led by André Mbida. In 1955, after rioting, the UPC was banned. In Dec. 1956, when elections were held prior to self-government, the UPC began guerilla war, but other parties took part in the elections and Mbida became prime minister in 1957. In Feb. 1958, Ahmadou Ahidjo, leader of the northern-based *Union Camerounais* (UC), became prime minister, while the UPC remained illegal and fought against the French and the new Cameroonian government. On 1 Jan. 1960 French Cameroun gained independence; elections were held, and Ahidjo became president. The UPC guerillas were largely defeated by 1963.

On 11 Feb. 1961, British Southern Cameroons voted in a referendum to join ex-French Cameroun, while British Northern Cameroons chose to join Nigeria. On 1 Oct. 1961, the Republic of Cameroon and British Southern Cameroons were united to form the Federal Republic of Cameroon.

On 2 June 1972, the limited powers of the West and East Cameroon governments were ended when the country became the United Republic of Cameroon.

Ahidjo resigned on 6 Nov. 1982 and was succeeded as president by Paul Biya, previously prime minister. After a crisis between Biya and his predecessor in 1983, and a *coup* attempt on 6 April 1984, Biya was confirmed in power. He was elected without opposition early in 1984 when the country's name was changed to the Republic of Cameroon.

TERRITORY AND POPULATION. Cameroon is bounded in the west by the Gulf of Guinea, north-west by Nigeria, east by Chad and the Central African Republic, and south by the Republic of the Congo, Gabon and Equatorial Guinea. The total area is 475,440 sq. km. On 29 March 1994 Cameroon asked the International Court of Justice to confirm its sovereignty over the Bakassi Peninsula, occupied by Nigerian troops. Population (1987 census) 10,494,000. Estimate (July 1996) 14,261,557 (7,150,420 females); density, 30·0 per sq. km. Population growth rate (1996): 2·89%; infant mortality, 78·7 per 1,000 live births; expectation of life (1996 est.): Males, 51·55 years; females, 53·68.

The areas, populations and chief towns of the 10 provinces were:

Province	Sq. km	Census 1987	Chief town	Estimate 1981
Adamaoua	63,691	495,185	Ngaoundéró	47,508
Centre	68,926	1,651,600	Yaoundé	649,000 [1]
Est	109,011	517,198	Bertoua	18,254
Extrême-Nord	34,246	1,855,695	Maroua	124,000 [1]
Littoral	20,239	1,354,833	Douala	810,000 [1]
Nord (Bénoué)	65,576	832,165	Garoua	142,000 [1]
Nord-Ouest	17,810	1,237,348	Bamenda	110,000 [1]
Ouest	13,872	1,339,791	Bafoussam	113,000 [1]
Sud	47,110	373,798	Ebolowa	22,222
Sud-Ouest	24,471	838,042	Buéa	29,953 [1]

[1] 1991

The population is composed of Sudanic-speaking people in the north (Fulani, Sao and others) and Bantu-speaking groups, mainly Bamileke, Beti, Bulu, Tikar, Bassa, Duala, in the rest of the country. The official languages are French and English.

CLIMATE. An equatorial climate, with high temperatures and plentiful rain, especially from March to June and Sept. to Nov. Further inland, rain occurs at all seasons. Yaoundé. Jan. 76°F (24·4°C), July 73°F (22·8°C). Annual rainfall 62" (1,555 mm). Douala. Jan. 79°F (26·1°C), July 75°F (23·9°C). Annual rainfall 160" (4,026 mm).

CONSTITUTION AND GOVERNMENT. The 1972 Constitution, subsequently amended, provides for a *President* as head of state and government. The President is directly elected for a 5-year term, and there is a Council of Ministers whose members must not be members of parliament.

Presidential elections were held on 12 Oct. 1997. The electorate in 1992 was 4,195,687. Paul Biya was elected against 2 opponents by 92·6% of votes cast.

The *National Assembly*, elected by universal adult suffrage for 5 years, consists of 180 representatives. After 1966 the sole legal party was the Cameroon People's Democratic Movement (RDPC), but in Dec. 1990 the National Assembly legalized opposition parties. At the elections of March 1992 751 candidates from 32 parties stood. Turn-out was 60·58%. The RDPC won 89 seats, the National Union for Democracy and Progress 65, the Cameroon People's Union 20, and the Democratic Movement for the Defence of the Republic 6. National Assembly elections were last held 13 May 1997. The RDPC won 109 seats, the Social-Democratic Front (SDF) 43, the Union Nationale pour la Démocratie et le Progrès (UNDP) 13, the Union

Démocratique du Cameroun (UDC) 5 and others won 3 seats. 3 constituencies (7 seats) were cancelled by the Supreme Court because of claims of fraudulent practices.

President: Paul Biya (assumed office 6 Nov. 1982, elected 14 Jan. 1984, re-elected 24 April 1988, re-elected 10 Oct. 1992 and sworn in 3 Nov. 1992, and once again re-elected 12 Oct. 1997).

Peter Musonge Mafani became *Prime Minister* in Sept. 1996 and formed a new government which comprises:

Minister for Agriculture: Zacharie Perevet. *Communication:* Rene Ze Nguele. *Culture:* Ferdinand Oyono. *Economy and Finance:* Edouard Mfoumou. *Employment, Labour and Social Insurance:* Pius Scurity Ondoua. *Environment and Forests:* Sylvestre Naah Ondoua. *External Relations:* Augustin Kontchou Kouomegni. *Industrial and Commercial Development:* Maigari Bello Bouba. *Justice and Keeper of the Seals:* Laurent Esso. *Livestock, Fisheries and Animal Industries:* Adjoudi Hamadjoda. *Mines, Water Resources and Energy:* Dr. Yves Mbele. *National Education:* Charles Etoundi. *Public Health:* Gotlieb Monekosso. *Social Affairs:* Madeleine Fouda. *Tourism:* Claude Joseph Mbafou. *Transport:* Joseph Tsanga Abanda. *Women's Affairs:* Aissatou Yaou. *Youth and Sport:* Joseph Owona. *Higher Education:* Antangana Mebara. *Posts and Telecommunication:* Mounchipou Seidou. *Public Works:* Jerome Etah. *Scientific and Technical Research:* Henri Hogbe Nlend. *Town Planning and Housing:* Pierre Hele. *Towns:* Antoine Zanga. *Public Investments and Territorial Development:* Justin Ndioro. *Public Service and Administrative Reform:* Sali Dairou. *Superior State Control:* Joseph Owona. *Territorial Administration:* Samson Ename Ename.

National anthem: 'O Cameroon, Thou Cradle of our Fathers/O Cameroun, Berceau de nos Ancêtres'; music by S. M. Bamba, tune by M. Nkoro.

Local Government: The 10 provinces are each administered by a governor appointed by the President. They are sub-divided into 49 departments (each under a prefect) and then into 336 communes (each under an under-prefect). Elections for councillors were held on 21 Jan. 1996. The electorate was 4·5m. 38 parties presented candidates. The RDPC gained a majority overall.

DEFENCE. The President of the Republic is C.-in-C. of the armed forces.

Army. There are 8 military regions. The Army consists of a Presidential Guard, 5 infantry battalions, 1 para-commando, 1 engineer, 1 artillery and 1 anti-aircraft battalion. Total strength (1997) 11,500; there is a Gendarmerie 9,000 strong.

Navy. The Navy, all French-built, operates 1 missile craft and 1 inshore patrol vessel. There are 2 landing craft and about 30 boats and service craft. Personnel in 1997 numbered 1,300. The marine wing of the Gendarmerie operates 10 inshore patrol craft.

Air Force. The Air Force has 2 Hercules turboprop transports, 4 Buffalo short-take-off-and-landing transports, 1 Puma and 1 Super Puma transport helicopters, 5 Magister armed jet basic trainers, 4 Alpha Jet close support/trainers, and 5 Alouette and 2 Bell 206 helicopters. Some of 4 Gazelle light helicopters are armed with anti-tank missiles. A small VIP transport fleet, maintained in civil markings, comprises 1 Boeing 727 jet aircraft, 1 Gulfstream III and 4 Aerospatiale helicopters. Radar-equipped Dornier 128-6 twin-turboprop aircraft serve for offshore patrol. Aircraft availability is low because of funding problems. Personnel (1997), 300.

INTERNATIONAL RELATIONS

Membership. Cameroon is a member of the UN, the Commonwealth and the OAU and is an ACP state of the EU.

ECONOMY

Policy. The Technical Commission for the Rehabilitation of Public Enterprises is overseeing both privatization and the restructuring of all state-owned companies. 18 companies were scheduled for privatization in 1997.

Performance. Real GDP growth was 3·3% in 1996.

Budget. The financial year ends on 30 June. Budget (in 1 bn. francs):

	1992	1993	1994	1995
Revenue	495·91	448·14	385·30	536·54
Expenditure	555·68	500·92	483·03	525·27

Currency. The unit of currency is the *franc CFA* (XAF), with a parity rate of 100 *francs CFA* to 1 French *franc*. Gold reserves were 30,000 troy oz. in 1992; foreign exchange reserves were US$20·4m. 155,560m. francs CFA were in circulation in 1992. Annualized inflation was 6% in 1996.

Banking and Finance. The Banque des Etats de l'Afrique Centrale is the sole bank of issue. There are 10, including 3 foreign, commercial banks.

Weights and Measures. The metric system is in use.

ENERGY AND NATURAL RESOURCES

Electricity. Installed capacity, 630,000 kW. Total production 2·7bn. kWh (95% hydro-electric).

Oil. Production (estimate, 1992) mainly from Kole oilfield was 7·46m. tonnes.

Minerals. Tin ore and limestone are extracted. There are deposits of bauxite, uranium, nickel, gold, cassiterite and kyanite. In 1993, 6·2m. metric tonnes of crude petroleum were produced.

Agriculture. In 1991 there were 5·95m. ha of arable land, 1·07m. ha of permanent crops and 8·3m. ha of permanent pasture. 30,000 ha were irrigated in 1991. The main food crops (with 1992 production in 1,000 tonnes): Cassava, 1,230; sorghum, 380; millet, 55; maize, 380; plantains, 860; yams, 80; groundnuts, 100; bananas, 520. Cash crops include: Palm oil, 107; palm kernels, 53; cocoa, 94; coffee, 85; rubber, 48; cotton lint, 48. Banana cultivation is being redeveloped.

Livestock (1991): 4·7m. cattle, 3·6m. sheep, 3·6m. goats, 1·4m. pigs.

Livestock products (in 1,000 tonnes), 1990: Beef, 78; pork, 16; mutton, 14; goat meat, 13; poultry meat, 14; cow's milk, 50; eggs, 12; honey, 2·7.

Forestry. Forests cover 24·65m. ha, ranging from tropical rain forests in the south (producing hardwoods such as mahogany, ebony and sapele) to semi-deciduous forests in the centre and wooded savannah in the north. In 1994, 15m. cu. metres of roundwood were cut.

Fisheries. In 1991 the total catch was 91,750 tonnes, of which 20,000 tonnes were freshwater fish.

INDUSTRY. Manufacturing is largely small-scale, with only some 30 firms employing more than 10 workers. Aluminium production in 1993 was 86,500 metric tonnes. There are also factories producing shoes, beer, soap, oil and food products, cigarettes. 1994 output included: sugarcane, 1·3m. metric tonnes; palm kernels, 54,000 metric tonnes; cassava, 1·3m. metric tonnes; cigarettes, 5m.

Labour. In 1990 the work-force numbered 4,351,000 of whom 61% were occupied in agriculture.

Trade Unions. The principal trade union federation is the *Organisation des syndicats des travailleurs camerounais* (OSTC) established on 7 Dec. 1985 to replace the former body, the UNTC.

FOREIGN ECONOMIC RELATIONS. Foreign debt was US$6,000m. in 1997.

Commerce. Imports and exports in US$1m.:

	1990	1991	1994(f.o.b.)
Imports	1,574	1,265	810
Exports	2,223	1,720	1,200

Principal exports (in 1,000m. francs CFA), 1991: Oil, 262·1; logs, 37·5; cocoa, 31·7; coffee, 31·5; aluminium, 24·1; timber products, 23·9; cotton, 17·4; bananas, 13·2.

Main export markets, 1992: France, 26·2%; Spain, 17·1%; Italy, 11·5%; Netherlands, 8·7%; Germany, 5·3%. Main import suppliers: France, 39·4%; Germany, 8·3%; Belgium, 5·3%; USA, 4·8%; Italy, 3·9%.

Tourism. There were 134,000 foreign visitors in 1995.

COMMUNICATIONS

Roads. There are about 64,626 km of classified roads, of which 2,666 km are paved. In 1991 there were 57,200 passenger cars and 30,900 commercial vehicles.

Railways. Cameroon Railways, *Regifercam* (1,104 km in 1995) link Douala with Nkongsamba and Ngaoundéré, with branches M'Banga–Kumba and Makak–M'Balmayo. In 1992-93 railways carried 1·9m. passengers and 1·2m. tonnes of freight.

Civil Aviation. There are 45 airports including 3 international airports at Douala, Garona and Yaoundé (Nsimalen). Cameroon Airlines (Camair), the national carrier, serves Dakar, Addis Ababa and destinations in Europe. In 1992–93 it carried 388,469 passengers and 1,059 tonnes of freight. In 1995 it operated 1 B-737-200 Adv, 2 B-737-200C Advs, 1 B-747-200B Combi, and 1 BAe(HS)-748. Cameroon is also served by Aeroflot, Air Afrique, Air France, Air Gabon, Ecuato Guineana, Nigeria Airlines, Sabena and Swissair.

Shipping. In 1995 the merchant marine totalled 40,194 GRT. Ports handled (1991–92) 3·78m. tonnes of cargo. The main port is Douala; other ports are Bota, Campo, Garoua (only navigable in the rainy season), Kribi and Limbo-Tiko.

Telecommunications. There were 36,737 telephone and fax subscribers in 1991. The state-controlled Cameroon Radio Television provides home, national, provincial and urban radio programmes and a TV service (colour by PAL). In 1995 there were about 2m. radio and 320,000 TV receivers.

Press. There was (1997) 1 national government-owned daily newspaper with a circulation of 66,000 and about 100 other periodicals, including 20 weeklies.

SOCIAL INSTITUTIONS

Justice. The Supreme Court sits at Yaoundé, as does the High Court of Justice (consisting of 9 titular judges and 6 surrogates all appointed by the National Assembly). There are magistrates' courts situated in the provinces.

Religion. In 1992 there were 4·43m. Roman Catholics, 2·79m. Moslems and 2·23m. Protestants. Some of the population follow traditional animist religions.

Education. In 1995, there were 1,061 pre-primary schools with 3,778 teachers for 91,242 pupils and 6,801 primary schools with 40,970 teachers for 1,896,722 pupils. In 1991, there were 500,272 secondary level pupils with 19,820 teachers at 425 general secondary and tertiary schools and 321 technical schools.

In 1991, 33,177 students were in higher education at 33 teacher training colleges and 5 new institutions of higher education. Total staff: 1,086. In 1994-95 there were 6 universities and 1 Roman Catholic university, 4 specialized *Ecoles Nationales*, an *Ecole Supérieure* for posts and telecommunications, 6 specialized institutes, a national school of administration and magistracy and a faculty of Protestant theology. In 1995-96 there were 15,220 university students and 830 academic staff. Adult literacy rate (1995 est.) 63·4%.

Health. In 1987 there were 251 hospitals and 809 health centres with 29,285 beds, 588 dispensaries, 177 pharmacies and 137 maternity clinics. In 1987 there were 888 doctors, 48 dentists, 201 pharmacists, 5,418 nurses and 6,520 auxiliary medical personnel.

DIPLOMATIC REPRESENTATIVES

Of Cameroon in Great Britain (84 Holland Pk., London, W11 3SB)
Ambassador: Samuel Libock Mbei.

Of Great Britain in Cameroon (Ave. Winston Churchill, BP 547, Yaoundé)
Ambassador: G. P. R. Boon.

Of Cameroon in the USA (2349 Massachusetts Ave., NW, Washington, D.C., 20008)
Ambassador: Jerome Mendouga.

Of the USA in Cameroon (Rue Nachtigal, BP 817, Yaoundé)
Ambassador: Charles Twining.

Of Cameroon to the United Nations
Ambassador: Vacant.

Of Cameroon to the European Union
Ambassador: Isabelle Bassong.

Further Reading

DeLancey, M. W., *Cameroon: Dependence and Independence.* London, 1989
DeLancey, M. W. and Schraeder, P. J., *Cameroon.* [Bibliography] Oxford and Santa Barbara (CA), 1986

National statistical office: Direction de la Statistique et de la Comptabilité Nationale, Ministère du Plan et de l'Aménagement du Territoire, Yaoundé

CANADA

Capital: Ottawa
Population: 30·29m.
GDP per head: (PPP$) 21,459
HDI/world rank: 0·960/1

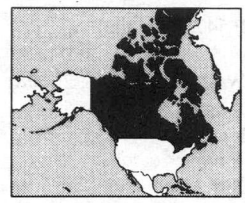

KEY HISTORICAL EVENTS. The first European in Canada was John Cabot in 1497. France claimed possession in 1534. The territories which now constitute Canada came under British power at various times by settlement, conquest or cession. For the most part such efforts were directed at gaining advantage over the indigenous Indian and Eskimo communities as well as displacing French colonial rule; conflict also broke out, however, with the fledgling United States in the Anglo-American war of 1812–14. Since then, Canadian-American relations have been described in terms of the world's longest undefended border. Nova Scotia was occupied in 1628 by settlement at Port Royal, was ceded back to France in 1632, and was finally ceded by France in 1713, by the Treaty of Utrecht; the Hudson's Bay Company's charter, conferring rights over all the territory draining into Hudson Bay, was granted in 1670; Canada, with all its dependencies, including New Brunswick and Prince Edward Island, was formally ceded to Great Britain by France in 1763; Vancouver Island was acknowledged to be British by the Oregon Boundary Treaty of 1846; and British Columbia was established as a separate colony in 1858. As originally constituted, Canada was composed of the provinces of Upper and Lower Canada (now Ontario and Quebec), Nova Scotia and New Brunswick. They were united under the British North America Act, 1867. The Act provided that the constitution of Canada should be 'similar in principle to that of the United Kingdom'; that the executive authority should be vested in the Sovereign, and carried out by a Governor-General and Privy Council; and that the legislative power should be exercised by a Parliament of two Houses, called the Senate, membership of which is by appointment, and the House of Commons, whose members are elected.

In 1931 the Statute of Westminster emancipated the Provinces as well as the Dominion from the operation of the Colonial Laws Validity Act, thus removing any remaining limitations on Canada's legislative autonomy.

Provision was made in the British North America Act for the admission of British Columbia, Prince Edward Island, the Northwest Territories and Newfoundland into the Union. In 1869 Rupert's Land, or the Northwest Territories, was purchased from the Hudson's Bay Company; the province of Manitoba was erected from this territory and admitted into the confederation on 15 July 1870. On 20 July 1871 the province of British Columbia was admitted, and Prince Edward Island on 1 July 1873. The provinces of Alberta and Saskatchewan were formed from the provisional districts of Alberta, Athabaska, Assiniboia and Saskatchewan, and admitted on 1 Sept. 1905. Newfoundland formally joined Canada as its 10th province on 31 March 1949.

In Feb. 1931 Norway formally recognized the Canadian title to the Sverdrup group of Arctic islands. Canada thus holds sovereignty in the whole Arctic sector north of the Canadian mainland.

In 1982 an amended constitution replaced the British North America Act to give Canada prerogative over all future constitutional changes. At the same time a charter of Rights and Freedoms was introduced recognizing the nation's multi-cultural heritage, affirming the existing rights of native peoples, and the principle of equality of benefits to the provinces.

TERRITORY AND POPULATION. Canada is bounded in the north-west by the Beaufort Sea, north by the Arctic Ocean, north-east by Baffin Bay, east by the Davis Strait, Labrador Sea and Atlantic Ocean, south by the USA and west by the

Pacific Ocean and USA (Alaska). The area is 9,970,610 sq. km, of which 755,180 sq. km are fresh water. Census population, 1996, 28,846,761. Estimate, July 1997, 30,286,596 (15,286,919 females). Population at previous censuses:

1851	2,436,297	1901	5,371,315	1951	14,009,429
1861	3,229,633	1911	7,206,643	1961	18,238,247
1871	3,689,257	1921	8,787,949	1971	21,568,311
1881	4,324,810	1931	10,376,786	1981	24,343,181
1891	4,833,239	1941	11,506,655	1991	27,296,859[1]

[1] Excludes data from incompletely enumerated Indian reserves and Indian settlements.

Of the total population in 1991, 13,842,300 were females, 20,907,135 urban, 22,343,315 Canadian born and 4,335,185 foreign born (249,075 of the latter being USA born and 2,364,700 European born).

The population (1991) born outside Canada in the provinces was in the following ratio (%): Newfoundland, 0·19; Prince Edward Island, 0·09; Nova Scotia, 0·89; New Brunswick, 0·55; Quebec, 13·6; Ontario, 54·6; Manitoba, 3·1; Saskatchewan, 1·3; Alberta, 8·8; British Columbia, 16·7; Yukon, 0·07; Northwest Territories, 0·06.

In 1991, figures for the population, according to ethnic origin, were[1]:

Single origins	19,199,790	Portuguese	246,890
Austrian	27,130	Romanian	28,650
Belgian	31,475	Russian	38,220
British	5,611,050	Scandinavian	174,370
Czech and Slovak	59,125	Spanish	82,675
Chinese	586,645	Swiss	23,610
Dutch (Netherlands)	358,180	Ukrainian	406,645
Finnish	39,230	Other single origins	3,104,400
French[2]	6,146,600		
German	911,560	*Multiple origins*	7,794,250
Greek	151,150	British and French	1,071,880
Hungarian	100,725	British and Other	2,516,840
Italian	750,055	French and Other	425,190
Japanese	48,595	Other multiple origins	835,990
Polish	272,810		

[1] Data on the ethnic origins for the 1991 Census excludes the population on incompletely enumerated Indian reserves and settlements. For Canada there were 78 such reserves and settlements and the total population was estimated to be about 38,000 in 1991.
[2] Includes the single origins of French, Acadian and Quebecois.

In 1991, 60·5% of the population gave their mother tongue as English, 23·8% as French.

The total aboriginal population single origins numbered 470,615 in 1991 and the Inuit population was 30,085 in 1991.

Populations of Census Metropolitan Areas (CMA), 1995 estimate, and Cities (proper), 1991 census:

	CMA	City proper		CMA	City proper
Toronto	4,344,300	635,395	Halifax	342,400	114,455
Montreal	3,337,200	1,017,666	Victoria	311,200	71,228
Vancouver	1,831,000	471,844	Windsor	285,700	191,435
Ottawa-Hull	1,022,700	—	Oshawa	275,800	129,344
Ottawa	—	313,987	Saskatoon	220,700	186,058
Hull	—	60,707	Regina	198,800	179,178
Edmonton	885,200	616,741	St John's	178,500	95,770
Calgary	831,800	710,677	Chicoutimi-		
Quebec	693,500	167,517	Jonquière	167,000	—
Winnipeg	677,700	616,790	Chicoutimi	—	62,710
Hamilton	643,000	318,499	Jonquière	—	57,933
London	413,000	303,165	Sudbury	166,400	92,884
Kitchener	395,400	168,282	Sherbrooke	148,300	76,429
St Catharines-			Trois Rivières	143,200	49,426
Niagara	386,300	—	Thunder Bay	131,000	113,946
St Catharines	—	129,300	Saint John	129,400	74,969
Niagara Falls	—	75,399			

Vital statistics:

	Live births	Deaths	Marriages
1993	388,394	204,909	161,610
1994	385,110	207,077	159,959
1995	383,145	212,990	160,616

Growth rate, 1993-96, 1·3%. Births, 1995-96, numbered 379,295; deaths, 215,740. Birth rate, 1995 (per 1,000 population), 12·9 (13·2 in 1994); death, 7·2 (7·1 in 1994); marriage, 1994, 5·5. Infant mortality (per 1,000 live births), 1993, 6·8. In 1993, life expectancy was: Males, 74·9 years; females, 81·2.

In 1995-96 there were 219,183 immigrants, of whom 142,535 were from Asia (including 28,317 from Hong Kong, 20,542 from India and 10,180 from the Philippines), 37,936 from Europe (including 5,483 from the UK), 13,962 from Africa, 8,295 from the West Indies, 5,657 from South America and 5,448 from the USA. In 1995 there were 46,416 emigrants.

CLIMATE. The climate ranges from polar conditions in the north to cool temperate in the south, but with considerable differences between east coast, west coast and the interior, affecting temperatures, rainfall amounts and seasonal distribution. Winters are very severe over much of the country, but summers can be very hot inland. *See* individual provinces for climatic details.

CONSTITUTION AND GOVERNMENT. In Nov. 1981 the Canadian government agreed on the provisions of an amended constitution, to the end that it should replace the British North America Act and that its future amendment should be the prerogative of Canada. These proposals were adopted by the Parliament of Canada and were enacted by the UK Parliament as the Canada Act of 1982. This was the final act of the UK Parliament in Canadian constitutional development. The Act gave to Canada the power to amend the Constitution according to procedures determined by the Constitutional Act 1982. The latter added to the Canadian Constitution a charter of Rights and Freedoms, and provisions which recognize the nation's multicultural heritage, affirm the existing rights of native peoples, confirm the principle of equalization of benefits among the provinces, and strengthen provincial ownership of natural resources.

Parliament consists of the Senate and the House of Commons. The members of the *Senate* are appointed until age 75 by summons of the Governor-General under the Great Seal of Canada. Members appointed before 2 June 1965 may remain in office for life. The Senate consists of 104 senators, namely, 24 from Ontario, 24 from Quebec, 10 from Nova Scotia, 10 from New Brunswick, 4 from Prince Edward Island, 6 from Manitoba, 6 from British Columbia, 6 from Alberta, 6 from Saskatchewan, 6 from Newfoundland, 1 from the Yukon Territory and 1 from the Northwest Territories. Each senator must be at least 30 years of age and reside in the province for which he or she is appointed. The *House of Commons* is elected by universal secret suffrage, by a first-past-the-post system, for 5-year terms. Representation is based on the population of all the provinces taken as a whole with readjustments made after each census.

The Special Joint Committee of the Senate and the House of Commons on a Renewed Canada released a unanimous report on 28 Feb. 1992 (Beaudoin-Dobbie Report). Another constitutional document was released on 16 July 1992 by the provincial premiers which summarized the multilateral meetings on the Constitution. A final constitutional accord was arrived at by the provinces and the federal government in Aug. 1992. At a national referendum on 26 Oct. 1992 proposed constitutional reforms were rejected by 54·4% of votes cast.

Indians have representation in the *Assembly of First Nations* (Chief, Ovide Mercredi).

The thirty-sixth Parliament, elected on 2 June 1997, comprises 301 members.

State of the parties in the Senate (1995): Progressive Conservatives, 51; Liberals, 42; Bloc Québécois, 8; Reform Party, 1; Independent Conservatives, 1; Vacant, 1.

The *Speaker* of the Senate is Gildas L. Molgat.

At the elections of 2 June 1997 the Liberal Party (Lib) gained 155 seats (177 in

1993) with 38·4% of votes cast, the Reform Party 60 (52) with 19·3%, the Bloc Québécois (BQ) 44 (54) with 10·7%, the New Democratic Party 21 (9) with 11·0%, the Progressive Conservative Party 20 (2) with 18·9%, ind 1.

The office and appointment of the Governor-General are regulated by letters patent of 1947. In 1977 the Queen approved the transfer to the Governor-General of functions discharged by the Sovereign. The Governor-General is assisted by a *Privy Council* composed of Cabinet Ministers.

Governor-General: Roméo Leblanc (b.1928; term of office, 1994–99).

The following is the list of ministers in the Liberal Cabinet in March. 1998:
Prime Minister: The Rt. Hon. Jean Chrétien.
Deputy Prime Minister: The Hon. Herbert Eser Gray. *Foreign Affairs:* The Hon. Lloyd Axworthy. *Transport:* The Hon. David Michael Collenette. *Fisheries and Oceans:* The Hon. David Anderson. *Natural Resources and Minister responsible for The Canadian Wheat Board:* The Hon. Ralph E. Goodale. *Canadian Heritage:* The Hon. Sheila Copps. *International Trade:* The Hon. Sergio Marchi. *Industry:* The Hon. John Manley. *International Cooperation and Minister responsible for Francophonie:* The Hon. Diane Marleau. *Finance:* The Hon. Paul Martin. *National Defence:* The Hon. Arthur C. Eggleton. *President of the Treasury Board and Minister responsible for Infrastructure:* The Hon. Marcel Massé. *Justice and Attorney General of Canada:* The Hon. Anne McLellan. *Health:* The Hon. Allan Rock. *Labour:* The Hon. Lawrence MacAulay. *Environment:* The Hon. Christine Stewart. *Public Works and Government Services:* The Hon. Alfonso Gagliano. *Citizenship and Immigration.* The Hon. Lucienne Robillard. *Veterans Affairs.* The Hon. Fred J. Mifflin. *Indian Affairs and Northern Development:* The Hon. Jane Stewart. *President of the Queen's Privy Council for Canada and Intergovernmental Affairs:* The Hon. Stephané Dion. *Human Resources Development:* The Hon. Pierre Pettigrew. *Leader of the Government in the House of Commons:* The Hon. Don Boudria. *Leader of the Government in the Senate:* The Hon. Bernard Alasdair Graham. *Agriculture and Agri-Food:* The Hon. Lyle Vanclief. *National Revenue:* The Hon. Herb Dhaliwal. *Solicitor General of Canada:* The Hon. Andy Scott.

The *Speaker* is Gilbert Parent (Lib).
The *Leader of the Opposition* is Michel Gauthier (BQ).

National anthem: 'O Canada, our home and native land'/'O Canada, terre de nos aïeux'; words by A. Routhier, tune by C. Lavallée.

Canadian Parliamentary Guide. Annual. Ottawa
Federalism and the Charter: Leading Constitutional Decisions. Edited and with an introduction by Peter H. Russell, 5th ed. Carleton Univ. Press, Ottawa, 1989
Laskin's Canadian Constitutional Law. 5th ed., Vol. 2, Neil Finkelstein. Toronto: Carswell, 1986
Bayefsky, A. F., *Canada's Constitution Act 1982 and Amendments: A Documentary History.* 2 vols. Toronto, 1989
Bejermi, J., *Canadian Parliamentary Handbook.* Ottawa, 1993
Cairns, A. C., *Charter versus Federalism: the Dilemmas of Constitutional Reform.* Montreal, 1992
Canada: The State of the Federation. Queen's Univ., annual
Cheffins, R. I. and Johnson, P. A., *The Revised Canadian Constitution: Politics as law.* Toronto, 1986
Forsey, E. A., *How Canadians Govern Themselves.* Ottawa, 1991
Fox, P. W. and White, G., *Politics Canada.* 7th ed. Toronto, 1991
Franks, C. E. S., *The Parliament of Canada.* Univ. of Toronto Press, 1987
Hogg, P. W., *Constitutional Law of Canada.* 3rd ed. Toronto, 1992
Kaplan, W. (ed.) *Belonging: the Meaning and Future of Canadian Citizenship.* McGill-Queen's Univ. Press, 1993
Kernaghan, K., *Public Administration in Canada: a Text.* Scarborough, 1991
Mahler, G., *Contemporary Canadian Politics, 1970–1994: an Annotated Bibliography.* 2 vols. Westport (CT), 1995
Osbaldston, G. F., *Organizing to Govern.* Toronto, 1992
Reesor, B., *The Canadian Constitution in Historical Perspective.* Scarborough, 1992
Tardi, G., *The Legal Framework of Government: a Canadian Guide.* Aurora, 1992
White, W. L., *Introduction to Canadian Politics and Government.* 5th ed. Toronto, 1990

Source: Library of Parliament

DEFENCE. The armed forces are unified and organized in functional commands: Mobile Command (land forces), Air Command (air forces) and Maritime Command (naval and naval air forces). There is a Tactical Air Group under the control of Mobile Command. In 1997 the armed forces numbered 61,600 (6,500 women); reserves, 72,100.

Army. The Land Forces numbered 21,900 in 1997 and were organized in 1 Task Force Headquarters, 3 mechanized infantry brigade groups (each with 1 Armoured regiment, 2 infantry battalions, 1 mechanized infantry battalion, 1 artillery regiment, 1 engineer regiment and 1 air defence battery), 1 Independent air defence regiment and 1 independent engineer support regiment. Reserves comprise a Militia of 20,100 and the Canadian Rangers, 3,250. Equipment includes 114 Leopard C-1 main battle tanks and 130 surface-to-air missiles.

Navy. The naval combatant force, which forms part of the Maritime Command of the unified armed forces, is headquartered at Halifax (Nova Scotia), and comprises 3 diesel submarines, 4 guided-missile destroyers and 16 helicopter-carrying frigates. Major auxiliaries include 3 helicopter-carrying replenishment tankers, 2 survey/research ships, 2 tugs and a diver support ship, and there are some 40 Minor auxiliaries, tenders and service craft. The Maritime Air Group includes 28 Sea King for embarked service.

Naval personnel in 1997 numbered about 9,400, with 4,000 reserves. The main bases are Halifax, where about two-thirds of the fleet is based, and Esquimault (British Columbia).

The Coast Guard numbers 4,000, and operates 17 icebreakers, numerous search-and-rescue and support craft, together with 2 fixed-wing aircraft, 37 helicopters and 5 hovercraft.

Air Force. The air forces numbered 17,600 in 1997 (825 women) with 190 combat aircraft and 150 helicopters. They are organized in the Air Combat and Mobility Group, the Maritime Air Group and Air Command HQ. The first controls air defence, tactical transport and helicopter units; the second oversees patrol, search-and-rescue and electronic countermeasures units; the third is responsible for training and logistics transports. Combat units include 5 squadrons of F-18 Hornet fighters, 4 of P-3 Orion patrol aircraft and 3 with Sea King anti-submarine helicopters.

INTERNATIONAL RELATIONS

Membership. Canada is a member of the UN, the Commonwealth, OAS, OECD, and NATO.

ECONOMY

Performance. GDP at market prices was $797,789m. in 1996 ($776,299m. in 1995).

Budget. Federal government revenue and expenditure (in $1m.):

	1992	1993	1994	1995
Revenue	135,540	134,306	138,635	146,566
Expenditure	163,783	168,301	166,120	172,397

In 1995 revenue comprised (in $1m.): Direct taxes from persons, 85,908; from businesses, 13,893; from non-residents, 1,696; indirect taxes, 30,255; other transfers, 20; investments, 14,794. Expenditure: Goods and services, 32,791; transfers to persons, 54,176; to businesses, 4,728; to non-residents, 2,303; to other governments, 32,125; interest on public debt, 46,274.

On 31 March 1994 the net public debt was $409,100m.

On 1 Jan. 1991 a 7% Goods and Services Tax (GST) was introduced, superseding a 13·5% manufacturers' sales tax.

Currency. The unit of currency is the *Canadian dollar* (CAD) of 100 *cents*. There are coins of 1, 5, 10, 25, 50 cents and $1, and notes of $2, $5, $10, $20, $50, $100 and $1,000. In June 1994, gold reserves were 5·03m. fine troy oz., and foreign exchange reserves totalled US$9,575m. $22,270m. were in circulation in April 1994.

Banking and Finance. The Bank of Canada (established 1935) is the central bank and bank of issue. The *governor* (in 1997 Gordon G. Thiessen) is appointed by the Bank's directors for 7-year terms. The Minister of Finance owns the capital stock of the Bank on behalf of Canada. Banks in Canada are chartered under the terms of the Bank Act, which imposes strict conditions on capital reserves, returns to the federal government, types of lending operations, ownership and other matters. In Aug. 1994 there were 60 chartered banks — 7 domestic and 53 foreign. The 6 biggest domestic banks had 7,971 branches serving over 1,600 communities in all provinces and both territories in Canada and 259 branches in 56 other countries. The foreign bank subsidiaries operate 269 offices in Canada. The First Nations Bank was founded in Dec. 1996 to provide finance to Inuit and Indian entrepreneurs.

Bank charters expire every 10 years which gives the federal government an opportunity to a review and amend sections of the Bank Act. Extensive changes were brought into force in June 1992. As a result of the substantial revision, bank charters were only renewed for 5 years. The chartered banks make regular detailed returns to and are subject to periodic inspection by the Superintendent of Financial Institutions, an official appointed by the Government.

The Bank Act of 1980 required chartered banks to maintain a statutory primary reserve of 10% on demand deposits, 3% on foreign-currency deposits and 2% on notice deposits, with an additional 1% on the portion of notice deposits exceeding $500m. This reserve is required to be maintained in the form of notes and deposits with the Bank of Canada. A secondary reserve of 4% in the form of treasury bills, government bonds, etc., is also required.

There are stock exchanges at Calgary (Alberta Stock Exchange), Montreal, Toronto, Vancouver and Winnipeg.

Weights and Measures. The legal weights and measures are in transition from the Imperial to the International system of units. The Metric Commission, established in June 1971, co-ordinates Canada's conversion to the metric system.

ENERGY AND NATURAL RESOURCES

Electricity. Generating capacity, 1995, 113m. MW. Net electricity generation in 1995 was 544m. MWh. 503m. MWh was to meet domestic demand. Of the total generated, 62% was from hydro generation, 21% from thermal generation and 17% from nuclear generation. Production, 1996, 440,063·5 GWh.

Oil and Natural Gas. Oil reserves at the beginning of 1995 were 656·1m. cu. metres (4,100m. bbls); gas, 1,812,000m. cu. metres. Production of petroleum crude and equivalent, 1996, 318,600 cu. metres a day; natural gas (1995), 149,600m. cu. metres. Canada's first off-shore field, 250 km off Nova Scotia, began producing in June 1992.

Minerals. Mineral production in 1995 (in 1,000 tonnes): Coal (1996), 75,675; iron ore, 37,130; copper, 705; lead, 203; zinc, 1,094; nickel, 167; uranium, 10·09; silver, 1·19; gold, 149,027 kg; salt, 10,772; asbestos, 511; cobalt, 2; lime, 2,516; gypsum, 7,974; peat, 1,010; sand and gravel, 239,871.

Agriculture. According to the census of 1991 the total land area was 2,278·6m. acres of which 167·4m. acres are agricultural land.

Grain growing, dairy farming, fruit farming, ranching and fur farming are all carried on. Total farm cash receipts (1995) $26,614m.

The following table shows the value of farm cash receipts for 1995, for selected agricultural commodities, in $1m.:

Crops	12,794	Livestock	
Wheat	2,795	and products	12,671
Barley	718	Beef	4,647
Canola	1,907	Hogs	2,253
Maize	708	Poultry	1,289
Flowers	869	Dairy	3,467
Vegetables	823		

Number of occupied farms (census of 1991) was 280,043; average farm size, 598 acres. In 1996, 252,839 census farms (of which 67,531 were beef cattle farms; 24,411 dairy; 29,526, wheat; 51,577 other grain and oilseed) reported total gross farm receipts of $2,500 or more.

Output (in 1,000 tonnes) and sown area (in 1,000 ha) of crops:

	Output		Sown Area	
	1992	1993	1992	1993
Wheat	29,871	27,825	13,830	12,626
Barley	10,919	13,342	3,790	4,240
Maize	4,883	6,300	858	950
Rye	265	314	138	159
Oats	2,823	3,615	1,238	1,357
Potatoes	3,588	3,333	124	125
Beans	53	120	54	82
Peas	505	1,000	277	482
Lentils	349	300	267	332
Soya beans	1,455	1,900	623	725
Sunflowers	65 [1]	79 [1]	74	85
Rape	3,872 [1]	5,400 [1]	3,045	4,027
Tomatoes	474	475	11	12
Carrots	299	310	7	8
Sugar beet	776	1,050	23	22
Hops	480	490	300	305
Tobacco	65	76	30	30

[1] Seeds

Livestock. In parts of Saskatchewan and Alberta stockraising is still carried on as a primary industry, but the livestock industry of the country at large is mainly a subsidiary of mixed farming. The following table shows the numbers of livestock (in 1,000) by provinces in July 1992:

Provinces	Milch cows	Total cattle and calves	Sheep and lambs	Pigs
Newfoundland	4·9	8·6	8·9	15·0
Prince Edward Island	18·5	94·0	3·2	103·0
Nova Scotia	28·3	128·0	30·0	126·0
New Brunswick	22·8	104·0	8·5	83·0
Quebec	505·0	1,430·0	116·0	3,068·0
Ontario	433·0	2,175·0	250·0	3,092·0
Manitoba	55·0	1,176·0	35·0	1,452·0
Saskatchewan	45·0	2,442·0	92·0	879·0
Alberta	105·0	4,866·0	311·0	1,868·0
British Columbia	75·0	773·5	72·5	213·5
Total	1,292·5	13,197·1	927·1	10,900·0

Livestock products. Slaughterings in 1993: Cattle, 3·37m.; sheep, 0·53m.; pigs, 15·4m. Production, 1993 (in 1,000 tonnes): Beef, 930; pork, 1,200; mutton, 11; horsemeat, 22; poultry meat, 735; cow's milk, 7,045; hens' eggs, 315; honey, 31; greasy wool, 1·52; rinsed wool, 0·96; hides, 85·84.

Fruit production in 1993 (and 1992), in 1,000 tonnes: Apples, 482 (553); pears, 16 (21); peaches and nectarines, 43 (40); plums, 3 (3); strawberries, 28 (29); raspberries, 15 (15).

Forestry. Forestry is of great economic importance, and forestry products (pulp, newsprint, building timber) constitute Canada's most valuable exports. As of 1986, the total area of land covered by forests was estimated at 453·3m. ha, of which 243·7m. ha were classed as productive forest land.

In 1995 the net merchantable volume (in 1,000 cu. metres) of roundwood harvested was 188,433; logs and bolts, 148,837; plywood, 31,089; fuelwood and firewood, 5,319; other industrial roundwood, 3,189.

Fur Trade. In 1995, 1,114,548 wild-life pelts valued at $25,141,280, and 0.95m. ranch raised pelts valued at $57,974,020 (including 917,300 mink pelts, value $55·1m.), were produced.

Fisheries. In 1993, the fishing fleet comprised 432 vessels totalling 169,900 GRT.

In 1994, Atlantic landings totalled 717,534 tonnes (of which 290,606 tonnes were shellfish and 206,777 tonnes herring); Pacific landings totalled 314,977 tonnes; freshwater landings totalled 27,300 tonnes.

INDUSTRY. Principal manufactures in 1993 (in 1,000 tonnes): Cement, 9,396; crude iron and alloys, 9,391; crude steel, 14,387; aluminium, 2,309; copper, 562; lead, 220; nickel, 141; zinc, 662; cadmium, 2; synthetic rubber, 199; passenger cars, 1·17m. units; lorries, 0·84m. (1992): Petroleum products, 31,293; heating oil, 28,336; mechanical wood pulp, 22,830; paper and cardboard, 16,585; newsprint, 8,931; sugar, 114; sawn timber, 56·3m. cu. metres; plywood, 1·84m. cu. metres; chipboard, 3·26m. cu. metres.

Labour. In 1996 the labour force was (in 1,000) 15,145·4 (6,844 females), of whom 13,676·2 (6,197·3) were in employment (2,589 part-time) distributed as follows: Business and personal services, 2,786·4; trade, 2,361·2; manufacturing, 2,082·5; health and social services, 1,425·7; educational services, 929; transport, storage and communication, 872·6; public administration, 820·1; finance, insurance and real estate, 799·9; primary industries, 733·2 (including agriculture, 453·3); construction, 718·6; utilities, 147. Unemployed, 1996, 1,469·2 (646·7 females).

Average weekly earnings in industry in Oct. 1996 were $592·64.

In 1995, 1,607,000 working days were lost in industrial disputes.

Trade Unions. Union membership in 1994 was 4,077,987 (4,089,000 in 1992), 29·2% of the workforce. 60·8% of the membership was affiliated to the Canadian Labour Congress, 6·3% to the Confédération des Syndicats Nationaux and 4·9% to the Canadian Confederation of Labour. 19·4% of unions were unaffiliated.

It is generally established by legislation, both federal and provincial, that a trade union to which the majority of employees in a unit suitable for collective bargaining belong, is given certain rights and duties. An employer is required to meet and negotiate with such a trade union to determine wage-rates and other working conditions of his employees. The employer, the trade union and the employees affected are bound by the resulting agreement. If an impasse is reached in negotiation conciliation services provided by the appropriate government board are available. Generally, work stoppages do not take place until an established conciliation or mediation procedure has been carried out and are prohibited while an agreement is in effect.

FOREIGN ECONOMIC RELATIONS. A North American Free Trade Agreement (NAFTA) between Canada, Mexico and the USA was signed on 7 Oct. 1992 and came into force on 1 Jan. 1994.

Commerce. In 1996 merchandise exports totalled $267,551m.; merchandise imports totalled $233,025m.

Main export markets, 1996 (in $1m.): USA, 221,854·7; Japan, 12,490·3; EU, 17,370; other OECD countries, 5,403·2. Main import suppliers: USA, 181,893·1; Japan, 7,235·7; EU, 20,617·2; other OECD countries, 8,950·7.

Main categories of exports, 1996 (in $1m.): Vehicles and parts, 63,357·2 (of which passenger cars and chassis, 33,736·3; motor vehicle parts, 17,154·5); machinery and equipment, 62,241 (industrial and agricultural machinery, 13,523·7; aircraft and other transport equipment, 12,453·1); industrial goods and materials, 52,086·5 (metals and alloys, 19,708·2; chemicals, plastics and fertilizers, 15,342·9); forestry products, 34,587·4 (lumber and sawmill products, 15,782·5; newsprint and other paper and paperboard products, 12,523·3). Imports: Machinery and equipment, 76,612·8 (of which industrial and agricultural machinery, 19,990·2; office machines and equipment, 13,372·8); vehicles and parts, 51,379·2 (motor vehicle parts, 30,475·8); industrial goods and materials, 46,507·7 (chemicals and plastics, 17,378·5; metals and metal ores, 11,752·4).

Tourism. The number of visitors to Canada in 1993 was 36,100,461 (1992, 35,730,803). In 1993, 32,622,740 came from the USA (1992, 32,427,324). Revenue from visitors was US$6,940m. in 1993.

COMMUNICATIONS

Roads. The total length of federal and provincial territorial roads and highways at the end of March 1991 was 290,194 km.

In general highways are controlled and maintained by the provinces who also have the responsibility of providing assistance to their municipalities and townships. Federal expenditures are directed largely to the maintenance of national park highways, Indian Reserve roads and designated provincial/territorial highway construction projects. The Alaska Highway is part of the Canadian highway system.

In 1991 intercity and rural bus services carried 15·3m. passengers 163·6m. vehicle-km, earning $408·2m.

Registered motor vehicles totalled 17,794,703 in 1994; they included 13,639,358 passenger cars and taxis, 3,697,792 trucks and truck tractors, 65,138 buses and 329,809 motor cycles and mopeds.

There were 4,210 fatalities in road accidents in 1990.

Railways. Canada has 2 great trans-continental systems: The Canadian National Railway system (CN), a body privatized in 1995 which operated 32,500 km (1994) of routes, and the Canadian Pacific Railway (CP), a joint-stock corporation operating 30,039 km (1994). A government-funded organization, VIA Rail, operates passenger services; 3·6m. passengers were carried in 1995. There are several provincial and private railways.

There are metros in Montreal, Toronto and Vancouver, and tram/light rail systems in Calgary, Edmonton and Toronto.

Civil Aviation. Civil aviation is under the jurisdiction of the federal government. The technical and administrative aspects are supervised by Transport Canada, while the economic functions are assigned to the National Transportation Agency.

In 1992 Canadian airports handled 40,405,937 revenue passengers on major scheduled services and 675,738,100 kg of cargo. Operating revenue for commercial air carriers (1992) was $7,459·7m.; operating expenditure, $7,698·8m.

The 2 major airlines are Air Canada (privatized in July 1989) and Canadian Airlines International. In 1995, Air Canada operated 34 A320-200s, 3 B-747-100s, 3 B-747-200B Combis, 3 B-747-400 Combis, 8 B-767-200s, 14 B-767-200ERs, 1 B-767-300ER, 8 Canadair RJs, 35 DC-9-30s, 1 L-1011-1 and 2 L-1011-100s; Canadian Airlines International, 12 A320-200s, 38 B-737-200 Advs, 1 B-737-200C, 7 B-737-200C Advs, 4 B-747-400s, 11 B-767-300ERs, 5 DC-10-30s and 5 DC-10-30ERs.

Shipping. In 1993 the merchant marine comprised 1,049 vessels over 100 GRT, including 31 oil tankers. Total tonnage, 1995, 0·66m. GRT, including oil tankers, 0·2m. GRT and container ships, 1,910 GRT. Total vessel arrivals and departures at Canadian ports in domestic shipping was 46,226 in 1991, totalling a cumulative GRT of 197,287,947. A total of 58,820 vessel movements in international shipping at Canadian ports in 1991 loaded and unloaded 234m. tonnes of cargo, totalling a GRT of 605,281,315.

The major canals are those of the St Lawrence–Great Lakes waterway. In 1992, traffic on the Montreal–Lake Ontario Section of the Seaway numbered 2,493 transits carrying 31·4m. cargo tonnes; on the Welland Canal Section, 3,140 transits with 33·2m. cargo tonnes.

Source: Statistics Canada and St. Lawrence Seaway Authority.

Telecommunications. At the end of the fiscal year 1995–96 Canada Post Corporation's retail network consisted of 18,500 retail locations. During fiscal year 1995–96, 11,800m. pieces of mail were processed. Total revenue (1995–96) was $4,900m.; income after expenditure, $28m.

In Oct. 1996 there were 17·96m. telephones in use; telephone provision was delivered by about 100 companies to 98·7% of households. There were 0·5m. fax machines in 1997.

The Canadian Radio-Television and Telecommunications Commission is an independent authority established by parliament in 1968 to regulate public and private radio and television. The Canadian Broadcasting Corporation operates 2 national TV networks, one in English and one in French, and there are 3 private TV networks. In 1995, 2,245 cable TV systems delivered programmes to 7·7m. households.

There were 841 originating radio stations operating in 1996, of which 333 were AM and 508 FM. There were also 968 radio rebroadcasters.

Sources: Statistics Canada, Canada Post Corporation, Canadian Radio-Television Telecommunication Commission.

Cinemas. (1991–92). There were 620 cinemas and 103 drive-in theatres.

Press. In 1991 there were 95 dailies in English (total circulation, 4·8m.) and 11 in French (1m.).

SOCIAL INSTITUTIONS

Justice. There is a Supreme Court in Ottawa, having general appellate jurisdiction in civil and criminal cases throughout Canada. The Exchequer Court (established in 1875) was replaced by the Federal Court in 1971. This has a Trial Division, consisting of the Associate Chief Justice and 9 other judges, and an Appeal Division, consisting of the Chief Justice and 3 other judges. Its seat is in Ottawa, but each Division may sit in any place in Canada. Decisions of the Trial Division may be appealed to the Appeal Division, those of the latter to the Supreme Court. There is a Superior Court in each province and county courts, with limited jurisdiction, in most of the provinces, all the judges in these courts being appointed by the Governor-General. Police, magistrates and justices of the peace are appointed by the provincial governments.

For the year ended 31 Dec. 1996, 2,624,148 Criminal Code Offences (excluding traffic) were reported, including 572 homicides. 203,900 cases were heard in Youth Courts in 1995.

Source: Statistics Canada

Royal Canadian Mounted Police (RCMP). The RCMP is a civil force maintained by the federal government. Established in 1873 as the North-West Mounted Police, it became 'Royal' in 1904. Its sphere of operations was expanded in 1918 to include all of Canada west of Thunder Bay. In 1920 the force absorbed the Dominion Police, its headquarters was transferred from Regina to Ottawa, and its title was changed to Royal Canadian Mounted Police. The force is responsible to the Solicitor-General of Canada and is controlled by a Commissioner who holds the rank of Deputy Minister. The Commissioner is empowered to appoint peace officers in all the provinces and territories of Canada.

The responsibilities of the RCMP are national in scope. The administration of justice within the provinces, including the enforcement of the Criminal Code of Canada, is the responsibility of provincial governments, but all the provinces except Ontario and Quebec have entered into contracts with the RCMP to enforce criminal and provincial laws under the direction of the respective Attorneys-General. In addition, in these 8 provinces the RCMP is under agreement to provide police services to municipalities. The RCMP is also responsible for all police work in the Yukon and Northwest Territories enforcing federal law and territorial ordinances. The 13 Divisions, alphabetically designated, make up the strength of the RCMP across Canada; they comprise 52 sub-divisions which include 723 detachments. Headquarters Division, as well as the Office of the Commissioner, is located in Ottawa.

Assisting the criminal investigation work of the RCMP is the Directorate of Identification Services; its services, together with those of divisional and sub-divisional units, and of 8 Crime Detection Laboratories, are available to police forces throughout Canada. The Canadian Police Information Centre at RCMP Headquarters, a national computer network, is staffed and operated by the RCMP. Law Enforcement agencies throughout Canada have access via remote terminals to information on stolen vehicles, licences and wanted persons.

In Feb. 1993, the Force had a total strength of 21,311 including regular members, special constables, civilian members and public service employees. It maintained 6,992 motor vehicles, 92 police service dogs and 156 horses.

The Force has 13 divisions actively engaged in law enforcement, 1 Headquarters Division and 1 training division. Marine services are divisional responsibilities and the Force currently has 402 boats at various points across Canada. The Air Directorate has stations throughout the country and maintains a fleet of 21 fixed-wing aircraft and 8 helicopters.

Source: Public Information Branch, RCMP Headquarters

Total police personnel in Canada at the end of 1994 numbered 74,902. Apart from the RCMP, Ontario and Quebec have police forces, as do most municipal centres. In 1995, 9% of police officers were women.

Religion. The most recent statistics available in 1997:

Religious body	Inclusive membership	Number of churches	Number of clergy
Anglican Church of Canada	780,897	2,499	3,240
Canadian Baptist Ministries	138,000	1,136	1,107
Evangelical Lutheran Church	290,846	1,006	1,230
Pentecostal Assemblies of Canada	226,678	1,075	. . .
Presbyterian Church	152,425	1,026	1,169
Roman Catholic Church	12,498,605	5,878	11,838
Ukrainian Greek Orthodox	120,000	270	. . .
United Church of Canada	2,018,808	4,044	3,939

Membership of other denominations: Mormons (1993), 118,000; Jehovah's Witnesses (1996), 110,659; Mennonites (1995), 114,000; Moslems (1996), 0·35m.; Jews (1996), 0·35m; Salvation Army (1996), 92,330.

Education. Under the Constitution the provincial legislatures have powers over education. These are subject to certain qualifications respecting the rights of denominational and minority language schools. School board revenues derive from local taxation on real property and government grants from general provincial revenue.

In 1996–97 there were 16,096 elementary and secondary public and private schools and 198 community colleges. There were 541,650 children in pre-elementary institutions; 4,969,317 children in elementary and secondary schools with 306,498 teachers; and 388,976 students in community colleges.

Enrolment for Indian and Inuit children, 1992-93: Federal schools, 5,096; band operated schools, 49,426; provincial schools, 44,418; private schools, 1,950.

In 1995-96 there were 48 universities, 1 technical university, 4 university colleges, 10 colleges, 1 Dominican college, 1 college of agriculture, 1 college of art and design, 2 open universities, 2 polytechnics, higher schools of business, public administration, and technology, and institutes of education, microbiology and virology, and scientific research.

In 1996-97 there were 572,179 full-time and 248,231 part-time university students with 36,035 teachers.

Health. Constitutional responsibility for health care services rests with the provinces and territories. Accordingly, Canada's national health insurance system consists of an interlocking set of provincial and territorial hospital and medical insurance plans conforming to certain national standards rather than a single national programme. These national standards, which are set out in the Canada Health Act, include: Provision of a comprehensive range of hospital and medical benefits; universal population coverage; access to necessary services on uniform terms and conditions; portability of benefits; and public administration of provincial and territorial insurance plans.

Provinces and territories satisfying these national standards are eligible for federal financial transfer payments. The provinces and territories are entitled to receive equal-per-capita federal health contributions escalated annually by the 3-year average increase in nominal GNP. These federal contributions, estimated at $3,734m. in 1993–94, are paid in the form of a combination of tax point and cash transfers. Over and above these health transfers, the federal government also provides financial support for such provincial and territorial extended health care service programmes as nursing home care, certain home care services, ambulatory health care services and adult residential care services. These supplementary equal-per-capita cash payments are estimated at $1,475m. in 1993–94.

The national health insurance programmes were introduced in stages. The Hospital Insurance and Diagnostic Services Act was passed in 1957, providing prepaid coverage to all Canadians for in-patient and, at the option of each province and territory, out-patient hospital services. The Medical Care Act was introduced in 1968 to extend universal coverage to all medically-equipped services provided by medical practitioners. The Canada Health Act, which took effect 1 April 1984, consolidated the original federal health insurance legislation and clarified the national standards provinces and territories are required to meet in order to qualify for full federal health contributions.

The approach taken by Canada is one of state-sponsored health insurance. Accordingly, the advent of insurance programmes produced little change in the ownership of hospitals, almost all of which are owned by non-government non-profit corporations, or in the rights and privileges of private medical practice. Patients are free to choose their own general practitioner. Except for a small percent of the population whose care is provided for under other legislation (such as serving members of the Canadian Armed Forces and inmates of federal penitentiaries), all residents are eligible, regardless of whether they are in the work force. Benefits are available without upper limit so long as they are medically necessary, provided any registration obligations are met.

In addition to the benefits qualifying for federal contributions, provinces and territories provide additional benefits at their own discretion. Most fund their portion of health costs out of general provincial and territorial revenues. There are no co-charges for medically necessary short-term hospital care or medical care. Most provinces and territories have charges for long-term chronic hospital care geared, approximately, to the room and board portion of this OAS–GIS payment mentioned under Social Welfare. In 1991, total health expenditures were about $66·77m., representing 10·2% of GNP. Public sector spending accounts for about 72·2% of total national health expenditure.

Social Welfare. The social security system provides financial benefits and social services to individuals and their families through a variety of programmes administered by federal, provincial and municipal governments, and voluntary organizations. Federally, Human Resources and Labour is responsible for research into the areas of social issues, provision of grants and contributions for various social services, and the administration of several income security programmes. These services are: The Old Age Security programme, introduced in 1952 and to which were added the Guaranteed Income Supplement in 1967 and the Spouse's Allowance in 1975; and the Canada Pension Plan and Canada Assistance Plan which came into being in 1966.

The Old Age Security (OAS) pension is payable to persons 65 years of age and over who satisfy the residence requirements stipulated in the Old Age Security Act. The amount payable, whether full or partial, is also governed by stipulated conditions, as is the payment of an OAS pension to a recipient who absents himself from Canada. OAS pensioners with little or no income apart from OAS may, upon application, receive a full or partial supplement known as the Guaranteed Income Supplement (GIS). Entitlement is normally based on the pensioner's income in the preceding year, calculated in accordance with the Income Tax Act. The spouse of an OAS pensioner, aged 60 to 64, meeting the same residence requirements as those stipulated for OAS, may be eligible for a full or partial Spouse's Allowance (SPA). SPA is payable, on application, depending on the annual combined income of the couple (not including the pensioner spouse's basic OAS pension or GIS). In 1979, the SPA programme was expanded to include a spouse, who is eligible for SPA in the month the pensioner spouse dies, until the age of 65 or until remarriage (Extended Spouse's Allowance). Since Sept. 1985, SPA has also been available to low income widow(er)s aged 60–64 regardless of the age of their spouse at death. For the third quarter of 1993, the basic OAS pension was $383·51 monthly; the maximum Guaranteed Income Supplement was $455·76 monthly for a single pensioner or a married pensioner whose spouse was not receiving a pension or a Spouse's

Allowance, and $296·87 monthly for each spouse of a married couple where both were pensioners. The maximum Spouse's Allowance for the same quarter was $680·38 monthly (equal to the basic pension plus the maximum GIS married rate), and $751·13 for widow(er)s. Total OAS/GIS/SPA benefit expenditures for 1991–92 were $18,921m.; in July 1992, over 3m. Canadians received benefits through these programmes.

The Canada Pension Plan (CPP) is designed to provide workers with a basic level of income protection in the event of retirement, disability or death. Benefits may be payable to a contributor, a surviving spouse or an eligible child. As of 1 Jan. 1992, payment of actuarially adjusted retirement benefits may begin as early as age 60 or as late as age 70. Benefits are determined by the contributor's earnings and contributions made to the Plan. Contribution is compulsory for most employed and self-employed Canadians 18 to 65 years of age. The CPP does not operate in Quebec, which has exercised its constitutional prerogative to establish a similar plan. In 1993, the maximum retirement pension payable under CPP was $667·36, the maximum disability pension was $812·85, and the maximum surviving spouse's pension was $400·42 (for survivors 65 years of age and over). For survivors under 65 years of age CPP pays a reduced flat rate. In 1993 CPP was funded by equal contributions of 2·5% of pensionable earnings from the employer and 2·5% from the employee (self-employed persons contribute the full 5%), in addition to the interest on the investment of excess funds. In 1993, the range of yearly pensionable earnings was from $3,300 to $33,400; a person who earned and contributed at less than the maximum level receives monthly benefits at rates lower than the maximum allowable under CPP. In July 1993, over 3·8m. Canadians received Canada or Quebec Pension Plan benefits. Total expenditures in 1992–93 for CPP were about $13,100m.

Social security agreements co-ordinate the operation of the Old Age Security and the CPP with the comparable social security programmes of certain other countries.

The Federal Government passed legislation in Nov. 1992, which replaced the Family Allowances programme with a new Child Tax Benefit, administered jointly by Human Resources and Labour and Revenue Canada. The programme delivered Canada its first payments in Jan. 1993.

Ismael, J. S., (ed.) *Canadian Welfare State: Evolution and Transition.* Univ. of Alberta Press, 1987

Source: Human Resources and Labour

DIPLOMATIC REPRESENTATIVES

Of Canada in Great Britain (Macdonald House., 1 Grosvenor Sq., London, W1X 0AB)
High Commissioner: Roy Maclaren, PC.

Of Great Britain in Canada (80 Elgin St., Ottawa, K1P 5K7)
High Commissioner: Sir Anthony Goodenough, KCMG.

Of Canada in the USA (501 Pennsylvania Ave., NW, Washington, D.C., 20001)
Ambassador: Raymond A. Chretien.

Of the USA in Canada (100 Wellington St., Ottawa, K1P 5TI)
Ambassador: Vacant.

Of Canada to the United Nations
Ambassador: Robert R. Fowler.

Of Canada to the European Union
Ambassador: Jean-Pierre Juneau

Further Reading

Statistics Canada. *The Canada Year Book.*
Cambridge History of the British Empire. Vol. VI. Canada and Newfoundland. Cambridge, 1930
Canadian Annual Review. From 1960
Canadian Encyclopedia. 2nd ed. 4 vols. Edmonton, 1988

Brown, R. C., *An Illustrated History of Canada*. Toronto, 1991
Cook, C., *Canada after the Referendum of 1992*. McGill-Queens Univ. Press, 1994
Dawson, R. M. and Dawson, W. F. *Democratic Government in Canada*. 5th ed. Toronto Univ. Press, 1989
Granatstein, J. L., *Twentieth-Century Canada*. Toronto, 1983
Harris, R. C., (ed.) *Historical Atlas of Canada*. Vol 1. Univ. of Toronto, 1987
Ingles, E., *Canada*. [Bibliography] Oxford and Santa Barbara, 1990
Jackson, R. J., *Politics in Canada: Culture, Institutions, Behaviour and Public Policy*. 2nd ed. Scarborough (Ont.), 1990
Leacy, F. H., (ed.) *Historical Statistics of Canada*. Government Printer, Ottawa, 1983
Longille, P., *Changing the Guard: Canada's Defence in a World in Transition*. Toronto Univ. Press, 1991
McCann, L. D., (ed.) *Heartland and Hinterland: A Geography of Canada*. Scarborough, Ontario, 1982
Silver, A. I. (ed.) *Introduction to Canadian History*. London, 1994
Smith, D. L., (ed.) *History of Canada: an Annotated Bibliography*. Oxford and Santa Barbara, 1983

Other more specialized titles are listed under CONSTITUTION AND GOVERNMENT *and* SOCIAL WELFARE, *above.*

National library: The National Library of Canada, Ottawa, Ontario. *Librarian:* Marianne Scott.
National statistical office: Statistics Canada, Ottawa, K1A 0T6. *Website:* http://statcan.ca/

CANADIAN PROVINCES

The 10 provinces each have a separate parliament and administration, with a Lieut.-Governor, appointed by the Governor-General in Council at the head of the executive. They have full powers to regulate their own local affairs and dispose of their revenues, provided only they do not interfere with the action and policy of the central administration. Among the subjects assigned exclusively to the provincial legislatures are: The amendment of the provincial constitution, except as regards the office of the Lieut.-Governor; property and civil rights; direct taxation for revenue purposes; borrowing; management and sale of Crown lands; provincial hospitals, reformatories, etc.; shop, saloon, tavern, auctioneer and other licences for local or provincial purposes; local works and undertakings, except lines of ships, railways, canals, telegraphs, etc., extending beyond the province or connecting with other provinces, and excepting also such works as the Canadian Parliament declares are for the general good; marriages, administration of justice within the province; education. On 18 July 1994 the federal and provincial governments signed an agreement easing inter-provincial barriers on government procurement, labour mobility, transport licences and product standards. Federal legislation of Dec. 1995 grants provinces a right of constitutional veto.

For the administration of the 2 territories *see* Northwest Territories, Yukon Territory *below*.

Areas of the 10 provinces and 2 territories (Yukon and Northwest Territory) (in sq. km) and population at recent censuses:

Province	Land area	Total land and fresh water area	Population, 1986	Population, 1991[1,2]	Population, 1996
Newfoundland (Nfld.)	371,634	405,720	568,349	568,474	551,792
Prince Edward Island (PEI)	5,660	5,660	126,646	129,765	134,557
Nova Scotia (NS)	52,840	55,490	873,199	899,942	909,282
New Brunswick (NB)	71,569	73,440	710,442	723,900	738,133
Quebec (Que.)	1,357,811	1,540,680	6,540,276	6,895,963	7,138,795
Ontario (Ont.)	916,733	1,068,580	9,113,515	10,084,885	10,753,573
Manitoba (Man.)	547,703	649,950	1,071,232	1,091,942	1,113,898
Saskatchewan (Sask.)	570,113	652,330	1,010,198	988,928	990,237

Province	Land area	Total land and fresh water area	Population, 1986	Population, 1991[1,2]	Population, 1996
Alberta (Alta.)	638,232	661,190	2,375,278	2,545,553	2,696,826
British Columbia (BC)	892,677	947,800	2,889,207	3,282,061	3,724,500
Yukon Territory (YT)	531,843	483,450	23,504	27,797	30,766
Northwest Territories (NWT)[3]	3,246,389	3,426,320	52,238	57,649	64,402

[1] Excludes data from incompletely enumerated Indian reserves and Indian settlements.
[2] Comparison of the 1991 census data with data from earlier censuses is affected by a change in the definition of the 1991 census population. Persons in Canada on student authorizations, Minister's permits, and as refugee claimants were enumerated in the 1991 census but not in previous censuses. These persons are referred to as non-permanent residents.
[3] For data on the new territory of Nunavut in course of formation *see* NORTHWEST TERRITORIES: Constitution and Government.

Local Government. Under the terms of the British North America Act the provinces are given full powers over local government. All local government institutions are, therefore, supervised by the provinces, and are incorporated and function under provincial acts.

The acts under which municipalities operate vary from province to province. A municipal corporation is usually administered by an elected council headed by a mayor or reeve, whose powers to administer affairs and to raise funds by taxation and other methods are set forth in provincial laws, as is the scope of its obligations to, and on behalf of, the citizens. Similarly, the types of municipal corporations, their official designations and the requirements for their incorporation vary between provinces. The following table sets out the classifications as at the 1991 census:

	Federal electoral districts	Sub-provincial regions	Census divisions
Nfld.	7	4	10
PEI	4	1	31
NS	11	5	18[1]
NB	10	5	15[1]
Que.	88	16	99[2]
Ont.	95	5	49[3]
Man.	14	8	23
Sask.	14	6	18
Alta.	21	8	19
BC	28	8	30[4]
YT	1	1	1[5]
NWT	2	1	5[5]

[1] Counties.
[2] 4 Census divisions, 3 communautés urbaines, 92 municipalités régionales de comté.
[3] 24 counties, 10 districts, 1 district municipality, 1 metropolitan municipality, 10 regional municipalities, 3 united counties. [4] 1 region, 29 regional districts. [5] Regions.

Justice. The administration of justice within the provinces, including the enforcement of the Criminal Code of Canada, is the responsibility of provincial governments, but all the provinces except Ontario and Quebec have entered into contracts with the Royal Canadian Mounted Police (RCMP) to enforce criminal and provincial law. In addition, in these 8 provinces the RCMP is under agreement to provide police services to municipalities.

ALBERTA

KEY HISTORICAL EVENTS. The southern half of Alberta was administered from 1670 as part of Rupert's land by the Hudson's Bay Company. Trading posts were set up after 1783 when the North West Company took a share in the fur trade. In 1869 Rupert's land was transferred from the Hudson's Bay Company (which had absorbed its rival in 1821) to the new Dominion, and in the following year this land was combined with the former Crown land of the North Western Territories to form the Northwest Territories.

In 1882 'Alberta' first appeared as a provisional 'district', consisting of the southern half of the present province. In 1905 the Athabasca district to the north was added when provincial status was granted to Alberta.

TERRITORY AND POPULATION. The area of the province is 661,185 sq. km; 644,389 sq. km being land area and 16,796 sq. km water area. The population at the 1996 census was 2,696,826; estimate, July 1997, 2,847,006. The urban population (1996), centres of 1,000 or over, was 79·5% and the rural 20·5%. Population (14 May 1996) of the 14 cities, as well as the 2 specialized municipalities (*see below under* Local Government for definition): Calgary, 768,082; Edmonton, 616,306; Lethbridge, 63,053; Red Deer, 60,075; St Albert, 46,888; Medicine Hat, 46,783; Grande Prairie, 31,140; Airdrie, 15,946; Leduc, 14,305; Spruce Grove, 14,271; Camrose, 13,728; Fort Saskatchewan, 12,408; Lloydminster (Alberta portion), 11,317; Wetaskiwin, 10,959; Specialized Municipality of Wood Buffalo (Fort McMurray), 35,213; Specialized Municipality of Strathcona County (Sherwood Park), 64,176.

Vital statistics, *see* CANADA: Territory and Population.

CLIMATE. A continental climate: Long, cold winters and mild summers. Rainfall amounts are greatest between May and Sept. Edmonton. Jan. 5°F (–15°C), July 63°F (17°C). Annual rainfall 13·6" (345·6 mm).

CONSTITUTION AND GOVERNMENT. The constitution of Alberta is contained in the British North America Act of 1867, and amending Acts; also in the Alberta Act of 1905, passed by the Parliament of the Dominion of Canada, which created the province out of the then Northwest Territories. All the provisions of the British North America Act, except those with respect to school lands and the public domain, were made to apply to Alberta as they apply to the older provinces of Canada. On 1 Oct. 1930 the natural resources were transferred from the Dominion to provincial government control. The province is represented by 6 members in the Senate and 26 in the House of Commons of Canada.

The executive is vested nominally in the Lieut.-Governor, who is appointed by the federal government, but actually in the Executive Council or the Cabinet of the legislature. Legislative power is vested in the Assembly in the name of the Queen.

Members of the Legislative Assembly are elected by the universal vote of adults over the age of 18 years.

There are 83 members in the legislature (elected 11 March 1997): 63 Progressive Conservative, 18 Liberal and 2 New Democrat.

Lieut.-Governor: H. A. Olson.

The members of the Ministry were as follows in March 1998:
Premier, President of Executive Council: Hon. Ralph Klein (b. 1942; Progressive Conservative).

Minister of Advanced Education and Career Development: Clint Dunford. *Energy:* Stephen C. West. *Family and Social Services:* Dr Lyle Oberg. *Provincial Treasurer:* Stockwell Day. *Environmental Protection:* Ty Lund. *Health:* Halvar Jonson. *Community Development:* Shirley McClellan. *Agriculture, Food and Rural Development:* Ed Stelmach. *Intergovernmental and Aboriginal Affairs:* David Hancock, QC. *Municipal Affairs:* Iris Evans. *Transportation and Utilities:* Walter Paszkowski. *Economic Development and Tourism:* Patricia Black. *Justice and Attorney General, Government House Leader:* Jon Havelock. *Education:* Gary G. Mar, QC. *Labour:* Murray Smith. *Public Works, Supply and Services:* Stan Woloshyn. *Without Portfolio responsible for Children's Services:* Pearl Calahasen.

Local Government. The local government units are City, Town, New Town, Village, Summer Village, County, Municipal District and Improvement District.

There are 14 cities (*see* TERRITORY AND POPULATION, *above*). These cities operate under the Municipal Government Act. The governing body consists of a mayor and a council of from 6 to 20 members. A city can be incorporated by order of the Lieut.-Governor-in-Council. A population of 10,000 is required on incorporation.

There are no limits of area specified in the statutes for any of the different local government units. The population requirement for a Town as specified in the Municipal Government Act is 1,000 people, and the area at incorporation is that of the original village.

A Village must contain 75 separate and occupied dwellings. The Municipal Government Act requires each dwelling to have been occupied continuously for a period of at least 6 months. A Summer Village must contain 50 separate dwellings.

A rural county area is an area incorporated through an order of the Lieut.-Governor-in-Council under the provisions of the County Act. One board of councillors deal with both municipal and school affairs.

A rural Municipal District is an area which has been incorporated under the Municipal Government Act. In Municipal Districts separate boards control municipal and school affairs.

Areas not incorporated as counties or Municipal Districts are termed Improvement Districts or Special Areas. Sparsely populated, such districts are administered and taxed by the Department of Municipal Affairs of the provincial government. There are no requirements as to the minimum number of residents of a County or Municipal District.

FINANCE. The budgetary revenue and expenditure (in $1m.) for years ending 31 March were as follows:

	1992–93	1993–94	1994–95	1995–96	1996–97
Revenue	14,173	15,308	16,082	15,504	16,651
Expenditure	17,497	16,679	15,144	14,353	14,162

Personal income *per capita* (1996), $23,511.

ENERGY AND NATURAL RESOURCES

Oil. In 1996, 90,353,000 cu. metres of crude oil were produced with gross sales value of $14,914,615,000. Alberta produced 76·8% of Canada's crude petroleum output in 1996.

Oil sands underlie some 60,000 sq. km of Alberta, the 4 major deposits being: The Athabasca, Cold Lake, Peace River and Buffalo Head Hills deposits. Some 7% (3,250 sq. km) of the Athabasca deposit can be exploited through open-pit mining. The rest of the Athabasca, and all the deposits in the other areas, are deeper reserves which must be developed through in situ techniques. These reserves reach depths of 760 metres.

Oil sands mining plants produced 16,317,500 cu. metres of synthetic crude oil in 1996.

Gas. Natural gas is found in abundance in numerous localities. In 1996, 127,903,000 cu. metres valued at $7,533,487,000 were produced. Production of natural gas by-products was 25,960,600 cu. metres, valued at $2,747·95m.

Minerals. Coal reserves are estimated at 2,300,000m. tonnes, of which 720,000m. tonnes are recoverable. Production in 1996 was 41·93m. tonnes.

Value of total mineral production increased from $20,700m. in 1995 to $26,000m. in 1996.

Agriculture. Total area of farms (1996), 51,964,360 acres; improved land, 35,617,109 acres (under crops, 23,590,033; improved pasture, 4,731,087; summer fallow, 3,550,265; other improved land, 3,745,724); unimproved land, 16,347,251 acres. Number of farms (1996), 59,007.

For particulars of agricultural production and livestock *see* CANADA: Agriculture. Farm cash receipts in 1996 totalled $6,391·74m., of which crops contributed $2,921·85m., livestock and products, $3,318·32m. and direct payments $151·57m.

Forestry. Forest land in 1991 covered some 203,000 sq. km. In Jan. 1995, 22,750,434 cu. metres was the net allowable cut from land managed by the Crown.

Fisheries. The largest catch in commercial fishing is whitefish. Perch, tullibee, walley, pike and lake trout are also caught in smaller quantities. In 1984 a provincial fish marketing policy was implemented and a new commercial fishery licensing system was implemented in 1987. Commercial fish production in 1990–91 was 2,210 tonnes, value $2·49m.

INDUSTRY. The leading manufacturing industries are food and beverages, petroleum refining, metal fabricating, wood industries, primary metal, chemical and chemical products and non-metallic mineral products industries. In 1995 there were 2,509 manufacturing establishments, in which were employed 99,225 persons who earned salaries and wages of $3,702,100,000.

Manufacturing shipments had a total value of $30,771·9m. in 1996. Chief among these shipments were (in $1m.): Food, 6,257·6; beverages, 584·2; chemicals and chemical products, 5,392·8; refined petroleum and coal products, 5,268·4; primary metals, 938·2; fabricated metal products, 1,578·4; wood, 1,915·1; printing, publishing and allied products, 882; machinery, 1,709; paper and allied products, 1,678·1; non-metal mineral products, 1,709; furniture and fixtures, 396·6; other, 350·7.

Total retail sales (1996) $23,141m.

Labour. In 1996 the labour force was 1,519,700 (681,000 females), of whom 1,412,700 (633,200) were employed.

Tourism. Tourism is important and in 1996 contributed an estimated $3,000m. to the economy.

COMMUNICATIONS

Roads. In 1997 there were 158,388 km of roads and highways, including 110,891 km gravelled and 23,146 km paved.

At 31 March 1997 there were 1,962,789 motor vehicles registered, including 1,549,662 passenger vehicles.

Railways. In 1997 the length of main railway lines was 8,395 km. There are light rail networks in Edmonton (12·8 km) and Calgary (29·3 km).

Telecommunications. The telephone system is owned and operated by the Telus Corporation (in which the Alberta Government holds 44% of the shares), except in the city of Edmonton (owned and operated by the City Council). There were 1,904,038 telephone subscriber lines in service in 1997.

SOCIAL INSTITUTIONS

Justice. The Supreme Judicial authority of the province is the Court of Appeal. Judges of the Court of Appeal and Court of Queen's Bench are appointed by the Federal Government and hold office until retirement at the age of 75. There are courts of lesser jurisdiction in both civil and criminal matters. The Court of Queen's Bench has full jurisdiction over civil proceedings. A Provincial Court which has jurisdiction in civil matters up to $2,000 is presided over by provincially appointed judges. Youth Courts have power to try boys and girls 12–17 years old inclusive for offences against the Young Offenders Act.

The jurisdiction of all criminal courts in Alberta is enacted in the provisions of the Criminal Code. The system of procedure in civil and criminal cases conforms as nearly as possible to the English system. In 1996, 248,296 Criminal Code offences were reported, including 46 homicides.

Education. Schools of all grades are included under the term of public school (including those in the separate school system which are publicly supported). The same board of trustees controls the schools from kindergarten to university entrance. In 1996–97 there were about 0·56m. pupils enrolled in grades 1-12, including private schools and special education programmes.

In 1998 Alberta had 35 post secondary institutions, 4 universities and 2 technical colleges with a total of approximately 80,000 students. The University of Alberta (in Edmonton), organized in 1907, had, in 1996–97, 26,130 full-time students; the University of Calgary, formerly part of the University of Alberta and autonomous from April 1966, had 19,714 and the University of Lethbridge, organized in 1966, had 5,160. The Athabasca University had in 1996–97, 11,689 part-time students.

Further Reading

MacGregor, J. G., *A History of Alberta*. 2nd ed. Edmonton, 1981
Masson, J., *Alberta's Local Governments and their Politics*. Univ. of Alberta Press, 1985
Richards, J., *Prairie Capitalism: Power and Influence in the New West*. Toronto, 1979
Wiebe, R., *Alberta: a Celebration*. Edmonton, 1979

Statistical office: Alberta Treasury, Statistics, Room 259, Terrace Bldg, 9515-107 St., Edmonton, AB T5K 2C3.

BRITISH COLUMBIA

KEY HISTORICAL EVENTS. British Columbia, formerly known as New Caledonia, was first administered by the Hudson's Bay Company. In 1849 Vancouver Island was given crown colony status and in 1853 the Queen Charlotte Islands became a dependency. The discovery of gold on the Fraser river and the following influx of population resulted in the creation in 1858 of the mainland crown colony of British Columbia, to which the Strikine Territory (established 1862) was later added. In 1866 the two colonies were united.

TERRITORY AND POPULATION. British Columbia has an area of 952,263 sq. km. The capital is Victoria. The province is bordered westerly by the Pacific Ocean and Alaska Panhandle, northerly by the Yukon and Northwest Territories, easterly by the Province of Alberta and southerly by the USA along the 49th parallel. A chain of islands, the largest of which are Vancouver Island and the Queen Charlotte Islands, affords protection to the mainland coast.

The 1996 census population was 3,724,500; estimate, July 1997, 3,933,273.

The principal cities and their 1996 census populations are as follows: Metropolitan Vancouver, 1,831,665; Metropolitan Victoria, 304,290; Abbotsford (amalgamated with Matsqui), 105,403; Kelowna, 89,442; Kamloops, 76,394; Prince George, 75,150; Nanaimo, 70,130; Chilliwack, 60,186; Vernon, 31,817; Penticton, 30,987; Mission, 30,519; Campbell River, 28,851; North Cowichan, 25,305; Port Alberni, 18,468; Cranbrook, 18,131.

Vital statistics, *see* CANADA: Territory and Population.

CLIMATE. The climate is cool temperate, but mountain influences affect temperatures and rainfall very considerably. Driest months occur in summer. Vancouver. Jan. 36°F (2·2°C), July 64°F (17·8°C). Annual rainfall 58" (1,458 mm).

CONSTITUTION AND GOVERNMENT. British Columbia (then known as New Caledonia) originally formed part of the Hudson's Bay Company's concession. In 1849 Vancouver Island and in 1858 British Columbia were constituted Crown Colonies; in 1866 the two colonies amalgamated. The British North America Act of 1867 provided for eventual admission into Canadian Confederation, and on 20 July 1871 British Columbia became the sixth province of the Dominion.

British Columbia has a unicameral legislature of 75 elected members. Government policy is determined by the Executive Council responsible to the Legislature. The Lieut.-Governor is appointed by the Governor-General of Canada, usually for a term of 5 years, and is the head of the executive government of the province.

Lieut.-Governor: His Honour the Hon. Garde B. Gardom, QC.

The Legislative Assembly is elected for a maximum term of 5 years. There are 75 electoral districts. Every Canadian citizen 18 years and over, having resided a minimum of 6 months in the province, duly registered, is entitled to vote. The province is represented in the Federal Parliament by 32 members in the House of Commons, and 6 Senators.

At the Legislative Assembly elections of 28 May 1996 the New Democratic Party

(NDP) gained 39% of votes cast and 39 seats, the Liberal Party gained 33 seats, the Reform Party 2 seats and the Progressive Democratic Alliance 1.

The 16-member NDP Executive Council comprised in Jan. 1998:
Premier and President of the Executive Council, and Minister Responsible for Youth: Hon. Glen Clark.
Deputy Premier and Minister of Employment and Investment: Hon. Dan Miller. *Aboriginal Affairs and Labour:* Hon. John Cashore. *Agriculture, Fisheries and Food:* Hon. Corky Evans. *Attorney General and Minister responsible for Multiculturalism, Human Rights and Immigration:* Hon. Ujjal Dosanjh. *Children and Families:* Hon. Penny Priddy. *Education, Skills and Training:* Hon. Paul Ramsey. *Environment, Lands and Parks:* Hon. Cathy McGregor. *Finance and Corporate Relations and Minister responsible for Intergovernmental Relations:* Hon. Andrew Petter. *Forests:* Hon. David Zirnhelt. *Health and Minister responsible for Seniors:* Hon. Joy MacPhail. *Human Resources:* Hon. Dennis Streifel. *Municipal Affairs and Housing:* Hon. Michael Farnsworth. *Small Business, Tourism and Culture:* Hon. Jan Pullinger. *Transportation and Highways:* Hon. Lois Boone. *Women's Equality:* Hon. Sue Hammell.

Local Government. Vancouver City was incorporated by statute and operates under the provisions of the Vancouver Charter of 1953 and amendments. This is the only incorporated area in British Columbia not operating under the provisions of the Municipal Act. Under this Act municipalities are divided into the following classes: *(a)* a village with a population between 500 and 2,500, governed by a council consisting of a mayor and 4 aldermen; *(b)* a town with a population between 2,500 and 5,000, governed by a council consisting of a mayor and 4 aldermen; *(c)* a city where the population exceeds 5,000 governed by a council consisting of a mayor and 6 or 8 aldermen depending on population; *(d)* a district where the area exceeds 810 hectares and the average density is less than 5 persons per hectare, governed by a council consisting of a mayor and 6 or 8 aldermen depending on population; *(e)* an Indian government district.

There are 2 other forms of local government: The Regional District covering a number of areas both incorporated and unincorporated, governed by a board of directors; and the improvement district governed by a board of 3 trustees.

Revenue for municipal services is derived mainly from real-property taxation, although additional revenue is derived from licence fees, business taxes, fines, public utility projects and grants-in-aid from the provincial government.

ECONOMY

Budget. Current provincial revenue and expenditure in $1m. for fiscal years ending 31 March:

	1994-95	1995-96	1996-97[1]	1997-98[2]
Revenue	19,547·3	20,401·6	20,207·0	20,286·0
Expenditure	19,993·7	20,170·0	20,602·0	20,471·0

[1] Forecast. [2] Estimate.

The main sources of current revenue are income taxes, sales taxes, contributions from the federal government, licences and fees, and natural resource taxes and royalties.

The main items of expenditure in 1997–98 (estimate) are as follows: Health, $7,297m.; education, $5,836m.; social services, $2,977·7m.; transportation, $804·9m.; natural resources and economic development, $868·5m.; protection of persons and property, $1,034·7m.; general government, $249·3m.

Banking and Finance. On 31 Dec. 1995, Canadian chartered banks maintained 906 branches and had total assets of $107,674m. in British Columbia. On 31 March 1996, credit unions at 100 locations had total assets of $18,500m. Several foreign banks have Canadian head offices in Vancouver and several others have branches.

ENERGY AND NATURAL RESOURCES

Electricity. Generation in 1996 totalled 70,733m. kWh of which 10,390m. kWh were exported. Available within the province was 74,021m. kWh (with imports 3,289m. kWh).

Minerals. Copper, coal, natural gas, crude oil, gold and molybdenum are the most important minerals produced. The 1996 total of mineral production was estimated at $4,399m. Total value of mineral fuels produced in 1996 was estimated at: Coal, $1,090m.; oil and gas, $1,304m.

Agriculture. Only 2·4m. ha or 4% of the total land area is arable or potentially arable. Farm cash receipts, in 1996, were $1,596m. of which livestock and products $897m., crops, $664m.

Forestry. About 55% of British Columbia's land is productive forest land, with 51·8m. hectares bearing commercial forest. Over 90% of the forest area is owned or administered by the provincial government. The total timber harvest in 1996 was 75·2m. cu. metres. Output of forest-based products, 1996: Lumber, 32·7m. cu. metres; plywood, 1·48m. cu. metres; pulp, 7·3m. tonnes; newsprint, paper and paperboard, 2·82m. tonnes.

Fisheries. In 1996, the total landed value of the catch was $572m., wholesale value $942m.

INDUSTRY AND TRADE

Industry. The value of shipments from all manufacturing industries reached $33,933m. in 1996.

Labour. In 1996 the labour force averaged 1,981,500 persons (898,300 females) with 1,805,800 (820,300) employed, of whom 715,000 were in service industries, 317,000 in trade, 207,000 in manufacturing, 138,000 in transportation and communications, 113,000 in finance, insurance and real estate, 106,000 in public administration, 127,000 in construction, 34,000 in agriculture, 28,000 in forestry, 16,000 in mining and 6,000 in fishing and trapping.

Commerce. Exports of British Columbia origin during 1996 totalled $25,682m. in value, while imports amounted to $19,600m. The USA is the largest market for products exported through British Columbia customs ports ($13,881m. in 1996) followed by Japan ($6,346m.) and South Korea ($866m.).

The leading exports in 1996 were: Wood products, $9,369m.; pulp, $3,407m.; coal, $1,932m.; metallic minerals, $1,594m.; newsprint, $1,284m.

Tourism. In 1996, 28m. tourists spent $6,967m.

COMMUNICATIONS

Roads. In 1995 there were 42,600 km of provincial roads and rights of way in the province, of which 23,300 km were paved. At 31 Dec. 1996, 1·6m. passenger cars and 560,792 commercial vehicles were licensed.

Railways. The province is served by two transcontinental railways, the Canadian Pacific Railway and the Canadian National Railway. Passenger service is provided by VIA Rail, a Crown Corporation and the publicly owned British Columbia Railway. In 1995 the American company Amtrak began operating a service between Seattle and Vancouver after a 14-year hiatus. British Columbia is also served by the freight trains of the B.C. Hydro and Power Authority, the Northern Alberta Railways Company and the Burlington Northern and Southern Railways Inc. The combined route-mileage of mainline track operated by the CPR, CNR and BCR totals 6,800 km. The system also includes CPR and CNR wagon ferry connections to Vancouver Island, between Prince Rupert and Alaska, and interchanges with American railways at southern border points. A metro line was opened in Vancouver in 1986 (29 km). A commuter rail service linking Vancouver and the Fraser Valley was established in 1995 (69 km).

Civil Aviation. International airports are located at Vancouver and Victoria. In 1996, total passenger arrivals and departures on scheduled services at Vancouver were 14m.

and at Victoria, 1m. Daily interprovincial and intraprovincial flights serve all main population centres. Small public and private airstrips are located throughout the province.

Shipping. The major ports are Vancouver, Prince Rupert and the Fraser River. Other coastal harbours include Nanaimo, Port Alberni, Campbell River, Powell River, Kitimat, Stewart and Squamish. Total cargo shipped through the port of Vancouver during 1996 was 72m. tonnes; from the port of Prince Rupert (1995), 11·2m. tonnes. 289 cruise ship voyages with 0·7m. passengers visited Vancouver in 1996.

The British Columbia Ferries connect Vancouver Island with the mainland and also provide service to other coastal points; in fiscal year 1996-97, 22·3m. passengers and 8·2m. vehicles were carried. Service by other ferry systems is also provided between Vancouver Island and the USA. The Alaska State Ferries connect Prince Rupert with centres in Alaska.

Telecommunications. The British Columbia Telephone Company had (1996) approximately 2·4m. telephones in service. In July 1996 there were 130 radio and 11 television stations originating in British Columbia. In addition there were 218 radio and 35 television re-broadcasting stations in the province.

SOCIAL INSTITUTIONS

Justice. The judicial system is composed of the Court of Appeal, the Supreme Court, County Courts, and various Provincial Courts, including Magistrates' Courts and Small Claims Courts. The federal courts include the Supreme Court of Canada and the Federal Court of Canada.

In 1996, 536,547 Criminal Code offences were reported, including 112 homicides.

Education. Education, free up to Grade XII levels, is financed jointly from municipal and provincial government revenues. Attendance is compulsory from the age of 5 to 16. There were approximately 623,317 pupils enrolled in 1,733 public schools from kindergarten to Grade 12 in the 1996-97 school year.

The universities had a full-time enrolment of approximately 68,005 for 1995-96. As of 1 Nov. 1996 they are the University of British Columbia, Vancouver; University of Victoria, Saanich; Simon Fraser University, Burnaby, and the University of Northern British Columbia, Prince George. The regional colleges are Camosun College, Victoria; Capilano College, North Vancouver; Cariboo College, Kamloops; College of New Caledonia, Prince George; Douglas College, New Westminister; East Kootenay Community College, Cranbrook; Fraser Valley College, Chilliwack/Abbotsford; Kwantlen College, Surrey; Malaspina College, Nanaimo; North Island College, Comox; Northern Lights College, Dawson Creek/Fort St John; Northwest Community College, Terrace/Prince Rupert; Okanagan College, Kelowna with branches at Salmon Arm and Vernon; Selkirk College, Castlegar; Vancouver Community College, Vancouver; Langara College, Vancouver. The colleges had a total enrolment of approximately 69,832 for 1995-96.

There are also the British Columbia Institute of Technology, Burnaby; Emily Carr College of Art and Design, Vancouver; Open Learning Institute, Richmond. The institutes had 26,720 persons enrolled in 1995-96. A televised distance education and special programmes through KNOW, the Knowledge Network of the West, is provided.

Health. The Government operates a hospital insurance scheme giving universal coverage after a qualifying period of 3 months' residence in the province. The province has come under a national medicare scheme which is partially subsidized by the provincial government and partially by the federal government.

Further Reading

Barman, J., *The West beyond the West: a History of British Columbia*. Toronto Univ. Press, 1991
Morley, J. T., *The Reins of Power: Governing British Columbia*. Vancouver, 1983

Statistical office: BC STATS, Ministry of Finance and Corporate Relations, Parliament Buildings, Victoria, V8V 1X4.

MANITOBA

KEY HISTORICAL EVENTS. Manitoba was known as the Red River Settlement before it entered the dominion in 1870. During the 18th century its only inhabitants were fur-trappers, but a more settled colonization began in the 19th century. The area was administered by the Hudson's Bay Company until 1869 when it was purchased by the new dominion. In 1870 it was given provincial status. It was enlarged in 1881 and again in 1912 by the addition of part of the North-West Territories.

TERRITORY AND POPULATION. The area of the province is 250,946 sq. miles (649,947 sq. km), of which 211,721 sq. miles are land and 39,225 sq. miles water. From north to south it is 1,225 km and at the widest point it is 793 km.

The 1996 census population was 1,113,898; estimate, July 1997, 1,145,242. Population (estimate 1996) of Winnipeg, the capital, 667,209; other municipalities with over 10,000 inhabitants: Brandon, 39,175; Thompson, 14,385; Portage la Prairie, 13,077; Springfield, 12,162; St Andrews, 10,144.

Vital statistics *see* CANADA: Area and Population.

CLIMATE. The climate is cold continental, with very severe winters but pleasantly warm summers. Rainfall amounts are greatest in the months May to Sept. Winnipeg. Jan. −3°F (−19·3°C), July 67°F (19·6°C). Annual rainfall 21" (539 mm).

CONSTITUTION AND GOVERNMENT. The provincial government is administered by a *Lieut.-Governor* assisted by an *Executive Council* (Cabinet) which is appointed from and responsible to a *Legislative Assembly* of 57 members elected for 5 years. Women were enfranchised in 1916. The Electoral Division Act, 1955, created 57 single-member constituencies and abolished the transferable vote. There are 26 rural electoral divisions, and 31 urban electoral divisions. The province is represented by 6 members in the Senate and 14 in the House of Commons of Canada.

Lieut.-Governor: Yvon Dumont (appointed 1993).

Elections to the Legislative Assembly were held on 25 April 1995. Party standings in autumn 1997: Progressive Conservative Party, 31 seats; New Democratic Party, 23; Liberal Party, 2; Independent,1.

The members of the Progressive Conservative Ministry in Jan. 1998 were:
Premier, President of the Executive Council, Minister of Federal-Provincial Relations: Hon. Gary Albert Filmon.
Deputy-Premier, Minister of Industry, Trade and Tourism: Hon. James Erwin Downey. *Family Services:* Hon. Bonnie Mitchelson. *Natural Resources:* Hon. Glen Cummings. *Education and Training:* Hon. Linda McIntosh. *Culture, Heritage and Citizenship:* Hon. Rosemary Vodrey. *Finance:* Hon. Eric Stefanson. *Highways and Transportation:* Hon. Glen Findlay. *Justice and Attorney General:* Hon. Victor Eric Toews, QC. *Consumer and Corporate Affairs:* Hon. Michael Radcliffe. *Agriculture:* Hon. Harry Enns. *Rural Development:* Hon. Leonard Derkach. *Health:* Hon. Darren Thomas Praznik. *Environment:* Hon. James McCrae. *Labour:* Hon. Harold Gilleshammer. *Urban Affairs and Housing:* Hon. Jack F. Reimer. *Energy and Mines and Northern Affairs:* Hon. David Newman. *Government Services:* Hon. Franklin Pitura.

Local Government. Rural Manitoba is organized into rural municipalities which vary widely in size. Some have only 4 townships (a township is 6 sq. miles), while the largest has 22 townships. The province has 117 rural municipalities, as well as 40 incorporated towns, 38 incorporated villages and 5 incorporated cities.

On 1 Jan. 1972, the cities and towns comprising the metropolitan area of Winnipeg were amalgamated to form the City of Winnipeg. A mayor and council are elected to a central government, but councillors also sit on 'community committees' which represent the areas or wards they serve. These committees are advised by non-elected residents of the area on provision of municipal services within the community committee jurisdiction. Taxing powers and overall budgeting rest with the central council. The mayor is elected at the same time as the councillors in a city-wide vote. Revisions to the City of Winnipeg Act came into effect with the municipal elections held in Oct. 1977.

Since Jan. 1945, 17 Local Government Districts were formed in the less densely populated areas of the province. In 1997, only two remained. They are administered by a provincially appointed person, who acts on the advice of locally elected councils.

In the extreme north, many communities have locally elected councils, while others are administered directly by the Department of Northern Affairs. This department provides most of the funding in all these northern settlements.

FINANCE. Provincial revenue and expenditure (current account, excluding capital expenditures) for fiscal years ending 31 March (in Canadian $1m.):

	1992–93	1993–94	1994–95	1995–96	1996–97[1]
Revenue	4,697	4,862	5,193	5,512	5,438
Expenditure	5,177	5,064	5,080	5,173	5,088

[1] Forecast.

ENERGY AND NATURAL RESOURCES

Electricity. In the year ending 31 March 1997, 31,800m. kWh of electricity was generated. The Manitoba Hydro System (generating capacity about 5 MW), owned by the province, produced 30,800m. kWh, of which 19,000m. kWh was delivered to its 391,000 customers in 1996-97. The city-owned Winnipeg Hydro (generating capacity about 0·8m. kWh) produced about 1m. kWh and also bought power from Manitoba Hydro to serve its 96,000 customers.

Oil. Crude oil production in 1996 was valued at $107m.

Minerals. Total value of mineral production in 1996 was about $1,020m. Principal minerals mined are nickel, zinc, copper, gold, and small quantities of silver.

Agriculture. Rich farmland is the main primary resource, although the area in farms is only about 14% of the total land area. In 1996 the total value of agricultural production was $2,800m., with more than $1,600m. from crops and more than $1,100m. from livestock; 22,456 census farms reported total gross farm receipts of $2,500 or more.

Forestry. About 51% of the land area is wooded, of which 334,460 sq. km is productive forest land. In 1995-96, about 140 primary wood producers with 2,200 direct employees were responsible for $440m. in shipments, including $300m. in export sales.

Fur Trade. The value of fur production to the trapper was $3·7m in the year ending 31 Aug. 1997; the estimated overall contribution of trapping to the provincial economy was about $20m.

Fisheries. From 57,000 sq. km of rivers and lakes, the value of fisheries production to fishers was about $23m. in 1995–96. Whitefish, sauger, pickerel and pike are the principal varieties of fish caught.

INDUSTRY AND TRADE

Industry. Goods producing industries accounted for about 25% of GDP in 1996, led by manufacturing at 11% or about $9,000m. Of this, food and beverages produced over $2,000m.; transport equipment (primarily aerospace parts and buses), $1,200m. and machinery (mainly farm equipment), $1,000m. worth of shipments. Manufacturing employed 68,000 people in Sept. 1997. Commercial services represented about 52% of GDP in 1996, led by the financial sector at 21%.

Labour. In 1996 the labour force was 568,200 (256,400 females), of whom 525,500 (237,300) were employed.

Trade. Products grown and manufactured in Manitoba find ready markets in other parts of Canada, in the USA, particularly the upper midwest region, and in other countries. Export shipments to foreign countries from Manitoba in 1996 were valued at $6,000m.

Tourism. In 1996, non-Manitoban tourists numbered an estimated 1·7m. Tourism contributed an estimated $1,100m. to the economy in 1996.

COMMUNICATIONS

Roads. Highways and provincial roads totalled 18,500 km, with 2,800 bridges and other structures, in 1997. In 1994 there were 796,368 motor vehicles registered, including 556,752 passenger cars.

Railways. In 1997 the province had about 4,350 km of commercial track, not including industrial track, yards and sidings. Canadian Pacific owns about 1,950 km and Canadian National about 2,400 km.

Civil Aviation. In 1997 a total of 96 licensed commercial air services operated from bases in Manitoba, as well as 16 regularly scheduled major national and international airlines.

Telecommunications. The Manitoba System provided service to over 475,000 individual customers in Sept. 1997.

SOCIAL INSTITUTIONS

Justice. In 1996, 121,167 Criminal Code offences were reported, including 37 homicides.

Education. Education is controlled through locally elected school divisions. There were 209,435 children enrolled in the province's nursery, kindergarten, elementary, secondary, independent (private) and home school system in the 1996–97 school year. The ratio of teachers to students in Sept. 1997 averaged 1:18·9. Manitoba has 4 universities with an enrolment (full- and part-time) of about 30,000 for the 1997–98 year; the University of Manitoba, founded in 1877, in Winnipeg, the University of Winnipeg, Brandon University and Collegiate University of Saint Boniface. Expenditure (estimate) on education in the 1996–97 fiscal year was $1,000m.

Community colleges, in Brandon, The Pas and Winnipeg, offer 2-year diploma courses in a number of fields, as well as specialized training in many trades. They also give a large number and variety of shorter courses, both at their campuses and in many communities throughout the province.

Further Reading

General Information: Inquiries may be addressed to Information Services, Room 29, Legislative Building, 450 Broadway, Winnipeg, R3C 0V8.The Department of Agriculture publishes: *Year Book of Manitoba Agriculture*
Manitoba Statistical Review. Manitoba Bureau of Statistics, Quarterly

Jackson, J. A., *The Centennial History of Manitoba.* Toronto, 1970
Morton, W. L., *Manitoba: A History.* Univ. of Toronto Press, 1967

NEW BRUNSWICK

KEY HISTORICAL EVENTS. Visited by Jacques Cartier in 1534, New Brunswick was first explored by Samuel de Champlain in 1604. With Nova Scotia, it originally formed one French colony called Acadia. It was ceded by the French in the Treaty of Utrecht in 1713 and became a permanent British possession in 1759. It was first settled by British colonists in 1764 and was separated from Nova Scotia and became a province in June 1784 as a result of the great influx of United Empire Loyalists. Responsible government came into being in 1848, and consisted of an executive council, a legislative council (later abolished) and a House of Assembly.

TERRITORY AND POPULATION. The area of the province is 28,354 sq.

miles (73,440 sq. km), of which 27,834 sq. miles (72.090 sq. km) is land area. The population at the 1996 census was 738,133; estimate, July 1997, 762,049. Of the individuals identifying a single ethnic origin (at the 1991 census), 33% were British and 32·8% French. Other significant ethnic groups were German, Dutch and Scandinavian. Among those who provided a multiple response 9·2% were of British and French descent and 5·4% British and other. In 1991 there were 11,835 Native People or Native People and other. Census 1996 population of urban centres: Saint John, 125,705; Moncton, 113,491; Fredericton (capital), 78,950; Bathurst, 25,415; Edmundston, 22,624; Campbellton, 16,867. The official languages are English and French.

Vital statistics *see* CANADA: Territory and Population.

CLIMATE. A cool temperate climate, with rain at all seasons but temperatures modified by the influence of the Gulf Stream. Saint John. Jan. 18°F (−7·8°C), July 62°F (16·7°C). Annual rainfall 57" (1,444·4 mm).

CONSTITUTION AND GOVERNMENT. The government is vested in a Lieut.-Governor and a Legislative Assembly of 55 members each of whom is individually elected to represent the voters in one constituency or riding. A simultaneous translation system is used in the Assembly. Any Canadian subject of full age and 6 months' residence is entitled to vote. The last provincial election was held on 11 Sept. 1995. As of Nov. 1997, the Legislative Assembly consists of 47 Liberals, 7 Progressive Conservatives, and 1 from the New Democratic Party. The province has 10 members in the Canadian Senate and 10 members in the federal House of Commons.

Lieut.-Governor: Hon. Dr Marilyn Trenholme Counsell (appointed April 1997).

The members of the Liberal government were as follows in Jan. 1998:
Premier, President of Executive Council: Hon. J. Raymond Frenette.
Justice, Attorney General: Hon. James Lockyer. *Finance:* Hon. Edmond Blanchard. *Supply and Services:* Hon. Peter LeBlanc. *Transportation:* Hon. Sheldon Lee. *Natural Resources and Energy:* Hon. Alan Graham. *Agriculture:* Hon. Doug Tyler. *Health and Community Services:* Hon. Russell King, MD. *Human Resources Development:* Hon. Marcelle Mersereau. *Advanced Education and Labour:* Hon. Roland MacIntyre. *Education:* Hon. Bernard Richard. *Municipalities, Culture and Housing:* Hon. Ann Breault. *Environment:* Hon. Joan Kingston. *Economic Development and Tourism:* Hon. Camille Thériault. *Fisheries and Aquaculture:* Hon. Danny Gay. *Solicitor General:* Hon. Jane Barry. *Minister Responsible for the Regional Development Corporation and Northern Development:* Hon. Jean Paul Savoie.

Local Government. Under the reforms introduced in 1967 the province has assumed complete administrative and financial responsibility for education, health, welfare and administration of justice. Local government is now restricted to provision of services of a strictly local nature. Under the new municipal structure, units include existing and new cities, towns and villages. Counties have disappeared as municipal units. Areas with limited populations have become local service districts. The former local improvement districts have become towns, villages or local service districts depending on their size.

FINANCE. The ordinary budget (in Canadian $1m.) is shown as follows (financial years ended 31 March):

	1994	1995	1996	1997
Gross revenue	4,022·9	4,300·0	4,426·3	4,470·5
Gross expenditure	4,272·9	4,368·6	4,375·1	4,345·1

Funded debt and capital loans outstanding (exclusive of Treasury Bills) as of 31 March 1997 was $6,472·5m. Sinking funds held by the province at 31 March 1997, $2,304·9m. The ordinary budget excludes capital spending.

ENERGY AND NATURAL RESOURCES

Electricity. Hydro-electric, thermal and nuclear generating stations of NB Power had an installed capacity of 4,116 MW at 31 March 1997, consisting of 15 generating stations. The Mactaquac hydroelectric development near Fredericton has a name plate capacity of 672 MW. The largest thermal generating station, Coleson Cove, near Saint John, has 1,006 MW of installed capacity. Atlantic Canada's first nuclear generating station, a 635 MW plant on a promontory in the Bay of Fundy, near Saint John, went into operation in 1983. New Brunswick is electrically inter-connected with utilities in neighbouring provinces of Quebec, Nova Scotia and Prince Edward Island, as well as the New England States of the USA. The sale of out-of-province power accounted for 17% of revenue in 1996–97. Total revenue amounted to $1,037·1m.

Minerals. In 1996, approximately 15 different metals, minerals and commodities were produced. These included lead, zinc, copper, cadmium, bismuth, gold, silver, antimony, potash, salt, lime, stone, coal, sand and gravel, peat and marl. The total value of minerals produced in 1996 reached $924·8m. The top 3 contributors to mineral production are zinc, silver and lead, accounting for 58·2% of total value in 1996. In Canada in 1996, New Brunswick ranked first in the production of zinc, second in lead and silver, and fourth in the production of copper. Not all of the province's minerals have been explored sufficiently and research continues. The Geological Survey of Canada and the New Brunswick Department of Natural Resources and Energy plan to commit $6·8m. over 5 years in exploration of the eastern part of the province.

Agriculture. The total area under crops is estimated at 135,008 ha. Farms numbered 3,405 and averaged 129 ha each (census 1996). Potatoes account for 22·3% of total farm cash income. Mixed farming is common throughout the province. Dairy farming is centred around the larger urban areas, and is located mainly along the Saint John River Valley and in the south-eastern sections of the province. Income from dairy products provides 19·9% of farm cash income. New Brunswick is self-sufficient in fluid milk and supplies a processing industry. For particulars of agricultural production and livestock, *see* CANADA: Agriculture. Farm cash receipts in 1996 were $317·9m.

Forestry. New Brunswick contains some 61,000 sq. km of productive forest lands. The value of manufacturing shipments for the wood related industries in 1996 was $3,066·9m., representing 36·2% of total shipments in the province. The paper and allied industry group is the largest component of the industry, contributing 64·7% of forestry output. In 1996 wood industries employed about 16,022 people for all aspects of the forest industry, including harvesting, processing and transportation. Practically all forest products are exported from the province's numerous ports and harbours near which many of the mills are located or sent by road or rail to the USA.

Fisheries. Commercial fishing is one of the most important primary industries of the province, in 1996 employing 7,757. Nearly 50 commercial species of fish and shellfish are landed, including scallop, shrimp, crab, herring and cod. Landings in 1996 (106,818 tonnes) amounted to $145·1m. In 1997 there were 114 fish processing plants employing an average of 6,509 people. In 1996 molluscs and crustaceans ranked first with a value of $122·7m., 84·6% of the total landed value; pelagic fish second, 13·1%, and groundfish third, 1·9%. Exports (1996) $416·1m., mainly to the USA and Japan.

INDUSTRY. In 1997 there were 1,443 manufacturing and processing establishments, employing on average 43,700 persons. New Brunswick's location, with deepwater harbours open throughout the year and container facilities at Saint John, makes it ideal for exporting. Industries include food and beverages, paper and allied industries, and timber products. Nearly 20% of the industrial labour force work in Saint John.

Labour. In 1996 the labour force was 354,100 (160,800 females), of whom 312,800 (143,800) were employed.

Tourism. Tourism is one of the leading contributors to the economy. In 1996, tourism revenues reached $705m.

COMMUNICATIONS

Roads. There are 1,541·9 km of arterial highways and 2,381·7 km of collector roads, all hard-surfaced, and 12,279·9 km of local roads provide access to most areas. The main highway system, including 596·4 km of the Trans-Canada Highway, links the province with the principal roads in Quebec, Nova Scotia, and Prince Edward Island, as well as the Interstate Highway System in the eastern seaboard states of the USA. Passenger vehicles, 31 March 1997, numbered 326,398; commercial vehicles, 184,244; motor cycles, 9,349.

Railways. New Brunswick is served by main lines of both Canadian Pacific and Canadian National railways.

Telecommunications. In 1995 the New Brunswick Telephone Co. Ltd had 527,317 access lines in service. The province is served by 28 radio stations, of which 3 are owned by the Canadian Broadcasting Corporation and 3 are university stations. 10 stations broadcast in French, 3 are bilingual. The province is served by 7 television stations, 2 of which broadcast in French.

Press. New Brunswick had (1997) 4 daily newspapers, 1 in French, and 18 weekly newspapers, 3 in French and 3 bilingual.

SOCIAL INSTITUTIONS

Justice. In 1996, 50,950 Criminal Code offences were reported, including 8 homicides.

Education. Public education is free and non-sectarian. There are 4 universities. The University of New Brunswick at Fredericton (founded 13 Dec. 1785 by the Loyalists, elevated to university status in 1823, reorganized as the University of New Brunswick in 1859) had 7,905 full-time students at the Fredericton campus and 1,969 full-time students at the Saint John campus (1996–97); Mount Allison University at Sackville had 2,209 full-time students; the Université de Moncton at Moncton, 3,751 full-time students, with 408 and 624 full-time students respectively at its satellite campuses at Shippegan and Edmundston; St Thomas University at Fredericton, 1,897 full-time students.

There were, in Sept. 1996, 133,276 students (including kindergarten) and 7,903 full-time equivalent/professional educational staff in the province's 376 schools. There are 18 school districts.

Further Reading

Industrial Information: Dept. of Economic Development and Tourism, Fredericton. *Economic Information:* Dept. of Finance, New Brunswick Statistics Agency, Fredericton. *General Information:* Communications New Brunswick, Fredericton.

Thompson, C., *New Brunswick Inside Out.* Ottawa, 1977
Trueman, S., *The Fascinating World of New Brunswick.* Fredericton, 1973

NEWFOUNDLAND AND LABRADOR

KEY HISTORICAL EVENTS. Archaeological finds at L'Anse-au-Meadow in northern Newfoundland show that the Vikings established a colony there at about AD 1000. This site is the only known Viking colony in North America. Newfoundland was discovered by John Cabot on 24 June 1497, and was soon frequented in the summer months by the Portuguese, Spanish and French for its fisheries. It was formally occupied in Aug. 1583 by Sir Humphrey Gilbert on behalf of the English Crown, but various attempts to colonize the island remained unsuccessful. Although British sovereignty was recognized in 1713 by the Treaty of Utrecht, disputes over fishing rights with the French were not finally settled till 1904.

By the Anglo-French Convention of 1904, France renounced her exclusive fishing rights along part of the coast, granted under the Treaty of Utrecht, but retained sovereignty of the offshore islands of St Pierre and Miquelon.

Self-governing from 1855, the colony remained out of the Canadian confederation in 1867 and continued to govern itself until 1934, when a commission of government appointed by the British Crown assumed responsibility for governing the colony and Labrador. This body controlled the country until union with Canada in 1949.

TERRITORY AND POPULATION. Area, 143,501 sq. miles (371,690 sq. km) of which freshwater, 13,139 sq. miles (34,030 sq. km). In March 1927 the Privy Council decided the boundary between Canada and Newfoundland in Labrador. This area, now part of the Province of Newfoundland and Labrador, is 102,699 sq. miles. The coastline is extremely irregular. Bays, fiords and inlets are numerous and there are many good harbours with deep water close to shore. The coast is rugged with bold rocky cliffs from 200 to 400 ft high; in the Bay of Islands some of the islands rise 500 ft, with the adjacent shore 1,000 ft above tide level. The interior is a plateau of moderate elevation and the chief relief features trend north-east and south-west. Long Range, the most notable of these, begins at Cape Ray and extends north-east for 200 miles, the highest peak reaching 2,673 ft. Approximately one-third of the area is covered by water. Grand Lake, the largest body of water, has an area of about 200 sq. miles. The principal rivers flow towards the north-east. On the borders of the lakes and water-courses good land is generally found, particularly in the valleys of the Terra Nova River, the Gander River, the Exploits River and the Humber River, which are also heavily timbered.

Census population, 1996, was 551,792; estimate, July 1997, 563,641.

The capital of Newfoundland is the City of St John's (1991 population, 171,859, metropolitan area). The other cities are Mt Pearl (23,689), Corner Brook (22,410); important towns are Conception Bay South (17,590), Grand Falls-Windsor (14,693), Gander (10,339), Labrador City (9,061), Happy Valley–Goose Bay (8,610), Stephenville (7,621), Marystown (6,739), Channel-Port aux Basques (5,644), Bay Roberts (5,474), Carbonear (5,259).

Vital statistics *see* CANADA: Territory and Population.

CLIMATE. The cool temperate climate is marked by heavy precipitation, distributed evenly over the year, a cool summer and frequent fogs in spring. St. John's. Jan. –4°C, July 15·8°C. Annual rainfall 1,240 mm.

CONSTITUTION AND GOVERNMENT. Until 1832 Newfoundland was ruled by the Governor under instructions of the Colonial Office. In that year a Legislature was brought into existence, but the Governor and his Executive Council were not responsible to it. Under the constitution of 1855, which lasted until its suspension in 1934, the government was administered by the Governor appointed by the Crown with an Executive Council responsible to the House of Assembly of 27 elected members and a Legislative Council of 24 members nominated for life by the Governor in Council. Women were enfranchised in 1925. At the Imperial Conference of 1917 Newfoundland was constituted as a Dominion.

In 1933 the financial situation had become so critical that the Government of Newfoundland asked the Government of the UK to appoint a Royal Commission to investigate conditions. On the strength of their recommendations, the parliamentary form of government was suspended and Government by Commission was inaugurated on 16 Feb. 1934.

A National Convention, elected in 1946, made, in 1948, recommendations to H. M. Government in Great Britain as to the possible forms of future government to be submitted to the people at a national referendum. Two referenda were held. In the first referendum (June 1948) the three forms of government submitted to the people were: Commission of government for 5 years, confederation with Canada and responsible government as it existed in 1933. No one form of government received a clear majority of the votes polled, and commission of government, receiving the fewest votes, was eliminated. In the second referendum (July 1948) confederation with Canada received 78,408 and responsible government 71,464 votes.

In the Canadian Senate on 18 Feb. 1949 Royal assent was given to the terms of union of Newfoundland and Labrador with Canada, and on 23 March 1949, in the House of Lords, London, Royal assent was given to an amendment to the British North America Act made necessary by the inclusion of Newfoundland and Labrador as the tenth Province of Canada.

Under the terms of union of Newfoundland and Labrador with Canada, which was signed at Ottawa on 11 Dec. 1948, the constitution of the Legislature of Newfoundland and Labrador as it existed immediately prior to 16 Feb. 1934 shall, subject to the terms of the British North America Acts, 1867 to 1946, continue as the constitution of the Legislature of the Province of Newfoundland and Labrador until altered under the authority of the said Acts.

The franchise was in 1965 extended to all male and female residents who have attained the age of 19 years and are otherwise qualified as electors.

The House of Assembly (Amendment) Act, 1979, established 52 electoral districts and 52 members of the Legislature.

Elections were held on 3 May 1993. In Nov. 1994 there were 35 Liberals, 16 Progressive-Conservatives and 1 New Democrat.

The province is represented by 6 members in the Senate and by 7 members in the House of Commons of Canada.

Lieut.-Governor: Hon. Frederick William Russell (assumed office 5 Nov. 1991).

The Liberal Executive Council was, in Jan. 1998, composed as follows:
Premier: Brian Tobin.

Development and Rural Renewal: Beaton Tulk. *Education:* Roger Grimes. *Environment and Labour:* Oliver Langdon. *Finance:* Paul Dicks. *Fisheries and Aquaculture:* John Efford. *Forest Resources and Agrifoods:* Kevin Aylward. *Government Services and Lands:* Ernest McLean. *Health:* Joan Aylward. *Human Resources and Employment:* Julie Bettney. *Industry, Trade and Technology:* Judy Foote. *Justice:* Chris Decker. *Municipal and Provincial Affairs:* Arthur Reid. *Tourism, Culture and Recreation:* Sandra Kelly. *Works, Services and Transportation:* Lloyd Matthews.

FINANCE. Budget in Canadian $1,000 for fiscal years ended 31 March:
Current account:

	1992–93	1993–94	1994–95[1]	1995–96[2]
Gross revenue	3,044,401	3,071,526	3,243,602	3,398,268
Gross expenditure	3,124,001	3,125,222	3,218,471	3,270,412

[1] Revised estimates.   [2] Estimates.

Capital account:

	1992–93	1993–94	1994–95[1]	1991–92[2]
Gross revenue	149,215	86,920	149,841	146,892
Gross expenditure	330,664	238,474	311,275	272,804

[1] Revised estimates. [2] Estimates.

Public debenture debt as at 31 March 1995 (estimate) was $5,623m.; sinking fund, $1,538m.

ENERGY AND NATURAL RESOURCES

Electricity. The electrical energy requirements of the province are met mainly by hydro-electric power, with petroleum fuels being utilized to provide the balance. The total amount of energy generated in the province in 1993 was 40,849,949 MWh, of which 96% was derived from hydro-electric facilities. The greater part of the energy produced in 1993 came from Churchill Falls, of which 29,942,214 MWh was sold to Hydro-Quebec under the terms of a long-term contract. Energy consumed in the province during 1993 totalled 10,907,775 MWh, with 9,251,443 MWh, or 85%, coming from hydro-electric facilities.

At Dec. 1994 total electrical generating capacity in the province was 7,343 MW, with hydro-electric plants accounting for 6,601 MW, or 90%. It is estimated that potential additional hydro-electric generating capacity of up to 4·5m. kW can be developed at various sites in Labrador.

Oil. Since 1965, 140 wells have been drilled on the Continental Margin of the Province. Only the Hibernia discovery had commercial capability with production starting in the early 1990's. In Sept. 1990 the governments of Canada and Newfoundland and a development consortium signed an agreement to start developing the Hibernia discovery from Oct. 1990.

Minerals. The mineral resources are vast but only partially documented. Large deposits of iron ore, with an ore reserve of over 5,000m. tons at Labrador City, Wabush City and in the Knob Lake area are supplying approximately half of Canada's production. Other large deposits of iron ore are known to exist in the Julienne Lake area. There are a variety of other minerals being produced in more limited amounts. The Central Mineral Belt, which extends from the Smallwood Reservoir to the Atlantic coast near Makkovik, holds uranium, copper, beryllium and molybdenite potential.

There is a gold mine at Hope Brook on the south coast east of Port aux Basques.

In 1994, a rich nickel, copper and cobalt discovery was made at Voisey's Bay, Labrador, with defined reserves of 31·7m. tonnes. Production in 1994 (preliminary): Iron ore, 20·9m. tonnes ($747,038,000); gold, 2,799,360 grammes ($47,219,000); sand and gravel, 3,128,000 tonnes ($14,202,000); stone, ($5,939,000); cement, 56,882 tonnes ($7,395,000); dolomite, 267,145 tonnes ($2,885,000).

Agriculture. The estimated value of agricultural products sold, including livestock, 1994, was $62·2m. In 1996, 573 census farms reported total gross farm receipts of $2,500 or more.

Forestry. The forestry economy in the province is mainly dependent on the operation of 3 newsprint mills. In 1994 the gross value of newsprint exported from these 3 mills totalled $472m. Lumber mills and saw-log operations produced 57m. flat bd ft in 1994–95.

Fisheries. The principal fish landings are cod, flounder, redfish, Queen crabs, lobster, salmon and herring. In 1994 (preliminary) a yearly average of some 2,800 persons were employed by the fish-processing industry and there were 22,045 licensed full-, part-time and casual fishermen engaged in harvesting operations. 207 processing operations were licensed in 1994. The production of fresh and frozen fish products was $490m. in 1994.

The total catch in 1993 was 245,942 tonnes valued at $197,125,873, including (in tonnes): Cod, 37,177 ($24,771,725); flounders and soles, 22,128 ($8,863,274); herring, 21,355 ($3,012,684); redfish, 26,284 ($7,253,497); capelin, 48,469 ($19,298,947); crab, 23,160 ($32,058,472); other, 41,612 ($31,499,911).

INDUSTRY. The total value of manufacturing shipments in 1993 was $1,324m. This consists largely of first-stage processing of primary resource products with two of the largest components being paper and fish products.

Labour. In 1996 the labour force was 235,500 (102,900 females) of whom 189,700 (85,600) were employed.

Trade Unions. There were 35 unions in 1993 representing 75,627 members of international and national unions and government employee associations.

COMMUNICATIONS

Roads. In 1993 there were 8,895 km, of which 6,356 were paved. In 1994 there were 322,652 motor vehicles registered, including 216,760 passenger cars.

Railways. In 1993 the Quebec North Shore and Labrador Railway operated 576 km of standard-gauge main railway track. The route runs from Sept-Iles, Quebec, to Shefferville, Quebec, with a branch at Ross Bay Junction to Wabush, Labrador. In 1995, 22m. tonnes of freight were carried.

Civil Aviation. The province is linked to the rest of Canada by regular air services provided by Air Canada, Canadian International Airways, Quebecair and a number of smaller air carriers.

Shipping. At 21 Dec. 1995 there were 1,624 ships on register in Newfoundland. In 1993 Marine Atlantic provided a freight and passenger service all year round to the south of the island and during the ice-free season as far north as Nain. There is a year-round ferry from Port-aux-Basques to North Sydney, Nova Scotia, and seasonal ferries connect Argentia with North Sydney, and Lewisporte with Goosebay, Labrador.

Telecommunications. There were 430 post offices in 1995. Telephone access lines numbered 262,856 in 1993 (193,987 private). There were 3,384 public pay phones.

SOCIAL INSTITUTIONS

Justice. In 1996, 33,828 Criminal Code offences were reported, including 7 homicides.

Education. The number of schools in 1994–95 was 479. The enrolment was 114,010; full-time teachers numbered 7,331. The Memorial University, offering courses in arts, science, engineering, education, nursing and medicine, had 17,226 full- and part-time students in 1994 (calendar year). Total expenditure for education by the Government in 1995–96 (estimate) was $716m.

Further Reading

Horwood, H., *Newfoundland.* Toronto, 1969
Perlin, A. B., *The Story of Newfoundland, 1497–1959.* St John's, 1959
Taylor, T. G., *Newfoundland: A Study of Settlement.* Toronto, 1946

Statistical office: Newfoundland Statistics Agency, POB 8700, St. John's, A1B 4J6.

NOVA SCOTIA

KEY HISTORICAL EVENTS. Nova Scotia was visited by John and Sebastian Cabot in 1497-98. In 1605 a number of French colonists settled at Port Royal. The old name of the colony, Acadia, was changed in 1621 to Nova Scotia. The French were granted possession of the colony by the Treaty of St-Germain-en-Laye (1632). In 1654 Oliver Cromwell sent a force to occupy the settlement. Charles II, by the Treaty of Breda (1667), restored Nova Scotia to the French. It was finally ceded to the British by the Treaty of Utrecht in 1713.

In the Treaty of Paris (1763) France resigned all claim, and in 1820 Cape Breton Island united with Nova Scotia. Representative government was granted as early as 1758 and a fully responsible legislative assembly was established in 1848. In 1867 the province entered the dominion of Canada.

TERRITORY AND POPULATION. The area of the province is 21,425 sq. miles (55,000 sq. km), of which 20,401 sq. miles are land area, 1,024 sq. miles water area. The population (census 1996) was 909,282; estimate (July 1997) 947,917.

Population of the principal cities (census 1996): Halifax, 113,910; Dartmouth, 65,629. Principal towns (census 1996): Bedford, 13,638; Truro, 11,938; New Glasgow, 9,812; Amherst, 9,669; Yarmouth, 7,568; Bridgewater, 7,351; Kentville, 5,551.

Vital statistics, *see* CANADA: Territory and Population.

CLIMATE. A cool temperate climate, with rainfall occurring evenly over the year. The Gulf Stream moderates the temperatures in winter so that ports remain ice-free. Halifax. Jan. 23·7°F (–4·6°C), July 63·5°F (17·5°C). Annual rainfall 54" (1,371 mm).

CONSTITUTION AND GOVERNMENT. Under the British North America Act of 1867 the legislature of Nova Scotia may exclusively make laws in relation to local matters, including direct taxation within the province, education and the administration of justice. The legislature of Nova Scotia consists of a Lieut.-Governor, appointed and paid by the federal government, and holding office for 5 years, and a House of Assembly of 52 members, chosen by popular vote at least every 5 years. The province is represented in the Canadian Senate by 10 members, and in the House of Commons by 11.

The franchise and eligibility to the legislature are granted to every person, male or female, if of age (19 years), a British subject or Canadian citizen, and a resident in the province for 1 year and 2 months before the date of the writ of election in the county or electoral district of which the polling district forms part, and if not by law otherwise disqualified. State of the parties in Nov. 1997: 39 Liberals, 9 Progressive Conservatives, 4 New Democrats.

Lieut.-Governor: Hon. John James Kinley.

The members of the Liberal Ministry were as follows in Jan. 1998:

Premier, President of the Executive Council, Minister of Intergovernmental Affairs, Minister responsible for Aboriginal Affairs and for Sable Offshore Resources: Hon. Russell MacLellan, QC.

Deputy Premier, Deputy President of the Executive Council, Minister of Finance, Minister responsible for the administration of Part I of the Gaming Control Act: Hon. J. William Gillis. *Economic Development and Tourism, Chair of the Priorities and Planning Committee, Minister responsible for Communications Nova Scotia, for the Innovation Corporation Act, for the Business Development Corporation Act, for the Nova Scotia Marketing Agency and for the Sydney Steel Corporation Act:* Hon. Manning MacDonald. *Health:* Hon. James A. Smith. *Transportation and Public Works:* Hon. Donald R. Downe. *Environment, Minister responsible for the Emergency Measures Act and for the Nova Scotia Boxing Authority:* Hon. F. Wayne Adams. *Education and Culture:* Hon. Robert S. Harrison. *Housing and Municipal Affairs, Minister in charge of the administration of the Heritage Property Act:* Hon. Guy A. C. Brown. *Fisheries and Aquaculture:* Hon. James A. Barkhouse. *Labour, Minister responsible for the Workers' Compensation Act:* Hon. Gerald J. O'Malley. *Human Resources, Minister responsible for Acadian Affairs and for the administration of the Youth Secretariat Act:* Hon. Allister Surette. *Attorney General and Justice, Minister responsible for the administration of the Human Rights Act, Minister in charge of the Regulations Act:* Hon. Alan E. Mitchell. *Business and Consumer Services, Minister in charge of the Residential Tenancies Act:* Hon. Wayne Gaudet. *Agriculture and Marketing, Minister responsible for the administration of Part II of the Gaming Control Act and for the administration of the Liquor Control Act:* Hon. Edward Lorraine. *Natural Resources:* Hon. Kenneth MacAskill. *Community Services, Minister responsible for the administration of the Advisory Council on the Status of Women Act and for the Disabled Persons Commission Act, Chair of the Senior Citizens Secretariat:* Hon. Francene Cosman. *Minister respon-sible for the Technology and Science Secretariat and for the Nova Scotia Sport and Recreation Commission:* Hon. Bruce Holland.

Local Government. In 1995 the new Cape Breton Regional Municipality was formed to amalgamate the former City of Sydney, the rural municipality of Cape Breton and 6 towns within the county. On 1 April 1996 a new Regional Municipality of Halifax incorporated the cities of Halifax and Dartmouth, the town of Bedford and the rural municipality of Halifax County. The other main divisions of the province for governmental purposes are 32 towns and 22 rural municipalities, each governed by a council and a mayor or warden. The cities have independent charters, and the various towns take their powers from and are limited by The Towns Act, and the various municipalities take their powers from and are limited by The Municipal Act as revised in 1967. The majority of municipalities comprise 1 county, but 6 counties are divided into 2 municipalities each. In no case do the boundaries of any municipality overlap county lines. The 18 counties as such have no administrative function.

Any incorporated town (of which there are 32) that lies within the boundaries of a municipality is excluded from any jurisdiction by the municipal council and has its own government.

FINANCE. Revenue is derived from provincial sources, payments from the federal government under the Federal-Provincial Fiscal Arrangements and Established Programs Financing Act. Recoveries consist generally of amounts received under various federal cost-shared programmes. Main sources of provincial revenues include income and sales taxes.

Revenue, expenditure and debt (in $1,000) for fiscal years ending 31 March:

	1996-97[1]	1997-98[2]	1997-98[3]
Ordinary Revenue	4,246,000	4,240,674	4,240,674
Net Programme Expenditures	3,550,528	3,509,422	3,549,437
Net Current Account	3,347,486	3,305,270	3,348,385
Restructuring Costs	35,600	31,510	31,510
Net Capital Account	167,442	172,642	169,542
Debt Servicing Costs	811,100	855,200	818,400
–Sinking Fund Earnings	123,900	127,900	128,300
Net Debt Servicing Costs	687,200	727,300	690,100

[1] Actual. [2] Estimate. [3] Forecast.

Banking and Finance. In the fourth quarter of 1995 total deposits with chartered banks totalled $7,951m.

NATURAL RESOURCES

Minerals. Principal minerals in 1996 were: Coal, 3·1m. tonnes, valued at $183m.; gypsum, 6·9m. tonnes, valued at $70·9m.; sand and gravel, 3·3m. tonnes, valued at $12·7m. Total value of mineral production in 1996 was $597·5m.

Agriculture. Dairying, poultry and egg production, livestock and fruit growing are the most important branches. Farm cash receipts for 1996 were estimated at $353·4m., with an additional $4·3m. going to persons on farms as income in kind. Cash receipts from sale of dairy products were $85·9m., with total milk and cream sales of 168,987,000 litres.

The production of poultry meat in 1996 was 28,912 tonnes, of which 26,531 tonnes were chickens and 2,381 tonnes were turkeys. Egg production was 17·1m. dozen.

The main 1996 fruit crops were apples, 48,263 tonnes; blueberries, 13,497 tonnes; strawberries, 2,320 tonnes.

Forestry. The estimated forest area of Nova Scotia is 15,830 sq. miles (40,990 sq. km), of which about 28% is owned by the province. The principal trees are spruce, balsam fir, hemlock, pine, larch, birch, oak, maple, poplar and ash. 5,608,000 cu. metres of round forest products were produced in 1996.

Fisheries. The fisheries of the province in 1995 had a landed value of $484m. of sea fish including scallop fishery, $79·2m., and lobster fishery, $194·9m. In 1995 there were 7,300 employees in the fish processing industry; the value of shipment of goods was $762m. in 1995.

INDUSTRY. The number of manufacturing establishments was 668 in 1994; the number of employees was 34,013; wages and salaries, $1,100m. The value of shipments in 1996 was $6,132m., and the leading industries were food, paper and allied, and beverage industries.

Labour. In 1996 the labour force was 440,600 (201,300 females) of whom 385,000 (177,900) were employed.

Trade Unions. Total union membership in 1997 was 102,352 belonging to 78 unions comprised of 653 individual locals. The largest union membership was in the service sector followed by public administration and defence.

COMMUNICATIONS

Roads. In 1997 there were 26,000 km of highways, of which 13,600 km were paved. The Trans Canada and 100 series highways are limited access, all-weather, rapid transit routes. The province's first toll road opened in Dec. 1997. In the fiscal year

1995–96, vehicle registrations numbered 368,119 passenger cars and 165,756 trucks and truck tractors.

Railways. The province has a 700 km network of mainline track operated predominantly by Canadian National Railways. The Cape Breton and Central Nova Scotia Railway operates between Truro and Cape Breton Island. The Windsor and Hantsport Railway operates in the Annapolis Valley region.

Civil Aviation. There is direct air service to all major Canadian points and international scheduled service to Boston, New York, Bermuda, London, Glasgow and Amsterdam. There are winter charter services to Florida and the Caribbean. In 1997, airlines providing national and international service from the major airports included Air Canada, Canadian Airlines International, Icelandair, Air Nova, Air Atlantic, Air St Pierre and Business Express. Charter air service is provided by Canada 3000, Air Transat, Royal Airlines, Air Europa and Can Air.

Shipping. Ferry services connect Nova Scotia to the provinces of Newfoundland, Prince Edward Island and New Brunswick as well as to the USA. The deep-water Port of Halifax handles about 13m. tonnes of cargo annually. Direct container service is provided to the USA, Europe, Asia, Australia/New Zealand and the Caribbean. There are numerous smaller ports.

SOCIAL INSTITUTIONS

Justice. The Supreme Court (Trial Division and Appeal Division) is the superior court of Nova Scotia and has original and appellate jurisdiction in all civil and criminal matters unless they have been specifically assigned to another court by Statute. An appeal from the Supreme Court, Appeal Division, is to the Supreme Court of Canada. The other courts in the Province are the Provincial Court, which hears criminal matters only, the Small Claims Court, which has limited monetary jurisdiction, Probate Court, County Court, which has jurisdiction in criminal matters as well as original jurisdiction over actions not exceeding $50,000, and Family Court. Young offenders are tried in the Family Court or the Provincial Court.

For the year ending 31 March 1995 there were 4,244 adult admissions to provincial custody; of these, 2,748 were sentenced. In 1996, 78,739 Criminal Code offences were reported, including 15 homicides.

Education. Public education in Nova Scotia is free, compulsory and undenominational through elementary and high school. Attendance is compulsory to the age of 16. There were 501 elementary-secondary public schools, with 8,938 full-time teachers and 168,670 pupils, in 1996–97, plus the Nova Scotia Youth Centres for young offenders in Shelburne and in Waterville; and the Nova Scotia Youth Training Centre in Truro for mentally handicapped children. The province has 12 degree-granting institutions, of which the largest is Dalhousie University in Halifax. The Nova Scotia Agricultural College is located at Truro. The Technical University of Nova Scotia at Halifax grants degrees in engineering and architecture. Through the Nova Scotia Community College, the Department of Education administers 19 college campuses, including 2 adult vocational training centres, 2 institutes of technology, a nautical institute, plus College de l'Acadie, the French component of the Nova Scotia Community College. There are also 7 teaching hospitals.

The Nova Scotia government offers financial support and organizational assistance to local school boards for provision of weekend and evening courses in academic and vocational subjects, and citizenship for new Canadians. It also provides local authorities with specialist support services to assist them in providing community workshops and it operates a correspondence study service for children and adults.

Total estimated expenditure on all levels of education for the year 1996–97 was $1,595·1m., of which 63·6% was borne by the provincial government.

Further Reading

Nova Scotia Fact Book. N. S. Department of Economic Development, Halifax, 1993
Nova Scotia Statistical Review. N. S. Department of Economic Development, Halifax, 1996
Nova Scotia Facts at a Glance. N. S. Department of Economic Development, Halifax, 1996

Atlantic Provinces Economic Council. *The Atlantic Vision, 1990.* Halifax, 1979
Beck, M., *The Evolution of Municipal Government in Nova Scotia, 1749–1973.* 1973
McCreath, P. and Leefe, J., *History of Early Nova Scotia.* Halifax, 1982
Vaison, R., *Nova Scotia Past and Present: A Bibliography and Guide.* Halifax, 1976

Statistical office: Statistics Branch, Department of Finance, POB 187, Halifax, Nova Scotia, B3J 2N3.

ONTARIO

KEY HISTORICAL EVENTS. The French explorer Samuel de Champlain explored the Ottawa River from 1613. The area was governed by the French, first under a joint stock company and then as a royal province, from 1627 and was ceded to Great Britain in 1763. A constitutional act of 1791 created there the province of Upper Canada, largely to accommodate loyalists of English descent who had immigrated after the United States war of independence. Upper Canada entered the Confederation as Ontario in 1867.

TERRITORY AND POPULATION. The area is 412,580 sq. miles (1,068,580 sq. km), of which some 344,100 sq. miles (891,190 sq. km) are land area and some 68,480 sq. miles (177,390 sq. km) are lakes and fresh water rivers. The province extends 1,050 miles (1,690 km) from east to west and 1,075 miles (1,730 km) from north to south. It is bounded on the north by the Hudson and James Bays, on the east by Quebec, on the west by Manitoba, and on the south by the USA.

The census population, 1996, was 10,753,573; estimate, July 1997, 11,407,691. Population of the principal cities (1996 census):

Toronto[1]	653,734	Kitchener	178,420	Thunder Bay	113,662
North York[1]	589,653	Markham	173,383	East York[1]	107,822
Scarborough[1]	558,960	York[1]	146,534	Gloucester	104,022
Mississauga	544,382	Burlington	136,976	Richmond Hill	101,725
Etobicoke[1]	328,718	Oshawa	134,364	Cambridge	101,429
London	325,646	Vaughan	132,549	Guelph	95,821
Ottawa	323,340	St Catharines	130,926	Sudbury	92,059
Hamilton	322,352	Oakville	128,405	Brantford	84,764
Brampton	268,251	Nepean	115,100	Sault Ste Marie	80,054
Windsor	197,694				

[1] Municipality of metropolitan Toronto.

There are over 1m. French-speaking people and 0·24m. native Indians. An agreement with the Ontario government of Aug. 1991 recognized Indians' right to self-government.

Vital statistics, *see* CANADA: Territory and Population.

CLIMATE. A temperate continental climate, but conditions can be quite severe in winter, though proximity to the Great Lakes has a moderating influence on temperatures. Ottawa. Jan. –10·8°C, July 20·8°C. Annual rainfall (including snow) 911 mm. Toronto. Jan. –4·5°C, July 22·1°C. Annual rainfall 818 mm.

CONSTITUTION AND GOVERNMENT. The provincial government is administered by a *Lieut.-Governor*, a cabinet and a single-chamber 130-member *Legislative Assembly* elected by a general franchise for a period of no longer than 5 years. The minimum voting age is 18 years.

Lieut.-Governor: Right Hon. Hilary Weston (b. 1942; appointed Dec. 1996).

At the elections on 8 June 1995 to the *Legislative Assembly*, the Progressive Conservative Party won 82 seats (20 in 1990), the Liberal Party, 31 (36), the New Democratic Party (NDP), 16 (74) and independents, 1. At 3 by-elections on 4 Sept. 1997, the Liberals won 2 seats and the NDP won 1 seat. The Party standings remain the same.

In Jan. 1998 the Executive Council comprised:
Premier and President of the Council: Michael Harris.

Deputy Premier, Minister of Finance: Ernie Eves. *Agriculture, Food and Rural Affairs, Minister responsible for Francophone Affairs:* Noble Villeneuve. *Consumer and Commercial Relations:* David Tsubouchi. *Environment and Government House Leader:* Norman Sterling. *Correctional Services and Solicitor-General:* Robert Runciman. *Education and Training:* David Johnson. *Attorney-General, Minister responsible for Native Affairs:* Charles Harnick. *Energy, Science and Technology:* Jim Wilson. *Northern Development and Mines, Chair of the Management Board of Cabinet:* Chris Hodgson. *Health:* Elizabeth Witmer. *Intergovernmental Affairs, Minister responsible for Women's Issues:* Dianne Cunningham. *Natural Resources:* John Snobelen.. *Economic Development, Trade and Tourism:* Al Palladini. *Community and Social Services:* Janet Ecker. *Transportation:* Tony Clement. *Labour:* James Flaherty. *Municipal Affairs and Housing:* Allan Leach. *Citizenship, Culture and Recreation:* Isabel Bassett. *Ministers without portfolio:* Rob Sampson *(responsible for Privatization)*; Cameron Jackson *(responsible for Seniors)*; Margaret Marland *(responsible for Children)*; David Turnbull *(Chief Government Whip)*.

Local Government. Local government is divided into 2 branches, one covering municipal institutions and the other education.

There are 2 levels of municipal government in the southern, settled part of Ontario. The upper level consists of 26 counties plus 13 restructured regional municipalities including metropolitan Toronto. As of 1 Jan. 1998, metropolitan Toronto and its area municipalities became the City of Toronto, a single-tier municipality. The local level comprises more than 700 cities, towns and townships. Cities with one exception in the traditional county system function independently of the county in which they lie, as do 4 towns and 1 township which have been separated for municipal purposes. There are no separated municipal units in regional governments.

Ontario's local municipalities are governed by councils elected by popular vote.

Lower tier municipal councils are composed of a head of council (mayor or reeve) and councillors. In the case of regional municipalities, one or more regional councillors represent the area municipalities on the regional council. Niagara and Ottawa-Carleton have their own directly elected upper level councils. Waterloo, Hamilton-Wentworth, Ottawa-Carleton and Sudbury have directly elected regional chairs.

County councils are federations. A county council consists of at least 1 representative of each local municipality, generally the head of the local council. The head of the county council is the warden, who is elected by the council from among its own members.

A regional council may include the heads of council of the local municipalities, as well as a varying number of regional councillors, who are elected on the basis of representation, either directly or indirectly.

No municipality may incur long-term debts over a reasonable level without the sanction of the tribunal created by the Provincial Legislature and known as the Ontario Municipal Board. Debenture obligations incurred by municipalities for utility undertakings are discharged out of revenues derived from the sale of utility services and do not fall upon the ratepayers.

Municipal councils have no jurisdiction for education beyond the collection of taxes for school purposes. Responsibility for providing, operating and maintaining school facilities, and for the supply of teachers, rests with elected local education authorities known as Boards of Education or School Boards. These Boards are now generally organized on a large regional basis.

Municipal institutions come under the jurisdiction of the Provincial Ministry of Municipal Affairs and Housing. One of the principal functions of the Ministry is to ensure municipalities have the legislative authority to respond to local needs and offer management and administrative support along with financial assistance to Ontario's 804 municipalities. Educational support and guidance at the provincial level is the responsibility of the Ministry of Education and Training, which deals with the training of teachers and the formulation of curriculum.

There are areas in the north where there is little or no settlement of population. Administration of such areas remains in the hands of the Provincial Government. Where there are municipalities in the north they are single lower tier, with the exception of the regional municipality of Sudbury.

FINANCE. Provincial revenue and expenditure (in $1m.) for years ending 31 March:

	1992–93	1993–94	1994–95	1995–96	1996–97
Gross revenue	41,807	43,674	46,039	49,473	49,450
Gross expenditure	54,235	54,876	56,168	58,273	56,355

Gross revenue and expenditure figures reflect accrual and consolidation accounting as recommended by the Public Sector Accounting and Auditing Board of the Canadian Institute of Chartered Accountants. Transactions on behalf of Ontario Hydro are excluded.

Personal income per capita, 1996, was $24,099.

ENERGY AND NATURAL RESOURCES

Electricity (1996). Ontario Hydro recorded for the calendar year an installed generating capacity of 29,844 MW. Primary energy made available 137,418m. kWh. In 1996 there were 69 hydro-electric, 5 nuclear and 6 fossil-fuel stations operating.

Minerals (1996). The total value of mine production was $5,643,611,881. The top 10 commodities (in $1m.) were: Nickel, 1,579·1; gold, 1,268·4; copper, 688·7; cement, 327·1; sand and gravel, 323·4; stone, 241·7; salt, 215·3; zinc, 167; cobalt, 139·7; platinum group (data confidential). Direct employment in the mining industry was 18,600 in 1996.

Agriculture. In 1996, 3,079,132 ha were under field crops with total farm receipts of $2,778,477,000.

Forestry. In 1996 the total area of productive forest was 60·9m. ha, of which the inventoried area was 40·3m. ha, comprising: Softwoods, 27·1m. ha; hardwoods, 13·1m. ha. The growing stock equals 5·34m. cu. metres.

INDUSTRY AND TRADE

Industry. Ontario is Canada's most industrialized province, with GDP in 1996 at $323,027m., or 40·5% of the Canadian total. Manufacturing accounts for 25·5% of Ontario GDP.

Leading manufacturing industries include: Motor vehicles and parts; office and industrial electrical equipment; food processing; chemicals; and steel.

Labour. In 1996 the labour force was 5,839,200 (2,675,400 females) of whom 5,310,700 (2,429,800) were employed. Total labour income was $178,659m.

Trade. In 1996 Ontario was responsible for about 51% ($139,964m.) of Canada's merchandise exports. Motor vehicles and parts accounted for about 45·1% of exports.

COMMUNICATIONS

Roads. There were, in 1995, 158,638 km of roads. Motor licences (on the road) numbered (1996) 8,262,926, of which 5,120,509 were passenger cars, 1,105,829 commercial vehicles, 27,518 buses, 1,438,481 trailers, 94,431 motor cycles and 361,596 snow vehicles.

Railways. In 1997 there were 10 provincial short lines plus the provincially-owned Ontario Northland Railway and 12 federal railways. The Canadian National and Canadian Pacific Railways operate in Ontario. Total track miles, approximately 12,500 km. There is a metro and tramway network in Toronto.

Telecommunications (1997). Telephone service is provided by 30 independent systems and Bell Canada.

SOCIAL INSTITUTIONS

Justice. In 1996, 893,824 Criminal Code offences were reported, including 174 homicides.

Education. There is a provincial system of publicly-financed elementary and secondary schools as well as private schools. In 1996–97 publicly-financed elementary and secondary schools had a total enrolment of 2,080,188 pupils.

There are 18 universities (Brock, Carleton, Dominicain, Guelph, Lakehead, Laurentian, McMaster, Nipissing, Ottawa, Queen's, Ryerson, Toronto, Trent, Waterloo, Western Ontario, Wilfred Laurier, Windsor and York) and 1 institute of equivalent status (Ontario College of Art and Design) with full-time enrolment in 1995 of 227,498. All receive operating grants from the Ontario government. There are also 25 publicly-financed Colleges of Applied Arts and Technology (CAAT), with a full-time enrolment of 134,127 in 1995.

Operating expense (including capital expenses) by the Ontario government on education for 1995–96 was $9,761·6m.

Further Reading

Statistical Information: Annual publications of the Ontario Ministry of Finance include: *Ontario Statistics; Ontario Budget; Public Accounts; Financial Report.*

PRINCE EDWARD ISLAND

KEY HISTORICAL EVENTS. The first recorded European visit was by Jacques Cartier in 1534, who named it Isle St-Jean. In 1719 it was settled by the French, but was taken from them by the English in 1758, annexed to Nova Scotia in 1763, and constituted a separate colony in 1769. Named Prince Edward Island in honour of Prince Edward, Duke of Kent, in 1799, it joined the Canadian Confederation on 1 July 1873.

TERRITORY AND POPULATION. The province lies in the Gulf of St Lawrence, and is separated from the mainland of New Brunswick and Nova Scotia by Northumberland Strait. The area of the island is 2,185 sq. miles (5,660 sq. km). Total population (census, 1996), 134,557; estimate, July 1997, 137,244. Population of the principal cities (1991): Charlottetown (capital), 15,396; Summerside, 7,474.

Vital statistics *see* CANADA: Territory and Population.

CLIMATE. The cool temperate climate is affected in winter by the freezing of the St. Lawrence, which reduces winter temperatures. Charlottetown. Jan. 3·4°C, July 23°C. Annual rainfall 869 mm.

CONSTITUTION AND GOVERNMENT. The provincial government is administered by a Lieut.-Governor-in-Council (Cabinet) and a Legislative Assembly of 27 members who are elected for up to 5 years. As of Dec. 5 1997 parties in the Legislative Assembly were: Progressive Conservatives, 18; Liberals, 8; Island New Democrats, 1.

Lieut.-Governor: Gilbert R. Clements (sworn in 30 Aug. 1995).

The Executive Council was composed as follows in Jan. 1998:
Premier and President of the Executive Council, Minister Responsible for Intergovernmental Affairs: Hon. Patrick G. Binns.
Agriculture and Forestry: Hon. J. Eric Hammill. *Community Affairs and Attorney-General:* Hon. P. Mitchell Murphy. *Economic Development and Tourism:* Hon. J. Weston MacAleer. *Education:* Hon. J. Chester Gillan. *Fisheries and Environment:* Hon. Kevin J. MacAdam. *Health and Social Services:* Hon. Mildred A. Dover. *Provincial Treasurer:* Hon. Patricia J. Mella. *Transportation and Public Works:* Hon. Michael F. Currie.

Local Government. The Municipalities Act provides for the incorporation of Towns and Communities. The City of Charlottetown, the Town of Cornwall and the Town of Stratford are incorporated under the Charlottetown Area Municipalities Act. The City of Summerside is incorporated under the City of Summerside Act.

FINANCE. Revenue and expenditure (in Canadian $1,000) for 5 financial years ending 31 March:

	1992–93	1993–94	1994–95	1995–96	1996–97
Revenue	676,028	738,855	812,461	802,579	801,143
Expenditure	793,328	810,199	821,422	797,937	818,747

Per capita personal income rose from $18,353 in 1995 to $18,708 in 1996.

ENERGY AND NATURAL RESOURCES

Electricity. In 1996, Prince Edward Island received 73,867 MWh of electricity from other provinces via an underwater cable which spans the Northumberland Strait. Net generation on Prince Edward Island was 483 MWh.

Agriculture. Total area of farmland occupies approximately half of the total land area of 566,177 ha. Farm cash receipts in 1996 were $294m. with cash receipts from potatoes accounting for about 50% of the total. Cash receipts from dairy products, cattle and hogs followed in importance. For particulars of agricultural production and livestock, see CANADA: Agriculture.

Forestry. Forests cover some 280,000 ha. or 48·6% of Prince Edward Island. In 1996 the forest produced 557,000 cu. metres of products with the commercial softwood component being 379,000 cu. metres. Sawlogs accounted for 65·2% of the commercial softwood harvest with pulpwood the other component. 70% of the sawlogs were processed on Prince Edward Island. The pulpwood shipments were to Quebec (40%), Newfoundland (26%), New Brunswick (20%), Nova Scotia (9%) and a small quantity was exported internationally. The rest of the forest products were primarily firewood (144,000 cu. metres) and wood chips for energy.

Fisheries. The total catch of 107m. lbs in 1996 had a landed value of $118m. Lobsters accounted for $79m., over two-thirds of the total value; other shellfish, $32m.; pelagic and estuarial, $5·2m.; groundfish, $0·8m.; seaplants, $1·7m.

INDUSTRY AND TRADE

Industry. Value of manufacturing shipments for all industries in 1996 was $641·6m. In 1996, provincial GDP in constant prices for manufacturing was $166·0m.; construction, $133·0m. In 1996 the total value of retail trade was $956·0m.

Labour. The average weekly wage (industrial aggregate) rose from $466·91 in 1995 to $491·04 in 1996. The labour force averaged 70,400 in 1995, while employment averaged 60,100.

Tourism. The value of the tourist industry was estimated at $150·8m. in 1996 with 298,693 tourist parties.

COMMUNICATIONS

Roads. At the end of 1995 there were 5,308 km of road, including 3,806 km of paved highway. A bus service operates twice daily to the mainland.

Civil Aviation (1995). Air Canada provides a daily service between Charlottetown and Toronto, Air Nova and Air Atlantic a service between Charlottetown and other centres, including Toronto, to connect with Air Canada and Canadian Airlines International flights at Halifax.

Shipping. Modern car ferries link the Island to New Brunswick and Nova Scotia. Service is provided year round to New Brunswick on schedules which vary from 14 to 20 return crossings daily, with ice-breaking ferries maintaining the service during the winter months. Ferry service is operated to Nova Scotia from late April to mid-Dec. on schedules ranging from 9 to 19 return crossings daily. A third ferry service, to the Magdalen Islands (Quebec), operates from 1 April to 31 Jan. There is also a substantial water movement of certain commodities, primarily through the ports of Summerside and Charlottetown.

Telecommunications. At the end of 1995 there were 83,104 telephone lines in service.

SOCIAL INSTITUTIONS

Justice. In 1996, 10,247 Criminal Code offences were reported, including no homicides.

Education (1995–96). Under the regional school boards there were 65 public schools, 1,434 teaching positions and 24,422 students. There is one undergraduate university (2,401 full-time and 7,477 part-time students), a veterinary college (197 students), and a Master of Science programme (25 students), all in Charlottetown. Holland College provides training for employment in business, applied arts and technology, with approximately 2,300 full-time students in post-secondary and vocational career programmes. The college offers extensive academic and career preparation programmes for adults.

Government expenditure on education, 1994–95, $174·7m.

Further Reading

Baldwin, D. O., *Abegweit: Land of the Red Soil.* Charlottetown, 1985
Bolger, F. W. P., *Canada's Smallest Province.* Charlottetown, 1973
Clark, A. H., *Three Centuries and the Island.* Toronto, 1959
Hocking, A., *Prince Edward Island.* Toronto, 1978
MacKinnon, F., *The Government of Prince Edward Island.* Toronto, 1951

QUEBEC—QUÉBEC

KEY HISTORICAL EVENTS. Quebec was known as New France from 1534 to 1763; as the province of Quebec from 1763 to 1790; as Lower Canada from 1791 to 1846; as Canada East from 1846 to 1867, and when, by the union of the four original provinces, the Confederation of the Dominion of Canada was formed, it again became known as the province of Quebec (Québec).

The Quebec Act, passed by the British Parliament in 1774, guaranteed to the people of the newly conquered French territory in North America security in their religion and language, their customs and tenures, under their own civil laws.

In a referendum on 20 May 1980, 59·5% voted against 'separatism'. At a further referendum on 30 Oct. 1995, 50·6% of votes cast were against Quebec becoming 'sovereign in a new economic and political partnership' with Canada. The electorate was 5m.; turn-out was 93%.

TERRITORY AND POPULATION. The area of Quebec (as amended by the Labrador Boundary Award) is 1,667,926 sq. km (594,860 sq. miles), of which 1,315,134 sq. km is land area and 352,792 sq. km water. Of this extent, 911,106 sq. km represent the Territory of Ungava, annexed in 1912 under the Quebec Boundaries Extension Act. The population (census 1996) was 7,138,795; estimate, July 1997, 7,419,890.

Principal cities: (1991 census populations): Quebec (capital), 167,517; Montreal, 1,017,666; Laval, 314,398; Longueuil, 129,874; Montreal North, 85,516; Sherbrooke, 76,429; Saint-Hubert, 74,027; LaSalle, 73,804; Sainte-Foy, 73,133; Saint-Laurent, 72,402, Charlesbourg, 70,788; Beauport, 69,158; Chicoutimi, 62,670; Verdun, 61,307; Hull, 60,707; Jonquière, 57,933.

Vital statistics, *see* CANADA: Territory and Population.

CLIMATE. Cool temperate in the south, but conditions are more extreme towards the north. Winters are severe and snowfall considerable, but summer temperatures are quite warm. Quebec. Jan. –12·5°C, July 19·1°C. Annual rainfall 1,123 mm. Montreal. Jan. –10·7°C, July 20·2°C. Annual rainfall 936 mm.

CONSTITUTION AND GOVERNMENT. There is a Legislative Assembly consisting of 125 members, elected in 125 electoral districts for 4 years. At the elections of 12 Sept 1994, the Parti Québécois won 77 seats with 44·7% of votes cast, the Liberal Party 47 with 44·3%. Action Démocratique won 1 seat.

Lieut.-Governor: The Hon. Lise Thibault.

Members of the Council of Ministers in Jan. 1998:
Premier and President of Executive Council: Lucien Bouchard.
Deputy Premier, Finance, Industry, Trade, Science and Technology, Revenue, and Minister of State for the Economy and Finance: Bernard Landry. *Education and Child and Family Welfare:* Pauline Marois. *Culture and Communications, Minister responsible for the French Language Charter:* Louise Beaudoin. *Justice:* Serge Ménard. *Transport, and Canadian Inter-Governmental Affairs:* Jacques Brassard. *Environment and Wildlife:* Paul Bégin. *Agriculture, Fisheries and Food:* Guy Julien. *Public Security:* Pierre Bélanger. *Labour:* Matthias Rioux. *Health and Social Services:* Jean Rochon. *International Relations, Minister responsible for Relations with French-Speaking Communities:* Sylvain Simard. *Municipal Affairs:* Rémy Trudel. *Administration and Public Service, Chairman of the Treasury Board:* Jacques Léonard. *Industry and Trade:* Roger Bertrand. *Electoral and Parliamentary Reform, and Government House Leader:* Jean-Pierre Jolivet. *Relations with the Citizens and Immigration:* André Boisclair. *Revenue:* Rita Dionne-Marsolais. *Tourism:* David Cliche. *Mines, Lands and Forests:* Denise Carrier-Perreault. *Minister responsible for Independent Community Action and for the Status of Women:* Louise Harel. *Minister responsible for Regional Development:* Guy Chevrette.

ECONOMY

Budget. Ordinary revenue and expenditure (in Canadian $1,000) for fiscal years ending 31 March:

	1991–92	1992–93	1993–94	1994–95	1995–96
Revenue	34,457,600	35,445,600	36,056,000	36,437,000	38,254,000
Expenditure	38,649,000	40,377,000	40,953,000	42,236,000	42,220,000

The total net debt at 31 March 1996 was $60,842m.

ENERGY AND NATURAL RESOURCES

Electricity. Water power is one of the most important natural resources of Quebec. Its turbine installation represents about 40% of the aggregate of Canada. At the end of 1994 the installed generating capacity was 38,909 MW. Production, 1994, was 193,000 GWh.

Minerals (1995). The value of mineral production (metal only) was $2,158,132,564. Chief minerals: Iron ore, (confidential); copper, $458,756,897; gold, $681,547,351; zinc, $242,782,635.

Non-metallic minerals produced include: Asbestos ($233,747,031; about 97% of Canadian production), titanium-dioxide (confidential), industrial lime, dolomite and brucite, quartz and pyrite. Among the building materials produced were: Stone, $197,833,920; cement, $172,687,663; sand and gravel, $82,735,967; lime, (confidential).

Agriculture. In 1995 the agricultural area was 3,445,000 ha. The yield of the principal crops was (1995 in 1,000 tonnes):

Crops	Yield	Crops	Yield
Tame hay	5,800	Fodder corn	760
Oats for grain	173	Corn for grain	2,000
Potatoes	429	Barley	350
Mixed grains	92	Buckwheat	88

About 38,000 farms were operating in 1995. Cash receipts, 1995, $4,382m. (dairy products, 31·9%; livestock, 30·1%; crops, 26·3%; poultry and eggs, 10·8%). In 1996, 33,906 census farms reported total gross farm receipts of $2,500 or more.

Forestry. Forests cover an area of 757,900 sq. km. 516,601 sq. km are classified as productive forests, of which 447,541 sq. km are provincial forest land and 65,991 sq. km are privately owned. Quebec leads the Canadian provinces in pulp and paper production, having nearly half of the Canadian estimated total.

In 1995 production of lumber was: Softwood and hardwood, 13,688,000 cu. metres; pulp and paper, 9,097,000 tonnes.

Fisheries. The principal fish are cod, herring, red fish, lobster and salmon. Total catch of sea fish, 1996, 47,070 tonnes, valued at $122,747m.

INDUSTRY AND TRADE

Industry. In 1994 there were 10,164 industrial establishments in the province; employees, 461,056; salaries and wages, $15,717·9m.; cost of materials, $51,774·34m.; value of shipments, $94,458·3m. Among the leading industries are petroleum refining, pulp and paper mills, smelting and refining, dairy products, slaughtering and meat processing, motor vehicle manufacturing, women's clothing, saw-mills and planing mills, iron and steel mills, commercial printing.

Labour. In 1996 the labour force was 3,642,500 (1,614,000 females) of whom 3,212,600 (1,434,000) were employed.

Commerce. In 1996 the value of Canadian exports through Quebec custom ports was $34,417·72m.; value of imports, $27,583·15m.

COMMUNICATIONS

Roads. In 1995 there were 28,898 km of roads and 4,275,429 registered motor vehicles.

Railways. There were (1996) 6,570 km of railway. There is a metro system in Montreal (64 km).

Civil Aviation. There are 2 international airports, Dorval (Montreal) and Mirabel (Montreal).

Telecommunications. Telephones numbered 4·1m. in 1994 and there were 29 television and 171 radio stations.

Newspapers (1996). There were 11 French- and 2 English-language daily newspapers.

SOCIAL INSTITUTIONS

Justice. In 1996, 510,375 Criminal Code offences were reported, including 143 homicides.

Education. Education is compulsory for children aged 6-16. Pre-school education and elementary and secondary training are free in some 2,670 public schools, which were managed by 156 school boards (135 Catholic, 18 Protestant and 3 serving mainly Native students) in 1996–97. Instruction is given in French only in 100 school boards, in French and English in 46, in English only in 7 and in French, English and aboriginal languages in 3. Just under 10% of the student population attends private schools: In 1996–97, 286 establishments were authorized to provide pre-school, elementary and secondary education. After 6 years of elementary and 5 years of secondary school education, students enter Cegeps, a post-secondary educational institution. In 1996–97, college, pre-university and technical training for young and adult students was provided by 47 Cegeps, 11 government schools and 70 private establishments.

In 1994–95, in pre-kindergartens, there were 14,023 pupils; in kindergartens, 89,912; in primary schools, 547,395; in secondary schools, 498,105; in colleges (postsecondary, non-university), 180,977; and in classes for children with special needs, 134,621. The school boards had a total of 65,541 teachers.

Expenditure of the Departments of Education for 1995–96, $9,176·41m. net. This included $1,709·01m. for universities, $5,329·95m. for public primary and secondary schools, $302·57m. for private primary and secondary schools and $1,190·99m. for colleges.

In 1994–95 the province had 10 universities: 3 English-language universities, McGill (Montreal, founded 1821), Bishop (Lennoxville, founded 1845) and the

Concordia University (Montreal, granted a charter 1975); 6 French-language universities: Laval (Quebec, founded 1852), Montreal University (opened 1876 as a branch of Laval, independent 1920), Sherbrooke University (founded 1954), University of Quebec (founded 1968) and 2 others; 1 French- and English-language university. In 1994 there were 134,933 full-time university students and 109,792 part-time students.

Further Reading

Dickinson, J. A. and Young, B., *A Short History of Quebec.* 2nd ed. Harlow, 1994
Jacobs, J., *The Question of Separatism: Quebec and the Struggle for Sovereignty.* London, 1981
McWhinney, E., *Quebec and the Constitution.* Univ. of Toronto Press, 1979
Wade, F. M., *The French Canadians, 1760–1967.* Toronto, 1968
Young, R. A., *The Secession of Quebec and the Future of Canada.* McGill-Queen's Univ. Press, 1995

Statistical office: Bureau de la Statistique du Québec, 117 rue Saint-André, Québec, G1K 3Y3

SASKATCHEWAN

KEY HISTORICAL EVENTS. Saskatchewan derives its name from its major river system, which the Cree Indians called 'Kis-is-ska-tche-wan', meaning 'swift flowing'. It officially became a province when it joined the Confederation on 1 Sept. 1905.

In 1670 King Charles II granted to Prince Rupert and his friends a charter covering exclusive trading rights in 'all the land drained by streams finding their outlet in the Hudson Bay'. This included what is now Saskatchewan. The trading company was first known as The Governor and Company of Adventurers of England; later as the Hudson's Bay Company. In 1869 the Northwest Territories was formed, and this included Saskatchewan. In 1882 the District of Saskatchewan was formed. By 1885 the North-West Mounted Police had been inaugurated, with headquarters in Regina (now the capital), and the Canadian Pacific Railway's transcontinental line had been completed, bringing a stream of immigrants to southern Saskatchewan. The Hudson's Bay Company surrendered its claim to territory in return for cash and land around the existing trading posts. Legislative government was introduced.

TERRITORY AND POPULATION. Saskatchewan is bounded on the west by Alberta, on the east by Manitoba, on the north by the Northwest Territories and on the south by the USA. The area of the province is 251,700 sq. miles (570,113 sq. km), of which 220,182 sq. miles is land area and 31,518 sq. miles is water. The population, 1996 census, was 990,237; estimate, July 1997, 1,023,483. Population of cities, 1996 census: Regina (capital), 180,400; Saskatoon, 193,647; Prince Albert, 34,777; Moose Jaw, 32,973; Yorkton, 15,154; Swift Current, 14,890; North Battleford, 14,051; Estevan, 10,752; Weyburn, 9,723; Lloydminster, 7,636; Melfort, 5,759; Melville, 4,646.

Vital statistics, *see* CANADA: Territory and Population.

CLIMATE. A cold continental climate, with severe winters and warm summers. Rainfall amounts are greatest from May to Aug. Regina. Jan. 0°F (−17·8°C), July 65°F (18·3°C). Annual rainfall 15" (373 mm).

CONSTITUTION AND GOVERNMENT. The provincial government is vested in a Lieut.-Governor, an Executive Council and a Legislative Assembly, elected for 5 years by universal suffrage. State of parties in Dec. 1997: New Democratic Party, 42; Saskatchewan Party, 8; Liberal Party, 6; Independent, 3.

Lieut.-Governor: Hon. Jack Wiebe.

The New Democratic Party Ministry in Jan. 1998 was composed as follows:
Premier, President of the Executive Council: Hon. Roy Romanow, QC (b. 1939).
Deputy Premier, Minister of Crown Investment Corporation: Hon. Dwain

Lingenfelter. *Intergovernmental and Aboriginal Affairs:* Hon. Bernhard Wiens. *Labour:* Hon. Robert Mitchell, QC. *Economic and Co-operative Development, Government House Leader:* Hon. Janice MacKinnon. *Provincial Secretary:* Hon. Ned Shillington. *Education:* Hon. Patricia Atkinson. *Social Services, Minister responsible for Seniors and for Disabilities Directorate:* Hon. Lorne Calvert. *Energy and Mines:* Hon. Eldon Lautermilch. *Northern Affairs:* Hon. Keith Goulet. *Post-Secondary Education and Skills Training, Minister responsible for Gaming:* Hon. Joanne Crofford. *Municipal Government:* Hon. Carol Teichrob. *Agriculture and Food:* Hon. Eric Upshall. *Finance:* Hon. Eric Cline. *Environment and Resource Management:* Hon. Lorne Scott. *Justice and Attorney General:* Hon. John Nilson, QC. *Health:* Hon. Clay Serby. *Highways and Transportation, Minister responsible for the Status of Women:* Hon. Judy Bradley. *Minister responsible for Saskatchewan Property Management Corporation:* Hon. Maynard Sonntag.

Local Government. The organization of a city requires a minimum population of 5,000 persons; that of a town, 500; that of a village, 100 people. No requirements as to population exist for the rural municipality. Cities, towns, villages and rural municipalities are governed by elected councils, which consist of a mayor and 6–20 aldermen in a city; a mayor and 6 councillors in a town; a mayor and 2 other members in a village; a reeve and a councillor for each division in a rural municipality (usually 6).

FINANCE. Budget and net assets (years ending 31 March) in Canadian $1,000:

	1993–94	1994–95	1995–96	1996–97
Budgetary revenue	4,631,800	4,841,700	5,165,200	5,345,400
Budgetary expenditure	4,928,142	5,030,424	5,140,849	4,987,602

ENERGY AND NATURAL RESOURCES. Agriculture used to dominate the history and economics of Saskatchewan, but the 'prairie province' is now a rapidly developing mining and manufacturing area. It is a major supplier of oil, has the world's largest deposits of potash and the net value of its non-agricultural production accounted for (1996 estimate) 88·6% of the provincial economy.

Electricity. The Saskatchewan Power Corporation generated 16,108m. kWh in 1996.

Minerals. 1996 mineral sales were valued at $5,387m., including (in $1m.): Petroleum, 3,137·1; natural gas, 369·1; coal and others, 145·8; potash, 936·9; salt, 19·9; uranium, 666·2; sodium sulphate, 31·5.

Agriculture. Saskatchewan produces normally about two-thirds of Canada's wheat. Wheat production in 1996 (in 1,000 tonnes), was 16,947 from 19m. acres; oats, 1,882 from 2·2m. acres; barley, 5,444 from 4·8m. acres; rye, 157 from 0·25m. acres; canola, 2,245 from 4m. acres; flax, 473 from 0·9m. acres. Livestock (1 July 1997): Cattle and calves, 2·9m.; swine, 888,000; sheep and lambs, 71,900. Poultry in 1996: Chickens, 12·4m.; turkeys, 757,000. Cash income from the sale of farm products in 1996 was $5,463m. At the June 1996 census there were 56,995 farms in the province, each being a holding of 1 acre or more with sales of $250 or more during the previous year. The South Saskatchewan River irrigation project, whose main feature is the Gardiner Dam, was completed in 1967. It will ultimately provide for an area of 0·2m. to 0·5m. acres of irrigated cultivation in Central Saskatchewan. As of 1996, 224,309 acres were intensively irrigated. Total irrigated land in the province, 319,798 acres.

Forestry. Half of Saskatchewan's area is forested, but only 115,000 sq. km are of commercial value at present. Forest products valued at $520m. were produced in 1996.

Fur Production. In 1995–96 wild fur production was estimated at $1,947,951 ($1,926,981 in 1994-95). Ranch-raised fur production amounted to $87,162 in 1994 and $109,887 in 1995.

Fisheries. The lakeside value of the 1995–96 commercial fish catch of 3m. kg was $4·5m.

INDUSTRY. In 1995 there were 725 manufacturing establishments, employing

17,216 persons. Manufacturing contributed $1,229·3m. and construction $966·3m. to total GDP at factor cost of $18,976·6m. in 1996.

Labour. In 1996 the labour force was 493,700 (221,200 females) of whom 461,200 (207,700) were employed.

Tourism. An estimated 1·5m. out-of-province tourists spent $288·3m. in 1996.

COMMUNICATIONS

Roads. In 1996 there were 25,390 km of provincial highways and 195,790 km of municipal roads (including prairie trails). Motor vehicles registered totalled (1995) 712,467. Bus services are provided by 2 major lines.

Railways. There were (1996) approximately 10,037 km of railway track.

Civil Aviation. There were 2 major airports,176 airports and landing strips in 1994.

Telecommunications. There were (1996) 458 post offices (excluding sub-post offices), 51 TV and re-broadcasting stations and 36 AM and FM radio stations. There were 607,092 telephone network access services to the Saskatchewan Telecommunications system in 1996.

SOCIAL INSTITUTIONS

Justice. In 1996, 118,961 Criminal Code offences were reported, including 27 homicides.

Education. The Saskatchewan education system in 1996–97 consisted of 115 school divisions and 5 comprehensive school boards, of which 22 were Roman Catholic separate school divisions, serving 147,233 elementary pupils, 44,554 high-school students and 2,094 students enrolled in special classes. In addition, the Saskatchewan Institute of Applied Science and Technology, established 1 Jan. 1988, had 11,842 full-time and 32,452 part-time students in 1995–96. There are also 10 regional colleges with an enrolment of approximately 41,784 students in 1995–96.

The University of Saskatchewan was established at Saskatoon in 1907. In 1996–97 it had 14,654 full-time students, 2,814 part-time students and 988 full-time academic staff. The University of Regina was established in 1974; in 1996–97 it had 8,188 full-time and 3,367 part-time students and 300 full-time academic staff.

Further Reading

Archer, J. H., *Saskatchewan: A History*. Saskatoon, 1980
Arora, V., *The Saskatchewan Bibliography*. Regina, 1980

Statistical office: Bureau of Statistics, 2350 Albert St., Regina, S4P 4A6.

THE NORTHWEST TERRITORIES

KEY HISTORICAL EVENTS. The Territory was developed by the Hudson's Bay Company and the North West Company (of Montreal) from the 17th century. The Canadian Government bought out the Hudson's Bay Company in 1869 and the Territory was annexed to Canada in 1870. The Arctic Islands lying north of the Canadian mainland were annexed to Canada in 1880.

A plebiscite held in March 1992 approved the division of the Northwest Territories into 2 separate territories. (For the new territory of Nunavut *see* CONSTITUTION AND GOVERNMENT, *below*).

TERRITORY AND POPULATION. The total area of the Territories is 3,426,320 sq. km, divided into 5 administrative regions: Fort Smith, Inuvik, Kitikmeot, Keewatin and Baffin. The population at the 1991 census was 57,649, 37% of whom were Inuit (Eskimo), 16% Dene (Indian) and 7% Metis. The population at the 1996 census was 64,402; estimate, July 1997, 67,528. The capital is Yellowknife, population (1991); 15,179. Other main centres (with population in 1991): Iqaluit

(3,552), Hay River (3,206), Inuvik (3,206), Fort Smith (2,480), Rankin Inlet (1,706), Rae-Edzo (1,521) and Arviat (1,323).

CLIMATE. Conditions range from cold continental to polar, with long hard winters and short cool summers. Precipitation is low. Yellowknife. Jan. mean high −24·7°C, low −33°C; July mean high 20·7°C, low 11·8°C. Annual rainfall 26·7 cm.

CONSTITUTION AND GOVERNMENT. The Northwest Territories comprises all that portion of Canada lying north of the 60th parallel of N. lat. except those portions within the Yukon Territory and the Provinces of Quebec and Newfoundland: It also includes the islands in Hudson Bay, James Bay and Ungava Bay except those within the Provinces of Manitoba, Ontario and Quebec.

The Northwest Territories is governed by a Premier, with a cabinet (the Executive Council) of 8 members including the Speaker, and a Legislative Assembly. The Assembly is composed of 24 members elected for a 4-year term of office. A Commissioner of the Northwest Territories acts as a lieutenant-governor and is the federal government's senior representative in the Territorial government. The seat of government was transferred from Ottawa to Yellowknife when it was named Territorial capital on 18 Jan. 1967. On 10 Nov. 1997 the Governments of Canada and the Northwest Territories signed an agreement so that the territorial government could assume full responsibility to manage its elections.

Commissioner: Helen Maksagak.

Premier: Don Morin.
Executive Council ministers in Jan. 1998:
Education: Charles Dent. *Finance:* John Todd. *Health and Social Services:* Kelvin Ng. *Justice:* Goo Arlooktoo. *Municipal and Community Affairs:* Manitok Thompson. *Public Works and Services and Transportation:* Jim Antoine. *Resources, Wildlife and Economic Development:* Stephen Kakfwi.

Legislative powers are exercised by the Executive Council on such matters as taxation within the Territories in order to raise revenue, maintenance of justice, licences, solemnization of marriages, education, public health, property, civil rights and generally all matters of a local nature.

The Territorial Government has assumed most of the responsibility for the administration of the Northwest Territories but political control of Crown lands and non-renewable resources still rests with the Federal Government. On 6 Sept. 1988, the Federal and Territorial Governments signed an agreement for the transfer of management responsibilities for oil and gas resources, located on- and off-shore, in the Northwest Territories to the Territorial Government. In a Territory-wide plebiscite in April 1982, a majority of residents voted in favour of dividing the Northwest Territories into two jurisdictions, east and west. In a plebiscite held in March 1992 residents voted in favour of an east-west boundary line. Constitutions for an eastern and western government have been under discussion since 1992. A referendum was held in Nov. 1992 among the Inuit on the formation of a third territory, **Nunavut** ('Our Land'), in the eastern Arctic, and comprising the present administrative regions of Kitikmeot, Keewatin and Baffin. The electorate was 9,648; turn-out was 80%. 69% of votes cast were in favour. An agreement was signed on 25 May 1993 by the federal Prime Minister beginning the process of establishing this territory. Its area of 2,201,400 sq. km is to be made over to the population of 22,000, of which some 80% are Inuit. The remainder will remain federal property. The capital is Iqaluit (formerly Frobisher Bay) with a 1991 population of 3,552. Rankin Inlet had 1,706 inhabitants in 1991.

ENERGY AND NATURAL RESOURCES

Oil and Gas. As of July 1993, 13 licences for oil and gas exploration were held for 1·4m. ha, 20 production licences were held for 64,578 ha and 108 significant discovery licences were retained on 695,473 ha.

Crude oil is produced at Norman Wells and piped to Alberta. Value of crude oil production in 1992 was $142·5m.; 1,850,379 cu. metres.

Minerals. Mineral production in 1992 was valued at $476·2m. 4·7% of Canada's total. The Northwest Territories yielded 12·3% of lead, 15·1% of zinc, 8·8% of gold, and 2% of silver produced in Canada in 1992.

Trapping and Game. The 39,629 pelts, furs and hides sold by 1,838 Northwest Territories hunters and trappers in the 1991–92 season were valued at $2,325,814. The pelts of highest value are those of the polar bear, black and brown bear, wolf, wolverine and lynx. There are some 1·3m. barren-ground caribou, 113,000 muskox and 12,700 polar bears. There are 2 protected herds of wood bison.

Forestry. Forest land area in the NWT consists of 61·4m. ha, about 18% of the total land area. The principal trees are white and black spruce, jack-pine, tamarack, balsam poplar, aspen and birch. In 1990–91, 56,000 cu. metres of timber, valued at $1·83m., was produced.

Fisheries. Commercial fishing, principally on Great Slave Lake, in 1991–92 produced 1,431,000 kg of fish valued at $912,000, principally trout, whitefish and pickerel.

CO-OPERATIVES. There are 39 active co-operatives, including 2 housing co-operatives and one central organization to service local co-operatives, in the Northwest Territories. They are active in handicrafts, furs, fisheries, retail stores, hotels and print shops. Total revenue in 1991 was about $41m.

COMMUNICATIONS

Roads. The Mackenzie Route connects Grimshaw, Alberta, with Hay River, Pine Point, Fort Smith, Fort Providence, Rae-Edzo and Yellowknife. The Mackenzie Highway extension to Fort Simpson and a road between Pine Point and Fort Resolution have both been opened.

Highway service to Inuvik in the Mackenzie Delta was opened in spring 1980, extending north from Dawson, Yukon as the Dempster Highway. The Liard Highway connecting the communities of the Liard River valley to British Columbia opened in 1984.

In 1994 there were 26,721 motor vehicles registered, including 9,582 passenger cars and 14,890 trucks and truck tractors.

Railways. There is one small railway system in the north which runs from Hay River, on the south shore of Great Slave Lake, 435 miles south to Grimshaw, Alberta, where it connects with the Canadian National Railways, but it is not in use.

Civil Aviation (1993). 9 certified airports are operated by the federal Department of Transport and there are 33 certified and 9 uncertified airports operated by the Government of the Northwest Territories. Numerous certified and uncertified airports are operated privately in support of military operations, mining and resource exploration, and tourism. There are also privately-owned float plane bases. Major communities receive daily jet service to southern points. Most smaller communities are served by scheduled turbo-prop air service several times weekly.

Shipping. A direct inland-water transportation route for about 1,700 miles is provided by the Mackenzie River and its tributaries, the Athabasca and Slave rivers. Subsidiary routes on Lake Athabasca, Great Slave Lake and Great Bear Lake total more than 800 miles. Communities in the eastern Arctic are resupplied by ship each summer via the Atlantic and Arctic Oceans or Hudson Bay.

Telecommunications (1993). There is a postal service in all communities. The CBC northern service operates radio stations at Yellowknife, Inuvik, Iqaluit and Rankin Inlet. All communities receive television via satellite. Telephone service is provided to nearly all communities in the Northwest Territories. Those few communities without service have high frequency or very high frequency radios for emergency use.

SOCIAL INSTITUTIONS

Education. In 1993–94 there were 8 divisional boards of education, which provide for more local and regional control of education. There were also 3 boards of education operating in Yellowknife: A separate school board, a public school board and a board of secondary education.

In 1993–94 there were 80 schools operating, with 1,091 teachers for 16,089 enrolled students. Residences in regional larger communities provide accommodation for students from smaller communities that cannot provide all education services up to grade 12. There is a full range of courses available in the school system: Academic, French immersion, native language and culture, commercial, technical and occupational training, post-secondary programmes, along with a first-year general arts university programme. Financial assistance (from the territorial government) is available to qualifying students for post-secondary studies.

Health. In 1988 complete responsibility for health services was transferred to the Territorial Government by the Government of Canada. There are (1993) 8 Boards of Management established to operate, manage and control the health services and programmes in their respective service regions. The health system is comprised of: 6 hospitals, providing both acute and long term care; 6 public health clinics; 43 community health centres; 8 lay dispensaries; 6 boarding homes for patients and escorts travelling.

Welfare. Welfare services are provided by professional social workers. Facilities included (1993) for children: 7 group homes and 2 residential treatment centres.

Further Reading

Annual Report of the Government of the Northwest Territories
Government Activities in the North, 1983–84. Indian and Northern Affairs, Canada
NWT Data Book 90/91. Yellowknife, 1991
Dawson, C. A., The New North-West. Toronto, 1947
MacKay, D., The Honorable Company. Toronto, 1949
Zaslow, M., The Opening of the Canadian North 1870–1914. Toronto, 1971

YUKON TERRITORY

KEY HISTORICAL EVENTS. The territory owes its fame to the discovery of gold in the Klondike at the end of the 19th century. Formerly part of the Northwest Territories, the Yukon was joined to the Dominion as a separate territory on 13 June 1898.

TERRITORY AND POPULATION. The Yukon is situated in the extreme north-western section of Canada and comprises 483,450 sq. km. of which 4,480 sq. km is fresh water. The census population in 1996 was 30,766; estimate, June 1997, 33,586. Principal centres (with 1997 populations) are Whitehorse, the capital, 24,031; Watson Lake, 1,791; Dawson City, 2,151; Faro, 1,266; Haines Junction, 862.

Vital statistics, *see* CANADA: Territory and Population.

CLIMATE. A cold climate in winter with moderate temperatures in summer provide a considerable annual range of temperature and moderate rainfall. Whitehorse. Jan. –5°F (–20°C), July 56°F (14·1°C). Annual rainfall 10" (261 mm). Dawson City. Jan. –22°F (–30°C), July 57°F (15·6°C). Annual rainfall 13" (306·1 mm).

CONSTITUTION AND GOVERNMENT. The Yukon was constituted a separate territory in June 1898. It is governed by a Cabinet (Executive Council) appointed from the majority party in the 17-member elected Legislative Assembly. The members are elected for terms not to exceed 4 years. In the territorial elections on 30 Sept. 1996 the New Democratic Party gained 11 seats, the Yukon Party 3 and the Liberal Party 3.

The seat of government is at Whitehorse. A federally appointed Commissioner serves in a similar capacity to the provincial lieutenant governors.

Commissioner: Judy Gingell (appointed 12 June 1995)

Government Leader: Hon. Piers McDonald.

The Yukon government consists of 12 departments, as well as a Women's Directorate and 4 Crown corporations, each taking direction from a responsible Cabinet Minister and generally from Cabinet. Government departments and agencies are responsible for a similar range of activities as found in Canadian provinces, including education, economic development, municipal affairs, housing, social services, transportation, tourism, justice, renewable resources, and finance. The administration of certain programmes, mostly in the natural resources field, remains under federal control. The Yukon government is, however, involved in negotiations with the federal government on the transfer of further responsibilities to its jurisdiction.

ECONOMY

Activities. GDP at market prices increased by 9·6% in 1996, to $1,037m. The key sectors of the economy are mining, tourism and government. Renewable resource industries' production was estimated at $9m. in 1995. Processing of renewable resources is an important source of economic diversification. In the manufacturing sector, manufacturers' shipments were valued at $47m. in 1995.

Finance. The Territorial Government's revenue and expenditure (in $1,000) for years ended 31 March was:

	1994–95	1995–96	1996–97[1]	1997–98[1]
Revenue	489,894	497,780	466,732	447,431
Expenditure	481,388	489,508	501,272	457,385

[1] Projected.

ENERGY AND NATURAL RESOURCES

Electricity. Hydro-generated power is supplied through plants at Whitehorse Rapids, Aishihik Lake, Fish Lake and Mayo. Diesel generated power is supplied from plants at several communities (including Whitehorse, Faro, Haines Junction, Ross River, Dawson City, Mayo and Watson Lake). Current capacity is 78 MW hydro and 52 MW diesel-generated power. Production, 1995, 390,035 MWh, of which 319,399 MWh hydroelectric.

Oil and Gas. In 1997, the Yukon Oil and Gas Act was passed, replacing the federal legislation. This Act provides for the transfer of responsibility for oil and gas resources to Yukon jurisdiction.

Minerals. Mining is the main industry. Lead, zinc and gold are the chief minerals. Production in tonnes (and value) in 1996 (preliminary): Gold, 5 ($76·9m.); zinc, 145,335 ($202·2m.); lead, 90,019 ($95·7m.); silver, 112 ($25·6m.)

Agriculture. Many areas have suitable soils and climate for the production of forages, cereal grains and vegetables, domestic livestock and game farming. In 1996 there were 160 farms operating full- and part-time. There were about 24,000 acres associated with farm operations, of which 13,000 acres were in production or under development. Farm receipts in 1996 were estimated at $3·5m. Total farm capital, 1996, was $45m.

Forestry. The forests, which cover 281,030 sq. km of the territory, are part of the great Boreal forest region of Canada which stretches from the east coast of Canada into Alaska and north well above the Arctic Circle. Vast areas are covered by coniferous stands in the southern portion of Yukon with white spruce and lodgepole pine forming pure stands on wet sites and in northern aspects. Deciduous species form pure stands or occur mixed with conifers throughout forest areas.

Production from forestry was 420,600 cu. metres in 1994–95.

Fisheries. Commercial fishing concentrates on chinook salmon, chum salmon, lake trout and whitefish.

Game and Furs. The country abounds with big game, such as moose, goat, caribou, mountain sheep and bear (grizzly and black). The fur trapping industry is considered vital to rural and remote residents and especially First Nations people wishing to maintain a traditional lifestyle. Fur production in 1996 (mostly beaver, lynx, marten, wolf and wolverine) was valued at $274,540.

Environment. The Yukon is recognized as a critical habitat for many species of rare and endangered flowers, big game animals, birds of prey and migratory birds. Three national parks (total area 36,572 sq. km), 3 territorial parks (297 sq. km), 3 protected areas (7,917 sq. km) and 2 wildlife sanctuaries (8,150 sq. km) had been established by 1996 to protect fragile and significant areas for the future.

TOURISM. In 1996 there were 244,960 foreign visitors.

COMMUNICATIONS

Roads. The Alaska Highway and branch highway systems connect Yukon's main communities with Alaska and the provinces and with adjacent mining centres. Interior roads connect the mining communities of Elsa (silver–lead), Faro (lead–zinc–silver) and Dawson City (gold) and mineral exploration properties (lead–zinc and tungsten) north of Ross River. The 735 km Dempster Highway north of Dawson City connects with Inuvik, on the Arctic coast; this highway, the first public road to be built to the Arctic Ocean, was opened in Aug. 1979. The South Klondike Highway links the tidewater port of Skagway, Alaska with the Yukon. It was opened in May 1979, providing a new access to the Pacific Ocean. In 1996-97 there were 4,680 km of roads maintained by the Yukon Territorial Government, of which 260 km were paved. The other major roads, including the Alaska Highway, have received a new surface treatment which resembles pavement and the rest are all-weather gravel of which 700 km are accessible during the summer months only. Vehicles registered in 1996 totalled 42,228, including 11,035 passenger cars and 21,027 trucks and truck tractors.

Railways. The 176-km White Pass and Yukon Railway connected Whitehorse with year-round ocean shipping at Skagway, Alaska, but was closed in 1982. A modified passenger service was restarted in 1988 to take cruise ship tourists from Skagway to Carcross, Yukon over the White Pass summit.

Civil Aviation. In 1997, Canadian International Airlines provided regular daily service between Whitehorse and Vancouver. Regular air service also extended beyond the Yukon to Yellowknife and Inuvik, Northwest Territories, and Juneau and Fairbanks, Alaska, with connecting service to other points in Alaska and other states in the USA. Regularly scheduled air services extend from Whitehorse to the Yukon communities of Dawson City, Old Crow and Watson Lake, with limited air service to Mayo. Commercial operations offering charter services are located throughout the Territory.

Shipping. The majority of goods are shipped into the Territory by truck over the Alaska and Stewart–Cassiar Highways. Some goods are shipped through the ports of Skagway and Haines, Alaska, and then trucked to Whitehorse for distribution throughout the Territory. The majority of goods are transported by road within the Territory, while a modest amount is shipped by air. Although navigable, the rivers are no longer used for shipping.

Telecommunications. There are 3 radio stations in Whitehorse and 15 low-power relay radio transmitters operated by CBC, and 6 operated by the Yukon Government. CHON-FM, operated by Northern Native Broadcasting, is broadcast to virtually all Yukon communities by satellite. Dawson City has its own community run radio station, CFYT-FM. There are also 27 basic and 36 extended pay-cable TV channels in Whitehorse, and private cable operations in Faro and Watson Lake. Live CBC national television and TVNC is provided by satellite and relayed to all communities. All telephone and telecommunications are provided by Northwestel, a subsidiary of Bell Canada Enterprises. Microwave stations, satellite ground stations and radio-telephone facilities provide most of the telephone transmission services to the communities.

Press. In 1997 there were 1 daily and 1 semi-weekly newspaper in Whitehorse, and semi-weekly and monthly papers in Dawson City. Other communities with local newspapers include Stewart Crossing, Haines Junction and Faro. There is also a monthly newspaper for francophones.

SOCIAL INSTITUTIONS

Education. The Yukon Department of Education operates (with the assistance of elected school councils) the Territory's 27 schools, both public and separate, from kindergarten to grade 12. There is also 1 private school and 1 French First Language school, which is under the governance of a school board. In Dec. 1996 there were 457 teachers and 6,241 pupils. French immersion is offered from kindergarten through grade 12. Yukon College provides adult education for young and mature students, 26% of whom are of First Nations ancestry. Ayamdigut Campus in Whitehorse is the administrative and programme centre for 13 other campuses located throughout the territory. In the 1996–97 academic year a total of 758 full-time and 4,318 part-time students enrolled in programmes and courses. The Yukon government provides financial assistance to students for post-secondary education whether they study at Yukon College or outside the Territory. Financial assistance is provided to First Nations students by the federal Department of Indian Affairs and Northern Development.

Health. In Dec. 1996 there were 2 hospitals with 69 staffed beds, 4 nursing stations, 8 health treatment centres, 3 public health centres, 112 doctors and 18 dentists. The territorial government operates a medical travel programme to send patients to Edmonton or Vancouver for specialized treatment not available in the Territory

Further Reading

Annual Report of the Government of the Yukon.
Yukon Executive Council, *Statistical Review.*
Berton, P., *Klondike.* (Rev. ed.) Toronto, 1987
Coates, K. and Morrison, W., *Land of the Midnight Sun: A History of the Yukon.* Edmonton, 1988
McClelland, C., *Part of the Land, Part of the Water.* Vancouver, 1987
Minter, R., *White Pass: Gateway to the Klondike.* Toronto, 1987

There is a Yukon Archive at Yukon College, Whitehorse.

CAPE VERDE

República de Cabo Verde

Capital: Praia
Population: 0·42m.
GDP per head: (PPP$) 1,862
GNP: US$0·3bn.
HDI/world rank: 0·547/123

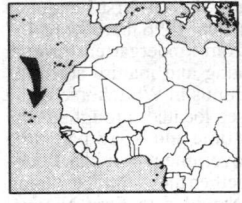

KEY HISTORICAL EVENTS. The Cape Verde Islands were uninhabited, except perhaps by some Lebou fishermen from Senegal, when first visited by Portuguese in 1456. During centuries of Portuguese rule the islands were gradually peopled with Portuguese, slaves from Africa, and people of mixed African-European descent who became the majority. While retaining some African culture, the Cape Verdians came to speak Portuguese or the Portuguese-derived Crioulo (Creole) language, and became Catholics.

Cape Verde included Portuguese Guinea until 1879, when that mainland territory was separated. Ruled as a colony and then, from 1951 to 1974, as an Overseas Territory of Portugal, Cape Verde had a governor, a government council, and latterly a partly elected legislative council. While many Cape Verdians were taken to São Tomé as labourers on cocoa plantations, because of their Portuguese culture and some degree of education Cape Verdians were in some ways privileged among Portuguese-ruled Africans; they held subordinate government positions in other colonies, such as Portuguese Guinea.

In 1956 nationalists from Cape Verde and Portuguese Guinea formed the *Partido Africano da Independência da Guiné e Cabo Verde* (PAIGC). In the 1960s the PAIGC led by Amilcar Cabral waged a successful guerilla war. While armed resist-ance was not possible in the Cape Verde Islands, the PAIGC won control there after the Portuguese revolution of 1974. On 5 July 1975 Cape Verde became independent, ruled by the PAIGC which was already the ruling party in ex-Portuguese Guinea-Bissau. Aristides Pereira became president of the new republic.

On 14 Nov. 1980 Luis Cabral, brother of the PAIGC's founder and president of Guinea-Bissau since 1974, was overthrown in a *coup d'état* caused partly by resentment at Cape Verdians' privileged position in Guinea-Bissau. Ensuing tension led to the end of the ties between the two countries' ruling parties. Although the PAIGC retained its name in Guinea-Bissau, in Jan. 1981 it was renamed the *Partido Africano da Independência do Cabo Verde* (PAICV), in Cape Verde. The Constitution of 1981 made the PAICV the sole legal party, but in Sept. 1990 the National Assembly abolished its monopoly and free elections were permitted.

TERRITORY AND POPULATION. Cape Verde is situated in the Atlantic Ocean 620 km off West Africa and consists of 10 islands (Boa Vista, Brava, Fogo, Maio, Sal, Santa Luzia, Santo Antão, São Tiago and São Vicente) and 5 islets. The islands are divided into 2 groups, named Barlavento (windward) and Sotavento (lee-ward). The total area is 4,033 sq. km (1,557 sq. miles). The population was 341,491 at the census of 1990 (29·7% urban). Estimate (1996) 417,000; density, 103·4 per sq. km. About 600,000 Cape Verdeans live abroad.

Areas, populations and chief towns of the islands and districts:

District/Island	Area (sq. km)	Population Census 1980	Population Census 1990	Chief town
Paul	54·3	7,983	8,121	Pombas
Porto Novo	558	13,236	14,873	Porto Novo
Ribeira Grande	166·7	22,102	20,851	Ponta do Sul
Santo Antão	779	43,321	43,845	
São Vicente[1]	227	41,594	51,277	Mindelo
São Nicolau	388	13,572	13,665	Ribeira Brava
Sal	216	5,826	7,715	Santa Maria
Boa Vista	620	3,372	3,452	Sal Rei
Barlavento	*2,230*	*107,685*	*119,954*	

District/Island	Area (sq. km)	Population Census 1980	Population Census 1990	Chief town
Maio	269	4,098	4,969	Porto Inglês
Praia	395·7	57,748	82,802	Praia
Santa Catarina	242·9	41,012	41,584	Assomada
Santa Cruz	149·3	22,995	25,892	Pedra Badejo
Tarrafal	203·1	24,202	25,413	Tarrafal
São Tiago	991	145,957	175,691	
Fogo	476	30,978	33,902	São Felipe
Brava	67	6,985	6,975	Nova Sintra
Sotavento	*1,803*	*188,018*	*221,537*	

[1] Including Santa Luzia island, which is uninhabited.

The main towns (1990 census) are Praia, the capital, on São Tiago (61,644) and Mindelo on São Vicente, 47,109). Ethnic groups: Mixed, 71%; Black, 28%; White, 1%. The official language is Portuguese; a creole (Crioulo) is in ordinary use.

Vital statistics, 1994: Birth rate, 33·0; death rate, 8·0. Natural increase 1995, 2%. Annual emigration varies between 2,000 and 10,000. Life expectancy, 1994, 65·3 years.

CLIMATE. The climate is arid, with a cool dry season from Dec. to June and warm dry conditions for the rest of the year. Rainfall is sparse, rarely exceeding 5" (127 mm) in the northern islands or 12" (304 mm) in the southern ones. There are periodic severe droughts. Praia. Jan. 72°F (22·2°C), July 77°F (25°C). Annual rainfall 10" (250 mm).

CONSTITUTION AND GOVERNMENT. The Constitution was adopted in Sept. 1992.

A constitutional referendum was held on 28 Dec. 1994; turn-out was 45%. 82·06% of votes cast favoured a reform extending the powers of the presidency and strengthening the autonomy of local authorities. The President is elected for 5-year terms by universal suffrage.

The National Assembly is elected for 5-year terms.

Elections for the *National Assembly* of 72 members elected domestically and 3 from Cape Verdeans living abroad were held on 17 Dec. 1995. The electorate was 190,000; turn-out was 70%. 5 parties stood. The Movement for Democracy (MPD) won 50 seats with 59% of votes cast, the PAICV 21 with 28% and the Party of Democratic Convergence 1 with 6%.

Presidential elections took place on 17 Feb. 1991. Antonio Mascarenhas Monteiro (b. 1943; MPD) was elected by 72% of votes cast, defeating the incumbent President Pereira.

An MPD government was formed in Dec. 1995, which in March 1998 comprised: *Prime Minister:* Carlos Veiga (b. 1949).

Foreign Affairs and Communities: Amílcar Spencer Lopes. *Health and Social Progress:* João Medina. *Education, Science and Culture:* José Luis Livramento de Brito. *Agriculture, Food and Environment:* José Pinto Monteiro. *Infrastructure and Transport:* Teofilo Silva. *Justice and Internal Administration:* Simão Monteiro. *Economic Co-ordination:* António do Rosário. *Defence:* Ulpio Fernandes. *Maritime Affairs:* Helena Semedo. *Assistant Minister to the Prime Minister, Minister of Youth, Sports, Public Administration, Labour and Communications:* José António dos Reis.

National anthem: 'Sol, suor, o verde e mar' ('Sun, sweat, the green and the sea'); words and tune by A. Lopes Cabral.

Local Government. There are 16 municipal councils. Local elections were held in Jan. 1996.

DEFENCE. There is selective conscription.

Army. The Army is composed of 2 battalions and had a strength of 1,000 in 1997.

Navy. The coast guard numbered 50 in 1997 and has 2 inshore patrol craft.

Air Force. The Air Force has 2 An-26 transport and 1 DO228 patrol aircraft and fewer than 100 personnel.

INTERNATIONAL RELATIONS

Membership. Cape Verde is a member of the UN, OAU and is an ACP state of the EU.

ECONOMY

Policy. The third National Development Plan (1992–95) emphasized rural development, balanced regional development and promotion of private enterprise.

Budget. The budget for 1996 envisaged revenue of 21,110m. escudos and expenditure of 21,020m. escudos.

Currency. The unit of currency is the *Cape Verde escudo* (CVE) of 100 *centavos*. There are coins of 20 and 50 centavos and of 1, 2$^1/_2$, 10, 20 and 50 escudos, and banknotes of 100, 200, 500, 1,000 and 2,500 escudos. Foreign exchange reserves were US$57·3m. in 1995.

Banking and Finance. The Banco de Cabo Verde is the central bank (*Governor*, Amaro Alexandre da Luz) and bank of issue and was also a commercial bank. Its latter functions have been taken over by the new Banco Comercial do Atlántico, mainly financed by public funds. Another new bank has been opened in Cape Verde (Tota Acores) and the Caixa Economica has been upgraded into a Bank. Two foreign banks have also been established there.

Weights and Measures. The metric system is in use.

ENERGY AND NATURAL RESOURCES

Electricity. Production in 1993 amounted to 40m. kWh.

Minerals. Salt is obtained on the islands of Sal, Boa Vista and Maio. Volcanic rock (pozzolana) is mined for export. There are also deposits of kaolin, clay, gypsum and basalt.

Agriculture. In 1993, agriculture contributed 14·5% of GDP. Some 10-15% of the land area is suitable for farming. Some 37,000 ha are cultivated, mainly confined to inland valleys. About 2,500 ha are irrigated. The chief crops (production, 1993, in 1,000 tonnes) are: Coconuts, 10; sugar-cane, 19; bananas, 6; potatoes, 3; cassava, 2; sweet potatoes, 4; maize, 6; beans, groundnuts and coffee. Bananas and coffee are mainly for export.

Livestock (1993): 128,000 goats, 21,000 cattle, 105,000 pigs and 11,000 asses.

Fisheries. In 1993 there were 64 large and 1,400 small fishing vessels. Annual average catch, 9,000 tonnes, mainly tuna. About 200 tonnes of lobsters are caught annually.

INDUSTRY. In 1993 industry accounted for 17·2% of GDP, services 81%.

Labour. In 1994 the workforce was 120,565 (44,779 females).

FOREIGN ECONOMIC RELATIONS. Foreign debt was US$169·6m. in 1994.

Commerce. Imports in 1994 totalled 17,133m. escudos, exports 408m. escudos. Exports: Fish, salt, pozzolana (volcanic rock) and bananas.

Main export markets, 1994: Portugal, 50%; Spain, 16·7%; UK, 16·7%. Main import suppliers: Portugal, 37·3%; France, 14·5%; Netherlands, 6·6%; Côte d'Ivoire, 5·4%.

Tourism. Tourism is in the initial stages of development. There were 25,000 visitors in 1994, mainly emigrants returning on holiday. Some 50% of tourists originate from Portugal, 15% from Germany and 7% from France.

COMMUNICATIONS

Roads. In 1995 there were 1,100 km of roads (858 km paved) and there were 2,860 private cars and 870 commercial vehicles.

Civil Aviation. Amilcar Cabral International Airport, at Espargos on Sal, is a major refuelling point on flights to Africa and Latin America. Transportes Aéreos (TACV) de Cabo Verde, the national carrier, provides services to most of the other islands, and internationally to Amsterdam, Dakar, Lisbon, Nouakchott and Paris. In 1995 it operated 6 aircraft. Scheduled flights are also provided by Aeroflot, American Airlines, SAA, TAP and TAAG.

Shipping. The main ports are Mindelo and Praia. In 1995, the merchant marine totalled 32,320 GRT. There is a state-owned ferry service between the islands.

Telecommunications. There were 19,000 telephones in 1996. There are 2 national radio stations and a national TV service. Portuguese and French international radio and TV services also broadcast to Cape Verde. There were (1995) 69,000 radio receivers and 1,000 television receivers.

Press. In 1996 there were 3 national newspapers. A state-owned bi-weekly, and a weekly and a fortnightly owned by political parties. Total circulation approximates 12,000, but publication is suspended from time to time due to shortage of paper.

SOCIAL INSTITUTIONS

Justice. There is a network of People's Tribunals, with a Supreme Court in Praia. The Supreme Court is composed of a minimum of 5 Judges, of whom 1 is appointed by the President, 1 elected by the National Assembly, and the other by the Supreme Council of Magistrates.

Religion. At the 1990 census 93·2% of the population were Roman Catholic and 6·8% were mainly Protestant (Nazarence Church).

Education. Adult literacy was 71·6% in 1995 (male, 81·4%; female, 63·8%). Primary schooling is followed by lower (13-15 years) and upper (16-18 years) secondary education options. In 1994, there were 370 primary schools with 2,657 teachers for 78,173 pupils; In 1990 there were 10,304 pupils and 321 teachers at 16 preparatory schools, 5,026 pupils and 170 teachers at 4 secondary schools, and 531 students and 52 teachers at a technical school. There were 211 students and 53 teachers in 3 teacher-training colleges and about 500 students were at foreign universities.

Health. Medical provision, 1992: 1 doctor per 4,270 inhabitants, 1 nurse per 670 inhabitants. In 1996 there were 2 central and 3 regional hospitals, 15 health centres, 22 dispensaries and 60 community health clinics.

DIPLOMATIC REPRESENTATIVES

Of Cape Verde in Great Britain
Ambassador: Vacant (resides in The Hague).

Of Great Britain in Cape Verde
Ambassador: David R. Snoxell (resides in Dakar).

Of Cape Verde in the USA (3415 Massachusetts Ave., NW, Washington, D.C., 20007)
Ambassador: Corentino Virgilio Santos.

Of the USA in Cape Verde (Rua Hojl Ya Yenna 81, Praia)
Ambassador: Lawrence N. Benedict.

Of Cape Verde to the United Nations
Ambassador: José Luis Leão Monteiro.

Of Cape Verde to the European Union
Ambassador: José Rocha.

Further Reading

Carreira, A., *The People of the Cape Verde Islands*. London, 1982

Foy, C., *Cape Verde: Politics, Economics and Society*. London, 1988

Shaw, C., *Cape Verde Islands:* [Bibliography]. Oxford and Santa Barbara (CA), 1990

National statistical office: Direcção Geral de Estatística, Praia.

CENTRAL AFRICAN REPUBLIC

République Centrafricaine

Capital: Bangui
Population: 3·27m.
GNP per capita: US$370
HDI/world rank: 0·355/148

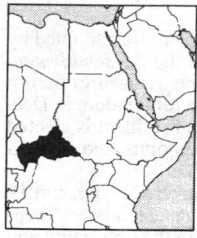

KEY HISTORICAL EVENTS. Central African Republic became independent on 13 Aug. 1960, after having been one of the 4 territories of French Equatorial Africa (under the name of Ubangi Shari) and from 1 Dec. 1958 a member state of the French Community. A Constitution of 1976 provided for the country to be a parliamentary democracy to be known as the Central African Empire. President Bokassa became Emperor Bokassa I. He was overthrown in a coup on 20–21 Sept. 1979 and the empire was abolished. On 15 March 1981 David Dacko was re-elected President but Army Chief General André Kolingba took power in a bloodless coup on 1 Sept. 1981 at the head of a Military Committee for National Recovery (CMRN), which held supreme power until 21 Sept. 1985 when President Kolingba dissolved it and initiated a return towards constitutional rule.

On 5 June 1996 following a mutiny in the army, President Patassé accepted an agreement brokered by France which amnestied the mutineers and led to the formation of a government of national unity. In Jan. 1997 mutineers demanded the replacement of President Patassé and killed 2 French soldiers. French forces retaliated, taking prisoner some 50 mutineers. France chaired a mediation committee of various neighbouring French-speaking states, and an agreement to end the mutiny was signed on 24 Jan. 1997 in Bangui and a peacekeeping force of neighbouring state, MISAB, was set up. Conflicts between the mutineers and MISAB continued well into 1997 despite a ceasefire concluded on 21 June 1997. A further ceasefire was concluded on 2 July 1997.

TERRITORY AND POPULATION. The republic is bounded in the north by Chad, east by Sudan, south by the Democratic Republic of the Congo and the Republic of the Congo, and west by Cameroon. The area covers 622,436 sq. km (240,324 sq. miles). The population at the 1988 census was 2,568,426; estimate, 1996, 3,274,000 (47% urban).

Vital statistics rates, 1996 estimates (per 1,000 population). Births, 40·0; deaths, 17·6. Infant mortality (per 1,000 live births), 111·7. Expectation of life in 1996 was 45·9 years (45·0 for males and 46·7 for females).

The areas, populations and capitals of the prefectures are as follows:

Prefecture	Sq. km	1988 census	Capital
Bangui[1]	67	451,690	Bangui
Ombella-M'poko	31,835	180,857	Bimbo
Lobaye	19,235	169,554	M'baiki
Sangha M'baéré	19,412	65,961	Nola
Mambere Kadéi	30,203	230,364	Berbérati
Nana-Mambere	26,600	191,970	Bouar
Ouham-Pendé	32,100	287,653	Bozoum
Ouham	50,250	262,950	Bossangoa
Nana Gribizi	19,996	95,497	Kaga-Bandoro
Bamingui-Bangoran	58,200	28,643	Ndele
Vakaga	46,500	32,118	Birao
Kemo	17,204	82,884	Sibut
Ouaka	49,900	208,332	Bambari
Basse-Kotto	17,604	194,750	Mobaye
Haute-Kotto	86,650	58,838	Bria
M'bomou	61,150	119,252	Bangassou
Haut-M'bomou	55,530	27,113	Obo

[1] Autonomous commune.

363

There are a number of ethnic groups, the main ones being Baya (34%) and Banda (27%).

French and Sango are the official languages.

CLIMATE. A tropical climate with little variation in temperature. The wet months are May, June, Oct. and Nov. Bangui. Jan. 31·9°C, July 20·7°C. Annual rainfall 1,289·3 mm. Ndele. Jan. 36·3°C, July 30·5°C. Annual rainfall 203·6 mm.

CONSTITUTION AND GOVERNMENT. Under the Constitution adopted by a referendum on 21 Nov. 1986, the sole legal political party was the *Rassemblement Démocratique Centrafricaine*. In Aug. 1992 the Constitution was revised to permit multi-party democracy. Further constitutional reforms followed a referendum in Dec. 1994, including the establishment of a *Constitutional Court*. The President is elected by popular vote for not more than 2 terms of 6 years, and appoints and leads a Council of Ministers. There is an 85-member *National Assembly.*

At the presidential and parliamentary elections held in 2 rounds on 22 Aug. and 19 Sept. 1993 there were 8 presidential and some 500 parliamentary candidates. Turn-out was 68·47%. Ange-Félix Patassé gained 37·8% of votes cast in the first round and 52·24% in the second. The Central African People's Liberation Movement (MLPC) gained 34 seats, the Democratic Central African Rally (DCAR) 13, the Patriotic Front for Progress 7, the Liberal Democratic Party 7, the Alliance for Democracy and Progress 6, the David Dacko Movement 6, the National Convention 3 and the Social Democratic Party 3, ind 2. 4 other parties gained 1 seat each.

President: Ange-Félix Patassé (MLPC; sworn in 22 Oct. 1993).

On 5 June 1996 an agreement was concluded between the government and opposition parties to form a government of national unity. Jean-Paul Ngoupandé (b. 1949; DCAR) replaced Jean Koyambonou as *Prime Minister* and was himself replaced on 30 Jan. 1997 by Michel Gbezzera-Bria (b. 1946; ind).

In March 1998 the government comprised:

Prime Minister: Michel Gbezzera-Bria.

Minister of Agriculture: Charles Massi. *Communications:* Thierry Ignifolo Vanden-Boss. *Economy, Planning and International Co-operation:* Christophe Bremaidou. *Environment:* Joseph Yomba. *Family and Social Affairs:* Eliane Mokodopo. *Finance and Budget:* Anicet Georges Doleguele. *Foreign Affairs:* Jean Mette-Yapende. *Higher Education and Research:* Theophile Touba. *Housing and Urban Development:* Clement Belibanga. *Human Rights, Culture and National Reconciliation:* Laurent Gomina Pampali. *Industry and Commerce:* Simon Bongolape. *Interior and Security:* Gen. François Ndjadder-Bedaya. *Justice:* Marcel Metefara. *Mines:* Joseph Agbo. *National Defence:* Dr Pascal Kado. *National Education:* Albert Mberio. *Parliamentary Relations:* Charles Armel Doubane. *Posts and Telecommunications:* Michel Bindo. *Public Function:* Jean-Claude Ngouandjia. *Public Health:* Dr Fernand Djemgbo. *Public Works:* Jackson Mazette. *Tourism, Arts and Culture:* Gaston Beina Gbandi. *Transport:* Andre Gombacko. *Youth and Sports:* Bertin Bea.

National anthem: 'La Renaissance' ('Rebirth'); words by B. Boganda, tune by H. Pepper.

Local Government: The Republic is divided into 16 prefectures (subdivided into 67 sub-prefectures and 2 administrative control posts) comprising 65 urban and 102 rural communes and 7 cattle-grazing communes. The 8 arrondissements of Bangui, the capital, have the status of communes. Local elected assemblies were inaugurated by the constitutional reforms of Dec. 1994.

DEFENCE. Selective national service for a 2-year period is in force. Some 1,200 French military personnel were stationed in 1993.

Army. The Army consisted (1997) of about 2,500 personnel, comprising a Republican Guard, 1 territorial defence, 1 combined arms and 1 support HQ regiment. Equipment includes 4 T-55 tanks. There are some 2,300 personnel in the para-military Gendarmerie.

Navy. The naval wing of the army has 9 river patrol craft and (1997) about 80 personnel.

Air Force. The Air Force has 2 Rallye light aircraft, 2 C-47 transports, 1 Falcon 20 VIP aircraft and 1 Ecureuil helicopter. Personnel strength (1997) about 150.

INTERNATIONAL RELATIONS

Membership. The Central African Republic is a member of the UN and OAU and is an ACP state of the EU.

ECONOMY

Budget. The budget for 1994 provided for expenditure of 54,406m. francs CFA, and for revenue of 43,904m. francs CFA.

Currency. The unit of currency is the *franc CFA* with a parity of 100 francs CFA to 1 French franc. There are coins of 1, 5, 10, 25, 50, 100 and 500 francs CFA, and banknotes of 500, 1,000, 2,000, 5,000 and 10,000 francs CFA. In 1992 42,800m. francs CFA were in circulation. Foreign exchange reserves were US$99·9m.; gold reserves, US$2·8m.

Banking and Finance. The Banque des Etats de l'Afrique Centrale (BEAC) acts as the central bank and bank of issue.

Weights and Measures. The metric system is in use.

ENERGY AND NATURAL RESOURCES

Electricity. Production in 1995 totalled 100,220 kWh (100,162 kWh hydro-electric).

Minerals. In 1994, 531,992 carats of gem diamonds, 95,957 carats of industrial diamonds and 138·18 kg of gold were mined. There are significant regions of uranium in the Bakouma area.

Agriculture. In 1993 1·9m. persons subsisted on agriculture, of whom 0·877m. were economically active. The main crops (production 1993, in 1,000 tonnes) are cassava, 610; groundnuts, 43; bananas, 96; plantains, 68; millet, 7; maize, 55; seed cotton, 20; coffee, 11; rice, 7.

Livestock, 1993, (in 1,000): Cattle, 2,781; goats, 1,334; sheep, 142; pigs, 474.

Forestry. There are 35·8m. ha of forest. The extensive hardwood forests, particularly in the south-west, provide mahogany, obeche and limba. Production (1995) 294,835 cu. metres.

Fisheries. Catch (1993) 13,500 tonnes.

INDUSTRY.

The small industrial sector includes factories producing cotton fabrics, footwear, beer and radios. Output in 1994: Beer, 258,149 hectolitres; cotton fabrics (1992), 5·32m. metres; soap, 1,896 tonnes; leather, 19 tonnes.

FOREIGN ECONOMIC RELATIONS

Commerce. Imports and exports in 1m. francs CFA:

	1991	1992	1993	1994	1995
Imports	44,770	43,211	35,559	73,263	94,582
Exports	30,750	28,328	31,073	79,541	96,981

In 1992, France took 74·4% of exports and provided 11% of imports. Main exports are coffee, diamonds, timber and cotton. Main imports include food, textiles, petroleum products, machinery, electrical equipment and motor vehicles.

COMMUNICATIONS

Roads. In 1994 there were 24,307 km of roads, of which 520 km were bitumenized. In 1992 46,982 vehicles were in use.

Civil Aviation. There is an international airport at Mpoko, near Bangui. The country is a member of Air Afrique, the regional carrier, with services to Paris and African capitals. Air Gabon and Air France also operate services.

Shipping. Timber and barges are taken to Brazzaville (Congo).

Telecommunications. There were 16,867 telephones in 1992. Broadcasting is provided by the state-controlled Radiodiffusion-Télévision Centrafricaine. There were 0·55m. radio and 7,500 TV (colour by SECAM) sets in 1993.

Cinemas. In 1992 there were 5 cinemas.

Press. In 1993 there was 1 daily newspaper.

SOCIAL INSTITUTIONS

Justice. The Criminal Court and Supreme Court are situated in Bangui. There are 16 high courts throughout the country.

Religion. In 1992 there were 1·44m. Protestants and 0·97m. Roman Catholics. Traditional animist beliefs are still current.

Education. A national education plan was initiated in 1994 to fund capital educational projects. Adult literacy rate was 60% in 1995. In 1990–91 there were 308,409 pupils at primary schools and 46,985 at secondary schools; technical schools had 1,862 students. There is a university at Bangui. It had 3,590 students and 140 academic staff in 1995–96.

Health. In 1990 there were 255 hospitals and health centres with 4,120 beds; there were also 170 doctors, 8 dentists, and 1,353 nursing personnel.

DIPLOMATIC REPRESENTATIVES

Of Central African Republic in Great Britain
Ambassador: Vacant (resides in Paris).

Of Great Britain in Central African Republic
Ambassador: Nicholas M. McCarthy, OBE (resides in Yaoundé).

Of Central African Republic in the USA (1618 22nd St., NW, Washington, D.C. 20008)
Ambassador: Henri Koba.

Of the USA in Central African Republic (Ave. David Dacko, Bangui)
Ambassador: Mosina Jordan.

Of Central African Republic to the United Nations
Ambassador: Antonio Deinde Fernandez.

Of Central African Republic to the European Union
Ambassador: Vacant.

Further Reading

Kalck, P., *Central African Republic* [Bibliography]. Oxford and Santa Barbara (CA), 1993

CHAD

République du Tchad

Capital: N'Djaména
Population: 6·98m.
GDP per head: (PPP$) 700
HDI/world rank: 0·288/164

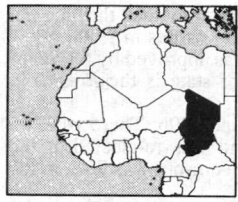

KEY HISTORICAL EVENTS. France proclaimed a protectorate over Chad on 5 Sept. 1900, and in July 1908 the territory was incorporated into French Equatorial Africa. It became a separate colony in 1920, and in 1946 one of the 4 constituent territories of French Equatorial Africa. On 28 Nov. 1958 it became an autonomous republic within the French Community and achieved full independence on 11 Aug. 1960.

Conflicts between the government and secessionist groups, particularly in the Moslem north and centre, began in 1965 and developed into civil war. In 1982 forces led by Hissène Habré gained control of the country. In June 1983 the Libyan-backed forces of former President Goukouni Oueddei re-occupied some territory, but by April 1987 they were forced back into the Aozou Strip in the north, occupied by Libyan forces since 1973. A ceasefire took effect in Sept. 1987. There was an attempted coup on 1 April 1989.

Rebel forces of the Popular Salvation Movement led by Idriss Déby entered Chad from Sudan in Nov. 1990 and, meeting little resistance, overcame the government forces of President Hissène Habré, who took refuge in Cameroon. On 4 Dec. 1990 Déby declared himself President.

TERRITORY AND POPULATION. Chad is bounded in the west by Cameroon, Nigeria and Niger, north by Libya, east by Sudan and south by the Central African Republic. In Feb. 1994 the International Court of Justice ruled that the Aouzou Strip along the Libyan border, occupied by Libya since 1973, was part of Chad. Area, 1,284,000 sq. km. At the 1993 census the population was 6,279,931 (5,929,192 settled, of whom 1,327,570 were urban and 359,069 nomadic). 1996 population estimate, 6,977,000. The capital is N'Djaména with 530,965 inhabitants (1993 census), other large towns being Moundou (282,103), Sarh (193,753), Bongor (196,713), Abéché (187,936) and Doba (185,461).

Vital statistics rates, 1996 estimates (per 1,000 population). Births, 44·2; deaths, 17·4. Infant mortality (per 1,000 live births), 120·4. Expectation of life in 1996 was 47·6 years (45·2 for males and 50·0 for females).

The areas, populations and chief towns of the 14 prefectures were:

Prefecture	Area sq. km	Population (1993 census)	Capital
Borkou-Ennedi-Tibesti	600,350	73,185	Faya (Largeau)
Biltine	46,850	184,807	Biltine
Ouaddaï	76,240	543,900	Abéché
Batha	88,800	288,458	Ati
Kanem	114,520	279,927	Mao
Lac	22,320	252,932	Bol
Chari-Baguirmi	82,910	1,251,906	N'Djaména
Guéra	58,950	306,253	Mongo
Salamat	63,000	184,403	Amtiman
Moyen-Chari	45,180	738,595	Sarh
Logone Oriental	28,035	441,064	Doba
Logone Occidental	8,695	455,489	Moundou
Tandjilé	18,045	453,854	Laï
Mayo-Kebbi	30,105	825,158	Bongor

The official languages are French and Arabic, but more than 100 different languages and dialects are spoken. The largest ethnic group is the Sara of southern Chad.

CLIMATE. A tropical climate, with adequate rainfall in the south, though Nov. to

April are virtually rainless months. Further north, desert conditions prevail. N'Djaména. Jan. 75°F (23·9°C), July 82°F (27·8°C). Annual rainfall 30" (744 mm).

CONSTITUTION AND GOVERNMENT. After overthrowing the regime of Hissène Habré, Idriss Déby proclaimed himself *President* and was sworn in on 4 March 1991.

A law of Oct. 1991 permits the formation of political parties provided they are not based on regionalism, tribalism or intolerance. There were 59 parties in 1996.

At a referendum on 31 March 1997 a new Constitution was approved by 63·5% of votes cast. It defines Chad as a unitary state. The head of state is the *President*, elected by universal suffrage.

A first round of presidential elections was held on 2 June 1996. There were 15 candidates. President Déby won 43·8% of votes cast, and was re-elected at the second round by 69·09% of votes cast against 1 opponent. Turn-out was 76% in the first round, but less than 50% in the second.

President: Idriss Déby (b. 1954; re-elected 3 July 1996).

The National Assembly has 125 members, elected for a four-year term in 25 single-member constituencies and 34 multi-member constituencies.

At the elections on 5 Jan. and 23 Feb. 1997 Idriss Déby's party, the Patriotic Salvation Movement, won 63 seats, the Union for Renewal and Democracy won 29 and the National Union for Democracy and Renewal won 15. Of the other 18 seats, 16 were won by 7 different parties and 2 were vacant.

In March 1998 the government comprised:
Prime Minister: Nassour Ouaïdou.
Minister of Agriculture: Mohktar Moussa. *Civil Service, Labour and Job Promotion:* Salibou Garba. *Commercial and Industrial Development and Promotion of Crafts:* Djitanger Djibangar. *Communication, Representative of Parliament and Government Spokesman:* Haroun Kabadi. *Culture, Youth and Sports:* Massouangaral Massingar. *Defence:* Oumar Kadjallmi. *Environment and Water:* Mariam Mahamat Nour. *Finance and the Economy:* Bichara Cherif Daoussa. *Foreign Affairs and Co-operation:* Mahamat Saleh Annadif. *Higher Education and Scientific Research:* Adoum Goudja. *Interior, Security and Decentralization:* Sallah Abderahmane. *Justice and Keeper of the Seals:* Limane Mahamat. *Livestock:* Mahamat Nouri. *Mines, Energy and Petroleum:* Saleh Kebzabo. *Planning and Development:* Ahmat Hamit. *Posts and Telecommunications:* Mahamat Ahmat Karambaye. *Primary, Secondary and Adult Education:* Abderahim Breme. *Public Health:* Kedellah Younouss Hamid. *Public Works, Transport, Habitat and Urbanization:* Ahmat Lamine. *Social Welfare and Family Support:* Agnes Allafi. *Tourism:* Pascal Yoadimnadji.

National anthem: 'Peuple tchadien, debout et à l'ouvrage' ('People of Chad, arise and to the task'); words by L. Gidrol, tune by P. Villard.

Local Government: The 14 prefectures are divided into 54 sub-prefectures and the Aouzou Strip.

DEFENCE. There are 8 military regions. Conscription is for 3 years.

Army. In 1996 the strength was 25,000 and there was a paramilitary Gendarmerie of 4,500 and a Republican Guard of 5,000. Equipment included 60 T-55 main battle tanks.

Air Force. The Air Force has 2 C-130 Hercules, 2 Turbo-Porters, 2 armed PC-7 aircraft and 2 Alouette helicopters.
Personnel (1995) about 350.

INTERNATIONAL RELATIONS

Membership. Chad is a member of the UN, OAU and is an ACP state of the EU.

ECONOMY

Budget. Budget revenue and expenditure (in 1m. francs CFA):

	1992	1993	1994	1995
Revenue:	31,422	42,694	39,042	42,704
Expenditure:	52,651	46,771	70,868	61,652

1993 revenue included: Income tax, 9,192; taxes on goods and services, 6,522; customs duties, 10,988; non-tax receipts, 6,383.

Currency. The unit of currency is the franc CFA with a parity value of 100 francs CFA to 1 French franc. The inflation rate for 1994 was 41%.

Banking and Finance. The Banque des Etats de l'Afrique Centrale is the bank of issue, and the principal commercial banks are the Banque de Développement du Tchad, the Banque Tchadienne de Crédit et de Dépôts and the Banque Commerciale du Chari.

ENERGY AND NATURAL RESOURCES

Electricity. Production (1994) amounted to 84·78m. kWh.

Oil. The oilfield in Kanem préfecture has been linked by pipeline to a new refinery at N'Djaména but production has remained minimal. There is a larger oilfield in the Doba Basin.

Minerals. Salt (about 4,000 tonnes per annum) is mined around Lake Chad, and there are deposits of uranium, gold, iron ore and bauxite. There are small-scale workings for gold and iron.

Agriculture. Some 80% of the workforce is involved in subsistence agriculture and fisheries. Cotton growing (in the south) and animal husbandry (in the central zone) are the most important branches. Production, 1994 (in 1,000 tonnes): Millet, 320; sugar-cane, 336; yams, 245; seed cotton, 160; groundnuts, 207; gum arabic, 7; dry beans, 24; sweet potatoes, 48; mangoes, 32; dates, 25; maize, 159; cotton lint, 39.

Livestock: Cattle (1995, in 1,000), 4,653; sheep and goats, 5,850; horses, 467; camels, 663.

Fisheries. Fish production, from Lake Chad and the Chari and Logone rivers, was estimated at 31,000 tonnes in 1993.

INDUSTRY. Output, 1994: Cotton fibre, 38,600 tonnes; edible oil, 5·41m. litres; sugar, 26,800 tonnes; beer, 1·1m. litres; cigarettes, 23·16m. packets; soap, 2,801 tonnes; bicycles, 1,827.

FOREIGN ECONOMIC RELATIONS

Commerce. Trade (in 1m. francs CFA):

	1992	1993	1994	1995
Imports	127,700	126,560	173,870	223,450
Exports	62,400	52,890	105,590	124,570

The main trading partners are France, Nigeria and Cameroon. Cotton exports in 1994, 28,857m. francs CFA; cattle, 15,401 francs CFA. Apart form cotton and cattle, other important exports are textiles and fish. The principal imports are machinery and transportation equipment, industrial goods, petroleum products and foodstuffs.

COMMUNICATIONS

Roads. In 1994 there were 32,000 km of roads, of which 0·82% were surfaced.

Civil Aviation. There is an international airport at N'Djaména, from which UTA and Air Afrique run 4 flights per week to Paris; there are also flights to Bangui and Kinshasa. There are also services by Camair, Ethiopian Airlines and Sudan Airlines. Air Tchad operates internal services to 12 secondary airports.

Telecommunications. In 1994 there were 4,733 telephones. The state-controlled Radiodiffusion Nationale Tchadienne broadcasts a national and 3 regional services in French, Arabic and Sara. There were estimated to be 1·26m. radio sets in 1993. Television is being developed (colour by SECAM) by the state-controlled Télé-Tchad.

SOCIAL INSTITUTIONS

Justice. There are criminal courts and magistrates courts in N'Djaména, Moundou, Sarh and Abéché, with a Court of Appeal situated in N'Djaména.

Religion. The northern and central parts of the country are predominantly Moslem. At the 1993 census there were 3,335,869 Moslems, 2,151,996 Christians and 456,064 animists.

Education. In 1994–95 there were 547,696 pupils in primary schools, 82,559 in secondary schools, 2,108 in technical schools and 2,000 at the university, with 120 academic staff. Adult literacy rate was 48·1% in 1995.

Health. In 1994 there were 3,962 hospital beds, 217 doctors, 878 nurses, 130 midwives and 10 pharmacists.

DIPLOMATIC REPRESENTATIVES

Of Chad in Great Britain
Ambassador: Vacant.

Of Great Britain in Chad
Ambassador: N. McCarthy, OBE (resides in Nigeria).

Of Chad in the USA (2002 R. St., NW, Washington, D.C., 20009)
Ambassador: Ahmat Mahamat Saleh.

Of the USA in Chad (Ave. Felix Eboue, N'Djaména)
Ambassador: David Halsted.

Of Chad to the United Nations
Ambassador: Ahmat A. Haggar.

Of Chad to the European Union
Ambassador: Ramadane Barma.

Further Reading

Joffe, G. and Day-Viaud, C. (eds.) *Chad.* [Bibliography]. Oxford and Santa Barbara (CA), 1995

National statistical office: Direction de la Statistique des Etudes Economiques et Démographiques, Ministère du Plan et de la Cooperation, N'Djaména.

CHILE

República de Chile

Capital: Santiago
Population: 14·66m.
GDP per head: (PPP$) 9,129
GNP: US$50·1bn.
HDI/world rank: 0·891/30

KEY HISTORICAL EVENTS. Magellan sighted what is now Chile in 1520. Subsequently Spaniards colonized the land in the 1530s and 1540s, defeating the Incas in the north and subjugating the Araucanian Indians in the South. Santiago, the capital, was founded in 1541, and Chile, as a colony, was attached to the viceroyalty of Peru.

In 1810 the Republic of Chile threw off allegiance to the Spanish crown, establishing a national government on 18 Sept. 1810. However, there were seven years of fighting before Chile was recognized as an independent republic in 1818. A constitution was adopted in 1883, and the country enjoyed stable government. Peru and Bolivia, which had been in dispute with Chile over their boundaries, were defeated in the War of the Pacific, 1879–1884. In 1925 the constitution was amended so as to strengthen the executive at the expense of the legislature.

1964 saw the election of the first Christian Democrat president, Eduardo Frei Montlava; but in 1970 Dr Salvador Allende Gossens was elected president as the Marxist leader of five left-wing parties which formed a coalition, the Popular Unity, to speed up social reform. This government was overthrown in 1973 by a *coup* of the three armed services and the *cabineros* (paramilitary police). These forces formed a government headed by a four-man junta. Gen. Augusto Pinochet Ugarte, C.-in-C. of the Army took over the presidency. President Allende died in the course of the *coup*. Tens of thousands of Popular Unity supporters were massacred and all political activities banned. The new government assumed wide-ranging powers, but the 'state of siege' ended in March 1978. A new constitution came into force on 11 March 1981 and provided for a return to democracy after a minimum period of eight years. Anti-government protests increased over the years while relations with the Roman Catholic church deteriorated. However, Gen. Pinochet continued as head of sate until 1989 when elections brought victory for the opposition. He remained army commander until March 1998 when he claimed his right, under the constitution, to become a senator for life. While clearing the way for much needed economic reforms, the Pinochet regime was responsible for wholesale human right abuses

TERRITORY AND POPULATION. Chile is bounded in the north by Peru, east by Bolivia and Argentina, and south and west by the Pacific Ocean. The area is 736,905 sq. km (284,520 sq. miles) excluding the claimed Antarctic territory. Many islands to the west and south belong to Chile: The Islas Juan Fernández (179 sq. km with 516 inhabitants in 1982) lie about 600 km west of Valparaíso, and the volcanic Isla de Pascua (Easter Island or Rapa Nui, 118 sq. km with 1,867 inhabitants in 1982), lies about 3,000 km WNW of Valparaíso. Small uninhabited dependencies include Sala y Goméz (400 km east of Easter Is.), San Ambrosio and San Félix (1,000 km northwest of Valparaíso, and 20 km apart) and Islas Diego Ramírez (100 km SW of Cape Horn).

In 1940 Chile declared, and in each subsequent year has reaffirmed, its ownership of the sector of the Antarctic lying between 53° and 90° W. long.; and asserted that the British claim to the sector between the meridians 20° and 80° W. long. overlapped the Chilean by 27°. Seven Chilean bases exist in Antarctica. A law of 1955 put the governor of Magallanes in charge of the 'Chilean Antarctic Territory' which has an area of 1,269,723 sq. km. and a population (1982) of 1,368.

The population at the census of 1992 was 13,231,803 (6,730,478 females). Estimate, 1997, 14,656,194 (83·5% urban in 1993; 7,416,492 females in 1997).

371

Vital statistics rates, 1996 (per 1,000 population): Birth, 18·09; death, 5·68; infant mortality (per 1,000 live births), 13·6. Growth rate, 1996, 1·24%. Life expectancy (1996), 74·49 years; male 71·26 years, female 77·76 years.

Area, population and capitals of the 13 regions:

Region	Sq. km	Population (1992 census)	Capital	Population (1992 census)
Tarapacá	58,786	341,112	Iquique	152,654
Antofagasta	125,253	407,409	Antofagasta	226,749
Atacama	74,705	230,786	Copiapó	100,946
Coquimbo	40,656	502,460	La Serena	120,336
Valparaíso	16,396	1,373,967	Valparaíso	276,736
Metropolitan	15,549	5,170,293	Santiago	5,180,757 [1]
Libertador	16,456	688,385	Rancagua	187,134
Maule	30,518	834,053	Talca	171,467
Bíobío	36,939	1,729,920	Concepción	330,448
Araucanía	31,946	774,959	Temuco	240,880
Los Lagos	67,247	953,330	Puerto Montt	130,737
Aysén	108,997	82,071	Coihaique	31,167 [2]
Magallanes	132,034	143,058	Punta Arenas	113,661

[1] Metropolitan area; city proper, 4,385,481. [2] 1982 census.

Other large towns (1992 census population) are: Viña del Mar (302,765), Puente Alto (254,534), Talcahuano (246,566), San Bernardo (188,850), Arica (169,217), Chillán (158,731), Los Angeles (142,136), Osorno (128,709), Coquimbo (122,872), Valdívia (122,436), Calama (120,602), Curicó (103,919) and Quilpué (102,824).79% of the population is mixed or *mestizo*, 20% are of European descent and 1% are indigenous Amerindians of the Araucanian, Fuegian and Chango groups. Language and culture remain of European origin, with the 675,000 Araucanian-speaking (mainly Mapuche) Indians the only sizeable minority.

The official language is Spanish.

CLIMATE. With its enormous range of latitude and the influence of the Andean Cordillera, the climate of Chile is very complex, ranging from extreme aridity in the north, through a Mediterranean climate in Central Chile, where winters are wet and summers dry, to a cool temperate zone in the south, with rain at all seasons. In the extreme south, conditions are very wet and stormy. Santiago. Jan. 67°F (19·5°C), July 46°F (8°C). Annual rainfall 15" (375 mm). Antofagasta. Jan. 69°F (20·6°C), July 57°F (14°C). Annual rainfall 0·5" (12·7 mm). Valparaíso. Jan. 64°F (17·8°C), July 53°F (11·7°C). Annual rainfall 20" (505 mm).

CONSTITUTION AND GOVERNMENT. A new Constitution was approved by 67·5% of the voters on 11 Sept. 1980 and came into force on 11 March 1981. It provided for a return to democracy after a minimum period of 8 years. Gen. Pinochet would remain in office during this period after which the Government would nominate a single candidate for President. At a plebiscite on 5 Oct. 1988 President Pinochet was rejected as a presidential candidate by 54·6% of votes cast.

The *President* is directly elected for a non-renewable 6-year term. Parliament consists of a 120-member *Chamber of Deputies* and a *High Assembly* of 39 senators.

Elections were held on 12 Dec. 1993 for the presidency, the Chamber of Deputies and 18 senators. Eduardo Frei was elected President by 58% of votes cast. The Christian Democratic Party (PDC) won 37 seats, the Socialist Party (PS) 33, National Renovation 31, the Independent Democratic Union 15 and ind 4.

A government was formed in Jan 1994 with the party composition: PDC, 10; PS, 4; Party for Democracy (PPD) and 4 ind. In the Congressional elections of 11 Dec. 1997 one Chilean adult in six did not register; of those who did 86% voted. President Eduardo Frei's Concertación alliance lost five points bringing its support down to 50·5%. With 70 seats the government still controls the 120-seat lower house.

In March 1998 the government comprised:
President: Eduardo Frei (b. 1943; PDC; sworn in 11 March 1994).
Agriculture: Carlos Mladinic Alonso (ind). *Promotion and Business:* Felipe

Sandoval. *Defence:* Raul Troncoso. *Trade and Industry:* Alvaro García (PPD). *Education:* José Arellano Marín (PDC). *Energy:* Alejandro Jadresic (ind). *Finance:* Eduardo Aninat (PDC). *Foreign Affairs:* José Miguel Insulzá (PS). *Health:* Alex Figueroa (PDC). *Housing:* Sergio Henriquez Diaz. *Interior:* Carlos Figueroa (PDC). *Justice:* Soledad Alvear (PDC). *Labour and Social Security:* Jorge Arrate (PS). *Minerals:* Sergio Jimenez Moraga. *National Resources:* Adriano del Piano (PPD). *Central Planning:* Roberto Pizarro Hofer (PS). *Public Works:* Ricardo Lagos (PS). *Transport:* Claudio Hohmann Barrientos (PDC). *Women's Affairs:* Josefina Bilbao (PDC). *General Secretary of the Government:* José Joaquín Brunner. *General Secretary of the Presidency:* Juan Villarzu Rohde.

National anthem: 'Dulce patria, recibe los votos' ('Sweet Fatherland, receive the vows'); words by E. Lillo, tune by Ramón Carnicer.

Local Government. There are 340 municipalities. Mayors and the 2,126 councillors are elected jointly and directly from the same list for 4-year terms, the most preferred candidate becoming mayor. Elections were held on 27 Oct. 1996. Concertación won 56·02% of votes cast; the Union for Chile coalition, 33%.

DEFENCE. Military service is for 1 year in the Army and 2 in the Navy and Air Force. Plans for weapons' modernization amounting to nearly US$2bn., which would benefit both the army and the air force, were announced in April 1998.

Army. A modernization plan of 1995 provides for the transformation of the 7 Army divisions into 3 garrisons: North, Centre-South and Austral, independent and adapted to the terrains in which they operate. Equipment includes 100 M4-A3 and 19 AMX-30 main battle tanks. The service operates 17 transport and 15 training aircraft and 7 helicopters. Strength (1997) 51,000 (28,000 conscripts) with 50,000 reserves. There is a 31,000-strong para-military force of Carabineros.

Navy. The principal ships of the Navy are the 4 ex-British 'County'-class guided missile armed destroyers of which 2 have had the missile launcher removed and replaced with an extended helicopter hangar and flight deck to operate 2 Super-Puma helicopters.

There are also 2 small modern West German-built diesel submarines, 2 British Oberon class submarines, 1 other British-built destroyer, 4 British Leander class frigates, 4 fast missile craft, 4 torpedo boats, 2 offshore patrol vessels and 8 coastal and 10 fast inshore patrol craft. There are 2 ex-US and 3 French-built landing ships. Major auxiliaries include 2 tankers, 1 submarine support vessel, 1 survey ship, 2 transports, and 1 Antarctic patrol ship. There are 11 service craft and numerous boats.

The Naval Air Service numbering 800 personnel operates 5 squadrons: 16 maritime patrol aircraft, 6 transport utility aircraft, 12 anti-submarine helicopters and 10 training aircraft.

Naval personnel in 1997 totalled 29,800 (3,800 conscripts) including 3,200 marines equipped with 30 light tanks and 60 artillery pieces and 1,500 Coast Guard who operate 15 patrol craft and 1 helicopter.

Air Force. Strength (1997) is 13,500 personnel (1,000 conscripts), with over 100 first-line and 150 second-line aircraft, divided among 13 groups, each comprising 1 squadron, within 4 combat and support brigades. Group 12 has twin-jet A-37Bs and Groups 1 and 3 have C-101CC Aviojets, all for strike duties. Group 2 is equipped for photo-reconnaissance with 3 Canberras. Group 4 has 14 Mirage 50 fighters. Group 5 has 14 Twin Otters for light transport and survey duties. Group 7 has 12 F-5E Tiger II fighter-bombers and 2 F-5F trainers. Group 8 fighter-bomber unit has 25 Mirage 5s. Group 10 is a transport wing, with 4 C-130 Hercules, 4 Aviocars, 4 Boeing 707s, including 1 equipped for airborne early warning and various helicopters. Group 9 has UH-1 Iroquois transport helicopters and Black Hawks. An aerial survey unit has 2 Learjets and 3 Beech twin-engined aircraft. Training aircraft include piston-engined Piper Dakota and T-35 Pillan basic trainers and licence-built CASA C-101BB Aviojets.

INTERNATIONAL RELATIONS

Membership. Chile is a member of the UN, OAS and LAIA, and is an associate member of Mercosur.

ECONOMY

Performance. In 1996, real GDP rose by 7·2%.

Budget. The fiscal year is the calendar year. 1995 government expenditure (in 1m. pesos): 4,443,188, including on health, 285,784; housing, 248,896; social security, 1,258,593; education, 741,913. The 1996 budget balanced at 6,267,200m. pesos. Total revenue (in 1,000m. pesos) 6,633·87, total expenditure 5,982·77. Sources of revenue included (in 1,000m. pesos): Taxes, 4,894·4; pension contributions, 389·3; sales of assets, 160·3; loan recoveries, 125·6. Expenditure included: Pensions, 1,644·3; personnel, 1,023·7; national investment, 760·1; consumer goods and services, 424·7; public debt service, 192·2. VAT is 16-18%.

Currency. The unit of currency is the *Chilean peso* (CLP) of 100 *centavos*. There are coins of 1, 5, 10, 50, 100, 2,000 and 10,000 pesos and notes of 10, 50, 100, 500, 1,000, 5,000 and 10,000 pesos. Inflation was 7·4% in 1996. In May 1996, 762,203m. pesos were in circulation. Gold reserves were US$700m. in 1993. Foreign exchange reserves were 6,980,787 pesos in May 1996. The peso was revalued 3·5% against the US dollar in Nov. 1994.

Banking and Finance. Banking is regulated by legislation of 1995. There is a Central Bank and a State Bank. The Central Bank was made independent of government control in March 1990. There were 12 domestic and 23 foreign banks in 1996. In May 1995, deposits in domestic banks totalled 8,623,323m. pesos; in foreign banks, 1,771,057m. pesos, and in other finance companies, 347,415m. pesos.

There are stock exchanges in Santiago and Valparaíso.

Weights and Measures. The metric system has been legally established since 1865, but the old Spanish weights and measures are still in use to some extent.

ENERGY AND NATURAL RESOURCES

Electricity. In 1995, production of electricity was 26,742m. kWh, of which 18,688m. kWh were hydro-electric.

Oil and Gas. Production of crude oil, 1995, was 605,100 cu. metres. Gas production, 1995, was 3,783·2m. cu. metres.

Minerals. The wealth of the country consists chiefly in its minerals. Copper is the most important source of foreign exchange and government revenues. Production, 1995, 2,448,100 tonnes. Coal is low-grade and difficult to mine, and mining is made possible by state subsidies. Production, 1995, 1,330,637 tonnes.

Output of other minerals, 1995 (in tonnes): Iron, 8,431,647; iron pellets, 3,859,700; limestone, 4,834,927; molybdenum, 16,694; zinc, 34,457; manganese, 70,450; gold, 44,233 kg; silver, 1,037,847 kg. Lithium, nitrate, iodine and sodium sulphate are also produced.

Agriculture. Agriculture and forestry contributed 6·9% of GDP in 1995. In 1991 4·13m. ha of land was arable, 0·25m. ha permanent crops and 13·6m. ha pasture. 1·3m. ha were irrigated in 1992. Some 35,000 tractors were in use in 1991.

Some principal crops were as follows:

Crop	Area harvested, 1,000 ha 1995	Production, 1,000 tonnes 1994	Crop	Area harvested, 1,000 ha 1994	Production, 1,000 tonnes 1992
Wheat	390	1,322	Potatoes	58	1,023
Oats	65	202	Dry beans	44	91
Barley	25	84	Lentils	10	16
Maize	104	899	Sugar-beet	52	2,978
Rice	30	131			

Fruit production, 1993 (in 1,000 tonnes): Apples, 870; grapes, 880; pears, 230;

peaches and nectarines, 160; plums, 130; oranges, 112; lemons and limes, 100. 0·32m. tonnes of wine were produced in 1992.

Livestock, 1992 (in 1,000): Cattle, 3,461; horses, 530; sheep, 6,600; goats, 600; pigs, 1,330; poultry, 35,000. Products, 1994 (in 1,000 tonnes): Beef, 247; mutton, 13; pork, 158; poultry, 310; milk, 1,222; eggs, 1,856m. Since 1985 agricultural trade has been consistently in surplus. Wine exports rose from US$50m. in 1990 to US$400m. in 1996.

Forestry. In 1995 there were 9m. ha of natural forest and woodland (eucalyptus, pine and poplar are important species) and 1·3m. ha of planted forest. 33m cu. metres of timber were cut in 1994.

Fisheries. Chile has 4,200 km of coastline and exclusive fishing rights to 1·6 m. sq. km. There are 220 species of edible fish. In 1990 the fishing fleet comprised 250 vessels over 100 GRT totalling 111,140 GRT. Catch in 1994 was 8·02m. tonnes. Fish farms produced 60,728 tonnes of salmon in 1992.

INDUSTRY. Manufacturing contributed 16·8% of GDP in 1995.

Output of major products in 1995 (in 1,000 tonnes): Fishmeal, 877; cellulose, 1,219·8; newsprint, 201·5; paper and cardboard, 198·7; motor tyres, 2,329,900 items; cement, 2,885·2; iron or steel plates, 294·1; copper wire, 5·6; beer, 331·7m. litres; motor vehicles, 21,574 items.

Labour. In 1996 the workforce numbered 5,294,100, of whom 240,100 were unemployed. In June 1996, 1,338,500 persons were employed in social or personal services, 770,900 in agriculture, forestry and fisheries, 907,900 in trade, 847,200 in manufacturing, 389,400 in transport and communications and 401,600 in building. In 1992 there was a monthly minimum wage of 38,600 pesos.

Trade Unions. Trade unions were established in the middle 1880s.

FOREIGN ECONOMIC RELATIONS. In Sept. 1991 Chile and Mexico signed the free trade Treaty of Santiago envisaging annual tariff reductions of 10% from Jan. 1992. On 1 Oct. 1996 Chile joined the Mercosur free trade zone, but continues to act unilaterally in trade with third countries.

Foreign debt was US$20,877m. on 30 June 1996.

Commerce. Imports and exports in US$1m.:

	1990	1991	1992	1993	1994	1995
Imports	7,272	7,686	9,670	10,869	11,501	15,348
Exports	8,580	9,048	10,126	9,416	11,645	16,446

In 1995 the principal exports were (in US$1m.): Agricultural products, 1,562; minerals, 7,984 (of which copper, 6,487); manufactures, 6,847. Major export markets (in US$1m.), 1995: Japan, 2,906; USA, 2,375; UK, 1,076; Brazil, 1,056; South Korea, 896; Germany, 837. Major import suppliers: USA, 3,793; Argentina, 1,385; Brazil, 1,195; Japan, 1,013; Germany, 790. External debt of the public sector shrank from US$7·5bn. to US$5·2bn. in the first half of 1996.

Tourism. There were 1·5m. foreign visitors in 1996. Tourist receipts were US$800m. in 1993.

COMMUNICATIONS

Roads. In 1997 there were about 80,000 km of roads, but only 20% were hard-surfaced. There were 65 km of motorways and 10,255 km of main roads. In 1991 there were 705,100 private cars, 60,500 taxis, 86,900 lorries, 281,700 vans, 30,400 buses and 52,500 motor cycles.

Railways. The total length of state railway (EFE) lines was (1995) 3,447 km, including 1,317 km electrified, of broad- and metre-gauge. EFE is now mainly a passenger carrier, and carried 10·1m. passengers in 1995. Freight operations are in the hands of the semi-private companies Ferronor, which carried 1·5m. tonnes in 1995, and Pacifico, which carried 4·3m. tonnes in 1995. The Antofagasta (Chili) and Bolivia

Railway (728 km, metre-gauge) links the port of Antofagasta with Bolivia and Argentina and carried 1·8m. tonnes in 1995.

There is a metro in Santiago (37·5 km).

Civil Aviation. There are 344 airports, with an international airport at Santiago (Comodoro Arturo Merino Benítez). The 2 major airlines merged in 1995: Línea Aérea Nacional Chile (Lan-Chile) operating (1995) 3 B-767-200ERs; 3 B-767-300ERs; 7 B-737-200s and 4 other aircraft; and Línea Aérea de Colore (Ladeco) operating (1995) 2 B-757-200ERs, 2 B-737-100s, 10 B-737-200s, 1 B-737-300 and 1 A300. Services are also provided by Aeroflot, Aerolíneas Argentinas, Aeroperú, Air France, Alitalia, American Airlines, Avianca, British Airways, Canadian Airlines, Cubana, Iberia, KLM, LACSA, LAPSA, Lloyd Aéreo Boliviano, Lufthansa, National Airlines, Pluna, Swissair, United Airlines and Varig. There are 3 domestic airlines operating internal flights.

Shipping. The mercantile marine in 1995 totalled 0·98m. GRT, including oil tankers, 71,150 GRT, but most of the fleet operates under flags of convenience. The 6 major ports, the largest being Valparaíso, San Antonio, Antofagasta, Arica and Iquique, are state-owned; there are 11 smaller private ports. In 1990 28·56m. tonnes of cargo were loaded, and 19·19m. unloaded.

Telecommunications. There are 1,486 post offices and agencies and in 1994 1·5m. telephones.

There are 168 radio stations grouped in the Asociación de Radiodifusores de Chile. There are 131 television broadcast stations. The state-controlled Televisión Nacional de Chile transmits from 23 stations (colour by NTSC). 4 universities also transmit programmes. In 1995 there were 4·95m. radio and 3m. TV sets.

Cinemas. Cinemas number 133. Total attendance, 1993, 7,733,407.

Press. (1995). There were 32 national daily newspapers with a combined circulation of 1·4m.

SOCIAL INSTITUTIONS

Justice. There are a High Court of Justice in the capital, 12 courts of appeal distributed over the republic, courts of first instance in the departmental capitals and second-class judges in the sub-delegations.

Religion. In 1990 there were 10·63m. Roman Catholics with 1 cardinal-archbishop, 5 archbishops, 22 bishops and 2 vicars apostolic. 15% of the population defined themselves as evangelical. There were 0·13m. Jews in 1991.

Education. In 1995 there were 4,779 pre-primary schools with 9,576 teachers for 283,061 pupils, 8,702 primary schools with 80,155 teachers for 2·1m. pupils and 51,042 teachers in secondary schools for 679,165 pupils. Adult literacy rate, 95·2%; male, 95·4%, female 95·0% (1995).

In 1996 there were 367,094 students in higher education. In the public sector there were 12 universities, 5 Roman Catholic universities, 2 universities of educational science and 1 technological university. In the private sector there were 33 universities, 2 Roman Catholic universities, 1 Adventist university, 2 technical universities, 2 maritime universities, 1 IndoAmerican university, 1 international university and 1 university for each of the following: arts, science and communications; arts and social science; Christian humanism; computer science; science and arts; teaching. There were also 83 other institutes of higher education.

Health. In 1988 there were 354 hospitals with (in 1991) 44,404 beds. In 1987 there were 5,744 doctors, 1,834 dentists, 232 pharmacists, 1,825 midwives and 2,461 other medical personnel.

Social Security. The Pension Fund Administration was founded in 1981. In Nov. 1995 its total assets were 9,974,787m. pesos. Employees are required to save 13% of their pay. In Oct. 1995 it had 5,193,590 members and assets of 9,974,787m. pesos. In 1995 about 25% of adults had private health insurance.

DIPLOMATIC REPRESENTATIVES

Of Chile in Great Britain (12 Devonshire St., London W1N 2DS)
Ambassador: Mario Artaza.

Of Great Britain in Chile (Av. El Bosque 0125, Casilla 72-D, Santiago 9)
Ambassador: Glynne Evans.

Of Chile in the USA (1732 Massachusetts Ave., NW, Washington, D.C., 20036)
Ambassador: John Biehl del Rios.

Of the USA in Chile (Agustinas 1343, Santiago)
Ambassador: Gabriel Guerra-Mondragon.

Of Chile to the United Nations
Ambassador: Juan Somavia Altamirano.

Of Chile to the European Union
Ambassador: Eduardo Gonzalo Arenas Valverde.

Further Reading

Banco Central de Chile. *Boletín Mensual.*

Bethell, L. (ed.) *Chile since Independence.* CUP, 1993
Blakemore, H., *Chile.* [Bibliography] Oxford and Santa Barbara (CA), 1988
Collier, S. and Sater, W. F., *A History of Chile, 1808–1994.* CUP, 1996
Garretón, M. A., *The Chilean Political Process.* London and Boston, 1989
Hojman, D. E., *Chile: the Political Economy of Development and Democracy in the 1990s.* London, 1993.—(ed.) *Change in the Chilean Countryside: from Pinochet to Aylwin and Beyond.* London, 1993
Oppenheim, L. H., *Politics in Chile. Democracy, Authoritarianism and the Search for Development.* Boulder (CO), 1993

National statistical office: Instituto Nacional de Estadísticas (INE), Santiago.
Website: http://ine.conicyt.cl:8020/

CHINA IN THE 21ST CENTURY

Richard Grant

The most populous country in the world with a huge geographical landmass, China today projects many contradictory images to the world. Over the last twenty years China's leaders, under the direction of the late Deng Xioaping, have undertaken an ambitious economic reform programme, which has astounded the world with growth rates of 9% to 10% per year during this period. Yet, China still claims to be only a developing country. By Western standards, China has a dismal human rights record, but calls for Beijing to make improvements are countered by the assertion that the Chinese people are more concerned about improved living standards—which the economic reform programme is delivering—than political rights. China claims to be a non-threatening power, seeking harmonious relations with the world, yet engages in provocative military exercises in the Taiwan Straits and lays territorial claims to large parts of the South China Sea.

These contradictions make predicting China's future course a difficult task. Some trends are worrisome. An authoritarian, economically successful China with a modernised military could be a source of instability and possible conflict. On the other hand, an economically successful China, in which personal freedoms are expanding and institutions of civil society are taking root, may well prove to be an attractive political and economic partner. These two projections of China's future are not the only possibilities, of course. China's economic reform process may run off course. The financial and currency turmoil in East Asia of late 1997, which so far has not affected China, was provoked by institutional failings which exist in China as well. Were China's economy to tumble into recession, social and political upheaval could well ensue, leading to chaos and instability. Finally, China might simply muddle through, continuing gradual economic reform with mixed results and maintaining internal stability, despite occasional outbreaks of tension. Such a China would not be threatening, but would most certainly be a prickly partner.

An assessment of China's future prospects requires an understanding of the realities of the contradictions and trends that shape her today. It is a truism, but a valid one nonetheless, that the forces dominant in China today will largely determine her future. Those elements which will contribute to China's positive development can be grouped under the label of modernization: economic development and reform, institutional development—both political and legal—and the development of civil society. These elements are countered by the forces of repression rooted in insecurity: fear of change, distrust of the outside world, and dread of instability. Modernization and repression are both at work in China today, and for the moment modernization seems to have the upper hand.

China's economic reform programme has been a remarkable success. Growth rates have averaged 8% to 10% for the period 1978-1997. Per capita GDP has more than doubled, and personal income has risen by 700%. Foreign Direct Investment (FDI) in China now totals over $100 billion and China now has hard currency reserves in excess of $140 billion.

These figures need to be put into perspective, however. China's GDP accounts for only 2·8% of the world total and China accounts for less than 3% of world trade. Per capita GDP in China still stands at only $625. Moreover the impact of economic reform has been felt unevenly. Most of this new wealth has been generated in the Southern coastal provinces, leaving much of China's hinterlands untouched. Rural areas, where the vast majority of the Chinese populace, 800 million people, reside, have seen the gains made in the initial period of reform in the 1980s erode. Importantly, China needs high growth rates to provide employment for its expanding population: 15 million babies are born in China each year.

The success of the market reforms in China have also cast a harsh light on the failure of the state owned enterprises (SOE). Well over 50% of the SOEs are loss-making and bad loans to them total 25% to 35% of GDP. As 40% of industrial workers are employed by the SOEs, large scale closure of loss making enterprises will result in unemployment in a country where the social welfare system is embryonic at best. Already workers in several SOEs have staged protests over non-payment of wages or job losses.

The plight of the SOEs is also threatening China's banking system. The percentage of unrecoverable loans to SOEs held by China's banks is high and a loss of confidence in the banking system would be disastrous. China has a high personal savings rate, 35% of GNP, most of which is held by China's banks.

As noted earlier, for the moment the forces of modernization have the upper hand in China. At the 15th Party Congress in October 1997 President Jiang Zemin announced an ambitious programme to reform the SOE system by the year 2000. Insolvent enterprises will be closed down or merged with viable entities and some form of share holding will be introduced. Similarly, the authorities are working to enhance the banking system. Regional branches of the People's Bank of China, the central bank, will be created along the lines of the Federal Reserve system in the United States. The goal is to distance banking authorities from the pressures exerted by local officials who often force loans to loss-making enterprises, and to bind regional banking authorities more closely to the centre.

These are very ambitious reforms and there is no guarantee of success. Hopes that viable SOEs could raise additional capital by issuing so-called "red shares" on the Hong Kong stock exchange will probably have to be deferred in light of the East Asian economic turmoil. The reform programme will without doubt generate unemployment and the government will be hard pressed to maintain social stability and cohesion. Failure of the SOE reform programme, or even modest success but accompanied by social unrest, could unleash new forces of repression.

China's leadership continues to maintain a firm grip on society. Even if it only plays lip service to the tenets of "Marxism, Leninism, Mao Zedong Thought" public criticism of the leadership or the Communist Party is not tolerated. The majority of the Chinese people seem willing to accept this, provided that their leaders continue to deliver economic success and that the growing prosperity is fairly widely spread. Large-scale unemployment in the industrial sector coupled with the perception that officials benefit unfairly from the reform process via corrupt practices might well provoke destabilising urban unrest.

This is particularly true because China is a much more open society than in 1978. Despite the crackdown that followed the crushing of the Tiananmen Square demonstrations in 1989, the average Chinese has much more freedom of personal choice since perhaps the 1930s. In urban areas in particular, it is relatively easy to change jobs, housing and schools. While public criticism of the leadership and party is not tolerated at the personal level discourse is relatively unfettered. Criticism of government policy can be heard in restaurants and offices, even among government employees.

China's political structures are also loosening. Most villages now elect their own officials, often in open multi-candidate elections. Candidates do not have to be Communist Party members. There are proposals to introduce similar elections at the township and municipal levels. These reforms have been introduced in part to eliminate the abuses committed by corrupt, appointed officials. They have also introduced notions of accountability into village governance practice and this will grow more widely throughout China if elections at higher levels of local government are more widely organised.

Legal reform is under way in China. The Criminal Justice system has been reformed, and now, for the first time, allows defendants access to legal counsel prior to trial. There is also growing recognition for the need for the rule of law. As the non-state sector expands there is growing frustration with a system characterized by the arbitrariness of the whim of officialdom and the strength of one's connections or "guanxi". The leadership in Beijing also sees legal reform as an important tool in the fight against corruption. There is, in short, demand for greater predictability and clarity.

These are all welcome developments but they will pose new challenges for China's leaders. As personal freedoms expand, accountability of officials grows, and as recourse to the law becomes a valid option to redress wrongs, tolerance of government failure or incompetence will decline. If the leadership perceives that these new freedoms are being used to challenge its legitimacy, there will be a crackdown.

Whether such a crackdown would succeed is questionable. The use of the People's Liberation Army (PLA) to suppress the 1989 demonstrators in Tiananmen Square was highly controversial at the time, even among some of the PLA's most senior leaders. Disquiet about those events has grown in the intervening years, and there is almost universal criticism of that action, even among some senior party cadres. There is no guarantee that the PLA would be willing to intervene against any future civilian unrest.

China's leaders are turning increasingly to pragmatic, non-ideological policies. There is keen awareness of the need to maintain international confidence, particularly in light of the Asian economic crisis. Hence, China has so far resisted temptations to devalue the currency, the yuan, despite devaluations by its neighbours which risk making Chinese exports less competitive. Beijing seems to realise that a devaluation of the yuan would only further aggravate regional economic woes. Similarly, despite intense downward pressure on Hong Kong's currency, stock and real estate markets, China has so far refrained from intervening in the Hong Kong government's efforts to stabilize the economy.

Beijing has also drawn at least one clear lesson from the economic upheaval in Asia; a weak, non-transparent banking system distorted by cronyism and political favouritism is a recipe for potential disaster. Hence the introduction of a more accountable banking system in China with stronger ties to the centre than to regional or provincial authorities. Whether these reforms will be successful remains to be seen. China, after all, has a long history of provincial authorities ignoring or defying instructions from Beijing. As an old Chinese proverb says "the mountains are high and the emperor is far away".

In any event, the Asian crisis is likely to delay any moves to make the yuan fully convertible. China has been able to insulate itself from recent turmoil precisely because its currency is not openly traded on world markets. A further opening to Western financial institutions will proceed more slowly than might have been the case had the Asian economic boom not faltered.

These policies are measured steps undertaken in order to mark a middle ground between on the one hand, the need to continue economic reform while, on the other hand, maintaining internal stability and shielding the Chinese economy from external instabilities. This pragmatism was demonstrated during the annual National People's Congress taking place in March 1998. China's economic czar and Deputy Prime Minister, Zhu Rongji, the man responsible for engineering China's "soft landing" in the mid 1990s—breaking inflation while maintaining economic growth—was made Premier, replacing the conservative Li Peng, who retired upon the completion of his second term of office. Zhu will push forward programmes to marketize and modernize the economy, seeking to ensure growing, if gradual, prosperity for the Chinese people.

Zhu will also be keeping a close eye on social and political instability. He is unlikely to introduce any large scale political reform. Despite his comments in June of 1989 when he was mayor of Shanghai during the repression in Tiananmen Square in Beijing: (". . . historical facts cannot be covered up by anybody. The truth will always come out."—comments which angered many conservatives), Zhu is not a Jeffersonian democrat. Zhu is first and foremost an economist and his priorities are firmly rooted in the pursuit of successful economic reform. Moreover, the collegial or collective leadership that now prevails in Beijing will require him to build coalitions that will include conservative elements of the leadership, such as Li Peng, who will take over as Chairman of the National People's Congress.

One area where Zhu may well prove more aggressive than his predecessors is in the fight against corruption. Anti-corruption drives have occurred frequently in recent years, but have often stopped short of hitting those in the higher echelons of the party or with close ties to them. Zhu is known to have little tolerance for corruption and incompetence and, as Deputy Prime Minister, dismissed officials who failed in their responsibilities. With the full powers of the premiership behind him, he may feel better equipped to cut out the rot which is hampering economic reform.

The challenges that confront Zhu are enormous: rising unemployment, vast over-capacity, environmental calamity, poor infrastructure, incompetent and corrupt bureaucrats to name the most obvious. He is, however, a man of vision, with a firm commitment to economic reform and, while he survives, will not waiver from that path. Political reality, however, will require him to proceed cautiously and he is highly unlikely to be the architect of a major restructuring of the Chinese system. More probably, Zhu Rongji will lay the ground work for the next generation, now in their forties and fifties (Zhu is seventy). It is they who will bring China fully into the twenty-first century.

The short term prognosis for China is therefore cautious management of the ups and downs that will be provoked by continued economic reform. China will continue to change, but not as dramatically as over the last decade. If Zhu and his colleagues orchestrate this process successfully they will have laid the foundation for a spectacular political and economic blossoming of China early in the next century.

Richard Grant is Head of the Asia Pacific Programme at the Royal Institute of International Affairs

CHINA

Zhonghua Renmin Gonghe Guo

(People's Republic of China)

Capital: Beijing (Peking)
Population: 1,224m.
GDP per head: (PPP$) 2,604
GNP: US$630·2bn.
HDI/world rank: 0·626/108

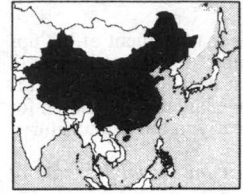

KEY HISTORICAL EVENTS. The Han dynasty (216 BC–220 AD) was founded by an official who retained the Ch'in bureaucracy and made Confucianism a state philosophy. The system of civil service recruitment by public competitive examination was instituted in this period, and Buddhism was introduced from India. The Han dynasty collapsed amid intrigues and was followed by centuries of division and disorder. Unity was restored under the T'angs (618–906), but was lost again until the Sung period (960–1279). Mongol invaders succeeded in imposing a foreign dynasty (Yuan) but were quickly assimilated to the higher cultural and technological level of the Chinese. A peasant rising drove the last Mongol from the throne in 1368 and ushered in the Ming dynasty.

Although unity and tradition were restored, the Ming empire was not as efficient as the T'ang nor as enlightened as the Sung. A new imperial capital was built at Beijing only 40 miles from the Wall and thus vulnerable to attack; preoccupation with the defence of this frontier contributed to a neglect of the defence of the sea, whence came the Portuguese in 1516, the Dutch in 1622, and the English in 1637. A wave of nomad invaders, the Manchus, breached the Wall to capture Beijing in 1644 and found the Ch'ing dynasty, which lasted until 1912. The Manchus, who used Dutch ships to subdue Taiwan in 1683, were not sea-going, and confined foreign trade to Canton after 1757. The court would not enter into diplomatic relations with Europe, and would receive foreigners only if they paid homage. Catholic missionaries were tolerated and even employed in state service, but outside ideas made little impression on the ossified and complacent traditionalism of the court and mandarins. Though gradually assimilated, the Ch'ing did not forget they were a foreign dynasty in an occupied country: a quota of posts was reserved for Manchus, and a system of garrison governorships was set up which degenerated into sinecures doing nothing to modernize the armed forces.

A British expeditionary force sent to overturn a Chinese ban on imports of opium forced the empire to cede Hong Kong and grant Britain economic and diplomatic privileges. Other western nations followed suit. Foreigners established concessions in 'treaty ports' administered by their own officials. In 1851 a neo-Protestant *T'ai P'ing* rebellion broke out, which was put down with western help in 1864. The British and French had seized Beijing in 1860 and burnt the imperial palace. In 1895 China was defeated by a modernized Japan and forced to cede Korea and Taiwan. The emperor became converted to the necessity for reforms, but these were blocked by court intrigue. An anti-foreigner *Boxer* rebellion was suppressed by western forces in 1900.

Sun Yat-sen founded the Kuomintang (Nationalist Party) in 1905. When troops at Hangchow mutinied in Oct. 1911 and proclaimed a republic, the emperor's mediator Yuan went over to them and made himself president; the infant emperor abdicated. Yuan attempted to make himself emperor but was overthrown in 1916 after acceding to Japan's demands which would have made China a virtual protectorate. The Beijing government lost all real authority and the country disintegrated into the hands of squabbling warlords. At Versailles the Allies failed to restore territory seized by Japan. Sun Yat-sen, who had formed a separatist government in Canton, turned to the Soviet regime. The Communist Party (founded in 1921) co-operated with the Kuomintang, led after 1926 by Chiang Kai-shek, in attacking both warlords and foreign concessions, but in 1937 Chiang turned on the Communists and suppressed them. Communism was then carried on by Mao Zedong's rural 'Soviet', at first in Kiangsi, and then, after the Long March, in Yenan. Chiang came to terms with the warlords and foreign concessionaries, but his aims to create a modern state were thwarted by Japanese invasions in 1931 and 1937, and by his campaign against the Communists. In 1936 he was forced (after being kidnapped) to declare a joint front with them against Japan, but hostilities continued.

After the Second World War full-scale civil war broke out. Chiang was defeated and took refuge on Taiwan where the Republic of China was set up. Mao proclaimed a People's Republic on 1 Oct. 1949. The Maoist period was marked by innovatory excesses: the agricultural communes (now abolished); the conscription of intellectuals to till the fields; the disastrous 'Great Leap Forward' with its backyard blast furnaces; the Thought (and cult) of Mao; the Cultural Revolution. After Mao's death in 1976 moderates within the Communist Party triumphed and the radical Gang of Four led by Mao's wife Chang Ch'ing were first publicly denounced and then arrested. China has since emerged as a major international power with a liberalized economy, firstly under Deng Xiaoping and more recently Jiang Zemin.

Denounced in the Cultural Revolution, Deng was formally rehabilitated in 1973 and became one of Mao's vice-premiers for a time in the 1970s. The keynote of his administration was political and economic pragmatism. He sought 'readjustment, restructuring, consolidation and improvement'. In 1979 China and the US established full diplomatic relations. From that time contacts with the west have grown considerably. Deng Xiaoping resigned from the Politburo in Nov. 1987 and from the chairmanship of the Military Commissions in Nov. 1989.

The funeral of the Communist party General secretary Hu Yaobang on 15 April 1989 sparked off mass student demonstrations which escalated into a popular 'pro-democracy' movement in Beijing, Shanghai and other provincial centres demanding reforms. The demonstrations gathered strength during the summit visit of the Soviet President Gorbachev (15–17 May) and culminated in a sit-in in Tiananmen Square, Beijing This was confronted by army units, at first peacefully. However, on 4 June troops opened fire on the demonstrators and tanks were sent in to disperse them. The official casualty figures were: 'over 200' demonstrators and 'dozens' of soldiers killed, and some 9,000 injured. A hard-line faction assumed control in the Party Politburo which appointed Jiang Zemin as General Secretary. Martial law was imposed from May 1989 to Jan. 1990. Since then, however, China has moved cautiously towards a more open society with an economy that makes allowance for market principles.

For the background to the handover of Hong Kong in 1997, see p.395.

TERRITORY AND POPULATION. China is bounded in the north by Russia and Mongolia, east by North Korea, the Yellow Sea and the East China Sea, with Hong Kong and Macao as enclaves on the south-east coast; south by Vietnam, Laos, Burma, India, Bhutan and Nepal; west by India, Pakistan, Afghanistan, Tajikistan, Kyrgyzstan and Kazakhstan The total area (including Taiwan) is estimated at 9,572,900 sq. km (3,696,100 sq. miles). A law of Feb. 1992 claimed the Spratly, Paracel and Diaoyutasi Islands. An agreement of 7 Sept. 1993 at prime ministerial level settled Sino-Indian border disputes which had first emerged in the war of 1962.

At the 1991 census the population was 1,130,510,638 (548,690,231 females). Population estimate, 1996: 1,223·89m. (601·89m. female; 359·5m. urban).

1979 regulations restricting married couples to a single child, a policy enforced by compulsory abortions and economic sanctions, have been widely ignored, and it was admitted in 1988 that the population target of 1,200m. by 2000 would have to be revised to 1,270m. Since 1988 peasant couples have been permitted a second child after 4 years if the first born is a girl, a measure to combat infanticide. The average number of live births per woman (married or otherwise) in 1996 was 1·42. The lowest and highest averages by region were Beijing with 0·84 and Hainan with 1·78. Only Beijing and Shanghai had averages less than 1. In 1996 the average Chinese woman had 1·39 living children.

Vital statistics, 1996: Birth rate (per 1,000), 16·98; death rate, 6·56; growth rate, 10·42. There were 9,339,615 marriages and 1,132,215 divorces in 1996. Expectation of life was 68 years for men and 71 for women in 1990.

43·2m. persons of Chinese origin lived abroad in 1993.

A number of widely divergent varieties of Chinese are spoken. The official 'Modern Standard Chinese' is based on the dialect of North China. The ideographic writing system of 'characters' is uniform throughout the country, and has under-gone systematic simplification. In 1958 a phonetic alphabet (*Pinyin*) was devised to transcribe the characters, and in 1979 this was officially adopted for use in all texts in the Roman alphabet. The previous transcription scheme (Wade) is still used in Taiwan and Hong Kong.

China is administratively divided into 22 provinces, 5 autonomous regions (originally entirely or largely inhabited by ethnic minorities, though in some regions now outnumbered by Han immigrants) and 4 government-controlled municipalities. These are in turn divided into 335 prefectures, 666 cities (of which 218 are at prefecture level and 445 at county level), 2,142 counties and 717 urban districts.

Government-controlled municipalities	Area (in 1,000 sq. km)	Population (1990 census, in 1,000)	Density per sq. km (in 1987)	Population (1996 estimate, in 1,000)	Capital
Beijing	17·8	10,870	644	12,590	—
Tianjin	4·0	8,830	777	9,480	—
Shanghai	5·8	13,510	2,152	14,190	—
Provinces					
Hebei[2]	202·7	60,280	301	64,840	Shijiazhuang
Shanxi	157·1	28,180	183	31,090	Taiyuan
Liaoning[2]	151·0	39,980	261	41,160	Shenyang
Jilin[2]	187·0	25,150	132	26,100	Changchun
Heilongjiang[2]	463·6	34,770	76	37,280	Harbin
Jiangsu	102·2	68,170	654	71,100	Nanjing
Zhejiang[2]	101·8	40,840	407	43,430	Hangzhou
Anhui	139·9	52,290	402	60,700	Hefei
Fujian	123·1	30,610	244	32,610	Fuzhou
Jiangxi	164·8	38,280	229	41,050	Nanchang
Shandong	153·3	83,430	551	87,380	Jinan
Henan	167·0	86,140	512	91,720	Zhengzhou
Hubei[2]	187·5	54,760	288	58,250	Wuhan
Hunan[2]	210·5	60,600	288	64,280	Changsha
Guangdong[2]	197·1	63,210	319	69,610	Guangzhou
Hainan[2]	34·3	6,420	191	7,340	Haikou
Sichuan[2]	569·0	106,370	188	114,300	Chengdu
Guizhou[2]	174·0	32,730	186	35,550	Guiyang
Yunnan[2]	436·2	36,750	85	40,420	Kunming
Shaanxi	195·8	32,470	168	35,430	Xian
Gansu[2]	366·5	22,930	61	24,670	Lanzhou
Qinghai[2]	721·0	4,430	6	4,880	Xining
Autonomous regions					
Inner Mongolia	1,177·5	21,110	18	23,070	Hohhot
Guangxi Zhuang	220·4	42,530	192	45,890	Nanning
Tibet[1]	1,221·6	2,220	2	2,440	Lhasa
Ningxia Hui	170.0	4,660	70	5,210	Yinchuan
Xinjiang Uighur	1,646·8	15,370	9	16,890	Urumqi

[1] See also paragraph on Tibet below.
[2] Also designated minority nationality autonomous area.

Population of largest cities in 1993: Shanghai, 8·76m.; Beijing (Peking), 6·56m.; Tianjin, 4·97m.; Shenyang, 3·86m.; Wuhan, 3·86m.; Guangzhou (Canton), 3·56m.; Chongqing, 3·78m.; Harbin, 3·1m.; Chengdu, 2·67m.; Zibo (1991), 2·46m.; Nanjing, 2·43m.; Xian, 2·36m.; Changchun, 2·4m.; Dalian, 2·33m.; Qingdao, 2·24m.; Jinan, 2·05m.; Hangzhou, 1·74m.; Taiyuan, 1·68m.; Zhengzhou, 1·53m.; Kunming, 1·45m.; Tangshan (1990), 1·5m.; Changsha, 1·48m.; Nanchang, 1·42m.; Anshan (1991), 1·39m.; Qiqihar (1991), 1·38m.; Fushun (1991), 1·35m.; Lanzhou, 1·32m.; Fuzhou, 1·29m.; Jilin (1991), 1·27m.; Shijiazhuang (1991), 1·21m.; Baotou (1991), 1·2m.; Huainan (1991), 1·2m.; Luoyang (1991), 1·19m.; Urumqi, 1·11m.; Datong (1991), 1·11m.; Handan (1991), 1·11m.; Guiyang, 1·07m.; Ningbo, 1·07m.

The autonomous regions and 14 provinces (*see table above*) have non-Han components in their populations ranging from 97·2% (in 1994) in Tibet to 9·9% in Zhejiang. Total minority population, 1994, 72,818,100. 55 ethnic minorities are identified. At the 1990 census the largest were: Zhuang, 15,555,820; Manchu, 9,846,776;

Hui, 8,612,001; Miao, 7,383,622; Uighur, 7,207,024; Yi, 6,578,524; Tujia, 5,725,049; Mongolian, 4,802,407; Tibetan, 4,593,072.

Li Chengrui, *The Population of China*. Beijing, 1992
The Population Atlas of China. OUP, 1988
Song, J. et al., *Population Control in China*. New York, 1985

Tibet. After the 1959 revolt was suppressed the Preparatory Committee for the Autonomous Region of Tibet (set up in 1955) took over the functions of local government, led by its Vice-Chairman, the Banqen Lama, in the absence of its Chairman, the Dalai Lama, who had fled to India in 1959. In Dec. 1964 both the Dalai and Banqen Lamas were removed from their posts and on 9 Sept. 1965 Tibet became an Autonomous Region. 301 delegates were elected to the first People's Congress, of whom 226 were Tibetans. The Chief of Government is Gyaincain Norbu. The senior spiritual leader, the Dalai Lama, is in exile. He was awarded the Nobel Peace Prize in 1989. The Banqen Lama died in Jan. 1989. In 1996 the population was 2·49m. In 1994 there were 2·22m. Tibetans living in Tibet out of a total population of 2·36m. Birth rate (per 1,000), 1996, 24·7; death rate, 8·5; growth rate, 16·2. Population of the capital, Lhasa, in 1992 was 124,000. Expectation of life was 65 years in 1990. 2m. Tibetans live outside Tibet, in China, and in India and Nepal. Chinese efforts to modernize Tibet include irrigation, road-building and the establishment of light industry: in 1991 there were 328 township and 123 village enterprises employing 21,168 persons; 12,000 persons worked in heavy industry, 16,000 in state-owned enterprises, 1990 output included 136,300 metres of woollen fabrics, 1,000 tonnes of salt, 1,900 tonnes of vegetable oil, 208,200 cu. metres of timber and 132,300 tonnes of cement. Electricity production in 1990 was 330m. kWh, of which 323m. kWh were hydroelectric.

In 1996 there were 953,000 rural labourers, including 886,000 in farming, forestry and fisheries. The total sown area was 220,100 ha, including 52,500 ha sown to wheat, 18,300 ha to rapeseed, 18,300 ha to oil-bearing crops and 14,500 ha to soya beans. Output (in 1,000 tonnes), 1996: Wheat, 261; soya beans, 41; oil-bearing crops, 35; rapeseeds, 35. There were 5·10m. cattle, 1·21m. draught animals, 0·36m. horses, 0·22m. pigs, 11·10m. sheep and 5·83m. goats in 1996.

In 1991 there were 21,842 km of roads, of which 6,240 km were paved. There are airports at Lhasa and Bangda providing external links. 30,000 tourists visited Tibet in 1986.

The borders were opened for trade with neighbouring countries in 1980. In July 1988 Tibetan was reinstated as a 'major official language', competence in which is required of all administrative officials.

Monasteries and shrines have been renovated and reopened. There were some 15,000 monks and nuns in 1987. In 1984 a Buddhist seminary in Lhasa opened with 200 students. On 8 Dec. 1995, the Chinese government designated Gyaincain Norbu (b. 1989) the tenth reincarnation of the Panchen Lama; this was repudiated by the Tibetan government-in-exile. In 1988 there were 2,437 primary schools, 67 secondary schools, 14 technical schools and 3 higher education institutes. The total number of primary school pupils in 1990–91 was 101,000. A university was established in 1985. In 1990 there were some 9,000 medical personnel and 1,006 medical institutions, with a total of about 5,000 beds.

Barnett, R. and Akiner, S. (eds.) *Resistance and Reform in Tibet*. Farnborough, 1994
Batchelor, S., *The Tibet Guide*. London, 1987
The Dalai Lama, *My Land and My People* (ed. D. Howarth). London, 1962:—*Freedom in Exile*. London, 1990
Grunfeld, A. T., *The Making of Modern Tibet*. London, 1987
Levenson, C. B., *The Dalai Lama: A Biography*. London, 1988
Pinfold, J., *Tibet:* [Bibliography]. Oxford and Santa Barbara, 1991
Schwartz, R. D., *Circle of Protest: Political Ritual in the Tibetan Uprising*. Farnborough, 1994
Shakabpa, T. W. D., *Tibet: A Political History*. New York, 1984
Sharabati, D., *Tibet and its History*. London, 1986
Smith, W. W., *A History of Tibet: Nationalism and Self-Determination*. Oxford, 1996

CLIMATE. Most of China has a temperate climate but, with such a large country, extending far inland and embracing a wide range of latitude as well as containing large areas at high altitude, many parts experience extremes of climate, especially in winter. Most rain falls during the summer, from May to Sept., though amounts decrease inland. Beijing (Peking). Jan. 24°F (−4·4°C), July 79°F (26°C). Annual rainfall 24·9" (623 mm). Chongqing. Jan. 45°F (7·2°C), July 84°F (28·9°C). Annual rainfall 43·7" (1,092 mm). Shanghai. Jan. 39°F (3·9°C), July 82°F (27·8°C). Annual rainfall 45·4" (1,135 mm). Tianjin. Jan. 24°F (−4·4°C), July 81°F (27·2°C). Annual rainfall 21·5" (533·4 mm).

CONSTITUTION AND GOVERNMENT. On 21 Sept. 1949 the *Chinese People's Political Consultative Conference* met in Beijing, convened by the Chinese Communist Party. The Conference adopted a 'Common Programme' of 60 articles and the 'Organic Law of the Central People's Government' (31 articles). Both became the basis of the Constitution adopted on 20 Sept. 1954 by the 1st National People's Congress, the supreme legislative body. The Consultative Conference continued to exist after 1954 as an advisory body. Its 8th session was convened in 1993. It has 2,093 members.

New Constitutions were adopted in 1975, 1978, 1982 and 1993, the latter embodying the principles of a 'Socialist market economy'.

The *National People's Congress* can amend the Constitution and nominally elects and has power to remove from office the highest officers of state. The Congress elects a *Standing Committee* (which supervises the State Council) and the *President* and *Vice-President* for a 5-year term. Congress has 2,978 deputies and is elected for a 5-year term and meets once a year for 2 or 3 weeks. When not in session, its business is carried on by its *Standing Committee*. It is composed of deputies elected on a constituency basis by direct secret ballot. Any voter, and certain organizations, may nominate candidates. Nominations may exceed seats by 50–100%. The 9th Congress was elected in March 1998.

The *State Council* is the supreme executive organ and comprises the Prime Minister, Deputy Prime Ministers and State Councillors.

President: Jiang Zemin (b. 1926; elected 27 March 1993 and sworn in April 1993).
Deputy President: Hu Jintao.

In March 1998 the government comprised:
Prime Minister: Zhu Rongji.
Deputy Prime Ministers: Li Lanqing, Qian Qichen, Wu Bangguo, Wen Jiabao.
Minister of Agriculture: Chen Yaobang. *Civil Affairs:* Doje Cering. *Communications:* Huang Zhendong. *Construction:* Yu Zhengsheng. *Culture:* Sun Jiazheng. *Education:* Chen Zhili. *Finance:* Xiang Huaicheng. *Foreign Affairs:* Tang Jiaxuan. *Foreign Trade and Economic Co-operation:* Shi Guangsheng. *Information Industry:* Wu Jichuan. *Justice:* Gao Changli. *Labour and Social Security:* Zhang Zuoji. *Land and Natural Resources:* Zhou Yongkang. *National Defence:* Chi Haotian. *Personnel:* Song Defu. *Public Health:* Zhang Wenkang. *Public Security:* Jia Chunwang. *Railways:* Fu Zhihuan. *State Security:* Xu Yongyue. *Supervision:* He Yong. *Water Resources:* Niu Maosheng.

Ministers heading State Commissions: *Economics and Trade*, Sheng Huaren. *Family Planning*, Zhang Weiqing. *Nationalities Affairs*, Li Dezhu. *Planning*, Zeng Peiyan. *Science, Technology and Industry for National Defence*, Liu Jibin.

National anthem: 'March of the Volunteers'; words by Tien Han, tune by Nieh Erh.

De facto power is in the hands of the Communist Party of China, which had 57m. members in 1997. There are 8 other parties, all members of the Chinese People's Political Consultative Conference.

The members of the Standing Committee of the Politburo in March 1998 were Jiang Zemin (*General Secretary*), Li Peng, Zhu Rongji, Hu Jintao, Li Ruihuan, Li Lanqing and Wei Jianxing.

Local Government. There are 4 administrative levels: (1) Provinces, Autonomous Regions and the municipalities directly administered by the Government; (2) prefectures and autonomous prefectures (*zhou*); (3) counties, autonomous counties and municipalities; (4) towns. Local government organs ('congresses') exist at provincial, county and township levels and in national minority autonomous prefectures, but not in ordinary prefectures which are just agencies of the provincial government. Up to county level congresses are elected directly. Elections take place every 3 years. Any person proposed by 10 electors may stand after political vetting. There are quotas for Party members and women. Multiple candidacies are permitted at local elections.

DEFENCE. President Jiang Zemin is chairman of the State and Party's Military Commissions. China is divided into 7 military regions. The military commander also commands the air, naval and civilian militia forces assigned to each region.

Conscription is compulsory but for organizational reasons selective: Only some 10% of potential recruits are called up. Service is 3 years with the Army and 4 years with the Air Force and Navy.

A military academy to train senior officers in modern warfare was established in 1985.

Army. The Army (PLA: 'People's Liberation Army') is divided into main and local forces. Main forces, administered by the 7 military regions in which they are stationed but commanded by the Ministry of Defence, are available for operation anywhere and are better equipped. Local forces concentrate on the defence of their own regions. There are 24 Integrated Group Armies comprising 78 infantry, 10 armoured and 5 artillery divisions; and 15 engineer regiments. Equipment includes some 700 T-34/85 and T-54, 6,000 T-59 and 200 T-69 main battle tanks. Land-based missile forces consisted of (1995 estimate): 17 intercontinental and 70 intermediate range. Military aviation has 8 Gazelle armed helicopters, 20 S-70 Black Hawk and 24 Mi-17 transport helicopters. Total strength in 1997 was 2·09m. including some 1·07m. conscripts.

There is a para-military force of 0·6m. People's Armed Police under PLA command.

Navy. The naval arm of the PLA comprises 1 nuclear-powered ballistic missile armed submarine, 5 nuclear-propelled fleet submarines, 1 diesel-powered cruise missile submarine and some 40 patrol submarines. Surface combatant forces include 18 missile-armed destroyers, 36 frigates, some 185 missile craft and 150 torpedo craft. There is a mixed coastal and inshore patrol force of some 500 vessels and 50 riverine craft. The mine warfare force consists of 40 ex-Soviet offshore minesweepers, some 12 inshore, and about 60 unmanned drones. There are 55 landing ships of various types and some 150 craft. Major auxiliaries number over 100, including 2 underway replenishment oilers and 1 fleet stores ship, and there are several hundred minor auxiliaries, yard craft and service vessels.

The land-based naval air force of about 620 combat aircraft, primarily for defensive and anti-submarine service, is organized into 3 bomber and 6 fighter divisions. The force includes some 120 H-5 torpedo bombers, about 100 Q-5 fighter/ground attack aircraft and 600 fighters, including J-5 (MiG-17), J-6 (MiG-19), and J-7 (MiG-21) types. Maritime patrol tasks are performed by 15 Be-6 and a small number of PS-5 flying boats, and anti-submarine operations by 40 Z-5 and 15 Super Frelon helicopters from shore and about 10 Z-9 afloat. There are also about 60 communications, training and transport aircraft.

Main naval bases are at Qingdao (North Sea Fleet), Shanghai (East Sea Fleet), and Zhanjiang (South Sea Fleet).

In 1997 personnel numbered some 280,000, including 25,000 in the naval air force, 29,000 coastal defence troops and 5,000 naval infantry.

Air Force. The Air Force has an estimated 3,500 front-line aircraft, organized in 100 regiments of jet-fighters and about 12 regiments of tactical bombers, plus reconnaissance, transport and helicopter units. Each regiment is made up of 3 or 4 squadrons (each 12 aircraft), and 3 regiments form a division.

Equipment includes about 500 J-7 (MiG-21) and 2,000 J-6 (MiG-19) interceptors and fighter-bombers, with about 500 H-5 (Il-28) jetbombers, about 120 H-6 Chinese-built copies of the Soviet Tu-16 twin-jet strategic bomber, plus 500 Q-5 twin-jet fighter-bombers, evolved from the MiG-19, while 50 Su-27 fighters have been supplied by Russia. About 100 of a locally-developed fighter designated J-8 (known in the west as 'Finback') are in service. Transport aircraft include about 500 Y-5 (An-2), Y-8 (An-12), Y-12, An-24/26, Il-76, Challenger and Il-14 fixed-wing types, plus 300 Z-5 (Mi-4) and Z-6 (Mi-8) helicopters, as well as 6 Super Puma VIP transport helicopters. Total strength (1997) 470,000 (160,000 conscripts), including 220,000 in air defence organization.

Joffe, E., *The Chinese Army after Mao*. London, 1987

INTERNATIONAL RELATIONS

Membership. The People's Republic of China is a member of UN (and its Security Council).

ECONOMY

Policy. A ninth 5-year plan covers 1996–2000; there is also a 15-year strategic plan 'Long-Term Target for 2010'. These plans envisage a continued opening to the outside world, an enhanced development of agriculture, the reduction of tariff barriers and the development of the poorer regions.

A Communist Party statement of Nov. 1993 declared that public ownership should remain the mainstay of the economy, but alongside a modern enterprise system suited to the demands of a market economy in which government control is separated from management.

Performance. In 1997 GDP growth was 8·8%, with a forecast for 1998 of 8%.

Budget. 1996 revenue was 740,799m. yuan; expenditure, 793,755m. yuan. Of this, local government revenue accounted for 374,692m. yuan and expenditure, 578,628m. yuan. Total debt incurred, 1996, 196,728m. yuan, of which 119,510m. yuan were foreign debts.

Sources of revenue, 1996 (in million yuan): Taxes, 690,982; industrial and commercial taxes, 527,004. Expenditure: Economic construction, 285,578 (1995); culture and education, 175,672 (1995); national defence, 63,672 (1995); government administration, 99,654 (1995); agriculture, 51,007; pensions and social welfare, 12,803; debt payments, 131,191.

Currency. The currency is called Renminbi (*i.e.,* People's Currency). The unit of currency is the *yuan* (CNY) which is divided into 10 *jiao*, the *jiao*, into 10 *fen*. Notes are issued for 1, 2 and 5 *jiao* and 1, 2, 5, 10, 50 and 100 *yuan* and coins for 1, 2 and 5 *fen*. Official foreign exchange reserves in 1996 were US$105,029m. Gold reserves in 1996 were 12·67m. troy oz. of gold. Annualized inflation was 6·1% in 1996. The yuan was floated to reflect market forces on 1 Jan. 1994 though remaining state-controlled, and the official rate of exchange was abolished. It became convertible for current transactions from 1 Dec. 1996.

Banking and Finance. The People's Bank of China is the central bank and bank of issue (*Director:* Dai Xianglong, b. 1945). There are a number of other banks, the largest of which are Agricultural Bank of China, Industrial and Commercial Bank of China, Construction Bank of China, Bank of China, Bank of Communications and Agricultural Development Bank of China. Legislation of 1995 permitted the establishment of commercial banks; credit co-operatives may be transformed into banks, mainly to provide credit to small businesses. Insurance is handled by the People's Insurance Company. There were also (1994) 350,813 credit co-operatives. The Bank of China is responsible for foreign banking operations.

Savings bank deposits were 2,151,880m. yuan in 1994.

611,566m. yuan was loaned from State Banks in 1996.

There are stock exchanges in the Shenzhen Special Economic Zone and in Shanghai. A securities trading system linking 6 cities (Securities Automated Quotations System) was inaugurated in 1990 for trading in government bonds.

Weights and Measures. The metric system is in general use alongside traditional units of measurement.

ENERGY AND NATURAL RESOURCES

Electricity. Installed capacity, 1996, 0·2m. MW. 1996 electricity output was 1,081,310m. kWh. Sources of energy in 1996 as percentage of total energy production: Coal, 74·8%; crude oil, 17·1%; hydro-electric power, 6·2%; natural gas, 1·9%. Generating is not centralized; local units range between 30 and 60 MW of output. Output in 1994: 928,100m. kWh.

Oil. There are on-shore fields at Daqing, Shengli, Dagang and Karamai, and 10 provinces south of the Yangtze River have been opened for exploration in co-operation with foreign companies. Crude oil production was 157·33m. tonnes in 1996.

Gas. Natural gas is available from fields near Canton and Shanghai and in Sichuan province. Production was 20,114m. cu. metres in 1996.

Minerals. *Coal.* Most provinces contain coal, and there are 70 major production centres, of which the largest are in Hebei, Shanxi, Shandong, Jilin and Anhui. Coal reserves were estimated at 1,000,850m. tonnes in 1996. Coal production was 1,397m. tonnes in 1996.

Iron. Iron ore reserves were 47,560m. tonnes in 1996. Deposits are abundant in the anthracite field of Shanxi, in Hebei and in Shandong and are found in conjunction with coal and worked in the north-east.

Tin. Tin ore is plentiful in Yunnan, where the tin-mining industry has long existed. Tin production was 40,000 tonnes in 1989.

Tungsten. China is a major producer of wolfram (tungsten ore). Mining of wolfram is carried on in Hunan, Guangdong and Yunnan.

Salt production was 29·96m. tonnes in 1994; gold production was 110 tonnes in 1992; output of other minerals in 1989 (in 1,000 tonnes): Aluminium, 770; copper, 540; nickel, 30; lead, 270; zinc, 430. Other minerals produced: Barite, bismuth, graphite, gypsum, mercury, molybdenum, silver. Reserves (in tonnes) of phosphate ore 15,766m.; sylvite, 458m.; salt, 402,400m.

Agriculture. In 1996 the sown area was 152·4m. ha comprising (in 1m. ha): rice, 31·41; wheat, 29·61; corn, 24·50; beans, 10·54; tubers, 9·8; oil-bearing crops, 12·56m. Intensive agriculture and horticulture have been practised for millennia. Present-day policy aims to avert the traditional threats from floods and droughts by soil conservancy, afforestation, irrigation and drainage projects, and to increase the 'high stable yields' areas by introducing fertilizers, pesticides and improved crops. In spite of this, 18·1m. ha of land were flooded in 1996 and 20·1m. ha were covered by drought. 50·38m. ha were irrigated in 1996.

'Township and village enterprises' in agriculture comprise enterprises previously run by the communes of the Maoist era, co-operatives run by rural labourers and individual firms of a certain size. There were 24·95m. such enterprises in 1994, employing 120·18m. persons. There were 2,157 state farms in 1994 with 5·18m. employees. In 1996 there were 234·38m. rural households. The rural workforce was 452·88m., of whom 322·6m. were employed in agriculture, fishing or land management. Net *per capita* annual peasant income, 1996: 1,926 yuan.

In 1992 there were 25,023 agricultural technical stations. There were 670,848 large and medium-sized tractors in 1996.

Agricultural production (in 1m. tonnes), 1996: Rice, 195·10; wheat, 110·57; corn, 127·47; beans, 17·90; tubers, 35·36; tea, 0·59; cotton, 4·20; oil-bearing crops, 22·11; sugar-cane, 66·88; fruit, 46·53. The gross value of agricultural output in 1996 was 2,342,866m. yuan.

Livestock, 1996 (in 1,000): Draught animals, 91,920; cattle, 139,813 (including 4,470 milk cows); goats, 170,680; pigs, 457,360; sheep, 132,690. Meat production in 1996 was 59·15m. tonnes; milk, 7·36m. tonnes; eggs, 19·54m. tonnes.

Powell, S. G., *Agricultural Reform in China: from Communes to Commodity Economy, 1978–1990.* Manchester Univ. Press, 1992

Forestry. Forest area in 1994 was 128·63m. ha, including 2·6m. ha of timber forest. Timber output in 1994 was 66·15m. cu. metres.

Fisheries. Total catch, 1996: 32·88m. tonnes, of which 12·75m. tonnes were freshwater produce.

INDUSTRY. Cottage industries persist into the late 20th century. Modern industrial development began with the manufacture of cotton textiles, and the establishment of silk filatures, steel plants, flour-mills and match factories. In 1996 there were 7,986,500 industrial enterprises. 113,800 were state-owned, 1,591,800 were collectives and 6,210,700 were individually owned. A law of 1988 ended direct state control of firms and provided for the possibility of bankruptcy.

Output of major products, 1996 (in tonnes): Cotton yarn, 5·12m.; paper, 26·38m.; sugar, 6·40m.; salt, 29·03m.; steel, 101·24m.; rolled steel, 93·38m.; cement, 491·1m.; chemical fertilizers, 28·09m.; aluminium ware, 159,100; silk, 94,900; woollen fabrics, 459·5m. metres; bicycles, 33·61m. units; TV sets, 35·41m. units; radios, 56·50m. units; cameras, 41·20m. units; refrigerators, 9·79m. units; motor vehicles, 1,470,000 units; locomotives, 1,050 units.

The gross value of industrial output in 1996 was 9,959,500m. yuan.

Labour. In 1991 the population of working age was 704·2m. The employed population at the 1990 census was 647·2m. (291·1m. female). By 1996 this is estimated to have risen to 688·5m., of whom 490·3m. were in rural areas and 198·2m. in urban areas. There were 329·1m. people working in agriculture, 97·6m. in manufacturing, 45·1m. in commerce, 34·1m. in construction and 20·1m. in communications. 109·4m. worked in state-owned enterprises, 29·5m. in urban collectives, and 50·2m. were self-employed. In 1994 there were 446·54m. working as individual rural labourers or in rural collectives and there were 15·57m. individual urban labourers. At the 1990 census there was a floating population of 21m. internal migrants who tour the country seeking seasonal employment. There were 5·53m. urban unemployed in 1996 (3% of the urban population). Almost one-third of unemployed people had not worked for a year. Only a quarter of the unemployed in 1996 were registered at employment services and only 1·7% received unemployment relief payments. In early 1998 the official unemployment rate was 3%, but was thought to be much higher. The average annual non-agricultural annual wage in 1996 was 6,210 yuan. Averages were: 4,302 yuan, urban collectives; 6,280 yuan, state-owned enterprises; 8,261 yuan, other enterprises. There is a 6-day 48-hour working week. Minimum working age was fixed at 16 in 1991. There were 19,098 labour disputes in 1994.

Trade Unions. The All-China Federation of Trade Unions is headed by Wei Jianxing. In 1991 there were 614,000 union branches with a total membership of 103·89m. (39·92m. female).

FOREIGN ECONOMIC RELATIONS. Foreign debt was US$116,275m. in 1996. Actual foreign investment totalled US$33,800m. by 1994. Direct foreign investment (in US$1m.) by 1995 by major countries of origin: Taiwan, 11,600; USA, 10,900; Japan, 10,500; Singapore, 3,900; South Korea, 2,300; UK, 2,200.

There are 6 Special Economic Zones at Shanghai and in the provinces of Guangdong and Fujian, in which concessions are made to foreign businessmen. The Pudong New Area in Shanghai is designated a special development area. Since 1979 joint ventures with foreign firms have been permitted. A law of April 1991 reduced taxation on joint ventures to 33%. There is no maximum limit on the foreign share of the holdings; the minimum limit is 25%. Contracts between Chinese and foreign firms are only legally valid if in writing and approved by the appropriate higher authority.

In June 1997 the US president extended most-favoured-nation status to China for a further year.

Commerce. Trade in 1996: Imports, US$138,840m.; exports, US$151,060m.

Major exports in 1996 (in 1,000 tonnes): Crude oil, 20,330; silk and satin, 147m.

metres; coal, 29,030; cotton cloth, 3,043m. metres; cement, 11,800. Imports: Wheat, 8,250; steel product, 15,840; chemical fertilizers, 18,570; iron ore, 43,870.

Exports to (and imports from) major trade partners in 1994 (in US$1m.): Hong Kong, 32,365 (9,457); Japan, 21,573 (26,231); USA, 21,461 (13,970); Germany, 4,762 (7,137); South Korea, 4,402 (7,318); Russia, 1,581 (3,496); Singapore, 2,558 (2,482). Customs duties with Taiwan were abolished in 1980.

Tourism. 51,128,000 tourists visited in 1996, including 44,229,000 from Hong Kong, Taiwan and Macao, and 155,000 other overseas Chinese. The World Tourism Organisation predicts that China will overtake France as the world's most visited destination by 2020 and become the world's 4th most important source of tourists to other countries. Income from tourists in 1996 was US$10,200m.

Lardy, N. R., *Foreign Trade and Economic Reform in China, 1978–1990.* CUP, 1992
Pearson, M. M., *Joint Ventures in the People's Republic of China: the Control of Foreign Direct Investment under Socialism.* Princeton Univ. Press, 1991
Wong, K. and Chu, D. (eds.) *Modernization in China: the Case of the Shenzhen Special Economic Zone.* OUP, 1986

COMMUNICATIONS

Roads. The total road length was 1,185,800 km in 1996. In 1994, 998,077 km were hard-surfaced. In 1996 there were 5·75m. lorries and 4·8m. passenger vehicles. 2·89m. vehicles were privately owned. The use of bicycles is very widespread. In 1996, 9,838m. tonnes of freight and 11,221m. persons were transported by road.

There were 253,537 traffic accidents in 1994, with 66,362 fatalities.

Railways. In 1996 there were 56,700 km of railway including 10,100 km electrified. Gauge is standard except for some 600 mm track in Yunnan.

In 1996 the railways carried 1,668m. tonnes of freight and 941m. passengers.

Civil Aviation. There are international airports at Beijing and Shanghai (Hongqiao). Altogether there were 142 civil airports in 1996, 106 of which can accommodate Boeing 737s or larger aircraft. The national and major airlines are state-owned, except Shanghai Airlines (75% municipality-owned, 25% private) and Shenzhen Airlines (private). In 1995 they operated the following numbers of aircraft:

Air China, 58 (including 2 B-707-320Cs, 18 B-737-300s, 3 B-747-200B Combis, 1 B-747-200F, 5 B-747-400s, 3 B-747-400 Combis, 4 B-747SPs, 6 B-767-200ERs, 4 B-767-300s); Air Great Wall, 8 (including 3 B-737-200 Advs); China Eastern Airlines, 46; China General Aviation, 25; China Northern Airlines, 46 (including 6 A300B4-600Rs); China Northwest Airlines, 33 (including 4 A300B4-600Rs, 4 A310-200s); China Southern Airlines, 78 (including 20 B-737-300s, 11 B-737-500s, 20 B-757-200s, 6 B-767-300ERs); China Southwest Airlines, 42 (including 1 B-707-320C, 20 B-737 300s, 13 D-757-200s); China United Airlines, 31 (including 4 B-737-300s); China Yunnan Airlines, 8 B-737-300s; Shanghai Airlines, 6 B-757-200s, 1 B-767-300; Shenzhen Airlines, 4 B-737-300s.

In 1996 airlines carried 55·55m. passengers (4·40m. international) and 1·15m. tonnes of freight.

Services are also provided by Aeroflot, Air Koryo, Air Macau, Air Ukraine, Alitalia, All Nippon Airways, Asiana, Austrian Airlines, British Airways, Canadian Airlines, Dragonair, El Al, Ethiopian Airlines, Finnair, Garuda Indonesia, Iran Air, JAL, Kazakhstan Airlines, Korean Air, LOT, Lufthansa, Malaysia Airlines, Mongolian Airlines, Pakistan International Airlines, Qantas, Royal Brunei Airlines, Royal Nepal Airlines, SAS, Singapore Airlines, Swan, Swissair, Tarom, Thai Airways, United Airlines and Uzbekistan Airways.

Shipping. In 1995 the ocean-going fleet consisted of 1,826 vessels totalling 34·27m. DWT, representing 5·18% of the world's total fleet tonnage. 308 vessels (35·22% of tonnage) were registered under foreign flags. Total tonnage registered, 15·83m. GRT, including oil-tankers, 2·28m. GRT, and container ships, 1·35m. GRT.

Cargo handled by the major ports in 1996 (in tonnes): Shanghai, 164m.; Qinhuangdao, 83m.; Ningbo, 76m.; Guangzhou (Canton), 75m.; Dalian, 64m.; Tianjin, 62m.; Qingdao, 60m. In 1993, 125·08m. tonnes of freight were carried.

Inland waterways totalled 110,593 km in 1994. 1,070·91m. tonnes of freight and 261·65m. passengers were carried.

Telecommunications. There were 72,496 post offices in 1996. In 1996 there were 70,467,500 telephones and in 1993 23,393 telex and 12,276 fax machines. At the end of 1996 there were 6·85m. mobile telephone subscribers (3·62m. at end of 1995). The use of *Pinyin* transcription of place names has been requested for mail to addresses in China (*e.g.*, 'Beijing' *not* 'Peking').

In 1994 there were 1,107 radio and 766 TV stations. The Central People's Broadcasting Station provides 2 central programmes, regional services, special services, a Taiwan service and external services. China Central Television (colour by PAL) transmits 3 programmes from Beijing, a programme from Shanghai, and an English-language programme. There are 29 regional programmes transmitted from 361 local stations. By 1995 about 600 cable TV systems had been licensed. In 1995 there were 225·5m. radio and 250m. TV receivers. In urban areas 96%, and in rural areas 48·5% of households possessed a TV set in 1994. The use of satellite receiving dishes was prohibited in 1993.

Cinemas. There were 4,639 cinemas in 1995. 148 feature films were made in 1994. In 1992 there were some 10,600m. cinema attendances.

Press. In 1994 there were 1,635 newspapers with a combined circulation of 125,200m. and 7,325 periodicals with 2,210m. The Party newspaper is *Renmin Ribao* (People's Daily), which had a daily circulation of 3m. in 1994. 103,836 book titles were produced in 6,007·75m. copies in 1994. There were 2,596 public libraries in 1993.

SOCIAL INSTITUTIONS

Justice. Six new codes of law (including criminal and electoral) came into force in 1980, to regularize the legal unorthodoxy of previous years. There is no provision for *habeas corpus*. The death penalty has been extended from treason and murder to include rape, embezzlement, smuggling, drug-dealing, bribery and robbery with violence. There were 2,535 executions in 1995 (2,050 in 1994). 'People's courts' are divided into some 30 higher, 200 intermediate and 2,000 basic-level courts, and headed by the Supreme People's Court. The latter tries cases, hears appeals and supervises the people's courts.

People's courts are composed of a president, vice-presidents, judges and 'people's assessors' who are the equivalent of jurors. 'People's conciliation committees' are charged with settling minor disputes.

There are also special military courts.

Procuratorial powers and functions are exercised by the Supreme People's Procuracy and local procuracies.

Religion. The government accords legality to 5 religions only: Buddhism, Islam, Protestantism, Roman Catholicism and Taoism. Confucianism, Buddhism and Taoism have long been practised. Confucianism has no ecclesiastical organization and appears rather as a philosophy of ethics and government. Taoism—of Chinese origin—copied Buddhist ceremonial soon after the arrival of Buddhism two millennia ago. Buddhism in return adopted many Taoist beliefs and practices. It is no longer possible to estimate the number of adherents to these faiths. A more tolerant attitude towards religion had emerged by 1979, and the Government's Bureau of Religious Affairs was reactivated.

Ceremonies of reverence to ancestors have been observed by the whole population regardless of philosophical or religious beliefs.

Moslems are found in every province of China, being most numerous in the Ningxia–Hui Autonomous Region, Yunnan, Shaanxi, Gansu, Hebei, Honan, Shandong, Sichuan, Xinjiang and Shanxi. They totalled 28m. in 1992.

Roman Catholicism has had a footing in China for more than 3 centuries. In 1992 there were about 3·5m. Catholics who are members of the Patriotic Catholic Association, which declared its independence of Rome in 1958. In 1979 there were about 1,000 priests. In 1977 there were 78 bishops and 4 apostolic administrators, not all of whom were permitted to undertake religious activity. This figure included 46 'democratically elected' bishops not recognized by the Vatican. A bishop of Beijing was consecrated in 1979 without the consent of the Vatican and 2 auxiliary bishops of Shanghai in 1984. Archbishop Gong Pinmei, arrested in 1955, was freed in 1988. Protestants are members of the All-China Conference of Protestant Churches. 2 Protestant bishops were installed in 1988, the first for 30 years.

Legislation of 1994 prohibits foreign nationals from setting up religious organizations.

Education. In 1996, 82·18% of the adult population were literate (89·88% of men and 74·46% of women). In 1994 98·4% of school-age children attended school. In 1993 maximum school fees were 10 yuan a term, to which other charges might be added. In 1996 there were 187,324 kindergartens with 26·66m. children and 889,000 teachers. An educational reform of 1985 is phasing in compulsory 9-year education consisting of 6 years of primary schooling and 3 years of secondary schooling, to replace a previous 5-year system. In 1996 there were 645,983 primary schools with 5,736,000 teachers and 136·15m. pupils, 79,967 secondary schools, with 3,465,000 teachers and 57·39m. pupils and 10,049 vocational schools with 308,000 teachers and 4·73m. students. There were 1,032 institutes of higher education, including universities, with 403,000 teachers and 3·02m. students. One-third of all higher education students study engineering.

There is an Academy of Sciences with provincial branches. An Academy of Social Sciences was established in 1977.

In 1995–96 in the private sector there were 3 general universities and 9 specialized universities (aeronautics and astronautics; agricultural engineering; agriculture; chemical technology; foreign studies; labour; medicine; traditional Chinese medicine; polytechnic). In the public sector there were 60 general universities, 2 for ethnic minorities and the following specialized universities: Agriculture, 12; agriculture and land reclamation, 1; land reclamation, 1; architecture, 2; architecture and technology, 1; chemical technology, 1; coal and chemical technology, 1; electronic science and technology, 1; engineering, 1; fisheries, 1; foreign languages, 1; forestry, 1; hydraulic and electrical engineering, 1; international business and economics, 1; international studies, 1; iron and steel technology, 1; maritime studies, 1; medicine, 11; traditional Chinese medicine, 2; mining and technology, 1; petroleum, 1; pharmacology, 1; political science and law, 1; polytechnic, 8; radio and television, 1; science and technology, 5; surveying and mapping, 1; teaching, 4; technology, 6; textiles, 1.

In 1996 there were also 893 teacher training schools. In 1994, 19,000 students were studying abroad. Fees were introduced for university students in 1996–97.

Health. Medical treatment is free only for certain groups of employees, but where costs are incurred they are partly borne by the patient's employing organization. In 1996 there were 1·94m. doctors, of whom 0·35m. practised Chinese medicine, and 1·16m. nurses. About 10% of doctors are in private practice.

In 1996 there were 67,964 hospitals (with 2·87m. beds), 528 sanatoria (with 109,000 beds) and 103,472 clinics.

Welfare. In 1996 there were 42,821 social welfare institutions with 769,348 inmates. Numbers (in 1,000) of beneficiaries of relief funds: Persons in poor rural households, 30,790; in poor urban households, 2,610; persons in rural households entitled to 'the 5 guarantees' (food, clothing, medical care, housing, education for children or funeral expenses), 2,675; retired, laid-off or disabled workers, 535. The major relief funds (in 1,000 yuan) in 1996 were: Families of deceased or disabled servicemen, 5,187,970; poor households, 712,270; orphaned, disabled, old and young persons, 1,856,680; welfare institutions, 1,551,000.

DIPLOMATIC REPRESENTATIVES

Of China in Great Britain (49-51 Portland Pl., London, W1N 3AH)
Ambassador: Ma Zhengang.

Of Great Britain in China (Guang Hua Lu 11, Jian Guo Men Wai, Beijing)
Ambassador: A. C. Galsworthy, CMG.

Of China in the USA (2300 Connecticut Ave., NW, Washington, D.C., 20008)
Ambassador: Li Xhaoxing.

Of the USA in China (Xiu Shui Bei Jie 3, Beijing)
Ambassador: James Sasser.

Of China to the United Nations
Ambassador: Qin Huasun.

Of China to the European Union
Ambassador: Mingjiang Song.

Further Reading

State Statistical Bureau. *China Statistical Yearbook*
China Directory [in Pinyin and Chinese]. Tokyo, annual

Baum, R., *Burying Mao: Chinese Politics in the Age of Deng Xiaoping.* Princeton Univ. Press,
    1994
Boorman, H. L. and Howard, R. C., (eds.) *Biographical Dictionary of Republican China.* 5 vols.
    Columbia Univ. Press, 1967–79
Brugger, B. and Reglar, S., *Politics, Economics and Society in Contemporary China.* London,
    1994
The Cambridge Encyclopaedia of China. 2nd ed. CUP, 1991
The Cambridge History of China. 14 vols. CUP, 1978 ff.
De Crespigny, R., *China this Century.* 2nd ed. OUP, 1993
Deng Xiaoping, *Speeches and Writings.* 2nd ed. Oxford, 1987
Dreyer, J. T., *China's Political System: Modernization and Tradition.* 2nd ed. London, 1996
Dietrich, C., *People's China: a Brief History.* OUP, 1986
Evans, R., *Deng Xiaoping and the Making of Modern China.* London, 1993
Fairbank, J. K., *The Great Chinese Revolution 1800–1985.* London, 1987.—*China: a New
    History.* Harvard Univ. Press, 1992
Fathers, M. and Higgins, A., *Tiananmen: the Rape of Peking.* London and New York, 1989
Glassman, R. M., *China in Transition: Communism, Capitalism and Democracy.* New York,
    1991
Goldman, M., *Sowing the Seeds of Democracy in China: Political Reform in the Deng Xiaoping
    Era.* Harvard Univ. Press, 1994
Goodman, D., *Deng Xiaoping and the Chinese Revolution: a Political Biography.* 2nd ed.
    London, 1994.—and Segal, G., (eds.) *China in the 90s: Crisis Management and Beyond.*
    Oxford, 1991
Gray, J., *Rebellions and Revolutions: China from the 1800s to the 1980s.* CUP, 1990
Hayford, C. W., *China.* [Bibliography] 2nd ed. Oxford and Santa Barbara (CA), 1997
Hinton, H. C., (ed.) *The People's Republic of China 1949–1979.* 5 vols. Wilmington, 1980
Huang, R., *China: a macro History.* 2nd ed. Armonk (NY), 1997
Jenner, W. J. F., *The Tyranny of History: the Roots of China's Crisis.* London, 1992
Lichtenstein, P. M., *China at the Brink: the Political Economy of Reform and Retrenchment in
    the Post-Mao Era.* New York, 1991
Lieberthal, K. G., *From Revolution through Reform.* New York, 1995.—and Lampton, D. M.
    (eds.) *Bureaucracy, Politics and Decision-Making in Post-Mao China.* California Univ. Press,
    1992
Lippit, V. D., *The Economic Development of China.* Armonk, 1987
Loewe, M. *The Pride that was China.* London, 1990
McCormick, B. L., *Political Reform in Post-Mao China: Democracy and Bureaucracy in a
    Leninist State.* California Univ. Press, 1990
MacFarquhar, R., (ed.) *The Politics of China: the eras of Mao and Deng.* 2nd ed. CUP, 1997.—
    The Origins of the Cultural Revolution. 3 vols. Columbia University Press, 1998
Mackerras, C. *et al., China since 1978: Reform, Modernization and Socialism with Chinese
    Characteristics.* New York, 1994.—and Yorke, A., *The Cambridge Handbook of
    Contemporary China.* CUP, 1991
Moise, E. E., *Modern China: A History.* London, 1986
Nathan, A. J., *Chinese Democracy.* London, 1986:—*China's Crisis: Dilemmas of Reform and
    Prospects for Democracy.* Columbia Univ. Press, 1990
Nolan, P., *State and Market in the Chinese Economy: Essays on Controversial Issues.* London,
    1993

Phillips, R. T., *China since 1911*. London, 1996
Riskin, C., *China's Political Economy: The Quest for Development since 1949*. OUP, 1987
Rodzinski, W., *A History of China*. Oxford, 1981–84
Schram, S., (ed.) *Mao's Road to Power: Revolutionary Writings 1912–1949*. 4 vols. Harvard, 1998
Sheng Hua, *et al.*, *China: from Revolution to Reform*. London, 1992
Shirk, S. L., *The Political Logic of Economic Reform in China*. Univ. of California Press, 1993
Spence, J. D., *The Search for Modern China*. London, 1990
White, G., (ed.) *The Chinese State in the Era of Economic Reform: the Road to Crisis*. London, 1991.—*Riding the Tiger: the Politics of Economic Reform in Post-Mao China*. London, 1993
Womack, B. (ed.), Contemporary Chinese Politics in Historical Perspective. CUP, 1992

Other more specialized titles are listed under TERRITORY AND POPULATION; TIBET; DEFENCE; AGRICULTURE; FOREIGN ECONOMIC RELATIONS.

National statistical office: State Statistical Bureau, 38 Yuetan Nanjie, Beijing.

HONG KONG

KEY HISTORICAL EVENTS. Hong Kong island and the southern tip of the Kowloon peninsula were ceded by China to Britain after the first and second Anglo-Chinese Wars by the Treaty of Nanking 1842 and the Convention of Peking 1860. The New Territories were leased to Britain for 99 years by China in 1898. Talks began in Sept. 1982 between Britain and China over the future of Hong Kong after the lease expiry in 1997. On 19 Dec. 1984, the two countries signed the Joint Declaration of the British and Chinese Governments on the Question of Hong Kong which entered into force on 27 May 1985. By the terms of this Hong Kong became, with effect from 1 July 1997, a Special Administrative Region of the People's Republic of China enjoying a high degree of autonomy, and vested with executive, legislative and independent judicial power, including that of final adjudication. It was agreed that the laws currently in force in Hong Kong would remain basically unchanged. The existing social and economic systems, and the present life-style, were to remain unchanged for another 50 years. This 'one country, two systems' principle, embodied in the Basic Law, which was enacted by the National People's Congress of the People's Republic of China in 1990, has become the constitution for the Hong Kong Special Administrative Region. In June 1991 the Legislative Council approved a Bill of Rights. China (People's Republic) objected to it.

China's selection on 21 Dec. 1996 of a provisional legislature which began functioning simultaneously with the Legislative Council in Jan. 1997 instead of after the latter's abolition on 30 June 1997 was protested by the UK as having no basis in the 1984 Joint Declaration.

TERRITORY AND POPULATION. Hong Kong island is situated off the southern coast of the Chinese mainland 32 km east of the mouth of the Pearl River. The area of the island is 79·99 sq. km. It is separated from the mainland by a fine natural harbour. On the opposite side is the peninsula of Kowloon (46·27 sq. km). Total area of the Territory is 1,091 sq. km, a large part of it being steep and unproductive hillside. Country parks and special areas cover over 40% of the land area. Since 1945, the Government has reclaimed over 5,400 ha from the sea, principally from the seafronts of Hong Kong and Kowloon, facing the harbour. The 'New Territories' are on the mainland, north of Kowloon.

The population was 5,674,100 at the 1991 census. Estimate (mid-1997) 6,502,100. Annual growth rate, 1996–97, 3·0%. Vital statistics, 1996: Known births, 63,000; known deaths, 31,000. Registered marriages (1994), 38,264. Rates (per 1,000, 1996): Birth, 10; death, 5; marriage, 6; infant mortality, 4 (per 1,000 live births). Life expectancy, 1996: Males, 76 years; females, 81. Some 43,100 persons emigrated in 1995. The British Nationality Scheme enables persons to acquire citizenship without leaving Hong Kong. There were 45,986 legal immigrants from China in 1995. 60% of the population was born in Hong Kong, 34% in China (1991 census). The population of Vietnamese migrants ('boat people') in Oct. 1996 was 12,710. All remaining 'boat people' were repatriated by Jan. 1997.

The official languages are Chinese and English.

CLIMATE. The climate is sub-tropical, tending towards temperate for nearly half the year, the winter being cool and dry and the summer hot and humid, May to Sept. being the wettest months. Jan. 60°F (15·8°C), July 84°F (28·8°C). Annual rainfall 87" (2,214·3 mm).

THE BRITISH ADMINISTRATION. Hong Kong was administered by the Hong Kong Government. The Governor was the head of Government and presided over the *Executive Council*, which advised the Governor on all important matters. The last British Governor was Chris Patten. In Oct. 1996, the Executive Council consisted of 3 ex-officio members and 10 appointed members, of whom 1 was an official member. The chief functions of the *Legislative Council* were to enact laws, control public expenditure and put questions to the administration on matters of public interest. The Legislative Council elected in Sept. 1995 was, for the first time, constituted solely by election. It comprised 60 members, of whom 20 were elected from geographical constituencies, 30 from functional constituencies encompassing all eligible persons in a workforce of 2·9m., and 10 from an election committee formed by members of 18 district boards. A president was elected from and by the members.

At the elections on 17 Sept. 1995, turn-out for the geographical seats was 35·79%, and for the functional seats (21 of which were contested), 40·42%. The Democratic Party and its allies gained 29 seats, the Liberal Party 10 and the pro-Beijing Democratic Alliance, 6. The remaining seats went to independents.

CONSTITUTION AND GOVERNMENT. In Dec. 1995 the Standing Committee of China's National People's Congress set up a Preparatory Committee of 150 members (including 94 from Hong Kong) to oversee the retrocession of Hong Kong to China on 1 July 1997. In Nov. 1996 the Preparatory Committee nominated a 400-member Selection Committee to select the Chief Executive of Hong Kong and a provisional legislature to replace the Legislative Council. The Selection Committee was composed of Hong Kong residents, with 60 seats reserved for delegates to the National People's Congress and appointees of the People's Political Consultative Conference. On 11 Dec. 1996 Tung Chee-hwa was elected Chief Executive by 80% of the Selection Committee's votes.

On 21 Dec. 1996 the Selection Committee selected a provisional legislature which began its activities in Jan. 1997 while the Legislative Council was still functioning. In Jan. 1997 the provisional legislature began repealing some civil rights legislation.

Theoretically Hong Kong is a Special Administrative Region of the People's Republic of China. It is supposed to retain a high degree of autonomy, and the legislative, judicial and administrative systems which were previously in operation are to remain in place. The Special Administrative Region Government is also empowered to decide on Hong Kong's monetary and economic policies independent of China.

In July 1997 the first-past-the-post system of electing the Legislative Council was replaced by proportional representation. Elections were scheduled for 1998.

Chief Executive: Tung Chee-hwa (b. 1937).
Chief Secretary: Anson Chan, CBE, JP.
Financial Secretary: Donald Tsang, OBE, JP.
The Chief Executive is aided by the Executive Council consisting of the Chief Secretary, the Financial Secretary and 12 other members.

Local Government. There are 2 municipal councils, the Urban Council and the Regional Council. With all appointed seats abolished in 1995, 59 of 80 seats were open to direct election in the March 1995 elections. Turn-out was 25·8%. Elections to the 18 Consultative District Boards set up in 1982 were held in Sept. 1994; turn-out was 33·1%.

At local council elections on 18 Sept. 1994 for 346 council seats turn-out was 33·1%. The United Democratic Party gained 77 seats; the Alliance for Democracy, 28; the Democratic Alliance for a Better Hong Kong (pro-Beijing), 37; the Liberal Party, 30, the United Democrats of Hong Kong won 11 out of 27 seats, independents 11, the Liberal Democratic Federation 3 and Communists 2.

ECONOMY

Budget. The total Government revenue and expenditure for financial years ending 31 March were as follows (in HK$1m.):

	1992–93	1993–94	1994–95	1995–96
Revenue	135,311	166,602	173,561	180,045
Expenditure	113,332	147,438	165,826	191,338

Estimated operating revenue (in HK$1m.) for 1995–96, 156,995; capital revenue, 32,605. Estimated operating expenditure, 124,540; capital expenditure, 45,200.

Currency. The unit of currency is the *Hong Kong dollar* (HKD) of 100 *cents*. Banknotes are issued by the Hongkong and Shanghai Banking Corporation and the Standard Chartered Bank, and, from May 1994, the Bank of China. There are coins of HK$10, HK$5, HK$2, HK$1, 50 cents, 20 cents and 10 cents. Currency in circulation in Aug. 1996, HK$83,174m. Fiscal reserves at 31 March 1997 stood at HK$163,000m.

Banking and Finance. As at Dec. 1995 there were 185 banks licensed under the Banking Ordinance, of which 31 were locally incorporated, 63 restricted licence banks and 154 representative offices of foreign banks. Licensed bank deposits were HK$2,601,971m. In June 1997; restricted licence bank deposits were HK$62,033m. There were 132 deposit-taking companies registered under the Banking Ordinance with total deposits of HK$18,419m. as at Nov. 1995.

There is a stock exchange. The summer of 1997 saw record highs on the Hang Seng index (16,365 in July 1997 compared with 10,681 in July 1996). In July 1997 the average daily turnover was HK$19,500m.

Weights and Measures. Metric, British Imperial, Chinese and US units are all in current use in Hong Kong. However, Government departments have now effectively adopted metric units; all new legislation uses metric terminology and existing legislation is being progressively metricated. Metrication is also proceeding in the private sector.

ENERGY AND NATURAL RESOURCES

Electricity. Production (1994) 25·14bn. kWh.

Water. Reservoirs are needed to store the summer rainfall in order to meet supply requirements. There are 17 impounding reservoirs with a total capacity of 586m. cu. metres. Water is also purchased (720m. cu. metres in 1996). Consumption in 1996 was 928m cu. metres.

Agriculture. Agriculture supplies about a quarter of domestic demand. Only 3·4% of the total land area is suitable for crop farming and most produce derives from intensive market gardening: 1,350 ha were under cultivation in 1995. In 1995, 88,000 tonnes of vegetables and 4,820 tonnes of fruit and nuts were produced. Poultry production was 24,921 tonnes; milk, 407 tonnes; eggs, 1,112 tonnes. There were 0·21m. pigs in 1995.

Fisheries. The fishing fleet of 4,800 vessels supplies about 62% of fresh marine fish consumed locally. In 1995 the marine fish catch was 203,300 tonnes. Inland freshwater farming and coastal marine farming provided 8,200 tonnes of fish.

INDUSTRY. An economic policy based on free enterprise and free trade; a skilled work force; an efficient commercial infrastructure; the modern and efficient sea-port (including container shipping terminals) and airport facilities; a geographical position relative to markets in North America; and traditional trading links with the UK all contributed to Hong Kong's success as a modern industrial territory. Links with China have been growing increasingly strong in recent years and will remain so.

In 1995 there were 31,114 manufacturing firms employing 386,106 persons. Firms by product type (and persons employed): Textiles and clothing, 7,046 (139,931); plastics, 2,250 (15,997); electronics, 1,109 (44,078); watches and clocks, 1,006 (12,119); electrical appliances, 136 (2,589); ship-building, 374 (4,510).

Labour. In 1996 the labour force (economically active population aged 15 and over) totalled 3·08m. (1·20m. female). The employed population included 1,047,000 people in wholesale, retail, restaurants and hotels, 391,000 in finance, insurance, business and real estate, 327,000 in manufacturing, 184,000 in the civil service and 77,000 manual labourers. The unemployment rate was 2·6% in 1996.

EXTERNAL ECONOMIC RELATIONS

Commerce. Industry is mainly export-oriented. The total value of domestic exports in 1996 was HK$212,200m.; re-exports, HK$1,185,000m. The major markets for domestic exports (in HK$1m.) were: People's Republic of China, 61,600; USA, 53,900; Germany, 11,400; and Japan, 11,300. Totals for the Asia-Pacific Economic Co-operation Group and the EU as a whole (in HK$1m.) were 162,200 and 37,000 respectively. The total value of imports in 1996 was HK$1,536,600m., the leading countries (in HK$1m.) being: People's Republic of China, 570,400; Japan, 208,220; Taiwan, 123,200; and USA, 121,100. Totals for the Asia-Pacific Economic Co-operation Group and the EU as a whole (in HK$1m.) were 1,287,000 and 170,600 respectively.

In 1996 domestic exports included (in HK$1m.): Clothing and accessories, 69,400; electrical machinery and parts, 30,400; textiles and fabrics, 13,700; watches and clocks, 12,000. The chief import items were consumer goods (573,000), raw materials (540,900); capital goods (324,000) and foodstuffs (65,200).

Visible trade normally carries an adverse balance which is offset by a favourable balance of invisible trade, in particular transactions in connection with air transportation, shipping, tourism and banking services.

Hong Kong has a free exchange market. Foreign merchants may remit profits or repatriate capital. Import and export controls are kept to the minimum, consistent with strategic requirements.

Tourism. There were about 11·7m. visitor arrivals in 1996 (2,380,000 from Japan, 751,000 from the USA).

COMMUNICATIONS

Roads. In 1996 there were 1,743 km of roads, more than 900 km of which were in the New Territories. There are 8 major road tunnels, including 2 under Victoria Harbour. In 1996 there were 475,000 licensed motor vehicles, including 293,000 private cars and 117,000 goods vehicles. There were 14,790 road accidents in 1995, 259 fatal. A total of 14·8m. tonnes of cargo were transported by road in 1996.

Railways. There is an electric tramway with a total track length of 33 km, and a cable tramway connecting the Peak district with the lower levels in Victoria. The electrified Kowloon-Canton Railway runs for 34 km from the terminus at Hung Hom in Kowloon to the border point at Lo Wu. It carried 232m. passengers in 1995. In 1996, 939,000 tonnes of cargo were transported by rail. A light rail system (32 km) is operated by the Kowloon-Canton Railway Corporation in Tuen Mun, Yuen Long and Tin Shui Wai; it carried 123m. passengers in 1995.

A metro, the Mass Transit Railway system comprises 43·2 km with 38 stations. It carried 812m. passengers in 1995.

In 1996 a total of 3·9m. passenger journeys were made on public transport (including local railways, buses etc.).

Civil Aviation. Hong Kong International Airport (Kai Tak) is situated on the north shore of Kowloon Bay. 61 airlines operate services. British Airways operates 14 flights per week to the UK. Cathay Pacific Airways, one of the 3 Hong Kong-based airlines, operates more than 365 passenger and cargo services weekly to Europe (including 16 passenger and 5 cargo services per week to the UK), the Far and Middle East, South Africa, Australasia and North America. In 1995, Cathay Pacific had a fleet of 2 A330-300s, 4 A340-200s, 7 B-747-200Bs, 1 B-747-200B(F), 3 B-747-200Fs, 6 B-747-300s, 19 B-747-400s, 1 B-747-400F and 14 other aircraft. Hong Kong Dragon Airlines Ltd operates A330 and A320 scheduled and non-scheduled services to a number of cities in Asia and the People's Republic of China. Air Hong Kong, an all-cargo operator, provides a scheduled service 5 times a week to Manchester, UK, and operates non-scheduled services around the region. In 1995–96, 150,118 aircraft arrived and departed. In 1996, 23·48m. passengers and 1·56m. tonnes of freight were carried on aircraft.

Shipping. The port of Hong Kong handled 12·6m. 20-ft equivalent units in 1995. The Kwai Chung Container Port has 31 berths with 6,059 metres of quay backed by 228 ha of cargo handling area. In 1995, more than 41,000 ocean-going vessels, 108,000 river trading vessels and 64,000 international passenger vessels called at Hong Kong. In 1996, 125·4m. tonnes of freight were handled.

Telecommunications. There were 126 post offices in March 1996. In March 1996 there were 4,216,800 telephones and over 284,000 fax lines. Basic local telephone services are provided by Hong Kong Telecom, which also offers fax services and value-added telephone services. The company also provides international voice, data and video transmission services, telex and telegram services, international private leased circuits, and shore-to-ship and ground-to-air communications. International facilities are provided through submarine cables, microwave and satellite radio systems.

Broadcasting is regulated by the Broadcasting Authority, a statutory body comprising 3 government officers and 9 non-official members. There is a government broadcasting station, Radio Television Hong Kong, which broadcasts on 7 channels (4 Chinese, 1 English and 1 bi-lingual service and 1 dedicated to BBC World Service), 6 of which provide a 24-hour service. Hong Kong Commercial Broadcasting Co. Ltd and Metro Broadcast Co. Ltd transmit commercial sound programmes on 6 channels. Television Broadcasts Ltd and Asia Television Ltd transmit commercial television in English and Chinese on 4 channels, in colour (by PAL). Hutchvision Hong Kong broadcasts by satellite to the entire Asian region on 14 TV and 2 radio channels and also carries the BBC World Service. There is also a cable TV network. In 1992 there were some 3m. radio; in 1995 there were over 2·3m. TV receivers.

Cinemas. In 1995 there were 184 cinemas; attendance was 27·4m. (57m. in 1990). 154 films were made in 1995.

Press. In 1995 there were 59 registered newspapers, including 36 dailies in Chinese and 5 in English, and 675 periodicals. A number of news agency bulletins are registered as newspapers.

SOCIAL INSTITUTIONS

Justice. The common law of England and the rules of equity were in force so far as they are applicable to the circumstances of Hong Kong. UK Acts of Parliament, however, were only binding if expressly applied to Hong Kong. By 1997 Hong Kong possessed a comprehensive body of law which owed its authority to its own legislature. The Hong Kong Act of 1985 provided for Hong Kong ordinances to replace English laws in specified fields.

The courts of justice comprise the Supreme Court (which includes the Court of Appeal and the High Court), the District Court (which includes the Family Court), the Magistracies, the Coroner's Court, the Juvenile Court and 4 tribunals. The Court of Appeal hears appeals on all matters, civil and criminal, from the lower courts. Pursuant to the Joint Declaration, the powers of final judgement were to be vested in the Court of Final Appeal, inaugurated in the territory in June 1997 to take over the functions of the UK Privy Council. While the High Court has unlimited jurisdiction in both civil and criminal matters, the District Court has limited jurisdiction. The maximum term of imprisonment it may impose is 7 years. Magistracies exercise criminal jurisdiction over a wide range of indictable and summary offences, and the powers of punishment are generally restricted to a maximum of 2 years' imprisonment. The Lands Tribunal determines on statutory claims for compensation over land and certain landlord and tenant matters. The Labour Tribunal provides a quick and inexpensive method of settling disputes between employers and employees. The Small Claims Tribunal deals with monetary claims involving amounts not exceeding HK$15,000.

After being in abeyance for 25 years, the death penalty was abolished in 1992.

79,050 crimes were reported in 1996, of which 15,191 were violent crimes. 47,157 people were arrested in 1996. The prison population was 13,117 in 1995.

Education. Free and compulsory education is available to all children aged from 6 to 15 years. In 1995–96 there were 180,317 pupils in 731 kindergartens (all private), 467,718 in 860 primary schools (some 10·1% in private schools) and 459,845 in 38 government, 337 aided and 91 private secondary schools.

There are 7 technical institutes with (in 1995–96) 13,972 full-time and 34,409 part-time students; 2 technical colleges with 9,300 students, and 5 teacher training colleges of education with 2,863 full-time students.

The University of Hong Kong (founded 1911) had 10,325 full-time and 2,618 part-time students in the academic year of 1995–96, the Chinese University of Hong Kong (founded 1963), 10,388 full-time and 2,536 part-time students, the Hong Kong University of Science and Technology (founded 1991), 5,792 full-time and 503 part-time students, the Hong Kong Polytechnic University (founded 1972 as the Hong Kong Polytechnic), 11,157 full-time and 9,289 part-time students, the City University of Hong Kong (founded 1984 as the City Polytechnic of Hong Kong), 10,061 full-time and 6,881 part-time students, the Hong Kong Baptist University (founded 1956 as the Hong Kong Baptist College), 4,146 full-time and 600 part-time students and the Lingnan College (founded 1967), 2,059 full-time and 2 part-time students.

Social Welfare. The Government co-ordinates and implements expanding programmes in social welfare, which include social security, family services, child care, services for the elderly, youth and community work, probation and corrections and rehabilitation. 170 non-governmental organizations are subsidized by public funds.

The Government gives non-contributory cash assistance to needy families, unemployed able-bodied adults, the severely disabled and the elderly. Caseload as at 31 Dec. 1995 totalled 623,029. Victims of natural disasters, crimes of violence and traffic accidents are financially assisted.

Health. In 1995 there were 8,122 doctors, 1,625 dentists and 29,328 hospital beds.

Further Reading

Statistical Information: The Census and Statistics Department is responsible for the preparation and collation of Government statistics. These statistics are published mainly in the *Hong Kong Monthly Digest of Statistics.* The Department also publishes monthly trade statistics, economic indicators and an annual review of overseas trade, etc. *Website:* http:/www.info.gov.hk/censtatd/

Hong Kong [various years] Hong Kong Government Press
Bonavia, D., *Hong Kong 1997.* London, 1984
Brown, J. M. (ed.), *Hong Kong's Transitions, 1842–1997.* London, 1997
Buckley, R., *Hong Kong: the Road to 1997.* CUP, 1997
Cameron, N., *An Illustrated History of Hong Kong.* OUP, 1991
Chill, H., *et al* (eds.) *The Future of Hong Kong: Toward 1997 and Beyond.* Westport, 1987
Cottrell, R., *The End of Hong Kong: the Secret Diplomacy of Imperial Retreat.* London, 1993
Courtauld, C. and Holdsworth, M., *The Hong Kong Story.* OUP, 1997
Endacott, G. B., *A History of Hong Kong.* 2nd ed. OUP, 1973.—*Government and People in Hong Kong, 1841–1962: a Constitutional History.* OUP, 1965
Flowerdew, J., *The Final Years of British Hong Kong: the Discourse of Colonial Withdrawal.* Hong Kong, 1997

Keay, J., *Last Post: the End of Empire in the Far East*. London, 1997

Lo, C. P., *Hong Kong*. London, 1992

Lo, S.-H., *The Politics of Democratization in Hong Kong*. London, 1997

Morris, J., *Hong Kong: Epilogue to an Empire*. 2nd ed. [of *Hong Kong: Xianggang*]. London, 1993

Patrikeeff, F., *Mouldering Pearl: Hong Kong at the Crossroads*. London, 1989

Roberti, M., *The Fall of Hong Kong: China's Triumph and Britain's Betrayal*. 2nd ed. Chichester, 1997

Roberts, E. V. *et al. Historical Dictionary of Hong Kong and Macau*. Metuchen (NJ), 1993

Scott, I., *Hong Kong:* [Bibliography]. Oxford and Santa Barbara (CA), 1990

Segal, G., *The Fate of Hong Kong*. London, 1993

Shipp, S., *Hong Kong, China: a Political History of the British Crown Colony's Transfer to Chinese Rule*. Jefferson (NC), 1995

Tsang, S. Y., *Hong Kong: an Appointment with China*. London, 1997

Wang, G. and Wong, S. L. (eds.) *Hong Kong's Transition: a Decade after the Deal*. OUP, 1996

Welsh, F., *A History of Hong Kong*. 3rd ed. London, 1997

Wilson, D., *Hong Kong, Hong Kong*. London, 1991

Yahuda, M., *Hong Kong: China's Challenge*. London, 1996

TAIWAN[1]

'Republic of China'

Capital: Taipei
Population: 21·6m.
GNP per capita: US$12,838

KEY HISTORICAL EVENTS. Taiwan, christened Formosa (beautiful) by the Portuguese, was ceded to Japan by China by the Treaty of Shimonoseki in 1895. After the Second World War the island was surrendered to Gen. Chiang Kai-shek in Sept. 1945, who made it the headquarters for his crumbling Nationalist Government. Chiang Kai-shek used the ideology of eventual Kuomintang victory as an excuse for authoritarian, military backed rule and the maintenance of a large standing army on the island. On Chiang Kai-shek's death in 1978 he was succeeded by his son, Chiang Ching-Kuo.

Until 1970 the US fully supported Taiwan's claims to represent all of China. Only in 1971 did the government of the People's Republic of China manage to replace that of Chiang Kai-shek at the UN. In Jan. 1979 the UN established formal diplomatic relations with the People's Republic of China, breaking off all formal ties with Taiwan.

Taiwanese fears that US recognition of China spelt the end of the island's independence were not realized. The US Congress in the Taiwan Relations Act subsequently authorized continuing economic and social ties with Taiwan. Taiwan itself has continued to reject all attempts at reunification, and although there have been frequent threats from mainland China to precipitate direct action (including military manoeuvres off the Taiwanese coast) the prospect of confrontation with the US supports the status quo.

TERRITORY AND POPULATION. Taiwan lies between the East and South China Seas about 100 miles from the coast of Fujian. The territories currently under the control of the Republic of China include Taiwan, Penghu (the Pescadores), Kinmen (Quemoy), and the Matsu Islands, as well as the archipelagos in the South China Sea. Off the Pacific coast of Taiwan are Green Island and Orchid Island. To the north-east of Taiwan are the Tiaoyutai Islets. The total area of Taiwan Island, the Penghu Archipelago and the Kinmen area (including the fortified offshore islands of Quemoy and Matsu) is 13,970 sq. miles (36,182 sq. km). Population (1997), 21,592,000. The indigenous Han Chinese are of Fujian origin. Of the population 15% is Hakka and 15% mainland Chinese who came with the Nationalist forces. There are also 381,204 aboriginals of Malay origin. Population density: 597 per sq. km.

[1] See note on transcription of names in CHINA: Territory and Population.

In 1997, the birth rate was 1·42%; death rate, 0·52%; rate of growth, 0·9% per annum (2000 target: 0·72% per annum). Life expectancy, 1996: Males, 71·87 years; females, 77·92 years. The death rate was 5·71 per 1,000 persons; infant mortality per 1,000 live births, 6·66.

Taiwan's administrative units comprise (with 1996 populations): 2 special municipalities: Taipei, the capital (2·61m.) and Kaohsiung (1·43m.); 5 cities outside the county structure: Chiayi (262,860), Hsinchu (345,954), Keelung (374,199), Taichung (876,384), Tainan (710,954); 16 counties (*hsien*): Changhwa (1,292,482), Chiayi (565,700), Hsinchu (414,932), Hualien (358,660), Ilan (465,120), Kaohsiung (1,208,128), Miaoli (560,099), Nantou (545,667), Penghu (90,087), Pingtung (912,850), Taichung (1,427,378), Tainan (1,088,986), Taipei (3,355,299), Taitung (253,831), Taoyuan (1,570,456), Yunlin (752,427).

CLIMATE. The climate is subtropical in the north and tropical in the south. The typhoon season extends from July to Sept. The average monthly temperatures of Jan. and July in Taipei are 59·5°F (15·3°C) and 83·3°F (28·5°C) respectively and average annual rainfall is 83·8" (2,128 mm). Kaohsiung's average monthly temperatures of Jan. and July are 65·5°F (18·6°C) and 83·3°F (28·5°C) respectively and average annual rainfall is 69" (1,752 mm).

CONSTITUTION AND GOVERNMENT. The ROC Constitution is based on the Principles of Nationalism, Democracy and Social Wellbeing formulated by Dr. Sun Yat-sen, the founding father of the Republic of China. The ROC government is divided into 3 main levels: central, provincial/municipal and county/city each of which has well-defined powers.

The central government consists of the Office of the President, the National Assembly and five governing branches called '*yuan*', namely the Executive Yuan, the Legislative Yuan, the Judicial Yuan, the Examination Yuan and the Control Yuan.

At the provincial level, the provincial governments exercise administrative responsibility. Since the ROC government administers only Taiwan Province and two counties in Fukien Province, only two provincial governments are currently operational—the Taiwan Provincial Government and the Fukien Provincial Government. Taipei and Kaohsiung are special municipalities which are under the direct jurisdiction of the central government. At the local level, under the Taiwan Provincial Government are five city governments: Keelung, Hsinchu, Taichung, Chiayi and Tainan; and 16 county governments with the governments of their subordinate cities. The Fukien Provincial Government oversees the regional affairs of Kinmen County and Lienchiang County. From 5 May to 23 July 1997 the *Additional Articles of the Constitution of the Republic of China* underwent yet another amendment. The roles of the provincial government and the Control Yuan have taken on drastic changes. Under the newest revision:

- The provincial government is to be streamlined and the popular elections of the governor and members of the provincial council are suspended.
- A resolution on the impeachment of the President or Vice President is no longer to be instituted by the Control Yuan but rather by the Legislative Yuan.
- The Legislative Yuan has the power to pass a no-confidence vote against the president of the Executive Yuan, while the president of the Republic has the power to dissolve the Legislative Yuan.
- The president of the Executive Yuan is to be directly appointed by the president of the Republic. Hence the consent of the Legislative Yuan is no longer needed.
- Educational, scientific and cultural budgets, especially the compulsory education budget, will be given priority, but no longer restricted by Article 164 of the Constitution to remain at least 15% of the total national budget.

President: Lee Teng-hui (b. 1923; sworn in 20 May 1996).
Vice President: Lien Chan (b. 1936).

Vincent C. Siew has served as the ROC president of the Executive Yuan since 1 Sept. 1997.

There are 8 ministries under the Executive Yuan. They are the ministries of the

Interior, Foreign Affairs, National Defence, Finance, Education, Justice, Economic Affairs, and Transportation and Communications.

The cabinet comprised the following in March 1998:
Prime Minister: Vincent Siew.
Vice Premier: Liu Chao-shiuan. *Foreign Affairs:* Jason Hu. *National Defence:* Chiang Chung-ling. *Interior:* Huang Chu-wen. *Finance:* Paul Chiu. *Education:* Lin Ching-chiang. *Economic Affairs:* Wang Chih-kang. *Justice:* Liao Cheng-hao.

In addition to the Mongolian and Tibetan Affairs Commission and the Overseas Chinese Affairs Commission, a number of commissions and subordinate organizations have been formed with the resolution of the Executive Yuan Council and the Legislature to meet new demands and handle new affairs. Examples include the Environmental Protection Administration, which was set up in 1987 as public awareness of pollution control rose; the Mainland Affairs Council, which was established in 1990 to handle the thawing of relations between Taiwan and the Chinese mainland; the Fair Trade Commission, which was established in 1992 to promote a fair trade system; and the Consumer Protection Commission, which was set up in July 1994 to study and review basic policies on consumer protection. Since 1995 even more commissions have been set up to provide a wider scope of services: the Public Construction Commission was set up in July 1995, the Council of Aboriginal Affairs in Dec. 1996, and the National Sports Council in July 1997.

These commissions and councils are headed by:
Aborigines Commission: Hua Chia-chih. *Agricultural Council:* Peng Tso-kuei. *Atomic Energy Council:* Hu Ching-piao. *Central Election Commission:* Lin Feng-cheng. *Consumers Protection Committee:* Hsu Li-teh. *Cultural Planning and Development Council:* Lin Chung-chih. *Economic Planning and Development Council:* Chiang Pin kung. *Fair Trade Commission:* Chao Ching-yang. *Labour Affairs Council:* Hsu Shieh-kwei. *Mainland Affairs Council:* Chang King-yuh. *Mongolian and Tibetan Affairs Commission:* Kao Koong-lian. *National Palace Museum:* Chin Hsiao-yi. *National Research, Development and Evaluation Commission:* Huang Ta-chou. *National Science Council:* Huang Chen-tai. *National Youth Commission:* Lee Chi-chu. *Overseas Chinese Affairs Commission:* Chiao Jen-ho. *Physical Education and Sports Commission:* Nancy Chao Li-yun. *Public Construction Commission:* Ou Chin-teh. *Research, Development and Evaluation Commission:* Yang Chou-hsiang. *Vocational Assistance for Retired Servicemen Commission:* Gen. Yang Ting-yung.

National anthem: 'San Min Chu I'; words by Dr Sun Yat-sen, tune by Cheng Mao-yun.

DEFENCE. Conscription is for 2 years.

Army. The Army numbered about 230,300 in 1997, including 21,000 military police. In 1997 it consisted of 10 infantry divisions, 2 mechanized infantry divisions, 2 airborne brigades, 6 independent armoured brigades, 1 tank group and 2 surface-to-air missile battalions. The aviation element comprises 6 squadrons with about 100 transport and 65 armed helicopters. Equipment includes 100 M-48A5, 450 M-48H and 20 M-60A3 main battle tanks.

Navy. The navy still includes a number of former US Navy ships over 40 years old although a major re-equipment programme is in progress, including new submarines, frigates and support ships. Current fleet strength is 2 new Netherlands-built diesel submarines, 18 ex-US 1940s destroyers, 5 new ROC-built guided-missile frigates, 2 new French-built La Fayette class, 6 ex-US Knox class and 2 older frigates, 52 fast missile craft, 45 other patrol craft and 16 minesweepers. The amphibious force includes 1 amphibious flagship, 2 dock landing ships, 20 landing ships and about 280 amphibious craft. Auxiliary craft include 1 combat support ship, 4 support tankers, 2 repair and salvage ships, 7 tugs and 3 survey ships. Main bases are at Tsoying, Makung and Keelung.

Active personnel in 1997 totalled 38,000 in the Navy and 30,000 in the Marine Corps. There are over 67,500 naval and marine reservists.

The Naval Air Command operates 31 S-2 Tracker aircraft, 12 small anti-submarine helicopters operated from the destroyers and 12 SH-2F and 10 S-70 Seahawk helicopters based ashore.

The Customs service operates 12 cutters.

Air Force. The Air Force is equipped mainly with aircraft of US design, including F-5E fighters built in Taiwan. It has 12 front-line squadrons of F-5E/F Tiger IIs, 2 of locally-produced Ching-kuo interceptors, 1 of locally-built AT-3 twin-jet light strike aircraft. The 6 transport squadrons are equipped with 4 Boeing 727s, 11 Beech 1900s, 3 Fokker 50s, a few remaining C-119Gs and 25 C-130H Hercules. 4 E-2 Hawkeye airborne early warning aircraft have been delivered. Search and rescue units operate S-70 and Iroquois helicopters, and there are other helicopter and large training elements, some equipped with AT-3 twin-jet trainers designed and built in Taiwan and others with US-supplied T-34Cs and T-38s. Deliveries of 60 Mirage 2000 and 150 F-16 fighters were made in 1997. Total strength in 1996, 68,000 personnel.

INTERNATIONAL RELATIONS. By a treaty of 1 Dec. 1954 the USA was pledged to protect Taiwan, but this treaty lapsed 1 year after the USA established diplomatic relations with the People's Republic of China on 1 Jan. 1979. In April 1979 the Taiwan Relations Act was passed by the US Congress to maintain commercial, cultural and other relations between USA and Taiwan through the American Institute on Taiwan and its Taiwan counterpart, the Taipei Economic and Cultural Representative Office in the USA, which were accorded quasi-diplomatic status in 1980.

The People's Republic took over the China seat in the UN from Taiwan on 25 Oct. 1971.

In May 1991 Taiwan ended its formal state of war with the People's Republic.

As of Oct. 1997 the ROC has formal diplomatic ties with 30 countries and maintains substantive relations with over 100 countries and territories around the globe.

In Sept. 1997 at the invitation of the Panamanian government, President Lee participated in the World Congress on the Panama Canal. In the wake of the visit to Panama, President Lee travelled to 3 other nations: Honduras, El Salvador and Paraguay. At a summit meeting with leaders of 6 Latin American nations held in El Salvador, the ROC was invited to join the System of Central American Integration, a regional grouping modelled after the European Union, which is known by its Spanish acronym SICA.

ECONOMY

Policy. As regional economic blocs take shape, Taiwan plans to develop itself into an operations centre for the Asia-Pacific region over the next 10 years. The plan calls for 6 operations centres to handle high value-added manufacturing, air and sea cargo and passenger transportation, and professional services.

Budget. There are 2 budgets, the central government's general budget together with some special defence and infrastructure appropriations and the provincial budget for Taiwan proper. For the fiscal year July 1997–June 1998 the central government's general budget was NT$1,243,464m. Expenditure planned: 20·9% on defence; 10·6% on economic development; 20·3% on social security; 15·3% on education, science and culture. Foreign exchange reserves were US$85,752m. in Sept. 1997.

Currency. The unit of currency is the *New Taiwan dollar* (TWD), of 100 *cents*. There are coins of NT$ 1, 5, 10 and 50 and notes of NT$ 50, 100, 500 and 1,000. Gold reserves were 13·57m. oz. in 1997.

Banking and Finance. The Central Bank of China (reactivated in 1961) regulates the money supply, manages foreign exchange and issues currency. *Governor:* Sheu Yuan-dong. The Bank of Taiwan is the largest commercial bank and the fiscal agent of the government. The number of financial institutions totalled 5,694 in 1996. There are 2 stock exchanges in Taipei.

ENERGY AND NATURAL RESOURCES

Electricity. Output of electricity in 1996 was 124,973m. kWh; total installed capacity was 23,763·5 MW, comprising 62% thermal, 21% nuclear and 17% hydroelectric. There are 3 nuclear power-stations (capacities 1·72m., 1·97m. and 1·9m. kW) and a fourth is envisaged.

Minerals. In 1996, coal production was 0·1m. tonnes; refined oil, 35·9m. kl; natural gas, 891m. cu. metres. Crude oil production (1996), 59,731 kl.

Agriculture. The cultivated area was 872,000 ha in 1996, of which 348,000 ha were paddy fields. Rice production totalled 1,580,000 tonnes in 1996.

In 1996 livestock production was valued at more than US$5,500m., accounting for 35·5% of Taiwan's total agricultural production value. However, the outbreak of foot and mouth disease in March 1997 posed a major threat to Taiwan's pork industry. A total of 22,433 hog farms in 14 cities and counties along Taiwan's west coast were stricken by the disease. The government soon exterminated all hogs at contaminated farms and imported 8m. doses of vaccine for healthy ones. Pork exports were banned and the outbound shipment of 105 kinds of products from cloven-hoofed animals were also prohibited. The government compensated pig farmers for their slaughtered animals and provided relief to both farmers and pork exporters in the form of US$970m. in low interest loans. The Executive Yuan also allocated a special budget of US$278m. for relevant government agencies to carry forward remedial measures. Accordingly, the disease was soon brought under control and the wholesale price of pork rebounded to the normal level.

Forestry. Forest area, 1996: 2,102,311 ha. Forest reserves: trees, 358,239,000 cu. metres; bamboo, 1,127m poles. Timber production, 35,603 cu. metres.

Fisheries. By 1996 Taiwan's fishing fleet totalled 28,111 vessels (of which 13,020 were powered craft); the catch was approximately 1m. tonnes. In 1996 Taiwan produced US$3,500m. worth of fish. Of this, 45% came from deep-sea fishing, 34% from aquaculture, 17% from offshore fishing and 4% from coastal fishing. More than 33% of the catch was exported, with the biggest items being skipjack and eel.

INDUSTRY. Output (in tonnes) in 1996 (and 1995): Steel bars, 6·8m. (7·7m.); sugar, 0·36m. (0·4m.); cement, 21·5m. (22·5m.); pulp, 0·31m. (0·37m.); cotton fabrics, 784·5m. metres (773·9m.); computers, 3·4m. portable (2·1m.) and 5·1m. desk-top (4·8m.).

Labour. In 1996 the labour force was 9·43m., of whom 0·88m. worked in agriculture, forestry and fisheries, 3·41m. in industry (including 2·5m. in manufacturing and 0·86m. in construction), 2·06m. in commerce, 465,000 in transport and communications, and 2·36m. in other services. 0·24m. were registered unemployed in 1996.

FOREIGN ECONOMIC RELATIONS. Restrictions on the repatriation of investment earnings by foreign nationals were removed in 1994.

Commerce. Total trade, in US$1m.:

	1991	1992	1993	1994	1995	1996
Imports	62,861	72,007	77,061	85,359	103,551	102,371
Exports	76,178	81,470	84,917	93,056	111,659	115,951

The USA, Japan and Hong Kong are Taiwan's major trade partners followed by Singapore, Germany, Thailand and Malaysia.

Principal exports in 1996, in US$1,000m.: Textiles, 15·67; base metals and articles, 10·25; machinery, 53·73; plastic and rubber products, 7·71; vehicles and transport equipment, 5·22; footwear, headwear and umbrellas, 1·65; toys, games, sports equipment, 2·67.

Principal imports in 1993, in US$1,000m.: Base metals and articles, 10·42; chemicals, 10·92; machinery, 35·97; minerals, 9·28 (8·7%); vehicles and transport equipment, 4·55; textile products, 3·63; precision instruments, clocks and watches, musical instruments, 5·33.

Tourism. In 1996, 2,358,221 tourists visited Taiwan, and 5,713,535 Taiwanese made visits abroad.

COMMUNICATIONS

Roads. In 1996 there were 19,634 km of roads. 14·3m. motor vehicles were registered including 3,874,203 passenger cars, 21,598 buses, 748,150 lorries and 8,517,024 motor cycles. 1,170m. passengers and 289·4m. tonnes of freight were transported (including urban buses).

Railways. Total route length in 1996 was 2,363·1 km (1,067 mm and 762 mm gauges). The state network consisted of 1,108 km as of Dec. 1996. Freight traffic amounted to 19·2m. tonnes and passenger traffic to 159m. in 1996.

Civil Aviation. There are 2 international airports: Chiang Kai-shek at Taoyuan near Taipei, and Kaohsiung in the south. In addition there are several domestic airports: Taipei, Hualien, Taitung, Taichung, Tainan, Chiayi, Pingtung, Makung, Chimei, Orchid Island, Green Island, Wangan, Kinmen and Peikan. In Oct. 1997 there were 17 domestic airlines, of which 4 are international carriers: China Airlines (CAL), EVE Airways Corp. (EVA AIR), Mandarin Airlines (MDA; CAL's subsidiary) and Trans Asia Airways (TNA) operate international services to 42 destinations in 27 countries. 35 foreign airlines also operate services. In 1996 52m. passengers and 1·2m. tonnes of freight were flown. To accommodate this heavier air passenger and cargo traffic a US$800m. expansion project at Chiang Kai-shek International Airport began in 1989. The project includes a second passenger terminal, aircraft bays, airport connection roads, car parks and the expansion of air freight facilities. It is scheduled for completion in June 1999. The planned facilities are designed to allow the airport to handle an additional 14m. passengers annually by the year 2010.

Shipping. Maritime transportation is vital to the trade-oriented economy of Taiwan. As of Dec. 1996 the ROC's shipping industry had a fleet of 256 vessels over 100 gross tons, for a total of 9·23m. dead weight tons. There are 4 international ports: Kaohsiung, Keelung, Hualien and Taichung. The first 2 are container centres. Suao port is an auxiliary port to Keelung.

Telecommunications. In 1997 there were 10,429,020 telephones, 1,253,987 mobile phones and 2,496,090 radio pager subscribers.

As of Sept. 1997 there were 65 radio stations, 4 commercial TV services and 117 cable systems. June 1997 saw the inauguration of a fourth over-the-air television station—The Kaohsiung-based Formosa Television—which is affiliated with the opposition Democratic Progressive Party and telecasts on VHF low-band. A Public Television Law was passed on 1 May 1997.

Cinemas (1996). Cinemas numbered 161, and 18 full-length films were made.

Press. There were 247 domestic news agencies, 341 newspapers and 5,400 periodicals in 1997.

SOCIAL INSTITUTIONS

Religion. There were 4·32m. Taoists in 1996 with 8,250 temples and 32,500 priests, 4·86m. Buddhists with 3,938 temples and 9,360 priests, 0·42m. Protestants and 0·3m. Catholics.

Education. Since 1968 there has been compulsory education for 9 years (6–15) with free tuition. The illiteracy rate dropped to 5·99 in 1995 and is still falling. In 1996–97, there were 2,519 elementary schools with 90,127 teachers and 1,934,736 pupils; 1,138 secondary schools with 98,437 teachers and 1,908,935 students; 137 schools of higher education, including 24 universities, 43 colleges and 70 junior colleges, with 37,779 teachers and 795,547 students. More than one-quarter of the total population attended an educational institution.

Health. In 1996 there was 1 physician serving every 868 persons, 1 doctor of Chinese medicine per 7,194 persons and 1 dentist per 2,967 persons. More than

114,000 beds were provided by the 95 public and 678 private hospitals, averaging nearly 54 beds per 10,000 persons. In addition to the 497 public and 15,375 private clinics, there were 865 health stations and health rooms serving residents in the sparsely populated areas. Acute infectious diseases were no longer the number one killer. Malignant neoplasms, cerebrovascular diseases, accidents and adverse effects, and heart diseases were the first 4 leading causes of death.

Social Security. A universal health insurance scheme came into force in March 1995 as an extension to the incorporation of 13 social insurance plans which only cover 59% of Taiwan's population. Premium shares among the government, employer and insured are varied according to the insured statuses. Up to May 1997 about 20·16m. people or 96·13% of the population were covered by the National Health insurance programme. The 7·99m. new beneficiaries are mainly the elderly, children, students and housewives.

Further Reading

Statistical Yearbook of the Republic of China. Taipei, annual
The Republic of China Yearbook. Taipei, annual
Taiwan Statistical Data Book. Taipei, annual
Annual Review of Government Administration, Republic of China. Taipei, annual
Arrigo, L. G. *et al. The Other Taiwan: 1945 to the Present Day.* New York, 1994
Cooper, J. F., *Historical Dictionary of Taiwan.* Metuchen (NJ), 1993
Gälli, A., *Taiwan ROC: A Chinese Challenge to the World.* London, 1987
Gold, T. B., *State and Society in the Taiwan Miracle.* Armonk, 1986
Hughes, C., *Taiwan and Chinese Nationalism: National Identity and Status in International Society.* London, 1997
Lee, S.-Y., *Money and Finance in the Economic Development of Taiwan.* London, 1990
Lee, W.-C., *Taiwan:* [Bibliography]. Oxford and Santa Barbara, 1990
Liu, A. P. L., *Phoenix and the Lame Lion: Modernization in Taiwan and Mainland China, 1950–1980.* Stanford, 1987
Long, S., *Taiwan: China's Last Frontier.* London, 1991
Moody, P. R., *Political Change in Taiwan: a Study of Ruling Party Adaptability.* New York, 1992
Tsang, S. (ed.) *In the Shadow of China: Political Developments in Taiwan since 1949.* Farnborough, 1994

National library: National Central Library, Taipei (established 1986).

COLOMBIA

República de Colombia

Capital: Bogotá
Population: 37·42m.
GDP per head: (PPP$) 6,107
GNP: US$58·9bn.
HDI/world rank: 0·848/51

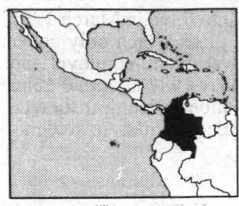

KEY HISTORICAL EVENTS. Columbus sighted what became Colombia in 1499. The conquest of the territory began in 1509; and 30 years later the Spaniards were well established. In 1564 the Spanish Crown appointed a President of New Granada, which included the territories of Colombia, Panama and Venezuela. In 1718 a viceroyalty of New Granada was created. This viceroyalty gained its independence from Spain in 1819, and together with the present territories of Panama, Venezuela and Ecuador was officially constituted on 17 Dec. 1819 as the state of 'Greater Colombia'. This new state lasted only until 1830 whent it split up into Venezuela, Ecuador and the republic of New Granada. The constitution of 22 May 1858 changed New Granada into a confederation of eight states, under the name of *Confederación Granadina*. Under the constitution of 8 May 1863 the country was renamed *Estados Unidos de Colombia,* which were nine in number. The revolution of 1885 led the National Council of Bogotá, composed of two delegates from each state, to promulgate the constitution of 5 Aug. 1886, forming the Republic of Colombia. The constitution abolished the sovereignty of the states, converting them into departments with governors appointed by the President of the Republic. The department of Panama, however, became an independent country in 1903.

Conservatives and Liberals have alternated in power. Both have faced unrest, rioting and civil war. Liberal governments were in power 1860–84, Conservatives 1884–1930, Liberals 1930–46, and Conservatives 1946–53. In 1953 Gen. Gustavo Rojas Pinilla established a dictatorship, but he was deposed in 1957.

The Conservatives and Liberals fought a civil war from 1948 to 1957 (*La Violencia*) during which some 300,000 people were killed. In a pebiscite in 1957 the two political parties agreed to support a single presidential candidate and to divide government posts equally. This arrangement was modified in 1974 and the growing strength of a third party, ANAPO (the *Allianza Nacional Popular*), led to it being abandoned in 1978. The Liberal, Virgilio Barco Vargas, was elected president in 1986 and although the transfer of power from the Conservatives was successful, powerful drugs lords have made violence endemic. Two Marxist guerrilla forces are active, the Colombian Revolutionary Armed Forces, and the Cuban-inspired National Liberation Army. They are opposed by a well armed paramilitary organization which emerged after the setting up of rural self-defence groups. The paramilitaries operate independently but are thought to have close links with the state security process. Killings and other abuses by paramilitary squads, guerrillas and the military in 1996 made it the most infamous year in the nation's history for human rights violations, according to a report by the Colombian Commission of Jurists. On average, 10 Colombians were slain every day for political or ideological reasons, while one person disappeared every two days. It has been estimated that no-one has been convicted in 97% of cases related to political violence, and impunity is virtually guaranteed in army courts.

The government deployed soldiers ahead of the March 1998 parliamentary and presidential elections and guerrillas of the Revolutionary Armed Forces claim to have killed 80 soldiers in the southern jungle.

TERRITORY AND POPULATION. Colombia is bounded in the north by the Caribbean Sea, north-west by Panama, west by the Pacific Ocean, south-west by Ecuador and Peru, north-east by Venezuela and south-east by Brazil. The estimated area is 1,141,748 sq. km (440,829 sq. miles). Population census, (1985) 29,481,852; estimate (1997), 37,418,290; density, 40·2 per sq. km. Bogotá, the capital, (census,

1985) 4,236,490; estimate (1990) 4,819,696. Vital statistics: Birth rate, 26·4; death rate, 5·1 (1997).

The following table gives population estimates for departments and their capitals for 1997.

Departments	Area (sq. km)	Population	Capital	Population
Antioquia	63,612	5,243,906	Medellín	1,970,691
Atlántico	3,388	1,984,910	Barranquilla	1,157,826
Bogotá[1]	—	6,004,782	—	—
Bolívar	25,978	1,843,630	Cartagena	812,595
Boyacá	23,189	1,351,829	Tunja	118,406
Caldas	7,888	1,084,081	Manizales	358,194
Caquetá	88,965	396,537	Florencia	114,848
Cauca	29,308	1,197,874	Popayán	218,057
César	22,905	873,044	Valledupar	296,624
Chocó	46,530	409,599	Quibdó	123,102
Córdoba	25,020	1,353,922	Montería	327,249
Cundinamarca	22,478	1,975,564	Bogotá[1]	—
Huila	19,890	894,109	Neiva	305,625
La Guajira	20,848	459,326	Riohacha	114,608
Magdalena	23,188	1,218,836	Santa Marta	343,038
Meta	85,635	659,825	Villavicencio	299,296
Nariño	33,268	1,558,045	Pasto	362,227
Norte de Santander	21,658	1,252,867	Cúcuta	589,196
Quindío	1,845	535,711	Armenia	283,842
Risaralda	4,140	905,780	Pereira	434,267
Santander	30,537	1,911,830	Bucaramanga	508,240
San Andrés y Providencia	44	65,700	San Andrés	61,309
Sucre	10,917	749,152	Sincelejo	213,916
Tolima	23,562	1,310,963	Ibagué	419,883
Valle del Cauca	22,140	3,970,302	Cali	1,985,906
Amazonas	109,665	60,251	Leticia	30,450
Arauca	23,818	206,151	Arauca	69,292
Casanare	44,460	226,896	Yopal	68,855
Guainía	72,238	31,148	Puerto Inírida	19,983
Guaviare	42,327	110,631	San José del Guaviare	53,667
Putumayo	24,885	273,981	Mocoa	29,946
Vichada	100,242	66,676	Puerto Carreño	12,063
Vaupés	54,135	26,865	Mitú	14,287

[1] Capital District.

The Amerindian population was 268,359 (131,192 females) in 1985. Ethnic divisions (1996): mestizo 58%, white 20%, mulatto 14%, black 4%, mixed black-Indian 3%, Indian 1%.

The official language is Spanish.

CLIMATE. The climate includes equatorial and tropical conditions, according to situation and altitude. In tropical areas, the wettest months are March to May and Oct. to Nov. Bogotá. Jan. 58°F (14·4°C), July 57°F (13·9°C). Annual rainfall 42" (1,052 mm). Baranquilla. Jan. 80°F (26·7°C), July 82°F (27·8°C). Annual rainfall 32" (799 mm). Cali. Jan. 75°F (23·9°C), July 75°F (23·9°C). Annual rainfall 37" (915 mm). Medellin. Jan. 71°F (21·7°C), July 72°F (22·2°C). Annual rainfall 64" (1,606 mm).

CONSTITUTION AND GOVERNMENT. Simultaneously with the presidential elections of May 1990, a referendum was held in which 7m. votes were cast for the establishment of a special assembly to draft a new constitution. Elections were held on 9 Dec. 1990 for this 74-member 'Constitutional Assembly' which operated from Feb. to July 1991. The electorate was 14·2m.; turn-out was 3·7m. The Liberals gained 24 seats, M19 (a former guerrilla organization), 19. The Assembly produced a new constitution which came into force on 5 July 1991. It stresses the state's obligation to protect human rights, and establishes constitutional rights to health care, social security and leisure. Indians are allotted 2 Senate seats. Congress may dismiss ministers, and representatives may be recalled by their electors.

The *President* is elected by direct vote for a term of 4 years, and is not eligible for re-election until 4 years afterwards. A vice-presidency was instituted in July 1991. The first round of presidential elections was held on 29 May 1994; turn-out was 35%. Ernesto Samper gained 45·2% of votes cast against 16 opponents. At the second round on 19 June Samper was elected by 50·3% of votes cast against 1 opponent. Turn-out was 45%.

The legislative power rests with a *Congress* of 2 houses, the *Senate*, of 102 members, and the *House of Representatives*, of 165 members, both elected for 4 years by proportional representation. Congress meets annually at Bogotá on 20 July. Congressional elections were held on 8 March 1998, President Samper's Liberal Party beating the Social Conservatives into second place amidst indications of large-scale vote burying. Hundreds of people were arrested with forged identity cards or other evidence of attempted fraud.

President: Ernesto Samper (b. 1951; sworn in 7 Aug. 1994).
Prior to the March 1998 election the government comprised:
Vice President: Carlos Simmonds Lemos. *Interior:* Alfonso Caballero Lopez. *Defence:* Gilberto Mejia Echeverri. *Finance:* José Antonio Urdinola. *Agriculture:* Antonio Merlano Gomez. *Economic Development:* Carlos Julio Gonzalez Gaitan. *Labour and Social Security:* Carlos Camacho Bula, *Health:* María Forero de Sade. *Mines and Energy:* Orlando Martinez Cabrales. *Education:* Jaime Diez Nino. *Communications:* Jose Fernando Bautista. *Foreign Trade:* Carlos Torres Ronderos. *Foreign Affairs:* Emma Maria Mejia. *Justice:* Almabeatriz Lopez Rengrifo. *Environment:* Eduardo de la Rosa Verano. *Transport:* Rodrigo Bernal Marin, *Culture:* Ramiro Fonseca Osorio.

National anthem: 'O! Gloria inmarcesible' ('Oh Glory unfading!'); words by R. Núñez, tune by O. Síndici.

Local government: The country is divided into 32 departments and the Capital District of Bogotá (properly, Santafé de Bogotá), and subdivided into 1,011 municipalities. The governor of each department is elected by universal suffrage, and each has also a directly-elected legislature. The departments are subdivided into municipalities. The mayors of these, and the Special District of Bogotá, are elected by direct vote for a 2-year term. Mayoral elections were held on 30 Oct. 1994.

Elections were held in March 1992. The largest number of seats was gained by the Liberal Party, followed by the Conservative Party and M19.

DEFENCE. Selective conscription at 18 years varies from 1 to 2 years of service. Manpower availability (1996): males age 15-49, 10,067,538; males fit for military service, 6,774,105; males reaching military age annually, 346, 372. Defence expenditure (1995): exchange rate conversion US$2bn., 2·8% of GDP.

Army. The Army consists of 16 infantry brigades, 2 counter-insurgency brigades, 1 Presidential Guard battalion and 1 air defence artillery battalion. Equipment includes 12 M-3A1 light tanks and 6 light transport aircraft. Personnel (1997) 121,000 (conscripts, 63,800); reserves 54,700. Number of national police (1997) 87,000.

Navy. The Navy has 2 German-built 1,200-tonne diesel powered submarines completed in 1975, 2 Italian-built midget submarines, 4 small German-built missile-armed frigates with helicopter decks, 4 offshore patrol vessels and 11 fast patrol craft. There are 3 river gunboats and 11 riverine patrol craft. Auxiliaries include 2 surveying vessels, 1 small transport and 1 training ship. Naval personnel in 1997 totalled 5,000. There are also 2 brigades of marines numbering 9,000. An air arm operates 7 light reconnaissance aircraft and 4 BO-105 helicopters for ship-borne anti-submarine and rescue duties. There is a shore-based Coastguard integrated with the Navy numbering 4,000.

Air Force. The Air Force has been independent of the Army and Navy since 1943, when its reorganization began with US assistance. It has about 90 combat aircraft, including 2 fighter-bomber squadrons, one with Mirage 5s and one with Kfirs. 2

squadrons of AC-47 armed transports and 1 with A-37B jets for counter-insurgency duties; a transport group equipped with 8 C-130, 8 C-47s, and a small number of Arava and Turbo-Porter light transports; a presidential F-28 Fellowship jet transport; 1 Boeing 707, 2 Bandeirante, UH-1B/H and UH-60 Black Hawk utility helicopters; and a reconnaissance unit with Iroquois, Lama, Hughes OH-6A, 300C and TH-55 helicopters. 10 Aviocars, 2 Boeing 727s, 1 F-28 and 2 HS.748 transports are flown by the Air Force operated airline SATENA. There are several dozen light transports, confiscated from drug-smugglers, in use. Cessna T-41D primary trainers, Tucanos, T-34s and 10 T-37C jet advanced trainers are in service. Total strength (1997) 7,300 personnel (3,500 conscripts).

INTERNATIONAL RELATIONS

Membership. Colombia is a member of the UN, OAS, the Andean Group and LAIA.

ECONOMY

Budget. Expenditure of central government in 1996, US$24bn. In 1993 revenue, 6,433·4bn. pesos; expenditure, 6,309·4bn. pesos. 1994 revenue was 9,894·8bn. pesos.

Currency. The unit of currency is the *Colombian peso* (COP) of 100 *centavos*. There are coins of 50 centavos and 1, 2, 5, 10, 20 and 50 pesos, and notes of 100, 200, 500, 1,000, 2,000, 5,000, 10,000 and 20,000 pesos. Money in circulation, May 1991: 773,691m. pesos. Inflation was 32·4% in 1990. The government target for 1991 was 22%.

Banking and Finance. In 1923 the Bank of the Republic was inaugurated as a semi-official central bank, with the exclusive privilege of issuing bank-notes. Its note issues must be covered by a reserve in gold of foreign exchange of 25% of their value. Its international reserves in May 1992 were US$7,315·2m.

There are 24 commercial banks, of which 18 are private or mixed, and 6 official. There is also an Agricultural, Industrial and Mining Credit Institute, a Central Mortgage Bank and a Social Savings Bank. Bank deposits totalled 1,446,686 pesos in May 1991.

There are stock exchanges in Bogotá, Medellín and Cali.

Weights and Measures. The metric system was introduced in 1857, but Spanish weights and measures are generally used, *e.g., botella* (750 grammes), *galón* (5 *botellas*), *vara* (70 cm), *arroba* (25 lb., of 500 grammes; 4 *arrobas* = 1 quintal).

ENERGY AND NATURAL RESOURCES

Electricity. Capacity of electric power (1995) was 10,583,700 kW. Electric power produced in 1995, 43·36bn. kWh.

Oil. Production in 1992 was 22·33m. tonnes.

Minerals. Output of gold, 1995, 193,530 troy oz. Other minerals found are silver (21,459 troy oz. in 1995; 187,025 troy oz. in 1994), copper, lead, mercury, manganese, emeralds (of which Colombia accounts for about half of world production) and platinum; production of platinum, 1995, 26,663 troy oz.

Salt production in 1995 was 119,092 tonnes of land salt and 162,315 tonnes of sea salt. Coal reserves were estimated at 20,963m. tonnes in 1986; production (1995) 13,471 tonnes. Iron ore production was 571,607 tonnes in 1995.

Agriculture. There is a wide range of climate and, consequently, crops. In 1992 there were 3·9m. ha of arable land, 1·54m. ha of permanent crops and 40·6m. ha of pasture.

Production, 1993 (in 1,000 tonnes): Coffee, 1,080; potatoes, 2,860; rice, 1,650; maize, 1,164; sorghum, 631.

Livestock (1993): 25,324,000 cattle, 2,635,000 pigs, 2,540,000 sheep, 62m. poultry. Meat production, 1991: Beef and veal, 651,000 tonnes; pork, 134,000 tonnes.

Fisheries. Total catch (1994) 123,700 tonnes.

Forestry. In 1994, 21m cu. metres of timber were cut.

INDUSTRY. Production (1991): Steel ingots, 332,485 tonnes; cement, 6,389,250 tonnes; motor cars, 35,286; industrial vehicles, 8,877; sugar, 1,633,353 tonnes. In 1987 there were 6,927 manufacturing establishments.

Labour. In 1990 46% of the labour force was employed in service industries; agriculture, 30%; industry, 24%. In 1996 the unemployment rate was 11·5%.

FOREIGN ECONOMIC RELATIONS. Foreign companies are liable for basic income tax of 30% and surtax of 7·5%. Since 1993 tax on profit remittance has started at 12%, reducing (except for oil companies) to 7% after 3 years. Foreign debt was US$20,000m. in Dec. 1994.

The Group of Three (G-3) free trade pact with Mexico and Venezuela came into effect on 1 Jan. 1995.

Commerce. In US$m.:

	1993	1994	1995	1996
Imports	9,085·7	11,040·0	11,806·7	11,754·7
Exports	7,428·5	8,753·7	9,370·6	9,708·5

The principal exports in 1991 were coffee (734,021 tonnes valued at US$1,336·4m. f.o.b.) and petroleum and other mineral products (29,480,329 tonnes). Main export markets, 1994: USA, 36·7%; EU, 27·7%; Andean Group, 13·1%; Japan, 4·3%. Main import suppliers: USA, 38·4%; EU, 16·9%; Andean Group, 13·1%; Japan, 8·3%.

COMMUNICATIONS

Roads. Total length of highways was estimated to be 106,600 km in 1995. Of the 2,300-mile Simón Bolívar highway, which runs from Caracas in Venezuela to Guayaquil in Ecuador, the Colombian portion is complete. Motor vehicles in 1990 numbered 1,461,476, of which 757,114 were passenger cars and 121,221 lorries.

Railways. The National Railways (2,532 km of route, 914 mm gauge) went into liquidation in 1990 prior to takeover of services and obligations by 3 new public companies in 1992. In 1994 railways carried 0·7m. tonnes of freight. Total rail track, 3,386 km.

Civil Aviation. There are 989 airports, with an international airport at Bogotá (Eldorado). The national carriers are Avianca, which operated 2 B-727-200 Advs, 4 B-757-200s, 2 B-767-200ERs, 1 B-767-300ER and 21 other aircraft in 1992; and ACES with 4 B-727s, 4 B-727-200Advs and 15 other aircraft. In 1995, 8,058,388 passengers and 130,255 tonnes of freight were carried. Services are also provided by Aerolíneas Argentinas, Aeroperu, Aerorepublica, Air Aruba, Air France, Aires, Alitalia, American Airlines, British Airways, Copa, Compania Mexicana, Continental Airlines and Air Micronesia, Cubana, Iberia, Intercontinental de Aviación, Ladeco, Lufthansa, Saeta and Varig.

Shipping. Vessels entering Colombian ports in 1995 unloaded 13,806,000 tonnes of imports and loaded 26,284,000 tonnes of exports. The merchant marine totalled 0·18m. GRT in 1995, including oil tankers, 9,681 GRT.

The Magdalena River is subject to drought, and navigation is always impeded during the dry season, but it is an important artery of passenger and goods traffic. The river is navigable for 900 miles; steamers ascend to La Dorada, 592 miles from Barranquilla.

Telecommunications. In 1993 there were 3,828,000 telephone main lines in use. There are 5 radio companies overseen by the Dirección General de Radio-comunicaciones. Instituto Nacional de Radio y Televisión transmits on 3 networks (colour by NTSC) and rents air time to 26 commercial companies. In 1993 there were 34,487,000 radio and 5·5m. TV sets. There are 33 television broadcast stations.

Press (1995). There were 34 daily newspapers, with daily circulation totalling 1·5m.

SOCIAL INSTITUTIONS

Justice. The July 1991 constitution introduced the offices of public prosecutor and public defence. There is no extradition of Colombians for trial in other countries. The Supreme Court, at Bogotá, of 20 members, is divided into 3 chambers—civil cassation (6), criminal cassation (8), labour cassation (6). Each of the 61 judicial districts has a superior court with various sub-dependent tribunals of lower juridical grade. 257,511 crimes were reported in 1988.

The police force numbered 73,176 in 1989.

Religion. The religion is Roman Catholic (33·92m. adherents in 1992), with the Cardinal Archbishop of Bogotá as Primate of Colombia and 9 other archbishoprics. There are also 44 bishops, 8 apostolic vicars, 5 apostolic prefects and 2 prelates. In 1990 there were 1,546 parishes and 4,020 priests. Other forms of religion are permitted so long as their exercise is 'not contrary to Christian morals or the law.'

Education. Primary education is free but not compulsory. Schools are both state and privately controlled. In 1995 there were 14,872 pre-primary schools with 35,031 teachers for 726,721 pupils; 47,663 primary schools with 189,123 teachers for 4,692,614 pupils; and 3m. secondary school pupils with 143,731 teachers. There were 235 higher education establishments with 562,716 students.

In 1995-96 in the public sector there were 20 universities, 1 open university, 3 technological universities and universities of education, educational technology and industry. There were also 2 colleges of public administration, 1 school of police studies, 1 institute of fine art, 1 polytechnic and 1 conservatory. In the private sector there were 25 universities, 4 Roman Catholic universities, 1 college of education and 1 school of administration. There were 8 public, and 44 private, other institutions of higher education. In 1994-95, there were 208,394 university students.

Adult literacy, 91·3%; male, 91·2%; female, 91·4% (1995).

Health. In 1988 there were 926 hospitals and clinics. There were also 861 health centres.

DIPLOMATIC REPRESENTATIVES

Of Colombia in Great Britain (3 Hans Cres., London, SW1X 0LN)
Ambassador: Carlos A. Lemos-Simmonds.

Of Great Britain in Colombia (Carrera 9 No 76 - 49, Piso 9, Bogotá)
Ambassador: Leycester Coltman, CMG

Of Colombia in the USA (2118 Leroy Pl., NW, Washington, D.C., 20008)
Ambassador: Carlos Lleras de la Fuente

Of the USA in Colombia (Calle 38, 8-61, Bogotá)
Ambassador: Myles R. Frechette.

Of Colombia to the United Nations
Ambassador: Julio Londoño-Paredes.

Of Colombia to the European Union
Ambassador: José Antonio Vargas Lleras.

Further Reading

Departamento Administrativo Nacional de Estadística. *Boletín de Estadística.* Monthly.
Davis, R. H., *Historical Dictionary of Colombia.* 2nd ed. Metuchen (NJ), 1994
Thorp, R., *Economic Management and Economic Development in Peru and Colombia.* London, 1991

National statistical office: Departamento Administrativo Nacional de Estadística (DANE), Avenida Eldorado, Bogotá.

COMOROS

République Fédérale
Islamique des Comores

Capital: Moroni
Population: 569,237
GDP per head: (PPP$) 1,366
GNP: US$0·2bn.
HDI/world rank: 0·412/140

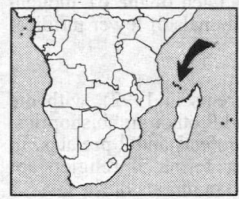

KEY HISTORICAL EVENTS. The 3 islands forming the present state became French protectorates at the end of the 19th century, and were proclaimed colonies in 1912. With neighbouring Mayotte they were administratively attached to Madagascar from 1914 until 1947, when the 4 islands became a French Overseas Territory, achieving internal self-government in Dec. 1961.

In referendums held on each island on 22 Dec. 1974, the 3 western islands voted overwhelmingly for independence, while Mayotte voted to remain French. The Comorian Chamber of Deputies unilaterally declared the islands' independence on 6 July 1975, but Mayotte remained a French dependency.

During a coup by the French mercenary Bob Denard in Sept. 1995, President Djohar was held prisoner by the insurrectionists. The coup was suppressed by French forces, and the President was released but not reinstated.

Recent years have been marked by political disruption. In 1997 the islands of Anjouan and Mohéli attempted to secede from the federation.

TERRITORY AND POPULATION. The Comoros consist of 3 islands in the Indian Ocean between the African mainland and Madagascar with a total area of 1,862 sq. km (719 sq. miles). The population at the 1991 census was 446,817; estimate, 1996, 569,237; density, 306 per sq. km. In 1995, 28% of the population were urban.

	Area (sq. km)	Population (1991 census)	Chief town
Njazídja (Grande Comore)	1,148	233,533	Moroni
Mwali (Mohéli)	290	24,331	Fomboni
Nzwani (Anjouan)	424	188,953	Mutsamudu

Birth rate per 1,000 population, 1996, 45·82; death, 10·28; infant mortality, 75·3 per 1,000 live births; population growth rate, 3·55%. Expectation of life was 58·7 years in 1996. Estimated population of the chief towns in 1988: Moroni, 22,000; Fomboni, 7,000; Mutsamudu, 14,000.

The indigenous population are a mixture of Malagasy, African, Malay and Arab peoples; the vast majority speak Comorian, an Arabised dialect of Swahili, but a small proportion speak Makua (a Bantu language) or one of the official languages, French and Arabic.

CLIMATE. There is a tropical climate, affected by Indian monsoon winds from the north, which gives a wet season from Nov. to April. Moroni. Jan. 81°F (27·2°C), July 75°F (23·9°C). Annual rainfall, 113" (2,825 mm).

CONSTITUTION AND GOVERNMENT. Under the Constitution approved by referendum on 1 Oct. 1978 (amended 1983), the Comoros were a Federal Islamic Republic. Mayotte had the right to join when it so chose. At a referendum on 7 June 1992 74·25% of votes cast were in favour of a new constitution. The electorate was 213,000; turn-out was 63·51%.

Under the 1992 constitution the *President* is Head of State, directly elected for a 5-year term (renewable once). He appoints Ministers to form the Council of Government, on which each island's Governor has a non-voting seat. The 42-member *Legislative Council* is directly elected for 4 years in 2 rounds. There is a 15-member *Senate* (5 members for each island) which is nominated for 6 years by an electoral college.

414

A first round of Presidential elections took place on 6 March 1996; turn-out was 64%. There were 15 candidates. Mohamed Taki Abdoulkarim gained 21·28% of votes cast, Abbas Djoussouf, 15·71%. A run-off round was held on 16 March, turn-out was 62%. Abdoulkarim was elected *President* by 64·29% of votes cast.

Elections for the Legislative Council were held in Jan. 1998. The Rally for Democracy and Renewal (RDR) won 15 seats; the Comoran Union for Progress (UDZIMA), 8; the Union for Democracy and Decentralization (UNDC), 5; Dialogue Proposition Action (DPA/MWANGAZA), 2; other smaller parties, 10. Two seats remained unfilled.

President: Mohamed Taki Abdoulkarim (b. 1936; National Union for Democracy; sworn in on 25 March 1996).

In March. 1998 a government reshuffle was under way.

National anthem: 'Udzima wa ya Masiwa' ('The union of the islands'); words by S. H. Abderamane, tune by K. Abdallah and S. H. Abderamane.

DEFENCE

Army. The Army was reorganized after the failed coup of Sept. 1995.

Navy. 1 landing craft with ramps was purchased in 1981. 2 small patrol boats were supplied by Japan in 1982. Personnel in 1996 numbered about 200.

Air Arm. 1 Cessna 402B communications aircraft and 1 Ecureuil helicopter were reported to be in operation.

INTERNATIONAL RELATIONS

Membership. Comoros is a member of the UN and Arab League and an ACP state of the EU.

ECONOMY

Budget. In 1994 current expenditure amounted to 14,783m. Comorian francs, revenue to 11,067m. Comorian francs.

Currency. The unit of currency is the *Comorian franc* (KMF) of 100 *centimes*. It is within France's Franc Zone (*see* FRANCE: Currency) and was devalued 25% in Jan. 1994. There are banknotes of 50, 100, 500, 1,000, and 5,000 Comorian francs. Foreign exchange reserves were US$29·02m.

Banking and Finance. The Central Bank is the bank of issue. The chief commercial banks are the Banque Internationale des Comores and the Banque de Développement des Comores.

Weights and Measures. The metric system is in force.

ENERGY AND NATURAL RESOURCES

Electricity. In 1991 installed capacity was 16,000 kW. Production was 25m. kWh in 1991.

Agriculture. 80% of the economically-active population depend upon agriculture, which (including fishing, hunting and forestry) contributes 40% to GDP. The chief product was formerly sugar-cane, but now vanilla, copra, maize and other food crops, cloves and essential oils (citronella, ylang, lemon-grass) are the most important products. Production (1991 in 1,000 tonnes): Cassava, 46; coconuts, 50; bananas, 52; sweet potatoes, 18; rice, 15; maize, 4 and copra, 4.

Livestock (1991): Cattle, 47,000; sheep, 14,000; goats, 125,000; asses, 5,000.

Forestry. The forested area has been severely reduced because of the shortage of cultivable land and ylang-ylang production.

Fisheries. Fishing is on an individual basis, without modern equipment. The catch was 7,000 tonnes in 1993.

INDUSTRY. Branches include perfume distillation, textiles, furniture, jewellery, soft drinks and the processing of vanilla and copra.

Labour. The workforce in 1991 was 238,000.

FOREIGN ECONOMIC RELATIONS. Total foreign debt was US$210m. in 1991.

Commerce. In 1993 imports amounted to US$409m.; exports to US$137m. France provided 34% of imports and took 40% of exports (the USA took 44%). The main exports are vanilla, cloves, ylang-ylang, essences, cocoa, copra and coffee. Rice accounts for 90% of imports.

Tourism. In 1993 there were about 24,000 foreign visitors (8,500 from France).

COMMUNICATIONS

Roads. In 1995 there were estimated to be 875 km of classified roads, of which 669 km were paved.

Civil Aviation. There is an international airport at Hahaya (on Njazídja). The state-owned Air Comores had no aircraft in 1995. Services are provided by Air Austral, Air France, Air Madagascar, Air Mauritius and South African Airways.

Shipping. In 1995 the merchant marine totalled 2,959 GRT.

Telecommunications. There were 4,000 telephones in 1993. The state-controlled Radio Comoro broadcasts in French and Comorian. Number of radios (1995), 84,000; television receivers, 400.

Press. There is 1 weekly newspaper.

SOCIAL INSTITUTIONS

Justice. French and Moslem law is in a new consolidated code. The Supreme Court comprises 7 members, 2 each appointed by the President and the Federal Assembly, and 1 by each island's Legislative Council. The death penalty is authorized for murder. The last execution was in 1996.

Religion. Islam is the official religion: 86% of the population are Sunni Moslems; 14% are Roman Catholics.

Education. After 2 pre-primary years at Koran school, which 50% of children attend, there are 6 years of primary schooling for 7- to 13-year-olds followed by a 4-year secondary stage attended by 25% of children. Some 5% of 17- to 20-year-olds conclude schooling at *lycées*. In 1995–96 there were 327 primary schools with 78,527 pupils and 1,237 teachers. 14,383 pupils attended secondary schools and *lycées* in 1991–92. There is a teacher training college.
   Adult literacy rate, 1998, 42·2%.

Health. In 1978 there were 20 doctors, 1 dentist, 2 pharmacists, 35 midwives and 124 nursing personnel. In 1980 there were 17 hospitals and clinics with 763 beds.

DIPLOMATIC REPRESENTATIVES

Of Great Britain in the Comoros
Ambassador: Robert Dewar (resides in Madagascar).

Of the Comoros in the USA
Ambassador: Mohamed Ahamada Djimbanaou.

Of the USA in the Comoros
Ambassador: Harold Geisel (resides in Mauritius).

Of the Comoros to the United Nations
Ambassador: Ahmed Djabir.

Of the Comoros to the European Union
Ambassador: Mahamoud Soilih.

Further Reading

Newitt, N., *The Comoro Islands*. London, 1985
Ottenheimer, M. and Ottenheimer, H. J., *Historical Dictionary of the Comoro Islands*. Metuchen (NJ), 1994

CONGO, DEMOCRATIC REPUBLIC OF THE (FORMERLY ZAÏRE)

République Démocratique du Congo

Capital: Kinshasa
Population: 47·44m.
GDP per head: (PPP$) 429
HDI/world rank: 0·381/142

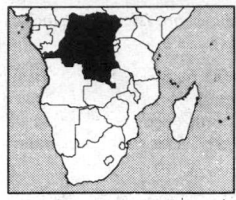

KEY HISTORICAL EVENTS. The area was visited by the Portuguese as early as the 14th century, but King Leopold II of the Belgians took the lead in exploring and exploiting the Congo Basin, and the Berlin Conference of 1884–85 recognized him as the sovereign head of the Congo Free State. In 1908 the country was annexed to Belgium as the Belgian Congo. After gaining independence in June 1960, the country's name was changed to Zaïre in 1971. Mobutu Sésé Séko came to power in a coup in 1965. At first he was seen as a strongman who could hold together a huge, unstable country comprising hundreds of tribes and language groups. In the 1970s he was feted by the USA, which used Zaïre as a springboard for operations into neighbouring Angola where western-backed Unita rebels were locked in civil war with a Cuban- and Soviet-backed government. Because Mobutu was useful in the fight against Communism, the brutality and repressiveness of his regime was ignored.

After armed insurrection by Tutsi rebels in the province of Kivu, the government alleged pro-Tutsi intervention by the armies of Burundi and Rwanda and on 25 Oct. 1996 declared a state of emergency. Following attacks on camps for Rwandan refugees, several hundred thousand of the occupants sought safety in flight. By the beginning of Nov. the eastern Zaïrean town of Goma was in the hands of Rwandan and rebel forces.

While the UN was deliberating the formation of a multinational intervention force in mid-Nov., a large number of the refugees began to return to Rwanda. On 15 Nov. the UN Security Council unanimously adopted a resolution authorizing the expedition of a temporary 15,000-strong force (largely composed of British, Canadian, French, Senegalese and US troops and under Canadian command) to permit the delivery of humanitarian aid and the repatriation of refugees in eastern Zaïre. Because of the spontaneous improvement in the situation, however, the dispatch of the force was first delayed and then eventually cancelled on 14 Dec.

By Dec. the secessionist forces of Laurent-Désiré Kabila, the Alliance of Democratic Forces for the Liberation of Congo-Zaïre (ADFL), had begun to drive the regular Zaïrean army out of Kivu, and an attempt was made to establish a rebel administration, 'Democratic Congo'. By the middle of Feb. 1997 large parts of eastern Zaïre were under rebel control, and the government began to mount air attacks. In the face of continuing rebel military successes and the disaffection of the army, the Government accepted a UN resolution demanding the immediate cessation of hostilities, and the Security Council asked the rebels also to make a public declaration of their acceptance. However, the latter continued in their victorious advance westwards, capturing Kisangani on 15 March 1997, then Kasai and Shaba, giving Kabila control of eastern Zaïre, and crucially the country's mineral wealth. Mobutu's attempts to cling to power looked hopeless. After another medical visit to France, and a futile attempt to deploy Serbian mercenaries, he succumbed to pressure—particularly from the US and South Africa—and agreed to meet Kabila in the presence of President Mandela on the South African ship, the *SAS Outeniqua*, offshore from the Republic of the Congo. Little happened but the meeting had all the trappings of a symbolic surrender. Mobutu still hoped for compromise but the final victory of Kabila's troops, east of Kinshasa at Kenge, dashed any remaining illusions, and the generals of Mobutu's own shell of an army told him that the situation was lost. In a state of indecision, he fled without warning or conditions on the night of 15–16 May 1997. He died of cancer 4 months later. Described as one of the most destructive tyrants of the African independence era, it is said that his personal fortune, if ever recovered, could wipe out his country's national debt. On coming to power Kabila changed the name of the country to the Democratic Republic of the Congo.

TERRITORY AND POPULATION. The Democratic Republic of the Congo is bounded in the north by the Central African Republic, north-east by Sudan, east by Uganda, Rwanda, Burundi and Lake Tanganyika, south by Zambia, south-west by Angola and north-west by the Republic of the Congo. There is a 37-km stretch of coastline which gives access to the Atlantic Ocean, with the Angolan exclave of Cabinda to the immediate north and Angola itself to the south. Area, 2,344,885 sq. km (905,365 sq. miles). At the 1988 census the population was 34·7m. Estimate (1997) 47,440,000 (29% urban).

Vital statistics rates (1997 estimates, per 1,000 population); Birth, 47·7; death, 16·6; growth rate, 2·3%. Infant mortality was 106 per 1,000 live births; expectation of life was 47·0 years (males, 45·2; females, 49·0).

More than 200,000 refugees who escaped the fighting between Hutus and Tutsis in Rwanda and Burundi in 1994 are still in the Democratic Republic of the Congo (out of 1m. who came originally), and there are also 100,000 Angolan and 100,000 Sudanese refugees in the country.

Area, populations (1994 estimate) and chief towns of the regions in 1994:

Region	Area (sq. km)	Population (in 1,000)	Chief town	Population
Bandundu	295,658	4,907	Bandundu	. . .
Bas-Zaïre	53,920	2,578	Matadi	172,730
Equateur	403,293	4,789	Mbandaka	169,841
Haut-Zaïre	503,239	5,432	Kisangani	417,517
Kasai Occidental	154,742	3,117	Kananga	393,030
Kasai Oriental	170,302	3,778	Mbuji-Mayi	806,475
Kinshasa City	9,965	4,655	Kinshasa	4,655,313
Maniema[1]	132,250	—	Kindu	—
Nord-Kivu[1]	59,483	—	Goma	109,094
Sud-Kivu[1]	65,130	—	Bukavu	201,569
Shaba	496,965	5,602	Lubumbashi	851,381

[1] Combined population of Maniema, Nord-Kivu and Sud-Kivu, 7,687,000.

Other large cities (with estimated 1994 population): Kolwezi (417,810), Likasi (299,118), Kikwit (182,142), Tshikapa (180,860).

The population is Bantu, with minorities of Sudanese (in the north), Nilotes (north-east), Pygmies and Hamites (in the east). French is the official language, but of more than 200 languages spoken, 4 are recognized as national languages: Kiswahili, Tshiluba, Kikongo and Lingala. Lingala has become the *lingua franca* after French.

CLIMATE. The climate is varied, the central region having an equatorial climate, with year-long high temperatures and rain at all seasons. Elsewhere, depending on position north or south of the Equator, there are well-marked wet and dry seasons. The mountains of the east and south have a temperate mountain climate, with the highest summits having considerable snowfall. Kinshasa. Jan. 79°F (26·1°C), July 73°F (22·8°C). Annual rainfall 45" (1,125 mm). Kananga. Jan. 76°F (24·4°C), July 74°F (23·3°C). Annual rainfall 62" (1,584 mm). Kisangani. Jan. 78°F (25·6°C), July 75°F (23·9°C). Annual rainfall 68" (1,704 mm). Lubumbashi. Jan. 72°F (22·2°C), July 61°F (16·1°C). Annual rainfall 50" (1,237 mm).

CONSTITUTION AND GOVERNMENT. Gen. Laurent-Désiré Kabila seized power on 17 May 1997 after the military defeat of Marshal Mobutu Sésé Séko and his government, and is both chief of state and head of government. Although parties other than the ADFL have been dissolved, a Constituent Assembly was due to be elected in June 1998, a constitutional referendum held in Dec. 1998, and presidential and parliamentary elections held in April 1999.

In March 1998 the government comprised:
President, Minister of Defence: Gen. Laurent-Désiré Kabila.
Minister of State for Economic Affairs and Petroleum: Pierre Victor Mpoyo.
Minister of State for Internal Affairs: Gaëtan Kakudji.

Minister of Agriculture and Livestock: Mawampanga Mwana Nanga. *Civil Service:* Paul Kapita Shabangi. *Commerce:* Paul Bandoma. *Education:* Kamara wa Kayika. *Energy:* Pierre Lokombe Kitete. *Environment and Tourism:* Eddy Angulu Mabengi. *Finance and Budget:* Fernand Tala Ngai. *Foreign Affairs:* Dr Bizima Karaha. *Health and Social Affairs:* Dr Jean-Baptiste Sondji. *Industry and Small and Medium-Sized Enterprises:* Babi Mbaye. *Information and Cultural Affairs:* Raphael Ghenda. *International Co-operation:* Célestin Lwangi. *Justice:* Mwenze Kongolo. *Labour:* Thomas Kanza. *Mines:* Fréderic Kibassa Maliba. *Planning and Development:* Etienne Richard Mbaya. *Post and Telecommunications:* Jean-Moreno Kinkela Vi Kan'sy. *Public Enterprises:* Florent Kambale Kabila Mututolo. *Public Works:* Anatole Bishikwabo Chubaka. *Transport:* Henri Mova Sakanyi. *Youth and Sports:* Vincent Mutombo Tshibal.

Local government: The Democratic Republic of the Congo is composed of Kinshasa (administered by a Governor) and 10 regions, each under a Regional Commissioner and 6 Councillors; all are appointed by the President. The regions are divided into 41 sub-regions.

DEFENCE

Following the overthrow of the Mobutu regime in May 1997, the former Zaïrean armed forces were in disarray. The insurgent Congo Liberation Army has between 20,000 and 40,000 fighters, equipped with small arms and some SA-7 SAM. Much of this equipment is believed to be non-operational.

In 1995 government expenditure on defence totalled 122,000m. zaïres.

INTERNATIONAL RELATIONS

Membership. The Democratic Republic of the Congo is a member of the UN, OAU and is an ACP state of the EU.

ECONOMY

Budget. Revenue for 1995 (1994 in brackets) was 2,120,000m. zaïres (208,000m.), and expenditure, 2,112,000m. zaïres (314,000m.). International economic aid has been made dependent on a coherent plan to revive the economy and progress on democracy and human rights.

Performance. GDP fell 0·7% in 1995 and was reported in Feb. 1998 to be 65% lower than it was in 1960 when it gained independence.

Currency. The unit of currency is the *zaïre* (ZRZ), notionally of 100 *makuta* replacing the former zaïre in Oct. 1993 at 1 new zaïre = 3m. old zaïre. There are notes of 1, 5, 10 and 50 makuta and 1, 5, 10, 20, 50, 100, 200 and 500 new zaïres. Foreign exchange reserves were US$151·77m. in 1993; gold reserves were US$6·99m. in 1992. Inflation was reported in Nov. 1997 to be 14%.

Banking and Finance. The central bank is Banque Centrale du Congo. A development bank with state backing is the Société Financière de Développement (SOFIDE). Commercial banks operating in the Democratic Republic of the Congo include Banque de Paris et des Pays-Bas, Banque de Kinshasa, National & Grindlays Bank, Barclays Bank SZPRL, First National City Bank, Banque du Peuple and Caisse Nationale d'Epargne et de Crédit Immobilier.

Since Aug. 1991 commercial banks have been able to trade foreign exchange freely at their own rates.

Weights and Measures. The metric system is in force.

ENERGY AND NATURAL RESOURCES

Electricity. Production (1994), 5,480m. kWh. A dam at Inga, on the River Congo near Matadi, has a potential capacity of 39,600 MW.

Oil. Offshore oil production began in Nov. 1975; estimated crude production (1992) was 1·35m. tonnes. There is an oil refinery at Kinlao-Muanda.

Minerals. Production in 1993 (in 1,000 tonnes): Copper, 48; zinc, 30; cobalt, 2·4; gold, 1,400 kg; diamonds, 15·6m. carats. Coal, tin and silver are also found. The most important mining area is in the region of Shaba (formerly Katanga).

Agriculture. There were (1992) 7·28m. ha of arable land and 15·0m. ha of permanent pasture. The main food crops (1993 production in 1,000 tonnes) are: Cassava, 20,835; plantains, 2,224; sugar-cane, 1,400; maize, 1,201; groundnuts, 604; bananas, 406; yams, 315; rice, 458. Cash crops (1993) include palm oil, 181; coffee, 78; palm kernels, 72; rubber, 5; seed cotton, 77. There are also pineapples, 145; mangoes, 212; oranges, 156; papayas, 210.

Livestock (1993, in 1,000): Cattle, 1,650; sheep, 985; goats, 4,120; pigs, 1,130; poultry, 35m.

Forestry. Equatorial rain forests cover 55% of the country. In 1994, 45m. cu. metres of roundwood were cut.

Fisheries. The catch for 1991 was 160,000 tonnes, almost entirely from inland waters.

INDUSTRY. The main manufactures are foodstuffs, beverages, tobacco, textiles, rubber, leather, wood products, cement and building materials, metallurgy and metal extraction, metal items, transport vehicles, electrical equipment and bicycles

Labour. In 1993 the workforce was 14·51m. Agriculture employs around 65% of the total workforce.

FOREIGN ECONOMIC RELATIONS. With Burundi and Rwanda, the Democratic Republic of the Congo forms part of the Economic Community of the Great Lakes. External debt was more than US$14,000m. in 1997.

Commerce. Exports in 1995 totalled US$1,470m., imports, US$1,250m. Main commodities for export are diamonds, copper, coffee, cobalt and crude oil; and for import, consumer goods, foodstuffs, mining and other machinery, transport equipment and fuels. Principal export markets are Belgium, USA, France, Germany, Italy, UK, Japan and South Africa. Principal import suppliers are Belgium, South Africa, USA, France, Germany, Italy, Japan and UK.

Tourism. There were some 46,000 foreign visitors in 1991.

COMMUNICATIONS

Roads. In 1993 there were almost 68,000 km of main, and 77,000 km of secondary, roads. Around 2,500 km were paved.

Railways. There was 5,138 km of track on 3 gauges in 1995, of which 858 km was electrified. However, the length of track in use was severely reduced by the civil strife in late 1996 and the early part of 1997.

Civil Aviation. There is an international airport at Kinshasa (Ndjili). Other major airports are at Lubumbashi (Luano), Bukavu, Goma and Kisangani.

Shipping. The River Congo and its tributaries are navigable to 300-tonne vessels for about 14,500 km. Regular traffic has been established between Kinshasa and Kisangani as well as Ilebo, on the Lualaba (*i.e.*, the river above Kisangani), on some tributaries and on the lakes. The Democratic Republic of the Congo has only 37 km of sea coast. The merchant marine in 1993 comprised 27 vessels over 100 GRT with a total tonnage of 14,900 GRT. Matadi, Kinshasa and Kalemie are the main seaports; in 1993, Matadi handled 0·6m. tonnes of freight.

Telecommunications. There are 362 post offices. Telephones numbered 34,000 in 1991. There is a ground satellite communications station outside Kinshasa. Broadcasting is provided by government-controlled radio and television stations (colour by SECAM). There is also an educational radio station. In 1995 there were 4·0m. radio and 100,000 TV receivers.

Press. In 1995 there were 9 daily newspapers with a combined circulation of 120,000.

SOCIAL INSTITUTIONS

Justice. There is a Supreme Court at Kinshasa, 11 courts of appeal, 36 courts of first instance and 24 'peace tribunals'.

Religion. In 1996 there were 21·9m. Roman Catholics, 13·1m. Protestants, 7·74m. Kimbanguistes (African Christians) and 0·63m. Moslems. Animist beliefs persist.

Education. In 1995 there were 14,885 primary schools with 121,054 teachers for 5·4m. pupils, 59,325 secondary teachers for 1·5m. pupils and 93,266 students at university level. In higher education there were 3 universities (Kinshasa, Kisangani and Lubumbashi) in 1994–95, 14 teacher training colleges and 18 technical institutes in the public sector; and 13 university institutes, 4 teacher training colleges and 49 technical institutes in the private sector. There were 20,130 university students and 1,630 academic staff in 1994–95. Adult literacy rate was 77·3% in 1995 (male, 86·6%; female, 66·7%). In 1995 government expenditure on education totalled 27,000m. zaïres.

Health. In 1990 there were 2,469 doctors, 41 dentists and 27,601 nurses. In 1995 government expenditure on health totalled 25,000m. zaïres.

DIPLOMATIC REPRESENTATIVES

Of the Democratic Republic of the Congo in Great Britain (26 Chesham Pl., London, SW1X 8HH)
Ambassador: Vacant.

Of Great Britain in the Democratic Republic of the Congo (Ave. de Trois Z, Gombe, Kinshasa)
Ambassador: Marcus L. H. Hope.

Of the Democratic Republic of the Congo in the USA (1800 New Hampshire Ave., NW, Washington, D.C., 20009)
Ambassador: Vacant.

Of the USA in the Democratic Republic of the Congo (310 Ave. des Aviateurs, Kinshasa)
Ambassador: Daniel H. Simpson.

Of the Democratic Republic of the Congo to the United Nations
Ambassador: André Kapanga.

Of the Democratic Republic of the Congo to the European Union
Ambassador: Kimbulu Moyanso wa Lokwa.

Further Reading

Leslie, W. J., *Zaïre: Continuity and Political Change in an Oppressive State.* Boulder (CO), 1993
Williams, D. B. *et al. Zaïre:* [Bibliography] 2nd ed. Oxford and Santa Barbara (CA), 1995

CONGO, REPUBLIC OF THE

République du Congo

Capital: Brazzaville
Population: 2·58m.
GDP per head: (PPP$) 2,410
GNP: US$1·6bn.
HDI/world rank: 0·500/130

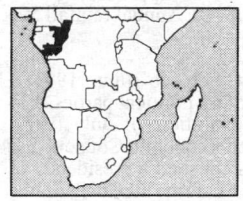

KEY HISTORICAL EVENTS. The Portuguese first reached the mouth of the Congo in the 15th century. Loango, in the Kouilou region, was one of the largest ports connected with slavery in the 18th century. Late in the 19th century Sir Henry Stanley and Savorgnan de Brazza (after whom the capital was named) multiplied the number of explorations and investigations. First occupied by France in 1882, the Congo became a territory of French Equatorial Africa from 1910–58, and then a member state of the French Community. Between 1940 and 1944, thanks to Equatorial Africa's allegiance to General de Gaulle, he named Brazzaville the capital of the Empire and Liberated France. Independence was granted in 1960.

The first President, Fulbert Youlou, was deposed on 15 Aug. 1963 by a coup led by Alphonse Massemba-Débat, who became President on 19 Dec. Following a second coup in Aug. 1968, the Army took power under the leadership of Major Marien Ngouabi, whose colleague, Major Alfred Raoul, was appointed President from 3 Sept. until 1 Jan. 1969, when Ngouabi himself became President. A Marxist-Leninist state was introduced in 1970. Ngouabi was assassinated on 18 March 1977, and succeeded by Col. Joachim Yhombi Opango, who in turn was replaced on 5 Feb. 1979 by Col. Denis Sassou-Nguesso. Free elections were restored in 1992 when the now Gen. Sassou-Nguesso was defeated by Pascal Lissouba, but violence erupted when in June 1997 President Lissouba tried to disarm the General's militia ahead of a fresh election. There followed 4 months of civil war with fighting concentrated on Brazzaville, which became a ghost town. In October Gen. Sassou-Nguesso proclaimed victory having relied upon military support from Angola. President Lissouba went into hiding in Burkina Faso.

TERRITORY AND POPULATION. The Republic of the Congo is bounded by Cameroon and the Central African Republic in the north, the Democratic Republic of the Congo to the east and south, Angola and the Atlantic Ocean to the south-west and Gabon to the west, and covers 341,821 sq. km. At the census of 1984 the population was 1,909,248.

Estimated population in 1997, 2,583,000; density, 7·6 per sq. km. In 1995 it was estimated that 40% of the population was urban. Estimated population of major cities in 1995: Brazzaville, the capital, 937,579; Pointe-Noire, 576,206; Loubomo, 83,605; N'Kayi, 42,465; Mossendjo, 16,405; Ouesso, 16,171.

Area, estimated population and county towns of the regions in 1992 were:

Region	Sq. km	Population	County town
Kouilou	13,694	665,502	Pointe-Noire
Niari	25,940	220,087	Loubomo
Lékoumou	20,950	74,420	Sibiti
Bouenza	12,266	219,822	Madingou
Pool	33,955	182,671	Kinkala
Capital District	100	937,579	Brazzaville
Plateaux	38,400	119,722	Djambala
Cuvette	74,850	151,839	Owando
Sangha	55,800	52,132	Ouesso
Likouala	66,044	70,675	Impfondo

Vital statistics rates, 1997 estimates (per 1,000 population). Births, 38·8; deaths, 17·3. Infant mortality (per 1,000 live births), 106·1. Expectation of life in 1997 was 45·7 years (44·25 for males and 47·3 for females). Growth rate, 2·15% per annum.

Main ethnic groups are: Kongo (48%), Sangha (20%), Teke (17%) and M'Bochi (12%).

French is the official language. Kongo languages are widely spoken. Monokutuba and Lingala serve as lingua francas.

CLIMATE. An equatorial climate, with moderate rainfall and a small range of temperature. There is a long dry season from May to Oct. in the south-west plateaux, but the Congo Basin in the north-east is more humid, with rainfall approaching 100" (2,500 mm). Brazzaville. Jan. 78°F (25·6°C), July 73°F (22·8°C). Annual rainfall 59" (1,473 mm).

CONSTITUTION AND GOVERNMENT. From Feb. to June 1991 a national conference was held consisting of representatives of 67 political parties, 134 associations and 30 specialists. This abolished the constitution of July 1979, dissolved the National Assembly, Constitutional Council and Economic Council, and adopted a basic law to regulate a period of transition. It established a presidency of the republic with newly-defined powers, a 153-member Supreme Council of the Republic and a prime ministership. At a referendum in March 1992 proposing multi-party democracy 96·32% of votes were in favour. Turn-out was 70·93%.

At the elections of 24 June and 19 July 1992 for the new 125-member *National Assembly*, the Pan-African Union for Social Democracy (UPADS) had gained 39 seats, the Congolese Movement for Democracy and Integral Development (MCDDI) 29, the Congolese Labour Party 19, the Democratic Rally for Social Progress 9 and the Rally for Democracy and Development 5.

In the 60-member *Senate*, UPADS gained 23 seats, MCDDI 13.

In Nov. 1992 the President dismissed the government of Stéphane Bongho-Nouarra and dissolved the National Assembly. At the first round of elections in May–June 1993 for 114 seats in the National Assembly, the Presidential Movement (PM; a coalition of some 60 parties) gained 62 seats, the Congolese Labour Party–Union for Democratic Renewal Coalition 49 and minor parties 3. At the second round in Oct. for the remaining 11 seats the PM gained 4 and CLP-UDR 7.

Having been sworn in as president in Oct. 1997, Gen. Sassou-Nguesso subsequently formed a transition government, which in March 1998 comprised:

President, Minister of National Defence: Denis Sassou-Nguesso.

Minister of Agriculture and Livestock: Célestin Nkoua Gongara. *Civil Service and Administrative Reforms:* Charles Dambenzet. *Communication and Government Spokesman:* François Ibovi. *Culture and Arts, in charge of Francophone Affairs:* Mambou Elie Niamy. *Energy and Water Resources:* Jean-Marie Tassoua. *Family Affairs, in charge of Integrating Women in Development Efforts:* Cécile Matigou. *Finance and Budget:* Mathias Dzon. *Fishing and Fish Resources:* Pierre Gassay. *Foreign Affairs and Co-operation:* Rodolphe Adada. *Forestry:* Henri Djombo. *Health and Population:* Mamadou Dekamo. *Higher Education and Scientific Research:* François Loumouamou. *Industry and Mines:* Michel Mampouya. *Interior, Security and Territorial Administration:* Pierre Oba. *Justice and Keeper of the Seals:* Pierre Nze. *Labour and Social Security:* Jean Martin Mbemba. *National Solidarity, Disasters and War Victims, in charge of Relief Actions:* Léon Alfred Opimba. *Organization of National Forum, in charge of Relations with National Council:* Firmin Ayessa. *Petroleum Affairs:* Jean-Baptiste Taty Loutard. *Posts and Telecommunications:* Jean Delo. *Primary and Secondary Education:* Pierre Tsiba. *Reconstruction and Urban Development:* Justin Itihi Lekoundzou Ossetoumba. *Small and Medium-Sized Enterprises, in charge of Handicrafts:* Boussoukou Pierre Damien Boumba. *Social Amenities and Public Works:* Col. Florent Tsiba. *State Control:* Gérard Bitsindou. *Technical Education and Vocational Training:* Okombi André Salissan. *Territorial and Regional Development:* Pierre Moussa. *Tourism and Environment:* Norbert Ngoua. *Trade, Consumer Affairs and Supplies:* Félix Ngoulou. *Transport and Civil Aviation, in charge of Merchant Navy:* Martin Mberi. *Youth Redeployment and Sports, in charge of Civic Education:* Ernest Claude Ndalla.

National anthem: La Congolaise; words and tune by Jean Royer and others.

Local Government: In compliance with a law of 18 Sept. 1995, the country was reorganized into 10 regions, which are themselves divided into 76 districts. In addition there are 6 urban councils. The regions are Kouilou, Niari, Lékoumou, Bouenza, Pool, Plateaux, Cuvette, Cuvette Ouest, Sangha and Likouala. Niari's county town, previously Loubomo, became Dolisie. Cuvette Ouest's county town is Ewo. (See also TERRITORY AND POPULATION, above.) The 6 distinct urban councils are Brazzaville, Dolisie, Mossendjo, Nkayi, Owando and Pointe-Noire.

DEFENCE

Army. The Army consists of 2 infantry battalion groups, 2 armoured and 1 infantry battalion, 1 artillery group, 1 engineer and 1 paracommando battalion. Equipment includes 25 T-54/-55 and 15 T-59 main battle tanks. Total personnel (1997) 8,000. There is a Gendarmerie of 2,000. The 'People's Militia' is being absorbed into the Army.

Navy. The combatant flotilla includes 3 modern Spanish-built and 3 ex-Soviet inshore patrol craft. There is also 1 French-built tug and some river patrol boats. Personnel in 1996 totalled about 600.

Air Force. The Air Force had (1997) about 1,200 personnel, 5 Antonov An-24/26 turboprop transports, 1 Noratlas piston-engined transport and 2 Mi-8 helicopters. Most of these aircraft are in store.

INTERNATIONAL RELATIONS

Membership. The Republic of the Congo is a member of the UN, OAU and is an ACP state of the EU.

ECONOMY

Policy. An economic and social recovery plan (Paséco) was launched in 1994.

Budget. Estimated figures for 1997 are: Revenue, US$870m.; expenditure, US$970m. (including capital expenditures).

Currency. The unit of currency is the *franc CFA* (BEAC) with a parity of 100 francs CFA to 1 French franc. There are coins of 1, 2, 5, 10, 25, 50, 100 and 500 francs CFA, and banknotes of 500, 1,000, 5,000 and 10,000 francs CFA. Currency in circulation, June 1993, 60,700m. francs CFA. Foreign exchange reserves, US$15,900m. Gold reserves, 11,000 troy oz.

Banking and Finance. The *Banque des États de l'Afrique Centrale* (BEAC) is the bank of issue. There are 3 commercial banks and a development bank in all of which the government has majority stakes. Inflation in 1996 was 3%.

Weights and Measures. The metric system is in use.

ENERGY AND NATURAL RESOURCES

Electricity. Total production in 1994 was 440m. kWh.

Oil and Gas. Oil was discovered in the mid-1960s when Elf Aquitaine was given exclusive rights to production. Elf still has the lion's share but Agip Congo is also involved in oil exploitation. In 1997 production was averaging 230,000 bbls. a day. Reserves are estimated at 500–1,000m. tonnes, including major off-shore deposits. Oil provides about 90% of government revenue and exports. There is a refinery at Pointe-Noire, the second largest city. Gas reserves are estimated at 71,000m. cu. metres.

Minerals. A government mine produces several metals; gold and diamonds are extracted by individuals. There are reserves of potash (4·5m. tonnes), and iron ore (1,000m. tonnes), and also clay, bituminous sand, phosphates, zinc and lead.

Agriculture. In 1991 agriculture produced 12·2% of GDP. Only 1,680 sq. km are cultivated. Production (1991, in thousand tonnes): Cassava, 780; bananas, 40; plantains, 80; yams, 12; maize, 25; groundnuts, 27; coffee, 1; cocoa, 2; rice, 1.

Livestock (1991, in 1,000): Cattle, 68; pigs, 52; sheep, 108; goats, 272; poultry, 2m. There were some 700 tractors in use in 1991.

Forestry. Equatorial forests cover 21m. ha from which (in 1994) 3m. cu. metres of timber were produced, mainly okoumé from the south and sapele from the north. Timber companies are required to replant, and to process at least 60% of their production locally. Before the development of the oil industry, forestry was the mainstay of the economy.

Fisheries. Annual catch by large companies is about 10,000 tonnes, by independent fishermen, 8,000 tonnes. Freshwater catch averages 12,000 tonnes annually.

INDUSTRY. There is a growing manufacturing sector, located mainly in the 4 major towns, producing processed foods, textiles, cement, metal goods and chemicals. Industry produced 37·4% of GDP in 1991, including 7·6% from manu-facturing. Production: Printed cloth (1990), 8·79m. metres; cement (1989), 121,000 tonnes; shoes (1989), 14,670 pairs; corrugated iron sheets (1990), 1·68m. tonnes; household goods (1990), 186 tonnes; nails (1990), 377 tonnes.

Trade Unions. In 1964 the existing unions merged into one national body, the Confédération Syndicale Congolaise. The 40,000-strong Confédération Syndicale des Travailleurs Congolais split off from the latter in 1993.

FOREIGN ECONOMIC RELATIONS. Foreign debt was US$5,300m. in 1996.

Commerce. Imports in 1994 totalled US$952m. and exports US$559m. Apart from crude oil, other significant commodities for export are lumber, plywood, sugar, cocoa, coffee and diamonds. Principal imported commodities are intermediate manufactures, capital equipment, construction materials, foodstuffs and petroleum products. Main export markets in 1995 were Belgium/Luxembourg, 24·3%, followed by Taiwan, the USA and Italy. Main import suppliers: France, 31·2%, followed by the Netherlands, Italy and the USA.

COMMUNICATIONS

Roads. In 1995 there were 12,760 km of roads, of which 1,238 km were bitum-enized. In 1991 there were 27,000 cars, 3,000 buses, 2,610 motor cycles and 9,618 commercial vehicles.

Railways. A railway (510 km, 1,067 mm gauge) connects Brazzaville with Pointe-Noire via Loubomo and Bilinga and a 285 km branch links Mont-Belo with Mbinda on the Gabon border. Total length is 795 km. In 1994 railways carried 285m. passenger-km and 223m. tonne-km of freight.

Civil Aviation. The principal airports are at Brazzaville (Maya Maya) and Pointe-Noire. The Republic of the Congo is a member of the multinational Air Afrique, which absorbed the former national carrier Lina-Congo in 1992. Services are also provided by Aeroflot, Air France, Cameroon Airlines, Ethiopian Airlines, Guinea Airlines, Sabena, Swissair, TAAG and TAP.

Shipping. The only seaport is Pointe-Noire, which handled 2·59m. tonnes of freight in 1990. The merchant marine totalled 11,010 GRT in 1995. There are some 5,000 km of navigable rivers, and river transport is an important service for timber and other freight as well as passengers. There are hydrofoil connections from Brazzaville to Kinshasa.

Telecommunications. Telephones (1990) numbered 15,900. Broadcasting is under the aegis of the government-controlled Radiodiffusion-Télévision Congolaise, which transmits a national and a regional radio programme and a programme in French. In 1993 there were 6 hours of TV broadcasting daily (colour by SECAM). There were 0·30m. radio and about 20,000 TV receivers in 1995.

Press. In 1995 there were 6 daily newspapers with a combined circulation of 20,000.

SOCIAL INSTITUTIONS

Justice. The Supreme Court, Court of Appeal and a criminal court are situated in Brazzaville, with a network of *tribunaux de grande instance* and *tribunaux d'instance* in the regions.

Religion. In 1990 there were 1·25m. Roman Catholics and 0·5m. Protestants. There are some Moslems and traditional animist beliefs are still practised.

Education. In 1996 there were 1,162 primary schools with 7,060 teachers for 497,305 pupils, 7,123 secondary school teachers for 214,650 pupils and 7,225 students at university level. Adult literacy rate (1995) 74·9% (male, 83·1%; female, 67·2%).

Health. There were (1988) 567 doctors, 2 dentists and 246 midwives.

DIPLOMATIC REPRESENTATIVES

Of the Republic of the Congo in Great Britain
Ambassador: Pierre-Michel Nguimbi (resides in Paris).

Of Great Britain in the Republic of the Congo
Chargé d'Affaires: Marcus L. H. Hope (resides in Kinshasa).

Of the Republic of the Congo in the USA (4891 Colorado Ave., NW, Washington D.C., 20011)
Ambassador: Dieudonné Ganga

Of the USA in the Republic of the Congo (PO Box 1015, Brazzaville)
Ambassador: Aubrey Hookes.

Of the Republic of the Congo to the United Nations
Ambassador: Daniel Abibi.

Of the Republic of the Congo to the European Union
Ambassador: Paul Mapingou.

Further Reading

Thompson, V. and Adloff, R., *Historical Dictionary of the People's Republic of the Congo.* 2nd ed. Metuchen (NJ), 1984

COSTA RICA

República de Costa Rica

Capital: San José
Population: 3·37m.
GNP: US$7·9bn.
HDI/world rank: 0·889/33

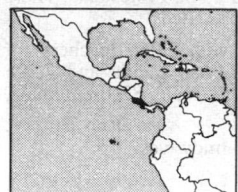

KEY HISTORICAL EVENTS. Discovered by Columbus in 1502 on his last voyage, Costa Rica (Rich Coast) was part of the Spanish viceroyalty of New Spain from 1540 and was thought to be rich in gold. Costa Rica became independent of Spain in 1821. From 1822 to 1823 it was part of Mexico and then part of the Central American Federation until 1838 when it left this confederation and achieved full independence. The first constitution was promulgated on 7 Dec. 1871.

Coffee was introduced in 1808 and became a main-stay of the economy, helping to create a peasant land-owning class. Bananas, another important crop, were introduced in 1878.

In 1917 Federico Tinoco overthrew the elected president but the USA intervened and Tinoco was deposed in 1919.

In 1948 accusations of election fraud led to a 6-week civil war, at the conclusion of which José Figueres Ferrer won power at the head of a revolutionary junta.

A new constitution was promulgated with, amongst other changes, the abolition of the army. Ferrer, the founder and leader of the *Partido de Liberación Nacional* (PLN), became the elected president from 1953 to 1958, and again in 1970-74. More conservative governments held office between Ferrer's 2 presidencies and again after Ferrer's PLN successor's single 4-year term. In 1982 the PLN candidate, Luis Alberto Monge, was elected president. In 1986 Oscar Arias Sánchez was elected to succeed Monge. He promised to prevent Nicaraguan anti-Sandinista (*contra*) forces using Costa Rica as a base. In 1987 he received the Nobel Peace Prize as recognition of his Central American peace plan, agreed to by the other Central American states.

Costa Rica was beset with economic problems in the early 1990s when several politicians, including President Calderón, were accused of profiting from drug traf-ficking.

TERRITORY AND POPULATION. Costa Rica is bounded in the north by Nicaragua, east by the Caribbean, south-east by Panama, and south and west by the Pacific. The area is estimated at 51,100 sq. km (19,730 sq. miles). The population at the census of 1 June 1984 was 2,416,809. Estimate (1995) 3,367,455 (44% urban); density, 66·2 per sq. km. There are 7 provinces (with 1995 population): Alajuela (607,674); Cartago (378,188); Guanacaste (266,198); Heredia (270,096); Limón (255,248); Puntarenas (375,639); San José (1,220,412).

Vital statistics for calendar years:

	Marriages	Births	Deaths
1994	21,520	80,391	13,313
1995	. . .	80,306	14,061

The population is mainly of Spanish (85%) and mixed (8%) descent. About 3% are Afro-Caribbean (including some 70,000 speakers of an English Creole along the Caribbean coast). There is a residual Amerindian population of about 10,000.

Spanish is the official language.

CLIMATE. The climate is tropical, with a small range of temperature and abundant rains. The dry season is from Dec. to April. San José. Jan. 66°F (18·9°C), July 69°F (20·6°C). Annual rainfall 72" (1,793 mm).

CONSTITUTION AND GOVERNMENT. The Constitution was promul-gated in Nov. 1949. The legislative power is vested in a single-chamber *Legislative Assembly* of 57 deputies elected for 4 years. The *President* and 2 Vice-Presidents are elected for 4 years; the candidate receiving the largest vote, provided it is over 40%

of the total, is declared elected, but a second ballot is required if no candidate gets 40% of the total. Elections are normally held on the first Sunday in February.

The President may appoint and remove members of the cabinet.

Presidential elections took place on 1 Feb. 1998. Miguel Angel Rodriguez was elected by 46·9% of votes cast.

At the simultaneous parliamentary elections the Social Christian Unity Party won 29 seats, the National Liberation Party 22 and others 6.

President: Miguel Angel Rodriguez.

National anthem: 'Noble patria, tu hermosa bandera' ('Noble fatherland, thy beautiful banner'); words by J. M. Zeledón Brenes, tune by M. M. Gutiérrez).

DEFENCE

Army. The Army was abolished in 1948, and replaced by a Civil Guard, 3,000 strong in 1996.

Navy. The para-military Civil Guard flotilla includes 1 150-tonne ex-US cutter, 1 fast patrol craft, 5 small coastguard cutters and some boats. Personnel (1996),400.

Air Wing. The Civil Guard operates a small air wing equipped with 10 light planes and helicopters and 2 Caribou transports.

INTERNATIONAL RELATIONS

Membership. Costa Rica is a member of the UN, CACM and OAS.

ECONOMY

Budget. In 1995 revenue was 260·17bn. colones (193·82bn. in 1994 and expenditure 285·42bn., colones (249·26bn. in 1994).

Currency. The unit of currency is the *Costa Rican colón* (CRC) of 100 *céntimos.* There are coins of 25 and 50 céntimos and C/5, 10 and 20, and notes of C/50, 100, 500, 1,000 and 5,000. The official rate is used for all imports on an essential list and by the Government and autonomous institutions and a free rate is used for all other transactions. 43,500m. colons were in circulation in 1993. Inflation was 11·53% in Oct. 1996.

Banking and Finance. The bank of issue is the Central Bank (founded 1950) which supervises the national monetary system, foreign exchange dealings and banking operations. The bank has a board of 7 directors appointed by the Government, including *ex officio* the Minister of Finance and the Planning Office Director. The *Governor* is Carlos Manuel Castillo.

Weights and Measures. The metric system is legally established, but in country districts the following old Spanish weights and measures may be found: *Libra* = 1·014 lb. avoirdupois; *arroba* = 25·35 lb. avoirdupois; *quintal* = 101·40 lb. avoirdupois, and *fanega* = 11 Imperial bushels.

ENERGY AND NATURAL RESOURCES

Electricity. Electricity output, derived from water power in the highlands, is around 4,000m. kWh.

Minerals. Gold output is about 3,000 troy oz. per year. Salt production was 50,000 tonnes in 1991.

Agriculture. Agriculture is the principal industry; the rural workforce was 335,300 in 1995, of whom 263,000 were economically active. The arable area is about 285,000 ha. The principal agricultural products are coffee, bananas, sugar and cattle.

Coffee production in 1995 (in tonnes) was 800,000; sugar-cane, 2·95m.; bananas (1994), 1·93m.; maize, 35,000; tobacco, 1,800; rice, 178,249; potatoes, 43,606.

In 1994 cattle numbered 1·69m. and pigs 252,000.

Forestry. The forest area (1·6m. ha. in 1988) is being depleted. 4·3m. cu. metres of timber were cut in 1993.

Fisheries. Total catch (1991) 18,000 tonnes.

INDUSTRY. The main manufactured goods are foodstuffs, textiles, fertilizers, pharmaceuticals, furniture, cement, tyres, canning, clothing, plastic goods, plywood and electrical equipment.

Trade Unions. There are two main trade unions, *Rerum Novarum* (anti-Communist) and *Confederación General de Trabajadores Costarricenses* (Communist).

FOREIGN ECONOMIC RELATIONS. A free trade agreement was signed with Mexico in March 1994. Some 2,300 products were freed from tariffs, with others to follow over 10 years.

Commerce. The value of imports and exports in US$1m.:

	1993	1994	1995
Imports	2,907	3,025	3,274
Exports	2,085	2,259	2,624

Chief exports: Manufactured goods and other products, coffee (mostly to Germany, USA, UK and Italy), bananas (to USA), sugar, cocoa.

Tourism. There was a total of 784,610 tourists in 1995.

COMMUNICATIONS

Roads. In 1992 there were about 35,560 km of all-weather motor roads open. On the Costa Rica section of the Inter-American Highway it is possible to motor to Panama during the dry season. The Pan-American Highway into Nicaragua is metalled for most of the way and there is now a good highway open almost to Puntarenas. Motor vehicles, 1995, numbered 477,778.

Railways. The nationalized railway system *(Incofer)* was closed in 1995 but was expected to be re-opened by private operators in 1999.

Civil Aviation. The national carrier is Líneas Aéreas Costarriquenses (LACSA), which in 1995 operated 4 A320-200s and 2 B-737-200 Advs.

Shipping. The chief ports are Limón on the Atlantic and Caldera on the Pacific. The merchant marine totalled 2,895 GRT in 1995.

Telecommunications. There were 364,000 telephones in 1994. The Government has 202 telegraph offices and 88 official telephone stations. In 1993 there were 844,000 radio and 465,000 television receivers (colour by NTSC).

Press. There are 4 national newspapers.

SOCIAL INSTITUTIONS

Justice. Justice is administered by the Supreme Court, 5 appeal courts divided into 5 chambers; the Court of Cassation, the Higher and Lower Criminal Courts, and the Higher and Lower Civil Courts. There are also subordinate courts in the separate provinces and local justices throughout the republic. Capital punishment may not be inflicted.

Religion. Roman Catholicism is the state religion; it had 2·55m. adherents in 1991. There is entire religious liberty under the constitution. The Archbishop of Costa Rica has 4 bishops at Alajuela, Limón, San Isidro el General and Tilarán. Protestants number about 40,000.

Education. Adult literacy was 92·8% in 1991. Primary instruction is compulsory and free from 6 to 15 years; secondary education (since 1949) is also free. Primary schools are provided and maintained by local school councils, while the national government pays the teachers, besides making subventions in aid of local funds. In

1996-97 there were 3,607 public and private primary schools with 17,554 teachers and administrative staff and 208,233 enrolled pupils and 358 public and private secondary schools with 11,114 teachers and 518,603 pupils. In 1995-96 there was 1 university and 1 technological institute in the public sector, and 8 universities, 1 Adventist university and 1 university of science and technology in the private sector. There were also 4 other institutions of higher education. In 1994-95 there were 48,354 university students and 3,687 academic staff.

Health. In 1995 there were 3,441 doctors, 201 dentists and 5,947 hospital beds.

DIPLOMATIC REPRESENTATIVES

Of Costa Rica in Great Britain (14 Lancaster Gate, London, W2 3LH)
Ambassador: Jorge Borbón.

Of Great Britain in Costa Rica (Edificio Centro Colón, Apartado 815, San José 1007)
Ambassador and Consul-General: A. S. Green, OBE, MVO.

Of Costa Rica in the USA (2112 Street, NW Washington D.C., 20008)
Ambassador: Sonia Picado Sotela.

Of the USA in Costa Rica (Pavas, Frente Centro Comercial, San José)
Ambassador: Peter J. De Vos.

Of Costa Rica to the United Nations
Ambassador: Fernando Berrocal Soto.

Of Costa Rica to the European Union
Ambassador: Mario Carvajal.

Further Reading

Ameringer, C. D., *Democracy in Costa Rica.* New York, 1982
Biesanz, R., *(et al), The Costa Ricans.* Hemel Hempstead, 1982
Bird, L., *Costa Rica: Unarmed Democracy.* London, 1984
Creedman, T. S. *Historical Dictionary of Costa Rica.* 2nd ed. Metuchen (N.J.), 1991
Stansifer, C., *Costa Rica.* 2nd ed. [Bibliography] Oxford and Santa Barbara (CA), 1991

National statistical office: Dirección General de Estadística y Censos, San José.

CÔTE D'IVOIRE

République de la
Côte d'Ivoire

(Republic of the Ivory Coast)

Capital: Yamoussoukro
Seat of Government: Abidjan
Population: 14·76m.
GNP: US$7·1bn.
HDI/world rank: 0·368/145

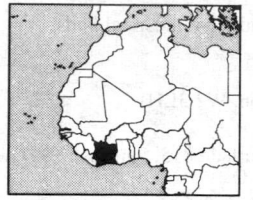

KEY HISTORICAL EVENTS. The Portuguese discovered Côte d'Ivoire (or the Ivory Coast as it was formerly known) in the 15th century, but there was little initial interest in the area. The dense forests which covered the southern half of the area that was to become Côte d'Ivoire formed barriers to large-scale socio-political organizations, and in the north dissimilar populations did not have the incentive to overcome ethnic differences and so forge a larger state. Even with the development in the 17th and 18th centuries of the Guinea coast gold and slave trades, Côte d'Ivoire generally lay too far to the west to be of significance.

France obtained rights on the coast in 1842, but did not actively and continuously occupy the territory until 1882. In the early 1870s the French ministry responsible for colonies even offered to exchange Côte d'Ivoire with the British for the Gambia, which bisected the French colony of Senegal, but the British refused. Rumours of gold later rekindled French interest, and on 10 Jan. 1889 Côte d'Ivoire was declared a French protectorate, becoming a colony on 10 March 1893. Over the next 20 years French administrators used the military to subdue African populations which openly resisted French intrusions. In 1904 Côte d'Ivoire became a territory of French West Africa.

The French administered Côte d'Ivoire in a direct style, and would routinely dismiss locally selected chiefs. Governors appointed from France administered the colony using a system of centralized rule that allowed little room for participation among the Ivorians.

In 1946 Côte d'Ivoire's first political party, the Democratic Party of Côte d'Ivoire, was created under the leadership of Félix Houphouët-Boigny, and after confrontations which nearly led to the ruin of the party, he eventually adopted a policy of practical co-operation with the French authorities. By the mid-1950s the country had become the wealthiest in French West Africa, and on 4 Dec. 1958 Côte d'Ivoire became an autonomous republic within the French Community.

Côte d'Ivoire achieved full independence on 7 Aug. 1960, with Félix Houphouët-Boigny as its first president. He was authoritarian yet his policies brought 2 decades of economic growth and political stability. Not until 1990 were opposition parties legalized, 3 years before his death. He was succeeded by Henri Konan Bédié, also of the Democratic Party of Côte d'Ivoire.

TERRITORY AND POPULATION. Côte d'Ivoire is bounded in the west by Liberia and Guinea, north by Mali and Burkina Faso, east by Ghana, and south by the Gulf of Guinea. It has an area of 320,783 sq. km and a population at the 1988 census of 10,812,782 (40% urban). Estimate (1996) 14·76m.; density, 46·0 per sq. km.

Vital statistics rates, 1996 estimates (per 1,000 population). Births, 42·5; deaths, 15·7. Infant mortality (per 1,000 live births), 82·4. Expectation of life in 1996 was 46·7 years (46·2 for males and 47·2 for females). Growth rate, 2·92% per annum.

Since 1991, the country has been divided into 10 regions (North-West, North, North-East, West, Centre-West, Centre-North, Centre, Centre-East, South-West, South) comprising 50 departments. Departments are named after their chief towns.

The areas and populations (1988 census) of the departments:

	Area (in sq. km)	Population		Area (in sq. km)	Population
Abengourou	5,200	214,162	Adzopé	5,230	237,265
Abidjan	8,550	2,492,513	Agboville	3,850	203,730
Aboisso	6,250	225,882	Agnibilekrou[1]	1,700	84,404

432

	Area (in sq. km)	Population		Area (in sq. km)	Population
Bangolo[2]	2,060	80,374	Korhogo	12,500	387,947
Béoumi[3]	2,860	91,062	Lakota	2,730	115,948
Biankouma	4,950	99,431	Man	4,990	286,860
Bondoukou	10,040	175,632	Mankono	10,660	123,723
Bongouanou	5,570	225,432	M'bahiakro[3]	5,460	102,774
Bouaflé	3,980	163,917	Odiénné	20,600	169,433
Bouaké	4,700	453,074	Oumé	2,400	140,166
Bouna	21,470	134,459	Sakassou[3]	1,880	59,494
Boundiali	7,895	127,231	San Pédro[7]	6,900	168,174
Dabakala	9,670	82,094	Sassandra	5,190	107,616
Daloa	5,450	361,472	Séguéla	11,240	121,120
Danané	4,600	222,045	Sinfra[8]	1,690	120,301
Daoukro[4]	3,610	86,425	Soubré	8,270	309,307
Dimbokro	4,920	141,934	Tabou[7]	5,440	59,708
Divo	7,920	389,530	Tanda[9]	6,490	203,129
Duékoué[5]	2,930	101,451	Tiassalé[6]	3,370	132,626
Ferkessedougou	17,728	172,850	Tingréla	2,200	55,251
Gagnoa	4,500	275,765	Touba	8,720	109,155
Grand-Lahou[6]	2,280	52,645	Toumodi[3]	2,780	80,909
Guiglo	11,220	169,660	Vavoua[10]	6,160	169,454
Issia	3,590	194,974	Yamoussoukro[3]	6,160	284,613
Katiola	9,420	131,221	Zuénoula	2,830	114,440

[1] Formerly part of Abengourou. [2] Formerly part of Man. [3] Formerly parts of Bouaké. [4] Formerly part of Dimbokro. [5] Formerly part of Guiglo. [6] Formerly parts of Abidjan. [7] Formerly parts of Sassandra. [8] Formerly part of Bouaflé. [9] Formerly part of Bondoukou. [10] Formerly part of Daloa.

Major towns (with 1988 census population): Abidjan, 1,929,079; Bouaké, 329,850; Daloa, 121,842; Korhogo, 109,445; Yamoussoukro, 106,786.

There are about 60 ethnic groups, the principal being the Baoulé, (23%), the Bété (18%) and the Sénoufo (15%).

French is the official language.

CLIMATE. A tropical climate, affected by distance from the sea. In coastal areas, there are wet seasons from May to July and in Oct. and Nov., but in central areas the periods are March to May and July to Nov. In the north, there is one wet season from June to Oct. Abidjan. Jan. 81°F (27·2°C), July 75°F (23·9°C). Annual rainfall 84" (2,100 mm). Bouaké. Jan. 81°F (27·2°C), July 77°F (25°C). Annual rainfall 48" (1,200 mm).

CONSTITUTION AND GOVERNMENT. The 1960 Constitution was amended in 1971, 1975, 1980, 1985 and 1986. The sole legal Party was the Democratic Party of Côte d'Ivoire, but opposition parties were legalized in 1990. There is a 175-member *National Assembly* elected by universal suffrage for a 5-year term. The President is also directly elected for a 5-year term (renewable). He and both his parents must be citizens born in Côte d'Ivoire. He appoints and leads a Council of Ministers.

In Nov. 1990 the National Assembly voted that its Speaker should become President in the event of the latter's incapacity, and created the post of Prime Minister to be appointed by the President. Following the death of President Houphouët-Boigny on 7 Dec. 1993 the speaker, Henri Konan Bédié, proclaimed himself head of state till the end of the presidential term in Sept. 1995. Presidential elections were held on 22 Oct. 1995; turn-out was 56·03%. President Konan Bédié was re-elected by 96·44% of votes cast against 1 opponent.

At the National Assembly elections of 26 Nov. 1995 the electorate was 3·8m. The Democratic Party won 148 seats; the Republican Rally, 14; the Ivorian Popular Front, 12. There was also 1 vacant seat.

In March 1998 the government comprised:

Prime Minister and Minister of Planning and Industrial Development: Daniel Kablan Duncan.

Minister of State in charge of Relations with Institutions: Timothée Ahoua N'Guetta. *Minister of State in charge of National Solidarity:* Laurent Dona-Fologo.

Minister of State for Religious Affairs and Dialogue with the Opposition: Leon Konan Koffi. *Minister of Defence:* Bandama N'Gatta. *Foreign Affairs:* Amara Essy. *Interior and National Integration:* Emile Constant Bombet. *Justice and Public Freedom, Keeper of the Seals:* Brou Kouakou. *Higher Education, Scientific Research and Technological Innovation:* Saliou Touré. *Agriculture and Animal Resources:* Lambert Kouassi Konan. *Commodities:* Guy Alain Gauze. *National Education and Basic Training:* Pierre Kipre. *Commerce:* Akon Kouassi. *Mines and Petroleum Resources:* Lamine Mohamed Fadika. *Energy:* Safiatou Ba-N'Daw. *Public Health:* Maurice Kacou Guikahue. *Communications:* Danielle Boni-Claverie. *Housing, Living Conditions and Environment:* Albert Kacou Tiapani. *Employment, Civil Service and Social Welfare:* Pierre Achi Atsain. *Security:* Marcel Dibona Kone. *Culture:* Bernard Zadi Zaourou. *Family and Promotion of Women:* Albertine Gnanazan Hepie. *Presidential Affairs:* Faustin Kouame. *Youth Promotion and Civic Education:* Faustin Vlami Bi Dou. *Technical Education, Professional Training and Handicrafts:* Komenan Zakpa. *Economic Infrastructure:* Ezan Akele. *Economy and Finance:* Niamien N'Goran. *Transport:* Adama Coulibaly. *Sports:* Sidibe Soumahoro.

The *Speaker* is Charles Donwahi.

National anthem: 'L'Abidjanaise' (words by M. Ekra and others, tune by P. M Pango).

Local government: There are 50 departments, each under an appointed Prefect and an elected General Council, sub-divided into 183 sub-prefectures. At the elections of 11 Feb. 1996 turn-out was low. The Democratic Party won control of 156 of the 196 councils contested.

DEFENCE. There is selective conscription for 6 months.

Army. There are 4 military regions. The Army consists of 1 armoured battalion, 3 infantry battalions, 1 artillery group and 1 airborne, 1 anti-aircraft and 1 engineer company. Equipment includes 5 AMX-13 light tanks. Total strength (1996), 6,800. Paramilitary forces, 7,800.

Navy. Offshore, riverine and coastal patrol squadrons include 2 fast missile craft, 2 patrol vessels, 1 riverine defence craft, 1 light amphibious transport and 2 minor landing craft. Personnel in 1996 totalled 900 and the force is based at Locodjo (Abidjan).

Air Force. There are 5 Alpha Jet light strike combat aircraft, though only 1 or 2 are operational. Transport aircraft include 5 fixed-wing and 4 rotary-wing aircraft. 4 Bonanzas are used for training and patrol. Personnel (1995) 700.

INTERNATIONAL RELATIONS

Membership. Côte d'Ivoire is a member of the UN, OAU and is an ACP state of the EU.

ECONOMY

Policy. Austerity measures were introduced in May 1990. A privatization programme was initiated in 1992. 30 companies had been privatized by 1997.

Performance. Real GDP growth was 7% in 1996.

Budget. 1993 budget (in 1,000m. francs CFA): Revenue, 621 (of which fiscal receipts, 533); expenditure, 996 (of which capital expenditure, 99).
VAT is 25%.

Currency. The currency is the *franc CFA* with a parity rate of 100 francs CFA to 1 French franc. In 1993 gold reserves were 45,000 troy oz; foreign exchange reserves were US$4m. In 1992 252,100m. francs CFA were in circulation. Inflation was an annualized 5% in 1996.

Banking and Finance. The regional *Banque Centrale des Etats de l'Afrique de* *l'Ouest* is the central bank and bank of issue. In 1994 there were 12 commercial banks; 3 other banks maintained representative offices. The African Development Bank is based in Abidjan. There is a stock exchange in Abidjan.

ENERGY AND NATURAL RESOURCES

Electricity. The electricity industry was privatized in 1990. Production in 1993 amounted to 1,800m. kWh, over half of which was from hydroelectric projects.

Oil and Gas. Petroleum has been produced (offshore) since Oct. 1977. Production (1992) 63,000 tonnes. Estimated gas reserves, 1996, 6,516,000m. cu. ft. Daily output, 1997, 75m. cu. ft.

Minerals. Diamond extraction was 20,000 carats in 1987. There are iron ore deposits at Bangolo and gold-mining began in Jan. 1990, reserves being estimated at 4,500 kg.

Agriculture. In 1992 some 8m. persons subsisted on agriculture in 0·56m. family smallholdings averaging 2 ha. In 1991 there were 2·4m. ha of arable land, 1·26m. ha of permanent crop land and 13m. ha of meadow and pasture. Côte d'Ivoire ranks among the world's largest producers and exporters of cocoa beans, coffee and palm-kernel oil. The main crops (production, 1991, in 1,000 tonnes) are coffee (240), cocoa (710), bananas (116), pineapples (189), palm oil (217), palm kernels (43), seed cotton (302), rubber (74), yams (269), cassava (1,435), plantains (1,110), rice (690), maize (510), millet (52), sugar-cane (1,600) and groundnuts (140).

Livestock, 1992: 1·18m. cattle, 1·2m. sheep, 0·92m. goats and 0·38m. pigs.

Forestry. In 1997 the rainforest covered 3m. ha (13m. ha in 1900). Products include teak, mahogany and ebony. In 1994, 14·4m. cu. metres of roundwood were cut.

Fisheries. In 1989 the fishing fleet comprised 32 vessels over 100 GRT totalling 9,386 GRT. The catch in 1988 amounted to 107,600 tonnes.

INDUSTRY. Industrialization has developed rapidly since independence, particularly food processing, textiles and sawmills. Output in 1988 (in 1,000 tonnes): Petrol, 311; paraffin, 237; fuel oil, 1,089; cement, 144; sawn timber, 775; veneer wood, 266; centrifugal sugar, 140; palm-oil (1989), 190; copra (1989), 75.

Labour. In 1996 the workforce was 5·7m.

Trade Unions. The main trade union is the *Union Générale des Travailleurs de Côte d'Ivoire*, with over 100,000 members.

FOREIGN ECONOMIC RELATIONS. External debt was 7,816,700m. francs CFA in Dec. 1995.

Commerce. Total exports, 1994, US$2,900m; imports, US$1,600m.

Principal exports, 1992 (in 1,000m. francs CFA): Cocoa, 256; petroleum products, 85; timber, 62; coffee, 56; cotton, 29; tinned tuna, 25. Principal imports: Crude oil, 116; machinery and vehicles, 96; pharmaceuticals, 34; fish, 27; plastics, 20. Main export markets, 1992: France, 15·1%; Germany, 9·9%; Italy, 7·6%; Netherlands, 7·4%; USA, 5·9%. Main import suppliers: France, 36%; Nigeria, 20·2%; Netherlands, 4·4%; USA, 3·9%; Italy, 3·8%.

Tourism. There were 0·23m. tourists in 1995 (0·19m. in 1994).

COMMUNICATIONS

Roads. In 1988 roads totalled 55,000 km (including 128 km of motorway) and there were (1994) about 311,000 motor vehicles.

Railways. From Abidjan a metre-gauge railway runs to Léraba on the border with Burkina Faso (655 km), and thence through Burkina Faso to Ouagadougou and Kaya. Operation of the railway in both countries is franchised to the mixed public-private company Sitarail. In 1991–92 the railways carried 0·9m. passengers and 0·5m. tonnes of freight. Route length in 1986, 1,177 km.

Civil Aviation. There are international airports at Abidjan-Port-Bouet and Yamoussoukro. The national carrier is the state-owned Air Ivoire, which provides domestic services to 10 regional airports and flights to Burkina Faso, Ghana, Guinea, Liberia and Mali. Air Ivoire had 3 aircraft in 1995. Services are also provided by Air Afrique, Air Burkina, Air France, Air Gabon, Air Guinée, Air Liberté, Cameroon Airlines, Egyptair, Ethiopian Airlines, Ghana Airways, Middle East Airlines, Nigeria Airways, Royal Air Maroc, Sabena, Swissair and TAP.

Shipping. The main ports are Abidjan and San Pédro. In 1992 Abidjan loaded 3·98m. tonnes of cargo and unloaded 6·18m. tonnes. In 1995 the merchant marine totalled 76,399 GRT, including oil-tankers, 1,170 GRT.

Telecommunications. There were 87,700 telephones in 1987 and 1,800 telex machines. The government-controlled Radiodiffusion Télévision Ivoirienne is responsible for broadcasting. In 1993 there were 810,000 television (colour by SECAM) and 1·5m. radio receivers.

Press. In 1992 there was 1 daily newspaper.

SOCIAL INSTITUTIONS

Justice. There are 28 courts of first instance and 3 assize courts in Abidjan, Bouaké and Daloa, 2 courts of appeal in Abidjan and Bouaké, and a supreme court in Abidjan. The death penalty is authorized, but has not been applied since independence in 1960.

Religion. In 1994 there were 5·2m. Moslems (mainly in the north) and 3·8m. Christians (chiefly Roman Catholics in the south). Traditional animist beliefs are also practised.

Education. In 1990 54% of the population over 15 were literate. There were, in 1992, 1,447,785 pupils in 6,844 primary schools, 289,510 pupils in 147 secondary schools and 3,094 students at 15 technical or teacher training institutes and 14,200 students in higher education. In 1986 there were 33,500 primary school teachers. In 1995-96 there was 1 university with 21,000 students and 730 academic staff, and 3 university centres. There were 6 other institutions of higher education.

Health. There were 93 hospitals and 669 health centres in 1984. In 1982 there were 10,062 hospital beds. In 1980 there were 591 doctors. In 1985 there were 60 dentists and 85 pharmacists.

DIPLOMATIC REPRESENTATIVES

Of Côte d'Ivoire in Great Britain (2 Upper Belgrave St., London, SW1X 8BJ)
Ambassador: Kouadio Adjoumani.

Of Great Britain in Côte d'Ivoire (Immeuble 'Les Harmonies', angle Blvd. Carde et Ave. Dr Jamot, Plateau, Abidjan)
Ambassador: H. B. Warren-Gash.

Of Côte d'Ivoire in the USA (2424 Massachusetts Ave., NW, Washington, D.C., 20008)
Ambassador: Koffi Moïse Koumoue.

Of the USA in Côte d'Ivoire (5 Rue Jesse Owens, Abidjan)
Ambassador: Lannon Walker.

Of Côte d'Ivoire to the United Nations
Ambassador: Youssoufou Bamba.

Of Côte d'Ivoire to the European Union
Ambassador: Nanan Koliabo N'zi Anet.

Further Reading

Direction de la Statistique. *Bulletin Mensuel de Statistique.*
Daniels, M., *Côte d'Ivoire.* [Bibliography]. Oxford and Santa Barbara (CA), 1996
Zartman, I. W. and Delgado, C., *The Political Economy of Ivory Coast.* New York, 1984

National statistical office: Direction de la Statistique, Ministère du Plan, Abidjan.

CROATIA

Republika Hrvatska

Capital: Zagreb
Population: 4·66m.
GDP per head: (PPP$) 3,960
HDI/world Rank, 0·760/77

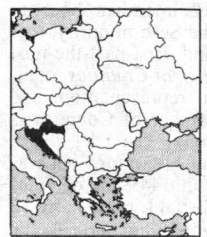

KEY HISTORICAL EVENTS. The original Croats migrated to their present territory in the 6th century and were converted to Roman Catholicism. Croatia was united with Hungary in 1091 and remained under Hungarian administration until the end of the first world war. On 1 Dec. 1918 Croatia became a part of the new Kingdom of Serbs, Croats and Slovenes, which was renamed Yugoslavia in 1929.

During the second world war an independent fascist (Ustaša) state was set up under the aegis of the German occupiers. During the Communist period Croatia became one of the 6 'Socialist Republics' constituting the Yugoslav federation led by Marshal Tito. With the collapse of Communism, an independence movement gained momentum.

In a referendum on 19 May 1991 94·17% of votes cast were in favour of Croatia becoming an independent sovereign state with the option of joining a future Yugoslav confederation as opposed to remaining in the existing Yugoslav federation. The Krajina, and other predominantly Serbian areas of Croatia, wanted union with Serbia and seized power by force of arms. Croatian forces and Serb insurgents backed by federal forces became embroiled in a conflict throughout 1991 until the arrival of a UN peace-keeping mission at the beginning of 1992 and the establishment of 4 UN ('pink zones') peace-keeping zones. Croatia obtained a reduction in the UN peace-keeping forces after 1 April 1995.

In early May 1995 Croatian forces retook Western Slavonia from the Serbs and opened the Zagreb-Belgrade highway. Serb rockets fell on Zagreb during the campaign, and civilians were killed. In a 60-hour operation mounted on 4 Aug. 1995 the former self-declared Serb Republic of Krajina was occupied, provoking an exodus of 0·18m. Serb refugees. Croats who had left the area in 1991 began to return. On 12 Nov. 1995 the Croatian government and Bosnian Serbs reached an agreement to place Eastern Slavonia, the last Croatian territory still under Bosnian Serb control, under UN administration until 15 July 1998.

TERRITORY AND POPULATION. Croatia is bounded in the north by Slovenia and Hungary and in the east by Yugoslavia and Bosnia-Hercegovina. It includes the areas of Dalmatia, Istria and Slavonia which no longer have administrative status. Its area is 56,538 sq. km. Population at the 1991 census was 4,784,265 (50·8% urban), of whom the predominating ethnic groups were Croats (3,736,356) and Serbs (581,663). Estimate, 1997, 4,664,710; population growth, 0·17%; density, 85·5 per sq. km. Principal towns (with 1991 census population): Zagreb (726,770), Split (189,388), Rijeka (167,964), Osijek (104,761).

At the beginning of 1991 there were some 0·6m. resident Serbs. A law of Dec. 1991 guaranteed the autonomy of Serbs in areas where they are in a majority after the establishment of a permanent peace.

Vital statistics: 1994: Birth, 10·9 per 1,000 population; death, 11·1; infant mortality, 10·2 per 1,000 live births.

The official language is the western variant of Serbo-Croat (in Croatia called Croato-Serb or, familiarly, Croatian).

CLIMATE. Inland Croatia has a Central European type of climate, with cold winters and hot summers, but the Adriatic coastal region experiences a Mediterranean climate with mild, moist winters and hot, brilliantly sunny summers with less than average rainfall. Jan./July temperature/annual rainfall: Dubrovnik, 9·2°C/24·7°C/1,006 mm. Zadar, 7·2°C/23·5°C/688 mm. Rijeka, 6·2°C/23°C/1,251 mm. Zagreb, 0°C/23·5°C/652 mm. Osijek, 0·6°C/20·8°C/541 mm.

CONSTITUTION AND GOVERNMENT. A new constitution was adopted on 21 Dec. 1990. The *President* is elected for renewable 5-year terms. Franjo Tudjman was elected President in May 1990, and re-elected on 3 Aug. 1992 against 7 opponents by 56·7% of votes cast. Presidential elections were last held 15 June 1997. There were 3 candidates. Turn-out was 56·2%. President Tudjman was re-elected with 61·41% of votes cast. Parliament consists of the 127-member *Sabor*, in which 12 seats are reserved for the Croat diaspora and 3 for the Serb minority. It is elected by a combination of proportional representation and first-past-the-post methods. There is also an upper house, the 68-member *Chamber of Counties*, composed of representatives of counties elected by proportional representation, and 5 members nominated by the President. The role of the Chamber of Counties is primarily consultative.

At elections to the Sabor on 29 Aug. 1995 the electorate was 3·6m.; turn-out was 66%. The Croatian Democratic Union (HDZ) won 75 seats with 44·82% of votes cast, the Peasant Party coalition 16 with 18·44%, the Croatian Social Liberal Party 12 with 11·62%, the Social Democratic Party 10, the Croat Right-Wing Party 4, the Istrian Democratic Diet 2, and the Independent Democrats 1. At elections to the Chamber of Counties in Feb. 1993 the HDZ gained 37 seats, the Social Liberals 16 and others 15.

President: Franjo Tudjman (b. 1922; CDU; sworn in 12 Aug. 1992).

The government comprised in March 1998:
Prime Minister: Zlatko Matesa.

Deputy Prime Ministers: Mate Granić (*also Foreign Minister*), Jure Radić (*also Minister for Reconstruction and Development*), Ivica Kostović (*also Minister for Humanitarian Issues and Science*), Borislav Skegro (*also Minister for the Economy and Finance*), Ljerka Mintas-Hodak (*also Minister for the Interior and Social Affairs*). *Defence:* Gojko Šušak. *Interior:* Ivan Penić. *Tourism:* Sergej Morsan. *Agriculture and Forestry:* Zlatko Dominiković. *Construction and Housing:* Marko Sirać. *Education and Sport:* Bozidar Pugelnik. *Health:* Andrija Hebrang. *Justice:* Miroslav Separović. *Administration:* Marijan Ramuscak. *Labour and Social Welfare:* Joso Škara. *Maritime Affairs, Transport and Communications:* Zeljko Lužavec. *Economy:* Nenad Porges. *Privatization and Property Management:* Milan Kovać. *Culture:* Božo Biskupić. *Immigration:* Marijan Petrović. *European Integration:* Ljerka Mintas-Hodak. *Homeland War Defenders and War Veterans:* Jurag Njavro. The *Speaker* is Nedjeljko Mihanović.

National anthem: 'Lijepa nasva domovino' ('Beautiful our homeland'); words by A. Mihanović, tune by J. Runjanin.

Local Government. The country is divided into 21 counties (*zvupanija*), 2 districts (Knin and Glina, at present under local Serbian control), 68 towns and 383 municipalities, all administered by elected councils. County councils elect as leader a prefect approved by the President. County councils have broad responsibilities in the spheres of economic development, health and education; town and municipal councils (the latter for areas with fewer than 10,00 population) are concerned with detailed administration. Elections were held in April 1997.

DEFENCE. Conscription is for 10 months.

Army. The country is divided into 6 operations zones. The Army consists of 10 infantry, 4 air defence, 3 special forces, 1 artillery-multiple rocket launcher, 3 anti-tank, 1 engineer and 1 mechanized brigade, 7 mixed and artillery divisions. Equipment includes 250 T-34, T-55 and M-84 main battle tanks. Personnel, 1997, 50,000 (33,500 conscripts). Paramilitary forces include an armed police of 40,000. There are also 10,000 reserves in 27 Home Defence regiments and 150,000 regular Army reservists.

Navy. In 1996 the fleet comprised 2 inshore submarines for special operations, 1 missile-armed corvette, 4 missile craft, 1 torpedo craft, 3 patrol craft, 2 minelayers and 2 small mine countermeasures vessels. There are 11 small amphibious craft and some 5 support vessels. A Marine service fields 7 independent infantry companies, and the coast defence force mans artillery batteries. Total personnel in 1997 numbered about 3,000 including marines.

Air Force. The Air Force has 7 squadrons, 2 with MiG-21 fighters, 1 with Mi-24 armed helicopters, 1 with Mi-8/17 transport helicopters, 1 with An-2, An-26 and An-32 fixed-wing transports, 1 fixed-wing training squadron with light aircraft and PC-9s and 1 with JetRanger helicopter trainer aircraft. Personnel, 1997, 5,000 (including Air Defence).

INTERNATIONAL RELATIONS. In Jan. 1994 relations with Yugoslavia were established with the opening of mutual representative offices. In late 1997 and early 1998 Croatia signed highway construction agreements with German, Italian and French companies worth US$800m.

Membership. Croatia is a member of the UN, the Council of Europe and the Central European Initiative.

ECONOMY

Performance. Real GDP growth was 4·0% in 1996 and 6·0% in 1997. Inflation is 4·6%.

Budget. Government revenue and expenditure (1m. kunas):

	1994	1995	1996	1997
Revenue	22,817·34	27,385·07	30,812·96	32,073·47
Expenditure	20,416·38	25,969·79	27,125·23	28,473·01

Expenditure by function (1997): Education, 3,558·52; Health, 7,837·70; Social Security and Welfare, 17,916·79. VAT at 22% was introduced in 1997.

Currency. On 30 May 1994 the *kuna* (HRK; a name used in 1941–45) of 100 *lipa*, replaced the Croatian dinar at 1 kuna = 1,000 dinars. There are coins of 1,2, 5,10, 20 and 50 lipa and 1,2 and 5 kuna, and notes of 5, 10, 20, 50, 100, 200, 500 and 1,000 kuna. Foreign exchange reserves were US$2,800m. in 1996.

Banking and Finance. The National Bank of Croatia (*governor*, Marko Skreb) is the bank of issue. In 1996 there were 57 domestic commercial banks and 1 foreign bank. Total savings deposits on 31 Dec. 1994 were 8,915m. kuna. Foreign exchange reserves (1996) US$2,314bn.

There are stock exchanges in Zagreb and Varazvdin.

Weights and Measures. The metric system is in use.

ENERGY AND NATURAL RESOURCES

Electricity. Output was 9,146m. kWh in 1995.

Oil and Gas. 1·50m. tonnes of crude oil were produced in 1995, and 1,966m. cu. metres of natural gas in 1995.

Minerals. Production, 1994 (in 1,000 tonnes): Coal, 96; brown coal and lignite, 37 (1991); bauxite, 1·3; salt, 21·7.

Agriculture. At the 1993 census 409,647 persons subsisted on agriculture. In 1995, agriculture contributed 11·6% of GDP. Agricultural land total 2·3m. ha (1·1m. ha arable, 0·77m. ha pasture, 55,000 ha vineyards). The cultivated area is 1·54m. ha. Yields (in 1,000 tonnes, 1994): Wheat, 750; maize, 1,687; potatoes, 563; plums, 36.

Livestock, 1994 (in 1,000): Cattle, 519 (milch cows, 347); sheep, 444; pigs, 1,347; poultry, 12,503. Animal products, 1994: Meat, 335,000 tonnes; honey, 844 tonnes; milk, 600m. litres; eggs, 0·88m.

Forestry. Forests covered 2,079,301 ha in 1994. 3·30m. cu. metres of timber were cut in 1994.

Fisheries. The total catch was 16,560 tonnes in 1994, of which 5,465 tonnes were freshwater fish.

INDUSTRY. Production, 1994 (in 1,000 tonnes): Crude steel, 63; cement, 2,055; cellulose, 127; cotton fabric, 23m. sq. metres; cotton cloth, 10m. sq. metres; woollen yarn, 4 tons; wine, 1·89m. hectolitres; beer, 3·1m. hectolitres.

Labour. The non-agricultural workforce was 1,022,000 in 1994, of whom 368,300 worked in industry (41% female). There were 241,000 registered unemployed in March 1996.

FOREIGN ECONOMIC RELATIONS. Croatia has accepted responsibility for 29·5% of the US$4,400m. commercial bank debt of the former Yugoslavia. Total foreign debt as a percentage of GDP, (1996) 26·6%; (1997) 31·0%.

Commerce. Exports in 1996 were valued at US$4,511m. and in 1997, US$4,800m. Imports for 1996 came to US$7,000m. and in 1997, US$7,540m.

The main exports are machinery and transport equipment, chemicals and food-stuffs. In 1996 the main export markets were Italy, 21·0%; Germany, 18·6%; Slovenia, 13·5%; Austria, 4·4%. Main import suppliers: Germany, 20·6%; Italy, 18·2%; Slovenia, 9·9%; Austria, 7·7%.

Tourism. 12·9m. tourist nights were spent in 1995. The tourist industry is now recovering with a 20% rise in receipts since 1995. Night stays are estimated at 21·6m. for 1996.

COMMUNICATIONS

Roads. There are 21,798 km of roads, including 302 km of motorways. In 1994 there were 698,391 passenger cars (667,881 private), 4,026 buses and 49,834 goods vehicles. 84m. passengers and 5·1m. tonnes of freight were carried by public transport in 1995.

There were 62,120 traffic accidents in 1994; 804 persons were killed.

Railways. There are 2,699 km of 1,435 mm gauge (1,213 km electrified). In 1995 railways carried 28·6m. passengers and 10·3m. tonnes of freight.

Civil Aviation. There are international airports at Zagreb (Pleso) and Dubrovnik. The national carrier is Croatia Airlines, which operated 5 B-737-200 Advs and 2 other air-craft in 1995. Services are also provided by Aeroflot, Air France, Austrian Airlines, CSA, LOT, Lufthansa, SAS and Swissair. 1,588,000 passengers were flown in 1995.

Shipping. The main port is Rijeka, which handled 3·8m. tonnes of freight in 1995. In 1995 there were 168 ocean-going vessels, totalling 3·29m. DWT. 132 of the vessels (94·09% of tonnage) were registered under foreign flags. Total GRT, 0·27m., including oil-tankers 30,549 GRT and container ships, 46,131 GRT. 5·8m. passengers and 22·39m. tonnes of cargo were transported.

Telecommunications. In 1994 there were 1,392,000 telephones. Broadcasting is controlled by the state Croatian Radio-Television (colour by PAL). In 1995 there were 1·2m. radio sets and 1·1m. television receivers.

Cinemas. There were 150 cinemas with a total of 55,000 seats in 1995. 3 feature films were made in 1995.

Press. In 1995 there were 12 dailies with an annual circulation of 225,000 and 603 other newspapers. There were 64 weeklies and 401 periodicals. An amendment of March 1996 to the criminal code makes it an offence for the press to defame the government.

SOCIAL INSTITUTIONS

Religion. At the 1991 census there were 76·5% Roman Catholics, 11·1% Orthodox, and 12·4% others (mainly Old Catholics and Moslems).

Education. In 1995–96 there were 902 pre-school institutions with 66,105 children and 5,531 childcare workers; 1,134 primary schools with 207,890 pupils and 10,605 teachers; 482 secondary schools with 417,475 pupils and 29,741 teachers. In 1994–95 there were 64 institutes of higher education with 80,185 students and 5,893 academic staff. In 1995–96 there were 3 universities with 86,357 students and 6,325 academic staff. Adult literacy rate, 97·0%.

Health. In 1994 there were 9,138 doctors and 1,798 dentists. There were 84 hospitals with 28,230 beds.

Social security. The health insurance scheme covered 4,591,341 persons in 1994, of whom 1,354,146 were contributing and 755,644 were receiving retirement pensions.

DIPLOMATIC REPRESENTATIVES

Of Croatia in Great Britain (21 Conway St., London W1P 5HL)
Ambassador: Andrija Kojakovic.

Of Great Britain in Croatia (Vlasvka 121/III, POB 454, 10000 Zagreb)
Ambassador: C. Munro.

Of Croatia in the USA (2343 Massachusetts Ave., NW, Washington, D.C., 20008)
Ambassador: Miomir Zuzul.

Of the USA in Croatia (Andrije Hebranga 2, Zagreb)
Ambassador: Peter W. Galbraith.

Of Croatia to the United Nations
Ambassador: Dr Ivan Šimonović.

Of Croatia to the European Union
Ambassador: Janko Vranyczany-Dobrinovic.

Further Reading

Central Bureau of Statistics. *Statistical Yearbook.—Monthly Statistical Report.*

Stallaerts, R. and Laurens, J., *Historical Dictionary of the Republic of Croatia.* Metuchen (NJ), 1995

Tanner, M. C.: *A nation forged in war.* Yale 1997.

National statistical office: Central Bureau of Statistics, 3 Ilica, Zagreb. *Director:* Ivan Rusan.
Website: http://www.dzs.hr/

CUBA

República de Cuba

Capital: Havana
Population: 10·95m.
*GDP per head: (*PPP$) 3,000
HDI/world rank: 0·723/86

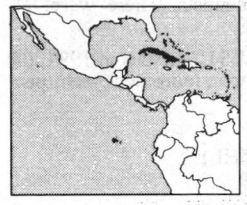

KEY HISTORICAL EVENTS. Cuba was discovered by Columbus in 1492 and, except for the brief British occupancy in 1762-63, remained a Spanish possession until 10 Dec. 1898. Sovereignty was then relinquished under the terms of the Treaty of Paris at the end of the Spanish-American War. Cuba became an independent republic in 1901, although the US continued to influence Cuban internal affairs and foreign policy until 1934. Since 1903 the USA has maintained a military and naval base at Guantánamo in Oriente province.

In 1933 Fulgencio Batista Zladivar led a successful military revolution. He ruled the country until 1944, as elected president from 1940, and again, after seizing power in a *coup*, from 1952 until 1959. A revolutionary movement against the corrupt Batista dictatorship, led by Dr Fidel Castro from 26 July 1953, was eventually successful and Batista fled the country on 1 Jan. 1959.

Under Castro, Cuba's relationship with the US deteriorated while relations with the USSR became closer. In Jan. 1961 the USA severed diplomatic relations after US business interests in Cuba had been expropriated without compensation for refusing to co-operate with the government's economic plans. On 17 April an invasion force of émigrés and adventurers, encouraged by the USA, landed in Cuba but was defeated at the Bay of Pigs. At the end of 1961 Castro declared Cuba to be a Communist state.

The US Navy imposed a blockade of Cuba from 22 Oct. until 22 Nov. 1962 to force the USSR to withdraw Soviet missile bases. Cuba continued to receive financial aid and technical advice from the USSR until the early '90s when subsidies of around US$4bn. a year were suspended. This led to a 40% drop in GDP between 1989 and 1993. The USA has maintained an economic embargo against the island and relations between Cuba and the USA have remained embittered. But in the wake of the Pope's visit to Cuba in Jan. 1998, President Clinton announced a package of measures to alleviate poverty including permission to allow Cuban Americans to send up to US$1,200 per family to relatives on the island.

TERRITORY AND POPULATION. The island of Cuba forms the largest and most westerly of the Greater Antilles group and lies 135 miles south of the tip of Florida, USA. The area is 110,860 sq. km, and comprises the island of Cuba, (104,945 sq. km.); the Isle of Youth (Isla de la Juventud, formerly the Isle of Pines; 2,200 sq. km.), and some 1,600 small isles ('cays'; 3,715 sq. km.). Population, census (1981) 9,723,605; estimate, 1996, 10,951,334; density, 99 per sq. km.

The area, population and density of population of the 14 provinces and the special Municipality of the Isle of Youth were as follows (1989 estimate):

	Area sq. km	Population		Area sq. km.	Population
Pinar del Río	10,860	681,500	Camagüey	14,134	727,700
La Habana	5,671	633,400	Las Tunas	6,373	481,500
Ciudad de La Habana	727	2,068,600	Holguín	9,105	927,700
Matanzas	11,669	599,500	Granma	8,452	777,300
Cienfuegos	4,149	356,700	Santiago de Cuba	6,343	974,100
Villa Clara	8,069	788,800	Guantánamo	6,366	487,900
Sancti Spíritus	6,737	422,300			
Ciego de Avila	6,485	355,500	Isla de la Juventud	2,199	70,900

Chief cities (1991 population estimate in 1,000): Havana, the capital (2,124), Santiago de Cuba (418), Camagüey (289), Holguín (206), Guantánamo (206), Santa

Clara (200); 1990, Bayamo (125,021), Cienfuegos (123,600), Pinar del Río (121,774), Las Tunas (119,400), Matanzas (113,724) and Manzanillo (107,650).

Vital statistics, 1996 (estimates): Birth rate, 13·4 per 1,000 population; death, 7·4; infant mortality rate, 9 per 1,000 live births; life expectancy, 75 years.

CLIMATE. Situated in the sub-tropical zone, Cuba has a generally rainy climate, affected by the Gulf Stream and the N.E. Trades, though winters are comparatively dry after the heaviest rains in Sept. and Oct. Hurricanes are liable to occur between June and Nov. Havana. Jan. 72°F (22·2°C), July 82°F (27·8°C). Annual rainfall 48" (1,224 mm).

CONSTITUTION AND GOVERNMENT. A Communist Constitution came into force on 24 Feb. 1976. It was amended in July 1992 to permit direct parliamentary elections.

Legislative power is vested in the *National Assembly of People's Power*, which meets twice a year and consists of 601 deputies elected for a 5-year term by universal suffrage. Lists of candidates are drawn up by mass organizations (trade unions, etc.). The National Assembly elects a 31-member *Council of State* as its permanent organ. The Council of State's President, who is head of state and of government, nominates and leads a Council of Ministers approved by the National Assembly.

President: Dr Fidel Castro Ruz (b. 1927) became *President* of the Council of State on 3 Dec. 1976; re-elected for 5 years on 24 Feb. 1998. He is also First Secretary of the Cuban Communist Party and C.-in-C. of the National Defence Council.

Elections to the National Assembly were held on 11 Jan. 1998. The electorate was 8m.; turn-out was 98·35%. All 601 candidates received the requisite 50% of votes for election.

In March 1998 the government comprised:
First Vice-President of the Council of State and of the Council of Ministers, Minister of the Revolutionary Armed Forces: Gen. Raúl Castro Ruz. *Vice-Presidents:* Dr Carlos Rodríguez Rodríguez, Osmani Cienfuegos Gorriarán, José Fernández Alvárez, Jaime Crombet Hernández-Baquero, Adolfo Díaz Suárez, Pedro Miret Prieto. *Minister of Agriculture:* Alfredo Jordán Morales. *Basic Industries:* Marcos Portal León. *Communications:* Gen. Silvano Colás Sánchez. *Construction:* Juan Junco del Pino. *Construction Materials Industry:* José Cañctc Alvárez. *Culture:* Abel Prieto Jiménez. *Domestic Trade:* Barbara Castillo Cuesta. *Economy and Planning:* José Rodríguez García. *Education:* Luís Gómez Gutiérrez. *Finance and Prices:* Manuel Millares Rodríguez. *Fishing Industry:* Orlando Rodríguez Romay. *Food Industry:* Alejandro Roca Iglesias. *Foreign Investment and Economic Co-operation:* Ibrahim Ferradez. *Foreign Relations:* Roberto Robaina González. *Foreign Trade:* Ricardo Cabrisas Ruíz. *Higher Education:* Fernando Vecino Alegret. *Interior:* Gen. Abelardo Colomé Ibarra. *Metallurgy and Electronics Industry:* Ignacio González Planas. *Justice:* Roberto Diaz Sotolongo. *Labour and Social Security:* Salvador Valdes Mesa. *Light Industry:* Jesús Pérez Othon. *Public Health:* Carlos Dotres Martínez. *Science, Technology and Environment:* Rosa Simeón Negrín. *Sugar Industry:* Nelson Torres Pérez. *Tourism:* Osmany Cienfuegos Gorriarán. *Transport:* Alvaro Perez Morales. *Without portfolio:* Wilfredo López Rodríguez.

The *Speaker* of the National Assembly is Ricardo Alarcón de Quesada.

Various left-wing parties and movements amalgamated as the Communist Party of Cuba (PCC).

The Congress of the PCC elects a Central Committee of 225 members, which in turn appoints a Political Bureau comprising 26 members.

National anthem: 'Al combate corred bayameses' ('Run, Bayamans, to the combat'); words and tune by P. Figueredo.

Local Government. The country is divided into 14 provinces, a special municipality (the Isle of Youth) and 169 municipalities. Elections are held for delegates to the Municipal Assemblies by universal suffrage for 2¹/₂ year terms; the municipal assemblies then elect the provincial assemblies for similar terms. Elections for 1,192 representatives to the 14 provincial assemblies were held on 11 Jan. 1998.

DEFENCE. The National Defence Council is headed by the President of the republic. Conscription is for 2 years.

Army. The strength was 38,000 (including conscripts and Ready Reservists) in 1997. There are 3 regional commands. The Army is organized in 5 armoured, 9 mechanized infantry, 1 airborne, 1 frontier guard, 1 surface-to-air missile and 14 reserve brigades; and 1 air defence regiment. Equipment includes 75 T-34 1,100 T-54/55 and 400 T-62 main battle tanks. Border Guard and State Security forces total 19,000 and the Territorial Militia, 1·3m. (reservists), all armed.

Navy. Naval combatants, all ex-Soviet, include 2 'Foxtrot' class diesel submarines, 2 'Koni' class frigates, 1 'Pauk' class corvette, 14 fast missile craft, 3 coastal mine-hunters and 12 inshore minesweepers. There is 1 medium landing ship and 6 craft. The major auxiliaries include 1 tanker and 1 electronic intelligence gatherer. Some 24 minor auxiliaries and service craft complete the total.

Personnel in 1997 totalled about 5,000 conscripts including about 550 marines. Main bases are at Cienfuegos, Havana and Mariel. The USA still occupies the Guantánamo naval base.

There is a coastal defence force equipped with artillery and some anti-ship missiles. A separate coast guard division of the Frontier Guards numbering 4,000 operates about 30 inshore patrol craft.

Air Force. The Air Force has been extensively re-equipped with aircraft supplied by USSR and in 1997 had a strength of some 10,000 and about 130 combat aircraft. About 10 interceptor and 3 ground-attack squadrons fly MiG-29, MiG-23 and MiG-21 jet fighters. There is a squadron of An-26 and An-32 twin-turboprop transports, some An-24 twin-turboprop transports, and about 20 Mi-24 armed helicopters, Mi-8 (some armed), Mi-17 and Mi-2 helicopters, Zlin 326 piston-engined trainers and L-39, MiG-21U, MiG-23U and MiG-29U jet trainers. 10 An-2M biplanes are operated by the Air Force, mainly on agricultural and liaison duties. Soviet-built surface-to-air ('Guideline', 'Goa' and 'Gainful') and coastal defence ('Samlet') missiles are in service.

INTERNATIONAL RELATIONS

Membership. Cuba is a member of the UN and SELA (Latin American Economic System).

ECONOMY

Policy. Prices were increased by at least 50% on 1 June 1994. The Central Planning Board was abolished in Jan. 1995. Since 1995 the government has been tolerant of some private enterprise, though the state sector remains dominant.

Performance. In 1995, real growth in GDP was 2·5% (0·7% in 1994).

Budget. The 1995 budget envisaged revenue of 11,680m. pesos and expenditure of 12,680m. pesos. Hard-currency earners and the self-employed became liable to a 10-50% income tax in Nov. 1995.

Currency. The unit of currency is the *Cuban peso* (CUP) of 100 *centavos*, which is not convertible although an official exchange rate is announced daily reflecting any changes in the strength of the US dollar. The US dollar has been legal tender since 1993. There are coins of 1, 5, 20 and 40 centavos and 1 peso, and notes of 3, 5, 10, 20 and 50 pesos. 11,750m. pesos were in circulation in 1994.

Banking and Finance. The Central Bank of Cuba (*Governor*, Francisco Soberón Valdés) replaced the National Bank of Cuba as the central bank in June 1997. On 14 Oct. 1960 all banks were nationalized. Changes to the banking structure beginning in 1996 divested the National Bank of its commercial functions, and created new commercial and investment institutions. There were 7 commercial banks in June

1997. 13 foreign banks had representative offices in 1997; foreign branches are not permitted.

All insurance business was nationalized in Jan. 1964. A National Savings Bank was established in 1983.

Weights and Measures. The metric system is legally compulsory, but the American and old Spanish systems are much used. The sugar industry uses the Spanish long ton (1·03 tonnes) and short ton (0·92 tonne). Cuba sugar sack = 329·59 lb. or 149·49 kg. Land is measured in *caballerías* (of 13·4 ha or 33 acres).

ENERGY AND NATURAL RESOURCES

Electricity. Production in 1993 was 12,000m. kWh.

Oil. Crude oil production (1995) 106m. tonnes.

Minerals. Iron ore abounds, with deposits estimated at 3,500m. tonnes. Output of copper concentrate (1989) was 2,800 tonnes; refractory chrome (1987), 52,400 tonnes. Other minerals are nickel (1995, 42,900 tonnes) and cobalt (1989, 46,500 tonnes), silica and barytes. Gold and silver are also worked. Salt output from the solar evaporation of sea water was 114,900 tonnes in 1989.

Agriculture. In 1959 all land over 30 *caballerías* was nationalized and eventually turned into state farms. Under legislation of 1993, state farms are being re-organized as 'units of basic co-operative production'. These units have the use of the land in perpetuity from the state. Unit workers select their own managers, and are paid an advance on earnings. 294,700 persons were employed in these units in 1995. In 1963 private holdings were reduced to a maximum of 5 *caballerías*. In Sept. 1984 there were 1,472 co-operatives comprising 70,000 *caballerías* of land. In 1994 farmers were permitted to trade on free market principles after state delivery quotas had been met.

The most important product is sugar and its by-products. 1996–97 production was 4·4m. tonnes (3·4m. tonnes in 1995–96). Production of other important crops in 1994 was (in 1,000 tonnes): Tobacco (leaves), 44; rice (paddy), 186; coffee, 21; maize, 90.

1994 fruit and vegetable production (in 1,000 tonnes): Oranges, 433; mangoes, 84; bananas, 180; grapefruit and pomelos, 317 and potatoes, 216.

In 1994 the livestock included 1,053,000 pigs; 0·58m. horses; 0·31m. sheep; 95,000 goats; 4·5m. cattle.

Forestry. Cuba has 2·7m ha of forests representing 25% of the land area. These forests contain valuable cabinet woods, such as mahogany and cedar, besides dye-woods, fibres, gums, resins and oils. Cedar is used locally for cigar-boxes, and mahogany is exported. 3m. cu. metres of roundwood were cut in 1994.

Fisheries. Fishing is the third most important export industry, after sugar and nickel. Catch (1993) 93,000 tonnes.

INDUSTRY. In 1996, manufacturing accounted for 27% of GDP. All industrial enterprises had been state-controlled, but in 1995 the economy was officially stated to comprise state property, commercial property based on activity by state enterprises, joint co-operative and private property. Production in 1989 was: Textiles, 218·6m. sq. metres (cotton fabrics 182·6m. sq. metres); cement (1989), 3,800m. tonnes; wheat flour, 398,000 tonnes; fuel oil (1989), 4,152,800 tonnes; diesel oil (1989), 1,178,500 tonnes; processed crude oil, 7,916,000 tonnes; steel, 314,200 tonnes; steel bars, 367,100 tonnes; nickel and cobalt, 46,500 tonnes; copper, 2,759,100 tonnes; 314,700 tyres; 231,200 inner tubes; leather shoes, 11·0m. pairs; paint (1989), 121,000 hectolitres; soft drinks (1989), 2,396,500 hectolitres; 308m. cigars; 16,519m. cigarettes; fertilizers, 898,600 tonnes; 2,345 buses; 172,700 radios; 70,500 TVs; 9,100 refrigerators; sulphuric acid, 381,500 tonnes; fine salt, 114,900 tonnes.

Labour. Self-employment was legalized in 1993; there were 0·21m. self-employed persons in 1996. Under legislation of Sept. 1994 employees made redundant must be assigned to other jobs or to strategic social or economic tasks; failing this, they are paid 60% of former salary.

Trade Unions. The Workers' Central Union of Cuba groups 23 unions.

FOREIGN ECONOMIC RELATIONS. Foreign debt to non-communist countries was US$10,400m. in 1997. Since July 1992 foreign investment has been permitted in selected state enterprises, and Cuban companies have been able to import and export without seeking government permission. Foreign ownership is recognized in joint ventures. A free-trade zone opened at Havana 1993. 3 more are envisaged in legislation of 1996. In 1994, the productive, real estate and service sectors were opened to foreign investment. Legislation of 1995 opened all sectors of the economy to foreign investment except defence, education and health services. 100% foreign-owned investments, and investments in property, are now permitted.

The Helms-Burton Law of March 1996 gives US nationals the right to sue foreign companies investing in Cuban estate expropriated by the Cuban government.

Commerce. In 1995, exports totalled US$1,600m., and imports US$2,400m. The principal exports are sugar, minerals, tobacco, citrus fruit and fish. In 1994-95, sugar exports totalled 2·76m. tonnes (3·19m. tonnes in 1993-94). In 1992 exports included (in 1m. pesos): Minerals, 210; fruit and vegetables, 150; fish, 130; tobacco, 95.

Tourism. Tourism is Cuba's largest foreign exchange earner. In 1995 there were 738,200 visitors, bringing US$1,100m. in net foreign exchange earnings. The age at which Cubans may obtain exit visas was lowered to 20 years in Aug. 1991.

COMMUNICATIONS

Roads. In 1996 there were some 26,500 km of roads, of which 14,575 km were paved.

Railways. There were (1992) 4,807 km of public railway (1,435 mm gauge) of which 147 km is electrified. In 1994 it carried 30·5m. passengers and 4·4m. tonnes of freight. In addition, the large sugar estates have 7,773 km of lines on 1,435, 914 and 760 mm gauges.

Civil Aviation. There is an international airport at Havana (Jose Martí). The state airline Cubana operates all services internally, and internationally from Havana to London, Madrid, Berlin, Prague, Paris, Zürich and Brussels, and also to Jamaica, Barbados, Trinidad and Tobago, Bahamas, Ecuador, Guyana, Canada, Argentina, Chile, Nicaragua and the Dominican Republic. It had 66 ex-Soviet aircraft in 1995. The other regular foreign services are Aeroflot, Aerorepublica, ALM, AOM, Bahamasair, Compania Mexicana, COPA, Iberia, KLM, LTU, LACSA, Ladeco, SAM and TAAG-Angola.

Shipping. There are 11 ports, the largest being Havana, Cienfuegos and Mariel. The merchant marine in 1995 totalled 0·54m. GRT of which 0·1m. GRT were oil-tankers.

Telecommunications. The national telephone system (1989) had 311,100 lines in use.

Broadcasting is the responsibility of the state-controlled Instituto Cubano de Radio y Televisión. There are 5 national radio networks, provincial and local stations and an external service, Radio Habana (Spanish, Arabic, Creole, English, Esperanto, French, Guaraní, Portuguese, Quechua). There are 2 TV channels (colour by NTSC). In 1995 there were 3·85m. radio and 2·5m. TV sets (colour by NTSC).

Cinemas and Theatres. In 1993 there were 461 cinemas with an attendance of 17·6m. There were 49 theatres with an attendance of 1,387,700 in 1989.

Press. There are (1998) 17 daily newspapers with a combined circulation of 1·3m.

SOCIAL INSTITUTIONS

Justice. There is a Supreme Court in Havana and 7 regional courts of appeal. The provinces are divided into judicial districts, with courts for civil and criminal actions, with municipal courts for minor offences. The civil code guarantees aliens the same property and personal rights as are enjoyed by nationals.

The 1959 Agrarian Reform Law and the Urban Reform Law passed on 14 Oct. 1960 have placed certain restrictions on both. Revolutionary Summary Tribunals have wide powers.

Religion. Religious liberty was constitutionally guaranteed in July 1992. 60% of the population were estimated to be Roman Catholics in 1996. In 1994 Cardinal Jaime Ortega (b. 1936) was nominated Primate by the Pope. In 1996 there were 260 Roman Catholic priests and monks, nearly half of them foreign nationals. There is a seminary in Havana which had 61 students in 1996. There is a bishop of the American Episcopal Church in Havana; there are congregations of Methodists in Havana and in the provinces as well as Baptists and other denominations. Cults of African origin still persist.

Education. Education is compulsory (between the ages of 6 and 14), free and universal. In 1995 there were 160,283 pre-primary pupils with 6,512 teachers; 9,864 primary schools with 90,565 teachers for 1·07m. pupils and 704,601 secondary level pupils with 74,139 teachers. There were 122,346 students at university level.

There are 4 universities, and 10 teacher training, 2 agricultural, 4 medical and 10 other higher educational institutions.

Health. There were (1989) 34,752 doctors, 6,482 dentists, 58,589 nursing personnel and 264 hospitals with 74,407 beds.

Free medical services are provided by the state polyclinics, though a few doctors still have private practices.

DIPLOMATIC REPRESENTATIVES

Of Cuba in Great Britain (167 High Holborn, London, WC1 6PA)
Ambassador: Rodney Alejandro López Clemente.

Of Great Britain in Cuba (Calle 34, No. 702/4, entre 7ma Avenida y 17 Miramar, Havana)
Ambassador: P. A. McLean, CMG.

Of Cuba to the United Nations
Ambassador: Bruno Rodríguez Parrilla.

Of Cuba to the European Union
Ambassador: René Mujica Cantelar.

The USA broke off diplomatic relations with Cuba on 3 Jan. 1961 but Cuba has an Interests Section in the Swiss Embassy in Washington, DC and the US has an Interests Section in the Swiss Embassy in Havana.

Further Reading

Bethell, L. (ed.) *Cuba: a Short History.* CUP, 1993
Bunck, J. M., *Fidel Castro and the Quest for a Revolutionary Culture in Cuba.* Pennsylvania State Univ. Press, 1994
Cabrera Infantye, G., *Mea Cuba*; translated into English from Spanish. London, 1994
Cardoso, E. and Helwege, A., *Cuba after Communism.* Boston (Mass.), 1992
Eckstein, S. E., *Back from the Future: Cuba under Castro.* Princeton Univ. Press, 1994
Fursenko, A., and Naftali, T., *'One Hell of a Gamble': Khrushchev, Castro, and Kennedy, 1958-64.* New York, 1997
May, E. R. and Zelikow, P. D., *The Kennedy Tapes: Inside the White House during the Cuban Missile Crisis.* Belknap Press/Harvard University Press, 1997
Mesa-Lago, C. (ed.) *Cuba: After the Cold War.* Pittsburgh Univ. Press, 1993
Ruttin, P., *Capitalism and Socialism in Cuba: a Study of Dependency, Development and Underdevelopment.* London, 1990
Stubbs, J., *et al., Cuba* [Bibliography]. Oxford and Santa Barbara (CA), 1996
Zimbalist, A. and Brundenius, C., *The Cuban Economy: Measurement and Analysis of Socialist Performance.* Johns Hopkins Univ. Press, 1990

CYPRUS

Kypriaki Dimokratia—
Kibris Çumhuriyeti

(Republic of Cyprus)

Capital: Nicosia
Population: 729,800
GDP per head: (PPP$) 13,071
HDI/world rank: 0·907/24

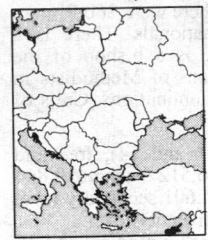

KEY HISTORICAL EVENTS. About the middle of the second millennium BC Greek colonies were established in Cyprus, and later it formed part of the Persian, Roman and Byzantine empires. In 1193 the island became a Frankish kingdom, in 1489 a Venetian dependency, and in 1751 was conquered by the Turks. The Turks retained possession of it until its cession to Britain for administrative purposes under a convention concluded with the Sultan of Constantinople in 1878. In 1914 the island was annexed by Great Britain, and on 1 May 1925 it was given the status of a Crown Colony.

In the 1930s the Greek Cypriots began to agitate for ENOSIS (Union with Greece). In 1955 they started a guerrilla movement (EOKA) against the British, with Archbishop Makarios, the head of the Greek Orthodox Church in Cyprus, as leader and Gen. Grivas in charge of military operations. As the British suspected Makarios of advocating violence, he was banished from the island. However, in 1959 the Greek and Turkish Cypriots agreed on a constitution for an independent Cyprus, and Makarios returned to be elected President. On 16 June 1960 Cyprus became an independent state.

In Dec. 1963 the Turkish Cypriots withdrew from the government. Fighting between Turkish and Greek Cypriots led to a UN peace-keeping force being sent in. On 15 July 1974 a military coup drove out Makarios and appointed as president, Nicos Sampson, an EOKA supporter. The coup was short-lived as Sampson resigned on 23 July and Makarios was recalled as President.

Turkey invaded the island on 20 July 1974, eventually occupying the northern part. 0·2m. Greek Cypriots fled to live as refugees in the south. The UN General Assembly unanimously adopted resolutions calling for the withdrawal of all foreign troops from Cyprus and the return of refugees to their homes, but without result.

On 13 Feb. 1975 a Turkish Cypriot Federated State was proclaimed. Rauf Denktaş was appointed President. On 15 Nov. 1983 the Turkish state unilaterally proclaimed itself the 'Turkish Republic of Northern Cyprus' (TRNC). In Nov. 1983 and May 1984 the UN Security Council declared all secessionist actions illegal. Several UN-inspired talks were held in 1985–91 without success.

In March 1991 the UN Security Council adopted unanimously a resolution rejecting new TRNC demands. In Sept. discussions were held between the UN Secretary-General's representatives, the Greek Cypriot president and Rauf Denktaş. In Oct. the UN Secretary-General rejected Rauf Denktaş's demands for the recognition of separate sovereignty for the TRNC including a right to secession.

Further talks were held without result in May–Aug. 1992. On 26 Aug. the UN Security Council adopted a resolution endorsing the Secretary-General's ideas and territorial adjustments as the basis for reaching an agreement. Talks were held in Oct. 1992 and in 1993 after the election of President Clerides without result. Cyprus has accepted confidence-building measures suggested by the UN but these were opposed by the TRNC. In July 1994 the UN Security Council adopted a resolution reaffirming its position that a settlement must be based on a single sovereignty and exclude any form of partition or succession. But recent talks between Rauf Denktaş and President Clerides have failed to overcome the 'legacy of distrust'.

TERRITORY AND POPULATION. The island lies in the Mediterranean, about 60 km off the south coast of Turkey and 90 km off the coast of Syria. Area, 3,572 sq. miles (9,251 sq. km). The Turkish-occupied area is 3,335 sq. km. Population by ethnic group:

Ethnic group	1946	1960	1973	1992
Greek Cypriot	361,199	447,901	498,511	599,000
Turkish Cypriot	80,548	103,822	116,000	95,000 [1]
Others	8,367	20,984	17,267	20,000
Total	450,114	572,707	631,778	714,000

[1] Revised to take into account Turkish Cypriots who have emigrated from the Turkish-occupied area since 1974 (estimated at over 41,000).

Principal towns with populations (1992 estimate): Nicosia (the capital), 177,451; Limassol, 136,741; Larnaca, 60,557; Paphos, 32,575.

As a result of the Turkish occupation of the northern part of Cyprus, 0·2m. Greek Cypriots were displaced and forced to find refuge in the south. The urban centres of Famagusta, Kyrenia and Morphou were completely evacuated. *See below* for details of the 'Turkish Republic of Northern Cyprus'.

Vital statistics rates, 1994 (per 1,000 population): Births, 16·4; deaths, 7·8; infantile mortality (per 1,000 live births), 9.

Life expectancy is 77·1 years.

Greek and Turkish are official languages. English is widely spoken.

CLIMATE. The climate is Mediterranean, with very hot, dry summers and variable winters. Maximum temperatures may reach 112°F (44·5°C) in July and Aug., but minimum figures may fall to 22°F (−5·5°C) in the mountains in winter when snow is experienced. Rainfall is generally between 10" and 27" (250 and 675 mm) and occurs mainly in the winter months, but it may reach 48" (1,200 mm) in the Troodos mountains. Nicosia. Jan. 50°F (10·0°C), July 83°F (28·3°C). Annual rainfall 15" (371 mm).

CONSTITUTION AND GOVERNMENT. Under the 1960 Constitution executive power is vested in a *President* elected for a 5-year term by universal suffrage and exercised through a Council of Ministers appointed by him or her. The *House of Representatives* exercises legislative power. It is elected by universal suffrage for 5-year terms, and consists of 80 members, of whom 56 are elected by the Greek Cypriot and 24 by the Turkish Cypriot community. Voting is compulsory, and is by preferential vote in a proportional representation system with reallocation of votes at national level. As from Dec. 1963 the Turkish Cypriot members have ceased to attend.

National anthem: 'Segnoriso apo tin kopsi' ('Always shall I know you'); words by D. Solomos, tune by N. Mantzaros.

Parliamentary elections were held on 26 May 1996. The Democratic Rally won 20 seats with 34·48% of votes cast, the Communist Progressive Party of the Working People (Akel) 19 with 33·03%, the Democratic Party 10 and the EDEK Party (Socialists) 5.

Presidential elections were held on 8 and 15 Feb. 1998. In the first round Glafcos Clerides won 40·1% of the vote as against 40·6% for his rival George Iakovou, a former foreign minister. The Socialist leader, Vassos Lyssarides, won 10·6%. In the run-off, Glafcos Clerides won 50·8% to 49·2% for George Iakovou. The turn-out was over 90%.

President: Glafcos Clerides (b. 1919; Democratic Rally).

The Council of Ministers in March 1998 was as follows:

Foreign Affairs: Ioannis Kasoulides. *Interior:* Dinos Michaelides. *Defence:* Yiannakis Omirou. *Agriculture, Natural Resources and Environment:* Costas Themistocleous. *Commerce, Industry and Tourism:* Nicos Rolandis. *Health:* Christos Solomis. *Communications, Public Works and Transport:* Leondios Ierodiaconou. *Finance:* Christodoulos Christodoulou. *Education and Culture:* Lykourgos Kappas. *Labour:* Andreas Moushouttas. *Justice:* Nicos Koshis.

The *Speaker* is Alexis Galanos.

DEFENCE. Conscription is for 26 months.

National Guard. Total strength (1997) 10,000 (8,700 conscripts) organized in 2 brigade HQ, 2 light infantry divisions, 2 light infantry and 1 armoured brigade, 2 light infantry regiments, 1 coastal defence surface-to-surface missile battery, and 1 special forces, 1 anti-tank and 7 artillery battalions. Equipment includes 52 AMX-30B-2 main battle tanks, 2 Islander transport/surveillance aircraft, 2 PC-9 trainers, and 3 Jet Ranger, 1 Bell 412, 2 W-3 Sokol and 4 armed Gazelle helicopters. In Jan. 1997 S-300 ground-to-air missiles were purchased from Russia. There is also a para-military force of 3,700 armed police.

There are 2 British bases (Army and Royal Air Force) and some 3,900 personnel. Greek (950) and UN peacekeeping (1,138; UNFICYP) forces are also stationed on the island.

Plans to install Russian-made air defence missiles have brought Turkish threats of retaliation.

INTERNATIONAL RELATIONS

Membership. Cyprus is a member of the UN, Commonwealth and Council of Europe. An application to join the EU was made in July 1990, but has stalled on the failure of Turks and Greeks to agree on a joint approach.

ECONOMY

Policy. There is a Central Planning Commission, headed by the President of the Republic and including the Council of Ministers. Its administrative arm is the Planning Bureau.

Performance. Real GDP growth in 1996 was an estimated 5%.

Budget. Total public revenue and expenditure for calendar years (in £C1m.):

	1991	1992	1993	1994	1995
Revenue	460·51	571·09	644·71	767·61	858·60
Expenditure	582·81	653·39	738·68	846·82	935·91

Main sources of ordinary revenue in 1995 (in £C1m.) were: Import duties, 101·40; excise duties, 99; income tax, 157·12; property taxes, 25·98; social security contributions, 180·97.

Main divisions of ordinary expenditure in 1995 (in £C1m.): Wages and salaries, 374·66; pensions and gratuities, 53; commodity subsidies, 37·74; expenditures on goods and services, 469·91; social insurance benefits, 312·91; education, 150·74; health, 81·14.

Development expenditure for 1994 (in £C1m.) included 15 for water development, 8 for agriculture, forests and fisheries, 10 for rural development and 39 for roads.

The outstanding long-term domestic debt as at 31 Dec. 1995 was £C1,583·40m. and the foreign debt £C479·27m.

Currency. The *Cyprus pound* (CYP) is divided into 100 *cents*. Notes of the following denominations are in circulation: £C20, £C10, £C5 and £C1. Coins in circulation: 20, 5, 2 and 1 cent. Inflation was 4·5% in 1995.

Banking and Finance. The Central Bank of Cyprus, established in 1963, is the bank of issue, regulates money supply, credit and foreign exchange and supervises the banking system.

In 1993 there were 7 commercial banks (3 foreign) and 4 specialized banks (cooperative, development, mortgage and savings). At 31 Dec. 1994 total deposits in banks were £C4,371m. The country's foreign exchange reserves at 31 Dec. 1994 were £C1,563m.

Weights and Measures. The metric (SI) system was introduced in 1986 and is now widely applied.

ENERGY AND NATURAL RESOURCES

Electricity. Production (1994) 2,681m. kWh.

Water Resources. In 1994, £C14·8m. was spent on water dams, water supplies, hydrological research and geophysical surveys. Existing dams had (1993) a capacity of 297m. cu. metres.

Minerals. The principal minerals extracted in 1994 were (in tonnes): Gypsum, 89,460; bentonite, 46,530; umber and other ochres, 8,630.

Agriculture. Chief agricultural products in 1994 (1,000 tonnes): Grapes, 155·4; potatoes, 135; milk, 167; cereals (wheat and barley), 162; citrus fruit, 135; meat, 81; carobs, 3; fresh fruit, 20; olives, 12; other vegetables, 82; eggs, 12m. dozen.

28% of the government-controlled area is cultivated. About 12% (1994) of the economically active population are engaged in agriculture.

Livestock in 1994 (in 1,000): Cattle, 64; sheep, 255; goats, 210; pigs, 356; poultry, 3,300.

Forestry. Total forest area, 1,754 sq. km. In 1994, 45,833 cu. metres of timber were produced.

Fisheries. Catch (1994) 3,082 tonnes.

INDUSTRY. The most important industries in 1995 were: Food, beverages and tobacco, textiles, wearing apparel and leather, chemicals and chemical petroleum, rubber and plastic products, metal products, machinery and equipment, wood and wood products including furniture. Manufacturing industry in 1993 contributed about £C407m. at current market prices to the GDP.

Labour. 45,336 persons were employed in industry in 1994. Unemployment was 2·7% at the end of 1994.

Trade Unions. About 80% of the workforce is organized and the majority of workers belong either to the Pancyprian Federation of Labour or the Cyprus Workers Confederation.

FOREIGN ECONOMIC RELATIONS. Equity capital for foreign investors must come from abroad, and the terms of foreign loans need approval by the Central Bank. Profits may be freely repatriated. Foreign debt was £C926m. in 1993.

Commerce. Trade figures for calendar years were (in £C1,000):

	1990	1991	1992	1993	1994
Imports	1,174,538	1,215,827	1,490,800	1,261,078	1,417,814
Exports[1]	435,599	441,789	443,045	431,462	475,978

[1] Including re-exports and ships' stores.

Chief civil imports, 1993 (in £C1m.):

Live animals and animal products	27·2	Machinery, electrical equipment, sound and television recorders	231·7
Vegetable products	47·4	Vehicles, aircraft, vessels and equipment	119·8
Prepared foodstuffs, beverages and tobacco	148·8		
Mineral products	132·5	Optical, photographic, medical, musical and other instruments, clocks and watches	30·7
Products of chemical or allied industries	89·6		
Plastics and rubber and articles thereof	52·0	Base metal and articles of base metal	100·8
Pulp, waste paper and paperboard and articles thereof	45·4	Wood and articles, charcoal, cork and articles, basketware, etc.	21·8
Textiles and textile articles	110·5	Pearls, precious stones and metals, semi-precious stones and articles	60·4
Footwear, headgear, umbrellas, prepared leathers, etc.	10·5		
Articles of stone, plaster, cement, etc., ceramic and glass products	31·9		

Chief domestic exports, 1994 (in £C1,000):

Grapes	2,124	Paper products	5,213
Citrus fruit	13,754	Cement	11,187
Potatoes	23,743	Clothing	44,623
Wine[1]	4,628	Footwear	6,930
Fruit, preserved and juices	9,161	Medicinal and pharmaceutical products	16,275
Cigarettes	2,680		

[1] 1993.

In 1994 the EU countries supplied 52·5% of the imports; Arab countries, 3·4%; others, 44·1%. Of the exports (1994), 35·96% went to EU countries and 23·5% to Arab countries.

Tourism. Foreign visitors (1994), 2,069,000 (long-stay). Tourist revenue amounted to some £C800m. in 1994.

COMMUNICATIONS

Roads. In 1994 the total length of roads in the government-controlled area was 10,117 km, of which 5,959 km were bituminous and 4,158 km were earth or gravel roads. The asphalted roads maintained by the Ministry of Communications and Works (Public Works Department) by the end of 1993 totalled 2,203 km, of which 287 km were within the municipal areas. Roads improved or constructed and asphalted in 1994 totalled 248 km. On 31 Dec. 1993, there were 412,944 motor vehicles including 2,856 buses, 99,130 goods vehicles, 71,127 motorcycles, and 10,385 tractors etc.

The area controlled by the Government of the Republic and that occupied by the TRNC are now served by separate transport systems, and there are no services linking the two areas.

Civil Aviation. Nicosia airport has been closed since Aug. 1974. During 1994, 4,391,417 persons travelled and 33,846 tonnes of commercial air-freight was handled through Larnaca and Paphos international airports. The national carrier is Cyprus Airways, which is 80·46% state-owned, and which in 1993 operated 2 A310-300s, 5 A320-200s and 2 BAC1-11-500s. Its subsidiary, Eurocypria, operated 3 A320-200s in 1993. Services are also provided by Aeroflot, Air Malta, Air Moldova, Air Ukraine, Air Zimbabwe, Alitalia, American Airlines, Austrian Airlines, Balkan, Belavia, British Airways, CSA, Donavia, Egyptair, El Al, Emirates, Finnair, Gulf Air, Hapag Lloyd, Iran Air, JAT, KLM, Kuwait Airways, Latvian Airlines, Libyan Airlines, Lithuanian Airlines, LOT, LTU, Lufthansa, Luxair, Malév, Middle East Airlines, Olympic, Royal Jordanian, Swissair, Syrian Airlines and Tarom.

Shipping. The 2 main ports are Limassol and Larnaca. In 1994, 4,983 ships of 15,350,000 net tonnes entered Cyprus ports carrying 7,094,801 tonnes of cargo from, to, and via Cyprus. Ships on the Cyprus open registry in 1995 totalled 35·79m. DWT (8% Cypriot-owned). Famagusta has been closed to international traffic since Aug. 1974.

Telecommunications. In 1993 there were 56 post offices and 722 postal agencies. In 1994 there were 330,364 telephone lines (45·3% per 100 population). The Cyprus Telecommunications Authority provides telephone and data transmission services nationally and to 190 countries.

Cyprus Broadcasting Corporation has 3 radio channels and broadcasts mainly in Greek, but also in Turkish, English and Armenian. The Corporation also broadcasts on 2 TV channels (colour by PAL). A law of June 1990 permits the operation of commercial radio and TV stations. In 1994 there were 2 independent radio stations broadcasting nationwide and numerous radio stations broadcasting locally. There were also 2 private TV stations operating and 1 private PAY-TV. There are also 2 foreign broadcasting stations. In 1993 there were 0·27m. radio and 234,000 TV sets.

Cinemas (1993). In the government-controlled area there were 16 cinemas and 17 screens.

Press (1994). There were 9 Greek, 7 Turkish and 1 English daily newspapers and 3 Greek, 3 Turkish weeklies and 2 English weeklies.

SOCIAL INSTITUTIONS

Justice. The administration of justice is exercised by a separate and independent judiciary. There is a Supreme Court, Assize Courts and District Courts.

The Supreme Court is composed of 13 judges one of whom is the President of the Court (in 1994, Demetrios Stylianides). There is a continuing Assize Court that holds sessions in every district according to the cases committed for trial before it. The Assize Courts have unlimited criminal jurisdiction and may order the payment of compensation up to £C3,000. The District Courts exercise original civil and criminal jurisdiction, the extent of which varies with the composition of the Bench.

There is a Supreme Council of Judicature, consisting of the President and Judges of the Supreme Court, entrusted with the appointment, promotion, transfers, termination of appointment and disciplinary control over all judicial officers, other than the Judges of the Supreme Court.

The Attorney-General (in 1994, Michalakis Triantafyllides) is head of the independent Law Office and legal advisor to the President and his Ministers.

Religion. The Greek Cypriots are Greek Orthodox Christians and the Turkish Cypriots are Moslems (mostly Sunnis of the Hanafi sect). There are also small groups of the Armenian Apostolic Church, Roman Catholics (Maronites and Latin Rite) and Protestants (mainly Anglicans). *See also* CYPRUS: Territory and Population.

Education. *Greek-Cypriot Education.* Elementary education is compulsory and is provided free in 6 grades to children between 5fi and 11fi years of age. There are also schools for the deaf and blind, and 10 schools for handicapped children. In 1992–93 the Ministry ran 218 kindergartens for children in the age group $2^1/_2$–5; there were 390 privately run pre-primary schools. There were 383 primary schools with 64,884 pupils and 3,498 teachers in 1994–95.

Secondary education is also free and attendance for the first cycle is compulsory. The secondary school is 6 years, 3 years at the gymnasium followed by 3 years at the *lykeion* (lyceum) or 3 years at one of the technical schools which provide technical and vocational education for industry. In 1994–95 there were 118 secondary schools with 4,341 teachers and 57,804 pupils.

Post-secondary education is provided at 6 public institutions: The Higher Technical Institute, which provides 3–4-year courses for technicians in civil, electrical, mechanical and marine engineering; a 2-year Forestry College (administered by the Ministry of Agriculture, Natural Resources and Environment); a Hotel and Catering Institute; the Mediterranean Institute of Management (Ministry of Labour and Social Insurance); the School of Nursing (Ministry of Health) which runs 2–3 year courses; the Cyprus Academy of Public Administration set up to help civil servants improve their management skills. There are also a number of private institutions that offer a variety of 1–4-year courses. Adult education is conducted through youth centres in rural areas, foreign language institutes in the towns and private institutions offering courses in business administration and secretarial work.

There is 1 university with 1,492 students and 128 academic staff in 1995–96.

The adult literacy rate is 94%.

Social Security. The administration of the social-security services is in the hands of the Ministry of Labour and Social Insurance, with the Ministry of Health providing medical services through public clinics and hospitals on a means test, except medical treatment for employment accidents, which is given free to all insured employees and financed by the Social Insurance Scheme.

DIPLOMATIC REPRESENTATIVES

Of Cyprus in Great Britain (93 Park St., London, W1Y 4ET)
High Commissioner: Vanias Markides.

Of Great Britain in Cyprus (Alexander Pallis St., Nicosia)
High Commissioner: David C. A. Madden, CMG.

Of Cyprus in the USA (2211 R. St., NW, Washington, D.C., 20008)
Ambassador: Andreas Jacovides.

Of the USA in Cyprus (Metochiou and Ploutarchou Streets, Engomi, Nicosia)
Ambassador: Kenneth Brill.

Of Cyprus to the United Nations
Ambassador: Sotirios Zackheos.

'TURKISH REPUBLIC OF NORTHERN CYPRUS (TRNC)'

KEY HISTORICAL EVENTS. *See* CYPRUS: KEY HISTORICAL EVENTS.

TERRITORY AND POPULATION. The Turkish Republic of Northern Cyprus occupies 3,355 sq. km (about 33% of the island of Cyprus) and its population in 1994 was estimated to be 177,120. Distribution of population by districts (1994): Nicosia, 82,424; Famagusta, 67,167; Kyrenia, 27,529.

CONSTITUTION AND GOVERNMENT. The Turkish Republic of Northern Cyprus was proclaimed on 15 Nov. 1983. Presidential elections were held in 2 rounds on 15 and 22 April 1995. Rauf Denktaş (b. 1924) failed to gain an outright majority against 6 opponents in the first round but, was re-elected at the second round against 1 opponent by 62·48% of the vote.

A 50-seat Legislative Assembly was elected in Dec. 1993. The position of the parties in Dec. 1996 was: Democratic Party (DP) 16, National Unity Party (NUP) 16, Republican Turkish Party (RTP) 13, Communal Liberation Party 5. The Council of Ministers consisted in March 1998 of:

Prime Minister: Derviş Eroğlu (NUP).

Minister of State and Deputy Prime Minister: Serdar Denktaş (DP). *Foreign and Defence:* Taner Etkin (DP). *Interior:* Ilkay Kamil (NUP). *Finance:* Salih Coşar (DP). *Economy:* Erdal Onurhan (NUP). *Education, Culture, Youth and Sport:* Günay Caymaz (NUP). *Agriculture and Forestry:* Kenan Akın (DP). *Communications and Works:* Mehmet Bayram (NUP). *Labour and Housing:* Özkan Altınısık (DP). *Health and Environment:* Ertuğrul Hasipoğlu (NUP).

The *Speaker* of the Legislative Assembly is Ayhan Acarkan.

Defence. In 1997, 30,000 members of Turkey's armed forces were stationed in the TRNC with 465 main battle tanks. TRNC forces comprise 7 infantry battalions and 3 patrol boats with a total personnel strength of 4,000. Conscription is for 2 years.

Budget. Revenue (in 1,000m. Turkish lira) in 1995 was 8,463·4; expenditure, 13,655·4.

Currency. The Turkish lira is used.

Banking and Finance. 50 banks, including offshore banks, were operating in 1995. Control is exercised by the Central Bank of the TRNC.

Agriculture. Agriculture accounted for 10·9% of GDP in 1994.

Foreign Economic Relations. Exports earned US$67·3m. in 1995. Imports cost US$366·1m. Customs tariffs with Turkey were reduced in July 1990. There is a free port at Famagusta.

Tourism. There were 385,759 tourists in 1995. Tourist earnings totalled US$388·3m.

Civil Aviation. There are international airports at Ercan and Geçitkale. Flights operate to Europe, the Middle East and the Gulf via Istanbul and Ankara.

Telecommunications. The local radio, Radio Bayrak (BRTK) broadcasts in several languages including Greek, Arabic and English. BRT Television broadcasts for an average of 10 hours a day (colour by PAL). In 1994 there were 108,800 TV and radio sets.

Press. In 1995 there were 7 daily and 4 weekly newspapers.

Education. In 1995–96 there were 15,526 pupils and 1,103 teachers in primary schools, and 14,816 pupils and 1,107 teachers in secondary and general high schools, 2,477 students and 348 teachers in technical and vocational schools, and 8,932 students in higher education. There are 3 private colleges and 6 universities.

Health. In 1995 there were 353 doctors, 120 dentists, 116 other specialists and 1,214 beds in state hospitals and private clinics.

Further Reading

Statistical Information: Statistics and Research Department, Nicosia.

North Cyprus Almanack, London, 1987

Christodolou, D., *Inside the Cyprus Miracle: the Labours of an Embattled Mini-Economy.* Univ. of Minnesota Press, 1992

Dodd, C. H. (ed.) *The Political, Social and Economic Development of Northern Cyprus.* Huntingdon, 1993

Hanworth, R., *The Heritage of Northern Cyprus.* Nicosia, 1993

Ioannides, C. P., *In Turkey's Image: the Transformation of Occupied Cyprus into a Turkish Province.* New Rochelle (N.Y.), 1991

Kitromilides, P. M. and Evriviades, M. L., *Cyprus,* [Bibliography]. 2nd ed. Oxford and Santa Barbara (CA), 1995

Salem N. (ed.) *Cyprus: a Regional Conflict and its Resolution.* London, 1992

Tamkoç, M., *The Turkish Cypriot State.* London, 1988

CZECH REPUBLIC

Ceská Republika

Capital: Prague
Population: 10·33m.
GDP per head: (PPP$) 9,201
HDI/world rank: 0·882/39

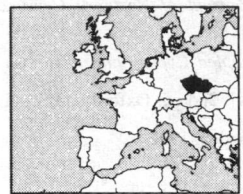

KEY HISTORICAL EVENTS. Although the name Bohemia is Celtic, Slav settlers were well established in the area by the 6th century. The Czech tribe rose to dominance in the 8th century. After the death of Charlemagne a Greater Moravian State emerged before being engulfed by Magyars around 905, though part was recovered by one of Přemysl ruling family (895-1306).

Dynastic squabbles, exacerbated by German interference, weakened the power of the dukes, but in 1212 Otakar I (1197-1230) received a hereditary kingship from the Holy Roman Emperor. A period of prosperity developed, aided by the immigration of German miners and merchants who were encouraged with special privileges. Bohemia expanded under the last Přemysl kings: Wenceslas I (1230-53) seized Austria in 1251, though it passed to the Hapsburgs when Otakar II was killed at the battle of Marchfeld in 1278; Wenceslas II was elected king of Poland in 1300. Wenceslas was assassinated in 1306 and was succeeded in 1310 by John of Luxemburg. His son, Charles (1346-78), became Holy Roman Emperor as Charles IV in 1355. Bohemia attained a high degree of prosperity and civilization at this time.

The clerical reform movement with which the name of Jan Hus is associated began as a protest against the corruption and venality of the church, but it had undertones of anti-German Czech nationalism and found support amongst the urban middle classes and lesser rural gentry as well as the urban poor and peasantry. Hus was burned at the stake in 1415, but the Hussite movement continued and repelled efforts to enthrone the Hungarian king Sigismund until 1436. There was some post-war recovery under the enlightened Hussite king, George of Poděbrad (1457-71). After his death the Jagiellonian dynasty succeeded, from 1490 ruling Hungary jointly, until the death of Louis against the Turks at Mohács in 1526. During this period the provincial diet of 3 estates (nobility, gentry, burgesses) acted to enhance the power of the nobility and diminish that of the burgesses.

In 1527 the diet elected the Hapsburg Ferdinand as king. The Hapsburgs gradually encroached upon Czech rights and religious freedom. In 1618 Protestants threw 2 Czech Catholic governors out of a window in Prague Castle. This incident sparked off the Thirty Years War. The estates deposed Emperor Ferdinand II in favour of the Calvinist Frederick V, but the latter's forces were defeated at the battle of the White Mountain on 8 Nov. 1620, and a period of Hapsburg hegemony ensued: The Czech nobility were replaced by German-speaking adventurers; the burgesses lost their rights; burdens were piled on to the peasantry and Catholicism was enforced. Risings were savagely repressed. Some relief came with the ideas of the Enlightenment: Amongst other reforms Emperor Joseph II granted the peasantry freedom of movement in 1781, a precondition for the burgeoning industrial revolution of the next century. At first Czech nationalism could find an outlet only in cultural activities. Uprisings in the revolutionary episode of 1848 were ineffective. The increasingly political aspirations of Czech nationalists were not for the resuscitation of the old Bohemia but for the formation of a new Czechoslovakia, an idea fostered by Thomas Masaryk. Manhood suffrage was granted in 1906, but the chamber of deputies was constantly bypassed by the emperor. The First World War brought a complete estrangement between the Czechs and the Germans, the latter supporting the war effort. Masaryk and other leaders went into exile and in 1916 a Czechoslovak National Council was set up under his chairmanship. In 1918 he secured the support of US president Woodrow Wilson for Czech and Slovak unity (*see* Slovakia). On 18 Oct. 1918 the National Council transformed itself into a provisional government, and was recognized by the Allies.

Austria accepted President Wilson's terms on 27 Oct. 1918, and the next day a republic was proclaimed with Masaryk as president and Edvard Beneš as foreign minister. On 29 Oct. the Slovak leaders declared Slovakia part of the Czechoslovak nation. In drawing up the frontiers of the new state it was impossible to apply strictly the principles of Wilsonian self-determination because of the ethnic mix; other criteria employed were the partial restoration of the historic provinces and the need to establish an economically viable and defensible state. Amongst the minorities were 3·25m. Sudeten Germans. The constitution of 1920 provided for a 2-chamber parliament elected by adult suffrage. The electoral system worked so that all governments were coalitions. Slovakia was granted an assembly in 1927, but the state was basically centralist, and the Slovaks maintained their own parties. Czechoslovakia developed into a prosperous democracy, but was hard hit by the economic depression of the 1930s. Nationalist agitation amongst the Sudeten Germans was fomented by Hitler. Czechoslovakia relied for her defence against the threat of German aggression on her treaty with France of 1925, but France sided with Britain in the Munich agreement of 29 Sept. 1938 which stipulated that all districts with a German population of more than 50% should be ceded to Germany. Beneš resigned the presidency and went into exile. On 14 March 1939 Slovakia declared itself independent under German hegemony and the next day the German army occupied the rest of the country and proclaimed the 'Protectorate of Bohemia-Moravia'. Czechoslovaks who managed to escape joined Beneš to form a government in exile. In Dec. 1943 Beneš signed a 20-year treaty of alliance with the USSR. In March 1945 he went to Moscow to talk to communists who had spent the war there about the nature of the post-war government, which was established in April at Košice in the wake of the Soviet Army. Liberation by the Soviet Army and US Forces was completed by May 1945 and territories taken by Germans, Poles and Hungarians were restored to Czechoslovak sovereignty. Subcarpathian Ruthenia was transferred to the USSR.

Elections were held in May 1946, at which the Communist Party obtained about 38% of the votes.

A coalition government under a Communist Prime Minister, Klement Gottwald, remained in power until 20 Feb. 1948, when 12 of the non-Communist ministers resigned in protest against infiltration of Communists into the police. In Feb. a predominantly Communist government was formed by Gottwald. In May elections resulted in an 89% majority for the government and President Beneš resigned.

In 1968 pressure for liberalization culminated in the overthrow of the Stalinist leader, Antonín Novotný, and his associates. The Communist Party introduced an 'Action Programme' of far-reaching reforms. Soviet pressure to abandon this programme was exerted between May and Aug. 1968, and finally, Warsaw Pact forces occupied Czechoslovakia on 21 Aug. The Czechoslovak government was compelled to accept a policy of 'normalization' (i.e., abandonment of most reforms) and the stationing of Soviet forces.

Mass demonstrations demanding political reform began in Nov. 1989. After the authorities' use of violence to break up a demonstration on 17 Nov., the Communist leader resigned. On 30 Nov. the Federal Assembly abolished the Communist Party's sole right to govern, and a new Government was formed on 3 Dec. The protest movement continued to grow, and on 10 Dec. another government was formed. Gustáv Husák resigned as President, and was replaced by Václav Havel on the unanimous vote of 323 members of the Federal Assembly on 29 Dec.

On 25 Nov. 1992 the Federal Assembly voted the dissolution of the Czech and Slovak Federal Republic. This came into effect at midnight on 31 Dec. 1992. Economic property was divided in accordance with a federal law of 13 Nov. 1992. Real estate became the property of the republic in which it was located. Other property was divided by specially-constituted commissions in the proportion of 2 (Czech Republic) to 1 (Slovakia) on the basis of population size. Military materiel was divided on the 2:1 principle. Regular military personnel were invited to choose which armed force they would serve in.

TERRITORY AND POPULATION. The Czech Republic is bounded in the west by Germany, north by Poland, east by Slovakia and south by Austria. Minor exchanges of territory to straighten their mutual border were agreed between the Czech Republic and Slovakia on 4 Jan. 1996, but the Czech parliament refused to ratify them on 24 April 1996. Its area is 78,864 sq. km. At the 1991 census the population was 10,302,215. 1996 estimate, 10,331,206 (51·4% female; 74·7% urban); density, 131 per sq. km. Vital statistics rates (per 1,000 population), 1995: Birth, 9·3; death, 11·4; marriage, 5·3; divorce, 3; infant mortality, (per 1,000 live births), 7·7. Expectation of life, 1995: Males, 64·8 years; females, 74·2 years.

There are 8 administrative regions *(Kraj)*, one of which is the capital, Prague (Praha).

Region	Chief city	Area in sq. km	Population 1991 census
Prague	—	496	1,212,010
Středočeský	Prague (Praha)	11,038	1,112,374
Jihočeský	České Budějovice	11,345	697,334
Západočeský	Plzeň (Pilsen)	10,873	860,311
Severočeský	Ustí nad Labem	7,777	1,173,681
Východočeský	Hradec Králové	11,240	1,232,646
Jihomoravský	Brno	15,027	2,048,867
Severomoravský	Ostrava	11,068	1,961,508

The population of the principal towns in 1993 (in 1,000):

Prague (Praha)	1,217	Liberec	159	Kladno	149
Brno	390	Hradec Králové	162	Most	120
Ostrava	327	České Budějovice	175	Karviná	286
Plzeň	172	Pardubice	163	Frýdek-Místek	229
Olomouc	225	Havírov	92		
Ustí nad Labem	118	Zlín	198		

At the 1991 census 81·2% of the population was Czech, 13·2% Moravian and 3·1% Slovak. There were also (in 1,000): Poles, 59; Germans, 48; Silesians, 44; Roma (Gypsies), 34; Hungarians, 21.

The official language is Czech.

CLIMATE. A humid continental climate, with warm summers and cold winters. Precipitation is generally greater in summer, with thunderstorms. Autumn, with dry, clear weather and spring, which is damp, are each of short duration. Prague. Jan. 29·5°F (−1·5°C), July 67°F (19·4°C). Annual rainfall 19·3" (483mm). Brno. Jan. 31°F (−0·6°C), July 67°F (19·4°C). Annual rainfall 21" (525mm).

CONSTITUTION AND GOVERNMENT. The Constitution of 1 Jan. 1993 provides for a parliament comprising a 200-member *House of Representatives*, elected for 4-year terms by proportional representation, and an 81-member *Senate* elected for 6-year terms in single-member districts, 27 senators being elected every 2 years. The main function of the Senate is to scrutinise proposed legislation. Senators must be at least 40 years of age, and are elected on a first-past-the-post basis, with a run-off in constituencies where no candidate wins more than half the votes cast. For the House of Representatives there is a 5% threshold; votes for parties failing to surmount this are redistributed on the basis of results in each of the 8 electoral districts.

There is a *Constitutional Court* at Brno whose 15 members are nominated by the President and approved by the Senate for 10-year terms.

The *President* of the Republic is elected for a 5-year term by both chambers of parliament. He or she must be at least 40 years of age. The President names the Prime Minister at the suggestion of the Speaker.

The *President* of the Republic is Václav Havel, elected by parliament on 26 Jan. 1993 against 2 opponents and sworn in on 2 Feb., re-elected 20 Jan. 1998.

Elections for the House of Representatives were held on 31 May–1 June 1996. The electorate was 8m.; turn-out was 75%. The Civic Democratic Party (ODS) won 68 seats with 29·62% of votes cast (72 with 29·73% in 1992); the Social Democratic Party (ČSSD), 61 with 26·44% (22 with 6·53%); the Communist Party (KSCM), 22 with 10·33% (10 with 14·05%); the Christian Democratic Union-Czech People's Party coalition (KDU/ČSL), 18 with 8·08% (24 with 6·28%); the Republican Party (SPR/RSC), 18 with 8·01% (5 with 5·98%); the Civic Democratic Alliance (ODA), 13 with 6·36% (16 with 5·93%).

Elections for the Senate were held on 15–16 Nov. and 22–23 Nov. 1996. The electorate was 7·9m.; turn-out was 35% and 30·6%. The ODS gained 32 seats; ČSSD, 25; KDU/ČSL, 13; ODA, 7; KSCM, 2; Democratic Union, 1; ind, 1.

An ODS-KDU/ČSL-ODA coalition government was formed in July 1996 which comprised in March 1998:

Prime Minister: Josef Tošovský.
Minister of Foreign Affairs: Jaroslav Šedivý. *Finance:* Ivan Pilip (ODS). *Agriculture:* Josef Lux (KDU/ČSL). *Justice:* Vlasta Parkanová. *Interior:* Cyril Svoboda (KDU/ČSL). *Industry and Trade:* Karel Kühnl (ODA). *Environment:* Jiři Skalický (ODA). *Health:* Zuzana Roithová. *Culture:* Martin Stropnický. *Labour and Social Welfare:* Stanislav Volák (ODS). *Education, Youth and Sport:* Jan Sokol. *Defence:* Michal Lobkowicz (ODS). *Transport and Communications:* Petr Moos. *Development of Regions, Towns and Municipalities:* Jan Černý (ODS).

Local Government. At elections on 18–19 Nov. 1994 turn-out was 60%. The Civic Democratic Party gained 25·4% of votes cast, ind 17%, the Party of Democratic Left 16·6%, the Christian Democratic Party 10·6% and the Social Democratic Party 8·1%. Local authorities have the power to raise local taxes and have responsibility for roads, schools, utilities and public health.

DEFENCE. Conscription is for 12 months.

Army. The Army comprises 2 Corps HQ, and 7 mechanized, 2 artillery and 2 engineer brigades. Equipment includes 469 T 54/-55 and 542 T-72M main battle tanks. Strength (1997) 27,000 (15,400 conscripts). There are also paramilitary Border Guards (4,000 strong) and Internal Security Forces (1,600).

Air Force. The Air Force has a strength of some 17,000 (including air defence troops) and operates a regiment of MiG-21s and MiG-23s. The Tactical Air Corps has a regiment of L-39, Su-22 and Su-25 strike aircraft, and a helicopter regiment with Mi-24 armed helicopters.

INTERNATIONAL RELATIONS. In 1974 the German Federal Republic and the then Czechoslovakia annulled the Munich agreement of 1938. On 14 Feb. 1997 the Czech parliament ratified a declaration of German-Czech reconciliation, with particular reference to the Sudeten German problems.

Membership. The Czech Republic is a member of the UN, the OECD, CEFTA, the Central European Initiative, and the NATO Partnership for Peace, and is an associate member of the EU and an associate partner of the WEU. An application to join the EU was made in Jan. 1996.

ECONOMY

Policy. By the end of 1992 assets valued at Kč. 470,000m. had been privatized. 21,400 small businesses were auctioned off in 1992, and some 900 enterprises privatized through the sale of vouchers. A second stage of privatization, affecting 770 enterprises, took place by vouchers on sale to all citizens in Oct.–Nov. 1993. This stage came to an end in Dec. 1994, by which time 80% of the Czech Republic's assets were in private hands. The privatization of shares in 53 large companies was announced in 1995, the state to retain some of these shares. The privatization of the remaining minor state companies is scheduled for 1997.

Performance. In 1997 real GDP growth was 1·0%, coompared to 4·5% in 1996.

Budget. Revenue and expenditure in Kč m.:

	1993	1994	1995	1996
Revenue	341,376	370,503	414,330	460,950
Expenditure	326,965	362,015	410,669	450,938

Expenditure by category, 1996: Defence, 30,604; education, 64,964; health, 95,416; social security and welfare, 139,433.

Currency. The unit of currency is the *koruna* (CEK) or crown of 100 *haler*, introduced on 8 Feb. 1993 at parity with the former Czechoslovakian koruna. Notes in circulation: Kč. 20, 50, 100, 500, 1,000 and 5,000. Coin: 5, 10, 20, 50 *halers*, and Kč. 1, 2, 5, 10, 20, 50. Gold reserves were 105 tonnes in 1992. Exchange reserves were US$15,000m. in Dec. 1996. Inflation was 8·8% in 1996. The koruna became convertible on 1 Oct. 1995. In May 1997 the koruna was devalued 10% and allowed to float.

Banking and Finance. The central bank and bank of issue is the Czech National Bank (*Governor*, Josef Tosovský), which also acts as banking supervisor and regulator. Decentralization of the banking system began in 1991, and private banks began to operate. The Commercial Bank and Investment Bank are privatized nationwide networks with a significant government holding. Specialized banks include the Czech Savings Bank and the Czech Commercial Bank (for foreign trade payments). Private banks tend to be on a regional basis, many of them agricultural banks. There are also subsidiaries of foreign banks, joint ventures with foreign participation and branches and representative offices of foreign banks. There were 59 banks in 1995. In Nov. 1997 the cabinet agreed to sell off large stakes in 3 major state-held banks.

Savings deposits were Kč. 289,163m. in 1993.

A stock exchange was founded in Prague in 1992.

Weights and Measures. The metric system is in force.

ENERGY AND NATURAL RESOURCES

Electricity. Output, 1993, 58,882 MWh. In 1993 76% of electricity was produced by thermal power stations using brown coal, 21% was nuclear (1 station) and the rest was hydro-electric. 29·2% of output was nuclear-generated in 1993.

Minerals. There are hard coal and lignite reserves (chief fields: Most, Chomutov, Kladno, Ostrava and Sokolov). Gold deposits were found near Prague in 1985.

Agriculture. In 1993 there were 4,282,000 ha of agricultural land (3,173,000 ha arable). 31·1% of agricultural land was state-owned, 61% co-operative, 4·4% private and 2·2% public.

A law of May 1991 returned land seized by the Communist regime to its original owners, to a maximum of 150 ha of arable to a single owner.

Livestock, 1994: Cattle, 2·16m. (including 0·83m. milch cows); pigs, 4·07m.; sheep, 196,000; poultry, 24·97m. In 1993 production of meat was 1,140,711 tonnes (live weight); milk, 3,350m. litres; 3,100m. eggs.

Forestry. In 1994 forests covered 2,628,628 ha. 12,910,000 cu. metres of timber were cut in 1994.

Fisheries. Ponds created for fish-farming number 21,800 and cover about 101,311 acres, the largest of them being 2 lakes in southern Bohemia.

INDUSTRY. In 1996 there were 1,123,804 small private businesses (of which 15,072 were incorporated), 117,040 companies (of which 8,002 were joint-stock companies), 6,332 co-operatives and 2,185 state enterprises. Output, 1993, included: Steel, 6·76m. tonnes; cement, 5·4m. tonnes; motor cars, 173,000.

Labour. Average employment in 1995 was 3,125,000. In 1993, 1·71m. persons were employed in mining, manufacture, electricity, gas and water; 609,000 in wholesale and retail trade and repairs; 453,000 in construction; 331,000 in agriculture; 263,000 in health and social work; and 65,000 in financial services. In March 1996, 159,000 persons were registered unemployed (3% of the economically active population). The average monthly wage was Kc. 8,500 in 1996. Pay increases are regulated in firms where wages grow faster than production. Fines are levied if wages rise by more than 15% over 4 years.

FOREIGN ECONOMIC RELATIONS. A memorandum envisaging a customs union and close economic co-operation was signed with Slovakia in Oct. 1992. An agreement of Dec. 1992 with Hungary, Poland and Slovakia abolished tariffs on raw materials and goods where exports do not compete directly with locally-produced items, and envisaged tariff reductions on agricultural and industrial goods in 1995–97.

Foreign debt was US$16,549m. at the beginning of 1996. There were 10,599 joint ventures in June 1993.

Commerce. Trade, 1995 (in US$1m.): Imports, 25,265 (of which 37·1% were machinery and transport equipment); exports, 21,650 (of which 32·2% were manufactures). Main export markets, 1995: Germany, 31·8%; Slovakia, 16·2%; Austria, 6·5%; Poland, 5·4%; Italy, 4%. Main import suppliers: Germany, 25·8%; Slovakia, 13·1%; Russia, 8·9% Austria, 6·9%; Italy 5·8%.

Tourism. There were 10·9m. forcign tourists in 1996. Foreign currency income from tourism in 1996 was US$4,100m. (65% of GDP).

COMMUNICATIONS

Roads. In 1995 there were 293 km of motorways. In 1995, passenger transport totalled 16,777m. passenger-km and freight, 8,713m. tonne-km.

Railways. In 1994 Czech State Railways had a route length of 9,316 km (1,435 mm gauge), of which 2,640 km were electrified. In 1994, 228·7m. passengers and 110·6m. tonnes of freight were carried. There is a metro (44 km) and tram/light rail system (496 km) in Prague, and tram/light rail networks in Brno, Liberec, Most, Olomouc, Ostrava, Plzen and Teplice-Trecianské.

Civil Aviation. The main airports are: Prague (Ruzyne), Brno (Cernovice) and Olomouc (Holice). The national carrier is Czech Airlines, 68·1% statc-owned, which in 1995 operated 2 A310-300s, 2 B-737-400s, 5 B-737-500s and 13 ex-Soviet aircraft. Services are also provided by Adria, Aeroflot, Air Algérie, Air France, Air Ukraine, Alitalia, Austrian Airlines, Balkan, British Airways, British Midland, Croatia Airlines, Crossair, Delta, El Al, Eurowings, Finnair, KLM, Libyan Airlines, Lithuanian Airlines, LOT, Lufthansa, Luxair, Malév, Orbi, Sabena, SAS, Swissair, Syrian Airlines and Tunis Air. 1·36m. passengers were transported by air in 1993.

Shipping. 4·9m. tonnes of freight were carried by inland waterways in 1993.

Telecommunications. In 1993 there were 2,334,000 main telephone lines. Broadcasting is the responsibility of the independent Board for Radio and Television. Czech Television (CTV; colour by SECAM) and Czech Radio are public corporations. The former federal Czechoslovakian broadcasting stations in the Czech Republic have become a second service. There is also a nationwide private TV company and 2 radio companies as well as local private stations.

Cinemas. In 1993, there were 1,900 screens. Attendance was 21,898,000 in 1993. 12 full-length films were made in 1994.

Press. There were 75 national and regional daily newspapers in 1995.

SOCIAL INSTITUTIONS

Justice. The post-Communist judicial system was established by a law of July 1991. This provides for a unified system of 4 types of court: civil, criminal, commercial and administrative. Commercial courts arbitrate in disputes arising from business activities. Administrative courts examine the legality of the decisions of state institutions when appealed by citizens. In addition, there are military courts which operate under the jurisdiction of the Ministry of Defence. There is a Supreme Court, and a hierarchy of courts under the Ministry of Justice at republic, region and district level. District courts are courts of first instance. Cases are usually decided by senates comprising a judge and 2 associate judges, though occasionally by a single judge. (Associate judges are citizens in good standing over the age of 25 who are elected for 4-year terms). Regional courts are courts of first instance in more serious cases and also courts of appeal for district courts. Cases are usually decided by a senate of 2 judges and 3 associate judges, although again occasionally by a single judge. There is also a Supreme Administrative Court. The Supreme Court interprets law as a guide to other courts and functions also as a court of appeal. Decisions are made by senates of 3 judges. Judges are appointed for life by the National Council.

There is no death penalty. In 1993, 398,505 crimes were reported, of which 31·7% were solved.

Religion. In 1991, 18 churches were registered. At a census in March 1991, church membership was: Roman Catholic, 1,038,720; Evangelical Church of the Czech Brethren, 182,693; Hussites, 173,232.

Miloslav Vlk (b. 1932) was installed as archbishop of Prague and primate of Czechoslovakia in 1991. The national Czech church, created in 1918, took the name 'Hussite' in 1972. In 1991 it had a patriarch, 5 bishops, 300 pastors (40% women) and some 0·8m. adherents. In 1991 there were also some 0·5m. adherents of a dozen Protestant churches, the largest being the Evangelical, which unites Calvinists and Lutherans and numbered about 0·2m.

Education. Elementary education up to age 15 is compulsory. 52% of children continue their education in vocational schools and 48% move on to secondary schools.

In 1995-96 there were 9 universities, 4 technical universities, 1 university for economics, 1 for agriculture, 1 for agriculture and forestry, 1 for veterinary and pharmaceutical sciences and 1 for chemical technology. There were also 4 academies (for performing arts, music and dramatic arts, fine arts and arts, architecture and industrial design) and a higher school of teacher training. Together, these 23 higher education institutions had 139,774 students in 1995-96 and 12,890 teaching staff in 1995.

DIPLOMATIC REPRESENTATIVES

Of the Czech Republic in Great Britain (26-30 Kensington Palace Gdns., London, W8 4QY)
Ambassador: Pavel Seifter.

Of Great Britain in the Czech Republic (Thunovská 14, 11800 Prague 1)
Ambassador: David S. Broucher.

Of the Czech Republic in the USA (3900 Linnean Ave., NW, Washington, D.C., 20008)
Ambassador: Alexander Vondra.

Of the USA in the Czech Republic (Trziste 15 12548, Prague)
Ambassador: Jennone Walker.

Of the Czech Republic to the United Nations
Ambassador: Vladimir Galuška.

Of the Czech Republic to the European Union
Ambassador: Josef Kreuter.

Further Reading

Czech Statistical Office. *Statistical Yearbook of the Czech Republic.*
Havel, V., *Disturbing the Peace.* London, 1990.—*Living in Truth: Twenty-Two Essays.* London, 1990.—*Summer Meditations.* London, 1992
Hermann, A. H., *A History of the Czechs.* London, 1975
Kalvoda, J., *The Genesis of Czechoslovakia.* New York, 1986
Leff, C. S., *National Conflict in Czechoslovakia: The Making and Remaking of a State, 1918–1987.* Princeton, 1988
Short, D., *Czechoslovakia.* [Bibliography] Oxford and Santa Barbara, 1986
Simmons, M., *The Reluctant President: a Political Life of Vaclav Havel.* London, 1992

National statistical office: Czech Statistical Office, Sokolovská 142, 186 04 Prague 8.
Website: http://infox.eunet.cz/csu/csu_e.html

DENMARK

Kongeriget Danmark

(Kingdom of Denmark)

Capital: Copenhagen
Population: 5·3m.
GDP per head: (PPP$) 21,431
HDI/world rank: 0·927/18

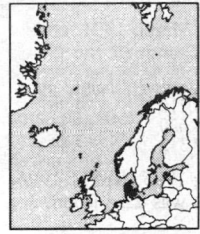

KEY HISTORICAL EVENTS. Denmark was first organized as a unified state in the 10th century, with a Christian monarchy. King Canute was also King of England and King of Norway in the 11th century, but the union of the three countries was soon dissolved. In 1363 a royal marriage united Denmark and Norway and these two countries joined with Sweden in 1397. Sweden separated herself in 1523 and thereafter was in conflict with Denmark until the Peace with Copenhagen in 1660. Denmark acquired approximately its present boundaries in 1815 at the end of the Napoleonic Wars. Having supported Napoleon, it was forced to cede Norway to Sweden by the Treaty of Kiel (1814); it lost its north German territory to Prussia 1864-66 and only in 1920 was North Schleswig returned to Denmark.

After 1815 there was much pressure for a more liberal form of government in preference to the traditional absolute monarchy and on 5 June 1849 the royal assent was given a new constitution. A parliament, the *Rigsdag*, was created, divided into an upper house, the *Landsting*, and a lower house, the *Folketing*. The franchise was granted to men over 30 years old.

During the First World War (1914-1918) Denmark remained neutral, and in 1939, at the commencement of the Second World War it again declared its neutrality. On this occasion, however, it was soon overwhelmed by the German forces which invaded on 9 April 1940. Throughout the war there was a considerable Danish resistance movement to which the Germans responded by imposing direct rule.

Immediately after the Second World War Denmark recognized the independence of Iceland. Home rule was granted to the Faroes in 1948 and to Greenland in 1979.

The constitution was amended in 1953 and this allowed for a female succession to the throne, abolished the *Landsting* (the upper house) and extended the franchise to all men and women over 18 years of age. Denmark joined NATO in 1949, took the lead in the formation of the consultative Nordic Council in 1953 and joined the EEC after a referendum held in 1972.

TERRITORY AND POPULATION. Denmark is bounded in the west by the North Sea, north-west and north by the Skagerrak and Kattegat straits (separating it from Norway and Sweden) and south by Germany.

Administrative divisions		Area (sq. km) 1997	Population Census 1970	Population 1 Jan. 1997	Population per sq. km
København (Copenhagen)	(city)	88	622,773	483,658	5,480·5
Frederiksberg	(borough)	9	101,874	89,230	1,0174·5
Københavns	(county)	526	615,343	609,123	1,158·5
Frederiksborg	,,	1,347	259,442	356,854	264·8
Roskilde	,,	891	153,199	226,683	254·3
Vestsjælland	,,	2,984	259,057	290,793	97·5
Storstrøm	,,	3,398	252,363	257,776	75·9
Bornholm	,,	588	47,239	45,018	76·5
Fyn	,,	3,486	432,699	471,422	135·2
Sønderjylland	,,	3,938	238,062	253,639	64·4
Ribe	,,	3,132	197,843	223,335	71·3
Vejle	,,	2,997	306,263	342,597	114·3
Ringkøbing	,,	4,853	241,327	271,483	55·9
Århus	,,	4,561	533,190	628,725	137·9
Viborg	,,	4,122	220,734	232,630	56·4
Nordjylland	,,	6,173	456,171	492,155	79·7
Total		43,094	4,937,579	5,275,121	122·4

In 1996, 94·2% of the inhabitants were born in Denmark, including the Faroe Islands and Greenland.

On 1 Jan. 1997 the population of the capital, Copenhagen (comprising Copenhagen, Frederiksberg and Gentofte municipalities), was 639,874 (including suburbs, 1,372,768); Århus, 215,045; Odense, 145,354; Aalborg, 119,118; Esbjerg, 73,333; Randers, 56,057; Kolding, 52,792; Horsens, 48,222; Vejle, 47,678; Helsingør, 44,485.

Vital statistics for calendar years:

	Live births	Still births	Marriages	Divorces	Deaths	Emigration	Immigration
1994	69,666	309	35,321	13,709	61,099	34,710	44,961
1995	69,771	318	34,736	12,976	63,127	34,630	63,187
1996	67,638	324	35,953	12,776	61,085	37,312	54,445

Single-parent births: 1992, 46·4%; 1993, 46·8%; 1994, 46·9%: 1995, 46·5%: 1996, 46·3%. Over 1990–95 the suicide rate (per 100,000 population) was 22·4 (men, 30; women, 15·1).

CLIMATE. The climate is much modified by marine influences, and the effect of the Gulf Stream, to give winters that may be both cold or mild and often cloudy. Summers may be warm and sunny or chilly and rainy. In general, the east is drier than the west. Long periods of calm weather are exceptional and windy conditions are common. Copenhagen. Jan. 33°F (0·5°C), July 63°F (17°C). Annual rainfall 650 mm. Esbjerg. Jan. 33°F (0·5°C), July 61°F (16°C). Annual rainfall 800 mm. 10% of rainfall precipitates as snow.

ROYAL HOUSE. The reigning Queen is **Margrethe II,** b. 16 April 1940; married 10 June 1967 to Prince Henrik, b. Count de Monpezat. She succeeded to the throne on the death of her father, King Frederik IX, on 14 Jan. 1972; *offspring:* Crown Prince Frederik, b. 26 May 1968; Prince Joachim, b. 7 June 1969, married 18 Nov. 1995 Alexandra Manley (b. 30 June 1964).

Mother of the Queen: Queen Ingrid, b. Princess of Sweden, 28 March 1910.

Sisters of the Queen: Princess Benedikte, b. 29 April 1944 (married 3 Feb. 1968 to Prince Richard of Sayn-Wittgenstein-Berleburg); Princess Anne-Marie, b. 30 Aug. 1946 (married 18 Sept. 1964 to King Constantine of Greece).

The crown was elective from the earliest times but became hereditary by right in 1660. The direct male line of the house of Oldenburg became extinct with King Frederik VII on 15 Nov. 1863. In view of the death of the king, without direct heirs, the Great Powers signed a treaty at London on 8 May 1852, by the terms of which the succession to the crown was made over to Prince Christian of Schleswig-Holstein-Sonderburg-Glücksburg, and to the direct male descendants of his union with the Princess Louise of Hesse-Cassel. This became law on 31 July 1853. Linked to the constitution of 5 June 1953, a new law of succession, dated 27 March 1953, has come into force, which restricts the right of succession to the descendants of King Christian X and Queen Alexandrine, and admits the sovereign's daughters to the line of succession, ranking after the sovereign's sons.

The Queen receives a tax-free annual sum of 43·5m. kroner from the state (1997).

CONSTITUTION AND GOVERNMENT. The present constitution is founded upon the Basic Law of 5 June 1953. The legislative power lies with the Queen and the *Folketing* (parliament) jointly. The executive power is vested in the monarch, who exercises authority through the ministers. The judicial power is with the courts. The monarch must be a member of the Evangelical-Lutheran Church, the official Church of the State and may not assume major international obligations without the consent of the Folketing. The Folketing consists of one chamber. All men and women of Danish nationality of more than 18 years of age and permanently resident in Denmark possess the franchise and are eligible for election to the Folketing, which is at present composed of 179 members; 135 members are elected by the method of proportional representation in 17 constituencies. In order to attain an equal representation of the different parties, 40 additional seats are divided among such parties which have not obtained sufficient returns at the constituency elections. 2 members are elected for the Faroe Islands and 2 for Greenland. The term of the legislature is 4 years, but a general election may be called at any time. The Folketing convenes every year on the first Tuesday in October. Besides its legislative functions, it appoints every 6 years judges who, together with the ordinary members of the Supreme Court, form the *Rigsret*, a tribunal which can alone try parliamentary impeachments.

At the elections on 21 Sept. 1994 the electorate was 3,988,787; turn-out was 84%. The Social Democratic Party (SD) won 62 seats with 34·6% of votes cast (69 with 37·4% in 1990); the Liberal Party, 42 with 23·3% (29 with 15·8%); the Conservative Party, 27 with 15% (30 with 16%); the Socialist Party, 13 with 7·3% (15 with 8·3%); the Progress Party, 11 with 6·4% (12 with 6·4%); the Social Liberal Party (SL; formerly Radical Liberal Party), 8 with 4·6% (7 with 3·5%); the Red-Green Alliance, 6 with 3·1%; the Centre Democrats (CD), 5 with 2·8% (9 with 5·1%); ind, 1 with 1%.

Following the 1994 elections a coalition government of the Social Democratic (S), Social Liberal (RV) and Centre Democratic (CD) Parties took office on 21 Sept. 1994, consisting in March 1998 of:

Prime Minister: Poul Nyrup Rasmussen (b. 1943; S). *Minister of Economic Affairs and Minister for Nordic Co-operation:* Marianne Jelved (RV). *Business and Industry:* Jan Trøjborg (S). *Finance:* Mogens Lykketoft (S). *Foreign Affairs:* Niels Helveg Petersen (RV). *Justice:* Frank Jensen (S). *Environment and Energy:* Svend Auken (S). *Education and Ecclesiastical Affairs:* Ole Vig Jensen (RV). *Development Co-operation:* Poul Nielson (S). *Interior:* Thorkild Simonsen (S). *Health.* Birte Weiss (S). *Labour:* Jytte Andersen (S). *Taxation:* Carsten Koch (S). *Defence:* Hans Haekkerup (S). *Culture:* Ebbe Lundgaard (RV). *Transport:* Bjørn Westh (S) *Social Affairs:* Karen Jespersen (S). *Housing and Building:* Ole Løvig Simonsen (S). *Research:* Jytte Hilden (S). *Food, Agriculture and Fisheries:* Henrik Dam Kristensen (S).

National anthem: 'Kong Kristian stod ved højen mast' ('King Christian stood by the lofty mast'); words by J. Ewald, tune by J. E. Hartmann.

European Parliament. Denmark has 16 representatives. At the June 1994 elections turn-out was 52·9%. The Liberal Party won 4 seats with 19% of votes cast (group in European Parliament: Liberal, Democratic and Reformist Group); the Conservative Party, 3 with 17·7% (Popular European Party); the SD, 3 with 15·8% (European Socialist Party); the June Movement, 2 with 15·2% (Europe of Nations); the People's Anti-EU Movement, 2 with 10·3% (Europe of Nations); the Socialist People's Party, 1 with 8·6% (Greens); the Radical Liberal Party, 1 with 8·5% (Liberal, Democratic and Reformist Group).

Local Government. For administrative purposes Denmark is divided into 275 communes; each of them has a district council of between 7 and 31 members, headed by an elected mayor. The city of Copenhagen forms a district by itself and is governed by a city council of 55 members, elected every 4 years, and an executive, consisting of the chief burgomaster and 6 burgomasters, appointed by the city council for 4 years. There are 14 counties, each of which is administered by a county council of between 13 and 31 members, headed by an elected mayor. All councils are elected directly by universal suffrage and proportional representation for 4-year terms. There are also about 2,100 parishes. Government at this level is administered by parish councils elected for 4 years.

The counties and Copenhagen are superintended by the Ministry of Interior Affairs. The municipalities are superintended by 14 local supervision committees, headed by a state county prefect who is a civil servant appointed by the Queen.

County and municipal elections were held on 16 Nov. 1993. The Social Democrats won 34·9% of votes cast, the Liberals 28·8% (county elections).

DEFENCE. The military defence is organized in accordance with the Defence Act of December 1993. The overall organization of the Danish Armed Forces comprises the Headquarter's Chief of Defence, the Army, the Navy, the Air Force and inter-service authorities and institutions. To this should be added the Home Guard, which is an indispensable part of Danish military defence. The Home Guard is based on the Home Guard Act of May 1982 as amended in December 1993.

In accordance with the Defence Act, the Chief of Defence is in full command of the three services: The Army, the Navy and the Air Force. The Chief of Defence and the Defence Staff constitute the Headquarter's Chief of Defence.

The Constitution of 1849 states that it is the duty of every fit man to contribute to the national defence. This provision is still in force. Selection of conscripts takes place at the age of 18–19 years, and the conscripts are normally called up for service $1/2$–$1 1/2$ years later. Conscripts may subsequently be recalled for refresher training or musters. The initial training period for conscripts is between 4 and 12 months.

Army. The Army is comprised of field army formations and the local defence forces. The peacetime strength of the army numbers 19,000 (including about 3,900 civilians and about 6,900 conscripts). The wartime strength is about 59,000. The Army is organized in a division and in brigades and regimental combat groups, headquarter units and support units. There are 4 mechanized infantry brigades including the Danish Reaction Brigade. The field army is equipped with approx. 350 battle tanks, about 530 armoured personnel carriers and 160 specialized light armoured vehicles as well as artillery including 76 self-propelled howitzers and one battery Multiple Launch Rocket System (MRLS). The Army has 12 AS-550 Fennec anti-armour helicopters and 12 Hughes 500 helicopters for observation and liaison. The local defence units are organized in infantry battalions and artillery units as well as a number of support units.

Navy. The Navy, some 6,000 strong (including 1,800 civilians and 500 conscripts) in 1997, is supported by 5,250 reservists. The wartime strength is 9,500. The fleet comprises 5 coastal submarines, 3 corvettes, 5 ocean patrol vessels with Lynx helicopters, 14 Standard Flex 300 multi-role ships, 10 fast missile patrol ships, 3 patrol cutters, 9 patrol boats, 4 coastal minelayers, 2 inshore minelayers and 1 coastal minesweeper. Furthermore, the fleet comprises 2 light auxiliary oilers, the Royal Yacht, and a number of smaller auxiliaries. The Naval Air Arm comprises 8 Lynx helicopters, and the Naval Home Guard operates 35 inshore patrol craft.

Coastal Defence forces comprise 1 permanent fortress armed with 150 mm guns and 2 mobile coastal batteries with Harpoon missiles.

Additionally the Navy man and control 4 icebreakers, 6 environment control vessels and 6 survey vessels.

The 2 main Naval bases are at Frederikshavn and Korsoer.

Air Force. The Air Force, in 1997, comprised some 7,900 (including 2,400 civilians and 400 conscripts). The wartime strength force is about 15,000.

The flying squadrons comprise 4 all-weather air-defence squadrons with a total of 69 F-16s. All squadrons have an air-defence and a fighter-bomber role. One squadron has an additional photo-reconnaissance role. The operational units also comprise 8 HAWK surface-to-air missile squadrons.

In addition the Air Force has a number of supplementary units, including 1 transport squadron (3 C-130 Hercules and 2 Gulfstream III), 1 helicopter search and rescue squadron (8 S-61As), and a control and warning system. T-17 Supporter aircraft are used for initial pilot training, and pilots continue training at EURO-NATO Joint Jet Pilot Training in the USA.

Home Guard. The overall Home Guard organization comprises the Home Guard Command, the Army Home Guard, the Navy Home Guard, the Air Force Home Guard and the Service Corps.

The personnel of the Home Guard is recruited on a voluntary basis. The personnel establishment of the Home Guard was in 1997 about 65,000 persons (51,000 in the Army Home Guard, 4,400 in the Navy Home Guard, 7,800 in the Air Force Home Guard and 1,800 in the Service Corps.).

INTERNATIONAL RELATIONS. In a referendum in June 1992 the electorate voted against ratifying the Maastricht Treaty for closer political union within the EU.

Turn-out was 82%. 50·7% of votes were against ratification, 49·3% in favour. However, a second referendum on 18 May 1993 reversed this result, with 56·8% of votes cast in favour of ratification and 43·2% against. Turn-out was 86·2%.

Membership. Denmark is a member of the UN, NATO, OECD, the EU, Council of Europe and the Nordic Council. On 19 Dec. 1996 Denmark acceded to the Schengen Accord of June 1990 which abolishes border controls between Denmark and Austria, Belgium, Finland, France, Germany, Greece, Iceland, Italy, Luxembourg, the Netherlands, Norway, Portugal, Spain and Sweden.

ECONOMY

Budget. The following shows the actual revenue and expenditure as shown in central government accounts for the calendar years 1995 and 1996, the approved budget figures for 1997 and the budget for 1998 (in 1,000 kroner):

	1995	1996	1997	1998
Revenue	355,220,200	363,334,500	379,771,800	397,122,900
Expenditure	382,790,500	379,709,500	379,804,200	385,202,200

Receipts and expenditures of special government funds and expenditures on public works are included.

The 1998 budget envisaged revenue of 118,960m. kroner from income and property taxes and 187,060m. from consumer taxes.

The central government debt on 31 Dec. 1996 amounted to 664,128m. kroner. VAT is 25%.

Currency. The monetary unit is the *Danish krone* (DKK) of 100 øre. There are notes of 1,000, 500, 100 and 50 kroner, and coins of 20, 10, 5 and 1 krone and 50 and 25 øre.

Banking and Finance. On 31 Dec. 1996 the accounts of the National Bank (*Governor*, Bodil Nyboe) balanced at 179,536m. kroner. The assets included official net foreign reserves of 85,219m. kroner. The liabilities included notes and coin of 36,613m. kroner. On 31 Dec. 1996 there were 117 commercial banks and savings banks, with deposits of 620,185m. kroner. On 31 Dec. 1996 the money supply was 439,800m. kroner.

There is a stock exchange in Copenhagen.

ENERGY AND NATURAL RESOURCES

Electricity. Production (1996), 45,387m. kWh. In 1996 some 3,500 wind turbines produced 4% of output.

Oil and Gas. Oil production was (1996) 10·3m. tonnes. Production of natural gas was (1996) 6·3m. cu. metres.

Agriculture. Land ownership is widely distributed. In June 1995 there were 64,426 holdings with at least 5 ha of agricultural area (or at least a production equivalent to that from 5 ha of barley). There were 12,118 small holdings (with less than 10 ha), 34,642 medium-sized holdings (10–50 ha) and 18,205 holdings with more than 50 ha.

There were 23,257 agricultural workers in 1996.

In 1996 the cultivated area was (in 1,000 ha): Grain, 1,545; pulses, 69; root crops, 154; other crops, 194; green fodder and grass, 563; set aside, 191; total cultivated area, 2716.

Chief crops	1993	Area (1,000 ha) 1994	1995	1996	Production (in 1,000 tonnes) 1993	1994	1995	1996
Wheat	619	572	607	681	4,334	3,725	4,599	4,758
Rye	78	88	96	72	356	423	500	343
Barley	709	700	714	738	3,369	3,446	3,898	3,953
Oats1	31	44	31	32	138	206	158	164
Potatoes	47	39	42	43	1,741	1,359	1,441	1,617
Other root crops	137	126	121	111	8,490	7,005	6,320	5,656

[1] Including mixed grain.

Livestock, 1996 (in 1,000): Horses, 20; cattle, 2,093; pigs, 10,842; poultry, 19,224.
Production (in 1,000 tonnes) in 1996: Milk, 4,495; butter, 57; cheese, 299; beef, 198; pork and bacon, 1,592; eggs, 88.

In 1996 tractors numbered 139,619 and combine harvesters, 28,609.

Fisheries. The total value of the fish caught was (in 1m. kroner): 1950, 156; 1955, 252; 1960, 376; 1965, 650; 1970, 854; 1975, 1,442; 1980, 2,888; 1985, 3,542; 1990, 3,439; 1991, 3,681; 1992, 3,398; 1993, 2,566; 1994, 2,835; 1995, 2,939; 1996, 2,960 (provisional figures).

INDUSTRY. The following table is of gross factor income (in 1m. kroner):

	1994*	1995*	1996*
Agriculture, fishing and quarrying	34,977	38,854	41,574
Agriculture, horticulture and forestry	25,223	28,857	29,190
Fishing	1,688	1,993	2,479
Mining and quarrying	8,067	8,004	10,905

* Provisional or estimated figures

In the following table 'number of employees' refers to 24,024 local activity units including single-proprietor units (Nov. 1995):

Branch of industry	Number of employees
Food, beverages and tobacco	93,105
Textiles, wearing apparel, leather	22,428
Wood and wood products	16,281
Paper products	62,960
Refined petroleum products	991
Chemicals and man-made fibres	28,069
Rubber and plastic products	21,365
Non-metallic mineral products	20,938
Basic metals	58,010
Machinery and equipment	76,294
Electrical and optical equipment	46,239
Transport equipment	23,066
Furniture, other manufactures	35,679
Total manufacturing	505,425

Labour. In 1996, 5% of the working population lived on agriculture, forestry and fishery, 19% on industries and handicrafts, 6% on construction, 18% on commerce, etc., 7% on transport and communication, and 45% on administration, professional services, etc. In 1995, 485,828 persons were employed in manufacturing. Retirement age is 67.

FOREIGN ECONOMIC RELATIONS

Imports and exports (in 1m. kroner) for calendar years:

	1995[1]		1996[1]	
Leading commodities	Imports	Exports	Imports	Exports
Live animals, meat and meat preparations	2,539	23,662	2,867	24,672
Dairy products, eggs	1,362	9,658	1,602	10,089
Fish, crustaceans, etc. and preparations	6,840	12,239	7,476	13,251
Cereals and cereal preparations	1,962	5,424	1,991	5,673
Sugar, sugar preparations and honey	970	1,748	1,230	1,778
Coffee, tea, cocoa, spices, etc.	2,279	689	2,277	773
Feeding stuff for animals	3,733	3,261	4,483	3,664
Wood and cork	3,826	810	3,817	810
Textile fibres, yarns, fabrics, etc.	6,210	5,311	6,729	727
Mineral fuels, lubricants, etc.	10,468	7,716	9,737	12,889
Medicine and pharmaceutical products	5,009	12,602	5,215	13,930
Fertilizers, etc.	1,983	1,065	1,034	409
Metals, manufacture of metals	21,923	13,547	21,111	14,316
Machinery, electrical, equipment, etc.	55,163	59,139	64,570	67,521
Transport equipment	21,963	11,017	21,306	13,090

[1] Excluding trade not distributed.

Distribution of foreign trade (in 1,000 kroner) according to countries of origin and destination, for 1996.

Countries	Imports [1]	Exports [1]
Belgium	9,090,396	5,936,065
Netherlands	19,243,822	13,209,693
Finland	7,216,469	8,036,638
France	14,248,654	15,326,981
Germany	59,519,751	66,663,212
Italy	11,854,391	10,935,507
Norway	13,332,282	19,205,034
Sweden	31,960,986	33,170,317
Switzerland	4,150,232	4,671,332
UK	19,959,055	26,403,711
Ireland	3,119,477	1,684,142
USA	12,576,926	11,973,825
Greece	423,725	2,261,646
Portugal	2,791,126	1,743,445
Spain	3,298,869	5,678,112
Iceland	871,965	1,354,632
Austria	2,534,513	3,025,917
Faroes	808,701	1,191,506
Lithuania	653,239	1,016,311
Poland	4,122,768	5,020,521
Russia	2,284,096	4,366,270
Saudi Arabia	12,920	1,570,640
India	1,144,873	1,243,285
Thailand	1,192,307	1,279,373
Singapore	553,587	1,351,992
China	4,721,673	1,788,615
South Korea	1,355,696	2,964,702
Japan	5,847,648	10,057,875
Taiwan	1,866,849	1,139,226
Hong Kong	1,369,583	2,721,315
Australia	567,014	1,628,445

[1] Excluding trade not distributed.

Tourism. In 1996, foreigners visiting Denmark spent some 19,859m. kroner. In 1996 foreigners spent 6,687,100 nights in hotels and 4,118,100 nights at camping sites.

COMMUNICATIONS

Roads. Denmark proper had (1 Jan. 1997) 825 km of motorways, 3,751 km of other state roads, 7,050 km of provincial roads and 59,710 km of commercial roads. Motor vehicles registered at 1 Jan. 1997 comprised 1,734,327 passenger cars, 47,430 lorries, 291,780 vans, 14,114 taxicabs (including 8,257 for private hire), 13,764 buses and 55,562 cycles.

Railways. In 1996 there were 2,346 km of State railways of 1,435 mm gauge (326 km electrified), which carried 145m. passengers and 9·5m. tonnes of freight. There were also 494 km of private railways.

Civil Aviation. There is an international airport at Copenhagen. The Scandinavian Airlines System (SAS) resulted from the 1950 merger of the 3 former Scandinavian airlines. Services are also provided by Adria, Aer Lingus, Aeroflot, Air China, Air France, Air India, Air Malta, Air UK, Alitalia, Atlantic Airways, Austrian Airlines, Balkan, British Airways, British Midland, Cimber Air, Continental Airlines and Air Micronesia, Croatia Airlines, Crossair, Czech Airlines, Delta, Egyptair, El Al, Estonian Air, Finnair, Iberia, Icelandair, JAT, KLM, Kenya Airways, Kuwait Airways, LOT, Lithuanian Airlines, Lufthansa, Luxair, Malév, Middle East Airlines, Northwest Airlines, Olympic, Pakistan International Airlines, Palair Macedonian, Royal Air Maroc, Sabena, Singapore Airlines, Swissair, TAP, Tarom, Thai Airways, Tunis Air, Turkish Airlines, United Airlines and Varig. In 1995 SAS flew 218·5m. km and carried 18,704,461 passengers.

On 1 Jan. 1997 Denmark had 1,094 aircraft with a capacity of 19,430 seats. In

1996 there were 266,341 take-offs and landings to and from abroad and 416,679 to and from Danish airports, excluding local flights.

Shipping. On 1 Jan. 1997 the merchant fleet consisted of 825 vessels (above 20 GRT) of 5,694,970 GRT.

In 1996, 50m. tonnes of cargo were unloaded and 33m. tonnes were loaded in Danish ports; traffic by passenger ships and ferries is not included.

Telecommunications. In 1996, there were 1,256 post offices. At 31 Dec. 1996 there were 3·25m. telephone subscribers; 1·32m. mobile telephones were in use.

Danmarks Radio is the government broadcasting station and is financed by licence fees. Television is broadcast by *Danmarks Radio* and *TV2* with colour programmes by PAL system. Number of receivers (1 Jan. 1996): TV, 2·08m., including 2m. colour sets; radio, 2·17m.

Cinemas. In 1996 there were 322 auditoria.

Press. In 1996 there were 37 daily newspapers with a combined circulation of 1·63m.

SOCIAL INSTITUTIONS

Justice. The lowest courts of justice are organized in 82 tribunals *(byretter)*, where minor cases are dealt with by a single judge. The tribunal at Copenhagen has one president and 44 other judges and Århus one president and 15 other judges; the other tribunals have 1 to 11 judges. Cases of greater consequence are dealt with by the 2 superior courts *(Landsretterne)*; these courts are also courts of appeal for the above-named minor cases. The Eastern superior court in Copenhagen has one president and 55 other judges and the Western in Viborg one president and 36 other judges. From these an appeal lies to the Supreme Court in Copenhagen, composed of a president and at present 17 other judges. Judges under 65 years of age can be removed only by judicial sentence.

In 1995, 14,916 men and 1,847 women were convicted of violations of the criminal code, fines not included. In 1995 the daily average population in penal institutions was 3,571, of whom 740 men and 54 women were on remand.

Religion. There is complete religious liberty. The state church is the Evangelical-Lutheran to which about 90% of the population belong. It is divided into 10 dioceses each with a Bishop. The Bishop together with the Chief Administrative Officer of the county make up the diocesan governing body, responsible for all matters of ecclesiastical local finance and general administration. Bishops are appointed by the Crown after an election by the clergy and parish council members. Each diocese is divided into a number of deaneries (107 in the whole country) each with its Dean and Deanery Committee, who have certain financial powers.

Education. Education has been compulsory since 1814. The *folkeskole* (public primary and lower secondary school) comprises a pre-school class *(børne-haveklasse)*, a 9-year basic school corresponding to the period of compulsory education and a 1-year voluntary tenth form. Compulsory education may be fulfilled either through attending the *folkeskole* or private schools or through home-instruction, on the condition that the instruction given is comparable to that given in the *folkeskole*. The *folkeskole* is mainly a municipal school and no fees are paid. In the year 1995–96, 2,295 primary and lower secondary schools had 587,291 pupils; they employed 56,323 teachers in 1992–93. 19·4% of the total number of schools were private schools and they were attended by 11·5% of the total number of pupils. The 9-year basic school is in practice not streamed. However, a certain differentiation may take place in the eighth and ninth forms.

On completion of the eighth and ninth forms the pupils may sit for the leaving examination of the *folkeskole (folkeskolens afgangsprøve)*. On completion of the tenth form the pupils may sit for either the leaving examination of the *folkeskole (folkeskolens afgangsprøve)* or the advanced leaving examination of the *folkeskole (folkeskolens udvidede afgangsprøve)*.

For 14–18 year olds there is an alternative of completing compulsory education at continuation schools, with the same leaving examinations as in the *folkeskole*. In the year 1995–96 there were 227 continuation schools with 19,197 pupils.

Under certain conditions the pupils may continue school either in the 3-year gymnasium (upper secondary school) or 2-year *studenterkursus* (adult upper secondary school) ending with *studentereksamen* (upper secondary school leaving examination) or in the 2-year or 3-year higher preparatory examination course ending with the *højere forberedelseseksamen*. There were (1995–96) 151 of these upper secondary schools with 73,436 pupils. Another way of continuing school is to attend HHX (*Hojere handelseksamen*) which are diploma courses within the field of trade and commerce (27,642 pupils were enrolled in 1995–96), or HTX (*Hojere teknisk eksamen*) which are technical diploma courses (6,233 pupils in 1995–96).

Vocational education and training consists of a $^1/_2$-year or 1-year basic course, followed by a second part of 2–4 years. Vocational education and training cover courses in commerce and trade, iron and metal industry, chemical industry, construction industry, graphic industry, service trades, food industry, agriculture, horticulture, forestry and fishery, transport and communication, and health related auxiliary programmes.

In 1995–96, 41,938 students were enrolled within trade and commerce. 80,153 students were enrolled within technical education.

Tertiary education comprises all education after the 12th year of education, no matter whether the 3 years after the 9th form of the *folkeskole* have been spent on a course preparing for continued studies (*studentereksamen, højere forberedelseseksamen* or *HHX/HTX*), or a course preparing for a vocation (*EUD*). Tertiary education can be divided into 2 main groups, short courses of further education and long courses of higher education. There was a total of 18,430 students at short courses of further education.

There were 18 teacher-training colleges with 11,545 students and 33 colleges for training of personnel for kindergartens, leisure-time and social care institutions with 16,051 students.

Degree-courses in engineering: The Technical University of Denmark had 6,387 students. 9 engineering colleges had 6,190 students.

Universities: The University of Copenhagen (founded 1479) 26,041 students. The University of Århus (founded in 1928) 16,768 students. The University of Odense (founded in 1964) 9,579 students. The University of Aalborg (founded in 1974) 8,857 students. Roskilde University Centre (founded in 1972) 4,806 students.

Other types of post-secondary education: The Royal Veterinary and Agricultural University has 2,934 students. The Danish School of Pharmacy, 1,017 students. 8 colleges of economics, business administration and modern languages, 24,120 students. 2 schools of architecture, 1,946 students. 7 academies of music, 1,147 students. 2 schools of librarianship, 806 students. The Royal Danish School of Educational Studies, 2,247 students. 5 schools of social work, 1,649 students. The Danish School of Journalism, 950 students. 10 colleges of physical therapy, 2,300 students. 2 schools of Midwifery Education, 206 students. 2 colleges of home economics, 513 students. The School of Visual Arts, 181 students. 28 schools of nursing, 9,397 students. 3 military academies, 592 students.

Of adult education institutions, the best-known are *Folkeskolehøjskoler*, folk high schools (with 54,923 students). Adult education includes, single subjects (96,878 students), labour market training courses for semi-skilled workers and for skilled workers (182,187 students) and courses in single subject education at vocational schools (108,845 students).

Social Security. The main body of Danish social welfare legislation is consolidated in 7 acts concerning (1) public health security, (2) sick-day benefits, (3) social pensions (for early retirement and old age), (4) employment injuries insurance, (5) employment services, unemployment insurance and activation measures, (6) social assistance including assistance to handicapped, rehabilitation, child and juvenile guidance, day-care institutions, care of the aged and sick, and (7) family allowances.

Public health security, covering the entire population, provides free medical care, substantial subsidies for certain essential medicines together with some dental care and a funeral allowance. Hospitals are primarily municipal and the hospital treatment is normally free. All employed workers are granted daily sickness allowances, others can have limited daily sickness allowances. Daily cash benefits are granted in the case of temporary incapacity because of illness, injury or child-birth to all persons in paid employment. The benefit is paid up to the rate of 100% of the average weekly earnings. There is however a maximum rate of 2,625 kroner a week.

Social pensions cover the entire population. Entitlement to the old-age pension at the full rate is subject to the condition that the beneficiary has been ordinarily resident in Denmark for 40 years. For a shorter period of residence, the benefits are reduced proportionally. The basic amount of the old-age pension in July 1996 was 131,616 kroner a year to married couples and 91,032 to single persons. Various supplementary allowances, depending on age and income, may be payable with the basic amount. Depending on health and income, persons aged 60–66 may apply for an early retirement pension. Persons over 67 years of age are entitled to the basic amount. The pensions to a married couple are calculated and paid to the husband and the wife separately. Early retirement pension to a disabled person is payable at ages 18–66 years, having regard to the degree of disability (physical as well as otherwise), at a rate of up to 143,976 kroner to a single person. Early retirement pensions may be subject to income regulation. The same applies to the basic amount of the old age pension to persons aged 67–69.

Employment injuries insurance provides for disablement or survivors' pensions and compensations. The scheme covers practically all employees.

Employment services are provided by regional public employment agencies. Insurance against unemployment provides daily allowances and covers about 85% of the unemployed. The unemployment insurance system is based on state subsidized insurance funds linked to the trade unions. The unemployment insurance funds had a membership of 2,202,969 in Aug. 1997.

The *Social Assistance Act* applies to individual benefits in contrast to the other fields of social legislation which apply to fixed benefits. Total social expenditure, including hospital and health services, statutory pensions etc. amounted in the financial year 1995 to 316,381·7m. kroner.

DIPLOMATIC REPRESENTATIVES

Of Denmark in Great Britain (55 Sloane St., London, SW1X 9SR)
Ambassador: Ole Lønsmann Poulsen.

Of Great Britain in Denmark (Kastelsvej 36–40, DK-2100, Copenhagen Ø
Ambassador: Andrew Bache, CMG.

Of Denmark in the USA (3200 Whitehaven St., NW, Washington, D.C.,
  20008-3683)
Ambassador: K. Erik Tygesen.

Of the USA in Denmark (Dag Hammarskjölds Allé 24, DK-2100, Copenhagen Ø
Ambassador: Edward E. Elson.

Of Denmark to the United Nations
Ambassador: Jørgen Bøjer.

Further Reading

Statistical Information: Danmarks Statistik (Sejrøgade 11, DK-2100 Copenhagen Ø. *Website:* http://www.dst.dk/) was founded in 1849 and reorganized in 1966 as an independent institution; it is administratively placed under the Minister of Economic Affairs. Its main publications are: *Statistisk Årbog* (Statistical Yearbook). From 1896; *Statistiske Efterretninger* (Statistical News). *Statistiske Månedsoversigt* (Monthly Review of Statistics), *Statistisk tiårsoversigt* (Statistical Ten-Year Review).

Dania polyglotta. Annual Bibliography of Books . . . in Foreign Languages Printed in Denmark. State Library, Copenhagen. Annual
Kongelig Dansk Hof og Statskalender. Copenhagen. Annual
Johansen, H. C., *The Danish Economy in the Twentieth Century.* London, 1987

Miller, K. E., *Denmark.* [Bibliography] Oxford and Santa Barbara, 1987.—*Denmark: a Troubled Welfare State.* Boulder (Colo.), 1991
Petersson, O., *The Government and Politics of the Nordic Countries.* Stockholm, 1994

National library: Det kongelige Bibliotek, P.O.B. 2149, DK-1016 Copenhagen K. *Director:* Erland Kolding Nielsen.

THE FAROE ISLANDS
Føroyar/Færøerne

KEY HISTORICAL EVENTS. A Norwegian province till the peace treaty of 14 January 1814, the islands have been represented by 2 members in the Danish parliament since 1851, and in 1852 they obtained an elected parliament of their own which in 1948 secured a certain degree of home-rule. The islands are not included in the EU, but left EFTA together with Denmark on 31 Dec. 1972.

TERRITORY AND POPULATION. The archipelago is situated due north of Scotland, 300 km from the Shetland Islands, 675 km from Norway and 450 km from Iceland, with a total land area of 1,399 sq. km (540 sq. miles). There are 17 inhabi-ted islands (the main ones being Stremoy, Eysturoy, Vágoy, Suðuroy, Sandoy and Borðoy) and numerous islets, all mountainous and of volcanic origin. Population in 1995 was 43,678. Birth rate per 1,000 inhabitants (1996 est.), 13·91; death rate, 8·69. Life expectancy at birth for total population (1996 est.), 77·83. The capital is Thórshavn (15,272) on Stremoy. The official languages are Faroese and Danish.

CONSTITUTION AND GOVERNMENT. The parliament comprises 32 members elected by proportional representation by universal suffrage at age 18. Parliament elects a government of at least 3 members which administers home rule. Denmark is represented in parliament by the chief administrator. At the general elections held on 7 July 1994, 8 seats were won by the Union Party, 6 by the People's Party, 5 by the Social Democratic Party, 4 by the Republican Party, 3 by the Workers' Front, 2 by the Home Rule Party, 2 by the Christian People's Progressive and Fishing Industry Party, and 2 by the Centre Party. A 4-party coalition of the Union, Social Democratic, Workers' and Home Rule Parties was formed on 15 Sept. 1994. In July 1995 the Social Democratic Party was replaced in the coalition by the People's Party.

Prime Minister: Edmund Joensen (Unionist).

Local government is vested in the 50 *kommunur,* which have 29 or more inhabitants and income taxes of their own.

ECONOMY

Budget. The 1995 Budget balanced at 2,805m. kr. As a result of an economic crash in the early 1990s, Denmark restructured the banks and lent money to the government to meet its international obligations. Since then the economy has improved but 5·5bn. Danish krone (£480m.) is still owed to the Danish state.

Currency. Since 1940 the currency has been the Faroese *króna* (kr.) which remains freely interchangeable with the Danish krone.

Banking and Finance. The largest bank is the state-owned Føroya Banki.

ENERGY AND NATURAL RESOURCES

Electricity. There are 5 hydro-electric stations at Vestmanna on Stremoy and one at Eiði on Eysturoy. Total production (1995) 174m. kWh, of which hydro-electric 76m. kWh.

Agriculture. Only 2% of the surface is cultivated; it is chiefly used for sheep and cattle grazing. Potatoes are grown for home consumption.

Fisheries. Deep sea fishing now forms the most important sector (90%) of the economy, primarily in the 200-mile exclusive zone but also off Greenland, Iceland, Svalbard and Newfoundland and in the Barents Sea. Total catch (1995) 284,971 tonnes, primarily cod, coalfish, redfish, mackerel, blue whiting, capelin, prawns and herring.

COMMERCE. Exports, mainly fresh, frozen, filleted and salted fish, amounted to 2,026m. kr. in 1995; imports to 1,776m. kr. In 1995 Denmark supplied 35% of imports, Norway 16% and UK 8%; exports were mainly to UK (26%), Denmark (22%), Germany (10%), France (8%) and Spain (5%).

COMMUNICATIONS

Roads. In 1995 there were 458 km of highways, 11,528 passenger cars and 2,901 commercial vehicles.

Civil Aviation. The airport is on Vágoy, from which there are regular services to Copenhagen, Reykjavík and Glasgow (in summer).

Shipping. The chief port is Tórshavn, with smaller ports at Klaksvik, Vestmanna, Skálafjørður, Tvøroyri, Vágur and Fuglafjørður.

Telecommunications. Radio and TV broadcasting (colour by PAL) are provided by Utvarp Føroya and Sjónvarp Føroya respectively. In 1994 there were 24,000 radio and 14,000 TV receivers registered.

SOCIAL INSTITUTIONS

Religion. About 80% are Evangelical Lutherans and 20% are Plymouth Brethren or belong to small communities of Roman Catholics, Pentecostal, Adventists, Jehovah Witnesses and Bahai.

Education. In 1994–95 there were 4,898 primary and 3,041 secondary school pupils with 554 teachers.

Health. In 1994 there were 90 doctors, 38 dentists, 10 pharmacists, 17 midwives and 355 nursing personnel. In 1994 there were 3 hospitals with 297 beds.

Further Reading

Árbók fyri Føroyar. Annual.
Rutherford, G. K., (ed.) *The Physical Environment of the Færoe Islands.* The Hague, 1982
West, J. F., *Faroe.* London, 1973
Wylie, J., *The Faroe Islands: Interpretations of History.* Lexington, 1987

GREENLAND

Grønland/Kalaallit Nunaat

KEY HISTORICAL EVENTS. A Danish possession since 1380, Greenland became an integral part of the Danish kingdom on 5 June 1953. Following a referendum in Jan. 1979, home rule was introduced from 1 May 1979.

TERRITORY AND POPULATION. Area 2,175,600 sq. km (840,000 sq. miles), made up of 1,833,900 sq. km of ice cap and 341,700 sq. km of ice-free land. The population, 1 Jan. 1997, numbered 55,971. In 1994, 44,657 persons were urban; 38,186 were Greenlanders and 6,471 Danes. 1993 population of West Greenland, 52,217; East Greenland, 2,644; North Greenland (Thule), 607, and 564 not belonging to any specific municipality. The capital is Nuuk (Godthåb), with a population in 1995 of 13,148. Birth rate per 1,000 inhabitants (1993), 20·0; death rate, 8·0. The predominant language is Greenlandic. Danish is widely used in matters relating to teaching, administration and business.

CONSTITUTION AND GOVERNMENT. There is a 31-member Home Rule Parliament, which is elected for 4-year terms and meets 2 or 3 times a year. At the elections of 4 March 1995 a Social Democratic Party (SDP)–Liberal Party (LP) coalition gained 22 seats, the Socialist Party, 6, the Centre Party 2 and the Union of Independents 1. The 7-member cabinet is elected by parliament. Ministers need not be members of parliament. In Dec. 1995 the cabinet comprised 5 SDP and 2LP ministers. Greenland elects 2 representatives to the Danish parliament (Folketing). Denmark is represented by an appointed High Commissioner. The *Prime Minister* is Jonathan Matzfeldt.

Local Government. Administratively Greenland is divided into 3 regions (North, East and West Greenland) and subdivided into 18 municipalities (1 in North, 2 in East and 15 in West Greenland). Town councils are elected for 4-year terms. There were elections in April 1997.

ECONOMY

Budget. Revenue, 1997: 4,049m. kroner; expenditure, 4,044m. kroner.

Currency. The Danish krone remains the legal currency.

Banking and Finance. There is 1 private bank, the Grønlandsbanken.

ENERGY AND NATURAL RESOURCES

Electricity. Production (1996) 279m. kWh.

Agriculture. Livestock, 1992: Sheep, 17,900; domesticated reindeer, 5,600. There are approximately 60 sheep-breeding farms in south-west Greenland. In 1993 a 2-year stop on the hunting of caribou was introduced.

Fisheries. Fishing and product-processing are the principal industry. In 1993 shrimps accounted for 80% of the country's economic output. Halibut and other fish made up the remaining 20%. In 1992 120 whales were caught (subject to the International Whaling Commission's regulations) and 69,000 sealskins sold.

INDUSTRY. Production of lead and zinc concentrates was in 1989 about 35,500 tonnes and 130,500 tonnes respectively. The mine closed down in 1990. 6 shipyards repair and maintain ships and produce industrial tanks, containers and steel constructions for building.

COMMERCE. Imports (c.i.f. Greenland) (in 1m. kroner): 1996, 2,705. Exports (f.o.b. Greenland) (in 1m. kroner): 1996, 2,141. Trade is mainly with Denmark.

COMMUNICATIONS

Civil Aviation. Greenland Air operates services to Denmark, Iceland and Frobisher Bay (Canada) and domestic services. Icelandair and SAS also serve Greenland. There are international airports at Søndre Srømfjord and Narsarsuaq, and 18 local airports/heliports with scheduled services. There were 66,135 international passengers in 1994.

Shipping. There are no overseas passenger services. In 1996, 88,195 passengers were carried on coastal services. There are cargo services to Denmark, Iceland and St John's (Canada).

Telecommunications. In 1996 there were 21,116 telephones. The government Kalaallit Nunaata Radioa provides broadcasting services, and there are also local services. In 1991 there were estimated to be 25,000 radio and 12,000 TV sets (colour by PAL). Several towns have local television stations.

Press. There are 2 daily newspapers.

SOCIAL INSTITUTIONS

Justice. The High Court in Nuuk comprises one professional judge and 2 lay magistrates, while there are 18 district courts under lay assessors.

Religion. About 99% of the population are Evangelical Lutherans. In 1995 there were 17 parishes with 83 churches and chapels and 25 ministers.

Education. Education is compulsory from 6 to 15 years. A further 3 years of schooling are optional. There were (1996–97) 10,719 pupils in 86 primary comprehensive schools. On 1 Sept. 1995 there were 1,221 students enrolled in vocational training and 548 in higher education.

Health. The medical service is free to all citizens. There is a central hospital in Nuuk and 18 smaller district hospitals. In 1996 there were 513 hospital beds.

Further Reading

The Greenland Home Rule Authority has published since 1989 *Greenland/Kalaallit Nunaat: Statistical Yearbook.*
Gad, F., *A History of Greenland.* 2 vols. London, 1970–1973
Miller, K. E., *Greenland* [Bibliography]. Oxford and Santa Barbara (CA), 1991
Greenland National Library, P.O. Box 1011, DK-3900 Nuuk
Greenland Statistical Office, Nuuk.

National statistical office: Statistics Greenland. *Website:* http://www.statgreen.gl/

DJIBOUTI

Jumhouriyya Djibouti

(Republic of Djibouti)

Capital: Djibouti
Population: 428,000
GDP per head: $1,270
HDI/world rank: 0·319/162

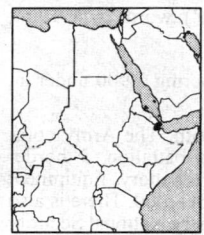

KEY HISTORICAL EVENTS. At a referendum held on 19 March 1967, 60% of the electorate voted for continued association with France rather than independence and the new statute for the territory came into being on 5 July 1967. France affirmed that the Territory of the Afars and the Issas was destined for independence but no date was fixed. Legislative elections were held on 8 May and independence as the Republic of Djibouti was achieved on 27 June 1977.

Afar rebels in the north belonging to the Front for the Restoration of Unity and Democracy (FRUD) signed a 'Peace and National Reconciliation Agreement' with the government on 26 Dec. 1994 envisaging the formation of a national coalition government, the redrafting of the electoral roll and the integration of FRUD militants into the armed forces and civil service.

TERRITORY AND POPULATION. Djibouti is in effect a city-state surrounded by a semi-desert hinterland bounded in the north-west by Eritrea, north-east by the Gulf of Aden, south-east by Somalia and south-west by Ethiopia. The area is 23,200 sq. km (8,958 sq. miles). The population was estimated in 1996 at 428,000 (81% urban), of whom about half were Somali (Issa, Gadaboursi and Issaq), 35% Afar and some Europeans (mainly French) and Arabs. Birth rate in 1996, 42·5%; infant mortality, 108 per 1,000 live births. Growth rate, 1996. 1·5% (estimate). Expectation of life, 1996, 48·24 for men, 52·12 for women. There are 5 administrative districts (areas in sq. km): Ali-Sabieh (2,600); Dikhil (7,800); Djibouti (600); Obock (5,700); Tadjoura (7,300). The capital is Djibouti (1995 population, 383,000).

CLIMATE. Conditions are hot throughout the year, with very little rain. Djibouti. Jan. 78°F (25·6°C), July 96°F (35·6°C). Annual rainfall 5" (130 mm).

CONSTITUTION AND GOVERNMENT. After a referendum at which turn-out was 70% a new constitution was approved on 4 Sept. 1992 by 96·63% of votes cast which permits the existence of up to 4 political parties. Parties are required to maintain an ethnic balance in their membership. The *President* is directly elected for a renewable 6-year term. Parliament is a 65-member *Chamber of Deputies* elected for 5-year terms.

At the presidential elections of 7 May 1993 the electorate was 150,487; turn-out was 50·26%. Hassan Gouled Aptidou was elected against 3 opponents by 60·71% of votes cast.

At the parliamentary elections of 19 Dec. 1997 the coalition of RPP and FRUD won 65 seats with 78·6% of votes cast, the Party of Democratic Renewal nil with 19·2% and the National Democratic Party nil with 2.3%.

President: Hassan Gouled Aptidon (b. 1916; elected 1977, re-elected 1981, 1987 and 1993).

The Council of Ministers in March 1998 was composed as follows:
Prime Minister, Planning and Territorial Administration: Barkat Gourad Hamadou.

Interior and Decentralization: Elmi Obsieh Wassi. *Justice, Islamic Affairs and Prisons:* Mohamed Dini Farah. *Foreign Affairs and International Co-operation:* Mohammed Moussa Chehem. *Defence:* Abdullah Chirwa Djibril. *Finance and Economy:* Yacin Elmi Boueh. *Industry, Energy and Mines:* Abdi Farah. *Labour and Training:* Mohamed Ali Mohamed. *Education:* Ahmed Guire Waberi. *Public Works, Urban Affairs and Housing:* Hassan Farah Mighil. *Health and Social Affairs:* Ali

Mohammed Daoud. *Transport and Telecommunications:* Abdallah Abdillahi Miguil. *Agriculture and Rural Reform:* Ibrahim Idris Djibril. *Youth, Sport and Culture:* Rifki Abdoulkader Bamakrama. *Civil Service and Administrative Reform:* Ougoureh Kifle Ahmed. *Commerce and Tourism:* Mohamed Abdillahi Barkat. *Environment:* Osman Robleh Daach. *Chief of Staff of the Presidency:* Ismail Omar Guelleh.

National anthem: 'Hinjinne u sara kaca' ('Arise with strength'); words by A. Elmi, tune by A. Robleh.

DEFENCE. France maintains a naval base and forces numbering 3,900 under an agreement renewed in Feb. 1991.

Army. There are 3 Army commands: North, Central and South. The Army comprises 1 infantry battalion, 1 armoured squadron, 1 support battalion, 1 border commando battalion and 1 parachute company, and 1 artillery battery. Equipment includes 31 armoured cars. The strength of the Army was (1996) 8,000. There is also a paramilitary Gendarmerie of some 1,200 and an Interior Ministry National Security Force of 3,000.

Navy. A coastal patrol is maintained consisting of 8 small inshore patrol craft and some boats. Personnel (1996), 200.

Air Force. There is a small air force. There are no combat aircraft. Fixed-wing aircraft comprise 1 An-28 transport and 2 Cessna 206s for liaison. There are also 3 Ecureuil, 3 Mi-8 and 2 Mi-2 helicopters. Personnel (1995), 200.

INTERNATIONAL RELATIONS

Membership. Djibouti is a member of the UN, OAU, the Arab League and is an ACP state of the EU.

ECONOMY

Performance. The IMF estimates that there was a decline of 2·9% in GDP in 1994.

Budget. Budget revenue for 1993 was 28,320m. Djibouti francs and expenditure 27,655m. Djibouti francs.

Currency. The currency is the *Djibouti franc* (DJF) notionally of 100 *centimes.* There are coins of 10, 20, 50, 100, 500 and notes of 1,000, 5,000 and 10,000 Djibouti francs. 10,693m. Djibouti francs were in circulation in 1994. Foreign exchange reserves were US$73·8m. in 1994.

Banking and Finance. The Banque Nationale de Djibouti is the bank of issue (*Governor*, Luc Aden). There are 6 commercial banks.

Weights and Measures. The metric system is in use.

ENERGY AND NATURAL RESOURCES

Electricity. Production (1991) 200m. kWh. Installed capacity, 115,000 kW.

Agriculture. Agricultural land was 674 ha in 1989, of which 407 ha were exploited, mainly by market gardening. Production is dependent on irrigation. Tomato production (1992) 1,000 tonnes. Livestock (1992): 180,000 cattle, 450,000 sheep, 506,000 goats, 61,000 camels.

Fisheries. In 1995 there were 140 individual fishing boats. The catch was about 500 tonnes.

INDUSTRY. In 1994 services provided 76% of GDP in 1993, industry 21% and agriculture 3%.

Labour. In 1991 the estimate labour force totalled 282,000, with 75% employed in agriculture, 14% in services and 11% in industry. A 40-hour working week is standard. In 1989 there was a minimum monthly wage of 15,850 Djibouti francs. Unemployment in 1994 was estimated at 30%.

FOREIGN ECONOMIC RELATIONS. Foreign debt totalled US$247m. in 1994.

Commerce. The main economic activity is the operation of the port; in 1990 only 36% of imports were destined for Djibouti. Exports are largely re-exports. The chief imports are cotton goods, sugar, cement, flour, fuel oil and vehicles; the chief exports are hides, cattle and coffee (transit from Ethiopia). Main export markets, 1995 (% of total trade): Somalia, 42%; Ethiopia, 35%; Yemen, 7%. Main import suppliers: Thailand, 15%; France, 13%; Ethiopia, 8%; Saudi Arabia, 6%.

Tourism. There were 46,595 tourists in 1994.

COMMUNICATIONS

Roads. There were (1993) 2,879 km of roads, of which 363 km were hard-surfaced. In 1987 there were 11,799 passenger cars and 1,501 commercial vehicles.

Railways. For the line from Djibouti to Addis Ababa, of which 97 km lie within Djibouti, *see* ETHIOPIA: Communications. Traffic carried is mainly in transit to and from Ethiopia.

Civil Aviation. There is an international airport at Djibouti (Ambouli). The national airlines are Daallo Airlines, which had 6 aircraft in 1995, and Puntavia Airlines, which operated 3 B-727-200s and 5 other aircraft. Services are also provided by Aeroflot, Air France, Air Tanzania, Ethiopian Airlines and Yemenia. In 1993 Djibouti airport handled 305,155 passengers and 15,000 tonnes of freight.

Shipping. Djibouti is a free port and container terminal. 950 ships berthed in 1989, (including 177 warships) totalling 3·87m. NRT. 3,211 passengers embarked or disembarked, and 0·87m. tonnes of cargo were handled (1·48m. tonnes in 1992). In 1995 the merchant marine totalled 4,800 GRT.

Telecommunications. Number of telephones (1989), 5,100. The state-run *Radiodiffusion-Télévision de Djibouti* broadcasts in French, Somali, Afar and Arabic. There is a television transmitter in Djibouti, broadcasting for 35 hours a week. Number of receivers (1993): Radio, 30,000; TV, 17,000 (colour by SECAM).

SOCIAL INSTITUTIONS

Justice. There is a Court of First Instance and a Court of Appeal in the capital. The judicial system is based on Islamic law.

Religion. In 1995, 96% of the population were Moslem, with about 12,000 Roman Catholics and 10,000 Protestant and Orthodox.

Education. Adult literacy in 1995 was estimated at 46·2% (60·3% of men; 32·7% of women). In 1991–92 there were 57 state primary schools (and 9 private) with 27,884 (2,895) pupils and 641 (66) teachers, 10 (6) secondary schools, with 6,892 (946) pupils and 307 teachers. There was an *école normale* with 112 pupils and 12 teachers. Professional education is all in private hands. In 1989–90 there were 11 institutions and 1,074 students.

Health. In 1993 there were 2 hospitals, 6 medical centres and 21 dispensaries. There were 91 doctors, 10 dentists and 14 pharmacists in 1989.

DIPLOMATIC REPRESENTATIVES

Of Djibouti in Great Britain
Ambassador: Ahmd Omar Farah (resides in Paris).

Of Great Britain in Djibouti
Ambassador: G. G. Wetherell (resides in Addis Ababa).

Of the USA in Djibouti (Plateau du Serpent Blvd., Djibouti)
Ambassador: Martin L. Cheshes.

Of Djibouti to the United Nations and in the USA
Ambassador: Roble Olhaye.

Further Reading

Direction Nationale de la Statistique. *Annuaire Statistique de Djibouti*

Schraeder, P. J., *Djibouti*. [Bibliography] Oxford and Santa Barbara, 1990

National statistical office: Direction Nationale de la Statistique, Ministère du Commerce, des Transports et du Tourisme, BP 1846, Djibouti

DOMINICA

Commonwealth of
Dominica

Capital: Roseau
Population: 66,633
GDP per head: (PPP$) 6,118
GNP: US$0·2bn.
HDI/world rank: 0·873/41

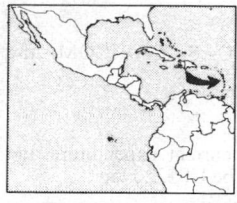

KEY HISTORICAL EVENTS. The earliest known inhabitants of this island in the Caribbean were two Amerindian tribes: the Arawaks who migrated from South America and the Caribs, who later drove them out. Dominica was discovered by Columbus on Sunday (hence the island's name), 3 Nov. 1493. Neither the Spanish nor the Earl of Carlisle, who was granted the island in 1672 by Charles I, established settlements, and instead it was French settlers who began to create plantations on the island. The island's strategic position, however, later caused it to become the centre of a threefold conflict between the Carib Indians, the British and French. Control of the island was contested between the British and French until it was ultimately awarded to the British in 1783.

Dominica became part of a federation on four occasions: in 1833 with the Leeward Islands, in 1871 in an extended Leeward Islands Colony, in 1940 as part of the Windward Islands group and in 1958-62 as a member of the Federation of the West Indies.

In March 1967 Dominica became an Associated State of the UK, allowed internal self-government, and became an independent republic as the Commonwealth of Dominica on 3 Nov. 1978.

TERRITORY AND POPULATION. Dominica is an island in the Windward group of the West Indies situated between Martinique and Guadeloupe. It has an area of 748·5 sq. km (289·5 sq. miles) and a population at the 1991 census of 71,794. 1997 estimate, 66,633. The chief town, Roseau, had 15,853 inhabitants in 1991.

The population is mainly of African and mixed origins, with small white and Asian minorities. There is a Carib settlement of about 500, almost entirely of mixed blood.

The official language is English, though 95% of the population speak a French Creole.

Life expectancy 77·4; male, 74·55, female, 80·4. Birth and death rate, per 1,000 (1996): birth rate, 18·38, death rate, 5·31.

CLIMATE. A tropical climate, with pleasant conditions between Dec. and March, but there is a rainy season from June to Oct., when hurricanes may occur. Rainfall is heavy, with coastal areas having 70" (1,750 mm) but the mountains may have up to 225" (6,250 mm). Roseau. Jan. 76°F (24·2°C), July 81°F (27·2°C). Annual rainfall 78" (1,956 mm).

CONSTITUTION AND GOVERNMENT. The head of state is the *President*, nominated by the Prime Minister and the Leader of the Opposition, and elected for a 5-year term (renewable once) by the House of Assembly. The *House of Assembly* has 21 elected and 9 members nominated by the President. Elections were held on 6 June 1995. The United Workers Party (UWP) won 11 seats (6 in 1990), the Dominica Labour Party (DLP), 5 (4) and the Dominica Freedom Party 5 (11).

President: Crispin Anselm Sorhaindo, OBE (elected 4 Oct. 1993, sworn in 25 Oct.).

The Cabinet in March 1998 was composed as follows:

Prime Minister and Minister of External Affairs, Legal Affairs, Trade, Marketing and Labour: Edison James (b. 1944; UWP).

Deputy Prime Minister and Minister of Finance, Industry and Planning: Julius Timothy. *Tourism, Ports and Employment:* Norris Prevost. *Health and Social Security:* Doreen Paul. *Community Development and Women's Affairs:* Gertrude Roberts. *Communications, Works and Housing:* Earl Williams. *Agriculture and the Environment:* Peter Carbon. *Education, Sports and Youth Affairs:* Ronald Green.

National anthem: 'Isle of beauty, isle of splendour'; words by W. Pond, tune by L. M. Christian.

Local Government. Roseau and Portsmouth have town councils with powers to raise property taxes. There are 25 rural districts administered by partially-elected village councils.

INTERNATIONAL RELATIONS

Membership. Dominica is a member of the UN, OAS, CARICOM, the Commonwealth and is an ACP state of the EU.

ECONOMY

Budget. The 1994–95 budget allocated US$106·1m. to current expenditure and US$41m. to capital expenditure. Revenue was expected to be US$220·8m.

Currency. The French *franc,* the £ sterling and the *East Caribbean dollar* are legal tender. Foreign exchange reserves were US$19·9m. in 1993.

Banking and Finance. In 1996 there were 4 foreign banks, 1 domestic bank, a development bank and a credit union.

ENERGY AND NATURAL RESOURCES

Electricity. There is a hydro-electric power station. Installed capacity was 13,500 kWh in 1995. Production (1994) 52m. kWh.

Agriculture. In 1994, agriculture provided 30% of GDP and employed 26% of the labour force. Production (1992): Bananas, 70,000 tonnes; coconuts, 12,000 tonnes. Livestock (1992): Cattle, 9,000; pigs, 5,000; sheep, 8,000; goats, 10,000.

INDUSTRY. Manufactures include clothing, soap, shampoo, cream, footwear, fruit juice, rum, electronic assemblies, candles and paint.

Labour. In 1994 the minimum wage was US$0·75 an hour.

FOREIGN ECONOMIC RELATIONS. Total external debt in 1994 was US$93·1m.

Commerce. In 1993 imports were worth US$98·8m. and exports US$48·3m. Chief products: Bananas, soap, fruit juices, essential oils, coconuts, vegetables, fruit and fruit preparations, and alcoholic drinks.

Tourism. In 1995, there were 134,921 cruise ship visitors and 60,471 staying visitors.

COMMUNICATIONS

Roads. In 1995 it was estimated there were 765 km of road of which 385 km were paved.

Civil Aviation. There are international airports at Melville Hall and Canefield. There are direct flights from Antigua, Barbados, Grenada, Guadeloupe, Puerto Rico, St Lucia, St Maarten, St Thomas, St Vincent, Trinidad and the US Virgin Islands. Services are provided by Air Anguilla, Air Caraïbes, Cardinal Airlines, Helenair, Air Guadeloupe, LIAT, American Eagle and Windward Island Airways.

Shipping. There are deep-water harbours at Roseau and Woodbridge Bay. Roseau has a cruise ship berth.

Telecommunications. Number of telephones, 1993, 14,613. Radio and television broadcasting is provided by the part government-controlled, part-commercial Dominica Broadcasting Corporation. There are also 2 religious radio networks, 2 commercial TV channels (colour by NTSC) and a commercial cable service. In 1995 there were 45,000 radio and 5,200 TV sets.

Cinemas. There is 1 cinema with a seating capacity of 1,000.

Press. In 1994 there were 3 newspapers, including 1 government and 1 independent weekly.

SOCIAL INSTITUTIONS

Justice. There is a supreme court and 12 magistrates' courts. Law is based on UK common law as exercised by the Eastern Caribbean Supreme Court on St Lucia. Final appeal lies to the UK Privy Council.

In 1995 the police force numbered 439; it has a residual responsibility for defence.

Religion. 77% of the population was Roman Catholic in 1995.

Education. In 1994 adult literacy was 90%. In 1993–94 there were 54 private kindergartens. Education is free and compulsory between the ages of 5 and 15 years. In 1993–94 there were 65 primary and 13 secondary schools, a teachers' training college and a Community College with academic and technical divisions.

Health. In 1994 there were 54 hospitals and health centres with 312 beds, 23 doctors, 6 dentists, 27 pharmacists and 265 nursing personnel.

DIPLOMATIC REPRESENTATIVES

Of Dominica in Great Britain (1 Collingham Gdns., London SW5 0HW)
High Commissioner: George E. Williams.

Of Great Britain in Dominica
High Commissioner: R. Thomas, CMG (resides in Barbados).

Of Dominica in the USA (3216 New Mexico Ave., NW, Washington, D.C. 20016)
Ambassador: Edward I. Watty (non-resident).

Of the USA in Dominica
Ambassador: Jeanette W. Hyde (resides in Barbados).

Of Dominica to the United Nations
Ambassador: Paul Richards.

Of Dominica to the European Union
Ambassador: Edwin Laurent.

Further Reading

Baker, P. L., *Centring the Periphery: Chaos, Order and the Ethnohistory of Dominica:* McGill-Queen's Univ. Press, 1994
Honychurch, L., *The Dominica Story: a History of the Island.* 2nd ed, London 1995
Myers, R. A., *Dominica.* [Bibliography] Oxford and Santa Barbara (CA), 1987

National statistical office: Central Statistical Office, Kennedy Avenue, Roseau

DOMINICAN REPUBLIC

República Dominicana

Capital: Santo Domingo
Population: 8·1m.
GDP per head: (PPP$) 3,933
GNP: US$101bn.
HDI/world rank: 0·718/87

KEY HISTORICAL EVENTS. Columbus discovered the island of Santo Domingo, which he called La Isla Española and which for a time was also known as Hispaniola. The city of Santo Domingo, founded by his brother, Bartholomew, in 1496, is the oldest city in the Americas. The western third of the island—now the Republic of Haiti—was later occupied and colonized by the French, to whom the Spanish colony of Santo Domingo was also ceded in 1795. In 1808 the Dominican population, under the command of Gen. Juan Sánchez Ramirez, routed an important French military force commanded by Gen. Ferrand at the battle of Palo Hincado. This battle was the beginning of the end for French rule in Santo Domingo and culminated in the successful siege of the capital. Eventually, with the aid of a British naval squadron, the French were forced to capitulate and the colony returned again to Spanish rule, from which it declared its independence in 1821. It was invaded and held by the Haitians from 1822 to 1844, when they were expelled, and the Dominican Republic was founded and a constitution adopted. In 1850 Great Britain was the first country to recognize the Dominican Republic.

Thereafter the rule was dictatorship interspersed with brief democratic interludes. Between 1916 and 1924 the country was under US military occupation. From 1930 until his assassination in 1961, Rafael Trujillo was one of Latin America's legendary dictators. The rise of radicalism following the election of Juan Bosch to the presidency in 1963 led, in 1965, to a further US invasion. The conservative pro-American Joaquin Balaguer was president from 1966 to 1978 when an opposition candidate, Antonio Guzuén, was elected. Resistance to repression of popular movements led to the election of the moderate leftist Salvador Jorge Blanco in 1982. In 1986 Balaguer returned to power at the head of the Socialist Christian Reform Party, leading the way to economic reforms. But there was violent opposition to spending cuts and general austerity. Balaguer was returned to power in 1994 by a narrow margin after accusations of electoral irregularity. The 1996 elections brought in a reforming government pledged to act against corruption.

TERRITORY AND POPULATION. The Dominican Republic occupies the eastern portion (about two-thirds) of the island of Hispaniola, the western division forming the Republic of Haiti. The frontier with Haiti is closed. The area is 48,442 sq. km (18,700 sq. miles). The 1990 area and population of the 29 provinces and National District (Santo Domingo area):

	Area (in sq. km)	Population		Area (in sq. km)	Population
La Altagracia	3,084	111,241	Pedernales	967	18,896
Azua	2,430	195,420	Peravia	1,622	186,810
Bahoruco	1,376	87,376	Puerto Plata	1,881	229,738
Barahona	2,528	152,405	La Romana	541	169,223
Dajabón	890	64,123	Salcedo	533	110,216
Distrito Nacional	1,477	2,411,895	Samaná	989	73,002
Duarte	1,292	261,725	Sánchez Ramírez	1,174	140,635
Espaillat	1,000	182,248	San Cristóbal	1,564	320,921
La Estrelleta	1,788	72,651	San Juan	3,561	266,628
Hato Mayor	1,330	77,823	San Pedro de Macorís	1,166	197,862
Independencia	1,861	43,077	Santiago	3,122	704,835
María Trinidad Sánchez	1,310	125,148	Santiago Rodríguez	1,020	61,570
Monseñor Nouel	1,004	124,794	El Seíbo	1,659	97,590
Monte Cristi	1,989	92,678	Valverde	570	111,470
Monte Plata	2,179	174,799	La Vega	2,373	303,047

Census population (1981) 5,647,977. Estimate (1996) 8,088,881 (58% urban in 1994). Vital statistics rates, 1996: Birth, 235 (per 1,000 population); death, 5·7; infant mortality, 47·7 (per 1,000 live births). Life expectancy, 1996, 69 years.

Population of the main towns (1991 estimate, in 1,000): Santo Domingo, the capital, 2,055; Santiago de los Caballeros, 375; La Vega, 189; San Francisco de Macorís, 162; San Pedro de Macorís, 137; La Romana, 136.

The population is mainly composed of a mixed race of European (Spanish) and African blood. The official language is Spanish; about 0·15m. persons speak a Haitian-French creole.

CLIMATE. A tropical maritime climate with most rain falling in the summer months. The rainy season extends from May to Nov. and amounts are greatest in the north and east. Hurricanes may occur from June to Nov. Santo Domingo. Jan. 75°F (23·9°C), July 81°F (27·2°C). Annual rainfall 56" (1,400 mm).

CONSTITUTION AND GOVERNMENT. The constitution dates from 28 Nov. 1966.

The *President* is elected for 4 years, by direct vote, and has executive power. A constitutional amendment of Aug. 1994 prohibits the President from serving consecutive terms. In 1994 the constitution was amended to allow for a second round of voting in a presidential election when no candidate secures an absolute majority in the first ballot. There is a bicameral legislature, the *Congress*, comprising a 30-member Senate (one member for each province and one for the National District of Santo Domingo) and a 120-member Chamber of Deputies, both elected for 4-year terms at the same date as the President. Citizens are entitled to vote at the age of 18, or less when married.

Presidential elections were held on 16 May 1996 with a run-off on 30 June 1996. Leonel Fernández Reyna was elected at the run-off by 51·25% of votes cast.

Parliamentary elections were held on 16 May 1994. The electorate was 3·3m.

President: Leonel Fernández Reyna (b. 1954; Dominican Liberation Party; sworn in 16 Aug. 1996).

Vice-President: Jaime Fernández Mirabal.

In March 1998 the government comprised the following Secretaries of State:

Agriculture: Frank Rodriguez. *Armed Forces:* Adm. Ruben Paulino Alvarez. *Education, Fine Arts, and Public Worship:* Ligia Amada Melo de Cardona. *Finance:* Daniel Toribio. *Foreign Relations:* Eduardo Latorre Rodriguez. *Industry and Commerce:* Luis Manuel Bonetti. *Interior and Police:* Norge Botello Fernandez. *Judicial Reform:* Ramon Andres Blanco Fernandez. *Labour:* Rafael Alburquerque de Castro. *Public Health and Social Welfare:* Altagracia Guzman. *Public Works and Communications:* Jaime Duran Hernando. *Sports, Physical Education, and Recreation:* Juan Marichal. *Tourism:* Felix Jimenez Jimenez. *The Presidency:* Danilo Medina. *Without Portfolio:* Lidio Cadet; Rafael Augusto Collado; Julian Serrule.

National anthem: 'Quisqueyanos valientes, alcemos' ('Valient Quisqueyans, Let us raise our voices'); words by E. Prud'homme, tune by J. Reyes.

Local Government. The 29 provinces have a governor appointed by the President. They and the National District are divided into 18 municipal districts and 72 municipalities run by elected councils. Elections for mayors took place simultaneously with the presidential and parliamentary elections of May 1994.

DEFENCE

Army. There are 3 defence zones. The Army has a strength (1997) of about 15,000. It is organized in 4 infantry brigades, 1 artillery, 1 engineer, 1 special forces and 1 armoured battalion and a Presidential Guard. Equipment includes 15 light tanks. There is a paramilitary National Police 15,000 strong.

Navy. The Navy is equipped with former US vessels. The combatant force consists of 1 frigate (built 1944) acting as the flagship, 6 offshore, 2 coastal and 8 inshore patrol craft. There is 1 utility landing craft and support is provided by 1 small oiler, 1 ocean tug and some 12 harbour and service craft. Personnel in 1997 totalled 4,000, based at Santo Domingo and Calderas.

Air Force. The Air Force, with HQ at San Isidoro, has 1 combat squadron with 8 Cessna A-37s; 1 squadron with 6 Bell 205A-1, 1 Dauphin and 1 OH-6A helicopters; 1 transport squadron with 3 C-47s, 5 Cessna 337s and some smaller communications aircraft, and 10 T-34B Mentor and 5 Cessna T-41 trainers. Personnel strength was (1997) 5,500.

INTERNATIONAL RELATIONS

Membership. The Dominican Republic is a member of the UN and OAS and an ACP member of the EU.

ECONOMY

Policy. In Jan. 1995 subsidies to the 33 state companies were discontinued. 20 state companies were put up for sale in Nov. 1995.

Performance. GDP grew by 4·8% in 1995.

Budget. Central government budgetary revenue and expenditure in RD$1m. for calendar years:

	1991	1992	1993	1994	1995
Revenue	10,053·8	17,516·4	19,677·8	21,076·4	24,781·7
Expenditure	8,094·8	12,968·4	18,887·0	21,025·4	21,784·8

Tax revenue in 1995 was RD$22,642·7m.; non-tax revenue, RD$2,079·6m.; capital revenue, RD$59·4m.

Currency. The unit of currency is the *peso oro* (DOP) of 100 *centavos.* There are coins of 1, 5, 10, 25 and 50 centavos and RD$1 peso oro, and notes of RD$1, 5, 10, 20, 50, 100, 500 and 1,000. RD$52,699m. were in circulation in 1993. Inflation was 9·2% in 1995. Gold reserves were US$6·8m. in 1995. Foreign exchange reserves were US$365·6m. in 1995.

Banking and Finance. In 1947 the Central Bank was established (*Governor*, Hector Váldez Albizú). Its total assets were RD$34,958·7m. in 1993. In 1993 there were 20 commercial banks (2 foreign); total assets, RD$30,765·5m.

The Santo Domingo Securities Exchange is a member of the Association of Central American Stock Exchanges (Bolcen).

Weights and Measures. The metric system was adopted on 1 Aug. 1913, but English and Spanish units have remained in common use.

ENERGY AND NATURAL RESOURCES

Electricity. Installed capacity, 1993, 1,500 MW, of which 356 MW was hydroelectric. Output, 1992, 4,626,147 MWh (660,907 MWh hydro-electric).

Minerals. Bauxite output in 1988 was 167,800 tonnes, but had declined to nil by 1992. Output, 1992: Ferro-nickel, 58,313 tonnes; gold, 76,349 troy oz.; silver, 478,320 troy oz.

Agriculture. Agriculture and processing are the chief source of income, sugar cultivation being the principal industry. There are 1m. ha of arable land, 0·45m. ha of permanent cropland and 2·09m. ha of pasture.

Production, 1994 (in 1,000 tonnes): Sugar-cane, 7,000 (6,916 in 1992); cocoa beans, 57; coffee, 39; bananas, 550; rice (paddy), 533; tobacco (leaves), 18 (20 in 1992); dry beans, 48; maize, 57; tomatoes, 102.

Livestock in 1994: 2·45m. cattle, 0·9m. pigs, 134,000 sheep. Livestock products, 1994 (in tonnes): Poultry meat, 0·13m.; beef and veal, 90,000; eggs, 43,900; milk, 385,000.

Forestry. Forests and woodlands cover 0·61m. ha. In 1994, 0·9m. tonnes of timber were cut.

Fisheries. The total catch (1994) was 14,100 tonnes.

INDUSTRY. Manufacturing contributed 17% of GDP in 1991. Production, 1992 (in tonnes): Raw sugar, 427,950; refined sugar, 90,021; cement, 1,364,877; paint, 16,328; beer, 195·64m. litres; rum, 43·41m. litres; cigarettes, 220,203 packets (of 20).

Labour. Average monthly wage, 1992, RD$2,136·98.

FOREIGN ECONOMIC RELATIONS. In 1994 there were 38 industrial free zones (employing 164,296 persons), which enjoy duty-free imports of raw materials and various tax exemptions. Legislation of 1995 allows foreign investments of 100% in all sectors except industries affecting the environment and arms production. Profits may be repatriated. Foreign debt was US$4,500m. in 1994.

Commerce. Total imports and exports in US$1m.:

	1991	1992	1993	1994	1995
Imports	1,729	2,174	2,118	2,276	2,588
Exports	658	562	530	644	765

Main exports, 1993 (in tonnes): Raw sugar, 342,197 (513,920 in 1988); molasses, 176,234; coffee, 18,079; cocoa, 42,077; tobacco, 11,410; ferro-nickel, 67,405; gold, 11,718 troy oz. (139,969 troy oz. in 1990); silver, 53,496 troy oz. (734,987 troy oz. in 1990). Main imports (in US$1m.): Oil and products, 453; coal, 10·3; foodstuffs, 11·6; wheat, 38·1.

Main export markets (% of trade), 1994: USA, 46·6%; Germany, 5·9%; Canada, 4·8%; Belgium, 4·6%. Main import suppliers: USA, 65·2%; Mexico, 7%; Venezuela, 6·8%; Japan, 6·3%.

Tourism. 2·04m. tourists visited in 1993, bringing foreign exchange earnings of US$1,233m.

COMMUNICATIONS

Roads. In 1991 there were 4,325 km of first- and second-class roads. In 1991 there were 242,038 motor vehicles.

Railways. In 1995 the total length was 757 km, comprising 375 km of the Central Romana Railroad, 142 km of the Dominican Government Railway between Guayubin and the port of Pepillo, and 240 km operated by the sugar industry.

Civil Aviation. There are international airports at Santo Domingo (Punta Caucedo), Puerto Plata, La Romana and Punta Cana. Dominican Airlines ceased operations in 1995 and was put up for privatization. Bavaro Sunlight operates scheduled domestic services.

Shipping. The main ports are Santo Domingo, Puerto Plata, La Romana and Haina. In 1995 the merchant marine totalled 2,833 GRT.

Telecommunications. There were 0·43m. telephone lines in 1994.

There were (1994) more than 170 broadcasting stations in Santo Domingo and other towns; this includes the 2 government stations. There were 7 television stations (colour by NTSC). In 1995 there were 1·3m. radio and 728,000 television receivers.

Press (1995). There were 11 dailies with a combined circulation of 264,000.

SOCIAL INSTITUTIONS

Justice. The judicial power resides in the Supreme Court of Justice, the courts of appeal, the courts of first instance, the communal courts and other tribunals created by special laws, such as the land courts. The Supreme Court consists of a president and 8 judges chosen by the Senate, and the procurator-general, appointed by the executive; it supervises the lower courts. Each province forms a judicial district, as does the National District, and each has its own procurator fiscal and court of first instance; these districts are subdivided, in all, into 97 municipalities, each with one or more local justices. The death penalty was abolished in 1924.

Religion. The religion of the state is Roman Catholic; there were 6·78m. adherents in 1992.

Education. Primary instruction is free and compulsory for children between 7 and 14 years of age; there are also secondary, normal, vocational and special schools, all of which are either wholly maintained by the State or state-aided. In 1995–96, there were 4,001 primary schools with 42,135 teachers for 1·4m. pupils, and 263,236 pupils at secondary level with 12,054 teachers. There are 4 universities, 3 Roman Catholic universities, 1 Adventist university, 3 technological universities and 1 Roman Catholic university college, and 5 other higher education institutions. Adult literacy was 82·1% in 1995 (male, 82%; female, 82·2%).

Health. There were, in 1980, 2,142 doctors and 8,953 hospital beds.

DIPLOMATIC REPRESENTATIVES

Of the Dominican Republic in Great Britain (15 Brechin Pl., London SW7 4QB)
Ambassador: Dr Pedro L. Padilla Tonos.

Of Great Britain in the Dominican Republic (Ave. 27 de Febrero 233, Santo Domingo)
Ambassador: R. Thomson.

Of the Dominican Republic in the USA (1715 22nd St., NW, Washington, D.C., 20008)
Ambassador: Bernardo Vega Boyrie.

Of the USA in the Dominican Republic (Calle Cesar Nicolas Penson, Santo Domingo)
Ambassador: Donna J. Hrinak.

Of the Dominican Republic to the United Nations
Ambassador: Cristina Aguiar.

Of the Dominican Republic to the European Union
Ambassador: Clara Quiñones.

Further Reading

Atkins, G. P., *Arms and Politics in the Dominican Republic.* London, 1981
Bell, I., *The Dominican Republic.* London, 1980
Black, J. K., *The Dominican Republic: Politics and Development in an Unsovereign State.* London, 1986
Schoenhals, K., *Dominican Republic:* [Bibliography]. London and Santa Barbara (CA), 1990
Wiarda, H. J. and Kryzanek, M. J., *The Dominican Republic: A Caribbean Crucible.* Boulder, 1982

National statistical office: Oficina Nacional de Estadistica.
Website: http://www.estadistica.gov.do/

ECUADOR

República del Ecuador

Capital: Quito
Population: 11·7m.
GDP per head: (PPP$) 4,626
GNP: US$14·7bn.
HDI/world rank: 0·775/72

KEY HISTORICAL EVENTS. The Incas of Peru conquered this territory in the 15th century but in 1532 the Spaniards, under Francisco Pizarro, founded a colony in Ecuador, then called Quito. This colony was in turn part of the viceroyalty of Peru and then of New Granada. Spanish rule was first challenged by the rising of Aug. 1809. In 1821 a revolt under Marshal Sucre led to the defeat of the Spaniards at Pichincha in 1821, and thus the winning of independence from Spain. In 1822 Bolivar persuaded the new republic to join the federation of Gran Colombia. However, in 1830 Ecuador left this federation and on 13 March 1830 became the Republic of Ecuador instead of the Presidency of Quito. For 100 years thereafter considerable difficulty was found in creating a stable régime as presidents and dictators followed one another. Since 1948 first President Galo Plazo Lasso (1948-52) and then President José Maria Velasco Ibarra (1934-35), 1944-47, 1952-56, 1960-61, 1968-72) gave more continuity to the presidential régimes, although the last named was deposed by military *coups* from four of his five presidencies.

From 1963 to 1966 and from 1976 to 1979 military juntas ruled the country. The last of these juntas produced a new constitution which was accepted by a national referendum in Jan. 1978 and came into force on 10 Aug. 1979. A new Congress was elected, and Jaime Roldós Aguilera was elected president. Since then presidencies have been more stable, although President Roldós Aguilera (1979-81) died in an air crash. A state of emergency was declared in March 1986 when Gen. Frank Vargas Pazos led an anti-government revolt at Quito air base but this ended quickly.

Following his election in July 1996, Congress deposed President Bucarám on 6 Feb. 1997 on the grounds of mental incompetence and elected the Speaker, Fabián Alarcón as President.

TERRITORY AND POPULATION. Ecuador is bounded on the north by Colombia, on the east and south by Peru and on the west by the Pacific ocean. The frontier with Peru has long been a source of dispute. The latest delimitation of it was in the treaty of Rio, 29 Jan. 1942, when, after being invaded by Peru, Ecuador lost over half her Amazonian territories. Ecuador unilaterally denounced this treaty in Sept. 1961. Fighting between Peru and Ecuador began again in Jan. 1981 over this border issue but a ceasefire was agreed in early Feb. Following a confrontation of soldiers in Aug. 1991 the foreign ministers of both countries signed a pact creating a security zone, and took their cases to the UN in Oct. 1991. Armed clashes with Peruvian forces broke out again in Jan. 1995. On 26 Jan. further armed clashes broke out with Peruvian forces in the undemarcated mutual border area ('Condor Cordillera'). On 2 Feb. talks were held under the auspices of the guarantor nations of the 1942 Protocol of Rio de Janeiro (Argentina, Brazil, Chile and the USA) but fighting continued. Ceasefires were agreed on 17 Feb. which were broken, and on 28 Feb. On 25 July 1995 an agreement between Ecuador and Peru established a demilitarized zone along their joint frontier. The frontier was re-opened on 4 Sept. 1995. Since 23 Feb. 1996 Ecuador and Peru have signed 3 further agreements to regulate the dispute.

No definite figure of the area of the country can yet be given. One estimate of the area of Ecuador is 275,830·0 sq. km, excluding the litigation zone between Peru and Ecuador, which is 190,807 sq. km, but including the **Galápagos** Archipelago (8,010 sq. km), situated in the Pacific ocean about 960 km west of Ecuador and comprising 13 islands and 19 islets. These were discovered in 1535 by Fray Tomás de Berlanga and had a population of 10,207 in 1996. They are a national park, and had about 80,000 visitors in 1995.

The population is an amalgam of European, Amerindian and African origins. Some 40% of the population is Amerindian: Quechua, Swiwiar, Achuar and Zaparo. In May 1992 they were granted title to the 1m. ha of land they occupy in Pastaza.
The official language is Spanish. Quechua and other languages are also spoken.
Census population in 1990, 9,648,189. Estimate, 1996, 11,698,496.
The population was distributed by provinces as follows in 1996:

Province	Sq. km	Population	Capital	Population[1]
Azuay	8,124·7	529,177	Cuenca	194,981
Bolívar	3,939·9	166,957	Guaranda	15,730
Cañar	3,122·1	194,529	Azogues	21,060
Carchi	3,605·1	146,343	Tulcán	37,069
Chimborazo	6,569·3	378,111	Riobamba	94,505
Cotopaxi	6,071·9	289,774	Latacunga	39,882
El Oro	5,850·1	441,025	Machala	144,197
Esmeraldas	15,239·1	327,931	Esmeraldas	98,558
Guayas	20,502·5	2,689,745	Guayaquil	1,508,444
Imbabura	4,559·3	286,155	Ibarra	80,991
Loja	11,026·5	392,877	Loja	94,305
Los Ríos	7,175·0	553,479	Babahoyo	50,285
Manabi	18,878·8	1,076,966	Portoviejo	132,937
Pichincha	12,914·7	1,893,744	Quito	1,100,847
Sucumbíos	18,327·5	90,222	Nueva Loja	13,165
Tungurahua	3,334·8	383,460	Ambato	124,166
Napo	33,930·9	114,380	Tena	7,873
Pastaza	29,773·7	46,095	Puyo	14,438
Morona-Santiago	25,690·0	104,737	Macas	8,246
Zamora-Chinchipe	23,110·8	73,383	Zamora	8,048
Galápagos	8,010·0	10,207	Puerto Baquerizo Moreno	3,023
Non-delimited zones	2,288·8	74,842		

[1] 1990 census population.

Vital statistics, 1995: Births, 408,983; deaths, 50,867; marriages, 70,480. Rates, 1994, (per 1,000 population): Birth, 31·3; death, 4·6; marriage, 6·4. Expectation of life, 1994, 69·3 years.

CLIMATE. The climate varies from equatorial, through warm temperate to mountain conditions, according to altitude which affects temperatures and rainfall. In coastal areas, the dry season is from May to Dec., but only from June to Sept. in mountainous parts, where temperatures may be 20°F colder than on the coast. Quito Jan. 59°F (15°C), July 58°F (14·4°C). Annual rainfall 44" (1,115 mm). Guayaquil. Jan. 79°F (26·1°C), July 75°F (23·9°C). Annual rainfall 39" (986 mm).

CONSTITUTION AND GOVERNMENT. A new Constitution came into force on 10 Aug. 1979. It provides for an executive President and a Vice-President to be directly elected for a non-renewable 4-year term by universal suffrage, with a further 'run-off' ballot being held between the two leading candidates where no-one has secured an absolute majority of the votes cast. The President appoints and leads a Council of Ministers. A referendum on constitutional reform was held in Nov. 1995.
Legislative power is vested in a unicameral 82-member *National Congress*, also directly elected, 12 members on a national basis for a 4-year term and 70 on a provincial basis for a 2-year term. Voting is obligatory for all literate citizens of 18–65 years. Mid-term Congressional elections were held on 19 May 1996. The Social Christian Party won 28 seats; the Roldosista Party, 19; Popular Democracy, 12; Pachacutik/New Country, 8.
On 19 May 1996 a first round of presidential elections was held. There were 9 candidates. The electorate was 5·5m. Jaime Nebot (Social Christian Party) won the first round with 29·8% of votes cast, but Abdalá Bucarám won the run-off round on 7 July with 51·2% of votes cast.
President Bucarám (b. 1952; Roldosista; sworn in 10 Aug. 1996) was deposed by Congress on 6 Feb. 1997.

President: Fabián Alarcón (b. 1948; Frente Radical Alfarista; elected by Congress 11 Feb. 1997).

Elections to the 70-member *Constitutional Assembly* (members of the *National Congress*) were held on 30 Nov. 1997. The Social Christian Party won 20 seats and the People's Democracy/Christian Democrat Union 10 seats, with the remaining 40 seats going to 15 other parties.

Presidential elections are scheduled for Aug. 1998. Pending these, President Alarcón formed an interim government in which Roldosistas and Social Democrats were not represented.

Vice President: Rosalía Arteaga Serrano. *Agriculture and Livestock:* Alfredo Saltos. *Education and Culture:* Mario Jaramillo. *Energy and Mines:* Raul Baca Carbo. *Environment:* Flor Maria Valverde. *Finance and Credit:* Marco Antonio Flores Troncoso. *Foreign Relations:* José Ayala Lasso. *Government, Police and Municipality:* Edgar Rivadeneira. *Industry, Commerce, Integration and Fisheries:* Benigno Sotomayor. *Information and Tourism:* Juana Vallejo de Navarro. *National Defence:* Ramiro Ricaurte Yanez. *Public Health:* Asdrubal de la Torre. *Public Works and Communications:* Homero Torres. *Urban Development and Housing:* Diego Ponce.

National anthem: 'Salve, Oh Patria, mil veces, Oh Patria' ('Hail, Oh Fatherland, a thousand times, Oh Fatherland'); words by J. L. Mera, music by A. Neumane.

Local Government. The country is divided administratively into 21 provinces. The provinces are administered by governors, appointed by the Government; their sub-divisions, or cantons, by political chiefs and elected cantonal councillors; and the parishes by political lieutenants. The 21 provinces are made up of 193 cantons, 322 urban parishes and 757 rural parishes. Elections for 54 provincial and 608 municipal councillors were held in June 1994. Elections for all provincial governorships were held on 19 May 1996.

DEFENCE. Military service is selective, with a 1-year period of conscription. The country is divided into 4 military zones, with headquarters at Quito, Guayaquil, Cuenca and Pastaza.

Army. The Army consists of 1 infantry division, 1 armoured, 2 infantry, 1 special forces and 3 'jungle' brigades, 1 aviation group, 1 air defence artillery group and 3 engineer battalions. Equipment includes 45 American M-3 and 108 French AMX-13 light tanks. The aviation element has about 30 transport and communications aircraft, including 12 helicopters. Strength (1997) 50,000, with about 100,000 reservists.

Navy. Navy combatant forces include 2 German-built diesel submarines, 2 ex-UK missile-armed Leander class frigates, 6 Italian-built missile corvettes (with helicopter deck) and 6 fast missile craft. Amphibious capability is 1 landing ship and 6 small craft. Auxiliaries consist of 1 ex-German depot ship, 1 small tanker, 1 survey ship, 1 armament carrier, 2 tugs and 1 training ship as well as some 8 harbour and service vessels. The Maritime Air Force has 11 aircraft, including 1 CN-235 transport, 3 Cessna light aircraft, 3 T-34C trainers, and 4 Jet Ranger helicopters. Naval personnel in 1997 totalled 4,100 including some 1,500 marines.

There are 6 inshore Coast Guard cutters and some 20 boats.

Air Force. The Air Force had a 1997 strength of about 3,000 personnel and 60 combat aircraft and includes a strike squadron equipped with 8 single-seat and 2 two-seat Jaguars; an interceptor squadron of 12 single-seat and 1 two-seat Mirage F.1; an interceptor squadron with 15 Kfirs; 3 counter-insurgency units equipped with 10 Cessna A-37B and 10 Strikemaster light jet attack and training aircraft, 1 squadron with 2 C-130, 1 Buffalo, 1 Twin Otter and 3 HS 748 turboprop transports; Alouette III, Bell 212, UH-1 Iroquois and SA 315B Lama helicopters; and Cessna 150, T-34C-1 and T-41A/D trainers. 1 F.28, 1 Boeing 737 and 3 Boeing 727 transports are operated by the military airline TAME.

INTERNATIONAL RELATIONS

Membership. Ecuador is a member of the UN, OAS, the Andean Group and LAIA.

ECONOMY

Policy. A reform programme was announced in 1992, including the privatization of 20 state-owned enterprises. Further privatization legislation followed in 1993. A new economic plan was promulgated in Nov. 1996, envisaging privatization of the oil and electricity sectors.

Budget. Revenue in 1995 was 8,030,429m. sucres and expenditure, 8,450,621m. sucres.

Currency. The monetary unit is the *sucre* (ECS), of 100 *centavos*. There are coins of 10, 20, 50, 100 and 500 sucres, and notes of 5,000, 10,000, 20,000 and 50,000 sucres. The sucre was devalued by 8% in Aug. 1996. Inflation was 24% in 1996. Foreign exchange reserves were US$1,761m. in Oct. 1996. Economic reforms of Nov. 1996 envisaged the convertibility of the currency as from 1 July 1997, with the sucre pegged to the US dollar at US$1 = 4 sucres. Under the reform programme foreign exchange reserves must at least match currency in circulation.

Banking and Finance. The Central Bank of Ecuador (*Governor*, Fidel Jaramillo), the bank of issue, with a capital and reserves of US$1,557m. at 31 Dec. 1995, is modelled after the Federal Reserve Banks of the USA: through branches opened in 16 towns it now deals in mortgage bonds. All commercial banks must be affiliated to the Central Bank. Legislation of May 1994 liberalized the financial sector.

There are stock exchanges in Quito and Guayaquil.

Weights and Measures. The metric system is the legal standard but English and old Spanish measures are still in use. A case (*caja*) of bananas = 18·14 kg.

ENERGY AND NATURAL RESOURCES

Electricity. In 1995, total capacity of hydro-electric and thermal plants was 2,469 MW. Output was 8,326 MWh.

Oil and Gas. Production of crude oil in 1995 was 141,151,000 bbls. Estimated reserves, 1995, 3,500m. bbls. In 1994, natural gas production was 6,284,900 bbls.

Minerals. Main products are silver, gold, copper and zinc. The country also has some iron, uranium, lead, coal, cobalt, manganese and titanium.

Agriculture. In 1991 3·23m. persons subsisted on agriculture, of whom 999,000 were economically active.

50,000 ha of rich virgin land in the Santo Domingo de los Colorados area has been set aside for settlement by medium and large landowners. A law of 1994 restricts the redistribution of land to small farmers to land which has lain fallow for more than 3 years.

The staple export products are bananas, cacao and coffee. Main crops, in 1,000 tonnes, in 1995: Rice, 1,291; potatoes, 477; maize, 613; barley (1994), 32; cocoa beans, 81; bananas, 5,086; coffee, 187; sugar-cane, 3,635.

Livestock, 1995 (in 1,000): Cattle, 4,994; sheep, 1,692; pigs, 2,620; goats, 295; poultry, 61,512.

Forestry. Excepting the agricultural zones and a few arid spots on the Pacific coast, Ecuador is a vast forest. 11·8m. ha, 43% of the land area is forested, but much of the forest is not commercially accessible.

Fisheries. In 1993 primary sea export products were valued at US$498·9m.

INDUSTRY. Production in 1994: Residual fuel oils, 3·0m. tonnes; cement, 2·1m. tonnes.

Trades Unions. The main trade union federation is the United Workers' Front.

FOREIGN ECONOMIC RELATIONS. Most restrictions on foreign investment were removed in 1992 and the repatriation of profits was permitted. Foreign debt was US$7,800m. in 1994.

Commerce. Imports and exports for calendar years, in US$1m.:

	1991	1992	1993	1994	1995
Imports (f.o.b.)	2,116	1,976	2,223	3,209	4,095
Exports (f.o.b.)	2,851	3,008	3,062	3,843	4,362

Ecuador is a major exporter of shrimps (US$673m. in 1995). Other major exports (1995, in US$1m.): Bananas, 845; coffee beans, 244; cocoa beans and products, 133; cut flowers, 79. Main export markets, 1995 (in US$1m.): USA, 1,847 (42%); Colombia, 246; Chile, 193; Germany, 166; Spain, 149. Main import suppliers: USA, 1,290 (32%); Colombia, 396; Japan, 328; Germany, 192; Brazil, 187.

Tourism. There were 442,042 visitors in 1995. Income from tourism, 1995, US$255m. (US$252m. in 1994).

COMMUNICATIONS

Roads. In 1995, there were estimated to be 43,106 km of roads. A trunk highway through the coastal plain will link Machala in the extreme south-west with Esmeraldas in the north-west and with Quito and the northern section of the Pan-American Highway; in 1994, 1,214 km had been built and 273 km were under construction. In 1992, there were 353,393 cars and 52,586 commercial vehicles.

Railways. The railway was closed in 1995.

Civil Aviation. There is an international airport at Quito (Mariscal Sucre). The national carriers are SAETA, SAN and TAME. In 1995, SAETA operated 2 A310-300s, 3 A320-200s, 1 B-727, 1 B-727-200 Adv, 1 B 737-200 Adv and 1 B-737-300. Services are also provided by Aeroperú, Air France, American Airlines, AOM, Avianca, Continental Airlines and Air Micronesia, COPA, Cubana, Iberia, KLM, LACSA, LAPSA, Lloyd Aereo Boliviano, Lufthansa, Servivensa and Varig.

Shipping. Ecuador has 3 major seaports, of which Guayaquil is the chief, and 6 minor ones. In 1995, the merchant navy totalled 0·36m. GRT of ocean-going vessels, including oil-tankers, 0·13m. GRT.

Telecommunications. In 1995 there were 1,046,462 telephones. In 1993 there were 3m. radios and 0·9m. TV receivers (colour by NTSC).

Press (1995). There were 75 daily, weekly and fortnightly newspapers.

SOCIAL INSTITUTIONS

Justice. The Supreme Court in Quito, consisting of a President and 30 Justices, comprises 6 chambers each of 5 Justices. It is also a Court of Appeal. There is a Superior Court in each province, comprising chambers (as appointed by the Supreme Court) of 3 magistrates each. The Superior Courts are at the apex of a hierarchy of various tribunals. There is no death penalty.

Religion. The state recognizes no religion and grants freedom of worship to all. In 1993 there were 10·21m. Roman Catholics.

Education. In 1995–96, there were 158,679 pre-primary pupils with 9,278 teachers. Primary education is free and compulsory. Private schools, both primary and secondary, are under some state supervision. In 1995 there were 16,868 primary schools and 2,965 secondary schools. In 1995–96 there were 1,793,882 pupils and 70,001 teachers in primary schools. In 1995–96, there were in the public sector: 9 universities, 3 Roman Catholic, 12 technical, 1 agricultural and 2 polytechnical universities, 2 institutes of technology and 1 military polytechnic; and in the private sector: 2 universities, 1 Roman Catholic and 1 technological university. 1994 adult literacy rate: 89·6%.

Health. In 1993 there were 12,149 doctors and 433 hospitals, 1,542 dentists and 906 pharmacists.

DIPLOMATIC REPRESENTATIVES

Of Ecuador in Great Britain (3 Hans Cres., London, SW1X 0LS)
Ambassador: Patricio Maldonado.

Of Great Britain in Ecuador (Calle González Suárez 111, Quito)
Ambassador: John William Forbes-Meyler, OBE.

Of Ecuador in the USA (2535 15th St., NW, Washington, D.C., 20009)
Ambassador: Alberto Maspons.

Of the USA in Ecuador (Avenida 12 de Octubre y Avenida Patria, Quito)
Ambassador: Leslie Alexander.

Of Ecuador to the United Nations
Ambassador: Luis Valencia Rodríguez.

Of Ecuador to the European Union
Ambassador: Alfredo Pinoargote Cevallos.

Further Reading

Corkill, D., *Ecuador.* [Bibliography] Oxford and Santa Barbara (CA), 1989
Hidrobo, J. A., *Power and Industrialization in Ecuador.* Boulder (CO), 1993
Martz, J. D., *Ecuador: Conflicting Political Culture and the Quest for Progress.* Boston, 1972.—
  Politics and Petroleum in Ecuador. New Brunswick, 1987

National statistical office: Instituto Nacional de Estadistica y Censos (INEC).
Website: http://www4.inec.gov.ec/

EGYPT

Jumhuriyat Misr al-Arabiya

(Arab Republic of Egypt)

Capital: Cairo
Population: 61·4m
GDP per head (PPP$): 3,846
GNP: US$41·0bn.
HDI/world rank: 0·614/109

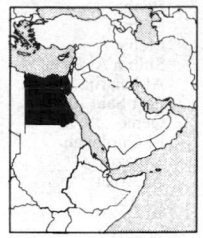

KEY HISTORICAL EVENTS. Egypt was part of the Ottoman Empire from 1517 until 1922, when it achieved independence, albeit qualified, from Britain, which had exercised direct control over Egyptian affairs since occupying the country in 1882. Muhammad Ali (1805–40) succeeded in establishing a hereditary dynasty of Khedives, yet with the opening of the Suez Canal in 1869 and Britain's purchase of the Khedives' shares, Egypt's strategic importance paved the way for foreign intervention and domination. In 1914 the country became a British protectorate and the Khedive was deposed. On 28 Feb. 1922, Egypt was declared an independent constitutional monarchy.

In the Second World War (1939–45) Egypt supported the Allies. Following a revolution in July 1952 led by Gen. Neguib, King Farouk abdicated in favour of his son, but in 1953 the monarchy was abolished. Neguib became president but encountered opposition from the military who attempted to move towards a parliamentary republic. Col. Gamal Abdel Nasser seized power and Neguib resigned. Nasser became head of state on 14 June 1954 (president from 1956), and remained in office until he died on 28 Sept. 1970. In 1956 Egypt nationalized the Suez Canal, a move which led Britain, France and Israel to mount military attacks against Egypt until forced by the UN and the USA to withdraw.

In 1958 Egypt and Syria united to form the United Arab Republic (UAR), but Syria withdrew in 1961. For ten years Egypt retained the name UAR, but a new constitution, approved by a referendum on 11 Sept. 1971 renamed the country the Arab Republic of Egypt.

The 1960s and 1970s saw constant conflict with Israel until President Muhammad Anwar Sadat, who succeeded Nasser, made a dramatic peace treaty with Israel in March 1979. Sadat was assassinated on 6 Oct. 1981, and was succeeded by the vice-president, Lieut.-Gen. Muhammad Hosni Mubarak.

TERRITORY AND POPULATION. Egypt is bounded in the east by Israel, the Gulf of Aqaba and the Red Sea, south by Sudan, west by Libya and north by the Mediterranean. The total area is 997,739 sq. km, but the cultivated and settled area, that is, the Nile Valley, Delta and oases, covers only 35,189 sq. km. Population density in this latter, 1992, 1,557·9 per sq. km. In 1997 the population was 61,404,000 (of whom 98% live in the Nile Valley and Delta). 2·3m. Egyptians were living abroad in 1997.

Vital statistics: Marriages, 1994, 0·53m. (rate per 1,000, 9·1); divorces, 90,000 (1.5); births (1994), 1·75m (26·8); deaths, 0·42m (7·6). Growth rate, 1995, 21·3 per 1,000 (it is government policy to reduce this to 21 per 1,000). Fertility rate, 1993, 3·9 births per woman. In 1991 the average family size was 4·3. 40% of the population was under 40 years. Life expectancy is 64·3 years.

Area, population and capitals of the governorates (1986 census and 1995 estimate):

Governorate	Area (in sq. km)	Population (1986 census)	1995 estimate (in 1,000)	Capital
Alexandria	2,679·36	2,917,327	3,431	Alexandria
Aswan	678·50	801,408	1,042	Aswan
Asyut	1,553·00	2,223,034	2,843	Asyut
Behera	10,129·49	3,257,168	3,973	Damanhur
Beni Suef	1,321·65	1,442,981	1,836	Beni Suef
Cairo	214·20	6,052,836	6,955	Cairo
Dakahlia	3,470·90	3,500,470	4,226	Mansura

Governorate	Area (in sq. km)	Population (1986 census)	1995 estimate (in 1,000)	Capital
Damietta	589·17	741,264	898	Damietta
Fayum	1,827·15	1,544,047	1,995	Fayum
Gharbia	1,942·21	2,870,960	3,437	Tanta
Giza	1,058·20	3,700,054	4,525	Giza
Ismailia	1,441·59	544,427	681	Ismailia
Kafr El Shaikh	3,437·12	1,800,129	2,266	Kafr El Shaikh
Kalyubia	1,001·09	2,514,244	3,045	Benha
Matruh	212,112·00	160,567	186	Matruh
Menia	2,261·72	2,648,043	3,372	Menia
Menufia	1,532·13	2,227,087	2,672	Shibin Al Kom
New Valley	376,505·00	113,838	136	Al Kharija
Port Said	72·01	399,793	467	Port Said
Qena	1,850·70	2,252,315	2,766	Qena
Red Sea	203,685·00	90,491	115	El Gurdakah
Sharkia	4,179·55	3,420,119	4,220	Zagazig
North Sinai	27,574·00	171,505	219	Al Arish
South Sinai	33,140·00	28,988	35	At Tur
Suez	17,840·42	326,820	411	Suez
Suhag	1,547·21	2,455,134	3,067	Suhag

Principal cities, with estimated 1990 populations (in 1,000): Cairo, 6,452; Alexandria, 3,170; Giza, 2,156; Shubra Al Khayma, 811; Port Said, 461; Suez, 392.

Smaller cities, with 1986 census populations: Mahalla Al Kubra, 358,844; Tanta, 334,505; Hulwan, 328,000; Mansura, 316,870; Asyut, 273,191; Zagazig, 255,000; Kafr Ad Dawwar, 223,000; Ismailia, 212,567; Fayum, 212,523; Aswan, 191,461; Damanhur, 190,840; Menia, 179,136; Beni Suef, 151,813; Uqsur (Luxor), 138,000; Suhag, 132,965; Shibin Al Kom, 132,751; Qena, 119,794; Benha, 115,571; Damietta, 113,000; Kafr Ash Shaikh, 102,910.

The official language is Arabic, although French and English are widely spoken.

CLIMATE. The climate is mainly dry, but there are winter rains along the Mediterranean coast. Elsewhere, rainfall is very low and erratic in its distribution. Winter temperatures are everywhere comfortable, but summer temperatures are very high, especially in the south. Cairo. Jan. 56°F (13·3°C), July 83°F (28·3°C). Annual rainfall 1·2" (28 mm). Alexandria. Jan. 58°F (14·4°C), July 79°F (26·1°C). Annual rainfall 7" (178 mm). Aswan. Jan. 62°F (16·7°C), July 92°F (33·3°C). Annual rainfall trace. Giza. Jan. 55°F (12·8°C), July 78°F (25·6°C). Annual rainfall 16" (389 mm). Ismailia. Jan. 56°F (13·3°C), July 84°F (28·9°C). Annual rainfall 1·5" (37 mm). Luxor. Jan. 59°F (15°C), July 86°F (30°C). Annual rainfall trace. Port Said. Jan. 58°F (14·4°C), July 78°F (27·2°C). Annual rainfall 3" (76 mm).

CONSTITUTION AND GOVERNMENT. The Constitution was approved by referendum on 11 Sept. 1971. It defines Egypt as 'an Arab Republic with a democratic, socialist system' and the Egyptian people as 'part of the Arab nation'. The *President* is nominated by the People's Assembly and confirmed by plebiscite for a 6-year term. The President may appoint 1 or more *Vice-Presidents.* The *People's Assembly* is a unicameral legislature consisting of 444 members directly elected from 222 constituencies for a 5-year term, and 10 members appointed by the President. There is a *Constitutional Court.*

The President appoints the Prime Minister and a Council of Ministers. It is traditional for 2 ministers to be Christian Copts.

A 210-member consultative body, the *Shura Council*, was established in 1980. Two-thirds of its members are elected and one-third appointed by the President.

Elections for the People's Assembly were held in 2 rounds on 29 Nov. and 6 Dec. 1995. The electorate was 21m.; turn-out was 50%. 3,980 candidates representing 14 parties stood. The National Democratic Party (NDP) gained 317 seats; ind (mainly NDP sympathizers), 113; Wafd, 6; Progressive Rally (former Communists), 5; Nasserites, 1; Liberal Socialists, 1, Islamic Workers, 1. 109 results were challenged by the Constitutional Court.

President: Hosni Mubarak (b. 1928; NDP; sworn in for a third term Oct. 1993).

A new government was formed on 4 Jan. 1996 which comprised in March 1998:
Prime Minister, Minister of Planning and International Co-operation: Dr Kamal El Ganzouri (b. 1934).
Deputy Prime Minister and Minister of Agriculture and Land Reclamation: Dr Youssouf Amin Wali. *Transport and Communication:* Suliman Metwalli Suliman. *Electricity and Energy:* Maher Abaza. *Defence and Military Production:* Field-Marshal Mohammed Hussein Tantawi. *Information:* Mohammed Safwat El-Sharif. *Foreign Affairs:* Amr Moussa. *Public Enterprises:* Dr Atef Mohammed Ebeid. *Justice:* Farouq Seif El-Nasr. *Culture:* Farouq Hosni. *Rural Development:* Dr Mahmoud Sharif. *Labour and Migration:* Ahmed El-Emawi. *Trade and Supply:* Ahmed Goweili. *Finance:* Dr Mohieddin Abu Bakr El-Gharib. *Cabinet Affairs and Follow-up:* Tala'at Sayed Hammad. *Religious Affairs (Waqfs):* Mahmoud Hamdi Zakzouk. *Industry and Mineral Resources:* Suliman Reda Suliman. *Health and Population:* Dr Ismail Awadallah Sallam. *Economy:* Youssef Boutros Ghali. *Education:* Dr Hussein Kamal Bahaeddin. *Oil:* Dr Hamdi El-Banbi. *Interior:* Gen. Habib El Adly. *Tourism:* Mamdouh El-Beltagi. *Public Works and Water Resources:* Mahmoud Abdul Halim Abu Zeid. *Housing, Utilities and New Communities:* Dr Mohammed Ibrahim Suliman. *Higher Education and Research:* Mofeed Shehab. *Social Insurance and Social Affairs:* Mervat Mehana El-Talawi. *Parliamentary Affairs:* Kamal El-Shazli. *Administrative Development:* Mohamed Abu Amer. *Environment:* Dr Nadia Riyad Makram Ebeid. *Local Administration:* Mahmud Sayid Ahmad Sharif.

National anthem: 'Biladi' ('My homeland'); words and tune by S. Darwish.

Local Government: The 26 governorates are divided into districts (*mudiriya*) and communes. Provincial governors are nominated by the President. Municipal elections were held on 3 Nov. 1992.

DEFENCE. Conscription is selective, for 3 years.

Army. There are 4 military districts and 2 Army headquarters. The Army comprises 1 infantry, 4 armoured and 7 mechanized infantry divisions; 1 Republican Guard, 4 independent armoured, 2 independent infantry, 4 independent mechanized, 1 air mobile, 1 parachute, 15 independent artillery and 2 surface-to-surface missile brigades and 6 commando groups. Equipment includes 840 T-54/-55, 500 T-62, 1,700 M-60 and 260 Ramses II (modified T-54/55) main battle tanks. Strength (1997) 320,000 (250,000 conscripts).

Navy. 2 of the current submarine force of 6 old ex-Soviet and ex-Chinese 'Romeo' class submarines have been modernized in the USA. Major surface combatants include 1 very old destroyer, 2 Spanish-built, 2 Chinese-built missile-armed frigates and 2 ex US Knox class. There are also 25 missile craft of mixed British, Soviet and Chinese origin and 18 coastal and inshore patrol craft. A small shore-based naval aviation branch operates 5 Sea King and 9 Gazelle helicopters. Mine warfare forces include 7 coastal minesweepers and 3 inshore minehunters. 3 ex-Soviet medium landing ships provide amphibious lift supported by 11 minor landing craft. There are 6 major auxiliaries and some 14 minor service vessels. There are naval bases at Alexandria, Port Said, Mersa Matruh, Port Tewfik, Hurghada and Safaqa. Naval personnel in 1997 totalled 20,000. An associated para-military coastguard about 2,000 strong operates 33 inshore cutters and numerous boats.

Air Force. Until 1979, the Air Force was equipped largely with aircraft of USSR design, but subsequent re-equipment involves aircraft bought in the West, as well as some supplied by China. Strength (1997) is about 80,000 personnel (50,000 conscripts), over 100 attack helicopters and 420 combat aircraft, of which the interceptors are operated by an independent Air Defence Command, in conjunction with many 'Guideline', 'Goa', 'Gainful', Hawk and Crotale missile batteries. The interceptor/ground attack fighter divisions are equipped with 150 F-16 Fighting Falcons, 50 Mirage 5s, 32 F-4E Phantoms, 19 Mirage 2000s, 70 F-6s (Chinese-built MiG-19s), 14 Alpha Jets and 60 F-7s (Chinese-built MiG-21s). Airborne early warning capability is provided by 5 E-2C Hawkeyes. Transport units have 22

C-130H Hercules turboprop heavy freighters, 5 An-12s, 9 twin-turboprop Buffaloes, 4 Beech 1900s, and over 175 Gazelle, AH-64 Apache, Mi-8, Commando and Agusta-built CH-47C helicopters; some Commando helicopters, Beech 1900s and 2 EC-130H Hercules are equipped for electronic warfare duties. Training units are equipped with Embraer Tucanos, Czech-built L-39 Albatros and French-designed Alpha Jet jet trainers, two-seat FT-6s, Mirage 5s and UH-12E helicopters. Main aircrew training centre is the Air Force Academy at Bilbeis.

INTERNATIONAL RELATIONS

Membership. Egypt is a member of the UN, OAU, Arab League and OAPEC.

ECONOMY

Policy. A privatization programme which began in 1993 envisaged the sale of 85 out of the 314 public sector companies by 1998. Foreign investment (US$900m. in 1996) has financed a huge development project in the Sinai Peninsula and Upper Egypt which aims to increase the inhabited area of the country from 6% to 20% in 20 years.

Performance. Real GDP growth was estimated at 5·7% in 1996–97 (2·2% in 1995), with a budget deficit of 0·8% of GDP.

Budget. The financial year runs from 1 July. The 1993–94 budget envisaged revenue of £E51,711m. and expenditure of £E55,325m. Sources of revenue (in £E1m.) included: Tax, 31,164; customs duties, 6,070; oil industry, 4,610; Suez Canal, 2,610. Items of expenditure included: Salaries, 11,026; pensions, 3,864; subsidies, 3,170; debt service, 16,426; defence, 5,892; public health (1992–93), 6,620.

Currency. The monetary unit is the *Egyptian pound* (EGP) of 100 *piastres*. There are coins of 5, 10 and 50 piastres, notes of 25 and 50 piastres and notes of £E1, 5, 10, 20, 50 and 100. Currency in circulation in 1994 was £E20,981m. In Feb. 1991 the official exchange rate was abolished, leaving a free rate, and a rate set by a panel of bankers. Annualized inflation was 5·4% in 1997. Foreign exchange reserves were US$16,719m. including gold.

Banking and Finance. The Central Bank of Egypt (founded 1960) is the central bank and bank of issue. The *Governor* is Ismail Hassan.

In 1994, 4 major public sector commercial banks accounted for some 70% of all banking assets: the National Bank of Egypt, the Banque Misr, the Bank of Alexandria and the Banque du Caïre. There were 40 other domestic commercial banks, 15 investment banks and 30 regional development banks, as well as foreign banks, branches and joint ventures.

Savings and term deposits in 1992 totalled £E83,034m.

There are stock exchanges in Cairo and Alexandria.

Weights and Measures. In 1951 the metric system was made official with the exception of the feddan and its subdivisions. However, other traditional measures are still in use: *Kadah* = 1/96th ardeb = 3·36 pints. *Rob* = 4 kadahs = 1·815 gallons. *Keila* = 8 kadahs = 3·63 gallons. *Ardeb* = 96 kadahs = 43·555 gallons, or 5·44439 bu., or 198 cu. decimetres. *Rotl* = 144 dirhems = 0·9905 lb. *Oke* = 400 dirhems = 2·75137 lb. *Qantar* or 100 rotls or 36 okes = 99·0493 lb. 1 *Qantar* of unginned cotton = 315 lb. 1 *Qantar* of ginned cotton = 99·05 lb. The approximate weight of the ardeb is as follows: Wheat, 150 kg; beans, 155 kg; barley, 120 kg; maize, 140 kg; cotton seed, 121 kg. *Feddan,* the unit of measure for land = 4,200·8 sq. metres = 7,468·148 sq. pics = 1·03805 acres. 1 sq. pic = 6·0547 sq. ft = 0·5625 sq. metre.

ENERGY AND NATURAL RESOURCES

Electricity. Electricity generated in 1996 was 54·4bn. kWh. Power used for domestic and commercial purposes in 1996 was 17·41m. kWh per hour. By 1995, 75% of power was gas-generated and use of solar energy is expanding.

Oil and Gas. Oil was discovered in 1909. Oil policy is controlled by the state-owned Egyptian General Petroleum Corporation, whole or part-owner of the production and refining companies. Production of crude (1995), 44·5m. tonnes. Gas reserves are estimated to be as high as 21,000,000m. cu. ft. Output was 9·1m. tonnes in 1993–94.

Minerals. Production (1993–94, in tonnes): Phosphate, 0·86m.; iron ore, 2·7m.; salt, 1·12m.; kaolin, 0·2m.; quartz, 84,000; asbestos and fermacolite, 916. Mining for uranium ore began near Aswan in May 1991.

Water. The Aswan High Dam, completed in 1970, allows for a perennial irrigation system.

Agriculture. Agriculture produced 22% of GDP in 1995. The cultivated area in 1996 was 7·6m. feddans, of which 1·4m. feddans were reclaimed desert. Irrigation is vital to agriculture and is being developed by government programmes; it now reaches most cultivated areas. 6·5% of the land area is arable. The Nile provides 85% of the water used in irrigation, some 55,000m. cu. metres annually.

In 1994 there were 5,214 agricultural co-operatives. 0·71m. feddan of land had been distributed by 1991 to 0·35m. families under an agrarian reform programme. In 1992 32·7% of the workforce worked in agriculture. Cotton, sugar-cane and rice are subject to government price controls and procurement quotas.

Output (in 1,000 tonnes), 1994: Barley, 130; broad beans, 357; chickpeas, 11; cotton seed (1993), 652; seed cotton (1993), 1,114; garlic, 150; lentils, 9; flax fibre and tow (1992), 11; maize, 5,550; dry onions, 481; peanuts, 194; potatoes, 1,032; rice, 4,583; sesame, 29; soya beans, 68; sugar-cane, 12,412; sugar-beet, 825; strawberries, 28; wheat, 4,437; sorghum (1992), 736.

Livestock (in 1,000), 1994: Cattle, 3,764; buffaloes, 2,592; sheep, 4,666; goats, 5,492; camels, 245; pigs, 134. There were 36·6m. chickens (egg production 2,214m.). 9,000 tonnes of honey were produced.

Forestry. In 1994 total removal of roundwood was 2·64m. cu. metres.

Fisheries. The catch in 1994 was 307,516 tonnes, of which 219,404 tonnes were freshwater fish.

INDUSTRY. Almost all large-scale enterprises are in the public sector and these account for about two-thirds of total output. The private sector, dominated by food processing and textiles, consists of about 150,000 small and medium businesses, most employing less than 50 workers. Industry production in 1995–96 showed a growth rate of 8% (£E74·1bn., compared to £E69·98bn. in 1994–95).

Production in 1993–94 (in 1,000 tonnes) included: White sugar crystal, 629; refined sugar, 481; tobacco, 50; cotton yarn, 299; jute yarn, 21; sulphuric acid, 112; paper, 200; fertilizers, 6,697; steel billets and sections, 368. 6,557 cars, 1,379 lorries, 100 tractors, 247,000 refrigerators, 209,000 washing machines, 24,000 bicycles, 13,000 radio (1992–93) and 281,000 TV sets were produced. Production of cotton textiles and synthetic textiles in 1990–91 was 1·38m. tonnes and 0·11m. tonnes respectively.

Labour. In 1996–97 the workforce was 17·4m. (from 16·9m in 1995–96). In 1992 32·7% of the workforce were employed in agriculture, forestry and fisheries, 29·7% in services, 21·4% in manufacturing, 15·5% in mining, 10·6% in business, 4·5% in transport and communications and 1·1% in tourism. 2,220 working days were lost through strikes in 1990. Unemployment was 11·8% in 1997.

FOREIGN ECONOMIC RELATIONS. Foreign debt totalled US$33bn. in 1997. Foreign investment in 1996 was £E2·6bn.

Commerce. In 1995–96, exports were valued at £E16·7bn. and imports at £E46·6bn.

Export of principal commodities (in £E1m.) in 1994: Crude oil; 2,684·98; raw cotton, 791·08; cotton yarn, 1,279·54; cotton fabrics, 409·03; clothing, 780; refined petroleum, 742·08; aluminium bars, etc., 405; oranges, 278·4; potatoes, 98·2. Imports: Wheat, 2,501·17; maize, 892·46; dairy products, 509·4; chemicals, 1,107·3; iron bars, 90·78; motor car parts, 762·05; motor cars, 746·46.

Main export markets, 1994: (percentage share of total trade): Italy, 19·8%; USA, 9·7%; Greece, 8·8%; UK, 6·3%; Spain, 4·8%; Germany, 4·7%. Main import suppliers: USA, 20·4%; Italy, 9·7%; Germany, 9·2%; UK, 4·1%.

Tourism. Terrorist attacks on tourists have reduced visitor numbers and revenue. In the first quarter of 1997 visitors totalled 931,405.

COMMUNICATIONS

Roads. In 1990 there were 30,105 km of highways and 22,690 km of desert roads. The road link between Sinai and the mainland across the Suez Canal was opened in 1996. Vehicles (in 1,000), 1994: Motor cars, 968; lorries, 399; motor cycles, 371; buses, 37.

Railways. In 1994 there were 5,024 km of state railways (1,435 mm gauge), of which 42 km were electrified. In 1994, 1,030m. passengers and 12·3m. tonnes of freight were carried.

There are tramway networks in Cairo and Alexandria, and a metro (11 km) opened in Cairo in 1996.

Civil Aviation. There are international airports at Cairo and Luxor. The national carrier is Egyptair, which in 1995 operated 4 A300B4-200s, 9 A300B4-600Rs, 7 A320-200s, 1 B-707-320C, 2 B-737-200 Advs, 4 B-737-500s, 2 B-747-300 Combis, 3 B-767-200ERs and 2 B-767-300ERs.

Services were also provided by Aeroflot, Air Algérie, Air France, Air Malta, Air Ukraine, Alitalia, Austrian Airlines, Balkan, British Airways, Cyprus Airways, Czech Airlines, El Al, Emirates, Ethiopian Airlines, Gulf Air, Iberia, JAT, KLM, Kenya Airways, Korean Air, Kuwait Airways, Libyan Airlines, LOT, Lufthansa, Malév, Middle East Airlines, Northwest Airlines, Olympic Airways, Pakistan International Airlines, Qatar Airways, Royal Air Maroc, Royal Jordanian, Saudia, Singapore Airlines, SAA, Sudan Airways, Swissair, Syrian Airlines, Tarom, TransWorld, Tunis Air, Turkish Airlines, United Airlines and Yemenia. 8·5m. passengers arrived or departed in 1996–97 (8·96m. in 1993–94). In 1993–94 107,207 tons of freight were carried.

Shipping. In 1995 the merchant marine totalled 1·9m. GRT, including oil tankers, 0·45m. GRT. Vessels arriving and leaving at major ports in 1995–96: 8,800; tonnes of freight: 427,333m. Dockyards for containerized shipping were constructed in Alexandria, Dekheila, Damietta and Port Said in 1995–96, with 2 more planned for Adabeya and the Suez Canal.

Suez Canal. The Suez Canal was opened for navigation on 17 Nov. 1869 and nationalized in June 1956. By the convention of Constantinople of 29 Oct. 1888 the canal is open to vessels of all nations and is free from blockade, except in time of war. It is 173 km long (excluding 11 km of approach channels to the harbours), connecting the Mediterranean with the Red Sea. It is being deepened from 16 to 17 metres and widened from 365 to 415 metres to permit the passage of vessels of 180,000 DWT.

In 1994 16,370 vessels (net tonnage, 364m. tonnes; cargo, 290m. tons; passengers, 15,800) went through the canal. Toll revenue in 1994 was US$1,897m. Tolls for tankers were reduced by 20% after Jan. 1996.

Telecommunications. There were, in 1993–94, 2,035 postal agencies, 1,972 mobile offices, 2,655 government and 2,472 private post offices. Number of telephones in 1994, 2,474,225. The internal telecommunications system is owned and operated by the Telecommunications Organization.

Broadcasting is conducted by the government-controlled Egyptian Radio and TV Union. Number of radio receivers in 1995, 19·4m.; TV sets, 6·8m. Colour is by SECAM.

Cinemas. In 1994 there were 138 cinemas. 72 films were made in 1995.

Press. In 1995 there were 14 dailies with a total circulation of 2·6m. To set up a newspaper requires permission from the prime minister.

SOCIAL INSTITUTIONS

Justice. The court system comprises: A Court of Cassation with a bench of 5 judges which constitutes the highest court of appeal in both criminal and civil cases;

5 Courts of Appeal with 3 judges; Assize Courts with 3 judges which deal with all cases of serious crime; Central Tribunals with 3 judges which deal with ordinary civil and commercial cases; Summary Tribunals presided over by a single judge which hear minor civil disputes and criminal offences.

The death penalty is in force.

Religion. Islam is constitutionally the state religion. In 1992 there were 50·4m. Moslems, mostly of the Sunni sect. Some 7% of the population are Coptic Christians, the remainder being Roman Catholics, Protestants or Greek Orthodox, with a small number of Jews. A Patriarch heads the Coptic Church, and there are 25 metropolitans and bishops in Egypt; 4 metropolitans for Ethiopia, Jerusalem, Khartoum and Omdurman, and 12 bishops in Ethiopia. The Copts use the Diocletian (or Martyrs') calendar, which begins in AD 284.

Education. Adult literacy is 50·5%. Free compulsory education is provided in primary schools (8 years). Secondary and technical education is also free. There are no private fee-paying schools except remedial classes, but private coaching is widespread. In 1995–96 there were 2,060 pre-primary schools with 266,502 pupils and 10,913 teachers; 16,188 primary schools with 7,470,437 pupils and 302,916 teachers; 2,753 secondary schools with 6,142,651 pupils and 369,107 teachers

Al Azhar institutes educate students who intend enrolling at Al Azhar University. In 1993–94 in the Al Azhar system there were 1,912 primary schools with 704,446 pupils, 1,030 preparatory schools with 147,762 pupils and 587 secondary schools with 165,829 pupils.

In 1993–94 there were 49,703 students in commerce institutes (24,906 women) and 31,259 in technical institutes (9,401 women). In 1995–96 there were 13 state universities, 1 American university and 1 academy of science and technology. There were 612,844 students (231,065 women) and 33,100 academic staff in 1993–94. 4 private universities opened in 1996.

Health. In 1992 there were 101,500 doctors, 15,150 dentists, 34,700 pharmacists and 98,500 other medical personnel. In 1994 there were 6,332 treatment units (including 330 general hospitals) with 113,020 beds.

DIPLOMATIC REPRESENTATIVES

Of Egypt in Great Britain (12 Curzon St., London, W1Y 7FY)
Ambassador: Adel El-Gazzar.

Of Great Britain in Egypt (Ahmed Ragheb St., Garden City, Cairo)
Ambassador: David E. S. Blatherwick, CMG, OBE.

Of Egypt in the USA (2310 Decatur Pl., NW, Washington, D.C., 20008)
Ambassador: Ahmed Maher El Sayed.

Of the USA in Egypt (Lazougi St., Garden City, Cairo)
Ambassador: Edward S. Walker.

Of Egypt to the United Nations
Ambassador: Nabil A. Elaraby.

Of Egypt to the European Union
Ambassador: Muhammad Chabane.

Further Reading

CAPMAS, *Statistical Year Book, Arab Republic of Egypt*
Hopwood, D., *Egypt: Politics and Society 1945–1990.* 3rd ed. London, 1992
King, J. W., *Historical Dictionary of Egypt.* 2nd ed. Revised by A. Goldschmidt. Metuchen (NJ), 1995
McDermott, A., *Egypt: From Nasser to Mubarak.* London, 1988
Makar, R. N., *Egypt.* [Bibliography] Oxford and Santa Barbara (CA), 1988
Malek, J. (ed.) *Egypt.* Univ. of Oklahoma Press, 1993
Vatikiotis, P. J., *History of Modern Egypt: from Muhammad Ali to Mubarak.* London, 1991

National statistical office: Central Agency for Public Mobilization and Statistics (CAPMAS), Nasr City, Cairo.

EL SALVADOR

República de El Salvador

Capital: San Salvador
Population: 5·79m.
GDP per head: (PPP$) 2,417
GNP: US$8·4bn.
HDI/world rank: 0·576/115

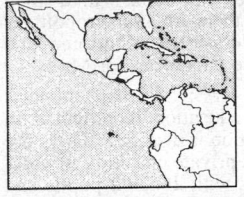

KEY HISTORICAL EVENTS. Conquered by Spain in 1526, El Salvador remained under Spanish rule until freeing itself in 1821. Thereafter, El Salvador was a member of the Central American Federation comprising the states of El Salvador, Guatemala, Honduras, Nicaragua and Costa Rica until this federation was dissolved in 1839. In 1841 El Salvador declared itself an independent republic.

The country's history has been marked by much political violence, and a number of enforced changes of rulers. The repressive dictatorship of President Maximiliano Hernandez Martinez lasted from 1931 to 1944 when he was deposed, as were his successors in 1948 and 1960. The military junta that followed gave way to more secure presidential succession, although there were charges of corruption at the election. Left-wing guerrilla groups became increasingly large and strong, and were engaged in constant fighting with government troops in the late 1970s. Many reports circulated of the violation of human rights, and in 1980 the Roman Catholic Archbishop of San Salvador, Oscar Romero y Galdames, an acknowledged advocate of human rights by government and army, was assassinated. As the guerrillas grew stronger and gained control over a part of the country, the USA sent economic aid and advisers to El Salvador and assisted in the training of Salvadorean troops. A new constitution was enacted in Dec. 1983 under which Agostín Duarte was elected president in May 1984, but it did nothing to pacify the situation. The presidential election was boycotted as a fraud by the main left-wing organization, the Favabundo Marti National Liberation Front (FMLN).

Talks between the government and the FMLN in April 1991 led to constitutional reforms in May, envisaging the establishment of civilian control over the armed forces and a reduction in their size. In May the UN Security Council sent a mission to observe the government-FMLN negotiations, initially for one year. An agreement reached in Sept. 1991 permitted the FMLN to participate in a newly created police force under civilian authority. On 16 Jan. 1992 the government and the FMLN signed a peace agreement and a ceasefire began on 1 Feb.

TERRITORY AND POPULATION. El Salvador is bounded in the north-east by Guatemala, north-east and east by Honduras and south by the Pacific Ocean. The area (including 247 sq. km of inland lakes) is 21,041 sq. km. Population (1992 census), 5,047,925 (female 52%); (1996 est., 5·79m.). Population density, 262·2 per sq. km. In 1995 1m. Salvadoreans were living abroad, mainly in the USA.

Vital statistics (1994, per 1,000 population): Birth, 29·5; deaths, 5·8; infant mortality (1992, per 1,000 births), 46. Life expectancy was 69·3 years in 1994.

The republic is divided into 14 departments. Areas (in sq. km) and 1992 census populations:

Department	Area	Population	Chief town	Population
Ahuachapán	1,240	260,563	Ahuachapán	83,885
Cabañas	1,140	136,293	Sensuntepeque	38,073
Chalatenango	2,017	180,627	Chalatenango	27,600
Cuscatlán	756	167,290	Cojutepeque	43,564
La Libertad	1,653	522,071	Nueva San Salvador	116,575
La Paz	1,224	246,147	Zacatecoluca	57,032
La Unión	2,074	251,143	La Unión	36,927
Morazán	1,447	166,772	San Francisco	20,497
San Miguel	2,077	380,442	San Miguel	182,817
San Salvador	886	1,477,766	San Salvador	422,570 [1]
San Vicente	1,184	135,471	San Vicente	45,842

Department	Area	Population	Chief town	Population
Santa Ana	2,023	451,620	Santa Ana	202,337
Sonsonate	1,226	354,641	Sonsonate	76,200
Usulatán	2,130	317,079	Usulután	62,967

[1] Greater San Salvador conurbation, 1,522,126.

The official language is Spanish.

CLIMATE. Despite its proximity to the equator, the climate is warm rather than hot, and nights are cool inland. Light rains occur in the dry season from Nov. to April, while the rest of the year has heavy rains, especially on the coastal plain. *San Salvador.* Jan. 71°F (21·7°C), July 75°F (23·9°C). Annual rainfall 71" (1,775 mm). *San Miguel.* Jan. 77°F (25°C), July 83°F (28·3°C). Annual rainfall 68" (1,700 mm).

CONSTITUTION AND GOVERNMENT. A new Constitution was enacted in Dec. 1983. Executive power is vested in a *President* and *Vice-President* elected for a non-renewable term of 5 years. There is a *Legislative Assembly* of 84 members elected by universal suffrage and proportional representation: 64 locally and 20 nationally, for a term of 3 years. Presidential elections were held on 20 March 1994, with a run-off for President on 24 April. The electorate was 2·7m. Armando Calderón Sol (Alianza Republicana Nacionalista, ARENA) was elected President. In parliamentary elections on 16 March 1997, ARENA gained 28 seats in the Legislative Assembly, the FMLN 27, and 6 other parties 29 seats between them.

In March 1998 the Cabinet comprised:

President: Dr Armando Calderón Sol (ARENA; sworn in 1 June 1994).

Vice-President and Minister of the Presidency: Dr Enrique Borgo Bustamente.

Minister of Agriculture: Ricardo Quiñones Avila. *Economy:* Eduardo Zablah Touche. *Education:* Maria Cecilia Gallardo de Cano. *Defence:* Gen. Jaime Guzmán Morales. *Public Security:* Hugo Cesar Barrera Guerrero. *Finance:* Manuel Enrique Hinds. *Foreign Affairs:* Ramón González Giner. *Health and Social Assistance:* Dr Eduardo Interiano. *Interior:* Mario Acosta Oertel. *Justice:* Dr Rubén Mejía Peña. *Labour and Social Security:* Dr Eduardo Tomasino. *Public Works:* Roberto Bará Osegueda.

National anthem: 'Saludemos la patria orgullosos' ('We proudly salute the Fatherland'); words by J. J. Cañas, tune by J. Aberle.

Local Government. Each of the 14 departments is under an appointed governor. There are 262 municipalities. ARENA has control of 161 municipalities, FMLN 48, the Christian Democratic Party 18.

DEFENCE. There is selective conscription for 2 years.

Army. There are 3 military zones. The Army comprises 1 special security and 6 infantry brigades, 8 infantry detachments, 1 mechanized cavalry regiment, 1 artillery brigade, 1 engineer command, 2 independent battalions including the Presidential Guard, and 1 special operations group. Equipment includes 68 armoured personnel carriers.

Strength (1997): 25,700 (4,000 conscripts). The National Civilian Police numbers 8,000.

Navy. A small coastguard force based largely at Acajutla, with 1,100 (1997) personnel, operates 5 inshore patrol craft, 2 landing craft and numerous boats. There was also (1996) 1 company of Naval Infantry numbering 150.

Air Force. The Air Force equipment includes 10 A-37B and 5 Magister attack aircraft, 2 Rallye armed trainers, 6 armed C-47 transports, 15 armed Cessna O-2s and 6 Hughes 500MD helicopters for counter-insurgency operations. Other aircraft include 2 C-47, 3 Arava, 1 DC-6 and 1 C-123 transports, 6 Cessna O-2 patrol aircraft, as well as 60 UH-1H helicopters. Training types include piston-engined Cessna light aircraft and 4 A-37s.

Strength (1997): 1,600 personnel (200 conscripts).

INTERNATIONAL RELATIONS

Membership. El Salvador is a member of the UN, CACM, LAIA and OAS.

ECONOMY

Policy. An economic liberalization programme aims at raising exports, foreign investment and domestic savings.

Budget. In 1994 current revenue was C/8,519m., current expenditure C/10,264m., capital revenue, C/135m. and capital expenditure C/2,605m.

Currency. The monetary unit is the *colón* (SVC) of 100 *centavos*. There are coins of 1, 5, 10, 25, 50 and 100 centavos and C/1, and notes of C/5, 10, 25, 50, 100 and 200. Inflation was 7·4% in 1996. Foreign exchange reserves were US$1,100m. in 1996; gold reserves (1993), 469,000 troy oz.

Banking and Finance. The bank of issue is the Central Reserve Bank (*Governor*, José Roberto Orellana Milla), formed in 1934 and nationalized in 1961. There are 15 commercial banks (2 foreign). Individual private holdings may not exceed 5% of the total equity.

There is a stock exchange in San Salvador, founded in 1992.

Weights and Measures. The metric system is standard but other units are still commonly in use, of which the principal are as follows: *Libra* = 1·014 lbs; *quintal* = 100 lbs; *arroba* = 25·35 lbs; *fanega* = 1·5745 bushels.

ENERGY AND NATURAL RESOURCES

Electricity. El Salvador has few mineral resources; its main source of power is hydroelectric. Installed capacity in 1992 was 751 MW (50% hydroelectric, 37% thermal, 13% geothermal). Production in 1996 was 3,340m. kWh.

Minerals. Production (1987, in tonnes): Salt, 3,100; limestone, 1·45m.; gypsum, 4,500.

Agriculture. 27% of the land surface is given over to arable farming. In 1993, 36% of the working population was engaged in farming. Large landholdings have been progressively expropriated and redistributed in accordance with legislation initiated in 1980. By 1994 some 12,000 individuals had received plots of 4–5 ha.

Since the mid-19th century, El Salvador's economy has been dominated by coffee. Cotton is the second main commercial crop. Production (1997, in 1,000 quintals): Coffee, 3,153; maize, 12,000; (1993, in 1,000 quintals): seed cotton, 207; beans, 1,354; rice, 1,564; sorghum, 4,656; sugar cane (in tonnes), 7,994.

Livestock (1994, in 1,000): 1,256 cattle, 310 pigs, 15 goats. Livestock products (1994, in 1,000 tonnes): Beef, 26; pork, 9; poultry, 44; milk, 280; eggs, 52.

Forestry. Forest area was 104,000 ha in 1988. In the national forests are found dye woods and valuable hardwoods including mahogany, cedar and walnut. Balsam trees abound: El Salvador is the world's principal source of this medicinal gum. 6·65m. cu. metres of roundwood were cut in 1994.

Fisheries. In 1989 there were 24 fishing vessels with a tonnage of 3,514 GRT. Total catch (1993): 13,000 tonnes.

INDUSTRY. Production (1988, in 1,000 tonnes): Petroleum, 136; fuel oil, 208; paper and products, 16. Traditional industries include food processing and textiles.

Labour. In 1992 the economically active population numbered 1·7m.

FOREIGN ECONOMIC RELATIONS. In May 1992 El Salvador, Guatemala and Honduras agreed to create a free trade zone for almost all goods and capital.

Commerce. Imports (including parcels' post) and exports in calendar years (in US$1m.):

	1992	1993	1994	1995	1996
Imports	1,855	2,145	2,574	3,329	3,223
Exports	796	1,032	1,249	1,652	1,789

The main export markets are the USA, Guatemala, Germany, Costa Rica, Nicaragua and Honduras. In 1991 139,000 quintals of coffee were exported. The main import suppliers are the USA, Guatemala, Mexico, Germany, Japan and Venezuela.

Tourism. There were 181,332 tourists in 1994.

COMMUNICATIONS

Roads. In 1995 there were estimated to be 12,320 km of national roads, including 1,712 km of paved roads. Vehicles registered (1992): Cars, 221,900; commercial vehicles, 33,200.

Railways. The railways are run by the National Railways of El Salvador. Route length (1994): 602 km. There is a link to the Guatemalan system. Total railway traffic in 1992 was 326,000 tonnes of freight and 408,000 passengers.

Civil Aviation. The international airport is at Comalapa, 40 km from San Salvador. The national carrier is TACA, which was operating 1 B-737-200, 2 B-737-200 Advs, 1 B-737-200C Adv, 4 B-737-300s, 1 B-767-200ER, 1 B-767-300ER and 1 other aircraft in 1995. It flies services to various destinations in the USA, Mexico and all Central American countries.

Shipping. The main ports are Acajutla and Cutuco. The merchant fleet numbered 14 vessels in 1989 with a total tonnage of 3,819 GRT.

Telecommunications. The telephone and telegraph systems are government-owned; the radio-telephone systems are partly private, partly government-owned. In 1993 there were 174,000 telephones. Broadcasting is under the control of the Administración Nacional de Telecomunicaciones. There are 6 commercial television channels, a government-owned channel and 2 educational channels sponsored by the Ministry of Education. In 1993 there were 1·93m. radio receivers and 0·5m. television sets (colour by NTSC).

Press. In 1995 there were 5 daily newspapers.

SOCIAL INSTITUTIONS

Justice. Justice is administered by the Supreme Court (6 members appointed for 3-year terms by the Legislative Assembly and 6 by bar associations), courts of first and second instance, and minor tribunals.

Following the disbanding of security forces in Jan. 1992 a new National Civilian Police Force was created which was planned to number 10,500 by 1997.

Religion. About 90% of the population is Roman Catholic. Under the 1962 Constitution, churches are exempted from the property tax; the Catholic Church is recognized as a legal person, and other churches are entitled to secure similar recognition. There is an archbishop in San Salvador and bishops at Santa Ana, San Miguel, San Vicente, Santiago de María, Usulután, Sonsonate and Zacatecoluca. There are about 200,000 Protestants.

Education. Adult literacy was 70·9% in 1994. Education, run by the state, is free and compulsory. In 1986 there were 72,500 pupils in nursery schools and 1,140,000 in primary and secondary schools. In 1995–96 in the public sector there were 3 universities; in the private sector there were 21 universities and 14 specialized universities (1 American, 3 Evangelical, 1 Roman Catholic, 1 Open and 1 each for business, integrated education, polytechnic, science and development, teaching, science and technology, technical studies and technology). In 1994–95, there were 63,413 university students and 3,983 academic staff.

Health. In 1986 there were 5,548 hospital beds and some 1,649 doctors.

Welfare. The Social Security Institute now administers the sickness, old age and death insurance, covering industrial workers and employees earning up to C/700 a month. Employees in other private institutions with salaries over this amount are included but are excluded from the medical and hospital benefits.

DIPLOMATIC REPRESENTATIVES

Of El Salvador in Great Britain (159 Great Portland St., London, W1N 5FD)
Ambassador: Manuel Gutiérrez Ruiz.

Of Great Britain in El Salvador (Paseo General Escalón 4828, POB 1591, San Salvador)
Ambassador and Consul General: Ian Gerken, LVO.

Of El Salvador in the USA (2308 California St., NW, Washington, DC., 20008)
Ambassador: Ana Cristina Sol.

Of the USA in El Salvador (Urbanización Santa Elena, Antiguo Cuscatlán, San Salvador)
Ambassador: Anne W. Patterson.

Of El Salvador to the United Nations
Ambassador: Dr Ricardo G. Castaneda-Cornejo.

Of El Salvador to the European Union
Ambassador: Rodezno Munguia.

Further Reading

Armstrong, R. and Shenk, J., *El Salvador: the Face of Revolution.* London, 1982
Baloyra, E. A., *El Salvador in Transition.* Univ. of North Carolina Press, 1982
Didion, J., *Salvador.* London, 1983
Kufeld, A., *El Salvador.* NY, 1991
Montgomery, T. S., *Revolution in El Salvador: Origins and Evolution.* Boulder (CO), 1982
North, L., *Bitter Grounds: Roots of Revolt in El Salvador.* London, 1981
Woodward, R. L., *El Salvador.* [Bibliography] Oxford and Santa Barbara (CA), 1988

National statistical office: Dirección General de Estadística y Censos, Calle Arce, San Salvador.

EQUATORIAL GUINEA

República de Guinea
Ecuatorial

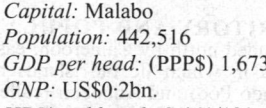

Capital: Malabo
Population: 442,516
GDP per head: (PPP$) 1,673
GNP: US$0·2bn.
HDI/world rank: 0·461/131

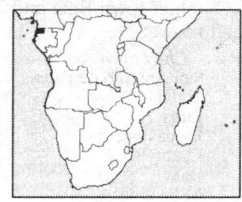

KEY HISTORICAL EVENTS. Equatorial Guinea consists of the island of Bioko, for centuries called Fernando Po; other, smaller islands, notably Annobón, formerly Pagalu; and the mainland territory of Rio Muni. The main ethnic group in Rio Muni is the Fang (or Pahouin), members of which also live in neighbouring Gabon; the Bubis, the original inhabitants of Fernando Po, still constitute the majority on Bioko. Fernando Po was called after the Portuguese navigator Fernão do Po who in 1471-72 became the first European visitor to the island; it was then ruled for 3 centuries by Portugal, but was in 1778 ceded to Spain, along with Annobon and a mainland area out of which Spain eventually retained a small area, Rio Muni, whose boundaries were recognized by other European countries in 1856.

For some decades after taking possession of Fernando Po, Spain did not effectively occupy it and allowed Britain to establish an important consulate and naval base at Clarence (later Santa Isabel), which dominated the island and were important for suppression of slave trading over a wide area in the 19th century. Spain asserted its rule from the 1840s. Fernando Po and Rio Muni were together called the Spanish Possessions in the Gulf of Guinea, or simply Spanish Guinea. African resistance to Spanish occupation of the interior of Rio Muni continued for a long time. In Rio Muni timber became the major export; on Fernando Po the Spanish developed cocoa cultivation on European-owned plantations, for which African labour was imported from the early 20th century. This labour traffic led to an international scandal in 1930 when Liberians were found to be sold to virtual slavery. Later many Nigerians were employed, often in poor conditions, and a large Nigerian community came to live on the island.

For much of Spanish rule Africans were kept in a subordinate position under the system called *patronato de indigenas* (patronage over natives). On 30 July 1959 it was announced that Spanish Guinea was to be a part of Spain and its people Spanish citizens. It became 2 provinces, represented in the *Cortes* in Madrid.

African nationalist movements began in the 1950s and 1960s. Internal self-government was granted in 1963, with a joint legislative assembly for the 2 provinces. Bonifacio Ondo Edu, leader of the *Movimiento de Unión Nacional de Guinea Ecuatorial* (MUNGE), became head of government. Other parties included the *Idea Popular de Guinea Ecuatorial* (IPGE), of which Francisco Macías Nguema became the leader. In 1969 Spain briefly suspended the constitution after rivalry among the parties, but then, under pressure to grant independence, agreed to this on condition of its approval by a referendum, which was given on 11 Aug. 1969. The 2 parts of Equatorial Guinea were united in a state which became independent on 12 Oct. 1968 with Macías Nguema as president.

President Macías established the rule of a single party, the *Partido Unico Nacional de los Trabajadores* (PUNT), in 1970. Under his dictatorship a third of the population was killed or else left the country. He was declared President-for-Life on 14 July 1972, but was overthrown by a military coup on 3 Aug. 1979, led by a relative of his, Col. Teodoro Obiang Nguema. The military régime ended the excesses of the rule of Macías, who was executed.

A constitution approved by a referendum on 3 Aug. 1982 restored some political institutions, but left the military régime in power, to stay until economic and social reconstruction was completed. A Supreme Military Council then created was the sole political body until constitutional rule was resumed on 12 Oct. 1982 and opposition parties legalized.

TERRITORY AND POPULATION. The mainland part of Equatorial Guinea is bounded north by Cameroon, east and south by Gabon, and west by the Gulf of Guinea in which lie the islands of Bioko (formerly Macías Nguema, formerly Fernando Póo) and Annobón (called Pagalu from 1973 to 1979). The total area is 28,051 sq. km (10,831 sq. miles) and the population at the last (1983) census was 304,000. Estimate (July 1997) 442,516. Another 110,000 are estimated to remain in exile abroad.

The 7 provinces are grouped into 2 regions, Continental (C), chief town Bata and Insular (I), chief town Malabo, with areas and populations as follows:

	Sq. km	Census 1983	Chief town
Annobón (I)	17	2,006	San Antonio de Palea
Bioko Norte (I)	776	46,221	Malabo
Bioko Sur (I)	1,241	10,969	Luba
Centro Sur (C)	9,931	52,393	Evinayong
Kié-Ntem (C)	3,943	70,202	Ebebiyin
Litoral (C)	6,665 [1]	66,370	Bata
Wele-Nzas (C)	5,478	51,839	Mongomo

[1] Including the adjacent islets of Corisco, Elobey Grande and Elobey Chico (17 sq. km).

In 1986 the largest towns were Bata (17,000) and the capital Malabo (10,000).

Vital statistics: Life expectancy (1997 estimate) 53·46 years (male, 51·2; female, 55·8). Birth rate (per 1,000 population, 1997 estimate): 39·33; death, 13·67; infant mortality, 95·7 deaths.

The main ethnic group on the mainland is the Fang, which comprises 85% of the total population; there are several minority groups along the coast and adjacent islets. On Bioko the indigenous inhabitants (Bubis) constitute 60% of the population there, the balance being mainly Fang and coast people. On Annobón the indigenous inhabi-tants are the descendants of Portuguese slaves and still speak a Portuguese patois. The official language is Spanish.

CLIMATE. The climate is equatorial, with alternate wet and dry seasons. In Rio Muni, the wet season lasts from Dec. to Feb.

CONSTITUTION AND GOVERNMENT. A Constitution was approved in Aug. 1982 by 95% of the votes cast in a plebiscite. It provided for an 11-member Council of State, and for a 41-member House of Representatives of the People, the latter being directly elected on 28 Aug. 1983 for a 5-year term and re-elected on 10 July 1988. The President appointed and leads a Council of Ministers.

On 12 Oct. 1987 a single new political party was formed as the *Partido Democrático de Guinea Ecuatorial*.

A referendum on 17 Nov. 1991 approved the institution of multi-party democracy, and a law to this effect was passed in Jan. 1992. The electorate is restricted to citizens who have resided in Equatorial Guinea for at least 10 years. A new parliament, the *National Assembly*, has 80 seats. At the elections on 21 Nov. 1993 candidates from 8 parties stood. The main opposition parties called for a boycott. Turn-out was 30%. Presidential elections were held on 25 Feb. 1996. It was announced that President Nguema Mbasogo had been re-elected by 99% of votes cast. Parliamentary elections were held on 26 Feb. 1996.

President of the Supreme Military Council, Minister of Defence: Brig.-Gen. Teodoro Obiang Nguema Mbasogo (b. 1943).

In March 1998 the government comprised:
Prime Minister: Serafin Seriche Dougan.
Deputy Prime Minister: Francisco Javier Ndongo Mbengono. *Agriculture, Fisheries and Food:* Alfredo Mokudi Nanga. *Culture, Tourism and Francophone Affairs:* Augustin Nse Nfumu. *Education:* Ricardo Obama Nfube. *Economy and Finance:* Anatolio Ndong Mba. *Foreign Affairs and Co-operation:* Miguel Oyono Ndong. *Health and Environment:* Bernabe Ngore. *Interior:* Júlio Ndong Ela Mangue. *Industry, Energy, and Small and Medium Industry Promotion:* Severino Obiang

Bengono. *Information:* Francisco Abaga Ndong. *Justice and Religion:* Francisco Javier Ndongo Mbengono. *Employment and Social Security:* Constantino Congue. *Mines and Hydrocarbons:* Juan Olo Mba Nseng. *Public Works, Housing and Urban Affairs:* Alejandro Envoro Ovono. *Social and Women's Affairs:* Balbina Nchama Nvo. *Transport:* Antonio Fernando Nve Ngu. *Territorial Administration and Local Government:* Julio Ndong Ela Mangue.

National anthem: 'Caminemos pisando las sendas' ('Let us journey treading the pathways'); words by A. N. Miyongo, tune anonymous.

Local Government. There are some 600 rural councils.

DEFENCE

Army. The Army consists of 3 infantry battalions with (1997) 1,100 personnel. There is also a paramilitary Guardia Civil.

Navy. A small force, numbering 120 in 1997, and based at Malabo, operates 4 inshore patrol craft.

Air Force. There is no formal air service but the National Guard Air Wing has 1 Yak-40 and 2 An-32 transports. Personnel (1997), 100.

INTERNATIONAL RELATIONS

Membership. Equatorial Guinea is a member of the UN and OAU and is an ACP state of the EU.

ECONOMY

Policy. Overseas investment, particularly in the oil industry, has transformed the economy which grew by more than 40% in 1996 and by 50% in 1997.

Budget. In 1995 the estimated total revenue was 13,542m. francs CFA and expenditure 13,400m. francs CFA, of which 12,170m. francs CFA were current expenditure.

Currency. On 2 Jan. 1985 the country joined the Franc Zone and the *epkwele* was replaced by the *franc CFA* which now has a parity value of 50 francs CFA to 1 French franc. There are coins of 1, 2, 5, 10, 25, 50, 100 and 500 francs CFA, and banknotes of 100, 500, 1,000, 5,000 and 10,000 francs CFA. Foreign exchange reserves were US$10·31m. at the end of 1992.

Banking and Finance. The *Banque des Etats de l'Afrique Centrale* became the bank of issue in Jan. 1985. There is 1 commercial bank.

ENERGY AND NATURAL RESOURCES

Electricity. There are 2 hydroelectric plants.

Minerals. There is some small-scale alluvial gold production.

Oil. Production started in 1992 and in 1997 topped 80,000 barrels a day. Mobil is the biggest operator in the country but other US-based oil companies are investing heavily. Oil production is estimated to be over 100,000 barrels a day by 2000.

Agriculture. Farming, forestry and fishing account for 50% of GDP. Subsistence farming predominates. Production (in 1,000 tonnes in 1994): Coconuts, 8; palm kernels, 3; bananas, 17; cassava, 48; sweet potatoes, 36. Plantations in the hinterland have been abandoned by their Spanish former owners and except for cocoa and coffee, commercial agriculture is under serious difficulties.

Forestry. 714,000 cu. metres of roundwood were cut in 1995.

Fisheries. The total catch in 1993 was 3,800 metric tonnes. Tuna and shellfish are caught.

INDUSTRY. The once-flourishing light industry collapsed under the Macías regime. Oil production is now the major activity. Food processing is also being developed.

Labour. The wage-earning non-agricultural workforce is small. The average monthly wage was 14,000 francs CFA in 1992.

FOREIGN ECONOMIC RELATIONS. Foreign debt was US$249·3m. in 1991.

Commerce. In 1995 imports amounted to US$52·3m. and exports to US$83·5m. Main export markets, 1995: USA, 34%; Japan, 16%; China, 12%. Main import suppliers: Spain, 51%; Cameroon, 21%; France, 6%; USA, 4%.

COMMUNICATIONS

Roads. Length (1993) 1,326 km of which 508 km were paved and 818 km laterite. There were also 1,356 km of dirt roads. Most roads are in a state of disrepair.

Civil Aviation. There are international airports at Malabo and Bata.

Shipping. Bata is the main port, handling mainly timber. The other ports are Luba, formerly San Carlos (bananas, cocoa), in Bioko and Malabo, Evinayong and Mbini on the mainland. Ocean-going shipping totalled 3,279 GRT in 1995.

Telecommunications. Telephone services are rudimentary. 2 radio programmes are broadcast by the state-controlled Radio Nacional de Guinea Ecuatorial and Televisión Nacional. There is also a commercial radio network, and a cultural programme produced with Spanish collaboration. In 1995 there were 170,000 radio and 24,000 TV receivers (colour by SECAM).

Press. There is one daily newspaper with a circulation of 2,000.

SOCIAL INSTITUTIONS

Justice. The Constitution guarantees an independent judiciary. The Supreme Tribunal is the highest court of appeal and is located at Malabo. There are Courts of First Instance and Courts of Appeal at Malabo and Bata.

Religion. Christianity was proscribed under President Macías but reinstated in 1979. In 1994 there were 0·3m. Roman Catholics and 8,000 Protestants.

Education. In 1994 there were 85 pre-primary schools with 171 teachers for 3,788 pupils; 281 primary schools with 1,381 teachers for 75,751 pupils and 16,616 secondary pupils with 588 teachers. In 1993 there were 2 teacher training colleges, 2 post-secondary vocational schools and 1 agricultural institute. Adult literacy was 78·5% in 1995 (male, 89·6%; female 68·1%).

Health. In 1989 there were 929 health workers including 100 doctors.

DIPLOMATIC REPRESENTATIVES

Of Equatorial Guinea in Great Britain
Ambassador: Lino-Sima Ekua Avomo (resides in Paris).

Of Great Britain in Equatorial Guinea
Ambassador and Consul-General: Nicholas M. McCarthy, OBE (resides in Cameroon).

Of Equatorial Guinea in the USA (Suite 405, 1511 K St., NW, Washington, D.C. 20005)
Ambassador: Pastor Micha Ondo Bile.

Of Equatorial Guinea to the United Nations
Ambassador: Pastor Micha Ondo Bile.

Of Equatorial Guinea to the European Union
Ambassador: Aurelio Mba Olo Andeme.

The USA does not have an embassy in Equatorial Guinea; US relations with
Equatorial Guinea are handled through the US Embassy in Yaoundé, Cameroon.

Further Reading

Fegley, R., *Equatorial Guinea, an African Tragedy.* New York, 1989.—*Equatorial Guinea:*
[Bibliography]. Oxford and Santa Barbara (CA), 1991
Liniger-Goumaz, M., *Guinea Ecuatorial: Bibliografía General.* Geneva, 1974–91.—*Historical
Dictionary of Equatorial Guinea.* 2nd ed. Metuchen (NJ), 1988.—*Small Is Not Always
Beautiful: the Story of Equatorial Guinea.* London, 1988
Molino, A. M. del, *La Ciudad de Clarence.* Madrid, 1994

ERITREA

Capital: Asmara
Population: 3·53m.
GDP per head: (PPP$) 960
HDI/world rank: 0·269/168

KEY HISTORICAL EVENTS. Italy was the colonial ruler of Eritrea from 1890 until 1941, when it fell to British forces in the Second World War and a British protectorate was set up. This ended in 1952 when the UN sanctioned its federation with Ethiopia. In 1962 Ethiopia became a unitary state and Eritrea was incorporated as a province. Eritreans began an armed struggle for independence under the leadership of the Eritrean People's Liberation Front (EPLF) which culminated successfully in the capture of Asmara on 24 May 1991. Thereafter the EPLF maintained a *de facto* independent administration recognized by the Ethiopian government. At a referendum on 23–25 April 1993 there was a 99·8% majority in favour of independence. Sovereignty was proclaimed on 24 May 1993.

TERRITORY AND POPULATION. Eritrea is bounded in the north-east by the Red Sea, south-east by Djibouti, south by Ethiopia and west by Sudan. Some 300 islands form the Dahlak Archipelago, most of them uninhabited. For the dispute with Yemen over the islands of Greater and Lesser Hanish *see* YEMEN: Territory and Population. Its area is 93,679 sq. km (36,171 sq. miles). Population, 1994 estimate, 3,525,000 (20% urban). 1m. Eritreans lived abroad in 1995, 0·5m. as refugees in Sudan. A UN Programme for Refugee Reintegration and Rehabilitation of Resettlement Areas in Eritrea (PROFERI) is in operation.

Annual population growth is about 3%. Infant mortality is 203 per 1,000 live births. Expectation of life is 46 years.

There are 10 provinces: Akele Guzai, Asmara, Barka, Denkel, Gash-Setir, Hamasien, Sahel, Semhar, Senhit and Seraye. The capital is Asmara (1991 population, 367,300). Other large towns (with 1989 populations) are Assab (39,569), Keren (32,110) and Massawa (19,404). An agreement of July 1993 gives Ethiopia rights to use the ports of Assab and Massawa.

48% of the population speak Tigrinya and 31% Tigré, and there are 7 other indigenous languages. Arabic is spoken on the coast and along the Sudanese border, and English is used in secondary schools. Arabic and Tigrinya are the official languages.

CLIMATE. Massawa. Jan. 78°F (25·6°C), July 94°F (34·4°C). Annual rainfall 8" (193 mm).

CONSTITUTION AND GOVERNMENT. A referendum to approve independence was held on 23–25 April 1993. The electorate was 1,173,506. 99·8% of votes cast were in favour.

The transitional government has a 4-year term and consists of the *President* and a 130-member *National Assembly.* The latter consists of the members of the People's Front for Democracy and Justice (PFDJ; until Feb. 1994 EPLF) Central Committee and 60 other deputies (including 11 seats reserved for women). It elects the President who in turn appoints the *State Council* made up of 14 ministers and the governors of the 10 provinces. The President chairs both the State Council and the National Assembly.

In the presidential and legislative elections in May 1997, President Afewerki was re-elected to office.

President: Issaias Afewerki (b. 1945; elected 22 May 1993).

In March 1998 the ministers in the State Council were:

Agriculture: Tesfai Ghermasien. *Commerce and Industry:* Ogbeh Abraha. *Construction:* Abraha Asfaha. *Culture and Information:* Baraki Gebreselassie. *Defence:* Mesfin Hafos. *Education:* Osman Saleh. *Energy, Mining and Water*

Resources: Tesfai Gebreselassie. *Finance and Development:* Haile Weldeteasae. *Foreign:* Petros Solomon. *Health:* Sebhat Ephrem. *Interior:* Ali Said Abdella. *Justice:* Fozia Hashim. *Marine Resources:* Saleh Meky. *Provincial Administration:* Mahmud Ahmed Sherifo. *Tourism:* Worku Tesfa Mikael. *Transport:* Giorgis Tekle Mikael.

Local Government. There are 10 provinces, each under a governor.

DEFENCE. Conscription for 18 months was introduced in 1994. The total strength of all forces was estimated at 35,000 in 1996.

Navy. Most of the former Ethiopian Navy is now in Eritrean hands. Strength is estimated as 1 small frigate, 1 fast torpedo craft, 6 patrol craft, 2 medium landing ships and 5 amphibious craft. The main bases and training establishments are at Massawa and Assab.

Air Force. There are 20 aircraft: 3 Y-12 transports, 2 Mi-8 helicopters, 8 L-90TP Redigo liaison/training machines, 1 Astra VIP transport and 6 MB-339 armed trainers.

INTERNATIONAL RELATIONS

Membership. Eritrea is a member of the UN and OAU.

ECONOMY

Budget. Government finance (in 1m. Ethiopian birr), 1991–92: Revenue, 154·5 (including sales taxes, 46·3; customs dues, 27·4; direct taxes, 21·4; sales, 8·3); expenditure, 128·6. Eritrea's resources are meagre, the population small and ill-educated, communications are difficult and there is a shortage of energy. But GDP grew by 8% a year from 1994 to 1996. Over 40 enterprises are scheduled for privatization.

Currency. A new currency, the nakfa, has replaced the Ethiopian currency, the birr. Inflation is 9%.

Banking and Finance. The central bank is the National Bank of Eritrea (*Governor*, Tequie Beyene). All banks and financial institutions are state-run. There is a Commercial Bank of Eritrea with 12 branches, an Agricultural and Industrial Bank, a Housing and Commercial Bank and an Insurance Corporation.

ENERGY AND NATURAL RESOURCES

Electricity. Installed capacity was 40 MW in 1993.

Minerals. There are deposits of gold, silver, copper, zinc, sulphur, nickel, chrome and potash. Basalt, limestone, marble, sand and silicates are extracted. Oil exploration is taking place in the Red Sea.

Agriculture. Several systems of land ownership (state, colonial, traditional) co-exist. In 1994 the PFDJ proclaimed the sole right of the state to own land. Sorghum is cultivated. Livestock includes goats and camels.

Fisheries. Current production is less than 4,000 tonnes but the Red Sea could sustain up to 100,000 tonnes.

INDUSTRY. Light industry was well developed in the colonial period but capability has declined. Processed food, textiles, leatherware, building materials, glassware and oil products are produced.

FOREIGN ECONOMIC RELATIONS. Eritrea is dependent on foreign aid for most of its capital expenditure, but there is no external debt.

Commerce. In 1995 exports were valued at US$24m. The main exports are drinks, leather and products, textiles and oil products. Most exports go to Ethiopia; principal import suppliers: Saudi Arabia, Ethiopia, UAE.

COMMUNICATIONS

Roads. There is a tarmac road from Asmara to Massawa and about 900 km of unsurfaced other roads. About 500 buses operate regular services.

Railways. The 117 km Asmara–Massawa line reopened in Jan. 1997.

Civil Aviation. There is an international airport at Asmara. Services are provided by Egyptair, Ethiopian Airlines, Lufthansa, Saudia, Sudan Airways, United Airlines and Yemenia.

Shipping. Massawa is the main port; Assab is used mainly for imports to Ethiopia: both are free ports for Ethiopia. Ethiopian Shipping Lines provide services.

Telecommunications. There is daily radio and TV broadcasting. International telephone links were restored in 1992.

Press. There is a government daily in Arabic and Tigrinya.

SOCIAL INSTITUTIONS

Justice. The legal system derives from a decree of May 1993.

Religion. Half the population are Sunni Moslems (along the coast and in the north), and half Coptic Christians (in the south).

Education. Adult literacy was about 25% in 1995. In 1993 there were 261 state primary schools and 52 secondary schools as well as some private schools. There were 0·25m. pupils and 6,965 teachers in 1994. There is 1 university, with 3,200 students and 250 academic staff in 1994–95.

Health. In 1993 there were 10 small regional hospitals, 32 health centres, 65 medical posts, 68 doctors, 488 nurses, 33 midwives and 850 auxiliary medical personnel.

DIPLOMATIC REPRESENTATIVES

Of Eritrea in Great Britain
Ambassador: Andebrhan Weldegiorgis (resides in Brussels).

Of Great Britain in Eritrea
Ambassador: G. G. Wetherell (resides in Ethiopia).

Of Eritrea in the USA
Ambassador: Amdemichael Kahsai.

Of the USA in Eritrea (Franklin D. Roosevelt St., POB 211, Asmara)
Ambassador: John F. Hicks.

Of Eritrea to the United Nations
Ambassador: Haile Menkerios.

Of Eritrea to the European Union
Ambassador: Andebrhan Weldegiorgis.

Further Reading

Connel, D., *Against All Odds: a Chronicle of the Eritrean Revolution.* Trenton (NJ), 1993
Fegley, R., *Eritrea.* [Bibliography]. Oxford and Santa Barbara (CA), 1995
Lewis, R., *Eritrea: Africa's Newest Country.* London, 1993

ESTONIA

Eesti Vabariik

(Republic of Estonia)

Capital: Tallinn
Population: 1·46m.
GDP per head: (PPP$) 4,294
HDI/world rank: 0·776/71

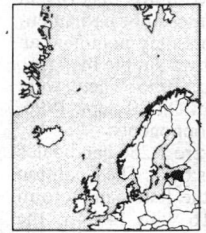

KEY HISTORICAL EVENTS. The early Estonians did not create state units and were subjected to Viking incursions. In 1346 the Danes relinquished Estonia to German rule, and it became part of the Holy Roman Empire and then a Swedish possession in the middle of the 17th century. On Sweden's defeat by Peter the Great, Estonia passed to the Russian Empire in 1721.

The workers' and soldiers' Soviets in Estonia took over power on 8 Nov. 1917, were overthrown by the German occupying forces in March 1918, and were restored to power as the Germans withdrew in Nov. 1918, establishing the 'Estland Labour Commune'. It was overthrown with the assistance of British naval forces in May 1919, and a democratic republic proclaimed. In March 1934 this régime was, in turn, overthrown by a fascist *coup*.

The secret protocol of the Soviet-German agreement of 23 Aug. 1939 assigned Estonia to the Soviet sphere of interest. An ultimatum (16 June 1940) led to the formation of a government acceptable to the USSR. On 21 July the Estonian parliament proclaimed the establishment of an Estonian Soviet Socialist Republic and applied to join the USSR; on 6 Aug. the Supreme Soviet of the USSR accepted the application.

On 30 March 1990 the Estonian Supreme Soviet proclaimed that the Soviet occupation of Estonia on 17 June 1940 had not disrupted the continuity of the former republic, and adopted, by 73 votes to nil with 3 abstentions, a declaration calling for the eventual re-establishment of full sovereignty. At a referendum in March 1991 77·8% of votes cast were in favour of independence. While an attempted coup was taking place in the USSR parliament declared independence on 20 Aug. 1991. A fully independent status was conceded by the USSR State Council on 6 Sept. 1991.

TERRITORY AND POPULATION. Estonia is bounded in the west and north by the Baltic Sea, east by Russia and south by Latvia. There are 1,541 offshore islands, of which the largest are Saaremaa and Hiiumaa, but only 14 are permanently inhabited. Area, 45,227 sq. km (17,462 sq. miles); population, 1,462,130 (1997 estimate). The 1989 census population was 1,565,662, of whom Estonians accounted for 61·5%, Russians 30·3%, Ukrainians 3·1%, Belorussians 1·8% and Finns 1·1%. A census is scheduled for Jan. 2000. Vital statistics rates (1996, per 1,000 population): Birth, 9·05, death, 12·95; infant mortality (per 1,000 live births), 10·4. There were 19,464 induced abortions in 1996 (25,587 in 1993). Expectation of life was 69·98 years in 1996.

The capital is Tallinn (1997 population, 420,470). Other large towns are Tartu (101,901), Narva (75,211), Kohtla-Järve (53,485) and Pärnu (51,807). There are 15 districts, 33 towns and 26 urban settlements.

The official language is Estonian.

CLIMATE. Because of its maritime location Estonia has a moderate climate, with cool summers and mild winters. Average daily temperatures in 1996: Jan. –7°C; July 15°C. Rainfall is heavy, 500–700 mm per year, and evaporation low.

CONSTITUTION AND GOVERNMENT. A draft constitution drawn up by a constitutional assembly was approved by 91·1% of votes cast at a referendum on 28 June 1992. Turn-out was 66·6%. The constitution came into effect on 4 July 1992. It defines Estonia as a 'democratic state guided by the rule of law, where universally recognized norms of international law are an inseparable part of the legal system.' It provides for a 101-member national assembly (*Riigikogu*) elected for 4-year terms. There are 11 electoral districts with 8 to 11 mandates each. Candidates may be elected a) by gaining more than 'quota', i.e. the number of votes cast in a district divided by the number of its mandates; b) by standing for a party which attracts for all of its candidates more than the quota, in order of listing; c) by being listed nationally for parties which clear a 5% threshold and eligible for the seats remaining according to position on the lists. The head of state is the *President*, elected by the Riigikogu for 5-year terms. Presidential candidates must gain the nominations of at least 20% of parliamentary deputies. If no candidate wins a two-thirds majority in any of 3 rounds, the Speaker convenes an electoral college composed of parliamentary deputies and local councillors. At this stage any 21 electors may nominate an additional candidate. The electoral college elects the President by a simple majority.

Presidential elections were held in 3 rounds on 26–27 Aug. 1996. There were 2 candidates. No candidate gained sufficient votes to be elected. On 20 Sept. 1996, President Meri was re-elected by an electoral college against 4 opponents.

Parliamentary elections were held on 5 March 1995. There were 1,256 candidates representing 16 parties. The electorate was 792,119; turn-out was 69%. The Coalition Party-Rural Union won 41 seats with 32·23% of votes cast; the Estonian Reform Party-Liberals, 19 with 16·19%; the Estonian Centre Party, 16 with 14·17%; the Fatherland Alliance, 8 with 7·85%; the Moderate Party, 6 with 5·99%; Our Home is Estonia (ethnic Russians), 6 with 5·87%; the Right Wing, 5 with 5%.

President: Lennart Meri (b. 1929; re-elected 20 Sept. 1996, sworn in 7 Oct. 1996).

A Coalition Party (K)-Reform Party (R)-Rural Union (M) coalition government was formed in Oct. 1995. In Dec. 1996 the Reform Party left the coalition government, which in March 1998 comprised:

Prime Minister: Mart Siimann.

Foreign Minister: Toomas Hendrik Ilves (ind). *Internal Affairs:* Olari Taal (ind). *Economics:* Jaak Leimann (ind). *Finance:* Mart Opmann (K). *Defence:* Andrus Öövel (K). *Social Affairs:* Tiiu Aro (K). *Transport and Communications:* Raivo Vare (ind). *Justice:* Paul Varul (K). *Education:* Mait Klaassen (ind). *Culture:* Jaak Allik (K). *Agriculture:* Andres Varik (M). *Environment:* Villu Reiljan (M). *Inter-Ethnic Affairs:* Andra Veidemann (Progressive Party). *Minister without portfolio for Regional Affairs:* Peep Aru (ind).

The *Speaker* is Toomas Savi (R).

Citizenship requirements are 2 years residence and competence in Estonian for existing residents. For residents immigrating after 1 April 1995, 5 years qualifying residence is required.

National anthem: 'Mu isamaa, mu õnn ja rõõm' ('My native land, my pride and joy'); words by J. V. Jannsen, tune by F. Pacius (same as Finland).

Local Government. There are 254 local municipalities, of which 207 are rural municipalities and 47 towns. The electorate consists of citizens and residents of 5 years' standing. Only citizens may stand for office. Elections were held on 20 Oct. 1996. Turn-out was 52%. Candidates contended for 3,453 seats.

DEFENCE. The President is the head of national defence, advised by the *National Security Council*, comprising the Prime Minister, the Speaker, the Commander of the Estonian Defence Forces, 3 ministers and various military officials. Conscription is 12 months for men and voluntary for women. Conscientious objectors may opt for 15 months civilian service instead.

Army. The Army comprises 3 motorized infantry battalions and 1 signal, 1 logistic and 1 guard battalion. Personnel (1997) 3,742.

Navy. The Navy consists of a Naval base, a Naval Staff and 1 Naval division, and operates 4 minesweepers, 2 patrol craft and 3 support craft. Personnel (1997) 344.

Air Force. The Air Force consists of an Air Force Staff, an air base at Ämari, and an air defence division, and has 2 Mi-2 helicopters and 2 AN-2 aeroplanes. Personnel (1997) 501.

Supporting units of the Armed Forces include a communications battalion and 1 background battalion. The Border Guards consist of 2,913 personnel (1997) with

10 ships, 25 launches and 37 motorboats. The Estonian Defence League consists of 8,500 volunteers.

INTERNATIONAL RELATIONS

Membership. Estonia is a member of the UN, the Council of Europe and the NATO Partnership for Peace, is an associate member of the EU and is an associate partner of the WEU. Estonia applied to join the EU in Nov. 1995.

ECONOMY

Policy. Privatization is being managed by the Estonian Privatization Agency under the jurisdiction of the Ministry of Finance. It is mainly achieved by direct sales, though there is some distribution by vouchers. By June 1997, 456 enterprises had been privatized realizing 3,300m. kroons.

Performance. GDP growth rate was 4% for 1996 and 10% in 1997. GDP in 1996 was 52,400m. kroons in current prices.

Budget. Budget estimates for 1995 balanced at 8,793m. kroons. Sources of revenue included sales tax, 2,260m. kroons; personal and corporate income tax, 2,000m. kroons. Items of expenditure: Education, culture, health and sport, 1,450m. kroons; economic reforms, 1,300m. kroons; justice and law enforcement, 713m. kroons; local government, 528m. kroons; social welfare, 385m. kroons. VAT is 18%.

Currency. The unit of currency is the *kroon* (EKR) of 100 *sents*. The kroon is pegged to the German mark within 3% of DM1 = 8 kroons. There are coins of 5, 10, 20 and 50 sents and 1 kroon, and notes of 1, 2, 5, 10, 25, 50, 100 and 500 kroons. There were 4,986·78m. kroons in circulation in Jan. 1997. Gold reserves were US$110m. in 1992. Foreign exchange reserves were 4,876m. kroons in May 1995. Inflation was an annualized 36% in 1993.

Banking and Finance. A central bank, the Bank of Estonia, was re-established in 1990 (*Governor:* Vahur Kraft). In 1997 there were 13 commercial banks. Since 1 Jan. 1996 banks have been required to have an equity of at least 50m. kroons. Assets (in 1,000m. kroons) of the largest banks in 1995: Hansapank, 3·3; North Estonian Bank, 1·4; Bank of Tallinn, 1·1; the state-owned Savings Bank, 2·9; Union Bank, 2·6. Total assets and liabilities of commercial banks at 30 Sept. 1997 were 34,0934m. kroons. The Estonian Investment Bank was established in 1992 to provide financing for privatized and private companies.

A stock exchange opened in Tallinn in 1996.

Weights and Measures. The metric system is in use.

ENERGY AND NATURAL RESOURCES

Electricity. Most electricity is produced by burning oil shale. A pilot wind turbine project was set up in 1996.

Oil and Gas. There are rich oil-shale deposits estimated at 3,700m. tonnes. A factory for the production of gas from shale and a 208 km-pipeline from Kohtla-Järve supplies shale gas to Tallinn and exports to St Petersburg.

Minerals. Oil shale is the most valuable mineral resource: Output was 133m. tonnes in 1995. There are extensive peat deposits. Phosphorites and super-phosphates are found and refined, and limestone, dolomite, clay, sand and gravel are mined.

Agriculture. Farming is concentrated on milk and meat production. Large state and collective farms are being converted into shareholding enterprises. The remainder are being divided into small private holdings for collective farm workers or former owners. At 1 Jan. 1997 there were 22,722 private farms averaging 22 ha, and 854 co-operatives and state farms. Minimum prices and the quantity of state purchases of agricultural produce were guaranteed by the government for 1997, along with agricultural supports of 332·81m. kroons.

At 1 Jan. 1997 there were 343,000 cattle (171,600 milch cows), 39,200 sheep and goats, 298,400 pigs and 2,324,900 poultry.

Output of main agricultural products (in 1,000 tonnes) in 1996: Wheat, 101·3; rye, 62·1; barley, 317·1; oats, 114·8; potatoes, 500·2; vegetables and greens, 54·7. Livestock products, 1996: Meat, 101,500 tonnes; milk, 674,800 tonnes; eggs, 300·8m.; wool, 159 tonnes.

Forestry. Some 47% of the land is covered by forests, which provide material for sawmills, furniture, match and pulp industries, as well as wood fuel. Private, municipal and state ownership of forests is allowed: In 1996 there were 162,300 ha of privately-owned forests out of a total of 2,016,200 ha. In 1995 the annual timber cut was 38m. cu. metres, of which 0·8m. cu. metres was from private forests.

INDUSTRY. Manufactures were valued at 14,610m. kroons before tax in 1993. Private firms employed 6% of the industrial workforce and produced 26·5% of total output. Output in 1989 included steel, 11,100 tonnes; timber, 2m. cu. metres; paper, 92,000 tonnes; cement, 1·1m. tonnes; fabrics, 235m. sq. metres; hosiery, 17m. pairs; footwear, 7·1m. pairs; knitwear, 23·6m. items; butter, 31,000 tonnes; preserves, 355m. standard jars. In 1990 there were some 5,600 enterprises of which 51% were state-owned, 32% co-operatives, 5% joint stock companies and 1·4% joint ventures.

Labour. In 1996 there was a monthly minimum wage of 680 kroons, and the average monthly wage was 2,986 kroons. Retirement age was 55 years for women and 60 for men in 1993, but is being extended to 60 and 65 respectively in 6-month stages by 2007. The official measure of unemployment is based on the number of job-seekers: There were 36,183 in May 1995. The registered unemployment rate was 3·6% in Sept. 1997.

15 commissions were set up in 1996 to deal with labour disputes.

FOREIGN ECONOMIC RELATIONS. On 12 April 1990 Estonia, Latvia and Lithuania concluded a Baltic Economic Co-operation Agreement. A free trade agreement came into force on 1 April 1994. Estonia also has free trade agreements with the EU, EFTA, the Czech Republic, Slovakia, Slovenia, Ukraine and Turkey.

Joint ventures are permitted, but non-Estonians may not own more than 50% of the equity without government permission. New ventures enjoy a 2-year tax exemption. Foreign investment by country of origin in 1996 (% of total): Finland, 30%; Sweden, 21%; Russia, 7%; USA, 7%; Denmark, 4%; UK, 4%. Direct foreign investments into the Estonian economy in 1996 totalled 1,800m. kroons.

Commerce. Exports (in 1m. kroons) in 1995 (and 1996) were valued at 21,048·8 (24,988·3); imports, 29,111·9 (38,552·6). Main export markets, 1996: Finland, 4,583·6 (18·3% of the total); Russia, 4,107·8 (16·4%); Sweden, 2,890·2 (11·6%); Latvia, 2,066·2 (8·3%); Germany, 1,764 (7·1%); Lithuania, 1,434·4 (5·7%); Ukraine, 1,254·7 (5%); Denmark, 885·3 (3·6%); UK, 866·6 (3·5%); Netherlands, 753·3 (3%); USA, 552·4 (2·2%). Main import suppliers: Finland, 11,257·4 (29·2% of total); Russia, 5,201·6 (13·5%); Germany, 3,843·3 (10%); Sweden, 3,149·8 (8·2%); UK, 1,275·6 (3·3%); Italy, 1,245·6 (3·2%); Netherlands, 1,098·7 (2·9%); Denmark, 1,088 (2·8%); USA, 882 (2·3%); Japan, 781·7 (2%); France, 779·1 (2%).

Tourism. There were 2·44m. foreign visitors in 1996 who spent 6,800m. kroons.

COMMUNICATIONS

Roads. At 1 Jan. 1997 there were 43,835 km of motor roads (10,080 km paved). The road network is being developed under a 10-year plan inaugurated in 1995.

Railways. Length of railways in 1996 was 1,021 km (1,520 mm gauge), of which 132 km was electrified. In 1996, 6·7m. passengers and 24·8m. tonnes of freight were carried.

Civil Aviation. There is an international airport at Tallinn (Ulemiste). In 1996 it handled 431,212 passengers and 3,997 tonnes of goods. The national carrier is

Estonian Air, 34% state-owned. It carried 164,886 passengers in 1996. It had 2 737-500, 2 Fokker 50 and 4 YAK-40 aircraft in 1996 and operated services to 11 countries. Services are also provided by Aeroflot, Drakk Air Lines, Finnair, Hamburg Airlines, Lithuanian Airlines, LOT, Lufthansa, SAS and United Airlines, and by Estonian Aviation (ELK) with flights to Helsinki, Kuressaare, Riga, Tartu and Turku.

Shipping. There are 2 major shipping companies, of which the Estonian Shipping Company is state-owned. It had 42 vessels totalling 428,466 DWT at 1 Jan. 1997. There are ice-free, deep-water ports at Tallinn and Muuga (state-owned). Tallinn handled 14m. tonnes of cargo and 443m. passengers in 1996. The ex-Soviet naval base at Paldiski is now vacant.

Telecommunications. There were 0·38m. telephone subscribers in 1994. Postal services are run by the state-owned Eesti Post. Estonian Radio operates under the aegis of the Broadcasting Council. There are also 3 commercial radio networks and the government's foreign service, Radio Estonia (Estonian, English, Esperanto, Finnish, German, Spanish). In 1997 there were 3 TV networks (colour by SECAM): Estonian State Television and 2 commercial channels. Programming ventures must be at least 51% Estonian-owned, and foreign programmes must not exceed 30% of output. In 1993 there were 0·6m. TV receivers.

Cinemas. Attendances were 2·1m. in 1993.

Press. In 1995 there were 4 national dailies in Estonian, 2 in Russian and 2 evening papers and 6 weeklies.

SOCIAL INSTITUTIONS

Justice. A post-Soviet criminal code was introduced in 1992. The death penalty is retained for murder and terrorism but there is a moratorium on it since 1991. There is a 3-tier court system with the State Court at its apex, and there are both city and district courts. The latter act as courts of appeal. The State Court is the final court of appeal, and also functions as a constitutional court. There are also administrative courts for petty offences. Judges are appointed for life. City and district judges are appointed by the President; State Court judges are elected by Parliament.

In 1996, 35,411 crimes were reported (including 268 murders) of which 32·5% were solved. There are 9 prisons; in July 1997, 4,785 persons were in custody.

Religion. There are about 0·35m. Lutherans and a Methodist Church. The Estonian Orthodox Church owed allegiance to Constantinople until it was forcibly brought under Moscow's control in 1940; a synod of the free Estonian Orthodox Church was established in Stockholm. Returning from exile, it registered itself in 1993 as the Estonian Apostolic Orthodox Church. By an agreement in 1996 between the Moscow and Constantinople Orthodox Patriarchates there are now 2 Orthodox jurisdictions in Estonia. In 1996 there were some 35,000 Orthodox in 84 congregations; 37 congregations had opted for allegiance to Constantinople.

Education. There are 9 years of comprehensive school starting at age 6, followed by 3 years secondary school. In 1996 pupils in 739 primary, secondary and special schools numbered 222,700; 602 of these general education schools were Estonian-language, 114 Russian-language and 23 mixed-language. In 1996, 59% of children between 1-6 years attended pre-school institutions. In 1996 there were 8 universities and 20 institutes of higher education with a total of 30,072 students, and 91 secondary vocational schools with 31,487 students.

Health. There were 79 state and 6 private hospitals in 1996. In 1996 there were 304 doctors and 765 hospital beds per 10,000 population.

Welfare. In 1997 there were 0·37m. pensioners. The average monthly pension was 1,037 kroons in 1997. An official poverty line was introduced in 1993 (then 280 kroons per month). Persons receiving less are entitled to state benefit. Unemployment benefit was 240 kroons a month in 1996.

DIPLOMATIC REPRESENTATIVES

Of Estonia in Great Britain (16 Hyde Park Gate, London SW7 5DG)
Ambassador: Raul Mälk.

Of Great Britain in Estonia (Kentmanni 20, Tallinn EE 0100)
Ambassador: Timothy James Craddock.

Of Estonia in the USA (1030 15th Street NW, Washington DC 20005)
Ambassador: Kalev Stoicescu.

Of the USA in Estonia (Kentmanni 20, Tallinn EE 0001)
Ambassador: Vacant.

Of Estonia to the United Nations
Ambassador: Trivimi Velliste.

Of Estonia to the European Union
Ambassador: Clyde Kull.

Further Reading

Statistical Office of Estonia. *Statistical Yearbook.*
Ministry of the Economy. *Estonian Economy.* Annual
Hood, N. *et al.* (eds.) *Transition in the Baltic States.* London, 1997
Lieven, A., *The Baltic Revolution: Estonia, Latvia, Lithuania and the Path to Independence.* 2nd ed. Yale Univ. Press, 1994
Misiunas, R.-J. and Taagepera, R., *The Baltic States: Years of Dependence 1940–1991.* 2nd ed, Farnborough, 1993
Raun, T. U., *Estonia and the Estonians.* Stanford, 1987
Smith, I. A. and Grunts, M. V. *The Baltic States.* [Bibliography]. Oxford and Santa Barbara, 1993
Taagepera, R., *Estonia: Return to Independence.* Boulder (CO), 1993

National library: The Estonian National Library was opened in 1993.
National statistical office: Statistical Office of Estonia, Tallinn.

ETHIOPIA

Federal Democratic Republic of Ethiopia

Capital: Addis Ababa
Population: 55m.
GNP: US$6·9bn.
HDI/world rank: 0·244/170

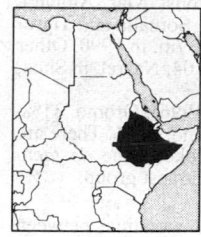

KEY HISTORICAL EVENTS. The ancient empire of Ethiopia has its legendary origin in the meeting of King Solomon and the Queen of Sheba. Historically, the empire developed at Askum in the north, in the centuries before and after the birth of Christ, as a result of Semitic immigration from South Arabia. The immigrants imposed their language and culture on the indigenous Hamitic people. Ethiopia's subsequent history is one of sporadic expansion southwards and eastwards, checked from the 16th to early 19th centuries by devastating wars with Moslems and Gallas. Modern Ethiopia dates from the reign of the Emperor Theodore (1855-68).

Menelik II (1889-1913) defeated the Italians in 1896 and thereby safeguarded the empire's independence in the scramble for Africa. By successful campaigns in neighbouring kingdoms within Ethiopia (Jimma, Kaffa, Harar, etc.) he united the country under his rule and created the empire as it is today.

In 1923 the heir to the throne, Ras Tafari (crowned Emperor Haile Selassie five years later), succeeded in getting Ethiopia admitted as an independent country to the League of Nations. However, the League was ineffective in preventing a second Italian invasion in 1936. The emperor fled the country, only returning when the Allied forces defeated the Italians in 1941.

In accordance with a resolution of the General Assembly of the UN, dated 2 Dec. 1950, the former Italian colony of Eritrea, from 1941 under British military administration, was handed over to Ethiopia on 15 Sept. 1952. Thereafter, a secessionist movement fought a guerrilla war for independence under the Eritrean Peoples' Liberation Front (EPLF). Another guerrilla campaign was waged in neighbouring Tigray, led by the Tigray Peoples' Liberation Front (TPLF).

A provisional military government, known as the Dirgue, assumed power in Ethiopia on 12 Sept. 1974 under the leadership of Lieut. Col. Mengistu Haile Miriam. It deposed the emperor, abolished the monarchy and as a means of abolishing rural feudalism mounted an agricultural collectivization programme.

In 1977 Somalia invaded Ethiopia and took control of the Ogaden region. After an offensive mounted with strong Soviet and Cuban support the area was recaptured and in March 1978 Somalia withdrew all troops from the area. Control was re-established by Ethiopia later in 1978 and nationalist guerrillas were pushed back. Sporadic fighting continued in the Ogaden and along the border. Talks about the normalization of relations between Ethiopia and Somalia commenced in 1986.

The Workers Party of Ethiopia (WPE), set up by the Dirgue in 1984, drew up a constitution for a Peoples' Democratic Republic of Ethiopia, which was approved by referendum in 1987. Elections took place in June and all central committee members were returned to office, including Mengistu who was elected President.

Following ever-increasing territorial gains by the insurgent Ethiopian People's Revolutionary Democratic Front (EPRDF) and the Eritrean People's Liberation Front (EPLF), Mengistu stepped down as president and fled the country. An interim EPRDF government led by Meles Zenawi took over after the flight of President Mengistu. In July 1991 a conference of 24 political groups called to appoint a transitional government agreed a democratic charter guaranteeing freedom of expression and association and the right to self-determination for ethnic groups. An 87-member Council of Representatives was formed which unanimously elected Meles President.

Eritrea seceded, and became independent, on 24 May 1993.

TERRITORY AND POPULATION. Ethiopia is bounded in the north-east by Eritrea, east by Djibouti and Somalia, south by Kenya and west by Sudan. It has a total area of 1·4m. sq. km. The secession of Eritrea in 1993 left Ethiopia without a coastline. An Eritrean-Ethiopian agreement of July 1993 gives Ethiopia rights to use the Eritrean ports of Assab and Massawa.

The first census was carried out in 1984: Population, 42,019,418 (without Eritrea, 39,570,266). Estimate (1994), 55m. (15% urban). Estimated expectation of life, (1997): Males, 45·48 years; females, 47·8.

The 1994 Constitution provides for a federation of 9 regions: Afar, Amhara, Benshangi, Gambella, Harar, Oromia, The Peoples of the South, Somalia and Tigre.

The population of the capital, Addis Ababa, was estimated at 1·7m. in 1990. Other large towns (population, May 1984): Dire Dawa, in Hararge, 98,104; Nazret, in Shoa, 76,284; Bahr Dar, 54,800; Debre Zeit, 51,143.

There are 6 major ethnic groups (in % of total population in 1996): Oromo, 31%; Amhara, 30%; Tigrinya, 7%; Gurage, 4·7%; Somali, 4·1%; Sidamo, 3·2%. There are also some 60 minor ethnic groups and 286 languages are spoken. The *de facto* official language is Amharic, though Oromo-speakers form the largest group.

CLIMATE. The wide range of latitude produces many climatic variations between the high, temperate plateaus and the hot, humid lowlands. The main rainy season lasts from June to Aug., with light rains from Feb. to April, but the country is very vulnerable to drought. Addis Ababa. Jan. 59°F (15°C), July 59°F (15°C). Annual rainfall 50" (1,237 mm). Harar. Jan. 65°F (18·3°C), July 64°F (17·8°C). Annual rainfall 35" (897 mm). Massawa. Jan. 78°F (25·6°C), July 94°F (34·4°C). Annual rainfall 8" (193 mm).

CONSTITUTION AND GOVERNMENT. A 548-member constituent assembly was elected on 5 June 1994; turn-out was 55%. The EPRDF gained 484 seats. On 8 Dec. 1994 it unanimously adopted a new federal Constitution which provides for the creation of a federation of 9 regions based (except the capital and the southern region) on a predominant ethnic group. These regions have the right of secession after a referendum. The *President*, a largely ceremonial post, is elected by parliament, the 548-member *Council of People's Representatives*. There is also an upper house, the 117-member *Federal Council*.

Parliamentary and regional elections were held in May and June 1995. The electorate was 24m. Candidates from 47 parties stood. The EPRDF won 593 seats.

President: Dr Negasso Gidada (b. 1950; EPRDF; elected 22 Aug. 1995).

A new government was formed on 24 Aug. 1995 which comprised in March. 1998:

Prime Minister: Meles Zenawi (b. 1955; EPRDF).

Deputy Prime Minister: Kassu Illala. *Agriculture:* Seifu Ketema. *Defence:* Tefera Walwa. *Education:* Genet Zewdie. *Finance:* Sufyan Ahmad. *Foreign Affairs:* Seyoum Mesfin. *Health:* Adem Ibrahim. *Information and Culture:* Wolde Michael Chamo. *Justice:* Worede-Wold Wolde. *Labour and Social Affairs:* Hassan Abdella. *Mines and Energy:* Ezaddin Ali. *Construction and Urban Development:* Haile Aseged. *Trade and Industry:* Kasahun Ayele. *Transport and Communications:* Abdulmejid Hussein. *Water Resources:* Shiferaw Jarso.

Speaker of the Council of Peoples' Representatives: Dawit Yohannes. *Speaker of the Federal Council:* Almaz Meko.

National anthem: 'Yazegennat keber ba-Ityop yachchen santo' ('In our Ethiopia our civic pride is strong'); words anonymous, tune by S. Lulu.

Local Government. Local authority elections were held on 21 June 1992. The electorate was about 33m.

DEFENCE

Army. Following the overthrow of President Mengistu's government Ethiopian armed forces were formed from former members of the Tigray Peoples' Liberation Front. Ethiopia auctioned off its naval assets in Sept. 1966. The strength of the armed forces is estimated at 120,000. Equipment includes some 350 T-54/-55 main battle tanks.

Air Force. Most of the Air Force is grounded and in the process of reorganization.

Surviving aircraft are reported to include 20 MiG-21 and some MiG-23 fighters, 18 Mi-24 armed helicopters and 25 Mi-8 transport helicopters. There were airfields at Debre Zeyit, Asmara, Gode, Dire Dawa and Deke.

INTERNATIONAL RELATIONS

Membership. Ethiopia is a member of the UN, OAU and is an ACP state of the EU.

ECONOMY

Policy. Following a long period of stagnation, the Ethiopian economy came to a turning point in 1991 when peace was restored. An Economic Reform Programme was instituted in 1992 aimed at stabilizing the economy and deregulating economic activities to prepare the ground for a free-market economy. An Economic Rehabilitation and Reconstruction Programme (ERRP) launched in 1991/92 eased foreign exchange regulations to allow for imports of raw materials and capital equipment. Over the 3-year period (1992/93 to 1994/95) real overall GDP growth averaged 6·5%. During the same period average growth rates of agricultural and industrial sectors were 2·4% and 14·5% respectively. Similarly, distributive and other services grew by 11·9% and 9·8%.

Budget. The fiscal year ends 6 July. Revenue, 1994–95 (in 1,000m. birr), 7·8. Government expenditure: 8·9.

Currency. The *birr* (ETB), of 100 *cents*, is the unit of currency. There are coins of 1, 5, 10, 25 and 50 cents, and notes of 1, 5, 10, 50 and 100 birr. The birr was devalued in Oct. 1992. Currency in circulation, 1992, 4,709m. birr. Foreign exchange reserves, 1993, US$414·3m.

Banking and Finance. The central bank and bank of issue is the National Bank of Ethiopia (founded 1964; *Governor*, Dubale Yale). There is an Agricultural and Industrial Development Bank, and a Housing and Savings Bank. On 1 Jan. 1975 the Government nationalized all banks, mortgage and insurance companies.

Weights and Measures. The metric system is officially in use. Traditional units include the *frasilla* = approximately 37½ lb., and the *gasha*, which can vary between 80 and 300 acres. The Julian calendar remains in use; the year has 13 months, and is 7 years behind the Gregorian calendar.

ENERGY AND NATURAL RESOURCES

Electricity. 98% of generation is hydro-electric. Output, 1995, 1·45m. kWh. Supply 220 volts; 50 Hz.

Minerals. Gold, cement and salt are produced.

Agriculture. Agriculture contributes over 50% of GDP. About 80% of the workforce are employed in agriculture. There are 85m. ha of arable land, of which 16m. ha were cultivated in 1994. By 1993 96% of agricultural land was worked by smallholdings averaging 0·5–1·5 ha. Land remains the property of the state, but individuals are granted rights of usage which can be passed to their children, and produce may be sold on the open market instead of compulsorily to the state at low fixed prices.

Coffee is by far the most important source of rural income. Teff (*Eragrastis abyssinica*) is the principal food grain, followed by barley, wheat, maize and durra. Cane sugar is an important crop.

Forestry. In 1994 forests covered 2·7% of the land area.

INDUSTRY.

Most public industrial enterprises are controlled by the state. Industrial activity is centred around Addis Ababa. Processed food, textiles and drinks are the main commodities produced.

Labour. The labour force in 1995 was 24·5m.; it was estimated by the UN that 30% were unemployed.

FOREIGN ECONOMIC RELATIONS. Foreign debt was US$4,354m. in 1992.

Commerce. Exports, 1992 (in 1,000m. birr), 309; imports, 669. Principal exports: Coffee, 188. Principal imports: Machinery and aircraft, 314; other vehicles, 179; oil, 553; textiles, 74. The main export markets: Germany, 32%; Japan, 14·5%; Saudi Arabia, 5·3%. Main import suppliers: USA, 12·3%; Germany, 7·9%; Italy, 11%; Saudi Arabia, 15%.

Tourism. There were 115,000 foreign visitors in 1997.

COMMUNICATIONS

Roads. There are 19,000 km of asphalt roads and 9,000 km of rural and gravel roads.

Railways. The Ethiopian-Djibouti Railway Corp. (782 km, metre-gauge) in 1993 carried 0·24m. tonnes of freight and 0·71m. passengers.

Civil Aviation. There are international airports at Addis Ababa (Bole) and Dire Dawa. A new airport at Mekele was scheduled for 1997. The national carrier is the state-owned Ethiopian Airlines, which in 1995 had a fleet of 1 B-707-320C, 1 B-737-200 Adv, 4 B-757-200s, 1 B-757-200PF, 3 B-767-200ERs and 10 other aircraft.

Telecommunications. The postal system serves 301 offices, mainly by air-mail. All the main centres are connected with Addis Ababa by telephone or radio telegraph.

The government-run Voice of Ethiopia broadcasts a national programme and an external service in English. Ethiopian Television (colour by PAL) transmits about 28 hours a week. In 1993 there were 10·2m. radio and 0·2m. TV receivers.

Press. There are 4 government-controlled daily newspapers with a combined circulation of about 60,000 and about 50 independent periodicals.

SOCIAL INSTITUTIONS

Justice. The legal system is said to be based on the Justinian Code. A new penal code came into force in 1958 and Special Penal Law in 1974. Codes of criminal procedure, civil, commercial and maritime codes have since been promulgated.

Provincial and district courts have been established, and High Court judges visit the provincial courts on circuit. The Supreme Court at Addis Ababa is presided over by the Chief Justice.

Religion. About 53% of the population are Christian, mainly belonging to the Ethiopian Orthodox Church, and 30% Sunni Moslems. Amhara, Tigreans and some Oromos are Christian. Somalis, Afars and some Oromos are Moslems. About 12% of the population follow traditional animist beliefs.

Education. Adult literacy was 34·5% in 1994. Primary education commences at 7 years and continues with optional secondary education at 13 years. Up to the age of 12 education is in the local language of the federal region. Pupil/teacher ratio: 33. In 1994–95 there was 1 university with 19,200 students and 900 academic staff, and 1 agricultural university with 1,551 students and 324 academic staff. There were also 2 institutes of health sciences and water technology; and 2 colleges, of teacher training and town planning.

Health. Population per hospital bed, 293,787; population per health centre, 22,242.

DIPLOMATIC REPRESENTATIVES

Of Ethiopia in Great Britain (17 Prince's Gate, London, SW7 1PZ)
Ambassador: Dr Solomon Gidada.

Of Great Britain in Ethiopia (Fikre Mariam Abatechan St., Addis Ababa)
Ambassador: G. G. Wetherell.

Of Ethiopia in the USA (2134 Kalorama Rd., NW, Washington D.C., 20008)
Ambassador: Berhane Gebre-Chirstos.

Of the USA in Ethiopia (Entoto St., Addis Ababa)
Ambassador: David Shinn.

Of Ethiopia to the United Nations
Ambassador: Duri Mohammed.

Of Ethiopia to the European Union
Ambassador: Peter Gabriel Robleh.

Further Reading

Alemneh Dejene. *Environment, Famine and Politics in Ethiopia: a View from the Village.* Boulder (Colo.), 1991

Araia, G., *Ethiopia: the Political Economy of Transition.* Univ. Press of America, 1995

Griffin, K. (ed.) *The Economy of Ethiopia.* London, 1992

Keller, E. J. *Revolutionary Ethiopia: From Empire to People's Republic.* Indiana Univ. Press, 1989

Marcus, H.G., *A History of Ethiopia.* California Univ. Press, 1994

Mekonnen, T. (ed.) *The Ethiopian Economy: Structure, Problems and Policy Issues.* Addis Ababa, 1992

Munro-Hay, S. and Pankhurst, R., *Ethiopia:* [Bibliography]. Oxford and Santa Barbara (CA), 1991

Tiruneh, A., *The Ethiopian Revolution: a Transformation from an Aristocratic to a Totalitarian Autocracy.* CUP, 1993

National statistical office: Central Statistical Office, Addis Ababa.

FIJI

Republic of Fiji

Capital: Suva
Population: 772,655
GDP per head: (PPP$) 5,763
GNP: (US$bn.) 1·8
HDI/world rank: 0·863/46

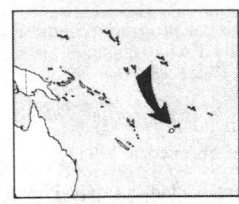

KEY HISTORICAL EVENTS. The Fiji Islands were discovered by Tasman in 1643 and visited by Capt. Cook in 1774, but first recorded in detail by Capt. Bligh after the mutiny of the Bounty (1789). In the 19th century the search for sandalwood, in which enormous profits were made, brought many ships. Deserters and shipwrecked men stayed on; firearms salvaged from wrecks were used in native wars, new diseases swept the islands, and rum and muskets became regular articles of trade. Tribal wars became bloody and general until Fiji was ceded to Britain on 10 Oct. 1874, after a previous offer of cession had been refused. Fiji gained independent status on 10 Oct. 1970.

Fiji remained an independent state within the Commonwealth with a Governor-General appointed by the Queen until 1987. In the general election of 12 April 1987 a left-wing coalition headed by Dr Timoci Bavadra defeated the ruling Alliance Party of Ratu Sir Kamisese Mara. The new government had the support of the Indian population who outnumber the indigenous Fijians at a rate of 50% to 44%. It was, however, overthrown in a military coup on 14 May led by Lieut.-Col. Sitiveni Rabuka.

After a period of uncertainty in which civil government was largely restored, Brigadier Rabuka led a second coup on 25 Sept. On 7 Oct. Fiji declared itself a Republic and Fiji's Commonwealth membership lapsed.

In 1990, a new coalition restored civilian rule but made it impossible for Fijian Indians to hold power. Recently, however, a rapprochement with Indian leaders has led to an agreement to restore multiracial government in 1998. Fiji rejoined the Commonwealth in 1997.

TERRITORY AND POPULATION. Fiji comprises 332 islands and islets (about one-third are inhabited) lying between 15° and 22° S. lat. and 174° E. and 177° W. long. The largest is Viti Levu, area 10,429 sq. km (4,027 sq. miles), next is Vanua Levu, area 5,556 sq. km (2,145 sq. miles). The island of Rotuma (47 sq. km, 18 sq. miles), about 12° 30' S. lat., 178° E. long., was added to the colony in 1881. Total area, 7,078 sq. miles (18,333 sq. km).

Total population (1996), 772,655.

Of Fiji's current population more than 60% live in rural areas. Population statistics for urban centres indicate that about 167,421 people live in the two major cities, Suva and Lautoka.

Vital statistics, 1994: Crude birth rate per 1,000 population, 23·0; crude death rate per 1,000 population, 4·5 Average life expectancy (1994), 71·8 years for males and 65·2 for females.

CLIMATE. A tropical climate, but oceanic influences prevent undue extremes of heat or humidity. The S. E. Trades blow from May to Nov., during which time nights are cool and rainfall amounts least. Suva. Jan. 80°F (26·7°C), July 73°F (22·8°C). Annual rainfall 117" (2,974 mm).

CONSTITUTION AND GOVERNMENT. The executive authority of the State is vested in the President, who is appointed by the Bose Levu Vakaturaga (Great Council of Chiefs). The Prime Minister is appointed by the President. The Prime Minister must establish a multi-party cabinet. The President's term of office is 5 years.

The Upper House or Senate will consist of 32 members of whom 14 are appointed by the President on the advice of Bose Levu Vakaturaga. 9 are appointed by the President on the advice of the Leader of the Opposition and 1 appointed by the President on the advice of the Council of Rotuma.

A new Constitution unanimously passed by Parliament and assented to by H.E. the President will come into force on 25 July 1998. The new Constitution does away with an indigenous Prime Minister and has a 71 seat House of Representatives (Lower House), with 46 elected on communal role and 25 from open electoral roll. Of the 46, 23 will be elected on Fijian roll, 19 from Indian roll, 3 from others and 1 from Rotuma.

In March 1998 the government comprised:

President: Ratu Sir Kamisese Mara, GCMG, KBE (sworn in 18 Jan. 1994).

Prime Minister, Minister with Special Responsibility for the Constitution, Multi-Ethnic Affairs, Regional Development: Maj.-Gen. Sitiveni Rabuka, OBE (b. 1948; SVT). *Deputy Prime Minister; Minister for Education and Technology:* Taufa Vakatale OF; *Minister for Agriculture, Fisheries and Forests:* Militoni Leveniqila. *Attorney-General:* Ratu Etuate Tavai. *Finance;* James Ah Koy. *Health:* Leo Smith. *Commerce, Industry, Co-operatives and Public Enterprises:* Isimeli Bose. *Justice and Home Affairs:* Col. Paul Manueli, OBE. *Foreign Affairs and External Trade:* Berenado Vunibobo. *Communications, Works and Energy:* Ratu Inoke Kubuabola. *Information, Women and Culture:* Seruwaia Hong Tiy. *National Planning:* Filipe Bole. *Local Government, Housing and Environment:* Vilisoni Cagimaivei. *Tourism, and Transport:* David Pickering. *Labour and Industrial Relations:* Vincent Lobendahn. *Youth, Employment Opportunities and Sports:* Jonetani Kaukimoce.

National anthem: 'Blessing grant, oh God of Nations, on the isles of Fiji'; words by M. Prescott, tune anonymous.

Local Government. 14 provinces subdivided into 188 *tikinas*, each with its own provincial council. Tikinas are composed of village units headed by a locally-elected or appointed chief. The number of tikina councils within a province varies from 4 to 22. Tikina councils have wide powers to make by-laws and levy rates to raise revenue. 50% of the rates collected is credited to the provincial council treasury for the running of the council and 50% is used for the financing of the tikina and village projects.

DEFENCE

Army. The Army consists of 7 infantry battalions and 1 engineer battalion. Personnel in (1996) numbered close to 3,796. More than 800 of these are actively involved in peace-keeping duties with the United Nations in the Middle East.

Navy. The naval division of the armed forces consists of 4 Israeli-built fast inshore patrol craft, 5 other patrol craft. Naval personnel in 1997 numbered 275.

Air Force. The Fiji Air Wing operates 1 Dauphin and 1 Ecureuil helicopter, both supplied by France.

INTERNATIONAL RELATIONS

Membership. Fiji is a member of the UN, the Commonwealth, the Colombo Plan, the Pacific Community, the South Pacific Forum and is an ACP state of the EU.

ECONOMY

Economic growth in 1996 was 3·1%. Operating revenue (1997) $F700·00m. Operating expenditure (1997) $F550·00m. Inflation rate (Oct. 1997) 3%.

Budget. The financial year corresponds with the calendar year. Government revenue and expenditure (in $F1m.):

	1992	1993	1994	1995	1996
Revenue	574·37	636·14	689·02	710·18	736·18
Expenditure	646·23	754·40	786·20	801·14	881·44

VAT of 10% was introduced in 1992.

Currency. The unit of currency is the *Fiji dollar* (FJD) of 100 *cents.* There are coins of 1, 2, 5, 10, 20 and 50 cents and $F1. There are notes of $F2, 5, 10, 20 and 50. $F85·8m. were in circulation in 1991. Foreign exchange reserves were $F480·64m. in 1992.

Banking and Finance. The central bank and bank of issue is the Reserve Bank of Fiji. Total assets were $F493·07m. in June 1996. The National Bank is a government owned commercial bank. The Fiji Development Bank has assets totalling $F356·01m. There are 5 foreign banks in the country. Total assets of commercial banks were $F1,797·92m. in June 1996.

ENERGY AND NATURAL RESOURCES

Electricity. The Fiji Electricity Authority is responsible for the generation, transmission and distribution of electricity in the country. It operates six separate supply systems. The largest energy project is one of hydro-electricity generating 95% of the main island's electric needs. Two rural hydro schemes have been completed, one generating 100 kilowatt and the other 800 kilowatt. In 1994 there were 7 thermal and 1 hydro-electric power stations. Production (1991) 474m. kWh.

Minerals. The main goldmine accounts for almost one tenth of Fiji's exports and employs about 1,700 people. Since the beginning of 1997 gold prices have continued to fall. However a total of 2,000 tonnes have been sold since 1991. Net sales in 1996 were 239 tonnes (gross sales were 588 tonnes).

Agriculture. With a total land area of 1·8m. ha, only 16% is suitable for farming. Arable land: 24% sugar cane, 23%, coconut, 53% other crops. In 1997 forecast for sugar production was at 460,000 tonnes. Copra production increased to 10,700 tonnes in 1995. Ginger is the most successful diversification crop to-date—1995 showed an increase of 1,000 tonnes, total export value for the 1995 crop was $F1,445,000. Rice production increased in 1995 with 18,500 tonnes. Fruits and vegetables were valued at $F1m. for 1,000 tonnes of export.

Livestock (1992, in 1,000): Cattle, 160; horses, 43; goats, 124; pigs, 15; poultry, 3,000. Products, 1991 (in tonnes): Beef, 2,847; pork, 715; goat meat, 660; chicken meat, 5,888; eggs, 2,191.

Dairy: total production in tonnes of milk increased in 1994, 1,621 tonnes.

Forestry. The forest covers about 935,000 ha and contributes around 1·5% of GDP. It is the fifth most important export commodity, valued at $F53m. in 1996. Hardwood plantations established 48,270 ha. By 2000, Fiji Pine Limited aims to establish 16,000 ha of plantation. Log production in 1996 was 556,986 cu. metres.

Fisheries. Accounts for 2% of GDP. Mainstay of export fisheries—the skipjack and albacore tuna for canning. Increase in export of fresh and chilled tuna from 53 tonnes (1989) to over 3,000 tonnes (1995).

INDUSTRY. The Tax Free Factory scheme was instituted in 1987 as an encouragement to industry. A total of 133 Tax Free Factories (TFF) were in operation in 1996, a decline from 144 in 1995. Of the total, 68 factories were engaged in garment manufacturing. Of the 8 new factories under the TFF scheme, 3 were involved in garment production. The garment industry earned $F141m. in 1996. Output, 1994 (in tonnes): Sugar, 475,000; (1991) coconut oil, 8,775; flour, 26,933; butter, 1,477; cigarettes, 585; animal feed, 25,377; cement, 78,800; soap, 7,068; beer, 18·31m. litres.

Labour. Approximately 301,500 persons were in paid employment in 1996.

FOREIGN ECONOMIC RELATIONS. The Tax-Free Factory/Tax-Free Zone Scheme was introduced in 1987 to stimulate investment and encourage export-oriented businesses.

Foreign debt was $F433·3m. in 1992.

Commerce. In 1995 the country's total imports were $F1,218·9m. and total exports were around $F869·9m. Chief exports are: Sugar, prepared and preserved fish, timber, ginger and molasses. Chief trading partners: Exports: Australia, Canada, Japan, Malaysia, New Zealand; Imports: Australia, China, Japan, New Zealand, Singapore, UK.

Tourism. Visitor arrivals in 1996 rose by 6·6% to a record 339,560 persons. The inauguration of new flight routes and their associated promotions contributed to this increase. In the first nine months of 1997, visitor arrivals increased by 8·1%.

COMMUNICATIONS

Roads. Total road length in 1996 was about 5,100 km, of which 1,030 km were sealed. A total of 95,554 vehicles were registered in Fiji in 1994.

Railways. Fiji Sugar Cane Corporation runs 600 mm gauge railways at four of its mills on Viti Levu and Vanua Levu, totalling 595 km.

Civil Aviation. There are international airports at Nadi and Nausori. The national carrier is Air Pacific (78% government owned). It provides services to Australia, Japan, New Zealand, USA and a number of Pacific island nations. Commercial domestic air operators include Sunflower Airlines, Air Fiji, Vanua Air, Air Wakaya, Turtle Airways and Pacific Crown Aviation (Helicopter Operator). In 1991 they handled 603,535 passengers.

Shipping. The 3 ports of entry are Suva, Lautoka and Levuka. Ocean-going shipping totalled 27,385 GRT in 1995, including oil tankers, 4,705 GRT. Inter-island shipping fleet is a mix of private and government vessels. A total of 620 foreign vessels called into the Suva port in 1995, 318 and 109 respectively in Lautoka and Levuka. Altogether 7,189 ships including local ships, yachts and foreign vessels called into the three major ports.

Telecommunications. The national telephone service has over 64,000 lines, standing at 8 lines per 100 population, of which 40% are business customers and 60% residential. There are over 500 cardphones located around the country and approximately 83 in rural areas. 19·6m. items were posted in Fiji for delivery to local addresses in addition to 4·76m. items posted for overseas destinations making total posting of 24·45m. items in 1995. There are currently 50 major post offices and 108 postal agencies.

There are two major radio stations, Island Network Corporation Ltd and Communications Fiji Ltd. Each has its own unique programmes to suit the culture, age and taste of the nation's radio audience. Fiji Television Company is a commercial network that has 1 free to air and 2 pay channels.

Press. There are 2 daily newspapers, *Fiji Times and Herald* and *The Daily Post*. Vernacular newspapers are also published by these two, including *Nai Lalakai*, *Nai Volasiga* and *Shanti Dut*. Other locally produced periodicals are the *Review, Island's Business, Fiji First, Pacific Islands Monthly* and *Marama Vou*.

SOCIAL INSTITUTIONS

Justice. An independent Judiciary is guaranteed under the Constitution of Fiji. The Constitution allows for a High Court of Fiji which has unlimited original jurisdiction to hear and determine any civil or criminal proceedings under any law.

The High Court also has jurisdiction to hear and determine constitutional and electoral questions including the membership of members of the House of Representatives.

The Chief Justice of Fiji is appointed by the President acting after consultation with the Prime Minister.

The Fiji Court of Appeal of which the Chief Justice is *ex officio* President is formed by three specially appointed Justices of Appeal. The Justices of Appeal are appointed by the President acting after consultation with the Judicial and Legal Services Commission. Generally any person convicted of any offence has a right of appeal from the High Court of Appeal. The final appellant court is the Supreme Court. Most matters coming before the Superior Courts originate in Magistrates' Courts.

Police. The Royal Fiji Police Force had (1997) a total strength of 1,915.

Religion. In 1996, the population consisted of 52% Christians, 39·4% Hindus, 7·8% Muslims, 0·7% Sikhs and 0·1% others.

Education. Of the total estimated population of Fiji in 1996 (mid-year), 26·4% were attending school full time. The number of registered schools totalled 1,261. Of these there were 391 pre-schools, 16 special schools, 698 primary schools, 151 secondary schools and 5 post secondary schools. The number of primary school teachers was 4,921. The number of civil servant teachers in secondary schools was 2,310.

The University of the South Pacific, which is located in Suva, serves 12 countries in the South Pacific region. Fiji also has a college of agriculture, school of medicine and nursing, an institute of technology, a primary school teacher training college and an advanced college of education.

Health. There are 409 village clinics, 100 nursing stations, 74 health centres, 3 area hospitals, 3 nursing homes, 16 sub-divisional hospitals, 3 divisional hospitals and 2 speciality hospitals.

Through its national health service system, the government continues to provide the bulk of health services both in the curative and public health programmes.

DIPLOMATIC REPRESENTATIVES

Of Fiji in Great Britain (34 Hyde Park Gate, London, SW7 5DN)
Ambassador: Filimone Jitoko.

Of Great Britain in Fiji (Victoria House, 47 Gladstone Rd., Suva)
High Commissioner. M. A. C. Dibben.

Of Fiji in the USA (2233 Wisconsin Ave., NW, Washington, D.C., 20007)
Ambassador: Ratu Napolioni Masirewa.

Of the USA in Fiji (31 Loftus St., Suva)
Chargé d'Affaires: Larry Dinger.

Of Fiji to the United Nations
Ambassador: Poseci Bune.

Of Fiji to the European Union
Ambassador: Kaliopate Tavola.

Further Reading

Bureau of Statistics. *Current Economic Statistics.* Quarterly
Reserve Bank of Fiji. *Quarterly Review*
Bain, K., *Fiji at the Crossroads.* London, 1989
Gorman, G. E. and Mills, J. J., *Fiji* [Bibliography]. Oxford and Santa Barbara (CA), 1994
Howard, M. C., *Fiji: Race and Politics in an Island State.* Univ. of British Columbia Press, 1991
Lal, B. J., *Broken Waves: a History of the Fiji Islands in the Twentieth Century.* Univ. of Hawaii Press, 1992
Lal, V., *Fiji: Coups in Paradise.* London, 1991
Ravuvu, A., *The Façade of Democracy: Fijian Struggles for Political Control.* Suva, 1991
Scarr, D., *Fiji: a Short History.* Sydney, 1984
Sutherland, W., *Beyond the Politics of Race: an Alternative History of Fiji to 1992.* Australian National Univ. Press, 1992
Wright, R., *On Fiji Islands.* London, 1987

National statistical office: Bureau of Statistics, POB 2221, Government Buildings, Suva.

FINLAND

Suomen Tasavalta—
Republiken Finland

Capital: Helsinki
Population: 5·12m.
GDP per head: (PPP$) 17,417
HDI/world rank: 0·940/8

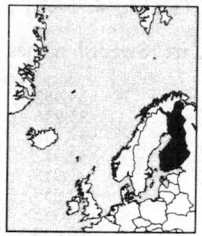

KEY HISTORICAL EVENTS. Finland was part of Sweden until the 18th century when the south-east territory was conquered by Russia. The rest of the country was ceded to Russia by the treaty of Hamina in 1809 when Finland became an autonomous grand-duchy retaining its laws and institutions under a grand duke, the Emperor of Russia. The Diet, elected since 1906 on universal suffrage, produced in 1916 a social democrat majority, the first in Europe. After the Russian revolution Finland declared itself independent but civil war broke out in Jan. 1918 between the 'whites' and 'reds', the latter supported by Russian Bolshevik troops. The defeat of the red guards in May 1918 freed the country from Russian troops. A peace treaty with Soviet Russia was signed in 1920.

On 30 Nov. 1939 Soviet troops invaded in what became known as the Winter War. The subsequent peace treaty of 12 March 1940 compelled Finland to cede 32,806 sq. km including the Carelian Isthmus, Viipuri and the shores of Lake Ladoga.

When the German attack on the USSR was launched in June 1941 Finland again became involved in war against the USSR. On 19 Sept. 1944 an armistice was signed in Moscow. Finland agreed to cede to the USSR the Petsamo area in addition to the cessions made in 1940 (total 42,934 sq. km) to lease to the USSR for 50 years the Porkkala headland as a military base and to pay 300m. gold dollars in reparations within six years (later extended to eight years). The peace treaty was signed in Paris on 10 Feb. 1947. The payment of reparations was completed on 19 Sept. 1952. The military base at Porkkala was returned to Finland on 26 Jan. 1956. To pacify the USSR, the post war premier and later president S. Passikivi pursued a policy of neutralism favourable to the Russians. This policy, known as Finlandization, was continued under Presidents V. Kekkonen (1956-81) and M. Koivisto (1981-94).

With the collapse of the Soviet Union, Finland was able to adopt an independent foreign policy which led to EU admission in 1995.

TERRITORY AND POPULATION. Finland, a country of lakes and forests, is bounded in the north-west and north by Norway, east by Russia, south by the Baltic Sea and west by the Gulf of Bothnia and Sweden. The area and the population of Finland on 31 Dec. 1995 (Swedish names in brackets):

Province	Area (sq. km)[1]	Population[2]	Population per sq. km[2]
Uusimaa (Nyland)	9,898	1,326,589	134·0
Turku-Pori (Åbo-Björneborg)	19,954	702,179	35·2
Ahvenanmaa (Åland)	1,527	25,202	16·5
Häme (Tavastehus)	19,226	730,472	38·0
Kymi (Kymmene)	10,780	331,892	30·8
Mikkeli (St Michel)	16,326	205,630	12·6
Pohjois-Karjala (Norra Karelen)	17,782	177,271	10·0
Kuopio	16,510	258,315	15·6
Keski-Suomi (Mellersta Finland)	16,249	258,078	15·9
Vaasa (Vasa)	26,418	447,939	17·0
Oulu (Uleåborg)	56,868	451,848	7·9
Lappi (Lappland)	93,057	201,411	2·2
Total	304,593	5,116,826	16·8

[1] Excluding inland water area which totals 33,551 sq. km. [2] Resident population.

The growth of the population, which was 421,500 in 1750, has been:

End of year	Urban	Rural	Total	Percentage urban
1800	46,600	786,100	832,700	5·6
1900	333,300	2,322,600	2,655,900	12·5
1950	1,302,400	2,727,400	4,029,800	32·3
1970	2,340,300	2,258,000	4,598,300	50·9
1980	2,865,100	1,922,700	4,787,800	59·8
1990	3,079,800	1,918,700	4,998,500	61·6
1994	3,279,195	1,819,559	5,098,754	64·3
1995	3,303,766	1,813,060	5,116,826	64·6

The population on 31 Dec. 1995 by language spoken: Finnish, 4,754,787; Swedish, 294,664; other languages, 65,649; Lappish, 1,726.

The principal towns with resident population, 31 Dec. 1995, are (Swedish names in brackets):

Helsinki (Helsingfors)–capital	525,031	Kokkola (Karleby)	35,552
Espoo (Esbo)	191,247	Rovaniemi	35,236
Tampere (Tammerfors)	182,742	Järvenpää	34,436
Vantaa (Vanda)	166,480	Mikkeli (St Michel)	32,812
Turku (Åbo)	164,370	Kouvola	32,078
Oulu (Uleåborg)	109,094	Imatra	32,057
Lahti	95,119	Kerava	29,385
Kuopio	84,733	Seinäjoki	29,039
Pori (Björneborg)	76,627	Savonlinna (Nyslott)	28,867
Jyväskylä	74,072	Nokia	26,287
Lappeenranta (Villmanstrand)	56,664	Riihimäki	25,838
Kotka	55,903	Kemi	24,696
Vaasa (Vasa)	55,502	Varkaus	24,160
Joensuu	50,431	Iisalmi	24,042
Hämeenlinna (Tavastehus)	44,891	Tornio	23,156
Hyvinkää (Hyvinge)	41,203	Salo	22,802
Rauma (Raumo)	38,162	Raisio	22,268
Kajaani	36,860	Kuusankoski	21,494

Vital statistics in calendar years:

	Living births	Of which outside marriage	Still-born	Marriages	Deaths (exclusive of still-born)	Emigration
1991	65,395	17,896	306	24,732	49,294	5,984
1992	66,731	19,257	288	23,560	49,844	6,055
1993	64,826	19,665	271	24,660	50,988	6,405
1994	65,231	20,439	249	24,898	48,000	8,672
1995	63,067	20,886	293	23,737	49,280	8,957

In 1995 the rate per 1,000 was: Births, 12; marriages, 5; deaths, 10; infantile deaths (per 1,000 live births), 3·9. Over 1990–95, the suicide rate per 100,000 population was 29·8 (men, 48·9; women, 11·7). Nearly 65% of the population live in urban areas. About one sixth of the total population lives in the Helsinki metropolitan region.

CLIMATE. A quarter of Finland lies north of the Arctic Circle. The climate is severe in winter, which lasts about 6 months, but mean temperatures in south and south-west are less harsh, 21°F (–6°C). In the north, mean temperatures may fall to 8·5°F (–13°C). Snow covers the ground for three months in the south and for over six months in the far north. Summers are short but quite warm, with occasional very hot days. Precipitation is light throughout the country, with one third falling as snow, the remainder mainly as convectional rain in summer and autumn. Helsinki (Helsingfors). Jan. 21°F (–6°C), July 62°F (16·5°C). Annual rainfall 24·7" (618 mm).

CONSTITUTION AND GOVERNMENT. Finland is a republic governed by the Constitution of 17 July 1919.

Parliament consists of one chamber of 200 members chosen by direct and proportional election by all citizens of 18 or over. The country is divided into 15 electoral districts with a representation proportional to their population. Every citizen over the age of 18 is eligible for Parliament, which is elected for 4 years, but can be dissolved sooner by the President.

The *President* is elected for 6 years by direct popular vote. In case no candidate wins an absolute majority, a second round is held between the 2 most successful candidates. Presidential elections were held in 2 rounds on 16 Jan. and 6 Feb. 1994. Martti Ahtisaari won the first round against 10 opponents with 25·9% of votes cast, and the second against 1 opponent with 53·9%. Turn-out at the second round was 82·3%.

President of Finland: Martti Ahtisaari (b. 1937; Social Democrat; sworn in 1 March 1994).

At the 19 March 1995 elections for the 200-member parliament, the electorate was 3·9m.; turn-out was 71·9%; 18 parties contested. The Social Democratic Party (SDP) won 63 seats with 28·3% of votes cast (48 seats in 1991); Centre Party (Cen), 44 with 19·8% (55); National Coalition Party (NCP), 39 with 17·9% (10); Left Wing Alliance (LWA), 22 with 11·2% (19); Swedish People's Party (SPP), 12 (including 1 for coalition of Åland) with 5·1% (12); Greens, 9 with 6·5% (10); Finnish Christian League (FCL), 7 with 3% (8); Progressive Finnish Party, 2 with 2·8%; Rural Party, 1 with 1·3% (7); Ecological Party 1 with 0·3%.

The Council of State (Cabinet) was composed as follows in March 1998:

Prime Minister: Paavo Lipponen (b. 1941; SDP).

Deputy Prime Minister, Minister of Finance: Sauli Niinistö (NCP). *Finance:* Jouko Skinnari. *Foreign Affairs:* Tarja Halonen (SDP). *Justice:* Jussi Järventaus (NCP). *Education:* Olli-Pekka Heinonen (NCP). *Culture.* Claes Andersson (LWA). *European Affairs and Foreign Trade:* Ole Norrback (SPP). *Interior:* Jan-Erik Enestam (SPP). *Trade and Industry:* Antti Kalliomäki (SDP). *Transport:* Matti Aura. *Social Affairs:* Sinikka Mönkäre (SDP). *Health and Sports:* Terttu Huttu-Juntunen (LWA). *Labour:* Liisa Jaakonsaari (SDP). *Defence:* Anneli Taina (NCP). *Environment:* Pekka Haavisto (Greens). *Administrative Affairs:* Jouni Backman (SDP). *Agriculture and Forestry:* Kalevi Hemilä (ind).

The *Speaker* is Riitta Uosukainen.

National anthem: 'Oi maamme Suomi, synnyinmaa'/'Vårt land, vårt land, vårt fosterland' ('Our land, Finland/our land, our native land'); words by J. L. Runeberg, tune by F. Pacius (same as Estonia).

Finnish and Swedish are the official languages. Sami is spoken in Lapland.

European Parliament. Finland has 16 representatives. At the Oct. 1996 elections turn-out was 60%. The Centre Party gained 24·4% of votes cast; the SDP, 21·5%; the LWA, 10·5%; the Greens, 7·6%.

Local Government. Finland is divided into 6 provinces (*lääni*, Sw.: *län*). The administration of each province is entrusted to a governor (*maaherra*, Sw.: *landshövding*) appointed by the President. The governor directs the activities of the provincial office (*lääninhallitus*, Sw.: *länsstyrelse*) and of local districts (*kihlakunta*, Sw.: *härad*). In 1997 the number of local districts was 90.

The unit of local government is the municipality (*kunta*, Sw.: *kommun*). Main fields of municipal activities are local planning, roads and harbours, sanitary services, education, health services and social aid. The municipalities raise taxes independent from state taxation. Two categories of municipalities are distinguished by names: Towns (*kaupunki*, Sw.: *stad*) and other municipalities. In 1997 there were altogether 452 municipalities of which 105 were towns. In all municipalities municipal councils are elected for terms of 4 years; all inhabitants (men and women) of the municipality who have reached their 18th year are entitled to vote and eligible. The executive power is in each municipality vested in a board which consists of members elected by the council. Several municipalities regularly form associations for the administration of common institutions, *e.g.*, a hospital or a vocational school, as well as for regional development and planning. Elections were held on 20 Oct. 1996. The SDP gained 24·5% of votes cast, the Centre Party, 21·8%.

The semi-autonomous province of **Åland Islands** occupies a special position as a demilitarized area. **Åland** elects a 30-member Legislature (*Lagting*), which in turn elects the provincial Executive Board. The capital is Mariehamn (Maarianhamina). It is 95% Swedish-speaking. At a referendum on 20 Nov. 1994 Åland voted to join the EU along with the rest of Finland.

DEFENCE. The period of military training is 240, 285 or 330 days with refresher training obligation of 40 to 100 days between conscript service and age 50 (officers and non-commissioned officers age 60). Total strength of trained and equipped reserves is about 700,000.

Army. The country is divided into 12 military provinces and 3 military commands. The Army consists of 1 armoured training brigade, 8 infantry training brigades, 1 artillery brigade, 2 special regiments, 2 independent infantry battalions, 1 independent signal battalion, 2 coastal artillery regiments, 3 independent coastal artillery battalions, 4 anti-aircraft regiments and Reserve Officer School, making a total strength of 27,300 (21,600 conscripts).

Frontier Guard. This comes under the purview of the Ministry of the Interior, but is militarily-organized to participate in the defence of the country. Personnel, 1997, 3,500.

Navy. The Navy is divided into 4 groups. About 50% of the combatant units are kept manned, with the others on short-notice reserve and re-activated on a regular basis. The inventory comprises 2 corvettes, 8 missile craft, 4 patrol craft, 10 minelayers and 6 inshore minesweepers. There are 4 landing craft and some 30 auxiliaries and tenders.

Naval bases exist at Upinniemi (near Helsinki) and Turku. Total personnel strength (1997) was 2,400 of whom 1,300 are conscripts.

The National Board of Navigation has 9 civil-manned icebreakers.

Air Force. The Air Force has 3 fighter squadrons, 1 support squadron, an air academy, a technical school, a signal school, 2 depots, and a signal equipment testing centre. Personnel (1996), 4,500 (1,600 conscripts).

INTERNATIONAL RELATIONS

Membership. Finland is a member of the UN, EU, Nordic Council, OECD, the NATO Partnership for Peace and the Council of Europe. Finland has acceded to the Schengen Accord, which abolishes border controls between Finland and Austria, Belgium, Denmark, France, Germany, Greece, Iceland, Italy, Luxembourg, the Netherlands, Norway, Portugal, Spain and Sweden.

ECONOMY

Budget. Revenue and expenditure for the calendar years 1990–97 in 1m. marks:

	1990	1991	1992	1993	1994	1995	1996	1997
Revenue	138,739	163,462	182,660	207,567	193,612	201,372	193,531	190,781
Expenditure	140,893	167,959	186,107	202,184	196,755	198,332	192,526	190,805

Of the total revenue, 1995, 18% derived from sales tax, 19% from income and property tax, 11% from excise duties, 7% from other taxes and similar revenue, 27% from loans and 19% from miscellaneous sources. Of the total expenditure, 1995, 14% went to education and culture, 4% to transport, 3% to communities and housing, 4% to promotion of industry, 25% to social security, 8% to agriculture and forestry, 10% to general administration, public order and safety, 4% to defence and 28% to other expenditure.

VAT is 22% (reduced rate, 12%).

At the end of Dec. 1995 the central government debt totalled 366,000m. marks. Domestic debt amounted to 193,700m. marks; foreign debt, 172,300m. marks.

Currency. The unit of currency is the *markka* (FIM) or mark of 100 *pennis*. There are coins of 10 and 50 pennis and 1, 5 and 10 marks, and notes of 10, 20, 50, 100, 500 and 1,000 marks. The mark was pegged to the ecu in June 1991 with a 3%

margin of fluctuation. It was devalued by 12·3% in Nov. 1991, and unpegged from the ecu in Sept. 1992.

Banking and Finance. The central bank is the Bank of Finland (founded in 1811), owned by the State and under the guarantee and supervision of Parliament. Its *Governor* is Sirkka Hämäläinen. It is the only bank of issue, and the limit of its right to issue notes is fixed equal to the value of its assets of gold and foreign holdings plus 1,500m. marks. Notes in circulation at the end of 1995 amounted to 15,611m. marks.

At the end of 1995 the deposits in banking institutions totalled 306,926m. marks and the loans granted by them 291,292m. marks.

The 3 largest banks are Merita, the state-owned Postipankki and Okobank.

There is a stock exchange in Helsinki.

Weights and Measures. The metric system is in use.

ENERGY AND NATURAL RESOURCES

Electricity. Electricity production was (in 1m. kWh) 62,180 in 1994 (18·8% hydro-electric) and 60,610 in 1995 (21·1%). In 1996 there were 4 nuclear power stations, which contributed 29·9% of production in 1995. Parliament has rejected the construction of a fifth.

Minerals. Notable of the mines are Pyhäsalmi (zinc, copper), Vammala (nickel) and Keminmaa (chromium); the zinc-copper mine at Vihanti closed in 1993. In 1995 (preliminary) the metal content (in tonnes) of the output of copper ore was 9,790, of zinc ore, 16,385; of nickel ore, 3,439; and of chromium, 247,264.

Agriculture. The cultivated area covers only 8% of the land, and of the economically active population 8% were employed in agriculture and forestry in 1995. The arable area was divided in 1995 into 169,707 farms, and the distribution of this area by the size of the farms was: Less than 5 ha cultivated, 54,198 farms; 5–20 ha, 72,695 farms; 20–50 ha, 36,238 farms; 50–100 ha, 5,773 farms; over 100 ha, 803 farms.

The principal crops (area in 1,000 ha, yield in 1,000 tonnes) were in 1996:

Crop	Area	Yield	Crop	Area	Yield
Rye	35·3	86·9	Oats	374·4	1,260·8
Barley	542·5	1,859·1	Potatoes	34·8	765·7
Wheat	112.5	459·3	Hay	243·6	1,047·3

The total area under cultivation in 1996 was 1,946,100 ha, about three-quarters of the entire country. Production of dairy butter in 1995 was 52,223 tonnes, and of cheese, 95,668 tonnes.

Livestock (1995): Horses, 25,700; cattle, 1,148,100; pigs, 1,400,300; poultry, 5,657,400; reindeer, 333,000.

Forestry. The total forest land (1996) amounts to 26·4m. ha. The productive forest land covers 20·1m. ha.

INDUSTRY. Last century Finland embarked on the road to industrialization by harnessing its forest resources. Today, forests are still Finland's most crucial raw material resource, although the metal and engineering industry has long been Finland's leading branch of manufacturing both in terms of value added and as an employer. Today, Finland is a typical advanced industrial economy: two-thirds of its total output is generated in the service sector.

GDP per head US$18,845.

Trade Unions. According to an incomes policy agreement reached by the central labour market organizations in Dec. 1997, which is in force until Jan. 2000, wages and salaries are raised by 1·6% in Jan. 1998 and by 1·6% in Jan. 1999. The Government has undertaken to cut taxes on wages and salaries in 1998 and 1999 in order to support moderate pay developments. Unemployment in 1996 was 16·3%.

FOREIGN ECONOMIC RELATIONS. For many years the Soviet Union was Finland's largest trading partner. Its share declined drastically, however, as that country's economy stagnated. In recent years trade with Russia and other parts of the former Soviet Union, especially Estonia, has resumed growth.

The export pattern has changed dramatically over the last 40 years. In 1960 wood and paper industry dominated exports with their 69% contribution. By 1995, the metal and engineering industry was the largest export sector. But as capital goods for the forest industry form a large proportion of machinery exports, "the forest cluster" can still be considered the dominant exporter.

Region	Exports 1996	Imports 1996
European Union	54%	60%
Other Europe	14%	11%
Developing Countries	13%	7%
EFTA	4%	6%
Other Countries	15%	16%

Industry	Exports 1996
Metal, Engineering, Electronics	50%
Forest Industry	31%
Chemical Industry	10%
Other	9%

Use of Goods	Imports 1996
Raw materials, production necessities	51%
Consumer goods	22%
Investment goods	16%
Fuels	9%
Other	2%

Tourism. In 1995 the total revenue from tourism was 7,536m. marks.

COMMUNICATIONS

Roads. In Jan. 1996 there were 78,403 km of public roads, of which 49,353 km were paved. At the end of 1995 there were 1,900,855 registered cars, 48,556 lorries, 203,476 vans and pick-ups, 8,083 buses and coaches and 20,269 special automobiles.

Railways. On 31 Dec. 1995 the total length of the line operated was 5,859 km (2,054 km electrified), of which all was owned by the State. The gauge is 1,524 mm. In 1995, 44m. passengers and 39·4m. tonnes of freight were carried. The total revenue in 1994 was 3,393m. marks and the total expenditure 3,064m. marks. There is a metro (17 km) and tram/light rail network (75 km) in Helsinki.

Civil Aviation. There is an international airport at Helsinki (Vantaa). The national carrier is Finnair, which in 1996 operated 2 A300s, 4 MD11s, 12 DC-9-51s and 34 other aircraft. Its scheduled traffic covered 70m. km in 1995. The number of passengers was 5·2m. and the number of passenger-km 8,562,000 in 1995; the air transport of freight and mail amounted to 227m. tonne-km. Services are also provided by Aeroflot, Air Botnia, Air France, Austrian Airlines, British Airways, El Al, Estonian Air, KLM, Karair, LOT, Lufthansa, Malév, Northwest Airlines, Sabena, SAS and Swissair.

Shipping. The total registered mercantile marine on 31 Dec. 1995 was 597 vessels of 1,581,360 gross tons. In 1995 the total number of vessels arriving in Finland from abroad was 23,699 and the goods discharged amounted to 37m. tonnes. The goods loaded for export from Finland ports amounted to 34·1m. tonnes.

The lakes, rivers and canals are navigable for about 6,300 km. Timber floating has some importance, and there are about 9,650 km of floatable inland waterways. In 1995 bundle floating was about 1·6m. tonnes.

Telecommunications. In 1995 there were 1,781 post offices. The number of telephone subscriber lines (1995), 2·79m.; 1,039,126 mobile telephones were in use. The net sales of Post Finland in 1994 were 4,874m. marks and of Telecom Finland, 4,927m. marks.

In 1995 the number of television licences was 1,915,000 (colour by PAL). The Finnish Broadcasting Company, YLE, is the biggest national radio and television service provider. YLE operates two television channels with full national coverage. The second biggest television broadcaster, the privately owned Commercial MTV3, has one nationwide channel. A new private TV channel, Ruutunelonen, started in 1997. Television programmes from TV Sweden are transmitted over YLE's channel 4. There are some 30 local TV stations that mainly relay foreign and domestic programmes over cable and radio waves in addition to locally produced material. The only radio broadcaster with full nationwide coverage is YLE. It transmits 3 national channels in Finnish and one in Swedish, as well as various regional channels, including 1 in Sami in Lapland. There are more than 60 private, local radio stations. Two of them, the news and music stations, Nova and Classic, cover almost 60% of the population.

Cinemas. In Dec. 1995 there were 330 cinema halls with a seating capacity of 58,400.

Press. Finland has 56 newspapers that are published 4 to 7 times a week and 172 with 1 to 3 issues per week. The total circulation of all newspapers is 3·6 million. In terms of a total circulation relative to population Finland ranks second in Europe and third in the world, after Norway and Japan. Most newspapers are bought on subscription rather than from newsstands. Only two newspapers depend entirely on newsstand sales. There are 2,585 registered periodicals with a total circulation of approximately 17·4 million. The five best selling newspapers in 1996 were:

Helsingin Sanomat	475,091
Ilta-Sanomat	209,490
Aamulehti	129,658
Turun Sanomat	111,615
Iltalehti	103,896

The best selling newspaper in the Swedish language is *Hufvudstadsbladet*, 59,206.

SOCIAL INSTITUTIONS

Justice. The lowest court of justice is the District Court. In most civil cases a District Court has a quorum with 3 legally-qualified members present. In criminal cases as well as in some cases related to family law the District Court has a quorum with a chair and 3 lay judges present. In the preliminary preparation of a civil case and in a criminal case concerning a minor offence a District Court is composed of the chair only. From the District Court an appeal lies to the courts of appeal in Turku, Vaasa, Kuopio, Helsinki, Kouvola and Rovaniemi. The Supreme Court sits in Helsinki. Appeals from the decisions of administrative authorities are in the final instance decided by the Supreme Administrative Court, also in Helsinki. Judges can be removed only by judicial sentence.

Two functionaries, the Chancellor of Justice, and the Ombudsman or Solicitor General, exercise control over the administration of justice. The former acts also as counsel and public prosecutor for the Government; the latter is appointed by Parliament.

At the end of 1995 the prison population numbered 3,103 men and 145 women; the number of convictions in 1994 was 359,656, of which 298,408 were for minor offences with a maximum penalty of fines and 22,122 with penalty of imprisonment. 9,186 of the prison sentences were unconditional.

Religion. Liberty of conscience is guaranteed to members of all religions. National churches are the Lutheran National Church and the Greek Orthodox Church of Finland. The Lutheran Church is divided into 8 bishoprics (Turku being the archiepiscopal see), 80 provostships and 595 parishes. The Greek Orthodox Church is divided into 3 bishoprics (Kuopio being the archiepiscopal see) and 27 parishes, in addition to which there are a monastery and a convent.

Percentage of the total population at the end of 1995: Lutherans, 85·8; Greek Orthodox, 1·1; others, 1; not members of any religion, 12·1.

Education (1995). *Primary and Secondary Education:*

	Number of institu- tions	Teachers	Students
First-level Education (Lower sections of the comprehensive schools, grades I–VI)			388,342
Second-level Education General education (Upper sections of the comprehensive schools, grades VII–IX, and senior secondary schools)	4,928	· · ·	325,661
Vocational education	458	22,194[1]	122,498

[1] Second and third level at vocational and professional institutions.

Higher Education. Education at the third level (including universities and third level education at vocational and professional institutions) was provided for 213,995 students. Education at universities was provided at 20 institutions with 7,552 teachers and 133,359 students.

University Education. Universities and university-type institutions with the number of teachers and students in 1995:

	Founded	Teachers	Students Total	Women
Universities				
Helsinki	1640	1,732	32,445	19,917
Turku (Swedish)	1919	326	5,340	3,155
Turku (Finnish)	1922	729	12,260	7,622
Jyväskylä	1958	540	9,417	5,946
Oulu	1958	820	11,605	5,711
Tampere	1966	591	12,770	8,149
Joensuu	1969	366	5,788	3,623
Kuopio	1972	318	3,809	2,564
Lapland	1979	121	2,344	1,443
Vaasa	1968	137	3,134	1,730
Universities of Technology				
Helsinki	1849	531	12,402	2,339
Lappeenranta	1969	185	3,479	740
Tampere	1972	296	7,415	1,281
Schools of Economics and Business Administration				
Helsinki (Finnish)	1911	165	3,814	1,756
Helsinki (Swedish)	1927	107	2,078	832
Turku (Finnish)	1950	89	1,911	955
Universities of Art				
Academy of Fine Arts	1848	142	1,407	854
Sibelius Academy	1939	270	1,445	794
University of Industrial Arts	1949	20	186	125
Theatre Academy	1979	67	310	163

General adult education (at folk high schools, adult education centres, music schools and colleges, sports institutes and study centres) had 607,000 students in 1995.

Health. In 1995 there were 13,771 physicians, 4,696 dentists and 50,850 hospital beds.

Welfare. The Social Insurance Institution administers general systems of old age pensions (to all persons over 65 years of age and disabled younger persons) and of health insurance. An additional system of compulsory old age pensions paid for by the employers is in force and works through the Central Pension Security Institute. Systems for other public aid are administered by the communes and supervised by the National Social Board and the Ministry of Social Affairs and Health.

The total cost of social security amounted to 189,601m. marks in 1994. Out of this 42,378m. (22·4%) was spent for health, 28,126m. (14·8%) for unemployment, 83,227m. (43·9%) for old age and disability, 27,259m. (14·4%) for family allowances and child welfare, 8,610m. (4·5%) for general welfare purposes and administration. Out of the total expenditure, 32% was financed by the State, 16% by local authorities, 34% by employers, 14% by the beneficiaries and 4% by users.

DIPLOMATIC REPRESENTATIVES

Of Finland in Great Britain (38 Chesham Pl., London, SW1X 8HW)
Ambassador: Pertti Salolainen.

Of Great Britain in Finland (Itäinen Puistotie, 17, Helsinki 00140)
Ambassador: G. W. Wallace, CMG.

Of Finland in the USA (3301 Massachusetts Ave., NW, Washington, D.C., 20008)
Ambassador: Jaakko Laajava.

Of the USA in Finland (Itäinen Puistotie 14A, Helsinki 00140)
Ambassador: Derek N. Shearer.

Of Finland to the United Nations
Ambassador: Wilhelm Breitenstein.

Further Reading

Statistics Finland. *Statistical Yearbook of Finland* (from 1879).—*Bulletin of Statistics* (monthly, from 1924).
Constitution Act and Parliament Act of Finland. Helsinki, 1984
Suomen valtiokalenteri—Finlands statskalender (State Calendar of Finland). Helsinki. Annual
Facts About Finland. Helsinki. Annual (Union Bank of Finland)
Finland in Figures. Helsinki, Annual
Arter, D., *Politics and Poltcy-Making in Finland.* Brighton, 1987
Jakobson, M. *Myth and Reality.* Helsinki, 1987
Jutikkala, E. and Pirinen, K., *A History of Finland.* 3rd ed. New York, 1979
Kekkonen, U., *President's View.* London, 1982
Kirby, D. G., *Finland in the Twentieth Century.* 2nd ed. London, 1984
Klinge, M., *A Brief History of Finland.* Helsinki, 1987
Mead, W. R., *Experience of Finland.* Farnborough, 1993
Petersson, O., *The Government and Politics of the Nordic Countries.* Stockholm, 1994
Screen, J. E. O., *Finland.* [Bibliography] Oxford and Santa Barbara (CA), 1981
Singleton, F., *The Economy of Finland in the Twentieth Century.* Univ. of Bradford Press, 1987
Tillotson, H. M., *Finland at Peace and War, 1918–1993.* London, 1993

National statistical office: Statistics Finland, Tilastokeskus, FIN-00022.
Website: http://www.stat.fi/

FRANCE
République Française

Capital: Paris
Population: 58·2m.
GDP per head: (PPP$) 20,510
HDI/world rank: 0·946/2

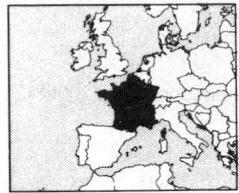

KEY HISTORICAL EVENTS. Gaul, the area that is now France, was conquered by Julius Caesar in the 1st century BC and became a part of the Roman Empire. In the 3rd and 4th centuries it was overrun by Germanic tribes, and in the 10th century Norsemen invaded. There was a long period of conflict with England, typified by the Hundred Years' War (1337-1453); and this was followed by rivalry with Spain in the latter part of the 15th and in the 16th century. The Reformation caused a long religious civil war between 1562 and 1598, at the end of which the Huguenot leader, Henry of Navarre, was converted to Catholicism and reigned as the first Bourbon king, Henry IV. The two powerful ministers of the 17th century, Cardinal Richelieu and Mazarin, successively ensured that France, and not Spain, established itself as the dominant country in Europe. Militarily, this was achieved by the treaties of Westphalia (which ended the Thirty Years' War in 1648) and of the Pyrenees (1659). There followed the brilliant reign of Louis XIV, the 'Sun King' (1643-1715).

The second half of the 18th century saw France defeated by England in the Seven Years' War (1756-63). The French Revolution began in 1789 when the 'Third Estate' assumed power as a National Assembly and overthrew the government. Riots and the storming of the Bastille were followed by the proclamation of a republic (1792) and the execution of the king, Louis XVI (1793). A Reign of Terror followed during which thousands were guillotined. After these excesses the Directory ruled from 1795 until 1799 when it was overthrown by Napoleon Bonaparte who became First Consul and then Emperor (1804) of the first French Empire. Napoleon went on to gain control of most of Europe until he was finally defeated at the Battle of Waterloo in 1815. The monarchy was restored, with the Bourbon family reigning (officially from 1814). A revolution in 1830 brought Louis Philippe, son of the Duke of Orleans, to the throne as a constitutional monarch. This 'July Monarchy' was overthrown in 1848 and superseded by the Second Republic, with Louis Napoleon (nephew of Napoleon I) elected president. In 1852 he took the title of Emperor Napoleon III, and hence began the Second Empire. However, the early military failures of France in the Franco-Prussian War (1870-71) led to Napoleon being deposed and the proclamation of the Third Republic in 1870. This survived both the First World War, which was fought chiefly on French soil, and also 44 successive governments from the end of the war in 1918 until 1940. In 1940 German troops invaded France, the French government capitulated, and a pro-German government was established at Vichy. Gen. Charles de Gaulle headed a Free French government in London, while in France the Resistance continued to harass the Germany Army of Occupation and give secret aid to the Allies.

When France was liberated in 1944 a provisional government under de Gaulle ruled the country until the Fourth Republic was established in 1946, and de Gaulle retired. The country now faced problems in Algeria and in Indo-China. There were changes of government up to 1958. In that year de Gaulle was recalled to be prime minister and then president as the Fifth Republic began in 1958. He granted independence to Algeria (1962) and was successful in establishing a firm and stable government until rioting and strikes by students and workers led to his resignation in 1969. He was succeeded by Georges Pompidou, who died in 1974 and was in turn succeeded by Giscard d'Estaing. Both presidents tended to continue Gaullist policies, but in 1981 François Mitterrand, a socialist candidate, was elected to the presidency but for a time had to govern in an uneasy relationship with a right-wing premier. Jacques Chirac. Mitterrand's period of office was clouded by charges of corruption. In 1995 Chirac was elected President in succession to the ailing Mitterrand.

TERRITORY AND POPULATION. France is bounded in the north by the English Channel *(La Manche)*, north-east by Belgium and Luxembourg, east by Germany, Switzerland and Italy, south by the Mediterranean (with Monaco as a coastal enclave), south-west by Spain and Andorra, and west by the Atlantic Ocean. The total area is 549,090 sq. km.

Population (1990 census), 56·6m. Growth rate (1994 estimate), 3·2 per 1,000; average density (1990), 104 persons per sq. km. Estimate (1996), 58·2m.; projection (2025), 61·2m.

The growth of the population has been as follows:

Census	Population	Census	Population	Census	Population
1801	27,349,003	1931	41,834,923	1968	49,778,540
1861	37,386,313	1946	40,506,639	1975	52,655,802
1901	38,961,945	1954	42,777,174	1982	54,334,871
1921	39,209,518	1962	46,519,997	1990	56,615,100

According to the 1990 census, there were 3·5m. people of foreign extraction in France (7·4% of the population). The largest groups of foreign residents (1992) were: Portuguese (649,714), Algerians (614,207) and Moroccans (572,652). 92,410 persons were naturalized in 1995 (126,337 in 1994).

Controls on illegal immigration were tightened in July 1991. Automatic right to citizenship for those born on French soil was restored in 1997 by the new left-wing coalition government. New immigration legislation, due to come into force early in 1998, will bring in harsher penalties for organized traffic in illegal immigrants and extend asylum laws to include people whose lives are at risk from non state as well as state groups. It will also extend nationality at the age of 18 to those born in France of non-French parents, provided they have lived a minimum of 5 years in France since the age of 11.

Vital statistics for calendar years:

	Marriages	Births	Deaths
1995	254,000	727,800	532,000
1996	279,000	734,000	536,000

Live birth rate (1994 estimate) was 12·2 per 1,000 inhabitants; death rate, 9·0; infant mortality, 6·1 per 1,000 live births. Marriage rate, 4·4; divorce rate, 1·9. Abortions were legalized in 1975; there were 162,620 in 1990. Expectation of life (1994): men, 73·1 years; women, 81·2. From 1990–95 the suicide rate per 100,000 population was 20·1 (men, 29·6; women, 11·1).

The areas, populations and chief towns of the 22 metropolitan regions at the 1990 census were as follows:

Regions	Area (sq. km)	Population	Chief town
Alsace	8,280	1,624,400	Strasbourg
Aquitaine	41,308	2,795,800	Bordeaux
Auvergne	26,013	1,321,200	Clermont-Ferrand
Basse-Normandie	17,589	1,391,300	Caen
Bourgogne (Burgundy)	31,582	1,609,700	Dijon
Bretagne (Brittany)	27,208	2,795,600	Rennes
Centre	39,151	2,371,000	Orléans
Champagne-Ardenne	25,606	1,347,900	Reims
Corse (Corsica)	8,680	250,400	Ajaccio
Franche-Comté	16,202	1,097,400	Besançon
Haute-Normandie	12,317	1,737,200	Rouen
Île-de-France	12,012	10,660,600	Paris
Languedoc-Roussillon	27,376	2,114,900	Montpellier
Limousin	16,942	722,800	Limoges
Lorraine	23,547	2,305,700	Nancy
Midi-Pyrénées	41,348	2,430,700	Toulouse
Nord-Pas-de-Calais	12,414	3,965,100	Lille
Pays de la Loire	32,082	3,059,200	Nantes
Picardie	19,399	1,810,700	Amiens
Poitou-Charentes	25,810	1,595,100	Poitiers
Provence-Alpes-Côte d'Azur	31,400	4,257,900	Marseille
Rhône-Alpes	43,698	5,350,800	Lyon

Populations of the principal conurbations (in descending order of size) and towns at the 1990 census:

	Conurbation	Town		Conurbation	Town
Paris	9,318,821[1]	2,152,423	Bayonne	164,378	41,846
Lyon	1,262,223[2]	415,487	Perpignan	157,873	105,983
Marseille-Aix-			Amiens	156,120	131,872
en-Provence	1,230,936[3]	800,550	Pau	144,674	82,157
Lille	959,234[4]	172,142	Nîmes	138,527	128,471
Bordeaux	696,364	210,336	Thionville	132,413	40,835
Toulouse	650,336	358,688	Saint-Nazaire	131,511	64,812
Nice	516,740	342,439	Annecy	126,729	51,143
Nantes	496,078	244,995	Troyes	122,763	59,271
Toulon	437,553	167,619	Besançon	122,623	113,828
Grenoble	404,733	150,758	Montbéliard	117,510	30,639
Strasbourg	388,483	252,338	Lorient	115,488	59,437
Rouen	380,161	102,723	Hagondange-Briey	112,061	9,091[5]
Valenciennes	338,392	39,276	Valence	107,965	63,437
Cannes	335,647	68,676	Melun	107,705	36,489
Nancy	329,447	99,351	Poitiers	107,625	78,894
Lens	323,174	35,278	Chambéry	103,283	54,120
Saint-Étienne	313,338	197,536	Angoulême	102,908	46,194
Tours	282,152	129,509	Maubeuge	102,772	35,225
Béthune	261,535	25,261	Calais	101,768	75,309
Clermont-Ferrand	254,416	136,181	La Rochelle	100,264	71,094
Le Havre	253,627	195,854	Forbach	98,758	27,357
Montpellier	248,303	207,996	Creil	97,119	32,501
Rennes	245,065	199,396	Bourges	94,731	75,609
Orléans	243,153	105,111	Cherbourg	92,045	28,773
Dijon	230,451	146,703	Boulogne-sur-Mer	91,249	44,244
Mulhouse	223,856	108,357	Chartres	85,933	41,850
Angers	208,282	141,404	Saint-Brieuc	83,861	47,370
Reims	206,437	180,620	Colmar	83,816	63,498
Brest	201,480	147,956	Saint-Chamond	81,795	39,262
Douai	199,562	44,195	Tarbes	80,680	50,228
Metz	193,117	119,594	Arras	79,607	42,715
Caen	191,490	112,846	Belfort	78,215	50,125
Dunkerque	190,879	70,331	Chalon-sur-Saône	77,764	54,575
Le Mans	189,107	145,502	Roanne	77,160	42,848
Mantes-la-Jolie	189,103	45,254	Alès	76,856	—
Avignon	181,136	86,939	Béziers	76,304	70,996
Limoges	170,065	133,464			

[1] Including Boulogne-Billancourt (101,743), Montreuil (94,754), Argenteuil (93,096), Versailles (87,789), Saint-Denis (89,988), Nanterre (84,565), Vitry-sur-Seine (82,400), Aulnay-sous-Bois (82,314), Créteil (82,088).
[2] Including Villeurbanne (116,872), Vénissieux (60,644).
[3] Including Aix-en-Provence (123,842).
[4] Including Roubaix (97,746), Tourcoing (93,765).   [5] 1982 census.

Languages. The official language is French. Breton and Basque are spoken in their regions. The *Toubon* legislation of 1994 seeks to restrict the use of foreign words in official communications, broadcasting and advertisements (a previous such decree dated from 1975). The Constitutional Court has since ruled that imposing such restrictions on private citizens would infringe their freedom of expression.

Monnier, A., *La Population de la France.* Paris, 1990

CLIMATE. The north-west has a moderate maritime climate, with small temperature range and abundant rainfall; inland, rainfall becomes more seasonal, with a summer maximum, and the annual range of temperature increases. Southern France has a Mediterranean climate, with mild moist winters and hot dry summers. Eastern France has a continental climate and a rainfall maximum in summer, with thunderstorms prevalent.

Paris. Jan. 37°F (3°C), July 64°F (18°C). Annual rainfall 22·9" (573 mm). *Bordeaux.* Jan. 41°F (5°C), July 68°F (20°C). Annual rainfall 31·4" (786 mm). *Lyon.* Jan. 37°F (3°C), July 68°F (20°C). Annual rainfall 31·8" (794 mm).

CONSTITUTION AND GOVERNMENT. The Constitution of the Fifth Republic, superseding that of 1946, came into force on 4 Oct. 1958. It consists of a preamble, dealing with the Rights of Man, and 92 articles.

France is a republic, indivisible, secular, democratic and social; all citizens are equal before the law (Art. 1). National sovereignty resides with the people, who exercise it through their representatives and by referendums (Art. 3). Constitutional reforms of July 1995 widened the range of issues on which referendums may be called. Political parties carry out their activities freely, but must respect the principles of national sovereignty and democracy (Art. 4).

A constitutional amendment of 4 Aug. 1995 deleted all references to the 'community' (*communauté*) between France and her overseas possessions, representing an important step towards the constitutional dismantling of the former French colonial empire.

The head of state is the President, who sees that the Constitution is respected; ensures the regular functioning of the public authorities, as well as the continuity of the state; is the protector of national independence and territorial integrity (Art. 5). The President is elected for 7 years by direct universal suffrage (Art. 6). The President appoints (and dismisses) a Prime Minister and, on the latter's advice, appoints and dismisses the other members of the Government (*Council of Ministers*) (Art. 8); presides over the Council of Ministers (Art. 9); may dissolve the National Assembly, after consultation with the Prime Minister and the Presidents of the two Houses (Art. 12); appoints to the civil and military offices of the state (Art. 13). In times of crisis, the President may take such emergency powers as the circumstances demand; the National Assembly cannot be dissolved during such a period (Art. 16). At the first round of presidential elections on 23 April 1995, Lionel Jospin gained the largest number of votes (23·31% of those cast) against 8 opponents. At the second round on 7 May 1995, the electorate was 39,976,944; turn-out was 79·77%. Jacques Chirac was elected President against Jospin by 52·64% of votes cast.

President: Jacques Chirac (RPR; sworn in 17 May 1995).

Parliament consists of the National Assembly and the Senate. The *National Assembly* is elected by direct suffrage by the second ballot system (by which candidates winning 50% or more of the vote in their constituencies are elected, candidates winning less than 12·5% are eliminated and other candidates go on to a second round of voting); the Senate is elected by indirect suffrage (Art. 24). Since 1996 the National Assembly has convened for an annual 9-month session. It comprises 577 deputies, elected by a two-ballot system for a 5-year term from single-member constituencies (555 in Metropolitan France, 22 in the overseas departments and dependencies); and may be dissolved by the President.

The *Senate* comprises 319 senators elected for 9-year terms (one-third every 3 years) by an electoral college in each Department or overseas dependency, made up of all members of the Departmental Council or its equivalent in overseas dependencies, together with all members of Municipal Councils within that area. Following the election held on 24 Sept. 1995, the Senate was composed of (by group, including affiliates): UDF, 129; RPR, 94; Socialist group, 75; Communist group, 15; ind, 8. The *Speaker* of the Senate deputizes for the President of the Republic in the event of the latter's incapacity. In Oct. 1995 René Monory was elected Speaker for a second 3-year term.

The *Constitutional Council* is composed of 9 members whose term of office is 9 years (non-renewable), one-third every 3 years; 3 are appointed by the President of the Republic, 3 by the President of the National Assembly, 3 by the President of the Senate; in addition, former Presidents of the Republic are, by right, life members of the Constitutional Council (Art. 56). It oversees the fairness of the elections of the President (Art. 58) and Parliament (Art. 59), and of referendums (Art. 60), and acts as a guardian of the Constitution (Art. 61). Its President is Roland Dumas (app. 1995).

The *Economic and Social Council* advises on Government and Private Members' Bills (Art. 69). It comprises representatives of employers', workers' and farmers' organizations in each Department and Overseas Territory.

At the elections of 25 May and 1 June 1997 to the National Assembly, there were 6,361 candidates; the electorate was 38,968,660. In the first round, turn-out was 68·93%. The Socialist Party (PS) and allies won 253 seats; the Rassemblement pour le République (RPR; Gaullists), 134; the Union for French Democracy (UDF), 108; the Communist Party (PCF), 38; Greens, 7; other left parties, 21; other right parties, 15; National Front, 1.

A new left-wing coalition government (including the anti-Euro Communist group) was formed on 4 June 1997, consisting in March 1998 of:

Prime Minister: Lionel Jospin (PS); *Minister of Justice and Keeper of the Seals:* Elisabeth Guigou (PS). *Foreign Affairs:* Hubert Védrine (PS). *Interior:* Jean-Pierre Chevènement (MDC). *Economy, Finance and Industry:* Dominique Strauss-Kahn (PS). *Defence:* Alain Richard (PS). *Labour and Social Affairs:* Martine Aubry (PS). *Education, Research and Technology:* Claude Allègre (PS). *Public Works, Transport and Housing:* Jean-Claude Gayssot (PC). *Relations with the Parliament:* Daniel Vaillant (PS). *Environment:* Dominique Voynet (Green). *Culture and Communication, and Government Spokeswoman:* Catherine Trautmann (PS). *Agriculture, Fisheries and Food:* Louis Le Pensec. *Civil Service, State Reform and Decentralization:* Emile Zuccarelli (PRS). *Youth and Sport*: Marie-Georges Buffet (PC).

Ministers-Delegate include*: European Affairs:* Pierre Moscovici (PS). *Foreign Trade:* Jacques Dondoux (PRS). *Overseas Territories*: Jean-Jack Queyranne (PS). *Industry:* Christian Pierret (PS). *Tourism:* Michelle Demessine (PC). *Housing:* Louis Besson (PS). *Education*: Ségolène Royal (PS). *Health:* Bernard Kouchner (PRS). *Budget:* Christian Sautter. *Veterans and War Victims:* Jean-Pierre Masseret (PS).

National anthem: La Marseillaise; words and tune by C. Rouget de Lisle.

European Parliament. France has 87 representatives. At the June 1994 elections turn-out was 53·5%. The RPR-UDF won 29 seats with 25·5% of votes cast (political affiliation in European Parliament: European Liberal, Democratic and Reformist Group; European People's Party); the PS, 16 with 14·5% (European Socialist Party); the Other Europe group, 13 with 12·3%; the Radical Energy group, 13 with 12%; the National Front, 10 with 10·5% (European Group of Nations); the Communist Party, 6 with 6·9%.

Regional Government. France is divided into 22 regions for national development, planning and budgetary policy. Many of these regions are broadly comparable with the provinces of pre-revolutionary France, and give a measure of recognition to the distinctive personalities of peripheral areas such as Alsace and Brittany.

By a law of 13 May 1991 Corsica became a territorial collectivity. After the regional elections of March 1992 it had an assembly which elects an executive council. Since Feb. 1995 the Pays Basque, which formed part of the department Pyrénées-Atlantique, has had an elected 65-member council bringing together parliamentary deputies, regional and general councillors and representatives of mayors.

Local Government. There are 96 departments within the 22 regions each governed by a directly elected *General Council.* In March 1982 state-appointed Regional Prefects were abolished and their executive powers transferred from the state to the presidents of the regional councils. Legislation of 1993 provides for the election every 3 years of half the members of the councils. Councillors elected in 1992 serve for 6 years. Those elected in March 1994 will serve for 7 years. Elections for 2,009 seats in the General Councils were held in 2 rounds on 20 and 27 March 1994. The electorate was 18,563,056; turn-out was 60·39% at the first round and 58·78% at the second. The PS gained 532 seats, the UDF 446, the RPR 382, various right-wing groups 309, various left-wing groups 171, the Communist Party 145, Greens 7, the National Front 3, others 12.

The unit of local government is the *commune,* the size and population of which vary much. There were, in 1995, in the 96 metropolitan departments, 36,763 communes (30,919 with fewer than 1,500 inhabitants). The local affairs of the commune are under a Municipal Council, composed of between 9 and 36 members elected by universal suffrage for 6 years. At the last municipal elections in 1995, there were

512,850 municipal councillors. Each municipal council elects a mayor who is both the representative of the commune and agent of the central government. Communes are associated in the *Assemblée des Districts et des Communautés de France*, and also co-operate in inter-commune public enterprise projects, of which there were some 1,200 in 1995.

In Paris the local council *(Conseil de Paris)* is composed of 109 members elected from the 20 *arrondissements*. It combines the functions of departmental General and Municipal Council.

In 1995 the *Pasqua* Law on Guidance for Territorial Management created a new territorial entity, the *pays*. These do not replace administrative divisions, but group regions, departments or communes according to historical, geographical or employment area criteria, with a view to their economic development. Some 200 *pays* had been formed by 1996.

Local revenue is raised from residence, business and property taxes, and amounted to 262,700m. francs in 1995 (250,000m. in 1994).

Ameller, M., *L'Assemblée Nationale.* Paris, 1994
Duhamel, O. and Mény, Y., *Dictionnaire Constitutionnel.* Paris, 1992
Elgie, R. (ed.) *Electing the French President: the 1995 Presidential Election.* London, 1996

DEFENCE. The President of the Republic is the supreme head of defence policy and exercises command over the Armed Forces. He is the only person empowered to give the order to use nuclear weapons. He is assisted by the Council of Ministers, which studies defence problems, and by the Defence Council and the Restricted Defence Committee, which formulate directives. The Prime Minister is responsible for national defence, exercising his military responsibilities and co-ordinating interministry defence activities through the General Secretariat of National Defence (SGDN). Under the Prime Minister's authority, the Minister of Defence is responsible for the execution of military policy, in particular the organization and administration of the Armed Forces.

The Ministry of Defence has overall responsibility for defence. The preparation and control of the Armed Forces is exercised by the Chief of Staff of the Armed Forces, the Chiefs of Staff of the 3 services—Army, Navy and Air—and the head of the *Gendarmerie.*

Legislation of 1996 inaugurated a wide-ranging reform of the defence system over 1997–2002, with regard to the professionalization of the armed forces (brought about by the ending of military conscription and consequent switch to an all-volunteer defence force), the modification and modernization of equipment and the restructuring of the defence industry. Defence was reported to be the main casualty of the Jospin administration's first budget. 1998 spending was due to fall by 4·5% in real terms from the 1997 level, with spending on equipment particularly affected. It is estimated under current plans that by 2002 the Army will have been reduced by more than 30%, the Navy by about 16%, the Air Force by almost 20%. Defence spending as a proportion of GDP has fallen from below 4% in 1988 to 3% in 1997 (compared with more than 4% of GDP in 1988 to 2·8% in 1997 in the UK).

French forces are not formally under the NATO command structure, although France signed the NATO strategic document on Eastern Europe in Nov. 1991. The Minister of Defence attends informal NATO meetings which have an agenda of French interest, but not the formal twice-yearly meetings. Since Dec. 1995 France has taken a seat on the NATO Military Committee. In 1996, 16,143 service personnel were stationed in Germany, 24,395 in the overseas departments and territories, 7,708 on UN peacekeeping missions and 1,336 constituted the 'French Maritime Presence' abroad.

The General Directorate for Armament (DGA) is responsible for all aspects of the procurement of defence equipment. It employs 48,800 personnel, and co-ordinates another 200,000 others employed in the defence industry. A reform programme for the GDA designed to modernize equipment and reduce costs was initiated in 1996.

Conscription is for 10 months. It is scheduled for abolition in 2000. Conscripts may not be compelled to serve abroad unless war is declared.

Army. The Army comprises 1 corps with 3 armoured and 1 infantry divisions,

1 armoured division in Eurocorps, 1 Franco-German brigade, 7 armoured, 6 mechanized infantry, 8 artillery, 3 mountain infantry and 4 motorized infantry regiments and 3 anti-tank and 3 reconnaissance squadrons, and corps units including 1 armoured reconnaissance, 1 parachute special forces, 1 motorized infantry, 1 missile-launching, 5 surface-to-air missile, 2 combat helicopter and 4 engineer regiments.

The *Rapid Action Force* (FAR) comprises 41,516 personnel organized, equipped and trained for rapid engagement either in Europe or over large distances elsewhere; it includes 1 parachute division, 1 air-portable marine division, a light armoured division, 1 mountain division and 1 air-mobile division, together with various specialized units.

Equipment includes 766 AMX-30/30B2 and 51 Leclerc main battle tanks, 337 AMX-10RC armoured vehicles, 1,364 other armoured vehicles, 1,435 pieces of artillery, 181 Roland surface-to-air missile systems and 1,440 Milan anti-tank weapons.

The *Aviation Légère de l'Armée de Terre* (ALAT) with about 7,000 personnel is an integral part of the Army, equipped with over 600 helicopters of various types for observation, reconnaissance, combat area transport, liaison and supply duties.

The *Foreign Legion* was formed in 1831 for duty in North Africa. It is officered by French nationals and based at Aubagne, near Marseilles. About half the other ranks are French. It numbered 8,500 in 1997.

The Army consisted in 1997 of 219,900 personnel, of whom 9,000 were women and 111,00 were conscripts.

Gendarmerie. The paramilitary police force exists to ensure public security and maintain law and order, as well as participate in the operational defence of French territory as part of the armed forces. It consisted in 1997 of 93,000 personnel including 12,000 conscripts, 2,600 women and 1,000 civilians. It comprises a territorial force of 57,000 personnel in 3,640 brigades throughout the country, a mobile force of 17,000 personnel in 128 squadrons and specialized formations including the Republican Guard, the Air Force and Naval Gendarmeries, and an anti-terrorist unit. It is equipped with 28 VBC-90 armoured gun-carriers, 121 light armoured cars, 155 armoured vehicles and 33 troop transport vehicles, as well as 40 helicopters.

Navy. The missions of the Navy are to provide the prime element of the French independent nuclear deterrent through its force of strategic submarines, to assure the security of the French offshore zones, to contribute to NATO's missions and to provide on-station and deployment forces overseas in support of French territorial interests and UN commitments.

French territorial seas and economic zones are organized into 3 maritime regions, each under the authority of a Maritime Prefect (with headquarters in Cherbourg, Brest and Toulon). Offshore, the seas and oceans are divided into 5 zones: Atlantic, Mediterranean, Indian Ocean, Pacific and Antilles-Guiana. Home-based forces are commanded by Commanders-in-Chief based in Brest and Toulon, those in the Indian Ocean and Pacific by Flag Officers based afloat in the Indian Ocean, and at Nouméa (in New Caledonia). Naval forces in the Caribbean come under a joint force commander based at Cayenne.

Pressures on public expenditure have dictated a phased reduction in fleet strength over 1997–2000, but following is a summary of the strength of the fleet at the end of the years shown:

	1991	1992	1993	1994	1995	1996
Aircraft carriers	2	1	1	1	1	2
Strategic-missile submarines	5	4	5	5	5	5
Other submarines	13	14	14	13	13	12
Cruisers	1	1	1	1	1	1
Destroyers	4	4	4	4	4	4
Frigates	34	34	35	36	35	35

The strategic deterrent force comprises 5 nuclear-powered strategic-missile submarines, including the first of 4 new-generation ships of a new, much larger, class of ships, *Le Triomphant*, which entered service in 1996, displaces 14,200 tonnes and deploys 16 M-45 missiles. The others comprise *L'Inflexible*, 9,100 tonnes, completed in 1985, together with 2 older vessels, *Le Foudroyant* and *L'Indomptable*, completed in 1974 and 1976, now converted to the same standard, and deploying 16 M-4 missiles. There are also six 2,700 tonne nuclear-powered submarines and 6 operational diesel submarines.

The principal surface ships are the aircraft carriers *Clemenceau* and *Foch* of 33,300 tonnes each, completed in 1961 and 1963, one of which is kept operational. The operational carrier embarks an air group typically comprising 16 Super-Etendard strike aircraft, 4 Etendard reconnaissance, 8 F-8P Crusader fighters, 6 Alize anti-submarine and warning and a flight of 4 utility helicopters. *Clemenceau* was to be withdrawn from service in 1997, *Foch* in 1999, when the nuclear-powered replacement, *Charles de Gaulle*, which was launched at Brest in 1994, is expected to commission. There is 1 cruiser, the helicopter cruiser *Jeanne d'Arc*, of 12,600 tonnes completed in 1963 and used in peacetime as a training vessel. She could perform amphibious or anti-submarine tasks in war. In these roles she could accommodate up to 8 Lynx helicopters, and 700 personnel. Her armament comprises 6 Exocet and 4 100 mm guns.

Other surface combatants include 4 guided-missile destroyers and 35 frigates of which 17 carry helicopters. A modern mine countermeasure force consists of 9 tripartite coastal minehunters and 5 others, and 4 diver support vessels. The amphibious force includes 4 dock landing ships, 5 medium landing ships, and some 30 craft. Patrol forces include 20 coastal and 2 inshore patrol vessels. The Navy deploys a substantial support force which includes 5 large and 1 small tankers, 15 other maintenance and logistic ships, 5 weapon system trials ships and 6 survey and research ships. There are several hundred minor auxiliaries.

All warships, and a proportion of naval weapons, are produced by the government armaments service, of which the naval element, *Direction des Constructions Navales* (DCN), operates the shipbuilding yards as well as dockyards. Building takes place at Cherbourg, Brest and Lorient.

The naval air arm, *Aéronautique Navale*, numbers some 7,500 personnel. Operational aircraft include 50 Super-Etendard nuclear-capable strike aircraft, 8 Etendard reconnaissance aircraft, 15 US-built Crusader F-8P all-weather fighters, 20 Alize turboprop anti-submarine aircraft, 8 Atlantic, 20 Atlantique and 5 Gardian maritime reconnaissance aircraft. The Crusaders' life has been extended to keep a carrier squadron operational until 1999, when the maritime Rafale combat aircraft will enter service on board the *Charles de Gaulle*. Rotary wing strength includes 16 commando Super Frelon, and 35 anti-submarine and search-and-rescue Lynx helicopters. Numerous training, utility and transport aircraft bring the total strength to about 300 comprising 200 fixed-wing aircraft and 100 helicopters. A small Marine force of 3,500 *Fusiliers Marins* provides 4 assault groups, an attack swimmer section as well as numerous naval base protection units.

Personnel in 1997 numbered 63,300, including 17,250 conscripts and 2,500 women.

Air Force. Created in 1934, the Air Force was reorganized in June 1994. France is divided into 3 air regions corresponding to the 3 military defence regions and 2 air defence zones. There are 2 operational commands (Strategic Air Forces Command—CFAS; Air Defence and Air Operations Command—CDAOA) and 5 organizational commands (Combat Air Force Command—CFAC; Projection Air Force Command—CFAP; Air Observation System, Information and Communication Command—CASSIC; Training Command—CEAA; Air Base Protection Infantry Command—CFCA). The CFAS is responsible for nuclear weapons; all other combat aircraft are operated by the CFAC under the authority of the CDAOA.

The Conventional Forces in Europe (CFE) agreement imposes a ceiling of 450 combat aircraft. Equipment summary (main types only) Combat: 125 Mirage 2000 B/C, 60 Mirage 2000 N, 30 Mirage 2000 D, 16 Mirage IV P, 30 Mirage F1 B/C, 40 Mirage F1 CT, 40 Mirage F1 CR, 80 Jaguar A/E. Airborne Early Warning: 4 E3F Awacs. Transport: 12 Hercules C 130, 4 DC8, 2 Airbus A 310, 60 C160 Transall, 20 Nord 262. Training: 105 Alphajet. Helicopters: 17 Alouette, 39 Fennec, 27 Puma, 4 Super Puma.

The organization and equipment of the Commands (bases in parentheses) is as follows:

Strategic Air Forces Command (CFAS): Strategic reconnaissance squadron 1/91 (Mont de Marsan) with 5 Mirages IV P. Fighter squadrons 1/4 and 2/4 with 40 Mirage 2000 N (Luxeuil), fighter squadrons 3/4 with 15 Mirage 2000 N (Istres). Flight refuelling squadron 93 with 11 C 135FR and 2 KC-135R (Istres). 59 Airborne strategic communication squadron (Evreux): 4 C 160 Transall Astarte V/UHF airborne relay posts (flown and maintained by COTAM). Tactical training centre: 3 Falcon 20, 6 Jaguar E (Luxeuil).

Combat Air Forces Command (CFAC): (Nancy): 3 squadrons with 45 Mirage 2000D. (Saint Dizier): 3 squadrons with 12 Jaguar A/E and 12 Jaguar E (two-seater). Fighter squadron (Toul) with 20 Jaguar A/E and 3 Jaguar E. (Colmar): 2 squadrons with 40 Mirage F1 CT. Recce squadrons 1/33, 2/33 with 40 Mirage F1 CR and 1 training squadron with 20 Mirage F1 B/C. (Dijon): 1 squadron with 10 Mirage F1C (Djibouti). 3 squadrons with 45 Mirage 2000 B/C. (Orange): 2 squadrons with 30 Mirage 2000 B/C. (Cambrai): 2 squadrons with 30 Mirage 2000 C and B. 54 electronic warfare squadrons. (Metz): 2 Transall Gabriel for SIGINT operations (flown and maintained by COTAM).

Projection Air Forces Command (CFAP): 3/60 Transport squadron (Creil): 4 DC8, 2 A 310. (Orléans): transport squadrons 1/61 and 3/61 with 29 C 160F Transall and 2/61 with 9 C130H-30 and 3 C 130H. Transport squadron 1/64: 10 C160 NG and Transport squadron 2/64: 11 C160 NG (Evreux). Transport squadron 1/65 (Villacoublay): 5 N 262, 8 Mystere 20, 4 TBM 700, 2 Falcon 900, 4 Falcon 50, 3 Twin Otters. 1/62 Transport squadron (Creil): 6 CASA 235, 3 Fennec, 3 Twin Otters. 56 special transport squadron (GAM 56) (Evreux): 3 C160, 3 Cougar. CIET 340 (Toulouse): 8 C160, 4 N 262. CIEH 341 (Toulouse): 6 Alouette II, 2 Alouette III, 9 Fennec, 4 Puma. ETE 41 (Metz): 2 N 262, 1 MS 760 Paris and 2 TBM 700. ETE 43 (Bordeaux): 3N 262, 2TBM 700. ETE 44 (Aix): 4 N 262 and 1 TBM 700. EH 1/67 (Cazaux): 5 Fennec, 4 Puma. EH 2/67 (Metz): 3 Alouette III, 5 Fennec. EH 3/67 (Villacoublay): 3 Alouette III, 3 Super Puma, 6 Ecureuil, 3 Fennec. EH 4/67 (Apt): 2 Fennec, 2 Puma. EH 5/67 (Aix): 5 Fennec, 4 Puma and 1 Super Puma. EH 6/67 (Solenzara): 2 Puma. Overseas transport squadron (ETOM 50) (Saint Denis la Réunion): 2 C 160, 2 Fennec. ETOM 52 (Nouméa): 2 C 160, 2 Fennec, 6 Puma. ETOM 55 (Dakar): 1 C 160, 1 Alouette III. ETOM 58 (Martinique): 2 C 160, 1 Alouette III, 2 Puma. ETOM 82 (Papeete): 2 CN 235, 3 Super Puma. ETOM 88 (Djibouti): 3 Alouette III, 1 C 160.

Air Observation System, Information and Communication Command (CASSIC): 36 AEW squadron (Avord: 2 flights with 4 E3F Awacs).

Air Training Command (CEAA): 1 ETO and 2 ETO 36 Alphajet (Cazaux). GE 312: Training group (Salon de Provence): 2 Paris MS 760, 30 Fouga, 12 Tucano. GE 314 (Tours): 55 Alphajet. GE 315 (Cognac): 98 Epsilon. GE 319 (Avord): 25 Xingu.

Personnel (1997) 83,420 (26,403 conscripts; 4,900 civilians).

INTERNATIONAL RELATIONS

Membership. France is a member of the UN, the Council of Europe, NATO, WEU, EU, OSCE, OECD and the Pacific Community, and is a signatory to the Schengen Accord (*see* EUROPEAN UNION *under* MAJOR POLICY AREAS).

At a referendum in Sept. 1992 to approve the ratification of the Maastricht treaty on European union of 7 Feb. 1992, 12,967,498 votes (50·81%) were cast for and 12,550,651 (49·18%) against.

France is the focus of the *Communauté Francophone* (French-speaking Community) which formally links France with many of its former colonies in Africa. A wide range of agreements, both with members of the Community and with other French-speaking countries, extend to economic and technical matters, and in particular to the disbursement of overseas aid.

ECONOMY

Performance. Real GDP growth was estimated at 2·3% in 1997 (1·5% in 1996); a rate of 2·9% was forecast for 1998. Contributory factors to economic growth in 1997 were a strong export market and weaker franc. Total GDP (1996, in US$): 1,539,000m. (1997 forecast: 1,358,300m.).

A second phase of privatization (the first being in 1986–87) involving some 20 state enterprises was initiated by legislation of May 1993, by which the state retained the right to acquire a 'golden share' to give itself veto powers in the national interest. In 1997 the sale of state assets included nearly a quarter of France Télécom and a majority stake in the CIC banking network. Other sell-offs in the pipeline in Feb. 1998 included Air France (49%) and a controlling stake in the defence electronics giant Thomson-CSF.

Budget. In 1997 public spending was cut by an extra 10,000m. francs when the new government came to power in June. The budget for 1998 envisages no further cuts in public spending (but an increase in line with inflation forecast at 1·5%); a reduction in the public deficit from 3·1% of GDP in 1997 (dramatically reduced in June from an estimated 3·5% and rising by the acquisition of 22,000m. francs in emergency corporate taxes) to 3% of GDP, which is the uppermost limit of the Maastricht criteria on budget deficits.

Receipts and expenditure in 1m. francs:

	1993	1994	1995	1996	1997
Revenue	1,142,698	1,154,165	1,291,700	1,264,162	1,194,700
Expenditure	1,410,129	1,436,333	1,595,700	1,551,969	1,480,800

In Nov. 1997 receipts were up by 18,700m. francs on the previous year; expenditure was up by 16,500m. The budget deficit at 30 Nov. 1997 was some 325,300m. francs (4,100m. francs less than at 31 Dec. 1996).

Breakdown of revenue and expenditure (in 1m. francs):

Receipts	1994	1995	1996
Income tax	296,328	303,525	314,100
Corporation tax	127,857	145,748	143,200
Other direct taxes	111,148	116,820	136,474
Stamp duty	77,758	83,400	81,745
Customs duties	155,080	158,801	158,986
VAT	648,393	673,216	761,627
Other indirect taxes	41,040	44,707	46,083
Non-fiscal receipts	161,661	150,365	115,564
Expenditure			
Public debt	199,834	198,983	226,369
Administration	506,410	524,275	
Subsidies	406,420	417,531	1,073,496[1]
Civil investments	89,111	86,172	
Defence	242,558	243,456	241,449

[1] Civil expenditure total.

The standard rate of VAT is 20·6% (reduced rate, 5·5%).

Ministère de l'Economie, des Finances et du Plan. *Le Budget de l'Etat: de la Préparation à l'Exécution*. Paris, 1995

Currency. The unit of currency is the franc (FRF) of 100 centimes. Coins are issued for 5, 10 and 20 centimes and 1, 2, 5 and 10 francs, and notes for 20, 50, 100, 200 and 500 francs. Notes in circulation at 29 Jan. 1998: 261,338m. francs. Reserves (minus gold) in 1995 (in US$): 26,853m.; total reserves at 29 Jan. 1998: 547,661·43m. francs. The annualized rate of inflation in 1997 was 1·4% (2% in 1996).

Franc Zone. 13 former French colonies (Benin, Burkina Faso, Cameroon, Central African Republic, Chad, Comoros, the Republic of the Congo, Côte d'Ivoire, Gabon, Mali, Niger, Senegal and Togo), the former Spanish colony of Equatorial Guinea and the former Portuguese colony of Guinea-Bissau are members of a Franc Zone, the CFA (*Communauté Financière Africaine*). Comoros uses the Comorian franc. From 1948 to 1994 1 French franc = 50 francs CFA. The franc CFA was devalued by 50% on 11 Jan. 1994, the Comorian franc by 25%. The franc CFP *(Comptoirs Français du Pacifique)* is the common currency of the French dependencies of French Polynesia, New Caledonia and Wallis and Futuna. It has a parity of CFP francs 18·18 to the French franc.

Banking and Finance. The central bank and bank of issue is the *Banque de France* (*Governor*: Jean-Claude Trichet, app. 1993), founded in 1800, and nationalized on 2 Dec. 1945. In 1993 it received greater autonomy in line with EU conditions. The Governor is appointed for a 6-year term (renewable once) and heads the 9-member Council of Monetary Policy.

The National Credit Council, formed in 1945 to regulate banking activity and consulted in all political decisions on monetary policy, comprises 45 members nominated by the Government; its president is the Minister for the Economy; its Vice-President is the Governor of the Banque de France.

In 1996 there were 1,445 banks and other credit institutions, including 400 share-holder-owned banks and 342 mutual or savings banks. 4 principal deposit banks were nationalized in 1945, the remainder in 1982; the latter were privatized in 1987. The banking and insurance sectors underwent a flurry of mergers, privatizations, foreign investment, corporate restructuring and consolidation in 1997, in both the national and international fields. Further flotations planned include the sale of the state-owned insurance company GAN (scheduled for 1998) and Crédit Lyonnais (by 2000).

The state savings organization *Caisse Nationale d'Epargne* is administered by the post office on a giro system. There are also commercial savings banks (*caisses d'epargne et de prévoyance*). Deposited funds are centralized by a non-banking body, the *Caisse de Dépôts et Consignations*, which finances a large number of local authorities and state-aided housing projects, and carries an important portfolio of transferable securities.

There is a stock exchange (Bourse) in Paris.

Weights and Measures. The metric system is in general use.

ENERGY AND NATURAL RESOURCES

Electricity. The state-owned monopoly Electricité de France is reponsible for power generation and supply under the Ministry of Industry. Electricity production (1995, in 1m. kWh): 470,974, of which 358,600 (76·14%) was nuclear. Hydroelectric power contributes about 20% of total electricity output (80,606m. kWh in 1994).

France, not rich in natural energy resources, is at the centre of Europe's nuclear energy industry. In 1997 there were 56 nuclear reactors in operation, with a capacity of 58·4m. kW, providing some 72·9% of the electricity output. Nuclear reactors accounted for 38% of total energy consumption in 1994. There were 4 new nuclear plants under construction in 1997, one of which (in western France) was cancelled mid-way through the year, and Electricité de France announced that it will not be considering any new plants before 2000. Also in 1997, following concern over its safety, it was decided that the 12-year-old Superphénix plant east of Lyons would be shut down.

Oil and Gas. In 1994, 2·8m. tonnes of crude oil were produced. The greater part came from the Parentis oilfield in the Landes. The importation and distribution of natural gas is the responsibility of the government monopoly Gaz de France. Production of natural gas was 37,263m. cu. metres in 1993. In 1994, 41·2% of total energy consumption came from oil; 13% from gas.

Minerals. Significant producer of nickel, uranium, iron ore, bauxite, potash, crude steel, pig iron, aluminium and coal. Société Le Nickel extracts in New Caledonia and is the world's third largest nickel producer; France is the world's seventh largest uranium producer. The mining sector contributed 1% of GDP in 1994, and employed 0·8% of the workforce.

Coal production (1995): 5·1m. tonnes. Coal power generators contributed 6·2% of total energy consumption in 1994. Coal reserves in Jan. 1996: 139m. tonnes. Production of other principal minerals and metals (1993, in 1,000 tonnes): crude steel, 17,106; iron ore, 3,549; pig iron, 12,396; aluminium, 1,264; potash salts, 960.

Agriculture. France is the world's largest food producer. The agricultural sector con-tributes about 4·6% of GDP, and employs about 6·1% of the workforce. In 1993 there were 801,000 holdings and 1·6m. persons employed in agriculture, hunting, fishing and forestry. Co-operatives account for between 30-50% of output. In 1990, crop production accounted for 54·4% of total agricultural output; animal production for 45·6%.

Of the total area of France (54·9m. ha), the utilized agricultural area comprised 29·99m. ha in 1996. 18·29m. ha were arable, 10·53m. ha were under pasture, and 1·16m. ha were under permanent crops including vines (0·91m. ha).

Area under cultivation and yield for principal crops:

| | Area (1,000 ha) | | | Produce (1,000 tonnes) | | |
	1994	1995	1996	1994	1995	1996
Wheat	4,580	4,744	5,040	30,549	30,879	35,948
Rye	45	46·3	48·6	176	190·7	220·8
Barley	1,405	1,339	1,485	7,646	7,492	9,276
Oats	166	148·8	139·5	685	601·2	621·9
Sugar-beet	437	458·2	456·7	29,037	30,571	30,943
Maize	1,660	1,650	1,733	12,943	12,739	14,529
Sorghum	. . .	45·6	54·7	. . .	256·4	343·1

Production of principal fruit crops (in 1,000 tonnes) as follows:

	1994	1995	1996		1994	1995	1996
Apples[1]	2,166	2,078	2,019	Melons	330	329	314
Pears	343	320	353	Nuts	27	38	39
Plums	221	299	364	Table grapes	69	107	95
Peaches	528	526	467	Strawberries	83	81	81·2
Apricots	155	100	174	Clementines	22	27	21

[1] Does not include apples for cider-making.

Total area under cultivation and yield (1996, in 1,000 tonnes) of grapes from the vine, 871,038 ha (7·57m.). Wine production (1996): 60,036,974 hectolitres.

The area under cultivation (and yield) for vegetables in 1996 was as follows: Leaf and stem, 130,544 ha (2·4m. tonnes); fruit vegetables, 39,882 ha (1·5m. tonnes); roots and bulbs, 44,782 ha (1·33m. tonnes); pods, 86,339 ha (657,461 tonnes); beans lentils and other dry, 10,213 ha (20,449 tonnes).

Livestock (1996, in 1,000s): Horses, 337; asses and mules, 13·7; cattle, 20,655; sheep, 10,457; goats, 1,202; pigs, 14,283; poultry, 231,003 (laying hens, 49,324); rabbits, 14,439. Livestock products (1996, in 1,000 tonnes): beef and veal, 1,470; pork, 2,038; lamb and mutton, 152; poultry, 2,103; rabbit, 90; horse, 14. Milk production: cows', 243,538,646 hectolitres; sheep's, 2,339,865 hl; goats', 4,574,176 hl. Eggs (1996, in 1,000s): 12,083m.

Forestry. Forestry is France's richest natural resource, with a revenue of about 8,000m. francs a year, and accounts for 0·55m. of the workforce. In 1996 forest covered some 16m. ha, about 29·3% of France. 73·7% of forest is private; 26% state-owned. Timber production (1995): 36m. cu. metres, of which 10m. cu. metres were for industry and 8·6m. tonnes for paper.

Fisheries. In 1996 there were 6,509 fishing vessels totalling 176,356 GRT, and 17,101 fishermen. Catch (1996, in tonnes): 868,572 (fish, 634,894; shellfish and molluscs, 233,678).

INDUSTRY. Contributes around 28% of GDP and employs about 27% of the workforce. In Nov. 1997 capacity utilization in industry was approaching 85%. Chief industries: steel, chemicals, textiles, aircraft, machinery, electronic equipment, tourism, wine and perfume.

Industrial production (1993, in 1,000 tonnes): Sulphuric acid, 2,357; caustic soda, 1,473; sulphur, 1,106; polystyrene, 481; polyvinyl, 1,176; polyethylene, 1,308; cement and lime, 20,133; wool, 56; cotton, 152; linen, 6; silk, 71.

Food products (1993, in 1,000 tonnes): cheese, 1,442; chocolate, 547; biscuits, 475; sugar, 4,599; fish preparations, 109; jams and jellies, 161.

Engineering production (in 1,000 units): Car tyres (1993), 50,475; motor vehicles (1994), 3,176; television sets (1994), 2,796.

Labour. According to the Employment Survey of March 1994, there was a working population of 25,136,598, including 13,898,272 men and 11,238,326 women; out of an economically active population of 22,074,700, 1,127,300 were engaged in agriculture, forestry and fishing, 1,525,600 in building, 1,422,500 in transport and telecommunications, 1,481,100 in manufacturing industries, 608,300 in banking and insurance, 4,278,700 in services, 2,614,100 in commerce. Some 5m. people work in the public sector at national and local level. It was estimated in 1997 that 51% of households have no-one working in the private sector.

A new definition of 'unemployed' was adopted in Aug. 1995, omitting persons who had worked at least 78 hours in the previous month. By this classification there were some 3·5m. unemployed in Jan. 1998, a rate of 12·4%. Under an 80% state-funded job creation programme announced in 1997, an extra 350,000 public-sector jobs will be created for the young by 2000.

Conciliation boards (*Conseils de Prud'hommes*) mediate in labour disputes. They are elected for 5-year terms by 2 colleges of employers and employees. In Jan. 1998 the minimum wage (SMIC) was 39·29 francs an hour (6,664 francs a month). SMIC affects about 1·5m. wage-earners. The average annual wage was 114,314 francs in 1994. Retirement age is 60. A 5-week annual holiday is statutory. Under controversial new government proposals announced in 1997, the basic working week (39 hours) is to be reduced to 35 hours.

Trade Unions. The main trade union confederations in 1997 were as follows: the Communist-led CGT (Confédération Générale du Travail), founded 1895; the CGT-FO (Confédération Générale du Travail–Force Ouvrière) which broke away from the CGT in 1948; the CFTC (Confédération Française des Travailleurs Chrétiens), founded in 1919 and divided in 1964, with a breakaway group retaining the old name and the main body continuing under the new name of CFDT (Confédération Française Démocratique du Travail); and the CGC (Confédération Générale des Cadres) formed in 1944 which represents managerial and supervisory staff. The main haulage confederation is the FNTR; the leading employers' association is the CNPF, often referred to as the *Patronat*. Unions are not required to publish membership figures, but in 1993 the 2 largest federations, the CGT and CFDT, had an estimated 0·63m. and 0·65m. members respectively.

Although France has the lowest rate of trade union membership in Europe, 9% in 1997 (compared to 29% in Germany, 33% in Britain and over 90% in Sweden), its trade unionists have considerable clout: they run France's welfare system; staff the country's dispute-settling industrial tribunals (*conseils de prud'hommes*); and fix national agreements on wages and working conditions. A union call to strike is invariably answered by more than a union's membership. Nearly 6m. working days were lost in French strikes in 1995 compared to 415,000 in Britain and 247,000 in Germany.

FOREIGN ECONOMIC RELATIONS. The trade balance showed a surplus of nearly 200,000m. francs in 1997 due to a strong export market, and a drop in imports owing to sluggish domestic demand. Trade balance (1997 estimate, in US$): 19,900m. (1998 forecast, 24,800m.). Main trading partners: Argentina, USA, Austria, Brazil, Canada, Egypt, Finland, Ghana, Japan, Uruguay, Philippines, Poland, Korea (Rep.) and Singapore.

Privatization legislation of May 1993 gave foreign nationals the right to acquire more than 20% of a firm's capital (the previous limit). In 1997, following intense activity on the equity market, approximately one third of French equity was owned by foreign investors.

Commerce. Total imports (1995, in US$): 273,100m.; total exports, 285,200m. Principal imports include: oil, machinery and equipment, chemicals, iron and steel, and foodstuffs. Major exports: metals, chemicals, industrial equipment, consumer goods and agricultural products.

Foreign trade by sector (1992, as % of total trade):

	% Imports	% Exports
Agriculture and agri-food	11·6	16·4
Energy	8·6	2·3
Raw materials and semi-products	24·9	23·7
Capital goods	24·2	27·6
Surface transport equipment	11·1	13·9
Consumer goods	16·9	15·3

In 1995, the chief import sources (as % of total imports) were as follows: Germany, 18·5%; Italy, 10%; Belgium-Luxembourg, 9%; UK, 8%; USA, 7·8%; Spain, 6·5%. The chief export markets (as % of total) were: Germany, 17·7%; UK, 9·3%; Italy, 9·6%; Belgium-Luxembourg, 8·5%; Spain, 7·3%; USA, 5·9%; Asia, 6·2%.

Tourism. In 1994 60·6m. foreigners visited France, bringing foreign exchange earnings of 137,010m. francs. Countries of origin (visitors, in 1,000) in 1993: Germany, 12,900; UK, 8,000; Netherlands, 7,100; Italy, 6,300; Spain, 3,000; Belgium, 2,000; USA, 1,900; Switzerland, 1,900; Portugal, 1,700; Sweden, 878; Canada, 694; Denmark, 687; Ireland, 475; Greece, 348; Austria, 329; Japan, 320; Norway, 320. There were 596,670 classified hotel rooms in 1994.

COMMUNICATIONS

Roads. In 1997 there were 806,000 km of road, including 7,100 km of motorway. France has the densest road network in the world, and longest in the EU. Around 90% of all freight is transported by road. In 1996 there were 24·4m. private cars and 4·9m. commercial vehicles (3·62m. lorries, about 42,000 buses and 0·87m. motorcycles and scooters). In 1993 there were 9,052 road deaths.

Railways. In 1938 all the independent railway companies were merged with the existing state railway system in a Société Nationale des Chemins de Fer Français (SNCF), which became a public industrial and commercial establishment in 1983. Legislation came into effect in 1997 which vested ownership of the railway infrastructure (track and signalling) in a newly established public corporation, the National Railway Network (RFN). The RFN is funded by payments for usage from the SNCF, government and local subventions and authority capital made available by the state derived from the proceeds of privatization. The SNCF remains responsible for maintenance and management of the rail network. The legislation also envisages the establishment of regional railway services which receive funds previously given to the SNCF as well as a state subvention. These regional bodies negotiate with SNCF for the provision of suitable services for their area. SNCF is the most heavily indebted and subsidized (38,000m. francs a year) company in France.

In 1997, SNCF totalled 33,769 km of track (one third of it electrified); it had an annual capacity of 58,000m. passengers-km and 45,900m. tonnes freight-km. High-speed TGV lines link Paris to the south and west of France, and Paris and Lille to the Channel Tunnel (Eurostar). The high-speed TGV line appeared in 1983; it had 1,860 km of track in 1997, and another 4,400 km planned by 2015. Services from London through the Channel Tunnel began operating in 1994.

The Paris transport network consisted in 1993 of 202 km of metro, 352 km of regional express railways, 91 km of light rail and 7 km of passenger stock. There are metros in Lille (29 km), Lyon (20·8 km), Toulouse (10 km) and Marseille (19·5 km), and tram/light railway networks in Grenoble (14·6 km), Lille (23 km), Marseille (3 km), Nantes (16·5 km), Rouen (17 km), St Étienne (7 km) and Strasbourg (11·4 km).

Civil Aviation. There are international airports at: Paris (Orly), Paris (Charles de Gaulle), Bordeaux (Mérignac), Lille (Lesquin), Lyon (Satolas), Marseille-Provence, Nice-Côte d'Azur, Strasbourg (Entzheim) and Toulouse (Blagnac). Air France is the national airline; Air Inter, the national domestic airline. Following their merger in 1990 (with UTA), between them these 2 airlines account for 97% of air traffic. In 1994 Air France and Air Inter flew 8,652m. tonne-km (excluding mail) and 52,435m. passenger-km.

Shipping. The merchant fleet of oceangoing steam and motor ships totalling 1,000 gross tonnes or more (excluding special ships such as cable, icebreakers, etc.) comprised in Jan. 1996 65 vessels of 1,564,000 GRT. In 1993 from a total of 215 vessels (all sizes; GRT: 3,928,000), 212m. tonnes of cargo were unloaded, including 130m. tonnes of crude and refined petroleum products, 93m. tonnes were loaded; total passenger traffic was 29·2m. Chief ports: Marseille, Le Havre, Nantes, Bordeaux and Rouen.

France has extensive inland waterways. Canals are administered by the public authority France Navigable Waterways (FVN). In 1993 there were 8,500 km of navigable rivers, waterways and canals (of which 1,647 km were accessible to vessels over 3,000 tons), with a total traffic of 59·8m. tonnes.

Telecommunications. There were 16,877 post offices in 1993. La Poste is a public enterprise under autonomous management responsible for mail delivery and financial services. France Télécom became a limited company on 1 Jan. 1997. In 1994 the telephone system had 31·6m. subscribers; in 1997 4·3m. mobile telephones were in use. In 1995 there were 1·7m. fax machines (including 0·4m. in working homes); and 6·5m. Minitel videotext terminals were rented out by France Télécom.

Radio and television broadcasting was reorganized under the Act of 7 Aug. 1974 which replaced the *Office de Radiodiffusion Télévision Française* with 4 broadcasting companies, a production company and an audio-visual institute. The broadcasting authority (an independent regulatory commission) is the *Conseil Supérieur de l'Audiovisuel (CSA)*. Radio programmes are broadcast from 874 VHF transmitters of which 418 belong to 4 stations: *France Info, France Inter, France Musique* and *France Culture*. An external service, *Radio-France Internationale*, was founded in 1931 (as 'Poste Coloniale'), and broadcasts in 20 languages.

There are 2 state-owned TV channels, *Antenne-2* and *FR3*, which are partly financed by advertising, and 5 commercial channels; colour is by SECAM. TV broadcasts must contain at least 60% EU-generated programmes and 50% of these must be French.

There were about 58m. radio receivers in use in 1997; 34·25m. TV sets (1995).

Cinemas. There were 4,414 screens in 1994; attendances totalled 126m. (133m. in 1993); and 115 full-length films were made. 360 new screens will be open by 2000.

Press. There were about 80 daily papers (10 nationals, 70 provincials) in 1997. Top dailies: *L'Equipe*; *Le Monde*; *Le Parisien-Aujourd'hui*; *Le Figaro-L'Aurore*; *Libération*; *France-Soir*; *Ouest France*; *Le Progrès*; *Centre France*; *Sud Ouest*; *Voix du Nord*. The *Journal de Dimanche* is the only national Sunday paper. In 1994, total national daily press circulation was 2·47m. copies.

SOCIAL INSTITUTIONS

Justice. The system of justice is divided into 2 jurisdictions: the judicial, and the administrative. Within the judicial jurisdiction are common law courts including 473 lower courts (*tribunaux d'instance*, 11 in overseas departments), 186 higher courts (*tribunaux de grande instance*, 5 *tribunaux de première instance* in the overseas territories), and 454 police courts (*tribunaux de police*, 11 in overseas departments).

The *tribunaux d'instance* are presided over by a single judge. The *tribunaux de grande instance* usually have a collegiate composition, but may be presided over by a single judge in some civil cases. The *tribunaux de police*, presided over by a judge on duty in the *tribunal d'instance*, deal with petty offences (*contraventions*); correctional chambers (*chambres correctionelles*, of which there is at least 1 in each *tribunal de grande instance*) deal with graver offences (*délits*), including cases involving imprisonment up to 5 years. Correctional chambers normally consist of 3 judges of a *tribunal de grande instance* (a single judge in some cases). Sometimes in cases of *délit*, and in all cases of more serious *crimes*, a preliminary inquiry is made in secrecy by one of 569 examining magistrates (*juges d'instruction*), who either dismisses the case or sends it for trial before a public prosecutor.

Within the judicial jurisdiction are various specialised courts, including 227 commercial courts (*tribunaux de commerce*), composed of tradesmen and manufacturers elected for 2 years initially, and then for 4 years; 271 conciliation boards (*conseils de prud'hommes*), composed of an equal number of employers and employees elected for 5 years to deal with labour disputes; 437 courts for settling rural landholding disputes (*tribunaux paritaires des baux ruraux*, 11 in overseas departments); and 116 social security courts (*tribunaux des affaires de sécurité sociale*).

When the decisions of any of these courts are susceptible of appeal, the case goes to one of the 35 courts of appeal (*cours d'appel*), composed each of a president and a variable number of members. There are 104 courts of assize (*cours d'assises*), each composed of a president who is a member of the court of appeal, and 2 other magistrates, and assisted by a lay jury of 9 members. These try crimes involving imprisonment of over 5 years. The decisions of the courts of appeal and the courts of assize are final. However, the Court of Cassation (*cour de cassation*) has discretion to verify if the law has been correctly interpreted and if the rules of procedure have been followed exactly. The Court of Cassation may annul any judgment, following which the cases must be retried by a court of appeal or a court of assizes.

The administrative jurisdiction exists to resolve conflicts arising between citizens and central and local government authorities. It consists of 34 administrative courts (*tribunaux administratifs*, 7 in overseas departments and territories) and 5 administrative courts of appeal (*cours administratives d'appel*). The Council of State is the final court of appeal in administrative cases, though it may also act as a court of first instance.

Cases of doubt as to whether the judicial or administrative jurisdiction is competent in any case are resolved by a *Tribunal de conflits* composed in equal measure of members of the Court of Cassation and the Council of State. In 1997 the new government restricted its ability to intervene in individual cases of justice.

Penal code. A revised penal code came into force on 1 March 1994, replacing the *Code Napoléon* of 1810. Penal institutions consist of: (1) *maisons d'arrêt*, where persons awaiting trial as well as those condemned to short periods of imprisonment are kept; (2) punishment institutions – (a) central prisons (*maisons centrales*) for those sentenced to long imprisonment, (b) detention centres for offenders showing promise of rehabilitation, and (c) penitentiary centres, establishments combining (a) and (b); (3) hospitals for the sick. Special attention is being paid to classified treatment and the rehabilitation and vocational re-education of prisoners including work in open-air and semi-free establishments. Juvenile delinquents go before special judges in 138 (11 in overseas departments and territories) juvenile courts (*tribunaux pour enfants*); they are sent to public or private institutions of supervision and re-education. Capital punishment was abolished in Aug. 1981. The population of the 187 penal establishments (3 for women) was, in 1996, 56,220 men and 2,396 women.

The first Ombudsman (*Médiateur*) was appointed for a 6-year period in Jan. 1973. The present incumbent is Jacques Pelletier (app. 1992).

Weston, M., *English Reader's Guide to the French Legal System.* Oxford, 1991

Religion. A law of 1905 separated church and state. In 1996 there were 95 Roman Catholic dioceses in metropolitan France and 112 bishops. In 1992 there were 43·77m. Roman Catholics (over 75% of the population), 0·8m. Protestants and 1·72m. Moslems.

Education The primary, secondary and higher state schools constitute the 'Université de France'. Its Supreme Council of 84 members has deliberative, administrative and judiciary functions, and as a consultative committee advises respecting the working of the school system; the inspectors-general are in direct communication with the Minister. For local education administration France is divided into 25 academic areas, each of which has an Academic Council whose members include a certain number elected by the professors or teachers. The Academic Council deals with all grades of education. Each is under a Rector, and each is provided with academy inspectors, 1 for each department.

Compulsory education is provided for children of 6–16. The educational stages are as follows:

1. Non-compulsory pre-school instruction for children aged 2–5, to be given in infant schools or infant classes attached to primary schools.

2. Compulsory elementary instruction for children aged 6–11, to be given in primary schools and certain classes of the *lycées*. It consists of 3 courses: preparatory (1 year), elementary (2 years), intermediary (2 years). Physically or mentally handicapped children are cared for in special institutions or special classes of primary schools.

3. Lower secondary education (*Enseignement du premier cycle du Second Degré*)

for pupils aged 11–15, consists of 4 years of study in the *lycées* (grammar schools), *Collèges d'Enseignement Technique* or *Collèges d'Enseignement Général*.

4. Upper secondary education (*Enseignement du second cycle du Second Degré*) for pupils aged 15–18: (1) *Long, général* or *professionel* provided by the *lycées* and leading to the *baccalauréat* or to the *baccalauréat de technicien* after 3 years; and (2) *Court*, professional courses of 3, 2 and 1 year are taught in the *lycées d'enseignement professionel*, or the specialized sections of the *lycées*, CES or CEG.

The following table shows the number of schools in 1994–95 and the numbers of pupils in full-time education:

	State		Private	
	Schools	Pupils	Schools	Pupils
Nursery	18,646	5,597,600	343	897,300
Primary	35,618		5,626	
Secondary	7,501	4,327,200	3,711	1,142,000

Higher education is provided by the state free of charge in the universities and in special schools, and by private individuals in the free faculties and schools. Legislation of 1968 redefined the activities and working of universities. Bringing several disciplines together, 780 units for teaching and research (*UER–Unités d'Enseignement et de Recherche*) were formed which decided their own teaching activities, research programmes and procedures for checking the level of knowledge gained. They and the other parts of each university must respect the rules designed to maintain the national standard of qualifications. The UERs form the basic units of the 69 state universities and 3 national polytechnic institutes (with university status), which are grouped into 25 *Académies*. There are also 5 Catholic universities in Paris, Angers, Lille, Lyon and Toulouse; and private universities. There were 1,475,181 students at state universities (1993–94); 21,355 at private universities (1991–92).

Outside the university system, higher education (academic, professional and technical) is provided by over 400 schools and institutes, including the 177 *Grandes Écoles*, which are highly selective public or private institutions offering mainly technological or commercial curricula. These have an annual output of about 17,000 graduates, and in 1994–95 there were also 71,271 students in preparatory classes leading to the *Grandes Écoles;* in 1993–94, 232,844 were registered in the Sections de Techniciens Supérieurs, 71,273 in the Écoles d'Ingénieurs.

Adult literacy rate: 99·0%.

Health. Ordinances of 1996 created a new regional régime of hospital administration and introduced a system of patients' records to prevent abuses of public health benefits. On 1 Jan. 1993 there were 158,968 doctors, 52,673 chemists, 38,868 dentists, 320,505 nurses and 11,479 midwives; and 3,810 hospitals with 680,888 beds.

Welfare. An order of 4 Oct. 1945 laid down the framework of a comprehensive plan of Social Security and created a single organization which superseded the various laws relating to social insurance, workmen's compensation, health insurance, family allowances, etc. All previous matters relating to Social Security are dealt with in the Social Security Code, 1956; this has been revised several times. The Chamber of Deputies and Senate, meeting as Congress on 19 Feb. 1996, adopted an important revision of the Constitution giving parliament powers to review annually the funding of social security (previously managed by the trade unions and employers' associations), and to fix targets for expenditure in the light of anticipated receipts.

In 1997 6m. people were dependent on the welfare system, which accounted for more than a quarter of GDP (US\$ 333,000m.). The Social Security budget had a deficit of some 17,000m. francs in 1996, and a cumulative debt (1992–96) of 250,000m. francs. A special levy, the new social debt repayment tax (RDS), at 0·5% on all incomes including pensions and unemployment benefit, has been introduced to clear the cumulative debt. A modest reform of the system was announced in June 1997 which will include a review of all welfare benefits.

Contributions. The general social security contribution (CSG) introduced in 1991 was raised by 4% to 7·5% in 1997 by the Jospin administration in an attempt to dramatically reduce the deficit on social security spending, effectively almost doubling the CSG. All wage-earning workers or those of equivalent status are insured regardless of the amount or the nature of the salary or earnings. The funds for the general scheme are raised mainly from professional contributions, these being fixed within the limits of a ceiling and calculated as a percentage of the salaries. The calculation of contributions payable for family allowances, old age and industrial injuries relates only to this amount; on the other hand, the amount payable for sickness, maternity expenses, disability and death is calculated partly within the limit of the 'ceiling' and partly on the whole salary. These contributions are the responsibility of both employer and employee, except in the case of family allowances or industrial injuries, where they are the sole responsibility of the employer.

Self-employed Workers. From 17 Jan. 1948 allowances and old-age pensions were paid to self-employed workers by independent insurance funds set up within their own profession, trade or business. Schemes of compulsory insurance for sickness were instituted in 1961 for farmers, and in 1966, with modifications in 1970, for other non-wage-earning workers.

Social Insurance. The orders laid down in Aug. 1967 ensure that the whole population can benefit from the Social Security Scheme; at present all elderly persons who have been engaged in the professions, as well as the surviving spouse, are entitled to claim an old-age benefit.

Sickness Insurance refunds the costs of treatment required by the insured and the needs of dependants.

Maternity Insurance covers the costs of medical treatment relating to the pregnancy, confinement and lying-in period; the beneficiaries being the insured person or the spouse.

Insurance for Invalids is divided into 3 categories: (1) those who are capable of working; (2) those who cannot work; (3) those who, in addition, are in need of the help of another person. According to the category, the pension rate varies from 30 to 50% of the average salary for the last 10 years, with additional allowance for home help for the third category.

Old-Age Pensions for workers were introduced in 1910 and are now fixed by the Social Security Code of 28 Jan. 1972. Since 1983 people who have paid insurance for at least $37^1/_2$ years (150 quarters) receive at 60 a pension equal to 60% of basic salary. People who have paid insurance for less than $37^1/_2$ years but no less than 15 years can expect a pension equal to as many 1/150ths of the full pension as their quarterly payments justify. In the event of death of the insured person, the husband or wife of the deceased person receives half the pension received by the latter. Compulsory supplementary schemes ensure benefits equal to 70% of previous earnings.

Family Allowances. A controversial programme of means-testing for Family Allowance was introduced in 1997 by the new administration. The Family Allowance benefit system comprises: (*a*) Family allowances proper, equivalent to 25·5% of the basic monthly salary for 2 dependent children, 46% for the third child, 41% for the fourth child, and 39% for the fifth and each subsequent child; a supplement equivalent to 9% of the basic monthly salary for the second and each subsequent dependent child more than 10 years old, and 16% for each dependent child over 15 years. (*b*) Family supplement for persons with at least 3 children or one child aged less than 3 years. (*c*) Ante-natal grants. (*d*) Maternity grant is equal to 260% of basic salary. Increase for multiple births or adoptions, 198%; increase for birth or adoption of third or subsequent child, 457%. (*e*) Allowance for specialized education of handicapped children. (*f*) Allowance for orphans. (*g*) Single parent allowance. (*h*) Allowance for opening of school term. (*i*) Allowance for accommodation, under certain circumstances. (*j*) Minimum family income for those with at least 3 children. Allowances (*b*), (*g*), (*h*) and (*j*) only apply to those whose annual income falls below a specified level.

Workmen's Compensation. The law passed by the National Assembly on 30 Oct. 1946 forms part of the Social Security Code and is administered by the Social Security

Organization. Employers are invited to take preventive measures. The application of these measures is supervised by consulting engineers (assessors) of the local funds dealing with sickness insurance, who may compel employers who do not respect these measures to make additional contributions; they may, in like manner, grant rebates to employers who have in operation suitable preventive measures. The injured person receives free treatment, the insurance fund reimburses the practitioners, hospitals and suppliers chosen freely by the injured. In cases of temporary disablement, the daily payments are equal to half the total daily wage received by the injured. In case of permanent disablement, the injured person receives a pension, the amount of which varies according to the degree of disablement and the salary received during the past 12 months.

Unemployment Benefits vary according to circumstances (full or partial unemployment) which are means-tested.

Ambler, J. S. (ed.) *The French Welfare State: Surviving Social and Ideological Change.* New York Univ. Press, 1992

DIPLOMATIC REPRESENTATIVES

Of France in Great Britain (58 Knightsbridge, London, SW1X 7JT)
Ambassador: Jean Gueguinou.

Of Great Britain in France (35 rue du Faubourg St Honoré, 75383 Paris Cedex 08)
Ambassador: Sir Michael Jay, KCMG.

Of France in the USA (4101 Reservoir Rd., NW, Washington, D.C., 20007)
Ambassador: François Bujon.

Of the USA in France (2 Ave. Gabriel, Paris)
Ambassador: Felix Rohatyn.

Of France to the United Nations
Ambassador: Alain Dejammet.

Of France to NATO
Ambassador: Gérard Errera.

Further Reading

Institut National de la Statistique et des Études Économiques: *Annuaire statistique de la France* (from 1878); *Bulletin mensuel de statistique* (monthly); *Documentation économique* (bi-monthly); *Economie et Statistique* (monthly); *Tableaux de l'Economie Française* (biennially, from 1956); *Tendances de la Conjoncture* (monthly).

Agulhon, M., *The French Republic, 1879–1992.* Oxford, 1993
Ardant, P., *Les Institutions de la Ve République.* Paris, 1992
Balladur, E., *Deux Ans à Matignon.* Paris, 1995
Braudel, F., *The Identity of France.* 2 vols. London, 1988-90
Caron, F., *An Economic History of Modern France.* London, 1979
Chambers, F. J., *France.* [Bibliography] Oxford and Santa Barbara (CA), (rev. ed.) 1990
Chazal, C., *Balladur.* [in French] Paris, 1993
Cubertafond, A., *Le Pouvoir, la Politique et l'État en France.* Paris, 1993
L'État de la France. Paris, annual
Gildea, R., *France since 1945.* OUP, 1996
Gouze, R., *Mitterrand par Mitterrand.* Paris, 1994
Hollifield, J. F. and Ross, G., *Searching for the New France.* London, 1991
Hudson, G. L., *Corsica.* [World Bibliographic Series, vol. 202] Oxford, 1997
Jones, C., *The Cambridge Illustrated History of France.* CUP, 1994
McMillan, J. F., *Twentieth-Century France: Politics and Society in France, 1898–1991.* 2nd ed. [of *Dreyfus to De Gaulle*]. London, 1992
Mendras, H. and Cole, A., *Social Change in Modern France: towards a Cultural Anthopology of the Fifth Republic.* CUP, 1991
Morris, P., *French Politics Today.* Manchester Univ. Press, 1994
Pinchemel, P., *France: A Geographical, Social and Economic Survey.* CUP, 1987
Popkin, J. D., *A History of Modern France.* New York, 1994
Price, R., *Concise History of France.* CUP, 1993
Schmidt, V. A., *Democratizing France: the Political and Administrative History of Decentralization.* CUP, 1991

Stevens, A., *The Government and Politics of France*. London, 1992
Todd, E., *The Making of Modern France: Politics, Ideology and Culture*. Oxford, 1991
Verdié, M. (ed.) *L'État de la France et de ses Habitants*. Paris, 1992
Vesperini, J.-P., *L'Économie de la France sous la Ve République*. Paris, 1993
Who's Who in France [in French]. Paris, annual
(Also see specialized titles listed under relevant selections, above.)

National statistical office: Institut National de la Statistique et des Etudes Economiques (INSEE), 75582 Paris Cedex 12.
Website: http://www.insee.fr/

DEPARTMENTS AND TERRITORIES OVERSEAS

Départements (DOM) et Territoires (TOM) d'Outre-Mer

These fall into 3 categories: *Overseas Departments* (French Guiana, Guadeloupe, Martinique, Réunion); *Territorial Collectivities* (Mayotte, St Pierre and Miquelon); and *Overseas Territories* (French Polynesia, New Caledonia, Southern and Antarctic Territories, Wallis and Futuna).

Further Reading

Aldrich, R. and Connell, J., *France's Overseas Frontier: Départements et Territoires d'Outre-Mer*. CUP, 1992

OVERSEAS DEPARTMENTS
GUADELOUPE

KEY HISTORICAL EVENTS. The islands were discovered by Columbus in 1493. The Carib inhabitants resisted Spanish attempts to colonize. A French colony was established on 28 June 1635, and apart from short periods of occupancy by British forces, Guadeloupe has since remained a French possession. On 19 March 1946 Guadeloupe became an Overseas Department.

TERRITORY AND POPULATION. Guadeloupe consists of a group of islands in the Lesser Antilles. The two main islands, Basse-Terre (to the west) and Grande-Terre (to the east), are joined by a bridge over a narrow channel. Adjacent to these are the islands of Marie Galante (to the south east), La Désirade (to the east), and the Îles des Saintes (to the south); the islands of St Martin and St Barthélemy lie 250 km to the north-west.

Island	Area (sq. km)	1990 Census	Chief town
St Martin[1]	54[2]	28,518	Marigot
St Barthélemy	21	5,038	Gustavia
Basse-Terre	848	149,943	Basse-Terre
Grande-Terre	590	177,570	Pointe-à-Pitre
Îles des Saintes	13	2,036	Terre-de-Bas
La Désirade	20	1,610	Grande Anse
Marie-Galante	158	13,463	Grand-Bourg
	1,705	378,178[3]	

[1] Northern part only; the southern third is Dutch.   [2] Includes uninhabited Tintamarre.   [3] Preliminary results.

Population at the last census (1990, final result), 386,987; 1995 estimate, 417,000. Population of principal towns: Basse-Terre, 14,082; Pointe-à-Pitre, 26,031; Les Abymes, 62,645. Basse-Terre is the seat of government, while larger Pointe-à-Pitre is the department's main economic centre and port; Les Abymes is a 'suburb' of Pointe-à-Pitre.

Vital statistics (1987): Live births, 6,855; deaths, 2,244; marriages, 1,880. French is the official language, but Creole is spoken by the vast majority, except on St Martin.

CLIMATE. Warm and humid. *Pointe-à-Pitre.* Jan. 74°F (23·4°C), July 80°F (26·7°C). Annual rainfall 71" (1,814 mm).

CONSTITUTION AND GOVERNMENT. Guadeloupe is administered by a General Council of 42 members directly elected for 6-year terms (assisted by an Economic and Social Committee of 40 members) and by a Regional Council of 41 members. It is represented in the National Assembly by 4 deputies; in the Senate by 2 senators; and on the Economic and Social Council by 1 councillor. There are 4 *arrondissements,* sub-divided into 42 cantons and 34 communes, each administered by an elected municipal council. The French government is represented by an appointed Prefect.

Prefect: Michel Diefenbacher.
President of the General Council: Dominique Larifla (DVG).
President of the Regional Council: Lucette Michaux-Chevry (RPR).

ECONOMY

Performance. In 1993 the GDP was 18,984m. French francs. GDP per capita (1993) was 46,484 French francs.

Currency. The French franc is in use.

Banking and Finance. The Caisse Française de Développement is the official bank of the department, and issues its bank-notes. The main commercial banks in 1995 (with number of branches) were: Banque des Antilles Françaises (6), Banque Régionale d'Escompte et de Depôts (5), Banque Nationale de Paris (8), Crédit Agricole (18), Banque Française Commerciale (8), Société Générale de Banque aux Antilles (5), Credit Lyonnais (6), Credit Martiniquais (3), Banque Inschauspé et Cie (1).

ENERGY AND NATURAL RESOURCES

Electricity. Total production (1993): 1,024m. kWh.

Agriculture. Chief products (1993): bananas, 105,400 tonnes; sugar-cane, 748,000 tonnes; flowers 8·9m. (1992). Other fruits and vegetables are also grown for both export and domestic consumption.
Livestock (1992): Cattle, 56,100; goats, 39,500; sheep, 3,500; pigs, 47,500.

Fisheries. Catch (1993), 7,950 tonnes; molluscs and shellfish, 650 tonnes.

INDUSTRY. The main industries are sugar refining, food processing and rum distilling, carried out by small and medium-sized businesses. Other important industries are cement production and tourism.

Labour. The economically active population in 1990 was 117,516. In 1993 there were 15,020 persons in the trade sector; 6,950 in transport and communications; and 34,223 in services. The minimum wage (SMIC) was 39·29 francs per hour (6,664 a month) in 1997. 46,360 persons were registered unemployed in 1994.

COMMERCE. Total imports (1994, in 1m. francs): 8,897; total exports: 845. Main export products (1993, with % of market share): bananas, 26%; sugar, 26%, rum, 7%. Trade with France (1993): 68% of all imports; 78% of exports.

Tourism. Tourism is the chief economic activity. 458,181 tourists visited in 1994, including 313,613 cruise visitors.

COMMUNICATIONS

Roads. In 1996 there were 3,200 km of roads.

Civil Aviation. Air France and a dozen or so other airlines call at Guadeloupe airport. In 1993 there were 37,065 arrivals and departures of aircraft, and 1,461,699 passengers at Raizet (Pointe-à-Pitre) airport. There are also airports at Marie-Galante, La Désirade, St Barthélemy and St Martin.

Shipping. In 1993, 2,812 vessels arrived to disembark 105,217 passengers and 1,933,000 tonnes of freight; and to embark 95,882 passengers and 431,000 tonnes of freight.

Telecommunications. In 1984 there were 47 post offices and 64,916 telephones. *Radiodiffusion Française d'Outre-Mer* broadcasts for 17 hours a day in French. There is a local region radio station, and several private stations. There are 2 television channels (1 regional; 1 satellite) broadcasting for 6 hours a day. There were (1993) 0·1m. radio and 0·15m. TV receivers.

Press. There was (1995) 1 daily newspaper with a circulation of 20,000.

SOCIAL INSTITUTIONS

Justice. There are 4 *tribunaux d'instance* and 2 *tribunaux de grande instance* at Basse-Terre and Pointe-à-Pitre; there is also a court of appeal and a court of assizes.

Religion. The majority of the population are Roman Catholic.

Education. Education is free and compulsory from 6 to 16 years. In 1994 there were 54,493 pupils at 321 pre-elementary and primary schools, and 46,176 at 20 *lycées* and 40 *collèges* at secondary level. In 1993 there were 4,308 students from Guadeloupe at the University of Antilles-Guyana (out of total number of 8,290).

Health. In 1995 there were 13 public hospitals and 16 private clinics.

FRENCH GUIANA

Guyane Française

KEY HISTORICAL EVENTS. A French settlement on the island of Cayenne was established in 1604 and the territory between the Maroni and Oyapock rivers finally became a French possession in 1817. Convict settlements were established from 1852, that on Devil's Island being the most notorious; all were closed by 1945. On 19 March 1946 the status of French Guiana was changed to that of an Overseas Department.

TERRITORY AND POPULATION. French Guiana is situated on the north-east coast of Latin America, and is bounded in the north-east by the Atlantic Ocean, west by Suriname, and south and east by Brazil. It includes the offshore Devil's Island, Royal Island and St Joseph, and has an area of 85,534 sq. km. Population at the 1990 census: 114,808 (including 34,087 of foreign origin); estimate (1995), 150,000. The chief towns are: the capital, Cayenne (41,600 inhabitants), Kourou (14,000) and Saint-Laurent-du-Maroni (13,900). About 58% of inhabitants are of African descent.

Vital statistics (1988): Live births, 2,700; deaths, 562; marriages, 365 (1987); birth rate, 30·7 per 1,000 inhabitants (1991).

CONSTITUTION AND GOVERNMENT. French Guiana is administered by a General Council of 19 members directly elected for 5-year terms, and by a Regional Council of 31 members. It is represented in the National Assembly by 2 deputies; in the Senate by 1 senator. The French government is represented by a Prefect. There are 2 *arrondissements* (Cayenne and Saint Laurent-du-Maroni) sub-divided into 22 communes and 19 cantons.

Prefect: Pierre Dartout.
President of the General Council: Stéphan Phinera (PS).
President of the Regional Council: Antoine Karam (PS).

ECONOMY

Performance. In 1993 the GDP was 7,989m. French francs. GDP per capita (1993) was 54,516 French francs.

Banking and Finance. The Caisse Centrale de Coopération Economique is the bank of issue. In 1995 commercial banks included the Banque Nationale de Paris-Guyane, Crédit Populaire Guyanais and Banque Française Commerciale.

ENERGY AND NATURAL RESOURCES

Electricity. Total production (1993): 445m. kWh.

Minerals. Placer gold mining is the most important industry in French Guiana. In 1993 2,795 kg of gold were produced.

Agriculture. Some 21,670 ha are estimated to be under cultivation. Principal crops (1993, in tonnes): rice, 26,962; manioc, 23,350; sugar-cane, 3,200.

Livestock (1993): 0·01m. cattle; 10,700 swine; 6,000 sheep and goats; 0·22m. poultry.

Forestry. The country has immense forests (about 83,000 sq. km in 1993) which are rich in many kinds of timber. Roundwood production (1993) 0·05m. cu. metres. The trees also yield oils, essences and gum products.

Fisheries. Total catch (1993): 3,431 tonnes of shrimps (from a fleet of 70 French boats); and 4,300 tonnes of fish.

INDUSTRY. Important products include rum, rosewood essence and beer. The island has sawmills and 1 sugar factory.

Labour. The economically active population (1989) was 31,183. In 1997 the minimum wage (SMIC) was 39·29 francs per hour (6,664 francs a month). 8,324 persons were registered unemployed in 1994.

COMMERCE. Total trade (1994, in 1m. francs): imports, 3,745; exports, 222.

Tourism. Total number of visitors (1993), 54,000.

COMMUNICATIONS

Roads. There were (1996) 356 km of national and 366 km of departmental roads. In 1989 there were 23,520 passenger cars, 1,568 trucks and 121 buses.

Civil Aviation. In 1993, 145,115 passengers and 3,656 tonnes of freight arrived, and 154,927 passengers and 1,533 tonnes of freight departed by air at Rochambeau International Airport (Cayenne). Services are provided by Air France, Cruzeiro do Sol and Suriname Airways. There are regular internal flights to 7 other airports. The base of the European Space Agency (ESA) is located near Kourou and has been operational since 1979.

Shipping. 359 vessels arrived and departed in 1993; 249,160 tonnes of petroleum products and 230,179 tonnes of other products were discharged, and 69,185 tonnes of freight loaded. Chief ports: Cayenne, St-Laurent-du-Maroni and Kourou. There are also inland waterways navigable by small craft.

Telecommunications. The number of telephones (1989) was 26,146. *Radiodiffusion Française d'Outre-Mer-Guyane* broadcasts for 133 hours each week on medium- and short-waves, and FM in French. Television is broadcast for 60 hours each week on 2 channels. In 1993 there were 44,000 radio and 6,500 TV receivers; colour is by SECAM.

Press. There was (1996) 1 daily newspaper with a circulation of 1,000, and a second paper published 4 times a week has a circulation of 5,500.

SOCIAL INSTITUTIONS

Justice. At Cayenne there is a *tribunal d'instance* and a *tribunal de grande instance*, from which appeal is to the regional *cour d'appel* in Martinique.

Religion. In 1984, 77·6% of the population was Roman Catholic, 4% Protestant.

Education. Primary education is free and compulsory. There were 24,000 children at primary schools in 1993; 12,000 at secondary schools; and (1988) a further 2,224 registered at private schools. In 1993 644 students from French Guiana attended the Henri Visioz Institute, which forms part of the University of Antilles-Guyana (8,290 students in 1993).

Health. In 1995 there were 2 hospitals with 567 beds, 3 private clinics and a care centre. There were (1986) 160 doctors, 44 dentists, 33 pharmacists, 29 midwives and 496 nursing personnel.

MARTINIQUE

KEY HISTORICAL EVENTS. Discovered by Columbus in 1502, Martinique became a French colony in 1635, and apart from brief periods of British occupation the island has since remained under French control. On 19 March 1946 its status was altered to that of an Overseas Department.

TERRITORY AND POPULATION. The island, situated in the Lesser Antilles between Dominica and St Lucia, occupies an area of 1,128 sq. km. Population at last census (1990), 359,579; estimate (July 1997), 402,984. Population of principal towns: the capital and main port Fort-de-France, 101,540; Le Lamentin, 30,026; Schoelcher, 19,825; Sainte-Marie, 19,683; Rivière-Pilote, 11,261; La Trinité, 10,330.

Vital statistics (1992): Live births 6,305; deaths 2,180; marriages 1,646.

French is the official language but the majority of people speak Creole.

CLIMATE. *Fort-de-France.* Jan. 74°F (23·5°C), July 78°F (25·6°C). Annual rainfall 72" (1,840 mm).

CONSTITUTION AND GOVERNMENT. The island is administered by a *General Council* of 45 members directly elected for 6-year terms, and by a Regional Council of 42 members. The French government is represented by an appointed Prefect. There are 4 *arrondissements*, sub-divided into 45 cantons and 34 communes, each administered by an elected municipal council. Martinique is represented in the National Assembly by 4 deputies, in the Senate by 2 senators, on the Economic and Social Council by 1 councillor.

Prefect: Jean-François Cordet.
President of the General Council: Claude Lise (PPM).
President of the Regional Council: Emile Capgras (PCM).

ECONOMY

Performance. In 1993 the GDP was 22,969m. French francs. GDP per capita (1993) was 60,861 French francs.

Banking and Finance. The Institut d'Émission des Départements d'Outre-Mer is the official bank. The Caisse Centrale de Développement is the government's vehicle for the promotion of economic development in the region. There were 4 commercial banks, 6 credit societies and 1 savings bank in 1995.

ENERGY AND NATURAL RESOURCES

Electricity. Total production (1993): 818m. kWh.

Agriculture. Chief products: bananas, rum, sugar, pineapples, food and vegetables. In 1993 there were 3,223 ha under sugar-cane, 8,500 ha under bananas and 600 ha under pineapples. Production (1993 in tonnes): sugar, 6,626; sugar-cane, 227,076; bananas (1992), 228,000; pineapples (1992), 28,500.

Livestock (1993): 36,000 cattle, 36,200 sheep, 21,200 pigs, 16,500 goats and 263,000 poultry.

Forestry. Forests comprise 42% of the land area. Production (1993): 5,000 cu. metres of wood.

Fisheries. Total catch (1992): 4,553 tonnes.

INDUSTRY. Some food processing and chemical engineering is carried out by small and medium-size businesses. There were 9,443 businesses in 1993 (30% in building). There is an important cement industry; 12 distilleries for rum; and an oil refinery, with an annual treatment capacity of 0·75m. tonnes. Martinique has 5 industrial zones.

Labour. The economically active population in 1994 was 164,870 (75% in trade and commerce; 10% in agriculture). In 1997 the minimum wage (SMIC) was 6,664 francs a month (39·29 an hour). 43,762 persons were registered unemployed in 1994.

COMMERCE. In 1994 imports were valued at 9,092m. francs; exports at 1,216m. The main imports are crude petroleum and foodstuffs; main exports (as % of total): petroleum products (14%, 1987), bananas (40%), rum (8%). Trade with France (1991): 62·1% of imports; 57% of exports; a further 31·5% of exports in 1991 went to Guadeloupe.

Tourism. In 1993 there were 816,423 tourists, including 428,695 cruise visitors.

COMMUNICATIONS

Roads. In 1995 there were 1,606 km of roads, of which 1,200 km were surfaced. 252 km were classified as national routes and 862 km as first-class roads. In 1992 there were 12,591 passenger cars and 2,443 commercial vehicles registered.

Civil Aviation. There is an international airport at Fort-de-France (Lamentin). In 1993, 1,488,834 passengers arrived. Services are provided by Air Canada, Air France, Air Guadeloupe, Air Liberté, Air Martinique, American Airlines, AOM and LIAT.

Shipping. The island is visited regularly by French, American and other lines. In 1993, 2,856 vessels called at Martinique and discharged 80,605 passengers and 1,612,000 tonnes of freight, and embarked 82,119 passengers and 789,000 tonnes of freight.

Telecommunications. There were estimated to be 209,672 telephones in 1994. *Radio Diffusion Française d'Outre-Mer* broadcasts on FM wave, and operates 2 channels (1 satellite). There are also 2 commercial TV stations. In 1993 there were 60,000 radio and 65,000 TV receivers (colour by SECAM).

Press. In 1996 there was 1 daily newspaper with a circulation of 30,000.

SOCIAL INSTITUTIONS

Justice. Justice is administered by 2 lower courts (*tribunaux d'instance*), a higher court (*tribunal de grande instance*), a regional court of appeal, a commercial court and an administrative court.

Religion. In 1997, 95% of the population was Roman Catholic.

Education. Education is compulsory between the ages of 6 and 16 years. In 1994, there were 51,824 pupils in 263 nursery and primary schools, and 43,384 pupils in 61 secondary schools. There were 29 institutes of higher education. In 1993, 3,670 students from Martinique were registered at the University of Antilles-Guyana (out of a total of 8,290).

Health. In 1994 there were 19 hospitals (including 1 central, 13 general and

5 maternity), 3 private clinics, 1 rest home and 1 rehabilitation centre. There were (1991) 3,747 hospital beds, 625 doctors, 199 pharmacists, 121 dentists and 130 midwives.

Further Reading

Crane, J., *Martinique*. [Bibliography]. Oxford and Santa Barbara (CA), 1995

RÉUNION

KEY HISTORICAL EVENTS. Réunion (formerly Île Bourbon) became a French possession in 1638 and remained so until 19 March 1946, when its status was altered to that of an Overseas Department.

TERRITORY AND POPULATION. The island of Réunion lies in the Indian Ocean, about 880 km east of Madagascar and 210 km south-west of Mauritius. It has an area of 2,504 sq. km. Population at the 1990 census: 597,828; 1996 estimate, 700,000; projection (2025), 900,000. The capital is Saint-Denis (population, 1995: 207,158); other large towns are Saint-Pierre (192,462), Saint-Paul (113,071) and le Tampon (47,577).

Vital statistics (1994): Live births, 13,330; deaths, 3,410; marriages, 3,284.

The islands of Juan de Nova, Europa, Bassas da India, Îles Glorieuses and Tromelin, with a combined area of 32 sq. km, are uninhabited and lie in the Indian Ocean adjacent to Madagascar. They remained French after Madagascar's independence in 1960, and are now administered by the Commissioner of Réunion. Both Mauritius and the Seychelles lay claim to Tromelin; and Madagascar claims all 5 islands.

CLIMATE. A sub-tropical maritime climate, free from extremes of weather, though the island lies in the cyclone belt of the Indian Ocean. Conditions are generally humid and there is no well-defined dry season. Saint-Denis. Jan. 80°F (26·7°C), July 70°F (21·1°C). Annual rainfall 56" (1,400 mm).

CONSTITUTION AND GOVERNMENT. Réunion is administered by a General Council of 44 members directly elected for 6-year terms, and by a Regional Council of 45 members. Réunion is represented in the National Assembly in Paris by 5 deputies; in the Senate by 3 senators; in the Economic and Social Council by 1 councillor. There are 4 *arrondissements* sub-divided into 47 cantons and 24 communes, each administered by an elected municipal council. The French government is represented by an appointed Commissioner.

Prefect: Hubert Fournier.
President of the General Council: Christophe Payet.
President of the Regional Council: Marguerite Demaiche-Sudre (SE).

ECONOMY

Performance. In 1994 the GDP was 35,266m. French francs. GDP per capita (1993) was 52,946 French francs.

Currency. The French franc is in use.

Banking and Finance. The Institut d'Émission des Départements d'Outre-mer has the right to issue bank-notes. Banks operating in Réunion are the Banque de la Réunion (Crédit Lyonnais), the Banque Nationale de Paris Intercontinentale, the Caisse Régionale de Crédit Agricole Mutuel de la Réunion, the Banque Française Commerciale (BFC) CCP, Trésorerie Générale, and the Banque de la Réunion pour l'Economie et la Développement (BRED).

ENERGY AND NATURAL RESOURCES

Electricity. Production (1996), 1,385·8m. kWh.

Agriculture. Production of sugar was 204,608 tonnes in 1996; rum, 70,005 hectolitres (pure alcohol) in 1994. Other important products (1994, in tonnes): tobacco, 37; potatoes, 335; geranium oil, 5·3; onions, 2,415; pineapples, 6,781; vanilla (1993), 114·8; maize (1992), 13,270.

Livestock (1992): 18,600 cattle, 94,480 pigs, 31,200 sheep and 366,700 poultry. Meat production (1993, in tonnes): beef 1,206, pork 9,850, goat (1989, 13,000) and poultry 14,080. Milk production (1993), 85,512 hectolitres.

Forestry. There were (1994) 101,000 ha of forest.

Fisheries. In 1994 the catch was 5,195 tonnes.

INDUSTRY. The major industries are electricity and sugar. Food processing, chemical engineering, printing and the production of perfume, textiles, leathers, tobacco, wood and construction materials are carried out by small and medium-sized businesses. At the beginning of 1994 there were 9,465 craft businesses employing about 20,000 persons.

Labour. The workforce was 264,200 in 1993. The minimum wage (SMIC) was 39·29 francs an hour (6,664 a month) In 1997. On 1 Jan. 1997, 96,330 persons were registered unemployed, a rate of 36·7%.

COMMERCE. Trade in 1m. French francs:

	1994	1995	1996
Imports	13,070	13,494	14,214
Exports	954	1,036	1,071

The chief export is sugar, accounting for 57% of total exports (1994). In 1994 67% of imports and 74% of exports were from and to France.

Tourism. Tourism is a major resource industry. There were 397,000 visitors in 1996 (82% French).

COMMUNICATIONS

Roads. There were, in 1994, 2,724 km of roads. In Jan. 1997 there were 208,300 registered vehicles.

Civil Aviation. Réunion is served by Air France, AOM French Airlines, Air Liberté, Corsair, Air Austral, Air Mauritius and Air Madagascar. In 1996, 629,034 passengers and 13,678 tonnes of freight arrived at, and 624,703 passengers and 4,396 tonnes of freight departed from, Roland Garros Saint-Denis airport.

Shipping. 585 vessels visited the island in 1995, unloading 1,961,000 tonnes of freight and loading 388,200 tonnes at Port-Réunion.

Telecommunications. There were (1994) 720 post offices and a central telephone office; number of telephones, 209,672. *Radiodiffusion Française d'Outre-Mer* broadcasts in French on medium- and short-waves for more than 18 hours a day. There are 4 television channels and 1 independent channel.

Cinemas. In 1995 there were 17 cinemas.

Press. There were (1994) 4 daily newspapers, 1 weekly, 1 monthly and 3 periodicals.

SOCIAL INSTITUTIONS

Justice. There are 3 lower courts (*tribunaux d'instance*), 2 higher courts (*tribunaux de grande instance*), 1 appeal, 1 administrative court and 1 conciliation board.

Religion. In 1990, 95% of the population was Roman Catholic.

Education. In 1994-95 there were 343 primary schools with 117,562 pupils. Secondary education was provided in 21 *lycées,* 64 colleges, and 16 technical *lycées,* with, together, 92,281 pupils. The *Université Française de l'Océan Indien* (founded 1971) had 11,291 students in 1994–95.

Health. In 1994 there were 19 hospitals with 2,902 beds, 1,119 doctors, 292 dentists, 250 pharmacists, 155 midwives and 2,684 nursing personnel.

Further Reading

Institut National de la Statistique et des Etudes Economiques: *Tableau Economique de la Réunion.* Paris (annual)
Bertile, W., *Atlas Thématique et Régional.* Réunion, 1990

TERRITORIAL COLLECTIVITIES

MAYOTTE

KEY HISTORICAL EVENTS. Mayotte was a French colony from 1843 until 1914, when it was attached, with the other Comoro islands, to the government-general of Madagascar. The Comoro group was granted administrative autonomy within the French Republic and became an Overseas Territory. When the other 3 islands voted to become independent (as the Comoro state) in 1974, Mayotte voted against this and remained a French dependency. In Dec. 1976, it became (following a further referendum) a Territorial Collectivity.

TERRITORY AND POPULATION. Mayotte, east of the Comoro Islands, consists of a main island (362 sq. km) with (1991 census) 94,385 inhabitants (estimate 1996, 121,700) containing the chief town, Mamoudzou (20,274 inhabitants); and the smaller island of Pamanzi (11 sq. km) lying 2 km to the east (9,775 in 1985) containing the old capital of Dzaoudzi (8,268). The whole territory covers 373 sq. km (144 sq. miles).

The spoken language is Mahorian (akin to Comorian, an Arabized dialect of Swahili), but French remains the official and commercial language.

CONSTITUTION AND GOVERNMENT. The island is administered by a General Council of 17 members, directly elected for a 6-year term. The French government is represented by an appointed Prefect. Mayotte is represented by 1 deputy in the National Assembly and by 1 member in the Senate. There are 17 communes, including 2 on Pamanzi.

Prefect: Philippe Boisadam.

ECONOMY

Currency. Since Feb. 1976 the currency has been the French franc.

Banking and Finance. The Institut d'Emission d'Outre-mer and the Banque Française Commerciale both have branches in Dzaoudzi and Mamoudzou.

ENERGY AND NATURAL RESOURCES

Electricity. Production (1993), 9·64m. kWh.

Agriculture. The area under cultivation in 1994 was 14,550 ha. The chief cash crops are: essence of ylang-ylang (23 tonnes, 1994), vanilla (5·9 tonnes, 1993), coffee (9·2 tonnes, 1985); other important crops are copra, cinnamon and cloves. The main food crops (1985, in tonnes): mangoes (1,500), bananas (1,300), breadfruit (700), cassava (500), pineapples (200).
Livestock (1991): Cattle, 12,000; goats, 15,000; sheep, 3,000; poultry, 30,000.

Forestry. There are some 20,000 ha of forests.

Fisheries. A lobster and shrimp industry was created. Catch (1992): 1,800 tonnes.

INDUSTRY

Labour. In 1994 18·5% of the active population was engaged in public building and works. In 1997 the minimum monthly wage (SMIC) was 39·29 francs an hour (6,664 a month).

COMMERCE. In 1993 exports totalled 15·13m. francs (mainly to France); imports, 573·6m.

Tourism. In 1994 there were 24,464 visitors.

COMMUNICATIONS

Roads. In 1994 there were 93 km of main roads and 137 km of local roads; and 1,528 motor vehicles.

Civil Aviation. There are regular services provided by Air Australe to Réunion and Madagascar, and by Air Comores.

Telecommunications. Broadcasting is conducted by *Radio-Télévision Française d'Outre-Mer* (RFO-Mayotte) with 1 hour a day in Mahorian. There are 2 private radio stations. In 1994 there were 30,000 radio and 3,500 TV receivers; colour is by SECAM.

Press. There was 1 weekly newspaper in 1997.

SOCIAL INSTITUTIONS

Justice. There is a *tribunal de première instance* and a *tribunal supérieur d'appel*.

Religion. The population is 97% Sunni Moslem, with a small Christian (mainly Roman Catholic) minority.

Education. In 1994 there were 25,805 pupils in nursery and primary schools, and 6,190 pupils at 7 *collèges* and 1 *lycée* at secondary level. There were also 1,922 pupils enrolled in pre-professional classes and professional *lycées*. There is a teacher training college.

Health. There were 2 hospitals with 100 beds in 1994. In 1985 there were 9 doctors, 1 dentist, 1 pharmacist, 2 midwives and 51 nursing personnel.

ST PIERRE AND MIQUELON

Îles Saint-Pierre et Miquelon

KEY HISTORICAL EVENTS. The only remaining fragment of the once-extensive French possessions in North America, the archipelago was settled from France in the 17th century. It was a French colony from 1816 until 1976, an overseas department until 1985, and is now a Territorial Collectivity.

TERRITORY AND POPULATION. The archipelago consists of 2 islands off the south coast of Newfoundland, with a total area of 242 sq. km, comprising the Saint-Pierre group (26 sq. km) and the Miquelon-Langlade group (216 sq. km). The population (1990 census) was 6,392, of whom 5,683 were on Saint-Pierre and 709 on Miquelon.1996 estimate, 6,660. The chief town is St Pierre.

Vital statistics (1995): Births, 75; marriages, 17; deaths, 45.

CONSTITUTION AND GOVERNMENT. The territorial collectivity is administered by a General Council of 19 members directly elected for a 6-year term. It is represented in the National Assembly in Paris by 1 deputy, in the Senate by 1 senator, in the Economic and Social Council by 1 councillor. The French government is represented by a Prefect. There are 2 municipal councils.

Prefect: Rémi Thuau.

ECONOMY

Budget. The budget (1995) balanced at 238m. francs.

Currency. The French franc is in use.

Banking and Finance. Banks include the Banque des Îles Saint-Pierre et Miquelon, the Crédit Saint-Pierrais and the Caisse d'Epargne.

ENERGY AND NATURAL RESOURCES

Electricity. Production (1995): 41·9m. kWh.; installed capacity, 23 MW.

Agriculture. The islands, being mostly barren rock, are unsuited for agriculture, but some vegetables are grown and livestock is kept for local consumption.

Fisheries. In June 1992 an international tribunal awarded France a 24-mile fishery and economic zone around the islands and a 10·5-mile-wide corridor extending for 200 miles to the high seas. A Franco-Canadian agreement regulating fishing in the area was signed in Dec. 1994. Catch (1995): 13,900 tonnes, chiefly cod, lumpfish and scallops.

INDUSTRY. In 1994 there were 351 businesses (including 144 services, 69 public works, 45 food trade, 8 manufacturing and 2 agriculture). The main industry, fish processing, resumed in 1994 after a temporary cessation due to lack of supplies in 1992. Aquaculture is in progress.

Labour. The economically active population in 1995 was 2,971. In 1997 the minimum wage (SMIC) was 39·29 francs per hour (6,664 a month). In 1996 11% of the labour force was registered as unemployed.

COMMERCE. Trade in 1m. French francs (1995): imports, 351 (48% from Canada); exports, 25·3 (10·4% to France).

Tourism. There were (1995) 13,760 foreign visitors, including 3,700 cruise visitors.

COMMUNICATIONS

Roads. In 1995 there were 114 km of roads, of which 69 km were surfaced, 2,216 passenger cars and 1,170 commercial vehicles.

Civil Aviation. Air Saint-Pierre connects St Pierre with Montreal, with Halifax and Sydney (Nova Scotia); and there are regular flights to and from St John's (Newfoundland) with Provincial Airlines. The opening of a new airport capable of receiving medium-haul aeroplanes is expected in 1998.

Shipping. St Pierre has regular services to Fortune and Halifax in Canada. In 1995 884 vessels called at St Pierre; 20,400 tonnes of freight were unloaded and 2,600 tonnes were loaded.

Telecommunications. There were 3,773 telephones in 1995. *Radio Télévision Française d'Outre-mer* (RFO) broadcasts in French on medium-waves, and on 2 television channels (1 satellite). There are 34 cable TV channels from Canada and the USA; and a private local radio station (*Radio Atlantique*). In 1995 there were about 4,800 radio and 3,200 TV sets in use.

SOCIAL INSTITUTIONS

Justice. There is a court of first instance and a higher court of appeal at St Pierre.

Religion. The population is chiefly Roman Catholic.

Education. Primary instruction is free. There were, in 1995, 3 nursery and 5 primary schools with 793 pupils; 3 secondary schools with 549 pupils; and 2 technical schools with 152 pupils.

Health. There was (1995) 1 hospital with 44 beds, 1 convalescent home with 20, 1 retirement home with 40; 17 doctors and 1 dentist.

Further Reading

De La Rüe, E. A., *Saint-Pierre et Miquelon*. Paris, 1963
Ribault, J. Y., *Histoire de Saint-Pierre et Miquelon: des Origines à 1814*. St Pierre, 1962

OVERSEAS TERRITORIES

SOUTHERN AND ANTARCTIC TERRITORIES

Terres Australes et Antarctiques Françaises (TAAF)

The Territory of the TAAF was created on 6 Aug. 1955. It comprises the Kerguelen and Crozet archipelagoes, the islands of Saint Paul and Amsterdam (formerly Nouvelle Amsterdam), all in the southern Indian ocean, and Terre Adélie. The administration has its seat in Paris. The Administrator is assisted by a 7-member consultative council which meets twice yearly in Paris; its members are nominated by the Government for 5 years. The 12 members of the Scientific Council are appointed by the Senior Administrator after approval by the Minister in charge of scientific research. The 15-member Polar Environment Committee, which in 1995 replaced the former Consultative Committee on the Environment (est. 1982), meets at least once a year to discuss all problems relating to the preservation of the environment.

The French Institute for Polar Research and Technology was set up to organize scientific research and expeditions in Jan. 1992. The staff of the permanent scientific stations of the TAAF (128 in 1997) is renewed every 6 or 12 months and forms the only population.

Administrateur Supérieur: Pierre Lise.

Kerguelen Islands Situated 48–50° S. lat., 68–70° E. long.; consists of 1 large and 85 smaller islands, and over 200 islets and rocks, with a total area of 7,215 sq. km (2,786 sq. miles) of which Grande Terre occupies 6,675 sq. km (2,577 sq. miles). It was discovered in 1772 by Yves de Kerguelen, but was effectively occupied by France only in 1949. Port-aux-Français has several scientific research stations (60 members). Reindeer, trout and sheep have been acclimatized.

Crozer Islands Situated 46° S. lat., 50–52° E. long.; consists of 5 larger and 15 tiny islands, with a total area of 505 sq. km (195 sq. miles). The western group includes Apostles, Pigs and Penguins islands; the eastern group, Possession and Eastern islands. The archipelago was discovered in 1772 by Marion Dufresne, whose mate, Crozet, annexed it for Louis XV. A meteorological and scientific station (20 members) at Base Alfred-Faure on Possession Island was built in 1964.

Amsterdam and **Saint-Paul Islands** Situated 38–39° S. lat., 77° E. long. Amsterdam, with an area of 54 sq. km (21 sq. miles) was discovered in 1522 by Magellan's companions; Saint-Paul, lying about 100 km to the south, with an area of 7 sq. km (2·7 sq. miles), was probably discovered in 1559 by Portuguese sailors. Both were first visited in 1633 by the Dutch explorer, Van Diemen, and were annexed by France in 1843. They are both extinct volcanoes. The only inhabitants are at Base Martin de Vivies (est. 1949 on Amsterdam Island), including several scientific research stations, a hospital, communication and other facilities (20 members). Crayfish are caught commercially on Amsterdam.

Terre Adélie Comprises that section of the Antarctic continent between 136° and 142° E. long., south of 60° S. lat. The ice-covered plateau has an area of about 432,000 sq. km (166,800 sq. miles), and was discovered in 1840 by Dumont d'Urville. A research station (30 members) is situated at Base Dumont d'Urville, which is maintained by the French Institute for Polar Research and Technology.

NEW CALEDONIA

Nouvelle Calédonie et Dépendances

KEY HISTORICAL EVENTS. New Caledonia was discovered by James Cook on 4 Sept. 1774. The first settlers (English Protestants and French Catholics) came in 1840. New Caledonia was annexed by France in 1853 and, together with most of its former dependencies, became an Overseas Territory in 1958.

TERRITORY AND POPULATION. The territory comprises the island of New Caledonia and various outlying islands, all situated in the south-west Pacific with a total land area of 18,576 sq. km (7,172 sq. miles). The population (1996 census) was 196,836, including 67,151 Europeans (majority French), 86,788 Melanesians (Kanaks), 7,825 Vietnamese and Indonesians, 5,171 Polynesians, 17,763 Wallisians, 15,715 others. Projected population (2025): 300,000. The capital Nouméa had 76,293 inhabitants in 1996.

Vital statistics (1996): Live births, 4,401; marriages, 937; divorces, 156; deaths, 1,020; growth rate, 17·1 (per 1,000 population).

There are 4 main islands (or groups of):

New Caledonia An area of 16,372 sq. km (about 400 km long, 50 km wide) with a population (1996 census) of 173,365. The east coast is predominantly Melanesian; the Nouméa region predominantly European; and the rest of the west coast is of mixed population.

Loyalty Islands 100 km (60 miles) east of New Caledonia, consisting of 3 large islands: Maré, Lifou and Uvéa, and many small islands, it has a total area of 1,981 sq. km and a population of 20,877, nearly all Melanesians, except on Uvéa which is partly Polynesian. The chief culture in the islands is coconuts; the chief export is copra.

Isle of Pines A tourist and fishing centre 50 km (30 miles) to the south-east of Nouméa, with an area of 152 sq. km and a population of 1,671.

Bélep Archipelago About 50 km north-west of New Caledonia, with an area of 70 sq. km and a population of 923.

The remaining islands are very small and have no permanent inhabitants. The largest are the Chesterfield Islands, a group of 11 well-wooded coral islets with a combined area of 10 sq. km, about 550 km west of the Bélep Archipelago. The Huon Islands, a group of 4 barren coral islets with a combined area of just 65 ha, are 225 km north of the Bélep Archipelago. Walpole, a limestone coral island of 1 sq. km, lies 150 km east of the Isle of Pines; Matthew Island (20 ha) and Hunter Island (2 sq. km), respectively 250 km and 330 km east of Walpole, are spasmodically active volcanic islands; and are also claimed by Vanuatu.

At the 1996 census there were 341 tribes (which have legal status under a high chief) living in 160 reserves, covering a surface area of 392,550 ha (21% of total land), and representing about 28·7 % of the population. 80,443 Melanesians belong to a tribe.

New Caledonia has a remarkable diversity of Melanesian languages (29 vernacular), divided into 4 main groups (Northern, Central, Southern and Loyalty Islands). There were 53,556 speakers (1996). The 3 most spoken forms are Drehu (11,338), Nengone (6,377) and Paicî (5,498). A ministerial decision in 1991 introduced local languages into the baccalauréat system. In 1997-98 6 Melanesian languages were taught in schools.

CLIMATE. Nouméa. Jan. 26·8°C, July 21°C (average temp., 24·1°; max., 35·8°; min., 14·5°). Annual rainfall 1,171 mm.

CONSTITUTION AND GOVERNMENT. Following constitutional changes introduced by the French government in 1985 and 1988, the Territory is administered by a High Commissioner assisted by a 4-member Consultative Committee, consisting of the President of the Territorial Congress (as President) and the Presidents of the 3 Provincial Assemblies. The French government is represented by the appointed High Commissioner.

There is a 54-member Territorial Congress consisting of the complete membership of the 3 Provincial Assemblies. Elections were held on 9 July 1995. The electorate was 102,487; turn-out was 70·23%. The Rally for Caledonia in the Republic (RPCR) won 22 seats with 36·41% of votes cast; the Kanak Socialist Front for National Liberation, 12 with 19·21%; New Caledonia for All, 9 with 15·27%, the National Union for Independence, 5 with 9·87%; the National Front, 2 with 3·29%; the Rally for New Caledonia within France, 2 with 3·2%; Socialist Kanak Liberation, 1 with 3·26%; and the Front for the Development of the Loyalty Isles, 1 with 2·12%.

New Caledonia is represented in the French National Assembly by 2 deputies, in the Senate by 1 senator, in the Economic and Social Council by 1 councillor. The Territory is divided into 3 provinces, Nord, Sud and Îles Loyauté, each under a directly elected Regional Council. They are sub-divided into 32 communes administered by locally elected councils and mayors.

In Sept. 1987 the electorate voted in favour of remaining a French possession. Agreement was reached in June 1988 between the French government and representatives of both the European and Melanesian communities on New Caledonia, and confirmed in Nov. 1988 by plebiscites in both France and New Caledonia, under which the territory has been divided into 3 autonomous provinces. A further referendum on full independence is scheduled for 1998.

High Commissioner: Dominique Bur.
President of the Territorial Congress: Harold Martin (RPCR).

ECONOMY

Performance. In 1993 GDP was 15,983m. French francs. GDP per capita (1993) was 86,631 French francs.

Budget. The budget for 1997 balanced at 70,037m. francs CFP.

Currency. The unit of currency is the franc CFP (XPF), with a parity of 18·18 to the French franc. 166,610m. francs CFP were in circulation in Dec. 1996.

Banking and Finance. There is a Banque Calédonienne d'Investissement, and branches of the Westpac Banking Corporation, the Banque Nationale de Paris, the Banque Paribas Pacifique, the Société Générale, Calédonienne de Banque, the Credit Agricole Mutuel and the Banque de la Nouvelle-Calédonie (Bank of Hawaii).

ENERGY AND NATURAL RESOURCES

Electricity. Production (1996): 1,475,807 kWh.

Minerals. The mineral resources are very great: nickel, chrome and iron abound; silver, gold, cobalt, lead, manganese, iron and copper have been mined at different times. The nickel deposits are of special value, being without arsenic. Production (1996, in 1,000 tonnes) of nickel ore, 7,266; the furnaces produced 11,239 tonnes of matte nickel and 42,173 tonnes of ferro-nickel.

Agriculture. 48,715 persons worked in agriculture in 1993, and 228,969 ha of land were under pasture. The chief products are beef, pork, poultry, coffee, copra, maize, fruit and vegetables. Production (1996, in tonnes): Cereals, 1,730; coffee, 37; copra, 345; potatoes, 2,165; squash, 1,508.

Livestock (1991): pigs, 38,252; goats, 16,498; horses, 11,245; deer, 12,523; poultry, 877,364; cattle (1994), 104,977.

Forestry. There are 0·98m. ha of forest. Timber production (1996), 1,244 tonnes.

Fisheries. In 1995 there were 302 fishing boats (1,768 GRT). Catch (1995): 5,292 tonnes. Aquaculture accounts for 25% (964·4 tonnes) of the world prawn market.

INDUSTRY.
Local industries include chlorine and oxygen plants, cement, barbed wire, nails, pleasure and fishing boats, clothing, pasta, household cleaners, beer and

soft drinks, confectionery and biscuits. The principal resource industries are nickel, fishing and tourism.

Labour. The working population (1996) was 64,377. The guaranteed monthly minimum wage was 76,207 francs CFP in Dec. 1997. In 1996 there were 30 industrial disputes and 13,826 working days were lost. There were 15,018 registered unemployed in 1997 (66% under 30 years of age).

COMMERCE. In 1996 the balance of trade showed a deficit of 42,863m. francs CFP. Imports and exports in 1m. francs CFP:

	1994	1995	1996	1997
Imports	87,305	86,896	93,088	97,700
Exports	41,706	51,235	50,225	55,912

In 1997 41·9% of imports came from France, 13·3% from Australia; and 28·2% of exports went to France. Refined minerals (mainly ferro-nickel and nickel) accounted for 52% of exports; nickel ore, 26·8%; mattes, 13·1%.

Tourism. Visitors (1996), 91,121 (30% French, 29% Japanese, 15·8% Australian). There were (1996) 76 hotels providing 2,075 beds.

COMMUNICATIONS

Roads. There were (1996) 5,764 km of road, and 70,000 vehicles. In 1996 there were 623 road accidents and 42 fatalities.

Civil Aviation. New Caledonia is connected by air routes with France and Tahiti (by Air France, AOM and Corsair), with Australia (Air France, Air Calédonie International and Qantas), with New Zealand (Air France, Air Calédonie International and Air New Zealand), with Fiji and Wallis and Futuna (Air Calédonie International), with Vanuatu (Air France) and Nauru (Air Nauru). Internal services connect Nouméa with 25 domestic airfields. In 1996, there were 3,197 international movements via La Tontouta international airport, near Nouméa, carrying 311,538 passengers and 4,462 tonnes of freight.

Shipping. 552 vessels entered Nouméa in 1996, unloading 1,091,400 tonnes of cargo and loading 4,950,700 tonnes.

Telecommunications. There were (1996) 42 post offices and 45,574 telephones. *Radio Télévision Française d'Outre-Mer* broadcasts in French on medium- and short-wave radio, and on 2 television channels; colour is by SECAM. There are also 3 commercial radio stations and 1 commercial TV channel (*Canal Plus*). There were 40,000 TV sets in 1996; 0·09m. radios in 1991.

Cinemas. There were 12 cinemas and 1 mobile cinema in 1994.

Press. In 1997 there was 1 daily newspaper.

SOCIAL INSTITUTIONS

Justice. There are courts at Nouméa, Koné and Wé (on Lifou Island), a court of appeal, a labour court and a joint commerce tribunal. There were 3,413 cases judged in the magistrates courts in 1996; 207 went before the court of appeal, 41 were sentenced in the court of assizes.

Religion. There were about 0·1m. Roman Catholics in 1994.

Education. In 1996 there were 36,139 pupils and 1,622 teachers in 279 primary schools; 26,276 pupils and 2,201 teachers in 69 secondary schools; and 1,749 students at university with 79 teaching staff; a further 68 were engaged in private further education. The state-funded French University of the Pacific (UFP) was founded in 1987 and comprises 2 campuses: 1 in New Caledonia (1,059 students in 1996); the other in French Polynesia. The South Pacific University Institute for Teacher Training, part of UFP, is based in Nouméa; there are 2 other colleges, in French Polynesia and Wallis and Futuna.

Welfare. There are 3 forms of social security cover: Free Medical Aid provides total sickness cover for non-waged persons and low-income earners; the Family Benefit, Workplace Injury and Contingency Fund for Workers (CAFAT); and numerous mutual benefit societies. In 1996 Free Medical Aid paid 53,055 beneficiaries a total of 8,298m. francs CFP; CAFAT paid 147,782 beneficiaries 12,874m. francs CFP in sickness cover.

Health. In 1996 there were 362 doctors, 107 dentists, 74 pharmacists, 61 midwives and 1,208 paramedical personnel; there were 26 socio-medical districts, with 4 hospitals, 3 private clinics and 1,173 beds.

Further Reading

Institut Territorial de la Statistique et des Etudes Economiques: *Journal Officiel de la Nouvelle Calédonie; Tableaux de l'Economie Calédonienne/New Caledonia: Facts & Figures (TEC 97)* (every 3 years); *Informations Statistiques Rapides de Nouvelle-Calédonie* (monthly).
Dommel, D., *La Crise Calédonienne: Démission ou Guérison?* Paris, 1993

Local statistical office: Institut Territorial de la Statistique et des Études Économiques, BP 823, 98845 Nouméa.

FRENCH POLYNESIA

Territoire de la Polynésie Française

KEY HISTORICAL EVENTS. French protectorates since 1843, these islands were annexed to France 1880–82 to form 'French Settlements in Oceania', which opted in Nov. 1958 for the status of an overseas territory within the French Community.

TERRITORY AND POPULATION. The total land area of these 5 archipelagoes comprising 120 islands and atolls, scattered over a wide area in the Eastern Pacific, is 4,167 sq. km. The population (1996 census) was 219,521 (105,587 females). Projected population (2025), 300,000.

Vital statistics (1987): Births, 5,384; marriages, 1,251; deaths, 980; annual growth rate (1995), 1·9%.

The official languages are French and Tahitian.

The islands are administratively divided into 5 *circonscriptions* as follows:

Windward Islands (Îles du Vent) (162,398 inhabitants in 1995) comprise Tahiti with an area of 1,042 sq. km and (1988) 115,820 inhabitants; Moorèa with an area of 132 sq. km and 7,059 inhabitants; Maio (Tubuai Manu) with an area of 9 sq. km and 190 inhabitants, and the smaller Mehetia and Tetiaroa. The capital is Papeete (78,814 inhabitants including suburbs).

Leeward Islands (Îles sous le Vent) comprise the volcanic islands of Raiatéa, Tahaa, Huahine, Bora-Bora and Maupiti, together with 4 small atolls, the group having a total land area of 404 sq. km and 25,745 inhabitants in 1995. The chief town is Uturoa on Raiatéa. The Windward and Leeward Islands together are called the Society Archipelago (Archipel de la Société). Tahitian, a Polynesian language, is spoken throughout the archipelago and used as a *lingua franca* in the rest of the territory.

Tuamotu Archipelago consists of 2 parallel ranges of 78 atolls lying north and east of the Society Archipelago, and has a total area of 690 sq. km (14,008 inhabitants in 1995). The most populous atolls are Rangiroa, Hao and Turéia. The Mururoa and Fangataufa atolls in the south-east of the group were ceded to France in 1964 by the Territorial Assembly, and were used by France for nuclear tests from 1966-96. The cessation of nuclear testing marked the end of activities of the Pacific Testing Centre in French Polynesia.

The *circonscription* also includes the Gambier Islands further east, with an area of 36 sq. km; the chief centre is Rikitea on the main island of Mangareva.

Austral or Tubuai Islands lying south of the Society Archipelago, comprise a 1,300 km chain of volcanic islands and reefs. They include Rimatara, Rurutu, Tubuai,

Raivaevae and, 500 km to the south, Rapa-Iti, with a combined area of 148 sq. km (7,219 inhabitants in 1995); the chief centre is Mataura on Tubuai.

Marquesas Islands lying north of the Tuamotu Archipelago, with a total area of 1,049 sq. km and 8,612 inhabitants in 1995, comprise Nukuhiva, Uapu, Uahuka, Hivaoa, Tahuata, Fatuhiva and 4 smaller (uninhabited) islands; the chief centre is Taiohae on Nukuhiva.

CLIMATE. Papeete. Jan. 81°F (27·1°C), July 75°F (24°C). Annual rainfall 83" (2,106 mm).

CONSTITUTION AND GOVERNMENT. Under the 1984 Constitution, the Territory is administered by a Council of Ministers, whose President is elected by the Territorial Assembly from among its own members; the President appoints a Vice-President and 9 other ministers. There is an advisory Economic and Social Committee. French Polynesia is represented in the French Assembly by 2 deputies, in the Senate by 1 senator, in the Economic and Social Council by 1 councillor. The French government is represented by a High Commissioner. The Territorial Assembly comprises 41 members elected every 5 years from 5 constituencies by universal suffrage, using the same proportional representation system as in metropolitan French regional elections. To be elected a party must gain at least 5% of votes cast. The Assembly elects a head of local government.

A statute drafted at the end of 1995 proposes to create French Polynesia as an Autonomous Overseas Territory in which the President of the Council of Ministers will become the President of the territory.

Elections were held on 12 May 1996. The electorate was 125,000. 412 candidates stood. Rassemblement pour le Peuple (RPP; affiliated to the French Rassemblement pour la République) won 18 seats with 31·41% of votes cast; Polynesian Union, 14 with 23·27%; New Fatherland (NF), 5 with 12·28%; Independent Liberation Front of Polynesia, 4 with 11·43%. An RPR-NF coalition was subsequently formed under Gaston Flosse (RPR).

High Commissioner: Paul Roncière.
President of the Council of Ministers: Gaston Flosse (RPR).

DEPENDENCY. The uninhabited Clipperton Island, 1,000 km off the west coast of Mexico, is administered by the High Commissioner for French Polynesia but does not form part of the Territory; it is an atoll with an area of 5 sq. km.

ECONOMY

Performance. In 1993 GDP was 18,110m. French francs. GDP per capita (1993) was 86,240 French francs.

Currency. The unit of currency is the franc CFP (XPF), with a parity of CFP francs 18·18 to the French franc.

Banking and Finance. Commercial banks include Indosuez, the Bank of Tahiti, Banque de Polynésie, Paribas Polynésie, Société de Crédit et de Développement de l'Océanie, and Westpac Banking Corp.

ENERGY AND NATURAL RESOURCES

Electricity. Production (1993): 323·4m. kWh (18% hydroelectric).

Agriculture. An important product is copra (coconut trees cover the coastal plains of the mountainous islands and the greater part of the low-lying islands); production (1993) 10,055 tonnes. Tropical fruits, such as bananas, pineapples and oranges, are grown for local consumption.

Livestock (1993): Cattle, 7,000; pigs, 16,800; goats, 12,000; (1990) sheep, 2,000; poultry, 1m.

Fisheries. There are about 400 traditional fishermen. Catch (1993 estimate): 3,240 tonnes. Industrial fishing is carried out by foreign fleets.

COMMERCE. Total exports (1993), 15,252m. francs CFP; total imports, 86,905m. francs CFP. The chief exports are coconut oil and cultured pearls (599,436 grammes of pearls were exported in 1990). Major trading partners: France and the USA, with France accounting for over 50% of imports, and around 44% of exports.

Tourism. Tourism is very important, earning almost half as much as visible exports. There were (1993) 147,800 visitors, including 49,200 from North America, 58,200 from Europe and 16,100 from Japan.

COMMUNICATIONS

Roads. There were estimated to be 792 km of roads in 1995.

Civil Aviation. Air France and 8 other international airlines connect Tahiti International Airport with Paris, Los Angeles, San Francisco and many Pacific locations. Local companies connect the islands with services from secondary airports at Bora-Bora, Rangiroa and Raiatea. In 1993, 473,903 international passengers arrived and departed via the airports at Faaa, and on Mooréa and Bora-Bora. Some 30 other airfields have regular domestic services.

Shipping. Several shipping companies connect France, San Francisco, New Zealand, Japan, Australia, South East Asia and most Pacific locations with Papeete.

Telecommunications. Number of telephones (1985), 28,192. *Radio Télévision Française d'Outre-mer* (RFO) broadcasts in French, Tahitian and English. There are also 9 private radio stations. Number of receivers (1991): radio, 90,000; TV, 26,500.

Press. In 1993 there were 2 daily newspapers.

SOCIAL INSTITUTIONS

Justice. There is a *tribunal de première instance* and a *cour d'appel* at Papeete.

Religion. In 1980 46·5% of inhabitants were Protestants, 39·4% Roman Catholic and 5·1% Mormon.

Education. There were (1991-92) 32,544 pupils in 235 primary schools and 12,933 pupils in 23 secondary schools. The French University of the Pacific (UFP), founded in 1987, has 2 campuses, one in French Polynesia (the other in New Caledonia). The South Pacific University Institute for Teacher Training, founded in 1992 (part of UFP) has 3 colleges: in French Polynesia, Wallis and Futuna, and in Nouméa (New Caledonia), where it is headquartered.

Health. There were (1991) 1 territorial hospital centre, 6 general hospitals, 1 psychiatric hospital and 22 medical centres and dispensaries; in 1987 there were 273 doctors, 88 dentists, 35 pharmacists, 24 midwives and 464 nursing personnel.

Further Reading

Bounds, J. H., *Tahiti.* Bend, Oregon, 1978
Luke, Sir Harry, *The Islands of the South Pacific.* London, 1961
O'Reilly, P. and Reitman, E., *Bibliographie de Tahiti et de la Polynésie française.* Paris, 1967
O'Reilly, P. and Teissier, R., *Tahitiens. Répertoire bio-bibliographique de la Polynésie française.* Paris, 1963

Local statistical office: Institut Territorial de la Statistique, Papeete.

WALLIS AND FUTUNA

KEY HISTORICAL EVENTS. French dependencies since 1842, the inhabitants of these islands voted on 22 Dec. 1959 by 4,307 votes out of 4,576 in favour of exchanging their status to that of an overseas territory, which took effect from 29 July 1961.

TERRITORY AND POPULATION. The territory comprises two groups of islands in the central Pacific (total area 240 sq. km, over 14,000 inhabitants in 1996). The Îles de Hoorn lie 255 km north-east of Fiji and consist of 2 main islands: Futuna (64 sq. km, 5,000 inhabitants) and uninhabited Alofi (51 sq. km). The Wallis Archipelago lies another 160 km further north-east, and has an area of 159 sq. km (9,000 inhabitants). It comprises the main island of Uvéa (60 sq. km; over 1,000 inhabitants) on Uvéa. Wallisian and Futunian are distinct Polynesian languages.

CONSTITUTION AND GOVERNMENT. A Prefect represents the French government and carries out the duties of head of the territory, assisted by a 20-member Territorial Assembly directly elected for a 5-year term, and a 6-member Territorial Council, comprising the 3 traditional chiefs and 3 nominees of the Prefect agreed by the Territorial Assembly. The territory is represented by 1 deputy in the French National Assembly, by 1 senator in the Senate, and by 1 member on the Economic and Social Council. There are 3 districts: Singave and Alo (both on Futuna), and Wallis; in each, tribal kings exercise customary powers assisted by ministers and district and village chiefs. Territorial Assembly elections were held in March 1992. The electorate was 6,972; 5,657 votes were cast.

Prefect: Léon Legrand.
President of the Territorial Assembly: Victor Brial (RPR).

ECONOMY

Budget. The budget for 1997 balanced at 120,100m. French francs.

Currency. The unit of currency is the franc CFP (XPF), with a parity of 18·18 to the French franc.

Banking and Finance. There is a branch of Indosuez at Mata-Utu.

ENERGY AND NATURAL RESOURCES

Electricity. There is a thermal power station at Mata-Utu.

Agriculture. The chief products are copra, cassava, yams, taro roots and bananas.
   Livestock (1993): 25,000 pigs; 7,000 goats.

COMMUNICATIONS

Roads. There are about 100 km of roads on Uvéa.

Civil Aviation. There is an airport on Wallis, at Hihifo, and another near Alo on Futuna. 3 flights a week link Wallis and Futuna. Air Calédonie International operates 2 flights a week to Nouméa.

Shipping. A regular cargo service links Mata-Utu (Wallis) and Singave (Futuna) with Nouméa (New Caledonia).

Telecommunications. There were (1986) 2 radio stations and 6 post offices, and 340 telephones (1985).

SOCIAL INSTITUTIONS

Justice. There is a court of first instance, from which appeals can be made to the court of appeal in New Caledonia.

Religion. The majority of the population is Roman Catholic.

Education. In 1993 there were 3,624 pupils in primary schools and 1,777 in secondary schools. The South Pacific University Institute for Teacher Training, founded in 1992 (part of the French University of the Pacific, UFP) has 3 colleges: in Wallis and Futuna, French Polynesia and Nouméa (New Caledonia), where it is headquartered.

Health. In 1991 there was 1 hospital with 60 beds, and 4 dispensaries.

GABON

République Gabonaise

Capital: Libreville
Population: 1·01m.
GDP per head: (PPP$) 3,641
GNP: US$3·7bn.
HDI/world rank: 0·562/120

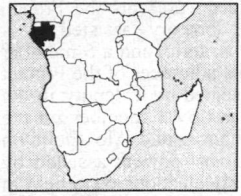

KEY HISTORICAL EVENTS. Between the 16th and 18th centuries, the Fang and other peoples in the region of present-day Gabon were part of a federation of chiefdoms. Some collaborated in the slave-trade, while others suffered from it. The country's capital, Libreville, grew from a settlement of slaves who were rescued from captivity by the French in 1849. Colonized by France around this period, the territory was annexed to French Congo in 1888. There was resistance by the indigenous people between 1905 and 1911 to the depredations of colonial rule, but the country became a separate colony in 1910 as one of the four territories of French Equatorial Africa. Gabon became an autonomous republic within the French Community on 28 Nov. 1958 and achieved independence on 17 Aug. 1960.

TERRITORY AND POPULATION. Gabon is bounded in the west by the Atlantic Ocean, north by Equatorial Guinea and Cameroon and east and south by the Republic of the Congo. The area covers 267,667 sq. km; its population at the 1993 census was 1,014,976 (73% urban); density, 3·8 per sq. km. The capital is Libreville (419,596 inhabitants, 1993 census), other large towns being Port-Gentil (79,225), Franceville (31,183), Oyem (22,404) and Moanda (21, 882).

Growth rate (1993): 2·5%; birth rate (per 1,000 population), 1993: 45·3; death, 16·1; infant mortality, 94 per 1,000 live births. Expectation of life was 52 years for men and 55 for women in 1990.

Provincial areas, populations (in 1,000) and capitals:

Province	Area in Sq. km	Population 1993 census	Capital
Estuaire	20,740	463,187	Libreville
Woleu-Ntem	38,465	97,271	Oyem
Ogooué-Ivindo	46,075	48,862	Makokou
Moyen-Ogooué	18,535	42,316	Lambaréné
Ogooué-Maritime	22,890	97,913	Port-Gentil
Nyanga	21,285	39,430	Tchibanga
Ngounié	37,750	77,781	Mouila
Ogooué-Lolo	25,380	43,915	Koulamoutou
Haut-Ogooué	36,547	104,301	Masuku

The largest ethnic groups are the Fang (25%) and Bapounou (24%) in the north. There are some 40 smaller groups. French is the official language.

CLIMATE. The climate is equatorial, with high temperatures and considerable rainfall. Mid-May to mid-Sept. is the long dry season, followed by a short rainy season, then a dry season again from mid-Dec. to mid-Feb., and finally a long rainy season once more. Libreville. Jan. 80°F (26·7°C), July 75°F (23·9°C). Annual rainfall 99" (2,510 mm).

CONSTITUTION AND GOVERNMENT. At a referendum on electoral reform on 23 July 1995, 96·48% of votes cast were in favour; turn-out was 63·45%. The 1991 Constitution provides for an Executive President directly elected for a 5-year term (renewable once only). The head of government is the Prime Minister who appoints a Council of Ministers. The unicameral *National Assembly* consists of 120 members, directly elected for a 5-year term. There is constitutional provision for the formation of an upper house.

Presidential elections were held on 5 Dec. 1993. The electorate was 484,319. President Bongo was re-elected against 12 opponents with 51·18% of votes cast.

Elections for the National Assembly were held in 2 rounds on 15 and 29 Dec. 1996. The Gabonese Democratic Party (PDG) gained the vast majority of seats.

President: Omar Bongo (PDG; succeeded 2 Dec. 1967, re-elected in 1973, 1979, 1986 and 1993; sworn in 22 Jan. 1994).

The Council of Ministers in March 1998 comprised:

Prime Minister: Dr Paulin Obame-Nguema.

Minister of State for Justice, Keeper of the Seals: Pierre-Louis Okawe. *Minister of State for Foreign Affairs and Co-operation:* Casimir Oye Mba. *Minister of State for Equipment and Construction:* Zacharie Myboto. *Minister of State for Habitat, Lands and Urban Planning and Welfare:* Jean-François Ntoutoume-Emane. *Minister of State for Labour, Human Resources and Training:* Jean-Remy Pendy Bouyiki. *Minister of State for Agriculture, Livestock and Rural Economy:* Emmanuel Ondo Methogo. *Minister of Public Health and Population:* Faustin Boukoubi. *National Defence, Security and Immigration:* Gen. Idriss Ngari. *Interior:* Antoine Mboumbou Miyakou. *Communication, Culture, Art, Education and Human Rights:* Jacques Adiahenot. *Transport and Civil Aviation:* Ndjave Ndjoy. *Finance, Economy and Participation:* Marcel Doupambi Matoka. *Civil Service and Administrative Reform:* Patrice Nziengui. *Commerce, Industry, Small and Medium Size Enterprises, Handicrafts, Reform of the Parastatal Sector and Privatization:* Martin Fidele Magnaga. *Mining, Energy and Oil:* Paul Toungui. *Higher Education and Scientific Research:* Gaston Mozogo Ovono. *Environment and Tourism:* Jean Ping. *Youth and Sports:* Alexandre Sambat. *National Education, Women's Affairs, Spokesperson for the Government:* Paulette Missambo. *Social Affairs and National Solidarity:* Zeng Emone. *Water and Forests:* Andre Berre.

National anthem: 'Uni dans la concorde' ('United in concord'); words and tune by G. Damas.

Local government: The 9 provinces, each administered by a governor appointed by the President, are divided into 37 departments, each under a prefect. Elections were held on 20 Oct. 1996 for departmental assemblies and municipal councils.

DEFENCE

Army. The Army consists of 1 all-arms Presidential Guard battalion group with support units and 8 infantry, 1 airborne commando and 1 engineer company, totalling (1997) 3,200. A referendum of 23 July 1995 favoured the transformation of the Presidential Guard into a republican guard. There is also a paramilitary Gendarmerie of 2,000. France maintains a 600-strong marine infantry battalion.

Navy. The small naval flotilla consists of 1 French-built fast missile craft and 2 coastal patrol craft. The flagship is a French-built medium landing ship, and there are about 3 minor service tenders. A separate Coast Guard operates some 10 small launches. Personnel in 1996 totalled 500.

Air Force. The Air Force has 6 single-seat, 2 two-seat Mirage 5 and 2 Magister ground-attack aircraft, and 1 EMB-111 maritime patrol aircraft. Transport duties are performed primarily by 2 Hercules and 1 EMB-110 Bandeirante turboprop aircraft and 1 CN-235. Single Falcon 900, Gulfstream III and DC-8 aircraft are used for VIP duties. Three T-34C-1 armed turboprop aircraft and a Super Puma are operated for the Presidential Guard. Also in service are 2 Puma, 3 Gazelle, 1 Bell 212, 1 Bell 412 and 2 Alouette III helicopters. Personnel (1996) 1,000.

INTERNATIONAL RELATIONS

Membership. Gabon is a member of the UN and OAU and is an ACP state of the EU.

ECONOMY

Policy. The *Economic and Social Council* was established in 1993 to advise the Council of Ministers. It comprises representatives of central government, local government, employers' groups, trade unions and other interest groups. 5-year development plans, of which there were 5 after 1966, have been replaced by 3-year rolling investment plans.

Budget. The 1994 budget provided for expenditure of 415,000m. francs CFA and revenue of 372,000m. francs CFA. Expenditure (in 1,000m. francs CFA): Current, 315 (administration, 246; debt servicing, 68); capital, 100.

Currency. The unit of currency is the *franc CFA*, with a parity value of 100 francs CFA to 1 French franc. There are coins of 1, 2, 5, 10, 25, 50, 100 and 500 *francs* CFA, and banknotes of 100, 500, 1,000, 5,000 and 10,000 *francs* CFA. 59,690m. francs CFA were in circulation in 1992. Foreign exchange reserves were 21,623m. francs CFA at the end of 1995. Gold reserves were 13,000 troy oz. in March 1992.

Banking and Finance. The *Banque des États de l'Afrique Centrale* is the bank of issue. There are 9 commercial banks. The *Banque Gabonaise de Développement* and the *Union Gabonaise de Banque* are Gabonese-controlled.

ENERGY AND NATURAL RESOURCES

Electricity. The semi-public *Société d'energie et d'eau du Gabon* produced 1,023·9m. kWh. in 1995. In 1994, 78% was from hydro-electric stations.

Oil and Gas. Proven oil reserves (1984) 490m. bbls. Crude oil production, 1995, 344,000 bbls. a day. Natural gas production (1994) was 129m. cu. metres.

Minerals. There are an estimated 200m. tonnes of manganese ore and 850m. tonnes of iron ore deposits; proven reserves of uranium, 35,000 tonnes. Gold, zinc and phosphates also occur. Output, 1995: Manganese ore, 1·9m. tonnes; uranium, 623 tonnes.

Agriculture. There are 0·46m. ha of cultivable land. The major crops (estimated production, 1995, in 1,000 tonnes) are: plantains, 247; cassava, 215; sugar-cane, 170 (1994); palm products, 73; taro, 56; maize, 28; groundnuts, 16. Other important crops include (1994 estimates in tonnes): soya, 1,792; palm oil, 4·9; cocoa, 718; coffee, 260 and rice, 166 (1995).

Livestock (1994): 38,000 cattle, 170,000 sheep, 83,000 goats, 165,000 pigs.

Forestry. Equatorial forests cover 20·4m. ha. 1·44m. cu. metres of timber were produced in 1993.

Fisheries. In 1992 there were 14 fishing vessels over 100 GRT, totalling 2,141 GRT. Industrial fleets account for about 25% of the catch. About 80,000 tonnes of tuna are caught annually.

INDUSTRY. Most manufacturing (5·2% of GDP in 1991) is based on the processing of food (particularly sugar), timber and mineral resources, cement and chemical production and oil refining.

Labour. The workforce in 1993 numbered 308,322 (140,077 female) of whom 41·6% were agricultural. In 1993 the legal minimum monthly wage was 1,200 francs CFA. There is a 40-hour working week.

FOREIGN ECONOMIC RELATIONS. Foreign debt was US$3,818m. in 1993. The government retains the right to participate in foreign investment in oil and mineral extraction.

Commerce. In 1994 imports totalled (in millions of francs CFA) 301,994 and exports 1,152,412. The main exports were worth: crude oil and natural gas, 1,004,387 (accounting for 74% of exports); timber and wood products, 195,677; manganese, 62,434; uranium, 20,069. Imports are mainly industrial goods. In 1991 the main export markets were: France, 31·1%; USA, 27·1%; Netherlands, 6·9%; Chile, 6%;

Japan, 5·4%. Main import suppliers: France, 45·7%; USA, 9·7%; Japan, 6·9%; UK, 6·2%.

Tourism. There were 115,000 foreign visitors in 1993. There were 5,598 tourist beds in 1990.

COMMUNICATIONS

Roads. There were (1992) 7,200 km of roads (614 km asphalted) and in 1990 there were some 22,000 passenger cars and in 1985 9,960 commercial vehicles. There were 896 road accidents in 1990 with 121 fatalities.

Railways. The 657-km standard gauge Transgabonais railway runs from the port of Owendo to Franceville. Total length of railways, 1994, 639 km. In 1995, 175,000 passengers and 3m. tonnes of freight were transported.

Civil Aviation. There are 3 international airports at Port-Gentil, Masuku and Libreville; internal services link these to 65 domestic airfields. The national carrier is Air Gabon (80% state-owned), which in 1995 operated 1 B-727-200 Adv, 1 B-737-200C Adv, 1 B-747-200B Combi, 2 F-28-2000s and 2 other aircraft. 580,168 passengers and 12m. tonnes of freight were carried in and out of Libreville in 1995. Services are also provided by Air Afrique, Air France, Air São Tomé e Príncipe, Cameroon Airlines, Nigeria Airways, Royal Air Maroc, Sabena and Swissair. 398,000 passengers were carried in 1991, including 120,000 on international routes.

Shipping. In 1995 vessels over 100 GRT totalled 37,000 GRT, including 2 tankers totalling 742 GRT. Owendo (near Libreville), Mayumba and Port-Gentil are the main ports. In 1994, 19·8m. tonnes of cargo were handled at the ports. Rivers are an important means of inland transport.

Telecommunications. In 1993 there were 30,000 telephones. Broadcasting is the responsibility of the state-controlled Radiodiffusion Télévision Gabonaise which transmits 2 national radio programmes and provincial services. There is also a commercial radio station and 2 TV channels. In 1993 there were 0·25m. radio and 40,000 TV sets (colour by SECAM).

Press. There was (1993) a government-run daily, *L'Union*, and 4 independent periodicals.

SOCIAL INSTITUTIONS

Justice. There are *tribunaux de grande instance* at Libreville, Port-Gentil, Lambaréné, Mouila, Oyem, Masuku and Koulamoutou, from which cases move progressively to a central Criminal Court, Court of Appeal and Supreme Court, all 3 located in Libreville. Civil police number about 900.

Religion. In 1993 there were 0·66m. Roman Catholics, 0·19m. Protestants and 0·12m. followers of African Christian sects. The majority of the remaining population following animist beliefs. There are about 10,000 Moslems.

Education. Adult literacy was 72·4% in 1993. Education is compulsory between 6–16 years. In 1993 there were 209,700 pupils and 5,242 teachers in primary schools; 36,600 pupils with 1,686 teachers in 73 secondary schools; 8,414 students with 421 teachers in 12 technical schools and 780 students with 43 teachers in 8 teacher-training establishments.

In 1994–95 there was 1 university and 1 university of science and technology, with a total of 2,950 students and 410 academic staff.

Health. In 1985 there were 565 doctors, and in 1977, 20 dentists, 28 pharmacists, 99 midwives and 823 nursing personnel. In 1988 there were 27 hospitals and 633 medical centres, with a total of 5,329 beds.

DIPLOMATIC REPRESENTATIVES

Of Gabon in Great Britain (27 Elvaston Place, London, SW7 5NL)
Ambassador: Honorine Dossou-Naki.

Of Great Britain in Gabon
Ambassador: Nicholas McCarthy, OBE (resides in Yaoundé).

Of Gabon in the USA (2034 20th St., NW, Washington, D.C., 20009)
Ambassador: Paul Boundoukou-Latha.

Of the USA in Gabon (Blvd de la Mer, Libreville)
Ambassador: Elizabeth Raspolic.

Of Gabon to the United Nations
Ambassador: Denis Dangue Rewaka.

Of Gabon to the European Union
Ambassador: Jean-Robert Goulongana.

Further Reading

Barnes, J. F. G., *Gabon: beyond the Colonial Legacy.* Boulder (Colo.), 1992
Gardiner, D. E. (ed.) *Historical Dictionary of Gabon.* 2nd ed. Metuchen (NJ), 1994
Saint Paul, M. A., *Gabon: the Development of a Nation.* London, 1989

National statistical office: Direction Générale de la Statistique et des Etudes Economiques, Ministère de la Planification, de l'Economie et de l'Aménagement du Territoire, Libreville.

THE GAMBIA

Republic of The Gambia

Capital: Banjul
Population: 1·09m.
GDP per head: (PPP$) 939
GNP: US$0·4bn.
HDI/world rank: 0·281/165

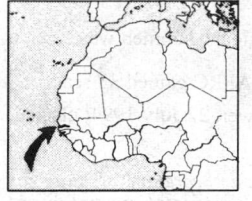

KEY HISTORICAL EVENTS. The Gambia was discovered by the early Portuguese navigators, but they did not settle. During the 17th century various companies of merchants obtained trading charters and established a settlement on the river, which, from 1807, was controlled from Sierra Leone; in 1843 The Gambia became an independent Crown Colony; in 1866 it formed part of the West African Settlements, but in Dec. 1888 it again became a separate Crown Colony. The boundaries were delimited only after 1890. The Gambia achieved full internal self-government on 4 Oct. 1963 and became an independent member of the Commonwealth on 18 Feb. 1965. The Gambia became a republic within the Commonwealth on 24 April 1970. The Gambia with Senegal formed the Senegambia Confederation on 1 Feb. 1982; this was officially dissolved on 21 Sept. 1989.

In a bloodless coup on 22 July 1994 a military junta seized power under the leadership of Lt. Yahya Jammeh; President Dawda Jawara left the country.

TERRITORY AND POPULATION. The Gambia takes its name from the River Gambia, and consists of a strip of territory never wider than 10 km on both banks. It is bounded in the west by the Atlantic Ocean and on all other sides by Senegal. The area is 10,689 sq. km, including 2,077 sq. km of inland water. Population (census, 1993), 1,025,867. Estimate, 1995, 1,087,000; density, 102 per sq. km.

Growth rate (1995) 2·9%; infant mortality (1991), 134 per 1,000 live births. Expectation of life, 1991, 45 years.

The largest ethnic group is the Mandingo, followed by the Wolofs, Fulas, Jolas and Sarahuley. The country is administratively divided into the capital, Banjul (1993 census, 42,326), and the surrounding urban area, Kombo St Mary (228,214), plus 5 other administratrive divisions in rural areas.

The 5 rural divisions, with their areas, populations and chief towns are (listed west to east, or upriver):

Division	Area in Sq. km	Population 1993 census	Chief town
Western	1,764	234,917	Brikama
North Bank	2,256	156,462	Kerewan/Farafenni
Lower River	1,618	65,146	Soma
Central River	2,894	156,021	Jangjangbureh
Upper River	2,069	155,059	Basse

The official language is English.

CLIMATE. The climate is characterized by two very different seasons. The dry season lasts from Nov. to May, when precipitation is very light and humidity moderate. Days are warm but nights quite cool. The SW monsoon is likely to set in with spectacular storms and produces considerable rainfall from July to Oct., with increased humidity. Banjul. Jan. 73°F (22·8°C), July 80°F (26·7°C). Annual rainfall 52" (1,295 mm).

CONSTITUTION AND GOVERNMENT. The 1970 constitution provided for an executive *President* elected directly for renewable 5-year terms. The then President appoints a *Vice-President* who is the government's chief minister. The single-chamber *House of Assembly* has 51 members: 36 elected, 8 nominated (these are from different fields of work and are selected by the Head of State), 5 Head Chief members (nominated by the Head of State), the Attorney-General and the Speaker (both of whom are nominated).

A referendum of 8 Aug. 1996 approved a new Constitution by 70·4% of votes cast. Under this the number of seats in parliament, now the *National Assembly*, is increased to 45 directly elected members and 4 nominated MPs, and the ban on political parties imposed in July 1994 is lifted. Members of the ruling Military Council resigned from their military positions before joining the Alliance for Patriotic Reorientation and Construction (APRC).

Presidential elections were held on 26 Sept. 1996. President Jammeh was elected against 3 opponents by 55·76% of votes cast.

Parliamentary elections were held on 2 Jan. 1997. The APRC gained 33 seats.

President: Rtd. Col. Yahya Jammeh (APRC; seized power, 22 July 1994; elected, 26 Sept. 1996).

In March 1998 the government comprised:

Head of State: Colonel Yahya Jammeh. *Vice-President, Secretary of State for Health and Social Affairs:* Isatou Njie Saidy. *Office of the President:* Captain Edward Singatey. *Local Government and Lands:* Lamine Bajo. *Interior:* Momodou Bojang. *Finance and Economic Affairs:* Famara Jatta. *Foreign Affairs:* Dr Momodou Lamin Sedat Jobe. *Information and Tourism:* Susan Waffa-Ogoo. *Trade, Industry and Employment:* Dominic Mendy. *Education:* Satang Jow. *Justice and Attorney General:* Hawa Sisay-Sabally. *Works and Communication:* Ebrima Ceesay. *Agriculture and Natural Resources:* Musa Mbenga. *Youth, Sports and Culture:* Yankuba Touray.

National anthem: 'For The Gambia, our homeland'; words by V. J. Howe, tune traditional.

Local Administration. The Gambia is divided into 35 districts, each traditionally under a Chief, assisted by Village Heads and advisers. These districts are grouped into 7 Area Councils containing a majority of elected members, with the Chiefs of the district as *ex-officio* members. The city of Banjul is administered by a City Council.

DEFENCE. The Gambia National Army, 800 strong, has 2 infantry battalions and 1 engineer squadron.

The marine unit of the Army consisted in 1996 of 70 personnel operating 2 ex-Chinese and 2 British-built inshore patrol craft and some boats, based at Banjul.

INTERNATIONAL RELATIONS

Membership. The Gambia is a member of the UN, OAU, Commonwealth, ECOWAS and is an ACP state of the EU.

ECONOMY

Budget. Revenue and expenditure for years ending 30 June are (in 1m. dalasis):

	1988–89	1989–90	1990–91	1991–92
Revenue	565·3	659·6	678·5	807·8
Expenditure	504·8	700·6	644·8	780·6

Currency. The unit of currency is the *dalasi* (GMD), of 100 *bututs*. There are coins of 1, 5, 10, 25 and 50 bututs and 1 dalasi, and notes of 1, 5, 10, 25 and 50 dalasis. Inflation was 5% in 1993. Currency in circulation, 1993, 207·1m. dalasis. Foreign exchange reserves were US$94·03m. in 1992.

Banking and Finance. The Central Bank of The Gambia (founded 1971) is the bank of issue. There are 5 commercial banks: Standard Chartered, BICI Trust Bank, Western Union Monetary Transfer, Arab Gambian Islamic Bank, Continent Bank.

Weights and Measures. The UK imperial system is in common use, but the metric system is being introduced.

ENERGY AND NATURAL RESOURCES

Electricity. Production (1991) 65m. kWh.

Minerals. Heavy minerals, including ilmenite, zircon and rutile, have been discovered in Sanyang, Batokunku and Kartong areas.

Agriculture. About 75% of the population depend upon agriculture, which in 1996/97 contributed 19·73% of GDP. Almost all commercial activity centres upon the marketing of groundnuts, which is the only export crop of financial significance; in 1996, 46,000 tonnes were produced. Cotton is also exported on a limited scale. Rice is of increasing importance for local consumption; production (1996) 18,185 tonnes.

Livestock (1996): 322,256 cattle, 231,398 goats, 166,170 sheep and 520,657 poultry.

Forestry. Forests cover 452,607 ha, 43% of the land area.

Fisheries. Total catch (1996) 38,900 tonnes, of which 2,700 tonnes were from inland waters.

FOREIGN ECONOMIC RELATIONS. Foreign debt was US$379·4m. in 1992.

Commerce. Exports and imports (in 1m. dalasis):

	1987–88	1988–89	1989–90	1990–91
Exports	218·5	316·2	248·2	291·0
Imports	861·6	1,054·2	1,447·3	1,932·7

Chief items of export: Groundnuts, groundnut oil, groundnut cake, cotton lint, fish and fish preparations, hides and skins.

Main export markets, 1992: Belgium, 51·5%; Italy, 19·7%; Japan, 14·3%. Main import suppliers: Hong Kong, 16%; China, 14·8%; UK, 10·1%.

Tourism. Tourism is The Gambia's biggest foreign exchange earner. In 1996/97, 82,207 air chartered tourists visited.

COMMUNICATIONS

Roads. There are 2,990 km of motorable roads, of which 1,718 km rank as allweather roads including 306 km of bituminous surface and 531 km of laterite gravel. Number of licensed motor vehicles (1985): 5,200 private cars, 700 buses, lorries and coaches, 2,000 motorcycles, scooters and mopeds.

Civil Aviation. There is an international airport at Banjul (Yundum). The national carrier is Gambia Airways. Services are also provided by Air Guinée, Air Mauritanie, Air Sénégal, Ghana Airways, Monarch Airlines, Nigeria Airways, Sabena, Swissair, Transportes Aéreos da Guiné-Bissau, Air Afrique, Air Dabia, and Cape Verde Airlines.

Shipping. The chief port is Banjul. Ocean-going vessels can travel up the Gambia River as far as Kuntaur. The merchant marine totalled 2,745 GRT in 1995.

Telecommunications. There are several post offices and agencies; postal facilities are also afforded to all towns. Telephones numbered about 8,000 in 1992.

Radio Gambia, a government owned station, broadcasts in English and some other local languages. There are 4 private commercial radio stations and 3 community radio station. Number of radio receivers (1993, estimate), 180,000. A television station carries programmes in English and some local languages. TV operations started in 1995 and programmes are transmitted countrywide and beyond.

Cinemas. In 1992 there were 15 cinemas.

Press. There is a government-owned daily; an independent newspaper appears 5 times a week, there are two weeklies and several news-sheets and a monthly.

SOCIAL INSTITUTIONS

Justice. Justice is administered by a Supreme Court consisting of a chief justice and puisne judges. The High Court has unlimited original jurisdiction in civil and criminal matters. The Supreme Court is the highest court of appeal and succeeds the judicial committee of the Privy Council in London. There are Magistrates Courts in each of the divisions plus one in Banjul and two in nearby Kombo St Mary's Division —8 in all. There are also resident magistrates in provincial areas. There are also Moslem courts, district tribunals dealing with cases concerned with customary law, and 2 juvenile courts.

The death penalty was abolished in 1993 but restored by decree in 1995.

Religion. About 90% of the population is Moslem. Banjul is the seat of an Anglican and a Roman Catholic bishop. There is a Methodist mission. A few sections of the population retain their original animist beliefs.

Education. Adult literacy was 27·2% in 1991.In 1991–92 there were about 600 primary schools, 16 secondary technical schools and 8 high schools. Higher education institutes comprise The Gambia College, a technical training institute, a management development institute, a multi-media training institute, a hotel training school, and centres for self-development and skills training, and continuing education.

Health. In 1994 there were 2 hospitals, 1 clinic, 10 health centres and some 60 dispensaries.

DIPLOMATIC REPRESENTATIVES

Of The Gambia in Great Britain (57 Kensington Ct., London, W8 5DG)
High Commissioner: John P. Bojang.

Of Great Britain in The Gambia (48 Atlantic Rd., Fajara, Banjul)
High Commissioner: John Wilde.

Of The Gambia in USA (1030, 15th St, NW, Washington, D.C. 2005)
Ambassador: Crispin Corey Johnson.

Of the USA in The Gambia (Fajara (East), Kairaba Ave., Banjul)
Ambassador: Gerald W. Scott.

Of The Gambia to the United Nations
Ambassador: Abdoulie Momodou Sallah.

Of The Gambia to the European Union
Ambassador: Ismaila Ceesay.

Further Reading

The Gambia since Independence 1965–1980. Banjul, 1980
Gamble, D. P., *The Gambia.* [Bibliography] Oxford and Santa Barbara (CA), 1988
Hughes, A. and Perfect, D., *Political History of The Gambia, 1816–1992.* Farnborough, 1993

GEORGIA

Sakartvelos Respublika

(Republic of Georgia)

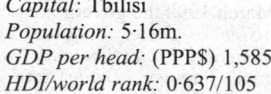

Capital: Tbilisi
Population: 5·16m.
GDP per head: (PPP$) 1,585
HDI/world rank: 0·637/105

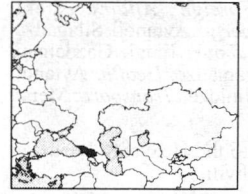

KEY HISTORICAL EVENTS. The independent Georgian Social Democratic Republic was declared on 26 May 1918 and was recognized by the Russian Soviet Federal Socialist Republic on 7 May 1920. A rising in Mingrelia, Abkhazia and Adjaria was put down by Soviet troops. On 25 Feb. 1921 the country was renamed the Georgian Soviet Socialist Republic. On 15 Dec. 1922 Georgia was merged with Armenia and Azerbaijan to form the Transcaucasian Soviet Federal Socialist Republic. In 1936 the Georgian Soviet Socialist Republic became one of the constituent republics of the USSR.

Following nationalist successes at elections in Oct. 1990, the Supreme Soviet resolved in Nov. 1990 to begin a transition to full independence and on 9 April 1991, following a 98·9% popular vote in favour, unanimously declared the republic an independent state based on the treaty of independence of May 1918.

President Zviad Gamsakhurdia was deposed by armed insurrection on 6 Jan. 1992 and a military council took control. After elections in which he gained 95% of votes cast, Eduard Shevardnadze became *de facto* head of state in Oct. 1992. On 22 Oct. 1993 Georgia joined the CIS, a move ratified by parliament on 1 March 1994. Supporters of the deposed president Gamsakhurdia were in intermittent armed conflict with the government, mainly in Mingrelia, but suffered heavy defeats once Russian support became available via the CIS. On 9 Feb. 1998 there was an unsuccessful attempt on the life of Eduard Shevardnadze. Later in the month UN military observers who had been held hostage by opposition forces were released after negotiations with representatives of former president Gamsakhurdia.

TERRITORY AND POPULATION. Georgia is bounded in the west by the Black Sea and south by Turkey, Armenia and Azerbaijan. Area, 69,700 sq. km (26,900 sq. miles). Its population in mid-July 1997 was estimated to be 5,160,000 (2,450,000 male). The capital is Tbilisi (1994 population estimate, 1·3m.). Other important towns (with 1991 population estimates) are Kutaisi (235,000), Rustavi (159,000), Batumi (136,000), Sukhumi (121,000), Poti (54,000), Gori (59,000).

Vital statistics rates, 1997 estimates: Birth, 11·8 per 1,000; death, 13·9 per 1,000; natural increase, −1·1%; infant mortality, 50·1 per 1,000 live births. Life expectancy 65·0 years (male, 62·0 years; female, 68·5 years).

Georgians accounted for 70·1% of the 1989 census population of 5,400,841; others included 8·1% Armenians, 6·3% Russians, 5·7% Azerbaijanis, 3% Ossetians, 1·9% Greeks, 1·8% Abkhazians and 1% Ukrainians. Georgia includes the Autonomous Republics of Abkhazia and Adjaria and the former Autonomous Region of South Ossetia.

CONSTITUTION AND GOVERNMENT. A new Constitution of 24 Aug. 1995 defines Georgia as a presidential republic with federal elements. The head of state is the *President*, elected by universal suffrage for not more than 2 5-year terms. The 235-member parliament is elected by a system combining 85 single-member districts with proportional representation based on party lists. There is a 5% threshold. Presidential and parliamentary elections were held on 5 Nov. 1995. Turnout was 69%. Eduard Shevardnadze was re-elected *President* with 74·9% of votes cast against 5 opponents.

54 parties presented parliamentary candidates. The Citizens' Union gained 106 seats; non-partisans, 45; the National Democratic Party, 34; the All-Georgia Revival Union, 29.

President: Eduard Shevardnadze (b. 1928; Citizens' Union of Georgia).

In March 1998 the government comprised:

Minister of State: Nikoloz Lekishvili. *Education:* Tamaz Kvachantiradze. *Environmental Protection and Natural Resources:* Nino Chkhobadze. *Economy:* Vladimer Papava. *Trade and Foreign Economic Relations:* Konstantine Zaldastanishvili. *Defence:* Varden Nadibaidze. *Communications and Posts:* Pridon Injia. *Culture:* Valeri Asatiani. *Refugees and Resettlement:* Valeri Vashakidze. *Urban Affairs and Construction:* Merab Chkhenkeli. *Foreign Affairs:* Irakli Menagharishvili. *Security:* Jemal Gakhokidze. *State Property:* Avtandil Silagadze. *Agriculture and Food:* Bakur Gulua. *Social Security and Labour:* Tengiz Gazdeliani. *Finance:* Mikheil Chkuaseli. *Internal Affairs:* Kakha Targamadze. *Health:* Avtandil Jorbenadze. *Energy:* David Zubitashvili. *Justice:* Tedo Ninidze. *Transport:* Merab Adeishvili.

National anthem: 'Dideba zetsit kurtheuls' ('Praise be to the Heavenly Bestower of Blessings'); words anonymous, tune by K. Potskhverashvili.

Local Government. Local administration was reorganized in Jan. 1991 into prefectures headed by prefects who report to the central government. Prefects may serve a maximum of two 4-year terms. Villages are administered by councils.

DEFENCE. Conscription is for 2 years. An 8-member *Defence Council* headed by the President was set up in Oct. 1992. In 1997 some 8,500 Russian troops and 2,100 peacekeeping forces were stationed in 3 military bases. The UN has some 117 observers from 23 countries.

Army. Forces of 24,000 are planned. There are 2 Corps HQ, some 6 infantry brigades, 1 artillery brigade and 1 peace-keeping battalion. Equipment includes 48 T-55 and 31 T-72 main battle tanks.

Navy. Former Soviet facilities at Poti have been taken over. The force comprises 2 small frigates, 4 torpedo boats and some 12 patrol vessels. Personnel, 1997, 2,000.

Air Force. Equipment includes 7 Su-25 fighter-bombers, 3 Mi-24 armed helicopters and 4 Mi-8/17 transport helicopters. Personnel, 1997, 3,000.

INTERNATIONAL RELATIONS. A Treaty of Friendship and Co-operation was signed with Russia in Feb. 1994.

Membership. Georgia is a member of the UN, CIS and the NATO Partnership for Peace.

ECONOMY

Policy. A privatization programme was inaugurated in 1995.

Performance. Real GDP growth was 14·3% in 1996.

Budget. The 1996 budget envisaged revenue of 555m. laris and expenditure of 784m. laris.

Currency. The unit of currency is the *lari* (GEL) of 100 *tetri*, which replaced coupons at 1 lari = 1m. coupons on 25 Sept. 1995. There are notes of 1, 2, 5, 10, 20, 50 and 100 lari. Inflation was an annualized 30% in 1996 (183% in 1995). No meaningful exchange rates were available in March 1997.

Banking and Finance. The *Governor* of the Central Bank is Nodar Javakhishvili. In 1996 there were 65 commercial banks. 1 foreign bank had a representative office.

ENERGY AND NATURAL RESOURCES

Electricity. The many fast-flowing rivers provide an important hydro-electric resource. Electricity production in 1996 was 7,100m. kWh.

Oil and Gas. Output (1993) of oil and gas concentrates, 0·1m. tonnes; natural gas (1995 estimate), 3·3m. cu. metres (excluding Abkhazia and South Ossetia). 200,000 tonnes of crude petroleum were produced in 1995.

Minerals. Manganese deposits are calculated at 250m. tonnes. Other important minerals are coal, barytes, clays, gold, diatomite shale, agate, marble, alabaster, iron and other ores, building stone, arsenic, molybdenum, tungsten and mercury. Output of coal in 1995 was estimated to be 42,700 tonnes (excluding Abkhazia and South Ossetia).

Agriculture. Land under cultivation was 4·6m. ha in 1986. Agriculture accounts for about 70% of GDP.

Output of main agricultural products (in 1,000 tonnes) in 1994 (estimates): Watermelons (including melons, pumpkins and squash), 800; grapes, 480; apples, 350; citrus fruits, 260; potatoes, 229; milk, 394 (1993); eggs, 138m. (1993 total).

Livestock on 1 Jan. 1994: Cattle, 1·05m.; pigs, 650,000; sheep and goats, 1·38m.

Forestry. Forest area, 2·4m. ha.

INDUSTRY. There is a metallurgical plant and a motor works. There are factories for processing tea, creameries and breweries. There are also textile and silk industries.

Production in 1993 (in tonnes): Rolled steel, 0·1m.; fertilizer, 0·06m.; cement, 0·3m.; processed meat, 0·7m.; textiles, 16·6m. cu. metres; footwear, 1·4m. pairs. Total output was valued at 129,000m. roubles in 1993.

Labour. The total labour force in 1996 was 2·2m. The unemployment rate was 21%.

FOREIGN ECONOMIC RELATIONS. Total foreign debt was estimated to be $1,600m. in 1996.

Commerce. In 1995 imports were valued at $647m. and exports at $356m. Major commodities imported are fuel, grain and other foods, machinery and parts, and transport equipment. Major commodities for export are iron and steel products, food and beverages, machinery, textiles and chemicals. The main partners for exports are Russia, Turkey, Armenia, Azerbaijan and Bulgaria; and for imports, Russia, Turkey and Azerbaijan. In addition humanitarian food shipments are sent by the EU and the USA.

COMMUNICATIONS

Roads. There were 21,000 km of motor roads in 1995 (19,635 km hard-surfaced).

Railways. Total length was 1,583 km of 1,520 mm gauge in 1994 (1,483 km electrified). In 1994, railways carried 2·7m. tonnes of freight and 9·8m. passengers.

Civil Aviation. The national carrier is Orbi.

Shipping. In 1995, sea-going shipping totalled 0·65m. GRT, of which oil tankers accounted for 0·34m. GRT.

Telecommunications. The government-controlled Georgian Radio broadcasts 2 national and 3 regional programmes, and a foreign service, Radio Georgia (English, Russian). There are local independent TV stations in 10 towns. In 1995 there were 3m. radio receivers and 2·5m. TV receivers.

Cinemas. In 1993 there were 289 cinemas.

Press. In 1995 there were 25 dailies and weeklies.

SOCIAL INSTITUTIONS

Religion. The Georgian Orthodox Church has its own organization under Catholicos (patriarch) Ilya II who is resident in Tbilisi.

Education. In 1996 there were 1,332 pre-primary schools with 10,491 teachers for 81,938 pupils and 3,187 primary schools with 17,950 teachers for 288,509 pupils. There were 441,753 pupils at secondary level and 155,033 students at 76 technical colleges and 23 institutions of higher education. There is 1 university and 1 technical university, with a total of 34,590 students and 6,464 academic staff. Adult literacy rate in 1994 was 94·9%.

Health. There were 29,900 doctors and 57,100 hospital beds in 1994.

Welfare. There were 804,000 age, and 355,000 other, pensioners in 1994.

ABKHAZIA

Area, 8,600 sq. km (3,320 sq. miles); population (Jan. 1990), 537,500. Capital Sukhumi (1990 population, 121,700). This area, the ancient Colchis, saw the establishment of a West Georgian kingdom in the 4th century and a Russian protectorate in 1810. In March 1921 a congress of local Soviets proclaimed it a Soviet Republic, and its status as an Autonomous Republic, within Georgia, was confirmed on 17 April 1930 and again by the Georgian Constitution of 1995.

Ethnic groups (1989 census) Georgians, 45·7%, Abkhazians, 17·8%, Armenians, 14·6% and Russians, 14·3%.

In July 1992 the Abkhazian parliament declared sovereignty under the presidency of Vladislav Ardzinba and the restoration of its 1925 constitution. Fighting broke out as Georgian forces moved into Abkhazia. On 3 Sept. and on 19 Nov. ceasefires were agreed, but fighting continued into 1993 and by Sept. Georgian forces were driven out. On 15 May 1994 Georgian and Abkhazian delegates under Russian auspices signed an agreement on a ceasefire and deployment of 2,500 Russian troops as a peacekeeping force. CIS economic sanctions were imposed in Jan. 1996.

On 26 Nov. 1994 parliament adopted a new Constitution proclaiming Abkhazian sovereignty. Parliamentary elections were held on 23 Nov. 1996 but were not recognized by the Georgian government or the international community.

President: Vladislav Ardzinba (elected by parliament 26 Nov. 1994).

The republic has coal, electric power, building materials and light industries. In 1985 there were 89 collective farms and 56 state farms; main crops are tobacco, tea, grapes, oranges, tangerines and lemons. Crop area 43,900 ha.

Livestock, 1 Jan. 1987: 147,300 cattle, 127,900 pigs, 28,800 sheep and goats.

In 1990–91 there were 16,700 children attending pre-school institutions. There is a university at Sukhumi with 3,000 students and 270 academic staff in 1995–96. In 1990 there were 2,100 students at colleges and 7,700 students at other institutions of higher education.

In Jan. 1990 there were 2,500 doctors and 6,600 junior medical personnel.

ADJARIA

Area, 3,000 sq. km (1,160 sq. miles); population (Jan. 1990), 382,000. Capital, Batumi (1990 population, 137,300). Adjaria fell under Turkish rule in the 17th century, and was annexed to Russia (rejoining Georgia) after the Berlin Treaty of 1878. On 16 July 1921 the territory was constituted as an Autonomous Republic within the Georgian SSR, a status confirmed by the Georgian Constitution of 1995.

Ethnic groups (1989 census): Georgians, 82·8%, Russians, 7·7% and Armenians 4%.

Acting President: Aslan Abashidze.

Elections were held in Sept. 1996. A coalition of the Citizens' Union of Georgia and the All-Georgian Union of Revival gained a majority of seats.

Adjaria specializes in sub-tropical agricultural products. These include tea, mandarines and lemons, grapes, bamboo, eucalyptus, etc. Livestock (Jan. 1990): 112,300 cattle, 6,200 pigs, 7,000 sheep and goats. In 1980 there were 69 collective farms and 21 state farms.

There are shipyards at Batumi, modern oil-refining plant (the pipeline from the Baku oilfields ends at Batumi), food-processing and canning factories, clothing, building materials, drug factories, etc.

The population is almost exclusively Sunni Moslem.

In 1990–91, 77,239 pupils were engaged in study at all levels.

In Jan. 1990 there were 1,700 doctors and 4,400 junior medical personnel.

SOUTH OSSETIA

Area, 3,900 sq. km (1,505 sq. miles); population (Jan. 1990), 99,800 (ethnic groups at the 1989 census, Ossetians, 66·2% and Georgians, 29%). Capital, Tskhinvali (34,000). This area was populated by Ossetians from across the Caucasus (North Ossetia), driven out by the Mongols in the 13th century. The region was set up within the Georgian SSR on 20 April 1922. Formerly an Autonomous Region, its administrative autonomy was abolished by the Georgian Supreme Soviet on 11 Dec. 1990, and it has been named the Tskhinvali Region.

Fighting broke out in 1990 between insurgents wishing to unite with North Ossetia (in the Russian Federation) and Georgian forces. By a Russo-Georgian agreement of July 1992 Russian peacekeeping forces moved into a 7-km buffer zone between South Ossetia and Georgia pending negotiations. An OSCE peacekeeping force has been deployed since 1992.

At elections not recognized by the Georgian government on 10 Nov. 1996 Lyudvig Chibirov (b. 1932) was elected *President*.

Though maintaining a commitment to independence, President Chibirov came to a political agreement with the Georgian government in 1996 that neither force nor sanctions should be applied.

Main industries are mining, timber, electrical engineering and building materials. Crop area, chiefly grains, was 21,600 ha in 1985; other pursuits are sheep-farming (128,500 sheep and goats on 1 Jan. 1987) and vine-growing. There were 14 collective farms and 18 state farms.

In 1989–90 there were 21,200 pupils in elementary and secondary schools. There were 6,525 children in pre-school institutions.

In Jan. 1987 there were 511 doctors and 1,400 hospital beds.

DIPLOMATIC REPRESENTATIVES

Of Georgia in Great Britain (3 Hornton Pl., London W8 4LZ)
Ambassador: Teimuraz Mamatsashvili.

Of Great Britain in Georgia (Metechi Palace Hotel, 380003 Tbilisi)
Ambassador: R. Jenkins, OBE.

Of Georgia in the USA
Ambassador: Tedo Djaparidze.

Of the USA in Georgia (25, Antoneli Street, 380026 Tbilisi)
Ambassador: William H. Courtney.

Of Georgia to the United Nations
Ambassador: Peter Chkheidze.

Of Georgia to the European Union
Ambassador: Zourab Abachidze.

Further Reading
Brook, S., *Claws of the Crab: Georgia and Armenia in Crisis.* London, 1992
Gachechiladze, R., *The New Georgia: Space, Society, Politics.* London, 1995
Lang, D. M., *A Modern History of Georgia.* London, 1962.—*The Georgians.* London, 1966
Nasmyth, P., *Georgia: a Rebel in the Caucasus.* London, 1992
Suny, R. G., *The Making of the Georgian Nation.* 2nd ed. Indiana Univ. Press, 1994

BRITAIN AND GERMANY.
A NEW PARTNERSHIP?

Jochen Thies

There are signs that the special relationship between Germany and France is over. The world has changed dramatically since 1989. Germany has recovered its central position in Europe forging close links with all its thirteen neighbours. France, on the other hand, has felt sidelined since the end of the Cold War and her politicians still have problems in coming to terms with German unification.

It seems inevitable, therefore, that sooner or later the European 'tandem' will be replaced by a vehicle which gives a seat to the United Kingdom. Even before Britain assumed the presidency of the European Union she was seen as a serious European player who in many ways dominated the European agenda while at the same time setting the pace for European development. It follows that the future of the British-German relationship looks good, even bright.

In the next few years Germany will change in ways which are favourable to the United Kingdom. The transfer of the German Parliament and of the government from Bonn to Berlin will transform German politics in mentality and in perceptions. Eastern Europe will be closer, new relationships will be set up and the problems of the Länder in what was East Germany will impress themselves on politicians in a way that would have been impossible had the government stayed in far off Bonn. Moreover, the longstanding domination of the Rhineland and the Catholic south on German politics which dates back to the days of Chancellor Konrad Adenauer, will be over. As Germany looks more towards the East and to the North of Europe so Protestant influences will dominate. Bridges and ferries between Germany and the Scandinavian and Baltic world will ease communications and set up new trade networks. Some people already speak of another Hansiatic League.

Germany will once more become a maritime country. This time, however, it will be for commercial not military purposes. With unification comes hundreds of miles of Baltic coastline. In Mecklenburg-Vorpommern, one of the five new Länder which stretches from Lübeck to the Polish border near Stettin, many ports and marinas will emerge during the coming years. Lakes and other inland waterways offer further opportunities. In a more leisure orientated society, millions of Germans will decide to spend their holidays at home instead of searching for coastal spots in the Netherlands, France or Spain. Maritime thinking in Germany will help towards a better understanding between Germany and the United Kingdom because it will broaden German horizons. A parochial view is no longer possible.

But the transition in Anglo-German relations will not be obstacle free, as anyone who reflects on the recent history of the two countries will readily acknowledge.

As one of the four occupying powers, Great Britain had a great influence on the start of the second German democracy. Even though many institutions are now seen as characteristically German it should be remembered that it was the British example that set the pattern for trade unions, local administration centred around the 'Oberstadtdirektor' and public service broadcasting.

But it was, of course, an enforced relationship, the result of a war which put Great Britain at the heart of continental affairs. It was not a role that Britain welcomed. Her politicians were more used to acting in a world scene and they looked to the USA as a natural partner. In any event, the problems of Empire and the first shrill cries for independence were of greater concern than Europe.

The Germans have always liked to compare themselves with the British and in the last century there have been many attempts by Germany to be accepted as a partner. The British resisted those demands. From their own perspective there was no need for a formal alliance with Bismarck's Kaiserreich even though Disraeli perceived it as more significant than the French Revolution. However, Britain did respond to the naval race which Admiral Tirpitz started in 1898 and half a generation later the two countries were at war. Any hope of restoring a constructive relationship with Germany was wrecked by Nazism. While nearly all the other nations of the continent travelled to Hitler's Berlin Chancellery in 1940 to discuss the new European order, only Churchill resisted.

Thus, a proud history has had a powerful effect on Britain's attitudes to Germany. At the same time Britain still has an apparently never-ending ability to think and act in global terms. Germany, in contrast, does not share this thinking. Recent examples of divergent attitude are the Falklands war, the British involvement in the Gulf and her strong military role in the Balkans just after the civil war. This has led, at least in the past, to an estrangement from Europe and also, therefore, from Germany.

One should not underestimate other factors that have set Britain apart from Germany: the reduction of the British military presence in Germany, the retreat from Berlin, the impact of war films and, not least, changes in the pattern of tourism. Thirty years ago, British tourists on their way to southern Mediterranean destinations crossed Germany by car. Today they take a plane. Educated British youth seems to prefer far flung parts of the world, mainly Asia and Australia, to the traditional European highlights of the Grand Tour. Knowledge of Germany and the German language is restricted to a small minority. Only the soccer stars are able to make Germany popular in the UK. Meanwhile, Great Britain under new Labour has renewed the special relationship with the United States. A younger generation of British politicians find it hard to accommodate themselves to their opposite members in Germany and in France where the post-war elders are still in office.

But Germany has parallel difficulties in focusing a realistic picture of Britain. Influenced by the British mass media even the German quality papers report more about the Royal family than about the political issues. The trend has been enforced by over fifteen years of Conservative politics which were never popular in Germany. 'Thatcherism' was a four letter word, standing for ultra-conservatism and anti-European sentiments, for civil confrontation and for the elbowing-society favoured by the Americans. The Germans were misled into believing that Thatcherism was driving the UK away from Europe. Until recently Germans were unaware that Great Britain under Margaret Thatcher had gone through a tough but relatively successful period. Great Britain today is fitter than Germany for the global challenges of the future. Investors from all over the world, Germany included, are attracted to the UK. As the premier financial centre of Europe, London has done much to secure this pre-eminence. The service sector is the big creator of new jobs and anyone familiar with the City and Docklands knows that these parts of London are more evocative of New York City than any other European capital.

These differences are not the full explanation as to why Germany and the UK have tended to keep their distance. One has to dig deeper into the relationship to find the obstacles. For the English one could argue that it must be hard for the moral winner of 1945 to find that the loser has become the European economic pace-maker. The truth is that Britain cannot forget the Second World War, a feature shared with many European countries such as the Netherlands which came under German rule. Additionally, the British strongly believe in their long-standing parliamentary traditions. They take a great pride in their well-proved institutions and believe that in this respect the Germans have little to offer or no record at all. Can one deny the British the right to be sceptical?

But the world at the millennium offers new opportunities to overcome these differences. Today, Germany is repeating the experiences of the UK in the 1980s. What happened to the British under Margaret Thatcher and to the American economy under Ronald Reagan will also happen in Germany where the realization is dawning that the welfare state cannot expand indefinitely and, indeed, may be unsustainable in its present form.

Germany is already finding it hard and will almost certainly find it harder in the future to hold its economic lead in Europe. At the same time, the United Kingdom is gaining confidence as an economic power. The inferiority complex seems to belong to the past. With monetary union approaching, the political influence of the UK in Europe will grow. The fact that the Germans have, at least in theory, accepted the Thatcher lessons will make it easier to achieve closer forms of cooperation between the two countries.

For Germany in an election year it is natural for the political parties, particularly the Social Democrats, to observe closely political developments in the UK. One of the two prominent figures of the German moderate left, Gerhard Schröder, the Ministerpräsident of Lower Saxony and leading challenger to Helmut Kohl, clearly tries to imitate Tony Blair. The German SDP is not 'New Labour', at least not for the time being. The party cannot simply turn away from the economic and political trends of the last 30 years. But the demands of globalization from which no country can escape will help to set German society and the German political system in the right direction.

In foreign policy Germany has moved forward since the days of the Gulf War and the outbreak of the Balkan civil war. German soldiers took part in about a dozen UN peace-keeping operations round the world. And the German Sfor-contingent in the Balkans is one of the strongest contributed by the West. The Germans have learned their lessons. They are ready to share the risks of those who work for a world free of aggression and dictatorial politics.

The future structure of Europe has still to be determined. But it is certain that the new Europe, in whatever form, cannot exist without the political experience and wisdom of the UK. When this is recognized on both sides of the Channel, Great Britain will play a prominent role together with Germany and France in bringing the West and East of the continent together. Poland, the Baltic states, Hungary and the Czech Republic, historical losers for a long time, must be allowed to enter the European stage. With their new energies and abilities Europe will thrive in the global society. A century dominated by two world wars and by their aftermath will have opened the way to a Europe based on true partnership.

Jochen Thies is head of political affairs at DeutschlandRadio Berlin. He has worked for German radio and television in Munich, Bonn and Cologne. He was deputy head of the speechwriting group of Chancellor Helmut Schmidt from 1980 to 1982 and became a well-known commentator writing for journals and newspapers. He is the author of several books on German history, international relations and European Affairs.

GERMANY

Bundesrepublik Deutschland

(Federal Republic of Germany)

Capital: Berlin
Seat of Government: Bonn/Berlin
Population: 81·90m.
GDP per head: (PPP$) 19,675
HDI/world rank: 0·924/19

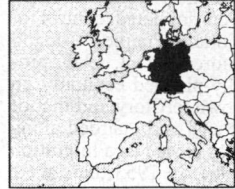

KEY HISTORICAL EVENTS. At the outbreak of the Napoleonic wars Germany consisted of many small states, independent but loosely bound by a common allegiance to the Holy Roman Emperor, a title which was hereditary in the Austrian royal house of Hapsburg. In 1806 the Holy Roman Empire was destroyed by Napoleon, who then combined 16 German states as the Confederation of the Rhine.

Following Napoleon's defeat in 1815, a larger Confederation was formed with 38 members (39 after 1817). Austria remained the dominant power with a permanent right to the presidency of the Confederation. Prussia held the vice-presidency. The other important states were: Bavaria, Saxony, Hanover, Württemberg, Baden, Hesse-Kassel, Hesse-Darmstadt, Holstein and Lauenberg, Brunswick, Nassau, Mecklenburg-Schwerin and Mecklenburg-Strelitz.

In 1848–50 attempts were made to draw up a constitution and elect a Confederation parliament. A constitution was published in Dec. 1848 but few states accepted it; a revised version was accepted in May 1849, but not by Austria or Bavaria. The parliament which sat from 20 March to 29 April 1850 was neither recognized by Austria nor powerful enough to control the other dominant state, Prussia. The Federal Diet therefore resumed power and held it until 1866.

In 1866 Prussia defeated Austria and formed the North German Confederation in 1867, under her own control. She had annexed Hanover, Hesse-Kassel and Nassau in 1866 together with the smaller states of Homburg and Frankfurt.

In 1870 Prussia went to war with France, rallied the German states in support and, following German victory, went on to the creation of the German Empire in 1871. The Empire included all German states except Austria and had, therefore, deep North-South, Protestant-Catholic divisions. It was dominated by Prussia, whose king became emperor. Conscious of arriving late on the world scene, Germany acquired colonies in West and South-West Africa in 1884 and at the end of the decade Zanzibar and Tanganyika in the East. The imperial government led Germany into the First World War in 1914 and when defeated, national unity collapsed. The emperor abdicated on 28 Nov. 1918.

After an anarchic period a republican government, with a constitution drawn up at Weimar in 1919, attempted under Chancellor Ebert to restore the economy and political stability. But the scale of reparations demanded by the Treaty of Versailles, the onset of world depression and the loss of resources and territory through warfare were too great.

In 1933 the National Socialist leader Adolf Hitler was appointed Chancellor. The National Socialist ('Nazi') party appealed to national pride and offered a return to self-respect after humiliation. Hitler became president of the Third Reich in 1934. His policies involved the wide expansion of German power and a theory of Aryan racial supremacy which meant in practice that non-Aryans were persecuted, murdered, and their assets confiscated. Hitler's expansionism led to his annexation of Austria and of German-speaking Czechoslovakia in 1938. In March 1939 he declared all of Czechoslovakia a German protectorate, and in Sept. invaded Poland, attempting to restore the authority exercised there by Prussia before 1918. This precipitated the Second World War.

The War ended in German defeat in 1945. The Allied forces occupied Germany; the UK, the USA and France holding the west and the USSR the east. By the Berlin Declaration of 5 June 1945 these governments assumed authority; each was given a zone of occupation, and the zone commanders-in-chief together made up the Allied Control Council in Berlin. The area of Greater Berlin was also divided into 4 sectors.

At the Potsdam Conference of 1945 northern East Prussia was transferred to the USSR. It was also agreed that, pending a final peace settlement, Poland should administer the areas east of the rivers Oder and Neisse, with the frontier fixed on the Oder and Western Neisse down to the Czechoslovak frontier.

By 1948 it had become clear that there would be no agreement between the occupying powers as to the future of Germany. Accordingly, the western allies united their zones into one unit in March 1948. In protest, the USSR withdrew from the Allied Control Council, blockaded Berlin until May 1949, and consolidated control of eastern Germany, establishing the German Democratic Republic. A People's Council appointed in 1948 drew up a constitution which came into force in Oct. 1949, providing for a communist state of five Länder with a centrally-planned economy. In 1952 the government made a physical division between its own territory and that of the Federal Republic, in the form of a three-mile cordon fenced and guarded along the frontier. This left Berlin as the only point of contact; it was closed as a migration route by the construction of a concrete boundary wall in 1961. In 1953 there were popular revolts against food shortages and the pressure to collectivize. In 1954 the government eased economic problems, the USSR ceased to collect reparation payments, and sovereignty was granted. The GDR signed the Warsaw Pact in 1955. Socialist policies were stepped up in 1958, leading to flight to the West of skilled workers.

Meanwhile, a constituent assembly met in Bonn in Sept. 1948 and drafted a Basic Law, which came into force in May 1949. In Sept. 1949 the occupation forces limited their own powers and the Federal Republic of Germany came into existence. The occupation forces retained some powers, however, and the Republic did not become a sovereign state until 1955 when the Occupation Statute was revoked.

The Republic consisted of the states of Schleswig-Holstein, Hamburg, Lower Saxony, Bremen, North Rhine-Westphalia, Hessen, Rhineland-Palatinate, Baden-Württemberg, Bavaria and Saarland, together with West Berlin.

The first chancellor, Konrad Adenauer (1949–63), was committed to the ultimate reunification of Germany and would not acknowledge the German Democratic Republic as a state. The two German states did not sign an agreement of mutual recognition and intent to co-operate until 1972, under Chancellor Willi Brandt.

The most marked feature of the post-war period was rapid population growth and the restoration of industry. Immigration from the German Democratic Republic, about 3m. since 1945, stopped when the Berlin Wall was built in 1961; however there was a strong movement of German-speaking people back into Germany from German settlements in countries of the Soviet bloc. Industrial growth also attracted labour from Turkey, Spain and the Balkans.

The Paris Treaty, which came into force in 1955, ensured the Republic's contribution to NATO, and NATO forces were stationed along the Rhine in large numbers, with consequent dispute about the deployment of nuclear missiles on German soil.

Even before sovereignty, the Republic had begun negotiations for a measure of European unity, and joined in creating the European Coal and Steel Community in 1951 and the European Economic Community in 1957. In Jan. 1957 the Saarland was returned to full German control. In 1973 the Federal Republic entered the UN.

In the autumn of 1989 movements for political liberalization in the GDR and re-unification with Federal Germany gathered strength. Erich Honecker and other long-serving Communist leaders were replaced in Oct.–Nov. The Berlin Wall was opened on 9 Nov.

Following the reforms in the GDR in Nov. 1989 the Federal Chancellor Helmut Kohl issued a plan for German confederation. The ambassadors of the 4 war-time allies met in Berlin in Dec. After talks with Chancellor Kohl on 11 Feb. 1990, President Gorbachev said the USSR had no objection to German re-unification. Allies agreed a formula ('two-plus-four') for re-unification talks to begin after the GDR elections on 18 March. 'Two-plus-four' talks began on 5 May 1990. On 18 May Federal Germany and the GDR signed a treaty transferring Federal Germany's currency, and its economic, monetary and social legislation, to the GDR as of 1 July. On 23 Aug. the Volkskammer by 294 votes to 62 'declared its accession to the jurisdiction of the Federal Republic as from 3 Oct. according to article 23 of the Basic

Law', which provided for the Länder of pre-war Germany to accede to the Federal Republic. On 12 Sept. the Treaty on the Final Settlement with Respect to Germany was signed by Federal Germany, the GDR and the 4 war-time allies: France, the USSR, the UK and the USA.

TERRITORY AND POPULATION. Germany is bounded in the north by Denmark and the North and Baltic Seas, east by Poland, east and south-east by the Czech Republic, south-east and south by Austria, south by Switzerland and west by France, Luxembourg, Belgium and the Netherlands. Area: 356,978 sq. km. Population estimate based on a microcensus of 1995: 81,538,603 (41,893,600 females); density, 228 per sq. km. 1996 estimate: 81,896m., of which 66,445m. live in the old Federal Republic of Germany and 15,451m. in the old German Democratic Republic. There were 37·28m. households in April 1996; 13·19m. were single-person, and 11·37m. had a female principal breadwinner.

On 14 Nov. 1990 Germany and Poland signed a treaty confirming Poland's existing western frontier and renouncing German claims to territory lost as a result of the Second World War.

The capital is Berlin; the Federal German government will move to Berlin in 1999.

The Federation comprises 16 Länder (states). Area and population:

Länder	Area in sq. km	Population (in 1,000) 1987 census	1995 estimate	Density per sq. km (1 Jan. 1996)
Baden-Württemberg (BW)	35,751	9,286	10,295	289
Bavaria (BY)	70,552	10,903	11,954	170
Berlin (BE)[1]	891	···	3,471	3,897
Brandenburg (BB)[2]	29,476	···	2,539	86
Bremen (HB)	404	660	680	1,682
Hamburg (HH)	755	1,593	1,707	2,262
Hessen (HE)	21,114	5,508	5,994	285
Lower Saxony (NI)	47,612	7,162	7,746	163
Mecklenburg-West Pomerania (MV)[2]	23,170	···	1,828	79
North Rhine-Westphalia (NW)	34,079	16,712	17,847	525
Rhineland-Palatinate (RP)	19,853	3,631	3,963	200
Saarland (SL)	2,570	1,056	1,084	422
Saxony (SN)[2]	18,413	···	4,575	248
Saxony-Anhalt (ST)[2]	20,446	···	2,750	134
Schleswig-Holstein (SH)	15,771	2,554	2,717	173
Thuringia (TH)[2]	16,171	···	2,511	155

[1] 1987 census population of West Berlin: 2,013,000.
[2] Reconstituted in 1990 in the GDR.

Vital statistics:

	Marriages	Live births	Of these to single parents	Deaths	Divorces
1992	453,428	809,114	120,448	885,443	135,179
1993	442,605	798,447	118,284	897,270	156,646
1994	440,244	769,603	118,460	884,661	166,496
1995	430,534	765,221	122,876	884,588	169,425

Of the 430,534 marriages in 1995, 26,554 were between foreign males and German females, and 28,306 vice-versa. The average age of bridegrooms in 1995 was 33·2, and of brides 30·3.

Rates (per 1,000 population), 1995: Birth, 9·4; marriage, 5·3; death, 10·8; infant mortality (per 1,000 live births): 5·3; Stillborn rate, 4·4 per 1,000 births. Expectation of life: Men, 72·99; women, 79·49. Suicide rates over 1990–95, per 100,000 population, 17·5 (men, 24·9; women, 10·7).

Legislation of 1995 categorizes abortions as illegal, but stipulates that prosecutions will not be brought if they are performed in the first 3 months of pregnancy after consultation with a doctor.

On 31 Dec. 1996 there were 7,314,000 resident foreigners, including 2,049,100 Turks, 754,300 Yugoslavs, 599,400 Italians and 362,500 Greeks. In 1996, 116,367 foreigners sought asylum (127,937 in 1995; 127,210 in 1994; 322,599 in 1993). Tighter controls on entry from abroad were applied as from 1993. 313,606 persons were naturalized in 1995, of whom 214,927 were from the former USSR. In 1995 there were 698,113 emigrants and 1,096,048 immigrants.

Populations of the 84 towns of over 100,000 inhabitants in 1995 (in 1,000):

Town (and Land)	Population (in 1,000)	Ranking by population	Town (and Land)	Population (in 1,000)	Ranking by population
Aachen (NW)	247·4	32	Koblenz (RP)	109·3	74
Augsburg (BY)	261·0	29	Krefeld (NW)	249·9	31
Bergisch Gladbach (NW)	105·2	79	Leipzig (SN)	478·2	14
Berlin (BE)	3,470·2	1	Leverkusen (NW)	161·9	49
Bielefeld (NW)	324·0	18	Lübeck (SH)	216·9	36
Bochum (NW)	400·5	16	Ludwigshafen am Rhein (RP)	168·0	46
Bonn (NW)	291·7	21	Magdeburg (ST)	263·0	28
Bottrop (NW)	119·9	66	Mainz (RP)	184·5	42
Braunschweig (NI)	253·6	30	Mannheim (BW)	315·1	19
Bremen (HB)	549·0	10	Moers (NW)	107·0	77
Bremerhaven (HB)	130·8	56	Mönchengladbach (NW)	266·0	26
Chemnitz (SN)	271·4	24	Mülheim a. d. Ruhr (NW)	176·7	45
Cologne (NW)	964·2	4	Munich (BY)	1,240·6	3
Cottbus (BB)	124·6	63	Münster (NW)	264·5	27
Darmstadt (HE)	139·1	52	Neuss (NW)	148·6	51
Dortmund (NW)	600·0	7	Nuremberg (BY)	494·1	13
Dresden (SN)	472·9	15	Oberhausen (NW)	224·9	35
Duisburg (NW)	535·2	11	Offenbach am Main (HE)	116·6	70
Düsseldorf (NW)	571·9	9	Oldenburg (NI)	150·5	50
Erfurt (TH)	212·6	38	Osnabrück (NI)	167·9	47
Erlangen (BY)	101·5	84	Paderborn (NW)	132·1	55
Essen (NW)	616·4	6	Pforzheim (BW)	118·4	67
Frankfurt am Main (HE)	651·2	5	Potsdam (BB)	137·6	54
Freiburg im Breisgau (BW)	198·3	40	Recklingshausen (NW)	127·2	58
Fürth (BY)	108·1	76	Regensburg (BY)	126·0	61
Gelsenkirchen (NW)	291·8	20	Remscheid (NW)	122·7	64
Gera (TH)	125·0	62	Reutlingen (BW)	108·4	75
Göttingen (NI)	127·2	58	Rostock (MV)	231·3	34
Hagen (NW)	212·7	37	Saarbrücken (SL)	187·8	41
Halle (ST)	287·4	22	Salzgitter (NI)	117·7	68
Hamburg (HH)	1,706·8	2	Schwerin (MV)	117·2	69
Hamm (NW)	183·7	43	Siegen (NW)	111·3	73
Hanover (NI)	524·6	12	Solingen (NW)	165·7	48
Heidelberg (BW)	138·4	53	Stuttgart (BW)	587·0	8
Heilbronn (BW)	121·7	65	Ulm (BW)	115·4	71
Herne (NW)	179·9	44	Wiesbaden (HE)	266·4	25
Hildesheim (NI)	106·0	78	Witten (NW)	105·0	80
Ingolstadt (BY)	111·9	72	Wolfsburg (NI)	126·8	60
Jena (TH)	101·8	83	Wuppertal (NW)	382·4	17
Kaiserslautern (RP)	102·0	82	Würzburg (BY)	127·7	57
Karlsruhe (BW)	276·6	23	Zwickau (SN)	103·9	81
Kassel (HE)	201·4	39			
Kiel (SH)	247·3	33			

The official language is German. Minor orthographical amendments were agreed in 1995. An agreement between German-speaking countries in Vienna on 1 July 1996 provides for minor orthographical changes to come into effect from 1998 and establishes a Commission for German Orthography in Mannheim.

CLIMATE. Oceanic influences are only found in the north-west where winters are quite mild but stormy. Elsewhere a continental climate is general. To the east and south, winter temperatures are lower, with bright frosty weather and considerable snowfall. Summer temperatures are fairly uniform throughout. Berlin. Jan. 31°F (−0·5°C), July 66°F (19°C). Annual rainfall 22·5" (563 mm). Dresden. Jan. 30°F (−0·1°C), July 65°F (18·5°C). Annual rainfall 27·2" (680 mm). Frankfurt. Jan. 33°F (0·6°C), July 66°F (18·9°C). Annual rainfall 24" (601 mm). Hamburg. Jan. 31°F (−0·6°C), July 63°F (17·2°C). Annual rainfall 29" (726 mm). Hanover. Jan. 33°F (0·6°C), July 64°F (17·8°C). Annual rainfall 24" (604 mm). Köln. Jan. 36°F (2·2°C), July 66°F (18·9°C). Annual rainfall 27" (676 mm). Munich. Jan. 28°F (−2·2°C), July

63°F (17·2°C). Annual rainfall 34" (855 mm). Stuttgart. Jan. 33°F (0·6°C), July 66°F (18·9°C). Annual rainfall 27" (677 mm).

CONSTITUTION AND GOVERNMENT. The Basic Law (*Grundgesetz*) was approved by the parliaments of the participating Länder and came into force on 23 May 1949. It is to remain in force until 'a constitution adopted by a free decision of the German people comes into being'. The Federal Republic is a democratic and social constitutional state on a parliamentary basis. The federation is constituted by the 16 Länder (states). The Basic Law decrees that the general rules of international law form part of the federal law. The constitutions of the Länder must conform to the principles of a republican, democratic and social state based on the rule of law. Executive power is vested in the Länder, unless the Basic Law prescribes or permits otherwise. Federal law takes precedence over state law.

Legislative power is vested in the *Bundestag* (Federal Assembly) and the *Bundesrat* (Federal Council). The Bundestag is currently composed of 672 members and is elected in universal, free, equal and secret elections for a term of 4 years. A party must gain 5% of total votes cast in order to gain representation in the Bundestag, although if a party gets 3 candidates elected directly, they may take their seats even if the party obtains less than 5% of the national vote. The electoral system combines relative-majority and proportional voting; each voter has 2 votes, the first for the direct constituency representative, the second for the competing party lists in the Länder. All directly elected constituency representatives enter parliament, but if a party receives more 'indirect' than 'direct' votes, the first name in order on the party list not to have a seat becomes a member—the number of seats is increased by the difference ('overhang votes'). Thus the number of seats in the Bundestag varies, but is usually around 670. The Bundesrat consists of 69 members appointed by the governments of the Länder in proportions determined by the number of inhabitants. Each *Land* has at least 3 votes.

The Head of State is the Federal *President* who is elected for a 5-year term by a *Federal Convention* specially convened for this purpose. This Convention consists of all the members of the Bundestag and an equal number of members elected by the Länder parliaments in accordance with party strengths, but who need not themselves be members of the parliaments. No president may serve more than 2 terms. Executive power is vested in the Federal Government, which consists of the Federal *Chancellor*, elected by the Bundestag on the proposal of the Federal President, and the Federal Ministers, who are appointed and dismissed by the Federal President upon the proposal of the Federal Chancellor.

The Federal Republic has exclusive legislation on: (1) foreign affairs (2) federal citizenship; (3) freedom of movement, passports, immigration and emigration, and extradition; (4) currency, money and coinage, weights and measures, and regulation of time and calendar; (5) customs, commercial and navigation agreements, traffic in goods and payments with foreign countries, including customs and frontier protection; (6) federal railways and air traffic; (7) post and telecommunications; (8) the legal status of persons in the employment of the Federation and of public law corporations under direct supervision of the Federal Government; (9) trade marks, copyright and publishing rights; (10) co-operation of the Federal Republic and the Länder in the criminal police and in matters concerning the protection of the constitution, the establishment of a Federal Office of Criminal Police, as well as the combating of international crime; (11) federal statistics.

In the field of finance the Federal Republic has exclusive legislation on customs and financial monopolies and concurrent legislation on: (1) excise taxes and taxes on transactions, in particular, taxes on real-estate acquisition, incremented value and on fire protection; (2) taxes on income, property, inheritance and donations; (3) real estate, industrial and trade taxes, with the exception of the determining of the tax rates. The Federal Republic can claim part of the income and corporation taxes to cover its expenditures not covered by other revenues. Financial jurisdiction is uniformly regulated by federal legislation.

Federal laws are passed by the Bundestag and after their adoption submitted to the Bundesrat, which has a limited veto. The Basic Law may be amended only upon the approval of two-thirds of the members of the Bundestag and two-thirds of the votes of the Bundesrat.

On 23 May 1994 Roman Herzog was elected President by the Federal Convention against 4 opponents.

Bundestag elections were held on 16 Oct. 1994; turn-out was 79·1%. The Christian Democratic Union/Christian Social Union (CDU/CSU; the CSU is a Bavarian party where the CDU does not stand) won 294 seats with 41·4% of votes cast, of which 7·3% were for the CSU (319 with 43·8% in 1990 and 7·1% for the CSU); the Social Democratic Party (SPD), 252 with 36·4% (239 with 33·5%); the Greens, 49 with 7·3% (8 with 5·1%); the Free Democratic Party (FDP), 47 seats with 6·9% (79 with 11%); the Party for Democratic Socialism (PDS; former Communists), 30 with 4·4% (17 with 2·4%).

Federal President: Roman Herzog (b. 1934; sworn in 1 July 1994).
Speaker of the Bundestag: Rita Süssmuth (elected Nov. 1988; re-elected Nov. 1994).

In March 1998 the government comprised:
Chancellor: Dr Helmut Kohl (b. 1930; CDU).
Deputy Chancellor and Foreign Minister: Dr Klaus Kinkel (FDP). *Special Tasks and Head of the Federal Chancellery:* Friedrich Bohl (CDU). *Interior:* Manfred Kanther (CDU). *Justice:* Eduard Schmidt-Jortzig (FDP). *Finance:* Dr Theo Waigel (CSU). *Economy:* Dr Günter Rexrodt (FDP). *Food, Agriculture and Forestry:* Jochen Borchert (CDU). *Labour and Social Affairs:* Dr Norbert Blüm (CDU). *Defence:* Volker Rühe (CDU). *Family, Youth, Women and Senior Citizens:* Claudia Nolte (CDU). *Health:* Horst Seehofer (CSU). *Transport:* Matthias Wissman (CDU). *Environment, Nature Conservation and Reactor Safety:* Dr Angela Merkel (CDU). *Regional Planning, Housing and Urban Development:* Eduard Uswald (CSU). *Education and Science, Research and Technology:* Dr Jürgen Rüttgers (CDU). *Economic Co-operation and Development:* Carl-Dieter Spranger (CSU).

National anthem: 'Einigkeit und Recht und Freiheit' ('Unity and right and freedom'); words by H. Hoffmann, tune by J. Haydn.

European Parliament. Germany has 99 representatives. At the June 1994 elections turn-out was 60%. The SPD won 40 seats with 32·2% of votes cast (group in European Parliament: European Socialist Party); the CDU, 39 with 32% (Popular European Party); the Greens, 12 with 10·1% (Greens); the CSU, 8 with 6·8% (Popular European Party).

Local Government. The 16 Länder are divided into a total of 29 administrative regions *(Regierungsbezirke)*. Below *Land* level local government is carried on by elected councils to 426 rural districts *(Landkreise)* and 117 urban districts *(Kreisfreie Städte)*, which form the electoral districts for the *Land* governments, and are subdivided into 16,043 communes *(Gemeinden)*.

Die Bundesrepublik Deutschland: Staatshandbuch. Cologne, annual
Hucko, E. M. (ed.) *The Democratic Tradition* [Texts of German constitutions]. Leamington Spa, 1987
Koch, J. W., *A Constitutional History of Germany in the Nineteenth and Twentieth Centuries.* London, 1984
König, K. *et al.* (eds.) *Public Administration in the Federal Republic of Germany.* Boston (MA), 1983

DEFENCE. Russian (ex-Soviet) forces had withdrawn from the territory of the former GDR by 1994.

Conscription is for 10 months. In July 1994, the Constitutional Court ruled that German armed forces might be sent on peacekeeping missions abroad.

Army. The Army is organized in the Army Forces Command, comprising 1 air-mobile division with 3 airborne brigades, 3 army aviation brigades, 1 signals/electronic intelligence brigade and 1 support brigade; and 8 military district commands grouped in 3 corps—2 with armoured divisions and 1 with an armed infantry division (I Corps: German-Netherlands), 2 with armoured divisions and 1 with a mountain division (II Corps), and 2 with armoured infantry divisions (IV Corps).The 8 military district commands control 6 armoured, 12 armoured infantry and 1 mountain brigade, and the German element of the German-French brigade. 1 armoured division is earmarked for Eurocorps. Corps units comprise 2 armoured reconnaissance battalions, 3 air defence regiments and 3 helicopter regiments. Equipment includes 731 Leopard 1A5 and 1,964 Leopard 2 main battle tanks and 1,511 surface-to-air missiles. The equipment of the former East German army is in store. An air component operates 205 BO 105P anti-armour helicopters, 107 CH-53G and 125 UH-1D Iroquois transport helicopters, as well as 40 Alouette II and 95 BO 105M liaison/observation helicopters. The Territorial Army is organized into 5 Military Districts, under 3 Territorial Commands. Its main task is to defend rear areas and remains under national control even in wartime. Total strength was (1997) 239,950 (conscripts 124,200).

Navy. The Fleet Commander operates from a modern Maritime Headquarters at Glücksburg, close to the Danish border.

The fleet includes 16 diesel coastal submarines, 3 US-built guided-missile destroyers, 10 frigates including 2 new guided-missile ships and 36 fast missile craft. There is a mine-warfare force of 42 vessels, comprising 32 coastal minesweepers and hunters, of which 10 are new combined minelayer/hunters and 6 control ships for TROIKA minesweeping drones, 5 inshore minesweepers and 1 diver support ship. Major auxiliaries include 4 repair ships, 4 transport oilers, 4 minesweeper/patrol craft support and HQ ships, 3 logistic transports, 8 large tugs, 3 intelligence collectors and 2 trial ships. There are several dozen minor auxiliaries and service craft.

The main naval bases are at Wilhelmshaven, Bremerhaven, Kiel, Eckernförde and Warnemünde.

The Naval Air Arm, 4,500 strong, is organized into 3 wings and comprises 54 missile-armed Tornado strike aircraft. 18 Atlantic long range, 20 shore-based Sea King helicopters, 17 Lynx (12 frigate-based) and 2 Do-228 anti-pollution patrol aircraft are also in service.

Procurement of 2 further new mine warfare craft is in hand. Personnel in 1997 numbered 27,760, including 5,460 conscripts.

Air Force. Since 1970, the *Luftwaffe* has comprised the following commands: German Air Force Tactical Command, German Air Force Support Command (including two German Air Force Regional Support Commands—North and South) and General Air Force Office. Personnel in 1995 was 75,300 (18,700 conscripts). Combat units, including 12 heavy fighter-bomber squadrons with Tornados and F-4Fs, 8 surface-to-surface missile squadrons, and an air defence force of 6 interceptor squadrons with F-4Fs and MiG-29s, 24 batteries of *Nike-Hercules* and 36 batteries of *Improved Hawk* surface-to-air missiles, are assigned to NATO. 3 wings operating both Transall C-160 aircraft and UH-1D Iroquois helicopters add to the air mobility of the *Bundeswehr*. There are also VIP, support and light transport aircraft. About 12 L-410 and Tu-154 transports and Mi-8 helicopters from the GDR air force are still in use, the single Tu-154 being assigned to arms control surveillance duties. Guided weapons in service include 8 squadrons of *Pershing* surface-to-surface missiles and 6 battalions of *Nike-Hercules* and 9 battalions of *Improved Hawk* surface-to-air missiles. Personnel in 1997 numbered 76,900, including 22,400 conscripts.

INTERNATIONAL RELATIONS. A treaty of friendship with Poland signed on 17 June 1991 recognized the Oder-Neisse border and guaranteed minorities' rights in both countries.

Membership. Germany is a member of the UN, OECD, EU, WEU, NATO and the Council of Europe, and is a signatory to the Schengen Accord which abolishes border controls between Germany, Austria, Belgium, Denmark, Finland, France, Greece, Iceland, Italy, Luxembourg, the Netherlands, Norway, Portugal, Spain and Sweden.

ECONOMY

Performance. Real GDP growth was 1·3% in 1996 (1·9% in 1995).

Budget. Since 1 Jan. 1979 tax revenues have been distributed as follows: Federal Government. Income tax, 42·5%; capital yield and corporation tax, 50%; turnover tax, 67·5%; trade tax, 15%; capital gains, insurance and accounts taxes, 100%; excise duties (other than on beer), 100%. Länder. Income tax, 42·5%; capital yield and corporation tax, 50%; turnover tax, 32·5%; trade tax, 15%; other taxes, 100%. Local authorities. Income tax, 15%; trade tax, 70%; local taxes, 100%.

VAT is 15% (reduced rate, 7%).

Budgets for 1996 and 1995 (in 1m. DM):

Revenue	All public authorities		Federal portion	
	1997	1996	1997	1996
	Current			
Taxes	832,013	827,586	382,696	376,235
Economic activities	30,141	30,382	9,017	9,005
Interest	8,072	8,288	2,563	2,792
Current allocations and subsidies	262,509	267,126	4,090	3,756
Other receipts	66,245	66,564	9,995	7,945
minus equalising payments	237,905	238,521	. . .	. . .
	961,075	961,425	408,361	399,733
	Capital			
Sale of assets	30,903	29,189	11,189	12,464
Allocations for investment	59,037	63,581	5	5
Repayment of loans	12,986	12,514	3,884	4,076
Public sector borrowing	1,310	1,383	. . .	. . .
minus equalising payments	50,861	55,166	. . .	. . .
	53,375	51,501	15,078	16,545
Totals	1,016,339	1,014,890	423,439	416,278

Expenditure				
	Current			
Staff	309,541	312,100	52,858	53,109
Materials	139,412	142,104	39,368	40,459
Interest	138,377	136,978	54,406	53,423
Allocations and subsidies	610,021	607,598	271,030	261,724
minus equalising payments	237,905	238,521	. . .	. . .
	959,446	960,259	417,662	408,715
	Capital			
Construction	70,255	76,063	10,594	10,142
Acquisition of property	17,377	18,347	2,406	2,285
Allocations and subsidies	97,829	106,343	35,209	39,934
Loans	30,787	34,507	11,749	13,834
Acquisition of shares	4,422	4,796	1,418	1,708
Repayments in the public sector	1,661	1,534	. . .	. . .
minus equalising payments	50,861	55,166	. . .	. . .
	171,470	186,424	61,376	67,903
Totals	1,125,998	1,141,731	476,859	476,348

Currency. The unit of currency is the *deutsche Mark* (DEM) of 100 *pfennig* (pf.). There are coins of 1, 2, 5, 10 and 50 pf. and 1, 2, 5 and 10 DM, and notes of 5, 10, 20, 50, 100, 200, 500 and 1,000 DM. Money in circulation in 1996, 261,765m. DM. Foreign exchange reserves in 1995 were 68,484m. DM; gold reserves were 13,688m. DM. Inflation was an 1·5% in 1996.

Banking and Finance. The Deutsche Bundesbank (German Federal Bank) is the central bank and bank of issue. Its duty is to protect the stability of the currency. It is independent of the government but obliged to support the government's general policy. Its Governor is appointed by the government for 8 years. The *Governor* is Hans Tietmayer (b. 1931). Its assets were 366,404m. DM in 1996. The largest private banks are the Deutsche Bank, Dresdner Bank and Commerzbank. The former GDR central bank Staatsbank has become a public commercial bank. In 1996 there were 3,517 credit institutes, including 331 banks, 607 savings banks, 34 mortgage lenders and 2,510 credit societies. They are represented in the wholesale market by the 12 public sector Länder banks. Total assets, 1996, 8,292,385m. DM. Savings deposits were 1,165,755m. DM in 1996. A single stock exchange, the Deutsche Börse, was created in 1992, based on the former Frankfurt stock exchange in a union with the smaller exchanges in Berlin, Bremen, Düsseldorf, Hamburg, Hanover, Munich and Stuttgart.

Gull, L. et al., The Deutsche Bank, 1870–1995. London, 1996
Marsh, D., The Bundesbank: the Bank that Rules Europe. London, 1992

Weights and Measures. The metric system is in force.

ENERGY AND NATURAL RESOURCES

Electricity. In 1994 there were 21 nuclear reactors producing 33% of electricity output. In 1994 output was 452,931,000 mWh, of which 151,203,000 mWh were nuclear and 20,711,000 mWh hydro-electric. There is a moratorium on further nuclear plant construction.

Oil and Gas. The chief oilfields are in Emsland (Lower Saxony). In 1996, 2·85m. tonnes of crude oil were produced. Gas production was 899,208,000 mWh in 1994, of which 818,034,000 mWh were natural gas.

Minerals. The main production areas are: North Rhine-Westphalia (for coal, iron and metal smelting-works), Central Germany (for lignite), and Lower Saxony (Salzgitter for iron ore; the Harz for metal ore).

Production (in tonnes), 1996: Coal, 48,197,000; lignite, 187,180,000.

Agriculture. Land in agricultural use, 1996 (in 1,000 ha). 17,246·0, including arable, 11,814·9; pasture, 5,213·1. Sown areas included: Wheat, 2,594·4; rye, 809·1; barley, 2,208·4; oats, 301·9; maize, 372·1; potatoes, 335·8; sugar-beet, 515·5; rape, 853·6; fodder, 1,817·1. Crop production, 1995 (and 1994) (in 1,000 tonnes): Wheat, 17,763·3 (16,480·5); rye, 4,521·3 (3,450·6); barley, 11,891·2 (10,902·5); oats, 1,420·4 (1,663·0); maize, 2,394·6 (2,446·0); potatoes, 9,898·3 (9,668·6); sugar-beet, 26,048·8 (24,211·3); rape, 3,103·3 (2,895·5); fodder, 53,935·1 (52,187·9).

In 1996 there were 539,975 farms, of which 68,023 were under 2 ha and 21,028 over 100 ha. In 1995 there were 561,900 farmers assisted by 586,400 household members and 263,000 hired labourers (84,800 seasonal). In the former GDR in 1990 state farms were leased to farmers until 2004 and will then be sold. Collective farms have continued operating as co-operatives or been turned over to their former members.

In 1996 wine production was 10,300,000 hectolitres.

Livestock, 1995 (in 1,000): Cattle, 16,097·9 (including milk cows, 5,232·6); sheep, 2,990·5; pigs, 24,515·9; horses, 598·8 (1994), poultry, 101,139 (1994). Livestock products, 1995 (in 1,000 tonnes): Milk, 28,621; meat, 4,884·4. 1992: Eggs, 15,525m. units.

Forestry. Forest area in 1992 was 8,033,600 ha, of which 4,419,200 ha were owned by the State. Timber production was 28·3m. cu. metres in 1993 and 34·6m. cu. metres in 1994.

In recent years depredation has occurred through pollution with acid rain.

Fisheries. In 1995 the yield of sea fishing was 137,630 tonnes live weight. The fishing fleet consisted of 51 ocean-going vessels and 2,324 coastal cutters.

INDUSTRY.
Public limited companies are managed on the 'co-determination' principle, and have 3 statutory bodies: a board of directors, a works council elected by employees, and a supervisory council which includes employee representatives but has an in-built management majority.

In 1994 there were 67,660 firms (with 20 and more employees) employing 8·9m. persons, made up of 363,000 in energy and water services, 174,000 in mining, 1·3m. in raw materials processing, 3·71m. in the manufacture of producers' goods, 1·28m. in the manufacture of consumer goods, 572,000 in food and tobacco production and 1·50m. in building.

Output of major industrial products, 1996 (in 1,000 tonnes): Cement, 35,845; pig-iron (1994), 29,923; crude steel (1994), 40,837; rolled steel (1994), 26,691; aluminium, 709; copper (1994), 1,926; nitrogenous fertilizers (1994), 1,199; plastics, 10,001; glassware (1994), 4,882; cotton yarn (1994), 108; synthetic fibre (1994), 85; flour, 3,851; paper, 10,636; passenger cars, 4,702,000 (units); refrigerators, 3,102,000; beer, 108·9m. hectolitres.

Labour. Retirement age is 63 years. In 1996 the workforce was 39·96m. (17·15m. females), of whom 33·81m. (13·68m. females) were working and 3·97m. (1·85m. females) were unemployed. In 1996 there were on average during the year 3·65m. self-employed or helping other family members, 2·51m. officials and 28·26m. employees. 2·98m. foreign workers were employed in 1994. Major categories (1996): Manufacturing industries, 11·94m.; services, 7·88m.; commerce and transport, 6·47m.; agriculture, forestry and fishing, 0·97m. In 1996 there were 327,278 unfilled vacancies. In Dec. 1997 there were 4,500,000 unemployed, a rate of 11·8%. In 1996 more than half the unemployed people had not had a job for over 6 months, and 12·4% of people who were unemployed were under 25 years old. Of unemployed people in the old Federal Republic of Germany, 17·3% were foreign nationals.

Trade Unions. The majority of trade unions belong to the *Deutscher Gewerkschaftsbund* (DGB, German Trade Union Federation), which had 9·4m. (2·86m. women) members in 1995, including 5·73m. (1·1m.) manual workers, 2·65m. (1·44m.) white-collar workers and 748,151 (179,170) officials. DGB unions are organized in industrial branches such that only one union operates within each enterprise. Outside the DGB are several smaller unions: The *Deutscher Beamtenbund* (DBB) or public servants' union with 1,075,652 (318,532) members, the *Deutsche Angestellten-Gewerkschaft* (DAG) or union of salaried staff with 507,478 (273,483) members and the *Christlicher Gewerkschaftsbund Deutschlands* (CGD, Christian Trade Union Federation of Germany) with 303,840 (76,387) members. The official GDR trade union organization (FDGB) was merged in the Deutscher Gewerkschaftsbund. Strikes are not legal unless called by a union with the backing of 75% of members. Certain public service employees are contractually not permitted to strike. 98,135 working days were lost through strikes in 1996; 247,460 in 1995.

FOREIGN ECONOMIC RELATIONS

Commerce. Imports and exports in 1m. DM:

	Imports				Exports		
1993	1994	1995	1996	1993	1994	1995	1996
566,495	616,955	634,271	669,060	628,387	690,573	727,732	771,913

Most important trading partners in 1996 (trade figures in 1m. DM). Imports: France, 71,035; Netherlands, 57,482; Italy, 55,010; USA, 48,980; UK, 45,625; Belgium with Luxembourg, 42,141; Japan, 34,098. Exports: France, 84,060; UK, 61,761; USA, 60,112; Netherlands, 57,323; Italy, 57,271; Belgium with Luxembourg, 48,113; Austria, 43,268; Switzerland, 37,793.

Distribution by commodities in 1996 (in 1m. DM). Imports and exports: Live animals, 1,000 and 840; foodstuffs, 57,057 and 31,785; drinks and tobacco, 9,719 and 6,833; raw materials, 35,629 and 6,687; semi-finished goods, 62,183 and 37,850; finished goods, 467,661 and 663,928.

Tourism. In 1996 there were 52,977 places of accommodation with 2,311,241 beds (including 12,887 hotels with 839,297 beds). 14,198,400 foreign visitors and 76,081,900 tourists resident in Germany spent a total of 299,991,800 nights in holiday accommodation. More foreign visitors were from the Netherlands (1,832,000) than any other country. In 1995 foreign visitors spent 17,600m. DM in Germany.

COMMUNICATIONS

Roads. In 1996 the total length of classified roads was 228,860 km, including 11,190 km of motorway *(Autobahn)*, 41,700 km of federal highways, 86,717 km of first-class and 89,253 km of second-class country roads. On 1 Jan. 1997 there were 48·5m.

motor vehicles, including (in 1,000): Passenger cars, 41,045; lorries, 2,296; buses, 84·7; motor cycles, 2,534. In 1995 7,877m. passengers were transported by long-distance road traffic.

687,745 motorists were arrested for driving offences in 1995.

Road casualties in 1996 (and 1995) totalled 492,967 injured (512,141) and 8,727 killed (9,454).

Railways. Legislation of 1993 provides for the eventual privatization of the railways. On 1 Jan. 1994 West German Bundesbahn and the former GDR Reichsbahn were amalgamated as the Deutsche Bahn, a joint-stock company in which track, long-distance passenger traffic, regional passenger traffic and goods traffic are run as 4 separate administrative entities. These are intended after 3–5 years to become themselves companies, at first under a holding company, and ultimately independent. Initially the government will hold all the shares. Length of railway in 1995 was 40,355 km (1,435 mm gauge) of which 18,164 km were electrified, and 148 km of narrow gauge. 1,334m. passengers were carried in 1995 and 302·2m. tonnes of freight.

There are metros in Berlin (136 km), Hamburg (95 km), Frankfurt am Main (51 km), Munich (63 km) and Nuremberg (23 km), and tram/light rail networks in 56 cities.

Civil Aviation. Lufthansa, the largest carrier, was set up in 1953 and is 36% state-owned. In 1995 it operated 11 A300B4-600s, 12 A312-300s, 33 A320-200s, 10 A321-100s, 6 A340-200s, 8 A340-300s, 19 B 737 200 Advs, 39 B 737 300s, 7 B-737-300QCs, 6 B-737-400s, 30 B-737-500s, 4 B-747-200Bs, 3 B-747-200B Combis, 10 B-747-400s, 7 B-747-400 Combis, 1 A310-200, 3 B-737-300s, 17 B-757-200s, 1 B-757-200ER, 8 B-767-300ERs and 5 DC-10-30s. Other airlines include Condor, Deutsche-British Airways and LTU International. In 1995 civil avia-tion had 444 aircraft over 20 tonnes (401 jets). In 1995 there were 54·89m. passenger arrivals and 55·2m. departures. 36·3m. passengers were carried to destinations abroad. International airports: Cologne-Bonn, Düsseldorf, Frankfurt am Main, Hamburg (Fuhlsbüttel), Hanover, Leipzig, Munich, Nuremberg, Stuttgart and 3 at Berlin (Tegel, Tempelhof and Schönefeld).

Shipping. At 31 Dec. 1996 the mercantile marine comprised 1,397 ocean-going vessels of 6,002,000 GRT. Sea-going ships in 1996 carried 206m. tonnes of cargo.

Navigable rivers have a total length of 4,842 km; canals, 2,087 km. The inland-waterways fleet on 31 Dec. 1995 included 1,477 motor freight vessels totalling 1·52m. tonnes and 355 tankers of 495,887 tonnes. 227m. tonnes of freight were transported in 1996.

Telecommunications. Telecommunications were deregulated in 1989. On 1 Jan. 1995, 3 state-owned joint-stock companies were set up: Deutsche Telekom, Postdienst and Postbank. The partial privatization of Deutsche Telekom began in Nov. 1996.

In 1995 there were 17,000 post offices and 3,000 affiliated agents, 40·4m. private telephones and 165,000 public telephones. In 1994 there were 1·45m. fax trans-mitters. 3·71m. mobile telephones were in use in 1996.

The national public broadcasters Deutschlandfunk, RIAS Berlin and Deutschlandsender Kultur form part of the *Nationaler Hörfunk.* The foreign service, Deutsche Welle, broadcasts in 30 languages, and there is a commercial European service. There are 12 regional radio and TV networks (colour by PAL). The *Arbeitsgemeinschaft der öffentlich-rechtlichen Rundfunkanstalten der Bundesrepublik Deutschland* (ARD) represents public-right broadcasters and organizes co-operation between them and also broadcasts a federal-wide TV pro-gramme of its own. There is another public TV channel, ZDF, and 4 commercial TV networks, as well as a sport channel, a pay-TV film channel and Deutsche Telekom's cable network. In 1996 there were 37m. radio and 33m. TV licences.

Cinemas. In 1995 there were 3,814 cinemas with a total seating capacity of 729,915. 63 feature films were made in 1995.

Press. 74,174 book titles were published in 1995, of which 53,359 were new works. The daily press is mainly regional. In 1996 the largest dailies with a national circulation were *Das Bild* (Hamburg, 4·5m. copies per day); *Süddeutsche Zeitung* (Munich, 0·4m.); *Frankfurter Allgemeine Zeitung* (0·4m.); *Die Welt* (Berlin, 0·22m.); *Frankfurter Rundschau* (0·2m.). In 1994, 381 newspapers and 9,093 periodicals were published with respective circulations of 30·6m. and 387·8m. In 1995 there were 1,260 academic and special libraries, and 13,032 public libraries, the latter with 9·39m. active users.

SOCIAL INSTITUTIONS

Justice. Justice is administered by the federal courts and by the courts of the Länder. In criminal procedures, civil cases and procedures of non-contentious jurisdiction the courts on the *Land* level are the local courts *(Amtsgerichte)*, the regional courts *(Landgerichte)* and the courts of appeal *(Oberlandesgerichte)*. Constitutional federal disputes are dealt with by the Federal Constitutional Court *(Bundesverfassungsgericht)* elected by the Bundestag and Bundesrat. The Länder also have constitutional courts. In labour law disputes the courts of the first and second instance are the labour courts and the *Land* labour courts and in the third instance, the Federal Labour Court *(Bundesarbeitsgericht)*. Disputes about public law in matters of social security, unemployment insurance, maintenance of war victims and similar cases are dealt with in the first and second instances by the social courts and the *Land* social courts and in the third instance by the Federal Social Court *(Bundessozialgericht)*. In most tax matters the finance courts of the Länder are competent and in the second instance, the Federal Finance Court *(Bundesfinanzhof)*. Other controversies of public law in non-constitutional matters are decided in the first and second instance by the administrative and the higher administrative courts *(Oberverwaltungsgerichte)* of the Länder, and in the third instance by the Federal Administrative Court *(Bundesverwaltungsgericht)*.

For the inquiry into maritime accidents the admiralty courts *(Seeämter)* are competent on the *Land* level and in the second instance the Federal Admiralty Court *(Bundesoberseeamt)* in Hamburg. The death sentence has been abolished.

Religion. In 1995 there were 27,922,000 Protestants in 18,243 parishes, 27,347,000 Roman Catholics in 13,328 parishes, and in 1996 61,203 Jews with 17 rabbis and 70 synagogues.

There are 5 Roman Catholic archbishoprics (Bamberg, Cologne, Freiburg, Munich and Freising, Paderborn) and 23 bishoprics. Chairman of the German Bishops' Conference is Cardinal Joseph Höffner, Archbishop of Cologne. A concordat between Germany and the Holy See dates from 10 Sept. 1933.

The Evangelical (Protestant) Church (EKD) consists of 24 member-churches including 7 Lutheran Churches, 8 United-Lutheran-Reformed, 2 Reformed Churches and 1 Confederation of United member Churches: 'Church of the Union'. Its organs are the Synod, the Church Conference and the Council under the chairmanship of Bishop Dr Eduard Lohse (Hanover). There are also some 12 Evangelical Free Churches.

Education. Education is compulsory for children aged 6 to 15. After the first 4 (or 6) years at primary school *(Grundschulen)* children attend post-primary *(Hauptschulen)*, secondary modern *(Realschulen)*, grammar *(Gymnasien)*, or comprehensive schools *(Integrierte Gesamtschulen)*. Secondary modern school comprises 6, grammar school 9, years. Entry to higher education is by the final Grammar School Certificate (Abitur-Higher School Certificate). There are special schools *(Sonderschulen)* for handicapped or maladjusted children.

In 1995–96 there were 4,183 kindergartens with 84,024 pupils and 5,471 teachers, 17,910 primary schools with 3,634,342 pupils and 199,623 teachers and 8,490 post-primary schools with 1,498,201 pupils and 100,156 teachers. There were also 3,397 special schools with 391,118 pupils and 62,541 teachers, 3,504 secondary modern schools with 1,175,168 pupils and 73,069 teachers; 3,168 grammar schools with 2,164,625 pupils and 154,379 teachers; 978 comprehensive schools with 571,590 pupils and 45,461 teachers.

In the 1995–96 academic year there were 670,107 working teachers, of whom 426,886 were female.

The adult literacy rate is 99·0%.

Vocational education is provided in part-time, full-time and advanced vocational schools (*Berufs-, Berufsaufbau-, Berufsfach-* and *Fachschulen,* including *Fachschulen für Technik* and *Schulen des Gesundheitswesens*). Occupation-related, part-time vocational training of 6 to 12 hours per week is compulsory for all (including unemployed) up to the age of 18 years or until the completion of the practical vocational training. Full-time vocational schools comprise courses of at least one year. They prepare for commercial and domestic occupations as well as specialized occupations in the field of handicrafts. Advanced full-time vocational schools are attended by pupils over 18. Courses vary from 6 months to 3 or more years.

In 1995–96 there were 9,245 full- and part-time vocational schools with 2,435,753 students and 107,548 teachers.

Higher Education. In the winter term of the 1996–97 academic year there were 335 institutes of higher education (*Hochschulen*) with 1,838,456 students including 84 universities (1,199,996 students), 7 polytechnics (*Gesamthochschulen*; 145,135), 6 teacher training colleges (18,659), 16 theological seminaries (2,540), 46 schools of art (30,108), 146 technical colleges (397,507) and 30 management schools (44,551). Only 12·1% of students were in their first year.

Health. In 1996 there were 279,335 doctors, 61,404 dentists and 45,534 pharmacists. In 1995 there were 2,325 hospitals (including 207 psychiatric and neurological and 373 private) with 609,123 beds.

Welfare. *Social Health Insurance* (introduced in 1883). Wage-earners and apprentices, salaried employees with an income below a certain limit and social insurance pensioners are compulsorily insured. Voluntary insurance is also possible.

Benefits: Medical treatment, medicines, hospital and nursing care, maternity benefits, death benefits for the insured and their families, sickness payments and outpatients' allowances. Economy measures of Dec. 1992 introduced prescription charges related to recipients' income.

50·83m. persons were insured in 1996 (29·8m. compulsorily). Number of cases of incapacity for work (1994) totalled 35·69m., and the number of working days lost were 317·6m. (men) and 243·78m. (women). Total disbursements, 234,274m. DM.

Accident Insurance (introduced in 1884). Those insured are all persons in employment or service, apprentices and the majority of the self-employed and the unpaid family workers.

Benefits in the case of industrial injuries and occupational diseases: Medical treatment and nursing care, sickness payments, pensions and other payments in cash and in kind, surviving dependants' pensions.

Number of insured in 1994, 53·84m.; number of current pensions, 1,185,850; total disbursements, 24,312m. DM.

Workers' and Employees' Old-Age Insurance Scheme (introduced in 1889). All wage-earners and salaried employees, the members of certain liberal professions and—subject to certain conditions—self-employed craftsmen are compulsorily insured. The insured may voluntarily continue to insure when no longer liable to do so or increase the insurance.

Benefits: Measures designed to maintain, improve and restore the earning capacity; pensions paid to persons incapable of work, old age and surviving dependants' pensions.

Number of insured in April 1995, 43·55m. (20·83m. women); number of current pensions (in July 1996), 20·30m.; pensions to widows and widowers, 5·06m. Total disbursements in 1995, 398,081m. DM.

There are also special retirement and unemployment pension schemes for miners and farmers, assistance for war victims and compensation payments to members of German minorities in East European countries expelled after the Second World War and persons who suffered damage because of the war or in connection with the currency reform.

Family Allowances. 37,285m. DM were dispensed to 8·45m. recipients (0·86m. foreigners) in 1996 on behalf of 14·11m. children. Paid child care leave is available for 3 years to mothers or fathers.

Unemployment Allowances. In 1996, 1·99m. persons (0·87m. women) were receiving unemployment benefit and 1·10m. (0·47m. women) earnings-related benefit. Total expenditure on these and similar benefits (e.g. short-working supplement, job creation schemes) was 105·59m. DM in 1996.

Public Welfare (introduced in 1962). In 1993, 48·92m. DM were distributed to 5·02m. recipients (2·67m. women).

Public Youth Welfare. For supervision of foster children, official guardianship, assistance with adoptions and affiliations, social assistance in juvenile courts, educational assistance and correctional education under a court order. Total expenditure in 1994, 24,880m. DM received by 788,562 people.

DIPLOMATIC REPRESENTATIVES

Of Germany in Great Britain (23 Belgrave Sq., London, SW1X 8PZ)
Ambassador: Gebhardt von Moltke.

Of Great Britain in Germany (Friedrich-Ebert-Allee 77, 53113 Bonn)
Ambassador: Paul Lever.

Of Germany in the USA (4645 Reservoir Rd, NW, Washington, D.C., 20007)
Ambassador: Jürgen Chrobog.

Of the USA in Germany (Deichmanns Ave., 5300 Bonn)
Ambassador: John Kornblum.

Of Germany to the United Nations
Ambassador: Antonius Eitel.

Further Reading

Statistisches Bundesamt. *Statistisches Jahrbuch für die Bundesrepublik Deutschland; Wirtschaft und Statistik* (monthly, from 1949); *Das Arbeitsgebiet der Bundesstatistik* (latest issue 1988; Abridged English version: *Survey of German Federal Statistics*).

Ardagh, J., *Germany and the Germans.* 2nd ed. London, 1991
Balfour, M., *Germany: the Tides of Power.* London, 1992
Bark, D. L. and Gress, D. R., *A History of West Germany, 1945–1991.* 2nd ed. 2 vols. Oxford, 1993
Betz, H. G., *Postmodern Politics in Germany.* London, 1991
Blackbourn, D., *Fontana History of Germany, 1780–1918, the long nineteenth century.* London, 1997
Blackbourn, D. and Eley, G., *The Peculiarities of German History.* 1984
Carr, W., *A History of Germany, 1815–1990.* 4th ed. London, 1991
Childs, D., *Germany in the 20th Century.* London, 1991
Dennis, M., *German Democratic Republic.* London, 1987
Detwiler, D. S. and Detwiler, I. E., *West Germany.* [Bibliography] Oxford and Santa Barbara, 1988
Edinger, L. J., *West German Politics.* New York, 1986
Eley, G., *From Unification to Nazism: Reinterpreting the German Past.* London, 1986
Fulbrook, M., *A Concise History of Germany.* CUP, 1991.—*The Divided Nation: a History of Germany, 1918–1990.* CUP, 1992
Glees, A., *Reinventing Germany: German political development since 1945.* Oxford, 1996
Huelshoff, M. G. *et al.* (eds.) *From Bundesrepublik to Deutschland: German Politics after Reunification.* Michigan Univ. Press, 1993
Kielinger, T., *Crossroads and Roundabouts, Junctions in German-British Relations.* Bonn, 1997
Loth, W., *Stalin's Unwanted Child – The Soviet Union, the German Question and the Founding of the GDR.* London, 1998
Maier, C. S., *Dissolution: The Crisis of Communism and the End of East Germany.* Princeton, N.J., 1997
Marsh, D., *The New Germany: at the Crossroads.* London, 1990
Marshall, B., *The Origins of Post-War German Politics.* London, 1988
Nicholls, A. J., *The Bonn Republic: West German Democracy, 1945–1990.* Harlow, 1998
Orlow, D., *The History of Modern Germany, 1871 to the Present.* 3rd ed. New York, 1994

Parkes, S., *Understanding Contemporary Germany*. London, 1996
Pulzer, P., *German Politics, 1945–1995*. OUP, 1995
Schmidt, H., *Handeln für Deutschland*. Berlin, 1993
Schweitzer, D.-C., (ed.) *Politics and Government in the Federal Republic of Germany: Basic Documents*. 2nd ed. Oxford, 1994
Sinn, G. and Sinn, H.-W., *Jumpstart: the Economic Reunification of Germany.* Boston (MA), 1993
Smyser, W.R., *The Economy of United Germany: Colossus at the Crossroads.* New York, 1992
Stürmer, M., *Die Grenzen der Macht.* Berlin, 1992
Taylor, R., *Berlin and its Culture.* Yale University Press, 1997
Thompson, W. C. *et al., Historical Dictionary of Germany.* Metuchen (NJ), 1995
Turner, H. A., *Germany from Partition to Reunification.* 2nd ed. [of *Two Germanies since 1945*]. Yale Univ. Press, 1993
Tusa, A., *The Last Division – A History of Berlin, 1945–1989.* Reading, Mass., 1997
Wallace, I., *East Germany: the German Democratic Republic.* [Bibliography]. Oxford and Santa Barbara (CA), 1987
Watson, A., *The Germans: Who Are They Now?* 2nd ed. London, 1994

Other more specialized titles are listed under CONSTITUTION AND GOVERNMENT *and* BANKING AND FINANCE, *above.*

National statistical office: Statistiches Bundesamt, 62 Wiesbaden 1, Gustav Stresemann Ring 11. *President:* Johann Hahlen. *Website:* http://www.statistik-bund.de
National libraries: Deutsche Bibliothek, Zeppelinallee 4–8; Frankfurt am Main. *Director:* K.-D. Lehmann; (Berliner) Staatsbibliothek Preussischer Kulturbesitz, Potsdamer Str., Postfach 1407 D-1000 Berlin 30. *Director:* Dr. Richard Landwehrmeyer.

THE LÄNDER

BADEN-WÜRTTEMBERG

KEY HISTORICAL EVENTS. The *Land* is a combination of former states. Baden (the western part of the present *Land*) became a united margravate in 1771, after being divided as Baden-Baden and Baden-Durlach since 1535; Baden-Baden was predominantly Catholic and Baden-Durlach, Protestant.

The margrave became an ally of Napoleon, ceding land west of the Rhine and receiving northern and southern territory as compensation. In 1805 Baden became a grand duchy and in 1806 a member state of the Confederation of the Rhine, extending from the Main to Lake Constance. In 1815 it was a founder-state of the German Confederation. A constitution was granted by the grand duke in 1818, but later rulers were less liberal and there was revolution in 1848, put down with Prussian help. The grand Duchy was abolished and replaced by a *Land* in 1919.

In 1949 Baden was combined with Württemberg to form three states; the three were brought together as 1 in 1952.

Württemberg, having been a duchy since 1495, became a kingdom in 1805 and joined the Confederations as did Baden. A constitution was granted in 1819 and the state remained liberal. In 1866 the king allied himself with Austria against Prussia, but in 1870 joined Prussia in war against France. The liberal monarchy came to an end with the abdication of William II in 1918, and Württemberg became a state of the German Republic. In 1945 the state was divided between different Allied occupation authorities but the divisions ended in 1952.

TERRITORY AND POPULATION. Baden-Württemberg comprises 35,751 sq. km, with a population (at 31 Dec. 1996) of 10,374,505 (5,297,785 females, 5,076,720 males).

The *Land* is divided into 4 administrative regions, 9 urban and 35 rural districts, and numbers 1,111 communes. The capital is Stuttgart.

Vital statistics for calendar years:

	Live births	Marriages	Divorces	Deaths
1993	117,982	59,885	19,108	98,572
1994	113,398	59,591	19,910	96,638
1995	112,459	58,198	19,921	97,733
1996	114,657	57,898	20,759	98,908

CONSTITUTION AND GOVERNMENT. The *Land* Baden-Württemberg is a merger of the 3 *Länder*, Baden, Württemberg-Baden and Württemberg-Hohenzollern, which were formed in 1952. The merger was approved by a plebiscite held on 9 Dec. 1951, when 70% of the population voted in its favour. It has 6 votes in the Bundesrat. At the elections to the 155-member Diet of March 1996, turn-out was 67·6%. The Christian Democrats won 69 seats with 41·3% of the vote, the Social Democrats 39 with 25·1%, the Republicans 14 with 9·1%, the Greens 19 with 9·5% and the Free Democrats 14 with 9·6%.

Erwin Teufel (CDU) is *Prime Minister* (Minister President).

AGRICULTURE. Area and yield of the most important crops:

	Area (in 1,000 ha)			Yield (in 1,000 tonnes)		
	1994	1995	1996	1994	1995	1996
Rye	14·0	15·5	12·7	67·2	73·0	71·9
Wheat	204·7	214·9	214·7	1,226·4	1,185·4	1,576·6
Barley	194·6	191·1	202·9	926·8	885·7	1,170·0
Oats	63·4	55·6	54·8	294·1	254·3	324·5
Potatoes	9·7	9·7	9·7	294·1	274·7	391·7
Sugar-beet	22·5	22·5	22·5	1,252·0	1,289·8	1,336·2

Livestock in 1,000 (Dec. 1996): Cattle, 1,382·0 (including 490·3 milk cows); pigs, 2,231·3; sheep, 286·3; poultry, 5,490·5.

INDUSTRY. In 1996, 8,585 establishments (with 20 and more employees) employed 1,228,010 persons; of these, 271,686 were employed in machine construction (excluding office machines, data processing equipment and facilities); 29,439 in the textile industry; 203,756 in electrical engineering; 195,201 in car manufacture.

LABOUR. Economically active persons totalled 4,764,400 at the 1%-EU-sample survey of April 1996. Of the total 539,900 were self-employed (including family-workers), 4·23m. employees: 119,700 were engaged in agriculture and forestry; 1,990,700 in power supply, mining, manufacturing and building; 961,800 in commerce and transport; 1,692,200 in other industries and services.

ROADS. On 1 Jan. 1997 there were 28,089 km of 'classified' roads, including 1,020 km of Autobahn, 4,979 km of federal roads, 10,016 km of first-class and 12,074 km of second-class highways. Motor vehicles, at 1 Jan. 1997, numbered 6,514,536, including 5,471,966 passenger cars, 9,466 buses, 250,491 lorries, 325,933 tractors and 365,540 motor cycles.

JUSTICE. There are a constitutional court *(Staatsgerichtshof)*, 2 courts of appeal, 17 regional courts, 108 local courts, a *Land* labour court, 9 labour courts, a *Land* social court, 8 social courts, a finance court, a higher administrative court *(Verwaltungsgerichtshof)*, 4 administrative courts.

RELIGION. On 1 Jan. 1997, 39·1% of the population were Protestants and 43·6% were Roman Catholics.

EDUCATION. In 1996–97 there were 2,679 primary schools *(Grund- und Hauptschulen)* with 34,895 teachers and 682,527 pupils; 549 special schools with 9,271 teachers and 49,647 pupils; 448 intermediate schools with 11,446 teachers and 205,711 pupils; 412 high schools with 18,850 teachers and 263,142 pupils; 41 *Freie Waldorf* schools with 1,381 teachers and 18,557 pupils. Other general schools had 597 teachers and 8,294 pupils in total; there were also 733 vocational schools with 359,032 pupils. There were 39 *Fachhochschulen* (colleges of engineering and others) with 58,865 students in winter term 1996–97.

In the winter term 1996–97 there were 9 universities (Freiburg, 22,073 students; Heidelberg, 26,587; Konstanz, 8,659; Tübingen, 23,076; Karlsruhe, 17,312; Stuttgart, 18,134; Hohenheim, 5,088; Mannheim, 11,498; Ulm, 5,201); 6 teacher-training colleges with 18,657 students; 5 colleges of music with 2,846 students and 3 colleges of fine arts with 1,214 students.

Statistical Information: Statistisches Landesamt Baden-Württemberg (P.O.B. 10 60 33, 70049 Stuttgart) (*President:* Dr Eberhard Leibing), publishes: *'Baden-Württemberg in Wort und Zahl'* (monthly); *Jahrbücher für Statistik und Landeskunde von Baden-Württemberg; Statistik von Baden-Württemberg* (series); *Statistisch-prognostischer Bericht* (latest issue 1997); *Statistisches Taschenbuch* (latest issue 1997).

State libraries: Württembergische Landesbibliothek, Konrad-Adenauer-Str. 8, 70173 Stuttgart. Badische Landesbibliothek Karlsruhe, Lamm-Str. 16, 76133 Karlsruhe.

BAVARIA

Bayern

KEY HISTORICAL EVENTS. Bavaria was ruled by the Wittelsbach family from 1180. The duchy remained Catholic after the Reformation, which made it a natural ally of Austria and the Hapsburg Emperors.

The present boundaries were reached during the Napoleonic wars, and Bavaria became a kingdom in 1805. Despite the granting of a constitution and parliament, radical feeling forced the abdication of King Ludwig I in 1848. Maximilian II was followed by Ludwig II who allied himself with Austria against Prussia in 1866, but was reconciled with Prussia and entered the German Empire in 1871.

In 1918 the King Ludwig III abdicated. The first years of republican government were filled with unrest, attempts at the overthrow of the state by both communist and right-wing groups culminating in an unsuccessful coup by Adolf Hitler in 1923.

The state of Bavaria included the Palatinate from 1214 until 1945, when it was taken from Bavaria and added to the Rhineland. The present *Land* of Bavaria was formed in 1948.

Munich became capital of Bavaria in the reign of Albert IV (1467–1508) and remains capital of the *Land*.

TERRITORY AND POPULATION. Bavaria has an area of 70,552 sq. km. The capital is Munich. There are 7 administrative regions, 25 urban districts, 71 rural districts, 260 unadopted areas and 2,056 communes, 1,021 of which are members of 325 administrative associations. The population (31 Dec. 1996) numbered 12,043,869 (5,876,744 males, 6,167,125 females).Vital statistics for calendar years:

	Live births	*Marriages*	*Divorces*	*Deaths*
1993	133,897	70,475	23,011	122,649
1994	127,828	69,401	23,087	121,581
1995	125,995	67,075	23,434	121,992
1996	129,376	66,767	24,259	123,329

CONSTITUTION AND GOVERNMENT. The Constituent Assembly, elected on 30 June 1946, passed a constitution on the lines of the democratic constitution of 1919, but with greater emphasis on state rights; this was agreed upon by the Christian Social Union (CSU) and the Social Democrats (SPD). Bavaria has 6 seats in the Bundesrat. The CSU replaces the Christian Democratic Party in Bavaria.

At the Diet elections on 25 Sept. 1994 the CSU won 120 seats with 52·8% of votes cast; the SPD, 70 with 30%, and Alliance '90/The Greens, 14 with 6·1%. The *Prime Minister* is Dr Edmund Stoiber (CSU).

At the *local government* elections of March 1996 the CSU won 43·1% of votes cast and the SPD 25·7%.

AGRICULTURE. Area and yield of the most important products:

	Area (in 1,000 ha)			*Yield (in 1,000 tonnes)*		
	1994	*1995*	*1996*	*1994*	*1995*	*1996*
Wheat	446·1	453·2	446·6	2,873·0	2,727·1	3,162·4
Rye	67·3	70·3	54·0	332·2	341·3	285·4
Barley	457·0	455·7	473·4	2,339·5	2,292·5	2,511·9
Oats	92·5	77·1	75·0	386·9	360·1	388·9
Potatoes	58·7	60·3	62·5	1,932·7	1,706·7	2,727·2
Sugar-beet	78·2	79·1	79·0	4,494·5	4,641·4	4,804·2

Livestock, 1996: 4,225,000 cattle (including 1,559,000 milk cows); 109,000 horses; 383,000 sheep; 3,521,000 pigs; 9,968,000 poultry.

INDUSTRY. In 1996, 8,306 establishments (with 20 or more employees) employed 1,198,378 persons; of these, 141,873 were employed in the manufacture of motor vehicles, 191,931 in the manufacture of machinery and equipment and 56,345 in the manufacture of textiles and textile products.

LABOUR. The economically active persons totalled 5,744,000 at the 1% sample survey of the microcensus of 1996. Of the total, 663,000 were self-employed, 130,000 unpaid family workers, 4,951,000 employees; 2,127,000 in power supply, mining, manufacturing and building; 1,278,000 in commerce and transport; 2,098,000 in other industries and services.

ROADS. There were, on 1 Jan. 1997, 41,622 km of 'classified' roads, including 2,192 km of Autobahn, 6,832 km of federal roads, 13,957 km of first-class and 18,621 km of second-class highways. Number of motor vehicles on 1 Jan. 1997 was 8,046,579, including 6,474,558 passenger cars, 314,613 lorries, 13,940 buses, 588,297 tractors, 541,297 motor cycles.

JUSTICE. There are a constitutional court *(Verfassungsgerichtshof)*, a supreme *Land* court *(Oberstes Landesgericht)*, 3 courts of appeal, 22 regional courts, 72 local courts, 2 *Land* labour courts, 11 labour courts, a *Land* social court, 7 social courts, 2 finance courts, a higher administrative court *(Verwaltungsgerichtshof)*, 6 administrative courts.

RELIGION. At the census of 25 May 1987 there were 67·2% Roman Catholics and 23·9% Protestants.

EDUCATION. In 1996–97 there were 2,841 primary schools with 47,407 teachers and 846,365 pupils; 375 special schools with 7,117 teachers and 57,338 pupils; 331 intermediate schools with 9,235 teachers and 142,196 pupils; 396 high schools with 21,142 teachers and 300,100 pupils; 239 part-time vocational schools with 7,903 teachers and 279,451 pupils, including 48 special part-time vocational schools with 843 teachers and 11,906 pupils; 592 full-time vocational schools with 4,463 teachers and 58,155 pupils including 264 schools for public health occupations with 1,381 teachers and 18,123 pupils; 374 advanced full-time vocational schools with 2,082 teachers and 25,847 pupils; 84 vocational high schools *(Berufsoberschulen, Fachoberschulen)* with 1,989 teachers and 29,411 pupils.

In 1996–97 there were 11 universities with 177,908 students (Augsburg, 13,569; Bamberg, 7,942; Bayreuth, 7,946; Eichstätt, 3,870; Erlangen-Nürnberg, 23,507; München, 57,681; Passau, 8,040; Regensburg, 16,229; Würzburg, 19,620; the Technical University of München, 17,488; München, University of the Federal Armed Forces *(Universität der Bundeswehr)*, 2,016); plus the college of politics, München, 657; the college of philosophy, München, 342, and 2 philosophical-theological colleges with 295 students in total (Benediktbeuern, 131; Neuendettelsau, 164). There were also 2 colleges of music, 2 colleges of fine arts and 1 college of television and film, with 2,454 students in total; 18 vocational colleges *(Fachhochschulen)* with 58,470 students including one for the civil service *(Bayerische Beamtenfachhochschule)* with 4,692 students.

Statistical Information: Bayerisches Landesamt für Statistik und Datenverarbeitung, Neuhauser Str. 8, 80331 Munich, was founded in 1833. *President:* Wolfgang Kupfahl. It publishes: *Statistisches Jahrbuch für Bayern.* 1894 ff.—*Bayern in Zahlen.* Monthly (from Jan. 1947).—*Zeitschrift des Bayerischen Statistischen Landesamts.* July 1869–1943; 1948 ff.—*Beiträge zur Statistik Bayerns.* 1850 ff.—*Statistische Berichte.* 1951 ff.—*Kreisdaten.* 1972 ff.—*Gemeindedaten.* 1973 ff.

Nawiasky, H. and Luesser, C., *Die Verfassung des Freistaates Bayern vom 2. Dez. 1946.* Munich, 1948; supplement, by H. Nawiasky and H. Lechner, Munich, 1953

State Library: Bayerische Staatsbibliothek, Munich. *Director:* Dr Hermann Leskin.

BERLIN

KEY HISTORICAL EVENTS. Greater Berlin was under 4-power (France, USSR, UK and USA) Allied government (the *Kommandatura*) from 5 June 1945 until 1 July 1948, when the Soviet element withdrew. On 30 Nov. 1948 a separate municipal government was set up in the Soviet sector. The French, UK and US sectors coalesced to form the administrative unit of 'West Berlin', covering 480 sq. km. With the establishment of the German Democratic Republic, the Soviet sector ('East Berlin', 403 sq. km) was designated its capital. East and West Berlin were amalgamated on the re-unification of Germany in Oct. 1990, and Berlin was declared the national capital. All except 6 federal ministries are scheduled to move to Berlin from Bonn in phases by 2000.

In April 1994 the *Land* governments of Berlin and Brandenburg agreed to merge the 2 *Länder* in 1999 or 2002, subject to the approval of their respective parliaments, and of their electorates in referendums held in May 1996. In Berlin 53·4% of votes were cast in favour, but in Brandenburg 62·8% were against.

TERRITORY AND POPULATION. The area is 891 sq. km. Population, 31 Dec. 1995, 3,471,418 (51·9% female), including 449,500 foreign nationals; density, 3,897 per sq. km.

Vital statistics for calendar years:

	Live births	Marriages	Divorces	Deaths
1992	29,667	17,895	6,644	42,001
1993	28,724	17,111	6,557	41,273
1994	28,503	17,269	8,108	40,738
1995	28,648	16,383	. . .	39,245

CONSTITUTION AND GOVERNMENT. According to the constitutions of Sept. 1950 and Oct. 1995, Berlin is simultaneously a *Land* of the Federal Republic and a city. It is governed by a House of Representatives (of at least 150 members); executive power is vested in a Senate, consisting of the Governing Mayor, the Mayor and not more than 16 senators.

After a proposed merger was rejected by Brandenburg in the 1996 referendum, a Joint Berlin-Brandenburg Co-operation Council was set up.

Berlin has 5 seats in the Bundesrat.

At the elections of 22 Oct. 1995 the Christian Democrats (CDU) won 87 seats in the House of Representatives with 37·4% of votes cast; the Social Democrats (SPD), 55, with 23·6%; the Party of Democratic Socialism (former Communists), 34, with 14·6%; and the Alliance '90/Greens, 30, with 13·2%.

In Jan. 1996 a CPU-SPD coalition government was formed.

Governing Mayor: Eberhard Diepgen (CDU).

INDUSTRY. In 1995 the main industries in terms of percentage of the labour force employed were: Electronics, 31·3%; food and tobacco, 13%; machine-building, 10·4%; chemicals, 8·5%; vehicle production, 6·6%; metallurgy, 6·3%; printing, 3·8%. There were some 25,000 business enterprises.

LABOUR. In 1995 the workforce was 1·6m., including 0·24m. craft workers. There were 216,000 persons registered unemployed in Jan. 1995 and 16,328 on short time in 1994. 12,509 jobs were available in 1995.

ROADS. In 1996 there were 249 km of roads, made up of 61 km of Autobahn and 188 km of federal roads. At Dec. 1995, 1,397,414 motor vehicles were registered, including 1,218,841 passenger cars, 89,103 lorries and buses, and 63,777 motor cycles. There were 26,294 road accidents in 1994.

JUSTICE. There are a court of appeal *(Kammergericht)*, a regional court, 9 local courts, a *Land* Labour court, a labour court, a *Land* social court, a social court, a higher administrative court, an administrative court and a finance court.

EDUCATION. In 1995–96 there were 413,449 pupils attending schools. There were 497 primary schools with 146,622 pupils, 551 post-primary schools with 83,098 pupils, 98 special schools with 13,297 pupils, 87 secondary modern schools with 31,346 pupils, 129 grammar schools with 84,726 pupils and 81 comprehensive schools with 54,360 pupils. In 1994–95 there were 2 universities and 1 technical university, 4 art colleges and 9 technical colleges. There was a total of some 147,000 students in higher education.

Statistical Information: The Statistisches Landesamt Berlin was founded in 1862 (Alt-Friedrichsfelde 60, 10315 Berlin (Lichtenberg)). *Director:* Prof. Günther Appel. It publishes: *Statistisches Jahrbuch* (from 1867): *Berliner Statistik* (monthly, from 1947).—*100 Jahre Berliner Statistik* (1962).

State Library: Amerika-Gedenkbibliothek-Berliner Zentralbibliothek, Blücherplatz 1, D-1000 Berlin 61. *Director:* Dr Klaus Bock.

Further Reading

Read, A., and Fisher, D., *Berlin, Biography of a City*. London, 1994
Taylor, R., *Berlin and its Culture*. London, 1997

BRANDENBURG

KEY HISTORICAL EVENTS. For the proposed merger with Berlin *see* BERLIN: Key Historical Events.

TERRITORY AND POPULATION. The area is 29,476 sq. km. Population on 31 Dec. 1996 was 2,554,441 (1,297,228 females). There are 4 urban districts, 14 rural districts and 1,696 communes. The capital is Potsdam.

Vital statistics for calendar years:

	Live births	Marriages	Divorces	Deaths
1993	12,238	7,901	3,341	29,024
1994	12,443	8,502	3,851	28,490
1995	13,494	8,775	3,949	27,401
1996	15,140	8,756	4,016	27,622

CONSTITUTION AND GOVERNMENT. The *Land* was reconstituted on former GDR territory on 14 Oct. 1990. Brandenburg has 4 seats in the Bundesrat.

After a proposed merger was rejected by Brandenburg in the 1996 referendum, a Joint Berlin-Brandenburg Co-operation Council was set up.

At the Diet elections on 11 Sept. 1994 the Social Democrats (SPD) won 52 seats with 54·1% of the vote; the Christian Democrats (CDU), 18, with 18·7%; the Party of Democratic Socialism (PDS, former Communists), 18, with 18·7%. At a referendum on 14 June 1992, 93·5% of votes cast were in favour of a new constitution guaranteeing direct democracy and the right to work and housing.

At the *local government* elections of Dec. 1993 the SPD won 34·53% of votes cast, the PDS 21·23%, the CDU 20·4%, the FDP 7·1% and the Greens, 4·2%.

The *Prime Minister* is Dr Manfred Stolpe (SPD).

AGRICULTURE. Livestock in Dec. 1996: Cattle, 716,436 (including 229,582 milk cows); pigs, 718,415; sheep, 120,617; horses, 21,541; poultry, 6,193,040.

Area and yield of the most important crops:

	Area (in 1,000 ha)			Yield (in 1,000 tonnes)		
	1994	1995	1996	1994	1995	1996
Rye	173·2	214·7	220·5	665·2	950·4	883·7
Wheat	94·9	108·0	101·7	507·5	647·5	551·2
Barley	93·5	108·4	90·2	459·5	596·4	332·2
Oats	17·4	13·8	18·2	53·7	59·8	76·9
Potatoes	15·8	16·7	17·8	304·0	320·1	542·3
Sugar-beet	13·5	14·7	14·2	453·0	565·3	663·0

INDUSTRY. In 1996, 960 establishments (20 and more employees) employed 92,299 persons; of these, 12,006 were employed in mining and quarrying; 6,622 in machine construction; 13,211 in vehicle construction; 5,452 in chemical industries.

LABOUR. In April 1996 at the 1%-sample of the microcensus, 1,009,700 persons were economically active, including 78,900 self-employed and family assistants, 482,500 manual and 538,200 white-collar workers, and 31,900 civil servants. In Dec. 1996 there were 195,526 unemployed persons.

ROADS. In Jan. 1996 there were 1,443,589 passenger cars, 102,263 lorries, 2,860 buses and 40,225 motor cycles.

EDUCATION. In 1996–97 there were 1,168 schools providing general education (including special schools) with 405,734 pupils, and (1991–92) 49 vocational schools with 48,340 pupils.

In the winter term 1996–97 there were 3 universities and 8 colleges with 22,230 students.

BREMEN

Freie Hansestadt Bremen

KEY HISTORICAL EVENTS. The state is dominated by the Free City of Bremen and its port, Bremerhaven.

In 1815, when it joined the German Confederation, Bremen was an autonomous city and Hanse port with important Baltic trade. In 1827 the expansion of trade inspired the founding of Bremerhaven, on land ceded by Hanover at the confluence of the Geest and Weser rivers. Further expansion followed the founding of the Norddeutscher Lloyd Shipping Company in 1857.

Merchant shipping, associated trade and fishing were dominant until 1940; there was diversification in post-war years. In 1939 Bremerhaven was absorbed by the Hanoverian town of Wesermünde. The combined port was returned to the jurisdiction of Bremen in 1947.

TERRITORY AND POPULATION. The area of the *Land*, consisting of the 2 urban districts and ports of Bremen and Bremerhaven, is 404 sq. km. Population, 31 Dec. 1995, 679,757 (327,323 males, 352,434 females).

Vital statistics for calendar years:

	Live births	Marriages	Divorces	Deaths
1993	6,656	3,969	1,736	8,643
1994	6,288	3,859	1,614	8,123
1995	6,429	3,561	1,799	8,378
1996	6,623	3,509	1,870	8,080

CONSTITUTION AND GOVERNMENT. Political power is vested in the 100-member House of Burgesses *(Bürgerschaft)* which appoints the executive, called the Senate. Bremen has 3 seats in the Bundesrat. At the elections of 14 May 1995 the Social Democratic Party won 37 seats with 33·4% of votes cast (41 with 38·8% in 1991); the Christian Democrats, 37 with 32·6% (32 with 30·7%); the Alliance '90/Greens, 14 with 13·1% (11 with 11·4%) and the AFB, 12 with 10·7%. The Free Democrats gained no seats with 3·4% (10 with 9·5%). The Senate president is Dr Henning Scherf (Social Democrat).

AGRICULTURE. Agricultural area comprised (1995) 9,400 ha. Livestock (2 Dec. 1996): 12,758 cattle (including 3,746 milk cows); 2,026 pigs; 253 sheep; 1,208 horses; 17,481 poultry.

INDUSTRY. In 1996, 338 establishments (20 and more employees) employed 67,164 persons; of these, 4,241 were employed in shipbuilding (except naval engineering); 5,528 in machine construction; 8,351 in electrical engineering; 1,591 in coffee and tea processing.

LABOUR. The economically active persons totalled 279,700 at the microcensus of April 1996. Of the total, 25,800 were self-employed, 253,900 employees; 83,200 in production industries, 77,100 in commerce, trade and communications, 117,100 in other industries and services.

ROADS. On 1 Jan. 1996 there were 112 km of 'classified' roads, including 48 km of Autobahn and 64 km of federal roads. Registered motor vehicles on 1 July 1997 numbered 331,139, including 290,940 passenger cars, 15,800 trucks, 2,766 tractors, 603 buses and 16,074 motor cycles.

SHIPPING. Vessels entered in 1996, 8,330 of 43,638,905 net tons; cleared, 8,365 of 43,931,175 net tons. Sea traffic, 1996, incoming 19,140,000 tonnes; outgoing, 12,360,000 tonnes.

JUSTICE. There are a constitutional court *(Staatsgerichtshof)*, a court of appeal, a regional court, 3 local courts, a *Land* labour court, 2 labour courts, a *Land* social court, a finance court, a higher administrative court, an administrative court.

RELIGION. On 25 May 1987 (census) there were 61% Protestants and 10% Roman Catholics.

EDUCATION. In 1996 there were 390 new system schools with 5,026 teachers and 70,521 pupils; 27 special schools with 591 teachers and 2,698 pupils; 26 part-time vocational schools with 17,792 pupils; 25 full-time vocational schools with 4,638 pupils; 8 advanced vocational schools (including institutions for the training of technicians) with 890 pupils; 10 schools for public health occupations with 856 pupils.

In the winter term 1996–97, 17,078 students were enrolled at the university. In addition to the university there were 4 other colleges in 1996–97 with 8,817 students.

Statistical Information: Statistisches Landesamt Bremen (An der Weide 14–16 (P.B. 101309), D-28195 Bremen), founded in 1850. *Director:* Reg. Dir. Jürgen Dinse. Its current publications include: *Statistisches Jahrbuch Bremen* (from 1992).—*Statistische Mitteilungen* (from 1948).— *Statistische Monatsberichte* (from 1954).—*Statistische Berichte* (from 1956).—*Statistisches Handbuch Bremen (1950–60*, 1961; *1960–64*, 1967; *1965–69*, 1971; *1970–74*, 1975; *1975–80*, 1982; *1981–85*, 1987).—*Bremen im statistischen Zeitvergleich 1950–1976*. 1977.—*Bremen in Zahlen*. 1997.

State and University Library: Bibliotheksstr., D-28359 Bremen. *Director:* Annette Rath-Beckmann.

HAMBURG

Freie und Hansestadt Hamburg

KEY HISTORICAL EVENTS. Hamburg was a free Hanse town owing nominal allegiance to the Holy Roman Emperor until 1806. In 1815 it became part of the German Confederation, sharing a seat in the Federal Diet with Lübeck, Bremen and Frankfurt. During the Empire it retained its autonomy. By 1938 it had become the third largest port in the world, and its territory was extended by the cession of land (3 urban and 27 rural districts) from Prussia. In 1945 Hamburg became a *Land* of the Federal Republic with its 1938 boundaries.

TERRITORY AND POPULATION. Total area, 755 sq. km (1996), including the islands Neuwerk and Scharhörn (7·6 sq. km). Population (1 Jan. 1996), 1,707,900 (822,600 males, 885,300 females). The *Land* forms a single urban district *(kreisfreie Stadt)* with 7 administrative subdivisions.

Vital statistics for calendar years:

	Live births	Marriages	Divorces	Deaths
1992	16,497	9,006	4,028	20,444
1993	16,257	8,575	4,303	20,703
1994	16,201	8,537	4,545	20,241
1995	15,872	8,242	4,652	20,276

CONSTITUTION AND GOVERNMENT. The constitution of 6 June 1952 vests the supreme power in the House of Burgesses *(Bürgerschaft)* of 121 members. The executive is in the hands of the Senate, whose members are elected by the Bürgerschaft. Hamburg has 3 seats in the Bundesrat. The elections of 21 Sept. 1997 had the following results: Social Democrats, 54 seats with 36·2% of votes cast; Christian Democrats, 46 with 30·7%; Green Alternatives 21, with 13·9%. The First Burgomaster is Ortwin Runde (Social Democrat).

AGRICULTURE. The agricultural area comprised 14,120 ha in 1996. Yield, 1996, in tonnes, of cereals, 15,000; potatoes, 700.

Livestock (3 Dec. 1996): Cattle, 8,715 (including 1,537 milk cows); pigs, 3,289; horses, 2,847; sheep, 1,634; poultry, 11,764.

INDUSTRY. In June 1996, 610 establishments (with 20 and more employees) employed 112,038 persons; of these, 21,451 were employed in manufacturing transport equipment (including motor vehicles, aircraft and ships), 17,699 in manufacturing machinery, 16,194 in manufacturing electrical and optical equipment, 8,700 in manufacturing chemical products and 6,677 in mineral oil industry.

LABOUR. The economically active persons totalled 769,300 at the 1%-sample survey of the microcensus of April 1996. Of the total, 89,400 were self-employed or unpaid family workers, 680,000 were employees; 6,600 were engaged in agriculture and forestry, 179,200 in power supply, mining, manufacturing and building, 219,100 in commerce and transport, 364,400 in other industries and services.

ROADS. In April 1997 there were 4,369 km of roads, including 82 km of Autobahn, 149 km of federal roads. Number of motor vehicles (1 July 1997), 812,652, including 714,446 passenger cars, 42,687 lorries, 1,446 buses, 5,598 tractors, 34,771 motor cycles and 13,704 other motor vehicles.

SHIPPING. Hamburg is the largest sea port in Germany.

Vessels	1994	1995	1996
Entered: Number	12,027	11,679	11,489
Tonnage	56,702,530	58,640,110	61,181,978
Cleared: Number	12,153	11,798	11,635
Tonnage	56,728,185	58,898,385	61,045,871

JUSTICE. There is a constitutional court *(Verfassungsgericht)*, a court of appeal *(Oberlandesgericht)*, a regional court *(Landgericht)*, 6 local courts *(Amtsgerichte)*, a *Land* labour court, a labour court, a *Land* social court, a social court, a finance court, a higher administrative court, an administrative court.

RELIGION. On 25 May 1987 (census) Evangelical Church and Free Churches 50·2%, Roman Catholic Church 8·6%.

EDUCATION. In 1995 there were 387 schools of general education (not including *Internationale Schule*) with 13,458 teachers and 172,796 pupils; 54 special schools with 1,256 teachers and 7,524 pupils; 44 part-time vocational schools with 33,593 pupils; 6 schools with 504 pupils in their vocational preparatory year; 28 schools with 2,624 pupils in manual instruction classes; 42 full-time vocational schools with 8,724 pupils; 10 economic secondary schools with 2,008 pupils; 2 technical *Gymnasien* with 381 pupils; 22 advanced vocational schools with 4,580 pupils; 38 schools for public health occupations with 2,489 pupils; 2 vocational introducing schools with 80 pupils and 24 technical superior schools with 1,423 pupils; all these vocational and technical schools had a total number of 3,249 teachers.

In the winter term 1994–95 there was 1 university with 42,542 students; 1 technical university with 3,300 students; 1 college of music and 1 college of fine arts with 2,041 students in total; 1 university of the *Bundeswehr* with 1,768 students; 1 university of economics and political sciences with 3,285 students; 3 professional colleges with a total of 15,931 students.

Statistical Information: The Statistisches Landesamt der Freien und Hansestadt Hamburg (Steckelhörn 12, D-20457 Hamburg) publishes: *Hamburg in Zahlen, Statistische Berichte, Statistisches Taschenbuch, Statistik des Hamburgischen Staates, Hamburger Statistische Porträts.*

Hamburgische Gesellschaft für Wirtschaftsförderung mbH, *Hamburg.* Oldenburg, 1993
Klessmann, E., *Geschichte der Stadt Hamburg.* 7th ed. Hamburg, 1994
Möller, I., *Hamburg-Länderprofile.* Hamburg, 1985
Schubert, D. and Harms, H., *Wohnen am Hafen.* Hamburg, 1993
Schütt, E. C., *Die Chronik Hamburgs.* Hamburg, 1991

State Library: Staats- und Universitätsbibliothek, Carl von Ossietzky, Von-Melle-Park 3, D-20146 Hamburg. *Director:* Prof. Dr Horst Gronemeyer.

HESSEN

KEY HISTORICAL EVENTS. The *Land* consists of the former states of Hesse-Darmstadt and Hesse-Kassel, and Nassau. Hesse-Darmstadt was ruled by the Landgrave Louis X from 1790. He became grand duke in 1806 with absolute power, having dismissed the parliament in 1803. However, he granted a constitution and bicameral parliament in 1820.

Hesse-Darmstadt lost land to Prussia in the Seven Weeks' War of 1866, but retained its independence, both then and as a state of the German Empire after 1871. In 1918 the grand duke abdicated, and the territory became a state of the German Republic. In 1945 areas west of the Rhine were incorporated into the new *Land* of Rhineland-Palatinate, areas east of the Rhine became part of the *Land* of Greater Hesse.

Hesse-Kassel was ruled by the Landgrave William IX from 1785 until he became Elector in 1805. In 1807 the Electorate was absorbed into the Kingdom of Westphalia (a Napoleonic creation), becoming independent again in 1815 as a state of the German Confederation. In 1831 a constitution and parliament were granted, but the Electors remained strongly conservative.

In 1866 the Diet approved alliance with Prussia against Austria; the Elector nevertheless supported Austria. He was defeated by the Prussians and exiled, and Hesse-Kassel was annexed to Prussia. In 1867 it was combined with Frankfurt and some areas taken from Nassau and Hesse-Darmstadt to form a Prussian province (Hesse-Nassau).

Nassau had been divided into northern and southern states since the 13th century. In 1801 Nassau west of the Rhine passed to France; Napoleon also took the northern state in 1806. The remnant of the southern states allied in 1803, and three years later they became a duchy. In 1866 the duke supported Austria against Prussia, and the duchy was annexed by Prussia as a result.

In 1944 the Prussian province of Hesse-Nassau was split in two: Nassau, and Electoral Hesse, also called Kurhessen. The following year these were combined with Hesse-Darmstadt as the *Land* of Greater Hesse, which became known as Hessen.

TERRITORY AND POPULATION. Area, 21,114 sq. km. Its capital is Wiesbaden. There are 3 administrative regions with 5 urban and 21 rural districts and 426 communes. Population, 31 Dec 1996, was 6,027,284 (2,949,768 males, 3,077,516 females).

Vital statistics for calendar years:

	Live births	Marriages	Divorces	Deaths
1993	61,610	35,070	12,852	64,028
1994	60,565	35,215	13,697	63,385
1995	59,858	34,517	13,387	63,346
1996	62,391	33,251	13,677	63,387

CONSTITUTION AND GOVERNMENT. The constitution was put into force by popular referendum on 1 Dec. 1946. Hessen has 5 seats in the Bundesrat. At the Diet elections on 19 Feb. 1995 the Christian Democrats gained 39·2% of votes cast, the Social Democrats 38%, the Alliance 90/The Greens 11·2% and the Free Democrats 7·4%. The Social Democrat/Green cabinet is headed by *Prime Minister* Hans Eichel (SPD).

AGRICULTURE. Area and yield of the most important crops:

	Area (in 1,000 ha)			Yield (in 1,000 tonnes)		
	1994	1995	1996	1994	1995	1996
Wheat	130·2	134·3	140·2	880·7	949·3	1,055·9
Rye	26·6	26·8	23·7	143·9	149·3	138·7
Barley	109·9	108·4	110·4	576·2	609·0	653·7
Oats	30·0	26·6	25·8	130·7	124·9	150·8
Potatoes	5·9	6·0	6·1	205·1	178·3	245·1
Sugar-beet	21·0	20·8	20·7	1,098·4	1,104·2	1,117·4
Rape	48·3	49·5	48·5	137·4	158·6	96·2

Livestock, Dec. 1996: Cattle, 598,397 (including 187,526 milk cows); pigs, 869,198; sheep, 158,772; horses, 46,018; poultry, 2·19m.

INDUSTRY. In June 1997, 3,222 establishments (with 20 and more employees) employed 479,536 persons; of these, 74,634 were employed in chemical industry; 71,354 in car building; 66,797 in electrical engineering; 64,852 in machine construction; 31,953 in food industry.

LABOUR. The economically active persons totalled 2·7m. at the 1% sample survey of the microcensus of April 1996. Of the total, 276,200 were self-employed, 29,600 unpaid family workers, 2,383,400 employees; 52,900 were engaged in agriculture and forestry, 864,600 in power supply, mining, manufacturing and building, 651,300 in commerce, transport, hotels and restaurants, 1,120,300 in other services.

ROADS. On 1 Jan. 1997 there were 16,684 km of 'classified' roads, comprising 956 km of Autobahn, 3,419 km of federal highways, 7,222 km of first-class highways and 5,087 km of second-class highways. Motor vehicles licensed on 1 July 1997 totalled 3,841,499, including 3,281,590 passenger cars, 5,987 buses, 150,591 trucks, 135,615 tractors and 193,219 motor cycles.

JUSTICE. There are a constitutional court *(Staatsgerichtshof)*, a court of appeal, 9 regional courts, 58 local courts, a *Land* labour court, 12 labour courts, a *Land* social court, 7 social courts, a finance court, a higher administrative court *(Verwaltungsgerichtshof)*, 5 administrative courts.

RELIGION. In 1987 (census) there were 52·7% Protestants and 30·4% Roman Catholics.

EDUCATION. In 1996 there were 1,239 primary schools with 295,945 pupils (including *Förderstufen*); 158 intermediate schools with 49,774 pupils; 18,770 teachers in primary and intermediate schools; 227 special schools with 3,348 teachers and 19,758 pupils; 161 high schools with 8,977 teachers and 129,991 pupils; 211 *Gesamtschulen* (comprehensive schools) with 11,618 teachers and 178,001 pupils; 118 part-time vocational schools with 125,580 pupils; 259 full-time vocational schools with 38,893 pupils; 112 advanced vocational schools with 10,338 pupils; 7,761 teachers in the vocational schools.

In the winter term 1996–97 there were 3 universities (Frankfurt/Main, 34,833 students; Giessen, 21,313; Marburg/Lahn, 17,028); 1 technical university in Darmstadt (14,758); 1 private *Wissenschaftliche Hochschule,* (755); 1 *Gesamthochschule* (17,697); 16 *Fachhochschulen* (42,385); 2 Roman Catholic theological colleges and 1 Protestant theological college with a total of 359; 1 college of music and 2 colleges of fine arts with 1,313 students in total.

Statistical Information: The Hessisches Statistisches Landesamt (Rheinstr. 35–37, D-65175 Wiesbaden). *President:* Eckart Hohmann. Main publications: *Statistisches Handbuch für das Land Hessen* (zweijährlich).—*Staat und Wirtschaft in Hessen* (monthly).— *Beiträge zur Statistik Hessens.*—*Statistische Berichte.*—*Hessische Gemeindestatistik* (annual, 1980 ff.).

State Library: Hessische Landesbibliothek, Rheinstr. 55–57, D-65185 Wiesbaden. *Director:* Dr Dieter Wolf.

LOWER SAXONY

Niedersachsen

KEY HISTORICAL EVENTS. The *Land* consists of the former state of Hanover, with Oldenburg, Schaumburg-Lippe and Brunswick. It does not include the cities of Bremen or Bremerhaven.

Oldenburg, Danish from 1667, passed to the bishopric of Lübeck in 1773; the Holy Roman Emperor made it a duchy in 1777. As a small state of the Confederation after 1815, it supported Prussia, becoming a member of the Prussian Zollverein (1853) and North German Confederation (1867). The grand duke abdicated in 1918 and was replaced by an elected government.

Schaumburg-Lippe was a very small sovereign principality. As such it became a member of the Confederation of the Rhine in 1807 and of the German Confederation in 1815. Surrounded by Prussian territory, it also joined the Prussian-led North German Confederation in 1866. Part of the Empire until 1918, it then became a state of the new republic.

Brunswick, a small duchy, was taken into the Kingdom of Westphalia by Napoleon in 1806 but restored to independence in 1814. In 1830 the duke, Charles II, was forced into exile and replaced in 1831 by his more liberal brother, William. The succession passed to a Hanoverian claimant in 913, but the duchy ended in 1918 with the Empire.

As a state of the republican Germany, Brunswick was greatly reduced under the Third Reich. Its boundaries were restored by the British occupation forces in 1945.

Hanover was an autonomous Electorate of the Holy Roman Empire, whose rulers were also kings of Great Britain from 1714 until 1837. After 1762 they ruled almost entirely from England. After Napoleonic invasions Hanover was restored in 1815. A constitution of 1819 made no radical change, and had to be followed by more liberal versions in 1833 and 1848.

Prussia annexed Hanover, despite its proclaimed neutrality, in 1866; it remained a Prussian province until 1946.

On 1 Nov. 1946 all four states were combined by the British military administration to form the *Land* of Lower Saxony.

TERRITORY AND POPULATION. Lower Saxony has an area of 47,612 sq. km, and is divided into 4 administrative regions, 9 urban districts, 38 rural districts and 1,030 communes; capital, Hanover.

Estimated population, on 31 Dec. 1996, was 7,795,149 (3,806,224 males, 3,988,925 females).

Vital statistics for calendar years:

	Live births	Marriages	Divorces	Deaths
1993	84,579	48,247	14,674	85,397
1994	81,520	47,349	15,342	85,700
1995	80,994	46,267	15,588	86,827
1996	83,655	46,669	16,761	85,574

CONSTITUTION AND GOVERNMENT. The *Land* Niedersachsen was formed on 1 Nov. 1946 by merging the former Prussian province of Hanover and the *Länder* Brunswick, Oldenburg and Schaumburg-Lippe. Lower Saxony has 7 seats in the Bundesrat. At the Diet elections on 13 March 1994 the electorate was 5·8m.; turn-out was 73·8%. The Social Democratic Party (SPD) won 81 seats with 44·3% of votes cast; the Christian Democratic Union, 67 with 36·4%; and the Greens, 13 with 7·5%.

The cabinet of the Social Democratic Party is headed by *Prime Minister* Gerhard Schröder (SPD), the SPD candidate for the general election to be held on 27 Sept. 1998.

AGRICULTURE. Area and yield of the most important crops:

| | Area (in 1,000 ha) | | | Yield (in 1,000 tonnes) | | |
	1994	1995	1996	1994	1995	1996
Wheat	303	318	336	2,325	2,537	2,678
Rye	138	160	157	699	923	936
Barley	299	302	326	1,583	1,779	1,794
Oats	52	38	34	228	174	185
Potatoes	117	125	136	4,257	4,386	5,230
Sugar-beet	131	132	134	6,291	6,523	6,576

Livestock, 3 Dec. 1996: Cattle, 2,992,719 (including 860,808 milk cows); pigs, 6,946,350; sheep, 226,237; horses, 113,479; poultry, 47,717,770.

FISHERIES. In 1995 the yield of sea and coastal fishing was 46,061 tonnes valued at 68m. DM.

INDUSTRY. In Sept. 1996, 3,909 establishments employed 552,259 persons; of these 53,666 were employed in machine construction; 56,056 in electrical engineering.

LABOUR. The economically active persons totalled 3,356,300 in April 1996. Of the total, 321,900 were self-employed, 48,400 unpaid family workers, 2,985,900 employees; 145,700 were engaged in agriculture and forestry, 1,095,700 in power supply, mining, manufacturing and building, 780,000 in commerce and transport, 1,335,000 in other industries and services.

ROADS. At 1 Jan. 1996 there were 28,282 km of 'classified' roads, including 1,325 km of Autobahn, 4,861 km of federal roads, 8,367 km of first-class and 13,729 km of second-class highways.Number of motor vehicles, 1 Jan. 1997, was 4,796,956 including 4,035,193 passenger cars, 200,693 lorries, 8,296 buses, 234,477 tractors, 253,319 motor cycles.

JUSTICE. There are a constitutional court *(Staatsgerichtshof)*, 3 courts of appeal, 11 regional courts, 79 local courts, a *Land* labour court, 15 labour courts, a *Land* social court, 8 social courts, a finance court, a higher administrative court and 4 administrative courts.

RELIGION. On 25 May 1987 (census) there were 66·12% Protestants and 19·6% Roman Catholics.

EDUCATION. In 1995 there were 1,862 primary schools with 342,006 pupils; 1,117 post-primary schools with 228,085 pupils; 305 special schools with 30,461 pupils; 438 secondary modern schools with 111,045 pupils; 262 grammar schools with 150,368 pupils; 38 comprehensive schools with 25,897 pupils. In 1993 there were 1,801 vocational training institutes (full and part-time) with 256,917 pupils and 213 public health schools with 11,952 pupils.

In the winter term 1996–97 there were 6 universities (Göttingen, 27,316 students; Hanover, 31,506; Oldenburg, 12,232; Osnabrück, 12,619; Hildesheim, 3,564; Lüneburg, 6,444); 2 technical universities (Braunschweig, 14,699; Clausthal, 2,887); the medical college of Hanover (3,419); the veterinary college in Hanover (1,841).

Statistical Information: The Niedersächsisches Landesamt für Statistik, Postfach 4460, D-30044 Hanover. *Head of Division:* President Karl-Ludwig Strelen. Main publications are: *Statistisches Jahrbuch Niedersachsen* (from 1950).—*Statistische Monatshefte Niedersachsen* (from 1947).—*Statistik Niedersachsen.—Statistisches Taschenbuch Niedersachsen 1996* Biennial.

State Libraries: Niedersächsische Staats- und Universitätsbibliothek, Prinzenstr. 1, D-37073 Göttingen. *Director:* Helmut Vogt; Niedersächsische Landesbibliothek, Waterloostr. 8, D-30169 Hanover. *Director:* Dr W. Dittrich.

MECKLENBURG-WEST POMERANIA

Mecklenburg-Vorpommern

TERRITORY AND POPULATION. The area is 23,170 sq. km. It is divided into 6 urban districts, 12 rural districts and 1,079 communes. Population on 31 Dec. 1996 was 1,817,196 (921,916 females). The capital is Schwerin.

Vital statistics for calendar years:

	Live births	Marriages	Divorces	Deaths
1993	9,432	5,458	2,126	19,563
1994	8,934	5,626	2,540	19,835
1995	9,878	6,113	3,128	19,290
1996	11,088	6,490	3,595	18,642

CONSTITUTION AND GOVERNMENT. The *Land* was reconstituted on former GDR territory in 1990. It has 3 seats in the Bundesrat.

At the Diet elections of Oct. 1994, the Christian Democrats (CDU) won 30 seats with 37·7% of the vote; the Social Democrats, 23, with 29·5%; and the Party of Democratic Socialism (former Communists), 18, with 22·7%. The *Prime Minister* is Berndt Seite (CDU).

AGRICULTURE. Area and yield of the most important crops:

	Area (in 1,000 ha)			Yield (in 1,000 tonnes)		
	1994	1995	1996	1994	1995	1996
Wheat	210·2	238·3	236·2	1,235·2	1,619·1	1,487·5
Rye	74·1	100·5	93·8	351·1	544·5	491·8
Barley	129·5	147·8	156·0	693·1	964·6	730·3
Oats	20·7	15·5	14·7	78·0	74·8	75·6
Potatoes	17·0	18·3	19·3	378·5	520·9	599·5
Sugar-beet	31·7	34·4	34·7	1,029·4	1,428·1	1,510·5

Livestock in 1996: Cattle, 636,135 (including 231,237 milk cows); pigs, 583,988; sheep, 68,495; horses, 19,030; poultry, 7,304,150.

FISHERIES. Sea catch, 1995: 19,039 tonnes. Freshwater catch, 1993: 1,140 tonnes (mainly carp, trout and eels).

INDUSTRY. At the end of 1996 there were 523 enterprises (with 20 or more employees) employing 47,611 persons.

LABOUR. 802,900 persons (354,100 females) were employed at the 1%-sample survey of the microcensus of April 1996, including 55,000 self-employed and family assistants, 354,800 manual and 361,400 white-collar workers. 31,800 persons were employed as officials. Employment by sector: Manufacturing and mining, 80,600; agriculture, forestry and fisheries, 52,800; trade and guest business, 139,700; transport and communications, 48,900; construction, 147,600; energy and water resources, 9,400.

ROADS. There were (Jan. 1997) 9,723 km of 'classified' roads, including 235 km of Autobahn, 2,079 km of federal roads, 3,224 km of first-class and 4,183 km of second-class highways. Number of motor vehicles, 1 Jan. 1997, 950,430, including 823,882 passenger cars, 64,991 lorries, 2,024 buses and 24,064 motor cycles.

SHIPPING. There is a lake district of some 660 lakes. The ports of Rostock, Stralsund and Wismar are important for ship-building and repairs. In 1996 the cargo fleet consisted of 83 vessels (including 4 tankers) of 659,000 GT. Sea traffic, 1996, incoming 12,907,901 tonnes; outgoing 10,755,758 tonnes.

JUSTICE. There is a court of appeal (*Oberlandesgericht*), 4 regional courts (*Landgerichte*), 31 local courts (*Amtsgerichte*), a *Land* labour court, 4 labour courts, a *Land* social court, 4 social courts, a finance court, a higher administrative court and 2 administrative courts.

RELIGION. In 1996 the Evangelical Lutheran Church of Mecklenburg had 246,600 adherents, 321 pastors and 383 parishes. Roman Catholics numbered 73,700, with 71 priests and 75 parishes. The Pomeranian Evangelical Church had 139,100 adherents, 178 pastors and 250 parishes in 1996.

EDUCATION. In 1996 there were 341 primary schools, 19 comprehensives, 481 secondary schools and 99 special needs schools. There are universities at Rostock and Greifswald with (in 1996–97) 14,475 students and 4,287 academic staff, and 5 institutions of equivalent status with 6,377 students and 844 academic staff.

Statistical Office: Statistisches Landesamt Mecklenburg-Vorpommern, Postfach 020135, D-19018 Schwerin. Main publications are: *Statistische Monatshefte Mecklenburg-Vorpommern* (since 1991); *Statistische Berichte* (since 1991; various); *Statistisches Jahrbuch Mecklenburg-Vorpommern* (since 1991); *Statistische Sonderhefte* (since 1992; various).

NORTH RHINE-WESTPHALIA

Nordrhein-Westfalen

KEY HISTORICAL EVENTS. Historical Westphalia consisted of many small political units, most of them absorbed by Prussia and Hanover before 1800. In 1807 Napoleon created a Kingdom of Westphalia for his brother Joseph. This included Hesse-Kassel, but was formed mainly from the Prussian and Hanoverian lands between the rivers Elbe and Weser.

In 1815 the kingdom ended with Napoleon's defeat. Most of the area was given to Prussia, with the small principalities of Lippe and Waldeck surviving as independent states. Both joined the North German Confederation in 1867. Lippe remained autonomous after the end of the Empire in 1918; Waldeck was absorbed into Prussia in 1929.

In 1946 the occupying forces combined Lippe with most of the Prussian province of Westphalia to form the *Land* of North Rhine-Westphalia. On 1 March 1947 the allied Control Council formally abolished Prussia.

TERRITORY AND POPULATION. The *Land* comprises 34,079 sq. km. It is divided into 5 administrative regions, 23 urban districts, 31 rural districts and 396 communes. Capital Düsseldorf. Population, 31 Dec. 1996, 17,947,715 (8,715,221 males, 9,232,494 females).

Vital statistics for calendar years:

	Live births	Marriages	Divorces	Deaths
1993	194,156	106,315	39,230	194,667
1994	186,079	104,200	40,523	192,669
1995	182,393	100,793	41,476	193,076
1996	188,493	99,922	42,839	194,548

CONSTITUTION AND GOVERNMENT. Since Oct. 1990 the North Rhine-Westphalia has had 6 seats in the Bundesrat. It is governed by Social Democrats (SPD); *Prime Minister*, Johannes Rau (SPD). The Diet, elected on 14 May 1995, consists of 108 Social Democrats (46% of votes cast), 89 Christian Democrats (37·7%) and 24 Greens (10%).

AGRICULTURE. Area and yield of the most important crops:

	Area (in 1,000 ha)			Yield (in 1,000 tonnes)		
	1994	1995	1996	1994	1995	1996
Wheat	244·8	250·9	255·5	1,877·1	2,035·2	2,185·9
Rye	39·4	41·0	37·7	223·0	260·2	263·8
Barley	190·8	192·8	195·8	1,022·7	1,220·9	1,259·9
Oats	40·0	30·7	28·2	181·5	134·0	151·4
Potatoes	26·3	29·9	33·4	999·0	1,047·8	1,467·3
Sugar-beet	76·4	77·0	78·0	3,942·6	4,018·0	4,295·7

Livestock, 3 Dec. 1996: Cattle, 1,711,178 (including 462,164 milk cows); pigs, 5,772,530; sheep, 231,377; horses, 116,709; poultry, 10,859,348.

INDUSTRY. In Sept. 1996, 10,320 establishments (with 20 and more employees) employed 1,579,776 persons; of these, 108,145 were employed in production of food and tobacco; 247,248 in machine construction; 331,723 in metal production and manufacture of metal goods; 157,501 in the chemical industry; 159,061 in manufacture of office machines, computers, electrical and precision engineering and optics; 105,011 in motor vehicle manufacture.

Output and/or production in 1,000 tonnes, 1996: Hard coal, 40,588; lignite, 102,779; pig-iron, 16,073; raw steel ingots, 20,130; rolled steel, 26,844; castings (iron and steel castings), 870; cement, 11,390; fireproof products, 616; sulphuric acid (including production of cokeries), 1,130; staple fibres and rayon, 250; machine tools, 286 (1,000 pieces); equipment for smelting works and rolling mills, 1,637; machines for mining industry, building and building material, 80 (1,000 pieces); cranes and hoisting machinery, 483; electricity distribution and control equipment, 8,236,019 (1,000 pieces); cables and electric lines, 182; springs of all kinds, 163; chains of all kinds, 36; locks and fittings, 231,265 (1,000 pieces); spun yarns, 90. Of the total population, 8·8% were engaged in industry.

LABOUR. The economically active persons totalled 7,341,000 at the 1%-sample survey of the microcensus of April 1996. Of the total, 637,000 were self-employed, 53,000 unpaid family workers, 6·65m. employees; 144,000 were engaged in agriculture, forestry and fishing, 2,607,000 in power supply, mining, manufacturing, water supply and building, 1,696,000 in commerce, hotel trade and transport, 2,894,000 in other industries and services.

ROADS. There were (1 Jan. 1997) 29,765 km of 'classified' roads, including 2,170 km of Autobahn, 5,107 km of federal roads, 12,604 km of first-class and 9,884 km of second-class highways. Number of motor vehicles, 1 July 1997, 10,340,683, including 8,951,585 passenger cars, 425,583 motor lorries/trucks, 17,152 buses, 212,142 tractors and 611,956 motor cycles.

JUSTICE. There are a constitutional court *(Verfassungsgerichtshof)*, 3 courts of appeal, 19 regional courts, 130 local courts, 3 *Land* labour courts, 30 labour courts, 1 *Land* social court, 8 social courts, 3 finance courts, a higher administrative court, 7 administrative courts.

RELIGION. On 25 May 1987 (census) there were 35·2% Protestants and 49·4% Roman Catholics.

EDUCATION. In 1996 there were 4,207 primary schools with 62,529 teachers and 1,107,857 pupils; 707 special schools with 14,424 teachers and 86,677 pupils; 516 intermediate schools with 15,462 teachers and 285,936 pupils; 246 *Gesamtschulen* (comprehensive schools) with 16,232 teachers and 206,951 pupils; 621 high schools with 34,587 teachers and 507,953 pupils; there were 261 part-time vocational schools with 285,665 pupils; vocational preparatory year 152 schools with 9,495 pupils; 241 full-time vocational schools with 68,714 pupils; 175 full-time vocational schools leading up to vocational colleges with 13,810 pupils; 244 advanced full-time vocational schools with 38,908 pupils; 662 schools for public health occupations with 16,356 teachers and 46,683 pupils; 42 schools within the scope of a pilot system of courses with 81,246 pupils and 3,673 teachers.

In the winter term 1996–97 there were 8 universities (Bielefeld, 19,723 students; Bochum, 35,495; Bonn, 35,894; Cologne, 57,027; Dortmund, 24,562; Düsseldorf, 21,253; Münster, 44,060; Witten, 716); the Technical University of Aachen (32,146); 3 Roman Catholic and 2 Protestant theological colleges with a total of 678 students. There were also 3 colleges of music, 4 colleges of fine arts and the college for physical education in Cologne with 10,708 students in total; 24 *Fachhochschulen* (vocational colleges) with 100,434 students, and 6 *Universitäten-Gesamthochschulen* with a total of 123,076 students.

Statistical Information: The Landesamt für Datenverarbeitung und Statistik Nordrhein-Westfalen (Mauerstr. 51, D-40476 Düsseldorf) was founded in 1946, by amalgamating the provincial statistical offices of Rhineland and Westphalia. *President:* Jochen Kehlenbach. The Landesamt publishes: *Statistisches Jahrbuch Nordrhein-Westfalen.* From 1949. More than 550 other publications yearly.

Först, W., *Kleine Geschichte Nordrhein-Westfalens.* Münster, 1986.

Land Library: Universitätsbibliothek, Universitätsstr. 1, D-40225 Düsseldorf. *Director:* Dr Niggemann.

RHINELAND-PALATINATE
Rheinland-Pfalz

KEY HISTORICAL EVENTS. The *Land* was formed from the Rhenisch Palatinate and the Rhine valley areas of Prussia, Hesse-Darmstadt, Hesse-Kassel and Bavaria.

The Palatinate was ruled, from 1214, by the Bavarian house of Wittelsbach; its capital was Heidelberg. In 1797 its land west of the Rhine was taken into France, and Napoleon divided the eastern land between Baden and Hesse. In 1815 the land taken by France was restored to Germany and allotted to Bavaria. The area and its neighbours formed the strategically-important Bavarian Circle of the Rhine.

The rule of the Wittelsbachs ended in 1918 but the Palatinate remained part of Bavaria until the American occupying forces detached it in 1946.

The new *Land,* incorporating the Palatinate and other territory, received its constitution in April 1947.

TERRITORY AND POPULATION. Rhineland-Palatinate has an area of 19,853 sq. km. It comprises 3 administrative regions, 12 urban districts, 24 rural districts and 2,305 communes. The capital is Mainz. Population (at 30 June 1997), 4,009,753 (2,045,872 females).

Vital statistics for calendar years:

	Live births	Marriages	Divorces	Deaths
1993	42,291	24,006	8,555	43,871
1994	40,539	23,182	9,003	42,857
1995	39,684	22,922	9,040	42,993
1996	40,926	22,741	9,385	43,752

CONSTITUTION AND GOVERNMENT. The constitution of the *Land* Rheinland-Pfalz was approved by the Consultative Assembly on 25 April 1947 and by referendum on 18 May 1947, when 579,002 voted for and 514,338 against its acceptance. It has 4 seats in the Bundesrat.

At the elections of 24 March 1996 the Social Democratic Party won 43 seats of the 101 in the state parliament with 39·8% of votes cast; the Christian Democrats 41 with 38·7%; the Free Democrats 10 with 8·9%; and the Greens, 7 with 6·9%.

The coalition cabinet is headed by Kurt Beck (b. 1949; Social Democrat).

AGRICULTURE. Area and yield of the most important products:

	Area (1,000 ha)			Yield (1,000 tonnes)		
	1994	1995	1996	1994	1995	1996
Wheat	77·7	85·3	86·9	484·0	543·2	587·7
Rye	19·0	20·6	15·6	94·3	107·6	93·5
Barley	118·8	113·3	121·1	541·0	542·7	681·7
Oats	22·8	18·3	17·1	87·1	74·0	84·0
Potatoes	10·6	11·1	11·0	329·1	329·7	372·6
Sugar-beet	22·9	23·1	22·6	1,228·1	1,261·5	1,440·0
Wine (1,000 hectolitres)	66·2	65·8	65·3	6,902·2	5,910·9	5,869·8

Livestock (1996, in 1,000): Cattle, 487·4 (including milk cows, 148·5); sheep, 132·4; pigs, 396·5; horses, 29·9; poultry, 1,874·4.

INDUSTRY. In 1996, 2,183 establishments (with 20 and more employees) employed 311,790 persons; of these 68,127 were employed in the chemical industry; 19,408 in electrical equipment manufacture; 7,443 in leather goods and footwear; 36,832 in machine construction; 23,717 in processing stones and earthenware.

LABOUR. The economically active persons totalled 1,713,600 in 1996. Of the total, 160,200 were self-employed, 18,400 were unpaid family workers, 1,535,100 employees; 48,300 were engaged in agriculture and forestry, 635,500 in power supply, mining, manufacturing and building, 367,000 in commerce, transport, hotels and restaurants, 662,700 in other industries and services.

ROADS. In 1997 there were 18,394 km of 'classified' roads, including 824 km of Autobahn, 3,029 km of federal roads, 7,139 km of first-class and 7,402 km of second-class highways. Number of motor vehicles, 1 July 1997, was 2,595,420, including 2,158,997 passenger cars, 103,402 lorries, 5,335 buses, 138,093 tractors and 158,010 motor cycles.

JUSTICE. There are a constitutional court *(Verfassungsgerichtshof)*, 2 courts of appeal, 8 regional courts, 47 local courts, a *Land* labour court, 5 labour courts, a *Land* social court, 4 social courts, a finance court, a higher administrative court, 4 administrative courts.

RELIGION. On 25 May 1987 (census) there were 37·7% Protestants and 54·5% Roman Catholics.

EDUCATION. In 1996 there were 984 primary schools with 9,257 teachers and 184,851 pupils; 751 secondary schools with 16,500 teachers and 265,193 pupils; 146 special schools with 2,096 teachers and 14,305 pupils; 113 vocational and advanced vocational schools with 4,898 teachers and 115,102 pupils.

In the winter term 1997–98 (provisional) there were the University of Mainz (28,277 students), the University of Kaiserslautern (8,068 students), the University of Trier (10,910 students), the University of Koblenz-Landau (8,542 students), the *Hochschule für Verwaltungswissenschaften* in Speyer (565 students), the *Wissenschaftliche Hochschule für Unternehmensführung* (Otto Beisheim Graduate School) in Vallendar (303 students), the Roman Catholic Theological College in Trier (181 students) and the Roman Catholic Theological College in Vallendar (104 students). There were also 9 *Fachhochschulen* with 22,248 students and 4 *Verwaltungsfachhochschulen* with 1,875 students.

Statistical Information: The Statistisches Landesamt Rheinland-Pfalz (Mainzer Str., 14–16, D-56130 Bad Ems) was established in 1948. *President:* Klaus Maxeiner. Its publications include: *Statistisches Jahrbuch für Rheinland-Pfalz* (from 1948); *Statistische Monatshefte Rheinland-Pfalz* (from 1958); *Statistik von Rheinland-Pfalz* (from 1949) 367 vols. to date; *Rheinland-Pfalz im Spiegel der Statistik* (from 1968); *Rheinland-Pfalz—seine kreisfreien Städte und Landkreise* (1992); *Rheinland-Pfalz heute* (from 1973); *Benutzerhandbuch des Landesinformationssystems* (1995); *Raumordnungsbericht 1993 der Landesregierung Rheinland-Pfalz* (Mainz, 1993).

SAARLAND

KEY HISTORICAL EVENTS. Long disputed between Germany and France, the area was occupied by France in 1792. Most was allotted to Prussia at the close of the Napoleonic wars in 1815.

In 1870 Prussia defeated France and when, in 1871, the German Empire was founded under Prussian leadership, it was able to incorporate Lorraine. This part of France was the Saar territory's western neighbour, so the Saar was no longer a vulnerable boundary state; it began to develop industrially, exploiting Lorraine coal and iron.

In 1919 the League of Nations took control of the Saar until a plebiscite of 1935 favoured return to Germany. In 1945 there was a French occupation, and in 1947 the Saar was made an international area, but in economic union with France. In 1954 France and Germany agreed that the Saar should be a separate and autonomous state, under an independent commissioner. This was rejected by referendum, and France agreed to return Saarland to Germany; it became a *Land* of the Federal Republic in June 1959.

TERRITORY AND POPULATION. Saarland has an area of 2,570 sq. km. Population, 31 Dec. 1996, 1,084,184 (525,592 males, 558,592 females). It comprises 6 rural districts and 52 communes. The capital is Saarbrücken.

Vital statistics for calendar years:

	Live births	Marriages	Divorces	Deaths
1993	10,653	6,528	2,907	13,053
1994	10,028	6,427	3,035	12,711
1995	9,727	6,095	2,785	12,647
1996	9,976	6,181	2,938	12,529

CONSTITUTION AND GOVERNMENT. Saarland has 3 seats in the Bundesrat.

The Saar Diet, elected on 16 Oct. 1994, is composed as follows: 27 Social Democrats, 21 Christian Democrats, 3 Greens.

Saarland is governed by Social Democrats in Parliament. *Prime Minister*: Oskar Lafontaine (Social Democrat).

AGRICULTURE AND FORESTRY. The cultivated area (1997) occupied 115,827 ha or 45·1% of the total area; the forest area comprises nearly 33·4% of the total (257,045 ha).

Area and yield of the most important crops:

	Area (in 1,000 ha)			Yield (in 1,000 tonnes)		
	1994	1995	1996	1994	1995	1996
Wheat	6·3	7·0	7·8	32·5	40·6	46·5
Rye	4·9	5·4	4·9	23·1	29·5	27·5
Barley	8·1	7·6	7·6	33·1	36·6	38·5
Oats	4·9	4·1	3·8	18·7	18·1	16·1
Potatoes	0·4	0·3	0·3	9·0	8·1	8·9

Livestock, Dec. 1996: Cattle, 63,315 (including 17,271 milk cows); pigs, 24,161; sheep, 16,786; horses, 6,115; poultry, 193,787.

INDUSTRY. In June 1997, 530 establishments (with 20 and more employees) employed 105,021 persons; of these 13,350 were engaged in coalmining, 17,171 in manufacturing motor vehicles, parts, accessories, 10,438 in iron and steel production, 15,000 in machine construction, 4,750 in electrical engineering, 4,668 in steel construction. In 1996 the coalmines produced 7·3m. tonnes of coal. 5 blast furnaces and 7 steel furnaces produced 3·3m. tonnes of pig-iron and 4·1m. tonnes of crude steel.

LABOUR. The economically active persons totalled 412,800 at the 1%-sample survey of the microcensus of April 1996 Of the total, 35,900 were self-employed, 372,800 employees; 4,500 were engaged in agriculture and forestry, 146,900 in power supply, mining, manufacturing and building, 95,300 in commerce and transport, 166,100 in other industries and services.

ROADS. At 1 Jan. 1997 there were 2,024 km of classified roads, including 226 km of Autobahn, 352 km of federal roads, 823 km of first-class and 623 km of second-class highways. Number of motor vehicles, 31 Dec. 1996, 673,995, including 585,185 passenger cars, 26,812 lorries, 1,416 buses, 13,991 tractors and 39,320 motor cycles.

JUSTICE. There are a constitutional court *(Verfassungsgerichtshof)*, a court of appeal, a regional court, 11 local courts, a *Land* labour court, 3 labour courts, a *Land* social court, a social court, a finance court, a higher administrative court, an administrative court.

RELIGION. In 1995, 70·5% of the population were Roman Catholics and 20·3% were Protestants.

EDUCATION. In 1997–98 there were 294 primary schools with 51,277 pupils; 41 special schools with 3,350 pupils; 103 *Realschulen, Erweiterte Realschulen* and *Sekundarschulen* with 26,512 pupils; 37 high schools with 27,503 pupils; 15 comprehensive high schools with 10,609 pupils; 4 *Freie Waldorfschulen* with 1,010 pupils; 4 evening intermediate schools with 218 pupils; 2 evening high schools and 1 Saarland College with 206 pupils; 39 part-time vocational schools with 21,002 pupils; year of commercial basic training: 53 institutions with 2,317 pupils; 22 advanced full-time vocational schools and schools for technicians with 2,185 pupils; 52 full-time vocational schools with 5,029 pupils; 1 *Berufsaufbauschule* (vocational extension school) with 23 pupils; 29 *Fachoberschulen* (full-time vocational schools leading up to vocational colleges) with 3,768 pupils; 43 schools for public health occupations with 2,255 pupils. The number of pupils visiting the vocational schools amounts to 36,579.

In the winter term 1997–98 (preliminary results) there was the University of the Saarland with 18,211 students; 1 academy of fine art with 248 students; 1 academy of music and theatre with 309 students; 1 vocational college (economics and technics) with 2,652 students; 1 vocational college for social affairs with 224 students; and 1 vocational college for public administration with 176 students.

Statistical Information: The Statistisches Landesamt Saarland (Virchowstrasse 7, D-66119 Saarbrücken) was established on 1 April 1938. As from 1 June 1935, it was an independent agency; its predecessor, 1920–35, was the Statistical Office of the Government Commission of the Saar. *Chief:* Direktor Josef Mailänder. The most important publications are: *Statistisches Handbuch für das Saarland,* from 1950.—*Statistisches Taschenbuch für das Saarland,* from 1959.—*Saarland in Zahlen* (special issues).—*Einzelschriften zur Statistik des Saarlandes,* from 1950.—*Statistik-Journal* (monthly), from 1996.

SAXONY

Freistaat Sachsen

TERRITORY AND POPULATION. The area is 18,413 sq. km. It is divided into 3 administrative regions, 7 urban districts, 22 rural districts and 809 communes. Population on 1 Jan. 1997 was 4,545,702 (2,354,368 females, 2,191,334 males); density, 247 per sq. km. The capital is Dresden.

Vital statistics for calendar years:

	Live births	Marriages	Divorces	Deaths
1993	23,423	13,808	5,116	59,900
1994	22,734	14,795	6,519	58,234
1995	24,004	15,474	7,043	57,550
1996	27,006	15,402	7,754	55,756

CONSTITUTION AND GOVERNMENT. The *Land* was reconstituted as the Free State of Saxony on former GDR territory in 1990. It has 4 seats in the Bundesrat.

At the Diet elections of Sept. 1994 the Christian Democrats won 77 seats, with 58·1% of the vote; the Social Democrats, 22, with 16·6%; the Party of Democratic Socialism (former Communists), 21, with 16·5%.

The *Prime Minister* is Kurt Biedenkopf (b. 1930; Christian Democrat).

AGRICULTURE. Area and yield of the most important crops:

	Area (in 1,000 ha)			Yield (in 1,000 tonnes)		
	1994	1995	1996	1994	1995	1996
Wheat	142·3	147·1	143·1	884·5	908·4	965·0
Rye	41·0	54·9	50·2	212·9	280·7	249·1
Barley	144·2	147·4	150·2	789·9	816·0	750·8
Maize	57·1	73·1	86·9	2,237·9	2,497·3	3,106·7
Potatoes	8·4	10·1	9·9	238·5	270·9	375·9
Fodder	195·9	198·3	196·3	1,661·7	1,854·6	1,682·1
Hops	0·5	0·5	0·4	0·4	0·6	0·6

Livestock in 1996 (in 1,000): Cattle, 630 (including milk cows, 248); pigs, 567; sheep, 116.

INDUSTRY. In Aug. 1997, 2,643 establishments (with 20 and more employees) employed 207,152 persons.

ROADS. On 1 Jan. 1997 there were 556 km of motorways and 2,467 km of main roads. There were, 1 July 1997, 2,467,099 registered motor vehicles, including 2,149,985 motor cars, 218,306 lorries and tractors, 4,341 buses and 74,519 motor cycles.

EDUCATION. In 1996–97 there were 1,227 primary schools with 216,345 pupils and 12,277 teachers; 657 secondary schools with 222,806 pupils and 14,171 teachers; 193 grammar schools with 149,323 pupils and 9,600 teachers and 208 high schools (*Förderschulen*) with 27,747 pupils and 3,863 teachers. There were 718 professional training schools with 158,647 students and 5,720 teachers. There were 6 universities with 49,089 students, 10 polytechnics with 17,411 students, 6 art schools with 2,225 students and 1 management college with 1,849 students.

Statistical office: Statistisches Landesamt des Freistaates Sachsen, Postfach 105, D-01911 Kamenz. It publishes *Statistisches Jahrbuch des Freistaates Sachsen* (since 1990).

SAXONY-ANHALT

Sachsen-Anhalt

TERRITORY AND POPULATION. The area is 20,446 sq. km. It is divided into 3 administrative regions, 3 urban districts, 21 rural districts and 1,299 communes. Population in 1996 was 2,723,620 (1,403,068 females). The capital is Magdeburg.

Vital statistics for calendar years:

	Live births	Marriages	Divorces	Deaths
1993	14,610	8,854	4,042	34,838
1994	14,280	9,415	4,287	33,816
1995	14,568	9,667	3,867	33,519
1996	16,152	9,534	3,432	32,639

CONSTITUTION AND GOVERNMENT. The *Land* was reconstituted on former GDR territory in 1990. It has 4 seats in the Bundesrat.

At the Diet elections on 26 June 1994 turn-out was 54·9%. The Christian Democrats won 37 seats, with 34·4% votes cast; the Social Democratic Party (SPD), 36, with 34%; the Party of Democratic Socialism (former Communists), 21 with 19·9%; Alliance '90/Greens, 5, with 5·1%.

The *Prime Minister* is Dr Manfred Höppner (SPD).

AGRICULTURE. Area and yield of the most important crops:

	Area (in 1,000 ha)			Yield (in 1,000 tonnes)		
	1994	1995	1996	1994	1995	1996
Cereals	494·0	539·7	563·8	3,133·9	3,607·5	3,473·1
Potatoes	14·9	17·5	18·2	429·6	521·8	710·1
Sugar-beet	56·0	61·5	61·4	2,343·7	2,716·8	2,869·5
Maize	60·2	66·3	78·8	1,896·7	2,299·1	3,420·3

Livestock in 1996 (in 1,000): Cattle, 439·0 (including milk cows, 168·6); pigs, 711·3; sheep, 125·8; poultry, 2,852.

INDUSTRY. In 1996, 1,748 establishments (with 20 or more employees) employed 114,582 persons; of these, 50,712 were employed in basic industry, 35,937 in capital goods industry and 15,963 in food and kindred industry. Major sectors are machine and transport equipment, electrical engineering, chemicals and energy and fuel.

LABOUR. In 1995 there were 1,110,450 economically-active persons. Of these, 467,864 worked in local authorities, social security and services, 198,120 in mining and manufacturing, 204,099 in building, 127,347 in trade, 75,273 in transport and communications and 37,747 in agriculture, forestry and fisheries.

ROADS. In 1996 there were 210 km of motorways, 2,330 km of main and 3,848 km of local roads. In 1997 there were 1,416,813 registered motor vehicles, including 1,237,657 passenger cars, 95,093 lorries, 2,772 buses and 37,275 motor cycles.

RELIGION. There are Saxon and Anhalt branches of the Evangelical Church. There were some 0·2m. Roman Catholics in 1990.

EDUCATION. In 1996–97 there were 1,528 schools with 385,429 pupils. There were 10 universities and institutes of equivalent status with 29,042 students.

Statistical office: Statistisches Landesamt Sachsen-Anhalt, Postfach 20 11 56, D-06012 Halle. It publishes *Statistisches Jahrbuch des Landes Sachsen-Anhalt* (since 1991).

SCHLESWIG-HOLSTEIN

KEY HISTORICAL EVENTS. The *Land* is formed from two states formerly contested between Germany and Denmark.

Schleswig was a Danish dependency ruled since 1474 by the King of Denmark as Duke of Schleswig. He also ruled Holstein, its southern neighbour, as Duke of Holstein, but he did so recognizing that it was a fief of the Holy Roman Empire. As such, Holstein joined the German Confederation which replaced the Empire in 1815.

Disputes between Denmark and the powerful German states were accompanied by rising national feeling in the duchies, where the population was part-Danish and part-German. There was war in 1848–50 and in 1864, when Denmark surrendered its claims to Prussia and Austria. Following her defeat of Austria in 1866 Prussia annexed both duchies.

North Schleswig (predominately Danish) was awarded to Denmark in 1920. Prussian Holstein and south Schleswig became the present *Land* in 1946.

TERRITORY AND POPULATION. The area of Schleswig-Holstein in 1996 was 15,771 sq. km. It is divided into 4 urban and 11 rural districts and 1,131 communes. The capital is Kiel. The population (estimate, 31 Dec. 1996) numbered 2,742,293 (1,339,326 males, 1,402,967 females).

Vital statistics for calendar years:

	Live births	Marriages	Divorces	Deaths
1993	28,632	18,451	6,250	31,223
1994	27,542	18,295	6,196	30,766
1995	27,430	17,671	6,679	31,288
1996	28,766	17,832	6,822	31,314

CONSTITUTION AND GOVERNMENT. The *Land* has 4 seats in the Bundesrat. At the elections of 24 March 1996 the Social Democrats won 33 seats with 39·8% of votes cast, the Christian Democrats 30 with 37·2%, the Greens 6 with 8·1%, the Free Democrats 4 with 5·7% and the (Danish) South Schleswig Association 2 with 2·5%.

Prime Minister: Heide Simonis (b. 1943; SPD).

AGRICULTURE. Area and yield of the most important crops:

| | Area (in 1,000 ha) | | | Yield (in 1,000 tonnes) | | |
	1994	1995	1996	1994	1995	1996
Wheat	157·2	155·8	166·4	1,223·3	1,333·5	1,433·4
Rye	32·6	35·1	30·5	188·0	207·6	190·9
Barley	67·5	74·8	84·8	430·3	541·4	554·0
Oats	16·9	9·6	8·6	76·4	50·6	50·2
Potatoes	4·8	5·2	5·8	146·3	154·1	192·9
Sugar-beet	15·0	15·3	15·4	699·5	715·3	716·6

Livestock, 3 Dec. 1996: 1,396,970 cattle (including 422,213 milk cows); 1,293,356 pigs; 222,495 sheep; 54,707 horses; 2,885,175 poultry.

FISHERIES. In 1996 the yield of small-scale deep-sea and inshore fisheries was 59,306 tonnes valued at 92·6m. DM.

INDUSTRY. In 1996 (average), 1,455 establishments (with 20 and more employees) employed 146,742 persons; of these, 6,976 were employed in shipbuilding (except naval engineering); 25,903 in machine construction; 20,187 in food and kindred industry; 10,368 in electrical engineering.

LABOUR. The economically active persons totalled 1,250,200 in 1996. Of the total, 128,900 were self-employed, 13,800 unpaid family workers, 1,107,600 employees; 42,800 were engaged in agriculture and forestry, 340,200 in power supply, mining, manufacturing and building, 340,100 in commerce and transport and 527,100 in other industries and services.

ROADS. There were (1 Jan. 1997) 9,886·1 km of 'classified' roads, including 447·9 km of Autobahn, 1,760·2 km of federal roads, 3,600·8 km of first-class and 4,077·2 km of second-class highways. Number of motor vehicles, 1 July 1997, was 1,706,336, including 1,432,722 passenger cars, 78,012 lorries, 2,940 buses, 69,981 tractors, 94,359 motor cycles.

SHIPPING. The Kiel Canal (*Nord-Ostsee-Kanal*) is 98·7 km (51 miles) long; in 1996, 37,055 vessels of 32·8m. NRT passed through it.

JUSTICE. There are a court of appeal, 4 regional courts, 28 local courts, a *Land* labour court, 5 labour courts, a *Land* social court, 4 social courts, a finance court, an upper administrative court and an administrative court.

RELIGION. On 25 May 1987 (census) there were 73·3% Protestants and 6·2% Roman Catholics.

EDUCATION. In 1996–97 there were 624 primary schools with 7,263 teachers and 119,937 pupils; 266 elementary schools with 2,772 teachers and 39,178 pupils; 171 intermediate schools with 2,863 teachers and 52,678 pupils; 102 grammar schools with 5,234 teachers and 63,234 pupils; 23 comprehensive schools with 1,236 teachers and 13,585 pupils; 162 other schools (including special schools) with 2,222 teachers and 16,254 pupils; 353 vocational schools with 4,170 teachers and 86,312 pupils.

In the winter term of the academic year 1997–98 there were 26,059 students at the three universities (Kiel, Flensburg and Lübeck) and 18,419 students at 11 further education colleges.

Statistical Information: Statistisches Landesamt Schleswig-Holstein (Fröbel Str. 15–17, D-24113 Kiel). *Director:* Dr Kirschner. Publications: *Statistisches Taschenbuch Schleswig-Holstein,* since 1954.—*Statistisches Jahrbuch Schleswig-Holstein,* since 1951.—*Statistische Monatshefte Schleswig-Holstein,* since 1949.—*Statistische Berichte,* since 1947.—*Beitrage zur historischen Statistik Schleswig-Holstein,* from 1967.—*Lange Reihen,* from 1977.

Baxter, R. R., *The Law of International Waterways.* Harvard Univ. Press, 1964
Brandt, O., *Grundriss der Geschichte Schleswig-Holsteins.* 5th ed. Kiel, 1957
Handbuch für Schleswig-Holstein. 28th ed. Kiel, 1996

State Library: Schleswig-Holsteinische Landesbibliothek, Kiel, Schloss. *Director:* Prof. Dr Dieter Lohmeier.

THURINGIA

Thüringen

TERRITORY AND POPULATION. The area is 16,171 sq. km. Population on 31 Dec. 1996 was 2,491,119 (1,280,397 females); density, 154 per sq. km. It is divided into 5 urban districts, 17 rural districts and 1,143 communes. The capital is Erfurt.

Vital statistics for calendar years:

	Live births	Marriages	Divorces	Deaths
1993	13,307	7,955	2,643	29,866
1994	12,721	8,581	3,795	28,877
1995	13,788	8,781	3,493	29,027
1996	15,265	8,646	3,955	28,468

CONSTITUTION AND GOVERNMENT. The *Land* was reconstituted on former GDR territory in 1990. It has 4 seats in the Bundesrat.

At the Diet elections of Oct. 1994 the Christian Democrats (CDU) won 42 seats, with 42·6% of the vote; the Social Democrats (SPD), 29 with 29·6%; the Party of Democratic Socialism (PDS), 17, with 16·6%.

The *Prime Minister* is Dr Bernhard Vogel (CDU).

AGRICULTURE. Area and yield of the most important crops:

	Area (in 1,000 ha)			Yield (in 1,000 tonnes)		
	1994	1995	1996	1994	1995	1996
Wheat	162·4	187·6	185·8	1,110·3	1,240·5	1,290·9
Rye	18·6	27·6	20·9	114·1	170·1	130·5
Barley	122·4	122·7	138·7	695·0	678·9	775·5
Oats	10·7	6·3	6·7	46·6	31·8	33·7
Potatoes	4·2	5·4	5·7	144·0	178·2	235·2
Sugar-beet	13·4	13·5	13·1	578·3	618·9	589·5

Livestock, 1 Jan. 1997: 458,932 cattle (including 164,066 milk cows); 641,031 pigs; 233,079 sheep; 14,048 horses; 4,065,825 poultry.

INDUSTRY. In 1996, 1,396 establishments (with 20 and more employees) employed 108,222 persons; of these, 46,720 were employed by producers of materials and supplies, 28,753 by producers of investment goods, 9,223 by producers of durables and 23,526 by producers of non-durables.

LABOUR. The economically active persons totalled 1,082,300 in April 1996, including 492,800 professional workers, 478,600 manual workers and 75,800 self-employed. 39,000 persons were engaged in agriculture and forestry, 395,800 in production industries, 225,300 in commerce, transport and communications and 422,200 in other sectors. There were 193,896 persons registered unemployed in Dec. 1996 (111,723 females), and 8,221 on short time; unemployment rate was 17·0%.

ROADS. In 1996 there were 7,905·6 km of 'classified' roads (310 km of Autobahn, 1,992·9 km of federal roads, 5,642·7 km of first- and second-class highways). Number of motor vehicles, Jan. 1997, 1,384,017, including 1,195,413 private cars, 95,280 lorries, 2,901 buses, 34,313 tractors and 43,804 motor cycles.

EDUCATION. In 1996–97 there were 660 primary schools with 123,835 pupils, 371 core curriculum schools with 122,425 pupils, 115 grammar schools with 86,869 pupils and 102 special schools with 18,696 pupils; there were 83,252 pupils in technical and professional education, and 4,520 in professional training for the disabled. In the winter term 1996–97 there were 11 universities and colleges with 29,274 students enrolled.

Statistical information: Thüringer Landesamt für Statistik (Postfach 900163, D-99104 Erfurt; Leipziger Str. 71, D-99085 Erfurt). *President:* Gerhard Scheuerer. Publications: *Statistisches Jahrbuch Thüringen,* since 1993. *Kreiszahlen für Thüringen,* since 1995. *Statistische Monatshefte Thüringen,* since 1994. *Statistische Berichte,* since 1991. *Faltblätter,* since 1991.

State library: Thüringer Universitäts- und Landesbibliothek, Jena.

GHANA

Republic of Ghana

Capital: Accra
Population: 18·1m.
GDP per head (PPP$): 2,120
GNP: US$7·3bn.
HDI/world rank: 0·468/132

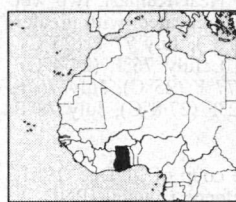

KEY HISTORICAL EVENTS. By the 17th century, several strong chiefdoms and warrior states, notably the powerful Ashanti state, ruled in the area. The Ashanti state was initially strengthened through its collaboration with the slave trade, but by 1874 it had been conquered by Britain and made a colony. The hinterland became a protectorate in 1901. A period of indirect British rule began, but was challenged after the Second World War by Kwame Nkrumah and Convention People's Party (CPP) formed in 1949. The state of Ghana came into existence on 6 Mar. 1957 when the former Colony of the Gold Coast and the Trusteeship Territory of Togoland attained Dominion status. In Dec. 1956 the UN General Assembly approved the termination of British administration in Togoland and the eventual union of Togoland with the Gold Coast.

The country was declared a Republic within the Commonwealth on 1 July 1960 with Dr Kwame Nkrumah as the first President. On 24 Feb. 1966 the Nkrumah regime was overthrown in a military coup and ruled by the National Liberation Council until 1 Oct. 1969 when the military regime handed over power to a civilian regime under a new constitution. On 13 Jan. 1972 the armed forces and police took over power again.

In Oct. 1975 the National Redemption Council was subordinated to a Supreme Military Council (SMC). In 1979 the SMC was toppled in a coup led by Flight Lieut. J. J. Rawlings. The new government permitted elections already scheduled and these resulted in a victory for Dr Hilla Limann and his People's National Party. However on 31 Dec. 1981 another coup led by Flight-Lieut. Rawlings dismissed the government and Parliament, suspended the constitution and established a Provisional National Defence Council to exercise all government powers.

A new pluralist democratic constitution was approved by referendum in April 1992. The Fourth Republic was proclaimed on 7 Jan. 1993.

TERRITORY AND POPULATION. Ghana is bounded west by Côte d'Ivoire, north by Burkina Faso, east by Togo and south by the Gulf of Guinea. The area is 238,537 sq. km. Census population, 1997 estimate, 18,100,703. Estimate (1995) 35% urban and an average population density of 69 per sq. km. 1m. Ghanaians lived abroad in 1995.

Vital statistics (1997 estimates): Growth rate, 2·21%; infant mortality, 78·9 per 1,000 live births; life expectancy, 54·47 for men, 58·57 for women.

Ghana is divided into 10 regions:

Regions	Area (sq. km)	Population census 1984	Capital
Eastern	19,977	1,680,890	Koforidua
Western	23,921	1,157,807	Sekondi-Takoradi
Central	9,826	1,142,335	Cape Coast
Ashanti	24,390	2,090,100	Kumasi
Brong-Ahafo	39,557	1,206,608	Sunyani
Northern	70,383	1,164,583	Tamale
Volta	20,572	1,211,907	Ho
Upper East	8,842	772,744	Bolgatanga
Upper West	18,477	438,008	Wa
Greater Accra	2,593	1,431,099	Accra

Chief cities with 1988 estimated populations: Accra, the capital, 949,113; Kumasi, 385,192; Tamale, 151,069; Tema, 109,975; Sekondi-Takoradi, 103,653.

About 44% of the population are Akan. Other tribal groups include Moshi-Dagomba (16%) Ewe (13%) and Ga (8%). About 75 languages are spoken; the official language is English.

CLIMATE. The climate ranges from the equatorial type on the coast to savannah in the north and is typified by the existence of well-marked dry and wet seasons. Temperatures are relatively high throughout the year. The amount, duration and seasonal distribution of rain is very marked, from the south, with over 80" (2,000 mm) to the north, with under 50" (1,250 mm). In the extreme north, the wet season is from March to Aug., but further south it lasts until Oct. Near Kumasi, two wet seasons occur, in May and June and again in Oct. and this is repeated, with greater amounts, along the coast of Ghana. Accra. Jan. 80°F (26·7°C), July 77°F (25°C). Annual rainfall 29" (724 mm). Kumasi. Jan. 77°F (25°C), July 76°F (24·4°C). Annual rainfall 58" (1,402 mm). Sekondi-Takoradi. Jan. 77°F (25°C), July 76°F (24·4°C). Annual rainfall 47" (1,181 mm). Tamale. Jan. 82°F (27·8°C), July 78°F (25·6°C). Annual rainfall 41" (1,026 mm).

CONSTITUTION AND GOVERNMENT. After the coup of 31 Dec. 1981, supreme power was vested in the Provisional National Defence Council (PNDC), chaired by Flight-Lieut. Jerry John Rawlings.

A new constitution was approved by 92·6% of votes cast at a referendum on 28 April 1992. The electorate was 8,255,690; turn-out was 43·8%. The constitution sets up a presidential system on the US model, with a multi-party parliament and an independent judiciary. The *President* is elected by universal suffrage for a 4-year term renewable once.

Presidential and parliamentary elections were held on 7 Dec. 1996. The electorate was 9m.; turn-out was 75%. President Rawlings was re-elected by 57·2% of votes cast against 2 opponents. There were some 700 parliamentary candidates. The National Democratic Congress (NDC) gained 130 seats.

In March. 1998 the government comprised the following:

President: Jerry John Rawlings (b. 1947; NDC; sworn in 7 Jan. 1997).

Vice-President: John Evans Atta Mills.

Secretary of State for Foreign Affairs: James Victor Gbeho. *Justice and Attorney-General:* Dr Obed Y. Asamoah. *Interior:* Nii Okaidja Adamafio. *Defence:* Mahama Iddrisu. *Finance and Economic Planning:* Richard Kwame Peprah. *Trade and Industries:* Dr John Abu. *Communications:* Ekow Spio-Garbrah. *Food and Agriculture:* Dr Kwabena Adjei. *Education:* Dr Chrstine Amoako-Nuama. *Health:* Eunice Brookman-Amissah. *Roads and Transport:* Edward Salia. *Local Government and Rural Development:* Kwamena Ahwoi. *Employment and Social Welfare:* Mohammed Mumuni. *Lands and Forestry:* Cletus Avoka. *Environment, Science and Technology:* J. E. Afful. *Parliamentary Affairs:* J. H. Owusu-Acheampong. *Tourism:* Michael Gizo. *Works and Housing:* Isaac Adjei-Mensah. *Youth and Sports:* Enoch T. Mensah.

The *Speaker* is Daniel Annan.

National anthem: 'God bless our Homeland, Ghana'; words by the government, tune by P. Gbeho.

Local government: The 10 Regions, each under a Regional Secretary appointed by the PNDC, are divided into 110 districts.

DEFENCE

Army. The Army consists of 2 brigades, 1 reconnaissance regiment, 1 airborne force, 1 field engineer battalion, and 1 mortar battalion, with armoured cars and ancillary units. Total strength, (1997) 5,000. There is a paramilitary People's Militia of 5,000, a part-time force with police duties, and a Presidential Guard comprising 1 infantry battalion.

Navy. The Navy, based at Sekondi and Tema, comprises 2 German-built coastal patrol, 2 inshore patrol craft and 2 small service craft. 2 unarmed F-27 aircraft are available for maritime patrol. Naval strength in 1997 was 1,000 including support personnel.

Air Force. The Ghana Air Force has 4 Italian-built Aermacchi M.B.326K light ground attack jets. It also operates, for training, transport, search and rescue, and air survey operations, 4 Fokker Friendship twin-turboprop transports and a twin-turbo-fan Fokker Fellowship for Presidential use, 4 Islander piston-engined light transports and 4 Shorts Skyvan twin-turboprop short-take-off-and-landing transports; 2 Bell 212 helicopters; 2 Alouette III helicopters, and 8 L-29 Delfin and 2 M.B.339 jet trainers. There are air bases at Takoradi and Tamale. Personnel strength (1997) 1,000.

INTERNATIONAL RELATIONS

Membership. Ghana is a member of the UN, the Commonwealth, OAU, ECOWAS and is an ACP state of the EU.

ECONOMY

Policy. A privatization programme was inaugurated in 1988. By 1996, 100 of the 260 enterprises in which the government had a majority stake had been sold.

Performance. Real GDP growth was 5·2% in 1996 (4·5% in 1995).

Budget. The 1996 budget provided for (in ₵ 1,000m.): Revenue, 2,328·3; expenditure, 2,169·5.VAT was abolished in 1995.

Currency. The monetary unit is the *cedi* (GHC) of 100 *pesewas* (P). There are coins of 0·5, 1, 5, 10, 20 and 50 pesewas and notes of ₵ 10, 20, 50, 100, 200, 500 and 1,000. Currency in circulation, Dec. 1995, ₵585,507·3m. In 1996, inflation was an annualized 50%. Inflation was 32·6% in Dec. 1996. Foreign exchange reserves were US$669m. in 1995.

Banking and Finance. The Bank of Ghana (*Chair*, Godfried K. Agama) was established in 1957 as the central bank and bank of issue. At Dec. 1995 its total assets were ₵3,272,946·6m. There are 3 large commercial banks, 7 secondary banks, 3 merchant banks and 100 rural banks. There are 2 discount houses. Banks are required to have a capital base of at least 6% of net assets. At Dec. 1995 assets of commercial banks totalled ₵1,900,327·1m.

There is a stock exchange in Accra.

ENERGY AND NATURAL RESOURCES

Electricity. Production (1994) 6·1bn. kWh, mainly from 2 hydro-electric stations operated by the Volta River Authority, Akosombo (6 units) and Kpong (4 units).

Minerals. In 1994 diamond production was officially estimated at 0·7m. carats; manganese (1993), 362,000 tonnes; bauxite (1994), 396,861 tonnes; gold (1994), 44·5 tonnes; (1993), 41·5 tonnes.

Agriculture. In 1996 agriculture contributed 43% of GDP. In southern and central Ghana main food crops are maize, rice, cassava, plantain, groundnuts, yam and cocoyam, and in northern Ghana groundnuts, rice, maize, sorghum, millet and yam.

Production of main food crops, 1993 (in 1,000 tonnes): Maize, 961; rice, 157; millet, 198; sorghum, 328; cassava, 4,200; cocoyam, 1,236; yam, 1,000; plantains, 1,322.

Cocoa is the main cash crop. Production (1995–96), 365,000 tonnes. Among other cash crops, tobacco and coffee are important, and improved types of palm oil and coconuts are being planted.

Livestock, 1994: Cattle, 1·6m.; sheep, 3·2m.; goats, 3·3m.; pigs, 0·5m.; poultry, 12m.

Forestry. The closed forest zone covers 8,225,900 ha (36% of the land area), of which 2,559,400 ha are reserves and 46,600 ha unreserved forest lands. In 1994, 2·7m. cu. metres of logs were produced.

Fisheries. Catch (1993) 371,000 tonnes (52,000 tonnes from inland waters).

INDUSTRY. Production of aluminium (1990) 174,000 tonnes.

FOREIGN ECONOMIC RELATIONS. Foreign debt was estimated at US$5·2bn. in 1996.

Commerce. In 1995 estimated exports were US$1·43bn.; imports valued at US$1·84bn. Principal exports, 1995: Gold, 1,539,000m. oz. valued at US$635·90m.; cocoa and products, 236,255 tonnes valued at US$364·63m.; timber valued at US$190m.; plus tuna, bauxite, aluminium, manganese ore and diamonds. Principal imported commodities: capital equipment, petroleum, consumer goods, food. Main export markets, 1995: UK, 14·1%; Germany, 11·6%; USA, 11·1%; Togo, 9·4%. Main import suppliers: UK, 16·7%; Nigeria, 15·6%; Germany, 7·8%; USA, 6·9%.

Tourism. In 1995 there were 335,000 foreign visitors, bringing in foreign exchange earnings of US$273m.

COMMUNICATIONS

Roads. In 1996 there were 14,700 km of trunk roads and 24,000 km of other roads. About 25% of all roads, including 21 km of expressway, are hard-surfaced. A Road Sector Strategy and Programme to develop the road network is running from 1995 to 2000.

Railways. Total length of railways in 1993 was 953 km of 1,067 mm gauge. In 1994 railways carried 0·7m. tonnes of freight and 2·3m. passengers.

Civil Aviation. There is an international airport at Accra (Kotoka). The national carrier is the state-owned Ghana Airways, which in 1995 operated 1 DC-10-30, 1 DC-9-50, 1 F-28-2000 and 1 F-28-4000. Services were also provided by Aeroflot, Air Afrique, Air Ivoire, Alitalia, British Airways, Egyptair, Ethiopian Airlines, KLM, Libyan Airlines, Lufthansa, Middle East Airlines, Nigeria Airways, Northwest Airlines, Sierra National and Swissair.

Shipping. The chief ports are Takoradi and Tema. In 1995, 1·2m. tonnes of cargo were unloaded at Takoradi and 3·9m. tonnes at Tema. There is inland water transport on Lake Volta. In 1996 the merchant marine had 4 cargo ships of 1,000 GRT or over, totalling 28,900 GRT. The Volta, Ankobra and Tano rivers provide 168 km of navigable waterways for launches and lighters.

Telecommunications. In 1995 there were 98,600 telephones. The Ghana Broadcasting Corporation is an autonomous statutory body. There are 5 national radio programmes. In 1994 there was 1 public national and 1 independent local TV network. In 1995 there were 4m. radio and 1·6m. TV receivers (colour by PAL).

Press. There were (1995) 4 daily newspapers with a combined circulation of 3·1m.

SOCIAL INSTITUTIONS

Justice. The Courts were constituted as follows:

Supreme Court. The Supreme Court consists of the Chief Justice who is also the President and not less than 4 other Justices of the Supreme Court. The Supreme Court is the final court of appeal in Ghana. The final interpretation of the provisions of the constitution has been entrusted to the Supreme Court.

Court of Appeal. The Court of Appeal consists of the Chief Justice together with not less than 5 other Justices of the Appeal court and such other Justices of Superior Courts as the Chief Justice may nominate. The Court of Appeal is duly constituted by 3 Justices. The Court of Appeal is bound by its own previous decisions and all courts inferior to the Court of Appeal are bound to follow the decisions of the Court of Appeal on questions of law. Divisions of the Appeal Court may be created, subject to the discretion of the Chief Justice.

High Court of Justice. The Court has jurisdiction in civil and criminal matters as well as those relating to industrial and labour disputes including administrative complaints. The High Court of Justice has supervisory jurisdiction over all inferior Courts and any adjudicating authority and in exercise of its supervisory jurisdiction has power to issue such directions, orders or writs including writs or orders in the nature of habeas corpus, certiorari, mandamus, prohibition and quo qarrantto. The High

Court of Justice has no jurisdiction in cases of treason. The High Court consists of the Chief Justice and not less than 12 other judges and such other Justices of the Superior Court as the Chief Justice may appoint.

The PNDC has established Public Tribunals in addition to the traditional courts of justice.

There is a Public Tribunal Board consisting of not less than 5 members and not more than 15 members of the public appointed by the PNDC, at least one of whom shall be a lawyer of not less than 5 years' standing as a lawyer. The Board is responsible for the administration of all tribunals.

A tribunal consists of at least three persons and not more than five persons, selected by the Board from among persons appointed by the Council as members of public tribunals.

Religion. An estimated 30% of the population are Muslim and 24% Christian, with 38% adherents to indigenous beliefs and 8% other religions.

Education. Schooling is free and compulsory, and consists of 6 years of primary, 3 years of junior secondary and 3 years of senior secondary education. In 1990 75% of eligible children attended primary, and 39% secondary, school. In 1991 there were 2·01m. pupils in primary and 829,518 in secondary schools. University education is free. There are 2 universities, 1 university each for development studies, and science and technology. In 1994–95 there were 11,225 university students and 779 academic staff. There were also 6 polytechnics, 7 colleges and 38 teacher training colleges. Adult literacy in 1995 was estimated at 64·5% (75·9% of men and 53·5% of women).

Health. Provision of doctors, 1994: 1 per 22,970 population. Provision of hospital beds, 1994: 1 per 638 population. At the end of 1995 there were 15,890 cases of AIDS, mainly women.

DIPLOMATIC REPRESENTATIVES

Of Ghana in Great Britain (13 Belgrave Sq., London SW1X 8PN)
High Commissioner: J. E. K. Aggrey-Orleans.

Of Great Britain in Ghana (Osu Link, off Gamel Abdul Nasser Ave., Accra)
High Commissioner: Ian W. Mackley, CMG.

Of Ghana in the USA (3512 International Dr., NW, Washington, D.C., 20008)
Ambassador: Harry Sawyers.

Of the USA in Ghana (Ring Rd. East, Accra)
Ambassador: Edward Brynn.

Of Ghana to the United Nations
Ambassador: Jacob Wilmot.

Of Ghana to the European Union
Ambassador: Alex Ntim Abankwa.

Further Reading

Carmichael, J., *Profile of Ghana.* London, 1992.—*African Eldorado: Ghana from Gold Coast to Independence.* London, 1993
Davidson, B., *Black Star.* London, 1973
Herbst, J., *The Politics of Reform in Ghana, 1982–1991.* California Univ. Press, 1993
Myers, R. A., *Ghana:* [Bibliography]. Oxford and Santa Barbara (CA), 1991
Petchenkine, Y., *Ghana in Search of Stability, 1957–1992.* New York, 1992
Ray, D. I., *Ghana: Politics, Economics and Society.* London, 1986
Rimmer, D., *Staying Poor: Ghana's Political Economy, 1950–1990.* Oxford, 1993
Rothchild., D. (ed.): *Ghana: the Political Economy of Recovery.* Boulder (Colo.), 1991

National statistical office: Statistical Service, Accra.

GREECE

Elliniki Dimokratia

(Hellenic Republic)

Capital: Athens
Population: 10·56m.
GDP per head: (PPP$) 11,265
HDI/world rank: 0·923/20

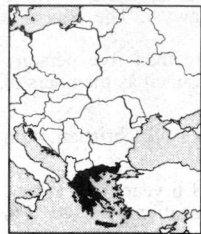

KEY HISTORICAL EVENTS. Greece gained independence from the Ottoman Empire between 1821-29, and by the Protocol of London of 3 Feb. 1830 was declared a kingdom under the protection of Great Britain, France and Russia. Many Greeks were left outside the new state and the cause of the union of all Greeks was championed by Otto I, a Bavarian who was enthroned on 18 Jan. 1833. After his overthrow on 23 Oct. 1862, a Danish prince was elected George I, King of the Hellenes, in 1863. The 1844 constitution was replaced by one based on popular sovereignty in 1864. Under the premier Venezelos a programme of domestic renewal was launched after 1910, including important land reforms in 1917. In 1864 Great Britain had ceded the Ionian Islands; in 1881 Thessaly and part of Epirus had been taken. Greece's area increased by 70%, the population growing from 2·8m. to 4·8 m. after the Treaty of Bucharest (1913) which recognized Greek sovereignty over Crete.

King Constantine who succeeded on his father's assassination on 18 March 1913 opted for neutrality in the First World War, while Venezelos favoured the Entente powers. This split or National Schism led to British and French intervention which deposed Constantine on 11 June 1917. When his son Alexander died on 25 Oct. 1920, he returned on 19 Dec. and reigned until 27 Sept. 1922. He was forced to abdicate by a *coup* after defeat by Turkey and the loss of Smyrna. The Treaty of Lausanne (1923) recognized Smyrna as Turkish with Eastern Thrace and the islands of Imvros and Tenedos, all of which had been ceded to Greece by the 1920 Treaty of Sevres.

An exchange of Christian and Moslem populations followed. Over 1m. immigrants caused social problems, despite an effective peasant settlement in the countryside. The newcomers contributed strongly to the fall of the monarchy in a plebiscite on 13 April 1924. George II was restored after a new plebiscite on 25 Nov. 1935.

The authoritarian Metaxas, premier since 1937, was unable to preserve neutrality after the Italian ultimatum of 28 Oct. 1940. The successful resistance of the Greek army forced the Germans to aid Italy on 6 April 1941. Surrender followed on 20 April and Athens was occupied on 27 April. The harsh occupation lasted till 15 Oct. 1944.

The popular front EAM and its military wing ELAS, both dominated by the communists, took a leading part in resistance to the Germans. The king had moved in April 1941 to Crete, then to Cairo and London. On 30 Dec. 1944 he appointed Archbishop Damaskinos as regent before, backed by Britain and approved in a plebiscite, he returned on 28 Sept. 1946. On his death on 1 April 1947 he was succeeded by his brother Paul. A conflict with ELAS developed into a civil war in 1946-47, which made refugees of 10% of the population. Britain handed responsibility to the USA which pledged support against the communists who received only short-lived Yugoslav aid. Peace came after 1949.

The adoption, under US pressure, of a simple majority system rather than proportional representation, and the growing industrialization of the economy brought stability, especially after 1955 under the pro-western Konstantinos Karamanlis. The late 1950s saw the emergence of the Left, capitalizing on the movement for union with Cyprus and unease over NATO membership (1952). On 9 Aug. 1954 Greece, Turkey and Yugoslavia signed a 20-year treaty of friendship and mutual aid.

The election of 1963, based on proportional representation, undermined the position of the Right, and led to conflict with the new king Constantine, who succeeded his father Paul on 6 March 1964. A military *coup* on 21 April 1967, with fear of communism its stated reason, led to the departure the following year of the king after an unsuccessful counter-*coup*. The authoritarian rule of the 'Colonels' was headed by George Papadopoulos, prime minister, regent (1972) and president after the republic was declared on 29 July 1973. The régime was overthrown in a bloodless *coup* by Gen. Chizikis on 25 Nov. 1973.

Inflation and the failure to defeat President Makarios of Cyprus or to prevent the Turkish invasion of the island led to the collapse of the military dictatorship on 23 July 1974. Karamanlis was recalled from exile to form a civilian government of national unity. On 17 Nov. 1974 he and his New Democracy Party won a large majority. The monarchy was abolished by a referendum on 8 Dec. 1974.

Hostility to the USA grew, especially as it was believed that America favoured Turkey, with whom conflicts persisted. The 1981 election brought Andreas Papandreou to power and the head of a socialist government. Earlier that year Greece had become the tenth member of the EC. Re-elected in 1985, Papandreou imposed economic austerity to combat inflation and soaring budgets. But industrial unrest and evidence of widespread corruption led to the fall of Papandreou and a succession of weak governments. Papandreou returned to power in Oct. 1993 but ill-health forced his resignation two years later. His successor Konstantinos Simitis took a more pro-European stance instituting economic reforms preparing the way for entry into EMU.

TERRITORY AND POPULATION. Greece is bounded in the north by Albania, the Former Yugoslav Republic of Macedonia (FYROM) and Bulgaria, east by Turkey and the Aegean Sea, south by the Mediterranean and west by the Ionian Sea. The total area is 131,957 sq. km (50,949 sq. miles), of which the islands account for 25,042 sq. km (9,669 sq. miles).

The population was 10,264,156 (5,234,446 females) according to the census of March 1991; (July 1994 est.: 10,564,630); density, 77·8 per sq. km. There were 166,031 resident foreign nationals.

In 1987 the territory of Greece was administratively reorganized into 13 *regions* comprising in all 51 *departments*. Areas and populations according to the 1991 census:

Region/Department	Area in sq. km	Population	Chief town
Attica[1]	3,808	3,523,407	Athens
Aegean North	3,836	199,231	*Mytilene*
Chios	904	52,184	Chios
Lesbos	2,154	105,082	Mytilene
Samos	778	41,965	Samos
Aegean South	5,286	257,481	*Hermoupolis*
Cyclades	2,572	94,005	Hermoupolis
Dodecanese	2,714	163,476	Rhodes
Crete	8,336	540,054	*Heraklion*
Canea	2,376	133,774	Canea
Heraklion	2,641	264,906	Heraklion
Lassithi	1,823	71,279	Aghios Nikolaos
Rethymnon	1,496	70,095	Rethymnon
Epirus	9,203	339,728	*Ioannina*
Arta	1,662	78,719	Arta
Ioannina	4,990	158,193	Ioannina
Preveza	1,036	58,628	Preveza
Thesprotia	1,515	44,188	Hegoumenitsa
Greece Central[2]	15,549	582,280	*Lamia*
Boeotia	2,952	134,108	Levadeia
Euboea	4,167	208,408	Chalcis
Evrytania	1,869	24,307	Karpenissi
Phocis	2,120	44,183	Amphissa
Phthiotis	4,441	171,274	Lamia
Greece West	11,350	707,687	*Patras*
Achaia	3,271	300,078	Patras
Elia	2,618	179,429	Pyrgos
Aetolia and Acarnania	5,461	228,180	Missolonghi
Ionian Islands	2,307	193,734	*Corfu*
Cephalonia	904	32,474	Argostoli
Corfu	641	107,592	Corfu
Leucas	356	21,111	Leucas
Zante	406	32,557	Zante

[1] Attica is both region and department.   [2] Without Attica.

Region/Department	Area in sq. km	Population	Chief town
Macedonia Central	*19,147*	*1,710,513*	*Thessaloniki*
Chalcidice	2,918	92,117	Polygyros
Imathia	1,701	138,934	Veroia
Kilkis	2,519	81,710	Kilkis
Mount Athos	336	1,536	—
Pella	2,506	138,761	Edessa
Pieria	1,516	116,763	Katerini
Serres	3,968	192,828	Serres
Thessaloniki	3,683	946,864	Thessaloniki
Macedonia East and			
Thrace	*14,157*	*570,496*	*Comotini*
Cavalla	2,111	135,937	Cavalla
Drama	3,468	96,554	Drama
Evros	4,242	143,752	Alexandroupolis
Rhodope	2,543	103,190	Comotini
Xanthi	1,793	91,063	Xanthi
Macedonia West	*9,451*	*293,015*	*Kozani*
Florina	1,924	53,147	Florina
Grevena	2,291	36,797	Grevena
Kastoria	1,720	52,685	Kastoria
Kozani	3,516	150,386	Kozani
Peloponnese	*15,490*	*607,428*	*Tripolis*
Arcadia	4,419	105,309	Tripolis
Argolis	2,154	97,636	Nauplion
Corinth	2,290	141,823	Corinth
Laconia	3,636	95,696	Sparta
Messenia	2,991	166,964	Calamata
Thessaly	*14,037*	*734,846*	*Larissa*
Karditsa	2,636	126,854	Karditsa
Larissa	5,381	270,612	Larissa
Magnesia	2,636	198,434	Volo
Trikala	3,384	138,946	Trikala

The largest cities (1991 census populations) are Athens (the capital), 772,072 (total conurbation of Greater Athens, 3,095,775); Thessaloniki, 739,998; Piraeus, 182,671; Patras, 172,763; Peristerion, 137,288; Heraklion, 127,600; Larissa, 113,426; Kallithea, 114,233.

The Monastic Republic of **Mount Athos** (or Agion Oros, i.e. 'Holy Mountain'), the easternmost of the three prongs of the peninsula of Chalcidice, is a self-governing community composed of 20 monasteries. The peninsula is administered by a Council of 4 members and an Assembly of 20 members, 1 deputy from each monastery. The Constitution of 1927 gives legal sanction to the Charter of Mount Athos, drawn up by representatives of the 20 monasteries on 20 May 1924, and its status is confirmed by the 1952 and 1975 Constitutions. Women are not permitted to enter. Population, 1997, 4,000.

Vital statistics (1994 est.): 103,763 live births; still births, 599; 2,982 births to unmarried mothers; 56,813 marriages; deaths, 97,807. Over 1990–95, the suicide rate per 100,000 population was 3·5 (men, 5·5; women 1·5).

The modern Greek language had 2 contesting literary standard forms, the archaizing *Katharevousa* ('purist'), and a version based on the spoken vernacular, 'Demotic'. In 1976 Standard Modern Greek was adopted as the official language, with Demotic as its core.

CLIMATE. Coastal regions and the islands have typical Mediterranean conditions, with mild, rainy winters and hot, dry, sunny summers. Rainfall comes almost entirely in the winter months, though amounts vary widely according to position and relief. Continental conditions affect the northern mountainous areas, with severe winters, deep snow cover and heavy precipitation, but summers are hot. Athens. Jan. 48°F (8·6°C), July 82·5°F (28·2°C). Annual rainfall 16·6" (414·3 mm).

CONSTITUTION AND GOVERNMENT. A new Constitution was introduced in June 1975. The 300-member *Chamber of Deputies* is elected for 4-year terms by proportional representation. There is a 3% threshold. Extra seats are awarded to the party which leads in an election. The Chamber of Deputies elects the head of state, the *President*, for a 5-year term.

President: Constantinos Stephanopoulos (elected 8 March 1995).

Parliamentary elections were held on 22 Sept. 1996. The electorate was 8,862,014. Seats gained (and % of vote): Pasok (i.e. Panhellenic Socialist Movement), 162 (41·5%); New Democracy, 108 (38·1%); Communist Party, 11 (5·6%); Coalition of Self-Management Left (SYN), 10 (5·1%); Dikki (dissident Pasok), 9 (4%).

A government was formed on 24 Sept. 1996, comprising in March 1998:
Prime Minister: Constantinos Simitis (b. 1937; Pasok).
Interior, Public Administration and Decentralization: Alexander Papadopoulos. *Defence:* Akis Tsohatsopulos. *Foreign Affairs:* Theodoros Pangalos. *Economy and Finance:* Yiannos Papantoniou. *Agriculture:* Stephanos Tzoumakas. *Labour and Social Security:* Militiade Papaioannou. *Health and Welfare:* Costas Geitonas. *Justice:* Evangelos Yannopoulos. *Education and Religious Affairs:* Gerasimos Arsenis. *Culture:* Evangelos Venizelos. *Merchant Marine:* Stavros Soumakis. *Public Order:* Georgios Romeos. *Macedonia and Thrace:* Phillipos Petsalnikos. *The Aegean:* Elizaveta Papazoi. *Environment, Town Planning and Public Works:* Costas Laliotis. *Development (Industry, Commerce and Tourism):* Vasso Papandreou. *Transport and Communications:* Tassos Mantelis. *Alternate Foreign Affairs Minister:* Georgios Papandreou. *Press, Mass Media and Media Government Spokesman:* Dimitris Reppas.

National anthem: Imnos eis tin Eleftherian (Hymn to Freedom); words by Dionysios Solomos, tune by N. Mantzaros.

European Parliament. Greece has 25 representatives. At the June 1994 elections turn-out was 71·9%. Pasok won 10 seats with 37·6% of votes cast (group in European Parliament: European Socialist Party); New Democracy, 9 with 32·7% (Popular European Party); left-wing coalition, 4 with 12·5%; others, 2 with 8·7%.

Local government: Departments are headed by prefects, elected for the first time in Oct. 1994. Mayoral elections were also held in 434 municipalities. Pasok and other socialists gained 213 municipalities and 37 departments with 45% of votes cast; New Democracy, 160 and 13 with 39%.

DEFENCE. Conscription is (Army) 19 months, (Navy) 23 months, (Air Force) 21 months.

Army. The Field Army is organized in 3 military regions, with 1 Army, 5 corps and 4 divisional headquarters. There are 9 infantry divisions, 5 independent armoured, 2 independent mechanized, 2 infantry and 1 marine brigade, 1 commando and 1 raider regiment, 4 reconnaissance, 10 field artillery, 8 air defence artillery, 2 surface-to-air missile and 2 army aviation battalions and 1 independent aviation company. There is also a Territorial Defence Force of 36,000, with 4 military command headquarters, comprising 1 infantry division, 1 parachute regiment and 8 field artillery, 4 air defence artillery and 1 army aviation battalion. Reserves of 35,000 form a National Guard whose role is internal security. Total Army strength (1997) 122,000 (95,000 conscripts, 2,900 women). There is also a paramilitary gendarmerie of 26,500.

Navy. The current strength of the Hellenic Navy includes 8 diesel submarines, 4 ex-US guided-missile destroyers, 11 frigates including 7 helicopter-equipped, 5 corvettes and 19 fast missile craft. Main bases are at Salamis, Patras, and Soudha Bay (Crete). Personnel in 1996 totalled 19,500 (9,800 conscripts, 1,300 women).
The Coastguard and Customs service is 4,000 strong.

Air Force. The Hellenic Air Force (HAF) had a strength (1996) of 26,800 (14,400 conscripts, 1,100 women). There are 3 squadrons of F-4E Phantom and 2 squadrons of Mirage 2000 air-superiority fighters, 2 squadrons of F-16 fighter-bombers, 4 squadrons of Mirage F.1 fighters, 4 squadrons of A-7H Corsair II attack aircraft, 2 squadrons of F-5 fighters, 1 squadron of RF-4E reconnaissance fighters and 1 squadron of P-3–Orion maritime reconnaissance aircraft (under Navy control).
The HAF is organized into Tactical and Air Support Commands.

INTERNATIONAL RELATIONS

Membership. Greece is a member of the UN, EU, WEU, Council of Europe and NATO.

ECONOMY

Policy. In 1990 the Government embarked on a large-scale privatization of state industries.

Performance. Real GDP growth was 2·6% in 1996.

Budget. Estimated revenue 1997 (in 1,000m. drachmas): 9,532; expenditure, 11,891. VAT is 18% (reduced rate, 8%).

Currency. The unit of currency is the *drachma* (GRD), notionally divided into 100 *lepta*. There are coins of 1, 2, 5, 10, 20, 50 and 100 and notes of 500, 1,000, 5,000 and 10,000 drachmas. Inflation was 7·5% in Dec. 1996 and 5·1% in Nov. 1997. Foreign exchange reserves (excluding gold) were US$17,501m. in 1996.

Banking and Finance. The central bank and bank of issue is the Bank of Greece. Its *Governor* is Loukas Papademos. There were 25 domestic banks in 1994, 8 private and the remainder in 4 state groupings. In 1995 the major banks (with profits in Dr 1,000m.) were: The private Alpha Credit Bank (50·7) and the State-owned National Bank (41·1), Ergobank (37·4), Commercial Bank (26·2), Mortgage Bank (20·6) and Ionian Bank (13·6). Total assets of all banks were US$15,421,377m. in 1994.

There is a stock exchange in Athens.

Weights and Measures. The metric system was made obligatory in 1959; the use of other systems is prohibited. The Gregorian calendar was adopted in Feb. 1923.

ENERGY AND NATURAL RESOURCES

Electricity. Total installed capacity was 9,150,155 kW as at 31 Dec. 1993. 72% of power is supplied by lignite-fired power stations. A national grid supplies the mainland, and islands near its coast. Power is produced in remoter islands by local generators. Total net production in 1993 was 34,391m. kWh.

Oil. Output, 1992, 5,008,368 bbls.

Minerals. Greece produces a variety of ores and minerals, including (with production, 1994, in tonnes) iron-pyrites (26,637), bauxite (2,193,971), nickel (1,944,018), magnesite (575,472), asbestos (4,647,033), chromite (5,650 in 1993), barytes (701), marble (white and coloured) and various other earths. There is little coal, and the lignite is of indifferent quality (57·5m. tonnes, 1994). Salt production (1994) 206,427 tonnes.

Agriculture. Of the total area (131,957 sq. km) 39,930 sq. km is arable and fallow. Another 52,101 sq. km is grazing land.

Production (1996, in 1,000 tonnes):

Wheat	2,288	Grapes	237
Rye	37	Wine must	439
Tobacco	189	Citrus fruit	1,429
Seed cotton	783	Other fruit	1,778
Sugar-beet	3,308	Milk	1,860
Raisins	90	Meat	505
Olive oil	396		

Olive production in 1996 was 282,000 tonnes. Rice, 1996, 149,478 tonnes. The main kinds of cheese produced are *fetta* (white cheese in brine, 118,225 tonnes in 1993), and hard cheese, 35,989.

Livestock (1996, in 1,000): 624 cattle, 1 buffaloes, 996 pigs, 8,660 sheep, 5,334 goats, 45 horses, 60 mules, 127 asses, 27,029 poultry.

Forestry. Forests covered 29,511 sq. km in 1991.

Fisheries. In 1996, 20,149 fishermen were active and landed 169,958 tonnes of fish. 2,500 kg of sponges were produced in 1994.

INDUSTRY. Manufacturing contributed an estimated 2,219,730m. drachmas to GDP in 1993. The main products are canned vegetables and fruit, fruit juice, beer, wine, alcoholic beverages, cigarettes, textiles, yarn, leather, shoes, synthetic timber, paper, plastics, rubber products, chemical acids, pigments, pharmaceutical products, cosmetics, soap, disinfectants, fertilizers, glassware, porcelain sanitary items, wire and power coils and household instruments.

Production, 1993 (1,000 tonnes): Textile yarns, 139; cement, 19,456; fertilizers, 998; ammonia, 57; iron (concrete-reinforcing bars), 799; alumina, 614; aluminium, 181; beer, 405; bottled wine, 187; chemical acids, 701; iron wire, 107; packing materials, 371; cigarettes (1,000 pieces), 29,437; petroleum, 7,773; detergents, 231.

Labour. Of the employed people in 1995, 781,934 were engaged in agriculture, 577,688 in manufacturing and 2,464,188 in other employment. Automatic index-linking of wages was abolished at the end of 1990. Wage increases of 8% were made in the public sector in 1991. In the private sector trade unions agreed to a 12% increase in 1991 and one of 9% in 1992. Since 1989 a statutory minimum of wage-bills must be spent on training. Retirement age is 65 years for men and 60 for women. Unemployment was 10% in Dec. 1996.

Trade Unions. The status of trade unions is regulated by the Associations Act 1914. Trade union liberties are guaranteed under the Constitution, and a law of June 1982 altered the unions' right to strike.

The national body of trade unions is the Greek General Confederation of Labour.

FOREIGN ECONOMIC RELATIONS. Following the normalization of their relations, Greece lifted its trade embargo (imposed in Feb. 1994) on Macedonia on 13 Oct. 1995. There are quarrels with Turkey over Cyprus, oil rights under the Aegean and ownership of uninhabited islands close to the Turkish coast.

Commerce. In 1996, exports were valued at US$6,100m. and imports at US$21,978m. In 1993 exports totalled (1m. drachmas) 2,539,265 including: Miscellaneous manufactured articles, 529,540; clothing and accessories (excluding footwear), 427,616; basic manufactures, 545,361; food and live animals, 460,193; vegetables and fruit, 294,658; mineral fuels, lubricants, etc., 165,290; petroleum and petroleum products, 162,214; refined petroleum products, 150,242; beverages and tobacco, 142,646; crude materials (inedible) except fuels, 180,244. Imports totalled 6,006,758 including: Machinery and transport equipment, 1,648,678; road vehicles and parts and other transport equipment (excluding tyres, engines and electrical parts), 643,795; basic manufactures, 1,192,862; food and live animals, 788,453; chemicals and related products, 791,163; mineral fuels, lubricants, etc., 434,295; petroleum and petroleum products, 412,564; miscellaneous manufactured articles, 610,665; crude petroleum, 331,430; ships, boats and floating structures, 99,547.

Exports in 1995 (in 1m. drachmas) were mainly to Germany (561,313), Italy (357,899), France (138,477), UK (154,731) and USA (79,664). Imports were mainly from Germany (993,859), Italy (1,024,901), France (488,019), Japan (158,073), the Netherlands (416,130) and UK (390,071).

Tourism. Tourists in 1995 numbered 10·7m. Tourist spending, US$3,905m. in 1994. In 1994 there were 508,408 hotel beds.

COMMUNICATIONS

Roads. There were, in 1992, 38,606 km of roads, of which 9,255 were national and 29,351 provincial roads. Number of motor vehicles in 1994: 2,946,654, of which 2,074,081 were passenger cars, 849,033 goods vehicles and 23,540 buses.

Railways. In 1994 the state network, Hellenic Railways (OSE), totalled 2,474 km including 1,565 km of 1,435 mm gauge, 887 km of 1,000 mm gauge, and 22 km of 750 mm gauge. Railways carried 3·4m. tonnes of freight and 11·2m. passengers.

Civil Aviation. There are international airports at Athens (Hellinikon) and Thessaloniki-Macedonia. In 1995 the state-owned Olympic Airways operated 4 A300B4-100s, 2 A300B4-200s, 2 A300B4-600Rs, 2 B-727-200s, 1 B-727-200 Adv, 11 B-737-200 Advs, 7 B-737-400s and 4 B-747-200Bs. 6m. passengers were carried in 1995. It operates routes from Athens to all important cities of the country, Europe, the Middle East and USA. Services are also provided by Aeroflot, Air France, Air Malta, Air Moldova, Air Ukraine, Alitalia, Armenian Airlines, Austrian Airlines, Azerbaijan Hava Yollary, Balkan, British Airways, Condor, Cyprus Airways, Czech Airlines, Delta, Egyptair, El Al, Ethiopian Airlines, Finnair, Gulf Air, Hamburg Airlines, Hapag Lloyd, Iberia, Iran Air, JAT, KLM, Kuwait Airways, Libyan Airlines, LOT, LTU, Lufthansa, Luxair, Malév, Middle East Airlines, Pakistan Airlines, Royal Air Maroc, Royal Jordanian, Sabena, SAS, Singapore Airlines, Swissair, Syrian Airlines, TAP, Tarom, Thai Airways, Trans World, Tunis Air, Turkish Airlines, Uzbekistan Airways and Virgin Atlantic.

Shipping. In 1995 the merchant navy comprised 2,128 vessels of 29,862,928 GRT. Greek-owned ships under foreign flags totalled 2,310,862 GRT. Totalled registered tonnage, 30·25m. GRT, including 13·45m. GRT of oil tankers and 0·64m. GRT of container ships.

There is a canal (opened 9 Nov. 1893) across the Isthmus of Corinth (about 4 miles).

Telecommunications. In 1995 there were 5,745 telephone exchanges and 6,235,512 telephones.

Elliniki Radiophonia Tileorasis (ERT), the Hellenic National Radio and Television Institute, is the government broadcasting station. There are 4 national and regional programmes, and an external service, Voice of Greece (16 languages). ERT broadcasts 2 TV programmes (colour by SECAM). Number of receivers in 1993: Radio, 4,085,000; television, 2·3m.

Cinemas. There were 236 screens in 1994. There were 6·2m. admissions in 1992. 11 full-length films were made in 1994.

Press There are 35 daily newspapers published in Athens, 6 in Piraeus and 76 elsewhere.

SOCIAL INSTITUTIONS

Justice. Judges are appointed for life by the President after consultation with the judicial council. Judges enjoy personal and functional independence. There are 3 divisions of the courts: Administrative, civil and criminal and they must not give decisions which are contrary to the Constitution. Final jurisdiction lies with a Special Supreme Tribunal.

Religion. The Christian Eastern (Greek) Orthodox Church is the established religion to which 98% of the population belong. It is under an archbishop and 67 metropolitans, 1 archbishop and 7 metropolitans in Crete, and 4 metropolitans in the Dodecanese. Roman Catholics have 3 archbishops (in Naxos and Corfu and, not recognized by the State, in Athens) and 1 bishop (for Syra and Santorin). The Exarchs of the Greek Catholics and the Armenians are not recognized by the State. There were 0·15m. Moslems in 1995.

Complete religious freedom is recognized by the Constitution of 1974, but proselytizing from, and interference with, the Greek Orthodox Church is forbidden.

Education. Public education is provided in nursery, primary and secondary schools, starting at $5^1/_2$–$6^1/_2$ years of age and free at all levels. Literacy was 93% in 1994.

In 1995–96 there were 5,598 nursery schools with 8,370 teachers and 127,089 pupils; 7,075 primary schools with 40,107 teachers and 673,409 pupils; 1,895 high schools with 31,353 teachers and 421,645 pupils; 1,192 lycea with 17,492 teachers and 252,945 pupils; 48 ecclesiastical and technical secondary schools of the first cycle with 291 teachers and 3,554 pupils, and 524 ecclesiastical and technical secondary schools of the second cycle with 10,210 teachers and 131,395 pupils. There was also 1 teacher training school with 5 teachers and 151 students;

12 technical education institutions (TEI) with 5,217 teachers and 51,910 students; 22 vocational and ecclesiastical schools with 432 teachers and 2,762 students and 1 technical teacher training school with 41 teachers (and 102 teachers shared with other institutions) and 2,477 students. In 1995–96 there were 18 universities, 2 technical universities and 3 specialized universities (agriculture; economics and business; economics and political science), 1 institute of home economics and 1 school of fine art. There were 184,516 students and 6,466 academic staff.

Health (1994). There were 362 hospitals and sanatoria with a total of 51,781 beds and 170 health centres. There were 40,487 doctors and 10,865 dentists.

DIPLOMATIC REPRESENTATIVES

Of Greece in Great Britain (1A Holland Park, London, W11 3TP)
Ambassador: Vassilis Zafiropoulos.

Of Great Britain in Greece (1 Ploutarchou St., 106 75 Athens)
Ambassador: Sir Michael Llewellyn Smith, KCVO, CMG.

Of Greece in the USA (2221 Massachusetts Ave., NW, Washington, D.C., 20008)
Ambassador: Loukas Tsilas.

Of the USA in Greece (91 Vasilissis Sophias Blvd., 10160 Athens)
Ambassador: Nicholas Barns.

Of Greece to the United Nations
Ambassador: Christos Zacharakis.

Further Reading

Clogg, R., *Greece in the 1980s.* London, 1983.—*A Concise History of Greece.* CUP, 1992
Clogg, M. J. and R., *Greece.* [Bibliography] Oxford and Santa Barbara (CA), 1980
Freris, A. F., *The Greek Economy in the Twentieth Century.* London, 1986
Jougnatos, G. A., *Development of the Greek Economy, 1950–91: an Historical, Empirical and Econometric Analysis.* London, 1992
Pettifer, J., *The Greeks: the Land and the People since the War.* London, 1994
Sarafis, M. and Eve, M. (eds.) *Background to Contemporary Greece.* London, 1990
Tsakalotos, E., *Alternative Economic Strategies: the Case of Greece.* Aldershot, 1991
Woodhouse, C. M., *Modern Greece: a Short History.* rev. ed. London, 1991

National statistical office: National Statistical Service; 14–16 Lycourgou St., Athens.
Website: http://thales.iacm.forth.gr/esye/

GRENADA

Capital: St George's
Population: 98,600
GDP per head:(PPP$) 5,137
GNP: US$0·2bn.
HDI/world rank: 0·843/54

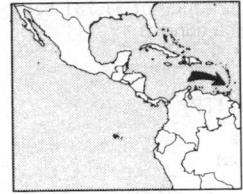

KEY HISTORICAL EVENTS. Grenada became an independent nation within the Commonwealth on 7 Feb. 1974. Grenada was formerly an Associated State under the West Indies Act, 1967. The 1973 Constitution was suspended in 1979 following a revolution.

On 19 Oct. 1983 the army took control after a power struggle led to the killing of Maurice Bishop, the Prime Minister. At the request of a group of Caribbean countries, Grenada was invaded by US-led forces on 25–28 Oct. On 1 Nov. a State of Emergency was imposed which ended on 15 Nov. when an interim government was installed. The 1973 Constitution was restored.

TERRITORY AND POPULATION. Grenada is the most southerly island of the Windward Islands with an area of 133 sq. miles (344 sq. km); the state also includes the Southern Grenadine Islands to the north, chiefly Carriacou (22·5 sq. miles) and Petit Martinique. The total population (Census, 1991) was 95,343 (48,169 females); density, 263 per sq. km. Estimated population (1996) 98,600; density, 287 per sq. km. The Borough of St George's, the capital, had 35,742 inhabitants. 85% of the population is of African descent, 11% of mixed origins, 3% Indian and 1% white.

Vital statistics (1994): Life expectancy, 72·0.

The official language is English. A French-African patois is also spoken.

CLIMATE. The tropical climate is very agreeable in the dry season, from Jan. to May, when days are warm and nights quite cool, but in the wet season there is very little difference between day and night temperatures. On the coast, annual rainfall is about 60" (1,500 mm) but it is as high as 150–200" (3,750–5,000 mm) in the mountains. Average temperature, 27°C.

CONSTITUTION AND GOVERNMENT. The British sovereign is represented by an appointed Governor-General. There is a bicameral legislature, consisting of a 13-member *Senate,* appointed by the Governor-General, and a 15-member *House of Representatives,* elected by universal suffrage. At the elections of 20 June 1995 for the House of Representatives, the New National Party (NNP) won 8 seats, the National Democratic Congress, 5 and the Grenada United Labour Party, 2.

Governor-General: Sir Daniel Williams.

In March 1998 the government comprised:
Prime Minister, Minister of Information, National Security, and Carriacou and Petite Martinique Affairs: Dr Keith Mitchell (NNP).

Minister of Health and the Environment: Dr. Roger Radix. *Minister of Agriculture, Lands and Forestry:* Mark Isaac. *Finance, Trade and Industry:* Patrick Bubb. *Fisheries:* Michael Baptiste. *Education and Labour:* Lawrence Joseph. *Legal Affairs, Local Government, Foreign Affairs:* Dr Raphael Fletcher. *Tourism, Civil Aviation and Co-operatives:* Joslyn Whiteman. *Social Security, Housing and Women's Affairs:* Laurina Waldron. *Youth, Sports, Culture and Community Development:* Adrian Mitchell. *Communication, Works and Public Utilities:* Gregory Bowen.

National anthem: 'Hail Grenada, land of ours'; words by I. M. Baptiste, tune by L. A. Masanto.

Local government: A Commissioner of Local Government was appointed in April 1996 to implement popular participation in local government.

DEFENCE

Royal Grenada Police Force. Modelled on the British system, the 730-strong police force includes an 80-member paramilitary unit and a 30-member coastguard.

INTERNATIONAL RELATIONS

Membership. Grenada is a member of the UN, OAS, Caricom, the Commonwealth and is an ACP state of the EU.

ECONOMY

Budget. In 1996, recurrent revenue was US$74·09m. and recurrent expenditure, US$68·8m. Capital expenditure was US$25·7m. Income tax has been abolished. VAT is 25% (reduced rate, 5%).

Currency. The unit of currency is the *Eastern Caribbean dollar* (EC$).

Banking and Finance. Grenada is a member of the Eastern Caribbean Central Bank. In 1995 there were 5 commercial banks (2 foreign). The Grenada Agricultural Bank was established in 1965 to encourage agricultural development; in 1975 it became the Grenada Agricultural and Industrial Development Corporation. In 1995, bank deposits were EC$666·8m. (US$249·7m.). Total foreign currency deposits in 1995 amounted to US$11·8m.

ENERGY AND NATURAL RESOURCES

Electricity. Production (1991) 59·9m. kWh. 68·9% of households had an electricity supply in 1991.

Agriculture. Agriculture contributed 10·4% of GDP in 1996. Principal crop production (1993): Cocoa, 2,000 tonnes; bananas, 10,000 tonnes and in 1991: nutmegs, 5,800·3 lbs; mace, 451·1 lbs. Corn and pigeon peas, citrus, sugar-cane, root-crops and vegetables are also grown, in addition to small scattered cultivations of cotton, cloves, cinnamon, pimento, coffee and fruit trees.

Livestock (1993): Cattle, 4,000; sheep, 12,000; goats, 11,000; pigs, 3,000.

Fisheries. The catch (1993) was 4·47m. lbs.

INDUSTRY

Labour. In 1993 the labour force was estimated at 27,820. Unemployment was 16·7%.

FOREIGN ECONOMIC RELATIONS

Commerce. 1993 exports (including re-exports) were valued at EC$55·1m., of which domestic imports, EC$45·3m. Imports, EC$309·4m. The principal exports are nutmeg, cocoa, bananas, mace and textiles. Exports were mainly to the UK, Trinidad and Tobago, the Netherlands and Germany.

Tourism. In 1996, there were 386,013 visitors, including 266,982 cruise ship passengers. Foreign exchange earnings from the sector were US$62m. in 1996.

COMMUNICATIONS

Roads. In 1995 there were 1,127 km of roads, of which 580 km were hard-surfaced.

Civil Aviation. Point Salines international airport is served by Aerotuy, Air Europe, American Airlines, BWIA, British Airways, British Caledonian and LIAT. 321,120 passengers travelled in 1995, and 3,010 tonnes of freight were carried. Lauriston Airport is on Carriacou.

Shipping. The main port is at St George's; there are 8 minor ports. Total number of containers handled in 1991 was 5,161; cargo landed, 187,039 tonnes; cargo loaded, 24,786 tonnes. Sea-going shipping totalled 555 GRT in 1995.

Telecommunications. At 30 Sept. 1993 there were 20,269 telephone lines. The government-owned Grenada Broadcasting Corporation operates Radio Grenada and Grenada Television. There are also 4 independent radio stations. Grenada Television transmits on 3 channels (colour by NTSC). A private cable TV company provides services on 25 channels, and there is a religious TV service. In 1993 there were 80,000 radio and 30,000 TV sets.

Press. In 1993 there were 5 weekly, 1 monthly and 2 bi-monthly newspapers.

SOCIAL INSTITUTIONS

Justice. The Grenada Supreme Court, situated in St George's, comprises a High Court of Justice, a Court of Magisterial Appeal (which hears appeals from the lower Magistrates' Courts exercising summary jurisdiction) and an Itinerant Court of Appeal (to hear appeals from the High Court). For police *see* DEFENCE, *above*.

Religion. At the 1991 census 53% of the population were Roman Catholic, 14% Anglican, 8·5% Seventh Day Adventists and 7·2% Pentecostal.

Education. Adult literacy was 95% in 1996. In 1992 there were 75 pre-primary schools with 3,916 pupils, 57 primary schools with 22,330 pupils and 18 secondary schools with 6,970 pupils. In 1991 there were 10 schools for special education and 12 day care centres caring for 249 children. The Grenada National College was established in 1988. There is also a branch of the University of the West Indies.

Health. In 1990 there was 1 main hospital with 2 subsidiaries. In 1990 there were 36 clinics, 52 doctors, 7 dentists, 28 pharmacists, 36 midwives, 296 nursing personnel and 28 medical technologists (laboratory, radiography and biomedical).

DIPLOMATIC REPRESENTATIVES

Of Grenada in Great Britain (1 Collingham Gdns., London, SW5 0HW)
High Commissioner: F. Marcelle Gairy.

Of Great Britain in Grenada
High Commissioner: R. Thomas, CMG (resides in Barbados).

Of Grenada in the USA (1701 New Hampshire Ave., NW, Washington, D.C., 20009)
Ambassador: Denis Antoine.

Of the USA in Grenada
Ambassador: Jeannette W. Hyde (resides in Barbados).

Of Grenada to the United Nations
Ambassador: Robert Millete.

Of Grenada to the European Union
Ambassador: Vacant.

Further Reading

Davidson, J. S., *Grenada: a Study in Politics and the Limits of International Law.* London, 1987
Ferguson, J., *Grenada: Revolution in Reverse.* London, 1991
Gilmore, W. G., *The Grenada Intervention: Analysis and Documentation.* London, 1984
Heine, J. (ed) *A Revolution Aborted: the Lessons of Grenada.* Pittsburgh Univ. Press, 1990
O'Shaughnessy, H., *Grenada: Revolution, Invasion and Aftermath.* London, 1984
Page, A., Sutton, P. and Thorndike, T., *Grenada and Invasion.* London, 1984
Sandford, G. and Vigilante, R., *Grenada: the Untold Story.* London, 1988
Schoenhals, K., *Grenada:* [Bibliography]. Oxford and Santa Barbara (CA), 1990
Sinclair, N., *Grenada: Isle of Spice.* London, 1987
Thorndike, T., *Grenada: Politics, Economics and Society.* London, 1985

GUATEMALA

República de Guatemala

Capital: Guatemala City
Population: 11·69m.
GDP per head: (PPP$) 3,208
GNP: US$12·2bn.
HDI/world rank: 0·572/117

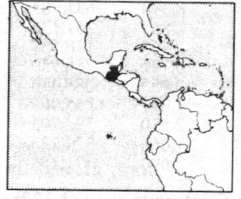

KEY HISTORICAL EVENTS. The Mayan civilisation flourished in the area now known as Guatemala from 2500 BC until 1000 AD. Their descendants were subjugated by the conquistadors from 1523. From 1524 until 1821 Guatemala was part of a Spanish captaincy-general, comprising the whole of Central America. It became independent in 1821 and formed part of the Confederation of Central America from 1823 to 1839 when Rafael Carrera dissolved the Confederation. Since then it has had a turbulent political history with periods of presidential dictatorship, democracy and military dictatorship. Boundary disputes with El Salvador, Honduras and Belize (formerly British Honduras) have caused intermittent fighting.

The economic crisis of the 1930s brought the right-wing dictator Jorge Ubico to power. His overthrow by a revolution in 1944 opened a decade of rising left-wing activity which alarmed the USA. In 1954 the leftist régime of Jacob Arbenz Guzmán was overthrown by a CIA-supported *coup*. A series of right-wing governments failed to produce stability while the toll on human life and the violation of human rights was such as to cause thousands of refugees to flee to Mexico. Over 50,000 people were killed in the 1970s.

On 23 March 1982, ignoring a presidential election of the same month, a junta consisting of Brig.-Gen. Efrain Rios Montt and other army officers took part in a bloodless *coup*. Gen. Rios Montt later became president. A further *coup* on 8 Aug. 1983 removed Montt from the presidency. Maj.-Gen. Oscar Humberto Meijia Victores became head of state. Elections to a National Constituent Assembly were held on 1 July 1984, and a new constitution was promulgated in May 1985. Amidst violence and assassinations, the presidential election was won by Marco Vinicio Cerezo Arévalo. On 14 Jan. 1986 Cerezo's civilian government was installed—the first for 16 years and only the second since 1954. Violence continued, however, and there were frequent reports of torture and killings by right-wing 'death squads' and various attempts to murder the government. Relations with the USA deteriorated and military and economic aid was suspended. By May 1993, President Serranto imposed martial law but was then forced into exile. There was a gradual return to constitutional rule and the first genuine efforts to investigate past violations of human rights.

The presidential and legislative elections of Nov. 1995 saw the return of the left-wing to open politics for the first time in over 40 years. Meanwhile the Guatemalan Revolutionary Unit (URNG) declared a ceasefire. On 6 May and 19 Sept. 1996 the government signed agreements with the URNG which envisaged reforms to military, internal security, judicial and agrarian institutions. A ceasefire was concluded in Oslo on 4 Dec. 1996 and a final peace treaty was signed on 29 Dec. 1996 in Guatemala. This final treaty consolidates earlier agreements to reform the electoral system and the economy, especially agriculture, and to guarantee human rights.

TERRITORY AND POPULATION. Guatemala is bounded on the north and west by Mexico, south by the Pacific ocean and east by El Salvador, Honduras and Belize, and the area is 108,889 sq. km (42,042 sq. miles). In March 1936 Guatemala, El Salvador and Honduras agreed to accept the peak of Mount Montecristo as the common boundary point.

The population was 11,277,614 in July 1996. Estimate (1997) 11,685,695. In 1996, 44% were Amerindian, of 21 different groups descended from the Maya; 56% Mestizo (mixed Amerindian and Spanish). 60% speak Spanish, with the remainder speaking one or a combination of the 23 Indian dialects.

Vital statistics: 1996, Birth rate, 36·4; death rate, 5·9; life expectancy, male 62·64, female 67·97.

Guatemala is administratively divided into 22 departments, each with a governor appointed by the President. Population, 1994:

Departments	Area (sq. km)	Population	Departments	Area (sq. km)	Population
Alta Verapaz	8,686	650,120	Petén	35,854	295,169
Baja Verapaz	3,124	200,019	Quezaltenango	1,951	606,556
Chimaltenango	1,979	374,898	Quiché	8,378	631,785
Chiquimula	2,376	268,379	Retalhuleu	1,858	261,136
El Progreso	1,922	115,469	Sacatepéquez	465	196,537
Escuintla	4,384	592,647	San Marcos	3,791	766,950
Guatemala City	2,126	2,188,652	Santa Rosa	2,955	285,456
Huehuetenango	7,403	790,183	Sololá	1,061	265,902
Izabal	9,038	359,056	Suchitepéquez	2,510	392,703
Jalapa	2,063	206,355	Totonicapán	1,061	324,225
Jutiapa	3,219	378,601	Zacapa	2,690	171,146

Populations of main towns, 1993 estimates (in 1,000): Guatemala City, 1,133; Quezaltenango, 98; Escuintla, 66; Mazatenango, 41; Puerto Barrios, 39; Retalhuleu, 38.

CLIMATE. A tropical climate, with little variation in temperature and a well marked wet season from May to Oct. Guatemala City. Jan. 63°F (17·2°C), July 69°F (20·6°C). Annual rainfall 53" (1,316 mm).

CONSTITUTION AND GOVERNMENT. A new Constitution, drawn up by the Constituent Assembly elected on 1 July 1984, was promulgated in June 1985 and came into force on 14 Jan. 1986. In 1993, 43 amendments were adopted, reducing *inter alia* the President's term of office from 5 to 4 years. The President and Vice-President are elected by direct election (with a second round of voting if no candidate secures 50% of the first-round votes) for a non-renewable 4-year term. The unicameral *Congress* comprises 80 members, 64 elected locally and 16 from a national list, for 4-year terms.

A referendum on constitutional reform was held on 30 Jan. 1994. The electorate was 3·4m.; turn-out was 17·5%. The reforms were approved by 83% of votes cast.

At the first round of the presidential elections on 12 Nov. 1995 the electorate was 3·7m.; turn-out was 40%. Alvaro Arzú gained 36·56% of votes cast against 18 opponents. At the second round on 7 Jan. 1996 Arzú was elected President against 1 opponent by 51·22% of votes cast.

Congressional elections were held on 12 Nov. 1995. The Party of National Advancement (PNA) won 42 seats, the Guatemalan Republic Front, 21 and the Guatemala New Democratic Front, 5. The next Presidential and Congressional elections are to be held in Nov. 2000.

President: Alvaro Arzú Irigoyen (PNA; sworn in 14 Jan. 1996).

Vice-President: Luis Flores Asturias.

In March 1998 the government comprised:

Minister of Agriculture: Mariano Ventura. *Communications, Transport and Public Works:* Fritz García Gallont. *Defence:* Brig.-Gen. Hector Mario Barrios Celada. *Economy and Commerce:* Juan Mauricio Wurmser. *Education:* Roberto Mareno Godoy. *Energy and Mining:* Leonel López Rodas. *Culture and Sports:* Augusto Vela. *Finance:* José Alejandro Arévalo. *Foreign Affairs:* Eduardo Stein. *Health and Social Welfare:* Marco Tulio Sosa Ramirez. *Government:* Rodolfo Mendoza Rosales. *Labour and Social Security:* Hector Cifuentes Mendoza.

National anthem: '¡Guatemala! Feliz' ('Happy Guatemala'); words by J. J. Palma, tune by R. Alvarez.

Local Government. Municipalities are autonomous under elected officials and are funded by 8% of the central government budget.

DEFENCE. There is selective conscription for 30 months.

Army. The Army numbered (1997) 38,500 (30,000 conscripts) and is organized in 19 military zones. There are 2 strategic reserve brigades, 1 special forces group, 39 infantry, 1 engineer and 2 airborne battalions, 6 armoured squadrons and a Presidential Guard battalion. Equipment includes 10 light tanks and armoured cars. There is a paramilitary national police of 9,800, Treasury police of 2,500 and a territorial militia of about 300,000.

Navy. A naval element of the combined armed forces operates 9 inshore patrol craft, as well as 20 river patrol boats. The force was (1997) 1,500 strong of whom 650 are marines for maintenance of riverine security. Main bases are Puerto Barrios (on the Atlantic Coast), Puerto Quetzal and Puerto San José (Pacific).

Air Force. There is a small Air Force with 8 A-37B light attack aircraft, 1 DC-6, 6 C-47, 3 F.27 and 6 Israeli-built Arava transports, 6 Pilatus PC-7 turboprop trainers, and a number of light aircraft and helicopters, including a few armed UH-1 Iroquois. Strength was (1997) 700.

INTERNATIONAL RELATIONS

Membership. Guatemala is a member of the UN and OAS.

ECONOMY

Policy. Policy targets are set out in the 'Government Programme 1996–2000'. Partial privatization of utilities, telecommunications and railways began in 1997.

Performance. The economy is based on family and corporate agriculture, which accounts for 25% of GDP, employs about 60% of the labour force, and supplies two-thirds of exports. GDP growth was 4·9% in 1995.

Budget. Government revenue and expenditure (in Q.1m.):

	1992	1993	1994	1995
Rev.	5,467·05	5,762·65	5,692·35	7,222·55
Exp.	5,607	6,229·55	6,648·98	7,579

VAT is 10%.

Currency. The unit of currency is the *quetzal* (CTQ) of 100 *centavos*, established on 7 May 1925. There are coins of 1, 5, 10 and 25 centavos and notes of 50 centavos and 1, 5, 10, 20, 50 and 100 quetzals. Q.4,017m. were in circulation at 31 Dec. 1995. Foreign exchange reserves were US$702m. in 1995; gold reserves, US$60·7m. Inflation was an annualized 8·7% in 1996.

Banking and Finance. The Banco de Guatemala is the central bank and bank of issue (*Governor*, Willy Zapata Sagastume). Constitutional amendments of 1993 placed limits on its financing of government spending. In 1996 there were 21 private banks, 3 state banks, 4 international banks and 18 foreign banks, of which latter 2 are authorized to operate as commercial banks.

There are 2 stock exchanges.

Weights and Measures. The metric system has been officially adopted, but traditional measures are still used locally.

ENERGY AND NATURAL RESOURCES

Electricity. Installed capacity in 1994 was 696 MW, of which 438 MW were hydro-electric. Output, 1995, 2,262m. kWh.

Oil. There are proven reserves of 36·2m. bbls. Production (1992), 0·29m. tonnes.

Minerals. There are deposits of gold, silver and nickel.

Agriculture. Agriculture contributed 24% of GDP in 1995. Production, 1993 (in 1,000 tonnes): Coffee, 177; bananas, 500; cotton lint, 23. Rubber development schemes are under way, assisted by US funds. Guatemala is one of the largest sources of essential oils (citronella and lemon grass). Arable land: 12%, permanent crops: 4%, meadows and pastures: 12%, forest and woodland: 40%, other: 32%.

Livestock (1993): Cattle, 2·1m.; pigs, 850,000; sheep, 430,000; horses, 116,000; poultry, 16m.

Forestry. Forests cover 36% of the land area. Mahogany and cedar are grown, and chick, a chewing gum base, is produced.

Fisheries. In 1995 the total catch was 11,927 tonnes.

INDUSTRY. Manufacturing contributed 14·1% of GDP in 1995. The principal industries are food and beverages, tobacco, chemicals, hides and skins, textiles, garments and non-metallic minerals. Raw sugar production in 1992 was 943,000 tonnes. New industries include electrical goods, plastic sheet and metal furniture.

Labour. In 1995, the workforce totalled 3,316,723 including: Agriculture, 1,513,600; commerce, 572,011; services, 439,719; manufacturing, 439,121; building, 214,102; transport and communications, 77,476; finance, 40,474.

The working week is 44 hours, with a 12-day paid holiday annually.

Trade Unions. There are 3 federations for private sector workers.

FOREIGN ECONOMIC RELATIONS. In May 1992 Guatemala, El Salvador and Honduras agreed to create a free trade zone and standardize import duties. External debt was US$2,080m. at 31 Aug. 1996.

Commerce. Values in US$1,000 were:

	1991	1992	1993	1994	1995
Imports (c.i.f.)	1,626	2,328	2,384	2,547	3,030
Exports (f.o.b.)	1,210	1,284	1,363	1,550	1,994

In 1995 the principal exports were (in US$1m.): Coffee, 550; sugar, 237; bananas, 138; cardamom, 41. Main export markets, 1995: USA, 31%; El Salvador, 13·8%; Honduras, 6·4%; Germany, 5·8%; Costa Rica, 5·2%. Main import suppliers: USA, 43%; Mexico, 9·3%; El Salvador, 5%; Venezuela, 4·6%; Japan, 3·7%.

Tourism. Tourism is an important source of foreign exchange (US$258m. in 1994). There were 537,374 visitors in 1994.

COMMUNICATIONS

Roads. In 1994 there were 26,429 km of roads, of which 2,850 km are paved. There is a highway from coast to coast via Guatemala City. There are 2 highways from the Mexican to the Salvadorean frontier: the Pacific Highway serving the fertile coastal plain and the Pan-American Highway running through the highlands and Guatemala City. Motor cars numbered about 155,000 in 1992; commercial vehicles, 140,000.

Railways. The state-owned Ferrocarriles de Guatemala operated 953 km of railway in 1996, linking east and west coast seaports to Guatemala City, with branch lines to the north and south borders.

Civil Aviation. There are 463 airports in total, with international airports at Guatemala City (La Aurora) and Tikal (Santa Elena). The 25%-government-owned airline, Aviateca, furnishes both domestic and international services. There are 6 other internal airlines. Aviateca had 3 B-737-200 Advs and 1 B-737-300 in 1995. Services are also provided by American Airlines, Compania Mexicana, Continental Airlines and Air Micronesia, COPA, Iberia, KLM, LACSA, LADECO, Sociedad Aeronáutica de Medellín, Taca International Airlines and United Airlines.

Shipping. The chief ports on the Atlantic coast are Puerto Barrios and Santo Tomás de Castilla: on the Pacific coast, Puerto Quetzal and Champerico.

Telecommunications. The Government own and operate the telecommunications services; there were 245,000 telephones in 1995, and 11,000 mobile phones. There are 5 government, 6 educational and 84 commercial radio broadcasting services.

Radio receiving sets in use, 1993, numbered about 0·4m. There are 4 commercial TV stations, 1 government station and about 475,000 TV receivers (colour by NTSC). There is also reception by US television satellite.

Press (1996). There were 4 independent dailies and 1 evening newspaper, 1 government daily and 2 weeklies.

SOCIAL INSTITUTIONS

Justice. Justice is administered in a Constitution Court, a Supreme Court, 6 appeal courts and 28 courts of first instance. Supreme Court and appeal court judges are elected by Congress. Judges of first instance are appointed by the Supreme Court.

The death penalty is authorized for murder and kidnapping. Executions were carried out in 1996.

There are 3 police forces (strengths in 1996) controlled respectively by the Ministry of the Interior (12,000), the Ministry of Finance (2,100) and the Ministry of Defence (4,000).

Religion. Roman Catholicism is the prevailing faith (7·1m. adherents in 1992) and there is a Roman Catholic archbishopric. Membership of the approximately 100 evangelical Protestant churches was estimated at 30% of the population in 1991 (75% Pentecostalist), with about 14,000 places of worship.

Education. In 1995 there were 1,430,254 pupils at 11,495 primary schools with 43,731 teachers; there were 372,006 pupils at secondary level with 23,807 teachers. 1995 adult literacy, 55·6%; male, 62·5%, female, 48·6%. In 1994–95 there were 5 universities with 70,233 students and 4,450 academic staff.

Health. In 1990 there were some 1,250 doctors, 275 dentists, 60 state hospitals and 100 dispensaries.

Welfare. A comprehensive system of social security was outlined in a law of 30 Oct. 1946.

DIPLOMATIC REPRESENTATIVES

Of Guatemala in Great Britain (13 Fawcett St., London, SW10 9HN)
Ambassador: Fernando Andrade Díaz-Durán.

Of Great Britain in Guatemala (7a Avenida 5-10, Zona 4, Guatemala City)
Ambassador: Peter M. Newton.

Of Guatemala in the USA (2220 R. St., NW, Washington, D.C., 20008)
Ambassador: Pedro Lamport.

Of the USA in Guatemala (7–01 Avenida de la Reforma, Zona 10, Guatemala City)
Ambassador: Donald J. Planty.

Of Guatemala to the United Nations
Ambassador: Julio Armando Martini Herrara.

Of Guatemala to the European Union
Ambassador: Claudio Riedel Telge.

Further Reading

Woodward, R. L., *Guatemala*. [Bibliography] Oxford and Santa Barbara (CA), 1992

National library: Biblioteca Nacional, 5a Avenida y 8a Calle, Zona 1, Guatemala City.

GUINEA

République de Guinée

Capital: Conakry
Population: 7·4m.
GDP per head: (PPP$) 1,103
GNP: US$3·3bn.
HDI/world rank: 0·271/167

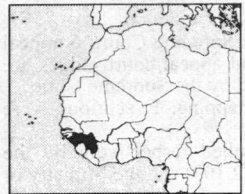

KEY HISTORICAL EVENTS. Present-day Guinea was historically a subordinate part of the broader Ghanaian empire in the 10th and 11th centuries and the Malinke empire (Mali-based) until the 16th century. A powerful feudal state of Guinea's Fulani people in the early 18th century resisted intrusions by both the French and the Moslem states to the north-east.

In 1888 Guinea became a French protectorate, in 1893 a colony and in 1904, a constituent territory of French West Africa. Forced labour and other colonial depredations ensued, although a form of representation was introduced in 1946. The independent Republic of Guinea was proclaimed on 2 Oct. 1958, after the territory of French Guinea had decided at the referendum of 28 Sept. to leave the French community rather than being self-governing within it. Ahmed Sékou Touré became the first president of the new republic. It became a single-party state. Ties with France were broken in 1965 and only restored in 1976. For a time Guinea was isolated, but in 1975 it joined its African neighbours in the Economic Community of West African States. Touré's strong measures to maintain his rule provoked riots in 1977. In 1977 and 1978, when a more liberal government policy was pursued, Touré spoke of his desire to co-operate with the West.

In 1980 Touré was elected for the fourth time for a 7-year term as president, but he died in 1984 when the armed forces staged a *coup* and dissolved the National Assembly and the *Parti démocratique de Guinée*. A Military Committee of National Rectification (CMRN) held power until Jan. 1991, when a Transitional Committee for National Rectification (CTRN) took over. Following popular disturbances a multi-party system was introduced in April 1992.

TERRITORY AND POPULATION. Guinea is bounded in the north-west by Guinea-Bissau and Senegal, north-east by Mali, south-east by Côte d'Ivoire, south by Liberia and Sierra Leone, and west by the Atlantic Ocean.

The area is 245,857 sq. km (94,926 sq. miles). Population estimate, 1997, 7,405,375 (3,768,311 female). A census of 1992 gave a figure of 5·04m.; it is officially acknowledged that this may be an under-count. Population growth rate, 1997, was 11%. The capital is Conakry. In 1995, 29·6% were urban.

The areas, populations and chief towns of the major divisions in 1991 were:

	Sq. km	1991 population	Chief town	Population (in year)
Conakry (city)	308	1,320,000	Conakry	950,000 (1992)
Guinée-Maritime	43,980	975,000	Kindia	80,000 (1986)
Moyenne-Guinée	51,710	1,262,000	Labé	110,000 (1986)
Haute-Guinée	92,535	1,147,000	Kankan	70,000 (1992)
Guinée-Forestière	57,324	1,033,000	Nzérékoré	55,356 (1983)

The country has since been divided into 7 administrative regions: Boké, Faranah, Kankan, Kindia, Labé, Mamou, Nzérékoré.

Vital statistics, 1997: Birth rate, 42 per 1,000 population; death, 18; infant mortality, 131·5 per 1,000 live births; life expectancy, 45·5 years.

The ethnic composition is Fulani (40·3%, predominant in Moyenne-Guinée), Malinké (or Mandingo, 25·8%, prominent in Haute-Guinée), Susu (11%, prominent in Guinée-Maritime), Kissi (6·5%) and Kpelle (4·8%) in Guinée-Forestière, and Dialonka, Loma and others (11·6%).

The official language is French.

CLIMATE. A tropical climate, with high rainfall near the coast and constant heat, but conditions are a little cooler on the plateau. The wet season on the coast lasts from

May to Nov., but only to Oct. inland. Conakry. Jan. 80°F (26·7°C), July 77°F (25°C). Annual rainfall 172" (4,293 mm).

CONSTITUTION AND GOVERNMENT. Presidential elections were held on 19 Dec. 1993. President Conté was re-elected against 7 opponents by 51·7% of votes cast. There is a 114-member *National Assembly*, 38 of whose members are elected on a first-past-the-post system, and the remainder from national lists by proportional representation. Elections were held on 11 June 1995. 21 parties or groups stood. The Party of Unity and Progress Party (PUP) gained 71 seats; the Guinean People's Rally, 19; the Renewal and Progress Party, 9; the Union for a New Republic, 9.

President: Gen. Lansana Conté (PUP; seized power 3 April 1984, re-elected 19 Dec. 1993).

In March 1998 the government comprised:
Prime Ministe: Sidya Touré.
Agriculture: Jean-Paul Sarr. *Communication and Culture:* Ibrahima Mongo Diallo. *Defence:* Dorank Assifat Diasseny. *Economic Affairs and Finance:* Ibrahima Kassory Fofana. *Employment and Civil Service, and Labour:* Almany Fode Sylla. *Energy, and Mines and Geology:* Facinet Fofana. *Fisheries and Animal Husbandry:* Boubacar Barry. *Foreign Affairs:* Lamine Camara. *Health:* Dr Kandjoura Dramé. *Industry and Commerce:* Madikaba Camara. *Justice:* Moussa Sampil. *Interior:* Zainoul Sanoussy. *National Education and Scientific Research:* Eugene Camara. *Planning and Co-operation:* Cellou Diallo. *Pro University Teaching:* Germain Doualamou. *Public Works, Environment, Transport, and Telecommunications:* Cellou Dalein Diallo. *Security:* Govreissi Conde. *Social and Women's Affairs:* Saran Daraba. *Technical Education and Training:* Almany Diaby. *Tourism and Hotels:* Kozo Zoumanigui. *Urban Affairs and Housing:* Ousmane Diallo. *Youth, Sport and Civic Education:* Koumba Diakité. *General Secretary to the Presidency:* Fode Bangoura.

National anthem: 'Peuple d'Afrique, le passé historique' ('People of Africa, the historic past'); words anonymous, tune by K. Fodeba.

Local Government. The administrative division comprises the capital Conakry and 33 prefectures grouped into 7 regions: Boké, Faranah, Kankan, Kindia, Labé, Mamou and Nzérékoré.

DEFENCE. Conscription is for 2 years.

Army. The Army of 8,500 (1997), comprises 1 armoured, 5 infantry, 1 commando and 1 engineer, 1 artillery, 1 air defence and 1 special forces battalion. Equipment includes 30 T-34 and 8 T-54 main battle tanks. There are also 3 paramilitary forces: People's Militia (7,000), Gendarmerie (1,000) and Republican Guard (1,000).

Navy. A small force of 400 (1997) operate 2 French-built, 1 US-built and 5 Soviet-built inshore patrol craft, and a number of riverine boats from bases at Conakry and Kakanda.

Air Force. The Air Force, formed with Soviet assistance, is reported to be equipped with a few MiG-21 jet fighters, 2 An-2 piston-engined transports and a Yak-40 jet aircraft for VIP duties, all Russian built, and 2 French-supplied helicopters are in service. Personnel (1997) 800.

INTERNATIONAL RELATIONS

Membership. Guinea is a member of the UN, OAU and is an ACP state of the EU.

ECONOMY

Performance. Real GDP growth in 1995 was officially estimated at 4·6% (4% in 1994).

Budget. Government revenue, 1994 (in 1,000m. Guinean francs): 608, of which taxes, 441·9; grants, 146·6. Expenditure: 730·3, of which current, 342. VAT was applied to non-essential goods in July 1996. In 1995 estimated revenue was US$519m. and expenditure US$947m.

Currency. The monetary unit is the *Guinean franc* (GNF). There are coins of 1, 5, 10, 25 and 50 and notes of 25, 50, 100, 500, 1,000 and 5,000 Guinean francs. At Dec. 1995, 153,200m. Guinean francs were in circulation. Inflation was 5·6% in 1995. At Nov. 1995 foreign exchange reserves (excluding gold) were US$69·9m.

Banking and Finance. In 1986 the Central Bank (*Governor*, Ibrahim Cherif Bah) and commercial banking were restructured, and commercial banks returned to the private sector. There were 6 commercial banks in 1993.

ENERGY AND NATURAL RESOURCES

Electricity. In 1996, installed capacity was 176 MW. Production was 300m. kWh in 1995.

Minerals. Mining produced 19·1% of GDP in 1994. Guinea possesses over 25% of the world's bauxite reserves. 1992 output: Bauxite, 16m. tonnes (17,054,000 tonnes in 1991); alumina, 603,000 tonnes (651,000 tonnes in 1991); diamonds, 0·1m. carats; gold, 2,100 kg. There are also deposits of granite, iron ore, chrome, copper, lead, manganese, molybdenum, nickel, platinum, uranium and zinc.

Agriculture. Subsistence agriculture supports about 70% of the population. Agriculture produced 24·1% of GDP in 1994. Some 25% of potential arable land is cultivated. The chief crops (production, 1993, in 1,000 tonnes) are: Cassava, 781; millet, 10; rice, 733; plantains, 429; sugar-cane, 225; bananas, 115; groundnuts, 105; sweet potatoes, 104; yams, 73; maize, 95; palm-oil, 40; palm kernels, 40; pineapples, 87; pulses, 60; coffee, 29; coconuts, 18.

Livestock (1993): Cattle, 1·65m.; sheep, 435,000; goats, 580,000; pigs, 33,000; poultry, 14m.

Forestry. 41% of the country is forested (10m. ha). In 1994, 4m. cu. metres of roundwood were cut.

Fisheries. Annual catch, 0·68m. tonnes, about half by industrial fishing.

INDUSTRY. Manufacturing accounted for 4·6% of GDP in 1994. Cement, beer, soft drinks and cigarettes are produced.

Labour. The agricultural sector employs 80% of the workforce.

FOREIGN ECONOMIC RELATIONS. Foreign debt was US$3,000m. in 1996. Imports require authorization and there are restrictions on the export of capital.

Commerce. In 1995 imports totalled US$775m. and exports US$725m. Main exports by value (US$1m.), 1994: Bauxite, 272; alumina, 103; gold, 84; coffee, 58. Main export markets, 1994: Belgium, 26·7%; USA, 15·1%; Ireland, 10%; Spain, 9·6%; Germany, 5·8%; Brazil, 5·4%. Main import suppliers: France, 19·5%; Côte d'Ivoire, 16%; USA, 7·1%; Belgium, 6·9%; Hong Kong, 6·3%.

COMMUNICATIONS

Roads. In 1995 there were about 5,000 km of main and national roads of which 1,200 km were hard-surfaced and about 9,200 km of other roads. In 1992 there were 23,155 cars and 13,000 commercial vehicles.

Railways. A railway connects Conakry with Kankan (662 km) and is to be extended to Bougouni in Mali. A line 134 km long linking bauxite deposits at Sangaredi with Port Kamsar was opened in 1973 (carried 12·5m. tonnes in 1993), a third line links Conakry and Fria (144 km; carried 1m. tonnes in 1993) and a fourth, the Kindia Bauxite Railway (102 km) linking Débéle with Conakry, carried 3m. tonnes in 1994.

Civil Aviation. There is an international airport at Conakry (Gbessia). The national carrier is the state-owned Air Guinée, which operated 1 B-737-200C, 1 DHC-7-102 and 2 ex-Soviet aircraft in 1995.

Shipping. There are ports at Conakry and for bauxite exports at Kamsar (opened 1973). There are 24 vessels of 5,600 GRT.

Telecommunications. The Société des Télécommunications de Guinée is 40% state-owned. Telephones, 1996, numbered about 18,000. Broadcasting is the responsibility of the state-controlled Radiodiffusion Télévision Guinéenne. There were 0·32m. radio and 65,000 television receivers in 1995 (colour by PAL).

Press. There is 1 daily newspaper (circulation 20,000).

SOCIAL INSTITUTIONS

Justice. There are *tribunaux du premier degré* at Conakry and Kankan, and a *juge de paix* at Nzérékoré. The High Court, Court of Appeal and Superior Tribunal of Cassation are at Conakry.

Religion. 85% of the population are Moslem, 5% Christian. Traditional animist beliefs are still found.

Education. In 1995, there were 543,441 pupils (193,140 girls) and 11,352 teachers in 3,118 primary schools, 91,921 pupils (23,874 girls) and 2,791 teachers in 239 secondary schools, 28,311 pupils (6,143 girls) and 1,407 teachers in 61 lycées and 8,569 pupils (3,013) and 1,268 teachers in 55 institutions of professional education. In 1996 there were 2 universities with 5,735 students and 525 academic staff.

Besides French, there are 8 official languages taught in schools: Fulani, Malinké, Susu, Kissi, Kpelle, Loma, Basari and Koniagi.

Adult literacy (1995) 35·9% (male, 49·9%; female, 21·9%).

Health. In 1991 there were 375 hospitals and dispensaries. In 1988 there were 3,382 beds; there were also 920 doctors (1991), 22 dentists (1988), 197 pharmacists (1991), 371 midwives (1991) and 1,243 trained nursing personnel (1988).

DIPLOMATIC REPRESENTATIVES

Of Guinea in Great Britain (resides in Paris)
Ambassador: Vacant.

Of Great Britain in Guinea
Ambassador: David R. Snoxell (resides in Senegal).

Of Guinea in the USA (2112 Leroy Pl., NW, Washington, D.C., 20008)
Ambassador: Mohammed Ali Thiam.

Of the USA in Guinea (Rue KA 038, Conakry)
Ambassador: Tibor P. Nagy, Jr.

Of Guinea to the United Nations
Ambassador: Mahawa Camara.

Of Guinea to the European Union
Ambassador: Naby Moussa Soumah.

Further Reading

Bulletin Statistique et Economique de la Guinée. Monthly. Conakry

Binns, M., *Guinea* [Bibliography]. Oxford and Santa Barbara (CA), 1996

GUINEA-BISSAU

Republica da Guiné-Bissau

Capital: Bissau
Population: 1·18m.
GDP per head: (PPP$) 793
GNP: US$0·3bn.
HDI/world rank: 0·291/163

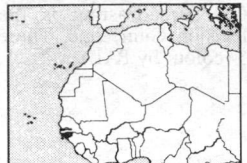

KEY HISTORICAL EVENTS. The area began to be settled with the break up of the ancient Ghanaian and Mali empires. The Portuguese explorer Nuno Tristão visited the coast in 1446. Portugal remained the major influence in the area and in the 19th century established its rule on the coast; however, Portuguese rule was not extended into the interior until later, and met African resistance well into the 20th century. Portuguese Guinea came under Cape Verde until 1879 when it became a separate colony. Portuguese Guinea became an Overseas Territory in 1951.

Amilcar Cabral, one of the many Cape Verdians working in government service in Portuguese Guinea, in 1956 joined other nationalists to form the *Partido Africano da Independência da Guiné e Cabo Verde* (PAIGC). From 1963 this party waged a successful guerrilla war against Portuguese rule in Guinea, Guineans and Cape Verdians working together and by 1973 evicting the Portuguese from much of the interior where the PAIGC set up its own administration. On 20 Jan. 1973 Cabral was murdered, but elections to a national assembly had already been held in liberated areas and on 23-24 Sept. 1973 the assembly proclaimed the independence of Guinea-Bissau. A Council of State was chosen with Luis Cabral, brother of Amilcar, as chairman.

In 1974, after the Portuguese revolution, Portugal abandoned the struggle to keep Guinea-Bissau, and independence was formally recognized on 10 Sept. 1974. In 1975 Cape Verde also became independent under the rule of the PAIGC, but the secretary-general of the party, President Pereira of Cape Verde, did not have authority over Guinea-Bissau and the two countries remained separate sovereign states.

On 14 Nov. 1980 Luis Cabral was overthrown in a *coup d'état* in part inspired by resentment in Guinea-Bissau over the privileges enjoyed by Cape Verdians, and Guineans obtained a more prominent role under the new government of Major João Bernardo Vieira, previously prime minister.

On 16 May 1984 a new constitution was approved which retained Marxist principles. But in Nov. 1986 the PAIGC Congress agreed a return to private enterprise in an attempt to solve critical economic problems and to lift the country out of poverty.

TERRITORY AND POPULATION. Guinea-Bissau is bounded by Senegal in the north, the Atlantic Ocean in the west and by Guinea in the east and south. It includes the adjacent archipelago of Bijagós. Area, 36,125 sq. km (13,948 sq. miles). Population (last census, 1979), 777,214, of whom 125,000 (estimate, 1988) resided in the capital, Bissau. Population (estimate, 1997) 1,178,584 (606,824 female); density, 32·6 per sq. km; growth rate, 2·33%

The area population, and chief town of the capital and the 8 regions:

Region	Area in sq. km	Population (1979 census)	Population (1985 estimate)	Chief town
Bissau City	78	109,214	126,900	—
Bafatá	5,981	116,032	134,100	Bafatá
Biombo	838	56,463	65,000	Bissau
Bolama	2,624	25,473	29,700	Bolama
Cacheu	5,175	130,227	150,500	Cacheu
Gabú	9,150	104,315	120,800	Gabú
Oio	5,403	135,114	156,600	Farim
Quinara	3,138	35,532	41,000	Fulacunda
Tombali	3,736	55,099	64,500	Catió

Vital statistics, 1997: Birth rate, 39·2 per 1,000 population; death, 15·9; infant mortality, 113·7 per 1,000 live births; life expectancy, 48·7 years.

The main ethnic groups were (1998) the Balante (30%), Fulani (20%), Manjaco (14%), Mandingo (13%) and Papeis (7%). Portuguese remains the official language, but Crioulo is spoken throughout the country.

CLIMATE. The tropical climate has a wet season from June to Nov., when rains are abundant, but the hot, dry Harmattan wind blows from Dec. to May. Bissau. Jan. 76°F (24·4°C), July 80°F (26·7°C). Annual rainfall 78" (1,950 mm).

CONSTITUTION AND GOVERNMENT. A new Constitution was promul gated on 16 May 1984. The Revolutionary Council, established following the 1980 coup, was replaced by a 15-member Council of State, while in April 1984 a new National People's Assembly was elected comprising 150 Representatives elected by and from the directly-elected regional councils for 5-year terms. The sole political movement was the *Partido Africano da Independência da Guiné e Cabo Verde* (PAIGC), but in Dec. 1990 a policy of 'integral multi-partyism' was announced, and in May 1991 the National Assembly voted unanimously to abolish the law making the PAIGC the sole party. The *President* is Head of State and Government and is elected for a 5-year term. The *National Assembly* has 100 members.

Presidential elections were held in 2 rounds on 3 July and 7 Aug. 1994. At the first round President Vieira gained 46·18% of votes cast against 7 opponents. At the second round turn-out was 70%. President Vieira was re-elected by 52 02% of votes cast against 1 opponent.

At the parliamentary elections on 3 July 1994 there were 1,136 candidates. The PAIGC gained 64 seats.

President: João Bernardo Vieira (b. 1939; seized power 1980; elected 1989; re-elected 1994).

In March 1998 the government comprised:
Prime Minister: Carlos Correia.
Minister at the Presidency in Charge of Parliamentary Affairs and Information: Malal Sané. *Defence:* Samba Lamine Mané. *Foreign Affairs and Co-operation:* Dr Fernando Delfin da Silva. *Justice and Labour:* Dr Daniel Ferreira. *Economy and Finance:* Issuf Sanha. *Equipment:* João Gomes Cardoso. *Interior:* Francesca Pereira. *Rural Development, Natural Resources, and Environment:* Jose Avito da Silva. *National Education:* Odette Semedo. *Public Health:* Brandao Gomes Co. *Social Affairs and Advancement of Women:* Nharebat Incaia Intchasso. *Territorial Administration:* Nicandro Barreto Pereira. *Veterans Affairs:* Arafam Mané.

National anthem: 'Sol, suor, o verde e mar' ('Sun, sweat, the green and the sea'); words and tune by A. Lopes Cabral.
(Same as Cape Verde.)

Local government. The administrative division is in 8 regions (each under a regional council elected for 5 years), in turn subdivided into 37 sectors; and the city of Bissau, an autonomous sector treated as a separate region.

DEFENCE. There is selective conscription.

Army. The Army consisted in 1997 of 1 armoured, 1 artillery and 5 infantry battalions and 1 engineer and 1 reconnaissance company. Equipment includes 10 T-34 main battle tanks. Personnel, 6,800. There is a paramilitary Gendarmerie 2,000 strong.

Navy. The naval flotilla, based at Bissau, is equipped with 8 inshore patrol craft of diverse origins and 1 utility landing craft. Personnel in 1997 totalled 350.

Air Force. Formation of a small Air Force began in 1978 with the delivery of a French-built Cessna FTB-337 twin-engined counter-insurgency and general-purpose light transport. It has been followed by 2 Alouette III helicopters and 1 Falcon 20 VIP transport. Personnel (1997) 100.

INTERNATIONAL RELATIONS

Membership. Guinea-Bissau is a member of the UN, OAU and is an ACP state of the EU.

ECONOMY

Performance. GDP growth was estimated by the IMF at 4·2% in 1995.

Budget. Estimated revenue in 1990 (in 1m. pesos) was 81,900, of which 40,600 were non-tax revenue; tax revenue included taxes on commerce (25,100), income tax (7,400) and indirect taxes (6,200). Current expenditure totalled 63,900, and included goods and services (31,900), salaries (21,700) and interest payments (3,000).

Currency. On 2 May 1997 Guinea-Bissau joined the French Franc Zone, and the *peso* was replaced by the franc CFA at 65 pesos = 1 franc CFA. The *franc CFA* (XOF) has a parity rate of 100 = 1 French franc. There are coins of 1, 2, 5, 10, 25, 50 and 100 francs CFA, and notes of 50, 100, 500, 1,000, 5,000 and 10,000 francs CFA. Inflation, 1995, 45·4% (15·2% in 1994).

Banking and Finance. The Banco da Guiné-Bissau, which replaced the Banco Nacional in 1989, is the central bank and bank of issue (*Governor* Luis Candido Ribeiro). A commercial bank was set up in 1990, with 51% of the capital held by the state and local companies and 49% by Portuguese banks. There is also a commercial bank.

ENERGY AND NATURAL RESOURCES

Electricity. Production (1991) 30m. kWh.

Minerals. Mineral resources are not exploited. There are estimated to be 200m. tonnes of bauxite and 112m. tonnes of phosphate.

Agriculture. Agriculture accounts for 45% of GDP and employs 80% of the labour force. Chief crops (production, 1993, in 1,000 tonnes) are: Groundnuts, 18; sugar-cane, 6; plantains, 34; coconuts, 25; rice, 126; palm kernels, 8; millet, 26; palm-oil, 5; sorghum, 14; maize, 13; cashew nuts, 30.

Livestock (1994): Cattle, 494,000; sheep, 263,000; goats, 276,000; pigs, 312,000; poultry, 1m.

Forestry. The forest area is 2·35m. ha. Timber output averages an annual 40,000 cu. metres of logs and 16,000 cu. metres of saw wood.

Fisheries. Total catch (1995) 5,595 tonnes.

INDUSTRY

Labour. The workforce in 1988 was 279,100 (9,300 females).

FOREIGN ECONOMIC RELATIONS. Foreign debt totalled US$816m. in 1994.

Commerce. Imports in 1994, US$52·4m.; exports, US$33·2m. Main exports in 1994 (in US$1m.) were: Cashew nuts, 31; frozen shrimps, 0·1; frozen fish, 0·1; saw timber, 0·3. Imports: Food, 16·4; transport equipment, 14·5; fuel, 6·3; machines, 6·5.

Main export markets, 1994: India, 48·1%; Portugal, 35·7%; China, 8·8%; Cape Verde, 5·5%. Main import suppliers: Portugal, 40·5%; Netherlands, 16·6%; Japan, 14·8%.

COMMUNICATIONS

Roads. In 1995 there were about 4,350 km of roads of which 444 km were paved and (1985) 2,700 passenger cars and 2,100 lorries.

Civil Aviation. There is an international airport serving Bissau at Bissalanca. The national carrier is the state-owned Air Bissau, which had 4 aircraft in 1995. There are services to Abidjan, Dakar, Lisbon, London, Luanda and São Tomé.

Shipping. The main port is Bissau; minor ports are Bolama, Cacheu and Catió. In 1995 the merchant marine totalled 1,846 GRT.

Telecommunications. In 1993 there were about 9,000 telephones and (in 1995) 45,000 radio receivers. An experimental TV service started in 1989.

Cinemas. There were 4 cinemas (1988) with a seating capacity of 950.

Press (1996). There were 3 newspapers, including 1 privately owned.

SOCIAL INSTITUTIONS

Religion. In 1998 about 30% of the population were Moslem and about 5% Christian (mainly Roman Catholic). The remainder held traditional animist beliefs.

Education. Adult literacy was estimated at 54·9% in 1995 (male, 68%; female, 42·5%). Some 60% of children of primary school age attend school.

Health. In 1993 there were 10 private, 2 national and 4 regional hospitals with a total of 1,300 beds. There were 125 dispensaries.

DIPLOMATIC REPRESENTATIVES

Of Guinea-Bissau in Great Britain
Chargé d'affaires: Maria Araujo Vieira (resides in Paris).

Of Great Britain in Guinea-Bissau
Ambassador: David R. Snoxell (resides in Senegal).

Of Guinea-Bissau in the USA (918 16th St., NW, Washington, D.C., 20006)
Ambassador: Rufino Mendes.

Of the USA in Guinea-Bissau (Bairro de Penha, 1067 Bissau)
Ambassador: Peggy Blackford.

Of Guinea-Bissau to the United Nations
Ambassador: Alfredo Lopes Cabral.

Of Guinea-Bissau to the European Union
Ambassador: Vacant.

Further Reading

Forrest, J. A., *Guinea-Bissau. Power, Conflict and Renewal in a West African Nation.* Boulder (CO), 1992
Galli, R., *Guinea-Bissau:* [Bibliography]. Oxford and Santa Barbara (CA), 1991

GUYANA

Co-operative Republic of Guyana

Capital: Georgetown
Population: 706,116
GDP per head: (PPP$) 2,729
GNP: US$0·4bn.
HDI/world rank: 0·649/104

KEY HISTORICAL EVENTS. First settled by the Dutch West Indian Company about 1620, the territory was captured by Britain to whom it was ceded in 1814 and named British Guiana. To work the sugar plantations African slaves were transported here in the 18th century and East Indian and Chinese indentured labourers in the 19th century. From 1950 the anti-colonial struggle was spearheaded by the Peoples Progressive Party (PPP) led by Cheddi Jagan and Forbes Burnham. But after its election with a left-wing programme in the elections of 1953, the British government suspended the constitution. By the time internal autonomy was granted in 1961 Burnham had split with Jagan to form the more moderate People's National Congress (PNC). After much conflict, instigated by Britain and the USA who tried to destabilise Jagan's PPP government of 1961–64, Guyana became an independent member of the Commonwealth in 1966 with Burnham as the first prime minister.

On 3 Feb. 1970 Guyana became the world's first Co-operative Republic, with Arthur Chung as its first non-executive president. In Oct. 1980 the prime minister, Forbes Burnham, declared himself the executive-president. Two months later his party, the PNC, won a large majority of votes at a rigged election for the National Assembly: Burnham was then declared duly elected as president. When he died in Aug. 1985 his prime minister, Desmond Hoyte, succeeded as president. Like his predecessor, Hoyte was declared duly elected when the PNC gained a large majority at another rigged election for the National Assembly in Dec. 1985. But desperate economic straits forced Guyana to seek outside help which came on condition of restoring free elections. Dr Jagan returned to power in 1992. Following his death in March 1997 his wife, Janet Jagan, was sworn in as President on 24 Dec. 1997.

TERRITORY AND POPULATION. Guyana is situated on the north-east coast of Latin America on the Atlantic Ocean, with Suriname on the east, Venezuela on the west and Brazil on the south and west. Area, 83,000 sq. miles (214,969 sq. km). Estimated population (1997), 706,116. Ethnic groups by origin: 49% Indian, 36% African, 7% mixed race, 7% Amerindian and 1% others. The capital is Georgetown; other towns are New Amsterdam, Linden, Rose Hall and Corriverton.

Venezuela demanded the return of the Essequibo region in 1963. It was finally agreed in March 1983 that the UN Secretary-General should mediate. There was also an unresolved claim (1984) by Suriname for the return of an area between the New river and the Corentyne river.

Vital statistics (1996): life expectancy 60·1, male, 57·55, female, 62·78, birth rate, 19·03, death rate, 9·55.

The official language is English.

CLIMATE. A tropical climate, with rainy seasons from April to July and Nov. to Jan. Humidity is high all the year but temperatures are moderated by sea-breezes. Rainfall increases from 90" (2,280 mm) on the coast to 140" (3,560 mm) in the forest zone. Georgetown. Jan. 79°F (26·1°C), July 81°F (27·2°C). Annual rainfall 87" (2,175 mm).

CONSTITUTION AND GOVERNMENT. A new Constitution was promulgated in Oct. 1980. There is an *Executive Presidency*, and a *National Assembly* which consists of 53 elected members and 12 members appointed by the regional authorities. Elections for 5-year terms are held under the single-list system of proportional representation, with the whole of the country forming one electoral area and each voter casting a vote for a party list of candidates.

Janet Jagan and the PPP won the presidential, parliamentary and regional elections of 15 Dec. 1997. The PPP won 220,667 or 55·3% of the national vote (29 seats in the National Assembly), compared to the 161,901 or 40·6% cast for the PNC (22 seats in the National Assembly). In the regional elections the PPP received 219,651 votes, the PNC 160,019 votes. The chief justice rejected the PNC's claims of election rigging. PNC supporters retaliated with looting and rioting in Georgetown.

President: Janet Jagan.

In March 1998 the government comprised:

Prime Minister: Samuel Hinds. *Vice-President, Minister of Agriculture and Parliamentary Affairs:* Reepu Baman Persaud.

Attorney-General and Minister of Legal Affairs: Charles Rishiram Ramson. *Cabinet Secretary:* Roger Luncheon. *(Senior Ministers) Finance:* Bharrat Jagdeo. *Foreign:* Clement Rohee. *Health, Labour and Social Services:* Henry Benfield Jeffrey. *Education and Cultural Development:* Dale Bisnauth. *Public Works and Home Affairs:* Samuel Hinds. *Communications and Regional Development:* Harripersaud Nokta. *Trade, Industry and Tourism:* Michael Shree Chand. *Amerindian Affairs:* Vibert D'Souza. *Housing:* Shaik Baksh. *Culture, Youth and Sports:* Gail Teixeira. *Information:* Moses Nagamootoo. *Local Government:* Harripersaud Nokta. *Human Services and Social Security:* Indra Chandrapal. *Marine Resources:* Satyadeow Sawah. *Public Service:* George Fung-On.

National anthem: 'Dear land of Guyana'; words by A. L. Luker, tune by R. Potter.

Local Government: There are 10 administrative regions: Barima/Waini, Pomeroon/Supernaam, Essequibo Islands/West Demerara, Demerara/Mahaica, Mahaica/Berbice, East Berbice/Corentyne, Cuyuni/Mazaruni, Potaro/Siparuni, Upper Takutu/Upper Essequibo, Upper Demerara/Berbice.

DEFENCE

Army. The Guyana Army had (1997) a strength of 1,400. It comprises 1 infantry battalion and 1 special forces, 1 support weapons and 1 engineer company. There is a paramilitary Guyana People's Militia 1,500 strong.

Navy. The Maritime Corps is an integral part of the Guyana Defence Force. In 1997 it had 17 personnel and 2 armed boats.

Air Force. The Air Command has no combat aircraft. It is equipped with light aircraft and helicopters, including 1 Islander twin-engined short take-off and landing transport, and 1 Bell 206, 1 Bell 212 and 2 Mı-8 helicopters. Personnel (1997) 100.

INTERNATIONAL RELATIONS

Membership. Guyana is a member of the UN, Commonwealth, CARICOM, OAS and is an ACP state of the EU.

ECONOMY

Policy. State control is being reduced, and some 30 enterprises were scheduled for privatization in 1991.

Performance. GDP growth in 1996 was estimated at 6·6%.

Budget. Current revenue and expenditure for calendar years (in G$1m.):

	1991	1992	1993	1994	1995
Revenue	11,823·5	17,769·5	21,778·0	23,809·1	28,961·4
Expenditure	15,273·4	23,070·7	17,716·8	19,360·8	22,422·3

In 1995, capital account receipts totalled G$3,151·2m.; expenditure, G$12,090·4m. Components of current revenue, 1995 (in G$1m.): Income taxes, 10,865·9; property taxes, 427·8; taxes on production and consumption, 7,351; taxes on international trade, 4,117·4; other taxes, 2,562·5; non-tax revenue, 1,479·5.

Currency. The unit of currency is the *Guyana dollar* (GYD) of 100 *cents*. There are notes of G$1, 5, 10, 20, 100 and 500, and coins of 1, 5, 10, 25 and 50 cents and G$1, 5 and 10. Inflation was an annualized 8% in 1996.

Banking and Finance. The bank of issue is the Bank of Guyana. Of the 6 commercial banks operating 2 are foreign-owned. At March 1996, the total assets of commercial banks were G$62,587,892,000. Savings deposits were G$26,564·2m.

ENERGY AND NATURAL RESOURCES

Electricity. Capacity in 1995 was estimated at 157,000 kW and production, 318m. kWh.

Minerals. Placer gold mining commenced in 1884, and was followed by diamond mining in 1887. Output of raw gold was 289,514 oz. in 1995. Other minerals include copper, tungsten, iron, nickel, quartz and molybdenum.

Agriculture. Production, 1993: Sugar, 243,000 tonnes; rice, 204,511 tonnes. Other products include coffee, cocoa, coconut and edible oils, copra, fruit, vegetables and tobacco.
Livestock estimate (1992): Cattle, 225,000; pigs, 60,000; sheep, 130,000; goats, 77,000; poultry, 13m. Livestock products, 1993 (in 1,000 kg): Beef, 3,840; pork, 1,137; poultry, 4,067. Dairy products, 1995: Eggs, 30·39m.; milk, 797,627 litres.

Forestry. In 1997, 75% of the land area was forested. 25% of the country's energy needs are met by wood fuel. Production (1996) 0·58m. cu. metres of timber.

Fisheries. Production (in tonnes): Fish (1995), 538,437; prawns (1994), 2,168; shrimps (1994), 6,013.

INDUSTRY. The main industries are agro-processing (sugar, rice, timber and coconut) and mining (gold and diamonds). There is a light manufacturing sector, and textiles and pharmaceuticals are produced by state and private companies. Production, 1995: Sugar, 253,870 tonnes; rum, 17,926 litres; beer, 8,470 litres; soft drinks, 3,032,130 cases; textiles, 322m. metres; footwear, 54,132 pairs; margarine, 1,262,420 kg.; edible oil, 2,388,120 litres; refrigerators, 2,763; paint, 923,847 litres.

FOREIGN ECONOMIC RELATIONS. External public debt was US$2,058·3m. at 31 Dec. 1995.

Commerce. In 1995, exports were valued at G$67,674·9m.; re-exports at G$2,384·1m. and imports at G$74,911·5m. Principal commodities exported, 1995 (in G$1m.): Sugar, 17,573; gold, 13,425·5; bauxite, 11,986·7; rice, 10,242·4; timber, 1,035·7; rum, 559·3; shrimps, 388·1. Exports by volume, 1995: Rice, 200,544 tonnes; sugar, 225,421 tonnes; bauxite, 1,971,063 tonnes; gold, 275,305 oz.; shrimps, 827 tonnes; timber, 35,873 cu. metres.

Tourism. There were 105,000 foreign visitors in 1996.

COMMUNICATIONS

Roads. In 1995 it was estimated there were 7,820 km of roads, of which 571 km were paved.

Railways. There is a government-owned railway in the North West District, while the Guyana Mining Enterprise operates a standard gauge railway of 133 km from Linden on the Demerara River to Ituni and Coomacka.

Civil Aviation. There is an international airport at Timehri. The national carrier is the state-owned Guyana Airways, which in 1995 operated 1 B-757-200 and 1 DHC-6-300. Services are also provided by BWIA, Carib Express, LIAT, Surinam Airways and TABA.

Shipping. The major port is Georgetown; there are 3 other ports. In 1995 sea-going shipping totalled 13,925 GRT. There are 217 nautical miles of river navigation. There are ferry services across the mouths of the Demerara, Berbice and Essequibo rivers.

Telecommunications. The inland public telegraph and radio communication services are operated by the Telecommunication Corporation. There are 57 post offices and 28 agencies. In 1988 telephone exchanges had 28,450 direct exchange lines with 20,000 telephones.

The Guyana Broadcasting Corporation has 2 radio programmes. In 1995 there were 0·41m. radio and 40,000 TV receivers (colour by NTSC). Guyana Television is government-controlled and there are 2 private stations relaying US satellite services.

Press In 1995 there were 2 daily newspapers with a combined circulation of 39,000.

SOCIAL INSTITUTIONS

Justice. The law, both civil and criminal, is based on the common and statute law of England, save that the principles of the Roman–Dutch law have been retained in respect of the registration, conveyance and mortgaging of land.

The Supreme Court of Judicature consists of a Court of Appeal, a High Court and a number of courts of summary jurisdiction.

Religion. In 1997, 57% of the population were Protestant and Roman Catholic, 33% Hindu, 9% Moslem and 1% other.

Education. In 1995 there were 363 pre-primary schools with 1,545 teachers for 30,004 pupils; 422 primary schools with 3,417 teachers for 99,664 pupils and 1,570 secondary school teachers for 63,838 pupils. There were 6,945 students at university level.

Adult literacy rate, 98·1%.

Health. In 1994 there were 30 hospitals (5 private), 162 health centres and 14 health posts. There were (1989) 111 doctors, 15 dentists, 29 pharmacists, 172 midwives and 854 nursing personnel.

DIPLOMATIC REPRESENTATIVES

Of Guyana in Great Britain (3 Palace Ct., London, W2 4LP)
High Commissioner: Laleshwar K. N. Singh.

Of Great Britain in Guyana (44 Main St., Georgetown)
High Commissioner: David J. Johnson, CMG, CVO.

Of Guyana in the USA (2490 Tracy Pl., NW, Washington, D.C., 20008)
Ambassador: Mohammed Ali Odeen Ishmael.

Of the USA in Guyana (31 Main St., Georgetown)
Ambassador: Vacant.

Of Guyana to the United Nations
Ambassador: Rudolph Insanally.

Of Guyana to the European Union
Ambassador: Havelock Brewster.

Further Reading

Baber, C. and Jeffrey, H. B., *Guyana: Politics, Economics and Society.* London, 1986
Braveboy-Wagner, J. A., *The Venezuela-Guyana Border Dispute: Britain's Colonial Legacy in Latin America.* London, 1984
Chambers, F., *Guyana.* [Bibliography] Oxford and Santa Barbara (CA), 1989
Daly, P. H., *From Revolution to Republic.* Georgetown, 1970
Daly, V. T., *A Short History of the Guyanese People.* 3rd. ed. London, 1992
Sanders, A., *The Powerless People.* London, 1987
Spinner, T. J., *A Political and Social History of Guyana, 1945–83.* Epping, 1985
Williams, B. F., *Stains on My Name, War in My Veins: Guyana and the Politics of Cultural Struggle.* Duke Univ. Press, 1992

National statistical office: Bureau of Statistics, Avenue of the Republic and Brickdam, Georgetown

HAITI

République d'Haïti

Capital: Port-au-Prince
Population: 7·0m.
GNP: US$1·5bn.
HDI/world rank: 0·338/156

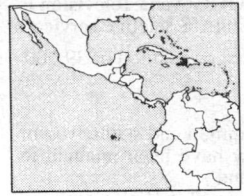

KEY HISTORICAL EVENTS. The island of Hispaniola was discovered by Christopher Columbus in 1492. Haiti occupies the western third. The Spanish colony was ceded to France in 1697. After the extirpation of the Indians by the Spaniards (by 1533) large numbers of African slaves were imported whose descendants now populate the country. The slaves obtained their liberation following the French Revolution, but Napoleon restored French authority and imprisoned Toussaint Louverture, the leader of the slaves who had been appointed a French general and governor. Subsequently the French surrendered to a blockading British squadron.

The country declared its independence on 1 Jan. 1804, and Gen. Jean-Jacques Dessalines proclaimed himself Emperor of the newly-named Haiti. After the assassination of Dessalines (1806) a separate régime was set up in the north under Gen. Henri Christophe who in 1811 had himself proclaimed King. In the south and west a republic was constituted, with Alexander Pétion as its first President. Pétion died in 1818 and was succeeded by Jean-Pierre Boyer, under whom the country became re-united after Henri Christophe had committed suicide in 1820. From 1822 to 1844 Haiti and the eastern part of the island (later the Dominican Republic) were united under Haitian rule. After one more monarchical interlude, under the Emperor Faustin (1847–59), Haiti has been a republic. From 1915 to 1934 Haiti was under United States occupation.

Dr François Duvalier was elected President on 22 Sept. 1957 and became president for life in 1964. He died on 21 April 1981 and was succeeded as president for life by his son, Jean-Claude Duvalier who fled the country on 7 Feb. 1986. Gen. Henry Namphy formed a Council of Government. In Jan. 1988 Leslie Manigat was elected president but Namphy again seized power in June 1988. In Sept. 1988 he was deposed and replaced by the military government of Lieut.-Gen. Prosper Avril. In March 1990 Ertha Pascal-Trouillot became head of an interim government. Father Jean-Bertrand Aristide was elected president in Dec. 1990.

On 30 Sept. 1991 President Aristide was deposed by a military junta and went into exile abroad. Under international diplomatic pressure parliament again recognized Aristide as president in June 1993. After 2 agreements brokered by the UN and OAS a new government was formed in Aug. President Aristide was scheduled to return on 30 Oct. However, the military régime prevented UN forces from landing on 11 Oct., and on 13 Oct. the UN Security Council voted to apply new sanctions if the agreements were not adhered to. On 14 Oct. the Minister of Justice was assassinated, and the USA and other UN members mounted a naval blockade.

The UN and OAS civil missions were expelled by the junta on 11 July 1994. Despite a full embargo under UN Resolution 917, the junta showed no sign of stepping down. On 15 Sept. US President Clinton demanded that the junta step down. Former US President Carter flew to Haiti on 17 Sept. to negotiate their removal. 20,000 US troops moved into Haiti on 19 Sept. in an uncontested occupation. President Aristide returned to office on 15 Oct. 1994. On 1 April 1995 a UN peacekeeping force (MANUH) took over from the US military mission. (All UN contingents were scheduled to leave by 30 Nov. 1996, but a UN Security Council resolution provided for an extension of MANUH, later MITNUH, to 30 Nov. 1997.)

TERRITORY AND POPULATION. Haiti is bounded in the east by the Dominican Republic, to the north by the Atlantic and elsewhere by the Caribbean Sea. The area is 27,750 sq. km (10,714 sq. miles). The Île de la Gonave, some 40 miles long, lies in the gulf of the same name. Among other islands is La Tortue, off the north peninsula. Population, (1994 est.) 7m. (UNICEF, Le Progrès des Nations).

Population density, 244 per sq. km. Infant mortality, 1992, 94 per 1,000 live births. Expectation of life, 1992, 54 years.

Areas, populations and chief towns of the 9 departments:

Department	Area (in sq. km)	Population	Chief town
Nord-Ouest	2,094	395,442	Port-de-Paix
Nord	2,175	724,084	Cap Haïtien
Nord-Est	1,698	239,734	Fort-Liberté
L'Artibonite	4,895	961,447	Gonaïves
Centre	3,597	467,514	Hinche
Ouest	4,595	2,285,044	Port-au-Prince
Sud-Est	2,077	444,323	Jacmel
Sud	2,602	630,007	Les Cayes
Grande Anse	3,100	616,151	Jérémie

The capital is Port-au-Prince (1,255,078); other towns are Cap-Haïtien (92,122); Gonaives (63,291), Les Cayes (45,904) and Jérémie (43,277). Most of the population is of African or mixed origin.

The official languages are French and Créole. Créole is spoken by all Haitians; French by only a small minority.

CLIMATE. A tropical climate, but the central mountains can cause semi-arid conditions in their lee. There are rainy seasons from April to June and Aug. to Nov. Hurricanes and severe thunderstorms can occur. The annual temperature range is small. Port-au-Prince. Jan. 77°F (25°C), July 84°F (28·9°C). Annual rainfall 53" (1,321 mm).

CONSTITUTION AND GOVERNMENT. The 1987 Constitution, ratified by a referendum, provides for a bicameral legislature (an 83-member *Chamber of Deputies* and a 27-member *Senate*), and an executive *President*, directly elected for a 5-year term, renewable once only.

At the presidential, parliamentary and local elections of Dec. 1990 the electorate was some 3m.; turn-out was estimated at 55% by international observers. Father Jean-Bertrand Aristide (b. 1957) was elected President by about 66% of votes cast. He was sworn in on 7 Feb. 1991 but deposed on 30 Sept. 1991 by a military junta. He returned to Haiti in Oct. 1994 to complete his term when the US military intervention forced the junta's departure.

Following the ouster of the junta, elections were held in 3 rounds on 25 June, 13 Aug. and 17 Sept. 1995. The electorate was 3·5m. Lavalas gained 17 Senate and 66 Chamber of Deputies seats. Presidential elections were held on 17 Dec. 1995. There were 14 candidates; turn-out was 28%. Rene Préval was elected with 88% of votes cast.

President: René Préval (b. 1943; Lavalas; sworn in 7 Feb. 1996).

A new government was formed in Feb. 1996, led by.

Prime Minister: Rony Smarth (b. 1941; Lavalas). The government resigned on 9 June 1997 but remained as a caretaker government until Smarth left office on 20 Oct. 1997. It was announced in Nov. 1997 that Hervé Denis had accepted President Préval's nomination to be the new Prime Minister.

The *Speaker* of the Senate is Edgard Leblanc, and of the Chamber of Deputies, Kelly Bastien.

National anthem: La Dessalinienne; words by J. Lhérisson, tune by N. Geffrard.

Local Government. Elections for 133 mayors and 565 3-member local councils were held on 17 Dec. 1995.

DEFENCE. After the restoration of civilian rule in 1994 the armed forces and police were disbanded and a 3,000-strong Interim Public Security Force formed in 1995. For Police, *see* JUSTICE, *below.*

INTERNATIONAL RELATIONS

Membership. Haiti is a member of the UN, CARICOM and OAS and is an ACP state of the EU.

ECONOMY

Budget. The budget for the fiscal year ending 30 Sept. 1997 was 13,400m. gourdes.

Currency. The unit of currency is the *gourde* (HTG) of 100 *centimes*. There are coins of 50, 20, 10 and 5 centimes and notes of 1, 2, 5, 10, 25, 50, 100, 250 and 500 gourdes. Money in circulation in Sept. 1996, 3,088m. gourdes.

Banking and Finance. The Banque Nationale de la République d'Haïti is the central bank and bank of issue (*Governor:* Leslie Delatour). In 1997 there were 11 commercial banks.

Weights and Measures. The metric system and British imperial and US measures are in use.

ENERGY AND NATURAL RESOURCES

Electricity. Rated output (1996), 166·5 MW. Maximum capability (1996), 119·2 MW.

Agriculture. The agricultural area is 1·4m. ha, of which 0·91m. ha are cultivated and 0·49m. ha pasture. 65% of the workforce, mainly smallholders, make a living by agriculture carried on in 7 large plains, from 0·2m. to 25,000 acres, and in 15 smaller plains down to 2,000 acres. Irrigation is used in some areas. The main crops are coffee, sugar, rice, maize, sorghum, millet, beans, cocoa, sweet potatoes, sisal, cotton, bananas and citrus fruits.

INDUSTRY. Manufacturing is largely based on the assembly of imported components: Toys, sports equipment, clothing, electronic and electrical equipment. Textiles, steel, soap, chemicals, paint, shoes and cement were also produced, but much of industry had to close down during the international embargo following President Aristide's deposal in 1991 and many jobs were lost to other Central American and Caribbean countries.

FOREIGN ECONOMIC RELATIONS. Foreign debt was US$893m. in Sept. 1996.

Commerce. In 1995 exports were US$137m. and imports, US$517m. The leading imports are petroleum products, foodstuffs, textiles, machinery, animal and vegetable oils, chemicals, pharmaceuticals, raw materials for transformation industries and vehicles.

COMMUNICATIONS

Roads. Total length of roads was estimated at 4,080 km in 1995, of which 987 km are surfaced.

Civil Aviation. There is an international airport at Port-au-Prince. Services are provided by Air Canada, Air France, American Airlines, Air Guadeloupe, COPA and ALM. Air services connecting Port-au-Prince with other Haitian towns are operated by Carib Inter.

Shipping. Port-au-Prince and Cap Haïtien are the principal ports, and there are 12 minor ports.

Telecommunications. There were about 60,000 telephones in 1995. The state telecommunications agency is Teleco.
   The aegis of the Conseil National des Télécommunications, Radio Nationale and Télévision Nationale broadcast radio and TV programmes (colour by NTSC). There is a privately-owned cable TV company, and several privately-owned radio stations. There were 3m. radio and 25,000 TV sets in 1993.

Cinemas. There are 10 cinemas in Port-au-Prince.

Press. There are 2 daily newspapers and several weekly news magazines.

SOCIAL INSTITUTIONS

Justice. The Court of Cassation is the highest court in the judicial system. There are 4 Courts of Appeal and 4 Civil Courts. Judges are appointed by the President. The legal system is basically French. A 4,000-strong police force has been re-recruited from former military personnel and others not implicated in human rights violations.

Religion. Since the Concordat of 1860 Roman Catholicism has been given special recognition, under an archbishop with 9 bishops. The Episcopal Church has one bishop. 90% of the population are nominally Roman Catholic, while other Christian churches number perhaps 10%. Probably two-thirds of the population to some extent adhere to African-derived traditional beliefs ('Voodoo'). A national Voodoo temple began construction in 1995.

Education. Education is divided into 9 years 'education fondamentale', followed by 4 years to 'Baccalaureate' and university/higher education. The school system is based on the French system and instruction is in French and Créole.

There are 360 primary schools (221 state, 139 religious), 21 public lycées, 123 private secondary schools, 18 vocational training centres and 42 domestic science centres.

There is a state university, several private universities and an Institute of Administration and Management.

Health. There are 944 doctors and 98 dentists, and 87 hospitals and health centres with 4,566 beds.

DIPLOMATIC REPRESENTATIVES

Of Haiti in Great Britain. The Embassy closed on 30 March 1987.

Of Great Britain in Haiti
Ambassador: Anthony R. Thomas, CMG (resides in Jamaica).

Of Haiti in the USA (2311 Massachusetts Ave., NW, Washington, D.C., 20008)
Ambassador: Jean Casimir.

Of the USA in Haiti (Harry Truman Blvd., Port-au-Prince)
Ambassador: William Lacy Swing.

Of Haiti to the United Nations
Ambassador: Pierre Lelong.

Of Haiti to the European Union
Ambassador: Yolette Azor-Charles.

Further Reading

Chambers, F. J., *Haiti*. [Bibliography] 2nd ed. Oxford and Santa Barbara (CA), 1994
Ferguson, J., *Papa Doc, Baby Doc: Haiti and the Duvaliers*. Oxford, 1987
Heinl, Robert & Nancy, revised by Michael Heinl *Written in Blood*. University Press of America, 1996
Laguerre, M. S., *The Complete Haitiana*. [Bibliography] London and New York, 1982.—*Voodoo and Politics in Haiti*. London, 1989
Lawless, R., *Haiti: a Research Guide*. New York, 1990
Lundahl, M., *The Haitian Economy: Man, Land and Markets*. London, 1983
Nicholls, D., *From Dessalines to Duvalier: Race, Colour and National Independence in Haiti*. 2nd ed. CUP, 1992.—*Haiti in Caribbean Context: Ethnicity, Economy and Revolt*. London, 1985
Thomson, I., *Bonjour Blanc: a Journey through Haiti*. London, 1992
Weinstein, B. and Segal, A., *Haiti: the Failure of Politics*. New York, 1992
Wilentz, A., *The Rainy Season: Haiti since Duvalier*. New York, 1989

National library: Bibliothèque Nationale, Rue du Centre, Port-au-Prince.

HONDURAS

República de Honduras

Capital: Tegucigalpa
Population: 5·6m.
GDP per head (PPP$) 2,050
GNP: US$3·2bn.
HDI/world rank: 0·575/116

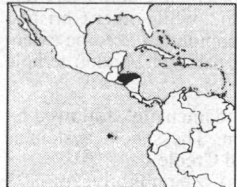

KEY HISTORICAL EVENTS. In pre-Columbian times the area which is now Honduras was part of the Mayan empire. Discovered by Columbus in 1502, Honduras was ruled by Spain as part of the Captain-Generalcy of Guatemala. In 1821 Honduras gained its independence from Spain, and from 1823 was part of the Central American Federation. On 5 Nov. 1838 the country declared itself an independent sovereign state, free from the Federation. Political instability became the rule, punctuated by a period of more serious administration from 1876 to 1891. The instability, with one period of US military occupation, continued until 1933. From 1933 to 1949 Gen. Tiburcio Carias Andino ruled as a dictator. There followed a disturbed period of presidential elections, depositions and military juntas. Dr Ramón Ernesto Cruz Velés was elected president in 1971, but a coup in 1972 led to his being superseded by Gen. López Arellano, who ruled by decree until 1975 when he too was ousted by army officers in favour of Col. Melgar Castro. In 1978 a military junta took control, with the commander of the army, Gen. Policarpo Paz Garcia nominated as head of state.

The end of military rule seemed to come in 1981 when a general election gave victory to the more liberal and non-military party, PLH (Partido Liberal de Honduras). The party's leader, Dr Roberto Svazo Cordova, became president. Considerable power, however, remained with the armed forces, led by their commander-in-chief, Gen. Gustavo Alvarez. The armed forces became more free from government control, fought the left-wing guerrillas, and also seemed to be responsible for the disappearance of some of their political opponents.

In 1984 junior army officers forced Gen. Alvarez and other senior officers into exile, and Gen. Walter López Reyes took over as commander-in-chief. There followed a period of less friendly relations with the USA and increasingly poor relations with Nicaragua, since the anti Sandinista (contra) rebels maintained bases in Honduras. Internal unrest continued into the 1990s, with politicians and military leaders at loggerheads, particularly over attempts to investigate violations of human rights.

TERRITORY AND POPULATION. Honduras is bounded in the north by the Caribbean, east and south-east by Nicaragua, west by Guatemala, south-west by El Salvador and south by the Pacific Ocean. The area is 112,088 sq. km (43,277 sq. miles). The estimated population in 1997 was 5,751,384 (2,870,740 female).

The chief cities (populations in 1,000, 1994) were Tegucigalpa, the capital (775·3), San Pedro Sula (368·5), El Progreso (81·2), Choluteca (72·8), Danlí (43·3) and the Atlantic coast ports of La Ceiba (86·0), Puerto Cortés (33·5) and Tela (24·8); other towns include Olanchito (17·9), Juticalpa (25·6), Comayagua (52·3), Siguatepeque (37·5) and Santa Rosa de Copán (23·4).

Areas and 1988 census populations of the 18 departments and the Central District (Tegucigalpa):

Department	Area (in sq. km)	Population	Department	Area (in sq. km)	Population
Atlántida	4,251	238,742	Francisco Morazán	6,298	251,613
Choluteca	4,211	295,484	Gracias a Dios	16,630	34,970
Colón	8,875	149,677	Intibucá	3,072	124,681
Comayagua	5,196	239,859	Islas de la Bahía	261	22,062
Copán	3,203	219,455	La Paz	2,331	105,927
Cortés	3,954	662,772	Lempira	4,290	177,055
El Paraíso	7,218	254,295	Ocotepeque	1,680	74,276

Department	Area (in sq. km)	Population	Department	Area (in sq. km)	Population
Olancho	24,350	283,852	Yoro	7,939	333,508
Santa Bárbara	5,115	278,868	Central District	1,648	576,661
Valle	1,565	119,645			

Vital statistics (1997 estimates): life expectancy, 66·4 years for men, 71·4 for women; birth rate, 32·6%; death rate 5·6%; infant mortality, 40·2 per 1,000 live births; populations growth rate, 2·55%.

The official language is Spanish. The Spanish-speaking population is of mixed Spanish and Amerindian descent (90%), with 7% Amerindians.

CLIMATE. The climate is tropical, with a small annual range of temperature but with high rainfall. Upland areas have two wet seasons, from May to July and in Sept. and Oct. The Caribbean Coast has most rain in Dec. and Jan. and temperatures are generally higher than inland. Tegucigalpa. Jan. 66°F (19°C), July 74°F (23·3°C). Annual rainfall 64" (1,621 mm).

CONSTITUTION AND GOVERNMENT. The present Constitution came into force in 1982. The *President* is elected for a 4-year term. Members of the *National Congress* (total 128 seats) and municipal mayors are elected simultaneously on a proportional basis, according to combined votes cast for the Presidential candidate of their party.

Elections were held on 30 Nov. 1997. The PLH gained 67 seats in Congress (49·7% of votes cast), with the remaining seats apportioned to the following parties: Nacional, 54 seats (41·3%), Inovación y Unidad 5 seats (4·2%), Unificación Democrática 1 seat (2·6%) and Demócrata Cristiano 1 seat (2·2%).

In March. 1998 the government consisted of:

President: Carlos Roberto Flores.

Agriculture and Livestock: Pedro Arturo Sevilla. *Culture, Arts and Sports:* Herman Allan Padgett. *Defence:* Col. Cristobál Corrales Calix. *Education:* Aristides Mejia Casco. *Finance:* Gabriela Nuñez. *Foreign Relations:* Fernando Martinez Jimenez. *Government and Justice:* Delmer Urbizo Panting. *Labour:* Andrés Victor Artiles. *Natural Resources and Environment:* Elvin Ernesto Santos. *Presidency:* Gustavo Adolfo Alfaro Zelaya. *Public Health:* Marco Antonio Rosa. *Public Works, Transportation and Housing:* Tomás Lozano Reyes. *Ministers without portfolio:* Jorge Arturo Reina, Nahun Valladares, Plutarco Castellanos, Roberto Leiva.

National anthem: 'Tu bandera' ('Thy Banner'); words by Λ. C. Coello, tune by C. Hartling.

Local Government: Honduras comprises a Central District (containing the cities of Tegucigalpa and Comayaguela) and 18 departments; (each administered by an appointed Governor), sub-divided into 293 municipalities. Mayors are elected simultaneously with Congressional deputies.

DEFENCE. Conscription was abolished in 1995.

Army. The Army consists of 3 infantry brigades, 1 special tactics group, 1 territorial force, 1 armed cavalry regiment and 1 artillery and 1 engineer battalion. Equipment includes 12 Scorpion light tanks. Strength (1997) 16,000 (12,000 conscripts). There is also a paramilitary Public Security Force of 5,500.

Navy. A small flotilla operates 5 US-built fast inshore patrol craft, some 6 other inshore craft, 4 landing craft and a number of boats. Personnel (1997), 1,000 including 400 marines. Bases are at Puerto Cortés and Amapala.

Air Force. Equipment includes 12 F-5E/F Tiger II fighters, 12 A-37B jet light attack aircraft, 4 Spanish-built CASA C-101BB armed jet trainers, 4 four-engined Lockheed transports, 5 C-47, 1 Israeli-built Arava transport, about 20 helicopters and Tucano and T-41D trainers. Total strength was (1997) about 1,800 personnel (700 conscripts).

INTERNATIONAL RELATIONS

Membership. Honduras is a member of the UN and OAS.

ECONOMY

Budget (1997 estimate). Expenditure was US$850m. (including capital expenditures of US$150m.); revenues totalled US$655m.

Currency. The unit of currency is the *lempira* (HNL) of 100 *centavos*. There are coins of 1, 2, 5, 10, 20 and 50 centavos and notes of 1, 2, 5, 10, 20, 50 and 100 lempiras. Cash in circulation 1994, 1,966m. lempiras. Foreign exchange reserves were US$61·9m. in 1994; gold reserves were US$5·4m. Year-end annual inflation was 13·7% in 1993.

Banking and Finance. The central bank of issue is the Banco Central de Honduras (*President:* Ermin Barjun). There is an agricultural development bank, Banadesa, for small grain producers, a state land bank and a network of rural credit agencies managed by peasant organizations. The Central American Bank for Economic Integration (BCIE) has its head office in Tegucigalpa. In 1993 there were 13 private banks, including 2 foreign.

There are stock exchanges in Tegucigalpa and San Pedro Sula.

Weights and Measures. The metric system has been legal since 1 April 1897, although there are still some minor traces of the Imperial and old Spanish systems.

ENERGY AND NATURAL RESOURCES

Electricity. Production (1995) 2·742bn. kWh (mainly hydro-electric).

Minerals. Output in 1993 (in 1,000 tonnes): Lead, 4·9; zinc, 26·5; silver, 24 tonnes. Small quantities of gold are mined, and there are also deposits of tin, iron, copper, coal, antimony and pitchblende.

Agriculture. In 1994 1·79m. ha were devoted to arable farming and permanent crop land, and 2·5m. ha to permanent pasture. Legislation of 1975 provided for the compulsory redistribution of land, but in 1992 the grounds for this were much reduced, and a 5-ha minimum area for land titles abolished. Members of the 2,800 co-operatives set up in 1975 received individual shareholdings which can be broken up into personal units. Since 1992 women may have tenure in their own right. The state monopoly of the foreign grain trade was abolished in 1992.

Crop production in 1994 (in 1,000 tonnes): Bananas, 411; coffee, 263; maize, 995; dry beans, 120; sorghum, 195.

Livestock (1994): Cattle, 2,286,000; sheep, 8,000; pigs, 603,000; goats, 28,000; horses, 246,000; poultry, 14m.

Forestry. Forests cover 4·1m. ha; another 2·5m. ha are suitable for re-afforestation. In 1994, 6·3m. cubic metres of roundwood were cut.

Fisheries. Shrimps and lobsters are important catches. Total catch (1995): 24,373 tonnes.

INDUSTRY. Industry is small-scale and local. 1994 output: Cement, 999·6 tonnes; fabrics, 11,286 yards. 217,835 bottles of beer and 5,300 litres of rum were produced in 1994.

Labour. The workforce was 1·3m. in 1996. In 1994 (in 1,000) 749·7 worked in agriculture, hunting and fishery; 203 in manufacturing; 183·9 in trade; 110·2 in building; 48·2 in transport and communications and 34·3 in finance. Unemployment rate (1996 estimate): 15%.

Trade Unions. About 346,000 workers were unionized in 1994.

FOREIGN ECONOMIC RELATIONS. In May 1992 Honduras, El Salvador and Guatemala agreed to create a free trade zone. Import duties are to be standardized. Foreign debt was US$4·6bn. in 1995.

Commerce. Imports in 1996 were valued at US$3·133bn. and exports at US$2·401bn.

Main exports are bananas, coffee, shrimps and lobsters, fruit, lead and zinc, timber, and refrigerated meats. Major trading partners are: USA, Germany, Belgium, UK, Japan, Spain, Netherlands and Italy.

Main imports are machinery and electrical equipment, industrial chemicals and mineral products and lubricants. Major trading partners are: USA, Japan, Guatemala, El Salvador, Germany, Mexico and Costa Rica.

Tourism. There were 237,985 foreign visitors in 1995.

COMMUNICATIONS

Roads. Honduras is connected with Guatemala, El Salvador and Nicaragua by the Pan-American Highway. Out of a total of 15,100 km of roads (1995), 3,050 km were paved. In 1995 there were 81,439 passenger cars in use, 170,006 commercial vehicles and 22,482 motorcycles and bicycles.

Railways. The small government-run railway was built to serve the banana industry and is confined to the northern coastal region and does not reach Tegucigalpa. In 1995 there were 595 km of track in 3 gauges, which in 1994 carried 1m. passengers and 1·2m. tonnes of freight.

Civil Aviation. There are 4 international airports: Tegucigalpa (Toncontín), San Pedro Sula, Roatún and La Ceiba, with over 80 smaller airstrips in various parts of the country. The national carrier is Servicio Aéreo de Honduras (Sahsa), which in 1995 operated 1 B-737-200 and 1 B-737-200 Adv. Services are also provided by American Airlines, Continental Airlines and Air Micronesia, Islena Airlines, LACSA and TACA.

Shipping. The largest port is Puerto Cortés on the Atlantic coast. There are also ports at Henecán (on the Pacific) and Puerto Castilla and Tela (northern coast). Ships of 1,000 GRT or over in 1996 were estimated at 251, including 153 cargo ships, 24 oil or chemical tankers and 5 container ships. Honduras is a flag of convenience registry.

Telecommunications. Hondutel, a government agency run by the military and scheduled in 1994 for privatization, operated 131,176 telephones in 1994. The telegraph remains important and there were 411 offices in the country in 1994.

In 1993, there were 6 commercial TV channels (colour by NTSC) and various radio stations (mostly local) operating. In 1995 there were 2·3m. radio and 0·5m. TV sets.

Press (1995). There are 5 national daily papers, with a combined circulation of 240,000.

SOCIAL INSTITUTIONS

Justice. Judicial power is vested in the Supreme Court, with 9 judges elected by the National Congress for 4 years; it appoints the judges of the courts of appeal, and justices of the peace.

Religion. Roman Catholicism is the prevailing religion, but the constitution guarantees freedom to all creeds, and the State does not contribute to the support of any. Evangelical movements from North America are spreading their influence.

Education. Adult literacy was 72·7% in 1995. Education is free, compulsory (from 7 to 12 years) and secular. There is a high drop out rate after the first years in primary education. In 1995 the 8,168 primary schools had 1,008,092 children (28,978 teachers); the 661 secondary, normal and technical schools had 184,589 pupils (12,480 teachers). There were 8 universities or specialized colleges, with a total of 54,293 students and 3,676 academic staff. In addition, 73,491 children attended pre-primary school.

Health. In 1990 there were about 2,900 doctors. In 1994 there were 29 public hospitals and 32 private, with 4,737 beds, and 849 health centres.

DIPLOMATIC REPRESENTATIVES

Of Honduras in Great Britain (115 Gloucester Pl., London, W1H 3PJ)
Ambassador: Ivan Romero-Martinez.

Of Great Britain in Honduras (Edificio Palmira, 3er Piso, Colonia Palmira, Tegucigalpa)
Ambassador: Peter R. Holmes.

Of Honduras in the USA (3007 Tilden St., NW, Washington, D.C., 20008)
Ambassador: Roberto Flores Bermúdez.

Of the USA in Honduras (Av. La Paz, Tegucigalpa)
Ambassador: James Creagan.

Of Honduras to the United Nations
Ambassador: Gerardo Martínez Blanco.

Of Honduras to the European Union
Ambassador: Ivan Romero Martínez.

Further Reading

Banco Central de Honduras. *Honduras en Cifras 1990–92.* Tegucigalpa, 1993
Howard-Reguindin, P., *Honduras.* [Bibliography]. Oxford and Santa Barbara (CA), 1991
Meyer, H. K. and Meyer, J. H., *Historical Dictionary of Honduras.* 2nd ed. Metuchen (NJ), 1994
Sheehan, E. R. F., *Agony in the garden: a Stranger in Central America.* New York, 1989

HUNGARY

Magyar Köztársaság

(Hungarian Republic)

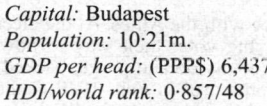

Capital: Budapest
Population: 10·21m.
GDP per head: (PPP$) 6,437
HDI/world rank: 0·857/48

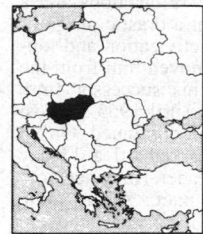

KEY HISTORICAL EVENTS. The Hungarians' name for themselves is "Magyars"; "Hungarian" derives from the Turkic name ("On ogur", i.e. ten arrows) of the tribal federation on the Don which Árpád and his horde left in order to settle the sparsely inhabited middle Danubian basin in 896. The horde spread terror by its forays, but was pacified by defeat at the hands of the Germans at Augsburg in 955. In 1000 Stephen adopted Roman Catholicism and received a crown from the Pope. Stephen replaced the tribal structure with a system of counties administered by royal officials. As nomadism gave way to agriculture a feudal society developed led by nobility descended from the original conquerors.

In 1301 Árpád's line died out. Henceforth, with two exceptions, the throne was held by foreigners, sometimes holding other thrones simultaneously. The Angevin king, Lájos the Great (1342-82), was also king of Poland; under him Hungary attained a golden age of prosperity, civilization and international significance.

In the 15th century the expansionist Ottoman empire reached the southern borders of Hungary. This first incursion was repelled by János Hunyádi. His son Matthias Corvinus, elected king in 1458, ruled as an enlightened renaissance despot. In 1526 the Turks again advanced on the Hungarians who were defeated at the battle of Mohács and their king killed. Southern and central Hungary were annexed and turned into a desert. The western rump came under Hapsburg rule, which was extended to most of Hungary with the expulsion of the Turks in 1699. A national rising in 1703 under Ferenc Rákoczi forced the crown to come to terms: Emperor Charles IV restored the constitution and the Hungarian assembly recognized the Emperor's claim to the Hungarian throne. The Hapsburgs imposed a centralizing Germanizing régime upon Hungary economically stagnating under protective tariffs designed to restrict industrialization to Austria. Nationalist sentiments led to the radical democracy of Lájos Kossuth, who set up a breakaway government in Debrecen in 1848-49. Ruthless repression followed but Austria's military defeats in Italy (1859) and against Prussia (1866) forced the emperor to moderate his absolutism. Under the Compromise (*Ausgleich*) of 1867 a Dual Monarchy was constituted; Hungary gained internal autonomy while foreign affairs and defence became joint Austro-Hungarian responsibilities.

Hungary entered the First World War on Austria's side but as hostilities drew to a close the ideas of Mihaly Károlyi, who stood for peace and independence, grew in popularity. After the armistice of 3 Nov. 1918 a National Council under his chairmanship proclaimed an independent republic. Political and social unrest, however, were compounded by a Romanian invasion. On 21 March 1919 Károlyi was replaced by Béla Kun's Soviet republic, a reign of red terror which antagonized most of the population. Kun fled on 4 Aug. and a counter-revolutionary government annulled all his and Károlyi's legislation and appointed Admiral Horthy as regent. Hungary was drastically reduced in size by the Peace Treaty.

The 1920s under the premiership of István Bethlen were a period of consolidation but Bethlen was forced to resign by the collapse of wheat prices in the world depression. Hungary's desire to revise the Versailles peace settlements brought her into alignment with Germany in the 1930s, and this was reinforced by her growing economic dependence on Germany. In 1940 Hungary adhered to the Tripartite pact and in June 1941 sent a force to join the German invaders of the Soviet Union. But pro-German sentiment was never wholehearted until Hitler occupied the country in March 1944. In Oct. Horthy was forced to abdicate in favour of a fascist "Arrow Cross" government but by then Soviet forces were well inside the frontiers.

The 4 democratic parties permitted by the Soviets formed a provisional government at Debrecen in Dec. 1944 which declared war on Germany and signed an armistice with the Allies. At the elections of Nov. 1945 the Communists polled only 17% of the vote; their way to power was to lie in their leader Rákosi's "salami tactics" of divide and purge, backed up by their acquisition of key ministries under Soviet pressure. In Feb. 1949 Catholic opposition was weakened by the arrest of cardinal Mindszenty, and all political parties were united in a People's Front whose single list of candidates gained 96% of the vote at the May 1949 elections and a Soviet-type constitution was adopted in Aug. Rákosi carried out a drastic purge of "Titoists" and embarked on a programme of such ruthless collectivization and top-heavy industrialization that the post-Stalin Soviet leadership removed him from the premiership. As party leader, however, he intrigued against his successor Imre Nagy's more liberal "new course" and took his place again in April 1955. Rákosi resigned the party leadership in July 1956 but popular discontent continued. On 23 Oct. the attempted suppression of a student demonstration sparked off a 13-day revolution. Nagy became prime minister and János Kádár party leader. Nagy declared Hungary's neutrality and withdrawal from the Warsaw pact. After some hesitation the Soviet army crushed the revolt on 4 Nov. and installed Kádár in power. Nagy was arrested and later executed; the gains of the uprising were harshly suppressed. Cautious economic reforms were introduced in the mid-60s when liberalization brought higher living standards.

A gathering reformist tendency within the Hungarian Socialist Workers' (i.e. Communist) Party led by Imre Pozsgay culminated in its self-dissolution in Oct. 1989 and reconstitution as the Hungarian Socialist Party. The People's Republic was abolished on 23 Oct. 1989.

Nagy was reburied with state honours on 16 Aug. 1989. The following year a multi-party democracy came into being.

TERRITORY AND POPULATION. Hungary is bounded in the north by Slovakia, north-east by Ukraine, east by Romania, south by Croatia and Yugoslavia and west by Austria. The peace treaty of 10 Feb. 1947 restored the frontiers as of 1 Jan. 1938. The area of Hungary is 93,032 sq. km (35,911 sq. miles).

At the census of 1 Jan. 1990 the population was 10,374,823 (5,389,919 females); estimate, 1996, 10,214,000 (5,330,000 females). 62·6% of the population was urban (18·7% in Budapest) in 1996; population density, 1996, 119·8 per sq. km. Ethnic minorities, 1995: Germans, 4%; Slovaks, 8%; Romanians, 7%; Gypsies, 4%; Serbs, 2%. A law of 1993 permits ethnic minorities to set up self-governing councils. There is a world-wide Hungarian diaspora, of 1·5m. in 1988 (730,000 in US; 220,000 in Israel; 140,000 in Canada), and Hungarian minorities (3·5m. in 1992) in Romania (2m.), Slovakia (0·6m.), Yugoslavia (Vojvodina, 0·4m.) and the Ukraine (0·16m.).

Vital statistics, 1995: Births, 112,000; marriages, 54,000 (14,000 remarriages); divorces, 24,000; deaths, 144,000; abortions, 77,000. There were 3,500 suicides. Rates (per 1,000), 1995: Birth, 10·9; death, 14·1; marriage, 5·3; divorce, 2·3; infant mortality, 10·7 (per 1,000 live births). Over 1990–95, the suicide rate per 100,000 population was 38·6 (men, 58; women, 20·7). Since 1981 the population has been decreasing, by 3 per 1,000 in 1995; expectation of life (1994): males, 64·8 years; females, 74·2.

Hungary is divided into 19 counties (*megyék*) and the capital, Budapest, which has county status.

Area (in sq. km) and population (in 1,000) of counties and county towns (estimate, 1 Jan. 1995):

Counties	Area	Population	Chief town	Population
Baranya	4,487	412	Pécs	163
Bács-Kiskun	8,362	541	Kecskemét	105
Békés	5,631	405	Békéscsaba	65
Borsod-Abaúj-Zemplén	7,247	750	Miskolc	182
Csongrád	4,263	429	Szeged	169
Fejér	4,373	426	Székesfehérvár	108
Győr-Moson-Sopron	4,062	426	Győr	127
Hajdú-Bihar	6,211	550	Debrecen	211
Heves	3,637	330	Eger	60
Jász-Nagykún-Szolnok	5,607	423	Szolnok	79
Komárom-Esztergom	2,251	31	Tatabánya	73

Counties	Area	Population	Chief town	Population
Nógrád	2,544	224	Salgótarján	46
Pest	6,394	973	Budapest	1,930
Somogy	6,036	338	Kaposvár	69
Szabolcs-Szatmár-Bereg	5,937	573	Nyíregyháza	113
Tolna	3,704	250	Szekszárd	36
Vas	3,336	273	Szombathely	84
Veszprém	4,639	379	Veszprém	65
Zala	3,784	302	Zalaegerszeg	62
Budapest	525	4,487	(has county status)	

The official language is Hungarian. Ethnic minorities have the right to education in their own language.

CLIMATE. A humid continental climate, with warm summers and cold winters. Precipitation is generally greater in summer, with thunderstorms. Dry, clear weather is likely in autumn, but spring is damp and both seasons are of short duration. Budapest. Jan. 32°F (0°C), July 71°F (21·5°C). Annual rainfall 25" (625 mm). Pécs. Jan. 30°F (–0·7°C), July 71°F (21·5°C). Annual rainfall 26·4" (661 mm).

CONSTITUTION AND GOVERNMENT. On 18 Oct. 1989 the National Assembly approved by an 88% majority a constitution which abolished the People's Republic, and established Hungary as an independent, democratic, law-based state.

The head of state is the *President*, who is elected for 5-year terms by the National Assembly. On 19 June 1995 Árpád Goncz was re-elected President.

The single-chamber *National Assembly* has 386 members, made up of 176 individual constituency winners, 152 allotted by proportional representation from county party lists and 58 from a national list. It is elected for 4-year terms. A *Constitutional Court* was established in Jan. 1990 to review laws under consideration.

Parliamentary elections were held in 2 rounds on 8 and 29 May 1994. Turn-out was 68·9% in the first round and 55·1% in the second. The Hungarian Socialist Party (HSP; former Communists) won 209 seats with 54·1% of votes cast (33 seats in 1990); the Alliance of Free Democrats (AFD), 70 with 18·13% (92); the Hungarian Democratic Forum (HDF), 37 with 9·58% (165); the Independent Smallholders (IS), 26 with 6·73% (43); the Christian Democratic People's Party (CDPP), 22 with 5·69% (21); the Federation of Young Democrats (FYD), 20 with 5·18% (21); the Agrarian Alliance, 1 with 0·26%; the Liberal Bloc, 1 with 0·26%.

President: Árpád Göncz (b. 1922; AFD; elected 3 Aug. 1990, re-elected 19 June 1995).

An HSP-AFD coalition government was formed, which in March 1998 consisted of:

Prime Minister: Gyula Horn (b. 1932; HSP).

Home Affairs: Gábor Kuncze (AFD). *Environmental Protection and Regional Development:* Ferenc Baja (HSP). *Finance:* Péter Medgyessy (HSP). *Culture and Education:* Bálint Magyar (AFD). *Defence:* György Keleti (HSP). *Foreign Affairs:* László Kovács (HSP). *Health and Welfare:* Kökény Mihály (HSP). *Labour:* Péter Kiss (HSP). *Transport, Telecommunications and Water Management:* Károly Lotz (AFD). *Agriculture:* Frigyes Nagy (HSP). *Industry and Trade:* Szabolcs Fazakas (Independent). *Justice:* Pál Vastagh (HSP). *Without portfolio (Secret Services):* István Nikolits (HSP). *Without Portfolio (Privatization):* Tamas Suchman.

National anthem: 'Isten áldd meg a magyart' ('God bless the Hungarians'); words by Ferenc Kölcsey, tune by Ferenc Erkel.

Local Government. Elections were held on 11 Dec. 1994 for mayors and local councils. 3,150 seats were contested. The HSP gained 32·3% of votes cast; the AFD, 15·67%; the FYD, 9·66%; the IS, 7·99%; the CDPP, 5·77%; the HDF, 4·33%

DEFENCE. The President of the Republic is C.-in-C. of the armed forces. Men between the ages of 18 and 23 are liable for 9 months' conscription.

Army. Hungary is divided into 4 army districts: Budapest, Debrecen, Kiskunfélegyháza, Pécs. The strength of the Army was (1997) 31,600 (including 19,000 conscripts). It is organized in 3 tank, 7 mechanized, 3 artillery, 1 engineer, 1 air defence artillery, 1 (Budapest) rivercraft and 1 anti-tank brigade, and 1 multiple rocket launcher, 2 anti-tank, 4 engineer and 2 air defence artillery regiments.

There are also 730 border guards.

Navy. The Danube Flotilla, the maritime wing of the Army, in 1996 consisted of some 300 personnel operating 6 river minesweepers and numerous boats and special-purpose vessels.

Air Force. The Air Force is under the control of the Army General Staff, with a strength (1996) of 17,500 (11,200 conscripts). The combat aircraft strength comprises 1 regiment of MiG-21 and MiG-23 fighters, 1 of MiG-29 interceptors and 1 of MiG-21 and Su-22 fighter-bombers and a regiment of Mi-8 and Mi-24 armed helicopters. Transport units are equipped with An-26 and L-410 aircraft. Other types in service include Mi-8/17 helicopters and L-39 Albatros and Yak-52 trainers.

In addition, 'Guideline' and 'Goa' surface-to-air missiles are operational.

INTERNATIONAL RELATIONS

Membership. Hungary is a member of the UN, Council of Europe, OECD, the Central European Initiative and the NATO Partnership for Peace, and is an Associate Member of the EU and an Associate Partner of the WEU. In April 1994 Hungary applied to join the EU.

ECONOMY

Policy. Privatization based on free market principles has been at the centre of economic policy since 1990. In 1995 the State Property Agency and the State Holding Company were merged in a new body charged with extending the private sector's share of former state assets to 80%. Legislation of June 1991 provides for compensating former owners or their descendants for property nationalized after May 1939. A Small Shareholder Programme of Privatization was launched in April 1994. Growing debt and balance of payments gap forced a Stabilization Programme.

Performance. Real GDP growth was estimated at 3% in 1997. The unemployment rate was estimated at 10·6% of a working population of 3·6m. (2·0m. males, 1·6m. females).

Budget. The budget for calendar years was as follows (in 1,000 forints):

	1995	1996
Revenue	1,811,247	2,287,536
Expenditure	1,968,375	2,206,101

Currency. A decree of 26 July 1946 instituted a new monetary unit, the *forint* (HUF) of 100 *fillér*. There are coins of 10, 20 and 50 fillér and 1, 2, 5, 10, 20 forints, and notes of 50, 100, 500, 1,000, 5,000 and 10,000 forints. The forint was made fully convertible in Jan. 1991. In 1996–97 the forint was devalued at a crawling peg exchange rate of 1·2% a month. Foreign exchange reserves were US$10,500m. in 1996. Annualized inflation was 21% in 1996.

Banking and Finance. In 1987 a two-tier system was established. The National Bank (*Director,* György Surányi) remained the central state financial institution, responsible for the circulation of money and foreign currency exchange, but also became a central clearing bank, with general (but not operational) control over commercial banks and development banks. There are over 40 commercial banks and 20 insurance companies based in Budapest. A law of June 1991 sets capital and reserve requirements, and provides for foreign investment in Hungarian banks. Permission is needed for investments of more than 10%. Privatization of the banking system is well under way.

The Hungarian International Trade Bank opened in London in 1973. In 1980 the Central European International Bank was set up in Budapest with 7 Western banks holding 66% of the shares. The National Savings Bank handles local government as well as personal accounts. Total savings deposits in 1994, 951,900m. forints.

A stock exchange was opened in Budapest in Jan. 1989.

Weights and Measures. The metric system is in use.

ENERGY AND NATURAL RESOURCES

Electricity. Installed capacity in 1991 was 6,403 mW (1,655 mW nuclear; 46 mW hydro-electric). There is an 880-mW nuclear power station at Paks which produced 41% of total output in 1995. 34,037m. kWh were produced in 1995 (14,026m. kWh by nuclear power), and 3,210m. kWh imported.

Oil and Gas. Oil and natural gas are found in the Szeged basin and Zala county. Production in 1995: Oil, 1,669,000 tonnes; gas, 5,365m. cu. metres.

Minerals. Production in 1995 (in 1,000 tonnes): Lignite, 7,153; brown coal, 6,458; hard coal (1994), 940; bauxite, 1,015.

Agriculture. Agriculture contributed 11% of GDP in 1992. Agricultural land was collectivized in 1950. It was announced in 1990 that land would be restored to its pre-collectivization owners if they wished to cultivate it. A law of April 1994 restricts the area of land that may be bought by individuals to 300 ha, and prohibits the sale of arable land and land in conservation zones to companies and foreign nationals. Today, although 90% of all cultivated land is in private hands, most farms are little more than smallholdings.

In 1996 the agricultural area was (in 1,000 ha) 6,179, of which 4,716 were arable, 1,148 meadows and pastures, 90 market gardens, and 225 orchards and vineyards.

Corn production dropped from 8·6m. tonnes in 1989 to below 6m. tonnes between 1994 and 1996. The annual maize yield has declined from 7m. tonnes to 3·5-4m. tonnes, potatoes from 0·9 to 0·6m. tonnes, and fruit from 1·6 to 1·3m. tonnes.

Livestock has drastically decreased since 1989 from 8·8m. pigs to 5m., from 1·8m. cattle to 1m., and from 1·9m. sheep to 1·5m. Thus the pig stock has declined to the 1938 level, the cattle stock to the 1945 level and the sheep stock to a level of the early 1930s.

The north shore of Lake Balaton and the Tokaj area are important wine-producing districts. Wine production in 1995 was 329m. litres.

Forestry. The forest area was 1,763,000 ha in 1995. 32,000 ha were afforested and 8·33m. cu. metres of timber were cut in 1989.

Fisheries. There are fisheries in the rivers Danube and Tisza and Lake Balaton. In 1993 there were 27,100 ha of commercial fishponds. Fish production was 23,404 tonnes.

INDUSTRY. In 1995 there were 18,921 limited liability companies, 1,475 co-operative societies and 81,433 individual businesses.

Output growth in 1996 saw highly variable trends among the individual sectors of the manufacturing industry. The most dynamic sector continues to be the engineering industry (116·3%). Its performance was driven by the 35·6 increase in exports. The manufacturing of non-ferrous mineral products went up by1·2% (exports rose by 11·1%). With the exception of the engineering industry and manufacturing of non-ferrous mineral products the output of each sector of manufacturing industry declined: the textile and clothing industry by 4·2% and chemical industry by 0·6%. Within this, the domestic sales of the textile and clothing industry dropped by 8·5% and that of the chemical industry by 6·7%, while the exports of both sectors rose (by 3·7% and 35·6%, respectively).

Labour. In 1995 the workforce (in 1,000) was 6,251·4, of whom 6,082 (2,918·5 females) were of working age. The economically active population was 4,564·8 (2,181·4 females) of whom 3,636·4 were active earners. Persons employed, 4,045·2. Employed persons by sector, 1995 (in 1,000, women in parentheses): Mining, manu-facturing, electricity, 1,029·4 (453); building, 190·5 (37·8); agriculture and forestry,

348·2 (108·4); transport and telecommunications, 333·2 (113·6); commerce, 550·8 (280); personal and business services, 394·4 (185·3); health, social and cultural services, 810·1 (593·7); public administration, 285 (131·7). Average monthly wages in 1995: 38,900 forints. Minimum monthly wage, 1996, 14,500 forints. The 10·9% unemployment rate in 1995 dropped to 10·6% by the end of 1996. In 1996, wage costs remained within originally set limits, resulting in a decrease of 5% in real wages. However, real wages increased 5% in the first half of 1997. Retirement age: Men, 60; women, 55.

Trade Unions. The former official Communist organization (National Council of Trade Unions), renamed the Confederation of Hungarian Trade Unions (MSZOSZ), groups 70 organizations and claimed 1m. members in 1993. A law of 1991 abolished its obligatory levy on pay packets; its assets derived from this period are to be distributed to other unions. Other unions are grouped in 6 federations (with 1993 membership): the Association of Autonomous Trade Unions (ASZOK, 0·3m.); Coalition of Christian Trade Unions (KESZOSZ, 0·15m.); Co-operation Forum of Trade Unions (SZEF, 0·5m.); Council of Intellectual Trade Unions (ÉSZT, 0·1m.); League of Independent Trade Unions (Liga, 0·25m.); Works Councils (60,000).

Social security benefits are administered jointly by elected representatives of trade unions and employers' organizations.

FOREIGN ECONOMIC RELATIONS. Hungary is a member of CEFTA, along with the Czech Republic, Poland, Slovakia and Slovenia. Foreign debt was US$31,820m. in 1996. At the end of 1995, foreign investments totalled US$11,500m. An import surcharge imposed in March 1995 was abolished in July 1997.

Commerce. In 1996, the value of exports was US$16 billion and that of imports US$18·6 billion; growth exceeded that of the previous year by 12 per cent in both cases. The trade deficit, including customs-free zones, totalled US$ 2·6 billion in 1996. In the first 8 months of 1997 exports totalled US$11·6 billion, 16% up on 1996, imports amounted to US$13·3 billion (15·2% up) while the trade balance showed a deficit of US$1·7 billion. 80% of exports go to OECD counties with EU members taking a 71% share. The share of CEFTA and CIS countries is around 7% each.

Tourism. In 1995, 39·2m. foreigners visited Hungary, of whom 20·7m. were tourists, and 13·1m. Hungarians travelled abroad. Revenue from foreign tourists in 1996 was US$2·2 billion.

COMMUNICATIONS

Roads. In 1995 there were 30,023 km of roads, including motorways, 293 km; highways, 85 km and other first class main roads, 2,054 km. Passenger cars numbered (1995) 2,245,000, trucks, vans and special-purpose vehicles, 292,000; buses, 20,000 and motorcycles, 157,327. 40·9m. tonnes of freight and 494·7m. passengers were transported by road in 1994 (excluding intra-urban passengers). In 1995 there were 19,817 road accidents with 589 fatalities.

Railways. Route length of public lines in 1995, 7,610 km, of which 2,283 km were electrified. 46·4m. tonnes of freight and 154·2m. passengers were carried. There is a metro in Budapest (30·1 km), and tram/light rail networks in Budapest (161·2 km), Debrecen, Miskolc and Szeged.

Civil Aviation. Budapest airport (Ferihegy) handled 2·94m. passengers in 1995. The national carrier is Malév, 65% state-owned, which carried 1·62m. passengers in 1995. Malév had 6 B-737-200 Advs, 4 B-737-300s, 2 B-737-400s, 2 B-767-200ERs and 11 ex-Soviet aircraft in 1995. Services are also provided by Aeroflot, Air France, Air Malta, Air Moldova, Air Ukraine, Alitalia, Austrian Airlines, Balkan, British Airways, Czech Airlines, Delta, Egyptair, El Al, Finnair, Kazakhstan Airlines, KLM, Libyan Airlines, Lithuanian Airlines, LOT, Lufthansa, Northwest Airlines, Sabena, SAS, Swissair, Syrian Airlines, Tarom, Tunis Air and United Airlines.

Shipping. Navigable waterways had (1993) a length of 1,622 km. In 1994 there were 3 sea-going ships. River craft included: Passenger ships, 63; tugs, 35; self-propelled barges and other ships, 21; barges, 170. In 1995, 3·52m. tonnes of cargo and 2·38m. passengers were carried. The Hungarian Shipping Company (MAHART) has agencies at Amsterdam, Alexandria, Algiers, Beirut, Rijeka and Trieste. It has 3 sea-going ships.

Telecommunications. In 1995 there were 2,599 post offices, 2,119,900 telephones, (1,711,500 private), and (1994) 9,275 telex subscribers. The government network *Magyar Rádió* broadcasts 4 programmes on medium-waves and FM and also regional programmes, including transmissions in German, Romanian and Serbo-Croat. There are 2 other networks, one of them commercial, and 2 further commercial channels were scheduled to start transmitting on 1 Sept. 1997. *Magyar Televizió* operates 2 TV channels (colour by PAL). *Duna Televizió* broadcasts to Hungarians abroad. In 1996 there were 31 independent radio and 26 independent TV stations. There were 6m. radios and 4,261,600 TV sets in use in 1993.

Cinemas (1995). There were 595 cinemas; attendance, 14m. 17 full-length feature films were made in 1994.

Press. In 1995 there were 12 national dailies with a combined circulation of 1,023m. copies, and 19 regional dailies (897m.). There were 28 weeklies. 8,749 book titles were published in 1995 in 62·98m. copies.

SOCIAL INSTITUTIONS

Justice. The administration of justice is the responsibility of the Procurator-General, elected by Parliament for 6 years. There are 111 local courts, 20 labour law courts, 20 county courts, 6 district courts and a Supreme Court. Criminal proceedings are dealt with by the regional courts through 3-member councils and by the county courts and the Supreme Court in 5-member councils. A new Civil Code was adopted in 1978 and a new Criminal Code in 1979.

Regional courts act as courts of first instance; county courts as either courts of first instance or of appeal. The Supreme Court acts normally as an appeal court, but may act as a court of first instance in cases submitted to it by the Public Prosecutor. All courts, when acting as courts of first instance, consist of 1 professional judge and 2 lay assessors, and, as courts of appeal, of 3 professional judges. Local government Executive Committees may try petty offences.

Regional and county judges and assessors are elected by the appropriate local councils; members of the Supreme Court by Parliament.

The Office of Ombudsman was instituted in 1993. He or she is elected by parliament for a 6-year term, renewable once.

There are also military courts of the first instance. Military cases of the second instance go before the Supreme Court.

The death penalty was abolished in Oct. 1990.

70,787 sentences were imposed on adults in 1994, including 21,404 of imprisonment. There were 14,321 juvenile offenders and 12,455 persons were in prison in 1995.

Religion. Church-state affairs are regulated by a law of Feb. 1990 which guarantees freedom of conscience and religion and separates church and state by prohibiting state interference in church affairs. Religious matters are the concern of the Department for Church Relations, under the auspices of the Prime Minister's Office. State aid to all churches was 2,800m. forints in 1993.

In 1995 67·5% of the population aged 14 and over were Roman Catholic, 20% Calvinist and 5% Lutheran.

The Primate of Hungary is Archbishop László Paskai, appointed Aug. 1986. There are 11 dioceses, all with bishops or archbishops. There is one Uniate bishopric.

In 1993 there were estimated to be 7m. Roman Catholics, 1·9m. Calvinists and 0·43m. Lutherans. 47 other sects had registered as churches. There were 4 Orthodox denominations with 40,000 members in 1979. The Unitarian Church had 10,000 members, 11 ministers and 6 churches. In 1991 there were 100,000 Jews (444,567 in 1937) with 136 synagogues, 26 rabbis and a rabbinical college which enrols 10 students a year.

Education. Education is free and compulsory from 6 to 14. Primary schooling ends at 14; thereafter education may be continued at secondary, secondary technical or secondary vocational schools, which offer diplomas entitling students to apply for higher education, or at vocational training schools which offer tradesmen's diplomas. Students at the latter may also take the secondary school diploma examinations after 2 years of evening or correspondence study. Optional religious education was introduced in schools in 1990.

In 1995–96 there were 4,720 kindergartens with 32,320 teachers and 399,300 pupils; 3,809 primary schools with 86,891 teachers and 974,800 pupils; 936 secondary schools with 28,684 teachers and 349,300 pupils; 197 schools for special needs with 41,924 pupils and 6,433 teachers, and 349 trade training schools, with 154,300 apprentices and 5,899 teachers and instructors. In 1994–95 there were 317 vocational training schools with 1,305 teachers and 22,241 trainees. In 1994–95 there were 91 higher education institutions, including 6 universities (Budapest, Pécs, Szeged, Debrecen, Miskolc and Veszprém). At these there were 18,098 teachers and 129,500 full-time students.

Schools for ethnic minorities, 1994–95: Kindergartens, 355, with 19,070 pupils and 882 teachers; primary schools, 397, with 49,679 pupils and 1,210 teachers; secondary schools, 18, with 4,348 pupils and 430 teachers.

Of nearly 2·5m. minors (aged 0–18), 40% live in poverty.

Health. In 1994 there were 41,562 doctors and dentists, 98,453 hospital beds and 1,479 pharmacies.

Social Security. Since 1993 social security and retirement pensions have been administered by the Social Security Administration, composed of members elected from the employers' organizations and trade unions (*which see*). Medical treatment is free. Patients bear 15% of the cost of medicines. Sickness benefit is 75% of wages, old age pensions (at 60 for men, 55 for women) 60–70%. In 1995, 582,200m. forints were paid out in pensions to 2·98m. pensioners (including old age, 1·6m.; disabled, 0·75m.; widows, 0·22m.). In 1995, 100,200m. forints in family allowances were paid to 1·4m. families on behalf of 2·36m. children. Monthly allowances (in forints) are: One child, 2,750; two, 3,250; three and more, 3,750 (more for single parents).

DIPLOMATIC REPRESENTATIVES

Of Hungary in Great Britain (35 Eaton Pl., London, SW1X 8BY)
Ambassador: Gábor Szentiványi.

Of Great Britain in Hungary (Harmincad Utca 6, Budapest 1051)
Ambassador: Christopher Long, CMG.

Of Hungary in the USA (3910 Shoemaker St., NW, Washington, D.C., 20008)
Ambassador: György Bánlaki.

Of the USA in Hungary (Szabadság Tér 12, Budapest V)
Ambassador: Donald M. Blinken.

Of Hungary to the United Nations
Ambassador: André Erdös.

Of Hungary to the European Union
Ambassador: Endre Juhász.

Further Reading

Central Statistical Office. *Statisztikai Évkönyv.* Annual since 1871.—*Magyar Statisztikai Zsebkönyv.* Annual.—*Statistical Yearbook.*—*Statistical Handbook of Hungary.*—*Monthly Bulletin of Statistics.*
Bako, E., *Guide to Hungarian Studies.* 2 vols. Stanford Univ. Press, 1973
Batt, J., *Economic Reform and Political Change in Eastern Europe: a Comparison of the Czechoslovak and Hungarian Experiences.* Basingstoke, 1988
Bölöny, J., *Magyarország Kormányai, 1848–1975.* Budapest, 1978. [Lists governments and politicians]

Bozóki, A., *et al.* (eds.) *Post-Communist Transition: Emerging Pluralism in Hungary.* London, 1992

Brown, D. M., *Towards a Radical Democracy: the Political Economy of the Budapest School.* Cambridge, 1988

Burawoy, M. and Lukács, J., *The Radiant Past: Ideology and Reality in Hungary's Road to Capitalism.* Chicago Univ. Press, 1992

Cox, T. and Furlong, A. (eds.) *Hungary: the Politics of Transition.* London, 1995

Geró, A., *Modern Hungarian Society in the Making: the Unfinished Experience*; translated from Hungarian. Budapest, 1995

Hann, C. M. (ed.), *Market Economy and Civil Society in Hungary.* London, 1990

Kabdebó, T., *Hungary.* [Bibliography] Oxford and Santa Barbara (CA), 1980

Kornai, J., *The Road to a Free Economy: Shifting from a Socialist System—the Example of Hungary.* New York and London, 1990

Lendvai, P., *Hungary: the Art of Survival.* London, 1989

Macartney, C. A., *Hungary: A Short History.* London, 1962

Mitchell, K. D. (ed.) *Political Pluralism in Hungary and Poland: Perspectives on the Reforms.* New York, 1992

Sugar, P. F. (ed.) *A History of Hungary.* London, 1991

Szekely, I. P., *Hungary: an Economy in Transition.* CUP, 1993

National statistical office: Központi Statisztikai Hivatal/Central Statistical Office, Keleti Károly u. 5/7, H-1024 Budapest. *Director:* Dr György Vukovich.

Website: Hungarian Central Statistics Office http://www.ksh.hu/
National library: Széchenyi Library, Budapest.

ICELAND

Lyðveldið Ísland

(Republic of Iceland)

Capital: Reykjavík
Population: 269,727
GDP per head: (PPP$) 20,566
HDI/world rank: 0·942/5

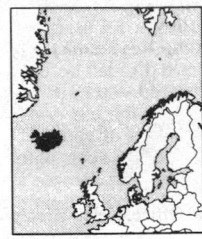

KEY HISTORICAL EVENTS. The first settlers came to Iceland in 874. Between 930 and 1262 Iceland was an independent republic, but by the 'Old Treaty' of 1262 the country recognized the rule of the King of Norway. In 1380 Iceland, together with Norway, came under the rule of the Danish kings, but when Norway was separated from Denmark in 1814, Iceland remained under the rule of Denmark. Since 1 Dec. 1918 it has been acknowledged as a sovereign state. It was united with Denmark only through the common sovereign until it was proclaimed an independent republic on 17 June 1944 following a referendum favouring severance from the Danish crown.

TERRITORY AND POPULATION. Iceland is an island in the North Atlantic, close to the Arctic Circle. Area, 103,000 sq. km (39,758 sq. miles).

There are 8 regions:

Region	Inhabited land (sq. km)	Mountain pasture (sq. km)	Waste-land (sq. km)	Total area (sq. km)	Popula-tion (1 Dec. 1996)
Capital area	} 1,266	716	–	1,982	{ 161,241
Southwest Peninsula					15,655
West	5,011	3,415	275	8,711	14,007
Western Peninsula	4,130	3,698	1,652	9,470	8,865
Northland West	4,867	5,278	2,948	13,093	9,995
Northland East	9,890	6,727	5,751	22,368	26,659
East	} 16,921	17,929	12,555	{ 21,991	12,680
South				25,214	20,625
Iceland	42,085	37,553	23,181	102,819	269,727

The census population (1980) was 229,187. In 1996, out of the population of 269,727, 21,800 were domiciled in rural districts and 247,927 in towns and villages (of over 200 inhabitants). Population density (1995), 2·6 per sq. km.

The population is almost entirely Icelandic. In 1996 foreigners numbered 5,148 (953 Danish, 576 US, 324 British, 288 Norwegian, 298 German).

The capital, Reykjavík, had on 1 Dec. 1996, a population of 105,458; other towns were: Akranes, 5,074; Akureyri, 115,015; Bolungarvík, 1,097; Dalvík, 1,505; Eskifjörður, 1,039; Garðabær, 7,831; Grindavík, 2,169; Hafnarfjörður, 17,935; Húsavík, 2,514; Ísafjörður, 3,042; Keflavík, 7,629; Kópavogur, 18,550; Neskaupstaður, 1,606; Njarðvík, 2,602; Ólafsfjörður, 1,168; Sauðárkrókur, 2,763; Selfoss, 4,216; Seltjarnarnes, 4,559; Seyðisfjörður, 831; Siglufjörður, 1,668; Vestmannaeyjar, 4,749.

Vital statistics for calendar years:

	Living births	Still-born	Marriages	Divorces	Deaths	Infant deaths	Net immigration
1994	4,442	15	1,310	489	1,717	14	760
1995	4,280	8	1,238	472	1,923	26	1,418
1996	4,329	22	1,371 (21 same sex)	530	1,879	16	1,418

Life expectancy (1995–96): Males, 76·5 years; females, 80·6.
The official language is Icelandic.

CLIMATE. The climate is cool temperate oceanic and rather changeable, but mild for its latitude because of the Gulf Stream and prevailing S.W. winds. Precipitation is high in upland areas, mainly in the form of snow. Reykjavík. Jan. 34°F (1°C), July 52°F (11°C). Annual rainfall 34" (860 mm).

CONSTITUTION AND GOVERNMENT. The President is elected by direct, popular vote for a period of 4 years. Presidential elections were held on 29 June 1996. The electorate was 195,000. Ólafur Ragnar Grímsson (b. 1943) was elected against 3 opponents and sworn in 1 Aug 1996.

An electoral law of 1984 provides for an *Alþingi* (parliament) of 63 members. Of these, 54 seats are distributed among the 8 constituencies as follows: 14 seats are allotted to Reykjavík, 8 to Reykjanes (i.e. the South-west excluding Reykjavík) and 5 or 6 to each of the remaining 6. From the 9 seats then left, 8 are divided before-hand among the constituencies according to the number of registered voters in the preceding elections. Finally, one seat is given to a constituency after the elections, to compensate the party with the fewest seats as compared to its number of votes.

At the elections on 8 April 1995 the Independence Party (IP) gained 25 seats with 37·1% of votes cast, the Progressive Party (PP) 15 with 23·3%, the People's Alliance 9 with 14·3%, the Social Democratic Party 7 with 11·4%, the People's Movement 4 with 7·2% and the Women's Alliance 3 with 4·9%.

An IP-PP coalition government was formed on 22 April 1995 which in March 1998 comprised:

Prime Minister, Minister for the Statistical Bureau: Davíð Oddsson (IP).

Foreign Affairs and Foreign Trade: Halldór Ásgrímsson (PP). *Finance:* Friðrik Sophusson (IP). *Social Affairs.* Páll Pétursson (PP). *Fisheries, Justice and Church:* Þorsteinn Pálsson (IP). *Agriculture and Environment:* Guðmundur Bjarnason (PP). *Health and Social Security:* Ingibjörg Pálmádottir (PP). *Education and Culture:* Björn Bjarnason (PP). *Trade and Industry:* Finnur Ingólfsson (PP). *Communications:* Halldór Blöndal (IP).

National anthem: 'Ó Guð vors lands' ('Oh God of Our Country'); words by M. Jochumsson, tune by S. Sveinbjörnsson.

Local Government. Iceland was on 1 Dec. 1995 divided into 170 communes, of which 31 had the status of a town. The commune councils are elected by universal suffrage, in towns and other urban communes by proportional representation, in rural communes by simple majority. For general co-operation the communes are free to form district councils. All the communes except 10 towns are members in 20 district councils. The communes appoint one or more representatives to the district councils according to their population size. The commune councils are supervised by the Ministry of Social Affairs. In 1992 the government administration and the jurisdictional system at local level were fundamentally reformed, so that the jurisdictional power was totally separated from the executive power, resulting in a new division of responsibilities and functions between the magistrates and the district courts. For national government there are 27 divisions exercised by the magistrates.

Municipal elections were held on 28 May 1994.

DEFENCE. Iceland possesses no armed forces. Under the North Atlantic Treaty, US forces are stationed in Iceland as the Iceland Defence Force. 3 armed offshore patrol craft and 1 smaller vessel for fishery protection are maintained by the National Coastguard, with 1 patrol aircraft and 1 helicopter. Coastguard Service personnel (1996), 120.

INTERNATIONAL RELATIONS

Membership. Iceland is a member of the UN, EFTA, OECD, the Council of Europe, NATO and the Nordic Council, and is an Associate Member of the WEU. Iceland has acceded to the Schengen Accord, which abolishes border controls between Iceland and Austria, Belgium, Denmark, Finland, France, Germany, Greece, Italy, Luxembourg, Norway, Portugal, Spain and Sweden.

ECONOMY

Budget. Total revenue and expenditure for calendar years (in 1m. kr.):

	1991	*1992*	*1993*	*1994*	*1995*	*1996*
Revenue	99,953	103,447	103,220	109,602	114,413	127,735
Expenditure	112,487	110,607	112,863	116,986	123,344	139,730

Central government debt was, on 31 Dec. 1996, 239,246m. kr, of which the foreign debt amounted to 132,218m. kr.

Currency. The unit of currency is the *króna* (ISK) of 100 *aurar*, (singular: *eyrir*). There are coins of 1, 5, 10, 50 and 100 kr. and notes of 500, 1,000, 2,000 and 5,000 kr. Foreign exchange markets were deregulated on 1 Jan. 1992. Note and coin circulation, 31 Dec. 1995, was 5,111m. kr. The krona was devalued 7·5% in June 1993.

Banking and Finance. The Central Bank of Iceland (founded 1961; *Governor:* Birgir Ísleifur Gunnarsson) is responsible for note issue and carries out the central banking functions which before 1961 were carried out by The National Bank of Iceland (owned entirely by the State), currently the largest commercial bank. There are 2 other commercial banks, 1 state-owned. Banking is being deregulated in stages.

On 31 Dec. 1996 the accounts of the Central Bank balanced at 60,026m. kr. Commercial bank deposits were 137,923m. kr. and deposits in the 29 savings banks, 36,246m. kr.

There is a stock exchange.

Weights and Measures. The metric system is obligatory.

ENERGY AND NATURAL RESOURCES

Electricity. The installed capacity of public electrical power plants at the end of 1995 totalled 1,048,932 kW; installed capacity of hydro-electric plants was 879,534 kW. Total electricity production in public-owned plants in 1995 amounted to 5,112m. kWh; in privately owned plants, 5m. kWh.

Agriculture. Of the total area, about six-sevenths is unproductive, but only about 1·3% is under cultivation, which is largely confined to hay, potatoes and turnips. Arable land totals 138 ha. In 1996 the total hay crop was 2,922,058 cu. metres; the crop of potatoes, 11,214 tonnes, and of turnips, 902 tonnes. Livestock (1996): Horses, 80,518; cattle, 74,816 (milch cows, 29,854); sheep, 463,935; pigs, 3,543; poultry, 166,300. Livestock products (1996, in tonnes): Milk, 106,692; butter and dairy margarines, 1,609; 1994: Cheese, 3,351; lamb, 8,798.

Fisheries. Fishing is of vital importance to the economy. Fishing vessels at the end of 1996 numbered 808 with a gross tonnage of 195,718 and GRT of 2,281 (9 ships). Total catch in 1992, 1,567,700 tonnes; 1993, 1,699,300 tonnes; 1994, 1,510,932 tonnes; 1995, 1,605,127 tonnes; 1996, 2,055,244 tonnes.

Fishery limits were extended from 12 to 50 nautical miles in 1972 and to 200 nautical miles in 1975.

INDUSTRY. Production, 1996, in 1,000 tonnes: Aluminium, 103·9; diatomite, 25·6; fertilizer (1995), 50·6; ferro-silicon, 71; sales of cement, 88 tonnes.

Labour. In 1996 the economically active population was 147,500, of which 3·7% were unemployed. In April 1997 the unemployment rate among the working population was 3·9%.

Trade Unions. In 1995 trade union membership was 85% of the workforce.

FOREIGN ECONOMIC RELATIONS. The economy is heavily trade-dependent.

Commerce. Total value of imports (c.i.f.) and exports (f.o.b.) in 1,000 kr.:

	1992	*1993*	*1994*	*1995*	*1996*
Imports	96,895,400	91,306,600	102,571,300	113,613,600	135,994,500
Exports	87,832,900	94,657,600	112,653.800	116,606,700	125,689,800

Main exports, 1996 (in 1m. kr.): Fish, crustaceans, molluscs and preparations thereof, 81,065; non-ferrous metals, 12,104; feeding stuff for animals (excluding unmilled cereals), 10,255; iron and steel, 3,835. Main imports: Road vehicles, 10,511; petroleum and products, 10,012; other transport equipment, 6,863.

Value of trade with principal countries for 3 years (in 1,000 kr.):

	1994		1995		1996	
	Imports (c.i.f.)	Exports (f.o.b.)	Imports (c.i.f.)	Exports (f.o.b.)	Imports (c.i.f.)	Exports (f.o.b.)
Austria	692,300	153,300	651,400	138,500	836,000	124,700
Belgium	2,037,200	1,993,300	2,259,100	2,040,900	2,581,500	1,552,500
Brazil	248,900	190,800	230,900	467,600	184,900	674,900
Canada	1,069,300	1,507,200	1,090,300	1,962,900	1,240,000	1,462,100
Czech Republic	332,500	58,900	402,900	42,900	483,700	74,300
Denmark	9,232,800	7,255,000	10,693,000	9,138,800	11,357,800	9,094,100
Faroe Islands	65,200	306,100	315,400	565,300	191,300	529,400
Finland	1,946,200	1,065,900	2,092,200	577,700	2,240,700	1,206,700
France	3,543,900	8,074,200	4,823,200	7,915,200	4,457,100	8,442,500
Germany	11,508	14,403,200	12,974,400	15,923,300	14,801,500	16,229,200
Greece	107,600	935,800	101,500	925,200	75,200	840,000
Hungary	85,000	1,800	92,000	2,400	135,400	26,900
India	281,200	32,500	335,500	52,100	375,300	55,000
Ireland	991,600	191,200	1,124,000	193,500	1,383,500	167,700
Israel	78,900	43,200	55,400	34,300	102,100	80,400
Italy	3,302,400	2,621,400	3,713,100	2,386,200	4,374,000	2,402,700
Japa	4,123,900	15,737,200	4,990,600	13,232,700	5,455,500	12,369,600
Netherlands	6,431,200	1,843,700	7,770,900	3,445,400	8,116,600	4,522,300
Nigeria	–	687,200	3,400	521,900	5,700	577,600
Norway	14,672,300	3,168,900	11,565,000	3,818,500	18,396,300	4,687,000
Poland	375,900	89,900	1,459,600	112,200	2,660,600	303,400
Portugal	1,229,700	1,420,900	990,700	2,119,500	980,200	3,237,600
Russia	2,283,200	686,800	2,653,200	676,800	3,372,700	1,285,200
Spain	1,423,400	5,272,800	1,831,900	4,267,800	2,356,400	4,881,400
Sweden	7,195,000	1,179,500	7,936,300	1,519,600	9,132,100	1,620,600
Switzerland	1,267,600	1,979,900	1,359,200	2,578,900	1,995,900	2,493,300
UK	10,121,600	23,085,400	10,948,800	22,474,900	13,874,300	23,949,000
USA	9,132,800	16,183,600	9,543,500	14,359,600	12,840,400	14,708,000

Tourism. There were 200,835 visitors in 1996.

COMMUNICATIONS

Roads. On 31 Dec. 1996 the length of the public roads (including roads in towns) was 12,342 km. Of these 8,206 km were national main roads and 4,136 km were provincial roads. Total length of surfaced roads was 3,176 km. A ring road of 1,400 km runs just inland from much of the coast; about 80% of it is smooth-surfaced. Motor vehicles registered at the end of 1996 numbered 141,532, of which 126,272 were passenger cars and 15,260 trucks; there were also 1,405 motor cycles. There were 10 fatal road accidents in 1996 with 10 persons killed.

Civil Aviation. Icelandair is the national carrier. It serves 20 destinations in west Europe and 5 in the USA. In 1996 it operated 4 B-737-400s, 4 B-757-200s and 3 other aircraft. In 1996 it carried 958,786 passengers on scheduled foreign flights and 280,922 on domestic routes. There are international airports at Reykjavík and Keflavík (Leifsstöd). Services are also provided by Greenlandair, Lufthansa and SAS.

Shipping. Total registered vessels, 989 (251,943 gross tonnage and 2,589 GRT) on 31 Dec. 1996; of these, 808 were sea-going fishing vessels.

Telecommunications. At the end of 1996 the number of post offices was 94 and telephone and telegraph offices 121; number of telephone subscribers, 155,400. The government-controlled Icelandic National Broadcasting Service broadcasts 2 national and 3 regional radio programmes and 1 TV channel. 13 privately owned radio stations and 5 TV stations were in operation in 1996. At 31 Dec. 1995, 96,600 TV sets were licensed (colour by PAL).

Cinemas (capital region only) There were 29 screens in 1995; attendances totalled 1,295,085 in 1996.

Press (1995). There are 5 daily newspapers, 4 in Reykjavík, with a combined circulation of about 0·1m.

SOCIAL INSTITUTIONS

Justice. In 1992 jurisdiction in civil and criminal cases was transferred from the provincial magistrates to 8 new district courts, separating the judiciary from the prosecution. From the district courts, there is an appeal to the Supreme Court in Reykjavík, which has 8 judges.

Religion. The national church, the Evangelical Lutheran, is endowed by the state. There is complete religious liberty. The affairs of the national church are under the superintendence of a bishop. In 1995, 91·5% of the population were members of it (93·2% in 1980). 11,082 persons (4·1%) were Dissenters and 5,257 persons (1·9%) did not belong to any religious community.

Education. Primary education is compulsory and free from 6–15 years of age. Optional secondary education from 16 to 19 is also free. In 1996–97 there were about 4,600 pupils in pre-schooling, 42,100 in primary schools, 17,200 in secondary schools and 7,400 tertiary-level students in Iceland. Some 25% of tertiary-level students study abroad.

There are 2 universities, Reykjavík (founded 1911) and Akureyri (1987). Total enrolment was 5,900 students in 1996–97. There are in Reykjavík a teachers' training and a technical college, and various other specialized institutions.

Health. On 31 Dec. 1994 there were 57 hospitals with 3,960 beds, 797 doctors, 273 dentists, 1,952 nurses, and 176 pharmacists.

Social Welfare. The main body of social welfare legislation is consolidated in 6 acts:

(i) The social security legislation (a) health insurance, including sickness benefits; *(b)* social security pensions, mainly consisting of old age pension, disablement pension and widows' pension, and also children's pension; *(c)* employment injuries insurance.

(ii) The unemployment insurance legislation, where daily allowances are paid to those who have met certain conditions.

(iii) The subsistence legislation. This is controlled by municipal government, and social assistance is granted under special circumstances, when payments from other sources are not sufficient.

(iv) The tax legislation. Prior to 1988 children's support was included in the tax legislation, according to which a certain amount for each child in a family was subtracted from income taxes or paid out to the family. Since 1988 family allowances are paid directly to all children age 0-15 years. The amount is increased with the second child in the family, and children under the age of 7 get additional benefits. Single parents receive additional allowances. The amounts are linked to income.

(v) The rehabilitation legislation.

(vi) Child and juvenile guidance.

Health insurance covers the entire population. Citizenship is not demanded and there is a 6 month waiting period. Most hospitals are both municipally and state run, a few solely state run and all offer free medical help. Medical treatment out of hospitals is partly paid by the patient, the same applies to medicines, except medicines of lifelong necessary use, which are paid in full by the health insurance. Dental care is partly paid by the state for children under 17 years old and also for old age and disabled pensioners. Sickness benefits are paid to those who lose income because of periodical illness. The daily amount is fixed and paid from the 11th day of illness.

The pension system is composed of the public social security system and some 90 private pension funds. The social security system pays basic old age and disablement pensions of a fixed amount regardless of past or present income, as well as supplementary pensions to individuals with low present income. The pensions are indexlinked, i.e. are changed in line with changes in wage and salary rates in the labour market. The private pension funds pay pensions that depend on past payments of premiums that are a fixed proportion of earnings. The payment of pension fund premiums is compulsory for all wage and salary earners. The pensions paid by the funds differ considerably between the individual funds, but are generally indexlinked. In the public social security system, entitlement to old age and disablement pensions at the full rates is subject to the condition that the beneficiary has been resident in Iceland for 40 years at the age period of 16–67. For shorter period of residence, the benefits are reduced proportionally. Entitled to old age pension are all those who are 67 years old, and have been residents in Iceland for 3 years of the age period of 16–67. Entitled to disablement pension are those who have lost 75% of their working capacity and have been residents in Iceland for 3 years before application or have had full working capacity at the time when they became residents. Old age and disablement pension are of equally high amount; in the year 1996 the total sum was 160,476 kr. for an individual. Married pensioners are paid 90% of two individuals' pensions. In addition to the basic amount, supplementary allowances are paid according to social circumstances and income possibilities. Widows' pensions are the same amount as old age and disablement pension, provided the applicant is over 60 when she becomes widowed. Women at the age 50–60 get reduced pension. Women under 50 are not entitled to widows' pensions.

The employment injuries insurance covers medical care, daily allowances, disablement pension and survivors' pension and is applicable to practically all employees.

Social assistance is primarily municipal and granted in cases outside the social security legislation. Domestic assistance to old people and disabled is granted within this legislation, besides other services.

Child and juvenile guidance is performed by chosen committees according to special laws, such as home guidance and family assistance. In cases of parents' disablement the committees take over the guidance of the children involved.

DIPLOMATIC REPRESENTATIVES

Of Iceland in Great Britain (1 Eaton Terrace, London, SW1W 8EY)
Ambassador: Benedikt Ásgeirsson.

Of Great Britain in Iceland (Laufásvegur 31, 101 Reykjavík)
Ambassador and Consul-General: James Ray McCulloch.

Of Iceland in the USA (2022 Connecticut Ave., NW, Washington, D.C., 20008)
Ambassador: Jón Baldwin Hannibalsson.

Of the USA in Iceland (Laufásvegur 21, 101 Reykjavík)
Ambassador: Day Oline Mount.

Of Iceland to the United Nations
Ambassador: Gunnar Palsson.

Of Iceland to the European Union
Ambassador: Gunnar Snorri Gunnarsson.

Further Reading

Statistics Iceland, *Landshagir* (Statistical Yearbook of Iceland).—*Hagtiindi* (Monthly Statistics)
Central Bank of Iceland. *Economic Statistics Quarterly.—The Economy of Iceland.* May 1994
McBride, *Iceland.* [Bibliography] 2nd ed. Oxford and Santa Barbara (CA), 1996

National statistical office: Statistics Iceland, Skuggasund 3, IS-150 Reykjavík.
Website: http://www.statice.is/
National library: Landsbókasafn Islands.—Háskólabókasafn, Reykjavík, *Librarian:* Einar Sigursson.

INDIA

Bharat

(Republic of India)

Capital: New Delhi
Population: 913·2m
GNP: US$278·7bn.
HDI/world rank: 0·446/138

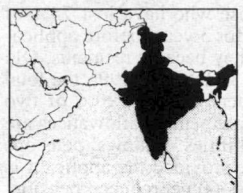

Map. Based upon Survey of India map with the permission of the Surveyor General of India. The responsibility for the correctness of internal details rests with the publisher. The territorial waters of India extend into the sea to a distance of 12 nautical miles measured from the appropriate base line. The external boundaries and coastlines of India agree with the Record/Master Copy certified by the Survey of India.

KEY HISTORICAL EVENTS. The Moghul emperors held power over most of north India and the Deccan (the central plateau of the Indian peninsula) by 1712, when the emperor Bahadur died and his sons weakened the dynasty by disputing the succession.

The power of the states within the empire then revived. The Mahratta rulers of central and western India were led by Shahu; it was he who created the hereditary office of chief minister (*peshwa*) and after his death in 1749 the *peshwas* became the effective rulers of the Mahratta states. In the Deccan, the Moghuls' viceroy of Hyderabad declared himself independent, becoming the founder of the Moslem dynasty of Nizams of Hyderabad. In the north-west in 1739 the Moghuls lost the Punjab to the Persians (who later lost it to the Afghans).

South of Hyderabad were the independent Hindu states of Mysore and Travancore, a number of small principalities and the territory around Madras where the British East India Company was the most powerful force. The Company had maintained a factory at Madras since 1639 and had since established other bases at Bombay (1668) and at Calcutta in Bengal.

In 1740 the Moghul governor (*nawab*) of Bengal rebelled successfully. In 1756, alarmed at the degree to which the Company (anticipating trouble with the French) was arming itself, he attacked and subdued the British base at Calcutta. In 1757 a large British force under Clive retaliated by defeating the Nawab at Plassey. The British were then able to install their own Nawab. Their hold on Bengal and Madras was soon complete and they defeated the French who presented the only serious European challenge. The East India Company thus became the rising power in India at the very time when Moghul power was in decline. Outside the remaining Moghul supremacy the other powers were the Mahrattas, the Punjab Sikhs (nominally under Afghan rule), Hyderabad and Mysore.

Mysore was a Hindu state until 1764 when the Moslem commander Hyder Ali usurped the throne. Having allied themselves to the Nizam of Hyderabad in 1766, the British attached Mysore in 1767; war was intermittent until 1799 when Hyder Ali's successor Tippoo was defeated and the Hindu dynasty restored.

In 1775 a confederacy of Mahratta chiefs, led by the chief of Pune, united against the British power spreading from Bombay and were successful. Mahadaji Sindhia emerged from the war as the leader of a Mahratta empire, to which he added the former Moghul fief of Rajputana.

In 1784 the British government imposed tighter controls on the Company by means of the India Bill.

In 1794 Mahadaji Sindhia died. His successors entered into treaty relations with the British in 1805, by which time the Moghul emperor in Delhi was under Mahratta domination. British-Mahratta relations deteriorated, however, and in 1818 the British annexed the Mahratta states and became the 'protectors' of Rajputana. In 1826 they drove the Burmese out of Assam and in 1830 they occupied Mysore.

In the north-west the Sikh ruler Ranjit Singh had driven the Afghans out of the Punjab and Kashmir by 1819. He died in 1839. Within a short time his strong state and army were highly unstable. Mutual mistrust between Sikhs and British led in 1845-46 to war, ending in British annexation of some Sikh territory. In 1848-49 a second war was fought and the whole Punjab was annexed. Nagpur and Oudh were taken in 1853 and 1856.

Since 1818 the East India Company had been the greatest power in India. Within its territory change had been rapid, and the mass of the Hindu population felt threatened by European attitudes, laws and religion. In 1857-58 there was a general rebellion, beginning with a revolt of Indian troops in the Company's army. The excesses of rebels and suppressing forces made the rebellion a national trauma for the British.

The immediate result was the India Act 1858, which transferred the Company's authority and territory to the Crown. The territory (excluding areas now forming Pakistan and Bangladesh) consisted of the Madras and Bombay presidencies; Bengal (which included Assam until 1874 when it became a separate province); the United Provinces and Oudh; the Central Provinces; the Punjab; Ajmere-Merwara; Coorg; and the Andaman Islands. The central government consisted of a viceroy and his executive, and an administrative council in England. This area under direct British rule (British *Raj*) co-existed with the independent states ruled by Indian princes; the viceroy claimed the right to interfere in the latter in emergency, and often did so.

In 1885 the Indian National Congress was founded by A. O. Hume and others, to work for more representative government. In 1892 the first Indian Councils Act added nominated Indian members to the central and provincial legislative councils.

In 1905-11 the experimental partition of Bengal into Hindu and Moslem provinces aroused violent opposition among Hindu Bengalis. This brought to the fore the question of national identity as opposed to religious identity. In 1906 the All-India Moslem League was founded to protect Moslem interests.

From 1909 there were further constitutional reforms, but the Congress thought them insufficient and began, especially after 1917, to work specifically for independence. The India Acts (1919 and 1935) defined and then revised the forms of parliamentary government. After 1930 Mohandas Gandhi led a campaign of civil disobedience for the end of British rule; his attempts at negotiation with Britain were abortive until the Second World War.

The war increased support for the independence movement, Congress being able to claim that Britain had involved India as a combatant state without consultation. In 1940, foreseeing a Hindu-dominated independent India, the Moslem League began to press for a separate Moslem state.

In June 1947 the scheme for partition was announced, after negotiations in which Gandhi had taken part. In Aug. India became independent within the Commonwealth, as a federal union of the former British provinces and the native states. Of the latter, Hyderabad had to be incorporated by force and was later dismembered.

Partition took place (*see* Pakistan), with mass movement of Hindus, Moslems and Sikhs, much violence and many deaths.

In 1950 India became a republic, within the Commonwealth, with Rajendra Prasad as the first president. In 1951 the Congress leader Pandit Nehru became prime minister, establishing a Congress domination which has lasted for all but brief periods. In 1966 his daughter Indira Gandhi became prime minister. She governed by Emergency Rule from 1975 but was defeated in the 1977 election, and re-elected again in 1979. Her son, Rajiv, succeeded her after her assassination by Sikh extremists on 31 Oct. 1984.

In 1956 the States Reorganization Act created a new structure of States and Territories with boundaries based on ethnic and language divisions.

There was an unresolved border war with China in 1962. But the status of Kashmir, disputed with Pakistan, has been the principal difficulty. The war of 1965, mediated at Tashkent by the USSR in 1966, left it divided between the two states. War again broke out when in Dec. 1971 India invaded East Pakistan and helped secure the independence of Bangladesh.

The Union was augmented by the annexation of Goa (a surviving Portuguese colony) in 1961 and of Sikkim in 1975.

In 1991 Rajiv Gandhi was assassinated by Tamil extremists after the government had imposed direct rule in Tamil Nadu. Throughout the early 1990s Hindu/Moslem violence was widespread.

TERRITORY AND POPULATION. India is bounded in the north-west by Pakistan, north by China, Tibet, Nepal and Bhutan, east by Myanmar, and south-east, south and south-west by the Indian Ocean. The far eastern states and territories are almost separated from the rest by Bangladesh. The area (excluding the Pakistan and China-occupied parts of Jammu and Kashmir) is 3,165,596 sq. km. A Sino-Indian agreement of 7 Sept. 1993 settled frontier disputes dating from the war of 1962. Population (excluding occupied Jammu and Kashmir), 1991 census: 846,302,688 (407,072,230 females; 217m. urban); density, 274 per sq. km. About 24·7% of the population was urban in 1991 (in Maharashtra, 35%; in Arunachal Pradesh, 6·6%). 1996 estimate: 913·2m. Many births and deaths go unregistered. The Registrar General's data suggests a birth rate for 1995–96 of 28·3 per 1,000 population, the death rate 9. In 1991 expectation of life was 60 years.

Marriages and divorces are not registered. The minimum age for a civil marriage is 18 for women and 21 for men; for a sacramental marriage, 14 for girls and 18 for youths.

Area and population of states and union territories:

	Area in sq. km	1991 census	Population 1994 estimate (in 1,000)	Density per sq. km
States				
Andhra Pradesh (And P)	275,045	66,508,008	71,800	261·0
Arunachal Pradesh (Arun P)	83,743	864,558	965	11·5
Assam (Ass)	78,438	22,414,322	24,200	308·5
Bihar (Bih)	173,877	86,374,465	93,080	535·3
Goa	3,702	1,169,793	1,235	333·5
Gujarat (Guj)	196,024	41,309,582	44,235	225·7
Haryana (Har)	44,212	16,463,648	17,925	405·4
Himachal Pradesh (Him P)	55,673	5,170,877	5,530	99·3
Jammu and Kashmir (J and K)[1]	100,569	7,718,700[2]	8,435	83·9
Karnataka (Kar)	191,791	44,977,201	48,150	251·1
Kerala (Ker)	38,863	29,098,518	30,555	786·3
Madhya Pradesh (MP)	443,446	66,181,170	71,950	162·2
Maharashtra (Mah)	307,713	78,937,187	85,565	278·1
Manipur (Man)	22,327	1,837,149	2,010	90·0
Meghalaya (Meg)	22,429	1,774,778	1,960	87·4
Mizoram (Miz)	21,081	689,756	775	36·7
Nagaland (Nag)	16,579	1,209,546	1,410	85·0
Orissa (Or)	155,707	31,659,736	33,795	217·0
Punjab (Pun)	50,362	20,281,969	21,695	430·8
Rajasthan (Raj)	342,239	44,005,990	48,040	140·4
Sikkim (Sik)	7,096	406,457	444	62·5
Tamil Nadu (TN)	130,058	55,858,946	58,840	452·4
Tripura (Tri)	10,486	2,757,205	3,055	291·4
Uttar Pradesh (UP)	294,411	139,112,287	150,695	511·9
West Bengal (WB)	88,752	68,077,965	73,600	829·3
Union Territories				
Andaman and Nicobar Islands (ANI)	8,249	280,661	322	39·0
Chandigarh (Chan)	114	642,015	725	6,359·7
Dadra and Nagar Haveli (DNH)	491	138,477	153	311·9
Daman and Diu (D and D)	112	101,586	111	990·7
Delhi (Del)	1,483	9,420,644	10,865	7,326·5
Lakshadweep (Lak)	32	51,707	56	1,764·2
Pondicherry (Pon)	492	807,785	894	1,816·3

[1] Excludes the area occupied by Pakistan and China.   [2] Projection.

Urban Agglomerations with populations over 1·6m., together with their core cities at the 1991 census:

	Urban Agglomeration	Core City		Urban Agglomeration	Core City
Bombay	12,596,243	9,925,891	Ahmedabad	3,312,216	2,954,526
Calcutta	11,021,915	4,309,819	Pune (Poona)	2,493,987	1,566,651
Delhi	8,419,084	7,206,704	Kanpur	2,029,889	1,879,420
Madras	5,421,985	3,841,396	Lucknow	1,669,204	1,619,115
Hyderabad	4,253,759	3,145,939	Nagpur	1,664,006	1,624,752
Bangalore	4,130,288	3,302,296			

Smaller Urban Agglomerations and cities with populations over 250,000 (with 1991 census populations, in 1,000):

Agra (UP)	892	Faridabad Complex (Har)	618	Moradabad (UP)	444
Ajmer (Raj)	403	Gaya (Bih)	292	Mysore (Kar)	481
Akola (Mah)	328	Ghaziabad (UP)	454	Nanded (Mah)	275
Aligarh (UP)	481	Gorakhpur (UP)	506	Nashik (Mah)	657
Allahabad (UP)	806	Gulbarga (Kar)	304	Nellore (And P)	316
Amravati (Mah)	422	Guntur (And P)	273	New Bombay (Mah)	308
Amritsar (Pun)	709	Guwahati (Ass)	584	New Delhi (Del)	301
Asansol (WB)	262	Gwalior (MP)	691	Panihati (WB)	276
Aurangabad (Mah)	573	Hubli-Dharwad (Kar)	648	Patna (Bih)	917
Bareilly (UP)	591	Indore (MP)	1,092	Raipur (MP)	439
Belgaum (Mah)	326	Jabalpur (MP)	742	Rajamundry (And P)	325
Bhagalpur (Bih)	253	Jaipur (Raj)	1,458	Rajkot (Raj)	559
Bhavnagar (Guj)	402	Jalandhar (Pun)	510	Ranchi (Bih)	599
Bhilainagar (MP)	386	Jamnagar (Guj)	342	Saharanpur (UP)	375
Bhiwandi (Mah)	379	Jamshedpur (Bih)	461	Salem (TN)	367
Bhopal (MP)	1,063	Jhansi (UP)	313	Sholapur (Mah)	604
Bhubaneswar (Or)	412	Jodhpur (Raj)	668	Srinagar (J and K)	595
Bikaner (Raj)	416	Kakinada (And P)	280	Surat (Guj)	1,499
Bokaro Steel City		Kharagpur (WB)	265	Thiruvananthapuram	
(Bih)	334	Kochi (Ker)	565	(Ker)	524
Chandigarh (Chan)	511	Kolhapur (Mah)	406	Tiruchirapalli (TN)	387
Coimbatore (TN)	816	Kota (Raj)	537	Udaipur (Raj)	309
Cuttack (Or)	403	Kozhikode (Ker)	420	Ujjain (MP)	362
Davangere (Kar)	266	Ludhiana (Pun)	1,043	Vadodara (Guj)	1,031
Dehra Dun (UP)	368	Madurai (TN)	941	Varanasi (UP)	932
Dhanbad (Bih)[1]	815	Malegaon (Mah)	342	Vijayawada (And P)	702
Dhule (Mah)	278	Mangalore (Kar)	273	Visakhapatnam (And P)	752
Durgapur (WB)	426	Meerut (UP)	850	Warangal (And P)	448

[1] Urban Agglomeration.

CLIMATE. India has a variety of climatic sub-divisions. In general, there are four seasons. The cool one lasts from Dec. to March, the hot season is in April and May, the rainy season is June to Sept., followed by a further dry season till Nov. Rainfall, however, varies considerably, from 4" (100 mm) in the N.W. desert to over 400" (10,000 mm) in parts of Assam.

Range of temperature and rainfall: New Delhi. Jan. 57°F (13·9°C), July 88°F (31·1°C). Annual rainfall 26" (640 mm). Bombay. Jan. 75°F (23·9°C), July 81°F (27·2°C). Annual rainfall 72" (1,809 mm). Calcutta. Jan. 67°F (19·4°C), July 84°F (28·9°C). Annual rainfall 64" (1,600 mm). Cherrapunji. Jan. 53°F (11·7°C), July 68°F (20°C). Annual rainfall 432" (10,798 mm). Darjeeling. Jan. 41°F (5°C), July 62°F (16·7°C). Annual rainfall 121" (3,035 mm). Hyderabad. Jan. 72°F (22·2°C), July 80°F (26·7°C). Annual rainfall 30" (752 mm). Kochi. Jan. 80°F (26·7°C), July 79°F (26·1°C). Annual rainfall 117" (2,929 mm). Madras. Jan. 76°F (24·4°C), July 87°F (30·6°C). Annual rainfall 51" (1,270 mm). Patna. Jan. 63°F (17·2°C), July 90°F (32·2°C). Annual rainfall 46" (1,150 mm).

CONSTITUTION AND GOVERNMENT. The Constitution was passed by the Constituent Assembly on 26 Nov. 1949 and came into force on 26 Jan. 1950. It has since been amended 85 times.

India is a republic and comprises a Union of 25 States and 7 Union Territories. Each State is administered by a Governor appointed by the President for a term of 5 years while each Union Territory is administered by the President through a Lieut.-Governor or an administrator appointed by him. The head of the Union is the *President* in whom all executive power is vested, to be exercised on the advice of ministers responsible to Parliament. The President, who must be an Indian citizen at least 35 years old and eligible for election to the House of the People, is elected by an electoral college of all the elected members of Parliament and of the state legislative assemblies, holds office for 5 years and is eligible for re-election. There is also a *Vice-President* who is *ex-officio* chairman of the Council of States.

Parliament consists of the President, the *Council of States* (*Rajya Sabha*) and the

House of the People (*Lok Sabha*). The Council of States, or the Upper House, consists of not more than 250 members; in Dec. 1996 there were 233 elected members and 5 members nominated by the President. The election to this house is indirect; the representatives of each State are elected by the elected members of the Legislative Assembly of that State. The Council of States is a permanent body not liable to dissolution, but one-third of the members retire every second year. The House of the People, or the Lower House, consists of 545 members, 543 directly elected on the basis of adult suffrage from territorial constituencies in the States, and the Union territories; in Dec. 1997 there were 541 elected members, 2 members nominated by the President to represent the Anglo-Indian community and 2 vacancies. The House of the People unless sooner dissolved continues for a period of 5 years from the date appointed for its first meeting; in emergency, Parliament can extend the term by 1 year.

State Legislatures. For every State there is a legislature which consists of the Governor, and *(a)* 2 Houses, a Legislative Assembly and a Legislative Council, in the States of Bihar, Jammu and Kashmir, Karnataka, Madhya Pradesh (where it is provided for but not in operation), Maharashtra and Uttar Pradesh, and *(b)* 1 House, a Legislative Assembly, in the other States. Every Legislative Assembly, unless sooner dissolved, continues for 5 years from the date appointed for its first meeting. In emergency the term can be extended by 1 year. Every State Legislative Council is a permanent body and is not subject to dissolution, but one-third of the members retire every second year. Parliament can, however, abolish an existing Legislative Council or create a new one, if the proposal is supported by a resolution of the Legislative Assembly concerned.

Legislation. The various subjects of legislation are enumerated in three lists in the seventh schedule to the constitution. List I, the Union List, consists of 97 subjects (including defence, foreign affairs, communications, currency and coinage, banking and customs) with respect to which the Union Parliament has exclusive power to make laws. The State legislature has exclusive power to make laws with respect to the 66 subjects in list II, the State List; these include police and public order, agriculture and irrigation, education, public health and local government. The powers to make laws with respect to the 47 subjects (including economic and social planning, legal questions and labour and price control) in list III, the Concurrent List, are held by both Union and State governments, though the former prevails. But Parliament may legislate with respect to any subject in the State List in circumstances when the subject assumes national importance or during emergencies.

Other provisions deal with the administrative relations between the Union and the States, interstate trade and commerce, distribution of revenues between the States and the Union, official language, etc.

Fundamental Rights. Two chapters of the constitution deal with fundamental rights and 'Directive Principles of State Policy'. 'Untouchability' is abolished, and its practice in any form is punishable. The fundamental rights can be enforced through the ordinary courts of law and through the Supreme Court of the Union. The directive principles cannot be enforced through the courts of law; they are nevertheless fundamental in the governance of the country.

Citizenship. Under the Constitution, every person who was on the 26 Jan. 1950, domiciled in India and *(a)* was born in India or *(b)* either of whose parents was born in India or *(c)* who has been ordinarily resident in the territory of India for not less than 5 years immediately preceding that date became a citizen of India. Special provision is made for migrants from Pakistan and for Indians resident abroad. Under the Citizenship Act, 1955, which supplemented the provisions of the Constitution, Indian citizenship is acquired by birth, by descent, by registration and by naturalization. The Act also provides for loss of citizenship by renunciation, termination and deprivation. The right to vote is granted to every person who is a citizen of India and who is not less than 18 years of age on a fixed date and is not otherwise disqualified.

Parliament. Parliament and the state legislatures are organized according to the following schedule (figures show distribution of seats in Dec. 1996):

| | Parliament | State Legislatures | |
	House of the People (Lok Sabha)	Council of States (Rajya Sabha)	Legislative Assemblies (Vidhan Sabhas)	Legislative Councils (Vidhan Parishads)
States:				
Andhra Pradesh	42	18	294	–
Arunachal Pradesh	2	1	60	–
Assam	14	7	126	–
Bihar	54	22	324	96
Goa	2	1	40	–
Gujarat	26	11	182	–
Haryana	10	5	90	–
Himachal Pradesh	4	3	68	–
Jammu and Kashmir	6	4	87[2]	36[3]
Karnataka	28	12	224	75
Kerala	20	9	140	–
Madhya Pradesh	40	16	320	–
Maharashtra	48	19	288	63
Manipur	2	1	60	–
Meghalaya	2	1	60	–
Mizoram	1	1	40	–
Nagaland	1	1	60	–
Orissa	21	10	147	–
Punjab	13	7	117	–
Rajasthan	25	10	200	–
Sikkim	1	1	32	–
Tamil Nadu	39	18	234	–
Tripura	2	1	60	–
Uttar Pradesh	85	34	425	108
West Bengal	42	16	294	–
Union Territories:				
Andaman and Nicobar Islands	1	–	–	–
Chandigarh	1	–	–	–
Dadra and Nagar Haveli	1	–	–	–
Delhi	7	3	70	–
Daman and Diu	1	–	–	–
Lakshadweep	1	–	–	–
Pondicherry	1	1	30	–
Nominated by the President under Article 80 (1) (a) of the Constitution	–	12	–	–
Total	5,45[1]	245	4,072	378[1]

[1] Includes 2 nominated members to represent Anglo-Indians.
[2] Excludes 24 seats for Pakistan-occupied areas of the State which are in abeyance.
[3] Excludes seats for the Pakistan-occupied areas.

The number of seats allotted to scheduled castes and scheduled tribes in the House of the People is 79 and 41 respectively. Out of the 4,072 seats allotted to the Legislative Assemblies, 557 are reserved for scheduled castes and 527 for scheduled tribes.

On 4 Dec. 1997 the House was dissolved and fresh elections ordered. Composition of the House of the People at dissolution: Congress (I) 138; Janata Dal, 29; Bharatiya Janata Party, 162; CPI (Marxist), 32; CPI, 12; DMK (Dravida Munnetra Kazagam), 17; Shiv Sena, 15; Samajwadi Party, 17; Rashtriya Janata Dal, 16; Revolutionary Socialist Party, 5; Bahujan Samaj Party, 11; Forward Bloc, 3; Moslem League, 2; Telugu Desam, 17; Tamil Maanila Congress (M), 20; Samata Party, 5; Shiromani Akali Dal, 8; Asom Gana Parishad, 5; Congress (T), 2; Haryana Vikas Party, 3; Independent and others, 21; nominated, 2; vacant, 2.

Composition of the Council of States in April 1997: Congress (I) 88; Communist Party of India (Marxist), 15; All-India Anna DMK, 14; Janata Dal, 23; Bharatiya Janata Party, 44; Telugu Desam (Naidu), 8; Samajwadi Party, 7; Communist Party, 6; Independent, 9; Moslem League, 2; Forward Bloc, 2; Shiv Sena, 4; Bahujan Samaj Patry, 3; J & K National Conference, 3; others, 8; nominated, 1; vacant, 8.

National anthem: 'Jana-gana-mana' ('Thou art the ruler of the minds of all people'); words and tune by Rabindranath Tagore.

Language. The Constitution provides that the official language of the Union shall be Hindi in the Devanagari script. It was originally provided that English should continue to be used for all official purposes until 1965. But the Official Languages Act 1963 provides that, after the expiry of this period of 15 years from the coming into force of the Constitution, English might continue to be used, in addition to Hindi, for all official purposes of the Union for which it was being used immediately before that day, and for the transaction of business in Parliament. According to the Official Languages (Use for official purposes of the Union) Rules 1976, an employee may record in Hindi or in English without being required to furnish a translation thereof in the other language and no employee possessing a working knowledge of Hindi may ask for an English translation of any document in Hindi except in the case of legal or technical documents.

The 58th amendment to the Constitution (26 Nov. 1987) authorized the preparation of a Constitution text in Hindi.

The following 18 languages are included in the Eighth Schedule to the Constitution (with 1994 estimate of speakers where over 5m.): Assamese (14·8m.), Bengali (68·3m.), Gujarati (44m.), Hindi (350·3m.), Kannada (35·7m.), Kashmiri, Konkani, Malayalam (34·4m.), Manipuri, Marathi (65·8m.), Nepali, Oriya (30·3m.), Punjabi (24·7m.), Sanskrit, Sindhi, Tamil (59·3m.), Telugu (71·9m.), Urdu (46·8m.).

The head of state is the *President.* There is a *Council of Ministers* to aid and advise the President; this comprises Ministers who are members of the Cabinet and Ministers of State and deputy ministers who are not. A Minister who for any period of 6 consecutive months is not a member of either House of Parliament ceases to be a Minister at the expiration of that period. The Prime Minister is appointed by the President; other Ministers are appointed by the President on the Prime Minister's advice. The salary of each Minister is Rs 27,000 per annum.

Presidential elections were held on 14 July 1997. Dr Kocheril Raman Narayanan was elected by 94·97% of votes cast against 1 opponent.

Parliamentary elections were held over 7 days from 27 April to 7 May 1996 (23 and 30 May in Jammu and Kashmir). The electorate was 590m. The Bharatiya Janata Party gained 160 seats; the Congress (I), 136. After the elections, a coalition government was formed, led by Bharatiya Janata Party with Atal Behari Vajpayee as Prime Minister. It lasted for 13 days. A 13-party Coalition government with H. D. Deve Gowda as Prime Minister took office, supported by Congress (I) from outside. When Congress (I) withdrew support in March 1997, Inder Kumar Gujral replaced Deve Gowda and formed the Government. Congress (I) again withdrew support in Nov. 1997 and the Gujral government resigned. The President accepted the resignation and dissolved the House of the People and ordered elections with Gujral heading the caretaker government. The elections were due to take place over a 3-week period between 16 Feb. and 7 March 1998.

President: Dr Kocheril Raman Narayanan (b. 1920; sworn in 25 July 1997).
Vice-President: Krishan Kant (elected 16 Aug. 1997).

The 13-party coalition government was composed as follows in March 1998:
Prime Minister: Inder Kumar Gujral (b. 1919; Janata Dal; sworn in 19 April 1997).
Portfolios held by the Prime Minister assisted by Ministers of State: *External Affairs, Personnel, Public Grievances and Pensions, Atomic Energy and Electronics, Ocean Development and Space, Health and Family Welfare, Planning and Programme Implementation, Jammu and Kashmir Affairs.*

Human Resources Development: S. R. Bommai. *Agriculture, excluding Animal Husbandry and Dairying:* Chaturanan Mishra. *Home Affairs:* Indrajit Gupta. *Rural Areas and Employment:* Yarran Naidu. *Industry:* Murasoli Maran. *Welfare:* Balwant Singh Ramoowalia. *Civil Aviation:* C. M. Ibrahim. *Petroleum and Natural Gas:* Janeshwar Mishra. *Parliamentary Affairs and Tourism:* Srikant Jena. *Finance and Company Affairs:* Palaniappan Chidambaram. *Chemicals and Fertilizers:* M. Arunachalam. *Communications:* Beni Prasad Verma. *Defence:* Mulayam Singh Yadav. *Railways:* Ram Vilas Paswan. *Steel and Mines:* Birendra Prasad Baishya.

Surface Transport: T. G. Venkataraman. *Environment and Forests:* Saifuddin Soz. *Information and Broadcasting:* S. Jaipal Reddy. *Textiles:* R. L. Jalappa.

There were also 9 Ministers of State with independent responsibilities and 12 Ministers of State.

Singh, V. B., *Elections in India: Data Handbook on Lok Sabha Elections, 1986–91.* Delhi, 1994
Thakur, R., *The Government and Politics of India.* London, 1995

Local Government. There were in 1989-90, 72 municipal corporations, 1,770 municipal committees/boards/councils, 663 town area committees and 337 notified area committees. The municipal bodies have the care of the roads, water supply, drainage, sanitation, medical relief, vaccination, education, street lighting, etc. Their main sources of revenue are taxes on the annual rental value of land and buildings, octroi and terminal, vehicle and other taxes. The municipal councils enact their own bye-laws and frame their budgets, which in the case of municipal bodies other than corporations generally require the sanction of the State government. All municipal councils are elected on the principle of adult franchise.

For rural areas there is a 3-tier system of *panchayati raj* at village, block and district level, although the 3-tier structure may undergo some changes in State legislation to suit local conditions. All *panchayati raj* bodies are organically linked, and representation is given to special interests. Elected directly by and from among villagers, the *panchayats* are responsible for agricultural production, rural industries, medical relief, maternity and child welfare, common grazing grounds, village roads, tanks and wells, and maintenance of sanitation. In some places they also look after primary education, maintenance of village records and collection of land revenue. They have their own powers of taxation. There are judicial *panchayats* or village courts.

Panchayati raj now cover almost all the States and Union Territories with variations in structural pattern. *Panchayati raj* involves a 3-tier arrangement: Village level, block level and district level. Tenure of *Panchayati raj* institutions range from 3–5 years.

The powers and responsibilities of *Panchayati raj* institutions are derived from State Legislatures, and from the executive orders of State governments.

DEFENCE. The Supreme Command of the Armed Forces vests in the President. Policy is decided at different levels by a number of committees, including the Political Affairs Committee presided over by the Prime Minister and the Defence Minister's Committee. Administrative and operational control rests in the respective Service Headquarters, under the control of the Ministry of Defence.

Army. The Army Headquarters functioning directly under the Chief of the Army Staff is divided into the following main branches: General Staff Branch; Adjutant General's Branch; Quartermaster-General's Branch; Master-General of Ordnance Branch; Engineer-in-Chief's Branch; Military Secretary's Branch.

The Army is organized into 5 commands each divided into areas, which in turn are subdivided into sub-areas.

The strength of the Army was (1997) 980,000. There are 3 armoured, 17 infantry and 10 mountain divisions and 5 independent armoured, 7 independent infantry, 3 independent artillery, 1 parachute, 1 mountain, 16 air defence and 3 engineer brigades, and 1 surface-to-surface missile regiment. An Aviation Corps operates 150 locally-built Alouette and Lama helicopters.

Equipment includes some 700 T-55, 1,100 T-72/-M1 and 1,700 Vijayanta main battle tanks.

Navy. The Navy has 3 commands; Eastern, Western and Southern, the latter a training and support command. The fleet is divided into 2 elements, Eastern and Western; and well-trained, all-volunteer personnel operate a mix of Soviet and Western vessels.

The principal ship is the light aircraft carrier, *Viraat*, formerly HMS *Hermes*, of 29,000 tonnes, completed in 1959 and transferred to the Indian Navy in 1987. *Viraat* embarks an air group of 12 Sea Harrier fighters and 6 Sea King anti-submarine helicopters. The *Vikrant* was decommissioned on 31 Jan. 1997.

The fleet includes 8 'Kilo' and 1 'Foxtrot' Soviet-built diesel submarines and 4 smaller new German-designed boats. 5 Soviet-built missile-armed destroyers, 3 heavily modified and 6 rather less modified 'Leander' class frigates, all built in India, together with 1 ex-British Batch 3 Leander class and 9 other Soviet-type frigates form the main surface force. Coastal forces include 14 Soviet-designed missile and 4 anti-submarine corvettes, 6 fast missile craft, 7 offshore and 10 inshore patrol craft. There are 12 Soviet-built offshore minesweepers, and 8 much smaller inshore vessels. Amphibious lift for the 1,000 strong marine force is provided by 1 tank landing ship and 8 medium landing ships, as well as about 8 craft. Support forces include 1 tanker, 1 submarine depot ship, 1 transport, 10 survey and research ships, 2 tugs and 1 training ship.

The Naval Air force, 5,000 strong, operates 20 Sea Harriers, 5 Il-38 'May', 8 Tu-142M 'Bear-F', 20 Dornier 228 and 13 Britten-Norman Islander maritime patrol aircraft. Armed helicopters include 26 Chetak, 7 Ka-25, 10 Ka-27 and 32 Sea King, and the inventory is completed with some 30 training and communications aircraft.

Main bases are at Bombay (HQ Western Fleet, and main dockyard), Goa, Visakhapatnam (HQ Eastern Fleet) and Calcutta on the sub-continent, Port Blair in the Andaman Islands and Lakhshadweep on the Laccadive Islands. HQ Southern Command is at Kochi.

Naval personnel in 1996 numbered 55,000 including 5,000 Naval Air Arm and 1,000 marines.

The Coast Guard is an independent para-military service 4,000 strong in 1996, which functions under Defence Ministry control, but is funded by the Revenue Department. The force comprises 10 offshore patrol vessels and 40 inshore patrol craft. Its 20 aircraft include Dornier-228, Fokker F-27 and Britten-Norman Islanders, and 13 Chetak helicopters.

Air Force. The Air Headquarters, under the Chief of Air Staff, consists of 4 main branches, viz., Air Staff, Administration, Policy and Plans, and Maintenance. Units of the IAF are organized into 5 operational commands—Western at Delhi, Central at Allahabad, Eastern at Shillong, Southern at Thiruvananthapuram and South-Western at Jodhpur. Training Command HQ is at Bangalore, Maintenance Command at Nagpur. Nominal strength in 1996 was 110,000 personnel, over 600 combat aircraft of all types, in over 40 squadrons of aircraft, 36 armed helicopters and about 30 squadrons of 'Guideline' and 'Goa' surface-to-air missiles, and close-range missiles such as 'Gainful' and Tigercat.

Air defence units include 2 squadrons of MiG-23 variable-geometry interceptors, 3 squadrons of MiG-29s, 16 squadrons of MiG-21s and 2 of Mirage 2000s. Other combat units include 8 squadrons of MiG-27s, 2 of Canberras, 4 of Jaguars, 4 of MiG-23 supersonic fighter-bombers and one of MiG-25 reconnaissance aircraft. Delivery of 40 Su-30 strike aircraft started in 1997.

The large transport force includes An-32s, Il-76s, Do 228s, HS 748s, 2 Boeing 737s, and smaller aircraft and helicopters for VIP and other duties. Helicopter units have Mi-8s and Mi-17s (10 squadrons), Mi-26s, and Mi-25 gunships. Main training types are the Hindustan HPT-32 and Kiran, Polish-built TS-11 Iskra, Hunter T.66, MiG-21UT1 and MiG-23U.

INTERNATIONAL RELATIONS

Membership. India is a member of the UN, the Commonwealth and the Colombo Plan.

ECONOMY

Policy. The highest economic decision-making body is the *National Development Council*, of which all state chief ministers are members. There is also a *Planning Commission*.

The eighth 5-year plan (1992–97) emphasized job creation and increased rural investment, and aimed at an annual growth of 5·6% of GDP, 3% in employment and a domestic savings rate of 21·6% of GDP. Indicative planning, however, is tending to take the place of centralized planning.

As a first step towards partial privatization of the 248 state-owned corporations, selected public sector enterprises are being allowed to raise funds through equity issues.

Requirements for government approval of investment decisions were reduced in 1990. The eighth plan (1992–97) envisaged an outlay of Rs 7,920,000m., with public sector investment of Rs 3,420,000m. Central plan outlay (1997–98), Rs 918,390m.

Performance. Real GDP growth at factor cost in 1996–97 was 6·8% (6·1% in 1995).

Budget. Revenue and expenditure (on revenue account) of the central government for years ending 31 March, in Rs 1m.:

	1995–96	1996–97[1]	1997–98[2]
Revenue	1,685,713	1,983,536	2,310.756
Expenditure	1,983,023	2,265,590	2,613,409

[1] Revised.   [2] Budget estimates.

Important items of revenue and expenditure on the revenue account of the central government for 1997–98 (estimates), in Rs 1m.:

Revenue		Expenditure	
Net tax revenue	1,379,568	General Services	1,167,096
Non-tax revenue	831,188	Defence	276,170
		Major subsidies	182,510

Total capital account receipts (1997–98 budget), Rs 2,774,893m.; capital account disbursements, Rs 2,777,284m. Total (revenue and capital) receipts, Rs 5,085,649m.; disbursements, Rs 5,390,693m.

Under the Constitution (Part XII and 7th Schedule), the power to raise funds has been divided between the central government and the states. Generally, the sources of revenue are mutually exclusive. Certain taxes are levied by the Union for the sake of uniformity and distributed to the states. The Finance Commission (Art. 280 of the Constitution) advises the President on the distribution of the taxes which are distributable between the centre and the states, and on the principles on which grants should be made out of Union revenues to the states. The main sources of central revenue are: customs duties; those excise duties levied by the central government; corporation, income and wealth taxes; estate and succession duties on non-agricultural assets and property, and revenues from the railways and posts and telegraphs. The main heads of revenue in the states are: taxes and duties levied by the state governments (including land revenues and agricultural income tax); civil administration and civil works; state undertakings; taxes shared with the centre; and grants received from the centre.

Currency. A decimal system of coinage was introduced in 1957. The Indian *rupee* (INR) is divided into 100 *paise*. There are coins of 1, 2, 3, 5, 10, 20, 25 and 50 *paise* and Rs 1, 2 and 5. The paper currency consists of: (1) Reserve Bank notes in denominations of Rs 2, 5, 10, 20, 50, 100 and 500; and (2) Government of India currency notes of denominations of Re 1 deemed to be included in the expression 'rupee coin' for the purposes of the Reserve Bank of India Act, 1934.

According to the Reserve Bank of India, the total money supply with the public on the last Friday of March 1997 was Rs 6,990,520m. Foreign exchange reserves, Oct. 1997, US$26,236m. (Rs 954,990m.). Wholesale price inflation was 8·5% in 1995.

The official exchange rate was abolished on 1 March 1993; the rupee now has a single market exchange rate and is convertible. The pound sterling is the currency of intervention.

Banking and Finance. The Reserve Bank, the central bank for India, was established in 1934 and started functioning on 1 April 1935 as a shareholder's bank; it became a nationalized institution on 1 Jan. 1949. It has the sole right of issuing currency notes. Its *Governor* is Chakravarty Rangarajan (b. 1932). The Bank acts as adviser to the Government on financial problems and is the banker for central and state governments, commercial banks and some other financial institutions. It manages the rupee public debt of central and state governments and is the custodian of the country's exchange reserve. The Bank has extensive powers of regulation of the banking system, directly under the Banking Regulation Act, 1949, and indirectly by the use of variations in Bank rate, variation in reserve ratios, selective credit controls and open market operations.

The commercial banking system consisted of 300 scheduled banks (*i.e.*, banks which are included in the 2nd schedule to the Reserve Bank Act) and 4 nonscheduled banks in Jan. 1993; scheduled banks included 196 Regional Rural Banks. Total deposits in commercial banks, March 1997, stood at Rs 5,035,960m. The business of non-scheduled banks forms less than 0·1% of commercial bank business. Of the 300 scheduled banks, 35 are foreign banks which specialize in financing foreign trade but also compete for domestic business. The State Bank of India acts as the agent of the Reserve Bank for transacting government business as well as undertaking commercial functions. The 27 public sector banks (which comprise the State Bank of India and its 7 associate banks and 19 nationalized banks) account for about 80·7% of deposits and about 78% of bank credit of all scheduled commercial banks.

There are stock exchanges in Ahmedabad, Bombay, Calcutta, Delhi, Madras and 17 other centres.

Weights and Measures. Uniform standards of weights and measures, based on the metric system, were established for the first time by the Standards of Weights and Measures Act, 1956.

A second Standards of Weights and Measures Act, 1976, recognizes the International System of Units and is in line with the recommendations of the International Organisation of Legal Metrology. This Act also protects consumers through proper indication of weight, quantity, identity, source, date and price on packaged goods.

While the Standards of Weights and Measures are laid down in the Central Act, enforcement of weights and measures laws is entrusted to the state governments; the central Directorate of Weights and Measures is responsible for co-ordinating activities so as to ensure national uniformity.

Calendar. The dates of the Saka era (named after the north Indian dynasty of the first century AD) are used alongside Gregorian dates in issues of the *Gazette of India*, news broadcasts by All-India Radio and government-issued calendars, from 22 March 1957, a date which corresponds with the first day of the year 1879 in the Saka era.

ENERGY AND NATURAL RESOURCES

Electricity. In Nov. 1996, 502,721 villages out of 579,132 had electricity. Production of electricity in 1995–96 was 380,084m. kWh, of which 299,606m. kWh came from thermal stations, 7,965m. kWh from nuclear stations and 72,513m. kWh from hydro-electric stations. 9 nuclear stations supplied 2·1% of output in 1995–96.

Oil and Gas. The Oil and Natural Gas Corporation Ltd and Oil India Ltd are the only producers of crude oil. Production 1996–97, 33·43m. tonnes, about 60% of consumption. The main fields are in Assam and Gujarat and offshore in the Gulf of Cambay (the Bombay High field). Natural gas production, 1995–96, 22,308m. cu. metres.

Water. 89·44m. ha (1995–96) irrigation potential had been created of which 79·89m. ha was utilized. Irrigation projects have formed an important part of all the Five-Year Plans. The possibilities of diverting rivers into canals being nearly exhausted, the emphasis is now on damming the monsoon surplus flow and diverting that. Ultimate potential of irrigation is assessed at 107m. ha, total cultivated land being 185m. ha.

Minerals. The coal industry was nationalized in 1973. Production, including lignite, 1996–97 (provisional), 319m. tonnes; reserves, including lignite, are estimated at (1995–96) 202,000m. tonnes. Production of other minerals, 1995–96 (in 1,000 tonnes): Iron ore, 66,578; bauxite, 5,444; chromite, 1,664; copper ore, 4,738; manganese ore, 1,797; gold, 2,038 kg. Other important minerals are lead, zinc, limestone, apatite and phosphorite, dolomite, magnesite and silver. Value of mineral production, 1996–97, Rs 330,204·3m. of which mineral fuels produced Rs 275,053m., metallic minerals Rs 24,295m. and non-metallic Rs 11,392·4m.

Agriculture. About 70% of the people are dependent on the land for their living. In 1990–91 agriculture provided about 35% of GDP. The farming year runs from July to June through three crop seasons: Kharif (monsoon); rabi (winter) and summer.

Agricultural production, 1996–97 (in 1,000 tonnes): Rice, 80,530; wheat, 64,660; total foodgrains, 192,120; maize, 9,440; pulses, 14,020; sugar-cane, 267,480; oilseeds, 24,210; cotton, 14·16m. bales (of 170 kg); jute is grown in West Bengal (70% of total yield), Bihar and Assam, total yield, 9·42m. bales (of 170 kg). The coffee industry is growing: The main cash varieties are Arabica and Robusta (main growing areas Karnataka, Kerala and Tamil Nadu).

The tea industry is important, with production concentrated in Assam, West Bengal, Tamil Nadu and Kerala. Total crop in 1996, 780m. tonnes from 414,232 ha; exports in 1995–96 valued at Rs 11,720m.

Livestock (1993): Cattle, 193m.; sheep, 45m.; pigs, 10·3m.; horses, 953,000; asses, 1,328,000; goats, 118m.; buffaloes, 79m.

Fertilizer consumption in 1996–97 was 14·31m. tonnes.

Land Tenure. There are three main traditional systems of land tenure: *Ryotwari* tenure, where the individual holders, usually peasant proprietors, are responsible for the payment of land revenues; *zamindari* tenure, where one or more persons own large estates and are responsible for payment (in this system there may be a number of intermediary holders); and *mahalwari* tenure, where village communities jointly hold an estate and are jointly and severally responsible for payment.

Agrarian reform, initiated in the first Five-Year Plan, being undertaken by the state governments includes: (1) The abolition of intermediaries under *zamindari* tenure. (2) Tenancy legislation designed to scale down rents to $^1/_4$-$^1/_5$ of the value of the produce, to give permanent rights to tenants (subject to the landlord's right to resume a minimum holding for his personal cultivation), and to enable tenants to acquire ownership of their holdings (subject to the landlord's right of resumption for personal cultivation) on payment of compensation over a number of years. (3) Fixing of ceilings on existing holdings and on future acquisition; the holding of a family is between 4·05 and 7·28 ha if it has assured irrigation to produce two crops a year; 10·93 ha for land with irrigation facilities for only one crop a year; and 21·85 ha for all other categories of land. Tea, coffee, cocoa and cardamom plantations have been exempted. (4) The consolidation of holdings in community project areas and the prevention of fragmentation of holdings by reform of inheritance laws. (5) Promotion of farming by co-operative village management.

The average size of holding for the whole of India is 2·63 ha. Andhra Pradesh, 2·87; Assam, 1·46; Bihar, 1·53; Gujarat, 4·49; Jammu and Kashmir, 1·43; Karnataka, 4·11; Kerala, 0·75; Madhya Pradesh, 3·99; Maharashtra, 4·65; Orissa, 1·98; Punjab, 3·85; Rajasthan, 5·5; Tamil Nadu, 1·49; Uttar Pradesh, 1·78; West Bengal, 1·56.

Of the total 71m. rural households possessing operational holdings, 34% hold on the average less than 0·2 ha of land each.

Opium. By international agreement the poppy is cultivated under licence, and all raw opium is sold to the central government. Opium, other than for wholly medical use, is available only to registered addicts.

Fisheries. Total catch (1995–96) was 4·95m. tonnes, of which Kerala, Tamil Nadu, and Maharashtra produced about half. Of the total catch in 1995–96, 2·71m. tonnes were marine fish. There were 46,918 mechanized boats (1994–95). There were also 31,726 motorized traditional crafts and 159,481 traditional crafts in 1994–95. There were 11,440 fishermen's co-operatives with 1,250,379 members in 1995–96; total sales, Rs 1,495m. (1994–95).

Forestry. The lands under the control of the state forest departments are classified as 'reserved forests' (forests intended to be permanently maintained for the supply of timber, etc., or for the protection of water supply, etc.), 'protected forests' and 'unclassed' forest land. In 1995 the total forest area was 639,622 sq. km. Main types are teak and sal. About 16% of the area is inaccessible, of which about 45% is potentially productive. Most states have encouraged planting small areas around villages.

INDUSTRY. In a number of industries new units are set up only by the state. Industries reserved for the public sector are arms and ammunition and allied items of defence equipment, military aircraft and warships, nuclear energy, coal and lignite, mineral oils and minerals specified in nuclear energy and railway transport. In a further group of industries (road transport, manufacture of chemicals such as drugs, dyestuffs, plastics and fertilizers) the state established new undertakings, but private enterprise may develop either on its own or with state backing.

Oil refinery installed capacity, Dec. 1996, was 60·55m. tonnes; production of petroleum refinery products (1995–96), 55·08m. tonnes. The Indian Oil Corporation was established in 1964 and had (1996) the major portion of the market.

There is expansion in petrochemicals, based on the oil and associated gas of the Bombay High field, and gas from Krishna-Godavari Basin, Rajasthan, Tripura, Assam and Bassein field. Small industries numbering 2·72m., (initial outlay on capital equipment of less than Rs 30m.) are important; they employ about 15·26m. and produced (1995–96) goods worth Rs 3,164,210m.

Industrial production, 1995–96 (in 1,000 tonnes): Steel ingots, 12,972; aluminium, 527; 2,2,588,004 motor cycles, mopeds and scooters; 293,172 commercial vehicles; petroleum products, 55,332; cement, 67,716; board and paper, 3,544; nitrogen fertilizer, 9,768; phosphate fertilizer, 3,792; jute goods, 1,114; man-made fibre and yarn, 468; diesel engines, 1,984,140; electric motors, 6·36m. h.p.; 361,488 passenger cars and jeeps; 19,044 railway wagons; pig-iron (saleable), 2,436; finished steel, 14,533.

Labour. At the 1991 census there were 285·9m. workers, of whom 110·7m. were cultivators, 74·6m. agricultural labourers; 28·7m. in manufacturing, processing, servicing and repairs, 5·5m. in construction and 8·02m. in transport, communications and storage. Workdays lost by industrial disputes, 1995, 14·29m., through strikes and lockouts. An ordinance of 1981 gave the government power to ban strikes in essential services; the ordinance was to remain in force for 6 months and would then be renewable.

Companies. The total number of companies limited by shares at work as on 31 Dec. 1996 was 409,142; aggregate paid-up capital was Rs 1,610,506m. At 31 Dec. 1996 there were 57,402 public limited companies with an aggregate paid-up capital of Rs 1,093,547m., and 351,740 private limited companies (Rs 516,959m.). There were also 392 companies with unlimited liability and 2,506 companies limited by guarantee and association not for profit.

During 1995–96, 56,433 new limited companies were registered in the Indian Union under the Companies Act 1956 with a total authorized capital of Rs 210,450m.; 11 were government companies (Rs 26,610m.) and 56,422 were non-government companies (Rs 183,840m.). There were 17 private companies with unlimited liability and 90 companies with liability limited by guarantee and association not for profit also registered in 1995–96. During 1995–96, 414 non-government companies with an aggregate paid-up capital of Rs 104m. went into liquidation or were struck off the register.

On 31 March 1996 there were 1,216 government companies at work with a total paid-up capital of Rs 767,665m.; 604 were public limited companies and 611 were private limited companies.

On 31 March 1996, 679 companies incorporated elsewhere were reported to have a place of business in India; 161 were of UK and 150 of US origin.

Co-operative Movement. In 1995–96 there were 411,000 co-operative societies with a total membership of 197·8m. These included Primary Cooperative Marketing Societies, State Co-operative Marketing Federations and the National Agricultural Co-operative Marketing Federation of India. There were also State Co-operative Commodity Marketing Federations, and 29 general purpose and 16 Special Commodites Marketing Federations.

There were, in 1995–96, 28 State Co-operative Banks, 362 Distirct Central Co-operative Banks, 90,783 Primary Agricultural Credit Societies, 20 State Land Development Banks, and 2,970 Primary Land Development Banks which provide long-term credits.

Agricultural credit is provided (31 Dec. 1993) through 32,641 rural and semi-rural branches of commercial banks and 14,543 branches of Regional Rural Banks, and (June 1993) 90,783 Primary Agricultural Credit Societies affiliated to 10,775 branches of District Central Co-operative Banks and 2,970 Primary units of Land Development Banks. Total agricultural credit disbursed by Co-operatives in 1995–96 was Rs 26,450m.

Value of agricultural produce marketed by Co-operatives in 1994–95 was about Rs 95,000m. Commercial and regional rural banks disbursed agricultural credit of Rs 136,840m. in 1995–96.

In 1994–95 there were 2,601 agro-processing units; 245 sugar factories produced 8·66m. tons; 137 spinning mills (capacity 3·2m. spindles) accounted for 12% of total spindleage in the country in 1995–96; there were 129 oilseed processing units; total storage capacity was 13·55m. tons on 31 March 1996.

In 1994–95 there were 76,500 retail depots distributing 4·12m. tons of fertilizers.

FOREIGN ECONOMIC RELATIONS. Foreign investment is encouraged by a tax holiday on income up to 6% of capital employed for 5 years. There are special depreciation allowances, and customs and excise concessions, for export industries. Proposals for investment ventures involving up to 51% foreign equity require only the Reserve Bank's approval under new liberalized policy. In Feb. 1991 India resumed trans-frontier trade with China, which had ceased in 1962.

Foreign debt was estimated at US$93,843m. in Sept. 1996.

Commerce. The external trade of India (excluding land-borne trade with Tibet and Bhutan) was as follows (in Rs 100,000):

	Imports	Exports and Re-exports
1994–95	8,870,502	8,233,80
1995–96	12,267,800	10,635,300
1996–97[1]	13,684,400	11,752,500

[1] Provisional.

The distribution of commerce by countries was as follows in the year ended 31 March 1996 (in Rs 100,000):

Countries	Exports to	Imports from	Countries	Exports to	Imports from
Argentina	12,571	43,900	Malaysia	131,500	302,000
Australia	125,700	341,800	Mexico	18,338	21,600
Austria	30,300	38,500	Morocco	8,967	100,700
Bahrain	19,842	287,700	Myanmar	10,094	54,300
Bangladesh	350,887	28,700	Nepal	53,536	16,400
Belgium	374,800	569,300	Netherlands	257,200	190,700
Canada	102,200	127,500	New Zealand	20,268	20,800
China	111,288	271,606	Nigeria	50,473	257,500
CIS	349,500	409,000	Pakistan	25,697	15,080
Czech Republic	9,835	29,800	Philippines	48,237	7,181
Denmark	48,800	90,300	Poland	29,271	43,800
Egypt	54,942	24,256	Qatar	11,777	37,800
Finland	17,900	57,100	Romania	10,005	49,600
France	249,900	281,200	Saudi Arabia	161,300	677,300
Germany	661,400	1,052,000	Singapore	301,600	365,200
Hong Kong	609,300	129,800	Spain	130,762	60,887
Hungary	7,587	5,600	Sri Lanka	134,400	13,864
Indonesia	221,570	154,300	Sweden	48,887	81,700
Iran	51,863	200,100	Switzerland	94,200	341,400
Israel	72,500	81,148	Taiwan	86,119	127,721
Italy	339,200	356,000	Thailand	158,200	56,800
Japan	741,100	825,400	UAE	477,800	537,411
Jordan	26,705	64,200	UK	672,600	641,483
South Korea	149,935	275,900	USA	1,846,600	1,291,622
Kuwait	45,322	659,000	Vietnam	41,600	5,182

The value (in Rs 100,000) of the leading articles of merchandise was as follows in the year ended 31 March 1996:

Exports	Value
Meat and meat preparations	62,700
Marine products	338,113
Processed foods (miscellaneous)	101,700

Exports	Value
Rice	456,808
Wheat	36,700
Vegetables and fruits	80,200
Nuts and seeds	123,700
Coffee and coffee substitutes	150,300
Tea and mate	117,111
Spices	79,353
Oil meals	234,861
Tobacco unmanufactured and tobacco refuse	29,700
Raw cotton	20,354
Iron ore	172,103
Ores and minerals (excluding iron, mica and coal)	208,500
Cotton yarn, fabrics and made-up articles	861,900
Ready-made garments, including clothing accessories of all textile materials	1,229,451
Jute manufactures including twist and yarn	62,084
Leather and leather manufactures	578,970
Natural silk textiles	44,500
Man-made textiles	251,100
Carpets, mill-made	49,900
Plastics and manufactures thereof	195,800
Sports goods	24,700
Gems and jewellery	1,764,400
Handicrafts	145,140
Handmade carpets	140,629
Electronic goods	252,000
Engineering goods	1,205,800
Petroleum products	151,775
Basic chemicals, pharmaceuticals and cosmetics, chemicals including residual	789,100

Imports	Value
Raw wool	48,580
Pulp and waste paper	92,082
Crude rubber including synthetic and reclaimed	71,921
Synthetic and regenerated fibre	50,210
Fertilizers, crude	52,444
Sulphur and unroasted iron pyrites	48,309
Metalliferous ores and metal scrap	275,101
Petroleum, petroleum products and related materials	2,517,360
Edible oil	226,192
Cashew nuts	76,008
Organic and inorganic chemicals	858,165
Medical and pharmaceutical products	135,796
Fertilizers, manufactured	462,100
Artificial resins, plastic materials etc	268,746
Chemical materials and products	82,109
Paper, paper board and manufactures thereof	158,331
Textile yarn, fabrics and made-up articles	119,982
Pearls, precious and semi-precious stones	704,467
Non-metallic mineral manufactures exclg. pearls	50,673
Iron and steel	483,755
Non-ferrous metal	302,351
Manufactures of metal	93,047
Machinery other than electric	2,236,890
Electrical machinery	129,239
Transport equipment	369,666
Professional, scientific, controlling instruments, photographic, optical goods, watches and clocks	223,798

In 1995–96 the main export markets (percentage of total trade) were: USA, 17·4%; Japan, 6·97%; Germany, 6·22%; UK, 6·3%. Main import suppliers: USA, 10·53%; Belgium, 4·64%; Germany, 8·66%; Saudi Arabia, 5·5%; Japan, 6·73%.

Tourism. There were 1·76m. visitors (excluding nationals of Pakistan and Bangladesh) in 1995 bringing about Rs 86,400m. in foreign exchange; 334,827 from UK, 203,343 from USA, 114,157 from Sri Lanka.

COMMUNICATIONS

Roads. In 1995–96 there were 3·29m. km of roads, of which 1·44m. km were surfaced. Roads are divided into 6 main administrative classes, namely, national highways, state highways, other public works department (PWD) roads, Panchayat Raj roads, urban roads and project roads. The national highways (34,298 km in 1996) connect capitals of states, major ports and foreign highways. The national highway system is linked with the UN Economic and Social Commission for Asia and the Pacific international highway system. The state highways are the main trunk roads of the states, while the other PWD roads and Panchayat Raj roads connect subsidiary areas of production and markets with distribution centres, and form the main link between headquarters and neighbouring districts.

There were (31 March 1996) 33,558,000 motor vehicles in India, comprising 4·19m. private cars, taxis and jeeps, 23·1m. motor cycles and scooters, 449,000 buses, 1,785,000 goods vehicles and 4,024,000 others.

Railways. The Indian railway system is government-owned (under the control of the Railway Board) and is divided into 9 zones; route-km 1995–96:

Zone	Headquarters	Route-km
Central	Bombay	7,047 km (2,892 km electrified)
Eastern	Calcutta	4,318 km (1,613 km)
Northern	Delhi	11,004 km (1,170 km)
North Eastern	Gorakhpur	5,107 km
North East Frontier	Guwahati	3,816 km
Southern	Madras	7,049 km (1,099 km)
South Central	Secunderabad	7,203 km (1,325 km)
South Eastern	Calcutta	7,351 km (2,905 km)
Western	Bombay	10,020 km (1,791 km)

A further 6 zones were proposed for creation in 1997.

The Konkan Railway (760 km of 1,676 mm gauge) linking Bombay and Mangalore opened in 1996. It is operated as a separate entity.

Principal gauges are 1,676 mm (40,620 km) and 1 metre (18,501 km), with networks also of 762 mm and 610 mm gauge (3,794 km).

Passengers carried in 1995–96 were 4,018m.; freight, 405·5m. tonnes. Revenue (1995–96) from passengers, Rs 61,244·9m.; from goods, Rs 152,904m.

Indian Railways pay to the central government a dividend on capital-at-charge at a rate fixed by the Convention Committee of Parliament. Railway finance in Rs1m.:

Financial years	Gross traffic receipts	Gross expenditure	Net revenues (receipts)	Net surplus or deficit (after dividend)
1995–96	224,179	185,249	41,351	+23,180
1996–97 revised	244,500	209,650	37,563	+22,410
1997–98 budget	270,550	251,350	30,037	+13,740

There is a metro (16·4 km) in Calcutta.

Civil Aviation. There are international airports at Bombay, Calcutta, Delhi (Indira Gandhi), Thiruvananthapuram and Madras. Air transport was nationalized in 1953 with the formation of 2 Air Corporations: Air India for long-distance international air services, and Indian Airlines for air services within India and to adjacent countries. A third airline, Vayudoot, formed in 1981 as an internal feeder, has been merged into Indian Airlines. Domestic air transport has been opened to private companies and by 1996–97 7 private airlines had been given scheduled status.

In Dec. 1996 Air India had 28 aircraft including B-747-200s, B-747-300 (Combi), B-747-400s, A-300-B4s and A-310-300s, and operated routes from Bombay, Delhi, Madras, Thiruvananthapuram, Hyderabad, Goa, Ahmedabad, Bangalore, Calicut, Amritsar and Calcutta to Africa (Nairobi, Dar-es-Salaam, Durban and Johannesburg); to Mauritius; to Europe (London, Paris, Frankfurt, Geneva, Moscow, Rome, Copenhagen and Manchester); to western Asia (Doha, Abu Dhabi, Dharan, Dubai, Bahrain, Kuwait, Muscat, Jeddah and Riyadh); to east Asia (Bangkok, Hong Kong, Tokyo, Osaka, Kuala Lumpur, Jakarta and Singapore); to North America (New York and Chicago) and to Australia (Perth). In addition, freight services are operated to

Zurich, Brussels, Dubai, Singapore and Luxembourg. Air India carried 2·8m. passengers and made a loss of Rs 2,718·4m. in 1995–96.

Indian Airlines has a fleet of 55 aircraft including 10 A-300s, 30 A-320s and 14 B-737s. It operates services to Bangkok, Chittagong, Colombo, Dhaka, Fujairah, Karachi, Khatmandu, Kuala Lumpur, Kuwait, Male, Muscat, Rangoon, Ras-al-Khaimah, Sharjah and Singapore. During 1995–96 the airline carried 7·74m. passengers.

Services are also provided by Aeroflot, Air Canada, Air France, Air Lanka, Air Maldives, Air Mauritius, Air Ukraine, Alitalia, All Nippon Airways, Alyemda, Ariana Afghan Airlines, Biman Bangladesh, British Airways, Cathay Pacific, Druk-Air, Egyptair, El Al, Emirates Air, Ethiopian Airlines, Gulf Air, Iran Air, JAL, Kazakhstan Airways, Kenya Airways, KLM, Korean Air, Kuwait Airways, Lufthansa, Malaysia Airlines, Oman Air, Pakistan International Airlines, Qatar Airways, Royal Brunei Airlines, Royal Jordanian, Royal Nepal Airlines, SAA, SAS, Saudia, Singapore Airlines, Swissair, Syrian Airlines, Tajikistan Airlines, Tarom, Thai Airways, Tower Air, Turkmenistan Airlines, United Airlines, Uzbekistan Airways and Yemenia Yemen Airways.

The Airports Authority of India maintains and operates 87 civil aerodromes, 28 civil enclaves and the 5 international airports at Bombay, Calcutta, Delhi, Madras and Thiruvananthapuram.

Shipping. In Oct. 1996, 481 ships totalling 7·02m. GRT were on the Indian Register. In Dec. 1995 219 ships of 0·61m. GRT were engaged in coastal trade, and 251 ships of 6·3m. GRT in overseas trade. Traffic of major ports, 1996–97, was as follows:

Port	Cargo ships cleared	Unloaded (1m. tonnes)	Loaded (1m. tonnes)
Kandla	1,527	27·08	4·48
Bombay	2,583	18·38	15·35
Mormugao	507	4·77	18·41
New Mangalore	644	4·45	7·97
Cochin	787	8·54	2·09
Tuticorin	905	7·61	1·58
Madras	1,660	21·42	9·40
Visakhapatnam	1,437	14·67	13·28
Paradip	556	3·89	7·72
Haldia	946 ⎫	11·99	5·06
Calcutta	822 ⎭		
Jawaharlal Nehru	601	4·68	3·39

There are about 3,700 km of major rivers navigable by motorized craft, of which 2,000 km are used. Canals, 4,300 km, of which 900 km are navigable by motorized craft.

Telecommunications. On 31 March 1995 there were 152,792 post offices and 42,766 telegraph offices.

The telephone system is in the hands of the Telecommunications Department, except in Delhi and Bombay, served by public corporation. In April 1996 the Department had 11,978,000 telephones, 417 telex exchanges and 43,900 subscribers.

In March 1997 there were 187 radio stations and 297 transmitters, 19 channels and 41 programme production centres. Television reached 85·8% of the population, through a network of 834 transmitters (colour by PAL). In 1991 there were estimated to be 55m. radio and 20m. TV sets.

Cinemas. In 1996 there were over 12,623 cinemas and 683 feature films were certified. Attendances totalled 90–100m. per week.

Press. There were 41,000 registered newspapers in March 1996, with a total circulation of 72·3m. In 1994 there were 369 dailies in 18 languages with a total circulation of 20m. There were 3,502 daily and 10,375 weekly papers. Hindi papers have the highest number and circulation, followed by English, then Urdu, Bengali and Marathi.

SOCIAL INSTITUTIONS

Justice. All courts form a single hierarchy, with the Supreme Court at the head, which constitutes the highest court of appeal. Immediately below it are the High Courts and subordinate courts in each state. Every court in this chain administers the whole law of the country, whether made by Parliament or by the state legislatures.

The states of Andhra Pradesh, Assam (in common with Nagaland, Meghalaya, Manipur, Mizoram, Tripura and Arunachal Pradesh), Bihar, Gujarat, Himachal Pradesh, Jammu and Kashmir, Karnataka, Kerala, Madhya Pradesh, Maharashtra (in common with Goa and the Union Territories of Daman and Diu and Dadra and Nagar Haveli), Orissa, Punjab (in common with the state of Haryana and the Union Territory of Chandigarh), Rajasthan, Tamil Nadu (in common with the Union Territory of Pondicherry), Uttar Pradesh, West Bengal and Sikkim each have a High Court. There is a separate High Court for Delhi. For the Andaman and Nicobar Islands the Calcutta High Court, for Pondicherry the High Court of Madras and for Lakshadweep the High Court of Kerala are the highest judicial authorities. The Allahabad High Court has a Bench at Lucknow, the Bombay High Court has Benches at Nagpur, Aurangabad and Panaji, the Gauhati High Court has Benches at Kohima, Aizwal, Imphal and Agartala, the Madhya Pradesh High Court has Benches at Gwalior and Indore, the Patna High Court has a Bench at Ranchi and the Rajasthan High Court has a Bench at Jaipur. Judges and Division Courts of the Guwahati High Court also sit in Meghalaya. Similarly, judges and Division Courts of the Calcutta High Court also sit in the Andaman and Nicobar Islands. Below the High Court each state is divided into a number of districts under the jurisdiction of district judges who preside over civil courts and courts of sessions. There are a number of judicial authorities subordinate to the district civil courts. On the criminal side magistrates of various classes act under the overall supervision of the High Court.

The Code of Criminal Procedure came into force with effect from 1 April 1974. It provides for complete separation of the Judiciary from the Executive throughout India.

In Oct. 1991 the Supreme Court upheld capital punishment by hanging.

Police. The states control their own police forces. The Home Affairs Minister of the central government co-ordinates the work of the states. The Indian Police Service provides senior officers for the state police forces. The Central Bureau of Investigation functions under the control of the Cabinet Secretariat.

The cities of Pune, Ahmedabad, Nagpur, Bangalore, Calcutta, Madras, Bombay, Delhi and Hyderabad have separate police commissionerates.

Religion. India is a secular state; any worship is permitted, but the state itself has no religion. The principal religions in 1991 (census) were: Hindus, 687·6m. (82%); Moslems, 101·6m. (12·1%); Christians, 19·6m. (2·34%); Sikhs, 16·3m. (1·94%); Buddhists, 6·4m. (0·76%); Jains, 3·4m. (0·4%).

Education. *Literacy.* According to the 1991 census the literacy percentage in the country (excluding age-group, 0-6 years) was 52·21% (43·67% in 1981): 64·13% among males, 39·29% among females. Of the states and territories, Kerala and Chandigarh have the highest rates.

Educational Organization. Education is the concurrent responsibility of state and Union governments. In the Union Territories it is the responsibility of the central government. The Union Government is also directly responsible for the central universities and all institutions declared by parliament to be of national importance; the promotion of Hindi as the federal language and co-ordinating and maintaining standards in higher education, research, science and technology. Professional education rests with the Ministry or Department concerned. There is a Central Advisory Board of Education to advise the Union and the State Governments on any educational question which may be referred to it.

School Education. The school system has 4 stages: Primary, middle, secondary and senior secondary.

Primary education is imparted either at independent primary (or junior basic) schools or primary classes attached to middle or secondary schools. The period of instruction varies from 4 to 5 years and the medium of instruction is in most cases the mother tongue of the child or the regional language. Free primary education is available for all children.

Legislation for compulsory education has been passed by some state governments and Union Territories but it is not practicable to enforce compulsion when the reasons for non-attendance are socio-economic. There are residential schools for country children.

The period for the middle stage varies from 2 to 3 years.

Higher Education. Higher education is given in arts, science or professional colleges, universities and all-India educational or research institutions. In 1995–96 there were 166 universities, 4 institutes established under state legislature act, 11 institutions of national importance and 37 institutions deemed as universities. Of the universities, 13 are central: Aligarh Muslim University; Banaras Hindu University; Delhi University; Hyderabad University; Jamia Millia Islamia, New Delhi; Jawaharlal Nehru University; North Eastern Hill University; Visva Bharati; Pondicherry University; Baba Sahib B. R. Ambedkar University; Assam University; Tezpur University; Nagaland University. The rest are state universities. Total enrolment at universities, 1995–96, 6,425,624, of which 5,667,400 were undergraduates. Women students numbered 2,191,138.

Grants are paid through the University Grants Commission to the central universities and institutions deemed to be universities for their maintenance and development and to state universities for their development projects only; their maintenance is the concern of state governments. During 1995–96 the University Grants Commission sanctioned grants of Rs 6,245·5m.

Technical Education. The number of institutions awarding degrees in engineering and technology in 1996–97 was 418, and those awarding diplomas, 1,029; the former admitted 328,399 students, the latter 357,891 including 58,454 girl students.

Adult Education. The Directorate of Adult Education, established in 1971, is the national resource centre.

There is also a National Literacy Mission.

Educational statistics for 1996–97:

Type of recognized institution	No. of institutions	No. of students on rolls	No. of teachers
Primary/junior basic schools	598,354	110,393,406	1,789,733
Middle/senior basic schools	176,772	41,064,849	1,195,845
High/higher secondary schools[1]	102,183	27,036,856	1,542,360
Training schools and colleges	1,931	237,509	–
Arts, Science and Commerce colleges	6,759	6,425,624	239,488

[1] Including Junior Colleges.

Expenditure. Total budgeted central expenditure on revenue account of education and other departments 1997–98 is estimated at Rs 46,383m. Total public expenditure on education, sport, arts and youth welfare during the Eighth (1992–97) Plan, Rs 212,170·2m.; Seventh Plan spending on adult education, Rs 3,007m. in the central and Rs 6,098m. in the state sectors.

Health. Medical services are primarily the responsibility of the states. The Union Government has sponsored major schemes for disease prevention and control which are implemented nationally.

Total central expenditure on health and family welfare in 1997–98 was Rs 14,166·2m. on revenue account.

DIPLOMATIC REPRESENTATIVES

Of India in Great Britain (India House, Aldwych, London, WC2B 4NA)
High Commissioner: Dr. L. M. Singhvi.

Of Great Britain in India (Chanakyapuri, New Delhi 110021)
High Commissioner: Sir David Gore-Booth, KCMG.

Of India in the USA (2107 Massachusetts Ave., NW, Washington, D.C., 20008)
Ambassador: Naresh Chandra.

Of the USA in India (Shanti Path, Chanakyapuri, New Delhi 110021)
Ambassador: Richard F. Celeste.

Of India to the United Nations
Ambassador: Kamalesh Sharma.

Of India to the European Union
Ambassador: Chandrashekhar Dasgupta.

Further Reading

Balasubramanyam, V. N., *The Economy of India*. London, 1985
Bardham, P., *The Political Economy of Development in India*. Oxford, 1984
Bhambhri, C. P., *The Political Process in India, 1947–91*. Delhi, 1991
Brown, J., *Modern India: The Origins of an Asian Democracy.* 2nd ed. OUP, 1994
Derbyshire, I. D., *India*. [Bibliography]. 2nd ed. Oxford and Santa Barbara (CA), 1995
Gupta, D. C., *Indian Government and Politics*. 3rd ed. London, 1992
Hall, A., *The Emergence of Modern India*. Columbia Univ. Press, *1981*
The Indian Annual Register. Calcutta, from 1953
Jaffrelot, C. (ed.) *L'Inde Contemporain de 1950 à nos Jours*. Paris, 1996
Jalan, B., *India's Economic Crisis: the Way Ahead*. OUP, 1991
Joshi, V. and Little, I. M. D., *India's Economic Reforms, 1991–2000*. Oxford, 1996
Kulke, H. and Rothermund, D., *A History of India*. rev. ed. London, 1990
Mehra, P., *A Dictionary of Modern Indian History, 1707–1947*. Delhi, 1987
Moon, P., *The British Conquest and Dominion of India*. London and Indiana Univ. Press, 1989
New Cambridge History of India. 2nd ed. 5 vols. CUP, 1994–96
Ray, R. K., *Industrialisation of India*. OUP, 1983
Smith, V. E., *Oxford History of India*. 3rd ed. OUP, 1958
Spear, P., *India: A Modern History*. 2nd ed. Univ. of Michigan Press, 1972

Other more specialized titles are listed under CONSTITUTION AND GOVERNMENT, *above.*

STATES AND TERRITORIES

The Republic of India is composed of the following 25 States and 7 centrally
administered Union Territories:

States	Capital	States	Capital
Andhra Pradesh	Hyderabad	Manipur	Imphal
Arunachal Pradesh	Itanagar	Meghalaya	Shillong
Assam	Dispur	Mizoram	Aizawl
Bihar	Patna	Nagaland	Kohima
Goa	Panaji	Orissa	Bhubaneswar
Gujarat	Gandhinagar	Punjab	Chandigarh
Haryana	Chandigarh	Rajasthan	Jaipur
Himachal Pradesh	Shimla	Sikkim	Gangtok
Jammu and Kashmir	Srinagar	Tamil Nadu	Madras
Karnataka	Bangalore	Tripura	Agartala
Kerala	Thiruvananthapuram	Uttar Pradesh	Lucknow
Madhya Pradesh	Bhopal	West Bengal	Calcutta
Maharashtra	Bombay		

Union Territories

Andaman and Nicobar Islands; Chandigarh; Dadra and Nagar Haveli; Daman and
Diu; Delhi; Lakshadweep; Pondicherry.

ANDHRA PRADESH

KEY HISTORICAL EVENTS. Andhra was constituted a separate state on 1
Oct. 1953, on its partition from Madras, and consisted of the undisputed Telugu-
speaking area of that state. To this region was added, on 1 Nov. 1956, the Telangana

area of the former Hyderabad State, comprising the districts of Hyderabad, Medak, Nizamabad, Karimnagar, Warangal, Khammam, Nalgonda and Mahbubnagar, parts of the Adilabad district and some taluks of the Raichur, Gulbarga and Bidar districts, and some revenue circles of the Nanded district. On 1 April 1960, 221·4 sq. miles in the Chingleput and Salem districts of Madras were transferred to Andhra Pradesh in exchange for 410 sq. miles from Chittoor district. The district of Prakasam was formed on 2 Feb. 1970. Hyderabad was split into 2 districts on 15 Aug. 1978 (Ranga Reddy and Hyderabad). A new district, Vizianagaram, was formed in 1979.

TERRITORY AND POPULATION. Andhra Pradesh is in south India and is bounded in the south by Tamil Nadu, west by Karnataka, north and north-west by Maharashtra, north-east by Madhya Pradesh and Orissa and east by the Bay of Bengal. The state has an area of 275,068 sq. km and a population (1991 census) of 66·5m. Density, 242 per sq. km. Growth rate 1981–91, 24·2%. The principal language is Telugu. Cities with over 250,000 population (1991 census), *see* INDIA: Territory and Population. Other large cities (1991): Nizamabad (241,034); Kurnool (236,800); Ramagundam (214,384); Eluru (212,866); Anantapur (174,924); Tirupati (174,369); Vizianagaram (160,359); Machilipatnam (159,110); Karimnagar (148,583); Tenali (143,726); Adoni (136,182); Proddutur (133,914); Chittoor (133,462); Khammam (127,992); Cuddapah (121,463); Bheemavaram (121,314).

CONSTITUTION AND GOVERNMENT. Andhra Pradesh has a unicameral legislature; the Legislative Council was abolished in June 1985. There are 294 seats in the Legislative Assembly. At the elections of Dec. 1994, the Telugu Desam Party gained 224 seats; Congress (I), 25. Party composition, Feb. 1997: Telugu Desam, 216 seats; Congress (I), 26.

For administrative purposes there are 23 districts in the state. The capital is Hyderabad.

Governor: Chakravarthy Rangarajan.
Chief Minister: N. Chandrababu Naidu.

BUDGET. Budget estimate, 1996–97: receipts on revenue account, Rs 114,516·3m.; expenditure, Rs 120,561·8m. Annual plan, 1997–98: Rs 35,330m.

ENERGY AND NATURAL RESOURCES

Electricity. There are 13 hydro-electric plants, 9 thermal stations and 2 gas-based units. Installed capacity, 1996–97, 6,800 MW, power generated 27,865m. kWh. In Nov. 1996 all 27,358 villages were electrified and 1·74m. electric pump sets energized.

Oil and Gas. Crude oil is refined at Visakhapatnam in Andhra Pradesh. Oil/gas structures are found in Krishna-Godavari basin which encompasses an area of 20,000 sq. km on land and 21,000 sq. km up to 200 metres isobath off-shore. Reserves of the land basin are estimated at 760 metric tonnes of oil and oil equivalent of gas.

Water. In 1997, 30 major and 75 medium irrigation projects had created irrigation potential of 5·7m. ha. The Telugu Ganga joint project with Tamil Nadu, now in execution, will irrigate about 233,000 ha, besides supplying drinking water to Madras city (Tamil Nadu).

Minerals The state is an important producer of asbestos and barytes. Other important minerals are copper ore, coal, iron and limestone, steatite, mica and manganese.

Agriculture. There were (1996) about 13·4m. ha of cropped land, of which 8·2m. ha were under food-grains. Irrigated area, 1996, 5·30m. ha. Production in 1996 (in tonnes): Foodgrains, 11·66m. (rice, 9·01m., wheat, 0·008m.); pulses, 0·77m.; sugarcane, 15·16m.; oil seeds, 3·03m.

Livestock (1993): Cattle, 10·95m.; buffaloes, 9·13m.; goats, 4·32m.; sheep, 7·77m.

Forestry. In 1996–97 it was estimated that forests occupy 23·2% of the total area of the state or 63,813 sq. km; main forest products are teak, eucalyuptus, cashew, casuarina, softwoods and bamboo.

Fisheries. Production 1996–97, 152,047 tonnes of marine fish and 207,312 tonnes of inland water fish. The state has a coastline of 974 km.

INDUSTRY. The main industries are textile manufacture, sugar-milling machine tools, pharmaceuticals, electronic equipment, heavy electrical machinery, aircraft parts and paper-making. There is an oil refinery at Visakhapatnam, where India's major shipbuilding yards are situated. A major steel plant at Visakhapatnam and a railway repair shop at Tirupathi are functioning.

At 31 March 1997 there were 1,536 large and medium industries employing 644,480 persons, and 124,209 small-scale industries employing 1m.

There are cottage industries and sericulture. District Industries Centres have been set up to promote small-scale industry.

Tourism is growing; the main centres are Hyderabad, Nagarjunasagar, Warangal, Arakuvalley, Horsley Hills and Tirupathi.

COMMUNICATIONS

Roads. In 1996–97 there were 2,949 km of national highways, 43,763 km of state highways and 103,971 km of major district roads. Number of vehicles as of 31 March 1997 was 2,783,220, including 2,287,029 motor cycles and scooters, 177,516 cars and jeeps and 187,863 goods vehicles.

Railways. There are 5,073 route-km of railway.

Civil Aviation. There are airports at Hyderabad, Tirupathi, Vijayawada and Visakhapatnam, with regular scheduled services to Bombay, Delhi, Calcutta, Bangalore and Chennai. International flights are operated from Hyderabad to Kuwait, Muscat, Sharjah and Jeddah.

Shipping. The chief port is Visakhapatnam. There are minor ports at Kakinada, Machilipatnam, Bheemunipatnam, Narsapur, Krishnapatnam, Nizampatnam, Vadarevu and Kalingapatnam.

SOCIAL INSTITUTIONS

Justice. The high court of Judicature at Hyderabad has a Chief Justice and 28 puisne judges.

Religion. At the 1991 census Hindus numbered 59,281,950; Moslems, 5,923,954; Christians, 1,216,348; Jains, 26,564; Sikhs, 21,910; Buddhists, 22,153

Education. In 1991, 44·09% of the population were literate (55·13% of men and 32·72% of women). There were, in 1996–97, 48,899 primary schools (7,898,481 students); 7,733 upper primary (2·30m.); 8,178 high schools (1,055,390). Education is free for children up to 14.

In 1995–96 there were 1,818 junior colleges (676,455 students). In 1996–97 there were 805 degree colleges (427,652 students); 52 oriental colleges (427,652 students in 1995–96), 46 oriented colleges and 13 universities: Osmania University, Hyderabad; Andhra University, Waltair; Sri Venkateswara University, Tirupathi; Kakatiya University, Warangal; Nagarjuna University, Guntur; Sri Jawaharlal Nehru Technological University, Hyderabad; Hyderabad University, Hyderabad; N. G. Ranga Agricultural University, Hyderabad; Sri Krishnadevaraya University, Anantapur; Smt. Padmavathi Mahila Vishwavidyalayam (University for Women), Tirupathi; Dr B. R. Ambedkar Open University, Hyderabad; Patti Sriramulu Telugu University, Hyderabad and N. T. R. University of Health Science, Vijayawada.

Health. There were (1996) 1,947 allopathic hospitals and dispensaries, 550 Ayurvedic hospitals and dispensaries, 193 Unani and 283 homeopathy hospitals and dispensaries. There were also 181 nature cure hospitals and (in 1996–97) 1,335 primary health centres. Number of beds in hospitals was 32,116.

ARUNACHAL PRADESH

KEY HISTORICAL EVENTS. Before independence the North East Frontier Agency of Assam was administered for the viceroy by a political agent working through tribal groups. After independence it became the North East Frontier Tract, administered for the central government by the Governor of Assam. In 1972 the area became the Union Territory of Arunachal Pradesh; statehood was achieved in Dec. 1986.

TERRITORY AND POPULATION. The state is in the extreme north-east of India and is bounded in the north by China, east by Burma, west by Bhutan and south by Assam and Nagaland. It has 13 districts and comprises the former frontier divisions of Kameng, Tirap, Subansiri, Siang and Lohit; it has an area of 83,743 sq. km and a population (1991 census) of 864,558; growth, 1981–91, 36·83%; density, 10 per sq. km.

The state is mainly tribal; there are 106 tribes using about 50 tribal dialects.

CONSTITUTION AND GOVERNMENT. There is a Legislative Assembly of 60 members. The capital is Itanagar (population, 1991, 16,545).

Governor: Mata Prasad.
Chief Minister: Gegong Apang.

BUDGET. Total estimated receipts, 1997–98, Rs 10,581m.; total estimated expenditure, Rs 10,302m. Plan outlay, 1997–98, Rs 6,000m.

ENERGY AND NATURAL RESOURCES

Electricity. Total installed capacity (1995–96), 43·85 MW. Power generated (1995–96): 70·8m. units. 2,188 out of 3,257 villages have electricity.

Oil and Minerals. Production, 1995–96, 28,000 tonnes of crude oil and 32m. cu. metres of gas. Crude oil reserves are estimated at 30m. tonnes; coal, 90·23m. tonnes; dolomite, 154·13m. tonnes; limestone, 409·35m. tonnes.

Agriculture. Production of foodgrains, 1995–96, 230,200 tonnes.

Forestry. Area under forest, 51,540 sq. km; revenue from forestry (1995–96) Rs 402m.

INDUSTRY. In 1996 there were 18 medium and 3,306 small industries, 80 craft or weaving centres and 225 sericulture centres. Most of the medium industries are forest-based.

COMMUNICATIONS. Total length of roads in the state, 12,250 km of which 9,855 km are surfaced. There were 14,821 vehicles in 1995–96. The state has 330 km of national highway. 4 towns are linked by air services.

SOCIAL INSTITUTIONS

Religion. At the 1991 census Hindus numbered 320,212; Moslems, 11,922; Christians, 89,013; Buddhists, 111,372.

Education. In 1991, 41·59% of the population were literate (51·45% of men and 29·69% of women). There were (1996–97) 1,256 primary schools with 147,676 students, 301 middle schools with 42,197 students, 157 high and higher secondary schools with 24,951 students, 6 colleges and 2 technical schools. Arunachal University, established in 1985, had 4 colleges and 3,240 students in 1994–95.

Health. There are (1996) 13 hospitals, 10 community health centres, 42 primary health centres and 260 sub-centres. There are 2 TB hospitals and 11 leprosy and other hospitals. Total number of beds, 2,539.

ASSAM

KEY HISTORICAL EVENTS. Assam first became a British Protectorate at the close of the first Burmese War in 1826. In 1832 Cachar was annexed; in 1835 the Jaintia Hills were included in the East India Company's dominions, and in 1839 Assam was annexed to Bengal. In 1874 Assam was detached from Bengal and made a separate chief commissionership. On the partition of Bengal in 1905, it was united to the Eastern Districts of Bengal under a Lieut.-Governor. From 1912 the chief commissionership of Assam was revived, and in 1921 a governorship was created. On the partition of India almost the whole of the predominantly Moslem district of Sylhet was merged with East Bengal (Pakistan). Dewangiri in North Kamrup was ceded to Bhutan in 1951. The Naga Hill district, administered by the Union Government since 1957, became part of Nagaland in 1962. The autonomous state of Meghalaya within Assam, comprising the districts of Garo Hills and Khasi and Jaintia Hills, came into existence on 2 April 1970, and achieved full independent statehood in Jan. 1972, when it was also decided to form a Union Territory, Mizoram (now a state), from the Mizo Hills district.

TERRITORY AND POPULATION. Assam is in north-east India, almost separated from central India by Bangladesh. It is bounded in the west by West Bengal, north by Bhutan and Arunachal Pradesh, east by Nagaland, Manipur and Myanmar, south by Meghalaya, Bangladesh, Mizoram and Tripura. The area of the state is now 78,438 sq. km. Population (census 1991) 22·4m. Density, 286 per sq. km. Growth rate 1981–91, 24·24%. Principal towns with population (1991) are; Guwahati, 584,342; Dibrugarh, 125,667; Silchar, 115,483; Nagaon, 93,350; Tinsukia, 73,918; Dhubri, 66,216; Jorhat, 58,358; Tezpur, 55,084. The principal language is Assamese.

The central government is surveying the line of a proposed boundary fence to prevent illegal entry from Bangladesh.

CONSTITUTION AND GOVERNMENT. Assam has a unicameral legislature of 126 members. In the 1996 elections an Asom Gana Parishad government was returned. The temporary capital is Dispur. The state has 23 districts.

Governor: Lt. Gen. (retd) S. K. Sinha.
Chief Minister: Prafulla Kumar Mahanta.

BUDGET. The budget estimates for 1997–98 showed receipts of Rs 72,312m. and expenditure of Rs 75,064·5m. Plan allocation, 1997–98, Rs 15,000m.

ENERGY AND NATURAL RESOURCES

Electricity. In 1996–97 there was an installed capacity of 597 MW. In March 1996, 21,887 villages (out of 21,995) had electricity. New power stations are under construction at Lakwa, and Karbi-Langpi hydro-electricity project.

Oil and Gas. Assam contains important oilfields and produces about 15% of India's crude oil. Production (1995–96): Crude oil, 5·04m. tonnes (including Nagaland); gas, 1,881m. cu. metres.

Water. Irrigation potential created up to 1994–95 was 0·67m. ha. 2 major and 10 medium projects were in hand.

Minerals. Coal production (1991), 982,000 tonnes. The state also has limestone, refractory clay, dolomite, and corundum.

Agriculture. There are 848 tea plantations, and growing tea is the principal industry. Production in 1990–91, 380m. kg, over 50% of Indian tea. Over 72% of the cultivated area is under food crops, of which the most important is rice. Total foodgrains, 1995–96, 3·56m. tonnes. Main cash crops: Jute, tea, cotton, oilseeds, sugar-cane, fruit and potatoes. Wheat production 95,100. tonnes in 1995–96; rice, 3·39m. tonnes; pulses, 57,100 tonnes. Cattle are important.

Forestry. In 1996 there were 18,242 sq. km of reserved forests under the administration of the Forest Department and 8,530 sq. km of unclassed forests, altogether about 39% of the total area of the state. Revenue from forests, 1993–94, Rs 213·1m.

INDUSTRY. Sericulture and hand-loom weaving, both silk and cotton, are important home industries together with the manufacture of brass, cane and bamboo articles. The main heavy industry is petro-chemicals; there are 3 oil refineries with 1 under construction in 1996. Other industries include manufacturing paper, nylon, electronic goods, cement, fertilizers, sugar, jute and plywood products, rice and oil milling.

There were 17,103 small-scale industries in 1994. The state in 1991 ran 480,622 enterprises employing 1·3m. persons.

COMMUNICATIONS

Roads. In March 1992 there were 65,605 km of road maintained by the Public Works Department. There were 2,033 km of national highway in 1990. There were 358,664 motor vehicles in the state in 1995–96.

Railways. The route km of railways in 1995–96 was 2,441 km.

Civil Aviation. Daily scheduled flights connect the principal towns with the rest of India. There are airports at Guwahati, Tezpur, Jorhat, North Lakhimpur, Silchar and Dibrugarh.

Shipping. Water transport is important in Lower Assam; the main waterway is the Brahmaputra River. Cargo carried in 1988–89 was 109,051 tonnes.

SOCIAL INSTITUTIONS

Justice. The seat of the High Court is Guwahati. It has a Chief Justice and 6 puisne judges.

Religion. At the 1991 census Hindus numbered 15,047,293; Moslems, 6,373,204; Christians, 744,367; Buddhists, 64,008; Jains, 20,645; Sikhs, 21,910.

Education. In 1991, 52·89% of the population were literate (61·87% of men and 43·03% of women). In 1996–97 there were 30,140 primary/junior basic schools with 3,816,603 students; 7,237 middle/senior basic schools with 1,304,504 students; 4,345 high/higher secondary schools with 664,422 students. There were 247 colleges for general education, 7 medical colleges, 3 engineering and 1 agricultural, 22 teacher-training colleges, and a fisheries college at Raha. There were 5 universities: Assam Agricultural University, Jorhat; Dibrugarh University, Dibrugarh with 86 colleges and 55,982 students (1992–93); Gauhati University, Guwahati with 128 colleges and 80,363 students (1992–93); and 2 central universities, at Silchar and Tezpur.

Health. In 1995–96 there were 161 hospitals (12,873 beds), 581 primary health centres and 316 dispensaries.

BIHAR

KEY HISTORICAL EVENTS. Bihar was part of Bengal under British rule until 1912 when it was separated together with Orissa. The two were joined until 1936 when Bihar became a separate province. As a state of the Indian Union it was enlarged in 1956 by the addition of land from West Bengal.

The state contains the ethnic areas of North Bihar, Santhal Pargana and Chota Nagpur. In 1956 certain areas of Purnea and Manbhum districts were transferred to West Bengal.

TERRITORY AND POPULATION. Bihar is in north India and is bounded north by Nepal, east by West Bengal, south by Orissa, south-west by Madhya Pradesh and west by Uttar Pradesh. The area of Bihar is 173,877 sq. km and its population (1991 census), 86,374,465, a density of 497 per sq. km. Growth rate since 1981,

23·54%. Population of principal towns, see INDIA: Territory and Population. Other large towns (1991): Muzaffarpur, 241,107; Darbhanga, 218,391; Biharsharif, 201,323; Arrah, 157,082; Dhanbad, 151,789; Munger, 150,112; Chapra, 136,877; Katihar, 154,367; Purnea, 114,912.

The state is divided into 14 divisions covering 55 districts. The capital is Patna.

The official language is Hindi (55·8m. speakers at the 1981 census), the second, Urdu (6·9m.), the third, Bengali (2m.).

CONSTITUTION AND GOVERNMENT. Bihar has a bicameral legislature. The Legislative Assembly consists of 324 elected members and the Council, 96. After the elections in 1995 the party composition of the Legislative Assembly was: Janata Dal, 31; Rashtriya Janata Dal, 136; Congress (I), 29; Bharatiya Janata Party, 41; Communist Party of India, 26; Jharkhand Mukti Morcha, 19; Communist-Marxist, 6; Samta Party, 6; Independent and others, 21.

Governor: A. R. Kidwai.
Chief Minister: Rabri Devi.

BUDGET. The budget estimates for 1997–98 showed total receipts of Rs 126,770m. and expenditure of Rs 121,216m. Plan allocation, 1997–98, Rs 22,000m.

ENERGY AND NATURAL RESOURCES

Electricity. Installed capacity (1996–97) 4,470 MW. Power generated (1994–95), 2,700m. kWh; there were (March 1996) 47,805 villages with electricity. Hydroelectric projects in hand will add about 149·2 MW capacity.

Minerals. Bihar is very rich in minerals, with about 40% of national production. There are huge deposits of copper, kyanite, coal, mica and china clay. Bihar is a principal producer of iron ore. Other important minerals: Manganese, limestone, graphite, chromite, asbestos, barytes, dolomite, bauxite, uranium ore, feldspar, columbite, pyrites, saltpetre, glass sands, slate, lead, silver, building stones and radioactive minerals. Revenue received from minerals (1994–95) Rs 7,039·3m.

Agriculture. The irrigated area was 4·13m. ha in 1993–94. Cultivable land, 11·6m. ha, of a total area of 17·4m. ha. Total cropped area, 1991–92, 9·79m. ha. Production (1995–96): Rice, 6·91m. tonnes; wheat, 4·18m.; total foodgrains, 13·07m. Other food crops are maize, rabi and pulses. Main cash crops are jute, sugar-cane, oilseeds, tobacco and potato.

Forests in 1995 covered 26,561 sq. km. There are 12 protected forests.

INDUSTRY. There are 28 industrial estates and 33 industrial areas. Iron and steel and aluminium are produced and there is an oil refinery. Other important industries are zinc and copper smelting, machine tools, fertilizers, electrical engineering, sugar-milling, paper-milling, silk-spinning, manufacturing explosives, chemicals and cement. There were 500 large and medium industries and 163,000 small and handicraft units in 1996–97.

TOURISM. The main tourist centres are Bodh Gaya, Patna, Nalanda, Jamshedpur, Sasaram, Hazaribagh, Rajgir, Ranchi and Vaishali.

COMMUNICATIONS

Roads. In March 1996–97 the state had 87,836 km of roads, including 2,118 km of national highway and 4,192 km of state highway, and 15,526 km of district roads. Passenger transport has been nationalized. There were 1,329,709 motor vehicles registered in March 1996.

Railways. The North Eastern, South Eastern and Eastern railways traverse the state; route-km, 1995–96, 5,283.

Civil Aviation. There are airports at Patna, Jamshedpur, Gaya and Ranchi with regular scheduled services to Calcutta and Delhi.

Shipping. The length of waterways open for navigation is 1,300 km.

SOCIAL INSTITUTIONS

Justice. There is a High Court (constituted in 1916) at Patna, and a bench at Ranchi, with a Chief Justice, 25 puisne judges and 4 additional judges.

Police. The police force is under a Director General of Police; in 1990 there were 1,097 police stations.

Religion. At the 1991 census Hindus numbered 71,193,417; Moslems, 12,787,985; Christians, 843,717; Sikhs, 78,212; Jains, 23,049; Buddhists, 3,518.

Education. At the census of 1991 the number of literates was 26·85m. (38·48%: males, 52·49%; females, 22·89%). There were, 1996–97, 4,149 high and higher secondary schools with 1,080,321 pupils, 13,834 middle schools with 2·42m. pupils and 53,652 primary schools with 9,626,855 pupils. Education is free for children aged 6–11.

There were 14 universities in 1996–97: Patna University (founded 1917) with 14,699 students (1994–95); Bihar University, Muzaffarpur (1952) with 95 colleges, and 84,873 students (1989–90); Bhagalpur University (1960) with 140,718 students (1990–91); Ranchi University (1960) with 106 colleges, 55,731 students (1994–95); Kameswar Singh Darbhanga Sanskrit University (1961); Magadh University, Gaya (1962) with 186 colleges and 122,019 students (1994–95); Lalit Narayan Mithila University (1972), Darbhanga; Bisra Agricultural University, Ranchi (1980); Rajendra Agricultural University, Samastipur (1970); Nalanda Open University, Nalanda and 4 others. There were 742 degree colleges, 11 engineering colleges, 31 medical colleges and 15 teacher training colleges.

Health. In 1986 there were 1,289 hospitals and dispensaries with 28,997 beds in 1992.

GOA

KEY HISTORICAL EVENTS. The coastal area was captured by the Portuguese in 1510 and the inland area was added in the 18th century. In Dec. 1961 Portuguese rule was ended and Goa incorporated into the Indian Union as a Territory together with Daman and Diu. Goa was granted statehood as a separate unit on 30 May 1987. Daman and Diu remained Union Territories.

TERRITORY AND POPULATION. Goa, bounded on the north by Maharashtra and on the east and south by Karnataka, has a coastline of 105 km. The area is 3,702 sq. km. Population, 1991 census, 1,169,793. Density, 316 per sq. km. Mormugao is the largest town; population (urban agglomeration, 1991) 90,429. The capital is Panaji; population (urban agglomeration 1991) 85,515. The state has 2 districts. There are 183 village Panchayats.The languages spoken are Konkani (official language), Marathi, Hindi and English.

CONSTITUTION AND GOVERNMENT. The Indian Parliament passed legislation in March 1962 by which Goa became a Union Territory with retrospective effect from 20 Dec. 1961. On 30 May 1987 Goa attained statehood. It is represented by 3 elected representatives in Parliament. There is a Legislative Assembly of 40 members. Elections were held in Nov. 1994.

Governor: P. C. Alexander.
Chief Minister: Pratap Singh Rane.

BUDGET. The total budget for 1996–97 was Rs 11,756·8m. Annual plan 1997–98, Rs 2,300m.

ENERGY AND NATURAL RESOURCES

Electricity. In 1996 installed capacity was 0·16m. MW, but Goa receives most of its power supply from the states of Maharashtra and Karnataka. In March 1996, 377 out of 386 villages were electrified.

Minerals. Resources include bauxite, ferro-manganese ore and iron ore, all of which are exported. Iron ore production (1992–93) 12,435,334 tonnes. There are also reserves of lime stone and clay.

Agriculture. Agriculture is the main occupation, important crops are rice, pulses, ragi, mango, cashew and coconuts. Area under rice (1995–96) 53,500 ha; production, 128,100 tonnes. Area under pulses 9,800 ha, sugar-cane 1,400 ha, groundnut 1,200 ha. Total production of foodgrains, 1995–96, 136,600 tonnes.

Government poultry and dairy farming schemes produced 94m. eggs and 29,000m. litres of milk in 1992–93.

Forests covered 1,250 sq. km in 1995.

Fisheries. Fish is the state's staple food. In 1995–96 the catch of seafish was 84,210 tonnes. There is a coastline of about 104 km and about 2,850 (1994–95) active fishing vessels.

INDUSTRY. In 1992–93 there were 52 large and medium industrial projects and 5,242 small units registered. Production included: Nylon fishing nets, ready made clothing, electronic goods, pesticides, pharmaceuticals, tyres, footwear, fertilizers, automotive components and shipbuilding.

In 1992–93, the 5,242 small-scale industry units employed 32,597 persons.

COMMUNICATIONS

Roads. In 1993–94 there were 7,419 km of roads (National Highway, 224 km). There were 211,756 motor vehicles in March 1996.

Railways. In 1995–96 there were 79 km of route.

Civil Aviation. An airport at Dabolim is connected with Bombay, Delhi and Bangalore.

Shipping. There are seaports at Panaji, Marmugao and Margao.

SOCIAL INSTITUTIONS

Justice. There is a bench of the Bombay High Court at Panaji.

Religion. At the 1991 census Hindus numbered 756,651; Christians, 349,225; Moslems, 61,455; Sikhs, 1,087.

Education. In 1991, 75·51% of the population were literate (83·64% of men and 67·09% of women). In 1996–97 there were 1,031 primary schools (126,425 students), 97 middle schools (77,275 students) and 445 high and higher secondary schools (73,216 students). There were also 2 engineering colleges, 4 medical colleges, 2 teacher-training colleges, 21 other colleges and 6 polytechnic institutes. Goa University, Taleigao (1985) had 33 colleges and 16,977 students in 1994–95.

Health. There were (1992–93) 129 hospitals (4,232 beds), 256 rural medical dispensaries, health and sub-health centres and 268 family planning units.

Hutt, A., *Goa: A Traveller's Historical and Architectural Guide.* Buckhurst Hill, 1988

GUJARAT

KEY HISTORICAL EVENTS. The Gujarati-speaking areas of India were part of the Moghul empire, coming under Mahratta domination in the late 18th century. In 1818 areas of present Gujarat around the Gulf of Cambay were annexed by the British East India Company. The remainder consisted of a group of small principalities, notably Baroda, Rajkot, Bhavnagar and Nawanagar. British areas became part of the Bombay Presidency.

At independence all the area now forming Gujarat became part of Bombay State except for Rajkot and Bhavnagar which formed the state of Saurashtra until incorporated in Bombay in 1956.

In 1960 Bombay State was divided and the Gujarati-speaking areas became Gujarat.

TERRITORY AND POPULATION. Gujarat is in western India and is bounded in the north by Pakistan and Rajasthan, east by Madhya Pradesh, south-east by Maharashtra, south and west by the Indian ocean and Arabian sea. The area of the state is 196,024 sq. km and the population at the 1991 census was 41,309,582; a density of 211 per sq. km. Growth rate 1981–91, 21·19%. The chief cities, *see* INDIA: Territory and Population. Other important towns (1991) are: Nadiad (167,051), Bharuch (133,102), Junagadh (130,484), Navsari (126,089), Gandhinagar (123,359), Porbandar (116,671), Anand (110,266), Gandhidham (104,585), Bhuj (102,376). Gujarati and Hindi in the Devanagari script are the official languages.

CONSTITUTION AND GOVERNMENT. Gujarat has a unicameral legislature, the *Legislative Assembly*, which has 182 elected members. After the elections in Feb. 1995 the Bharatiya Janata Party came to power. The party suffered a split and the Mahagujarat Janata Party, supported by Congress (I), formed a government. The Legislative Assembly was then dissolved on 24 Dec. and an election ordered. Party composition of the Legislative Assembly in Dec. 1997: Bharatiya Janata Party, 77 seats; Maha-Gujarat Janata Party, 45; Congress (I), 45; independents and others, 15.

The Government was dismissed and the state brought under presidential rule on 21 Sept. 1996.

The capital is Gandhinagar. There are 19 districts.

Governor: Krishna Pal Singh.
Chief Minister: Dilip Parikh.

BUDGET. The budget estimates for 1997–98 showed revenue receipts of Rs 107,559m. and revenue expenditure of Rs 107,325·5m. Plan outlay for 1997–98, Rs 45,000m.

ENERGY AND NATURAL RESOURCES

Electricity. In Sept. 1996 total installed capacity was 6,452 MW. In March 1996 17,985 villages were electrified.

Oil and Gas. There are large crude oil and gas reserves. Production, 1995–96: Crude oil, 6·2m. tonnes; gas, 2,461m. cu. metres.

Water. Water resources are limited. In 1995 irrigation potential was 6·49m. ha.

Minerals. Chief minerals produced in 1995–96 (in tonnes) included lime stone (8·73m.), agate stone (530), calcite (694), quartz and silica (262,000), bauxite (572,000), crude china clay (61,007), refined china clays (7,229), dolomite (452,000), crude fluorite (165,000), calcareous and sea sand (225,000) and lignite (4·15m.). Value of production (1995–96) Rs 27,621m. Reserves of coal lie under the Kalol and Mehsana oil and gas fields. The deposit, mixed with crude petroleum, is estimated at 100,000m. tonnes.

Agriculture. 3·09m. ha of the cropped area was irrigated in June 1995.

Production of principal crops, 1995–96: Rice, 0·83m. tonnes from 570,000 ha; foodgrains, 4·1m. tonnes (wheat, 1·12m. tonnes); pulses, 457,000 tonnes; cotton, 2·2m. bales of 170 kg. Tobacco and groundnuts are important cash crops.

Livestock (1992): Buffaloes, 5·27m.; other cattle, 6·8m.; sheep and goats, 6·27m.; horses and ponies (1988), 16,015.

Forests covered 18,872 sq. km in 1995.

Fisheries. There were (1993) 123,000 people engaged in fisheries. In 1995–96 there were 22,663 fishing vessels (14,017 motor vessels). The catch for 1995–96 was 0·66m. tonnes.

INDUSTRY. Gujarat is one of the 4 most industrialized states. In 1996 there were 184,120 small-scale units and (1995) 16,532 factories including 1,300 cotton textile factories, 2,752 chemical and chemical products factories, 1,965 non-metallic mineral products factories, 1,678 machinery, machine tools and parts factories and 1,075 rubber, plastic, petroleum and coal products factories. There were 167 industrial estates in 1992–93. Principal industries are textiles, general and electrical engineering, oil-refining, fertilizers, petrochemicals, machine tools, automobiles, heavy chemicals, pharmaceuticals, dyes, sugar, soda ash, cement, man-made fibres, salt, sulphuric acid, paper and paperboard.

State production of soda-ash is 90·4% of national output, and of salt, about 60%. Salt production (1995) 8·7m. tonnes; cement, 5·85m. tonnes.

COMMUNICATIONS

Roads. In 1995–96 there were 71,260 km of roads. Gujarat State Transport Corporation operated 17,254 routes. Number of vehicles, Oct. 1996, 3,602,370.

Railways. In 1995–96 the state had 5,320 route km of railway line.

Civil Aviation. Ahmedabad is the main airport. There are regular services between Ahmedabad and Bombay, Jaipur and Delhi. There are 9 other airports: Bhavnagar, Bhuj, Jamnagar, Kandla, Keshod, Porbandar, Rajkot, Surat and Vadodara.

Shipping. The largest port is Kandla. There are 40 other ports, 11 intermediate, 29 minor.

Telecommunications. There were (1995–96) 8,949 post offices, 1,770 telegraph offices. There were 915,563 telephone connexions in the state.

SOCIAL INSTITUTIONS

Justice. The High Court of Judicature at Ahmedabad has a Chief Justice and 30 puisne judges.

Religion. At the 1991 census Hindus numbered 36,964,228; Moslems, 3,606,920; Jains, 491,331, Christians, 181,753; Sikhs, 33,044; Buddhists, 11,615.

Education. In 1991 the number of literates was 21·28m. (60·91%; male, 72·45%, female 48·5%). Primary and secondary education up to Standard XI are free. Education above Standard XII is free for girls. In 1996–97 there were 14,163 primary schools with 5·81m. students, 19,278 middle schools with 2,143,570 students and 5,792 secondary schools (including 1,831 higher secondary schools) with 1,387,000 students.

There are 10 universities in the state. Gujarat University, Ahmedabad, founded in 1950, is teaching and affiliating; it has 119 affiliated colleges. The Maharaja Sayajirao Universityof Vadodara (1949) is residential and teaching; it has 3 colleges and 32,498 students (1992–93). The Sardar Patel University, Vallabh-Vidyanagar, (1955) has 20 constituent and affiliated colleges; Saurashtra University at Rajkot (1968) has 87 affiliated colleges and 70,044 students (1992–93); South Gujarat University at Surat (1967) has 53 colleges. Bhavnagar University (1978) is residential and teaching with 12 affiliated colleges. North Gujarat University was established at Patan in 1986 and has 20 colleges. Gujarat Vidyapith at Ahmedabad is deemed a university under the University Grants Commission Act. There are also Gujarat Agricultural University, Banaskantha and Gujarat Ayurved University, Jamnagar.

There are 14 engineering and technical colleges, 29 polytechnics, 26 medical colleges and 6 agricultural colleges. There are also 303 arts, science and commerce colleges, 42 teacher-training colleges and 32 law colleges. There were 0·4m. students enrolled in 1993–94 in all colleges.

Health. In 1996 there were 2,528 hospitals (63,417 beds), 957 primary health centres and 7,284 sub-centres. In 1994, 10,776 medical institutions treated 31·37m. patients.

Desai, I. F., *Untouchability in Rural Gujarat*. Bombay, 1977

HARYANA

KEY HISTORICAL EVENTS. The state of Haryana, created on 1 Nov. 1966 under the Punjab Reorganization Act, 1966, was formed from the Hindi-speaking parts of the state of Punjab (India). It comprises the districts of Hissar, Mahendragarh, Gurgaon, Rohtak, Yamunanagar, Rewari, Kaithal, Karnal; Bhiwani, Faridabad, Jind, Kurukshetra, Sirsa, Sonipat, Ambala.

TERRITORY AND POPULATION. Haryana is in north India and is bounded north by Himachal Pradesh, east by Uttar Pradesh, south and west by Rajasthan and north-west by Punjab. Delhi forms an enclave on its eastern boundary. The state has an area of 44,212 sq. km and a population (1991) of 16,463,648; density, 372 per sq. km. Growth rate, 1981–91, 27·41%. Principal cities, *see* INDIA: Territory and Population. Other large towns (1991) are: Rohtak (216,096), Panipat (191,212), Hisar (181,255), Karnal (173,751), Yamunanagar (144,346), Sonipat (143,922), Ambala (139,889), Gurgaon (135,884), Bhiwani (121,629), Sirsa (112,841). The principal language is Hindi.

CONSTITUTION AND GOVERNMENT. The state has a unicameral legislature with 90 members. After the 1996 elections Haryana Vikas Party held 32 seats; Samata Party, 24; Bharatiya Janata, 11; Congress (I), 9; independents and others, 13; vacant, 1. The state shares with Punjab (India) a High Court, a university and certain public services. The capital (shared with Punjab) is Chandigarh. Its transfer to Punjab, intended for 1986, has been postponed. There are 19 districts.

Governor: Mahabir Prasad.
Chief Minister: Bansi Lal.

BUDGET. Budget estimates for 1997–98 show revenue income of Rs 74,426m. and revenue expenditure of Rs 81,560m. Annual plan 1997–98, Rs 15,750m.

ENERGY AND NATURAL RESOURCES

Electricity. Approximately 1,000 MW are supplied to Haryana, mainly from the Bhakra Nangal system. In 1996–97 installed capacity was 2,382 MW and all the villages had electric power.

Minerals. Minerals include placer gold, barytes and rare earths. Value of production, 1987–88, Rs 40m.

Agriculture. Haryana has sandy soil and erratic rainfall, but the state shares the benefit of the Sutlej-Beas scheme. Agriculture employs over 82% of the working population; in 1981 there were about 0·9m. holdings (average 3·7 ha), and the gross irrigated area was 2·05m. ha in 1993–94. Area under foodgrains, 1995–96, 4·02m. ha. Foodgrain production, 1995–96, 10·21m. tonnes (rice 1·86m. tonnes, wheat 7·35m. tonnes); pulses, 416,400 tonnes; cotton, 1·5m. bales of 170 kg; sugar (gur) and oilseeds are important.

Forests covered 603 sq. km in 1995.

INDUSTRY. Haryana has a large market for consumer goods in neighbouring Delhi. In 1996–97 there were 916 large and medium scale industries and 138,759 small units providing employment to about 1m. persons, and 56,012 rural industrial units. The main industries are cotton textiles, agricultural machinery and tractors, woollen textiles, scientific instruments, glass, cement, paper and sugar milling, cars, tyres and tubes, motor cycles, bicycles, steel tubes, engineering goods, electrical and electronic goods. An oil refinery is being set up at Panipat.

COMMUNICATIONS

Roads. There were (1996–97) 22,757 km of metalled roads, linking all villages. Road transport is nationalized. There were 954,563 motor vehicles in 1995–96. In 1996–97 road transport carried 1·65m. passengers daily with a fleet of 3,818 buses.

Railways. The state is crossed by lines from Delhi to Agra, Ajmer, Ferozepur and Chandigarh. Route km, 1995–96, 1,452. The main stations are at Ambala and Kurukshetra.

Civil Aviation. There is no airport within the state but Delhi is on its eastern boundary.

SOCIAL INSTITUTIONS

Justice. Haryana shares the High Court of Punjab and Haryana at Chandigarh.

Religion. At the 1991 census Hindus numbered 14,686,512; Moslems, 763,775; Sikhs, 956,836; Christians, 15,699; Jains, 35,296.

Education. In 1991 the number of literates was 7·43m. (55·85%); 69·1% of men and 40·47% of women. In 1996–97 there were 5,651 primary schools with 1,981,993 students, 3,233 high and higher secondary schools with 511,377 students, 1,631 middle schools with 832,886 students and 129 colleges of arts, science and commerce, 9 engineering and technical colleges and 10 medical colleges. There are 3 universities: Haryana Agricultural University, Hisar; Kurukshetra University, Kurukshetra with 70 colleges and 70,000 students (1993–94), and Maharshi Dayanand University, Rohtak.

Health. There were (1996–97) 111 hospitals (11,061 beds) and community health centres, 399 primary health centres and 2,416 sub-centres, and 442 Ayurvedic and Unani institutions.

HIMACHAL PRADESH

KEY HISTORICAL EVENTS. Thirty small hill states were merged to form the Territory of Himachal Pradesh in 1948; the state of Bilaspur was added in 1954 and parts of the Punjab in 1966. The whole territory became a state in Jan. 1971. The state is a Himalayan area of hill-tribes, rivers and forests. Its main component areas are Chamba, a former princely state, dominated in turn by Moghuls and Sikhs before coming under British influence in 1848; Bilaspur, an independent Punjab state until it was invaded by Gurkhas in 1814 (the British East India Company forces drove out the Gurkhas in 1815); Simla district around the town built by the Company near Bilaspur on land reclaimed from Gurkha troops (the summer capital of India from 1865 until 1948); Mandi, a princely state until 1948; Kangra and Kulu districts, originally Rajput areas which had become part of the British-ruled Punjab; they were incorporated into Himachal Pradesh in 1966 when the Punjab was reorganized.

TERRITORY AND POPULATION. Himachal Pradesh is in north India and is bounded north by Kashmir, east by Tibet, south-east by Uttar Pradesh, south by Haryana, south-west and west by Punjab. The area of the state is 55,673 sq. km and it had a population at the 1991 census of 5,170,877. Density, 93 per sq. km. Growth rate, 1981–91, 20·79%. Principal languages are Hindi and Pahari. The capital is Shimla, population (1991 census) of the urban agglomeration, 110,360.

CONSTITUTION AND GOVERNMENT. Full statehood was attained, as the 18th State of the Union, on 25 Jan. 1971. On 1 Sept. 1972 districts were reorganized and 3 new districts created, Solan, Hamirpur and Una, making a total of 12.

There is a unicameral *Legislative Assembly*. After the elections in Nov. 1993 a Congress (I) government came to power. Total seats, 68: Congress (I), 52; Bharatiya Janata Party, 8; others, 8. The Legislative Assembly was dissolved on 25 Dec. 1997 and new elections ordered.

Governor: V. S. Rama Devi.
Chief Minister: Virbhadra Singh.

BUDGET. Budget estimates for 1997–98 showed receipts of Rs 27,064·2m. and expenditure of Rs 28,905·4m. Annual plan, 1997–98, Rs 10,080m.

ENERGY AND NATURAL RESOURCES

Electricity. In 1991, all the 16,807 villages had electricity. Installed capacity (1995–96), 288·7 MW. Electricity generated (1995–96), 1,286m. kWh.

Water. An artificial confluence of the Sutlej and Beas rivers has been made, directing their united flow into Govind Sagar Lake. Other major rivers are Ravi, Chenab and Yamuna.

Minerals. The state has rock salt, slate, gypsum, limestone, barytes, dolomite and pyrites.

Agriculture. Farming employs 71% of the people. Irrigated area is 17% of the area sown. There are 1,660 tea planters cultivating 2,000 ha. Main crops are seed potatoes, wheat, maize, rice and fruits such as apples, peaches, apricots, nuts, pomegranates; 0·35m. tonnes of fruits were produced in 1996–97.

   Production (1994–95): Rice, 112,200 tonnes; wheat, 412,800 tonnes; pulses, 10,300 tonnes. Total foodgrains, 1·21m. tonnes.

   Livestock (1992 census): Buffaloes, 701,000; other cattle, 2,152,000; goats and sheep, 2·19m.

Forestry. Himachal Pradesh forests cover 63·8% of the state and supply the largest quantities of coniferous timber in northern India. The forests also ensure the safety of the catchment areas of the Yamuna, Sutlej, Beas, Ravi and Chenab rivers. Commercial felling of green trees has been totally halted and forest working nationalized. Area under forests in 1995–96, 35,318 sq. km, of which 1,896 sq. km are reserved and 31,541 sq. km are protected.

INDUSTRY. The main sources of employment are the forests and their related industries; there are factories making turpentine and rosin. The state also makes fertilizers, cement, electronic items and TV sets. There is a foundry and a brewery. Other industries include salt production and handicrafts, including weaving. The state has 161 large and medium units, 25,000 small scale units, 5 industrial estates, 10 industrial areas and 7 electronic complexes.

COMMUNICATIONS

Roads. The national highway from Chandigarh runs through Shimla; other main highways from Shimla serve Kullu, Manali, Kangra, Chamba and Pathankot. The rest are minor roads. Pathankot is also on national highways from Punjab to Kashmir. Length of roads (March 1996), 24,665 km; number of vehicles (1995–96), 119,037; number of transport buses (1995–96), 1,692.

Railways. There is a line from Chandigarh to Shimla, and the Jammu-Delhi line runs through Pathankot. A Nangal-Talwara rail link has been approved by the central government. There are 2 narrow gauge lines, from Shimla to Kalka (96 km) and Jogindernagar to Pathankot (113 km), and a broad gauge line from Una to Nangal (16 km). Route-km in 1995–96, 266 km.

Civil Aviation. The state has airports at Bhuntar near Kullu, at Jubbarhatti near Shimla and at Gaggal in Kangra district.

SOCIAL INSTITUTIONS

Justice. The state has its own High Court at Shimla.

Religion. At the 1991 census Hindus numbered 4,958,560; Moslems, 89,134; Sikhs, 52,050; Buddhists, 64,081; Christians, 4,435.

Education. In 1991, 63·86% of the population were literate (75·36% of men and 52·32% of women). There were (1996–97) 7,732 primary schools with 728,870 students, 1,037 middle schools with 371,622 students, 1,228 high and higher secondary schools with 271,596 students, 62 (including 18 private) arts, science and commerce colleges, 1 engineering college, 2 medical colleges, 1 teacher training college and 3 universities. The universities are Himachal Pradesh University, Shimla (1970) with 48 affiliated colleges and 32,773 students (1992–93), Himachal Pradesh Agricultural University, Palampur (1978) and Dr Y. S. Parmar University of Horticulture and Forestry, Solan (1985).

Health. There were (Dec. 1996) 80 hospitals (9,525 beds), 286 primary and community health centres and 1,831 sub-health centres, and 838 allopathic and Ayurvedic dispensaries.

JAMMU AND KASHMIR

KEY HISTORICAL EVENTS. The state of Jammu and Kashmir, which had earlier been under Hindu rulers and Moslem sultans, became part of the Mogul Empire under Akbar from 1586. After a period of Afghan rule from 1756, it was annexed by the Sikh rulers of the Punjab in 1819. In 1820 Ranjit Singh made over the territory of Jammu to Gulab Singh. After the decisive battle of Sobraon in 1846 Kashmir also was made over to Gulab Singh under the Treaty of Amritsar. British supremacy was recognized until the Indian Independence Act, 1947, when all states decided on accession to India or Pakistan. Kashmir asked for standstill agreements with both. Pakistan agreed, but India desired further discussion with the Government of Jammu and Kashmir State. In the meantime the state became subject to armed attack from the territory of Pakistan and the Maharajah acceded to India on 26 Oct. 1947, by signing the Instrument of Accession. India approached the UN in Jan. 1948; India-Pakistan conflict ended by ceasefire in Jan. 1949. Further conflict in 1965 was followed by the Tashkent Declaration of Jan. 1966. Following further hostilities between India and Pakistan a ceasefire came into effect on 17 Dec. 1971, followed by the Simla Agreement in July 1972, whereby a new line of control was delineated bilaterally through negotiations between India and Pakistan and came into force on 17 Dec. 1972.

TERRITORY AND POPULATION. The state is in the extreme north and is bounded north by China, east by Tibet, south by Himachal Pradesh and Punjab and west by Pakistan. The area is 222,236 sq. km, of which about 78,932 sq. km is occupied by Pakistan and 42,735 sq. km by China; the population of the territory on the Indian side of the line, 1991 projection, was 7,718,700. Growth rate, 1981–91, 28·92%. Srinagar (population, 1991, 892,506) is the summer and Jammu (1,207,996) the winter capital. The official language is Urdu; other commonly spoken languages are Kashmiri (3·1m. speakers at 1981 census), Hindi (1m.), Dogri, Gujri, Pahari, Ladakhi and Punjabi.

CONSTITUTION AND GOVERNMENT. The Maharajah's son, Yuvraj Karan Singh, took over as Regent in 1950 and, on the ending of hereditary rule (17 Oct. 1952), was sworn in as Sadar-i-Riyasat. On his father's death (26 April 1961) Yuvraj Karan Singh was recognized as Maharajah by the Indian Government. The permanent Constitution of the state came into force in part on 17 Nov. 1956 and fully on 26 Jan. 1957. There is a bicameral legislature; the Legislative Council has 36 members and the Legislative Assembly has 87. Since the 1967 elections the 6 representatives of Jammu and Kashmir in the central House of the People are directly elected; there are 4 representatives in the Council of States. After a period of President's rule, a National Conference–Indira Congress coalition government was formed in March 1987. The government was dismissed and the state was brought under President's rule on 18 July 1990. Elections were held in Sept.-Oct. 1996 and National Conference formed a government. Total seats, 87: National Conference, 57; Bharatiya Janata Party, 8; Congress (I), 7; Janata Dal, 5; Independent and others, 10.

The state has 14 districts.

Governor: Gen. K. V. Krishna Rao.
Chief Minister: Dr Farooq Abdullah.

BUDGET. Budget estimates for 1997–98 show total receipts of Rs 53,628·9m. and total expenditure of Rs 52,748·1m. Annual Plan (1997–98) Rs 15,500m.

ENERGY AND NATURAL RESOURCES

Electricity. Installed capacity (1996–97) 365·8 MW; 6,252 villages had electricity in 1995–96.

Minerals. Minerals include coal, bauxite and gypsum.

Agriculture. About 80% of the population are supported by agriculture. Rice, wheat and maize are the major cereals. The total area under foodgrains (1995–96) was estimated at 887,000 ha. Total foodgrains produced, 1995–96, 1·37m. tonnes (rice, 0·51m. tonnes; wheat, 0·35m. tonnes); pulses, 22,900 tonnes. Fruit is important: Production, 1994–95, 0·9m. tonnes; exports, 0·76m. tonnes.

Irrigated area, 1993–94, 442,000 ha.

Livestock (1982): Cattle, 2,325,200; buffaloes, 5,631,000; goats, 1,003,900; sheep, 1,908,700; horses, 973,000, and poultry, 2,406,760.

Forestry. Forests cover about 20,443 sq. km (1995), forming an important source of revenue, besides providing employment to a large section of the population.

INDUSTRY. There are 2 central public sector industries and 30 medium-scale. There are 35,576 small units (1994–95) employing over 125,000. There are industries based on horticulture; traditional handicrafts are silk spinning, wood-carving, papier-maché and carpet-weaving. 750 tonnes of silk cocoons were produced in 1994–95.

The handicraft sector employed 0·26m. persons and had a production turnover of Rs 2,500m. in 1995–96.

COMMUNICATIONS

Roads. Kashmir is linked with the rest of India by the motorable Jammu-Pathankot road. The Jawahar Tunnel, through the Banihal mountain, connects Srinagar and Jammu, and maintains road communication with the Kashmir Valley during the winter months. In 1994–95 there were 12,252 km of roads.

There were 195,125 motor vehicles in 1995–96.

Railways. Kashmir is linked with the Indian railway system by the line between Jammu and Pathankot; route km of railways in the state, 1995–96, 88 km.

Civil Aviation. Major airports, with daily service from Delhi, are at Srinagar and Jammu. There is a third airport at Leh.

Telecommunications. There were 1,583 post offices in 1994, and 202 telephone exchanges and 54,644 telephones in 1994–95.

SOCIAL INSTITUTIONS

Justice. The High Court, at Srinagar and Jammu, has a Chief Justice and 4 puisne judges.

Religion. The majority of the population, except in Jammu, are Moslems. At the 1981 census Moslems numbered 3,843,451; Hindus, 1,930,448; Sikhs, 133,675; Buddhists, 69,706; Christians, 8,481; Jains, 1,576.

Education. The proportion of literates was 32·68% in 1991 (44·18% of men and 19·55% of women). Education is free. There were (1996–97) 1,351 high and higher secondary schools with 227,699 students, 3,104 middle schools with 405,598 students and 10,483 primary schools with 893,005 students. Jammu University (1969) has 5 constituent and 13 affiliated colleges, with 15,278 students (1992–93); Kashmir University (1948) has 18 colleges (17,000 students, 1992–93); the third university is Sher-E-Kashmir University of Agricultural Sciences and Technology. There are 4 medical colleges, 2 engineering and technology colleges, 4 polytechnics, 8 oriental colleges and an Ayurvedic college, 34 arts, science and commerce colleges and 4 teacher training colleges.

Health. In 1993–94 there were 43 hospitals with 9,256 beds, 264 primary health centres and 1,740 sub-centres, and 35 community health centres. There is a National Institute of Medical Sciences.

Lamb, A., *Kashmir: a Disputed Legacy, 1846–1990*. Hertingfordbury, 1991.
Wirsing, R. G., *India, Pakistan and the Kashmir Dispute: on Regional Conflict and its Resolution*. London, 1995

KARNATAKA

KEY HISTORICAL EVENTS. The state of Karnataka, constituted as Mysore under the States Reorganization Act, 1956, brought together the Kannada-speaking people distributed in 5 states, and consisted of the territories of the old states of Mysore and Coorg, the Bijapur, Kanara and Dharwar districts and the Belgaum district (except one taluk) in former Bombay, the major portions of the Gulbarga, Raichur and Bidar districts in former Hyderabad, the South Kanara district (apart from the Kasaragod taluk) and the Kollegal taluk of the Coimbatore district in Madras. The state was renamed Karnataka in 1973.

TERRITORY AND POPULATION. The state is in south India and is bounded north by Maharashtra, east by Andhra Pradesh, south by Tamil Nadu and Kerala, west by the Indian ocean and north-east by Goa. The area of the state is 191,791 sq. km, and its population (1991 census), 44,977,201, an increase of 21·82% since 1981. Density, 235 per sq. km. Principal cities, *see* INDIA: Territory and Population. The capital is Bangalore. Other large towns (1991) are: Bellary (245,391), Bijapur (186,939), Shimoga (178,882), Raichur (157,551), Timkur (138,903), Gadag-Betigeri (134,051), Mandya (120,265), Hospet (114,154), Bidar (108,016).

Kannada is the language of administration and is spoken by about 66% of the people. Other languages include Telugu (8·17%), Urdu (9%), Marathi (4·5%), Tamil (3·6%), Tulu and Konkani.

CONSTITUTION AND GOVERNMENT. Karnataka has a bicameral legislature. The Legislative Council has 75 members. The Legislative Assembly consists of 224 elected members. At the elections in Nov. 1994 the Janata Dal gained 116 seats; the Bharatiya Janata Party, 40; Congress (I), 35; the Karnataka Congress Party, 10; independents and others, 23. Janata Dal formed a government.

The state has 20 districts grouped in 4 divisions: Bangalore, Belgaum, Gulbarga and Mysore. The capital is Bangalore.

Governor: Khurshid Alam Khan.
Chief Minister: J. H. Patel.

BUDGET. Budget estimates, 1997–98: Revenue receipts, Rs 117,664·5m.; revenue expenditure, Rs 119,654·5m. Plan allocation 1997–98, Rs 41,300m.

ENERGY AND NATURAL RESOURCES

Electricity. In 1995–96 the state's installed capacity was 3,377·5 MW. Electricity generated, 1994–95, 16,830m. kWh. 26,483 villages had electricity in March 1996.

Water. About 2,327,193 ha were irrigated in 1993–94.

Minerals. Karnataka is an important source of gold and silver. The estimated reserves of high grade iron ore are 8,798m. tonnes. These reserves are found mainly in the Chitradurga belt. The National Mineral Development Corporation of India has indicated total reserves of nearly 332m. tonnes of magnesite and iron ore (with an iron content ranging from 25 to 40) which have been found in Kudremukh Ganga-

Mula region in Chickmagalur District. Value of production (1992–93) Rs 2,590m. The estimated reserves of manganese are over 320m. tonnes.

Limestone is found in many regions; deposits (1992–93) are about 5,892m. tonnes.

Karnataka is the largest producer of chromite. It is one of the only two states of India producing magnesite. The other minerals of industrial importance are corundum and garnet.

Agriculture. Agriculture forms the main occupation of more than three-quarters of the population. Physically, Karnataka divides into 4 regions—the coastal region, the southern and northern plains, comprising roughly the districts of Bangalore, Tumkur, Chitradurga, Kolar, Bellary, Mandya and Mysore, and the hill country, comprising the districts of Chickmagalur, Hassan and Shimoga. Rainfall is heavy in the hill country, and there is dense forest. The greater part of the plains are cultivated. Coorg district is essentially agricultural.

The main food crops are rice paddy and jowar, and ragi which is also about 30% of the national crop. Total foodgrains production (1995–96), 8·77m. tonnes (rice 3·02m. tonnes, wheat 150,200 tonnes); pulses 0·72m. tonnes. Sugar, groundnut, castor-seed, safflower, mulberry silk and cotton are important cash crops. The state grows about 70% of the national coffee crop.

Production, 1995–96: Sugar-cane, 24·92m. tonnes; cotton (1993–94), 773,279 bales (each 170 kg).

Livestock (1992–93): Buffaloes, 4·07m.; other cattle, 10·18m.; sheep, 4·73m.; goats, 3·89m.

Forestry. Total forest in the state (1995) is 30,382 sq. km, producing sandalwood, bamboo and other timbers.

Fisheries. Production, 1995–96, 304,870 tonnes.

INDUSTRY. There were 7,765 factories, 125 industrial estates and 5,176 industrial sheds employing 818,000 in March 1994. In 1994–95, 163,524 small industries employed 1,076,312 persons. The Vishveshwaraiah Iron and Steel Works is situated at Bhadravati, while at Bangalore are national undertakings for the manufacture of aircraft, machine tools, telephones, light engineering and electronics goods. The Kudremukh iron ore project is of national importance. An oil refinery is in operation at Mangalore. Other industries include textiles, vehicle manufacture, cement, chemicals, sugar, paper, porcelain and soap. In addition, much of the world's sandalwood is processed, the oil being one of the most valuable productions of the state. Sericulture is a more important cottage industry giving employment, directly or indirectly, to about 2·7m. persons; production of raw silk, 1992–93, 7,147 tonnes, over two-thirds of national production.

COMMUNICATIONS

Roads. In 1993–94 the state had 134,832 km of roads, including 1,997 km of national highway. There were (31 March 1996) 2,249,890 motor vehicles.

Railways. In 1995–96 there were 3,124 km of railway (including 149 km of narrow gauge) in the state.

Civil Aviation. There are airports at Bangalore, Hubli, Mysore, Mangalore, Bellary and Belgaum, with regular scheduled services to Bombay, Calcutta, Delhi and Madras.

Shipping. Mangalore is a deep-water port for the export of mineral ores. Karwar is being developed as an intermediate port.

SOCIAL INSTITUTIONS

Justice. The seat of the High Court is at Bangalore. It has a Chief Justice and 21 puisne judges.

Religion. At the 1991 census there were 38,432,027 Hindus; 5,234,023 Moslems; 859,478 Christians; 326,114 Jains; 73,012 Buddhists; 10,101 Sikhs.

Education. The number of literates, according to the 1991 census, was 21·08m. (56·04%; 67·26% of men and 44·34% of women). In 1996–97 the state had 22,870 primary schools with 6,507,805 students, 18,485 middle schools with 2,158,487 students, 7,644 high and higher secondary schools with 1,270,794 students, 172 polytechnic and 125 medical colleges, 49 engineering and technology colleges, 761 arts, science and commerce colleges and 12 universities. Education is free up to pre-university level.

Universities: Mysore (1916); Karnataka (1949) at Dharwar; University of Agricultural Sciences (1964) at Hebbal, Bangalore; Gulbarga; Mangalore; University of Agricultural Sciences, Dharwad; Kuvempu University, Shimoga; Kannada University and National Law School of India. Mysore has 6 university and 125 affiliated colleges; Karnataka, 5 and 240; Bangalore, 204 affiliated; Hebbal, 8 constituent colleges.

The Indian Institute of Science, Bangalore, has the status of a university.

Health. There were in 1993–94, 306 hospitals, 208 dispensaries, 1,459 primary health centres and 459 family welfare centres. Total number of beds in 1993–94, 43,308.

KERALA

KEY HISTORICAL EVENTS. The state of Kerala was created in 1956, bringing together the Malayalam-speaking areas. It includes most of the former state of Travancore Cochin and small areas from the state of Madras.

Cochin, an exceptionally safe harbour, was an early site of European trading in India. In 1795 the British took it from the Dutch and British influence remained dominant.

Travancore was a Hindu state which became a British protectorate in 1795, having been an ally of the British East India Company for some years.

Cochin and Travancore were combined as one state in 1947, reorganized and renamed Kerala in 1956.

TERRITORY AND POPULATION. Kerala is in south India and is bounded north by Karnataka, east and south-east by Tamil Nadu, south-west and west by the Indian ocean. The state has an area of 38,863 sq. km. The 1991 census showed a population of 29,098,518; density of population was 749 per sq. km. Growth rate, 1981–91, 14·32%. Chief cities, *see* INDIA: Territory and Population. Other principal towns (1991): Alappuzha (174,666), Kollam (139,852), Palakkad (123,289), Thalassery (103,577).

Languages spoken in the state are Malayalam, Tamil and Kannada.

CONSTITUTION AND GOVERNMENT. The state has a unicameral legislature of 140 elected (and one nominated) members including the Speaker. After the elections of April–May 1996 the Left Democratic Front led by CPI (M) and allies held 80 seats, the United Democratic Front led by Congress (I), 59.

The state has 14 districts. The capital is Thiruvananthapuram.

Governor: Sukhdev Singh Kang.
Chief Minister: E. K. Nayanar.

BUDGET. Budget estimates for 1997–98 showed revenue receipts of Rs 75,534m. expenditure Rs 87,957m. Annual Plan expenditure, 1997–98, Rs 28,500m.

ENERGY AND NATURAL RESOURCES

Electricity. Installed capacity (1995–96), 1,505 MW; energy generated in 1995–96 was 6,662m. kWh. The Idukki hydro-electric plant produced 3,064m. kWh, the Sabarigiri scheme 1,674m. kWh. All villages are electrified.

Minerals. The beach sands of Kerala contain monazite, ilmenite, rutile, zircon, sillimanite, etc. There are extensive whiteclay deposits; other minerals of commercial importance include magnesite, china clay, limestone, quartz sand and lignite. Iron ore has been found at Kozhikode (Calicut).

Agriculture. Area under irrigation in 1995–96 was 644,000 ha; 6 irrigation projects were under execution in 1996–97. The chief agricultural products are rice, tapioca, coconut, arecanut, cashewnut, oilseeds, pepper, sugar-cane, rubber, tea, coffee and cardamom. About 98% of Indian black pepper and about 95% of Indian rubber is produced in Kerala. Production of principal crops, 1994–95: Total foodgrains, 1·1m. tonnes (of which rice 953,026 tonnes from 471,000 ha); pulses, 16,800 tonnes; sugar-cane, 464,000 tonnes; rubber, 475,000 tonnes; tea, 64,794 tonnes; coffee, 42,600 tonnes; cashewnuts, 96,780 tonnes.

Livestock (1987); Buffaloes, 329,000; other cattle, 3·4m.; goats, 1·6m. In 1995–96 milk production was 2·24m. tonnes; egg production, 1,991m.

Forestry. Forest occupied 10,336 sq. km in 1995, including teak, sandal wood, ebony and blackwood and varieties of softwood. Net forest revenue, 1995–96, Rs 1,607·7m.

Fisheries. Fishing is a flourishing industry; the total catch in 1995–96 was 582,000 tonnes (of which marine, 532,000 tonnes). Fish exports, 78,896 tonnes in 1995–96.

INDUSTRY. There are numerous cashew and coir factories. Important industries are rubber, tea, coffee, tiles, automotive tyres, watches, electronics, oil, textiles, ceramics, fertilizers and chemicals, pharmaceuticals, zinc-smelting, sugar, cement, rayon, glass, matches, pencils, monazite, ilmenite, titanium oxide, rare earths, aluminium, electrical goods, paper, shark-liver oil, etc. The state has a refinery and a shipyard at Kochi (Cochin).

The number of factories registered under the Factories Act 1948 on 31 Dec. 1995 was 15,965, with daily average employment of 0·41m. There were 143,23 small-scale units employing 0·78m. persons on 31 March 1996.

COMMUNICATIONS

Roads. In 1995–96 there were 144,636 km of roads in the state; national highways, 1,011 km. There were 1·17m. motor vehicles at 31 March 1996.

Railways. There is a coastal line from Mangalore in Karnataka which connects with Tamil Nadu. In 1995–96 there were 1,053 route-km of track.

Civil Aviation. There are airports at Kozhikode, Kochi and Thiruvananthapuram with regular scheduled services to Delhi, Bombay and Madras; international flights leave from Thiruvananthapuram.

Shipping. Port Kochi, administered by the central government, is one of India's major ports; in 1983 it became the out-port for the Inland Container Depot at Coimbatore in Tamil Nadu. There are 12 other ports and harbours.

SOCIAL INSTITUTIONS

Justice. The High Court at Ernakulam has a Chief Justice and 21 puisne judges.

Religion. At the 1991 census there were 16,668,587 Hindus; 6,788,364 Moslems; 5,621,510 Christians; 3,641 Jains; 2,224 Sikhs.

Education. Kerala is the most literate Indian State with 22·66m. literates at the 1991 census (89·81%); 93·62% of men and 86·13% of women. Education is free up to the age of 14.

In 1996–97 there were 6,725 primary schools with 2·79m. students, 2,998 middle schools with 1·84m. students and 3,125 high and higher secondary schools with 1·07m. students. There were also 169 junior colleges with 210,074 pupils.

Kerala University (established 1937) at Thiruvananthapuram is affiliating and teaching; in 1995–96 it had 52 affiliated colleges with 113,569 students. The University of Kochi is federal, and for post-graduate studies only. The University of Calicut (established 1968) is teaching and affiliating and has 95 affiliated colleges with 122,343 students (1995–96). Kerala Agricultural University (established 1971) has 7 constituent colleges. Mahatma Gandhi University at Kottayam was established in 1983 and has 64 affiliated colleges with 112,992 students (1995–96). There are 2 other universities, Sree Sankaracharya University and Malabar University. There were also (1995–96) 6 medical colleges, 15 engineering and technology colleges, 19 teacher training colleges and 211 arts and science colleges.

Health. There were 149 allopathic hospitals, 961 primary health centres, 60 community health centres, 53 dispensaries, 21 TB centres/clinics and 15 leprosy control units, with 42,569 beds, in 1995–96. There were also 108 Ayurvedic hospitals with 2,529 beds and 31 homeopathy hospitals with 394 beds.

Further Reading

Jeffrey, R., *Politics, Women and Well-Being: How Kerala became a Model.* London, 1992

MADHYA PRADESH

KEY HISTORICAL EVENTS. The state was formed in 1956 to bring together the Hindu-speaking districts of the area including most of the former state of Madhya Bharat, the former states of Bhopal and Vindhya Pradesh and a former Rajput enclave, Sironj.

This was an area which the Mahrattas took from the Moghuls between 1712 and 1760. The British overcame Mahratta power in 1818 and established their own Central Provinces. Nagpur became the Provinces capital and was also the capital of Madhya Pradesh until in 1956 boundary changes transferred it to Maharashtra.

The present capital, Bhopal, was the centre of a Moslem princely state from 1723. An ally of the British against the Mahrattas, Bhopal (with neighbouring small states) became a British-protected agency in 1818. After independence Bhopal acceded to the Indian Union in 1949. The states of Madhya Bharat and Vindhya Pradesh were then formed as neighbours, and in 1956 were combined with Bhopal and Sironj and renamed Madhya Pradesh.

TERRITORY AND POPULATION. The state is in central India and is bounded north by Uttar Pradesh, east by Bihar and Orissa, south by Andhra Pradesh and Maharashtra, west by Gujarat and Rajasthan. Madhya Pradesh is the largest Indian state in size, with an area of 443,446 sq. km. In respect of population it ranks fifth. Population (1991 census), 66,181,170, an increase of 26·84% since 1981. Density, 149 per sq. km.

Cities with over 250,000 population, *see* INDIA: Territory and Population. Other large cities (1991): Ratlam, 195,776; Sagar, 195,346; Bilaspur, 192,396; Burhanpur, 172,710; Dewas, 164,364; Murwara, 163,431; Satna, 160,500; Durg, 150,645; Morena, 147,124; Khandwa, 145,133; Rewa, 128,981; Rajnandgaon, 125,371; Korba, 124,501; Bhind, 109,755; Shivpuri, 108,271; Guna, 100,490.

The number of persons speaking each of the more prevalent languages (1981 census) were: Hindi, 43,870,242; Urdu, 1,131,288; Marathi, 1,184,128; Gujarati, 581,084. In April 1990 Hindi became the sole official language.

CONSTITUTION AND GOVERNMENT. Madhya Pradesh is one of the 9 states for which the Constitution provides a bicameral legislature, but the Vidhan Parishad or Upper House (to consist of 90 members) has yet to be formed. The Vidhan Sabha or Lower House has 320 elected members. Following the election in Nov. 1993, Congress (I) came to power. Congress (I), 177; Bharatiya Janata Party, 112; Bahujan Samaj Party, 11; Janata Dal, 4; independents and others, 16.

For administrative purposes the state has been split into 12 divisions with a Commissioner at the head of each; the headquarters of these are located at Bhopal, Bilaspur, Gwalior, Hoshangabad, Indore, Jabalpur, Jagdalpur, Morena, Raipur, Rewa, Sagar and Ujjain. There are 45 districts.

The seat of government is at Bhopal.

Governor: Mohammad Shafi Qureshi.
Chief Minister: Digvijay Singh.

BUDGET. Budget estimates for 1996–97 showed revenue receipts of Rs 102,771m. and expenditure of Rs 108,426m. Annual plan, 1997–98, Rs 34,000m.

ENERGY AND NATURAL RESOURCES

Electricity. Madhya Pradesh is rich in low-grade coal suitable for power generation, and also has immense potential hydro-electric energy. Total installed capacity, 1995–96, 3,863·4 MW. Power generated, 17,599m. kWh in 1995–96. There are 6 hydro-electric power station of 848 MW installed capacity. 67,741 out of 71,352 villages were electrified by 1995–96.

Water. Major irrigation projects include the Chambal Valley scheme (started in 1952 with Rajasthan), the Tawa project in Hoshangabad district, the Barna and Hasdeo schemes, the Mahanadi canal system and schemes in the Narmada valley at Bargi and Narmadasagar.

Minerals. The state had (1996) extensive mineral deposits, including 8,001m. tonnes of limestone, 126·8m. tonnes of bauxite, 26,853m. tonnes of coal and 2,186·2m. tonnes of iron ore.
In 1995–96 the output of major minerals was (in tonnes): Limestone, 27·45m.; diamonds, 30,000 carats; iron ore, 17·43m.; manganese ore, 0·4m. Revenue from minerals, 1996–97, Rs 8,500m. Coal output was 79·97m. tonnes in 1995–96.

Agriculture. Agriculture is the mainstay of the state's economy and 76·8% of the people are rural. 43·7% of the land area is cultivable, of which 16·6% is irrigated. Production of principal crops, 1994–95 (in tonnes): Foodgrains, 18·86m. (rice, 6m., wheat, 7·17m.); pulses, 3·4m.; cotton, 0·35m. bales of 170 kg.
Livestock (1992): Buffaloes, 7·97m.; other cattle, 30·34m.; sheep and goats, 7·3m.

Forestry. Forested area total 154,000 sq. km, or about 34·8% of the state. The forests are chiefly of sal, saja and teak species. They are the chief source in India of best-quality teak; they also provide firewood for about 60% of domestic fuel needs, and form valuable watershed protection. Forest revenue, 1995–96, Rs 5,250m.

INDUSTRY. The major industries are steel, aluminium, paper, cement, motor vehicles, ordnance, textiles and heavy electrical equipment. Other industries include sugar, fertilizers, straw board, vegetable oil, refractories, potteries, textile machinery, steel casting and rerolling, industrial gases, synthetic fibres, drugs, biscuit manufacturing, engineering, electronics, optical fibres, plastics, tools, rayon and art silk. The number of heavy and medium industries in the state is 759, with 600 ancillary industries; the number of small-scale establishments in production is 414,000. 39 out of 45 districts in the state are categorized as industrially backward.
There are 23 'growth centres' in operation, and 5 under development.

COMMUNICATIONS

Roads. Total length of roads in 1995–96 was 97,343 km. In 1995–96 there were 2,286,000 motor vehicles.

Railways. Bhopal, Bilaspur, Katni, Khandwa and Ratlam are junctions for the central, south, eastern and western networks. Route length (1995–96), 5,761·5 km.

Civil Aviation. There are airports at Bhopal, Gwalior, Indore, Khajuraho and Raipur with regular scheduled services to Bombay and Delhi, Varanasi, Nagpur, Raipur and Bhubaneswar.

SOCIAL INSTITUTIONS

Justice. The High Court of Judicature at Jabalpur has a Chief Justice and 21 puisne judges. Its benches are located at Gwalior and Indore.

Religion. At the 1991 census Hindus numbered 61,412,898; Moslems, 3,282,800; Christians, 426,598; Buddhists, 216,667; Sikhs, 161,111; Jains, 490,324.

Education. The 1991 census showed 23·49m. people to be literate (44·28%; 58·42% of men; 28·86% of women). Education is free for children aged up to 14.

In 1996 there were 75,000 primary schools with 8·97m. students, 17,800 middle schools with 3·42m. students, 2,582 high schools with 1·1m. students and 3,039 higher secondary schools with 0·61m. students.

There are 14 universities in Madhya Pradesh: Dr. Hari Singh Gour University (established 1946), at Sagar, had 97 affiliated colleges and 74,386 students in 1992–93; Rani Durgavati University at Jabalpur (1957) had 46 affiliated colleges and 45,315 students; Vikram University (1957), at Ujjain, had 83 affiliated colleges and 39,723 students; Indira Kala Sangeet Vishwavidyalaya (1956), at Khairagarh, had 33 affiliated colleges and (1991–92) 6,720 students on roll (this university teaches music and fine arts); Devi Ahilya University at Indore (1964) had 32 affiliated colleges and 28,196 students; Jiwaji University (1963), at Gwalior, had 60 affiliated colleges and (1991–92) 58,825 students; Jawaharlal Nehru Krishi University (1964), at Jabalpur, had 10 constituent colleges and 2,053 students; Ravishankar University (1964), at Raipur, had 89 affiliated colleges; Indira Gandhi Krishi Vishwavidyalaya, Raipur; A. P. Singh University, Rewa had 81 colleges and 24,960 students; Barkatullah Vishwavidyalaya, Bhopal had 44 colleges and 18,817 students; Guru Ghasidas University, Bilaspur had 58 colleges and 34,717 students; Makhanlal Chaturvedi Rashtriya Patrakarita Vishwavidhyalaya Bhopal; Chitrakoot Gramodoya Vishwavidhayalaya Chitrakoot. In 1994–95 there were 448 colleges of arts, science and commerce, 20 teacher-training colleges, and 14 engineering and technology colleges, 7 medical colleges, 41 polytechnics and 69 technical-industrial arts and craft schools.

Health. In March 1996 there were 620 hospitals and dispensaries, and 1,615 primary and mini-primary health centres and 11,936 sub-health centres.

MAHARASHTRA

KEY HISTORICAL EVENTS. The Bombay Presidency of the East India Company began with a trading factory, made over to the Company in 1668. The Presidency expanded, overcoming the surrounding Mahratta chiefs until Mahratta power was finally conquered in 1818.

After independence Bombay State succeeded the Presidency; its area was altered in 1956 by adding Kutch and Saurashtra and the Marathi-speaking areas of Hyderabad and Madhya Pradesh, and taking away Kannada-speaking areas (which were added to Mysore).

In 1960 the Bombay Reorganization Act divided Bombay State between Gujarati and Marathi areas, the latter becoming Maharashtra.

The state of Maharashtra consists of the following districts of the former Bombay State: Ahmednagar, Akola, Amravati, Aurangabad, Bhandara, Bhir, Buldana, Chanda, Dhulia (West Khandesh), Greater Bombay, Jalgaon (East Khandesh), Kolaba, Kolhapur, Nagpur, Nanded, Nasik, Osmanabad, Parbhani, Pune, Ratnagiri, Sangli, Satara, Sholapur, Thane, Wardha, Yeotmal; certain portions of Thane and Dhulia districts have become part of Gujarat.

TERRITORY AND POPULATION. Maharashtra is in central India and is bounded north and east by Madhya Pradesh, south by Andhra Pradesh, Karnataka and Goa, west by the Indian ocean and north-west by Daman and Gujarat. The state has an area of 307,713 sq. km. The population at the 1991 census was 78,937,187 (an increase of 25·73% since 1981), of whom about 30m. were Marathi-speaking. Density, 257 per sq. km. The area of Greater Bombay was 603 sq. km. and its population 9·93m. For other principal cities, *see* INDIA: Territory and Population. Other large towns (1991): Jalgaon (242,193), Chandrapur (226,105), Ichalkaranji (214,950), Latur (197,408), Sangli (193,197), Parbhani (190,255), Ahmadnagar (181,339), Jalna (174,958), Bhusawal (145,143), Miraj (125,407), Bid (112,434), Gondiya (109,470), Yavatmul (108,578), Wardha (102,985).

CONSTITUTION AND GOVERNMENT. Maharashtra has a bicameral legislature. The Legislative Council has 78 members. The Legislative Assembly has 288 elected members and 1 member nominated by the Governor to represent the Anglo-Indian community. Following the election of Feb. 1995 Shiv Sena and Bharatiya Janata formed a coalition government. The party composition of the Legislative Council was: Congress (I), 81; Shiv Sena, 73; Bharatiya Janata Party, 65; Janata Dal, 11; People's and Workers' Party, 6; independents and others, 52.

The Council of Ministers consists of the Chief Minister, 16 other Ministers, and 19 Ministers of State.

The capital is Bombay. The state has 30 districts.

Governor: P. C. Alexander.
Chief Minister: Manohar Joshi.

BUDGET. Budget estimates, 1995–96: Revenue receipts, Rs 151,802m.; revenue expenditure, Rs 167,657m. Plan outlay, 1997–98, Rs 83,250m.

ENERGY AND NATURAL RESOURCES

Electricity. Installed capacity, 1995–96, 10,039 MW (7,155 MW thermal, 1,602 MW hydro-electric, 1,092 MW gas and 190 MW nuclear). All villages are electrified. Electricity generated, 1996–97, 39,599m. kWh.

Oil and Gas. Bombay High (offshore) produced 22·7m. tonnes of crude oil and 16,579,000 cu. metres of natural gas in 1995–96.

Minerals. The state has coal, silica sand, dolomite, kyanite, chromite, limestone, iron ore, manganese, bauxite. Value of mineral production, 1995, Rs 11,590m.

Agriculture. 3·3m. ha of the cropped area of 21·4m. ha are irrigated. In normal seasons the main food crops are rice, wheat, jowar, bajra and pulses. Main cash crops: Cotton, sugar-cane, groundnuts. Production, 1994–95 (in tonnes): Foodgrains, 11·5m. (rice, 2·4m.; wheat, 1·11m.); pulses, 1·7m.; cotton, 401,300; sugar-cane, 42·68m.; groundnuts, 0·63m.

Livestock (1992 census, in 1,000): Buffaloes, 5,447; other cattle, 17,441; sheep and goats, 13,015; poultry, 32,189.

Forestry. Forests occupied 64,300 sq. km. in 1995–96. Value of forest products in 1996–97, Rs 2,820m.

Fisheries. In 1995–96 the marine fish catch was estimated at 424,000 tonnes and the inland fish catch at 84,000 tonnes; 18,038 boats, including 8,552 mechanized, were used for marine fishing.

INDUSTRY. Industry is concentrated mainly in Bombay, Nashik, Pune and Thane. The main groups are chemicals and products, textiles, electrical and non-electrical machinery, petroleum and products, aircraft, rubber and plastic products, transport equipment, automobiles, paper, electronic items, engineering goods, pharmaceuticals and food products. The state industrial development corporation invested Rs 77,020m. in 21,452 industrial units in 1994–95. In June 1995 there were 26,642 working factories employing 1·2m. people. In Dec. 1996 there were 203,882 small scale industries employing 1·63m. people.

COMMUNICATIONS

Roads. On 31 March 1996 there were 223,000 km of roads, of which 187,090 km were surfaced. There were 4,359,029 motor vehicles on 1 Jan. 1997, of which 17% were in Greater Bombay. Passenger and freight transport has been nationalized.

Railways. The total length of railway on 31 March 1996 was 5,462 km; 66% was broad gauge, 14% metre gauge and 20% narrow gauge. The main junctions and termini are Bombay, Dadar, Manmad, Akola, Nagpur, Pune and Sholapur.

Civil Aviation. The main airport is Bombay, which has national and international flights. Nagpur airport is on the route from Bombay to Calcutta and there are also airports at Pune and Aurangabad.

Shipping. Maharashtra has a coastline of 720 km. Bombay is the major port, and there are 48 minor ports.

SOCIAL INSTITUTIONS

Justice. The High Court has a Chief Justice and 45 judges. The seat of the High Court is Bombay, but it has benches at Nagpur, Aurangabad and Panaji (Goa).

Religion. At the 1991 census Hindus numbered 64,033,213; Moslems, 7,628,755; Buddhists, 5,040,785; Christians, 885,030; Jains, 965,840; Sikhs, 161,184. Other religions, 99,768; religion not stated, 106,560.

Education. The number of literates, according to the 1991 census, was 42·8m. (64·87%; men, 76·56%, women, 52·32%). In 1996–97, there were 13,225 high and higher secondary schools with 2,795,567 pupils; 21,969 middle schools with 4,753,257 pupils and 41,005 primary schools, with 11,685,598 pupils. There are 111 engineering and technology colleges, 156 medical colleges (including dental and Ayurvedic colleges), 244 teacher training colleges, 152 polytechnics and 820 arts, science and commerce colleges.

Bombay University, founded in 1857, is mainly an affiliating university. It has 276 colleges with a total (1993–94) of 234,469 students. Nagpur University (1923) is both teaching and affiliating. It has 258 colleges with 95,664 students. Poona University, founded in 1948, is teaching and affiliating; it has 167 colleges and 151,990 students. The SNDT Women's University had 33 colleges with a total of 33,343 students. Dr B. R. Ambedkar Marathwada University, Aurangabad, was founded in 1958 as a teaching and affiliating body to control colleges in the Marathwada or Marathi-speaking area, previously under Osmania University; it has 190 colleges and 195,806 students. Shivaji University, Kolhapur, was established in 1963 to control affiliated colleges previously under Poona University. It has 205 colleges and 115,553 students. Amravati University has 130 colleges and 74,484 students. Other universities are: Marathwada Krishi Vidyapeeth, Parbhani; Y. Chavan Maharashtra Open University, Nashik; North Maharashtra University, Jalgaon, with 101 colleges and 66,092 students; Mahatma Phule Krishi University, Rahuri; Punjabrao Krishi University, Akola; Konkan Krishi University, Dapoli; Dr Babasaheb Ambedkar Technological University; North Maharashtra University and Swami Ramanand Teerth Marathwad University.

Health. In 1995 there were 736 hospitals (124,701 beds), 1,418 dispensaries and 1,695 primary health centres, 161 primary health units and 2,154 TB hospitals and clinics.

MANIPUR

KEY HISTORICAL EVENTS. Formerly a state under the political control of the Government of India, Manipur, on 15 Aug. 1947, entered into interim arrangements with the Indian Union and the political agency was abolished. The administration was taken over by the Government of India on 15 Oct. 1949 under a merger agreement, and it was centrally administered by the Government of India through a Chief Commissioner. In 1950–51 an Advisory form of Government was introduced. In 1957 this was replaced by a Territorial Council of 30 elected and 2 nominated members. Later in 1963 a Legislative Assembly of 30 elected and 3 nominated members was established under the Government of Union Territories Act 1963. Because of the unstable party position in the Assembly, it had to be dissolved on 16 Oct. 1969 and President's Rule introduced. The status of the administrator was raised from Chief Commissioner to Lieut.-Governor with effect from 19 Dec. 1969. On the 21 Jan. 1972 Manipur became a state and the status of the administrator was changed from Lieut.-Governor to Governor.

TERRITORY AND POPULATION. The state is in north-east India and is bounded north by Nagaland, east by Myanmar, south by Myanmar and Mizoram, and west by Assam. Manipur has an area of 22,327 sq. km and a population (1991) of 1,837,149. Density, 82 per sq. km. Growth rate, 1981–91, 29·29%. The valley, which is about 1,813 sq. km, is 2,600 ft above sea-level. The hills rise in places to nearly 10,000 ft, but are mostly about 5,000–6,000 ft. The average annual rainfall is 65 in. The hill areas are inhabited by various hill tribes who constitute about one-third of the total population of the state. There are about 30 tribes and sub-tribes falling into two main groups of Nagas and Kukis. Manipuri and English are the official languages. A large number of dialects are spoken.

CONSTITUTION AND GOVERNMENT. With the attainment of statehood, Manipur has a Legislative Assembly of 60 members, of which 19 are from reserved tribal constituencies. There are 9 districts. Capital, Imphal. Following the elections in Feb. 1995, Congress (I) formed a government with the support of other parties. The party composition of the Legislative Assembly in Dec. 1997 was: Congress (I), 13; Manipur State Congress, 23; Manipur People's Party, 11; Federal Party of Manipur, 2; independents, 2; others, 4; vacant, 5.

Governor: O. N. Srivastava.
Chief Minister: W. Nipamacha Singh.

BUDGET. Budget estimates for 1995–96 show revenue of Rs 6,437·6m. and expenditure of Rs 7,542·4m. Plan allocation 1997–98, Rs 4,100m.

ENERGY AND NATURAL RESOURCES

Electricity. Installed capacity (1995–96) is 12 MW from diesel and hydro-electric generators. This has been augmented since 1981 by the North Eastern Regional Grid. In March 1996 there were 2,015 villages with electricity.

Water. The main power, irrigation and flood-control schemes are the Loktak Lift Irrigation scheme (irrigation potential, 40,000 ha); the Singda scheme (potential 4,000 ha, and improved water supply for Imphal); the Thoubal scheme (potential 34,000 ha), and 4 other large projects. By 1994–95 59,100 ha had been irrigated.

Agriculture. Rice is the principal crop; with wheat, maize and pulses. Total food-grains, 1995–96, 0·48m. tonnes (rice, 338,100 tonnes).

Agricultural work force, 453,040. Only 0·21m. ha are cultivable, of which 134,900 ha are under paddy. Fruit and vegetables are important in the valley, including pineapple, oranges, bananas, mangoes, pears, peaches and plums. Soil erosion, pro-duced by shifting cultivation, is being halted by terracing. Fruit production in 1993–94, 0·11m. tonnes.

Forestry. Forests occupied about 17,588 sq. km in 1995. The main products are teak, jurjan, pine; there are also large areas of bamboo and cane, especially in the Jiri and Barak river drainage areas, yielding about 0·3m. tonnes annually. Total revenue from forests, 1990–91, Rs 9·95m.

Fisheries. Landings in 1995–96, 12,500 tonnes.

INDUSTRY. Handloom weaving is a cottage industry. Larger-scale industries include the manufacture of bicycles and TV sets, sugar, cement, starch, vegetable oil and glucose. Sericulture produces about 45 tonnes of raw silk annually. Estimated non-agricultural work force, 229,408.

COMMUNICATIONS. A national highway from Kaziranga (Assam) runs through Imphal to the border with Myanmar. A railway link was opened in 1990. There is an airport at Imphal with regular scheduled services to Delhi and Calcutta. Length of road (1995), 7,003 km; number of vehicles (1996–97) 65,223.

SOCIAL INSTITUTIONS

Religion. At the 1991 census Hindus numbered 1,059,470; Christians, 626,669; Moslems, 133,535.

Education. The 1991 census gave the number of literates as 895,223 (59·89%; men 71·63%, women 47·6%). In 1996–97 there were 2,548 primary schools with 230,230 students, 555 middle schools with 106,200 students, 553 high and higher secondary schools with 66,160 students, 50 colleges, 1 medical college, 2 teacher training colleges, 3 polytechnics, Manipur University with 62 colleges and 52,352 students (1997–98), and an agricultural university.

Health. In 1996–97 there were 93 hospitals and public health centres, 52 dispensaries, 16 community health centres, 420 sub-centres and 58 other facilities.

MEGHALAYA

KEY HISTORICAL EVENTS. The state was created under the Assam Reorganization (Meghalaya) Act 1969 and inaugurated on 2 April 1970. Its status was that of a state within the State of Assam until 21 Jan. 1972 when it became a fully-fledged state of the Union. It consists of the former Garo Hills district and United Khasi and Jaintia Hills district of Assam.

TERRITORY AND POPULATION. Meghalaya is bounded in the north and east by Assam, south and west by Bangladesh. In 1991 (census figure) the area was 22,429 sq. km and the population 1,774,778. Density, 79 per sq. km. Growth rate, 1981–91, 32·86%. The people are mainly of the Khasi, Jaintia and Garo tribes.

CONSTITUTION AND GOVERNMENT. Meghalaya has a unicameral legislature. The Legislative Assembly has 60 seats. Party position in Feb. 1993: Congress (I), 24; Hill People's Union, 11; Independents, 10; others, 15.

There are 7 districts. The capital is Shillong (population, 1991, 131,719).

Governor: Madhukar Dighe.
Chief Minister: Salseng C. Marak.

BUDGET. Budget estimates for 1996–97 showed revenue receipts of Rs 7,758m. and expenditure of Rs 6,502m. Annual Plan outlay, 1997–98, Rs 3,820m.

ENERGY AND NATURAL RESOURCES

Electricity. Total installed capacity (1995–96) was 186·71 MW. 2,408 villages out of 4,902 had electricity in March 1996.

Minerals. The Khasi Hills, Jaintia Hills and Garo Hills districts produce coal, sillimanite (95% of India's total output), limestone, fire clay, dolomite, feldspar, quartz and glass sand. The state also has deposits of coal (estimated reserves 600m. tonnes), limestone (3,000m.), fire clay (6m.) and sandstone which are so far virtually untapped.

Agriculture. About 83% of the people depend on agriculture. Principal crops are rice, maize, potatoes, cotton, oranges, ginger, tezpata, areca nuts, jute, mesta, bananas and pineapples. Production 1995–96 (in tonnes) of principal crops: Rice, 118,900; wheat, 6,400; pulses, 2,400; Potatoes, 146,941; maize, 20,800; jute, 43,444; cotton, 5,432; rape and mustard, 4,200.

Forestry. Forests covered 9,496 sq. km in 1995–6. Forest products are the state's chief resources.

INDUSTRY. Apart from agriculture the main source of employment is the extraction and processing of minerals; there are also important timber processing mills and cement factories. Other industries include electronics, tantalum capacitors, beverages and watches. The state has 5 industrial estates, 2 industrial areas and 1 growth centre. In 1995–96 there were 58 registered factories and 2,533 small-scale industries. There were also, in 1994–95, 1,812 sericultural villages, 6 sericultural farms and 8 silk units and, in 1995–96, 5,400 *khadi* and village industrial units.

COMMUNICATIONS. Three national highways run through the state for a distance of 460 km. The state has only 1 km of railways. Umroi airport (25 km from Shillong) connects the state with main air services. In 1995–96 there were 6,572 km of surfaced and unsurfaced roads. Total number of motor vehicles, 1995–96, 44,715.

SOCIAL INSTITUTIONS

Justice. The Guwahati High Court is common to Assam, Meghalaya, Nagaland, Manipur, Mizoram, Tripura and Arunachal Pradesh. There is a bench of the Guwahati High Court at Shillong.

Religion. At the 1991 census Hindus numbered 260,306; Moslems, 61,462; Christians, 1,146,092; Buddhists, 2,934; Sikhs, 2,612.

Education. In 1991, 38·2% of the population were literate (55·58% of men and 44·42% of women). In 1996–97 the state had 4,235 primary schools with 299,961 students, 851 middle schools with 78,858 students, 431 high and higher secondary schools with 44,221 students, 10 teacher training schools and 1 college, 1 polytechnic and 28 colleges. The North-eastern Hill University started functioning at Shillong in 1973; in 1993–94 it had 41 colleges and 54,803 students.

Health. In 1995–96 there were 9 government hospitals, 77 primary health centres, 20 government dispensaries and 325 sub-centres. Total beds (hospitals and health centres), 2,352.

MIZORAM

KEY HISTORICAL EVENTS. On 21 Jan. 1972 the former Mizo Hills District of Assam was created a Union Territory. A long dispute between the Mizo National Front (originally Separatist) and the central government was resolved in 1986. Mizoram became a state by the Constitution (53rd Amendment) and the State of Mizoram Acts, July 1986.

TERRITORY AND POPULATION. Mizoram is one of the eastern-most Indian states, lying between Bangladesh and Myanmar, and having on its northern boundaries Tripura, Assam and Manipur. The area is 21,081 sq. km and the population (1991 census) 689,756. Density, 33 per sq. km; growth rate 1981–91, 39·7%.

CONSTITUTION AND GOVERNMENT. Mizoram has a unicameral Legislative Assembly with 40 seats: Congress (I), 16; Mizo National Front, 14; Mizo Janata Dal, 8; Independents, 2. The capital is Aizawl (population, 1991, 155,240).

Governor: P. R. Kyndiah.
Chief Minister: Lal Thanhawla.

BUDGET. Budget estimates for 1997–98 show revenue receipts of Rs 6.769·7m. and expenditure of Rs 5,865·9m. Annual plan outlay, 1997–98, Rs 2,900m.

ENERGY AND NATURAL RESOURCES

Electricity. Installed capacity (1993–94), 24·45 MW. 617 out of 721 villages had electricity in March 1996.

Agriculture. About 60% of the people are engaged in agriculture, either on terraced holdings or in shifting cultivation. Total production of foodgrains, 1995–96, 122,700 tonnes (rice, 101,500 tonnes).
    Total forest area, 1995, 18,576 sq. km.

INDUSTRY. Handloom weaving and other cottage industries are important. The state has (1992) 2,300 small scale industrial units, including furniture industries, steel fabrication, TV manufacturing, truck and bus body building.

COMMUNICATIONS. Aizawl is connected by road and air with Silchar in Assam and by air with Calcutta. Total length of roads, 31 March 1992, 5,095 km. There were 18,238 motor vehicles in 1995–96.

SOCIAL INSTITUTIONS

Religion. At the 1991 census Christians numbered 591,342; Buddhists, 54,024; Hindus, 34,788; Moslems, 4,538.

Education. The number of literates in 1991 was 462,246 (82·27%; 85·61% of men and 78·68% of women). In 1996–97 there were 1,263 primary schools with 129,662 students, 702 middle schools with 44,186 students and 346 high and higher secondary schools with 23,140 students; there were 29 colleges, 1 teacher training college, 3 teacher training schools, 1 polytechnic and 29 junior colleges.

Health. In 1993–94 there were 11 hospitals, 38 primary and 22 subsidiary health centres, and 314 health sub-centres. Total beds, 1,444.

NAGALAND

KEY HISTORICAL EVENTS. The state was created in 1961, effective 1963. It consisted of the Naga Hills district of Assam and the Tuensang Frontier Agency.

The agency was a British-supervized tribal area on the borders of Myanmar Its supervision passed to the Government of India at independence, and in 1957 Tuensang and the Naga Hills became a Centrally Administered Area, governed by the central government through the Governor of Assam.

A number of Naga leaders fought for independence until a settlement was reached with the Indian Government at the Shillong Peace Agreement of 1975.

TERRITORY AND POPULATION. The state is in the north-east of India and is bounded in the north by Arunachal Pradesh, west by Assam, east by Myanmar and south by Manipur. Nagaland has an area of 16,579 sq. km and a population (1991 census) of 1,209,546. Density, 73 per sq. km. Growth rate, 1981–91, 56·08%. The major towns are the capital, Kohima (1991 population, 51,418) and Dimapur (57,182). Other towns include Wokha, Mon, Zunheboto, Mokokchung and Tuensang. The chief tribes in numerical order are: Angami, Ao, Sumi, Konyak, Chakhesang, Lotha, Phom, Khiamngan, Chang, Yimchunger, Zeliang-Kuki, Rengma, Sangtam and Pochury.

CONSTITUTION AND GOVERNMENT. An Interim Body (Legislative Assembly) of 42 members elected by the Naga people and an Executive Council (Council of Ministers) of 5 members were formed in 1961, and continued until the State Assembly was elected in Jan. 1964. The Assembly has 60 members, and after the elections of Feb. 1993 includes: Congress (I), 41; Nagaland People's Council, 10; independents, 7; others, 1; vacant, 1. The Governor has extraordinary powers, which include special responsibility for law and order.

The state has 7 districts (Kohima, Mon, Zunheboto, Wokha, Phek, Mokokchung and Tuensang). The capital is Kohima.

Governor: Om Prakash Sharma.
Chief Minister: S. C. Jamir.

BUDGET. Budget estimates for 1996–97 showed total receipts of Rs 9,604·4m. and expenditure of Rs 9,937·8m. Annual Plan, 1997–98, Rs 3,500m.

ENERGY AND NATURAL RESOURCES

Electricity. Installed capacity (1995–96) 6·82 MW; all towns and villages are electrified. In 1995–96, 7 electricity generation schemes were under implementation.

Minerals. Oil has been located in 3 districts. Other minerals include: Coal, limestone, chromite, magnesite, iron ore, copper ore, clay, glass sand and slate.

Agriculture. 90% of the people derive their livelihood from agriculture. The Angamis, in Kohima district, practise a fixed agriculture in the shape of terraced slopes, and wet paddy cultivation in the lowlands. In the other two districts a traditional form of shifting cultivation (*jhumming*) still predominates, but some farmers have begun tea and coffee plantations and horticulture. About 61,000 ha were under terrace cultivation and 74,040 ha under *jhumming* in 1994–95. Production of rice (1995–96) was 0·185m. tonnes, total foodgrains 238,300 tonnes, pulses 12,300 tonnes. Forests covered 8,625 sq. km in 1995–96.

INDUSTRY. There is a forest products factory at Tijit; a paper-mill (100 tonnes daily capacity) at Tuli, a distillery unit and a sugar-mill (1,000 tonnes daily capacity) at Dimapur, and a cement factory (50 tonnes daily capacity) at Wazeho. Bricks and TV sets are also made, and there are 1,850 small units. There is a ceramics plant and sericulture is also important.

COMMUNICATIONS. There is a national highway from Kaziranga (Assam) to Kohima and on to Manipur. There are state highways connecting Kohima with the district headquarters. Total length of roads in 1992, 14,933 km. Dimapur has a railhead and a daily air service to Calcutta. Railway route-km in 1995–96, 13 km. There were 95,020 motor vehicles registered in 1994–95.

SOCIAL INSTITUTIONS

Justice. A permanent bench of the Guwahati High Court has been established in Kohima.

Religion. At the 1991 census there were 1,057,940 Christians; 122,473 Hindus; 20,642 Moslems; 1,202 Jains; 732 Sikhs.

Education. The 1991 census records 621,048 literates, or 61·65%: 67·62% of men and 54·75% of women. In 1996–97 there were 1,414 primary schools with 271,932 students, 416 middle schools with 63,437 students, 244 high and higher secondary schools with 24,547 students, 36 colleges, 2 teacher training colleges and 2 polytechnics. The North Eastern Hill University opened at Kohima in 1978. Nagaland University was established in 1994.

Health. In 1995–96 there were 32 hospitals (1,051 beds), 27 primary and 5 community health centres, 65 dispensaries, 243 sub-centres, 5 TB centres and 30 leprosy centres.

Aram, M., *Peace in Nagaland,* New Delhi, 1974

ORISSA

KEY HISTORICAL EVENTS. Orissa was divided between Mahratta and Bengal rulers when conquered by the British East India Company, the Bengal area in 1757 and the Mahratta in 1803. The area which now forms the state then consisted of directly controlled British districts and a large number of small princely states with tributary rulers.

The British districts were administered as part of Bengal until 1912 when, together with Bihar, they were separated from Bengal to form a single province. Bihar and Orissa were separated from each other in 1936.

In 1948 a new state government took control of the whole state, including the former princely states (except Saraikella and Kharswan which were transferred to Bihar, and Mayurbhanj which was not incorporated until 1949).

TERRITORY AND POPULATION. Orissa is in eastern India and is bounded north by Bihar, north-east by West Bengal, east by the Bay of Bengal, south by Andhra Pradesh and west by Madhya Pradesh. The area of the state is 155,707 sq. km, and its population (1991 census), 31,659,736, density 203 per sq. km. Growth rate, 1981–91, 20·06%. Cities with over 250,000 population at 1991 census, *see*

INDIA: Territory and Population. Other large cities (1991): Rourkela (urban agglomeration), 398,864; Brahmapur, 210,418; Sambalpur, 131,138; Puri, 125,199. The principal and official language is Oriya.

CONSTITUTION AND GOVERNMENT. The Legislative Assembly has 147 members. After the elections in Feb. 1995 Congress (I) formed a government. Parties in the Legislative Assembly: Congress (I), 80 seats; Janata Dal, 17; Niju Janata Dal, 29; Bharatiya Janata Party, 10; Jharkhand Mukti Morcha, 4; independents and others, 7.

The state consists of 30 districts.

The capital is Bhubaneswar (18 miles south of Cuttack).

Governor: G. Ramanujan.
Chief Minister: Janaki Ballav Patnaik.

BUDGET. Budget estimates, 1996–97, showed total receipts of Rs 79,812m. and total expenditure of Rs 84,683m. Annual plan outlay, 1997–98, Rs 25,000m.

ENERGY AND NATURAL RESOURCES

Electricity. The Hirakud Dam Project on the river Mahanadi irrigates 628,000 acres and has an installed capacity of 307·5 MW. There are other projects under construction; hydro-electric power is now serving a large part of the state. Other hydro-power projects are Balimela (360 MW), Upper Kolab (320 MW) and Rengali (250 MW). Total installed capacity (1995–96) 2,152 MW. In 1994–95 the state generated 5,967m. units. There were 32,068 electrified villages in March 1996.

Minerals. Orissa is India's leading producer of chromite (95% of national output), dolomite (50%), manganese ore (25%), graphite (80%), iron ore (16%), fire-clay (34%), limestone (20%), and quartz-quartzite (18%). Production in 1995–96 (1,000 tonnes): Iron ore, 9,330; manganese ore, 630; chromite, 1,650; coal, 32,660; limestone, 2,380; dolomite, 1,350; bauxite, 2,420. Value of production in 1995–96 was Rs 16,340m.

Agriculture. The cultivation of rice is the principal occupation of about 80% of the workforce, and only a very small amount of other cereals is grown. Production of foodgrains (1994–95) totalled 7·2m. tonnes from 7·9m. ha (rice 6·4m. tonnes, wheat 58,000 tonnes); pulses, 0·58m. tonnes; oilseeds, 0·27m. tonnes; sugar-cane, 781,000 tonnes. Turmeric is cultivated in the uplands of the districts of Ganjam, Phulbani and Koraput, and is exported.

Livestock (1993): Buffaloes, 1·04m.; other cattle, 9·2m.; sheep, 1·87m.; goats, 5·4m.; 15·91m. poultry including ducks (1995).

Forestry. Forests occupied 56,059·5 sq. km in 1995–96. The most important species are sal, teak, kendu, sandal, sisu, bija, kusum, kongada and bamboo.

Fisheries. There were, in March 1996, 603 fishery co-operative societies. Fish production in 1995–96 was 258,040 tonnes. The state has 4 fishing harbours.

INDUSTRY. 289 large and medium industries are in operation (1995–96), mostly based on minerals: steel, pig-iron, ferrochrome, ferromanganese, ferrosilicon, aluminium, cement, automotive tyres and synthetic fibres.

Other industries of importance are sugar, glass, paper, fertilizers, caustic soda, salt, industrial explosives, heavy machine tools, a coach-repair factory, a re-rolling mill, textile mills and electronics. An oil refinery is under implementation. Also, there were 49,611 small-scale industries employing 349,800 persons. There were 1,342,561 artisan units providing employment to 2·33m. persons; handloom weaving and the manufacture of baskets, wooden articles, hats and nets; silver filigree work and hand-woven fabrics are specially well known.

TOURISM. Tourist traffic is concentrated mainly on the 'Golden Triangle', Konark, Puri and Bhubaneswar, and its temples. Tourists also visit Gopalpur, the

Similipal National Park, Nandankanan and Chilka Lake, Bhitar-Kanika and Ushakothi Wildlife Sanctuary.

COMMUNICATIONS

Roads. On 31 March 1996 length of roads was: State highway, 4,360 km; national highway, 1,625 km; other roads, 212,490 km. There were 658,401 motor vehicles in 1995–96. A 144-km expressway, part national highway, connects the Daitari mining area with Paradip Port.

Railways. The route-km of railway in 1995–96 was 2,191 km, of which 143 km was narrow gauge.

Civil Aviation. There is an airport at Bhubaneswar with regular scheduled services to New Delhi, Calcutta, Visakhapatnam and Hyderabad.

Shipping. Paradip was declared a 'major' port in 1966; it handled 11·2m. tonnes of traffic in 1995–96. There are minor ports at Bahabalpur and Gopalpur.

SOCIAL INSTITUTIONS

Justice. The High Court of Judicature at Cuttack has a Chief Justice and 13 puisne judges.

Religion. At the 1991 census Hindus numbered 29,971,257; Christians, 666,220; Moslems, 577,775; Sikhs, 17,296; Buddhists, 9,153; Jains, 6,302.

Education. The percentage of literates in the population in 1991 was 49·09% (males, 63·09%, females, 34·68%).

In 1996–97 there were 42,104 primary schools with 3·95m. students, 12,096 middle schools with 1·3m. students and 6,198 high and higher secondary schools with 945,000 students. There are 10 engineering and technology colleges, 20 medical colleges, 13 teacher training colleges, 15 engineering schools/polytechnics, 497 arts, science and commerce colleges and 440 junior colleges.

Utkal University was established in 1943 at Cuttack and moved to Bhubaneswar in 1962; it is both teaching and affiliating. It has 368 affiliated colleges and 14,000 students (1993–94). Berhampur University has 33 affiliated colleges with 33,755 students, and Orissa University of Agriculture and Technology has 8 constituent colleges with 641 students. Sambalpur University has 97 affiliated colleges and 43,982 students. Sri Jagannath Sanskrit Viswavidyalaya at Puri was established in 1981 for oriental studies.

Health. There were (1995–96) 180 hospitals, 150 dispensaries, 885 primary health centres and 402 health centres/units. There were also 478 homeopathic and 537 Ayurvedic dispansaries.

PUNJAB (INDIA)

KEY HISTORICAL EVENTS. The Punjab was constituted an autonomous province of India in 1937. In 1947, the province was partitioned between India and Pakistan into East and West Punjab respectively, under the Indian Independence Act, 1947, the boundaries being determined under the Radcliffe Award. The name of East Punjabwas changed to Punjab (India) under the Constitution of India. On 1 Nov. 1956 the erstwhile states of Punjab and Patiala and East Punjab States Union (PEPSU) were integrated to form the state of Punjab. On 1 Nov. 1966, under the Punjab Reorganization Act, 1966, the state was reconstituted as a Punjabi-speaking state comprising the districts of Gurdaspur (excluding Dalhousie), Amritsar, Kapurthala, Jullundur, Ferozepore, Bhatinda, Patiala and Ludhiana; parts of Sangrur, Hoshiarpur and Ambala districts; and part of Kharar tehsil. The remaining area comprising an area of 18,000 sq. miles and an estimated (1967) population of 8·5m. was shared between the new state of Haryana and the Union Territory of Himachal Pradesh. The existing capital of Chandigarh was made joint capital of Punjab and

Haryana; its transfer to Punjab alone (due in 1986) has been delayed while the two states seek agreement as to which Hindi-speaking districts shall be transferred to Haryana in exchange.

TERRITORY AND POPULATION. The Punjab is in north India and is bounded at its northernmost point by Kashmir, north-east by Himachal Pradesh, south-east by Haryana, south by Rajasthan, west and north-west by Pakistan. The area of the state is 50,362 sq. km, with census (1991) population of 20,281,969. Density, 403 per sq. km. Growth rate, 1981–91, 20·81%. Cities with over 250,000 population at 1991 census, *see* INDIA: Territory and Population. Other principal towns (1991): Bathinda (159,042), Pathankot (123,930), Moga (108,304), Abohar (107,163). The official language is Punjabi.

CONSTITUTION AND GOVERNMENT. Punjab (India) has a unicameral legislature, the Legislative Assembly, of 117 members. Presidential rule was imposed in May 1987 after outbreaks of communal violence. In March 1988 the Assembly was officially dissolved. Elections were held in Feb. 1997. The electorate was 15m.; turn-out was 68%. Shiromani Akali Dal (SAD) gained 75 seats; the Bharatiya Janata Party, 18; Congress (I), 14; the Communist Party, 2; independents and others, 8.

There are 16 districts. The capital is Chandigarh. There are 106 municipalities, 118 community development blocks and 9,331 elected village councils (*panchayats*). Elections took place for 95 municipalities on 6 Sept. 1992, and for the 11,500 village councils in Jan. 1993.

Governor: Lieut.-Gen. Bakshi K. N. Chibber.
Chief Minister: Prakash Singh Badal (SAD).

BUDGET. Budget estimates, 1995–96, showed revenue receipts of Rs 72,634·7m. and revenue expenditure of Rs 75,076·4m. Plan outlay, 1997–98, Rs 21,000m.

ENERGY AND NATURAL RESOURCES

Electricity. Installed capacity, 1996–97, was 3,511 MW; all villages had electricity.

Agriculture. About 75% of the population depends on agriculture which is technically advanced. The irrigated area rose from 2·21m. ha in 1950–51 to 4·2m. ha in 1996–97. In 1994–95, wheat production was 13·6m. tonnes; rice, 7·7m.; 1992–93: maize, 333,000; oilseeds, 90,000; cotton, 2·3m. bales of 170 kg.

Livestock (1977 census): Buffaloes, 4,110,000; other cattle, 3·31m.; sheep and goats, 1,219,600; horses and ponies, 75,900; poultry, 5·5m.

Forestry. In 1995 there were 1,342 sq. km of forest land.

INDUSTRY. In March 1997 the number of registered industrial units was 194,208, employing about 1·04m. people. In 1996–97 there were 586 large and medium industries. On 31 March 1997 there were 0·19m. small industrial units, investment Rs 25,050m. The chief manufactures are textiles (especially hosiery), sewing machines, sports goods, sugar, bicycles, electronic goods, machine tools, hand tools, automobiles and vehicle parts, surgical goods, vegetable oils, tractors, chemicals and pharmaceuticals, fertilizers, food processing, electronics, railway coaches, paper and newsprint, cement, engineering goods and telecommunications items. An oil refinery is under construction.

COMMUNICATIONS

Roads. The total length of roads on 31 March 1997 was 47,000 km. State transport services cover 1·9m. effective km daily with a fleet of 3,426 buses carrying a daily average of over 1·2m. passengers. Coverage by private operators is estimated as 40%. There were 1,915,059 vehicles in 1995–96.

Railways. The Punjab possesses an extensive system of railway communications, served by the Northern Railway. Route-km (1995–96) 2,121 km.

Civil Aviation. There is an airport at Amritsar, and Chandigarh airport is on the north-eastern boundary; both have regular scheduled services to Delhi, Jammu, Srinagar and Leh. There are also Vayudoot services to Ludhiana.

SOCIAL INSTITUTIONS

Justice. The Punjab and Haryana High Court exercises jurisdiction over the states of Punjab and Haryana and the territory of Chandigarh. It is located in Chandigarh. It consists (1988) of a Chief Justice and 21 puisne judges.

Religion. At the 1991 census Hindus numbered 6,989,226; Sikhs, 12,767,697; Moslems, 239,401; Christians, 225,163; Jains, 20,763.

Education. Compulsory education was introduced in April 1961; at the same time free education was introduced up to 8th class for boys and 9th class for girls as well as fee concessions. The aim is education for all children of 6-11. In 1991, 58·51% of the population were literate (65·66% of men and 50·41% of women).

In 1996–97 there were 12,590 primary schools with 2,081,965 students, 2,545 middle schools with 9968,762 students, 2,159 high schools with 490,888 students and 1,134 higher secondary schools with 259,718 students.

Punjab University was established in 1947 at Chandigarh as an examining, teaching and affiliating body (in 1993–94 it had 94 colleges and 77,868 students). In 1962 Punjabi University was established at Patiala (it had 66 colleges and 40,712 students) and Punjab Agricultural University at Ludhiana. Guru Nanak Dev University has been established at Amritsar to mark the 500th anniversary celebrations for Guru Nanak Dev, first Guru of the Sikhs (it had 85 colleges and 80,330 students, 1992–93). Altogether there are 237 affiliated colleges, 190 for arts, science and commerce, 18 for teacher training, 6 medical and 11 engineering, and 30 polytechnic institutes.

Health. There were (1992–93) 219 hospitals, 2,151 allopathic, homeopathic, Ayurvedic and Unani dispensaries, 446 primary health centres and 38 community health centres. Total number of beds (1991–92), 24,742.

Singh, Khushwant, *A History of the Sikhs.* 2 vols. Princeton and OUP, 1964–67
Singh Tatla, D. and Talbot, I., *Punjab.* [Bibliography]. Oxford and Santa Barbara (CA), 1995

RAJASTHAN

KEY HISTORICAL EVENTS. The state is in the largely desert area formerly known as Rajputana. The Rajput princes were tributary to the Moghul emperors when they were conquered by the Mahrattas' leader, Mahadaji Sindhia, in the 1780s. In 1818 Rajputana became a British protectorate and was recognized during British rule as a group of princely states including Jaipur, Jodhpur and Udaipur.

After independence the Rajput princes surrendered their powers and in 1950 were replaced by a single state government. In 1956 the state boundaries were altered; small areas of the former Bombay and Madhya Bharat states were added, together with the neighbouring state of Ajmer.

Ajmer had been a Moghul power base; it was taken by the Mahrattas in 1770 and annexed by the British in 1818. In 1878 it became Ajmer-Merwara, a British province, and survived as a separate state until until 1956.

TERRITORY AND POPULATION. Rajasthan is in north-west India and is bounded north by Punjab, north-east by Haryana and Uttar Pradesh, east by Madhya Pradesh, south by Gujarat and west by Pakistan. The area of the state is 342,239 sq. km and its population (census 1991), 44,005,990, density 129 per sq. km. Growth rate, 1981–91, 28·44%. For chief cities, *see* INDIA: Territory and Population. Other major towns (1991): Alwar (205,086), Bhilwara (183,965), Ganganagar (161,482), Bharatpur (148,519), Sikar (148,272), Pali (136,842), Beawar (105,363).

CONSTITUTION AND GOVERNMENT. There is a unicameral legislature, the Legislative Assembly, having 200 members. After the election in Nov. 1993 the

Bharatiya Janata Party came to power. Bharatiya Janata Party, 100; Congress (I), 73; Janata Dal, 4; Independents and others, 23.The capital is Jaipur. There are 30 districts. *Governor:* Bali Ram Bhagat. *Chief Minister:* Bhairon Singh Shekhawat.

BUDGET. Estimates for 1997–98 show total revenue receipts of Rs 89,894·1m., and expenditure of Rs 91,469·2m. Annual plan, 1997–98, Rs 35,000m.

ENERGY AND NATURAL RESOURCES

Electricity. Installed capacity in 1995–96, 1,981 MW; 30,620 villages (March 1996) and 514,758 wells had electric power.

Water. In 1994 the Bhakra Canal irrigated 0·3m. ha, the Chambal Canal, 0·2m. ha and the Rajasthan Canal, 0·94m. ha. The Indira Gandhi canal is the main canal system, of which (1994) 189 km. of main canal, 204 km of feeder and 3,400 km of distributors had been built, creating an irrigation potential of 582,000 ha. There were 36,397 villages with full or partial drinking water facilities in Dec. 1993, out of 37,124.

Minerals. The state is rich in minerals, including silver, tungsten, granite, marble, dolomite, lignite, lead, zinc, emeralds, soapstone, asbestos, feldspar, copper, limestone and salt. Total revenue from minerals in 1995–96, Rs 2,145·2m. 4 blocs are being explored for mineral oils and gas.

Agriculture. The state has suffered drought and encroaching desert for several years. The cultivable area is (1995–96) about 25·6m. ha, of which 4·65m. ha is irrigated. Production of principal crops (in tonnes), 1995–96: Pulses, 1·46m.; total foodgrains, 9·57m. (rice, 117,600; wheat, 5·49m.); cotton, 1m. bales of 170 kg.

Livestock (1992): Buffaloes, 7·75m.; other cattle, 11·6m.; sheep, 12·17m.; goats, 15·06m.; horses and ponies, 28,000; camels, 731,000.

Forests covered 12,320 sq. km in 1995.

INDUSTRY. In 1993–94 there were 167,400 small industrial units with an investment of Rs 13,163·1m. and employment of 0·64m. There were 212 industrial estates. Total capital investment (1993–94) Rs 13,160m. Chief manufactures are textiles, cement, glass, sugar, sodium, oxygen and acetylene units, pesticides, insecticides, dyes, caustic soda, calcium, carbide, synthetic fibres, fertilizers, shaving equipment, automobiles and automobile components, tyres, watches, nylon tyre cords and refined copper. In 1993–94 there were 583 large and medium industries.

COMMUNICATIONS

Roads. In 1995–96 there were 116,667 km of roads including 61,520 km of good and surfaced roads in Rajasthan; there were 2,846 km of national highway. Motor vehicles numbered 1,768,709 in 1995–96.

Railways. Jodhpur, Marwar, Udaipur, Ajmer, Jaipur, Kota, Bikaner and Sawai Madhopur are important junctions of the north-western network. Route km (1995–96) 5,924.

Civil Aviation. There are airports at Jaipur, Jodhpur, Kota and Udaipur with regular scheduled services by Indian Airlines.

SOCIAL INSTITUTIONS

Justice. The seat of the High Court is at Jodhpur. There is a Chief Justice and 11 puisne judges. There is also a bench of High Court judges at Jaipur.

Religion. At the 1991 census Hindus numbered 39,201,099; Moslems, 3,525,339; Jains, 562,806; Sikhs, 649,174; Christians, 47,989; Buddhists, 4,467.

Education. The proportion of literates to the total population was 38·55% at the 1991 census; men 54·99% and women 20·44%.

In 1996–97 there were 33,801 primary schools with 6,665,000 students, 12,642 middle schools with 2,091,000 students, 3,439 high schools with 682,600 students and 1,404 higher secondary schools with 500,000 students. Elementary education is free but not compulsory.

In 1996–97 there were 206 colleges. Rajasthan University, established at Jaipur in 1947, is teaching and affiliating; in 1993–94 it had 135 colleges and 160,000 students. There are 5 other universities: Rajasthan Agricultural University, Bikaner; Mohanlal Sukhadia University, Udaipur; Maharishi Dayanand Saraswati University, Ajmer; Jai Narayan Vyas University, Jodhpur; Kota Open University, Kota. There are also 22 medical colleges, 7 engineering colleges, 21,436 adult and other education centres, 32 sanskrit institutions, 39 teacher-training colleges and 27 polytechnics.

Health. In 1995–96 there were 266 hospitals, 283 dispensaries, 1,453 primary health centres, 384 family welfare centres, 1,104 upgraded sub-centres and 118 maternity centres. There were 34,066 beds in hospitals.

SIKKIM

KEY HISTORICAL EVENTS. A small Himalayan kingdom between Nepal and Bhutan, Sikkim was independent in the 1830s although in continual conflict with larger neighbours. In 1839 the British took the Darjeeling district. British political influence increased during the 19th century, as Sikkim was the smallest buffer between India and Tibet. However, Sikkim remained an independent kingdom ruled by the 14th-century Namgyal dynasty.

In 1950 a treaty was signed with the Government of India, declaring Sikkim an Indian Protectorate. Indian influence increased from then on.

Internal political unrest came to a head in 1973, and led to the granting of constitutional reforms in 1974. Agitation continued until Sikkim became a 'state associated with the Indian Union' later than year. In 1975 the king was deposed and Sikkim became an Indian state, a change approved by referendum.

TERRITORY AND POPULATION. Sikkim is in the Eastern Himalayas and is bounded north by Tibet, east by Tibet and Bhutan, south by West Bengal and west Nepal. Area, 7,096 sq. km. It is inhabited chiefly by the Lepchas, a tribe indigenous to Sikkim, the Bhutias, who originally came from Tibet, and the Nepalis, who entered from Nepal in large numbers in the late 19th and early 20th century. Census population (1991), 406,457, of whom 25,024 lived in the capital, Gangtok. Density, 57 per sq km. Growth rate, 1981–91, 28·47%.

CONSTITUTION AND GOVERNMENT. The Assembly has 32 members. After the election of Nov. 1994 the Sikkim Democratic Front formed a government.

Governor: Chaudhury Randhir Singh.
Chief Minister: Pawan Kumar Changling.

The official language of the Government is English. Lepcha, Bhutia, Nepali and Limboo have also been declared official languages.

Sikkim is divided into 4 districts for administration purposes, Gangtok, Mangan, Namchi and Gyalshing being the headquarters for the Eastern, Northern, Southern and Western districts respectively. Each district is administered by a District Collector. Within this framework are the Panchayats or Village Councils.

ECONOMY

Budget. Budget estimates for 1996–97 showed a budget of Rs 61,800m. Annual plan outlay for 1997–98 is Rs 2,200m.

ENERGY AND NATURAL RESOURCES

Electricity. Installed capacity (1995–96) 33·6 MW. There are 4 hydro-electric power stations. All villages had electricity in 1991.

Minerals. Copper, zinc and lead are mined.

Agriculture. The economy is mainly agricultural; main food crops are rice, maize, millet, wheat and barley; cash crops are cardamom (a spice), mandarin oranges, apples, potatoes, and buckwheat. Foodgrain production, 1995–96, 104,200 tonnes (rice, 21,900 tonnes, wheat, 15,300 tonnes); pulses, 5,700 tonnes. Tea is grown. Forests occupied about 3,127 sq. km. in 1995 and the potential for a timber and wood-pulp industry is being explored. Medicinal herbs are exported.

INDUSTRY AND TRADE

Industry. Small-scale industries include cigarettes, distilling, tanning, fruit preservation, carpets and watchmaking. Local crafts include carpet weaving, making handmade paper, wood carving and silverwork. The State Trading Corporation of Sikkim stimulates trade in indigenous products.

Tourism. There is great potential for the tourist industry, which has been stimulated by the opening of new roads.

COMMUNICATIONS

Roads. There are 1,615 km. of roads, all on mountainous terrain, and 18 major bridges under the Public Works Department. Public transport and road haulage is nationalized. There were 8,997 motor vehicles in 1995–96.

Railways. The nearest railhead is at Siliguri (115 km from Gangtok).

Civil Aviation. The nearest airport is at Bagdogra (128 km from Gangtok), linked to Gangtok by helicopter service.

Telecommunications. There are 1,445 telephones (1987) and 37 wireless stations. A radio broadcasting station, Akashvani Gangtok, was built in 1982, and a permanent station in 1983. Gangtok also has a low-power TV transmitter.

SOCIAL INSTITUTIONS

Religion. At the 1991 census there were 277,881 Hindus; 3,849 Moslems; 13,413 Christians; 110,371 Buddhists; 375 Sikhs; 40 Jains.

Education. At the 1991 census there were 186,789 literates (56·94%; men 65·74% and women 46·69%). Sikkim had (1996–97) 723 pre-primary schools with 19,946 students, 341 primary schools with 83,410 students, 117 middle schools with 21,955 students, 72 high schools with 8,295 students and 27 higher secondary schools with 3,368 students. Education is free up to class XII; text books are free up to class V. There are 500 adult education centres. There is also a training institute for primary teachers, 2 degree colleges and a teacher training college.

TAMIL NADU

KEY HISTORICAL EVENTS. The first trading establishment made by the British in the Madras State was at Peddapali (now Nizampatnam) in 1611 and then at Masulipatnam. In 1639 the English were permitted to make a settlement at the place which is now Madras, and Fort St George was founded. By 1801 the whole of the country from the Northern Circars to Cape Comorin (with the exception of certain French and Danish settlements) had been brought under British rule.

Under the provisions of the States Reorganization Act, 1956, the Malabar district (excluding the islands of Laccadive and Minicoy) and the Kasaragod district taluk of South Kanara were transferred to the new state of Kerala; the South Kanara district (excluding Kasaragod taluk and the Amindivi Islands) and the Kollegal taluk of the Coimbatore district were transferred to the new state of Mysore; and the Laccadive, Amindivi and Minicoy Islands were constituted a separate Territory. Four taluks of the Trivandrum district and the Shencottah taluk of Quilon district were transferred from Travancore-Cochin to the new Madras State. On 1 April 1960, 405 sq. miles from the Chittoor district of Andhra Pradesh were transferred to Madras in exchange for 326 sq. miles from the Chingleput and Salem districts. In Aug. 1968 the state was renamed Tamil Nadu.

TERRITORY AND POPULATION. Tamil Nadu is in south India and is bounded north by Karnataka and Andhra Pradesh, east and south by the Indian Ocean and west by Kerala. Area, 130,058 sq. km. Population (1991 census), 55,858,946, density of 429 per sq. km. Growth rate, 1981–91, 15·39%. Tamil is the principal language and has been adopted as the state language with effect from 14 Jan. 1958. For the principal towns, *see* INDIA: Territory and Population. Other large towns (1991): Ambattur (215,424), Thanjavur City (202,013), Tuticorin (199,854), Nagercoil City (190,084), Avadi (183,215), Dindigul City (182,477), Vellore (175,061), Thiruvottir (168,642), Erode (159,232), Kanchipuram (144,955), Cuddalore City (144,561), Tirunelveli (135,825), Alandur (125,244), Neyveli (118,080), Rajapalaiyam City (114,202), Pallavaram (111,866), Tambaran (107,187). There are 21 districts. The capital is Madras.

CONSTITUTION AND GOVERNMENT. There is a unicameral legislature; the Legislative Assembly has 235 members: Dravida Munnetra Kazagam (DMK), 172; Tamil Maanila Congress, 39; Communist Party, 8; others, 16.

Governor: Meera Sahib Fathima Beevi.
Chief Minister: K. Muthuvel Karunanidhi.

BUDGET. Budget estimates for 1997–98, revenue receipts, Rs 126,410·5m., revenue expenditure, Rs 143,776·2m. Annual plan, 1997–98, Rs 40,000m.

ENERGY AND NATURAL RESOURCES

Electricity. Installed capacity in 1995–96 was 5,067 MW, of which 1,948 MW was hydro-electricity and 2,970 MW thermal. All villages were supplied with electricity. The Kalpakkam nuclear power plant became operational in 1983; capacity, 330 MW.

Water. A joint project with Andhra Pradesh was agreed in 1983, to supply Madras with water from the Krishna river, also providing irrigation, *en route,* for Andhra Pradesh. In 1993–94, 3·54m. ha were irrigated.

Minerals. Value of mineral production, 1987, Rs 1,760m. The state has magnesite, salt, coal, lignite, chromite, bauxite, limestone, manganese, mica, quartz, gypsum and feldspar.

Agriculture. The land is a fertile plain watered by rivers flowing east from the Western Ghats, particularly the Cauvery and the Tambaraparani. Temperature ranges between 6°C. and 40°C., rainfall between 442 mm. and 934 mm. Of the total land area (13m. ha), 7,158,464 ha were cropped and 298,659 ha of waste were cultivable in 1996. The staple food crops grown are paddy, maize, jawar, bajra, pulses and millets. Important commercial crops are sugar-cane, oilseeds, cashew-nuts, cotton, tobacco, coffee, tea, rubber and pepper. Production, 1995–96 (in tonnes): Total food-grains, 9·16m. (rice, 7·56m.); pulses, 359,700.

Livestock (1993): Buffaloes, 3,116,647; other cattle, 9,318,666; sheep, 5,865,989; goats, 5,938,475; poultry, 21,454,890.

Forestry. Forest area, 1993–94, 2·14m. ha, of which 1,948,627 ha were reserved forest. Forests cover about 17·21% of land area. Main products are teak, soft wood, wattle, sandalwood, pulp wood, cashew and cinchona bark.

Fisheries. In 1995–96, 448,000 tonnes of fish were produced; marine, 340,000 tonnes.

INDUSTRY AND TRADE

Industry. The number of working factories was 18,480 in 1994, employing 1m. workers. In 1993–94 there were 178,114 small industries employing over 1·6m.

persons. The biggest central sector project is Salem steel plant. Cotton textiles is one of the major industries. There were 449 cotton textile mills in 1991–92 and many spinning mills supplying yarn to the decentralized handloom industry. Other important industries are cement, sugar, manufacture of textile machinery, power-driven pumps, bicycles, electrical machinery, tractors, motor-cars, rubber tyres and tubes, bricks and tiles and silk.

Main exports: Cotton goods, tea, coffee, spices, engineering goods, motor-car ancillaries, leather and granite.

In 1994 there were 5,981 registered trade unions. Work-days lost by strikes and lockouts in 1994, 1,668,484.

Tourism. In 1992, 203,985 foreign tourists visited the state.

COMMUNICATIONS

Roads. On 31 March 1992 the state had 172,936 km of national and state highways, major and other district roads. In 1995–96 there were 2,771,845 registered motor vehicles.

Railways. On 31 March 1996 there were 4,005 route km. Madras and Madurai are the main centres.

Civil Aviation. There are airports at Madras, Tiruchirapalli and Madurai, with regular scheduled services to Bombay, Calcutta and Delhi. Madras is an international airport and the main centre of airline routes in South India.

Shipping. Madras and Tuticorin are the chief ports. Important minor ports are Cuddalore and Nagapattinam. Madras handled 26·5m. tonnes of cargo in 1993–94, Tuticorin, 6·7m. The Inland Container Depot at Coimbatore has a capacity of 50,000 tonnes of export traffic; it is linked to Cochin (Kerala).

SOCIAL INSTITUTIONS

Justice. There is a High Court at Madras with a Chief Justice and 26 judges. *Police:* Strength of police force, 1 Jan. 1995, 76,447.

Religion. At the 1991 census Hindus numbered 49,532,052 (88·67%), Christians, 3,179,410 (5·69%); Moslems, 3,052,717 (5·47%).

Education. At the 1991 census 30·38m. people were literate (62·66%; men 73·75% and women 51·33%).

Education is free up to pre-university level. In 1996–97 there were 30,619 primary schools with 6·8m. students, 5,503 middle schools with 3·51m. students, 3,574 high schools with 1,465,631 students and 2,734 higher secondary schools with 0·69m. students. There are also 78 medical colleges, 74 engineering and technology colleges, 22 teacher training colleges and 280 general education colleges.

There are 13 universities. Madras University (founded in 1857) is affiliating and teaching (it had 119 colleges and 125,082 students in 1993–94); Annamalai University, Annamalainagar (founded 1929) is residential; Madurai Kamaraj University (founded 1966) is an affiliating and teaching university; 10 others include one agricultural university, Mother Theresa Women's University, and Tamil University, Tanjavur. There are 4 institutions which are deemed to be universities.

Health. There were (1993–94) 427 hospitals, 484 dispensaries (of which 56 were Indian medicine and homeopathy), 1,683 primary health centres and 8,681 health sub-centres; total number of beds, 48,128.

Statistical Information: The Department of Statistics (Fort St George, Madras) was established in 1948 and reorganized in 1953. *Director:* C. Sethu. Main publications:

Annual Statistical Abstract; Decennial Statistical Atlas; Season and Crop Report; Quinquennial Wages Census; Quarterly Abstract of Statistics.

TRIPURA

KEY HISTORICAL EVENTS. A Hindu state of great antiquity having been ruled by the Maharajahs for 1,300 years before its accession to the Indian Union on 15 Oct. 1949. With the reorganization of states on 1 Sept. 1956 Tripura became a Union Territory, and was so declared on 1 Nov. 1957. The Territory was made a State on 21 Jan. 1972.

TERRITORY AND POPULATION. Tripura is bounded by Bangladesh, except in the north-east where it joins Assam and Mizoram. The major portion of the state is hilly and mainly jungle. It has an area of 10,486 sq. km and a population of 2,757,205 (1991 census); Density, 263 per sq. km. Growth rate, 1981–91, 34·3%.

The official languages are Bengali and Kokbarak. Manipuri is also spoken.

CONSTITUTION AND GOVERNMENT. The territory has 4 districts, divided into 14 administrative subdivisions, namely: Sadar, Khowai, Kailasahar, Dharmanagar, Sonamura, Udaipur, Gandachhara, Belonia, Kamalpur, Sabroom, Bishalgarh, Longthorai Velly, Kanchanpur and Amarpur. The capital is Agartala (population, 1991, 157,358).

The Communist Party won the elections of 6 April 1993.

Governor: Siddheshwar Prasad.
Chief Minister: Dasaratha Deb.

BUDGET. Budget estimates, 1994–95, show an expenditure of Rs 3,605m. Annual plan outlay for 1997–98 is Rs 4,370m.

ENERGY AND NATURAL RESOURCES

Electricity. Installed capacity (1995–96), 69·36 MW; there were (March 1996) 3,640 electrified villages out of a total of 4,856.

Agriculture. About 24% of the land area is cultivable. The tribes practise shifting cultivation, but this is being replaced by modern methods. The main crops are rice, wheat, jute, mesta, potatoes, oilseeds and sugar-cane. Foodgrain production (1995–96), 477,100 tonnes. There are 55 registered tea gardens producing 5,432,000 kg per year, and employing 14,170 in 1994–95.

Forestry. Forests covered 5,538 sq. km in 1995, about 53% of the land area. They have been much depleted by clearance for shifting cultivation and, recently, for refugee settlements of Bangladeshis. About 8% of the forest area still consists of dense natural forest; losses elsewhere are being replaced by plantation. Commercial rubber plantation has also been encouraged. In 1994–95, 30,328 ha were under new rubber plantations.

INDUSTRY. Tea is the main industry. There is also a jute mill producing about 15 tonnes per day and employing about 2,000. The main small industries: Aluminium utensils, rubber, saw-milling, soap, piping, fruit canning, handloom weaving and sericulture. There were 1,174 registered factories which employed 31,912 persons, and 700 notified factories with 3,000 workers in 1995–96. 330,980 persons were employed in handloom, handicrafts and sericulture industries in 1995–96.

COMMUNICATIONS

Roads. Total length of roads (1995–96) 5,760 km, of which 2,258 km were surfaced. Vehicles registered, 31 March 1996, 34,683 of which 4,701 were lorries.

Railways. There is a railway between Kumarghat and Kalkalighat (Assam). Route-km in 1995–96, 45 km.

Civil Aviation. There is 1 airport and 3 airstrips. The airport (Agartala) has regular scheduled services to Calcutta.

SOCIAL INSTITUTIONS

Religion. At the 1991 census Hindus numbered 2,384,934; Moslems, 196,495; Christians, 46,472; Buddhists, 128,260; Sikhs, 740; Jains, 301.

Education. In 1991, 60·44% of the population were literate (70·58% of men and 49·65% of women). In 1996–97 there were 2,045 primary schools (434,143 pupils); 411 middle schools (126,129); 558 high and higher secondary schools (82,273). There were 14 colleges of general education, 1 engineering college, 1 teacher training college and 1 polytechnic. Tripura University, established in 1987, has 20 affiliated colleges with 20,000 students.

Health. There were (1995–96) 27 hospitals, with 2,171 beds, 548 dispensaries, 818 doctors and 729 nurses. There were 53 primary health centres and 67 family planning centres.

UTTAR PRADESH

KEY HISTORICAL EVENTS. In 1833 the then Bengal Presidency was divided into two parts, one of which became the Presidency of Agra. In 1836 the Agra area was styled the NorthWest Province and placed under a Lieut.-Governor. The two provinces of Agra and Oudh were placed, in 1877, under one administrator, styled Lieut.-Governor of the North-West Province and Chief Commissioner of Oudh. In 1902 the name was changed to 'United Provinces of Agra and Oudh', under a Lieut.-Governor, and the Lieut.-Governorship was altered to a Governorship in 1921. In 1935 the name was shortened to 'United Provinces'. On Independence, the states of Rampur, Banaras and Tehri-Garwhal were merged with United Provinces. In 1950 the name of the United Provinces was changed to Uttar Pradesh.

TERRITORY AND POPULATION. Uttar Pradesh is in north India and is bounded north by Himachal Pradesh, Tibet and Nepal, east by Bihar, south by Madhya Pradesh and west by Rajasthan, Haryana and Delhi. The area of the state is 294,411 sq. km. Population (1991 census), 139,112,287, a density of 473 per sq. km. Growth rate, 1981–91, 25·48%. Cities with more than 250,000 population, *see* INDIA: Territory and Population. Other important towns (1991): Rampur (243,742), Muzaffarnagar (240,609), Shahjahanpur (237,717), Mathura (226,691), Firozabad (215,128), Farrukhabad-Cum-Fatehgarh (194,567), Mirzapur-Cum-Vindhyachal (169,336), Sambhal (150,819), Hardwar (147,305), Noida (146,514), Hapur (146,262), Amroha (137,061), Maunath Bhanjan (136,697), Jaunpur (136,062), Bahraich (135,400), Rae Bareli (129,904), Bulandshahr (127,201), Faizabad (124,437), Etawah (124,072), Sitapur (121,842), Fatehpur (117,675), Budaun (116,695), Hathras (113,285), Unnao (107,425), Pilibhit (106,605), Haldwani-Cum-Kathgodam (104,195), Modinagar (101,660). The sole official language has been Hindi since April 1990.

CONSTITUTION AND GOVERNMENT. Uttar Pradesh has had an autonomous system of government since 1937. There is a bicameral legislature. The Legislative Council has 108 members; the Legislative Assembly has 426, of which 425 are elected. The state was brought under presidential rule on 18 Oct. 1995 and the Legislative Assembly dissolved on 27 Oct. 1995. Elections were held in Oct. 1996. Bharatiya Janata Party, 174; Samajwadi Party, 110; Bahujan Samaj Party, 67; Congress (I), 33; Janata Dal, 7; independent and others, 34. As no party was in a position to form a stable government, presidential rule was reimposed.

There are 14 administrative divisions, each under a Commissioner, and 68 districts.

The capital is Lucknow.

Governor: Romesh Chandra Bhandari.
Chief Minister: Kalyan Singh.

BUDGET. Budget estimates 1996–97 showed revenue receipts of Rs 155,963·2m.; expenditure, Rs 194,039·9m. Annual plan outlay, 1997–98, Rs 70,800m.

ENERGY AND NATURAL RESOURCES

Electricity. The state had, 1995–96, an installed capacity of 6,049 MW. There were 85,657 villages with electricity in March 1996, out of a total 112,804.

Minerals. The state has magnesite, china-clay, coal, granite, sandstone, copper-lead-zinc, dolomite, limestone, soapstone, bauxite, diaspore, ochre, phosphorite, pyrophyllite, silica sand and steatite among others. In 1995–96 about 13m. tonnes of minerals were produced.

Agriculture. Agriculture occupies 78% of the work force. 10·13m. ha are irrigated. The state is India's largest producer of foodgrains; production (1995–96), 38·94m. tonnes (rice 10·4m. tonnes, wheat 22·2m. tonnes); pulses, 2·25m. tonnes. The state is one of India's main producers of sugar; production of sugar-cane (1995–96), 119·9m. tonnes. There were (1995–96) 1,965 veterinary centres for cattle.

Forests cover (1995) about 51,663 sq. km.

INDUSTRY. Sugar production is important; other industries include oil refining, aluminium smelting edible oils, textiles, distilleries, brewing, leather working, agricultural engineering, paper, automobile tyres, fertilizers, cement, jute, glass, heavy electricals, chemicals, automobiles and synthetic fibres. Large public-sector enterprises have been set up in electrical engineering, pharmaceuticals, locomotive building, general engineering, electronics and aeronautics. Village and small-scale industries are important; there were 0·64m. small units in 1995–96 providing employment to 1·19m. people. The state had 1,661 large and medium industries with an investment of Rs 223,002m. and employing 0·57m. persons in 1995–96.

COMMUNICATIONS

Roads. There were, 31 March 1995, 185,575 km of roads. In 1995–96 there were 2,977,275 motor vehicles of which 2,057,408 were two-wheelers.

Railways. Lucknow is the main junction of the northern network; other important junctions are Agra, Kanpur, Allahabad, Mughal Sarai, Dehra Dun and Varanasi. Route-km in 1995–96, 8,934 km.

Civil Aviation. There are airports at Lucknow, Kanpur, Varanasi, Allahabad, Agra, Gorakhpur and 7 other places.

SOCIAL INSTITUTIONS

Justice. The High Court of Judicature at Allahabad (with a bench at Lucknow) has a Chief Justice and 63 puisne judges including additional judges. There are 63 sessions divisions in the state.

Religion. At the 1991 census Hindus numbered 113,712,829; Moslems, 24,109,684; Sikhs, 675,775; Christians, 383,477; Jains, 176,259; Buddhists, 221,443.

Education. At the 1991 census 46·87m. people were literate (41·6%; 55·73% of men and 25·31% of women). In 1996–97 there were 91,093 primary schools with 16·26m. students, 19,917 middle schools with 5·63m. students, 2,628 high schools with 2,329,904 students and 4,375 higher secondary schools with 1,167,552 students.

Uttar Pradesh has 20 universities including: Allahabad University (founded 1887); Agra University (1927); the Banaras Hindu University, Varanasi (1916); Lucknow University (1921); Aligarh Muslim University (1920) with 4 colleges and 13,437 students in 1993–94; Roorkee University (1949), formerly Thomason College of Civil Engineering (established in 1847); Gorakhpur University (1957) with 33 colleges and 96,504 students; Sampurnanand Sanskrit Vishwavidyalaya, Varanasi (1958); Kanpur University (1966); Ch. Charan Singh University (1966), with 82 colleges and 96,004 students in 1993–94; Govind Ballabh Pant University of Agriculture and Technology, Pantnagar (1960); H. N. Bahuguna Garhwal University, Srinagar, (1973). C. S. Azad University of Agriculture and Technology, Kanpur, Narendra Deva University of Agriculture and Technology, Faizabad, and Dr Ram Manohar Lohia Awadh (32 colleges and 64,142 students), Kumaon, Rohilkhand (32 colleges and 86,996 students) and Bundelkhand Universities were founded in 1975. Jaunpur University (Purvanchal Vishwavidyalaya) was founded in 1987. There are also 6 institutions with university status: Gurukul Kangri Vishwavidyalaya, Hardwar, Indian Veterinary Research Institute, Central Institute of Higher Tibetan Studies, Forest Research Institute, Sanjay Gandhi Post-Graduate Institute of Medical Sciences and Dayal Bagh Educational Institute. There are 35 medical colleges, 18 engineering colleges, 62 teacher training colleges and 550 arts, science and commerce colleges.

Health. In 1994–95 there were 5,011 allopathic, 2,690 Ayurvedic and Unani and 1,149 homoepathic hospitals and dispensaries. There were also 3,766 primary health centres and 20,153 sub-centres, and TB hospitals and clinics.

WEST BENGAL

KEY HISTORICAL EVENTS. Bengal was under the overlordship of the Moghul emperor and ruled by a Moghul governor (*nawab*) who declared himself independent in 1740. The British East India Company based at Calcutta was in conflict with the *nawab* from 1756 until 1757 when British forces defeated him at Plassey and installed their own *nawab* in 1760. The French were also in Bengal; the British captured their trading settlement at Chandernagore in 1757 and in 1794, restoring it to France in 1815.

The area of British Bengal included modern Orissa and Bihar, Bangladesh and (until 1833) Uttar Pradesh. Calcutta was the capital of British India from 1772 until 1912.

The first division into East and West took place in 1905-11 and was not popular. However, at Partition in 1947 the East (Moslem) chose to join what was then East Pakistan (now Bangladesh), leaving West Bengal as an Indian frontier state and promoting a steady flow of non-Moslem Bengali immigrants from the East. In 1950 West Bengal received the former princely state of Cooch Behar and, in 1954, Chandernagore. Small areas were transferred from Bihar in 1956.

TERRITORY AND POPULATION. West Bengal is in north-east India and is bounded north by Sikkim and Bhutan, east by Assam and Bangladesh, south by the Bay of Bengal, south-west by Orissa, west by Bihar and north-west by Nepal. The total area of West Bengal is 88,752 sq. km. At the 1991 census its population was 68,077,965, an increase of 24·73% since 1981, the density of population 767 per sq. km. Population of chief cities, *see* INDIA: Territory and Population. Other major towns (1991): Barddhaman (245,079), South Dum Dum (232,811), Baranagar (224,821), Siliguri (216,950), Bally (181,978), Burnpur (174,933), Uluberia (155,172), Hugli-Chinsura (151,806), Raiganj (151,045), North Dum Dum (149,965), Dabgram (147,217), English Bazar (139,204), Serampur (137,028), Barrackpur (133,265), Naihati (132,701), Medinipur (125,498), Nabadwip (125,037), Krishnanagar (121,110), Chandannagar (120,378), Balurghat (119,796), Baharampur (115,144), Bankura (114,876), Titagarh (114,085), Halisahar (114,028), Santipur (109,956), Kulti-Barakar (108,518), Basirhat (101,409), Haldia (100,347), Habra (100,223), Kanchrapara (100,194). The principal language is Bengali.

CONSTITUTION AND GOVERNMENT. The state of West Bengal came into existence as a result of the Indian Independence Act, 1947. The territory of Cooch-Behar State was merged with West Bengal on 1 Jan. 1950, and the former French possession of Chandernagore became part of the state on 2 Oct. 1954. Under the States Reorganization Act, 1956, certain portions of Bihar State (an area of 3,157 sq. miles with a population of 1,446,385) were transferred to West Bengal.

The Legislative Assembly has 295 seats (294 elected and 1 nominated). Distribution after the 1996 elections, Dec. 1996: Communist Party of India (Marxist), 150; Indian National Congress, 82; All India Forward Bloc, 21; Revolutionary Socialist Party, 18; Communist Party of India, 6; Independents and others, 17.

The capital is Calcutta.

For administrative purposes there are 3 divisions (Jalpaiguri, Burdwan and Presidency), under which there are 18 districts, including Calcutta. The Calcutta Metropolitan Development Authority has been set up to co-ordinate development in the metropolitan area (1,350 sq. km). For the purposes of local self-government there are 16 *zila parishads* (district boards) excluding Darjeeling, 328 *panchayat samities* (regional boards), and 3,222 *gram* (village) *panchayats*. There are 113 municipalities, 3 Corporations and 11 Notified Areas. The Calcutta Municipal Corporation is headed by a mayor in-Council.

Governor: K. V. Raghunatha Reddy.
Chief Minister: Jyoti Basu.

BUDGET. Budget estimates for 1997–98, revenue receipts Rs 102,582·9m. and expenditure Rs 120,329·1m. Plan outlay for 1997–98 was Rs 29,456m.

ENERGY AND NATURAL RESOURCES

Electricity. Installed capacity, 1995–96, 5,481·5 MW; 29,237 villages had electricity in November 1996.

Water. The largest irrigation and power scheme under construction is the Teesta Barrage (irrigation potential, 533,520 ha). Other major irrigation schemes are the Mayurakshi Reservoir, Kangsabati Reservoir, Mahananda Barrage and Aqueduct and Damodar Valley. In 1995–96 there were 9,171 tubewells, 7,170 open dugwells and 3,170 riverlift irrigation schemes.

Minerals. Value of production, 1995, Rs 10,094m. The state has coal (the Raniganj field is one of the 3 biggest in India) including coking coal. Coal production (1995) 17·56m. tonnes.

Agriculture. About 5·95m. ha were under rice-paddy in 1995–96. Total foodgrain production, 1995–96, 12·99m. tonnes (rice 11·89m. tonnes, wheat 850,000 tonnes); pulses, 125,900 tonnes; oilseeds, 415,500 tonnes; jute, 5·7m. bales of 180 kg; tea (1995), 160·3m. kg. The state produces 63·4% of the national output of jute and *mesta* (1994–95).

Livestock (1989 census): 16,509,487 cattle; 965,517 buffaloes; 1,459,771 sheep; 11,890,278 goats and 35,542,444 poultry.

The recorded forest area (1995–96) was 11,879 sq. km.

Fisheries. Landings, 1995–96, 0·89m. tonnes, of which inland 740,000 tonnes. During 1996–97 Rs 407·1m. was invested in fishery schemes. The state is the largest inland fish producer in the country.

INDUSTRY. The total number of registered factories, 1995, was 10,236 (excluding defence factories); average daily employment, 1995, 920,763. The coalmining industry, 1993, had 110 units with average daily employment of 107,000.

There is a large automobile factory at Uttarpara, and an aluminium rolling-mill at Belur. There is a steel plant at Burnpur (Asansol) and a spun pipe factory at Kulti. Durgapur has a large steel plant and other industries under the state sector—a thermal power plant, coke oven plant, fertilizer factory, alloy steel plant and ophthalmic glass plant. There is a locomotive factory at Chittaranjan and a cable factory at Rupnarayanpur. A refinery and fertilizer factory are operating at Haldia. Other industries include chemicals, engineering goods, electronics, textiles, automobile tyres, paper, cigarettes, distillery, aluminium foil, tea, pharmaceuticals, carbon black, graphite, iron foundry, silk and explosives.

Small industries are important; 453,831 units were registered at 31 March 1996, employing 3m. persons. The silk industry is also important; 376,000 persons were employed in handloom industry in the organized sector in 1995–96.

COMMUNICATIONS

Roads. In 1995 the total length of roads was 68,375 km. On 31 March 1996 the state had 1,198,733 motor vehicles.

Railways. The route-km of railways within the state (1995–96) is 3,817 km. The main centres are Asansol, New Jalpaiguri and Kharagpur. There is a metro in Calcutta (16·4 km).

Civil Aviation. The main airport is Calcutta which has national and international flights. The second airport is at Bagdogra in the extreme north, which has regular scheduled services to Calcutta and Delhi.

Shipping. Calcutta is the chief port: A barrage has been built at Farakka to control the flow of the Ganges and to provide a rail and road link between North and South Bengal. A second port has been developed at Haldia, between the present port and the sea, which is intended mainly for bulk cargoes. West Bengal possesses 779 km of navigable canals.

SOCIAL INSTITUTIONS

Justice. The High Court of Judicature at Calcutta has a Chief Justice and 45 puisne judges. The Andaman and Nicobar Islands come under its jurisdiction.

Police. In March 1995 the police force numbered about 56,550, under a director-general and an inspector-general. Calcutta has a separate force under a commissioner directly responsible to the Government; its strength was about 22,000 in March 1995.

Religion. At the 1991 census Hindus numbered 50,866,624; Moslems, 16,075,836, Christians, 383,477; Buddhists, 203,578; Sikhs, 55,392; Jains, 34,355.

Education. In 1996 70·64% of the total population were literate (Men, 78·62%; women, 61·67%). In 1996–97 there were 51,021 primary schools with 10,117,000 students, 3,156 junior high schools with 4,603,000 students and 6,728 high and higher secondary schools with 1,881,226 students. Education is free up to higher secondary stage. There are 10 universities.

The University of Calcutta (founded 1857) is affiliating and teaching; in 1993–94 it had 212 colleges and 150,000 students. Visva Bharati, Santiniketan, was established in 1951 and is residential and teaching; it had 5,226 students in 1993–94. The University of Jadavpur, Calcutta (1955), had 7,087 students in 1992–93. Burdwan University was established in 1960; in 1992–93 there were 91,379 students. Kalyani University was established in 1960 (2,520 students in 1993–94). The University of North Bengal (1962) had 34,000 students in 1993–94. Rabindra Bharati University had 8,309 students in 1992–93. Bidhan Chandra Krishi Viswavidyalaya (1974) had 389 students in 1992–93. There is also Vidyasagar University, Medinipur. Bengal Engineering College has university status. There are 12 engineering and technology colleges, 19 medical colleges, 24 teacher training colleges, 41 polytechnics and 308 arts, science and commerce colleges.

Health. As at 31 March 1996 there were 402 hospitals, 1,352 clinics, 1,266 health centres and 8,126 sub-centres with a total of 68,901 beds, and 566 dispensaries.

UNION TERRITORIES

ANDAMAN AND NICOBAR ISLANDS. The Andaman and Nicobar Islands are administered by the President of the Republic of India acting through a Lieut.-Governor. There is a 30-member Pradesh Council, 5 members of which are selected by the Administrator as advisory counsellors. The seat of administration is at Port Blair, which is connected with Calcutta (1,255 km away) and Madras (1,190 km) by steamer service which calls about every 10 days; there are air services from Calcutta and Madras. Roads in the islands, 733 km black-topped and 48 km others. There are 2 districts.

The population (1991 census) was 280,661; Area, 8,249 sq. km; density 34 per sq. km. Growth rate 1981–91, 48·7%. Port Blair (1991), 74,955.

The climate is tropical, with little variation in temperature. Heavy rain (125" annually) is mainly brought by the south-west monsoon. Humidity is high.

Budget figures for 1997–98 show total revenue receipts of Rs 819m., and total expenditure on revenue account of Rs 3,027m. Plan outlay, 1997–98, Rs 2,550m.

In 1996–97 there were 188 primary schools with 41,976 students, 45 middle schools with 22,862 students, 38 high schools with 11,151 students and 42 higher secondary schools with 3,858 students. There is a teachers' training college, 2 polytechnics and 2 colleges. Literacy (1991 census), 73·02% (78·99% of men and 65·46% of women).

Lieut.-Governor: Rajendra Kumari Bajpai.

The **Andaman Islands** lie in the Bay of Bengal, 193 km from Cape Negrais in Myanmar, 1,255 from Calcutta and 1,190 from Madras. Five large islands grouped together are called the Great Andamans, and to the south is the island of Little Andaman. There are some 204 islets, the two principal groups being the Ritchie Archipelago and the Labyrinth Islands. The Great Andaman group is about 467 km long and, at the widest, 51 km broad.

The original inhabitants live in the forests by hunting and fishing. The total population of the Andaman Islands (including about 430 aboriginals) was 240,089 in 1991. Main aboriginal tribes: Andamanese, Onges, Jarawas and Sentinelese.

The Great Andaman group, densely wooded (forests covered 7,615 sq. km in 1995), contains hardwood and softwood and supplies the match and plywood industries. Annually the Forest Department export about 25,000 tons of timber to the mainland. Coconut, coffee and rubber are cultivated. The islands are slowly being made self-sufficient in paddy and rice, and now grow approximately half their annual requirements. Livestock (1982): 27,400 cattle, 9,720 buffaloes, 17,600 goats and 21,220 pigs. Fishing is important. There is a sawmill at Port Blair and a coconut-oil mill. Little Andaman has a palm-oil mill.

The islands possess a number of harbours and safe anchorages, notably Port Blair in the south, Port Cornwallis in the north and Elphinstone and Mayabandar in the middle.

The **Nicobar Islands** are situated to the south of the Andamans, 121 km from Little Andaman. The British were in possession 1869–1947. There are 19 islands, 7 uninhabited; total area, 1,841 sq. km. The islands are usually divided into 3 subgroups (southern, central and northern), the chief islands in each being respectively, Great Nicobar, Camorta with Nancowrie and Car Nicobar. There is a harbour between the islands of Camorta and Nancowrie, Nancowrie Harbour.

The population numbered, in 1991, 39,208, including about 22,200 of Nicobarese and Shompen tribes. The coconut and areca nut are the main items of trade, and coconuts are a major item in the people's diet.

CHANDIGARH. On 1 Nov. 1966 the city of Chandigarh and the area surrounding it was constituted a Union Territory. Population (1991), 642,015; density, 5,632 per sq. km.; growth rate, 1981–91, 42·16%. Area, 114 sq. km. It serves as the joint capital of both Punjab (India) and the state of Haryana, and is the seat of a High Court. The city will ultimately be the capital of just the Punjab; joint status is to last while a new capital is built for Haryana.

Budget for 1997–98 showed revenue of Rs 3,412m. and expenditure of Rs 3,989m.

There is some cultivated land and some forest (27·5% of the territory).

In 1992 there were 15 large and medium scale industries and about 2,800 small scale industries.

In 1996–97 there were 44 primary schools (60,012 students), 33 middle schools (34,095 students), 50 high schools (18,510 students) and 47 higher secondary schools (16,710 students). There were also 2 engineering and technology colleges, 12 arts, science and commerce colleges, 2 polytechnic institutes and a university.

In 1991, 77·81% of the population were literate (82·04% of men and 72·34% of women).

Administrator: Lieut.-Gen. Bakshi K. N. Chibber.

DADRA AND NAGAR HAVELI. Formerly Portuguese, the territories of Dadra and Nagar Haveli were occupied in July 1954 by nationalists, and a pro-India administration was formed; this body made a request for incorporation into the Union, 1 June 1961. By the 10th amendment to the constitution the territories became a centrally administered Union Territory with effect from 11 Aug. 1961, forming an enclave at the southernmost point of the border between Gujarat and Maharashtra. Area 491 sq. km.; population (census 1991), 138,477; density 282 per sq. km; growth rate, 1981–91, 33·57%. There is an Administrator appointed by the Government of India. The day-to-day business is done by various departments, co-ordinated by the Resident Deputy Collector, Collector or Assistant Secretary. Headquarters are at Silvassa. 78·82% of the population is tribal and organized in 72 villages. Languages used are Bhilli, Gujarati, Bhilodi (91·1%), Marathi and Hindi.

Administrator: S. P. Aggarwal.
Collector: S. P. Marwah.

Budget. Budget for 1996–97 shows revenue receipts of Rs 285m. and revenue expenditure of Rs 1,140m.

Electricity. Electricity is supplied by Gujarat, and all villages have been electrified.

Water. As the result of a joint project with the governments of Gujarat, Goa and Daman and Diu there is a reservoir at Damanganga with irrigation potential of 7,044 ha.

Agriculture. Farming is the chief occupation, and 22,899 ha were under crops in 1994–95. Much of the land is terraced and there is a 100% subsidy for soil conservation. The major food crops are rice and ragi; wheat, small millets and pulses are also grown. There is little irrigation (4,790 ha). There are 9 veterinary aid centres, a veterinary hospital, an agricultural research centre and breeding centres to improve strains of cattle and poultry. During 1996–97 the Administration distributed 179 tonnes of high-yielding paddy and wheat seed and 1,458 tonnes of fertilizer.

Forestry. 19,967 ha or 40·8% of the total area is forest, mainly of teak, sadad and khair. There was (1985) a moratorium on commercial felling, to preserve the environmental function of the forests and ensure local supplies of firewood, timber and fodder. The moratorium still continued in 1997.

Industry. There is no heavy industry, and the Territory is a 'No Industry District'. Industrial estates for small and medium units have been set up at Piparia, Masat and Khadoli. There were (1996) 552 small units, and 170 medium scale, employing 12,500. Concessions (15 years' sales tax holiday) are available for small industries.

Tourism. The territory is a rural area between the industrial centres of Bombay and Surat-Vapi. The Tourism Department is developing areas of natural beauty to promote acceptable tourism.

Communications. There were (1997) 461 km of roads. The railway line from Bombay to Ahmedabad runs through Vapi near Silvassa. The nearest airport is Bombay (now renamed Mumbai). There were 11,272 motor vehicles in 1996–97.

Justice. The territory is under the jurisdiction of the Bombay (Maharashtra) High Court. There is a District and Sessions Court and one Junior Division Civil Court at Silvassa.

Education. Literacy was 40·71% of the population at the 1991 census (53·56% of men and 26·98% of women). In 1996–97 there were 150 adult education centres (4,500 students); there were 191 primary and middle schools and 15 high and higher secondary schools. Total primary and middle school enrolment was 26,702; high-school and higher secondary, 4,996.

Health. The territory had (1995–96) 1 cottage hospital, 5 primary health centres and 4 dispensaries; there is also a mobile dispensary. A Community Health Centre has been established at Khanvel, 20 km from Silvassa.

DAMAN AND DIU. Daman (Damão) on the Gujarat coast, 100 miles (160 km) north of Bombay, was seized by the Portuguese in 1531 and ceded to them (1539) by the Shar of Gujarat. The island of Diu, captured in 1534, lies off the south-east coast of Kathiawar (Gujarat); there is a small coastal area. Former Portuguese forts on either side of the entrance to the Gulf of Cambay, in Dec. 1961 the territories were occupied by India and incorporated into the Indian Union; they were administered as one unit together with Goa, to which they were attached until 30 May 1987, when Goa was separated from them and became a state.

Territory and Population. Daman, 72 sq. km, population (1991) 62,101; Diu, 40 sq. km, population 39,485. Density, 907 per sq. km. Growth rate 1981–91, 28·62%. The main language spoken is Gujarati.

The chief towns are Daman (population, 1991, 26,905) and Diu (20,643).

Daman and Diu have been governed as parts of a Union Territory since Dec. 1961, becoming the whole of that Territory on 30 May 1987.

The main activities are tourism, fishing and tapping the toddy palm. In Daman there is rice-growing, some wheat and dairying. Diu has fine tourist beaches, grows coconuts and pearl millet, and processes salt.

Administrator: S. P. Aggarwal.

Budget. Budget for 1997–98 shows revenue receipts of Rs 397·7m. and revenue expenditure of Rs 312·2m. Plan outlay, 1995–96, Rs 230m.

Education. In 1991, 71·2% of the population were literate (82·66% of men and 59·4% of women). In 1996–97 there were 53 primary schools with 14,531 students, 20 middle schools with 6,834 students, 20 high schools with 3,220 students and 3 higher secondary schools with 1,202 students. There is a degree college and a polytechnic.

DELHI. Delhi became a Union Territory on 1 Nov. 1956 and was designated the National Capital Territory in 1995.

Territory and Population. The territory forms an enclave near the eastern frontier of Haryana and the western frontier of Uttar Pradesh in north India. Delhi has an area of 1,483 sq. km. At the 1991 census its population was 9,420,644 (density per sq. km, 6,352). Growth rate, 1981–91, 51·45%. In the rural area of Delhi there are 231 villages and 27 census towns. They are distributed in 5 community development blocks.

Government. The Lieut-Governor is the Administrator. Under the New Delhi Municipal Act 1994 New Delhi Municipal Council is nominated by central government and replaces the former New Delhi Municipal Committee.

Elections for the 70-member Legislative Assembly were held in Nov. 1993 and Bharatiya Janata Party formed the government. Bharatiya Janata Party, 49; Congress (I), 14; Janata Dal, 4; Independent and others, 3.

Lieut.-Governor: Tejendra Khanna.
Chief Minister: Sahib Singh Verma.

Budget. Estimates for 1996–97 show revenue receipts of Rs 25,911·2m. and expenditure of Rs 37,624·7m. Plan outlay (1997–98) Rs 23,250m.

Agriculture. The contribution to the economy is not significant. In 1995–96 about 53,900 ha were cropped (of which 36,000 ha were irrigated). Animal husbandry is increasing and mixed farms are common. Chief crops are wheat, bajra, paddy, sugarcane and vegetables.

Industry. The modern city is the largest commercial centre in northern India and an important industrial centre. Since 1947 a large number of industrial units have been established; these include factories for the manufacture of razor blades, sports goods, electronic goods, bicycles and parts, plastic and PVC goods including footwear, textiles, chemicals, fertilizers, medicines, hosiery, leather goods, soft drinks, hand tools. There are also metal forging, casting, galvanising, electro-plating and printing enterprises. The number of industrial units functioning was about 126,218 in 1996–97; average number of workers employed was 1·14m. Production was worth Rs 63,100m. and investment was about Rs 25,240m. in 1996–97.

Some traditional handicrafts, for which Delhi was formerly famous, still flourish;

among them are ivory carving, miniature painting, gold and silver jewellery and papier mâché work. The handwoven textiles of Delhi are particularly fine; this craft is being successfully revived.

Delhi publishes major daily newspapers, including the *Times of India, Hindustan Times, The Hindu, Indian Express, National Herald, Patriot, Economic Times, The Pioneer, The Observer of Business and Politics, Financial Express, Statesman, Asian Age* and *Business Standard* (all in English); *Nav Bharat Times, Rashtriya Sahara, Jansatta* and *Hindustan* (in Hindi) and 3 Urdu dailies.

Roads. 5 national highways pass through the city. There were (1995–96) 2,629,545 registered motor vehicles. The Transport Corporation had 3,206 buses in 1995–96.

Railways. Delhi is an important rail junction with 3 main stations. There is an electric ring railway for commuters (route-km in 1995–96, 214).

Civil Aviation. Indira Gandhi International Airport operates international flights; Palam airport operates internal flights.

Religion. At the 1991 census Hindus numbered 7,882,164; Sikhs, 455,657; Moslems, 889,641; Jains, 94,672; Christians, 83,152; Buddhists, 13,906; others, 1,452.

Education. The proportion of literates to the total population was 75·29% at the 1991 census (82·01% of males and 66·99% of females). In 1996–97 there were 2,184 primary schools with 1,146,691 students, 559 middle schools with 535,511 students, 324 high schools with 676,209 students and 994 higher secondary schools with 460,334 students. There are 9 engineering and technology colleges, 9 medical colleges and 25 polytechnics.

The University of Delhi was founded in 1922; it had 66 affiliated colleges and 189,332 students in 1994 95. There are also Jawahar Lal Nehru University, Indira Gandhi National Open University and the Jamia Millia Islamia University; the Indian Institute of Technology at Hauz Khas; the Indian Agricultural Research Institute at Pusa; the All India Institute of Medical Science at Ansari Nagar and the Indian Institute of Public Administration are the other important institutions.

Health. In 1992 there were 82 hospitals including 46 general, 27 special, 6 Ayurvedic, 1 Unani, 2 Homeopathic. There were 656 dispensaries.

LAKSHADWEEP. The territory consists of an archipelago of 36 islands (10 inhabited), about 300 km off the west coast of Kerala. It was constituted a Union Territory in 1956 as the Laccadive, Minicoy and Amindivi Islands, and renamed in Nov. 1973. The total area of the islands is 32 sq. km. The northern portion is called the Amindivis. The remaining islands are called the Laccadives (except Minicoy Island). The inhabited islands are: Androth (the largest), Amini, Agatti, Bitra, Chetlat, Kadmat, Kalpeni, Kavaratti, Kiltan and Minicoy. Androth is 4·8 sq. km, and is nearest to Kerala. An Advisory Committee associated with the Union Home Minister and an Advisory Council to the Administrator assist in the administration of the islands; these are constituted annually. Population (1991 census), 51,707, nearly all Moslems. Density, 1,616 per sq. km.; growth rate, 1981–91, 28·4%. The language is Malayalam, but the language in Minicoy is Mahl. Budget for 1997–98 showed revenue of Rs 73·1m. and expenditure of Rs 1,255·7m. Plan outlay, 1990–91, Rs 211·3m. In 1991, 81·78% of the population were literate (90·18% of men and 72·89% of women). There were, in 1996–97, 9 high schools (2,043 students) and 9 nursery schools (1,197 students), 19 junior basic schools (9,015 students), 4 senior basic schools (4,797 students) and 2 junior colleges. There are 2 hospitals and 7 primary health centres. The staple products are copra and fish; coconut is the only major crop. There is a tourist resort at Bangarem, an uninhabited island with an extensive lagoon. Headquarters of administration, Kavaratti Island. An airport, with Vayudoot services, opened on Agatti island in April 1988. The islands are also served by ship from the mainland and have helicopter inter-island services.

Administrator: Rajeev Talwar.

PONDICHERRY. Formerly the chief French settlement in India, Pondicherry was founded by the French in 1673, taken by the Dutch in 1693 and restored to the French in 1699. The English took it in 1761, restored it in 1765, re-took it in 1778, restored it a second time in 1785, retook it a third time in 1793 and finally restored it to the French in 1816. Administration was transferred to India on 1 Nov. 1954. A Treaty of Cession (together with Karaikal, Mahé and Yanam) was signed on 28 May 1956; instruments of ratification were signed on 16 Aug. 1962 from which date (by the 14th amendment to the Indian Constitution) Pondicherry, comprising the 4 territories, became a Union Territory.

Territory and Population. The territory is composed of enclaves on the Coromandel Coast of Tamil Nadu and Andhra Pradesh, with Mahé forming an enclave on the coast of Kerala. The total area of Pondicherry is 492 sq. km, divided into 4 Districts. On Tamil Nadu coast: Pondicherry (293 sq. km; population, 1991 census (provisional), 607,600, Karaikal (160; 145,723). On Kerala coast: Mahé (9; 33,425). On Andhra Pradesh coast: Yanam (30; 20,297). Total population (1991 census), 807,785; density, 1,642 per sq. km.; growth rate, 1981–91, 33·64%. Pondicherry Municipality had (1991) 203,065 inhabitants. The principal languages spoken are Tamil, Telugu, Malayalam, French and English.

Government. By the Government of Union Territories Act 1963 Pondicherry is governed by a Lieut.-Governor, appointed by the President, and a Council of Ministers responsible to a Legislative Assembly. A DMK led government was formed after the election in June 1996. Total seats, 30: Congress (I), 9; DMK, 7; Ramil Maanila Congress, 6; All India Anna DMK, 3; CPI, 2; Independents and others, 3.

> *Governor:* Rajendra Kumari Bajpai.
> *Chief Minister:* R. V. Janakiraman.

Budget. Budget estimates for 1996–97 showed expenditure of Rs 5,354·8m. Plan outlay, 1996–97, Rs 2,000m.

Electricity. Power is bought from neighbouring states. All 292 villages have electricity. Consumption, 1991–92, 747 units per head. Peak demand, 130 MW; total consumption, 607·73m. units.

Agriculture. Nearly 45% of the population is engaged in agriculture and allied pursuits; 90% of the cultivated area is irrigated. The main food crop is rice. Foodgrain production, 71,600 tonnes in 1995–96. Rice production, 67,100 tonnes from 26,600 ha in 1995–96; principal cash crops are cotton (10,934 bales of 180 kg), sugar-cane (258,400 tonnes) and groundnuts; minor food crops include ragi, bajra and pulses.

Industry. There were, 1994–95, 23 large and 73 medium-scale enterprises manufacturing items such as textiles, sugar, cotton yarn, spirits and beer, potassium chlorate, rice bran oil, vehicle parts, soap, amino acids, paper, plastics, steel ingots, washing machines, glass and tin containers and bio polymers. There were also 5,197 small industrial units engaged in varied manufacturing.

Roads. There were (1992–93) 3,282 km of roads of which 1,248 km were surfaced. Motor vehicles (March 1996) 119,290.

Railways. Pondicherry is connected to Villupuram Junction. Route-km in 1995–96, 11.

Civil Aviation. The nearest main airport is Madras. Vayudoot domestic airline connects Pondicherry with Madras.

Education. In 1991, 74·74% of the population were literate (83·68% of men and 65·63% of women). There were, in 1996–97, 178 pre-primary schools (15,107 pupils), 350 primary schools (103,201), 120 middle schools (64,617), 89 high schools (28,731) and 52 higher secondary schools (11,168). There were (1996–97) 7 general education colleges, 2 medical colleges, a law college, an engineering college, an agricultural college and a dental college, and 4 polytechnics. Pondicherry University had, in 1994–95, 19 colleges and 9,910 students.

Health. In 1995–96 there were 9 hospitals, 55 health centres and dispensaries and 79 sub-centres. In 1990 family schemes had reduced the birth rate to 19·9 per 1,000 and the infant mortality rate to 34·79 per 1,000 live births.

INDONESIA

Republik Indonesia

Capital: Jakarta
Population: 195·28m.
GDP per head: (PPP$) 3,740
GNP: US$167·6bn.
HDI/world rank: 0·668/99

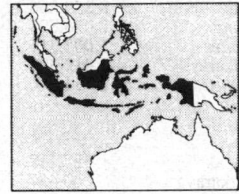

KEY HISTORICAL EVENTS. In the 16th century Portuguese traders settled in some of the islands which now comprise Indonesia, but were ejected by the British, who in turn were ousted by the Dutch in 1595. From 1602 the Netherlands East India Company conquered the area and ruled until the dissolution of the Company in 1798. The Netherlands government then ruled the colony from 1816 until 1941, when it was occupied by the Japanese until 1945. On 17 Aug. 1945 an independent republic was proclaimed by Dr Sukarno and Dr Hatta, the nationalist leaders. The republic was not, however, recognized by the Netherlands with whom negotiations and fighting continued until 1949. On 27 Dec. 1949 complete and unconditional sovereignty was transferred to the Republic of the United States of Indonesia.

A settlement of the New Guinea (Irian Jaya) question was, however, delayed until 15 Aug. 1962, when through the offices of the UN, an agreement was concluded for the transfer of the territory to Indonesia on 1 May 1963.

In 1950 the federal form of government which had sprung up in 1946–48 was abolished, and Indonesia was again made a unitary state. On 5 July 1959, by presidential decree, the constitution of 1945 was reinstated.

On 12 Jan. 1960 President Sukarno issued a decree enabling him to control and dissolve the political parties. He also set up a mass organization, the National Front, and a supreme state body called the Provisional People's Consultative Assembly. On 6 March 1960 he prorogued parliament to be reorganized on the basis of the 1945 constitution with the local administrations nominating members to the new 'Mutual Co-operation House of Representatives'.

On 11–12 March 1966 the military commanders under the leadership of Lieut.-Gen. Suharto took over executive power while leaving President Sukarno as the head of state. The Communist party, which had twice attempted to overthrow the government and had killed six generals in 1965, was at once outlawed; the National Front was dissolved in Oct. 1966. On 22 Feb. 1967 Sukarno handed over all his powers to Gen. Suharto who has been continually re-elected president at five-year intervals, most recently on 10 March 1998.

TERRITORY AND POPULATION. Indonesia, with a land area of 741,098 sq. miles (1,919,443 sq. km), consists of 17,508 islands (6,000 of which are inhabited) extending about 3,200 miles east to west through three time-zones (East, Central and West Indonesian Standard time) and 1,250 miles north to south. The largest islands are Sumatra, Java, Kalimantan (Indonesian Borneo), Sulawesi (Celebes) and Irian Jaya (the western part of New Guinea). Most of the smaller islands except Madura and Bali are grouped together. The two largest groups of islands are Maluku (the Moluccas) and Nusa Tenggara (the Lesser Sundas).

Population at the 1990 census was 179,378,946. Estimate, 1995, 195·28m. (42% urban).

Area, population and chief towns of the provinces, autonomous districts and major islands at the 1990 census:

	Area (in sq. km)	*Population*	*Chief town*	*Population*
Aceh[1]	55,392	3,416,156	Banda Aceh	143,409
Sumatera Utara	70,787	10,256,027	Medan	1,685,972
Sumatera Barat	49,778	4,000,207	Padang	477,344
Riau	94,561	3,303,976	Pakanbaru	341,328
Jambi	44,800	2,020,568	Jambi[2]	301,359
Sumatera Selatan	103,688	6,313,074	Palembang	1,084,483

	Area (in sq. km)	Population	Chief town	Population
Bengkulu	21,168	1,179,122	Bengkulu	146,439
Lampung	33,307	6,016,573	Tanjungkarang	284,275[3]
Sumatra	473,481	36,505,703		
Jakarta Raya[1]	590	8,259,266	Jakarta	8,259,266
Jawa Barat	46,300	35,384,352	Bandung	2,026,893
Jawa Tengah	34,206	28,520,643	Semarang	1,005,316
Yogyakarta[1]	3,169	2,913,054	Yogyakarta	412,392
Jawa Timur	47,921	32,503,991	Surabaya	2,421,016
Java and Madura	132,186	107,581,306		
Kalimantan Barat	146,760	3,229,153	Pontianak	387,112
Kalimantan Tengah	152,600	1,396,486	Palangkaraya	60,447[3]
Kalimantan Selatan	37,660	2,597,572	Banjarmasin	443,738
Kalimantan Timur	202,440	1,876,663	Samarinda	335,016
Kalimantan	539,460	9,099,874		
Sulawesi Utara	19,023	2,478,119	Menado	275,374
Sulawesi Tengah	69,726	1,711,327	Palu	298,584[3]
Sulawesi Selatan	72,781	6,981,646	Ujung Padang	913,196
Sulawesi Tenggara	27,686	1,349,619	Kendari	41,021[3]
Sulawesi	189,216	12,520,711		
Bali	5,561	2,777,811	Denpasar	261,263[3]
Nusa Tenggara Barat	20,177	3,369,649	Mataram	141,387[3]
Nusa Tenggara Timur	47,876	3,268,644	Kupang	403,110[3]
Timor Timur[4]	14,874	747,750	Dili	60,150[4]
Maluku	74,505	1,857,790	Amboina	206,260
Irian Jaya	421,981	1,648,708	Jayapura	149,618[3]
Pulau—Pulau Lain	584,974	13,670,352		

[1] Autonomous District. [2] Formerly Telanaipura. [3] 1980 census. [4] See section below.

The capital, Jakarta, had a population of 9m. in 1993. Other major cities (census 1990 in 1m.): Surabaya, 2·5; Bandung, 2; Medan, 1·7; Semarang, 1·3; Palembang, 1·1.

Vital statistics, 1994: Birth rate, 23·5 per 1,000; death rate, 8·0. Life expectancy in 1996 was 63 years.

The principal ethnic groups are the Acehnese, Bataks and Minangkabaus in Sumatra, the Javanese and Sundanese in Java, the Madurese in Madura, the Balinese in Bali, the Sasaks in Lombok, the Menadonese, Minahasans, Torajas and Buginese in Sulawesi, the Dayaks in Kalimantan, Irianese in Irian Jaya, the Ambonese in the Moluccas and Timorese in Timor Timur. There were some 6m. Chinese resident in 1991.

Bahasa Indonesia is the official language; Dutch is spoken as a colonial inheritance.

East Timor. Portugal abandoned its former colony, whose population is largely Roman Catholic, in 1975, when it was occupied by Indonesia and claimed as the province of Timor Timur. The UN does not recognize Indonesian sovereignty over the territory. An independence movement, FRETILIN, has maintained a guerilla resistance to the Indonesian government which has resulted in large-scale casualties and alleged atrocities.

Carey, P. and Bentley, G. C. (eds.) *East Timor at the Crossroads: the Forging of a Nation.* London, 1995

CLIMATE. Conditions vary greatly over this spread of islands, but generally the climate is tropical monsoon, with a dry season from June to Sept. and a wet one from

Oct. to April. Temperatures are high all the year and rainfall varies according to situation on lee or windward shores. Jakarta. Jan. 78°F (25·6°C), July 78°F (25·6°C). Annual rainfall 71" (1,775 mm). Padang. Jan. 79°F (26·1°C), July 79°F (26·1°C). Annual rainfall 177" (4,427 mm). Surabaya. Jan. 79°F (26·1°C), July 78°F (25·6°C). Annual rainfall 51" (1,285 mm).

CONSTITUTION AND GOVERNMENT. The political system is based on *pancasila*, in which deliberations lead to a consensus. 425 members of the *House of People's Representatives* are elected every 5 years, and the remaining 75 are appointed from the armed forces. Together with 500 government appointees they make up the *People's Consultative Assembly* which meets every 5 years to choose a president. There is no limit to the number of presidential terms. The military perform a dual function enshrined in law, combining conventional defence duties with participation in all areas of political and social life. Golkar is a 'functional group'. There are 2 officially-sanctioned parties also in the House of People's Representatives: the United Development Party (UDP, largely Moslem), and the Indonesian Democratic Party (IDP nationalist Christian).

General elections to the 425 elected seats in the House of Representatives were held on 29 May 1997. The electorate was 124·7m.; turn-out was 93%. Golkar won 425 seats with 74% of votes cast (68% in 1992), UDP received 22·5% of the votes (17·5% in 1992) and IDP 3% (15% in 1992).

The Cabinet was as follows in March. 1998:

President and Prime Minister: Gen. Suharto (b. 1921; elected in 1968, 1973, 1978, 1983, 1988, 1993 and 1998). *Vice-President:* B. J. Habibie (elected 1998).

Co ordinating Ministers. (Defence and Security) Gen. Feisal Tanjung; (*Economy, Finance, Industry and Supervision of Development*) Ginanjar Kartasasmita; (*Welfare*) Haryono Suyono; (*Production and Distribution*) Ir Hartarto.

Internal Affairs: R. Hartono. *Foreign Affairs:* Ali Alatas. *Defence and Security:* Gen. Wiranto. *Justice:* Dr H. Muladi. *Information:* Alwi Dahlan. *Finance:* Fuad Bawazir. *Trade and Industry:* Muhammad Hasan. *Agriculture:* Syarifuddin Baharsyah. *Mines and Energy:* Kuntoro Mangkusubroto. *Public Works:* Rachmadi Bambang Sumadio. *Co-operatives and Small Business:* Subiakto Cakrawerdaya. *Manpower:* Theo Sambuaga. *Transmigration:* Abdullah Hendropriyono. *Tourism, Arts and Culture:* Abdul Latief. *Communications:* Giri Suseno Hadihardjono. *Education and Culture:* Wiranto Arismunandar. *Health:* Farid Antara Muluk. *Religious Affairs:* Qureisy Syihab. *Social Affairs:* Siti Hardiyanti Rukmana. *Forestry:* Sumohadi. *Secretary of State:* Saadillah Mursyid.

National anthem: 'Indonesia, tanah jang mulia' ('Indonesia, our native land'); words and tune by W. R. Supratman.

Local government: There are 27 provinces, 3 of which are special territories (the capital city of Jakarta, Yogyakarta and Aceh), each administered by a Governor appointed by the President; they are divided into 246 districts (*kabupatens*), each under a district head (*bupati*), and 55 municipalities (*kotamadya*), each under a mayor (*wali kota*). The districts are divided into 3,592 sub-districts (*kecamtans*), each headed by a *camat*. There were 66,594 villages in 1988.

DEFENCE. There is selective conscription for 2 years.

Army. The Army is organized in a strategic reserve, with 2 infantry divisional headquarters, 3 infantry and 3 airborne brigades, 2 field artillery and 1 air defence artillery regiment and 2 engineer battalions; and 10 military area commands, with 62 infantry, 8 cavalry, 11 field artillery, 10 air defence and 8 engineer battalions, and 1 composite aviation and 1 helicopter squadron. Equipment includes 275 AMX-13, 30 PT-76 and 26 Scorpion light tanks. The Army has about 100 aircraft, including 1 Islander, 4 Aviocars and 12 other fixed-wing types, 30 Bell 205, 12 BO 105, 9 Hughes 300, 24 locally-built Bell 412 helicopters. There is a paramilitary police some 177,000 strong, and 2 part-time local auxiliary forces: KAMRA (People's Security) and WANRA (People's Resistance). Army personnel in 1997 numbered 220,000.

Navy. The Navy in 1996 numbered about 43,000, including 12,000 in the Commando Corps, and 1,000 in the Naval Air Arm. Combatant strength includes 2 German-built diesel submarines (1 in long refit) and 13 frigates of which 6 are former Dutch Van Speijk class, and 3 former British Ashanti class each equipped with 1 helicopter. Delivery of 16 ex-East German Parchim class anti-submarine corvettes completed in 1996. There are also 4 fast missile craft, 2 torpedo-armed craft and 35 miscellaneous patrol craft as well as 2 Dutch-built tripartite coastal minehunters and 11 other minesweepers. Amphibious lift is provided by 14 tank landing ships (4 with helicopter facilities), 14 smaller ex-East German units and 50 craft. The auxiliary force includes 2 replenishment tankers, 2 transport tankers, 6 surveying vessels, 1 command and submarine support ship, 1 repair ship, 3 training ships and some dozens of minor auxiliaries and service craft.

The Naval Air Arm operates 60 aircraft, including 15 Searchmaster maritime reconnaissance and 8 NC-212 Aviocar transport aircraft, and 10 anti-submarine helicopters as well as miscellaneous communications and utility aircraft.

The Marine Commando Force of 12,000 comprises 2 brigades and is equipped with some 100 light tanks and 48 artillery pieces.

A separate Military Sealift Command operates about 25 inter-island transport ships (which number includes 3 of the tank landing ships in the navy listing) totalling approximately 30,000 tonnes. The Maritime Security Agency operates 10 cutters, the Customs about 70 and the armed Marine Police 60 craft.

Air Force. Operational combat units comprise 3 squadrons of British Aerospace Hawk and 1 of A-4E Skyhawk attack aircraft, and single squadrons of F-5E Tiger II and of F-16 fighters. There are 5 transport squadrons, equipped with turboprop C-130 Hercules, Nurtanio/CASA NC-212 Aviocar and CN-235 and F27 Friendship aircraft, as well as 3 specially-equipped Boeing 737 dual-purpose maritime surveillance/transports; and an assortment of other aircraft in transport, helicopter and training units including 15 Hawks, 15 T-34C-1 armed turboprop trainers, and 36 Swiss-built AS 202 Bravo piston-engined primary trainers. Personnel (1996) approximately 21,000.

INTERNATIONAL RELATIONS

Membership. Indonesia is a member of the UN, OPEC and ASEAN.

ECONOMY

Policy. The Government's plan for growth has been hit by financial instability in the Asian money markets and international concern about corruption, a shaky banking system and the slow pace of deregulation and privatization. But this is not to deny the economic successes of the Suharto administration. Since 1970 the economy has grown, on average, by more than 6% a year.

Performance. Economic growth was 8·1% in 1995 (7·5% in 1994).

Budget. By law the budget must balance. The fiscal year starts 1 April. Revenue and expenditure for 1995–96 were 78,000,000m. rupiahs. Current revenue (in 1,000m. rupiahs), 1993–94, 52,280; current expenditure, 38,799; capital revenue, 10,372; capital expenditure, 25,661.

Currency. The monetary unit is the *rupiah* (IDR) notionally of 100 *sen*. There are coins of 5, 10, 25, 50, 100 and 500, and notes of 100, 500, 1,000, 5,000, 10,000, 20,000 and 50,000 rupiahs. In July 1995, 19,109,000m. rupiahs were in circulation. Inflation was 8·64% in 1995 (9·24% in 1994). Foreign exchange reserves were US$13,399m. at April 1995.

Banking and Finance. The Bank Indonesia, successor to De Javasche Bank established by the Dutch in 1828, was made the central bank of Indonesia on 1 July 1953. Its *Governor* is Sudradjat Djiwandono. It had an original capital of Rp. 25m.; a reserve fund of Rp. 18m. and a special reserve of Rp. 84m. Total assets and liabilities as at Dec. 1992, Rp. 123,689,000m. Total savings deposits at July 1996 were 41,858,000m. rupiahs.

There are 117 commercial banks, 28 development banks and other financial institutions, 8 development finance companies and 9 joint venture merchant banks. Commercial banking is dominated by 7 state-owned banks: Bank Rakyat Indonesia provides services to smallholder agriculture and rural development; Bank Bumi Daya, estate agriculture and forestry; Bank Negara Indonesia 1946, industry; Bank Dagang Negara, mining; and Bank Expor-Impor Indonesia, export commodity sector. All state banks are authorized to deal in foreign exchange.

There are 70 private commercial banks owned and operated by Indonesians. The 11 foreign banks specialize in foreign exchange transactions and direct lending operations to foreign joint ventures. The government owns 1 Savings Bank, Bank Tabungan Negara, and 1,000 Post Office Savings Banks. There are also over 3,500 rural and village savings bank and credit co-operatives. At least 16 banks closed in the wake of the 1997 financial crisis.

There is a stock exchange in Jakarta.

Weights and Measures. The metric system is in use.

The following are the old weights and measures: *Pikol* = 136·16 lb. avoirdupois; *Katti* = 1·36 lb. avoirdupois; *Bau* = 1·7536 acres; *Square Pal* = 227 hectares = 561·16 acres; *Jengkal* = 4 yd; *Pal* (Java) = 1,506 metres; *Pal* (Sumatra) = 1,852 metres.

ENERGY AND NATURAL RESOURCES

Electricity. There were 7 hydro-electric plants in 1989; 19,044 out of 66,594 villages are supplied with electricity in Java and Sumatra. Installed capacity was 9m. MW in 1993. Electricity produced (1991) 37,700m. kWh.

Oil and Gas. The importance of oil in the economy is declining. The 1995 output of crude oil was 1,476,000 bbls. Natural gas production, 1994, was 2,949,635m. cu. ft.

Water. In 1988–89, 23,677 ha of new irrigation networks were constructed and 377,461 ha rehabilitated and maintained.

Minerals. The high cost of extraction means that little of the large mineral resources outside Java is exploited; however, there is copper mining in Irian Jaya, nickel mining and processing on Sulawesi, aluminium smelting in northern Sumatra. Open-cast coal mining has been conducted since the 1890s, but since the 1970s coal production has been developed as an alternative to oil. Reserves are estimated at 28,000m. tonnes. Coal production (1994, in tonnes) 28·6m. tonnes; bauxite, 1,342,400 tonnes; iron ore, 334·9; copper, 1,065·5; silver, 105,961 kg; gold, 44,843 kg; nickel ore, 2,302; tin, 30·6.

Agriculture. Agriculture contributed 19·5% of GDP in 1990. Production (1994, in 1,000 tonnes): Rice, 46,641; cassava, 15,729; maize, 6,869; sweet potatoes, 1,845; sugar-cane (1993), 32,400; coconuts (1993), 14m.; copra (1993), 1,100; palm oil, 1,930; palm kernels, 472; soybeans, 1,565; rubber (1993), 1,370; coffee, 43·7; groundnuts, 632; vegetables (1993), 4,912; fruits (1993), 7,341; tea, 97·4; tobacco (1993), 85. In 1991, 6,750 tonnes of nutmeg were produced, about 75% of world production.

Livestock (1993): Cattle, 11·0m.; buffaloes, 3·5m.; horses, 705,000; sheep, 6·3m.; goats, 11·8m.; pigs, 8·2m.; poultry, 620m.

Forestry. The forest area was (1993) 144m. ha, 75% of the land area. Of this, 66m. ha is scheduled for selective logging, 48m. ha for preservation for national parks and watersheds and 30m. ha for removal for agriculture, industry and settlement. Production (1991–92): Sawn timber, 3m. cu. metres; plywood, 9·1m. cu. metres.

Fisheries. In 1991 the catch of sea fish was 2,537,612 tonnes; inland fish was 811,989 tonnes. In 1991 there were 130,712 motorized and 373,086 other fishing vessels.

INDUSTRY. Manufacturing contributed 14·9% of GDP in 1990. There are shipyards at Jakarta Raya, Surabaya, Semarang and Amboina. There were (1985) more than 2,000 textile factories (total production in 1987–88, 2,925·6m. metres), large paper factories (817,200 tonnes, 1986–87), match factories, automobile and bicycle assembly works, large construction works, tyre factories, glass factories, a caustic soda and other chemical factories. Production (1987–88): Cement, 22,419,000 tonnes; fertilizers, 5,811,000 tonnes; 160,372 motor vehicles and 249,573 motorcycles; 2·36m. boxes of matches; glasses and bottles, 126,060 tonnes; steel ingots, 1,337,000 tonnes; 640 TV sets and 159,020 refrigerators.

Labour. Reforms announced in Nov. 1994 included an annual review of regional minimum wages, enhanced enforcement of salary, safety and health regulations, and an improved dispute resolution process. National daily average wage, 1996, 4,073 rupiahs.

Trade Unions. Workers have a constitutional right to organize. Unions are expected to affiliate to the Indonesian Welfare Labour Union (SBSI) which enjoys government approval, but in Nov. 1990 an independent union, Setia Kawan (Solidarity) was set up. About 40% of the labour force belong to unions. In 1993 (and 1992) there were 169 (197) strikes involving 97,807 (98,764) workers and resulting in the loss of 857,845 (1,044,519) working hours. Strikes are forbidden by law.

FOREIGN ECONOMIC RELATIONS. Since 1992 foreigners have been permitted to hold 100% of the equity of new companies in Indonesia with more than US$50m. part capital, or situated in remote provinces. Foreign investment in 1994 totalled US$23,724·3m. (including from Hong Kong, US$6,041·7m.; UK, US$2,957·1m.; Taiwan, US$2,487·5m.). Foreign debt was US$85,000m. in Dec. 1992.

Pressure on Indonesia's currency and stock market led to an appeal to the IMF and World Bank for long-term support funds in Oct. 1997. A bail-out package worth $38,000m. was eventually agreed on condition that Indonesia tightened financial controls and instituted reforms, including the establishment of an independent privatization board, liberalizing foreign investment, cutting import tariffs and phasing out export levies.

Commerce. In June 1994 import duties were cut on 739 commodities, surcharges on 108 imports were removed and non-tariff barriers on 27 items abolished. Imports and exports (including oil and gas) in US$1m.:

	1991	1992	1993	1994
Imports f.o.b.	25,869	27,280	28,328	31,984
Exports f.o.b.	29,142	33,967	36,823	40,053

Main export items: Gas and oil, forestry products, manufactured goods, rubber, coffee, fishery products, coal, copper, tin, pepper, palm products and tea. In 1993 main trade partners were Japan (21·3% of imports, 30·4% of exports), USA (11·7%, 13%), Singapore (6·5%, 9·9%) and South Korea (5·6%, 6·6%).

Tourism. In 1995, 4·32m. tourists visited, bringing a total revenue of US$5,900m.

COMMUNICATIONS

Roads. In 1991 there were 137,060 km of asphalted, of which 103,622 km were in good condition. Motor vehicles, 1994: Passenger cars, 1,890,340; buses, 651,608; lorries, 1,251,986; motorcycles, 8,134,903.

Railways. In 1992 the national railways totalled 6,458 km of 1,067 mm gauge, comprising 4,967 km on Java (of which 125 km electrified) and 1,491 km on Sumatra. In 1992 they carried 66m. passengers and 13·4m. tonnes of freight.

Civil Aviation. Garuda Indonesia is the state-owned national flag carrier, in 1995 operating 1 A300B4-200, 10 A300B4-600Rs, 8 B-737-300s, 7 B-737-400s, 6 B-747-200Bs, 3 B-747-400s 6 DC-10-30s, 6 DC-9-30s, 12 F-28-4000s and 6 other aircraft. Merpati Nusantara Airways is their domestic subsidiary. There are international airports at Jakarta (Sukarno-Hatta), Denpasar (on Bali), Medan (Sumatra), Pekanbaru (Sumatra), Ujung Pandang (Sulawesi), Solo (Java), Manado, Ambon (Maluku), Biak (Irian Jaya) and Batu Ampar (Batam). Air traffic, 1994: Domestic passenger arrivals, 10,824,204; departures, 10,851,352. International passenger arrivals, 4,090,771; departures, 4,211,233. Services are also provided by Aeroflot Russian Airlines, Air China, Air Lanka, Balkan Bulgarian, British Airways, Cathay Pacific, China Airlines, China Southern Airlines, CSA, Emirates, Eva Airways, JAL, KLM, Korean Air, Lufthansa, Malaysia Airlines, Myanma Airways, Philippine Airlines, Qantas, Royal Brunei Airlines, Royal Jordanian, Saudia, Silk Air, Singapore Airlines, Thai Airways and UTA.

Shipping. There are 16 ports for ocean-going ships, the largest of which is Tanjung Priok, which serves the Jakarta area and has a container terminal. The national shipping company Pelajaran Nasional Indonesia (PELNI) maintains inter-island communications. The Jakarta Lloyd maintains regular services between Jakarta, Amsterdam, Hamburg and London. In 1995, the merchant marine comprised 535 ocean-going ships totalling 4·13m. DWT. 95 vessels (36·22% of total tonnage) were registered under foreign flags. Total tonnage registered, 2·69m. GRT, including oil tanker, 0·65m. GRT, and container ships, 154,518 GRT. In 1992, 216,924,300 tonnes of freight were loaded and 150,117,400 tonnes discharged.

Telecommunications. In 1996, telephone supply was 1·7 per 100 population. There were 0·2m. mobile phones.

Radio Republik Indonesia, under the Department of Information, operates 49 stations. In 1988–89 there were 8,948,195 TV receivers, and 54,318 public TV sets had been placed in villages within reach of the state-owned Televisi Republik Indonesia telecast

Cinemas. There were 2,173 cinemas in 1990.

Press. In 1988–89 there were 252 newspaper publishers with an estimated circulation of 10,783,009, of which 3,716,056 were dailies. There were 270 publishers of weekly papers and magazines with a circulation (1988–89) of 3,444,802 and 1,721,130 respectively. 1,396 book titles were published in 1989.

SOCIAL INSTITUTIONS

Justice. There are courts of first instance, high courts of appeal in every provincial capital and a Supreme Court of Justice for the whole of Indonesia in Jakarta.

In civil law the population is divided into three main groups: Indonesians, Europeans and foreign Orientals, to whom different law systems are applicable. When, however, people from different groups are involved, a system of so-called 'inter-gentile' law is applied.

The present criminal law, which has been in force since 1918, is codified and is based on European penal law This law is equally applicable to all groups of the population.

Religion. Religious liberty is granted to all denominations. In 1992 there were 160·62m. Moslems, 11·94m. Protestants and 5·78m. Roman Catholics. There were also 1·81m. Buddhists, probably for the greater part Chinese, and 3·59m. Hindus, of whom 2·5m. were on Bali.

Education. The adult literacy rate was 83·2% in 1997. In 1991–92 there were 26,325,701 pupils in primary schools, 5,510,287 students in junior high schools and, in 1990–91, 3,910,115 students in senior high schools, vocational schools, higher training and sports teachers' training colleges. Number of students in higher education (1991–92) 1,773,459. In 1994–95 in the state sector there were 31 universities and 1 open university, and 13 institutes of higher education, including 10 teacher training colleges. In the private sector there were 66 universities and the following specialized universities: Adventist, 1; Christian, 7; Islamic, 10; Methodist, 1; Roman Catholic, 5; Veterans', 1. There were 19 institutes of higher education in the private sector, including 12 teacher training colleges. In 1994–95 there were 694,152 university students and 44,014 academic staff.

Health. In 1990 there were 25,752 doctors, 98,842 nurses and in 1991, 5,976 public health centres, 12,944 sub-public health centres and 3,521 mobile units.

DIPLOMATIC REPRESENTATIVES

Of Indonesia in Great Britain (38 Grosvenor Sq., London W1X 9AD)
Ambassador: Rahardjo Jamtomo.

Of Great Britain in Indonesia (Jalan M.H. Thamrin 75, Jakarta 10310)
Ambassador: D. R. C. Christopher CMG.

Of Indonesia in the USA (2020 Massachusetts Ave., NW, Washington, D.C., 20036)
Ambassador: Arifin Mohamad Siregar.

Of the USA in Indonesia (Medan Merdeka Selatan 5, Jakarta)
Ambassador: J. Stapleton Roy.

Of Indonesia to the United Nations
Ambassador: Makarim Wibosono.

Of Indonesia to the European Union
Ambassador: Poedji Koentarso.

Further Reading

Central Bureau of Statistics. *Statistical Yearbook of Indonesia.—Monthly Statistical Bulletin: Economic Indicator.*

Cribb, R., *Historical Dictionary of Indonesia.* Metuchen (NJ), 1993.—and Brown, C., *Modern Indonesia: a History since 1945.* Harlow, 1995

International Commission of Jurists, *Indonesia and the Rule of Law.* London, 1987

Kim, T. J. *et al.*, *Spatial Development in Indonesia.* Aldershot, 1992

Krausse, G. H. and Krausse, S. C. E., *Indonesia* [Bibliography]. Oxford and Santa Barbara (CA), 1994

Palmier, L., *Understanding Indonesia.* London, 1986

Ricklefs, M. C., *A History of Modern Indonesia since 1300.* 2nd ed. London, 1993

Schwartz, A., *A Nation in Waiting: Indonesia in the 1990s.* London, 1994

Thoolen, H., *Indonesia and the Rule of Law.* London, 1987

Vatikiotis, M.R.J., *Indonesian Politics under Suharto: Order, Development and Pressure for Change.* 2nd ed. London, 1994

See also **East Timor**, *above.*

National statistical office: Central Bureau of Statistics, POB1003, Jakarta, 10010.
Website: http://www.bps.go.id/

IRAN

Jomhuri-e-Eslami-e-Iran

(Islamic Republic of Iran)

Capital: Tehran
Population: 60·1m.
GDP per head: (PPP$) 5,766
HDI/world rank: 0·780/70

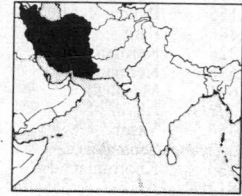

KEY HISTORICAL EVENTS. Persia was ruled by the Shahs as an absolute monarchy from the 16th century until 30 Dec. 1906, when the first constitution was granted and a national assembly established. After a coup in 1921, Reza Khan began his rise to power which culminated in his deposing the last Shah of the Qajar Dynasty on 31 Oct. 1925. He was declared Shah as Reza Shah Pahlavi on 12 Dec. 1925 and the country's name was changed to Iran on 21 March 1935. When in the Second World War Iran supported Germany, the Allies occupied the country and forced Reza Shah to abdicate on 16 Sept. 1941 in favour of his son, Muhammad Reza Pahlavi.

Iran's oil industry was nationalized in March 1951. This was an important part of the policy of the National Front Party, whose leader, Dr Muhammad Mussadeq, became prime minister in April 1951. He was opposed by the Shah, but although ousted in 1952, quickly regained power. The Shah fled the country temporarily until Aug. 1953 when the monarchists staged a coup which led to Mussadeq finally being deposed.

The Shah's policy, which included the redistribution of land to small farmers and the enfranchisement of women, was opposed by the Shia religious scholars who considered it to be contrary to Islamic teaching. This group was considered responsible for the assassination of the prime minister, Hassan Ali Mansur, in 1965.

Despite economic growth, the country suffered considerable unrest because of opposition to the Shah's harsh repressive measures and his extensive use of the Savak, the secret police. The opposition was widespread, and that led by Ayatollah Ruhollah Khomeini, the Shia Moslem spiritual leader who had been exiled in 1965, was particularly successful. Following intense civil unrest in Tehran, the Shah left Iran with his family on 17 Jan. 1979 (and died in Egypt on 27 July 1980). The Ayatollah Khomeini returned from exile on 1 Feb. 1979 and appointed a provisional government on 5 Feb. The Shah's government resigned and parliament dissolved itself on 11 Feb. Following a referendum in March, an Islamic Republic was proclaimed on 1 April 1979. The constitution of the Islamic Republic, approved by a national referendum in Dec. 1979, gave supreme authority to a religious leader (*wali faqih*), a position to be held by Ayatollah Khomeini for the rest of his life. In Sept. 1980 war began with Iraq with destruction of some Iranian towns and damage to the oil installations at Abadan. A UN-arranged ceasefire took place on 20 Aug. 1988, and UN-sponsored peace talks continued in 1989. On 15 Aug. 1990 the Iraqi President Saddam Hussein offered peace terms and began the withdrawal of troops from Iranian soil.

TERRITORY AND POPULATION. Iran is bounded in the north by Armenia, Azerbaijan, the Caspian Sea and Turkmenistan, east by Afghanistan and Pakistan, south by the Gulf of Oman and the Persian Gulf, and west by Iraq and Turkey. It has an area of 1,648,000 sq. km (634,293 sq. miles), but a vast portion is desert. Population (1996 census): 60·1m. (1994, 58% urban). Population density: 36 per sq. km. By 1992 there were 2m. refugees from Afghanistan in Iran; repatriation began in 1993.

Vital statistics: Births (1994, per 1,000), 36·4; deaths, 6·4; life expectancy, 68·2 years. Abortion is illegal, but a family planning scheme was inaugurated in 1988.

The areas, populations and capitals of the 26 provinces *(ostan)* were:

767

Province	Area (sq. km)	Census 1991	Census 1996	Capital
Ardabil	18,451	1,141,625	1,168,011	Ardabil
Azarbayejan, East	44,767	3,278,718	3,325,540	Tabriz
Azarbayejan, West	37,599	2,284,208	2,496,320	Orumiyeh
Bushehr	25,360	694,252	743,675	Bushehr
Chahar Mahal and Bakhtyari	14,820	747,297	761,168	Shahr-e-Kord
Esfahan	105,805	3,682,444	3,923,255	Esfahan
Fars	120,006	3,543,828	3,817,036	Shiraz
Gilan	14,820	2,204,047	2,241,896	Rasht
Hamadan	19,445	1,651,320	1,677,957	Hamadan
Hormozgan	65,379	924,433	1,062,155	Bandar-e-Abbas
Ilam	19,086	440,693	487,886	Ilam
Kerman	185,675	1,862,542	2,004,328	Kerman
Kermanshah	23,622	1,622,159	1,778,596	Kermanshah
Khorasan	315,687	6,013,200	6,047,661	Mashhad
Khuzestan	66,532	3,175,852	3,746,772	Ahvaz
Kohgiluyeh and Boyer Ahmad	13,699	496,739	544,356	Yasuj
Kordestan	27,858	1,233,480	1,346,383	Sanandaj
Lorestan	28,560	1,501,778	1,584,434	Khorramabad
Markazi	29,530	1,182,611	1,228,812	Arak
Mazandaran	46,645	3,793,149	4,028,296	Sari
Semnan	91,544	458,125	501,447	Semnan
Sistan and Baluchestan	181,471	1,455,102	1,722,579	Zahedan
Tehran	42,689	9,982,309	11,176,239	Tehran
Yazd	69,605	691,119	750,769	Yazd
Zanjan	11,152	1,776,133	1,936,873	Zanjan
Qom	10,762	616,963	853,044	Qom

At the 1996 census the populations of the principal cities were:

	Population		Population
Tehran	6,758,845	Arak	380,755
Mashhad	1,887,405	Ardabil	340,386
Esfahan	1,266,072	Yazd	326,776
Tabriz	1,191,043	Qazvin	291,117
Shiraz	1,053,025	Zanjan	286,295
Karaj	940,968	Sanandaj	277,808
Ahvaz	804,980	Bandar-e-Abbas	273,578
Qom	777,677	Khorramabad	272,815
Kermanshah	692,986	Eslamshahr	265,450
Orumiyeh	435,200	Borujerd	217,804
Zahedan	419,518	Abadan	206,073
Rasht	417,748	Dezul	202,639
Hamadan	401,281	Khorramshahr	105,636
Kerman	384,991		

The national language is Farsi or Persian, spoken by 45% of the population in 1986. 28% spoke related languages, including Kurdish (9%) and Luri in the west, Gilaki and Mazandarami in the north, and Baluchi in the south-east; 22% speak Turkic languages, primarily in the north-west.

CLIMATE. Mainly a desert climate, but with more temperate conditions on the shores of the Caspian Sea. Seasonal range of temperature is considerable, as is rain (ranging from 2" in the south-east to 78" in the Caspian region). Winter is normally the rainy season for the whole country. *Abadan*. Jan. 54°F (12·2°C), July 97°F (36·1°C). Annual rainfall 8" (204 mm). *Tehran*. Jan. 36°F (2·2°C), July 85°F (29·4°C). Annual rainfall 10" (246 mm).

CONSTITUTION AND GOVERNMENT. The Constitution of the Islamic Republic was approved by a national referendum in Dec. 1979. It gives supreme authority to the *Spiritual Leader* (*wali faqih*), which position was held by Ayatollah Khomeini until his death on 3 June 1989. Ayatollah Seyed Ali Khamenei was elected to succeed him on 4 June 1989. Following the death of the previous incumbent, Ayatollah Ali Khamenei was proclaimed the *Source of Knowledge* (*Marja e Taghlid*) at the head of all Shi'ite Moslems in Dec. 1994.

The 83-member *Assembly of Experts* was established in 1982. It is popularly elected every 8 years. Its mandate is to interpret the constitution and select the Spiritual Leader. Candidates for election are examined by the *Council of Guardians.* At the last election of Oct. 1990 turn-out was 46%.

The *Islamic Consultative Assembly* has 270 members, elected for a 4-year term in single-seat constituencies. All candidates have to be approved by the *Council of Guardians.* At elections on 8 March and 19 April 1996 the Jameh-ye Ruhaniyat Mobarez (Combatant Clergy Association) won 110 seats, the Servants of Iran's Construction won 80 and others 58, with 22 vacant.

The *President* of the Republic is popularly elected for not more than 2 4-year terms and is head of the executive; he appoints Ministers subject to approval by the *Islamic Consultative Assembly (Majlis).* Presidential elections held on 23 May 1997 produced a landslide vote for Mohammad Khatami, who favours greater freedom and adherence to the rule of law. There were 4 candidates. Turn-out was 14m. Mohammad Khatami was elected with 69% of votes cast.

The Cabinet was composed as follows in March 1998:
President: Seyyed Mohammad Khatami.
Vice-President: Hasan Ebrahim Habibi.
Atomic Energy: Gholamreza Aghazedeh. *Foreign Affairs:* Kamal Kharrazi. *Oil:* Bijan Namdar Zanganeh. *Interior:* Abdollah Nouri. *Economic Affairs and Finance:* Hossein Namazi. *Agriculture:* Issa Kalantari. *Commerce:* Mohammad Shariatmadar. *Energy:* Habibollah Bitaraf. *Roads and Transport:* Mahmoud Hojjati. *Construction Jihad:* Mohammad Saidi Kya. *Industry:* Gholamreza Shafei. *Housing and Urban Development:* Ali Abdolalizadeh. *Labour:* Hossein Kamali. *Posts, Telephones and Telegraphs:* Mohammad Reza Aref. *Health and Medical Treatment:* Mohammad Farhadi. *Education:* Hossein Mozaffar. *Higher Education:* Mostafa Moin. *Justice:* Mohammad Esmael Shoushtari. *Defence:* Ali Shamkhani. *Intelligence and Security:* Qorbanali Dorri Najafabadi. *Islamic Culture and Guidance:* Ataollah Mohajerani. *Mines and Metals:* Eshaq Jahangiri. *Co-operatives:* Morteza Haji. *Executive Affairs:* Mohammad Hashemi. *Environmental Protection:* Mrs Masoomeh Ebtekar.

Legislative power is held by the 270-member Islamic Consultative Assembly, directly elected on a non-party basis for a 4-year term by all citizens aged 15 or over. Voting is secret but ballot papers are not printed; electors must write the name of their preferred candidate themselves. 5 seats are reserved for religious minorities. All legislation is subject to approval by a 12-member *Council of Guardians* who ensure it is in accordance with the Islamic code and with the Constitution. Six members are appointed by the Spiritual Leader and 6 by the judiciary.

Elections for the Majlis were held on 8 March 1996 with a run-off on 19 April 1996. The Council of Guardians annulled 13 results which were subsequently filled by by-elections. The electorate was 32m.; 3,231 candidates stood

National anthem: 'Sar zad az ofogh mehr-e khavaran' ('Rose from the horizon the affectionate sun of the East'); words by a group of poets; tune by Dr Riahi.

Local Government. The country is divided into 26 provinces *(ostan).* These are subdivided into 195 counties, each under a governor, and thence into 500 districts, each under a district head. The districts are subdivided into *dehistan* (groups of villages), each under a *dehdar,* each village having its elected headman.

DEFENCE. Two years' military service is compulsory.

Army. The Army is organized in 4 armoured, 2 special force and 7 infantry divisions, 1 airborne brigade, some independent armoured, infantry and commando brigades, and 5 artillery groups. Equipment includes some 110 T-54/-55, 220 Chinese T-59, 150 T-62, 200 T-72, 250 Chieftain Mk 3/5, 150 M-47/-48, 160 M-60A1 and 200 Chinese T-69 main battle tanks and 664 multiple rocket launchers. The Army is estimated to have an inventory of 50 fixed-wing aircraft and over 200 helicopters but the effective strength is not known. There are reports of Iran developing non-conventional long-range missiles.

Strength (1997): 350,000 (about 250,000 conscripts). There is also a paramilitary gendarmerie of 120,000, including border guards.

Revolutionary Guard. The ground forces are loosely organized in battalions of no fixed size, and are grouped into 13 infantry and 2 armoured divisions plus other independent units. It controls the *Basij*, a volunteer 'popular mobilization army' of about 0·2m., which may reach 1m. strong in wartime.

Strength (1996): 100,000 ground forces and 20,000 naval.

Navy. The Navy received the first 2 Soviet-built 'Kilo' class submarines before the end of 1993, but these have suffered battery problems and the third was not delivered until the end of 1996. The remainder of the fleet comprises 2 ex-US 'Sumner' class destroyers, 3 UK-built frigates, 2 very old ex-US patrol frigates, and 10 French-built and 10 new Chinese-built missile craft. Other units include 35 inshore patrol craft (some of them hovercraft), 3 small minesweepers, 7 tank landing ships and 3 tank landing craft. Auxiliaries include 3 replenishment tankers, 1 repair ship, 4 water tankers and 2 accommodation ships.

Naval Aviation comprises 1 anti-submarine helicopter squadron with 9 Sea King and AB-212 helicopters, a mine counter-measures squadron with 2 RH-53D helicopters, a transport squadron with about a dozen various aircraft and about 20 AB-205 and AB-206 transport and liaison helicopters. The main naval bases are at Bandar-e-Abbas, Bushehr and Chah Bahar.

Strength (1996): 18,000, including naval air and 3 battalions of Marines.

Air Force. Combat aircraft include some Chinese-built F-6 fighter-bombers and F-7 interceptors, surviving US fighters that include F-14 Tomcat, F-5E Tiger II and F-4D/E Phantom II fighter-bombers, as well as a few RF-4E reconnaissance-fighters, and a number of MiG-29 interceptors and Su-24 strike aircraft purchased from Russia. Transport aircraft include F27s, C-130 Hercules, PC-6 Turbo-Porters, Boeing 707s and 747s, some equipped as flight refuelling tankers. The status of the large fleet of CH-47C Chinook, Bell Model 214 and other helicopters is not known; but two P-3F Orion maritime patrol aircraft remain operational. Training aircraft include Pakistani-built Mushshak and Bonanza basic trainers and French-built Socata light aircraft, 30 PC-7 Turbo-Trainers and 15 Tucanos for advanced training.

Strength (1996): 30,000 personnel (about 12,000 air defence).

INTERNATIONAL RELATIONS

Membership. Iran is a member of the UN, OPEC, ECO and the Colombo Plan.

ECONOMY

Policy. A 5-year plan, the Second Five-Year Development Plan (SFYDP), is running from March 1995. At the beginning of 1991 about 70% of industry was state-owned, much of it nationalized after the 1979 revolution, but the government is now committed to partial privatization. Strategic heavy industry will remain in the public sector.

Budget. Total revenue and expenditure for 1998–99 (in 1,000m. rials) is put at 231,200, an increase of 20% over the 1997–98 budget. The annual inflation rate is 50% plus. The accuracy of budget figures is questionable given the policy of dividing the budget into 2 parts: the first covering ministerial expenditure, the second dealing with state banks and industries, which receive allocations by the expediency of printing money.

Currency. The unit of currency is the *rial* (IRR) of which 10 = 1 *toman*. There are notes of 100, 200, 500, 1,000, 2,000, 5,000 and 10,000 rials, and coins of 1, 2, 5, 10, 20, 50, 100 and 250 rials. The value of the rial has fallen from IRR 70 to the US$ in 1979 to a low of IRR 4,630 in 1997. Currency in circulation (1996, in 1,000m. rials): 14,228·9.

Banking and Finance. The Central Bank is the note-issuing authority and government bank. Its *Governor* is Moshen Nurbakhach. All other banks and insurance companies were nationalized in 1979, and re-organized into new state banking corporations, of which there were 5 in 1994. Private banks were permitted to operate

from 1994; their initial capital must be at least 5,000m. rials. The 'Law for Usury-Free Banking' dates from 1983. In 1985 interest on accounts was abolished.
A stock exchange re-opened in Tehran in 1992.

Weights and Measures. The metric system is in force.

Calendar. The Iranian year is a solar year running from 21 March to 20 March. The current solar year is 1376 (21 March 1997 to 20 March 1998). The Islamic *hegira* (622 AD, when Mohammed left Mecca for Medina) year 1418 corresponds to 9 May 1997–29 April 1998, and is the current lunar year.

ENERGY AND NATURAL RESOURCES

Electricity. Total installed capacity (1994): 25,117,000 kW. Production (1996): 85,825m. kWh (62,364m. steam, 15,475m. gas and combined, 7,376m. hydroelectric, 610m. diesel).

Oil. Iran has 8·9% of proven global oil reserves. Oil is its chief source of revenue. The main oilfields are in the Zagros Mountains where oil was first discovered in 1908. Oil companies were nationalized in 1979 and operations of crude oil and natural gas exploitation are now run by the National Iranian Oil Company. Refining operations of crude oil are run by the National Company for Refining and Distribution of Oil Products.

Crude oil production (1995): 3,625,000 bbls a day. Refining capacity (1990): 766·9 bbls a day. Petroleum production (1996): 3,595,000 bbls a day.

Gas. Iran has nearly one fifth of proven global gas reserves. A deal between Gazprom, the Russian gas company, and Total, the French energy group, is to put US$2,000m. into the development of a gas field.

In Dec. 1997 the first national gas pipeline linking Iran with the Caspian Sea via Turkmenistan was opened. The 200-km line links gas fields in western Turkmenistan to industrial markets in northern Iran.

Natural gas production (1994): 95,691m. cu. metres.

Minerals. Output (1994, in tonnes): Iron ore, 5,017,145; coal, 1,293,263; zinc and lead, 148,606; copper, 393,611; manganese, 96,115; chromite, 354,163; salt, 865,927; bauxite, 144,206; decorative stone, 5,386,656.

Agriculture. In 1994 cultivable land totalled 13,958,500 ha: 12,336,500 ha were under annual crops (of which 5,697,000 ha were irrigated). In 1994 there were 1,524,700 ha and 97,200 ha of productive and non-productive orchards and nurseries respectively. Crop production (1993, in tonnes): Wheat, 10,869,560; barley, 3,044,695; rice (paddy), 2,258,969; sugar beet, 5,294,729; tobacco, 9,887. Wool (1991): 32,000 tonnes greasy; 17,600 tonnes scoured.

Livestock (1991): 40,707,000 sheep, 22,244,000 goats, 6,126,000 cattle, 155,172 horses, 86,000 camels, 289,000 buffaloes, 1,422,672 donkeys.

Forestry. Approximately 11% of Iran is forested, much of it in the Caspian region.

Fisheries. Total catch (1994): 350,000 tonnes.

INDUSTRY. Production of selected commodities in large-scale manufacturing establishments with 50 workers and more (1994): Sugar, 829,748 tonnes; stockings, 16·3m. pairs; machine-made bricks, 3,054m.; cement, 15,726,936 tonnes. In 1994 there were 2,263 large-scale manufacturing establishments and the number of workers was 651,362. The textile industry uses local cotton and silk; carpet manufacture is an important industry. The country's steel industry is the largest in the Middle East.

Labour. The economically active population numbered 16m. in 1996-97, of which 14·6m. were employed.

FOREIGN ECONOMIC RELATIONS. There had been a limit on foreign investment, but legislation of 1995 permits foreign nationals to hold more than 50% of the equity of joint ventures with the consent of the Foreign Investment Board. Foreign debt was US$13,250m. in 1993.

Commerce. Iran's main trading partners are Germany, Japan and Italy for imports; and Japan, the UK and USA for exports. Exports (1996, in US$m.) totalled 22,496; imports 14,973. Petroleum and crude oil exports (1996): 2,620,000 bbls a day.

Imports and exports for calendar years (in US$m., excluding oil and gas):

	1991/92	1992/93	1993/94
Imports	29,677	29,870	20,037
Exports	2,987	3,746	4,455

Tourism. The total number of visitors in 1994 was 470,647.

COMMUNICATIONS

Roads. In 1995 the total length of roads was 156,507 km, of which 463 km were free-ways, 22,314 km main roads, 42,177 km by-roads, 80,320 km rural roads and 11,436 km other roads. In 1991-95 registered motor vehicles numbered 784,274, including 367,900 passenger cars, 8,900 buses, 19,250 minibuses, 135,641 vans and trucks, 41,491 lorries, 15,180 articulated lorries. There were also 195,912 motorcycles.

Railways. The State Railways totalled 5,612 km of main lines in 1996, of which 149 km were electrified. In 1996 the railways carried 8·9m. passengers and 22·7m. tonnes of freight. An isolated 1,676 mm gauge line (96 km) in the south-east links with Pakistan Railways. A rail link to Turkmenistan was opened in May 1996.

Civil Aviation. There is an international airport at Tehran (Mehrabad). 5·9m. passengers and 46,459 tonnes of freight were carried in 1995 (the state-owned air-line, Iran Air, carried 5·8m. passengers, 30,342 tonnes of freight). In 1995 Iran Air operated 5 A300B2-200s, 2 A300B4-600Rs, 4 B-707-320Cs, 2 B-727s, 5 B-727-200 Advs, 1 B-737-200 Adv, 2 B-737-200C Advs, 1 B-747-100B, 2 B-747-200B Combis, 2 B-747SPs and 6 others. Services are also provided by Aeroflot, Air France, Air Ukraine, Alitalia, Ariana, Armenian Airlines, Austrian Airlines, Azerbaijan Hava Yollary, British Airways, Emirates, Gulf Air, KLM, Kuwait Airways, Lufthansa, Malaysia Airlines, Pakistan Airlines, Swissair, Syrian Airlines and Turkish Airlines.

Shipping. In 1995 the merchant fleet comprised 146 vessels totalling 6·71m. DWT, representing 1·01% of the world's total fleet tonnage. Total tonnage registered: 3·8m. GRT, including oil tankers: 2·14m. GRT, and container ships: 1,593 GRT. In 1996, 3,334 ships with a capacity of 16·8m. tonnes entered commercial ports, loading 5·5m. tonnes of goods (excluding oil products).

Telecommunications. In 1993 the number of telephones was 3·67m. Broadcasting is controlled by the government agency, Islamic Republic of Iran Broadcasting (IRIB). Both television and radio operate under a single organization, the National Iranian Radio and Television Organization (NIRT) established by an Act of Parliament in 1967, which in 1990 employed some 11,620 people. There are 2 national radio stations (Radio One and Radio Two) and 27 regional radio stations, including a Koran service and an external service (Voice of the Islamic Republic of Iran which publishes in 20 languages). There are no commercial radio stations; radio broadcasting is a state monopoly. There were (1997) 138 radio transmitters in operation. There are 4 television networks (colour by SECAM). A 3-year ban on TV satellite receiver dishes was imposed in Jan. 1995.

Cinemas. There were 280 cinemas with 171,723 seats in 1993.

Press. In 1990 25 newspapers were issued nationwide. Approximately 80% of the Iranian press is printed in Farsi; much of the remaining 20% is in English or Arabic.

SOCIAL INSTITUTIONS

Justice. A legal system based on Islamic law (*Sharia*) was introduced by the 1979 constitution. A new criminal code on similar principles was introduced in Nov. 1995. The President of the Supreme Court and the public Prosecutor-General are appointed by the Spiritual Leader. The Supreme Court has 16 branches and 109 offences carry the death penalty. To these were added economic crimes in 1990.

Religion. The official religion is the Shi'a branch of Islam. Adherents numbered 93·8% of the population in 1990; 6% were Sunni Moslems.

Education. In 1991 adult literacy was 80·6% for men and 67·1% for women. Most primary and secondary schools are state schools. Elementary education in state schools and university education is free; small fees are charged for state-run secondary schools. In 1988–89 there were 8,262,441 pupils in primary schools, 2,724,606 in orientation schools and 1,363,130 in high schools; there were 209,887 students in technical and vocational schools, 41,884 in teacher training schools, 29,127 gifted children, and 921,152 in adult education courses.

In 1994–95 there were 30 universities, 30 medical universities, 12 specialized universities (1 agriculture, 1 art, 1 oil engineering, 4 teacher training, 5 technology) and 2 open (distance-learning) universities. There were 289,392 students and 10,745 academic staff.

Health. There were (1988) 77,804 hospital beds in 609 hospitals. Medical personnel included 13,898 physicians and 954 dentists.

DIPLOMATIC REPRESENTATIVES

Of Iran in Great Britain (16 Prince's Gate, London, SW7 1PT)
Chargé d'Affaires: Gholamreza Ansari.

Of Great Britain in Iran (143 Ferdowsi Ave., Tehran 11344)
Chargé d'Affaires: N. W. Browne.

Of Iran to the United Nations
Ambassador: Vacant.

Of Iran to the European Union
Ambassador: Hamid Aboutalebi.

Further Reading

Abrahamian, E., *Khomeinism: Essays on the Islamic Republic.* Univ. of California Press, 1993
Amuzegar, J., *Iran's Economy under the Islamic Republic.* London, 1992
Bina, C. and Zanganeh, H. (eds.), *Modern Capitalism and Islamic Ideology in Iran.* London, 1991
Cambridge History of Iran. 7 vols. CUP, 1968–91
Daneshvar, P., *Revolution in Iran.* London, 1996
Ehtesami, A., *After Khomeini: the Iranian Second Republic.* London, 1994
Foran, J., *Fragile Resistance: Social Transformation in Iran from 1500 to the Revolution.* Boulder (Colo.), 1993
Fuller, G. E., *Centre of the Universe: Geopolitics of Iran.* Boulder (Colo.), 1992
Hunter, S. T., *Iran after Khomeini.* New York, 1992
Hussain, A., *Islamic Iran: Revolution and Counter-Revolution.* London, 1985
Kamrava, M., *Political History of Modern Iran: from Tribalism to Theocracy.* London, 1993
Karshenas, M., *Oil, State and Industry in Iran.* CUP, 1990
Katouzian, H., *The Political Economy of Iran.* London, 1981
Lahsaelzadeh, A., *Contemporary Rural Iran.* London, 1993
Modaddel, M., *Class, Politics and Ideology in the Iranian Revolution.* Columbia Univ. Press, 1992
Navabpour, A. R., *Iran.* [Bibliography] Oxford and Santa Barbara (CA), 1988
Omid, H., *Islam and the Post-Revolutionary State in Iran.* London, 1994
Rahnema, A. and Nomani, F., *The Secular Miracle: Religion, Politics and Economic Activity.* London, 1990.—and Behdad, S. (eds.) *Iran after the Revolution: the crisis of an Islamic State.* London, 1995

National statistical office. Statistical Centre of Iran, Dr Fatemi Avenue, Tehran, Iran, 14144.

IRAQ

Jumhouriya al 'Iraqia

(Republic of Iraq)

Capital: Baghdad
Population: 22·22m.
GDP per head: (PPP$) 3,159
HDI/world rank: 0·531/126

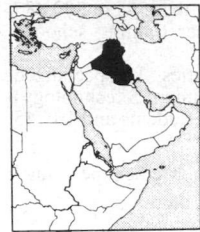

KEY HISTORICAL EVENTS. Iraq, formerly
Mesopotamia, was part of the Ottoman Empire from 1534
until it was captured by British forces in 1916. Under a
League of Nations mandate, administered by Britain, Amir
Faisal Ibn Hussain was crowned king in 1921. On 3 Oct.
1932 Britain's mandate expired, and Iraq became an independent country. The pro-British policy was continued, and
in Jan. 1943 Iraq declared war on the Axis powers.

The ruling Hashemite dynasty was overthrown by an
armed coup led by a group of army officers on 14 July
1958. King Faisal II and his uncle, the ex-Regent the Emir
Abdul Ilah, and Nuri al Said, the prime minister, were killed. A republic was established, controlled by a military-led Council of Sovereignty under Gen. Qassim. The
republican regime terminated the adherence of Iraq to the Arab Federation, which
Iraq and Jordan had formed in Feb. 1958.

In 1963 Qassim was overthrown, and Gen. Abdul Salam Aref became president,
with a partial return to a civilian government. In 1966 Abdul Rahman Aref
succeeded his brother as president, but on 17 July 1968 a successful coup was
mounted by the Ba'ath Party and Gen. Ahmed Al Bakr became president, prime
minister, and chairman of a newly established ruling 9-member Revolutionary
Command Council. In July 1979 Saddam Hussein, the vice-president, became
president in a peaceful transfer of power.

In Sept. 1980 Iraq invaded Iran in a dispute over territorial rights in the Shatt-al-
Arab waterway which developed into a full-scale war. A UN-arranged ceasefire took
place on 20 Aug. 1988 and UN-sponsored peace talks continued in 1989. On 15 Aug.
1990 Iraq offered peace terms and began the withdrawal of troops from Iranian soil.

Early on 2 Aug. 1990 Iraqi forces without warning invaded and rapidly overran
Kuwait, meeting little resistance. The Amir escaped to Saudi Arabia. President
Saddam declared the annexation of Kuwait on 8 Aug.

On 6 Aug. the UN Security Council voted by 13 to nil with 2 abstentions (Cuba
and Yemen) to impose total economic sanctions on Iraq until it withdrew from
Kuwait. On 7 Aug. the USA announced it was sending a large military force to Saudi
Arabia at the latter's request to prevent a further Iraqi invasion of the area, and the
UK made a similar commitment the following day. Various other countries
announced the despatch of forces and equipment to this coalition force, including 12
Arab League countries on 10 Aug.

Measures to secure Iraq's withdrawal from Kuwait were given international legal
sanction by a UN Security Council Resolution of 25 Aug. (by 13 votes to nil),
authorizing a naval blockade of Iraq under UN auspices. Further Security Council
resolutions included (25 Sept., by 14 votes to 1) an air embargo of Iraq and (29 Oct.,
13–nil), a call for compensation to be paid by Iraq to states for losses resulting from
the invasion of Kuwait. A 12th resolution of 29 Nov. (12 in favour, Cuba and Yemen
against, China abstaining) authorized the use of military force if Iraq did not
withdraw by 15 Jan. 1991.

On the night of 16–17 Jan. coalition forces began an air attack on strategic targets
in Iraq. A land offensive followed on 24 Feb. The Iraqi army was routed and
sustained massive destruction. Kuwait City was liberated on 27 Feb. and on 28 Feb.
Iraq agreed to the conditions of a provisional ceasefire, including withdrawal from
Kuwait.

On 3 April 1991 the UN Security Council adopted a permanent ceasefire resolu-
tion by 12 votes to 1 (Cuba) with 2 abstentions (Ecuador, Yemen). This provided for
Iraq and Kuwait to respect the disputed border, the UN to demarcate it, and the
Security Council to guarantee it. A UN observer force was to monitor a demilitarized

zone extending 10 km into Iraq and 5 km into Kuwait. Iraq accepted the destruction of all chemical and biological weapons and nuclear weapons-usable material, under international supervision, and liability for damages arising from its invasion of Kuwait.

Insurrections amongst Shi'ites in the south and Kurds in the north were put down by government forces. A massive exodus of Kurdish refugees to the borders of Iran and Turkey followed. International relief operations were succeeded in April by the establishment of 'safe havens' for refugees within Iraqi borders policed by US and other coalition troops. Kurdish opposition leaders began talks with the Iraqi government at the end of April, and refugees began to move from the border areas into camps in north Iraq under the supervision of US, UK and other coalition forces. In May 1991 a UN Security Council resolution adopted by 14 votes to 1 (Cuba) provided for a fund to compensate victims for damage caused during the Iraqi invasion of Kuwait. The fund is based at Geneva, administered by a council of representatives of all the Security Council members, and supplied from not more than 30% of Iraqi oil-export earnings. Iraq denounced the resolution as illegal, but said it would comply with it as it had no choice. Following a UN-Iraqi agreement, about 500 UN security guards were brought in to protect Kurds in the north in June 1991. Coalition forces in Iraq withdrew in 1991, leaving only air forces based in Turkey.

In Sept. a UN Security Council resolution adopted by 13 votes to 1 (Cuba) with 1 abstention (Yemen) permitted Iraq to sell oil worth US$1,600m. to pay for food and medical supplies and start a reparations fund. In Oct. the Security Council voted unanimously to prohibit Iraq from all nuclear activities except medical. Imports of materials used in the manufacture of nuclear, biological or chemical weapons are banned, and UN inspectors have received wide powers to examine and retain data throughout Iraq.

In Aug. 1992 the USA, UK and France began to enforce an air exclusion zone over southern Iraq in response to the government's persecution of Shi'ite Moslems. Following Iraqi violations of this zone, and incursions over the Kuwaiti border, US, British and French forces made air and missile attacks on Iraqi military targets in Jan. 1993. On 27 June 1993 US forces made a missile attack on an intelligence centre in Baghdad in retaliation for an attempt on former US President Bush's life while he was visiting Kuwait in April.

On 10 Nov. 1994 Iraq recognized the independence and boundaries of Kuwait.

An agreement between the UN and Iraq of 20 May 1996 (renewed in June 1997) permitted Iraq to export crude oil worth US$2,000m. in order to purchase foodstuffs and medicine.

At the beginning of Sept. 1996 Iraqi troops occupied the town of Arbol in a Kurdish safe haven in support of the Kurdish Democratic Party faction which was at odds with another Kurdish faction, the Patriotic Union of Kurdistan. On 3 Sept. 1996 US forces fired missiles at targets in southern Iraq and extended the no-fly area northwards to the southern suburbs of Baghdad (33rd parallel).

Relations with the USA deteriorated still further in 1997 when Iraq refused co-operation with UN weapons inspectors. On 29 Oct. the Iraqi Revolutionary Command Council announced that it had 'postponed' a decision to stop working with UNSCOM, the UN commission responsible for the destruction of Iraq's ballistic, chemical and biological weapons programmes, but it went on to demand that there should be no American nationals among the UN inspectors. The UN team suspended its operations in Iraq and the Security Council warned Saddam Hussein of 'serious consequences' if he carried out his threat to expel the Americans.

While the USA and the UK threatened retaliatory action, the larger Arab countries with Russia, China and France urged compromise. However, a renewal of hostilities looked probable until late February 1998 when Kofi Annan, the UN Secretary General, forged an agreement in Baghdad allowing for 'immediate, unconditional and unrestricted access' to all suspected weapons sites.

TERRITORY AND POPULATION. Iraq is bounded in the north by Turkey, east by Iran, south-east by the Persian (Arabian) Gulf, south by Kuwait and Saudi Arabia, and west by Jordan and Syria. In April 1992 the UN Boundary Commission redefined Iraq's border with Kuwait, moving it slightly northwards in line with an agreement of 1932. Area, 438,317 sq. km. Population, 1987 census, 16,335,198; 1997 estimate, 22·22m.; density, 50·7 per sq. km.

Vital statistics rates, 1997 estimates (per 1,000 population). Births, 42·5; deaths, 6·3. Infant mortality (per 1,000 live births), 57·5. Expectation of life in 1997 was 67·4 years (66·3 for males and 65·8 for females). Growth rate, 3·62% per annum.

The areas, populations and capitals of the governorates:

Governorate	sq. km	Population (1987 census)	Capital	Population (1987 census)
Al-Anbar	138,501	820,690	Ar-Ramadi	192,556
Babil (Babylon)	6,468	1,109,574	Al-Hillah	268,834
Baghdad	734	3,841,268	Baghdad	3,841,268
Al-Basrah	19,070	872,176	Al-Basrah	406,296
Dahuk	6,553	293,304	Dahuk	19,736[2]
Dhi Qar	12,900	921,066	An-Nasiriyah	265,937
Diyala	19,076	961,073	Ba'qubah	114,516[3]
Irbil	14,471	770,439	Irbil	485,968
Karbala	5,034	469,282	Karbala	296,705
Maysan	16,072	487,448	Al-Amarah	208,797
Al-Muthanna	51,740	315,815	As-Samawah	33,473[1]
An-Najaf	28,824	590,078	An-Najaf	309,010
Ninawa (Nineveh)	37,323	1,479,430	Mosul	664,221
Al-Qadisiyah	8,153	559,805	Ad-Diwaniyah	196,519
Salah ad-Din	24,751	726,138	Samarra	62,008[2]
As-Sulaymaniyah	17,023	951,723	As-Sulaymaniyah	364,096
Ta'mim	10,282	601,219	Kirkuk	418,624
Wasit	17,153	564,670	Al-Kut	183,183

[1] Census 1965.   [2] Estimate 1970.   [3] Estimate 1985.

In 1993 there were 3,688,000 Kurds, 270,000 Turkmens. The national language is Arabic.

CLIMATE. The climate is mainly arid, with small and unreliable rainfall and a large annual range of temperature. Summers are very hot and winters cold. Al-Basrah. Jan. 55°F (12·8°C), July 92°F (33·3°C). Annual rainfall 7" (175 mm). Baghdad. Jan. 50°F (10°C), July 95°F (35°C). Annual rainfall 6" (140 mm). Mosul. Jan. 44°F (6·7°C), July 90°F (32·2°C). Annual rainfall 15" (384 mm).

CONSTITUTION AND GOVERNMENT. The Provisional Constitution was promulgated on 16 July 1970. The highest state authority is the Revolutionary Command Council (RCC) but some legislative power has now been given to the 220-member *National Assembly*. National Assembly elections were held on 24 March 1996. There were 689 candidates. The Ba'ath Party gained a majority of seats.

The only legal political grouping was the National Progressive Front (founded 1973) comprising the Arab Socialist Renaissance (Ba'ath) Party and various Kurdish groups, but a law of Aug. 1991 legalized political parties provided they are not based on religion, racism or ethnicity.

The President and Vice-President are elected by the RCC; the President appoints and leads a Council of Ministers responsible for administration.

On 15 Sept. 1995 a referendum was held to determine whether President Saddam Hussein should remain in office for a further 7 years. The electorate was 8·4m. It was announced that turn-out was 99·47% and 99·96% of votes cast were in favour.

President: Saddam Hussein at-Takriti (b. 1937; assumed office 17 July 1979; re-investiture, 17 Oct. 1995).

Vice-Presidents: Taha Yassin Ramadhan; Mohieddin Masarouf.

In Nov. 1996 the RCC comprised: President Saddam (*Chairman*); Ezzat Ibrahim (*Vice-Chairman*); Ahmed Hussein Al Khodair (*Head of the President's Office*); Mohieddin Masarouf; Tariq Aziz; Taha Yassin Ramadhan; Mohammed Hamza Al Zubaidi; Gen. Ali Hassan Al Majid; Mizban Khider Hadi.

In March 1998 the Cabinet comprised:

Prime Minister: President Saddam Hussein.

Deputy Prime Ministers: Tariq Aziz; Taha Yassin Ramadhan; Mohammed Hamza Al Zubaidi.
Trade: Mohamed Mehdi Saleh. *Oil:* Lieut.-Gen. Amir Mohammed Rashid. *Culture and Information:* Humam Abd Al Khaliq Abd Al Ghafur. *Defence:* Lieut.-Gen. Sultan Hashim Ahmed. *Higher Education and Scientific Research:* Abduljabbar Tawfiq Mohammed. *Industry and Minerals:* Adnan Abdul-Majid Jassim. *Justice:* Shabib Al Malki. *Education:* Fahd Salim Shaqrah. *Labour and Social Affairs:* Latif Nasif Jassim. *Awqaf (Religious Endowments) and Religious Affairs:* Abdul-Muneim Ahmed Saleh. *Finance:* Aikmet Mezban Ibrahim. *Interior:* Mohammed Zammam Abdel-Razzak. *Foreign Affairs:* Mohammed Said Al Sahhaf. *Health:* Umeed Madhat Mubarak. *Housing and Reconstruction:* Maan Abdullah Sarsam. *Transport and Communications:* Ahmed Murtada Ahmed Khalil. *Agriculture:* Abdullah Hamid Mahmoud Saleh. *Irrigation:* Mahmoud Diyab Al Ahmed.

National anthem: 'Watanum Mede, al alufqi janalia' ('A homeland which extended its wings over the horizon'); words by S. Jabar Al Kamali, tune by W. G. Gholmieh.

Local Government. Iraq is divided into 18 governorates *(liwa),* each administered by an appointed Governor; three of the governorates form a (Kurdish) Autonomous Region, with an elected 57-member Kurdish Legislative Council. Each governorate is divided into *qadhas* (under Qaimaqams) and *nahiyahs* (under Mudirs).

DEFENCE. Conscription is 18-24 months. Military service is waived on payment of the equivalent of US$800.

Army. The Army is organized into 19 armoured/mechanized/infantry divisions, 7 Republican Guard divisions and 10 special forces brigades. Equipment includes 2,700 main battle tanks, including T-54/-55/M-77, Chinese T-59/-69, T-62, T-72 and Chieftain. Strength (1997 estimate) 350,000, including 100,000 active reserves.

Navy. The Iraqi Navy continues to lack operational capability. Current strength is believed to comprise 1 training frigate (currently non-operational), 1 missile craft, 7 small patrol craft and 4 inshore minesweepers.

In 1997 naval personnel were estimated at about 2,500. Bases exist at Basra and Az Zubayr (exit controlled by Kuwait).

Air Force. The Iraqi Air Force suffered heavy losses during the Gulf War; over 60 aircraft were destroyed by the opposing Allied forces, many more were damaged beyond repair on the ground in Iraq and at least 100 aircraft are impounded in Iran. Reliable data on the status of the service are not available and the following are estimates. The combat aircraft are mostly of Soviet manufacture (MiG-21/23/29, Su-22/25), although there are French supplied Mirage F1-E/B fighters, Alouette, Super Frelon and Super Puma helicopters, F-6 and F-7 fighters from China, Bell 214ST helicopters from the USA, Czech-built L-39 light attack/trainer aircraft, and BO 105 and BK-117 helicopters from Germany.

The combat helicopter inventory comprises anti-armour Gazelles, Mi-24s and BO 105s, and Super Pumas equipped for anti-shipping duties. Transports include fixed-wing An-12s, An-26s and Il-76s, and Puma, Bell 214ST, BO 105, BK-117, Mil, Mi-6, Mi-8/17, AB.212 and AS-61 transport and liaison helicopters. Training aircraft comprise AS.202 Bravo primary trainers, Tucano, PC-7 and PC-9 basic trainers and two-seat models of most combat types. Personnel (1997), about 35,000 (including 17,000 air defence).

INTERNATIONAL RELATIONS

Membership. Iraq is a member of the UN and Arab League.

ECONOMY

Budget. Before UN sanctions were applied, oil revenues accounted for nearly 50% and customs and excise for about 26%, of the total revenue.

Currency. The monetary unit is the *Iraqi dinar* (IQD) of 1,000 *fils*. There are coins for 100, 50, 25, 10, 5 and 1 fils. Notes are for /, fi and 1 dinar, and for 5, 10, 25, 50, 100 and 250 dinars.

Banking and Finance. All banks were nationalized on 14 July 1964. The Central Bank of Iraq is the sole bank of issue. In 1941 the Rafidain Bank, financed by the Iraqi Government, was instituted to carry out normal banking transactions. Its head office is in Baghdad and it has 239 branches, 11 abroad, including London. Its assets were US$47,000m. in Sept. 1990. In addition, there are 4 government banks which are authorized to issue loans to companies and individuals: the Industrial Bank, the Agricultural Bank, the Estate Bank, and the Mortgage Bank.

There is a stock exchange in Baghdad.

Weights and Measures. The metric system is in general use.

ENERGY AND NATURAL RESOURCES

Electricity. Production in 1996 was 31,800m. kWh.

Oil. Crude oil production was 3·6m. tonnes in 1995. Natural gas, 123 petajoules. Since 1991 sanctions against Iraq have held back oil sales of some US$100,000m.

Agriculture. There are 5·45m. ha of arable land and 4m. ha of permanent cropland. Production (1994 estimates, in 1,000 tonnes): Wheat, 1,008; barley, 1,002; tomatoes, 750; dates, 600; watermelons, 460.

Livestock (1994): Cattle, 1·1m.; buffaloes, 100,000; sheep, 6·3m.; goats, 1·05m.; asses, 162,000; chickens (1991), 50m.

Fisheries. Catch (1995) 22,550 tonnes.

Forestry. 155,000 cu. metres of roundwood were cut in 1994.

INDUSTRY. Iraq is still relatively under-developed industrially but work has begun on new industrial plants.

Labour. The total workforce in 1989 was 4·4m., with 48% employed in services, 30% in agriculture and 22% in industry.

FOREIGN ECONOMIC RELATIONS

Commerce. Imports and exports (in US$1m.):

	1988	1989	1990	1991
Imports	9,311	10,170	6,605	International embargo
Exports	9,613	12,408	10,353	International embargo

Crude oil is the main export commodity, with Jordan and Turkey being significant export partners in 1996. Manufactures and food are the main import commodities, with major partners in 1996 being France, Turkey, Jordan, Vietnam and Australia.

Tourism. An estimated 400,000 tourists visited Iraq in 1993.

COMMUNICATIONS

Roads. In 1995 there were 46,500 km of roads, of which 39,990 km were paved. Vehicles registered in 1989 totalled 672,205 passenger cars and 128,550 commercial vehicles.

Railways. In 1993 railways comprised 2,032 km of 1,435 mm gauge route. In 1993 they carried 1,566m. passenger-km and 1,649m. tonne-km of freight.

Civil Aviation. The national carrier is Iraqi Airways, which in 1992 operated 3 B-707-320Cs, 2 B-737-200s, 6 B-727s, 3 B-747s and 1 B-747SP.

Shipping. The merchant fleet in 1995 had a total tonnage of 1·55m. GRT, including oil tankers, 1·35m. GRT. 1980. A 565-km canal was opened in 1992 between

Baghdad and the Persian (Arabian) Gulf for shipping, irrigation, the drainage of saline water and the reclamation of marsh land.

Telecommunications. Telephones, 1987 estimate, 632,000. Broadcasting is controlled by the government Broadcasting Service, and Baghdad Television. In 1995 there were 4·5m. radio and 1·6m. TV receivers (colour by SECAM).

Press. In 1995 there were 4 main daily newspapers (one of which is in English) with a combined circulation of 530,000.

SOCIAL INSTITUTIONS

Justice. For civil matters: The court of cassation in Baghdad; 6 courts of appeal at Baghdad (2), Basra, Babylon, Mosul and Kirkuk; 18 courts of first instance with unlimited powers and 150 courts of first instance with limited powers, all being courts of single judges. In addition, 6 peace courts have peace court jurisdiction only. 'Revolutionary courts' deal with cases affecting state security.

For religious matters: The Sharia courts at all places where there are civil courts, constituted in some places of specially appointed Qadhis (religious judges) and in other places of the judges of the civil courts. For criminal matters: The court of cassation; 6 sessions courts (2 being presided over by the judge of the local court of first instance and 4 being identical with the courts of appeal). Magistrates' courts at all places where there are civil courts, constituted of civil judges exercising magisterial powers of the first and second class. There are also a number of third-class magistrates' courts, powers for this purpose being granted to municipal councils and a number of administrative officials.

The death penalty was introduced for serious theft in 1992; amputation of a hand for theft in 1994.

Religion. The constitution proclaims Islam the state religion, but also stipulates freedom of religious belief and expression. In 1993 there were 11·9m. Shi'ite Moslems and 6·6m. Sunni Moslems (including 3·5m. Kurds). There were 0·72m. Christians in 14 sects, including: 0·48m. Chaldean (Eastern rite Roman Catholic) Church, with some 100 priests in 9 dioceses; 0·15m. Apostolic Assyrian (Nestorian) Church, with 29 priests in 3 dioceses and 80,000 Syriac Orthodox in 2 dioceses. There were some 10,000 in various Protestant sects.

Education. Primary and secondary education is free and primary education became compulsory in 1976. Primary school age is 6–12. Secondary education is for 6 years, of which the first 3 are termed intermediate. The medium of instruction is Arabic; Kurdish is used in primary schools in northern districts.

There were, in 1995, 576 pre-primary schools with 4,972 teachers for 93,028 pupils. In 1993 there were 8,003 primary schools with 131,271 teachers for 2,857,467 pupils and 57,117 secondary level teachers for 1·14m. pupils. Adult literacy rate was 58·0% in 1995 (male, 70·7%; female, 45·0%). In 1994–95 there were 10 universities and 1 technological university, 1 institute of administration, 1 institute of applied arts, 1 technical teacher training institute and 22 technical institutes.

Health. In 1991 there were 9,366 doctors, 1,577 dentists, 1,552 pharmacists and 177 hospitals with 31,227 beds.

DIPLOMATIC REPRESENTATIVES

On 6 Feb. 1991 Iraq broke off diplomatic relations with Great Britain and the USA.

Of Iraq to the United Nations
Ambassador: Nizar Hamdoon.

Further Reading

Abdulrahman, A. J., *Iraq* [Bibliography]. Oxford and Santa Barbara, 1984
Al-Khalil, S., *Republic of Fear: the Politics of Modern Iraq.* Univ. of California Press, 1989

Baram, A., *Cultural History and Ideology in the Formation of Ba'athist Iraq, 1968–89*. London, 1991

Bleaney, C. H., *Iraq*. [Bibliography]. 2nd ed. Oxford and Santa Barbara (CA), 1995

Bulloch, J. and Morris, H., *Saddam's War: the Origins of the Kuwait Conflict and the International Response*. London, 1991

Chubin, S. and Tripp, C., *Iran and Iraq at War*. London, 1988

Farouk-Sluglett, M., and Sluglett, P., *Iraq since 1958: from Revolution to Dictatorship*. London, 1991

National statistical office: Central Statistical Organization, Ministry of Planning, Baghdad.

IRELAND

Republic of Ireland—

Poblacht na hÉireann

Capital: Dublin
Population: 3·63m.
GDP per head: (PPP$) 16,061
HDI/world rank: 0·929/17

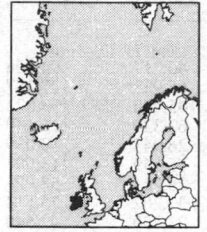

KEY HISTORICAL EVENTS. In April 1916 an insurrection against British rule took place and a republic was proclaimed. The armed struggle was renewed in 1919 and continued until 1921. The independence of Ireland was reaffirmed in Jan. 1919 by the Irish Parliament (*Dáil Éireann*), elected in Dec. 1918.

In 1920 an Act was passed by the British Parliament, under which separate Parliaments were set up for 'Southern Ireland' (26 counties) and 'Northern Ireland' (6 counties). The Unionists of the 6 counties accepted this scheme, and a Northern Parliament was duly elected on 24 May 1921. The rest of Ireland, however, ignored the Act.

On 6 Dec. 1921 a treaty was signed between Great Britain and Ireland by which Ireland accepted dominion status subject to the right of Northern Ireland to opt out. This right was exercised, and the border between the Irish Free State (26 counties) and Northern Ireland (6 counties) was fixed in Dec. 1925 as the outcome of an agreement between Great Britain, Ireland and Northern Ireland.

Subsequently the constitutional links between Ireland and the UK were gradually removed by the *Dáil*. The remaining formal association with the British Commonwealth by virtue of the External Relations Act, 1936, was severed when the Republic of Ireland Act, 1948, came into operation on 18 April 1949.

TERRITORY AND POPULATION. The Republic of Ireland lies in the Atlantic Ocean, separated from Great Britain by the Irish Sea to the east, and bounded in the north-east by Northern Ireland (UK). The population at the 1996 census was 3,626,087 (1,825,855 females).

The capital is Dublin (Baile Átha Cliath). Town populations, 1996: Greater Dublin, 952,692; Cork, 179,954; Limerick, 75,729; Galway, 57,363; Waterford, 44,155.

Vital statistics for 6 calendar years:

	Births	Marriages	Deaths		Births	Marriages	Deaths
1991	52,718	17,441	31,305	1994	48,255	16,621	30,948
1992	51,089	16,636	30,931	1995[1]	48,530	15,623	31,711
1993	49,304	16,824	32,148	1996[1]	50,390	16,255	31,514

[1] Provisional figures—based on year of registration.

Over 1991–96 the suicide rate per 100,000 population was 10·2 (men, 16·6; women, 3·9).

At a referendum on 24 Nov. 1995 on the legalization of civil divorce the electorate was 1,628,580; 818,852 votes were in favour, 809,728 against.

Counties and county boroughs	Area in ha[1]	Population, 1996[2]		Total
		Males	Females	
Province of Leinster				
Carlow	89,655	21,086	20,530	41,616
Dublin County Borough	11,758	228,401	253,453	481,854
Dun Laoghaire-Rathdown	12,638	90,435	99,564	189,999
Fingal	45,467	82,720	84,963	167,683
South Dublin	22,364	107,410	111,318	218,728
Kildare	169,540	68,007	66,985	134,992
Kilkenny	207,289	38,144	37,192	75,336
Laoighis	171,990	27,160	25,785	52,945
Longford	109,116	15,468	14,698	30,166
Louth	82,613	45,641	46,525	92,166
Meath	234,207	55,340	54,392	109,732
Offaly	200,117	30,003	29,114	59,117
Westmeath	183,965	31,599	31,715	63,314

[1] Area Details Provided by Ordnance Survey.   [2] Revised Based on 1996 Census of Population.

Counties and county boroughs	Area in ha[1]	Population, 1996[2]		Total
		Males	Females	
Province of Leinster—contd.				
Wexford	236,685	52,432	51,939	104,371
Wicklow	202,662	50,823	51,860	102,683
Total of Leinster	1,980,066	944,669	980,033	1,924,702
Province of Munster				
Clare	345,004	47,789	46,217	94,006
Cork County Borough	3,953	61,254	65,933	127,187
Cork	746,042	147,923	145,400	293,323
Kerry	480,689	63,801	62,329	126,130
Limerick County Borough	2,087	25,092	26,947	52,039
Limerick	273,504	57,454	55,549	113,003
Tipperary, N. R.	204,627	29,290	28,731	58,021
Tipperary, S. R.	225,845	38,312	37,202	75,514
Waterford County Borough	4,103	20,790	21,750	42,540
Waterford	181,556	26,512	25,628	52,140
Total of Munster	2,467,410	518,217	515,686	1,033,903
Province of Connacht				
Galway County Borough	5,057	26,973	30,268	57,241
Galway	609,820	67,556	64,057	131,613
Leitrim	159,003	13,044	12,013	25,057
Mayo	558,605	56,371	55,153	111,524
Roscommon	254,819	26,695	25,280	51,975
Sligo	183,752	27,748	28,073	55,821
Total of Connacht	1,771,056	218,387	214,844	433,231
Province of Ulster (part of)				
Cavan	193,177	27,263	25,633	52,944
Donegal	486,091	65,520	64,474	129,944
Monaghan	129,508	26,158	25,155	51,313
Total of Ulster (part of)	808,776	118,959	115,292	234,251
Total	7,027,308	1,800,232	1,825,855	3,626,087

[1] Area Details Provided by Ordnance Survey.   [2] Based on 1996 Census of Population.

The official languages are Irish (the national language) and English; according to the National Survey of Languages of 1994, Irish is spoken as a mother tongue only by 2% of the population, in certain western areas (Gaeltacht), and is no longer a compulsory subject at school.

CLIMATE. Influenced by the Gulf Stream, there is an equable climate with mild south-west winds, making temperatures almost uniform over the whole country. The coldest months are Jan. and Feb. (39–45°F, 4–7°C) and the warmest July and Aug. (57–61°F, 14–16°C). May and June are the sunniest months, averaging 5·5 to 6·5 hours each day, but over 7 hours in the extreme S.E. Rainfall is lowest along the eastern coastal strip. The central parts vary between 30–44" (750–1,125 mm), and up to 60" (1,500 mm) may be experienced in low-lying areas in the west. Dublin. Jan. 40°F (4·7°C), July 59°F (15°C). Annual rainfall 30" (750 mm). Cork. Jan. 42°F (5·6°C), July 61°F (16°C). Annual rainfall 41" (1,025 mm).

CONSTITUTION AND GOVERNMENT. Ireland is a sovereign independent, democratic republic. Its parliament exercises jurisdiction in 26 of the 32 counties of the island of Ireland. The first Constitution of the Irish Free State came into operation on 6 Dec. 1922. Certain provisions which were regarded as contrary to the national sentiments were gradually removed by successive amendments, with the result that at the end of 1936 the text differed considerably from the original document. On 14 June 1937 a new Constitution was approved by Parliament and enacted by a plebiscite on 1 July 1937. This Constitution came into operation on 29 Dec. 1937. Under it the name Ireland (Éire) was restored. It states that the whole island of Ireland is the national territory, but that, pending its reintegration, laws enacted by Parliament have the same area and extent of application as those of the former Irish Free State.

The head of state is the *President*, whose role is largely ceremonial, but who has the power to refer proposed legislation which might infringe the Constitution to the Supreme Court.

The *Oireachtas* or National Parliament consists of the President, a House of Representatives, (*Dáil Éireann*) and a Senate (*Seanad Éireann*). The *Dáil*, consisting of 166 members, is elected by adult suffrage on the Single Transferable Vote system in constituencies of 3, 4 or 5 members. Of the 60 members of the Senate, 11 are nominated by the *Taoiseach* (Prime Minister), 6 are elected by the universities and the remaining 43 are elected from 5 panels of candidates established on a vocational basis, representing the following public services and interests: (1) national language and culture, literature, art, education and such professional interests as may be defined by law for the purpose of this panel; (2) agricultural and allied interests, and fisheries; (3) labour, whether organized or unorganized; (4) industry and commerce, including banking, finance, accountancy, engineering and architecture; (5) public administration and social services, including voluntary social activities. The electing body comprises members of the *Dáil*, Senate, county boroughs and county councils.

A maximum period of 90 days is afforded to the Senate for the consideration or amendment of Bills sent to that House by the *Dáil*, but the Senate has no power to veto legislative proposals.

No amendment of the Constitution can be effected except with the approval of the people given at a referendum.

President: Mary McAleese (b. 1951), elected out of 5 candidates on 30 Oct. 1997 and inaugurated 11 Nov. 1997.

A general election was held on 6 June 1997: Fianna Fáil (FF) gained 76 seats with 39·33% of votes cast (in 1992, 68 seats); Fine Gael (FG), 54 with 27·95% (45); Labour Party (L), 17 with 10·4% (33); Progressive Democrats (PD), 4 with 4·68% (10); Democratic Left (DL), 4 with 2·51%; Green Party (G), 2 with 2·76%; Socialist Party, 1 with 0·7%; Sinn Fein, 1 with 2·55%; others, 6 with 6·88%.

A new coalition Government was formed on 26 June 1997 between Fianna Fáil (FF) and The Progressive Democrats (PD). In March 1998 it comprised:

Taoiseach (Prime Minister): Bertie Ahern (b. 1951; FF). *Tánaiste (Deputy Prime Minister), Minister for Enterprise, Trade and Employment:* Mary Harney (b. 1953; PD). *Finance:* Charlie McCreevy (b. 1949; FF) *Social Community and Family Affairs:* Dermot Ahern (b. 1955; FF). *Justice, Equality and Law Reform:* John O'Donoghue (b. 1956; FF). *Environment and Local Government:* Noel Dempsey (b. 1953; FF). *Defence:* Michael Smith (b. 1940; FF). *Agriculture, Forestry and Food:* Joe Walsh (b. 1943; FF). *Tourism, Sport and Recreation:* Jim McDaid (b. 1949; FF). *Public Enterprise:* Mary O'Rourke (b. 1937; FF). *Arts, Heritage, Gaeltacht and the Islands:* Síle de Valera (b. 1954; FF). *Health and Children:* Brian Cowen (b. 1960; FF). *Education and Science:* Micheal Martin (b. 1960; FF). *Marine and Natural Resources:* Michael Woods (b. 1935; FF). *Foreign Affairs:* David Andrews (b. 1935; FF).

There are 17 Ministers of State.
Attorney-General: David Byrne, SC.

National anthem: Amhrán na bhFiann (The Soldier's Song); words by P. Kearney, tune by P. Heeney.

European Parliament. Ireland has 15 representatives. At the June 1994 election turn-out was 44%. Fianna Fáil gained 7 seats (group in European Parliament: Union for Europe); Fine Gael, 4 (European People's Party); Greens, 2 (Green Group); Labour, 1 (European Socialist Party); independent, 1.

Local Government. The elected local authorities comprise 29 county councils, 5 county borough corporations, 5 borough corporations, 49 urban district councils and 26 Boards of Town Commissioners. All the members of these authorities are elected under a system of proportional representation, normally every 5 years. All residents of an area who have reached the age of 18 and whose names appear on the register of electors are entitled to vote in the local election for their area. Elected members are not paid, but provision is made for the payment of travelling expenses and subsistence allowances.

The range of services for which local authorities are responsible is broken down into 8 main programme groups as follows: Housing and Building; Road Transportation and Safety; Water Supply and Sewerage; Development Incentives and Controls; Environmental Protection; Recreation and Amenity; Agriculture, Education, Health and Welfare; Miscellaneous Services. Because of the small size of their administrative areas the functions carried out by town commissioners and some of the smaller urban district councils have tended to become increasingly limited, and the more important tasks of local government have tended to become the responsibility of the county councils.

The local authorities have a system of government which combines an elected council and a whole-time manager. The elected members have specific functions reserved to them which include the striking of rates (local tax), the borrowing of money, the adoption of development plans, the making, amending or revoking of bye-laws and the nomination of persons to other bodies. The managers, who are paid officers of their authorities, are responsible for the performance of all functions which are not reserved to the elected members, including the employment of staff, making of contracts, management of local authority property, collection of rates and rents and the day-to-day administration of local authority affairs. The manager for a county council is manager also for every borough corporation, urban district council and board town commissioners whose functional area is wholly within the county.

At the elections of June 1991, at city and county council level, 883 seats were contested. Fianna Fáil won 357 seats with 38% of votes cast. Fine Gael 270 with 26%. Labour 90 with 11%, the Progressive Democrats 37 with 5%, the Workers' Party 24 with 4%, the Greens 13 with 2%, and Sinn Fein 7 with 2%. Independents gained 85 seats.

DEFENCE. Supreme command of the Defence Forces is vested in the President. Exercise of the supreme command is regulated by law (Defence Act 1954). Military Command is exercised by the government through the Minister for Defence who is the overall commander of the Defence Forces.

The Defence Forces comprise the Permanent Defence Force (the regular Army, the Air Corps and the Naval Service) and the Reserve Defence Force (comprising a First Line Reserve of members who have served in the Permanent Defence Force, a second-line Territorial Army reserve and a second-line Naval reserve). The total strength of the Permanent Defence Force in 1997 averaged 11,750. The total strength of the Reserve in 1997 was about 15,350.

Army. The Army is organized in 4 territorial commands and has 4 infantry brigades and an infantry force of 2 battalions. Three of the brigades have 2 battalions and 1 brigade has 3 battalions. Each brigade has a field artillery regiment and a squadron/company-size unit for each of the support corps (cavalry, engineer, signals, supply and transport, military police, medical). Equipment includes 14 Scorpion light tanks. Average army strength in 1997 was 9,700 personnel.

Navy. The Naval Service, based at Haulbowline in Cork, comprises 6 offshore patrol vessels and 1 helicopter patrol vessel. Two Dauphin helicopters (operated by the Air Corps) for use from the helicopter patrol vessel and 2 maritime reconnaissance aircraft are deployed for fishery protection and other duties. Average Naval Service strength in 1997 was 1,000 personnel.

Air Corps. The Air Corps has its headquarters in Dublin and has 2 other bases. Most of the Corps' technical and administrative services are located at Casement Aerodrome which is also the main centre for flying and technical training. Fixed-wing aircraft types in service include 4 Fouga Magister armed jet trainers, 7 SIAI Marchetti SF 260W armed piston-engined trainers, 7 Cessna F 172 reconnaissance aircraft, 2 CASA CN 235 maritime patrol aircraft and 1 Beech Super Kingair and 1 Gulfstream G IV aircraft for VIP transport. The Corps also has 7 Alouette III, 5 Dauphin and 2 Gazelle helicopters in use. Average Air Corps strength in 1997 was 1,050 personnel.

INTERNATIONAL RELATIONS

Membership. Ireland is a member of the UN, OECD, the Council of Europe and the EU.

ECONOMY

Performance. GDP growth was 7·7% in 1996.

Budget. Current revenue and expenditure (in IR£1m.):

Current revenue	1997[1]	1998[2]
Customs duties	180	176
Excise duties	2,507	2,659
Capital taxes	225	198
Stamp duties	429	467
Income tax	5,218	5,522
Income levy	1	–
Corporation tax	1,699	1,926
Value-added tax	3,718	4,017
Agricultural levies (EU)	9	9
Motor vehicle duties	100[3]	–
Employment and training levy	189	193
Tax Amnesty proceeds	–	–
Non-Tax Revenue	345	330
Total	14,619	15,497

Current expenditure		
Debt service	2,755	2,625
Industry and Labour	572	632
Agriculture	624	589
Fisheries, Forestry, Tourism	91	101
Health	2,678	2,943
Education	2,361	2,351
Social Welfare	4,568	4,866
Other (excl. Balances)	3,317	3,392
Less: Receipts, e.g. social security	( )2,939	(–)3,091
Total (including other items)	14,027	14,408

[1] Provisional outturn. [2] Budget targets. [3] Now retained by Local Authorities.

VAT is 21% (reduced rate 12·5%).

Total Public Capital Programme Expenditure amounted to IR£3,640m. in 1997, with provision for IR£4,324m. in 1998. On 31 Dec. 1996 the National Debt amounted to IR£29,912m. of which IR£21,193m. was denominated in Irish pounds and IR£8,718m. in foreign currencies. The official external reserves of the Central Bank of Ireland amounted to IR£5,092m. at end June 1997.

Currency. The unit of currency is the *Irish pound* (IEP) or *punt Éireannach* of 100 *pence.* From 10 Sept. 1928 when the first Irish legal-tender notes were issued, the Irish currency was linked to Sterling on a one-for-one basis. This relationship was discontinued on 30 March 1979 when, following Ireland's adherence to the EMS (which it had joined on its inception on 13 March 1979), it became inconsistent with Ireland's obligations. The Central Bank has the sole right of issuing legal tender notes; token coinage is issued by the Minister for Finance through the Bank. Notes are currently issued in denominations of IR£5, 10, 20, 50 and 100. There are 1, 2, 5, 10, 20, 50 pence and IR£1 coins. The volume of legal-tender notes outstanding on 30

June 1997 was IR£2,213m. The Irish pound was realigned within the ERM on 30 Jan. 1993 with bilateral central rates of the IR£ against other ERM currencies being reduced by 10% effective 1 Feb. Inflation was an annualized 1·5% in 1997.

Banking and Finance. The Central Bank (founded in 1943), replaced the Currency Commission as the note-issuing authority. The Central Bank has the power of receiving deposits from banks and public authorities, of rediscounting Exchequer bills and bills of exchange, of making advances to banks against such bills or against Government securities, of fixing and publishing rates of interest for rediscounting bills, or buying and selling certain Government securities and securities of any international bank or financial institution formed wholly or mainly by governments. The Bank also collects and publishes information relating to monetary and credit matters. The Central Bank Acts, 1971, 1989 and 1997, together with the Building Societies Act, 1989, the Investment Intermediaries Act, 1995 and the Stock Exchange Act, 1995, give further powers to the Central Bank in the regulation and supervision of financial institutions and payment systems. The capital of the Bank is IR£40,000, of which IR£24,000 has been paid up and is held by the Minister for Finance.

The Board of Directors of the Central Bank consists of a Governor, appointed for a 7-year term by the President on the advice of the Government, and 9 directors, all appointed by the Minister for Finance. The Governor is Maurice O'Connell (b. 1937; appointed 1994).

At 31 Dec. 1996 there were 42 credit institutions authorized to carry on banking business in the State; 5 building societies and 3 State banks, ICC Bank, ACC Bank and the Trustee Savings Bank. In addition there were 13 credit institutions authorized in another Member State of the European Union operating in Ireland.

At 31 Dec. 1996 total assets of within-the-State offices of all credit institutions amounted to IR£67bn.

The Dublin stock exchange has been affiliated to the London exchange since 1973.

Weights and Measures. Conversion to the metric system is in progress; with some exceptions which are confined to the domestic market, all imperial units of measurement ceased to be legal, for general use, after 31 Dec. 1994.

ENERGY AND NATURAL RESOURCES

Electricity. The total generating capacity was (1996) 4,297 MW. In 1996 the total sales of electricity amounted to 15,707m. units supplied to 1,442,416 customers.

Oil. Over 0·6m. sq. km of the Irish continental shelf has been designated an exploration area for oil and gas; at the furthest point the limit of jurisdiction is 520 nautical miles from the coast. It has been established that there is potential for discoveries both offshore and onshore. In the offshore there is a vast Continental Shelf in which 13 major basins and troughs have been identified. Much of the shelf remains unexplored but from 1971 to date, 129 exploration wells have been drilled, and since 1965 a total of 348 separate surveys have been carried out from which approximately 316,000 line kilometres of seismic data has been produced since 1985.

A number of encouraging oil and gas flows have been recorded, including the Corrib North Prospect in the Slyne/Erris Trough and '7 Heads' and 'Helvick' fields which are located in the Celtic Sea. In Nov. 1992 revised licensing terms were issued which allowed for a range of generous allowances against tax. In 1994 a Frontier Licensing Round in the Erris and Slyne Troughs resulted in the award of five licences over 28 blocks. A further 8 licences over 32 blocks were awarded under the Porcupine Basin Frontier Licensing Round in 1995.

Eleven licences were awarded over 58 full and part blocks under the Petroleum Exploration round in the Rockall Trough in June 1997. The area in the Round covered 615 full and 35 part blocks in an area of almost 150,000 sq. kilometres. The Rockall Trough lies some 100 to 650 kilometres west of Ireland with water depths ranging from 500 metres to 2,500 metres.

Comprehensive work programmes will be undertaken that will ensure licensed areas are fully explored. Up to 18,000 kilometres of new 2D seismic, and up to 2,000 sq. kilometres of 3D seismic data will be acquired and assessed by the end of the first four years of the licences.

An invitation was issued to interested petroleum companies to apply for a Lease Undertaking over the 'Seven Heads' oil and gas accumulation in the Celtic Sea. The area which covers almost 520 sq. kilometres has been closed to the granting of authorizations since March 1997.

At the same time details of a Petroleum Licensing Round in the South Porcupine Basin was also announced. The acreage on offer covers 156 blocks in the Irish offshore—an area of over 5,000 sq. kilometres. Due to the special difficulties created by the physical environment of the area, it has been designated as a Frontier Area. Long term licences for a period of 15 years will be granted.

The South Porcupine Basin lies off the south-west coast of Ireland. Water depths vary from 200 metres in the east to over 2,500 metres in the south-west.

An Onshore Petroleum Prospecting Licence was issued for a three year period from 1 Dec. 1997 covering 1,960 kilometres of the Northwest Carboniferous Basin in counties Sligo, Leitrim, Roscommon, Cavan and Monaghan.

These steps in conjunction with the maintenance of Ireland's 'open door' approach to licensing, its favourable environment and existing tax regime achieves a risk/reward balance which reflects Ireland's circumstances and acknowledges the realities of competition for internationally mobile exploration and production investment.

Gas. (1995) Consumption of natural gas was 2,900m. cu. metres, of which 95% came from the Kinsale Head gas field, 50 km off the south coast, and the smaller Ballycotton field about 16 km north-west of Kinsale Head field, which was discovered in 1989 and which went into production in July 1991. These gas reserves are expected to be exhausted by the year 2003. Gas transmission and distribution is carried on by the Irish Gas Board (BGE). A gas pipeline from County Dublin to south-west Scotland was completed in 1994. 5% of gas used in 1995 was imported.

Peat. The country has very little indigenous coal, but possesses large reserves of peat, the development of which is handled largely by Bord na Mona (Peat Board). To date, the Board has acquired and developed 88,000 ha of bog and has 20 locations around the country. In the year ending 31 March 1996, the Board sold 86,000 tonnes of sod peat and 3,145,000 tonnes of milled peat for use in 5 milled peat electricity generating stations. 294,000 tonnes of briquettes were produced for sale to the domestic heating market. The Board also sold 1·7m. cu. metres of horticultural peat.

Minerals. Lead and zinc concentrates are important. In 1997 mineable resources stood at over 6m. tonnes of zinc and over 1m. tonnes of lead. Metal content of concentrates production, 1996: Zinc, 164,500 tonnes; lead, 45,300 tonnes. Gypsum, limestone and aggregates are important, and there is some production of silver (contained in lead) and dolomite. Exploration is centred on base metals, but with interest also in gold, gem minerals, industrial minerals and coal, and about 50 companies are involved. There is a thriving sand, gravel and aggregate extraction industry, employing some 7,500 people.

Agriculture. The CSO's Labour Force Survey shows in 1997 134,000 people whose primary source of income is from agriculture. A total of 301,000 people work on farms on a regular basis, working the equivalent of 223,400 full-time jobs. There are 149,500 farm holdings in Ireland, almost all of which are family farms. Average farm size is 29·2 ha. 48% of farms are under 20 ha. 12% of farmers are under 35 and 45% are over 55.

Agriculture represented 6·3% of GDP in 1997. The total area used for agricultural and forestry purposes is almost 5m. ha. Over 90% of the agricultural area is devoted to grass, and beef and milk production currently account for two-thirds of gross agricultural output.

At June 1997 the total area used for crops was 308,800 ha, of which wheat accounted (in ha.) for 91,300; oats, 21,300; barley, 190,000; other cereals, 6,100; potatoes, 20,400.

Gross agricultural output (including changes in stock) for the year 1997 was estimated at IR£3·3bn.; aggregate income from agriculture is IR£2bn. Direct income payments, financed of co-financed by the EU, amounted to IR£941m. or 47% of aggregate income. Livestock (June 1997): Cattle, 7,625,800; sheep, 8,210,100; pigs, 1,717,000.

Forestry. Current forest area cover amounts to 11% of the agricultural and forestry area, or about 8% of total land area.

Fisheries. In 1992 approximately 16,000 people were engaged full- or part-time in the sea fishing industry. The quantities and values of fish landed during 1996 were: Demersal fish, 46,881 tonnes, value IR£50,951,328·16; Pelagic fish, 256,901·7 tonnes, value IR£50,410,690·08; Shellfish, 43,667·6 tonnes, value IR£43,101,889·86. Total quantity: 347,450·03 tonnes; total value, IR£144,463,908·10.

INDUSTRY. The census of industrial production for 1995 gives the following details of the values (in IR£1m.) of gross and net output for the principal manufacturing industries. The figures for net output are those of gross output minus cost of materials, including fuel, light and power, repairs to plant and machinery and amounts paid to others in connection with products made.

	Gross output	Net output
Slaughtering, preparing and preserving meat	1,994·4	251·2
Manufacture of dairy products	2,257·6	405·2
Bread, biscuit and flour confectionery	320·5	143·1
Cocoa, chocolate and sugar confectionery	421·6	148·7
Animal and poultry foods	495·4	123·7
Brewing and malting	582·5	435·5
Spirit distilling and compounding	545·1	299·6
Paper and paper products	467·3	222·3
Printing and publishing	2,573·0	1,960·4
Manufacture of metal articles	993·2	389·3
Manufacture of non-metallic mineral products	716·5	402·2
Chemicals, including manmade fibres	5,446·2	3,857·4
Manufacture of machinery and equipment n.e.c.	1,072·3	518·7
General mechanical engineering	11·2	6·0
Office machinery and data-processing machinery	5,993·8	2,162·8
Electrical engineering	2,160·6	865·0
Manufacture and assembly of motor vehicles, parts and accessories	280·0	116·1
Manufacture of other means of transport	245·2	133·4
Instrument engineering	1,004·9	618·1
Textiles	442·3	189·3
Manufacture of footwear and clothing	352·3	168·5
Timber and wooden furniture	321·9	115·1
Processing rubber and plastics	734·2	348·8
Gas, water and electricity	1,471·7	835·6
All other industries	4,760·3	2,727·6
Total (all industries)	35,566·0	17,443·6

Labour. The total labour force for 1997 was estimated to be 1,517,000, of which an estimated 0·179m. were out of work. Of those at work, 134,000 were employed in the Agricultural sector, 386,000 in Industrial sector and 818,000 in the Services sector. The retirement age is 65 years.

Trade Unions. The number of trade unions in Dec. 1996 was 56; total membership, 540,000. The six largest unions accounted for almost two thirds of total membership. There were 11 employers' associations holding negotiation licences, with membership of 9,747. A series of three year social pacts, which, in addition to covering a range of economic and social policy measures, include provision for pay increases, have been negotiated between the Government, trade unions and employers' organizations since 1987. The fourth such agreement concluded in Jan. 1997, Partnership 2000, provides pay increases of 7·25% of basic pay in the public and private sectors of the economy over the period of the agreement, 1997–1999. In addition, employers and unions may engage in local level bargaining for a further increase, which must not exceed 2% of the basic pay cost of the particular group of employees.

Forbairt. Forbairt is the organization established by the Government to provide support services to Irish Industry across a wide range of commercial activities including management development, innovation, R&D, finance and technology transfer. A key part of the Forbairt mission is to bring science, technology and innovation into the mainstream of economic development in Ireland.

IDA Ireland. The IDA was established by the Irish Government in 1969 but its remit was altered in 1993 when responsibility for development of indigenous industry was moved to Forbairt. The objective of IDA Ireland is to create employment in Ireland by influencing foreign enterprises to start new businesses or expand their existing businesses in Ireland.

Today, companies choose Ireland as a base for a wide range of activities, from product and process development to manufacturing, marketing and international distribution logistics, from financial management to customer care and technical support services. Over 1,200 such enterprises have already established businesses in Ireland.

Exports. Ireland is one of the most trade-dependent countries in the world. Exports constitute an increasing share of the economy's output of goods and services. In 1996, the total value of merchandise exports amounted to just over IR£30bn. and generated a trade surplus of IR£7·7bn. In employment terms, taking the economy as a whole, one job in four is directly dependent on exports. When indirect influences are taken into account, almost one job in two depends on exports. Exports of goods and services in 1996 contributed over 80% of GDP.

FOREIGN ECONOMIC RELATIONS

Commerce. Value of imports and exports of merchandise for calendar years (in IR£1m.):

	1993	1994	1995	1996
Imports	14,884·7	17,283·4	20,619·1	22,469·9
Exports	19,829·7	22,753·4	27,824·7	30,315·8

The values of the chief imports and total exports are shown in the following table (in IR£1m.):

	Imports		Exports	
	1995	1996	1995	1996
Live animals and food	1,475·3	1,543·7	4,850·0	4,143·9
Raw materials	408·6	406·8	564·2	556·6
Mineral fuels and lubricants	670·2	823·8	120·5	116·4
Chemicals	2,636·6	2,763·7	5,272·5	6,726·7
Manufactured goods	2,374·3	2,418·0	1,351·2	1,356·6
Machinery and transport equipment	8,826·2	9,443·3	9,597·8	10,532·0
Manufactured articles	2,442·8	2,858·0	4,326·9	4,599·3
Beverages and tobacco	209·4	233·2	483·3	517·6

Exports, in IR£1m., for 1996 (and 1995): UK, 7,463 (7,099); Germany, 3,911 (4,038); France, 2,500 (2,621); USA, 2,816 (2,240); Netherlands, 2,042 (1,936); Belgium and Luxembourg, 1,443 (1,240); Italy, 1,088 (1,072); Japan, 861 (815); Spain, 700 (679); Sweden, 548 (546); Switzerland, 561 (494); Denmark, 387 (353); Norway, 336 (294); Canada, 247 (209);.

Imports: UK, 7,808 (7,296); USA, 3,460 (3,629); Germany, 1,527 (1,459); Japan, 1,206 (1,063); Singapore, 988 (808); France, 876 (786); Netherlands, 672 (602); Italy, 463 (405); Norway, 276 (279); Taiwan, 270 (266); Belgium and Luxembourg, 292 (257); Sweden, 303 (227); China, 253 (219).

Tourism. Total number of overseas tourists in 1996 was 4,682,000. These, together with cross-border visitors, spent IR£1,889m.

COMMUNICATIONS

Roads. At 31 October 1997 there were 94,900 km of public roads, consisting of 2,739 km of National Primary Roads (including 90 km of motorway), 2,686 km of National Secondary Roads, 11,607 km of Regional Roads and 77,868 km of Local Roads.

Number of licensed motor vehicles at 21 December 1996: Private cars, 1,057,383; Public-Service Vehicles, 14,754; Goods Vehicles, 146,601; Agricultural Vehicles, 74,280; Motor Cycles, 23,847; Other Vehicles, 21,751.

Railways. The total length of railway open for traffic at 31 Dec. 1996 was 1,872 km (38 km electrified), all 1,600 mm gauge.

Railway statistics for years ending 31 Dec.	1995	1996
Passengers (journeys)	27,124,000	27,930,000
Km run by passenger train	9,966,000	11,052,000
Freight (tonne-km)	602,457,000	569,885,000
Km run by freight trains	4,417,000	4,335,000
Receipts (IR£)	86,372,000	89,451,000
Expenditure (IR£)	*202,577,000	*223,116,000

*Expenditure figures include exceptional restructuring costs of IR£10·1m. (1995) and IR£37·1m. (1996).

Civil Aviation. Aer Lingus was incorporated in 1936 as a State-owned enterprise. Its principal business is the provision of passenger and cargo services to a range of points in the UK, Europe and the United States. In 1993, the company was restructured into the present Aer Lingus Group plc. Within the Group there are three airline operating companies: Aer Lingus which operates services to London and Europe; Aer Lingus Shannon, which operates services to the United States; Aer Lingus Commuter, which operates domestic services within Ireland and to UK provincial points.

During the year ended 31 March 1997 Aer Lingus carried almost 5 million passengers and 32,000 tonnes of cargo.

Aer Lingus currently operates 5 Airbus A330s, 6 Boeing 737-400s, 10 Boeing 737-500s, 6 Fokker 50s and 5 British Aerospace 146-300s.

In addition to Aer Lingus, there were in 1996 16 independent air transport operators including Cityjet, Ryanair and Translift Airways which operate scheduled and/or charter services to and from Ireland. Services are also provided by Aeroflot, AB Shannon, Air France, Air Malta, Air Ukraine, Alitalia, Belavia, British Airways, British Midland, Croatia Airlines, Crossair, Delta, Finnair, Hamburg Airlines, Iberia, KLM, Lauda, Lufthansa, Manx, Sabena, SAS, Swiss Regional, TAP, Tarom and Viva Air. The principal airports are at Dublin, Shannon and Cork; there are also 6 privately-owned airports.

Shipping. The merchant fleet totalled 193,934 GRT in 1996, including oil tankers, 191 GRT and container ships, 17,276 GRT. Total cargo traffic passing through the country's ports amounted to 33,918,000 tonnes in 1996.

Inland Waterways. The principal inland waterways open to navigation are the Shannon Navigation (270 km), which includes the Shannon-Erne Waterway (Ballinamore/Ballyconnell Canal), and the Grand Canal and Barrow Navigation (249 km). The Waterways Service of the Department of Arts, Culture and the Gaeltacht is responsible for the waterways system as a public amenity. Merchandise traffic has now ceased and navigation is confined to pleasure craft operated either privately or commercially. The Royal Canal (146 km) from Dublin to Mullingar (53 km) was reopened for navigation in 1995.

Telecommunications. Ireland's telecommunications sector is currently undergoing a process of liberalization with the provision of certain voice services (excluding voice telephony), fax and data services, satellite services and mobile telephony services having been liberalized to date. In addition liberalized services may be provided over cable TV and satellite networks or independently established networks. The areas of voice telephony and provision of the PSTN (Public Switched Telephone Network) remain for the present within the area of exclusive privilege of Telecom Eireann, (the dominant operator in majority state ownership) and are due to be fully liberalized on 1 January 2000, in line with the derogation granted to Ireland by the European Commission. An independent regulator for the sector—the Office of the Director of Telecommunications Regulation—was established in June 1997.

Telecom Eireann—Operational Information. The dominant operator in the telecommunications sector is Telecom Eireann, a statutory body set up under the Postal and Telecommunications Services Act, 1983. In 1996 20% of the State's holding was sold to KPN/Telia, a Dutch-Swedish consortium.

Number of working lines (April 1997), 1·39m; data lines, 24,600; Eircell (mobile telephone network), 314,000 customers approx. (Dec. 1997). Number of telex lines, 2,000 customers approx.; Eirpac (public packet-switched network), 2,500 customers approx.; Eirpage (radio paging network), customer base 40,175 (October 1997).

Other Telecommunications Operators. In addition to Telecom Eireann, 47 other companies are licensed to provide telecommunications services other than voice telephony. In the mobile phone market there is a second GSM operator, Esat Digifone (90,000 customers), and applications have been sought for the provision of a third mobile phone service, to be operational in 1998.

Postal services are provided by An Post, a statutory body established under the Postal and Telecommunications Services Act, 1983. Number of Post Offices as of 31 Dec. 1996, 1,921; delivery points, 1,261,000. Number of items delivered in the year ended 31 Dec. 1996, 578·0m. An Post also offers a range of services to the business community through a dedicated unit, Special Delivery Services, subsidiaries PostGEM, Printpost and Precision Marketing Information. A range of services are provided through the Post Office network including Savings and Investments, passport applications, bill payments, National Lottery products and the payment of Social Welfare benefits on an agency basis for the State.

Public service broadcasting is provided by Radio Telefis Éireann (RTÉ), a statutory body established under the Broadcasting Authority Acts 1960–93. RTÉ is financed principally by TV licence and advertising. In 1996 a total of 972,069 TV licences were issued. Legislation enacted in 1988 provided for the establishment of the Independent Radio and Television Commission to arrange provision of independent commercial radio stations and an independent TV service. There were (1996) 21 local commercial radio stations, 10 community radio stations, 2 special interest Irish language radio stations, 1 independent national radio station and 4 hospital radio stations. The IRTC have recently awarded the contract for the first independent TV service which they estimate is due to come on air in Sept. 1988. An Irish-language TV channel, Teilifis na Gaeilge, began broadcasting for 4 hours a day in 1996.

Cinemas. There were 197 screens in 1995.

Press (1997). There are 8 weekday newspapers and 5 Sunday newspapers (all in English) with a combined circulation of 1,310,411 for Jan. to June 1997.

SOCIAL INSTITUTIONS

Justice. The Constitution provides that justice shall be administered in public in Courts established by law by Judges appointed by the President on the advice of the Government. The jurisdiction and organization of the Courts are dealt with in the Courts (Establishment and Constitution) Act, 1961 and the Courts (Supplemental Provisions) Acts, 1961–91. These Courts consist of Courts of First Instance and a Court of Final Appeal, called the Supreme Court. The Courts of First Instance are the High Court with full original jurisdiction and the Circuit and the District Courts with local and limited jurisdictions. A judge may not be removed from office except for stated misbehaviour or incapacity and then only on resolutions passed by both Houses of the Oireachtas. Judges of the Supreme and High Courts are appointed from among practising barristers or serving Circuit Court judges. Judges of the Circuit and District Courts may be appointed from among practising barristers or practising solicitors.

The Supreme Court, which consists of the Chief Justice (who is ex officio an additional judge of the High Court) and 7 ordinary judges, may sit in two Divisions and has appellate jurisdiction from all decisions of the High Court. The President may, after consultation with the Council of State, refer a Bill, which has been passed by both Houses of the Oireachtas (other than a money bill and certain other bills), to the Supreme Court for a decision on the question as to whether such Bill or any provision thereof is repugnant to the Constitution.

The High Court, which consists of a President (who is ex officio an additional Judge of the Supreme Court) and 22 ordinary judges, has full original jurisdiction in and power to determine all matters and questions, whether of law or fact, civil or criminal. In all cases in which questions arise concerning the validity of any law having regard to the provisions of the Constitution, the High Court alone exercises original jurisdiction. The High Court on Circuit acts as an appeal court from the Circuit Court.

The Court of Criminal Appeal consists of the Chief Justice or an ordinary Judge of the Supreme Court, together with either 2 ordinary judges of the High Court or the President and one ordinary judge of the High Court. It deals with appeals by persons convicted on indictment where the appellant obtains a certificate from the trial judge that the case is a fit one for appeal, or, in case such certificate is refused, where the court itself, on appeal from such refusal, grants leave to appeal. The decision of the Court of Criminal Appeal is final, unless that court, the Attorney-General or the Director of Public Prosecutions certifies that the decision involves a point of law of exceptional public importance, in which case an appeal is taken to the Supreme Court.

The Offences against the State Act, 1939 provides in Part V for the establishment of Special Criminal Courts. A Special Criminal Court sits without a jury. The rules of evidence that apply in proceedings before a Special Criminal Court are the same as those applicable in trials in the Central Criminal Court. A Special Criminal Court is authorized by the 1939 Act to make rules governing its own practice and procedure. An appeal against conviction or sentence by a Special Criminal Court may be taken to the Court of Criminal Appeal. On 30 May 1972 Orders were made establishing a Special Criminal Court and declaring that offences of a particular class or kind (as set out) were to be scheduled offences for the purposes of Part V of the Act, the effect of which was to give the Special Criminal Court jurisdiction to try persons charged with those offences.

The High Court exercising criminal jurisdiction is known as the Central Criminal Court. It consists of a judge or judges of the High Court, nominated by the President of the High Court. The Court sits in Dublin and tries criminal cases which are outside the jurisdiction of the Circuit Court.

The Circuit Court consists of a President (who is ex officio an additional judge of the High Court) and 25 ordinary judges. The country is divided into 8 circuits. The jurisdiction of the court in civil proceedings is subject to a financial ceiling, save by consent of the parties, in which event the jurisdiction is unlimited. In criminal matters it has jurisdiction in all cases except murder, treason, piracy, rape, aggravated sexual assault and allied offences. The Circuit Court acts as an appeal court from the District Court.

The District Court, which consists of a President and 48 ordinary judges, has summary jurisdiction in a large number of criminal cases where the offence is not of a serious nature. In civil matters the Court has jurisdiction in contract and tort (except slander, libel, seduction, slander of title and false imprisonment) where the claim does not exceed IR£5,000; in proceedings founded on hire-purchase and credit-sale agreements, the jurisdiction is IR£5,000.

All criminal cases, except those of a minor nature, and those tried in the Special Criminal Court, are tried by a judge and a jury of 12. A majority vote of the jury (10 must agree) is necessary to determine a verdict.

Religion. According to the census of population taken in 1991 the principal religious professions were as follows:

	Leinster	Munster	Connacht	Ulster (part of)	Total
Roman Catholics	1,685,334	941,675	397,848	203,470	3,228,327
Church of Ireland (Anglican)	50,912	15,758	5,321	10,849	82,840
Protestants	3,391	1,385	516	1,055	6,347
Presbyterians	3,799	548	333	8,519	13,199
Methodists	2,815	1,185	286	751	5,037
Jewish	1,439	111	21	10	1,581
Other religious denominations	24,829	9,192	3,208	1,514	38,743
Not stated or no religion	88,430	39,679	15,498	6,038	149,645

Sean Brady (b. 1939) is the Roman Catholic Cardinal of Armagh and Primate of All Ireland.

In May 1990 the General Synod of the Church of Ireland voted to ordain women.

Education. *Elementary.* Elementary education is free and was given in about 3,317 national schools (including 116 special schools) in 1995–96. The total number of pupils on rolls in 1995–96 was 473,506, including pupils in special schools and classes; the number of teachers of all classes was about 21,052 in 1995–96, including remedial teachers and teachers of special classes. The total salaries for teachers for 1995, including superannuation etc., of teachers was IR£601,100,000.

Special. Special provision is made for handicapped and deprived children in special schools which are recognized on the same basis as primary schools, in special classes attached to ordinary schools and in certain voluntary centres where educational services appropriate to the needs of the children are provided. Integration of handicapped children in ordinary schools and classes is encouraged wherever possible, if necessary with special additional supports. There are also part-time teaching facilities in hospitals, child guidance clinics, rehabilitation workshops, special 'Saturday-morning' centres and home teaching schemes. Special schools (1995–96) numbered 116 with approximately 7,652 pupils. There were also some 5,186 pupils enrolled in about 413 special classes, and 1,188 remedial teachers were employed for backward pupils in ordinary national schools. There is a National Education Officer for travelling children.

Secondary. Voluntary secondary schools are under private control and are conducted in most cases by religious orders. These schools receive grants from the State and are open to inspection by the Department of Education. The number of recognized secondary schools during the school year 1996–97 was 434, and the number of pupils in attendance was 220,100.

Vocational Education Committee schools provide courses of general and technical education. The number of vocational schools during the school year 1996–97 was 246, and the number of full-time students in attendance was 95,500. These schools are controlled by the local Vocational Education Committees; they are financed mainly by state grants and also by contributions from local rating authorities and Vocational Education Committee receipts.

Comprehensive and Community Schools. Comprehensive schools which are financed by the State combine academic and technical subjects in one broad curriculum so that each pupil may be offered educational options suited to his needs, abilities and interests. Pupils are prepared for State examinations and for entrance to universities and institutes of further education. The number of comprehensive and community schools during the school year 1996–97 was 80 and the number of students in attendance was 53,500. These schools also provide adult education facilities for their own areas and make facilities available to voluntary organizations and to the adult community generally.

The net non capital State expenditure for second level and further education for 1997 was IR£807,274,000.

Education Third-Level. University education is provided by the National University of Ireland, founded in Dublin in 1908, by the University of Dublin (Trinity College), founded in 1592, and by the Dublin City University and the University of Limerick established in 1989. The National University comprises 4 constituent universities, NUI Dublin, NUI Cork, NUI Galway and NUI Maynooth.

St Patrick's College, Maynooth, Co. Kildare, is a national seminary for Catholic priests and a pontifical university with the power to confer degrees up to doctoral level in philosophy, theology and canon law.

Besides the University medical schools, the Royal College of Surgeons in Ireland (a long-established independent medical school) provides medical qualifications which are internationally recognized. Courses to degree level are available at the National College of Art and Design, Dublin.

Regional Technical Colleges/Institutes of Technology in 12 centres (Athlone,

Carlow, Cork, Dundalk, Dun Laoghaire, Limerick, Tallaght, Galway, Letterkenny, Sligo, Tralee and Waterford) provide vocational and technical education and training for trade and industry from craft to professional level through certificate, diploma and some degree courses. These colleges (with the exception of Dun Laoghaire) were established on a statutory basis on 1 Jan. 1993. Prior to this they operated under the aegis of the Vocational Education Committees (VECs) for their areas. Dun Laoghaire College of Art and Design was designated under the RTC Act 1992, from 1 April 1997. The Dublin Institute of Technology (DIT) was also established on a statutory basis on 1 Jan. 1993. Prior to this it operated under the aegis of City of Dublin VEC. The DIT provides certificate, degree and diploma level courses in engineering, architecture, business studies, catering, music, etc. The Hotel and Catering College in Killybegs continues to operate under the aegis of Co. Donegal VEC.

Total full-time enrolments in the 1996–97 academic year were approximately 39,335.

There are 5 Colleges of Education for training primary school teachers. For degree awarding purposes, 3 of these colleges are associated with Trinity College, 1 with Dublin City University and 1 with The University of Limerick. There are also 2 Home Economics Colleges for teacher training, 1 associated with Trinity College and the other with The National University of Ireland, Galway.

The total full-time enrolment at third-level in institutions aided by the Department of Education and Science in 1995–96 was 95,099. The total current expenditure from public funds on third level education during the financial year ended 31 December 1995 was approximately IR£440,200,000. The National Council for Educational Awards, established on a statutory basis in 1979, is the validating and awarding authority for courses in the third-level sector outside the universities.

Agricultural. Teagasc, the Agriculture and Food Development Authority, is the state agency responsible for providing advisory, training, research and development services for the agriculture and food industries. Full-time instruction in agriculture is provided for all sections of the farming community. There are 4 agricultural colleges, administered by Teagasc, and 7 private Teagasc-aided agricultural colleges. Courses in commercial horticulture are also offered, and short courses for adults already farming.

Coolahan, J., *Irish Education: its History and Structure.* Dublin, 1981

Health Services. Everybody ordinarily resident in Ireland has either full or limited eligibility for the public health services.

(i) A person who satisfies the criteria of a means test receives a medical card which confers Category 1 or full eligibility on them and their dependants. This entitles the holder to the full range of public health and hospital services, free of charge, i.e. family doctor, drugs and medicines, hospital and specialist services as well as dental, aural and optical services. Maternity care and infant welfare services are also provided.

(ii) The remainder of the population have Category 2 or limited eligibility. Category 2 patients receive public consultant and public hospital services subject to certain charges. They are not entitled to free drugs or medicines but receive reimbursement of their drug expenditure in excess of IR£90 in any quarter commencing Jan., April, July and Oct. or a refund of all drug expenditure over IR£32 per month if they suffer from a long term medical condition requiring ongoing medication.

Persons in Category 2 are liable for a hospital in-patient charge of IR£25 per night up to a maximum of IR£250 in any 12 consecutive months (with effect from 1 January 1998). There is no charge for out-patient services. However persons in Category 2 are liable for a charge of IR£12 if they attend the Accident and Emergency Department of a hospital without a letter of referral from a General Practitioner.

The Long Term Illness Scheme entitles persons to free drugs and medicines which are prescribed in respect of sixteen specific illnesses. The needs of individuals with significant or ongoing medical expenses are met by a range of other schemes which provide assistance towards the cost of prescribed drugs and medicines. The *Drug*

Cost Subsidization Scheme caters for people who do not have a medical card or a long term illness book and are certified as having a medical condition with a regular and ongoing requirement for prescribed drugs and medicines. Persons who qualify for inclusion in this scheme will not have to spend more than IR£32 in any month on prescribed medication. Under the *Drugs Refund Scheme* which covers expenditure by the whole family, any expenditure on prescribed medication above IR£90 in a calendar quarter is refunded by the Health Board.

Where an individual or a family is subjected to a significant level of ongoing expenditure on medical expenses, such as general practitioner fees or prescribed drugs due to a long term medical condition, these expenses may be reckoned in determining eligibility for a medical card. Eligibility for a medical card is solely a matter for the Chief Executive Officer of the relevant health board to decide.

Services for Children: Health Boards provide, with the co-operation of a wide range of voluntary organizations, comprehensive child welfare and protection services including adoption, fostering, residential care, day care, social work and family support services.

Welfare Services: There are various services provided for the elderly, the chronic sick, the disabled and families in stress, such as social support service, day care services for children, home helps, home nursing, meals-on-wheels, day centres, cheap fuel, etc. Health Boards also provide disabled persons, without charge, with training for employment and place them in jobs.

Grants and Allowances: The Department of Health and Children provide, through the Health Boards, a wide range of services for people with disabilities. These include day care, therapy services, training, employment, sheltered work, residential as well as transport to and from these services.

Blind welfare allowance—provides a supplementary weekly allowance to recipients of the following allowances from the Department of Social, Community and Family Affairs, Disability Allowance, Blind pension or Old Age Pension.

A grant of up to IR£2,718 is payable, subject to a means test, to disabled persons towards the purchase of a car, in order that they might obtain or retain employment.

Health contributions: A health contribution of 1·25% of income is payable by those with Category 2 eligibility. Employers meet the levy in respect of those employees who have a medical card.

Social Welfare Services (SWS) is the executive arm of the Department of Social, Community and Family Affairs and is responsible for the day to day administration and management of social welfare schemes and services through a network of local, regional and decentralized offices. The Department's local delivery of services is structured on a regional basis. There is a total of 10 regions with offices in Waterford, Cork, Limerick, Galway, Longford, Sligo, Dundalk and three in Dublin.

The Social Welfare Appeals Office (SWAO) is an independent office responsible for determining appeals against decisions on social welfare entitlements.

There are in addition, three statutory agencies under the aegis of the Department:
– *the Combat Poverty Agency* which has responsibilities in the areas of advice to the Minister, research, action programmes and public information in relation to poverty;
– *the Pensions Board* which has the function of promoting the security of occupational pensions, their development and the general issue of pensions coverage;
– *the National Social Service Board* which has the function of ensuring that all citizens have easy access to the highest quality of information, advice and advocacy on social services.

Social Welfare Schemes. The social welfare supports can be divided into three categories:
Social Insurance (Contributory) payments made on the basis of a Pay Related Social Insurance (PRSI) record. Such payments are funded by employers, employees and the self-employed. Any deficit in the fund is met by Exchequer subvention.
Social Assistance (Non Contributory) payments made on the basis of satisfying a means test. These payments are financed entirely by the Exchequer.

Universal services such as Child Benefit or Free Travel which do not depend on PRSI or a means test.

DIPLOMATIC REPRESENTATIVES

Of Ireland in Great Britain (17 Grosvenor Pl., London, SW1X 7HR)
Ambassador: Edward Barrington.

Of Great Britain in Ireland (29 Merrion Rd., Dublin, 4)
Ambassador: Veronica Sutherland, CMG.

Of Ireland in the USA (2234 Massachusetts Ave., NW, Washington, D.C., 20008)
Ambassador: Seán Ó Huiginn.

Of the USA in Ireland (42 Elgin Rd., Ballsbridge, Dublin)
Ambassador: Jean Kennedy Smith (until Aug. 1998; replacement not known at time of going to press).

Of Ireland to the United Nations
Ambassador: John H. Campbell.

Further Reading

Central Statistics Office. *National Income and Expenditure* (annual), *Statistical Abstract* (annual), *Census of Population Reports* (quinquennial), *Census of Industrial Production Reports* (annual), *Trade and Shipping Statistics* (annual and monthly), *Trend of Employment and Unemployment, Reports on Vital Statistics* (annual and quarterly), *Statistical Bulletin* (quarterly), *Labour Force Surveys* (annual), *Trade Statistics* (monthly), *Economic Series* (monthly).

Ardagh, J., *Ireland and the Irish: a Portrait of a Changing Society.* London, 1994
Chubb, B., *Government and Politics in Ireland.* 3rd ed. London, 1992
Collins, N. (ed.), *Political Issues in Ireland Today.* Manchester, Univ. Press, 1994
Eager, A. R., *A Guide to Irish Bibliographical Material.* 2nd ed. London, 1980
Delanty, G. and O'Mahony, P., *Rethinking Irish History, Nationalism, Identity and Ideology.* London, 1997
Encyclopaedia of Ireland. Dublin, 1968
Fitzgerald, G., *All in a Life: an Autobiography.* London, 1991
Foster, R. F., *Modern Ireland 1600–1972.* London, 1988.—(ed.) *The Oxford Illustrated History of Ireland.* OUP, 1991
Garvin, T., *1922 The Birth of Irish Democracy.* Dublin, 1997
Harkness, D., *Ireland in the Twentieth Century: a Divided Island.* London, 1995
Hickey, D. J. and Doherty, J. E., *A Dictionary of Irish History since 1800.* Dublin, 1980
Hussey, G., *Ireland Today: Anatomy of a Changing State.* Dublin, 1993
Institute of Public Administration, *Ireland: a Directory.* Dublin, annual
Kostick, C., *Revolution in Ireland – Popular Militancy 1917-1923.* London, 1997
Lee, J. J., *Ireland 1912-1985: Politics and Society.* CUP, 1989
Munck, R., *The Irish Economy: Results and Prospects.* London, 1993
A New History of Ireland. 6 vols. Oxford, 1996
O'Beirne Ranelagh, J., *A Short History of Ireland.* 2nd ed. CUP, 1994
O'Hagan, J. W. (ed.) *The Economy of Ireland: Policy and Performance of a Small European Country.* London, 1995
Shannon, M. O., *Irish Republic.* [Bibliography] Oxford and Santa Barbara (CA), 1986
Vaughan, W. E. (ed.), *A New History of Ireland,* 6 vols. Oxford, 1997
Wiles, J. L. and Finnegan, R. B., *Aspirations and Realities: a Documentary History of Economic Development Policy in Ireland since 1922.* London, 1992.

A more specialized title is listed under EDUCATION, *above.*

National statistical office: Central Statistics Office, Skehard Road, Cork. *Director-General:* Donal Murphy, M.Sc., M.Econ.Sc., M.Sc.(Mgt).
Website: http://www.cso.ie/

ISRAEL

Medinat Israel

(State of Israel)

Capital: Jerusalem
Population: 5·53m.
GDP per head: (PPP$) 16,023
HDI/world rank: 0·913/23

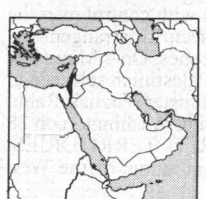

KEY HISTORICAL EVENTS. The area once designated as Palestine, of which Israel forms part, was formerly part of Turkey's Ottoman Empire. During the First World War, when Turkey was allied with Germany, the Arabs under Ottoman rule rebelled and Palestine was occupied by British forces. In 1917 the British Government issued the Balfour Declaration, stating that it viewed 'with favour the establishment in Palestine of a national home for the Jewish people'. In 1922 the League of Nations recognized 'the historical connection of the Jewish people with Palestine' and 'the grounds for reconstituting their national home in that country,' and Britain assumed a mandate over Palestine, pending the establishment there of such a national home. In accord-ance with the mandate, Jewish settlers were admitted to Palestine, under the direction of Zionist settlement agencies, where the population had remained almost entirely Arab. There were anti-Zionist riots in 1921 and 1929. In the 1930s the Nazi persecution of the Jews led to escalated immigration into Palestine.

In Nov. 1947 the UN General Assembly passed a resolution calling for the establishment of a Jewish and an Arab state in Palestine. On 14 May 1948 the British Government terminated its mandate, and the Jewish leaders proclaimed the State of Israel. No independent Arab state was established in Palestine. Instead the neighbouring Arab states invaded the new Israel on 15 May 1948. The Jewish state defended itself successfully, and the ceasefire in Jan. 1949 left Israel with one-third more land than had been originally assigned by the UN. The Suez crisis of 1956 saw Israel joined with Britain and France in a tripartite attack on Egypt in an effort to topple Nasser's regime which they each regarded as inimical to their own interests in the region.

In 1967, following some years of uneasy peace, local clashes on the Israeli–Syrian border were followed by Egyptian mass concentration of forces on the borders of Israel. The UN emergency force in Gaza was expelled and a blockade of shipping to and from Israel was imposed by Egypt in the Red Sea. Israel struck out at Egypt on land and in the air on 5–9 June 1967. Jordan joined in the conflict which spread to the Syrian borders. By 11 June the Israelis had occupied the Gaza Strip and the Sinai peninsula as far as the Suez Canal in Egypt, West Jordan as far as the Jordan valley and the heights east of the Sea of Galilee, including Quneitra in Syria.

A further war broke out on 6 Oct. 1973 when Egyptian and Syrian offensives were launched. Following UN Security Council resolutions a ceasefire finally came into being on 24 Oct. In Dec. Egypt and Israel signed a disengagement agreement; as did Israel and Syria on 31 May 1974. A further disengagement agreement was signed between Israel and Egypt in Sept. 1975.

Developments in 1977 included President Sadat of Egypt's visit to Israel and peace initiative and in March 1978 Israeli troops entered southern Lebanon but later withdrew after the arrival of a UN peace-keeping force. In Sept. 1978 US President Carter convened the Camp David conference at which Egypt and Israel agreed on frameworks for peace in the Middle East with treaties to be negotiated between Israel and her neighbours. Negotiations began in the USA between Egypt and Israel in Oct. 1978 and a treaty was signed in Washington on 26 March 1979. Under this treaty Israel withdrew from the Sinai Desert in two phases; part was achieved on 26 Jan. 1980 and the final withdrawal by 26 April 1982.

In June 1982 Israeli forces once again invaded the Lebanon, this time in massive strength, and swept through the country, laying siege to and devastatingly bombing Beirut. On 16 Feb. 1985 the Israeli forces stared a complete withdrawal, leaving behind an Israeli trained and equipped Christian Lebanese force to act as a control over and buffer against Moslem Shi'a or Palestinian guerrilla attacks.

In 1993 following declarations by Prime Minister, Yitzhak Rabin, recognizing the Palestine Liberation Organization (PLO) as representative of the Palestinian people, and Yasser Arafat, leader of the PLO, renouncing terrorism and recognizing the State of Israel, an agreement was signed in Washington providing for limited Palestinian self-rule in the Gaza Strip and Jericho. A further agreement, signed by the Foreign Minister, Shimon Peres, and Yasser Arafat on 9 Feb. 1994 dealt with control over the Egypt–Gaza Strip and Jericho–Jordan border crossings, and security arrangements for Jewish settlers in Gaza which would divide the strip into 3 zones. On 4 May 1994 in Cairo an Israeli–Palestinian agreement on the first phase of Palestinian self-rule in the Gaza Strip and Jericho was signed by the Israeli Prime Minister Yitzhak Rabin and Yasser Arafat. An Israeli–Palestinian agreement was signed in Washington on 28 Sept. 1995. (For details *see* PALESTINIAN-ADMINISTERED TERRITORIES: Key Historical Events, *below*). Negotiations on the permanent status of the West Bank and Gaza began in 1996.

On 4 Nov. 1995 the Prime Minister, Yitzhak Rabin, was assassinated by a Jewish religious extremist. In the subsequent election, a right wing coalition led by Binyamin Netanyahu took office. Peace talks with the Palestinians then stalled, partly as a result of Palestinian terrorism but also because it became clear that Israel balked at the basic conditions for a settlement. In Feb. 1998 plans were announced to construct a new Jewish settlement in East Jerusalem, a move which Palestinians said could kill the peace progress.

TERRITORY AND POPULATION. The area of Israel, including the Golan Heights (1,150 sq. km) and East Jerusalem (70 sq. km), is 21,946 sq. km (8,473 sq. miles), with a population estimated in 1997 to be 5·53m., including East Jerusalem, the Golan Heights and Israeli settlers in the occupied territories.

Crude birth rate per 1,000 population of Jewish population (1995), 18·1; non-Jewish: Moslems, 37·9; (1994): Christians, 18·7; Druzes, 29·2. Crude death rate (1994), Jewish, 6·9; non-Jewish: Moslems, 3; Christians, 4·3; Druzes, 3·2. Infant mortality rate per 1,000 live births (1995), Jewish, 6·3; non-Jewish: Moslems, 13; (1994): Christians, 10·4; Druzes, 8·7. Life expectancy (1997), 78·2 (males, 76·3 years; females, 80·2). Average population growth rate, 1983–93, 2·6%. Growth rate in 1997 was estimated to be 2·0%.

Immigration. The following table shows the numbers of Jewish immigrants entering Palestine/Israel.

1990	199,516	1992	77,057	1994	79,844
1991	176,100	1993	76,805	1995	76,361

Population by place of origin as of 1995: Europe and America, 1·8m.; former USSR, 0·66m.; Morocco, 0·5m.; Poland, 0·25m.; Romania, 0·25m.; Iraq, 0·25m.; Yemen, 0·15m.; Iran, 0·13m.; Algeria and Tunisia, 0·12m.

The Jewish Agency, which, in accordance with Article IV of the Palestine Mandate played a leading role in establishing the State of Israel, continues to organize immigration.

Israel is administratively divided into 6 districts:

District	Area (sq. km)	Population[1]	Chief town
Northern	4,501	952,100	Nazareth
Haifa	854	740,300	Haifa
Central	1,242	1,213,200	Ramla
Tel Aviv	170	1,141,900	Tel Aviv
Jerusalem[2]	627	662,700	Jerusalem
Southern	14,107	770,200	Beersheba

[1] 31 Dec. 1995. [2] Includes East Jerusalem.

On 23 Jan. 1950 the Knesset proclaimed Jerusalem the capital of the State and on 14 Dec. 1981 extended Israeli law into the Golan Heights. Population of the main towns (1995): Jerusalem, 591,400; Tel Aviv/Jaffa, 355,900; Haifa, 252,300; Holon, 163,900; Petach Tikva, 153,100; Bat Yam, 142,300; Rishon le-Ziyyon, 165,300; Netanya, 148,400; Beersheba, 152,600; Ramat Gan, 121,700; Bene Berak, 128,600.

The official languages are Hebrew and Arabic.

CLIMATE. From April to Oct., the summers are long and hot, and almost rainless. From Nov. to March, the weather is generally mild, though colder in hilly areas, and this is the wet season. Jerusalem. Jan. 12·8°C, July 28·9°C. Annual rainfall, 657 mm. Tel Aviv. Jan. 17·2°C, July 30·2°C. Annual rainfall, 803 mm.

CONSTITUTION AND GOVERNMENT. Israel is an independent sovereign republic, established by proclamation on 14 May 1948.

In 1950 the Knesset (*Parliament*), which in 1949 had passed the Transition Law dealing in general terms with the powers of the Knesset, President and Cabinet, resolved to enact from time to time fundamental laws, which eventually, taken together, would form the Constitution. The 9 fundamental laws that have been passed: The Knesset (1958), Israel Lands (1960), the President (1964), the Government (1968), the State Economy (1975), the Army (1976), Jerusalem, capital of Israel (1980), the Judicature (1984) and the Electoral System (1996).

The *President* (head of state) is elected by the Knesset by secret ballot by a simple majority; his term of office is 5 years. He may be re-elected once.

The Knesset, a one-chamber Parliament, consists of 120 members. It is elected for a 4-year term by secret ballot and universal direct suffrage. Under the system of election introduced in 1996, electors vote once for a party and once for a candidate for Prime Minister. To be elected Prime Minister, a candidate must gain more than half the votes cast, and be elected to the Knesset. If there are more than 2 candidates and none gain half the vote, a second round is held 15 days later. The Prime Minister forms a cabinet (no fewer than 8 members and no more than 18) with the approval of the Knesset.

At the elections of 29 May 1996, 20 parties put up candidates. Binyamin Netanyahu (Likud) was elected Prime Minister against 1 opponent by 50·4% of votes cast. Labour gained 34 seats (44 in 1992); Likud-Tsomet-Gesher (L), 32 (Likud alone, 32); Shas (Oriental Religious Jews), 10 (6); Meretz, 9 (12); National Religious Party (NRP), 9 (6); Yisrael ba-Aliyah, 7; Hadash, 5 (2); Third Way, 4; United Torah-Jewry, 4 (4); United Arab List, 4; Moledet, 2 (3).

President: Ezer Weizman (b. 1924; elected 24 March 1993, sworn in 13 May 1993).

Following the elections of May 1996 a Likud-led coalition government was formed in June. In March 1998 the government comprised:

Prime Minister, Minister of Foreign Affairs, Minister of Housing and Construction: Binyamin Netanyahu (b. 1940; L).

Deputy Prime Minister, Minister of Agriculture and the Environment: Rafael Eitan (Tsomet). *Deputy Prime Minister, Minister of Tourism:* Moshe Katsav (L). *Defence:* Yitzhak Mordechai (L). *Finance:* Yaakov Neeman (no affiliation). *Justice:* Tzachi Hanegbi (L). *Internal Security:* Avigdor Kahalani (Third Way). *Labour and Social Affairs:* Ellyahu Yishai (Shas). *Interior:* Eli Suissa (Shas). *Transport:* Shaul Yahalom (NRP). *Infrastructure:* Ariel Sharon (L). *Trade and Industry:* Natan Sharansky (Israel with Immigration). *Immigrant Absorption:* Yuli Edelstein (Israel with Immigration). *Communications:* Limor Livnat (L). *Health:* Yehoshua Matza (L). *Education and Culture, Religious Affairs:* Yitzhak Levi (NRP). *Science and Technology:* Michael Eitan (L).

National anthem: Hatikvah (The Hope); words by N. H. Imber.

Local Government. In 1995 there were 57 municipalities (5 Arab), 138 local councils (66 Arab or Druze) and 78 regional councils. Regional councils are local authorities set up in agricultural areas and include all the agricultural settlements in the area under their jurisdiction. All local authorities exercise their authority mainly by means of bye-laws approved by the Minister of the Interior. Their revenue is derived from rates and a surcharge on income tax. Local authorities are elected for a 4-year term. Elections were held for 158 municipal councils in Nov. 1993. The electorate was 3·3m.; turn-out was 36%.

Sayer, S., *The Parliamentary System of Israel.* Syracuse Univ. Press, 1986

DEFENCE. Conscription (for Jews and Druze only) is 3 years (usually 4 years for officers; 2 years for women).

The Israel Defence Force is a unified force, in which army, navy and air force are subordinate to a single chief-of-staff. The Minister of Defence is *de facto* C.-in-C. The cabinet usually forms a defence committee with authority to make decisions on military operations. In 1996 government expenditure on defence totalled 26,489m. shekels.

Army. The Army is organized in 3 territorial and 1 home front command, and has 3 corps headquarters, 2 divisional headquarters, 3 armoured divisions, 3 regional infantry divisions, 4 mechanized infantry brigades and 3 artillery battalions. The Reserves are organized in 9 armoured divisions, 1 mechanized (air mobile) division, 10 regional infantry and 4 artillery brigades. Equipment includes 1,080 Centurion, 325 M-48A5, 400 M-60, 600 M-60A1, 200 M-60A3, 150 Magach 7, 300 T-54/-55, 110 T-62 and 930 Merkava main battle tanks. Strength (1997) 134,000 (conscripts 114,700). There are also 430,000 reservists available on mobilization.

Navy. The Navy, tasked primarily for coastal protection and based at Haifa, Ashdod and Eilat, includes 3 small diesel submarines, 3 well-armed Sa'aR-5 corvettes of 1,200 tonnes, 22 missile craft of the smaller evolving Sa'aR types, from 250 to 500 tonnes, 40 fast inshore patrol craft, 1 tank landing ship, 4 amphibious craft and a few minor auxiliaries. The first of 3 new German-built diesel submarines commences sea trials in 1996.

Naval personnel in 1997 totalled 9,000 including a Naval Commando of 300, of whom 3,000 are conscripts. There are also 10,000 naval reservists available on mobilization.

Air Force. The Air Force (including air defence) has a personnel strength (1997) of 32,000 (21,800 conscripts), with about 600 first-line aircraft, all jets, of Israeli and US manufacture. There are 4 squadrons with about 70 F-15s, and 8 squadrons with 240 F-16s in an interceptor role; 3 squadrons with 80 F-4E Phantoms, supported by 4 Boeing 707 airborne early warning and control aircraft, RC-12 electronic intelligence aircraft. There are transport squadrons of turboprop C-130/KC-130 Hercules, C-47, Arava, Islander, and Boeing 707 (some equipped for tanker duties) aircraft, helicopter squadrons of UH-60 Black Hawk, CH-53, AH-64A Apache, AH-1 Huey-Cobra, JetRanger, Agusta-Bell 205, 206 and 212 aircraft, SOCATA Trinidad and DO-28 communications aircraft and training units with locally-built Magister jet trainers, which can be used also in a light ground attack role. Missiles in service include surface-to-air Hawks and surface-to-surface Lances.

INTERNATIONAL RELATIONS. A 46-year old formal state of hostilities with Jordan was brought to an end by a peace agreement on 26 Oct. 1994.

Membership. Israel is a member of the UN.

ECONOMY

Policy. 30 to 40 of some 150 state-owned companies are scheduled for privatization under a scaled-down programme of 1991. Over 1986–95, the proceeds of privatization totalled US$2,000m. (target, US$5,000m.). In 1996, the Prime Minister inaugurated an acceleration of the privatization process, and took over privatization powers from the Ministry of Finance. Efforts to generate some 0·5m. jobs are being made to cope with the influx of Soviet immigrants.

Performance. Real GDP growth was 4·6% in 1996.

Budget. The budget year runs from 1 Jan to 31 Dec. beginning with 1992. (Previously it ran from 1 April to 31 March).

Budget revenue and expenditure (in 1m. shekels):

	1992	1993	1994	1995	1996[1]
Revenue:	58,994	68,457	82,515	95,489	108,701
Expenditure:	68,094	74,232	87,016	102,311	121,471

[1] Provisional

Currency. The unit of currency is the *shekel* (ILS) of 100 *agorot*. There are coins of 5 and 50 agorot and 1, 5 and 10 shekels, and notes of 10, 20, 50, 100 and 200 shekels.

Foreign exchange reserves were US$6,500m. in July 1996. Inflation in 1997 was 7% (10·6% in 1996).

Banking and Finance. The Bank of Israel was established by law in 1954 as Israel's central bank. Its *Governor* is appointed by the President on the recommendation of the Cabinet for a 5-year term. He acts as economic adviser to the Government and has ministerial status. The *Governor* is Jacob Frenkel. There are 26 commercial banks headed by Bank Leumi Le Israel, Bank Hapoalim and Israel Discount Bank, 2 merchant banks, 1 foreign bank, 15 mortgage banks and 9 lending institutions specifically set up to aid industry and agriculture. The government holds a majority stake in the 4 largest banks, but these are now (1997) in process of privatization.

There is a stock exchange in Tel Aviv.

Weights and Measures. The metric system is in general use. The (metrical) *dunam* = 1,000 sq. metres (about 0·25 acre).

Jewish Year. The Jewish year 5758 corresponds to 2 Oct. 1997–20 Sept. 1998; 5759 to 21 Sept. 1998–10 Sept. 1999; 5760 to 11 Sept. 1999–29 Sept. 2000.

ENERGY AND NATURAL RESOURCES

Electricity. Electric-power production amounted during 1995 to 30,425m. kWh.

Oil and Gas. The only significant hydrocarbon is oil shale.

Water. In the northern Negev farming has been aided by the Yarkon–Negev water pipeline. This has become part of the overall project of the 'National Water Carrier', which is to take water from the Sea of Galilee (Lake Kinnereth) to the south. The plan includes a number of regional projects such as the Lake Kinnereth–Negev pipeline which came into operation in 1964; it has an annual capacity of 320m. cu. metres.

Minerals. The most valuable natural resources are the potash, bromine and other salt deposits of the Dead Sea. Potash production in 1995 was 2,214,000 tonnes.

Agriculture. In the coastal plain mixed farming, poultry raising, citriculture and vineyards are the main agricultural activities. The Emek (the Valley of Jezreel) is the main agricultural centre of Israel. Mixed farming is to be found throughout the valleys; the sub-tropical Beisan and Jordan plainlands are also centres of banana plantations and fish breeding. In Galilee mixed farming, olive and tobacco plantations prevail. The Hills of Ephraim are a vineyard centre; many parts of the hill country are under afforestation.

The area under cultivation (in 1,000 dunams) in 1994 was 4,344, of which 1,930 were under irrigation. Of the total cultivated area (1994) 2,129 dunams were under field crops, 550 under vegetables, potatoes, pumpkins and melons, 830 under citrus and plantations, 32 under fish ponds and the rest under miscellaneous crops. Production, 1995 (in 1,000 tonnes): Wheat, 242; barley, 7·2; maize grain, 2·5; potatoes, 281; melons, 79·4; tomatoes, 503·7; citrus fruit, 942·3; grapefruit, 404·4; cotton, 42·8.

Livestock (1993) included 357,000 cattle, 0·33m. sheep, 1m. goats, 27m. poultry.

Types of rural settlement: (1) The *Kibbutz* and *Kvutza* (communal collective settlement), where all property and earnings are collectively owned and work is collectively organized. (124,600 people lived in 269 *Kibbutzim* in 1995). (2) The *Moshav* (workers' co-operative smallholders' settlement) which is founded on the principles of mutual aid and equality of opportunity between the members, all farms being equal in size. (160,000 in 411). (3) The *Moshav Shitufi* (co-operative settlement), which is based on collective ownership and economy as in the *Kibbutz*, but with each family having its own house and being responsible for its own domestic services. (13,100 in 43). (4) Other rural settlements in which land and property are privately owned and every resident is responsible for his own well-being. In 1996 there were 233 villages with a population of 141,500.

INDUSTRY. Products include chemicals, metal products, textiles, tyres, diamonds, paper, plastics, leather goods, glass and ceramics, building materials, precision instruments, tobacco, foodstuffs, electrical and electronic equipment.

Labour. The workforce was 2·2m. in 1996. A 'social-economic pact' between government, employers and trade unions in May 1991 aimed to create some 32,000 new jobs to lessen the impact of increased immigration. Unemployment was 7·2% of the workforce in July 1996.

Trade Unions. The General Federation of Labour (Histadrut) founded in 1920, had, in 1987, 1·6m. members (including 0·17m. Arab and Druze members); including workers' families, this membership represents 71·5% of the population covering 87% of all wage-earners. Several trades unions also exist representing other political and religious groups.

FOREIGN ECONOMIC RELATIONS. Total foreign debt amounted to US$34,000m. in July 1996.

Commerce. External trade, in US$1m., for calendar years:

	1991	1992	1993	1994	1995	1996
Imports	16,688	18,007	20,209	23,369	27,982	28,300[1]
Exports	11,219	12,444	14,083	16,051	17,897	20,300[1]

[1] Estimates

The main exportable commodities are citrus fruit and by-products, fruit-juices, flowers, wines and liquor, sweets, polished diamonds, chemicals, tyres, textiles, metal products, machinery, electronic and transportation equipment. The main exports were, in 1995 (US$1m.): Diamonds, 4,921·6; chemicals and chemical products, 2,369·7; agricultural products including citrus fruit, 740·5; machinery and equipment, 958·9. Of exports in 1995, US$6,529·8m. went to EU and EFTA countries and US$5,735·9m. to USA. In 1995 the main export markets were: USA, 30·1%; UK, 6·1%; Germany, 5·5%; Belgium, 5·4%. Main import suppliers: USA, 18·6%; Belgium, 12·1%; Germany, 9·7%; UK, 8·3%.

Tourism. In 1995 there were 2·2m. tourists.

COMMUNICATIONS

Roads. There were 14,700 km of paved roads in 1995. Registered motor vehicles in 1995 totalled 1,459,000, including 10,794 buses, 246,696 trucks and 1,112,281 private cars.

Railways. There were 526 km of standard gauge line in 1995. In 1995, 4·3m. passengers and 9·4m. tonnes of freight were carried.

Civil Aviation. There are international airports at Tel Aviv (Ben Gurion) and Eilat. In 1995, 23,952 planes landed at Israeli airports on international flights; 3,434,200 passengers arrived, 3,367,300 departed. In 1995, 142,515 tons of freight were loaded and 113,785 tons unloaded. In 1995 the state-owned airline El Al operated 1 B-747-100, 4 B-747-200Bs, 3 B-747-200Cs, 2 B-747-200Fs, 3 B-747-400s, 2 B-757-200s, 4 B-757-200ERs, 2 B-767-200s and 3 B-767-200ERs. Services are also provided by the Israeli airline Arkia, which flew 16 aircraft in 1995, and by Aeroflot, Air Canada, Air France, Air Malta, Air Moldova, Air Ukraine, Alitalia, Austrian Airlines, Azerbaijan Hava Yollary, Balkan, Belavia, British Airways, Cyprus Airways, Czech Airlines, Iberia, JAT, Kazakhstan Airlines, KLM, Korean Air, LOT, Lufthansa, Malév, Olympic Airways, Orbi Airways, SAA, SAS, Sabena, Swissair, TAP, Tarom, Tower Air, Trans World, Turkish Airlines, Uzbekistan Airways and World Airways.

Shipping. Israel has 3 commercial ports, Haifa, Ashdod and Eilat. In 1995, 6,145 ships departed from Israeli ports; 38m. tons of freight were handled. The merchant fleet consisted in 1995 of 65 vessels, totalling 1·5m. GRT.

Telecommunications. The Ministry of Communications supervises the postal service, and a public company responsible to the Ministry administers the telecommunications service. In 1995 there were 662 post offices and postal agencies, 48 mobile post offices and 2·3m. direct telephone lines.

Television and the state radio station, Kol Israel (Voice of Israel), are controlled by the Israel Broadcasting Authority. There is a national programme, 2 commercial programmes, a music programme and a service in Arabic. In 1995 there were 2·7m. radio and 1·6m. TV sets (colour by PAL).

Cinemas. There were 266 screens in 1994; attendances totalled 10·0m.

Press (1992). There were 31 daily newspapers.

SOCIAL INSTITUTIONS

Justice. *Law.* Under the Law and Administration Ordinance, 5708/1948, the first law passed by the Provisional Council of State, the law of Israel is the law which was obtaining in Palestine on 14 May 1948 in so far as it is not in conflict with that Ordinance or any other law passed by the Israel legislature and with such modifications as result from the establishment of the State and its authorities.

Capital punishment was abolished in 1954, except for support given to the Nazis and for high treason.

The law of Palestine was derived from Ottoman law, English law (Common Law and Equity) and the law enacted by the Palestine legislature, which to a great extent was modelled on English law.

Civil Courts. Municipal courts, established in certain municipal areas, have criminal jurisdiction over offences against municipal regulations and bye-laws and certain specified offences committed within a municipal area. Magistrates courts, established in each district and sub-district, have limited jurisdiction in both civil and criminal matters. District courts, sitting at Jerusalem, Tel Aviv and Haifa, have jurisdiction, as courts of first instance, in all civil matters not within the jurisdiction of magistrates courts, and in all criminal matters, and as appellate courts from magistrates courts and municipal courts. The 14-member Supreme Court has jurisdiction as a court of first instance (sitting as a High Court of Justice dealing mainly with administrative matters) and as an appellate court from the district courts (sitting as a Court of Civil or of Criminal Appeal).

In addition, there are various tribunals for special classes of cases. Settlement Officers deal with disputes with regard to the ownership or possession of land in settlement areas constituted under the Land (Settlement of Title) Ordinance.

Religious Courts. The rabbinical courts of the Jewish community have exclusive jurisdiction in matters of marriage and divorce, alimony and confirmation of wills of members of their community and concurrent jurisdiction with the civil courts in all other matters of personal status of all members of their community with the consent of all parties to the action.

The courts of the several recognized Christian communities have a similar jurisdiction over members of their respective communities.

The Moslem religious courts have exclusive jurisdiction in all matters of personal status over Moslems who are not foreigners, and over Moslems who are foreigners, if under the law of their nationality they are subject in such matters to the jurisdiction of Moslem religious courts.

Where any action of personal status involves persons of different religious communities, the President of the Supreme Court will decide which court shall have jurisdiction, and whenever a question arises as to whether or not a case is one of personal status within the exclusive jurisdiction of a religious court, the matter must be referred to a special tribunal composed of 2 judges of the Supreme Court and the president of the highest court of the religious community concerned in Israel.

In 1996 government expenditure on public order and safety totalled 4,481m. shekels.

Religion. Religious affairs are under the supervision of a special Ministry, with departments for the Christian and Moslem communities. The religious affairs of each community remain under the full control of the ecclesiastical authorities concerned: in the case of the Jews, the Sephardi and Ashkenazi Chief Rabbis, in the case of the Christians, the heads of the various communities, and in the case of the Moslems, the

Qadis. The Druze were officially recognized in 1957 as an autonomous religious community.

In 1995 there were: Jews, 4,549,500; Moslems, 813,000; Christians, 162,600; Druze, 94,000.

The Chief Rabbi is Israel Meir Lau.

Education. The adult literacy rate in 1992 was 95% (male, 97%; female, 93%). There is free and compulsory education from 5 to 16 years and optional free education until 18. There is a unified state-controlled elementary school system with a provision for special religious schools. The standard curriculum for all elementary schools is issued by the Ministry with a possibility of adding supplementary subjects comprising not more than 25% of the total syllabus. Most schools in towns are maintained by municipalities, a number are private and some are administered by teachers' co-operatives or trustees.

Statistics relating to schools under government supervision, 1995–96:

Type of School[1]	Schools	Teachers	Pupils
Hebrew Education			
Primary schools	1,365	42,946	528,429
Schools for handicapped children	203	5,276	12,392
Schools of intermediate division	371	19,945	150,804
Secondary schools	621	⎫	240,990
Vocational schools	313	⎬ 31,803	102,716
Agricultural schools	23	⎭	6,513
Arab Education			
Primary schools	326	8,802	150,083
Schools for handicapped children	43	549	2,461
Schools of intermediate division	104	3,828	44,984
Secondary schools	101	⎫	43,510
Vocational schools	62	⎬ 3,543	12,765
Agricultural schools	2	⎭	621

[1] Schools providing more than one type of education are included more than once.

There are also a number of private schools maintained by religious foundations—Jewish, Christian and Moslem—and also by private societies.

The Hebrew University of Jerusalem, founded in 1925, comprises faculties of the humanities, social sciences, law, science, medicine and agriculture. In 1995–96 it had 20,290 students. The Technion in Haifa had 10,370 students. The Weizmann Institute of Science in Rehovoth, founded in 1949, had 760 students.

Tel Aviv University had 26,100 students. The religious Bar-Ilan University at Ramat Gan, opened in 1965, had 19,110 students. The Haifa University had 12,820 students. The Ben Gurion University had 12,250 students.

In 1996 government expenditure on education totalled 20,630m. shekels.

Health. In 1995 there were 259 hospitals with 33,159 beds and (1990) 9,500 doctors. In 1996 government expenditure on health totalled 15,052m. shekels.

Social Welfare. The National Insurance Law of 1954 provides for old-age pensions, survivors' insurance, work-injury insurance, maternity insurance, family allowances and unemployment benefits. In 1996 government expenditure on social security and welfare totalled 38,082m. shekels.

DIPLOMATIC REPRESENTATIVES

Of Israel in Great Britain (2 Palace Green, London, W8 4QB)
Ambassador: Moshe Raviv.

Of Great Britain in Israel (192 Hayarkon St., Tel Aviv 63405)
Ambassador: David G. Manning, CMG.

Of Israel in the USA (3514 International Dr., NW, Washington, D.C., 20008)
Ambassador: Eliahu Ben Elissar.

Of the USA in Israel (71 Hayarkon St., Tel Aviv)
Ambassador: Vacant.

Of Israel to the UN
Ambassador: Dore Gold.

Of Israel to the European Union
Ambassador: Efraïm Halevy.

Further Reading

Central Bureau of Statistics. *Statistical Abstract of Israel.* (Annual).—*Statistical Bulletin of Israel.* (Monthly).
Atlas of Israel. 3rd ed. 1985
Aharoni, Y., *The Israeli Economy: the Dreams and Realities.* London, 1991
Ben-Gurion, D., *Ben-Gurion Looks Back.* London, 1965.—*The Jews in Their Land.* London, 1966.—*Israel: A Personal History.* New York, 1971
Beitlin, Y., *Israel: a Concise History.* London, 1992
Bleaney, C. H., *Israel* [Bibliography]. 2nd ed. Oxford and Santa Barbara (CA), 1994
Freedman, R. (ed.) *Israel under Rabin.* Boulder (CO), 1995
Garfinkle, A., *Politics and Society in Modern Israel: Myths and Realities.* Armonk (NY), 1997
Gilbert, Martin, *Israel: A History.* New York, 1998
Harkabi, Y., *Israel's Fateful Decisions.* London, 1989
Louis, W. R. and Stookey, R. W., *The End of the Palestine Mandate.* London, 1986
Peres, S., *Battling for Peace: Memoirs.* London and New York, 1995
Reich, B., *Israel: Land of Tradition and Conflict.* London, 1986.— and Kieval (eds.) *Israeli Politics in the 1990s: Key Domestic and Foreign Policy Factors.* London, 1991
Sachar, H. M., *A History of Israel.* 2 vols. OUP, 1976–87
Segev, T., *1949: The First Israelis.* New York, 1986
Sharkansky, I., *The Political Economy of Israel.* Oxford and Santa Barbara (CA), 1986

Other more specialized titles are entered under PALESTINIAN-ADMINISTERED TERRITORIES *and* CONSTITUTION AND GOVERNMENT, *above.*

National statistical office: Central Bureau of Statistics, Prime Minister's Office, POB 13015, Jerusalem 91130. *Website:* http://www.cbs.gov.il/
National library: The Jewish National and University Library, Jerusalem.

PALESTINIAN-ADMINISTERED TERRITORIES

Key Historical Events. Under the Israeli–Palestinian agreement of 28 Sept. 1995 the Israeli army redeployed from 6 of the 7 of the largest Palestinian towns in the West Bank and from 460 smaller towns and villages. Following this in April 1996 an 82-member *Palestinian Council* was elected and also a head (*Rais*) of the executive authority of the Council. The rest of the West Bank stayed under Israeli army control with some progressive redeployments at 6-month intervals, although Palestinian civil affairs here too were administered by the Palestinian Council. Negotiations on the permanent status of the West Bank and Gaza began in May 1996. Issues reserved for these included the position of 0·14m. Israelis in 144 settlements, the status of Jerusalem, military locations and water supplies.

Following the opening of an archaeological tunnel in Jerusalem, armed clashes broke out at the end of Sept. 1996 between demonstrators and Palestinian police on the one hand and Israeli troops. On 18 Nov. 1996 the Israeli Minister of Defence approved plans for an expansion of Jewish settlement in the West Bank. Under an agreement brokered by King Hussein of Jordan and signed by the Prime Minister of Israel and the President of the Palestinian Authority on 15 Jan. 1997 Israeli troop withdrawals from 80% of Hebron and all rural areas of the West Bank were scheduled to take place in 3 phases between 28 Feb. 1996 and 31 Aug. 1998.

The Israeli decision in Feb. 1997 to continue to promote Jewish settlement in the Jerusalem suburb of Har Homa was perceived by the Palestinian authorities as a hostile move and caused a setback to peace negotiations.

Constitution and Government. In April 1996 the Palestinian Council removed from its Charter all clauses contrary to its recognition by Israel, including references to armed struggle as the only means of liberating Palestine, and the elimination of Zionism from Palestine. The *President* is directly elected and heads the executive organ, the Palestinian National Authority, one fifth of whose members he appoints, while four fifths are elected by the *Legislative Council*. The latter comprises 88 members and is directly elected by the first-past-the-post system from 16 electoral districts.

Elections for *President* and *Legislative Council* were held on 20 Jan. 1996. The electorate was 1,013,200; turn-out was 84%. 672 candidates stood for the Council. Yasser Arafat was elected *President* against 1 opponent by 88·1% of votes cast, and was sworn in on 12 Feb. 1996.

Following an Israeli–Palestinian agreement on customs duties and VAT in Aug. 1994 the Palestinians set up their own customs and immigration points into Gaza and Jericho. Israel collects customs dues on Palestinian imports through Israeli entry points and transfers these to the Palestinian treasury.

Israeli currency is in use. Banking is regulated by the Palestinian Monetary Authority. *Governor:* Fouad Hamdi.

There is a Palestinian *Council for Reconstruction and Development.*

There is a Palestinian police of some 15,000; they are not empowered to arrest Israelis, but may detain them and hand them over to the Israeli authorities. A securities exchange opened in Nablus in Feb. 1997.

The **West Bank** (preferred Palestinian term, Northern District) has an area of 5,879 sq. km (2,270 sq. miles) and a population (1994) of 1,122,900. 97% of the population in 1988 were Palestinian Arabs of whom some 85% were Moslems, 7·4% Jewish and 8% Christian. In 1995 there was a Palestinian diaspora of 3·3m. In 1994, there were 77,604 private cars and 21,714 commercial vehicles and trucks registered. There were (1988) 183,041 pupils in primary schools and 105,007 in secondary schools, while (1983) there were 7,066 students in higher education. In 1993 there were 17 hospitals and clinics with 1,418 beds.

The **Gaza Strip** (preferred Palestinian term, Gaza District) has an area of 363 sq. km (140 sq. miles) and a population (1993) of 748,400. The chief town is Gaza itself, with (1979) 0·12m. inhabitants. In 1984, over 98% of the population were Arabic-speaking Moslems; the birth rate was 4·8% and the death rate 0·8%. Citrus fruits, wheat and olives are grown, with farm land covering 193 sq. km (1980) and occupying most of the active workforce. In 1993 there were 20,434 private cars and 4,518 commercial vehicles and trucks registered. There were (1988) 112,959 pupils in primary schools and 64,699 in secondary schools, with (1983) 2,387 students in higher education. In 1993 there were 6 hospitals and clinics with 957 beds.

Further Reading

Kimmerling, B. and Migdal J. S., *Palestinians: the Making of a People.* Harvard Univ. Press, 1994

Robinson, G. E., *Building a Palestinian State: the Incomplete Revolution.* Indiana Univ. Press, 1997

Rubin, B., *Revolution until Victory? The Politics and History of the PLO.* Harvard Univ. Press, 1994

Stendel, O., *The Arabs in Israel.* Brighton, 1996

Tessler, M., *A History of the Israeli-Palestinian Conflict.* Indiana Univ. Press, 1994

ITALY

Repubblica Italiana

Capital: Rome
Population: 57·46m.
GDP per head: (PPP$) 19,363
HDI/world rank: 0·921/21

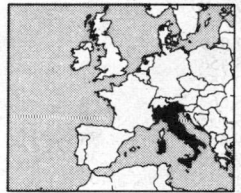

KEY HISTORICAL EVENTS. From 1815 a strong movement grew throughout the Italian states for *risorgimento* (unification) and for independence from Austrian control. Victor Emmanuel II, King of Sardinia-Piedmont from 1849, his prime minister from 1852, Count Cavour, and Giuseppe Garibaldi, an Italian soldier, together achieved success for the movement. The first Italian parliament assembled in Feb. 1861, and on 17 March declared Victor Emmanuel King of Italy.

During the remaining years of the 19th century, Italy acquired an African colonial empire composed of Eritrea, Somaliland and Libya. For her support of the allies in the First World War (1914-18) Italy gained the Trentino and the Istrian peninsula on the North Adriatic.

Fascism spread rapidly after the war and in 1922 Benito Mussolini, leader of the Fascist Party, was appointed prime minister. In 1924 he established himself as dictator with the title *Duce.* His internal policy, with a programme of public works, greater efficiency and better law and order, was successful. In 1929 the Lateran Treaties with the Papacy ended over a century of tension between Church and State. However, his aggressive foreign policy as evinced by the invasion of Ethiopia in 1935 and his alliance with Nazi Germany in 1936 was eventually to lead to his downfall. During the Second World War (1939-45) British forces captured much of Italy's colonial empire, and in 1942 occupied Libya. The allies conquered Sicily and Mussolini was compelled to resign in July 1943. In 1945 he was captured and killed by Italian partisans.

June 1946 saw the end of the reign of the House of Savoy, whose kings had ruled over Piedmont for nine centuries and as Kings of Italy since 1861. The Crown Prince Umberto, son of King Victor Emmanuel III, had become Lieut-Gen. (ie Regent) of the kingdom on 5 June 1944. Following the abdication and retirement to Egypt of his father on 9 May 1946, Umberto was declared King Umberto II, but his reign only lasted until 13 June when he left the country. Three days before, on 10 June 1946, Italy had become a republic, following a referendum.

In the post war years the ruling Christian Democrat Party resisted the challenge of the Communists to pursue a strongly pro-West and European policy. But no single government was able to reform an ailing economy or face up to lawlessness and corruption. Changes of administration were frequent. From 1947 to the early 1990s, Italy had no less than 57 governments. In 1992, in the wake of Italy's humiliating exit from Europe's Exchange Rate Mechanism (ERM), the old political establishment was driven out of office. Several prominent politicians were accused of links to organised crime and some went to prison. A new era for Italian politics opened the way for a radical modernization of the country's economic and social structure.

TERRITORY AND POPULATION. Italy is bounded in the north by Switzerland and Austria, east by Slovenia and the Adriatic Sea, south-east by the Ionian Sea, south by the Mediterranean Sea, south-west by the Tyrrhenian Sea and Ligurian Sea and west by France. The area is 301,308 sq. km. Populations at successive censuses were as follows:

10 Feb. 1901	33,370,138	4 Nov. 1951	47,158,738
10 June 1911	35,694,582	15 Oct. 1961	49,903,878
1 Dec. 1921	37,403,956	24 Oct. 1971	53,744,737
21 April 1931	40,582,043	25 Oct. 1981	56,243,935
21 April 1936	42,302,680	20 Oct. 1991	56,778,031

Population estimate, 1997: 57,460,977 (29,567,628 females).

Vital statistics (and rates per 1,000 population), 1996: Births, 525,640 (9·2); deaths, 547,404 (9·5); marriages, 272,049 (4·7); natural increase, −21,764 (−0·3);

infant deaths, 1994 (up to 1 yr of age) 3,436 (6·5 per 1,000 live births). Expectation of life: 77·8.

In 1996 the suicide rate was 4,587 (8·0 per 100,000 population); 73·7% were men.

The following table gives area and population of the Autonomous Regions (census 1991 and estimate 1996):

Regions	Area in sq. km (1996)	Resident pop. census, 1991	Resident pop. 1 Jan. 1995	Density per sq. km
Piedmont	25,399	4,302,565	4,297,989	169
Valle d'Aosta[1]	3,263	115,938	118,456	36
Lombardy	23,861	8,856,074	8,910,451	372
Trentino-Alto Adige[1]	13,607	90,360	908,667	66
Bolzano-Bozen	7,404	440,508	449,055	60
Trento	6,207	449,852	459,612	73
Veneto	18,338	4,380,797	4,422,290	239
Friuli-Venezia Giulia[1]	7,844	1,197,666	1,191,248	152
Liguria	5,421	1,676,282	1,663,696	308
Emilia Romagna	22,122	3,909,512	3,922,604	177
Tuscany	22,993	3,529,946	3,526,031	154
Umbria	8,456	811,831	822,480	96
Marche	9,694	1,429,205	1,441,031	148
Lazio	17,207	5,140,371	5,193,233	300
Abruzzi	10,795	1,249,054	1,267,694	116
Molise	4,438	330,90	332,155	75
Campania	13,595	5,630,280	5,745,761	417
Puglia	19,363	4,031,885	4,075,802	209
Basilicata	9,992	610,528	610,699	61
Calabria	15,080	2,070,203	2,076,128	138
Sicily[1]	25,707	4,966,386	5,082,697	194
Sardinia[1]	24,090	1,648,248	1,659,466	69

[1] With special statute.

In 1997 there were 1m. legal immigrants living in Italy, plus an estimated 250,000 illegal immigrants.

Communes of more than 100,000 inhabitants, with population resident at the census of 20 Oct. 1991 and on 31 Dec.1995:

	1991	1995		1991	1995
Rome	2,775,250	2,654,187	Foggia	156,268	156,032
Milano	1,369,231	1,306,494	Salerno	148,932	143,863
Naples	1,067,365	1,050,234	Perugia	144,732	151,118
Turin	962,507	923,106	Ferrara	138,015	135,135
Palermo	698,556	689,301	Ravenna	135,844	137,216
Genoa	678,771	659,116	Reggio nell'Emilia	132,030	135,406
Bologna	404,376	386,491	Rimini	127,960	129,598
Florence	403,294	383,594	Syracuse	125,941	127,448
Bari	342,309	336,560	Sassari	122,339	121,639
Catania	333,075	341,623	Pescara	122,236	118,764
Venice	309,422	298,915	Monza	120,651	119,658
Verona	255,824	254,145	Bergamo	114,936	116,990
Taranto	232,334	212,650	Forli	109,541	108,017
Messina	231,693	263,092	Terni	108,248	108,435
Trieste	213,100	223,611	Vicenza	107,454	107,786
Padua	215,137	212,731	Latina	106,203	110,233
Cagliari	204,237	174,543	Piacenza	102,268	99,962
Brescia	194,502	190,208	Trento	101,545	103,181
Reggio di C.	177,580	179,623	La Spezia	101,442	98,316
Modena	176,990	174,518	Torre del Greco	101,361	98,749
Parma	170,520	167,516	Ancona	101,285	99,732
Livorno	167,512	164,569	Novara	101,112	102,219
Prato	165,707	167,991	Lecce	100,884	100,046

The official language is Italian, spoken by 94·1% of the population in 1991. There are 0·3m. German-speakers in Bolzano and 30,000 French-speakers in Valle d'Aosta.

CLIMATE. The climate varies considerably with latitude. In the south, it is warm temperate, with little rain in the summer months, but the north is cool temperate with rainfall more evenly distributed over the year.

Florence, Jan. 44°F (6·8°C), July 74°F (23·3°C). Annual rainfall 32" (807 mm). Milan, Jan. 35°F (1·9°C), July 69°F (20·8°C). Annual rainfall 23" (573 mm). Naples, Jan. 48°F (8·9°C), July 77°F (25·6°C). Annual rainfall 34" (850 mm). Palermo, Jan. 54°F (12·3°C), July 79°F (26·1°C). Annual rainfall 14" (352 mm). Rome, Jan. 45°F (7·5°C), July 77°F (24·9°C). Annual rainfall 26" (657 mm). Venice, Jan. 38°F (3·2°C), July 75°F (23·9°C). Annual rainfall 8" (207 mm).

CONSTITUTION AND GOVERNMENT. The Constitution dates from 1948. Italy is 'a democratic republic founded on work'. Parliament consists of the *Chamber of Deputies* and the *Senate*. The Chamber is elected for 5 years by universal and direct suffrage and consists of 630 deputies. The Senate is elected for 5 years on a regional basis by electors over the age of 25; each Region having at least 7 senators, consisting of 315 elected senators; the Valle d'Aosta is represented by 1 senator only, the Molise by 2. The President of the Republic can nominate 11 senators for life from eminent persons in the social, scientific, artistic and literary spheres. The President may become a senator for life. The *President* is elected in a joint session of Chamber and Senate, to which are added 3 delegates from each Regional Council (1 from the Valle d'Aosta). A two-thirds majority is required for the election, but after a third indecisive scrutiny the absolute majority of votes is sufficient. The President must be 50 years or over; term of office, 7 years. The Speaker of the Senate acts as the deputy President. The President can dissolve the chambers of parliament, except during the last 6 months of the presidential term.

A *Constitutional Court*, consisting of 15 judges who are appointed, 5 each by the President, Parliament (in joint session) and the highest law and administrative courts, can decide on the constitutionality of laws and decrees, define the powers of the State and Regions, judge conflicts between the State and Regions and between the Regions, and try the President and Ministers.

The reorganization of the Fascist Party is forbidden. Direct male descendants of King Victor Emmanuel are excluded from all public offices, have no right to vote or to be elected, and are banned from Italian territory; their estates are forfeit to the State. Titles of nobility are no longer recognized, but those existing before 28 Oct. 1922 are retained as part of the name.

A referendum was held in June 1991 to decide whether the system of preferential voting by indicating 4 candidates by their listed number should be changed to a simpler system, less open to abuse, of indicating a single candidate by name. The electorate was 46m. Turn-out was 62·5% (there was a 50% quorum). 95·6% of votes cast were in favour of the change. As a result, an electoral reform of 1993 provides for the replacement of proportional representation by a system in which 475 seats in the Chamber of Deputies are elected by a first-past-the-post single-round vote and 155 seats by proportional representation in a separate single-round vote on the same day. There are 27 electoral regions. There is a 4% threshold for entry to the Chamber of Deputies.

At a further referendum in April 1993, turn-out was 77%. Votes favoured the 8 reforms proposed, including a new system of election to the Senate and the abolition of some ministries. 75% of the Senate is now elected by a first-past-the-post system, the remainder by proportional representation; no party may present more than 1 candidate in each constituency. In July 1997 an all-party parliamentary commission on constitutional reform proposed a directly elected president with responsibility for defence and foreign policy, the devolving of powers to the regions, a reduction in the number of seats in the Senate and in the lower house and the creation of a third chamber to speak on behalf of the regions.

Parliamentary elections were held on 21 April 1996. There were 1,574 candidates. The Olive Tree Alliance gained 284 seats in the Chamber of Deputies and 157 in the Senate with 41·2% of the national vote, the Freedom Alliance 246 and 116 with 37·3%, the Northern League 59 and 27 with 37·3%, the Refounded Communists 35 and 10 with 8·6%. In the Chamber of Deputies minor parties won 6 seats. In the Senate the Pannella List won 27 seats and minor parties won 4.

President: Oscar Luigi Scalfaro (b. 1919; DC; sworn in 28 May 1992).

A government was formed on 17 May 1996 which in March 1998 comprised (PDS = Democratic Party of the Left; PPI = Popular Party; RI = Italian Renewal): *Prime Minister:* Romano Prodi (b. 1940; PPI; sworn in 18 May 1996).

Deputy Prime Minister and Minister of Culture: Walter Veltroni (PDS). *Foreign Affairs:* Lamberto Dini (RI). *Finance:* Vincenzo Visco (PDS). *Defence:* Beniamino Andreatta (PPI). *Interior:* Giorgio Napolitano (PDS). *Agriculture:* Michele Pinto (PPI). *Education and University:* Luigi Berlinguer (PDS). *Environment:* Edo Ronchi (Greens). *Foreign Trade:* Augusto Fantozzi (RI). *Health:* Rosaria Bindi (PPI). *Industry and Tourism:* Pierluigi Bersani (PDS). *Justice:* Giovanni Flick (ind). *Labour and Social Welfare:* Tiziano Treu (RI). *Post and Telecommunications:* Antonio Maccanico (Democratic Union). *Public Works:* Paolo Costa (ind). *Transport:* Claudio Burlando (PDS). *Treasury and Budget:* Carlo Azeglio Ciampi (ind). *Ministers Without Portfolio: Family and Social Affairs:* Livia Turco (PDS). *Equal Opportunities:* Anna Finocchiaro (PDS). *Civil Service and Regional Affairs:* Franco Bassanini (PDS).

The *Speaker* is Luciano Voilante (PDS). The *Speaker of the Senate* is Nicola Mancini (PPI).

In Oct. 1997 the Refounded Communists withdrew support from the Government when Prime Minister Prodi refused to underwrite the continuation of a pension system which allows Italians to retire as early as 50. The Government resigned. However, the threat of fresh elections brought the Communists back into the coalition and Romano Prodi continued as Prime Minister.

National anthem: Fratelli d'Italia ('Brothers of Italy'; words by G. Mameli; tune by M. Novaro, 1847).

European Parliament. Italy has 87 representatives. At the June 1994 elections turnout was 74·8%. Forza Italia gained 27 seats with 30·6% of votes cast; the Party of the Democratic Left (former Communists), 16 with 19·1% (group in European Parliament: European Socialist Party); the National Alliance, 11 with 12·5%; the Popular Party (former Christian Democrats), 8 with 10% (Popular European Party); the Northern League, 6 with 6·6%; the Reformed Communists, 5 with 6·1%; the Greens, 3 with 3·2% (Greens); Segni, 3 with 3·2%; the Pannella Reformers, 2 with 2·1%; the Socialist Party, 2 with 1·8% (European Socialist Party); Rete, 1 with 1·1%; the Republican Party, 1 with 0·7% (Liberals, Democrats, Reformers); the Social Democratic Party, 1 with 0·7% (European Socialist Party); the South Tyrol People's Party, 1 with 0·6% (Popular European Party).

Regional and Local Government. Italy is administratively divided into 15 autonomous regions and 5 autonomous regions with a special constitutional status; these are subdivided into 94 provinces and 1,230 municipalities. The regions have their own councils and governments with certain legislative and administrative functions adapted to the circumstances of each region. A government commissioner co-ordinates regional and national activities. Since 1993 mayors have been directly elected for 4-year terms in towns of more than 15,000 inhabitants and allot 60% of seats on municipal councils, the remainder being apportioned according to party vote.

Measures for the autonomy of the largely German-speaking **Alto Adige** (South Tyrol) were granted in Jan. 1992 and accepted by Austria in June 1992.

A powerful separatist movement, the Northern League, campaigns for autonomy for the regions around the Po Valley. Local government elections were held on 27 April 1997 and 11 May 1997, involving 11 provinces and 1,192 communes. The electorate was 14·4m.. Regional elections held in Nov. 1997 resulted in landslide victories for the ruling centre-left coalition.

DEFENCE. Head of the armed forces is the Defence Chief of Staff. There is conscription for 12 months.

Army. The Field Army is organized into 3 corps headquarters (1 mountain), consisting of 3 mechanized, 2 armoured and 4 mountain brigades, 2 armoured cavalry, 2 heavy artillery and 2 amphibious battalions, 3 aviation groups, 3 artillery regiments and 2 anti-aircraft regiments; an air defence command with surface-to-air missiles; and an aviation group. There is a territorial defence force of 8 independent mechanized brigades deployed in 7 military regions, and a rapid intervention force and a support brigade with missiles. Equipment includes 167 M-60A1, 910 Leopard and 242 Centauro main battle tanks. The Army air corps operates 8 DO228 transports, over 40 light aircraft and 360 helicopters. Strength (1997) 188,300 (127,550 conscripts). The paramilitary Carabinieri number 113,200.

Navy. The principal ships of the Navy are the light aircraft carrier *Giuseppe Garibaldi* and the helicopter-carrying cruiser *Vittorio Veneto*. The *Giuseppe Garibaldi*, 13,450 tonnes, was completed in 1985 and operates an air group of 10 SH-3D Sea King anti-submarine helicopters and 5 AV8-B Harrier aircraft. She is also armed with 4 Teseo anti-ship missiles. The *Vittorio Veneto*, completed in 1969, is of 9,650 tonnes, and operates a squadron of 6 AB-212 anti-submarine helicopters as well as a twin launcher for anti-submarine rockets and US Standard SM-1 surface-to-air missiles, and Teseo anti-ship missiles.

The combatant forces also include 8 diesel submarines, 4 guided-missile destroyers armed with Standard SM-I, 26 frigates, of which 18 carry one or more AB-212 helicopters and 6 missile-armed patrol hydrofoils. Mine countermeasure forces comprise 12 coastal minehunters. There are 4 new helicopter-carrying offshore patrol vessels for the protection of economic resources. Amphibious lift for the San Marco commando group (1,000 men) is provided by 3 dock landing ships and 35 craft. Auxiliaries include 2 replenishment oilers, 4 water carriers, 3 survey ships, 4 trial vessels, 2 training ships and 8 large tugs.

The Naval Air Arm, 1,600 strong, operates 75 anti-submarine and training helicopters and has acquired the first 8 operational and 2 training Harrier-type TAV-8B short take off/vertical landing aircraft for the carrier squadron.

There is a Special Forces commando of some 600 assault swimmers.

Main naval bases are at Spezia, Naples, Taranto and Ancona, with minor bases at Brindisi and Venice. The personnel of the Navy in 1997 numbered 44,000, including the naval air arm and the marine battalion.

Paramilitary maritime tasks are carried out by the Financial Guards fleet of some 70 patrol craft and a harbour control force with 12 inshore patrol craft and numerous boats.

Air Force. Control is exercised through 2 regional headquarters near Taranto and Milan. Units assigned to NATO comprise the 1st air brigade of Nike-Hercules surface-to-air missiles, 9 fighter-bomber, 7 interceptor and 1 tactical reconnaissance squadron, with supporting transport, search and rescue, and training units. 4 of the fighter-bomber squadrons have Tornados, and 5 squadrons operate AM-X Centauros. F-104S Starfighters have been standardized throughout the 7 interceptor squadrons.

One transport squadron has turboprop C-130H Hercules aircraft; 2 others have turboprop Aeritalia G222s, Piaggio PD-808s and Boeing 707s. There is a VIP and personnel transport squadron, equipped with AS-61, DC-9, Gulfstream III and Falcon 50 aircraft.

Electronic warfare duties are performed by specially equipped G222s, PD-808s and MB 339s. Two land-based anti-submarine squadrons operate Breguet Atlantics. Search and rescue are performed by 30 Agusta-Sikorsky HH-3F helicopters and smaller types. There are also strong support and training elements; some MB 339 jet trainers have armament provisions for secondary close air support and anti-helicopter roles.

Air Force strength in 1997 was about 63,600 (19,500 conscripts).

INTERNATIONAL RELATIONS

Membership. Italy is a member of the UN, NATO, EU, WEU and the Central European Initiative. Italy is a signatory to the Schengen Accord of June 1990 which abolishes border controls between Italy and Austria, Belgium, Denmark, Finland, France, Germany, Greece, Iceland, Luxembourg, the Netherlands, Norway, Portugal, Spain and Sweden.

ECONOMY

Policy. The government is committed to a reduction in borrowing, a strong currency and low inflation. It has embarked on an ambitious privatization programme to reduce radically its presence in industry and banking. In 1997 the government completed its biggest privatization to date with the 26,000bn. lire flotation of Telecom Italia. It also sold a third tranche in the Eni oil and gas group, privatized the Banca di Roma, Italy's second largest banking group, and pledged to pursue this programme with further sell-offs in 1998.

Performance. GDP growth was 0·7% in 1997.

Budget. Total revenue and expenditure for fiscal years, in 1,000m. lire:

	Revenue	Expenditure		Revenue	Expenditure
1991	458,122	579,966	1994	511,789	635,915
1992	514,013	627,578	1995	552,709	692,681
1993	480,973	632,567	1996	503,973	705,486

1996: Direct taxes, 293,955,000m. lire; taxes on goods and services, 138,827,000m. lire; consumer taxes, 37,101,000m. lire; and business taxes, 34,090,000m. lire.

The proposed 1998 budget provides for an increase in value-added tax. Some reforms due to take place in 1988 are meant to reallocate the existing tax burden in a more business-friendly way. The rate of corporation tax will come down from 53·2% to 37%. Other measure include reducing social security contributions, and a new two-tier income tax, brought in to encourage entrepreneurs to reinvest in profits and issue equity.

VAT is 19% (reduced rate, 10%).

The public debt at 31 Dec. 1996 totalled 2,077,170,000m. lire, including consolidated debt of 37,000m. lire and the floating debt of 549,630,000m. lire. During the last five years the public deficit has come down from more than 10% to 3%, or possibly less, of gross domestic product. Inflation, which was running close to 7%, has fallen below 2%. Interest rates have also declined significantly.

Currency. The unit of currency is the *lira* (ITL), notionally of 100 *centesimi*. There are coins of 10, 20, 50, 100, 200 and 500, and notes of 1,000, 2,000, 5,000, 10,000, 50,000 and 100,000 lire. The lira left the ERM in Sept. 1993 and rejoined in Nov. 1996. Circulation of money at 31 Dec.1996, 100,113,000m. lire.

Banking and Finance. The bank of issue is the Bank of Italy (founded 1893). It is owned by public-sector banks. Its *governor* (Antonio Fazio, b. 1936) is selected without fixed term by the 13 directors of the Bank's non-executive board. In 1991 it received increased responsibility for the supervision of banking and stock exchange affairs, and in 1993 greater independence from the government. Its gold reserve amounted to 38,366,000m. lire in Dec. 1996; the foreign credit reserves of the Exchange Bureau (*Ufficio Italiano Cambi*) amounted to 45,566,000m. lire.

Credit institutions are under the control of the state's 'Inspectorate of Credit'. Other credit institutions, totalling 1,024, are classified as: (1) 217 commercial banks including 126 private and 40 branches of foreign banks; (2) 102 co-operative banks; (3) 700 rural and artisans' banks; (4) 5 Istituti di Categoria.

The 'Amato' law of July 1990 gave public sector banks the right to become joint stock companies and permitted the placing of up to 49% of their equity with private shareholders.

On 31 Dec. 1996 the post office savings banks had deposits and current accounts of 221,597,000m. lire; credit institutions, 913,300,000m. lire.

Legislation reforming stock markets came into effect in Dec. 1990. In 1996 local stock exchanges, relics of pre-unification Italy, were closed, and stock exchange activities concentrated in Milan.

Weights and Measures. The metric system is in use. 1 quintal = 100 kg.

ENERGY AND NATURAL RESOURCES

Electricity. In 1996 the total power generated was 244,424m. kWh., of which 47,111 m. kWh. were generated by hydro-electric plants.

Oil and Gas. Oil production, 1995, 5,207,980 tonnes. In 1995, natural gas production in 1,000 cu. ft was 719,282.

Minerals. Fuel and mineral resources are inadequate to needs. Only sulphur and mercury yield a substantial surplus for exports.

Production of metals and minerals (in tonnes) was as follows:

	1992	1993	1994	1995	1996
Bentonite	402,478	150,503	326,992	590,845	471,535
Cement	13,123,662	13,902,392	12,285,703	11,733,556	12,480,388
Zinc	70,046	62,558	7,379	43,669	20,137
Sulphur	3,503,891	3,365,946	3,021,427	3,430,374	3,528,120
Lead	20,042	27,475	8,011	22,658	20,260
Feldspar	1,354,191	1,387,968	1,534,421	2,199,315	2,287,086

Agriculture. In 1993, 1,984,100 persons were dependent on agriculture, of whom 1,329,900 were economically active. In 1993 there were 205,819 sq. km of agricultural and forest lands, distributed as follows (in 1,000 ha.): Forage and pasture, 6,746; woods, 5,874; cereals, 4,214; olive trees, 1,106; vines, 899; garden produce, 597; leguminous plants, 97.

At the 1991 census agricultural holdings numbered 3,023,344 and covered 22,702,356 ha. 2,893,145 owners (95·7%) farmed directly 15,961,093 ha (70·3%); 118,020 owners (3·9%) worked with hired labour on 6,603,522 ha (29·1%); 95,045 share-croppers (3·1%) tilled 1,208,337 ha (5·3%); the remaining 12,179 holdings (0·4%) of 137,740 ha (0·6%) were operated in other ways. In 1990 persons engaged in agriculture numbered 1·9m. (0·68m. females).

In 1993 1,464,322 farm tractors were being used.

The production of the principal crops (in 1,000 metric quintals) in 1995: Sugar beet, 131,883; maize, 84,403; wheat, 79,555; tomatoes, 51,826; potatoes, 20,808; oranges, 15,968; barley, 14,216; rice, 13,281; olive oil, 6,128; lemons, 5,431; tangerines, mandarines and clementines, 4,509; other citrus fruit, 152; oats, 3,013; rye, 198; wine, 56,201 (in 1,000 hectolitres); tobacco (in tonnes, 1994), 1,206.

Livestock, 1 Dec. 1995 (in 1,000): Cattle, 7,417; sheep, 10,668; pigs, 8,061; goats, 1,373; horses, 315; donkeys, 26; mules, 12.

Livestock products, 1995 (in 1,000 quintals): Milk, 111,578; meat, 36,574; cheese, 9,818; wool, 110; eggs, 6,760 (1,000 pieces).

Forestry. In 1996 forests covered 127,787 ha.

Fisheries. The fishing fleet comprised, in 1994, 15,798 motor boats of 245,637 gross tonnes. The catch in 1995 was 3,586,143 metric quintals.

INDUSTRY. The main branches of industry are: (% of industrial value added at factor cost in 1992) Textiles, clothing, leather and footwear (14·2%), food, beverages and tobacco (8·3%), energy products (10·7%), agricultural and industrial machines (8·6%), metal products except machines and means of transport (8·9%), mineral and non-metallic mineral products (7%), timber and wooden furniture (5·2%), electric plants and equipment (6·7%), chemicals and pharmaceuticals (7·9%), means of transport (6·2%).

Production, 1995: Motor vehicles, 163,676; artificial and synthetic fibres (including staple fibre and waste), 680,901 tonnes. Figures for 1996 (in tonnes): Cement, 33,327,194; steel, 24,284,985; polyethylene resins, 1,055,421.

Labour. In 1996 the workforce was 22,851,000 (8,615,000 females) of whom 20,088,000 were employed. 2,763,000 (1,428,000 females) were unemployed, a rate of 12·1%. In the relatively poor South, unemployment is estimated at 25%. Over 50% of Italy's jobless have been out of work for more than a year. Pensionable retirement age was 60 for men and 55 for women in 1991, but this is being progressively raised to 65 for both sexes. Agreements between the government, employers and trade unions in 1992 and 1993 ended automatic wage indexation and regulated labour relations and wage increases.

Trade Unions. There are 3 main groups: the Confederazione Generale Italiana del Lavoro (CGIL; no longer Communist-dominated), the Confederazione Italiana Sindacati Lavoratori (CISL; Catholic), and the Unione Italiana del Lavoro (UIL). Membership in 1994: CGIL, 5·2m. (2·7m. retired); CISL, 3·7m. (1·5m. retired); UIL, 1·7m. (0·5m. retired). In referendums held in June 1995 the electorate voted to remove some restrictions on trade union representation, end government involvement in public sector trade unions and end the automatic deduction of trade union dues from wage packets.

FOREIGN ECONOMIC RELATIONS. Foreign debt in Dec. 1996 was 68,013bn. lire.

Commerce. The territory covered by foreign trade statistics includes Italy and San Marino, but excludes the municipalities of Livigno and Campione.
The following table shows the value of Italy's foreign trade (in 1,000m. lire):

	1992	1993	1994	1995	1996
Imports	232,111	232,911	272,382	335,661	319,396
Exports	219,436	266,214	308,046	381,175	386,946

Percentage of trade with EU countries in 1996: Exports, 55·3%; imports, 60·8%. Principal export markets, 1996 (% of total trade): Germany, 17·4%; France, 12·5%; USA, 7·3%; UK, 6·5%; Spain, 4·9%. Principal import suppliers: Germany, 18·5%; France, 13·5%; UK, 6·6%; Netherlands, 6%; USA, 4·9%; Belgium and Luxembourg, 4·8%.
Exports/imports by category, 1996 (in 1,000m. lire):

	Exports	Imports
Metal products and machinery	139,378	76,762
Textiles and leather goods	65,045	23,097
Wood, paper and rubber goods	49,126	319,396
Transport equipment	38,743	35,375
Chemical products	31,962	44,896
Foodstuffs, beverages and tobacco	16,451	24,361
Metallic minerals	15,425	28,317
Non-metallic minerals and products	15,199	5,781
Agricultural, forestry and fish products	9,961	19,033
Energy	5,736	35,253

Tourism. In 1996, 56,300,496 foreigners visited Italy; they included Swiss, 8,374,527; Germans, 8,752,281; French, 9,303,490; Austrians, 6,147,073. Foreign tourist revenue was 46,249,264m. lire in 1996.

COMMUNICATIONS

Roads. Roads totalled (1994) 306,445 km, of which 6,469 km were motorway and 113,073 km were provincial roads; there were 45,237 km state roads (1993) and 141,666 km communal roads (1977). In 1993 there were 38,706,899 motor vehicles, including: Cars, 29,652,024; buses, 76,974; vans, 2,569,008; motor cycles, 5,889,740; lorries, 444,125. There were 6,512 fatalities in traffic accidents in 1995 (6,578 in 1994).

Railways. Total of railways (1994), 19,527 km. The state-run railway (*Ferrovie dello Stato*) was 16,000 km (10,122 km electrified). In 1996 the state railways carried 468,300,000 passengers and 77,299,000 tonnes of freight. There are metros in Milan (68 km) and Rome (33·5 km), and tram/light rail networks in Genoa (2·3 km), Milan (240 km), Naples (23 km), Trieste and Turin (119 km).

Civil Aviation. There are major international airports at Bologna (G. Marconi), Genoa (Cristoforo Colombo), Milan (Linate and Malpensa), Naples (Capodichino), Pisa (Galileo Galilei), Rome (Leonardo da Vinci), Turin and Venice (Marco Polo). The national carrier Alitalia is 89·3% owned by the state, and in 1993 operated 2 A300B2-200s, 4 A300B4-100s, 8 A300B4-200s, 7 A321-100s, 7 B-747-200Bs,

4 B-747-200B Combis, 1 B-747-200F, 2 B-767-300ERs and 114 other aircraft. Passenger arrivals, 1996: Domestic, 16,569,832; international, 15,515,432. Departures: Domestic, 16,569,646; international, 15,649,188. Freight embarked (in quintals): Domestic, 549,922; international, 2,500,701. Discharged: Domestic, 549,941; international, 1,762,978.

Shipping. The mercantile marine in 1995 consisted of 614 vessels of 11·88m. DWT, representing 1·79% of the world's tonnage. 112 vessels (26·42% of tonnage) were registered under foreign flags. Total tonnage registered was 6·82m. GRT, including oil tankers, 2·18m. GRT and container ships, 0·14m. GRT. In 1995, 234,115,000 tonnes of cargo were unloaded, and 48,254,000 were loaded. 2,039,697 passengers embarked, and 2,185,645 departed in 1995.

Telecommunications. In 1991 there were 14,412 post offices and 13,918 telegraph offices. In 1995 there were 29,407,629 telephones. In 1995, 4m. mobile telephones were in use. Broadcasting is regulated by the Public Radio-Television Administration Council. This consists of 8 members elected by parliament who choose a ninth member as chair for 3-year terms. *Radiotelevisione Italiana* broadcasts 3 radio programmes and additional regional programmes. It also broadcasts 2 TV programmes. There are 12 national and about 820 local independent TV networks. In 1993 there were 15m. radio and 17m. TV sets (colour by PAL). In 1996 16,114,572 television licences were bought.

Cinemas. In 1995 there were 3,816 screens (1,200 full-time) and 90·7m. admissions.

Press. There were (1995) 113 dailies (76 are general information) and 62 weeklies. The combined circulation of the dailies (including unsold copies) is 2,263·2m., and of the weeklies is 921·2m.

SOCIAL INSTITUTIONS

Justice. Italy has 1 court of cassation, in Rome, and is divided for the administration of justice into 28 appeal court districts, subdivided into 164 tribunal *circondari* (districts), and these again into about 617 districts each with its own magistracy (*Pretura*). There are also 90 first degree assize courts and 28 assize courts of appeal. For civil business, besides the magistracy above mentioned, *Conciliatori* have jurisdiction in petty plaints (those to a maximum of 1m. lire).

2,422,991 crimes were reported in 1996; 546,591 persons were indicted. In 1996 there were 89,517 persons in prison (7,061 females).

Religion. The treaty between the Holy See and Italy, of 11 Feb. 1929, confirmed by article 7 of the Constitution of the republic, lays down that the Catholic Apostolic Roman Religion is the only religion of the State. Other creeds are permitted, provided they do not profess principles, or follow rites, contrary to public order or moral behaviour.

The appointment of archbishops and of bishops is made by the Holy See; but the Holy See submits to the Italian Government the name of the person to be appointed in order to obtain an assurance that the latter will not raise objections of a political nature.

Catholic religious teaching is given in elementary and intermediate schools. Marriages celebrated before a Catholic priest are automatically transferred to the civil register. Marriages celebrated by clergy of other denominations must be made valid before a registrar.

There were 47·56m. Catholics in 1993.

Education. 5 years of primary and 3 years of secondary education are compulsory from the age of 6. In 1996-97 there were 26,047 pre-school institutions with 1,580,414 pupils (including 13,738 state-run institutions with 891,981pupils); 20,006 primary schools with 2,801,407 pupils (including 18,624 state schools with 2,597,907 pupils); 9,215 compulsory secondary schools (*scuole medie*) with 1,893,476 pupils (including 8,400 state schools with 1,792,676 pupils); and 7,875 higher secondary schools with 2,644,291 pupils (including 5,957 state-run with 2,462,157 pupils). Numbers of teachers: Pre-primary institutions, 1992–93, 118,943;

primary schools, 1992–93, 283,762; compulsory secondary schools, 1993–94, 249,604; higher secondary schools, 1993–94, 324,000.

Higher secondary education is subdivided into classical (*ginnasio* and classical *liceo*), scientific (scientific *liceo*), language lyceum, professional institutes and technical education: agricultural, industrial, commercial, technical, nautical institutes, institutes for surveyors, institutes for girls (5-year course) and teacher-training institutes (4-year course).

In 1994–95 there were 47 universities, 2 universities of Italian studies for foreigners and 3 specialized universities (commerce; education; Roman Catholic), 3 polytechnical university institutes and 7 other specialized university institutes: (architecture; bio-medicine; modern languages; naval studies; oriental studies; social studies; teacher training). In 1995–96 there were 1,617,140 university students and 58,111 academic staff.

The adult literacy rate is 98·1%.

Health. The provision of health services is a regional responsibility, but they are funded by central government. Medical consultations are free, but a portion of prescription costs are payable. In 1995 there were 1,036 public hospitals with 270,598 beds, 777 private hospitals with 85,644 beds. In 1994 there were 81,348 doctors in public hospitals and 218,378 auxiliary medical personnel.

Welfare. Social expenditure is made up of transfers which the central public departments, local departments and social security departments make to families. Payment is principally for pensions, family allowances and health services. Expenditure on subsidies, public assistance to various classes of people and people injured by political events or national disasters are also included.

State pensions are indexed to prices; 21,445,199 pensions were paid in 1995 with contributions totalling 207,959,000m. lire.

DIPLOMATIC REPRESENTATIVES

Of Italy in Great Britain (14 Three Kings Yard, London, W1Y 2EH)
Ambassador: Paolo Galli.

Of Great Britain in Italy (Via XX Settembre 80A, 00187, Rome)
Ambassador: Tom Richardson, CMG.

Of Italy in the USA (1601 Fuller St., NW, Washington, D.C., 20009)
Ambassador: Ferdinando Salleo.

Of the USA in Italy (Via Veneto 119/A, Rome)
Ambassador: Reginald Bartholomew.

Of Italy to the United Nations
Ambassador: Francesco Fulci.

Further Reading

Istituto Nazionale di Statistica. *Annuario Statistico Italiano.—Compendio Statistico Italiano.* (Annual).—*Italian Statistical Abstract* (Annual).—*Bollettino Mensile di Statistica* (Monthly).

Absalom, R., *Italy since 1880: a Nation in the Balance?* Harlow, 1995
Baldassarri, M. (ed.) *The Italian Economy: Heaven or Hell?* London, 1993
Clark, M., *Modern Italy 1871–1982.* London, 1984
Di Scala, S. M., *Italy from Revolution to Republic: 1700 to the Present.* Boulder (CO), 1995
Duggan, C., *A Concise History of Italy.* CUP, 1994
Frei, M., *Italy: the Unfinished Revolution.* London, 1996
Furlong, P., *Modern Italy: Representation and Reform.* London, 1994
Gilbert, M. *Italian Revolution: the Ignominious End of Politics, Italian Style.* Boulder (CO), 1995
Ginsborg, P., *A History of Contemporary Italy: Society and Politics, 1943–1988.* London, 1990
Gundie, S. and Parker, S. (eds.) *The New Italian Republic: from the Fall of the Berlin Wall to Berlusconi.* London, 1995
Hearder, H., *Italy: a Short History.* CUP, 1991
McCarthy, P., *The Crisis of the Italian State: from the Origins of the Cold War to the Fall of Berlusconi.* London, 1996

Putnam, R. *et al., Making Democracy Work: Civic Traditions in Modern Italy.* Princeton Univ. Press, 1993
Richards, C., *The New Italians.* London, 1994
Smith, D. M., *Modern Italy, A Political History.* Yale University Press, 1997
Sponza, L. and Zancani, D., *Italy.* [Bibliography]. Oxford and Santa Barbara (CA), 1995

National statistical office: Istituto Nazionale di Statistica (ISTAT), 16 Via Cesare Balbo, 00184 Rome. *Website:* http://www.istat.it/
National library: Biblioteca Nazionale Centrale, Vittorio Emanuele II, Viale Castro Pretorio, Rome.

JAMAICA

Capital: Kingston
Population: 2·5m.
GDP per head: (PPP$) 3,816
GNP: US$3·6bn.
HDI/world rank: 0·736/83

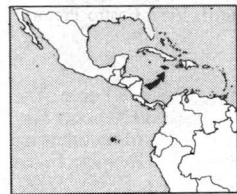

KEY HISTORICAL EVENTS. Jamaica was discovered by Columbus in 1494, and was occupied by the Spaniards from 1509 until 1655 when the island was captured by the English. Their possession was confirmed by the Treaty of Madrid of 1670. In 1661, a representative constitution was established consisting of a governor, privy council, legislative council and legislative assembly. The slave production introduced by the Spanish was augmented as sugar production increased in value and extent in the 18th century. The plantation economy collapsed with the abolition of the slave trade in in the late 1830s. The 1866 Crown Colony government was introduced, with a legislative council consisting of official and unofficial members. In 1884, a partially elective legislative council was instituted. Women were enfranchised in 1919. By the late 1930s, demands for self-government increased and the constitution of Nov. 1944 stated that the governor was to be assisted by a house of representatives of 32 elected members, a legislative council (the upper house) of 15 members, and an executive council. Every person over 21 years of age was granted the right to vote.

In 1958, Jamaica joined with Trinidad, Barbados, the Leeward Islands and the Windward Islands to create the West Indies Federation; but Jamaica withdrew in 1961. In 1959, internal self-government had been achieved, and in 1962 Jamaica became an independent state within the British Commonwealth.

TERRITORY AND POPULATION. Jamaica is an island which lies in the Caribbean Sea about 150 km south of Cuba. The area is 4,411 sq. miles (11,425 sq. km). The population at the census of 7 April 1991 was 2,374,193. Estimated population in 1995 was 2,500,025, distributed on the basis of the 13 parishes of the island as follows: Kingston and St Andrew, 683,700; St Thomas, 88,600; Portland, 78,300; St Mary, 111,200; St Ann, 155,800; Trelawny, 72,100; St James, 167,100; Hanover, 67,600; Westmoreland, 133,800; St Elizabeth, 148,200; Manchester, 173,500; St Catherine, 398,600; Clarendon, 221,500.

Chief towns (population, 1995): Kingston and St Andrew, 538,100, metropolitan area; Spanish Town, 110,400; Portmore, 93,800; Montego Bay, 82,000; May Pen, 45,900; Mandeville, 39,900.

The population is about 75% of African ethnic origin.

Vital statistics (1995): Births, 57,607 (23·0 per 1,000 population); deaths, 12,776 (5·1); marriages, 16,515 (6·6); divorces, 1,332 (0·5). There were 17,669 emigrants in 1995, mainly to the USA.

CLIMATE. A tropical climate but with considerable variation. High temperatures on the coast are usually mitigated by sea breezes, while upland areas enjoy cooler and less humid conditions. Rainfall is plentiful over most of Jamaica, being heaviest in May and from Aug. to Nov. The island lies in the hurricane zone. Kingston. Jan. 76°F (24·4°C), July 81°F (27·2°C). Annual rainfall 32" (800 mm).

CONSTITUTION AND GOVERNMENT. Under the Constitution of Aug. 1962 the Crown is represented by a Governor-General appointed by the Crown on the advice of the Prime Minister. The Governor-General is assisted by a Privy Council of 6 appointed members. The Legislature comprises the *House of Representatives* and the *Senate*. The Senate consists of 21 senators appointed by the Governor-General, 13 on the advice of the Prime Minister, 8 on the advice of the Leader of the Opposition. The House of Representatives (60 members) is elected by universal adult suffrage for a period not exceeding 5 years. Electors and elected must be Jamaican or

Commonwealth citizens resident in Jamaica for at least 12 months before registration. It is likely that Jamaica will become a republic in the next five years. Queen Elizabeth II will be replaced as head of state by a ceremonial president.

At the elections of Dec. 1997 the People's National Party (PNP) gained 60 seats and the Jamaica Labour Party, 8.

Governor-General: Sir Howard Felix Cooke.

The Cabinet in March 1998 comprised:

Prime Minister and Minister of Defence: Percival Patterson, QC (b. 1935; PNP).

Deputy Prime Minister and Minister of Foreign Affairs and Trade: Seymour Mullings. *National Security and Justice:* K. D. Knight. *Education, Youth and Culture:* Burchell Whiteman. *Health:* John Junor. *Labour, Social Security and Sport:* Portia Simpson. *Mining and Energy:* Robert Pickersgill. *Local Government, Youth and Community Development:* Arnold Bertram. *Industry and Investment:* Dr Paul Robertson. *Transportation and Works:* Peter Phillips. *Commerce and Technology* Phillip Paulwell. *Housing and the Environment:* Easton Douglas. *Agriculture:* Roger Clarke. *Water:* Karl Blythe. *Finance and Planning:* Omar Davies. *Tourism:* Francis Tulloch. *Without portfolio:* Maxine Henry-Wilson.

National anthem: Eternal Father, bless our land (words by H. Sherlock, tune by R. Lightbourne).

DEFENCE

Army. The Jamaica Defence Force consists of a Regular and a Reserve Force. The Regular Force is comprised of the 1st battalion, Jamaica Regiment and Support Services which include the Air Wing and Coast Guard. The Coast Guard, numbering 150 in 1995, operates 5 inshore patrol craft based at Port Royal. The Reserve Force consists of the 3rd battalion, Jamaica Regiment. Total strength (army, 1996), 3,000. Reserves, 800.

Navy. The Coast Guard, numbering 150 in 1996, operates 5 inshore patrol craft based at Port Royal.

Air Force. The Air Wing of the Jamaica Defence Force was formed in July 1963 and has since been expanded and trained successively by the British Army Air Corps and Canadian Air Force personnel. There are no combat aircraft. Equipment for army liaison, search and rescue, police co-operation, survey and transport duties includes 2 Defender armed STOL transports; 1 Beech King Air and 1 Cessna 210 light transports; 4 JetRanger, 4 Bell 205 and 2 Bell 212 helicopters. Personnel (1997), 170.

INTERNATIONAL RELATIONS

Membership. Jamaica is a member of the UN, the Commonwealth, OAS, CARICOM and is an ACP state of the EU.

ECONOMY

Budget. Revenue and expenditure for fiscal years ending 31 March (in J$1m.):

	1992–93	1993–94	1994–95	1995–96
Revenue	21,029	34,243	43,636	59,438
Expenditure	26,871	41,256	68,384	73,869

The chief items of current revenue are income tax; consumption, customs and stamp duties. The other major share of current resources is generated by the Bauxite Production Levy. The chief items of current expenditure are public debt, education and health.

Currency. The unit of currency is the *Jamaican dollar* (JMD) of 100 *cents.* The Jamaican dollar was floated in Sept. 1990. There are coins of 1, 5, 10, 20, 25 and 50 cents and J$1, and notes of J$1, 2, 5, 10, 20, 50, 100 and 500. Currency in circulation in 1995 was J$10,775·3m. Inflation was 19·9% in 1995.

Banking and Finance. The central bank and bank of issue is the Bank of Jamaica. In 1997 there were 9 commercial banks with 208 branches and agencies in operation. 5 of these banks are subsidiaries of major British and North American banks, of which 4 are incorporated locally. Total assets of commercial banks in 1995 were J$121,324·9m.; deposits were J$89,135·4m.

There is a stock exchange in Kingston, which participates in the regional Caribbean exchange.

ENERGY AND NATURAL RESOURCES

Electricity. The Jamaica Public Service Co. is the public supplier. Total installed capacity, 1995, 624·9 MW. Production (1995) 2,417m. kWh.

Minerals. Jamaica is a major producer of bauxite. Ceramic clays, marble, silica sand and gypsum are also commercially viable. Production in 1996 (in tonnes): Bauxite ore, 10·8m.; gypsum, 208,017; marble, 2,800; sand and gravel, 1·8m.; industrial lime, 3·4m.

Agriculture (1995). Production (in tonnes): Sugar-cane, 2,295,000; bananas for export, 85,303; citrus fruit, 27,693; cocoa, 6,186; coconuts, 18,135.

Livestock (1991): Cattle, 0·3m.; goats, 0·44m.; pigs, 0·25m.; poultry, 8m. Slaughtered livestock in 1994: Cattle, 72,717 head; goats, 41,240; pigs, 111,297; poultry, 44,900 tonnes.

INDUSTRY. Alumina production, 1995, 3m. tonnes. Output of other products, 1995 (in tonnes): Sugar, 207,000; molasses, 95,900; cornmeal, 13,400; flour, 146,000; edible oils, 6m. litres; condensed milk, 15,800; fertilizer, 57,500; petrol, 852·8m. litres; glass bottles, 20,588; cement, 523,000; cigarettes, 989·8m. units. There is an oil refinery in Kingston. In 1995, manufacturing contributed J$28,775m. to the total GDP at current prices.

Labour. Average total labour force (1995), 1·15m., of whom 963,300 were employed. 551,400 were employed in services (including 201,400 in trade and catering, 51,600 in business), 223,200 in agriculture, forestry and fisheries, 104,700 in manufacturing, 76,000 in building and 7,000 in mining.

FOREIGN ECONOMIC RELATIONS. Foreign debt was US$3,451·9m. in 1995.

Commerce. Value of imports and domestic exports for calendar years (in US$1m.):

	1991	1992	1993	1994	1995
Imports	1,809	1,693	2,165	2,177	2,773
Exports	1,151	1,053	1,045	1,220	1,430

Principal imports in 1995 (in US$1m.): Consumer goods, 686 (24·7%), of which food including beverages, 197 (7·1%); raw materials, 1,548 (55·8%); capital goods, 539 (19·4%), of which construction materials, 144 (5·2%) and machinery and equipment, 284 (10·3%).

Principal domestic exports in 1995 (in US$1m.): Traditional exports, 916 (64%), of which bauxite, 72 (5%), alumina, 632 (44·2%), gypsum, 1 (0·1%), sugar, 96 (6·7%) and bananas, 48 (3·4%); non-traditional exports, 464 (32·5%), of which food, 77 (5·4%), beverages and tobacco, 22 (1·5%), mineral fuels, lubricants and related materials, 7 (0·5%), crude materials, 7 (0·5%), chemicals, 36 (2·5%), manufactured goods, 16 (1·1%), machinery and transport equipment, 4 (0·3%) and miscellaneous manufactures, 294 (20·5%).

Tourism. In 1995, 1,752,179 visitors (including 605,178 cruise ship arrivals) arrived, spending about US$965m.

COMMUNICATIONS

Roads (1993). The island has 3,000 miles of main roads, and over 7,000 miles of secondary and tertiary roads. In 1995 there were 135,059 licensed vehicles (including 86,791 passenger cars). There were 7,379 traffic accidents in 1995 with 367 fatalities.

Civil Aviation. International airlines operate through the Norman Manley and Sangster airports at Palisadoes and Montego Bay. In 1995 Norman Manley airport had 20,879 aircraft movements, handled 1·4m. passengers and 28,800 tonnes of freight. Sangster had 21,916 aircraft movements, with 2·3m. passengers. Trans-Jamaica Airlines Ltd operates internal flights. Air Jamaica, originally set up in conjunction with BOAC and BWIA in 1966, became a new company, Air Jamaica (1968) Ltd. In 1969 it began operations as Jamaica's national airline. In 1993 Air Jamaica carried 1m. passengers. In 1995 it operated 5 A300B4-200s, 5 B-727-200 Advs and 2 A310s.

Services are also provided by Air Canada, ALM, American Airlines, British Airways, BWIA, Cayman Airways, COPA, Cubana and KLM.

Shipping. In 1995 the merchant marine totalled 10,545 GRT, including oil tankers, 3,292 GRT. In 1995 there were 3,275 visits to all ports; 13·9m. tonnes of cargo were handled. Kingston had 2,120 visits and handled 4·4m. tonnes.

Telecommunications. In 1995 there were 316 post offices and 477 postal agencies. In 1995 there were 411,777 telephones.

There were (1995) 7 commercial and 1 publicly owned broadcasting stations; the latter also operates a television service (colour by NTSC), and there was 1 commercial television station. In 1991 there were 1,481,000 radio and 484,000 TV sets.

Cinemas. In 1993 there were 35 cinemas and 2 drive-in cinemas.

SOCIAL INSTITUTIONS

Justice. The Judicature comprises a Supreme Court, a court of appeal, resident magistrates' courts, petty sessional courts, coroners' courts, a traffic court and a family court which was instituted in 1975. The Chief Justice is head of the judiciary. 54,595 crimes were reported in 1995, of which 33,889 were cleared up. The daily average prison population, 1995, was 3,289.

Police. The Constabulary Force in 1995 stood at approximately 5,861 officers, subofficers and constables (men and women).

Religion. Freedom of worship is guaranteed under the Constitution. The main Christian denominations are Anglican, Baptist, Roman Catholic, Methodist, Church of God, United Church of Jamaica and Grand Cayman (Presbyterian–Congregational–Disciples of Christ), Moravian, Seventh-Day Adventist, Pentecostal, Salvation Army and Quaker. Pocomania is a mixture of Christianity and African survivals. Non-Christians include Hindus, Jews, Moslems, Bahai followers and Rastafarians.

Education. Education is free in government-operated schools. Schools and colleges in 1994–95 (government-operated and grant-aided): Basic, 1,694; infant, 29; primary, 792; primary with infant department, 83; all-age, 430; primary and junior high, 20; new secondary, 47; secondary high, 56; comprehensive high, 23; technical high, 12; agricultural/vocational, 6; special, 11; (independent): Kindergarten/preparatory, 126; secondary high with preparatory department, 28; high/vocational, 5; business education, 29; (tertiary): Teacher-training, 13.

Numbers of pupils and students, 1994–95: Basic schools, 116,390; infant, 9,710; infant departments in primary schools, 6,737; primary, 172,510; all-age and primary and junior high (grades 1 to 6), 132,728; all-age and primary and junior high (grades 7 to 9), 54,371; new secondary, 30,797; secondary high, 70,613; technical high, 14,199; comprehensive high, 45,332; agricultural/vocational, 1,699. Numbers of teachers, 1994–95: Infant schools, 299; primary, 5,399; all-age and primary and junior high (grades 1 to 9), 6,424; new secondary, 1,852; secondary high, 4,132; technical high, 831; comprehensive high, 2,393; agricultural/vocational, 119.

The University of the West Indies is at Kingston. In 1994–95 it had 12,630 students, 800 external students and about 900 academic staff. The University of Technology in Kingston had 6,374 students, and the College of Agriculture, Science and Education in Portland, 533 students. Adult literacy rate: 84·4%.

Health. In 1995 the public health service had 4,058 staff in medicine, nursing and pharmacology; 326 in dentistry; 260 public health inspectors; 70 in nutrition. In 1995 there were 371 primary health centres, 5,021 public hospital beds and 305 private beds.

DIPLOMATIC REPRESENTATIVES

Of Jamaica in Great Britain (1-2 Prince Consort Rd., London, SW7 2BZ)
High Commissioner: Derick R. Heaven.

Of Great Britain in Jamaica (Trafalgar Rd., Kingston 10)
High Commissioner: Richard Thomas, CMG.

Of Jamaica in the USA (1850 K. St., NW, Washington, D.C., 20006)
Ambassador: Richard L. Bernal.

Of the USA in Jamaica (2 Oxford Rd., Kingston 5)
Ambassador: Jerome Gary Cooper.

Of Jamaica to the United Nations
Ambassador: M. Patricia Durrant, CD.

Of Jamaica to the European Union
Ambassador: Douglas A. C. Saunders.

Further Reading

Planning Institute of Jamaica. *Economic and Social Survey, Jamaica.* Annual.—*Survey of Living Conditions.* Annual
Statistical Institute of Jamaica. *Statistical Abstract.* Annual.—*Demographic Statistics.* Annual.—*Production Statistics.* Annual.

Bakan, A. B. *Ideology and Class Conflict in Jamaica: the Politics of Rebellion.* Montreal, 1990
Goulbourne, H., *Teachers, Education and Politics in Jamaica, 1892–1972.* London, 1988
Ingram, K. E., *Jamaica.* [Bibliography] Oxford and Santa Barbara (CA), 1997
Manley, M., *A Voice at the Workplace.* London, 1975.—*Jamaica: Struggle in the Periphery.* London, 1983
Payne, A. J., *Politics in Jamaica.* London and New York, 1988

National library: National Library of Jamaica, Kingston.
National statistical office: Statistical Institute of Jamaica (STATIN), POB 643, Kingston 5.
   Director General, Vernon James.

JAPAN

Nihon (or Nippon[1]) Koku

(Land of the Rising Sun)

Capital: Tokyo
Population: 125·86m.
GDP per head: (PPP$) 21,581
HDI/world rank: 0·940/7

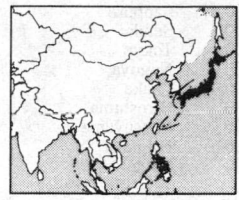

KEY HISTORICAL EVENTS. The house of Yamato united the nation in about 200 AD. The present imperial family are their direct descendants. From 1186 until 1867 successive families of the military Shoguns exercised the temporal power. In 1867 the Emperor Meiji recovered the imperial power after the abdication on 14 Oct. 1867 of the fifteenth and last Tokugawa Shogun Keiko. In 1871 the feudal system (*Hōken Seido*) was abolished and in the early 1890's constitutional government was introduced by the Emperor.

Japan's victory over Russia in the war of 1904 prevented Russian expansion into Korea and consolidated Japan' position as the strongest military power in Asia. Japan used the pretext of the Anglo-Japanese alliance to attack Chinese territory during the First World War. Bad feelings over the terms of the subsequent peace treaty led to continuing hostility between the two countries.

Economic distress, population growth (from 30m. in 1868 to 65m. in 1930) and a sense of dissatisfaction with the 'unjapanese' system of constitutional government led to the emergence between the wars of extremist nationalist and militarist movements in Japan. Plots among the young army officers, a revolt in Manchuria and the assassination of two prime ministers (a third only escaped when his brother-in-law was shot by mistake) highlighted the weaknesses of central government. In 1936 a military revolt in Tokyo gave the premiership to Konoe Fumimaro, a popular but ineffective figure, who failed to prevent further militarization of the country. In 1938 a national mobilization law was passed and in 1940 all political parties merged into the Imperial Rule Assistance Association.

On 27 Sept. 1940 Germany, Italy and Japan signed a 10 year pact to assure their mutual co-operation in the establishment of a 'new world order', with Japanese leadership recognized in Asia. In 1940 Japan invaded North Indochina and on 7 Dec. 1941 attacked the United States (principally at Pearl Harbour) and British bases in the Pacific, and then declared war on these two countries. Japanese forces eventually surrendered in Aug. 1945 after the dropping of atomic bombs on Hiroshima and Nagasaki. The country was placed under US military occupation, and in a new constitution in 1947 the Japanese people renounced the war and pledged themselves to uphold democracy and peace. The Emperor became a constitutional monarch instead of a divine ruler.

At San Francisco on 8 Sept. 1951 a Treaty of Peace was signed by Japan and representatives of 48 countries. A security treaty with the US provided for the stationing of American troops in Japan until the latter was able to undertake its own defence. The peace treaty came into force on 28 April 1952, when Japan regained her sovereignty. Of the islands under US administration since 1945, the Bonin (Ogasawara), Volcano, and Daito groups and Marcus Island were returned to Japan in 1968, and the southern Ryuku Islands (Okinawa) in 1972.

TERRITORY AND POPULATION. Japan consists of 4 major islands, Honshu, Hokkaido, Kyushu and Shikoku, and many small islands, with an area of 377,819 sq. km. Census population (1 Oct. 1995) 125,568,504 (males 61,575,570, females 63,992,934); density, 337 per sq. km. Population estimate, 1996, 125·86m. Foreigners registered 31 Dec. 1996 were 1,415,136 of whom 657,159 were Koreans, 234,264 Chinese, 201,795 Brazilians, 84,569 Filipinos, 44,168 Americans, 37,099 Peruvians, 18,187 Thais, 13,328 British, 10,228 Vietnamese, 8,418 Iranians, 8,023 Canadians, 8,742 Indonesians, 6,290 Australians, 6,343 Indians and 2,109 stateless persons.

[1] Both forms are valid, and derive from different pronunciations of a Chinese character.

Japanese overseas, Oct. 1996, 763,977; of these 273,779 lived in the USA, 89,005 in Brazil, 55,372 in the UK, 26,545 in Canada, 24,117 in Germany, 25,688 in Australia, 25,355 in Singapore, 23,292 in Thailand, 24,500 in Hong Kong, 20,060 in France, 19,379 in China.

The areas, populations and chief cities of the principal islands (and regions) are:

Island/Region	Sq. km	Census 1995	Chief cities
Hokkaido	83,452	5,692,000	Sapporo
Honshu/Tohoku	66,946	9,834,000	Sendai
Honshu/Kanto	32,419	39,518,000	Tokyo
Honshu/Chubu	66,780	21,400,000	Nagoya
Honshu/Kinki	33,097	22,468,000	Osaka
Honshu/Chugoku	31,909	7,775,000	Hiroshima
Shikoku	18,799	4,183,000	Matsuyama
Kyushu	42,157	13,424,000	Fukuoka
Okinawa	2,266	1,274,000	Naha

The leading cities, with population, 1 Oct. 1995 (in 1,000), are:

Akashi	288	Kasugai	278	Omiya	434
Akita	312	Kawagoe	323	Osaka	2,602
Amagasaki	489	Kawaguchi	449	Otsu	276
Aomori	294	Kawasaki	1,203	Sagamihara	571
Asahikawa	361	Kitakyushu	1,020	Sakai	803
Chiba	857	Kobe	1,424	Sapporo	1,757
Fujisawa	369	Kochi	322	Sasebo	245
Fukui	256	Koriyama	327	Sendai	971
Fukuoka	1,285	Koshigaya	298	Shimonoseki	260
Fukushima	286	Kumamoto	650	Shizuoka	474
Fukuyama	375	Kurashiki	423	Suita	343
Funabashi	541	Kyoto	1,464	Takamatsu	331
Gifu	407	Machida	361	Takatsuki	362
Hachioji	503	Maebashi	285	Tokorozawa	320
Hakodate	299	Matsudo	462	Tokushima	269
Hamamatsu	562	Matsuyama	461	Tokyo	7,968
Higashiosaka	517	Miyazaki	300	Toyama	325
Himeji	471	Nagano	359	Toyohashi	353
Hirakata	400	Nagasaki	439	Toyonaka	399
Hiroshima	1,109	Nagoya	2,152	Toyota	341
Ibaraki	258	Naha	302	Urawa	453
Ichihara	277	Nara	359	Utsunomiya	435
Ichinomiya	267	Neyagawa	258	Wakayama	395
Ichikawa	441	Niigata	495	Yao	277
Iwaki	361	Nishinomiya	390	Yokkaichi	286
Kagoshima	546	Oita	427	Yokohama	3,307
Kanazawa	454	Okayama	616	Yokosuka	432
Kashiwa	318	Okazaki	323		

Vital statistics (in 1,000) for calendar years:

	1990	1991	1992	1993	1994	1995	1996
Births	1,222	1,224	1,228	1,204	1,229	1,221	1,203
Deaths	820	830	854	882	877	924	896

Crude birth rate of Japanese nationals in present area, 1995, was 9·6 per 1,000 population (1947: 34·3); crude death rate, 7·4; crude marriage rate, 6·4; infant mortality rate per 1,000 live births, 4·3. Population growth rate was 2·1 per 1,000 in 1995. Expectation of life was 76·36 years for men, 82·84 years for women in 1995.

The suicide rate per 100,000 population in 1996 was 17·7 (men, 24·1; women, 11·3).

CLIMATE. The islands of Japan lie in the temperate zone, north-east of the main monsoon region of South-East Asia. The climate is temperate with warm, humid summers and relatively mild winters except in the island of Hokkaido and northern parts of Honshu facing the Japan Sea. There is a month's rainy season in June-July, but the best seasons are spring and autumn, though Sept. may bring typhoons. There is a summer rainfall maximum. Tokyo. Jan. 5·2°C, July 25·2°C. Annual rainfall

1,405mm. Hiroshima. Jan. 4°C, July 25·7°C. Annual rainfall 1,555 mm. Nagasaki. Jan. 6·4°C, July 26·6°C. Annual rainfall 1,945 mm. Osaka. Jan. 5·5°C, July 27°C. Annual rainfall 1,318 mm. Sapporo. Jan. –4·6°C, July 20·2°C. Annual rainfall 1,130mm.

IMPERIAL HOUSE. The Emperor is **Akihito** (b. 23 Dec. 1933), who succeeded his father, Hirohito on 7 Jan. 1989 (enthroned, 12 Nov. 1990); married 10 April 1959, to Michiko Shoda (b. 20 Oct. 1934). *Offspring:* Crown Prince Naruhito (Hironomiya; b. 23 Feb. 1960), married Masako Owada (b. 9 Dec. 1963) 9 June 1993; Prince Fumihito (Akishinomiya; b. 30 Nov. 1965); Princess Sayako (Norinomiya; b. 18 April 1969). The succession to the throne is fixed upon the male descendants.

CONSTITUTION AND GOVERNMENT. The 1947 constitution supersedes the Meiji constitution of 1889. In it the Japanese people pledge themselves to uphold the ideas of democracy and peace. The Emperor is the symbol of the States and of the unity of the people. Sovereign power rests with the people. The Emperor has no powers related to government. Fundamental human rights are guaranteed.

Legislative power rests with the *Diet*, which consists of the *House of Representatives*, elected by men and women over 20 years of age for a 4-year term, and an upper house, the *House of Councillors* of 252 members (100 elected by party list system with proportional representation according to the d'Hondt method and 152 from prefectural districts), one-half of its members being elected every 3 years.

Elections to 126 seats of the House of Councillors were held on 23 July 1995; turn-out was 44%. The LDP gained 49 seats, Shinshinto 40, the SDP 16, the Communists 8, the NHP 3 and others 13.

In Nov. 1994 the Diet adopted electoral reforms changing the number of members in the House of Representatives from 511 to 500, of whom 300 are to be elected from single-seat constituencies, and 200 by proportional representation on a base of 11 regions. There is a 2% threshold to gain one of the latter seats. Donations to individual politicians are to be supplanted over 5 years by state subsidies to parties.

Elections to the House of Representatives were held on 20 Oct. 1996. Turn-out was 59·6%. The Liberal Democratic Party (LDP) gained 239 seats; New Frontier Party, 156; Democratic Party of Japan, 52; Japan Communist Party, 26; Social Democratic Party, 15; New Harbinger Party, 2; minor parties and ind, 10.

The largest opposition party, Shinshinto, was dissolved in Dec. 1997 and at the beginning of Jan. 1998, 6 new parties emerged.

A new government was formed on 11 Sept. 1997 comprising in March 1998:
Prime Minister: Ryutaro Hashimoto (b. 1912; LDP).
Minister of Justice: Kokichi Shimoinaba. *Foreign Affairs:* Kiezo Obuchi. *Finance:* Hikaru Matsunaga. *Education:* Nobutaka Machimura. *Health and Welfare:* Junichiro Koizumi. *Agriculture, Forestry and Fisheries:* Yoshinobu Shimamura. *International Trade and Industry:* Mitsuo Horiuchi. *Transport:* Takao Fujii. *Posts and Telecommunications:* Shozaburo Jimi. *Labour:* Bunmei Ibuki. *Construction:* Tsutomu Kawara. *Home Affairs:* Mitsuhiro Uesugi. *Chief Cabinet Secretary:* Kanezo Muraoka. *Director General, Management and Co-ordination Agency:* Sadatoshi Ozato. *Director General, Hokkaido Development Agency and Okinawa Development Agency:* Muneo Suzuki. *Director General, Defence Agency:* Fumio Kyuma. *Director General, Economic Planning Agency:* Koji Omi. *Director General, Science and Technology Agency:* Sadakazu Tanizaki. *Director General, Environment Agency:* Hiroshi Oki. *Director General, National Land Agency:* Hisaoki Kamei.

National anthem: 'Kimi ga yo wa'('May your peaceful reign long last'); words 9th century, tune by Hiromori Hayashi.

Local Government. The country is divided into 47 prefectures, each with an elected governor. Each prefecture, city, town and village has a representative elected assembly. There were 3,233 local authorities at 1 Oct. 1995. Elections were held on 9 and 22 April 1995 for 13 prefectural governorships, 43 prefectural assemblies and

86 mayorships. Turn-out was 60%. 60% of prefectural assembly seats were won by independents.

DEFENCE. Japan has renounced war as a sovereign right and the threat or the use of force as a means of settling disputes with other nations. Its troops had not been able to serve abroad, but in 1992 the House of Representatives voted to allow up to 2,000 troops to take part in UN peacekeeping missions. A law of Nov. 1994 authorizes the Self-Defence Force to send aircraft abroad in rescue operations where Japanese citizens are involved.

In Jan. 1991 Japan and the USA signed a renewal agreement under which Japan pays 40% of the costs of stationing US forces and 100% of the associated labour costs. US forces in Japan totalled 47,000 in 1997, of whom 28,000 were on Okinawa. A US-Japanese agreement of Dec. 1996 stipulates that one fifth of the territory on Okinawa occupied by the US military is to be returned to local landowners by 2008.

Army. The 'Ground Self-Defence Force' is organized in 5 regional commands and had in 1997 an authorized strength of 148,000 (5,200 women) and a reserve of 46,000 men. The Army is organized in 12 infantry divisions, 1 armoured division, 1 airborne brigade, 2 air defence brigades, 1 artillery, 2 combined, 5 engineer and 1 helicopter brigade in addition to 4 training brigades. Equipment includes 190 T-61, 870 T-74 and 100 T-90 main battle tanks, approximately 90 AH-1S attack helicopters, as well as some 200 transport helicopters and 16 MU-2H fixed-wing aircraft.

Navy. The 'Maritime Self-Defence Force' is tasked with coastal protection and defence of the sea lanes to 1,000 nautical miles range from Japan. The modern and well-equipped combatant forces are mainly fitted with American weapon systems, which in many cases have been re-engineered and improved in Japan.

The combatant fleet, all home-built, includes 17 diesel submarines and 1 trials and training boat. There are 3 Aegis-equipped guided-missile destroyers, 5 other guided-missile destroyers armed with US Standard SM-1 surface-to-air missiles, 25 helicopter-carrying frigates and 27 other frigates of which 2 are employed on non-military tasks. Light forces comprise 3 missile hydrofoils and 3 small inshore patrol craft. There are 39 mine warfare vessels: 1 minelayer, 1 layer/command ship, 3 1,200-tonne offshore mine countermeasure vessels, 27 coastal minesweepers and 2 smaller vessels. A substantial amphibious capability is provided by 6 tank landing ships supported by some 40 smaller craft. 12 major auxiliaries include 4 combined oiler/ammunition ships, 8 survey vessels and 5 training support vessels, and there are several hundred minor auxiliaries and service craft.

The Air Arm, organized into 7 operational Air Groups, includes 88 Orion anti-submarine patrol aircraft, 7 US-1A rescue flying boats, 60 Sea King anti-submarine helicopters, 10 mine countermeasures helicopters as well as about 100 transport, training and utility aircraft.

The main elements of the fleet are organized into 4 escort flotillas based at Yokosuka (2), Sasebo and Maizuru. The submarines are based at Sasebo and Kure.

Personnel in 1996 numbered 43,000 including about 12,000 in the Naval Air Arm.

Coastguard. This is administered by the Ministry of Transport. For details *see under* COMMUNICATIONS *below.*

Air Force. An 'Air Self-Defence Force' was inaugurated on 1 July 1954. Its equipment includes 7 interceptor squadrons of F-15J/DJ Eagles and 3 of F-4EJ Phantoms; 3 squadrons of Mitsubishi F-1 close-support fighters; 1 squadron of RF-4E reconnaissance fighters; 13 E-2C Hawkeye AWACS aircraft; ECM flight with 2 YS-11Es; 2 squadrons of turbofan Kawasaki C-1 and 1 with turboprop C-130H Hercules and NAMC YS-11 transports. About 90 KV-107, CH-47 Chinook and Black Hawk helicopters, and MU-2 twin-turboprop aircraft perform search, rescue and general duties. Training units use piston-engined Fuji T-3 basic trainers, Fuji T-1 jet intermediate trainers, Kawasaki T-4 jet trainers and supersonic Mitsubishi T-2 jet advanced trainers. 6 surface-to-air missile groups (19 squadrons) are in service. Strength (1996) 44,500.

INTERNATIONAL RELATIONS

Membership. Japan is a member of the UN, Colombo Plan, APEC and OECD.

ECONOMY

Policy. The head of the Economic Planning Agency (Koji Omi) has cabinet rank. The real growth rate for 1998 was estimated at 1·9% and the nominal at 2·4%. In Dec. 1996 the Government adopted a 5-year economic and financial reform plan centred on the relaxing of state controls and the creation of jobs. Its implementation is co-ordinated by the Ministry of International Trade and Industry. In late 1997 the economy was thrown off course by the collapse of three leading financial institutions which had been saddled with bad debts following the stock market and property crash in 1990. Following a period of recession, this raised fears of another but more severe downturn. Economic growth in 1998 was set to turn negative for the first time since the oil crisis of 1974 savaged the economy. Yet, for all the financial blues, Japan remains one of the world's strongest economies with a highly trained workforce and the talent to exploit profitable export markets.

Performance. The real growth rate for 1996 was estimated at 2·5% and the nominal at 2·7%.

Budget. Ordinary revenue and expenditure for fiscal year ending 31 March 1998 balanced at 77,390,000m. yen.

Of the proposed revenue (in yen) in 1996, 57,802,000m. was to come from taxes and stamps, 16,707,000m. from public bonds. Main items of expenditure: Social security, 14,550,100m.; public works, 9,744,700m.; local government, 15,481,000m.; education, 6,343,600m.; defence, 4,947,500m.

The outstanding national debt incurred by public bonds was estimated in March 1996 to be 227,975,000m. yen.

The estimated 1997 budgets of the prefectures and other local authorities forecast a total revenue of 87,060,000m. yen, to be made up partly by local taxes and partly by government grants and local loans.

Currency. The unit of currency is the *yen* (JPY). There are coins of 1, 5, 10, 50, 100 and 500 yen and notes of 1,000, 5,000 and 10,000 yen.

In Dec. 1996 the currency in circulation consisted of 50,671,000m. yen Bank of Japan notes and 3,918,000m. yen subsidiary coins.

Banking and Finance. The Nippon Ginko (Bank of Japan), founded 1882, finances the government and the banks, its function being similar to that of a central bank in other countries. The Bank undertakes the management of Treasury funds and foreign exchange control. Its *Governor* is Yasuo Matsushita (b. 1926; appointed Jan. 1995 for a 5-year term). Its gold bullion and cash holdings at 31 Dec. 1996 stood at 464,000m. yen.

There were on 31 Dec. 1996, 10 city banks, 64 regional banks, 33 trust banks, 3 long-term credit banks, 65 member banks of the second association of regional banks, 412 Shinkin banks (credit associations), 365 credit co-operatives, and 92 foreign banks. There are also various governmental financial institutions, including postal savings which amounted to 231,306,200m. yen in Sept. 1997. Total savings by individuals, including insurance and securities, stood at 1,018,873,400m. yen on 30 Sept. 1997, and about 64% of these savings were deposited in banks and the post-office.

1997 saw the disappearance of Yamaichi Securities, Japan's fourth largest stockholder; also Sanyo Securities and the Hokkaido Takushoku bank.

There are 8 stock exchanges, the largest being in Tokyo, Osaka and Nagoya.

Weights and Measures. The metric system is obligatory.

ENERGY AND NATURAL RESOURCES

Electricity. Japan is poor in energy resources, and nuclear power generation is important in reducing dependence on foreign supplies. In 1995 generating facilities were capable of an output of 227·0m. kW; electricity produced was 989,966m. kWh. There were 50 nuclear reactors in 19 power plants, producing 29·4% of electricity, and 6 more were under construction in 1995. 10 regional publicly-held supply companies produce 74·5% of output.

Oil and Gas. Output of crude petroleum, 1995, was 861,000 kl, almost entirely from oilfields on the island of Honshu, but 266·9m. kl crude oil had to be imported. Output of natural gas, 1995, 2,209m. cu. metres.

Minerals. Ore production in tonnes, 1995, of coal, 6,317,000; iron, 2,959; zinc, 95,274; copper, 2,376; lead, 9,659; tungsten, 66 (1993); silver, 100,078 kg; gold, 9,185 kg.

Agriculture. Agricultural workers in 1996 on farms with 0·3 ha or more of cultivated land or 0·5m. yen annual sales were 4·0m., including 0·3m. subsidiary and seasonal workers; 5·2% (1994) of the labour force as opposed to 24·7% in 1962. The arable land area in 1996 was 4,994,000 ha. Rice is the staple food, but its consumption is declining. Rice cultivation accounted for 1,977,000 ha in 1996. The area planted with industrial crops such as rapeseed, tobacco, tea, rush, etc., was 205,000 ha in 1995.

Average farm size was 1·5 ha in 1996. Farmers are represented by the co-operative organization in Nokyo.

In 1995 there were 3,467,000 power cultivators and tractors and 1,650,000 rice power planters. (1990): 1,871,000 power sprayers and dusters.

Output of rice (in 1,000 tonnes), was 11,981 in 1994, 10,748 in 1995 and 10,344 in 1996.

Production in 1996 (in 1,000 tonnes) of barley was 234; wheat, 478; soybeans, 148. Sweet potatoes, which in the past mitigated the effects of rice famines, have, in view of rice over-production, decreased from 4,955,000 tonnes in 1965 to 1,109,000 tonnes in 1996. Domestic sugar-beet and sugar-cane production accounted for only 31% of requirement in 1994. In 1995, 1·75m. tonnes were imported, 42·8% of this being imported from Australia, 32·6% from Thailand, 10·1% from South Africa and 9·7% from Cuba.

Fruit production, 1995 (in 1,000 tonnes): Mandarins, 1,378; apples, 963; pears, 401; grapes, 250; peaches, 163 and persimmons, 254.

Livestock (1996): 4·88m. cattle (including about 1·93m. milch cows), 28,000 horses (1994), 9·9m. pigs, 25,000 sheep (1994), 31,000 goats (1994), 309m. chickens. Milk (1995), 8·38m. tonnes.

Forestry. Forests and grasslands covered about 25m. ha of the whole land area in 1993, with an estimated timber stand of 3,483m. cu. metres in 1995. In 1994, 31,349,000 cu. metres were felled.

Fisheries. The catch in 1995 was 7·49m. tonnes, excluding whaling.

INDUSTRY. The industrial structure is dominated by corporate groups (*keiretsu*) either linking companies in different branches or linking individual companies with their suppliers and distributors.

Japan's industrial equipment, 1994, numbered 382,825 plants of companies with 4 or more employees, employing 10·42m. production workers.

Output in 1996 includes: Television sets 7·57m., radio sets 3·5m., cameras 12·26m., computers 9·2m. The chemical industry ranks fourth in shipment value after machinery, metals and food products. Production, 1996, included (in tonnes): Sulphuric acid, 6·9m.; caustic soda, 3,940,000; ammonium sulphate, 1·81m.; calcium superphosphate, 328,000.

Output (1996), in 1,000 tonnes, of pig iron was 74,597; crude steel, 98,801; ordinary rolled steel, 78,266.

In 1996 paper production was 17,767,000 tonnes; paperboard, 12·25m. tonnes.

Output of cotton yarn, 1996, 196,000 tonnes, and of cotton cloth, 916m. sq. metres.

Output, 1996, 65,000 tonnes of woollen yarns and 247m. sq. metres of woollen fabrics.

Output, 1996, of rayon woven fabrics, 401m. sq. metres; synthetic woven fabrics, 1,997m. sq. metres; silk fabrics, 58m. sq. metres.

Shipbuilding has been decreasing and in 1995, 8,678,000 GRT were launched, of which 2,350,000 GRT were tankers.

Labour. Total labour force, 1996, was 64·9m., of which 3·3m. were in agriculture and forestry, 0·26m. in fishing, 60,000 in mining, 6·7m. in construction, 14m. in manufacturing, 17·19m. in commerce and finance, 4·48m. in transport and other public utilities, 15·98m. in services (including the professions) and 2·14m. in government work. Retirement age is being raised progressively from 60 years to reach 65 by 2013.

In 1996, 2·25m. (3·4%) were unemployed. In 1996, 43,000 working days were lost in industrial stoppages. In 1996 the average working week was 39·98 hours.

Trade Unions. In 1996 there were 12,451,000 workers organized in 70,699 unions. In Nov. 1989, the 'Japanese Private Sector Trade Union Confederation' (Rengo), which was organized in 1987, was reorganized into the 'Japan Trade Union Confederation' (Rengo) with the former 'General Council of Japanese Trade Unions' (Sohyo) and other unions, and was the largest federation with 7,658,000 members in 1996. The 'National Confederation of Trade Unions' (Zenroren) had 281,000 members in 1996 and the 'National Trade Union Council' (Zenrokyo) 298,000 members in 1994.

FOREIGN ECONOMIC RELATIONS

Commerce. Trade (in US$1m.):

	1991	1992	1993	1994	1995	1996
Imports	236,737	233,021	240,670	274,742	336,094	333,832
Exports	314,525	339,650	360,911	395,600	442,937	393,035

Distribution of trade by countries (customs clearance basis) (US$1m.):

	Exports		Imports	
	1995	1996	1995	1996
Africa[1]	7,524	5,874	4,713	5,062
Australia	8,104	7,082	14,569	13,604
Canada	5,827	4,898	10,834	9,670
China	21,931	20,933	35,922	38,658
Germany	20,317	17,405	13,705	13,539
Hong Kong	27,775	24,251	2,739	2,461
Latin America	19,696	17,919	11,924	11,487
ASEAN[2]	77,633	73,096	48,288	52,388
Korea, Republic of	31,291	28,050	17,269	15,248
Taiwan	28,969	24,823	14,366	14,302
UK	14,141	11,933	7,151	6,853
USA	120,859	106,993	75,408	75,837

[1] Figures are not comparable to those through 1994 because of change in the coverage of survey. Data until 1994 exclude South Africa and some countries included in the Middle East.
[2] Data of Asia and ASEAN have been published instead of those of Southeast Asia since 1995.

Principal items in 1996, with value in 1m. yen were:

Imports, c.i.f.		Exports, f.o.b.	
Mineral fuels	6,588,000	Machinery and transport	
Foodstuffs	5,523,000	equipment	33,163,000
Raw materials	3,304,000	Metals and metal products	2,779,000
Metal ores and scrap	898,000	Textile products	930,000
Machinery and transport		Chemicals	3,139,000
equipment	10,461,000		

The importation of rice was prohibited, but in 1993–94 there was an emergency importation of 1m. tonnes from Australia, China, Thailand and the USA to offset a poor domestic harvest. The prohibition was lifted in line with WTO agreements. Till 2000 rice imports will have limited access; thereafter the market will be fully open.

Tourism. In 1996, 4,244,529 foreigners visited Japan, 606,652 of whom came from USA, 283,838 from UK. Japanese travelling abroad totalled 16,694,769 in 1996.

COMMUNICATIONS

Roads. The total length of roads (including urban and other local roads) was 1,142,308 km at 1 April 1995. There were 53,327 km of national roads, of which 52,545 km were paved. Motor vehicles, at 31 Dec. 1996, numbered 67,200,000, including 46,868,000 passenger cars and 20,089,000 commercial vehicles. The world's longest undersea road tunnel spanning Tokyo Bay was opened in Dec. 1997. The Tokyo Bay Aqualine built at a cost of 1·44 trillion yen (US$11·3bn.) consists of a 4·4 kilometre (2·7 mile) bridge and a 9·4 kilometre tunnel that allows commuters to cross the bay in about 15 minutes.

Railways. The first railway was completed in 1872, between Tokyo and Yokohama (29 km). Most railways are of 1,067 mm, but the high-speed 'Shinkansen' lines are standard 1,435 mm gauge. In April 1987 the Japanese National Railways was reorganized into 7 private companies, the Japanese Railways (JR) Group—6 passenger companies and 1 freight company. Total length of railways, in March 1996, was 27,258 km, of which the JR had 20,135 km and other private railways, 7,123 km. In 1995 the JR carried 8,982m. passengers (other private, 13,648m.) and 51m. tons of freight (other private, 25m.). An undersea tunnel linking Honshu with Hokkaido was opened to rail services in 1988.

There are metros in Tokyo (2 systems, total 230 km in 1995), Fukuoka (18 km), Kobe (2 systems total 30 km), Kyoto (11 km), Nagoya (77 km), Osaka (106 km), Sapporo (45 km), Sendai (15 km) and Yokohama (33 km), and tram/light rail networks in 19 cities.

Civil Aviation. There are international airports at Tokyo (Narita), Fukuoka, Kagoshima, Kansai, Nagoya Komaki and Osaka. The principal airlines are Japan Airlines (JAL), Japan Air System and All Nippon Airways. In 1995 their fleets were as follows: JAL: 1 B-737-400, 2 B-747-100s, 3 B-747-100Bs, 2 B-747-100B Suds, 21 B-747-200Bs, 1 B-747-200B(F), 6 B-747-200Fs, 9 B-747-300s, 24 B-747-400s, 8 B-747-400Ds, 4 B-747-SR-300s, 3 B-767-200s, 17 B-767-300s and 20 other aircraft; Japan Air System: 9 A300B2-200s, 8 A300B4-200s, 14 A300B4-600Rs and 51 other aircraft; All Nippon Airways: 14 A320-200s, 6 B-747-200Bs, 7 B-747-400s, 10 B-747-400Ds, 14 B-747SRs, 25 B-767-200s, 32 B-767-300s, 5 B-767-300ERs and 3 other aircraft. In the financial year 1995 Japanese companies carried 78,10m. passengers in domestic services and 14·47m. passengers in international services.

Shipping. On 1 July 1996 the merchant fleet consisted of 6,824 vessels of 100 GRT and over; total tonnage 18m. GRT; there were 199 ships for passenger transport (245,000 GRT), 2,148 cargo ships (1,107,000 GRT) and 1,063 oil tankers (5·81m. GRT).

Coastguard. The 'Maritime Safety Agency' (Coastguard) consists of 1 headquarters, 11 regional headquarters, 66 offices, 1 maritime guard and rescue office, 51 stations, 14 air stations, 1 special rescue station, 10 district communications centres, 5 traffic advisory service centres, 4 hydrographic observatories, 1 Loran navigation system centre, and 97 navigation aids offices (with 5,429 navigation aids facilities) and controls 48 large patrol vessels, 47 medium patrol vessels, 19 small patrol vessels, 225 patrol craft, 13 hydrographic service vessels, 5 large firefighting boats, 10 medium firefighting boats and 77 guard and rescue boats, and 1 aids to navigation evaluation vessel, 4 buoy tenders, 66 aids to navigation tenders (as of May 1, 1996). Personnel in 1996 FY numbered 12,204.

The Coastguard aviation service includes 26 fixed-wing aircraft and 44 helicopters.

Telecommunications. Telephone services have been operated by private companies (NTT and others) since 1985. In 1995 there were 71m. subscribers, including 10m. mobile telephones.

Broadcasting is under the aegis of the public Japan Broadcasting Corporation (Nippon Hoso Kyokai) and the National Association of Commercial Broadcasters

(Minporen). The former transmits 2 national networks and an external service, Radio Japan (22 languages). There is also a university station and a religious broadcasting station. Nippon Hoso Kyokai transmits a general and an educational TV programme, and there are 5 commercial networks. In 1994 there were 114m. radio and 85m. TV sets (colour by NTSC).

Cinemas (1996). Cinemas numbered 1,828 with an annual attendance of 120m. (1960: 1,014m.).

Press (1995). Daily newspapers numbered 121 with aggregate circulation of 72·05m., including 4 major English-language newspapers. 72m. newspapers were sold a day in 1996.

SOCIAL INSTITUTIONS

Justice. The Supreme Court is composed of the Chief Justice and 14 other judges. The Chief Justice is appointed by the Emperor, the other judges by the Cabinet. Every 10 years a justice must submit himself to the electorate. All justices and judges of the lower courts serve until they are 70 years of age.

Below the Supreme Court are 8 regional higher courts, district courts in each prefecture (4 in Hokkaido) and the local courts.

The Supreme Court is authorized to declare unconstitutional any act of the Legislature or the Executive which violates the Constitution.

The police are under central government control.

Religion. State subsidies have ceased for all religions, and all religious teachings are forbidden in public schools. In Dec. 1995 Shintoism claimed 117m. adherents, Buddhism 87·48m.; these figures obviously overlap. Christians numbered 1·45m.

Education. Education is compulsory and free between the ages of 6 and 15. Almost all national and municipal institutions are co-educational. On 1 May 1996 there were 14,724 kindergartens with 103,518 teachers and 1,798,051 pupils; 23,857 elementary schools with 425,714 teachers and 8,105,629 pupils; 11,192 junior high schools with 270,972 teachers and 4,527,400 pupils; 5,353 senior high schools with 278,879 teachers and 4,547,497 pupils; 598 junior colleges with 20,294 teachers and 473,279 pupils.

There were also 893 special schools for handicapped children (52,723 teachers, 86,293 pupils).

Japan has 7 main state universities: Tokyo University (1877); Kyoto University (1897); Tohoku University, Sendai (1907); Kyushu University, Fukuoka (1910); Hokkaido University, Sapporo (1918); Osaka University (1931), and Nagoya University (1939). In addition, there are various other state and municipal as well as private universities. There are 576 colleges and universities altogether with (1 May 1996) 2,596,667 students and 139,608 teachers.

Health. Hospitals on 1 Oct. 1995 numbered 9,606 with 1,669,951 beds. Physicians at the end of 1994 numbered 230,519; dentists, 81,055.

Social Welfare. There are in force various types of social security schemes, such as health insurance, unemployment insurance and age pensions. Citizens over 60 receive pensions of 70% of the average wage. In 1995 the basic retirement pension was 214,300 yen per month, funded by contributions of 17·35% of salary. There was a total of 27m. pensioners in 1994.

In 1995, 10,586,753 persons and 7,223,101 households received some form of regular public assistance, the total of which came to 1,428,071m. yen.

14 weeks maternity leave is statutory.

DIPLOMATIC REPRESENTATIVES

Of Japan in Great Britain (101-104 Piccadilly, London, W1V 9FN)
Ambassador: Sadayuki Hayashi.

Of Great Britain in Japan (1 Ichiban-cho, Chiyoda-ku, Tokyo 102)
Ambassador: Sir David Wright, KCMG, LVO.

Of Japan in the USA (2520 Massachusetts Ave., NW, Washington, D.C., 20008)
Ambassador: Kunihiko Saito.

Of the USA in Japan (10–5, Akasaka 1-chome, Minato-ku, Tokyo)
Ambassador: Vacant.

Of Japan to the United Nations
Ambassador: Hisashi Owada.

Of Japan to the European Union
Ambassador: Atsushi Tokinoya.

Further Reading

Statistics Bureau of the Prime Minister's Office: *Statistical Year-Book* (from 1949).— *Statistical Abstract* (from 1950).—*Monthly Bulletin* (from April 1950)
Economic Planning Agency: *Economic Survey* (annual), *Economic Statistics* (monthly), *Economic Indicators* (monthly)
Ministry of International Trade: *Foreign Trade of Japan* (annual)

Allinson, G. D., *Japan's Postwar History*. London, 1997
Argy, V. and Stein, L., *The Japanese Economy*. London, 1996
Bailey, P. J., *Post-war Japan: 1945 to the Present*. Oxford, 1996
Beasley, W. G., *The Rise of Modern Japan: Political, Economic and Social Change since 1850*. 2nd ed. London, 1995
The Cambridge Encyclopedia of Japan. CUP, 1993
Cambridge History of Japan. vols. 1-5. CUP, 1990–93
Campbell, A. (ed.) *Japan: an Illustrated Encyclopedia*. Tokyo, 1994
Clesse, A. *et al*, (eds.) *The Vitality of Japan: Sources of National Strength and Weakness*. London, 1997
Cortazzi, H., *The Japanese Achievement*. London, 1990
Francks, P., *Japanese Economic Development: Theory and Practice*. London, 1991
Gordon, A., *Postwar Japan as History*. Univ. of California Press, 1993
Horsley, W. and Buckky, R., *Nippon, New Superpower: Japan since 1945*. London, 1990
Ito, T., *The Japanese Economy*. Boston (Mass.), 1992
Jain, P. and Inoguchi, T., *Japanese Politics Today*. London, 1997
Japan: an Illustrated Encyclopedia. London, 1993
Japan Times Year Book. Tokyo, first issue 1933
Johnson, C., *Japan: Who Governs? The Rise of the Developmental State*. New York, 1995
Martineau, L., *Caught in a Mirror: Reflections on Japan*. London, 1993
Nakano, M., *The Policy-making Process in Contemporary Japan*. London, 1996
Okabe, M., (ed.) *The Structure of the Japanese Economy: Changes on the Domestic and International Fronts*. London, 1994
Perren, R., *Japanese Studies From Pre-History to 1990*. Manchester Univ. Press, 1992
Reischauer, E. O., *The Japanese Today: Change and Continuity*. Harvard Univ. Press, 1991
Schirokauer, C., *Brief History of Japanese Civilization*. New York, 1993
Shulman, F. J., *Japan*. [Bibliography] Oxford and Santa Barbara (CA), 1990
Woronoff, J., *The Japanese Economic Crisis*. 2nd ed. London, 1996

National statistical office: Statistics Bureau, Prime Minister's Office, Tokyo.
Website: http://www.stat.go.jp/

JORDAN

Al-Mamlaka Al-Urduniya
Al-Hashemiyah

(Hashemite[1] Kingdom
of Jordan)

Capital: Amman
Population: 4·3m.
GDP per head (PPP$): 4,187
GNP: US$5·8bn.
HDI/world rank: 0·730/84

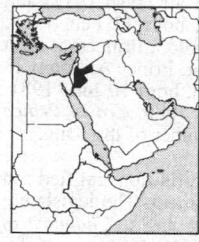

KEY HISTORICAL EVENTS. During the first World War (1914–18) the Arabs of Transjordan and Palestine rebelled against the suzerainty of Turkey, which had become an ally of Germany. Britain supported the rebellion, occupied the areas and in 1920 was given a League of Nations mandate for Transjordan and Palestine. In April 1921 the Amir Abdullah Ibn Hussein (brother of King Feisal of Iraq) became the ruler of Transjordan, which was officially separated from Palestine in 1923. On 20 Feb. 1928 an agreement was signed between Transjordan and Britain whereby the latter, (with the approval of the League of Nations) recognized the existence of an independent government in Transjordan under the rule of the Amir Abdullah.

By a treaty signed in London on 22 Mar. 1946 Britain recognized Transjordan as a sovereign independent state. On 25 May 1946 the Amir Abdullah assumed the title of king; and when the treaty was ratified on 17 June 1949 the name of the territory was changed to that of the Hashemite Kingdom of Jordan. On 13 Mar. 1957 the Anglo-Transjordan treaty of Mar. 1948 was terminated by mutual consent, and all British troops were withdrawn.

The part of Palestine remaining to the Arabs under the armistice with Israel on 3 April 1949, with the exception of the Gaza Strip on the Mediterranean coast, was in Dec. 1949 placed under Jordanian rule and formally incorporated in Jordan on 24 April 1950. In June 1967 this territory ('the West Bank') was occupied by Israel. On 31 July 1988 King Hussein announced the dissolution of Jordan's legal and administrative ties with the West Bank.

King Hussein, who became king in 1953 at the age of 17 because his father was mentally unfit to rule, has remained in executive control in the face of attempted assassinations and constant changes of prime ministers.

TERRITORY AND POPULATION. Jordan is bounded in the north by Syria, east by Iraq, south-east and south by Saudi Arabia and west by Israel. It has an outlet to an arm of the Red Sea at Aqaba. Its area is 91,860 sq. km. Its estimated population in 1997 was 4,324,638. Population of the 12 governorates:

Governorate	1995	Governorate	1995
Ajloun	98,600	Jerash	128,700
Amman	1,613,000	Ma'an	85,800
Aqaba	85,800	Madaba	111,400
Balqa	287,400	Mafraq	184,500
Irbid	776,600	Tafilah	64,300
Karak	175,900	Zarqa	661,000

The largest towns with suburbs, with estimated population, 1994: Amman, the capital, 1,300,042; Irbid, 379,844; Zarqa, 608,626.

Vital statistics (1997 estimates): birth rate, 3·6%; death rate, 0·38%; population growth, 2·6%; life expectancy, 72·7 years (70·8 for men, 74·7 for women). Jordan has a young population: 1997 estimates showed 44% aged under 15, 53% aged 15–64 and 3% aged 65 and over.

The official language is Arabic.

[1] 'Hashemite' denotes a descendant of the prophet Mohammed.

833

CLIMATE. Predominantly a Mediterranean climate, with hot dry summers and cool wet winters, but in hilly parts summers are cooler and winters colder. Those areas below sea-level are very hot in summer and warm in winter. Eastern parts have a desert climate. Amman. Jan. 46°F (7·5°C), July 77°F (24·9°C). Annual rainfall 12" (290 mm). Aqaba. Jan. 61°F (16°C), July 89°F (31·5°C). Annual rainfall 1·5" (35 mm).

ROYAL HOUSE. The Kingdom is a constitutional monarchy headed by HM King **Hussein**, GCVO, born 14 Nov. 1935, and married Princess Dina Abdul Hamid on 19 April 1955 (divorced 1957), Toni Avril Gardiner (Muna al Hussein) on 25 May 1961 (divorced 1972), Alia Toukan on 26 Dec. 1972 (died in air crash 1977) and Elizabeth Halaby on 15 June 1978. *Offspring:* Princess Alia, born 13 Feb. 1956; Prince Abdulla, born 30 Jan. 1962; Prince Faisal, born 11 Oct. 1963; Princesses Zein and Aisha, born 23 April 1968; Princess Haya, born 3 May 1974; Prince Ali, born 23 Dec. 1975; Prince Hamzah, born 1 April 1980; Prince Hashem, born 10 June 1981; Princess Iman, born 4 April 1983; Princess Raya, born 9 Feb. 1986. *Crown Prince* (appointed 1 April 1965): Prince Hassan (b. 1947), younger brother of the King.

CONSTITUTION AND GOVERNMENT. The Constitution ratified on 8 Dec. 1952 provides that the Cabinet is responsible to Parliament. The legislature consists of a *Senate* of 40 members appointed by the King and a *Chamber of Deputies* of 80 members elected by universal suffrage. 9 seats are reserved for Christians, 6 for Bedouin and 3 for Circassians. A law of 1993 restricts each elector to a single vote, replacing a system in which electors had several votes depending on the number of seats in the constituency.

The lower house was dissolved in 1976 and elections postponed because no elections could be held in the West Bank under Israeli occupation. Parliament was reconvened on 9 Jan. 1984. By-elections were held in March 1984 and 6 members were nominated for the West Bank bringing Parliament to 60 members. Women voted for the first time in 1984. On 9 June 1991 the King and the main political movements endorsed a national charter which legalized political parties in return for the acceptance of the constitution and monarchy. Movements linked to, or financed by, non-Jordanian bodies are not allowed.

Elections were held on 4 Nov. 1997. Of the 80 seats, 76 went to non-partisans of various orientations, 3 to the National Constitutional Party and 1 to the BAATH Party. After a cabinet reshuffle in March 1998 the government consisted of:

Prime Minister, Minister of Defence: Abd-al-Salam al-Majali.

Deputy Prime Minister for Service Affairs, Minister for Information: Abdallah al-Nusur.

Deputy Prime Minister for Development Affairs, Minister of Foreign and Cabinet Affairs: Jawad al-Anani.

Higher Education: Munthir al-Masri. *Interior:* Nadir Rashid. *Public Works and Housing:* Nasir al-Lawzi. *Justice:* Riyad al-Shakah. *Communications:* Bassam al-Sakit. *Water and Irrigation:* Munthir Haddadin. *Industry, Trade and Supply:* Hani al-Mulki. *Tourism and Antiquities:* Akil Biltaji. *Municipal and Rural Affairs and the Environment:* Tawfik Kurayshan. *Health and Healthcare:* Ashraf al-Kurdi. *Awqaf (Religious Endowments), Islamic Affairs and Holy Places:* Abd-al-Salam al-Abbadi. *Planning:* Rima Khalaf. *Energy and Mineral Resources:* Muhammad Salih al-Hurani. *Parliamentary and Legal Affairs:* Khaled al-Zoubi. *Cabinet Affairs:* Sad-al-Din Jumah. *Social Development:* Muhammad Khayr. *Labour:* Mahdi al-Farhan. *Culture and Youth:* Talal al-Hassan. *Agriculture:* Mijhim al-Khurayshah. *Education:* Mohammed Hamdan. *Finance:* Sulayman Hafiz. *Supply:* Hani al-Mulki. *Transport:* Sami Gammo. *Administrative Affairs:* Bassam al-Emmoush.

The *Speaker* is Sa'd Hayel Srour.

National anthem: 'Asha al Malik' ('Long Live the King'); words by A. Al Rifai, tune by A. Al Tanir.

Local Government. The 12 governorates are divided into cities, towns, districts and sub-districts. Municipal elections were held in July 1995; turn-out was low.

DEFENCE

Army. The Army is organized in 2 armoured and 2 mechanized infantry divisions, 1 Royal Guard, 1 special force, and 1 field artillery brigade. Equipment includes 270 M-47/-48A5, 218 M-60A1/3, 360 Khalid Chieftain and 293 Tariq (Centurion) main battle tanks. Total strength (1997) 90,000.

Navy. The Royal Jordanian Naval Force numbered 650 in 1997 and operates 3 fast inshore patrol boats, 2 ex-East German patrol craft and some boats all based at Aqaba.

Air Force. The Air Force has 1 interceptor and 4 ground attack squadrons equipped with Mirage F1 and F-5E Tiger II fighters, and 2-seat F-5Fs. Two anti-armour squadrons have Bell AH-1S Huey Cobra helicopters. There are 4 C-130H Hercules and 2 CASA Aviocar turboprop transports, S-70 Blackhawk, Gazelle, and Hughes 500D helicopters, piston-engined Bulldog basic trainers and CASA Aviojet jet trainers. Hawk surface-to-air missiles equip 14 batteries. Strength (1997) 13,400 personnel, 60 combat aircraft and 24 armed helicopters, with 16 F-16s to be delivered in 1997-98.

INTERNATIONAL RELATIONS. A 46-year-old formal state of hostilities with Israel was brought to an end by a peace agreement on 26 Oct. 1994.

Membership. Jordan is a member of the UN and the Arab League.

ECONOMY

Policy. An economic adjustment programme has been adopted for 1992-98.

Performance. Nominal total GDP was JD.5,120m. in 1996. Real GDP growth was 4·1% in 1996 (6·4% in 1995).

Budget. Revenue and expenditure over a 5-year period (in millions of dinar):

	1991	1992	1993	1994	1995
Revenue	761·5	1,109·4	1,119·6	1,162·4	1,332·6
Expenditure	1,055·7	1,081·2	1,235·1	1,312·8	1,471·5

Estimated total revenue (in US$) in 1997 was 2·7bn; expenditure 2·8bn.

Currency. The unit of currency is the *Jordan dinar,* (JD) of 1,000 *fils.* There are coins of 1, 5, 10, 20, 25, 50, 100, 250, 500 and 10,000 fils, and notes of 500 fils and JD.1, 5, 10 and 20. Foreign currency reserves were JD.1,001·1m. in 1992. The annual inflation rate was 1% in 1992 (8·2% in 1991). Foreign exchange controls were abolished in July 1997.

Banking and Finance. The Central Bank of Jordan was established in 1964 (*Governor,* Dr Ziad Fariz). In 1993 there were 28 licensed banks with a total of 410 branches and 95 offices. Assets and liabilities of the banking system (including the Central Bank, commercial banks, the Housing Bank and investment banks) totalled JD.10,641·5m. in 1994.

There is a stock exchange in Amman (Amman Financial Market).

Weights and Measures. The metric system is in force. Land area is measured in *dunums* (1 dunum = 0·1 ha).

ENERGY AND NATURAL RESOURCES

Electricity. Production (1994) 4·76bn. kWh.

Minerals. Phosphates production in 1994 was 4·08m. tonnes; potash, 1·55m. tonnes.

Agriculture. In 1995 agriculture produced an estimated 6% of GDP. The country east of the Hejaz Railway line is largely desert; northwestern Jordan is potentially of agricultural value and an integrated Jordan Valley project began in 1973. In 1993 about 15% of land was given over to agricultural use (including 9% permanent pasture and 4% arable crops). In 1993 it was estimated that there was 630 sq. km of irrigated land. The agricultural cropping pattern for irrigated vegetable cultivation was introduced in 1984 to regulate production and diversify the crops being cultivated. In 1986 the government began to lease state-owned land in the semi-arid southern regions for agricultural development by private investors, mostly for wheat and barley.

Production in 1994 (in tonnes): wheat, 50,000; barley, 65,000; tomatoes, 550,000; potatoes, 70,000; olives, 70,000; citrus fruits, 187,000; grapes, 50,000; aubergines, 50,000; watermelons, melons and squashes, 105,000.

Livestock (1994): 2·1m. sheep; 555,000 goats; 42,000 cattle; 22,000 asses and mules; 18,000 camels; 77m. poultry. Total meat production was 102,000 tonnes in 1993; milk, 96,000 tonnes.

There were 5,850 tractors in 1992.

Forestry. There were 70,000 ha of forest and woodland in 1992, from which 11,000 cubic metres of wood was harvested.

INDUSTRY. In 1995 service industries accounted for 66% of GDP and industry 28%. The number of industrial units in 1994 was 18,980, employing more than 0·1m. persons. The principal industrial concerns are the production or processing of phosphates, potash, fertilizers, cement and oil.

Production (1994, in 1,000 tonnes): Phosphate, 4,215; petroleum products, 2,815; cement, 3,437; potash, 1,370; chemical acids, 846; fertilizers, 470.

Labour. The workforce in 1996 was 935,000. In 1993, 434,806 persons worked in social and public administration, 91,087 in mining and manufacturing, 129,754 in commerce, 57,573 in transport and communications and 54,995 in agriculture. In 1987 277,200 Jordanians worked abroad. Unemployment was 16% in 1994.

FOREIGN ECONOMIC RELATIONS. Foreign debt was US$7,006m. in 1996. Legislation of 1995 eases restrictions on foreign investment and makes some reductions in taxes and customs duties.

Commerce. Imports in 1995 were valued at JD.3,550m. and exports at JD.1,440m. Major exports are phosphate, potash, fertilizers, foodstuffs, pharmaceuticals, fruit and vegetables, textiles, cement, plastics, detergent and soap.

Exports in 1994 (in JD.1m.) were mainly to India, 88; Saudi Arabia, 72; Iraq, 78; Indonesia, 28; United Arab Emirates, 39. Imports were mainly from USA, 232; Germany, 184; Japan, 94; Italy, 139; UK, 120; Turkey, 62.

Tourism. In 1995 there were 842,000 tourists. Earnings from tourism in 1994 amounted to US$560·8m. (12·7% of GDP).

COMMUNICATIONS

Roads. Total length of roads, 1995 estimate, 6,750 km, of which 2,820 km were main roads. Motor vehicles in 1993 included 175,325 motor cars (154,294 private), 901 motorcycles, 1,235 buses, 7,521 lorries and 38,595 vans. There were 26,837 road accidents in 1994.

Railways. The 1,050 mm gauge Hejaz Jordan and Aqaba Railway runs from the Syrian border at Nassib to Ma'an and Naqb Ishtar and Aqaba Port (total, 618 km). In 1994 it carried 2·5m. tonnes of freight. The state railway is only minimally operational.

Civil Aviation. The Queen Alia International airport is at Zizya, 30 km south of Amman. There are also international airports at Amman and Aqaba. The national carrier is the state-owned Royal Jordanian, which carried 1·2m. passengers and 54,062 tonnes of freight in 1994, and operated 1 A310-200, 4 A310-300s, 2 A320-200s, 3 B-707-320Cs, 2 B-727-200 Advs and 5 other aircraft in 1995.

Services are also provided by Aeroflot, Air Algérie, Air Canada, Air France, Air Lanka, Alitalia, Alyemda, Austrian Airlines, British Airways, British Mediterranean Airways, Cyprus Airways, Egyptair, Emirates, Gulf Air, JAT, KLM, Libyan Airlines, Malaysia Airlines, Middle East Airlines, Northwest Airlines, Olympic Airways,

Pakistan International Airlines, Qatar Airways, Saudia, Sudan Airways, Tarom, Tunis Air, Turkish Airlines and Yemenia.

Shipping. In 1995 sea-going shipping totalled 0·11m. GRT, including oil tankers, 97,286 GRT. 11m. tonnes of cargo were handled by the port of Aqaba in 1994.

Telecommunications. In 1996 there were 836 post offices and agencies. In 1994 there were 317,330 telephones and 2,094 telexes. Broadcasting is the responsibility of the Jordan Radio and Television Corporation, which transmits 2 national radio services (1 in English), a Koran service and an external service, Radio Jordan. There are 2 television services (colour by PAL). In 1995, 430,000 radio and 2·2m. TV sets were in use.

Cinemas. In 1993 there were 35 cinemas with an annual attendance of 0·2m.

Press (1996). There are 4 daily (including 1 in English) and 22 weekly papers. Newspapers were denationalized in 1990, though government institutions still hold majority ownership.

SOCIAL INSTITUTIONS

Religion. About 96% of the population are Sunni Moslems.

Education. Adult literacy in 1995 was 86·6% (93·4% of men and 79·4% of women). Basic primary and secondary education is free and compulsory. In 1994 there were 664 kindergartens (662 private) with 2,422 teachers and 55,996 pupils; 2,482 basic schools (322 private) with 48,158 teachers and 1,036,079 pupils; 741 secondary schools (77 private) with 4,572 teachers and 93,773 pupils and 54 vocational schools with 2,519 teachers and 30,052 pupils. In 1996–97 there were 6 state and 11 private universities. 22,500 Jordanians were studying abroad in 1994.

Health In 1994 there were 11,842 doctors, 2,670 dentists and 3,300 nurses. In 1995 there was a total of 6,800 hospital beds in 63 hospitals.

DIPLOMATIC REPRESENTATIVES

Of Jordan in Great Britain (6 Upper Phillimore Gdns., London, W8 7HB)
Ambassador: Fouad Ayoub.

Of Great Britain in Jordan (Abdoun, Amman)
Ambassador: Christopher Battiscombe, CMG.

Of Jordan in the USA (3504 International Dr., NW, Washington, D.C., 20008)
Ambassador: Marwan Muashir.

Of the USA in Jordan (Abdoun, Amman)
Ambassador: Wesley W Egan.

Of Jordan to the United Nations
Ambassador: Hassan Abu Nam'eh.

Of Jordan to the European Union
Ambassador: Umayya Toukan.

Further Reading

Department of Statistics. *Statistical Yearbook*
Central Bank of Jordan. *Monthly Statistical Bulletin*
Gubser, P., *Jordan.* Boulder (CO), 1982
Rogan, E. and Tell, T. (eds.) *Village, Steppe and State: the Social Origins of Modern Jordan.* London, 1994
Salibi, K., *A Modern History of Jordan.* London, 1992
Satloff, R. B., *From Abdullah to Hussein: Jordan in Transition.* OUP, 1994
Seccombe, I., *Jordan.* [Bibliography] Oxford and Santa Barbara, 1984
Wilson, M. C., *King Abdullah, Britain and the making of Jordan.* CUP, 1987

National statistical office: Department of Statistics, Amman

KAZAKHSTAN

Kazak Respublikasy

Capital: Akmola
Population: 16·5m.
GDP per head: (PPP$) 3,284
HDI/world rank: 0·709/93

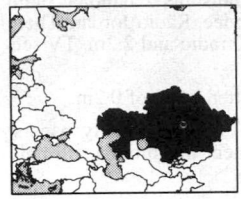

KEY HISTORICAL EVENTS. What was Soviet Central Asia embraced the Kazakh Soviet Socialist Republic, the Uzbek Soviet Socialist Republic and the Kirghiz Soviet Socialist Republic.

Turkestan (by which name part of this territory was then known) was conquered by the Russians in the 1860s. In 1866 Tashkent was occupied and in 1868 Samarkand, and subsequently further territory was conquered and united with Russian Turkestan. In the 1870s Bokhara was subjugated, the emir, by an agreement of 1873, recognizing the suzerainty of Russia. In the same year Khiva became a vassal state to Russia. Until 1917 Russian Central Asia was divided politically into the Khanate of Khiva, the Emirate of Bokhara and the Governor-Generalship of Turkestan.

In the summer of 1919 the authority of the Soviet Government was established in these regions. The Khan of Khiva was deposed in Feb. 1920, and a People's Soviet Republic was set up, the medieval name of Khorezm being revived. In Aug. 1920 the Emir of Bokhara suffered the same fate, and a similar régime was set up in Bokhara. The former Governor-Generalship of Turkestan was constituted an Autonomous Soviet Socialist Republic within the RSFSR on 11 April 1921.

In the autumn of 1924 the Soviets of the Turkestan, Bokhara and Khiva Republics decided to redistribute the territories of these republics on a nationality basis; at the same time Bokhara and Khiva became Socialist Republics. The redistribution was completed in May 1925, when the new states of Uzbekistan, Turkmenistan and Tadzhikistan were accepted into the USSR as Union Republics. The remaining districts of Turkestan populated by Kazakhs were united with Kazakhstan which was established as an Autonomous Soviet Republic in 1925 and became a constituent republic in 1936.

Independence was declared on 16 Dec. 1991 when Kazakhstan joined the CIS.

TERRITORY AND POPULATION. Kazakhstan is bounded in the west by the Caspian Sea and Russia, in the north by Russia, in the east by China and in the south by Uzbekistan and Kyrgyzstan. The area is 2,717,300 sq. km (1,049,155 sq. miles). The 1989 census population was 16,464,464, of whom Kazakhs accounted for 39·7%, Russians 37·8%, Germans 5·8%, Ukrainians 5·4%, Uzbeks and Tatars 2% each. In 1997 there were 0·5m. Germans. Since 1992 a further 0·5m. had emigrated to Germany. Estimate, Jan. 1996, 16·5m. (51·4% female; 57·2% urban) with a population density of 6·1 per sq. km.. Vital statistics rates, 1993 (per 1,000 population): Births, 18·6; deaths, 9·2; natural increase, 9·4; infant mortality (per 1,000 live births), 28·4.

It consists of 19 provinces as follows, with area and population:

	Area (sq. km)	Population (1996)		Area (sq. km)	Population (1996)
Akmola[1]	92,000	808,600	Kzyl-Orda	226,000	679,000
Aktube	300,600	750,400	Mangyshlak	165,600	340,100
Almaty[2]	105,700	2,141,100	North Kazakhstan	45,000	575,600
Atyrau[3]	118,600	463,200	Pavlodar	124,800	921,000
East Kazakhstan	97,500	918,800	South Kazakhstan	117,300	2,029,100
Jeskazgan	312,600	479,600	West Kazakhstan	151,300	668,500
Karaganda	115,400	1,234,100	Zhambyl[4]	144,300	1,037,000
Kostanay	113,900	1,022,800			

[1] Formerly Tselinograd. [2] Formerly Alma-Ata. [3] Formerly Gurev.
[4] Formerly Dzhambul.

The capital is Akmola (moved from Almaty in 1995). In all there are 82 towns, 197 urban settlements and 221 rural districts.

The official language is Kazakh.

CONSTITUTION AND GOVERNMENT. Relying on a judgement of the Constitutional Court that the 1994 parliamentary elections were invalid, President Nazarbaev dissolved parliament on 11 March 1995 and began to rule by decree. A referendum on the adoption of a new constitution was held on 30 Aug. 1995. The electorate was 8·8m.; turn-out was 80%. 89% of votes cast were in favour. The Constitution thus adopted allows the President to rule by decree and to dissolve parliament if it holds a no-confidence vote or twice rejects his nominee for Prime Minister. It establishes a parliament consisting of a 47-member Senate, 40 senators being elected by some 4,000 representatives of local authorities and 7 appointed by the President; and a lower house of 67, directly elected, though heads of families may cast votes for all of their family members. Candidates must gain an absolute majority of votes to be elected, and are not permitted to disclose their political affiliation.

At the elections of 9 Dec. 1995 turn-out was 78%. 43 candidates were elected. A second round of voting was held in Jan. 1996. A new Constitution was adopted on 28 Jan. 1993. A Constitutional Court was set up in Dec. 1991.

President Nazarbaev abolished the Constitutional Court in 1995.

At the presidential elections of 2 Dec. 1991 Nursultan Nazarbaev (the sole candidate) was elected with 99% of votes cast. Turn-out was 88%. At a referendum in April 1995, 95.4% of votes cast favoured extending his term of office until 2000. Turn-out was 90%.

President: Nursultan Nazarbaev (b. 1940).

In March 1998 the government comprised:

Prime Minister: Nurlan Balgimbayer.

First Deputy Premier: Uraz Zhandosov. *Deputy Premiers:* Zhanybek Karibzhanov, Aleksandr Pavlov. *Agriculture:* Sergey Vitaliyevich Kulagin. *Defence:* Lt.-Gen. Mukhtar Altynbayev. *Ecology and Natural Resources:* Serikbek Daukeyev. *Education, Culture and Health:* Krimbek Kysherbayev. *Energy, Industry and Trade:* Asigat Zhabagin. *Finance:* Sauat Mynbayev. *Foreign Affairs:* Kasymzhomart Tokaev. *Information and Public Accord:* Altynbek Sarsenbayev. *Internal Affairs:* Lt.-Gen. Kairbek Suleymenov. *Justice:* Bayurzhan Mukhamedzhanov. *Labour and Social Security:* Natalya Korzhova. *Science:* Vladimir Shkolnik. *Transport and Communications:* Yerkin Kaliyev.

The *Speaker* is Abish Kekilbaev.

National anthem: A competition for a new anthem had no result, and the old Soviet anthem is retained.

Local Government. Elections were held in Dec. 1989. Local government was directly subordinated to the President in Jan. 1992.

DEFENCE. In 1991 the former Soviet Union transferred some 2,680 T-64/-720, 2,428 ACVs and 6,900 artillery to storage bases in Kazakhstan. The equipment is deteriorating. A USA funded programme for nuclear dismantlement and demilitarization continues.

Army. The Army is organized in 1 tank and 2 motor rifle divisions; 1 independent motor rifle, 1 artillery, 1 multiple rocket launcher and 1 surface-to-surface missile regiment; and 1 artillery and 1 airborne brigade. Equipment includes 624 T-62 and T-72 main battle tanks. Personnel, 1996, 25,000. Paramilitary units: Republican Guard (2,500), Ministry of the Interior Security Troops (20,000), Frontier Guards (12,000).

Navy. Formally constituted in Aug. 1996, a force of 9 inshore patrol craft with further craft on order from Germany operates on the Caspian Sea. Personnel, 250.

Air Force. In 1995 there was an Air Force division with about 15,000 personnel with some 150 combat aircraft, including MiG-29 and Su-27 interceptors and MiG-27 and Su-24 strike aircraft.

INTERNATIONAL RELATIONS. In Jan. 1995 agreements were reached for closer integration with Russia, including the combining of military forces, currency convertibility and a customs union.

Membership. Kazakhstan is a member of the UN, CIS and the NATO Partnership for Peace.

ECONOMY

Policy. A National Council for Economic Reform was instituted in Jan. 1993. A privatization programme for 1993–95 envisaged the sale of most state enterprises with more than 200 employees by a combination of cash and vouchers. Enterprises of national importance remain controlled by the government through holding companies. A privatization programme started in April 1994 involving the auctioning of 3,500 medium-size enterprises. Coupons are issued to citizens to be exchanged for shares in investment funds. Foreign nationals may participate in trading after the auctions. Large (i.e. with over 2,000 employees) and small (i.e. with fewer than 500) enterprises are being sold for cash.

Performance. Real GDP growth was nil in 1996 (–8·9 in 1995).

Budget. Budgetary income in 1996 (and 1997) was 218,278m. tenge (278,737m. tenge); expenditure was 259,564m. tenge (300,945m. tenge).

Currency. The unit of currency is the *tenge* of 100 *tiyn*, which was introduced on 15 Nov. 1993 at 1 tenge = 500 roubles. It became the sole legal tender on 25 Nov. 1993. There are notes of 50 tiyn, and 1, 3, 5, 10, 20, 50 and 100 tenge. Inflation was running at nearly 130% in 1997, but it is hoped that it will be around 17% by the end of 1998. In Jan. 1997 foreign exchange reserves were US$2,700m.

Banking and Finance. The central bank and bank of issue is the National Bank (*Governor,* Uraz Djandosov). In 1995 there were 180 commercial banks, 60 privately owned.

ENERGY AND NATURAL RESOURCES

Electricity. Output in 1996 was 58,600m. kWh. (1997 – 61,000m. kWh. estimate). There is 1 nuclear power station.

Minerals. Kazakhstan is extremely rich in mineral resources, including coal, bauxite, chromium, copper, Iceland spar, lead, manganese, molybdenum, nickel, tungsten and zinc. Coal production (1996 estimate), 76·6m. tonnes; iron ore (1995), 7·21m. tonnes; gold (1993), 14·6 tonnes; steel (1996), 3·22m. tonnes; refined copper (1997 estimate), 0·30m. tonnes.

Oil and Gas. Proven oil reserves in 1996 were 2,000m. tonnes. The Tengiz field has estimated oil reserves between 6,000m. and 9,000m. bbls; the Karachaganak field has oil reserves of 2,000m. bbls, and gas reserves of 20,000,000m. cu. feet. Output of crude oil (including gas concentrates), 1996, 22·9m. tonnes (1997 estimate, 26·2m. tonnes); natural gas, 6,396m. cu. metres (1997 estimate, 7,300m. cu. metres). In Sept. 1997 Kazakhstan signed oil agreements with China worth US$9·5bn. and includes a 3,000 km. pipeline to Xinjiang province in western China.

Agriculture. Kazakh agriculture has changed from primarily nomad cattle breeding to production of grain, cotton and other industrial crops. In 1993, 181·3m. ha were under cultivation, of which private subsidiary agriculture accounted for 0·3m. ha and commercial farming 6·3m. ha in 16,300 farms. Private and commercial agriculture accounted for 35% of output by value in 1992; agricultural output was valued at 13,700m. roubles (in constant 1983 prices) in 1993, 97% of the 1992 figure.

Tobacco, rubber plants and mustard are also cultivated. Kazakhstan has rich orchards and vineyards, which accounted for 95,000 ha of cultivated land in 1985. Kazakhstan is noted for its livestock, particularly its sheep, from which excellent quality wool is obtained. Livestock on 1 Jan. 1994 included 9·3m. cattle, 34·2m. sheep and goats and 2·4m. pigs.

Output of main agricultural products (in 1m. tonnes) in 1997 (estimate): Grain, 14·2; sugar-beet, 0·4; cotton, 0·2; vegetables, 0·8; meat (cattle and poultry), 1·4 (1996); milk, 3·7; and 1,400m. eggs.

Forestry. In 1997, 0·29m. cu. metres of timber were cut.

INDUSTRY. Kazakhstan was heavily industrialized in the Soviet period, with non-ferrous metallurgy, heavy engineering and the chemical industries prominent. Output was valued at 30,000m. tenge in current prices in 1996 and 35,000m. tenge in 1997. Production (in tonnes) in 1997 (estimate) included ferroalloy, 680,000; mineral fertilizer, 200,000; chemical fibre, 1,900 (1993); cardboard, 7,400 (1996); lead, 85,000; fabrics, 24·6m. sq. metres; leather footwear, 0·8m. pairs; forge-press machines, 180; tractors, 3,100; radio sets, 600; refrigerators and freezers, 12,900 (1993); washing machines, 23,200.

Labour. In 1996 the population of working age was estimated as 7·4m. In Jan. 1997 3% of the labour force were registered unemployed, of whom 15,400 were receiving benefits. Average monthly salaries in 1993 were 134·9 tenge.

FOREIGN ECONOMIC RELATIONS. In Jan. 1994 an agreement to create a single economic zone was signed with Kyrgyzstan and Uzbekistan. Since Jan. 1992 individuals and enterprises have been able to engage in foreign trade without government permission, except for goods 'of national interest' (fuel, minerals, mineral fertilizers, grain, cotton, wool, caviar and pharmaceutical products) which may be exported only by state organizations. Foreign nationals may be licensed to purchase Kazakh assets for privatization. Foreign debt was US$4,500m. in 1997.

Commerce. In 1997 imports were valued at US$6,656m. and exports at US$6,015m. Main export markets (% of trade in 1996): CIS countries, 55·7%; Europe, 26·4%; Asia, 16·2%; America, 1·5%. Main import suppliers: CIS, 69·6%; Europe, 18·3%; Asia, 9·4%; America, 2·5%.

COMMUNICATIONS

Roads. In 1997 there were estimated to be 115,400 km of motor roads with hard cover. In 1997, an estimated 1,000m. passengers used public transport and 1,000m. tonnes of freight were carried.

Railways. In 1997 there were estimated to be 14,400 km of 1,520 mm gauge railways (3,528 km electrified 1994). In 1997, about 37·5m. passengers and 150m. tonnes of freight were carried.

Civil Aviation. The national carrier is Kazakhstan Airways, which operated 11 ex-Soviet aircraft in 1995. In 1997, around 1·5m. passengers and 0·02m. tonnes of freight were carried. Services are also provided by Aeroflot, Aerosweet, Arax, Austrian Airlines, Belavia, Iran Air, KLM, Lufthansa, Mongolian Airlines, Pakistan Airlines, Siberia Airlines, Swissair, Transaero, Turkish Airlines, United Airlines, Uzbekistan Airways and Xinjiang Airlines.

Shipping. There is 1 large port, Aktau. In 1993, 1·2m. passengers and 4m. tonnes of freight were carried on inland waterways.

Telecommunications. Broadcasting is the responsibility of the Kazakh State Radio and Television Co. There are 3 national and 13 regional radio programmes, a Radio Moscow relay and a foreign service, Radio Alma-Ata (Kazakh, English). There is 1 TV channel (colour by SECAM).

Press. In 1995 there were 472 periodicals in Kazakh, 511 in Russian and 60 in both languages.

SOCIAL INSTITUTIONS

Justice. In 1994, 201,796 crimes were reported, including 2,549 murders or attempted murders.

Religion. There were some 4,000 mosques in 1996 (63 in 1990). An Islamic Institute opened in 1991 to train imams. A Roman Catholic diocese was established in 1991. In 1995, the Union of Evangelical Baptist Churches had 140 communities, the Russian Orthodox Church, 177, and the Evangelical Lutheran Church, 112.

Education. In Jan. 1994, 0·7m. children (39% of those eligible) were attending pre-school institutions. In 1993–94 there were 3,114,000 pupils at 8,700 elementary and secondary schools, 247 technical colleges with 222,100 students, 68 higher educational institutions with 272,100 students, and 207 research institutes. Adult literacy rate is 97·5%.

Health. In Jan. 1994 there were 66,900 doctors, 187,000 junior medical personnel and 1,899 hospitals with 225,000 beds.

Welfare. In Jan. 1994 there were 2·1m. age, and 0·9m. other pensioners. Pension contributions are 20% of salary and are payable to the State Pension Fund. The Fund is scheduled for privatization in 1998, when half the mandatory 20% contribution from salary will go into private pension schemes.

DIPLOMATIC REPRESENTATIVES

Of Kazakhstan in Great Britain (33 Thurlowe Sq., London, SW7 2DS)
Ambassador: Kanat B. Saudabaev.

Of Great Britain in Kazakhstan (ul. Furmanova 173, Almaty)
Ambassador: Douglas B. McAdam.

Of Kazakhstan in the USA
Ambassador: Bulat Nurgaliyev.

Of the USA in Kazakhstan (99 Furmanova St., Alma-Ata, 480012)
Ambassador: A. Elizabeth Jones.

Of Kazakhstan to the United Nations
Ambassador: Akmaral Arystanbekova.

Of Kazakhstan to the European Union
Ambassador: Aoueskhan Kyrbassov.

Further Reading

Olcott, M. B., *The Kazakhs.* Stanford, 1987

KENYA

Jamhuri ya Kenya

(Republic of Kenya)

Capital: Nairobi
Population: 26·44m.
GDP per head: (PPP$) 1,404
GNP: US$6·6bn.
HDI/world rank: 0·463/134

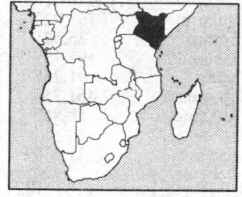

KEY HISTORICAL EVENTS. Prior to colonialism, the area covered by Kenya comprised African farming communities, notably the Kikuyu and the Masai. From the 16th century through to the 19th, they were loosely controlled by the Arabic rulers of Oman (whose base moved to Zanzibar in the early 19th century). In 1895, the British declared part of the region the East Africa Protectorate, including the mainland dominions of the Sultan of Zanzibar as well as Mau, Kipini, the island of Lamu and all adjacent islands between the rivers Umba and Tana. In 1905 the colony and the protectorate, formerly known as the East African Protectorate, was transferred from the Foreign Office to the Colonial Office. In Nov. 1906 the protectorate, excluding the Sultan of Zanzibar's dominions, was placed under the control of a governor and annexed to the Crown, and known from 1920 as the Colony of Kenya. It was only in Dec. 1963 that the Sultan ceded his coastal strip to Kenya.

In the First World War the Germans in East Africa invaded the south of Kenya but the British army, under Gen. Smuts, counter-attacked and captured much of German East Africa.

The influx of European settlers was resented by Africans not only for the whites' land holdings, but also for their exclusive political representation in the colonial Legislative Council. A state of emergency existed between Oct. 1952 and Jan. 1960 during the period of the Mau Mau uprising caused by discontent, particularly among the Kikuyu people, over colonial rule and land policy. Over 13,000 Africans and 100 Europeans were killed. The Kenya African Union was banned and its president, Jomo Kenyatta, imprisoned. When the state of emergency ended in 1960 political activity resumed, to pave the way to independence, and two political parties emerged.

On his release from imprisonment Jomo Kenyatta became president of the Kenya Africa National Union, while the Kenya African Democratic Union, which favoured a regional form of government, was led by Ronald Ngala and Daniel T. arap Moi.

Full internal self-government was achieved in 1962 and in Dec. 1963 Kenya became an independent member of the Commonwealth.

Before independence the East African High Commission had been administering services of an inter-territorial nature for Kenya, Tanzania and Uganda and this continued after independence. The arrangement was changed to the East African Community in 1967. The Community practically ceased to function after 30 June 1977, chiefly because of the failure to agree a budget and the refusal of President Nyerere of Tanzania to negotiate with President Amin of Uganda.

In 1964 and 1965 constitutional amendments provided for Kenya to become a republic with a president as head of state, and a further change in 1966 required members who changed their parties to seek re-election. Later that year another amendment amalgamated the Senate and the House of Representatives to form a unicameral National Assembly.

In 1982 Kenya became a one-party state and in 1986 party preliminary elections were instituted to reduce the number of parliamentary candidates at general elections. Only those candidates obtaining over 30% of the preliminary vote were eligible to stand.

On the death of Kenyatta in Aug. 1978 Daniel T. arap Moi, the vice president, became acting president and was elected in 1979 and re-elected in 1983, 1988, 1992 and 1997. An attempted coup in 1982 was unsuccessful. A multi-party election was permitted in 1992 and again in 1997, the first genuinely competitive elections since 1963.

TERRITORY AND POPULATION. Kenya is bounded by Sudan and Ethiopia in the north, Uganda in the west, Tanzania in the south and Somalia and the Indian Ocean in the east. The total area is 582,646 sq. km, of which 571,416 sq. km is land area. In the 1989 census, the population was 21,443,636, (19% urban). Estimate (1995), 26·44m. (20% urban); density, 50·3 per sq. km. Growth rate, 1993, 4·2%. Expectation of life, 1992, 58·6 years.

The land areas, populations and capitals of the provinces are:

Province	Sq. km	Census 1989	Estimate 1993	Capital	Census 1989
Rift Valley	182,413	4,981,613	6,107,900	Nakuru	163,927
Eastern	154,354	3,768,677	4,940,900	Embu	26,525
Nyanza	12,507	3,507,162	4,804,500	Kisumu	192,733
Central	13,236	3,116,703	4,152,600	Nyeri	91,258
Coast	84,113	1,829,191	2,430,700	Mombasa	461,753
Western	8,285	2,544,329	3,176,000	Kakamega	58,862
Nairobi	693	1,324,570	1,758,900		
North-Eastern	126,186	371,391	741,400	Garissa	31,319

Other towns (1989): Machakos (116,293), Meru (94,947), Eldoret (111,882), Thika (57,603).

Most of Kenya's 26·44m. people belong to 13 tribes, the main ones including Kikuyu (about 22% of the population), Luhya (14%), Luo (13%), Kalenjin (12%), Kamba (11%), Gusii (6%), Meru (5%) and Mijikenda (5%).

Swahili is the official language, but people belonging to the different tribes will have their own language as their mother tongue. English is spoken in commercial centres.

CLIMATE. The climate is tropical, with wet and dry seasons, but considerable differences in altitude make for varied conditions between the hot, coastal lowlands and the plateau, where temperatures are very much cooler. Heaviest rains occur in April and May, but in some parts there is a second wet season in Nov. and Dec. Nairobi. Jan. 65°F (18·3°C), July 60°F (15·6°C). Annual rainfall 39″ (958 mm). Mombasa. Jan. 81°F (27·2°C), July 76°F (24·4°C). Annual rainfall 47″ (1,201 mm).

CONSTITUTION AND GOVERNMENT. There is a unicameral *National Assembly*, which until the Dec. 1997 elections had 200 members, comprising 188 elected by universal suffrage for a 5-year term, 10 members appointed by the President, and the Speaker and Attorney-General ex-officio. Following a review of constituency boundaries, the National Assembly now has 210 elected members, 12 members appointed and the two ex-officio members, making 224 in total. The President is also directly elected for 5 years; he appoints a Vice-President and other Ministers to a Cabinet over which he presides. A constitutional amendment of Aug. 1992 stipulates that the winning presidential candidate must receive a nation-wide majority and also the vote of 25% of electors in at least 5 of the 8 provinces. The sole legal political party had been the Kenya African National Union (KANU), but after demonstrations by the pro-reform lobby which led to extreme violence, KANU agreed to legalize opposition parties.

The last presidential and parliamentary elections were held on 29 Dec. 1997. In the presidential election Daniel T. arap Moi was opposed by 14 candidates including Charity Ngilu for the Social Democratic Party (SDP), who aims to become Africa's first elected female head of state. In the event, Daniel T. arap Moi benefited from an opposition split along tribal lines and won comfortably, with a 40·4% show of the vote, passing the 25% threshold in 5 out of 8 provinces. Mwai Kibaki (Democratic Party) came next with 30·9% and Raila Odinga (National Development Party) third, with 10·8%.

At the National Assembly elections of 29 Dec. 1997, KANU gained 107 seats, the Democratic Party (DP) 39, the National Development Party 21, the Forum for the Restoration of Democracy (FORD)-Kenya 17, the Social Democratic Party 15, and 5 other parties won 11 seats between them. Of the 12 members appointed by the president, 6 were from KANU and 2 from DP, plus 1 each from 4 other parties.

President: Daniel T. arap Moi (b. 1924).

In March 1998 the government comprised:
Finance: Simeon Nyachae. *Planning and National Development:* George Saitoti.
East African and Regional Co-operation: Nicholas Biwott. *Education and Human
Resource Development:* Stephen Musyoka. *Agriculture:* Musalia Mudavadi. *Foreign
Affairs:* Bonaya Godana. *Water Resources:* Kipng'eno arap Ngeny. *Energy:*
Chrisanthus Okemo. *Natural Resources:* Francis Lotodo. *Transport and
Communications:* William Ole Ntimama. *Industrial Development:* Y. F. Masakhalia.
Tourism and Wildlife: Henry Kosgey. *Health:* Jackson Kalweo. *Local Authorities:*
Sam Ongeri. *Lands and Settlement:* Noah Katama Ngala. *Labour and Manpower
Development:* Joseph Ngutu. *Information and Broadcasting:* Joseph Nyagah.
Co-operative Development: Amukowa Anangwe. *Public Works and Housing:*
Kipkalya Kones. *Environment and Conservation:* Francis Nyenze. *Home Affairs,
Culture and Social Services:* Shariff Nassir. *Research and Technology:* Andrew
Kiptoon. *Trade:* Joseph Kamotho. *Attorney-General:* Amos Wako.

National anthem: 'Ee Mungu nguvu yetu' ('Oh God of all creation'); words by a
collective, tune traditional.

Local government. The country is divided into the Nairobi Municipality and 7
provinces and there are 53 districts.

DEFENCE

Army. The Army consists of 1 armoured, 1 engineer, 1 artillery and 2 infantry
brigades and 1 air defence, 1 airborne, 1 independent air cavalry and 2 engineer
battalions. Equipment includes 80 Vickers Mk3 main battle tanks. Total strength
(1997) 20,500.

Navy. The Navy, based in Mombasa, in 1996 consisted of 2 56-metre fast missile
craft, 4 smaller missile craft, and 1 inshore patrol craft, all built in Britain, and 1 tug.
Personnel in 1997 totalled 1,200.

The Marine police and Customs operate an additional 15 patrol boats.

Air Force. An air force, formed 1 June 1964, was built up with RAF assistance.
Equipment includes 8 F-5E/F-5F supersonic combat aircraft/trainers, 12 Hawk light
jet attack/trainers, 11 twin-turboprop Buffaloes and Dash-8s for transport, air
ambulance, anti-locust spraying and security duties, 6 Skyservant light twins, 10
Bulldog piston-engined primary trainers, 12 Tucano turbo-prop basic trainers and
Puma, Gazelle and Hughes 500 helicopters. Personnel (1997) 2,500, with 18 combat
aircraft and 20 armed helicopters.

INTERNATIONAL RELATIONS

Membership. Kenya is a member of the UN, Commonwealth, OAU and is an ACP
member state of the ACP-EU relationship.

ECONOMY

Policy. Since a privatization programme was launched in 1992, the government has
completed the sale of 145 enterprises of the 207 originally targeted. Privatization of
the remaining 62 is set to be completed by the end of 1998. In 1996 a Presidential
Economic Commission was set up to implement reforms to public companies over
1996–98. A US$215m. IMF loan agreement signed in April 1995 has been suspend-
ed while the government considers measures against corruption.

Budget. The fiscal year ends on 30 June. Government revenue, 1994–95, 90,211m.
shillings; expenditure, 113,721m. shillings.

Currency. The monetary unit is the *Kenya shilling* (KES) of 100 *cents.* There are
notes of Ksh.5, 10, 20, 50, 100, 200 and 500 and coins of 5, 10 and 50 cents and
Ksh.1 and 5. Inflation was 28·8% in 1994. Foreign exchange reserves were 58,400m.
shillings in 1993. The currency became convertible in May 1994. The shilling was
devalued by 23% in April 1993.

Banking and Finance. The central bank and bank of issue is the Central Bank of Kenya. (*Governor*, Micah Cheserem). There are 50 banks, 40 non-banking financial institutions and a couple of building societies. In March 1995 their combined assets totalled KSh.£268,811m. On 15 Oct. 1997 the government announced its decision to offload a further 25% of its stake in the Kenya Commercial Bank, which lowers its shareholding to 35%. Savings deposits totalled KSh.£724m. in March 1990.

There is a stock exchange in Nairobi.

ENERGY AND NATURAL RESOURCES

Electricity. Installed generating capacity was 807 MW in 1994; 80% was provided by hydropower from power stations on the Tana river, 20% by oil-fired power stations and the rest by geothermal power. Production (1994) 3,538m. kWh.

Oil. Kenya signed an oil and gas exploration deal in 1997 with Canada's Tornado Resources Ltd, who will commit a minimum of US$7m. over the next 3 years.

Minerals. In 1989 there were 49 mines and quarries. Production, 1994 (in 1,000 tonnes): Soda ash, 224; fluorspar, 89; salt, 75·8. Other minerals included gold, raw soda, lime and limestone, diatomite, garnets and vermiculite.

Agriculture. As agriculture is possible from sea-level to altitudes of over 9,000 ft, tropical, sub-tropical and temperate crops can be grown and mixed farming is pursued. Agriculture produces 30% of GDP. There are 1·93m. ha of arable land, 520,000 ha of permanent crop land and 38·1m. ha of pasture. Four-fifths of the country is range-land which produces mainly livestock products and the wild game which is a major tourist attraction.

Tea and coffee are the two big foreign exchange earners, ahead of tourism. Horticultural products, particularly flowers, are in fourth position.

Kenya has about 110,000 ha under tea production, and is the world's largest exporter of tea. The production is high quality tea, raised in near-perfect agronomic conditions. It is plucked the whole year round, and almost exclusively by hand. In 1996 production reached a record 257m. kg (244·5m. in 1995) and earned about US$350m. in exports.

Coffee production in 1996–97 is estimated at between 75,000 and 78,000 tonnes (97,500 tonnes in 1995–96 and 96,000 tonnes in 1994–95). Arabica coffee covers 176,500 ha of land under coffee in Kenya. Some 70% of the total hectarage under coffee is cultivated by 335,000 smallholders, although their production has been in decline in recent years.

Fresh horticultural exports were 84,824 tonnes in 1996, up 18% on the 71,758 tonnes in 1995, earning about US$340m. By the year 2000 Kenyan horticultural exports are expected to pass the 100,000 tonnes mark, with increases in pre-packed vegetables, salads, cut flowers, avocados, passion fruit and mangoes. The biggest growth has been in cut flowers, up 20% from 29,374 tonnes in 1995 to 35,212 tonnes in 1996. Around two-thirds of the flowers are destined for the Netherlands, largely for re-export. 1996 vegetable exports totalled 32,742 tonnes and fruit 16,869 tonnes, both up on 1995.

Maize is Kenya's most important food crop with about 1·4m. ha under cultivation and production in excess of 2m. tonnes. Sisal, pyrethrum, maize and wheat are crops of major importance in the Highlands, while coconuts, cashew nuts, cotton, sugar, sisal and maize are the principal crops grown at the lower altitudes.

Livestock (1993): Cattle, 11m.; sheep, 5·5m.; goats, 7·3m.; pigs, 105,000; poultry, 25m.

More than half the agricultural labour force is employed in the livestock sector, accounting for 10% of GDP.

Forestry. Forest reserves are 16,800 sq. km, mainly between 6,000 and 11,000 ft above sea-level. There are coniferous, broad-leaved, hardwood and bamboo forests. The forest area is 1·7m. ha. Production (1994) 40·3m. cu. metres.

Fisheries. Landings in 1994 were 179,000 tonnes of fresh water fish, 5,194 tonnes of marine fish, 403 tonnes of crustaceans and 127 tonnes of other marine products; total value K£212,145,000. While the aggregate landings from Kenya's inland waters (more than 90% from Lake Victoria) have grown over the past 20 years, marine fishing has not reached its full potential, despite a coastline of 680 km. Fish landed from the sea totals between 5,000 and 7,000 tonnes annually, but there is an estimated potential of 200,000 tonnes in tuna and similar species.

INDUSTRY. In 1994 there were 648 manufacturing firms employing more than 50 persons. The main products are textiles, chemicals, vehicle assembly and transport equipment, leather and footwear, printing and publishing, food and tobacco processing and oil refining. Production in 1994 included (in tonnes): Sugar, 303,000; maize meal, 233,200; wheat flour, 191,400; animal feed (1988), 184,266; cotton yarn, 4,767; cotton fabrics, 45·69m. sq. metres.

Labour. In 1997 the unemployment level was close to 3m.

FOREIGN ECONOMIC RELATIONS. Foreign debt was US$7·1m. in 1993. Foreign investment on the stock exchange has been permitted since 1 Jan. 1995. Export Processing Zones were introduced in 1990, offering foreign companies exemption from taxes and duties for 10 years.

Commerce. Exports were valued at 85,643m. shillings in 1994; imports, 115,080m. shillings. Exports are estimated to have increased by 13·7% in 1995 and by 21·4% in 1996. The estimated growth for 1997 is 25%.

Principal exports (in 1,000m. shillings) 1994: Tea, 16·9; coffee, 13; horticultural produce, 8·3. Imports: Petroleum, 18·6; machinery and transport equipment, 31·8; chemicals (1993), 19·9; manufactures, 14·7.

Main export markets: Uganda, Tanzania, UK. Main import suppliers: UK, United Arab Emirates, Japan, Germany, France.

The UK is the largest foreign investor in Kenya with over US$1,500m. in more than 60 enterprises.

Tourism. In 1996 there were 670,000 holiday visitors. Receipts were US$465m.

COMMUNICATIONS

Roads. Of some 67,000 km of classified roads, only about 8,900 km, or 14%, have been tarred. More than 80,000 km of roads are unclassified. The network has seriously deteriorated in the past 15 years through poor maintenance. Urban roads comprise around 7,000 km, or about 5% of the total road network, but less than half of them are classified as 'good' or in 'fair' condition. Yet more than 70% of all vehicles in the country use urban roads because of the heavy concentration of economic activities in urban areas. Overall, more than 80% of passengers and freight are carried on the roads. There were, in 1994, 171,569 motor cars, 32,317 motor cycles, 100,178 vans, 32,413 lorries and 29,681 buses. There were 11,785 road accidents in 1994 (2,424 fatal).

Railways. In 1994 route length was 2,506 km of metre-gauge. In 1994–95, 1·6m. passengers and 2·1m. tonnes of freight were carried.

Civil Aviation. There are international airports at Mombasa (Moi) and Nairobi (Jomo Kenyatta). The national carrier is the now privatized Kenya Airways, which in 1995 operated 3 A310-300s, 2 B-737-200 Advs and 3 other aircraft. KLM has a 26% share of Kenya Airways. Services are also provided by Aero Zambia, Aeroflot, Air Afrique, Air Austral, Air Botswana, Air Burundi, Air France, Air India, Air Madagascar, Air Malaŵi, Air Mauritius, Air Seychelles, Air Tanzania, Air Zimbabwe, Alitalia, Alyemda, Balkan, British Airways, Cameroon Airlines, Egyptair, El Al, Emirates, Ethiopian Airlines, Gulf Air, KLM, LTU, Lufthansa, Northwest Airlines, Olympic Airways, Pakistan Airlines, Royal Swazi, SAA, Sabena, Saudia, Sudan Airways, Swissair and Uganda Airways. In 1994, 2,768, 200 passengers and 65,500 tonnes of freight were carried.

Shipping. The main port is Mombasa, which averages 7·8m. tonnes of cargo a year. Container traffic has nearly doubled since 1990 to 217,028 TEUs (twenty foot equivalent units) in 1996. The merchant marine totalled 15,579 GRT in 1995, including oil tankers, 6,412 GRT.

Telecommunications. In 1994 there were 445,673 telephones. The government aims to improve telephone availability in rural areas from the present 0·16 lines to 1 line per 100 people, and in urban areas from 4 lines to 20 lines per 100 people, by 2015. Broadcasting is the responsibility of KBC, which transmits the following services: National (in Swahili), General (English), Central (4 languages), Western (6 languages), North-Eastern and Coastal (4 languages). KBC also provides television programmes, mainly in English and Swahili. There are several private broadcasting stations, including Kenya Television Network (which broadcasts CNN), Stellavision (which broadcasts Sky News), Capital Radio and Metro FM. The BBC has been awarded a licence to broadcast on the FM frequency. In 1995, 2·6m. radio and 500,000 TV sets were in use.

Cinemas. In 1993 there were 17 cinemas.

Press. In 1995 there were 5 daily papers with a total circulation of 450,000.

SOCIAL INSTITUTIONS

Justice. The courts of Justice comprises the court of Appeal, the High Court and a large number of subsidiary courts. The court of Appeal is the final Apellant court in the country and is based in Nairobi. It comprises of 7 Judges of Appeal. In the course of its Appellate duties the court of Appeal visits Mombasa, Kisumu, Nakuru and Nyeri. The High court with full jurisdiction in both civil and criminal matters comprises of a total of 28 puisne Judges. Puisne Judges sit in Nairobi (16), Mombasa (2), Nakuru, Kisumu, Nyeri, Eldoret Meru and Kisii (1 each).

The Magistracy consists of approximately 300 magistrates of various cadres based in all provincial, district and some divisional centres. In addition to the above there are the Kadhi courts established in areas of concentrated Moslem populations: Mombasa, Nairobi, Malindi, Lamu, Garissa, Kisumu and Marsabit. They exercise limited jurisdiction in matters governed by Islamic Law.

There were 17,589 criminal convictions in 1993; the prison population was 130,393 in 1994.

Religion. In 1992 there were 7·12m. Roman Catholics, 1·94m. Protestants and 1·62m. Moslems. Traditional beliefs persist.

Education. Adult literacy is 77·8%. In 1994 there were 19,083 pre-primary schools with 27,829 teachers and 951,997 pupils; 15,906 primary schools with 5,544,998 pupils and 181,975 teachers; 2,834 secondary schools with 619,839 pupils and 38,307 teachers; 20 teacher training schools with 16,461 students; 20 technical training institutes with 8,148 students. There were 3 polytechnics with 10,836 students, and 5 universities (Nairobi, Moi, Kenyatta, Egerton and Jomo Kenyatta University College of Agriculture and Technology) with 39,340 students.

Health. In 1994 there were 4,558 doctors and 630 dentists. There were 324 hospitals (with 37,271 beds), 522 health centres and 2,868 sub-centres and dispensaries. Free medical service for all children and adult out-patients was launched in 1965.

DIPLOMATIC REPRESENTATIVES

Of Kenya in Great Britain (45 Portland Pl., London, W1N 4AS)
High Commissioner: Mwanyengela Ngali.

Of Great Britain in Kenya (Lower Hill Road, Nairobi)
High Commissioner: Sir Jeffrey James, CMG.

Of Kenya in the USA (2249 R. St., NW, Washington, D.C., 20008)
Ambassador: S. Chemai.

Of the USA in Kenya (Moi/Haile Selassie Ave., Nairobi)
Ambassador: Prudence Bushnell.

Of Kenya to the United Nations
Ambassador: Njuguna Mahugu.

Of Kenya to the European Union:
Ambassador: Philip Mwanzia.

Further Reading

Coger, D., *Kenya.* [Bibliography] 2nd ed. London and Santa Barbara (CA), 1996
Haugerud, A., *The Culture of Politics in Modern Kenya.* CUP, 1995
Miller, N. N., *Kenya: the Quest for Prosperity.* 2nd ed. Boulder (CO), 1994
Ochieng, W. R., (ed.) *Themes in Kenyan History.* Nairobi and Ohio Univ. Press, 1990
Ogot, B. A. and Ochieng, W. R. (eds.) *Decolonization and Independence in Kenya, 1940–93.* London, 1995
Widner, J. A., *The Rise of a Party State in Kenya: from 'Harambee' to 'Nayayo'.* Univ. of California Press, 1993

National statistical office: Central Bureau of Statistics, Ministry of Planning and National Development, POB 30266, Nairobi

KIRIBATI

Ribaberikin Kiribati

(Republic of Kiribati)

Capital: Bairiki (Tarawa)
Population: 82,449
GDP: US$62m.

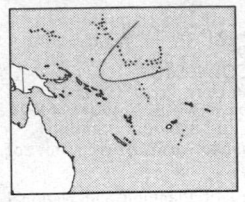

KEY HISTORICAL EVENTS. The islands that now constitute Kiribati were first settled by early Austronesian-speaking peoples long before the 1st century AD. Fijians and Tongans arrived about the 14th century and subsequently merged with the older groups to form the traditional I-Kiribati Micronesian society and culture. The Gilbert and Ellice Islands were proclaimed a British protectorate in 1892 and annexed at the request of the native governments as the Gilbert and Ellice Islands Colony on 10 Nov. 1915 (effective on 12 Jan. 1916). Formally part of the British Colony of Gilbert and Ellice Islands, which separated into two parts in 1976, the Gilberts achieved full independence as Kiribati in 1979. Internal self-government was obtained on 1 Nov. 1976 and independence achieved on 12 July 1979 as the Republic of Kiribati. On 1 Oct. 1975 the former Ellice Islands severed constitutional links with the Gilbert Islands and took on a new name, Tuvalu.

TERRITORY AND POPULATION. Kiribati (pronounced Kiribass) consists of 3 groups of coral atolls and one isolated volcanic island, spread over a large expanse of the Central Pacific with a total land area of 717·1 sq. km (276·9 sq. miles). It comprises **Banaba** or Ocean Island (5 sq. km), the 16 **Gilbert Islands** (295 sq. km), the 8 **Phoenix Islands** (55 sq. km), and 8 of the 11 **Line Islands** (329 sq. km), the other 3 Line Islands (Jarvis, Palmyra and Kingman Reef) being uninhabited dependencies of the USA. The capital is the island of Bairiki in Tarawa.

Population, 1990 census, 72,298. 1997 estimate, 82,449. Between 1988 and 1993 4,700 people were resettled on Teraina and Tabuaeran atolls because the main island group was overcrowded. Banaba, all 16 Gilbert Islands, Kanton (or Abariringa) in the Phoenix Islands and 3 atolls in the Line Islands (Teraina, Tabuaeran and Kiritimati—formerly Washington, Fanning and Christmas Islands respectively) are inhabited; their populations in 1990 (census) were as follows:

Banaba (Ocean Is.)	284	Abemama	3,218	Onotoa	2,112
Makin	1,762	Kuria	985	Tamana	1,396
Butaritari	3,786	Aranuka	1,002	Arorae	1,440
Marakei	2,863	Nonouti	2,766	Kanton	45
Abaiang	5,314	North Tabiteuea	3,275	Teraina	936
North Tarawa	3,648	South Tabiteuea	1,325	Tabuaeran	1,309
South Tarawa	25,154	Beru	2,909	Kiritimati	2,537
Maiana	2,184	Nikunau	2,048		

The remaining 11 atolls have no permanent population; the 7 Phoenix Islands comprise Birnie, Rawaki (formerly Phoenix), Enderbury, Manra (formerly Sydney), Orona (formerly Hull), McKean and Nikumaroro (formerly Gardner), while the others are Malden and Starbuck in the Central Line Islands, and Caroline, Flint and Vostok in the Southern Line Islands. The population is almost entirely Micronesian.

Vital statistics (1997 est.): birth rate, 26·79 per 1,000 population; death rate, 7·71 per 1,000; infant mortality rate, 51·5 per 1,000 live births; life expectancy, 62·35 years.

English is the official language; Gilbertese is also spoken.

CLIMATE. The Line Islands, Phoenix Islands and Banaba have a maritime equatorial climate, but the islands further north and south are tropical. Annual and daily ranges of temperature are small; mean annual rainfall ranges from 50" (1,250 mm) near the equator to 120" (3,000 mm) in the north. Typhoons are prevalent (Nov-March) and there are occasional tornadoes. Tarawa. Jan. 83°F (28·3°C), July 82°F (27·8°C). Annual rainfall 79" (1,977 mm).

CONSTITUTION AND GOVERNMENT. Under the constitution founded 12 July 1979 the republic has a unicameral legislature, the *House of Assembly* (Maneaba ni Maungatabu), comprising 41 members, 39 of whom are elected by popular vote, and 2 (the Attorney-General *ex-officio* and a representative from the Banaban community) appointed for a 4-year term. The *President* is directly elected and is both Head of State and Government. The last general election of 22 July 1994 was won by the Maneaban te Mauri and its allies, with the National Progressive Party becoming the opposition.

In March 1998 the government comprised:
President, Minister of Foreign Affairs and *International Trade:* Teburoro Tito (since 1 Oct. 1994, with 51·2% of the parliamentary vote).

Vice-President, Minister of Home Affairs and *Rural Development:* Tewareka Tentoa. *Minister of Education, Science and Technology:* Willie Tokataake. *Finance and Economic Planning:* Beniamina Tinga. *Environment and Natural Resource Development:* Anote Tong. *Health, Family Planning and Social Welfare:* Kataotika Tekee. *Transport, Communications and Tourism:* Manraoi Kaiea. *Commerce, Industry and Employment:* Tanieru Awerika. *Works and Energy:* Emile Schutz. *Line and Phoenix Islands Development:* Teiraoi Tatabea.

National anthem: 'Teirake kain Kiribati' ('Stand up, Kiribatians'); words and tune by U. Ioteba.

INTERNATIONAL RELATIONS

Membership. Kiribati is a member of the Commonwealth, South Pacific Forum and the Pacific Community (formerly the South Pacific Commission), and is an ACP state of the EU.

ECONOMY

Budget. Foreign financial aid, mainly from the UK and Japan, has amounted to 25-50% of GDP in recent years. Budget estimates for 1995 showed revenue at US$32·5m.; expenditure at US$54·3m.

Currency. The currency in use is the Australian *dollar.*

ENERGY AND NATURAL RESOURCES

Electricity. Capacity (1994), 5,000 kW; production (1994), 10m. kWh.

Agriculture. Copra and fish represent the bulk of production and exports. The principal tree is the coconut; other food-bearing trees are the pandanus palm and the breadfruit. The only vegetable which grows in any quantity is a coarse calladium (alocasia) with the local name 'bwabwai', which is cultivated in pits; taro and sweet potatoes are also grown. Copra production (1994), 12,216 tonnes; coconuts, 65,000 tonnes. Principal livestock: pigs and fowl.

Fisheries. Tuna fishing is an important industry; licenses are held by the USA, Japan and the Republic of Korea.

INDUSTRY Mostly fishing and handicrafts.

Labour. The economically active population in paid employment (not including subsistence farmers) totalled 11,167 in 1990. In 1994 11% were employed in agriculture, 4% in industry, 85% in services. Some 70% of the labour force are under-employed; 2% unemployed.

FOREIGN ECONOMIC RELATIONS

Commerce. Total exports (1995 est.), US$6·3m.; imports, US$38·6m. Main trading partners: Denmark, Fiji, US, Australia, Japan and New Zealand. Principal exports: copra, seaweed, fish; imports: foodstuffs, machinery and equipment, manufactured goods and fuel.

Tourism. Tourism is in the early stages of development.

COMMUNICATIONS

Roads. There were (1995) 655 km of roads, of which 483 km were suitable for vehicles.

Civil Aviation. There were (1996) 20 airports (9 paved). Air Kiribati is the national carrier; it had 2 aircraft in Oct. 1997. It operates services from Tarawa to the outer islands, with one or two flights a week.

Shipping. The main port is at Betio (Tarawa). Other ports of entry are Banaba, English Harbor and Kanton. There is also a small network of canals in the Line Islands. The merchant marine fleet (1996) had 2 vessels totalling 3,248 GRT.

Telecommunications. In 1991 there were 12,000 telephones on South Tarawa and Betio, and a direct link service for 7 other islands. *Radio Kiribati*, a division of the Broadcasting and Publications Authority, transmits daily in English and I-Kiribati from Tarawa. A satellite link to Australia was established in 1985. There were (1993) 15,000 radio receivers.

Cinemas. There are no cinemas. There is a private-owned projector with film shows once a week in every village on South Tarawa.

Press. There was (1991) 1 bilingual weekly newspaper.

SOCIAL INSTITUTIONS

Justice. In 1989 Kiribati had a police force of 232 under the command of a Commissioner of Police. The Commissioner of Police is also responsible for prisons, immigration, fire service (both domestic and airport) and firearms licensing. There is a Court of Appeal and High Court, with judges at all levels appointed by the President.

Religion. In 1990 53% of the population were Roman Catholic, 39% Protestant (Congregational); there are also small numbers of Seventh-Day Adventists, Mormons (6%), Baha'i and Church of God.

Education. In 1990 the government-maintained boarding school had 593 pupils. There were 104 primary schools, with 14,709 pupils; 8 secondary schools with 2,713 pupils; and 1 high school with 117 pupils. There is also a teachers' training college with 39 students (1990) and a marine training centre offering training for about 100 merchant seamen a year. The Tarawa Technical Institute at Betio (389 students in 1986) offers part-time technical and commercial courses.

Welfare. The government maintains free medical and other services. In 1990 there were 16 doctors and 1 hospital on Tarawa with 283 beds, and dispensaries on other islands.

DIPLOMATIC REPRESENTATIVES

Of Great Britain in Kiribati
High Commissioner: Vacant.

Of the USA in Kiribati (assigned from Majuro in the Marshall Islands)
Ambassador: Joan M. Plaisted.

Further Reading

Bailey, E., *The Christmas Island Story.* London, 1977
Kiribati: Aspects of History. University of South Pacific, 1979
Sabatier, E., *Astride the Equator.* Melbourne, 1978
Tearo, T., *Coming of Age.* Tarawa, 1989
Whincup, T., *Nareau's Nation.* London, 1979

KOREA

Daehan Min-kuk

(Republic of Korea)

Capital: Seoul
Population: 44·61m.
GDP per head: (PPP$) 10,656
HDI/world rank: 0·890/32

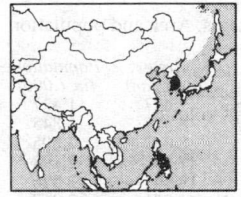

KEY HISTORICAL EVENTS. Korea was united in a single kingdom under the Silla dynasty from 668. China, which claimed a vague suzerainty over Korea, recognized the latter's independence in 1895. Korea concluded trade agreements with the USA in 1882 and with Great Britain and Germany in 1883. After the Russo-Japanese war of 1904–05, Korea was virtually a Japanese protectorate. On 29 Aug. 1910 it was formally annexed by Japan, thus ending 600 years of Confucian rule under the Yi dynasty.

Following the collapse of Japan in 1945, American and Soviet forces entered Korea to enforce the surrender of the Japanese troops, dividing the country into portions separated by the 38th parallel of latitude. Negotiations between the Americans and the Russians regarding the future of Korea broke down in May 1946. In 1948 two separate states were proclaimed. In the south, Syngman Rhee, former president of the Korean government in exile, was elected president of the Republic of Korea, which was recognized by the UN as the only legal government of Korea. In the north, Kim Il-sung, a major in the Red Army who had marched back into Korea with the Soviet forces, was proclaimed premier of the Democratic Peoples' Republic of Korea—which was recognized by the USSR as the only legal government of Korea

The US occupation forces withdrew from South Korea in June 1949. Military equipment promised by the US as part of their aid programme was still on its way to Korea when the North Koreans launched, in June 1950, a full-scale invasion across the 38th parallel. The next day the Security Council of the UN approved a resolution condemning the invasion and asking all member-states to assist in the restoration of peace.

The war, in which North Korea received support from the Chinese army and South Korea from the UN forces and the US, lasted for three years, killed some 5m. people and destroyed an estimated 43% of Korea's industrial plant and 33% of her homes. It was concluded by an armistice signed on 27 July 1953 which implicitly recognized the 38th parallel and the *de facto* boundary between North and South Korea.

Twelve years of Syngman Rhee's authoritarian rule collapsed after student demonstrations brought the country to the brink of civil war in April 1960. There followed nine months of multi-party parliamentary government. A military coup in May 1961 led to the dissolution of the National Assembly, the introduction of martial law and the establishment of Gen Park Chung Hee as president for the next 17 years. Park's assassination in Oct. 1979 threw the country again into a state of crisis. The prime minister, Choi Kyu Hah, became President until Aug. 1980. He was succeeded by Gen. Chun Doo Hwan who was re-elected under a revised constitution in March 1981 and retained his majority again in Feb. 1985. A new, more democratic, constitution, approved by both ruling and opposition parties came into force in 1988.

On 13 Dec. 1991 the prime ministers of North and South Korea signed a declaration of non-aggression and reconciliation, agreeing to respect each other's political systems, not to interfere in each other's internal affairs or slander each other.

The Four-Party Meeting to Promote Peace on the Korean Peninsula, participated in by South Korea and North Korea, the USA and China, held the first plenary session in Dec. 1997

TERRITORY AND POPULATION. South Korea is bounded in the north by the demilitarized zone (separating it from North Korea), east by the Sea of Japan (East Sea), south by the Korea Strait (separating it from Japan) and west by the Yellow Sea. The area is 99,263 sq. km. The population (census, 1 Nov. 1990) was 43,412,000 (urban, 74·4%). Results of an official survey in Nov. 1995, 44,606,000 (22,209,000 females) (84% urban); density, 443 per sq. km. Population estimate, July

1997, 45·99m. Vital statistics rates per 1,000 in 1996: Birth, 16; death, 6; growth, 0·94%. Expectation of life, 77·4 years for females and 69·5 for males. In 1955 life expectancy had been 47.

In 1996, 12,949 South Koreans emigrated. Between 1962 and 1996 a total of 821,256 Koreans emigrated, 78·2% of them to the USA. 5·3m. Koreans lived abroad in 1996.

There are 9 provinces (*do*) and 6 cities with provincial status. Area and population in 1994:

Province	Area (in sq. km)	Population (in 1,000)	Province	Area (in sq. km)	Population (in 1,000)
Seoul (city)	605	10,799	North Chungchong	7,437	1,427
Pusan (city)	526	3,847	South Chungchong	8,317	1,845
Taegu (city)	456	2,347	North Cholla	8,052	2,005
Inchon (city)	313	2,208	South Cholla	11,812	2,198
Kwangju (city)	501	1,274	North Kyongsang	19,443	2,876
Taejon (city)	537	1,235	South Kyongsang	11,771	3,968
Kyonggi	10,769	7,438	Cheju	1,825	514
Kangwon	16,898	1,531			

Cities with over 400,000 inhabitants (census 1990):

Seoul	10,627,790	Taejon	1,062,084	Chonchu	517,104
Pusan	3,797,566	Ulsan	682,978	Chongchu	497,429
Taegu	2,228,834	Puchon	667,777	Masan	496,639
Inchon	1,818,293	Suweon	644,968	Anyang	480,668
Kwangchu	1,144,695	Seongnam	540,764		

CLIMATE. The extreme south has a humid warm temperate climate while the rest of the country experiences continental temperate conditions. Rainfall is concentrated in the period April to Sept. and ranges from 40" (1,020 mm) to 60" (1,520 mm). Pusan. Jan. 36°F (2·2°C), July 76°F (24·4°C). Annual rainfall 56" (1,407 mm). Seoul. Jan. 23°F (–5°C), July 77°F (25°C). Annual rainfall 50" (1,250 mm).

CONSTITUTION AND GOVERNMENT. The 1988 Constitution provides for a *President*, directly elected for a single 5-year term, who appoints and heads a *State Council*, and a *National Assembly* (299 members) directly elected for 4 years (253 from constituencies and 46 from party lists in proportion to the overall vote).

Presidential elections were held on 18 Dec. 1997. In the closest political contest in Korea's history, Kim Dae-Jung, the standard-bearer of a generation of pro-democracy campaigners, was elected with 40·4% of votes against 38·6% for Lee Hoi Chang, the candidate of the governing party.

Elections to the National Assembly were held on 11 April 1996. 1,389 candidates stood. The electorate was 31,526,918; turn-out was 63·9%. The New Korea Party (since renamed the Grand National Party) won 139 seats with 34·5% of votes cast; the National Congress for New Politics, 79 with 25·3%; the United Liberal Democrats, 50 with 16·2%; the Democratic Party, 15 with 11·2%; ind, 16 with 11·9%. In Feb. 1998 the Grand National Party held 161 seats, the National Congress for New Politics 78, the United Liberal Democrats 43 and independents 12 (with 5 vacant), but with the new president being from the National Congress for New Politics it was expected that disillusioned members of the Grand National Party would defect.

The minimum voting age is 20, an age upheld by the Constitutional Court after a challenge in 1997.

President: Kim Dae-Jung (b. 1925; National Congress for New Politics; sworn in 25 Feb. 1998).

On 23 Feb. 1998 Kim Dae-Jung nominated his former political rival Kim Jong-pil as his Prime Minister. The nomination was subject to confirmation by the National Assembly.

National anthem: 'Aegukka' ('A Song of Love for the Country'); words anonymous, tune by An Ik Tae.

Local Government. The 15 provinces are divided into 136 districts *(Gun)* and 68 cities *(Shi)*. Elections were held on 27 June 1995 for the 9 provinces and 6 cities of provincial status and 5,700 other local government posts. The DLP gained 5 governorships, the DP 4, the UPP 4 and ind 2.

DEFENCE. Peacetime operational control, which had been transferred to the Combined Forces Command (CFC) under a US general in July 1950 on the outbreak of the Korean War, was restored to South Korea in Dec. 1994. In the event of a new crisis, operational control over the Korean armed forces will revert to CFC. Conscription is 26 months in the Army and 30 months in the Navy and Air Force. Conscripts may choose or be required to exchange military service for civilian work.

Army. The Army is organized in 19 infantry and 3 mechanized infantry divisions, 2 independent infantry brigades, 7 special forces brigades, 3 air defence artillery brigades, 3 counter-infiltration brigades, 1 army aviation command, 5 surface-to-air and 3 surface-to-surface missile battalions. Equipment includes 800 Type 88, 400 M-47 and 850 M-48A5 main battle tanks. Army aviation equipment includes 250 Hughes 500 and McDonnell Douglas 530 and 60 AH-1F helicopters for anti-armour operations, observation and liaison, and 18 CH-47D transport helicopters and 70 Bell UH-1 utility helicopters. Delivery of 150 UH-60 Black Hawk transport helicopters began in 1991 and is scheduled to continue until 1998. Strength (1997) 548,000 (140,000 conscripts). Paramilitary Civilian Defence Corps, 3·5m.

Navy. A substantial force of 60,000 (19,000 conscripts), including 25,000 marines (1996), continues its steady modernization programme. Current strength includes 4 German-designed ocean-going diesel submarines, 3 midget submarines (175 tonnes), 7 aged (1943–46) ex-US destroyers, 33 locally-built frigates with modern US and European weapons, 4 corvettes, 11 fast missile craft, together with a patrol force of 100 inshore craft. There are 14 coastal mine counter-measure vessels and an amphibious force of 8 tank landing ships, 7 medium landing ships, together with 35 amphibious craft. Major auxiliaries include 2 replenishment and 2 transport tankers, 2 large tugs, 4 survey vessels and 35 service craft. The Navy aviation element operates 8 P-3-C Orion, 15 shore-based S-2E Tracker anti-submarine aircraft and 25 Hughes 500MD, 12 Super-Lynx and 10 Alouette helicopters, some of which embark in frigates and destroyers.

Main bases are at Chinhae, Inchon and Pusan.

The Coastguard numbering some 5,000 (mostly shore-based) operates 10 offshore, 26 coastal and 38 inshore patrol craft as well as 9 light helicopters.

Air Force. In 1996 the Air Force had a strength of 52,000 men and 450 combat aircraft. Its combat aircraft include 100 F-16C/D Fighting Falcons, about 180 F-4D/E Phantoms, 200 F-5E/F tactical fighters, 15 RF-4E Phantom reconnaissance fighters, 10 O-2A and 10 OV-1 forward air control aircraft and 10 Hughes 500 Defender helicopters. There are also 12 CN-235, 10 C-130 Hercules turboprop-engined transports, 2 HS.748s, 1 Boeing 737 for VIP transport; UH 1, Bell 212 and Bell 412 transport helicopters, and Hawk T-41, T-33, T-37C and T-38 trainers.

INTERNATIONAL RELATIONS

Membership. The Republic of Korea is a member of the UN and OECD.

ECONOMY

Policy. The seventh 5-year social and economic plan (1993–97) aimed at controlling growth and strengthening national competitiveness. Part of the plan ('the core industrial sector system') was to make the powerful commercial conglomerates (*chaebol*) more competitive by restricting the industrial areas in which they may engage. The major conglomerates selected their core industries and companies early in 1994. Restrictions on chaebols were relaxed in 1995 where family owners reduced their holdings to less than 20%.

40 state-owned or state-invested companies are scheduled for privatization between 1995 and 1998.

After thirty years of impressive economic growth, South Korea was hit by financial crisis in 1997 when it became clear that the *chaebol* had been allowed to borrow too heavily against inadequate returns. In Dec. 1997, Korea's international debts were estimated at US$200,000m. An IMF and World Bank rescue was tied to undertakings to transform the economy into one based on market principles instead of state directives. Reforms so far approved by the National Assembly include greater monetary policy independence for the central bank, a new structure for financial negotiations and the lifting of the 50% ceiling on foreign ownership of listed Korean companies.

Performance. GDP growth rate was 7% in 1996 (9% in 1995). The rate is liable to fall to under 3% for 1997/98.

Budget. Revenue and expenditure (in 1,000,000m. won) at the 1997 budget: 67,770 and 71,600. Sources of revenue: National tax, 64,230; non-tax, 3,540. Expenditure includes defence, 14,270; infrastructure, 10,130; education, 18,630; agriculture and fisheries, 6,670; technology, 3,220; environment, 2,110.

Currency. The unit of currency is the *won* (KRW). Notes are in denominations of 10,000, 5,000 and 1,000 won and coins in denominations of 500, 100, 50, 10, 5 and 1 won. Notes and coins to the value of 9,234,600m. won were in circulation in 1993. In June 1995 foreign exchange reserves were US$28,380m.; gold reserves were US$34m. Inflation was 4·5% in 1996.

Banking and Finance. The central bank and bank of issue is the Bank of Korea (*Governor*, Lee Kyung Shik). In June 1996 bank deposits totalled 326,030,000m. won, of which 146,850,000m. won were savings and time deposits.

There are 23 national and provincial commercial banks, the 6 largest being Cho Hung, Commercial Bank, Korea First, Hanil, Bank of Seoul and Korea Exchange. There were 52 foreign banks in 1994, granted parity of treatment with domestic banks in July 1991, when the ceiling on their funds was lifted.

In addition, there are non-bank financial institutions including insurance companies, the Land Bank of Korea, the Credit Guarantee Fund, 32 short-term financial companies, plus merchant banks.

The use of real names in financial dealings has been required since 1994.

There is a stock exchange in Seoul.

Weights and Measures. The metric system is in use alongside traditional measures. 1 *sok* = 144 kg. 1 *pyong* = 3·3 sq. metres.

ENERGY AND NATURAL RESOURCES

Electricity. Electricity generated (1994) was 188,348m. kWh; installed capacity (1993) was 27·65 kW. Sources of power in 1993: Nuclear, 40%; oil, 28·5%; coal, 15%; liquefied natural gas, 12·3%; hydro-electric, 4·2%.

Minerals. In 1991, 1,788 mining companies employed 60,983 people. Mineral deposits are small except tungsten. Output, 1993, included (in tonnes): Anthracite coal, 9·44m.; iron ore, 0·2m.; tungsten ore (1990), 2,451; limestone, 77m.; graphite, 59,100; lead ore, 14,818; zinc ore, 27,616.

Agriculture. Cultivated land was 2·07m. ha in 1992, of which 1·31m. ha were rice paddies. In 1995, the farming population was 5·16m. and there were 1·55m. farms. There were some 65,000 farms over 10 ha. The agricultural workforce was 2·8m. in 1994.

In 1995, 1·06m. ha were sown to rice. Production (1993, in tonnes): Rice, 5,315,000; barley, 354,389; wheat, 552,000; potatoes, 243,000; beans, 212,000. There were 64,159 tractors in 1992.

Livestock in 1992 (in 1,000): Draught cattle, 2,019; milk cows, 508; pigs, 5,463; sheep, 505; chickens, 73,324; ducks, 1,000.

Forestry. Forest area was 6·47m. ha in 1992. Total stock (1995) was 257·3m. cu. metres. In 1995, 71% of the national forest was privately owned. Timber output was 1·7m. cu. metres in 1992.

Fisheries. In 1992, there were a total of 94,135 boats (959,056 gross tonnes). 783 deep-sea fishing vessels were operating overseas in 1991. The fish catch (inland and marine) was 3·34m. tonnes in 1993.

INDUSTRY. Manufacturing industry is concentrated primarily on oil, petrochemicals, chemical fibres, construction, iron and steel, cement, machinery, shipbuilding, automobiles and electronics. Tobacco manufacture is a government monopoly. Industry is dominated by giant conglomerates (*chaebol*). There were 2·77m. businesses in 1995, of which 224,654 were incorporated. 521,496 businesses were in catering, 314,283 in manufacturing, 298,136 in services and 211,425 in transport and communications.

Production in 1992 (in 1,000 tonnes): Paper and products, 2,568; artificial fertilizers, 3,077; plastic products, 727; pig-iron, 19,238; steel bars, 1,055; steel angles, 1,999; (in 1,000 sq. metres): Cotton fabrics, 18; synthetic fabrics, 469; silk fabrics, 18; synthetic fabrics, 3,434; petrol, 5,476,000 kilolitres; shoes, 19·4m. pairs; 1·6m. cars; 0·3m. lorries; 7·17m. microwave ovens; 1·3m. electronic calculators.

South Korea is the world's largest producer of ships and memory chips and the fifth largest car maker, with 2,526,000 cars being manufactured in 1995.

Labour. In 1996 the population of working age (15 to 59 years) was 33·56m. The economically-active population was 20·79m., of whom 0·42m. were registered unemployed. In 1995, 4·77m. persons were employed in manufacturing, 11·22m. in services, 1·93m. in building, 27,000 in mining and 1·74m. in agriculture, fisheries and forestry. 5·84m. persons were self-employed in 1995. An annual legal minimum wage is set by the *Minimum Wage Council* each Sept. applicable to firms with more than 10 employees; in 1995–96 it was 288,250 won per month. In Sept. 1996 the average monthly wage was 1,334m. The working week averaged 49·2 hours in 1995. There were 235 labour disputes in 1992; 1,520,364 working days were lost.

Legislation abolishing security of job tenure and giving employers powers to introduce flexible working hours and use substitute labour in the event of strikes was rushed through parliament in Dec. 1996, provoking public protests and a general strike. However, in the wake of the 1997 financial crisis, the trade unions agreed to support labour reforms including job dismissals in return for improved social benefits and new rights to organize.

Trade Unions. In 1993 there were 7,531 unions with a total membership of 1,735,000. The government-recognized Federation of Korean Trade Unions groups 1·4m. of these. Since 1997 unions have been permitted to engage in political activities, and the ban on more than one union in one work place is being abolished in 1998.

FOREIGN ECONOMIC RELATIONS. Foreign debt was US$78,440m. in 1995. Since 1991 foreign partners in joint ventures holding less than 50% of the capital have needed only to report, instead of seek approval for, their projects. Tax concessions for foreign investments have been reduced. Since 1994 foreign investors have been able to buy 15% of the equity of most Korean companies. Since June 1995 South Korean businesses and individuals have been permitted to make investments and set up branch offices in North Korea. South Korea donated 0·15m. tonnes of rice to North Korea in 1995.

Commerce. In 1995 exports were US$125,058m., imports, US$135,119m. Trade in 1994 with major partners (in US$1m.): Imports: Japan, 25,390; USA, 21,578; China, 5,463; Germany, 5,159. Exports: USA, 20,553; Japan, 13,523; Hong Kong, 8,015; China, 6,203.

Major exports in 1994 included (in US$1m.): Transistors and chips, 11,848; textiles, 7,838; clothing, 5,653; ships, 4,945; motor cars, 4,470; iron and steel, 4,456; telecommunications equipment, 3,687; office machines, 3,607; chemicals, 2,116. Major imports included: Machinery and transport equipment, 37,408; mineral fuels, 15,415; chemicals, 9,763; inedible raw materials, 9,405; food, 4,761. Rice imports were prohibited until 1994, but following the GATT Uruguay Round the rice market opened to foreign imports in 1995.

Tourism. In 1995, 3,818,740 Koreans travelled abroad and 3,753,197 foreign nationals visited South Korea (3,580,024 in 1994).

COMMUNICATIONS

Roads. In 1993 there were 61,295 km of roads. 11·6m. passengers and 345·8m.

tonnes of freight were carried in 1994. In 1997 motor vehicles registered totalled 9,964,000 including 2,021,000 lorries, 688,000 buses and 7,220,000 passenger cars. There were 11,585 road deaths in 1992 (13,429 in 1991).

Railways. In 1995 the National Railroad totalled 3,120 km of 1,435 mm gauge (557 km electrified) and 20 km of 762 mm gauge. In 1995 railways carried 817m. passengers and 57·4m. tonnes of freight.

There are metros in Seoul (132 km) and Pusan (26·1 km).

Civil Aviation. There are international airports at Seoul (Kimpo), Kimhae and Chaeju. The national carrier is Korean Air which in 1995 operated 6 A300B4-200s, 5 A300B4-600s, 16 A300B4-600Rs, 2 A300F4-200s, 3 B-727-200 Advs, 4 B-747-200Bs, 2 B-747-200B(F)s, 1 B-747-200C, 8 B-747-200Fs, 2 B-747-300s, 1 B-747-300 Combi, 16 B-747-400s, 1 B-747-400 Combi, 2 B-7475Ps and 34 other aircraft. Asiana Airlines also provides services, and the foreign airlines Aeroflot, Air Canada, Air China, Air France, Air New Zealand, Alitalia, All Nippon Airways, British Airways, Cathay Pacific, China Eastern Airlines, China Northern Airlines, Continental Airlines and Air Micronesia, Delta, Garuda Indonesia, JAL, Japan Air System, KLM, Lufthansa, Malaysia Airlines, Northwest Airlines, Philippine Airlines, Qantas, Singapore Airlines, Swissair, Thai Airways, United Airlines, Uzbekistan Airways, VASP and Vietnam Airlines. In 1994, 18·4m. passengers and 0·31m. tonnes of cargo were carried on domestic routes and 13·08m. passengers and 1·11m. tonnes of cargo on international routes.

Shipping. In 1992 there were 48 ports, including 27 for international trade. In 1995 the merchant marine comprised 684 vessels totalling 19·49m. DWT, representing 2·95% of the world's tonnage. 234 vessels (49·56% of tonnage) were registered under foreign flags. Total GRT, 7·01m., including oil tankers, 0·52m. GRT and container ships, 1·15m. GRT. 7·87m. passengers and 234m. tonnes of freight were carried on domestic routes in 1994, and 0·41m. passengers and 353·42m. tonnes of cargo on international routes.

Telecommunications. Post offices totalled 3,390 in 1995; public telephones, 310,451; telephone subscribers, 18·08m.; telex subscribers, 4,006. 1·65m. mobile phones were in use in 1995. The Korean Broadcasting System (KBS) is a public corporation which broadcasts 4 national radio programmes (1 commercial), regional programmes and a service for Koreans living abroad. An external service, Radio Korea, broadcasts in 10 languages. There is also a commercial network, an educational service and 4 religious networks. KBS transmits 3 TV channels (1 educational); colour by NTSC) and there is a commercial channel. Local commercial TV based on major cities began in 1994. Cable TV was inaugurated in March 1995 and had 1m. subscribers in June 1996. There were 42m. radio and 8·7m. television receivers in 1993.

Cinemas. In 1988 there were 696 with a seating capacity of 240,000. 96 full-length films were produced in 1992.

Press. In 1992 there were 77 dailies and 4,994 periodicals.

SOCIAL INSTITUTIONS

Justice. Judicial power is vested in the Supreme Court, High Courts, District Courts and Family Court. The 14 Justices of the Supreme Court are appointed by the President for renewable 6-year terms; the Chief Justice appoints other judges. The President appoints the Prosecutor-General. The death penalty is authorized.

Religion. The main religions have been Shamanism, Buddhism (introduced AD 372) and Confucianism, which was the official faith from 1392 to 1910. Catholic converts from China introduced Christianity in the 18th century, but a ban on Roman Catholicism was not lifted until 1882. The Anglican Church was introduced in 1890 and became an independent jurisdiction in 1993 under the Archbishop of Korea. In 1995 it had 84 churches, 110 priests and some 52,000 faithful. Religious affiliations of the population in 1991 (and 1985): Buddhism, 23·7% (27·7%); Protestantism, 16·3% (18·6%); Roman Catholicism, 4·8% (5·7%); Confucianism, 1·5% (1%); others, 0·9% (1%); no religion, 52·9% (46%).

Education. After 1 or 2 years of kindergarten, education is compulsory from 6 to 12, followed by the options of middle school till 15 and general or vocational high school to 18.

In 1992–93 there were 8,526 kindergartens with 263,562 pupils and 21,117 teachers; 6,122 elementary schools with 4,561,078 pupils and 137,819 teachers; 2,539 middle schools with 2,336,206 pupils and 93,439 teachers; 1,735 high schools with 2,123,621 pupils and 95,208 teachers; 126 junior colleges with 294,412 students and 10,146 teachers; 11 teacher training colleges with 14,347 students and 603 teachers; 121 colleges and universities with 814,426 students and 37,031 teachers; 9 open colleges with 231,197 students and 1,179 teachers; and 287 other institutions with 185,370 students and 8,199 teachers.

The adult literacy rate is 97·9%.

106,458 South Koreans were studying abroad in 1994.

Health. In 1992 there were 236 general hospitals (with 76,619 beds), 337 other hospitals (36,425), 4,901 oriental medical hospitals and clinics (2,096) and 6,639 dental hospitals and clinics. There were 48,390 physicians, 6,839 oriental medical doctors, 11,285 dentists, 8,012 midwives, 101,140 nurses, and 39,564 pharmacists.

Social Security. In 1992 5·02m. persons were covered by the National Pension System introduced in 1988. Employers and employees make equal contributions; persons joining by choice or in rural areas pay their own contributions. The System covers age pensions, disability payments and survivors' pensions. Recipients of benefit in 1992 included: Public livelihood aid, 2·42m.; veterans, 174,100.

Under a system of unemployment insurance introduced in July 1996, workers laid off after working at least 1 year for a member employer are entitled to benefits averaging 50% of their previous wage for a period of 30 to 210 days.

DIPLOMATIC REPRESENTATIVES

Of Korea in Great Britain (60 Buckingham Gate, London, SW1E 6AJ)
Ambassador: Dong-Jin Choi.

Of Great Britain in Korea (4 Chung-Dong, Chung-Ku, Seoul)
Ambassador: Stephen D. R. Brown.

Of Korea in the USA (2370 Massachusetts Ave., NW, Washington, D.C., 20008)
Ambassador: Kun Woo Park.

Of the USA in Korea (Sejong-Ro, Seoul)
Ambassador: Stephen W. Bosworth.

Of Korea to the United Nations
Ambassador: Park Soo Gil.

Of Korea to the European Union
Ambassador. Jai-Chun Lee.

Further Reading

National Bureau of Statistics. *Korea Statistical Yearbook*
Bank of Korea. *Economic Statistics Yearbook*
Castley, R., *Korea's Economic Miracle.* London, 1997
Cumings, B., *Korea's Place in the Sun: A Modern History.* New York, 1997
Das, D. K., *Korean Economic Dynamism.* London, 1991
Eckert, C. J. *et al., Korea Old and New: a History.* Harvard Univ. Press, 1991
Gibney, F., *Korea's Quiet Revolution: from Garrison State to Democracy.* New York, 1992
Hoare, James E., *Korea.* [Bibliography]. Oxford and Santa Barbara (CA), 1997
Kang, M.-H. *The Korean Business Conglomerate: Chaebol Then and Now.* Univ. of California Press, 1996
Kim, D.-H. and Tat, Y.-K. (*eds.*) *The Korean Peninsula in Transition.* London, 1997
Simons, G., *Korea: the Search for Sovereignty.* London, 1995
Song, P.-N., *The Rise of the Korean Economy.* 2nd ed. OUP, 1994
Tennant, R., *A History of Korea.* London, 1996

National statistical office: National Bureau of Statistics, Economic Planning Board, Seoul
Website: http://www.nso.go.kr/

NORTH KOREA

Chosun Minchu-chui
Inmin Konghwa-guk

(People's Democratic Republic
of Korea)

Capital: Pyongyang
Population: 23·26m.
GDP per head: (PPP$) 3,965
HDI/world rank: 0·765/75

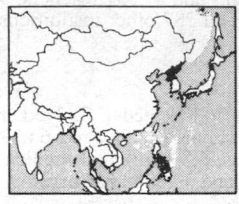

KEY HISTORICAL EVENTS. Following the
collapse of Japan in 1945, Soviet forces arrived in North
Korea, one month ahead of the Americans, and established a Communist-led provisional government. The
newly created Korean Workers' (i.e. Communist) Party,
with other pro-Communist groups and individuals,
formed the United Democratic front. On 25 Aug. 1948
the Communists organized elections for a Supreme
People's Assembly, both in the Soviet-occupied north
and the American-occupied south; some southern
deputies went to the north and took their seats. A People's Democratic Republic was
proclaimed on 9 Sept. 1948, and Kim Il-sung became premier, purging all rivals.

On 25 June 1950 North Korea invaded the south; its advance was stopped with the
aid of UN forces. Chinese Communist 'volunteers' joined the war in Oct. 1950. Truce
negotiations were begun in 1951 and concluded on 27 July 1953. A demilitarized
zone was set up along the final battle line between North and South Korea.

On 13 Dec. 1991 the prime ministers of North and South Korea signed a declaration of non-aggression, agreeing not to interfere in each other's internal affairs.
3 agreements were reached between the North and South Korean prime ministers in
1992 on proposals for military, economic, political and social co-operation.

Kim Il-sung, head of state, Communist Party and the military since 1948, died on
8 July 1994, and was succeeded by his son, Kim Jong Il, who was formally elected
general-secretary of the ruling North Korean Workers' Party in Oct. 1997.

In June 1993, after negotiations with the USA, North Korea reversed its decision
to withdraw from the Nuclear Non-Proliferation Treaty. On 21 Oct. 1994 an agreement to restrict nuclear power to peaceful purposes in Korea was signed by North
Korea and the USA. Talks on setting up a four-way peace conference involving the
USA, China and North and South Korea broke down in Sept. 1997 on the question
of food aid as a precondition of negotiations. Initial problems were subsequently
resolved and the Four-Party Meeting to Promote Peace on the Korean Peninsula, with
representatives from the four countries, held the first plenary session in Dec. 1997.

Although food aid has been stepped up, the UN World Food Programme estimates
that 2m. North Koreans face starvation. But with Kim Jong Il now personally in
control a gradual opening up of what has been described as 'the world's most
mysterious country' is widely anticipated. However, as controls are relaxed, a flood
of refugees across the border into South Korea is expected.

TERRITORY AND POPULATION. North Korea is bounded in the north by
China, east by the sea of Japan, west by the Yellow Sea and south by South Korea,
from which it is separated by a demilitarized zone of 1,262 sq. km. Its area is 122,762
sq. km. Population estimate in 1995, 23,261,000 (64% urban); density, 187·6 per sq.
km. Growth rate, 1994, 1·7%; birth rate, 22·4%; death rate, 5·5%. Marriage is
discouraged before the age of 32 for men and 29 for women. Expectation of life in
1994 was 71·4 years.

The area, 1987 population (in 1,000) and chief towns of the provinces and cities
with provincial status:

	Area in sq. km	*Population*	*Chief Town*
North Hamgyong	17,570	2,003	Chongjin
South Hamgyong	18,970	2,547	Hamhung
Yanggang	14,317	628	Hyesan

	Area in sq. km	Population	Chief Town
Chagang	16,968	1,156	Kanggye
North Pyongan	12,191	2,408	Sinuiju
South Pyongan	11,577	2,653	Pyongsan
Pyongyang (city)	2,000	2,355	
Nampo (city)	753	715	
Kangwon	11,152	1,227	Wonsan
North Hwanghae	8,007	1,409	Sariwon
Kaesong (city)	1,255	331	
South Hwanghae	8,002	1,914	Haeju

Large towns (estimate, 1984): Pyongyang, the capital (2,639,448); Chongjin (754,128); Nampo (691,284); Sinuiju (500,000); Wonsan (350,000); Kaesong (345,642); Kimchaek (281,000); Haeju (131,000); Sariwon (130,000); Hamhung (775,000 in 1981).

CLIMATE. There is a warm temperate climate, though winters can be very cold in the north. Rainfall is concentrated in the summer months. Pyongyang. Jan. 18°F (−7·8°C), July 75°F (23·9°C). Annual rainfall 37" (916 mm).

CONSTITUTION AND GOVERNMENT. The political structure is based upon the Constitution of 27 Dec. 1972. Constitutional amendments of April 1992 delete references to Marxism-Leninism but retain the Communist Party's monopoly of rule. The Constitution provides for a *Supreme People's Assembly* of 687 delegates elected every 5 years by universal suffrage. Citizens of 17 years and over can vote and be elected. Elections were held in April 1990. It was claimed that 99·78% of the electorate voted for the list of single candidates presented. There are 687 deputies. The government consists of the *Administration Council* directed by the Central People's Committee (*Secretary,* Chi Chang Ik).

The head of state is the *President*, elected for 4-year terms. On the death of Kim Il-sung on 8 July 1994 his son and designated successor, Kim Jong Il (b. 1942) assumed all his father's posts. The *Vice Presidents* are Kim Yong Ju, Pak Song Chol, Li Jong Ok and Kim Pyong Sik.

In Feb. 1997 Hong Song Nam became *Prime Minister*.

In March 1998 the government included:

Deputy Prime Ministers: Chang Chol (*Culture and Art*), Choe Yong Nim (*Metallurgy*), Kim Bok Sin (*Light Industry*), Kim Chang Chu, Kim Hwan (*Chemicals Industry*), Kim Yong Nam (*Foreign Affairs*), Kim Yun Hyok, Kong Chin Tae (*Public Welfare*).

In practice the country is ruled by the Korean Workers' (*i.e.*, Communist) Party which elects a Central Committee which in turn appoints a Politburo.

By Nov. 1995 the Presidium of the Politburo was headed by Kim Jong Il, *(General Secretary of the Party, President of the Republic, Chairman of the Central People's Committee, Supreme Commander of the Armed Forces).*

Party membership was 2m. in 1995. There are also the puppet religious Chongu and Korean Social Democratic Parties and various organizations combined in a Fatherland Front.

National anthem: 'A chi mun bin na ra i gang san' ('Shine bright, o dawn, on this land so fair'); words by Pak Se Yong, tune by Kim Won Gyun.

Local Government. The country is divided into 12 administrative units: 3 cities (Pyongyang, Nampo and Kaesong) and 9 provinces. These are sub-divided into 152 counties. There are 26,539 deputies in People's Assemblies at city/province, county and commune level. Elections were held in Nov. 1991. Turn-out was said to be 99·5%.

DEFENCE. The Supreme Commander of the Armed Forces is Kim Jong Il. Military service is compulsory at the age of 16 for periods of 5–8 years in the Army, 5–10 years in the Navy and 3–4 years in the Air Force, followed by obligatory part-time service in the Pacification Corps to age 40.

Army. One of the world's biggest, the Army is organized in 26 infantry divisions (some motorized); 14 armoured, 23 motorized infantry and 5 independent infantry brigades; 1 special purpose corps numbering 88,000; 6 heavy artillery brigades with multiple rocket launchers, 1 independent surface-to-surface missile brigade and 1 regiment. Equipment includes some 3,400 T-34, T-54/55, T-62 and Type-59 main battle tanks, chemical weapons and possibly nuclear warheads. Strength (1996) 1m., with 0·75m. reserves. There is also a paramilitary worker-peasant Red Guard of some 3·8m. and a Ministry of Public Security force of 115,000 including border guards.

Navy. The Navy, principally tasked to coastal patrol and defence, comprises 24 diesel submarines (20 of Chinese design and 4 ex-Soviet) and 12 small coastal submarines. Surface forces include 3 small missile-armed frigates, 4 corvettes, 42 missile craft, 200 fast torpedo craft, 18 anti-submarine patrol craft and some 180 inshore patrol craft. Amphibious forces consist of some 130 small craft. Support is provided by 2 ex-Soviet ocean tugs and 100 service craft. There is a coastal defence element equipped with 6 missile batteries and old 122 mm, 130 mm and 152 mm guns. Personnel in 1996 totalled about 46,000 with 40,000 reserves.

Air Force. The Air Force had a total of 700 combat aircraft and 80 armed helicopters and 82,000 personnel in 1995. Combat aircraft include 60 MiG-23 and 30 MiG-29 interceptors, 40 Su-25 fighter-bombers and more than 100 F-6s (Chinese-built MiG-19s) for ground attack and reconnaissance, as well as 40 Chinese-built A5 fighter-bombers. There are 200 An-2 light transport aircraft, about 20 larger fixed-wing transports, 50 Mi-8 transport helicopters and 80 US Hughes 300 and 500 helicopters.

INTERNATIONAL RELATIONS

Membership. North Korea is a member of the UN.

ECONOMY

Policy. In Dec. 1993 it was officially admitted that the third 7-year plan had failed to achieve its industrial targets owing to the disappearance of Communist markets and aid. Policy now concentrates on the development of agriculture, light industry and foreign trade.

Performance. GDP growth rate was negative in 1996 at –4·6%.

Budget. Revenue, 1991, US$17,300m.; expenditure, US$17,170m. The 1992 budget balanced at US$18,550m.

Currency. The monetary unit is the *won* (KPW) of 100 *chon*. There are coins of 1, 5, 10 and 50 chon and 1, 5, 10, 50 and 100 won. Banknotes were replaced by a new issue in July 1992. Exchanges of new for old notes were limited to 500 won.

Banking and Finance. The bank of issue is the Central Bank of Korea (*governor*, Chong Song Taek).

Weights and Measures. While the metric system is in force traditional measures are in frequent use. The *jungbo* = 1 ha; the *ri* = 3,927 metres. A new yearly calendar was announced on 9 July 1997 based on Kim Il-sung's birthday on 15 April 1912. Thus 15 April 1998–14 April 1999 is Year 87.

ENERGY AND NATURAL RESOURCES

Electricity. There are 3 thermal power stations and 4 hydro-electric plants. A nuclear power plant is being built. Output in 1993 was 21,100m. kWh. Installed capacity was 7·1m. kW in 1993. Hydro-electric potential exceeds 8m. kW. A hydro-electric plant and dam under construction on the Pukhan near Mount Kumgang has been denounced as a flood threat by the South Koreans, who constructed a defensive 'Peace Dam' in retaliation.

Oil. Oilwells went into production in 1957. An oil pipeline from China came on stream in 1976. Crude oil refining capacity was 70,000 bbls. a day in 1990.

Minerals. North Korea is rich in minerals. Estimated reserves in tonnes: Iron ore, 3,300m.; copper, 2·15m.; lead, 6m.; zinc, 12m.; coal, 11,990m.; uranium, 26m.; manganese, 6,500m. 27·1m. tonnes of coal were mined in 1993, 8m. tonnes of iron ore and 15,000 tonnes of copper ore in 1986. 1986 production of gold was 160,000 fine troy oz; silver, 1·6m. fine troy oz; salt, 570,000 tonnes.

Agriculture. In 1992 there were 1·71m. ha. of arable land, 305,000 ha of permanent crop land and 50,000 ha of pasture. In 1991 there were 0.68m. ha of paddy fields. In 1992, 7·14m. persons subsisted on agriculture.

Collectivization took place between 1954 and 1958. 90% of the cultivated land is farmed by co-operatives. Land belongs either to the State or to co-operatives, and it is intended gradually to transform the latter into the former, but small individually-tended plots producing for 'farmers' markets' are tolerated as a 'transition measure'. Livestock farming is mainly carried on by large state farms.

There is a large-scale tideland reclamation project. In 1992 1·46m. ha were under irrigation, making possible 2 rice harvests a year. In 1992 there were 75,000 tractors. The technical revolution in agriculture (nearly 95% of ploughing, etc., is mechanized) has considerably increased the yield of wheat (sown on 90,000 ha). Production (1993, in 1,000 tonnes): Wheat, 100; rice, 2,940; maize, 1,960; potatoes, 1,750; soya beans, 380. Total grain production was 2·52m. tonnes in 1996.

Livestock, 1993: Cattle, 1·3m.; pigs, 3·3m.; sheep, 0·39m.; goats, 0·3m.; 22m. poultry.

A chronic food shortage has led to repeated efforts by UN agencies to stave off famine. In Jan. 1998, the UN launched an appeal for US$378m. for food for North Korea, the largest ever relief effort mounted by its World Fund Programme.

Forestry. Forest area in 1991 was 6,468,000 ha. 4·6m. cu metres of timber were cut in 1986.

Fisheries. Catch in 1993, 1·09m. tonnes. There is a fishing fleet of 30,600 vessels including 20,000 motor vessels.

INDUSTRY. Industries were intensively developed by the Japanese occupiers, notably cotton spinning, hydro-electric power, cotton, silk and rayon weaving, and chemical fertilizers. Production in 1986: Cement, 9m. tonnes; textiles, 600m. metres; motor-cars (1993), 10,000; TV sets, 240,000; ships, 50,000 GRT. Annual steel production capacity was 4·3m. tonnes in 1987.

Labour. The economically-active population was 10·08m. in 1991. Industrial workers make up some 60% of the work force.

FOREIGN ECONOMIC RELATIONS. Joint ventures with foreign firms have been permitted since 1984. A law of Oct. 1992 revised the 1984 rules: Foreign investors may now set up wholly-owned facilities in special economic zones, repatriate parts of profits and enjoy tax concessions. Economic zones have been set up at the ports of Sonbong and Najin. In 1996 foreign debt was estimated at US$11,830m. The USA imposed sanctions in Jan. 1988 for alleged terrorist activities. Since June 1995 South Korean businesses and individuals have been permitted to make investments and set up branch offices in North Korea. South Korea donated 0·15m. tonnes of rice to North Korea in 1995 and a further 50,000 tonnes in 1997.

Commerce. Exports in 1995 were US$740m.; imports, US$1,310m. In 1992 China was the biggest trade partner (total trade US$620m.), followed by Japan, CIS and Iran. The chief exports are metal ores and products, the chief imports machinery and petroleum products.

Tourism. A 40-year ban on non-Communist tourists was lifted in 1986.

COMMUNICATIONS

Roads. There were 23,219 km of road in 1993, including 240 km of motorways. There were 248,000 motor cars in 1990.

Railways. In 1990 the railway network totalled 8,533 km of which 3,250 km were electrified. In 1990 38·5m. tonnes of freight and 35m. passengers were carried.

There is a metro and tramway in Pyongyang.

Civil Aviation. The national carrier is Air Koryo which had 25 ex-Soviet aircraft in 1995 and flew services to Moscow, Khabarovsk, Beijing, Tokyo and Hong Kong. There are domestic flights from Pyongyang to Hamhung and Chongjin.

Shipping. The leading ports are Chongjin, Wonsan and Hungnam. Pyongyang is connected to the port of Nampo by railway and river. In 1995 the ocean-going merchant fleet totalled 1·08m. GRT, including oil tankers, 0·23m. GRT.

The biggest navigable river is the Yalu, 698 km up to the Hyesan district.

Telecommunications. In 1993 the provision of telephones was 3.5 per 100 inhabitants. An agreement to share in Japan's telecommunications satellites was reached in Sept. 1990. The government-controlled Korean Central Broadcasting Station and Korean Central Television Station are responsible for radio and TV broadcasting. In 1991 there were 34 radio and 11 TV stations (colour by PAL). There were 4·7m. radio and 2m. TV sets in 1993.

Cinemas. There were 1,778 cinemas in 1985 and 3,515 mobile cinemas.

Press. There were 3 national and 12 local newspapers in 1994. The party newspaper is *Nodong* (or *Rodong*) *Sinmun* (Workers' Daily News). Circulation about 600,000.

SOCIAL INSTITUTIONS

Justice. The judiciary consists of the Supreme Court, whose judges are elected by the Assembly for 3 years; provincial courts; and city or county people's courts. The procurator-general, appointed by the Assembly, has supervisory powers over the judiciary and the administration; the Supreme Court controls the judicial administration.

Religion. The Constitution provides for 'freedom of religion as well as the freedom of anti-religious propaganda'. In 1986 there were 3m. Chondoists, 400,000 Buddhists and 200,000 Christians. Another 3m. followed traditional beliefs.

Education. Free compulsory universal technical education lasts 11 years: 1 preschool year, 4 years primary education starting at the age of 6, followed by 6 years secondary. In 1994-95 there were 37 universities, 32 specialized universities (agriculture, 2; chemical industry; cinema; coal mining; construction; economics, 2; education, 5; fine arts; foreign studies; geology; hydraulics and dynamics; light industry; mechanical engineering; medicine; mining and metallurgy; music and dance; pharmacy; physical education; printing; railways; science; sea transport; technology, 2; veterinary science) and 108 specialized colleges.

The adult literacy rate is 95%.

Health. Medical treatment is free. In 1982 there were 1,531 general hospitals, 979 specialized hospitals and 5,414 clinics. The doctor/inhabitant ratio was 1:370 in 1993.

DIPLOMATIC REPRESENTATIVE

Of North Korea to the United Nations
Ambassador: Li Hyong Chol.

Further Reading

North Korea Directory. Tokyo, annual since 1988

Kihl, Y. W., *Politics and Policies in Divided Korea.* Boulder, 1984

Park, J. K. and Kim, J.-G., *The Politics of North Korea.* Boulder (CO), 1979

Scalapino, R. A. and Lee, C.-S., *Communism in Korea.* Univ. of California Press, 1972—and Kim, J-Y. (eds.), *North Korea Today: Strategic and Domestic Issues.* Univ. of California Press, 1983

Smith, H. *et al.* (eds.) *North Korea in the New World Order.* London, 1996

Suh, D.-S., *Korean Communism, 1945–1980: A Reference Guide to the Political System.* Honolulu, 1981

National statistical office: Central Statistics Bureau, Pyongyang.

KUWAIT

Dowlat al Kuwait

(State of Kuwait)

Capital: Kuwait
Population: 2·02m.
GDP per head: (PPP$) 21,875
GNP: US$314·3bn.
HDI/world rank: 0·844/53

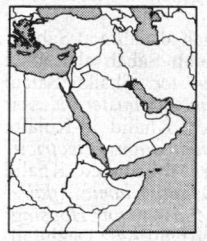

KEY HISTORICAL EVENTS. The ruling dynasty was founded by Shaikh Sabah al-Awwal, who ruled from 1756 to 1772. In 1899 the then ruler, Shaikh Mubarak, concluded a treaty with Great Britain wherein, in return for the assurance of British protection, he undertook to support British interests. In 1914 the British Government recognized Kuwait as an independent government under British protection. On 19 June 1961 an agreement reaffirmed the independence and sovereignty of Kuwait and recognized the Government of Kuwait's responsibility for the conduct of internal and external affairs; the agreement of 1899 was terminated.

In 1990 Iraqi forces overran the country, meeting little resistance, and President Saddam of Iraq declared the annexation of Kuwait on 8 Aug. Following the expiry of the date required by the UN for the withdrawal of Iraqi forces on 15 Jan. 1991, an air offensive was launched by coalition forces against targets in Kuwait, followed by a land attack on 24 Feb. Iraqi forces were routed, and Kuwait City was liberated on 26 Feb. Iraq withdrew all its forces from Kuwait. On 10 Nov. 1994 Iraq recognized the independence and boundaries of Kuwait.

TERRITORY AND POPULATION. Kuwait is bounded in the east by the Arabian (Persian) Gulf, north and west by Iraq and south and south-west by Saudi Arabia, with an area of 17,818 sq. km. In 1992-93 the UN Boundary Commission redefined Kuwait's border with Iraq, moving it slightly northwards in conformity with an agreement of 1932. The population at the census of 1995 was 1,590,013 (96% urban), of whom about 56% were non-Kuwaitis. Population density, 80 per sq. km. Estimate, 1996, 2,016,037 (64·36% non-Kuwaiti). Life expectancy was 75·2 years in 1994, with a birth rate (per 1,000) of 22·9 and death rate 2·0.

Following the Iraqi occupation of 1990-91, the government announced plans to reduce its population to about 1m. to ensure that Kuwaitis formed a majority at about 0·55m. Many foreign workers who fled during the occupation would not be permitted to return.

The country is divided into 5 governorates: The capital (comprising Kuwait City, Kuwait's 9 islands and territorial and shared territorial waters) (population 237,892, 1993 estimate); Hawalli (386,953); Ahmadi (266,433); Jahra (178,688) and Farwaniya (363,255).

The chief cities are (1993 population estimate) Kuwait, the capital (31,241), and its suburbs Hawalli (84,478), as-Salimiya (116,104), Jahra (139,476) and Farwaniya (47,106).

The Neutral Zone (Kuwait's share, 2,590 sq. km), jointly owned and administered by Kuwait and Saudi Arabia from 1922 to 1966, was partitioned between the two countries in May 1966, but the exploitation of the oil and other natural resources continues to be shared.

Over 78% speak Arabic, the official language. English is also used as a second language.

CLIMATE. Kuwait has a dry, desert climate which is cool in winter but very hot and humid in summer. Rainfall is extremely light. Kuwait. Jan. 56°F (13·5°C), July 99°F (36·6°C). Annual rainfall 5" (125 mm).

RULER. HH Shaikh Jaber al-Ahmed al-Jaber al-Sabah the 13th Amir of Kuwait, succeeded on 31 Dec. 1977.

CONSTITUTION AND GOVERNMENT. In 1990 the *National Council* was established, consisting of 50 elected members and 25 appointed by the Amir. The franchise, limited to men over 21 whose families have been of Kuwaiti nationality since before 1920 and the sons of persons naturalized since 1992, produced an electorate of 107,169 at the elections of 7 Oct. 1996. There were 230 candidates. Turn-out was 80%.

Executive authority is vested in the *Council of Ministers*, which in March 1998 comprised:

Prime Minister: HRH Crown Prince Shaikh Saad al-Abdullah al-Salim al-Sabah.
First Deputy Prime Minister and Foreign Minister: Shaikh Sabah al-Ahmed al-Jaber al-Sabah. *Deputy Prime Minister and Defence Minister:* Shaikh Salem Sabah al-Salem al-Sabah. *Deputy Prime Minister and Finance Minister:* Nassar Abdullah al-Roudhan. *Social Affairs and Labour:* Ahmed Khalid al-Kulaib. *Commerce and Industry:* Jasim Mohammed al-Mudhaf. *Communications, Electricity and Water:* Jasim Mohammed al-Aoun. *Interior:* Shaikh Mohammed Khalid al-Hamad al-Sabah. *Justice, Religious Endowments (Awqaf) and Islamic Affairs:* Mohammed Dhaifallah Sharar. *Public Works and State Minister for Housing:* Abdullah Rashed al-Hajri. *State Minister for Cabinet Affairs:* Abdul Aziz Dakhil al-Dakhil. *Education and Higher Education:* Abdullah Yousef al-Ghunaim. *Planning and State Minister for Administrative Development Affairs:* Ali Fahd al-Zumeih. *Oil:* Issa Mohammed al-Mazidi. *Information and Health:* Shaikh Soud Nassar al-Sabah.

National anthem: There are no words, tune by Ibrahim Nassar al-Soula.

DEFENCE. In Sept. 1991 the USA signed a 10-year agreement with Kuwait to store equipment, use ports and carry out joint training exercises. In Feb. 1992 the UK signed an agreement with Kuwait to provide advisers and equipment. Conscription is for 2 years.

Army. The army consists of 2 mechanized, 2 armoured, 1 reserve; 1 engineer and 1 artillery brigade, 1 commando battalion and the Amiri Guard brigade. Equipment includes 150 M-84, 50 M-1A2 and 20 Chieftain main battle tanks. Strength (1997) about 11,000.

Navy. The navy operates 2 German-built fast missile craft, 4 Australian-built inshore patrol craft together with 1 logistic support craft. Some 50 boats are operated by the Coast Guard. Personnel in 1997 numbered 1,800, including 400 Coast Guard personnel.

Air Force. From a small initial combat force the Air Force has grown rapidly, although it suffered heavy losses after the Iraqi invasion of 1990–91. It has 2 squadrons with 40 F/A-18 Hornet strike aircraft. Other equipment includes 1 DC-9 and 1 MD-83 jet transport, 3 L-100-30 Hercules turboprop transports and 12 Hawk jet trainers, 9 Puma, 3 Exocet missile-armed Super Puma and 16 missile-armed Gazelle helicopters. 16 Tucano aircraft are in use. Hawk surface-to-air missiles are in service. Personnel strength (1996) 2,500, with 40 Combat aircraft and 16 armed helicopters.

INTERNATIONAL RELATIONS

Membership. Kuwait is a member of the UN, Arab League, Gulf Co-operation Council and OPEC.

ECONOMY

Policy. The 4-year reconstruction and development plan covers 1995-2000.

Performance. GDP growth in 1996 was 1·6%.

Budget. The fiscal year begins on 1 July. Revenue and expenditure over a 5-year span (in millions of dinar):

	1992	1993	1994	1995	1996
Revenue	586	2,285	2,545	2,987	3,306
Expenditure	5,022	3,610	3,847	3,790	3,426

Expenditure by function (in 1996): defence, 1,163; public order and safety, 331; education, 476; health, 247; social security and welfare, 656.

Currency. The unit of currency is the *Kuwaiti dinar* (KD) of 1,000 *fils*. There are coins of 1, 5, 10, 20, 50 and 100 fils and notes of KD 20, 10, 5, 1, $^1/_2$ and $^1/_4$. In 1994 KD 365·3m. were in circulation. Inflation in 1996 was 1·8%. Foreign exchange reserves were US$3,892m. in June 1995; gold reserves were US$730·1m.

Banking and Finance. The *Governor* of the Central Bank is Shaikh Salem Abdel-Aziz al-Sabah. There is also the Kuwait Finance House. In 1995 there were 8 local banks. Total assets of commercial banks as at 31 Dec. 1994 were KD 8,671·9m.; private deposits were KD 5,562m., of which KD 582m. were in savings accounts.

There is a stock exchange, linked with those of Bahrain and Oman.

Weights and Measures. The metric system is in force.

ENERGY AND NATURAL RESOURCES

Electricity. There are 4 power stations with a total installed capacity of 6,898 MW in 1994. 20,173m. kWh were produced in 1993.

Oil and Gas. Estimated crude oil production in 1997, 2·5m bbls. a day. Gas production was 5,170m. cu. metres in 1993.

Water. The country depends upon desalination plants. In 1993 there were 4 plants with a daily total capacity of 216m. gallons. Fresh mineral water is pumped and bottled at Rawdhatain. Underground brackish water is used for irrigation, street cleaning and livestock. Production, 1993, 68,379m. gallons (46,409m. gallons fresh, 21,970m. gallons brackish).

Agriculture. In 1992 there were 5,000 ha of arable land, and 137,000 ha of permanent pasture. Production of main crops, 1993 (in tonnes): Melons, 4,000; tomatoes, 35,000; onions, 16,000; dates, 1,000.

Livestock (1993): Cattle, 12,000; sheep, 150,000; goats, 15,000; camels, 1,000; poultry, 10m. Milk production (1993) 15,000 tonnes.

Fisheries. Shrimp fishing was important, but has declined since the 1990-91 war through oil pollution of coastal waters. Total catch in 1995: 8,706 tonnes. Pearl fishing is now on a small scale.

INDUSTRY. Industries, apart from oil, include boat building, fishing, food production, petrochemicals, gases and construction.

Labour. In 1994 the labour force totalled 990,518 (including 824,658 non-Kuwaitis) distributed by sector as follows: Social services, 469,645 (non-Kuwaitis, 333,743); commerce and catering, 184,284 (181,371); building, 128,813 (128,171); industry, 70,659 (64,979); transport and communications, 38,706 (33,939); finance and business, 35,341 (30,297); agriculture and fishing, 15,985 (15,939); mining, 7,017 (3,615); public utilities, 7,017 (3,383); others, 33,051 (29,221). Registered unemployment was 1·4% in 1996.

Trade Unions. In 1986 there were 16 trade unions and 17 labour federations.

FOREIGN ECONOMIC RELATIONS

Commerce. Imports were valued at KD 1,988·2m. in 1994 and exports at KD 3,341·6m. (including oil exports, KD 3,112m.). The main non-oil export is chemical fertilizer.

Main export markets, 1994 (in KD 1m.): France, 36; Saudi Arabia, 33·31; UAE, 31·64; India, 30·93. Main import suppliers: USA, 289·1; Japan, 233·1; Germany, 163·5; UK, 138; France, 126·2.

COMMUNICATIONS

Roads. There are 4,741 km of roads. Number of vehicles (1994) was 747,000. There were 15,921 road accidents in 1993 with 290 fatalities.

Civil Aviation. There is an international airport. The national carrier is the state-owned Kuwait Airways, which operated 5 A300B4-600Rs, 1 A300C4-600, 3 A310-300s, 3 A320-200s, 2 A340-300s, 2 B-707-320Cs, 4 B-747-200B Combis, and 1 B-747-400 Combi in 1995. Services are also provided by Aeroflot, Air China, Air France, Air India, Air Lanka, Alitalia, Balkan, Biman Bangladesh, British Airways, Czech Airlines, Egyptair, Emirates, Gulf Air, Indian Airlines, Iran Air, KLM, Lufthansa, Middle East Airlines, Northwest Airlines, Olympic Airways, Oman Air, Pakistan Airlines, Qatar Airways, Saudia, Syrian Airlines, Tarom, Turkish Airlines, United Airlines and Zas.

Shipping. The port of Kuwait formerly served mainly as an entrepôt, but this function is declining in importance with the development of the oil industry. The largest oil terminal is at Mina Ahmadi. 3 small oil ports lie to the south of Mina Ahmadi: Mina Shuaiba, Mina Abdullah and Mina Al-Zor. The main ports for other traffic are at Shuwaikh, Shuiaba and Doha. The merchant fleet totalled 7,783,000 GRT in 1990, of which 593,000 GRT were tankers.

Telecommunications. There were (1993), 615,000 telephones. The government-controlled Radio Kuwait and Kuwait Television broadcast a main and a second radio programme, a Koran programme and a service in English and 2 TV programmes (colour by PAL). In 1995 there were 625,000 TV receivers and 800,000 radios.

Cinemas. In 1996 there were 6 cinemas, with a total annual attendance of 800,000.

Press. In 1995 there were 7 daily newspapers in Arabic and 2 in English, with a combined circulation of about 655,000. Formal press censorship was lifted in Jan. 1992.

SOCIAL INSTITUTIONS

Justice. In 1960 Kuwait adopted a unified judicial system covering all levels of courts. These are: Courts of Summary Justice, Courts of the First Instance, Supreme Court of Appeal, Court of Cassation, Constitutional Court and State Security Court. Islamic Sharia is a major source of legislation. The death penalty was imposed for drug smuggling in April 1995.

Religion. In 1995 about 78% of the population were Sunni Moslems, 14% Shia Moslems, 6% Christians and 2% others.

Education. Education is free and compulsory from 6 to 14 years. In 1996 there were 201 pre-primary schools with 3,145 teachers for 49,393 pupils; 266 primary schools with 9,747 teachers for 141,841 pupils and 19,087 teachers in secondary schools for 206,934 pupils. There were 28,705 students in higher education, of which 14,884 were at university level. Adult literacy rate in 1995 was 78·6% (82·2% men, 74·9% women). Total expenditure on education: 5·6% of GDP.

Health. Medical services are free to all residents. There are 16 hospitals and sanatoria with 6,104 beds, 88 clinics and 25 health centres, with 2,641 doctors, 320 dentists and 7,977 nursing staff.

DIPLOMATIC REPRESENTATIVES

Of Kuwait in Great Britain (2 Albert Gate, London, SW1X 7JU)
Ambassador: Khaled al-Duwaisan.

Of Great Britain in Kuwait (Arabian Gulf St., Kuwait)
Ambassador: Graham H. Boyce, CMG.

Of Kuwait in the USA (2940 Tilden St., NW, Washington, D.C., 20008)
Ambassador: Dr M. Sabah al-Salem al-Sabah.

Of the USA in Kuwait (PO Box 77, Safat, Kuwait)
Ambassador: Ryan C. Crocker.

Of Kuwait to the United Nations
Ambassador: Mohammad A. Abulhasan.

Of Kuwait to the European Union
Ambassador: Ahmad Al-Ebrahim.

Further Reading

Al-Yahya, M.A., *Kuwait: Fall and Rebirth.* London, 1993
Clements, F. A., *Kuwait.* [Bibliography] 2nd ed. Oxford and Santa Barbara (CA), 1996
Crystal, J., *Kuwait: the Transformation of an Oil State.* Boulder (Colo.), 1992
Finnie, D. H., *Shifting Lines in the Sand: Kuwait's Elusive Frontier with Iraq.* London, 1992

KYRGYZSTAN

Kyrgyz Respublikasy

Capital: Bishkek
Population: 4·51m.
GDP per head: (PPP$) 1,930
HDI/world rank: 0·635/107

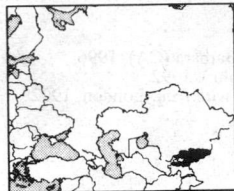

KEY HISTORICAL EVENTS. After the establishment of the Soviet regime in Russia, Kyrgyzstan became part of Soviet Turkestan, which itself became an Autonomous Soviet Socialist Republic within the Russian Soviet Federal Socialist Republic (RSFSR) in April 1921. In 1924, when Central Asia was reorganized territorially on a national basis, Kyrgyzstan was separated from Turkestan and formed into an autonomous region within the RSFSR. On 1 Feb. 1926 the Government of the RSFSR transformed Kyrgyzstan into an Autonomous Soviet Socialist Republic within the RSFSR, and finally in Dec. 1936 Kyrgyzstan was proclaimed one of the constituent Soviet Socialist Republics of the USSR. With the collapse of the Soviet Empire, the republic asserted its claim to sovereignty in 1990 and declared independence in Sept. 1991.

It became a member of the CIS in Dec. 1991.

TERRITORY AND POPULATION. Kyrgyzstan is situated on the Tien-Shan mountains and bordered in the east by China, west by Kazakhstan and Uzbekistan, north by Kazakhstan and south by Tajikistan. Area, 199,900 sq. km (77,180 sq. miles). Population (estimate, July 1997), 4,512,809. Vital statistics rates, 1997 estimate (per 1,000 population): Birth, 22·27; death, 8·59; infant mortality (per 1,000 live births), 73·6. Life expectancy, 1997 estimate, 63·97 years.

The republic comprises 6 provinces: Djalal-Abad, Issyk-Kul, Naryn, Osh, Talas and Chu. There are 18 towns, 31 urban settlements and 40 rural districts. Its capital is Bishkek (formerly Frunze; 1991 population estimate, 641,400). Other large towns are Osh (238,200), Djalal-Abad (74,200), Tokmak (71,200), Przhevalsk (64,300) and Kyzyl-Kiya.

The Kyrgyz are of Turkic origin and formed 52·4% of the 1989 census population of 4,257,755; the rest include Russians (21·5%), Uzbeks (12·9%), Ukrainians (2·5%), Germans, (2·4%) and Tatars (1·6%).

The official language is Kyrgyz, and also Russian in provinces where Russians are in a majority. The Roman alphabet (in use 1928–40) was re-introduced in 1992.

CLIMATE. The climate varies from dry continental to polar in the high Tien-Shan, to sub-tropical in the south-west (Fergana Valley) and temperate in the northern foothills.

CONSTITUTION AND GOVERNMENT. A new Constitution was adopted on 5 May 1993. The Presidency is executive, and directly elected for renewable 5-year terms. At a referendum on 30 Jan. 1994, 96% of votes cast favoured President Akaev's serving out the rest of his term of office; turn-out was 95%. At a referendum on 22–23 Oct. 1994 turn-out was 87%. 75% of votes cast were in favour of instituting referendums as a constitutional mechanism, and 73% were in favour of establishing a new bicameral parliament (*Jogorku Kenesh*), with a 35-member directly-elected legislature, and a 70-member upper house elected on a regional basis and meeting twice a year. Elections were held in 2 rounds on 5 and 19 Feb. 1995. 94·5% of votes cast at a referendum on 10 Feb. 1996 were in favour of giving the President the right to appoint all ministers except the Prime Minister without reference to parliament.

Presidential elections were held on 24 Dec. 1995. President Akaev was re-elected by 71·6% of votes cast against 2 opponents. Turn-out was 82%.

President: Askar Akaev (b. 1945).

A new government was appointed in March 1996 which in March 1998 comprised:

Prime Minister: Kubanychbeck Jumaliyev.
First Deputy Prime Minister: Kemilbek Nanaev. *Deputy Prime Ministers:* Karimshev Abdimomunov *(Agriculture)*; Mira Jangaracheva *(Social Issues)*. *Foreign Affairs:* Muratbek Imanaliev. *Interior:* Omurbek Kutuev. *Architecture and Construction:* Aleksandr Moiseev. *Finance and Economy:* Tolobek Koychumanov. *Agriculture and Water Resources:* Jumkadyr Akineev. *Geology and Mineral Resources:* Baiseit Tursungaziev. *Defence:* Murzakan Subanov. *National Security:* Feliks Kulov. *Co-operation with CIS States:* Yan Fisher. *Emergency Situations and Civil Defence:* Mambetzhunus Abylov. *Industry and Trade:* Andrei Yordan. *Tourism and Sport:* Myrza Kaparov. *Justice:* Larisa Gutchenko. *Labour and Social Welfare:* Asylgul Abdurekhmenov. *Health:* Naken Kasiev. *Culture:* Cholponbek Bazarbaev. *Education and Science:* Askar Kakeev.

The *Speaker* is Almanbet Matubraimov.

Local Government. Elections were held on 25 Feb. 1990. The appointment of leaders of local councils is approved or vetoed by the President of the Republic.

DEFENCE. Conscription is for 18 months.

Army. The Army consists of 1 motor rifle division and 1 mountain brigade. Equipment includes 204 T-72 main battle tanks. Personnel, 1997, 9,800.

Air Force. There is an aviation element with MiG-21 fighters and a variety of other ex-Soviet equipment, including L-29 and L-39 trainers. The Government is selling aircraft to other countries to finance the operation of its remaining equipment. Personnel, 1997, 2,400.

INTERNATIONAL RELATIONS

Membership. Kyrgyzstan is a member of the UN, CIS and the NATO Partnership for Peace.

ECONOMY

Budget. Budgetary revenue in 1995 (excluding grants received, 54·6m. soms) was 2,653·6m. soms; expenditure (excluding lending minus repayments, 556m. soms) was 4,327·2m. soms.

Currency. On 10 May 1993 Kyrgyzstan introduced its own currency unit, the *som* (KGS), of 100 *tyiyn*, at a rate of 1 som = 200 rubles. There are notes of 50 tyiyn, and 1, 5, 10 and 20 som. Inflation was 0·7% in Sept. 1994.

Banking and Finance. The central bank and bank of issue is the National Bank. (*Chairman:* Narat Sultanov). There were 13 commercial banks and 1 German-Kyrgyz industrial bank in 1996.

ENERGY AND NATURAL RESOURCES

Electricity. Output was 12,280m. kWh (91% hydro-electric) in 1995.

Oil and Gas. Output of oil (including gas concentrate), 1995, 179m. tonnes; natural gas, 36m. cu. metres.

Water. Kyrgyzstan's most valuable natural resource is water.

Minerals. In 1995, 474,000 tonnes of coal were produced. Some gold is mined.

Agriculture. Kyrgyzstan is famed for its livestock breeding. On 1 Jan. 1995 there were 1,061,000 cattle, 165,000 pigs, 7,077,000 sheep and 219,000 goats. Yaks are bred as meat and dairy cattle, and graze on high altitudes unsuitable for other cattle. Crossed with domestic cattle, hybrids give twice the yield of milk. The small Kyrgyz horse is famed.

Area under cultivation (1993), 16m. ha, of which private subsidiary agriculture accounted for 0·15m. ha and commercial farming 3·3m. ha in 12,800 farms. Private and commercial agriculture accounted for 46% of output by value in 1993. Total output was valued at 2,400m. roubles (in constant 1983 prices) in 1993, 92% of the 1992 figure.

Kyrgyzstan raises wheat sufficient for its own use and other grains and fodder, particularly lucerne; also sugar-beet, hemp, kenaf, kendyr, tobacco, medicinal plants and rice. Sericulture, fruit, grapes and vegetables and bee-keeping are major branches.

Output of main agricultural products (in 1,000 tonnes) in 1995: Grain, 776; cottonseed, 40; sugar-beet, 110; potatoes, 431; tomatoes, 159; apples, 65; tobacco (leaves), 58; beef and veal, 68; mutton and lamb, 50; milk, 864; and 83m. eggs.

Fisheries. The total catch in 1995 was 364 tonnes.

INDUSTRY. Industrial enterprises include sugar refineries, tanneries, cotton and wool-cleansing works, flour-mills, a tobacco factory, food, timber, textile, engineering, metallurgical, oil and mining enterprises. Output was valued at 3,300m. som in current prices in 1993, 75·8% of the 1992 figure.

Production, 1995: Cement, 0·31m. tonnes; textile fabrics, 23,208,000 sq. metres; carpets, 0·98m. sq. metres; footwear, 728,000 pairs; 4,000 washing machines.

Labour. In 1993 the population of working age was 2·3m., of whom 1·7m. were employed, 54·1% in the state sector, 28·5% in the private sector and 14·6% in co-operatives. In Jan. 1994 there were 2,900 registered unemployed (0·2% of the labour force), of whom 1,700 were receiving benefits. Average monthly salaries in 1993 were 85·90 som.

FOREIGN ECONOMIC RELATIONS. In Jan. 1994 an agreement to create a single economic zone was signed with Kazakhstan and Uzbekistan. In March 1996 Kyrgyzstan joined a customs union with Russia, Kazakhstan and Belarus.

Commerce. In 1995 imports were valued at US$522·3m. and exports at US$408·9m.

Principal imports in 1995 (in US$1m.): Petroleum and gas, 162·4; machinery and metalworking, 103·6; food and beverages, 96·7. Principal exports: Food and beverages, 82·8; light industry, 82·6; non-ferrous metallurgy, 62·7.

Main import suppliers in 1995 (in US$1m.): Russia, 114·3; Kazakhstan, 112·5; Uzbekistan, 88·9; Turkey, 38·3; Cuba, 22·7. Main export markets: Russia, 104·8; Uzbekistan, 70; People's Republic of China, 68·5; Kazakhstan, 66·8; UK, 27·4.

COMMUNICATIONS

Roads. There were 18,560 km of roads (16,890 km paved) in 1997. In 1993, 219·5m. passengers and 14·6m. tonnes of freight were carried.

Railways. In the north a railway runs from Lugovaya through Bishkek to Rybachi on Lake Issyk-Kul. Towns in the southern valleys are linked by short lines with the Ursatyevskaya–Andizhan railway in Uzbekistan. Total length of railway, 1994, 318 km. In 1994, 1·1m. passengers and 1·1m. tonnes of freight were carried.

Civil Aviation. There is an international airport at Bishkek Manas. The national carrier is Kyrgyzstan Airlines. Services are also provided by Azerbaijan Hava Yollery, Siberia Airlines and Uzbekistan Airways. In 1993, 0·3m. passengers and 800 tonnes of freight were carried.

Inland Waterways. Total length was 600 km in 1990. In 1993, 0·1m. tonnes of freight were carried.

Telecommunications. There were an estimated 342,000 telephones in 1991. Kyrgyz Radio and Kyrgyz Television are state-controlled. There are 2 national radio programmes, with some broadcasting in English and German. There is 1 commercial radio station. In 1993 there were 3 hours of TV broadcasting a day (colour by SECAM). In 1995 there were 0·51m. radio and 0·15m. television receivers.

Cinemas. In 1995 there were 343 cinemas with an annual attendance of 0·6m.

Press. In 1995 there were 3 daily newspapers with a combined circulation of 53,000.

SOCIAL INSTITUTIONS

Justice. In 1994, 41,155 crimes were reported, including 546 murders or attempted murders.

Religion. In 1996, 70% of the population was Sunni Moslem. There were some 1,000 mosques, 30 Russian Orthodox, 17 Evangelical, 9 Seventh Day Adventist and 8 Lutheran, churches.

Education. In 1996 there were 453 pre-primary schools with 4,013 teachers for 35,254 pupils; 1,885 primary schools with 24,086 teachers for 473,077 pupils; 42,286 secondary teachers for 530,854 pupils, and 3,691 university level teachers for 49,744 students. There are 21 higher educational institutions and 51 technical and teachers' training colleges, as well as music and art schools. Kyrgyz University had 7,300 students in 1994–95.

Health. In Jan. 1994 there were 14,800 doctors, 42,600 junior medical personnel and 348 hospitals with 48,900 beds.

Welfare. In Jan. 1994 there were 443,000 age and 196,000 other pensioners.

DIPLOMATIC REPRESENTATIVES

Of Kyrgyzstan in Great Britain (119 Crawford St., London W1H 1AF)
Ambassador: Roza I. Otunbaeva.

Of Great Britain in Kyrgyzstan
Ambassador: Douglas B. McAdam (resides in Kazakhstan).

Of Kyrgyzstan in the USA (1732 Wisconsin Ave., NW, Washington, D.C., 20007)
Ambassador: Baktybek Abdrisaev.

Of the USA in Kyrgyzstan (66 Erkindik Prospekt, Bishkek 720002)
Ambassador: Eileen A. Malloy.

Of Kyrgyzstan to the United Nations
Ambassador: Zamira Eshmambetova.

Of Kyrgyzstan to the European Union
Ambassador: Tchinguiz Aitmatov.

LAOS

Saathiaranarath Prachhathipatay
Prachhachhon Lao

(Lao People's Democratic
Republic)

Capital: Vientiane
Population: 5·12m.
GDP per head: (PPP$) 2,484
GNP: US$1·5bn.
HDI/world rank: 0·459/136

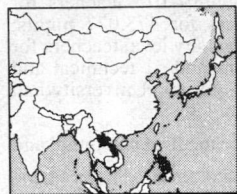

KEY HISTORICAL EVENTS. The Kingdom of Laos, once called Lanxang (the Land of a Million Elephants), was founded in the 14th century. The kingdom has always depended on the maintenance of good relations with its more powerful neighbours, Thailand, Myanmar and Vietnam.

In 1893 Laos became a French protectorate and in 1907 acquired its present frontiers. In 1945, after French authority had been suppressed by the Japanese, an independence movement known as Lao Issara (Free Laos) set up a government under Prince Phetzarath, the viceroy of Luang Prabang. This government collapsed with the return of the French in 1946, its leaders fleeing to Thailand.

Under a new constitution of 1947 Laos became a constitutional monarchy under the Luang Prabang dynasty, and in 1949 became an independent sovereign state within the French Union. A few Lao Issara leaders remained in dissidence under Prince Souphanouvong who allied himself with the Vietminh and subsequently formed the 'Pathet Lao' (Lao state) rebel movement.

An almost continuous state of war began in 1953 between the Royal Lao Government, supported by American bombing and Thai mercenaries, and the Patriotic Front Pathet Lao, supported by North Vietnamese troops. Peace talks from 1972 resulted in an agreement on 21 Feb. 1973 providing for the formation of a provisional government of national union, and the withdrawal of foreign troops. A provisional coalition government was duly formed in 1974. However, after the Communist victories in neighbouring Vietnam and Cambodia in April 1975, the Pathet Lao took over the running of the whole country, maintaining only a façade of a coalition. On 29 Nov. 1975 HM King Savang Vatthana abdicated and the People's Congress proclaimed a People's Democratic Republic of Laos on 2 Dec. 1975.

TERRITORY AND POPULATION. Laos is a landlocked country of about 91,400 sq. miles (236,800 sq. km) bordered on the north by China, the east by Vietnam, the south by Cambodia and the west by Thailand and Myanmar. Apart from the Mekong River plains along the border of Thailand, the country is mountainous, particularly in the north, and in places densely forested.

The population (census, 1995) was 4,581,258 (2,315,931 females); density, 19 per sq. km. Population 1997 estimate, 5,116,959, growth rate, 2·78%. Population density, 19·4 per sq. km. Vital statistics, 1997 estimate: Birth rate, 41·25 per 1,000 population; death rate, 13·4; infant mortality, 94·3 per 1,000 live births; life expectancy, 53·63 years.

There are 17 provinces divided into 133 districts and 1 special region. Area, population and administrative centres in 1996:

Province	Sq. km	Population (in 1,000)	Administrative centre
Vientiane (town)	3,920	531·8	—
Vientiane	19,990	286·8	
Phongsaly	16,270	153·4	Phongsaly
Luang Nam Tha	9,325	115·2	Luang Nam Tha
Oudomsai	21,190	211·3	Ban Nahin
Bokeo	4,970	114·9	Ban Honei Sai
Luang Prabang	16,875	367·2	Luang Prabang
Houaphan	16,500	247·3	Sam Neua
Sayaboury	11,795	293·3	Sayaboury
Xiang Khouang	17,315	201·2	Xiang Khouang

Province	Sq. km	Population (in 1,000)	Administrative centre
Bolikhamsai	16,470	164·9	Paksane
Khammouane	16,315	275·4	Thakhek
Savannakhet	22,080	674·9	Savannakhet
Saravane	10,385	258·3	Saravane
Sekong	7,665	64·2	Sekong
Champassak	15,415	503·3	Pakse
Attopei	10,320	87·7	Attopei

The Special Region had a population of 54,200 in 1995.

The capital and largest town is Vientiane, with a population of (census 1985) 377,409. Other important towns are Savannakhet, 96,652; Luang Prabang, 68,399; Pakse, 47,323.

The population is divided into 3 groups: about 67% Lao-Lum (Valley-Lao); 17% Lao-Theung (Lao of the mountain sides); and 5% Lao-Soung (Lao of the mountain tops), who comprise the Meo and Yao. Lao is the official language. French and English are spoken.

CLIMATE. A tropical monsoon climate, with high temperatures throughout the year and very heavy rains from May to Oct. Vientiane. Jan. 70°F (21·1°C), July 81°F (27·2°C). Annual rainfall 69" (1,715 mm).

CONSTITUTION AND GOVERNMENT. On 14 Aug. 1991 the National Assembly adopted a new constitution. The head of state is the President, elected by the National Assembly.

Under the constitution the Lao People's Revolutionary Party (LPRP) remains the 'central nucleus' of the 'people's democracy'; other parties are not permitted. The LPRP's Politburo comprises 9 members, including Khamtay Siphandone (*LPRP, President*).

President: Khamtay Siphandone (elected 24 Feb. 1998).
Vice President: Oudom Khattigna.
In March 1998 the government consisted of:
Prime Minister: Sisavath Keobounphanh.
Deputy Prime Ministers: Boungnang Vorachith, Choummaly Sayasone (also *Minister of Defence*), Somsavat Lengsavad (also *Foreign Affairs*), Khamphoui Keoboualapha (also *Finance*). *Commerce:* Phoumy Thipphavone. *Communications, Transport, Posts, and Construction:* Phao Bounnaphol. *Education:* Phimmasone Leuangkhamma. *Interior:* Asang Laoly. *Information and Culture:* Sileua Bounkham. *Industry and Handicrafts:* Soulivong Daravong. *Labour and Social Welfare:* Somphanh Phengkhammy. *Justice:* Kham Ouane Boupha. *Public Health:* Ponemek Daraloy. *Agriculture and Forestry:* Siene Saphangthong.

The *Speaker* is Samane Vignaket.

National anthem: 'Xatlao tangtae dayma lao thookthuana nentxoo sootchay' ('For the whole of time the Lao people have glorified their Fatherland'); words by Sisana Sisane, tune by Thongdy Sounthonevichit.

DEFENCE. Military service is compulsory for a minimum of 18 months.

Army. There are 4 military regions. The Army is organized in 5 infantry divisions; 3 engineering regiments, 7 independent infantry regiments and 65 independent infantry companies; and 5 artillery and 9 anti-aircraft battalions. Equipment includes 30 T-54/-55 main battle tanks. Strength (1997) about 25,000.

Navy. There is a riverine force of about 500 personnel (1997) organized into 4 squadrons running some 12 patrol craft, 4 landing craft and 40 smaller river patrol for operations on the Mekong.

Air Force. The Air Force has about 50 aircraft, including 20 MiG-21 fighters, 6 An-2, 6 An-24, 3 An-26, 2 Y-12 and 2 Yak-40 transports and 10 Mi-8 helicopters. Personnel strength, about 3,500 in 1997.

INTERNATIONAL RELATIONS

Membership. Laos is a member of the UN and ASEAN.

ECONOMY

Policy. The fourth 5-year plan (1996–2000) aims at an annual growth of 8%.

Performance. Real GDP growth over 1990–94 averaged 6%. Estimates for 1995 and 1996, between 7% and 7·5%.

Budget. In 1993 revenue was 144,526m. kip and expenditure 170,514m. kip. Revenue included 85,928m. kip raised from taxation. Current expenditure was 61·5% of the total.

Currency. The unit of currency is the *kip* (LAK). There are notes of 10, 20, 50, 100, 500 and 1,000 kip. In 1991, 20,233m. kip were in circulation. Inflation was 12% in 1996 (21·4% in 1995). Foreign exchange reserves were US$55·1m., gold US$0·6m.

Banking and Finance. The central bank and bank of issue is the State Bank (*Governor*, Cheuang Somboukhanh). There were 12 commercial banks in 1995 (6 foreign). Total savings and time deposits in 1991 amounted to 4,075m. kip.

ENERGY AND NATURAL RESOURCES

Electricity. Total installed capacity in 1996 was 217,000 kW, of which 93% was hydroelectric. Production (1990) 870m. kWh (825m. kWh hydro-electric). In 1996, 16% of households had electricity, mainly in Vientiane.

Minerals. 1991 output (in tonnes): Coal, 1,250; baryte, 4,500; 1995: Tin, 687; gypsum, 0·11m.

Agriculture. Agriculture accounted for 54·6% of GDP in 1996. In 1992 there were 78,000 ha of arable land, 25,000 ha, permanent crop land and 800,000 ha, pasture. The chief products (1995 output in 1,000 tonnes) are rice 1,423; tobacco, 62; coffee, 10; and sweet potatoes and cassava, 164; maize, 79; seed-cotton, 84; sugar-cane, 123; soya beans, 72; tea 17. Opium is produced but its manufacture is controlled by the state.

Livestock (1995): Cattle, 1,145,900; buffaloes, 1,191,600; horses (1993), 29,000; pigs, 1,723,600; goats and sheep, 153,100; poultry, 11,338,400.

Forestry. The forests, which cover 12·7m. ha, produce valuable woods such as teak. Timber production, 1995, 512,000 cu. metres.

Fisheries. The total catch in 1995 was 40,250 tonnes.

INDUSTRY. Industry accounted for 16% of GDP in 1995. Production in 1995: Corrugated iron, 1m. sheets; nails, 58 tonnes; oxygen, 13,000 cylinders; detergent, 800 tonnes; cigarettes, 40m. packets; beer, 126,000 hectolitres; soft drinks, 108,000 hectolitres; reinforced concrete, 24,000 cu. metres; plastic, 500 tonnes; salt, 12,000 tonnes.

Labour. The working age is 16–55 for females and 16–60 for males. At the 1995 census there were 1,086,172 females and 1,051,112 males within those age groups.

FOREIGN ECONOMIC RELATIONS. Since 1988 foreign companies have been permitted to participate in Lao enterprises. In 1990 foreign investments amounted to US$189m., mainly in hotels and textiles. Total foreign debt was US$1,2021m. at 31 Dec. 1993.

Commerce. In 1995 imports amounted to US$587m. and exports to US$348m. The main imports in 1995 were: Electricity, 43·1m. kWh; lorries, 105; motor cars, 1,390; motorcycles, 4,288; bicycles, 17,501; (in tonnes) fuel, 43,200; cement, 4,400; iron, 4,900; paper, 617; fabrics, 2,098; medicines, 3,621; sugar, 2,433; rice, 1,172. Main exports: Electricity, 705·2m. kWh; timber, 86,100 cu. metres; lumber, 88,200 cu. metres; plywood, 1,512,000 sheets; coffee, 2,830 tonnes; gypsum, 110,000 tonnes; tin, 653 tonnes. Main import suppliers, 1991 (in US$1,000): Thailand, 76,622; Japan, 21,360; China, 11,154; Italy, 6,093. Main export markets, 1995: Thailand, 142,300; Vietnam, 87,700; France, 23,600; USA, 11,200; Russia, 11,200; China, 9,500; Germany, 5,000.

Tourism. There were 16,023 foreign visitors in 1994.

COMMUNICATIONS

Roads. In 1996 there were 16,760 km of roads (14% hard-surfaced) classified as: National highways, 4,460 km (38% hard-surfaced); provincial roads, 6,380 km (9% hard-surfaced); district roads, 5,920 km. 955,000 tonnes of freight were transported by road in 1995. In 1992 there were 20,233 cars, 11,551 lorries, 1,435 buses and 105,921 motorcycles. There were 1,820 traffic accidents with 600 fatalities. A bridge over the River Mekong, providing an important north-south link, was opened in 1994.

Railways. The Thai railway system extends to Nongkhai, on the Thai bank of the Mekong River. A 20 km-spur to Vientiane across the bridge here is proposed.

Civil Aviation. There is an international airport at Vientiane (Wattay). Air Lao provides services to Bangkok, Phnom Penh and Hanoi. It had 9 Chinese aircraft in 1995. Services are also provided by Aeroflot, Air Vietnam and Thai Airways. 115,000 passengers were carried in 1991 (28,000 on international flights) and 0·8m. tonnes of freight.

Shipping. The River Mekong and its tributaries are an important means of transport. 898,000 tonnes of freight were carried on inland waterways in 1995.

Telecommunications. In 1995 there were 15,757 (10,743 private or business) telephones. The government-controlled National Radio of Laos broadcasts a national and 6 regional programmes and an external service (6 languages). Lao National TV transmits for 3 hours daily. There were (1995) about 0·63m. radio and 45,000 television receivers.

Cinemas. In 1993 there were 5 cinemas with an annual attendance of 10,000.

Press. In 1996 there were 3 dailies (1 in English).

SOCIAL INSTITUTIONS

Justice. Criminal legislation of 1990 established a system of courts and a prosecutor's office. Polygamy became an offence.

Religion. In 1992 some 2·55m. were Buddhists (Hinayana), but about a third of the population follow tribal religions.

Education. In 1995–96 there were 685 kindergartens with 33,500 pupils and 1,900 teachers, 8,425 primary schools with 724,100 pupils and 24,600 teachers, 705 secondary schools with 117,900 pupils and 7,700 teachers and 129 higher secondary schools with 44,600 pupils and 2,800 teachers. There is 1 teachers' training college, 1 college of education, 1 school of medicine, 1 agricultural college and an advanced school of Pali.

In 1994–95 there was 1 university of medical science, 1 institute of pedagogy and 1 national polytechnic institute, and 8 other institutes of higher education. There were 4,507 university students and 494 academic staff.
Adult literacy (1995) 56·6% (male, 69·4%; female, 44·4%).

Health. In 1995 there were 25 hospitals, 131 health centres, 542 dispensaries and 3,100 doctors.

DIPLOMATIC REPRESENTATIVES

Of Laos in Great Britain (resides in Paris)
Ambassador: Khamphan Simmalavong.

Of Great Britain in Laos
Ambassador: Sir James W. Hodge, KCVO, CMG (resides in Thailand).

Of Laos in the USA (2222 S. St., NW, Washington, D.C., 20008)
Ambassador: Hiem Phommachanh.

Of the USA in Laos (Rue Bartholonie, Vientiane)
Ambassador: Wendy Jean Chamberlin.

Of Laos to the United Nations
Ambassador: Alounkeo Kittikhoun.

Of Laos to the European Union
Ambassador: Khamphan Simmalavong.

Further Reading

National Statistical Centre. *Basic Statistics about the Socio-Economic Development in the Lao P.D.R.* Annual.

Cordell, H., *Laos*. [Bibliography] Oxford and Santa Barbara (CA), 1990
Stuart-Fox, M., *History of Laos*. Cambridge University Press, 1998
Stuart-Fox, M., *Laos: Politics, Economics and Society*. London, 1986
Zasloff, J. J., and Unger, L. (eds.) *Laos: Beyond the Revolution*. London, 1991

National statistical office: National Statistical Centre, Vientiane.

LATVIA

Latvijas Republika

Capital: Riga
Population: 2·48m.
GDP per head: (PPP$) 3,332
HDI/world rank: 0·771/92

KEY HISTORICAL EVENTS. The territory that is now Latvia was controlled by crusaders, primarily the German Order of Livonian Knights, until 1561, when Latvia fell into Polish and Swedish hands. Between 1721 and 1795 Latvia was absorbed into the Russian empire. In the part of Latvia unoccupied by the Germans during the First World War, the Bolsheviks won 72% of the votes in the Constituent Assembly elections (Nov. 1917). Soviet power was proclaimed in Dec. 1917, but was overthrown when the Germans occupied all Latvia (Feb. 1918). Restored when they withdrew (Dec. 1918), it was overthrown once more by combined British naval and German military forces (May–Dec. 1919), and a democratic government set up. This régime was in turn replaced when a coup took place in May 1934.

The secret protocol of the Soviet–German agreement of 23 Aug. 1939 assigned Latvia to the Soviet sphere of interest. An ultimatum (16 June 1940) led to the formation of a government acceptable to the USSR. On 21 July a People's Diet proclaimed the establishment of the Latvian Soviet Socialist Republic and applied to join the USSR, whose Supreme Soviet accepted the application on 5 Aug.

On 4 May 1990 the Latvian Supreme Soviet declared, by 138 votes to nil with 58 abstentions, that the Soviet occupation of Latvia on 17 June 1940 was illegal, and resolved to re-establish the authority of the Constitution of 1922. A transition period was set for the restoration of independence. In a referendum in March 1991 the principle of independence was supported by 73·6% of votes cast. A fully independent status was conceded by the USSR State Council in Sept. 1991.

TERRITORY AND POPULATION. Latvia is situated in north-eastern Europe. It is bordered by Estonia on the north, by Lithuania on the south-west, while on the east there is a frontier with the Russian Federation and to the south-east with Belarus. Territory, 64,600 sq. km. (larger than Denmark, the Netherlands, Belgium and Switzerland). Population (1996), 2,479,870. Nationalities: Latvians 55·3%, Russians 32·5%, Belarussians 4%, Ukrainians 2·9%, Poles 2·2%, Lithuanians 1·3%, Jews 0·4%, Gypsies 0·3%, Estonians 0·1%, Germans 0·1%.

Vital statistics, 1996: Births,19,782 (7·9% per 1,000 inhabitants); deaths, 34,320 (13·8 per 1,000 inhabitants); marriages, 9,634 (3·9 per 1,000 inhabitants); infant deaths, 15·8 per 1,000 births.. In 1996 life expectancy was: Males, 63·9 years; females, 75·6. Divorce, 6,051 (2·4 per 1,000 inhabitants). In 1995 there were 2,799 immigrants and 13,346 emigrants.

Citizenship is conferred upon all residents of pre-1940 Latvia and their descendants, and is open to immigrants of at least 16 years residence. Further legislation of July 1994 provides for the naturalization of non-citizens born in Latvia over the following 6 years and of those born outside Latvia from 2000. There were 1,764,968 citizens registered as of Jan. 1996.

There are 26 districts, 56 towns and 37 urban settlements. The capital is Riga (820,577 in 1996); other principal towns are Daugavpils (117,835), Liepāja (97,917), Jelgava (70,943), Jurmala (58,959) and Ventspils (46,567).

The official language is Latvian.

CLIMATE. Owing to the influence of maritime factors, the climate is relatively temperate but changeable. Average temperatures in January range from –2·8°C in the western coastal town of Liepāja, to –6·6°C in the inland town of Daugavpils. The average summer temperature is 20°C.

CONSTITUTION AND GOVERNMENT. The Declaration of the Renewal of the Independence of the Republic of Latvia dated 4 May 1990, and the 21 August 1991 declaration re-establishing de facto independence, proclaimed the authority of the Constitution *(Satversme)*. The Constitution was fully re-instituted as of 6 July 1993, when the 5th Parliament *(Saeima)* was elected.

The head of state in Latvia is the *President*, elected by parliament for a period of 3 years. H.E. Mr Guntis Ulmanis (LZS) was elected President of the Republic of Latvia on 7 July 1993 and re-elected for a second term on 18 June 1996.

The highest legislative body is the one-chamber parliament comprised of 100 deputies and elected in direct, proportional elections by citizens 18 years of age and over. Deputies serve for three years and parties must receive at least 5% of the national vote to gain seats in parliament. Elections for the Republic of Latvia 6th Parliament were held on 30 Sep.-1 Oct. 1995 and 19 parties, movements and pre-election coalitions submitted their candidate lists to the electorate. It was estimated that 71·9% of eligible voters went to the polls.

At the parliamentary elections of 30 Sept.-1 Oct. 1995, the number of seats, percents, party and chair were as follows: Democratic Party "Saimnieks" (DPS) *(Demokrātiska Partija "Saimnieks")* won 18 seats with 15·1% of votes cast, Ziedonis Cevers; Latvia's Way (LC) *(Latvijas Celš)*, 17 with 14·6%, Andrejs Pantelējevs; For Latvia (L) *(Latvijas)*, 16 with 14·9%, Odiejs Kostanda; Fatherland and Freedom (TB) *(Tēvzemei un Brīvībai)*, 14 with 11.9%, Jānis Straume; Latvia's Farmer's Union, Latvia's Christian Democratic Union and Latgale's Democratic Party *(Latvijas Zemnieku Savienība, Latvijas Kristīgo Demokrātu Savienība, Latgale's Demokrātiskā Partija)* (LZS, KDS, LDP), 18 with 6·3%, Kārlis Jūlijs Druva; Unity Party (UP) *(Vienības Partija)*, 8 with 6·3%; Latvia's National Conservative party "LNNK" and Latvia's Green Party coalition *(Latvijas Nacionāli Konservatīvā Partija* and *Latvijas Zaļā partija)*, 8 with 6·3%, Aleksandrs Kiršteins; People Unity Party *(Tautas Saskaņas Partija)*, 6 with 5·55%, Jānis Jurkāns; Socialist Party *(Sociālistikā Partija)*, 5 with 5·58%, Olegs Denisovs.

A 7-member *Constitutional Court* was established in 1996 with powers to invalidate legislation not in conformity with the constitution. Its members are appointed by parliament for 10-year terms.

In 6th Parliamentary elections on 1 Dec. 1997 the number of seats won was as follows:

Democratic Party "Samnieks" (DPS), 20; For Fatherland and Freedom (TB) and Latvia's National Conservative Party "LNNK" coalition, 17; Latvia's Way (LC), 16; Latvia's Farmer's Union and Christian Democratic Union (LZS, KDS) coalition, 13; For Latvia (L), 9; Latvia's National Reform Party *(Latvijas Nacionālā Reformu Partija)* and Green Party coalition, 6; People Unity Party, 5; People Group "Freedom" *(Tautas Kopa "Brīvība")*, 5; Independent MP, 15. The *speaker* is Alfrēds Cepānis (DPS). Next Parliamentary elections will be held in Oct. 1998.

Executive power is held by the *Cabinet of Ministers*. On 21 Dec. 1995 parliament voted to support a Cabinet headed by Andris Skele. The Prime Minister submitted his resignation on 20 Jan. 1997, but was renamed as a prime ministerial candidate by President Ulmanis after discussions with all parliamentary parties. On 13 Feb. 1997 the parliament confirmed the second government of the 6th Parliament under Prime Minister Andris Skele. On 28 July 1997, Prime Minister Andris Skele handed in the letter of resignation to the President.

The *new government*, headed by former Minister of Economy, Guntars Krasts, was confirmed by the Saeima on 7 Aug. 1997. In March 1998 it comprised:

Prime Minister: Guntars Krasts (TB/LNNK).

Deputy PM: Juris Kaksētis (DPS). *Minister of Education and Science:* Juris Celmiņš (DPS). *Minister of Defence:* Tālavs Jundzis (KDS). *Minister of Agriculture:* Andris Rāviņš (LZS). *Minister of Environmental Protection and Regional Development:* Anatolijs Gorbunovs (LC). *State Minister for the Environment:* Indulis Emsis (LZP, Green Party). *State Minister for Local Governments:* Eriks Zunda (DPS). *Minister of Foreign Affairs:* Valdis Birkavs (LC). *Minister of Economy:* Atis Saunītis (DPS). *Minister of Finance:* Roberts Zīle (TB/LNNK). *State Minister for State Revenues:* Aija Poca (LC). *Minister of the Interior:* Ziedonis Cevers (DPS).

Minister of Transport: Vilis Krištopāns (LC). *Minister of Welfare:* Vladimirs Makārovs (TB/LNNK). *State Minister for Health:* Viktors Jaksons (TB/LNNK). *Minister of Justice:* Dzintars Rasnacs (TB/LNNK). *Minister of Culture:* Ramona Umblija.
N.B. State Ministers cannot be regarded as fully fledged cabinet members, but have voting rights in the Issues concerning their field.

National anthem: 'Dievs, svēti Latviju' ('God bless Latvia'); words and tune by Kārlis Baumanis.

Local Government. There are 2 tiers of local authorities: Regional, which are appointed, and county, which are elected for 4-year terms. Citizens of 21 years or over who have resided in a locality for 12 months may stand for election. Last elections took place on 9 March 1997 for 77 city and 489 town councils. There were 11942 candidates from 1454 registers of candidates which represented 29 political parties. Next elections will be held on March 2001.

DEFENCE. Since Latvia gained its independence in Aug. 1991, a renewal process for Latvia's armed forces, including the National Armed forces, the Home Guard and Border Guard, has been underway. Military service is compulsory for male citizens from the age of 19 (women and men 18 years and older can join the National defence Forces voluntarily) and the duration of military service is 18 months. Conscientious objectors have the option of serving in non-military service. Latvia has signed a defence co-operation treaty with Lithuania and Estonia to co-ordinate Baltic States' defence and security activities. A joint Baltic peace-keeping force has been established (BALTBAT) as well as joint navy fleet (BALTRON), and joint air control system (BALNET) will be introduced in 1998. A sub-unit of Latvia's National Armed Forces is participating in the NATO led IFOR operations in the former Yugoslavia as a part of a joint Latvian-Danish military battalion.

Army. The Army is organized in 1 infantry, 1 reconnaissance and 1 engineer battalion, and was 1,500 strong in 1996. There is a Home Guard reserve of 5 brigades, and a paramilitary Frontier Guard of 4,300.

Navy. A small coastal protection force numbered 1,000 in 1996 and operates 18 patrol vessels of Swedish, German and Soviet origins based at Riga and Liepāja. There is a coastal defence battalion numbering 350, and a coastguard operates 9 small craft.

Air Force. Personnel numbered 150 in 1995. There are 1 L-410 and 2 An-2 transports and 6 Mi-2 helicopters.

INTERNATIONAL RELATIONS

Membership. Latvia is a member of the UN, OSCE, the Council of Europe and the NATO Partnership for Peace (and is looking for full NATO membership), an Associate Partner in WEU, and an Associate Member of the EU. Latvia will become a member of WTO at the end of 1997.

ECONOMY. The Latvian Privatization Agency, established in 1994 to oversee the entire privatization process, has adopted a case-by-case approach in determining the privatization method for each entity earmarked for privatization. The privatization of state owned companies will be completed in mid-1998. Latvian citizens, local and state authorities and legal persons which are either majority owned by Latvian citizens or foreign nationals from countries with which Latvia has mutual investment protection agreements can freely purchase both industrial and agricultural land that has been entered in the Land Book.

Policy. By 1994 70% of industrial capacity was still in state ownership, and a Privatization Agency was set up to accelerate the transfer to private hands. By Jan. 1995 86·9% of residents had taken out privatization vouchers. 230 state enterprises were privatized in 1995, realising 37·3m. lats, of which 21·8m. lats were provided by vouchers.

Performance. In 1997 growth was expected almost in all sectors of national economy. It was expected to achieve 4-5% growth of GDP. The share of the private sector exceeded 60% by mid-1997.

Budget. The financial year is the calendar year. The 1997 budget balanced at US$993,211m. Main items of expenditure, 1995 (in 1m. lats): Social and cultural, 226; economic development, 47; administration, 36; defence, 23.

Budgets for 1997 and 1998 have been adopted by the parliament as non-deficit budgets. Revenues of the general government budget exceeded expenditure by 7·3 m. lats in the first quarter of 1997.

Currency. The unit of currency is the *lats* (LVL) of 100 *santims*. The lats has been pledged to the SDR basket. There are coins of 1, 2, 5, 10, 20 and 50 santims and 1 and 2 lats, and notes of 5, 10, 20, 50, 100 and 500 lats. In March 1997 274m. lats were in circulation. Inflation was an annualized 23·1% in 1995.

Banking and Finance. The Bank of Latvia both legally and practically is a completely independent institution. Governor of the Bank and Council members are appointed by Parliament for the office for 6 years (*present governor*, Einārs Repše). In 1997, 35 licensed banks, 4 savings and loan associations, Riga branch of Société Generale, Vereinsbank and a representative office of Dresdner Bank were functioning. Law on credit institutions stipulates a gradual increase of minimal foundation capital up to 5m. ECU. The only bank fully owned by the state is Latvijas Hipoteku un Zemes Banka.

There is a stock exchange in Riga.

ENERGY AND NATURAL RESOURCES

Electricity. Electricity supply for 1996 was 6·56bn. kWh, of which 3·12bn. kWh was produced domestically and 3·44bn. kWh imported. Total electricity power supply in 1997 is forecasted at 6·2-6·4bn. kWh. Output of electrical power as follows (in 1bn. kWh): hydroelectric, 2-2·4; thermoelectric, 1·3-1·5; block stations, 0·1; small hydroelectric, 0·005; wind generators, 0·001.

Minerals. Peat deposits extend over 645,000 ha or about 10% of the total area, and it is estimated that total deposits are 3,000-4,000m. tons. The average annual output of peat at the moment reaches 450-550 thousand tonnes.

Resources:

	deposits (in m.)	production (in 1,000) 1995	1996
Dolomite (metres³)	661·3	379·7	429·4
Clay for bricks (metres³)	218·5	70·5	72·9
Clay for cement (tonnes)	416·6	85·8	120·0
Sand and gravel mix (metres³)	413·2	534·5	775·4
Sand (metres³)	72·8	184·3	153·5
Limestone for cement (tonnes)	477·5	324·0	367·0

Agriculture. Area under cultivation was 3·9m. ha in 1990. Cattle and dairy farming are the chief agricultural occupations. Oats, barley, rye, potatoes and flax are the main crops.

On 1 Jan. 1989 there were 248 state farms and 331 (including 11 fishery) collective farms. There were 38,100 tractors and 7,400 grain combine harvesters. Large state and collective farms are being converted into shareholding enterprises; the remainder are being divided into small private holdings for collective farm workers or former owners. There were 52,000 such farms in 1993 averaging 16 ha and 99,000 smallholdings averaging 4·4 ha.

Livestock (1995, in 1,000): Cattle, 537 (of which milch cows, 292); sheep, 72; pigs, 553; poultry, 4,198.

Output of crops (in 1,000 tonnes), 1995: Wheat, 244; sugar-beet, 250; potatoes, 864; rye, 71; vegetables, 224. Livestock products (1995): Meat, 0·17m. tonnes; milk, 0·9m. tonnes; eggs, 421·0m.

Persons employed in agriculture, 13·6%.

In 1996 there were 24% state farms, collective farms and statutory companies, 35% peasant farms, 41% household plots and private subsidiary farms. The total area of agricultural land was 2·52 m. ha.

Output of crops (in 1,000 tonnes) 1996: Grain 969 (made up of: wheat, 279·7; rye, 112·9; barley, 366·6; oats 101·4); flax 0·8; sugar beet 257·8; potatoes 1,082; vegetables 179·5.

Livestock (in 1,000) 1996: Cattle, 509·4 (of which cows, 277·4); sheep, 55·5; pigs, 459·6; poultry, 3,790·7.

Livestock products (1,000 tonnes): Meat, 75·7; milk, 922·7; eggs, 470·8; wool, 134.

Forestry. In 1995, forest covered 2·7m. ha, with wood resources of 426m. cu. metres. 6·5m. cu. metres are cut annually. In 1996 the total forested area was 2·86m. ha (44·3% of the total territory of Latvia) of which 0·377m. ha were privately owned.

To provide the protection of forests there are three forest categories: protected forests, 11%; restricted management forests, 18·6%; commercial forests, 70·4%.

Fisheries. There are 7 fishing ports in Latvia. In 1995, the total catch (in 1,000 tonnes) was 149·2 (146·2 marine). In 1996 the total catch (in 1,000 tonnes) was 135·7, comprised of: freshwater fish, 0·9 and marine fish, 134·8. Fish catch by fishing ground (1,000 tonnes): inland waters, 0·9; northwest Atlantic, 1; northeast Atlantic 71 of which Baltic Sea, 69·7; East central Atlantic, 63·7; southwest Atlantic, 4·1.

INDUSTRY. In 1996 the decline of production in manufacturing has been stopped for the first time since the beginning of economic reforms. Structure of sectors of industry by outputs, current prices in %, 1996: Food products and beverages, 44·3%; textile 8·2%; wood products, 8·2%; chemicals, 7·6%; motor vehicles 0·9%; publishing 2·5%; radio and communication equipment, 1·2%; building materials, 2·5%.

Labour. In June 1996, 1,170,000 persons were employed. In 1995 there was a monthly minimum wage of 50-60 lats. Average monthly salary was 120 lats in 1995. Retirement age is 60 years for men and 55 for women, but flexible retirement ages will be possible under a new contributory pension scheme introduced in 1995. There were 89,345 registered unemployed in Sept. 1996.

Registered non working persons 6·8% in Oct 1997. The average monthly wage in the public sector was 135·64 lats.

Trade Unions. The Latvian Free Trade Union has Andris Siliņš as chairman.

FOREIGN ECONOMIC RELATIONS. External debt of Latvia at the end of 1996 was 227·3 m. lats, 8·2% of GDP. The free trade agreements on industrial and agricultural goods are in force among the Baltic states; the Baltic Customs Union will be the next step to be implemented. Foreign trade policy envisaged accession of Latvia into the WTO at the end of 1997. In 1996 Latvia established free trade regimes with the EU and EFTA. In June 1997 the competition Act was adopted on the EU directives. Direct foreign investments in 1996 was US$65 per capita; total amount was 369·2m. lats.

Commerce. The main exports are wood and products, textiles and foodstuffs. In 1995 the main export markets were: Russia, 25%; Germany, 14·5%; Sweden, 9·3%. Main import suppliers: Russia, Lithuania, Finland, Estonia.

Total imports and exports (in 1,000 lats).

	Imports	Exports
1995	959,636	688,413
1996	1,278,169	795,172

The main export markets were: EU, 355,457; CIS, 326,279.

COMMUNICATIONS

Roads. In 1995 there were estimated to be 60,046 km of roads. In 1995, 4,926,700 tonnes of freight were carried by road. In 1995 there were 4,056 traffic accidents with

611 fatalities. In 1996 the number of road accidents with casualties decreased by 8·5% with 3,711 accidents and 550 deaths. In 1996 213·5 km of road was repaired and 13·1 km of new road built.

Railways. In 1996 there were 2,413 km of 1,520 mm gauge route (271 km electrified). In 1995 44·53m. passengers and 28·8m. tonnes of freight were carried. In 1996 freight turnover was 35·26m tonnes.

Civil Aviation. There is an international airport at Riga. A new national carrier, Air Baltic, assumed control of Latavio and Baltic International Airlines in 1995 and began flying in Oct. to Amsterdam, Copenhagen, Frankfurt, Geneva, Helsinki, Kiev, London, Minsk, Moscow, St Petersburg, Stockholm, Tallinn, Vilnius and Warsaw. It is 51% state-owned, and in 1995 operated 2 B-727s and 2 ex-Soviet aircraft. Services are also provided by Aeroflot, Aerosweet, Air Express, Austrian Airlines, British Airways, Czech Airlines, Delta, Estonian Air, Finnair, Hamburg Airlines, LOT, Lufthansa, SAS, Transaero and Transeast Airlines. In 1996, 497,000 passengers arrived and departed and 3,912,000 tonnes of freight (including mail) were handled.

Shipping. There are 3 large ports (with 38·89m. tonnes of cargo handled, 1995): Riga (7·5), Ventspils (29·62) and Liepāja (1·4). 4,600 ships in all docked at Riga and Ventspils in 1994. In 1995, 10·59m. tonnes of cargo were transported. In 1995 the merchant marine totalled 1·18m. GRT, including oil tankers, 0·73m. GRT. In 1996 a total of 45·03m tonnes of cargo were loaded and unloaded at Latvia's ports: Riga, 7·9; Ventspils, 35·74, Liepāja, 1·6 and the cargo turnover by sea was 10·06m tonnes.

Telecommunications. In 1995 there were 1,018 post offices. Telecommunications are conducted by companies in which the government has a 51% stake, under the aegis of the state-controlled Lattelecom. In 1995 there were 0·7m. telephones and 14,983 mobile telephones.

Broadcasting is overseen by the 9-member National Radio and Television Council appointed by parliament for 4-year terms. Latvijas Radio broadcasts 3 programmes and an external service (English, German, Swedish). There are also 1 municipal and 3 commercial broadcasters. The government-controlled Latvijas Televizija transmits on 2 networks (colour by SECAM; 1 commercial channel uses PAL). Russian television broadcasting ceased in 1996. In 1993 there were over 100 regional, commercial and municipal TV stations. There were 1·2m. TV sets in use.

Cinema. In 1995 there were 268 cinemas; attendances totalled 1·02m.

Press. In 1995 there were 307 newspapers and 229 periodicals, including 3 national dailies (1 in Russian) and 1 English-language weekly. 1,966 book titles were published.

SOCIAL INSTITUTIONS

Justice. The criminal code is inherited from the former USSR. Judges are appointed for life. There are a Supreme Court, regional and district courts and administrative courts. The death penalty is retained, but has been subject to a moratorium since Oct. 1996. 39,141 crimes were reported in 1995 (40,983 in 1994), 35·3% of which were solved.

Religion. In order to practise in public, religious organizations must be licensed by the Department of Religious Affairs attached to the Ministry of Justice. New sects are required to demonstrate loyalty to the state and its traditional religions over a 3-year period. Traditionally, Lutherans constituted the largest church, but their numbers have declined from some 0·6m. in 1956 to 0·1m. in 1991. Estimates of Roman Catholics in 1991 varied from 0·3m. to 0·5m. Congregations in Jan. 1996: Lutherans, 297; Roman Catholics, 196; Russian Orthodox, 118; Old Believers, 55; Baptists, 77; Adventists, 33; Jews, 5; others, 43.

Education. The Soviet education system has been restructured on the UNESCO model. Education may begin in kindergarten. From the age of 6 or 7 education is compulsory for 9 years in comprehensive schools. This may be followed by 3 years in special secondary school or 1 to 6 years in art, technical or vocational schools. In 1995–96 there were 716 comprehensive schools with 0·35m. pupils, 52 special secondary schools with 17,200 pupils, with a combined total of 34,700 teachers. 174,100 pupils were attending Latvian-language schools, 114,000 Russian and 40,900 mixed. 25,000 pupils were attending vocational schools. Schools for ethnic minorities were established in 1990: there were 8 in 1994–95.

In 1995–96 in the whole field of higher education there were 17 state institutions with 45,828 students and 10 private institutions with 3,112 students. There were 1 university and 4 specialized universities (agriculture; aviation; pedagogy; technical) and academies of arts, medicine and music, and 7 other institutions of higher education, with 31,400 full-time students in all.

Health. In 1995 there were 8,400 doctors, 18,300 paramedics and 166 hospitals with 27,800 beds.

Social Security. Benefits are paid from the State Social Insurance Fund and the government budget. It is a statutory requirement that the rate of pensions be reviewed twice a year, taking inflation into account. A compulsory contributory health insurance scheme was inaugurated on 1 Jan. 1997. In 1995 there were 666,000 pensioners, including retirement, 497,000; disability, 103,400; survivors, 38,400; social, 19,600. The average monthly pension was 36 lats in 1996. Legislation of 1995 provides for the phasing in of a new retirement pension scheme which links benefits to contributions made during working years and average life expectancy.

DIPLOMATIC REPRESENTATIVES

Of Latvia in Great Britain (45 Nottingham Place, London, W1M 3FE)
Ambassador: Normans Penke.

Of Great Britain in Latvia (Aluana ielā 5, LV-1010, Riga)
Ambassador: Nicholas Jarrold.

Of Latvia in the USA (4325 17th St., NW, Washington DC 20011)
Ambassador: Ojars Kalnins.

Of the USA in Latvia (7 Raina Bulevard, Riga, 226050)
Ambassador: Larry C. Napper.

Of Latvia to the United Nations
Ambassador: Jānis Priedkalns.

Of Latvia to the European Union
Ambassador: Juris Kanels.

Further Reading

Central Statistical Bureau. *Statistical Yearbook of Latvia.—Latvia in Figures.* Annual.
Bilmanis, A., *A History of Latvia.* Princeton Univ. Press, 1951
Dreifeld, J., *Latvia in Transition.* Riga, 1997
Lieven, A., *The Baltic Revolution: Estonia, Latvia, Lithuania and the Path to Independence.* 2nd ed. Yale UP, 1994
Misiunas, R. J. and Taagepera, R., *The Baltic States: the Years of Dependence, 1940–91.* 2nd ed. Farnborough, 1993
Spekke, A., *History of Latvia.* Stockholm, 1951
Smith, I. A. and Grunts, M. V., *The Baltic States.* [Bibliography]. Oxford and Santa Barbara, 1993
Who Is Who in Latvia. Riga, 1996

National statistical office: Central Statistical Bureau, Lācplēša ielā 1, 1301 Riga.
Website: http://www.csb.lv/

LEBANON

Jumhouriya al-Lubnaniya

(Republic of Lebanon)

Capital: Beirut
Population: 3·45m.
HDI/world rank: 0·794/65

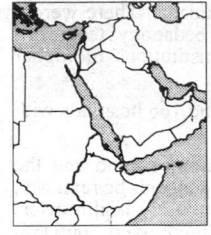

KEY HISTORICAL EVENTS. The Ottomans invaded Lebanon, then part of Syria, in 1516-17 and held nominal control until 1918. After 20 years' French mandatory regime, Lebanon was proclaimed independent on 26 Nov. 1941. On 27 Dec. 1943 an agreement was signed between representatives of the French National Committee of Liberation and of Lebanon, by which most of the powers and capacities exercised hitherto by France were transferred as from 1 Jan. 1944 to the Lebanese Government. The evacuation of foreign troops was completed in Dec. 1946.

In early May 1958 the Moslem opposition to President Chamoun rose in insurrection· and for 5 months the Moslem quarters of Beirut, Tripoli, Sidon and the northern Bekaa were in insurgent hands. On 15 July the US Government acceded to President Chamoun's request and landed a force of army and marines who re-established Government authority.

Internal problems were exacerbated by the politically active Palestine population and by the deeply divisive question of the Palestinian problem itself. An attempt to regulate the activities of Palestinian fighters through the secret Cairo agreement of 1969 was frustrated both by the inability of the Government to enforce its provisions, and by an influx of battle-hardened fighters expelled from Jordan in Sept. 1970. A further attempt to control the guerrillas in 1973 also failed. From March 1975, Lebanon was beset by civil disorder by which the economy was brought to a virtual standstill.

By Nov. 1976 however, large-scale fighting had been brought to an end by the intervention of the Syrian-dominated Arab Deterrent Force which ensured sufficient security to permit Lebanon to establish quasi-normal conditions under President Sarkis. Large areas of the country, however, remained outside governmental control, including West Beirut, which was the scene of frequent conflict between opposing militia groups. The south, where the Arab Deterrent Force could not deploy, remained unsettled and subject to frequent Israeli attacks. In March 1978 there was an Israeli invasion following a Palestinian attack inside Israel. Israeli troops eventually withdrew in June, but instead of handing over all their positions to UN Peacekeeping Forces, they installed Israeli-controlled Christian Lebanese militia forces in border areas. Severe disruption continued in the south. In June 1982 Israeli forces once again invaded, this time in massive strength, and swept through the country, eventually laying siege to and bombing Beirut. In Sept. Palestinian forces, together with the PLO leadership, evacuated Beirut. On 23 Aug. 1982 Bachir Gemayel was elected President of Lebanon. On 14 Sept. he was assassinated. There followed a period of 'no peace, no war' with intermittent clashes between various *de facto* forces on the ground. Israeli forces started a complete withdrawal on 16 Feb. 1985. Western forces pulled out after a peace agreement was signed by the leaders of the Druse, Amal and (Christian) Lebanese Forces to end the civil war on 28 Dec. 1985 but it was not until the end of 1990 that the various militias which had held sway in Beirut withdrew. A new Gov   nt of National Reconciliation was announced on 24 Dec. 1990. The dissolution or all militias was decreed by the National Assembly in April 1991, but the Shi'ite Moslem militia Hizbollah was allowed to remain active and deploy heavy weapons. In July the army defeated the Palestine Liberation Organization at Sidon, depriving the latter of their territorial base in South Lebanon, and bringing the army up to the Israeli-occupied southern strip ('security zone').

Following a 17-day Israeli bombardment of Hizbollah positions and South Lebanon generally in April 1996, a US-brokered unsigned 'understanding' of 26 April 1996 guaranteed that Hizbollah guerrillas and Palestinian radical groups would cease attacks on civilians in northern Israel and granted Israel the right to self-defence and return of fire. Hizbollah maintained the right to resist Israel's occupation of Lebanese soil.

TERRITORY AND POPULATION. Lebanon is mountainous, bounded on the north and east by Syria, on the west by the Mediterranean and on the south by Israel. The area is 10,452 sq. km (4,036 sq. miles). Population (1997 estimate), 3·45m. (88% urban); density, 306 per sq. km. The principal towns, with estimated population (1991), are: Beirut (the capital), 1·5m.; Tripoli, 0·2m.; Saida (Sidon), 0·1m.; Tyre, 70,000. Infant mortality was 29 per 1,000 live births in 1997; expectation of life, 69·9 years.

The official language is Arabic. French and, increasingly, English are widely spoken in official and commercial circles. Armenian is spoken by a minority group.

CLIMATE. A Mediterranean climate with short, warm winters and long, hot and rainless summers, with high humidity in coastal areas. Rainfall is largely confined to the winter months and can be torrential, with snow on high ground. Beirut. Jan. 55°F (13°C), July 81°F (27°C). Annual rainfall 35·7" (893 mm).

CONSTITUTION AND GOVERNMENT. The first Constitution was established under the French Mandate on 23 May 1926. It has since been amended in 1927, 1929, 1943 (twice), 1947 and 1990. It is based on a separation of powers, with a President, a single-chamber *National Assembly* elected by universal suffrage at age 21 in 12 electoral constituencies, and an independent judiciary. In Oct. 1995 the National Assembly extended the President's term of office from 6 to 9 years. The executive consists of the President and a Prime Minister and Cabinet appointed after consultation between the President and the National Assembly. The system is adapted to the communal balance on which Lebanese political life depends by an electoral law which allocates deputies according to the religious distribution of the population, and by a series of constitutional conventions whereby, *e.g.,* the President is always a Maronite Christian, the Prime Minister a Sunni Moslem and the Speaker of the Assembly a Shia Moslem. There is no party system. In Aug. 1990, and again in July 1992, the National Assembly voted to increase its membership, and now has 128 deputies with equal numbers of Christians and Moslems.

On 21 Sept. 1990 President Hrawi established the Second Republic by signing constitutional amendments which had been negotiated at Taif (Saudi Arabia) in Oct. 1989. These institute an executive collegium between the President, Prime Minister and Speaker, and remove from the President the right to recall the Prime Minister, dissolve the Assembly and vote in the Council of Ministers.

5-stage elections were held in Aug.–Sept. 1996; turn-out averaged 45%.

President: Elias Hrawi (Maronite; elected 24 Nov. 1989).

In Nov. 1996 a new government was formed, comprising in March 1998:

Prime Minister, Minister of Finance and Minister of Post and Telecommunications: Rafik Hariri (b. 1944).

Deputy Prime Minister, Minister of the Interior: Michel Murr. *Justice:* Bahij Tabbarah. *Displaced Persons:* Walid Jumblatt. *Defence:* Mohsen Dalloul. *Agriculture:* Shawki Fakhouri. *Labour:* Asaad Hardan. *Foreign Affairs:* Fares Boueiz. *Water and Electricity:* Elias Hobeika. *Health:* Sleiman Franjieh. *Emigrants:* Talal Arslan. *Industry and Oil:* Shahi Barsoumian. *Transport:* Omar Meskaoui. *Tourism:* Nicholas Fattouch. *Administrative Reform:* Bcharah Merhej. *Housing and Co-operatives:* Mahmoud Abou Hamdan. *Municipalities and Rural Affairs:* Hagop Damarjian. *Education:* Jem Obeid. *Economy and Trade:* Yassine Jaber. *Public Works:* Ali Harajli. *Culture and Higher Education:* Fawzi Hobeish. *Information:* Basem Sabaa. *Environment:* Akram Shouhayyeb. *Social Affairs:* Ayoub Houmayed. *Vocational and Technical Education:* Farouk Barbir.

The *Speaker* is Nabih Berri.

National anthem: 'Kulluna lil watan lil 'ula lil 'alam' ('All of us for our country, flag and glory'); words by Rashid Nachleh, tune by W. Sabra.

Local Government: The 6 governorates (including the city of Beirut) are subdivided into 26 districts.

DEFENCE. There were 30,000 Syrian troops in the country in 1995. In the Israeli-occupied southern strip the pro-Israeli South Lebanese Army is estimated to number 2,500 and has 30 main battle tanks.

Conscription is for 12 months.

Army. The strength of the Army was 53,300 in 1997. It is organized into a Presidential Guard, 11 infantry brigades, 2 artillery and 3 special forces regiments, and 1 ranger and 1 air assault regiment. Its equipment includes 100 M48A1/A5 and 200 T-54/-55 main battle tanks. There is an internal security force, run by the Ministry of the Interior, some 13,000 strong.

Navy. The flotilla consists of 14 inshore patrol craft, 2 tank landing craft and some armed boats, manned and supported by about 1,000 personnel (1997).

Air Force. The Air Force had (1997) about 800 personnel. About 30 Alouette, Gazelle, Puma and AB.212 helicopters survived the civil war, while the US government supplied 16 UH-1H Iroquois helicopters in 1994. No combat aircraft are operated.

INTERNATIONAL RELATIONS. A Treaty of Brotherhood, Co-operation and Co-ordination with Syria of May 1991 provides for close relations in the fields of foreign policy, the economy, military affairs and security. The treaty stipulates that Lebanese government decisions are subject to review by 6 joint Syrian-Lebanese bodies.

Membership. Lebanon is a member of the UN and Arab League.

ECONOMY

Policy. The semi-autonomous Council of Development and Reconstruction, originally set up in 1977, was revived in 1991 to oversee a post-civil war rehabilitation programme, 'Horizon 2000'. In 1995 this programme was revised and extended up to 2007.

Performance. Total GDP was US$9·5bn. in 1995.

Budget. The fiscal year is the calendar year. Budget for 1997: Revenue, £Leb.4,100,000m.; expenditure, £Leb.6,433,000m.

Currency. The unit of currency is the *Lebanese pound* (LBP) of 100 *piastres.* There are coins of 1, 2·5, 5, 10, 25 and 50 piastres and £Leb.1, and notes of £Leb.50, 100, 250, 500, 1,000, 5,000, 10,000, 25,000, 50,000 and 100,000. Inflation was an annualized 15% in 1995. Foreign exchange reserves were US$4,533m. in June 1995; gold reserves were US$3,541·2m. in 1994. Currency in circulation, 1994, £Leb.938,800m. There is a fluctuating official rate of exchange, fixed monthly; it in practice is used only for the calculation of *ad-valorem* customs duties on Lebanese imports and for import statistics. For other purposes the free market is used.

Banking and Finance. The Bank of Lebanon (*Governor*, Riad Salameh) is the bank of issue. In 1994 there were 52 domestic banks, 14 subsidiaries and 12 foreign banks, with 590 branches in all. Commercial bank deposits in 1995 totalled £Leb.24,900,400m. There is a stock exchange in Beirut (closed 1983-95).

Weights and Measures. The use of the metric system is legal.

ENERGY AND NATURAL RESOURCES

Electricity. Generating capacity was 1,200,000 kW in 1993. Output, 1995, 1,857m. kWh.

Minerals. There are no commercially viable deposits.

Agriculture. In 1992 there were 216,000 ha of arable land, 90,000 ha of permanent crop land and 10,000 ha of pasture. Crop production (in 1,000 tonnes), 1993: Total fruits excluding melons, 1,332; apples, 160; grapes, 365; potatoes, 280; sugar-beet, 190; wheat, 55; bananas, 62; olives, 103.

Livestock (1993): Goats, 450,000; sheep, 250,000; cattle, 77,000; pigs, 40,000; asses, 23,000; mules, 8,000.

Forestry. The forests of the past have been denuded by exploitation and in 1991 covered 80,000 ha.

Fisheries. Total catch (1990) was 2,200 tonnes (90% from seafishing).

INDUSTRY. In 1994 there were 23,518 factories operating.

Labour. The workforce was some 650,000 in 1995, of whom 72,000 worked in agriculture. Following considerable labour unrest, an agreement on wage increases and social benefits was concluded between the government and the GCLW in Dec. 1993.

Trade Unions. The main unions are the General Confederation of Lebanese Workers (GCLW) and the General Confederation of Sectoral Unions.

FOREIGN ECONOMIC RELATIONS. Foreign and domestic trade is the principal source of income. Foreign debt was US$2,500m. in 1996.

Commerce. Imports, 1995: US$7,286·6m.; exports, US$825·2m.

In 1994 the main export markets (in % of total trade) were: UAE, 18·1; Saudi Arabia, 15·3; Syria, 10·6; Kuwait, 5·7; France, 4·6; Jordan, 4. Main import suppliers: Italy, 13·4; Germany, 10·1; USA, 9·3; France, 9; Syria, 4·4.

COMMUNICATIONS

Roads. There were (1997) 7,370 km of roads of which 6,265 km are paved.

Railways. Railways are state-owned. There is 222km. of standard gauge track.

Civil Aviation. Beirut International Airport is served by Aeroflot, Air Algérie, Air France, Alitalia, Armenian Airlines, Austrian Airlines, Balkan, British Airways, British Mediterranean Airways, Cyprus Airways, Czech Airlines, Egyptair, Emirates, Gulf Air, Iberia, JAT, KLM, Kuwait Airways, LOT, Malaysia Airlines, Malév, Olympic Airways, Qatar Airways, Royal Jordanian, Saudia, Swissair, Syrian Airlines, Tarom, Turkish Airlines and Yemenia. It handled 1·43m. passengers in 1994. There are 2 national airlines, the state-owned Middle East Airlines, which in 1995 operated 2 A310-200s, 2 A310-300s, 1 B-707-320B, 7 B-707-320Cs, 2 B-720Bs, and 3 B-747-200B Combis, and Trans-Mediterranean Airways, which had 7 aircraft in 1995. There are 7 airports in total

Shipping. Beirut is the largest port, followed by Tripoli, Jounieh and Sidon. Total GRT, 1995, 0·41m., including oil tankers 2,431 GRT and container ships, 1,162 GRT. There are 58 ships in total (1,000 GRT or over).

Telecommunications. In 1996 there were 1m. telephones. 2 companies are operating a mobile telephone network with 0·1m. subscribers.

The government-controlled Radio Lebanon transmits in Arabic, French, English and Armenian. In 1992 there were 2·37m. radios. Télé-Liban, which is government-owned, transmits programmes from 13 stations. Colour is by SECAM. There were 1·1m. TV sets in 1993 and 2·15m. radios.

Press (1994). There were about 30 daily newspapers in Arabic, 2 in French, 1 in English and 4 in Armenian, and 60 weekly periodicals. A 2nd English language newspaper began publication in 1997.

SOCIAL INSTITUTIONS

Religion. In 1994 it was estimated that the population was 55·3% Moslem (34% Shi'ite and 21·3% Sunni), 37·6% Christian (mainly Maronite) and 7·1% Druze. In 1996 there were 119 Roman Catholic bishops.

Education. There are state and private primary and secondary schools. There are 13 universities, including 2 American and 1 French, and 10 other institutions of higher education. In 1994-95 there were 64,055 university students and 4,449 academic staff. The literacy rate is more than 75%.

There is an Academy of Fine Arts.

Health. There were 24 government-run hospitals in 1993.

DIPLOMATIC REPRESENTATIVES

Of Lebanon in Great Britain (21 Kensington Palace Gdns., London, W8 4QM)
Ambassador: Mahmoud Hammoud.

Of Great Britain in Lebanon (8th St., Rabieh, Beirut)
Ambassador: David R. MacLennan.

Of Lebanon in the USA (2560 28th St., NW, Washington, D.C., 20008)
Ambassador: Riad Tabbarah.

Of the USA in Lebanon (POB 70-840, Antelias, Beirut)
Ambassador: Richard H. Jones.

Of Lebanon to the United Nations
Ambassador: Samir Moubarak.

Of Lebanon to the European Union
Ambassdor: Jihad Mortada.

Further Reading

Bleaney, C. H., *Lebanon.* [Bibliography]. 2nd ed. Oxford and Santa Barbara (CA), 1991
Choueiri, Y. M., *State and Society in Syria and Lebanon.* Exeter Univ. Press, 1994
Cobban, H., *The Making of Modern Lebanon.* London, 1985
Fisk, R., *Pity the Nation: Lebanon at War.* 2nd ed. OUP, 1992
Gemayel, A., *Rebuilding Lebanon.* New York, 1992
Hiro, D., *Lebanon Fire and Embers: a History of the Lebanese Civil War.* New York, 1993
Shehadi, N. and Mills, D.H., *Lebanon: A History of Conflict and Consensus.* London, 1988
Weinberger, N. J., *Syrian Intervention in Lebanon.* New York, 1986

National library: Dar el Kutub, Parliament Sq., Beirut.
National statistical office: Service de Statistique Générale, Beirut.

LESOTHO

Kingdom of Lesotho

Capital: Maseru
Population: 2·11m.
GDP per head: (PPP$) 1,109
GNP: US$1·4bn.
HDI/world rank: 0·457/137

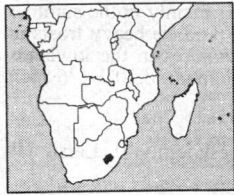

KEY HISTORICAL EVENTS. The Basotho nation was constituted in the 19th century under the leadership of Moshoeshoe I, bringing together refugees from disparate tribes scattered by Zulu expansionism in southern Africa. War with land-hungry Boer settlers in 1856 (and again in 1886) cost the Basotho significant territory, and Moshoeshoe appealed for British protection. This was granted in 1868, and in 1871 the territory was annexed to the Cape Colony (now Republic of South Africa), but in 1883 it was restored to the direct control of the British government through the High Commissioner for South Africa.

In 1955, the Basutoland Council, which had been established in 1903, sought and obtained the right to pass its own laws for its internal affairs. In 1965, full internal self-government was achieved and the paramount chief became King Moshoeshoe II. On 4 Oct. 1966, Basutoland became an independent and sovereign member of the British Commonwealth as the Kingdom of Lesotho.

Chief Leabua Jonathan, leader of the Basotho National Party and prime minister from 1965, forced the king to refrain from trying to gain some executive power in 1967, and suspended the constitution when the elections of 1970 were declared invalid. Parliamentary rule, with a national assembly of nominated members, was reintroduced in April 1973; although there was subsequent talk of elections, these were constantly postponed.

On 20 Jan. 1986, after a border blockade by the Republic of South Africa, Chief Jonathan was deposed in a bloodless military *coup* led by Maj.-Gen. Justin Lekhanya who became the chairman of a newly formed military council, banned political parties and granted significant powers to the king. South Africa embarked on a major scheme to develop Lesotho's water resources.

King Moeshoeshoe II was deposed by the Military Council in Nov. 1990 and replaced by King Letsie III. Maj.-Gen. Lekhanya was deposed from the chairmanship of the Military Council in a bloodless coup on 30 April 1991. The Military Council was dissolved and a democratic constitution promulgated in April 1993.

TERRITORY AND POPULATION. Lesotho is an enclave within South Africa. The area is 11,720 sq. miles (30,355 sq. km). Vital statistics rates, 1995: Birth (per 1,000 population), 37; death, 10; growth, 2·6%.

The census in 1986 showed a total population of 1,577,536 persons. Estimate (1996) 2,110,000 (20·9% urban in 1993); density, 69·5 per sq. km.

There are 10 districts, all named after their chief towns, except Berea (chief town, Teyateyaneng). Area and population:

Region	Area (in sq. km.)	Population (1986 census, in 1,000)	Population (1995 estimate, in 1,000)
Berea	2,222	194·6	206·2
Butha-Buthe	1,767	100·6	135·4
Leribe	2,828	258·0	349·5
Mafeteng	2,119	195·6	259·0
Maseru	4,279	311·1	400·2
Mohale's Hoek	3,530	164·4	231·3
Mokhotlong	4,075	74·7	100·3
Qacha's Nek	2,349	64·0	86·8
Quthing	2,916	110·4	151·9
Thaba-Tseka	4,270	104·1	136·2

The chief towns (with 1986 census population) are: Maseru, 109,382; Qacha's Nek, 10,000 (1992 estimate); Teyateyaneng, 14,251; Mafeteng, 12,667; Hlotse, 9,595.

891

The official languages are Sesotho and English.

The population is more than 98% Basotho and less than 1% Zulu. The rest is made up of Xhosas, approximately 3,000 expatriate Europeans and several hundred Asians. Vital statistics; life expectancy 52·9.

CLIMATE. A healthy and pleasant climate, with variable rainfall, but averaging 29" (725 mm) a year over most of the country. The rain falls mainly in the summer months of Oct. to April, while the winters are dry and may produce heavy frosts in lowland areas and frequent snow in the highlands. Temperatures in the lowlands range from a maximum of 90°F (32·2°C) in summer to a minimum of 20°F (−6·7°C) in winter.

ROYAL HOUSE. Following the death of his father, Moeshoeshoe II, **Letsie III** succeeded to the throne in Jan. 1996.

CONSTITUTION AND GOVERNMENT. Lesotho is a constitutional monarchy with the King as Head of State. The 1993 constitution provides for a *National Assembly* comprising an elected 65-member lower house and a *Senate* of 22 principal chiefs and 11 members nominated by the King.

Parliamentary elections were held on 28 March 1993 for the *National Assembly.* The Basotho Congress Party won 65 seats, the Basotho National Party, nil.

Following the elections the King swore allegiance to a new constitution and the Military Council was dissolved.

In March 1998 the Council of Ministers comprised:

Prime Minister, Minister of Public Service, Minister of Defence: Ntsu Mokhehle (sworn in 2 April 1993).

Deputy Prime Minister, Minister for Home Affairs, Local Government and Rural and Urban Development: Pakalitha Mosisili. *Foreign Affairs:* Kelebone Maope. *Trade and Industry:* Lira Motete. *Agriculture, Co-operatives and Youth Affairs:* Mopshatla Mabitle. *Health and Social Welfare:* Tefo Mabote. *Natural Resources:* Shakhane R. Mokhehle. *Transport and Communications:* Mamoshebi Kabi. *Information and Broadcasting:* Monyane Moleleki. *Justice, Human Rights, Law and Constitutional Affairs:* Sephiri Motanyane. *Employment and Labour:* Not'si Molopo. *Works:* Mohaila Mohale. *Education:* Lesao Lehohla. *Tourism, Sport and Culture:* Pasho Mochesane. *Finance and Economic Planning:* Viktor Ketso.

The *College of Chiefs* settles the recognition and succession of Chiefs and adjudicates cases of inefficiency, criminality and absenteeism among them.

National anthem: 'Lesotho fatsela bontat'a rona' ('Lesotho, land of our fathers'); words by F. Coillard, tune by L. Laur.

Local Government. The country is divided into 10 districts, subdivided into 22 wards. Most of the wards are presided over by hereditary chiefs.

DEFENCE. The Royal Lesotho Defence Force has 2,000 personnel and is organized in 7 infantry and 1 support company and 1 air squadron with 2 Aviocar transports, 1 Bell 47, 1 Bell 412 and 2 BO-105 helicopters and 1 Cessna 182 light aircraft.

INTERNATIONAL RELATIONS

Membership. Lesotho is a member of the UN, OAU, the Commonwealth, the SADC and is an ACP state of the EU.

ECONOMY

Policy. The Lesotho National Development Corporation promotes industrial and tourist trade development.

Budget. Expenditure (1992–93) 474·8m. maloti; revenue, 537·1m. maloti.

Currency. The unit of currency is the *loti* (plural *maloti*) (LSL) of 100 *lisente* at par with the South African rand, which is legal tender. There are coins of 1, 2, 5, 10, 25 and 50 lisente and 2 maloti, and notes of 5, 10, 20 and 50 maloti. Currency in circulation, 1993, was 43·80m. maloti. Annualized inflation was 8·4% in July 1994. Foreign exchange reserves were US$94·8m. in 1991.

Banking and Finance. The Central Bank of Lesotho is the bank of issue, founded in 1982 to succeed the Lesotho Monetary Authority. There are 3 commercial banks and an Agricultural Development Bank. Savings deposits totalled 342·8m. maloti in 1993.

Weights and Measures. The metric system is in use.

ENERGY AND NATURAL RESOURCES

Electricity. Capacity (1993) 13,400 kWh. (98% supplied by South Africa.)

Minerals. Diamonds are the main product. 1990 output was 11,400 carats.

Agriculture. Agriculture contributes about 15% of GDP and employs two-thirds of the workforce. The chief crops were (1993 production in 1,000 tonnes): Wheat, 9; maize, 92; sorghum, 52; beans, 2; peas and other vegetables are also grown. Soil conservation and the improvement of crops and pasture are matters of vital importance. Area sown to crops, 1993, 264,000 ha.

Livestock (1993): Cattle, 658,000; horses, 107,000; pigs, 60,000; sheep, 1·18m.; goats, 811,000; poultry, 1m.

INDUSTRY. Manufacturing contributed 15·1% of GDP in 1991.

Labour. In 1991 the workforce numbered 826,000 (351,000 females). In 1993 117,600 were working in mines in South Africa.

FOREIGN ECONOMIC RELATIONS. Lesotho, Botswana and Swaziland are members of the South African customs union, by agreement dated 29 June 1910. Foreign debt was US$427·7m. in 1991.

Commerce. In 1992 imports were valued at US$933m. and exports at US$109m. In 1993 exports were valued at 410,725,000 maloti.

Principal exports in 1993 (in 1,000 maloti): Cattle, 8,409; wheat flour, 1,717; canned vegetables, 2,275; wool, 16,853; mohair, 5,131; manufactures, 13,426; machinery and transport equipment, 25,540.

The bulk of international trade is with South Africa.

Tourism. In 1993 there were 349,185 foreign visitors.

COMMUNICATIONS

Roads. In 1992 there were 1,005 km of tarred, and 4,319 km of untarred roads, 2,337 km gravelled and 1,806 earth. In 1983 there were 10,200 commercial vehicles and 4,359 passenger cars. In 1993 there were 1,650 traffic accidents with 286 fatalities.

Railways. A branch line built by the South African Railways, 1 mile long, connects Maseru with the Bloemfontein–Natal line at Marseilles.

Civil Aviation. The national carrier is Air Lesotho, which had 3 aircraft in 1995 and operates services twice daily to Maseru and Johannesburg. Air Lesotho also has regular internal flights to remote districts of Lesotho. 21,657 passengers were carried on international, and 57,256 on domestic flights in 1993.

Telecommunications. There were 11,456 telephones in 1992. Radio Lesotho transmits daily in English and Sesotho. The broadcasting authority is the Lesotho National Broadcasting Service. In 1992 there were 420,000 radio and 50,000 TV sets (colour by PAL).

Press. There are 3 daily newspapers.

SOCIAL INSTITUTIONS

Justice. The legal system is based on Roman-Dutch law. The Lesotho High Court and the Court of Appeal are situated in Maseru, and there are Magistrates' Courts in the districts. 5,888 criminal offences were reported in 1993.

Religion. In 1995 there were 0·88m. Roman Catholics, 0·6m. Evangelical Protestants, 0·44m. other Christians. 0·14m. of other faiths.

Education. Education levels: Pre-school, 3 to 5 years; first level (elementary), 6 to 12; second level (secondary or teacher training or technical training), 7 to 13; third level (university or teacher training college). In 1993–94 there were 354,275 pupils in 1,201 primary schools with 7,292 teachers; 55,312 pupils in 187 secondary schools with 2,526 teachers; 751 students in the National Teacher-Training College with 117 teachers; and 1,575 students in 8 technical schools with 108 teachers. The National University of Lesotho was established in 1975 at Roma; enrolment in 1992–93, 1,612 students and 190 teaching staff. Literacy rate, 70·5%.

Health. Provision of doctors, 1993, 1 per 14,306 population.

DIPLOMATIC REPRESENTATIVES

Of Lesotho in Great Britain (7 Chesham Pl., London, SW1 8HN)
High Commissioner: Benjamin M. Masilo.

Of Great Britain in Lesotho (PO Box Ms 521, Maseru 100)
High Commissioner: Peter J. Smith, OBE.

Of Lesotho in the USA (2511 Massachusetts Ave., NW, Washington, D.C., 20008)
Ambassador: Eunice Bulane.

Of the USA in Lesotho (PO Box 333, Maseru, 100)
Ambassador: Bismarck Myrick.

Of Lesotho to the United Nations
Ambassador: Percy Mangoaela.

Of Lesotho to the European Union
Ambassador: R. V. Lechesa.

Further Reading

Bureau of Statistics. *Statistical Reports.* Occasional
Bardill, J. E. and Cobbe, J. H., *Lesotho: Dilemmas of Dependence in South Africa.* London, 1986
Johnston, D., *Lesotho* [Bibliography]. Oxford and Santa Barbara (CA), 1997
Murray, C., *Families Divided: The Impact of Migrant Labour in Lesotho.* OUP, 1981
Willet, S. M. and Ambrose, D. P., *Lesotho.* [Bibliography] Oxford and Santa Barbara, 1981

National statistical office: Bureau of Statistics, PO Box 455, Maseru.

The Political World

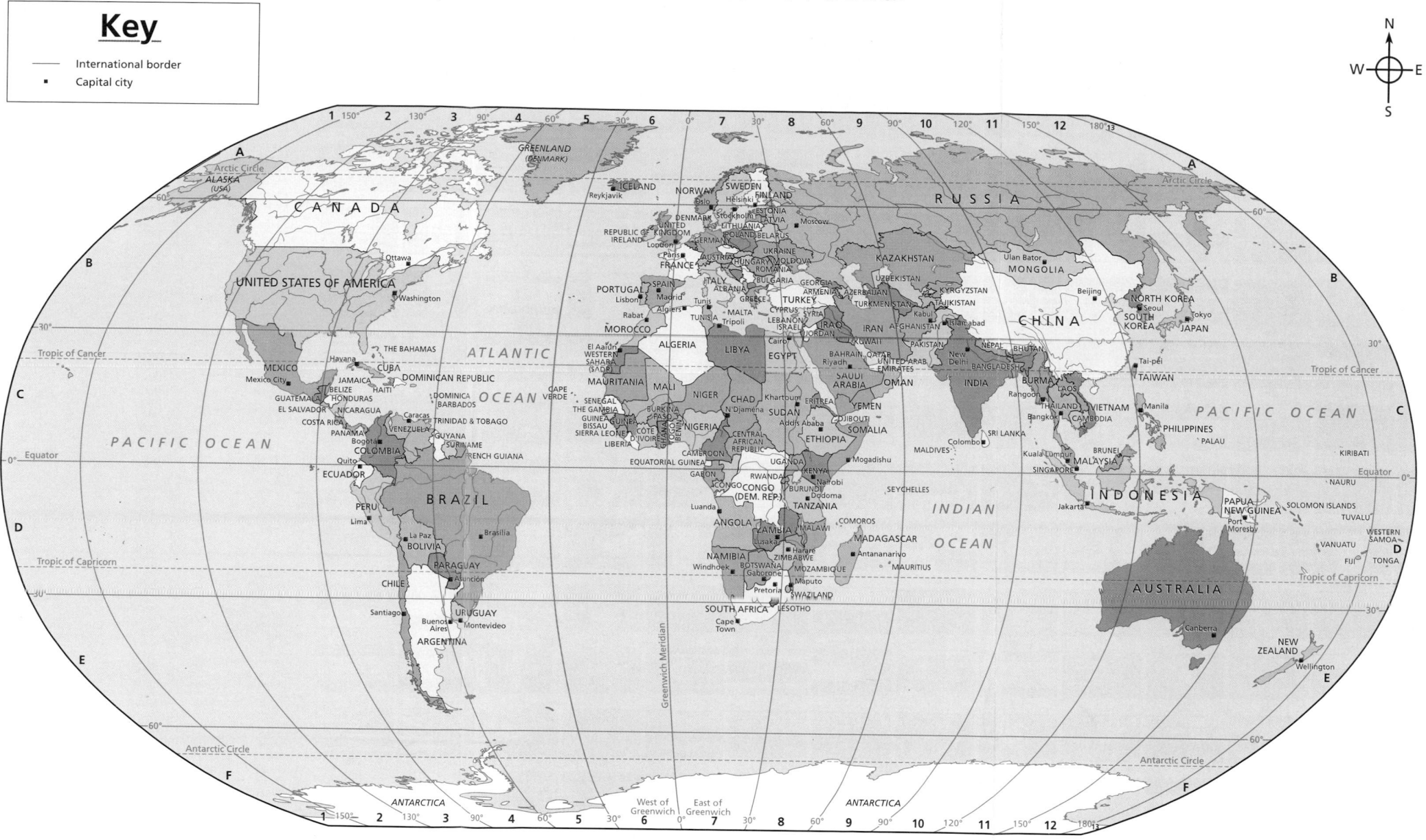

0   4000 km

KEY

LIBERIA

Republic of Liberia

Capital: Monrovia
Population: 2·60m.

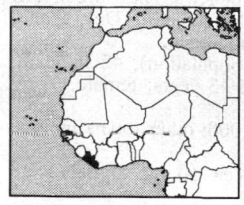

KEY HISTORICAL EVENTS. The Republic of Liberia had its origin in the efforts of several American philanthropic societies to establish freed American slaves in a colony on the West African coast. In 1822 a settlement was formed near the spot where Monrovia now stands. On 26 July 1847 the State was constituted as the Free and Independent Republic of Liberia.

On 12 April 1980, President Tolbert was assassinated and his government overthrown in a coup led by Master-Sergeant Samuel Doe, who was later installed as Head of State and Commander-in-Chief of the army.

At the beginning of 1990 rebel forces entered Liberia from the north and fought their way successfully southwards to confront President Doe's forces in Monrovia. The rebels comprised the National Patriotic Front of Liberia (NPFL) led by Charles Taylor, and the hostile breakaway Independent National Patriotic Front led by Prince Johnson. A peacekeeping force dispatched by the Economic Community of West African States (ECOWAS) disembarked at Monrovia on 25 Aug. 1990, and attempts to form a new provisional government were made.

On 9 Sept. 1990 President Doe was assassinated by Prince Johnson's rebels. At an ECOWAS summit at Bamako (Mali) on 28 Nov. government forces and the two rebel factions signed a ceasefire. ECOWAS installed a provisional government led by Amos Sawyer. Charles Taylor also declared himself president, as did the former vice-president, Harry Moniba.

On 13 Feb. 1991 Taylor, Johnson and the commander of the Liberian armed forces signed a second ceasefire. After a West African 12-nation summit meeting from July to Oct. 1991 Taylor signed an agreement to allow ECOWAS to disarm his troops and organize elections. However, fighting continued. A UN Security Council resolution in Nov. 1992 imposed an arms embargo and expressed support for ECOWAS's action.

Peace negotiations opened in Geneva in July 1993 between the interim government, the armed forces, the NPFL and the United Liberation Movement (ULIMO) under OAU auspices. A peace agreement was signed on 25 July.

On 12 Sept. 1994 the leaders of the 3 military factions, Charles Taylor (NPFL), Alhaji Kromah (ULIMO) and Gen. Hezekiah Bowen, commander of the Armed Forces, met in Ghana and agreed to form a new Council of State, but other warring factions and civilian forces in Monrovia repudiated this.

On 21 Dec. 1994 at Accra under Ghanaian auspices the factions concluded an agreement providing for a ceasefire on 28 Dec. 1994, the establishment of safe zones and buffer zones under ECOWAS control, elections on 14 Nov. 1995 and a new 5-member transitional executive. However, factional fighting continued into 1995.

On 19 Aug. 1995 an eleventh peace agreement was signed in Abuja by Taylor, Kromah and George Boley (Council for Peace in Liberia, CPL).

Fighting broke out in April 1996 between the Krahn and Mandingo branches of ULIMO, terminated on 31 July 1996 by an unconditional ceasefire between all factions.

A peace agreement was signed on 17 Aug. 1996 under the auspices of ECOWAS in Abuja which provided for the disarmament of all factions by the end of Jan. 1997 and the election of a president on 31 May 1997. ECOWAS's peacekeeping force, ECOMOG, was increased from 8,500 to 18,000 troops.

By the end of Jan. 1997 some 20,000 out of perhaps 60,000 insurgents had surrendered their arms. Possession of arms after that date became a criminal offence.

The civil war is reckoned to have killed up to 200,000 people, and made 1m. homeless. A presidential election was held in July 1997. Charles Taylor was elected by an overwhelming majority.

895

TERRITORY AND POPULATION. Liberia is bounded in the north-west by Sierra Leone, north by Guinea, east by Côte d'Ivoire and south-west by the Atlantic ocean. The total area is 99,067 sq. km. At the census (1984) the population was 2,101,628. Estimate (1997) 2,602,068, of whom some 25% were refugees abroad. English is the official language spoken by 15% of the population. The rest belong in the main to 3 linguistic groups: Mande, West Atlantic, and the Kwa. These are in turn subdivided into 16 ethnic groups: Bassa, Bella, Gbandi, Mende, Gio, Dey, Mano, Gola, Kpelle, Kissi, Krahn, Kru, Lorma, Mandingo, Vai and Grebo.

Vital statistics (1997 estimate): Birth rate (per 1000 population), 42·3; death, 11·53. Life expectancy at birth (1997 estimate): Male, 56·43 years; female, 61·69 years.

Monrovia, the capital, had (1984) a population of 425,000; other towns include Buchanan (24,000).

There are 13 counties, whose areas, populations (1984 census) and capitals were as follows:

County	Sq. km	1984	Chief town
Bomi	1,955	66,420	Tubmanburg
Bong	8,099	255,813	Gbarnga
Grand Bassa	8,759	159,648	Buchanan
Grand Cape Mount	5,827	79,322	Robertsport
Grand Gedeh	17,029	102,810	Zwedru
Lofa	19,360	247,641	Voinjama
Margibi	3,263	97,992	Kakata
Maryland	5,351	132,058	Harper
Montserrado	2,740	544,878	Bensonville
Nimba	12,043	313,050	Saniquillie
Rivercess	4,385	37,849	Rivercess
Sinoe	10,254	64,147	Greenville

The county of Grand Kru (chief town, Barclayville) was created in 1985 from the former territories of Kru Coast and Sasstown.

CLIMATE. An equatorial climate, with constant high temperatures and plentiful rainfall, though Jan. to May is drier than the rest of the year. Monrovia. Jan. 79°F (26·1°C), July 76°F (24·4°C). Annual rainfall 206" (5,138 mm).

CONSTITUTION AND GOVERNMENT. A Constitution was approved by referendum in July 1984 and came into force on 6 Jan. 1986. Under it the National Assembly consisted of a 26-member Senate and a 64-member House of Representatives.

Presidential and parliamentary elections were held in July 1997. The electorate was 700,000; turnout was 85%. Charles Taylor was elected President with 75% of the vote. His closest rival, Ellen Johnson-Sirleaf, won 10% of the vote.

In March 1998 the Liberian government comprised:
President: Charles Taylor
Agriculture Minister: Roland Massaquoi. *Commerce/Industry:* Luseni Kaba. *Defence:* Daniel Chea. *Education:* Evelyne Kandakai. *Finance:* Elias Saleeby. *Foreign Affairs:* Monie Captan. *Health and Social Welfare:* Fineboy Darkinah. *Information, Culture and Tourism:* Joe W. Mulbah. *Internal Affairs:* Edward Komo Sackor. *Justice:* Eddington Varmah. *Employment:* Thomas Woewiyu. *Land, Mines and Energy:* Jenkins Dunbar. *National Security:* Philip Kammah. *Planning and Economic Affairs:* Amelia Ward. *Posts and Telecommunications:* Maxwell Kaba. *Public Works:* John T. Richardson. *Rural Development:* Roosevelt Johnson. *Minister of State for Presidential Affairs:* Ernest Eastman. *Transport:* Larmin Kawai. *Youth and Sports:* François Massaquoi.

National anthem: 'All hail, Liberia, hail!'; words by President Daniel Warner, tune by O. Lucas.

DEFENCE. The Armed Forces of Liberia are confined to the capital, Monrovia, and number about 2,000. ULIMO, NPFL and CPL forces control most of the country with combat strengths of 7,000, 12,000 and 2,000 respectively.

An ECOWAS peacekeeping force (ECOMOG, with forces from Ghana, Guinea, Nigeria and Sierra Leone) of some 8,600 is deployed. There is also a 70-strong UN Observer Mission (UNOMIL).

INTERNATIONAL RELATIONS

Membership. Liberia is a member of the UN, OAU, ECOWAS and is an ACP state of the EU.

ECONOMY

Currency. US currency is legal tender. There is a *Liberian dollar* (LRD), in theory at parity with the US dollar. There are coins of 1, 5, 10, 25 and 50 cents and $1, and notes of $5. Since 1993 different notes have been in use in government-held Monrovia and the rebel-held country areas.

Banking and Finance. The National Bank of Liberia opened on 22 July 1974 to act as a central bank. The Governor of the bank is Charles Bright.

Weights and Measures. Weights and measures are the same as in UK and USA.

ENERGY AND NATURAL RESOURCES

Electricity. Production, 1991, 430,000 kWh.

Minerals. Iron ore production was 1·1m. tonnes in 1992. Gold production (1991) 600 kilogrammes and diamond production (1992) 150,000 carats.

Agriculture. Over 65% of the labour force is engaged in agriculture. The soil is productive, but due to excessive rainfall there are large swamp areas. Principal crops (1995) in 1,000 metric tonnes: Cassava, 450; rice, 50; sugar cane, 234; bananas, 82; vegetables and melons, 76. Coffee, cocoa and palm-kernels are produced mainly by the traditional agricultural sector. Livestock (1995), in 1,000s: Cattle, 36; pigs, 120; sheep, 210; goats, 220.

Forestry. In 1994, 6·1m. cubic metres of roundwood were cut. There are rubber plantations.

Fisheries. Catch (1995) 7,700 tonnes.

INDUSTRY. There are a number of small factories.

FOREIGN ECONOMIC RELATIONS. Foreign debt was US$1,989m. in 1991.

Commerce. Imports in 1991 totalled L$4,081·2m. (1990, L$4,186·8m.) and exports L$556·5m. (1990, L$1,940·6m.). Liberia's main trading partners in 1991 were Norway, South Korea, Spain and Belgium.

In 1987, iron ore accounted for about 70% of total export earnings, rubber 15% and sawn timber over 5%. Other exports were coffee, cocoa, palm-kernel oil, diamonds and gold.

COMMUNICATIONS

Roads. There are 10,300 km of public roads (628 paved, 9,672 unpaved). In 1995, there were 10,300 cars and 28,300 goods vehicles.

Railways. There is a total of 490 km single track. A 148-km freight line connects iron mines to Monrovia. There is a line from Bong to Monrovia (78 km). All railways were out of use in 1997 because of the civil war.

Civil Aviation. There is an international airport (Roberts) at Monrovia. The national carrier is Air Liberia. Air services are also maintained by Air Afrique, Air Guinée, Ethiopian Airways and Nigerian Airways.

Shipping. There are ports at Buchanan, Greenville, Harper and Monrovia. Over 2,000 vessels enter Monrovia each year. The Liberian Government requires only a modest registration fee and an almost nominal annual charge and maintains no control over the operation of ships flying the Liberian flag. In 1995, shipping registered totalled 91·76m. DWT, all foreign-owned.

Telecommunications. There were 5,000 telephones in 1993. There were (1995) 675,000 radio and 56,000 television receivers.

Press. There are 8 daily newspapers with a combined circulation of 35,000.

SOCIAL INSTITUTIONS

Justice. Justice was administered by a Supreme Court of 5 judges, 14 circuit courts and lower courts.

Religion. There were (1993) about 0·85m. Sunni Moslems, and some 125,000 Roman Catholics, 50,000 Methodists, 40,000 Baptists, 32,000 Lutherans and 25,000 Anglicans.

Education. Schools are classified as: (1) Public schools, maintained and run by the Government; (2) Mission schools, supported by foreign Missions and subsidized by the Government, and operated by qualified Missionaries and Liberian teachers; (3) Private schools, maintained by endowments and sometimes subsidized by the Government. There are no up to date figures for schools, teachers or pupils. Adult literacy (1995) is 38·3%; 53·.9% male, 32·4% female.

DIPLOMATIC REPRESENTATIVES

Of Liberia in Great Britain (2 Pembridge Pl., London, W2 4XB)
Ambassador: Vacant.

Of Great Britain in Liberia
Ambassador: H. B. Warren-Gash (resides in Côte d'Ivoire).

Of Liberia in the USA (5201 16th St., NW, Washington, D.C., 20011)
Ambassador: Konah K. Blackett.

Of the USA in Liberia (111 United Nations Drive, Monrovia)
Ambassador: Vacant.

Of Liberia to the United Nations
Ambassador: William Bull.

Of Liberia to the European Union
Ambassador: Vacant.

Further Reading

Daniels, A., *Monrovia Mon Amour: a Visit to Liberia.* London, 1992
Elwood Dunn, D., *Liberia.* [Bibliography]. Oxford and Santa Barbara (CA), 1995
Sawyer, A., *The Emergence of Autocracy in Liberia: Tragedy and Challenge.* San Francisco, 1992

LIBYA

Jamahiriya Al-Arabiya
Al-Libiya Al-Shabiya
Al-Ishtirakiya Al-Uzma

(Great Socialist People's
Libyan Arab Republic)

Capital: Tripoli
Population: 5·59m.
GDP per head: (PPP$) 6,125
HDI/world rank: 0·801/64

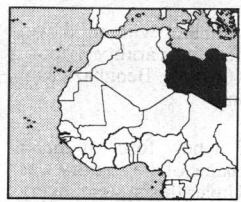

KEY HISTORICAL EVENTS. Tripoli fell under Ottoman domination in the 16th century, and though in 1711 the Arab population secured some measure of independence, the country came under the direct rule of Turkey in 1835. In 1911, Italy occupied Tripoli and in 1912, by the Treaty of Ouchy, Turkey recognized the sovereignty of Italy in Tripoli.

During the Second World War, the British army expelled the Italians and their German allies, and Tripolitania and Cyrenaica were placed under British, and Fezzan under French, military administration. This continued until 1950 under a UN directive. Libya became an independent, sovereign kingdom with the former Amir of Cyrenaica, Muhammad Idris al Senussi, as king on 24 Dec. 1951.

King Idris was deposed in Sept. 1969 by a group of army offices, 12 of whom formed the Revolutionary Command Council which, chaired by Col. Muammar Qadhafi, proclaimed the Libyan Arab Republic.

Qadhafi favoured Arab unity, but his efforts in that direction have been abortive. The Federation of the Arab Republics formed in 1972 with Libya, Egypt and Syria as members; an agreement to merge Libya and Egypt in 1973; a proposed union with Tunisia in 1974; and a union with Syria in 1980 have all proved unsuccessful.

In 1977 the country's name was changed to the Socialist People's Libyan Arab Jamahiriya. At the same time the Revolutionary Command Council was superceded by a more democratic system of People's Congress and Popular Committees. Qadhafi remained head of state.

Throughout the 1980s Libya had constant disagreements with her neighbours, and her relations with the USA and other Western countries deteriorated, culminating in the US bombing of the capital in April 1987, in an attempt to punish Qadhafi for his alleged support of international terrorism.

A US trade embargo has been in force since 1986. In 1992 the USA banned international flights and the sale of defence equipment to Libya because it refused to surrender suspects in the 1988 bombing of a Pan Am flight over Lockerbie in Scotland. In 1996 US sanctions were widened to penalize any foreign company that invested more than US$40m. in Libya's oil industry.

TERRITORY AND POPULATION. Libya is bounded in the north by the Mediterranean Sea, east by Egypt and Sudan, south by Chad and Niger and west by Algeria and Tunisia. The area is estimated at 1,759,540 sq. km (679,358 sq. miles). The population, at the census on 31 July 1984, was 3,637,488; estimate (1996), 5·59m. (86% urban; 47·9% female); density, 3·18 per sq. km. Life expectancy (1997 estimate), 65·05. Birth rate (per 1000 population), 43·94; death rate, 7·49; growth rate, 3·64%.

The country is administratively divided into 13 regions (baladiyat):

Region	Area in sq. km	1988 population	Chief town
Benghazi	15,000	512,200	Benghazi
Jabal al-Akhdar	37,000	308,300	Bayda
Jabal al-Gharbi	87,000	204,300	Gharyan
Khalij Surt	376,000	382,100	Surt
Kufrah	484,000	23,800	Kufrah
Margib	29,000	408,900	Khums

Region	Area in sq. km	1988 population	Chief town
Marzuq	350,000	45,200	Marzuq
Nikat al-Khums	101,000	196,000	Zuwarah
Sabha	82,000	121,700	Sabha
Tripoli	3,000	1,083,100	Tripoli
Tobruk	84,000	110,900	Tobruk
Wadi al-Hait	105,000	49,600	Awbari
Zawiyah	4,000	326,500	Zawiyah

The official language is Arabic.

CLIMATE. The coastal region has a warm temperate climate, with mild wet winters and hot dry summers, though most of the country suffers from aridity. Tripoli. Jan. 52°F (11·1°C), July 81°F (27·2°C). Annual rainfall 16" (400 mm). Benghazi. Jan. 56°F (13·3°C), July 77°F (25°C). Annual rainfall 11" (267 mm).

CONSTITUTION AND GOVERNMENT. In 1977 a new form of direct democracy, the state of the masses, was promulgated and the name of the country was changed to Great Socialist People's Libyan Arab Republic. Under this system, every adult is supposed to be able to share in policy making through the Basic People's Congresses of which there are some 2,000. These Congresses appoint People's Committees to execute policy. Provincial and urban affairs are handled by People's Committees responsible to Municipality People's Congresses, of which there are 13. Officials of these Congresses and Committees form at national level the 3,000-member General People's Congress which normally meets for about a week early each year (usually in March). This is the highest policy-making body in the country. The General People's Congress appoints its own General Secretariat and the General People's Committee, whose members (the equivalents of ministers elsewhere) head the government departments which execute policy at national level.

Until 1977 Libya was ruled by a Revolutionary Command Council (RCC) headed by Col. Muammar Qadhafi. Upon its abolition in that year the 5 surviving members of the RCC became the General Secretariat of the General People's Congress, still under Qadhafi's direction. In 1979 they stood down to be replaced by officials elected by the Congress. Since then, Col. Qadhafi has retained his position as Leader of the Revolution. Neither he nor his former RCC colleagues have any formal posts in the present administration, although they continue to wield considerable authority.

Leader: Col. Muammar Abu Minyar al-Qadhafi.
In March 1998 the General People's Congress comprised:
Secretary: Muhammad al-Zanati. *Assistant:* Ali Mursi al-Shairi.
In March 1998 the General People's Committee comprised:
Secretary: Muhammad Ahmad al-Manqush. *Agriculture:* Ali bin Ramadan. *Animal Wealth:* Masud Abu-Suwa. *Arab Unity:* Juma Fazani. *Communications and Transport:* Izz al-Din al-Muhammad al-Hinshiri. *Economy and Trade:* Abd al-Hafidh Mahmud Zalitni. *Education and Scientific Research:* A-Mahdi Muftah al-Birish. *Energy:* Abdallah Salim al-Badri. *Finance:* Muhammad Bayt al-Mal. *Health and Social Security:* Sulayman al-Ghamari Abdallah. *Housing and Utilities:* Mubarak al-Shamikh. *Industry and Mines:* Muftah Azzouz. *Information, Culture and Mass Mobilization:* Fawziyah al-Shalabi. *Justice and Public Security:* Muhammad Mahmud al-Hijazi. *Marine Resources:* Bashir Ramadan Abu-Jinah. *People's Control and Follow-Up:* Mahmud Badi. *People's External Liaison and International Co-operation Bureau:* Omar Mustafa al-Montassir. *Planning:* Jadallah Azzouz al-Talhi. *Tourism:* Al-Bukhair Salem Huda. *Youth and Sport:* Ali Mursi al-Shairi.
The *Speaker* of the Congress is Abd Al-Raziq Sawsa.

National anthem: 'Allah Akbar' ('God is Great'); words by Abdullah Al-Din, tune by Mahmoud Al-Sharif.

Local Government. An administrative decentralizing reform of 1992 divided the country into some 1,500 self-managing communes, each with an elected 13-member People's Committee, grouped into 13 administrative regions (*baladiyat*).

DEFENCE. There is selective conscription for 1–2 years.

Army. There are 7 military districts. The Army is organized into 5 elite and 5 surface-to-surface missile brigades and 21 infantry, 8 mechanized infantry, 22 artillery, 8 air defence, 10 tank and 15 parachute commando battalions. Equipment includes 1,600 T-54/-55, 350 T-62 and 260 T-72 main battle tanks. Strength (1997) 35,000 (25,000 conscripts).

Navy. The fleet, a mixture of Soviet and West European-built ships, comprises 4 old Soviet-built diesel submarines, 2 missile-armed frigates, 4 missile-armed corvettes, 24 fast missile craft, 8 inshore patrol craft and 8 offshore minesweepers. There are 2 tank landing ships and 3 medium landing ships as well as 3 landing craft. Auxiliaries include 1 logistic support ship, 1 salvage ship, 6 transports and 1 diving support ship.

There is a small Naval Aviation wing operating 25 Mi-14 Haze and 5 Super-Frelon helicopters from shore bases.

Personnel in 1997 totalled 8,000, including coastguard. The forces are based at Tripoli, Benghazi, Derna, Tobruk, Sidi Bilal and Al Khums.

Air Force. The Air Force has over 300 combat aircraft but most are in storage. About 100 MiG-23, MiG-25 and Su-22 aircraft can be flown and there are also some armed Gazelle and Mi-24 helicopters. Other equipment includes 10 C-130/L-100 Hercules, 10 An-26, 12 Il-76 and 20 Aeritalia G222T transports, 8 Super Frelon and 6 Agusta-built CH-47C Chinook heavy-lift helicopters, and a total of 16 Bell 212, Bell 47, Alouette III and Mi-8 helicopters. Training is performed on piston-engined SF.260Ms (some of which are armed for light attack duties) from Italy; L-39 Albatros, Galeb and Magister jet aircraft; and twin-engined L-410s built in the former Czechoslovakia. Personnel total (1997) about 22,000, with some of the combat aircraft operated by Syrian aircrew.

INTERNATIONAL RELATIONS

Membership. Libya is a member of the UN, OAU, OPEC and the Arab League.

ECONOMY

Policy. An enactment of the People's General Congress in Sept. 1992 authorizes the privatization of enterprises.

Currency. The unit of currency is the *Libyan dinar* (LYD) of 1,000 *millemes*. There are notes of LD 0·25, 0·50, 1, 5 and 10. The dinar was devalued 15% in Nov. 1994, and alongside the official exchange rate a new rate was applied to private sector imports.

Banking and Finance. A National Bank of Libya was established in 1955; it was renamed the Central Bank of Libya in 1972. The *Governor* is Tahii al-Jihimi. All foreign banks were nationalized by Dec. 1970. In 1972 the government set up the Libyan Arab Foreign Bank whose function is overseas investment and to participate in multinational banking corporations. The National Agricultural Bank has been set up to give loans and subsidies to farmers to develop their land and to assist them in marketing their crops.

Weights and Measures. Although the metric system has been officially adopted and is obligatory for all contracts, the following weights and measures are still used: *oke* = 1·282 kg; *kantar* = 51·28 kg; *draa* = 46 cm; *handaza* = 68 cm.

ENERGY AND NATURAL RESOURCES

Electricity. Production (1994) 16·73bn. kWh.

Oil. Oil revenues provided 28·2% of GDP in 1990. Crude oil production (1995) 1,426,000 bbls. a day. Reserves 23,000m. bbls. The Libyan National Oil Corporation (NOC) is the state's organization for the exploitation of oil resources. Since US oil companies withdrew due to sanctions, European rivals have been quick to move in.

Gas. Reserves 620,000m. cu. metres. Agip, the Italian oil company, is investing US$3bn. in a project to export natural gas to Europe. Production (1995) 246 petajoules.

Water. Since 1984 a major project has been under way to bring water from wells in southern Libya to the coast. This scheme, called the 'Great Man-Made River', is planned, on completion, to irrigate some 185,000 acres of land with water brought along some 4,000 km of pipes. Phase I was completed in Aug. 1991 at a cost of US$3,300m; Phase II of the project (covering the west of Libya) was announced in Sept. 1989.

Minerals. Cement production (1994) 2·3m. tonnes. Iron ore deposits have been found in the south.

Agriculture. Only the coastal zone, which covers an area of about 17,000 sq. miles, is really suitable for agriculture. Of some 25m. acres of productive land, nearly 20m. are used for grazing and about 1m. for static farming. The sub-desert zone produces the alfalfa plant. The desert zone and the Fezzan contain some fertile oases.

Cyrenaica has about 10m. acres of potentially productive land and is suitable for grazing. Certain areas are suitable for dry farming; in addition, grapes, olives and dates are grown. About 143,000 acres are used for settled farming; about 272,000 acres are covered by natural forests. The Agricultural Development Authority plans to reclaim 6,000 ha each year for agriculture. In the Fezzan there are about 6,700 acres of irrigated gardens and about 297,000 acres are planted with date palms.

Production (1995, in tonnes): Wheat, 167,000; barley, 148,000; olives, 62,000; dates, 68,000.

Livestock (1995):4·4m. sheep, 0·8m. goats, 0·1m. cattle, 0·13m. camels, 17m. poultry.

Forestry. In 1994, 650,000 cu. metres of roundwood were cut.

Fisheries. The catch in 1995 was 7,700 tonnes.

INDUSTRY. Industry is nationalized. Small scale private sector industrialization in the form of partnerships is permitted. Output (1994) per 1,000 metric tonnes: Residual fuel oils, 4,900; distillate fuel oils, 4,100.

FOREIGN ECONOMIC RELATIONS. Since 1986 the USA has applied a trade embargo on the grounds of Libya's alleged complicity in terrorism. In 1992 UN sanctions were imposed for Libya's refusal to deliver suspected terrorists for trial in the UK or USA. In Feb. 1989 Libya signed a treaty of economic co-operation with the 4 other Maghreb countries, Algeria, Mauritania, Morocco and Tunisia.

Commerce. Some 80% of GDP derives from trade. Oil accounts for over 95% of exports worth annually about US$10,000m. Total imports in 1995 were estimated at US$7·3bn. and exports at US$8·4bn. Main trading partners in 1995: Exports, Italy, Germany, Spain, France, UK, Turkey; imports, Italy, Germany, UK, France, Spain, Turkey.

COMMUNICATIONS

Roads. There are 25,675 km of roads.

Civil Aviation. A national airline, the Jamahiriya Libyan Arab Airlines, links Benghazi and Tripoli to Athens, Rome, Madrid, Malta, Moscow, Frankfurt, Paris, Amsterdam, Vienna and Zurich. In 1995 it operated 2 B-707-320Cs, 1 B-727-200, 8 B-727-200 Advs and 48 other aircraft (including 21 ex-Soviet).

Shipping. Sea-going vessels totalled 1·22m. GRT in 1995, including oil tankers, 1·09m. GRT.

Telecommunications. In 1993 some 240,000 telephones were in use. Broadcasting is controlled by the government Libyan Jamihiriya Broadcasting and People's Revolution Broadcasting-Television. Radio has a home service, external services in English, French and Arabic and a Holy Koran programme. In 1995 there were estimated to be 1·2m. radio and 0·55m. TV receivers (colour by PAL).

Press. In 1995 there were 4 daily newspapers with a combined circulation of 71,000.

SOCIAL INSTITUTIONS

Justice. The Civil, Commercial and Criminal codes are based mainly on the Egyptian model. Matters of personal status of family or succession matters affecting Moslems are dealt with in special courts according to the Moslem law. All other matters, civil, commercial and criminal, are tried in the ordinary courts, which have jurisdiction over everyone.

There are civil and penal courts in Tripoli and Benghazi, with subsidiary courts at Misurata and Derna; courts of assize in Tripoli and Benghazi, and courts of appeal in Tripoli and Benghazi.

Religion. Islam is declared the State religion, but the right of others to practise their religions is provided for. In 1990, 97% were Sunni Moslems.

Education. There were (1986) 1·01m. primary pupils in 4,164 schools with 63,122 teachers; 143,113 secondary level pupils with 10,765 teachers. In 1994-95 there were 3 universities and 1 medical and 1 technological university. There were 3 other institutes of higher education. In 1994-95 there were 31,140 university students and 1,710 academic staff. Adult literacy (1995) 76·2%; male, 87·9%; female, 63%.

Health. In 1981 there were 74 hospitals with 15,375 beds, 4,690 physicians, 314 dentists, 420 pharmacists, 1,080 midwives and 5,346 nursing personnel.

DIPLOMATIC REPRESENTATIVES

UK broke off diplomatic relations with Libya on 22 April 1984. Saudi Arabia looks after Libyan interests in UK and Italy looks after UK's interests in Libya.

USA suspended all embassy activities in Tripoli on 2 May 1980.

Of Libya to the United Nations
Ambassador: Abuzed Omar Dorda.

Of Libya to the European Union
Ambassador: Hamed Elhouderi.

Further Reading

Bearman, J., *Qadhafi's Libya*. London, 1986
Blundy, D. and Lycett, A., *Qadhafi and the Libyan Revolution*. London, 1987
Davis, J., *Libyan Politics: Tribe and Revolution*. London, 1988
Harris, L. C., *Libya: Qadhafi's Revolution and the Modern State*. Boulder (CO) and London, 1986
Lawless, R. I., *Libya*. [Bibliography] Oxford and Santa Barbara (CA), 1987
Simons, G., *Libya: the Struggle for Survival*. London, 1993
Vandewalle, D. (ed.) *Qadhafi's Libya 1969-1994*. London, 1995
Wright, J., *Libya: a Modern History*. London, 1982

LIECHTENSTEIN

Fürstentum Liechtenstein

(Principality of Liechtenstein)

Capital: Vaduz
Population: 30,923

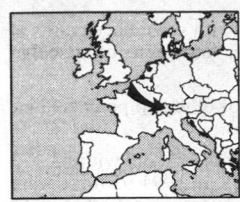

KEY HISTORICAL EVENTS. Liechtenstein is a sovereign state whose history dates back to 3 May 1342, when Count Hartmann III became ruler of the county of Vaduz. Additions were later made to the count's domains, and by 1434 the territory reached its present boundaries. It consists of the two former counties of Schellenberg and Vaduz (until 1806 immediate fiefs of the Holy Roman Empire). The former in 1699 and the latter in 1712 came into the possession of the house of Liechtenstein. On 23 Jan. 1719 the Emperor Charles VI constituted the two counties as the Principality of Liechtenstein. In 1862 the constitution established an elected diet which was to participate in the legislative process. After the First World War, Liechtenstein severed its treaties with Austria in 1919 and turned towards Switzerland, adopting Swiss currency in 1921. Liechtenstein has been represented abroad by Switzerland since 1919. On 5 Oct. 1921 a new constitution based on that of Switzerland extended democratic rights. It also stated that the head of government must be a Liechtenstein citizen.

TERRITORY AND POPULATION. Liechtenstein is bounded on the east by Austria and the west by Switzerland. Area, 160 sq. km (61·8 sq. miles); population (census 1990), 28,777; estimate, 1995, 30,923 (15,823 females), including 12,083 resident foreigners. In 1995 there were 358 births and 206 deaths. Population of Vaduz (census 1990), 4,870; estimate, 1995, 5,085. The language is German.

PRINCELY HOUSE. The reigning Prince is **Hans-Adam II,** b. 14 Feb. 1945; succeeded his father Prince Francis-Joseph, 13 Nov. 1989 (he exercised the prerogatives to which the Sovereign is entitled from 26 Aug. 1984); married on 30 July 1967 to Countess Marie Kinsky. *Offspring:* Hereditary Prince Alois (b. 11 June 1968), married Duchess Sophie of Bavaria on 3 July 1993 (*Offspring:* Prince Joseph Wenzel, b. 16 May 1995; Marie Caroline, b. 17 Oct. 1996); Prince Maximilian (b. 16 May 1969); Prince Constantin (b. 15 March 1972); Princess Tatjana (b. 10 April 1973). The monarchy is hereditary in the male line.

CONSTITUTION AND GOVERNMENT. Liechtenstein is a constitutional monarchy ruled by the princes of the House of Liechtenstein. The present constitution of 5 Oct. 1921 provided for a unicameral parliament (*Landtag*) of 15 members elected for 4 years, but this was amended to 25 members in 1988. Election is on the basis of proportional representation. The prince can call and dismiss the parliament. On parliamentary recommendation, he appoints the prime minister and the 4 councillors for a 4-year term. Any group of 1,000 persons or any 3 communes may propose legislation (initiative). Bills passed by the parliament may be submitted to popular referendum. A law is valid when it receives a majority approval by the parliament and the prince's signed concurrence. The capital is Vaduz.

At the elections on 2 Feb. 1997 the Fatherland Union (VU) gained 13 seats; the Progressive Citizens' Party, 10; Free List, 2.

Head of Government and Minister of Finance and Justice: Dr Mario Frick (b. 1965; VU; sworn in 14 April 1997). On becoming prime minister following the election of 24 Oct. 1993, he became the world's youngest prime minister, at the age of 28.

Parliamentary: Paul Kindle.

National anthem: 'Oben am jungen Rhein' ('Up above the young Rhine'); words by H. H. Jauch; tune, 'God save the Queen'.

Local government. There are 11 communes, fully independent administrative bodies within the laws of the principality. They levy additional taxes to the state taxes.

INTERNATIONAL RELATIONS

Membership. Liechtenstein is a member of the UN, EFTA, EEA and the Council of Europe.

ECONOMY

Liechtenstein is one of the world's richest countries with a well diversified economy. Low taxes and strict bank secrecy laws have made Liechtenstein a successful offshore financial centre.

Budget. Budget (in Swiss francs), 1997: Revenue, 605,594,000; expenditure, 572,675,000. There is no public debt.

Currency. Swiss currency has been in use since 1921.

Banking and Finance. There were (1995) 5 banks. Combined total assets were 27,398m. Swiss francs in 1996.

Weights and Measures. The metric system is in force.

ENERGY AND NATURAL RESOURCES

Electricity. Electricity produced in 1996 was 75,096 MWh.

Agriculture. In 1990 there were 3,890 ha of cultivated land and 2,510 ha of Alpine pasture. The rearing of cattle on the Alpine pastures is highly developed. In 1996 there were 5,905 cattle (including 2,652 milch cows), 319 horses, 3,352 sheep, 275 goats, 2,392 pigs. Total production of dairy produce, 1995, 12,801,216 kg.

Forestry. In 1995 there were 5,560 ha of forest. 18,087 cu. metres of timber were cut in 1994.

INDUSTRY. The country is highly industrialized, and has a great variety of light industries (textiles, ceramics, steel screws, precision instruments, canned food, pharmaceutical products, heating appliances, etc.).

Labour. The farming population has gone down from 70% in 1930 to 1·5% in 1996. The rapid change-over has led to the immigration of foreign workers (Austrians, Germans, Italians, Spaniards). The workforce was 15,741 in 1996, excluding employees commuting from abroad (8,231 in 1996). Industrial undertakings affiliated to the Liechtenstein Chamber of Commerce in 1996 employed 6,666 workers earning 447m. Swiss francs.

FOREIGN ECONOMIC RELATIONS. Liechtenstein has been in a customs union with Switzerland since 1923.

Commerce. Exports of home produce in 1996 (in Swiss francs), for member companies affiliated to the Chamber of Industry and Commerce, amounted to 3,045m. Swiss francs: 440·6m. (14·5%) went to Switzerland, 1,382m. (45·4%) went to EU countries and 1,222m. (40·1%) went to other countries. Imports in 1995 amounted to 1,071·8m. Swiss francs.

Tourism. In 1996, 56,751 visitors arrived in Liechtenstein.

COMMUNICATIONS

Roads. There are 250 km of roads. Postal buses are the chief means of public transportation within the country and to Austria and Switzerland. There were 19,310 cars in 1996. There were 404 road accidents in 1996 (3 fatal).

Railways. The 18·5 km of main railway passing through the country is operated by Austrian Federal Railways.

Telecommunications. In 1996 there were 19,916 telephones and 129 telex, 12,134 radios and 11,785 TV sets. Post and telegraphs are administered by Switzerland.

Cinemas. There were 2 cinemas in 1995.

Press. In 1997 there were 2 daily newspapers with a total circulation of 17,900, and 1 weekly with a circulation of 13,900.

SOCIAL INSTITUTIONS

Justice. The principality has its own civil and penal codes. The lowest court is the county court, *Landgericht*, presided over by one judge, which decides minor civil cases and summary criminal offences. The criminal court, *Kriminalgericht*, with a bench of 5 judges is for major crimes. Another court of mixed jurisdiction is the court of assizes (with 3 judges) for misdemeanours. Juvenile cases are treated in the Juvenile Court (with a bench of 3 judges). The superior court, *Obergericht*, and Supreme Court, *Oberster Gerichtshof*, are courts of appeal for civil and criminal cases (both with benches of 5 judges). An administrative court of appeal from government actions and the State Court determines the constitutionality of laws.

The death penalty was abolished in 1989.

Police. The principality has no army. 1997: Police force, 55, auxiliary police, 14.

Religion. In 1997 there were 24,748 Roman Catholics and 2,138 Protestants.

Education (1995–96). In 14 primary, 3 upper, 5 secondary and 1 grammar schools there were 3,728 pupils and 226 teachers. There is also an evening technical school, a music school and a children's pedagogic-welfare day school.

Health. There is an obligatory sickness insurance scheme. In 1989 there was 1 hospital, but Liechtenstein has an agreement with the Swiss cantons of St Gallen and Graubünden and the Austrian Federal State of Vorarlberg that her citizens may use certain hospitals.

DIPLOMATIC REPRESENTATIVES

In 1919, Switzerland agreed to represent the interests of Liechtenstein in countries where it has diplomatic missions and where Liechtenstein is not represented in its own right. In so doing Switzerland always acts only on the basis of mandates of a general or specific nature, which it may either accept or refuse, while Liechtenstein is free to enter into direct relations with foreign states or to set up its own additional diplomatic missions.

Of Liechtenstein to the European Union
Ambassador: Prince Nicolas of Liechtenstein

Further Reading

Amt für Volkswirtschaft. *Statistisches Jahrbuch.* Vaduz

Rechenschaftsbericht der Fürstlichen Regierung. Vaduz. Annual, from 1922
Jahrbuch des Historischen Vereins. Vaduz. Annual since 1901
National library: Landesbibliothek, Vaduz

National statistical office: Amt für Volkswirtschaft, Vaduz

LITHUANIA

Lietuvos Respublika

Capital: Vilnius
Population: 3·71m.
GDP per head: (PPP$) 3,960
HDI/world rank: 0·762/76

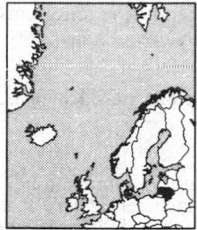

KEY HISTORICAL EVENTS. Lithuanian tribes organized into state units in the 9th century, unified in the face of encroachment by the German order of Teutonic Knights. At the time of Tatar-Mongol domination of Russia, Lithuania annexed Russian lands until by the middle of the 15th century Belorussia, parts of Russia and the Ukraine as far as the Black Sea were under its rule. Lithuania united with Poland dynastically in 1385 and politically in 1569. During the partitions of the Polish-Lithuanian Commonwealth by Russia, Prussia and Austria in the 18th century, Lithuania yielded its Russian territories and was absorbed into the Russian empire in 1795.

Following the German occupation during the First World War and the Russian revolution on 16 Feb. 1918, the Lithuanian Council proclaimed the restoration of the Lithuanian state. The Soviets attempted re-capturing the lost lands and heavy fighting occurred between the Soviet, German, Polish and Lithuanian forces. In April 1919, the Soviets withdrew and the re-formed Lithuanian government established a democratic republic. Lithuanian independence was recognized by the Treaty of Versailles. The peace treaty between Lithuania and the Soviet Union was signed in July 1920. In Oct. 1919, Poland occupied Vilnius, the capital of the historic Lithuanian state, and incorporated it into Poland in 1923 (this was acknowledged by Lithuania only in 1938). In Dec. 1926, the democratic régime was overthrown by a coup.

The secret protocol of the Soviet-German frontier treaty of 23 Sept. 1939 assigned the greater part of Lithuania to the Soviet sphere of influence. In Oct. 1939, the province and city of Vilnius (in Polish occupation 1920-39) were ceded by the USSR. An ultimatum (14 June 1940) led to the formation of a government acceptable to the USSR. Lithuania became a Soviet Socialist Republic of the USSR on 3 Aug. 1940.

On 11 March 1990 the newly-elected Lithuanian Supreme Soviet, by 120 votes to nil, proclaimed independence based on the continuing validity of the act of independence of 16 Feb. 1918. This decision was not accepted by the USSR government.

Massive price rises in Jan. 1991 triggered demonstrations from ethnic Russians and led the Prime Minister, Kazimiera Prunskiene, to resign. Initially dispatched to Vilnius to enforce conscription, Soviet army units occupied key buildings in the face of mounting popular unrest. On 13 Jan. the army fired on demonstrators and there were fatal casualties. A referendum on independence was held in Feb. 1991 at which 90·5% voted in favour. A fully independent status was conceded by the USSR State Council on 6 Sept. 1991.

TERRITORY AND POPULATION. Lithuania is bounded in the north by Latvia, east and south by Belarus, and west by Poland, the Russian enclave of Kaliningrad and the Baltic Sea. The total area is 65,300 sq. km (25,170 sq. miles) and the population (Aug. 1997) 3,707,200 (1,958,200 females; 2,534,500 urban); den-sity, 56·8 per sq. km. The 1989 census population was 3,674,802, of whom Lithuanians accounted for 79·6%, Russians 9·4%, Poles 7%, Belorussians 1·7% and Ukrainians 1·2%. In 1997 there were the following ethnic groups (in 1,000): Russians, 324·9; Poles, 256·6; Belorussians, 54·4; Ukrainians, 36·9; Jews, 5·2; others, 24·9. Vital statistics, 1994: Births, 42,832; deaths, 46,486; marriages, 23,337; divorces, 11,061; infant deaths, 603. Rates (per 1,000 population): Growth, –1; birth, 11·5; death, 12·5; marriage, 6·3; divorce, 3·0; infant mortality (per 1,000 live births), 13·9. 4,607 births were registered to unmarried mothers in 1994. There were 1,703 suicides in 1994 (262 women). In 1994 there were 30,326 legally induced abortions.

907

Expectation of life, 1994: Males, 62·8 years; females, 74·9. In 1994 there were 4,246 emigrants and 1,664 immigrants.

There are 10 provinces (with capitals of the same name): Alytus; Kaunas; Klaipėda; Marijampolė; Panevėžys; Šiauliai; Tauragė; Telšiai; Utena; Vilnius.

The capital is Vilnius (1997 population, 580,100). Other large towns are Kaunas (418,700), Klaipėda (203,300), Šiauliai (147,000) and Panevėžys (133,300).

The official language is Lithuanian, but ethnic minorities have the right to official use of their language where they form a substantial part of the population. All residents who applied by 3 Nov. 1991 received Lithuanian citizenship, requirements for which now are 10 years residence and competence in Lithuanian.

CLIMATE. Vilnius. Jan. –2°C, July 15·6°C. Annual rainfall 826 mm. Klaipėda. Jan. 0·9°C, July 16·5°C. Annual rainfall 685 mm.

CONSTITUTION AND GOVERNMENT. A referendum to approve a new constitution was held on 25 Oct. 1992. Parliament is the 141-member *Seimas*. It is elected by a system partly proportional and partly constituency-based. 70 seats are allocated to parties according to their share of the vote (with a 5% threshold). The 71 constituency seats require candidates to poll more than 50% of the vote, otherwise there are run-offs.

The *Constitutional Court* is empowered to rule on whether proposed laws conflict with the constitution or existing legislation. It comprises 9 judges who serve 9-year terms, one third rotating every 3 years.

Presidential elections were held in two rounds, 21 Dec. 1997 and 4 Jan. 1998. In the run off vote Valdas Adamkus defeated Arjuras Pauluska by 11,000 votes, 49·9% against 49·29%. President Adamkus lived in the USA for 50 years, having fled Lithuania as a teenager in 1944 when Soviet troops occupied its Baltic states.

Parliamentary elections were held in 2 rounds on 20 Oct. and 10 Nov. 1996. 28 parties stood. The electorate was 2,501,886; turn-out in the first round was 54%, in the second, 40%. The Homeland Union (HU) gained 70 seats, the Christian Democrats (CD) 16, the Lithuanian Centre Union (LCU) 13, the Lithuanian Social Democratic Party 12, the Lithuanian Democratic Labour Party 12, the Lithuanian Democratic Party 2; 7 other parties gained 1 seat each, independents gained 4.

President: Valdas Adamkus.

Gediminas Vagnorus (HU) was appointed *Prime Minister* by the President with the approval of the parliament on 26 Nov. 1996 and formed an HU-CD coalition government in Dec. which in March 1998 comprised:

Minister of Finance: Algirdas Gediminas Semeta. *Economy:* Vincas Babilius. *Social Security:* Irena Degutiene. *Interior:* Vidmantas Ziemelis. *Health:* Laurynas Stankevicius. *Justice:* Vytautas Pakalniskis. *Agriculture:* Edvardos Makelis. *Foreign Affairs:* Algirdas Saudargas. *Defence:* Ceslovas Stankevicius. *Environmental Protection:* Algis Caplikas. *Transport:* Algis Zvaliauskas. *Government Reform and Local Government:* Kestutis Skrebys. *Culture:* Saulius Saltenis.

The *Speaker* is Vytautas Landsbergis (HU).

National anthem: 'Lietuva tėvynė mūsu' ('Lithuania land of heroes'); words and tune by V. Kurdirka.

Local Government: There are 10 provinces administered by governors comprising 92 towns, 19 urban districts, 44 regions and 427 rural districts, each with an appropriate authority. Elections were held 23 March 1997 for 1,484 seats in 56 districts. Turn-out was 39·92%. 24 parties stood for about 1,000 council seats. HU won 34% of votes cast, the Lithuanian Democratic Labour Party 16% and the Christian Democrats 13%.

DEFENCE. Conscription is for 12 months.

Army. The Army consists of 1 motorized infantry brigade with separate battalion and

1 peacekeeping company, and in 1997 numbered 4,300. There is a 12,000-strong volunteer Home Guard reserve.

Navy. A small coastal defence flotilla numbering some 350 in 1996 mans 2 ex-Soviet light frigates, 1 ex-Norwegian fast patrol boat, 1 auxiliary vessel and several harbour patrol craft. It is based at Klaipéda.

Air Force. A combat squadron has L-39 unarmed trainers, while 2 transport squadrons operate Antonov aircraft, Mi-8 helicopters and a few L-410s. Personnel (1997), 250.

INTERNATIONAL RELATIONS

Membership. Lithuania is a member of the UN, Council of Europe, OSCE, EBRD, IMF, UNESCO, FAO, IMO, the NATO Partnership for Peace and EAPC, is an Associate Member of the EU and Associate Partner of the WEU. In Dec. 1995 Lithuania applied to join the EU.

ECONOMY

Policy. The first stage of privatization in Lithuania enabling Lithuanian subjects to purchase state-owned assets for 'compensation vouchers' was completed in 1995.

Generally, the privatization process in Lithuania is close to completion as currently as much as 70% of GDP in Lithuania is generated by the private entities. The restructuring of priority sectors of the Lithuanian economy is presently facilitated by the second stage of privatization: privatization for cash, giving equal rights to local and foreign investors. The Ministry of European Affairs of the Republic of Lithuania co-ordinates the privatization process in Lithuania and directly organizes privatization of the largest state-controlled entities in industry and infrastructure. Privatization of these enterprises is carried out by a competitive procedure of international tenders, prepared and executed by internationally renowned advisors.

Budget. The 1997 budget envisaged revenue of 7,600m. litas and expenditure of 6,400m. litas. Revenue in 1996 included (in 1m. litas): VAT, 2,280; personal income tax, 2,087; tax on corporate profit, 587. Expenditure in 1996 included: General public services, 553; defence, 178; public order, 830; education, 1,713; health, 1,703; social welfare, 746; housing and community amenities, 353; recreational, cultural and religious affairs, 290; fuel and energy, 297; agriculture, forestry and fishing, 632; transport and communications, 168.

VAT is 18%

Currency. The unit of currency is the *litas* of 100 *cents*, which was introduced on 25 June 1993 and became the sole legal tender on 1 Aug. There are coins of 1, 2, 5, 10, 20 and 50 cents and 1, 2 and 5 litas, and notes of 1, 2, 4, 10, 50, 100 and 200 litas. The litas was pegged to the US dollar on 1 April 1994 at US$1 = 4 litas. Inflation was 25% in 1996. Consumer Price index was 6·9% in Oct. 1997. 2,395·5m. litas were in circulation in Sept. 1997.

Standard & Poor's assigned Lithuania an investment grade rating of BBB+ for local currency and BBB– for foreign currency in July 1997.

Banking and Finance. The central bank and bank of issue is the Bank of Lithuania (*Governor*, Reinoldijas Šarkinas). There are three state banks—the Savings Bank, the Agricultural Bank and the State Commercial Bank. State banks have been partially privatized. A programme to restructure and privatize three state banks was started in 1996. There were 8 commercial banks in Sept. 1997. Lithuanian Development Bank jointly owned by the government and the EBRB, in the proportions 2:1, was founded in 1994. Four representatives offices of the foreign banks are registered in Lithuania.

A stock exchange opened in Vilnius in 1993. In Oct. 1997 its capitalization was US$2·5bn. and it had 541 companies listed.

ENERGY AND NATURAL RESOURCES

Electricity. Output was 17·1m. kWh in 1996. A nuclear power station in Ignalina is responsible for 80% of total output, and there are also 2 hydro-electric and 5 thermal plants.

Oil. Production started from a small field at Kretinga in 1990. In 1996 recoverable reserves were estimated at 4·7m. tonnes.

Minerals. Peat reserves total 127·7m. tonnes. Output, 1996, 233,000 tonnes.

Agriculture. In 1996, agriculture contributed 10·4% of GDP and employed about 24% of the workforce. As of 1 Jan. 1997 the agricultural land area was 3,513,000 ha, of which 2,958,000 ha were arable, 495,900 ha pasture and 58,800 ha orchards. 390,100 persons were employed in agriculture and forestry in 1994. Output of main agricultural products (in 1,000 tonnes) in 1996: grain, 2,702·5; potatoes, 2,044·3; sugar-beet, 795·5; vegetables, 432·6; meat, 198·6; milk, 1,831·5; eggs, 750·9m. units; flax fibre, 6·2. Value of agricultural production, 1996 (in 1m. litas), reached 6,963·5, of which from agricultural partnerships and enterprises, 2,237·5, and from individual farm holdings, 4,726·0.

Livestock, 1996 (in 1,000): Cattle, 1,054·1 (of which milch cows, 589·9); pigs, 1,127·6; sheep and goats, 45·1; horses, 81·4; poultry, 7,775·4. 91,261 tractors were in use in 1996.

Forestry. Forests cover 30·2% of Lithuania's territory and consists of conifers, mostly pine. Output of timber, 1996, 4,771·1m. cu. metres.

Fisheries. In 1996 the fishing fleet comprised 167 vessels totalling 230,610 GRT.

INDUSTRY. Industry accounted for 28·3% of GDP in 1996. Industrial output included, in 1996 (in 1,000 tonnes): extraction of peat, 233; quarrying of stone, clay and sand, 1·2m. cu. metres; sulphuric acid, 424; mineral fertilizers, 459; paper, 16·8; petrol, 3,748; television picture tubes, 1,695,000; silk, 7·8m. sq. metres; linen, 13·5m. sq. metres; woollen fabrics, 12·6m. sq. metres; cotton fabrics, 39·9m. cu. metres; TV sets, 54,600; bicycles, 142,900; refrigerators, 143,800.

Labour. Total population in 1996 was 3·7m., of which the workforce was 1·8m., employed were 1·7m. (66·6% in private enterprises and 34·4% in the public sector). Employed population by activity (in per cent): Manufacturing, 17·4; construction, 7·2; education, 8·9; transport and communications, 5·7; wholesale and retail trade, 12·7; health and social work, 6·2; real estate, 2·4. Employment skills, 17·9% with higher degrees, 44·1% with a specialized education. In July 1997 average monthly wage was US$215·36. Legal minimum wage was 400 litas (=US$100).

Up to 1995, old age pension for men and women started at 55. Starting with 1995, this age has been increased by 2 months per year for men and 4 months for women until it reaches 62 years 6 months for men and 60 years for women. Average number of persons entitled to pensions in 1996 was 879,800. Unemployment rate as of July 1997 was 5·3%.

Trade Unions. In 1996 there were 44 unions grouped in 4 federations: Trade Union Centre; Workers' Union; Trade Unions' Association; Trade Union Society.

FOREIGN ECONOMIC RELATIONS. In order to foster export growth, Lithuania maintains rather a liberal foreign trade régime. There is no quantitative import restriction and the import duties are one of the lowest throughout Central Europe. By the end of 1996 free trade agreements with the European Union, European Free Trade Association (EFTA) countries, neighbouring Latvia and Estonia, as well as with a number of Central European Free Trade Agreement countries (CEFTA), and Ukraine were signed. Meanwhile, to trade with Russia, most favoured-nation régime is applied.

Foreign investors may purchase up to 100% of the equity companies in Lithuania. By mid 1997, US$762m. of foreign capital has been invested.

Total foreign debt was US$1,203m. in 1996.

As of present, the individual laws on 3 free economic zones (namely the laws on Šiauliai, Klaipėda and Kaunas) had been cleared by Lithuania's Parliament, the Seimas. All referred zones presently are in different stages of development.

Commerce. In 1996, exports were valued at US$3,356·4m. and imports at US$4,558·6m. Main export markets, 1996 (% of trade): Russia, 24·0%; Germany, 12·8%; Latvia, 9·2%. Main import suppliers: Russia, 25·5%; Germany, 15·8%; Ukraine, 3·3%. Main exports are meat, dairy produce, spirits, electricity, wood and wooden articles, iron and steel and TV sets.

Tourism. There were 59,394 foreign visitors in 1996. In 1995 visitors brought in a revenue of US$124m.

COMMUNICATIONS

Roads. In 1996 there were 45,340 km of surfaced roads. The Via Baltica, the US$180m. project, will upgrade a 1,000 km. (620 miles) an international highway linking Finland, Estonia, Latvia, Lithuania and Poland, and there are plans to continue the link to Western and Southern Europe.

In 1996 there were 785,088 motor cars, 16,026 buses and trolley buses, 81,291 goods vehicles and 19,402 motor cycles. In 1996, road transport carried 593·1m. passengers and 123·1m. tonnes of freight. There were 3,902 traffic accidents in 1994, with 765 fatalities.

Railways. There are 2,898 km of railway track in Lithuania. Lithuania's railroads are used considerably for both passenger and freight traffic. The majority of rail traffic is diesel propelled, though 350 km of track are electrified. In 1996, 13·2m. passengers and 29·14m. tonnes of freight were carried.

Civil Aviation. The main international terminal is based in the capital, Vilnius. The largest airline, a state-owned joint stock company Lithuanian Airlines (on the list of privatization), has regularly scheduled flights to most of Europe's main transit hubs, while a number of other international airlines (Finnair, Lufthansa, LOT, Austrian Airlines, Estonian Air, SAS, United Airlines, Delta) run regular scheduled flights into the country as well. Other international airports are at Kaunas, Palanga, Šiauliai.

Shipping. The ice-free port of Klaipėda plays a dominant role in sea traffic. It has the second largest tonnage in the Baltic region. A 1,028 ha site has been set aside as a *Free Economic Zone,* which will offer a number of attractive conditions to foreign investors, including a five year exemption from profit taxes.

In 1996 the merchant fleet numbered 96 ships totalling 372,967 GRT and 6 tankers totalling 7,036 GRT. The port has a cargo capacity of 20m. tonnes; the turnover of the port in 1996 was almost 15m. tonnes (up from almost 13m. in 1995).

The port's planned annual capacity will increase to 30m. tonnes by the year 2000 after the completion of several modernization projects. In 1994 there were 788 km of navigable inland waterways. The inland fleet comprised 94 vessels.

Telecommunications. In 1996, telephone provision was 26·1 per 100 inhabitants (31·4 urban, 16·8 rural). A majority stake in Lithuanian Telecom will be privatized in an inernational tender in 1998. At present, over 40,000 subscribers use the services of mobile digital connection (GSM). By 2000 this number should exceed 130,000. There are 12 commercial and 10 TV companies.

In 1996, there were 77 radio and 78 TV sets per 100 households. Approaching 120,000 households have cable television. This comprises 13% of the total number of households in Lithuania.

On average, there are three computers per 100 inhabitants, about 20% of these are connected to the telecommunications network.

Cinemas. There were 93 cinemas in 1996; attendance, 470,200.

Press In 1996 there were 443 (including 6 dailies) newspapers (389 in Lithuanian, 37 in Russian, 8 in Polish, 5 in English, 3 in German, 1 in Yiddish) and 351 periodicals. 3,645 book titles were published.

SOCIAL INSTITUTIONS

Justice. The Supreme Court is at the apex of the court system. In 1996 there were 54 local courts, 5 district courts and the Court of Appeal. Trial by jury has been introduced for capital offences. The death penalty is retained for premeditated murder but there is a moratorium on it. 68,053 crimes were reported in 1996, of which 41·3% were solved. In 1996 there were 366 murders and 39 attempted murders. 16,983 persons were convicted. 10 prisons hold 9,742 inmates (502 women).

Religion. Under the Constitution, the state supports religious groups which have been active in Lithuania for 400 years, i.e., the Roman Catholic, Evangelical Lutheran, Evangelical Re-formats and Orthodox Churches. 90% of the population are Roman Catholic. As of 1 Jan. 1997, there were 691 Roman Catholic churches with 743 priests, and 44 Orthodox churches with 31 priests. There is an archbishopric of Vilnius and 10 bishops. In 1997, the Lutheran Church had 41 churches, 54 parishes, 17 pastors headed by a bishop.

Education. Education is compulsory from 7 to 16. In 1996-97, there were 729 pre-school establishments with 93,800 pupils and 2,561 schools (including 36 private) with 67,324 teachers and 688,000 pupils, in the following categories:

Type of School	No. of Schools	No. of Pupils
Nursery	151	16,500
Primary	828	37,000
Junior	21	2,100
Elementary	597	59,200
Special	53	7,500
Secondary	698	418,400
College type	68	26,500
Vocational	105	51,700
Adult	25	10,500

58,800 students (33,100 females) attended 15 institutions of higher education in 1996-97, including 8 universities. The adult literacy rate is 98·4%.

Health. In 1996 there were 14,763 physicians, 1,709 dentists and 39,585 para-medical personnel. There were 197 hospitals with 39,182 beds, and 643 pharmacies.

Welfare. The social security system is financed by the State Social Insurance Fund. As of 31 Dec. 1996, 879,800 persons were eligible for pensions, including (in 1,000): retirement, 655·3; disability, 147·0; loss of breadwinner, 47·8; widow's/widower's and orphan's, 27·3. Average monthly pensions (in litas in 1996) was 180·10.

DIPLOMATIC REPRESENTATIVES

Of Lithuania in Great Britain, Ireland and Portugal (84 Gloucester Place, London, W1H 3HN)
Ambassador: Justas V. Paleckis.

Of Great Britain in Lithuania (2 Antakalnio., 2055 Vilnius)
Ambassador: Thomas T. Macan.

Of Lithuania in the USA (2622 16th St., NW, Washington, D.C., 20009)
Ambassador: Stasys Sakalauskas.

Of the USA in Lithuania (Ak Menu 6, Vilnius)
Ambassador: Keith C. Smith.

Of Lithuania to the United Nations
Ambassador: Oskaras Jusys.

Of Lithuania to the European Union
Ambassador: Jonas Cicinscas.

Further Reading

Department of Statistics to the Government. *Statistical Yearbook of Lithuania – Economic and Social Development in Lithuania.* Monthly.

Hood, N. et al (eds.), *Transition in the Baltic States.* 1997

Jurgéla, C. R., *History of the Lithuanian Nation.* New York, 1948

Kantantas, A. and F., *A Lithuanian Bibliography.* Univ. of Alberta Press, 1975

Lieven, A., *The Baltic Revolution: Estonia, Latvia, Lithuania and the Path to Independence.* 2nd ed. Yale UP, 1994

Misiunas, R. J. and Taagepera, R., *The Baltic States: the Years of Dependence, 1940–91.* 2nd ed. Farnborough, 1993

Smith, I. A. and Grunts, M. V., *The Baltic States.* [Bibliography], Oxford and Santa Barbara (CA), 1993

Vardys, V. S. and Sedaitis, J. B., *Lithuania: the Rebel Nation.* Boulder (CO), 1997

National statistical office: Department of Statistics to the Government, Gedimino Pr. 29, 2746 Vilnius. *Director:* Kestutis Zaborskas.

LUXEMBOURG

Grand-Duché de
Luxembourg

Capital: Luxembourg
Population: 418,300
GDP per head: (PPP$) 34,155
GNP: US$16·3bn.
HDI/world rank: 0·899/27

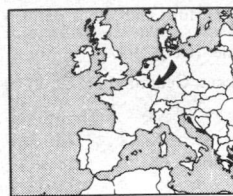

KEY HISTORICAL EVENTS. The country formed part of the Holy Roman Empire until it was conquered by the French in 1795. In 1815 the Grand Duchy of Luxembourg came under the house of Orange-Nassau, also sovereigns of the Netherlands. In 1839 the Walloon-speaking area was joined to Belgium. In 1890 the personal union with the Netherlands ended with the accession of a member of another branch of the house of Nassau, Grand Duke Adolphe of Weilburg. In both world wars (1914–18 and 1939–45) Luxembourg was invaded and occupied by German forces. From May 1940 until Sept. 1944 the government carried on an independent administration in London.

In 1948 a Benelux customs union formed by Belgium, the Netherlands and Luxembourg allowed for standardization of prices, taxes and wages, and the free movement of labour among the three countries.

TERRITORY AND POPULATION. Luxembourg has an area of 2,586 sq. km (999 sq. miles) and is bounded on the west by Belgium, south by France, east by Germany. The population (1997) was 418,300 (including 142,800 foreigners). The capital, Luxembourg, had (1997) 78,300 inhabitants; Esch-sur-Alzette, the centre of the mining district, 24,600; Differdange, 16,500; Dudelange, 16,200, and Pétange, 13,200.

Vital statistics (figures in parentheses indicate births and deaths of resident foreigners):

	Births	Deaths	Marriages	Divorces
1995	5,421 (2,270)	3,797 (502)	2,079	727
1996	5,689 (2,401)	3,895 (516)	2,105	817

Life expectancy is 72·6 years for men and 79·1 years for women.

Letzebuergesch is spoken by most of the population, and since 1985 has been an official language with French and German.

CLIMATE. Cold, raw winters with snow covering the ground for up to a month are features of the upland areas. The remainder resembles Belgium in its climate, with rain evenly distributed throughout the year. Jan. 0·8°C, July 17·5°C. Annual rainfall 782·2 mm.

DUCAL HOUSE. The reigning Grand Duke is **Jean**, b. 5 Jan. 1921, son of the late Grand Duchess Charlotte and the late Prince Felix of Bourbon-Parma; succeeded 12 Nov. 1964 on the abdication of his mother; married to Princess Joséphine-Charlotte of Belgium, 9 April 1953. *Offspring:* Princess Marie-Astrid, b. 17 Feb. 1954, married Christian of Habsbourg-Lorraine 6 Feb. 1982 (*Offspring:* Marie Christine, b. 31 July 1983; Imre, b. 8 Dec. 1985; Christophe, b. 2 Feb. 1988; Alexander, b. 26 Sept. 1990); Prince Henri, *heir apparent,* b. 16 April 1955, married Maria Teresa Mestre 14 Feb. 1981; (*Offspring:* Prince Guillaume, b. 11 Nov. 1981, Prince Felix, b. 3 June 1984, Prince Louis, b. 3 Aug. 1986, Princess Alexandra, b. 16 Feb. 1991, Prince Sebastian, b. 16 April 1992). Prince Jean, b. 15 May 1957, married Hélène Vestur; Princess Margaretha, b. 15 May 1957, married Prince Nikolaus of Liechtenstein 20 March 1982; Prince Guillaume, b. 1 May 1963, married Sibilla Weiller 24 Sept. 1994.

CONSTITUTION AND GOVERNMENT. The Grand Duchy of Luxembourg is a constitutional monarchy. The constitution of 17 Oct. 1868 was revised in 1919, 1948, 1956, 1972, 1983, 1988, 1989, 1994 and 1996.

The country forms 4 electoral districts. Voters choose between party lists of candidates in multi-member constituencies. The parliament is the *Chamber of Deputies*, which consists of a maximum of 60 members elected for 5 years. There is a *Council of State* of 21 members appointed by the Sovereign for life. It advises on proposed laws and any other question referred to it.

The head of state takes part in the legislative power, exercises executive power and has a part in the judicial power. The constitution leaves to the sovereign the right to organize the Government, which consists of a Minister of State, who is Prime Minister, and of at least 3 Ministers.

At the elections of June 1994 the electorate was 217,131; turn-out was 82·5%. The Christian Social Party (CS) gained 21 seats, the Socialist Workers' Party (S) 17, the Democratic Party 12, the Action Committee for Democracy 5 and Déi Gréng GLEI-GAP 5. A Christian Social-Socialist coalition was formed which in March 1998 comprised:

Prime Minister, Minister of State, Employment, Finance and the Exchequer: Jean-Claude Juncker (b. 1945; CS; sworn in 20 Jan. 1995).

Deputy Prime Minister, Minister of Foreign Affairs, Trade, Overseas Aid and Development: Jacques Poos (S). *Agriculture, Viticulture, Rural Development, Small Business, Housing and Tourism:* Fernand Boden (CS). *Justice:* Luc Frieden (CS). *Budget, Relations with Parliament:* Marc Fischbach (CS). *The Family, Women, the Disabled:* Marie-Josée Jacobs (CS). *Education, Cultural and Religious Affairs:* Erna Hennicot-Schoepges (CS). *Home Affairs, Civil Service and Administrative Reforms:* Michel Wolter (CS). *Economy, Public Works, Energy:* Robert Goebbels (S). *Environment, Health, Physical Education and Sport:* Georges Wohlfahrt (S). *Land Planning and Defence:* Alex Bodry (S). *Social Security, Transport, Post and Communication:* Mady Delvaux-Stehres (S). *Secretary of State (Foreign Affairs, Foreign Trade and Co-operation):* Lydie Err (S).

The *Speaker* is Jean Spautz.

National anthem: Ons Hemecht (Our Homeland); words by M. Lentz, tune by J. A. Zinnen.

European Parliament. Luxembourg has 6 representatives. At the June 1994 elections turn-out was 90%. CS won 2 seats with 31·4% of votes cast (group in European Parliament: Popular European Party); S, 2 with 24·8% (European Socialist Party); the Democratic Party, 1 with 18·8% (Liberal, Democratic and Reformist Group); the Greens, 1 with 10·9% (Greens).

DEFENCE. There is a volunteer light infantry battalion of (1996) 800, and a Gendarmerie of 560.

INTERNATIONAL RELATIONS

Membership. Luxembourg is a member of the UN, Benelux, the EU, OECD, the Council of Europe, NATO and WEU. The Schengen Accord of June 1990 abolished border controls between Luxembourg, Belgium, Denmark, Finland, France, Germany, Greece, Iceland, Italy, the Netherlands, Norway, Portugal, Spain and Sweden.

ECONOMY

Performance. Real GDP growth was estimated at 2·5% in 1996 (3·2% in 1995). Total GDP in 1995 was US$16,300m.

Budget. Revenue and expenditure (including extraordinary) for years ending 30 April (in 1m. francs):

	1994	1995	1996	1997
Revenue	136·2	149·8	155·8	163·9
Expenditure	137·8	148·8	156·6	163·3

VAT is 15%, with a reduced rate of 6%.

Public debt in June 1997 was LUF23·7bn., of which LUF23·6bn. was domestic debt.

Currency. The unit of currency is the *Luxembourg franc* (LUF) notionally of 100 *centimes*, at parity with the Belgian franc. There are coins of 1, 5, 20 and 50 francs and notes of 100, 500, 1,000, 2,000, 5,000 and 10,000 francs. Belgian francs are legal tender. Foreign exchange reserves (excluding gold) were US$75,000m. in 1995.

Banking and Finance. Luxembourg's equivalent of a central bank is its Monetary Institute (*Director-General*, Pierre Jans). In 1996 there were 221 banks and 74 other credit institutions established in Luxembourg, which has become an international financial centre. Total deposits in 1996 were LUF7,579·0bn.; net assets in unit trusts, LUF7,560·7bn.; net assets in investment companies, LUF4,754·9bn. There is a stock exchange. The financial sector accounted for 14·4% of GDP in 1994 and in 1996 the banks showed a net profit of LUF71·6bn. In 1995 the total number of approved insurance companies was 81 with reinsurance companies numbering 234; the amount of premiums due was LUF130,267·0m.

Weights and Measures. The metric system is in force.

ENERGY AND NATURAL RESOURCES

Electricity. Power production was 1,166m. kWh in 1994.

Minerals. In 1994 production (in tonnes) of pig-iron, 1,926,890; of steel, 3,073,268.

Agriculture. There were 5,700 workers engaged in agricultural work (including wine-growing and forestry) in 1996 (1,600 wage-earners), and 3,060 farms with an average area of 48·06 ha; 126,765 ha were under cultivation in 1994. Production, 1996 (in tonnes) of main crops: Maize, 476,400; roots and tubers, 28,790; bread crops, 66,720; forage crops, 105,860; pulses, 1,920; grassland, 160,260. Production, 1996 (in 1,000 tonnes) of meat, 28·1; milk, 265·5; butter, 3·1; cheese, 3. In 1995/96, 149,700 hectolitres of wine were produced. In 1994 there were 8,177 tractors, 1,074 harvester-threshers, 2,036 manure spreaders and 2,241 gatherer-presses.

Livestock (1996): 2,198 horses, 217,927 cattle, 72,494 pigs, 7,152 sheep.

Forestry. In 1994 there were 88,620 ha of forests, which produced 166,018 cu. metres of broadleaved and 245,582 cu. metres of coniferous wood.

INDUSTRY. Production, 1996 (in 1,000 tonnes); Steel, 2,502; rolled steel products, 3,438. In 1994 there were 2,501 industrial enterprises, of which 1,487 building industry.

Labour. In 1996 the estimated total workforce was 219,000, of which 121,100 worked in the service industries The government fixes a legal minimum wage. Retirement is at 65. In 1996 the unemployment rate was 3·3%.

FOREIGN ECONOMIC RELATIONS.

Commerce. Exports in 1996 (provisional figures) totalled LUF220,997m., and imports LUF292,778m. Principal imports and exports by type of goods:

	Exports		Imports	
	1995	1996	1995	1996
Food, beverages, tobacco	5,648	5,842	17,108	18,332
Minerals	2,977	2,249	27,392	28,831
Chemicals	10,622	7,797	24,324	23,371
Plastics/rubber goods	32,212	31,164	17,199	17,604
Textiles, clothing	15,101	13,549	15,183	15,486
Iron, steel	81,344	71,057	53,921	49,037
Mechanical/electrical equipment	37,001	43,096	49,649	51,813
Transport equipment	9,444	11,455	32,906	34,176

Trade with selected countries (in LUF1m.)

	Exports		Imports	
	1995	1996	1995	1996
Austria	3,357	3,317	2,373	2,294
Belgium	30,434	29886	110,824	115,444
France	45,829	44,574	35,302	35,083

	Exports		Imports	
	1995	1996	1995	1996
Germany	65,005	61,317	86,310	86,225
Italy	11,275	11,374	6,172	6,565
Netherlands	12,230	11,315	13,647	15,188
Spain	4,359	4,563	1,602	1,530
UK	14,446	14,362	5,372	4,355
Total EU	196,482	189,850	265,464	270,018
Japan	1,365	995	3,981	2,652
USA	7,168	6,074	9,796	7,335

Tourism. In 1996 there were 667,000 tourists.

COMMUNICATIONS

Roads. In 1996 there were 2,855 km of roads of which 118 km were motorways. Motor vehicles registered in 1996 included 236,834 passenger cars, 16,277 trucks, 915 coaches, 8,716 motorcycles, 23,254 tractors and special vehicles.

Railways. In 1996 there were 274 km of railway (standard gauge) of which 262 km were electrified. Railways carried (1996) 12·6m. passengers.

Civil Aviation. Findel is the airport for Luxembourg. 1,262,000 passengers and 335,168 tonnes of freight were handled in 1996. The national carrier is Luxair, 23·1% state-owned, which in 1995 operated 2 B-737-400s, 2 B-737-500s and 7 other aircraft. Services are also provided by Aeroflot, Air Berlin, Air France, Balkan Bulgarian, British Airways, Condor, Crossair, Hapag Lloyd, Iberia, Icelandair, KLM, Lufthansa, Malév, Sabena, Sterling Airways, TAP, Transavia and Tunis Air.

Shipping. A shipping register was set up in 1990. 59 vessels were registered at Sept. 1995.

Telecommunications. In 1996 there were 244,205 telephones and 106 post offices. The commercial Radio-Télé-Luxembourg broadcasts 1 programme in Letzebuergesch on FM. There are commercial and religious programmes in French, German, English and Italian. Ten TV programmes are broadcast. Colour transmission is by the SECAM system. In 1995 there were 155,000 TV sets in use and 260,000 radio receivers.

Cinemas. In 1994 there were 17 cinemas.

Press. There were 5 daily newspapers with a circulation of 135,000.

SOCIAL INSTITUTIONS

Religion. The population is 95% Roman Catholic.

Education. Education is compulsory for all children between the ages of 6 and 15. In 1995 there were 10,398 children in pre-primary school with 539 teachers; 27,082 pupils in primary schools; 25,607 pupils in secondary schools (including vocational training). In higher education (1993–94) the Higher Institute of Technology had 320 students and 973 students pursued university studies. In 1995–96 there were 271 students in teacher training. In 1994–95 the University Centre of Luxembourg had 1,100 students and 200 academic staff. Total expenditure on education, LUF18m.

Health. In 1996 there were 975 doctors and 229 dentists.

DIPLOMATIC REPRESENTATIVES

Of Luxembourg in Great Britain (27 Wilton Crescent, London, SWIX 8SD)
Ambassador: Joseph Weyland.

Of Great Britain in Luxembourg (14 Blvd Roosevelt, L-2450 Luxembourg)
Ambassador and Consul-General: J. N. Elam, CMG.

Of Luxembourg in the USA (2200 Massachusetts Ave., NW, Washington, D.C., 20008)
Ambassador: Alphonse Berns.

Of the USA in Luxembourg (22 Blvd. Emmanuel Servais, Luxembourg)
Ambassador: Clay Constantinou.

Of Luxembourg to the United Nations
Ambassador: Jean-Louis Wolzfeld.

Further Reading

STATEC. *Annuaire Statistique.*

The Institutions of the Grand Duchy of Luxembourg. Information and Press Service, Luxembourg, 1989

Calmes, C., *The Making of a Nation from 1815 up to our Days.* Luxembourg, 1989

Hury, C. and Christophory, J., *Luxembourg.* [Bibliography] Oxford and Santa Barbara, 1981

Newcomer, J., *The Grand Duchy of Luxembourg: the Evolution of Nationhood, 963 A.D. to 1983.* Washington, 1983

Trausch, G., *The Significance of the Historical Date of 1839.* Luxembourg, 1989

National Library: 37 Boulevard Roosevelt, Luxembourg City.

National statistical office: Service Central de la Statistique et des Etudes Economiques (STATEC), CP 304, Luxembourg City

Website: http://statec.gouvernement.lu/

MACEDONIA

Republika Makedonija

The Republic of Macedonia

(Former Yugoslav Republic of
Macedonia)

Capital: Skopje
Population: 1·98m.
GDP per head: (PPP$) 3,965
HDI/world rank: 0·748/80

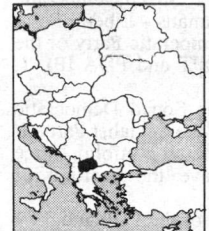

KEY HISTORICAL EVENTS. The history of
Macedonia can be traced to the reign of King Karan
(808–778 BC), but the country was at its most powerful at
the time of Philip II (359–336 BC) and Alexander the Great
(336–323 BC). At the end of the 6th century AD, Slavs
began to settle in Macedonia. There followed a long period
of internal fighting but the spread of Christianity led to consolidation and the creation of the first Macedonian Slav
state, the Kingdom of Samuel, 976–1018. In the 14th
century it fell to Serbia, and in 1355 to the Turks. After the
Balkan wars of 1912–13 Turkey was ousted, and Serbia
received part of the territory, the rest going to Bulgaria and Greece. In 1918 Yugoslav
Macedonia was incorporated into Serbia as South Serbia, becoming a republic in the
Socialist Federal Republic of Yugoslavia. Claims to the historical Macedonian
territory have long been a source of contention with Bulgaria and Greece. Macedonia
declared its independence on 20 Nov. 1992, and was admitted to the UN on 8 April
1993.

TERRITORY AND POPULATION. Macedonia is bounded in the north by
Yugoslavia, in the east by Bulgaria, in the south by Greece and in the west by
Albania. Its area is 25,713 sq. km. According to the 1994 census final results, the
population on 20 June 1994 was 1,945,932. The ethnic groups were Macedonians
(1,295,964), Albanians (441,104), Turks (78,019), Rhomas (43,707), Serbs (40,228),
Vlachs (8,601). There were 36,427 others and 1,882 not stated. Ethnic Albanians
predominate on the western side of Macedonia. Minorities are represented in the
Council for Inter-Ethnic Relations. 1996 population estimate, 1·98m.

The major cities (with 1994 census population) are: Skopje, the capital, 444,299;
Bitola, 77,464; Prilep, 68,148; Kumanovo, 71,853; Tetovo, 50,344.

Migration within the Republic of Macedonia, 1996: Emigrated persons, 11,653;
immigrated persons, 12,283; net migration 630. International (external) migration:
Emigrated persons, 220; immigrated persons 850.

Vital statistics, 1996; Births, 31,403; deaths, 16,063; marriages, 14,089; divorces,
705; infant deaths, 515. Rates (per 1,000 population): Birth, 15·8; death, 8·1;
marriage, 7·1; divorce, 0·3; natural increase, 7·7; infant mortality (per 1,000 live
births), 16·4. Expectation of life, 1994: Men, 69·56 years; women 74·01.

The official language is Macedonian, which uses the Cyrillic alphabet.

CLIMATE. Macedonia has a mixed Mediterranean-continental type climate, with
cold moist winters and hot dry summers. Skopje, Jan. –0·4°C, July 23·1°C.

CONSTITUTION AND GOVERNMENT. At a referendum held on 8 Sept.
1991 turn-out was 74%; 99% of votes cast were in favour of a sovereign Macedonia.
On 20 Nov. 1991 parliament promulgated a new constitution which proclaimed
Macedonia's independence.

The *President* is directly elected for 5-year terms. Candidates must be citizens
aged at least 40 years. The parliament is a 120-member single-chamber *Assembly*
(*Sobranie*), elected by universal suffrage for 4-year terms. There is a *Constitutional
Court* whose members are elected by the assembly for non-renewable 8-year terms,
and a *National Security Council* chaired by the President. Laws passed by the
Assembly must be countersigned by the President, who may return them for recon-
sideration, but cannot veto them if they gain a two-thirds majority.

Political Parties. The new Law on Political Parties makes a distinction between a political party and an association of citizens. The signatures of 500 citizens with the right to vote must be produced for a party to be legally registered. Presently the country has 34 legally registered parties.

Parliamentary composition (May 1997). Social Democratic League of Macedonia (SDSM), 61 members; Liberal-Democratic Party (LDP), 26; Party of Democratic Prosperity of the Albanians in Macedonia (PDP-A), 4; Party of Democratic Prosperity (PDP), 11; Socialist Party (SP), 6; National Democratic Party (NDP), 2; Party for the Complete Emancipation of the Romanies (PCER), 1; Social Democratic Party of Macedonia (SDP), 1; Democratic League of the Albanians - Liberal Party (DSA - LP), 1; Democratic Party of Macedonia (DPM), 1; Democratic Party of the Turks and the Party of Democratic Action - Islamic Way (DPT and PDA IP), 1; independent MPs, 5.

The present Cabinet has 20 members who come from the Social Democratic League of Macedonia, the Party of Democratic Prosperity, and the Socialist Party. It is composed of a Premier, 15 ministers with and 4 ministers without portfolio. Three of the ministers, one from each coalition party, also have the position of Vice-Premiers.

12 posts are held by members of the SDSM, 5 by members of the PDP and 3 by members of the SP. 15 ministers are Macedonian and 5 Albanian.

President: Kiro Gligorov (b. 1917)

The Liberal Party left the coalition in Feb. 1996, necessitating the formation of a new government, which comprised in March 1998:

Prime Minister: Branko Crvenkovski (b. 1962)

Deputy Prime Ministers: Jane Miljovski, Bekir Zuta, Naser Ziberi (also *Minister of Labour and Social Affairs*).

Members of the Government: Minister of Defence: Lazar Kitanovski; *Internal Affairs:* Tomislav Cokrevski; *External Affairs:* Blagoja Handziski; *Justice:* Gjorgi Spasov; *Finance:* Taki Fiti; *Economy:* Boris Rikalovski; *Development:* Abdimenaf Neziri; *Urbanism, Construction and Ecology:* Tome Trombov; *Transport and Communications:* Abdelmenaf Bedzheti; *Agriculture, Forestry and Water:* Kiro Dokuzovski; *Education and Sports:* Dr Sofija Todorova; *Science:* Aslan Selmani; *Culture:* Slobodan Unkovski; *Health:* Dr Petar Iliovski; *Ministers without Portfolio:* Dzemail Hajdari, Vlado Naumovski.

National anthem: 'Denes nad Makedonija se radja novo sonce na slobodata' ('Today a new sun of liberty appears over Macedonia').

Local government. Macedonia is administratively divided into 125 communes.

DEFENCE. The President is the C.-in-C. of the armed forces. There is conscription for 9 months. The Army numbered 15,400 (8,000 conscripts) in 1997, and was operating at least 4 Mi-8 transport helicopters, 3 Zlin 242 trainers and some light communications aircraft. There is a paramilitary police force of 7,500.

INTERNATIONAL RELATIONS. On 13 Sept. 1995 under the auspices of the UN, Macedonia and Greece agreed to normalize their relations.

Membership. Macedonia is a member of the UN, the Council of Europe and the Central European Initiative.

ECONOMY

Policy. According to the Privatization Agency, by the end of 1996 914 firms had been privatized, 257 were in the process of transformation, and 45 were awaiting privatization.

At the same time, a number of firms which had been experiencing heavy losses were obliged by law to embark on a re-structuring programme. Comprehensive measures were taken for a well-planned financial and ownership re-structuring of 25 large firms which had experienced extremely heavy losses.

Most of the firms in the country, ie 95·9%, are privately owned, 1·3% are publicly owned, 1·6% have mixed ownership, and 1·2% are co-operatives.

By the end of January 1997, 90,543 legal entities were registered in the Institute of Statistics.

Budget. In 1996 revenue and expenditure balanced at 46,364m. denars.

Currency. The national currency of Macedonia is the denar (MKD), of 100 deni. There are six banknotes—10, 50, 100, 500, 1,000 and 5,000 denars respectively—and coins of 50 deni, and 1, 2 and 5 denars. As of 31 Oct. 1997, gold reserves were US$25·1m. Inflation was 0·2% for 1996, and 4·55% for the first 10 months of 1997.

Banking and finance. The central bank and bank of issue is the National Bank of Macedonia. Its *Governor* is Dr Ljube Trpevski. As of 30 Sept. 1997, commercial banks' total non-government deposits were 17,774m. denars, and non-government savings deposits were 11,959m. denars.

A stock exchange opened in Skopje in 1996.

Weights and measures. The metric system is in use.

ENERGY AND NATURAL RESOURCES

Electricity. Output in 1996: 6,629,485 MWh, of which 1,435,852 MWh were hydro-electric.

Minerals. Macedonia is relatively rich in minerals, including lead, zinc, copper, iron, chromium, nickel, antimony, manganese, silver and gold. Output in 1996 (in tonnes): Lead-zinc ore 846,244; lead-zinc concentrates 53,561; copper ore 3,887,400; copper concentrate 47,219; chromium concentrate 919; refined silver 21.

Agriculture. At the 1994 census the active agricultural population was 91,354. In 1996, there were 657,689 ha of arable land and 631,704 ha of pasture. 143,276 ha of arable land were owned by agricultural organizations, and 460,684 ha by individual farmers.

Crop production, 1996 (in 1,000 tonnes): Wheat, 269; barley, 97; maize, 142; rice, 22; sugar-beet, 78; sunflower, 21; tobacco, 15; lucerne, 107; potatoes, 157; beans, 11; tomatoes, 146; peppers, 121; apples, 65; pears, 13; plums, 31; grapes, 215.

Livestock, 1996 (in 1,000): Cattle, 295; horses, 66; sheep, 1,814; pigs, 192. Livestock products, 1996 (in 1,000 tonnes): Beef, 7; pork, 9; mutton, 10; poultry, 2; wool, 3; honey, 1; cow's milk, 133m. litres; sheep's milk, 53m. litres; eggs (total), 435m.

There were 53,977 tractors in use in 1995.

Forestry. In 1996, the forest area was 1,021,139 ha, chiefly oak and beech. In 1996, 1,118,428 cu. metres of timber were cut.

Fisheries. Total catch of freshwater fish in 1995 was 1,500 tonnes live weight.

INDUSTRY. In 1996, there were 86,309 enterprises (82,658 private, 1,254 public, 1,005 co-operative, 1,366 mixed and 26 state-owned). Production (in tonnes): Ferro-alloys, 92,638; steel ingots, 1,617; buses, 608 (units); refrigerators, 22,337 (units); sulphuric acid, 99,545; medicines, 41; detergents, 20,229; wood pulp, 754; cotton yarn, 6,270.

Labour. At the 1994 census the population of working age was 1,247,481. In 1995, 356,617 persons were employed and 35,314 were self-employed. 216,222 persons (101,284 women) were seeking employment; unemployment rate, 35·6%.

FOREIGN ECONOMIC RELATIONS. The foreign debt of Macedonia, including debt taken over from the former Yugoslavia, was US$1,172.4m. on 31 Dec. 1996.

Commerce. Imports and exports (in US$1,000)

	1993	1994	1995	1996
Imports	1,199,351	1,484,092	1,718,904	1,147,440
Exports	1,055,298	1,086,341	1,204,048	1,626,917

Main export markets, 1996: Germany, Yugoslavia, Slovenia, Greece, Italy, Russia, Bulgaria, USA, Netherlands, Croatia.

Tourism. In 1996, 476,205 tourists spent 1·6m. nights in Macedonia.

COMMUNICATIONS

Roads. In 1996 there were 909 km of main roads, 3,058 km of regional roads and 5,656 km of local roads: 1,081 km of roads were macadamized, and 5,622 km asphalted. 17m. passengers and 2·2m. tonnes of freight were transported. There were 231,163 cars and 15,404 lorries.

Railways. In 1996 there were 699 km of railways (233 km electrified). 1·5m. passengers and 1·8m. tonnes of freight were transported.

Civil aviation. There are international airports at Skopje and Ohrid. Services are provided by Adria, Aeroflot, Albanian Airlines, Balkan, Croatia Airlines, Hamburg Airlines, Hemus and JAT. In 1996, 536,000 passengers and 3,807 tonnes of freight were carried.

Telecommunications. In 1996 there were 291 post offices and 514,769 telephones. The national Macedonian Radio and Television is government-funded. It broadcasts on 3 TV channels. There are also state-owned and private local TV stations. There were 89 local radio stations (56 private) in 1996, and 306,159 TV subscribers (colour by PAL).

Cinemas. There were 40 cinemas and 278,197 admissions in 1996.

Press. There were 4 national newspapers in 1996, 2 in Macedonian, 1 in Albanian and 1 in Turkish, and 142 other newspapers and periodicals.

SOCIAL INSTITUTIONS

Justice. Courts are autonomous and independent. Judges are tenured and elected for life on the proposal of the *Judicial Council*, whose members are themselves elected for renewable 6-year terms. The highest court is the Supreme Court. There are 28 courts of first instance and 3 higher courts.

Religion. Macedonia is traditionally Orthodox but the church is not established and there is freedom of religion. At the 1994 census 66·3% of the population were Orthodox, 30% Moslem and 0·4% Roman Catholic. In 1967 an autocephalous Orthodox church split off from the Serbian. Its head is the Archbishop of Ohrid and Macedonia whose seat is at Skopje. It has 5 bishoprics in Macedonia and representatives in USA, Canada and Australia. It has some 300 priests.

The Moslem Religious Union has a superiorate at Skopje. The Roman Catholic Church has a seat at Skopje.

Education. Education is free and compulsory for 8 years. In 1996, 37,506 children attended 52 pre-school institutions and 365 infant schools of elementary education. In 1996 there were 259,594 pupils enrolled in 1,044 primary, 83,402 in 91 secondary and (in 1995-96) 1,237 in higher schools, and 29,517 students in higher education. There are universities at Skopje (Cyril and Methodius, founded in 1949; 25,593 students and 1,177 academic staff in 1996-97) and Bitola (founded 1979; 5,161 students and 164 academic staff in 1996-97).

Health. In 1996 there were 4,464 doctors and 58 hospitals with 10,311 beds.

Welfare. In 1994 there were 216,838 pensioners (116,617 old age). 75,227 adults and 66,522 children received social benefits in 1993.

DIPLOMATIC REPRESENTATIVES

Of Macedonia in Great Britain (Harcourt House, 19A, Cavendish Sq., London, W1M 9AD)
Ambassador: Stevo Crvenkovski.

Of Great Britain in Macedonia (26 Ulica Veljko Vlahovic, 91000 Skopje)
Ambassador: Mark Dickinson.

Of Macedonia in the USA
Ambassador: Lubica Acevska.

Of the USA in Macedonia (Bd. Linden, 91000 Skopje)
Ambassador: Christopher R. Hill.

Of Macedonia to the United Nations
Ambassador: Naste Čalovski.

Of Macedonia to the European Union
Ambassador: Jovan Tegovski.

Further reading

Danforth, L. M., *The Macedonian Conflict: Ethnic Nationalism in a Transnational World.* Princeton Univ. Press, 1996
Poulton, H., *Who Are the Macedonians?* Farnborough, 1996

National statistical office. Republic of Macedonia Statisitical Office, Dame Gruev 4, Skopje.

MADAGASCAR

Repoblikan'i
Madagasikara

Capital: Antananarivo
Population: 14·1m.
GDP per head: (PPP$) 694
GNP: US$3·1bn.
HDI/world rank: 0·350/152

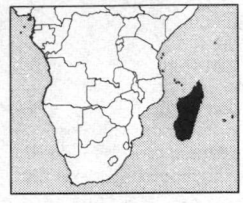

KEY HISTORICAL EVENTS. Evidence of human inhabitants on Madagascar dates back 2,000 years, and the island was settled by people of African and Indonesian origin when it was visited by the Portuguese explorer, Diego Diaz, in 1500. The island was unified under the Imérina monarchy between 1797 and 1861, but French claims to a protectorate led to hostilities culminating in the establishment of a French protectorate on 30 Sept. 1895. The monarchy was abolished and Madagascar became a French colony on 6 Aug. 1896.

Madagascar became an Overseas Territory of France in 1946, and on 14 Oct. 1958, following a referendum, was proclaimed the autonomous Malagasy Republic within the French community, achieving full independence on 26 June 1960.

In Feb. 1975 Col. Richard Ratsimandrava, Head of State, was assassinated. A National Military Directorate was established on 12 Feb. On 15 June it handed over power to a Supreme Revolutionary Council under Didier Ratsiraka. The 1975 Constitution instituted a 'Democratic Republic' in which only a single political party was permitted.

After 6 months of anti-government unrest, during which the opposition formed an alternative 'government', in Oct. 1991 the government and the Committee of Living Forces, a coalition of 16 opposition parties led by Albert Zafy, agreed to form an 18-month transitional administration. However, Zafy refused to join a government formed on 13 Nov., and was instead appointed chairman of the High State Authority for a Provisional Government formed on 23 Nov.

A new Constitution instituted the Third Republic in Sept. 1992.

TERRITORY AND POPULATION. Madagascar is situated off the south-east coast of Africa, from which it is separated by the Mozambique channel. Its area is 587,041 sq. km (226,658 sq. miles). At the 1993 census the population was 12,092,157 (50·45% female); density, 20·6 per sq. km. Estimate (1997), 14,062,000 (25% urban in 1994). Population density, 24·0 per sq. km.

Province	Area in Sq. km	Population (1993 census)	Chief town	Population (1993 census)
Antsiranana	43,046	942,410	Antsiranana	54,418 [1]
Mahajanga	150,023	1,330,612	Mahajanga	100,807
Toamasina	71,911	1,935,330	Toamasina	127,441
Antananarivo	58,283	3,483,236	Antananarivo	1,052,835
Fianarantsoa	102,373	2,671,150	Fianarantsoa	99,005
Toliary	161,405	1,729,419	Toliary	61,460 [1]

[1] 1990 estimate.

Vital statistics rates, 1997 estimates (per 1,000 population). Births, 42·3; deaths, 14·1. Infant mortality (per 1,000 live births), 92. Expectation of life in 1997 was 52·5 years (51·4 for males and 53·7 for females). Growth rate, 2·82% per annum.

The indigenous population is of Malayo–Polynesian stock, divided into 18 ethnic groups of which the principal are Merina (26%) of the central plateau, the Betsimisaraka (15%) of the east coast, and the Betsileo (12%) of the southern plateau. Foreign communities include Europeans, mainly French (30,000), Indians (15,000), Chinese (9,000), Comorians and Arabs.

The official language is Malagasy. French is the language of international communication.

CLIMATE. A tropical climate, but the mountains cause big variations in rainfall, which is very heavy in the east and very light in the west. Antananarivo. Jan. 70°F (21·1°C), July 59°F (15°C). Annual rainfall 54" (1,350 mm). Toamasina. Jan. 80°F (26·7°C), July 70°F (21·1°C). Annual rainfall 128" (3,256 mm).

CONSTITUTION AND GOVERNMENT. Following a referendum, a Constitution came into force on 30 Dec. 1975 establishing a Democratic Republic. It provided for a National People's Assembly elected by universal suffrage from the single list of the *Front National pour la Défense de la Révolution Socialiste Malgache.* Executive power was vested in the President with the guidance of a Supreme Revolutionary Council.

Under a convention of 31 Oct. 1991 the powers of the National People's Assembly and the Supreme Revolutionary Council were delegated to a High State Authority for a Provisional Government. Following a referendum on 19 Aug. 1992 at which turnout was 77·68% and 75·44% of votes cast were in favour a new Constitution was adopted on 21 Sept. 1992 establishing the Third Republic. Under this the *National Assembly* has 138 seats. Elections were held on 16 June 1993; the electorate was 6m. The Living Forces coalition gained 75 seats; the Movement for Proletarian Power, 59; others, 4.

A referendum on 17 Sept. 1995 was in favour of the President appointing and dismissing the Prime Minister, hitherto elected by parliament. The electorate was 6m.; turn-out was 50%.

At the first round of presidential elections on 3 Nov. 1996 there were 15 candidates. The electorate was 6,453,612, turn-out was 58·41%. President Albert Zafy gained 36·61% of votes cast. At the second round on 29 Dec. 1996 turn-out was 49·66%. Didier Ratsiraka was elected by 50·71% of votes cast

President: Didier Ratsiraka (b. 1935; sworn in 9 Feb. 1997).

In March 1998 the government comprised: *Prime Minister:* Pascal Rakotomavo.

Deputy Prime Minister in charge of Decentralization and Budget: Pierrot Rajaonarivelo. *Deputy Prime Minister in charge of the Economy and Finance:* Tantely Andrianarivo. *Deputy Prime Minister in charge of Foreign Affairs:* Herzio Razafimahaleo. *Minister of Agriculture:* M. Ranjakason. *Applied Research for Development:* Mantasoa Soloniaina Rakotonavahy. *Armed Forces:* Brig. Gen. Marcel Ranjeva. *Civil Service, Labour and Social Laws:* Jean Désiré Ratovonelinjafi. *Commerce and Consumption:* Auguste Paraina. *Energy and Mines:* Charles Rasoza. *Environment:* Colette Vaohita. *Fisheries and Ocean Resources:* Abdallah Houssen. *Health:* Henriette Rahantalalao. *Higher Education:* Ange Randrianarisoa. *Industrialization and Crafts:* Manassé Esoavelomandroso. *Information, Culture and Communication:* Fredo Betsimifira. *Interior:* Col. Jean-Jacques Rasolondraibe. *Justice:* Anaclet Imbiky. *Livestock:* Capt. Corvette Ndrianasolo. *Population and Solidarity:* Ernest Njara. *Posts and Telecommunications:* Ny Hasina Andriamanjato. *Public Works:* Col. Emile Tsaranazy. *Private Sector and Privatization:* Horace Constant. *Scientific Research:* Lila Ratsifandramanana. *Secondary and Primary Education:* Simon Jacquit. *Technical and Professional Education:* Boniface Levolo. *Tourism:* Juliette Raharisoa. *Transport and Meteorology:* Naivo Ramamonjisoa. *Urban and Territorial Development:* Herivelona Ramanantsoa. *Water Resources and Forests:* Rija Rajohnson. *Youth and Sports:* Lina Andriamifidimanana.

National anthem: 'Ry tanindrazanay malala ô!' ('O our beloved Fatherland'); words by Pastor Rahajason, tune by N. Raharisoa.

Local Government: The 6 provinces (*faritany*) are sub-divided into 113 *fivondronana*, which in turn are divided into 13,476 *fokontany* (the traditional communal divisions). Each level is governed by an elected council.

DEFENCE. There is conscription (including civilian labour service) for 18 months. In 1996 government expenditure on defence totalled MGFr151,200m.

Army. The Army is organized in 2 battalion groups, and 1 engineer regiment. Equipment includes 12 PT-76 light tanks. Strength (1997) 20,000 and gendarmerie, 7,500.

Navy. In 1997 the maritime force had a strength of 500 (including 100 marines), and was equipped with 1 250-tonne patrol craft, 1 medium landing ship, 4 landing craft, together with a 1,200-tonne former trawler used for transport and training.

Air Force. Equipment includes 1 Britten-Norman Defender armed transport, 2 C-47s, and 1 Yak-40 for VIP use, 1 Aztec, 2 Cessna Skymasters, 4 Cessna 172Ms and 4 Mi-8 helicopters. Personnel (1997), 500. The 12 MiG-17 and MiG-21 combat aircraft are grounded.

INTERNATIONAL RELATIONS

Membership. Madagascar is a member of the UN, OAU and is an ACP state of the EU.

ECONOMY

Budget. Budget revenue and expenditure (in MGFr1,000m.):

	1992	1993	1994	1995	1996
Revenue:	503·6	556·0	748·5	1,148·7	1,404·6
Expenditure:	817·3	996·4	1,379·7	1,921·0	2,177·5

Currency. The unit of currency is the *Malagasy franc* (MGFr). 1 *ariary* = MGFr5. There are coins of MGFr1, 2, 5, 10, 20, 25, 50, 100 and 250 banknotes of MGFr500, 1,000, 2,500, 5,000, 10,000 and 25,000. MGFr317,230m. were in circulation in 1992. In 1996 foreign exchange reserves were US$240·8m. Inflation in 1996 was 19·8%.

Banking and Finance. A Central Bank was formed in 1973, replacing the former *Institut d'Emission Malgache* as the central bank of issue. All commercial banking and insurance was nationalized in 1975 and privatized in 1988. Industrial development is financed through the *Bankin'ny Indostria*. Other commercial banking is undertaken by the *Bankin'ny Tantsaha Mpamokatra*, the *Banky Fampandrosoana ny Varotra*. The Malagasy Bank of the Indian Ocean was set up in Sept. 1990 as part of a bank privatization programme.

Weights and Measures. The metric system is in use.

ENERGY AND NATURAL RESOURCES

Electricity. Production (1992) 484m. kWh (303m. kWh hydro-electric).

Oil and Gas. Annual crude oil production is 37,000 tonnes. Natural gas production is 2,500 tonnes per annum.

Minerals. Mining production in 1995 (provisional figures) included: Salt, 80,000 tonnes; chromite, 74,000 tonnes; graphite, 13,900 tonnes.

Agriculture. 80–85% of the workforce is employed in agriculture. The principal agricultural products in 1995 were (estimates in 1,000 tonnes): Rice, 2,596; cassava, 2,420; sugar-cane, 1,980; sweet potatoes, 560; vegetables and melons, 333; potatoes, 270; bananas, 210; mangoes, 200.

Cattle breeding and agriculture are the chief occupations. There were, in 1995, an estimated 10,309,000 cattle, 1,592,000 pigs, 1,300,000 goats and 740,000 sheep.

Forestry. The forests cover 14·7m. ha (about 25% of the land surface) and contain many valuable woods, while gum, resins and plants for tanning, dyeing and medicinal purposes abound. Production (1994) 10·6m. cu. metres.

Fisheries. In 1989 the fishing fleet numbered 44 vessels over 100 GRT totalling 6,852 GRT. The catch of sea fish in 1995 was 120,140 tonnes.

INDUSTRY. Industry, hitherto confined mainly to the processing of agricultural products, is now extending to cover other fields.

Labour. In 1995 the workforce was estimated to be 7,020,000.

FOREIGN ECONOMIC RELATIONS. Foreign debt was US$4,200m. in 1995.

Commerce. Exports, 1996 estimate, US$493m.; imports, US$612m. Chief exports (1995) were coffee (45%), vanilla (20%), plus cloves, shellfish (especially prawns), sugar and petroleum products. Principal imports in 1995 were intermediate manufactures (30%), capital goods (28%), plus petroleum products, consumer goods and foodstuffs. France is the leading partner for both exports and imports, with other important markets for exports being the USA, Germany and Japan and major suppliers of imports being Japan, the Southern African Customs Union and the USA.

Tourism. There were an estimated 78,800 tourists in 1995.

COMMUNICATIONS

Roads. In 1995 there were 49,837 km of roads (5,731 km paved). In 1995 there were 58,100 passenger cars, 11,000 lorries and vans and 4,340 buses and coaches.

Railways. In 1994 there were 883 km of railways, all metre gauge. In 1994, 0·6m. passengers and 0·3m. tonnes of freight were transported.

Civil Aviation. There are international airports at Antananarivo (Ivato) and Mahajanga (Amborovy). The national carrier is Air Madagascar, which is 89·5% state-owned, and in 1995 operated 1 B-737-200, 1 B-737-200 Adv, 1 B-737-300, 1 B-747-200B Combi and 7 other aircraft. There are also services by Air France and Air Mauritius. In 1988, 452,000 passengers and 9,169 tonnes of cargo arrived and departed.

Shipping. In 1989, 760,100 tonnes were loaded and 1,062,900 tonnes unloaded at Toamasina, Mahajanga, Antsiranana and Nosy-Be. In 1995, registered merchant marine totalled 37,721 GRT, including oil tankers, 13,859 GRT.

Telecommunications. There are 724 post offices and agencies. There were (1993) about 35,000 main telephones. The government-controlled Radio-Television Malagasy is responsible for broadcasting. There are radio programmes in Malagasy and French, and 3–4 hours TV transmission a day (colour by SECAM). In 1995 there were 2·8m. radio and 0·29m. TV sets.

Cinemas. In 1991 there were 11 cinemas with an annual attendance of 0·4m.

Press. In 1995 there were 6 daily newspapers with a total circulation of 59,000.

SOCIAL INSTITUTIONS

Justice. The Supreme Court and the Court of Appeal are in Antananarivo. In most towns there are Courts of First Instance for civil and commercial cases. For criminal cases there are ordinary criminal courts in most towns. In 1996 government expenditure on public order and safety totalled MGFr59,200m.

Religion. About 50% of the population practise the traditional religion, 43% are Christians (of whom approximately half are Roman Catholic and half are Protestant, mainly belonging to the Fiangonan'i Jesosy Kristy eto Madagasikara) and 7% Moslem.

Education. Education is compulsory from 6 to 14 years of age. In 1994 there were 13,624 primary schools with 37,676 teachers for 1·5m. pupils, 298,241 pupils at secondary level with 15,118 teachers and (1993) 42,681 students at university level. In 1994–95 there were 6 universities. In 1996 government expenditure on education totalled MGFr255,500m. Adult literacy rate (1995) was 45·7% (male, 59·8%; female, 32%).

Health. There are 249 state hospitals and 1,904 health centres. In 1996 government expenditure on health totalled MGFr191,300m.

Welfare. In 1996 government expenditure on social security and welfare totalled MGFr26,000m.

DIPLOMATIC REPRESENTATIVES

Of Madagascar in Great Britain
Ambassador: Vacant (resides in Paris)

Of Great Britain in Madagascar (Immeuble 'Ny Havana', Cite de 67 Ha, Antananarivo)
Ambassador: Robert S. Dewar.

Of Madagascar in the USA (2374 Massachusetts Ave., NW, Washington, D.C., 20008)
Ambassador: Pierrot J. Rajaonarivelo.

Of the USA in Madagascar (14 rue Rainitovo, Antsahavola, Antananarivo)
Ambassador: Vicki Huddleston.

Of Madagascar to the United Nations
Ambassador: Vacant.

Of Madagascar to the European Union
Ambassador: Jean Beriziky.

Further Reading

Banque des Données de l'Etat. *Bulletin Mensuel de Statistique*
Allen, P. M., *Madagascar*. Boulder (CO), 1995
Brandt, H., *Guide to Madagascar*. Chalfont St Peter, 1988
Bradt, H. and Brown, M., *Madagascar*. [Bibliography]. Oxford and Santa Barbara, 1993
Deschamps, H., *Histoire de Madagascar*. Paris, 4th ed. 1972
Rabetafika, R., *Réforme Fiscal et Révolution Socialiste à Madagascar*. Paris, 1990
Rajoelina, P. and Ramelet, A., *Madagascar, la Grande Ile*. Paris, 1989
Ramahatra, O., *Madagascar: une Economie en Phase d'Ajustement*. Paris, 1989

National statistical office: Banque des Données de l'Etat, Antananarivo.

MALAŴI

Dziko la Malaŵi—

Republic of Malaŵi

Capital: Lilongwe
Population: 11m.
GDP per head: (PPP$) 694
GNP: US$1·6bn.
HDI/world rank: 0·320/161

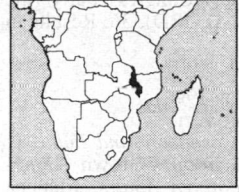

KEY HISTORICAL EVENTS. A powerful kingdom dominated much of Malaŵi and the surrounding area from the 15th to the 18th centuries, based on the Bantu-speaking people who began settling there 200 years earlier. However, by the beginning of the 19th century, this had disintegrated into many small entities, and occupation by Ngoni people from the south facilitated European control. The explorer David Livingstone reached Lake Nyasa, now Lake Malaŵi, in 1859 and it was the land along the lake's western shore that became, in 1891, the British Protectorate of Nyasaland. The name was changed to British Central Africa Protectorate in 1893 but reverted to Nyasaland in 1907.

In 1884 the British South Africa Company applied for a charter to trade. Within a few years the slavery and the slave trade had been suppressed. Pressure on land, the colour bar and other grievances about colonial rule generated Malaŵian resistance which was only checked by 1915. After the Second World War, the Nyasaland African Congress was formed to lead a new wave of resistance, particularly against the impending federation of the country to two neighbouring British colonies.

In 1953 Nyasaland was joined with Southern Rhodesia (Zimbabwe) and Northern Rhodesia (Zambia) to form the Federation of Rhodesia and Nyasaland, under British control. This union was dissolved in 1963 when Nyasaland was for a year self-governing, until on 6 July 1964 it became independent, adopting the name of Malaŵi. In 1966 Malaŵi was declared a republic and Dr Hastings Banda became the first president. Jailed in 1959–60 for his activities in the resistance, Banda had led the Malaŵi Congress Party to victory in elections in 1961 and established a one party dictatorship which lasted for 30 years. In 1994, with the election of Bakili Muluzi, Malaŵi returned to multi-party democracy.

TERRITORY AND POPULATION. Malaŵi lies along the southern and western shores of Lake Malaŵi (the third largest lake in Africa), and is otherwise bounded in the north by Tanzania, south by Mozambique and west by Zambia. Area (including the inland water areas of Lake Malombe, Chilwa, Chiuta and the Malaŵi portion of Lake Malaŵi, which total 24,208 sq. km), 118,484 sq. km (45,747 sq. miles).

Population at census 1987, 7,982,607. Estimate (1996), 11m. (12% urban). Population of main towns (census 1987): Blantyre, 331,588; Lilongwe, 233,973; Mzuzu, 44,238; Zomba, 42,878. Population of the regions, census 1987 (and census 1977): Northern, 907,121 (648,853); Central, 3,116,038 (2,143,716); Southern, 3,959,448 (2,754,891).

The birth rate is 50·2 per 1,000 population and the death rate 22·7. Expectation of life is 41·1 years.

The official languages are Chichewa, spoken by over 50% of the population, and English.

CLIMATE. The tropical climate is marked by a dry season from May to Oct. and a wet season for the remaining months. Rainfall amounts are variable, within the range of 29–100" (725–2,500 mm), and maximum temperatures average 75–89°F (24–32°C), and minimum temperatures 58–67°F (14·4–19·4°C). Lilongwe. Jan. 73°F (22·8°C), July 60°F (15·6°C). Annual rainfall 36" (900 mm). Blantyre. Jan. 75°F (23·9°C), July 63°F (17·2°C). Annual rainfall 45" (1,125 mm). Zomba. Jan. 73°F (22·8°C), July 63°F (17·2°C). Annual rainfall 54" (1,344 mm).

CONSTITUTION AND GOVERNMENT. The *President* is also head of

Government. Malaŵi was a one-party state, but following a referendum on 14 June 1993, in which 63% of votes cast were in favour of reform, a new Constitution was adopted on 17 May 1994 which ended Hastings Banda's life presidency and provided for the holding of multi-party elections. At these Bakili Muluzi was elected President by 47·16% of votes cast against President Banda and 2 other opponents.

Parliament is composed of 177 members. At the elections of 17 May 1994 the United Democratic Front (UDF) won 84 seats; the Malaŵi Congress Party (the former single party), 55; and the Alliance for Democracy (AFORD), 36. Results in the remaining 2 seats were nullified.

In March 1998 the government comprised:
President: Bakili Muluzi (b. 1943; UDF; sworn in 21 May 1994).
First Vice-President and Minister of Finance: Justin Malewezi.
Minister of Agriculture and Irrigation: Aleka Banda. *Commerce and Industry:* Matembo Nzunda. *Defence:* Joseph Kubwalo. *Education:* Brown James Mpinganjira. *Energy and Mining:* Dr Jombo Lemani. *Foreign Affairs:* Mapopa Chipeta. *Forestry, Fisheries and Environmental Affairs:* Mayinga Mkandawire. *Health and Population:* Harry Thompson. *Home Affairs:* Melvin Moyo. *Information and Broadcasting, Posts and Telecommunications:* Sam Mpasu. *Justice and Attorney-General:* Cassim Chilumpha. *Labour and Vocational Training:* Dr Kaliyoma Phumisa. *Lands, Housing, Physical Planning and Surveys:* Peter Fachi. *Local Government and Sports:* Chakakala Chaziya. *National Heritage:* Richard Sombereka. *Tourism, Parks and Wildlife:* Patrick Mbewe. *Transport and Civil Aviation:* Kamangadazi Chambalo. *Water Development:* Edward Bwanali. *Women, Children's Affairs, Community Development and Social Welfare:* Lilian Patel. *Works and Supplies:* Abdul Pillane.

National anthem: 'O God Bless our Land of Malaŵi'; words and tune by M.-F. Sauka.

Local Government. There are 3 regions and 24 districts, each administered by a district commissioner.

DEFENCE. All services form part of the Army.

Army. The army is organized into 3 infantry battalions, 1 support battalion and 1 commando battalion. Personnel (1997) 5,000.

Navy. 3 patrol craft, 2 landing craft and some boats operated by about (1997) 220 personnel based at Chilumba on Lake Nyasa.

Air Wing. To support the infantry battalion, the Air Wing has 2 C-47 and 4 Do 228 light transports, and 2 Ecureuil helicopters. An HS 125 jet is used for VIP transport. Personnel (1997), 80. There is also a paramilitary police force numbering 1,000.

INTERNATIONAL RELATIONS

Membership. Malaŵi is a member of the UN, the Commonwealth, OAU and SADC and is an ACP state of the EU.

ECONOMY

Policy. The government operates a 3-year 'rolling' public-sector investment programme, revised annually to take into account changing needs and the expected level of resources available. The greatest part of the development programme is annually financed from external aid. Some 200 state enterprises are marked down for privatization. Inflation has fallen from 98·2% in 1994 to 7% in 1997 and interest rates have come down from 37% to 24%.

Budget. Revenue Account receipts and expenditure (in K.1,000) for years ending 31 March:

	1993–94	1994–95	1995–96	1996–97
Revenue	1,569,270	2,194,590	4,355,830	5,728,170
Expenditure	3,263,930	4,286,030	7,101,930	8,877,000

Currency. The unit of currency is the *kwacha* (MWK) of 100 *tambala*. There are coins of 1, 2, 5, 10, 20 and 50 tambalas, and notes of 1, 5, 10, 20, 50 and 100 kwachas. In 1991 currency in circulation totalled K.240·88m. Foreign exchange reserves were K.390·7m. in 1991. Foreign exchange controls were abolished in Feb. 1994.

Banking and Finance. The central bank and bank of issue is the Reserve Bank of Malaŵi (founded 1964). There are 2 commercial banks and an Investment Development Bank.

Weights and Measures. The metric system is in use.

ENERGY AND NATURAL RESOURCES

Electricity. The Electricity Supply Commission of Malaŵi is the sole supplier. Capacity is 220 MW with demand at 180 MW. In 1997 Malaŵi and Mozambique came to an agreement on the construction of an oil pipeline between the two countries.

Minerals. The main product in 1976 was marble (149,254 tonnes) for the manufacture of cement. Coal mining began in 1985.

Agriculture. Malaŵi is predominantly an agricultural country. In 1997 agriculture contributed about 40% to the GDP, and agricultural produce accounted for 90% of export earnings. Maize is the main subsistence crop and is grown by over 95% of all smallholders; production, 1995, 2,033m. tonnes. Tobacco is the chief cash crop, providing 70% of export earnings. Also important are groundnuts, cassava, millet and rice. There are large plantations which produce sugar, tea and coffee. Production (1995): Tobacco, 129,630 tonnes; sugar-cane, 1,980,000 tonnes; tea, 34,160 tonnes.

Livestock in 1993: Cattle, 0·97m.; sheep, 0·2m.; goats, 0·89m.; pigs, 0·24m.; chickens, 9m.

Forestry. There are 4·3m. ha of forests; 46% of the land area. Production, 1997, 10·2m. cu. metres.

Fisheries. Landings in 1995 were 45,427 tonnes.

INDUSTRY. Index of manufacturing output in 1995 (1984 = 100): manufacturing for domestic consumption, excluding mining and quarrying, 114·9; of this consumer goods were at 127 and intermediate goods for building and construction were at 85·2. Manufacturing for export, 116·7.

FOREIGN ECONOMIC RELATIONS

Commerce. Major exports 1995 (in K.1m.): Tobacco, 4,051; tea, 427·8; sugar, 481·7; cotton, 57·7; groundnuts, 4·0. Major imports: Petroleum products, 214,820 cu. metres.

Trade statistics for calendar years are (in K.1m.):

	1992	1993	1994	1995
Imports	2,066·8	2,349·8	3,295·7	6,318·8
Exports	1,427·1	1,396·6	3,253·7	6,559·2

Tourism. There were 230,000 tourists in 1997.

COMMUNICATIONS

Roads. There are 4,520 km of main roads (2,564 km bitumen, 1,956 km earth or gravel); 2,768 km of secondary roads (285 km bitumen, 2,483 km earth or gravel); 6,789 km of district roads (all earth or gravel); and 517 km of other roads. A major repair programme is under way.

Railways. Malaŵi Railways and its subsidiary the Central Africa Railway operate 797 km on 1,067 mm gauge, providing links to the Mozambican ports of Beira and Nacala. In 1995 railways carried 0·4m. passengers and 0·3m. tonnes of freight.

Civil Aviation. The national carrier is the state-owned Air Malaŵi (soon to be privatized), which operates 2 Boeing 737s, an ATR 45-seater, a 19-seater Dornier and a 14-seater Cessna Caravan. Air Malaŵi flies to a number of regional centres in Mozambique, Zambia, Zimbabwe, South Africa, Tanzania and Kenya and operates a service to Dubai. There are airports at Lilongwe (Kamuzu International Airport) and Chileka. In 1995 315,595 passengers and 6,463 tonnes of freight were handled. Services are also provided by Air Zimbabwe, British Airways, Ethiopian Airways, Kenya Airways, KLM, Northwest Airlines and SAA.

Shipping. In 1995 lake ships carried 169,000 passengers and 6,000 tonnes of freight.

Telecommunications. Number of telephones (1995) 42,000. The Malaŵi Broadcasting Corporation, a statutory body, broadcasts in English and Chichewa. There were 2·45m. radio sets in 1994.

Press *The Daily Times* (English, Monday to Friday); 17,000 copies daily. *Malaŵi News* (English and Chichewa, Saturdays); 23,000 copies weekly. *Odini* (English and Chichewa); 8,500 copies fortnightly. *Boma Lathu* (Chichewa); 80,000 copies monthly. *Za Alimi* (English and Chichewa); 10,000 copies monthly.

SOCIAL INSTITUTIONS

Justice. Justice is administered in the High Court, the magistrates' courts and traditional courts. There are 23 magistrates' courts, 176 traditional courts and 23 local appeal courts. Appeals from traditional courts are dealt with in the traditional appeal courts and in the national traditional appeal court. Appeals from magistrates' courts lie to the High Court, and appeals from the High Court to Malaŵi's Supreme Court of Appeal.

Religion. In 1992 there 6·12m. Christians and 1·54m. Moslems. In 1988 the Roman Catholic Church claimed 1·5m. members.

Education. Adult literacy is 55·8%. Fees for primary education were abolished in 1994. In 1995–96 the number of pupils in primary schools was 3m. The primary school course is of 8 years' duration, followed by a 4-year secondary course. English is taught from the 1st year and becomes the general medium of instruction from the 4th year.

The University of Malaŵi had 3,657 students and 366 academic staff in 1994–95. There were also 4 colleges and 1 polytechnic.

Health. There are two central hospitals, one general hospital, one mental hospital, two leprosaria and 45 hospitals of which 21 are government district hospitals.

DIPLOMATIC REPRESENTATIVES

Of Malaŵi in Great Britain (33 Grosvenor St., London, W1X 0DE)
High Commissioner: T. Jake Muwamba.

Of Great Britain in Malaŵi (PO Box 30042, Lilongwe, 3)
High Commissioner: J. F. R. Martin, CMG.

Of Malaŵi in the USA (2408 Massachusetts Ave., NW, Washington, D.C., 20008)
Ambassador: Willie Chokani.

Of the USA in Malaŵi (PO Box 30016, Lilongwe, 3)
Ambassador: Peter Chaveas.

Of Malaŵi to the United Nations
Ambassador: David Rubadiri.

Of Malaŵi to the European Union
Ambassador: Julie Mphande.

Further Reading

National Statistical Office. *Monthly Statistical Bulletin*
Ministry of Economic Planning and Development. *Economic Report.* Annual
Decalo, S., *Malaŵi.* [Bibliography]. 2nd ed. Oxford and Santa Barbara (CA), 1995

National statistical office: National Statistical Office, POB 333, Zomba.

MALAYSIA

Persekutuan Tanah Malaysia

(Federation of Malaysia)

Capital: Kuala Lumpur
Population: 21·7m.
GDP per head: (PPP$) 8,865
GNP per capita: US$68·7bn.
HDI/world rank: 0·832/60

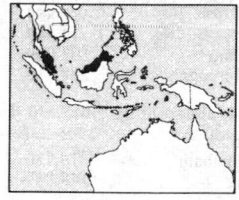

KEY HISTORICAL EVENTS. Malaysia is a federation consisting of the eleven States of Peninsular Malaysia and the two states of Sabah and Sarawak.

The Portuguese were the first Europeans to settle in the area and Malacca became a Portuguese possession in 1541. The Dutch took Malacca in 1641 and held it until 1794 when it was occupied by the British who had established three trading posts at the end of the 18th century. Although Malacca was returned to the Dutch in 1814, it was finally ceded to Britain in 1824. At the same time (1814-24) Stamford Raffles established a settlement and Singapore became British territory.

In 1826 Singapore and Malacca were incorporated with Penang to form the Straits Settlements. In 1896 Negri Sembilan, Penang, Perak and Selangor became the Federated Malay States; these were 'protected' states and were not part of the Straits Settlements. The remaining five Malay states became known as the Unfederated Malay States.

Singapore and what is now Malaysia were occupied by the Japanese from 1941 to 1945. Soon thereafter, in Jan. 1946, plans were published to create a Malaysian Union excluding Singapore but including the four Federated and the five Unfederated Malay States and the Settlements of Penang and Malacca. The Union came into being in April 1946 but was soon abandoned in the face of opposition. However, in Jan. 1948 the Union was reconstituted as the Federation of Malaya.

From 1948 to 1960 a State of Emergency existed in order to counter revolt by Malayan Communists aimed at the disruption of the country's economy. Commonwealth forces supported the Federation's own armed forces.

Following lengthy negotiations independence was granted to the Federation of Malaya on 31 Aug. 1857.

On 31 Aug. 1963 Malaysia was created from the Federation of Malaya, Singapore, North Borneo (renamed Sabah) and Sarawak. Brunei was also invited to join but no agreement could be reached. The UK relinquished sovereignty over Singapore, North Borneo and Sarawak from independence day and extended the 1957 defence agreement with Malaya to apply to Malaysia. Malaysia became a member of the Commonwealth. Singapore left Malaysia on 9 Aug. 1965 to become an independent sovereign state.

TERRITORY AND POPULATION. The federal state of Malaysia comprises the 11 states and 1 federal territory of Peninsular Malaysia, bounded in the north by Thailand, and with the island of Singapore as an enclave on its southern tip; and, on the island of Borneo to the east, the state of Sabah (which includes the federal territory of the island of Labuan), and the state of Sarawak, with Brunei as an enclave, both bounded in the south by Indonesia and in the north-west and north-east by the South China and Sulu Seas.

The area of Malaysia is 329,758 sq. km (127,317 sq. miles) and the population (1997 estimate) is 21·7m.; density, 62 per sq. km. The growth of the population has been:

Year	Peninsular Malaysia	Sarawak	Sabah/Labuan	Total Malaysia
1980	11,426,613	1,307,582	1,011,046	13,745,241
1990	14,127,556	1,648,217	1,791,209	17,566,982
1997	17,047,300	1,954,300	2,663,800	21,665,400

933

The areas, populations and chief towns of the states and federal territories are:

Peninsular States	Area (in sq. km)	Population (1997 estimate)	Chief Town	Population (1996 census)
Johor	18,986	2,554,100	Johor Baharu	328,436
Kedah	9,426	1,530,100	Alor Setar	124,412
Kelantan	14,943	1,447,000	Kota Baharu	219,582
Kuala Lumpur[1]	243	1,231,500	Kuala Lumpur	1,145,342
Malacca	1,650	582,000	Malacca	75,909
Negeri Sembilan	6,643	810,500	Seremban	182,869
Pahang	35,965	1,239,000	Kuantan	199,484
Penang	1,031	1,222,100	Penang (Georgetown)	219,603
Perak	21,005	2,094,800	Ipoh	382,853
Perlis	795	217,400	Kangar	14,247
Selangor	7,956	2,999,800	Shah Alam	102,019
Terengganu	12,955	975,800	Kuala Terengganu	228,119

Other states		Population (1997 estimate)		
Labuan[1]	91	70,400	Victoria	. . .
Sabah	73,711	2,593,400	Kota Kinabalu	76,120
Sarawak	124,449	1,954,300	Kuching	148,059

[1] Federal territory.

Other large cities (1997 estimate): Petaling Jaya (254,350), Kelang (243,355), Taiping (183,261), Sibu (126,381), Sandakan (125,841) and Miri (87,167).

Vital statistics rates, 1996 (per 1,000 population): Birth, 26·1, (25·9 in 1997); death, 4·6; infant mortality rate 9·8 per 1,000 live births (9·3 in 1997); natural increase, 21·7 per 1,000 (21·4 in 1997). Life expectancy: Males, 69·3 (1996), 69·5 (1997); females, 74·1 (1996), 74·3 (1997).

CLIMATE. Malaysia lies near the Equator between latitudes 1° and 7° North and longitudes 100° and 119° East. Malaysia is subject to maritime influence and the interplay of wind systems which originate in the Indian Ocean and the South China Sea. The year is generally divided into the South-East and the North-East Monsoon seasons. The average daily temperature throughout Malaysia varies from 21° C to 32° C. Humidity is high.

CONSTITUTION AND GOVERNMENT. The Constitution of Malaysia is based on the Constitution of the former Federation of Malaya, but includes safeguards for the special interests of Sabah and Sarawak. It was amended in 1983.

The Constitution provides for one of the Rulers of the Malay States to be elected from among themselves to be the *Yang di-Pertuan Agong* (Supreme Head of the Federation). He holds office for a period of 5 years. The Rulers also elect from among themselves a Deputy Supreme Head of State, also for a period of 5 years.

In Feb. 1993 the Rulers accepted constitutional amendments abolishing their legal immunity.

Supreme Head of State (Yang di-Pertuan Agong): HM Tuanku Ja'afar ibni Al-Marhum Tuanku Abdul Rahman, D.K., D.K.M., D.M.N., D.K.M.B., elected as 10th *Yang di-Pertuan Agong* on 4 Feb. 1994, crowned 26 April 1994.

Deputy Supreme Head of State, Sultan of Selangor: HRH Sultan Salahuddin Abdul Aziz Shah ibni Al-Marhum Sultan Hisamuddin 'Alam Shah Al-Haj, D.K., D.M.N., S.P.M.S., S.S.S.A., D.K.M.B., S.P.D.K., D.P., D.U.N.M., P.J.K., acceded 3 Sept. 1960.

Raja of Perlis: HRH Tuanku Syed Putra ibni Al-Marhum Syed Hassan Jamalullail, D.K., D.K.M., D.M.N., S.M.N., S.P.M.P., S.P.D.K., D.K.M.B., acceded 12 March 1949.

Sultan of Kedah: HRH Tuanku Haji Abdul Halim Mu'adzam Shah ibni AlMarhum Sultan Badlishah, D.K., D.K.H., D.K.M., D.M.N., D.U.K., S.P.M.K., S.S.D.K., D.P., D.U.N.M., D.H.M.S., acceded 20 Feb. 1959.

Sultan of Johor: HRH Sultan Mahmood Iskandar ibni Al-Marhum Sultan Ismail, D.K., S.P.M.J., S.P.D.K., D.K. (Brunei), S.S.I.J., P.I.S., B.S.I., acceded 11 May 1981 (Supreme Head of State from 26 April 1984 to 25 April 1989), returned as Sultan of Johor 26 April 1989.

Sultan of Perak: HRH Sultan Azlan Shah Muhibbuddin Shah ibni Almarhum Sultan Yussuf Izzuddin Ghafarullahu-lahu Shah, D.K., D.M.N., P.M.N., S.P.C.M., S.P.M.P., D.K.M., D.K.M.B., S.S.M., P.S.M., S.P.T.S., S.I.M.P.

Regent of Negeri Sembilan: HRH Tengku Naquiyuddin, D.K.Y.R., S.P.N.S., P.P.T., appointed 26 April 1994.

Sultan of Kelantan: HRH Sultan Ismail Petra ibni Al-Marhum Sultan Yahya Petra, D.K., S.P.M.K., S.J.M.K., S.P.S.M., D.M.N., D.K.M.B., D.P.S.S., S.P.K.K., S.P.S.K., D.P., appointed 29 March 1979.

Sultan of Trengganu: HRH Sultan Mahmud Al-Marhum ibni Al-Marhum Tuanku Al-Sultan Ismail Nasiruddin Shah, D.K., S.P.M.T., S.P.C.M., D.M.N., S.S.M.T., D.K.M.B., D.P. appointed 2 Sept. 1979.

Sultan of Pahang: Sultan Haji Ahmad Shah Al-Musta'in Billah ibni Al-Marhum Sultan Abu Bakar Ri'Ayatuddin Al-Mu'Adzam Shah, D.K.M., D.K.P., D.K., S.S.A.P., S.P.C.M., S.P.M.J., S.I.M.P., D.M.N.

Yang di-Pertua Negeri Pulau Pinang: HE Tun Haji Hamdan Sheikh Tahir, S.M.N., P.S.M., D.U.P.N., D.P., D.M.P.N., appointed 2 May 1989.

Yang di Pertua Negeri Melaka: HE Tun Datuk Seri Utama Syed Ahmad Al-Haj bin Syed Mahmud Shahabudin, S.S.M., P.S.M., D.U.N.M., S.P.M.K., S.S.D.K., P.G.D.K., P.N.B.S., J.M.N., J.P., S.M.N., S.P.M.S., D.P., appointed 4 Dec. 1984.

Yang di-Pertua Negeri Sarawak: HE Datuk Patinggi Haji Ahmad Zaidi Adruce bin Muhammed Noor, S.S.M., D.P., D.U.N.M., P.N.B.S., B.M. Adipradana (Indonesia), S.M.N., D.U.P.N., appointed 2 April 1985.

Yang di-Pertua Negeri Sabah: HE Tan Sri Sakaran Dandai, P.M.N., S.P.D.K., D.S.M., S.S.A.P., P.G.D.K., A.D.K., J.P., appointed 31 Dec. 1994.

The federal parliament consists of the *Yang di-Pertuan Agong* and two *Majlis* (Houses of Parliament) known as the *Dewan Negara* (Senate) of 69 members (26 elected, 2 by each state legislature; and 43 appointed by the Yang di-Pertuan Agong) and *Dewan Rakyat* (House of Representatives) of 192 members (BN 168, DAP 9, PAS 7, PBS 7, STAR 1). Appointment to the Senate is for 3 years. The maximum life of the House of Representatives is 5 years, subject to its dissolution at any time by the *Yang di-Pertuan Agong* on the advice of his Ministers.

Parliamentary and 11 state assembly elections were held on 24–25 April 1995. The 14-party National Front Coalition, in which the United Malays National Organization was the predominant partner, gained 162 seats with 63% of votes cast. The Democratic Action Party gained 9 seats. The National Front Coalition also gained a majority in every state assembly except Kelantan, which was won by the Islamic Party of Malaysia.

In March 1998 the government comprised:
Prime Minister and Minister for Home Affairs: Dato Seri Dr Mahathir Mohamad (b. 1926).
Deputy Prime Minister and Minister of Finance: Datuk Seri Anwar Ibrahim.
Transport: Dato Seri Dr Ling Liong Sik. *Energy, Telecommunications and Posts:* Datuk Seri Leo Moggie Anak Irok. *Primary Industries:* Dato Seri Dr Lim Keng Yaik.
Works: Datuk Seri S. Samy Vellu. *International Trade and Industry:* Dato Seri Rafidah Aziz. *Education:* Datuk Seri Najib Tun Razak. *Rural Development:* Datuk Annuar Musa. *Agriculture:* Datuk Amar Dr Sulaiman Daud. *Domestic Trade and Consumer Affairs:* Dato Seri Megat Junid Megat Ayob. *Health:* Chua Jui Meng.
Foreign Affairs: Dato Abdullah bin Haji Ahmad Badawi. *Defence:* Datuk Syed Hamid Albar. *Information:* Dato Mohamed bin Rahmat. *Culture, Arts and Tourism:* Dato Sabbaruddin bin Chik. *National Unity and Community Development:* Datin

Paduka Zaleha Ismail. *Entrepreneur Development:* Datuk Mustapha Mohamed. *Human Resources:* Dato Lim Ah Lek. *Science, Technology and Environment:* Datuk Law Hieng Ding. *Housing and Local Government:* Dato Dr Ting Chew Peh. *Land and Co-operative Development:* Osu bin Haji Sukam. *Youth and Sports:* Muhyiddin Yassin. *Ministers in the Prime Minister's Department:* Datuk Abang Abu Bakar bin Datu Bandar Abang Haji Mustapha, Datuk Chong Kah Kiat, Dr Abdul Hamid Othman.

National anthem: Negara-Ku (My Country); words collective, tune by Pierre de Béranger.

Regional and Local Government. States have elected single-chamber legislative assemblies. The ruler appoints an executive council on the advice of the chief minister. In Peninsular Malaysia each state is divided into districts under a district officer. Each district is divided into *mukims* under a chief, and each village in the *mukim* has a headman.

DEFENCE. The Constitution provides for the Head of State to be the Supreme Commander of the Armed Forces who exercises his powers in accordance with the advice of the Cabinet. Under their authority the Armed Forces Council is responsible for all matters relating to the Armed Forces, other than those relating to their operational use. The Council is chaired by the Minister of Defence and its membership consists of the chief of the Defence Forces, the 3 Service Chiefs and 2 other senior military officers, the Secretary-General of the Ministry of Defence, a representative of State Rulers and an appointed member.

The chief of the Armed Forces Staff is the professional head of the Armed Forces and the senior military member in the Armed Forces Council. He chairs the Armed Forces Staff's committee, the highest level at which joint planning and co-ordination with the Armed Forces are carried out.

Malaysia is a member of the Five Powers Defence Arrangement with Australia, New Zealand, Singapore and the UK.

Army. The Army is organized into 2 military regions, 1 corps and 5 divisional headquarters. There are 10 infantry brigades made up of 35 infantry battalions, 4 armoured, 5 field artillery, 1 air defence artillery, 1 special forces and 5 engineer regiments, and 1 Rapid Deployment Force. Equipment includes 26 Scorpion light tanks. Strength (1996) about 85,000. There is a paramilitary Police Field Force of 18,000.

Navy. The Royal Malaysian Navy is commanded by the Chief of the Navy from the integrated Ministry of Defence in Kuala Lumpur. There are 4 operational areas: No. 1, covering the eastern peninsular coast (headquarters Kuantan); No. 2, Sabah (headquarters Labuan); No. 3, the western peninsular coast (headquarters Lumut); and No. 4, Sarawak (headquarters Kuching). The peace-time tasks include fishery protection and anti-piracy patrols.

The combatants include 2 German-built and 2 British-built frigates all with helicopter platforms, 8 fast missile craft and 2 offshore and 27 inshore patrol craft. There are also 4 Italian-type offshore mine countermeasure vessels and 4 tank landing ships normally employed in support of patrol and missile craft. Auxiliaries include 2 multipurpose support ships, 1 survey ship, 1 diving support ship and 33 amphibious craft. The first of 2 new well-equipped British-built frigates were expected to be delivered in 1996.

A Naval aviation squadron operates 12 ex-British Wasp helicopters. Navy personnel in 1995 totalled 12,000 and 2,700 reserves.

Paramilitary maritime forces include 50 armed patrol launches, 48 operated by the Royal Malaysian Police and 2 by the Government of Sabah which also operates 4 other patrol boats, 1 landing craft and a yacht.

Air Force. Formed on 1 June 1958, the Royal Malaysian Air Force is equipped primarily to provide air defence and air support for the Army, Navy and Police. Its secondary role is to render assistance to Government departments and civilian organizations. There are 16 squadrons, of which 9 operate transport aircraft and helicopters. Some 18 MiG-29s equip 2 squadrons. Other equipment includes 25 Hawk strike/trainer aircraft, 10 F-5E Tiger II jet fighterbombers, 2 RF-5E reconnaissance-fighters, and 3 F-5F trainers, 1 F.28 Fellowship and 1 Falcon 900 VIP transports, 14 C-130 Hercules four-engined transport and patrol aircraft, 12 Caribou twin-engined short-take-off-and-landing transports, 2 HU-16 amphibians, 31 Sikorsky S-61A-4 Nuri heavy troop and cargo transport helicopters, 20 Alouette III, and 6 Bell 47 helicopters, 9 Cessna 402Bs for twin-engine training and liaison, 39 PC-7 Turbo-Trainers, 11 MB.339 jet trainers, 2 H.S. 125 Merpati twin-jet executive transports, 2 AS-61 VIP transport helicopters, and 20 MD30160 primary trainers. Personnel (1995) totalled about 12,500, with 120 combat aircraft.

INTERNATIONAL RELATIONS

Membership. Malaysia is a member of the UN, the Commonwealth, the Colombo Plan, Organization of Islamic Conference and ASEAN.

ECONOMY

Policy. The government's Economic Planning Unit produces economic development plans. The Second Outline Perspective Plan of 1991 set targets for the coming decade to be implemented by the New Development Policy. The seventh Malaysia Plan covers 1996–2000 and is the second of two 5-year programmes under the Policy. There are privatization programmes involving telecommunications, railways, airports, electricity and shipping. Manufacturing is expected to lead economic growth. The Plan aims for an annual real GDP growth of 8%. However, in March 1998 Malaysia revised its economic growth projection for the year down to 2–3%.

Performance. During the sixth 5 year plan (1991–95) economic growth averaged 8·7% a year (target, 8·1%).

Budget. 1997 budget: Revenue, RM60,780m.; expenditure, RM59,980m. Revenue and expenditure for calendar years, in RM1m.:

	1993	1994	1995	1996	1997[1]
Revenue	41,231	44,730	50,953	56,549	60,947
Operating expenditure	32,315	32,285	36,573	43,268	43,304

[1] Forecast.

Sources of revenue in 1996: Direct taxes, 45·6% (45·8%—1997 est.); indirect taxes, 36% (36·2—1997 est.); non-tax revenue, 18·4 % (18·0%—1997 est.).

Federal government net development (in addition to operating) expenditure in 1996: RM11,156m. (RM 12,525m. 1997), of which economic services 49·9% (47·4%—1997 est.), social services, 25·3% (30%—1997 est.), security, 19·0% (16·6%—1997 est.) and general administration, 5·8% (6·0%—1997 est.).

Currency. The unit of currency is the Malaysian *ringgit* (MYR) of 100 *sen*. Currency notes are of denominations of RM1, 2, 5, 10, 20, 50, 100, 500 and 1,000. Coins are of denominations of 1 sen, 5, 10, 20, 50 sen and RM1, 5 and 100. Currency in circulation at the end of 1996 totalled RM21,065,609,098.

Banking and Finance. The central bank and bank of issue is the Bank Negara Malaysia (*Governor*, Ahmad Mohamad Don). 37 commercial banks were operating at 31 Dec. 1996 (including 16 foreign) with a total of 1,433 branches. Number of employees 69,154. Total deposits with commercial banks at 31 Dec. 1996 were RM194,974m. There were 12 merchant banks at 31 Dec. 1996. Number of employees 2,592. Their total assets were RM34m. The Islamic Bank of Malaysia began operations in July 1983. There were 40 finance companies in 1996 with 1,096 offices. Number of employees 26,728.

There is a stock exchange at Kuala Lumpur.

The economy suffered from the financial crisis that hit South-East Asia in Nov. 1997. But while the *ringgit* lost nearly 30% of its value in the second half of 1997, the underlying strength of the economy (a modest foreign debt and few non-performing loans) is expected to lead to an early recovery.

Weights and Measures. The metric system is standard, but British imperial units are still in residual use.

ENERGY AND NATURAL RESOURCES

Electricity. Installed capacity in 1995, 11,427 MW. In 1995, 41,961m. kWh were generated.

Oil and Gas. Estimated oil production (1995) 706,000 bbls. a day. Natural gas reserves, 1987, 1,400,000m. cu. metres. Production of liquefied natural gas in 1995 was an estimated 11·68m. tonnes.

Minerals. In 1992 mining contributed 8·6% of GDP. Tin production was an estimated 6,500 tonnes in 1995.

Agriculture. In 1995 agriculture contributed 13·6% of GDP. Production (1995 estimates): Rubber, 1,106,000 tonnes; palm oil, 7,813,000 tonnes.

Forestry. In 1990 there were 19·6m. ha of forests. The total output of saw logs in 1995 (estimate) was 32·2m. cu. metres.

Fisheries. Total landings of marine fish, 1990, 907,300 tonnes.

INDUSTRY. In 1995 manufacturing contributed 33·1% of GDP.

Labour. In 1996 the workforce was 8·4m. (47·2% female), of whom 8,181,000 were employed (16·8% in agriculture, 27% in manufacturing and 8·6% in building). Unemployment was 2·8%.

Trade Unions. Membership was 737,484 at 30 Sept. 1997, of which the Malaysian Trades Union Congress, an umbrella organization of 158 unions, accounted for 0·4m. Number of unions was 536.

FOREIGN ECONOMIC RELATIONS. Privatization policy permits foreign investment of 25–30% generally; total foreign ownership is permitted of export-oriented projects.

Commerce. In 1996 exports totalled RM197,707m. with an estimated rise to RM221,550 in 1997, and imports RM198,580m. (RM219,394 in 1997 est.).

In 1996 imports of consumer goods totalled RM27,801m.; intermediate goods, RM89,361m.; capital goods, RM80,425m.

Chief exports, 1996 (in RM1m.): Rubber, 2,719; palm oil, 8,345; saw logs and sawn timber, 4,756; crude oil, 6,917; manufactures of metal, 5,480; manufacturing products, 160,068.

In 1996 imports (in RM1m.) came chiefly from Japan (48,399), USA (30,495) and Singapore (26,340). Exports went chiefly to USA (35,821), Singapore (40,289) and Japan (26,378).

Tourism. 7·5m. tourists visited Malaysia in 1995, producing revenue of RM9,200m.

COMMUNICATIONS

Roads. Total road length in 1997 was 67,608 km (estimate), of which 51,700 km were paved and 15,908 km were unpaved. In 1996, there were 750,811 motor vehicles.

Railways. In 1997 there were 2,227 km of railway tracks. It was estimated about 33·7m. passenger journeys were made in that year and 4·9m. tonnes of freight were carried.

Civil Aviation. There are a total of 19 airports of which 5 are international airports and 14 are domestic airports at which regular public air transport is operated. *International airports;* Kuala Lumpur, Pulau Pinang, Kota Kinabalu, Kuching and Langkawi. *Domestic airports;* Johor Bahru, Alor Setar, Ipoh, Kota Bharu, Kuala Terengganu, Kuantan, Melaka, Sandakan, Lahat Datu, Tawau, Labuan, Bintulu, Sibu and Miri. There are 39 Malaysian airstrips of which 10 are in Sabah, 15 in Sarawak and 14 in peninsular Malaysia.

33 international airlines operate through Kuala Lumpur (Subang). Malaysia Airlines, the national airline, is 39% state-owned, and operates domestic flights

within Peninsular Malaysia as well as between Kuala Lumpur and Sabah and Sarawak, and flies to Australia, Austria, Belgium, Cambodia, China, France, Germany, Hong Kong, India, Indonesia, Iran, Japan, Jordan, South Korea, Mauritius, Mexico, Myanmar, Netherlands, New Zealand, Pakistan, Philippines, Singapore, Spain, Sri Lanka, Switzerland, Taiwan, Thailand, Turkey, UAE, UK, USA and Vietnam. In 1995 its fleet comprised 2 A300B4-200s, 5 A330-300s, 2 B-737-300(F)s, 35 B-737-400s, 9 B-737-500s, 2 B-747-200Bs, 1 B-747-300 Combi, 10 B-747-400s, 2 B-747-400 Combis, and 22 other aircraft. Services are also provided by Aeroflot, Air India, Air Lanka, Air Maldives, Air Mauritius, All Nippon Airways, Ansett Australia, Berjaya Air, Biman Bangaldesh, British Airways, Canadian Airlines, Cathay Pacific, China Airlines, China Southern Airlines, Eva Airways, Garuda Indonesia, Gulf Air, Indian Airlines, Iran Air, JAL, KLM, Korean Air, Kuwait Airways, Lufthansa, Myanma Airways, Pakistan Airlines, Philippine Air, Qantas, Royal Air Cambodge, Royal Brunei Airlines, Royal Jordanian, Saudia, Singapore Airlines, Thai Airways, Uzbekistan Airways, Vietnam Airlines and Virgin Atlantic.

Shipping. The major ports are Port Kelang, Penang, Johor, Tg. Bruas, Miri, Rajang, Pel Pel Sabah, Port Dickson Kemaman, Teluk Ewa, Kuantan, Kuching and Bintulu. In 1996 there were 2,429 marine vessels including 118 oil tankers (0·73m. GRT), 198 passenger carriers (0·03m. GRT) and 426 general cargo ships (0·76m. GRT), with a total GRT of 4·27m. In 1996, 167·9m. tonnes of cargo were loaded and unloaded. The figure in 1997 is estimated to be 185·6m. tonnes.

Telecommunications. Postal services are the responsibility of the Ministry of Energy, Telecommunications and Post.

At the end of October 1997, there were 6,036 postal services networks established in Malaysia, including 620 post offices, 290 mini posts and 493 post representatives.

In 1995 there were 3·32m. telephones, 755,000 mobile telephones and 6,578 telex and (1994) 58,090 fax subscribers.

The Government-controlled Radio, Television Malaysia broadcasts radio and TV programmes nationally. The Voice of Malaysia (broadcasting in 8 languages) is beamed internationally. System TV Malaysia Berhad transmits from Kuala Lumpur and is also beamed throughout the country.

Press. The Malaysian Media Agencies are comprised of the press, magazine and press agencies/local media, which are further divided into home and foreign news. In 1996 there were a total of 143 press and liaison divisions.

SOCIAL INSTITUTIONS

Justice. The judicial power is vested in the Federal Court, the High Court of Malaya, the High Court of Borneo and subordinate courts: Sessions Courts, Magistrates' Courts and *Mukim* chiefs' Courts.

The head of the Judiciary is the Lord President of the Federal Court which consists of himself, the Chief Justices of the High Courts and Judges of the Federal Court. The Federal Court has jurisdiction to determine the validity of any law made by Parliament or by a State legislature and disputes between States or between the Federation and any State. It also has jurisdiction to hear and determine appeals from the High Courts.

Religion. One of the unique features of Malaysia is its multi-racial population which practises various religions such as Islam, Buddhism, Taoism, Hinduism and Christianity. Each ethnic group has its own beliefs. Under the Federal constitution, Islam is the official religion of Malaysia but there is freedom of worship. Churches, temples and mosques all stand side by side as testimony to the perfect harmony that prevails in the country. In 1992 there were 9·86m. Moslems, 3·22m. Buddhists, 2·16m. adherents of Chinese traditional religions and 1·3m. Hindus.

Language. Malay is the National Language of the country. The government promotes the use of the national language to foster national unity. However, the people are free to use their mother tongue and other languages. English as the second language is widely used in business.

Education. School education is free; tertiary education is provided at a nominal fee. There are 6 years of primary schooling starting at age 6, 3 years of universal lower secondary, 2 years of selective upper secondary and 2 years of pre-university education. During the Seventh Plan period, a number of major changes will be introduced to the education and training system with a view to strengthening and improving the system. These efforts are expected to improve the quality and increase the quantity of output to meet the manpower needs of the nation, particularly in the fields of science and technology. In addition, continued emphasis will be given to expand educational opportunities for those in the rural and remote areas. Under the Seventh Plan, the education Ministry allocated RM8,437,200 on this education programme and RM1,661,600 for training purposes.

Health. In 1995, medical professionals numbered 12,917 of which 9,504 were doctors, 1,791 dentists and 1,622 pharmacists, whereas allied health professionals were 42,878. These were divided into dental, paramedics and auxiliary (2,720), medical assistants and laboratory technologists (5,392), nurses (32,401), occupational therapists and physiotherapists (410), public health inspectors (1,418) and radiographers (537). At the end of 1995 the Ministry of Health ran a total of 1,375 dental clinics. In the same year there were 39,738 beds in hospitals, clinics and other medical institutions.

Social Security. The Employment Injury Insurance Scheme provides medical and cash benefits and the Invalidity Pension Scheme provides protection to employees against invalidity due to disease or injury from any cause. Other supplementary measures are the Employees' Provident Fund, the pension scheme for government employees, free medical benefits for all who are unable to pay and the provision of medical benefits particularly for workers under the Labour Code.

DIPLOMATIC REPRESENTATIVES

Of Malaysia in Great Britain (45 Belgrave Sq., London, SW1X 8QT)
High Commissioner: Dato Kamarudin Abu.

Of Great Britain in Malaysia (185, Jalan Semantan, Ampang 50450, Kuala Lumpur)
High Commissioner: D. J. Moss, CMG.

Of Malaysia in the USA (2401 Massachusetts Ave., NW, Washington, D.C., 20008)
Ambassador: Dato Dali Mahmud Hashim.

Of the USA in Malaysia (376 Jalan Tun Razak, Kuala Lumpur)
Ambassador: John Malott.

Of Malaysia to the United Nations
Ambassador: Tah Sri Razali Ishmail.

Of Malaysia to the European Union
Ambassador: Dato M. M. Sathiah.

Further Reading

Department of Statistics. *Yearbook of Statistics.*

Prime Minister's Department. Economic Planning Unit. *Malaysian Economy in Figures.* Annual
Brown, I. and Ampalavanar, R., *Malaysia.* [Bibliography] Oxford and Santa Barbara (CA), 1986
Gullick, J., *Malaysia: Economic Expansion and National Unity.* Boulder and London, 1982
Information Malaysia Yearbook. Kuala Lumpur
Jomo, K. S., *Growth and Structural Change in the Malaysian Economy.* London, 1990
Kahn, J. S. and Wah, F. L. K., *Fragmented Vision: Culture and Politics in Contemporary Malaysia.* Sydney, 1992
King, V. T. and Parnwell, M. J. (eds), *Margins and Minorities: the Peripheral Areas and People of Malaysia.* Hull Univ. Press, 1990
Means, G. P., *Malaysian Politics: the Second Generation.* OUP, 1991
Zakaria, A., *Government and Politics in Malaysia.* OUP, 1987

National statistical office: Department of Statistics, Wisma Statistik, Jalan Cenderasari, 50514 Kuala Lumpur.
Website: http://spl.pnm.my/~stat/

MALDIVES

Divehi Raajjeyge
Jumhooriyyaa

(Republic of the Maldives)

Capital: Malé
Population: 253,298
GNP: US$0·2bn.
HDI/world rank: 0·611/111

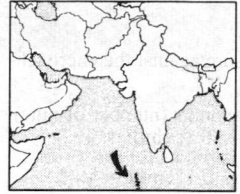

KEY HISTORICAL EVENTS. The islands were under British protection from 1887 until complete independence was achieved on 26 July 1965. The Maldives became a republic on 11 Nov. 1968.

TERRITORY AND POPULATION. The republic, some 400 miles to the south-west of Sri Lanka, consists of 1,200 low-lying (the highest point is 6 feet above sea-level) coral islands, grouped into 26 atolls. 199 are inhabited. Area 115 sq. miles (298 sq. km). At the 1995 census, the population was 244,644 (119,592 females). Estimate (1996), 253,298. Population growth rate, 1995, 2·5%. Expectation of life was 65·5 years in 1995. Capital, Malé (1995 population, 62,973).

The official language is Divehi.

CLIMATE. The islands are hot and humid, and affected by monsoons. Malé: Average temperature 81°F (27°C), annual rainfall 59" (1,500 mm).

CONSTITUTION AND GOVERNMENT. There is a Citizens' *Majlis* (Parliament) which consists of 48 members, 8 of whom are nominated by the President and 40 directly elected (2 each from Malé and the 19 administrative districts) for a term of 5 years. There are no political parties. The President of the Republic is elected by the Citizens' Majlis.

In March 1998 the Government consisted of:

President, Minister of Defence and National Security, Minister of Finance and Treasury: Maumoon Abdul Gayoom (b. 1937; re-elected unopposed for a fourth 5-year term on 23 Aug. 1993; sworn in, 1 Oct. 1993).

Atolls Administration: Abdullah Hameed. *Foreign Affairs:* Fathullah Jameel. *Youth and Sports:* Mohamed Zahir Hussain. *Minister of Home Affairs and Housing:* Abdullah Jameel. *Construction and Public Works:* Umar Zahir. *Justice:* Ahmed Zahir. *Transport and Communications:* Ismail Shafeeu. *Planning, Human Resources and Environment:* Abdul Rasheed Hussain. *Health:* Ahmed Abdullah. *Tourism:* Ibrahim Hussain Zaki. *Fisheries and Agriculture:* Hassan Sabir. *Education:* Dr Mohamed Latheef. *Information, Arts and Culture:* Ibrahim Manik. *Trade, Industries and Labour:* Abdullah Yameen. *Women's Affairs and Social Welfare:* Rashida Yoosuf. *Attorney General:* Dr Mohamed Munawwar.

Speaker of Citizens' Majlis: Abdulla Hameed.

The official and spoken language is Divehi.

National anthem: 'Gavmii mi ekuverikan matii tibegen kuriime salaam' ('In national unity we salute our nation'); words by M. J. Didi, tune by W. Amaradeva.

Local government: The Maldives is divided into the capital and 19 other administrative districts, each under an appointed governor assisted by appointed local chiefs.

INTERNATIONAL RELATIONS

Membership. The Maldives is a member of the UN, the Commonwealth and the Colombo Plan.

ECONOMY

Budget. 1996 provisional estimates: Revenue, 1,557·8m. Rufiyaa (including grant,

237·8m. Rufiyaa); current expenditure 926·2m. Rufiyaa; capital expenditure, 738·8m. Rufiyaa.

Currency. The unit of currency is the *rufiyaa* (MVR) of 100 *laari*. There are coins of 1, 2, 5, 10, 25 and 50 laari and 1 rufiyaa, and notes of 2, 5, 10, 20, 50, 100 and 500 rufiyaa.

ENERGY AND NATURAL RESOURCES

Electricity. Production, 1996, 68·33m. kWh.

Minerals. Inshore coral mining has been banned as a measure against the encroachment of the sea.

Agriculture. Principal crops in 1993 (in 1,000 tonnes): Coconuts (number of nuts), 15,324,732; maize, 9; cassava, 8; sweet potatoes, 44; onions, 0·1; chillies, 40·3.

Fisheries. Catch, 1996 (1,000 metric tonnes), 105·5.

INDUSTRY. The main industries are fishing, tourism, shipping, lacquerwork and garment manufacturing.

FOREIGN ECONOMIC RELATIONS

Commerce. In 1996 imports amounted to 3,551,289,000 Rufiyaa and exports to 699,191,000 Rufiyaa. Bonito ('Maldive fish') is the main export commodity. It is exported principally to Thailand, Singapore, Sri Lanka, Japan, and some European markets.

Tourism. Tourism is the major foreign currency earner. There were 338,733 visitors in 1996.

COMMUNICATIONS

Roads. In 1996 there were 787 cars, 5,319 motorbikes/auto cycles, 377 lorries/trucks/tractors, 209 vans/buses, 658 jeeps/land rovers/pickups, 271 taxis and 274 other vehicles.

Civil Aviation. There are direct flights from Colombo, Thiruvananthapuram, Dubai, Karachi, Singapore, Frankfurt, Munich, Düsseldorf, Zurich and Bucharest. In 1996, 7,710 aircraft, 1,153,750 passengers and 13,370,436 kg of mail and air freight were handled at Malé International Airport. There are 4 domestic airports. Air Maldives operates domestic and international flights.

Shipping. The Maldives Shipping Line operated (1992) 10 vessels.

Telecommunications. There were (1996) 15,172 telephones. Voice of Maldives and Television Maldives are government-controlled. There were (1995) 29,484 radio receivers and (1995) 9,879 television sets (colour by PAL).

Press. There were (1996) 3 daily newspapers, 2 weekly, 2 fortnightly and a number of monthly periodicals.

SOCIAL INSTITUTIONS

Justice. Justice is based on the Islamic Shari'ah.

Religion. The State religion is Islam.

Education. Education is not compulsory. In 1996, there were 60 government schools (40,935 pupils) and 32 private schools (40,153 pupils) and 171 community schools (9,509 pupils) with a total of 3,278 teachers.

Health. In 1996 there were 193 beds at the Indhira Ghandi Memorial Hospital in Malé, 4 regional hospitals (125 beds) and 27 health centres. In 1996 there were 99 doctors and 303 nurses.

DIPLOMATIC REPRESENTATIVES

Of the Maldives in Great Britain (22 Nottingham Pl., London W1M 3FB)
High Commissioner: Vacant.

Of Great Britain in the Maldives
High Commissioner: David Tatham, CMG (resides in Sri Lanka).

Of the USA in the Maldives
Ambassador: Vacant.

Permanent Representative of the Maldives to the United Nations
Ambassador: Vacant.

Further Reading

Reynolds, C. H. B., *Maldives*. [Bibliography] Oxford and Santa Barbara (CA), 1993

MALI

République du Mali

Capital: Bamako
Population: 9·79m.
GDP per head: (PPP$) 543
GNP: US$2·4bn.
HDI/world rank: 0·229/171

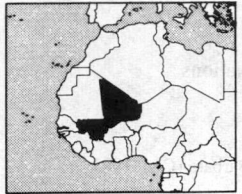

KEY HISTORICAL EVENTS. Mali's political organization and power reached their peak between the 11th and 13th centuries when its gold-based empire controlled much of the surrounding area. It declined thereafter and the French began invading from Senegal in the mid-19th century, fully annexing the country by 1904. The region became the territory of French Sudan as part of French West Africa. The Sudanese Union, led by Modibo Keita, gained strength in the 1950s and took over the internal running of the country after winning elections in 1957. The country became an autonomous state within the French Community on 24 Nov. 1958, and on 4 April 1959 joined with Senegal to form the Federation of Mali. The Federation achieved independence on 20 June 1960, but Senegal seceded on 22 Aug. and Mali proclaimed itself an independent republic on 22 Sept., with Keita as president. Much later, in March 1982, Guinea and Mali were to agree to pursue gradual unification. The National Assembly was dissolved on 17 Jan. 1968 by President Modibo Keita, whose government was then overthrown by an army coup on 19 Nov. 1968; power was assumed by a Military Committee for National Liberation led by Lieut. Moussa Traoré, who became president on 19 Sept. 1969. He ruled on the basis of tight control during the severe drought of the 1970s. Traoré formed a political party in 1976, the *Union démocratique du peuple malien* (UDPM), and was confirmed as president in elections in June 1979. He was deposed on 26 March 1991 in a military coup. Lieut.-Col. Amadou Touré was named head of a Transitional Committee of Public Safety.

In Jan. 1991 a ceasefire was signed with Tuareg insurgents in the north, but sporadic skirmishing continued. A further agreement was reached at a Special Conference on the North held in Dec. 1991, and in April 1992 a national pact was concluded providing for a special administration for the Tuareg north. A further accord with Tuareg insurgents under which their northern bases would be dismantled was signed in May 1994.

Under its current president, Alpha Oumar Konaré, 2 elections for the National Assembly have been held, but the first (April 1997) was cancelled by the Constitutional Court and the second, in July 1997, was boycotted by opposition parties which are weakened by internal fighting.

TERRITORY AND POPULATION. Mali is bounded in the west by Senegal, north-west by Mauritania, north-east by Algeria, east by Niger and south by Burkina Faso, Côte d'Ivoire and Guinea. Its area is 1,248,574 sq. km (482,077 sq. miles) and had a population of 7,696,348 at the 1987 census (20·3% urban). Estimate, 1997, 9,789,000; density, 7·8 per sq. km.

Vital statistics rates, 1997 estimates (per 1,000 population). Births, 50·3; deaths, 19·5. Infant mortality (per 1,000 live births), 124. Expectation of life in 1997 was 46·6 years (45·25 for males and 47·9 for females). Growth rate, 3·18% per annum.

The areas, populations and chief towns of the regions are:

Region	Sq. km	Census 1987	Chief town
Kayes	197,760	1,058,575	Kayes
Koulikoro	89,833	1,180,260	Koulikoro
Capital District	267	646,153	Bamako
Sikasso	76,480	1,308,828	Sikasso
Ségou	56,127	1,328,250	Ségou
Mopti	88,752	1,261,383	Mopti
Tombouctou	408,977	453,032	Tombouctou
Gao	321,996	383,734	Gao

An 8th region, Kidal (chief town, Kidal), was instituted in the north in 1991.

944

In 1996 the principal ethnic groups numbered (in 1,000): Bambara, 2,930; Fulani, 1,290; Senufo, 1,100; Soninke, 800; Tuareg, 675; Songhai, 660; Malinke, 610; Dogon, 370. The official language is French; Bambara is spoken by about 60% of the population.

CLIMATE. A tropical climate, with adequate rain in the south and west, but conditions become increasingly arid towards the north and east. Bamako. Jan. 76°F (24·4°C), July 80°F (26·7°C). Annual rainfall 45" (1,120 mm). Kayes. Jan. 76°F (24·4°C), July 93°F (33·9°C). Annual rainfall 29" (725 mm). Tombouctou. Jan. 71°F (21·7°C), July 90°F (32·2°C). Annual rainfall 9" (231 mm).

CONSTITUTION AND GOVERNMENT. A constitution was approved by a national referendum in 1974; it was amended by the National Assembly on 2 Sept. 1981. The sole legal party was the *Union démocratique du peuple malien* (UDPM).

A national conference of 1,800 delegates agreed a draft constitution enshrining multi-party democracy in Aug. 1991, and this was approved by 99·76% of votes cast at a referendum in Jan. 1992. Turn-out was 43%.

The *President* is elected for not more than 2 terms of 5 years.

A *Constitutional Court* was established in 1994.

Elections were held in July–Aug. 1997 for the 160-member National Assembly. The Alliance for Democracy in Mali (ADEMA) won 128 seats.

In the presidential elections on 11 May 1997 Alpha Oumar Konaré was re-elected against a single opponent. As with the elections to the National Assembly, many parties boycotted the elections.

President: Alpha Oumar Konaré (b. 1946; sworn in, 8 June 1997).

In March 1998 the government comprised:

Prime Minister: Boubacar Keita (b. 1945; ADEMA).

Minister of Foreign Affairs and Malians Abroad: Modibo Sidibe. *Culture and Tourism:* Aminata Drame Traoré. *Industry, Artisanry and Trade:* Fatou Haidara. *Communications:* Ascofare Ouleymatou Tamboura. *Finance:* Soumeyla Cissé. *Economic Affairs, Planning and Integration:* Ahmed el Madani Diallo. *Youth:* Boubacar Karamoko Coulibaly. *Sports:* Adama Kone. *Health, Solidarity and the Elderly:* Diakite Fatoumata Ndiaye. *Mines and Energy:* Yoro Diakite. *Rural Development and Water Resources:* Modibo Traoré. Environment: Mohamed Ag Erlaf. *Employment, Civil Service and Labour:* Ousmane Oumarou Sidibe. *Primary Education and Government Spokesman:* Adama Sammassekou. *Secondary Education, Higher Education and Scientific Research:* Younouss Hamaye Dicko. *Promotion of Women, Children and Family Affairs:* Diarra Hafsatou Thierro. *Justice and Keeper of the Seals:* Hamidou Diabate. *Territorial Administration and Security:* Lieut.-Col. Sada Samake. *Public Works and Transportation.* Ibrchima Siby. *Relations with Institutions and Political Parties:* Hassane Diallo. *Armed Forces and Veterans:* Mohammed Salia Sokona. *Defence:* Mamodou Ba. *Urban Development and Housing:* Sy Kadiatou Sow.

National anthem: 'A ton appel, Mali' ('At your call, Mali'); words by S. Kouyate, tune by B. Sissoko.

Local Government: Mali is divided into the Capital District of Bamako and 8 regions, sub-divided into 46 *cercles* and then into 279 *arrondissements*.

At the elections of Jan. 1992 turn-out was 35%. The Alliance for Democracy in Mali (ADEMA) gained 214 of the 751 seats contested, the Sudanese Union-RDA (US-RDA), 130, and the National Committee for Democratic Initiative (CNID), 96.

DEFENCE. There is a selective system of 2 years' conscription, for civilian or military service.

Army. The Army consists of 4 infantry 2 tank, 1 engineer, 1 parachute, 1 special force, 2 artillery battalions and 2 air defence and 1 surface-to-air missile battery. Equipment includes 21 T-34 main battle tanks. Strength (1997) 7,000. There are also paramilitary forces of 4,800.

Air Force. The Air Force MiG fighters are withdrawn from use. There are 2 An-24, 2 An-26 and 1 Mi-8 helicopter. A twin-turbofan Corvette is used for VIP transport. Personnel (1997) total about 400.

INTERNATIONAL RELATIONS

Membership. Mali is a member of the UN, OAU and is an ACP state of the EU.

ECONOMY

Performance. The economy was virtually ruined by the Traoré regime, but with IMF and World Bank help has recovered rapidly. Real GDP growth was 6% in 1996.

Budget. Revenues for 1997 were estimated to be US$730m. and expenditures US$770m.

Currency. The unit of currency is the *franc CFA*, which replaced the Mali franc in 1984. There are coins of 1, 2, 5, 10, 25, 50 and 100 francs CFA, and notes of 50, 100, 500, 1,000, 5,000 and 10,000 francs CFA. There were 60,800m. francs CFA in circulation in 1992. Foreign exchange reserves were US$309·5m. in 1995; gold reserves were US$7·3m. in 1995. Annualized inflation was 3% in 1996.

Banking and Finance. There are 4 domestic and 2 French-owned banks.

ENERGY AND NATURAL RESOURCES

Electricity. Production (1995) totalled 235m. kWh, much of it hydro-electric.

Minerals. There are deposits of iron ore, uranium, diamonds, bauxite, manganese, copper and lithium. 7·8 tonnes of gold were extracted in 1994.

Agriculture. About 80% of the population depends on agriculture, mainly carried on by small peasant holdings. It contributes 44% of GDP. Mali is second only to Egypt among African cotton producers. In 1992 there were 2·2m. ha of arable land, 3,000 ha, permanent cropland and 30m. ha, pasture. Production in 1995 included (estimates, in 1,000 tonnes): Millet, sorghum and fonio, 1,604; rice, 469; maize, 322, vegetables, 267; sugar cane, 262; groundnuts, 215; cottonseed, 150; cotton (lint), 110.

Livestock, 1995 estimates: Cattle, 5,542,000; horses, 101,000; asses, 611,000; sheep, 5,173,000; goats, 7,380,000; camels, 260,000; chickens, 23m.

0·21m. ha were irrigated in 1992.

Forestry. There are 8·52m. ha. of forest. 6·3m. cu. metres of roundwood were cut in 1994.

Fisheries. In 1995, 133,000 tonnes of fish were caught in the rivers.

INDUSTRY. Manufacturing accounted for 11% of GDP in 1991. The main branch is food processing, followed by cotton processing, textiles and clothes. Cement and pharmaceuticals are also produced.

Labour. In 1990 the workforce comprised 2,959,000 persons (479,000 females). Large numbers of Malians emigrate temporarily to work abroad, principally in Côte d'Ivoire.

FOREIGN ECONOMIC RELATIONS. Foreign debt was US$2,800m. in 1995.

Commerce. Exports in 1994 totalled US$320m.; imports, US$422m. Principal export commodities are cotton, livestock and gold. The main export markets are the franc zone, western Europe and the People's Republic of China. Principal import commodities are machinery and equipment, foodstuffs, construction materials, petroleum and textiles. Main import suppliers are also the franc zone (in particular Côte d'Ivoire and France), western Europe and the People's Republic of China.

Tourism. There were 28,000 foreign tourists in 1994.

COMMUNICATIONS

Roads. There were (1995 estimate) 14,776 km of classified roads, of which 1,773 km were paved. In 1992 there were 23,209 passenger cars and 6,802 commercial vehicles.

Railways. Mali has a railway from Kayes to Koulikoro by way of Bamako, a continuation of the Dakar–Kayes line in Senegal. Total length 642 km (metre-gauge) and in 1987 carried 196m. passenger-km and 199m. tonne-km of freight.

Civil Aviation. Air services connect the republic with Paris, Dakar and Abidjan. There are international airports at Bamako (Senou) and Mopti, and Air Mali operates domestic services to 10 other airports. It had 2 aircraft in 1995.

Shipping. For about 7 months in the year small steamboats operate a service from Koulikoro to Tombouctou and Gao, and from Bamako to Kouroussa.

Telecommunications. There were, in 1993, 14,000 telephones. Broadcasting is the responsibility of the autonomous Radiodiffusion Télévision du Mali. In 1993 there were 7 independent radio networks, 6 private and 1 public. In 1995 there were 500,000 radio and 20,000 TV sets (colour by SECAM).

Press. In 1995 there were 2 daily newspapers with a circulation of 41,000.

SOCIAL INSTITUTIONS

Justice. The Supreme Court was established at Bamako in 1969 with both judicial and administrative powers. The Court of Appeal is also at Bamako, at the apex of a system of regional tribunals and local *juges de paix*.

Religion. The state is secular, but predominantly Sunni Moslem. About 15% of the population follow traditional animist beliefs and there is a small Christian minority.

Education. Adult literacy was 29·3% in 1994. In 1994 there were 151 pre-primary schools with 503 teachers for 15,908 pupils. In 1995 there were 1,996 primary schools with 8,738 teachers for 608,444 pupils. In 1991 there were 78,523 secondary level pupils with 5,748 teachers, and 6,703 students at university level.

Health. In 1984 there were 12 hospitals, 333 health centres, 592 maternity homes and 590 dispensaries, with a total of 3,430 beds. In 1987 there were 114 doctors, 2 dentists, 23 pharmacists, 238 midwives and 1,219 nursing personnel.

DIPLOMATIC REPRESENTATIVES

Of Mali in Great Britain (resides in Brussels)
Ambassador: N'Tji Laico Traoré.

Of Great Britain in Mali (resides in Senegal)
Ambassador: David R. Snoxell.

Of Mali in the USA (2130 R. St., NW, Washington, D.C., 20008)
Ambassador: Cheick Oumar Diarrah.

Of the USA in Mali (Rue Rochester and Rue Mohamed V, Bamako)
Ambassador: David P. Rawson.

Of Mali to the United Nations
Ambassador: Moctar Ouane.

Of Mali to the European Union
Ambassador: N'Tji Laico Traoré.

MALTA

Repubblika ta' Malta

Capital: Valletta
Population: 374,718
GDP: (PPP$) 13,009
HDI/world rank: 0·887/34

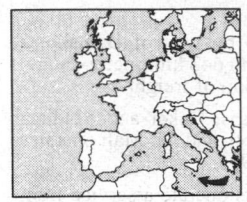

KEY HISTORICAL EVENTS. Malta was held in turn by Phoenicians, Carthaginians and Romans, and was conquered by Arabs in 870. From 1090 it was subject to the same rulers as Sicily until 1530, when it was handed over to the Knights of St John, who ruled until dispersed by Napoleon in 1798. The Maltese rose in rebellion against the French and the island was subsequently blockaded by the British aided by the Maltese from 1798 to 1800. The Maltese people requested the protection of the British Crown in 1802 on condition that their rights and privileges be preserved. The islands were finally annexed to the British Crown by the Treaty of Paris in 1814. On 15 April 1942, in recognition of the fortitude of the people of Malta during the Second World War, King George VI awarded the George Cross to the island. Malta became independent on 21 Sept. 1964 and a republic within the Commonwealth on 13 Dec. 1974.

TERRITORY AND POPULATION. The 3 Maltese islands and minor islets lie in the Mediterranean 93 km (at the nearest point) south of Sicily and 288 km east of Tunisia. The area of Malta is 246 sq. km (94·9 sq. miles); Gozo, 67 sq. km (25·9 sq. miles) and the virtually uninhabited Comino, 3 sq. km (1·1 sq. miles); total area, 316 sq. km (121·9 sq. miles). Population, 31 Dec. 1996, 373,958 (Malta island, 345,338; Gozo and Comino, 28,620). 1997 estimate, 374,718. Chief town and port, Valletta, population (1996) 7,172 but the inner harbour area, 87,380. Other towns: Birkirkara, 21, 551; Qormi, 17,928; Mosta, 15,887; Sliema, 13,823; Zabbar, 13,772. Vital statistics, 1996: Births, 4,944; deaths, 2,765; marriages, 2,370; emigrants (1995), 737; returned emigrants (1995), 622.

The constitution provides that the national language and language of the courts is Maltese, but both Maltese and English are official languages. Italian is also spoken.

CLIMATE. The climate is Mediterranean, with hot, dry and sunny conditions in summer and very little rain from May to Aug. Rainfall is not excessive and falls mainly between Oct. and March. Average daily sunshine in winter is 6 hours and in summer over 10 hours. Valletta. Jan. 12·8°C (55°F), July 25·6°C (78°F). Annual rainfall 578 mm (23").

CONSTITUTION AND GOVERNMENT. Malta is a parliamentary democracy. The Constitution of 1964 provides for a *President*, a *House of Representatives* of members elected by universal suffrage and a Cabinet consisting of the Prime Minister and such number of Ministers as may be appointed. The Constitution makes provision for the protection of fundamental rights and freedom of the individual, and for freedom of conscience and religious worship, and guarantees the separation of executive, judicial and legislative powers. In 1996 the House of Representatives had 65 members directly elected on a plurality basis. At the elections of 26 Oct. 1996 the electorate was 0·27m. Turn-out was 96·2%. The Labour Party (MLP) gained 31 seats with 50·72% of votes cast; the Nationalist Party (NP), 34 seats with 47·8%. A constitutional amendment of March 1996 rules that where more than 2 parties stand, but only 2 parties gain seats, the party with the most votes is allocated extra seats. Thus, in Nov. 1996 the party composition of the House of Representatives was: MLP, 35; NP, 34.

President: Dr Ugo Mifsud Bonnici (b. 1932; sworn in April 1994).

The MLP Cabinet was in March 1998:
Prime Minister: Alfred Sant.
Deputy Prime Minister, Minister of Foreign Affairs and the Environment: George

Vella. *Education and National Culture:* Evarist Bartolo. *Finance and Commerce:* Leo Brincat. *Tourism:* Karmenu Vella. *Justice and Local Councils:* Charles Mangion. *Economic Affairs and Industry:* John Attard Montalto. *Transport and Ports:* Joe Debono Grech. *Without portfolio in the Office of the Prime Minister:* Joseph Mizzi. *Public Works and Construction:* Charles Buhagiar. *Health, Care of the Elderly and Family Affairs:* Michael Farrugia. *Social Welfare:* Edwin Grech. *Housing:* Freddie Portelli. *Agriculture and Fisheries:* Noel Farrugia.

Speaker: Myriam Spiteri Debono.

National flag: 2 equal vertical stripes, white in the hoist and red in the fly, with a representation of the George Cross medal edged with red in the canton.

National anthem: 'Lil din l'art helwa, l'omm li tatna isimha' ('Guard her, O Lord, as ever Thou hast guarded'); words by Dun Karm Psaila, tune by Dr Robert Samut.

Local Government: Legislation of 1993 provides for the election of 67 local councils on Malta and Gozo.

DEFENCE. In 1997 the Armed Forces of Malta (AFM) had a strength of about 2,000 and consisted of the Headquarters and 3 Regiments. 1st Regiment AFM is an Infantry Battalion, 2nd Regiment AFM comprises an Air Defence Battery, an Air Squadron and the Maritime Squadron. 3rd Regiment AFM consists of the logistics and support element and a Revenue Security Corps.

In addition to infantry and low-level air defence artillery weapons, AFM are equipped with helicopters (Alouette IIIs and NH500s), fixed-wing aircraft (PBN Islander and Cessna Birdogs), and a number of patrol craft for inshore and offshore duties, including 3 Kondor Class 52 metre patrol boats.

Apart from normal military duties, AFM are also responsible for Search and Rescue, airport security, surveillance of Malta's territorial and fishing zones, harbour traffic control and anti-pollution duties.

INTERNATIONAL RELATIONS

Membership. Malta is a member of the UN, the Commonwealth, the Council of Europe, the Organization for Security and Co-operation in Europe, the International Atomic Energy Agency, the Organization for the Prohibition of Chemical Weapons, the Comprehensive Test-Ban Treaty Organization and the Inter-Parliamentary Union. Malta's application to join the EU made in July 1990 by the nationalist government is now on hold, though the present administrations wants a 'special relationship' with the EU spanning 10–15 years.

ECONOMY

The Maltese economy has developed and expanded significantly over the past two decades. The manufacturing and tourism industries have become the pillars of the domestic economy. Malta's industrial strategy encourages the need for technologies that promote high quality manufactured products and increased value-added output. Direct investment by both local and foreign entrepreneurs is actively promoted and supported, while particular importance is attached to the development of small- and medium-sized companies.

In line with the policy of developing Malta as an international financial centre, active steps are being taken in the financial servies sector in order to enhance Malta's potential in this field. Other teritary sectors, notably freeport activities, are also being encouraged and promoted to ensure that they effectively become mainstays of the domestic economy.

Malta is committed to develop closer ties with the EU through the establishment of a free trade zone with the Union, together with co-operation in financial, political, security and other matters. Malta also actively supports the Euro-Mediterranean Partnership as a means towards political, social and economic development in the region.

Performance. Annual GDP growth averaged 4·7% over 1992–97.

Budget. Revenue and expenditure (in Lm1m.):

	1992	1993	1994	1995	1996
Revenue	358·2	396·6	429·0	487·3	468·3
Expenditure	372·3	410·9	450·9	498·1	548·9

The most important sources of revenue are VAT, customs and excise duties, income tax, social security and receipts from the Central Bank of Malta.

Currency. The unit of currency is the *Maltese lira* (formerly *pound*) (MTL) of 100 *cents*. Central Bank of Malta notes are issued in denominations of Lm2, 5, 10 and 20, and there are coins of 1, 2, 5, 10, 25 and 50 cents and Lm1. Total notes and coins in circulation on 30 Nov. 1997, Lm376·6m. (Lm362m. notes, Lm14·6m. coins). Annualized inflation was 2·82% as at Oct. 1997.

Banking and Finance. The Central Bank of Malta (*Governor*, Emanuel Ellul) was founded in 1968. In 1997 there were 4 domestic and 1 foreign bank undertaking business in the local market. 10 local financial institutions, licensed in terms of the Financial Institutions Act 1994, also provided services that ranged from exchange bureau-related business to merchant banking.

During 1997 Malta continued to establish itself as a financial international business centre. The Malta Financial Services Centre is the autonomous government authority set up in 1994 as the primary regulator of financial services. The financial services framework available provides the necessary legal structure for the setting up of international business operations including unit trusts, mutual funds, captive insurance, international trading and holding companies and other investment products.

ENERGY AND NATURAL RESOURCES

Electricity. Electricity is generated at 2 interconnected power stations located at Marsa (272 MW) and Delimara (195 MW). The primary transmission voltages are 132,000, 33,000 and 11,000 volts while the low-voltage system is 414/240V, 50Hz with neutral point earthed.

Oil. Intensive negotiations with AGIP led to the successful conclusion of an exploration agreement in an offshore area of approximately 9,000 sq. km. Onshore exploration was revived and a deep stratigraphic well will be drilled by the government onshore on Gozo in 1998.

Agriculture. Despite the dry climate and the lack of fertile land, a wide-range of fruits and vegetables are cultivated. The two main crops are potatoes and tomatoes. The former is the country's primary export crop whilst the latter are the main input for the local canning industry. Peaches, plums, nectarines and apricots are Malta's main fruits produced during the summer. Sugar-melons, water-melons and strawberries are grown intensively and have significant export potential. Cereals and sulla are mainly grown for hay and straw for livestock feeding.

The livestock sector is very important. Malta is self-sufficient in chicken, eggs, pork and fresh milk. During 1997 export of pork was initated and it appears that there is a significant potential in such a venture. Livestock produce accounted for 65% of the total value of agricultural production during 1997.

During 1997 the contribution of agriculture to GDP was estimated at Lm31m. or 3%. There are about 2,500 full-time farmers.

Fisheries. In Dec. 1996 the fishing industry employed 1,619 power-propelled and 9 other fishing boats, engaging some 340 full-time and 1,379 part-time fishermen. The catch for 1996 was 841 tonnes, valued at Lm1,404,481. Production from fish farms was 1,552 tonnes. It is estimated that during 1997 the local aquaculture industry produced a total of about 1,800 tonnes of sea bass and sea bream valued at Lm3·8m. 95% of local production was harvested for export, mainly to Italy. The production forecast for the marine hatchery at the National Aquaculture Centre in 1998 is 1·1m. It is estimated that all the aquaculture industry employs about 120 full-timers and around 60 part-timers.

INDUSTRY.
Besides manufacturing (food, clothing, chemicals, electrical machinery parts and electronic components and products), the mainstays of the economy are ship repair and shipbuilding, agriculture, small crafts units, tourism and

the provision of other services such as the freeport facilities. The majority of state-aided manufacturing enterprises operating in Malta are foreign-owned or with foreign interests. The Malta Development Corporation is the Government agency responsible for promoting investment, while the Malta Export Trade Corporation serves as a catalyst to the export of local products.

Labour. The labour supply in Sept. 1997 was 145,654 (females, 40,207), including 37,312 in private direct production (agriculture and fisheries, 2,533; manufacturing, 29,082; oil drilling, construction and quarrying, 5,697), 45,163 in private market services, 50,155 in the public sector (including government departments, armed forces, revenue security corps, airport company, independent statutory bodies and companies with public sector majority shareholding), and 6,123 in temporary employment. Registered unemployed were 6,901 in Sept. 1997 (4·7% of labour supply).

Trade Unions. There were 38 trade unions registered as at 1 Dec. 1997, with a total membership of 80,560, and 25 employers' associations with a total membership of 8,510.

FOREIGN ECONOMIC RELATIONS. Imports are being liberalized. Marsaxlokk is an all-weather freeport zone for transhipment activities.

Commerce. Imports and exports including bullion and specie (in Lm1,000):

	1991	1992	1993	1994	1995	1996
Imports	684,000	747,770	830,920	918,766	1,037,657	1,007,616
Exports	405,453	490,903	518,325	592,422	674,947	624,154

In 1996 the principal items of imports were: Semi-manufactures, Lm141·8m.; machinery and transport equipment, Lm486·1m.; foodstuffs, Lm91·8m.; fuels, Lm53·8m.; manufactures, Lm19·4m.; chemicals, Lm74·3m. Of domestic exports: Manufactures, Lm143·5m.; machinery and transport equipment, Lm354·6m.; semi-manufactures, Lm42·1m.; beverages and tobacco, Lm2·9m.; foodstuffs, Lm10·7m.; chemicals, Lm14·3m.

In 1996, imports valued at Lm196·7m. came from Italy, Lm159·8m. from France, Lm143·9m. from UK, Lm94·8m. from Germany, Lm69·6m. from USA. Main export markets: France, Lm91·9m.; Germany, Lm86·4m.; USA, Lm81·3m.; Singapore Lm75·6m.; Italy, Lm71·9m.; UK, Lm42·7m.

Tourism. Tourism is the major foreign currency earner. In 1997 an estimated 1·1m. tourists (38·7% from the UK) generated earnings of Lm194m. (Jan.–Sept. 1997). Cruise passenger visits totalled 115,604. Employment in hotel and catering establishments was 9,296 in 1997.

COMMUNICATIONS

Roads. There is a car ferry between Malta and Gozo. In 1997 there were 1,742 km of roads, including 1,560 km of main roads. About 94% of roads are paved. Motor vehicles registered at the end of 1995: Private cars, 173,259; commercial vehicles, 40,835; cars for hire, 7,592; buses and minibuses, 1,014; motor cycles, 17,411.

Civil Aviation. The national carrier is Air Malta, which is 96·4% state-owned, and in 1997 operated 2 Airbus A320-200s, 2 B-737-200 Advs, 3 B-737-300s and 4 AVRO RJ70 aircraft. Services are also provided by Aeroflot, Air France, Alitalia, Austrian Airlines, Balkan, Condor, Corsair, Czech Airlines, Egyptair, GB Airways JAT, LTU, Lufthansa, Romavia, Sudan Airways, Swissair, Transavia and Tuninter. In 1997 there were scheduled services to Austria, Bahrain, Bulgaria, Cyprus, Czech Republic, Egypt, France, Germany, Greece, Ireland, Israel, Italy, Morocco, Netherlands, Norway, Portugal, Romania, Russia, Spain, Sweden, Switzerland, Syria, Tunisia, Turkey, UAE, UK, USA and Yugoslavia. In 1996 there were 27,048 commercial aircraft movements at Malta International Airport. 2,267,019 passengers and 10,311 tonnes of freight and 877 tonnes of mail were handled.

Shipping. The number of vessels registered on 31 Dec. 1996 was 2,807 totalling 20,265,745 GT. Ships entering harbour, excluding yachts and fishing vessels, during 1995–96, 5,760. 15 cruise vessels put in during 1996.

Telecommunications. Telecommunications are operated by MaltaCom plc. There are 15 telephone exchanges and 7 remote switching exchanges with a total installed capacity of 213,000 lines. There is a digital data transmission network. Radio and TV services are under the control of the Broadcasting Authority, an independent statutory body. The government-owned Public Broadcasting Services Ltd was set up in 1991 and operates 2 radio stations and a TV station (colour by PAL). Legislation of 1991 introduced private commercial broadcasting. In 1997 there were 12 radio and 3 TV services and a cable TV network. On 31 Dec. 1995 there were some 160,000 licensed television sets.

Cinemas (1996). There were 22 cinemas with a seating capacity of 4,237.

Press. There were (1997) 3 English and 2 Maltese dailies, 5 Maltese and 2 English weeklies, 1 financial weekly in English and 1 fortnightly in Maltese.

SOCIAL INSTITUTIONS

Justice. The number of persons convicted of crimes in 1995 was 1,743; those convicted for contraventions against various laws and regulations numbered 5,761. 133 persons were committed to prison and 7,371 awarded fines and other punishments.

On 31 Dec. 1997, police numbered 90 officers (5 women) and 1,710 other ranks (190 women).

Religion. 98% of the population belong to the Roman Catholic Church, which is established by law as the religion of the country, though full liberty of conscience and freedom of worship are guaranteed.

Education. Education is compulsory between the ages of 5 and 16 and free in government schools from kindergarten to university. Kindergarten education is provided for 3- and 4-year old children. The primary school course lasts 6 years. In Oct. 1997, there were 6,105 children in state kindergartens and 23,000 (12,000 boys and 11,000 girls) in 80 state primary schools. There are education centres for children with special needs, but these are taught in ordinary schools if possible.

Secondary schools, trade schools and junior lyceums provide secondary education in the state sector. At the end of their primary education, pupils sit for the 11+ examination to start a secondary education course. Pupils who qualify are admitted in the junior lyceum, while the others attend secondary schools. In 1997, 11 junior lyceums had a total of 9,300 students (5,800 and 3,500 boys). 5 centres cater for 1,370 children (450 girls and 920 boys) at secondary level whose cultural capital is low or negligible. Secondary schools and junior lyceums offer a 5-year course leading to the Secondary Education Certificate and the General Certificate of Education, Ordinary Level. At the end of the third year of secondary education, students may opt for a course with a technology bias in a trade school, where the full course may last 6 years. Trade School students generally come from the secondary schools. Courses run by Trade Schools lead to a Journeyman's Certificate and/or a City and Guilds of London Institute certificate. In Oct. 1997, there were 2,500 students (100 girls) enrolled in trade schools. At the end of the 5-year secondary course, students may opt to follow a higher academic or technical or vocational course of from 1 to 4 years. The academic courses generally lead to Intermediate and Advanced Level examinations set by the British universities. The junior college, administered by the University, prepares students specifically for a university course. The Matriculation Certificate, which qualifies students for admission to university, is a broad-based holistic qualification covering the humanities, sciences and operacy subjects, together with systems of knowledge. About 3,000 students (1,400 females) attend state higher secondary educational institutions; 2,069 students attend the junior college. Students following higher secondary courses who qualify for the Extended Skill Training Scheme or Technician Apprenticeship Scheme or the Sixth Form Students' Scheme receive an allowance.

About 30% of the student population attend non-state schools, from kindergarten to higher secondary level. In Oct. 1997 there were about 26,000 pupils attending non-state schools, 17,600 of whom were in schools run by the Roman Catholic Church, while 8,200 students were attending private schools. Under an agreement between the Government and the Church, the Government subsidizes Church schools and students attending these schools do not pay any fees.

Nearly 7,000 students (3,540 females) were following courses at the University in 1997. University students receive a stipend.

In Oct. 1997 about 5,800 students were attending adult or evening courses covering a very wide spectrum of studies at different levels. Many of these courses lead to a recognized certification.

Health. In 1996 there were 925 doctors, 122 dentists, 648 pharmacists, 200 midwives and 4,000 nursing personnel. There were 7 hospitals (2 private) with 2,140 beds and 8 health centres.

Welfare. Legislation provides a national contributory insurance scheme and also for the payment of non-contributory allowances, assistances and pensions. It covers the payment of marriage grants, maternity benefits, child allowances, parental allowances, handicapped child allowance, family bonus, sickness benefit, injury benefits, disablement benefits, unemployment benefit, contributory pensions in respect of retirement, invalidity and widowhood, and non-contributory medical assistance, free medical aids, social assistance, a carer's pension and pensions for the handicapped, blind and the aged.

DIPLOMATIC REPRESENTATIVES

Of Malta in Great Britain (36-38 Piccadilly, London, W1V 0PQ)
High Commissioner: Richard A. Matrenza.

Of Great Britain in Malta (7 St Anne St., Floriana)
High Commissioner: Graham Archer.

Of Malta in the USA (2017 Connecticut Ave., NW, Washington, D.C., 20008)
Ambassador: Dr Mark Anthony Micallef.

Of the USA in Malta (Development Hse., St Anne St., Floriana)
Ambassador: Ms Kathryn H. Proffitt.

Of Malta to the United Nations
Ambassador: George Saliba.

Of Malta to the European Union
Ambassador: Victor Camilleri.

Further Reading

Central Office of Statistics. *Statistical Abstracts of the Maltese Islands*, a quarterly digest of statistics, quarterly and annual trade returns, annual vital statistics and annual publications on shipping and aviation, education, agriculture, industry, National Accounts and Balance of Payments.

Department of Information (3 Castille Place, Valletta). *The Malta Government Gazette, Malta Information, Economic Survey [year], Reports on the Working of Government Departments, The Maltese Economy in Figures, 1986–1995, Business Opportunities on Malta, Acts of Parliament and Subsidiary Legislation, Laws of Malta, Constitution of Malta 1992.*

Berg, W. G., *Historical Dictionary of Malta.* Metuchen (NJ), 1995
Central Bank of Malta. *Annual Reports.*
Chamber of Commerce (annual). *Trade Directory.*
Blouet, B., *The Story of Malta.* London, Rev. ed. 1981
Cremona, J. J., *The Constitutional Developments of Malta under British Rule.* Malta Univ. Press, 1963.—*Human Rights Documentation in Malta.* Malta Univ. Press, 1966
Gerada, E. and Zuber, C., *Malta: an Island Republic.* Paris, 1979
The Malta Yearbook. Valletta
Thackrah, J. R., *Malta* [Bibliography]. Oxford and Santa Barbara (CA), 1985

National statistical office: Central Office of Statistics, Auberge d'Italie, Valletta.
Website: http://www.magnet.mt/home/cos/

MARSHALL ISLANDS

Republic of the
Marshall Islands

Capital: Dalap-Uliga-Darrit
Population: 60,000
GNP: US$88m.

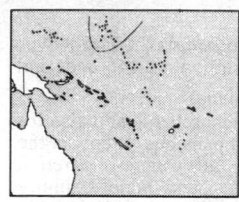

KEY HISTORICAL EVENTS. A German protectorate was formed in 1886 which was occupied at the beginning of the First World War by Japan. Japan was awarded a mandate by the League of Nations in 1919. During the Second World War the Islands were occupied by Allied forces in 1944, and became part of the UN Trust Territory of the Pacific Islands created on 18 July 1947 and administered by the USA. On 21 Oct. 1986 the islands gained independence and a Compact of Free Association with the USA came into force. The UN recognized the termination of the US Trusteeship on 22 Dec. 1990, and the Islands became a full UN member state on 17 Sept. 1991.

TERRITORY AND POPULATION. The Marshall Islands lie in the North Pacific Ocean north of Kiribati and east of Micronesia, and consist of an archipelago of 31 coral atolls, 5 single islands and 1,152 islets strung out in 2 chains, eastern and western. The land area is 181 sq. km (70 sq. miles). The capital is Dalap-Uliga-Darrit on Majuro in the eastern chain (population, 1990, 20,000). The principal atoll in the western chain is Kwajalein containing the only other town, Ebeye (population, 1992, 10,000). The two archipelagic island chains of Bikini and Enewetak are former US nuclear test sites; Kwajalein is now used as a US missile test range. The islands lay claim to the US territory of Wake Island. At the census of 1988 the population was 43,380 (48% urban); 1997 estimate, 60,652; density, 335 per sq. km. About 97% of the population are Marshallese, a Micronesian people.

Vital statistics (1997 est.): Population growth rate, 3·85%; birth rate, 45·54 per 1,000 population; death rate, 7·05 per 1,000; infant mortality rate, 45·7 per 1,000 live births; life expectancy, 64·14 years.

English is universally spoken and is the official language. Two major Marshallese dialects from the Malayo-Polynesian family, and Japanese, are also spoken.

CLIMATE. Hot and humid, with wet season from May-November. The islands border the typhoon belt. Jaluit. Jan. 81°F (27·2°C), July 82°F (27·8°C). Annual rainfall 161" (4,034 mm).

CONSTITUTION AND GOVERNMENT. Under the constitution which came into force on 1 May 1979, the Marshall Islands form a republic with a *President* as head of state and government, who is elected for 4-year terms by the parliament. The parliament consists of a 33-member *House of Assembly* (Nitijela), directly elected by popular vote for 4-year terms. There is also a 12-member appointed *Council of Chiefs* (Iroij) which has a consultative and advisory capacity on matters affecting customary law and practice. The last election was held on 14 Jan. 1997.

In March 1998 the government comprised:

President: Imata Kabua (since 14 Jan. 1997), with 63% of the parliamentary vote.
Minister of Finance: Ruben Zackhras. *Foreign Affairs:* Phillip Muller. *Transport and Telecommunications:* Kunio Lemari. *Resources, Development and Public Works:* Jiba Kabua. *Education:* Justin de Brum. *Internal and Social Welfare:* Brenson Wase. *Health and Environment:* Thomas D. Kijiner. *Justice:* Lomes McKay. *Interior and Outer Island Affairs:* Brenson Wase. *Minister without Portfolio, Ralik Island Chain:* Christopher Loeak. *Minister without Portfolio, Ratak Island Chain:* Litokwa Tomeing. *Chief Secretary:* Philip Kabua. *Attorney General:* Gerald Zackhras.

DEFENCE. The Compact of Free Association gave the USA responsibility for

954

defence in return for US assistance. There is a police force, and a coast guard may be established.

INTERNATIONAL RELATIONS

Membership. The Marshall Islands are a member of the UN, Pacific Community (formerly the South Pacific Commission) and the South Pacific Forum.

ECONOMY

Budget. 1995 estimate: revenue, US$67·2m.; expenditure: US$79·6m. Under the terms of the Compact of Free Association, the USA provides approximately US$4m. a year in aid.

Currency. US currency is used.

ENERGY AND NATURAL RESOURCES

Electricity. Total installed capacity (1994), 16,000 kW. Production (1994), 57m. kWh.

Minerals. High-grade phosphate deposits are mined on Ailinglaplap Atoll. Deep-seabed minerals are an important natural resource.

Agriculture. A small amount of agricultural produce is exported: coconuts, tomatoes, melons and breadfruit. Other important crops include copra, taro, cassava and sweet potatoes. Pigs and chicken constitute the main livestock.

Fisheries. There is a commercial tuna-fishing industry with a canning factory on Majuro. Seaweed is cultivated.

INDUSTRY. The main industries are copra, fish, tourism, handicrafts (items made from shell, wood and pearl), mining, manufacturing, construction and power.

Labour. The working population numbered 4,800 in 1986. An estimated 16% were unemployed in 1991. In 1994, agriculture accounted for 16% of the working population; industry, 14%; services, 70%.

FOREIGN ECONOMIC RELATIONS

Commerce. Imports (mainly oil) were estimated at US$69·9m. in 1995; exports, US$21·3m. Main trading partners: USA, Japan and Australia. Main exports: fish, coconut oil, trochus shells, live animals. Main imports: foodstuffs, machinery and equipment, fuel, beverages and tobacco.

COMMUNICATIONS

Roads. There are paved roads on major islands (Majuro, Kwajalein); roads are otherwise stone-, coral- or laterite-surfaced.

Civil Aviation. There are 9 paved and 7 unpaved airports (1996). Air Marshall Islands operates flights to Fiji, Kiribati and Tuvalu as well as domestic services. It had 4 aircraft in 1992. 44,000 passengers were carried in 1993.

Shipping. Majuro is the main port. There were 94 ships in 1996, totalling over 4m. GRT.

Telecommunications. In 1997 there were nearly 3,500 telephones in use. There is a US satellite communications system on Kwajalein and 2 Intelsat satellite earth stations (Pacific Ocean). There is 1 TV and 3 radio stations.

SOCIAL INSTITUTIONS

Justice. The Supreme Court is situated on Majuro. There is a High Court and Traditional Rights Court for customary disputes.

Religion. The population is mainly Protestant, but there are Roman Catholic and Bahai communities.

Education. In 1994 there were 13,565 pupils in 104 primary schools, and 2,483 pupils in 11 secondary schools. There is a College of the Marshall Islands, and a subsidiary of the University of the South Pacific, on Majuro.

Health. In 1987 there were 19 doctors, 88 nurses and 2 hospitals with 54 beds.

DIPLOMATIC REPRESENTATIVES

Of Great Britain in the Marshall Islands (resides in Fiji)
Ambassador: Vernon M. Scarborough.

Of the Marshall Islands in the USA (2433 Massachusetts Ave., NW, Washington, D.C., 20008)
Ambassador: Banny de Brum.

Of the USA in the Marshall Islands (Oceanside Mejen Weto, Long Island, Majuro)
Ambassador: Joan M. Plaisted.

Of the Marshall Islands to the United Nations
Ambassador: Laurence N. Edwards.

MAURITANIA

República Islamique Arabe
et Africaine de Mauritanie

Capital: Nouakchott
Population: 2·33m.
GDP per head: (PPP$) 1,593
GNP: US$1·1bn.
HDI/world rank: 0·355/150

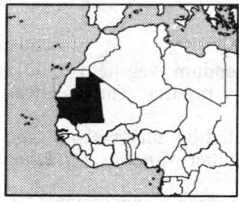

KEY HISTORICAL EVENTS. Mauritania became a French protectorate in 1903 and a colony in 1920. It became an autonomous republic within the French Community on 28 Nov. 1958 and achieved full independence on 28 Nov. 1960. Under its first President, Moktar Ould Daddah, Mauritania became a one-party state in 1964.

Following a coup on 10 July 1978, power was placed in the hands of a Military Committee for National Recovery (CMRN); the constitution was suspended and the 70-member National Assembly dissolved. On 6 April 1979 the CMRN was renamed the Military Committee for National Salvation (CMSN). A coup in Jan. 1980 installed Lieut.-Col. Mohammed Haidalla in power, and under his rule slavery was finally abolished in Mauritania. In Feb. 1984 he recognized Polisario's declaration of a Sahrawi Arab Democratic Republic. He was overthrown in Dec. 1984 when his prime minister, Lieut.-Col. Maaouiya Ould Sidi Ahmed Taya, seized power.

The 1980s were characterized by territorial disputes with Morocco and Senegal. In April 1991 Taya announced a new constitution allowing for a multi-party political system, but which also gave extensive powers to the president. The proposed constitution was approved by referendum in July 1991. Taya was re-elected in Jan. 1992 but legislative elections in March were boycotted by opposition parties who accused the government of electoral fraud. Subsequent elections were dominated by President Taya and his Democratic and Socialist Republican Party.

TERRITORY AND POPULATION. Mauritania is bounded west by the Atlantic Ocean, north by Western Sahara, north-east by Algeria, east and south-east by Mali, and south by Senegal. The total area is 1,030,700 sq. km (398,000 sq. miles) of which 47% is desert, and the population at the census of 1988 was 1,864,236. Estimate, 1996, 2,332,000 (54% urban); density, 2·26 per sq. km.

Vital statistics rates, 1996 estimates (per 1,000 population). Births, 46·9; deaths, 15·2. Infant mortality (per 1,000 live births), 81·7. Expectation of life in 1996 was 49·0 years (46·1 for males and 52·1 for females). Growth rate, 3·2%.

Area, population and chief towns of the Nouakchott Capital District and 12 regions at the 1988 census:

Region	Area (sq. km)	Population (1992 estimate)	Chief town
Nouakchott District	1,000	324,037	Nouakchott
Hodh ech-Chargui	182,700	234,011	Néma
Hodh el-Gharbi	53,400	175,089	Aïoun el Atrouss
Açâba	36,600	185,574	Kiffa
Gorgol	13,600	201,301	Kaédi
Brakna	37,100	207,590	Aleg
Trarza	67,800	217,867	Rosso
Adrar	215,300	62,906	Atâr
Dakhlet Nouâdhibou	22,300	83,246	Nouâdhibou
Tagant	95,200	67,939	Tidjikdja
Guidimaka	10,300	129,797	Sélibaby
Tiris Zemmour	252,900	37,534	Zouérate
Inchiri	46,800	13,630	Akjoujt

Principal towns (1992 population): Nouakchott, 480,408 including suburbs; Nouâdhibou, 72,305; Kaédi, 35,241.

In 1987 there were also 0·43m. nomads.

957

The major ethnic groups are (with numbers in 1993): Moors (of mixed Arab, Berber and African origin), 1,513,400; Wolof, 147,000; Tukulor, 114,600; Soninke, 60,000.

Arabic is the official language. French no longer has official status. Pulaar, Soninke and Wolof are national languages.

CLIMATE. A tropical climate, but conditions are generally arid, even near the coast, where the only appreciable rains come in July to Sept. Nouakchott. Jan. 71°F (21·7°C), July 82°F (27·8°C). Annual rainfall 6" (158 mm).

CONSTITUTION AND GOVERNMENT. A referendum was held in July 1991 to approve a new constitution instituting multi-party politics. Turn-out was 85·34%; 97·94% of votes cast were in favour.

The new constitution envisages that the President is elected by universal suffrage for renewable 6-year terms. There is a *Senate* and a 72-member *National Assembly*. Parties specifically Islamic are not permitted.

Presidential elections were held on 12 Dec. 1997. There were 5 candidates. Col. Maaouiya Ould Sidi Ahmed Taya was re-elected with 90·2% of votes cast, compared to 62·8% in the elections of 24 Jan. 1992.

Elections for the National Assembly were held on 19 Oct. 1996. 21 parties stood. The Democratic and Socialist Republican Party (PRDS) gained 72 seats.

President: Maaouiya Ould Sidi Ahmed Taya (assumed office 12 Dec. 1984; re-elected 1992 and 1997).

In March 1998 the government comprised:
Prime Minister: Mohamed Lamine Ould Guig.

Minister of National Defence: Kaba Ould Elewa. *Interior, Posts and Telecommunications:* Col. Ahmed Ould Minnih. *Foreign Affairs and Co-operation:* Mohamed El Hacen Ould Lebatt. *Justice:* Mohamed Ould Ahmed Lemine. *Planning:* Mohamedou Ould Michel. *Finance:* Camara Aly Gueladio. *Fisheries and Maritime Economy:* Mohamed El Moctar Ould Zamel. *Commerce, Artisans and Tourism:* Sidi Mohamed Ould Mohamed Vall. *Mines and Industry:* N'Gaide Lamine Kayo. *Health and Social Affairs:* Diye Ba. *Culture and Islamic Orientation:* Moustaph Ould sid 'El Isselmou. *Civil Service, Labour, Youth and Sports:* Baba Ould Sidi. *Equipment and Transportation:* Sghair Ould M'Bareck. *Education:* Ahmedou Ould Moustapha Senhoury. *Rural Development and the Environment:* Lemrabott Sidi Mahmoud Ould Cheikh Ahmed. *Hydraulics and Energy:* Mohamed Salem Ould Merzoug. *Communications and Relations with Parliament:* Rachid Ould Saleh.

National anthem: No words, tune by T. Nikiprowetzky.

Local Government: Mauritania is divided into a capital district and 12 regions. These are sub-divided into 49 departments and 208 communes. At the municipal elections of Jan.–Feb. 1994 the PRDS won a majority in 172 communes.

DEFENCE. Conscription is authorized for 2 years.

Army. There are 6 military regions. The Army consists of 7 motorized infantry, 1 parachute, 1 Presidential security, 3 artillery, 8 infantry and 2 Camel Corps battalions, 1 armoured car squadron, 4 air defence artillery batteries and 1 engineer company. Equipment includes 35 T-54/-55 main battle tanks. Strength 15,000 in 1997.

Navy. The Navy, some 500 strong in 1997, is based at Nouâdhibou and consists of 2 offshore patrol craft for fishery protection, 9 inshore patrol craft and a few boats.

Air Force. The Air Force has 5 Britten-Norman Defender armed light transports, 2 Maritime Surveillance Cheyennes for coastal patrol, 1 Buffalo transport, 2 Y-12 transports, 4 Reims-Cessna 337 Milirole twin-engined counter-insurgency, forward air control and training aircraft and 2 Hughes 500 helicopters for communications. Personnel (1997), 150 with 7 combat aircraft.

INTERNATIONAL RELATIONS

Membership. Mauritania is a member of the UN, OAU, the Arab League and is an ACP state of the EU.

ECONOMY

Budget. 1994 revenue (in 1,000m. ouguiya), 29·46 (including tax receipts, 22·72); expenditure, 35·20.

Currency. The monetary unit is the *ouguiya* (MRO) which is divided into 5 *khoums*. There are notes of 1,000, 500, 200 and 100 ouguiya and coins of 20, 10, 5 and 1 ouguiya and 1 and 0·2 khoum. 7,898m. ouguiya were in circulation in 1992. Foreign exchange reserves were US$61·1m. in 1994. Gold reserves were 12,000 troy oz. in 1989. In Oct. 1992 the ouguiya was devalued 28%. Inflation was 3·5% in 1995.

Banking and Finance. The Central Bank (created 1973) is the bank of issue, and there are 4 commercial banks. Bank deposits totalled 12,304m. ouguiya in 1992.

Weights and Measures. The metric system is in use.

ENERGY AND NATURAL RESOURCES

Electricity. Installed public-sector capacity was 129 MW in 1990. Production (1993) was 135m. kWh.

Minerals. There are reserves of copper, gold, phosphate and gypsum. Iron ore production (1993) was 9·20m. tonnes. Mining contributed 11·4% of GDP in 1994.

Agriculture. Only 1% of the country receives enough rain to grow crops, so agriculture is mainly confined to the south, in the Senegal river valley. Production in tonnes (1995) of millet and sorghum, 165,000; rice, 79,000; dates, 25,000; pulses, 17,000; watermelons, 6,000; yams, 3,000; groundnuts, 2,000; sweet potatoes, 2,000.
   Herding is the main occupation of the rural population and accounted for 16% of GDP in 1992. In 1995 there were 5,288,000 sheep, 3,526,000 goats, 1,125,000 cattle, 1,087,000 camels, 155,000 asses, 18,000 horses.

Forestry. There are 15m. ha of forests, chiefly in the southern regions, where wild acacias yield the main product, gum arabic. In 1994, 13,000 cu. metres of roundwood were cut.

Fisheries. Total catch (1995) was 90,000 tonnes.

INDUSTRY. Output, 1988 (in tonnes): Fish products, 352,200; cheese, 1,754; butter, 647.

Labour. In 1994 the workforce was 687,000, of whom 430,000 worked in agriculture, forestry and fishing, 177,000 in services and 80,000 in industry.

FOREIGN ECONOMIC RELATIONS. Total foreign debt was US$2,467m. at the end of 1995. In Feb. 1989 Mauritania signed a treaty of economic co-operation with the 4 other Maghreb countries, Algeria, Libya, Morocco and Tunisia.

Commerce. In 1994 imports (in US$) totalled 390m. and exports 355m. Main exports are fish and fish products (57% of total exports) and iron ore (40%). Main imports are foodstuffs, consumer goods, petroleum products and capital goods. Principal export markets in 1994 were Japan (27%), followed by Italy and Belgium. Main import suppliers were Algeria (15%), followed by China and the USA.

Tourism. In 1986 there were 13,000 tourists.

COMMUNICATIONS

Roads. There were 8,150 km of roads in 1988, of which 1,710 km were asphalted. In 1995 there were 17,300 passenger cars and 9,200 commercial vehicles.

Railways. A 704-km railway links Zouérate with the port of Point-Central, 10 km south of Nouâdhibou, and is used primarily for iron ore exports. In 1995 it carried 11·3m. tonnes of freight.

Civil Aviation. There are international airports at Nouakchott and Nouâdhibou. Air Mauritanie had 3 aircraft in 1995. A total of 215,000 passengers were carried in 1993.

Shipping. In 1995 the merchant fleet totalled 20,311 GRT. The major ports are at Point-Central (for mineral exports), Nouakchott and Nouâdhibou.

Telecommunications. There were, in 1993, 8,000 telephones. The government-controlled Office de Radiodiffusion-Télévision de Mauritanie is responsible for broadcasting. There are 2 radio and 1 TV networks. In 1995 there were estimated to be 34,000 radio and 57,000 TV sets (colour by SECAM).

Press. In 1995 there was 1 daily newspaper with a circulation of 1,000.

SOCIAL INSTITUTIONS

Justice. There are courts of first instance at Nouakchott, Atâr, Kaédi, Aïoun el Atrouss and Kiffa. The Appeal Court and Supreme Court are situated in Nouakchott. Islamic jurisprudence was adopted in 1980.

Religion. Over 99% of Mauritanians are Sunni Moslem, mainly of the Qadiriyah sect.

Education. In 1993 there were 36 pre-primary schools with 108 teachers for 800 pupils; in 1995 there were 1,854 primary schools with 5,648 teachers for 289,945 pupils. In 1994 there were 45,810 secondary level pupils with 1,038 teachers, and 7,501 students at university level. The University of Nouakchott had 2,850 students and 70 academic staff in 1994–95. Adult literacy rate (1995), 37·7% (male, 49·6%; female, 26·3%).

Health. There were about 200 doctors in 1994.

DIPLOMATIC REPRESENTATIVES

Of Mauritania in Great Britain
Ambassador: Dah Ould Abdi (resides in Paris).

Of Great Britain in Mauritania
Ambassador: William H. Fullerton, CMG (resides in Morocco).

Of Mauritania in the USA (2129 Leroy Pl., NW, Washington, D.C., 20008)
Ambassador: Bilal Ould Werzeg.

Of the USA in Mauritania (PO Box 222, Nouakchott)
Ambassador: Dorothy Myers Sampas.

Of Mauritania to the United Nations
Ambassador: Mahfoudh Ould Deddach.

Of Mauritania to the European Union
Ambassador: Boullah Ould Mogueye.

Further Reading

Belvaud, C., *La Mauritanie*. Paris, 1992
Calderini, S. *et al., Mauritania*. [Bibliography]. Oxford and Santa Barbara (CA), 1992

MAURITIUS

Republic of Mauritius

Capital: Port Louis
Population: 1·13m.
GNP: US$3·5bn.
HDI/world rank: 0·831/61

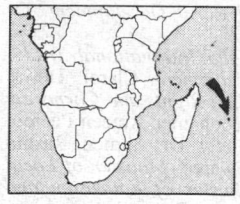

KEY HISTORICAL EVENTS. Mauritius was known to Arab navigators probably not later than the 10th century. Malays almost certainly visited in the 15th century, and it was discovered by the Portuguese between 1507 and 1512, but the Dutch were the first settlers in 1598, who named it after their stadtholder, Count Maurice. In 1710 they abandoned the island, which was occupied by the French under the name of Ile de France in 1715. The British occupied the island in 1810, and it was formally ceded to Great Britain by the Treaty of Paris, 1814.

The majority of the population were descendants of slaves brought by the French from Madagascar and East Africa, and indentured Indian labourers brought by Britain. European settlers unsuccessfully opposed calls for independence, and the elections in August 1967 provided an overwhelming mandate; independence was attained within the Commonwealth on 12 March 1968. Mauritius became a republic on 12 March 1992.

TERRITORY AND POPULATION. Mauritius, the main island, lies 500 miles (800 km) east of Madagascar. Rodrigues is 350 miles (560 km) east. The outer islands are Agalega and the St Brandon Group. Area and population:

Island	Area in sq. km	Census 1990	Estimate 1st July 1997
Mauritius	1,865	1,024,571	1,112,636
Rodrigues	104	34,204	35,070
Outer Islands	71	167	170
Total	2,040	1,058,942	1,147,876

The population growth rate in 1996 was 1·2%. Port Louis is the capital (146,322). Other towns: Beau Bassin-Rose Hill: 99,069, Quatre Bornes: 75,554, Curepipe: 78,516 and Vacoas-Phoenix: 96,928.

Vital statistics, 1996: Births: 20,763 (18·3 per 1,000); deaths: 7,670 (6·8 per 1,000); marriages: 10,697 (18·9 per 1,000).

Ethnic composition, 1996: Hindus, 52% 'General Population' (i.e. European, African, Creole), 33%; Moslems, 10%; Chinese, 5%.

The official language is English, although French is widely used. Creole and Bhojpuri are vernacular languages.

CLIMATE. The sub-tropical climate is humid. Most rain falls in the summer. Rainfall varies between 40" (1,000 mm) on the coast to 200" (5,000 mm) on the central plateau, though the west coast only has 35" (875 mm). Mauritius lies in the cyclone belt, whose season runs from Nov. to April, but is seldom affected by intense storms. Port Louis: Jan. 73°F (22·8°C), July 81°F (27·2°C). Annual rainfall 40" (1,000 mm).

CONSTITUTION AND GOVERNMENT. The head of state is the *President* elected by a simple majority of members of the National Assembly.

The *National Assembly* consists of 62 elected members (3 each for the 20 constituencies of Mauritius and 2 for Rodrigues) and 8 additional seats in order to ensure a fair and adequate representation of each community within the Assembly. Elections are held every 5 years on the basis of universal adult suffrage.

Parliamentary elections were held on 20 Dec. 1995. 481 candidates representing 42 parties stood.The electorate was 567,810; turn-out was 79·39%. All 62 elected seats were won by a coalition of the Labour Party (Parti Travailliste; LP) and the Mauritian Militant Movement with 65·2% of votes cast. The coalition split in mid 1997 and the Mauritian Militant Movement is now in opposition.

President: Cassam Uteem.

The Cabinet was composed as follows in March 1998:

Prime Minister, Minister of Defence and Home Affairs, External Communications and the Outer Islands, Civil Service Affairs, Urban and Rural Development: Dr Navinchandra Ramgoolam (b. 1947; LP).

Deputy Prime Minister, Minister of Foreign Affairs, and International Trade: Rajkeswur Purryag. *Minister of Housing and Land Development:* Clarel Désiré Malherbe. *Attorney-General and Minister of Justice, Human Rights and Corporate Affairs, Labour and Industrial Relations:* Abdool Razack Mohamed Ameen Peeroo. *Minister of Land Transport, Shipping and Public Safety:* Dr Ahmed Rashid Beebeejaun. *Minister of Finance:* Dr Vasant Kumar Bunwaree. *Minister of Local Government and Environment:* James Burty David. *Minister of Education and Human Resource Development:* Ramsamy Chedumbarum Pillay. *Minister of Agriculture, Fisheries and Co-operatives:* Dr Arvin Boolell. *Minister of Economic Development and Regional Co-operation:* Rundheersing Bheenick. *Minister of Arts and Culture:* Tsang Fan Hin Tsang Mang Kin. *Minister of Public Infrastructure:* Dr Mohummud Siddick Chady. *Minister of Public Utilities:* Devanand Virahswamy. *Minister of Women, Family Welfare and Child Development:* Indira Savitree Thacoor-Sidaya. *Minister of Youth and Sports:* Sachindev Mahess Kumar Soonarane. *Minister of Tourism and Leisure:* Joseph Jacques Chasteau de Balyon. *Minister of Health and Quality of Life:* Dr Nankeswarsingh Deerpalsingh. *Minister of Industry and Commerce:* Sathiamoorthy Sunassee. *Minister of Telecommunications and Information Technology, Social Security and National Solidarity:* Sarat Dutt Lallah. *Minister for Rodrigues:* Benoit Jolicoeur.

National anthem: 'Glory to thee, Motherland'; words by J. G. Prosper, tune by P. Gentille.

Local Government: The Island of Mauritius (only) is divided into 5 municipalities and 4 district councils.

DEFENCE. The Police Department, which is responsible for defence, is equipped with arms, 1 offshore patrol vessel, 4 inshore patrol craft, 1 Dornier and 1 Defender aircraft, 4 helicopters and 32 boats; its strength was (1997) 8,500.

INTERNATIONAL RELATIONS

Membership. Mauritius is a member of the UN, Commonwealth, OAU, La Francophonie, SADC and is an ACP state of the EU. Mauritius is also a founder member of the Indian Ocean Rim Association for Regional Co-operation.

ECONOMY

Budget. Revenue and expenditure (in Rs 1m.) for years ending 30 June:

	1994–95	1995–96	1996–97	1997–98 (Estimate)
Revenue	12,862	12,612	16,410	18,375
Expenditure	15,559	17,208	19,150	20,500

Principal sources of revenue, 1997–98 (Estimate): Direct taxes, Rs 3,662m.; indirect taxes, Rs 12,453m.; receipts from public utilities, Rs 277m.; receipts from public services, Rs 516,842m.; rental of government property, Rs 44m.; interest and royalties, Rs 1,248·7m.; reimbursement, Rs 173·6m. On 30 June 1997, the public debt of Mauritius was Rs 4,505m.

Currency. The unit of currency is the *Mauritius rupee* (MUR) of 100 *cents*. There are: (i) Bank of Mauritius notes of Rs 1,000, 500, 200, 100, 50, 10; (ii) cupro-nickel coins of 10 rupees, 5 rupees and 1 rupee; (iii) nickel-plated steel coins of 50 cents, 25 cents, 20 cents and 10 cents; (iv) copper-plated steel coins of 5 cents and 1 cent.

Banking and Finance. The Bank of Mauritius (founded 1967) is the central bank. The *Governor* is Mitrajeet Dhaneswar Maraye. There are 10 commercial banks. Non-bank financial intermediaries are the Post Office Savings Bank, the State Investment Corporation Ltd, the Mauritius Leasing Company, the National Mutual Fund, the National Investment Trust and the National Pension Fund. Other financial institutions are the Mauritius Housing Company and the Development Bank of Mauritius. There is also a stock exchange.

ENERGY AND NATURAL RESOURCES

Electricity. Electric power production (1996) was 2,173m. kWh.

Agriculture. In 1996, 76,812 hectares were planted with sugar cane. There were 17 factories, and sugar production (1996, in tonnes) was 588,455. Main secondary crops (1996, in tonnes): tea (1,109 ha) from which 2,497 were produced, tobacco 878, potatoes 10,639, and maize 438.

Livestock 1996: cattle, 12,525; goats 12,955; and pigs, 15,925.

Livestock products (1996) in tonnes: beef, 2,321; pork, 1,112; goat meat and mutton, 140.

Forestry. The total forest area was estimated (1995) at 65,400 ha including some 12,400 ha of plantations. In 1995 production totalled 21,000 cu. metres of timber, poles and fuel wood.

Fisheries. Production (1996) 11,010 tonnes.

INDUSTRY. Manufacturing includes: textile products, footwear and other leather products, diamond cutting, jewellery, furniture, watches and watchstraps, sunglasses, plastic ware, chemical products, electronic products, pharmaceutical products, electrical appliances, ship models and canned food.

Labour. In 1996, the Labour Force was estimated at 492,800. Manufacturing employed the largest proportion, with 27·9% of total employment; community, social and personal services, 26%; agriculture and fishing, 13·6%; trade, restaurants and hotels, 15·6%. The unemployment rate was estimated at 5·5% (provisional).

Trade Unions. In 1996 there were 330 registered trade unions with a total membership of about 110,000.

FOREIGN ECONOMIC RELATIONS

Commerce. Total trade (in Rs 1m.) for calendar years:

	1994	1995	1996 (provisional)
Imports c.i.f	34,548	34,363	40,892
Exports f.o.b.	24,097	27,326	31,991

In 1996, Rs 4,554m. of the imports came from France, Rs 4,893m. from the Republic of South Africa, Rs 2,648m. from the UK, and Rs 1,1811m. from Australia. In 1996, Rs 10,799m. of the exports went to the UK, Rs 6,109m. to France, Rs 4,092m. to the USA, and Rs 1,748m. to Germany.

Sugar exports in 1996 were 612,000 tonnes, Rs 8,024m. Other major exports (1996) included articles of apparel and clothing, Rs 270m.; chemicals and related products, Rs 159m.; cut flowers and foliage, Rs 126m. Major imports included (1996) manufactured goods (paper, textiles, iron and steel), Rs 13,715m.; machinery and transport equipment, Rs 8,917m.; food and live animals, Rs 5,922m.

Tourism. In 1996, there were 486,867 tourists bringing foreign exchange earnings of Rs 9,050m.

COMMUNICATIONS

Roads. In 1996 there were 31 km of motorway, 902 km of main roads, 966 km of secondary and other roads. At 31 December 1996, there were 45,563 cars, 2,348 buses, 22,229 motor cycles, 79,524 auto cycles, and 20,482 lorries and vans.

Civil Aviation. In 1996, 630,240 passengers arrived at Sir Seewoosagur Ramgoolam International Airport and 16,856 tonnes of freight were unloaded. The national carrier is Air Mauritius, which is partly state-owned and in 1996 operated 4 A340-300s, 2 B-767-200ERs, 2 ATR 42-300s and 2 Bell 206B helicopters. Services are also provided by Aeroflot, Air Austral, Air France, Air Madagascar, Air Zimbabwe, British Airways, Cathay Pacific, Condor, SAA and Singapore Airlines.

Shipping. A free port was established at Port Louis in September 1991. In 1996, 1,300 vessels entered Port Louis with a total gross registered tonnage of 5m tonnes.

Telecommunications. Mauritius Telecom, formed in 1992, provides telephone services to 183,902 subscribers (1996) through 58 exchanges. There were 23,000 cellular mobile telephone subscribers in 1996. Communication with other parts of the world is by satellite and microwave links. Broadcasting is run by the commercial Mauritius Broadcasting Corporation. At 31 Dec 1996 there were 172,080 television sets (colour by SECAM) and 0·3m. radio sets.

Cinemas (1997). There are 25 cinemas, with a seating capacity of about 25,000.

Press There are (1997) 7 daily papers in French (with occasional articles in English) with a combined circulation of about 100,000.

SOCIAL INSTITUTIONS

Justice. There is an Ombudsman. The death penalty was abolished in 1995.

Religion. At the 1990 Census (excluding Rodrigues) there were 287,726 Roman Catholics, 4,399 Protestants, 530,456 Hindus and 172,047 Moslems.

Education. Primary and secondary education is free, primary education being compulsory. About 91% of children aged 5-11 years attend schools. In 1996, there were 119,655 pupils in 269 primary schools, and 90,120 pupils in 127 secondary schools in the island of Mauritius, and 4,934 pupils in 12 primary schools and 2,917 in 3 secondary schools in Rodrigues. In 1996, 3,061 teachers were enrolled for training at the Mauritius Institute of Education.

In 1997-98, there were 3,462 students and 193 academic staff at the University of Mauritius.

Health. In 1996 (provisional) there were 1,008 doctors, 15 hospitals with 3,420 beds, 156 health centres and 12 private clinics with about 300 beds.

The life expectancy years at birth for the period 1993-95 was 66·5 years for males and 74·0 for females.

DIPLOMATIC REPRESENTATIVES

Of Mauritius in Great Britain (32/33 Elvaston Pl., London, SW7 5NW)
High Commissioner: Sir Satcam Boolell, QC.

Of Great Britain in Mauritius (Les Cascades Bldg., Edith Cavell St., Port Louis)
High Commissioner: James Daly.

Of Mauritius in the USA (4301 Connecticut Ave., NW, Washington, D.C., 20008)
Ambassador: C. Jesseramsing.

Of the USA in Mauritius (Rogers Bldg., John Kennedy St., Port Louis)
Ambassador: H. W. Geisel.

Of Mauritius to the United Nations
Ambassador: T. W. Wan Chat Kwong.

Of Mauritius to the European Union
Ambassador: Parrwiz Hossen.

Further Reading

Central Statistical Information Office. *Bi-annual Digest of Statistics*.
Bennett, P. R., *Mauritius*. [Bibliography] Oxford and Santa Barbara (CA), 1992
Bowman, L. W., *Mauritius: Democracy and Development in the Indian Ocean*. Aldershot, 1991
Mathur, H., *Parliament in Mauritius*. Rose Hill, 1991

National statistical office: Central Statistical Information Office, Rose Hill.

MEXICO

Estados Unidos Mexicanos
(United States of Mexico)

Capital: Mexico City
Population: 95·5m.
GDP per head: (PPP$) 7,384
GNP: US$368·7bn.
HDI/world rank: 0·853/50

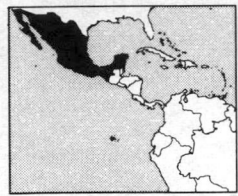

KEY HISTORICAL EVENTS. Mexico's history falls into four epochs: the era of the Indian empires (before 1521), the Spanish colonial phase (1521-1810), the period of national formation (1810-1910), and the present period which began with the social revolution of 1910-21.

Mexico was conquered for Spain by Cortés in 1521, and became part of the viceroyalty of New Spain. In 1810 began the fight for independence which was eventually achieved in 1821. A substantial part of Mexico's territory (including the present state of California) was lost to the USA by the Mexican War of 1846-48. In the 1860s France, Britain and the USA declared war on Mexico; France invaded the country and declared Maximilian, Archduke of Austria, to be Emperor of Mexico. When the French withdrew in 1867, Maximilian was executed by the Mexicans. The leader of the opposition to the French, Benito Juárez, again became president. In 1876 began the long presidency of Porfirio Diaz (1876-80, 1884-1911) who established himself as a dictator.

The latest period of Mexican history—regarded as one of social and national consolidation—began with the social revolution of 1910-21 led by Francisco Madero. The constitution of 1917 established a representative, democratic and federal republic, comprising 31 states and a federal district. There is a complete separation of legislative, executive and judicial powers. The president, who is the supreme executive authority, is directly elected for a single six year term. Women were enfranchised in 1958.

Despite democratic elections, the PRI (Partido Revolucionario Institucional) has been in power for 60 years; in 1982 the PRI won all 64 seats in the Senate, and in 1985, 289 of the 300 single-member seats in the Chamber of Deputies. The chief opposition party, PAN (Partido de Acción Nacional), has caused civil disturbances, claiming illegalities in the elections.

TERRITORY AND POPULATION. Mexico is bounded in the north by the USA, west and south by the Pacific Ocean, south-east by Guatemala, Belize and the Caribbean Sea, and north-east by the Gulf of Mexico. It comprises 1,967,183 sq. km (759,529 sq. miles), including uninhabited islands (5,073 sq. km) offshore. Population density, 41·3 per sq. km.

Population at recent censuses: 1970, 48,225,288; 1980, 66,846,833; 1990, 81,249,645. Estimate, 1995, 91,120,433; 46,242,875 (females). 1997 est., 95·5m.

Area, population and capitals of the Federal District and 31 states:

	Area (Sq. km)	Population (1990 census)	Population (1995 counting)	Capital
Federal District	1,499	8,235,744	8,489,007	Mexico City
Aguascalientes	5,589	719,659	862,720	Aguascalientes
Baja California	70,113	1,660,855	2,112,140	Mexicali
Baja California Sur	73,677	317,764	375,494	La Paz
Campeche	51,833	535,185	642,516	Campeche
Coahuila	151,571	1,972,340	2,173,775	Saltillo
Colima	5,455	428,510	488,028	Colima
Chiapas	73,887	3,210,496	3,584,786	Tuxtla Gutiérrez
Chihuahua	247,087	2,441,873	2,793,537	Chihuahua
Durango	119,648	1,349,378	1,431,748	Victoria de Durango
Guanajuato	30,589	3,982,593	4,406,568	Guanajuato
Guerrero	63,794	2,620,637	2,916,567	Chilpancingo
Hidalgo	20,987	1,888,366	2,112,473	Pachuca de Soto
Jalisco	80,137	5,302,689	5,991,176	Guadalajara
México	21,461	9,815,795	11,707,964	Toluca de Lerdo

	Area (Sq. km)	Population (1990 census)	Population (1995 counting)	Capital
Michoacán	59,864	3,548,199	3,870,604	Morelia
Morelos	4,941	1,195,059	1,442,662	Cuernavaca
Nayarit	27,621	824,643	896,702	Tepic
Nuevo Léon	64,555	3,098,736	3,550,114	Monterrey
Oaxaca	95,364	3,019,560	3,228,895	Oaxaca de Juárez
Puebla	33,919	4,126,101	4,624,365	Puebla de Zaragoza
Querétaro	11,769	1,051,235	1,250,476	Querétaro
Quintana Roo	50,350	493,277	703,536	Chetumal
San Luis Potosí	62,848	2,003,187	2,200,763	San Luis Potosí
Sinaloa	58,092	2,204,054	2,425,675	Culiacán Rosales
Sonora	184,934	1,823,606	2,085,536	Hermosillo
Tabasco	24,661	1,501,744	1,748,769	Villahermosa
Tamaulipas	79,829	2,249,581	2,527,328	Ciudad Victoria
Tlaxcala	3,914	761,277	883,924	Tlaxcala
Veracruz	72,815	6,228,239	6,737,324	Jalapa Enríquez
Yucatán	39,340	1,362,940	1,556,622	Mérida
Zacatecas	75,040	1,276,323	1,336,496	Zacatecas

At the 1980 census 33,039,307 were males, 33,807,526 females. The official language is Spanish, the mother tongue of over 92% of the population, but there are some indigenous language groups (of which Náhuatl, Maya, Zapotec, Otomi and Mixtec are the most important) spoken by 5,282,347 persons over 5 years of age (1990 census).

The populations (1990 Census) of the largest cities were:

Mexico City[1]	15,047,685	Hermosillo	448,966	Ensenada	259,979
Guadalajara[1]	2,987,194	Saltillo	440,920	Guasave	258,130
Monterrey[1]	2,603,709	Victoria de Durango	413,835	Tepic	241,463
Puebla de Zaragoza	1,057,454	Irapuato	362,915	Gómez Palacio	232,742
Léon de los Aldama	867,920	Villa Hermosa	361,231	Coatzacoalcos	233,115
Ciudad Juárez	798,499	Veracruz Llave	328,607	Tapachula	222,405
Tijuana	721,285	Atizapán de		Nuevo Laredo	219,468
Mexicali	601,938	Zaragoza	315,192	Uruapán	217,068
Culiacán Rosales	601,123	Mazatlán	314,345	Oaxaca de Juárez	213,985
Acapulco de Juárez	593,212	Ciudad Obregón	311,443	Ciudad Victoria	207,923
Mérida	556,819	Celaya	310,569	Salamanca	204,311
Chihuahua	530,783	Los Mochis	303,558	Minatitlán	195,523
San Luis Potosí	525,733	Matamoros	303,293	Pachuca de Soto	180,630
Morelia	492,901	Tuxtla Gutiérrez	295,608	Monclova	178,606
Toluca de Lerdo	487,612	Xalapa	288,454	Campeche	173,645
Aguascalientes	479,659	Reynosa	282,667	Ciudad Madero	160,331
Torreón	464,825	Cuernavaca	281,294	Poza Rica de Hidalgo	151,739
Querétaro	456,458	Tampico	272,690	Córdoba	150,454

[1] Metropolitan Area

1995 population (in 1,000): Mexico City, 16,674; Guadalajara, 3,461; Monterrey, 3,022; Puebla de Zaragoza, 1,222; Léon de los Aldama, 1,042; Ciudad Juárez, 1,011; Tijuana, 991; Mexicali, 696.

Vital statistics for calendar years:

	Births	Deaths	Marriages	Divorces
1993	2,839,686	416,335	659,567	32,483
1994	2,904,389	419,074	671,640	35,029
1995	2,750,444	430,278	658,114	37,455

Infant mortality was 36 per 1000 live births in 1996. Life expectancy, 72 years.

CLIMATE. Latitude and relief produce a variety of climates. Arid and semi-arid conditions are found in the north, with extreme temperatures, whereas in the south there is a humid tropical climate, with temperatures varying with altitude. Conditions on the shores of the Gulf of Mexico are very warm and humid. In general, the rainy season lasts from May to Nov. Mexico City. Jan. 55°F (12·6°C), July 61°F (16·1°C). Annual rainfall 30" (747 mm). Guadalajara. Jan. 59°F (15·2°C), July 69°F (20·5°C). Annual rainfall 36" (902 mm). La Paz. Jan. 64°F (17·8°C), July 85°F (29·4°C). Annual rainfall 6" (145 mm). Mazatlán Jan. 66°F (18·9°C), July 82°F (27·8°C).

Annual rainfall 33" (828 mm). Mérida. Jan. 72°F (22·2°C), July 83°F (28·3°C). Annual rainfall 38" (957 mm). Monterrey. Jan. 58°F (14·4°C), July 81°F (27·2°C). Annual rainfall 23" (588 mm). Puebla de Zaragoza. Jan. 54°F (12·2°C), July 63°F (17·2°C). Annual rainfall 34" (850 mm).

CONSTITUTION AND GOVERNMENT. A new Constitution was promulgated on 5 Feb. 1917 and has been amended from time to time. Mexico is a representative, democratic and federal republic, comprising 31 states and a federal district, each state being free and sovereign in all internal affairs, but united in a federation established according to the principles of the Fundamental Law. The head of state and supreme executive authority is the *President*, directly elected for a non-renewable 6-year term.

There is complete separation of legislative, executive and judicial powers (Art. 49). Legislative power is vested in a General Congress of 2 chambers, a *Chamber of Deputies* and a *Senate*. The Chamber of Deputies consists of 500 members directly elected for 3 years, 300 of them from single-member constituencies and 200 chosen under a system of proportional representation. In 1990 Congress voted a new Electoral Code. This establishes a body to organize elections (IFE), an electoral court (TFE) to resolve disputes, new electoral rolls and introduce a voter's registration card. Priests were enfranchised in 1991.

The Senate comprises 128 members, 4 from each state and 4 from the federal district, directly elected for 6 years. After the elections of Aug. 1994, the party composition of the Senate was: PRI, 95; PAN, 25; PRD, 8. The PRI won 60 seats and the FDN 4 seats. Members of both chambers are not immediately re-eligible for election. Congress sits from 1 Sept. to 31 Dec. each year; during the recess there is a permanent committee of 15 deputies and 14 senators appointed by the respective chambers.

At the presidential and parliamentary elections of Aug. 1994 the electorate was 45·7m. Ernesto Zedillo was elected President by 48·77% of votes cast against 2 opponents. In the Chamber of Deputies 277 of the single-member seats were won by the Institutional Revolutionary Party (PRI) and 27 by proportional representation (PR); 18 by the Party of National Action (PAN) and 101 by PR; 5 by the Revolutionary Democratic Party (PRD) and 66 by PR; and 10 by the Workers' Party (PT), all by PR. At the mid-term elections of Aug. 1991 for 300 electoral districts, 32 Senate seats and 6 governorships, the PRI gained 61·4% of votes cast and won 290 Congress seats, 31 Senate seats and all 6 governorships. PAN gained 17·7% of votes cast, and the Party of Democratic Revolution, 8·3%.

Elections were held 6 July 1997 for the Chamber of Deputies, 32 members of the Senate, 6 State Governors and the Mayor of Mexico City. In the Chamber of Deputies PRI gained 239 seats, PRD 125, PAN 122, the Ecology Party 8 and the Labour Party 6. Following the election the composition of the Senate was: PRI, 77 seats; PAN, 33; PRD, 13. The PRI gained 4 State Governorships and the PAN 2. This was the first time the PRI had lost its overall majority in the lower house.

In March 1998 the government comprised:
President: Ernesto Zedillo Ponce de León (b. 1952; PRI; sworn in 1 Dec. 1994).
Minister of Government: Francisco Labastida Ochoa. *Foreign Affairs:* Rosario Green. *Defence:* Gen. Enrique Cervantes Aguirre. *Naval Affairs:* Adm. José Ramón Lorenzo Franco. *Finance and Public Credit:* José Angel Gurría Treviño. *Social Development:* Carlos Rojas Guitiérrez. *Comptroller-General:* Arsenio Farell Cubillas. *Energy:* Luis Téllez Kuenzler. *Trade and Industry:* Herminio Blanco Mendoza. *Agriculture, Rural Development and Livestock:* Romarico Arroyo Marroquin. *Communication and Transport:* Carlos Ruiz Sacristán. *Education:* Miguel Limón Rojas. *Health:* Juan Ramón de la Fuente Ramírez. *Labour and Social Welfare:* Javier Bonilla García. *Agrarian Reform:* Arturo Warman Gryj. *Tourism:* Oscar Espinosa Villarreal. *Fishing, Environment and Natural Resources:* Julia Caravias Lillo. *Attorney-General:* Jorge Madrazo Cuéllar. *Attorney of Justice for Mexico City:* José Antonio González. *Mexico City Mayor:* Cuauhtémoc Cárdenas Solórzano. *Private Secretary to the President:* David Melo Alvarado. *Head of the Co-ordination Office of the Presidency:* Roger Iván Recio. *Social Communication of the Presidency:* Fernando Lerdo de Tejada. *Presidential Chief of Staff:* Gen. Roberto

Miranda. *Director of PEMEX:* Adrian Lajous. *Director of Federal Electricity Commission:* Rogelio Gasca Neri. *Director of Mexican Social Security Institute:* Genaro Borrego Estrada. *Director of the Institute of Security and Social Services for the State Workers:* Manuel Aguilera Gómez.

National anthem: 'Mexicanos, al grito de guerra' ('Mexicans, at the war-cry'); words by F. González Bocanegra, tune by Jaime Nunó.

Local Government. Mexico is divided into 31 states and a Federal District. The latter is co-extensive with Mexico City and is administered by a Governor directly elected for a 6 year term. Each state has its own constitution, with the right to legislate and to levy taxes (but not inter-state customs duties); its Governor is directly elected for 6 years and its unicameral legislature for 3 years; judicial officers are appointed by the state governments. Mexico City is sub-divided into 16 districts and the 31 states into 2,428 municipalities.

DEFENCE

Army. Enlistment into the regular army is voluntary, but there is also one year of conscription (4 hours per week) by lottery. The army consists of 36 zonal garrisons, 1 armoured, 1 motorized infantry, 2 infantry, 2 airborne and 1 Presidential Guard brigade, and air defence, engineer and support units. Equipment includes 50 M-8 light tanks and 110 armoured cars. Strength of the regular army (1996) 130,000 (60,000 conscripts).

Navy. The Navy is primarily equipped and organized for offshore and coastal patrol duties. It comprises 3 very old ex-US destroyers, 2 modern and 2 very old ex-US frigates, 10 modern offshore patrol vessels with small helicopter decks and hangars, and 29 older offshore ships, mostly ex-US. There are also 44 inshore patrol vessels and 20 small riverine patrol craft. There are 2 ex-US landing ships, and auxiliaries include 3 support tankers, 3 survey ships, 1 repair ship, 4 logistic support ships, 2 training ships, 6 tugs and 24 service craft.

The naval air force, 1,100 strong, operates 9 Aviocars for maritime patrol, 12 Bo-105 helicopters for service afloat, and 20 fixed wing and 12 helicopters for transport, training and liaison duties.

Naval personnel in 1997 totalled 37,000, including the naval air force and 8,500 marines comprising 1 airborne brigade and 21 regionally-based battalions.

Air Force. The Air Force had (1997) a strength of about 8,000 with over 90 combat aircraft and 25 armed helicopters, and has 4 operational groups, each with 1 or 2 squadrons. No. 1 Group comprises No. 209 Squadron with Bell 205A, 206B JetRanger, 212 and MD-530 helicopters as well as PC-6 Turbo-Porter transports, and No. 216 Squadron with MD-530 and S-70 helicopters. No. 2 Group has 2 Squadrons (Nos. 206 and 207) of Swiss-built Pilatus PC-7 Turbo-Trainers for light attack duty. No. 3 Group (203 and 204 Squadrons) also operates PC-7s; No. 4 Group (201 and 205 Squadrons) is equipped with PC-7s. No. 5 Group consists of No. 101 communications Squadron and a photo-reconnaissance unit, both equipped with Aero Commander 500S piston-engined light twins. Nos. 301 and 302 Squadrons, in No. 6 Group, operate a total of 9 turboprop-powered Lockheed C-130 Hercules and 6 C-118A piston-engined transports. The main combat Group, No. 7, comprises No. 401 Squadron with 11 F-5E Tiger II and F-5F 2-seat fighters, and No. 202 Squadron with AT-33A jet trainer/fighter-bombers. No. 8 Group has a variety of VIP transports and 2 S-70 helicopters. No. 9 Group operates the Air Force's remaining 10 C-47s in Nos. 311 and 312 transport Squadrons, and No. 208 Squadron with Arava transports. No. 10 Group comprises 3 squadrons (Nos. 210, 211 and 212) of T-33 trainers. No. 11 Group has 1 squadron (No. 214) with Bell 212 and MD-530 helicopters, and PC-6 Turbo-Porter transports. The Aviation College has Maute Mx-7 and Beech Bonanza trainers.

INTERNATIONAL RELATIONS

Membership. Mexico is a member of the UN, OAS, APEC and OECD.

ECONOMY

Policy. Following a deep recession in 1994, the government aimed to reduce inflation and provided tax concessions to stimulate investment. After the peso was devalued in Dec. 1994 an emergency economic plan was introduced to include an agreement between labour and employers to contain inflation, a fiscal adjustment to reduce the current account deficit, further privatization of infrastructural enterprises and the establishment of an international assistance fund. In 1997 the economy grew by 7% and 800,000 new jobs were created. An economic programme to attack 'the roots of poverty' was announced.

Performance. Real GDP declined by 5·1% in 1996 (1995 showed a decline rate of –6·2%).

Budget. In 1996 revenue was 392,566m. new pesos; expenditure, 372,874m. new pesos.

Currency. The unit of currency is the *Mexican peso* (MXP) of 100 *centavos*. A new peso was introduced on 1 Jan. 1993: 1 new peso = 1,000 old pesos. There are coins of 50, 100, 200, 500, 1,000 and 5,000 old pesos; and banknotes of 2,000, 5,000, 10,000, 20,000 and 50,000 old pesos. Notes for new and old pesos circulated jointly. There are coins for 1, 2, 5, 10 and 20 new pesos and notes for 20, 50, 100, 200 and 500 new pesos. The peso was devalued by 13·94% in Dec. 1994. International exchange reserves were US$13,543m. in Aug. 1995. Gold reserves were 947,000 troy oz. in 1991. Total currency in circulation (1993) was 43,228m. new pesos. Inflation was 52% in 1995 (7% in 1994).

Banking and Finance. The Bank of Mexico, established 1 Sept. 1925, is the central bank of issue (*Governor*, Miguel Mancera, b. 1933). It gained autonomy over monetary policy in 1993. Exchange rate policy is determined jointly by the bank and the Finance Ministry. Banks were nationalized in 1982, but in May 1990 the government approved their reprivatization. The state continues to have a majority holding in foreign trade and rural development banks. Foreign holdings are limited to 30%. There were 23 banks in 1993; deposits were 4,500,000m. old pesos in 1992.

There is a stock exchange in Mexico City.

Weights and Measures. The metric system is legal.

ENERGY AND NATURAL RESOURCES

Electricity. Output in 1996 was 145·7m. kWh. Installed capacity, 1995, 32,737 MW.

Oil and Gas. Crude petroleum output was 2,858,000 bbls. a day in 1996. Natural gas, 1996, 4,195m. cu. ft.

Minerals. Output, (in 1,000 tonnes) 1996: Lead, 167·1; copper, 328·0; zinc, 348·3; gypsum, 3,758·9; silica, 1,424·8; fluorite, 524·66; iron, 6,109·5; sulphur, 921·3; manganese, 173·4; barite, 470·0; graphite, 40·4; silver, 2,536·1; gold, 24,083 kg; coal, 8,779·5; feldspar, 140·0.

Agriculture. Mexico has 20·3m. ha of arable land and 52·2m. ha of meadows and pastures. Agriculture provided 7% of GDP in 1992. Some 60% of agricultural land belongs to about 30,000 *ejidos* (with 15m. members), communal lands with each member farming his plot independently. *Ejidos* can now be inherited, sold or rented. A land-titling programme (PROCEDE) is establishing the boundaries of 4·6m. plots of land totalling 102m. ha. Other private farmers may not own more than 100 ha of irrigated land or an equivalent in unirrigated land. There is a theoretical legal minimum of 10 ha for holdings, but some 60% of private farms were less than 5 ha in 1990. Laws abolishing the *ejido* system were passed in 1992.

Sown areas, 1995 (in 1,000 ha) included: Maize, 9,082; beans, 2,367; sorghum, 1,592; wheat, 964; cotton-seed, 297; barley, 272; soya, 151; safflower, 107; rice, 90.

Production in 1995 (in 1,000 tonnes): Wheat, 3,468; rice (washed), 367; beans, 1,271; soya, 190; barley, 487; maize, 18,353; sorghum, 4,170; cotton-seed, 369; grapes, 550; apples, 427; oranges, 3,922; lemons, 961; mangoes, 1,088; pineapples, 229 (1994); bananas, 2,069; melons, 404; watermelons, 402; avocado pears, 787.

Livestock (1994): Cattle, 23·2m.; sheep, 3·9m.; pigs, 10m.; goats, 6m.; (1992) horses, 6·17m.; mules, 3·18m.; donkeys, 3·18m.; poultry, 315m. Meat production, 1994 (in 1,000 tonnes): Beef, 1,364·7; pork, 807·5; goat meat, 40·1; sheep meat, 31·4. Dairy production, 1995 (in tonnes): Milk, 7,537,647; eggs, 1,241,987; honey, 49,228; wool, 4,045.

Forestry. Forests extended over 44m. ha in 1984, representing 23% of the land area, containing pine, spruce, cedar, mahogany, logwood and rosewood. There are 14 forest reserves (nearly 0·8m. ha) and 47 national park forests of 0·75m. ha. In 1995 total roundwood production amounted to 6,295,000 cu. metres.

Fisheries. Total catch, 1996, 1,379,219 tonnes (freshwater, 1993, 1,133,665 tonnes).

INDUSTRY. In 1996 manufacturing industry provided 18·7% of GDP. Output in 1996 (in 1,000 tonnes): Petrol, 16,975; cement, 28,168; crude iron, 6,109; crude steel, 5,867; aluminium, 95·8; copper, 328; lead, 167·1; zinc, 348·3; wheat flour, 1,835; butter, 34; passenger cars (units), 782,743; lorries, 429,843.

Labour. In 1996 the workforce was 24,063,283 (5,644,588 female). The daily minimum wage in 1996 was 24·3 new pesos. Registered unemployment rate, 1997, 4·3% (1996, 5·5%).

Trade Unions. The Mexican Labour Congress (CTM) is incorporated into the Institutional Revolutionary Party, and is an umbrella organization numbering some 5m. An agreement, 'Alliance for Economic Recovery', was reached in Nov. 1995 between the government, trade unions and business, providing for an increase in the minimum wage of 10·1%, increased unemployment benefits, tax incentives, the staggering of price increases, and a commitment to reduce public spending. A breakaway from CTM took place in 1997 when rebel labour leaders set up the National Union of Workers (UNT) to combat what they saw as a sharp drop in real wages.

FOREIGN ECONOMIC RELATIONS. In Sept. 1991 Mexico signed the free trade Treaty of Santiago with Chile, envisaging an annual 10% tariffs reduction from Jan. 1992. The North American Free Trade Agreement (NAFTA), between Canada, Mexico and the USA, was signed on 7 Oct. 1992. A free trade agreement was signed with Costa Rica in March 1994. Some 8,300 products were freed from tariffs, with others to follow over 10 years. The Group of Three (G3) free trade pact with Colombia and Venezuela came into effect 1 Jan. 1995. Total foreign debt was US$170,100m. at the end of 1995.

Commerce. Trade for calendar years in US$1m.:

	1992	1993	1994	1995	1996
Imports	62,129	65,367	79,346	72,453	89,469
Exports	46,196	51,886	60,882	79,542	96,030

Of total imports in 1996, 75·4% came from USA, 4·4% from Japan, 3·5% from Germany and 0·8% from UK.

Of total exports in 1996, 83% went to USA, 1·4% to Spain, 1·0% to Japan and 0·6% to UK.

The in-bond (*maquiladora*) assembly plants along the US border generate the largest flow of foreign exchange with oil (11·2% of exports in 1996) and tourism.

Tourism. In 1996, there were 8·98m. tourists; gross revenue, including border visitors, amounted to US$4,647m.

COMMUNICATIONS

Roads. Total length, (1994) 307,142 km, of which 48,960 km were main roads, 57,364 km were secondary roads and 200,818 km by-roads. In 1994, 8,433,709 motor vehicles (8,080,419 private), 3,839,369 lorries, 105,390 buses and 264,650 motorcycles were registered.

Railways. The National Railway, *Ferrocarriles Nacionales de Mexico*, was split into 5 companies in 1996 as a preliminary to privatization. It comprises 20,445 km of 1,435 mm gauge (246 km electrified). In 1996 it carried 59·1m. tonnes of freight and in 1996, 6m. passengers. There is a 178 km metro in Mexico City. There are light rail lines in Guadalajara (48 km) and Monterrey (35 km).

Civil Aviation. There is an international airport at Mexico City (Benito Juárez) and 49 other international and 33 national airports. Each of the larger states has a local airline which links it with main airports. The national carriers are Aeromexico, Mexicana, Taesa, Aerocalifornia and Aerolineas Internacionales. In 1995, Aeromexico operated 6 B-757-200s, 2 B-767-300ERs and 47 other aircraft; and Mexicana, 12 A320-200s, 25 B-727-200 Advs and 12 other aircraft. Services are also provided by Aeroflot, Aeroperu, Air France, Alitalia, American West, American Airlines, Avensa, Aviacsa, Avianca, Aviateca, British Airways, Canadian Airlines, Continental Airlines and Air Micronesia, COPA, Cubana, Delta, Iberia, JAL, KLM, LACSA, Ladeco, Lan-Chile, Lloyd Aereo Boliviano, LTU, Lufthansa, Malaysia Airlines, Northwest Airlines, Taca, Transworld, United Airlines and Varig. In 1994, there were 19,151,345 domestic passenger and 7,466,352 international passenger arrivals; 18,768,136 domestic passenger and 7,168,476 international passenger departures.

Shipping. Mexico has 49 ocean ports, of which, on the Gulf coast, the most important include Coatzacoalcos, Ciudad del Carmen (Campeche), Tampico, Veracruz and Tuxpan. On the Pacific Coast are Salina Cruz, Isla de Cedros, Guaymas, Santa Rosalia, Manzanillo, Lázaro Cárdenas and Mazatlán. It was announced in 1992 that ports would be privatized.

Merchant shipping loaded 139·5m. tonnes and unloaded 62m. tonnes of cargo in 1996. In 1995, the merchant marine had a total tonnage of 1·55m. GRT, including oil tankers, 0·71m. GRT, and container ships, 0·14m. GRT.

Telecommunications. Telmex, previously a state-controlled company, was privatized in 1991. It controls about 98% of all the telephone service. There were 8·83m. telephone lines in 1996.

There are over 1,500 stations licensed by the Dirección General de Concesiones y Permisos de Telecomunicaciones. Most carry the 'National Hour' programme. Television services are provided by the recently privatized Televisión Azteca and Azteca Televisa. In 1991 there were 16,325,000 radio and 12·35m. TV sets (colour by NTSC).

Cinemas. In 1993 there were 1,777 screens and 113m. admissions.

Press. In 1992 there were 292 daily newspapers.

SOCIAL INSTITUTIONS

Justice. Magistrates of the Supreme Court are appointed for 6 years by the President and confirmed by the Senate; they can be removed only on impeachment. The courts include the Supreme Court with 21 magistrates, 12 collegiate circuit courts with 3 judges each and 9 unitary circuit courts with 1 judge each, and 68 district courts with 1 judge each.

The penal code of 1 Jan. 1930 abolished the death penalty, except for the armed forces.

Religion. 93·5% of the population was Roman Catholic in 1992, with (1983) 3 cardinals, 12 archbishops and 87 bishops. The Church is separated from the State, and the constitution of 1917 provided strict regulation of this and all other religions. In Nov. 1991 Congress approved an amendment to the 1917 constitution permitting the recognition of churches by the state, the possession of property by churches and the enfranchisement of priests. Church buildings remain state property. Diplomatic relations with the Vatican were established in Sept. 1992. At the 1990 census there were also 4·9% Protestants, and 5·4% members of other religions. There were 711,000 Mormons in 1994.

Education. In 1990 12·7% of the population over 15 were illiterate. Primary and secondary education is free and compulsory, and secular, although religious instruction is permitted in private schools.

In 1996–97 there were:

	Establishments	Teachers	Students (in 1,000)
Pre-school	63,319	146,247	3,238·3
Primary	95,855	524,922	14,650·5
Secondary	24,402	275,331	4,809·3
Vocational training	4,710	27,543	498·8
Professional	1,900	36,131	383·8
Higher education	1,786	142,952	1,329·7
Postgraduate education	860	12,674	94·3

In 1994–95 in the public sector there were 36 universities, 1 technical institute and 3 specialized universities (1 agricultural; 2 pedagogical). In the private sector there were 48 universities, 1 institute of technical and higher educational studies, 1 women's university and 1 technical university.

The adult literacy rate is 89·2%.

Health. In 1992 there were 833 general hospitals with 71,500 beds. There were 39,578 general practitioners, 29,796 specialist doctors and 4,730 dentists.

Welfare. In 1997 there were 11·28m. workers insured as permanent beneficiaries with the Social Security Institute.

DIPLOMATIC REPRESENTATIVES

Of Mexico in Great Britain (42 Hertford Street, London, W1Y 7TF)
Ambassador: Santiago Oñate Laborde.

Of Great Britain in Mexico (Rio Lerma 71, Col. Cuauhtémoc, Mexico City 06500, D.F.)
Ambassador: A. J. Beamish, CMG.

Of Mexico in the USA (1911 Pennsylvania Ave., NW, Washington, D.C., 20006)
Ambassador: Jesús Reyes Heroles.

Of the USA in Mexico (Paseo de la Reforma 305, México City 5, D.F.)
Ambassador: Vacant.

Of Mexico to the United Nations
Ambassador: Manuel Tello.

Of Mexico to the European Union
Ambassador: Armendariz Etchegaray.

Further Reading

Instituto Nacional de Estadística, Geografía e Informática. *Anuario Estadístico de los Estados Unidos Mexicanos. Mexican Bulletin of Statistical Information.* Quarterly.

Aspe, P., *Economic Transformation: the Mexican Way.* Cambridge (MA), 1993
Bailey, J. J., *Governing Mexico: The Statecraft of Crisis Management.* London and New York, 1988
Bartra, R., *Agrarian Structure and Political Power in Mexico.* Johns Hopkins Univ. Press, 1993
Bazant, J., *A Concise History of Mexico.* CUP, 1977
Bethell, L. (ed.) *Mexico since Independence.* CUP, 1992
Camp, R. A., *Politics in Mexico.* 2nd ed. OUP, 1996
Grayson, G. W., *Oil and Mexican Foreign Policy.* Univ. of Pittsburgh Press, 1988
Hamilton, N. and Harding, T. F., (eds.) *Mexico: State, Economy and Social Conflict.* London, 1986
Krauze, E., *Mexico, Biography of Power: A History of Modern Mexico, 1810-1996.* London 1997
Philip, G., (ed.) *Politics in Mexico.* London, 1985.—*The Presidency in Mexican Politics.* London, 1991.—*Mexico* [Bibliography]. 2nd ed. Oxford and Santa Barbara, 1993

Riding, A., *Distant Neighbours*. London, 1985.—*Mexico: Inside the Volcano*. London, 1987
Rodríguez, J. E., *The Evolution of the Mexican Political System*. New York, 1993
Robbins, N. C., *Mexico*. [Bibliography] Oxford and Santa Barbara, 1984
Ruíz, R. E., *Triumphs and Tragedy: a History of the Mexican People*. New York, 1992
Whiting, V. R., *The Political Economy of Foreign Investment in Mexico: Nationalism, Liberalism, Constraints on Choice*. Johns Hopkins Univ. Press, 1992

National statistical office: Instituto Nacional de Estadística, Geografía e Informática (INEGI), Aguascalientes.
Website: http://www.inegi.gob.mx/paginamenu.html

MICRONESIA

Federated States of Micronesia

Capital: Kolonia
Population: 127,616
GDP: US$205m.

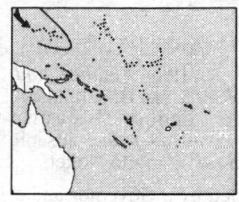

KEY HISTORICAL EVENTS. Spain acquired sovereignty over the Caroline Islands in 1886, but sold the archipelago to Germany in 1899. Japan occupied the Islands at the beginning of the First World War, and in 1921 they were mandated to Japan by the League of Nations. Captured by Allied Forces in the Second World War in 1944, the Islands became part of the UN Trust Territory of the Pacific Islands created on 18 July 1947 and administered by the USA. The Federated States of Micronesia came into being on 10 May 1979 comprising all of the Caroline Islands except the Belau (Palau) group. Its trusteeship was terminated on 3 Nov. 1986 by the UN Security Council and on the same day it entered into a 15-year Free Association with the USA. The UN recognized the termination of the Trusteeship Agreement on 22 Dec. 1990, and Micronesia became a full UN member state on 17 Sept. 1991.

TERRITORY AND POPULATION. The Federated States lie in the North Pacific Ocean between 137° and 163° E, comprising 607 islands with a total land area of 702 sq. km (271 sq. miles). The population (1994 census) was 104,724; 1997 estimate, 127,616; density, 181 per sq. km; population growth rate, 1997 estimate, 3·33%

The areas and populations of the 4 major groups of island states (east to west) are as follows:

State	Area (sq. km)	Population (1994 census)	Headquarters
Kosrae	109	7,354	Tofol
Pohnpei	344	33,372	Kolonia
Chuuk	127	52,870	Weno
Yap	119	11,128	Colonia

Kosrae consists of a single island. Its main town is Lele (2,422 inhabitants in 1989).

Pohnpei comprises a single island (covering 334 sq. km with 30,000 inhabitants in 1994) and 8 scattered coral atolls. Its main town Kolonia (6,169 inhabitants in 1989) is the national capital of the Federated States. A new capital is being built about 10 km southwest in the Palikir valley.

Chuuk consists of a group of 14 islands within a large reef-fringed lagoon (44,000 inhabitants in 1994); the state also includes 12 coral atolls (8,000 inhabitants), the most important being the Mortlock Islands. The chief town is Weno (15,253 inhabitants in 1989).

Yap comprises a main group of 4 islands (covering 100 sq. km with 7,000 inhabitants in 1994) and 13 coral atolls (4,000 inhabitants), the main ones being Ulithi and Woleai. Colonia is its chief town (3,456 inhabitants in 1989).

Vital statistics (1997 est.): birth rate, 27·75 per 1,000 population; death rate, 6·14 per 1,000; infant mortality rate, 35·11 per 1,000 live births; life expectancy, 68·18 years.

English is used in schools and is the official language. Trukese, Pohnpeian, Yapese and Kosrean are also spoken.

CLIMATE. Tropical, with heavy year-round rainfall, especially in the eastern islands, and occasional typhoons (June-Dec.). Kolonia. Jan. 80°F (26·7°C), July 79°F (26·1°C). Annual rainfall 194" (4,859 mm).

CONSTITUTION AND GOVERNMENT. Under the Constitution founded on 10 May 1979, there is an executive presidency and a 14-member National

975

Congress, comprising 10 members elected for 2-year terms from single-member constituencies of similar electorates, and 4 members elected one from each State for a 4-year term. The Federal President and Vice-President first run for the Congress before they are elected by members of Congress for a 4-year term. The last election was held on 11 May 1995.

In March 1998 the government comprised:
President: Jacob Nena (app. May 1997).
Vice-President: Leo A. Falcam. *Foreign Affairs:* Epel K. Ilon. *Finance and Administration:* John Ehsa. *Health, Education and Social Affairs:* Dr Eliuel K. Pretrick. *Economic Affairs:* Sebastian Anefal. *Justice:* Emilio Musrasrik. *Transportation and Communication:* Lukner Weilbacher. *Public Defence:* Joseph Phillip. *Postmaster-General:* Bethwell Henry. *Attorney-General:* Camillo Noket.

State Government. Each State has an executive branch headed by a Governor and a unicameral State Legislature (except Chuuk which has a bicameral legislature), all directly elected for a 4-year term.

INTERNATIONAL RELATIONS

Membership. Micronesia is a member of the UN, Pacific Community (formerly the South Pacific Commission) and the South Pacific Forum.

ECONOMY

Policy. The modern sector of the economy consists of a small private sector supported by public service incomes and demand. The traditional sector is based on subsistence farming and fishing.

Budget. US compact funds are an annual US$100m. Revenue (1995 estimate), US$45m.; expenditure, US$31m.

Currency. US currency is used.

ENERGY AND NATURAL RESOURCES

Electricity. Capacity (1995), 38,500 kW.

Minerals. The islands have few mineral deposits except for high-grade phosphates.

Agriculture. Consists mainly of subsistence farming: coconuts, breadfruit, bananas, sweet potatoes and cassava. A small amount of crops are produced for export, including copra, tropical fruits, peppers and taro. Pigs and chickens constitute the main livestock.

Fisheries. In 1995 the catch amounted to 21,150 tonnes. Fishing licence fees were US$20m. in 1993 and are a primary revenue source.

INDUSTRY. The chief industries are construction, fish processing, tourism and handicrafts (items from shell, wood and pearl).

Labour. Two-thirds of the labour force are government employees. In 1989 unemployment was 27%.

FOREIGN ECONOMIC RELATIONS

Commerce. Total exports (1994 est.), US$29·1m.; imports, US$141·1m. Major trading partners: USA, Japan, Australia and Guam. The main exports are copra, bananas, black pepper, fish and garments. Main imports: foodstuffs and beverages, manufactured goods, machinery and equipment.

Tourism. In 1990 there were 20,475 visitors.

COMMUNICATIONS

Roads. In 1995 there were 235 km of roads (41 km paved).

Civil Aviation. There are international airports on Pohnpei, Chuuk, Yap and Kosrae. Services are provided by Air Nauru, Continental Airlines and Air Micronesia. There were 5 airports in 1996 (4 paved).

Shipping. The main ports are Kolonia (Pohnpei), Colonia (Yap), Lepukos (Chuuk), Okat and Lele (Kosrae).

Telecommunications. In 1994 there were 7,000 telephone lines in use. The islands are interconnected by shortwave radiotelephone. There are 4 earth stations linked to the Intelsat satellite system. There were 5 radio and 6 TV stations, and 22,000 radio and 19,800 TV sets in 1996.

SOCIAL INSTITUTIONS

Justice. There is a Supreme Court headed by the Chief Justice with 2 other judges, and a State Court in each of the 4 states with 13 judges in total.

Religion. Predominantly Christian. Yap is mainly Roman Catholic; Protestantism is prevalent elsewhere.

Education. In 1987 there were 25,139 pupils in 177 primary schools, with 1,051 teachers; 5,385 pupils in 17 high schools, with 314 teachers; and 861 students (1986) at the College of Micronesia in Pohnpei. The Micronesia Maritime and Fisheries Academy in Yap (est. 1990) provides education and training in fisheries technology at secondary and tertiary levels.

Health. In 1993 there were 50 doctors, 7 dentists, 7 pharmacists, 230 nurses and 4 hospitals with 325 beds.

DIPLOMATIC REPRESENTATIVES

Of Great Britain in Micronesia (resides in Fiji)
Ambassador: Vernon M. Scarborough.

Of Micronesia in the USA (1725 N St., NW, Washington, D.C., 20036)
Ambassador: Jesse B. Marehalau.

Of the USA in Micronesia (POB 1286, Kolonia, Pohnpei)
Chargé d'Affaires: Cheryl Martin.

Of Micronesia to the United Nations
Ambassador: Vacant.

Further Reading

Kluge, P. F., *The Edge of Paradise: America in Micronesia.* New York, 1991
Wuerch, W. L. and Ballendorf, D. A., *Historical Dictionary of Guam and Micronesia.* Metuchen (NJ), 1995

MOLDOVA

Republica Moldova

Capital: Chişinau
Population: 4·5m.
GDP per head: (PPP$) 1,576
GNP per capita: US$870
HDI/world rank: 0·612/120

KEY HISTORICAL EVENTS. The Moldavian SSR (in 1990 renamed Moldova) was formed by the union of part of the former Moldavian ASSR (organized 12 Oct. 1924), formerly included in the Ukrainian SSR, and the areas of Bessarabia (ceded by Romania to the USSR, 28 June 1940) with a mainly Moldovan population. As from 2 Aug. 1940 the Moldavian SSR included the following regions of the former Moldavian ASSR: Grigoriopol, Dubasari, Camenca, Rybnitsa, Slobozia and Tiraspol, and the following districts of Bessarabia: Beltsi, Bender (Tighina), Chişinau (*then* Kishinev), Cahul, Orhey and Soroca.

In Dec. 1991 Moldova became a member of the CIS, a decision ratified by parliament in April 1994.

Fighting took place in 1992 between government forces and separatists in the (largely Russian and Ukrainian) area east of the River Nistru (Transnistria).

An agreement signed by the presidents of Moldova and Russia on 21 July 1992 brought to an end the armed conflict and established a 'security zone' controlled by the 'peace-keeping forces' formed by military from Russia, Moldova and Transnistria. On 21 Oct. 1994, a Moldo-Russian agreement was signed in compliance with which the Russian Federation was obliged to withdraw its troops (former 14th Soviet army) from the territory of Moldova over 3 years. But the agreement was not ratified by the State Russian Duma.

On 8 May 1997, an agreement between Transnistria and the Moldovan government to end the separatist conflict was signed in Moscow, brokered by the presidents of Russia and Ukraine, and stipulated that Transnistria would remain part of Moldova as it was territorially constituted in Jan. 1990.

In 1997 some 7,000 Russian troops were stationed in Transnistria.

TERRITORY AND POPULATION. Moldova is bounded in the east and south by Ukraine and on the west by Romania. The area is 33,700 sq. km (13,000 sq. miles). In Jan. 1994 the population was 4,353,000 (52·3% female; 46·9% urban). Estimate, July 1997, 4·5m. The 1989 census population was 4,335,360, of whom Moldovans accounted for 64·5%, Ukrainians 13·9%, Russians 13%, Gagauzi 3·5%, Bulgarians 2% and Jews 1·5%. Vital statistics rates, 1993 (per 1,000 population): Births, 15·2; deaths, 10·7; natural increase, 4·5; infant mortality (per 1,000 live births), 21·5. Life expectancy, 67·7 years (1994).

Apart from Chişinau, the capital (0·7m. population in 1994), larger towns are Tiraspol (186,000), Beltsy (161,000) and Bender (133,000). The official Moldovan language (i.e., Romanian) was written in Cyrillic prior to the restoration of the Roman alphabet in 1989. It is spoken by 75% of the population; the use of other languages (Russian, Gagauz) is safeguarded by the Constitution.

CONSTITUTION AND GOVERNMENT. A declaration of republican sovereignty was adopted in June 1990 and in Aug. 1991 the republic declared itself independent. A new Constitution came into effect on 27 Aug. 1994, which defines Moldova as an 'independent, democratic and unitary state'. At a referendum on 6 March 1994 turn-out was 75·1%; 95·4% of votes cast favoured 'an independent Moldova within its 1990 borders'. The referendum (and the Feb. parliamentary elections) were not held by the authorities in Transnistria.

Presidential elections were held on 17 Nov. 1996. President Snegur won the first round with 38·24% of votes cast. A run-off round was held on 1 Dec. 1996 between President Snegur and the Speaker, Petru Lucinschi. Turn-out was 72%. Lucinschi was elected by 54% of votes cast.

Parliament has 104 seats and is elected for 4-year terms. There is a 4% threshold for election; votes falling below this are re-distributed to successful parties. The *President* is elected for 4-year terms.

At the elections on 27 Feb. 1994 turn-out was 74%. The Agrarian Democratic Party won 56 seats with 43·2% of votes cast, the Socialist/Unity Bloc 28 with 22%, the Bloc of Peasants and Intellectuals 11 with 9·2% and the Popular Front Alliance 9 with 7·5%.

President: Petru Lucinschi (ind; elected 1 Dec. 1996).

In March 1998 the government comprised:

Prime Minister: Ion Ciubuc.

Deputy Prime Ministers: Valeriu Bulgari, Ion Gutu. *Minister of Agriculture:* Gheorghe Lungu. *Information and Telecommunications:* Ion Casian. *Culture:* Ghenadie Ciobanu. *Defence:* Valeriu Pasat. *Economy and Reforms:* Ion Gutu. *Education, youth and sport:* Iacob Popovici. *Finance:* Valeriu Chitan. *Foreign Affairs:* Nicolae Tabacaru. *Health:* Mihai Magdei. *Industry and Trade:* Andrei Cucu. *Internal Affairs:* Mihail Plamadeala. *Justice:* Vasile Sturza. *Social Welfare:* Vasile Vartic. *National Security:* Tudor Botnaru. *Privatization:* Iurie Badir. *Minister of State:* Nicolae Cernomaz. *Transport and Roads:* Vasile Iovv. *Utilities:* Mihai Severovan.

National anthem: The Romanian anthem was replaced in Aug. 1994 by a traditional tune, *Lîmbă noastră (Our Language).*

Local and Regional Government. There are local authorities at district, municipality and town/village level. Prefects and mayors of districts and municipalities are appointed by the President on the nomination of the local councils; mayors of towns and villages are elected. Local elections were held on 16 April 1995. The Agrarian Democratic Party gained most seats.

The 1994 Constitution makes provision for the autonomy of Transnistria and the Gagauz (Gagauzi Yeri) region.

Transnistria. In the predominantly Russian-speaking areas of Transnistria a self-styled republic was established in Sept. 1991, and approved by a local referendum in Dec. 1991. A Russo-Moldovan agreement of 21 July 1992 provided for a special statute for Transnistria and a guarantee of self-determination should Moldova unite with Romania. The population in 1995 was 0·72m. Romanian here is still written in the Cyrillic alphabet. At a referendum on 24 Dec. 1995, 81% of votes cast were in favour of adopting a new constitution proclaiming independence.

On 17 June 1996 the Moldovan government granted Transnistria a special status as 'a state-territorial formation in the form of a republic within Moldova's internationally recognized border'.

Elections for chief regional executive were held on 22 Dec. 1996. The electorate was 428,000; turn-out was 57·3%. Igor Smirnov (b. 1941) was re-elected for a further 5-year term against 1 opponent by 71·9% of votes cast.

A Transnistrian rouble was introduced on 17 Jan. 1994.

Gagauz Yeri. This was created an autonomous territorial unit by Moldovan legislation of 13 Jan. 1995. In 1995 the population was 153,000. There is a 35-member *Popular Assembly* directly elected for 4-year terms and headed by a *Governor*, who is a member of the Moldovan cabinet. At the elections of 28 May and 11 June 1995 turn-out was 68%.

Governor: Gheorghi Tabunshchik (b. 1939).

DEFENCE. Conscription is up to 18 months.

Army. The Army is organized in 3 motor rifle and 1 artillery brigade and 1 reconnaissance battalion. Personnel, 1997, 9,300 (5,200 conscripts). There is also a paramilitary Interior Ministry force of 2,500 and riot police numbering 900.

Air Force. The Air Force has a small number of MiG-29 fighters, Antonov transport and Ilyushin aircraft and Mi-8 transport helicopters. Personnel (including air defence), 1997, 1,730.

INTERNATIONAL RELATIONS

Membership. Moldova is a member of the UN, OCSE, CIS, the Council of Europe and the NATO Partnership for Peace.

ECONOMY

Policy. Starting in April 1993, 33% of state property, mainly small and medium-sized firms in construction, light industry, commerce and services, were being privatized through the distribution of vouchers to citizens. This phase was completed in Nov. 1995 with the sale of 657 state-owned enterprises. The second phase aims to attract foreign investment for the sale of two thirds of state property.

Performance. There was no economic growth in 1997, following a fall of 9% in 1996.

Budget. For the first half of 1997 revenue, 105·7m. lei, expenditure, 138·1m. lei.

Currency. A new unit of currency, the *leu* (MDL), replaced the rouble in Nov. 1993. There are notes of 1, 5, 10, 20, 50, 100 and 200 lei. Inflation was 11·2% in 1997, compared to 16% in 1996.

Banking and Finance. The central bank and bank of issue is the National Bank (*Governor*, Leonid Talmaci). In 1996 there were 26 commercial banks and 1 foreign branch office (Romanian).

ENERGY AND NATURAL RESOURCES

Electricity. Output was 10·2m. kWh in 1993.

Minerals. There are deposits of lignite, phosphorites, gypsum and building materials.

Agriculture. Agriculture contributed 43% of GDP in 1996 and employs about 700,000. Land under cultivation in 1997 was 2·5m. ha, of which 0·3m. ha was accounted for by private subsidiary agriculture and 6,700 ha (in 1993) by commercial agriculture in 3,100 farms. Private and commercial agriculture accounted for 31% of the value of all output in 1993. The free sale of land is not permitted.

Output of main agricultural products (in 1,000 tonnes) in 1994: Grain, 2,900; sugar-beet, 2,400; sunflower seeds 210; potatoes, 300; vegetables, 900; fruit and berries (1992), 511; processed meat, 178; milk, 896; and 540m. eggs. Livestock included (1 Jan. 1994) 0·9m. cattle, 1·2m. pigs and 1·4m. sheep and goats.

Fisheries. The south is rich in sturgeon, mackerel and brill.

INDUSTRY. There are canning plants, wine-making plants, woodworking and metallurgical factories, a factory of ferro-concrete building materials, footwear, dairy products and textile plants. Output was valued at 1,200m. lei in 1993. Production, 1993 (in tonnes): Rolled ferrous metals (1992), 0·5m.; cement, 0·6m.; processed meat, 56,100; fabrics, 31·1m. sq. metres; footwear, 11·9m. pairs; 4,200 tractors; 167,000 TV sets; 57,600 refrigerators and freezers; 123,000 washing machines.

Labour. In 1993 there were 2·45m. persons of working age, of whom 2·03m. were employed, 57·6% in the state sector, 16·4% in the private sector and 21·9% in co-operatives. In Jan. 1994 there were 14,100 registered unemployed (0·7% of the labour force), of whom 4,100 were receiving benefits. Average monthly salaries in 1993 were 21,582 roubles.

FOREIGN ECONOMIC RELATIONS

Commerce. In 1993 imports were valued at US$181·2m. and exports at US$174·3m. Chief export markets are CIS countries - 68·1% (of which Russia takes 53·7%, Ukraine 6·0%, Belarus 4·3% and Kazakhstan 1·0%). Central and Eastern European countries take 16·5% (of which Romania 9·3%, Lithuania 1·9%, Latvia 1·8%, Bulgaria 1·6% and Hungary 0·4%).

Trade with the EU amounts to 9·8% (of which Germany 3·7%, Italy 2·6%,

Netherlands 1·1%, Austria 0·5%). 61·5% of imports come from CIS countries with Central and Eastern Europe's share at 16·6% and that of EU countries at 15·1%.

Basic Exports: Alimentation industry products, beverages and tobacco, vegetative origin products, livestock and cattle farming products, textile and textile based articles, machines, electrical equipment, articles made from stone, gypsum, cement and glass.

Basic Imports: Power resources, industrial equipment, fortified alcoholic beverages and wines, plastics and articles made from plastics, natural cork, furniture, rolled metal, steel pipes and motor transport.

COMMUNICATIONS

Roads. There were 20,100 km of motor roads (14,000 km with hard surface) in 1990. In 1993, 71m. passengers and 7·8m. tonnes of freight were carried.

Railways. Total length in 1996 was 1,318 km of 1,520 mm gauge. In 1994, 14·9m. passengers and 4·5m. tonnes of freight were carried.

Civil Aviation. The national carrier is Air Moldova, which operated 15 ex-Soviet aircraft in 1995. In 1993, 0·2m. passengers and 1,500 tonnes of freight were carried.

Inland Waterways. In 1993, 0·3m. passengers and 0·3m. tonnes of freight were carried.

Telecommunications. The government authority Radioteleviziunea Nationala is responsible for broadcasting. There are 2 national radio programmes, a Radio Moscow relay and a foreign service, Radio Moldova International. There is a national state TV service and a private TV network. Romanian and Russian channels are also broadcast.

Press Moldova has 567 newspapers and magazines. Of these 323 are published in Moldovan, 4 in English and the rest in Russian.

SOCIAL INSTITUTIONS

Justice. 47,515 crimes were reported in 1994.

Education. In 1996 there were 1,880 pre-schools, 736,000 pupils in 1,698 primary, secondary and special schools, 43,000 students in 97 vocational secondary schools and 54 technical colleges and 47,000 students in 9 higher educational institutions including the state university. In Jan. 1994, 0·2m. children (52% of those eligible) attended pre-school institutions. Adult literacy rate, 96%.

Health. In Jan. 1996 there were 17,400 doctors, 48,400 junior medical personnel and 312 hospitals with 54,300 beds.

Welfare. In Jan. 1994 there were 649,000 age pensioners and 267,000 other pensioners.

DIPLOMATIC REPRESENTATIVES

Of Moldova in Great Britain (resides in Brussels)
Ambassador: Anatol Arapu.

Of Great Britain in Moldova (resides in Moscow)
Ambassador: Sir Andrew Wood, KCMG

Of Moldova in the USA
Ambassador: Nicolae Tau

Of the USA in Moldova (103 strada Alexei Matveevici, Chişinau)
Ambassador: John T. Stewart.

Of Moldova to the United Nations
Ambassador: Vacant.

Of Moldova to the European Union
Ambassador: Tudor Botnaru.

MONACO

Principauté de Monaco

Capital: Monaco
Population: 31,515

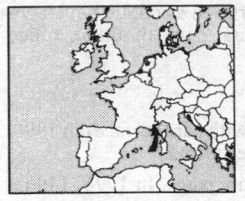

KEY HISTORICAL EVENTS. From 1297 Monaco belonged to the house of Grimaldi. In 1731 it passed into the female line, Louise Hippolyte, daughter of Antoine I, heiress of Monaco, marrying Jacques de Goyon Matignon, Count of Torigni, who took the name and arms of Grimaldi. The Principality was placed under the protection of the Kingdom of Sardinia by the Treaty of Vienna, 1815, and under that of France in 1861. Prince Albert I (reigned 1889–1922) acquired fame as an oceanographer; and his son Louis II (1922–49) was instrumental in establishing the International Hydrographic Bureau.

TERRITORY AND POPULATION. Monaco is bounded in the south by the Mediterranean and elsewhere by France (Department of Alpes Maritimes). The area is 195 ha. The Principality is divided into 4 districts: Monaco-Ville, la Condamine, Monte-Carlo and Fontvieille. Population (1990), 29,972, of whom 5,070 were Monegasques; (1995 estimate) 31,515. A census was scheduled for 1997. Vital statistics, 1995: Births, 830; deaths, 560; marriages, 190; divorces, 80.

The official language is French.

CLIMATE. A Mediterranean climate, with mild moist winters and hot dry summers. Monaco. Jan. 50°F (10°C), July 74°F (23·3°C). Annual rainfall 30" (758 mm).

PRINCELY HOUSE. The reigning Prince is **Rainier III**, b. 31 May 1923, son of Princess Charlotte, Duchess of Valentinois, daughter of Prince Louis II, 1898–1977 (married 19 March 1920 to Prince Pierre, Comte de Polignac, who had taken the name Grimaldi, from whom she was divorced 18 Feb. 1933). Prince Rainier succeeded his grandfather Louis II, who died on 9 May 1949. He married on 19 April 1956 Miss Grace Kelly, a citizen of the USA (died 14 Sept. 1982). *Issue:* Princess Caroline Louise Marguerite, b. 23 Jan. 1957; married Philippe Junot on 28 June 1978, divorced, 9 Oct. 1980, married Stefano Casiraghi on 29 Dec. 1983 (died, 3 Oct. 1990). Offspring: Andrea, b. 8 June 1984, Charlotte, b. 3 Aug. 1986, Pierre, b. 7 Sept. 1987. Prince Albert Alexandre Louis Pierre, b. 14 March 1958 *(heir apparent)*. Princess Stéphanie Marie Elisabeth, b. 1 Feb. 1965, married Daniel Ducruet on 1 July 1995, divorced 4 Oct. 1996. Offspring Louis, b. 27 Nov. 1992, Pauline, b. 4 May 1994.

CONSTITUTION AND GOVERNMENT. On 17 Dec. 1962 a new constitution was promulgated. It maintains the hereditary monarchy, though Prince Rainier renounces the principle of divine right. Executive power is exercised jointly by the Prince and a 4-member *Council of Government*, headed by a Minister of State (Michel Leveque). An 18-member *National Council* is elected for 5-year terms. At the election held on 2 Feb. 1998 all 18 seats were won by the National and Democratic Union (UND).

The constitution can be modified only with the approval of the National Council. A law of 1992 permits Monegasque women to give their nationality to their children.

National anthem: 'Principauté Monaco ma patrie' ('Principality of Monaco my fatherland'); words by T. Bellando de Castro, tune by C. Albrecht.

INTERNATIONAL RELATIONS. Monegasque relations with France are based on conventions of 1963. French citizens are treated as if in France.

Membership. Monaco is a member of the UN.

982

ECONOMY

Policy. A 22-ha site reclaimed from the sea at Fontvieille has been earmarked for office and residential development. The present industrial zone is to be reorganized and developed with a view to attracting new light industry.

Budget. The budget (in 1,000 francs) was as follows:

	1994	1995	1996
Revenue	3,052,412	2,851,699	3,205,310
Expenditure	2,883,897	2,923,434	3,258,380

Currency. Monaco is a member of the French Franc Zone.

Banking and Finance. There were 38 banks in 1996.

Weights and Measures. The metric system is in use.

ENERGY AND NATURAL RESOURCES

Electricity. Production (1996), 13·4m. kWh.

INDUSTRY. Light industry made up 9·9% of economic activity in 1995. There were some 700 small businesses, including chemicals, plastics, electronics, engineering and paper in 1993.

Labour. There were 30,520 persons employed in Sept. 1995. On 1 July 1995 the minimum wage (SMIC) was 36·98 francs an hour.

Trade Unions. Membership of trade unions was estimated at 2,000 out of a work force of 25,600 (1989).

FOREIGN ECONOMIC RELATIONS

Commerce. There is a customs union with France. Exports for 1996 totalled 1,798m. FF; imports, 1,909m. FF.

Tourism. In 1996, 226,421 foreign visitors, including 25,734 visitors from the USA and 39,000 from France, spent a total of 642,558 nights. There are 3 casinos run by the state, including the one at Monte Carlo attracting 0·4m. visitors a year.

COMMUNICATIONS

Roads. There were estimated to be 43 km of roads in 1995 and 28,757 motor vehicles.

Railways. The 1·7 km of main line passing through the country are operated by the French National Railways (SNCF).

Civil Aviation. The nearest airport is at Nice, France. At the Heliport of Monaco (Fontvieille) there were 109,209 passengers in 1995 (104,345 in 1994).

Shipping. In 1995 there were 1,024 vessels registered, of which 7 were over 100 tonnes. 1,573 yachts put in to the port of Monaco and 618 at Fontvieille in 1995.

Telecommunications. In 1996 there were 31,687 telephones.

Radio Monte Carlo broadcasts FM commercial programmes in French (long- and medium-waves). Radio Monte Carlo owns 55% of Radio Monte Carlo Relay Station on Cyprus. The foreign service is dedicated exclusively to religious broadcasts and is maintained by voluntary contributions. It operates in 36 languages under the name 'Trans World Radio' and has relay facilities on Bonaire, West Indies, and is planning to build relay facilities in the southern parts of Africa. *Télé Monté-Carlo* broadcasts TV programmes in French, Italian and English. There is a 30-channel cable service.

Cinemas. In 1996 there were 2 cinemas.

SOCIAL INSTITUTIONS

Justice. There are the following courts, *Juge de Paix*, Tribunal of the First Instance, a Court of Appeal, Criminal Tribunal, *Cour de Révision Judiciaire* and a Supreme Tribunal. There is no death penalty.

Police: There is an independent police force *(Sûreté Publique)* which comprised (1993) 500 personnel.

Religion. 90% of the resident population are Roman Catholic. There is a Roman Catholic archbishop.

Education. In 1996, in the public sector there were 7 pre-school institutions with 734 pupils; 4 primary schools with 1,271 pupils and 125 teachers; 3 secondary schools with 1,738 pupils and 1 technical school with 503 pupils; total secondary school teachers, 266. In the private sector there were 4 pre-school and primary schools with 622 pupils; 3 secondary schools with 707 pupils. The University of southern Europe is in Monaco with 117 students at the end of academic year 1996.

Health. In 1996 there were 503 hospital beds and 194 doctors, 22 dentists and 22 nurses.

DIPLOMATIC REPRESENTATIVES

British Consul-General (resident in Marseilles)*:* I. Davies.
British Honorary Consul: Eric G. Blair.
Consul-General for Monaco in London: I. B. Ivanovic.

Of Monaco to the United Nations
Ambassador: Jacques Louis Boisson.

Further Reading

Journal de Monaco. Bulletin Officiel. 1858 ff.

Hudson, G. L. *Monaco.* [Bibliography]. Oxford and Santa Barbara (CA), 1990

MONGOLIA

Mongol Uls

Capital: Ulan Bator
Population: 2·4m.
GNP: US$0·8bn.
HDI/world rank: 0·661/101 (1994)

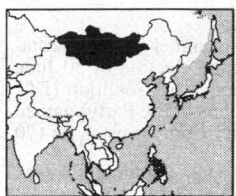

KEY HISTORICAL EVENTS. Temujin became khan of Hamag Mongolia in 1190, and having united by conquest various Tatar and Mongolian tribes, was confirmed as 'Universal' ('Genghis', 'Chingiz') khan in 1206. The expansionist impulse of his nomadic empire (Beijing captured 1215; Samarkand, 1220) continued after his death in 1227, though the empire was by then administratively divided among his sons. Tamurlaine (died 1405) was the last of the conquering khans. In 1368 the Chinese drove the Mongols from Beijing, and for the next two centuries Sino-Mongolian relations alternated between war and trade. Lamaism spread from Tibet in the 16th century. The last Mongol khan, Ligden (1604-34), failed to stem the tide of Manchu expansion; southern (Inner) Mongolia was conquered in 1636 and Beijing in 1644. In 1691 Outer Mongolia accepted Manchu rule. The head of the Lamaist faith became the symbol of national identity, and his seat ('Urga', now Ulan Bator) was made the Mongolian capital.

When the Manchu dynasty was overthrown in 1911 Outer Mongolia declared its independence under its spiritual ruler and turned to Russia for support against China. 'Autonomy' (not independence) was agreed by the Sino-Russo-Mongolian agreement of May 1915. In 1919 China re-established central rule, but Soviet and Mongolian revolutionary forces set up a provisional government in March 1921. On the death of the spiritual ruler (the 'Urga Living Buddha') a people's republic and new constitution were proclaimed in May 1924.

With Soviet help Japanese invaders were fended off during the Second World War. The Mongols then took part in the successful Soviet campaign against Inner Mongolia and Manchuria.

On 5 Jan. 1946 China recognized the independence of Outer Mongolia after a plebiscite in Mongolia (20 Oct. 1945) had resulted in an overwhelming vote for independence. A Sino-Soviet treaty of 14 Feb. 1950 guaranteed this independence. In Aug. 1986 a consular agreement, in June 1987 a boundary agreement, and in Nov. 1988 a border treaty, were signed with China.

Until 1990 sole power was in the hands of the Mongolian People's Revolutionary (Communist) Party (MPRP), but an opposition Mongolian Democratic Party, founded in Dec. 1989, achieved tacit recognition and held its first congress in Feb. 1990. Following demonstrations and hunger-strikes, on 12 March the entire MPRP Politburo resigned and political opposition was legalized.

TERRITORY AND POPULATION. Mongolia is bounded in the north by the Russian Federation, and in the east and south and west by China. Area, 1,565,008 sq. km (604,250 sq. miles). Population (1989 census), 2,095,600; 1997 estimate, 2,356,000 (52% urban; 49·7% male). Density, 1·5 per sq. km. Birth rate (1995), 23·7 per 1,000; death rate, 7·3 per 1,000; marriage rate, 12 per 1,000; divorce rate, 0·7 per 1,000. Rate of increase, 16·4 per 1,000. Infant mortality rate, 1997, 468 per 1,000 live births. Expectation of life in 1997 was 63·7 years. The population is predominantly made up of Mongolian peoples (78·8% Halh). There is a Turkic Kazakh minority (5·9% of the population) and 20 Mongol minorities. The official language is Halh Mongol.

The republic is administratively divided into 3 cities: Ulan Bator, the capital, (1996 population, 619,200), Darhan, (89,900) and Erdenet (65,600), and 18 provinces *(aimag)*. The provinces are sub-divided into 334 districts or counties *(suums)*.

CLIMATE. A very extreme climate, with six months of mean temperatures below freezing, but much higher temperatures occur for a month or two in summer. Rainfall is very low and limited to the months mid-May to mid-Sept. Ulan Bator. Jan. −14°F (−25·6°C), July 61°F (16·1°C). Annual rainfall 8" (208 mm).

CONSTITUTION AND GOVERNMENT. The Constitution of 12 Feb. 1992 abolished the 'People's Democracy', introduced democratic institutions and a market economy and guarantees freedom of speech.

The *President* is directly elected for renewable 4-year terms.

Since June 1992, the legislature has consisted of a single-chamber 76-seat parliament, *the Great Hural*, which elects the Prime Minister. At the election of 30 June 1996 the electorate was 1·2m.; turn-out was 90%. The Democratic Coalition (DC, consisting of the National Democratic Party and the Social Democratic Party) gained 50 seats; the Mongolian People's Revolutionary Party (former Communists), 25 (70 in 1992); ind, 1.

At the presidential election on 18 May 1997 Natsagiin Bagabandi obtained 60·8% of the votes cast, against 29·8% for President Punsalmaagiyn Ochirbat.

President: Natsagiin Bagabandi (b. 1940; Mongolian People's Revolutionary Party, elected May 1997).

A DC government was formed in July 1996 which comprised in March 1998:

Prime Minister: Tsakhiagiin Elbegdorj (b. 1962; Mongolian National Democratic Party).

External Relations: S. Altangerel. *Environment:* T. Adiyasuren. *Defence:* D. Dorligjav. *Finance:* P. Tsagaan. *Infrastructure and Development:* G. Nyamdavaa. *Justice:* J. Amarsanaa. *Health and Social Security:* L. Zorig. *Education:* C. Lhagvajav. *Agriculture and Industry:* L. Nyamsambuu. *Administration:* L. Enebish.

The *Speaker* is Radnaasumbereliyn Gonchidorj (Social Democratic Party).

National anthem: 'Darkhan manai khuvsgalt uls' ('Our sacred revolutionary republic'); words by Tsendiyn Damdinsüren, tune by Bilegin Damdinsüren and Luvsanjamts Murjorj.

Local government is carried out by 380 local authorities. Some 13,000 deputies were elected in July 1990.

DEFENCE. Conscription is for 1 year for males aged 18-28 years.

Army. The Army comprises 4 motorized infantry divisions (3 under strength), 1 artillery and 1 air defence brigade and 1 airborne and 2 independent infantry battalions. Equipment includes 650 T-54/-55/-62 main battle tanks. Strength (1997) 15,500 (11,000 conscripts). There is a border guard of 5,000 and some 1,000 internal security troops.

Air Force. The Air Force had a strength of 2,000 in 1996 (500 conscripts). There are 24 Antonov An-24 and An-26 transports used mainly on civil air services, 10 Mi-8 helicopters and a few Yak-18 trainers.

INTERNATIONAL RELATIONS

Membership. Mongolia is a member of the UN.

ECONOMY

Policy. Mongolia has had for centuries a traditional nomadic pastoral economy, which the Government aims to transform into a market economy. An Agency for National Development, whose head has cabinet rank, co-ordinates economic policy. A law of May 1991 envisages privatization by the issue of vouchers worth 10,000 tugriks to all citizens to acquire holdings in large privatizations or to buy small business or livestock.

Performance. Real GDP growth was 6·3% in 1995 (2·3% in 1994).

Budget (in 1m. tugriks):

	1991	1992	1993	1994	1995	1996
Revenue	6,497	8,378	44,310	57,797	94,811	112,983
Expenditure	8,929	7,111	34,850	45,230	66,834	88,470

Sources of revenue, 1995 (in 1m. tugriks): Taxes, 109,269·5 (comprising: Income, Profits and Capital Gains Tax, 49,999·4; Social security contributions, 18,906·1; payroll taxes, 43·5; taxes on goods and services, 27,364·7; taxes on foreign trade, 9,630·5; other, 3,325·3); non-tax revenue, 18,243·2; capital revenue, 3,751·2; grants, 5,010·5. Items of expenditure: Current, 105,536·2 (comprising: Goods and services, 75,083·5; wages, 25,542·5; employer contributions, 7,161·1; other purchases, 42,379·9); interest payments, 1,794·4; subsidies, 28,658·5; capital, 22,559·3; foreign amortization, 16,836.

Currency. The unit of currency is the *tugrik* (MNT) of 100 *möngö*. Notes are issued for 1, 2, 5, 10, 20, 50, 100, 500 and 1,000 *tugriks*; and coins for 1, 2, 5, 10, 15, 20, 50 *möngö* and 1 *tugrik*. The tugrik was made convertible in 1993. Foreign exchange reserves were nil in July 1993. Inflation was 35% in 1995 (55% in 1994).

Banking and Finance. The Mongolian Bank (established 1924) is the bank of issue, being also a commercial, savings and development bank: the *Governor* is J. Unenbat. It has 21 main branches. There are also a Trade and Industry Bank, an Insurance Bank and a Co-operative Bank.

A stock exchange opened in Ulan Bator in 1992.

Weights and Measures. The metric system is in use.

ENERGY AND NATURAL RESOURCES

Electricity. There are 6 thermal electric power stations. Production of electricity, 1995, 2,053m. kWh.

Minerals. There are large deposits of copper, nickel, zinc, molybdenum, phosphorites, tin, wolfram and fluorspar; production of the latter in 1995, 526,900 tonnes. There are major coalmines near Ulan Bator and Darhan. Coal (mainly lignite) production in 1995 was 5m. tonnes. Copper production, 0·35m. tonnes.

Agriculture. The prevailing Mongolian style of life is pastoral nomadism. 73% of agricultural production derives from cattle-raising. In 1995 there were 2·6m. horses, 3·3m. cattle, 13,718,600 sheep, 367,500 camels, 8,520,700 goats and 23,500 pigs. In 1995 there were 99,300 poultry.

Production 1995 (in 1,000 tonnes): Meat, 216 (249 in 1990); cow's milk, 343; fermented mare's milk (1992), 25m. litres.

The total agricultural area in 1995 was 118·5m. ha. 96% was sown to cereals, 1·6% to fodder and 0·9% to vegetables. In 1995 there was 1·3m. ha of arable land, 1,000 ha of permanent crop land and 117·1m. ha of pasture. The 1995 crop was 256,700 tonnes of wheat; 52,000 tonnes of potatoes; (1993) 10,000 tonnes of oats; 18,000 tonnes of barley. In 1992 there were 11,700 tractors (15 h.p. units) and 2,600 combine harvesters.

Forestry. Forests, chiefly larch, cedar, fir and birch, occupy 15·1m. ha. Production, 1995: 61,200 cu. metres of sawn wood.

INDUSTRY. Industry is still small in scale and local in character. The food
industry accounts for 25% of industrial production. The main industrial centre is Ulan Bator; others are at Erdenet and Baga-Nur, and a northern territorial industrial complex is being developed based on Darhan and Erdenet to produce copper and molybdenum concentrates, lime, cement, machinery and wood- and metal-worked products. Production figures (1995): Scoured wool, 1,200 tonnes; cement, 108,800 tonnes; leather footwear, 0·25m. pairs; meat, 11,300 tonnes; soap, 600 tonnes.

Labour. The labour force was 1,103,100 in 1995, including 108,100 in industry, 354,300 in agriculture, 29,500 in building, 31,600 in transport and communications and 64,800 in trade. Average wage was 16,000 tugriks per month in 1995. As of 1 Feb. 1997, 57,900 people were officially registered as unemployed.

Trade Unions. Membership was 0·53m. in 1988.

FOREIGN ECONOMIC RELATIONS. Mongolia is dependent on foreign aid. The largest donor in 1992 was Japan. Foreign debt was US$12,000m. in 1993.

Joint ventures with foreign firms are permitted. Foreign investors may acquire up to 49% of the equity in Mongolian companies. Foreign companies (except in precious metal mining) have a 5-year tax holiday and a further 5 years at 50% of the tax rate.

Commerce. Value of exports, 1995: US$512m.; imports, US$384m. Main exports (in tonnes): Copper concentrate, 435,000; molybdenum concentrate, 3,438; wheat, 8,300; sawn wood, 37,200 cu. metres; 62,000 horse skins; 1,818,500 sheepskins; 314,600 goatskins; 20,600 woollen blankets.

Main export markets, 1995 (trade in US$1m.): Japan, 95·6; Kazakhstan, 77·7; China, 73·2; Switzerland, 67·6; Russia, 66·9; USA, 29·9; South Korea, 25·5; UK, 19·4. Main import suppliers: Russia, 202; Japan, 44·5; China, 39·4; South Korea, 20·3; USA, 14·1.

Tourism. 147,200 tourists visited Mongolia in 1990.

COMMUNICATIONS

Roads. There are 1,185 km of surfaced roads running around Ulan Bator, from Ulan Bator to Darhan, at points on the frontier with the Russian Federation and towards the south. Truck services run where there are no surfaced roads. 1·6m. tonnes of freight were carried in 1995, and 107·2m. passengers.

Railways. The Trans-Mongolian Railway (1,928 km of 1,524 mm gauge in 1992) connects Ulan Bator with the Russian Federation and China. There are spur lines to Erdenet and to the coalmines at Nalayh and Sharyn Gol. A separate line connects Choybalsan in the east with Borzaya on the Trans-Siberian Railway. 2·8m. passengers and 7·3m. tonnes of freight were carried in 1995.

Civil Aviation. In 1995, Mongolian Airlines (MIAT) had 1 B-727-200, 2 B-200-Advs, 5 Chinese and 19 ex-Soviet aircraft. It operates internal services, a flight to Irkutsk which links with a stopping service to Moscow, and a daily non-stop service to Moscow from Ulan Bator. There are also flights to Beijing. 2,676 tonnes of freight were carried in 1995 and 0·2m. passengers. Ulan Bator airport (Buyant Uhaa) was modernized and expanded in 1985.

Shipping. There is a steamer service on the Selenge River and a tug and barge service on Hövsgöl Lake. 70,000 tonnes of freight were carried in 1990.

Telecommunications. There were, in 1995, 391 post offices and (in 1990) 341 telephone exchanges. Number of telephones (1995), 75,300.

The government-controlled Ulaanbaatar Radio broadcasts 2 national programmes and an external service (English, Chinese, Japanese, Russian). Mongol Televiz transmits a daily programme and a Moscow relay (colour by SECAM). In 1995 153,442 radio and 142,800 TV sets were in use.

Cinemas. In 1990 there were 30 cinemas, 522 mobile cinemas and 30 theatres.

Press. In 1995 there was 1 government daily with a circulation of 50,000, and a police-run weekly. About 300 other titles were registered, but few were actually publishing. 717 book titles were published in 1990 in 6·4m. copies.

SOCIAL INSTITUTIONS

Justice. The Procurator-General is appointed, and the Supreme Court elected, by parliament for 5 years. There are also courts at province, town and district level. Lay assessors sit with professional judges.

Religion. Tibetan Buddhist Lamaism is the prevalent religion; the Dalai Lama is its spiritual head. In 1995 there were about 100 monasteries and 2,500 monks.

Education. In 1995 there were 711 nurseries with 68,100 children. Schooling begins at the age of 7. In 1995 there were 664 general education schools with 403,800 pupils and 19,400 teachers. In 1990–91 there were 31 specialized secondary schools with 18,500 students and 1,300 teachers and 44 vocational technical schools with 29,100 pupils.

In 1994-95 there were 1 university and 4 specialized universities (agricultural; medical; pedagogical; technical). There were also colleges of commerce and business, economics, and railway engineering, and an institute of culture and art.

Health and Welfare. In 1995, 102·8m. tugriks were spent on maternity benefits.

Annual average per capita consumption (in kg) of foodstuffs in 1995: Meat, 97; milk and products, 126; sugar, 8·7; flour, 94; potatoes, 11; fresh vegetables, 8. In 1995 there were 250 doctors and 96 hospital beds per 10,000 population.

DIPLOMATIC REPRESENTATIVES

Of Mongolia in Great Britain (7 Kensington Ct., London, W8 5DL)
Ambassador: Tsedenjavyn Suhbaatar.

Of Great Britain in Mongolia (30 Enkh Taivny Gudamzh, Ulan Bator 13)
Ambassador: John Durham.

Of Mongolia in the USA
Ambassador: Vacant.

Of the USA in Mongolia
Ambassador: Vacant.

Of Mongolia to the United Nations
Ambassador: Jargalsaikhany Enkhsaikhan.

Of Mongolia to the European Union
Ambassador: Jagvaralin Hanibal.

Further Reading

State Statistical Office: *Mongolian Economy and Society in [year]: Statistical Yearbook.—National Economy of the MPR, 1924–1984: Anniversary Statistical Collection.* Ulan Bator, 1984

Akiner. S. (ed.) *Mongolia Today.* London, 1992
Bawden, C. R., *The Modern History of Mongolia.* London, 1968
Becker, J., *The Lost Country.* London, 1992
Bruun, O. and Odgaard, O. (eds.) *Mongolia in Transition.* Richmond, 1996
Griffin, K. (ed.) *Poverty and the Transition to a Market Economy in Mongolia.* London, 1995
Jagchid, S. and Hyer, P., *Mongolia's Culture and Society.* Folkestone, 1979
Lattimore, O., *Nationalism and Revolution in Mongolia.* Leiden, 1955.—*Nomads and Commissars.* OUP, 1963
Nordby, J., *Mongolia in the Twentieth Century.* Farnborough, 1993
Sanders, A. J. K., *Mongolia: Politics, Economics and Society.* London, 1987
Shirendev, B. and Sanjdorj, M. (eds.) *History of the Mongolian People's Republic.* Vol. 3 (vols. 1 and 2 not translated). Harvard Univ. Press, 1976

National Statistical Office: State Statistical Office, Ulan Bator

MOROCCO

Mamlaka al-Maghrebia

(Kingdom of Morocco)

Capital: Rabat
Population: 28·3m.
GDP per head: (PPP$) 3,681
GNP: US$30·3bn.
HDI/world rank: 0·566/119

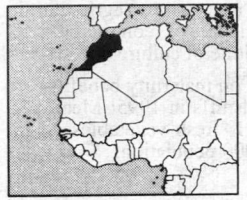

KEY HISTORICAL EVENTS. The native people of Morocco are the Berbers, an ancient race who, throughout history, have seen their country invaded by a succession of foreign powers. In the 12th century BC the first of these foreign invaders were the Phoenicians, who established trading posts at several points along the North African coast. The Carthaginians later took over these Phoenician colonies and expanded them as part of the mighty Carthaginian Empire. When the city of Carthage fell to Rome in the second century BC, the African Mediterranean coast was under Roman dominance for almost six hundred years. When the Roman Empire in turn fell into decline, the area was invaded first by the Vandals in AD 429 and later by Byzantium in AD 533. An Arab invasion of Morocco in AD 682 marked the end of Byzantium dominance, and the first Arab rulers, the Idrisid dynasty, ruled for 150 years.

Arab and Berber dynasties succeeded the Idrisids; notably the Almoravids (1062–1147) and the Almohads (1147–1258). The Almohad Empire declined after the defeat of the Moroccans by the Spanish at the Battle of Las Navas de Tolosa in 1212. By 1250 its power had completely collapsed and the country was plunged into bitter civil war between Arab and Berber factions. The reign of Ahmed I al-Man-sur in the first Sharifian dynasty stabilized and unified the country between 1579 and 1603. Moors and Jews expelled from Spain settled in Morocco during this time and the country flourished and prospered. It became a centre for the arts and this period was known as Morocco's golden age.

Portuguese and Spanish power had been growing in the Mediterranean region since the beginning of the 15th century, and in 1415 the Moroccan port of Ceuta was captured by Portugal. Moroccan forces defeated the Portuguese in 1578, and by 1700 had regained control of many coastal towns which had previously been in Portuguese hands. During the 18th and early 19th centuries, the Barbary Coast became the scene of widespread piracy. Ships which traded in the Mediterranean were plundered and protection money was extorted from several sea-going nations.

Morocco shared possession of the Straits of Gibraltar with Spain, resulting in a focus of attention from the maritime powers in Europe, particularly France and Britain. By the beginning of the 20th century Britain had recognized Morocco as a French sphere of influence and in 1904 Morocco was divided between France and Spain, with the former receiving the larger area. These arrangements were regarded as spurious by Imperial Germany and, despite the Act of Algeciras (an agreement signed by the major powers in 1906, which guaranteed equal economic rights in Morocco), Germany was still dissatisfied.

In 1911, a German gunboat was dispatched to the Moroccan port of Agadir, in an attempt to excite further nationalist unrest against the French. From 1912 to 1956 Morocco was divided into three areas: a French protectorate, established by the Treaty of Fez of 1912 concluded between France and the Sultan; a Spanish protectorate, established by the Franco-Spanish Convention of 1912; and the international zone of Tangier which was established by France, Great Britain and Spain in 1923.

Gen. Lyautey, the first French resident-general, was responsible for much modernization and by 1934 had pacified the country. However, as tribesmen were defeated so nationalism in various forms developed.

On 2 March 1956 France and the Sultan terminated the Treaty of Fez and on 7 April 1956 Spain relinquished her protectorate. On 29 Oct. 1956 the international status of the Tangier Zone was abolished by common consent and Morocco became a kingdom on 18 Aug. 1957, with the Sultan taking the title Mohammed V.

The country became territorially complete when the northern strip of Spanish Sahara was ceded by Spain on 10 April 1958 and the former Spanish province of Ifni was returned to Morocco on 30 June 1969.

Crown Prince Moulay Hassan succeeded his father on 3 March 1961 as Hassan II. King Hassan tried to combine the various parties in government and he established an elected House of Representatives, but political unrest led him to discard any attempt at a parliamentary government, and to rule autocratically from 1965 to 1977. In 1977 a new Chamber of Representatives was elected, and under the constitution Morocco became a constitutional monarchy with a single elected chamber.

In 1974 Morocco embarked on a campaign aimed at forcing Spain to withdraw from the Western region of the Sahara (now known as the Moroccan Sahara), an area rich in phosphates. The International Court of Justice, meeting in the Hague in 1975, rejected Morocco's claim for full sovereignty over the region. Morocco ignored this decision and resolved to continue the fight alone, organizing a massive demonstration known as the Green March. Spain entered into secret negotiations and a deal was struck, whereby the region was divided into three, and administered by Morocco, Spain and Mauritania.

The Polisaro front, a Saharan nationalist movement, hotly disputed Morocco's right to the territory and guerrilla fighting ensued. In 1978, the Polisaro Front succeeded in forcing Mauritania to relinquish its Saharan interests, but was unable to do the same with Morocco.

The United Nations continued to mediate in this dispute throughout the eighties, and by 1990 a referendum proposed self-determination by both sides. Negotiations between the Moroccan government and Polisaro brokered by the USA opened in Lisbon 23 June 1997 but were immediately adjourned so that UN and US proposals could be considered. Talks reopened in London on 19 July 1997.

TERRITORY AND POPULATION. Morocco is bounded by Algeria to the east and south-east, Mauritania to the south, the Atlantic Ocean to the north-west and the Mediterranean to the north. Excluding the Western Saharan territory claimed and retrieved since 1976 by Morocco, the area is 458,730 sq. km and population at the 1982 census was 20,255,687. Western Sahara had an area of 252,120 sq. km and 163,868 population. The Moroccan superficie is 710,850 sq. km. Population in 1994: Morocco 26m. (50% urban); Density, 36·7 per sq. km. Estimate, 1995, 28·3m. There was a census in Sept. 1994. Vital statistics rates, 1993 (per 1,000 population): Birth, 27·3; death, 7·0; growth, 20·3; life expectancy 65·3.

The 49 provinces and 22 prefectures are grouped into 7 economic regions (in parentheses). Area and population in 1994:

Province	Area in sq. km	Population in 1,000	Province	Area in sq. km	Population in 1,000
(South)			Ben Slimane	2,760	213
Agadir	5,910	921	Aïn Chok-Hay Hassani		516
Boujdour	100,120	22	Aïn Sebaâ-Hay		
Es-Semara	61,760	40	Mohammadi		521
Guelmim	28,750	147	Ben Msik-Sidi Othmane	1,615	704
El-Aaiún	39,360	154	Casablanca-Anfa		523
Ouarzazate	41,550	695	Mohammadia-Znata		170
Oued Eddahab	50,880	37	El Jadida	6,000	971
Tan-Tan	17,295	58	Khouribga	4,250	481
Taroudannt	16,460	694	Settat	9,750	847
Tata	25,925	119			
Tiznit	6,960	348	(North-West)		
			Chefchaouen	4,350	439
(Tensift)			Kénitra	4,745	979
El Kelâa Srahna	10,070	682	Khémisset	8,305	486
Essaouira	6,335	434	Rabat		623
Marrakesh	14,755	1,608	Salé	1,275	632
Safi	7,285	823	Skhirate-Témara		245
			Sidi Kacem	4,060	646
(Centre)			Tangiers	1,195	628
Azilal	10,050	455	Tétouan	6,025	537
Béni Mellal	7,075	870	Larache		

Province	Area in sq. km	Population in 1,000	Province	Area in sq. km	Population in 1,000
(Centre-North)			Nador	6,130	684
Al Hoceima	3,550	383	Oujda	20,700	968
Boulemane	14,395	162			
Fes	5,400	1,161	(Centre-South)		
Taounate	5,585	629	Errachidia	59,585	522
Taza	15,020	708	Ifrane	3,310	128
			Khenifra	12,320	465
(Eastern)			Meknès	3,995	789
Figuig	55,990	117			

The chief cities (with estimated populations in 1,000, 1993) are as follows:

Casablanca	3,200	Oujda	331	Mohammedia	156
Rabat	1,220	Tangiers	307	Beni Mellal	139
Marrakesh	602	Safi	278	Agadir	137
Fez	564	Tétouan	272	El Jadida	125
Salé	521	Kénitra	234		
Meknès	401	Khouribga	190		

The official language is Arabic, spoken by 75% of the population; the remainder speak Berber. French and Spanish are considered subsidiary languages and, more recently, English.

CLIMATE. Morocco is dominated by the Mediterranean climate which is made temperate by the influence of the Atlantic Ocean in the northern and southern parts of the country. Central Morocco is continental while the south is desert. Rabat. Jan. 55°F (12·9°C), July 72°F (22·2°C). Annual rainfall 23" (564 mm). Agadir. Jan. 57°F (13·9°C), July 72°F (22·2°C). Annual rainfall 9" (224 mm). Casablanca. Jan. 54°F (12·2°C), July 72°F (22·2°C). Annual rainfall 16" (404 mm). Marrakesh. Jan. 52°F (11·1°C), July 84°F (28·9°C). Annual rainfall 10" (239 mm). Tangier. Jan. 53°F (11·7°C), July 72°F (22·2°C). Annual rainfall 36" (897 mm).

ROYAL HOUSE. The ruling King is **Hassan II,** born on 9 July 1929, succeeded on 3 March 1961, on the death of his father Mohammed V, who reigned 1927–61. The royal style was changed from 'His Sherifian Majesty the Sultan' to 'His Majesty the King' on 18 Aug. 1957. *Heir apparent:* Crown Prince Sidi Mohammed, born 21 Aug. 1963. The King holds supreme civil and religious authority, the latter in his capacity of Emir-el-Muminin or Commander of the Faithful. He resides usually at Rabat, but occasionally in one of the other traditional capitals, Fez (founded in 808), Marrakesh (founded in 1062), or at Skhirat.

CONSTITUTION AND GOVERNMENT. A new Constitution was approved by referendum in March 1972 and amendments were approved by referendum in May 1980 and Sept. 1992. The Kingdom of Morocco is a constitutional monarchy. Parliament consists of a *Chamber of Representatives* composed of 325 deputies directly elected for 6-year terms. A referendum on 13 Sept. 1996 established a second *Chamber of Counsellors,* of whom 60% are elected for 9-year terms in tranches of one-third of the members by local councils, 20% by employers' associations and 20% by trade unions. The Chamber of Counsellors has power to initiate legislation, issue warnings of censure to the government and ultimately to force the government's resignation by a two-thirds majority vote. The electorate was 12·3m. and turn-out was 82·95%. The King, as sovereign head of State, appoints the Prime Minister and other Ministers, has the right to dissolve Parliament and approves legislation.

A new electoral code of March 1997 fixed voting at 20 and made enrolment on the electoral roll compulsory.

The new Chamber of Representatives was elected on 14 November 1997 during the General Elections. At this election, the USFP (Socialist Opposition) won 57 seats, UC (Constitutional Union) won 50 and PI (Istiqlat; Independence Party) won 32. These General Elections showed that no party can constitute a government without the support of the other parties. The opposition parties won 102 seats, the coalition of ruling parties won 100, and the centre won 91. The opposition and the centre will probably make an arrangement to constitute the next government.

Prime Minister: Abderrahmane Youssoufi.
In March 1998 a new government was still under construction.

National anthem: 'Manbit al Ahrah, mashriq al anwar' ('Fountain of freedom, source of light'); words by Ali Squalli Houssaini, tune by Leo Morgan.

*Local Government.*The country is administratively divided into 49 provinces and 22 prefectures divided into 159 circles, which are subdivided into 248 urban and 1,297 rural communes.

Elections were held on 13 June 1997. The Democratic Bloc (Koutla) gained 102 seats, the Right Bloc 100 and the Rassemblement National des Indépendants 97 seats. There were 3,000 candidates and turnout was 58·3%. Two women were elected.

DEFENCE. Conscription is authorized for 18 months.

Army. The Army is deployed in 2 commands: Northern Zone and Southern Zone. It comprises 3 mechanized infantry, 1 light security and 2 parachute brigades; 8 mechanized infantry regiments; 1 air defence group; 37 infantry, 3 camel corps, 2 cavalry, 1 mountain, 10 armoured, 12 artillery, 7 engineer and 2 airborne battalions and 4 commando units. There is also a Royal guard of 1,500. Equipment includes 224 M-48A5 and 300 M-60 main battle tanks. Strength (1997), 175,000 (100,000 conscripts). There is also a Royal Gendarmerie of 12,000 and an Auxiliary Force of 30,000.

Navy. The Navy includes 1 missile-armed Spanish-built frigate, 2 Italian-built missile-armed corvettes, 4 fast missile craft, 14 coastal patrol craft and 6 inshore patrol craft. There are additionally 1 ex-US tank landing ship, 3 medium landing ships of French origin, 2 transports and 1 Ro-Ro ferry in naval use. Personnel in 1996 numbered 7,800, including a 1,500 strong brigade of Naval Infantry. Bases are located at Casablanca, Agadir, Al-Hoceima and Dakhla.

The Coast Guard wing of the Royal Gendarmerie operates 12 patrol craft.

Air Force. Equipment in current use includes 32 Mirage F1s, a total of 32 F-5A/B/E/F fighter-bombers and RF-5A reconnaissance-fighters, 3 OV-10 Bronco counter-insurgency aircraft, 2 Falcon 20s for electronic warfare, and 18 Gazelle armed helicopters, 20 Alpha Jet advanced trainers, 20 Magister armed jet basic trainers, 10 T-34C-1 turboprop basic trainers, 10 Swiss-built Bravo primary trainers, 2 Mudry CAP 10B and 4 CAP 230 aerobatic trainers, 70 Agusta-Bell 205 and 212, Puma and JetRanger helicopters, 2 Do 28D Skyservants for coastal patrol, 9 CH-47C heavy-lift helicopters, 15 C-130H turboprop transport aircraft, 2 KC 130H tanker/transports, 2 Citation V, a Falcon 50 and a Gulfstream III VIP transport, 2 Boeing 707s (1 modified as a tanker), 7 CN-235s, 10 turboprop King Air light transports and 14 T-37 trainers. Personnel strength (1996) about 13,500, with 87 combat aircraft and 18 armed helicopters.

INTERNATIONAL RELATIONS

Membership. Morocco is a member of the UN and the Arab League.

ECONOMY

Policy. There is a programme of privatization involving 112 companies. 30 had been privatized by mid-1995.

Performance. Economic growth was 11·8% in 1996.

Budget. 1991 revenue was DH57,562m.; expenditure, DH46,451m. VAT is 20%.

Currency. The unit of currency is the *dirham* (MAD) of 100 *centimes*, introduced in 1959. There are coins of 5, 10, 20 and 50 centimes and 1 and 5 dirhams, and notes of 10, 50, 100 and 200 dirhams. Foreign exchange reserves were US$3,400m. in 1993.

DH42,080m. were in circulation at the end of 1994. Since 1993 the dirham has been convertible for current account operations. Inflation was 3% in 1996.

Banking and Finance. The central bank is the Bank Al Maghrib, which had assets of DH60,968m. on 31 Dec. 1993. There are 14 commercial banks (11 foreign). There are also 3 development banks, specializing respectively in industry, housing and agriculture.

There is a stock exchange at Casablanca. The global volume, in 1989, was DH672m.; in 1996, it was DH23·9bn.

Weights and Measures. The metric system is legal.

ENERGY AND NATURAL RESOURCES

Electricity. Installed capacity was 2,646,100 kW in 1993. Production was 9,276·6m. kWh. (855·1m. hydro-electric) in 1994.

Minerals. The principal mineral exploited is phosphate, the output of which was 20·68m. tonnes in 1995. Other minerals (in tonnes, 1995) are: Lead (101,545), zinc (150,160), silver (259·1), copper (33,685), iron ore (33,500), manganese (22,000), barytine (273,809), salt (182,000).

Agriculture. In 1996, agriculture contributed 78·8% of GDP. Agricultural production is subject to drought; about 1m. ha are irrigated. 85% of farmland is individually owned. Only 1% of farms are over 50 ha; most are under 3 ha. Land suitable for cultivation, 1993, 9·26m. ha, of which (in 1,000 ha): Cereals, 6,074; leguminous vegetables, 347; market gardening, 204; oil-producing, 98, industrial crops, 151; fodder, 168; dense fruit plantations, 664; fallow, 2,687.

Production in 1995/96 (in 1,000 tonnes): Wheat, 22,697; barley, 38,311; maize, 2,350; fruit, 2,890 (of which citrus fruits, 1,324); pulses, 276·7; sunflower seeds, 60·8; groundnuts, 30; sugar beets, 3,144; sugar-cane, 925; cotton, 31·2.

Dairy production in 1994 included: Milk, 490m. litres; butter, 5,600 tonnes. Meat production, 454,000 tonnes.

Livestock (in 1,000 head), 1994: Cattle, 2,238; sheep, 13,902; goats, 4,060; camels, 41; horses (1993), 156.

Forestry. Natural forests covered (1993) 8·97m. ha. 520,364 ha were reafforested in 1992–93. Produce includes firewood, building and industrial timber and some cork and charcoal.

Fisheries. The fishing fleet numbered 2,564 coastal vessels in 1993 and 462 deep-sea vessels, the latter totalling 152,417 GRT. Total catch in 1994 was 748,886 tonnes (deep-sea, 132,800 tonnes). Total catch value was DH3,195m.

INDUSTRY. In 1992 there were 5,855 industrial firms employing 351,149 persons. 1,785 of these employed fewer than 10 persons; 80, more than 500. 1,434 firms were engaged in food production, 789 in clothing, 723 in textiles and 397 in paper- and board-making and printing. Production, 1993 (in tonnes): Sugar, 497,767; olive oil, 38,000; cement, 6,175,000. In 1995, the industrial investment was DH14·2bn. of which 92% came from the private sector.

Labour. Amongst the total urban population in 1993 of 13,149,000, 3,659,319 persons were employed (784,963 females; 68,193 under 15 years) and 680,801 registered unemployed. The monthly non-agricultural minimum wage was DH1,510. The agricultural minimum was DH37·60 per day in 1994.

Trade Unions. In 1996 there were 8 trade unions: UMT (Union Marocaine de Travail), CDT (Confédération Démocratique du Travail), UGTM (Union Générale des Travailleurs Marocaine), UNTM (National Union of Moroccan Workers), USP (Union of Popular Workers) and the SNP (National Popular Union).

FOREIGN ECONOMIC RELATIONS. In 1989 Morocco signed a treaty of economic co-operation with the 4 other Maghreb countries: Algeria, Libya,

Mauritania and Tunisia. In 1995, Morocco signed an association agreement with the EU to create a free trade zone in 12 years. Foreign debt was US$22,000m. in 1995.

Commerce. In 1996 imports were US$7,999m. and exports, US$4,628m. Imports in 1994 included (in 1,000 tonnes): Crude oil, 6,855; grain, 1,191; sulphur, 2,653; chemicals, 588; sawn wood, 663. Exports included: Foodstuffs and tobacco, 1,310; phosphates, 9,527; other mineral products (1993), 2,063; natural and artificial fertilizers, 1,674.

Main export markets in 1995 (in DH1m.): France, 11,940; Spain, 3,779; India, 2,640; Italy, 2,291; Japan, 3,085. Main import suppliers: France, 15,915; Spain, 6,215; Italy, 4,470; Germany, 4,563; USA, 4,770.

Tourism. In 1994, 2,293,744 foreign visitors stayed 11·54m. nights. Tourist revenue (1993), DH11,222m.

COMMUNICATIONS

Roads. In 1994 there were 60,449 km of classified roads, of which 30,374 km were surfaced and including 9,584 km of surfaced main roads. A motorway links Rabat to Casablanca. 3·4m. passengers and 16·1m. tonnes of freight were carried in 1993. In 1993 there were 316,722 commercial vehicles, 849,344 private cars and 19,689 motor cycles. There were 43,681 road accidents in 1994 (3,605 fatalities).

Railways. In 1995 there were 1,907 km of railways, of which 1,003 km were electrified. In 1995 the railways carried 1,645m. passenger-km and 4,621m. tonne-km of freight.

Civil Aviation. The national carrier is Royal Air Maroc, which in 1995 operated 6 B-727-200 Advs, 4 B-737-200 Advs, 2 B-737-200C Advs, 6 B-737-400s, 5 B-737-500s, 1 B-747-200B Combi, 1 B-747-400, 2 B-757-200s and 2 other aircraft. Services are also provided by Aeroflot, Air Algérie, Air France, Air Inter, Air Malta, Air Mauritanie, Alitalia, Balkan, British Airways, Gulf Air, Iberia, KLM, Kuwait Airways, Libyan Airlines, Lufthansa, Royal Jordanian, Sabena, Saudia, Swissair, Tunis Air and Zas. The major international airport is Mohammed V at Casablanca; there are 8 other airports. 4,488,507 passengers and 48,243 tonnes of freight were carried in 1994. Morocco launched in July its first private air company 'Regional Air Lines' to serve the major regions of the kingdom, in addition to Southern Spain and the Canary Islands.

Shipping. There are 12 ports, the largest being Casablanca, Tangiers and Jorf Lasfar. 1·56m. passengers and 40·6m. tonnes of freight were handled in 1994. In 1995 seagoing shipping totalled 0·39m. GRT, including oil tankers, 25,092 GRT, and container ships, 10,071 GRT. The Fleet: No. of boats; 3,200 units. Inshore fishing, 2,921 (70,000 tonnes per day), offshore fishing, 470 (150,000 tonnes per day).

Telecommunications. In 1994 there were 621 main post offices. Telephone subscribers totalled 1m. in 1995.

The government-controlled Radiodiffusion Télévision Marocaine broadcasts 3 national (1 in French, English and Spanish) and 8 regional radio programmes and 1 TV channel (colour by SECAM). Broadcasting in Berber languages commenced in 1994. There is also a government commercial radio service and an independent TV channel. In 1993 there were 4·5m. radio and 1·21m. TV sets in use.

Cinemas. There were 218 cinemas in 1995 and 22·014m. attendances. 5 full-length films were made.

Press. In 1984 there were 19 daily newspapers (7 Arabic, 5 French). In 1995, the number of newspapers was 475, including dailies, weeklies and periodicals, of which 314 come out in Arabic, 150 in French and 1 in English.

SOCIAL INSTITUTIONS

Justice. The legal system is based on French and Islamic law codes. There are a Supreme Court, 21 courts of appeal, 65 courts of first instance, 196 centres with resident judges and 706 communal jurisdictions for petty offences.

Religion. Islam is the established state religion. 98% of the population are Sunni Moslems of the Malekite school and 0·16% are Christians, mainly Roman Catholic, and there is a small Jewish community (0·05%).

Education. Adult literacy was 50% in 1996. Education in Berber languages has been permitted since 1994. Education is compulsory from the age of 7 to 13. In 1993–94 there were 28,335 Koranic schools (33,721 in 1990) with 30,367 teachers and 611,729 pupils; 3,563 modern pre-primary schools (343 in 1990) with 5,836 teachers and 171,727 pupils; 4,349 primary schools (392 private) with 91,487 teachers and 2,769,323 pupils; 1,168 secondary schools with (in the public sector) 75,407 teachers and 1,226,194 pupils (38,692 private). There were 13 universities with 7,566 teachers and 218,516 students (89,223 women), 8,390 students (1,761 women) in teacher training and (1992–93) 8,967 students and 1,145 teachers in other higher education institutions. An English-language university was opened at Ifrane in Jan. 1995, initially with a staff of 35 and 300 students (scheduled to rise to 3,500).

Health. In the public sector in 1994 there were 4,422 doctors, and 72 dentists; in the private sector there were 4,416 doctors and 1,132 dentists. In 1994 there were 2,470 pharmacists. In 1993 in the public sector there were 98 hospitals with 24,725 beds, 103 health centres with 1,548 beds and 1,220 dispensaries.

DIPLOMATIC REPRESENTATIVES

Of Morocco in Great Britain (49 Queen's Gate Gdns., London, SW7 5NE)
Ambassador: Khalil Haddaoui.

Of Great Britain in Morocco (17 Blvd de la Tour Hassan, Rabat)
Ambassador: William H. Fullerton, CMG.

Of Morocco in the USA (1601 21st St., NW, Washington, D.C., 20009)
Ambassador: Mohammed Beneissa.

Of the USA in Morocco (2 Ave. de Marrakech, Rabat)
Ambassador: Vacant

Of Morocco to the United Nations
Ambassador: Ahmed Snoussi.

Of Morocco to the European Union
Ambassador: Rachad Bouhlal.

Further Reading

Direction de la Statistique. *Annuaire Statistique du Maroc.—Conjoncture Économique.* Quarterly *Bulletin Official.* Rabat. Weekly
Findlay, A. M., *Morocco.* [Bibliography]. 2nd ed. Oxford and Santa Barbara (CA), 1995

National library: Bibliothèque Générale et Archives, Rabat.
National statistical office: Direction de la Statistique, BP178, Rabat.

WESTERN SAHARA

Area 266,769 sq. km (102,680 sq. miles). The population at the census held by Morocco in Sept. 1982 was 163,868; estimate (July 1997) 228,138. Another estimated 196,000 Saharawis live in refugee camps around Tindouf in south-west Algeria. The main towns (1982 census) are El-Aaiún, the capital (96,784), Dakhla (17,822) and Es-Semara (17,753). The population is Arabic-speaking, and virtually entirely Sunni Moslem.

President: Mohammed Abdelaziz.

Rich phosphate deposits were discovered in 1963 at Bu Craa. Morocco holds 65% of the shares of the former Spanish state-controlled company. While production reached 5·6m. tonnes in 1975, exploitation has been severely reduced by guerrilla activity but in 1984 produced 1m. tonnes. After a nearly complete collapse, production and transportation of phosphate resumed in 1978, ceased again, and then resumed in 1982. There are about 6,100 km of motorable tracks, but only about 500 km of paved roads. There are airports at El-Aaiún and Dakhla. As most of the land is desert, less than 19% is in agricultural use, with about 2,000 tonnes of grain produced annually. In 1989 there were 27 primary schools with 14,794 pupils and 18 secondary schools with 9,218 pupils.

Further Reading

Damis, J., *Conflict in Northwest Africa: The Western Sahara Dispute*. Stanford, 1983
Hodges, T., *Western Sahara: The Roots of a Desert War*. London and Westport, 1984
Pazzanita, A. G., *Western Sahara* [Bibliography]. Oxford and Santa Barbara (CA), 1996
Sipe, L. F., *Western Sahara: A Comprehensive Bibliography*. New York, 1984
Thompson, V. and Adloff, R., *The Western Saharans: Background to Conflict*. London, 1980
Zoubir, Y. H. and Volman, D. (eds.) *The International Dimensions of the Western Sahara Conflict*. New York, 1993

MOZAMBIQUE

República de Moçambique

Capital: Maputo
Population: 16m.
GDP per head: (PPP$) 986
GNP: US$1·3bn.
HDI/world rank: 0·281/166

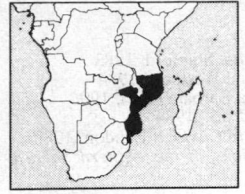

KEY HISTORICAL EVENTS. In 1506 Sofala was occupied by the Portuguese. Mozambique was at first ruled as part of Portuguese India, but a separate administration was created in 1752. In 1951 Mozambique became an Overseas Province of Portugal. Following a decade of guerrilla activity, Portugal and the nationalists jointly established a transitional government on 20 Sept. 1974. Independence was achieved on 25 June 1975. A one-party state dominated by the Mozambique Liberation Front (FRELIMO) was set up, but armed insurgency led by the Mozambique National Resistance (RENAMO) continued until on 4 Oct. 1992 President Chissano and Afonso Dhlakama, leader of RENAMO, signed a treaty in Rome ending the civil war. The treaty provided for all weapons to be handed over to the UN, and all armed groups to be disbanded within 6 months. In 1994 the country held its first multi-party elections won by the Frelimo Party and a new Parliament was inaugurated with 250 seats. The UN presence ended in Jan. 1995.

TERRITORY AND POPULATION. Mozambique is bounded east by the Indian ocean, south by South Africa, south-west by Swaziland, west by South Africa and Zimbabwe and north by Zambia, Malawi and Tanzania. It has an area of 799,380 sq. km (308,642 sq. miles) and a population, according to the preliminary results of the 1997 census, of 15·7m. Up to 1·5m. refugees abroad and 5m. internally displaced persons during the Civil War have begun to return home. UN estimate, 1995, 16,004,000. Infant mortality per 1,000 live births, 1995, 147. Life expectancy was 46·8 years in 1995. The areas, populations and capitals of the provinces are:

Province	Sq. km	1 Jan 1987	Estimate 1991	Capital
Cabo Delgado	82,625	1,109,921	1,202,200	Pemba
Niassa	129,056	607,670	686,700	Lichinga
Nampula	81,606	2,837,856	2,841,400	Nampula
Zambézia	105,008	2,952,251	2,619,300	Quelimane
Tete	100,724	981,319	734,600	Tete
Manica	61,661	756,886	609,500	Chimoio
Sofala	68,018	1,257,710	1,427,500	Beira
Inhambane	68,615	1,167,022	1,157,000	Inhambane
Gaza	75,709	1,138,724	1,401,500	Xaixai
Province of Maputo	25,756	544,692	840,800	Maputo
City of Maputo	602	1,006,765	931,600	

The capital is Maputo (estimated population, 1993, 2m.). Other large cities are Beira (1991 population, 294,197), Nampula (232,670) and Nacala (125,208).

The main ethnolinguistic groups are the Makua/Lomwe (52% of the population), the Nyanja and Sena (12%), Shona (6%) and Tsonga (24%). Portuguese remains the official language, but vernaculars are widely spoken throughout the country.

CLIMATE. A humid tropical climate, with a dry season from June to Sept. In general, temperatures and rainfall decrease from north to south. Maputo. Jan. 78°F (25·6°C), July 65°F (18·3°C). Annual rainfall 30" (760 mm). Beira. Jan. 82°F (27·8°C), July 69°F (20·6°C). Annual rainfall 60" (1,522 mm).

CONSTITUTION AND GOVERNMENT. On 2 Nov. 1990 the People's Assembly unanimously voted a new Constitution, which came into force on 30 Nov. This changed the name of the state to 'Republic of Mozambique', legalized opposition parties, provided for universal secret elections and introduced a bill of rights including the right to strike, press freedoms and habeas corpus. The head of state is the *President*, directly elected for a 5-year term. Parliament is a 250-member *National Assembly*.

Presidential and parliamentary elections were held on 27-29 Oct. 1994. The electorate was 6·5m.; turn-out was 90%. President Chissano was re-elected by 53·3% of votes cast against 1 opponent. FRELIMO gained 44·3% of votes cast for the National Assembly, and RENAMO 37·7%.

A new government was formed on 16 Dec. 1994 which in March 1998 comprised:
President: Joaquim A. Chissano (FRELIMO; sworn in 9 Dec. 1994).
Prime Minister: Dr Pascoal M. Mocumbi. *Economic and Social Affairs (President's Office):* Dr Eneas C. Comiche. *Parliamentary Affairs (President's Office):* Francisco C. J. Madeira. *Defence and Security Affairs (President's Office) and Home Affairs:* Almerinho Manherje. *Foreign Affairs and Co-operation:* Dr Leonardo S. Simão. *National Defence:* Aguiar J. R. Mazula. *Justice:* Jose I. Abudo. *Planning and Finance:* Tomas A. Salomão. *Education:* Arnaldo V. Nhavoto. *Health:* Aurelio A. Zilhao. *Culture, Youth and Sports:* Mateus M. Kathupa. *Industry, Trade and Tourism:* Oldemiro J. Baloi. *Mineral Resources and Energy:* John W. Katchamila. *Labour:* Guilherme L. Mavila. *Environmental Action Co-ordinator:* Bernardo P. Ferraz. *State Administration:* Alfredo M. S. C. Gamito. *Agriculture and Fisheries:* Carlos A. Rosario. *Public Construction and Housing:* Roberto C. White. *Transport and Communication:* Paulo Muxanga. *Social Action:* Alcinda Albreu.

National anthem: 'Viva, viva a Frelimo' ('Long live Frelimo'); words and tune by J. Sigaulane Chemane.

Local Government. The capital of Maputo and 10 provinces, each under a Governor, are sub-divided into 112 districts.

DEFENCE. The President of the Republic is C.-in-C. of the armed forces.

Army. Equipment includes about 80 T-54/-55 main battle tanks. Personnel 4-5,000.

Navy. A small flotilla based principally at Maputo, with subsidiary bases at Beira, Nacala, Pemba and Inhambane, comprises 3 ex-Soviet inshore patrol craft, 2 ex-Soviet inshore minesweepers and 2 landing craft, but none is believed operational. Some boats are based at Metangula on Lake Nyasa. Naval personnel in 1997 were believed to total 100.

Air Force. The Air Force was reported to have about 40 MiG-21 fighters and 5 An-26 turboprop transports. About 4 Mi-24 armed helicopters and 5 Mi-8 transport helicopters, 4 Cherokee primary trainers and 4 Cessna light aircraft. Personnel (1997) 1,000 (including air defence units), with 40 combat aircraft and 5 armed helicopters.

INTERNATIONAL RELATIONS

Membership. Mozambique is a member of the UN, Commonwealth, OAU, SADC, Non-Aligned Movement, Organization of the Islamic Conference, Indian Ocean Rim, Organization of the Portuguese Language Countries and is an ACP state of the EU.

ECONOMY

Policy. In 1990 the government abandoned economic planning in favour of a market economy. In Dec. 1993 the National Reconstruction Plan was launched to repair the rural economic and social infrastructure. Its implementation is dependent upon foreign aid.

Performance. Real GDP growth was 6% annually between 1990 and 1996.

Budget. Revenue (in 1,000m. meticais), 1994, 1,525·7; 1993, 1,092·6 (including income tax; 156; non-fiscal receipts, 97·6). Expenditure, 1994, 4,096; 1993, 2,307·8 (including capital expenditure, 1,137). Budget estimates for 1994: Domestic revenue, 1,100; current expenditure, 1,300; capital expenditure, 1,200.

Currency. The unit of currency is the *metical* (MZM) of 100 *centavos*. There are coins of 1, 2·5, 5, 10 and 20 and notes of 50, 100, 500, 1,000, 5,000 and 10,000 meticais. Inflation was 17% in 1996.

Banking and Finance. Most banks had been nationalized by 1979. The central bank and bank of issue is the Bank of Mozambique, which hived off its commercial functions in 1992 to the newly-founded Commercial Bank of Mozambique. There is a state Development Bank.

Weights and Measures. The metric system is in force.

ENERGY AND NATURAL RESOURCES

Electricity. Production (1992) 490m. kWh. Capacity (1992) 2,358,000 kW.

Minerals. There are deposits of pegamite, tantalite, graphite, apatite, tin, iron ore and bauxite. Other known reserves are: nepheline syenite magnelite, copper, garnet, kaolin, asbestos, bentonite, limestone, gold, titanium and tin.

Output (in 1,000 tonnes), 1991: Coking coal, 584; lignite, 167; charcoal, 572; salt, 3,839; marble, 118; gold, 5,773 kg.

Agriculture. All land is owned by the state but concessions are given. In 1996 there were 20m. ha of arable land, of which 10% was cultivated. Production in tonnes (1994): Cereals, 819,000; maize, 526,000; bananas (1992), 80,000; rice, 98,000; groundnuts, 74,000; copra (1992), 72,000; vegetables (1992), 115,000; potatoes (1992), 72,000; cashews, 54,000; sunflower seed, 10,000; cotton (lint) (1992), 13,000; sugar cane (1994) 234,000; raw cotton (1994) 29,400.

Livestock 1994: 1·25m. cattle, 389,000 goats, 119,000 sheep, 174,000 pigs, 20,000 asses.

Forestry. There are 19m. ha of productive woodland, including eucalyptus, pine and rare hardwoods. Production of logs (1993) 31,411,000 cu. metres of cut timber.

Fisheries. Prawns and shrimps are the major export at 14,000 tonnes per year, with a sustainable annual catch estimated at 500,000 tonnes of fish (anchovies, 300,000 tonnes, the rest mainly mackerel).

INDUSTRY. Although the country is overwhelmingly rural, there is some substantial industry in and around Maputo (steel, engineering, textiles, processing, docks and railways).

Trade Unions. The main trade union confederation is the Organização dos Trabalhadores de Moçambique, but several unions have broken away.

FOREIGN ECONOMIC RELATIONS. Foreign debt was US$5,781m. in 1995.

Commerce. Imports in 1995 totalled US$784m. and exports US$170m. Principal exports, 1995 (in US$1m.): Prawns, 70; cashew nuts, 3; cotton, 19; sugar, 11. Main export markets, 1994: Spain, 22·7%; South Africa, 17%; USA, 10%; Japan, 16%; Portugal, 14·7%. Main import suppliers: South Africa, 42·8%; Portugal, 4·6%; Zimbabwe, 6·7%; France, 2·6%.

COMMUNICATIONS

Roads. In 1994 there were 5,000 km of paved and 23,000 km of unpaved roads, but most were in bad condition or mined.

Railways. The state railway consists of 5 separate networks, with principal routes on 1,067 mm gauge radiating from the ports of Maputo (950 km), Beira (994 km) and Nacala (914 km). Total length in 1995 was 2,983 km of 1,067 mm gauge and 140 km of 762 mm gauge. In 1995, 5·4m. passengers and 3·1m. tonnes of freight were carried.

Civil Aviation. There are international airports at Maputo, Beira and Nampula. The national carrier is the state-owned Linhas Aéreas de Moçambique (LAM), which in 1995 operated 1 B-767-200ER, 1 B-737-200, 1 B-737-200C Adv, 1 B-767-200ER and 6 other aircraft. Services are also provided by Air France, Air Zimbabwe, Metavia Airlines, Royal Swazi, SAA and TAP.

Shipping. The principal ports are Maputo, Beira, Nacala and Quelimane. In 1995 sea-going shipping totalled 26,080 GRT.

Telecommunications. Number of telephones (1993), 62,000. Radio Moçambique is part state-owned and part commercial. There are 3 national programmes in Tsonga and Portuguese and an external service in English. Television is at a trial stage (colour by PAL). In 1992 there were about 0·7m. radio and 44,000 TV receivers.

Cinemas. There were 60 in 1987.

Press. There are 2 daily newspapers (Noticias and Diário in Maputo and Beira respectively).

SOCIAL INSTITUTIONS

Justice. The 1990 Constitution provides for an independent judiciary, habeas corpus, and an entitlement to legal advice on arrest. The death penalty was abolished in Nov. 1990.

Religion. About 40% of the population follow traditional animist religions. In 1992 there were 4·72m. Christians (mainly Roman Catholic) and 1·95m. Moslems.

Education. Adult literacy was 40% in 1997. In 1997 there were 1,750,000 pupils in 5,600 primary schools and (1991) 145,800 in 216 secondary schools. Private schools and universities were permitted to function in 1990. Eduardo Mondlane University had 3,470 students and 390 academic staff in 1995–96.

Health. There were (1997) 10 hospitals, 418 health centres and 996 medical posts. There were 2 psychiatric hospitals. In 1990 there were 387 doctors, 1,139 midwives, 3,533 nursing personnel, 108 dentists and 353 pharmacists. Private health care was introduced alongside the national health service in 1992.

DIPLOMATIC REPRESENTATIVES

Of Mozambique in Great Britain (21 Fitzroy Sq., London W1P 5HJ)
High Commissioner: Dr Eduardo Koloma.

Of Great Britain in Mozambique (Ave. Vladimir I. Lenine 310, Maputo)
High Commissioner: Bernard Everett.

Of Mozambique in the USA (1990 M. St., NW, Washington, D.C., 20036)
Ambassador: Marcos Namashulua.

Of the USA in Mozambique (Ave Kaunda 193, Maputo)
Ambassador: Vacant.

Of Mozambique to the United Nations
Ambassador: Carlos Dos Santos.

Of Mozambique to the European Union
Ambassador: Trindade O Da Silva.

Further Reading

Andersson, H., *Mozambique: a War against the People.* London, 1993
Darch, C., *Mozambique.* [Bibliography] Oxford and Santa Barbara (CA), 1987
Finnegan, W., *A Complicated War: the Harrowing of Mozambique.* California Univ. Press, 1992
Newitt, M., *A History of Mozambique.* Farnborough, 1996

MYANMAR

Myanmar Naingngandaw

(Union of Myanmar)

Capital: Rangoon (Yangon)
Population: 44·74m.
GDP per head: (PPP$) 1,051
HDI/world rank: 0·475/131

KEY HISTORICAL EVENTS. In 1785 the Alaugpaya dynasty of Burma conquered Arakan in the south-west. Arakanese refugees fled into India in large numbers and turned Chittagong into a base for guerrilla raids on Burma, thus provoking reprisal raids into India by Burmese forces.

This was followed by Burma's invasions of the kingdom of Assam. The British East India Company then took action in defence of its Indian interests and in 1826 finally drove the Burmese out of India and annexed territory in south Burma. The kingdom of Upper Burma, ruled from Mandalay in the north, remained independent. A second war with Britain in 1852 ended with the British annexation of the Irrawaddy Delta.

In 1862 and 1867 trade treaties were concluded with Upper Burma. However, in 1885 the British invaded, deposed the king and occupied Upper Burma. In 1886 all Burma became a province of the Indian empire. The Chin tribes of the Burmese-Indian borderlands were subdued in 1889-90. The Indian system of administration was not suitable for the country and exacerbated resentment at imperial economic policies and Britain's refusal to support Buddhism as the state religion. There were violent uprisings in the 1930s and in 1937 Burma was separated from India and some degree of self-government was introduced.

Following the Japanese invasion and occupation of 1942-45, Britain and Burma began to negotiate the establishment of independence, which was achieved in 1948 with the creation of the Union of Burma, an independent republic outside the Commonwealth. The president was Sao Shwe Thaike.

In 1958 there was an army *coup*, and another in 1962 led by Gen. Ne Win, who installed a Revolutionary Council and dissolved parliament. The Council lasted until March 1974 when the country become a one-party socialist republic, a new constitution having been approved by referendum in Dec. 1973. The name was changed to Socialist Republic of the Union of Burma. U Ne Win became president, serving until 1982, when he was succeeded by U San Yu. On 18 Sept. 1988, the Armed Forces seized power and set up the State Law and Order Restoration Council (SLORC). On 19 June 1989 the government changed the official name of the country in English to the Union of Myanmar.

The leader of the party which won the 1990 elections, Aung San Suu Kyi, was under house arrest from July 1989 to July 1995. She is still under restraint, and many of her followers, friends and relations have been arrested. She was awarded the Nobel Peace Prize in 1991.

TERRITORY AND POPULATION. Myanmar is bounded in the east by China, Laos and Thailand, and west by the Indian Ocean, Bangladesh and India. Three parallel mountain ranges run from north to south; the Western Yama or Rakhine Yama, the Bagu Yama and the Shaun Plateau. The total area of the Union is 261,228 sq. miles (676,577 sq. km). The population in 1983 (census) was 35,313,905. Estimate (1996) 44·74m. (22·52m. female). Growth rate in 1996, 1·87%. Birth rate (1994 estimate), 27·9 per 1,000 population; death rate, 10·5; infant deaths, 47·5 per 1,000 live births; still births, 10·3 per 1,000 live births. Expectation of life was 58·4 years in 1994.

The leading towns are: Rangoon (Yangon), the capital (1983), 2,458,712; other towns, Mandalay, 532,985; Moulmein, 219,991; Pegu, 150,447; Bassein, 144,092; Sittwe (Akyab), 107,907; Taunggye, 107,607; Monywa, 106,873.

The population of the 7 states and 7 administrative divisions at the 1983 census: Kachin State, 903,982; Kayah State, 168,355; Karen State, 1,057,505; Chin State, 368,985; Sagaing Division, 3,855,991; Tenasserim Division, 917,628; Pegu Division,

3,800,240; Magwe Division, 3,241,103; Mandalay Division, 4,580,923; Mon State, 1,682,041; Rakhine State, 2,045,891; Rangoon Division, 3,973,782; Shan State, 3,718,706; Irrawaddy Division, 4,991,057. Myanmar is inhabited by many ethnic nationalities. There are as many as 135 national groups with the Bamars, comprising about 68·96% of the population, forming the largest group.

The official language is Burmese; English is also in use.

CLIMATE. The climate is equatorial in coastal areas, changing to tropical monsoon over most of the interior, but humid temperate in the extreme north, where there is a more significant range of temperature and a dry season lasting from Nov. to April. In coastal parts, the dry season is shorter. Very heavy rains occur in the monsoon months May to Sept. Rangoon. Jan. 77°F (25°C), July 80°F (26·7°C). Annual rainfall 104" (2,616 mm). Akyab. Jan. 70°F (21·1°C), July 81°F (27·2°C). Annual rainfall 206" (5,154 mm). Mandalay. Jan. 68°F (20°C), July 85°F (29·4°C). Annual rainfall 33" (828 mm).

CONSTITUTION AND GOVERNMENT. In elections in May 1990 the opposition National League for Democracy (NLD), led by Aung San Suu Kyi (b. 1945), won 392 of the 485 People's Assembly seats contested with some 60% of the valid vote. Turn-out was 72%, but 12·4% of ballots cast were declared invalid. The ruling State Law and Order Restoration Council (SLORC) said it would hand over power after the People's Assembly had agreed on a new constitution, but in July 1990 it stipulated that any such constitution must conform to guidelines which it would itself prescribe.

In May 1991 48 members of the NLD were given prison sentences on charges of treason. In July 1991, opposition members of the People's Assembly were unseated for alleged offences ranging from treason to illicit foreign exchange dealing. Such members, and unsuccessful candidates in the May 1990 elections, are forbidden to stand in future elections.

On 28 Nov. 1995 the government re-opened a 706-member Constitutional Convention in which the NLD was given 107 places. The NLD withdrew on 29 Nov.

In Nov. 1997 the country's ruling generals changed the name of the government to the State Peace and Development Council (SPDC), and reshuffled the cabinet. In Dec. 1997, following a period when the national currency fell to a record low, there were further changes to the cabinet, while corruption investigations were begun against some former ministers.

In March 1998 the government comprised:
Prime Minister and Minister of Defence: Senior Gen. Than Shwe.
Deputy Ministers: Vice-Admiral Maung Maung Khin; Lieut.-Gen. Tin Tun.
Agriculture and Irrigation: Maj. Gen. Nyunt Tin. *Industry:* Aung Thaung; Maj.-Gen. Hla Myint Swe. *Foreign Affairs:* Ohn Gyaw. *National Planning and Economic Development:* Soe Tha. *Transport:* Lieut.-Gen. Tin Ngwe. *Labour:* Vice-Adm. Tin Aye. *Co-operatives:* Aung San. *Rail Transportation:* Pan Aung. *Energy:* Brig.-Gen. Lun Thi. *Education:* Than Aung. *Health:* Maj.-Gen. Ket Sein. *Commerce:* Maj.-Gen. Kyaw Than. *Hotels and Tourism:* Maj.-Gen. Saw Lwin. *Communications, Posts and Telegraphs:* Brig.-Gen. Win Tin. *Finance and Revenue:* Khin Maung Thein. *Religious Affairs:* Maj.-Gen. Sein Htwa. *Construction:* Maj.-Gen. Saw Tun. *Science and Technology:* U Thaung. *Culture:* Win Sein. *Immigration and Population:* Saw Tun. *Information:* Maj.-Gen. Kyi Aung. *Border Area, National Races and Development Affairs:* Col. Thein Nyunt. *Electric Power:* Maj.-Gen. Tin Htut. *Sports:* Brig.-Gen. Sein Wit. *Forestry:* Aung Phone. *Home Affairs:* Col. Tin Hlaing. *Mines:* Brig.-Gen. Ohn Myint. *Social Welfare, Relief and Resettlement:* Brig.-Gen. Pyi Sone. *Livestock and Fisheries:* Brig.-Gen. Maung Maung Thein. *Office of the Chairman of the State Peace and Development Council:* Lieut.-Gen. Min Thein; Brig.-Gen. Maung Maung; Brig.-Gen. David Oliver Abel. *Office of the Prime Minister:* Brig.-Gen. Lun Maung; Than Shwe; Maj.-Gen. Tin Ngwe.

National anthem: 'Gba majay Bma' ('We shall love Burma for ever'); words and tune by Saya Tin.

Local government: Myanmar is divided into 7 states and 7 administrative divisions; these are sub-divided into 314 townships and then into villages and wards.

DEFENCE

Army. The strength of the Army reported to be about 300,000 in 1997. The Army is organized into 10 regional commands comprising 10 light infantry divisions. Combat units comprise 3 armoured, 245 infantry and 7 artillery battalions, and 1 anti-aircraft artillery battalion. Equipment includes 26 Comet and 36 Ch T-69II main battle tanks. There are 2 paramilitary units: People's Police Force (50,000) and People's Militia (35,000).

Navy. The fleet includes 2 old escort patrol vessels (ex-USA PCE and MSF types) and about 50 patrol craft, half sea-going and half riverine. Auxiliaries include 1 patrol craft support ship, 2 survey ships and 15 small landing craft. Personnel in 1996 totalled about 14,000 including 800 naval infantry.

The Fishery Protection Service (under the Pearl and Fishery Department) operates 3 coastal and 8 inshore patrol craft.

Air Force. The Air Force is intended primarily for internal security duties. Its combat force comprises 10 G-4 Super Galeb supplied by Yugoslavia, 30 F-7 fighters and 24 A-5 fighter-bombers received from China, 18 turboprop Pilatus PC-7s and PC-9s. Transport and second-line units are equipped with 10 Mi-17 helicopters, 4 FH-227, 1 Turbo-Porter, 2 Chinese-built Y-8s, 1 Citation and 6 Cessna 180 aircraft, 10 Polish-built W-3 Sokol, 12 Bell UH-1, and 10 Alouette III helicopters. Personnel (1996) 9,000.

INTERNATIONAL RELATIONS

Membership. Myanmar is a member of the UN, Colombo Plan and ASEAN.

ECONOMY

Policy. A short-term plan ran from 1992–93 to 1995–96. There were within it annual plans with targets. Liberalization measures to promote a market economy were introduced in 1990. 1992–93 was designated 'Economic Year'.

Budget. The fiscal year ends 31 March. Estimates for 1995–96: Revenue, K.129,507m.; current expenditure, K.122,904m., capital expenditure, K.39,620m.

State budget estimates are classified into 3 parts, *viz.* State Administrative Organizations, State Economic Enterprises and Town and City Development Committees.

Receipts included: Tax revenue, K.19,945m.; receipts from state economic enterprises, K.92,899·6m.

Currency. The unit of currency is the *kyat* (MMK) of 100 *pyas*. There are notes of kyat 500, 200, 100, 90, 50, 45, 15, 10, 5 and 1 and pyas 50, and coins of kyat 1 and pyas 50, 25, 10, 5 and 1. In 1995 K.110,866m. were in circulation. Foreign exchange reserves were K.2,016m. in Sept. 1995; gold reserves were K.74·8m. in Sept. 1994. Inflation was about 40% in 1994. Since 1 June 1996 import duties have been calculated at a rate US$1 = K.100.

Banking and Finance. The Central Bank of Myanmar was established in 1990. Its *Governor* is Kyi Aye. In 1995 there were 15 private domestic banks. Since 1996 foreign banks with representative offices (there were 31 in 1996) have been permitted to set up joint ventures with Burmese banks. The foreign partner must provide at least 35% of the capital. The state insurance company is the Myanmar Insurance Corporation. Deposits in savings banks were K.30,963m. in 1994.

A stock exchange opened in Rangoon in 1996.

Weights and Measures. The British system of weights and measures is generally used. The metric system has also been introduced in many areas. But in the markets the use of Myanmar weights and measures, as outlined below, is common:

1 viss (peit-tha)	= 3·6 lbs	= 1·633 kilograms
1 tical (kyat-tha)	= 0·576 oz	= 16·33 grams
622·22 viss	= 1 long ton (2,240 lbs)	= 1·016 metric ton
612·39 viss	= 2,204·62 lbs	= 1 metric ton

ENERGY AND NATURAL RESOURCES

Electricity. In 1995–96 the installed capacity of Myanma Electric Power was 1,000 MW, of which 328 MW was hydro-electric, 62 MW thermal, 530 MW natural gas and 80 MW diesel. Capacity of other networks was 344 MW. Total generated, 3,922m. kWh.

Oil. Production (1995–96) of crude oil was 6·9m. bbls.; natural gas, 69,540m. cu. feet.

Minerals. Production in 1995–96 (in tonnes): Zinc concentrates, 6,070; nickel speiss, 60; antimonial lead, 210; refined lead, 4,250; tin concentrates, 492; tungsten concentrates, 95; tin, tungsten and scheelite mixed, 1,400; refined silver, 260,000 fine oz; gold, 22,496 troy oz; refined tin metal, 310; copper concentrates, 42,500; coal, 49.

Agriculture. In 1995–96 4·5m. peasant families cultivated 24·9m. acres. Liberalization measures of 1990 permit farmers to grow crops of their choice. The total sown area in 1995–96 was 22·5m. acres. 4·76m. acres were irrigated. In 1995–96 429,864 tonnes of fertilizer were distributed. Production (1995–96, in 1,000 tonnes): Paddy, 19,568; sugar-cane, 3,060; maize, 212; jute, 43; cotton, 214; wheat, 109; butter beans, 29; soya beans, 64; rubber, 28; groundnuts, 569.

Livestock (1995–96): Cattle, 12m.; buffaloes, 2·3m.; pigs, 3·2m.; sheep and goats, 1·5m.; poultry, 31·9m. In 1995–96 there were 6·8m. draught cattle and about 8,000 tractors.

Net output of agriculture for 1993–94 was valued at K.23,595m.

Forestry. Forest area in 1994–95 was 80·04m. acres (25·52m. acres reserved), covering more than 50% of the total land area. Teak resources cover about 6m. hectares (15m. acres). Teak extracted in 1995–96, 256,000 cu. tons; hardwood, 1,109,000 cu. tons.

Fisheries. In 1995–96 sea fishing produced 371·4m. viss and freshwater fisheries 138·4m. viss. Aquacultural fish production was 48·9m. viss. Cultured pearls and oyster shells are produced.

INDUSTRY. Of the 48,601 industrial enterprises in 1995–96, 1,607 were state-owned, 636 were co-operatives and 46,358 were private. Production (1995–96) in 1,000 tonnes: Cement, 524; fertilizers, 300; sugar, 67·6; paper, 15·5; 1,429 motor cars, 597 tractors; (1994–95) cotton yarn, 16·8; 35,042 bicycles were produced. In 1995–96 manufacturing output was valued at K.6,556m.

Labour. The population of working age (15 to 59) in 1995–96 was 26·34m. Economically active persons in 1995–96: 17·59m., of whom 11·27m. were employed in agriculture, 1·34m. in services, 1·48m. in manufacturing and 1·72m. in trade.

FOREIGN ECONOMIC RELATIONS. In Aug. 1991 the USA imposed trade sanctions in response to alleged civil rights violations. Foreign debt was some US$4,200m. in 1990, of which US$2,000m. was owed to Japan. A law of 1989 permitted joint ventures, with foreign companies or individuals able to hold 100% of the shares.

Commerce. Since 1990 in line with market-oriented measures firms have been able to participate directly in trade.

Imports and exports (K.1m.) for 1994–95: Imports 9,117·0; exports 4,772·6. Main imports (in K.1m.), 1994–95: Raw materials, 1,854·3; transport equipment, 1,251; tools and spares, 303·5; machinery, 1,099·9; construction materials, 472. Main exports: Teak, 953·1; pulses and beans, 799·4; rubber, 443·1; hardwood, 107·8; rice,

1,165·8. Main export markets: India, 695·4; Singapore, 883·5; Thailand, 542·7; China, 277·5; Hong Kong, 269·1.

Tourism. There were 105,863 tourists in 1995 (91,859 in 1994), bringing a revenue of K.203,791m.

COMMUNICATIONS

Roads. There were 16,770 miles of road in 1993–94, of which 2,452 miles were union highway. In 1995–96 the state service ran 951 buses, 197 taxis and 1,969 lorries. There were also 155,107 buses and 29,694 lorries in private co-operative ownership. In 1995–96 121·28m. passengers and 1·19m. tonnes of freight were carried by road.

Railways. In 1995 there were 3,955 km of route on metre gauge. In 1995–96 Myanma Railways carried 3·28m. tonnes of freight and 53·4m. passengers.

Civil Aviation. Myanma Airways maintains international services to Bangkok, Hong Kong and Singapore. In 1995 it had 8 Fokker F-27 and 3 F-28 aircraft. There were, in 1995, 43 civil airfields. In 1995–96 0·72m. passengers were carried on domestic, and 138,000 on international, flights (121,000 in 1994–95). Services are also provided by Aeroflot Russian Airlines, Air China, Biman Bangladesh, Silk Air and Thai Airways.

Shipping. There are 60 miles of navigable canals. The Irrawaddy is navigable up to Myitkyina, 900 miles from the sea, and its tributary, the Chindwin, is navigable for 390 miles. The Irrawaddy delta has nearly 2,000 miles of navigable water. The Salween, the Attaran and the Gíyne provide about 250 miles of navigable waters around Moulmein. In 1995–96 24·5m. passengers and 1·03m. tonnes of freight were carried on inland waterways. The ocean-going fleet of the state-owned Myanma Five Star Line in 1995 comprised 11 liners, 4 short-haul vessels and 3 coastal passenger/cargo vessels. In 1995–96 60,000 passengers and 1,030,000 tonnes of freight were transported coastally and overseas. The port is Rangoon.

Telecommunications. In 1995–96 there were 1,205 post offices, 168,399 telephones, 405 telegraph offices, 227 telexes and 1,362 fax machines. The government runs a TV and a radio station. In 1993 there were 3·2m. radio and 1m. television receivers (colour by NTSC).

Press. There are 4 daily newspapers, one of which is in English.

SOCIAL INSTITUTIONS

Justice. The highest judicial authority is the Chief Judge, appointed by the government.

Religion. About 89·4% of the population—mainly Bamars, Shans, Mons, Rakhines and some Kayins—are Buddhists, while the rest are Christians, Muslims, Hindus and Animists. The Christian population is composed mainly of Kayins, Kachins and Chins. Islam and Hinduism are practised mainly by people of Indian origin.

Education. Education is free in primary, middle and vocational schools; fees are charged in senior secondary schools and universities. In 1995–96 there were 36,499 primary schools with 187,344 teachers and 5,995,015 pupils; 1,578 monastic primary schools (permitted since 1992) with 80,863 pupils; 2,112 middle schools with 60,759 teachers and 1,417,189 pupils and 927 high schools with 19,120 teachers and 402,411 pupils.

In higher education in 1995–96 there were 12 teacher training schools with 315 teachers and 2,067 students, 5 teacher training institutes with 304 teachers and 2,170 students, 17 technical high schools with 498 teachers and 7,145 students, 11 technical institutes with 668 teachers and 12,080 students, 10 agricultural high schools with 100 teachers and 1,053 students, 7 agricultural institutes with 162 teachers and 1,844 students, 41 vocational schools with 369 teachers and 6,532 students, 6 universities with 3,050 teachers and 154,680 students, 6 degree colleges with 705 teachers and 53,362 students and 10 colleges with 629 teachers and 40,327 students.

There was also a University for the Development of the National Races of the Union and institutes of medicine (3), dentistry, paramedical science, pharmacy, nursing, veterinary science, economics, technology (2), agriculture, education (2), foreign languages, computer science and forestry. An institute of remote education maintains a correspondence course at university level.

The adult literacy rate is 82·7%.

Health. In 1995–96 there were 12,950 doctors, 860 dentists, 9,851 nurses, 8,143 midwives and 737 hospitals with 28,372 beds.

Welfare. In 1995–96 contributions to social security totalled (K.1m.) 117·5 (from employers, 73·2; from employees, 43·9). Benefits paid totalled 82·6, and included: Sickness, 12·9; maternity, 3·9; disability, 3·7; survivors' pensions, 1·3.

DIPLOMATIC REPRESENTATIVES

Of Myanmar in Great Britain (19A Charles St., London, W1X 8ER)
Ambassador: U Win Aung.

Of Great Britain in Myanmar (80 Strand Rd., Rangoon)
Ambassador: Robert A Gordon, OBE.

Of Myanmar in the USA (2300 S. St., NW, Washington, D.C., 20008)
Ambassador: U Tin Win.

Of the USA in Myanmar (581 Merchant St., Rangoon)
Ambassador: Kent Wiedemann.

Of Myanmar to the United Nations
Ambassador: Win Mra.

Of Myanmar to the European Union
Ambassador: Vacant.

Further Reading

Carey, P. (ed.): *Burma: The Challenge of Change in a Divided Society.* London, 1997
Herbert, P., *Burma* [bibliography]. Santa Barbara and Oxford, 1991
Lintner, B., *Outrage: Burma's Struggle for Democracy.* 2nd ed. London, 1990
O'Brien, H., *Forgotten Land: a Rediscovery of Burma.* London, 1991
Silverstein, Josef: *Burma, Military Rule and the Politics of Stagnation.* Cornell, 1977
Smith, M., *Burma: Insurgency and the Politics of Ethnicity.* London, 1991
Suu Kyi, Aung San, *Freedom from Fear and Other Writings.* London, 1991
Taylor, R. H., *The State in Burma.* London, 1988

National statistical office: Ministry of National Planning and Economic Development, Rangoon.

NAMIBIA

Republic of Namibia

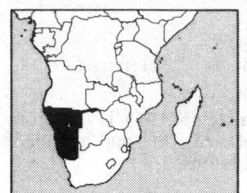

Capital: Windhoek
Population: 1·7m.
GNP: US$3·0bn.
HDI/world rank: 0·570/11

KEY HISTORICAL EVENTS. Namibia's first inhabitants were the Bushmen (Sands). Around 1300, the Namas and the Damaras came from the north pushing the Bushmen towards the Kalahari Desert. Around 1500, the Owambos settled on the high plateau and in the Okavongo delta. Around 1600, Herero herdsmen arrived from the north.

German migration accelerated from 1850 onwards. In 1884 South West Africa was declared a German protectorate. Germany then introduced racial segregation and the exploitation of the diamond mines began. In 1915 the Union of South Africa occupied German South West Africa at the request of the Allied powers. On 17 Dec. 1920 the League of Nations entrusted South West Africa as a Mandate to the Union of South Africa, to be administered under the laws of the mandatory power. After World War II South Africa refused to place the territory under the UN Trusteeship system, and formally applied for its annexation to the Union. In Oct. 1966 the General Assembly of the UN terminated South Africa's mandate, and established a UN Council for South West Africa in May 1967. However, South Africa continued to administer the territory, in defiance of various UN resolutions. In June 1968 the UN changed the name of the territory to Namibia. In 1971 the International Court of Justice ruled in an advisory opinion that South Africa's presence in Namibia was illegal. In Dec. 1973 the UN appointed a UN Commissioner for Namibia.

After negotiations between South Africa and the UN, a multi-racial Advisory Council was appointed in 1973. Representatives of all the population groups assembled in Windhoek for the Constitutional Conference, which in Aug. 1976 resolved that a multi-racial interim government be formed by early 1977, and that the country should become independent by 31 Dec. 1978. This resolution was rejected by the UK, the USA, the Federal Republic of Germany, France and Canada, after which South Africa agreed to universal suffrage elections. An Administrator-General was appointed in Sept. 1977 to govern the territory until independence, and he moved to abolish all laws based on racial discrimination – a precondition for elections. In April 1978 South Africa accepted a plan for UN-supervised elections leading to independence, which was endorsed in UN Security Council Resolution 435 of 27 July 1978. After the final plans for the UN-supervised elections were published, South Africa announced on 20 Sept. 1978 that it was going ahead with internally sponsored elections for a Constituent Assembly. In the elections held on 4-8 Dec. 1978 the Democratic Turnhalle Alliance (DTA) gained 41 of the 50 seats in a percentage poll of 82%, in spite of the fact that the South West Africa People's Organization (SWAPO) instructed its members not to take part in the elections.

A 12-member Ministers' Council was instituted, and in Sept. 1981 it was enlarged to 15 members and given executive authority on all matters except constitutional issues, security and foreign affairs. On 11-13 Nov. 1980 elections were held for the second-tier Representative Authorities, which each controlled certain administrative functions for a specific ethnic group, but no specific geographical area. In Jan. 1983 the Ministers' Council and the National Assembly were dissolved and executive and legislative powers reverted to the Administrator-General.

In Sept. 1983 the Multi-Party Conference (MPC) of internal parties was formed. In May 1984 talks were held in Lusaka between the MPC and SWAPO. SWAPO refused to take part in further constitutional talks with the MPC. The MPC then petitioned South Africa for a form of self-government for Namibia, and on 17 June 1985 the Transitional Government of National Unit was installed. Negotiations began again in May and July 1988 between Angola, Cuba and South Africa. A peaceful settlement was agreed and the Geneva Protocol was signed on 5 Aug. 1988. In Dec. it was agreed that Cuban troops should withdraw from Angola and South African troops from Namibia by 1 April 1989. The Transitional Government of National Unity resigned on 28 Feb. 1988 to make provision for the implementation of UN Security Council Resolution 435. The UN Transition Assistance Group (UNTAG) supervised elections for the constituent assembly in Nov. 1989. Independence was achieved on 21 March 1990.

TERRITORY AND POPULATION. Namibia is bounded in the north by Angola and Zambia, west by the Atlantic Ocean, south and south-east by South Africa and east by Botswana. The Caprivi Strip (Caprivi Region), about 300 km long, extends eastwards up to the Zambezi river, projecting into Zambia and Botswana and touching Zimbabwe. The area, including the Caprivi Strip and Walvis Bay, is 824,269 sq. km. South Africa transferred Walvis Bay to Namibian jurisdiction on 1 March 1994. Census population, 1991, 1,401,711 (720,784 females; urban, 32·76%). Estimate, 1996, 1,677,243.

Population by ethnic group at the censuses of 1970 and 1981 and estimates for 1991:

	1970	1981	1991
Ovambos	342,455	506,114	665,000
Whites	90,658	76,430	85,000
Damaras	64,973	76,179	100,000
Hereros	55,670	76,296	100,000
Namas	32,853	48,541	64,000
Kavangos	49,577	95,055	124,000
Caprivians	25,009	38,594	50,000
Coloureds	28,275	42,254	...
Basters	16,474	25,181	
Bushmen	21,909	29,443	...
Tswanas	4,407	6,706	...
Other	...	12,403	...
	732,260	1,033,196	1,401,711

Namibia is administratively divided into 13 regions. Area, estimated population and chief towns in 1997:

Region	Area (in sq. km)	Population	Chief town
Caprivi	19,532	92,000	Katima Mulilo
Okavango	43,417	136,000	Rundu
Otjozondjupa	105,327	85,000	Grootfontein
Oshikoto	26,607	176,000	Tsumeb
Omusati	13,637	158,000	Outapi
Oshana	5,290	159,000	Oshakati
Ohangwena	10,582	178,000	Oshikango
Kunene	144,254	58,500	Opuwo
Erongo	63,719	98,500	Swakopmund
Khomas	36,804	174,000	Windhoek
Omaheke	84,731	55,600	Gobabis
Hardap	109,888	80,000	Mariental
Karas	161,324	73,000	Keetmanshoop

Towns with populations over 5,000 (1990): Windhoek, 125,000; Swakopmund, 15,500; Rehoboth, 15,000; Rundu, 15,000; Keetmanshoop, 14,000; Tsumeb, 13,500; Otjiwarongo, 11,000; Grootfontein, 9,000; Okahandja, 8,000; Mariental, 6,500; Gobabis, 6,500; Khorixas, 6,500; Lüderitz, 6,000.

Vital statistics: rates (1996 estimate) per 1,000 population: Birth, 37·29; death, 7·98; infant mortality rate, 47·2. Expectation of life, 1996 estimate: Males, 62·85; females, 66·16.

English is the official language. Afrikaans and German are also spoken.

CLIMATE. The rainfall increases steadily from less than 50 mm in the west and south-west up to 600 mm in the Caprivi Strip. The main rainy season is from Jan. to March, with lesser showers from Sept. to Dec. Namibia is the driest African country south of the Sahara.

CONSTITUTION AND GOVERNMENT. On 9 Feb. 1990 with a unanimous vote the Constituent Assembly approved the Constitution which stipulated a multi-party republic, an independent judiciary and an executive *President* who may serve a maximum of two 5-year terms. The bicameral legislature consists of a 78-seat *National Assembly*, 72 members of which are elected for 5-year terms by proportional representation and up to 6 appointed, and a *National Council* consisting of 2 members from each Regional Council elected for 6-year terms.

Presidential and parliamentary elections were held on 7-8 Dec. 1994. The electorate was 0·65m.; turn-out was 76%. Sam Nujoma was re-elected President by 76·3% of votes cast against 1 opponent. The South West Africa People's Organization (SWAPO) won 53 of the electable National Assembly seats; the Democratic Turnhalle Alliance, 15; the United Democratic Front, 2; others, 2.

President: Sam Nujoma (b. 1928; SWAPO, elected Feb. 1990; re-elected Dec. 1994; sworn in 21 March 1995).

In March 1998 the government comprised:

Prime Minister: Hage Geingob.

Deputy Prime Minister: Hendrik Witbooi. *Home Affairs:* Jerry Ekandjo. *Foreign Affairs:* Theo-Ben Gurirab. *Defence:* Erikki Nghimtina. *Finance:* Nangolo Mbumba. *Tertiary Education and Vocational Training:* Nahas Angula. *Information and Broadcasting:* Ben Amathila. *Health and Social Services:* Dr Libertine Amathila. *Labour and Manpower Development:* Moses Garoeb. *Mines and Energy:* Andimba Toivo Ya Toivo. *Justice:* Ngarikutuke Tjiriange. *Regional and Local Government and Housing:* Nicky Iyambo. *Agriculture, Water and Rural Development:* Helmut Angula. *Trade and Industry:* Hidipo Hamutenya. *Environment and Tourism:* Philemon Malima. *Works, Transport and Communication:* Hampie Plichta. *Lands, Resettlement and Rehabilitation:* Pendukeni Iithana. *Youth and Sport:* Richard Kapelwa-Kabajani. *Fisheries and Marine Resources:* Abraham Iyambo. *Prisons and Correctional Services:* Marco Hausiku. *Basic Education and Culture:* John Mutorwa.

National anthem: 'Namibia, land of the brave'; words and tune by Axali Doeseb.

Local Government. There are 13 elected regional and 93 local authority councils. Elections to regional councils and local authorities took place in Dec. 1992. SWAPO gained 70 regional seats with 67·3% of votes cast; DTA, 20 with 27·1%.

A *Council of Traditional Chiefs* advises the President on the utilization and control of communal land.

DEFENCE

Army. The army consists of 1 Presidential Guard, 4 motorized infantry, 1 artillery, 1 air defence artillery and 1 anti-tank battalion. An Air Wing has 6 Cessna 337 patrol aircraft, along with 2 Alouette and 2 Lama helicopters. Personnel (1997), 5,700.

Coastguard. A force of 100 (1996) operates 2 offshore and 1 inshore patrol craft based at Walvis Bay. There is 1 Cessna Caravan II maritime patrol aircraft.

INTERNATIONAL RELATIONS

Membership. Namibia is a member of the UN, Commonwealth, SADC and OAU.

ECONOMY

Policy. The National Development Plan aims for annual average growth of 5% up to 2000.

Performance. Real GDP growth was 3% in 1996.

Budget. The financial year runs from 1 April. In 1996-97 revenue was N$4,489m. and expenditure, N$5,073m. Tax revenue totalled N$3,988m.; re-current expenditure was N$4,099m.

Currency. The unit of currency is the *Namibia dollar* (NAD) of 100 *cents*, introduced on 14 Sept. 1993 and pegged to the South African rand. The rand is also legal tender at parity. There are coins of 1, 5, 10 and 50 cents and N$1 and 5, and notes of N$1, 2, 5, 10, 50, 100 and 200.

Banking and Finance. The Bank of Namibia is the central bank. Its *Governor* is Tom Alweendo. Commercial banks include First National Bank of Namibia, Namibia Banking Corporation, Standard Bank Namibia, Commercial Bank of Namibia and Bank Windhoek (the only locally-owned bank). There is a state-owned Agricultural Bank. Total assets of commercial banks were R2,383·2m. at 31 Dec. 1991.

There are 2 building societies with total assets (31 March 1990) R424.9m. A Post Office Savings Bank was established in 1916. In March 1991 its total assets were R21·8m. A stock exchange (NSE) is in opeation.

ENERGY AND NATURAL RESOURCES

Electricity. Installed capacity was 606,000 kW in 1990. In 1992 output was 1,714m. kWh.

Water. The 12 most important dams have a total capacity of 589·2m. cu. metres. The Kunene, the Okavango, the Zambezi, the Kwando or Mashi and the Orange River are the only permanently running rivers but water can generally be obtained by sinking shallow wells. Except for a few springs, mostly hot, there is no surface water.

Minerals. There are diamond deposits off the coast, which produce a third of diamond production. Namibia produces 1·3m. carats per year, accounting for around 8% of world diamond production. 1991 output (in tonnes): Uranium oxide (1990), 2,849; copper, 31,928; lead, 33,367; zinc, 68,099; silver, 91,293 kg; tin, 17; gold, 1,851,150 grammes; diamonds, 1,186,870 carats.

Agriculture. Namibia is essentially a stock-raising country, the scarcity of water and poor rainfall rendering crop-farming, except in the northern and north-eastern parts, almost impossible. Generally speaking, the southern half is suited for the raising of small stock, while the central and northern parts are more suited for cattle. In 1989 there were 4,460 farms and 6,327 other agricultural enterprises raising stock on 34,887,659 ha. Guano is harvested from the coast, converted into fertilizer in South Africa and most of it exported to Europe. In 1991, 15% of the active labour force worked in the agricultural sector, while 70% of the population was directly or indirectly dependent on agriculture for their living.

In 1991, 13m. litres of milk and (in 1988) 70,000 tonnes of cheese were produced. Principal crops (1991 in tonnes): Wheat, 6,400; maize, 35,065; sunflower seed, 108; sorghum (1990), 8,000; vegetables (1990), 32,000.

Forestry. Forests cover 18m. ha (20% of the land area).

Fisheries. Pilchards, mackerel and hake are the principal fish caught. Since 1993 there has been a dearth of fish. Conservation policies are in place.

INDUSTRY. Manufacturing contributed 12% of GDP in 1996. Of the estimated total of 400 undertakings, the most important branches are food production (accounting for 29·3% of total output), metals (12·7%) and wooden products (7%). The supply of specialized equipment to the mining industry, the assembly of goods from predominantly imported materials and the manufacture of metal products and construction material play an important part. Small industries, including home industries, textile mills, leather and steel goods, have expanded. Products manufactured locally include chocolates, beer, cement, leather shoes and delicatessen meats and game meat products.

Labour. In 1991 there were 0·75m. economically active persons. The estimated unemployment rate was 46·4%. The main employers were government services, agriculture and mining.

FOREIGN ECONOMIC RELATIONS. Total foreign debt was US$140m. in

1996. Export Processing Zones were established in 1995 to grant companies with EPZ status some tax exemptions and other incentives.

Commerce. Trade in 1991 (in R1m.): Imports, 3,410·6; exports, 3,236·2, including cattle (112·4), karakul pelts (15), small stock (104·9), unprocessed fish (324·2), diamonds (1,216·5), uranium (340·8), fish products (368) and meat products (189). The largest import supplier in 1996 was South Africa with 87%; largest export markets: UK, 34%; South Africa, 27%.

Tourism. In 1991 there were 318,028 visitors who spent R21,059,590.

COMMUNICATIONS

Roads. In 1991 the total national road network was 41,815 km, including 4,572 km of tarred roads. In 1991 there were 132,331 registered motor vehicles.

Railways. The Namibia system connects with the main system of the South African railways at Ariamsvlei. The total length of the line inside Namibia was 2,382 km of 1,065 mm gauge in 1996. In 1995–96 railways carried 124,000 passengers and 1·7m. tonnes of freight.

Civil Aviation. The national carrier is the state-owned Air Namibia, which in 1995 operated 1 B-737-200 Adv, 1 B-747SP and 3 other aircraft. In 1990–91 the 2 major airports, Windhoek (international) and Eros (domestic), handled about 215,175 passengers and 2·8m. kg of freight on international flights and 7,117 passengers and 211,218 kg of freight on internal flights. Windhoek is also served by Air Botswana, Air Zimbabwe, Commercial Airways, LTU, Lufthansa, SAA and TAAG.

Shipping. The main port is Walvis Bay. During 1991–92 820 ships called and 1m. tonnes of cargo were unloaded. There is a harbour at Lüderitz which handles mainly fishing vessels.

Telecommunications. Namibia Post and Telecom Namibia are the responsible corporations. In 1992 there were 72 post offices and 15 postal agencies which served 46,328 private box renters and 961 private bag services distributed by rail or road transport.

There were (1992) 89,722 telephones. There were 466 telex users.

The Namibian Broadcasting Corporation operates a national radio service from 3 stations and vernacular services. It also operates 10 TV stations (colour by PAL). In 1993 there were 27,000 TV sets and (1992) 195,000 radios in use.

Press (1993). There were 5 daily and 6 weekly newspapers.

SOCIAL INSTITUTIONS

Justice. There is a Supreme Court, a High Court and a number of magistrates' and lower courts. An Ombudsman is appointed. Judges are appointed by the president on the recommendation of the Judicial Service Commission.

Religion. About 90% of the population is Christian.

Education. Literacy was 60% in 1997. Primary education is free and compulsory. In 1988 there were 1,153 schools for all races, 374,269 pupils and 12,525 teachers. This included 1,118 primary and senior secondary schools, 3 centres for the handicapped, 1 technical school and 2 agricultural schools, 3 technical institutes and 3 agricultural colleges. There were 4 teachers' training colleges and an academy. The University of Namibia had 2,240 students and 160 academic staff in 1994–95.

Health In 1992 there were 47 hospitals (4 private) and 238 clinics and health centres. There were 324 doctors, 51 dentists and 4,471 nursing staff.

DIPLOMATIC REPRESENTATIVES

Of Namibia in Great Britain (6 Chandos St., London W1M 0LQ)
High Commissioner: Ben Ulenga.

Of Great Britain in Namibia (116 Robert Mugabe Ave., 9000 Windhoek)
High Commissioner: Glyn Davis.

Of Namibia in the USA (1605 Hampshire Ave., NW, Washington DC 20009)
Ambassador: Veiccoh K. Nghiwete.

Of the USA in Namibia (14 Lossen St., Private Bag 12029, Windhoek)
Ambassador: George F. Ward.

Of Namibia to the United Nations
Ambassador: Martin Andjaba.

Of Namibia to the European Union
Ambassador: Zedekia Ngavirue.

Further Reading

Gupta, V., *Independent Namibia: Problems and Prospects.* Delhi, 1990

Herbstein, D. and Evenston, J., *The Devils are Among Us: the War for Namibia.* London, 1989

Kaela, L. C. W., *The Question of Namibia.* London, 1996

Katjavivi, P.H., *A History of Resistance in Namibia.* London, 1988

Schoeman, Elna and Stanley, *Namibia.* [Bibliography] Oxford and Santa Barbara (CA), 1997

Sparks, D.L. and Green, D., *Namibia: the Nation after Independence.* Boulder, (CO), 1992

National statistical office: Central Statistics Office, Windhoek.

NAURU

Republic of Nauru

Population: 10,390
GDP: $100m.

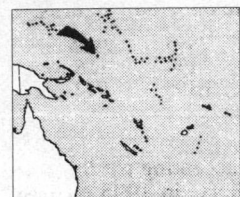

KEY HISTORICAL EVENTS. The island was discovered by Capt. Fearn in 1798, annexed by Germany in Oct. 1888, and surrendered to Australian forces in 1914. It was administered by the UK under a League of Nations mandate from 1920 until 1947, when the UN approved a trusteeship agreement with Australia, New Zealand and the UK as joint administering authorities. Independence was gained on 31 Jan. 1968.

TERRITORY AND POPULATION. Nauru is a coral island surrounded by a reef situated 0° 32' S. lat. and 166° 56' E. long. Area, 21·3 sq. km. At the 1983 census the population totalled 8,100, of whom 5,285 were Nauruans. Estimated population in July 1997: 10,390. Vital statistics (1995 estimate): Births, 18 (per 1,000 population); deaths, 5; infant mortality, 41 (per 1,000 live births).

CLIMATE. A tropical climate, tempered by sea breezes, but with a high and irregular rainfall, averaging 82" (2,060 mm). Jan. 81°F (27·2°C), July 82°F (27·8°C). Annual rainfall 75" (1,862 mm).

CONSTITUTION AND GOVERNMENT. A Legislative Council was inaugurated on 31 Jan. 1966. An 18-member Parliament is elected on a 3-yearly basis.

The government in March 1998 comprised:
Chief of State (and Head of Government), Minister for Island Development and Industry, Civil Aviation and Education: Bernard Dowiyogo (b. 1947).
Finance, External Affairs and Public Service: Kinza Clodumar. *Internal Affairs and Sports:* Vinson Detenamo. *Health:* Ludwig Scotti. *Justice:* Vassal Gadoengin. *Works and Community Service:* Derog Gioura.

National anthem: 'Nauru bwiema, ngabena ma auwe' ('Nauru our homeland, the country we love'); words by a collective, tune by L. H. Hicks.

INTERNATIONAL RELATIONS

Membership. Nauru is a member of the Pacific Community, the South Pacific Forum and has a special relationship with the Commonwealth.

ECONOMY

Currency. The Australian dollar is in use.

ENERGY AND NATURAL RESOURCES

Minerals. A central plateau contained high-grade phosphate deposits. The interests in the phosphate deposits were purchased in 1919 from the Pacific Phosphate Company by the UK, Australia and New Zealand. In 1967 the British Phosphate Corporation agreed to hand over the phosphate industry to Nauru for approximately $A20m. over 3 years. Nauru took over the industry in July 1969. It is estimated that the deposits will be exhausted by 2000. In May 1989 Nauru filed a claim against Australia for environmental damage caused by the mining. In Aug. 1993 Australia agreed to pay compensation of $A73m. In March 1994 New Zealand and the UK each agreed to pay compensation of $A12m.

FOREIGN ECONOMIC RELATIONS

Commerce. The export trade consists almost entirely of phosphate shipped to Australia, New Zealand, the Philippines and Japan. Imports: food, building construction materials, machinery for the phosphate industry and medical supplies.

COMMUNICATIONS

Civil Aviation. There is an airfield on the island capable of accepting medium size jet aircraft. Air Nauru, a wholly owned government subsidiary, in 1995 operated 2 B-737-400s to Melbourne, Sydney, Honiara, Guam, Tarawa, Port Vila, Suva, Nadi, Manila, Truk, Palau and Auckland.

Shipping. Deep offshore moorings can accommodate medium-size vessels. The Nauru Local Government Council, through its agency the Nauru Pacific Shipping Line, owns 3 ships and 1 fishing boat. These ships ply between Australia, the Pacific Islands, the USA, New Zealand, Japan and Singapore. Other shipping coming to the island consists of vessels under charter to the phosphate industry.

Telecommunications. There were 1,000 telephones in 1992. International telephone, telex and fax communications are maintained by satellite. A satellite earth station was commissioned in 1990. The government-controlled Nauru Broadcasting Service broadcasts a home service in Nauruan and English for 3 hours daily. There were 4,000 radio sets in use in 1993. New Zealand television programmes are received.

Cinemas. In 1989 there were 3 cinemas with seating capacity of 500.

SOCIAL INSTITUTIONS

Justice. The highest Court is the Supreme Court of Nauru. It is the Superior Court of record and has the jurisdiction to deal with constitutional matters in addition to its other jurisdiction. There is also a District Court which is presided over by the Resident Magistrate who is also the Chairman of the Family Court and the Registrar of Supreme Court. The laws applicable in Nauru are its own Acts of Parliament. A large number of British statutes and much common law has been adopted insofar as is compatible with Nauruan custom.

Religion. The population is mainly Roman Catholic or Protestant.

Education. Attendance at school is compulsory between the ages of 6 and 17. In 1989 there were 10 infant and primary schools and 2 secondary schools with a total of 165 teachers and 2,707 pupils. There is also a trade school with 4 instructors and an enrolment of 88 trainees. Scholarships are available for Nauruan children to receive secondary and higher education and vocational training in Australia and New Zealand.

DIPLOMATIC REPRESENTATIVES

Of Great Britain in Nauru
High Commissioner: Michael J. Peart, CMG, LVO (resides in Fiji).

Of the USA in Nauru
Ambassador: Don Lee Gevirtz (resides in Fiji).

Further Reading

Macdonald, B., *Trusteeship and Independence in Nauru.* Wellington, 1988
Weeremantry, C., *Nauru: Environmental Damage under International Trusteeship.* OUP, 1992
Williams, M. and Macdonald, B., *The Phosphateers.* Melbourne Univ. Press, 1985

NEPAL

Nepal Adhirajya

(Kingdom of Nepal)

Capital: Káthmandu
Population: 23·11m.
GDP per head: (PPP$) 1,137
GNP: US$4·2bn.
HDI/world rank: 0·347/154

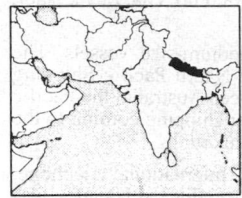

KEY HISTORICAL EVENTS. Nepal is an independent Himalayan Kingdom located between India and the Tibetan region of China. Until relatively recently, the history of Nepal was the struggle of rival chiefs for the consolidation of the surrounding area into a unified kingdom and its role as an asylum for refugees from the plains of India. Buddhism was introduced in about 639 AD.

From the 8th to the 11th centuries, many Buddhists fled to Nepal from India, which had been invaded by Muslims. In the 18th century Nepal was a collection of small principalities (many of Rajput origin) and the three kingdoms of the Malla dynasty: Káthmandu, Pátan and Bhádgaon. In central Nepal lay the principality of Gurkha (or Gorkha); its ruler after 1742 was Prithvi Náráyan Sháh, who conquered the small states which were his neighbours. Fearing his ambitions, in 1767 the Mallas brought in forces lent by the British East India Company to keep him in check. In 1769, these forces were withdrawn and Gurkha was then able to conquer the Malla kingdoms and unite Nepal as one state with its capital at Káthmandu.

Prithvi Náráyan also enlarged Nepal by annexing Sikkim and the Tarai, Kumáon, Garhwál and Simla areas of India. He died in 1775 and his successors were beset by internal rivalry. Most of the Indian annexations were lost to the British.

In 1846, the Ráná family became the effective rulers of Nepal, establishing the office of the prime minister as hereditary. In 1860, Nepal reached agreement with the British in India whereby Nepali independence was preserved and the recruitment of Gurkhas to the British army was sanctioned.

In 1950, the Sháh royal family allied itself with Nepalis abroad to end the power of the Ránás. The last Ráná prime minister resigned in Nov. 1951, the king having proclaimed a constitutional monarchy in Feb. 1951. A new constitution, approved in 1959, led to confrontation between the king and his ministers; it was replaced by one less liberal in 1962.

King Mahendra died in Jan. 1972 and was succeeded by his son Birendra Bir Bikram Sháh Dev.

Following pro-democracy demonstrations, on 16 April 1990 when 45 people died, King Birendra dismissed the government and proclaimed the abolition of the *panchayat* system of nominated councils. But continuing pressure from pro-democracy activists persuaded the King to concede a new constitution. In Nov. 1990, he relinquished his absolute power. A general election held the following year was won by the Nepali Congress Party. The present government is a coalition led by the United Marxist-Leninist Party. Nepal remains one of the poorest countries, but a five year plan encompasses economic reform with the hope of ending illiteracy among the young by 2005.

TERRITORY AND POPULATION. Nepal is bounded in the north by China (Tibet) and the east, south and west by India. Area 140,800 sq. km; population (estimate, July 1997), 23,107,000; (census, 1991) 18,462,081 (9,241,167 females; 9·6% urban). Density (1992), 125·4 per sq. km. Growth rate, 1997 estimate 2·53%; infant mortality, 78·4 per 1,000 live births. Expectation of life was 57·61 years for males and 57·13 years for females in 1996.

The country is divided into 5 regions and subdivided into 14 zones. Area, population and administrative centres in 1990:

Zone/Region	Sq. km	Population (in 1,000)	Administrative centre
Mechi	8,196	1,268	Ilam
Koshi	9,669	1,885	Biratnagar (Morang)
Sagarmatha	10,591	1,597	Rajbiraj
East Region	28,456	4,750	Dhankuta
Janakpur	9,669	2,052	Jaleswar
Narayani	8,313	1,923	Birganj
Bagmati	9,428	2,093	Káthmandu
Central Region	27,410	6,068	Káthmandu
Gandaki	12,275	1,320	Pokhara
Lumbini	8,975	2,056	Butwal
Dhanlagiri	8,148	508	Baglung
West Region	29,398	3,884	Pokhara
Rapti	10,482	1,035	Tulsipur
Bheri	10,545	1,153	Nepalganj
Karuali	21,351	281	Jumla
Mid-West Region	42,378	2,469	Surkhet
Seti	12,550	724	Dhangarhi
Mahakali	6,989	1,022	Mahendra Nagar
Far West Region	19,539	1,746	Dipayal

Capital, Káthmandu; population (census 1991) 419,073. Other towns include Patan (Lalitpur), 117,203; Biratnagar (Morang), 130,129; Bhadgaon (Bhaktapur), 61,122.

The indigenous people are of Tibetan origin with a considerable Hindu admixture. The Gurkha clan became predominant in 1559 and has given its name to men from all parts of Nepal. There are 18 ethnic groups, the largest being: Newars, Indians, Tibetans, Gurungs, Mogars, Tamangs, Bhotias, Rais, Limbus and Sherpas. The official language is Nepalese but there are 20 new languages divided into numerous dialects.

CLIMATE. Varies from cool summers and severe winters in the north to sub-tropical summers and mild winters in the south. The rainfall is high, with maximum amounts from June to Sept., but conditions are very dry from Nov. to Jan.

ROYAL HOUSE. The sovereign is HM Maharajadhiraja **Birendra Bir Bikram Sháh Dev** (b. 1946), who succeeded his father Mahendra Bir Bikram Sháh Dev on 31 Jan. 1972.

CONSTITUTION AND GOVERNMENT. Under the constitution of 9 Nov. 1990 Nepal became a constitutional monarchy based on multi-party democracy, Parliament has 2 chambers; a 205-member House of Representatives (Pratinidhi Sabha) elected for 5-year terms, and a 60-member National Council (Rastriya Sabha), of which 10 members are nominated by the king.

Elections were held on 15 Nov. 1994. The electorate was 12·3m.; turn-out was 58%. 24 parties stood. The Communist Party of Nepal-United Marxist-Leninist Party (CPN-UML) won 88 seats, the Nepali Congress, 75, and the National Democratic Party, 20. A Nepali Congress-Rastriya Prajatantra-Nepal Sadhavana coalition government was formed on 11 Sept. 1995, which in March 1998 comprised:

Prime Minister: Sher Bahadur Deuba (b. 1946; Nepali Congress).
Minister of Labour: Palten Gurung. *Forest and Soil Conservation:* Hrideyesh Tripathi. *Agriculture:* Prakash Chandra Lohani. *Industry:* Surya Bahadur Thapa. *Information and Communications:* Mahanta Thakur. *Housing and Physical Planning:* Balaram Gharti Magar. *Education:* Krishna Bahadur Gurung. *Water:* Pashupati Shumshere Rana. *Science and Technology:* Rajib Parajuli. *Finance:* Rabindra Nath Sharma. *Foreign Affairs:* Kamal Thapa. *Works and Transport:* Bijaya Gachhedar. *Health:* Bipen Koirala. *Commerce:* Ram Bilas Yadav. *Law and Justice:* Siddha Raj Ojha. *Local Development:* Gajendra Narayan Singh. *Supply:* Moti Prasad Pahadi. *Land Reform and Management:* Buddhi Man Tamang. *Youth, Sport and Culture:* Sharat Singh Bhandari. *Population and Environment:* Prakash Man Singh.

National anthem: 'Sri man gumbhira nepali prachanda pratapi bhupati' ('May glory crown our illustrious sovereign, the gallant Nepalese'); words by C. Chalise, tune by B. Budhapirthi.

Local Government. The country is administratively divided into 14 zones, subdivided into 75 districts and over 3,500 villages. Elections were held in May 1992. The Nepali Congress gained a majority of seats.

DEFENCE. The King is commander-in-chief of the armed forces, but shares supreme military authority with the National Defence Council, of which the Prime Minister is chairman.

Army. The Army consists of 1 Royal Guard brigade and 5 infantry and 1 support brigade. Strength (1997) 46,000, and there is also a 40,000-strong paramilitary police force.

Air Force. Independent of the army since 1979, the Air Force has 1 Twin Otter and 2 Skyvan transport aircraft, 1 Puma helicopter and 3 Chetak helicopters. An H.S. 748 turboprop transport and 1 Super Puma and 1 Puma helicopter are operated by the Royal Flight. There are no combat aircraft. Personnel, 1997, 215.

INTERNATIONAL RELATIONS

Membership. Nepal is a member of the UN and the Colombo Plan.

ECONOMY

Budget. Revenue US$645m., expenditure US$1·05bn. Agriculture is the mainstay of the economy, providing a livelihood for over 80% of the population and accounting for about one-half of GDP. Industrial activity is limited, mainly involving the processing of agricultural produce (jute, sugarcane, tobacco, and grain). Production of textiles and carpets has expanded recently and accounts for 85% of foreign exchange earnings. Apart from agricultural land and forests, exploitable natural resources are mica, hydropower and tourism. Agricultural production in the late 1980s grew by about 5%, as compared with annual population growth of 2·6%. More than 40% of the population is undernourished. Since May 1991, the government has been moving forward with economic reforms, particularly those that encourage trade and foreign investment, e.g., by eliminating business licenses and registration requirements in order to simplify investment procedures. The government has also been cutting public expenditures by reducing subsidies, privatizing state industries, and laying off civil servants. Prospects for foreign trade and investment, particularly in areas other than power development and tourism, are limited by the small size of the economy, its remoteness and its susceptibility to natural disaster. The international community provides funding for 62% of Nepal's developmental budget and for 34% of total budgetary expenditures.

Currency. The unit of currency is the *Nepalese rupee* (NPR) of 100 *paisas.* 50 *paisas* = 1 *mohur.* There are coins of 1, 2, 5, 10, 25 and 50 paisas and 1 rupee, and notes of 1, 2, 5, 10, 20, 50, 100, 500 and 1,000 rupees. Currency in circulation, 1994, NRs 21,511·8m. Inflation was 30% in mid-1993. In 1994 foreign exchange reserves totalled US$806·0m. and gold reserves 153,000 troy oz.

Banking and Finance. The Central Bank is the bank of issue. There were 438 commercial bank branches in 1994 with total deposits of NRs 52,327·7m.

ENERGY AND NATURAL RESOURCES

Electricity. Production, 920m. kWh, almost entirely hydro-electric.

Minerals. Production (in tonnes), 1994: Lignite, 290; talcum, 1,363; magnesite (1990), 25,000; limestone, 295,000.

Agriculture. Arable land accounts for 17% of land use; forest and woodland 33%. In 1994 agriculture accounted for about 41% of GDP. Crop production (1994 in 1,000 tonnes): Rice, 2,928; maize, 1,273; wheat, 914; sugar-cane, 1,500; potatoes, 840; millet, 268.

Livestock (1993): Cattle, 6,237,000; buffaloes, 3,073,000; sheep, 911,000; goats, 5,452,000; pigs, 630,000; poultry, 7m.

Forestry. There are 8 national parks, covering 1m. ha, 5 wildlife reserves (170,490 ha) and 2 conservation areas (349,000 ha). 18·22m. cu. metres of wood were cut in 1990, 17,657m. cu. metres for fuel. Expansion of agricultural land has led to widespread deforestation.

Fisheries. 17,580 tonnes of fish were caught in 1994.

INDUSTRY. In 1992 there were 4,271 firms employing 10 or more persons in which 223,463 persons were working. Production, 1994: Cement, 326,839 tonnes; electrical cable, 9·3m. metres; soap, 18,600 tonnes; paper, 8,863 tonnes; leather, 1,369,750 sq. metres; shoes, 0·69m. pairs; jute goods, 20,187 tonnes; cotton fabrics, 5·1m. metres; synthetic textiles, 14·7m. metres; sugar, 49,227 tonnes; tea, 2,351 tonnes; beer, 16,776 litres; animal feed, 19,500 tonnes.

Labour. In 1992 the workforce (persons over 10 years old) was 8·66m., of whom 7·25m. worked in agriculture, forestry or fisheries, 0·69m. in services, 0·23m. in mining, 0·18m. in commerce, 0·18m. in communications and 0·1m. in building.

FOREIGN ECONOMIC RELATIONS. Foreign debt was US$1,705m. in 1991.

Commerce. Principal exports are food grains, jute, timber, oilseeds, ghee (clarified butter), potatoes, medicinal herbs, hides and skins, cattle.

Exports: US$430m. (1995 est.) but does not include unrecorded border trade with India. *Commodities:* carpets, clothing, leather goods, jute goods, grain. *Partners:* India, USA, Germany, UK.

Imports: US$1·4bn. (1995 est.). *Commodities:* petroleum products 20%, fertilizer 11%, machinery 10%. *Partners:* India, Singapore, Japan, Germany.

External debt: US$2·3bn. (1994/95 est.).

Tourism. There were 363,395 tourists in 1995, bringing revenue of NRs 8,973·2m.

COMMUNICATIONS

Roads. In 1995 there were 9,933 km of roads, of which 3,421 km were macadamized and 6,512 km unpaved.

Railways. 101 km (762 mm gauge) connect Jayanagar on the North Eastern Indian Railway with Janakpur and thence with Bizalpura (54 km). 653,000 passengers and 9,151 tonnes of freight were carried in 1994.

Civil Aviation. There is an international airport (Tribhuvan) at Kathmandu. The national carrier is the state-owned Royal Nepal Airlines, which in 1995 operated 1 A310-300, 1 B-757-200, 1 B-757-200 Combi and 11 other aircraft. In 1994 1,273,506 passengers (803,222 on international flights) and 16·99m. tonnes of freight were flown. Services are also provided by Aeroflot, Biman Bangladesh, China Southwest Airlines, Druk-Air, Everest Air, Indian Airlines, Lufthansa, Necon Air, Pakistan Airlines, Singapore Airlines and Thai Airways.

Telecommunications. In 1994 there were 2,493 post offices. There were 82,774 telephones in 1995. Radio Nepal is part government-owned and part commercial. It broadcasts in Nepali and English from 3 stations. The government-owned Nepal Television Corporate transmits from 1 station (colour by PAL). In 1993 there were 690,000 radio and 45,000 TV sets.

Press. In 1997 there were 59 daily newspapers, including the official English-language *Rising Nepal*, 3 bi-weeklies, 454 weeklies and 48 fortnightlies. Press censorship was relaxed in June 1991.

SOCIAL INSTITUTIONS

Justice. The Supreme Court Act, established a uniform judicial system, culminating in a supreme court of a Chief Justice and no more than 6 judges. Special courts to deal with minor offences may be established at the discretion of the Government. The Chief Justice is appointed by the king on recommendation of the Constitutional Council. Other judges are appointed by the king on the recommendation of the Judicial Council.

Religion. Nepal is a Hindu state. Hinduism was the religion of 90% of the people in 1992. Buddhists comprise 5% and Moslems 3%. Christian missions are permitted, but conversion is forbidden.

Education. In 1997, 26% of the male and 13% of the female population were literate. In 1994–95 there were 21,102 primary schools with 3,191,000 pupils and 81,544 teachers (33,536 trained); 4,739 lower secondary schools, with 0·67m. pupils and 15,358 teachers (4,820 trained); and 2,482 secondary schools, with 274,000 pupils and 13,820 teachers (5,865 trained). The Tribhuvan University had 93,800 students and 4,300 academic staff in 1995–96. There is also a Sanskrit University.

Health. There were 872 doctors and 4,606 nurses in 1996. There were 82 hospitals with 3,604 beds, 17 health centres and 775 medical posts.

DIPLOMATIC REPRESENTATIVES

Of Nepal in Great Britain (12A Kensington Palace Gdns., London, W8 4QU)
Ambassador: Dr Singha B. Basnyat.

Of Great Britain in Nepal (Lainchaur, Káthmandu, POB 106)
Ambassador: Lloyd B. Smith.

Of Nepal in the USA (2131 Leroy Pl., NW, Washington, D.C., 20008)
Ambassador: Basuden Prasad Dhungana.

Of the USA in Nepal (Pani Pokhari, Káthmandu)
Ambassador: Sandra L. Vogelgesang.

Of Nepal to the United Nations
Ambassador: Narendra Bikram Shah.

Of Nepal to the European Union
Ambassador: Vacant.

Further Reading

Central Bureau of Statistics. *Statistical Pocket Book.* [Various years]

Borre, O. et al., *Nepalese Political Behaviour.* Aarhus Univ. Press, 1994
Ghimire, K., *Forest or Farm?: The Politics of Poverty and Land Hunger in Nepal.* OUP, 1993
Pant, Y. P., *Trade and Co-operation in South Asia: a Nepalese Perspective.* Delhi, 1991
Sanwal, D. B., *Social and Political History of Nepal.* London, 1993
Wadwha, D.N., *Nepal.* [Bibliography]. Oxford and Santa Barbara (CA), 1986

National statistical office: Central Bureau of Statistics, National Planning Commission Secretariat, Kathmandu

THE NETHERLANDS

Koninkrijk der Nederlanden

(Kingdom of the Netherlands)

Capital: Amsterdam
Seat of Government: The Hague
Population: 15·49m.
GDP per head: (PPP$) 19,238
HDI/world rank: 0·940/6

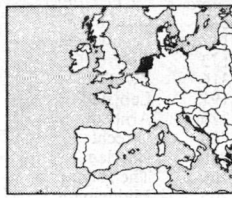

Source for statistics (*except* Climate *and* Defence): Netherlands Central Bureau of Statistics.

KEY HISTORICAL EVENTS. As the German Count of Nassau, William of Orange (1533–84) inherited vast possessions in the Netherlands and the Princedom of Orange in France. He was the initiator of the struggle for independence from Spain. The Revolt of the Netherlands began in 1568, and by the Union of Utrecht the more easily defensible seven provinces of the North—Holland, Zeeland, Utrecht, Overijssel, Groningen, Drenthe and Friesland—declared themselves independent. At the end of the Thirty Years War, by the Treaty of Westphalia (1648), Spain recognized the independence of the Republic of the United Netherlands. Members of the Orange-Nassau family became in succession the 'first servant of the Republic' with the title of 'Stadhouder' (governor). In 1689 Willem III acceded to the throne of England, becoming joint sovereign with his wife Mary. Willem III died in 1702 without issue, and there was no stadhouder until a member of the Frisian branch of Orange–Nassau was nominated hereditary stadhouder in 1747. His successor, Willem V, had, however, to take refuge in England in 1795 when the French Army invaded. The country was freed from French domination in Nov. 1813.

The Congress of Vienna (1815) joined the Belgian provinces, called the 'Spanish' or the 'Austrian Netherlands' before the French Revolution, to the Northern Netherlands. The son of the former stadhouder, Willem V, was proclaimed King of the Netherlands as King Willem I on 16 March 1815. The union was dissolved by the Belgian revolution of 1830, and in 1839 Belgium and the Netherlands were recognized as two separate independent kingdoms.

In 1840 Willem I abdicated in favour of his son, Willem II, who was liberal in his outlook and who moved the Netherlands towards a constitutional monarchy, developing ministerial responsibility and electoral equality among direct tax payers. Willem II was succeeded by Willem III in 1849 under whom the liberal development continued. In 1890 Wilhelmina, the first of three successive queens, ascended the throne (the Netherlands is a hereditary monarchy with the succession in the direct male or female line in the order of primogeniture).

The Netherlands followed a policy of non-participation in the European conflicts of the early 20th century and during the First World War remained neutral. In the Second World War, however, the Netherlands was occupied by Germany from 1940 until 1945. After liberation in 1945, the country abandoned its traditional policy of neutrality. In 1948 the Netherlands joined with Belgium and Luxembourg to form the Benelux economic union; in 1957 it was a founder member of the EEC, and in 1949 joined NATO.

Since the Second World War the Netherlands has granted independence to her overseas possessions of Indonesia (in 1949 after much fighting) and Suriname (in 1975), leaving the Netherlands Antilles and Aruba as the only remaining Dutch dependencies.1

In April 1980 Queen Juliana, who had reigned since 1948, abdicated in favour of her daughter Beatrix.

TERRITORY AND POPULATION. The Netherlands is bounded in the north and west by the North Sea, south by Belgium and east by Germany. The area (1996) is 41,526 sq. km, of which 33,889 sq. km is land. Projects of sea-flood control and land reclamation (polders) by the construction of dams and drainage schemes have continued since 1920.

The population was 13,060,115 at the census of 1971. On-going 'rolling' censuses have replaced the former decennial counts.

Area, estimated population and density, and chief towns of the 12 provinces on 1 Jan. 1996:

	Area 1995 (in sq. km)	Population 1996	Density 1996 per sq. km land area	Chief Town
Groningen	2,967·10	558,100	238	Groningen
Friesland	5,740·75	612,000	182	Leeuwarden
Drenthe	2,680·49	457,300	172	Assen
Overijssel	3,420·06	1,054,000	316	Zwolle
Flevoland	2,412·29	272,800	191	Lelijstad
Gelderland	5,143·36	1,876,300	376	Arnhem
Utrecht	1,434·24	1,070,600	789	Utrecht
Noord-Holland	4,059·09	2,468,400	928	Haarlem
Zuid-Holland[1]	3,445·75	3,332,900	1,166	The Hague
Zeeland	2,931·91	367,400	205	Middelburg
Noord-Brabant	5,016·11	2,290,400	464	's-Hertogenbosch
Limburg	2,195·98	1,133,700	523	Maastricht
Total	41,447·18	15,493,900[2]	457	

[1] Since 29 Sept. 1994 includes inhabitants of the municipality of The Hague formerly registered in the abolished Central Population Register.
[2] 7,662,300 males; 7,831,600 females.

Vital statistics for calendar years:

	Live births		Marriages	Divorces	Deaths	Net migration
	Total	Outside marriage				
1993	195,74	825,648	88,273	30,496	137,795	+59,932
1994	195,61	127,899	82,982	36,182	133,471	+37,156
1995	190,51	329,561	81,469	34,170	135,675	+32,800

Over 1990–95 the suicide rate per 100,000 population was 9·7 (men, 12·3; women, 7·2).

Population of municipalities with over 50,000 inhabitants on 1 Jan. 1996:

Alkmaar	93,052	Gouda	70,935	Oosterhout	51,046
Almelo	65,211	Groningen	169,627	Oss	63,199
Almere	112,704	Haarlem	147,617	Purmerend	65,604
Alphen a/d Rijn	67,583	Haarlemmermeer	106,095	Roosendaal en	
Amersfoort	114,884	The Hague	442,503	Nispen	63,854
Amstelveen	75,869	Heerlen	96,015	Rotterdam	592,745
Amsterdam	718,119	Den Helder	60,573	Schiedam	74,162
Apeldoorn	150,915	Helmond	74,918	Smallingerland	50,199
Arnhem	135,026	Hengelo	77,440	Spijkenisse	70,515
Assen	53,480	's-Hertogenbosch	125,044	Tilburg	164,380
Breda	130,033	Hilversum	83,272	Utrecht	234,254
Capelle a/d Ijssel	61,421	Hoorn	61,800	Veenendaal	55,325
Delft	93,229	Kerkrade	52,617	Velsen	65,509
Deventer	69,023	Leeuwarden	88,239	Venlo	64,781
Dordrecht	116,196	Leiden	116,224	Vlaardingen	74,271
Ede	99,927	Lelystad	60,707	Zaanstad	133,817
Eindhoven	197,374	Maastricht	118,518	Zeist	59,188
Emmen	94,114	Nieuwegein	59,214	Zoetermeer	106,581
Enschede	147,832	Nijmegen	147,600	Zwolle	100,835

Urban agglomerations as at 1 Jan. 1996: Amsterdam, 1,101,850; Rotterdam, 1,076,878; The Hague, 694,895; Utrecht, 548,464; Eindhoven, 398,359; Arnhem, 315,321; Heerlen-Kerkrade, 271,134; Enschede-Hengelo, 254,414; Nijmegen, 250,891; Tilburg, 238,643; Dordrecht/Zwijndrecht, 216,007; Haarlem, 211,139; Groningen, 209,494; 's-Hertogenbosch, 202,173; Leiden, 196,066; Geleen-Sittard, 186,695; Breda, 166,899; Maastricht, 164,813; Zaanstreek, 148,301; Velsen-Beverwijk, 136,297; Hilversum, 101,633.

CLIMATE. A cool temperate maritime climate, marked by mild winters and cool summers, but with occasional continental influences. Coastal temperatures vary from 37°F (3°C) in winter to 61°F (16°C) in summer, but inland the winters are slightly colder and the summers slightly warmer. Rainfall is least in the months Feb. to May, but inland there is a well-defined summer maximum in July and Aug.

The Hague. Jan. 37°F (2·7°C), July 61°F (16·3°C). Annual rainfall 32·8" (820 mm). Amsterdam. Jan. 36°F (2·3°C), July 62°F (16·5°C). Annual rainfall 34" (850 mm). Rotterdam. Jan. 36·5°F (2·6°C), July 62°F (16·6°C). Annual rainfall 32" (800 mm).

ROYAL HOUSE. The reigning Queen is **Beatrix Wilhelmina Armgard,** born 31 Jan. 1938, daughter of Queen Juliana and Prince Bernhard; married to Claus von Amsberg on 10 March 1966; succeeded to the crown on 1 May 1980, on the abdication of her mother. *Offspring:* Prince Willem-Alexander, born 27 April 1967; Prince Johan Friso, born 25 Sept. 1968; Prince Constantijn, born 11 Oct. 1969.

The Queen receives an allowance from the civil list. This was 6·3m. guilders in 1992; that of Prince Claus was 1·2m. guilders and that of Crown Prince Willem Alexander, 1·5m. guilders.

Mother of the Queen: Queen Juliana Louise Emma Marie Wilhelmina, born 30April 1909, daughter of Queen Wilhelmina (born 31 Aug. 1880, died 28 Nov. 1962) and Prince Henry of Mecklenburg-Schwerin (born 19 April 1876, died 3 July 1934); married to Prince Bernhard Leopold Frederik Everhard Julius Coert Karel Godfried Pieter of Lippe-Biesterfeld (born 29 June 1911) on 7 Jan. 1937. Abdicated in favour of her daughter, the Reigning Queen, on 30 April 1980.

Sisters of the Queen: Princess Irene Emma Elisabeth, born 5 Aug. 1939, married to Prince Charles Hugues de Bourbon-Parma on 29 April 1964, divorced 1981 (*sons:* Prince Carlos Javier Bernardo, born 27 Jan. 1970; Prince Jaime Bernardo, born 13 Oct. 1972; *daughters:* Princess Margarita Maria Beatriz, born 13 Oct. 1972; Princess Maria Carolina Christina, born 23 June 1974); Princess Margriet Francisca, born in Ottawa, 19 Jan. 1943, married to Pieter van Vollenhoven on 10 Jan. 1967 (*sons:* Prince Maurits, born 17 April 1968; Prince Bernhard, born 25 Dec. 1969; Prince Pieter-Christiaan, born 22 March 1972; Prince Floris, born 10 April 1975); Princess Maria Christina, born 18 Feb. 1947, married to Jorge Guillermo on 28 June 1975 (*sons:* Bernardo, born 17 June 1977; Nicolas, born 6 July 1979; *daughter:* Juliana, born 8 Oct. 1981).

The royal succession is in the direct female or male line in order of birth.

CONSTITUTION AND GOVERNMENT. According to the Constitution (promulgated 1814; last revision, 1983), the Kingdom consists of the Netherlands, Aruba and the Netherlands Antilles. Their relations are regulated by the 'Statute' for the Kingdom, which came into force on 29 Dec. 1954. Each part enjoys full autonomy; they are united, on a footing of equality, for mutual assistance and the protection of their common interests.

The Netherlands is a constitutional and hereditary monarchy.

The central executive power of the State rests with the Crown, while the central legislative power is vested in the Crown and Parliament (the *States-General*), consisting of 2 Chambers. The upper *First Chamber* is composed of 75 members, elected by the members of the Provincial States (*see* LOCAL GOVERNMENT, *below*). The 150-member *Second Chamber* is directly elected by proportional representation for 4-year terms. Members of the States-General must be Netherlands subjects of 21 years of age or over.

The *Council of State*, appointed by the Crown, is composed of a vice-president and not more than 28 members. The monarch is president, but the day-to-day running of the Council is in the hands of the vice-president. The Council can be consulted on all legislative matters.

The Hague is the seat of the Court, Government and Parliament; Amsterdam is the capital.

The Sovereign has the power to dissolve either Chambers, subject to the condition that new elections take place within 40 days, and the new Chamber be convoked within 3 months.

Both the Government and the Second Chamber may propose Bills; the First Chamber can only approve or reject them without inserting amendments. The meetings of both Chambers are public, though each of them may by a majority vote decide on a secret session. A Minister or Secretary of State cannot be a member of Parliament at the same time.

The Constitution can be revised only by a Bill declaring that there is reason for introducing such revision and containing the proposed alterations. The passing of this Bill is followed by a dissolution of both Chambers and a second confirmation by the new States-General by two-thirds of the votes. Unless it is expressly stated, all laws concern only the realm in Europe, and not the overseas part of the kingdom, Aruba and the Netherlands Antilles.

Party affiliation in the First Chamber as elected in 1995: Liberals (VVD), 23 seats; Christian Democrats (CDA), 19; Democrats (PVDA), 14; Democrats '66 (D66), 7; Green Left, 4; Party for the Elderly (AOV), 2; Political Calvinists (SGP), 2; Reformed Political Association (GPV), 1; Calvinist Evangelical Party (RPF), 1; Socialist Party (SP), 1; List Kuperus (regional parties and Green Party), 1.

Elections to the Second Chamber were held on 3 May 1994. Turn-out was 78·3%. PVDA won 37 seats with 24% of votes cast (49 seats in 1989); CDA, 34 with 22·2% (54); VVD, 31 with 20% (22); D66, 24 with 15·5% (12); AOV, 6 with 3 (nil); Green Left, 5 with 3·5% (6); CD (Extreme Right), 3 with 2·5% (1); RPF, 3 with 1·8% (1); SGP, 2 with 1·7% (3); GPV, 2 with 1·3% (2); SP, 2 with 1·3% (nil); Union 55+, 1 with 0·9%.

A PVDA/VVD/D66 coalition government was sworn in on 22 Aug. 1994 and in March 1998 comprised:

Prime Minister, Minister for General Affairs: Wim Kok (PVDA).

Deputy Prime Minister, Minister for Home Affairs: Hans Dijkstal (VVD). *Deputy Prime Minister, Minister for Foreign Affairs:* Hans van Mierlo (D66). *Minister of Agriculture, Management of Nature and Fisheries:* J. van Aartsen (VVD). *Development Co-operation:* Jan Pronk (PVDA). *Defence, Netherlands Antilles and Aruba Affairs:* Dr Joris Voorhoeve (VVD). *Economic Affairs:* Dr G. J. Wijers (D66). *Foreign Trade:* A. van Dok-van Weele (PVDA). *Education, Cultural Affairs and Science:* Dr Jo M. Ritzen (PVDA). *Finance:* Gerrit Zalm (VVD). *Housing, Planning and Environment:* M. de Boer (PVDA). *Justice:* Winnie Sorgdrager (D66). *Social Affairs and Employment:* Ad Melkert (PVDA). *Transport and Public Works:* Annemarie Jorritsma-Lebbink (VVD). *Welfare, Health and Sport:* Dr E. Borst-Eilers (D66).

National anthem: Wilhelmus van Nassaue; words by Philip Marnix van St Aldegonde, tune anonymous.

European Parliament. The Netherlands has 31 representatives. At the June 1994 elections turn-out was 35·6%. The CDA won 10 seats with 30·8% of votes cast (group in European Parliament: Popular European Party); the PVDA, 8 with 22·9% (European Socialist Party); the VVD, 6 with 17·9% (Liberal, Democratic and Reformist Group); D66, 4 with 11·7% (Liberal Democratic and Reformist Group); GPV/RPF/SGP, 2 with 7·8%; Greens, 1 with 3·7% (Greens).

Local Government. The kingdom is divided into 12 provinces and 636 municipalities.

Each province has its own representative body, the Provincial States. The members must be 21 years of age or over; they are directly elected for 4 years. The electoral register is the same as for the Second Chamber. Membership varies according to the population of the province. The Provincial States are entitled to issue ordinances concerning the welfare of the province, and to raise taxes pursuant to legal provisions. The provincial budgets and the provincial ordinances and resolutions relating to provincial property, loans, taxes, etc., must be approved by the Crown. The members of the Provincial States elect the First Chamber of the States-General. They meet twice a year, as a rule in public. A permanent commission composed of 6 of their members, called the 'Deputy States', is charged with the executive power and, if required, with the enforcement of the law in the province. Deputy as well as Provincial States are presided over by a Commissioner of the Queen, appointed by the Crown, who in the former assembly has a deciding vote, but attends the latter in only a deliberative capacity. He is the chief magistrate in the province. Elections to the Provincial States were held in March 1995; turn-out was 50%. VVD gained 27·2% of all votes cast; CDA, 22·9%; PVDA, 17%; D66, 9·2%.

Each municipality is governed by a Municipal Council, directly elected by residents who are 18 years of age or over, for 4 years. All Netherlands inhabitants and non-Netherlands inhabitants who meet certain requirements aged 21 or over are eligible to stand, the number of members varying according to the population. The Municipal Council may issue bye-laws and levy taxes pursuant to legal provisions; these must be approved by the Crown. The Municipal Budget and resolutions to alienate municipal property require the approbation of the Deputy States of the province. The Council meets in public as often as may be necessary, and is presided over by a Burgomaster, appointed by the Crown. The day-to-day administration is carried out by the Burgomaster and Aldermen, elected by and from the Council; this body is also charged with the enforcement of the law. In maintaining public order, the Burgomaster acts as the chief of police. Municipal Council elections were held on 2 March 1994; turn-out was 64%. CDA gained 21·6% of all votes cast; PVDA, 16·9%; local independent parties, 16·4%; VVD, 15·5%.

DEFENCE. Conscription ended on 30 Aug. 1996.

Army. The 1st Netherlands Army Corps is assigned to NATO. It consists of 10 brigades and Corps troops. The active part of the Corps comprises 2 armoured brigades and 4 armoured infantry brigades, grouped in two divisions and 40% of the Corps troops.

The mobilizable part of the Corps comprises 1 armoured brigade, 2 armoured infantry brigades, 1 infantry brigade and the remaining Corps troops.

The mechanized brigades comprise tank battalions (Leopard I improved and Leopard 2), armoured infantry battalions (YPR-765), medium artillery battalions (155 mm self-propelled), armoured engineer units and armoured anti-armour units. Equipment includes 298 Leopard 1A4 and 445 Leopard 2 main battle tanks. Personnel in 1996 numbered 43,200 (24,700 conscripts).

The National Territorial Command forces consist of territorial brigades, security forces, some logistical units and staffs. Some units in the Netherlands may be assigned to the UN as peace-keeping forces. The army is responsible for the training of these units.

There is a paramilitary Royal Military Constabulary, 3,600 strong (500 conscripts).

Navy. The principal headquarters and main base of the Royal Netherlands Navy is at Den Helder, with minor bases at Vlissingen (Flushing), Curaçao (Netherlands Antilles) and Oranjestad (Aruba). Command and control in home waters is exercised jointly with the Belgian Navy (submarines excepted).

The combatant fleet includes 4 diesel submarines of the new Zeeleeuw class, 4 guided-missile destroyers armed with US Standard SM1-MR surface-to-air missiles, 12 frigates each with 1 or 2 Lynx anti-submarine helicopters, 10 coastal minehunters and 2 coastal minesweepers.

In 1996 personnel totalled 14,000, including 1,100 in the Naval Air Service and 2,900 in the Royal Netherlands Marine Corps.

Air Force. The Royal Netherlands Air Force (RNLAF) strength is 9,000 (3,300 conscripts). It has a first-line combat force of 7 squadrons of aircraft and 2 groups of surface-to-air missiles in Germany. All squadrons are operated by Tactical Air Command.

INTERNATIONAL RELATIONS

Membership. The Netherlands is a member of the UN, EU, OECD, Council of Europe, WEU and NATO, and is a signatory of the Schengen Accord which abolishes border controls between the Netherlands and Austria, Belgium, Denmark, Finland, France, Germany, Greece, Iceland, Italy, Luxembourg, Norway, Portugal, Spain and Sweden.

ECONOMY

Budget. The revenue and expenditure of the central government (ordinary and extraordinary) were, in 1m. guilders, for calendar years:

	1990	1991	1992	1993	1994	1995
Revenue	155,227	171,639	171,528	180,824	170,955	168,474
Expenditure	182,330	189,932	195,398	196,924	190,441	225,262

VAT is 17·5% (reduced rate, 6%).

Currency. The monetary unit is the *gulden* (NLG; written as fl[orin]; in English, 'guilder') of 100 *cents*. There are coins of 5, 10 and 25 cents and 1, 2·5 and 5 guilders, and notes of 10, 25, 50, 100, 250 and 1,000 guilders. It is tied to the German Deutschmark.

Banking and Finance. The central bank and bank of issue is the Netherlands Bank (*President*, Willem F. Duisenberg), founded in 1814 and nationalized in 1948. Its Governor is appointed by the government for 7-year terms. The capital amounts to 75m. guilders.

There is a stock exchange in Amsterdam.

Weights and Measures. The metric system is in use.

ENERGY AND NATURAL RESOURCES

Electricity. Production of electrical energy in 1996, 88,503m. kWh (6% nuclear). 790 windmills were installed in 1994 to produce 238m. kWh.

Gas. Production of natural gas in 1995, 80,164m. cu. metres.

Agriculture. The total area of cultivated land in 1996 was 1,981,700 ha: Grassland, 1,052,100 ha; arable crops, 807,200 ha; horticultural crops, 108,400 ha, of which 18,600 ha was flowering bulbs and tubers including 8,700 ha of tulips; fallow land, 13,900 ha.

The yield of the more important arable crops, in 1,000 tonnes, was as follows:

Crop	1994	1995	1996
Wheat	981·0	1,166·7	1,268·9
Rye	26·5	42·5	38·2
Barley	227·6	202·5	234·8
Oats	27·9	15·5	10·7
Kidney beans	4·8	5·4	7·8
Peas	9·4	4·6	7·6
Colza	4·2	4·5	3·1
Flax	32·9	34·4	...
Potatoes	7,088·4	7,340·4	8,055·9
Sugar-beet	6,149·4	6,499·4	6,415·7
Sown onions	464·7	479·1	623·2
Fodder maize	2,728·1	2,527·4	2,694·6

Livestock, 1996 (in 1,000) included: 4,551 cattle, 8,793 fattening pigs and breeding sows; 106 horses and ponies; 803 lambs; 92,691 turkeys and chickens.

Animal products in 1995 (in 1,000 tonnes) included: Butter, 132; cheese, 692; hens' eggs, 621; beef, 386; horsemeat, 1.

Fisheries. Marine catch in 1995: 533,691 tonnes; chiefly scad, herring and mackerel.

INDUSTRY. The three largest industrial sectors are chemicals, food processing and metal, mechanical and electrical engineering.

At 31 Dec. 1995 there were 6,672 enterprises in the manufacturing industry (excepting construction), of which 3,269 had 20-49 employees and 198 had 500 employees or more; total annual sales for 1995 were 280,571m. guilders.

In 1994 there were 6,710 enterprises with 20 or more employees. The food products and beverages industry employed 114,185 people at 30 Sept. 1994 (annual sales for 1994 in 1m. guilders, 71,040); tobacco products, 5,524 (4,673); chemicals and chemical products, 76,260 (48,486); electrical machinery and apparatus, 82,450

(18,663); transport equipment, 45,928 (18,006); machinery and equipment, 67,793 (17,711); publishing, printing and reproduction of recorded media, 61,058 (17,501); other fabricated metal products, 65,789 (17,028).

In 1994, total annual sales for mining and quarrying were 17,748m. guilders and for public utilities, 24,434m. guilders.

Labour. The total labour force in 1995 was 6,596,000 persons (2,529,000 women) of whom 533,000 (281,000) were unemployed, with 464,000 (204,000) registered unemployed. By education level, the 1995 labour force included (in 1,000): Primary education, 585; junior general secondary, 467; pre-vocational secondary, 1,010; senior general secondary, 349; senior vocational secondary, 2,539; vocational colleges, 1,120; university, 513.

In Oct. 1994 the weekly working hours (excluding overtime) of employees were 36·6 for men and 26·5 for women. In 1994, full-time employees' working hours (excluding overtime) totalled 1,732; part-time, 923 and flexible, 853. Employees in the private sector worked a total of 1,471 hours, those in the public sector 1,465 hours and those in the subsidized sector 1,292 hours (all excluding overtime). The working hours of employees ranged from a total of 1,698 in mining and quarrying, 1,662 in public utilities, 1,649 in construction and 1,635 in manufacturing to 1,209 in health and social work and 1,017 in hotels and restaurants (all excluding overtime). Average annual gross earnings of employees in 1994 were 53,800 guilders for men and 29,900 guilders for women. In 1995, gross hourly wage earnings (in guilders) by type of employment ranged from 41·71 in mining and quarrying, 37·75 in education and 35·63 in public utilities to 20·20 in hotels and restaurants and 15·23 for domestic personnel in private households.

Trade Unions. Trade unions are grouped in 4 central federations. Total membership was 1,865,000 in 1995. In Nov. 1993 an agreement on wage restraint was concluded between the trade unions and the employers' federations, in return for an enhancement of the roles of works committees and professional training for employees.

FOREIGN ECONOMIC RELATIONS. On 5 Sept. 1944 and 14 March 1947 the Netherlands signed agreements with Belgium and Luxembourg for the establishment of a customs union. On 1 Jan. 1948 this union came into force and the existing customs tariffs of the Belgium–Luxembourg Economic Union and of the Netherlands were superseded by the joint Benelux Customs Union Tariff. It applied to imports into the 3 countries from outside sources, and exempted from customs duties all imports into each of the 3 countries from the other two.

Commerce. Imports and exports for calendar years (in 1m. guilders):

	Imports	Exports		Imports	Exports
1969	39,955	36,205	1992	236,597	246,540
1979	134,885	127,689	1993	231,643	258,342
1989	221,412	229,409	1994	256,439	287,452
1991	237,117	249,051	1995	282,384	313,545

Value of trade with major partners (in 1m. guilders):

Country	Imports		Exports	
	1994	1995	1994	1995
Belgium–Luxembourg	30,687	33,360	38,067	40,548
France	19,438	20,986	30,851	34,930
Germany	59,758	66,024	82,881	89,816
Italy	9,506	10,194	15,988	17,404
Japan	9,148	9,288	2,943	3,188
Spain	4,653	5,414	7,535	9,090
Sweden	5,723	7,786	4,433	6,583
Switzerland	3,402	3,454	4,805	5,041
UK	24,525	28,598	28,738	30,511
USA	19,975	22,586	11,348	10,344

The main imports in 1995 (in 1m. guilders) included machines (including electrical machines), 60,143; road vehicles, 19,311; crude petroleum, 12,241; organic chemicals, 9,361; iron and steel, 8,152; clothing, 8,035; non-ferrous metals,

4,968; paper and paperboard, 4,743; oil products, 4,172. Main exports included machines (including electrical machines), 59,795; organic chemicals, 14,780; oil products, 12,920; fruit and vegetables, 12,386; road vehicles, 11,864; crude vegetable materials, 8,303; meat, 7,436; beverages and tobacco, 7,407; iron and steel, 6,907; natural and manufactured gas, 6,542.

Tourism. There were 6,043,000 foreign visitors in 1993-4, of whom 4,045,000 spent 8,555,000 nights in hotels. Total income from tourism in 1995, 9,277m. guilders.

COMMUNICATIONS

Roads. In 1996 the length of the Netherlands network of surfaced inter-urban roads was 58,133 km, of which 2,207 km were motorways. Number of private cars (1996), 5·74m.; lorries and vans, 597,000; motor cycles, 335,000.

Railways. All railways are run by the mixed company 'N.V. Nederlandse Spoorwegen'. Route length in 1995 was 2,739 km, of which 1,991 km were electrified. Passengers carried (1995), 305m.; goods transported, 20·9m. tonnes. There is a metro (23 km) and tram/light rail network (153 km) in Amsterdam and in Rotterdam (28 km and 141 km). Tram/light rail networks operate in The Hague (122 km) and Utrecht (28 km).

Civil Aviation. There are international airports at Amsterdam (Schiphol), Rotterdam, Maastricht and Eindhoven. The Royal Dutch Airlines (KLM) was founded on 7 Oct. 1919 and had a fleet of 66 aircraft in 1994. Revenue traffic, 1995–96: Passengers, 12·34m.; freight and mail, 598m. kg. Services are also provided by 83 foreign airlines.

Sea-going Shipping. Survey of the Netherlands mercantile marine as at 1 Jan. (capacity in 1,000 GRT):

	1995		1996	
Ships under Netherlands flag	*Number*	*Capacity*	*Number*	*Capacity*
Passenger ships[1]	6	147	6	147
Freighters (100 GRT and over)	326	2,140	322	2,056
Tankers	53	616	51	592
	385	2,903	379	2,795

[1] With accommodation for 13 or more cabin passengers.

In 1995, 43,556 sea-going ships of 486·64m. gross tons entered Netherlands ports. Total goods traffic by sea-going ships in 1994 (with 1993 figures in brackets), in 1m. tonnes, amounted to 287 (277) unloaded, of which 129 (130) tankshipping, and 88 (88) loaded, of which 24 (24) tankshipping; total seaborne goods traffic in 1995 (and 1994) at Rotterdam was 291·2 (293·4) and at Amsterdam 31·4 (29·3).

The number of containers (including flats) at Rotterdam in 1995 (and 1994) was: Unloaded from ships, 1·56m. (1,516,000) and 1,535,000 (1·48m.) loaded into ships.

Inland Shipping. The total length of navigable rivers and canals is 5,046 km, of which 2,398 km is for ships with a capacity of 1,000 and more tonnes. On 1 Jan. 1996 the inland fleet used for transport (with carrying capacity in 1,000 tonnes) was composed as follows:

	Number	*Capacity*
Self-propelled barges	4,439	4,159
Dumb barges	377	263
Pushed barges	743	1,675
	5,559	6,097

In 1995, 208·4m. tonnes of goods were transported on rivers and canals, of which 131·6m. tonnes was by international shipping. Goods transport on the Rhine across the Dutch-German frontier near Lobith amounted to 139·5m. tonnes.

Telecommunications. On 1 Jan. 1993 there were 6·9m. telephone connections (46 per 100 inhabitants). Number of telex lines, 22,000. *Nederlandse Omroepprogramma*

Stichting (NOS) provides 5 programmes on medium-waves and FM in co-operation with broadcasting organizations. Regional programmes are also broadcast.

Advertisements are transmitted. NOS broadcasts 3 TV programmes (colour by PAL). At 31 Dec. 1995 there were 5,837,000 registered owners of television and radio sets and 123,000 of radio only.

Cinemas (1995). There were 484 cinemas with a seating capacity of 94,000. Total attendance was 17m.

Press (1994). There were 64 daily newspapers with a total circulation of 4·6m.

SOCIAL INSTITUTIONS

Justice. Justice is administered by the High Court (Court of Cassation), by 5 courts of justice (Courts of Appeal), by 19 district courts and by 63 cantonal courts. The Cantonal Court, which deals with minor offences, comprises a single judge; more serious cases are tried by the district courts, comprising as a rule 3 judges (in some cases one judge is sufficient); the courts of appeal are constituted of 3 and the High Court of 5 judges. All judges are appointed for life by the Sovereign (the judges of the High Court from a list prepared by the Second Chamber of the States-General). They can be removed only by a decision of the High Court.

At the district court the juvenile judge is specially appointed to try children's civil cases and at the same time charged with administration of justice for criminal actions committed by young persons between 12 and 18 years old, unless imprisonment of more than 6 months ought to be inflicted; such cases are tried by 3 judges.

Number of sentences, and cases in which prosecution was evaded by paying a fine to the public prosecutor (excluding violation of economic and tax laws):

Major offences		*Minor offences*[1]	
1992	112,815	1990	814,675
1993	132,432	1991	837,900
1994	136,943	1992	582,799
		1993	351,484
		1994	248,568

[1] Excluding an estimated 2m. minor traffic violations.

The population in penal institutions at 31 Dec. 1995 was 9,921, of which 4,612 were convicted. The total number of inmates during the year was 32,523 (30,935 men).

Police. In 1994 the police force was divided into 25 regions. There is also a National Police Service which includes the Central Criminal Investigation Office, which deals with serious crimes throughout the country, and the International Criminal Investigation Office, which informs foreign countries of international crimes.

Religion. Entire liberty of conscience is granted to the members of all denominations. The royal family belong to the Dutch Reformed Church.

According to survey estimates of 1995, the distribution of the population aged 18 years and over was: Roman Catholics, 33%; Dutch Reformed Church, 14%; Calvinist, 7%; other creeds, 7%; no religion, 40%. The government of the Reformed Church is Presbyterian. On 1 July 1992 the Dutch Reformed Church had 1 synod, 9 provincial districts, 75 classes, about 160 districts and about 2,000 parishes. Their clergy numbered 1,735. The Roman Catholic Church had, Jan. 1992, 1 archbishop (of Utrecht), 6 bishops, 4 assistant bishops and about 1,750 parishes and rectorships. The Old Catholics had (1 July 1992) 1 archbishop (Utrecht), 1 bishop and 28 parishes. The Jews had, in 1992, 40 communities. At 1 Jan. 1996 there were an estimated 667,900 Moslems and 79,100 Hindus.

Education. Statistics for the scholastic year 1995–96:

	Schools	Full-time Pupils/Students (in 1,000) Total
Primary education	7,411	1,477
Special education	975	119

	Schools	Full-time Pupils/Students (in 1,000) Total
General secondary education	690	661
Pre-vocational education	434	207
Senior vocational secondary education	141	289
Vocational colleges	77	230
University education	20	178

Academic Year 1994–95

	Schools	Full-time Students		Part-time Students	
		Total	Female	Total	Female
University education:					
Agriculture		5,253	2,226	30	8
Science		13,449	4,375	278	52
Engineering		26,346	4,138	65	5
Health	20	17,424	10,201	643	409
Economics		27,995	7,074	657	131
Law		24,716	12,569	3,490	1,586
Behaviour and Society		30,625	19,426	4,113	2,679
Language and Culture		27,139	17,993	2,244	1,241
Education		681	370	67	23

In 1994, there were 138,454 participants in adult basic education, and 27,156 Open University students (39% women). In 1995, 176,943 people participated in private correspondence courses, with subjects including the humanities (23,415 people), commerce (21,683), business administration (18,701), service trades (15,384), retail trade (15,178), technical (13,116) and public order and security (10,128).

Health. On 1 Jan. 1995 there were 7,125 general practitioners, 13,337 specialists, 7,328 dentists, 1,276 midwives, 11,701 physiotherapists and 2,544 pharmacists; there were 60,623 licensed hospital beds (excluding mental hospitals).

Welfare. At 31 Dec. 1995 there were 2,186,200 persons entitled to receive an old age pension, and 195,700 a pension under the General Widows and Orphans Act; 1,814,000 parents were receiving benefits under the General Family Allowances Act; 326,800 persons were receiving assistance under the State Group Regulations for the Unemployed; there were 860,700 persons claiming disablement insurance under the General and Industrial Disablement Acts.

Culture. In 1994 there were 741 museums open to the public, to which visits totalled 21,582,000. In 1994 there were 602 public libraries with 4,587,000 registered users (2,157,000 children). In 1994-95 there were 9,447 music and theatre performances of which 2,843 were of plays, 2,041 concerts, 306 opera and operetta and 1,307 ballet and dance, with a total attendance of 2,981,000.

DIPLOMATIC REPRESENTATIVES

Of the Netherlands in Great Britain (38 Hyde Park Gate, London, SW7 5DP)
Ambassador: Jan Hermann R. D. van Roijen.

Of Great Britain in the Netherlands (Lange Voorhout 10, 2514 ED The Hague)
Ambassador: Rosemary Spencer, CMG.

Of the Netherlands in the USA (4200 Linnean Ave., NW, Washington, D.C., 20008)
Ambassador: Adriaan de Szeged.

Of the USA in the Netherlands (Lange Voorhout, 102, The Hague)
Ambassador: K. Terry Dornbush.

Of the Netherlands to the United Nations
Ambassador: Jaap P. Ramaker.

Further Reading

Centraal Bureau voor de Statistiek. *Statistical Yearbook of the Netherlands.* From 1923/24.—*Statistisch Jaarboek.* From 1899/1924.—*CBS Select (Statistical Essays).* From 1980.—*Statistisch Bulletin.* From 1945; weekly.—*Maandschrift.* From 1944; monthly bulletin.—*90 Jaren Statistiek in Tijdreeksen* (historical series of the Netherlands 1899–1989)
Nationale Rekeningen (National Accounts). From 1948–50.—*Statistische onderzoekingen.* From 1977.—*Regionaal Statistisch Zakboek* (Regional Pocket Yearbook). From 1972.—*Environmental Statistics of the Netherlands*, 1987
Staatsalmanak voor het Koninkrijk der Nederlanden. Annual. The Hague, from 1814
Staatsblad van het Koninkrijk der Nederlanden. The Hague, from 1814
Staatscourant (State Gazette). The Hague, from 1813

Anderweg, R. B. and Irwin, G. A., *Dutch Government and Politics.* London, 1993
Cox, R. H., *The Development of the Dutch Welfare State: from Workers' Insurance to Universal Entitlement.* Pittsburgh Univ. Press, 1994
Gladdish, K., *Governing from the Centre: Politics and Policy-Making in the Netherlands.* London, 1991
King, P. K. and Wintle, M., *The Netherlands.* [Bibliography] Oxford and Santa Barbara, 1988

National library: De Koninklijke Bibliotheek, Prinz Willem Alexanderhof 5, The Hague.
National statistical office: Centraal Bureau voor de Statistiek, Netherlands Central Bureau of Statistics, POB 959, 2270 AZ Voorburg.
Website: *Statistics Netherlands* http://www.cbs.nl

ARUBA

KEY HISTORICAL EVENTS. Discovered by Alonzo de Ojeda in 1499, the island of Aruba was claimed for Spain but not settled. It was acquired by the Dutch in 1634, but apart from garrisons was left to the indigenous Caiquetios (Arawak) Indians until the 19th century. From 1828 it formed part of the Dutch West Indies and, from 1845, part of the Netherlands Antilles, with which on 29 Dec. 1954 it achieved internal self-government.

Following a referendum in March 1977, the Dutch government announced on 28 Oct. 1981 that Aruba would proceed to independence separately from the other islands. Aruba was constitutionally separated from the Netherlands Antilles from 1 Jan. 1986, and full independence had been promised by the Netherlands after a 10-year period. However, an agreement with the Netherlands government in June 1990 deletes, at Aruba's request, references to eventual independence.

TERRITORY AND POPULATION. The island, which lies in the southern Caribbean 29 km north of the Venezuelan coast and 68 km west of Curaçao, has an area of 193 sq. km (75 sq. miles) and a population at the 1995 census of 65,974; density, 369 per sq. km. Estimate, 1996, 72,100; density, 377 per sq. km. The chief towns are Oranjestad, the capital (1996 population estimate, 21,000) and Sint Nicolaas. Dutch is the official language, but the language usually spoken is Papiamento, a creole language. Over half the population is of Indian stock, with the balance of Dutch, Spanish and mestizo origin.

CLIMATE. Aruba has a tropical marine climate, with a brief rainy season from Oct. to Dec. Oranjestad. Jan. 79°F (26·0°C), July 84°F (29·0°C). Annual rainfall 17" (432 mm).

CONSTITUTION AND GOVERNMENT. Under the separate constitution inaugurated on 1 Jan. 1986, Aruba is an autonomous part of the Kingdom of the Netherlands with its own legislature, government, judiciary, civil service and police force. The Netherlands is represented by a Governor appointed by the monarch (in 1997, Governor General Olindo Koolman). The unicameral legislature *(Staten)* consists of 21 members.

Elections were held on 29 July 1994. The electorate was some 46,000; turn-out was 85%. The Arubaanse Volkspartij (AVP) won 10 seats, the Movimento Electoral di Pueblo, 9, and the Organización Liberal Arubianco (OLA), 2.

An AVP-OLA coalition government was formed on 8 Aug. 1994:

Prime Minister: Jan H. Eman (AVP).

Economy: R. R. Croes. *Education and Labour:* P. E. Croes. *Finance:* A. W. Engelbrecht. *Health, Social Affairs, Culture and Sport:* L. G. Beck Martínez. *Justice and Public Works:* E. J. Vos. *Representative in the Netherlands:* A. G. Croes. *Transport and Communications:* G. F. Croes.

ECONOMY

Budget. The 1991 budget totalled 495m. florins tax revenue.

Currency. Since 1 Jan. 1986 the currency has been the *Aruban florin,* at par with the Netherlands Antilles guilder. There are notes of 5, 10, 25, 50 and 100 florins. There were 76·2m. Aruban florins in circulation in 1992. Inflation was 6·9% in 1994. Foreign exchange reserves in 1992 were US$142m.

Banking and Finance. There were 5 domestic and Dutch banks, and 1 foreign bank in 1995. There is a special tax regime for offshore banks. The *President* of the Central Bank of Aruba is J. H. du Marchie Sarvaas.

ENERGY AND NATURAL RESOURCES

Electricity. Generating capacity totalled 114 MW in 1995.

Water. There is a desalination plant with an annual capacity of 22,000 tonnes.

INDUSTRY. The government has established 6 industrial sites at Oranjestad harbour. An oil refinery closed in 1985 was re-opened in 1993 with a capacity in 1997 of 0·14m. bbls. a day.

EXTERNAL ECONOMIC RELATIONS. There are 2 Free Zones at Oranjestad.

Exports. US$1·3 billion (1993 estimate).

Imports. US$1·6 billion (1993 estimate).

Tourism. In 1994 there were 582,136 staying tourists and (1993) 251,000 cruise-ship visitors. Tourist revenue was US$464m. in 1993.

COMMUNICATIONS

Roads. In 1984 there were 380 km of surfaced highways. In 1991 there were 26,710 passenger cars and 3,704 commercial vehicles.

Civil Aviation. There is an international airport (Queen Beatrix). Air Aruba operated 1 B-767-200, 2 B-737-300s and 1 other aircraft in 1992. Services are also provided by Aerorepublica, Air France, Alitalia, ALM, Aserca, Avenza, Avianca, British Airways, BWIA, Continental Airlines and Air Micronesia, KLM, SAM, SAS, Servivensa, TAP, United Airlines, VASP and VIASA.

Shipping. Oranjestad has a container terminal and cruise ship port. The port at Barcadera services the offshore and energy sector and a deep-water port at Sint Nicolas services the oil refinery.

Telecommunications. In 1996 there were 25,000 telephones. In 1995 there were 9 radio stations and 1 commercial television station (colour by NTSC). In 1993 there were 40,000 radio and 19,000 TV sets.

Press. In 1995 there were 1 Dutch-language (circulation 3,500), 1 English (circulation 5,000), 4 Papiamento dailies and 5 other newspapers.

SOCIAL INSTITUTIONS

Justice. There is a Common Court of Justice with the Netherlands Antilles. Final Appeal is to the Supreme Court in the Netherlands.

Religion. In 1990, 89% of the population were Roman Catholic and 7% Protestant.

Education. In 1991 there were 30 elementary schools with 7,191 pupils, 10 junior high schools with 3,094 pupils and 16 schools and colleges for vocational education with 2,520 students.

Health. In 1991 there were 74 doctors, 19 dentists, 11 pharmacists, 515 nursing personnel and one hospital with 263 beds.

Further Reading

Schoenhals, K., *Netherlands Antilles and Aruba.* [Bibliography] Oxford and Santa Barbara, 1993

THE NETHERLANDS ANTILLES

De Nederlandse Antillen

KEY HISTORICAL EVENTS. Bonaire and Curaçao islands, originally populated by Arawak Indians, were discovered in 1499 by Alonso de Ojeda, and claimed for Spain. They were settled in 1527, and the indigenous population exterminated and replaced by a slave-worked plantation economy. The 3 Windward Islands, inhabited by Caribs, were discovered by Columbus in 1493. They were taken by the Dutch in 1632 (Saba and Sint Eustatius), 1634 (Curaçao and Bonaire) and 1648 (the southern part of Sint Maarten, with France acquiring the northern part). With Aruba, the islands formed part of the Dutch West Indies from 1828, and the Netherlands Antilles from 1845, with internal self-government being granted on 29 Dec. 1954. Aruba was separated from 1 Jan. 1986. At a referendum in Nov. 1993 Curaçao voted to remain part of the Netherlands Antilles.

TERRITORY AND POPULATION. The Netherlands Antilles comprise two groups of islands, the Leeward group (Curaçao and Bonaire) being situated 100 km north of the Venezuelan coast and the Windward group (Saba, Sint Eustatius and the southern portion of Sint Maarten) situated 800 km away to the north-east, at the northern end of the Lesser Antilles. The total area is 800 sq. km (308 sq. miles) and the census population in 1995 was 207,333. Willemstad is the capital.

The areas, populations and chief towns of the islands are:

Island	Sq. km	1995 Census	Chief town
Bonaire	288	14,218	Kralendijk
Curaçao	444	151,448	Willemstad
Saba	13	1,200	The Bottom
Sint Eustatius	21	1,900	Oranjestad
Sint Maarten[1]	43	38,567	Philipsburg

[1] The northern portion (St Martin) belongs to France.

Dutch is the official language, but the languages usually spoken are Papiamento (derived from Dutch, Spanish and Portuguese) on Curaçao and Bonaire, and English in the Windward Islands.

Vital statistics (1995), Live births, 3,753; marriages, 1,056; divorces, 521; deaths, 1,363.

CLIMATE. All the islands have a tropical marine climate, with very little difference in temperatures over the year. There is a short rainy season from Oct. to Jan. Willemstad. Feb. 27·7°C, Aug. 29°C. Annual rainfall 499 mm.

CONSTITUTION AND GOVERNMENT. On 29 Dec. 1954, the Netherlands Antilles became an integral part of the Kingdom of the Netherlands but are fully autonomous in internal affairs, and constitutionally equal with the Netherlands and Aruba. The Sovereign of the Kingdom of the Netherlands is Head of State and Government, and is represented by a Governor.

The executive power in internal affairs rests with the Governor and the Council of Ministers, who together form the Government. The Ministers are responsible to a unicameral legislature *(States)* consisting of 27 members (13 from Curaçao, 3 from Bonaire, 3 from Sint Maarten, and 1 each from Saba and Sint Eustatius) elected by universal suffrage. In general elections held for the States on 25 Feb. 1994, in Curaçao 8 seats were won by the *Partido Antia Restrukturá* (PAR), 3 by the *Nationale Volkspartij* (NVP) and 2 by the *Movemiento Anti Nobo* (MAN); in Bonaire 2 by the *Partido Demokrátiko Boneriano* (PDB) and 1 by the *Union Patriótiko Boneriano* (UPB); in Sint Maarten 2 by the *Sint Maarten Patriotic Alliance* (SPA) and 1 by the *Democratic Party of Sint Maarten* (DP of Sint Maarten); in Saba 1 by the *Windward Island People's Movement* (WIPM); and in Sint Eustatius 1 by the *Democratic Party of Sint Eustatius.*

The executive power in external affairs is vested in the Council of Ministers of the Kingdom, in which the Antilles is represented by a Minister Plenipotentiary with full voting powers. On each of the insular communities, local autonomous power is divided between an Island Council (elected by universal suffrage), the Executive Council and the Lieut.-Governor, responsible for law and order.

At a referendum in Curaçao on 19 Nov. 1993, 73% of votes cast favoured maintaining the status quo of Curaçao as part of the Netherlands Antilles. The other options were: Autonomy (18%), unification with the Netherlands (8%) or complete independence (1%). At a referendum in Oct. 1994 Sint Maarten, Sint Eustatius and Saba voted to remain part of the Netherlands Antilles.

Governor: Dr Jaime M. Saleh.

The Cabinet installed in March 1994 was composed as follows in Nov. 1996:
Prime Minister: Miguel A. Pourier (PAR).
Deputy Prime Minister and Traffic and Transport: Leo A. I. Chance (SPA).
Justice: Pedro J. Atacho (PAR). *Finance:* Harold Henriquez (PAR). *Labour and Social Affairs:* Mike Willen (PAR). *Co-operation for Development, Women's and Humanitarian Affairs:* Edith Strauss-Mercera (PDB). *Public Health and Environmental Affairs:* Beatrice Doran Schoop (MAN). *Education, Sport, Culture and Youth Affairs:* Marta B. Dijkhoff (PAR).

ECONOMY

Budget. The central government budget for 1995 envisaged 470·5m. NA guilders revenue and 565·5m. NA guilders expenditure.

Currency. The unit of currency is the *Netherlands Antilles guilder, gulden* (ANG) or *florin* (NAfl.) divided into 100 *cents.* There are notes of 500, 250, 100, 50, 25, 10 and 5 guilder, and coins of 1 guilder and 25, 10, 5 2¹/₂ and 1 cent. The NA guilder has been pegged to the US dollar at US$1 = 1·79 NA guilder since 12 Dec. 1971.

Banking and Finance. At 31 Dec. 1994 the Bank of Netherlands Antilles had total assets and liabilities of 514·4m. NA guilders; commercial banks, 3,913m. NA guilders.

ENERGY AND NATURAL RESOURCES

Electricity. Production (1995) totalled 1000m. kWh.

Oil. The economy was formerly based largely on oil refining at the Shell refinery on Curaçao, but following an announcement by Shell that closure was imminent, this was sold to the Netherlands Antilles government in Sept. 1985, and leased to Petróleos de Venezuela to operate on a reduced scale.

Minerals. Calcium carbonate (limestone) has been mined since 1980; production (1991), 0·32m. tonnes. Production of limestone, 1990 (estimate), 0·36m. tonnes.

Agriculture. Livestock (1992 estimate): Cattle, 1,000; goats, 13,000; pigs, 3,000. (Curaçao, 1991 estimate: Cows, 290; goats, 46,000; pigs, 6,100; sheep, 10,500).

Fisheries. Catch (1991 estimate) 7,700 tonnes.

INDUSTRY AND TRADE

Industry. Curaçao has an oil refinery and a large ship-repair dry docks. Bonaire has a textile factory and a modern equipped salt plant. Sint Maarten's industrial activities are primarily based on a rum factory and a fishing factory.

Labour. In 1992 (census) the economically active population numbered 87,756; unemployment rate 15·3% (Curaçao, 1995: 62,236; unemployment rate 13·1%).

Commerce. There is a Free Zone on Curaçao. Total imports (1994) amounted to 2,622m. (crude and petroleum products, 1,302m.) NA guilders, total exports to 1,835m. (crude and petroleum products, 1,484m.) NA guilders.

Tourism. In 1995, 752,000 tourists visited the islands (Sint Maarten, Curaçao and Bonaire) and there were 757,000 cruise passengers.

COMMUNICATIONS

Roads. In 1989, the Netherlands Antilles had 845 km of surfaced highway distributed as follows: Curaçao, 590; Bonaire, 226; Sint Maarten, 19. Number of motor vehicles registered in 1994, 166,392.

Civil Aviation. There are international airports on Curaçao (Curaçao International Airport), Bonaire (Flamingo Airport) and Sint Maarten (Princess Juliana Airport). In 1995 Curaçao handled 1,196,935 passengers, Bonaire 286,117, Sint Maarten 1,497,359, Sint Eustatius 49,369 and Saba (1994) 45,457. The local carrier, ALM, had 6 aircraft in 1995.

Shipping (1995). 5,152 ships (totalling 31,785,000 GRT) entered the port of Curaçao; 1,011 ships (15,911,000 GRT) entered the port of Bonaire; 1,400 ships entered the port of Sint Maarten. In 1995 Curaçao handled 171,854 passengers; in 1994 Bonaire handled 12,736 and Sint Maarten 718,550.

Telecommunications. Number of telephones, 1995, 75,868. In 1995 there were 32 radio transmitters (8 on Bonaire, 17 on Curaçao, 2 on Saba, 1 on Sint Eustatius and 4 on Sint Maarten) and each island had 1 cable television station. These stations broadcast in Papiamento, Dutch, English and Spanish and are mainly financed by income from advertisements. Broadcasting is administered by Landsradio, Telecommunication Administration and Tele Curaçao. In 1992 there were estimated to be 125,000 radio and 64,000 TV sets (colour by NTSC) in use. In addition, Radio Nederland and Trans World Radio have powerful relay stations operating on medium- and short-waves from Bonaire.

Press. In 1995 there were 9 daily and 2 weekly newspapers.

SOCIAL INSTITUTIONS

Justice. There is a Court of First Instance, which sits in each island, and a Court of Appeal in Willemstad.

Religion. In 1992, 73% of the population were Roman Catholics, 10% were Protestants (Sint Maarten and Sint Eustatius being primarily Protestant).

Education. In 1994–95 there were 23,007 pupils in primary schools, 1,859 pupils in special schools, 8,678 pupils in general secondary schools, 6,685 pupils in junior and senior secondary vocational schools, and 848 students in vocational colleges and universities.

Health. In 1996 there were 314 doctors, 67 dentists, 11 hospitals with 1,466 beds and 1,498 nursing personnel.

DIPLOMATIC REPRESENTATIVE

US Consul-General: James L. Williams (J. B. Gorsiraweg 1, Curaçao).

Further Reading

Central Bureau of Statistics. *Statistical Yearbook of the Netherlands Antilles*

Bank of the Netherlands Antilles. *Annual Report.*

Schoenhals, K., *Netherlands Antilles and Aruba.* [Bibliography] Oxford and Santa Barbara, 1993

NEW ZEALAND

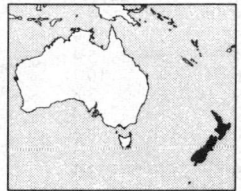

Capital: Wellington
Population: 3·77m.
GDP per head: (PPP$) 16,851
HDI/world rank: 0·937/9

KEY HISTORICAL EVENTS. New Zealand was first called *Aotearoa* by the Maori who migrated from other northern islands in Polynesia, sometime around the 14th century. The first European to discover New Zealand was Tasman in 1642. The coast was explored by Capt. Cook in 1769. From about 1800 onwards, New Zealand became a resort for whalers and traders, chiefly from Australia. New Zealand's European constitutional history can be traced back to 1840 when the Maori entered into an agreement with the Crown under the Treaty of Waitangi and New Zealand became a British colony with the Maori retaining full rights of self-governance. However, the effective administration of the country became the province of European settlers within 12 years, although there were movements for Maori self-government. These movements declined in the early 1900s but the struggle for self-determination has re-emerged over the past decade which has also seen a relative decline in the number of immigrants from England, Scotland and Ireland.

TERRITORY AND POPULATION. New Zealand lies south-east of Australia in the south Pacific, Wellington being 1,983 km from Sydney. There are two principal islands, the North and South Islands, besides Stewart Island, Chatham Islands and small outlying islands, as well as the territories overseas.

New Zealand (*i.e.*, North, South and Stewart Islands) extends over 1,750 km from north to south. Area, excluding territories overseas, 270,534 sq. km comprising North Island, 115,777 sq. km; South Island, 151,215 sq. km; Stewart Island, 1,746 sq. km; Chatham Islands, 963 sq. km. The minor islands (total area, 320 sq. miles, 829 sq. km) included within the geographical boundaries of New Zealand (but not within any local government area) are the following: Kermadec Islands (34 sq. km), Three Kings Islands (8 sq. km), Auckland Islands (606 sq. km), Campbell Island (114 sq. km), Antipodes Islands (62 sq. km), Bounty Islands (1 sq. km), Snares Islands (3 sq. km), Solander Island (1 sq. km). With the exception of meteorological station staff on Raoul Island in the Kermadec Group and Campbell Island there are no inhabitants.

The **Kermadec Islands** were annexed to New Zealand in 1887, have no separate administration and all New Zealand laws apply to them. Situation, 29° 10' to 31° 30' S. lat., 177° 45' to 179° W. long., 1,000 miles NNE of New Zealand. The largest of the group is Raoul or Sunday Island, 29 sq. km, smaller islands being Macaulay and Curtis, while Macaulay Island is 3 miles in circuit.

Growth in census population, exclusive of territories overseas:

	Total population	Average annual increase %		Total population	Average annual increase %
1858	115,462	—	1936	1,573,810	1·13
1878	458,007	7·33	1945[1]	1,702,298	0·83
1881	534,030	5·10	1951[1]	1,939,472	2·37
1886	620,451	3·05	1956[1]	2,174,062	2·31
1891	668,632	1·50	1961[1]	2,414,984	2·12
1896	743,207	2·13	1966[1]	2,676,919	2·10
1901[1]	815,853	1·89	1971[1]	2,862,631	1·34
1906	936,304	2·75	1976[1]	3,129,383	1·71
1911	1,058,308	2·52	1981[1]	3,175,737	0·20
1916[1]	1,149,225	1·50	1986[1]	3,307,084	0·82
1921	1,271,644	2·27	1991[1]	3,434,950	0·77
1926	1,408,139	2·06	1996[1]	3,681,546	7·20

The census of New Zealand is quinquennial, but the census falling in 1931 was abandoned as an act of national economy, and owing to war conditions the census due in 1941 was not taken until 25 Sept. 1945.

[1] Excluding members of the Armed Forces overseas.

The populations of regional councils (all data conforms with boundaries redrawn after the 1989 re-organization of local government) at the 1996 census:

| | Total Population | | Percentage change |
Local Government Region	1991 census	1996 census	1991-96 (%)
Northland	131,620	141,865	7·8
Auckland	953,980	1,077,205	12·9
Waikato	338,959	357,294	5·4
Bay of Plenty	208,163	230,465	10·7
Gisborne	44,387	46,089	3·8
Hawke's Bay	139,479	144,292	3·4
Taranaki	107,222	106,570	–0·6
Manuwatu-Wanganui	226,616	229,989	1·5
Wellington	402,892	416,019	3·3
Total North Island	2,553,413	2,749,788	7·7
Tasman	34,416	40,036	9·9
Nelson	38,003	42,073	10·7
Marlborough	36,765	40,242	9·4
West Coast	33,961	35,671	5·0
Canterbury	446,114	478,912	7·4
Otago	186,067	193,132	3·8
Southland	103,442	100,758	–2·6
Total South Island	881,537	930,824	5·7
Remainder New Zealand[1]	864	934	8·1
Total New Zealand	3,435,814	3,681,546	7·2

[1] Includes Kermadec, Campbell and Chatham Islands and oil rigs.

1997 population estimate, 3·77m.

Between 1986 and 1996, the number of people who identified as of European ethnicity dropped from 81·2% to 71·7%. Pacific Island people made up 4·8% of population in 1996 (3·7% in 1986), Asian ethnic groups went from 1·5% to 4·4% in 1996.

Maori population: 1896, 42,113; 1936, 82,326; 1945, 98,744; 1951, 115,676; 1961, 171,553; 1971, 227,414; 1981, 279,255; 1986, 294,201; 1991, 324,000; 1996, 523,374. This is an increase of 20·4% since 1991. In addition, 579,714 people said they have Maori ancestry, up 13·4% on 1991. There were estimated in 1995 to be 10,123 fully fluent speakers of Maori and a further 12,153 who were at the medium to high fluency level. In the 1996 Census, 153,669 New Zealanders said they could hold a conversation about everyday matters in Maori.

From the 1970s organizations were formed to pursue Maori grievances over loss of land and resources. The Waitangi Tribunal was set up in 1975 as a forum for complaints about breaches of the Treaty of Waitangi, and in 1984 empowered to hear claims against Crown actions since 1840. Direct negotiations with the Crown have been offered to claimants and a range of proposals to resolve historical grievances launched for public discussion in Dec. 1994. These proposals specify that all claims are to be met over 10 years with treaty rights being converted to economic assets. There have been four recent major Treaty settlements: NZ$170m. each for Tainui and Ngai Tahu, the NZ$150m. Sealord fishing agreement and NZ$40m. for Whakatohea in the Bay of Plenty. The Maori Land Court has jurisdiction over Maori freehold land and some general land owned by Maoris under the Te Ture Whenue Maori Act 1993.

Populations of main urban areas as at the 1996 census were as follows:

Auckland	997,940	Invercargill	49,306
Christchurch	331,443	Nelson	52,348
Dunedin	112,279	New Plymouth	49,079
Hamilton	159,234	Rotorua	56,928
Hastings and		Tauranga	82,832
Napier	113,719	Wanganui	41,320
Palmerston North	73,862	Wellington	335,468
Gisborne	32,653	Whangarei	45,785

Vital statistics for calendar years:

	Total live births	Single-parent births	Deaths	Marriages	Divorces (decrees absolute)
1993	58,867	22,355	27,248	22,056	9,193
1994	57,435	22,180	27,092	21,858	9,213
1995	57,791	23,499	27,960	21,579	9,574
1996	57,082	23,722	28,206	21,506	10,009

Birth rate, 1996, 15·50 per 1,000 population; death rate, 7·60; marriage rate, 17·1; infant mortality, 6·68 per 1,000 live births. Population increase 1996, 1·5%. Expectation of life, 1996: Males, 73·7 years; females, 79·1.

In 1996 there were 80,288 immigrants (77,563 in 1995) and 54,212 emigrants (49,077 in 1995).

CLIMATE. Lying in the cool temperate zone, New Zealand enjoys very mild winters for its latitude owing to its oceanic situation, and only the extreme south has cold winters. The situation of the mountain chain produces much sharper climatic contrasts between east and west than in a north-south direction. Observations for mid-summer and mid-winter daily averages in 1990:

	Jan (°C)	July (°C)	Annual rainfall (mm) in 1996
Auckland	23·4	7·8	1,105
Christchurch	21·7	1·5	645
Dunedin	19·1	3·1	800
Hokitika	19·3	2·8	2,810
New Plymouth	21·5	5·4	1,455
Wellington	20·1	5·6	1,270

CONSTITUTION AND GOVERNMENT. Definition was given to the status of New Zealand by the (Imperial) Statute of Westminster of Dec. 1931, which had received the antecedent approval of the New Zealand Parliament in July 1931. The Governor-General's assent was given to the Statute of Westminster Adoption Bill on 25 Nov. 1947.

The powers, duties and responsibilities of the Governor-General and the Executive Council are set out in Royal Letters Patent and Instructions thereunder of 11 May 1917. In the execution of the powers vested in him the Governor-General must be guided by the advice of the Executive Council.

At a referendum on 6 Nov. 1993 a change from a first-past-the-post to a proportional representation electoral system was favoured by 53·9% of votes cast.

Parliament is the *House of Representatives*, since 1996 consisting of 120 members: 60 for general seats, 55 for party list seats and 5 for Maori seats, elected by universal adult suffrage on the mixed-member-proportional system (MMP) for 3-year terms. The 5 Maori electoral districts cover the whole country. Maori and people of Maori descent are entitled to register either for a general or a Maori electoral district. As at Sept. 1997, there were 163,310 persons on the Maori electoral roll. At the next general election there will be six Maori seats.

At the elections on 12 Oct. 1996 the electorate was 2,418,587; turn-out was 88%. 27 parties stood. The National Party (NP) gained 44 seats with 34·13% of votes cast (83·31% in 1993), the Labour Party 37 with 28·27% (34·68%), New Zealand First (NZF) 17 with 13·13% (8·4%), the Alliance coalition 13 with 10·12% (18·21%), Association of Consumers and Tax Payers (ACT) 8 with 6·17%, United Party 1 with 0·91%. In Dec. 1997, Prime Minister Jim Bolger was ousted as leader of the National Party. He was replaced by Jenny Shipley who became the country's first woman prime minister.

Governor-General: Sir Michael Hardie Boys, GCMG, GNZM (b. 1931; sworn in March 1996).

An NP-NZF coalition government was formed on 16 Dec. 1996 which in March 1998 consisted of:

Prime Minister: Jenny Shipley (b. 1952; NP).

Deputy Prime Minister, Treasurer: Winston Peters (NZF). *Minister of Foreign*

Affairs and Trade, Pacific Island Affairs, Disarmament and Arms Controls: Don McKinnon (NP). *Finance, Revenue:* Bill Birch (NP). *State Services, State-owned Enterprises, Audit Department and Radio NZ:* Tony Ryall (NP). *Attorney General, Justice, Courts, Treaty of Waitangi Negotiations:* Doug Graham. *Maori Affairs, Racing:* Tau Henare (NZF). *Defence, Labour, Immigration, Energy and Business Development:* Max Bradford (NP). *Agriculture, Forestry, International Trade:* Lockwood Smith (NP). *Employment:* Peter McCardle (NP). *Education, Courts, Ministerial Services and Leader of the House:* Wyatt Creech (NP). *Environment, State Services, Cultural Affairs and Crown Research Institutes:* Simon Upton (NP). *Police, Civil Defence, Internal Affairs:* Jack Elder (NZF). *Health,:* Bill English (NP). *Commerce, Fisheries, Lands, Biosecurity, Industry:* John Luxton (NP). *Transport, Research, Science and Technology, Communications, Information Technology, Local Government, Statistics:* Maurice Williamson (NP). *Minister in charge of the Valuation Department, Customs and Public Trust Office:* John Delamere (NZF). *Housing, Tourism, Sport, Fitness and Leisure, Accident Rehabilitation and Compensation Insurance:* Murray McCully (NP). *Social Welfare, War Pensions:* Roger Sowry. *Conservation, Corrections:* Dr Nick Smith (NP).

There are also 1 NP and 3 NZF ministers outside the Cabinet.

National anthem: God Defend New Zealand; words by T. Bracken, tune by J. J. Woods. There is a Maori version, Aotearoa, words by T. H. Smith. The UK national anthem has equal status.

Local Government. Since the reform of local government in Nov. 1989 it comprises 12 regional councils, 74 territorial authorities (15 city councils, 58 district councils and the Chatham Islands council), 155 community boards and 6 special authorities. Territorial authorities and regional councils are directly elected. A city must have a minimum of 50,000 persons, be predominantly urban in character, be a distinct entity and a major centre of activity within the region. A district, on the other hand, serves a combination of rural and urban communities. There is no distinction in structural status or responsibility between a city council and a district council. There are a few other local authorities created for specific functions.

Local elections were held on 14 Oct. 1995.

Bush, G., *Local Government and Politics in New Zealand.* Auckland, 1995
Joseph, P. A., *Constitutional Law in New Zealand.* Sydney, 1993.—(ed.) *Essays on the Constitution.* Sydney, 1995
McGee, D. G., *Parliamentary Practice in New Zealand.* 2nd ed. Wellington, 1994
Ringer, J. B., *An Introduction to New Zealand Government.* Christchurch, 1992
Vowles, J. and Aimer, P. (eds.) *Double Decision: the 1993 Election and Referendum in New Zealand.* Victoria (Wellington) Univ. Press, 1994

DEFENCE. The control and co-ordination of defence activities is obtained through the Ministry of Defence.

The total expenditure for defence in 1995-96 was NZ$1,382,778 (1·5% of GDP). New Zealand forces serve abroad in Australia and Singapore, and with UN peace-keeping missions.

Army. The Army is organized into Land Command, 2 Land Force Groups, 1 armoured regiment, 2 infantry battalions, 1 artillery, 1 engineer regiment and 2 special forces squadrons. Major equipment of the NZ Army includes: 8 Scorpion armoured reconnaissance vehicles, 78 armoured personnel carriers, 491 Land-Rover 4x4, 351 Unimog 4 tonne trucks, 18 105-mm Howitzer guns and 5 very low level air defence ground to air missile systems will be introduced.

Personnel total: regular force 4,540 (540 women), territorial force 3,539 and civilian employees 832.

Navy. On 1 Jan. 1998, the Navy comprised 1 Anzac class frigate (Te Kaha) with a second (Te Mana) due to enter service in 1999, 3 Leander frigates (Canterbury, Wellington, Waikato - the latter to be decommissioned in June 1998), 1 12,400-tonne fleet replenishment tanker (Endeavour), 1 naval sea-lift vessel (Charles Upham), 1 diving support vessel (Manawanui), 1 oceanographic survey and 2 inshore survey vessels plus 4 inshore patrol craft. Wasp helicopters are currently embarked but are being replaced by 4 Kaman SH 2G helicopters during 1998, which in turn will be replaced by 5 Kaman SH 2F helicopters in 2000. The main base and Fleet headquarters is at Auckland.

At 1 Jan. 1998, the Royal New Zealand Navy personnel totalled 2,080 uniformed plus 405 Reserve personnel and 562 civilians.

Air Force. Maritime (P-3K Orion), long and medium-range transport (Boeing 727 and C-130H Hercules), and helicopter (UH-1H Iroquois and HAS1 Wasp) squadrons are based at RNZAF Base Auckland, and air attack force (A-4) Skyhawk at RNZAF Base Ohakea and RANAS Nowra (Australia). Flying training is conducted at Ohakea, (CT/4B) Airtrainer and (MB 339CB) Macchi, and Auckland (Andover and Sioux). Ground training is carried out at RNZAF Base Woodbourne.

The uniform strength in 1997 was 3,235 (560 women), and 480 civilian personnel, with 38 combat aircraft.

Rolfe, J., *Defending New Zealand.* Wellington, 1993

INTERNATIONAL RELATIONS

Membership. New Zealand is a member of the UN, the Commonwealth, OECD, the Pacific Community, South Pacific Forum and the Colombo Plan.

ECONOMY

Performance. GDP at current prices grew 4·4% to NZ$95,816m. in the year ended March 1997, an increase of 2·4% in constant prices. The previous year's growth was respectively 3·1% and 6·9%.

Budget. The following tables of revenue and expenditure relate to the Consolidated Account, which covers the ordinary revenue and expenditure of the government— *i.e.*, apart from capital items, commercial and special undertakings, advances, etc. Total revenue and expenditure of the Consolidated Account, in NZ$1m., year ended 30 June:

	1993	1994	1995	1996	1997
Revenue	29,835	30,183	33,648	35,059	34,778
Expenditure	31,429	29,639	30,400	31,743	32,953

1997 tax revenue included (in NZ$1m.): Income tax, NZ$15,324; company tax, NZ$3,233; withholding taxes, NZ$1,932; domestic goods and services, NZ$7,725. Non-tax revenue was NZ$2,862m.

The gross public debt at June 1997 was NZ$35,972m., of which NZ$29,625m. was held in New Zealand currency and NZ$6,347m. in foreign currency. The gross annual interest charge on the public debt at June 1997 was NZ$3,072m. (1996 NZ$3,703m.).

New Zealand System of National Accounts. National Accounts aggregates for 5 years are given in the following table (in NZ$1m.):

Year ended 31 March	Gross domestic product	Gross national product	National income
1992	73,213	69,700	62,839
1993	77,067	74,281	67,090
1994	80,864	77,644	70,506
1995	86,304	82,145	73,865
1996	91,045	85,561	77,072

Currency. The monetary unit is the *New Zealand dollar* (NZD), of 100 *cents*. There are notes of NZ$5, 10, 20, 50 and 100; and coins of 5c, 10c, 20c, 50c, NZ$1 and NZ$2. Inflation was 1·1% at 30 June 1997.

Banking and Finance. The central bank and bank of issue is the Reserve Bank (*Governor*, Dr Don Brash).

The financial system comprises a central bank (the Reserve Bank of New Zealand), registered banks, and other financial institutions. Registered banks include banks from abroad, which have to satisfy capital adequacy and managerial quality requirements. Other financial institutions include the regional trustee banks, now grouped under Trust Bank, building societies, finance companies, merchant banks and stock and station agents. The number of registered banks was 18 in 1997. Around 99% of the assets of the New Zealand banking system were under the ownership of a foreign bank parent.

The primary functions of the Reserve Bank are the formulation and implementation of monetary policy to achieve the economic objectives set by the Government, and the promotion of the efficiency and soundness of the financial system, through the registration of banks, and supervision of financial institutions. Since 1996 supervision has been conducted on a basis of public disclosure by banks of their activities every quarter.

On 30 June 1996 the funding (financial liabilities including deposits) and claims (financial assets including loans) for all registered banks and other financial institutions were: Funding, NZ$119,028m. (foreign currency, NZ$11,800m.); claims, NZ$104,053m. (foreign currency, NZ$3,690m.).

The stock exchange in Wellington conducts on-screen trading, unifying the 3 former trading floors in Auckland, Christchurch and Wellington.

Weights and Measures. The metric system of weights and measures operates.

ENERGY AND NATURAL RESOURCES

Electricity. On 1 April 1987 the former Electricity Division of the Ministry of Energy became a state-owned enterprise, the Electricity Corporation of N.Z. Ltd. In 1995 it had 40 power stations (31 hydro-electric and 9 thermal, with a total nominal capacity of 7,268 MW) producing almost 100% of the country's electricity. The remainder is generated by the Electrical Supply Authorities from 23 small plants.

A wind farm was opened in 1996.

Statistics for 6 years ended 31 March are:

	1991	1992	1993	1994	1995	1996
Total sales revenue (NZ$1m.)	1,580	1,589	1,543	1,700	1,520	1,383
Total sales volume (gwh)	27,892	28,660	27,753	29,228	29,780	. . .
Generation (gwh) (nett)	29,556	30,339	29,569	32,453	33,415	32,653
Number of employees	3,974	3,096	2,861	2,835	. . .	. . .
Production/total staff employed (gwh/person)	7·46	8·89	9·93	10·95	. . .	. . .

With privatization much of this material is no longer attainable.

Oil. Crude oil production was 69 petajoules in 1996.

Natural Gas. In 1996 there were 5 gasfields in production, with an output of 180 petajoules.

Agriculture. Two-thirds of the land area is suitable for agriculture and grazing. The total area under cultivation at 30 June 1994 was 16,606,969 ha (including residential area and domestic orchards). There were 13,535,699 ha of grassland, lucerne and tussock, 103,789 ha of land for horticulture and 1,488,082 ha of plantations of exotic timber.

The largest freehold estates are held in the South Island. The number of occupied holdings as at 30 June 1995 were as follows:

Regional Council	No. of farms	Total area of farms 1,000 ha)	Regional Council	No. of farms	Total area of farms 1,000 ha)
Northland	5,770	862	Marlborough	1,413	702
Auckland	5,298	310	Nelson	132	15
Waikato	11,954	1,734	West Coast	890	407
Bay of Plenty	5,511	628	Canterbury	9,381	3,408
Gisborne	1,394	699	Otago	3,895	2,507
Hawke's Bay	3,860	1,086	Southland	4,575	1,257
Taranaki	3,963	497	Tasman	1,919	272
Wanganui and Manawatu	6,612	1,611	*Total South Island*	*22,165*	*8,638*
Wellington	2,249	512			
Total North Island	*46,611*	*7,940*	*Total New Zealand*	*68,776*	*16,578*

The area and yield for each of the principal crops are given as follows (area and yield for threshing only, not including that grown for chaff, hay, silage, etc.):

	Wheat		Maize		Barley	
Crop years	Area (1,000 ha)	Yield (1,000 tonnes)	Area (1,000 ha)	Yield (1,000 tonnes)	Area (1,000 ha)	Yield (1,000 tonnes)
1992	37·8	191·0	18·0	163·8	67·4	318·8
1993	40·9	219·4	15·9	133·1	79·8	389·5
1994	44·7	241·9	14·7	142·8	76·9	395·5
1995	52·4	245·2	16·5	160·8	68·2	302·8

In 1996, a total of 2,205,568 (provisional) tonnes of fertilizer were sold.

Livestock 1995 (in 1,000): Dairy cattle, 4,090; beef cattle, 5,182; sheep, 48,816; deer, 1,179; goats, 283; pigs, 431. Total meat produced in the year ended 30 Sept. 1996 was estimated at 1·4m. tonnes (including 619,000 tonnes of beef and 378,000 tonnes of lamb). Total liquid milk produced in the year ended March 1995 was 8,997m. litres.

Production of wool for 1995–96, 199,000 (rounded figure) tonnes.

Forestry. Forests cover 7·9m. ha of New Zealand's land area. Of this, about 6·4m. ha are indigenous forest and 1·5m. ha planted productive forest. New planting has increased from 15,000 ha in 1991 to 71,000 ha in 1995. Introduced pines form the bulk of the large exotic forest estate and among these radiata pine is the best multi-purpose tree, reaching log size in 25–30 years. Other species planted are Douglas fir and Eucalyptus species. The table below shows production of rough sawn timber in 1,000 cu. metres for years ending 31 March:

	Indigenous			Exotic			All Species
	Rimu and Miro	Beech	Total	Exotic Pines	Douglas Fir	Total	Total
1991–92	51	4	63	1,935	221	2,238	2,301
1992–93	55	4	67	2,281	160	2,567	2,634
1993–94	66	4	79	2,497	123	2,736	2,810
1994–95	66	7	79	2,591	128	2,870	2,949
1995–96	44	4	55	2,631	104	2,849	2,904

In March 1996, forest industries consisted of 440 saw-mills, 13 plywood and veneer plants, 3 particle board mills, 6 pulp and paper mills and 5 fibreboard mills.

The basic products of the pulp and paper mills are mechanical and chemical pulp which are converted into newsprint, kraft and other papers, paperboard and fibreboard. Production of woodpulp, 31 March 1996, amounted to 1·40m. tonnes and of paper (including newsprint paper and paperboard) to 892,969 tonnes.

Fisheries. The total value of New Zealand Fisheries exports during the year ended 30 June 1995 was NZ$1,105·5m. Exports: Fish, 175,400 tonnes, value NZ$705·6m.; crustaceans, 3,157 tonnes, value NZ$131·5m.

INDUSTRY. Statistics of manufacturing industries:

			Stocks (NZ$1m.)			Ratio of
Production year	Hours worked	Salaries and wages paid (NZ$1m.)	Materials	Finished goods	Sales and other income (NZ$1m.)	total stocks to sales
1995–96	498·2m.	8,083	10,864	15,342	51,341	...

The following is a statement of the provisional value of the products (including repairs) of the principal industries for the year 1994–95 (in NZ$1m.):

Industry group	Purchases and operating expenses	Sales and other income	Additions to fixed tangible assets
Primary food	9,495	10,791	467
Textiles, apparel and leathergoods	2,298	3,171	88
Wood and wood products (including furniture)	2,884	4,056	186
Paper and paper products, printing and publishing	3,217	4,886	346
Chemicals and chemical, petroleum, coal, rubber and plastic products	4,313	6,103	463

Industry group	Purchases and operating expenses	Sales and other income	Additions to fixed tangible assets
Non-metallic mineral products	908	1,344	61
Basic metal industries	1,503	1,849	105
Fabricated metal products, machinery and equipment	7,642	10,477	338
Other manufacturing industries	296	418	15
Total	37,865	49,954	2,373

Labour. There were 1,690,200 persons employed in the June quarter 1997, 753,200 females. Unemployment was 6·6% of the workforce in the same quarter. Seasonally adjusted unemployment figures for the Sept. quarter 1997, 124,000.

In the 1996 March year 39,500 had been unemployed for longer than 6 months. The weekly average wage in the Aug. quarter 1997 was NZ$736·82 for men, NZ$547·18 for women. A minimum wage is set by the government annually. In 1997 it was NZ$7 an hour. In 1997 a minimum wage was fixed for 16-19 year old workers, NZ$4·20 an hour. In 1997, the year to Aug., there were 62 industrial stoppages (73 in 1996) with 47,719 working days lost (42,690 in 1996).

Trade Unions. In 1997, 22 industrial unions of workers (representing 80% of all union members) were affiliated to the council of Trade Unions (*President*, Ken Douglas). Compulsory trade union membership was made illegal in 1991, and the national wage award system was replaced by local wage agreements under the Employment Contracts Act 1991. In Dec. 1996, 339,327 persons (19·9% of the workforce) belonged to trade unions (409,112 in Dec. 1993, 603,118 in May 1991).

FOREIGN ECONOMIC RELATIONS. Total overseas debt was NZ$7,550m. in March 1997. In 1990 New Zealand and Australia completed the Closer Economic Relations Agreement (initiated in 1983), which provides for mutual free trade in goods.

Commerce. Trade (excluding specie and bullion) in NZ$1m. for 12 months ended 30 June:

	Total merchandise imported (v.f.d.)[1]	Exports of domestic produce	Re-exports	Total merchandise exported (f.o.b.)
1992–93	15,979·4	18,240·4	730·3	18,970·8
1993–94	17,019·3	19,166·4	660·7	19,827·1
1994–95	19,746·4	20,199·8	725·1	20,924·9
1995–96	21,352·5	19,958·8	586·9	20,545·7

[1] Value for duty.

The principal imports for the 12 months ended 30 June 1997:

Commodity	Value (NZ$1m. v.f.d.)
Fruit	132·5
Sugar and sugar confectionery	139·3
Beer, wine and spirits	152·9
Crude petroleum oil	754·2
Inorganic chemicals (excluding aluminium oxide)	160·8
Aluminium oxide	190·2
Knitted or crocheted fabrics and articles	283·5
Glass and glassware	127·8
Iron and steel	346·3
Articles of iron and steel	320·7
Copper and articles of copper	101·8
Aluminium and articles of aluminium	202·3
Tools, implements and articles of base metals	206·6
Machinery and mechanical appliances	3,102·5
Organic chemicals	254·8
Pharmaceutical products	531·3
Plastics and articles of plastic	829·3
Rubber and articles of rubber	248·8
Paper, paperboard and articles thereof	568·8

Commodity	Value (NZ$1m. v.f.d.)
Printed books, newspapers etc.	314·4
Cotton yarn and fabrics	88·1
Man-made filaments and fibres	177·8
Electrical machinery and equipment	2,124·2
Motor cars, station wagons, utilities	1,647·9
Trucks, buses and vans	374·3
Aircraft	303·4
Ships and boats	298·2
Optical, photographic, technical and surgical equipment	649·8

The principal exports of New Zealand produce for the 12 months ended 30 June 1997 were:

Commodity	Value (NZ$1m. f.o.b.)	Commodity	Value (NZ$1m. f.o.b.)
Live animals	125·3	Fish, fresh, chilled or frozen	688·6
Meat, fresh, chilled or frozen		Vegetables	270·9
Beef and veal	992·7	Fresh kiwifruit	376·8
Lamb and mutton	1,502·5	Fresh apples	342·0
Dairy products		Forest products	
Milk, cream and yoghurt	1,738·1	Sawn timber and logs	1,140·4
Butter	917·4	Paper and paper products	365·4
Cheese	838·4	Wood pulp	356·7
Raw hides, skins and leather	662·2	Iron and steel and	
Wool	946·3	articles thereof	416·7
Aluminium and		Machinery and	
articles thereof	810·9	mechanical appliances	759·1
Casein and caseinates	569·4	Electrical machinery and	
Plastic materials and		equipment	575·6
articles thereof	261·1		
Sausage casings	127·6		

The following table shows the trade with different countries for the year ended 30 June (in NZ$1m.):

Countries	Imports v.f.d. from		Exports and re-exports f.o.b. to		
	1994	1995	1994	1995	1996
Total EU countries	3,073·9	3,555·0	3,058·2	3,263·1	3,423·3
Australia	3,656·9	4,146·4	4,162·2	4,342·4	4,275·7
Belgium	122·9	135·5	239·1	224·1	307·3
Canada	263·1	280·9	361·9	334·6	313·1
China	516·6	644·2	528·6	544·7	559·7
Fiji	—	—	215·7	193·3	188·1
France	295·1	331·6	211·6	232·1	191·2
Germany	754·2	910·6	490·8	507·8	512·1
Hong Kong	207·0	213·1	481·9	595·6	574·9
Iran	—	—	72·8	68·1	67·1
Italy	448·4	427·8	265·3	290·4	300·9
Japan	2,693·9	2,916·1	2,886·8	3,416·6	3,137·7
Korea, Republic of	272·6	308·7	928·6	398·5	978·3
Malaysia	202·7	257·2	392·8	120·6	491·6
Netherlands	195·3	214·5	123·1	89·3	114·8
Peru	—	—	88·4	194·7	80·5
Philippines	—	—	202·1	168·6	293·6
Saudi Arabia	339·0	254·9	215·9	281·3	192·2
Singapore	279·6	377·5	269·6	—	283·0
Sweden	301·3	340·1	—	—	—
Switzerland	200·7	187·9	—	623·3	—
Taiwan	487·1	536·6	507·3	260·6	552·9
Thailand	134·4	142·3	192·2	192·2	282·4
UK	1,036·5	1,233·2	1,182·3	1,290·5	1,358·8
USA	3,072·5	4,022·4	2,228·7	2,168·3	2,085·7

Tourism. There were 1,441,838 tourists in the year to March 1996 (including 409,326 from Australia, 151,823 from the USA, 157,970 from Japan and 126,076 from the UK). International visitor expenditure for 1996 was NZ$3,554m.

COMMUNICATIONS

Roads. Total length of maintained roads at 30 June 1996 was 91,864 km, of which 55,855 sealed and 36,009 gravel. There were 15,800 bridges. There were 74 national and provincial state highways comprising 10,453 km of roadway, including the principal arterial traffic routes.

Total expenditure on roads, streets and bridges by the central government and local authorities combined for the financial year 1995–96 amounted to NZ$624m.

At 31 March 1996 motor vehicles licensed numbered 2,540,006, of which 1,635,718 were cars and 14,981 omnibuses, public taxis and 47,196 motor cycles. Included in the remaining numbers were 2,102 power cycles, 342,246 lorries and 341,841 trailers and caravans.

In 1997 there were 539 deaths in road accidents (513 in 1996).

Railways. New Zealand Rail was privatized in 1993 and is now known as Tranz Rail. In 1996 there were 4,439 km of 1,067 mm gauge railway open for traffic (524 km electrified). In 1995–96, NZ rail carried 10·3m. tonnes and 10·9m. passengers. Operating profit in 1997 was NZ$86·1m. Three rail/road ferries maintain a regular service between the North and South Islands, and in 1994 a 24-hour freight link was introduced between Auckland and Christchurch.

Civil Aviation. There are international airports at Wellington, Auckland and Christchurch. The national carrier is Air New Zealand, which in 1997 operated 11 B-737-200, 5 B-747-200, 5 747-400, 2 B-767-200 and 8 B-767-300. Ansett New Zealand also provides services, as do Aerolíneas Argentinas, Air Calédonie International, Air Pacific, Air Vanuatu, American Airlines, Ansett Australia, British Airways, Canadian Airlines, Cathay Pacific, EVA, Evergreen International, Garuda Indonesia, JAL, Korean Air, Lufthansa, Malaysia Airlines, Mandarin Airlines, Polynesian Airlines, Qantas, Royal Tongan Airlines, Singapore Airlines, Solomon Airlines, Thai Airways, Lan Chile, Polar Air, Asian Express and United Airlines. Trans-Tasman air travel is subject to agreement between Air New Zealand and Qantas.

Air New Zealand and Ansett New Zealand are the major domestic carriers.

Shipping. In 1995 sea-going shipping totalled 0·26m. GRT, including oil tankers, 94,169 GRT.

Telecommunications. The provision of postal and telecommunication services is the responsibility of the state-owned New Zealand Post, which began operations on 1 April 1987; the Telecom Corporation of New Zealand, formed in 1987 and privatized in 1990; and CLEAR Communications, which began operations in Dec. 1990. In 1996-7, there were 1·719m. main lines, 477 per 1,000 people. New Zealand Post ran the only telegram service in 1996. In 1996 there were 288 post shops, 683 post centre franchises and 3,599 stamp resellers.

Legislation of 1995 split the state-owned Radio New Zealand into a government-owned public radio broadcasting company and some 40 commercial stations. Television New Zealand operates 2 channels. 2 other channels, TV3 and TV4, are commercial. There are also regional TV networks. Pay television was introduced in May 1990 – Sky Entertainment operates on 5 channels. The New Zealand Public Radio Service also includes the Radio New Zealand International, a short-wave which broadcasts to the South Pole. In Nov. 1996, there were over 180 radio stations including 21 regional Maori stations for the promotion of Maori culture and 10 community access radio stations. Number of TV receiving licences was approximately 1,126,000.

Cinemas. There were 217 screens in 1993; attendances totalled 13·3m. in 1994.

Press. There were, in 1996, 28 daily newspapers. The *New Zealand Herald* published in Auckland has the largest daily circulation of 226,702. Other dailies range from 2,200–100,000 copies.

SOCIAL INSTITUTIONS

Justice. The judiciary consists of the Court of Appeal, the High Court and District

Courts. All exercise both civil and criminal jurisdiction. Final appeal lies to the Privy Council in London. Special courts include the Maori Land Court, the Maori Appellate Court, Family Courts, the Youth Court, Environment Court and the Employment Court. During 1996 prisons contained an average 4,216 prisoners. Some 515,809 offences, including 52 murders were reported in the year ending June 1996. The death penalty for murder was replaced by life imprisonment in 1961.

The Criminal Injuries Compensation Act, 1963, which came into force on 1 Jan. 1964, provided for compensation of persons injured by certain criminal acts and the dependants of persons killed by such acts. However, this has now been phased out in favour of the Accident Compensation Act, 1982, except in the residual area of property damage caused by escapees. The Offenders Legal Aid Act 1954 provides that any person charged or convicted of any offence may apply for legal aid which may be granted depending on the person's means and the gravity of the offence etc. Since 1970 legal aid in civil proceedings (except divorce) has been available for persons of small or moderate means. The Legal Services Act 1991 now brings together in one statute the civil and criminal legal aid schemes.

Police. The police are a national body maintained by the central government. Legislation of 1994 permits the private management of prisons and prisoner escort services. The total authorized establishment at June 1996 was 6,589. The total cost of law and order for the year 1995–96 was NZ$1,237m. (NZ$581m. for the police). In 1991 1,100 traffic officers merged with the police, who previously did not control traffic.

Ombudsmen. The office of Ombudsman was created in 1962. From 1975 additional Ombudsmen have been authorized. There are currently two. Ombudsmen's functions are to investigate complaints under the Ombudsman Act, the Official Information Act and the Local Government Official Information and Meetings Act from members of the public relating to administrative decisions of central, regional and local government.

During the year ended 30 June 1996, a total of 5,167 complaints were received, 49 of which were sustained and 593 were still under investigation.

Religion. No direct state aid is given to any form of religion. For the Church of England the country is divided into 7 dioceses, with a separate bishopric (Aotearoa) for the Maori. The Presbyterian Church is divided into 23 presbyteries and the Maori Synod. The Moderator is elected annually. The Methodist Church is divided into 10 districts; the President is elected annually. The Roman Catholic Church is divided into 4 dioceses, with the Archbishop of Wellington as Metropolitan Archbishop.

	Number of adherents	
Religious denomination	1991 census	1996 census
Church of England	732,048	631,764
Presbyterian	541,050	458,289
Roman Catholic (including 'Catholic' undefined)	498,612	473,112
Methodist	139,494	121,650
Baptist	70,155	53,613
Brethren	20,337	19,950
Ratana	47,592	36,450
Buddhist	12,765	28,131
Salvation Army	19,992	14,625
Latter-day Saints (Mormon)	48,009	41,166
Pentecostal	25,368	39,228
Seventh-day Adventist	13,005	12,324
Hindu	17,661	25,293
Jehovah's Witnesses	19,182	19,524
Assemblies of God	17,226	17,520
All other religious affiliations	164,687	273,732
No religion	672,654	893,910
Not specified	56,286	187,881
Object to state	251,709	256,593
Total	3,373,926	3,618,303

Education. New Zealand has 7 universities, the University of Auckland, University of Waikato (at Hamilton), Victoria University of Wellington, Massey University (at Palmerston North), the University of Canterbury (at Christchurch), the University of Otago (at Dunedin) and Lincoln University (near Christchurch). The number of students in 1996 was 105,690. There were 5 teachers' training colleges with 12,390 students in 1996.

In 1996 there were 320 state secondary schools with 14,119 full-time teachers and 206,153 pupils. There were also 51 state composite area schools with 4,509 scholars in the secondary division. 95,346 students were enrolled in polytechnic courses in 1996, of these 51,568 were part-time. In 1996, 3,364 pupils received tuition from the secondary department of the correspondence school. There were 19 registered private secondary schools with 553 teachers and 11,249 pupils.

In 1996, there were 2,240 state primary schools (including intermediate and state contributing schools), with 422,596 pupils; the number of teachers was 21,177. A correspondence school for children in remote areas and those otherwise unable to attend school had 4,629 primary and secondary pupils. There were 61 registered private primary and intermediate schools with 446 teachers and 12,765 pupils.

Education is compulsory between the ages of 6 and 15. Children aged 3 and 4 years may enrol at the 594 free kindergartens maintained by Free Kindergarten Associations, which receive government assistance. There are also 557 play centres which also receive government subsidy. In 1996 there were 46,960 and 17,596 children on the rolls respectively. There are also 1,213 child care centres with 57,582 children, 767 *kohanga reo* (providing early childhood education in the Maori language) with 14,302 children, and a number of other smaller providers of early childhood care and education.

Total budgeted expenditure in 1996–97 on education was NZ$5,353m.

The universities are autonomous bodies. All state-funded primary and secondary schools are controlled by boards of trustees. Education in state schools is free for children under 19 years of age. All educational institutions are reviewed every 3 years by teams of educational reviewers.

A series of reforms is being implemented by the government following reports of 18 working groups on tertiary education. These include a new funding system, begun in 1991 and based solely on student numbers.

Health. At 30 June 1996 there were 11,557 doctors on the medical register. In 1996 there were 15,270 public hospital beds. There are 4 regional health authorities, but these are being amalgamated into one transitional health authority. Total expenditure on health in 1995–96 was NZ$5,163m.

Social Welfare. Non-contributory old-age pensions were introduced in 1898. Large reductions in welfare expenditure were introduced by the government in Dec. 1990.

At 1 April 1997 Family Support for families on the lowest incomes was NZ$44·50 for the first child aged under 16, NZ$37·50 for subsequent children aged 13–15, and NZ$29·50 under 13. Child allowance for single persons with one child was NZ$209·30 per week; with 2 or more children, NZ$244·12 per week.

The weekly unemployment benefit in April 1997 for a single person aged 25 and over was NZ$146·13, aged 16–17 NZ$97·97 and aged 18–24 NZ$121·77. Persons made redundant become eligible for benefit after 26 weeks. In 1991 subsidized housing was replaced by cash subsidies.

In 1993 earners of NZ$17,500 a year and less received subsidized health care; a lesser subsidy applied up to NZ$27,000; over that health care was paid for by patients.

In the budget of July 1991 it was announced that current rates of Guaranteed Retirement Income Scheme (GRI) payment would be frozen until 1 April 1993, thereafter to be on the previous year's consumer price index. On 1 April 1992 GRI was replaced by the National superannuation scheme which is income-tested. Eligibility will be gradually increased to 65 years by 2001. Universal eligibility is available at 70 years. At 1 April 1997 a married couple received NZ$379·04 per week, a single person NZ$252·82 per week.

Social Welfare Benefits and War Pensions:

Benefits	Number in force at 30 June 1995	Total payments 1995–96 (NZ$1,000)
SOCIAL WELFARE:		
Monetary—		
National Superannuation	459,901	5,170,506
Widows	9,047	85,008
Invalids	42,450	494,849
Miners	n/a	n/a
Orphans	4,662	22,929
Domestic purposes	108,789	1,440,122
Unemployment	134,133	1,276,540
Sickness	33,386	378,850
War pensions	6,559	60,612
Training	11,389	96,973
Total	810,316	9,026,389

Health benefits in 1996: Payments for primary services, NZ$322·2m.; pharmaceutical, NZ$695·93m.

Reciprocity with Other Countries. There are reciprocal arrangements between New Zealand and Australia in respect of age, invalids', widows', family, unemployment and sickness benefits, and between New Zealand and the UK in respect of family, age, superannuation, widows', orphans', invalids', sickness and unemployment benefits. Some of these payments are also available to former New Zealand residents living in Canada (effective 1 May 1997) and New Zealand pays people eligible for New Zealand Superannuation or veterans' pensions who live in the Cook Islands, Niue or Tokelau.

DIPLOMATIC REPRESENTATIVES

Of New Zealand in Great Britain (New Zealand Hse., Haymarket, London, SW1Y 4TQ)
High Commissioner: Dr Richard Grant.

Of Great Britain in New Zealand (44 Hill St., Wellington, 1)
High Commissioner: Robert J. Alston, CMG.

Of New Zealand in the USA (37 Observatory Cir., NW, Washington, D.C., 20008)
Ambassador: L. John Wood.

Of the USA in New Zealand (29 Fitzherbert Terr., Wellington)
Ambassador: Josiah Beeman.

Of New Zealand to the United Nations
Ambassador: Michael J. Powles.

Of New Zealand to the European Union
Ambassador: Derek Leask.

Further Reading

Statistics New Zealand. *New Zealand Official Yearbook.—Key Statistics: a monthly Abstract of Statistics.—New Zealand in Profile: annual publication.*
Dictionary of New Zealand Biography. vol 1 (to 1868). Wellington, 1990
Encyclopaedia of New Zealand. 3 vols. Wellington, 1966
Alley, R., *New Zealand and the Pacific.* Boulder (CO), 1984
Belich, J., *Making peoples: a History of the new Zealanders from Polynesian Settlement to the end of the Nineteenth century.* London, 1997
Grover, R. R., *New Zealand.* [Bibliography] Oxford and Santa Barbara, 1981
Harland, B., *On Our Own: New Zealand in a Tripolar World.* Victoria Univ. Press, 1992
Harris, P. and Levine, S. (eds.) *The New Zealand politics source book.* 2nd ed. Palmerston North, 1994
Hawke, G. R., *The Making of New Zealand: an Economic History.* CUP, 1985
Massey, P., *New Zealand: Market Liberalization in a Developed Economy.* London, 1995

Oliver, W. H. (ed.) *The Oxford History of New Zealand.* OUP, 1981
Sinclair, K., *A History of New Zealand.* 2nd ed. London, 1980 —. (ed.) *The Oxford Illustrated History of New Zealand.* 2nd ed. OUP, 1994

For other more specialized titles see under CONSTITUTION AND GOVERNMENT and DEFENCE, *above.*

National statistical office: Statistics New Zealand, POB 2922, Wellington, 1.
Website: http://www.stats.govt.nz/statsweb.nsf

TERRITORIES OVERSEAS

Territories Overseas coming within the jurisdiction of New Zealand consist of Tokelau and the Ross Dependency.

Tokelau. Situated some 500 km to Samoa's north and comprises three dispersed atolls, Atafu, Fakaofo and Nukunonu. The land area is 12 sq. km. and the population at the 1996 census was 1,487.

The British Government transferred administrative control of Tokelau to New Zealand in 1925. Formal sovereignty was transferred to New Zealand in 1948 by act of the New Zealand Parliament. New Zealand statue law however does not apply to Tokelau unless it is expressly extended to Tokelau. In practice New Zealand legislation is extended to Tokelau only with its consent.

Tokelau's three villages are its foundation, and have remained largely autonomous. There has never been any resident New Zealand administration. At the national level Tokelau's needs remain formally the responsibility of the New Zealand Government, and in particular, the Administration of Tokelau.

Under a programme agreed in 1992, the role of Tokelau's political institutions is being better defined and expanded. The process under way enables the base of Tokelau government to be located within Tokelau's national level institutions rather than as before, within a public service located largely in Samoa. In 1994, the Administrator's powers were delegated to the General Fono (the national representative body), and when the General Fono is not in session, to the Council of Faipule. The Tokelau Amendment Act 1996 conferred on the General Fono a power to make rules for Tokelau, including the power to impose taxes.

Development prospects are restricted by the small land area and population, geographic isolation, and the relatively high cost of providing education, health and other services including telecommunications and shipping, to three widely separated communities. For these reasons Tokelau relies substantially on external financial support, particularly from New Zealand. Nonetheless the development of government structures at the national level has promoted a wish for Tokelau to be self-reliant to the greatest extent possible.

Tokelau affirmed to the United Nations in 1994 that it had under active consideration both the Constitution of a self-governing Tokelau and an act of self-determination. It also expressed a strong preference for a future status of free association with New Zealand.

Ross Dependency. By Imperial Order in Council, dated 30 July 1923, the territories between 160° E. long. and 150° W. long. and south of 60° S. lat. were brought within the jurisdiction of the New Zealand Government. The region was named the Ross Dependency. From time to time laws for the Dependency have been made by regulations promulgated by the Governor-General of New Zealand.

The mainland area is estimated at 400,000–450,000 sq. km and is mostly ice-covered. In Jan. 1957 a New Zealand expedition under Sir Edmund Hillary established a base in the Dependency. In Jan. 1958 Sir Edmund Hillary and 4 other New Zealanders reached the South Pole.

The main base—Scott Base, at Pram Point, Ross Island—is manned throughout the year, about 12 people being present during winter. Temporary accommodation facilities provide support for specific activities in the Dry Valleys and elsewhere in the Ross Sea Region. The annual activities of 200-300 scientists and support staff are managed by a crown agency, Antarctica New Zealand, based in Christchurch.

SELF-GOVERNING TERRITORIES OVERSEAS

THE COOK ISLANDS

KEY HISTORICAL EVENTS. The Cook Islands, which lie between 8° and 23° S. lat., and 156° and 167° W. long., were proclaimed a British protectorate in 1888, and on 11 June 1901 were annexed and proclaimed part of New Zealand. In 1965 the Cook Islands became a self-governing territory in 'free association' with New Zealand.

TERRITORY AND POPULATION. The islands fall roughly into two groups—the scattered islands towards the north (Northern group) and the islands towards the south (Lower group). The islands with their populations at the census of 1996:

Lower Group—	Area sq. km	Population	Northern Group—	Area sq. km	Population
Rarotonga	67·2	10,322	Nassau	1·2	98
Mangaia	51·8	1,081	Palmerston (Avarau)	2·0	49
Atiu	26·9	941	Penrhyn (Tongareva)	9·8	604
Aitutaki	18·0	2,272	Manihiki (Humphrey)	5·4	656
Mauke (Parry Is.)	18·4	638	Rakahanga (Reirson)	4·1	249
Mitiaro	22·3	317	Pukapuka (Danger)	5·1	777
Manuae and To au o tu	6·2	—	Suwarrow (Anchorage)	0·4	4
			Total	293	18,008

The population in 1994 was 18,500. Birth rate (1994, per 1,000 population), 23·22; death rate, 5·2.

CONSTITUTION AND GOVERNMENT. The Cook Islands Constitution of 1965 provides for internal self-government but linked to New Zealand by a common Head of State and a common citizenship, that of New Zealand. It provides for a ministerial system of government with a Cabinet consisting of a Prime Minister and not more than 8 nor fewer than 6 other Ministers. The New Zealand Government is represented by a New Zealand Representative and the Queen, as head of state, by the Queen's Representative. The capital is Rarotonga.

The unicameral *Parliament* comprises 25 members elected for a term of 5 years. At the elections of March 1994 the Cook Islands Party (CIP) gained 20 seats, the Democratic Coalition Party 3 and the Alliance Party, 2. Subsequently the Democratic and Alliance Parties merged to form the Democratic-Alliance Party (DAP). DAP has won two by-elections— one for the seat of Nikao on Rarotonga held on 2 July 1996 and another for the seat of Ivirua on Mangaia held on 2 Dec. 1997. DAP now holds 7 seats and the CIP 18. There is also an advisory council composed of hereditary chiefs, the 15-member House of Ariki, without legislative powers.

Prime Minister: Sir Geoffrey A. Henry (CIP; re-elected March 1994).

ECONOMY AND TRADE

Policy and Performance. A package of economic reforms including privatization and deregulation was initiated in July 1996 to deal with a national debt of US$141m., 120% of GDP.

Budget. Revenue, 1996–97, NZ$45·8m.; expenditure, NZ$44·8m. Revenue is derived chiefly from customs duties which follow the New Zealand customs tariff, income tax and stamp sales.

Grants from New Zealand, mainly for medical, educational and general administrative purposes, totalled NZ$11·3m. in 1996–97.

Currency. The Cook Island *dollar* was at par with the New Zealand *dollar*, but was replaced in 1995 by New Zealand currency.

Electricity. 19·84m. kWh were generated in 1996.

Agriculture. Livestock (1996): 21,988 pigs, 3,697 goats.

Commerce. Exports, mainly to New Zealand, were valued at NZ$7·15m. in 1993. Main items exported were fresh fruit and vegetables, clothing and footwear. Imports totalled NZ$124·24m.

COMMUNICATIONS

Roads. In 1992 there were 320 km of roads and, in 1991, 5,015 vehicles.

Civil Aviation. New Zealand has financed the construction of an international airport at Rarotonga which became operational for jet services in 1973. There are 9 useable airports.

Shipping. A fortnightly cargo shipping service is provided between New Zealand, Niue and Rarotonga.

Telecommunications. Seven Satellite Earth Stations are located at seven of the most populated islands with HF Radio provided as backup. In the remaining islands HF radio is the only means of communication. In March 1997 there were 5,141 telephone lines in service. There are 2 radio stations (AM and FM) operating in the Cook Islands with 3,693 radio receivers (Dec. 1996) of which 2,525 are located on Rarotonga.

Press. The *Cook Islands News* (circulation 1,800 (1996)) is the sole daily newspaper.

SOCIAL INSTITUTIONS

Justice. There is a High Court and a Court of Appeal, from which further appeal is to the Privy Council in the UK.

Religion. Some 58% of the population belong to the Cook Islands Christian Church; about 17% are Roman Catholics, and the rest chiefly Latter Day Saints and Seventh-Day Adventists.

Education. In March 1997 there were 29 primary schools with 139 teachers and 2,882 pupils, and 24 secondary schools with 132 teachers and 1,904 pupils, and 28 pre-schools with 29 teachers and 447 pupils.

Health. A user pay scheme was introduced in July 1996 where all Cook Islanders pay a fee of NZ$5·00 for any medical or surgical treatment including consultation. Those under the age of 16 years or over the age of 60 years are exempted from payment of this charge. The dental department is privatized except for the school dental health provision. This service continues to be free to all schools.

The Rarotonga Hospital, which is the referral hospital for the outer islands, consists of 80 beds. The hospital has 8 doctors, 33 registered nurses and 11 hospital aides.

Further Reading

Local statistical office: Ministry of Finance and Economic Management, P.O. Box 41, Rarotonga, Cook Islands.

NIUE

Key Historical Events. Captain James Cook sighted Niue in 1774 and called it Savage Island. Christian missionaries arrived in 1846. Niue became a British Protectorate in 1900 and was annexed to New Zealand in 1901. Internal self-government was achieved in free association with New Zealand on 19 Oct. 1974, New Zealand taking responsibility for external affairs and defence. Niue is a member of the South Pacific Forum.

Territory and Population. Niue is the largest uplifted coral island in the world. Distance from Auckland, New Zealand, 1,343 miles; from Rarotonga, 580 miles.

Area, 258 sq. km; height above sea-level, 220 ft. Population (census, 1991) 2,239 (1,134 males, 1,105 females); (July 1997 estimate) 1,708. During 1992 births registered numbered 31, deaths 12. Migration to New Zealand is the main factor in population change. The capital is Alofi (682 inhabitants in census, 1991).

Constitution and Government. There is a Legislative Assembly (*Fono*) of 20 members, 14 elected from 14 constituencies and 6 elected by all constituencies. There was an election on 16 Feb. 1996. Frank Lui's party gained 11 seats.

Prime Minister and Minister of Finance: Frank Lui (re-elected 16 Feb. 1996).

Budget. Financial aid from New Zealand, 1995–96, totalled NZ$8·4m.

Agriculture. The main commercial crops of the island are coconuts, taros and yams. In 1989 there were 450 agricultural holdings with 1,527 pigs and 9,716 chickens.

Commerce. Exports, 1993, NZ$0·42m.; imports, NZ$3·52m.

Civil Aviation. A weekly commercial air service links Niue with New Zealand.

Tourism. In 1992 there were 2,329 visitors (1,668 tourists).

Telecommunications. There is a wireless station at Alofi, the port of the island. Cable television is available. A weekly newspaper is published in English and Niuean; circulation about 400. Telephones (1992) 276.

Justice. There is a High Court under a Chief Justice, with a right of appeal to the New Zealand Supreme Court.

Religion (1991 census). 1,487 belong to the Congregational (Ekalesia Niue); Latter Day Saints (213), Roman Catholics (90), Jehovah's Witness (47), Seventh Day Adventists (27), other (63), No religion (34), not stated (1).

Education. In 1991 there was 1 primary school with 22 teachers and 337 pupils, and 1 secondary school with 27 teachers and 304 pupils.

Health. In 1992 there were 4 doctors, 1 dentist, 6 midwives and 19 nursing personnel. There is a 24-bed hospital at Alofi.

NICARAGUA

República de Nicaragua

Capital: Managua
Population: 4·39m.
GDP per head: (PPP$) 1,580
GNP: US$1·4bn.
HDI/world rank: 0·530/127

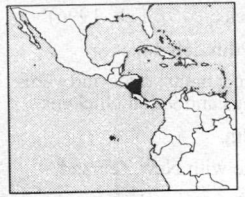

KEY HISTORICAL EVENTS. Colonization of the Nicaraguan Pacific coast was undertaken by Spaniards from Panama, beginning in 1523. France and Britain however, and later the USA, have all tried to play a colonial or semi-colonial role in Nicaragua. Between 1740 and 1786 Britain attempted to organize a colony on the Miskito Coast and from 1848 to 1860 the British occupied the port of San Juan de Norte. After links with other Central American territories and with Mexico, Nicaragua became an independent republic in 1838. Its independence was often threatened by US intervention. William Wolber, the filibuster from Tennessee, conquered the country and declared himself President in 1856-57. Between 1910 and 1930 the country was under almost continuous US military occupation.

In 1914 the Bryan-Chamarro Treaty between Nicaragua and the USA was signed, under which the USA, in return for US$3m., acquired a permanent option for a canal route through Nicaragua, a 99-year option for a naval base in the Bay of Fonseca on the Pacific coast, and the Corn Islands on the Atlantic coast. The Bryan-Chamarro Treaty was ratified in 1916 and was not abrogated until 14 July 1970 when the Corn Islands returned to Nicaragua.

The Samoza family held political domination of Nicaragua from 1933 to 1979. Through a brutal dictatorship imposed through the National Guard, they secured for themselves a large share of the national wealth. In 1962 the radical Sandanista National Liberation Front was formed with the object of overthrowing the Samozas. After 17 years of civil war the Sandanistas triumphed. On 17 July 1979 President Samoza was overthrown and fled into exile. A Government Junta of National Reconstruction was established by the revolutionary government on 20 July, and a 51-member Council of State was later created.

The USA made efforts to unseat the revolutionary government by supporting the Contras (counter-revolutionary forces). In March 1984 the Nicaraguan government filed a case against the USA in the International Court of Justice; the court's subsequent ruling was, however, ignored by the USA.

The elections that were expected after the 1979 revolution did not take place until Nov. 1984. The Government Junta of National Reconstruction and the Council of State were dissolved on 10 Jan. 1985 following the presidential and legislative elections; the Constituent Assembly which replaced them drew up a constitution within two years as instructed. On 9 Jan. 1987 the Sandanista president, Daniel Ortega, signed the new constitution, but immediately reimposed a state of emergency, suspending many of the liberties granted under the constitution. The state of emergency was lifted early in 1988 as part of the Central American peace process.

Rebel Sandinista activities had ceased by 1990; the last organized insurgent group negotiated an agreement with the government in April 1994.

TERRITORY AND POPULATION. Nicaragua is bounded in the north by Honduras, east by the Caribbean, south by Costa Rica and west by the Pacific. Area, 130,671 sq. km (121,428 sq. km dry land). The coastline runs 450 km on the Atlantic and 305 km on the Pacific. Population: July 1996, 4,272,352 (1997 estimate, 4,386,399). Population growth rate, 2·67%.

Vital statistics: 1996, life expectancy 65·72 years, male 63·41, female 68·13. birth rate, 35, death rate 6·01.

16 administrative departments are grouped in 3 zones. Areas (in sq. km.), populations (in 1,000) and chief towns in 1993:

	Area	Population	Chief town
Pacific Zone	18,429	2,622·5	
Chinandega	4,926	357·7	Chinandega
León	5,107	373·4	León
Managua	3,672	1,188·1	Managua
Masaya	590	225·1	Masaya
Granada	929	165·2	Granada
Carazo	1,050	165·2	Jinotepe
Rivas	2,155	147·8	Rivas
Central-North Zone	35,960	1,417·0	
Chontales	6,378	276·6	Juigalpa
Boaco	4,244	129·0	Boaco
Matagalpa	8,523	403·7	Matagalpa
Jinotega	9,755	190·1	Jinotega
Estelí	2,335	181·2	Estelí
Madriz	1,602	104·4	Somoto
Nueva Segovía	3,123	132·0	Ocotal
Atlantic Zone	67,039	225·3	
Rio San Juan	7,473	37·6	San Carlos
Zelaya	59,566	187·7	Bluefields

The capital is Managua with (1985) 682,111 inhabitants. Other cities: León, 100,982; Granada, 88,636; Masaya, 74,946; Chinandega, 67,792; Matagalpa, 36,983; Estelí, 30,635; Tipitapa, 30,078; Chichigalpa, 28,889; Juigalpa, 25,625; Corinto, 24,250; Jinotepe, 23,538.

The population is of Spanish and Amerindian origins with an admixture of Afro-Americans on the Caribbean coast. Ethnic groups in 1997: Mestizo (mixed Amerindian and white), 69%; white, 17%; black, 9%; Amerindian, 5%. The official language is Spanish.

CLIMATE. The climate is tropical, with a wet season from May to Jan. Temperatures vary with altitude. Managua. Jan. 81°F (27°C), July 81°F (27°C). Annual rainfall 38" (976 mm).

CONSTITUTION AND GOVERNMENT. A new Constitution was promulgated on 9 Jan. 1987. It provides for a unicameral *National Assembly* comprising 93 members directly elected by proportional representation, together with unsuccessful presidential election candidates obtaining a minimum level of votes.

The *President* and *Vice-President* are directly elected for a 5-year term commencing on the 10 Jan. following their date of election. The President may stand for a second term, but not consecutively.

Presidential and parliamentary elections were held on 20 Oct. 1996. The electorate was 2·4m. There were 23 presidential candidates. Arnoldo Alemán was elected by 49·34% of votes cast. At the parliamentary elections the Liberal Alliance gained 42 seats; the Sandinista National Liberation Front, 36; the Christian Way Party, 4; 8 minor parties, 11.

President: Arnoldo Alemán (Liberal Alliance; sworn in on 10 Jan. 1997).

In March 1998 the government included:

Minister of Agriculture and Livestock: Mario de Franco. *Minister of Construction and Transportation:* Edgar Qunitana. *Minister of Culture:* Blanca Rojas. *Minster of Defence:* Jaime Cuadra Somarriba. *Minster of Economy and Development:* Noel Sacasa. *Minister of Education:* Humberto Belli Pereira. *Minister of Environment and Natural Resources:* Roberto Stadhagen. *Minister of Finance:* Esteban Duque Estrada. *Minister of Foreign Affairs:* Emilio Alvarez Montalvan. *Minister of Foreign Cooperation:* David Robleto Lang. *Minister of Interior:* Jose Antonio Alvarado. *Minister of Health:* Lombaro Martinez Cabezas. *Minister of Labour:* Wilfredo Navarro Moreira. *Minister of Social Action:* Jamileth Bonilla. *Minister of Sports:* Carlos Garcia. *Minister of Tourism:* Pedro Joaquin Chamorro Barrios.

National anthem: 'Salve a ti Nicaragua' ('Hail to thee, Nicaragua'); words by S. Ibarra Mayorga, tune by L. A. Delgadillo.

Local government. There are 16 departments and 143 municipalities.

DEFENCE

Army. The Army is being reorganized. There are 5 regional commands, and in 1996 the Army comprised 2 military detachments, 1 light mechanized and 1 special forces brigade, 1 infantry, 1 security and 3 special forces battalions. Equipment included 130 T-54/-55 main battle tanks. Strength (1997) 15,000.

Navy. The Nicaraguan Navy was some 800 strong in 1997 and operates 12 inshore patrol craft of mixed Soviet and North Korean origins and 2 small inshore minesweepers.

Air Force. The Air Force has been semi-independent since 1947. Personnel (1997) 1,200, with no combat aircraft and 16 armed helicopters. There are 10 transport and trainer aircraft.

INTERNATIONAL RELATIONS

Membership. Nicaragua is a member of the UN, OAS, SELA and the Central American Common Market.

ECONOMY

Budget. (Millions of Córdobas)

	1992	1993	1994	1995
Rev.	1,893·92	2,162·38	2,476·72	3,136·35
Exp.	2,497·27	2,982·56	3,514·57	4,176·86

Expenditure by function (1994): Defence 231·56, public order 316·29, education 615·86, health 531·36, social security 584·43.

Currency. The monetary unit is the *córdoba* (NIO), of 100 *centavos*, which replaced the córdoba oro in 1991 at par. There are coins and notes of 1, 5, 10, 25 and 50 centavos and notes of ½, 1, 5, 10, 20, 50 and 100 córdobas. Inflation was 3·5% in 1992.

Banking and Finance. The Central Bank of Nicaragua came into operation on 1 Jan. 1961 as an autonomous bank of issue, absorbing the issue department of the National Bank. Its *Governor* is José Evenor Taboada. There were 9 private commercial banks in 1994.

Weights and Measures. The metric system is recommended.

ENERGY AND NATURAL RESOURCES

Electricity. Installed capacity was 460,000 kW in 1994 (401,900 kW in 1993: 43·7% thermal; 25·8% hydroelectric; 17·5% geothermal; 10·5% gas turbine; 2·5% Aislado system). In 1995 it was estimated that 1·713bn. kWh were produced.

Minerals. Production of gold in 1993 was 39,900 troy oz.; silver, 71,900 troy oz; limestone, 12,000 cu. metres.

Agriculture. In 1991 there were 1·1m. ha arable land, 155,000 ha permanent crop-land and 1·57m. ha pasture. 86,000 ha were irrigated. Production (in 1,000 tonnes) in 1993-94: Rice, 106; maize, 254; sorghum, 105; dry beans, 73; soya beans, 13; sesame seed, 8; cotton seed, 2; raw sugar, 173; bananas, 68; green coffee, 49; green tobacco, 1; raw cotton, 4.

There were about 1·68m. head of cattle in 1992 and 0·7m. pigs. Animal products (in 1,000 tonnes), 1993: Beef, 49; pork, 4; poultry, 23; milk, 47m. gallons; eggs, 34.

Forestry. The forest area in 1992 was 4·3m. ha, of which 2·1m. ha were commercially utilizable.

Fisheries. In 1995 the catch was 13,503 tonnes.

INDUSTRY. Production in 1993 (in 1,000 tonnes): Vegetable oil, 27; wheat flour, 48; main chemical products, 13; cement, 258; metallic products, 2,483; rum, 9,868 litres; processed leather, 309 sq. yards.

Labour. The workforce in 1993 was 1,489,500 (303,000 females in 1990, 52,000 between 10 and 15 years of age). 0·43m. worked in agriculture and forestry, 0·17m. in manufacturing, 0·34m. in services and 0·19m. in trade. There were 0·32m. unemployed in 1993.

FOREIGN ECONOMIC RELATIONS. Foreign debt was US$11,000m. in 1994.

Commerce. Foreign trade in US$1m. (1993): Exports, 267, consisting of cotton, coffee, chemical products, meat, sugar; imports, 728.

Main import suppliers in 1993 (in US$1m.): USA, 168·1; Venezuela, 83; Costa Rica, 79; Guatemala, 70·8; Japan, 46·3. Main export markets: USA, 100·9; Canada, 28·4; Costa Rica, 24·6; Germany, 21·6; El Salvador, 15·3.

Nicaragua signed a letter of intent with the IMF for an enhanced structural adjustment facility up to 2000 and hopes to secure assistance of up to US$1·5bn. from a meeting in April 1998 of a consultative group of donor countries.

Tourism. In 1994 there were 238,000 tourist arrivals.

COMMUNICATIONS

Roads. Road length in 1995 was estimated at 17,146 km, of which 1,715 km were asphalted. In 1992 there were 72,102 motor cars, 3,408 buses, 60,553 lorries and 21,678 motor cycles.

Civil Aviation. The national carrier is Nica, which in 1995 operated 1 B-737-200 Adv. 47,051 passengers were carried in 1993. The Augusto Sandino international airport at Managua handled 398,010 passengers in 1993.

Shipping. The merchant marine totalled 1,483 GRT in 1995. The Pacific ports are Corinto (the largest), San Juan del Sur and Puerto Sandino through which pass most of the external trade. The chief eastern ports are El Bluff (for Bluefields) and Puerto Cabezas. In 1993, 0·2m. tonnes of cargo were loaded, and 1·07m. tonnes discharged.

Telecommunications. In 1993 there were 66,810 telephones. Broadcasting is administered by the Instituto Nicaragüense de Telecomunicaciones y Correos (Telcor). Number of radio sets in 1995 was 1·1m. and television sets 300,000. There were 7 television stations at Managua (colour by NTSC) in 1994.

Press. In 1995 there were 4 daily newspapers in Managua, with a total circulation of 130,000.

SOCIAL INSTITUTIONS

Justice. The judicial power is vested in a Supreme Court of Justice at Managua, 5 chambers of second instance and 153 judges of inferior tribunals.

Religion. The prevailing form of religion is Roman Catholic (3·75m. adherents in 1992), but religious liberty is guaranteed by the Constitution. There is 1 archbishopric and 7 bishoprics.

Education. Adult literacy rate (1995) 65·7%; male, 64·6%; female, 66·6%. In 1995 there were 5,251 primary schools with 20,116 teachers for 264,582 pupils. In 1995 there were 203,962 pupils at secondary level and 32,464 students at university level.

In 1994–95 there were 2 universities and 3 specialized universities (agriculture; engineering; polytechnic) with 1,260 academic staff.

Health. In 1993 there were 30 hospitals with 3,460 beds, 152 health centres (26 with beds), 247 medical posts and 475 health posts. There were 2,554 doctors, 332 dentists and 1,753 qualified nurses.

DIPLOMATIC REPRESENTATIVES

Of Nicaragua in Great Britain
Embassy closed in 1997.

Of Great Britain in Nicaragua (Plaza Churchill Reparto 'Los Robles', Apartado 1-168, Managua)
Ambassador: Roy Osborne.

Of Nicaragua in the USA (1627 New Hampshire Ave., NW, Washington, D.C., 20009)
Ambassador: Francisco Aguirre Sacasa.

Of the USA in Nicaragua (Km. 4$^{1}/_{2}$ Carretera Sur., Managua)
Ambassador: Luis Gutierrez.

Of Nicaragua to the United Nations
Ambassador: Enrique Paguaga Fernández.

Of Nicaragua to the European Union
Ambassador: Rojer Guevara Mena.

Further Reading

Dematteis, L. and Vail, C., *Nicaragua: a Decade of Revolution.* New York, 1991
Dijkstra, G., *Industrialization in Sandinista Nicaragua: Policy and Party in a Mixed Economy.* Boulder (CO), 1992
Walker, T. W., *Nicaragua: the Land of Sandino.* 2nd ed. Boulder (Colo.), 1991
Woodward, R. L., *Nicaragua.* [Bibliography] Oxford and Santa Barbara (CA), 1983

National statistical office: Dirección General de Estadística y Censos, Managua

NIGER

République du Niger

Capital: Niamey
Population: 9·39m.
GDP per head: (PPP$) 787
GNP: US$2bn.
HDI/world rank: 0·206/173

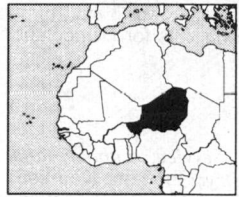

KEY HISTORICAL EVENTS. Niger was occupied by France between 1883 and 1899. It was constituted a military territory in 1901, and became a part of French West Africa in 1904. It became an autonomous republic within the French Community on 18 Dec. 1958 and achieved full independence on 3 Aug. 1960.

Guerilla activity by Tuaregs of the Armed Resistance Organization (ORA) seeking local autonomy in the north continued into 1995. On 15 April a peace agreement between the Government and the ORA was initialled under the auspices of Algeria, Burkina Faso and France, but the ORA suspended the agreement on 27 Nov. 1995.

On 27 Jan. 1996 in a bloodless coup the army chief of staff Gen. (then Col.) Barré Maïnassara deposed President Ousmane Mahamane, dissolved parliament and began to rule through a National Security Council which he headed. On 30 Jan. Boukari Adji was named Prime Minister. In a statement on 13 Feb. the deposed president, prime minister and speaker recognized the necessity of the military 'intervention'.

TERRITORY AND POPULATION. Niger is bounded in the north by Algeria and Libya, east by Chad, south by Nigeria, south-west by Benin and Burkina Faso, and west by Mali. Area, 1,186,408 sq. km, with a population at the 1988 census of 7,250,383. Estimate (1997), 9,388,859. Vital statistics, 1997 estimate: Birth rate, 53·73 (per 1,000 population); death, 23·98; fertility, 11·6; infant mortality, 124 (per 1,000 live births); expectation of life, 41·09 years; growth rate, 2·98%.

The country is divided into the capital, Niamey, an autonomous district, and 7 departments. Area, population and chief towns at the 1988 census:

Department	Sq. km	Population	Chief town	Population
Niamey	670	398,265	Niamey	392,169
Agadez	634,209	203,959	Agadez	49,361
Diffa	140,216	189,316	Diffa	–
Dosso	31,002	1,019,997	Dosso	–
Maradi	38,581	1,388,999	Maradi	109,386
Tahoua	106,677	1,306,652	Tahoua	49,941
Tillabéry	89,623	1,332,398	Tillabéry	–
Zinder	145,430	1,410,797	Zinder	119,838

The population is composed chiefly of Hausa (53%), Songhai and Djerma (21%), Tuareg (10·5%), Fulani (10%) and Kanuri-Manga (4·5%). The official language is French. Hausa, Djerma and Fulani are national languages.

CLIMATE. Precipitation determines the geographical division into a southern zone of agriculture, a central zone of pasturage and a desert-like northern zone. The country lacks water, with the exception of the south-western districts, which are watered by the Niger and its tributaries, and the southern zone, where there are a number of wells. Niamey, 95°F (35°C). Annual rainfall varies from 22" (560 mm) in the south to 7" (180 mm) in the Sahara zone. The rainy season lasts from May till Sept., but there are periodic droughts.

CONSTITUTION AND GOVERNMENT. Theoretically, Niger is a unitary multi-party democracy. The *President* is directly elected for a 5-year term renewable once. There is an 83-member *National Assembly* elected for a 5-year term by proportional representation.

At a referendum on 12 May 1996 90% of votes cast were in favour of a new constitution; turn-out was 33%. The ban on political parties which had been in force since 27 Jan. was lifted on 20 May 1996.

Presidential elections were held on 7–8 July 1996. Before they ended the National Security Council dissolved the Independent National Electoral Commission and replaced it with a body of its own nomination. Turn-out was 70%. Gen Maïnassara was elected *President* by 52·22% of votes cast against 4 opponents, one of whom was the deposed president, Ousmane Mahamane, who polled 19·75% of votes cast. Parliamentary elections were held on 23 Nov. 1996. The electorate was 3·8m.; turn-out was 27%. The pro-presidential National Union of Independents for Democratic Renewal gained a majority of seats.

President: Gen. Ibrahim Bare Maïnassara.

In March 1998 the government comprised:

Prime Minister: Ibrahim Assane Mayaki.

Agriculture and Livestock: Idi Ango Omar. *Civil Service, Labour, and Employment:* Moussa Oumarou. *Commerce and Industry:* Ibrahim Koussou. *Communication and Culture:* Issa Moussa. *Foreign Affairs and African Integration:* Mamane Sambo Sidikou. *Economic Reform, Finance, and Privatization:* Ide Niandou. *Education:* Aissata Moumouni. *Equipment and Infrastructure:* Cherif Chako. *Higher Education, Research and Technology:* Oumarou Boube. *Interior and Territorial Administration:* Abdoulaye Souley. *Justice, Human Rights, and Keeper of the Seals:* Issoufou Aba Moussa. *Mines and Energy:* Mai Manga Boukar. *National Defence:* Yahaya Tounkara. *Planning:* Yacouba Nabassoua. *Public Health:* Illo Almoustapha. *Social Development, Population, and Promotion of Women and Children:* Mariama Sambo Abdoulaye. *Tourism and Crafts:* Aissa Abdoulaye Diallo. *Transportation:* Oubandawaki Issofou Ousmane. *Water Resources and Environment:* Harouna Niandou. *Youth, Sports, National Solidarity and Government Spokesman:* Abdourauhamane Saidou.

National anthem: 'Auprès du grand Niger puissant' ('By the banks of the mighty great Niger'); words by M. Thiriet, tune by R. Jacquet and N. Frionnet.

Local government. The 8 departments are each under a prefect, sub-divided into 32 *arrondissements*, each under a sub-prefect, and some 150 communes.

DEFENCE. Selective conscription for 2 years operates.

Army. There are 3 military districts. The Army consists of 4 armoured reconnaissance squadrons, 7 infantry, 1 engineer and 2 parachute companies. Equipment includes 90 AML-90 armoured cars. Strength (1997) 5,200. There are additional paramilitary forces of some 5,400.

Air Force. The Air Force had (1997) 100 personnel, 1 C-130H transport, 1 Boeing 737 VIP transport, 2 Cessna Skymasters and 2 Do 28D Skyservants and 1 Do 228 for communications duties. There are no combat aircraft.

INTERNATIONAL RELATIONS

Membership. Niger is a member of the UN, OAU and is an ACP state of the EU.

ECONOMY

Budget. In 1995 (estimates) revenue (in 1,000m. francs CFA) was 115·7 and expenditure, 143·6. Revenue included: Tax revenue, 63·9; grants, 45·4. Current expenditure, 102·7; capital expenditure, 44·1.

Currency. The unit of currency is the *franc CFA* (XAF), with a parity rate of 100 francs CFA to 1 French franc. In 1991 42,110m. francs CFA were in circulation. Foreign exchange reserves were US$225m. in 1992; gold reserves were 11,000 troy oz.

Banking and Finance. The regional Central Bank of West African States (BCEAO) functions as the bank of issue, and there were 6 commercial banks in 1994.

Weights and Measures. The metric system is legal, but traditional units are still in use.

ENERGY AND NATURAL RESOURCES

Electricity. Production (1994) amounted to 178m. kWh.

Minerals. Large uranium deposits are mined at Arlit and Akouta. Concentrate production (1992), 2,504 tonnes. Phosphates are mined in the Niger valley, and coal reserves are being exploited by open-cast mining (production of hard coal in 1994 was an estimated 172,000 tonnes). Tin ore production in 1994 was 20 tonnes; salt, 3,000 tonnes.

Agriculture. Production is dependent upon adequate rainfall. In 1992 there were 36·1m. ha of arable land and 80·0m. ha of permanent pasture. 45,000 ha were irrigated. Production in 1993 (in 1,000 tonnes): Millet, 1,430; maize, 1,000; sorghum, 305; groundnuts, 60; cassava, 220; sugar-cane, 140; sweet potatoes, 35·0; cotton, 3·0.

Livestock (1993): Cattle, 1·8m.; horses, 82,000; asses, 462,000; sheep, 3·5m.; goats, 5·4m.; pigs, 39,000; camels, 370,000; chickens, 2m.

Livestock products (in 1,000 tonnes), 1993: Butter, 4·4; cheese, 12.

There were 180 tractors in 1991.

Forestry. There is a government programme of afforestation as a protection from desert encroachment. There are 2·06m. ha of forest. Production (1994) 5,671,000 cu. metres, mainly for fuel.

Fisheries. There are fisheries on the River Niger and along the shores of Lake Chad. Catch (1995) 3,586 tonnes.

INDUSTRY. Some small manufacturing industries, mainly in Niamey, produce textiles, food products, furniture and chemicals. Output of cement in 1994, 29,000 tonnes.

Labour. In 1990 the workforce was 3,619,000 (1,690,000 women). Employment (in 1,000) by branch, 1989: Agriculture, forestry and fisheries, 1·8; energy and water supply, 3·5; mining, 4·1; manufacturing, 2·9; building, 3·6; trade and tourism, 3·1; finance, 1·2; transport and communications, 2·3; public service, 5·8. In 1989 there were 24,600 registered unemployed (1,300 women).

Trade Unions. The national confederation is the *Union Syndicale des Travailleurs du Niger*, which has 15,000 members in 31 unions.

FOREIGN ECONOMIC RELATIONS. Foreign debt was US$1,711m. in 1992.

Commerce. In 1991 imports were valued at 77,100m. francs CFA and exports at 80,100m. francs CFA. Uranium and livestock are the principal exports. Major trading partners are France and Nigeria.

Tourism. There were 11,000 tourists in 1994.

COMMUNICATIONS

Roads. In 1995 there were 9,863 km of all-weather roads and 779 km of paved roads. Niamey and Zinder are the termini of two trans-Sahara motor routes; the Hoggar–Aïr–Zinder road extends to Kano and the Tanezrouft–Gao–Niamey road to Benin. A 648-km 'uranium road' runs from Arlit to Tahoua. There were (1987), 27,254 private cars, 2,253 buses, 5,687 lorries and 8,925 motorcycles. There were 422 traffic accidents in 1987 with 148 fatalities.

Civil Aviation. There are international airports at Niamey and Agadez. Niger is a member of Air Afrique, and there are services by Air Algérie, Air France, Air Mali, Ethiopian Airlines, Libyan Airlines and Royal Air Maroc. 84,752 passengers and 3,951 tonnes of freight passed through Niamey Airport in 1991 (174,000 passengers in 1990).

Shipping. Sea-going vessels can reach Niamey (300 km inside the country) between Sept. and March.

Telecommunications. There are 159 post offices and (1994) about 5,000 telephones. La Voix du Sahel and Télé-Sahel under the government's Office de Radiodiffusion Télévision du Niger are responsible for radio and TV broadcasting (colour by SECAM). In 1995 there were estimated to be 0·62m. radio and 105,000 TV sets.

Press. In 1998 there were 2 daily newspapers with a combined circulation of 4,000.

SOCIAL INSTITUTIONS

Justice. There are Magistrates' and Assize Courts at Niamey, Zinder and Maradi, and justices of the peace in smaller centres. The Court of Appeal is at Niamey.

Religion. In 1997 there were 9·34m. Sunni Moslems. There are some Roman Catholics, and traditional animist beliefs survive.

Education. In 1996 there were 105 pre-primary schools with 417 teachers for 9,013 pupils and 2,908 primary schools with 11,978 teachers for 44,058 pupils. In 1991 there were 108 secondary schools with 2,725 teachers for 76,758 pupils. In 1988–89 there were 5 teacher training colleges with 1,578 students, and in 1989–90 there were 2 professional training colleges with 859 students (61 women) and 69 teachers. There is a university and an Islamic university, with a total in 1994–95 of 3,980 students and 281 academic staff.

Adult literacy (1995) 13·6% (male, 20·9%; female, 6·6%).

Health. In 1987 in government service there were 13 hospitals, 39 medical centres and 205 dispensaries. In 1987 there were 93 doctors, 1 dentist, 7 pharmacists, 217 midwives and 1,402 nursing personnel (577 state-registered).

DIPLOMATIC REPRESENTATIVES

Of Niger in Great Britain (resides in Paris)
Ambassador: Vacant.

Of Great Britain in Niger
Ambassador: Margaret I. Rothwell, CMG (resides in Côte d'Ivoire).

Of Niger in the USA (2204 R. St., NW, Washington, D.C., 20008)
Ambassador: Joseph Diatta.

Of the USA in Niger (PO Box 11201, Niamey)
Ambassador: Charles O. Cecil.

Of Niger to the United Nations
Ambassador: Joseph Diatta.

Of Niger to the European Union
Ambassador: Houseïni Abdou Saleye.

Further Reading

Fugelstad, F., *A History of Niger, 1850–1960.* OUP, 1984
Zamponi, L. F., *Niger* [Bibliography]. Oxford and Santa Barbara (CA), 1994

National statistical office: Direction de la Statistique et de l'Informatique, Ministère du Plan, Niamey.

NIGERIA

Federal Republic of Nigeria

Capital: Abuja
Population: 107·1m.
GDP per head: (PPP$) 1,351
GNP: US$30·0bn.
HDI/world rank: 0·393/141

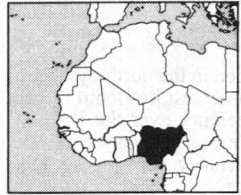

KEY HISTORICAL EVENTS. Farming communities settled in the area of present-day Nigeria 4,000 years ago, which was previously occupied by hunter-gatherers. They developed the large centralized state of Kanem-Bornu in the 8th century, based on control of trans-Saharan trade. Adjacent states, notably the Hausa, Oyo and Benin empires arose later, and became caught up in the slave trade by the 18th century. British occupation aimed at enforcing the abolition of the trade.

The port of Lagos was captured by Britain in 1851 and annexed in Aug. 1861, administered first from Sierra Leone and then from the Gold Coast. Growing British involvement in the Lagos hinterland and in the Niger Delta led to the establishment of protectorates in the former in Jan. 1886 with Lagos itself becoming a separate colony, and in the latter, known as the Oil Rivers Protectorate, in June 1885. British commercial interests among the Moslem emirates of the north led in July 1886 to the chartering of the Royal Niger Company which established its own political administration over a wide territory.

In 1893 the Oil Rivers Protectorate was expanded and renamed the Niger Coast Protectorate. On 1 Jan. 1900 the Royal Niger Company transferred its territory to the British Crown, and the southern parts of this were amalgamated with the Niger Coast Protectorate to form the Protectorate of Southern Nigeria (to which the colony and protectorate of Lagos was added in Feb. 1906), while the remainder was constituted as the Protectorate of Northern Nigeria. On 1 Jan. 1914 the two territories were merged to form the 'colony and protectorate of Nigeria'.

Through the system of indirect rule, Africans were excluded from political power until the end of the Second World War. A constitution was promulgated in 1947, and on 1 Oct. 1954 Nigeria vested in a federal system of government comprising Eastern, Western and Northern Regions; the first two of these secured internal self-government in 1956 and the Northern Region in 1959. Full independence was achieved by the Federation of Nigeria on 1 Oct. 1960 and it became a republic on 1 Oct. 1963.

The republic was overthrown by a military coup on 15 Jan. 1966, and a military government established. In May 1967 a decree replaced the existing regions by 12 new states. Ethnic and regional conflict ensued, with Hausa northerners fearing domination by the Ibo people from the east of the country. The Chairman of the Supreme Military Council, Johnson Aguiyi-Ironsi, was killed in an army mutiny and replaced by Lieut.-Col. Yakubu Gowon. He restored the federal system, but the Eastern Region decided to secede as the Republic of Biafra in May 1967. This set off a bloody civil war, prolonged by international involvement, and a severe famine. Federal forces re-established control in Jan. 1970. Besides the political problems, Gowon also faced economic problems related to Nigeria's new oil wealth, and he was ousted in a coup on 27 July 1975. He was succeeded by Brig. Murtala Muhammed who was, however, assassinated the following year. Lieut.-Gen. Olusegun Obasanjo replaced him, and returned the country (by now organized in 19 states) to civilian rule in Oct. 1979 when Shehu Shagari was elected president. Shagari was re-elected in Sept. 1983, but overthrown by the military later that year. In Aug. 1985, Maj.-Gen. Ibrahim Babangida replaced Maj.-Gen. Muhammadu Buhari as head of the Armed Forces Ruling Council. This was dissolved in Jan. 1993 and replaced by a transitional civilian council. Presidential elections held in June 1993 were annulled. President Babangida stepped down from office on 26 Aug., nominating Chief Ernest Shonekan as interim head of state.

On 17 Nov. 1993 Gen. Sani Abacha forced Shonekan to resign, and assumed the function of head of state himself. Moshood Abiola, who claims to have won the annulled 1993 presidential election, proclaimed himself head of state in June 1994 and was arrested for treason.

Following the execution of Ogoni separatist Ken Saro-wiwa and 8 other civil rights activists in Nov. 1995, Nigeria was suspended from the Commonwealth. The 1997 Commonwealth Conference gave Nigeria a further year to restore democratic government. Failure to comply could lead to expulsion from the Commonwealth and possible oil sanctions. Gen. Abacha has promised to restore constitutional government by Oct. 1998.

TERRITORY AND POPULATION. Nigeria is bounded in the north by Niger, east by Chad and Cameroon, south by the Gulf of Guinea and west by Benin. It has an area of 356,669 sq. miles (923,773 sq. km). For sovereignty over the Bakassi Peninsula *see* CAMEROON: Territory and Population. Census population, 1991, 88,514,501 (43,969,970 females, urban, 36%); population density, 95·8 per sq. km. Official estimate, 1997, 107,115,000. Density, 116 per sq. km.

Vital statistics rates, 1995: Birth, 49 (per 1,000 population); death, 14. Infantile mortality, 195 (per 1,000 live births). Growth rate, 1995, 2·1%. Expectation of life, 1995, 52 years.

There were 30 states and a Federal Capital Territory (Abuja) in 1991.

Area, population and capitals of these states:

State	Area (in sq. km)	Population (1991 census)	Capital
Sokoto	} 102,535	{ 4,392,391	Sokoto
Kebbi		2,062,226	Birnin-Kebbi
Niger	65,037	2,482,367	Minna
Kwara	} 66,869	{ 1,566,469	Ilorin
Kogi		2,099,046	Lokoja
Benue	45,174	2,780,398	Makurdi
Plateau	58,030	3,283,704	Jos
Taraba	} 91,390	{ 1,480,590	Jalingo
Adamawa		2,124,049	Yola
Borno	} 116,400	{ 2,596,589	Maiduguri
Yobe		1,411,481	Damaturu
Bauchi	64,605	4,294,413	Bauchi
Jigawa	} 43,285	{ 2,829,929	Dutse
Kano		5,632,040	Kano
Katsina	} 70,245	{ 3,878,344	Katsina
Kaduna		3,969,252	Kaduna
Federal Capital Territory	7,315	378,671	Abuja
Total North	*730,885*	*47,261,959*	

State	Area (in sq. km)	Population (1991 census)	Capital
Oyo	} 37,705	{ 3,488,789	Ibadan
Osun		2,203,016	Oshogbo
Ogun	16,762	2,338,570	Abeokuta
Lagos	3,345	5,685,781	Ikeja
Ondo	20,959	3,884,485	Akure
Edo	} 35,500	{ 2,159,848	Benin City
Delta		2,570,181	Asaba
Rivers	21,850	3,983,857	Port-Harcourt
Abia	} 11,850	{ 2,297,978	Umuahia
Imo		2,485,499	Owerri
Anambra	} 17,675	{ 2,767,903	Awka
Enugu		3,161,295	Enugu
Cross River	} 27,237	{ 1,865,604	Calabar
Akwa Ibom		2,359,736	Uyo
Total South	*192,883*	*41,252,542*	

6 new states were created in 1996, 3 in the north and 3 in the south. In the north, Zamfara State was created from Sokoto, with its headquarters at Gusau; Nassarawa State was created from Plateau, with its headquarters at Lafia; and Gombe State was

created from Bauchi, with its headquarters at Gombe. In the south, Ekiti State was created from Ondo, with its capital at Ado-Ekiti; Bayelsa State was created from Rivers, with its headquarters at Yenagoa; and Ebonyi State was created by merging Abia and Enugu, with its headquarters at Abakaliki.

Abuja replaced Lagos as the federal capital and seat of government in Dec. 1991.

Estimated population of the largest cities, 1992:

Lagos	1,347,000	Aba	270,500	Akure	146,900
Ibadan	1,295,000	Ife	268,600	Gusau	143,000
Kano	699,900	Ila	238,900	Ijebu-Ode	141,600
Ogbomosho	660,600	Oyo	237,400	Effon-Alaiye	138,600
Oshogbo	441,600	Ikerre	221,400	Kumo	134,000
Ilorin	430,600	Benin City	207,200	Shomolu	133,700
Abeokuta	386,800	Iseyin	197,100	Oka	129,600
Port Harcourt	371,000	Katsina	186,900	Ikare	127,500
Zaria	345,200	Jos	185,600	Sapele	126,000
Ilesha	342,400	Sokoto	185,500	Minna	125,900
Onitsha	336,600	Ilobu	180,100	Deba Habe	125,300
Iwo	335,200	Offa	178,400	Warri	114,100
Ado-Ekiti	325,300	Ikorodu	167,300	Bida	113,600
Kaduna	309,600	Ilawe-Ekiti	166,900	Ikire	111,500
Abuja (capital)	305,900	Owo	166,100	Makurdi	111,410
Mushin	301,500	Ikirun	164,300	Lafia	110,900
Maiduguri	289,100	Shaki	161,200	Inisa	108,300
Enugu	286,100	Calabar	157,800	Shagamu	106,000
Ede	277,900	Ondo	153,500	Awka	100,700

There are about 250 ethnic groups. The 3 largest are Hausa-Fulani, Yoruba and Igbo. These, together with the Kamuri, Tiv, Edo, Nupe, Ibibio and Ijaw groups, constitute 80% of the population. The official languages are English and (since 1997) French, but 50% of the population speak Hausa as a lingua franca.

CLIMATE. Lying wholly within the tropics, temperatures everywhere are high. Rainfall varies very much, but decreases from the coast to the interior. The main rains occur from April to Oct. Lagos. Jan. 81°F (27·2°C), July 78°F (25·6°C). Annual rainfall 72" (1,836 mm). Ibadan. Jan. 80°F (26·7°C), July 76°F (24·4°C). Annual rainfall 45" (1,120 mm). Kano. Jan. 70°F (21·1°C), July 79°F (26·1°C). Annual rainfall 35" (869 mm). Port Harcourt. Jan. 79°F (26·1°C), July 77°F (25°C). Annual rainfall 100" (2,497 mm).

CONSTITUTION AND GOVERNMENT. Under the 1978 Constitution, Nigeria is a sovereign, federal republic comprising states and a federal capital district. As part of the process of demilitarization and democratization, in 1993 the government created 2 parties, the Social Democratic Party (SDP) and the National Republican Convention (NRC). Voting has not been secret since March 1991; voters indicate a poster of the candidate of their choice. At the legislative and gubernatorial elections of Dec. 1991 the NRC gained 16 state governorships and the SDP 14. Parliament consists of a 593-member *House of Representatives* and a 91-member *Senate.* At the elections of 4 July 1992 the SDP gained 44 seats in the Senate and 305 in the House of Representatives, the NRC 32 and 260. Presidential primary elections in Aug. and Sept. 1992 were annulled on grounds of fraud and corruption. Primaries were eventually held on 6 March 1993. Presidential elections were held on 16 June 1993 and won by Moshood Abiola (SDP), but the results were annulled.

On stepping down from all his offices on 26 Aug. 1993 President Babangida nominated an interim government of national unity headed by Ernest Shonekan (ING).

On 17 Nov. 1993 the Minister of Defence, Gen. Sani Abacha, assumed the functions of head of state and set up an 11-member Provisional Ruling Council headed by himself. Parliament, the 30 state Executive Councils and the 2 political parties were dissolved. A 33-member cabinet, the Federal Executive Council, was appointed, chaired by Gen. Abacha. In June 1994 a Constitutional Conference opened with 360 participants, 90 of whom were appointed by the government. In Oct. 1994 the Conference recommended the introduction of a plurality of political parties, and the rotation of the presidency between North and South to overcome the bitter hostility between the two regions. In June 1995 the Conference submitted a proposal for a new constitution to the head of state, and the latter lifted the ban on political parties. 5 parties gained government recognition in Oct. 1996. However, by March 1998 the proposed new constitution was still on the drawing board. In Nov. 1997 Gen. Abacha dismissed the cabinet only to reappoint about half of them.

In March 1998 the Federal Executive Council comprised:
Chair, Minister of Defence: Sani Abacha.

Agriculture: Dr Malami Buwal. *Minister of State for Agriculture:* Frank Adejuwon. *Aviation:* Air Commodore Udo Imeh. *Commerce and Tourism:* Dr Emmanuel Odogu. *Communications:* Maj.-Gen. Patrick Aziza. *Education:* Dauda Birma. *Minister of State for Education:* Rose Adunine. *Federal Capital Territory:* Lieut.-Gen. Jeremiah Useni. *Minister of State for Federal Capital Territory:* Alhassan Kpaki. *Finance:* Anthony Ani. *Minister of State for Finance:* Abu Gidado: *Foreign Affairs:* Tom Ikimi. *Minister of State for Foreign Affairs:* Buhari Bala. *Health:* Rear Adm. Jubril Ayinla. *Minister of State for Health:* Prof. Iyowose Hagher. *Industry:* O. Akande. *Information and Culture:* Ike Mokelu. *Internal Affairs:* Bashir Dalhatu. *Justice:* Abdulahi Ibrahim. *Labour and Productivity:* Uba Ahmed. *National Planning:* Ayo Ogunlade. *Petroleum:* Dan Etete. *Minister of State for Petroleum:* Umaru Dembo: *Power and Steel:* Baba Gana Kingibe. *Minister of State for Power and Steel:* Kunle Oluwasemi. *Science and Technology:* Maj.-Gen. Samuel Momah. *Solid Minerals:* Kaloma Ali. *Transport:* Maj.-Gen. Ibrahim Gumel. *Water Resources:* Hamza Sakwa. *Works and Housing:* Brig.-Gen. Garba Mohammed. *Minister of State for Works and Housing:* Elias Okete. *Women's Affairs:* Hajo Sani. *Youth and Sports:* Air Commodore Samson Omeruah.

National anthem: 'Arise, O compatriots, Nigeria's call obey'; words by a collective, tune by B. Odiase.

Local Government. Each state is administered by a directly-elected governor, who appoints and presides over a State Executive Council. The states are subdivided into local government areas, and there is a Federal Capital Territory, Abuja. Local elections were held on 15 March 1997. The electorate was 55m. 5 parties were registered. The Unified Congress Party and the Democratic Party gained a majority of seats.

DEFENCE

Army. The Army consists of 1 armoured division, 2 mechanized divisions, 1 air defence brigade and 1 composite division (motorized infantry, airborne amphibious), each with supporting artillery and engineer and reconnaissance units. Equipment includes 60 T-55 and 150 Vickers Mk 3 main battle tanks. Strength (1997) 62,000.

Navy. The Navy comprises 1 German-built MEKO-type frigate with a helicopter and 1 frigate-type training ship (both beyond economic repair), 1 British-built corvette, 2 fast missile craft, 2 minehunters, and some 45 inshore patrol craft. There are also 2 German-built tank landing ships, 1 survey ship and some 15 service craft. The Navy has a small aviation element equipped with 2 Lynx anti-submarine helicopters. Naval personnel in 1997 totalled 5,500, including Coastguard. The main bases are at Apapa (Lagos) and Calabar.

The Coastguard operate 10 patrol craft launches, and the police numerous boats.

Air Force. The Air Force has been built up with the aid of a German mission; much first-line equipment was received from the former Soviet Union. It has 12 MiG-21 supersonic jetfighters and MiG-21U fighter-trainers, and 22 Alpha Jet light attack/trainers. About 15 BO 105 twin-turbine helicopters serve for search and rescue, while 1 F.27MPA is used for maritime patrol. Transport units operate 7 C-130H-30 and C-130H Hercules 4-turboprop heavy transports, 5 twin-turboprop Aeritalia G222s, 4 Super Puma helicopters, 18 Dornier 128-6 twin-turboprop and 18 DO 28D twin-piston utility aircraft, 2 Navajos and a Navajo Chieftain. Training types include 20 Bulldog primary trainers, 12 MB 339 jets for instrument training, 12 Hughes 300 helicopters and 30 L-39 Albatros advanced trainers. Personnel (1997) total about 9,500, with 62 combat aircraft.

INTERNATIONAL RELATIONS

Membership. Nigeria is a member of the UN, ECOWAS, OAU, OPEC and is an ACP state of the EU. Membership of the Commonwealth was suspended in Nov. 1995. Involvement in Sierra Leone where Nigeria supported the exiled government of President Ahmed Tejan Kabbah led to a full-scale attack in Feb. 1998 and the routing of the Sierra Leone military junta.

ECONOMY

Policy. After 1985, 5-year plans gave way to 3-year rolling plans against a background of 15–20-year plans. There is a privatization programme. An Economic Planning Committee was set up in 1996 to draft a development plan, 'Vision 2010'.

Performance. Real GDP growth in 1996 was 3·25% (2·2% in 1995). The projected growth for 1998 is 5·5% but this is based on an oil price estimate of US$17 a barrel. In March 1998 the price was closer to US$15.

Budget. The financial year is the calendar year. 1995 revenue, ₦350,700m. (of which ₦150,000m. from oil); expenditure, ₦204,200m. (of which ₦44,500m. capital expenditure, ₦57,000m. debt service).

Currency. The unit of currency is the *naira* (NGN) of 100 *kobo*. There are coins of 1, 10, 25 and 50 kobo and 1 naira, and notes of 1, 5, 10, 20 and 50 naira. In Dec. 1995 currency in circulation totalled ₦106,768m. Foreign exchange reserves were US$4,100m. in Dec. 1996, but a dual exchange rate allows the government to purchase US dollars for 25% of the market price; gold reserves were 687 troy oz. in June 1992. Government figures showed inflation at 28% at the end of 1996.

Banking and Finance. The Central Bank of Nigeria is the bank of issue (*Governor*, Paul Ogwuma). There were 65 commercial banks (with 2,403 branches) and 51 merchant banks in 1995 (with 144 branches), in 20 of which central or state governments held a controlling interest. Total assets of commercial banks, 1995, ₦463,671m.; merchant banks, ₦91,803m. Total saving deposits, Dec. 1995, ₦121,026m.

There is a stock exchange.

Weights and Measures. The metric system is in force.

ENERGY AND NATURAL RESOURCES

Electricity. Installed capacity, 1991, 4,548m. kW. Output, 1995, 14,482·6m. kWh (5,500·2 kWh hydro-electric).

Oil. Nigeria depends on oil for more than 90% of its overseas earnings. The cumulative income from oil over 25 years exceeds US$220,000m. Production, 1995, 2,059,000 bbls. a day (total for the year: 92,130m. tonnes). There are 4 refineries.

Gas. Natural gas reserves, 1995, were estimated at 3,114,870m. cu. metres. Production, 1991, 31,300m. cu. metres.

Water. 11 River Basin Development Authorities have been established for water resources development.

Minerals. Production, 1995 (in tonnes): Columbite, 37; coal, 20,000; limestone, 3·66m.; marble, 22,460; cassiterite, 203. There are large deposits of iron ore, coal (reserves estimate 245m. tonnes), lead and zinc. There are small quantities of gold and uranium. Lead production was 3,000 tonnes in 1990, tin, 149 tonnes in 1992.

Agriculture. Agriculture accounts for about 30% of GDP. Of the total land mass, 75% is suitable for agriculture, including arable farming, forestry, livestock husbandry and fisheries. 29·8m. ha are arable, 2·54m. ha permanent cropland and 40m. ha permanent pasture. 0·87m. ha are irrigated. Main food crops are millet and sorghum in the north, plantains and oil palms in the south, and maize, yams, cassava and rice in much of the country, the north being, however, the main food producing area. Output, 1995 (in 1,000 tonnes): Millet, 4,900; sorghum, 6,377; plantains, 1,604; maize, 7,240; yams, 24,370; groundnuts, 1,523; cotton seed, 308; palm kernel, 543,000; palm oil, 871,000; cassava, 31,404; rice, 2,920; cocoa, 331.

Livestock: Cattle, 16·3m.; sheep, 14m.; goats, 24·5m.; pigs, 6·7m.; 120m. poultry. Products (in 1,000 tonnes), 1995: Beef and veal, 192; pork, 31; mutton and lamb, 94; goat meat, 88; poultry meat, 73; milk, 961; eggs, 399.

Forestry. There are 11·9m. ha of woodland. The most important timber species include mahogany, iroko, obeche, abwa, ebony and camwood. 1995 output (in 1,000 cu. metres): Roundwood, 116,053; saw logs, 1,325; panels, 111.

Fisheries. The total catch (1995) was (in 1,000 tonnes): Coastal fishing, 142; deep-sea, 11; fish farms, 21; other freshwater, 127.

INDUSTRY. Manufacturing contributes about 9% of GDP. 1994 production (in 1,000 tonnes) included: Sugar, 55; paper and products, 43; cement, 3,086; cigarettes, 9,228. Also plywood, 72,000 cu. metres.

Labour. In 1990 the workforce (over 10 years old) was 41·86m. (14·55 females). There were 196 work stoppages in 1995 with 235·1m. working days lost. Unemployment was 1·8% in 1995.

Trade Unions. All trade unions are affiliated to the Nigerian Labour Congress.

FOREIGN ECONOMIC RELATIONS. Nigeria's estimated debt (1997) exceeded US$34,000m. Rescheduling the debt depends on an IMF agreement which requires the ending of a two-tier exchange rate.

Commerce. Exports in 1995 were valued at ₦748,368m.; imports at ₦656,572m. Principal exports, 1992 (in ₦1m.): Oil, 201,349; cocoa, 1,345; rubber, 766; urea and ammonia, 447; fish, 400. Principal imports: Machinery and transport equipment, 61,841; other manufactures, 35,072; chemicals, 22,904; foodstuffs, 12,597.

The main export markets are: USA, 44·1%; Germany, 6·8%; Spain, 6%; India, 5·9%; France, 5·9%. Main import suppliers: UK, 14%; USA, 13·1%; Germany, 10·1%; France, 8·3%; Japan, 7·3%.

Tourism. Arrivals are about 200,000, mostly from other African countries.

COMMUNICATIONS

Roads. There are 142,837 km of maintained roads. In 1995 there were 663,000 motor cars and 68,000 trucks and vans. In 1995 there were 12,212 road accidents with 4,908 fatalities.

Railways. There are 3,505 route-km of line 1,067 mm gauge, which in 1995 carried 108,000 tonne-kilometres of freight and 1,729,000 passengers.

Civil Aviation. There is an international airport at Lagos (Murtala Muhammed). In 1995, 335,000 passengers were carried on domestic flights and 192,000 on international flights. The national carrier is the state-owned Nigeria Airways, which in 1995 operated 2 A310-200s, 5 B-737-200 Advs and 1 DC-10-30. In 1992, 229,000 international and 415,000 domestic passengers were carried. Services are also provided by Air Afrique, Air Gabon, Air Zaïre, Alitalia, American Trans Air, Balkan Bulgarian, British Airways, Cameroon Airlines, Egyptair, Ethiopian Airlines, Ghana Airways, KLM, Lufthansa, Middle East Airlines, Nigeria Airways, Sabena, Swissair, UTA and Varig.

Shipping. In 1995 the merchant marine totalled 0·7m. GRT, including oil tankers, 0·47m. GRT. The principal ports are Lagos, Port Harcourt, Warri and Calabar. In 1990 938,000 tonnes of cargo were loaded and 5,917,000 tonnes unloaded; 2,886 ships arrived and 2,855 departed. There is an extensive network of inland waterways.

Telecommunications. In 1995 there were 3,651 post offices. There were 405,991 telephones in 1995 and 6,767 telex sets.

The Federal Radio Corporation of Nigeria, a statutory body, broadcasts 3 national radio programmes in English, Yoruba, Hausa and Igbo, and an international service, Voice of Nigeria (5 languages). The government Nigerian Television Authority transmits a national service (colour by PAL), and 10 states have services. In 1994 there were an estimated 21m. radio and 4·1m. TV sets.

Press. In 1995 there were 27 daily newspapers with a combined circulation of 1,950,000.

SOCIAL INSTITUTIONS

Justice. The highest court is the Federal Supreme Court, which consists of the Chief Justice of the Republic, and up to 15 Justices appointed by the government. It has original jurisdiction in any dispute between the Federal Republic and any State or between States; and to hear and determine appeals from the Federal Court of Appeal, which acts as an intermediate appellate Court to consider appeals from the High Court.

High Courts, presided over by a Chief Justice, are established in each state. All judges are appointed by the government. Magistrates' courts are established throughout the Republic, and customary law courts in southern Nigeria. In each of the northern States of Nigeria there are the Sharia Court of Appeal and the Court of Resolution. Moslem Law has been codified in a Penal Code and is applied through Alkali courts.

Religion. Moslems, 48%; Christians, 34% (17% Protestants and 17% Roman Catholic); others, 18%. Northern Nigeria is mainly Moslem; Southern Nigeria is predominantly Christian and Western Nigeria is evenly divided between Christians, Moslems and animists.

Education. Adult literacy was 44·4% in 1995. In 1994 there were 38,649 primary schools with 16·19m. pupils and 435,210 teachers, and 6,987 secondary and tertiary schools with 4·64m. students and 162,242 teachers.

In 1995 there were 13 universities, 2 agricultural and 5 technological universities, 21 polytechnics, 7 colleges and 2 institutes. There were 150,072 university students and 10,742 academic staff.

Health. Health provision, 1995: 1 doctor per 3,707 population; 1 nurse per 605; 1 hospital bed per 1,477.

DIPLOMATIC REPRESENTATIVES

Of Nigeria in Great Britain (Nigeria Hse., 9 Northumberland Ave., London, WC2N 5BX)
Acting High Commissioner: Uche Okeke.

Of Great Britain in Nigeria (11 Eleke Cres., Victoria Island, Lagos)
High Commissioner: Mr G. S. Burton, CMG.

Of Nigeria in the USA (1333 16th St., NW, Washington, D.C., 20036)
Ambassador: Wakili Hassan Adamu.

Of the USA in Nigeria (2 Eleke Cres., Lagos)
Ambassador: William Twaddell.

Of Nigeria to the United Nations
Ambassador: Ibrahim Gambari.

Of Nigeria to the European Union
Ambassador: Vacant.

Further Reading

Achebe, C., *The Trouble with Nigeria*. Heinemann, 1983
Adamolekun, L., *Politics and Administration in Nigeria*. Ibadan, 1986
Burns, A., *History of Nigeria*. 8th ed. London, 1978

Crowder, M. and Abdullahi, G., *Nigeria: an Introduction to its History*. London, 1979
Forrest, T., *Politics and Economic Development in Nigeria*. Boulder (CO), 1993
Myers, R. A., *Nigeria*. [Bibliography] Oxford and Santa Barbara, 1989
Oyovbaine, S. E., *Federalism in Nigeria: A Study in the Development of the Nigerian State*. London, 1985

Further information

Nigeria High Commission Library, London WC2
National statistical office: Federal Office of Statistics.

NORWAY

Kongeriket Norge

(Kingdom of Norway)

Capital: Oslo
Population: 4·4m.
GDP per head: (PPP$) 21,346
HDI/world rank: 0·943/3

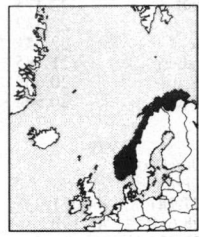

KEY HISTORICAL EVENTS. Norway was under Danish domination from the 14th century. By a Treaty of 14 Jan. 1814, the King of Denmark ceded Norway to the King of Sweden, but the Norwegian people declared themselves independent and elected Prince Christian Frederik of Denmark as their king. The foreign Powers refused to recognize this election, and on 14 Aug. a convention proclaimed the independence of Norway in a personal union with Sweden. This was followed on 4 Nov. by the election of Karl XIII (II) as King of Norway. Norway declared this union dissolved on 7 June 1905 and Sweden agreed to the repeal of the union on 26 Oct. 1905. The throne was offered to a prince of the reigning house of Sweden, who declined. After a plebiscite, Prince Carl of Denmark was formally elected King on 18 Nov. 1905, and he took the name of Haakon VII, reigning for 52 years, after which he was succeeded by his son.

From 1940 to 1944, during the Second World War, Norway was occupied by the Germans who set up a widely resented pro-German government under Vidkun Quisling.

Apart from this wartime episode, the Labour Party held office, and the majority in the Storting (parliament), from 1935 to 1965. From 1965 coalitions of minority governments held power until a Labour government again took office on 9 May 1986, succeeding a Conservative and Centre coalition. Thereafter, a left wing coalition held to power by a narrow margin until a centre right coalition took over in 1988. In 1990, Labour regained power.

TERRITORY AND POPULATION. Norway is bounded in the north by the Arctic Ocean, east by Russia, Finland and Sweden, south by the Skagerrak Straits and west by the North Sea. The total area of mainland Norway is 323,758 sq. km, including 17,506 sq. km of fresh water.

There are 19 counties (*folk*). Land area, population and densities:

	Land area (sq. km)	Population (1990 census)	Population (1997 estimate)	Density per sq. km 1997
Oslo (City)	427	461,190	494,793	1,159
Akershus	4,587	417,653	446,296	97
Østfold	3,889	238,296	241,151	62
Hedmark	26,120	187,276	186,003	7
Oppland	23,827	182,578	182,433	8
Buskerud	13,856	225,172	230,805	17
Vestfold	2,140	198,399	206,119	96
Telemark	14,186	162,907	163,449	12
Aust-Agder	8,485	97,333	100,582	12
Vest-Agder	6,817	144,917	151,580	22
Rogaland	8,553	337,504	360,403	42
Hordaland	14,962	410,567	427,003	29
Sogn og Fjordane	17,864	106,659	107,989	6
Møre og Romsdal	14,596	238,409	241,530	17
Sør-Trøndelag	17,839	250,978	258,283	14
Nord-Trøndelag	20,777	127,157	127,223	6
Nordland	36,302	239,311	240,255	7
Troms	25,147	146,716	151,242	6
Finnmark	45,879	74,524	75,575	2
Mainland total	306,253[1]	4,247,546	4,392,714	14

Svalbard and Jan Mayen have an area of 61,606 sq. km. Persons staying on Svalbard and Jan Mayen are registered as residents of their home Norwegian municipality.

[1] 118,244 sq. miles.

Population of the principal towns at the census of 3 Nov. 1990:

Oslo	459,292	Sandefjord	36,095	Halden	25,873
Bergen	212,944	Ålesund	35,862	Moss	24,683
Trondheim	137,846	Karmoy	35,087	Rana	24,650
Stavanger	98,109	Skedsmø	34,110	Lillehammer	22,850
Baerum	90,333	Tonsberg	31,551	Børre	22,568
Kristiansand	65,543	Ringsaker	31,377	Harstad	22,375
Drammen	51,880	Porsgrunn	31,268	Ski	22,337
Tromsø	51,218	Haugesund	27,736	Molde	22,251
Skien	47,870	Ringerike	27,384	Kongsberg	21,185
Sandnes	44,798	Fredrikstad	26,546	Oppegard	20,669
Asker	41,848	Lorensko	26,454	Steinkjer	20,665
Bodø	36,890	Gjøvik	26,207		

Vital statistics for calendar years:

	Marriages	Divorces	Births	Still-born	Outside marriage[1]	Deaths
1994	20,605	10,934	60,092	276	27,581	44,071
1995	21,677	10,360	60,292	236	28,680	45,190
1996	...	...	60,927	276	29,435	...

[1] Excluding still-born.

Over 1990–95, the suicide rate per 100,000 population was 15·5 (men, 23·3; women, 8).

Expectation of life, 1995: Males, 74·8 years; females, 80·82.

At 1 Jan. 1997 the immigrant population totalled 232,200, of whom 39% held Norwegian citizenship.

The official language is Norwegian, which has 2 versions: Bokmål (or Riksmål) and Nynorsk (or Landsmål).

The Sami, the indigenous people of the far north, number some 30,000 and form a distinct ethnic minority with their own culture and language.

CLIMATE. There is considerable variation in the climate because of the extent of latitude, the topography and the varying effectiveness of prevailing westerly winds and the Gulf Stream. Winters along the whole west coast are exceptionally mild but precipitation is considerable. Oslo. Jan. 24°F (−4·7°C), July 63°F (17·3°C). Annual rainfall 29·1" (740 mm). Bergen. Jan. 35°F (1·4°C), July 60°F (15·3°C). Annual rainfall 83" (2,108 mm). Trondheim. Jan. 26°F (−3·5°C), July 57°F (14°C). Annual rainfall 32·1" (870 mm).

ROYAL HOUSE. The reigning King is **Harald V,** born 21 Feb. 1937, married on 29 Aug. 1968 to Sonja Haraldsen. He succeeded on the death of his father, King Olav V, on 21 Jan. 1991. *Offspring:* Princess Märtha Louise, born 22 Sept. 1971; Crown Prince Haakon Magnus, born 20 July 1973. The king receives a tax-free annual allowance of 19·8m. kroner from the civil list. Women have been eligible to succeed to the throne since 1990. There is no coronation ceremony. The royal succession is in direct male line in the order of primogeniture. In default of male heirs the King may propose a successor to the Storting, but this assembly has the right to nominate another, if it does not agree with the proposal.

CONSTITUTION AND GOVERNMENT. Norway is a constitutional and hereditary monarchy. The Constitution, voted by a constituent assembly on 17 May 1814 and modified at various times, vests the legislative power of the realm in the *Storting* (Parliament). The royal veto may be exercised; but if the same Bill passes two Stortings formed by separate and subsequent elections it becomes the law of the land without the assent of the sovereign. The King has the command of the land, sea and air forces, and makes all appointments.

The 165-member Storting is directly elected by proportional representation. The country is divided into 19 districts, each electing from 4 to 15 representatives.

The Storting, when assembled, divides itself by election into the *Lagting* and the *Odelsting.* The former is composed of one-fourth of the members of the Storting, and the other of the remaining three-fourths. Each Ting (the Storting, the Odelsting and the Lagting) nominates its own president. Most questions are decided by the Storting, but questions relating to legislation must be considered and decided by the Odelsting and the Lagting separately. Only when the Odelsting and the Lagting disagree, the Bill has to be considered by the Storting in plenary sitting, and a new law can then only be decided by a majority of two-thirds of the voters. The same majority is required for alterations of the Constitution, which can only be decided by the Storting in plenary sitting. The Storting elects 5 delegates, whose duty it is to revise the public accounts. The Lagting and the ordinary members of the Supreme Court of Justice (the *Høyesterett*) form a High Court of the Realm (the *Riksrett*) for the trial of ministers, members of the *Høyesterett* and members of the Storting. The impeachment before the *Riksrett* can only be decided by the Odelsting.

The executive is represented by the King, who exercises his authority through the Cabinet. Cabinet ministers are entitled to be present in the Storting and to take part in the discussions, but without a vote.

At the elections for the Storting held on 16 Sept. 1997 the following parties were elected: Labour Party, 65 (with 35% of the vote); Christian Democratic Party, 25; Progress Party 25; Conservative Party, 23; Centre Party, 11; Socialist Left Party, 9; Liberal Party, 6; Coastal Party, 1.

During the election campaign, Prime Minister Thorbjørn Jagland announced his decision to resign if the Labour Party failed to attract at least 36·9% of the vote, the same share that the party received in 1993. He resigned on 14 Oct. 1997 and on 17 Oct. Kjell Magne Bondevik formed a coalition government of the 3 centrist parties (Christian Democratic, Centre and Liberal) with a combined 261% of the vote.

In March 1998 the minority Coalition government comprised:

Prime Minister: Kjell Magne Bondevik (b. 1947).

Culture· Anne Enger Lahnstein. *Children and Family Affairs:* Valgerd Svarstad Haugland. *Industry and Trade:* Lars Sponheim. *Foreign Affairs:* Knut Vollebæk. *Fisheries:* Peter Angelsen. *Finance:* Gudmund Restad. *Local Government and Regional Development:* Ragnhild Queseth Haarstad. *Agriculture:* Kåre Gjønnes. *Justice:* Aud Inger Aure. *Labour and Government Administration:* Eldbjørg Løwer. *Transport and Communications:* Odd Einar Dørum. *Education, Research and Church Affairs:* Jon Lilletun. *Defence:* Dag Jostein Fjærvoll. *Social Affairs:* Magnhild Meltveit Kleppa. *Health:* Dagfinn Høybråten. *Oil and Energy:* Marit Arnstad. *Environment:* Guro Fjellanger. *Development Co-operation and Human Rights:* Hilde Frafjord Johnson.

National anthem: 'Ja, vi elsker dette landet' ('Yes, we love this land'); words by B. Bjørnson, tune by R. Nordraak.

Local Government. There are 18 counties and the urban district of Oslo, in each of which the central government is represented by a county governor. The counties are divided into 435 municipalities, each of which usually corresponds in size to a parish. The municipalities are administered by municipal councils, whose membership may vary between 25 and 85 directly-elected councillors. Elections were held in Sept. 1995; turn-out was 62·8%. The Labour Party gained 30·5% of all votes cast; the Conservative Party, 20·2%; the Centre Party, 11·6%; the Progress Party, 10·5%.

DEFENCE. Conscription is for 12 months, with 4 to 5 refresher training periods.

Army. There are a Northern and a Southern command, and within these the Army is organized in 4 district commands, 1 divisional headquarters and 14 territorial commands. North Command consists of 1 brigade group. South Command consists of 2 infantry battalions, including the Royal Guard. Equipment includes 170 Leopard main battle tanks. Strength (1997) 14,700 (including 9,200 conscripts). The fast mobilization reserve numbers 255,000.

Navy. The Royal Norwegian Navy has 3 components: The Navy, Coast Guard and Coastal Artillery. Main Naval combatants include 12 coastal submarines (including 6 new German-built Ula class), 4 frigates, 28 missile craft, 3 coastal minesweepers, 6 minehunters and 2 minelayers. Auxiliaries comprise 1 submarine/missile craft support ship, 1 Royal Yacht and some 10 small general-purpose tenders. The Coastal Artillery man 26 coastal batteries and other static defence systems.

The personnel of the navy totalled 6,400 in 1996, of whom 3,600 were conscripts. 1,000 served in Coastal Artillery and 700 in the Coast Guard. The main naval base is at Bergen (Håkonsvern), with subsidiary bases at Horten, Ramsund and Tromsø.

The naval elements of the Home Guard on mobilization can muster some 6,000 personnel, and man 2 tank landing craft, 7 torpedo craft and about 400 requisitioned fishing vessels.

The 12 Coast Guard offshore patrol vessels (of which 3 are armed, and of frigate capability) are Navy-subordinated, and assist other government agencies in rescue service, environmental patrols, surveillance and police duties.

Air Force. The Royal Norwegian Air Force comprises the Air Force and the Antiair Artillery. The Air Force consists of 4 squadrons of F-16 Fighting Falcons, 1 squadron of F-5 fighter-bombers, 1 maritime patrol squadron of P-3N and P-3C Orions, 1 squadron of C-130 Hercules transports, 1 squadron of Falcon 20s equipped for EW duties, 1 squadron with DHC-6 Twin Otter light transports and 2 squadrons of Bell 412SP helicopters. The Anti-air Artillery deploy 4 Nike surface-to-air missile batteries and several light anti-aircraft artillery units. 6 NOAH (Norwegian adapted Hawk missiles) batteries provide area and airfield defence co-ordinated with 10 SAM batteries with the mobile missile system RBS-70. Finally 27 batteries with 40 mm Bofors AA-guns and 12·7 mm machine guns. 12 Westland Sea King helicopters are used for search and rescue duties; 5 Lynx helicopters are operated for the Coast Guard; 17 Saab Safaris are used for primary training; pilots then go to the USA for advanced training.

Total strength (1996) is about 7,900 personnel, including 4,100 conscripts.

Home Guard. The Home Guard is organized in small units equipped and trained for special tasks. Service after basic training is 1 week a year. The Home Guard consists of the Land Home Guard (strength, 1996, 71,000), Sea Home Guard and Anti-Air Home Guard organized in 18 districts. *See also under* NAVY, *above.*

INTERNATIONAL RELATIONS

Membership. Norway is a member of the UN, NATO, EFTA, OECD, the Council of Europe and the Nordic Council, and an Associate Member of the WEU. Norway has acceded to the Schengen Accord abolishing border controls between Norway and Austria, Belgium, Denmark, Finland, France, Germany, Greece, Iceland, Italy, Luxembourg, Netherlands, Portugal, Spain and Sweden.

In a referendum on 27-28 Nov. 1994 52·2% of votes cast were against joining the EU. The electorate was 3,266,182; turn-out was 88·88%.

ECONOMY

Performance. Real GDP growth was estimated at 3·3% in 1997 (4·8% in 1996).

Budget. Current central government revenue and expenditure (in 1m. kroner) for years ending 31 Dec.:

	1994	1995	1996	1997
Revenue	347,260	381,849	423,676	429,000
Expenditure	345,046	350,667	365,247	374,600

All state income from oil and gas is put into the Petroleum Fund. The Government uses the Fund to finance the gap between state spending and conventional state revenues.

Currency. The unit of currency is the *Norwegian krone* (NOK) of 100 *øre*. There are coins of 10 and 50 øre and 1, 5 and 10 kroner, and notes of 50, 100, 200, 500 and 1,000 kroner. On 31 Dec. 1996 the nominal value of notes and coins in circulation was 43,569m. kroner. After Oct. 1990 the krone was fixed to the ecu in the EMS of the EU in the narrow band of 2·25%, but it was freed in Dec. 1992. Annualized inflation was 1·2% in 1996.

Banking and Finance. Norges Bank is the central bank and bank of issue. Supreme authority is vested in the Executive Board consisting of 7 members appointed by the King and the Supervisory Council consisting of 15 members elected by the Storting. The *Governor* is Kjell Storvik (b. 1930).

There are 3 major commercial banks: Den Norske Bank, Christiana and Fokus. Total assets and liabilities of the 20 commercial banks at 31 Dec. 1996 were 552,348m. kroner.

At the end of 1992 there were 23 private joint-stock banks. Their total amount of capital and funds was 21,284m. kroner (capital 12,029m., funds 9,255m.). Deposits at the end of 1995 amounted to 248,187m. kroner.

The number of savings banks at 31 Dec. 1996 was 132; ordinary deposits totalled 247,678m. kroner.

There is a stock exchange in Oslo.

Weights and Measures. The metric system is obligatory.

ENERGY AND NATURAL RESOURCES

Electricity. Norway is a large producer of hydro-electric energy. The potential total hydro-electric power is estimated at 170,000m. kWh annually. Installed capacity in 1989 was 251 MW (thermo-electric) and 25,841 MW (hydro-electric). Output, 1996, 104,756m. kWh (123,011m. kWh in 1995, of which 122,484m. kWh hydro-electric).

Oil and Gas. There are enormous oil reserves in the Norwegian continental shelf. In 1966 the first exploration well was drilled. Production of crude oil, 1996 (provisional), 156,788,000 tonnes. Output of natural gas, 1996 (provisional), 41,289m. cu. metres. Norway is the world's second biggest oil exporter after Saudi Arabia.

Minerals. Production, 1996 (in tonnes): Iron ore, 1,554,599; ferrotitanium ore, 758,711; copper concentrates, 31,736; lead ore (1995), 3,721; zinc ore, 8,619.

Agriculture. Norway is barren and mountainous. The arable area is in strips in valleys and around fiords and lakes.

In 1996 the agricultural area[1] was 1,031,200 ha, of which 609,300 ha were meadow and pasture, 174,600 ha were sown to barley, 97,000 ha to oats, 58,800 ha to wheat and 18,100 ha to potatoes. Production (in 1,000 tonnes) in 1995: Barley, 547; oats, 354; wheat, 312; potatoes, 400; hay, 3,274; vegetables, 132; meat, 240.

Livestock, 1996[1]: 1,005,800 cattle (342,700 milch cows), 1,032,300 sheep, 57,900 goats, 1,328,500 pigs, 3,460,600 hens. 1995: 0·1m. silver and platinum fox, 0·52m. blue fox, 0·33m. mink, 203,900 reindeer.

[1] Holdings with at least 50 ha agricultural area in use.

Forestry. Productive forest area, 1997, approximately 67,375 sq. km. About 80% of the productive forest area consists of conifers and 20% of broadleaves. The annual increment (in 1993) was 20,332,000 cu. metres with bark. In 1995–96, 7·8m. cu. metres of roundwood were cut: 37m. cu. metres were special and saw timber and 36m. cu. metres pulpwood.

Fisheries. The total number of fishermen in 1996 was 23,397, of whom 6,310 had another chief occupation. In 1996, the number of registered fishing vessels (all with motor) was 13,944, and of these 5,290 were open boats.

The catch in 1996 totalled 2,632,867 tonnes. 16,737 seals were caught in 1996. Commercial whaling was prohibited in 1988, but recommenced in 1993: 388 whales were caught in 1996.

Environment. In 1996 there were 18 national parks (total area, 1,378,840 ha), 1,293 nature reserves (228,895 ha), 82 landscape protected areas (467,117 ha) and 75 other areas with protected flora and fauna (10,869 ha).

INDUSTRY. Industry is chiefly based on raw materials. Paper and paper products, industrial chemicals and basic metals are important export manufactures. In the following table are given figures for industrial establishments in 1995. The values are given in 1m. kroner.

Industries	Establish-ments	Number of Employees	Gross value of produc-tion	Value added
Coal and peat	12	325	165	32
Metal ores	8	1,161	1,118	348
Other mining and quarrying	333	2,868	3,336	1,464
Food products	1,712	45,503	79,500	13,481
Beverages and tobacco	56	5,942	12,705	9,460
Textiles	307	4,777	3,520	1,298
Clothing, etc.	154	2,465	1,431	514
Leather and leather products	45	776	527	179
Wood and wood products	959	14,469	14,737	4,173
Pulp, paper and paper products	115	10,869	22,230	7,236
Printing and publishing	1,785	36,033	25,927	11,616
Basic chemicals	65	8,439	20,785	7,251
Other chemical products	97	5,422	8,748	3,492
Coal and refined petroleum products	78	1,636	13,425	870
Rubber and plastic products	337	6,312	6,507	2,294
Other non-metallic mineral products	500	8,349	9,906	3,840
Basic metals	116	15,107	37,113	9,867
Metal products, except machinery/equipment	1,150	16,891	13,793	5,564
Machinery and equipment	1,123	21,972	23,812	8,084
Office machinery and computers	21	889	1,292	352
Electrical machinery and apparatus	304	9,325	10,673	3,828
Radio, television, communication equipment	66	4,171	5,672	1,976
Medical, precision and optical instruments	285	5,155	5,859	2,187
Oil platforms	99	18,006	16,486	6,728
Motor vehicles and trailers	91	4,553	4,404	1,464
Other transport equipment	483	17,827	19,611	5,381
Other manufacturing industries	720	12,428	9,296	3,441
Total (all industries)	11,021	281,490	372,578	116,419

Income at factor cost (in 1m. kroner):

	1990	1991	1992
Net domestic product	561,727	584,224	598,762
Less Indirect taxes	111,089	115,617	121,441
Add Subsidies	39,992	42,770	44,395
	490,630	511,377	521,718

Labour. The labour force (i.e. employed persons plus non-employed persons seeking work aged 16–74) averaged 2,246,000 persons in 1996 (1·03m. females).

The total number of employed persons averaged 2,137,000 in 1996 (0·98m. females), of whom 1,952,000 were salaried employees and wage earners, 165,000 self-employed and 19,000 family workers.

Distribution of employed persons by occupation in 1995 showed 560,000 in technical, physical science, humanistic and artistic work; 146,000 administrative executive work; 197,000 clerical; 222,000 sales; 105,000 agriculture, forestry, fishing etc.; 8,000 mining and quarrying; 131,000 transport and communication; 385,000 manufacturing; 285,000 service; and 39,000 military and occupation not specified.

There were 90,983 registered unemployed in 1996 (40,589 females).

There were 18 work stoppages in 1996: 549,842 working days were lost.

Trade Unions. There were 1,426,837 union members in 1996.

FOREIGN ECONOMIC RELATIONS

Commerce. Total imports and exports in calendar years (in 1m. kroner):

	1992	1993	1994	1995	1996
Imports	161,931	170,991	192,963	208,626	229,720
Exports	218,374	226,626	244,475	265,883	320,128

Major import suppliers in 1996 (value in 1m. kroner): Sweden, 37,857·4; Germany, 30,106·7; UK, 22,630·6; Denmark, 17,136·4; USA, 15,376·2; Japan, 10,512·6; Netherlands, 9,877·7; France, 9,424·1; Italy, 9,2657; Finland, 7,9457.

Imports from economic areas: EU, 160,759·5; Nordic countries, 63,599·3; EFTA, 3,641·6.

Major export markets in 1996: UK, 62,885·1; Netherlands, 36,432·6; Germany, 35,596·5; Sweden, 29,176·9; France, 27,753·9; USA, 22,670·1; Denmark, 14,514·7; Canada, 12,917·7; Belgium, 10,219·2; Italy, 8,490·8; Finland, 7,171·1. Exports to economic areas: EU, 245,387·2; Nordic countries, 52,968·1; EFTA, 3,115·9.

Principal imports in 1996 (in 1m. kroner): Machinery, 24,263·3; motor vehicles, 23,010·2; electrical machinery, 12,121·4; iron and steel, 10,169; office machines and computers, 10,096·8; metalliferous ores and metal scrap, 9,319·1; clothing and accessories, 8,903·8; telecommunications and sound apparatus and equipment, 7,351·1; ships over 100 tonnes, 6,091·5; paper, paperboard and products, 6,054·6; petroleum and products, 5,532·9. Principal exports in 1996 (in 1m. kroner): Crude petroleum, 135,729·5; fish, crustaceans and molluscs, and preparations thereof, 21,383·4; natural gas, 20,959·5; non-ferrous metals, 20,554·1; paper, paperboard and products, 9,490·3; iron and steel, 9,311·9; ships over 100 tonnes, 7,512·9.

Tourism. In 1996, foreign visitors spent 5·05m. nights in the 1,186 hotels and 1,936,000 nights in the 744 camping sites.

COMMUNICATIONS

Roads. In 1997 the length of public roads (including roads in towns) totalled 91,346 km. Of these, 61,101 km were hard-surfaced in 1991. Total road length included: National roads, 26,535 km; provincial roads, 27,127 km; local roads, 37,684 km. Number of registered motor vehicles, 1996: 1,661,247 passenger cars (including station wagons and ambulances), 33,959 buses, 186,523 vans, 102,233 combined vehicles, 69,372 goods vehicles, 218,552 tractors, 39,809 snow scooters, 50,661 motor cycles and 114,114 mopeds. In 1996 there were 8,779 road accidents with 255 fatalities.

Railways. The length of state railways in 1996 was 4,021 km (2,420 km electrified); of private companies in 1995, 16 km (electrified). Total receipts of the state railways in 1995 were 5,560m. kroner; total expenses, 5,328m. kroner. The state railways carried 14,559,000 tonnes of freight and 40,701,000 passengers in 1996.

There is a metro (98 km) and tram/light rail line (54 km) in Oslo.

Civil Aviation. There are international airports at Oslo (Fornebu), Bergen (Flesland) and Stavanger (Sola). Denmark and Norway each hold two-sevenths and Sweden three-sevenths of the capital of SAS (Scandinavian Airlines System), but they have joint responsibility towards third parties. At 31 Dec. 1996 there were 864 registered aircraft. 23,744,601 passengers, 87,489 tonnes of freight and 50,154 tonnes of mail were carried on all domestic and international flights in 1996.

Services are also provided by Aeroflot, Air France, Air Malta, Air Stord, Air UK, Alitalia, Austrian Airlines, Braathens, British Airways, British Midland, Coast Air, Continental Airlines & Air Micronesia, Finnair, Hemus Air, Icelandair, KLM, Lufthansa, Muk Air, Newair, Northwest Airlines, Sabena, Sun Air, Swissair, TAP, Teddy Air, United Airlines and Wideroe's.

Shipping. The Norwegian International Ship Register was set up in 1987. At 31 Dec. 1996, 664 ships were registered (438 Norwegian) totalling 18,886,000 GRT. There were also 923 ships totalling 2,385,000 GRT on the Norwegian Ordinary Register. These figures do not include fishing boats, tugs, salvage vessels, icebreakers and similar special types of vessels.

Goods (in 1,000 tonnes) in 1993 discharged, 18,929; loaded, 108,268.

In 1995, 43,213,000 passengers were carried by coastwise shipping on long distance, local and ferry services, and in 1993 (excluding long distance except Bergen-Stavanger) 34·6m. tonnes of cargo.

Telecommunications. There were 2,091 post offices in 1996. Number of telephone connexions on 31 Dec. 1996 was 2,440,185. There were 1,261,445 mobile telephones in use in 1996. The Norwegian Broadcasting Corporation is a non-commercial enterprise operated by an independent state organization and broadcasts 1 programme (P1) on long-, medium-, and short-waves and on FM and 1 programme (P2) on FM. Local programmes are also broadcast. It broadcasts 1 TV programme from 2,259 transmitters. Colour programmes are broadcast by PAL system. Number of television licences, 1996, 1,637,172.

Press. There were 64 daily newspapers with a combined average net circulation of 2·22m. in 1996, and 90 weeklies and semi-weeklies with 725,000.

SOCIAL INSTITUTIONS

Justice. The judicature is common to civil and criminal cases; the same professional judges preside over both. These judges are state officials. The participation of lay judges and jurors, both summoned for the individual case, varies according to the kind of court and kind of case.

The 96 city or district courts of first instance are in criminal cases composed of one professional judge and 2 lay judges, chosen by ballot from a panel elected by the local authority. In civil cases 2 lay judges may participate. These courts are competent in all cases except criminal cases where the maximum penalty exceeds 6 years imprisonment.

In every community there is a Conciliation Board composed of 3 lay persons elected by the district council. A civil lawsuit usually begins with mediation by the Board which can pronounce judgement in certain cases.

The 5 high courts, or courts of second instance, are composed of 3 professional judges. Additionally, in civil cases 2 or 4 lay judges may be summoned. In serious criminal cases, which are brought before high courts in the first instance, a jury of 10 lay persons is summoned to determine whether the defendant is guilty according to the charge. In less serious criminal cases the court is composed of 2 professional and 3 lay judges. In civil cases, the court of second instance is an ordinary court of appeal. In criminal cases in which the lower court does not have judicial authority, it is itself the court of first instance. In other criminal cases it is an appeal court as far as the appeal is based on an attack against the lower court's assessment of the facts when determining the guilt of the defendant. An appeal based on any other alleged mistakes is brought directly before the Supreme Court.

The Supreme Court *(Høyesterett)* is the court of last resort. There are 18 Supreme Court judges. Each individual case is heard by 5 judges. Some major cases are determined in plenary session. The Supreme Court may in general examine every aspect of the case and the handling of it by the lower courts. However, in criminal cases the Court may not overrule the lower court's assessment of the facts as far as the guilt of the defendant is concerned.

The Court of Impeachment *(Riksretten)* is composed of 5 judges of the Supreme Court and 10 members of Parliament.

All serious offences are prosecuted by the State. The Public Prosecution Authority consists of the Attorney General, 18 district attorneys and legally qualified officers of the ordinary police force. Counsel for the defence is in general provided for by the State.

Religion. There is freedom of religion, the Church of Norway (Evangelical Lutheran), however, being the national church, endowed by the State. Its clergy are nominated by the King. Ecclesiastically Norway is divided into 11 bishoprics, 96 archdeaconries and 626 clerical districts. There were 237,733 members of registered and unregistered religious communities outside the Evangelical Lutheran Church, subsidized by central government and local authorities in 1996. At 1 Jan. 1997 there were 59 Moslem congregations with 46,500 members. The Roman Catholics are under a Bishop at Oslo, a Vicar Apostolic at Trondheim and a Vicar Apostolic at Tromsø.

Education. Free compulsory schooling in primary and lower secondary schools was extended to 10 years from 9, and the starting age lowered to 6 from 7, in July 1997. All young people between the ages of 16 and 19 have the statutory right to 3 years of upper secondary education. In 1995 there were 6,261 nursery schools for children under 7 with 188,213 children and 51,832 staff. In 1995–96 there were 3,285 primary and lower secondary schools with 477,236 pupils and 37,966 teachers; (1991–92) 75 special schools with 1,980 pupils and (1990–91) 1,099 teachers; 730 upper secondary schools with 216,126 pupils and 20,849 teachers; and 74 colleges, with 93,788 students and 5,116 teachers.

There are 4 universities: Bergen, founded 1946; Oslo, 1811; Tromsø, 1968; and the Norwegian University of Science and Technology, 1996 (formerly the University of Trondheim and the Norwegian Institute of Technology); and 10 specialized institutions of equivalent status. In 1995–96 these had 82,957 students and 6,031 academic staff. The University of Tromsø is responsible for Sami language and studies.

Health. The health care system, which is predominantly publicly financed (mainly by a national insurance tax), is run on both county and municipal levels. Persons who fall ill are guaranteed medical treatment, and health services are distributed according to need. In 1996 there were 15,368 doctors, 5,222 dentists and 65,232 nurses.

Social Security. In 1996 there were 625,940 old age pensioners who received a total of 50,426m. kroner, 239,429 disability pensioners who received 23,473·7m. kroner, 30,895 widows and widowers who received 1,774·8m. kroner and 45,529 single parents who received 2,425·4m. kroner. In 1996, 910,009 children received family allowances. Maternity leave is for 1 year on 80% of previous salary; unused portions may pass to a husband. In 1996 sickness benefits totalling 24,784·9m. kroner were paid: 13,220·5m. kroner in sickness allowances and 11,564·4m. kroner in medical benefits. Expenditure on benefits at childbirth and adoption totalled 6,262·5m. kroner to 87,714 cases in 1996.

Culture. There were 557 museums in 1995 (41 art, 447 social history, 15 natural history and 54 mixed social and natural history), with 8,880,924 visitors.

There were 6,639 theatre and opera performances attended by 1,287,026 people at 20 theatres in 1995.

There were 393 cinemas in 1995, with a seating capacity of 90,290.

In 1995 there were 1,157 public libraries, 3,667 school libraries, and 342 special and research libraries (8 national).

DIPLOMATIC REPRESENTATIVES

Of Norway in Great Britain (25 Belgrave Sq., London, SW1X 8QD)
Ambassador: Kjell Colding, CMG.

Of Great Britain in Norway (Thomas Heftyesgate 8, 0244 Oslo, 2)
Ambassador: M. Elliott, CMG.

Of Norway in the USA (2720 34th St., NW, Washington, D.C., 20008)
Ambassador: Tom Eric Vraalsen, GCVO.

Of the USA in Norway (Drammensveien 18, 0244 Oslo, 2)
Ambassador: Thomas Loftus.

Of Norway to the United Nations
Ambassador: Ole Peter Kolby.

Of Norway to the European Union
Ambassador: Einar Bull.

Further Reading

Central Bureau of Statistics. *Statistisk Årbok; Statistical Yearbook of Norway.—Economic survey* (annual, from 1935; with English summary from 1952, now published in *Økonomiske Analyser*, annual).—*Historisk Statistikk; Historical Statistics.—Statistisk Månedshefte* (with English index)

Norges Statskalender. From 1816; annual from 1877

Arntzen, J. G. and Knudsen, B. B., *Political Life and Institutions in Norway.* Oslo, 1981

Derry, T. K., *A History of Modern Norway, 1814–1972.* OUP, 1973.—*A History of Scandinavia.* London, 1979

Petersson, O., *The Government and Politics of the Nordic Countries.* Stockholm, 1994

Sather, L. B., *Norway.* [Bibliography] Oxford and Santa Barbara (CA), 1986

Selbyg, A., *Norway Today: An Introduction to Modern Norwegian Society.* Oslo, 1986

National library: The University Library, Drammensvein 42b, 0255 Oslo.
National statistical office: Central Bureau of Statistics, PB 8131 Dep., N-0033 Oslo.
Website: http://www.ssb.no/

SVALBARD

An archipelago situated between 10° and 35° E. long. and between 74° and 81° N. lat. Total area, 61,229 sq. km (23,640 sq. miles). The main islands are Spitsbergen, Nordaustlandet, Edgeøya, Barentsøya, Prins Karls Forland, Bjørnøya, Hopen, Kong Karls Land and Kvitøya. The Arctic climate is tempered by mild winds from the Atlantic.

The archipelago was probably discovered by Norsemen in 1194 and rediscovered by the Dutch navigator Barents in 1596. In the 17th century whale-hunting gave rise to rival Dutch, British and Danish–Norwegian claims to sovereignty. But when in the 18th century the whale-hunting ended, the question of the sovereignty of Svalbard lost its significance; it was again raised in the 20th century, owing to the discovery and exploitation of coalfields. By a treaty, signed on 9 Feb. 1920 in Paris, Norway's sovereignty over the archipelago was recognized. On 14 Aug. 1925 the archipelago was officially incorporated in Norway.

Total population on 1 Jan. 1997 was an estimated 3,231, of whom 1,739 were Norwegians, 1,482 Russians, and 10 Poles. Coal is the principal product. There are 2 Norwegian and 2 Russian mining camps. 292,094 tonnes of coal were produced from Norwegian mines in 1995 valued at 73,275,000 kroner.

There were 2,104 motor vehicles and trailers registered at 31 Dec. 1996, including 1,168 snow scooters.

There are research and radio stations, and an airport near Longyearbyen (Svalbard Lufthavn) opened in 1975.

Greve, T., *Svalbard: Norway in the Arctic.* Oslo, 1975
Hisdal, V., *Geography of Svalbard.* Norsk Polarinstitutt, Oslo, rev. ed., 1984

JAN MAYEN

This bleak, desolate and mountainous island of volcanic origin and partly covered by glaciers, is situated 71° N. lat. and 8° 30' W. long., 300 miles NNE of Iceland. The total area is 377 sq. km (146 sq. miles). Beerenberg, its highest peak, reaches a height of 2,277 metres. Volcanic activity, which had been dormant, was reactivated in Sept. 1970.

The island was possibly discovered by Henry Hudson in 1608, and it was first named Hudson's Tutches (Touches). It was again and again rediscovered and renamed. Its present name derives from the Dutch whaling captain Jan Jacobsz May, who indisputably discovered the island in 1614. It was uninhabited, but occasionally visited by seal hunters and trappers, until 1921 when Norway established a radio and meteorological station. On 8 May 1929 Jan Mayen was officially proclaimed as incorporated in the Kingdom of Norway. Its relation to Norway was finally settled by law of 27 Feb. 1930. A LORAN station (1959) and a CONSOL station (1968) have been established.

BOUVET ISLAND

Bouvetøya

This uninhabited volcanic island, mostly covered by glaciers and situated 54° 25' S. lat. and 3° 21' E. long., was discovered in 1739 by a French naval officer, Jean Baptiste Loziert Bouvet, but no flag was hoisted till, in 1825, Capt. Norris raised the Union Jack. In 1928 Great Britain waived its claim to the island in favour of Norway, which in Dec. 1927 had occupied it. A law of 27 Feb. 1930 declared Bouvetøya a Norwegian dependency. The area is 59 sq. km (23 sq. miles). Since 1977 Norway has had an automatic meteorological station on the island.

PETER I ISLAND
Peter I Øy

This uninhabited island, situated 68° 48' S. lat. and 90° 35' W. long., was sighted in 1821 by the Russian explorer, Admiral von Bellingshausen. The first landing was made in 1929 by a Norwegian expedition which hoisted the Norwegian flag. On 1 May 1931 Peter I Island was placed under Norwegian sovereignty, and on 24 March 1933 it was incorporated in Norway as a dependency. The area is 249 sq. km (96 sq. miles).

QUEEN MAUD LAND
Dronning Maud Land

On 14 Jan. 1939 the Norwegian Cabinet placed that part of the Antarctic Continent from the border of Falkland Islands dependencies in the west to the border of the Australian Antarctic Dependency in the east (between 20° W. and 45° E.) under Norwegian sovereignty. The territory had been explored only by Norwegians and hitherto been ownerless. In 1957 it was given the status of a dependency.

OMAN

Saltanat 'Uman

(Sultanate of Oman)

Capital: Muscat
Population: 2·14m.
GNP: US$10·8bn.
HDI/world rank: 0·718/88

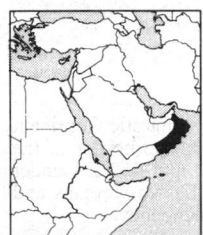

KEY HISTORICAL EVENTS. Little is known about Oman's pre-Islamic past but it is clear from recent archaeological discoveries and research that early civilizations existed at least 5,000 years ago. The ancestors of present day Oman are believed to have arrived in two waves of migration over a number of years, the first from the Yemen and the second from northern Arabia at a time when various parts of the country were occupied by the Persians. In the 9th century maritime trade flourished and Sohar became the greatest sea port in the Islamic world. In the early 16th century after the Portuguese under Vasco de Gama had discovered the sea route round the Cape of Good Hope to India, they occupied Muscat and its trade until they were expelled in 1650. The Ya'aruba dynasty introduced a period of renaissance in Omani fortunes both at home and abroad, uniting the country and bringing prosperity. But, on the death in 1718 of Sultan bin Saif II, civil war broke out over the election of his successor. Persian troops occupied Muttrah and Muscat but failed to take Sohar which was defended by Ahmad bin Said, who continued to fight the Persians and drive them from Oman after the civil war had ended.

In 1744, the Al bu Said family assumed power and has ruled to the present day. The early part of this century saw a period of decline and, at the time of the First World War, Oman's share of international commercial activities was very limited. Indeed, Oman remained largely isolated from the rest of the world until 1970 when Said bin Taimur was deposed by his son Qaboos in a bloodless *coup*. Sultan Qaboos bin Said introduced reforms including the setting up of an advisory council of regional representatives.

TERRITORY AND POPULATION. Situated at the south-east corner of the Arabian peninsular, Oman is bounded in the north-east by the Gulf of Oman and south-east by the Arabian Sea, south-west by Yemen and north-west by Saudi Arabia and the United Arab Emirates. There is an enclave at the northern tip of the Musandam Peninsula between the United Arab Emirates of Ras al-Khaimah in the west and Fujairah in the south-east. An agreement of June 1995 completed the demarcation of the border with Yemen, and an agreement with Saudi Arabia of July 1995 permits the demarcation of their mutual border.

With a coastline of 1,700 sq. km. from the Strait of Hormuz in the north to the borders of the Republic of Yemen, the Sultanate is strategically located overlooking ancient maritime trade routes linking the Far East and Africa with the Mediterranean.

The Sultanate of Oman occupies a total area of 309,500 sq. km. and includes different terrains that vary from plain to highlands and mountains. The coastal plain overlooking the Gulf of Oman and the Arabian Sea forms the most important and fertile plain in Oman.

The **Kuria Muria** islands were ceded to the UK in 1854 by the Sultan of Muscat and Oman. On 30 Nov. 1967 the islands were retroceded to the Sultan of Muscat and Oman, in accordance with the wishes of the population.

At the 1993 census the population was 2,018,000. Estimated population (1995), 2,135,000, chiefly Arabs, and including 0·53m. foreign workers. Birth rate, 3·5%; infant mortality rate, 20 per 1,000 live births. Expectation of life was 67·4 years in 1995.

The official language is Arabic; English is in commercial use.

CLIMATE. Oman has a desert climate, with exceptionally hot and humid months from April to Oct., when temperatures may reach 47°C. Light monsoon rains fall in the south from June to Sept., with highest amounts in the western highland region. Muscat. Jan. 28°C, July 46°C. Annual rainfall 101 mm. Salalah. Jan. 29°C, July 32°C. Annual rainfall 98 mm.

RULER. The present Sultan is Qaboos bin Said (born Nov. 1940).

CONSTITUTION AND GOVERNMENT. Oman is a hereditary absolute monarchy. The Sultan legislates by decree and appoints a Cabinet to assist him; and he is nominally Prime Minister and Minister of Foreign Affairs, Defence and Finance. The other Ministers were in March 1998:

Personal Representative of the Sultan: Saiyid Thuwainy bin Shihab Al Said.
Prime Minister: Ahmed bin Abdul-Nabi Maki.
Deputy Prime Minister: Sayyid Fahad bin Mahmoud Al Said (*Council of Ministers*). *Agriculture and Fisheries:* Ahmad bin Khalfan bin Muhammad al-Rawahi. *Civil Service:* Abdul Aziz bin Matar bin Salim al-Azizi. *Commerce and Industry:* Maqbool bin Ali bin Sultan. *Transportation:* Salim bin Abdullah al-Ghazali. *Education:* Sayyid Saud bin Ibrahim al-Busaidi. *Electricity and Water:* Mohamed bin Ali al-Qatabi. *Regional Municipalities and Environment:* Khamis bin Mubarak bin Isa al-Alawi. *National Economy:* Ahmed bin Abdul Nabi Macki. *Health:* Ali bin Mohammed bin Moosa. *Housing:* Malik bin Suleiman al-Ma'mari. *Information:* Abdul Aziz bin Mohammed al-Rowas. *Interior:* Sayyid Badr bin Saud bin Hareb Al Busai'di. *Justice:* Muhammaad bin Abdallah bin Zahir al-Hinai. *National Heritage and Culture:* Sayyid Faisal bin Ali Al Said. *Petroleum and Minerals:* Muhammad bin Hamad bin Sayf al-Rumhi. *Posts, Telegraphs and Telephones:* Ahmed bin Suwaidan al-Balushi. *Social Affairs and Labour:* Amir bin Shuwayn al-Alawi. *Awqaf and Religious Affairs:* Abdallah bin Muhammad bin Abdallah al-Salimi. *Minister of the Diwan of the Royal Court:* Sayyid Saif bin Hamad bin Saud. *Minister of the Palace Office Affairs and Head of the Office of the Supreme Commander of the Armed Forces:* Fariq Awal Ali bin Majid al-Ma'amiri. *Water Resources:* Hamed bin Said al-Aufi. *Minister of State and Governor of Dhofar:* Sayyid Mussallam bin Ali al-Busaidi. *Minister of State, Governor of Muscat:* Sayyid al Mutasim bin Hamoud al-Busaidi. *Minister of State for Foreign Affairs:* Yusuf bin Alawi bin Abdullah. *Higher Education:* Yahya bin Mahfudh al-Mantheri. *Legal Affairs:* Mohammed bin Ali al-Alawi. *Development Affairs:* Mohammed bin Moosa al-Yousef.

In 1991 a new consultative assembly, the *Majlis al Shura*, replaced the former State Consultative Chamber. The Majlis consists of a president and 59 representatives (including 2 women) who are nominated one from each governorate, and ultimately approved by the Sultan. It debates domestic issues, but has no legislative or veto powers.

National anthem: 'Ya Rabbana elifidh lana jalalat al Saltan' ('O Lord, protect for us his majesty the Sultan'); words and tune anonymous.

Local Government. Oman is divided into 8 regions and 59 governorates *(wilayats)*.

DEFENCE

Army. The Army consists of 1 divisional and 2 brigade headquarters, 2 armoured, 1 armoured reconnaissance, 4 artillery, 1 air defence, 8 infantry, 1 infantry reconnaissance, 1 field engineer and 1 airborne regiment and a security force. Equipment includes 6 M-60A1, 43 M-60A3, 24 Chieftain and 18 Challenger 2 main battle tanks. Strength (1997) about 25,000. (Regiments are of battalion size). The armed forces include 6,500 Royal Household troops, and the Musandam Security Force, an independent rifle company. A paramilitary tribal home guard numbers 4,000.

Navy. The Navy, which is based principally at Seeb (HQ) and Wudam includes 2 new British-built missile corvettes, 4 fast missile craft, 3 coastal and 6 inshore patrol craft. Naval personnel in 1996 totalled 4,200.

The marine police coastguard, 400 strong in 1996, operates 10 coastal patrol craft.

The wholly separate Royal Yacht Squadron consists of a 3,800-tonne yacht and an 11,000-tonne support ship with helicopter and troop-carrying capability.

Air Force. The Air Force, formed in 1959, has 46 combat aircraft including in 1996 two strike/interceptor squadrons of Jaguars, a ground attack squadron of Hawk 200s and a squadron of Strikemaster light jet training/attack aircraft. The defence force has batteries of Rapier low-level surface-to-air missiles. Personnel (1996) about 4,100.

INTERNATIONAL RELATIONS. A 1982 Memorandum of Understanding with the UK provided for regular consultations on international and bilateral issues.

Membership. Oman is a member of the UN, the Arab League, the Organization of the Islamic Conference and the Gulf Co-operation Council.

ECONOMY

Policy. The fifth 5-year development plan (1996-2000) projects that total public expenditure during the period will reach RO 10,630 m. The deficit will be reduced to RO 538m., compared with the RO 2,247m. deficit of the fourth 5-year development plan. The non-oil revenue is estimated at RO 2,639m. of total revenue compared with the RO 2,111m. non-oil revenue of the previous plan. The current plan is based on an estimated oil production average of 880,000 bbls. a day valued at US$15 per barrel. If oil revenues exceed the projected barrel price of US$15-17, the surplus will be placed in the State General Reserve Fund. Total revenues are expected to increase by 17% from RO 8,614m. to 10,092m. Oil revenues are expected to constitute 73·9% of total revenues.

Operating expenditure will amount to RO 8,696m. (81·8% of total Government expenditure) and capital expenditure will amount to RO 1,854m. (17·4%). Contributions and loans to the private sector will amount to about RO 80m.

The public debt will be maintained at RO 1,500m. over the period of the plan. It is expected to range between 20-22% of GDP as the latter expands. The aim is to attain a GDP annual average growth rate of 4·6% at current prices and to increase the GDP share of the non-oil sectors to 69% by the year 2000.

Privatization of water and electricity is underway.

Performance. GDP, 1995: RO 5,288·2m.; growth rate, 3·4%.

Budget. Revenue (1996) RO 1,934m., of which RO 1,473m. from oil; expenditure, RO 2,152m.

Currency. The unit of currency is the *Omani rial* (OMR). It is divided into 1,000 *baiza*. There are notes of 100, 200, 250 and 500 baiza and RO 1, 5, 10, 20 and 50 and coins of 5, 10, 25, 50, 100, 250 and 500 baiza. The rial is pegged to the US dollar. Foreign exchange reserves were US$908m. in 1993.

Banking and Finance. The bank of issue is the Central Bank of Oman, which commenced operations in 1975 (*President*, Hamid Sangur Hasim). All banks must comply with BIS capital adequacy ratios and have a minimum capital of OR 10m. In 1995 there were 21 commercial banks, of which 11 were foreign. There are 3 specialized banks.

There is a stock exchange in Muscat, which is linked with those in Bahrain and Kuwait.

Weights and Measures. The metric system is in operation.

ENERGY AND NATURAL RESOURCES

Electricity. Production (1995) 6,500m. kWh. The mountains of the Sultanate of Oman are rich in mineral deposits; these include copper ore, chromite, coal, asbestos, manganese, gypsum, limestone and marble. The government is studying the exploitation of gold, platinum and suphide.

Oil. The economy is dominated by the oil industry, which provided 83% of Government revenue in 1990 and 49·2% of GDP. Oil in commercial quantities was discovered in 1964 and production began in 1967. Production in 1996 was 853,000 bbls. a day. Total proven reserves were estimated in 1991 to be 5·2m. bbls.

Gas. Gas is likely to become the second major source of income for the country. Oman's estimated gas reserves are 25 trillion cu. ft, of which 16 trillion ft are proven, with exploration continuing.

Water Resources. Oman relies on a combination of aquifers and desalination plants for its water, augmented by a construction programme of some 60 recharge dams. Desalination plants at Ghubriah and Wadi Adai provide most of the water needs of the capital area. In 1995 water production was 16,755m. gallons.

Minerals. Production of refined copper at the smelter at Sohar was 12,015 tonnes in 1990.

Agriculture. Agriculture and fisheries are the traditional occupations of Omanis and remain important to the people and economy of Oman to this day. The country now produces a wide variety of fresh fruit, vegetables and field crops. The country is rapidly moving towards its goal of self-sufficiency in agriculture with the total area under cultivation standing at over 70,000 hectares and total output more than 1m. tonnes. This effort has not been achieved without effort. In a country where water is a scarce commodity it has meant educating farmers on efficient methods of irrigation and building recharge dams to make the most of infrequent rainfall.

The coastal plain (Batinah) north-west of Muscat is fertile, as are the Dhofar highlands in the south. In the valleys of the interior, as well as on the Batinah coastal plain, date cultivation has reached a high level, and there are possibilities of agricultural development. The crop of dates was 625,000 tonnes in 1995. Vegetable and fruit production are also important, and livestock are raised in the south where there are monsoon rains. Camels (92,000 in 1992) are bred by the inland tribes. Live animals and meat constitute more than 25% of the country's non-oil exports.

Fisheries. The catch, which is the largest in the Arabian Gulf, is (1992) 112,313 tonnes. 15,267 tonnes were taken by industrial ships, the rest by some 85,000 self-employed fishermen. Agriculture and fisheries now contribute more than 5% to Oman's GDP.

INDUSTRY. In 1990 manufacturing accounted for only 3·7% of GDP. Apart from oil production, copper mining and smelting and cement production, there are light industries, mainly food processing and chemical products. The government gives priority to import substitute industries.

Labour. In 1995 there were 619,351 employees in the private sector and 110,444 persons in government service. The employment of foreign labour is being discouraged following 'Omanization' regulations of 1994.

FOREIGN ECONOMIC RELATIONS. Total foreign debt was US$2,661m. in 1993. A royal decree of 1994 permits up to 65% foreign ownership of Omani companies with a 5-year tax and customs duties exemption.

Commerce. Total imports, 1995: RO 1,683·6m.; exports, RO 2,333·2m. (of which oil: RO 1,829·3m.). Principal non-oil exports are metal, metal goods, animals and products and textiles. Main export markets (% of total trade); 1993: UAE, 33·4; Japan, 19·5; South Korea, 14; China, 7. Main import suppliers: UAE, 23·7; Japan, 20·8; UK, 11·9.

COMMUNICATIONS

Roads. A network of adequate graded roads links all the main sectors of population, and only a few mountain villages are not accessible by motor vehicles. In 1995 there were 6,213 km of asphalt roads and 24,276 km of graded roads. In Dec. 1995 there were 298,726 cars registered.

Civil Aviation. Oman has a 25% share in Gulf Air with Bahrain, Qatar and the UAE. For details *see* BAHRAIN: Civil Aviation. Gulf Air run regional services in and out of Seeb international airport (20 miles from Muscat) to Bahrain, Doha, Abu Dhabi, Dubai, Karachi and Bombay and operate daily flights to and from London. Other airlines serving Muscat are Air France, Air India, Air Lanka, Air Tanzania, Balkan Bulgarian, Biman Bangladesh, British Airways, Egyptair, Ethiopian Airlines, KLM, Kuwait Airways, Pakistan Airlines, Royal Jordanian, Saudia, Sudan Airways, Thai Airways and UTA. Domestic flights are provided by Oman Aviation Services.

Shipping. In Mutrah a deep-water port (named Mina Qaboos) was completed in 1974. The annual handling capacity is 1·5m. tonnes. Mina Raysut, the port of Salalah, has a capacity of 1m. tonnes per year. Sea-going shipping totalled 10,604 GRT in 1995.

Telecommunications. In 1995 there were 90 post offices. The General Telecommunications Organization maintains a telegraph office at Muscat and an automatic telephone exchange (177,655 lines, 1995).

The government-owned Radio Oman broadcasts in Arabic and English. A colour (PAL) television service, the government-owned Oman Television, covering Muscat and the surrounding area, started transmission in 1974. A television service for Dhofar opened in 1975. In 1991 there were 7 television stations. Total number of televisions, 1,000,033 and radios, 0·9m. in 1991.

Press. There are 2 Arabic-language and 2 English-language daily newspapers.

SOCIAL INSTITUTIONS

Religion. In 1995, 87·7% of the population were Moslem.

Education. Adult literacy was 41% in 1994. In 1995–96, there were 965 schools with 490,482 pupils and 22,504 teachers. Plans have been implemented for the development of technical and agricultural training and craft training at intermediate and secondary level. Oman's first university, the Sultan Qaboos University, opened in 1986 and in 1994–95 there were 4,331 students and 483 academic staff.

Health. In 1995 there were 53 hospitals with 4,411 beds, 121 health centres, 2,476 doctors, 142 dentists (1992), 370 pharmacists and 6,036 nursing staff.

DIPLOMATIC REPRESENTATIVES

Of Oman in Great Britain (167 Queen's Gate, London, SW7 5HE)
Ambassador: Hussain Ali Abdullatif.

Of Great Britain in Oman (PO Box 300, Muscat)
Ambassador: R. J. S. Muir, CMG.

Of Oman in the USA (2342 Massachusetts Ave., NW, Washington, D.C., 20008)
Ambassador: Abdalla Bin Mohamed Al-Dhahab.

Of the USA in Oman (PO Box 202 Madinat Qabos, Muscat)
Ambassador: Frances D. Cook.

Of Oman to the United Nations
Ambassador: Salim Bin Mohammed Al-Khussaiby.

Further Reading

Carter, J. R. L., *Tribes of Oman*. London, 1981
Clements, F. A., *Oman: The Reborn Land*. London and New York, 1980.—*Oman*. [Bibliography] 2nd ed. Oxford and Santa Barbara (CA), 1994
Hawley, D., *Oman and its Renaissance*. London, 1977
Peterson, J. E., *Oman in the Twentieth Century*. London and New York, 1978
Peyton, W. D., *Oman before 1970: The End of an Era*. London, 1985
Pridham, B. R., (ed.) *Oman: Economic, Social and Strategic Developments*. London, 1987
Shannon, M. O., *Oman and South-Eastern Arabia: A Bibliographic Survey*. Boston, 1978
Skeet, I., *Muscat and Oman: The End of an Era*. London, 1974.—*Oman: Politics and Development*. London, 1992
Wilkinson, J. C., *The Imamate Tradition of Oman*. CUP, 1987

National statistical office: Directorate General of National Statistics, POB 881, Muscat 113.

PAKISTAN

Islami Jamhuriya e Pakistan

(Islamic Republic of
Pakistan)

Capital: Islamabad
Population: 137·4m.
GDP per head: (PPP$) 2,154
GNP: US$55·6bn.
HDI/world rank: 0·445/139

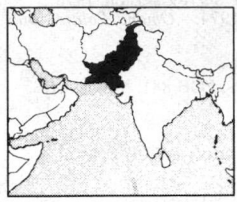

KEY HISTORICAL EVENTS. The State of Pakistan was created on 14 Aug. 1947 by the Partition of India and consisted of the former East Bengal (with a district of Assam), the North West Frontier, Sind, the West Punjab and Baluchistan. Kashmir was disputed between Pakistan and India.

Pakistan was a deliberate creation, formed in order to provide Indian Moslems with their own state. This aim had been expressed by the All-India Moslem League since 1940 and was successfully pressed by Mohammad Ali Jinnah (1876-1948) despite initial strong opposition from the predominantly Hindu Indian National Congress.

East Bengal acceded to Pakistan in 1947 and seceded after civil war in Dec. 1971 when it became the independent republic of Bangladesh.

The North West Frontier was created by the government of British India as a military buffer zone to protect its Indian empire from Tsarist Russian expansion through central Asia; it was administered as a tribal agency, and included parts of the Punjab across the Indus River, the Peshawar valley and the mountain areas between Chitrál and the Vihowa River. The people were Moslem Pathan hill tribes; government contact with them was often difficult, but essential in order to protect the vital routes across the province through the Khyber, Kuram, Tochi and Gomal passes. The centre was Peshawar, an ancient city on a caravan route.

Sind was a tributary state of the Mughal empire from 1592, its people having previously come under Persian and Arabian influence. The British took Sind in 1843 and governed it as part of the Bombay Presidency, developing Karachi as a supply port.

The western Punjab was part of the Sikh homeland annexed by the British in 1849 (*see* India).

Baluchistan was an independent state which entered into treaty relations with British India in 1854 and 1876. The British then obtained a small area around Quetta, British Baluchistan. They also received the right to fortify and administer Quetta and Bolan, and to bring troops into the territory of the paramount Baluch chief, the Khan of Kalat, who in return received a subsidy. Outside Quetta, Bolan and British Baluchistan there was Kalat as an independent state and an independent northern area which was not ruled by the khan and was mainly Pathan. In 1887 British Baluchistan was incorporated into British India.

In 1947 Pakistan came into being, with Jinnah as its first governor-general. The state incorporated the whole of Baluchistan, an action which is still the cause of unrest. Pakistan's status was that of a Dominion within the Commonwealth; it became a republic in 1956 and left the Commonwealth in 1972. Efforts to rejoin were opposed by India until 1989 when Pakistan once more became a full member of the Commonwealth.

The first of several periods of martial law began in 1958, followed by the rule of Field Marshal Mohammad Ayub Khan (until 1969) and Maj.-Gen. Agha Mohammad Yahya Khan (until 1971).

During the latter's term, differences between East and West Pakistan came to a head. The East Pakistan Awami League won the majority of seats in the general election of 7 Dec. 1970, pressing for autonomy. Martial law continued while attempts were made to negotiate, but civil war broke out in March 1971 and ended in Dec. 1971 with the creation of Bangladesh. President Yahya Khan resigned and was succeeded by Zulfiquar Ali Bhutto.

A new constitution came into force on 14 Aug. 1973, providing a federal parliamentary government with a president as head of state and a prime minister as head of the government. Mr Bhutto became prime minister, relinquishing the post of president. His government was thought by traditionalists to be too Western and not sufficiently Islamic. There was an army *coup* led by Gen. Mohammad Zia ul-Haq in July 1977. The prime minister, Zulfiquar Ali Bhutto was hanged for conspiring to murder. Gen. Zia ul-Haq became president in 1978.

The constitution of 1973 was held in abeyance and national elections were not held until Feb. 1985. The president set up a National Security Council to control the elected government in March 1985; in April 1985 this was replaced by a Federal Cabinet. Martial law ended on 30 Dec. 1985.

The Constitution (Ninth Amendment) Bill, 1986, confirmed that Islamic teaching is the basis of national law.

On 6 Aug. 1990 the President, accusing the government of corruption and under-mining the constitution, dismissed the Prime Minister, Benazir Bhutto, and all her cabinet, dissolved the National Assembly and declared a state of emergency. New governors were appointed for all 4 provinces.

On 18 April 1993 President Ghulam Ishaq Khan dismissed the next Prime Minister, Nawaz Sharif, but he was reinstated by the Constitutional Court. Both President and Prime Minister resigned on 18 July 1993, and new elections took place.

On 5 Nov. 1996 the President, Farooq Leghari, accusing the government of corruption and mismanaging the economy, again dismissed the Prime Minister, Benazir Bhutto, and all her cabinet, and dissolved the National Assembly, paving the way for Nawaz Sharif's re-election on 3 Feb. 1997.

Relations between Pakistan and India have foundered on the issue of Kashmir, a disputed territory divided by a cease-fire line negotiated by the UN in 1949. In March 1997 the two countries held talks for the first time in three years.

The invasion of neighbouring Afghanistan by Soviet forces in 1979 caused a flow of Afghan refugees in Pakistan, chiefly into the North West Frontier Province which still functions as a military buffer zone.

TERRITORY AND POPULATION. Pakistan is bounded in the west by Iran, north-west by Afghanistan, north by China, east by India and south by the Arabian Sea. The area (excluding the disputed area of Kashmir) is 307,293 sq. miles (796,095 sq. km); population (1981 census, excluding Azad, Kashmir, Baltistan, Diamir and Gilgit), 84,253,644 (females, 40·02m.). Estimate (1997) 137·386m., a growth rate of 2·7% per annum. Vital statistics, 1997 (rates per 1,000 population): Birth, 36; death, 9; infant mortality (per 1,000 live births), 90. Formal registration of marriages and divorces has not been required since 1992. Expectation of life was 63·7 years in 1997.

The population of the principal cities:

1994 estimates

Islamabad	340,286	Lahore	5,500,000	Rawalpindi	928,000
Karachi	10,000,000	Faisalabad	2,000,000	Hyderabad	800,000

Population of the provinces (census of 1981) was (1,000):

	Area (sq. km)	1981 census population				1981 density per sq. km (number)	Estimated total 1985
		Total	Male	Female	Urban		
North-West Frontier Province	74,521	11,061	5,761	5,300	1,665	148	12,287
Federally administered Tribal Areas	27,219	2,199	1,143	1,056	–	81	2,467
Federal Capital Territory Islamabad	907	340	185	155	204	376	379
Punjab	205,344	47,292	24,860	22,432	13,051	230	53,840
Sind	140,914	19,029	9,999	9,030	8,243	135	21,682
Baluchistan	347,190	4,332	2,284	2,048	677	12	4,908

In 1994 there were still some 1·5m. Afghan refugees, mainly in the North-West Frontier Province.

Urdu is the national language, though only spoken by 7·6% of the population at the

1981 census; English is used in business, higher education and in central government. In 1981 48% of the population spoke Punjabi.

CLIMATE. A weak form of tropical monsoon climate occurs over much of the country, with arid conditions in the north and west, where the wet season is only from Dec. to March. Elsewhere, rain comes mainly in the summer. Summer temperatures are high everywhere, but winters can be cold in the mountainous north. Islamabad. Jan. 50°F (10°C), July 90°F (32·2°C). Annual rainfall 36" (900 mm). Karachi. Jan. 61°F (16·1°C), July 86°F (30°C). Annual rainfall 8" (196 mm). Lahore. Jan. 53°F (11·7°C), July 89°F (31·7°C). Annual rainfall 18" (452 mm). Multan. Jan. 51°F (10·6°C), July 93°F (33·9°C). Annual rainfall 7" (170 mm). Quetta. Jan. 38°F (3·3°C), July 80°F (26·7°C). Annual rainfall 10" (239 mm).

CONSTITUTION AND GOVERNMENT. Under the 1973 Constitution, the *President* is elected for a 5-year term by a college of parliamentary deputies, senators and members of the Provincial Assemblies. Parliament is bi-cameral, comprising a *Senate* of 87 members and a *National Assembly* of 217. The 4 Provincial Assemblies each elect 19 senators, the tribal areas are represented by 8 senators elected by the National Assembly and the Federal Capital has 3 representatives. About half the senators are elected for 6-year terms every 3 years. The National Assembly is directly elected with 10 religious minority representatives.

During the period of martial law (1977–85) the Constitution was in abeyance, but not abrogated. In 1985 it was amended to extend the powers of the President, including those of appointing and dismissing ministers and vetoing new legislation until 1990. Legislation of 1 April 1997 abolishes the President's right to dissolve parliament, appoint provincial governors and nominate the heads of the armed services.

The Constitution obliges the Government to enable the people to order their lives in accordance with Islam and consolidates Islam.

Following the President's dismissal of Benazir Bhutto's government in Nov. 1996, elections were held on 3 Feb. 1997 for the 217 contestable seats in the National Assembly. The electorate was 54m.; turn-out was 38%. The Moslem League gained 142 seats; the Pakistan People's Party, 18. 6 women were elected to the National Assembly. The *Speaker* of the Assembly is Illahi Bukhsh Soomro.

Elections to 46 of the 87 seats of the Senate were held on 21 March 1997. The Moslem League and its sympathizers held 30 seats, the Pakistan People's Party, 19 seats. The Senate has 2 women members. Wasim Sajjad is Chairman of the Senate for the fourth consecutive period.

President: Farooq Leghari (b. 1940; PPP; elected 13 Nov. 1993; sworn in 14 Nov. 1993).

A Moslem League government was formed on 26 Feb. 1997 which in March 1998 included:

Prime Minister: Nawaz Sharif (b. 1949; sworn in 17 Feb. 1997).

Minister of Finance: Sartaj Aziz. *Foreign Affairs, Kashmir and the Northern Areas:* Gohar Ayub Khan. *Interior, Railways and Narcotics Control:* Chaudhry Shujaat Hussain. *Commerce and Industries:* Mohammad Ishaq Dar. *Water, Power, Petroleum and Natural Resources:* Chaudhry Nisar Ali Khan. *Population and Welfare:* Syed Abida Hussain. *Education:* Azghar Ali Shah. *Communications:* Muhammad Azam Khan Hoti.

National anthem: 'Pak sarzamin shadbad' ('Blessed be the sacred land'); words by A. Hafeez Jullandhuri, tune by A. Ghulamali Chagla.

Provincial and Local Government. Pakistan comprises the Federal Capital Territory (Islamabad), the provinces of the Punjab, the North-West Frontier (NWFP), Sind and Baluchistan, and the tribal areas of the north-west. The provincial capitals are Peshawar (NWFP), Lahore (Punjab), Karachi (Sind) and Quetta (Baluchistan). Provincial governors are appointed by the President and are assisted by elected provincial assemblies. That of Punjab has 248 seats (8 reserved for non-Moslems); Sind, 99; Baluchistan, 40; NWFP, 80. Elections were held on 8 Oct. 1993. Seats gained in the Punjab assembly: PML 106, PPP 94, PML-Junejo 18, ind 17, minor parties 5; Sind: PPP 56, Mohajir 27, PML 8, ind 5, minor parties 3; Baluchistan: minor parties 21, ind 9, PML 6, PPP 3, Awami 1; NWFP: PPP 22, Awami 20, PML 15, ind 11, minor parties 7, PML-Junejo 4. Municipal elections were held in the Punjab in Dec. 1991. Direct rule was imposed in Punjab in Sept. 1995.

Within the provinces there are divisions administered by Commissioners appointed by the President; the divisions are divided into districts and agencies administered by Deputy Commissioners or Political Agents who are responsible to the Provincial Governments.

The tribal areas (Khyber, Kurram, Malakand, Mohmand, North Waziristan, South Waziristan) are administered by political agents responsible to the federal government.

DEFENCE. A *Council for Defence and National Security* was set up in Jan. 1997, comprising the President, the Prime Minister, the Ministers of Defence, Foreign Affairs, Interior, Finance and the military chiefs of staff. The Council advises the Government on the determination of national strategy and security priorities.

Army. The Army is organized into 9 corps headquarters and 1 area command, and consists of 2 armoured and 19 infantry divisions; 7 independent armoured, 9 independent infantry, 9 artillery and 7 engineer brigades; 3 armoured reconnaissance regiments, 1 air defence command and 1 Special Services Group. Equipment includes 120 M-47, 50 T-54/-55, 280 M-48, 1,200 Chinese Type-59, 200 Chinese Type-69 and 200 Chinese Type-85 main battle tanks, 850 surface-to-air and 18 surface-to-surface missiles. The Army has an air component with about 140 fixed-wing aircraft for transport, reconnaissance and observation duties and 150 helicopters for anti-armour operations, transport, liaison and training. Strength (1997) 520,000. There are also 257,000 personnel in paramilitary units: National Guard, Frontier Corps and Pakistan Rangers.

Navy. The combatant fleet comprises 6 French-built diesel submarines, 3 midget submarines for swimmer delivery, 3 ex-US Second World War vintage destroyers and 6 ex-British Amazon and 2 Leander class frigates, 8 fast missile craft, 1 coastal and 4 inshore patrol craft, 3 French-built tripartite minehunters and 2 coastal mine-sweepers. Auxiliaries include 2 fleet replenishment tankers, 1 survey ship and 1 salvage tug. There are about a dozen minor auxiliaries.

The Air Force operates the first of 3 P-3C Orion and 4 Atlantic aircraft under naval control for maritime patrol duties and 3 F-27 patrol aircraft, whilst the Navy operates 6 Sea King helicopters, 2 Lynx and 4 Alouette III anti-submarine and liaison helicopters.

The principal naval base and dockyard are at Karachi. Naval personnel in 1996 totalled 22,000. There is a marine force of 1,200.

A navy-subordinated Maritime Safety Agency 2,000 strong (1996) operates 1 ex-naval destroyer and 6 fast coastal patrol craft on economic exclusion zone protection duties.

Air Force. The Pakistan Air Force came into being on 14 Aug. 1947. It has its head-quarters at Peshawar and is organized within 3 air defence sectors, in the northern, central and southern areas of the country. Air defence units include 3 squadrons of F-16 Fighting Falcons, 5 squadrons of F-7P Skybolts and 3 squadrons of Chinese-built F-6s (MiG-19). Tactical units include 2 squadrons of Mirage 5 supersonic fighters and 3 with A-5 fighter-bombers, 1 squadron equipped with Mirage III strike and reconnaissance aircraft, and 1 with C-130 Hercules turboprop transports. Flying training schools are equipped with Mashshaq (Saab Supporter) armed piston-engined primary trainers, T-33 and T-37B/C jet trainers supplied by the USA, Mirage III-DPs and Chinese-built FT-5s (two-seat MiG-17s) and FT-6s (two-seat MiG-19s). A VIP transport squadron operates the Presidential F27 turboprop aircraft and Boeing 737 jet, 3 four-jet Boeing 707s, 3 twin-jet Falcon 20s and a Puma helicopter. There is a flying college at Risalpur and an aeronautical engineering college at Korangi Creek. Total strength in 1996 was 430 combat aircraft and 45,000 personnel.

INTERNATIONAL RELATIONS

Membership. Pakistan is a member of the UN, the Commonwealth (not 1972-89) and the Colombo Plan.

ECONOMY

Policy. The 8th Five-Year Plan runs from 1993 to 1998. Growth targets: GDP, 7%; agriculture, 4·9%; manufacturing, 9·9%; services, 6·7%. There is also a Perspective Plan for 1993-2008. There is a Privatization Commission.

Performance. The pace of growth maintained by the economy during the last several years of around 6% accelerated sharply to 7·7% in 1991-92 but this growth trend was interrupted in 1992-93 and GDP growth estimates were revised down to 2·3%. The agriculture sector sank to a negative growth rate of 5·3% from 9·5% achieved in 1992-93. Manufacturing sector with 8·1% growth in 1991-92 came down to 5·4% in 1992-93. This downward drift seems to have been checked in 1993-94. GDP growth is estimated at 4·0% with 2·6% growth in agriculture and 5·6% in the manufacturing sector during 1993-94. But the economy remains vulnerable with low reserves of foreign exchange and sluggish industrial growth. Inflation is estimated at 11·8% as against 9·26% during the same period last year.

Budget. The financial year ends on 30 June. The consolidated federal and provincial budget for 1995-96 envisaged revenue of Rs 361,717m. (Rs 259,215m. from taxation) and expenditure of Rs 361,005m. (current expenditure, Rs 334,722m.; development, Rs 26,283m.). Provincial revenue, Rs 149,638m. (including federal transfers of Rs 96,522m.). Defence spending, Rs 115,254m.

Currency. The monetary unit is the *Pakistan rupee* (PKR) of 100 *paisas*. There are notes of R1, 2, 5, 10, 50, 100, 500 and 1,000; and coins of 5, 10, 25 and 50 paisas. Currency in circulation in June 1995, Rs 215,579m. Gold reserves in 1995 were Rs 24,002m., approved foreign exchange reserves, Rs 70,009m. Inflation was 10% in 1996. The rupee was devalued 3·79% in Sept. and 8% in Oct. 1996.

Banking and Finance. In Jan. 1985, banks and financial institutions abandoned, in conformity with Islamic doctrine, the payment of interest on new transactions. This does not apply to international business, but does apply to the domestic business of foreign banks operating in Pakistan. Investment partnerships, between bank and customer, replaced straight loans at interest. In Dec. 1991 the Federal Shariat Court pronounced that interest or usury (*riba*) is un-Islamic and therefore illegal.

The State Bank of Pakistan is the central bank (*Governor*, Mohammad Yaqub); it came into operation as the Central Bank on 1 July 1948 and was nationalized in 1974. It was granted greater autonomy in Sept. 1993. In June 1995 total assets of the issue department amounted to Rs 230,613m. and those of the banking department Rs 241,329m.; total deposits, Rs 135,593m. It is the bank of issue, custodian of foreign exchange reserves and banker for the federal and provincial governments and for scheduled banks. It also manages the rupee public debt of federal and provincial governments. The Bank's subsidiary Federal Bank for Co-operatives makes loans to provincial co-operative banks. The National Bank of Pakistan acts as an agent of the State Bank where the State Bank has no offices of its own.

Banks were nationalized in 1974, but a federal government decision of Dec. 1990 again allows banks in the private sector. It was announced in Nov. 1990 that 51% of the equity of state-owned banks was to be privatized in 2 phases. In June 1995 there were 40 banks (21 foreign) with total assets of Rs 1,654,094m.

There are stock exchanges at Islamabad, Karachi and Lahore.

Weights and Measures. The metric system is in general use.

ENERGY AND NATURAL RESOURCES

Electricity. Installed capacity of the state power system in 1990 was 8,430 MW. Total generated electrical energy in 1994-95, 53,312m. kWh; in 1993-94, 19,386m.

kWh of output was hydro-electric, 30,006m. kWh thermal and 497m. kWh nuclear. By 1996, 64,568 villages (of a total of 125,083) had access to electric power.

Oil and Gas. Oil production in 1995 was 19,859,000 bbls. Exploitation is mainly through government incentives and concessions to foreign private sector companies. Gas production, 1992–93, 14,200m. cu. metres.

Minerals. Production (tonnes, 1994–95): Coal, 3·01m.; chromite, 13,513; limestone, 9·68m.; gypsum, 0·62m.; rock salt, 0·89m.; fire clay, 151,889; feldspar, 20,267; bauxite, 4,456; barytes, 20,079; china clay, 30,986; dolomite, 228,090; fullers' earth, 15,154. Other minerals of which useful deposits have been found are magnesite, sulphur, marble, antimony ore, bentonite, celestite, fluorite, phosphate rock, silica sand and soapstone.

Agriculture. The north and west are covered by mountain ranges. The rest of the country consists of a fertile plain watered by 5 big rivers and their tributaries. Agriculture is dependent almost entirely on the irrigation system based on these rivers. Area irrigated, 1994, 17·1m. ha. Agriculture employs half the workforce and in 1989–90 contributed 26% of GDP.

Pakistan is self-sufficient in wheat, rice and sugar. Areas harvested, 1994: Wheat, 8·03m. ha; rice, 2·19m. ha; sugar-cane, 0·96m. ha; cotton, 2·8m. ha and maize, 0·88m. ha. Production, 1994 (1,000 tonnes): Rice, 3,995; wheat, 15,213; sugar-cane, 44,427; cotton, 1,517; maize, 1,213; (1993) millet, 126; sorghum, 218 and dates, 320.

An ordinance of Jan. 1977 reduced the upper limit of land holding to 100 irrigated or 200 non-irrigated acres. A new agricultural income tax was introduced in 1995, from which holders of up to 25 irrigated or 50 unirrigated acres are exempt. Of about 4m. farms, 89% are of less than 25 acres. In 1992, 20·65m. ha were arable land, 0·46m. ha were cropland and 12·80m. ha were pasture.

Livestock, 1993 (in 1m.): Cattle, 17·8; buffaloes, 18·7; sheep, 27·6; goats, 40·2; camels, 1·1; poultry, 95m.

Dairy products, 1993 (in 1,000 tonnes): Mutton and lamb, 288; beef and buffalo, 844; wool, 50·5; eggs, 231·9; milk, 13,192.

Forestry. In 1993–94 the forest area was 3m. ha, some 3·8% of the total land area. The government considers a 20-25% coverage desirable for economic growth and environmental stability. 0·34m. cu. metres of timber and 0·4m. cu. metres of firewood were produced by state-owned forests in 1993–94.

Fisheries. In 1993 the catch totalled 621,700 tonnes.

INDUSTRY. Industry is based largely on agricultural processing, with engineering and electronics. Government policy is to encourage private industry, particularly small industry. The public sector, however, is still dominant in large industries. Steel, cement, fertilizer and vegetable ghee are the most valuable public sector industries.

Production 1994–95 (tonnes): Sugar, 3,001,275; vegetable products, 678,050; jute textiles, 67,254; soda ash, 184,636; sulphuric acid, 82,063; caustic soda, 92,746; paper and board, 19,555; bicycles, 474,445 units; cotton cloth, 314·9m. sq. metres (1993–94); cotton yarn, 130·96m. kg (1993–94); cement, 8·1m. (1993–94); steel billets, 343,500; hot-rolled steel sheets and coils, 467,642; cold-rolled, 170,766; pig-iron, 1,044,710; motor cars, 20,955 items; tractors, 17,144 items; tea, 59,313.

Labour. In 1992 the workforce was 33·71m. (5·02m. females). 1·6m. were unemployed (0·52m. females). In 1994 50·04% were engaged in agriculture, forestry and fishing, 10·3% in manufacturing; the textile industry was the largest single manufacturing employer. Services employed 13·2%; commerce, 12·78%; construction, 6·5%; transport, storage and communication, 4·95%. At the end of 1993, 183,801 job seekers were registered at labour exchanges.

In 1994 there were 25 industrial disputes and 341,196 working days were lost.

FOREIGN ECONOMIC RELATIONS. Foreign debt was US$28,600m. in 1996. Most foreign exchange controls were removed in Feb. 1991. Foreign investors may repatriate both capital and profits, and tax exemptions are available for companies set up before 30 June 1995.

Commerce. In 1994–95 imports were valued at Rs 320,892m., exports at Rs 251,173m., and re-exports at Rs 1,091m. Major exports: raw cotton and cotton products, rice, fish and fish products, carpets and rugs, leather and leather goods, sports and surgical goods. Major imports: tea, petroleum and its products, edible oils, chemical fertilizers, milk and milk food, agricultural machinery, transport equipment, medicines, iron and steel. Cotton and related items account for 60% of Pakistan's export earnings. Major trading partners: USA, Japan, Germany, UK, Hong Kong, Saudi Arabia, China.

Tourism. In 1994 there were 454,353 tourist arrivals. Foreign exchange receipts were US$126·2m. in 1994.

COMMUNICATIONS

Roads. According to officially revised figures, in 1993 there were 86,597 km of roads, of which 60,154 km were 'high type' roads. In 1994 there were 118,389 lorries, 107,440 buses, 52,444 taxis, 902,654 motor cars, 1,679,259 motor cycles and 683,680 other vehicles. There were 10,916 road accidents in 1993–94, with 4,511 fatalities.

All traffic in Pakistan drives on the left-hand side. All cars must be insured and registered. Minimum age for driving: 18 years.

Railways. Pakistan Railways had (1996) a route length of 7,344 km (of which 293 km electrified) mainly on 1,676 mm gauge, with some metre gauge line. In 1994–95 66·47m. passengers and 7·36m. tonnes of freight were carried.

Civil Aviation. There are international airports at Karachi, Islamabad, Lahore, Peshawar and Quetta. In 1993–94 9,107,405 domestic and 4,093,250 international passengers were handled, and 83,914 and 136,147 tonnes of freight.

The national carrier is Pakistan International Airlines (PIA; founded 1955; 56% of shares are held by the Government), which in 1995 operated 9 A300B4-200s, 6 A310-300s, 2 B-707-320Cs, 7 B-737-300s, 6 B-747-200Bs, 2 B-747-200B Combis, and 15 other aircraft. Services are also provided by Aero Asia, Aeroflot, Air China, Air Lanka, Air Liberté, Azerbaijan Hava Yollary, Bhoja Air, Biman Bangladesh, British Airways, Egyptair, Emirates, Ethiopian Airlines, Gulf Air, Indian Airlines, Iran Air, Kenya Airways, KLM, Kuwait Airways, Libyan Airlines, Lufthansa, Malaysia Airlines, Northwest Airines, Oman Air, Philippine Airlines, Qatar Airways, Royal Jordanian, Saudia, Shaheen Air, Singapore Airlines, Swissair, Syrian Airlines, Tarom, Thai Airways, Turkish Airlines, Uzbekistan Airways and Yemenia.

Shipping. In 1995, ocean-going shipping totalled 0·58m. tonnes, including oil tankers, 90,821 GRT. There are ports at Karachi and Port Qasim. Cargo handled, 1994–95, 23·21m. and 9·20m. tonnes respectively. In 1994–95 2,322 international vessels entered, and 2,323 cleared, these ports.

Telecommunications. The telegraph and telephone system is government-owned. Telephones, 1995, numbered 2,492,000. There were 13,450 telex machines in 1991. In 1995 there were 13,320 post offices. The Pakistan Broadcasting Corporation is a government body responsible for broadcasting a national radio programme in English, 3 home services and an external service, Radio Pakistan (15 languages). A separate government authority, Azad Kashmir Radio, broadcasts in Kashmir. The commercial Pakistan Television Corporation transmits on 8 channels (colour by PAL). In 1994, 10m. radio and 2·5m. TV sets were in use.

Cinemas. There were 703 screens in 1994. 92 full-length films were made in 1994.

Press. In 1994 there were 130 dailies, 269 weeklies, 68 fortnightlies and 390 period-icals of greater frequencies. 690 titles were in Urdu, 69 in English and 62 in more than one language. Average circulation of all dailies in 1993 was 1,031,727.

SOCIAL INSTITUTIONS

Justice. The Federal Judiciary consists of the Supreme Court of Pakistan, which is a court of record and has three-fold jurisdiction, namely, original, appellate and advisory. There are 4 High Courts in Lahore, Peshawar, Quetta and Karachi. Under the Constitution, each has power to issue directions of writs of *Habeas Corpus, Mandamus, Certiorari* and others. Under them are district and sessions courts of first instance in each division; they have also some appellate jurisdiction. Criminal cases not being sessions cases are tried by judicial magistrates. There are subordinate civil courts also.

The Constitution provides for an independent judiciary, as the greatest safeguard of citizens' rights. There is an Attorney-General, appointed by the President, who has right of audience in all courts and the Parliament, and a Federal Ombudsman.

A Federal Shariat Court at the High Court level has been established to decide whether any law is wholly or partially un-Islamic. In Aug. 1990 a presidential ordinance decreed that the criminal code must conform to Islamic law (Shariah), and in May 1991 parliament passed a law incorporating it into the legal system.

320,807 crimes were reported in 1994 (290,255 in 1993). Execution of the death penalty for murder, in abeyance since 1986, was resumed in 1992. There were 8,303 murders in 1994 (7,258 in 1993).

Religion. Pakistan was created as a Moslem state. The Moslems are mainly Sunni, with an admixture of 15–20% Shi'ite. Religious groups: Moslems, 97%; Christians, 2%; Hindus, Parsees, Buddhists, and others. There is a Minorities Wing at the Religious Affairs Ministry to safeguard the constitutional rights of religious minorities.

Education. Adult literacy was 35% in 1992. Adult literacy programmes have been strengthened.

The principle of free and compulsory primary education has been accepted as the responsibility of the state; duration has been fixed provisionally at 5 years. About 60% of children aged 5-9 are enrolled at school. Present policy stresses vocational and technical education, disseminating a common culture based on Islamic ideology. Figures for 1994–95:

	Students (in 1,000)	Teachers (in 1,000)	Institutions
Primary	16,722	412·2	123,119[3]
Middle	4,140	109·9	13,615[3]
Secondary	1,563	217·9	13,236[3]
Secondary vocational	56·8[1]	4·9[2]	477[1]
Colleges	77·7	4·8	100
Universities	87·4	6·4	24

[1] 1992-93 [2] 1991-92 [3] 1993-94

Health. In 1994 there were 814 hospitals and 4,280 dispensaries (with a total of 80,908 beds) and 820 maternity and child welfare centres. There were 66,199 doctors, 2,590 dentists and 21,419 nurses.

DIPLOMATIC REPRESENTATIVES

Of Pakistan in Great Britain (35-36 Lowndes Sq., London, SW1X 9JN)
High Commissioner: Mian Riaz Samee.

Of Great Britain in Pakistan (Diplomatic Enclave, Ramna 5, Islamabad)
High Commissioner: Sir David Dain, KCVO, CMG.

Of Pakistan in the USA (2315 Massachusetts Ave., NW, Washington, D.C., 20008)
Ambassador: Maleeha Lodhi.

Of the USA in Pakistan (Diplomatic Enclave, Ramna, 5, Islamabad)
Ambassador: Thomas W. Simons.

Of Pakistan to the United Nations
Ambassador: Ahmad Kamal.

Of Pakistan to the European Union
Ambassador: Riaz M. Khan.

Further Reading

Government Planning Commission. *Eighth Five Year Plan, 1993–1998.* Karachi, 1994
Federal Bureau of Statistics.—*Pakistan Statistical Yearbook.—Statistical Pocket Book of Pakistan.* (annual)
Ahmen, A. S., *Jinnah, Pakistan and Islamic Identity - The Search for Saladin.* London, 1997
Ahsan, A., *The Indus Saga and the Making of Pakistan.* Oxford, 1997
Akhtar, R., *Pakistan Year Book.* Karachi-Lahore
Bhutto, B., *Daughter of the East.* London, 1988
Burki, S. J., *Historical Dictionary of Pakistan.* Metuchen (NJ), 1991.—*Pakistan: the Continuing Search for Nationhood.* 2nd ed. Boulder (Colo.), 1992
Choudhury, G. W., *Pakistan: Transition from Military to Civilian Rule.* London, 1988
Gilmartin, D., *Empire and Islam: Punjab and the making of Pakistan.* London, 1988
Hyman, A. et al., *Pakistan: Zia and After.* London, 1989
James, W. E. and Roy, S. (eds.) *The Foundations of Pakistan's Political Economy: towards an Agenda for the 1990s.* London, 1992
Joshi, V. T., *Pakistan: Zia to Benazir.* Delhi, 1995
Kapur, A., *Pakistan in Crisis.* London, 1991
Lamb, C., *Waiting for Allah: Pakistan's Struggle for Democracy.* London, 1991
Low, D. A. (ed.) *The Political Inheritance of Pakistan.* London, 1991
Malik, I. H., *State and Civil Society in Pakistan: the Politics of Authority, Ideology and Ethnicity.* London, 1996
Taylor, D., *Pakistan.* [Bibliography] Oxford and Santa Barbara, 1989

National library: National Library of Pakistan, Islamabad.
National statistical office: Federal Bureau of Statistics, Statistics Division, Karachi.

PALAU

Republic of Palau

Capital: Koror
Population: 17,000

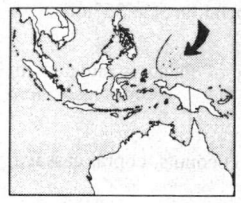

KEY HISTORICAL EVENTS. The actual origin of the first Palauans is uncertain, but archaeological and linguistic studies have shown that Malays from Indonesia, Melanesians from New Guinea and some Polynesians formed the basic genetic stock, resulting in a diversity of facial types. Palauan money consisting of orange and yellow glass beads, similar to money found in Indonesia, helps in tracing the origins of Palauans to the Malay region. Ancient village sites on one of the islands which make up Palau have been carbon-dated to 1000 BC.

The most noteworthy first foreign contact occurred in 1783 when the vessel *Antelope*, under the command of its English captain Henry Wilson, was shipwrecked. With the assistance of the local High Chief, he and his men were able to stay for three months to rebuild the ship.

Spain acquired sovereignty over the Palau Islands in 1886, but sold the archipelago to Germany in 1899. Japan occupied the islands in 1914, and in 1921 they were mandated to Japan by the League of Nations. Captured by Allied Forces in 1944, the islands became part of the UN Trust Territory of the Pacific Islands created on 18 July 1947 and administered by the USA. Following a referendum in July 1978 in which Palauans voted against joining the new Federated States of Micronesia, the islands became an autonomous republic from 1 Jan. 1981, but acquisition of a free-association status with the USA was delayed by disputes over US intentions to base nuclear weapons on the islands. At a referendum in Nov. 1993 (the ninth of a series) 68% of votes cast favoured a Compact of Free Association with the USA, which provides US$450m. over 15 years in return for military facilities.

Palau became an independent republic on 1 Oct. 1994.

TERRITORY AND POPULATION. The archipelago lies in the Western Pacific and has a total area of 1,632 sq. km (630 sq. miles); water covers 1,124 sq. km (434 sq. miles). It comprises 26 islands and over 300 islets. Only 8 of the islands are inhabited, the largest being Babelthuap (368 sq. km), but most inhabitants live on the small island of Koror (8 sq. km) to the south, containing the present headquarters (a new capital is being built in eastern Babelthuap). Koror had an estimated population of 11,500 in 1995. The total population at the time of the 1990 Census was 15,122; 1996 estimate, 17,000. Some 6,000 Palauans live abroad. The local language is Palauan; both Palauan and English are official.

Vital statistics rates, 1996 (per 1,000 population): Births, 21·6; deaths, 6·6; infant mortality (per 1,000 live births), 25·1. Expectation of life: Males, 69; females, 73.

CLIMATE. Palau has a pleasantly warm climate throughout the year with temperatures averaging 81°F (27°C). The heaviest rainfall is between July and October.

CONSTITUTION AND GOVERNMENT. The Constitution was adopted on 2 April 1979 and took effect from 1 Jan. 1981. The Republic has a bicameral legislature, the *Olbiil era Kelulau* (National Congress), comprising a 16-member *Senate* (one from each of the Republic's 16 component states) and an 18-member *House of Delegates*, both elected for a term of 4 years as are the *President* and *Vice-President.* Customary social roles and land and sea rights are allocated by a matriarchal 16-clan system.

At the elections on 12 Nov. 1992 Kuniwo Nakamura was elected *President* by 4,841 votes to 4,707 against a single opponent. He was re-elected in 1996, defeating two other candidates.

Vice-President: Tommy Remengesau.

INTERNATIONAL RELATIONS

Membership. Palau is a member of the UN, the South Pacific Forum and the Pacific Community.

ECONOMY

Budget. Revenues for 1995 are estimated at $17m. and expenditures at $57m.

Currency. US currency is used.

Banking and Finance. The National Development Bank of Palau is situated in Koror.

ENERGY AND NATURAL RESOURCES

Agriculture. The main agricultural products are bananas, coconuts, copra, cassava and sweet potatoes.

Fisheries. Catch (1992) 4,000 tonnes, mainly tuna.

INDUSTRY. There is little industry, but the principal activities are food-processing and boat-building.

FOREIGN ECONOMIC RELATIONS

Commerce. Imports (1989) US$24·6m. Exports (1989) $600,000. The main trading partners are the USA and Japan for exports and the USA for imports.

Tourism. Tourism is a major industry, particularly marine-based. There are about 40,000 visitors a year.

COMMUNICATIONS

Roads. There are 61 km of roads of which 36 km are paved. In 1986 there were 1,687 motor vehicles.

Civil Aviation. Continental Micronesia flies daily to Guam and there are also scheduled services to Manila. Palau has 3 airports, with internal flights operated by Paradise Air.

Shipping. In 1985, 56,000 tonnes of cargo were discharged and 2,000 tonnes were loaded.

Telecommunications. In 1988 there were 1,500 telephones. There is a radio station (WSZB) which broadcasts daily on AM and FM, and ICTV Cable TV presents 12 channels with CNN. In 1993 there were an estimated 1,600 televisions and 9,000 radios.

Press. The local newspaper *Tia Belau* is published bi-weekly.

SOCIAL INSTITUTIONS

Justice. There is a Supreme Court and various subsidiary courts.

Religion. The majority of the population are Roman Catholic.

Education. In 1987 there were 2,784 pupils in 26 primary schools, 1,009 pupils in 6 secondary schools and 382 students (1984) in a technical school. The adult literacy rate is 92%.

Health. In 1986 there were 10 doctors, 3 dentists, 1 pharmacist, 82 nursing personnel and a hospital with 70 beds.

DIPLOMATIC REPRESENTATIVES

Of Great Britain in Palau
Ambassador: Vernon M. Scarborough (resides in Fiji)

Of the USA in Palau
Ambassador: Thomas C. Hubbard (resides in The Philippines)

Of Palau at the United Nations
Ambassador: Vacant.

PANAMA

República de Panamá

Capital: Panama City
Population: 2·7m.
GNP: US$6·9bn.
HDI/world rank: 0·864/45

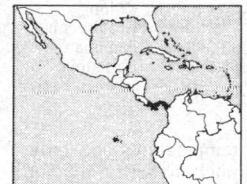

KEY HISTORICAL EVENTS. A revolution, inspired by the USA, led to the separation of Panama from the United States of Colombia and the declaration of its independence on 3 Nov. 1903. The *de facto* government was recognized by the USA on 5 Nov., and soon afterwards by the other major powers. Diplomatic relations between Colombia and Panama were finally established on 8 May 1924.

On 18 Nov. 1903 a treaty between the USA and the Republic of Panama was signed making it possible for the USA to build and operate a canal connecting the Atlantic and Pacific oceans through the Isthmus of Panama. The treaty granted the USA in perpetuity the use, occupation and control of a Canal Zone, in which the USA would possess full sovereign rights. In return the USA guaranteed the independence of the republic and agreed to pay the republic US$10m. and an annuity of US$250,000. The USA purchased the French rights and properties—the French had been labouring from 1879 to 1899 in an effort to build the canal—for US$40m. and in addition paid private landholders within what would be the Canal Zone a mutually agreeable price for their properties. The Canal was opened on 15 Aug. 1914.

The US domination of Panama has provoked frequent anti-American political actions. In 1968 a more independently minded president, Col. Omar Torryas Herrera, took power in a *coup* and attempted to negotiate a more advantageous treaty with the USA. Two new treaties between Panama and the USA were agreed on 10 Aug. and signed on 7 Sept. 1977. One deals with the operation and defence of the Canal until the end of 1999 and the other guarantees permanent neutrality.

The USA maintains operational control over all lands, waters and installations, including military bases, necessary to manage, operate and defend the Canal until 31 Dec. 1999. Six months after the exchange of instruments of ratification Panama assumed general territorial jurisdiction over the former Canal Zone and became able to use portions of the area not needed for the operation and defence of the Canal.

Torryas vacated the presidency in 1978 but maintained his power as head of the National Guard until his death in an air crash in 1981. Subsequently Gen. Manuel Noriega, Torryas' successor as head of the National Guard, became the strong man of the régime. His position was threatened by some internal political opposition and economic pressure applied by the USA but in Oct. 1989 a US-backed coup attempt failed. On 15 Dec. Gen. Noriega, declared a 'state of war' with the USA. On 20 Dec. the USA invaded Panama to remove Gen. Noriega from power and he surrendered on 3 Jan. 1990. Accused as a drug dealer he was convicted by a court in Miami and is now serving a 40-year jail sentence. Currently, Panama is preparing for life without America. By 31 Dec. 1999 all American troops—10,000 a few years ago—will have left.

TERRITORY AND POPULATION. Panama is bounded in the north by the Caribbean Sea, east by Colombia, south by the Pacific Ocean and west by Costa Rica. The area is 75,517 sq. km). Population at the census of 1990 was 2,329,329 (49% urban). July 1997 estimate, 2·7m.

Vital statistics (1994): Births, 59,947; marriages, 13,523; deaths, 10,983. Crude birth rate (per 1,000): 23·0. In 1994 infant mortality was 14·7 per 1,000 live births; life expectancy was 73·2 years.

The largest towns (1995) are Panama City, the capital, on the Pacific coast (658,102); its suburb San Miguelito (290,919); Colón, the port on the Atlantic coast (156,289); and David (113,527).

The areas and populations of the 9 provinces and the Special Territory were:

Province	Sq. km	Census 1980	1995 (est.)	Capital
Bocas del Toro	9,506	53,579	119,336	Bocas del Toro
Chiriquí	8,924	287,801	407,849	David
Veraguas	11,226	173,195	219,049	Santiago
Herrera	2,185	81,866	101,198	Chitré
Los Santos	4,587	70,200	79,935	Las Tablas
Coclé	4,981	140,320	189,579	Penonomé
Colón	7,205	166,439	226,139	Colón
San Blas (Special Territory)	3,206			El Porvenir
Panama	11,400	830,278	1,232,390	Panama City
Darién	15,458	26,497	55,538	La Palma

The official language is Spanish.

CLIMATE. A tropical climate, unvaryingly with high temperatures and only a short dry season from Jan. to April. Rainfall amounts are much higher on the north side of the isthmus. Panama City. Jan. 79°F (26·1°C), July 81°F (27·2°C). Annual rainfall 70" (1,770 mm). Colón. Jan. 80°F (26·7°C), July 80°F (26·7°C). Annual rainfall 127" (3,175 mm). Balboa Heights. Jan. 80°F (26·7°C), July 81°F (27·2°C). Annual rainfall 70" (1,759 mm). Cristóbal. Jan. 80°F (26·7°C), July 81°F (27·2°C). Annual rainfall 130" (3,255 mm).

CONSTITUTION AND GOVERNMENT. The 1972 Constitution, as amended in 1978 and 1983, provides for a *President*, elected for 5 years, 2 *Vice-Presidents* and a 72-seat *Legislative Assembly* to be elected for 5-year terms by a direct vote. To remain registered, parties must have attained at least 50,000 votes at the last election. A referendum held on 15 Nov. 1992 rejected constitutional reforms by 64% of votes cast. Turn-out was 40%.

Presidential and parliamentary elections were held on 8 May 1994. The electorate was 1,499,848; turn-out was 73·7%. Ernesto Pérez Balladares was elected President by 33·3% of votes cast against 6 opponents. Representatives of 16 parties stood for election to the Legislative Assembly, 13 grouped in alliances. The Revolutionary Democratic Party (RDP) gained 31 seats in the 'United People' alliance with the Liberal Republican Party (LRP; 1) and the Labour Party (1); the Arnulfist Party (AP) gained 15 in the 'Democratic Alliance' with the Authentic Liberal Party (4), the National Liberal Party (1) and the Democratic Independent Union (1); the Papá Egoró Movement gained 6; the Liberal Republican Nationalist Movement (MORILENA) gained 5 in the 'Change 94' alliance with the Civil Renovation Party (3) and the National Renovation Party (1); the Solidarity Party gained 2; the Christian Democrat Party gained 1.

President: Ernesto Pérez Balladares (RDP; sworn in 1 Sept. 1994).

First Vice-President: Tomas Altamirano Duque; *Second Vice-President:* Felipe Virzi.

In March 1998 the government comprised:

Interior and Justice: Raul Montenegro. *Foreign Affairs:* Ricardo Arias. *Public Works:* Luis Blanco. *Finance and Treasury:* Miguel Heras Castro. *Agricultural Development:* Carlos Sousa Lennox. *Commerce and Industry:* Raúl Arango. *Health:* Aida Libia de Rivera. *Labour and Social Welfare:* Mitchel Doens. *Education:* Dr Pablo Thalassinos. *Housing:* Dr Francisco Sánchez Cardenas. *Planning and Economic Policy:* Dr Guillermo Chapman. *Minister of the Presidency:* Olmedo Miranda. *Canal Affairs:* Jorge Ritter.

National anthem: 'Alcanzamos por fin la victoria' ('We achieve victory in the end'); words by J. de la Ossa, tune by Santos Jorge.

Local Government: The 9 provinces and a Special Territory are divided into 67 municipal districts and sub-divided into 511 local authorities.

DEFENCE. The armed forces were disbanded in 1990 and constitutionally abolished in 1994. Divided between both coasts, the National Maritime Service, a coast guard rather than a navy, comprises 5 inshore patrol craft and 1 LCM amphibious craft. In 1996 personnel totalled 400. For Police see JUSTICE, below.

INTERNATIONAL RELATIONS

Membership. Panama is a member of the UN, OAS Non-aligned Movement, WTO.

ECONOMY

Policy. A 5 year programme of trade liberalization aims to attract foreign investment. Hopes of diversifying an economy heavily dependent on the Canal rest largely on shipping services, mining and tourism.

Budget. The 1995 budget provided for revenue of 1,729m. balboas, current expenditure of 1,702m. balboas, capital expenditure of 381m. balboas and debt service of 493m. balboas. Public sector debt was US$3,771m. in 1989.

Currency. The monetary unit is the *balboa* (PAB) of 100 *centesimos*, at parity with the US dollar. There are coins of 1, 5, 10, 25 and 50 centesimos and 1 and 100 balboas. The only paper currency used is that of the USA. US coinage is also legal tender. Inflation was 0·9% in Dec. 1995.

Banking and Finance. There is no statutory central bank. Banking is supervised and promoted by the National Banking Commission. Government accounts are handled through the state-owned *Banco Nacional de Panama*. There are 2 other state banks. The number of commercial banks was 108 in 1996. Total assets, June 1996, US$33,400m., total deposits, US$25,000m. (including offshore, US$15,900m.).

Weights and Measures. US Customary weights and measures are in general use; the metric system is the official system.

ENERGY AND NATURAL RESOURCES

Electricity. In 1995 capacity was 921 MW. Output, 1995, 551 MWh.

Minerals. Limestone, clay and salt are produced. There are known to be copper deposits.

Agriculture. Production in 1995 (in 1,000 quintales; 1 quintal = 46 kg): Rice, 4,935; maize, 2,335; dry beans, 138; raw sugar, 1,516; coffee, 244; tobacco, 244. Livestock (1995): 1,456,000 cattle, 261,000 pigs and 10m. poultry.

Forestry. Forest and woodland covered 3·9m. ha in 1994. There are great timber resources, notably mahogany. Production (1986) 2·05m. cu. metres.

Fisheries. The catch in 1994 was 276,662 tonnes. Shrimps are the principal species caught.

INDUSTRY. The main industry is agricultural produce processing. Other areas include oil refining, chemicals and paper-making.

Labour. In 1996 the workforce (persons 15 years and over) numbered 1,001,439, of whom 870,622 were employed.

Trade Unions. 77,500 workers belonged to trade unions in 1994, of whom 27,000 were members of the Confederación de Trabajadores de la República de Panamá.

FOREIGN ECONOMIC RELATIONS. The Colón Free Zone is an autonomous institution set up in 1953. 1,556 companies were operating there in 1997. Factories in export zones are granted tax exemption on profits for 10–20 years and exemption from the provisions of the labour code. Foreign debt was US$5,605m. in Dec. 1995.

Commerce. Trade in 1995 (in 1m. balboas): Exports, 565·4; imports, (1994) 2,404·1. Main exports: Bananas, 190·3; shellfish, 104·2; sugar, 18·0. Chief export markets: USA, 37·5%; Germany, 12·2%; Sweden, 9%; Costa Rica, 7·1%; Belgium, 7%. Chief import suppliers: USA, 38%; Japan, 7·1%; Ecuador, 4%; Costa Rica, 3%.

Tourism. In 1993, 327,000 people visited Panama. Revenue from tourism was US$270m. in 1995.

COMMUNICATIONS

Roads. In 1995 there were 10,792 km of roads, about one-third paved or tarred. The road from Panama City westward to the cities of David and Concepción and to the Costa Rican frontier, with several branches, is part of the Pan-American Highway. The Trans-Isthmian Highway connects Panama City and Colón. In 1995 there were 250,319 registered motor vehicles.

Railways. The 1,524 mm gauge *Ferrocarril de Panama*, which connects Ancón on the Pacific with Cristóbal on the Atlantic along the bank of the Panama Canal, is the principal railway. 43,000 tonnes of freight were carried in 1994. The United Brands Company runs 376 km of railway, and the Chiriquí National Railroad 171 km.

Civil Aviation. There is an international airport at Panama City (Tocumén). The national carrier is COPA, which in 1995 operated 6 B-737-200 Advs, 1 B-737-200C and 1 B-737-200C Adv. In 1996 COPA flew to 22 destinations in 16 countries and carried 0·7m. passengers. Services are also provided by Aces, Aeroflot, Aeroperlas, Aeroperú, Aerotour Dominicano, American Airlines, Avensa, Avianca, Aviateca, Continental Airlines & Air Micronesia, Cubana, Eva, Iberia, KLM, LACSA, Lloyd Aéreo Boliviano, Mexicana, SAETA, SAM, Servivensa and Taca.

Shipping. Ships under Panamanian registry in 1995 totalled 86·46m. DWT, all foreign-owned. As at Sept. 1996, 13,618 vessels were registered. Most of these ships elect Panamanian registry because fees are low and labour laws lenient. Revenue from the registry was US$44m. in 1996. All the international maritime traffic for Colón and Panama runs through the Canal ports of Cristóbal, Balboa and Bahia Las Minas (Colón); Almirante is used for both the provincial and international trade. There is an oil transfer terminal at Puerto Armuelles on the Pacific coast.

Panama Canal. The Panama Canal Commission is concerned primarily with the operation of the Canal. Since 1 Oct. 1995, tolls assessment has been based on the Panama Canal/Universal Measurement System (PC/UMS), which incorporates the principles of the 1969 International Convention on Tonnage Measurement of Ships. Toll rates are US$2·21 a PC/UMS ton for vessels carrying passengers or cargo and US$1·90 per ton for vessels in transit in ballast. The toll rate for warships, hospital ships and supply ships, which pay on a displacement basis, is US$1·33 a ton.

The rates are set to continue the approximately break-even financial operating results after paying its own expenses.

Administrator of the Panama Canal Commission: Alberto Alemán Zubieta.

US military personnel: Army, 4,090; Navy, 700; Marines, 120; Air Force, 2,050.

Particulars of the ocean-going commercial traffic through the canal are given as follows (vessels of 300 PC/UMS tons net and 500 displacement tons and over; cargo in long tons):

Fiscal year ending 30 Sept.	No. of vessels transiting	PC/UMS net tonnage	Cargo in long tons	Tolls levied (in US$)
1995	13,459[1]	215,355,914	190,303,065	460,043,676
1996	13,700	228,000,000	198,000,000	486,000,000

[1] 6,933 Atlantic to Pacific; 6,526 Pacific to Atlantic.

In the fiscal year ending 30 Sept. 1996, 15,187 ships of all sizes passed through the Canal. Most numerous transits by flag: Panama, 2,560; Liberia, 1,663; Bahamas, 1,242; Greece, 999; Cyprus, 956; Norway, 393.

Statistical Information: The Panama Canal Commission Office of Public Affairs.
Annual Reports on the Panama Canal, by the Administrator of the Panama Canal Commission.
Rules and Regulations Governing Navigation of the Panama Canal. The Panama Canal Commission, Miami, Florida *or* Washington, DC
Cameron, I., *The Impossible Dream.* London, 1972
Le Feber, W., *The Panama Canal: The Crisis in Historical Perspective.* OUP, 1978

McCullough, D., *The Path Between the Seas*. New York and London, 1978
Major, J., *Prize Possession: the United States and the Panama Canal, 1903–1979*. CUP, 1994

Telecommunications. There were 0·3m. telephones in 1995. There are about 60 broadcasting stations, mostly commercial, grouped in the Asociación Panameña de Radiodifusión. There are 4 television channels (colour by NTSC), an educational channel, and a radio and TV network for US forces. In 1995 there were 0·2 radio and 204,539 TV sets in use.

Press. In 1994 there were 8 dailies (1 in English).

SOCIAL INSTITUTIONS

Justice. The Supreme Court consists of 9 justices appointed by the executive. There is no death penalty. The police force numbered 11,000 in 1996, and includes a Presidential Guard.

Religion. 85% of the population is Roman Catholic, 5% Protestant, 4·5% Moslem. There is freedom of religious worship and separation of Church and State. Clergymen may teach in the schools but may not hold public office.

Education. Adult literacy was 90% in 1992. Elementary education is compulsory for all children from 7 to 15 years of age. In 1995 there were 3 universities and 1 technological university with a total of 75,951 students and 4,106 academic staff. There were also a nautical school, a business school and institutes of teacher training and tourism.

Health. In 1995 there were 3,074 doctors, 656 dentists and 2,823 nursing personnel. There were 59 hospitals, 174 health centres and 443 health sub-centres with a total of 7,138 beds.

DIPLOMATIC REPRESENTATIVES

Of Panama in Great Britain (48 Park St., London, W1Y 3PD)
Ambassador: Vacant.

Of Great Britain in Panama (Torre Swiss Bank, Calle 53, Apartado 889, Panama City 1)
Ambassador and Consul-General: William Sinton.

Of Panama in the USA (2862 McGill Terr., NW, Washington, D.C., 20008)
Ambassador: Eduardo Morgan González.

Of the USA in Panama (Apartado 6959, Panama City 5)
Ambassador: William J. Hughes.

Of Panama to the United Nations
Ambassador: Aquilino Boyd de la Guardia.

Of Panama to the European Union
Ambassador: Vilma Ramírez.

Further Reading

Statistical Information: The Comptroller-General of the Republic (Contraloria General de la República, Calle 35 y Avenida 6, Panama City) publishes an annual report and other statistical publications.

Jorden, W. J., *Panama Odyssey.* Univ. of Texas Press, 1984
Langstaff, E. DeS., *Panama.* [Bibliography]. Oxford and Santa Barbara (CA), 1982
Ropp, S. C., *Panamanian Politics.* New York, 1982
Sahota, G. S., *Poverty Theory and Policy: a Study of Panama.* Johns Hopkins Univ. Press, 1990

Other titles are listed under PANAMA CANAL, above.

National library: Biblioteca Nacional, Departamento de Información. Calle 22, Panama.

PAPUA
NEW GUINEA

Capital: Port Moresby
Population: 3·85m.
GDP per head: (PPP$) 2,821
GNP: US$4·9bn.
HDI/world rank: 0·525/128

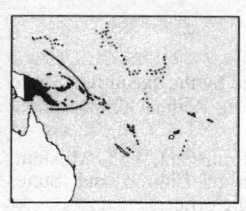

KEY HISTORICAL EVENTS. New Guinea, especially the eastern half (Irian Jaya), was known to Indonesian and Asian seafarers centuries before it was known to the Europeans. In 1512 the Portuguese sighted the New Guinea coast but made no landing until 1527. Spanish first claimed the island in 1545 but the first attempt at colonization was made in 1793 by the British. The Dutch, however, claimed the west half of the island as part of the Dutch East Indies in 1828.

In order to prevent that portion of the island of New Guinea not claimed by the Netherlands or Germany from passing into the hands of another foreign power, the government of Queensland annexed Papua in 1883. This step was not sanctioned by the Imperial Government, but on 6 Nov. 1884 a British Protectorate was proclaimed over the southern portion of the eastern half of New Guinea, and in 1887 Queensland, New South Wales and Victoria undertook to defray the cost of administration, and the territory was annexed to the Crown the following year. By 1884 the south-east of New Guinea had been annexed to Britain and the German New Guinea Company took over the north-east of the country. The Australian federal government took over control in 1901; the political transfer was completed by the Papua Act of the federal parliament in Nov. 1905, and on 1 Sept. 1906 the Governor-General of Australia declared that British New Guinea was to be known henceforth as the Territory of Papua. The northern portion of New Guinea was a German colony until 1914, when Australian armed forces occupied it and it remained under their administration for the next seven years. It became a League of Nations mandated territory in 1921, administered by Australia, and later a UN Trust Territory (of New Guinea).

The Papua New Guinea Act 1949–72 provided for the administration of the UN Australian Trust Territory of New Guinea in an administrative union with the Territory of Papua, under the title of Papua New Guinea. Australia granted Papua New Guinea self-government on 1 Dec. 1973, and on 16 Sept. 1975 Papua New Guinea became a fully independent state.

What began in 1988 as an armed campaign by tribes claiming traditional land rights against the Australian owner of the massive Panguna copper field soon escalated into a civil war for the secession of the island of Bougainville. Fighting between the government and the secessionist Bougainville Revolutionary Army (BRA) continued until 3 Sept. 1994, when a peace agreement was signed. This provides for 4 neutral zones to be occupied by a Pacific peacekeeping force drawn from Fiji, Tonga and Vanuatu with logistic support from Australia and New Zealand. The agreement also set up a provisional Bougainville government. The ceasefire was broken by the rebels in mid-1995, and the provisional government leader was assassinated in Oct. 1996, after which the situation deteriorated further. In March 1997 the Government began to employ foreign mercenaries.

TERRITORY AND POPULATION. Papua New Guinea extends from the equator to Cape Baganowa in the Louisiade Archipelago to 11° 40' S. lat. and from the border of West Irian to 160° E. long. with a total area of 462,840 sq. km. According to the census the 1990 population was 3,529,538 (excluding North Solomons, estimated 1990 population 159,500). Estimate, 1992, 3·85m. Population of main towns (1990 census): Port Moresby (National Capital District), 193,242; Lae, 80,655; Rabaul, 17,022; Madang, 27,057; Wewak, 23,224; Goroka, 17,855; Mount Hagen, 17,392. Area and population of the provinces:

Provinces	Sq.km	Census 1980	Census 1990	Capital
Milne Bay	14,000	127,975	157,288	Alotau
Northern	22,800	77,442	96,762	Popondetta
Central	29,500	116,964	140,584	Port Moresby
National Capital District	240	123,624	193,242	—
Gulf	34,500	64,120	68,060	Kerema
Western	99,300	78,575	108,705 [1]	Daru
Southern Highlands	23,800	236,052	302,724	Mendi
Enga	12,800	164,534	238,357	Wabag
Western Highlands	8,500	265,656	291,090	Mount Hagen
Chimbu	6,100	178,290	183,801	Kundiawa
Eastern Highlands	11,200	276,726	299,619	Goroka
Morobe	34,500	310,622	363,535	Lae
Madang	29,000	211,069	270,299	Madang
East Sepik	42,800	221,890	248,308	Wewak
West Sepik	36,300	114,192	135,185 [2]	Vanimo
Manus	2,100	26,036	32,830	Lorengau
West New Britain	21,000	88,941	127,547	Kimbe
East New Britain	15,500	133,197	184,408	Rabaul
New Ireland	9,600	66,028	87,194	Kavieng
North Solomons	9,300	128,794	· · ·	Arawa

[1] Excludes 3 census divisions, estimated total 1,500.
[2] Excludes 2 census divisions, estimated total 3,000.

Vital statistics (1994, estimate): Crude birth rate, 33·4 per 1,000; crude death rate, 10·4. Life expectancy was 56·4 years in 1994.

The principal local languages are Neo-Melanesian (or Pidgin, a creole of English) and Hiri Motu. English is in official use.

CLIMATE. There is a monsoon climate, with high temperatures and humidity the year round. Port Moresby is in a rain shadow and is not typical of the rest of Papua New Guinea. Jan. 82°F (27·8°C), July 78°F (25·6°C). Annual rainfall 40" (1,011 mm).

CONSTITUTION AND GOVERNMENT. A single legislative house, known as the *National Parliament*, is made up of 109 members from all parts of the country. The members are elected by universal suffrage; elections are held every 5 years. All citizens over the age of 18 are eligible to vote and stand for election. Voting is by secret ballot and follows the preferential system. The Governor-General is nominated by parliament for 6-year terms.

Governor-General: Silas Atopare.

At the elections of June 1997 no party held a majority. Following coalition negotiations, William Skate of the People's National Congress was elected prime minister, heading a government composed of representatives from the five main parties (People's National Congress, People's Progress Party, Pangu Pati, People's Democratic Movement and People's Resource Party).

In March 1998 the government comprised:
Prime Minister, Minister of Defence: William Skate (elected 22 July 1997).
Deputy Prime Minister: Michael Nali. *Senior Minister for State:* Sir Rabbie Namaliu. *Minister for National Planning and Implementation:* Sir Mekere Morauta. *Agriculture and Livestock:* Tukape Masani. *Petroleum and Energy:* Masket Iangalio. *Mining and Energy:* Philemon Embel. *Forests:* Dr Fabian Pol. *Provincial and Local Government Affairs:* Simon Kaumi. *Transport:* Vincent Auali. *Justice:* Jacob Wama. *Information and Communications:* Simeon Wai. *Trade and Industry:* Michael Nali. *Fisheries:* Kala Swokin. *Correctional Services:* Peter Arul. *Environment:* Herowa Agiwa. *Education, Culture and Science:* Muki Taranupi. *Lands:* Viviso Seravo. *Health:* Ludger Mondo. *Police:* Thomas Pelika. *Youth and Employment:* Mathias Karani. *Family and Church Affairs:* Titus Philemon. *Works:* Yauwe Riyong. *Housing:* Mao Zeming. *Public Service:* Peter Waieng. *Finance:* Digbara Yagbo. *Works:* Yauwe Riyong. *Foreign Affairs:* Roy Yaki. *Bougainville Affairs:* Sam Akoitai.
The *Speaker* is John Pundari.

National anthem: 'Arise, all you sons of this land'; words and tune by T. Shacklady.

Local Government: In 1950 the first village council was formed which established the basis of an extensive local government system. A system of provincial government was introduced in 1976 and the importance of lower-level local government diminished. However, lower-level community government had replaced local government councils in some provinces by 1991. Each of the 19 provinces has its own government which may levy taxes to supplement grants received from the national government.

DEFENCE. The Papua New Guinea Defence Force has a total strength of 3,800 (1996) consisting of land, maritime and air elements. The Army is organized in 2 infantry and 1 engineer battalion. The Navy, based at Port Moresby and Manus, is all of Australian build and comprises 4 inshore patrol craft, 2 tank landing craft and some boats. Personnel numbered 400 in 1996. The Defence Force has an Air Transport Squadron, grounded through shortage of funds in 1996. Current equipment comprises 2 CN-235 transports and 3 Arava, 1 Australian-built N22B Nomad and 4 Iroquois helicopters.

INTERNATIONAL RELATIONS

Membership. Papua New Guinea is a member of the UN, the Commonwealth, the Colombo Plan, the South Pacific Commission and the Pacific Community and is an observer at ASEAN and an ACP state of the EU.

ECONOMY

Budget. Budgetary income (in K1m.) for calendar years was:

Source	1996	1997[1]
Tax revenue	1,526·3	1,555·7
Non-tax revenue	201·2	200·8
Foreign grants	170·1	125·5
Total	1,897·7	1,882·0
Expenditure:		
National departmental	720·6	742·8
Provincial governments	521·8	568·3
Interest	257·1	328·6
Other grants & expenditure	112·2	120·3
Net lending & investment	−4·0	−5·1
Development	252·8	246·2
Total	1,860·7	2,001·1

[1] Estimates.

Currency. The unit of currency is the *kina* (PGK) of 100 *toea*. There are coins of 1, 2, 5, 10, 20 and 50 toea and 1 kina, and notes of 2, 5, 10, 20 and 50 kina. K141·2m. were in circulation in 1992. The kina was floated in Oct. 1994. Foreign exchange reserves were K231m. in 1992; gold reserves K11·1m.

Banking and Finance. The Bank of Papua New Guinea assumed the central banking functions formerly undertaken by the Reserve Bank of Australia on 1 Nov. 1973. A national banking institution, the Papua New Guinea Banking Corporation, has been established. This bank has assumed the Papua New Guinea business of the Commonwealth Trading Bank of Australia.

There are 5 commercial banks, 3 Australian and 2 with 51% Papuan ownership. Total deposits, 1992, K1318·2m. Total savings account deposits, 1992, K226·8m.

In addition, the Agriculture Bank of Papua New Guinea had assets of K82·6m. in 1992, and finance companies and merchant banks had total assets of K198·4m.

Weights and Measures. The metric system is in force.

ENERGY AND NATURAL RESOURCES

Electricity. Production in 1990 was 1,362·3m. kWh (490·3m. kWh hydro-electric).

Oil. The Iagifu field in the Southern Highlands had (1988) potential recoverable reserves of 500m. bbls. Crude oil production (1992), 2·12m. tonnes.

Minerals. In 1991 mining produced 15% of GDP. Copper is the main mineral product. Gold, copper and silver are the only minerals produced in quantity. The Misima open-pit gold mine, was opened in 1989. Production was forecast at 0·21m. oz a year with a life of 10 years. The Porgera gold mine opened in 1990 with an expected life of 20 years; in the first quarter of 1997 it produced 121,000 oz. Major copper deposits in Bougainville have proven reserves of about 800m. tonnes; mining was halted by secessionist rebel activity. Copper and gold deposits in the Star Mountains of the Western Province are being developed by Ok Tedi Mining Ltd at the Mt. Fubilan mine. Production of gold commenced in 1984 and of copper concentrates in 1987. In 1996 Ok Tedi Mining Ltd produced 47 tons of gold, 127,700 tons of copper and 39m. barrels of crude oil. Figures for 1997 point to a 50% increase in copper and 10% increase in gold. Gold mining also began at Lihir in 1997. Total yields for export in 1996 were: gold, 47 tonnes; copper, 127,700 tonnes; crude petroleum, 39·3m bbls.

Agriculture. In 1991 agriculture, forestry and fishery produced 27% of GDP and employed 75% of the workforce. At 31 Dec. 1988 there were 1,024 large holdings with a total area of 415,000 ha. In 1992 there were 40,000 ha of arable land, 0·37m ha of permanent cropland and 80,000 ha of permanent pasture. Minor commercial crops include pyrethrum, tea, peanuts and spices. Locally consumed food crops include sweet potatoes, maize, taro, bananas, rice and sago. Tropical fruits grow abundantly. There is extensive grassland. The sugar industry has made the country self-sufficient in this commodity while a beef-cattle industry is being developed.

Production for export (1996, in tonnes): coffee, 62,300; copra, 99,200; copra oil, 49,600; cocoa, 41,000.

Livestock (1993): Cattle, 105,000; pigs, 1·02m.; sheep, 4,000; goats, 2,000; poultry, 3m.

Forestry. The forest area totals 36m. ha of which about 15m. ha of high quality tropical hardwoods are considered suitable for development. Timber production is important for both local consumption and export. In 1997 577,300 cu. metres of logs were exported.

Fisheries. Tuna is the major resource. In 1996 the fish catch for export was 2,800 tonnes.

INDUSTRY. Secondary and service industries are expanding for the local market. The main industries were (1988) food processing, beverages, tobacco, timber products, wood, and fabricated metal products. In 1988 there were 692 factories employing 30,503 persons. Value of output K768m.

Labour. In 1996 formal employment in the building and construction industries rose by 27·5%, but around 85% of the population is dependent on non-monetarized agriculture.

FOREIGN ECONOMIC RELATIONS. Australian aid amounts to an annual $A300m. The 'Pactra II' agreement of 1991 establishes a free trade zone with Australia and protects Australian investments. Foreign debt was K863·3m. in 1993.

Commerce. Imports (in K1,000) for calendar years:

	1988	1989	1990
Food and live animals	181,789	190,853	194,624
Beverages and tobacco	15,456	14,957	14,764
Crude materials, inedible, except fuels	8,577	7,769	8,712
Mineral fuels, lubricants and related materials	98,175	63,704	80,132
Oils and fats (animal and vegetable)	3,350	3,387	4,793
Chemicals	84,403	78,588	81,563

	1988	1989	1990
Manufactured goods, chiefly by material	205,654	253,251	223,045
Machinery and transport equipment	424,587	524,966	423,019
Miscellaneous manufactured articles	99,113	109,776	97,560
Commodities and transactions of merchandise trade, not elsewhere specified	12,356	12,877	13,711
Total imports	1,133,459	1,260,128	1,141,922

Exports (in K1,000) for calendar years:

	1995	1996
Cocoa	47,700	66,200
Coffee beans	214,500	190,300
Tea	5,400	12,700
Copra and copra oil	57,100	100,400
Palm oil	142,200	182,400
Logs	436,700	464,800
Crude petroleum	827,700	1,073,900
Gold	840,100	773,600
Copper	754,500	387,000
Fish	12,300	10,400

Of exports in 1993, Japan took 21%, Germany, 6·4% and Australia, 36%; of imports (1990), Australia furnished about 47%, Singapore, 8·5% and Japan, 13·3%.

Tourism. In 1995, there were 42,328 foreign tourist arrivals.

COMMUNICATIONS

Roads. In 1992 there were 21,433 km of roads. Motor vehicles numbered (1992) about 95,000 (65,000 commercial).

Civil Aviation. Jacksons International Airport is at Port Moresby. The state-owned national carrier, Air Niugini, operated 2 A310-300s and 12 other aircraft in 1995. Services are also provided by Qantas and Solomon Airlines. There are a total of 177 airports and airstrips with scheduled services.

Shipping. There are 12 entry and 4 other main ports served by 5 major shipping lines; the Papua New Guinea Shipping Corporation is state-owned. Sea-going shipping totalled 51,051 GRT in 1995, including oil tankers, 5,044 GRT.

Telecommunications. Telephones numbered 40,000 in 1994. The National Broadcasting Commission operates 3 networks: national, provincial and commercial. A national service is relayed throughout the country. Each province has a broadcasting service, while the larger urban centres are also covered by a commercial network relayed from Port Moresby. 2 commercial television stations broadcast from Port Moresby (colour by PAL). In 1990 there were 10,000 television and 235,000 radio receivers.

Press. In 1993 there was 1 daily newspaper and a number of weeklies and monthlies.

SOCIAL INSTITUTIONS

Justice. In 1983, over 1,500 criminal and civil cases were heard in the National Court and an estimated 120,000 cases in district and local courts. The discretionary use of the death penalty for murder and rape was introduced in 1991.

Religion. In 1992 there were 2·24m. Protestants and 1·26m. Roman Catholics.

Education. Obligatory universal primary education is a government objective. In 1990 about two-thirds of eligible children were attending school. In 1990-91 there were 2,606 primary schools with 413,089 pupils, 135 secondary schools with 56,638 pupils, 101 vocational schools with 5,395 students, 7 technical colleges with 1,043 students, 9 teacher training colleges with 1,686 students and 2 universities (the University of Papua New Guinea and the Papua New Guinea University of Technology) with 5,007 students. Adult literacy rate is 71·2%.

Health. In 1986, there were 19 hospitals, 459 health centres and 2,231 aid posts. In 1991 there was 1 doctor per 12,870 inhabitants.

DIPLOMATIC REPRESENTATIVES

Of Papua New Guinea in Great Britain (14 Waterloo Pl., London, SW1R 4AR)
High Commissioner: Sir Kina Bona, KBE.

Of Great Britain in Papua New Guinea (PO Box 212, Waigani NCD 131)
High Commissioner: C. D. S. Drace-Francis, CMG.

Of Papua New Guinea in the USA (1615 New Hampshire Ave., NW, Washington D.C., 20036)
Ambassador: Sir Nagora Bogan, KBE.

Of the USA in Papua New Guinea (Armit St., Port Moresby)
Ambassador: Arma Jane Karaer.

Of Papua New Guinea to the United Nations
Ambassador: Utula Utuoc Samana, CMG.

Of Papua New Guinea to the European Union
Ambassador: Gabriel Pepson.

Further Reading

National Statistical Office. *Summary of Statistics.* Annual. *Abstract of Statistics.* Quarterly. — *Economic Indicators.*
Monthly Bank of Papua New Guinea. *Quarterly Economic Bulletin.*
McConnell, F., *Papua New Guinea.* [Bibliography] Oxford and Santa Barbara, 1988
Ryan, P. (ed.) *Encyclopaedia of Papua and New Guinea.* Melbourne Univ. Press, 1972
Turner, A., *Historical Dictionary of Papua New Guinea.* Metuchen (NJ), 1995
Waiko, J. D., *Short History of Papua New Guinea.* OUP, 1993

National statistical office: National Statistical Office, PO Wards Strip.

PARAGUAY

República del Paraguay

Capital: Asunción
Population: 5·65m.
GNP: US$7·6bn.
HDI/world rank: 0·706/94

KEY HISTORICAL EVENTS. A landlocked territory bordered by Brazil, Argentina and Bolivia, Paraguay was occupied by the Spanish in 1537 and became a Spanish colony as part of the viceroyalty of Peru. The Guarani-speaking population gained some protection from the powerful Jesuit mission stations until the expulsion of the Jesuits in 1767. In 1776 the area became part of the vice-royalty of Rio de la Plata, gaining its independence from Spain, as the Republic of Paraguay, on 14 May 1811. Paraguay was then ruled by a succession of dictators, the first being Dr José Gaspar Rodriguez de Francia who was elected dictator in 1814 by the national assembly and became perpetual dictator in 1816; he died in 1840. In 1844 a new constitution was adopted under which Carlos Antonio López (nephew of Dr Francia) and his son, Francisco López, ruled until 1870.

During a devastating war, fought from 1865 to 1870, between Paraguay and a coalition of Argentina, Brazil and Uruguay, Paraguay's population was reduced from about 600,000 to 233,000. Further severe losses were incurred during the war with Bolivia (1932-35) over territorial claims in the Chaco inspired by the unfounded belief that minerals existed in the territory. A peace treaty by which Paraguay obtained most of the area her troops had conquered was signed in July 1938.

The dictatorship of Gen. Higinio Moringo was ended following a civil war in which the right-wing party (*Partido Colorado*) defeated the Liberals. A period of unrest ensued until Gen. Alfredo Stroessner Mattiauda, the C.-in-C. of the Army, assumed power in a military *coup* in 1954. He was deposed in a further coup in Feb. 1989.

A new constitution took effect in Feb. 1968 under which executive power is discharged by an executive president. In 1977 the constitution was amended to enable the president to stand for more than two consecutive terms of office. Gen. Stroessner was, in fact, re-elected 7 times between 1958 and 1988. Since then, Paraguay has been under democratic government. The third consecutive general democratic elections were held in May 1998.

TERRITORY AND POPULATION. Paraguay is bounded in the north-west by Bolivia, north-east and east by Brazil and south-east, south and south-west by Argentina. The area is 406,752 sq. km (157,042 sq. miles).

The population (census 1992) was 4·12m. (51% urban); estimate (July 1997) 5·65m.; density, 13·9 per sq. km.

Vital statistics rates, 1997 estimates (per 1,000 population): Birth, 30·47; death, 4·24; growth, 2·62%; expectation of life, 74·1 years.

At the 1992 census the capital, Asunción (and metropolitan area), had 637,737 inhabitants and Ciudad del Este (formerly Presidente Stroessner), 133,893.

There are 17 departments and the capital city. Area and population at the 1992 census:

Department	Area in sq. km	Population	Department	Area in sq. km	Population
Asunción (city)	117	502,426	Caazapá	9,496	128,550
Central	2,465	864,540	Canendiyú	14,667	96,826
Caaguazú	11,474	383,319	Amambay	12,933	97,158
Alto Paraná	14,895	403,858	Misiones	9,556	88,624
Itapúa	16,525	375,748	Neembucú	12,147	69,884
San Pedro	20,002	277,110	*Oriental*	*159,827*	*4,026,342*
Paraguari	8,705	203,012	Presidente Hayes	72,907	59,100

Department	Area in sq. km	Population	Department	Area in sq. km	Population
Cordillera	4,948	206,097	Boquerón[1]	91,669	26,292
Concepción	18,051	166,946	Alto Paraguay[2]	83,349	11,816
Guairá	3,846	162,244	*Occidental*	*246,925*	*97,208*

[1] Incorporates former department of Nueva Asunción.
[2] Incorporates former department of Chaco.

The population is mixed Spanish and Guaraní Indian. There are some 46,700 unassimilated Indians of other tribal origin, in the Chaco and the forests of eastern Paraguay. 40·1% of the population speak only Guaraní; 48·2% are bilingual (Spanish/Guaraní); and 6·4% speak only Spanish.

Mennonites who arrived in 3 groups (1927, 1930 and 1947) are settled in the Chaco and eastern Paraguay. There are also Korean and Japanese settlers.

CLIMATE. A tropical climate, with abundant rainfall and only a short dry season from July to Sept., when temperatures are lowest. Asunción. Jan. 81°F (27°C), July 64°F (17·8°C). Annual rainfall 53" (1,316 mm).

CONSTITUTION AND GOVERNMENT. On 18 June 1992 a Constituent Assembly approved a new constitution. The head of state is the *President,* elected for a non-renewable 5-year term. Parliament consists of an 80-member *Chamber of Deputies,* elected from departmental constituencies, and a 45-member *Senate,* elected from a single national constituency.

Presidential and parliamentary elections were held on 9 May 1993. Juan Carlos Wasmosy was elected President against 2 opponents with 39·5% of votes cast. The electorate was 1·6m. At the parliamentary elections the Colorado Party gained 40 seats in the Chamber of Deputies (and 20 in the Senate), the Authentic Radical Liberal Party 32 (and 17) and National Encounter 8 (and 8).

President: Juan Carlos Wasmosy (b.1938; Colorado Party; sworn in 15 Aug. 1993).

The Cabinet in March 1998 comprised:

Foreign Affairs: Dr Ruben Melgarejo Lanzoni. *Interior:* Carlos Garcette. *Finance:* Gustavo Facetti. *Health:* Dr Andres Vidovich. *Justice:* Dr Sebastian Gonzalez Insfran. *Public Works and Communications:* Gustavo Pedrozo. *Industry and Commerce:* Dr Atilio Fernández. *Education:* Dr Vicente Sarubbi. *Defence:* Dr Hugo Estigarribia. *Agriculture and Livestock:* Cayo Franco. *Integration:* Dr Gustavo Diaz de Vivar. *Women:* Nilda Cabrera.

National anthem: 'Paraguayos, república o muerte!' ('Paraguayans, republic or death!'); words by F. Acuña de Figueroa, tune by F. Dupuy.

Local Government. There are 17 departments with directly-elected councils and governors, and 212 municipalities.

DEFENCE. The army, navy and air forces are separate services under a single command. The President of the Republic is the active C.-in-C. Conscription is for 12 months (2 years in the navy).

Army. The Army is organized into 3 corps and 9 divisional headquarters and consists of 1 armoured, 2 mechanized and 4 horsed cavalry regiments, 7 infantry regiments (of battalion strength), 6 artillery groups (of battalion strength), 1 air defence and 4 engineer battalions and 20 frontier detachments. Equipment includes 5 M-4A3 main battle tanks. Strength (1997) 14,900 (10,400 conscripts).

Navy. The flotilla includes 7 armed river defence gunboats (the average age of which exceeds 50 years), 7 river patrol boats, and about 12 service craft. Personnel in 1996 totalled 3,600 including 900 marines.

Air Force. The Air Force has 3 combat units, 1 with Xavante light jet strike/training aircraft, 1 with armed T-33 trainers and the other with armed Tucano turboprop trainers. HQ and flying school are at Campo Grande, Asunción. Personnel (1996) 1,700 (600 conscripts).

INTERNATIONAL RELATIONS

Membership. Paraguay is a member of the UN, OAS, Mercosur and LAIA.

ECONOMY

Policy. There is a privatization programme for large state enterprises.

Budget. In 1995 revenue (in 1m. guaranís) was 2,078,993 and expenditure, 2,971,354; in 1994 revenue was 2,253,138 and expenditure, 2,038,193.

Revenue items, 1995: Import duties, 369,650; domestic taxes, 587,572; income tax, 308,584. Items of expenditure: Public debt service, 293,632; public works, 445,570; education, 579,754; defence, 267,373; agriculture, 283,794; health, 192,151.

Currency. The unit of currency is the *guaraní* (PYG), notionally divided into 100 *céntimos*. There are coins of 1, 5, 10, 50 and 100, and notes of 100, 500, 1,000, 5,000, 10,000 and 50,000 guaranís. 1,036m. guaranís were in circulation in 1995. In 1995 foreign exchange reserves were US$1,107m.; gold reserves were US$14m. in 1995. Inflation was 8·2% in 1996.

Banking and Finance. The Central Bank is a state-owned autonomous agency with the sole right of note issue, control over foreign exchange and the supervision of commercial banks (*Governor*, Hermes Gomez). In 1994 there were 28 commercial banks (mostly foreign), 2 other banking institutions, 1 investment bank, 1 development bank and 6 building societies.

There is a stock exchange in Asunción.

Weights and Measures. The metric system was officially adopted in 1901, but some traditional measures continue in use.

ENERGY AND NATURAL RESOURCES

Electricity. There is a vast hydro-electric potential; only 2% of output is thermal. Installed capacity was 8,500 MW in 1993. Output (1995), 41·63bn. kWh.

Minerals. The country is poor in minerals. Limestone, gypsum, kaolin and salt are extracted. Deposits of bauxite, iron ore, copper, manganese and uranium exist.

Agriculture. In 1992 agriculture produced 25·7% of GDP and employed 45% of the workforce. 23·8m. ha were in farming use, of which 4m. ha were cultivated.

At the agrarian census of 1991 there were 307,221 farms working 23,799,737 ha. 122,750 farms had fewer than 5 ha; 884 had over 5,000 ha.

Output (in 1,000 tonnes), 1995: Soybeans, 2,200; maize, 816; wheat, 250; cotton, 438; sugar-cane, 2,000; 1993: Cassava, 2,680; rice, 50; tobacco, 11. *Yerba maté*, or strongly flavoured Paraguayan tea, continues to be produced but is declining in importance.

Livestock (1993); 8,074,000 cattle, 330,000 horses, 2,915,000 pigs, and 371,000 sheep.

Forestry. In 1993 15m. ha were forested. Palm and tung oil are produced. In 1988, 629,700 tonnes of sawtimber were produced.

INDUSTRY. In 1994 industry produced 15·1% of GDP. Production, 1994 (1,000 tons): Frozen meat, 45·8; cotton fibre, 136·8; sugar, 110·8; rice, 81·9; wheat flour, 47·8; edible oil, 78·9; industrial oil, 10·0; tung oil, 6·8; cement, 528·8; soybean, peanut and coconut flour, 468; cigarettes (1988) (1m. packets), 46,598; matches (1,000 boxes), 8,979.

Labour. In 1993 there was a monthly minimum wage of 269,445 guaranís.

Trade Unions. Trade unionists number about 30,000 (*Confederación Paraguaya de Trabajadores* and *Confederación Cristiana de Trabajadores*).

FOREIGN ECONOMIC RELATIONS. Foreign debt was US1,233m. in 1994. In 1992 direct foreign investment totalled US$117m. (40% from Brazil, 19% from France, 12% from USA).

Commerce. Imports and exports (in US$1m.):

	1991	1992	1993	1994	1995
Imports	1,669·1	1,421·7	1,477·5	2,140·4	3,400
Exports	1,117·3	656·5	725·2	816·8	2,000

Main exports in 1994 (in US$1m.): Cotton fibre, 170·9; soya, 222·3; timber, 78·6; hides, 63; meat, 55·4. Main imports: Machinery, 476·2; vehicles, 276·8; fuel and lubricants, 159·4; beverages and tobacco, 179; chemicals, 145; foodstuffs, 99·1.

Main export markets in 1994 (in US$1m.): Brazil, 323·7; Netherlands, 160; Argentina, 90·7; USA, 56·9; Italy, 24·2; Germany, 13·2. Main import suppliers: Brazil, 555; Argentina, 308·1; USA, 243·3; Japan, 193·3; UK, 58·2.

Tourism. Visitors numbered 406,000 in 1994.

COMMUNICATIONS

Roads. In 1995 there were 28,900 km of roads, of which 2,717 were paved.

Railways. The President Carlos Antonio López (formerly Paraguay Central) Railway runs from Asunción to Encarnación, on the Río Alto Paraná, with a length of 441 km (1,435 mm gauge), and connects with Argentine Railways over the Encarnación-Posadas bridge opened in 1989. In 1994, traffic amounted to 182,000 tonnes and 24,000 passengers.

Civil Aviation. There is an international airport at Asunción (Silvio Pettirossi). The national carrier is Air Paraguay, which had 1 B-737-200 Adv in 1995. Services are also provided by Aerolineas Argentinas, Aeroperu, American Airlines, Iberia, Ladeco, Lloyd Aérea Boliviano, National Airlines, Pluna, TAM and Varig.

Shipping. Asunción, the chief port, is 950 miles from the sea. In 1995, ocean-going shipping totalled 32,226 GRT, including oil tankers, 2,850 GRT.

Telecommunications. In 1985 there were 382 post offices and 88,730 telephones. In 1993 there were 30 commercial radio stations and 2 TV stations. In 1994 there were 400,000 television and 830,000 radio receivers.

Cinemas. There are 6 cinemas in Asunción.

Press. There are 5 daily and 6 weekly newspapers.

SOCIAL INSTITUTIONS

Justice. The 1992 constitution confers a large measure of judicial autonomy. The highest court is the Supreme Court with 9 members. Nominations for membership must be backed by 6 of the 8 members of the Magistracy Council, which appoints all judges, magistrates and the electoral tribunal. The Council comprises elected representatives of the Presidency, Congress and the bar. There are special Chambers of Appeal for civil and commercial cases, and criminal cases. Judges of first instance deal with civil, commercial and criminal cases in 6 departments. Minor cases are dealt with by Justices of the Peace.

The Attorney-General represents the State in all jurisdictions, with representatives in each judicial department and in every jurisdiction.

Religion. Religious liberty was guaranteed by the 1967 constitution. Article 6 recognized Roman Catholicism as the official religion of the country. It had 4·34m. adherents in 1992. There are Mennonite, Anglican and other communities.

Education. Adult literacy was 90·8% in 1992. Education is free and nominally compulsory. In 1994 there were 5,318 primary schools (public and private) with 835,089 pupils and 34,580 teachers. In 1990 there were 801 secondary schools with 220,000 students and 17,688 teachers. There were 11 universities (1 Roman Catholic) in 1994–95 and 1 institute of education catering for 43,000 students.

Health. In 1982 there were 2,201 doctors, 855 dentists, 860 pharmacists, 783 midwives and 2,636 nursing personnel. In 1985 there were 3,380 hospital beds.

DIPLOMATIC REPRESENTATIVES

Of Paraguay in Great Britain (Braemar Lodge, Cornwall Gdns, London, SW7 4AQ)
Ambassador: Vacant.

Of Great Britain in Paraguay (Calle Presidente Franco, 706, Asunción)
Ambassador and Consul-General: Graham Pirnie.

Of Paraguay in the USA (2400 Massachusetts Ave., NW, Washington, D.C., 20008)
Ambassador: Jorge Prieto.

Of the USA in Paraguay (1776 Mariscal López Ave., Asunción)
Ambassador: Robert E. Service.

Of Paraguay to the United Nations
Ambassador: Hugo Saguier Caballero.

Of Paraguay to the European Union
Ambassador: Manuel María Cáceres Cardozo.

Further Reading

Gaceta Official, published by Imprenta Nacional, Estrella y Estero Bellaco, Asunción
Anuario Daumas. Asunción
Anuario Estadístico de la República del Paraguay. Asunción. Annual
Lewis, P. H., *Paraguay under Stroessner.* Univ. of North Carolina Press, 1980
Nickson, R. A., *Paraguay.* [Bibliography] Oxford and Santa Barbara, 1987

National Library: Biblioteca Nacional, De la Rosidenta, Asunción.

PERU

República del Perú

Capital: Lima
Population: 24·4m.
GDP per head: (PPP$) 3,645
GNP: US$44·1bn.
HDI/world rank: 0·717/89

KEY HISTORICAL EVENTS. The Incas of Peru were conquered by the Spanish in the 16th century, and subsequent Spanish colonial settlement made Peru the most important of the Spanish viceroyalties in South America. On 28 July 1821 Peru declared its independence, but it was not until after a war which ended in 1824 that the country gained its freedom. The two presi-dential terms served by Gen. Ramón Castilla (1845–51 and 1855–62) were prosperous ones for Peru; but in a disastrous war with Chile (1879–83) Peru's capital, Lima, was captured and she lost some of her southern territory to Chile under the peace treaty. Tacna remained in Chilean control from 1880 until 1929.

In 1924 Dr Victor Raúl Haya de la Torre founded the *Alianza Popular Revolucionaria Americana* to oppose the dictatorial government then in power. The party was banned between 1931 and 1945, and between 1948 and 1956 its leader failed regularly in the presidential elections but it was at times the largest party in Congress.

In Oct. 1948 Gen. Manuel Odria deposed President José Luis Bustamante y Rivera and became president in 1950. He was succeeded by an elected president, Dr Manuel Prado y Ugarteche in 1956; but the closeness of the 1962 elections led Gen. Ricardo Pérez Godoy, Chairman of the Joint Chiefs-of-Staff, to seize power. A *coup* led by Gen. Nicolás Lindley López deposed him in 1963. There followed, after elections, a period of civilian rule under President Fernando Belaúnde Terry, who enacted important legislation and measures to promote agrarian reforms. The military staged yet another *coup* in 1968, and the Army Chief-of-staff, Gen. Juan Valasco Alvarado, usurped the presidency and dissolved Congress. He in turn was overthrown and superseded by Gen. Francisco Morales Bermudez in 1975. In 1978-79 a constituent assembly drew up a new constitution, after which a civilian government was installed and President Fernando Belaúnde Terry again took office on 28 July 1980. He was succeeded in a constitutional process of election by President Alan Garcia Pérez in July 1985.

On 6 April 1992 the President suspended the constitution and dissolved the parliament. A new constitution was promulgated on 29 Dec. 1993.

On 17 Dec. 1996 Tupac Amaru Revolutionary Movement guerrillas seized the residence of the Japanese ambassador, holding 72 hostages in a demand for the release of guerrilla prisoners. The standoff continued until the following April when the Peruvian army launched an assault to liberate the hostages.

TERRITORY AND POPULATION. Peru is bounded in the north by Ecuador and Colombia, east by Brazil and Bolivia, south by Chile and west by the Pacific Ocean. Area, 1,285,216 sq. km.

For an account of the border dispute with Ecuador *see* ECUADOR: Territory and Population.

Census population, 1997, 24,371,043 (estimate). Urban 17,484,470; rural 6,886,573. Vital statistics 1996 (in 1,000s): Births, 615·3; deaths, 156·8; infant deaths (under 1 year), 58·3. Growth rate, 1990–95, 2%; infant mortality, 1996, 47·9 per 1,000 live births. Expectation of life in 1996: males, 65·5 years; females, 70·4.

Area and 1993 census population of the 24 departments and the constitutional province of Callao, together with their capitals:

Department	Area (in sq. km)	Population	Capital	Population
Amazonas	39,249	336,665	Chachapoyas	15,785
Ancash	35,826	955,023	Huaraz	66,888

1115

Department	Area (in sq. km)	Population	Capital	Population
Apurímac	15,666	381,997	Abancay	46,997
Arequipa	63,345	916,806	Arequipa	619,156
Ayacucho	43,814	492,507	Ayacucho	105,918
Cajamarca	33,247	1,259,808	Cajamarca	92,447
Callao[1]	147	639,729	Callao	369,768
Cusco	71,892	1,028,763	Cusco	255,568
Huancavelica	22,131	385,162	Huancavelica	31,068
Huánuco	36,938	654,489	Huánuco	118,814
Ica	21,328	565,686	Ica	161,406
Junín	44,410	1,035,841	Huancayo	258,209
La Libertad	25,570	1,270,261	Trujillo	509,312
Lambayeque	14,231	920,795	Chiclayo	411,536
Lima	34,802	6,386,308	Lima	5,706,127
Loreto	368,852	687,282	Iquitos	274,759
Madre de Dios	85,183	67,008	Puerto Naidona	31,249
Moquegua	15,734	128,747	Moquegua	38,837
Pasco	25,320	226,295	Cerro de Pasco	62,749
Piura	35,892	1,388,264	Piura	277,964
Puno	71,999	1,079,849	Puno	91,877
San Martín	51,253	552,387	Moyobamba	24,800
Tacna	16,076	218,353	Tacna	174,336
Tumbes	4,669	155,521	Tumbes	74,085
Ucayali	102,411	314,810	Pucallpa	72,286

[1] Constitutional province.

In 1991 there were some 100,000 Peruvians of Japanese origin.

The official languages are Spanish (spoken by 80·3% of the population in 1993), Quechua (16·5%) and Aymara (3%).

CLIMATE. There is a very wide variety of climate, ranging from equatorial to desert (or perpetual snow on the high mountains). In coastal areas, temperatures vary very little, either daily or annually, though humidity and cloudiness show considerable variation, with highest humidity from May to Sept. Little rain is experienced in that period. In the Sierra, temperatures remain fairly constant over the year, but the daily range is considerable. There the dry season is from April to Nov. Desert conditions occur in the extreme south, where the climate is uniformly dry, with a few heavy showers falling between Jan. and March. Lima, Jan. 74°F (23·3°C), July 62°F (16·7°C). Annual rainfall 2" (48 mm). Cuzco, Jan. 56°F (13·3°C), July 50°F (10°C). Annual rainfall 32" (804 mm). El Niño is the annual warm Pacific current which moves to the coasts of Peru and Ecuador. The last big El Niño in 1982-83 resulted in agricultural production down by 8·5% and fishing output down by 40%. El Niño in 1991-94 was unusually long. El Niño which began in summer 1997 and is expected to last until at least May 1998 has resulted in a sudden rise in the surface temperature of the Pacific by 5°C.

CONSTITUTION AND GOVERNMENT. The 1980 Constitution provided for a legislative *Congress* consisting of a *Senate* (60 members) and a *Chamber of Deputies* (180 members) and an Executive formed of the President and a Council of Ministers appointed by him. Elections were held every 5 years with the President and Congress elected, at the same time, by separate ballots. All citizens over the age of 18 are eligible to vote. Voting is compulsory.

On 5 April 1992 President Fujimori suspended the 1980 constitution and dissolved Congress. Elections were held on 22 Nov. 1992 for an 80-member Constituent Assembly. Elections were held on 9 April 1995 for President and a new 120-member single-chamber Congress to replace the Constituent Assembly. The electorate was 12m. President Fujimori was re-elected by 64·42% of votes cast. In the Congressional elections, Change 90-New Mayoralty won 67 seats with 52·1% of votes cast, Pérez de Cuellar's movement gained 17 seats, APRA 8, Popular Action 4 and the United Left 2.

A referendum was held on 31 Oct. 1993 to approve the twelfth constitution, including a provision for the president to serve a consecutive second term. 52·24% of votes cast were in favour. The constitution was promulgated on 29 Dec. 1993. In Aug. 1996 Congress voted for the eligibility of the President to serve a third consecutive term of office.

President Fujimori estimates that El Niño has caused US$12m worth of infrastructure damage, killed over 100 people and resulted in tens of thousands becoming homeless. The government has declared a state of emergency in 9 out of the country's 24 regions. President Fujimori has regained popularity due to his efforts against El Niño.

President: Alberto Fujimori (b. 1938; Change 90 Movement; sworn in 28 July 1990).

The President formed a new government in July 1995 which in March 1998 comprised:

Prime Minister: Alberto Pandolfi Arbulú.

Minister of Fisheries: Ludwig Meier Cornejo. *Minister of Foreign Affairs:* Eduardo Ferrero Costa. *Economy and Finance:* Jorge Camet Dickman. *Interior:* José Villanueva Ruesta. *Justice:* Álfredo Quispe Correa. *Defence:* César Saucedo Sánchez. *Health:* Marino Costa Bauer. *Labour and Social Mobility:* Jorge González Izquierdo. *Agriculture:* Rodolfo Muñante Sanguinetti. *Energy and Mines:* Daniel Hokama Tokashiki. *Industry, Tourism, Integration and International Commercial Negotiations:* Gustavo Caillux Zazzali. *Transport, Communications, Housing and Construction:* Antonio Paucer Carbajal. *Education:* Domingo Palermo Cabrejos. *Minister at the Presidency:* Tomas Gonzalez Reatuegui. *Minister for the Promotion of Women and Human Development:* Miriam Schenone Ordinola.

National anthem: 'Somos libres, seámoslo siempre' ('We are free, let us always be so'); words by J. De La Torre Ugarte, tune by J. B. Alcedo.

Local Government. There are 24 departments and 1 constitutional province divided into 192 provinces and 1,812 districts. There are also 14 administrative regions with their own authorities. Municipal elections were held on 12 Nov. 1995.

DEFENCE. There is selective conscription for 2 years.

Army. There are 6 military regions. The Army comprises (1997) approximately 85,000 personnel (60,000 conscripts) and 188,000 reserves. There are 3 armoured, 1 cavalry, 7 infantry, 1 airborne and 1 jungle division with supporting artillery, engineer and helicopter battalions, 1 Presidential Escort regiment and 1 air defence artillery group. There is an air element of 50 Mil Mi-8 and Mi-17 and 25 other helicopters, as well as about 14 fixed-wing transport and liaison aircraft. Equipment includes 300 T-54/-55 main battle tanks (perhaps 50 operational).

There is a para-military national police force of 60,000 personnel.

Navy. The principal ships of the Navy are the former Netherlands cruisers *Almirante Grau* and *Aguirre* built in 1953. *Almirante Grau's* main armament is 8 152 mm guns and 8 Otomat surface-to-surface missiles. *Aguirre* has been converted to a helicopter cruiser and mounts only 4 152 mm guns, the two after-turrets having been removed in favour of a hangar and flight deck capable of supporting 4 SH-3D Sea King helicopters. There are 6 diesel submarines built in West Germany (1974–82). Other combatants include 1 modernized former British Daring class destroyer, 4 Italian Lupo class frigates, 6 French-built fast missile craft and 3 tank landing ships. Major auxiliaries include 1 transport, 1 Antarctic patrol ship, 2 replenishment and 1 freighting tankers, 1 survey ship and 1 ocean tug, and 30 minor auxiliaries and service craft. A river flotilla of 9 patrol craft police the Upper Amazon, based at Puerto Maldonado and Iquitos.

The Naval Aviation branch comprises 6 S-2 Trackers and 3 EMB-111 anti-submarine aircraft based ashore, 8 Sea King and 6 AB-212 anti-submarine helicopters for service afloat and over 30 miscellaneous transport and utility aircraft.

Callao is the main base, where the dockyard is located and most training takes place. Smaller ocean bases exist at Paita and Talara.

Naval personnel in 1997 totalled 25,000 (12,500 conscripts) including 700 Naval Air Arm and 3,000 Marines. There are 3 batteries of coastal defence artillery.

The Coast Guard, 600 strong in 1996, includes 5 coastal patrol craft, 3 inshore and 8 river patrol craft.

Air Force. The operational force consists of 5 combat groups. No. 6 Group has 1 squadron of Mirage 5 jet fighters; No. 9 Group has 1 squadron of Canberra jet bombers; No. 7 Group has 2 squadrons of A-37B light attack aircraft; No. 11 Group has Soviet-built Su-22 variable-geometry fighter bombers in 1 operational squadron; No. 4 Group has one squadron of Su-22s and one with Mirage 2000s. MiG-29 interceptors were bought from Belarus in 1997. Other aircraft in service include medium transports (1 F.28 Fellowship, 20 An-32, 10 C-130/L-100 Hercules), light transports (16 Twin Otter, 5 Y-12, 1 twin-jet Falcon and 12 Turbo-Porter), helicopters (40 Mi-8/17, 25 Mi-24 gunships, Bell 206, 212, 214ST, 412 and UH-1, BO 105 and Ecureuil), 60 training aircraft (including Aermacchi MB 339, Tucano and T-41D) and a small number of miscellaneous types for photographic and communications duties. There are military airfields at Talara, Chiclayo, Piura, Pisco, Lima (2), Iquitos and La Joya, and a floatplane base at Iquitos. In 1997 there were some 15,000 personnel (2,000 conscripts) and 90 combat aircraft and 20 armed helicopters.

INTERNATIONAL RELATIONS

Membership. Peru is a member of the UN, OAS, the Andean Group and LAIA.

ECONOMY

Policy. Privatization began in 1991 under the aegis of the Privatization Commission (COPRI). By early 1995 95 state companies had been sold bringing revenue of US$4,400m. In 1996 31 state companies were sold, bringing in US$871m. In 1994 a 'citizen participation' scheme was initiated to increase the extent of private shareholding in state enterprises; retirement pensions may also be taken as shares.

Performance. Forecasts for GDP growth for 1998 range from 2·5% to 6%. In 1997 the GDP growth (Jan. to Aug.) was 7·2%.

Budget. At US$10·2bn., the 1998 budget is 10% higher in real terms than for 1997. There was a trade deficit of US$1·7bn. for 1997. In 1997 the World Bank approved a US$150m. loan to help Peru overcome expected problems associated with El Niño.

Currency. The monetary unit is the *nuevo sol* (PES), of 100 *centimos*, which replaced the inti in 1990 at a rate of 1m. intis = 1 nuevo sol. There are coins of 1, 5, 10, 20 and 50 centimos and 1 sol, and notes of 10, 20, 50 and 100 sols. Inflation was 5·7% in 1997. Foreign exchange reserves were US$8,470m. in Sept. 1997.

Banking and Finance. The bank of issue is the Banco Central de Reserva (*Governor*, Germán Suárez Chávez), which was established in 1922. The government's fiscal agent is the Banco de la Nación. There were in addition, in 1995, 17 domestic commercial, 1 foreign and 4 multinational banks. Legislation of April 1991 permitted financial institutions to fix their own interest rates and reopened the country to foreign banks. The Central Reserve Banks sets the upper limit.

There are stock exchanges in Lima and Arequipa.

Weights and Measures. The metric system is in use.

ENERGY AND NATURAL RESOURCES

Electricity. In 1996 output was 16,541·6m. kWh (13,222·7m. kWh hydro-electric). Total generating capacity was 4,771·7 MW. 66·1% of the population were supplied with electricity in 1996. Peru's reliance on hydro-generated electricity means that electricity production is likely to be affected by the drought brought on by the 1997/8 El Niño.

Oil. Proven oil reserves in 1996 amounted to 340·3m. bbls. Output, 1996, 43·91m. bbls.

Minerals. Mining accounts for some 8·4% of GDP (1996). Lead, copper, iron, silver, zinc and petroleum are the chief minerals exploited. Mineral production, 1996 (in 1,000 tonnes): Iron, 2,875·6; zinc, 760·6; copper, 484·2; lead, 248·8; silver, 1,970·2; gold, 64·8. Early in 1998 Southern Peru Copper, the country's largest mining company, estimated that 3,000 tonnes of copper production had been lost due to flooding caused by El Niño.

Agriculture. There are 4 natural zones: The Coast strip, with an average width of 80 km; the Sierra or Uplands, formed by the coast range of mountains and the Andes proper; the Montaña or high wooded region which lies on the eastern slopes of the Andes; and the jungle in the Amazon Basin, known as the Selva. 2·7m. ha were cultivated in 1991. Legislation of 1991 permits the unrestricted sale of agricultural land. Workers in co-operatives may elect to form limited liability companies and become shareholders.

Production in 1996 (in 1,000 tonnes): Potatoes, 2,327·3; wheat, 130; seed cotton, 268·6; coffee, 106·5; rice, 1,203; maize, 559·4; beans, 68·9; sugar-cane 6,119.

Livestock (in 1,000), 1996: Alpacas, 2,663; cattle, 4,646; pigs, 2,533; sheep, 12,713; poultry, 77,226. Livestock products (in 1,000 tonnes), 1996: Poultry meat, 310·5; mutton and lamb, 20·3; pork, 83; beef, 110·1.

Arable land (in 1,000 ha), 1996: 35,381·8, of which 5,477 was given over to agricultural production, of which 4,314·4 was cultivated, 892·3 was permanent crops and 270·3 was permanent pasture. 29,904·8 of the arable land was not used for agricultural production, with 16,906·4 natural pasture, 9,053·7 left wild and 3,944·7 was other types of earth.

Forestry. There are 84·5m. ha of forest area, made up of 74m. ha of natural forest, 253,646 ha of planted forest and 10·25m. ha of land suitable for reforestation. The forests contain valuable hardwoods; oak and cedar account for about 40%. In 1994 roundwood removals totalled 12m. cu. metres. In Nov. 1997 more than 3,000 ha of farmlands were washed away in floods caused by El Niño.

Fisheries. Sardines and anchovies are caught offshore to be processed into fishmeal, of which Peru is a major producer. Fishing in deeper waters is being developed, subject to government conservation by the imposition of quotas and fishing bans. Production, 1995, 8·99m. tonnes with a value of US$936·7m. (1994, 11·58m. tonnes, US$901·5m.). In the first 9 months of 1997 1·3m tonnes of fishmeal was produced, up 3·4% over the same period for 1996. The central bank forecasts that El Niño will shrink the fishing industry by 14% in 1998/9.

INDUSTRY. About 70% of industries are located in the Lima/Callao metropolitan area. Products include pig-iron, blooms, billets, largets, round and round-deformed bars, wire rod, black and galvanized sheets and galvanized roofing sheets.

Labour. At the 1993 census the workforce (persons aged 15 and over) numbered 7,109,527 (2,104,755 females). 505,767 (157,892 females) were unemployed. In 1993 1,852,800 worked in agriculture, 72,200 in mining, 783,900 in manufacturing, 18,700 in electricity production, 255,000 in building, 1,167,000 in commerce, 347,500 in transport and 599,700 in services. In Dec. 1994 the minimum monthly wage was 132 sols.

Trade Unions. Trade unions have about 2m. members (approximately 1·5m. in peasant organizations and 500,000 in industrial). The major trade union organization is the *Confederación de Trabajadores del Perú*, which was reconstituted in 1959 after being in abeyance for some years. The other labour organizations recognized by the Government are the *Confederación General de Trabajadores del Perú*, the *Confederación Nacional de Trabajadores* and the *Central de Trabajadores de la Revolución Peruana*.

FOREIGN ECONOMIC RELATIONS. An agreement of 1992 gives Bolivia duty-free transit for imports and exports through a corridor leading to the Peruvian Pacific port of Ilo from the Bolivian frontier town of Desaguadero, in return for

Peruvian access to the Atlantic via Bolivia's roads and railways. Foreign debt was US$26,890m. in June 1997.

Commerce. The value of trade has been as follows (in US$1m.):

	1990	1991	1992	1993	1994	1995	1996
Imports	2,930	3,630	4,090	4,123	5,596	7,761	7,897
Exports	3,323	3,391	3,594	3,536	4,598	5,591	5,897

In 1996 the main export markets (in US$1m.) were: USA, 1,154·4; UK, 424·2; Japan, 388; China, 419·4; Germany, 300·7. Main import suppliers: USA, 1,858·4; Japan, 317·8; Brazil, 328·6; Colombia, 633·2, Venezuela, 528·7. Main exports, 1996 (in US$1m.): Fishmeal, 834·9; gold, 579·3; refined copper, 715·6, zinc, 273·3.

The central bank predicts that the combined effects of the Asian economic crisis of 1997 and El Niño will result in lower export earnings and increased food imports to compensate for lost agricultural production.

Tourism. There were 635,000 foreign visitors in 1996 (485,169 in 1995), bringing foreign exchange earnings of US$631m.

COMMUNICATIONS

Roads. In 1996 there were 73,766 km of roads, of which 8,565 km were paved, 13,280 km was gravel, 16,876 was without a surface and 35,045 were narrow roads. In 1996 there were 936,501 registered motor vehicles, including 483,413 cars, 73,629 station wagons, 233,166 vans, 43,154 buses and 83,084 lorries.

Railways. Total length (1996), 1,992 km on 1,435- and 914-mm gauges. In 1996 railways carried 6·1m. tonnes of freight and 1·2m. passengers.

Civil Aviation. There is an international airport at Lima (Jorge Chávez). The national carrier is Faucett Perú, which in 1995 operated 4 B-727s, 3 B-727-200 Advs, 1 B-727C and 2 B-757-200s. In 1996 there were 32 airports. 180 civil aircraft were registered in 1996, of which 87 were in commercial use, 13 were in tourist use and 80 were for private use. Services are also provided by the domestic airlines Aero Continente and Imperial Air, and by Aeroflot, Aerolíneas Argentinas, Aeromexico, Aerosanta, Air Paraguay, Alitalia, American Airlines, AOM, Avianca, COPA, Cubana, Expresso Aereo, Iberia, KLM, LACSA, Lan-Chile, Lloyd Aereo Boliviano, Lufthansa, SAETA, Servivensa, United Airlines and Varig.

Shipping. In 1994 there were 30 sea-going vessels and 519 lake and river craft. In 1995, sea-going shipping totalled 0·32m. GRT, including oil tankers, 0·13m. GRT.

Telecommunications. In 1990 there were 1,363 post offices. In 1996 there were 1,435,147 telephones and 3,100 teleprinters. Radio broadcasting is conducted by hundreds of national, provincial and local stations grouped in the Asociación de Radiodifusores del Perú and the Unión de Radioemisores de Provincias del Perú. There are 59 TV companies (colour by NTSC). In 1995 there were 6·1m. radio and 2·5m. TV sets in use.

Press. There were 48 dailies in 1995 with a combined circulation of 2m.

SOCIAL INSTITUTIONS

Justice. The judicial system is a pyramid at the base of which are the justices of the peace who decide minor criminal cases and civil cases involving small sums of money. The apex is the Supreme Court with a President and 12 members; in between are the judges of first instance, who usually sit in the provincial capitals, and the superior courts.

The police had some 85,000 personnel in 1991.

Religion. Religious liberty exists, but the Roman Catholic religion is protected by the State, and since 1929 only Roman Catholic religious instruction is permitted in schools, state or private. There were 21·56m. adherents in 1992.

Education. Adult literacy was 87·2% at the 1993 census. In 1996 adult literacy was 88·3%. Elementary education is compulsory and free between the ages of 7 and 16; secondary education is also free. In 1994–95 there were 597,800 children in preschool education, 4,085,000 pupils in primary and 1,996,200 in secondary schools. In 1993 the number of students at the 28 state and 23 private universities was 727,200. There were 251,700 students in other forms of further education.

Health. There were, in 1992, 455 hospitals and 1,083 health centres.

Social Security. An option to transfer from state social security (IPSS) to privately-managed funds was introduced in 1993.

DIPLOMATIC REPRESENTATIVES

Of Peru in Great Britain (52 Sloane St., London, SW1X 9SP)
Ambassador: J. Eduardo Ponce-Vivanco.

Of Great Britain in Peru (Edificio El Pacifico Washington, Ave. Arequipa, Lima 100)
Ambassador: John Illman.

Of Peru in the USA (1700 Massachusetts Ave., NW, Washington, D.C., 20036)
Ambassador: Ricardo V. Luna.

Of the USA in Peru (PO Box 1995, Lima)
Ambassador: Dennis C. Jett.

Of Peru to the United Nations
Ambassador: Dr Fernando Guillén Salas.

Of Peru to the European Union
Ambassador: José Antonio Arróspide-del Busto.

Further Reading

Instituto Nacional de Estadística e Informática.—*Anuario Estadístico del Perú.*—*Perú: Compendio Estadístico.* Annual.—*Boletín de Estadística Peruana.* Quarterly
Banco Central de Reserva. Monthly Bulletin.—*Renta Nacional del Perú.* Annual, Lima

Cameron, M. A., *Democracy and Authoritarianism in Peru: Political Coalitions and Social Change.* London, 1995
Daeschner, J., *The War of the End of Democracy: Mario Vargas Llosa vs. Alberto Fujimori.* Lima, 1993
Figueroa, A., *Capitalist Development and the Peasant Economy of Peru.* CUP, 1984
Fisher, J., *Peru:* [Bibliography]. Oxford and Santa Barbara (CA), 1989
Stokes, S. C., *Cultures in Conflict: Social Movements and the State in Peru.* California Univ. Press, 1995
Strong, S., *Shining Path.* London, 1993
Thorp, R., *Economic Management and Economic Development in Peru and Colombia.* London, 1991
Vargas Llosa, A., *The Madness of Things Peruvian: Democracy under Siege.* Brunswick (NJ), 1994

National statistical office: Instituto Nacional de Estadística e Informática, Avenida 28 de Julio, 1056 Lima
Website: http://www.inei.gob.pe:8081/

PHILIPPINES

Republika ng Pilipinas

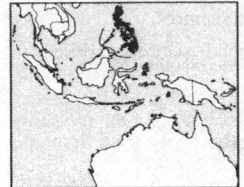

Capital: Manila
Population: 73·36m.
GDP per head: (PPP$) 2,681
GNP: US$63·3bn.
HDI/world rank: 0·672/98

KEY HISTORICAL EVENTS. Discovered by Magellan in 1521, the Philippine islands were conquered by Spain in 1565 and named after the Spanish king, Philip. The independence of the Philippines was declared in June 1898 but in Dec. 1898 at the signing of the Treaty of Paris, following the Spanish-American War, the Philippines were ceded to the USA. A four-year war followed with considerable loss of life of Filipinos.

The Philippines acquired self-government as a Commonwealth of the USA in March 1934. This Act provided for complete independence after a ten year transitional period. The islands were occupied by the Japanese from 1942 to 1945. Independence was achieved in July 1946. From independence until 1972, the Philippines were governed under a constitution based largely on the US pattern, consisting of a president with a fixed four-year term of office, a bicameral legislature and an independent judiciary. Two political parties dominated the political scene during this period, the Liberals and the Nationalists.

In 1971, changes were planned for the constitution. However, in Sept. 1972 before the constitution could be ratified, President Ferdinand Marcos declared martial law. Following the death sentence on Benigno Aquino, Jr (the main opposition leader, in Nov. 1977) criticism of Marcos increased. A stay of execution was allowed and in May 1980, Aquino was released from prison to go to the USA for medical treatment. Jan. 1981 saw the lifting of martial law and in Aug. 1983 Aquino returned to the Philippines after three years' in exile and was shot dead on arrival at Manila airport. This action united the opposition parties against Marcos.

At the presidential elections of Feb. 1986 Ferdinand Marcos was opposed by Corazón Aquino, widow of Benigno Aquino. Though Marcos was proclaimed president by parliament, the elections proved to be fraudulent and Aquino became president. Marcos fled the country, but was subsequently elected president in May 1992.

Insurgent activities carried out since 1972 by the Moro National Liberation Front (Moslems) were ended by a peace agreement of 2 Sept. 1996. The agreement provides for the establishment of a Moslem autonomous region covering 14 provinces and 9 cities in Mindanao, Palawan, Sulu and Basilan under the administrative council. But Moslem rebels continue their guerrilla war against the state.

TERRITORY AND POPULATION. The Philippines is situated between 21° 25' and 4° 23' N. lat. and between 116° and 127° E. long. It is composed of 7,100 islands and islets, 2,773 of which are named. Approximate land area, 300,000 sq. km (115,830 sq. miles). The largest islands (in sq. km) are Luzon (104,688), Mindanao (94,630), Samar (13,080), Negros (12,710), Palawan (11,785), Panay (11,515), Mindoro (9,735), Leyte (7,214), Cebu (4,422), Bohol (3,865), Masbate (3,269).

Census population (1995) was 68,614,162. Estimate, 1997, 73·36m.; density, 244·5 per sq. km.

The area (in 1,000) and population of the 16 regions (from north to south):

Region	Sq. km	1995	Region	Sq. km	1995
Ilocos	12,840	3,803,890	Central Visayas	14,952	5,014,588
Cordillera[1]	18,294	1,254,838	Eastern Visayas	21,432	3,366,917
Cagayan Valley	26,838	2,536,035	Northern Mindanao	14,033	2,483,272
Central Luzon	18,231	6,932,570	Southern Mindanao	27,141	4,604,158
National Capital	636	9,454,040	Central Mindanao	14,373	2,359,880
Southern Tagalog	46,924	9,940,722	Western Mindanao	16,042	2,794,659
Bicol	17,633	4,325,307	Moslem Mindanao[2]	11,638	2,020,903
Western Visayas	20,223	5,776,938	Caraga	18,847	1,942,687

[1] Administrative region.   [2] Autonomous region

1122

City populations (1995 census, in 1,000) are as follows; all on Luzon unless indicated in parenthesis.

Manila (the capital)[1]	1,655	Malabon[2]	347
Quezon City[1]	1,989	Taguig[2]	355
Davao (Mindanao)	1,191	General Santos (Mindanao)	327
Caloocan[1]	1,023	Mandaluyong[1]	287
Cebu (Cebu)	662	Angeles	234
Makati[1]	484	Butuan (Mindanao)	247
Zamboanga (Mindanao)	511	Iligan (Mindanao)	273
Pasig[1]	471	Olongapo[1]	180
Muntilupa[1]	400	Navotas[2]	229
Bacolod (Negros)	402	Batangas[1]	212
Pasay[1]	409	Baguio[1]	227
Cagayan de Oro (Mindanao)	428	Mandaue (Cebu)	195
Valenzuela[2]	437	Cabanatuan	201
Iloilo (Panay)	335	San Pablo	184
Marikina[2]	357	Lipa	178
Parañaque[2]	391	Lucena	178
Las Piñas[2]	413		

[1] City within Metropolitan Manila   [2] Municipality within Metropolitan Manila

Vital statistics, 1992: Births, 1,684,400 (rate per 1,000 population, 25·8); deaths, 319,600 (4·9); marriages, 454,200 (14); natural increase, (20·9); infant mortality (per 1,000 live births), 21·9. Expectation of life in 1995: Males, 64·4 years; females, 67·8.

Filipino (based on Tagalog) is spoken by 55% of the population, but as a mother tongue by only 27·9%; among the 76 other indigenous languages spoken, Cebuano is spoken as a mother tongue by 24·3% and Ilocano by 9·8%. English is widely spoken.

CLIMATE. Some areas have an equatorial climate while others experience tropical monsoon conditions, with a wet season extending from June to Nov. Mean temperatures are high all year, with very little variation. Manila. Jan. 77°F (25°C), July 82°F (27·8°C). Annual rainfall 82" (2,083 mm).

CONSTITUTION AND GOVERNMENT. A new Constitution was ratified by referendum in 1987 with the approval of 78·5% of voters. The head of state is the executive *President*, directly elected for a non-renewable 6-year term. At the elections on 11 May 1992 the electorate was 32m. Fidel Ramos was elected President against 2 opponents with 23·6% of votes cast.

Congress consists of a 24-member upper house, the *Senate*, and a 250-member *House of Representatives*. Elections were held on 8 May 1995 for 12 Senate seats and the 204 constituency-based seats in the House of Representatives. The electorate was 34m.; turn-out was 80%. A majority in both houses was gained by the pro-government coalition of National Union of Christian Democrats, Lakas ng Edsa and Laban ng Demokratikong Filipino.

A campaign led by President Ramos to amend the constitution to allow him to stand for a second term was voted down by the Senate by 23 to one in Dec. 1996.

In March. 1998 the government comprised:
President: Fidel Ramos (sworn in 30 June 1992).
Vice President: Joseph Estrada.
Secretary for Foreign Affairs: Domingo Siazon. *Justice:* Silvestre Bello. *Defence:* Fortunato Abat. *Commerce and Industry:* Cesar Bautista. *Finance:* Salvador Enriquez. *Agriculture:* Salvador Escudero. *Works and Highways:* Gregorio Vigilar. *Energy:* Francisco Viray. *Education, Culture and Sport:* Erlinda Perfianco. *Labour and Employment:* Crecenciano Trajano. *Health:* Carmencita N. Reodica. *Social Welfare and Development:* Lina Laigo. *Agrarian Reform:* Ernesto Garilao. *Interior and Local Government:* Epimaco Velasco. *Tourism:* Mina T. Gabor. *Budget and Management:* Emilia Boncodin. *Transport and Communications:* Josefina Lichauco. *Science and Technology:* William Padolina. *Director-General, National Economic Development Authority:* Cielito Habito. *Environment and Natural Resources:* Victor Ramos. *Government Spokesman:* Hector Villanueva. *Executive Secretary:* Ruben Torres.

Speaker: José de Venecia.
Presidential elections are due on 11 May 1998.

National anthem: Land of the Morning, lyric in English by M. A. Sane and C. Osias, tune by Julian Felipe; *Bayang magiliw*; Tagalog lyric by the Institute of National Language.

Local Government. The country is divided administratively into 16 regions, 76 provinces, 65 cities, 1,547 municipalities and 40,824 *barangays* (units of no fewer than 1,000 inhabitants administered by elected officials). Local government authorities are directly elected for 3-year terms. A reform of Oct. 1991 devolved more power to local authorities, giving them 40% of local tax revenues to deliver local services. Elections were held simultaneously with the national elections on 8 May 1995 for provincial governors, city and municipal mayors and councillors.

DEFENCE. An extension of the 1947 agreement granting the USA the use of several army, navy and air force bases was rejected by the Senate in Sept. 1991. An agreement of Dec. 1994 authorizes US naval vessels to be revictualled and repaired in Philippine ports. The Philippines is a signatory of the South-East Asia Collective Defence Treaty.

Army. The Army is organized into 5 area joint-service commands, and comprises 8 infantry divisions, 3 engineer brigades, 1 special services regiment, 1 light armoured brigade, 1 scout ranger regiment, the Presidential Security Group and 8 artillery battalions. Equipment includes 41 Scorpion light tanks.

Strength (1997) 20,000, with reserves totalling 100,000.

Navy. The Navy consists principally of ex-US ships completed in 1944 and 1945, and serviceability and spares are a problem. The modernization programme in progress has been revised and delayed, but the first 30 inshore patrol craft of US and Korean design have been delivered.

The present fleet includes 1 ex-US frigate, 9 offshore patrol vessels (ex-US minesweepers and escorts) and about 50 inshore patrol craft. There are 5 tank landing ships and 2 medium landing ships, and some 30 landing craft. Auxiliaries include 1 repair ship, 2 small oilers, 3 survey ships and 2 water tankers, as well as some 20 minor auxiliaries. 8 BN Defender maritime patrol aircraft and 10 BO-105 helicopters are in use.

Navy personnel in 1997 totalled 24,000 including 9,500 marines.

Coastguard. The Coastguard is no longer part of the Navy. In 1996 there were some 60 patrol and search-and-rescue craft. Personnel, 2,000.

Air Force. The Air Force had (1997) a strength of 16,500, with 40 combat aircraft and 104 armed helicopters, but serviceability is impaired due to shortage of funds. Its fighter-bomber wing is equipped with 1 squadron of F-5As (only 3 or 4 operational). A strike wing includes 1 squadron having OV-10 Broncos and 1 squadron, T-28s. There are 7 transport and counter-insurgency squadrons (1 with C-130/L-100 Hercules, 1 with F27s, 1 with Nomads, 1 with C-47s, 2 with UH-1 Iroquois helicopters, 1 with MD-500 helicopters and 1 with S-76 helicopters). Training aircraft include SF.260TPs, T-41s, T-34s, S.211 and T-33 jets. 2 Pumas and 1 S-70 helicopter are used as VIP transports.

Constabulary. Public order is maintained partly through the Philippine Constabulary and partly through the local police forces. The Constabulary is part of the armed forces and has some 45,000 personnel.

INTERNATIONAL RELATIONS

Membership. The Philippines is a member of the UN, ASEAN and the Colombo Plan.

ECONOMY

Policy. In 1992–95 most state industrial assets were privatized. In 1996, a 'third wave' of privatization was initiated involving state pensions and social security funds. Monopolies have been dismantled in telecommunication, oil, civil aviation, shipping, water and power industries. In Dec. 1997 a comprehensive tax reform was approved, setting an exemption level of 98,400 pisos for a family of six.

Performance. Real GDP growth was 4·9% in 1995 and 6·8% in 1996. Export growth was 18%.

Budget. Government revenue and expenditure (in 1m. pisos):

	1991	1992	1993	1994	1995	1996
Revenue	220,287	242,714	260,405	335,200	370,000	417,200
Expenditure	293,161	286,603	339,359	479,500	586,300	615,300

Expenditure (1996) included (in 1,000m. pisos): Defence, 36·7; economic services, 106·8; social services, 128·8; general public administration, 71·4.

Total internal public debt was 624,700m. pisos in 1994.

Currency. The unit of currency is the *piso* (PHP) of 100 *sentimos*. There are notes of 5, 10, 20, 50, 100, 500 and 1,000 pisos and coins of 1, 5, 10, 25 and 50 sentimos and 1, 2 and 5 pisos. Total money supply, Dec. 1993, was 133,877m. pisos. Inflation was 6·5% in 1997. Foreign exchange reserves were US$7,500m. in 1995.

Banking and Finance. The Central Bank (*Chairman*, Gabriel Singson) issues the currency, manages foreign exchange reserves and supervises the banking system. In 1995 there were 28 domestic commercial and 14 foreign banks. A law of May 1994 allows the entry of up to 10 foreign banks with 6 branches each in the subsequent 5 years, after which banking will be closed to further foreign participation. 70% of total bank resources must remain in Filipino hands. In 1993 there were also 653 thrift banks (for savings and mortgages) with total deposits of 33,303m. pisos, and 1,045 rural banks (for savings and agricultural loans) with deposits of 13,422m. pisos In June 1995 the total number of banking institutions was 5,269, with total assets of 1,509,600m. pisos and total deposits of 860,900m. pisos.

There is a stock exchange in Manila.

The financial crisis that struck south-east Asia in 1997 led to the floating of the piso in July. It subsequently lost 36% of its value against the dollar.

Weights and Measures. The metric system was established by law in 1869 and since 1916 has come into general use, but there are local units including the picul (63·25 kg) for sugar and fibres, and the cavan (16·5 gallons) for cereals.

ENERGY AND NATURAL RESOURCES

Electricity. Total installed capacity, 6,927m. MW (1993). Output, 1993, 26,592m. kWh.

Gas. The recent discovery of a gas field off the island of Palawan is expected to yield up to 2·6 trillion cu. feet of natural gas. It is estimated that reserves of up to 34 trillion cu. feet are waiting to be discovered.

Minerals. Mineral production in 1994, (in tonnes): Copper, 547,400; coal, 1,458,100; gold, 27,100 kg; silver, 29,600 kg; chromite refractory ore, 64,100; 1992: Nickel metal, 14,000; salt, 495,800; silica sand, 500,300. Other minerals include cement, rock asphalt, sand and gravel. Total value of mineral production, 1994, 18,773m. pisos.

Agriculture. In 1991 there were 4·61m. farms with a total area of 9,975m. ha, of which 55·01% was arable land, 41·83% permanent cropland and 1·31% pasture. 37·76% of farms were less than 3 ha in size. In Oct. 1995, 12,465,340 persons were employed in agriculture (44·5% of the working population).

Output (in 1,000 tonnes) in 1995: Rough rice, 10,541; coconuts, 12,183; sugarcane, 18,679; bananas, 3,082; corn, 4,128; pineapple, 1,397. Minor crops are fruits, nuts, vegetables, coffee, cacao, peanuts, ramie, rubber, maguey, kapok, abaca and tobacco.

Livestock, 1995 (in 1,000): Water buffaloes (carabao), 2,500; cattle, 2,000; pigs, 8,900; goats, 2,800 and poultry, 84m.

Forestry. In 1994 forest land covered 15·9m. ha, of which 21·8% was forest reserves and 66·8% timberland. 19,211 ha were reafforested in 1993. Wood production, 1994 (in 1,000 cu. metres): Logs, 957; timber, 407; plywood, 258; veneer, 39.

Fisheries. Fish production from all sources was 2,686,600 tonnes in 1994.

INDUSTRY. Leading sectors are foodstuffs, oil refining and chemicals. In June 1993 there were about 11,000 large manufacturing establishments employing 908,700 persons.

Labour. In Oct. 1995 the total workforce was 28,012,000, of whom 25,672,000 were employed (15,546,600 in non-agricultural work). Employees by sector, 1994: 11·8m. in agriculture, forestry and fisheries, 4·3m. in services, 3·53m. in commerce, 2·58m. in manufacturing, 1·41m. in transport and communications and 1·23m. in building work. 2·34m. persons (1m. females) were registered unemployed in Oct. 1995. 363,983 persons worked overseas in 1994.

The 1997 unemployment rate was 8·3% (8·5% in 1996).

Trade Unions. In 1994 there were 6,442 trade unions with a total membership of 978,894.

FOREIGN ECONOMIC RELATIONS. Foreign debt was 51·8% of GDP in 1997 (51·0% in 1996). A law of June 1991 gave foreign nationals the right to full ownership of export and other firms, considered strategic for the economy.

Commerce. Values of imports and exports (f.o.b.) in US$1m.:

	1993	1994	1995	1996	1997
Imports	17,597	21,333	26,538	32,312	37,097
Exports	11,375	13,484	17,447	20,491	40,577

Principal exports: electronics, garments, coconut oil, woodcraft and furniture, ignition wiring sets.

Main imports: electronics and components, mineral fuels, lubricants and related materials, industrial machinery and equipment, telecommunications equipment, transport equipment.

Main export markets, 1995: USA, 35·3%; Japan, 15·7%; Singapore, 5·7%; UK, 5·3%; Hong Kong, 4·7%. Main sources of import: Japan, 22·4%; USA, 18·9%; Singapore, 5·9%; Hong Kong, 4·8%.

Tourism. In 1997, 2,300,000 foreign visitors brought foreign exchange receipts of US$2,300m. (1,900m. in 1996).

COMMUNICATIONS

Roads. In 1995 roads totalled 187,608 km; of these, 21,019 km were concrete, 19,492 km asphalt, 8,716 km earth and 138,380 km gravel. In 1993 there were 26,594 km of national highway. In 1995, 2,581,300 motor vehicles were registered, including 626,600 passenger cars, 192,800 lorries, 28,200 buses and 708,000 motor cycles. In 1993 there were 13,292 road accidents, with 581 fatalities.

Railways. In 1995 the National Railways totalled 429 km (1,067 mm gauge). In 1995, 4·6m. passengers and 14,000 tonnes of freight were carried. There is a light railway in Manila.

Civil Aviation. There is an international airport at Manila (Ninoy Aquino). The national carrier Philippine Airlines is 33% state-owned, and in 1995 operated 2 A300B4-100s, 7 A300B4-200s, 1 A300C4-200, 12 B-737-300s, 9 B-747-200Bs, 2 B-747-200B Combis, 3 B-747-400s and 11 other aircraft, and in 1993 carried 5,671,630 international and domestic passengers. Services were also provided by Air France, Air Nauru, Air Niugini, Alitalia, Asiana, British Airways, Cathay Pacific, China Airlines, China Southern Airlines, Continental Airlines & Air Micronesia, Egyptair, Emirates, Eva Airways, Garuda Indonesia, Grand International Airways, Gulf Air, JAL, KLM, Korean Air, Kuwait Airways, Lufthansa, Malaysia Airlines,

Northwest Airlines, Pakistan Airlines, Qantas, Royal Brunei Airlines, Saudia, Singapore Airlines, Swissair, Thai Airways, United Airlines and Vietnam Airlines.

Shipping. In 1995 there were 415 ports; the main ones are Manila, Cebu, Iloilo and Zamboanga. In 1993 there were 958 registered Philippine vessels totalling 3,815,261 GRT, and including 33 passenger ships, 302 cargo vessels and 27 tankers. In 1991, 139,969 vessels on domestic routes totalling 71,819 NRT, and in 1993, 10,714 vessels on international routes totalling 61,426 NRT, entered and cleared all ports.

Telecommunications. In 1995 there were 1,948 post offices and in 1994, 1,186,000 telephones.

In 1995 there were 370 AM and FM radio stations and 120 television stations. In 1993 there were 7m. TV sets in use.

Press. In 1995 there were 31 daily newspapers.

SOCIAL INSTITUTIONS

Justice. There is a Supreme Court which is composed of a chief justice and 14 associate justices; it can declare a law or treaty unconstitutional by the concurrent votes of the majority sitting. There is a Court of Appeals, which consists of a presiding justice and 50 associate justices. There are 15 regional trial courts, one for each judicial region, with a presiding regional trial judge in its 720 branches. There is a metropolitan trial court in the Metropolitan Manila Area, a municipal trial court in each of the other cities or municipalities and a municipal circuit trial court in each area defined as a municipal circuit comprising one or more cities and/or one or more municipalities.

The Supreme Court may designate certain branches of the regional trial courts to handle exclusively criminal cases, juvenile and domestic relations cases, agrarian cases, urban land reform cases which do not fall under the jurisdiction of quasijudicial bodies and agencies and/or such other special cases as the Supreme Court may determine. The death penalty, abolished in 1987, was restored in 1993 for 13 offences. No one can be executed until a year after final appeal.

In 1994 there were 96,365 police. Local police forces are supplemented by the Philippine Constabulary, which is part of the armed forces.

In 1995 the prison population was 17,850.

Religion. In 1990 there were 50,217,801 Roman Catholics, 3,287,355 Protestants, 2,769,643 Moslems, 1,590,208 Aglipayans, 1,414,393 Iglesia ni Kristo, 323,789 Born Again Christians and 736,239 members of other religions. There were 338,000 Mormons in 1994.

The Roman Catholics are organized with 2 cardinals, 23 archbishoprics, 91 bishoprics, 79 diocese, 2,328 parishes and some 20,873 chapels or missions.

Education. Public elementary education is free and schools are established almost everywhere. The majority of secondary and post-secondary schools are private. Formal education consists of an optional 1 to 2 years of pre-school education; 6 years of elementary education; 4 years of secondary education; and 4 to 5 years of tertiary or college education leading to academic degrees. 3-year post-secondary non-degree technical/vocational education is also considered formal education. In 1994–95 there were 6,362 pre-school institutions (1,892 private) with, in 1990–91, 9,644 teachers; 35,671 elementary schools (2,052 private) with 10·9m. pupils and 6,055 secondary schools (2,294 private) with 4·8m. pupils; and 2,563 tertiary schools with 2·2m. students. In 1993–94 there were 10,731,453 pupils in elementary schools, 4,590,037 in secondary schools and 1,564,763 students in tertiary education.

Non-formal education consists of adult literacy classes, agricultural and farming training programmes, occupation skills training, youth clubs, and community programmes of instructions in health, nutrition, family planning and co-operatives.

In 1994–95 in the public sector there were 20 universities, 1 technological university, 1 polytechnic and 1 technological institute, and 123 other institutions of higher education. In the private sector there were 49 universities, 4 specialized universities (1 Christian; 1 Roman Catholic; 1 medical; 1 for women) and 405 other institutions of higher education. The adult literacy rate is 94·4%.

Health. In 1993 there were 1,723 hospitals (1,095 private) with 77,434 beds. There were 1,895 dentists, 8,849 nurses and 10,831 midwives. In 1993 there were 76,913 doctors.

Welfare. The Social Security System (SSS) is a contributory scheme for employees. Disbursements in 1994 (in 1m. pisos): SSS (sickness, maternity, disability, survivors'; benefits), 14,861; medicare (hospitalization), 1,754; employees' compensation (occupational accidents or sickness), 596.

DIPLOMATIC REPRESENTATIVES

Of the Philippines in Great Britain (9A Palace Green, London, W8 4QE)
Ambassador: Jesus P. Tambunting.

Of Great Britain in the Philippines (6752 Ayala Avenue, Makati, Metro Manila)
Ambassador: Adrian Charles Thorpe, CMG.

Of the Philippines in the USA (1617 Massachusetts Ave., NW, Washington, D.C., 20036)
Ambassador: Raul Rabe.

Of the USA in the Philippines (1201 Roxas Blvd., Manila)
Ambassador: Thomas C. Hubbard.

Of the Philippines to the United Nations
Ambassador: Felipe Mabilangan.

Of the Philippines to the European Union
Ambassador: Pacifico A. Castro.

Further Reading

National Statistics Office. *Philippine Statistical Yearbook.*
Boyce, J. K., *The Political Economy of Growth and Impoverishment in the Marcos Era.* London, 1993
Bresnan, J., (ed.) *Crisis in the Philippines: The Marcos Era and Beyond.* Princeton Univ. Press, 1986
Karnow, S., *In Our Image: America's Empire in the Philippines.* New York, 1989
Kerkvliet, B. J. and Mojares, R. B. (eds.), *From Marcos to Aquino: Local Perspectives on Political Transition in the Philippines.* Hawaii Univ. Press, 1992
Larkin, J. A., *Sugar and the Origins of Modern Philippine Society.* California Univ. Press, 1993
Richardson, J. A., *Philippines.* [Bibliography] Oxford and Santa Barbara, 1989
Vob, R. and Yap, J. T., *The Philippine Economy: East Asia's Stray Cat? Structure, Finance and Adjustment.* London and The Hague, 1996

National statistical office: National Statistics Office, POB 779, Manila
Website: http://www.census.gov.ph/

POLAND

Rzeczpospolita Polska
(Polish Republic)

Capital: Warsaw
Population: 38·61m.
GDP per head: (PPP$) 5,002
HDI/world rank: 0·834/58

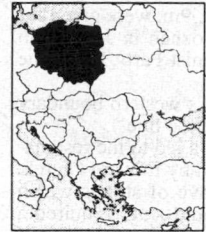

KEY HISTORICAL EVENTS. Poland takes its name from the Polanie ('plain dwellers'), whose ruler Mieszko I had achieved a federation by 966, a date taken as that of the foundation of the Polish state. He placed Poland under the Roman Holy See around 990. His son Bolesław I (992–1025) continued his father's territorial expansionism until by the time of his coronation in 1024 Poland's boundaries were much as they are today. The tendency of this state to fragment under German pressure was formalized by Bolesław III (1102–38), whose sons divided the kingdom into 3 duchies. In the 13th century Poland was laid waste by incursions from the pagan proto-Russians and Mongols. In 1320 Władysław of Kraków succeeded in being crowned king of Poland. The work of unification was consolidated by his son, Kazimierz III (1333–70), whose reign brought prosperity and administrative efficiency. A descendant of his married the pagan duke of Lithuania, Jagiełło, who was converted to Catholicism and became king of Poland in 1386, uniting Poland and Lithuania in a vast multi-ethnic empire which was able to break the power of the Teutonic Knights at Tannenberg in 1410.

The Jagiełłonian period to 1572 is regarded as an economic and cultural 'golden age'. In 1648 a Cossack revolt in the Ukraine resulted in a Russian victory and acquisition of territory; immediately afterwards Sweden occupied and devastated the whole country. Turkish inroads were only finally quelled by King Jan Sobieski's victory at Vienna in 1683. Poland's involvement in the Russo-Swedish wars of 1700–09 brought not only further economic ruin but also the political dependence of the Polish king on the might of Peter the Great. In 1701 the Hohenzollern prince Frederick assumed the title of King of Prussia; his descendant, Frederick the Great, brought Prussia to the position of European power. In the 'First Partition' of 1772 Russia and Prussia in conjunction with Austria took over a third of Poland's territory on the pretext of a Polish uprising at Bar (1768). Poland was wiped off the map by the Second and Third partitions (1793, 1795), except for a brief independent interlude under Napoleon.

Risings in 1830, 1846, 1848 and 1863 were unsuccessful. Thereafter nationalist efforts were channelled more into cultural and economic development. Political parties were formed: the National Democrats under Roman Dmowski campaigned for autonomy; the Socialists under Józef Piłsudski joined the 1905 uprising in search of independence. With the impending collapse of the partitioning powers in the First World War, a Polish National Committee was formed in Paris in 1917 and recognized by the Allies. The thirteenth of President Woodrow Wilson's 'Fourteen Points' guaranteed Poland's independence and access to the sea. A Polish army was organized in France in 1918. Inside Poland Piłsudski had formed a fighting force of his own, the 'Polish legions', and he set up a rival government. The breach was healed by the appointment to the premiership of the neutral Jan Paderewski, with Piłsudski remaining chief of state.

A constitution was voted in March 1921. Poland's frontiers were not established until 1923, after plebiscites in Silesia and East Prussia and a war with Soviet Russia in 1920 which Poland nearly lost. Piłsudski took power in a coup in May 1926. His dictatorship endured until 1935. In foreign affairs Poland attempted to maintain a balance between Germany and the USSR, but after Munich it accepted a British guarantee of its independence in April 1939. In Aug. Hitler signed a non-aggression pact with Stalin which provided for a partition of Poland; this took place a few days after the outbreak of war.

Poland was rapidly overrun, but Polish forces were able to reform on Allied soil under a government-in-exile. Moscow broke off relations with the 'London' Poles in

1943 and recognized the Polish Committee of National Liberation (the 'Lublin committee') which proclaimed itself the sole legal government when Lublin was liberated in July 1944. In Aug. and Sept. the Soviet army stopped short of the city while the resistance forces were destroyed in the Warsaw uprising. At the Yalta conference Stalin agreed that the Lublin government should be extended to include non-Communists, and the 'London' Polish leader Mikolajczyk with 3 colleagues joined the cabinet in July 1945.

Elections were held on 19 Jan. 1947. Of the 12·7m. votes cast, 9m. were given for the Communist-dominated 'Democratic Bloc'. After riots in Poznań in June 1956 nationalist anti-Stalinist elements gained control of the Communist Party, under the leadership of Władysław Gomułka.

In 1970 the Federal Republic of Germany recognized Poland's western boundary as laid down by the Potsdam Conference of 1945 (the 'Oder-Neisse line').

In Dec. 1970 strikes and riots in Gdańsk, Szczecin and Gdynia led to the resignation of a number of leaders including Gomułka. He was replaced by Edward Gierek.

The raising of meat prices on 1 July 1980 resulted in a wave of strikes which broadened into generalized wage demands and eventually by mid-Aug. acquired a political character. Workers in Gdańsk, Gdynia and Sopot elected a joint strike committee, led by Lech Wałęsa demanding the right to strike and to form independent trade unions, the abolition of censorship, access to the media and the release of political prisoners.

On 31. Aug. the government and Wałęsa signed the 'Gdańsk Agreements' permitting the formation of independent trade unions.

On 5 Sept. Gierek suffered a heart attack and retired from the party leadership. On 17 Sept. various trade unions decided to form a national confederation ('Solidarity') and applied for legal status, which was granted on 24 Oct. after some government resistance.

On 9 Feb. 1981 the Defence Minister, Gen. Wojciech Jaruzelski, became Prime Minister. On 13 Dec. 1981 the Government imposed martial law and set up a Military Council of National Salvation. Solidarity was proscribed.

Following strikes and demands for the reinstatement of Solidarity, the government resigned in Sept. 1988. After the parliamentary elections of June 1989 the Communists were unable to form a government against the opposition of Solidarity and Tadeusz Mazowiecki, a Solidarity member, was elected Prime Minister by the Sejm on 24 Aug. Unconditionally free parliamentary elections were held in Oct. 1991.

TERRITORY AND POPULATION. Poland is bounded in the north by the Baltic Sea and Russia, east by Lithuania, Belarus and the Ukraine, south by the Czech Republic and Slovakia and west by Germany. Poland comprises an area of 312,685 sq. km (120,628 sq. miles).

At the census of 7 Dec. 1988 the population was 37,879,000 (18·47m. males; 61·2% urban). Population in May 1996, 38,612,000 (51·3% female; 61·8% urban), density, 125 per sq. km. Vital statistics, 1996 (in 1,000): Marriages, 203·6; births, 428·2; deaths, 385·5; infant deaths, 5·2. Rates (per 1,000 population): Marriage, 5·3; birth, 11·1; death, 10; infant mortality (per 1,000 live births), 12·2; growth rate, 1·1. A law prohibiting abortion was passed in 1993, but an amendment of Aug. 1996 permits it in cases of hardship or difficult personal situation. Expectation of life in 1995 was 67·6 years for males and 76·4 for females. In 1994 there were 25,900 emigrants and 6,900 immigrants. Suicide rates, 1990–95 (per 100,000): All, 13·9; males, 23·9; females, 4·4.

The country is divided into 49 voivodships (*wojewodztwo*). Area (in sq. km) and population (in 1,000) in 1993 (% urban in brackets).

Voivodship	Area	Population		Voivodship	Area	Population	
Biała Podlaska	5,348	309	(37)	Częstochowa	6,182	782	(52·9)
Białystok	10,055	699	(62·8)	Elblag	6,103	488	(62·6)
Bielsko-Biała	3,704	912	(48·8)	Gdańsk	7,394	1,445	(75·9)
Bydgoszcz	10,349	1,127	(65·1)	Gorzów	8,484	508	(62·8)
Chełm	3,866	250	(43·4)	Jelenia Góra	4,379	523	(66·9)
Ciechanów	6,362	435	(38·7)	Kalisz	6,512	720	(46·8)

Voivodship	Area	Population		Voivodship	Area	Population	
Katowice	6,650	3,954	(86·9)	Przemyśl	4,437	413	(39·1)
Kielce	9,211	1,136	(47·4)	Radom	7,294	761	(47·7)
Konin	5,139	477	(41·9)	Rzeszów	4,397	740	(41·9)
Koszalin	8,470	517	(63·8)	Siedlce	8,499	659	(32·1)
Kraków (Cracow)	3,254	1,235	(68·7)	Sieradz	4,869	412	(37·7)
Krosno	5,702	504	(35·1)	Skierniewice	3,960	423	(47·9)
Legnica	4,037	522	(70·7)	Słupsk	7,453	423	(55·4)
Leszno	4,154	394	(48·4)	Suwałki	10,490	482	(56·2)
Łódź	1,523	1,126	(93·0)	Szczecin	9,982	985	(76·3)
Łomża	6,684	353	(41·5)	Tarnobrzeg	6,283	608	(39·6)
Lublin	6,792	1,024	(59·4)	Tarnów	4,151	687	(35·6)
Nowy Sącz	5,576	721	(35·7)	Toruń	5,348	668	(63·1)
Olsztyn	12,327	766	(60)	Wałbrzych	4,168	742	(74·1)
Opole	8,535	1,027	(53·2)	Warsaw	3,788	2,413	(88·8)
Ostrołęka	6,498	406	(35·5)	Włocławek	4,402	434	(47·3)
Piła	8,205	490	(56·4)	Wrocław	6,287	1,134	(74·1)
Piotrków	6,266	645	(50·0)	Zamość	6,980	493	(30·3)
Płock	5,117	521	(49·0)	Zielona Góra	8,868	670	(61·9)
Poznań	8,151	1,347	(71·0)				

Population (in 1,000) of the largest towns (1995):

Warsaw	1,638·3	Katowice	354·2	Gliwice	214·0
Łódź	825·6	Lublin	353·3	Kielce	213·7
Kraków (Cracow)	745·4	Białystok	277·8	Toruń	204·3
Wrocław (Breslau)	642·7	Częstochowa	259·5	Żabrze	201·6
Poznań	581·8	Gdynia	251·4	Bielsko-Biała	180·7
Gdańsk	462·8	Sosnowiec	249·0	Olsztyn	167·4
Szczecin (Stettin)	419·3	Radom	232·3	Ruda Śląska	166·3
Bydgoszcz	385·8	Bytom	227·6	Rzeszów	160·3

Ethnic minorities are not identified. There were estimated to be 1·2m. Germans in 1984, and there are Ukrainians, Belorussians and Lithuanians. A movement for Silesian autonomy has attracted sufficient support to suggest that further moves towards decentralization may soon be considered. A Council of National Minorities was set up in March 1991. There is a large Polish diaspora, some 65% in USA.

CLIMATE. Climate is continental, marked by long and severe winters. Rainfall amounts are moderate, with a marked summer maximum. Warsaw. Jan. 25°F (−3·9°C), July 66°F (18·9°C). Annual rainfall 22·1" (550 mm). Gdańsk. Jan. 29°F (−1·7°C), July 63°F (17·2°C). Annual rainfall 22" (559 mm). Kraków. Jan. 27°F (−2·8°C), July 67°F (19·4°C). Annual rainfall 29" (729 mm). Poznań. Jan. 30°F (−1·1°C), July 67°F (19·4°C). Annual rainfall 21" (523 mm). Szczecin. Jan. 30°F (−1·1°C), July 65°F (18·3°C). Annual rainfall 22" (550 mm). Wroclaw. Jan. 30°F (−1·1°C), July 66°F (18·9°C). Annual rainfall 23" (574 mm).

CONSTITUTION AND GOVERNMENT. The present Constitution was adopted on 22 July 1952. Amendments were adopted in 1976 and 1983. Constitutional amendments of Aug. 1992 (the 'Small Constitution') redefined relations between the President, Government and Sejm, enhancing the powers of the President and the Prime Minister. The head of state is the *President*, who is directly elected for a 5-year term (renewable once). The President may appoint, but may not dismiss, cabinets.

The authority of the republic is vested in the *Sejm* (Parliament of 460 members), elected by proportional representation for 4 years by all citizens over 18. There is a 5% threshold for parties and 8% for coalitions, but seats are reserved for representatives of ethnic minorities even if their vote falls below 5%. 69 of the Sejm seats are awarded from the national lists of parties polling more than 7% of the vote. The Sejm elects a *Council of State* and a *Council of Ministers*. There is also an elected 100-member upper house, the *Senate*. The President and the Senate each has a power of veto which only a two-thirds majority of the Sejm can override. The Prime Minister is chosen by the President with the approval of the Sejm.

A Political Council consultative to the presidency consisting of representatives of all the major political tendencies was set up in Jan. 1991.

At the first round of the presidential elections on 5 Nov. 1995, 13 candidates stood; turn-out was 64·7%. Aleksander Kwaśniewski gained 35·11% of votes cast, President Lech Wałęsa, 33.11%. At the run-off round on 19 Nov. 1995 Kwaśniewski was elected by 51·72% of votes cast; turn-out was 68%.

A referendum was held on 25 May 1997. 52·71% of votes cast were in favour of a new constitution which diminishes the powers of the president in favour of the Sejm. Turn-out was 42·86%.

Parliamentary elections held on 21 Sept. 1997 led to the defeat of the reformed communist government and the return of a coalition led by Solidarity Electoral Action (AWS) and the Federal Union (UW). The AWS won 34% of the votes and the Federal Union 13% against the Communist Democratic Left Alliance with 27%. On 15 Oct. Jerzy Buzek was nominated by AWS to be prime minister. In Dec. Józef Oleksy, leader of the former communists, was replaced by Leszek Miller.

President: Aleksander Kwaśniewski (b. 1954; SLD; elected Nov. 1995).

In March 1998 the government was:

Council of Ministers

Prime Minister: Jerzy Buzek (AWS).

Deputy Prime Minister and Minister of Finance: Leszek Balcerowicz (UW). *Deputy Prime Minister and Minister of Internal Affairs and Administration:* Janusz Tomaszewski (AWS). *Foreign Affairs:* Bronislaw Geremek (UW). *Defence:* Janusz Onyszkiewicz (UW). *Treasury:* Emil Wąsacz (AWS). *Economy:* Janusz Steinhoff (AWS). *Justice:* Hanna Suchocka (UW). *Labour and Social Policy:* Longin Komolowski (AWS). *National Education:* Miroslaw Handke (AWS). *Culture and Arts:* Joanna Wnuk-Nazarowa (UW). *Agriculture:* Jacek Janiszewski (AWS). *Health:* Wieslaw Maksymowicz (AWS). *Transport and Maritime Economy:* Eugeniusz Morawski (UW). *Environmental Protection, National Resources and Forestry:* Jan Szyszko (AWS). *Telecommunications:* Marek Zdrojewski (AWS). *Head of Scientific Research Committee:* Andrzej Wiszniewski (AWS). *Head of European Integration Committee:* Ryszard Czarnecki (AWS).

Without portfolio

Minister without portfolio in charge of Social Reforms: Teresa Kamińska (AWS). *Minister without portfolio, head of Government Centre for Strategic Studies:* Jerzy Kropiwnicki (AWS). *Minister without portfolio in charge of co-ordinating the Council of Ministers' assignment:* Wiesław Walendziak (AWS). *Minister without portfolio in charge of Security Services:* Janusz Pałubicki (AWS).

Speaker of the Sejm: Maciej Płażyński (AWS).

National anthem: 'Jeszcze Polska nie zginęla' ('Poland has not yet perished'); words by J. Wybicki; tune by M. Ogiński.

Local government The 49 voivodships (regions) are administratively divided into 267 districts and subdivided into 2,483 urban wards (*gmina*) and 39,277 rural wards (*sołectwo*). Local government is carried out by councils elected every 4 years at every level. Local government is financed partly by local taxes and partly by central government taxes. There are also district agencies which form a link between local and central government. Communities of fewer than 40,000 inhabitants elect councils on a first-past-the-post system; larger communities have a proportional party-list system. Elections were held on 19 June 1994 for 52,173 seats on 2,465 councils; turn-out was 35·8%. Administrative reforms introduced as from 1993 devolve responsibility for education and health from voivodships to wards.

Further reforms to decentralize government and to make it more democratic should be in place in time for the municipal elections in Sept. 1998. The number of regions will be reduced from 49 to 13 or 14. Governors will act as 'supervisors' of regional government but real power will belong to elected assemblies and to their chairmen who will become the new regions' chief executives. They will control 30% of income tax and 15% of VAT raised within their regions. A new level of government, 320 elected counties (*powiaty*), will administer much state welfare including health and education beyond primary level.

DEFENCE. Poland is divided into 4 military districts: Warsaw, Pomerania, Kraków and Silesia.

Conscription is for 18 months. 3-year civilian duty as a conscientious alternative to conscription was introduced in 1988.

Army. The Army includes 9 mechanized divisions, 1 coastal defence, 4 artillery, 4 engineer, 1 air assault, 1 mountain infantry and 4 missile brigades; and 4 missile, 2 anti-tank and 1 artillery regiment. Equipment includes 892 T-55 and 809 T-72 main battle tanks. An aviation element has been formed by taking over the attack and troop support helicopters of the Air Force. There are 80 Mi-24 armed helicopters, 60 Mi-8 transports and 50 Mi-2 communications helicopters, as well as a small number of W-3 Sokol transports. Strength (1997) 168,650 (including 101,670 conscripts).

Navy. The fleet comprises 3 ex-Soviet diesel submarines, 1 ex-Soviet guided missile destroyer armed with SA-N-1 Goa surface-to-air and SS-N-2C Styx anti-ship missiles, 1 small frigate, 4 missile corvettes, 7 smaller fast missile craft, 3 coastal and 19 inshore patrol craft, 6 coastal and 18 inshore minesweepers, 5 medium landing ships and about 3 landing craft. Auxiliaries include 1 command ship, 4 support tankers, 2 intelligence vessels, 2 survey vessels, and 3 training ships together with about 60 minor auxiliaries.

The Fleet Air Arm comprises 2 regiments, one with 14 Iskra patrol aircraft the other with 30 Mig-21 fighter bombers, 1 squadron with 4 Mi-14 Haze and 6W-3 Sokol helicopters, and 1 squadron with 7 An-2 and 2 An-28 transports. Naval-manned coast defences provide 6 artillery battalions and 3 missile batteries.

Personnel in 1997 totalled 17,000 including 9,500 conscripts. 2,460 of these serve in naval aviation and 3,000 in coast defence. Bases are at Gdynia, Gdańsk and Świnoujscie.

A para-military border guard service operates 28 inshore patrol craft and some 30 boats.

Air Force. The Air Force had a strength (1997) of 56,100 (30,430 conscripts). There are 7 air defence regiments (16 squadrons)with about 180 MiG-21, MiG-23 and MiG-29 supersonic interceptors, and 4 tactical regiments (11 squadrons) operating variable-geometry Su-22 close-support fighters. There are also reconnaissance, ECM, transport, helicopter (including Mi-2s for observation and Mi-24 gunships) and training units. Soviet 'Guideline' 'Goa', 'Ganef', 'Gainful' and 'Gaskin' surface-to-air missiles are operational.

INTERNATIONAL RELATIONS. A treaty of friendship with Germany signed 17 June 1991 renounced the use of force, recognized Poland's western border as laid down at the Potsdam conference of 1945 (the 'Oder-Neisse line') and guaranteed minority rights in both countries.

Membership. Poland is a member of the UN, the Council of Europe, OECD, CEFTA, the Central European Initiative and the NATO Partnership for Peace, an associate partner of the WEU and an associate member of the EU. Full membership of the EU is likely soon after 2000.

ECONOMY

Policy. The Central Planning Office was absorbed by the newly created Economies Ministry in Jan. 1997. An economic plan ran from 1994 to 1997. In 1995 15 National Investment Funds were set up to oversee the privatization of 444 state enterprises. All citizens may purchase titles to participate in these funds for 10% of their annual salary, which will enable them to buy shares in the enterprises when privatized (Mass Privatization Scheme). By May 1997, 25·9m. persons had purchased titles to participate. As of Jan. 1997, 4,107 enterprises had been privatized and 1,900 wound up.

Performance. Real GDP growth was 5·5% in 1997 (6·1% in 1996). Poland's economy is growing faster than any of the other ex-communist countries in Europe. The private sector accounts for more than 60% of GDP. Inflation has dropped from 249% in 1990 to 14·5% in 1997.

Budget. Figures for recent years (in 1m. złotys)

	1994	1995	1996
Revenue	61,636	81,240	96,048
Expenditure	46,227	65,813	80,521

Currency. The currency unit is the *złoty* (PLZ) of 100 *groszy*. A new złoty was introduced on 1 Jan. 1995 at 1 new złoty = 10,000 old złotys. There are coins of 1, 2, 5, 10, 20 and 50 grosz and 1 and 5 złotys, and notes of 10, 20, 50, 100 and 200 złotys. Old złoty notes were valid until 1997. In 1995, currency in circulation totalled 19,529·4m. złotys. Inflation was 19% in 1996. The złoty became convertible on 1 Jan. 1990. In 1995 the złoty was subject to a creeping devaluation of 1·2% per month; it was allowed to float in a 7% band from 16 May 1995. Foreign exchange reserves were US$3,500 in Aug. 1993.

Banking and Finance. The National Bank of Poland (established 1945) is the central bank and bank of issue. Its Governor is nominated by the President and approved by the Sejm. (*Governor*, Hanna Gronkiewicz-Waltz). 72 commercial banks were operating in 1996. 68% of the sector was still state-owned. The General Savings Bank (Powszechna Kasa Oszczędności) exercises central control over savings activities.

There is a stock exchange in Warsaw.

Weights and Measures. The metric system is in general use.

ENERGY AND NATURAL RESOURCES

Electricity. Electricity production (1995) 138,990m. kWh.; installed capacity in 1991 was 31,952 MW.

Oil and Gas. Total oil reserves amount to some 100m. tonnes. Crude oil production was 292,000 tonnes in 1995, natural gas, 4,820 cu. metres. *Petrochemia Plock*, the country's largest oil refinery, and CPN, the petrol distribution network, are to be privatized.

Minerals. Poland is a major producer of coal (reserves of some 120,000m. tonnes), copper (56m. tonnes) and sulphur. Production in 1995 (in tonnes): Coal, 136·16m.; brown coal, 63·55m.

Agriculture. In 1997 there were 18·66m. ha of agricultural land, comprising: Arable, 14·29m. ha; meadows, 2·42m. ha; pasture, 1·63m. ha; orchards, 0·29m. ha. In 1995, 15·2m. ha were owned by private farmers, 1·37m. ha by state farms and 0·54m. ha by co-operatives. 6·69m. ha were irrigated in 1993. Poland has 4m. small farmers.

Some government subsidies and guaranteed prices were restored in 1992.

Output in 1995 (in 1,000 tonnes): Wheat, 8,668; rye, 6,288; barley, 3,278; oats, 1,495; potatoes, 24,891; sugar-beet, 13,309.

Livestock, 1995 (in 1m.): Cattle, 7·3 (including cows, 3·58); pigs, 20·38; sheep, 0·71; horses, 0·64; chickens, 44m. Milk production was 12,401m. litres; meat, 1·02m. tonnes; eggs, 6,217m.

Tractors in use in 1995: 1,319,000 (in 15-h.p. units).

Forestry. In 1996, 8·96m. ha were forests (predominantly coniferous). In 1995, 72·62m. ha were in the public domain and 14·94m. ha were private. In 1995, 77,800 ha were afforested, and 22·49m. cu. metres of timber gained.

Fisheries. The catch was 451,346 tonnes in 1995.

INDUSTRY. In March 1996 there were 4,197 state firms, 101,687 limited liability companies, 220,234 other companies and 19,834 co-operatives. Production in 1995 (in 1,000 tonnes): Rolled steel, 8,959; cement, 13,884; electrolytic copper, 407; fertilizers, 2,129; paper, 1,327; refined petroleum products, 13,444; plastics, 715; metal-working machines, 7,378; cars, 366,000 units; lorries, 30,572 units; buses, 1,404 units; sulphur, 2,419.

Output of light industry in 1995: Cotton fabrics, 219m. cu. metres; woollen fabrics, 33·2m. metres; synthetic fibres, 134,000 tonnes; shoes, 54·9m. pairs; cleaning agents, 253,000 tonnes; washing machines, 419,000; refrigerators, 586,000, and TV sets, 1,086,000.

Labour. In Dec. 1993 the population of working age was 28·38m. (14·92m. females). In Jan. 1996, the economically active population was 22,647,000 (10,945,000 females). In July 1996 there were 2·51m. registered unemployed and 78,000 job vacancies. In March 1996, 2·66m. persons worked in industry, 0·59m. in building, 0·71m. in transport and communications, 0·81m. in trade, 0·89m. in education, 0·25m. in financial services and 0·98m. in health and social services. Workers made redundant are entitled to one month's wages. Retirement age is 60 for women and 65 for men.

Trade Unions. In 1980 under Lech Wałęsa, Solidarity was an engine of political reform. Dissolved in 1982 it was re-legalized in 1989 and successfully contested the parliamentary elections, but was defeated in 1993. It had 2·3m. members in 1991. The official union, OPZZ, had 5m. members in 1990; there were also about 4,000 small unions not affiliated to it.

FOREIGN ECONOMIC RELATIONS. Since Jan. 1989 foreign investors may own 100% of companies on Polish soil. There were 11,473 joint ventures in May 1993. Legislation of 1991 removed limits on the repatriation of profits, reduced the number of cases needing licences and ended a 10% ceiling on share purchases. Licenses are required for investment in ports, airports, arms manufacture, estate agency and legal services. In June 1997 foreign investments totalled US$13,900m.

Foreign debt was US$43,957m. in Jan. 1996.

An agreement of Dec. 1992 with the Czech Republic, Hungary and Slovakia abolished tariffs on raw materials and goods where exports do not compete directly with locally-produced items, and envisaged tariff reductions on agricultural and industrial goods in 1995–97.

Commerce. Exports (in US$1m.), 1995: 22,894·9; imports, 29,049·7.

Imports in 1993 included (in tonnes): Crude oil, 13·67m.; iron ore, 8·78m.; fertilizers, 0·81m.; wheat, 0·82m.; machinery and transport equipment, 14,966. Exports (in tonnes): Coal, 22·98m.; coke, 1·89m.; copper, 267,000; sulphur, 2·29m.; cement, 3·24m.; paper and products, 0·27m.

Main export markets, 1995: Germany, 38·3%; Netherlands, 5·6%; Russia, 5·6%; Italy, 4·9%; UK, 4%. Main import suppliers: Germany, 26·6%; Italy, 8·5%; Russia, 6·7%; UK, 5·2%; France, 4·9%.

Tourism. There were 82·24m. foreign visitors in 1995.

COMMUNICATIONS

Roads. In 1995 there were 237,000 km of hard-surfaced roads. In 1995 there were 257 km of motorways. There were 7·52m. passenger cars, 1·35m. lorries; 85,000 buses and 0·93m. motor cycles. Public road transport carried 1,132m. passengers and 319m. tonnes of freight in 1995. There were 48,901 road accidents in 1993 (6,341 fatal).

Railways. In 1995 railways comprised 22,598 km of 1,435 mm gauge (11,627 km electrified, 14,660 km single-track) and 1,388 km of narrow gauge. In 1995 railways carried 465·9m. passengers and 225·35m. tonnes of freight. Some regional railways are operated by local authorities. A 12 km metro opened in Warsaw in 1995, and there are tram/light rail networks in 13 cities.

Civil Aviation. There is an international airport at Warsaw (Okęcie). The national carrier is LOT-Polish Airlines, state-owned but with 49% of its equity scheduled for privatization. Its fleet in 1995 comprised 4 B-737-400s, 6 B-737-500s, 2 B-767-200ERs, 2 B-767-300ERs and 7 other aircraft. 1,847,000 passengers and 22,000 tonnes of freight were flown in 1995. Services are also provided by Aeroflot, Air France, Air Moldova, Air Ukraine, Alitalia, Austrian Airlines, Balkan Belavia, British

Airways, Czech Airlines, Delta, El Al, Finnair, KLM, Libyan Airlines, Lithuanian Airlines, Lufthansa, Malév, Sabena, SAS, Swissair, Tarom and Tunis Air.

Shipping. The principal ports are Gdynia, Gdańsk and Szczecin. 49·18m. tonnes of cargo were handled in 1995. Ocean-going services are grouped into Polish Ocean Lines based on Gdynia and operating regular liner services, and the Polish Shipping Company based on Szczecin and operating cargo services. Poland also has a share in the Gdynia America Line. In 1995, 24·97m. tonnes of freight and 458,000 passengers were carried. In 1995 the merchant marine comprised 167 ships totalling 3·56m. GRT, including oil tankers, 0·15m. GRT. 524,000 GRT of shipping completed building in 1995.

In 1995 there were 3,980 km of navigable inland waterways. 9·31m. tonnes of freight were carried in 1995 (including coastal traffic).

Telecommunications. In 1995 there were 8,011 post offices. There were 5,728,000 telephone and 24,000 telex subscribers in 1995 and 23,000 fax subscribers in 1992.

Polskie Radio i Telewizja broadcasts 3 radio programmes and 2 TV programmes. There is also a commercial TV channel. Colour programmes are transmitted by the SECAM system. Links with the West are provided through the Eutelstat satellite. In 1992 independent radio and TV broadcasting were introduced under the aegis of a 9-member National Council of Radiophonics and Television. Radio licences in 1995, 17·5m.; TV licences, 12·0m.

Telekomunikacia Polska (TP), the state telecoms operator, is to be privatized.

Cinemas. In 1995 there were 681 cinemas; admissions, 22·6m. 20 full-length films were made in 1995.

Press. In 1995 there were 65 newspapers with an overall circulation of 5·4m.

SOCIAL INSTITUTIONS

Justice. The penal code was adopted in 1969. Espionage and treason carry the severest penalties. For minor crimes there is provision for probation sentences and fines. In 1995 the death penalty was suspended for 5 years; it had not been applied since 1988. A new penal code abolishing the death penalty was adopted in June 1997.

There exist the following courts: 1 Supreme Court, 2 high administrative courts, 10 appeal courts, 95 voivodship courts, 898 district courts, 66 family consultative centres and 34 juvenile courts. Judges and lay assessors are elected. Judges for higher courts are appointed by the President of the Republic from candidatures proposed by the National Council of the Judiciary. Judges have life tenure. An ombudsman's office was established in 1987.

Family consultative centres were established in 1977 for cases involving divorce and domestic relations, but divorce suits were transferred to ordinary courts in 1990. 273,892 criminal sentences were passed in 1995. There were 533 convictions for murder in 1994. 61,136 persons were in prison as at 31 Dec. 1995.

Religion. Church–State relations are regulated by laws of 1989 which guarantee religious freedom, grant the Church radio and TV programmes and permit it to run schools, hospitals and old age homes. The Church has a university (Lublin), an Academy of Catholic Theology and seminaries. On 28 July 1993 the government signed a Concordat with the Vatican regulating mutual relations. The archbishop of Warsaw is the primate of Poland (since 1981, Cardinal Józef Glemp). The religious capital is Gniezno, whose archbishop will be the future primate. In Oct. 1978 Cardinal Karol Wojtyla, archbishop of Cracow, was elected Pope as John Paul II.

Statistics of major churches as at Dec. 1994:

Church	Congregations	Places of Worship	Clergy	Adherents
Roman Catholic	9,363	16,032	26,341	35,000,261
Uniate	63	101	72	110,380
Old Catholics	146	148	154	90,576
Polish Orthodox	243	410	254	543,200
Protestant (31 sects)	976	855	1,789	155,971
Moslem	6	8	11	5,303
Jewish	24	17	3	1,410
Jehovah's Witnesses	1,494	—	—	115,778

Education. Basic education from 7 to 15 is free and compulsory. Free secondary education is then optional in general or vocational schools. Primary schools are organized in complexes based on wards under one director ('ward collective schools'). In 1995–96 there were: Nursery schools, 20,618 with 984,000 pupils and 74,200 teachers; primary schools, 19,823 with 5,372,000 pupils and 323,500 teachers; secondary schools, 1,705 with 683,000 pupils and 34,700 teachers; vocational schools, 7,455 with 1,568,300 pupils and 88,700 teachers, 1,432 tertiary (post-lycée) schools with 161,000 students and 179 institutions of higher education (including 12 universities, 30 polytechnics, 9 agricultural schools, 51 schools of economics, 14 teachers' training colleges, 11 theological colleges and 11 medical schools) with 794,600 students and 71,300 teaching staff.

The adult literacy rate is 99%.

Religious (Catholic) instruction was introduced in all schools in 1990; for children of dissenting parents there are classes in ethics.

Health. Medical treatment is free and funded from the state budget. Medical care is also available in private clinics. In Jan. 1996 there were 705 hospitals and 48 psychiatric hospitals with 243,036 beds. In 1995 there were 88,523 doctors, 17,619 dentists, 19,450 pharmacists and 210,425 nurses.

Social Security. Social security benefits are administered by the State Insurance Office and funded 45% by a payroll tax and 55% from the state budget. Pensions, disability payments, child allowances, survivor benefits, maternity benefits, funeral subsidies, sickness compensation and alimony supplements are provided. In June 1996 age and disability pensions were paid to 9·2m. recipients; these are index-linked to the average wage. Unemployment benefits are paid from a fund financed by a 3% payroll tax. It is indexed in various categories to the average wage and payable for 12 months. Social assistance is administered and partly-funded by local government. It provides last-resort benefits in cash and kind.

DIPLOMATIC REPRESENTATIVES

Of Poland in Great Britain (47 Portland Pl., London, W1N 3AG)
Ambassador: Ryszard Stemplowski.

Of Great Britain in Poland (Aleje Roz No. 1, 00-556 Warsaw)
Ambassador: Christopher O. Hum, CMG.

Of Poland in the USA (2640 16th St., NW, Washington, D.C., 20009)
Ambassador: Jerzy Kosmiński.

Of the USA in Poland (Aleje Ujazdowskie 29/31, Warsaw)
Ambassador: Nicholas A. Rey.

Of Poland to the United Nations
Ambassador: Eugeniusz Wyzner.

Of Poland to the European Union
Ambassador: Jan Truszczynski.

Further Reading

Central Statistical Office, *Rocznik Statystyczny.* Annual.—*Concise Statistical Yearbook of Poland.—Statistical Bulletin.* Monthly.

Bromke, A., *The Meaning and Uses of Polish History.* New York, 1987
Davies, N., *Poland, Past and Present: a Select Bibliography of Works in English.* Newtonville, 1977.—*God's Playground: a History of Poland.* 2 vols. OUP, 1981.—*Heart of Europe: a Short History of Poland.* OUP, 1984
Halecki, O., *A History of Poland.* 4th ed. London, 1983
Kaminski, B., *The Collapse of the State of Socialism: the Case of Poland.* Princeton Univ. Press, 1991
Kanka, A. G., *Poland: an Annotated Bibliography of Books in English.* New York, 1988
Kurski, J., *Lech Wałęsa: Democrat or Dictator?* Boulder (CO), 1993
Leslie, R. F., (ed.) *The History of Poland since 1863.* CUP, 1980

Mitchell, K. D. (ed.) *Political Pluralism in Hungary and Poland: Perspectives on the Reforms.* New York, 1992

Sikorski, R., *The Polish House: An Intimate History of Poland.* London, 1997; US title: *Full Circle.* New York, 1997

Sanford, G. and Gozdecka-Sanford, A., *Poland:* [Bibliography]. Oxford and Santa Barbara, 1993

Slay, B., *The Polish Economy: Crisis, Reform and Transformation.* Princeton Univ. Press, 1994

Staar, R. F., (ed.) *Transition to Democracy in Poland.* New York, 1993

Staniszkis, J., *The Dynamics of the Breakthrough in Eastern Europe: the Polish Experience.* California Univ. Press, 1991

Wałęsa, L., *A Path of Hope.* London, 1989

Wedel, J., *The Unplanned Society: Poland during and after Communism.* Columbia Univ. Press, 1992

National library: Biblioteka Narodowa, Rakowiecka 6, Warsaw.

National statistical office: Central Statistical Office, Aleje Niepodległości 208, 00-925 Warsaw.

Website: http://www.stsp.gov.pl/

PORTUGAL

República Portuguesa

Capital: Lisbon
Population: 9·9m.
GDP per head: (PPP$) 12,326
HDI/world rank: 0·890/31

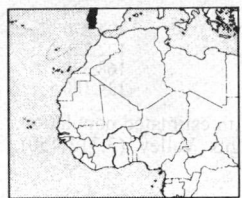

KEY HISTORICAL EVENTS. Portugal has been an independent state since the 12th century apart from one period of Spanish rule (1580-1640). It became a kingdom in 1139 under Alfonso I. During the 15th century Portugal played a leading role in oceanic exploration, opening up new trade routes and establishing colonies. Portuguese influence spread in Guinea, Brazil, the Indies and on the African coast.

In 1807, during the Napoleonic wars, the Spaniards again invaded Portugal, but were driven out by the Duke of Wellington and Portuguese guerrillas during the peninsula war. Brazil, where the king had fled during the French invasion, became independent in 1822.

During much of the 19th century liberal governments, led by financial and agrarian oligarchs and chosen by an electorate composed of fewer than one percent of the population, were in office. The excluded nationalistic republicans finally deposed King Manual II on 5 Oct. 1910. Another *coup* on 28 May 1926 removed the unstable parliamentary republic which had fought from 1916 on the Allied side in the First World War. The military government established on 1 June 1926 was succeeded in 1932 when Dr Antonio de Oliveira Salzaar became Prime Minister. The corporalist constitution of the New State was adopted on 19 March 1933 under which a civil dictatorship governed in a one party state. The Iberian Pact with Spain was signed on 17 March 1939.

In the 1960s Portugal faced economic stagnation at home and rebellion in her colonies. Goa was seized by India in 1961. War raged in the African colonies. In Sept. 1968 Salzaar was succeeded by Dr Caetano, but the government party, from 1970 called the *Acção Nacional Popoular*, remained in power.

There was a fresh *coup* on 25 April 1974, establishing a junta of National Salvation. Gen. Antonio Ribeiro de Spinola became president. When he resigned in Sept. he was succeeded by Gen. Francisco de Costa Gomes. During 1974-75 most of the Portuguese overseas possessions, notably the African colonies, gained independence.

Following an attempted revolt on 11 March 1975, the junta was dissolved and a Supreme Revolutionary Council formed which ruled until 25 April 1976 when constitutional government was resumed. The Supreme Revolutionary Council was renamed the Council of the Revolution, becoming a consultative body chaired by the president. The transit to full civilian government was completed in 1982 when the constitution of 1976 was revised to abolish the Council of the Revolution and to reduce the powers of the president.

TERRITORY AND POPULATION. Mainland Portugal is bounded in the north and east by Spain and south and west by the Atlantic Ocean. The Atlantic archipelagoes of the Azores and of Madeira form autonomous but integral parts of the republic, which has a total area of 91,905 sq. km. Population (1991 census), 9,862,700 (5,107,500 females). Density (1995 estimate), 107·9 per sq. km. (North, 165·9; Central, 72·3; Lisbon and Tagus Valley, 277·5, Alentejo, 19·5, Algarve, 16·2; Azores, 103·7; Madeira, 330·3). Resident population (1996 estimate), 9,934,110 (5,150,500 females).

The areas and populations (in1,000) of the districts and Autonomous Regions:

Areas	Resident Population	Areas	Resident Population
North		*North–contd.*	
Minho-Lima	249,650	Tâmega	531,540
Cávado	371,000	Entre Douro e Vouga	263,080
Ave	477,210	Douro	234,670
Grande Porto	1,191,740	Alto Trás os Montes	225,890

Areas	Resident Population	Areas	Resident Population
Central		*Lisbon and Tagus Valley*	
Baixo Vouga	360,200	Oeste	362,710
Baixo Mondego	326,710	Grande Lisboa	1,833,140
Pinhal Litoral	228,700	Península de Setúbal	662,380
Pinhal Interior Norte	133,520	Médio Tejo	230,370
Dão Lafões	281,450	Lezíria do Tejo	230,370
Pinhal Interior Sul	46,150	*Alentejo*	
Serra da Estrela	52,340	Alentejo Litoral	94,270
Beira Interior Norte	113,050	Alto Alentejo	122,220
Beira Interior Sul	78,180	Alentejo Cental	168,370
Cova da Beira	89,770	Baixo Alentejo	134,180

In 1996 mainland Portugal was divided into 5 regions, with estimated population: North (3,544,780); Central (1,710,070); Lisbon and Tagus Valley (3,313,450); Alentejo (519,040); Algarve (346,110).

Vital statistics for calendar years:

	Marriages	Live births	Still births	Deaths	Separations	Dissolutions
1992	69,887	115,018	909	101,161	192	58,181
1993	68,176	114,030	887	106,384	229	59,670
1994	66,003	109,287	825	99,621	292	58,443
1995	65,776	107,184	747	103,939	360	59,140

Vital statistics rates, 1995 (per 1,000 population): Birth, 10·8; death, 10·4; natural increase, 0·04; rate of population increase, 0·09; infant mortality (per 1,000 live births), 7·4. Life expectancy at birth, 1995: Males, 71·52 years; females 78·61.

In 1996 the births comprised 57,374 boys and 52,989 girls; deaths, 56,444 males and 50,815 females.

In 1994, 157,073 foreigners were legally registered: 68,945 African; 18,612 Brazilian; 10,731 British; 8,352 USA. There were 5,653 immigrants. In 1996 there were 3,637 immigrants in total.

Origin	Immigrants	Origin	Immigrants	Origin	Immigrants
Europe	*2,149*	United Kingdom	456	Guinea-Bissau	89
EU	1,946	*North America*	*263*	Mozambique	15
Germany	485	USA	227	São Tomé e Príncipe	24
Spain	276	*Africa*	*593*	*Central South America*	*468*
France	239	Angola	123	Brazil	339
Netherlands	143	Cape Verde	260	*Asia*	*164*

The total number of emmigrants was 7,286 comprised as follows:

Destination	Emigrants
Europe	*6,682*
EU	4,849
Germany	1,425
Spain	498
France	2,063
United Kingdom	436
Africa	*604*

The chief cities are Lisbon, the capital, Oporto, Amadora, Setúbal and Coimbra.

The **Azores** islands lie in the mid-Atlantic Ocean, between 1,200 and 1,600 km west of Lisbon. They are divided into 3 widely separated groups with clear channels between, São Miguel (759 sq. km) together with Santa Maria (97 sq. km) being the most easterly; about 100 miles north-west of them lies the central cluster of Terceira (382 sq. km), Graciosa (62 sq. km), São Jorge (246 sq. km), Pico (446 sq. km) and Faial (173 sq. km); still another 150 miles to the north-west are Flores (143 sq. km) and Corvo (17 sq. km), the latter being the most isolated and primitive of the islands. São Miguel contains over half the total population of the archipelago.

Madeira comprises the island of Madeira (745 sq. km), containing the capital, Funchal; the smaller island of Porto Santo (40 sq. km), lying 46 km to the north-east of Madeira; and two groups of uninhabited islets, Ilhas Desertas (15 sq. km), being 20 km. south-east of Funchal and Ilhas Selvagens (4 sq. km), near the Canaries.

CLIMATE. Because of westerly winds and the effect of the Gulf Stream, the climate ranges from the cool, damp Atlantic type in the north to a warmer and drier Mediterranean type in the south. July and Aug. are virtually rainless everywhere. Inland areas in the north have greater temperature variation, with continental winds blowing from the interior. Lisbon. Jan. 52°F (11°C), July 72°F (22°C). Annual rainfall 27·4" (686 mm). Porto. Jan. 48°F (8·9°C), July 67°F (19·4°C). Annual rainfall 46" (1,151 mm).

CONSTITUTION AND GOVERNMENT. A new Constitution, replacing that of 1976, was approved by the Assembly of the Republic (by 197 votes to 40) on 12 Aug. 1982 and promulgated in Sept. It abolished the (military) Council of the Revolution and reduced the role of the President under it. Portugal is a sovereign, unitary republic. Executive power is vested in the *President*, directly elected for a 5-year term (for a maximum of 2 consecutive terms). The President appoints a Prime Minister and, upon the latter's nomination, other members of the Council of Ministers.

The 230-member *National Assembly* is a unicameral legislature elected for 4-year terms by universal adult suffrage under a system of proportional representation.

At the presidential elections of 14 Jan. 1996 Jorge Sampãio was elected President by 53·8% of votes cast against former prime minister Anibal Cavaco Silva (Social Democrat).

At the parliamentary elections of 1 Oct. 1995 turn-out was 68%. The Socialist Party won 112 seats with 42·9% of votes cast (72 with 29·1% in 1991); the Social Democratic Party, 88 with 34% (135 with 50%); the Christian Democratic Party, 15 with 5·1% (5 with 4·4%); and the Communist Alliance, 15 with 8·6% (17 with 8·8%).

President: Jorge Sampãio (Socialist; sworn in 9 March 1996).

The Socialist government was composed in March 1998 of:

Prime Minister: António Guterres. *Minister of Agriculture, Rural Development and Fisheries:* Fernando Gomes da Silva. *Culture:* Manuel Carrilho. *Defence and the Presidency:* Veiga Simão. *Economy:* Piano Moura. *Education:* Marçal Grilo. *Environment:* Elisa Ferreira. *Finance:* António Sousa Franco. *Foreign Affairs:* Jaime Gama. *Health:* Maria de Belém. *Home Affairs:* Alberto Costa. *Justice:* José Vera Jardím. *Labour:* Ferro Rodrigues. *Science and Technology:* Mariano Gago. *Social Security:* Ferro Rodrigues. *Territorial Planning:* João Cravinho. *Without portfolio:* Jorge Coelho.

The *Speaker* is António Almedia Santos (Socialist).

European Parliament. Portugal has 25 representatives. At the June 1994 elections turn-out was 35·7%. The Socialist Party won 10 seats with 34·7% of votes cast (Group in European Parliament: European Socialist Party); The Social Democratic Party, 9 with 34·3% (Popular European Party: Liberal, Democratic and Reformist Group); the Social Democratic Centre, 3 with 12·4% (European Democrats' Rally); the United Democratic Alliance, 3 with 11·2%.

Local Government: Since 1976, the archipelagoes of the **Azores** and of **Madeira** are Autonomous Regions with their own legislatures and governments. Elections were held in Oct. 1992. The Social Democrats gained 28 seats out of 51 in the Azores and 39 out of 55 in Madeira. Pending the formation of other regional governments, Continental Portugal is divided into 18 districts. Regions and districts are divided into 305 municipal councils and sub-divided into 4,209 parishes. Each level is governed by an assembly elected by direct universal suffrage under a system of proportional representation, with an executive body responsible to the assembly. Elections for municipal 305 councils were held on 14 Dec. 1997. The Socialist Party achieved victories in Lisbon, Oporto and other big cities, with 39·9% of votes cast (up from 36·1% in 1993), and the opposition Social Democrats 32·9% (33·7%). In Lisbon the Socialist candidate won 50·56% of the vote, while in Oporto, the party had 58–64%.

DEFENCE. Conscription is 4–18 months.

Army. There are 5 territorial commands. The Army consists of 1 composite and 1 airborne brigade and 2 armoured cavalry, 11 infantry, 2 field, 1 military police, 1 tank and 2 engineer regiments. Equipment includes 24 M-47, 86 M-48A5 and 88 M-60A3 main battle tanks. Strength (1997) 32,100 (11,800 conscripts). Paramilitary forces are the National Republican Guard (20,900), Public Security Police (20,000), and the Border Guard (8,900).

Navy. The combatant fleet comprises 3 French-built Daphne class diesel submarines, 3 missile-armed frigates of the Vasco da Gama class of West German MEKO design which can embark 2 Lynx helicopters, 8 other small frigates, 6 offshore, 10 coastal and 12 inshore patrol vessels. Auxiliaries include 1 tanker, 2 survey ships, 1 sail training ship and 1 ocean tug. There are 10 small amphibious craft and some 20 service vessels. Naval personnel in 1997 totalled 14,800 (900 conscripts) including 1,700 marines.

Air Force. The Air Force in 1997 had a strength of about 7,700 (14,800 conscripts). Equipment comprises 1 interceptor unit with 20 F16s, 2 strike squadrons with 30 A-7P Corsair IIs; 1 squadron of P-3P Orion maritime patrol aircraft; 1 squadron of C-130H Hercules and 3 squadrons of CASA 212 Aviocars for transport and search and rescue operations; 12 Cessna 337 Skymasters and a force of Puma and Alouette III helicopters. Other aircraft in service include 1 Falcon 20 and 3 Falcon 50 VIP transports, 16 Epsilon piston-engined trainers and 40 AlphaJet advanced trainers.

INTERNATIONAL RELATIONS

Membership. Portugal is a member of the UN, EU, OECD, NATO, WEU and the Council of Europe. Portugal is a signatory to the Schengen Accord abolishing border controls between Belgium, Denmark, Finland, France, Germany, Iceland, Italy, Norway, Portugal, Spain and Sweden.

The Community of Portuguese-speaking Countries (CPLP, comprising Angola, Brazil, Cape Verde, Guinea-Bissau, Mozambique, Portugal and São Tomé e Príncipe) was founded in July 1996 with headquarters in Lisbon, primarily as a cultural and linguistic organization.

ECONOMY

Policy. Large-scale privatization has been in train since 1989. 22 companies were offered for privatization in 1996–97.

Portugal has introduced a wide range of structural reform to deregulate and liberalize the economy starting with a programme of privatization. Transactions associated with more than 43 companies during the period 1989–95 has reached 1·243m. contos (1 conto = 1,000 escudos). The Government intends to accelerate the privatization programme. The Privatization Programme for 1998–99 focuses on 7 major companies: ANA (Airports and Air Navigation), BRISA (Motorways), CIMPOR (Cements—3rd phase), PETROGAL (Oil—last phase), PORTUCEL (Wood-Pulp), TABAQUEIRA (Tobaccos—2nd/3rd phase), Comanhia das Lez'rias (Agriculture).

Performance. Real GDP growth was 1·9% in 1995 (0·7% in 1994). Total GDP was US$100,800m.

	1997 Estimates	1998 Forecasts
Total GDP, nominal (US$1bn.)	104·6	108·0
Real GDP growth (annual % change	3·3	3·5
Inflation (annual % change in CPI)	2·2	2·4
Wage Rates (annual % change)	4·5	4·5
Industrial Production (annual % change)	3·5	3·5
Unemployment Rate (% workforce)	7·1	7·0
Government Deficit (% GDP)	2·9	2·5
Gross External Debt (% GDP)	15·7	14·9
Current Account Balance (US$1bn.)	−1·6	−1·9

Budget. 1996 budget (in 1m. escudos): Total income, 7,281,569·3; current income, 3,967,485·9; capital income, 3,111,834·7.

Currency. There are notes of 10,000, 5,000, 2,000, 1,000, 500 escudos and coins of 200, 100, 50, 20, 10, 5, 2·5 and 1 escudos.

Banking and Finance. The central bank and bank of issue is the Bank of Portugal, founded in 1846 and nationalized in 1974. Its *Governor* is António de Sousa.

In 1991 there were 26 commercial banks (9 foreign), 4 investment banks and 3 savings banks.

There are stock exchanges in Lisbon and Oporto.

Since the privatization of the Bank sector in 1984/5 and the entrance of Portugal to the European Union, the financial system registered significant structural alterations. The Finance Authorities (Bank of Portugal and The Finance Ministry) are creating a less restrictive and more transparent legal system through the creation of new institutions and financial instruments.

On 31 Dec. 1995 there were 46 banks. The major ones are: Caixa Geral de Depósitos, Banco Comercial Português do Atlântico. Total assets: 40,437,218m. contos, credits: 16,787,999m. contos, resources: 72,747,082m. contos, capital surplus: 1,912,602m. contos and gross proceeds 833,177m. contos.

Weights and Measures. The metric system is the legal standard.

ENERGY AND NATURAL RESOURCES

Electricity. Total production of electrical power in 1995 was 752,672 tonnes of oil equivalent.

In 1994:

	Coal	Oil	Electricity	Others	Total
Imports	3,277,904	17,731,141	194,102	—	21,153,147
Domestic Production	60,333		924,672	1,116,791	2,101,796
Exports	8,047	5,274,826	117,734	—	5,400,607
Primary Energy Consumption	3,328,203	12,636,709	1,001,040	1,116,791	18,082,743
Final Energy Consumption	657,171	8,637,970	2,318,130	993,950	12,607,221

Minerals. Portugal possesses considerable mineral wealth. Production in tonnes (1987): Gold (refined) 0·320; uranium, 167; wolframite, 2,011; coal, 228,648; tin ore, 90; kaolin, 66,736. (1992): Tungsten, 1,870; (1993): Copper, 615,189; non-crystalline limestone, 32,176,852; granite, 17,771,910; marble, 896,315.

Agriculture. The following figures show the production (in 1,000 tonnes) of the chief crops on the mainland:

	1990/1994				1990/1994		
Crop	Average	1994	1995	Crop	Average	1994	1995
Wheat	431·9	462·3	359·8	Fruits			
Maize	655·0	719·6	759·6	apples	257·1	208·4	231·4
Rye	75·4	63·8	36·3	pears	99·8	116·1	73·1
Rice	127·4	131·7	124·6	oranges	168·2	180·0	199·9
Oats	69·8	79·2	57·6	peaches	94·3	91·5	89·6
Barley	92·1	96·2	53·1	Tomatoes	672·4	879·0	838·9
Potatoes	1,323·1	1,265·8	1,378·3	Sunflower	46·2	40·0	26·1
Wine	7,784·1	6,316·0	7,000·0	Tobacco	4·2	4·5	4·8
Olive Oil	370·7	345·4	427·1				

Livestock (1,000 head):

	1993	1994	1995
Cattle	1,323	1,329	1,324
Pigs	2,664	2,416	2,402
Sheep	3,305	3,416	3,428
Goats	836	819	799

Animal products (mainland) in 1996 (1,000 tonnes): Meat, 668·5; milk, 1,437·9; eggs, 87·1; cheese, 51·1.

Forestry. Portugal is a major producer of cork. Estimated production, 1993, 143,000 tonnes. Production of resin was 20,000 tonnes in 1993.

Fisheries. The fishing industry is important. In 1995 there were 12,162 registered fishing vessels (9,402 with motors) (12,620/9,609 in 1994). Registered catches of fish, 1994, 231,710 tonnes.

Species	1994		1995	
	tonnes	escudos	tonnes	escudos
Total	245,956	58,563,219	244,447	61,528,225
Tuna	12,990	2,253,031	22,429	3,569,163
Codfish	4,832	1,496,030	4,494	1,486,011
Mackerel	22,250	3,906,033	20,525	3,650,813
Swordfish	15,921	4,542,898	16,743	4,668,062
Sardine	94,469	5,485,631	87,711	5,345,050
Shellfish	25,541	10,614,753	22,108	12,341,204

INDUSTRY. Output of major industrial products: (in tonnes unless otherwise specified):

Product	1993	1994
Tungsten	615,189	534,553
Ornamental rocks	50,845,077	51,492,899
Rice	108,010	145,253
Refined sugar	303,063	294,126
Compound feedstuff	3,580,956	3,755,207
Beer (hectolitres)	6,661,940	6,901,582
Discontinuous synthetic fibre fabric	62,354	57,055
Knitted fabrics	72,585	73,716
Footwear with leather vamp (1,000 pairs)	70,302	66,104
Wood pulp	1,288,685	1,334,634
Paper and cardboard	817,781	854,740
Petrol	2,742,778	3,532,413
Diesel fuel	3,269,218	4,199,222
Fuel oil	4,994,899	4,694,797
Glass bottles (1,000)	1,889,980	2,290,310
Ready-mix concrete	7,298,558	7,540,566

Ammonia, raw steel, tin, plate and matches are also produced.

Labour. The maximum working week was reduced to 40 hours in 1997. A minimum wage is fixed by the government. Retirement is at 65 years for men and 62 for women. In 1995, out of a working population of 4,754,300 (2,141,100 female), 4,415,900 (1,960,400 female) were employed. Unemployment was 7·1% (8·1% female). Employment (in 1,000) by sector, 1995 (females in parentheses): Agriculture, forestry and fishing, 508·9 (248·0); industry, construction, energy and water, 1,415·3 (446·2); services, 2,491·7 (1,274·2).

Employment by sector (in 1,000):

Sector (Mainland)	4th quarter 1995		4th quarter 1996	
	Total	Men	Total	Men
Total	4,228·8	2,329·0	4,248·9	2,341·1
Agriculture, forestry, hunting and fishing	476·0	238·9	526·3	255·9
Mining and quarrying	17·4	15·8	15·2	14·3
Manufacturing	962·4	562·1	920·0	530·8
Electricity, gas and water	32·0	25·9	31·6	28·0
Construction	337·0	326·2	358·3	341·9
Retail and wholesale trade, repairs, hotels and restaurants	821·4	461·0	831·1	476·8
Transport, storage and communication	171·6	132·5	168·1	132·4
Financial intermediation	332·0	196·8	339·8	203·6
Public administration	312·2	181·0	288·4	171·9
Education	306·9	74·6	284·5	65·6
Health and social work	194·1	53·9	198·6	48·5
Other service activities	265·8	60·3	286·7	71·1

Trade Unions. In 1994 there were 390 unions. An agreement between trade unions, employers and the government for 1997 involved employment, social security, investment, tax reform and education.

FOREIGN ECONOMIC RELATIONS. As at 31 Dec. 1995 the foreign debt was 1,887,300m. escudos and the total debt was 9,223,000m. escudos.

Commerce. In 1995 exports totalled US$22,800m. and imports US$32,600m.

Principal imports, 1994, (in 1m. escudos): Chemical, petroleum, coal, rubber and plastic products, 706,899; transport equipment, 713,835; machinery except electrical, 420,298; electrical machinery and apparatus, 456,091; textiles, 321,262; food, beverages and tobacco, 334,779; crude petroleum and natural gas, 261,758; industrial chemicals, 250,087; other chemical products, 234,451; iron and steel, 134,644.

Principal exports, 1994 (in 1m. escudos): Metal products, machinery and equipment, 782,860; textiles, 425,214; clothing, 376,896; electrical machinery and apparatus, 357,226; footwear, 290,141; chemical, petroleum, coal, rubber and plastic products, 333,142; transport equipment, 204,355; food, beverages and tobacco, 195,021; wood and cork, 189,260; wood products except furniture, 156,120; paper, 164,862; china, pottery and earthenware, 74,623.

Imports and exports to main trade partners, 1994-95 (in 1m. escudos):

| | Imports (c.i.f.) | | Exports (f.o.b.) | |
From or to	1994	1995	1994	1995
EU	3,218,000	3,748,000	2,245,000	2,823,000
Belgium/Luxembourg	152,220	167,000	108,367	108,000
France	574,502	594,000	437,848	494,000
Germany	653,480	742,000	562,788	754,000
Italy	383,685	421,000	99,739	119,000
Japan	127,543	111,000	22,512	27,000
Netherlands	193,328	227,000	160,045	185,000
Spain	890,355	1,064,000	430,771	524,000
EFTA	256,000	143,000	222,000	104,000
OPEC	257,000	258,000	25,000	23,000
UK	295,000	332,000	345,129	389,000
USA	161,991	111,000	153,760	158,000

Tourism. In 1997 tourist revenue increased to 667bn. escudos. Number of visitors, 9·9m. In 1995 there were (in 1,000) 22,875 foreign visitors (21,759 in 1994), including from Spain, 17,141; UK, 1,574; Germany, 1,072; the Netherlands, 407; Italy, 319. There were 1,733 hotel establishments with 204,051 accommodation capacity in 1995.

COMMUNICATIONS

Roads (1995). There were 9,742 km of national roads on the mainland, including 587 km of motorways. On 31 Dec. 1995 the number of light and heavy motor vehicles registered was 4,984,457; motorcycles, 233,182; tractors, 280,012. In 1995 there were 47,785 road accidents with 2,104 victims (1,966 in 1994).

The 11 mile Vasco da Gama bridge across the River Tagus north of Lisbon is the longest in Europe. It opened in March 1998.

Railways. In 1994 total railway length was 3,072 km (1,668 mm and metre gauges), of which 461 km of broad-gauge was electrified. In 1994, 201·4m. passengers were carried and 7·1m. tonnes of freight. There is a metro (19 km) and tramway (94 km) in Lisbon.

Civil Aviation. There are international airports at Portela (Lisbon), Pedras Rubras (Porto), Faro (Algarve), Santa Maria and Lages (Azores) and Funchal (Madeira). The national carrier is the state-owned TAP-Air Portugal, which in 1995 operated 5 A310-300s, 6 A320-200s, 4 A340-300s, 7 B-737-200 Advs, 1 B-737-200C Adv 8 B-737-300s and 5 other aircraft. Airlines in 1994 carried 3·92m. passengers and 61,769 tonnes of freight. Services are also provided by Aeroflot, Aero Lloyd, Air Afrique, Air Belgium, Air France, Air Inter, Air Liberté, Air Malta, Air Toulouse, Alitalia, British Airways, Condor, Delta, El Al, Finnair, Hamburg Airlines, Hapag Lloyd, Iberia, KLM, LAM, Lauda Air, LTU, Lufthansa, Luxair, Royal Air Maroc, Sabena, Swissair, TAAG, Trans World, Transavia, Transportes Aéreos de Cabo Verde, Tunis Air, Varig and Zas.

Shipping. In 1994, 14,190 vessels of 85·44m. tonnes entered the ports; 152,161 passengers embarked and 150,032 disembarked. 16·94m. tonnes of cargo were loaded and 40·92m. tonnes unloaded. On 31 Dec. 1993 there were 323 merchant vessels of 903,604 GRT.

Telecommunications. The number of post offices was 1,015 in 1994. Portugal Telecom (PT) was formed from a merger of 3 state-owned utilities in 1994. It is 51% state-owned. In 1994 there were 3,444,269 main and 32,760 public telephones. There were 5,794 public telexes.

Radiodifusão Portuguesa broadcasts 3 programmes on medium-waves and on FM as well as 3 regional services and an external service, Radio Portugal (English, French, Italian). There are 2 state-owned TV channels (Canal 1 and Radiotelevisão Portuguesa 2) and 2 independent channels, including 1 religious (colour by PAL). Radio Trans Europe is a high-powered short-wave station, retransmitting programmes of different broadcasting organizations. Number of receivers: Radio (1993), 2·2m.; TV set licences (1993), 1,686,513.

Cinemas (1994). There were 175 cinemas and 7·13m. admissions.

Press (1994). There were 23 daily newspapers with a combined circulation of 137,301,000 including 6 in the Azores and 2 on Madeira. There were 988 other periodicals with a combined circulation of 311,545,000.

SOCIAL INSTITUTIONS

Justice. There are 4 judicial districts (Lisbon, Porto, Coimbra and Evora) divided into 47 circuits. In 1994 there were 370 common courts, including 324 of the first instance (71 specialized). There are also 29 administration and fiscal courts.

There are 4 courts of appeal in each district, and a Supreme Court in Lisbon.

Capital punishment was abolished completely in the Constitution of 1976.

In 1994 there were 51 prisons. The prison population as at 1 Jan. 1994 was 11,062 including 10,191 men and 954 inmates aged under 21 years.

Religion. There is freedom of worship, both in public and private, with the exception of creeds incompatible with morals and the life and physical integrity of the people. There were 9·86m. Roman Catholics in 1992.

Education. Compulsory education has been in force since 1911. Adult literacy was 80% in 1990 according to official figures. In 1993–94 there were 5,388 pre-school establishments (3–6 years) with 183,298 pupils. There were 10,308 basic primary establishments (6–10 years) with 586,034 pupils and 43,070 teachers (669 private with 44,647 pupils and 2,257 teachers). There were 1,758 preparatory establishments (6–8 years) with 343,437 pupils.

In 1993–94, secondary education: General Unified schools, 446,676 pupils aged 11–14 years, complementary secondary, 171,409 pupils aged 14–16 years and 104,555 pupils aged 17–18 years; 1,860 lycées with 99,842 pupils aged 14–17 years; 31,975 pupils aged 14–16 years in technical schools (in 1992–93); 22,339 pupils aged 15 onwards in professional schools. There are also establishments for students aged 17–20 years for teaching kindergarten and basic primary pupils.

In 1994–95 there were in the public sector 12 universities, an open university, a technical university, an institute of dentistry and an institute of industrial and business studies. In the private sector there were 4 universities and 1 Roman Catholic university. There were 125,483 students and 10,066 academic staff (not including the open university).

In 1994–95 there were 62 other higher education establishments with 300,573 registered students distributed as follows: University institutions, 139,027; Polytechnics, 49,048, Nursing schools, 4,787; Military and police institutions, 1,190; Other institutions, 1,353; Universities, 46,066; Other establishments, 59,102.

Welfare. In 1994, 2,653,882m. escudos were paid in social security benefits. Cash payments in escudos (and types): 906,880m. (sickness), 297,724m. (disability), 65,538m. (accidents at work), 873,326m. (age), 191,343m. (widows), 20,500m.

(maternity), 116,945m. (family), 13,681m. (promotion of employment), 139,584m. (unemployment), 449m. (accommodation), 6,928m. (destitution).

Health. In 1995 there were 200 hospitals (4·1 hospital beds per 1,000 inhabitants), 383 clinics and 463 medical centres. In 1994 there were 29,031 doctors, 1,197 dentists, 341 dental surgeons and 6,319 pharmacists.

DIPLOMATIC REPRESENTATIVES

Of Portugal in Great Britain (11 Belgrave Sq., London, SW1X 8PP)
Ambassador: José Gregóro Faria.

Of Great Britain in Portugal (35-37 Rua de São Bernardo 33, 1299 Lisbon)
Ambassador: Roger Westbrook, CMG.

Of Portugal in the USA (2125 Kalorama Rd., NW, Washington, D.C., 20008)
Ambassador: Fernando Andresen Guimarães.

Of the USA in Portugal (Ave. das Forcas Armadas, 1600 Lisbon)
Ambassador: Elizabeth Frawley Bagley.

Of Portugal to the United Nations
Ambassador: António Monteiro.

Further Reading

Instituto Nacional de Estatística. *Anuário Estatístico de Portugal/Statistics Year-Book.—Estatísticas do Comércio Externo.* 2 vols. Annual from 1967

Birmingham, D., *A Concise History of Portugal.* CUP, 1993
Corkill, D., *The Portuguese Economy since 1974.* Edinburgh UP, 1993
Laidlar, J., *Lisbon.* [Bibliography] Oxford and Santa Barbara, 1997
Maxwell, K., *The Making of Portuguese Democracy.* CUP, 1995
Opello, W., *Portugal: from Monarchy to Pluralist Democracy.* Boulder (Colo.), 1991
Saraiva, J. H., *Portugal: A Companion History.* Manchester, 1997
Unwin, P. T. H., *Portugal.* [Bibliography] Oxford and Santa Barbara, 1987
Wheeler, D. L., *Historical Dictionary of Portugal.* Metuchen (NJ), 1994

National library: Biblioteca Nacional de Lisboa, Campo Grande, Lisbon.
National statistical office: Instituto Nacional de Estatística (INE), Avenida António José de Almeida, 1000 Lisbon.

MACAO

KEY HISTORICAL EVENTS. Macao was visited by Portuguese traders from 1513 and became a Portuguese colony in 1557. It was soon a principal entrepôt for international trade with China and Japan. Initially sovereignty remained vested in China, with the Portuguese paying an annual rent. In 1848-49 the Portuguese declared Macao a free port and established jurisdiction over the territory. A Sino-Portuguese treaty of 1 Dec. 1887 confirmed Portuguese rights to the territory. Diversion of its trade to Hong Kong, and the opening of the treaty ports by China, left Macao handling only local distributive trade, although its entrepôt role was briefly revived during the closure of the Hong Kong/China border in 1939. It was an Overseas Province of Portugal from 1951-74. In 1976 it became a Territory under Portuguese administration. On 6 Jan 1987 Portugal agreed to return Macao to China in 1999 under a plan in which it would become a special administrative zone of China, with considerable autonomy.

TERRITORY AND POPULATION. The territory, which lies at the mouth of the Pearl River, comprises a peninsula (7·84 sq. km) connected by a narrow isthmus to the People's Republic of China, on which is built the city of Santa Nome de Deus de Macao, and the islands of Taipa (5·79 sq. km), linked to Macao by a 2-km bridge, and Colôane (7·82 sq. km) linked to Taipa by a 2-km causeway (total area, 17·31 sq. km). The total area of Macau 21·45 sq. km. Land is being reclaimed from the sea.

The population (1991 census) was 339,464 (174,858 females). Population as on 31 Dec. 1997 415,850 (215,700 females). The official language is Portuguese, but Cantonese is used by virtually the entire population.

Vital statistics, 1997: Births, 5,468 (13·2 per 1,000 population); marriages, 2,106 (5·1); deaths, 1,413 (3·4); divorces, 320 (0·8); natural increase rate, 1%.

In Dec. 1993, 19,305 foreigners were legally registered including 12,731 from Hong Kong.

CLIMATE. Sub-tropical tending towards temperate. The number of rainy days is more than a third of the year. It is very humid from May to September.

CONSTITUTION AND GOVERNMENT. By agreement with Beijing in 1974, Macao is a Chinese territory under Portuguese administration. An 'organic statute' was published on 17 Feb. 1976. It defined the territory as a collective entity, *pessoa colectiva,* with internal legislative authority which, while remaining subject to Portuguese constitutional laws, would otherwise enjoy administrative, economic and financial autonomy. The Governor is appointed by the Portuguese President, who also appoints up to 7 Under-Secretaries on the Governor's nomination. The Legislative Assembly of 23 deputies, chosen for a 3-year term, comprises 8 members directly elected by universal suffrage, 8 indirectly elected by economic, cultural and social bodies and 7 appointed by the Governor. In April 1990 the Portuguese parliament unanimously approved laws passed by the Legislative Assembly to widen its powers and those of the governor.

At the elections held on 30 Sept. 1992 the electorate was 48,137; turn-out was 55·5%. 50 candidates stood.

Governor: Gen. Vasco Rocha Vieira.

ECONOMY

Budget. In 1995, revenue was 11,033·8m. patacas and expenditure 10,314·9m. patacas. Provisional figures for 1996 are revenue, 8,569·3m; expenditure, 8,545·1m.

Currency. The unit of currency is the *pataca* (MOP) of 100 *avos* which is tied to the Hong Kong dollar at parity. There are coins of 10, 20 and 50 avos and 1 and 5 patacas, and notes of 5, 10, 50, 100, 500 and 1,000 patacas. Inflation was 8·6% in 1995.

Banking and Finance. The bank of issue is the Banco Nacional Ultramarino. The Monetary and Foreign Exchange Authority functions as a central bank (*Director,* António dos Santos Ramos). Commercial business is handled (1993) by 20 banks with 112 branches in Macao, 6 of which are local and 14 foreign (including 4 off-shore banking units). Total banks' deposits, 1993, 53,232·6m. patacas (including 4,679·7m. patacas in current and 15,198·3m. patacas in savings accounts).

ENERGY AND NATURAL RESOURCES

Electricity. Gross production (1993), 1,073m. kWh. In 1996 the electricity consumption per capita was 3,250 kWh. The net import was 174·0m. kWh.

Fisheries. Total catch (1993) was 1,964 tonnes valued at 30,959,470 patacas.

INDUSTRY. The economy is based on gambling and tourism with a light industrial base of textiles and toy-making. In 1996 the number of firms was 1,265 (509 in textiles and clothing). In 1992, output was valued at 14,301,883 patacas. Number of firms (and value of output in 1m. patacas) per sector: textiles, 237 (2,924·40); clothing, 644 (7,316·18); food products, beverages and tobacco, 133 (214·58); paper, paper products, printing and publishing, 137 (306·91); wood and cork, 36 (20·26).

Labour. In 1991, there were 53,536 people declared employed, including 52,427 employed in manufacturing and 1,073 in services. Unemployment was 2·5% in May 1995. In 1996 there was 66·7% employment of which 30·6% were employed in

Public, social and private services; 27·5%, Restaurants and hotels; 20·6%, Manufacturing; 7·5%, Construction and public works; 6·6%, Banks, insurance and services to companies and 7·2% in other employment. Unemployment stood at 4·3%.

FOREIGN ECONOMIC RELATIONS

Commerce. The trade, mostly transit, is handled by Chinese merchants. Imports, in 1994, were US$2,126·2m.; exports, US$1,866m., of which textiles and garments, US$1,371·6m.

In 1995, 29% of imports came from Hong Kong and 22% from China. 42% of exports went to USA, 32% to the EU (mainly Germany, France and UK); clothing accounted for 68·2% of exports, textiles for 10·5% and toys 3·6%.

In 1996 exports were valued at 15,898·5m. patacas of which the main products were: textiles and garments, toys, electronics, footwear, cement, travelling articles, ceramic articles and optical products. The main markets were the EU, USA, China, Japan, Hong Kong and Australia. The total imports were 15,930·7m. pastacas of which the main products were: foodstuff, beverage and tobacco, other consumer goods, raw materials and semi-manfactured goods, capital goods, fuels and lubricants. The main origins were: EU, USA, China, Japan and Hong Kong.

Tourism. In 1995 there were 7·8m. visitors, but only 2·2m. spent one night or more. In 1996 there were 8·2m visitors.

COMMUNICATIONS

Roads. In 1994 there were 90 km of roads. In 1993 there were 63,745 vehicles, of which 32,580 were passenger cars and 2,148 vans and 3,676 lorries. There were 6,185 traffic accidents. In 1996 there were 45,206 registered vehicles of which 41,403 were light load and 3,803 heavy load. There were 5,787 vehicles registered during the year. There are 109 cars per 1,000 inhabitants.

Civil Aviation. An international airport opened in Dec. 1995. There are flights to Vietnam and an air services agreement with Germany.

Shipping. Macao is served by Portuguese, British and Dutch steamship lines. Regular services connect Macao with Hong Kong, 65 km to the north-east.

Telecommunications. There were 206,154 telephones in 1996 and 188 telex instruments. One government and a private commercial radio station are in operation on medium-waves broadcasting in Portuguese and Chinese. Number of receivers (1992), 0·25m. Macao receives television broadcasts from Hong Kong and in 1984 a public bilingual TV station began operating. There were (1992) 70,000 receivers (colour by PAL).

Press. In 1993, there were 11 daily newspapers (4 in Portuguese and 7 in Chinese) and 16 periodicals (5 in Portuguese and 11 in Chinese).

SOCIAL INSTITUTIONS

Justice. There is a judicial district court, a criminal court and an administrative court with 13 magistrates in all. Appeals lie to the Court of Appeal and then the Supreme Court, both in Lisbon.

In 1996 (1995) there were 8,576 (7,181) cases of crimes known to the police, of which 5,460 (4,618) were against property. There were 625 persons in prison in 1996 (482 in 1995).

Religion. The majority of the Chinese population are Buddhists. About 6% are Roman Catholic.

Education. In 1992–93 there were 108 schools and colleges and 3,536 teachers. Numbers of schools and colleges by category: pre-primary, 16 (7 private); pre-primary and primary, 38 (36); private pre-primary, primary and secondary, 14; primary, 10 (3); primary and secondary, 10 (8); private primary and secondary technical, 2; secondary, 8 (6); secondary and teacher training, 1; secondary and tertiary, 1; private secondary and teacher training, 1; teacher training and tertiary, 1; nurses training, 2 (1); tertiary, 7 (1). There were 9 special schools with 72 teachers and 211 enrolments. The University of East Asia, established in 1981 on Taipa, had 1,647 students and 155 teachers in 1991–92

	1994–5	1995–6		1994–5	1995–6
Total students	93,587	96,846	teacher training	318	338
pre-primary	20,476	19,770	nurses training	172	177
primary	45,153	46,703	Higher education	5,655	6,418
secondary	20,624	22,277	Special education	349	359
secondary technical	1,189	1,163	Adult education	38,456	38,506

Health. In 1993 there were 2 general hospitals (1 private) and 41 health centres (26 private) with 892 beds. There were 319 doctors, 13 dentists, 720 nurses and 38 pharmacists. In 1996 there were 517 inhabitants per doctor and 428 per hospital bed.

Further Reading

Direcção de Serviços de Estatística e Censos. *Anuário Estatístico/Yearbook of Statistics Macau in Figures.* Macao, Annual.

Edmonds, R. L., *Macau.* [Bibliography] Oxford and Santa Barbara (CA), 1989

Porter, J., *Macau, the Imaginary City: Culture and Society, 1557 to the Present.* Oxford, 1996

Roberts, E. V., *Historical Dictionary of Hong Kong and Macau.* Metuchen (NJ), 1993

QATAR

Dawlat Qatar

(State of Qatar)

Capital: Doha
Population: 548,000
GDP per head: (PPP$) 18,403
HDI/world rank: 0·840/55

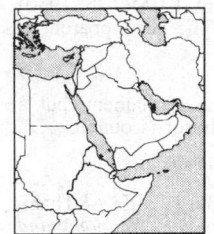

KEY HISTORICAL EVENTS. There is evidence of human habitation in Qatar dating as far back as the 5th or 6th centuries BC. The Greek historian, Herodotus, refers to the seafaring Canaanites as being the original inhabitants of the country. Qatar embraced Islam in the 7th century AD, and since then it has been noticed regularly in the accounts of Arab historians and writers.

Like all of the countries in the area, it eventually came under Turkish rule and control for several centuries. Ottoman power was in fact mostly nominal, with real power being in the hands of local sheikhs and tribal leaders. In 1915 the Turks withdrew, and on 3 Nov. 1916 Qatar signed a protection treaty with Britain. However, British influence was restricted to the supervision of administrative matters.

The dominant economic activity had traditionally been pearl diving, but around 1930 the pearl market collapsed, affecting the whole economy of the country. It was at this time that initial suggestions were being made that oil might be found, and in 1939 oil was discovered in commercial quantities. Although the Second World War delayed progress, exporting began in 1949. This was to change Qatar dramatically. Qatar declared its independence from Britain on 3 Sept. 1971, ending the Treaty of 1916 which was replaced by a Treaty of friendship between the 2 countries. In 1974 the Qatar General Petroleum Corporation was set up, resulting in petroleum extraction coming under national control.

The ruling family, the Al-Thani, arrived in Qatar in the early 18th century and in the mid-19th century moved to the capital, Doha. The family's ancestor, Thani bin Mohammed, was the father of the first Al-Thani sheikh to rule over the entire Qatari peninsula, in the mid-19th century. On 27 June 1995 the Heir Apparent, Sheikh Hamad, deposed his father, the Amir Sheikh Khalifa bin Hamad Al-Thani, while Khalifa was travelling abroad.

TERRITORY AND POPULATION. Qatar is a peninsula running north into the Persian/Arabian Gulf. It is bounded in the south by the United Arab Emirates. An agreement of 26 Oct. 1996 with Saudi Arabia provides for a definitive delimitation of the common frontier by 1998. The territory includes a number of islands in the coastal waters of the peninsula, the most important of which is Halul, the storage and export terminal for the offshore oilfields. Area, 11,437 sq. km; population census (1986) 369,079; estimate, 1996, 548,000; density 47·1 per sq. km.

Area and estimated population of municipalities, 1993:

Municipality	Area (in sq. km)	Population	Municipality	Area (in sq. km)	Population
Doha	131·8	339,471	Al Shamal	901·3	5,347
Al Rayyan	889·2	143,046	Al Ghwayriyah	622·3	2,517
Al Wakra	1,114·0	30,976	Al Jumayliyah	2,564·8	8,674
Umm Salal	492·6	16,785	Jarian Al Batnah	3,714·7	2,518
Al Khour	996·3	10,234			

The capital is Doha, which is the main port. Other towns are Dukhan, the centre of oil production, Umm Said, oil-terminal of Qatar, and Ruwais, Wakra, Al-Khour, Umm Salal Mohammad and Umm-Bab.

Vital statistics rates, 1996 estimates (per 1,000 population). Births, 21·0; deaths, 3·6. Infant mortality (per 1,000 live births), 19·6. Expectation of life in 1996 was 73·3 years (70·75 for males and 75·8 for females). Growth rate, 2·39% per annum.

About 40% of the population are Arabs, 18% Indian, 18% Pakistani and 10% Iranian. Other nationalities make up the remaining 14%.

The official language is Arabic.

CLIMATE. The climate is hot and humid. Doha. Jan. 62°F (16·7°C), July 98°F (36·7°C). Annual rainfall 2·5" (62 mm).

RULER. *The Amir:* HH Sheikh Hamad bin Khalifa Al-Thani, KCMG (b. 1950) assumed power after deposing his father on 27 June 1995. The heir apparent is Sheikh Hamad's third son, Jassem (b. 1978).

CONSTITUTION AND GOVERNMENT. There is no Parliament, but a *Council of Ministers* is assisted by a 30-member nominated Advisory Council.

In March 1998 the government comprised:
Minister of Defence and C.-in-C. of the Armed Forces: The Amir.
Prime Minister, Minister of the Interior: Sheikh Abdullah bin Khalifa Al-Thani.
Deputy Prime Minister: Muhammad bin Khalifa Al-Thani. *Finance, Economy and Trade:* Yusif Husayn Al-Kamal. *Foreign Affairs:* Sheikh Hamad bin Jassem bin Jabr Al-Thani. *Education and Higher Education:* Dr Mohammed Abdulrahim Kafoud. *Justice (Acting):* Ahmed bin Muhammad Ali Al-Subai. *Minister of State for Interior Affairs:* Sheikh Abdullah bin Khalid Al-Thani. *Minister of State for Foreign Affairs:* Ahmed Abdullah Al-Mahmoud. *Minister of State for Cabinet Affairs:* Ali bin Muhammad Al-Khatir. *Minister of Endowments and Islamic Affairs:* Ahmed Abdullah Al-Merri. *Municipal Affairs and Agriculture:* Ali bin Said Al-Khayarin. *Communications and Transport:* Sheikh Ahmed bin Nasser Al-Thani. *Public Health:* Dr Abdulrahman Salem Al-Kawari. *Civil Service Affairs and Housing:* Sheikh Falah bin Jassem bin Jabr Al-Thani. *Electricity and Water:* Ahmed bin Muhammad Ali Al-Subai. *Energy and Industry:* Abdullah bin Hamad Al-Attiyah.

National anthem: There are no words, and the tune is anonymous.

Local government. Qatar is divided into 9 municipalities.

DEFENCE

Army. The Army consists of 1 Royal Guard regiment, 1 tank and 4 mechanized infantry battalions, 1 special forces company and 1 field artillery regiment. Equipment includes 24 AMX-30 main battle tanks. Personnel (1996) 8,500.

Navy. The navy operates 4 new British-built 380-tonne and 3 390-tonne French-built fast missile craft. There is 1 tank landing craft and some 30 boats. There are also 4 quadruple shore-based Exocet missile batteries. Personnel in 1996 totalled 1,800 and the base is at Doha.

Air Force. The Air Force has 6 Mirage F1 fighters and 12 Commando and 14 Gazelle helicopters and 6 Alpha Jet armed trainers and Tigercat surface-to-air missile systems. Personnel (1996) 800 with 11 combat aircraft and 20 armed helicopters.

INTERNATIONAL RELATIONS

Membership. Qatar is a member of the UN, the Arab League and the Gulf Co-operation Council.

ECONOMY

Budget. Revenue (1995–96) US$2,500m.; expenditure US$3,500m.

Currency. The unit of currency is the *Qatari riyal* (QAR) of 100 *dirhams*, introduced in 1973. There are coins of 1, 5, 10, 25 and 50 dirhams, and banknotes of 1, 5, 10, 50, 100 and 500 riyals. The inflation rate in 1993 was 3%.

Banking and Finance. The Qatar Monetary Agency, which functioned as a bank of issue, became the Central Bank in 1995. In 1993 there were 6 domestic and 8 foreign banks with total deposits of 18,870·7m. riyals.

A stock exchange was established in Doha by the Amir's decree in 1995, initially to trade only in Qatari stocks.

Heavy investment in energy development has increased foreign debt from US$1,300m. in 1991 to US$10,400m. in 1997.

Weights and Measures. The metric system is in general use.

ENERGY AND NATURAL RESOURCES

Electricity. Production from main power stations (1993) 5,425·8m. kWh.

Oil. Proven reserves (1995) 3,700m. bbls. Output, 1997, 600,000 bbls. a day. Production is likely to increase to 700,000 bbls. a day by 2000.

Gas. The North Field, the world's biggest single reservoir of gas and containing 12% of the known world gas reserves, is half the size of Qatar itself. Development cost is estimated at US$25m.

Water Resources. 2 main desalination stations have a daily capacity of 167·6m. gallons of drinkable water. A third station is planned, with a capacity of 40m. gallons a day. Total water production in 1993 (well field and distillate) was 20,136·1m. gallons.

Agriculture. 10% of the working population is engaged in agriculture. Percentage of total agricultural area under various crops in 1993: Vegetables, 28%; green fodder, 23%; cereals, 22%; palm dates, 20% and fruits, 7%. Government policy aims at ensuring self-sufficiency in agricultural products. In 1993 there were 875 farms. Production (1993) in tons: Cereals, 5,368; dates, 10,723; fruits, 1,038; vegetables, 36,851; meat, 2,595; poultry meat, 3,672; milk and dairy products, 29,917; eggs, 3,303.

Livestock (1993): Cattle, 11,651; camels, 42,906; sheep, 165,500; goats, 142,270; chickens, 3·0m.; horses, 1,273.

Fisheries. Catch, 1993, 6,994 tonnes. The state-owned Qatar National Fishing Company has 3 trawlers and its refrigeration unit processes 10 tonnes of shrimps a day.

INDUSTRY. 1993 output (in 1,000 tonnes): Ammonia, 763·0; urea, 825·0; reinforcing steel bars, 608·6; ethylene, 351·6; polyethylene, 181·5; sulphur, 68·2; flour, 33·0; bran, 11·5; butane, 454·7; propane, 646·1. There is an industrial zone at Umm Said.

Labour. In 1993, 604 manufacturing and mining firms with more than 10 employees employed a total of 36,456 persons.

FOREIGN ECONOMIC RELATIONS

Commerce. Imports in 1995, US$2,900m.; exports, US$2,000m. The main exports are petroleum products (75%), steel and fertilizers. Main imports are machinery and equipment, consumer goods, food and chemicals. The principal partners for exports in 1994 were Japan (61%), Australia (5%), followed by the United Arab Emirates and Singapore, and for imports, Germany (14%), Japan (12%), UK (11%), USA (9%) and Italy (5%).

Tourism. In 1994 there were 241,000 tourists.

COMMUNICATIONS

Roads. In 1995 there were about 1,210 km of roads, of which 1,089 km were paved. In 1993 there were 205,852 registered vehicles including 2,851 motorcycles and 76 fatal accidents with 84 deaths.

Civil Aviation. Gulf Air (owned equally by Qatar, Bahrain, Oman and the UAE. For details *see* BAHRAIN: Civil Aviation), operates daily services from Bahrain. There is also a Qatari airline, Qatar Airways. Services are also provided by Air India, Air Lanka, Alyemda, American Airlines, Balkan, Biman Bangladesh, Egyptair, Emirates, Iran Air, Kuwait Airways, Middle East Airlines, Pakistan Airlines, Royal Jordanian, Saudia, Sudan Airways, Syrian Airlines and Yemenia. In 1993, 704,105 passengers arrived, 702,447 departed and 346,045 were in transit; 12,607 aircraft arrived and departed, 22,873 tons of cargo and mail were received and 7,852 tons were dispatched.

Shipping. In 1995, sea-going vessels totalled 0·92m. GRT, including oil tankers, 0·33m. GRT, and container ships, 91,536 GRT. In 1993, 1,383 vessels with a total tonnage of 66,255,841 GRT and 2,697,629 tonnage of cargo was discharged.

Telecommunications. There were 28 post offices in Doha and other towns in 1993. There were 177,130 telephones and 450 telex subscribers in 1992. Broadcasting is the responsibility of the state-run Qatar Broadcasting Service and Qatar Television Service. There were 175,000 radios in 1991 and 205,000 television receivers in 1992 (colour by PAL).

Cinemas. In 1993 there were 3 cinemas with 281,128 attendance.

Press. In 1993 there were 4 daily, 1 weekly newspaper and 9 magazines.

SOCIAL INSTITUTIONS

Justice. The Judiciary System is administered by the Ministry of Justice which comprises three main departments: Legal affairs, courts of justice and land and real estate register. There are 5 Courts of Justice proclaiming sentences in the name of H. H. the Amir: The Court of Appeal, the Labour Court, the Higher Criminal Court, the Civil Court and the Lower Criminal Court. The death penalty is in force.

All issues related to personal affairs of Moslems under Islamic Law embodied in the Holy Quran and Sunna are decided by Sharia Courts.

Religion. The population is almost entirely Moslem.

Education. Adult literacy rate was 79·4% in 1995 (79·2% among males and 79·9% among females). There were, in 1992–93, 34,163 pupils at 105 primary schools, 16,150 pupils at 50 preparatory schools, 10,987 pupils at 38 secondary schools and 782 male students at 3 specialist schools. There were 48 Arab and foreign private schools with 27,895 pupils and 1,692 teachers in 1992–93. The University of Qatar had 7,294 students and 881 academic staff in 1993–94.

Students abroad (1993–94) numbered 1,262. In 1992–93, 3,567 men and 2,639 women attended night schools and literacy centres.

Health. There were 3 public hospitals (including 1 for women and 1 for gynaecology and obstetrics) with a total of 1,103 beds in 1993. There were 24 health centres in 1993. In 1993 there were 644 doctors, 71 dentists, 160 pharmacists and 1,718 qualified nurses.

DIPLOMATIC REPRESENTATIVES

Of Qatar in Great Britain (1 South Audley St., London, WIY 5DQ)
Ambassador: Ali M. Jaidah.

Of Great Britain in Qatar (POB 3, Doha, Qatar)
Ambassador: David A. Wright.

Of Qatar in the USA (600 New Hampshire Ave., NW, Washington, D.C., 20037)
Ambassador: Saad Muhammad Al-Kubaysi.

Of the USA in Qatar (Fariq Bin Omran, Doha)
Ambassador: Patrick N. Theros.

Of Qatar to the United Nations
Ambassador: Nasser Bin Hamad Al-Khalifa.

Of Qatar to the European Union
Ambassador: Vacant.

Further Reading

Central Statistical Organization. *Annual Statistical Abstract.*
Unwin, P. T. H., *Qatar.* [Bibliography] Oxford and Santa Barbara (CA), 1982

National statistical office: Central Statistical Organization, Presidency of the Council of Ministers, Doha.

ROMANIA

România

Capital: Bucharest
Population: 22·73m.
GDP per head: (PPP$) 4,037
HDI/world rank: 0·748/79

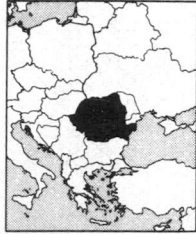

KEY HISTORICAL EVENTS. The Romanians cherish their Latin origins and language, which date from Trajan's occupation of Dacia. The foundation of the feudal 'Danubian Principalities' of Wallachia and Moldavia in the late 13th and early 14th centuries marks the beginning of an era. (Transylvania, also part of the modern Romania by this time, was in the hands of the Magyars). The Orthodox church and quarrelsome nobility were nearly as powerful as the princes, a balance of power which the expansionist Turks were able to manipulate after the 14th century. Wallachia and Moldavia became tribute-paying vassals without ever being formally incorporated into the Ottoman Empire. The nobility acted as the Turks' agents until 1711 when, suspected of pro-Russian sentiments (Peter the Great was on their northern doorstep), they were replaced by Greek merchant adventurers, the Phanariots.

The Phanariot period of ruthless extortion and corruption was ameliorated by Russian interference. Bessarabia was annexed and Russian support after the rebellion of Tudor Vladimirescu in 1821 brought about the restoration of Romanian princes. Between 1829 and 1834 the foundations of the modern state were laid under a Russian protectorate, but in the revolutionary episode of 1848 Russian interference became repressive. After the Crimean War, Bessarabia was restored to Moldavia, and under the auspices of the great powers elections were held in both principalities which resulted in the election of Alexandru Cuza to both thrones in Jan. 1859; the Moldavian and Wallachian assemblies were fused in 1862. Cuza's reforms brought him into conflict with the nobility, who deposed him in 1866. Carol of Hohenzollern was brought to the throne, and a constitution adopted based on that of Belgium of 1831. Romania was formally declared independent by the Treaty of Berlin of 1878, and became a kingdom (the 'Old Kingdom') in 1881. Romania regained Bessarabia by the Treaty, and gained Dobrudja from Bulgaria in the Balkan wars of 1913.

This was a period of expansion for an economy firmly in the hands of the land-owners (represented by the Conservative party) and nascent industrialists (of the Liberal party). The condition of the peasantry remained miserable, and the rebellion of 1907 was an expression of their discontent. Romania joined the First World War on the allied side in 1916. The spoils of victory brought Transylvania (with large Hungarian and German populations), Bessarabia, Bukovina and Dobrudja into the union with the 'Old Kingdom'. The centralizing constitution of 1923 reduced the autonomy of the Transylvanian Romanians; the National Peasant party of Iuliu Maniu was formed in 1926 in protest. The Liberals had broken the power of the Conservatives by the land reform of 1920, and continued in office until the (relatively fair) elections of 1928, at which the Peasants gained 330 seats to the Liberals' 13. Carol II's advent to the throne was delayed by a sexual scandal; when he acceded in 1930 Maniu resigned. Hit by the world recession, Romania was increasingly drawn into Germany's economic orbit. Against this background the fascist Iron Guard assassinated the Liberal leader in 1934. Carol himself adopted increasingly totalitarian modes of rule, banning political parties by his constitution of 1938. Following Nazi and Soviet annexations of Romanian territory in 1940, he abdicated in favour of his son Michael. The government of the fascist Ion Antonescu declared war on the USSR on 22 June 1941. On 23 Aug. 1944, Michael with the backing of a bloc of opposition parties deposed Antonescu and switched sides.

The armistice of Sept. 1944 gave the Soviet army control of Romania's territory.

This, and the 'spheres of influence' diplomacy of the Allies, predetermined the establishment of communism in Romania. A government under the pro-communist peasant leader Petru Groza was installed in March 1945. Transylvania was restored to Romania (though it lost Bessarabia and Southern Dobrudja), and large estates were broken up for the benefit of the peasantry. Elections in Nov. 1946 were held in an atmosphere of intimidation and fraudulence; the communist bloc received 376 seats, the Peasants 33, the Liberals 3. In 1947, the latter parties were abolished, Michael was forced to abdicate and a people's republic was proclaimed. The communist leader, Gheorghe Gheorghiu-Dej purged himself of his fellow leaders in the early 1950s. Under his successor, Nicolae Ceausescu, Romania took a relatively independent stand in foreign affairs while becoming increasingly repressive and impoverished domestically.

An attempt by the authorities on 16 Dec. 1989 to evict a Protestant pastor, László Tökés, from his home in Timişoara, provoked a popular protest which escalated into a mass demonstration against the government. Despite the use of armed force against the demonstrators, the uprising spread to other areas. On 21 Dec. the government called for an official rally in Bucharest, but this turned against the régime. A state of emergency was declared but the Army went over to the rebels and Nicolae and Elena Ceausescu fled the capital. A dissident group which had been active before the uprising, the National Salvation Front (NSF), proclaimed itself the provisional government.

The Ceausescus were captured and after a secret two hour trial by military tribunal, summarily executed on 25 Dec. on four charges of genocide, undermining the power of the state, undermining the economy and embezzlement. Fighting by pro-Ceausescu 'Securitate' forces continued until 27 Dec. It is estimated that 7,689 people were killed in the uprising.

On 26 Dec. 1989 Ion Iliescu, leader of the National Salvation Front, and Petre Român, were sworn in as President and Prime Minister respectively. But the Iliescu led administration, while committed to reform, was inhibited by its communist origins. The economy stalled and the debts piled up. After seven years, Iliescu was voted out of office and his government replaced by a four party coalition led by President Emil Constantinescu and Prime Minister Victor Ciorbea.

TERRITORY AND POPULATION. Romania is bounded in the north by Ukraine, in the east by Moldova, Ukraine and the Black Sea, south by Bulgaria, south-west by Yugoslavia and north-west by Hungary. The area is 237,500 sq. km (91,699 sq. miles). Population (1994), 22,730,622 (11,573,815 females; 54·7% urban); density, 95·4 per sq. km.

Vital statistics, 1994: Births, 246,736; deaths, 266,101; stillborn, 1,623; infant deaths, 5,894; marriages, 154,221; divorces, 39,663. Rates (per 1,000 population): Live births, 10·9; deaths, 11·7; marriages, 6·8; divorces, 1·7; stillborn (per 1,000 live births), 6·5; infant mortality (per 1,000 live births), 23·9. Growth rate, −0·8 per 1,000. Expectation of life in 1994: Males, 65·9 years; females, 73·3. Measures designed to raise the birthrate were abolished in 1990, and abortion and contraception legalized. There were 0·62m. abortions in 1992.

Romania is divided into 41 counties (*judeţ*), of which the capital, Bucharest (Bucuresti), is one.

County	Area in sq. km	Population (1994)	Capital	Population (1994)
Bucharest	1,820	2,339,156		
Alba	6,231	408,457	Alba Iulia	72,962
Arad	7,652	482,144	Arad	187,876
Argeş	6,801	679,868	Piteşti	184,171
Bacău	6,606	742,901	Bacău	207,730
Bihor	7,535	633,629	Oradea	221,885
Bistriţa-Năsăud	5,305	328,786	Bistriţa	87,646
Botoşani	4,965	462,370	Botoşani	128,322
Braşov	5,351	642,764	Braşov	324,210
Brăila	4,724	391,923	Brăila	235,763
Buzău	6,072	515,202	Buzău	149,610

County	Area in sq. km	Population (1994)	Capital	Population (1994)
Caraş-Severin	8,503	370,058	Reşiţa	96,197
Călăraşi	5,074	336,657	Călărasi	78,874
Cluj	6,650	727,033	Cluj-Napoca	326,017
Constanţa	7,055	747,441	Constanţa	348,575
Covasna	3,705	232,951	Sf. Gheorghe	68,073
Dîmboviţa	4,036	558,518	Tîrgovişte	99,235
Dolj	7,413	758,895	Craiova	306,825
Galaţi	4,425	642,983	Galati	326,728
Giurgiu	3,511	305,661	Giurgiu	73,997
Gorj	5,641	397,927	Tîrgu Jiu	98,050
Harghita	6,610	347,145	Miercurea-Ciuc	46,854
Hunedoara	7,016	547,180	Deva	77,218
Ialomiţa	4,449	305,454	Slobozia	56,719
Iaşi	5,469	815,368	Iaşi	339,889
Maramureş	6,215	539,718	Baia Mare	149,975
Mehedinţi	4,900	330,017	Drobeta-Turnu Severin	118,383
Mureş	6,696	607,355	Tîrgu Mureş	166,315
Neamţ	5,890	584,364	Piatra-Neamţ	125,622
Olt	5,507	520,871	Slatina	87,012
Prahova	4,694	874,219	Ploieşti	254,136
Satu Mare	4,405	398,401	Satu Mare	131,431
Sălaj	3,850	264,448	Zalău	70,358
Sibiu	5,422	448,474	Sibiu	170,528
Suceava	8,555	708,571	Suceava	117,314
Teleorman	5,760	477,527	Alexandria	59,414
Timiş	8,692	691,797	Timişoara	327,830
Tulcea	8,430	269,311	Tulcea	97,616
Vaslui	5,297	463,832	Vaslui	80,316
Vâlcea	5,705	436,989	Râmnicu Vâlcea	114,286
Vrancea	4,863	394,257	Focşani	100,900

At the 1992 census the following ethnic minorities numbered over 100,000: Hungarians, 1,624,959 (mainly in Transylvania); Gipsies, 401,087; Germans, 119,462. A *Council of National Minorities* made up of representatives of the government and ethnic groups was set up in 1993.

The official language is Romanian.

CLIMATE. A continental climate with a large annual range of temperature and rainfall showing a slight summer maximum. Bucharest. Jan. 27°F (−2·7°C), July 74°F (23·5°C). Annual rainfall 23·1" (579 mm). Constanţa. Jan. 31°F (−0·6°C), July 71°F (21·7°C). Annual rainfall 15" (371 mm).

CONSTITUTION AND GOVERNMENT. A new Constitution was approved by a referendum on 8 Dec. 1991. Turn-out was 66%, and 77·3% of votes cast were in favour. The Constitution defines Romania as a republic where the rule of law prevails in a social and democratic state. Private property rights and a market economy are guaranteed.

The head of state is the *President*, who must not be a member of a political party, elected by direct vote for a maximum of 2 4-year terms. The President is empowered to veto legislation unless it is upheld by a two-thirds parliamentary majority. The National Assembly consists of a 343-member *Chamber of Deputies* and a 143-member *Senate*; both are elected for 4-year terms from 41 constituencies by modified proportional representation, the number of seats won in each constituency being determined by the proportion of the total vote. 15 seats in the Chamber of Deputies are reserved for ethnic minorities. There is a 3% threshold for admission to either house. Votes for parties not reaching this threshold are redistributed.

There is a *Constitutional Court*.

The first rounds of the presidential and parliamentary elections were held on 3 Nov. 1996. Turn-out was 77%. There were 7 presidential candidates. President Iliescu won with 32·3% of votes cast. At the second run-off round of the presidential elections on 17 Nov. turn-out was 75·9%. Emil Constantinescu was elected with 54·41% of votes cast.

At the parliamentary elections 6 parties passed the 3% threshold. The Democratic Convention of Romania (CDR) bloc won 31% of votes cast; the Party of Social Democracy in Romania, 22%; the Social Democratic Union bloc (USD), 13%; the Hungarian Democratic Union of Romania (UDMR), 6·7%; the Greater Romania Party, 4·5%; the Romanian National Unity Party, 4·2%. Seats gained:

Party	Chamber of Deputies seats	Senate seats
Democratic Convention of Romania		
Christian Democratic National Peasants Party (PNTCD)	88	31
National Liberal Party (PNL)	25	17
Romanian Ecological Party	5	1
Romania's Alternative (PAR)	3	1
Romanian Ecological Federation	1	1
Party of Social Democracy of Romania (PDSR)	91	41
Social Democratic Union		
Democratic Party (PD)	43	22
Romanian Social Democratic Party	10	1
Hungarian Democratic Union of Romania (UDMR)	25	11
Greater Romania Party	19	8
Romanian National Unity Party	18	7

President: Emil Constantinescu (b. 1939; CDR; sworn in 29 Nov. 1996).

On 30 March 1998 the *Prime Minister*, Victor Ciorbea, and his Cabinet resigned after concerted pressure from coalition partners.

National anthem: 'Deșteaptă-te, Române, din somnul cel de moarte' ('Wake up, Romanians, from your deadly slumber'); words by A. Muresianu, tune by A. Pann.

Local government. Councils are elected at county (*județ*) level (on a proportional representation system) and municipal level (on a first-past-the-post system), and mayors are also elected. Elections were held in June 1996; turn-out was 56·4%. The PDSR won 26·49% of the mayoral vote, the CDR 26·45%, but the latter gained more county council seats.

DEFENCE. Military service is compulsory for 12 months in the Army and Air Force and 18 months in the Navy.

Army. The 4 Army Areas consist of 2 tank and 8 motor rifle divisions; 4 mountain, 2 artillery, 3 anti-aircraft and 2 surface-to-surface missile brigades; and 4 artillery, 3 anti-tank and 4 airborne regiments. Equipment includes 146 T-34, 822 T-55, 30 T-72, 620 TR-85 and 225 TR-580 main battle tanks. Strength (1997) 129,350 (90,000 conscripts), and 400,000 reservists. The Ministry of the Interior operates a paramilitary Frontier Guard (22,300 strong), a Gendarmerie (10,000) and a Security Guard (46,800).

Navy. The fleet comprises 1 ex-Soviet diesel submarine, 1 Romanian-built missile-armed destroyer with a hangar for 2 helicopters, 5 frigates, 3 missile-armed corvettes, 6 fast missile craft, 32 fast torpedo craft, 4 offshore, and 8 inshore patrol vessels, 2 minelayer/mine countermeasure support ships and 35 small minesweepers. The Danube flotilla counts 4 river monitors (100 mm guns) and some 20 river patrol craft. Auxiliaries include 2 logistic ships, 3 small tankers, 2 oceanographic ships, 1 training ship and 2 tugs. A force of naval infantry some 8,000 strong in 1996 is equipped with 120 tanks and some 120 artillery pieces, but lacks amphibious transport.

There is a coastal defence force numbering 800 (1996) organized into 4 main batteries of artillery with 32 130 mm guns and 10 anti-aircraft batteries.

Headquarters of the Navy is at Mangalia with the main base at Constanța, and of the Danube flotilla at Braila. Personnel in 1997 totalled 17,500 (9,500 conscripts).

Air Force. The Air Force numbered some 47,600, with 300 combat aircraft and 80 armed helicopters in 1997. These were organized into 12 interceptor squadrons with MiG-21, MiG-23 and MiG-29 fighters, 3 ground-attack and close-support squadrons with IAR-93 fighter-bombers, and 1 reconnaissance squadron of L-39s. There were also more than 150 training aircraft, 28 An-24/26/30 transports and about 200 helicopters (Mi-8, Alouette and Puma), some armed. 'Guideline' and 'Gainful' surface-to-air missiles were operational, and short-range surface-to-surface missiles have been displayed.

INTERNATIONAL RELATIONS

Membership. Romania is a member of the UN, the Council of Europe, the Central European Initiative, the NATO Partnership for Peace and is an Associate Partner of the WEU and an Associate Member of the EU.

ECONOMY

Policy. By 1995 some 4,000 of the 6,200 state companies were offered for privatization, but only 18% of these had been sold. Legislation of 1995 offered 60% of shares in state companies to citizens in exchange for privatization coupons, and 40% to foreign investors.

With the change of government, the pace of reform has accelerated. There are more than 80 economic reform laws in the planning stage. Privatization of the banks has begun with the Romanian Development Bank. Foreign investment is actively encouraged. Most of the companies still in state hands will be privatized by the end of 1998. The liquidation of bankrupt state enterprises is proceeding slowly. Even so, the freeing of prices and ending of many subsidies has pushed up inflation to 20% plus. Also, there is the risk of a political breakdown which could damage the fragile economy.

Legislation of Nov. 1995 compensates former owners of 0·2m. nationalized properties. Compensation is limited to the ownership of 1 home if lived in or 50m. lei.

Performance. Real GDP growth was 4·5% in 1996 (−2·0% in 1997).

Budget. Revenue and expenditure (in 1m. lei) for calendar years:

	1991	1992	1993	1994
Revenue	496,779	1,363,884	3,792,352	8,860,117
Expenditure	537,875	1,626,908	4,128,779	10,930,320

In 1994 sources of revenue (in 1m. lei) included: Fiscal revenues, 8,318,838; profits tax, 1,904,144; tax on wages, 3,220,600; tax on commodity circulation, 774,488; customs duties, 562,698; non-fiscal revenues, 532,052; capital revenue, 9,227. Expenditure: Socio-cultural, 3,216,891; education, 1,490,795; health, 997,982; arts, 101,155; social assistance, 15,231; child benefit, 364,226; pensions, 213,837; defence, 1,184,676; public order, 661,398; state power, 496,521; economy, 3,648,099.

VAT was introduced in July 1993.

Currency. The monetary unit is the *leu*, pl. *lei* (ROL) notionally of 100 *bani*. There are coins of 1, 3, 5, 10, 25, 50 and 100, and notes of 100, 200, 500, 1,000, 5,000 and 10,000 lei. Foreign exchange reserves (excluding gold) were US$1,705m. in 1995. Inflation was 151% in 1997 (57% in 1996).

Banking and Finance. The National Bank of Romania (founded 1880, nationalized 1946; *governor*, Mugur Isarescu) is the central bank and bank of issue under the Minister of Finance. It manages monetary policy. In May 1996 total assets of commercial banks were 37,000,000m. lei, 67% of which were controlled by 4 state-owned banks: Bancorex (for foreign trade), Banca Agricola, Romanian Commercial Bank and Romanian Development Bank. Total assets, 1994, 20,415,121m. lei. Savings were 617,692m. lei in 1993.

A stock exchange re-opened in Bucharest in 1995.

Weights and Measures. The Gregorian calendar was adopted in 1919. The metric system is in use.

ENERGY AND NATURAL RESOURCES

Electricity. Installed electric power 1994: 22,060,000 kW.; output, 1994, 55,136m. kWh (13,046m. kWh hydroelectric). A nuclear power plant at Cernavoda began working in April 1996.

Oil. Oil production in 1994 was 6·7m. tonnes.

Minerals. The principal minerals are oil and natural gas, salt, brown coal, lignite, iron and copper ores, bauxite, chromium, manganese and uranium. Output, 1994 (in 1,000 tonnes): Iron ore, 951; coal, 6,307; lignite, 36,385; methane gas (cu. metres, 1991), 17,252m.

Agriculture. Romania has the biggest agricultural area in Eastern Europe after Poland. In 1997, 30% of the workforce was employed in agriculture, which contributed 22% of GDP. There were 14,797,500 ha of agricultural land in 1994, including (in 1,000 ha): Arable, 9,338; meadows, 1,494; pasture, 3,378; vineyards, 2,398 and orchards and nurseries, 289. There were 3,205,200 ha of irrigated land.

Production (in 1,000 tonnes): Wheat and rye, 7,000; barley, 2,134; oats, 497; maize, 9,343; potatoes, 2,947; sunflower seeds, 764; sugar-beet, 2,764.

Livestock, 1995 (in 1,000): Cattle, 3,481 (including milch cows, 1,963); pigs, 7,758; sheep, 10,897; goats, 745; horses, 784; poultry, 70,157. There were 161,223 tractors in 1994.

A law of Feb. 1991 provided for the restitution of collectivized land to its former owners or their heirs up to a limit of 10 ha. Land may be resold, but there is a limit of 100 ha on total holdings. Landless peasants received a distribution from the residue. There are 74 state farms; peasants receive shares in their equity worth up to 10 ha. Collective farms may become private co-operative associations. By 1997 72% of farmed land was in private hands. The government has pledged an end to state ownership of farms.

Forestry. Total forest area was 6·37m. ha in 1994 including 1·91m. ha coniferous, 1·9m. ha beech and 1·14m. ha oak. 14,744 ha were afforested in 1994.

INDUSTRY. In 1994 there were 33,824 industrial enterprises, of which 2,182 were state-controlled, 374 local government-controlled and 554 co-operatives. 50 enterprises employed more than 5,000 persons; 31,043 fewer than 100.

Output of main products in 1994 (in tonnes): Pig-iron, 3,496; steel, 5,800; steel tubes, 472; rolled steel, 4,510; chemical fertilizers, 1,163; sulphuric acid, 491; caustic soda, 291; paper, 288; cement, 5,998; sugar, 231; edible oils, 194; plastics, 304; chemical fibres, 83. In 1,000 units: Tractors, 14; TV sets, 452; washing machines, 109.

Labour. The employed population in 1994 was 10·0m., of whom 3·6m. worked in agriculture and 3·4m. in industry and building. In 1994 46% of the total workforce, and 39·4% of the industrial workforce, were women. Men retire at 62, women at 57. A law of 1991 established an unemployment fund and provides for retraining unemployed persons. A minimum monthly wage was set in 1993; it was 45,000 lei in 1994. The average monthly wage was 141,951 lei in 1994. Unemployment was 8·9% in Dec. 1996.

Trade Unions. In 1994 the National Confederation of Free Trade Unions-Fratia had 65 branch federations and 3·7m. members. The other major confederations were Alfa Cartel and the National Trade Union Bloc.

FOREIGN ECONOMIC RELATIONS. Foreign debt was US$6,600m. in 1995. In Nov. 1993 the USA granted most-favoured-nation status.

Foreign investors may establish joint ventures or 100%-owned domestic companies in all but a few strategic industries. After an initial 2-year exemption, profits are taxed at 30%, dividends at 10%. Foreign investors register with the Romanian Development Agency. The 1991 constitution prohibits foreign nationals from owning real estate.

Commerce. In 1996 exports totalled US$7,200m. and imports US$9,000m. In 1997, exports totalled US$8,000m. and imports US$9,2000m.

In 1996 Romania's main export markets were: Germany (18·7%); Netherlands (4·2%); Italy (16·7%); France (5·6%); Turkey (5·0%); Eastern Europe (7·4%). Romania's main import markets were: Germany (17·1%); Italy (15·6%); France (5%); Russia (12·6%); Eastern Europe (6·8%).

Tourism. In 1994 5·9m. foreign nationals visited Romania.

COMMUNICATIONS

Roads. There are 72,828 km of roads (113 km of motorways, 14,683 km of main roads). At least two-thirds of the main roads are in urgent need of repair.

Railways. Length of standard-gauge route in 1994 was 10,887 km, of which 3,866 km were electrified; there were 427 km of narrow-gauge lines and 60 km of 1,524 mm gauge. Freight carried in 1995, 105·1m. tonnes; passengers, 211m. There is a metro (57 km) and tram/light rail network (353 km) in Bucharest, and tramways in 13 other cities.

Civil Aviation. Tarom (*Transporturi Aeriene Române*), the 70%-state-owned airline, operated 2 A310-300s, 1 B-707-320C, 5 B-737-300s, 26 ex-Soviet and 10 other aircraft in 1995. It also provided internal services and services to Amsterdam, Athens, Beijing, Beirut, Belgrade, Berlin, Brussels, Budapest, Cairo, Cologne, Copenhagen, Düsseldorf, Frankfurt, Istanbul, London, Moscow, Paris, Prague, Rome, Sofia, Tel Aviv, Vienna, Warsaw and Zürich. Services are also provided by Aeroflot, Air France, Alitalia, Austrian Airlines, Balkan, British Airways, Czech Airlines, Delta, El Al, Hemus Air, Iberia, JAT, KLM, Lufthansa, Malév, Royal Jordanian, Swissair, Syrian Airlines and Turkish Airlines.

Bucharest's airports are at Baneasa (internal flights) and Otopeni (international flights). Air transport in 1994 carried 1·98m. passengers and 46,000 tonnes of freight.

Shipping. In 1995 the merchant marine comprised 297 vessels totalling 4·81m. DWT, of which 30 (20·78% of tonnage) were registered under foreign flags. Total GRT was 2·69m., including oil tankers, 0·44m. GRT, and container ships, 15,160 GRT. The main ports are Constanţa and Agigea on the Black Sea and Galati and Braila on the Danube. In 1994 sea-going transport carried 30·2m. tonnes of freight; river transport, 7·99m. tonnes and 0·99m. passengers.

Telecommunications. There were 10,802 post offices in 1994. Number of telephone subscribers, 1994, 2,750,000. Mobile phones were introduced in 1997, with 2 private operators. A law of June 1994 puts broadcasting under parliamentary control through the supervision of the National Audiovisual Council. *Radio-televiziunea Română* broadcasts 3 radio programmes on medium-waves and FM. In March 1995, 436 cable TV stations, 66 local TV stations and 135 local radio stations were registered. There is also radio and TV transmission in Hungarian and German. There are 2 independent TV channels. Radio licences, 1994, 3·93m.; TV (colour by PAL), 4·05m.

Cinemas. There were, in 1994, 713 cinemas, of which 394 were for standard-sized films. These latter had 162,442 seats; admissions were 24·72m. 18 full-length films were made in 1994 (4 in 1990).

Press. There were, in 1994, 97 daily papers and 870 periodicals, including 13 dailies and 92 periodicals in minority languages. 4,074 book titles were published in 1994 in 50·2m. copies (33 titles in minority languages).

SOCIAL INSTITUTIONS

Justice. Justice is administered by the Supreme Court, the 41 county courts, 81 courts of first instance and 15 courts of appeal. Lay assessors (elected for 4 years) participate in most court trials, collaborating with the judges. In 1994 there were 2,471 judges. The *Procurator-General* exercises 'supreme supervisory power to ensure the observance of the law'. The Procurator's Office and its organs are independent of any organs of justice or administration, and only responsible to the Grand National Assembly, which appoints the Procurator-General for 4 years. The death penalty was abolished in Jan. 1990 and is forbidden by the 1991 constitution. In 1994 criminal sentences were awarded to 95,795 persons (11,710 females, 9,121 juveniles) and 31,190 persons were imprisoned.

Religion. The State Secretariat for Religious Denominations oversees religious affairs. Churches' expenses and salaries are paid by the State. There are 14 Churches, the largest being the Romanian Orthodox Church. It is autocephalous, but retains dogmatic unity with the Eastern Orthodox Church. It is organized into 12 dioceses grouped into 5 metropolitan bishoprics and headed by Patriarch Teoctist Arapasu. There are some 11,800 churches, 2 theological colleges and 6 'schools of cantors', as well as seminaries. The Uniate (Greek Catholic) Church (which severed its connection with the Vatican in 1698) was suppressed in 1948 but in 1990 was re-legalized. Property seized by the state in 1948 was restored to it, but not property which had passed to the Orthodox Church.

Religious affiliation at the 1992 census: Romanian Orthodox, 19,762,135; Roman Catholic, 1,144,820; Protestant, 801,577; Uniate, 228,377; Pentecostal, 220,051; Baptist, 109,677; Seventh Day Adventist, 78,658; Unitarian, 76,333; Moslem, 55,988.

Education. Education is free and compulsory from 6 to 16, consisting of 8 years of primary school and 2 years of secondary (gymnasium). Further secondary education is available at *lycées*, professional schools or advanced technical schools.

In 1994–95 there were 12,665 kindergartens with 37,603 teachers and 715,514 children; 13,963 primary and secondary schools with 168,702 teachers and 2,532,169 pupils, 1,276 *lycées* with 60,514 teachers and 757,673 pupils; 761 professional schools with 7,313 teachers and 288,221 pupils; and 596 advanced technical institutes with 1,728 teachers and 45,321 students. In 1994–95 primary and secondary education in Hungarian was given to 154,222 pupils by 11,555 teachers and in German to 13,586 pupils by 808 teachers.

In 1994–95 there were 19 universities, 16 specialized universities (agriculture, 4; medicine and pharmacy, 5; petroleum and gas, 1; technical, 6), a polytechnic institute, a merchant navy institute, a school of political and administrative studies and 9 specialized academies (architecture; dramatic art; economics; fine arts; 2 music; physical education and sport; theatre and film; visual arts). The adult literacy rate is 96·9%.

Health. In 1994 there were 174,900 hospital beds and 47,990 doctors (including 6,163 dentists).

Social Security. In 1994 pensioners comprised 3·44m. old age and retirement, 374,000 disability, 585,000 successor allowance, 58,000 war invalidity and dependants, 20,000 social assistance and 1,478,000 retired farmers. These drew average monthly pensions ranging from 12,254 to 77,960 lei. In 1997 social security spending was raised by more than 2% of GDP to 10·4%.

DIPLOMATIC REPRESENTATIVES

Of Romania in Great Britain (4 Palace Green, London, W8 4QD)
Ambassador: Radu Onofrei.

Of Great Britain in Romania (24 Strada Jules Michelet, 70154 Bucharest)
Ambassador: Christopher D. Crabbe, CMG.

Of Romania in the USA (1607 23rd St., NW, Washington, D.C., 20008)
Ambassador: Mircea Geoana.

Of the USA in Romania (7–9 Strada Tudor Arghezi, Bucharest)
Ambassador: Alfred H. Moses.

Of Romania to the United Nations
Ambassador: Ion Gorița.

Of Romania to the European Union
Ambassador: Constantin Ene.

Further Reading

Comisia Nationala pentru Statistica. *Anuarul Statistic al României/Romanian Statistical Yearbook.* Bucharest, annual.—*Revista de Statistica.* Monthly

Deletant, A. and D., *Romania* [Bibliography]. Oxford and Santa Barbara (CA), 1985
Gallagher, T., *Romania after Ceausescu; the Politics of Intolerance.* Edinburgh Univ. Press, 1995
Rady, M., *Romania in Turmoil: a Contemporary History.* London, 1992
Ratesh, N., *Romania: the Entangled Revolution.* New York, 1991

National statistical office: Comisia Nationala pentru Statistica, 16 Libertatii Ave., sector 5, Bucharest
Website: http://www.kappa.ro/clients/cns/

THE PROSPECTS FOR DEMOCRACY IN RUSSIA

Margot Light

In 1946 George Orwell pointed out that 'in the case of a word like democracy not only is there no agreed definition, but the attempt to make one is resisted ... it is almost universally felt that when we call a country democratic, we are praising it: consequently the defenders of every kind of regime claim that is a democracy...'[1] However, few people in the socialist states and even fewer in Western liberal democracies took the word democracy in the term *socialist democracy* at face value. Even if there was no single agreed definition of democracy, therefore, there was general consensus about what it was *not*: one-party states, elections (no matter how regularly they took place) which offered no choice between candidates, and the absence of opportunity to exercise elementary civil rights (which may or may not have been guaranteed in the constitution) did not qualify. By the same count, these were the things which would have to change in states which wanted to become democratic.

The process of transition from an authoritarian system is called democratization. Those states which succeed in making the transition become consolidated democracies. It is a hazardous process, and failure can result in reversion to authoritarianism or dictatorship. Democratization is particularly difficult when it has to be accompanied by the replacement of a centralized state-dominated economic system with a market economy, and where there is no previous history or experience of democracy. This was the situation in the Russian Federation when the Soviet Union disintegrated in 1991. The president and government of Russia declared that their aim was the establishment of democracy and a market economy. This article considers the progress they have made in achieving their goal. It evaluates whether Russia has moved beyond the transition stage of democratization towards democratic consolidation. It also examines what the major challenges are to the further development of Russian democracy in the next few years.

Democratization in Russia

The meaning of democracy is still contested. Moreover, there is little agreement about what type of constitution (parliamentary, semi-presidential or presidential) will best ensure its survival. The democratic progress of the post-socialist states, however, is usually evaluated according to the extent to which they have established representative liberal democracy. This means that they should have a political system in which elected officials are chosen and peacefully removed in relatively frequent, fair and free elections in which practically all adults are eligible to participate. The elected officials should have constitutionally vested control over government policy. Most adults should quality to run for public office. Citizens should be guaranteed political rights and civil liberties, including access to sources of information which are not monopolized by the government (or by any other single group), an effectively enforced right to freedom of expression (including the right to criticize officials, government conduct, the prevailing political, economic and social system, and the dominant ideology), and the right to form and join autonomous associations (including political associations, such as political parties and interest groups).

If one applies these criteria of representative liberal democracy, Russia has certainly embarked upon democratic transition. Relatively free elections have been held on a number of occasions. Most adults can run for public office and a large number of candidates from a variety of different political parties have contested the elections on the basis of universal adult suffrage. Many Russians criticize the government and its policies, the prevailing system and the market ideology. Russians have access to various sources of information (although very few of them are objective or balanced). On the face of it, therefore, Russia is well on the way to democratic consolidation.

In fact, Russia's democratic journey began in March 1990, well before the disintegration of the Soviet Union in December 1991, when the first free elections for national-level office took place. After March 1990, however, Russia's democratic progress was patchy. The Soviet Union was dissolved in December 1991 without reference to the Soviet government, the constitution, or Soviet citizens. President Yeltsin suspended and then bombarded the Russian Supreme Soviet in September/October 1993. Both acts were, in effect, *coups d'état*. Freedom of association has sometimes been denied to certain Russian citizens (for example, the communist party was suspended and then banned between August 1991 and February 1993), and so has freedom of the press (the publication of the communist newspaper *Pravda* was obstructed in the run up to the December 1993 election). The attack on Chechnya in December 1994 bore little resemblance to democratic process. Elections may be free, but they are not always fair. Contenders in the 1996 presidential elections had unequal access to the media. In the hope of further gain, financiers who had already been enriched by economic reform subsidised the election campaigns of some candidates in the 1995 and 1996 elections, giving them great advantage over those who had no private funding.

Many of these actions have been defended in the name of democracy. Until the end of 1993 Russia operated under an unsatisfactory, much amended constitution which dated from Soviet times. The Supreme Soviet, responsible for day-to-day legislation, was indirectly elected by delegates to the Congress of People's Deputies, themselves elected by universal suffrage and charged with setting the direction of policy and approving members of government. The constitution was vague about the division of power both between these two bodies and the government, and between them, the government, and the executive president, elected by popular national poll in June 1991. This semi-presidential system with its lack of clarity about the separation of power proved inadequate when living conditions deteriorated as a result of economic reform. The Supreme Soviet and Congress were determined to obstruct further change, and turned into an intractable opposition to the president and government. As long as the president had temporary emergency powers to rule by decree, he could ignore parliament's opposition. When the Congress revoked his emergency powers in March 1993, however, Russia became virtually ungovernable. The president abrogated the constitution, dissolved the Congress and the Supreme Soviet and dismissed all locally elected councils. He decided that Russia needed a strong presidential system and set about framing a new constitution to institute it.

The constitution adopted in December 1993 established a bicameral Federal Assembly. It is responsible for approving the budget and confirming the president's appointment of the prime minister and some members of his cabinet (however, the ministers of defence, interior, foreign affairs and the intelligence services were made directly responsible to the president). The Duma, the lower house, can initiate legislation, but the president can veto their laws. He can also rule by decree. If the Duma persistently opposes government policy or attempts to remove the government, the president can dissolve it and call new elections. Thus it is extremely difficult for elected parliamentarians to exercise the kind of control over government policy envisaged in a representative democracy. The president, elected by national poll, can be impeached, but only by a two-thirds majority in both the Duma and the upper house, the Council of the Federation. Amending the constitution is even more difficult: in addition to a two-thirds majority of both houses, it requires the approval of two-thirds of the 89 constituent territories of the federation. The judiciary in Russia is not independent. Judges are appointed by the president and funded by the federal budget. The judicial system is inefficient and slow and many judges are alleged to be corrupt. The chairman of the Constitutional Court is also appointed by the president, although parliament has to approve him. It would be difficult, therefore, for the legislature to change the constitution to gain more control over government policy, or to remove a president who had lost his commitment to democratic change. In short, so much political authority is concentrated in the hands of the president and his government that Russia has been called a 'superpresidential system'.

Despite the overwhelming power accorded to the central executive branch of government by the constitution, the Russian government frequently has difficulty in implementing its policies. Russia is a curious federation. Although there is a federal treaty which is intended to apply to all the 89 units which constitute the federation, many of the units have signed separate power-sharing agreements with the central government which give them considerable autonomy. But even those regions which have not yet negotiated their own treaties frequently ignore laws which are applicable across the country. The more prosperous federal units have gained the right to retain a significant proportion of their assets for local use instead of paying them into the central budget. That leaves the federal government with insufficient income to assist the poorer regions. Their consequent disillusion with market reforms is reflected in the fact that they tend to vote against reformist parties in elections. A further cause of hardship is the fact that the government has immense difficulty in collecting taxes, and often has too little revenue to pay its suppliers, its employees or state pensions. The government seems incapable of imposing law and order, and crime and corruption have risen to unprecedented rates in Russia. The constitution may accord great power to the executive, therefore, but the authority of the central government simply does not reach many of its constituents.

The major reason for disbanding the Supreme Soviet in 1993 was the hope that new elections would produce a parliament more amenable to the government's reform policies. The 1993 and 1995 elections failed to do this. The Duma is frequently bitterly opposed to the president and the government and it uses what little power it has to obstruct legislation, wielding its budgetary powers and adopting resolutions which contradict government policy. They are not binding resolutions, but they embarrass the government and president and often make Russian domestic policy and foreign affairs seem inconsistent and confusing.

In short, confrontational politics predominates in Russia, and the negotiations and compromise among political elites that make democracies governable occur only intermittently, and usually after a period of bitter dispute. There is little understanding or acceptance by the ruling elite and its supporters of the concept of loyal opposition. Similarly, those who are opposed to government policy, including the people who call for stronger government, do not seem to acknowledge the legitimate right of government to govern.

The mass participation in political activity which was a striking feature of the early period of Soviet and Russian democratization has subsided into widespread apathy. Opinion polls reveal that the public has no respect for politicians, little trust in the political process, and it dislikes president and government only slightly less than it despises parliament. Although freedom of expression is guaranteed, media ownership favours the ruling political elite and a small group of very wealthy businessmen. This not only limits the opportunity for others to exercise their right to express their opinions, but effectively rules out objective non-partisan journalism. Furthermore, the regular cooption of financiers into prominent political positions attests to the political power of big business. In other words, inequalities of financial and social resources have an increasing political impact in Russia, suggesting that what is becoming established is not democracy, but oligarchy.

Despite this dismal record, some elements of democracy were instituted in Russia between December 1991 and September 1993, and a more sustained process of democratization began after the December 1993 election. Government and opposition have made some concessions in the past two years, and periods of defiance have alternated with attempts to cooperate. Although both ruling elites and opposition forces frequently warn of impending civil strife and war, the extreme confrontation of 1993 has not been repeated. The 1995 parliamentary and 1996 presidential elections both took place, notwithstanding many demands to postpone them. At the very least, this suggests general acceptance that political leaders should be chosen through competitive elections and recognition that policy conflicts must be settled through parliamentary procedure. It seems that procedural democracy, however flawed, has been institutionalized in Russia. The transition stage has, therefore, been successfully concluded.

Nevertheless, Russia has not yet achieved democratic consolidation. Successful democratic consolidation can be judged by the 'two-turnover test', according to which democracy is considered established if, after democratic transition, the incumbents lose the first election and give up power peacefully, and their successors lose the second election and also voluntarily relinquish power.[2] The results of the elections in 1995 and 1996, and particularly the re-election of President Yeltsin, mean that political power has not yet changed hands peacefully after electoral defeat. Russia has instituted procedural democracy, therefore, but its democratic consolidation is not yet assured. Moreover, there are a number of challenges to democracy in Russia that will have to be met if liberal democracy is to survive.

Challenges to Russian Democracy

As we have seen, a number of undemocratic actions have been justified in Russia on the grounds that they were the only way to defend democracy. This is one of the gravest dangers to democratic consolidation in Russia. Whether or not the threats were real, the argument that the ends justify the means is one that can be wielded by those opposed to democracy as well as those who wish to defend it. Orwell once pointed out that if totalitarian methods are employed, the time may come when they will be used against, rather than for, democracy. Neither president nor opposition have resorted to force since 1993, but the easy recourse in Russia by both government and opposition to threats of impending civil strife and war serves to exacerbate confrontation and to discourage respect for democratic procedure.

The 1993 Russian constitution aggravates this danger. The concentration of power in the hands of the president, and the extraordinary difficulty of removing him by constitutional means might have been considered necessary in 1993, but it places responsibility for the future fate of Russian democracy in the hands of one person and it encourages the use of unconstitutional means to remove him. It also means that the task of amending the constitution is urgent: it can only be done by a president who is committed to democracy and who has the capacity to understand why the present provisions are dangerous. Waiting for a generally unacceptable president to be elected will be too late.

There is another reason why the 1993 constitution is inimical to democratic consolidation. It gives too little legislative power and insufficient responsibility to the Duma. This is not just a question of counterbalancing executive power and holding government to account. Being a legislator requires competence, and negotiating and learning to compromise need practice. Balancing between obligations to constituents and the interests of the country is a delicate art. The present constitution neither enables parliamentarians to acquire these capabilities nor instils the habits of democracy. On the contrary, Duma delegates are encouraged to be irresponsible, to oppose for the sake of opposition and to put their own short-term interests before those of their constituents or the country.

The absence of strong political parties is a feature common to many democratizing states. The lack of a functioning multi-party system hampers democratic development. Without national parties little aggregation of interests takes place. Numerous small parties lead to fragmented parliaments in which unstable coalitions are formed. This can make it difficult to pass coherent legislation, or to offer concerted opposition to the government. Furthermore, political parties enable their members to hold their leaders accountable for their actions. Russia displays these features. It has weak and ineffective political parties. What makes it different from other post-socialist states, however, is that no reformist communist party with a social democratic programme has been established. The absence of centrist parties produces a polarization of politics in Russia. The Communist Party of the Russian Federation is the country's only strong political party with a national-level organization, and its leader, Gennady Zyuganov, consistently tops the opinion polls. The Communist Party tends to ally itself with fundamentalist nationalist groups, and nationalism can be a pernicious force in a multinational country. Russian nationalism arouses non-Russian nationalism, with the attendant danger that secessionist movements will cause the disintegration of the Russian Federation. The government response to further drives for secession is likely to be as harsh as it was in the case of Chechnya. Democracy is bound to be the victim.

Many of the calls to abandon the 1995 and 1996 elections were provoked by fear that the 'red-brown coalition' would gain power and reverse the reforms. Other appeals to cancel the elections came from wealthy businessmen who were afraid they would lose their often ill-gotten gains. In return for their financial support during the elections many were rewarded with official positions within the government or the presidential bureaucracy. This interweaving of political and financial power is antithetical to democratic development. Similarly, corruption within the political elite and suspicion that there are connections between big business, political leaders and organized crime discredit government and increase the public's disillusion with the political process.

Rising crime and corruption interfere with democratic consolidation because they are used to justify undemocratic laws. But the absence of law and order also fuels an aspect of Russian political culture which is among the greatest threats to democracy. Many Russians admire strong leadership and believe that it is the only way to reimpose law and order. They combine this with the conviction that Russia has a unique route to democracy which goes via authoritarian rule. The danger, therefore, is not so much that democracy will fail of its own accord, but that Russians will deprive themselves of it in the mistaken belief that an authoritarian ruler will promote democracy when the time is right, rather than simply entrench his power.

There is, therefore, a long way to go before Russian democratic consolidation is secure and there are many challenges and pitfalls along the way. However, the imminent demise of Russian democracy has been regularly predicted since the attempted putsch of August 1991. Democracy may have become misshapen, but it has not yet fallen. There is room, therefore, for cautious optimism about Russia's democratic prospects, just as long as Russians continue to defend their democracy—using only democratic means.

Margot Light is Reader in International Relations at the London School of Economics and Political Science

[1] George Orwell, 'Politics and the English Language', *The Collected Essays, Journalism and Letters of George Orwell*, Volume 4, London, Secker & Warburg, 1968, pp 132-3.

[2] Samuel P. Huntington, *The Third Wave: Democratization in the Late Twentieth Century*, Norman and London: University of Oklahoma Press, 1991, p. 267.

RUSSIA

Rossiiskaya Federatsiya

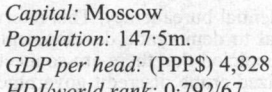

Capital: Moscow
Population: 147·5m.
GDP per head: (PPP$) 4,828
HDI/world rank: 0·792/67

KEY HISTORICAL EVENTS. At the end of the 17th century the Russian Empire embraced much of eastern Europe and northern and central Asia. The Empire was governed as an autocracy under the Romanovs who had ruled since 1613.

On 8 March 1917 a revolution broke out. The Duma parties, on 12 March, set up a Provisional Committee of the State Duma, while the factory workmen and the insurgent garrison of Petrograd elected a Council (Soviet) of Workers' and Soldiers' Deputies. Soviets were also elected by the workmen in other towns, in the Army and Navy and, as time went on, by the peasantry. On 15 March 1917 Tsar Nicholas II abdicated, and the Provisional Committee, by agreement with the Petrograd Soviet, appointed a Provisional Government and, on 14 Sept., proclaimed a republic. However, a political struggle went on between the supporters of the Provisional Government—the Mensheviks and the Socialist Revolutionaries—and the Bolsheviks who advocated the assumption of power by the Soviets. When they had won majorities in the Soviets of the principal cities and of the armed forces on several fronts, the Bolsheviks organized an insurrection through a Military-Revolutionary Committee of the Petrograd Soviet. On 7 Nov. 1917 the Committee arrested the Provisional Government and transferred power to the second All-Russian Congress of Soviets. This elected a new government, the Council of People's Commissars, headed by Lenin.

On 25 Jan. 1918 the third All-Russian Congress of Soviets issued a Declaration of Rights of the Toiling and Exploited People, which proclaimed Russia a Republic of Soviets of Workers', Soldiers' and Peasants' Deputies; and on 10 July 1918 the fifth Congress adopted a constitution for the Russian Soviet Federal Socialist Republic (RSFSR). In the course of the following civil war other Soviet republics were set up in the Ukraine, Belorussia and Transcaucasia. These first entered into treaty relations with the RSFSR and then, in 1922, joined with it in a closely integrated Union.

The Union of Soviet Socialist Republics (USSR) was formed by the union of the RSFSR, the Ukrainian Soviet Socialist Republic, the Belorussian Soviet Socialist Republic and the Transcaucasian Soviet Socialist Republic; the Treaty of Union was adopted by the first Soviet Congress of the USSR on 30 Dec. 1922. In Oct. 1924 the Uzbek and Turkmen Autonomous Soviet Socialist Republics and in Dec. 1929 the Tadzhik Autonomous Soviet Socialist Republic were declared constituent members of the USSR, becoming Union Republics.

From about 1929 Stalin's authority was supreme. Resistance to agricultural collectivization was ruthlessly suppressed. A series of Five-Year Plans (1928, 1933, 1937, 1946 and 1951) transformed the USSR into a powerful industrial state. Opposition in party and government was crushed by the purges of 1933 and 1936-38.

At the eighth Congress of the Soviets on 5 Dec. 1936, a new constitution of the USSR was adopted. The Transcaucasian Republic was split up into the Armenian Soviet Socialist Republic, the Azerbaijan Soviet Socialist Republic and the Georgian Soviet Socialist Republic, each of which became constituent republics of the Union. At the same time the Kazakh Soviet Socialist Republic and the Kirghiz Soviet Socialist Republic, previously autonomous republics within the RSFSR, were proclaimed constituent republics of the USSR.

In Sept. 1939 (under a secret clause of the 10-year non-aggression signed with Nazi Germany on 23 Aug. 1939) Soviet troops occupied eastern Poland as far as the 'Curzon line', which in 1919 had been drawn on ethnographical grounds as the eastern frontier of Poland, and incorporated it into the Ukrainian and Belorussian

Soviet Socialist Republics. In Feb. 1951 some districts of the Drogobych Region of the Ukraine and the Lublin Voivodship of Poland were exchanged.

On 31 March 1940 territory ceded by Finland was joined to that of the Autonomous Soviet Socialist Republic of Karelia to form the Karelo-Finnish Soviet Socialist Republic, which was admitted into the Union as the 12th Union Republic. On 16 July 1956 the Supreme Soviet of the USSR altered the status of the Karelo-Finnish Republic from that of a Union Republic of the USSR to that of an Autonomous (Karelian) Republic within the RSFSR.

On 2 Aug. 1940 the Moldavian Soviet Socialist Republic was constituted as the 13th Union Republic. It comprised the former Moldavian Autonomous Soviet Socialist Republic and Bessarabia (44,290 sq. km, ceded by Romania on 28 June 1940), except for the districts of Khotin, Akerman and Izmail, which together with Northern Bukovina (10,440 sq. km), were incorporated in the Ukrainian Soviet Socialist Republic. The Soviet-Romanian frontier thus constituted was confirmed by the peace treaty with Romania, signed on 10 Feb. 1947. On 29 June 1945 Ruthenia (Sub-Carpathian Russia, 12,742 sq. km) was by treaty with Czechoslovakia incorporated into the Ukrainian Soviet Socialist Republic.

On 3, 5 and 6 Aug. 1940 Lithuania, Latvia and Estonia were incorporated in the Soviet Union as the 14th, 15th and 16th Union Republics respectively. The change in the status of the Karelo-Finnish Republic reduced the number of Union Republics to 15.

After the defeat of Nazi Germany it was agreed by the governments of the UK, the USA and the USSR that part of East Prussia should be embodied in the USSR. The area (11,655 sq. km), which includes the towns of Königsberg (renamed Kaliningrad), Tilsit (renamed Sovyetsk) and Insterburg (renamed Chernyakhovsk), was joined to the RSFSR by decree of 7 April 1946.

By the peace treaty with Finland, signed on 10 Feb. 1947, the province of Petsamo (Pechenga), ceded to Finland on 14 Oct. 1920 and 12 March 1946, was returned to the Soviet Union. On 19 Sept. 1955 the Soviet Union renounced its treaty rights to the naval base of Porkkala-Udd and on 26 Jan. 1956 completed the withdrawal of its forces from Finnish territory.

In 1945, after the defeat of Japan, the southern half of Sakhalin (36,000 sq. km) and the Kurile Islands (10,200 sq. km) were, by agreement with the Allies, incorporated in the USSR. However, Japan has since asked for the return of the Etorofu and Kunashiri Islands as not belonging to the Kurile Islands proper. The Soviet government informed Japan on 27 Jan. 1960 that the Habomai Islands and Shikotan would be handed back to Japan on the withdrawal of American troops from Japan.

Nikita Khruschev, Secretary-General of the Party, criticized the regime of Stalin who died in 1953 at the Twentieth Party Congress in 1956. This encouraged a liberalizing of the Russian-backed communist regimes of Hungary and Poland, and later Czechoslovakia (1968) which the USSR crushed with its forces and those of the Warsaw Pact (established 1955). A policy of 'peaceful co-existence' with the West, especially after the war scare with the USA in 1962 over Cuban missles, led to years of strained relations with China. After 1985, with Mikhail Gorbachev as Secretary-General of the Communist Party, a new period of *glasnost* (openness) and *perestroika* (reconstruction) was inaugurated. But desperate economic problems helped to accelerate liberalization and in 1991 the Soviet Union broke up into its constituent parts.

After the dissolution of the USSR in Dec. 1991, Russian became one of the founding members of the Commonwealth of Independent States. Boris Yeltsin was elected President in June 1991. A period of confrontation in 1992-93 between President Yeltsin and parliament culminated on 21 Sept. in a presidential decree on 'gradual constitutional reform' which suspended the operations of parliament, called new parliamentary elections for Dec. and assumed emergency executive powers. Parliament and the Constitutional Court rejected this action, and parliament proclaimed Vice-President Rutskoi acting president. The USA, the EC and other countries expressed support for President Yeltsin, as did Ukraine and Belarus. Many deputies refused to leave the parliament building and mounted an armed guard which was cordoned off by pro-Yeltsin forces. Public demonstrations and counter-demonstrations began on 26 Sept. After a week in which deputies remained in the parliament building, some thousands of armed anti-Yeltsin demonstrators assembled on 3 Oct. and were urged to seize the Kremlin and television centre. Shots were fired and there were fatal casualties. On 4 Oct. troops took the parliament building by storm after a 10-hour assault in which 140 people died. Vice-President Rutskoi and Speaker Khasbulatov were stripped of their offices and arrested.

In Feb. 1994 parliament amnestied not only those arrested after the occupation of the parliament building in Sept.-Oct. 1993, but also the instigators of the failed *coup* against the Soviet government in Aug. 1991.

TERRITORY AND POPULATION. Russia is bounded in the north by various seas (Barents, Kara, Laptev, East Siberian) which join the Arctic Ocean, and in which is a fringe of islands, some of them large. In the east Russia is separated from the USA (Alaska) by the Bering Strait; the Kamchatka peninsula separates the coastal Bering and Okhotsk Seas. Sakhalin Island, north of Japan, is Russian territory. Russia is bounded in the south by North Korea, China, Mongolia, Kazakhstan, the Caspian Sea, Georgia, the Black Sea and Ukraine, and in the west by Belarus, Latvia, Estonia, the Baltic Sea and Finland. Kaliningrad (the former East Prussia) is an exclave on the Baltic Sea between Lithuania and Poland in the west. Russia's area is 17,075,400 sq. km. Its 1989 census population was 147,021,869 (53·3% female, 73·6% urban), of whom 81·5% were Russians, 3·8% Tatars, 3% Ukrainians, 1·2% Chuvash, 0·9% Bashkir, 0·8% Belorussians, and 0·7% Mordovians. Chechens, Germans, Udmurts, Mari, Kazakhs, Avars, Jews and Armenians all numbered 0·5m. or more. Population estimate, 1997, 147·501m. (female, 53%; urban, 73%). Age structure: 16-29 years, 34%; 30-44, 42%; 45+, 24%.

Vital statistics rates, 1996 (per 1,000 population): Birth, 8·9; death, 15·7; natural increase, −5·5; 1995: marriage, 7·3; divorce, 4·5; infant mortality, 18·1. There were 3·1m. induced abortions in 1994. There were 61·9 divorces per 100 marriages in 1995.

There were 915,000 immigrants in 1995, mainly from the former Soviet republics. In Jan. 1995 there were 702,451 refugees, mostly from Tajikistan, Georgia, Azerbaijan, Chechnya and Ingushetia.

The 2 principal cities are Moscow, the capital, with a population (in 1m.) of 8·6 and St Petersburg (formerly Leningrad), 4·8. Administrative breakdown of the Russian Federation, population and territory, 1 Jan. 1997:

	Population (in 1,000)	Territory (in 1,000 sq. km)		Population (in 1,000)	Territory (in 1,000 sq. km)
North	5,833	1,466	Tula Oblast	1,800	26
Arkhangelsk Oblast	1,506	587	Vladimir Oblast	1,637	29
Nenets Autonomous			Yaroslavl Oblast	1,443	36
Okrug	55	178	*Volgo-Vyatka*	8,404	263
Republic of Karelia	780	172	Republic of Chuvash	1,359	18
Republic of Komi	1,172	416	Kirov Oblast	1,623	121
Murmansk Oblast	1,030	145	Republic of Mary-El	764	23
Vologda Oblast	1,344	146	Mordovian Republic	950	26
North-west	8,017	197	Nizhy Novgorod Oblast	3,710	75
St Petersburg City	4,774	n/a	*Central Black Earth*	7,863	168
Leningrad Oblast	1,677	86	Belgorod Oblast	1,477	27
Novgorod Oblast	738	55	Kirsk Oblast	1,341	30
Pskov Oblast	827	55	Lipetsk Oblast	1,248	24
Central	29,751	485	Tambov Oblast	1,301	34
Bryansk Oblast	1,473	35	Voronezh Oblast	2,495	52
Ivanovo Oblast	1,256	24	*Volga*	16,890	536
Kaluga Oblast	1,096	30	Astrakhan Oblast	1,029	44
Kostroma Oblast	801	60	Republic of Kalmykia	317	76
Moscow Oblast	6,573	47	Penza Oblast	1,555	43
Moscow City	8,637	n/a	Samara Oblast	3,763	54
Orel Oblast	910	25	Saratov Oblast	2,726	100
Ryazan Oblast	1,316	40	Republic of Tatarstan	3,763	68
Smolensk Oblast	1,166	50	Ulianovsk Oblast	1,490	37
Tver Oblast	1,642	84	Volgograd Oblast	2,702	114

	Population (in 1,000)	Territory (in 1,000 sq. km)		Population (in 1,000)	Territory (in 1,000 sq. km)
North Caucasus	17,778	355	Yamal-Nenets		
Republic of Dagestan	2,121	50	Autonomous Okrug	493	750
Chechen Republic	862	19	*Eastern Siberia*	9,407	4,123
Ingush Republic	303	n/a	Republic of Buryatia	1,050	351
Kabaardino-Balkar			Chita Oblast	1,288	432
Republic	789	13	Aginskoe Buryat		
Krasnodarsk Krai	5,066	76	Autonomous Okrug	78	19
Republic of Adygeya	449	8	Irkutsk Oblast	2,785	768
North-Osetian Republic	664	8	Ust-Orda Buryat		
Rostov Oblast	4,415	101	Autonomous Okrug	138	22
Stavropol Krai	2,672	67	Krasnoyarsk Krai	3,095	2,340
Karachevo-Cherkess			Taimyr (Dolgano-Nenets)		
Republic	436	14	Autonomous Okrug	54	862
Urals	20,410	824	Evenk Autonomous		
Republic of			Okrug	25	768
Bashkortostan	4,134	144	Republic of Khakasia	584	62
Chelyabinsk Oblast	3,675	88	Republic of Tuva	310	171
Kurgan Oblast	1,105	71	*Far East*	7,421	6,216
Orenburg Oblast	2,226	124	Amur Oblast	1,016	364
Perm Oblast	2,997	161	Kamchatka Oblast	402	472
Komi-Permyatsk			Koriak Autonomous		
Autonomous Okrug	160	33	Okrug	40	302
Sverdlovsk Oblast	4,668	195	Khabarovsk Krai	1,555	825
Udmurt Republic	1,636	42	Jewish Autonomous		
Western Siberia	15,087	2,427	Area	207	36
Altai Krai	2,675	169	Magadan Oblast	251	1,199
Republic of Altai	202	93	Chukchi Autonomous		
Kemerovo Oblast	3,042	96	Okrug	87	738
Novosibirsk Oblast	2,745	178	Primorskii Krai	2,239	166
Omsk Oblast	2,174	140	Sakhalin Oblast	632	87
Tomsk Oblast	1,072	317	Republic of Sakha		
Tyumen Oblast	3,177	1,435	(Yakutia)	1,032	3,103
Khanty-Mansy			Kaliningrad Oblast	935	15
Autonomous Okrug	1,314	523	Russian Federation	147,501	17,075

CLIMATE. Moscow. Jan. −9·4°C, July 18·3°C. Annual rainfall 630 mm. Arkhangelsk. Jan. −15°C, July 13·9°C. Annual rainfall 503 mm. St. Petersburg. Jan. −8·3°C, July 17·8°C. Annual rainfall 488 mm. Vladivostok. Jan. −14·4°C, July 18·3°C. Annual rainfall 599 mm.

CONSTITUTION AND GOVERNMENT. The Russian Soviet Federative Socialist Republic (RSFSR) adopted a constitution in April 1978. In June 1990, pending the promulgation of a new constitution, it adopted a declaration of sovereignty by 544 votes to 271. It became a founding member of the CIS in Dec. 1991, and adopted the name 'Russian Federation'. A law of Nov. 1991 extended citizenship to all who lived in Russia at the time of its adoption and to those in other Soviet republics who requested it.

There is a 19-member *Constitutional Court*, whose functions under the 1993 Constitution include making decisions on the constitutionality of federal laws, presidential and government decrees, and the constitutions and laws of the subjects of the Federation. It is governed by a Law on the Constitutional Court, adopted in July 1994. Judges are elected for non-renewable 12-year terms.

At a referendum on 25 April 1993 the electorate was 107·3m.; turn-out was 69·2m. 4 questions were put: Confidence in President Yeltsin (58·7% of votes cast); approval of economic reforms (53% of votes cast); early presidential elections (31·7% of the electorate); early parliamentary elections (43·1% of the electorate). This referendum had no constitutional effect, however.

Voting was held on 12 Dec. 1993 on the adoption of a new constitution and the election of a new parliament for a 2-year term. The electorate was 106,170,335; turn-out was 54·8%. The constitution was approved by 58·4% of votes cast, and came into effect on 24 Dec. 1993.

According to the 1993 Constitution the Russian Federation is a 'democratic federal legally-based state with a republican form of government'. The state is a secular one, and religious organizations are independent of state control. Individuals have freedom of movement within or across the boundaries of the Federation; there is freedom of assembly and association, and freedom to engage in any entrepreneurial activity not forbidden by law. All citizens have a right to housing, to free medical care, and to a free education. The state itself is based upon a separation of powers and upon federal principles, including a Constitutional Court. The most important matters of state are reserved for the federal government, including socio-economic policy, the budget, taxation, energy, foreign affairs and defence. Other matters, including the use of land and water, education and culture, health and social security, are for the joint management of the federal and local governments, which also have the right to legislate within their spheres of competence. A central role is accorded to the *President*, who defines the 'basic directions of domestic and foreign policy' and represents the state inter-nationally. The President is directly elected for a 4-year term, and for not more than 2 consecutive terms; he or she must be at least 35 years old, a Russian citizen, and a resident in Russia for at least the previous 10 years. 1m. signatures are needed to validate a presidential candidate, no more than 7% of which may come from any one region or republic. The President has the right to appoint the prime minister, and (on his nomination) to appoint and dismiss deputy prime ministers and ministers, and may dismiss the government as a whole. In the event of the death or incapacity of the President, the Prime Minister becomes head of state.

Boris Yeltsin became President for a 5-year term at the elections of 12 June 1991, gaining 57·3% of the votes cast against 5 opponents. Presidential elections took place in 2 rounds in 1996. In the first round on 16 June 11 candidates stood. The electorate was 104m.; turn-out was 69·8%. President Yeltsin won 35·28% of votes cast, Gennadi Zyuganov (Communist) 32·08% and Aleksandr Lebed, 14·52%. In the second run-off round on 3 July turn-out was 68·8%. Yeltsin was re-elected with 53·8% of votes cast.

Parliament is known as the *Federal Assembly.* The 'representative and legislative organ of the Russian Federation', it consists of 2 chambers: the *Council of the Federation* and the *State Duma.* The Council of the Federation, or upper house, consists of 178 deputies, 2 from each of the 89 subjects of the Federation. The State Duma, or lower house, consists of 450 deputies chosen for a 4-year term. 225 of these are elected from single-member constituencies on the first-past-the-post system, the remainder from party lists by proportional representation. To qualify for candidacy an individual must obtain signatures from at least 1% of voters in the constituency; a party or electoral alliance must obtain a minimum of 100,000 supporting signatures from at least 7 regions, but not more than 15% from any one region. There is a 5% threshold for the party-list seats. Parties which gain at least 35 seats may register as a faction, which gives them the right to join the Duma Council and chair committees. Any citizen aged over 21 may be elected to the State Duma, but may not at the same time be a member of the upper house or of other representative bodies, and all deputies work on a 'permanent professional basis'. Both houses elect a chair, committees and commissions. The Council of the Federation considers all matters that apply to the Federation as a whole, including state boundaries, martial law, and the deployment of Russian forces elsewhere. The Duma approves nominations for prime minister, and adopts federal laws (they are also considered by the Council of the Federation, but any objection may be overridden by a two-thirds majority; objections on the part of the President may be overridden by both houses on the same basis). The Duma for its part can reject nominations for prime minister, but after the third such rejection it is automatically dissolved. It is also dissolved if it twice votes a lack of confidence in the government as a whole, or if it refuses to express confidence in the government when the matter is raised by the prime minister.

Elections for the State Duma were held on 17 Dec. 1995. The electorate was 107·5m.; turn out was 64·4%. 2,687 candidates stood representing 43 parties or groups. 4 parties exceeded the 5% threshold for party-list seats: Communist Party, 99 seats; Liberal Democratic Party (of Vladimir Zhirinovsky), 50; Our Home is Russia,

45; Yabloko, 31. Total seats gained: Communist Party, 157 with 22·3% of votes cast (48 with 12·4% in 1993); Our Home is Russia, 55 with 10·13%; Liberal Democratic Party, 51 with 11·18% (64 with 22·92% in 1993); Yabloko, 45 with 6·89% (23 with 7·86% in 1993); Agrarian Party, 20 with 3·78% (33 wtih 7·99% in 1993); Power to the People, 9 with 1·61%, Russia's Democratic Choice, 9 with 3·86% (70 with 15·51% in 1993); Congress of Russian Communities, 5 with 4·31%; Women of Russia, 3 with 4·61% (23 with 8·13% in 1993); Forward Russia, 3 with 1·94%; Ivan Rybkin's Bloc, 3 with 1·11%; Pamfilova-Gurev-Lysenko, 2 with 1·6%. 78 seats went to independents (141 in 1993) and 10 to minor parties. The Communist Party delegated some seats to the Agrarian Party to enable it to register as a faction. Registered factions (with seats held) in Jan. 1996: Communist Party (149), Our Home is Russia (55), Liberal Democratic Party (51), Yabloko (46), Russian Regions (42), Power to the People (37), Agrarian Party (35).

President: Boris Yeltsin (b. 1931; sworn in 9 Aug. 1996).

On 23 March 1998 President Yeltsin dismissed the government, and appointed Sergei Kiriyenko, formerly Minister for Energy, as acting Prime Minister.

National anthem: No words, tune from an opera by M. Glinka.

Regional and Local Government: There are 49 provinces, 6 territories, 21 republics (including Cechnya) and 10 autonomous areas. The republics are homelands of non-Russian minorities and as such enjoy a high degree of autonomy including the right to elect a president. Provinces (*oblasts*) and territories (*krais*) are led by governors, formerly presidential appointments but now elected. Local councils include 24,230 rural settlements, 2,048 urban settlements, 318 urban districts, 1,086 towns and 1,863 sub-regions.

A presidential decree of Oct. 1993 established a new regime for local authorities. Their membership is limited to 50. During 1996, 47 of the 89 federal units held elections for presidents or governors, these being areas where regional heads had been appointed before elections were instituted in 1995.

DEFENCE. The President of the Republic is C.-in-C. of the armed forces. Conscription was raised from 18 months to 2 years in April 1995.

Army. A Russian Army was created by presidential decree in March 1992. In 1997 forces numbered 420,000 (170,000 conscripts). The Army is deployed in 8 military districts and 1 Group of Forces, and comprises: 14 Army and 8 Corps headquarters, 12 tank, 28 motor rifle, 5 airborne, 4 machine gun/artillery and 4 artillery divisions, and some 47 artillery, 4 heavy artillery, 7 airborne, 8 special forces, 23 surface-to-surface missile, 2 independent tank, and 17 independent motor rifle brigades, and 19 anti-tank and 28 surface-to-air missile regiments. Equipment includes some 16,800 main battle tanks, including T-54/ 55, T-62, T-64A/-B, T-72L/-M and T-80/-M9, 200 PT 76 light tanks, 1,962 multiple rocket launchers, 144 surface-to-surface nuclear-capable missile launchers and 2,300 surface-to-air missiles.

The Army air element has some 2,450 helicopters in the inventory, including 2,000 Mi-8/17 transport, assault and battlefield electronic countermeasures and electronic intelligence machines and 950 armed Mi-24s. There are a small number of Mi-6 and Mi-26 heavy-lift helicopters as well as a small number of fixed-wing transport and communications aircraft. Funding shortages have reduced serviceability drastically.

Strategic Nuclear Ground Forces. In 1995 there were 5 rocket armies, each with launcher groups, 10 silos and 1 control centre. Inter-continental ballistic missiles numbered 928. Personnel, 100,000 (50,000 conscripts).

Navy. The Russian Navy continues to reduce steadily and levels of sea-going activity remain very low with activity concentrated on a few operational units in each fleet. The safe deployment and protection of the reduced force of strategic missile-firing submarines remains its first priority; and the defence of the Russian homeland its second. The strategic missile submarine force operates under command of the Strategic Nuclear Force commander whilst the remainder come under the Main Naval Staff in Moscow, through the Commanders of the fleets.

The Northern and Pacific fleets count the entirety of the ballistic missile submarine force, all nuclear-powered submarines, the sole operational aircraft carrier and most major surface warships. The Baltic Fleet organization is based in the St Petersburg area and in the Kaliningrad exclave. Some minor war vessels have been ceded to the Baltic republics. The Black Sea Fleet continues to be the object of wrangling between Russia and Ukraine, and remains operationally paralyzed by the dispute. While a political decision has been made to divide the fleet between the nations, the practical and personnel issues remain unresolved. The small Caspian Sea flotilla, formerly a sub-unit of the Black Sea Fleet, has been divided between Azerbaijan (25%), and Russia, Kazakhstan and Turkmenistan, the littoral republics (75%).

The material state of all the fleets is suffering from continued inactivity and lack of spares and fuel. The nuclear submarine refitting and refuelling operations in the Northern and Pacific Fleets remain in disarray, given the large numbers of nuclear submarines awaiting defuelling and disposal. The strength of the submarine force has now essentially stabilized, but there are still large numbers of decommissioned vessels awaiting their turn for scrapping in a steadily deteriorating state.

The aircraft carrier *Admiral Kuznetsov* is now operational, albeit with a limited aviation capability, and she deployed to the Mediterranean in Dec. 1995.

The overall strength of the Navy at the end of the indicated year was as follows:

Category	1991	1992	1993	1994	1995	1996
Strategic Submarines	59	55	50	46	38	34
Nuclear Attack Submarines	100	95	80	63	66	62
Diesel Submarines	80	75	70	62	55	26
Aircraft Carriers	5	4	3	1	1	1
Cruisers	38	33	31	25	26	24
Destroyers	29	26	22	22	21	20
Frigates	146	129	114	112	101	101

The strength of the disputed Black Sea Fleet at the end of 1996 was 12 diesel-powered submarines, 4 cruisers, 3 destroyers and 22 frigates, as well as some 30 mine warfare amphibious ships and 100 support units. The force of Strategic Submarines is constituted as follows:

Class	No.	Tonnage	Speed	Missiles	Other Weapons
Typhoon	6	27,000	27	20 SS-N-20	Torpedoes
Delta-IV	7	12,350	24	16 SS-N-23	Torpedoes
Delta-III	13	11,900	24	16 SS-N-18	Torpedoes
Delta-II	4	11,500	24	16 SS-N-8	Torpedoe
Delta-I	8	11,000	25	12 SS-N-8	Torpedoes

Some other non-operational strategic submarines continue to be counted to START totals.

The SS-N-20 'Sturgeon' missile carried by the Typhoon carries 6 warheads to a maximum range of 4,500 nautical miles, while the SS-N-23 'Skiff' in the other modern class, the 'Delta-IV', carries 10 warheads over the same range. The other older missiles carry 1 to 3 warheads over ranges varying between 1,300 and 4,000 nautical miles.

The attack submarine fleet comprises a wide range of classes, from the enormous 16,250 tonne 'Oscar' nuclear-powered missile submarine to diesel boats of around 2,000 tonnes. The inventory of anti-ship missile-firing submarines comprises 13 'Oscar I' and 'II' built 1982–1994, 24 SS-N-19 'Shipwreck' missiles, 2 'Charlie-II', 1972–75, 8 SS-N-7 'Starbright'; and 1 'Echo-II', 1961–67, 8 SS-N-3 'Shaddock' or SS-N-12 'Sandbox', all nuclear-propelled. Finally, there are 3 former strategic 'Yankee'-class submarines converted to fire the SS-N-21 'Sampson' land-attack cruise missile, which has a range of 1,600 nautical miles. Torpedo-firing boats currently building are the 'Akula' class, nuclear-powered and of 8,100 tonnes, of which there are 13, and the 'Sierra' class, nuclear-powered, 7,700 tonnes now numbering 4. The 'Victor-III' class, nuclear-powered, 6,400 tonnes, totals 26 units. The diesel-powered 'Kilo' class, of which the Navy operates 17, is still building at a reduced rate mostly for export. There are a further 9 diesel submarines nominally on the active list.

Cruisers (7,500–8,000 tonnes full load and upwards) are divided into 2 categories; those optimized for anti-submarine warfare (ASW) are classified as 'Large Anti-Submarine Ships' and those primarily configured for anti-surface ship operations are classified 'Rocket Cruisers'. The principal surface ships of the Russian Navy include the following classes:

Aircraft Carrier. The *Admiral Kuznetsov* of 65,000 tonnes was completed in 1989, is capable of 30 knots, and armed with 12 SS-N-19 'Shipwreck' anti-ship missiles and SA-N-9 anti-air missiles; it is capable of embarking 25–30 aircraft and 8–10 helicopters. All other aircraft carriers have been decommissioned or scrapped.

Anti-Shipping Rocket Cruisers. The ships of this classification are headed by the 4 ships of the Admiral Ushakov (formerly Kirov) class, the largest combatant warships, apart from aircraft carriers, to be built since the Second World War. *Admiral Ushakov* (1980), *Admiral Lazarev* (1984), *Admiral Nakhimov* (1988) and *Petr Velikii* (1995). They displace 28,400 tonnes and are capable under combined nuclear and oil-fired steam propulsion of 33 knots and are armed with 20 SS-N-19 anti-ship missiles, 12 batteries of SA-N-6 anti-air missiles, 3 helicopters and a wide range of lesser armaments. There are 4 Slava class: *Slava* (1982), *Marshal Ustinov* (1986), *Chervona Ukraina* (1988) and *Admiral Lobov* (1995), each of 12,700 tonnes capable of 34 knots, and armed with 16 SS-N-12 anti-ship missiles, 8 batteries of SA-N-6 anti-air missiles, 8 torpedo tubes and a single helicopter.

Anti-Submarine Cruisers. There are 4 ships of the Nikolaev ('Kara') class, displacing 9,800 tonnes, capable of 34 knots, completed 1973–79, and armed with SS-N-14 anti-submarine missiles with a secondary anti-ship role, SA-N-3 anti-air missiles, torpedo-tubes and a single helicopter and 12 newer Udaloy class, the first of which entered service in 1981. These displace 8,600 tonnes, are capable of 30 knots and are armed with SS-N-14 missiles, torpedo tubes and 100 mm guns, and carry 2 helicopters.

Smaller ships include the 17 Sovremenny class guided missile destroyers and the single remaining 'modified Kashin' class. There are a further 2 'Kashin', 26 large frigates including the first of a new class, the *Neustrashimy*, and 75 smaller frigates.

The coastal defence force includes 80 missile corvettes, 16 fast missile craft, 25 hydrofoil fast torpedo craft and 15 patrol craft (many more are laid up). Mine warfare forces include 3 minelayers and 33 offshore, 80 coastal and about 65 inshore mine countermeasure vessels.

Amphibious ships include 3 large dock landing ships of the Ivan Rogov class, 22 Ropucha and 7 Alligator class tank landing ships, 20 medium landing ships, and some 80 minor craft. Amphibious landing forces are found from the Naval Infantry, 14,000 strong, units of which are assigned to all fleets. Organized into a single division, 7,000 strong, and 3 active independent brigades, its principal equipment includes 240 main battle tanks, 100 amphibious light tanks, 300 artillery pieces and about 900 armoured personnel carriers. A separate force of 6,000 Coastal Defence troops mans artillery and missile batteries as well as conventional mechanized units positioned to defend the main naval bases and ports.

There is 1 multi-purpose underway replenishment ship, the *Berezina*, an additional 6 dual-purpose stores and fuel replenishment ships, 6 purpose-built tankers, and 18 other tankers converted from a commercial design with limited underway replenishment capability. Second line support is provided by 12 tankers, and about 230 maintenance and logistic ships, 60 electronic intelligence gatherers, 70 other special-purpose auxiliaries, and 210 survey, research and space support ships.

The Russian Naval Air Force includes some 100 bombers, 170 maritime patrol and anti-submarine aircraft, 175 fighter/ground attack aircraft and 280 helicopters. Maritime reconnaissance and anti-submarine tasks are performed by 65 Tu-95 and Tu-142 'Bear' with numerous shorter range aircraft tasked to anti-submarine operations, electronic countermeasures, intelligence gathering, and tankers. The helicopter force includes 200 anti-submarine, 25 combat assault, and 15 mine countermeasures aircraft.

Personnel in 1997 numbered 220,000, of whom 142,000 were conscripts. Some

13,000 serve in the strategic submarine force, 40,000 in naval aviation, 14,000 marines or naval infantry, and 6,000 in coastal artillery and coastal defence troops.

Coastguard, customs and border patrol duties are performed by the substantial maritime element of the Committee for the Protection of State Borders, which operates some 7 large helicopter-carrying frigates of a modified naval 'Krivak' class, 18 small frigates, 40 coastal and 150 inshore patrol craft divided among all the Russian coastal areas.

Air Force. Russia has both Air Force (1996: 145,000 personnel) and Air Defence Forces (175,000). Under the terms of the Conventional Forces in Europe (CFE) treaty, Russia is allowed to have up to 3,450 combat aircraft, 890 helicopters and 300 naval combat aircraft.

The Air Force is organized into 4 main Commands: Long-Range Aviation, Frontal Aviation, Military Transport Aviation and Reserve and Training Command.

Long-Range Aviation is reported to have 10 Tu-160, 100 Tu-22M, 120 Tu-95 bombers, some equipped to carry nuclear weapons. There are 150 MiG-25s and Su-24s equipped for electronic countermeasures and electronic intelligence missions and 30 Il-78 tanker aircraft. Frontal Aviation has over 3,500 combat and 1,800 support aircraft and is divided into 8 Air Armies, 7 in Russia and 1 in Trans-Caucasia. The main bomber type is the Su-24 of which 500 are available. The MiG-23/27, Su-17/20 and Su-25 serve for fighter and attack missions. There are also MiG-29s for air defence duties. The MiG-21 and most older combat aircraft have been withdrawn from service. Military Transport Aviation has over 300 Il-76s, which are replacing An-12s for heavy-lift operations. The other main transport type is the An-2 of which 300 are available, although there are about 100 An-24/26/32 medium transports and 15 An-124 and 30 An-22 very heavy-lift aircraft. 30-plus Il-62, Tu-134, Tu-154 and Yak-40 aircraft are assigned to VIP transport. Reserve and Training Command uses Yak-18 and Yak-52 primary trainers and L-29s and L-39s for jet conversion, plus two-seat models of many front-line types, such as the MiG-23, MiG-25, MiG-29, Su-17/20 and Su-25. It is being reorganized and slimmed down. Strength (1997), 130,000.

The Border Guards have their own aviation component to patrol Russia's borders. It has An-24 fixed-wing aircraft, now being succeeded by armed An-72Ps and Mi-8 and armed Mi-24 helicopters.

INTERNATIONAL RELATIONS

Membership. Russia is a member of the UN (Security Council), CIS, the Council of Europe and the NATO Partnership for Peace. On 16 May 1997 NATO ratified a 'Fundamental Act on Relations, Co-operation and Mutual Security' with Russia.

ECONOMY

Policy. In Oct. 1991 the President announced an economic programme whose aim was the establishment of a 'healthy mixed economy with a powerful private sector'. As part of this programme the prices of most commodities were freed on 2 Jan. 1992.

A bankruptcy law of Nov. 1992 permits the winding-up of indebted enterprises; further legislation came into force in April 1993. Centralized distribution of resources to enterprises was abolished from 1993.

Privatization is overseen by the State Committee on the Management of State Property, and began with small and medium-sized enterprises. A state programme of privatization of state and municipal enterprises was approved by parliament in June 1992, and vouchers worth 10,000 roubles each began to be distributed to all citizens in Oct. 1992. These may be sold or exchanged for shares. Employees have the right to purchase 51% of the equity of their enterprises. 25 categories of industry (including raw materials and arms) remain in state ownership. The voucher phase of privatization ended on 30 June 1994. A post-voucher stage authorized by presidential decree of 22 July 1994 provides for firms to be auctioned for cash following the completion of the sale of up to 70% of manufacturing industry for vouchers. By Dec. 1997 a total of 127,000 enterprises had been privatized, 33% of which were in manufacturing, construction, transport and communications, 2·4% in agriculture and 59% in trade, public catering and personal services.

Performance. GDP grew by at least 0·4% in 1997, the first expansion since the Soviet Union's collapse in 1991. But many economists believe that the booming informal economy adds over 25% to the value of GDP.

Budget. Budgetary incomes were valued at 459,224bn. roubles in 1996. The main sources of revenue (in roubles) were: taxes on profits (82,365bn.), value added tax (116,222bn.), income tax (49,185bn.), income from foreign trade (37,016bn.) and excise duties (41,281bn.). Budgetary expenditures were valued at 542,060bn. roubles. Items of expenditure (in roubles) included: National economy, 136,500bn.; socio-cultural (including education, health and social security), 121,335bn.; defence, 53,170bn.; foreign trade 18,315bn.

Currency. The unit of currency is the *rouble* (RUR), of 100 *kopeks*. Banknotes are in denominations of 100, 200, 500, 1,000, 5,000, 10,000, 20,000 and 50,000 roubles. In Jan. 1998 the rouble was redenominated by a factor of a thousand. Gold and currency reserves were valued at US$18bn. in Jan. 1998. In 1997 the rouble was tied to the US dollar on a sliding scale ranging from US$1 = 5,500–6,100 roubles on 1 Jan. 1997 to 6 roubles on 31 Jan. 1998. Inflation was 15% in 1997 and 22% in 1996. It was an annualized 197·4% in 1995 and in that year the total external debt was US$120,461m., most of it inherited from the Soviet Union.

Banking and Finance. The central bank and bank of issue is the State Bank of Russia (*Governor*, Sergei Dubinin). The Russian Bank for Reconstruction and Development and the State Investment Company were created in 1993 to channel foreign and domestic investment. In Jan. 1997 there were some 2,603 commercial banks, about 80% of which were state-owned through ministries or state enterprises. In 1997, the top 6 banks in terms of assets (in US$m.) were: Sberbank, 29·1; Vneshtorgbank, 3·9; Uneximbank, 3·6; Inkombank, 3·4; National Reserve Bank, 2·0. Sberbank is the only Russian bank to appear in the world top 20. Foreign bank branches have been operating since Nov. 1992.

By 1995 the number of registered commercial banks had increased to around 5,000 but following the Aug. 1997 liquidity crisis, due to the ensuing bankruptcies, mergers and the Central Bank's revoking of licences, the number fell to 2,500. By mid-1997 a further 571 licences were still being revoked. However, licences are still being revoked at an estimated rate of 5 or 6 per week.

By Jan. 1995, 166 exchanges were in operation, and 28,700 firms of brokers.

In 1994 all forms of investment were valued at 108,809,000m. roubles, of which 30·3% was invested in industry, 25·5% in housing and 10·9% in transport; 64·2% was provided by enterprises themselves, 13·4% by the federal budget and 10·6% by regional budgets.

There are stock exchanges in St Petersburg and Vladivostok.

Weights and Measures. The metric system is in use. The Gregorian Calendar was adopted as from 14 Feb. 1918.

ENERGY AND NATURAL RESOURCES

Electricity. There were 9 nuclear plants in 1997.

Minerals. Russia contains great mineral resources: Iron ore, coal, gold, platinum, copper, zinc, lead, tin and rare metals. Output (in tonnes), 1995: Coal, 262m.; iron ore, 78m.; gold ores and concentrates, 131·9.

Oil and Gas. Output of oil was 301m. tonnes in 1996. Output of natural gas in 1996 was 590,000m. cu. metres.

Agriculture. A presidential decree of Dec. 1991 authorized the private ownership of land on a general basis; a further decree of March 1996 authorized its free sale. Collective and state farms which wish to start private farming are required to re-register as co-operatives or share companies. Members of collectives may withdraw with a certificate of land ownership and a share of the collective's equipment or compensation in lieu; members may also elect to remain in co-operatives voluntarily. The decree permits foreign nationals to own land through joint ventures.

In Jan. 1995 there were 26,900 agricultural enterprises including 6,000 collective farms, 3,600 state farms and 17,300 commercial farms; 6·4m. were employed in agriculture, and output was valued at 38,491,000m. roubles. In 1995, 220,800m. ha were in cultivation, of which 105,100m. ha were in the hands of companies and co-operatives, 32,200m. ha in collective farms, 18,500m. ha in state farms, 10,100m. ha in commercial farms, and 5,700m. ha in individual private plots.

Output in 1996 (in tonnes) included: Grain, 6·9m.; sunflower seeds, 2·8m.; potatoes, 38·5m.; other vegetables, 10·7m.; Sugarbeet, 16·1m.; fruit and berries (1995), 2·5m.

Livestock, Jan. 1997: Cattle, 35·8m.; sheep and goats, 23·6m.; pigs, 19·6m. Livestock products in 1996 (in tonnes): Meat, 5·3m.; milk, 35·8m.; (in units) eggs, 31,902m.; wool (1995), 98,000.

Forestry. 119m. cu. metres of timber were produced in 1994.

INDUSTRY. Output in 1994 (in tonnes) included: Cast-iron, 36·5m.; steel, 48·8m.; rolled iron, 35·9m.; steel pipe, 3·6m.; caustic soda, 1·1m.; synthetic fibre, 198,000; soap, 56,300; cellulose, 3·3m.; paper, 2·2m.; cement, 37·2m.; confectionery, 1·5m.; (in sq. metres) glass, 58·6m.; (in units) bricks, 14,700m.; tractors, 28,700; combine harvesters, 12,100; bulldozers, 2,200; tins of food, 2,817m.; personal computers, 82,100; watches, 25·9m.; televisions, 2·2m. (colour, 1·2m.); refrigerators, 2·7m.; motor cars, 798,000; cigarettes, 94,300m.; liquor, 125m. decalitres. Total output in physical terms was 79% of the 1993 total, and 51% of 1990.

Labour. In 1997 subsistence minimum was estimated at 393,600 roubles; 22% of the population fell below it. In Jan. 1997 the official monthly minimum wage was 83,490 roubles; the average monthly wage was 870,000 roubles. The state Federal Employment Service was set up in 1992. Unemployment benefits are paid for 15 months: 3 months at full salary, 3 months at 75% and a final 9 months at a progressively reducing rate. Annual paid leave is 24 working days. The workforce was 73·1m. on 31 March 1996. In 1994, 30·6m. were in the state or municipal and 22·6m. in the private sector; 27·1% were employed in industry, 15·4% in agriculture and 10·8% in education and culture. In the third quarter of 1997 6·6m. persons (9·2% of the workforce) were unemployed, of whom 3·4% were registered with the Federal Employment Service. In 1996, 4,007 man-days were lost through strikes. In 1996 84·3m. people were of working age and 30·5m. people were above working age. Retirement age is 55 years for women, 60 for men.

Trade Unions. The Federation of Independent Trade Unions (founded 1990) is the successor to the former Communist official union organization. In 1993 it comprised 77 regional and 46 sectoral trade unions, with a total membership of 60m. There are also free trade unions.

FOREIGN ECONOMIC RELATIONS. Most CIS republics have given up claims on Soviet assets in return for Russia's assuming their portion of foreign debt. A Foreign Investment Agency was set up in Dec. 1992. In Jan. 1994 there were 6,359 joint enterprises in operation, employing 304,000 and accounting for 8% of foreign trade.

Commerce. In 1996, exports were valued at US$87,008·1m. (to other CIS states, US$15,617·3m.), and imports at US$45,438·7m. (from other CIS states, US$14,090·6m.). In 1995 Germany was the main trading partner outside the CIS, followed (for exports) by the USA, Switzerland, China, Italy and the Netherlands, and (for imports) by the USA, Finland, Italy and the Netherlands. In 1995, of exports, 26·4% by value were minerals and 29·8% metals and precious stones. Of imports, 38·9% by value was machinery, 29·2% foodstuffs and 11·5% chemical products.

Tourism. In 1995 there were 5,311,000 foreign visitors (2·2m. on business and 1·8m. tourists).

COMMUNICATIONS

Roads. In 1995 there were 945,000 km of which 80% were hard surfaced; 22,817m. passengers were carried by bus services, 8,547m. by trolley buses and 7,564m. by trams. 40% of villages cannot be reached by road.

Railways. Length of railways in 1996 was 87,000 km of 1,520 mm gauge (of which 44% were electrified). 908·3m. tonnes of freight were carried. There are metro services in 6 cities. It is estimated that 10% of all railways are in some way defective.

Civil Aviation. There are international airports at Moscow (Sheremetevo) and St Petersburg (Pulkovo). The national carrier is Aeroflot International Russian Airlines, which is 51% state- and 49% employee-owned. In 1995 it had a fleet of 2,643 ex-Soviet aircraft. There are 11 other Russian airlines. Services are also provided by Adria, Aerosweet, Air Algérie, Air China, Air France, Air India, Air Koryo, Air Moldova, Air Ukraine, Alitalia, All Nippon Airways, Arax, Austrian Airlines, Azerbaijan Hava Yollary, Balkan, Bashkir Airlines, Belavia, British Airways, Croatia Airlines, Cubana, Cyprus Airways, Czech Airlines, Delta, Donavia, Egyptair, El Al, Estonian Air, Finnair, Iberia, Iran Air, JAL, JAT, Kazakhstan Airlines, KLM, Korean Air, Libyan Airlines, Lithuanian Airlines, LOT, Lufthansa, Malév, Mongolian Airlines, Northwest Airlines, Orbi, Pakistan Airlines, Palair Macedonian, Royal Jordanian, SAS, Swissair, Syrian Airlines, TAAG, Tarom, Transaero, Turkish Airlines, Uzbekistan Airways, Vietnam Airlines, Xinjiang Airlines and Yemenia. In 1994, 34m. passengers and 0·7m. tonnes of freight were carried on domestic flights, and 4·7m. passengers and 0·2m. tonnes of freight on international flights.

Shipping. In 1995, the merchant fleet comprised 2,991 vessels totalling 20·38m. DWT, and representing 3·08% of the world's total fleet tonnage. 236 vessels (24% of tonnage) were registered under foreign flags, Total GRT, 16·54m., including oil tankers, 2·38m. GRT, and container ships, 0·46m. GRT. In 1994, 155m. tonnes of freight and 40m. passengers were carried on the 94,000 km of inland waterways; about two-thirds was building materials. Kaliningrad was opened to shipping in May 1991. In 1994, 70m. tonnes of cargo were carried by the merchant marine.

Telecommunications. In mid-1995 there were 51,800 post office (35,400 in rural areas) and 27·5m. telephones (18 lines per 1,000 people). In 1994 there were 27,700 cellular mobile phone subscribers, 242 internet networks and (1995) 70,200 fax machines. Telephone density: Moscow, 50%; St Petersburg, 39%; Nizhni Novgorod, 18%. In 1997, 56m. households had TVs.

Television broadcasting is still largely state-controlled, although an independent service began in 1993. There are 2 major channels, Ostankino and Russian Television (colour by SECAM). In 1994, 98·8% of the population could receive TV broadcasts. There are also local city channels (e.g. 6 in Moscow in 1993). Access to cable TV varies with locality; satellite TV reached about 5% of the population in 1993. As well as state radio, 24% of the population in 1995 could receive commercial broadcasts.

Culture. In 1995 there were 54,400 public libraries, 470,000 theatres and 1,725,000 museums.

Cinemas. There were about 0·12m. screens in 1993; attendances totalled about 2,000m. in 1993.

Press. In 1994 there were 4,526 newspapers, 4,197 of them in Russian. Daily circulation of Russian-language newspapers, 84m.; other languages, 2m. A presidential decree of 22 Dec. 1993 brought the press agencies ITAR-TASS and RIA-Novosti under state control. In 1996, 30,200 titles (books and brochures) were published.

SOCIAL INSTITUTIONS

Justice. The Supreme Court is the highest judicial body on civil, criminal and administrative law. The Supreme Abritration Court deals with economic cases. The KGB, and the Federal Security Bureau which succeeded it, were replaced in Dec. 1992 by the Federal Counter-Intelligence Service.

A new civil code was introduced in 1993 to replace the former Soviet code. It guarantees the inviolability of private property and includes provisions for the freedom of movement of capital and goods.

12-member juries were introduced in a number of courts after Nov. 1993. A new criminal code came into force on 1 Jan. 1997, based on respect for the rights and freedoms of the individual and the sanctity of private property. The death penalty is retained for 5 crimes against the person. It is not applied to minors, women or men over 65.

In 1996, 2,625,000 crimes were reported; 29·4 thousand were cases of murder or attempted murder; 53·4 thousand were cases of GBH and 10·9 thousand were cases of rape. In 1994, 924,600 sentences were passed, of which 36% involved imprisonment. In 1996 there were 56 executions (86 in 1995; 1 in 1992). Organized crime groups control up to 40,000 commercial organizations.

Religion. The Russian Orthodox Church, represented by the Patriarchate of Moscow, had, in 1996, an estimated 35-40m. adherents, over 14,000, 136 monasteries, and 26 secondary and higher educational institutions. There are still many Old Believers, whose schism from the Orthodox Church dates from the 17th century. The Russian Church is headed by the Patriarch of Moscow and All Russia (Metropolitan Aleksei II (b. 1929) of St Petersburg and Novgorod, elected June 1990), assisted by the Holy Synod, which has 7 members—the Patriarch himself and the Metropolitans of Krutitsy and Kolomna (Moscow), St Petersburg and Kiev *ex officio*, and 3 bishops alternating for 6 months in order of seniority from the 3 regions forming the Moscow Patriarchate. The Patriarchate of Moscow maintains jurisdiction over 119 eparchies, of which 59 are in Russia; there are parishes of Russian Orthodox abroad, in Belarus, Ukraine, Kazakhstan, Moldova, Uzbekistan, the Baltic states, and in Damascus, Geneva, Prague, New York and Japan. There is a spiritual mission in Jerusalem, and a monastery at Mt Athos in Greece. There are Jewish communities in Moscow and St Petersburg.

Education. In 1995 there were 21·5m. pupils in 68,400 primary and secondary day schools; 2·7m. students in 559 higher educational establishments (including 746,800 correspondence students), 3·6m. students in 6,800 technical colleges of all kinds (including correspondence students); 5·6m. children in 68,600 pre-school institutions. In 1994–95 there were 822 grammar schools and 505 *lycées* with a combined total of 1m. students. In addition there were 447 private schools with 40,000 pupils. Adult literacy rate, 98·7%.

In 1957 a Siberian branch of the Academy of Sciences was organized. Pre-dating the foundation of a Russian Academy of Sciences, St Petersburg and Urals branches were founded in 1990 and 1991 respectively. The Soviet became the Russian Academy of Sciences in Dec. 1991. There were 3,968 scientific institutes, of which 2,166 are independent research institutes.

Health. Doctors in Jan. 1995 numbered 663,100 (1996, 650,000), and hospital beds 1·9m. There were 12,300 hospitals. In Jan. 1995 there were 863 recorded cases of HIV (156 of whom had AIDS). Respiratory diseases are the chief killer.

Welfare. Vouchers are issued to cover basic health care and pensions contributions. These may be topped up to buy better services. A transition from state-financed to insurance-based health care is taking place.

There were 37·1m. pensioners in 1996. A lump sum of 2,700 roubles was payable in 1992 to parents on the birth of a child. From Dec. 1996 the minimum pension was 75,900 roubles a month. The average monthly pension in June 1995 was 201,874 roubles.

Personal pensions conferred by the former Communist régime conferring special benefits on party or state personnel or awarded for services rendered were abolished in 1992.

There are an estimated 52·1m. private households (based on 1994 micro-census).

In 1995, percentage of households which have: Running water, 71; sewerage, 66; central heating, 68; bathroom, 61; gas, 69; hot running water, 54; electric cooker, 15.

Consumer expenditure in 1995 (%): Household services, 19·3; public transport, 28; communications, 7·6; housing services, 19·4; childcare, 2·5; culture, 1·1; tourism/excursions, 1·3; sport, 0·3; healthcare, 2·6; sanatoriums, 3·4; legal services, 8·1; other, 6·4.

Over 80m. Russians live in areas where concentrations of air pollutants are well in excess of permissible levels. 30-40% of children's diseases are caused by air pollution; respiratory diseases such as asthma have increased sixfold since the early 1990s.

DIPLOMATIC REPRESENTATIVES

Of Russia in Great Britain (13 Kensington Palace Gdns., London W8 4QX)
Ambassador: Yuri Fokine.

Of Great Britain in Russia (Sofiiskaya Naberezhnaya 14, 109072 Moscow)
Ambassador: Sir Andrew Wood, KCMG.

Of Russia in the USA (1125 16th St., NW, Washington, D.C., 20036)
Ambassador: Yuli Vorontsov.

Of the USA in Russia (Novinski Bulvar 19, Moscow)
Ambassador: Vacant.

Of Russia to the United Nations
Ambassador: Sergei Lavrov.

Of Russia to the European Union
Ambassador: Vacant.

Further Reading

Rossiiskii Statisticheskii Ezhegodnik. Moscow, annual (title varies)

Acton, E. *et al. Critical Companion to the Russian Revolution.* Indiana University Press, 1997
Aslund, A. (ed.) *Economic Transformation in Russia.* New York, 1994
Cambridge Encyclopedia of Russia and the Former Soviet Union. CUP, 1995
Dukes, P., *A History of Russia: Medieval, Modern, Contemporary.* 2nd ed. London, 1990
Freeze, G. (ed), *Russia: A History.* OUP, 1997
Kochan, L., *The Making of Modern Russia.* 2nd ed, revised by R. Abraham. London, 1994
Lloyd, J., *Rebirth of a Nation.* London, 1998
McCauley, M., *Who's Who in Russia since 1900.* London 1991
Paxton, J., *Encyclopedia of Russian History.* Denver (CO), 1993
Pitman, L., *Russia/USSR.* [Bibliography]. 2nd ed. Oxford and Santa Barbara (CA), 1994
Riasanovsky, N. V., *A History of Russia.* 5th ed. OUP, 1993
Sakwa, R., *Russian Politics and Society.* 2nd ed. London, 1996
Service, R., *A History of Twentieth-Century Russia.* London, 1997
Treadgold, D. W., *Twentieth Century Russia.* 6th ed. Boston, 1987
Westwood, J.N., *Endurance and Endeavour: Russian History, 1812–1992.* 4th ed. OUP, 1993
White, S. *et al. How Russia Votes.* Chatham House (NJ), 1997.—(eds.) *Developments in Russian Politics.* London, 1997
Yeltsin, B., *The View from the Kremlin* (in USA *The Struggle for Russia*). London and New York, 1994

National statistical office: Gosudarstvennyi Komitet po Statistike (*Goskomstat*), Moscow.

THE REPUBLICS

Status. The 21 republics that with Russia itself constitute the Russian Federation were part of the RSFSR in the Soviet period. On 31 March 1992 the federal government concluded treaties with the then 20 republics, except Checheno-Ingushetia and Tatarstan, defining their mutual responsibilities. The *Council of the Heads of the Republics* is chaired by the Russian President and includes the Russian Prime Minister. Its function is to provide an interaction between the federal government and the republican authorities.

ADYGEYA

Part of Krasnodar Territory. Area, 7,600 sq. km (2,934 sq. miles); population (Jan. 1995), 451,000. Capital, Maikop (149,000). Established 27 July 1922; granted republican status in 1991.

President: Aslan Dzharimov.

Chief industries are timber, woodworking, food processing and there is some engineering. Agriculture consists primarily of crops (beets, wheat, maize), on partly irrigated land. Industrial output was valued in 1993 at 112,000m. roubles, agricultural output at 68,000m. roubles.

In 1994–95 there were 174 schools with 67,000 pupils, 3 technical colleges with 5,200 students and 2 higher educational institutions with 6,200 students.

In 1995 there were 32·7 doctors and 113 hospital beds per 10,000 population.

ALTAI

Part of Altai Territory. Area, 92,600 sq. km (35,740 sq. miles); population (Jan. 1995), 0·2m. Capital, Gorno-Altaisk (39,000). Established 1 June 1922 as Oirot Autonomous Region; renamed 7 Jan. 1948; granted republican status in 1991 and renamed in 1992.

Chairman of the State Assembly (El-Kurultai): Vladilen Vladimirovich Volkov. *Chairman of the Government:* Valery Ivanovich Chaptynov.

Chief industries are clothing and footwear, foodstuffs, gold mining, timber, chemicals and dairying. Cattle breeding predominates; pasturages and hay meadows cover over 1m. ha, but 142,000 ha are under crops. Industrial output was valued at 19,900m. roubles in 1993, agricultural output at 43,000m. roubles.

In 1994–95 there were 39,000 pupils in 194 schools; 4 technical colleges had 3,100 students and 3,700 students were attending a pedagogical institute.

In 1995 there were 32·7 doctors and 153 hospital beds per 10,000 population.

BASHKORTOSTAN

Area 143,600 sq. km (55,430 sq. miles), population (Jan. 1995) 4·08m. Capital, Ufa (1989 census population 1·1m.). Bashkiria was annexed to Russia in 1557. It was constituted as an Autonomous Soviet Republic on 23 March 1919. A declaration of republican sovereignty was adopted in 1990, and a declaration of independence on 28 March 1992. A treaty of Aug. 1994 with Russia preserves the common legislative framework of the Russian Federation while defining mutual areas of competence. The population, census 1989, was 39·3% Russian, 28·4% Tatar, 21·9% Bashkir, 3% Chuvash and 2·7% Mari.

A constitution was adopted on 24 Dec. 1993. It states that Bashkiria conducts its own domestic and foreign policy, that its laws take precedence in Bashkiria, and that it forms part of the Russian Federation on a voluntary and equal basis.

President: Murtaza Gubaidullovich Rakhimov. *Chairman of the State Assembly:* Mikhail Alexeyevich Zaitsev. *Prime Minister:* Rim Sagitovich Bakiev.

Industrial production was valued at 4,188,000m. roubles in 1993, agricultural output at 617,000m. roubles. The most important industries are oil and oil products; there are also engineering, glass and building materials enterprises. Agriculture specializes in wheat, barley, oats and livestock.

In 1994–95 there were 658,000 pupils in 3,317 schools. There is a state university and a branch of the Academy of Sciences with 8 learned institutions (511 research workers). There were 59,800 students in 75 technical colleges and 49,800 in 11 higher educational establishments.

In 1995 there were 40·1 doctors and 131 hospital beds per 10,000 population.

BURYATIA

Area is 351,300 sq. km (135,650 sq. miles). The Buryat Republic, situated to the south of Sakha, adopted the Soviet system 1 March 1920. This area was penetrated by the Russians in the 17th century and finally annexed from China by the treaties of Nerchinsk (1689) and Kyakhta (1727). The population (Jan. 1995) was 1,053,000. Capital, Ulan-Ude (1989 census population, 353,000). The population (1989 census) was 69·9% Russian, 24% Buryat, 2·2% Ukrainian, 1% Tatar and 0·5% Belorussian.

There is a 65-member parliament, the *People's Hural.*

President: Leonid Potapov

The main industries are engineering, brown coal and graphite, timber, building materials, sheep and cattle farming. Industrial production was valued at 384,000m. roubles in 1993, agricultural output at 181,000m. roubles.

In 1994–95 there were 615 schools with 196,000 pupils, 20 technical colleges with 13,400 students and 4 higher educational institutions with 19,300 students. A branch of the Siberian Department of the Academy of Sciences had 4 institutions with 281 research workers.

In 1995 there were 37·4 doctors and 114 hospital beds per 10,000 population.

CHECHNYA

The area of the former Checheno-Ingush Republic was 19,300 sq. km (7,350 sq miles); population (Jan. 1995, estimate), 904,000. Capital, Grozny (1989 census population, 401,000). The Chechens and Ingushes were conquered by Russia in the late 1850s. In 1918 each nationality separately established its 'National Soviet' within the Terck Autonomous Republic, and in 1920 (after the Civil War) were constituted areas within the Mountain Republic. The Chechens separated out as an Autonomous Region on 30 Nov. 1922 and the Ingushes on 7 July 1924. In Jan. 1934 the two regions were united, and on 5 Dec. 1936 constituted as an Autonomous Republic. This was dissolved in 1944 and the population was deported en masse, allegedly for collaboration with the German occupation forces. It was reconstituted on 9 Jan. 1957. 232,000 Chechens and Ingushes returned to their homes in the next 2 years. The population (1989 census) included 70·7% Chechens and Ingushes, 23·1% Russians, 1·2% Armenians and 1% Ukrainians.

A Chechen Republic declared its independence in Nov. 1991. (A separate Ingush Republic was declared in June 1993).

In April 1993 President Dudaev dissolved parliament. Hostilities continued throughout 1994 between the government and forces loosely grouped under the 'Provisional Chechen Council'. The Russian government, which had never recognized the Chechen declaration of independence of Nov. 1991, moved troops and armour into Chechnya on 11 Dec. 1994 'to re-establish constitutional order'. Grozny was bombed and attacked by Russian ground forces at the end of Dec. 1994 and the presidential palace was captured on 19 Jan. 1995, but fighting continued. On 30 July 1995 the Russian and Chechen authorities signed a ceasefire. On 8 Dec. 1995 an agreement between the Russian and Chechen prime ministers amnestied insurgents who laid down their arms. However, hostilities, raids and hostage-taking continued. The Chechen President was killed during fighting in April 1996. A further ceasefire was concluded on 30 Aug. 1996, and it was agreed that the status of Chechnya would be determined by a referendum in 2001. On 23 Nov. 1996 the Russian President decreed the withdrawal of all Russian troops by the end of 1996.

Presidential and a first round of parliamentary elections were held on 27 Jan. 1997. The electorate was 513,000. There were 14 presidential candidates. There were some 150 foreign observers, including 72 from OSCE. The second round of parliamentary elections was declared invalid because turn-out failed to reach the necessary 50%. A third round was held in 1997.

President: Aslan Maskhadov. *Prime Minister:* Doku Zavgaev. *Minister of Information:* Movladi Udugov. *Finance:* Taimaz Abubakarov.

Ingush desire to separate from Chechnya led to fighting along the Chechen-Ingush border and a deployment of Russian troops. An agreement to withdraw was reached between Russia and Chechnya on 15 Nov. 1992. The separation of Chechnya and Ingushetia was formalized by an amendment of Dec. 1992 to the Russian Constitution.

Checheno-Ingushetia had a major oilfield, and a number of engineering works, chemical factories, building materials works and food canneries. There was a timber, woodworking and furniture industry. Industrial output in the two republics was valued at 213,000m. roubles in 1993, agricultural output at 79,000m. roubles.

There were, in the Chechen and Ingush republics in 1993–94, 548 schools with 251,000 pupils, 12 technical colleges with 8,700 students and 3 places of higher education with 13,100 students.

In 1992 it was decided to revert to the Roman alphabet (which had replaced Arabic script in 1927 and been itself replaced by Cyrillic in 1938).

In 1993 there were 21·1 doctors and 91 hospital beds per 10,000 population in the Chechen and Ingush republics.

CHUVASHIA

Area, 18,300 sq. km (7,064 sq. miles); population (Jan. 1995), 1,361,000. Capital, Cheboksary (1989 census population, 0·42m.). The territory was annexed by Russia in the middle of the 16th century. On 24 June 1920 it was constituted as an Autonomous Region, and on 21 April 1925 as an Autonomous Republic. The population (1989 census) was 67·8% Chuvash, 26·7% Russian, 2·7% Tatar and 1·4% Mordovian. Republican sovereignty was declared in Sept. 1990.

President: Nikolai Fedorov

The timber industry antedates the Soviet period. Other industries include railway repair works, electrical and other engineering industries, building materials, chemicals, textiles and food industries. Grain crops account for nearly two-thirds of all sowings and fodder crops for nearly a quarter. Industrial output was valued at 641,000m. roubles in 1993, agricultural output at 224,000m. roubles.

In 1994–95 there were 218,000 pupils at 719 schools, 20,000 students at 27 technical colleges and 18,900 students at 3 higher educational establishments.

In 1995 there were 37·9 doctors and 124 hospital beds per 10,000 population.

DAGESTAN

Area, 50,300 sq. km (19,416 sq. miles); population (Jan. 1995), 2,067,000. Capital, Makhachkala (1989 census population, 315,000). Over 30 nationalities inhabit this republic apart from Russians (9·2% at 1989 census); the most numerous are Dagestani nationalities (80·2%), Azerbaijanis (4·2%), Chechens (3·22%) and Jews (0·5%). Annexed from Persia in 1723, Dagestan was constituted an Autonomous Republic on 20 Jan. 1921. In 1991 the Supreme Soviet declared the area of republican, rather than autonomous republican, status.

Chairman of the State Council, Head of the Republic: Magomedali Magomedovich Magomedov. *Chairman of the People's Assembly:* Mukhu Gimbatovich Aliyev.

There are engineering, oil, chemical, woodworking, textile, food and other light industries. Agriculture is varied, ranging from wheat to grapes, with sheep farming and cattle breeding. Industrial output was valued at 136,000m. roubles in 1993, agricultural output at 155,000m. roubles.

In 1994–95 there were 1,609 schools with 413,000 pupils, 17,700 students at 27 technical colleges and 6 higher education establishments with 28,400 students. In 1995 there were 36·5 doctors and 88 hospital beds per 10,000 population.

INGUSHETIA

The history of Ingushetia is interwoven with that of Chechnya (*see above*). Ingush desire to separate from Chechnya led to fighting along the Chechen-Ingush border and a deployment of Russian troops. The separation of Ingushetia from Chechnya was formalized by an amendment of Dec. 1992 to the Russian Constitution. On 15 May 1993 an extraordinary congress of the peoples of Ingushetia adopted a declaration of state sovereignty within the Russian Federation.

The capital is Nazran.

Estimated population, 1996, 0·28m.

There is a 27-member parliament. On 27 Feb. 1994 presidential elections and a constitutional referendum were held. Turn-out was 70%. At the referendum 97% of votes cast approved a new constitution stating that Ingushetia is a democratic law-based secular republic forming part of the Russian Federation on a treaty basis.

President: Ruslan Sultanovich Aushev. *Vice President:* Boris Nikolaevich Agapov. *Chairman of the People's Assembly (of the Parliament):* Arsamak Arsamakovich Malsagov. *Prime Minister:* Belan Bagaudinovich Khamchiyev.

A special economic zone for Russian residents was set up in 1994, and an 'offshore' banking tax haven in 1996.

In 1995 there were 19·6 doctors and 59 hospital beds per 10,000 population.

KABARDINO-BALKARIA

Area, 12,500 sq. km (4,825 sq. miles); population (Jan. 1995) 0·79m. Capital, Nalchik (1989 census population, 235,000). Kabarda was annexed to Russia in 1557. The republic was constituted on 5 Dec. 1936. Population (1989 census) included Kabardinians (48·2%), Balkars (9·4%), Russians (31·9%), Ukrainians (1·7%), Ossetians (1·3%) and Germans (1·1%).

A treaty with Russia of 1 July 1994 defines their mutual areas of competence within the legislative framework of the Russian Federation.

President: Valeri Kokov.

Main industries are ore-mining, timber, engineering, coal, food processing, timber and light industries, building materials. Grain, livestock breeding, dairy farming and wine-growing are the principal branches of agriculture. Industrial output was valued at 176,000m. roubles in 1993, agricultural output at 113,000m. roubles.

In 1994–95 there were 252 schools with 139,000 pupils, 6,900 students in 8 technical colleges and 12,900 students at 3 higher educational establishments. In 1995 there were 44·8 doctors and 120 hospital beds per 10,000 population.

KALMYKIA

Area, 76,100 sq. km (29,382 sq. miles); population (Jan. 1995), 0·32m. Capital, Elista (85,000). The population (1989 census) was 45·4% Kalmyk, 37·7% Russian, 2·6% Chechen, 1·9% Kazakh and 1·7% German.

The Kalmyks migrated from western China to Russia (Nogai Steppe) in the early 17th century. The territory was constituted an Autonomous Region on 4 Nov. 1920, and an Autonomous Republic on 22 Oct. 1935; this was dissolved in 1943. On 9 Jan. 1957 it was reconstituted as an Autonomous Region and on 29 July 1958 as an Autonomous Republic once more. In Oct. 1990 the republic was renamed the Kalmyk Soviet Socialist Republic; it was given its present name in Feb. 1992.

President: Kirsan Nikolaevich Ilyumzhinov.

In April 1993 the Supreme Soviet was dissolved and replaced by a professional parliament consisting of 25 of the former deputies. On 5 April 1994 a specially-constituted 300-member constituent assembly adopted a 'Steppe Code' as Kalmykia's basic law. This is not a constitution and renounces the declaration of republican sovereignty of 18 Oct. 1990. It provides for a *President* elected for 5-year terms with the power to dissolve parliament, and a 27-member parliament, the *People's Hural,* elected every 4 years. It stipulates that Kalmykia is an equal member and integral part of the Russian Federation, functioning in accordance with the Russian constitution.

Main industries are fishing, canning and building materials. Cattle breeding and irrigated farming (mainly fodder crops) are the principal branches of agriculture.

Industrial output was valued at 35,600m. roubles in 1993, agricultural output at 89,000m. roubles.

In 1994–95 there were 59,000 pupils in 252 schools, 4,200 students in 6 technical colleges and 5,100 in higher education. In 1995 there were 48·8 doctors and 151 hospital beds per 10,000 population.

KARACHAI-CHERKESSIA

Area, 14,100 sq. km (5,442 sq. miles); population (Jan. 1995), 436,000. Capital, Cherkessk (113,000). A Karachai Autonomous Region was established on 26 April 1926 (out of a previously united Karachaevo-Cherkess Autonomous Region created in 1922), and dissolved in 1943. A Cherkess Autonomous Region was established on 30 April 1928. The present Autonomous Region was re-established on 9 Jan. 1957. The Region declared itself a Soviet Socialist Republic in Dec. 1990.

Head of the Republic: Vladimir Islamovich Khubiev. *Chairman of the People's Assembly:* Igor Vladimirovich Ivanov. *Chairman of the Government:* Anatoly Galimzhanovich Ozov.

There are ore-mining, engineering, chemical and woodworking industries. The Kuban-Kalaussi irrigation scheme irrigates 200,000 ha. Livestock breeding and grain growing predominate in agriculture. Industrial output was valued at 114,000m. roubles in 1993, agricultural output at 92,000m. roubles.

In 1994–95 there were 74,000 pupils in 188 secondary schools, 6 technical colleges with 4,800 students and 2 institutes with 6,200 students. In 1995 there were 29 doctors and 102 hospital beds per 10,000 population.

KARELIA

The Karelian Republic, capital Petrozavodsk (1989 census population, 0·27m.), covers an area of 172,400 sq. km, with a population of 789,000 (Jan. 1995). Karelians represent 10% of the population, Russians, 73·6%, Belorussians 7% and Ukrainians 3·6% (1989 census).

Karelia (formerly Olonets Province) became part of the RSFSR after 1917. In June 1920 a Karelian Labour Commune was formed and in July 1923 this was transformed into the Karelian Autonomous Soviet Socialist Republic (one of the autonomous republics of the RSFSR). On 31 March 1940, after the Soviet–Finnish war, practically all the territory (with the exception of a small section in the neighbourhood of the Leningrad area) which had been ceded by Finland to the USSR was added to Karelia and the Karelian Autonomous Republic was transformed into the Karelo-Finnish Soviet Socialist Republic as the 12th republic of the USSR. In 1946, however, the southern part of the republic, including its whole seaboard and the towns of Viipuri (Vyborg) and Keksholm, was attached to the RSFSR, reverting in 1956 to autonomous republican status within the RSFSR. In Nov. 1991 it declared itself the 'Republic of Karelia'.

Chairman of the Government: Viktor Nikolaevich Stepanov. *Chairman of the Chamber of the Republic of the Legislative Assembly:* Ivan Petrovich Alexandrov. *Chairman of the Chamber of Representatives of the Legislative Assembly:* Valentina Nikolaevna Pivmenko.

Karelia has a wealth of timber, some 70% of its territory being forest land. It is also rich in other natural resources, having large deposits of mica, diabase, spar, quartz, marble, granite, zinc, lead, silver, copper, molybdenum, tin, baryta and iron ore. Its lakes an rivers are rich in fish.

There are timber mills, paper-cellulose works, mica, chemical plants, power stations and furniture factories. Industrial output was valued at 520,000m. roubles in 1993, agricultural output at 97,000m. roubles.

In 1994–95 there were 0·12m. pupils in 341 schools. There were 9,700 students in 3 institutions of higher education and 11,300 in 16 technical colleges.

In 1995 there were 47·2 doctors and 135 hospital beds per 10,000 population.

KHAKASSIA

Area, 61,900 sq. km (23,855 sq. miles); population (Jan. 1995), 584,000. Capital, Abakan (1989 census, 154,000). Established 20 Oct. 1930; granted republican status in 1991.

Chairman of the Government: Alexei Ivanovich Lebed.

There are coal- and ore-mining, timber and woodworking industries. The region is linked by rail with the Trans-Siberian line. Industrial output was valued at 545,000m. roubles in 1993, agricultural output at 83,000m. roubles.

In 1994–95 there were 97,000 pupils in 282 secondary schools, 6,200 students in 7 technical colleges and 5,600 students at a higher education institution.

In 1995 there were 36 doctors and 132 hospital beds per 10,000 population.

KOMI

Area, 415,900 sq. km (160,540 sq. miles); population (Jan. 1995), 1,202,000. Capital, Syktyvkar (1989 census population, 233,000). Annexed by the princes of Moscow in the 14th century, the territory was constituted as an Autonomous Region on 22 Aug. 1921 and as an Autonomous Republic on 5 Dec. 1936. The population (1989 census) was 57·7% Russian, 23·3% Komi, 8·3% Ukrainian and 2·1% Belorussian.

A declaration of sovereignty was adopted by the republican parliament in Sept. 1990, and the designation 'Autonomous' dropped from the republic's official name.

Head of the Republic, Chairman of the Government: Yury Alexeyevich Spiridonov. *Chairman of the State Council:* Vladimir Alexandrovich Torlopov.

There are coal, oil, timber, gas, asphalt and building materials industries, and light industry is expanding. Livestock breeding (including dairy farming) is the main branch of agriculture. Crop area, 92,000 ha. Industrial output was valued at 1,038,000m. roubles in 1993, agricultural output at 134,000m. roubles.

In 1994–95 there were 196,000 pupils in 595 schools, 11,300 students in 3 higher educational establishments, 14,200 students in 20 technical colleges; and a branch of the Academy of Sciences with 4 institutions (297 research workers).

In 1995 there were 39·6 doctors and 134 hospital beds per 10,000 population.

MARI EL

Area, 23,200 sq. km (8,955 sq. miles); population (Jan. 1995), 766,000. Capital, Yoshkar-Ola (1989 census population, 242,000). The Mari people were annexed to Russia, with other peoples of the Kazan Tatar Khanate, when the latter was overthrown in 1552. On 4 Nov. 1920 the territory was constituted as an Autonomous Region, and on 5 Dec. 1936 as an Autonomous Republic. The republic renamed itself the Mari Soviet Socialist Republic in Oct. 1990, and adopted a new constitution in June 1995. In Dec. 1991 Vladislav Zotin was elected the first president. The population (1989 census) was 47·5% Russian, 43·3% Mari, and 5·9% Tatar.

President, Head of the Government: Vyacheslav Alexandrovich Kislitsyn. *Chairman of the State Assembly:* Mikhail Mikhailovich Zhukov.

Coal is mined. The main industries are metalworking, timber, paper, woodworking and food processing. Crops include grain, flax, potatoes, fruit and vegetables. Industrial output was valued at 257,000m. roubles in 1993, agricultural output at 153,000m. roubles.

In 1994–95 there were 432 schools with 128,000 pupils; 14 technical colleges and 3 higher education establishments had 8,900 and 13,100 students respectively.

In 1995 there were 38 doctors and 126 hospital beds per 10,000 population.

MORDOVIA

Area, 26,200 sq. km (10,110 sq. miles); population (Jan. 1995), 959,000. Capital, Saransk (1989 census population, 312,000). By the 13th century the Mordovian tribes had been subjugated by Russian princes. In 1928 the territory was constituted as a Mordovian Area within the Middle-Volga Territory, on 10 Jan. 1930 as an Autonomous Region and on 20 Dec. 1934 as an Autonomous Republic. The population (1989 census) was 60·8% Russian, 32·5% Mordovian and 4·9% Tatar.

President: Nikolai Merkushkin.

Industries include wood-processing and the production of building materials, furniture, textiles and leather goods. Agriculture is devoted chiefly to grain, sugar-beet, sheep and dairy farming. Industrial output was valued at 457,000m. roubles in 1993, agricultural output at 185,000m. roubles.

In 1994–95 there were 139,000 pupils in 828 schools, 12,600 students in 21 technical colleges and 22,900 attending 2 higher educational institutions.

In 1995 there were 45·2 doctors and 155 hospital beds per 10,000 population.

NORTH OSSETIA (ALANIA)

Area, 8,000 sq. km (3,088 sq. miles); population (Jan. 1995), 659,000. Capital, Vladikavkaz (1989 census population, 0·3m.). North Ossetia was annexed by Russia from Turkey and named the Terek region in 1861. On 4 March 1918 it was proclaimed an Autonomous Soviet Republic, and on 20 Jan. 1921 set up with others as the Mountain Autonomous Republic, with North Ossetia as the Ossetian (Vladikavkaz) Area within it. On 7 July 1924 the latter was constituted as an Autonomous Region and on 5 Dec. 1936 as an Autonomous Republic. A new Constitution was adopted on 12 Nov. 1994 under which the republic reverted to its former name, Alania. The population (1989 census) was 53% Ossetian, 29% Russian, 5·2% Chechen, 1·9% Armenian and 1·6% Ukrainian.

President: Aleksandr Dzasokhov.

The main industries are non-ferrous metals (mining and metallurgy), maize processing, timber and woodworking, textiles, building materials, distilleries and food processing. There is also a varied agriculture. Industrial output was valued at 167,000m. roubles in 1993, agricultural output at 175,000m. roubles.

There were in 1994–95, 104,000 children in 214 schools, 10,800 students in 14 technical colleges and 18,100 students in 5 higher educational establishments.

In 1995 there were 68·3 doctors and 127 hospital beds per 10,000 population.

SAKHA

The area is 3,103,200 sq. km (1,197,760 sq. miles); population (Jan. 1995), 1,036,000. Capital, Yakutsk (187,000). The Yakuts were subjugated by the Russians in the 17th century. The territory was constituted an Autonomous Republic on 27 April 1922. The population (1989 census) was 50·3% Russian, 33·4% Yakut, 7% Ukrainian and 1·6% Tatar.

President: Mikhail Nikolaev. *Vice-President and Prime Minister:* Vyacheslav Shtyrov.

The principal industries are mining (gold, tin, mica, coal) and livestock-breeding. Silver- and lead-bearing ores and coal are worked. Large diamond fields have been opened up; Sakha produces most of the Russian Federation's output. Timber and food industries are developing. Trapping and breeding of fur-bearing animals (sable, squirrel, silver fox) are an important source of income. Industrial production was valued at 1,771,000m. roubles in 1993, agricultural output at 373,000m. roubles.

In 1994–95 there were 193,000 pupils in 715 secondary schools, 10,400 students at 19 technical colleges and 9,700 attending 3 higher education institutions.

In 1995 there were 41·3 doctors and 156 hospital beds per 10,000 population.

TATARSTAN

Area, 68,000 sq. km (26,250 sq. miles); population (Jan. 1995), 3,755,000. Capital, Kazan (1989 census population 1·1m.). From the 10th to the 13th centuries this was the territory of the Volga-Kama Bulgar State; conquered by the Mongols, it became the seat of the Kazan (Tatar) Khans when the Mongol Empire broke up in the 15th century, and in 1552 was conquered again by Russia. On 27 May 1920 it was constituted as an Autonomous Republic. The population (1989 census) was 48·5% Tatar, 43·3% Russian, 3·7% Chuvash, 0·9% Ukrainian and 0·8% Mordovian.

In Oct. 1991 the Supreme Soviet adopted a declaration of independence. At a referendum in March 1992 61·4% of votes cast were in favour of increased autonomy. A Constitution was adopted in April 1992, which proclaims Tatarstan a sovereign state which conducts its relations with the Russian Federation on an equal basis. On 15 Feb. 1994 the Russian and Tatar presidents signed a treaty defining Tatarstan as a state united with Russia on the basis of the constitutions of both, but the Russian parliament has not ratified it.

President: Mintimer Sharipovich Shaimiyev. *Chairman of the State Council:* Vassily Nikolayevich Likhachev. *Prime Minister:* Farid Khairullovich Mukhametshin.

The republic has engineering, oil and chemical, timber, building materials, textiles, clothing and food industries. Industrial production was valued at 2,955,000m. roubles in 1993, agricultural output at 532,000m. roubles.

In 1994–95 there were 2,463 schools with 0·56m. pupils, 65 technical colleges with 52,500 students and 16 higher educational establishments with 63,000 students (including a state university). There is a branch of the USSR Academy of Sciences with 5 institutions (512 research workers).

In 1995 there were 42·3 doctors and 124 hospital beds per 10,000 population.

TUVA

Area, 170,500 sq. km (65,810 sq. miles); population (Jan. 1995), 308,000. Capital, Kyzyl (80,000). Tuva was incorporated in the USSR as an autonomous region on 11 Oct. 1944 and elevated to an Autonomous Republic on 10 Oct. 1961. The population (1989 census) was 64·3% Tuvans and 32% Russian. Tuva renamed itself the 'Republic of Tuva' in Oct. 1991.

A new constitution was promulgated on 22 Oct. 1993 which adopts the name 'Tyva' for the republic. This constitution provides for a 32-member parliament (*Supreme Hural*) and a *Grand Hural* alone empowered to change the constitution, asserts the precedence of Tuvan law and adopts powers to conduct foreign policy It was approved by 62·2% of votes cast at a referendum on 12 Dec. 1993.

President: Sherig-ool Dizizhikovich Oorzhhak.

Tuva is well-watered and hydro-electric resources are important. The Tuvans are mainly herdsmen and cattle farmers and there is much good pastoral land. There are deposits of gold, cobalt and asbestos. The main exports are hair, hides and wool. There are mining, woodworking, garment, leather, food and other industries. Industrial production was valued at 25,800m. roubles in 1993, agricultural output at 44,000m. roubles.

In 1994–95 there were 167 schools with 62,000 pupils; 6 technical colleges with 3,800 students, and 1 higher education institution with 2,800 students.

In 1995 there were 36·7 doctors and 187 hospital beds per 10,000 population.

UDMURTIA

Area, 42,100 sq. km (16,250 sq. miles); population (Jan. 1995), 1,641,000. Capital, Izhevsk (1989 census population 635,109). The Udmurts (formerly known as 'Votyaks') were annexed by the Russians in the 15th and 16th centuries. On 4 Nov. 1920 the Votyak Autonomous Region was constituted (the name was changed to Udmurt in 1932), and on 28 Dec. 1934 was raised to the status of an Autonomous

Republic. The population (1989 census) was 58·9% Russian, 30·9% Udmurt, 6·9% Tatar, 0·9% Ukrainian and 0·6% Mari. A declaration of sovereignty and the present state title were adopted in Sept. 1990.

A new parliament was established in Dec. 1993 consisting of a 50-member upper house, the *Council of Representatives*, and a full-time 35-member lower house.

Chairman of the State Council: Alexander Alexandrovich Volkov. *Chairman of the Council of Ministers:* Pavel Nikolayevich Vershinin.

Heavy industry includes the manufacture of locomotives, machine tools and other engineering products, most of them for the defence industries, as well as timber and building materials. There are also light industries: Clothing, leather, furniture and food. Industrial production was valued at 958,000m. roubles in 1993, agricultural output at 368,000m. roubles.

In 1994–95 there were 902 schools with 263,000 pupils; there were 19,900 students at 30 technical colleges and 24,800 at 5 higher educational institutions.

In 1995 there were 48·1 doctors and 129 hospital beds per 10,000 population.

JEWISH AUTONOMOUS REGION (BIROBIJAN)

Part of Khabarovsk Territory. Area, 36,000 sq. km (13,895 sq. miles); population (Jan. 1995), 212,000 (1989 census, Russians, 83·2%; Ukrainians, 7·4%; Jews, 4·2%). Capital, Birobijan (82,000). Established as Jewish National District in 1928, became an Autonomous Region 7 May 1934. In Oct. 1991 the region declared itself an Autonomous Republic.

Chief industries are non-ferrous metallurgy, building materials, timber, engineering, textiles, paper and food processing. There were 161,000 ha under cultivation in 1983; main crops are wheat, soya, oats, barley. Industrial production was valued at 74,500m. roubles in 1993, agricultural output at 73,000m. roubles.

In 1991–92 there were 35,000 pupils in 111 schools; students in 6 technical colleges numbered 4,900. There are a Yiddish national theatre, newspaper and broadcasting service.

In 1995 there were 38·3 doctors and 175 hospital beds per 10,000 population.

AUTONOMOUS AREAS

Agin-Buryat Situated in Chita region (Eastern Siberia); area, 19,000 sq. km, population (Jan. 1995), 79,000. Capital, Aginskoe. Formed 1937, its economy is basically pastoral.

Chukot Situated in Magadan region (Far East); area, 737,700 sq. km. Population (Jan. 1995), 0·1m. Capital, Anadyr. Formed 1930. Population chiefly Russian, also Chukchi, Koryak, Yakut, Even. Minerals are extracted in the north, including gold, tin, mercury and tungsten.

Evenki Situated in Krasnoyarsk territory (Eastern Siberia); area, 767,600 sq. km, population (Jan. 1995) 21,000, chiefly Evenks. Capital, Tura. Formed 1930.

Khanty-Mansi Situated in Tyumen region (Western Siberia); area, 523,100 sq. km, population (Jan. 1995) 1,326,000, chiefly Russians but also Khants and Mansi. Capital, Khanti-Mansiisk. Formed 1930.

Komi-Permyak Situated in Perm region (Northern Russia); area, 32,900 sq. km, population (Jan. 1995) 159,000, chiefly Komi-Permyaks. Formed 1925. Capital, Kudymkar. Forestry is the main occupation.

Koryak Situated in Kamchatka; area, 301,500 sq. km, population (Jan. 1995) 34,000. Capital, Palana. Formed 1930.

Nenets Situated in Archangel region (Northern Russia); area, 176,700 sq. km, population (Jan. 1995) 49,000. Capital, Naryan-Mar. Formed 1929.

Taimyr Situated in Krasnoyarsk territory, this most northerly part of Siberia comprises the Taimyr peninsula and the Arctic islands of Severnaya Zemlya. Area, 862,100 sq. km, population (Jan. 1995) 47,000, excluding the mining city of Norilsk which is separately administered. Capital, Dudinka. Formed 1930.

Ust-Ordyn-Buryat Situated in Irkutsk region (Eastern Siberia); area, 22,400 sq. km, population (Jan. 1995) 143,000. Capital, Ust-Ordynsk. Formed 1937.

Yamalo-Nenets Situated in Tyumen region (Western Siberia); area, 750,300 sq. km, population (Jan. 1995) 0·48m. Capital, Salekhard. Formed 1930.

RWANDA

Republika y'u Rwanda

Capital: Kigali
Population: 5·1m.
GDP per head: (PPP$) 352
HDI/world rank: 0·187/174

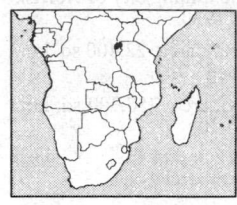

KEY HISTORICAL EVENTS. From the 16th century to 1959 the Tutsi kingdom of Rwanda shared the history of Burundi. In 1959 an uprising of the Hutu destroyed the Tutsi feudal hierarchy and overthrew the monarchy. Elections and a referendum under the auspices of the UN in Sept. 1961 resulted in an overwhelming majority for the republican party, the Parmehutu (*Parti du Mouvement de l'Emancipation du Bahutu*), and the rejection of the monarchy. The republic proclaimed by the Parmehutu on 28 Jan. 1961 was recognized by the Belgian administration (but not by the UN) in Oct. 1961. Internal self-government was granted on 1 Jan. 1962, and by decision of the General Assembly of the UN the Republic of Rwanda became independent on 1 July 1962.

Conflict between the Hutu and Tutsi in 1963 was renewed, and again trouble broke out, with much bloodshed, in 1972–73. A coup on 5 July 1973 deposed the first president, Gregoire Kayibanda, and a military government was established. The military leader of this coup, Gen. Juvénal Habyarimana, became president. There was gradual return to civilian rule. In 1978 a new constitution was accepted by a national referendum. President Habyarimana was confirmed in office in elections in 1978 and again in 1983, when candidates from the country's sole political party, the National Revolutionary Democratic Movement, were also returned. However, for much of the time since then the country has contended with the problem of refugees fleeing repression and war in neighbouring Uganda.

In Oct. 1990 rebel Tutsi forces of the Rwandan Patriotic Front (RPF) invaded from Uganda. An agreement was signed on 14 Aug. 1992 to end the civil war, but fighting continued. Rebels and government agreed to merge their forces at peace talks in March 1993. A peace agreement was signed on 4 Aug. 1993 at Arusha (Tanzania). On 5 Oct. the UN Security Council unanimously decided to send a peacekeeping force to oversee the establishment of transitional organs in line with the Aug. agreement. However, President Habyarimana was killed, possibly assassinated, on 6 April 1994. Fatalities in the fighting which broke out included the Prime Minister and UN personnel. Rebel Tutsi forces of the RPF began an attack from the north of the country.

An interim government was formed on 10 April with the Speaker Théodore Sindikubwabo (National Republican Movement for Development; MRND) as President and Jean Kambada (Democratic Republican Movement; MDR) as Prime Minister.

Most UN forces were withdrawn during the fighting and massacres of April 1994, but following a UN Security Council resolution of 17 May 1994 a new force of 5,500 was sent in.

On 22 June 1994 the UN Security Council approved France's dispatch of 2,000 troops on a humanitarian mission. The RPF, however, said it would treat the force as invaders. The French forces maintained a 'safe zone' for refugees in the south-west of Rwanda until their withdrawal on 21 Aug. 1994. Under the aegis of the OAU at Tunis representatives of the Rwandan interim government and the RPF agreed a ceasefire. At the request of the RPF on 6 July 1994 in Brussels Faustin Twagiramungu agreed to form a 22-member government of national unity in which 8 posts were held by the RPF.

It is estimated that more than 1m. Rwandans were killed in 1994 through genocide and the civil war, and that more than 2m. were forced to flee to neighbouring countries.

On 8 Nov. 1994 the UN Security Council resolved by 13 votes (China abstaining and Rwanda opposing) to set up an international tribunal to try crimes of genocide in Rwanda. It was inaugurated on 27 June 1995 and subsequently merged with that for Yugoslavia.

UN forces (UNAMIR) left Rwanda on 8 March 1996, and although progress has been made since then, the civil strife between the two factions continues, particularly in the north-west of the country. In Dec. 1997 over 300 Tutsis were killed at a large refugee camp.

TERRITORY AND POPULATION. Rwanda is bounded south by Burundi, west by the Democratic Republic of the Congo, north by Uganda and east by Tanzania. A mountainous state of 26,338 sq. km (10,169 sq. miles), its western third drains to Lake Kivu on the border with the Democratic Republic of the Congo and thence to the Congo river, while the rest is drained by the Kagera river into the Nile system.

The population was 7,164,994 at the 1991 Census, of whom over 90% were Hutu, 9% Tutsi and 1% Twa (pygmy); estimate (1996) 5,100,000 (8% urban); density, 193·6 per sq. km. Expectation of life, 1994, 22·6 years. Birth rate (per 1,000 population, 1994), 43·5; death rate, 52·2.

The areas and populations of the 10 prefectures are:

Prefecture	Area (in sq. km)	Population (1991 census)	Prefecture	Area (in sq. km)	Population (1991 census)
Cyangugu	1,845	515,129	Kigali	3,118	1,156,651
Kibuye	1,705	470,747	Kibungo	4,046	655,368
Gisenyi	2,050	734,697	Gitarama	2,189	851,516
Ruhengeri	1,663	766,112	Gikongoro	2,057	464,585
Byumba	4,761	783,350	Butare	1,837	766,839

Kigali, the capital, had 234,500 inhabitants in 1993; other towns being Butare, Ruhengeri and Gisenyi

Kinyarwanda, the language of the entire population, French and English (since 1996) are the official languages. Swahili is spoken in the commercial centres.

CLIMATE. Despite the equatorial situation, there is a highland tropical climate. The wet seasons are from Oct. to Dec. and March to May. Highest rainfall occurs in the west, at around 70" (1,770 mm), decreasing to 40–55" (1,020–1,400 mm) in the central uplands and to 30" (760 mm) in the north and east. Kigali. Jan. 67°F (19·4°C), July 70°F (21·1°C). Annual rainfall 40" (1,000 mm).

CONSTITUTION AND GOVERNMENT. Under the 1978 Constitution the MRND was the sole political organization.

A new Constitution was promulgated in June 1991 which permits multi-party democracy.

The Arusha Agreement of Aug. 1994 provided for a transitional 70-member National Assembly, which began functioning in Nov. 1994. The seats won by the MRNDD (formerly MRND) were taken over by other parties on the grounds that the MRNDD was culpable of genocide.

President: Pasteur Bizimungu (b. 1950; RPF; installed 19 July 1994).

In March. 1998 the government comprised:
Vice President and Minister of Defence: Paul Kagame (RPF).
Prime Minister: Pierre-Célestin Rwigema (MDR).
Minister of Agriculture: Augustin Iyamuremye. *Civil Service and Labour:* Joseph Nsengimana. *Commerce, Industry and Co-operatives:* Bonaventure Niyibizi. *Communications:* Charles Ntakirutinka. *Crafts, Mines and Tourism:* Marc Rugenera. *Education:* Joseph Karemera. *Family and Women's Affairs:* Aloysia Inyumba. *Finance and Planning:* Donat Kaberuka. *Foreign Affairs:* Anastase Gasana. *Health:* Vincent Biruta. *Information:* Jean Nepomcene Nayinzira. *Interior and Communal Development:* Sheik Abdelkarim Harelimana. *Justice:* Faustin Nteziryayo. *Public Works and Energy:* Laurien Ngirabanzi. *Youth:* Jacques Bihozagara.

National anthem: 'Rwanda rwacu, Rwanda gihugu cyambyage' ('My Rwanda, Rwanda who gave me birth'); words by a collective, tune traditional.

Local government. The 10 prefectures, each under an appointed Prefect, are divided into 143 communes, each with an appointed Burgomaster and an elected Council.

DEFENCE

Army. The Army consisted of 1 commando battalion, 1 reconnaissance, 8 infantry and 1 engineer company. Equipment included 12 AML-60 armoured cars. Strength (1997) about 55,000. There was a paramilitary gendarmerie of some 7,000.

INTERNATIONAL RELATIONS

Membership. Rwanda is a member of the UN, OAU and is an ACP state of the EU.

ECONOMY

Budget. In 1993 total revenue (in 1m. Rwanda francs) was 27,746; expenditure was 66,171.

Currency. The unit of currency is the *Rwanda franc* (RWF) notionally of 100 *centimes*. There are coins of 1, 2, 5, 10, 20 and 50 and notes of 100, 500, 1,000 and 5,000 Rwanda francs. On 3 Jan. 1995 500-, 1,000- and 5,000-Rwanda franc notes were replaced by new issues, demonetarizing the currency taken abroad by exiles. The currency is not convertible. Foreign exchange reserves were US$40m. in July 1994. There are no gold reserves. Inflation in 1994 was 64%.

Banking and Finance. The central bank is the National Bank of Rwanda (founded 1960; *Governor* Augustin Ruzidana) which became the bank of issue in 1964. There are 4 commercial banks (independent with state equity participation, the Economic Community of the Great Lakes Bank, and a state-run savings bank and development bank).

ENERGY AND NATURAL RESOURCES

Electricity. 4 hydro-electric installations and 1 thermal plant produced 110m. kWh in 1986, but over half of the country's needs come from the Democratic Republic of the Congo.

Minerals. Production (1991): Cassiterite, 871 tonnes; wolfram, 212 tonnes. About 1m. cu. metres of natural gas are obtained from under the lake each year.

Agriculture. Subsistence agriculture accounts for most of the GNP. Staple food crops (production 1995, in 1,000 tonnes) are plantains (2,600), sweet potatoes (1,100), cassava (250), potatoes (150), dry beans (118), sorghum (72), maize (71), taro (30), dry peas (12) and groundnuts (8). The main cash crops are coffee (22), tea (5) and pyrethrum. There is a pilot rice-growing project.

Long-horned Ankole cattle play an important traditional role. Efforts are being made to improve their present negligible economic value. There were (1995) 465,000 cattle, 920,000 goats, 250,000 sheep and 80,000 pigs.

Forestry. 5·6m. cu. metres of roundwood were cut in 1994.

INDUSTRY. There are about 100 small-sized modern manufacturing enterprises in the country. Food manufacturing is the dominant industrial activity (64%) followed by construction (15·3%) and mining (9%). There is a large modern brewery.

FOREIGN ECONOMIC RELATIONS. With Burundi and the Democratic Republic of the Congo, Rwanda forms part of the Economic Community of the Great Lakes. Foreign debt was 95,817m. Rwanda francs in 1992.

Commerce. In 1994 exports amounted to US$52m. and imports US$37m. Major exports are coffee, tea and tin. Main export markets, 1991: Germany, 21·3%; Netherlands, 18·8%; Belgium, 11·8%; UK, 6·4%. Main import suppliers: Belgium, 17·1%; Kenya, 13·4%; South Africa, 10·4%; France, 6·8%.

COMMUNICATIONS

Roads. There were (1993) 3,100 km of main roads and 4,900 km of secondary roads (979 km asphalt). There are road links with Burundi, Uganda, Tanzania and the Democratic Republic of the Congo. In 1990 there were 7,868 cars and 18,600 other vehicles.

Civil Aviation. There are international airports at Kanombe, for Kigali, and at Kamembe. The national carrier is Air Rwanda, which operated 1 B-707-320C and 1 other aircraft in 1995.

Telecommunications. Telephone provision, 1993, 1 per 1,000 population. The state-controlled Radiodiffusion de la République Rwandaise is responsible for broadcasting. There is no television. There were about 525,000 radio sets in 1995.

Press. In 1995 there was 1 daily newspaper with a circulation of 5,000.

SOCIAL INSTITUTIONS

Justice. A system of Courts of First Instance and provincial courts refer appeals to Courts of Appeal and a Court of Cassation situated in Kigali.

Religion. In 1997 there were 65% Roman Catholics, 9% Protestants and 1% Moslems. Some of the population follow traditional animist religions. Before the civil war there were 9 Roman Catholic bishops and 370 priests. By the end of 1994, 3 bishops had been killed and 3 reached retiring age; 106 priests had been killed and 130 had sought refuge abroad.

Education. In 1992 there were 1,710 primary schools with 18,937 teachers for 1·1m. pupils; 94,586 secondary pupils with 3,413 teachers; and 3,389 students at university level. Adult literacy rate, 1995, 60·5% (male, 69·8%; female, 51·6%).

Health. In 1983 there were 170 hospitals and health centres with (1980) 9,015 beds; there were also 164 doctors, 1 dentist, 10 pharmacists, 464 midwives and 525 nursing personnel.

There were 10,786 reported cases of AIDS by Nov. 1993, and 1·38m. reported of malaria in 1992.

DIPLOMATIC REPRESENTATIVES

Of Rwanda in Great Britain (Uganda Hse., 58-59 Trafalgar Sq., London WC2N 5DX)
Ambassador: Dr Zac Nsenga.

Of Great Britain in Rwanda (Parcelle No. 1131, Blvd. De l'Umuganda, Kacyira-Sud, POB 576, Kigali)
Ambassador: Kaye W. Oliver, OBE.

Of Rwanda in the USA (1714 New Hampshire Ave., NW, Washington, D.C., 20009)
Ambassador: Theogene Rudasingwa.

Of the USA in Rwanda (Blvd. de la Révolution, Kigali, POB28)
Ambassador: Robert Gribbin.

Of Rwanda to the United Nations
Ambassador: Gideon Kayinamura.

Of Rwanda to the European Union
Ambassador: Manzi Bakuramutsa.

Further Reading

Braeckman, C., *Rwanda: Histoire d'un Génocide.* Paris, 1994
Dorsey, L., *Historical Dictionary of Rwanda.* Metuchen (NJ), 1995
Prunier, G., *The Rwanda Crisis: History of a Genocide.* Farnborough, 1995

ST KITTS AND NEVIS

Federation of St Kitts and Nevis

Capital: Basseterre
Population: 45,000
GDP per head: (PPP$) 6,437
GNP: US$0·2bn.
HDI/world rank: 0·853/49

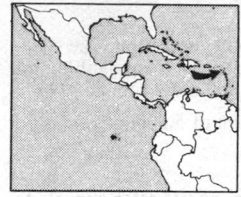

KEY HISTORICAL EVENTS. The islands of St Kitts (formerly St Christopher) and Nevis were discovered and named by Columbus in 1493. They were settled by Britain in 1623 and 1628 respectively, but ownership was disputed with France until 1783. They formed part of the Leeward Islands Federation from 1871 to 1956, and part of the Federation of the West Indies from 1958 to 1962. In Feb. 1967 the colonial status was replaced by an 'association' with Britain, giving the islands full internal self-government. St Kitts and Nevis became fully independent on 19 Sept. 1983.

In Oct. 1997 the 5-person Nevis legislature voted to end the federation with St Kitts. If successful this could lead to the creation of one of the smallest nations in the world.

TERRITORY AND POPULATION. The 2 islands of St Kitts and Nevis are situated at the northern end of the Leeward Islands in the Eastern Caribbean. Nevis lies 3 km to the south-east of St Kitts. Population, census (1991) 40,618. Estimate, 1997, 45,000 (9,000 on Nevis).

Vital statistics rates, 1997 estimates (per 1,000 population). Births, 23·1; deaths, 8·85. Infant mortality (per 1,000 live births), 18·4. Expectation of life in 1997 was 67·2 years (64·2 for males and 70·4 for females). Growth rate, 1·1% per annum.

	sq. km	Census 1980	Census 1991	Chief town	1994 estimate
St Kitts	168·4	33,881	31,824	Basseterre	12,605
Nevis	93·2	9,428	8,794	Charlestown	1,411
	261·6	43,309	40,618		

In 1991, 94·9% of the population were Black. English is the official and spoken language.

CLIMATE. Temperature varies between 17–33°C, with a sea breeze throughout the year, low humidity. Average annual rainfall is 1,300 mm.

CONSTITUTION AND GOVERNMENT. The 1983 Constitution described the country as 'a sovereign democratic federal state'. The Queen of the UK is the head of state, represented by a Governor-General. It allowed for a unicameral Parliament consisting of 11 elected Members (8 from St Kitts and 3 from Nevis) and 3 appointed Senators. Nevis was given its own Island Assembly and the right to secession from St Kitts. At the elections on 3 July 1995 the Labour Party gained 7 seats, the People's Action Movement 1, the Concerned Citizens Movement 2 and the Nevis Reformation Party 1.

Governor-General: Sir Cuthbert Montraville Sebastian, GCMG, OBE.

In March 1998 the government comprised:
Prime Minister and Minister of National Security, Foreign Affairs Finance, Planning and Information: Dr Denzil L. Douglas.

Deputy Prime Minister and Minister of Trade, Industry and CARICOM Affairs, Youth, Sports and Community Affairs: Sam Condor. *Health and Women's Affairs:* Dr Earl Asim Martin. *Tourism, Culture and Environment:* G. A. Dwyer Astaphan. *Education, Labour and Social Security:* Rupert Herbert. *Communications, Works, Public Utilities and Posts:* Cedric Liburd. *Agriculture, Lands and Housing:* Timothy Harris. *Attorney General:* Delano Bart.

The *Speaker* is Walford Gumbs.

The Premier of *Nevis* is Vance Amory.

The *Nevis Island* legislature comprises an Assembly of 3 nominated members and elected members from each electoral district on the Island, and an Administration consisting of the Premier and 2 other persons appointed by the Deputy Governor-General.

National anthem: 'O Land of beauty! Our country where peace abounds'; words and tune by K. A. Georges.

Local government: There are 14 parishes.

INTERNATIONAL RELATIONS

Membership. St Kitts and Nevis is a member of the UN, the OAS, the Commonwealth and is an ACP state of the EU.

ECONOMY

Performance. Real GDP growth in 1996 was estimated to be 4%.

Budget. Budget revenue and expenditure (in 1m. EC$):

	1990	1991	1992	1993	1994[1]
Revenue:	105·47	99·05	114·11	131·95	153·62
Expenditure:	115·24	118·35	127·07	146·17	165·29

[1] Provisional

Currency. The East Caribbean *dollar* (XCD) (of 100 *cents*) is in use. There are notes of EC$5, 10, 20, 50 and 100, and coins of 1, 2, 5, 10 and 25 cents and EC$1. Inflation was 3% in 1995.

Banking and Finance. The East Caribbean Central Bank (*Governor,* K. Dwight Venner) is the bank of issue. It operates 4 branches in St. Kitts and Nevis. The main office is located in Basseterre. There are 7 commercial banks, including 3 foreign. Commercial banks' assets (Dec. 1992) EC$646·47m.; deposits EC$481·28. Nevis has some 9,000 offshore businesses registered.

ENERGY AND NATURAL RESOURCES

Electricity. Production (1995) 42m. kWh.

Agriculture. The main crops are sugar, coconut, copra and cotton. In 1995, 3,327 ha were sown to sugar-cane. Most of the farms are small-holdings and there are a number of coconut estates amounting to some 400 ha under public and private ownership. Production, 1995 (in tonnes): Sugar, 20,760; sugar-cane, 19,960; coconuts, 2,000; fruit and vegetables, 3,000; cotton (1994), 4,783 lbs of clean lint; copra (1990), 12 tons.

Livestock (1995 in 1,000): Sheep, 14; goats, 11; pigs, 2; cattle (1992), 5; poultry, (1987) 50·12.

Fisheries. Catch (1994) 212,000 tonnes.

INDUSTRY. In 1996 industry accounted for 22% of GDP. There are 3 industrial estates on St Kitts and 1 on Nevis. Export products include electronics and data processing equipment, and garments for the US market. Other small enterprises include food and drink processing, particularly sugar and cane spirit, and construction. 180,285 tonnes of sugar were produced in 1995.

FOREIGN ECONOMIC RELATIONS

Commerce. Exports, 1995, EC$76m.; imports, EC$359·2m. Main trading partners are the USA, the UK and other CARICOM members. The chief export is sugar. Other significant exports are machinery, food, electronics, beverages and tobacco. Main imports include machinery, manufactures, food and fuels.

Tourism. In 1995 there were 214,415 visitors, including 123,148 cruise ship passengers. There were 31 hotels with 1,593 rooms.

COMMUNICATIONS

Roads. There were (1996) about 250 km of roads, of which 200 km were surfaced (124 km paved), and (1994) 6,941 licensed vehicles.

Railways. There are 58 km of railway operated by the sugar industry.

Civil Aviation. The airport is the Robert Llewelyn Bradshaw International Airport (just over 3 km from Basseterre). 123,195 passengers arrived by air in 1992. Services are provided by American Eagle, BWIA, Cruisin Air, LIAT and WinAir. There is also an airport on Nevis (Newcastle).

Shipping. There is a deep-water port at Bird Rock (Basseterre). 169,042 tons of cargo were unloaded in 1995 and 30,832 tons loaded. The government maintains a commercial motor boat service between the islands.

Telecommunications. There are 2 post offices with 7 branches. There were 14,000 telephone subscribers in 1994. There are 3 AM radio stations and 2 TV stations. Cable television is also available. In 1994 there were 9,000 television (colour by NTSC) and 27,000 radio receivers.

Press. In 1996 there were 2 weekly and 1 twice weekly newspapers.

SOCIAL INSTITUTIONS

Justice. Justice is administered by the Supreme Court and by Magistrates' Courts. They have both civil and criminal jurisdiction.

Religion. In 1994, 27·5% of the population were Anglican, 25·3% Methodist, 6·9% Roman Catholic, 5·5% Pentecostal, 3·9% Baptist and 3·9% Church of God.

Education. Adult literacy was 95% in 1996. Primary education is compulsory between the ages of 5 and 14, but no pupil is required to leave school before the age of 16. In 1993–94 there were 2,203 pupils and 156 teachers in 45 pre-primary schools. In 1994–95 there were 5,802 pupils and 290 teachers in 23 primary schools, 4,541 pupils and 326 teachers in 7 secondary schools, and (1993) 1,299 pupils and 76 teachers in 8 private schools. There is an Extra-Mural Department of the University of the West Indies, a Technical College and a Teachers' Training College.

Health. In 1990 there were 28 doctors, 4 hospitals with 258 beds and 17 health clinics.

DIPLOMATIC REPRESENTATIVES

Of St Kitts and Nevis in Great Britain (10 Kensington Ct., London W8 5DL)
High Commissioner: Aubrey E. Hart.

Of Great Britain in St Kitts and Nevis
High Commissioner: R. Thomas, CMG (resides in Antigua).

Of St Kitts and Nevis in the USA (OECS Building, 3216 New Mexico Ave., NW, 3rd Floor, Washington, D.C., 20016)
Ambassador: Dr Osbert Liburd

Of the USA in St Kitts and Nevis
Ambassador: Jeanette Hyde (resides in Barbados).

Of St Kitts and Nevis to the United Nations
Ambassador: Lee L. Moore, QC.

Of St Kitts and Nevis to the European Union
Ambassador: Edwin Laurent.

Further Reading

Statistics Division. *National Accounts.* Annual.—*St Kitts and Nevis Quarterly.*
Gordon, J., *Nevis: Queen of the Caribees.* London, 1985
Moll, V. P., *St Kitts and Nevis.* [Bibliography]. Oxford and Santa Barbara (CA), 1995

National library: Public Library, Basseterre.
National statistical office: Statistics Division, Ministry of Development, Basseterre.

ST LUCIA

Capital: Castries
Population: 150,600
GDP per head: (PPP$) 6,182
GNP: US$0·5bn.
HDI/world rank: 0·838/56

KEY HISTORICAL EVENTS. An island state of the lesser Antilles in the eastern Caribbean, St Lucia is believed to have been settled by the Arawaks, Amerindians who were subsequently driven out by the warlike Caribs. The island was probably discovered by Columbus in 1502. An unsuccessful attempt to colonize by the British took place in 1605, and again in 1638 when settlers were soon murdered by the Caribs who inhabited the island. France claimed the right of sovereignty, and ceded it to the French West India Company in 1642. The French settlers fought constant battles with the Caribs until peace was established in 1660. St Lucia regularly and constantly changed hands between Britain and France, until it was finally ceded to Britain in 1814 by the Treaty of Paris.

Since 1924 the island has had representative government. It was a part of the federal government of the Windward Islands until, in Jan. 1960, along with the colonies in the group, it was given its own administrator. In March 1967 St Lucia gained full control of its internal affairs while Britain remained responsible for foreign affairs and defence; the Administrator became the Governor, and a House of Assembly replaced the Legislative Council. On 22 Feb. 1979 St Lucia achieved independence, opting to remain in the British Commonwealth.

TERRITORY AND POPULATION. St Lucia is an island of the Lesser Antilles in the Eastern Caribbean between Martinique and St Vincent, with an area of 238 sq. miles (617 sq. km). Population (census, 1991) 133,308. Estimate, 1997, 150,600 (46% urban in 1995); density, 244·1 per sq. km.

Area and estimated population of the 10 administrative districts in 1992 were:

Districts	Sq. km	Population estimate	Districts	Sq. km	Population estimate
Ane-la-Raye }	47	{ 5,218	Gros Inlet	101	13,996
Canaries }		{ 1,864	Laborie	38	7,763
Castries	79	53,883	Micoud	78	15,636
Choiseul	31	6,638	Soufrière	51	7,962
Dennery	70	11,574	Vieux Fort	44	13,617

The official language is English, but 80% of the population speak a French creole.

In 1990 over 90% of the population was black, 6% were of mixed race and 3% of south Asian ethnic origin.

Vital statistics rates, 1997 estimates (per 1,000 population). Births, 23·3; deaths, 5·7. Infant mortality (per 1,000 live births), 17·3. Expectation of life in 1997 was 71·3 years (67·7 for males and 75·2 for females). Growth rate, 1·14% per annum.

Growth rate, 1995, 1·4%. Life expectancy (1992) was 69·3 (men) and 74 (women). The capital is Castries (population, 1991, 2,063).

CLIMATE. The climate is tropical, with a dry season from Jan. to April. Most rain falls in Nov.–Dec.; annual amount varies from 60" (1,500 mm) to 138" (3,450 mm). Temperature is about 80°F (26·7°C).

CONSTITUTION AND GOVERNMENT. There is a 17-seat *House of Assembly* elected for 5 years and an 11-seat *Senate* appointed by the Governor-General. At the elections of 23 May 1997 the St Lucia Labour Party gained 16 seats and the United Workers' Party 1.

Governor-General: Dr Perlette Louisy.

In March 1998 the government comprised:
Prime Minister and Minister of Finance, Planning, Information and the Public Service: Dr Kenny Anthony.
Deputy Prime Minister and Minister of Education, Human Resource Development, Youth and Sports: Mario Michel. *Tourism, Civil Aviation and Offshore Financial Services:* Phillip Pierre. *Agriculture, Fisheries, Forestry and the Environment:* Cassius Elias. *Community Development, Culture, Local Government and Co-operatives:* Damian Greaves. *Health, Family Affairs, Human Services and Women:* Sarah Flood. *Commerce, Industry and Consumer Affairs:* Walter François. *Communications, Works, Transport and Public Utilities:* George Calixte. *Legal Affairs, Home Affairs and Labour:* John Velon. *Foreign Affairs and International Trade:* George Odlum.
Attorney-General: Petrus Compton.

National anthem: 'Sons and daughters of St Lucia'; words by C. Jesse, tune by L. F. Thomas.

Local Government. There are 10 administrative districts.

INTERNATIONAL RELATIONS

Membership. St Lucia is a member of the UN, OAS, CARICOM, the Commonwealth and is an ACP state of the EU.

ECONOMY

Budget. 1995 estimates are: Expenditures, US$311m.; revenues, US$361·5m.

Banking and Finance. There are 3 domestic and 4 foreign banks. Inflation in 1996 was 3%.

ENERGY AND NATURAL RESOURCES

Agriculture. Bananas, cocoa, breadfruit and mango are the principal crops, but changes in the world's trading rules and changes in taste are combining to depress the banana trade. Farmers are experimenting with okra, tomatoes and avocados to help make up for the loss.
   Livestock (1992): Cattle, 3,000; pigs, 8,000; sheep, 5,000; goats, 3,000.

Fisheries. In 1995 the total catch was 1,023 tonnes.

INDUSTRY. The main products are clothing, assembly of electronic components, beverages, corrugated cardboard boxes, tourism, lime processing and coconut processing.

FOREIGN ECONOMIC RELATIONS. Foreign debt was US$115m. in 1996.

Commerce. Value of imports (1995), US$270·5m.; of exports, US$104·1m. Bananas accounted for 60% of exports. The main export markets in 1991 were the UK (56%), followed by the USA (22%) and CARICOM countries (19%). In 1995 manufactured goods accounted for 21% of imports, as did machinery and transportation equipment. Main partners in 1991 for imports were the USA (34%), followed by CARICOM countries (17%) and the UK (14%).

Tourism. The total number of visitors during 1994 was 394,000 (219,000 stop-over visitors and 175,000 cruise-ship passenger arrivals).

COMMUNICATIONS

Roads. The island has 500 miles of main and secondary roads.

Civil Aviation. There is an international airport at Hewanorra. The island is served by Air Canada, Air Martinique, American Airlines, British Airways, BWIA, Condor, Helenair and LIAT.

Shipping. There are 2 ports, Castries and Vieux Fort.

Telecommunications. There were (1994) 27,000 telephones, 68 telex and 560 fax machines. In 1993 there were 2 private radio stations, 2 privately-owned local TV stations and a cable TV service. There were 30,000 TV and 108,000 radio receivers in 1995.

Press. In 1993 there were 3 newspapers with a nation-wide circulation.

SOCIAL INSTITUTIONS

Justice. The island is divided into 2 judicial districts, and there are 9 magistrates' courts. Appeals lie to the Eastern Caribbean Supreme Court of Appeal.

Religion. In 1997 over 80% of the population was Roman Catholic.

Education. Primary education is free and compulsory. In 1993 there were 88 primary schools with 1,204 teachers for 32,545 pupils, and 14 secondary schools with 10,356 pupils and 558 teachers. There is a community college. Adult literacy rate is 82%.

Health. In 1992 there were 64 doctors, 6 dentists and 256 nursing personnel employed by the government, 4 hospitals with 435 beds and 34 health centres.

DIPLOMATIC REPRESENTATIVES

Of St Lucia in Great Britain (10 Kensington Ct., London, W8 5DL)
High Commissioner: Aubrey E. Hart.

Of Great Britain in St Lucia (Derek Walcott Sq., Castries)
(Acting) High Commissioner: P. J. Hughes.

Of St Lucia in the USA (2100 M St., NW, Washington, D.C., 20037)
Ambassador: Dr Joseph E. Edmunds.

Of the USA in St Lucia
Ambassador: Jeanette Hyde (resides in Barbados).

Of St Lucia to the United Nations
Ambassador: Vacant.

Of St Lucia to the European Union
Ambassador: Edwin Laurent.

Further Reading

Mommsen, J. H., *St Lucia.* [Bibliography]. Oxford and Santa Barbara (CA), 1996

ST VINCENT AND THE GRENADINES

Capital: Kingstown
Population: 118,344
GDP per head: (PPP$) 5,650
GNP: US$0·2bn.
HDI/world rank: 0·836/57

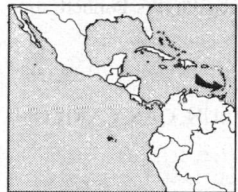

KEY HISTORICAL EVENTS. These islands in the eastern Caribbean were originally inhabited by the Carib tribes. St Vincent was discovered by Columbus on 22 Jan. (St Vincent's Day) 1498. British and French settlers occupied parts of the islands after 1627.

In 1773 the Caribs recognized British sovereignty and agreed to a division of territory between themselves and the British. Resentful of British rule, the Caribs rebelled in 1795, aided by the French, but the revolt was subdued within a year. Most of the Carib population was deported to islands in the Gulf of Honduras and the surviving population was further reduced by eruptions of the volcano Santiere in 1812 and 1902.

The islands were part of the federal government of the Windward Islands until, in Jan. 1960, along with other colonies in the group, they were given their own Administrator. Universal adult suffrage had been in existence on the islands since 1951. On 27 Oct. 1969 St Vincent became an Associated State with the UK responsible only for foreign policy and defence, while the islands were given full internal self-government. The Administrator became the Governor-General, and a House of Assembly replaced the Legislative Council. On 27 Oct. 1979 the colony acquired full independence as St Vincent and the Grenadines.

TERRITORY AND POPULATION. St Vincent is an island of the Lesser Antilles, situated in the Eastern Caribbean between St Lucia and Grenada, from which latter it is separated by a chain of small islands known as the Grenadines. The total area of 389 sq. km (150 sq. miles) comprises the island of St Vincent itself (345 sq. km) and those of the Grenadines attached to it, of which the largest are Bequia, Mustique, Canouan, Mayreau and Union.

The population at the 1991 Census was 106,499, of whom 8,367 lived in the St Vincent Grenadines. 1996 estimate, 118,344 (24·6% urban in 1994); density 304 per sq. km. The capital, Kingstown, had 26,223 inhabitants in 1991 (including suburbs). The population is mainly of black (82%) and mixed (13·9%) origin, with small white, Asian and American minorities.

Vital statistics (1996): Birth rate, 19·4 per 1,000 population; death, 5·4; infant mortality, 16·8 per 1,000 live births; life expectancy, 73 years.

CLIMATE. The climate is tropical marine, with north-east Trades predominating and rainfall ranging from 150" (3,750 mm) a year in the mountains to 60" (1,500 mm) on the south-east coast. The rainy season is from June to Dec., and temperatures are equable throughout the year.

CONSTITUTION AND GOVERNMENT. The head of state is Queen Elizabeth II, represented by a *Governor.* Parliament is unicameral and consists of a 21-member *House of Assembly,* 15 of which are directly elected for a 5-year term from single-member constituencies. The remaining 6 are senators appointed by the Governor (4 on the advice of the Prime Minister and 2 on the advice of the Leader of the Opposition). At the elections in Feb. 1994, the New Democratic Party won 12 seats and the alliance of the St Vincent Labour Party and the Movement for National Unity (which in 1995 merged to form the Unity Labour Party) 3.

Governor-General: Sir Charles Antrobus.

In March 1998 the government comprised:
Prime Minister and Minister of Finance: Rt Hon. Sir James Fitz-Allen Mitchell, KCMG.

Labour, and Fisheries: Bernard Wyllie. *Communications and Works:* Jeremiah C. Scott. *Education, Ecclesiastical Affairs, and Cultural Affairs:* Alpian Allen. *Foreign Affairs, Tourism, and Information:* Allan Cruickshank. *Health and the Environment:* Stephanie Browne. *Housing and Community Development, Youth and Sports:* Louis Jones. *Trade, Industry and Commerce:* John Horne. *Attorney General and Justice:* Carl Joseph.

National anthem: 'St Vincent, land so beautiful'; words by Phyllis Punnett, tune by J. B. Miguel.

INTERNATIONAL RELATIONS

Membership. St Vincent and the Grenadines is a member of UN, OAS, CARICOM, the Commonwealth and is an ACP state of the EU.

ECONOMY

Budget. Central government consolidated revenue and expenditure in US$1m. for calendar years:

	1992	1993	1994	1995	1996
Revenue	175·9	185·1	195·6	204·1	217·7
Expenditure	217·6	208·3	204·4	207·8	240·8

Expenditure by function in 1996 (and 1997) in US$1m.: Education, 387 (434); health, 317 (333); social security and welfare, 196 (139); public order and safety, 187 (198); housing and community amenities, 5 (5).

Currency. The currency in use is the *East Caribbean dollar* (XCD). Foreign exchange reserves were US$27·9m. in Sept. 1993.

Banking and Finance. The East Caribbean Central Bank is the bank of issue. There are branches of Barclays Bank PLC, the Caribbean Banking Corporation, the Canadian Imperial Bank of Commerce, the Bank of Nova Scotia. Locally-owned banks: First St Vincent Bank, the National Commercial Bank and St Vincent Co-operative Bank.

ENERGY AND NATURAL RESOURCES

Electricity. Production (1995) was 73m. kWh.

Agriculture. Agriculture accounted for 12·7% of GDP in 1995. According to the 1985–86 census of agriculture, 29,649 acres of the total acreage of 85,120 were classified as agricultural lands; 5,500 acres were under forest and woodland and all other lands accounted for 1,030 acres. The total arable land was about 8,932 acres, of which 4,016 acres were under temporary crops, 2,256 acres under temporary pasture, 2,289 acres under temporary fallow and other arable land covering 371 acres. 16,062 acres were under permanent crops, of which approximately 5,500 acres were under coconuts and 7,224 acres under bananas; the remainder produce cocoa, citrus, mangoes, avocado pears, guavas and miscellaneous crops. The sugar industry was closed down in 1985 although some sugar-cane is grown for rum production. Production (1995, in 1,000 tonnes): Bananas, 55; sugar-cane, 44; coconuts, 23; (1990, in tonnes): Nutmeg and mace, 111; arrowroot starch, 56; ginger, 834; taro, 5,240.

Livestock (1995, in 1,000): Cattle, 6; pigs, 9; sheep, 13; goats, 6.

Fisheries. Total catch, 1994, 1,743 tonnes.

INDUSTRY. Industries include assembly of electronic equipment, manufacture of garments, electrical products, animal feeds and flour, corrugated galvanized sheets, exhaust systems, industrial gases, concrete blocks, plastics, soft drinks, beer and rum, wood products and furniture, and processing of milk, fruit juices and food items. Rum production, 1994, 0·4m. litres.

Labour. The Department of Labour is charged with looking after the interest and welfare of all categories of workers, including providing advice and guidance to employers and employees and their organizations and enforcing the labour laws. In 1991 the total labour force was 41,682, of whom 33,355 (11,699 females) were employed.

FOREIGN ECONOMIC RELATIONS. Foreign debt was US$74·9m. in 1993.

Commerce (1996). Imports, EC$323·6m.; exports, EC$125·2m.

Principal exports, 1995 (in US$1m., preliminary): Dasheen, 15; bananas, 219; manufactured goods, 232 (flour, 87; rice, 64). Principal imports: Manufactured goods, 448; food, 24; machinery and transport equipment, 21; chemicals, 165.

Main export markets, 1995 (in US$1m., preliminary): UK, 9; St Lucia, 71; USA, 54; Trinidad and Tobago, 5. Main import suppliers: USA, 436; Trinidad and Tobago, 203; UK, 154.

Tourism. There were 218,014 visitors (85,258 cruise-ship passengers) in 1995.

COMMUNICATIONS

Roads. There were (1991) 60 miles of highway, 34 miles of concrete road, 296 miles of oiled asphalt road and 196 miles of earth track. Vehicles in use (1994): 5,700 passenger cars; 3,200 commercial vehicles.

Civil Aviation. There is an airport (E. T. Joshua) on mainland St Vincent. Scheduled services are operated daily by LIAT and Air Martinique. Airports on Bequia, Union, Mustique and Canouan have regular scheduled services.

Shipping. In 1994 there were some 200 ships in the Vincentian open register. In 1991 943 motor vessels of 919,846 NRT entered and cleared and 73 tankers of 84,367 NRT bringing 23,974 tons of fuel entered.

Telecommunications. There is a General Post Office at Kingstown and 56 district post offices. There is a fully digital automatic telephone system with (1992) 14,600 subscribers; 17,500 stations and digital radio links to Bequia, Mustique, Union, Petit St Vincent and Palm Island. The telephone network has almost 100% geographical coverage. The National Broadcasting Corporation is part government-owned and part commercial. In 1995 there were 75,000 radio and 18,000 TV sets (colour by NTSC).

SOCIAL INSTITUTIONS

Justice. Law is based on UK common law as exercised by the Eastern Caribbean Supreme Court on St Lucia. Final appeal lies to the UK Privy Council. In 1995 there were 4,700 criminal matters disposed of in the 3 magisterial districts which comprise 11 courts. 62 cases were dealt with in the Criminal Assizes in the High Court. Strength of police force (1995), 663 (including 19 gazetted officers).

Religion. At the 1980 Census, 42% of the population was Anglican, 21% Methodist and 12% Roman Catholic.

Education. In 1994 there were 97 pre-primary schools with 175 teachers for 2,500 pupils and 65 primary schools with 1,080 teachers for 21,386 pupils. In 1991 there were 10,719 secondary pupils with 431 teachers and 677 students at university level. Adult literacy (1994) 82%.

Health. In 1992 there was a general hospital in Kingstown with 207 beds, 6 rural hospitals, 2 private hospitals and 38 clinics. There were 40 doctors, 6 dentists, 224 registered nurses, 144 nursing assistants and 39 community health aides.

Library: St Vincent Public Library, Kingstown. *Librarian:* Mrs Pearl Herbert.

DIPLOMATIC REPRESENTATIVES

Of St Vincent and the Grenadines in Great Britain (10 Kensington Ct, London, W8 5DL)
High Commissioner: Aubrey E. Hart.

Of Great Britain in St Vincent and the Grenadines (POB 132, Granby St., Kingstown)
High Commissioner: R. Thomas, CMG (resides in Barbados).

Of St Vincent and the Grenadines in the USA
Ambassador: Kingsley C. A. Layne.

Of the USA in St Vincent and the Grenadines
Ambassador: Jeanette Hyde (resides in Barbados).

Of St Vincent and the Grenadines to the United Nations
Ambassador: Herbert G. Young.

Of St Vincent and the Grenadines to the European Union
Ambassador: Edwin Laurent.

Further Reading

Jenkins, D. and Bobrow, J., *St Vincent and the Grenadines: a Plural Country.* St Vincent, 1985
Potter, R. B., *St Vincent and the Grenadines.* [Bibliography]. Oxford and Santa Barbara (CA), 1992
Price, N., *Behind the Planter's Back.* London, 1988
Sutty, L., *St Vincent and the Grenadines.* London, 1993

SAMOA

O le Malo Tutoatasi o Samoa—

Independent State of Samoa

Capital: Apia
Population: 219,509
GDP per head: (PPP$) 2,726
HDI/world rank: 0·684/96

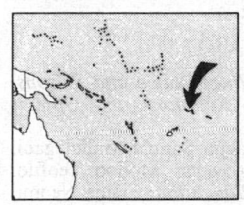

KEY HISTORICAL EVENTS. Polynesians settled in the Samoan group of islands in the southern Pacific from about 1000 BC. Shortly before European arrival, stratified society with paramount chiefs and fortified settlements developed. Although probably sighted by the Dutch in 1722, the first European visitor was French in 1768. Treaties were signed between the Chiefs and European nations in 1838–39.

Continuing strife among the chiefs was compounded by British, German and US rivalry for influence. In the Treaty of Berlin 1889 the three powers agreed to Western Samoa's independence and neutrality. When strife continued, the treaty was annulled and the Samoan group was annexed.

Western Samoa became a German protectorate until in 1914 it was occupied by a New Zealand expeditionary force. The island was administered by New Zealand from 1920 to 1961, at first under a League of Nations Mandate and from 1946 under a United Nations Trusteeship Agreement. In May 1961 a plebiscite held under the supervision of the UN on the basis of universal adult suffrage voted overwhelmingly in favour of independence. In Oct. 1961 the General Assembly of the United Nations passed a resolution to terminate the trusteeship agreement as from 1 Jan. 1962, on which date Western Samoa became an independent sovereign state. In July 1997 the country renamed itself as the Independent State of Samoa.

TERRITORY AND POPULATION. Samoa lies between 13° and 15° S. lat. and 171° and 173° W. long. It comprises the two large islands of Savai'i and Upolu, the small islands of Manono and Apolima, and several uninhabited islets lying off the coast. The total land area is 1,093 sq. miles (2,830·8 sq. km), of which 659·4 sq. miles (1,707·8 sq. km) are in Savai'i, and 431·5 sq. miles (1,117·6 sq. km) in Upolu; other islands, 2·1 sq. miles (5·4 sq. km). The islands are of volcanic origin, and the coasts are surrounded by coral reefs. Rugged mountain ranges form the core of both main islands. The large area laid waste by lava-flows in Savai'i is a primary cause of that island supporting less than one-third of the population of the islands despite its greater size than Upolu.

Population at the 1991 census, 161,298. July 1997 estimate, 219,509. The population at the 1986 census was 112,228 in Upolu (including Manono and Apolima) and 44,930 in Savai'i. The capital and chief port is Apia in Upolu (population 32,196 in 1986). Expectation of life was 69·09 years in 1997.

The official languages are Samoan and English.

CLIMATE. A tropical marine climate, with cooler conditions from May to Nov. and a rainy season from Dec. to April. The rainfall is unevenly distributed, with south and east coasts having the greater quantities. Average annual rainfall is about 100" (2,500 mm) in the drier areas. Apia. Jan. 80°F (26·7°C), July 78°F (25·6°C). Annual rainfall 112" (2,800 mm).

CONSTITUTION AND GOVERNMENT. HH Malietoa Tanumafili II is the sole Head of State for life. Future Heads of State will be elected by the Legislative Assembly and hold office for 5-year terms.

The executive power is vested in the *Head of State*, who swears in the *Prime Minister* (who is elected by the Legislative Assembly) and, on the Prime Minister's advice, the Ministers to form the Cabinet. The Constitution also provides for a *Council of Deputies* of 3 members, of whom the chairman is the Deputy Head of State.

Before 1991 the 49-member *Legislative Assembly* was elected exclusively by *matai* (customary family heads). At the elections of April 1991 the suffrage was universal, but only the approximately 20,000 *matai* could stand as candidates. The electorate was 56,000. At the most recent elections, in April 1996, the Human Rights Protection Party won 24 seats; the Samoan National Development Party, 11; Non-partisans, 13; and others, 1.

Head of State: HH Malietoa Tanumafili II, GCMG, CBE.
Deputy Head of State: Mataafa Faasuamaleaui Puela.
The cabinet in March 1998 was composed as follows:
Prime Minister, Minister of Foreign Affairs, Broadcasting, Police and Prisons, Attorney General, Public Service Commission Public Relations and Official Information: Tofilau Eti Alesana (re-elected in 1996).
Deputy Prime Minister and Minister of Finance: Tuilaepa Sailele Malielegaoi. *Agriculture, Forestry, Fisheries and Meteorological Services:* Molioo Teofilo. *Works:* Luagalau Levaula Kamu. *Health:* Misa Telefoni. *Education:* Fiame Naomi. *Posts and Telecommunication:* Leafa Vitale. *Lands, Survey and Environment:* Tuala Sale Tagaloa. *Justice:* Solia Papu Vaai. *Youth, Sports and Cultural Affairs:* Leota Lu Il. *Women's Affairs:* Leniu Tofaeono Avamagalo. *Labour:* Polataivao Fosi. *Transport:* Hans Joachim Keil.

National anthem: 'Samoa, tula'i ma sisi ia laufu'a/Samoa, Arise and Raise your Banner'; words and tune by S. I. Kuresa.

INTERNATIONAL RELATIONS. Samoa, as an independent state, deals directly with other governments and international organizations. It has diplomatic relations with a number of countries.

Membership. Samoa is a member of the UN, the Commonwealth, the South Pacific Forum and is an ACP member state of the ACP-EU relationship.

ECONOMY

Budget. For 1996–97 revenue was WS$288·4m.; expenditure, WS$312·7m. For 1997–98 budgeted revenue was WS$292·6m. and expenditure WS$306·6m.

Currency. The unit of currency is the *tala* (WST) of 100 *sene*. There are coins of 1, 2, 5, 20 and 50 sene and 1 tala, and notes of 2, 5, 10, 20, 50 and 100 talas.

Banking and Finance. The Central Bank of Samoa (founded 1984) is the bank of issue.

ENERGY AND NATURAL RESOURCES

Electricity. Production (1995) 69m. kWh.

Agriculture. The main products (1993, in 1,000 tonnes) are coconuts (130), taro (37), copra (11), bananas (10), papayas (10), mangoes (5), pineapples (6) and cocoa beans (1, in 1991).
    Livestock (1993): Horses, 3,000; cattle, 25,000; pigs, 178,000; poultry 1m. (1991).

Fisheries. The total catch (1994) was 1,500 tonnes.

INDUSTRY. Some industrial activity is being developed associated with agricultural products and forestry.

FOREIGN ECONOMIC RELATIONS

Commerce. In 1995, exports were valued at WS$65,844,800. Principal exports in 1995 were beer (WS$12·00m.) coconut cream (WS$4·20m.); coconut oil (WS$5·51m.) and kava (WS$1·06m.).

Tourism. There were 66,343 visitors in 1995 (62,608 in 1994).

COMMUNICATIONS

Roads. There are 2,085 km of roads, 400 km surfaced, and 1,200 km plantation roads. In 1993 there were 1,269 private cars, 1,936 pick-up trucks, 472 trucks, 334 buses, 936 taxis and 67 motor cycles.

Civil Aviation. There is an international airport at Apia (Faleolo). The national carrier is Polynesian Airlines, which in 1995 operated 1 B-737-300 and 1 other aircraft. Services are also provided by Air New Zealand and Air Pacific. Samoa Air provides international services between Samoa and American Samoa (a US Trust Territory) and domestic services to Upolu and Savai'i.

Shipping. Sea-going shipping totalled 6,501 GRT in 1995. Samoa is linked to Japan, USA, Europe, Fiji, Australia and New Zealand by regular shipping services.

Telecommunications. There are 3 radio communication stations at Apia. Radio telephone service connects Samoa with American Samoa, Fiji, New Zealand, Australia, Canada, USA and UK. Telephone subscribers numbered 3,452 in 1985. Broadcasting is the responsibility of the government-run commercial Western Samoa Broadcasting Department, which transmits radio programmes in Samoan and English. In 1995 there were 80,000 radio receivers and about 7,000 television sets.

Cinemas. In 1995 there were 3 cinemas.

Press. There are 4 weeklies (circulation 12,000) and 2 monthlies (8,000); all are in Samoan and English.

SOCIAL INSTITUTIONS

Religion. At the 1991 census, 43% of the population were Congregationalist, 21% Roman Catholic, 17% Methodist, 10% Mormon and 3% Seventh Day Adventist.

Education. In 1994 the total number of pupils in primary, junior and secondary schools was 48,507. The University of the South Pacific has a School of Agriculture in Samoa, at Apia. A National University was established in 1984. In 1994–95 it had 614 students and 30 academic staff. There is also a Polytechnic Institute which provides mainly vocational and training courses.

The adult literacy rate is 98·0%.

Health. In 1994 there were 2 national hospitals, 14 district hospitals, 9 health centres and 22 subcentres. There were 44 doctors in 1990.

DIPLOMATIC REPRESENTATIVES

Of Samoa in Great Britain and to the European Union
High Commissioner: Tauiliili Uili Meredith (resides in Brussels).

Of Great Britain in Samoa
High Commissioner: Robert J. Alston, CMG (resides in Wellington)

Of the USA in Samoa
Ambassador: Josiah H. Beeman (resides in Wellington).

Of Samoa in the USA and to the United Nations (1115 15th St., NW, Washington D.C. 20005)
Ambassador: Tuiloma Neroni Slade.

Further Reading

Hughes, H. G. A. *American Samoa, Western Samoa, Samoans Abroad.* [Bibliography]. Oxford and Santa Barbara (CA), 1997

SAN MARINO

Repubblica di San Marino

Capital: San Marino
Population: 25,515

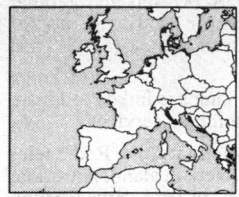

KEY HISTORICAL EVENTS. San Marino is a small republic situated on the Adriatic side of central Italy. According to tradition, St Marinus and a group of Christians settled there to escape persecution. By the 12th century San Marino had developed into a commune ruled by its own statutes and consul. Unsuccessful attempts were made to annex the republic to the papal states in the 18th century and when Napoleon invaded Italy in 1797 he respected the rights of the republic and even offered to extend its territories.

In 1815 the Congress of Vienna recognized the independence of the republic. On 22 March 1862 San Marino concluded a treaty of friendship and co-operation, including a *de facto* customs union, with the Kingdom of Italy, thus preserving its ancient independence although completely surrounded by Italian territory. This treaty was renewed in 1872, 1879 and 1939, with several amendments between 1942 and 1987.

TERRITORY AND POPULATION. San Marino is a land-locked state in central Italy, 20 km from the Adriatic. Area is 61·19 sq. km (23·6 sq. miles) and the population (1996), 25,515 (90·5% urban); some 13,360 citizens live abroad. Population density, 396 per sq. km. The capital, San Marino, has 4,372 inhabitants (1996); the largest town is Serravalle (8,026 in 1996), an industrial centre in the north.

CONSTITUTION AND GOVERNMENT. The legislative power is vested in the *Great and General Council* of 60 members elected every 5 years by popular vote, 2 of whom are appointed every 6 months to act as *Captains Regent*, who are the heads of state.

At the elections of 30 May 1993 the Christian Democrats gained 41·4% of votes cast and the Socialist Party 23·7%, forming a coalition government with 40 seats in the Great and General Council. The Progressive Democrats (former Communists) gained 18·6% of votes cast and 11 seats, the Popular Democratic Alliance 4 seats, the Democratic Movement 3 seats and the Refounded Communists 2.

Executive power is exercised by the 10-member *Congress of State*, presided over by the Captains Regent. The *Council of Twelve*, also presided over by the Captains Regent, is appointed by the Great and General Council to perform administrative functions and is a court of third instance.

In March 1998 the Congress of State comprised:

Minister of Foreign and Political Affairs: Gabriele Gatti. *Finance, Budget, Planning and Information:* Clelio Galassi. *Home Affairs:* Antonio Volpinari. *Industry and Handicraft:* Fiorenzo Stolfi. *Territory, Environment and Agriculture:* Luciano Ciavatta. *Commerce and Relations with Local Councils:* Ottaviano Rossi. *Health and Social Security:* Sante Canducci. *Education, Culture and Justice:* Pier Marino Menicucci. *Labour and Co-operation:* Claudio Podeschi. *Communications, Transport, Tourism and Sport:* Augusto Casali.

National anthem: No words, tune monastic, transcribed by F. Consolo.

Local Government. There are 9 districts (*castelli*), each run by a board elected every 5 years.

DEFENCE. Military service is not obligatory, but all citizens between the ages of 16 and 55 can be called upon to defend the State. They may also serve as volunteers in the Military Corps. There is a paramilitary Gendarmerie.

INTERNATIONAL RELATIONS. San Marino maintains a traditional neutrality, and remained so in the First and Second World Wars. It has diplomatic and consular relations with over 70 countries.

Membership. San Marino is a member of the UN, the Council of Europe, the OSCE and various UN specialised agencies.

ECONOMY. The budget (ordinary and extraordinary) for the financial year ending 31 Dec. 1996 balanced at 699 billion lire. 3,940 ha of land area are arable. Wheat, barley, maize and vines are grown. The chief exports are wood machinery, wine, textiles, tiles, varnishes and ceramics.

Italian currency is in use, but the republic issues its own coins.

In 1996, 3·5m. tourists visited San Marino.

FOREIGN ECONOMIC RELATIONS

Commerce. Export commodities are building stone, lime, wood, chestnuts, wheat, wine, baked goods, hides and ceramics. Import commodities are a wide range of consumer manufactures and foodstuffs.

COMMUNICATIONS

Roads. A bus service connects San Marino with Rimini. There are 237 km of roads and (1996) 24,408 passenger cars and 4,246 commercial vehicles.

Telecommunications. In 1996 there were 16,000 telephones and 9 post offices. In 1996 there were 12,000 television receivers. San Marino RTV is the state broadcasting company.

Cinemas. In 1996 there were 4 cinemas with a seating capacity of 1,800.

SOCIAL INSTITUTIONS

Justice. Judges are appointed permanently by the Great and General Council; they may not be San Marino citizens. Petty civil cases are dealt with by a justice of the peace; legal commissioners deal with more serious civil cases and all criminal cases and appeals lie to them from the justice of the peace. Appeals against the legal commissioners lie to an appeals judge, and the Council of the Twelve functions as a court of third instance.

Religion. The great majority of the population are Roman Catholic.

Education. Education is compulsory up to 16 years of age. In 1996 there were 15 nursery schools with 854 pupils and 96 teachers, 14 elementary schools with 1,170 pupils and 211 teachers, 3 junior high schools with 753 pupils and 148 teachers, and 1 high school with 310 pupils and 44 teachers. The University of San Marino began operating in 1988.

Health. In 1996 there were 160 hospital beds and 65 doctors.

DIPLOMATIC REPRESENTATIVES

British Consul-General (resides at Florence): R. J. Griffiths, OBE.

Of San Marino to the United Nations
Ambassador: Gian Nicola Filippi Balestra.

Further Reading

Edwards, A. and Michaelides, C., *San Marino* [Bibliography]. Oxford and Santa Barbara (CA), 1996
Matteini, N., *The Republic of San Marino*. San Marino, 1981

Information: Office of Cultural Affairs and Information of the Department of Foreign Affairs.

SÃO TOMÉ E PRÍNCIPE

República Democrática de
São Tomé e Príncipe

Capital: São Tomé
Population: 147,865
GDP per head: (PPP$) 1,704
HDI/world rank: 0·534/125

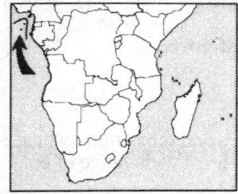

KEY HISTORICAL EVENTS. The islands of São Tomé and Príncipe off the west coast of Africa were colonized by Portugal for 5 centuries after being first visited by Portuguese navigators on 21 Dec. 1470. There may have been a few African inhabitants or visitors earlier, but most of the population arrived during the centuries when the islands served as an important slave-trading depot for South America and some slaves were kept on the islands to work on the sugar plantations. In the 19th century the islands became the first parts of Africa to grow cocoa. Although in 1876 Portugal abolished slavery in name, in practice it continued thereafter with many Angolans, Mozambicans and Cape Verdians being transported to work on the cocoa plantations. Because the slave-descended population was cut off from African culture, São Tomé had a higher proportion than other Portuguese colonies of *assimilados* (Africans acquiring full Portuguese culture and certain rights).

After becoming an Overseas Province of Portugal in 1951, São Tomé saw serious riots against Portuguese rule in 1953. From 1960 a Committee for the Liberation of São Tomé e Príncipe operated from neighbouring African territories. There was, however, no armed resistance on the islands, where in 1970 Portugal introduced some reforms and formed a 16-member legislative council and a provincial consultative council. Following the Portuguese revolution of 1974, the Movement for the Liberation of São Tomé e Príncipe, headed by Manoel Pinto da Costa, held talks with Portugal. A transitional government was formed later that year and, after a period of tension due to landowners' resistance to decolonization and the temporary retention of Portuguese troops, independence came on 12 July 1975. Pinto da Costa became the first president and was re-elected for a further 5 years in 1985.

Independent São Tomé e Príncipe officially proclaimed Marxist-Leninist policies, but it maintained a non-aligned foreign policy and has received aid from Portugal.

TERRITORY AND POPULATION. The republic, which lies about 200 km off the west coast of Gabon, in the Gulf of Guinea, comprises the main islands of São Tomé (845 sq. km) and Príncipe and several smaller islets including Pedras Tinhosas and Rolas. It has a total area of 1,001 sq. km (387 sq. miles). Population (census, 1991) 120,146. Estimate (1997), 147,865.

The areas and populations of the 2 provinces:

Province	Sq. km	Census 1991	Estimate 1995	Chief town	Census 1991
São Tomé	859	114,507	125,200	São Tomé	43,420
Príncipe	142	5,639	5,900	São António	1,000

Vital statistics (1997 estimate): Birth rate per 1,000 population, 33·77; death rate, 8·4; infant mortality (per 1,000 live births), 60·2. Expectation of life, 64·09.

The official language is Portuguese. Lungwa São Tomé, a Portuguese creole, and Fang, a Bantu language, are the spoken languages.

CLIMATE. The tropical climate is modified by altitude and the effect of the cool Benguela current. The wet season is generally from Oct. to May, but rainfall varies very much, from 40" (1,000 mm) in the hot and humid north-east to 150–200" (3,800–5,000 mm) on the plateau. São Tomé. Jan. 79°F (26·1°C), July 75°F (23·9°C). Annual rainfall 38" (951 mm).

CONSTITUTION AND GOVERNMENT. The 1990 constitution was approved by 72% of votes at a referendum of Aug. 1990. It abolished the monopoly of the Movement for the Liberation of São Tomé e Príncipe (MLSTP). The *President* must be over 34 years old, and is elected by universal suffrage for one or two (only) 5-year terms. He or she is also head of government and appoints a Council of Ministers. The 55-member *National Assembly* is elected for 4 years.

At the presidential elections on 21 July 1996 President Trovoada was re-elected by 52·2% of votes cast against 1 opponent.

At the elections on 2 Oct. 1994 the electorate was some 57,000; turn-out was 79%. The MLSTP/Social Democratic Party won 27 seats, the Democratic Convergence Party (DCP), 14 and Independent Democratic Action (IDA), 14.

President, C.-in-C.: Miguel Trovoada (b. 1946; IDA; re-elected 21 July 1996).

The government comprised in March 1998:

Prime Minister Raul Wagner Conceição Braganca Neto.

Minister of Agriculture and Fisheries: Hermenilgido de Assunção Sousa Santos. *Commerce, Industry and Tourism:* Cosme Afonso da Trindade Rita. *Defence and Internal Order:* Capt. Joao Quaresma Viegas Bexigas. *Education, Culture and Sport:* Albertino Homem dos Santos Sequeira. *Equipment and Environment:* Arlindo Afonso Carvalho. *Foreign Affairs and São Tomé Communities Abroad:* Homero Jeronimo Salvaterra. *Health:* Eduardo do Carmo Ferreira de Matos. *Justice, Labour and Public Administration:* Amaro Pereira de Couto. *Planning and Finance:* Acacio Elba Bonfim.

National anthem: 'Independência total, glorioso canto do povo' ('Total independence, glorious song of the people'); words by A. N. do Espírito Santo, tune by M. de Sousa e Almeida.

Local Government. São Tomé province comprises 6 districts. Districts have assemblies elected universally for 3-year terms. In elections in Dec. 1992 the MLSTP won 38 of the 59 district assembly seats with 70% of votes cast, the DCP won 15 seats, IDA 6.

Since April 1995 **Príncipe** has enjoyed internal self-government, with a 5-member regional government and an elected assembly.

INTERNATIONAL RELATIONS

Membership. São Tomé e Príncipe is a member of the UN, OAU and is an ACP state of the EU.

ECONOMY

Policy. Most branches of the economy were nationalized after independence, but economic liberalization began in 1985 and was increased in 1991.

Budget. The 1995 budget set revenue at 11,000m. dobras and expenditure at 50,000m. dobras.

Currency. The unit of currency is the *dobra* (STD) of 100 *centimos*. There are coins of 50 centimos and 1, 2, 5, 10 and 20 dobras, and notes of 50, 100, 500, 1,000, 2,000 and 5,000 dobras.

Banking and Finance. In 1991 the Banco Central de São Tomé e Príncipe replaced the Banco Nacional as the central bank and bank of issue. A private commercial bank, the Banco Internacional de São Tomé e Príncipe, began operations in 1993.

Weights and Measures. The metric system is in use.

ENERGY AND NATURAL RESOURCES

Electricity. Installed capacity, 1992, 7·2m. kW; output, 4·6m. kWh. 30% of supply is hydroelectric.

Agriculture. Agriculture accounts for 25% of GDP. After independence all land-holdings over 200 ha were nationalized into 15 state farms. These were partially privatized in 1985 by granting management contracts to foreign companies, and distributing some state land as small private plots. Production (1995 in tonnes): Coconuts, 22,000; cocoa, 4,500; copra, 500; bananas, 3,000; palm oil, 250. Food crops include cassava, sweet potatoes and yams. In 1994 there were 30,000 goats, 2,000 sheep and 7,000 pigs.

Forestry. Forests cover 60% of the land area. In 1994, 9,000 cu. metres of timber were cut.

Fisheries. There are rich tuna shoals. Catch (1994) 3,000 tonnes.

INDUSTRY. Manufacturing contributes less than 10% of GDP. There are a few small factories in agricultural and timber processing, bricks, ceramics, printing, textiles and soap-making.

Labour. In 1994 the economically active population was 54,000. There were 15,000 registered unemployed.

FOREIGN ECONOMIC RELATIONS. Foreign debt was US$189·9m. in 1992.

Commerce. Imports in 1992 amounted to 10,089·4m. dobras and exports to 1,739·8m. dobras, the main exports being cocoa (80%), copra (15%), coffee, bananas and palm-oil.

Main export markets: Germany, 44·8%; Netherlands, 31·1%. Main import suppliers: Portugal, 39·5%; Spain, 12·3%; Belgium, 12·1%.

Tourism. There were about 5,000 arrivals in 1994.

COMMUNICATIONS

Roads. There were 380 km of roads in 1994, 250 km asphalted.

Civil Aviation. São Tomé airport is linked by regular services to Lisbon, Luanda, and Libreville. There is a light aircraft service to Príncipe. The national carrier is Air São Tomé in which the government has a 35% stake. 40% is owned by TAP-Air Portugal, who operate most international routes.

Shipping. São Tomé is the main port, but it lacks a deep water harbour. Neves handles oil imports and is the main fishing port. Portuguese shipping lines run routes to Lisbon, Oporto, Rotterdam and Antwerp.

Telecommunications. There were (1991) 3,105 telephones. Radio broadcasting is conducted by the government-controlled Rádio Nacional. There is a Voice of America radio station, a religious station and a private German station. There were about 35,000 radio sets in 1994. There is an experimental TV service at weekends.

Press. There are 4 weekly newspapers.

SOCIAL INSTITUTIONS

Justice. Members of the Supreme Court are appointed by the National Assembly. There is no death penalty.

Religion. About 90% of the population are Roman Catholic. There is a small Protestant church and a Seventh Day Adventist school.

Education. Adult literacy was 67·1% in 1994. Education is free and compulsory. In 1993 there were 85 primary and 5 secondary schools. 90% of primary age children were attending school. There is a vocational centre, a school of agriculture and a pre-university *lycée*.

Health. In 1988 there were 50 doctors.

DIPLOMATIC REPRESENTATIVES

Of São Tomé e Príncipe in Great Britain (resides in Brussels)
Ambassador: Vacant.

Of Great Britain in São Tomé e Príncipe
Ambassador: Roger D. Hart (resides in Angola).

Of São Tomé e Príncipe in the USA
Ambassador: Vacant.

Of the USA in São Tomé e Príncipe
Ambassador: Elizabeth Raspolic.

Of São Tomé e Príncipe to the United Nations
Ambassador: Vacant.

Of São Tomé e Príncipe to the European Union
Ambassador: Vacant.

Further Reading

Shaw, C. S., *São Tomé e Príncipe.* [Bibliography] Oxford and Santa Barbara (CA), 1994

SAUDI ARABIA

Mamlaka al-'Arabiya
as-Sa'udiya

(Kingdom of Saudi Arabia)

Capital: Riyadh
Population: 17·8m.
GDP per head: (PPP$) 9,338
GNP: US$126·6bn.
HDI/world rank: 0·774/73

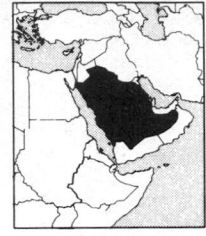

KEY HISTORICAL EVENTS. In the 6th century AD Makkah, now in western Saudi Arabia, was a thriving commercial centre. Around 610 the Prophet Mohammed began receiving revelations of the oneness of God through the Angel Gabriel, and he began to attract a following. In 622, learning of an assassination plot against him, he led his followers to the town of Yathrib (now Madinah). This was the *Hijrah*, or migration, which marks the beginning of the Islamic calendar. Battles ensued between Mohammed's followers and the pagans of Makkah, but by 628 Mohammed had united the tribes so successfully he and his followers entered Makkah without bloodshed. Less than 100 years from the advent of Islam, its empire extended from Spain to areas of India and China. Islamic rule thrived well into the 17th century.

Today the Kingdom of Saudi Arabia is a union of two regions, Nejd and Hejaz. In the 18th century, Nejd was an autonomous region governed from Diriya, the stronghold of the Wahhabis, a puritanical Islamic sect. It subsequently fell under Turkish rule, but in 1913 Abdulaziz Ibn Abdul Rahman Al-Saud defeated the Turks and also captured the Turkish province of al Hasa. In 1920 he captured the Asir, and in 1921 by force of arms he added to his dominions the Jebel Shammar territory of the Rashid family. In 1925 he completed the conquest of the Hejaz.

Great Britain recognized Abdulaziz as an independent ruler, King of the Hejaz and of Nejd and its dependencies, by the Treaty of Jiddah on 20 May 1927. The name was changed to the Kingdom of Saudi Arabia in Sept. 1932. King Abdulaziz ruled until his death in Nov. 1953. During his rule there was considerable development of the oil resources of the country. Although begun before the Second World War, oil exploitation grew greatly with the support of the USA after 1945.

King Abdulaziz was succeeded by his sons, Saud, Faisal, Khalid and Fahd. Saud succeeded to the throne in 1953 but in March 1964 abdicated in favour of Faisal Ibn Abdulaziz who had carried considerable power during the older brother's reign, being for a time prime minister with control over foreign and economic policy. Faisal was assassinated in 1975, and was succeeded by his brother, Khalid Ibn Abdulaziz. On Khalid's death in 1982, Fahd Ibn Abdulaziz became king. In 1995, after King Kahd suffered a stroke, he appointed his half-brother Crown Prince Abdullah Ibn Abdulaziz to act on his behalf.

TERRITORY AND POPULATION. Saudi Arabia, which occupies nearly 80% of the Arabian peninsula, is bounded in the west by the Red Sea, east by the Arabian/Persian Gulf and the United Arab Emirates, north by Jordan, Iraq and Kuwait and south by Yemen and Oman. An agreement with Qatar of 26 Oct. 1996 provided for the definitive delimitation of their common frontier by 1998. For the border dispute with Yemen *see* YEMEN: Territory and Population. The total area is estimated to be 849,400 sq. miles (2·2m. sq. km). Riyadh is the political, and Makkah the religious, capital.

The total population was (1974 census) 7,012,642, of which 5,128,655 were categorized as settled and 1,883,987 as nomadic. Estimate (1992), 16,929,294 (7,462,753 females), of whom 12,304,835 were Saudi Arabians. 1994 estimate, 17·8m.

Annual growth rate of the indigenous population was 3·7% in 1990. Expectation of life was 70·3 years in 1994. Birth rate (1994) was 34·6; death rate, 4·4.

Principal cities with 1991 population estimates (in 1m.): Riyadh, 1·8; Jiddah, 1·5; Makkah, 0·63; Taif, 0·41;Madinah, 0·4; Dammam, 0·35.

The Neutral Zone (3,560 sq. miles, 5,700 sq. km.), jointly owned and administered by Kuwait and Saudi Arabia from 1922 to 1966, was partitioned between the two countries in 1966, but the exploitation of the oil and other natural resources continues to be shared.

CLIMATE. A desert climate, with very little rain and none at all from June to Dec. The months May to Sept. are very hot and humid, but winter temperatures are quite pleasant. Riyadh. Jan. 58°F (14·4°C), July 108°F (42°C). Annual rainfall 4" (100 mm). Jiddah. Jan. 73°F (22·8°C), July 87°F (30·6°C). Annual rainfall 3" (81 mm).

ROYAL HOUSE. The reigning King is **Fahd Ibn Abdulaziz Rahman Al-Saud** (b. 1923), Custodian of the two Holy Mosques, succeeded in May 1982, after King Khalid's death. *Crown Prince:* Prince Abdullah Ibn Abdulaziz, half-brother of the King.

CONSTITUTION AND GOVERNMENT. Constitutional practice derives from Sharia law. There is no formal Constitution, but 3 royal decrees of 1 March 1992 established a Basic Law which defines the systems of central and municipal government, and set up a 60-man Consultative Council (*Majlis Al-Shura*) of royal nominees in Aug. 1993. *Chairman* is Mohammed Ibn Uthman Ibn Jubair.

In July 1997 the King decreed an increase of the Consultative Council to chairman plus 90 members, selected from men of science and experience.

Saudi Arabia is an absolute monarchy; executive power is discharged through a *Council of Ministers,* consisting of the King, Deputy Prime Minister, Second Deputy Prime Minister and Cabinet Ministers.

The King has the post of *Prime Minister,* and can veto any decision of the Council of Ministers within 30 days.

In March 1998 the Council of Ministers comprised:
Deputy Prime Minister and Commander of the National Guard: Crown Prince Abdullah Ibn Abdulaziz Al-Saud (b. 1924). *Second Deputy Prime Minister and Minister of Defence and Aviation, and Inspector-General:* Prince Sultan Ibn Abdulaziz Al-Saud. *Housing and Public Works:* Prince Met'eb Ibn Abdulaziz Al-Saud. *Interior:* Prince Naif Ibn Abdulaziz Al-Saud. *Foreign Affairs:* Prince Saud Al-Faisal Ibn Abdulaziz Al-Saud. *Labour and Social Affairs:* Musaid Ibn Mohammed Al-Sanani. *Communications:* Dr Nasir Ibn Mohammed Al-Salloum. *Finance and National Economy:* Dr Ibrahim Ibn Abdulaziz Ibn Abdullah Al-Assaf. *Information:* Dr Fouad Ibn Abdul Salaam Ibn Mohammed Farsi. *Industry and Electricity:* Dr Hashim Ibn Abdullah Ibn Hashim Al-Yamani. *Commerce:* Osama Ibn Jafar Ibn Ibrahim Faqih. *Justice:* Dr Abdullah Ibn Mohammed Ibn Ibrahim Al-Ashaik. *Education:* Dr Mohammed Ibn Ahmed Al-Rasheed. *Higher Education:* Dr Khalid Al-Angary. *Petroleum and Mineral Resources:* Ali Ibn Ibrahim Al-Naimi. *Islamic Affairs, Endowments, Call and Guidance:* Dr Abdullah Ibn Abdulmohsen Al-Turki. *Pilgrimage:* Dr Mahmoud Ibn Mohammed Safar. *Municipal and Rural Affairs:* Dr Mohammed Ibin Ibrahim Al-Jarallah. *Planning:* Dr Abdul Wahab Ibn Abdul Salam Attar. *Agriculture and Water:* Dr Abdullah Ibin Abdulaziz Ibin Mu'amar. *Health:* Dr Osama Ibin Abdul Majeed Shobokshi. *Posts, Telegraphs and Telephones:* Dr Ali Ibin Talal Al-Jahani.

National anthem: 'Sarei lil majd walaya' ('Onward towards the glory and the heights'); words by Ibrahim Khafaji, tune by Abdul Rahman al Katib.

Local Government. 13 provinces were designated in 1993, each governed by an emir with ministerial rank appointed by the King. Each province has a consultative council which meets every 3 months and consists of provincial government officials *ex officio* and at least 10 Saudi citizens recommended by the emir for the King's appointment. Council members serve 4 years and meet once every 2 weeks.

DEFENCE. The USA stations Air Force units on rotational detachment. The Peninsular Shield Force of about 7,000 comprises units from all Gulf Co-operation Council countries.

Army. The Army comprises 3 armoured brigades, 5 mechanized brigades, 1 airborne brigade, 1 Royal Guard regiment and 8 artillery battalions. Equipment includes 315 M-1A2, 290 AMX-30, 450 M-60A3 main battle tanks and 10 surface-to-surface missiles. The Army Aviation Command disposes of nearly 50 Blackhawk, Dauphin and armed AH-64A Apache and Bell 406 helicopters. Strength (1997) was approximately 70,000. There is a para-military Frontier Force (approximately 10,500).

Navy. The Royal Saudi Naval Forces comprise 4 French-built 2,900-tonnes frigates armed with Otomat anti-ship missiles, 4 smaller US-built missile frigates, 9 US-built fast missile craft, 3 German-built torpedo craft, 4 US-built coastal minesweepers and the first 3 of 6 UK-built Sandown class minehunters. Auxiliaries include 2 French-built replenishment tankers each embarking 2 helicopters, 3 ocean tugs and a Royal Yacht. There are numerous minor auxiliaries and boats.

Naval Aviation forces operate 6 Super Puma armed with Exocet missiles, 6 for search and rescue and 21 Dauphin helicopters, both ship and shore based.

The main naval bases are at Jiddah (Red Sea) and Jubail (The Gulf). Naval personnel in 1997 totalled 13,500, including 3,000 marines.

The Coast Guard operates some 35 inshore patrol craft, 24 hovercraft and over 300 boats of various types.

Air Force. Current combat units include 4 squadrons of F-15 Eagle interceptors, 4 squadrons of F-5E Tiger II supersonic fighter-bombers and RF-5E Tigereye reconnaissance aircraft, supported by a conversion unit with F-5B/F combat trainers. 2 squadrons operate Tornado strike aircraft and another 2 have Tornado interceptors. There is a squadron with Boeing E-3 Sentry airborne early-warning aircraft and KE-3 flight refuelling tankers. 1 squadron of Hawk light jet attack/trainers is based at the Al Kharj and a second at King Faisal Air Academy, Riyadh, together with 12 Reims/Cessna FR172 piston-engined primary trainers, PC-9 basic trainers and Jetstream navigation trainers. Other types in current service include 60 C-130E/H and KC-130H Hercules transports and tankers, 1 Boeing 747 SP, 1 Boeing 747-200, 1 Boeing 737, 3 Boeing 707, 4 CN-235s, 12 BAe-125s, 3 Learjets and 2 JetStar VIP jet transports, more than 80 Agusta-Bell 205, 212 and JetRanger and KV-107 helicopters, 2 Agusta AS-61A-4 VIP transport helicopters and communications aircraft. Personnel (1995), about 18,000 with 295 combat aircraft.

Air Defence Force. This separate Command was formerly part of the Army, which retains a point air defence capability. In 1995 it had 33 surface-to-air missile batteries and a strength of 4,000.

National Guard. The National Guard comprises 2 mechanized and 6 infantry brigades and 1 ceremonial cavalry squadron. Additionally there are a number of regular and irregular units, the total strength of the National Guard amounting to approximately 77,000 (57,000 active, 20,000 tribal levies). The National Guard's primary role is the protection of the Royal Family and vital points in the Kingdom. It is directly under royal command. The UK provides small advisory teams to the National Guard in the fields of general training and communications.

INTERNATIONAL RELATIONS

Membership. Saudi Arabia is a member of the UN, the Arab League, the Gulf Cooperation Council and OPEC.

ECONOMY

Policy. The sixth 5-year development plan (1995–99) continues the emphasis on developing the private sector, and aims to increase and indigenize the workforce, enhance defence capacity, achieve a balanced economic development and protect the environment. The 1998 budget emphasises expenditure and capital projects such as roads and schools. 80% of the budget goes on public sector salaries.

Performance. Real GDP growth was 8·6% in 1996.

Budget. In 1986 the financial year became the calendar year. Estimated revenue,

1996: SAR177,000m. 1997 budget: Revenue, SAR164,000m.; expenditure, SAR181,000m. Revenues for 1998 are forecast at SAR178,000m., and expenditure at SAR196,000m.

Oil sales account for 80% of state income. Estimated 1993 expenditure (in 1m. rials): Defence and security, 61·6; education, 34·1; health and social welfare, 14·1; economic and social subsidies, 9·2; transport and communications, 9·1.

Currency. The unit of currency is the *rial* (SAR) of 100 *halalahs*. There are coins of 5, 10, 25, 50 and 100 halalahs, and notes of 1, 5, 10, 50, 100 and 500 rials. In Oct. 1994, foreign exchange reserves totalled US$7,241m.; gold reserves in 1993 were US$1,290m. Inflation was 0·9% in 1996.

Banking and Finance. The Saudi Arabian Monetary Agency (*governor*, Hamad Saud al Sayari), established in 1953, functions as the central bank and the government's fiscal agent. There were 12 commercial banks with 1,160 branches, 5 special credit institutions and a variety of other financial institutions in 1995. Sharia forbids the charging of interest; Islamic banking is based on sharing clients' profits and losses and imposing service charges. The Saudi Arabian Agricultural Bank with 70 branches and offices extended 755m. rials in credit services to farmers during 1989. At 30 Sept. 1995 total assets of commercial banks were 323,900m. rials.

There is a stock exchange.

ENERGY AND NATURAL RESOURCES

Electricity. By 1995 the over 100 electricity producers had been amalgamated into 4 companies. Installed capacity was 21,901 MW in 1994. All electricity is thermally generated. 63,632m. kWh. were generated in 1990-91.

Oil. Proven reserves (1996) 260,100m. bbls (26% of world resources). Oil production began in 1938 by Aramco, which is now 100% state-owned and accounts for about 97% of total crude oil production.

Saudi Arabia's 1997 OPEC quota was 8·76m. bls. a day.

Production comes from 14 major oilfields, mostly in the Eastern Province and offshore, and including production from the Neutral Zone.

Gas. In 1996, gas reserves were estimated at 190,100,000m. cu. feet.

Water. Efforts are underway to provide adequate supplies of water for urban, industrial, rural and agricultural use. Most investment has gone into sea-water desalination. In 1996, 33 plants produced 1·9m. cu. metres a day, meeting 70% of drinking water needs. Total annual consumption was 18,200m. cu. metres in 1995. Irrigation for agriculture consumes the largest amount, from fossil reserves (the country's principal water source), and from surface water collected during seasonal floods. In 1996 there were 183 dams with a holding capacity of 450m. cu. metres. Treated urban waste water is an increasing resource for domestic purposes; in 1996 there were 2 recycling plants in operation.

Minerals. Production began in 1988 at Mahd Al-Dahab gold mine. In 1993, 189,353 tonnes of ore were extracted. Deposits of iron, phosphate, bauxite, uranium, silver, tin, tungsten, nickel, chrome, zinc, lead, potassium ore and copper have been found.

Agriculture. Since 1970 the Government has spent substantially on desert reclamation, irrigation schemes, drainage and control of surface water and control of moving sands. Undeveloped land has been distributed to farmers and there are research and extension programmes. Large scale private investment has concentrated on wheat, poultry and dairy production.

In 1990 agriculture contributed 8% of GDP. 1·2m. ha of land were cultivated and 85m. ha in pastoral use. There were some 152,000 farms in 1992; the agricultural workforce was 1,877,000 in 1993.

Date production in 1994 was 568,000 tonnes; wheat (1993), 3·6m. tonnes. About 2m. tonnes of barley are produced annually as animal fodder. Estimated production of other crops, 1994 (in 1,000 tonnes): Vegetables, 2,500; fruit, 1,088. Livestock products: Milk, 587; poultry and red meat, 453; eggs, 126.

Livestock estimates (1993, in 1,000) include 210 cattle, 420 camels, 7,100 sheep and 3,400 goats.

Fisheries. Production, 1994, 62,000 tonnes, including fish farming and an offshore fishing catch of 51,000 tonnes.

INDUSTRY. The Government encourages the establishment of manufacturing industries. Its policy focuses on establishing industries that use petroleum products, petrochemicals and minerals. Petrochemical and oil-based industries have been concentrated at 8 new industrial cities, with the 2 principal cities at Jubail and Yanbu. In 1996, there were 15 major plants and other industrial facilities, a dedicated desalination plant, a vocational training institute and a college at Jubail, and 3 major refineries, a petrochemical complex and many manufacturing and support enterprises at Yanbu. Products include chemical, plastics, industrial gases, steel and other metals. In 1995 there were 2,234 factories employing 196,000 workers.

Labour. In 1988, 95% of the total labour force was employed in the non-oil sector. There were 4m. foreign workers in 1995.

FOREIGN ECONOMIC RELATIONS. In 1992, foreign debt totalled US$17,089m.

Commerce. In 1993 imports totalled 127,926m. rials and exports 174,996m. rials (154,867m. rials oil and products). Exports in 1994 were some 155,500m. rials (oil, 139,800m. rials). The principal export is crude oil; refined oil, petro-chemicals and wheat are other major exports. Share of exports: Japan, 17·1%; USA, 16·2%; Singapore, 5·7%; France, 5·2%. Imports: USA, 20·6%; Japan, 12·7%; UK, 8·5%; Germany, 7·2%.

Tourism. In 1989 there were 774,560 pilgrims to Makkah from abroad.

COMMUNICATIONS

Roads. In 1996 there were 43,200 km of primary roads and 96,000 km of secondary roads. A causeway links Saudi Arabia with Bahrain. In 1991, 5m. vehicles were registered. Women may not drive.

Railways. 1,435 mm gauge lines link Riyadh and Dammam with stops at Hofuf and Abqaiq. This line is being extended to Jubail. In 1994–95 railways carried 453,000 passengers and 1·9m. tonnes of freight.

Civil Aviation. The national carrier is the state-owned Saudia, which in 1995 operated 11 A300B4-600s, 17 B-737-200 Advs, 2 B-737-200C Advs, 2 B747-100s, 8 B-747-100Bs, 1 B-747-200B(F), 1 B-747-200F, 10 B-747-300s, 1 B-747SP and 33 other aircraft. In 1994 it carried 12·5m. passengers on international and domestic flights. Services are also provided by 42 foreign airlines. There are 3 major international airports at Jiddah (King Abdulaziz), Dhahran and Riyadh (King Khaled) and 22 domestic airports. King Fahd International Airport in Eastern Province is under construction. In 1990, 21·3m. passengers passed through Saudi airports.

Shipping. The ports of Dammam and Jubail are on the Arabian/Persian Gulf and Jiddah, Yanbu and Jizan on the Red Sea. There is a deepwater oil terminal at Ras Tanura, and 16 minor ports. In 1994 the ports handled 86·8m. tonnes of cargo. In 1995 the merchant marine comprised 110 vessels totalling 8·2m. DWT, representing 1·24% of the world's total fleet tonnage. 49 vessels (89·13% of tonnage) were registered under foreign flags. GRT totalled 1·08m; including oil tankers, 210,370 GRT, and container ships, 67,599 GRT.

Telecommunications. Number of telephones (1995), 1·78m., including 15,590 mobile. There were 10,100 telex machines. Number of post offices (1988) 603. The government-controlled Broadcasting Service of the Kingdom of Saudi Arabia and Saudi Arabian Television are responsible for broadcasting. Radio programmes include 2 home services, 2 religious services, services in English and French and an external service. Aramco Oil have a private station. There are TV programmes in Arabic and English; Channel 3 TV is a non-commercial independent. Colour is by SECAM and PAL. In 1993 there were estimated to be 5m. radio and 4·5m. TV sets.

Press. In 1991 there were 3 daily newspapers in Arabic and 3 in English and 2 Arabic and 2 English weeklies.

SOCIAL INSTITUTIONS

Justice. The religious law of Islam (Sharia) is the common law of the land, and is administered by religious courts, at the head of which is a chief judge, who is responsible for the Department of Sharia Affairs. Sharia courts are concerned primarily with family inheritance and property matters. The Committee for the Settlement of Commercial Disputes is the commercial court. Other specialized courts or committees include one dealing exclusively with labour and employment matters; the Negotiable Instruments Committee, which deals with cases relating to cheques, bills of exchange and promissory notes, and the Board of Grievances, whose preserve is disputes with the government or its agencies and which also has jurisdiction in trade-mark-infringement cases and is the authority for enforcing foreign court judgements.

The death penalty is in force for murder, rape, sodomy, armed robbery, sabotage, drug trafficking, adultery and apostasy; executions may be held in public. There were 58 executions in 1994.

Religion. About 92% are Sunni Moslems and 8% Shiites. The *Grand Mufti*, Abdul Aziz ben Baz, has cabinet rank. A special police force, the Mutaween, exists to enforce religious norms.

Education. The educational system provides students with free education, books and health services. General education consists of kindergarten, 6 years of primary school and 3 years each of intermediate and high school. Students can attend either high schools offering programmes in arts and sciences, or vocational schools. Girls' education is administered separately. In 1995 there were 815,000 students in intermediate schools and 447,000 in high schools; 9,578 students were enrolled in vocational training. In 1996 there were more than 30 special schools for the handicapped with about 4,550 students. The adult literacy rate is 61·8%.

In 1996 there were 2,343 adult education centres.

In 1995-96 there were 4 universities, 2 Islamic universities and 1 university of petroleum and minerals. There were 90,207 students and 7,352 academic staff.

Health. In 1995 there were 3,254 primary health care centres and clinics and 279 hospitals with 41,923 beds. 29,227 doctors, 61,627 nursing and 32,167 technical staff were employed at these facilities. At Jiddah there is a quarantine centre for pilgrims.

DIPLOMATIC REPRESENTATIVES

Of Saudi Arabia in Great Britain (30 Charles St., London, W1X 7PM)
Ambassador: Dr Ghazi A. Algosaibi.

Of Great Britain in Saudi Arabia (PO Box 94351, Riyadh 11963)
Ambassador: Andrew F. Green, CMG.

Of Saudi Arabia in the USA (601 New Hampshire Ave., NW, Washington, D.C., 20037)
Ambassador: HRH Prince Bandar bin Sultan.

Of the USA in Saudi Arabia (PO Box 9041, Riyadh)
Ambassador: Wyche Fowler.

Of Saudi Arabia to the United Nations
Ambassador: Vacant.

Of Saudi Arabia to the European Union
Ambassador: Nassir Alassaf.

Further Reading

Azzam, H., *Saudi Arabia: Economic Trends, Business Environment and Investment Opportunities*. London, 1993

Clements, F. A., *Saudi Arabia*. [Bibliography] Oxford and Santa Barbara (CA), 1988

Holden, D. and Johns, R., *The House of Saud*. London and New York, 1981

Kostiner, J., *The Making of Saudi Arabia: from Chieftaincy to Monarchical State*. OUP, 1994

Peterson, J. E., *Historical Dictionary of Saudi Arabia*. Metuchen (NJ), 1994

Wright, J. W. (ed.) *Business and Economic Development in Saudi Arabia: Essays with Saudi Scholars*. London, 1996

National statistical office: Ministry of Finance and National Economy, Department of Statistics, Riyadh.

SENEGAL

République du Sénégal

Capital: Dakar
Population: 9·09m.
GDP per head: (PPP$) 1,596
GNP: US$5·0bn.
HDI/world rank: 0·326/160

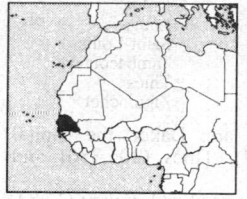

KEY HISTORICAL EVENTS. The major ethnic groups of Senegal are the Wolof, Serer, Tukulor (or Toucouleur), Soninke (or Sarakole), Mandinka and Diola peoples. Some of them had important traditional kingdoms. In Fouta Toro in the east there was the state of Tekrur and then an Islamic state founded in 1776 by Muslim Tukulors. Islam reached the Senegal river valley by the 11th century, and later the Fulanis (whose migration all over West Africa began from Senegal) and the related Tukolors helped spread Islam over a large area.

For several centuries, starting in the 14th, the Wolofs had a supreme ruler, the Bourba Jolof, and several important kingdoms under him, notably the kingdom of Kayor (Kajoor) ruled by 30 kings or *damels* from the 16th century to 1886. The last *damel*, the Muslim Lat Dior, was famous for his resistance to French rule.

While in the mid-1400s the Portuguese were the first Europeans to reach the area around the Senegal river estuary; in succeeding centuries the French became the dominant Europeans on the coast in that area, except for the Gambia, where the British were installed. The French founded Saint-Louis in 1659 and also occupied the island of Goree, an important slave-trading depot. By the 18th century Saint-Louis had an important small elite community, partly African, called the *habitants*. In the 19th century French rule, interrupted earlier by occasional British occupation, was confirmed over Saint-Louis and Goree. Free Africans received the vote in 1833, and the franchise was further extended in 1848 when slavery was abolished in all French colonies. The Africans in Saint-Louis and Goree, and also in Dakar and Rufisque, were in the 19th century called the *originaires* and had the rights of French citizens. They elected a deputy to the French national Assembly and voted for local government councils (or *communes*).

From the late 1870s France began a sustained push up the river and into the interior. Here, groundnuts were already being grown for export to France, but African monarchs still ruled, including the new Islamic conqueror, El Hadj Umar and, after his death in 1864, his son Ahmadu. There was strong resistance to the French, notably that led by Lat Dior from 1882 until his death in action in 1886. French rule was established by the mid-1890s, while the British then consolidated their rule inland in The Gambia. French efforts to obtain cession of that territory, entirely surrounded by Senegal, did not succeed.

The normal French colonial system prevailed, one of its features being the breaking up of traditional kingdoms (completed in Senegal by the 1920s). Senegal was part of French West Africa *(Afrique Occidentale Française)* from 1902 and became an autonomous state within the French Community on 25 Nov. 1958. On 4 April 1959 Senegal joined with French Sudan to form the Federation of Mali, which achieved independence on 20 June 1960, but on 22 Aug. Senegal withdrew from the Federation and became a separate independent republic. Senegal was a one-Party state from 1966 until 1974, when a pluralist system was re-established.

TERRITORY AND POPULATION. Senegal is bounded by Mauritania to the north and north-east, Mali to the east, Guinea and Guinea-Bissau to the south and the Atlantic to the west with The Gambia forming an enclave along that shore. Area, 196,190 sq. km; population (census, 1988), 6,982,084; (estimate, 1996) 9·09m. (40% urban). Population density, 40·5 per sq. km. Growth rate (1992), 2·9%; infant mortality (1996), 64 per 1,000 live births; birth rate (1991) per 1,000 population, 43; death rate, 16. Life expectancy in 1996 was 53·75 years for men and 59·3 for women. Age structure : 1–14 years, 48%; 15–64, 49%; 65 and over, 3%.

The areas, populations and capitals of the 10 regions:

Region	Area (in sq. km)	1988 Census	Capital
Dakar	550	1,571,614	Dakar
Diourbel	4,359	620,197	Diourbel
Fatick	7,935	507,651	Fatick
Kaolack	16,010	805,859	Kaolack
Kolda	21,011	593,199	Kolda
Louga	29,188	507,572	Louga
Saint-Louis	44,127	656,941	Saint-Louis
Tambacounda	57,602	383,572	Tambacounda
Thiès	6,601	937,412	Thiès
Ziguinchor	7,339	398,067	Ziguinchor

The largest cities (with 1992 estimated population) are: Dakar, the capital (1,729,823), Kaolack (179,894), Saint-Louis (125,717), Thiès (201,350) and Ziguinchor (148,831).

Ethnic groups are the Wolof (36% of the population), Serer (17%), Fulani (17%), Tukulor (9%), Diola (9%), Malinké (6%), Bambara (6%) and Sarakole (2%).

The official language is French; Wolof is widely spoken.

CLIMATE. A tropical climate with wet and dry seasons. The rains fall almost exclusively in the hot season, from June to Oct., with high humidity. Dakar. Jan. 72°F (22·2°C), July 82°F (27·8°C). Annual rainfall 22" (541 mm).

CONSTITUTION AND GOVERNMENT. The 1963 constitution was revised in 1991. The head of state is the *President*, elected by universal suffrage for not more than two 7-year terms. For the unicameral 120-member National Assembly 60 members are elected in single-member constituencies and 60 by a form of proportional representation for 5-year terms. It was announced in Dec. 1995 that a senate would be established to represent territorial collectives in parliament.

At the presidential elections of 21 Feb. 1993 there were 8 candidates; turn-out was 51·46%. Abdou Diouf was re-elected with 58·4% of votes cast.

President: Abdou Diouf (took office in Jan. 1981, re-elected 1983, 1988 and 1993).

At the elections of 9 May 1993 the electorate was 2·5m.; turn-out was 40·74%. 1,282 candidates representing 6 parties stood. The Socialist Party (SP) gained 84 seats, the Senegalese Democratic Party 27, the Democratic League 3, the Japoo coalition 3, the African Party of Independence and Labour 2 and the Senegalese Democratic Union—Renovation 1.

The Cabinet appointed in April 1991 was composed as follows in March 1998:
Prime Minister: Habib Thiam.
Ministers of State: Moustapha Niasse (*Foreign Affairs and Expatriates*); Robert Sagna (*Agriculture*); Lamine Cisse (*Interior*); Abdoulaye Wade (*Without Portfolio*); Ousmane Dieng (*Presidential Services*). Minister of the *Armed Forces*: Cheikh Hamidou Kane. *Communications:* Serigne Diop. *Culture:* Abdoulaye Kane. *Economy, Finance and Planning:* Mamadou Lamine Loum. *Employment, Labour and Professional Training:* Assane Diop. *Education:* André Sonko. *Energy, Mining and Industry:* Magued Diouf. *Environment and Conservation of Nature:* Abdoulaye Bathily. *Equipment and Land Transport:* Landing Sane. *Fisheries and Marine Transport:* Alassane Ndiaye. *Justice:* Jacques Baudin. *Modernization:* Nene Mbaye. *Tourism and Civil Aviation:* Tidiane Sylla. *Towns:* Daour Cisse. *Trades and Crafts:* Idrissa Seck. *Water Resources:* Mamadou Faye. *Women, Children and Family Welfare:* Aminata Ndiaye. *Youth and Sport:* Ousmane Paye. *Urban Planning and Housing:* Abdourahmane Sow. *Health and Social Action:* Ousmane Ngom. *Research and Technology:* Marie-Louise Correa.

The *Speaker* is Sheikh Abdul Khadre Cissokho (SP).

National anthem: 'Pincez tous vos koras, frappez les balafos'('All pluck the koras, strike the balafos'); words by Léopold Sédar Senghor, tune by Herbert Pepper.

Local Government. Senegal is divided into 10 regions, each with an appointed governor and an elected regional assembly. They are divided into 30 departments, each under an appointed prefect, and thence into 99 *arrondissements.* Legislation of 1996 increased the powers of local authorities. Local elections were held on 1 Dec. 1996; SP gained a large majority of seats.

DEFENCE. There is selective conscription for 2 years.

Army. There are 4 military zones. The Army had a strength of 12,000 (mostly conscripts) in 1996, organized in 6 infantry battalions, 1 engineer, 1 armoured, 1 airborne, 1 commando and 1 artillery battalion, 1 horsed Presidential Guard and 3 construction companies. Equipment includes 67 armoured cars. There is also a paramilitary force of gendarmarie and customs.

Navy. The flotilla includes 2 coastal patrol craft, 8 inshore patrol craft, 1 tank landing craft, 2 smaller amphibious craft, and about 6 service craft. Personnel (1996) totalled 700, and bases are at Dakar and Casamance.

Air Force. The Air Force, formed with French assistance, has 3 Rallye Guerrier and 5 Magister armed trainers, 5 F.27 twin-turboprop transports, 2 Puma, 1 Gazelle and 2 Alouette II helicopters, plus 2 Rallye trainers, but serviceability is low. Personnel (1995) 650, with 8 combat aircraft.

INTERNATIONAL RELATIONS

Membership. Senegal is a member of the UN, OAU and is an ACP state of the EU.

International disputes: short section of the boundary with The Gambia is indefinite; boundary with Mauritania is in dispute.

ECONOMY

Policy. Privatization began in 1987 and by 1996 20 companies had been sold off. An austerity programme was adopted in 1993 and the following year Senegal embarked on a structural adjustment aimed to exploit a 50% devaluation of the currency in the 14 francophone African countries. A start has been made on liberalizing labour laws, closing tax loopholes and ending monopolies. With IMF targets met, the second part of a loan facility was approved in 1995.

Performance. Real GDP growth was 4·5% in 1996 (4% in 1995).

Budget. The 1996 budget is estimated to have produced revenues of US$836m. and an expenditure of US$1,970m.

Currency. The currency is the *franc CFA* (XOF) at a parity of 100 *francs CFA* to 1 French *franc.* Currency in circulation, 1992: 96,610m. francs CFA. In 1992 gold reserves were 29,000 troy oz., and foreign exchange reserves US$8·7m. The inflation rate was 6·1% in 1995.

Banking and Finance. The Banque Centrale des États de l'Afrique de l'Ouest is the bank of issue of the franc CFA for all the countries of the West African Economic and Monetary Union (Benin, Burkina Faso, Côte d'Ivoire, Mali, Niger, Senegal and Togo) but has had its headquarters in Dakar since 1973. Its *governor* is Charles Konan Banny. There are few major banks, the largest including the Banque Internationale pour le Commerce et l'Industrie and Banque de l'Habitat (9% state-owned).

ENERGY AND NATURAL RESOURCES

Electricity. In 1996 installed capacity was 230 MW. Output was 720m. kWh.

Minerals. 1,128,000 tonnes of calcium phosphate were produced in 1992 and 93,000 tonnes of aluminium phosphate in 1989. There are gold deposits and exploration was under way by 1996.

Agriculture. Because of erratic rainfall 25% of agricultural land needs irrigation. Most land is owned under customary rights and holdings tend to be small. In 1992 2·35m. ha were used as arable land, 0·16m. ha for permanent crops and 3·1m. ha for permanent pasture. Production, 1993 (in tonnes): Groundnuts, 628,000; cotton, 50,000; sorghum, 98,000; rice paddy, 89,000; millet, 657; maize, 125,000; cassava, 43,000.

Livestock (1993, in 1,000): 4,400 sheep, 3,118 goats, 2,750 cattle, 320 pigs, 364 asses, 15 camels and 498 horses. Animal products, 1993 (1,000 tonnes): Beef and veal, 45; pork, 7; horseflesh, 6; mutton and lamb, 15; goat meat, 13; poultry meat, 52; milk, 103; eggs, 27. In 1992 there were 550 tractors.

Forestry. There are 10·55m. ha of forest, accounting for 31% of the land surface. Production (1994) amounted to 5·10m. cu. metres.

Fisheries. The fishing fleet comprises 167 vessels totalling 40,600 GRT. In 1994 the total catch was 388,000 metric tonnes.

INDUSTRY. Predominantly agricultural and fish processing, phosphate mining, petroleum refining and contruction materials.

Labour. The workforce (10 years and over) in 1996 was 2,509,000, of whom 77% were engaged in subsistence farming; 60% of the workforce is in the public sector.

Trade Unions. There are two major unions, the *Union Nationale des Travailleurs Sénégalais* (government-controlled) and the *Confédération Nationale des Travailleurs Sénégalais* (independent) which broke away from the former in 1969 and in 1994 comprised 75% of salaried workers.

FOREIGN ECONOMIC RELATIONS

Commerce. In 1994 imports totalled US$1·1m. and exports US$940m. Chief exports: fish, groundnuts, petroleum products, phosphates and cotton. Chief imports: food and beverages, capital goods. Main trading partners are: France, other EU countries, Algeria, Côte d'Ivoire and Mali.

Tourism. In 1995 there were 0·4m. foreign visitors.

COMMUNICATIONS

Roads. The length of roads (1995) was 13,850 km of which 3,900 km were bitumenized. In 1987 there were 81,855 passenger cars, 30,454 lorries and 8,843 buses.

Railways. There are 4 railway lines: Dakar-Kidira (continuing in Mali), Thiès-Saint-Louis (193 km), Guinguinéo-Kaolack (22 km), and Diourbel-Touba (46 km). Total length (1993), 1,225 km (metre gauge). In 1993 railways carried 3·7m. passengers and 2·3m. tonnes of freight.

Civil Aviation. The international airport is Dakar Yoff. 603,000 passengers passed through Yoff in 1991. Air Sénégal is 50% state-owned, had 3 aircraft in 1995. Services are also provided by Aeroflot, Air Afrique, Air Algérie, Air France, Air Gabon, Air Guinée, Air Liberté, Air Mauritanie, Alitalia, Condor, Ethiopian Airlines, Gambia Airways, Ghana Airways, Iberia, Royal Air Maroc, Sabena, Saudia, Swissair, TAP and Tunis Air.

Shipping. In 1995 the merchant marine totalled 27,640 GRT. 5·5m. tonnes of freight were handled in the port of Dakar in 1995. There is a river service on the Senegal from Saint-Louis to Podor (363 km) open throughout the year, and to Kayes (924 km) open from July to Oct. The Senegal River is closed to foreign flags. The Saloum River is navigable as far as Kaolack, the Casamance River as far as Ziguinchor.

Telecommunications. There were, in 1983, 530 post offices. Telephones in 1993 numbered 55,000. The government-owned Office de Radio-Télévision du Sénégal broadcasts a national and an international radio service from 10 main transmitters. There are also regional services. There is also a TV service (colour by SECAM). In 1993 there were 0·85m. radio and 61,000 TV sets.

Press. The main daily is *Le Soleil,* circulation (1989) 30,000.

SOCIAL INSTITUTIONS

Justice. There are *juges de paix* in each *département* and a court of first instance in each region. Assize courts are situated in Dakar, Kaolack, Saint-Louis and Ziguinchor, while the Court of Appeal resides in Dakar. The death penalty is authorized.

Religion. The population is 90% Sunni Moslem, the remainder being Christian (mainly Roman Catholic) or animist.

Education. Adult literacy is 32·1%. In 1992 there were 738,556 pupils and 1,711 teachers in 2,454 primary schools and 182,140 pupils in secondary schools, and 7,301 students in vocational training schools. There are 14,833 students (3,136 female) and 770 teachers at university level. There are 2 universities with 16,654 students and 889 academic staff in 1995-96, and 19 other institutions of higher education.

Health. In 1988 there were 16 government hospitals with 4,064 beds, 529 maternity homes, 47 health centres, 661 clinics and 13 leprosy clinics. There were 407 doctors (258 in government service), 58 dentists (27), 474 midwives (458), and 934 other medical personnel (879). There were 200 pharmacists.

DIPLOMATIC REPRESENTATIVES

Of Senegal in Great Britain (21-24 Cockspur Street, London, SW1Y 5BN)
Ambassador: Gabriel Alexandre Sar.

Of Great Britain in Senegal (20 Rue du Docteur Guillet, Dakar)
Ambassador: David R. Snoxell.

Of Senegal in the USA (2112 Wyoming Ave., NW, Washington, D.C., 20008)
Ambassador: Mamadou Mansour Seck.

Of the USA in Senegal (Ave. Jean XXIII, Dakar)
Ambassador: Mark Johnson.

Of Senegal to the United Nations
Ambassador: Ibra Ka.

Of Senegal to the European Union
Ambassador: Saloum Kande.

Further Reading

Centre Français du Commerce Extérieur. *Sénégal: un Marché.* Paris, 1993
Adams, A. and So, J., *A Claim in Senegal, 1720–1994.* Paris, 1996
Delgado, C. L. and Jammeh, S., *The Political Economy of Senegal under Structural Adjustment.* New York, 1991
Dilley, R. M. and Eades, J. S., *Senegal.* [Bibliography] Oxford and Santa Barbara (CA), 1994
Gellar, S., *Senegal.* Boulder (Colo.), 1982.—*Senegal: an African Nation between Islam and the West.* Aldershot, 1983
Phillips, L. C., *Historical Dictionary of Senegal.* 2nd ed, revised by A. F. Clark. Metuchen (NJ), 1995

National statistical office: Direction de la Statistique, BP 116, Dakar.

SEYCHELLES

Republic of Seychelles

Capital: Victoria
Population: 76,417
GNP: US$0·5bn.
HDI/world rank: 0·845/52

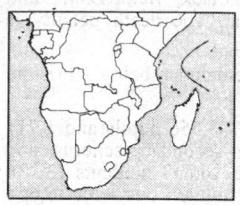

KEY HISTORICAL EVENTS. The Seychelles were first colonized by the French in 1756 in order to establish plantations for growing spices to compete with the Dutch monopoly. The islands were captured by the English in 1794. During discussions before the Treaty of Paris was signed, Britain offered to return Mauritius and its dependencies which included the Seychelles to France if that country would renounce all claims to her possessions in India. France refused and the Seychelles were formally ceded to Britain as a dependency of Mauritius. In Nov. 1903 the Seychelles archipelago became a separate British Crown Colony. Internal self-government was achieved on 1 Oct. 1975 and independence as a republic within the British Commonwealth on 29 June 1976.

The first president, James Mancham, was deposed in a *coup* on 5 June 1977 and replaced by his prime minister, Albert René. The National Assembly was dissolved and the constitution suspended. A new constitution came into force on 5 June 1979, under which the Seychelles People's Progressive Front became the sole legal party and nominates all candidates for election. There is a unicameral People's Assembly consisting of 33 seats, of which 22 are directly elected and 11 are allocated on a proportional basis, and an executive president directly elected for a 5-year term. In 1979 and 1984 Albert René was the only candidate in the presidential elections. Under the new constitution approved in June 1993, President René was re-elected against two opponents with 59·5% of the vote.

TERRITORY AND POPULATION. The Seychelles consists of 115 islands in the Indian Ocean, north of Madagascar, with a combined area of 175 sq. miles (455 sq. km) in two distinct groups. The Granitic group of 32 islands cover 92 sq. miles (239 sq. km); the principal island is Mahé, with 59 sq. miles (153 sq. km) and 59,500 inhabitants at the 1987 census, the other inhabited islands of the group being Praslin, La Digue, Silhouette, Fregate and North, which together had 7,100 inhabitants.

The Outer or Coralline group comprises 83 islands spread over a wide area of ocean between the Mahé group and Madagascar, with a total land area of 83 sq. miles (214 sq. km) and a population of about 400. The main islands are the Amirante Isles (including Desroches, Poivre, Daros and Alphonse), Coetivy Island and Platte Island, all lying south of the Mahé group; the Farquhar, St Pierre and Providence Islands, north of Madagascar; and Aldabra, Astove, Assumption and the Cosmoledo Islands, about 1,000 km south-west of the Mahé group. Aldabra (whose lagoon covers 55 sq. miles), Farquhar and Desroches were transferred to the new British Indian Ocean Territory in 1965, but were returned by Britain to the Seychelles on the latter's independence in 1976. Population, 76,417 (1996). Births, 1,611; deaths, 566; infant mortality, 9·3 per 1,000 births.

The official languages are Creole, English and French but 95% of the population speak Creole.

CLIMATE. Though close to the equator, the climate is tropical. The hot, wet season is from Dec. to May, when conditions are humid, but south-east trades bring cooler conditions from June to Nov. Temperatures are high throughout the year, but the islands lie outside the cyclone belt. Victoria. Jan. 80°F (26·7°C), July 78°F (25·6°C). Annual rainfall 95" (2,287 mm).

CONSTITUTION AND GOVERNMENT. Under the 1979 Constitution the Seychelles People's Progressive Front (SPPF) was the sole legal Party. A constitutional amendment of Dec. 1991 legalized other parties. A commission was elected in July 1992 to draft a new constitution. The electorate was some 50,000; turn-out was

90%. The SPPF gained 14 seats on the commission, the Democratic Party, 8; the latter, however, eventually withdrew. At a referendum in Nov. 1992 the new draft constitution failed to obtain the necessary 60% approval votes. The commission was reconvened in Jan. 1993. At a further referendum on 18 June 1993 the constitution was approved by 73·6% of votes cast.

At the presidential and parliamentary elections of 23 July 1993 turn-out was 60%. President René was re-elected against 2 opponents by 59·5% of votes cast. The SPPF gained 28 seats, the Democratic Party, 4 and the United Opposition, 1.

The Government in March 1998 comprised:

President: France Albert René (b. 1935; SPPF; re-elected for a 4th term and sworn in 26 July 1993).

Vice-President: James Michel. *Minister of Administration:* Noellie Alexander. *Agriculture and Marine Resources:* Ronny Jumeau. *Education:* Danny Faure. *Foreign Affairs, Planning and Environment: :* Jeremie Bonnelame. *Health:* Jacqueline Dugasse. *Industry and International Business:* Joseph Belmont. *Land Use and Habitat:* Dolor Ernesta. *Local Government and Sports:* Sylvette Pool. *Youth and Culture:* Patrick Pillay. *Social Affairs and Manpower Development:* William Herminie. *Tourism and Civil Aviation:* Simone de Comarmond.

National anthem: Koste Seselwa.

DEFENCE. The Defence Force comprises all services. Personnel (1996) Army, 200; Paramilitary, 250; Coast Guard, 200; Air Wing, 20; 1 infantry battalion and 2 artillery troops. The Coast Guard, based at Port Victoria, operates 4 fast inshore patrol craft, 1 tank landing craft and 1 Defender patrol craft.

INTERNATIONAL RELATIONS

Membership. Seychelles is a member of the UN, Commonwealth and OAU and is an ACP state of the EU.

ECONOMY

Policy. A gradual move from socialism to a free market economy anticipates Seychelles becoming an international offshore financial centre.

Budget. Budget in 1m. rupees, for calendar years:

	1991	1992	1993	1994	1995
Recurrent revenue	961·5	1,097·6	1,209·5	1,319·5	1,158·4
Recurrent expenditure	870·5	1,014·7	1,122·2	1,126 7	1,276 5

Currency. The unit of currency is the *Seychelles rupee* (SCR) divided into 100 *cents.* There are coins of 5, 10 and 25 cents and 1 and 5 rupees, and notes of 10, 25, 50 and 100 rupees.

Inflation. (1996) 0·0%.

Banking and Finance. Central Bank of Seychelles (the bank of issue), Development Bank of Seychelles, Seychelles Savings Bank and Seychelles International Mercantile Banking Cooperation have head offices and Barclays Bank, Banque Française Commerciale, Habib Bank and Bank of Baroda, have branches in Victoria and Mahé.

ENERGY AND NATURAL RESOURCES

Electricity. Production (1996) 135·2. kWh.

Agriculture. Coconuts are the main cash crop (production, 1995, 3,000 tonnes). Other main crops produced for export are cinnamon bark (1996, 318 tonnes) and copra (1995, 353 tonnes). Tea production, 1995, 226 tonnes (green leaf). Crops grown for local consumption include cassava, sweet potatoes, yams, sugar-cane, bananas and vegetables. The staple food crop, rice, is imported.

Fisheries. Seychelles is located in abundant tuna fishing grounds. Catch (1996) 4,508 tonnes.

INDUSTRY. Local industry is expanding, the largest development in recent years being the brewery (output, 1996, 6,365,000 litres of beer and stout and 7,852,000 litres of soft drinks). Other main activities include production of cigarettes (62m. in 1996), tuna canning (12,708 tonnes in 1996) and paints, dairy, processing of cinnamon and coconuts.

FOREIGN ECONOMIC RELATIONS

Commerce. Total trade, in 1m. rupees, for calendar years:

	1991	1992	1993	1994	1995
Imports (less re-exports)	910·4	980·9	1,234·9	1,042·4	1,319·4
Domestic exports	87·6	93·2	78·8	114·3	113·7

Principal imports (1996): Manufactured goods, Rs 277·7m.; food, beverages and tobacco, Rs 330·7m.; petroleum products, Rs 143·6m., machinery and transport equipment, Rs 327·2m., mainly from UK (13·3%), Singapore (13·1%), South Africa (12·8%), USA (7·7%) and France (6·2%). Principal exports (1996): Fresh and frozen fish, Rs 11·0m.; canned tuna, Rs 170·0m.; frozen prawns, Rs 11·0m.; cinnamon bark, Rs 4·7m. mainly to UK, France, Réunion and Singapore.

Tourism. Tourism is the main foreign exchange earner. Visitor numbers were 131,000 in 1996.

COMMUNICATIONS

Roads. In 1996 there were 277 km of surfaced roads and 68 km of earth roads. In 1996 there were 8,460 vehicles registered.

Civil Aviation. There is an international airport on Mahé. 385,000 passengers were handled in 1995. Air Seychelles operated 1 B-757-200ER, 1 B-767-200ER and 4 other aircraft in 1995. Services are also provided by Aeroflot, Air Austral, Air France, British Airways, Condor and Kenya Airways.

Shipping. The main port is Victoria, which is also a tuna-fishing and fuel and services supply centre. Sea freight (1996), 363,000 tonnes.

Telecommunications. Services operated by Cable & Wireless Ltd provide telegraphic communications with all parts of the world by satellite. Telephone lines in 1996 numbered 15,712. Broadcasting is under the auspices of the Seychelles Broadcasting Corporation, an independent body. There is a radio programme in English, French and Creole. There is also a religious station. TV colour is by PAL. In 1991 there were 30,000 radio and 8,200 TV sets.

Press. There is 1 daily and 2 weekly newspapers.

SOCIAL INSTITUTIONS

Justice. In 1996, 3,710 criminal and other offences were recorded by the police.

Religion. 92% of the inhabitants are Roman Catholic and 8% Anglican.

Education. Adult literacy was 84% in 1996. Education is free from 5 to 15 years in primary schools, 16 to 18 in secondary schools and 18 to 21 in polytechnics. In 1996 there were 9,588 pupils and 562 teachers in primary schools, 6,192 pupils and 412 teachers in secondary schools and 1,437 students and 145 teachers at polytechnic level.

Health. In 1996 there were 84 doctors, 9 dentists, 346 nurses and 414 hospital beds. The health service is free.

DIPLOMATIC REPRESENTATIVES

Of Seychelles in Great Britain (111 Baker St., London, W1M 1FE)
High Commissioner: Vacant. (Chargé d'Affaires *ad interim* Mrs S. Williamson)

Of Great Britain in Seychelles (Victoria Hse., Victoria, Mahé)
High Commissioner: J. W. Yapp.

Of Seychelles in the USA
Ambassador: Vacant.

Of the USA in Seychelles
Ambassador: Harold Geisel (resides in Comoros)

Of Seychelles to the United Nations
Ambassador: Vacant.

Of Seychelles to the European Union
Ambassador: Claude Morel

Further Reading

Statistical Information: Information Office, 52 Kingsgate House, Victoria, Mahé.
Seychelles in Figures. Statistics Division, Mahé, 1989

Benedict, M. and Benedict, B., *Men, Women and Money in Seychelles.* Univ. of California Press, 1983
Bennett, G. and Bennett, P. R., *Seychelles.* [Bibliography] Oxford and Santa Barbara, 1993
Franda, M., *The Seychelles: Unquiet Islands.* Boulder (CO), 1982
Lionnet, G., *The Seychelles.* Newton Abbot, 1972
Mancham, J. R., *Paradise Raped: Life, Love and Power in the Seychelles.* London, 1983

SIERRA LEONE

Republic of Sierra Leone

Capital: Freetown
Population: 4·46m.
GDP per head: (PPP$) 643
GNP: US$0·7bn.
HDI/world rank: 0·176/175

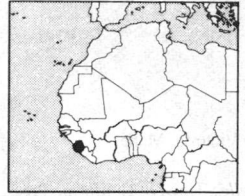

KEY HISTORICAL EVENTS. The Colony of Sierra Leone originated in 1787, when English settlers bought a piece of land intended as a home for natives of Africa who were waifs in London. The land was later used as a settlement for Africans rescued from slaveships. The hinterland was declared a British protectorate on 21 Aug. 1896.

The first constitution was introduced in 1951 and this removed the political component from the privileged status of the Creoles of the colony by giving power to the majority. Sierra Leone became independent as a member state of the British Commonwealth on 27 April 1961. In a general election in March 1967, Dr Siaka Stevens' All People's Congress came to power and was installed despite a military coup to prevent his taking office. Sierra Leone became a republic on 19 April 1971, with Dr Siaka Stevens as executive president.

Following a referendum in June 1978, a new constitution was instituted under which the ruling All People's Congress became the sole legal party.

Stevens remained president until 1985 when he handed over to Maj.-Gen. Dr Joseph Saidu Momoh, the army C.-in-C., who was the only candidate in the presidential election that year and received 99% of the votes cast.

A military coup on 29 April 1992 deposed the president and set up a National Provisional Ruling Council. The chairman of this, Captain Valentine Strasser, was in turn deposed in a bloodless military coup on 16 Jan. 1996, and Gen. Julius Maada Bio assumed power. Presidential and parliamentary elections in Feb.–March 1996 resulted in a new government led by President Ahmed Tejan Kabbah. In May 1997 he was overthrown by a group of junior officers calling themselves the Armed Forces Ruling council (AFRC) in alliance with the Revolutionary United Front (RUF), a rebel gang that had terrorized the south-east of the country in the early 1990s. In Feb. 1998 a Nigerian-led intervention force launched an air and artillery offensive against the military junta. On 10 March President Kabbah returned from exile in Guinea, promising a 'new beginning'.

TERRITORY AND POPULATION. Sierra Leone is bounded on the north-west, north and north-east by Guinea, on the south-east by Liberia and on the south-west by the Atlantic Ocean. The area is 27,925 sq. miles (73,326 sq. km). Population (census 1985), 3,517,530, of whom about 2,000 were Europeans, 3,500 Asiatics and 30,000 non-native Africans. Estimate (1993), 4,460,000 (32% urban); density, 64·3 per sq. km. The capital is Freetown, with 469,776 inhabitants in 1985.

Vital statistics rates (1993, per 1,000 population); Birth, 48·2; death, 21·6; growth rate, 2·7%. Infant mortality was 143 per 1,000 live births in 1990; expectation of life was 43 years.

Sierra Leone is divided into 4 provinces:

	Sq. km	Census 1985	Capital	Estimate 1988
Western Province	557	554,243	Freetown	469,776
Southern Province	19,694	740,510	Bo	26,000
Eastern Province	15,553	960,551	Kenema	13,000
Northern Province	35,936	1,262,226	Makeni	12,000

The provinces are divided into districts as follows: Bo, Bonthe, Moyamba, Pujehun (Southern Province); Kailahun, Kenema, Kono (Eastern Province); Bombali, Kambia, Koinaduga, Port Loko, Toukolili (Northern Province).

The principal peoples are the Mendes (34% of the total) in the south, the Temnes

(31%) in the north and centre, the Konos, Fulanis, Bulloms, Korankos, Limbas and Kissis. English is the official language; a Creole (Krio) is spoken.

CLIMATE. A tropical climate, with marked wet and dry seasons and high temperatures throughout the year. The rainy season lasts from about April to Nov., when humidity can be very high. Thunderstorms are common from April to June and in Sept. and Oct. Rainfall is particularly heavy at Freetown because of the effect of neighbouring relief. Freetown. Jan. 80°F (26·7°C), July 78°F (25·6°C). Annual rainfall 135" (3,434 mm).

CONSTITUTION AND GOVERNMENT. In a referendum in Sept. 1991 some 60% of the 2·5m. electorate voted for the introduction of a new constitution instituting multi-party democracy. There is a 68-member *National Assembly.*

There is a *Supreme Council of State (SCS),* and a *Council of State Secretaries.*

Presidential and National Assembly elections were held on 26–27 Feb. 1996.

13 parties stood. Turn-out was 60%. Ahmed Tejan Kabbah gained 35·8% of votes cast for the presidency in a first round. There was a qualifying threshold of 55% of votes for outright election in this round. At the second round on 17 March 1996 Kabbah was elected by 59·49% of votes cast against 1 opponent.

At the National Assembly elections the Sierra Leone People's Party (SLPP) won 36·1% of votes cast, the United People's Party 21·6% and the People's Democratic Party 15·3%.

President: Ahmed Tejan Kabbah (b. 1931; SLPP; elected 17 March 1996).

National anthem: 'High We Exalt Thee, Realm of the Free'; words by C. Nelson Fyle, tune by J. J. Akar.

Local Government. The provinces are administered through the Ministry of Internal Affairs and divided into 148 Chiefdoms, each under the control of a Paramount Chief and Council of Elders known as the Tribal Authorities, who are responsible for the maintenance of law and order and for the administration of justice (except for serious crimes). All of these Chiefdoms have been organized into local government units, empowered to raise and disburse funds for the development of the Chiefdom concerned.

DEFENCE

Army. Following the civil war, no details of the force structure or numbers can be given.

INTERNATIONAL RELATIONS

Membership. Sierra Leone is a member of the UN, OAU, ECOWAS and the Commonwealth and is an ACP state of the EU.

ECONOMY

Budget. In 1m. leones:

	1992	1993	1994	1995	1996
Revenue	35,384	54,294	67,414	61,743	69,713
Expenditure	56,993	78,695	104,654	107,312	128,167

Currency. The unit of currency is the *leone* (SLL) of 100 *cents.* There are notes of 1, 2, 5, 10, 20, 50 100, 500, 1,000 and 5,000 leones, and coins of 1, 5, 10, 20 and 50 *cents.* 15,650m. leones were in circulation in 1992. Foreign exchange reserves were US$34·8m. in 1993. Exchange controls were liberalized in 1993.

Banking and Finance. The bank of issue is the Bank of Sierra Leone (established 1964). There are 4 commercial banks (2 foreign).

Weights and Measures. The metric system is in use.

ENERGY AND NATURAL RESOURCES

Electricity. Installed capacity was 126 MW in 1991. Production (1990) 224m. kWh.

Minerals. The chief minerals mined are gold (12,900 troy oz, 1994), diamonds (197,000 metric carats), bauxite (729,000 tonnes), and rutile (144,000 tonnes). The presence of rich diamond deposits partly explains the close interest of neighbouring countries in the politics of Sierra Leone.

Agriculture. Agriculture contributed 31·7% of GDP in 1990, and engaged 65% of the workforce, mainly in small-scale peasant production. Cattle production is important in the north. Production (1995, in 1,000 tonnes): Rice, 284; cassava, 219; palm oil, 45·2; palm kernels, 29·2; coffee, 25; cocoa, 10.

Livestock (1995): Cattle, 360,000; goats, 166,000; sheep, 302,000; pigs, 50,000; chickens, 6m.

Fisheries. In 1995, 62,313 tonnes of fish were caught.

INDUSTRY. Manufacturing contributed 6% of GDP in 1990. There are palm-oil and rice mills; sawn timber, joinery products and furniture are produced.

Labour. The workforce was 1,438,000 in 1990. 14,800 persons were registered unemployed in 1992. About 125,000 workers are in wage-earning employment.

FOREIGN ECONOMIC RELATIONS. Foreign debt was US$1,291m. in 1991.

Commerce. Total trade (in 1m. leones) for 1994: Imports, 183,550; exports, 67,930.
Main exports are bauxite, diamonds, gold, coffee and cocoa.

Main export markets, 1994 (in 1,000 leones): USA, 30,431; UK, 11,767; Belgium, 11,412; Germany, 1,328. Main import suppliers, 1994 (in 1,000 leones): USA, 78,288; Netherlands, 26,050; UK, 10,453.

COMMUNICATIONS

Roads. There are about 7,500 miles of main roads, of which 1,500 miles are surfaced with bitumen. In 1995 there were 20,860 passenger cars and 11,014 commercial vehicles.

Civil Aviation. Freetown Airport (Lungi) is the international airport.

Shipping. The port of Freetown has a very large natural harbour. Iron ore is exported through Pepel, and there are small ports at Bonthe and Sulima. In 1995 the merchant fleet totalled 15,100 GRT, including oil tankers, 1,835 GRT. 1·8m. tonnes of cargo were loaded in 1990 and 0·53m. tonnes discharged.

Telecommunications. Telephone provision, 1994, 16,000 main lines. There are 37 post offices and 76 postal agencies. Broadcasting is under the auspices of the government-controlled Sierra Leone Broadcasting Service and Sierra Leone Television, which is part commercial. In 1995 there were 1,050,000 radio and 49,000 TV sets (colour by PAL).

Press. In 1995 there was one daily newspaper with a circulation of 20,000.

SOCIAL INSTITUTIONS

Justice. The High Court has jurisdiction in civil and criminal matters. Subordinate courts are held by magistrates in the various districts. Native Courts, headed by court Chairmen, apply native law and custom under a criminal and civil jurisdiction. Appeals from the decisions of magistrates' courts are heard by the High Court. Appeals from the decisions of the High Court are heard by the Sierra Leone Court of Appeal. Appeal lies from the Sierra Leone Court of Appeal to the Supreme Court which is the highest court.

Religion. There were 1·72m. Moslems in 1992. Traditional animist beliefs persist.

Education. Adult literacy was 30·3% in 1994. Primary education is partially free but not compulsory. In 1990–91 there were 2,072 primary schools with 414,200 pupils and 14,972 teachers, 227 secondary schools with 116,648 pupils and 5,610 teachers, 19 vocational training colleges with 4,530 students and 326 staff, and 6 teacher training schools. There were 5 institutes of higher education with 4,742 students and 600 teachers. Fourah Bay College and Njala University College are the 2 constituent colleges of the University of Sierra Leone. They had 2,571 students and 257 academic staff in 1990–91.

Health. In 1988 there were 300 doctors and 4,025 hospital beds.

DIPLOMATIC REPRESENTATIVES

Of Sierra Leone in Great Britain (33 Portland Pl., London, W1N 3AG)
High Commissioner: Prof. Cyril P. Foray.

Of Great Britain in Sierra Leone (Spur Rd., Freetown)
High Commissioner: Peter A. Penfold, CMG.

Of Sierra Leone in the USA (1701 19th St., NW, Washington, D.C., 20009)
Ambassador: John E. Leigh.

Of the USA in Sierra Leone (Corner Walpole and Siaka Stevens St., Freetown)
Ambassador: John L. Hirsch.

Of Sierra Leone to the United Nations
Ambassador: James O. Jonah.

Of Sierra Leone to the European Union
Ambassador: Peter J. Kuyembeh.

Further Reading

Binns, M. and Binns, T., *Sierra Leone* [Bibliography]. Oxford and Santa Barbara (CA), 1992
Fyfe, C., *A History of Sierra Leone*. OUP, 1962

SINGAPORE

Republic of Singapore

Population: 3·3m.
GDP per head: (PPP$) 20,987
GNP: US$65·8bn.
HDI/world rank: 0·900/26

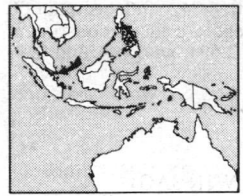

KEY HISTORICAL EVENTS. Singapore Island became part of the Javanese Majapahit Empire in the 14th century. The Portuguese established hegemony in the area in the 16th century, followed by the Dutch a hundred years later. In 1819 Sir Thomas Stamford Raffles, the British East India Administrator, established a trading settlement there. The original lease of the site of a factory to the British East India Company by the Sultan of Johore was followed by the treaty of 2 Aug. 1824 ceding the entire island in perpetuity to the company. In 1826 Penang, Malacca and Singapore were combined as the Straits Settlements in an Indian presidency. On 1 April 1867 the settlements were transferred from the control of the Indian government to that of the British Secretary of State for the Colonies. With the opening of the Suez Canal in 1869 and the advent of the steamship, an era of prosperity began for Singapore. Growth continued with the export of tin and rubber from the Malay peninsula.

Thought to be impregnable by land, Singapore fell to the Japanese in 1942 whose occupation continued until the end of the Second World War. In 1945 Singapore became a Crown Colony, being separated from Penang and Malacca. In June 1959 the state was granted complete internal self-government. When the Federation of Malaysia was formed in Sept. 1963, Singapore became one of the 14 states of the newly created country.

On 7 Aug. 1965, by agreement with the Malaysian government, Singapore left the Federation of Malaysia and became an independent sovereign state. The name of the state was changed to 'Republic of Singapore' with a president as its head. Singapore and Malaysia agreed to enter into a treaty for external defence and mutual assistance. The British military presence was withdrawn from Singapore in 1971. Continuing economic prosperity has made Singapore a powerful influence in ASEAN.

TERRITORY AND POPULATION. The Republic of Singapore consists of Singapore Island itself, and 64 islets. Singapore Island is situated off the southern extremity of the Malay peninsula, to which it is joined by a 1,056-metre causeway carrying a road, railway and water pipeline. The Straits of Johore between the island and the mainland are 914 metres wide. The island is 647·5 sq. km in area, including the 64 adjacent islets, 20 of which are inhabited.

Census of population (1990): 2,089,400 Chinese, 380,600 Malays, 191,000 Indians and 29,200 others; total 2,690,200. In June 1996 Chinese residents numbered 2,352,700 (77·3%), Malays 430,900 (14·1%), Indians 222,100 (7·3%) and others 38,600 (1·3%); total 3,044,300. 1997 estimate, 3·3m.; density, 5,097 per sq. km. Resident growth rate, 1·9%; infant mortality, 1996, 3·8 per 1,000 live births; life expectancy, 1996, 74·4 years for males and 78·9 years for females.

Malay, Chinese (Mandarin), Tamil and English are the official languages; Malay is the national language and English is the language of administration.

CLIMATE. The climate is equatorial, with relatively uniform temperature, abundant rainfall and high humidity. Rain falls throughout the year but tends to be heaviest from Nov. to Jan. Jan. 78·1°F (25·6°C), July 80·8°F (27·1°C). Annual rainfall 2,353 mm.

CONSTITUTION AND GOVERNMENT. *Parliament* is unicameral consisting of 83 members, elected by secret ballot from single-member and group representation constituencies. With the customary exception of those serving criminal sentences, all citizens over 21 are eligible to vote. Voting in an election is compulsory. Group representation constituencies may return up to 6 Members of Parliament

(4 before 1996), one of whom must be from the Malay community, the Indian and other minority communities. Opposition parties are constitutionally guaranteed 3 seats between them. There is a common roll without communal electorates.

A Presidential Council to consider and report on minorities' rights was established in 1970.

At the elections of 2 Jan. 1997 opposition parties contested only 36 seats. The People's Action Party (PAP) won 81 seats with 65% of votes cast (77 and 61% in 1991); the Singapore People's Party gained 1 seat and the Workers' Party 1 seat. Under the 3-opposition-seats guarantee, a further non-constituency seat was awarded to the Workers' Party.

At the presidential elections of 28 Aug. 1993 there were 2 PAP candidates. Ong Teng Cheong was elected by 58·7% of votes cast.

President: Ong Teng Cheong (sworn in 1 Sept. 1993).

The Cabinet in March 1998 was composed as follows:

Prime Minister: Goh Chok Tong (b. 1941; PAP).

Senior Minister, Prime Minister's Office: Lee Kuan Yew, GCMG, CH. *Deputy Prime Ministers:* Lee Hsien Loong; Dr Tony Tan Keng Yam (*Defence*). *Health and Environment:* Yeo Cheow Tong. *Finance:* Dr Richard Hu Tsu Tau. *Education:* Teo Chee Hean. *Law and Foreign Affairs:* S. Jayakumar. *Labour:* Dr Lee Boon Yang. *Home Affairs:* Wong Kan Seng. *Information and the Arts:* George Yeo Yong Boon. *Community Development:* Abdullah Tarmugi. *Communications:* Mah Bow Tan. *National Development:* Lim Heng Kiang. *Trade and Industry:* Lee Yock Suan. *Without portfolio:* Lim Boon Heng.

National anthem: Majulah Singapura (*May Singapore Progress*); words and tune by Zubir Said.

DEFENCE. The Ministry of Defence is organized into the Defence Administration Group, which oversees the manpower, financial and administrative aspects of defence, the Defence Technology Group, and the Defence Policy Group, which is also responsible for information and security. Compulsory military service in peacetime for all male citizens and permanent residents was introduced in 1967. Periods of service are officers and non-commissioned officers 30 months, other ranks 24 months. Reserve liability is to age 40 for men, 50 for officers.

An agreement with the USA in Nov. 1990 provided for an increase in US use of naval and air force facilities.

Singapore is a member of the Five Powers Defence Arrangement, with Australia, New Zealand, Malaysia and the UK.

Army. The Army consists of 3 Combined Arms Divisions, 2 People's Defence Force (PDF) Commands and some non-divisional units. Strength (1997) 55,000 (including 35,000 conscripts) and 250,000 reserves.

Navy. The Royal Singapore Navy comprises 4 commands: Fleet, Coastal Command, Naval Logistics Command and Training Command. The Fleet has 6 German-designed fast missile corvettes, 6 missile gunboats, 6 patrol craft, 1 ex-UK and 4 ex-US tank landing ships and fast craft. Coastal Command operates 4 coastal patrol craft, 12 inshore patrol boats and 1 diving support ship. Naval personnel in 1997 numbered 2,700 (1,800 conscripts) and the naval bases are on Pulau Brani and at Jurong.

The Marine Police operates 4 inshore patrol craft and some 80 patrol boats, some armed.

Air Force. The Air Force has 2 squadrons of F-5 Tigers; 3 squadrons of A4-SU Super Skyhawks; a squadron each of Hawker Hunter/RF5 and F-16 Fighting Falcons; 2 squadrons of Super Pumas; a squadron each of UH-1Hs; 2 squadrons of the Fennecs; 1 squadron of 4 Grumman E-2C Hawkeyes; a squadron each of Skyvans/Fokker-50 and C-130 Hercules; a squadron each of Siai-Marchetti SF-260s for air grading, the Siai-Marchetti S-211s for basic training and the A4-SU for advanced training. Personnel strength (1997) about 6,000 (3,000 conscripts), with 155 combat aircraft and 20 armed helicopters.

INTERNATIONAL RELATIONS

Membership. Singapore is a member of the UN, the Commonwealth, the Colombo Plan and ASEAN.

ECONOMY

Performance. Real GDP growth was 7% in 1996 (8·8% in 1995).

Budget. Public revenue and expenditure for financial years (in S$1m.):

	1993	1994	1995	1996
Revenue	19,527·2	23,280·3	24,781·6	. . .
Expenditure	12,554·3	14,118·1	15,555·0	19,174·3

Currency. The unit of currency is the *Singapore dollar* (SGD) of 100 *cents*. There are coins of 1, 5, 10, 20 and 50 cents and S$1, and notes of S$1, 2, 5, 10, 20, 50, 100, 500, 1,000 and 10,000. Gross circulation at Dec. 1996 was S$11,276·22m. Inflation was an annualized 1·4% in 1996. Foreign exchange reserves in Dec. 1996 were S$107,800·0m.

Banking and Finance. The Monetary Authority of Singapore performs the functions of a central bank, except the issuing of currency which is the responsibility of the Board of the Commissioners of Currency.

The Development Bank of Singapore was established as a fully licensed bank in 1968, and is the largest local bank in terms of assets. Primarily it provides long-term financing of manufacturing and other industries. At 31 Dec. 1995 it had a paid up capital of S$1,300m. and shareholders' funds amounting to S$6,100m.

There were 149 commercial banks (1996 estimate) with 446 banking offices operating in 1995. The total assets/liabilities amounted to S$252,700·0m. in 1996 (estimate). Total deposits of non-bank customers amounted to S$108,885·5m. and advances including bills financing, totalled S$108,974m. in 1995. There were 79 merchant banks as at 31 Dec. 1995.

At 31 Dec. 1996, the Singapore Post Office Savings Bank had 4·9m. savings accounts and a total deposit balance amounting to S$24,898m.

There is a stock exchange.

Weights and Measures. The metric system is in use.

ENERGY AND NATURAL RESOURCES

Electricity. In 1995 Singapore Power Pte. Ltd. took over from the Public Utilities Board the responsibility for the provision of electricity and gas. Electrical power is generated by 4 oil-fired power stations, with a total generating capacity of more than 5,600 MW in 1996. Production (1995) 22,057·4m. kWh.

Agriculture. Only about 1·43% of the total area is used for farming. Most food is imported but egg production meets about 35% of local demand, and 7,336 tonnes of vegetables were produced for domestic consumption in 1995.

Agro-technology parks house large-scale intensive farms to improve production of fresh food. In 1996 there were 6 parks with a total area of 1,137 ha.

Fisheries. The total local supply of fresh fish in 1996 was 9,700 tonnes.

INDUSTRY. The largest industrial area is at Jurong, with 33 modern industrial estates housing over 6,500 companies in 1996, and 333,099 workers employed in 1994.

Production, 1996 (in S$1m.), totalled 113,358·0, including electronic products, machinery and appliances, 66,804·4; petroleum, 10,603·3; chemicals and chemical products, 6,834·9; transport equipment, 5,208·9; fabricated metal products, 6,546·4; food, beverages and tobacco, 3,747·2; paper products and printing, 3,595.

Labour. In June 1996, 1,748,100 persons were employed, of whom 53,800 were unemployed. The majority were employed in manufacturing, 406,300; community, social and personal services, 367,700; commerce, 405,900; financial, insurance, real estate and business services, 246,000.

Legislation regulates the principal terms and conditions of employment such as hours of work, sick leave and other fringe benefits. Youths of 14–16 years may work in industrial establishments, and children of 12–14 years may be employed in approved apprenticeship schemes. A trade dispute may be referred to the Industrial Arbitration Court.

The Ministry of Labour operates an employment service and provides the handicapped with specialized on-the-job training. The Central Provident Fund was established in 1955 to make provision for employees in their old age. At the end of 1995 there were 2,683,525 members with S$66,035·4m. standing to their credit in the fund.

Trade Unions. There were 83 registered trade unions comprising 79 employee unions and 3 employer unions, and 1 federation of trade unions (the National Trades Union Congress) in 1996. The total membership of the trade unions numbered 255,020.

FOREIGN ECONOMIC RELATIONS. Foreign investment in up to 40% of the equity of domestic banks is permitted. Net foreign investment commitments in the manufacturing sector totalled S$5,716·2m. in 1996 (preliminary) (S$4,852·4m. in 1995).

In Jan. 1998 Singapore's Trade Development Board projected that trade growth in 1998 would be between 3·5% and 5·5% but warned there could be a revision because of 'volatility of development in the region'. The Board said Singapore's full-year, non-oil domestic exports increased 5·3% to S$91·6bn. in 1997, with growth already slowed by the regional economic turmoil.

Commerce. Imports and exports (in S$1m.), by country, 1995:

	Imports (c.i.f.)	Exports (f.o.b.)
Australia	2,556·0	3,674·0
China	5,729·5	3,910·6
France	3,964·0	2,852·0
Germany	6,127·2	5,666·3
Hong Kong	5,820·8	14,352·2
Italy	2,510·0	1,091·0
Japan	37,288·4	3,066·2
Korea (South)	7,652·4	4,596·5
Malaysia	27,285·0	32,124·9
Saudi Arabia	5,380·0	461·0
Taiwan	7,250·9	6,822·3
Thailand	9,096·6	9,671·8
UK	4,680·8	4,351·8
USA	26,470·3	30,546·5

The major export markets for 1995 were Malaysia (19%), USA (18%), EU (13%), Hong Kong (8·6%) and Japan (7·8%). Total imports increased to S$176,313·5m. in 1995 from S$156,395·8m. in 1994. Exports increased to S$167,514·7m. in 1995 from S$147,327·2m. in 1994.

Exports (1995, in S$1m.): Machinery and transport equipment, 110,007 (of which electrical machinery, 54,427; transport equipment, 3,156; non-electric machinery, 52,424); mineral fuels, 13,858; raw materials, 2,405 (including rubber); chemicals, 9,999; food, beverages and tobacco, 5,828; clothing, 2,075; animal and vegetable oils, 718; textiles, 2,119; scientific and optical instruments, 3,704; metal goods, 1,820; iron and steel, 1,212.

Imports (1995, in S$1m.): Machinery and transport equipment, 102,055 (of which electrical machinery, 56,194; transport equipment, 8,719; non-electric machinery, 37,143); mineral fuels, 14,204; food, beverages and tobacco, 7,177; chemicals, 11,385; crude materials, 2,086 (of which rubber, 684); textiles, 2,987; iron and steel, 3,910; animal and vegetable oils, 753; metal goods, 3,006; scientific and optical instruments, 5,359; non-metal mineral goods, 2,662; paper and paperboard and related articles, 1,674.

Tourism. There were 7,292,500 visitors in 1996 (preliminary). In 1996 there were 89 gazetted hotels with a total of 29,073 rooms.

COMMUNICATIONS

Roads. There were (1996) 3,072 km of public roads, of which 2,988 km are asphalt-paved. In 1996 motor vehicles numbered 668,304, of which 367,593 were private cars, 10,998 buses, 132,344 motor cycles and scooters, 16,857 taxis and 140,512 goods and other vehicles.

Railways. A 25·8-km main line runs through Singapore, connecting with the States of Malaysia and as far as Bangkok. Branch lines serve the port of Singapore and the industrial estates at Jurong. The Mass Rapid Transit metro extended to 83 km in 1997.

Civil Aviation. In 1997 the SIA Group (Singapore Airlines and Silk Air Services) (54% state-owned) flew to 79 destinations in 43 countries. At March 1996 it operated 2 B-747-200s, 5 B-747-300s, 3 B-747-300 Combis, 32 B-747-400s, 17 A310-300s and 6 A310-200s. 69 international airlines operated more than 3,100 scheduled flights a week, totalling 156,334 commercial aircraft movements at Singapore International Airport in Changi ('Airtropolis') in 1996, from which routes were flown to 130 destinations in 54 countries. Services are provided by Aeroflot, Air China, Air France, Air India, Air Lanka, Air Mauritius, Air New Zealand, Air Niugini, Air Seychelles, Alitalia, All Nippon Airways, Asiana, Buman Bangladesh, British Airways, Cathay Pacific, China Airlines, China Eastern Airlines, China Southern Airlines, China Southwest Airlines, Czech Airlines, Delta, Egyptair, Emirates, Eva, Finnair, Garuda Indonesia, Gulf Air, Indian Airlines, JAL, JAT, KLM, Korean Air, Kuwait Airways, Lauda Air, Lufthansa, Malaysia Airlines, Middle East Airlines, Myanma Airways, Northwest Airlines, Pakistan Airlines, Philippine Airlines, Qantas, Royal Air Cambodge, Royal Brunei Airlines, Royal Jordanian, Royal Nepal Airlines, SAA, SAS, Saudia, Swissair, Thai Airways, Turkish Airlines, United Airlines, Vietnam Airlines and Yunnan Airlines. In 1996, 24,514,248 passengers and 1,190,457 tonnes of freight were handled.

Shipping. Singapore is a large container port. The economy is dependent on shipping and entrepôt trade. An estimated total of 127,242 vessels of 832·5m. GRT entered Singapore during 1996. In 1996 3,157 vessels with a total of 18,238,813 GRT were registered in Singapore The fleet ranks 11th among the principle merchant fleets of the world. In 1995 202 vessels (31·88% of total tonnage) were registered under foreign flags. Total GRT, 11·89m., including oil tankers, 4·96m. GRT, and container ships, 1·33m. GRT.

Telecommunications. In 1996, there were 1,423 postal outlets in operation, comprising 150 post offices 1,135 stamp vendors. Telephones numbered approximately 1,530,000 at 31 Dec. 1996 and fax machines 39,354 in 1992. In 1997, Singapore Telecom, one of the largest companies in Asia, lost its monopoly.

On 1 Oct. 1994, Singapore Broadcasting Corporation was privatized with the formation of a group of companies, Singapore International Media, within which Television Corporation of Singapore broadcasts mainly English and Chinese programmes and Television 12 broadcasts Malay and Tamil programmes as well as sports, documentaries and arts programmes. In 1994 there were 210,370 radio and (1995) 652,970 TV licences (colour by PAL).

Cinemas. (1995). There were 108 cinemas with a total seating capacity of 49,000.

Press. (1996). There were 8 daily newspapers, in 4 languages, with a total daily circulation of 1,008,100.

SOCIAL INSTITUTIONS

Justice. There is a Supreme Court in Singapore which consists of the High Court and the Court of Appeal. The Supreme Court is composed of a Chief Justice and 13 Judges. The High Court has unlimited original jurisdiction in both civil and criminal cases. The Court of Appeal is the final appellate court. It hears appeals from any judgement or order of the High Court in any civil matter. The Subordinate Courts consist of 30 district courts, 7 magistrates' courts, 1 juvenile and 1 coroner's court and a small claims tribunal. The right of appeal to the UK Privy Council was abolished in 1994.

Penalties for drug trafficking and abuse are severe, including a mandatory death penalty.

Religion. In 1995, 53·9% of the population aged 10 years and above were Buddhists and Taoists, 12·9% Christians, 14·9% Moslems and 3·3% Hindus.

Education. The general literacy rate rose from 84% in 1980 to an estimated 92·2% in 1996. Kindergartens are private and fee-paying. Compulsory primary state education starts at 6 years and culminates at 11 or 12 years with an examination which influences choice of secondary schooling. There are 18 autonomous and 8 private fee-paying secondary schools. Tertiary education at 16 years is divided into 3 branches: Junior colleges leading to university; 4 polytechnics with 51,254 students at 30 June 1996; and 11 technical institutes with 8,233 students in 1996.

Statistics of schools in June 1996:

	Schools	Pupils	Teachers
Primary schools	198	269,688	10,163
Secondary schools	153	185,324	8,779
Pre-university centres and Junior colleges	21	22,395	1,575

There are 2 universities: the National University of Singapore (established 1905) with 17,960 students in 1996–97, and the Nanyang Technological University (established 1991) with 12,186 in 1996–97.

Health. There were 24 hospitals (4 government, 6 government-structured and 14 private) with 10,694 beds in 1996. There were 4,661 doctors, 835 dentists and 13,193 nurses registered.

Social Security. The Central Provident Fund makes provision for retired employees. At 31 Dec. 1995 there were 2,683,525 members with S$66,035·4m. standing to their credit in the Fund.

DIPLOMATIC REPRESENTATIVES

Of Singapore in Great Britain (9 Wilton Cres., London, SW1X 8RW)
High Commissioner: J. Y. Pillay.

Of Great Britain in Singapore (Tanglin Rd, Singapore 247919)
High Commissioner: A. C. Hunt, CMG.

Of Singapore in the USA (3501 International Pl., NW, Washington, D.C., 20008)
Ambassador: Chan Heng Chee.

Of the USA in Singapore (27 Napier Rd, Singapore 258508)
Ambassador: Timothy Chorba.

Of Singapore to the United Nations
Ambassador: Bilahari Kausikan.

Of Singapore to the European Union
Ambassador: Eng Fong Pang.

Further Reading

Department of Statistics. *Monthly Digest of Statistics.— Yearbook of Statistics.*
The Constitution of Singapore. Singapore, 1992
Information Division, Ministry of Information and the Arts. *Singapore* [*year*]: a Review of [*the previous year*].
Ministry of Trade and Industry, *Economic Survey of Singapore.* (Quarterly and Annual)

Chew, E. C. T., *A History of Singapore.* Singapore, 1992
Clammer, J. R., *Singapore: Ideology, Society, Culture.* Singapore, 1985

Huff, W. G., *Economic Growth of Singapore: Trade and Development in the Twentieth Century*. CUP, 1994

Myint, S., *The Principles of Singapore Law*. 2nd ed. Singapore, 1992

National Library. *Books about Singapore*. Singapore, irregular

Quah, J. S. T., *Government and Politics of Singapore*. OUP, 1985

Quah, S. R. and Quah, J. S. T., *Singapore* [Bibliography] Oxford and Santa Barbara (CA), 1988

Tan, C. H., *Financial Markets and Institutions in Singapore*. 7th ed. Singapore, 1992

Turnbull, C. M., *A History of Singapore, 1819–1988*. 2nd ed. OUP, 1989

Vasil, R. K., *Governing Singapore*. Singapore, 1992

National library: National Library, Stamford Rd, Singapore, 178896.

National statistical office: Department of Statistics, Minister of Trade and Industry, Singapore 068811.

Website: http://www.singstat.gov.sg/

SLOVAKIA

Slovenská Republika

Capital: Bratislava
Population: 5·37m.
GDP per capita: (PPP$) 6,389
HDI/world rank: 0·873/42

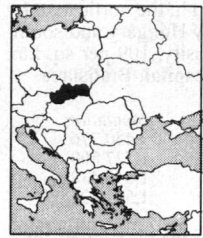

KEY HISTORICAL EVENTS. The Czechoslovak State came into existence on 28 Oct. 1918, when the Czech *Národni Výbor* (National Committee) took over the government of the Czech lands upon the dissolution of Austria-Hungary. Two days later the Slovak National Council manifested its desire to unite politically with the Czechs. On 14 Nov. 1918 the first Czechoslovak National Assembly declared the Czechoslovak State to be a republic with T. G. Masaryk as President (1918-35).

The Treaty of St Germain-en-Laye (1919) recognized the Czechoslovak Republic, consisting of the Czech lands (Bohemia, Moravia, part of Silesia) and Slovakia. To these lands were added as a trust the autonomous province of Subcarpathian Ruthenia.

This territory was broken up for the benefit of Germany, Poland and Hungary by the Munich agreement (29 Sept. 1938) between UK, France, Germany and Italy.

In March 1939 the German-sponsored Slovak government proclaimed Slovakia independent, and Germany incorporated the Czech lands into the Reich as the 'Protectorate of Bohemia and Moravia'. A government-in-exile, headed by Dr Beneš, was set up in London in July 1940.

Liberation by the Soviet Army and US Forces was completed by May 1945.

Territories taken by the Germans, Poles and Hungarians were restored to Czechoslovak sovereignty. Subcarpathian Ruthenia was transferred to the USSR.

Elections were held in May 1946 at which the Communist Party obtained about 38% of the votes.

A coalition government under a Communist Prime Minister, Klement Gottwald, remained in power until 20 Feb. 1948, when 12 of the non-Communist ministers resigned in protest against infiltration of Communists into the police.

In Feb. a predominantly Communist government was formed by Gottwald. In May elections resulted in an 89% majority for the government and President Beneš resigned.

In 1968 pressure for liberalization culminated in the overthrow of the Stalinist leader, Antonín Novotný , and his associates. The Communist Party introduced an 'Action Programme' of far-reaching reforms.

Soviet pressure to abandon this programme was exerted between May and Aug 1968, and finally, Warsaw Pact forces occupied Czechoslovakia on 21 Aug. The Czechoslovak government was compelled to accept a policy of 'normalization' (*i.e.*, abandonment of most reforms) and the stationing of Soviet forces.

Mass demonstrations demanding political reform began in Nov. 1989. After the authorities' use of violence to break up a demonstration on 17 Nov. , the Communist leader resigned. On 30 Nov. the Federal Assembly abolished the Communist Party's sole right to govern, and a new Government was formed on 3 Dec. The protest movement continued to grow, and on 10 Dec. another Government was formed. Gustáv Husák resigned as President, and was replaced by Václav Havel on the unanimous vote of 323 members of the Federal Assembly on 29 Dec.

At the June 1992 elections the Movement for Democratic Slovakia led by Vladimír Meciar campaigned on the issue of Slovak independence, and on 17 July the Slovak National Council adopted a declaration of sovereignty by 113 to 24 votes. President Havel resigned as Federal president on 20 July.

On 1 Sept. 1992 the Slovak National Council adopted, by 114 votes to 16 with 4 abstentions (and a boycott by the Hungarian deputies), a Constitution for an independent Slovakia to come into being on 1 Jan. 1993.

Economic property was divided between Slovakia and the Czech Republic in accordance with a Czechoslovakian law of 13 Nov. 1992. Real estate became the property of the republic in which it was located. Other property was divided by specially-constituted commissions in the proportion of 2 (Czech Republic) to 1 (Slovakia) on the basis of population size. Military materiel was divided on the 2:1 principle. Regular military personnel were invited to choose which armed force they would serve in.

TERRITORY AND POPULATION. Slovakia is bounded in the north-west by the Czech Republic, north by Poland, east by Ukraine, south by Hungary and south-west by Austria. Estimated population in 1995, 5,368,000; density, 109 per sq. km. There are 4 administrative regions *(Kraj)*, one of which is the capital, Bratislava.

Region	Chief city	Area in sq. km	Population
Bratislava	—	368	450,776
Západoslovenský	Bratislava	14,492	1,727,800
Stredoslovenský	Banská Bystrica	17,982	1,615,438
Východoslovenský	Košice	16,193	1,503,421

Vital statistics rates (per 1,000 population), 1995: Birth, 11·2; death, 10; marriage, 5·4; divorce, 1; infant mortality (per 1,000 live births), 13·6. Expectation of life in 1995 was 68·4 years for males and 76·3 for females.

The population of the principal towns in 1993 (in 1,000): Bratislava, 448; Banská Bystrica, 85; Zilina, 86; Trnava, 72; Košice, 239; Nitra, 87; Prešov, 91; Martin, 60.

There was a Hungarian minority of 567,000 in 1996.

A law of Nov. 1995 makes Slovak the sole official language.

CLIMATE. A humid continental climate, with warm summers and cold winters. Precipitation is generally greater in summer, with thunderstorms. Autumn, with dry, clear weather and spring, which is damp, are each of short duration. Bratislava, Jan. −0·7°C. June 19·1°C. Annual rainfall 649 mm.

CONSTITUTION AND GOVERNMENT. Parliament is the *National Council*. It has 150 members elected by proportional representation.

There is a *Constitutional Court* whose judges are normally nominated by the President.

Citizenship belongs to all citizens of the former federal Slovak Republic; other residents of 5 years standing may apply for citizenship. Slovakia grants dual citizenship.

Elections to the National Council were held on 30 Sept.–1 Oct. 1994. The electorate was 3·9m.; turn-out was 75·7%. The Movement for a Democratic Slovakia (HZDS) gained 61 seats with 35% of votes cast; the Common Choice Coalition (Party of the Democratic Left and Social Democrats and Greens and Peasant Movement), 18 with 10·4%; the Hungarian Coalition, 17 with 10·2%; the Christian Democratic Movement, 17 with 10·1%; the Democratic Union, 15 with 8·6%; the Union of Slovak Workers (ZRS), 13 with 7·3%; the Slovak National Party (SNS), 9 with 5·4%.

The next Parliamentary election is scheduled for 1998.

President: Mihal Kovác (b. 1936; ind; elected unopposed by the National Council on 15 Feb. 1993 sworn in on 2 March).

A coalition government was appointed on 13 Dec. 1994 composed of members of the Movement for a Democratic Slovakia (HZDS), the Workers' Association of Slovakia (ZRS) and the Slovak National Party (SNS). In March 1998 this comprised:
Prime Minister: Vladimír Meciar (b. 1942; HZDS).
Deputy Prime Minister for Legislature and Media Policy: Katarína Tóthová (HZDS). Deputy Prime Minister for the Economy:* Sergej Kozlík (HZDS). *Deputy Prime Minister for Social and Spiritual Development, National Minorities and European Integration:* Jozef Kalman (ZRS). *Minister of Foreign Affairs:* Zdenka Kramplova (HZDS). Finance:* Miroslav Maxon (HZDS). *Defence:* Ján Sitek (SNS). The Economy:* Karol Cesnek (HZDS). *Privatization:* Peter Bisák (ZRS). *Interior;* Gustáv Krajcí (HZDS). *Labour, Social Affairs and the Family:* Olga Keltošová. *Culture:* Ivan Hudec (HZDS). *Justice:* Jozef Liščák (ZRS). *Education and Science:* Eva Slavkovská (SNS). *Health:* Lubomír Javorský (HZDS). *Agriculture:* Peter Baco

(HZDS). *Transport and Communications:* Ján Jasovský (HZDS). *Environment:* Jozef Zlocha (ZRS). *Construction and Public Works:* Ján Mráz (ZRS).

The *Speaker* is Ivan Gáspárovič.

National anthem: 'Nad Tatrou sa blýska' ('Over Tatra it lightens'); words by J. Matuška, tune anonymous.

Local Government. The local authorities are the district bureaux with the power to raise local taxes and with responsibility for roads, schools, utilities and public health. Elections for 2,853 mayors and 35,524 municipal councillors were held on 18–19 Nov. 1994. Turn-out was 52%. Independents gained 28·5% of the mayoralties, the Democratic Left 17·9%; HZDS 15·9%; Christian Democrats 14·8%. HZDS gained 22·8% of the councillor posts; Christian Democrats 19·7%; Party of the Democratic Left 15·7%. Local Government elections are scheduled for 1998.

DEFENCE. Conscription is for 12 months.

Army. There are 3 tank and 3 mechanized infantry brigades. Equipment includes 478 T-72M and T-54/-55 main battle tanks. Personnel (1997), 23,800 (including 15,000 conscripts).

Air Force. There are 72 combat aircraft, including 20 Su-22 and 12 Su-25, 16 MiG-21 and 24 MiG-29 fighters and 19 attack helicopters. Transport equipment includes 13 fixed-wing aircraft and 30 Mi-8/17 helicopters, while 18 Mi-2s are used for liaison duties. Personnel (1997), 12,000.

INTERNATIONAL RELATIONS

Membership. Slovakia is a member of the UN, CEFTA, the Central European Initiative, the NATO Partnership for Peace and is an associate member of the EU and an associate partner of the WEU. An application to join the EU was made in June 1995. A referendum on whether Slovakia should apply to join NATO took place on 23–24 May 1997. Turn-out was 9·8% and the results were declared invalid. 55% of votes cast were against participation

ECONOMY

Policy. Privatization was proceeding by the issue of vouchers and direct sale. By the end of 1992, 503 large joint stock companies had been privatized by the voucher scheme, and 330 large firms and 9,676 small businesses had been sold off. 3·2m. persons had invested in privatization vouchers by the end of 1994. Legislation of July 1995 ended privatization by vouchers, which became exchangeable instead against state securities. At the end of 1995 the private sector share of total GDP reached 64.9%.

Performance. Real GDP growth was 6·9% in 1996 and 6% in 1997 (estimate). Inflation was 5·8% in 1996/97.

Budget. In 1995, revenue was Ks. 163,100m. and expenditure, Ks. 171,400m.

VAT, personal and company income tax, real estate taxes and inheritance taxes came into force in Jan. 1993.

Currency. The unit of currency is the *Slovak koruna* or crown (SKK) of 100 *haliers*, introduced on 8 Feb. 1993. There are coins of 10, 20 and 50 haliers and Ks. 1, 2, 5 and 10, and notes of Ks. 20, 50, 100, 200, 500, 1,000, 2,000 and 5,000. The koruna was revalued 4% in May 1995. Foreign exchange reserves were US$3,000m. in Dec. 1995.

Banking and Finance. The central bank and bank of issue is the Slovak National Bank, founded in 1993 (*Governor,* Vladímir Masár). It has an autonomous statute modelled on the German Bundesbank, with the duties of maintaining control over monetary policy and inflation, ensuring the stability of the currency, and supervising commercial banks. However, it is now proposed to amend the central bank law to allow the government to appoint half the members of the board and force the bank to increase its financing of the budget deficit. Decentralization of the banking system began in 1991, and private banks began to operate. Foreign investors may acquire up to 25% of major banks' assets (100% of small banks), but no single investor may acquire more than 10%. There were 26 commercial banks in 1993, and 9 foreign bank branches. Total subscribed bank capital was Ks. 11,800m. in 1993. Savings accounts totalled Ks. 94,859m. in 1992.

There is a stock exchange in Bratislava.

Weights and Measures. The metric system is in force.

ENERGY AND NATURAL RESOURCES

Electricity. There is a nuclear power station at Bohunice, and a hydro-electric dam at Gabcikovo on the Danube, from which Hungary has withdrawn. Output, 1993, 24,429 MWh. In 1995 about 55% of electricity was nuclear-generated.

Minerals. In 1993 2·81m. tonnes of brown coal and in 1991 1·34m. tonnes of lignite were produced. 1·09m. tonnes of iron ore were extracted in 1993.

Agriculture. In 1993 there were 1·48m. ha of arable land. In 1993 agriculture produced about 20% of GDP.

A federal law of May 1991 returned land seized by the Communist regime to its original owners, to a maximum of 150 ha of arable to a single owner.

Livestock in the state and co-operative sectors in 1993: Cattle, 1·89m. (0·34m. milch cows); pigs, 1·62m.; sheep, 0·23m.; poultry, 3·99m. Livestock products, 1993: Meat, 477,565 tonnes; eggs, 1,527,000; milk, 1,214,000 litres.

INDUSTRY. In Czechoslovakia Slovakia was less industrialized than the Czech Republic, though there are concentrations of heavy engineering and munitions plants. Consumer industries include textiles and footwear. 1993 output included (in 1m. tonnes): Pig iron, 3·21; crude steel, 3·92; iron and steel plates, 2·86; zinc (1991), 0·81; plastics, 0·37; TV receivers (1991), 201,851.

Labour. In 1993, 2,166,000 persons were employed. 539,711 persons were employed in industry, 259,000 in agriculture, forestry and hunting, 250,000 in commerce and 133,000 in building. In March 1996, 342,700 persons were registered unemployed (13·3% of the economically active population). The average monthly wage in Oct. 1993 was Ks. 5,348. Unemployment was 12·3% in Sept. 1996.

FOREIGN ECONOMIC RELATIONS. A memorandum envisaging a customs union and close economic co-operation was signed with the Czech Republic in Oct. 1992. An agreement of Dec. 1992 with the Czech Republic, Hungary and Poland abolishes tariffs on raw materials and goods where exports do not compete directly with locally-produced items, and envisaged tariff reductions on agricultural and industrial goods in 1995–97.

Tax holidays of up to 7 years are available to foreign investors.

Foreign debt was US$5,854m. in Jan. 1996. By Sept. 1994 total foreign investments since 1990 amounted to US$416m.

Commerce. While keen to join the EU, Slovakia is currently excluded from Brussels' list of East European countries scheduled for early negotiations because of 'shortcomings' in the functioning of its democracy.

The major foreign trade partner, the Czech Republic, accounts for 28·2% of all exports from Slovakia and 23·2% of all imports into the country. The EU accounts for 45·4% of exports and 38% of imports; OECD for 87% of exports and 73·6% of imports. Russia provides 17·1% of imports (mainly crude oil, gas and other raw materials) and takes 2·3% of exports.

Basic figures in US$bn. (March 1998):

Foreign trade turnover	Slovak exports	Slovak imports	Foreign trade balance (deficit)
4·73	2·12	2·61	–0·49

Leading foreign trade partners as of March 1997:

Country	% of total exports	% of total imports
Czech Republic	28·2	23·2
Germany	24·5	17·1
Austria	6·2	14·9
Poland	5·7	5·4
Italy	5·3	4·6
UK	1·7	2·4

COMMUNICATIONS

Roads. In 1995 there were 198 km of motorways and 17,869 km of main roads. In 1995 there were 1,015,794 passenger cars, 16,930 vans, 85,704 lorries, 11,812 buses and 229,119 motorcycles.

Railways. In 1995 the length of railway routes was 3,665 km of 1,435 mm gauge (1,473 km electrified) with short sections on 3 other gauges. In 1995 railways carried 89·5m. passengers and 60·8m. tonnes of freight. There are tram/light rail networks in Bratislava and Košice.

Civil Aviation. There is an international airport at Bratislava (M. R. Stefánik). Services are provided by Aeroflot, Czech Airlines, Hemus and Tatra Air.

Telecommunications. In 1995 there were 1,617 post offices and 1,616,565 telephones. Broadcasting is the responsibility of the government-controlled Slovak Broadcasting Council. The state-run Slovak Radio broadcasts on 4 wavelengths, and there are 12 private regional stations. Slovak Television is a public corporation. It transmits on 2 channels (colour by SECAM), the second being shared with a commercial station. There are several independent local TV stations, and 2 cable networks. In 1994 there were 1·6m. TV sets in use.

Cinemas. There were 472 cinemas in 1995. 57 films were completed in 1995, out of which 4 were full-length feature films.

Press (1995). There were 20 daily newspapers and 78 weeklies.

SOCIAL INSTITUTIONS

Justice. The post-Communist judicial system was established by a federal law of July 1991. This provided for a unified system of 4 types of court: civil, criminal, commercial and administrative. Commercial courts arbitrate in disputes arising from business activities. Administrative courts examine the legality of the decisions of state institutions when appealed by citizens. In addition, there are military courts which operate under the jurisdiction of the Ministry of Defence. There is a Supreme Court, and a hierarchy of courts under the Ministry of Justice at republic, region and district level. District courts are courts of first instance. Cases are usually decided by senates comprising a judge and 2 associate judges, though occasionally by a single judge. (Associate judges are citizens in good standing over the age of 25 who are elected for 4-year terms). Regional courts are courts of first instance in more serious cases and also courts of appeal for district courts. Cases are usually decided by a senate of 2 judges and 3 associate judges, although again occasionally by a single judge. The Supreme Court interprets law as a guide to other courts and functions also as a court of appeal. Decisions are made by senates of 3 judges. The judges of the Supreme Court are nominated by the President; other judges are appointed by the National Council.

Religion. A federal Czechoslovakian law of July 1991 provides the basis for church-state relations and guarantees the religious and civic rights of citizens and churches. Churches must register to become legal entities but operate independently of the state. A law of 1993 restored confiscated property to churches and religious communities unless it had passed into private hands, co-operative farms or trading companies. An official poll of Oct. 1995 showed that 73% of the population were religious. Of these, 75% were Roman Catholic, 12% Protestant and 7% Uniate.

Education. In 1995 there were 3,322 pre-school institutions with 161,697 children and 14,933 teachers and 2,485 primary schools with 661,082 pupils and 39,224 teachers. There were 190 grammar schools with 76,380 students and 5,457 teachers and 364 vocational schools with 119,853 pupils and 9,558 teachers. There were 357 secondary vocational apprentice training centres with 139,688 pupils and 6,056 teachers and 400 special schools with 29,914 children and 3,862 teachers. 14 universities or university-type institutions with 74,322 students.

Health. In 1995 there were 14,447 doctors. Population per doctor: 371. 62,634 beds in health establishments in total, out of which 41,727 were in hospitals.

DIPLOMATIC REPRESENTATIVES

Of Slovakia in Great Britain (25 Kensington Palace Gdns., London W8 4QY)
Ambassador: Igor Slobodnik.

Of Great Britain in Slovakia (Panska 16, 81109 Bratislava)
Ambassador: Peter Harborne.

Of Slovakia in the USA (220 Wisconsin Ave., NW, Washington DC, 20007)
Ambassador: Dr Branislav Lichardus.

Of the USA in Slovakia (4 Hviezdoslavovo Namestie, 81102 Bratislava)
Ambassador: Ralph R. Johnson.

Of Slovakia to the United Nations
Ambassador: Vacant.

Of Slovakia to the European Union
Ambassador: Emil Kuchár.

Further Reading

Kirschbaum, S. J., *A History of Slovakia: the Struggle for Survival.* London and New York, 1995
Krejcí, J., *Czechoslovakia at the Crossroads of History.* London, 1990
Leff, C. S., *National Conflict in Czechoslovakia: The Making and Remaking of a State, 1918–1987.* Princeton Univ. Press, 1988
Short, D., *Czechoslovakia.* [Bibliography] Oxford and Santa Barbara (CA), 1986
Stone, N. and Strouhal, E., (eds.) *Czechoslovakia: Crossroads and Crises, 1918-88.* London, 1989
Wheaton, B. and Kavan, Z., *Velvet Revolution: Czechoslovakia 1988-91.* Boulder (CO), 1992

National statistical office: Statistical Office of the Slovak Republic, Miletičova 3, 82467 Bratislava.
Website: http://www.statistics.sk/

SLOVENIA

Republika Slovenija

Capital: Ljubljana
Population: 1·99m.
GDP per head: (PPP$) 10,404
HDI/World Rank: 0.886/35

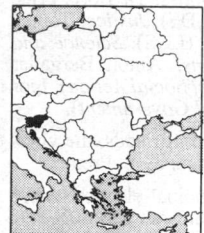

KEY HISTORICAL EVENTS. The lands originally settled by Slovenes in the 6th century were steadily encroached upon by Germans. Slovenia developed as part of Austria-Hungary, after the defeat of the latter in the First World War becoming part of the Kingdom of the Serbs, Croats and Slovenes (Yugoslavia) on 1 Dec. 1918.

In Oct. 1989 the Slovene Assembly voted a constitutional amendment giving it the right to secede from Yugoslavia. On 2 July 1990 the Assembly adopted a 'declaration of sovereignty' by 187 votes to 3, and in Sept. proclaimed its control over the territorial defence force on its soil. At a referendum on 23 Dec. 88·5% of participants voted for independence. On 25 June 1991 Slovenia declared independence, but agreed to suspend this for 3 months at peace talks sponsored by the EU. Federal troops moved into Slovenia on 27 June to secure Yugoslavia's external borders, but after some fighting withdrew by the end of July. After the agreed 3-month moratorium Slovenia (and Croatia) declared their independence from the Yugoslav Federation on 8 Oct. 1991.

TERRITORY AND POPULATION. Slovenia is bounded in the north by Austria, in the north-east by Hungary, in the south-east by Croatia and in the west by Italy. There is a small strip of coast south of Trieste. Its area is 20,253 sq. km. The capital is Ljubljana (1997) population, 330,000. Population (30 June 1995), 1,987,505 (females, 1,021,855), density per sq. km, 98·1. 1998 estimate, 1,987,100; density per sq. km, 98·1.

Vital statistics:

	Live births	Marriages	Deaths	Growth rate per 1,000
1990	22,368	8,517	18,555	1·9
1993	19,793	9,022	20,012	−0·1
1994	19,463	8,314	19,359	0·1

Rates, 1995 (per 1,000 population): Birth, 11·5; death, 9·8; marriage, 5·1; divorce, 1·7; infant mortality, 11 (per 1,000 live births). Expectation of life in 1994 was 69·6 years for males and 77·4 for females.

The population is predominantly Slovene. The official language is Slovene.

CONSTITUTION AND GOVERNMENT. There is a bicameral parliament consisting of a 90-member *National Assembly*, elected for 4-year terms by proportional representation with a 3% threshold; and a 40-member *State Council*, elected for 5-year terms by interest groups. It has veto powers over the National Assembly. Presidential elections were held on 23 Nov. 1997. The electorate was 1·6m; turn-out was 68%. Milan Kučan was re-elected President against 7 opponents by 56% of votes cast.

Elections were held for the National Assembly on 10 Nov. 1996. The electorate was 1·53m.; turn-out was 74%. The Liberal Democratic Party (LDS) won 25 seats with 27·05% of votes cast; the Slovenian People's Party (SLS), 19 with 19·6%; the Social Democratic Party, 16 with 16%; the Christian Democratic Party, 10 with 9·5%; the United List of Social Democrats (former Communists) gained 9 seats; the Pensioners Democratic Party (DeSUS), 5; the National Party, 4. According to the constitution the Hungarian and Italian authorities are entitled to 1 seat each.

President: Milan Kucan (b. 1941; elected 23 Nov. 1997).

In Feb. 1997 an LDS-SLS-DeSUS coalition government was formed which in March 1998 comprised:

Prime Minister: Janez Drnovšek (b. 1950; LDP).

Deputy Prime Minister in charge of Co-ordination of Ministries of Vital Importance: Marjan Podobnik (SLS). *Minister of Agriculture, Food and Forestry:* Ciril Smrkolj (SLS). *Culture:* Jozef Školč (LDS). *Defence:* Alojz Krapez (SLS). *Economic Affairs:* Metod Dragonja (LDS). *Economic Relations and Development:* Marjan Senjur (SLS). *Education and Sport:* Slavko Gaber (LDS). *Environment:* Pavle Gantar (LDS). *Finance:* Mitja Gaspari (ind). *Foreign Affairs:* Dr Boris Frlec (LDS). *Health:* Marjan Jereb (SLS). *Interior:* Mirko Bandelj (LDS). *Justice:* Tomaž Marušič (SLS). *Labour, Family and Social Affairs:* Tone Rop (LDS). *Science and Technology:* Lojze Marinček. *Transport and Communications:* Anton Bergauer (SLS). *Without portfolio:* Janko Kušar (DeSUS; *Co-ordination of Social Action*); Igor Bavčar (LDS; *European Affairs*); Božo Grafenauer (SLS; *Local Government*).

National anthem: 'Prijateli obrodile so trte vince nam sladko' ('Friends, the vines have produced wine sweet to us'); words by France Prešeren, tune by S. Premrl.

Local Government. There are 62 administrative districts. Municipal elections were held in 2 rounds on 4 and 18 Dec. 1994 for 147 mayoralties. Turn-out was 50%.

DEFENCE. There is conscription for 7 months.

Army. There are 6 military districts. The Army is organized in 7 infantry and 1 surface-to-air missile brigades and 2 independent mechanized battalions. Equipment includes some 42 M-84 and 40 T-55 main battle tanks. Personnel (1996), 8,400 (5,500 conscripts). There is a paramilitary police force of 4,500 with 5,000 reserves.

INTERNATIONAL RELATIONS

Membership. Slovenia is a member of the UN, CEFTA, the Central European Initiative and the NATO Partnership for Peace, and is an Associate Partner of the WEU and an Associate Member of the EU. Intensive negotiations regarding Slovenia's accession to full membership of the EU begin in April 1998. Slovenia hopes to become a full member of the Union by the year 2002.

ECONOMY

Policy. Privatization is being carried out in 2 stages, beginning with small businesses, by transferring the capital to an investment fund to act as intermediary. 20% of the capital is to be transferred to savings banks, 10–20% to commercial banks, 20% to wage-earners and 10% to former owners.

Performance. GDP growth rate was 3·25% in 1997 (3·1% in 1996). In 1997, preliminary figures indicate that real exports and imports of goods will have increased by around 7·8% and 7·6%, respectively. The trade deficit is estimated to be US$940m.

Budget. The 1997 Budget was adopted by the Parliament in the beginning of December 1997. It sets expenditure at 743·6bn. tolars. Due to this delay, the government has proposed to extend the budgetary year until the end of January 1998. In view of this budgetary expenditure, public finance expenditure will amount to 46·5% of GDP. Revenue in 1997 was 1,295,107m. tolars; expenditure, 1,335,442m. tolars. Items of revenue (in 1m. tolars) comprised: Tax revenues, 726,327 (corporate income tax, 32,906; personal income tax, 193,540; taxes on goods and services, 394,013; custom duties and import taxes, 59,350; other income taxes, 1,216); social security contributions, 452,299 (contributions for unemployment, 2,428; health care, 190,524; pension fund, 259,347); non-tax revenues, 101,781; proceeds of privatization, 14,700. Items of expenditure: Central government, 483,575; local government, 137,964; pensions, 387,447; health care, 195,583; privatization expenditure, 14,800.

Currency. The unit of currency is the *tolar* (SLT) of 100 *stotinas*, which replaced the Yugoslav dinar. There are coins of 10, 20 and 50 stotinas and 1, 2 and 5 tolars, and notes of 1, 2, 5, 10, 50, 100, 200, 500, 1,000, 5,000 and 10,000 tolars. It is based on the ecu according to a floating exchange rate, and became convertible on 1 Sept.

1995. Inflation was 9·5% in 1997 and is expected to drop in 1998 to around 8%. Foreign exchange reserves were US$4,467m. in October 1997.

Banking and Finance. A central bank and bank of issue, the Bank of Slovenia, was founded in June 1991. Its *Governor* is Franc Arhar. In 1996 there were 31 commercial banks (3 foreign) and 7 savings banks.

There is a stock exchange in Ljubljana (LSE).

ENERGY AND NATURAL RESOURCES

Electricity. Output in the first ten months of 1997 was 9,647·6m. kWh. There is 1 nuclear power station. In the first ten months of 1997 3,886m. kWh were nuclear-produced, 3,465m. kWh thermal and 2,297m. kWh hydro-electric.

Minerals. Brown coal production was 967,000 tonnes in 1995.

Agriculture. Agriculture contributed 4·5% (estimate) of GDP in 1997 (4·6% in 1996). In 1994 agricultural land totalled 791,000 ha (640,000 ha arable, 148,000 ha pasture, 22,000 ha vineyards). The cultivated area was 649,285 ha. Yields (in tonnes) in 1995: Wheat, 233,200; maize, 305,900; sugar-beet, 265,100; potatoes, 448,700; grapes, 101,500.

Livestock in 1995 (in 1,000): Cattle, 477; sheep, 18; pigs, 571; poultry, 10,194. Livestock products, 1996: Meat, 123,000 tonnes; milk, 590m. litres.

Forestry. 2·09m. cu. metres of timber were cut in 1991.

Fisheries. There were 46 sea fishing vessels in 1989. Total catches in marine waters was 2,200 tonnes (1996).

INDUSTRY. There were 51,647 enterprises and companies at March 1996, of which 55 were public, 955 social, 185 private, 84 financial and 1 co-operative. Industry contributed 32·8% of GDP in 1996. Traditional industries are metallurgy, furniture-making and sports equipment. The manufacture of electric goods and transport equipment is being developed.

Production (in 1,000 tonnes): crude steel, 297 (1992); cement, 991 (1995); aluminium, 84·8 (1992); paper and allied products, 278 (1995); machinery, 22·7 (1992); cotton fabrics, 108m. sq. metres (1992); woollens, 13·1m. sq. metres (1992).

Labour. Registered labour force was 870,600 in September 1997. There were 125,400 registered unemployed in September 1997, which is fractionally higher than in 1996. However, using international standards the level of unemployment was 7·1% in the second quarter of 1997, which is slightly less than a year earlier (7·3%). In September 1997 the average monthly gross wage per employee was 145,362 tolars.

FOREIGN ECONOMIC RELATIONS. Foreign debt amounted to US$4,117m. in September 1997. Slovenia has accepted 18% of the US$4,400m. commercial bank debt of the former Yugoslavia.

Commerce. Exports of goods and services in 1996 were worth US$10,497m. and imports, US$10,675m. Major exports in 1995 included: Raw materials, semi-finished goods, machinery, electric motors, transport equipment, foodstuffs, clothing, pharmaceuticals and cosmetics. Major imports: Raw materials, semi-finished goods, machinery, foodstuffs. Share of exports to principal markets in 1996: Germany, 30·6%; Italy, 13·3%; Croatia, 10·3%; France, 7·2%; Austria, 6·6%. Imports: Germany, 21·7%; Italy, 16·9%; France, 9·8%; Croatia, 6·3%.

Tourism. 2,551,000 nights were spent by foreign visitors in 1996.

COMMUNICATIONS

Roads. In 1994 there were 14,810 km of roads, including 11,512 km of modern roadways. There were, in 1995, 293 km of motorways. There were 698,211 passenger cars in 1995. In 1995 there were 2,467 buses, 37,739 lorries and 8,430 motorcycles. 122m. passengers and 4·4m. tonnes of freight were carried in 1995. There were 6,540 traffic accidents in 1995 in which 506 persons were killed.

Railways. In 1995 there were 1,201 km of 1,435 mm gauge, of which 499 km were electrified. In 1995, 89·5m. passengers and 14·9m. tonnes of freight were carried.

Civil Aviation. There are international airports at Ljubljana (Brnik) and Maribor. The national carrier is Adria Airways. In 1995 it had 2 A320-200s, and 6 other aircraft. Services were also provided by Aeroflot, Air France, Austrian Airlines, Croatia Airlines, Czech Airlines, Macedonian Airlines and Swissair. In 1995, 647,000 passengers and 3,877 tonnes of freight were flown.

Shipping. There is a port at Koper. Sea-going shipping totalled 9,061 GRT in 1995.

Telecommunications. In 1992 there were 505 post offices and in 1994 577,173 telephone subscribers. The government-controlled Radiotelevizija Slovenija broadcasts 1 national and local radio programme, and also programmes in German and Italian. In all there were in 1995 6 nationwide radio networks as well as regional and local stations. Public television transmission is carried out by the 2 stations of Televizija Slovenija (colour by PAL). There are also a national independent TV network, a network serving Ljubljana and district and several local stations.

Cinemas. There were 158 cinemas with a total of 45,000 seats in 1989.

Press. In 1997 there were 6 national dailies, 1 national evening and 20 weekly newspapers

SOCIAL INSTITUTIONS

Justice. There are 8 courts of first instance, 4 higher courts and a supreme court.

Religion. 75% of the population were Roman Catholic in 1996.

Education. In 1995–96 there were 823 primary schools with 207,975 pupils and 15,364 teachers and 151 secondary schools with 104,827 pupils and 8,053 teachers. In 1995–96 there were 37 institutions of higher education with 45,951 students and 2,102 academic staff. There were 2 universities with 54,582 students and approximately 2,422 academic staff in 1997–98.

Health. In 1995 there were 4,183 doctors and 11,607 hospital beds.

Welfare. There were 454,722 pensioners in 1995, including 259,253 old age pensioners. Benefits totalled 625,353m. tolars in the first 10 months of 1997.

DIPLOMATIC REPRESENTATIVES

Of Slovenia in Great Britain (11-15 Wigmore St., London W1H 9LA)
Ambassador: Marjan Setinc.

Of Great Britain in Slovenia (3 Trg Republike, 61000 Ljubljana)
Ambassador: David Lloyd.

Of Slovenia in the USA
Ambassador: Dr Dimitrij Rupel

Of the USA in Slovenia (4 Prazakova, 61000 Ljubljana)
Ambassador: Victor Jackovich.

Of Slovenia to the United Nations
Ambassador: Danilo Türk.

Of Slovenia to the European Union
Ambassador: Boris Cizelj.

Further Reading

Benderly, J. and Kraft, E. (eds.) *Independent Slovenia: Origins, Movements, Prospects.* London, 1995
Carmichael, C., *Slovenia* [Bibliography]. Oxford and Santa Barbara (CA), 1996

National statistical office: National Statistical Office, Vožarski Pot 12, 1000 Ljubljana.
Website: http://www.sigov.si/zrs/

SOLOMON ISLANDS

Capital: Honiara
Population: 426,855
GDP per head: (PPP$) 2,118
GNP: US$0·3bn.
HDI/world rank: 0·556/122

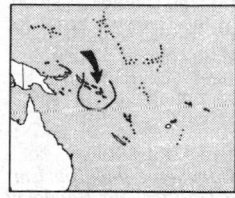

KEY HISTORICAL EVENTS. The Solomon Islands were discovered by Europeans in 1568; 200 years passed before contact was made again. The southern Solomon Islands were placed under British protection in 1893; the eastern and southern outliers were added in 1898 and 1899. Santa Isabel and the other islands to the north were ceded by Germany in 1900. Full internal self-government was achieved on 2 Jan. 1976 and independence on 7 July 1978.

TERRITORY AND POPULATION. The Solomon Islands lie within the area 5° to 12° 30' S. lat. and 155° 30' to 169° 45' E. long. The group includes the main islands of Guadalcanal, Malaita, New Georgia, San Cristobal (now Makira), Santa Isabel and Choiseul; the smaller Florida and Russell groups; the Shortland, Mono (or Treasury), Vella La Vella, Kolombangara, Ranongga, Gizo and Rendova Islands; to the east, Santa Cruz, Tikopia, the Reef and Duff groups; Rennell and Bellona in the south; Ontong Java or Lord Howe to the north; and many smaller islands. The land area is estimated at 10,954 sq. miles (28,370 sq. km). The larger islands are mountainous and forest clad, with flood-prone rivers of considerable energy potential. Guadalcanal has the largest land area and the greatest amount of flat coastal plain. Population (1997 estimate), 426,855; life expectancy, 71·5 years; birth rate (per 1,000 population), 37·3; death rate, 4·3. Population growth rate estimated at 3·3% (1997).

The islands are administratively divided into a Capital Territory and 7 provinces. Area and population:

Province	Sq.km	Census 1986	Estimate 1991	Capital
Western	9,312	55,250	64,732	Gizo
Isabel	4,136	14,616	16,526	Buala
Central	1,286	18,457	20,914	Tulagi
Capital Territory	22	30,413	36,919	. . .
Guadalcanal	5,336	49,831	60,692	Honiara
Malaita	4,225	80,032	86,710	Auki
Makira and Ulawa	3,188	21,796	25,307	Kirakira
Temotu	895	14,781	16,500	Lata (Santa Cruz)

The capital, Honiara, on Guadalcanal, is the largest urban area, with an estimated population in 1989 of 33,749. 93% of the population are Melanesian; other ethnic groups include Polynesian, Micronesian, European and Chinese.

English is the official language, and is spoken by 1-2% of the population. All together 120 indigenous languages are spoken; Melanesian languages are spoken by 85% of the population, Papuan languages by 9% and Polynesian languages by 4%.

CLIMATE. An equatorial climate with only small seasonal variations. South-east winds cause cooler conditions from April to Nov., but north-west winds for the rest of the year bring higher temperatures and greater rainfall, with annual totals ranging between 80" (2,000 mm) and 120" (3,000 mm).

CONSTITUTION AND GOVERNMENT. The Solomon Islands is a constitutional monarchy with the British Sovereign (represented locally by a Governor-General, who must be a Solomon Island citizen) as Head of State. Legislative power is vested in the single-chamber *National Parliament* composed of 47 members, elected by universal adult suffrage for 4 years. Executive authority is effectively held by the Cabinet, led by the Prime Minister.

The Governor-General is appointed for up to five years, on the advice of

Parliament, and acts in almost all matters on the advice of the Cabinet. The Prime Minister is elected by and from members of Parliament. Other Ministers are appointed by the Governor-General on the Prime Minister's recommendation, from members of Parliament. The Cabinet is responsible to Parliament. Emphasis is laid on the devolution of power to provincial governments, and traditional chiefs and leaders have a special role within the arrangement.

At the elections of 26 May 1993 the electorate was 165,000; 280 candidates stood. A coalition of the People's Alliance Party, the United Party, the National Front for Progress and the Liberation Party gained 24 seats.

Governor General: Sir Moses Pitakaka, GCMG.

In March 1998 the government comprised:
Prime Minister: Bartholomew Ulufa'alu.
Deputy Prime Minister: Sir Baddeley Devesi.
Minister of Agriculture and Fisheries: Steve Aumanu. *Commerce and Tourism:* Enele Kwainairara. *Communication, Transport, Works and Utilities:* Sir Baddeley Devesi. *Education and Training:* Ronnie Mannie. *Finance:* Manassah Sogavare. *Foreign Affairs and Trade:* Patterson Oti. *Forests, Environment and Conservation:* Hilda Kari. *Health and Medical Services:* Dick Warakohia. *Home Affairs:* Rev. Leslie Boseto. *Lands and Housing:* Jackson Piasi. *Mines and Energy:* Walton Naeson. *National Planning and Development:* Fred Fono. *Police and National Security:* Lester Saomasi. *Provincial Government:* Japhet Waipora. *Women, Youth and Sports:* Roben Mesepitu.

National anthem: 'God save our Solomon Islands from shore to shore'; words and tune by P. Balekana.

DEFENCE. The marine wing of the police operates 4 inshore patrol craft and 2 small landing craft with about 80 personnel in 1997.

INTERNATIONAL RELATIONS

Membership. The Solomon Islands is a member of the UN, the Commonwealth, the Pacific Community, South Pacific Forum and is an ACP state of the EU.

ECONOMY

Policy. The Government of the Solomon Islands has a deficit far higher than the US$20m. forecasted in the 1996 budget, and in 1997 had taken few steps to restrain expenditure. In mid-1995 the central bank suspended interest and principal payments on government bonds and treasury bills held by financial institutions and the general public.

Budget. The budget estimate for 1997 was a total expenditure of SI$602·2m.; total revenue SI$444·7m.

Currency. The *Solomon Island dollar* (SBD) of 100 *cents* was introduced in 1977. There are coins of 1, 2, 5, 10, 20 and 50 cents and SI$1, and notes of SI$2, 5, 10, 20 and 50.

Banking and Finance. The Central Bank of Solomon Islands is the bank of issue. There are 3 commercial banks.

Weights and Measures. The metric system is in force.

ENERGY AND NATURAL RESOURCES

Electricity. Capacity (1994) was 20,000 kW; production 55m. kWh.

Minerals. The islands are rich in undeveloped mineral resources such as lead, zinc, nickel and gold. Gold earned SI$1.3m. in 1991, decreasing to SI$0·3m. for 8 kg in 1994. The Gold Ridge gold mining project was due to begin operations in March 1998, hoping to produce 100,000 oz per year for 10 years.

Agriculture. Land is held either as customary land (88% of holdings) or registered land. Customary land rights depend on clan membership or kinship. Only Solomon Islanders own customary land; only Islanders or government members may hold perpetual estates of registered land. Coconuts, cocoa, rice and other minor crops are grown. Main food crops: coconut, cassava, sweet potato, yam, taro and banana. Production of copra (1994), 20,724 tonnes; palm oil, 25,855; cocoa, 2,063; palm kernels, 5,690.

Livestock (1991): Cattle, 13,000; pigs, 53,000.

Forestry. Forests cover about 2·4m. ha. Production (1994) of sawn timber, 372 cu. metres.

Fisheries. Total catch, 1995, 46,462 tonnes.

INDUSTRY. Industries include palm oil milling, rice milling, fish canning, fish freezing, saw milling, food, tobacco and soft drinks. Other products include wood and rattan furniture, fibreglass articles, boats, clothing and spices.

FOREIGN ECONOMIC RELATIONS. The Government's Programme of Action for 1990–94 aimed to encourage foreign investment, particularly in manufacturing and tourism.

Commerce. Imports (1994), SI$468·12m.; exports, SI$467·88m. Main imports (in SI$1,000): Rice, 25,840; distillate, 21,408; motor spirits, 6,891; outboard motors, 3,770; passenger cars, 3,675; cement, 3,463; meat preparations, 3,360; refined sugar, 3,209. Main exports: Timber, 276,856; fish products, 99,068; oil palm products, 44,215; copra, 19,770; cocoa, 12,549; coconut oil, 2,013. In 1994 the principal suppliers were Australia (37·2%), Japan (17·1%), New Zealand (9·6%) and Singapore (8·4%); the principal export markets were Japan (41·1%), South Korea (14·1%) and UK (13·1%).

Tourism. In 1994 there were 16,902 visitor arrivals.

COMMUNICATIONS

Roads. In 1995 there was estimated to be a total of 2,100 km of roads, of which 32 km were paved. The unpaved roads included 800 km of private plantation roads. In 1986 there were 3,376 vehicles, of which about 2,026 were commercial vehicles.

Civil Aviation. The international airport at Honiara (Henderson) is served by Air Nauru, Air Niugini, Air Pacific, Qantas and Western Pacific. The national carrier is the state-owned Solomon Airlines, which in 1995 operated 2 aircraft. There are 27 airfields. Solomon Airlines also provides inter-island transport and scheduled flights to Kieta in Papua New Guinea.

Shipping. There are international ports at Honiara, and Yandina in the Russell group. In 1995 the merchant marine totalled 5,746 GRT.

Telecommunications. There are 14 post offices and 95 postal agencies. Number of telephones (1994) 6,000. Solomon Islands Broadcasting Corporation is a statutory authority which broadcasts radio programmes from Honiara, Gizo and Lata. In 1994 there were 45,000 radio receivers and 2,000 televisions.

Press. There are 3 weekly newspapers.

SOCIAL INSTITUTIONS

Justice. Civil and criminal jurisdiction is exercised by the High Court of Solomon Islands, constituted 1975. A Solomon Islands Court of Appeal was established in 1982. Jurisdiction is based on the principles of English law (as applying on 1 Jan. 1981). Magistrates' courts can try civil cases on claims not exceeding SI$2,000, and criminal cases with penalties not exceeding 14 years' imprisonment. Certain crimes, such as burglary and arson, where the maximum sentence is for life, may also be tried by magistrates. There are also local courts, which decide matters concerning customary titles to land; decisions may be put to the Customary Land Appeal Court. There is no capital punishment.

Religion. 34% of the population are Anglican, 19% Roman Catholic, 17·6% Baptist, 11% United (Methodist/Presbyterian), 10% Seventh-Day Adventist, 5% other Protestant and 4% traditional beliefs.

Education. In 1994 there were 12,627 pre-primary pupils, and 65,493 primary pupils, with 2,514 teachers. There were 7,811 pupils at secondary level. Adult literacy (1994) is 62·0%.

Training of teachers and trade and vocational training is carried out at the college of Higher Education. The University of the South Pacific Centre is at Honiara.

Health. In 1988 there were 8 hospitals, 31 doctors, 464 registered nurses and 283 nursing aides.

DIPLOMATIC REPRESENTATIVES

Of the Solomon Islands in Great Britain (resides in Brussels).
High Commissioner: Robert Sisilo.

Of Great Britain in the Solomon Islands (Telekon House, Mendana Ave., Honiara)
High Commissioner: Brian N. Connelly.

Of the USA in the Solomon Islands
Ambassador: Richard W. Teare (resides in Papua New Guinea).

Of the Solomon Islands in the USA and to the United Nations
Ambassador: Rex Horoi.

Of the Solomon Islands to the European Union
Ambassador: Robert Sisilo.

Further Reading

Bennett, J. A., *Wealth of the Solomons: A History of a Pacific Archipelago, 1800–1978*. Univ. of Hawaii Press, 1987
Kent, J., *The Solomon Islands*. Newton Abbot, 1972

SOMALIA

Jamhuriyadda Dimugradiga
ee Soomaaliya
(Somali Democratic Republic)

Capital: Mogadishu
Population: 6·59m.

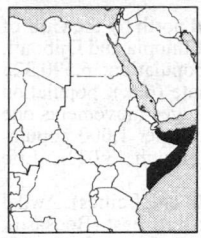

KEY HISTORICAL EVENTS. The origins of the Somali people can be traced back 2,000 years when they migrated to the region, displacing and absorbing an earlier Arabic people. They converted to Islam in the 10th century and were organized in loose Islamic states by the 19th century. The northern part of Somaliland was created a British protectorate in 1884. The southern part belonged to two local rulers who, in 1889, accepted Italian protection for their lands. The Italian invasion of Ethiopia in 1935 was launched from Somaliland and in 1936 Somaliland was incorporated with Eritrea and Ethiopia to become Italian East Africa. In 1940 Italian forces invaded British Somaliland but in 1941 the British, with South African and Indian troops, recaptured this territory as well as occupying Italian Somaliland. After the Second World War British Somaliland reverted to its colonial status and ex-Italian-Somaliland became the UN Trust Territory of Somaliland, administered by Italy.

The independent Somali Republic came into being on 1 July 1960 as a result of the merger of the British Somaliland Protectorate, which first became independent on 26 June 1960, and the Italian Trusteeship Territory of Somaliland. Aden Abdullah Osman was elected president of the new republic, and the legislatures of the two territories were merged to create a single national assembly.

On 21 Oct. 1969 Maj.-Gen. Mohammed Siyad Barre, the C.-in-C. of the armed forces, took power in a *coup*. He suspended the constitution and formed a Supreme Revolutionary Council to administer the country, which was renamed the Somali Democratic Republic.

Various insurgent forces combined to oppose the Barre regime in a bloody civil war. Barre fled on 27 Jan. 1991. Ali Mahdi Muhammad, of the United Somali Congress, became president in Aug. 1991, but interfactional fighting continued. In Aug. 1992 a new coalition government agreed a UN military presence to back up relief efforts to help the estimated 1·5-2m. victims of famine. In accordance with a unanimous UN Security Council resolution of 3 Nov. 1992, troops from the USA and other countries mounted a mission to ensure the supply of aid to victims of the civil war and drought. On 11 Dec. 1992 the leaders of the two most prominent of the warring factions, Ali Mahdi Muhammad and Muhammad Farah Aidid, agreed to a peace plan under the aegis of the UN, and a pact was signed on 15 Jan. 1993. At the end of March, the warring factions agreed to disarm and form a 74-member National Transitional Council.

Following the killing of 24 Pakistani soldiers of the UN 29-nation peacekeeping force on 17 June 1993, UN troops attacked and seized the stronghold of Muhammad Aidid and sought his arrest. After an escalation of violence in which hundreds of Somalis were killed, an envoy from the US President negotiated the release of hostages from Gen. Aidid and it was agreed to set up an independent commission of enquiry. After Dec. 1993 various national contingents began to leave the peace-keeping force, including US forces in March 1994. A unanimous UN National Security Council resolution of 4 Feb. 1994 laid stress on the need for reconciliation and the promotion of democratic government, and scaled down the number of UN forces in the country. On 4 Nov. 1994 the UN Security Council unanimously decided to withdraw UN forces; the last of these left on 2 March 1995.

The principal insurgent group in the north of the country, the Somali National Movement, declared the secession of an independent **'Somaliland Republic'** on 17 May 1991, based on the territory of the former British protectorate, with a capital at Hargeisa and a port at Berbera. Its president is Muhammad Ibrahim Egal. The

Somalian government rejected the secession. Clan warfare broke out in Hargeisa in Nov. 1994, and Muhammad Aidid's forces launched a campaign to reoccupy the 'Republic' in Jan. 1996.

Muhammad Farah Aidid was assassinated in July 1996 and succeeded by his son Hussein Aidid (b. 1965). Fighting between the Ali Mahdi Muhammad and the Hussein Aidid factions broke out in Dec. 1996 in Mogadishu, but on 20 Jan. 1997 the factions agreed to unify the city.

TERRITORY AND POPULATION. Somalia is bounded north by the Gulf of Aden, east and south by the Indian ocean, and west by Kenya, Ethiopia and Djibouti. Total area 637,657 sq. km (246,201 sq. miles). Estimated population: 6,590,325 (1997). Aid and relief agencies have produced a lower estimate (6m.); population counting is complicated due to large number of nomads and refugee movements due to famine and clan warfare. Vital statistics, 1997 estimate (rates per 1,000 population): Birth, 45·49; death, 18·34; infant mortality, 125·8; growth, 3·03%. Life expectancy in 1997, 46·23 years.

The country is administratively divided into 18 regions (with chief cities): Awdal (Saylac), Bakol (Xuddur), Bay (Baydhabo), Benadir (Mogadishu), East (Boosaso), Galgudug (Duusa Marreeb), Gedo (Garbahaarrey), Hiran (Beledweyne), Central Juba (Jilib), Lower Juba (Kismaayo), Mudug (Gaalkacyo), Nogal (Gaarowe), North-West (Hargeysa), Sanaag (Ceerigabo), Central Shabele (Jawhar), Lower Shabele (Marka), Sol (Las Anod), Togder (Burao). The capital is Mogadishu (1987 population, 1m.). Other large towns are Hargeysa (0·4m.), Kismayo (0·2m.), Marka (0·1m.) and Berbera.

The national language is Somali. Arabic is also an official language and English and Italian are spoken extensively.

CLIMATE. Much of the country is arid, though rainfall is more adequate towards the south. Temperatures are very high on the northern coasts. Mogadishu. Jan. 79°F (26·1°C), July 78°F (25·6°C). Annual rainfall 17" (429 mm). Berbera. Jan. 76°F (24·4°C), July 97°F (36·1°C). Annual rainfall 2" (51 mm).

CONSTITUTION AND GOVERNMENT. The Constitution of 1984 authorized a sole legal party, the Somali Revolutionary Socialist Party. There was an elected President and People's Assembly.

A conference of national reconciliation in July 1991 and again in March 1993 allowed for the setting up of a transitional government charged with reorganizing free elections, but inter-factional fighting and anarchy have replaced settled government.

Local Government. The 18 regions are sub-divided into 84 districts.

DEFENCE. With the breakdown of government following the 1991 revolution armed forces broke up into clan groupings, four of those in the north and six in the south.

INTERNATIONAL RELATIONS

Membership. Somalia is a member of the UN, OAU and the Arab League and is an ACP state of the EU.

ECONOMY

Budget. Budget for 1990: Revenue, Som.Sh. 49,264m.; expenditure, Som.Sh. 68,970m.

Currency. The unit of currency is the *Somali shilling* (SOS) of 100 *cents.* There are notes of 5, 10, 20, 100, 500 and 1,000 shillings and coins of 1, 5, 10, 50 cents and 1 shilling.

Banking and Finance. The bank of issue is the Central Bank of Somalia (founded in 1960 as the Somali National Bank). All banks were nationalized in 1970. The

Somali Development Bank (founded 1983) and the Commercial Bank of Somalia are the only banks.

Weights and Measures. The metric system is in use.

ENERGY AND NATURAL RESOURCES

Electricity. Capacity: 144,000 kW prior to the civil war, now largely shut down; some localities operate their own generating plants. Production (1991): 60 m. kWh.

Minerals. There are deposits of chromium, coal, copper, gold, gypsum, lead, limestone, manganese, nickel, silver, titanium, tungsten, uranium and zinc.

Agriculture. Somalia is essentially a pastoral country, and about 80% of the inhabitants depend on livestock-rearing (cattle, sheep, goats and camels). Half the population is nomadic. Arable and permanent crop land in 1990 were 1·0m. ha and 0·01m. ha. Estimated production, 1995 (in 1,000 tonnes): Sugar-cane, 200; bananas, 45; maize, 146; sorghum, 136; grapefruit, 19.

Livestock (1995): 12·5m. goats; 13·5m. sheep; 6·2m. camels; 5·2m. cattle; 24,000 asses and 21,000 mules.

Forestry. 60% of the country is woodland. In 1994, 8·6m. cubic metres of round-wood were cut. Wood and charcoal are the main energy sources. Frankincense and myrrh are produced.

Fisheries. In 1988 the fishing fleet comprised 28 vessels totalling 5,188 DWT. 15,500 tonnes were caught in 1995.

INDUSTRY. A few small industries existed in 1986 including sugar refining, food processing, textiles and petroleum refining.

Labour. 2,143,000 persons (828,000 females) were employed in 1990. 167,000 were between 10 and 15 years of age. 34·6% were labourers, 21·4% worked in trade and 14·3% in services.

FOREIGN ECONOMIC RELATIONS. Foreign debt was US$2,447m. in 1992.

Commerce. Exports in 1991 totalled US$52·3m.; imports, US$238·1m.

Principal exports: Livestock, hides and skins, bananas. Main export markets in 1992 (trade in US$1m.): Saudi Arabia, 24·9; Italy, 11. Main import suppliers: Saudi Arabia, 12·9; USA, 10·9; Italy, 10·6.

COMMUNICATIONS

Roads. In 1993 there were estimated to be 18,000 km of roads, of which 2,700 km were paved.

Civil Aviation. There are international airports at Mogadishu and Berbera and 5 domestic airports. The national airline, Somali Airlines, which transported 105,000 passengers in 1988, had 1 aircraft in 1995. Mogadishu airport was used by Air Tanzania, Alitalia, Alyemda, Kenya Airways, PIA and Saudia.

Shipping. There are deep-water harbours at Kismayo, Berbera, Marka and Mogadishu. The merchant fleet (1995) totalled 17,288 GRT.

Telecommunications. Number of telephones (1991), about 9,000. The state radio stations transmit in Somali, Arabic, English and Italian from Mogadishu and Hargeysa. The television station was destroyed in fighting in 1991; there are estimated to be 400,000 radios and 124,000 televisions.

Press. In 1995 there was one daily newspaper, with a circulation of 10,000.

SOCIAL INSTITUTIONS

Justice. There are 84 district courts, each with a civil and a criminal section. There are 8 regional courts and 2 Courts of Appeal (at Mogadishu and Hargeysa), each with a general section and an assize section. The Supreme Court is in Mogadishu.

Religion. The population is almost entirely Sunni Moslems.

Education. The nomadic life of a large percentage of the population inhibits education progress. In 1990 adult literacy was estimated at 24%. In 1985 there were 194,335 pupils and 9,676 teachers in primary schools, there were 37,181 pupils and 2,320 teachers in secondary schools, and in 1984 613 students with 30 teachers at teacher-training establishments. The National University of Somalia in Mogadishu (founded 1959) had 4,650 students and 550 academic staff in 1994–95.

Health. In 1986 there were 88 hospitals, 358 doctors, 113 pharmacists, 2 dentists, 556 midwives and 1,834 nursing personnel.

DIPLOMATIC REPRESENTATIVES

The Embassy of Somalia in Great Britain closed on 2 Jan. 1992.

Of Great Britain in Somalia (Waddada Xasan Geedd Abtoow 7/8, Mogadishu) Staff temporarily withdrawn.

The Embassy of Somalia in the USA closed on 8 May 1991. A liaison office opened in March 1994, and withdrew to Nairobi in Sept. 1994.

Of Somalia to the United Nations
Ambassador: Vacant.

Of Somalia to the European Union
Ambassador: Vacant.

Further Reading

Abdisalam, M. I.-S., *The Collapse of the Somali State*. London, 1995
DeLancey, M. W., *et al. Somalia*. [Bibliography] Oxford and Santa Barbara (CA), 1988
Ghalib, J. M., *The Cost of Dictatorship: the Somali Experience*. New York, 1995
Lewis, I. M., *Blood and Bone: the Call of Kinship in Somali Society*. Lawrenceville (NJ), 1995.—*Understanding Somalia: a Guide to Culture, History and Social Institutions*. 2nd ed. London 1995
Omar, M. O., *The Road to Zero: Somalia's Self-Destruction*. London, 1995
Samatar, A. I. (ed.) *The Somali Challenge: from Catastrophe to Renewal?* Boulder (CO), 1994

National statistical office: Central Statistical Department, State Planning Commission, Mogadishu.

SOUTH AFRICA

Republic of South Africa

Capitals: Pretoria (Administrative), Cape Town (Legislative), Bloemfontein (Judicial)
Seats of Parliament: Cape Town
Seats of Government: Cape Town, Pretoria
Population: 41·5m
GDP per head: (PPP$) 4,291
GNP: US$125·2bn.
HDI/world rank: 0·716/90

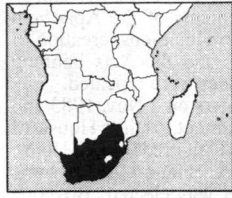

KEY HISTORICAL EVENTS. The Dutch first established a trading post at the Cape in 1652. The hinterland was then inhabited by the Khoisan peoples and, further east and north, by Bantu-speaking peoples. There was some white settlement over the next century. During the Napoleonic Wars, Britain took possession of the Cape and later many Boer (Dutch) settlers migrated north-east in the Great Trek. In the mid-19th century Britain ruled the Cape Colony and Natal along the coast of southern African, while in the interior the Afrikaners or Boers, descendants of Dutch settlers, established their own independent republics in the Transvaal and the Orange Free State. Some Bantu African peoples remained unconquered, notably the Xhosas east of the Cape Colony and, north of Natal, the Zulus, whose leader Shaka (died 1828) had formed a powerful kingdom in a great political and demographic upheaval called the *Mfecane*. The Sothos, who formed another new state under Moshoeshoe, resisted the Boers' encroachment on their land, until in 1868 Britain granted Moshoeshoe's request for a protectorate over Basutoland. Meanwhile, British settlers emigrated to Cape Colony and Natal in the 19th century, and from the 1860s many Indians were brought to Natal as indentured labourers on the sugar plantations. The population of the Cape Colony included many Afrikaners as well as the 'Coloured' community, descendants of Dutch settlers and indigenous Khoisan women and of Malay slaves. Most coloureds spoke Afrikaans, the offshoot of Dutch spoken by the Boers.

Britain annexed the Transvaal in 1877, and fought in 1879 with the Zulus who, under King Ketshwayo, won a victory at Isandhlwana but were then defeated at Ulundi. Britain restored independence to the Transvaal (South African Republic) in 1884 but annexed Zululand in 1887. Both the British and the Boers fought African resistance for many years, the last major rising being in Natal in 1906. However, the British and Boers were also rivals for supremacy, especially after the discovery of diamonds at Kimberley in 1867 and of gold in the Transvaal in 1884. This led to an economic boom and wealth for many, of whom Cecil Rhodes, for a time prime minister of the Cape, was the dominant entrepreneurial figure.

In the South African War of 1899–1902, the British defeated and annexed the Boer republics. The Boer republics were given self-government again in 1907, and on 31 May 1910 Cape Colony, Natal, the Transvaal and the Orange Free State combined to form the Union of South Africa, a self-governing dominion under the British Crown. The Union was ruled by the white minority; the franchise accorded to some non-whites in Cape Colony was kept, but not extended to the other three provinces.

The Union's economy was based on gold and diamond mining, for which there was organized recruitment of migrant African labourers from Union territory and other parts of Africa. Pass Laws were in operation, controlling Africans' movements in the towns and industrial areas, where they were regarded officially as temporary residents and segregated in 'townships'. By an Act of 1913 87% of the land was reserved for white ownership only, much of it being owned by white farmers while Africans farmed as tenants or squatters.

African protests at segregation and lack of political rights were led by the African National Congress (ANC). From 1918 there were also many African labour protests. African rights were further suppressed after the coming to power in 1924 of the

Afrikaner Nationalist Party, led by J. B. Hertzog. Hertzog's government secured recognition of full independence for South Africa by the Statute of Westminster on 11 Dec. 1931. It also promoted the status of the Afrikaans language and introduced new segregation measures. From 1948 the National Party government reinforced the segregation system, developing it into the system of Apartheid, enforced under prime ministers Malan (1948–54), Strijdom (1954–58), Verwoerd (1958–66) and Voerster (1966–78). The shooting by police of protesters against the Pass Laws at Sharpeville on 21 March 1960 led to a major crisis from which, however, the government emerged only stronger. The ANC and the Pan African Congress were banned, and the leaders forced to operate from exile after internal ANC leaders, including Nelson Mandela, were gaoled in 1964.

On 31 May 1961 South Africa became a Republic outside the Commonwealth.

When P. W. Botha became prime minister in 1978, elements of the Apartheid system were modified. Africans were allowed to form legal trade unions, creation of Black local government authorities in cities was enacted, and the Acts banning marriage and sexual relations between people of different races were repealed.

A new constitution, approved in a referendum of white voters on 2 Nov. 1983 and in force from 3 Sept. 1984, created a new three-part parliament, with a House of Assembly for the Whites, a House of Representatives for the Coloureds, and a House of Delegates for the Indians; Africans remained without representation. At the same time an executive presidency was created, to which Botha was elected. Boycotts ensured low polls in the elections for the Coloured and Indian houses held on 22 and 28 Aug. 1984 respectively. The Whites retained their House of Assembly as elected in 1981 with its massive National Party majority.

From late 1984 Blacks in the cities and industrial areas staged large-scale protests, including strikes. Largely spontaneous—though the gaoled ANC leader Mandela was seen as the Africans' hero—the protests involved large-scale violence. In June 1986 a state of emergency was imposed. Foreign condemnation of this led to the first economic sanctions against South Africa imposed by a number of countries including the USA.

By 1989 the restrictions of Apartheid began to be removed, and the government announced its willingness to consider the extension of Black South Africans' political rights. In Feb. 1990 a 30-year ban on the African National Congress (ANC) was lifted and its leader, Nelson Mandela, released from prison.

At the Whites-only referendum on 17 March 1992 on the granting of constitutional equality to all races turn-out was 85·6%. 1,924,186 (68·7%) votes were in favour; 875,619 against.

On 22 Dec. 1993 parliament approved (by 237 votes to 45) a Transitional Constitution paving the way for a new multi-racial parliament which was elected on 26–29 April 1994 and South Africa rejoined the Commonwealth. On 9 May 1994 Nelson Mandela was elected President and sworn in the following day. A new Constitution was signed into law in Dec. 1996. Also in Dec. 1996, South Africa set up the Truth and Reconciliation Commission in an effort to rescue the country from denial and lies about the past, to give dignity to those who had suffered, and to extend a hand of forgiveness to the perpetrators of civil crimes.

TERRITORY AND POPULATION. South Africa is bounded in the north by Namibia, Botswana and Zimbabwe, north-east by Mozambique and Swaziland, east by the Indian Ocean and south and west by the South Atlantic with Lesotho forming an enclave. Area: 1,224,691 sq. km. This area includes the uninhabited Prince Edward Island (41 sq. km) and Marion Island (388 sq. km) lying 1,900 km south-east of Cape Town and taken possession of in Dec. 1947. In 1994 Walvis Bay was ceded to Namibia and Transkei, Bophuthatswana, Venda and Ciskei were re-integrated into South Africa.

At the census of 1991 the population was 37,713,951 (19,055,846 females; 5,061,242 Whites). Official population estimate, Oct. 1995, (in 1,000): 41,544 (females, 21,167; urban, 20,647; Whites, 5,224; Coloureds, 3,508; Asians, 1,015; Blacks, 31,461). Growth rate, 1995, 1·9%. Urban population in Oct. 1995 was 49·7% (20,647,000).

Vital statistics for calendar years:

	Births	Still Births	Deaths	Marriages	Immigrants	Emigrants
1994	677,107	6,968	213,279	133,309	6,398	10,235
1995	809,439	8,946	268,028	148,148	5,064	8,725
1996	...	...	...	...	5,407	9,708

Due to under-registration and the high percentage of late registration, the collection of Black birth information was discontinued in 1981–89. As from 1991 no distinction between racial groups was made. The 1994 live birth figure includes 430,762 late registrations of births which actually took place between 1987–93.

Infant deaths in 1995, 22,865. Divorces in 1995: Whites, 16,788; Coloureds, 5,029; Asians, 1,601; Blacks, 8,174.

Of the 5,407 immigrants in 1996, 2,315 were from Europe (of whom 1,052, UK); 1,020 from Asia (of whom 244, Taiwan); 1,549 from Africa, 257 from the Americas and 86 from Oceania. Of the 9,708 emigrants in 1996, 3,198 went to Europe (of whom 2,243 to UK); 3,035 to Oceania (of whom 1,767, Australia); 1,786 to the Americas; 1,151 to Africa and 136 to Asia.

In 1995 there were also estimated to be 8·5m. illegal immigrants, 3m. of whom had arrived since 1994.

Urban areas, according to the 1991 census:

Urban Area	Total	White	Coloured	Asian	Black
Johannesburg/Randburg	1,916,063	538,728	131,047	66,176	1,180,112
Cape Peninsula	2,350,157	612,200	1,256,290	27,058	454,609
Durban/Pinetown/Inanda/ Chatsworth	1,137,378	328,183	64,876	575,268	169,051
East Rand	1,378,792	445,160	37,289	17,951	878,392
Pretoria/Wonderboom/ Soshanguve	1,080,187	529,732	25,728	20,516	504,211
Port Elizabeth/Uitenhage	853,204	183,901	204,504	9,548	455,251
West Rand	870,066	263,168	30,473	24,812	551,613
Vanderbijlpark/Vereeniging/ Sasolburg	773,594	187,771	24,794	7,962	553,067
Bloemfontein	300,150	111,374	25,100	442	163,234
Pietermaritzburg	228,549	61,104	15,862	64,506	87,077
Free State Goldfields	427,569	77,200	8,159	129	342,081
Kimberley	167,060	34,066	57,853	1,475	73,666
East London/Bisho	270,127	90,486	35,880	4,125	139,635

There are 11 official languages (with numbers of home speakers at the 1991 census): Zulu (8,457,022); Xhosa (6,596,882); Afrikaans (5,689,131); Pedi (3,694,950); English (3,417,263); Tswana (2,715,419); Sotho (2,604,048); Tsonga (1,603,364); Swazi (975,827); Venda (645,315); Ndebele (562,463). The use of any of these is a constitutional right 'wherever practicable'. Each province may adopt any of these as its official language. English is the sole language of command and instruction in the armed forces.

At the 1991 census 67,387 persons declared themselves bilingual in Afrikaans and English, and 685,120 spoke other languages, 8 of which are recognized by the Constitution and promoted by a special board.

CLIMATE. There is abundant sunshine and relatively low rainfall. The south-west has a Mediterranean climate, with rain mainly in winter, but most of the country has a summer maximum, though quantities show a decrease from east to west. Pretoria. Jan. 72·5°F (22·5°C), July 52·3°F (11·3°C). Annual rainfall 29·5" (750 mm). Bloemfontein. Jan. 73°F (22·8°C), July 47°F (8·3°C). Annual rainfall 23" (564 mm). Cape Town. Jan. 69°F (20·6°C), July 54°F (12·2°C). Annual rainfall 20" (508 mm). Johannesburg. Jan. 68°F (20°C), July 51°F (10·6°C). Annual rainfall 28" (709 mm).

CONSTITUTION AND GOVERNMENT. A Transitional Constitution was adopted on 27 April 1994 to be in force for 5 years. Under it the National Assembly and Senate form a *Constitutional Assembly* (chaired by Cyril Ramaphosa, b. 1952; ANC) which had the task of adopting a definitive constitution by a two-thirds majority. This was adopted on 9 May 1996 and signed into law in Dec. 1996. The 1994 Constitution provides for an executive *President*, elected by parliament, *Deputy Presidents*, nominated one each by parties gaining at least 20% of electoral votes, and a parliament of 2 houses: a National Assembly and a National Council of Provinces. The 1999 Constitution defines the powers of the President, Parliament, the national executive, the judiciary, public administration and the security services. It incorporates a Bill of Rights appertaining to education, housing, the food and water supply and security as well as political rights. A section defines the relationship between central and provincial aspect; this section was challenged by the Constitutional Court and is being re-drafted.

A *Constitutional Court*, consisting of a president, a deputy president and 9 other judges, was inaugurated in Feb. 1995. Of the Court's judges, 6 are appointed by the President of the Republic on the advice of the Judicial Service Commission, and 4 are appointed from among the judges of the Supreme Court. A Constitutional Court judge is appointed for a non-renewable term of 12 years, but must retire at the age of 70. The Court reviews the actions of the legislature, executive and judiciary in the light of the Bill of Rights, and can overturn legislation. Its remit includes approval of the post-1999 constitution prior to its adoption by parliament.

The *National Assembly* is a legislature consisting of 400 members directly elected for 5 years, 200 from a national list, and 200 from provincial lists in the following proportions: Eastern Cape, 28; Free State, 14; Gauteng, 44; KwaZulu-Natal, 42; Mpumalanga, 11; Northern Cape, 4; Northern Province, 25; North-West, 12; Western Cape, 20. Parties gaining at least 5% of votes are entitled to Cabinet representation. The 9 provincial parliaments are elected at the same time, and candidates may stand for both, choosing if elected to both whether to sit in the national or provincial assembly; in the former case the runner-up is elected to the provincial assembly. The *Senate* consists of 90 members (10 from each province) indirectly elected by the provincial legislatures by proportional representation.

Bills may be introduced in either house, but must be passed by both. If a bill is rejected by one house, it is referred back to both after consideration by a joint National Assembly-Senate committee. Bills relating to the provinces must be passed by the Senate.

Parliamentary elections were held on 26–28 April 1994 (extended to 29 April in some areas). The electorate was 22·7m.; turn-out was 86%. 19 parties stood. The African National Congress (ANC) gained 252 seats with 62·7% of votes cast, the National Party (NP) 82 with 20·4%, the Inkatha Freedom Party 43 with 10·5%, the Freedom Front (FF) 9 with 2·2%, the Democratic Party 7 with 1·7%, the Pan-Africanist Congress (PAC) 5 with 1·2% and the African Christian Democratic Party 2 with 0·5%.

The party composition of the Senate in Dec. 1994 was: ANC, 10; NP, 17; Inkatha, 5; FF, 5; DP,3. Its *President* is Dr Kobie Coetsee.

A Government of National Unity took office on 6 May 1994 which, after the withdrawal of NP members, in March 1998 comprised:

President: Nelson Mandela (b. 1918; ANC; elected 9 May 1994, sworn in 10 May).

Executive Deputy President: Thabo Mbeki (ANC). *Minister of Land and Agriculture:* Derek Hanekom (ANC). *Arts, Culture, Science and Technology:* L. P. H. M. Mtshali (IFP). *Correctional Services:* Dr Sipho Mzimela (Inkatha). *Defence:* Joe Modise (ANC). *Education:* Sibusiso Bengu (ANC). *Environmental Affairs and Tourism:* Dr Pallo Jordan. *Finance:* Trevor Manuel (ANC). *Foreign Affairs:* Alfred Nzo (ANC). *Health:* Dr Nkosazana Zuma (ANC). *Home Affairs:* Dr Mangosuthu Buthelezi (Inkatha). *Housing:* Sankie Mthembi-Mahanyele (ANC). *Justice:* Dr Dullah Omar (ANC). *Labour:* Tito Mboweni (ANC). *Mineral and Energy Affairs:* Penuell Maduna (ANC). *Posts, Telecommunications and Broadcasting:* Jay Naidoo (ANC). *Provincial Affairs and Constitutional Development:* Valli Moosa (ANC). *Public Enterprises:* Stella Sigcau (ANC). *Public Services and Administration:* Dr Zola Skweyiya (ANC). *Public Works:* Jeff Radebe (ANC). *Safety and Security:* F. Sidney Mufamadi (ANC). *Sport and Recreation:* Steve Tshwete (ANC). *Trade and Industry:* Alec Erwin (ANC). *Transport:* S. 'Mac' Maharaj (ANC). *Water Affairs and*

Forestry: Kadar Asmal (ANC). *Welfare and Population Development:* Geraldine Fraser-Moleketi (ANC).

The *Speaker* is Dr Frene Ginwala.

National anthem: A combination of shortened forms of *Die Stem van Suid-Afrika/The Call of South Africa* (words by C. J. Langenhoven; tune by M. L. de Villiers) and the ANC anthem *Nkosi sikelel' iAfrika/God bless Africa*.

Provincial Government. The 1994 Transitional Constitution provides for 9 provinces, which may with a two-thirds majority adopt a constitution for the province in question. A provincial constitution may not be inconsistent with the provisions of the transitional Constitution except that different legislative and executive structures may be provided for. A provincial constitution only becomes effective after the Constitutional Court has certified that it is in accordance with the provisions of the Constitution. Each province has a provincial legislature in which the legislative authority of that province vests and which accordingly has the power to make laws for the province. A provincial legislature must consist of a minimum of 30 and a maximum of 100 members elected by proportional representation. A provincial legislature is elected for 5 years or less in certain circumstances. If a legislature adopts a motion of no-confidence in the executive council of the province, including the Premier, the Premier must resign or dissolve the legislature for an election.

The executive council of a province consists of the Premier as chairperson and a maximum of 10 members who are proportionately divided between all parties holding at least 10% of the seats in the provincial legislature. The Premier allocates portfolios to the parties in question after consultation with the respective leaders and appoints members of the council.

A provincial legislature has legislative authority and an executive council has executive authority with regard to the following functional areas or topics: Agriculture, education (excluding universities and technikons), health service, welfare services, housing, local government, police, cultural affairs, nature conservation, soil conservation, the environment, animal control and diseases, abattoirs, markets and pounds, gambling, language policy, public media, regional airports, transport, road traffic, regional planning and development, provincial sport and recreation, tourism, trade and industrial promotion, consumer protection, indigenous law and customary law, traditional authorities, and urban and rural development. A province does not automatically enjoy authority over these matters. Existing laws on these topics are administered by the national government until a province requests a transfer of them. The condition for such a transfer is that the province must have the administrative capacity to perform the powers and functions in question.

(For details of the individual provinces *see below*).

Local Government. Elections were held on 1 Nov. 1995 for 688 metropolitan, town and rural councils. The electorate was 12·3m.; it is estimated that only 75% of eligible voters were registered. The ANC gained 66·37% of all votes cast and a majority in some 400 councils; the NP, 16·22%; the Freedom Front, 5%. Elections in Western Cape and KwaZulu-Natal were postponed until 29 May and 26 June 1996 respectively.

DEFENCE. The Department of Defence (DoD) is in the process of radical change involving its design, structure and force levels. Transformation is being driven by a White Paper on Defence and a major Defence Review which, in turn, has resulted from dramatic changes in the strategic environment. The country has been welcomed back into many regional and international organizations and is now expected to play an active role in peace and security in Africa and Southern Africa in particular. The Defence Review will consist of three reports, of which the first two have been completed and approved by Parliament.

The first report presented options for the design of a core force. The recommended option was styled 'The Growth Core Force Design'. This provided for a combat element consisting of 22,000 full-time component members and 69,400 members of the part-time component. It was costed at a little over R5bn. In addition the combat element will be backed by approximately 44,000 full-time civilian and military members in the support and command and control roles. The provision of new equipment for the SANDF formed part of the recommendations. This includes submarines and corvettes for the Navy, fighter, maritime control and transport aircraft for the Air Force and new armoured vehicles. Further planning and decisions will take place to determine what is militarily, fiscally and industrially viable.

The second report dealt with the structure of the Department. The structure of the DoD has been redesigned so that the top structure, incorporates the Minister, Deputy Minister and the DoD Head Office, collectively known as the Ministry of Defence. The Head Office will combine as an integrated whole the former Arms of Service Headquarters, Defence Headquarters and the Defence Secretariat. The divisions aim to be fully operational on or as soon as possible after 1 April 1998. The main divisions will formulate policy and be responsible for the provision, preparation and support of the forces necessary to fulfil any DoD assignments. As a new feature, and following certain international trends, the employment of these forces will fall under a Joint Operations Division.

The new structure of the DoD will still contain four Arms of the Service, namely the SA Army, SA Air Force, SA Navy and SA Medical Service. However, there will be new intermediate structures, progressively replacing the present territorial commands, for which various options have been approved in principle. The number of units on the ground and their shape and functions will be determined in the final planning stages of the Defence Review and the transformation process. It is not possible at this stage to provide specific details on the organization, strength, armaments and equipment of each individual arm of the service.

The full-time and part-time components of the DoD are being embodied in a 'one force concept' and the SANDF will be an all volunteer force.

The final force design and shape of the DoD and its human resource content has yet to be decided. A key element is a major improvement in the ration of combat troops to support troops. It has been recommended that a strength of some 70,000 personnel, including civilians, will provide a viable full-time force component. The present regular content of the DoD is approximately 95,000 personnel.

It will be necessary, therefore, to proceed with a rationalization programme to bring the force strength down to the approved level. This will be accomplished in part by normal attrition, voluntary severance packages, demobilization, the termination of contracts and transfers to other departments. However, there will inevitably be an element of retrenchment for which the procedures, including compensation, are being formulated.

The establishment of the Service Corps is designed to assist with the re-integration of ex-service members into civil society with appropriate vocational and life skills. Planning is in hand to set up Service Corps centres in each province of South Africa in conjunction with the relevant authorities.

The Part-time Component is an integral and essential element of the SANDF and will form a key part of the core defence capability. The PTC has two main elements; conventional units and territorial units. The conventional units will be trained and prepared to conduct the land battle in conjunction with the regular combat units. The Part-time Conventional Force will now consist of one division, with divisional troops and three similarly organized brigades.

The territorial units are responsible for area defence and provide assistance to the SA Police Service in the prevention of crime and violence and the maintenance of public order.

Army. Currently, equipment includes some 250 Mk 1A Olifant main battle tanks and about 180 Rooikat armoured combat vehicles. The Army numbered 54,300 in 1998. There is a paramilitary South African Police Service 140,000 strong.

Navy. The Navy includes 3 French-built diesel submarines of which 1 is fully operational, 6 fast missile armed patrol craft (3 more in reserve), 8 coastal minesweepers, 3 inshore patrol craft, 1 British-built survey ship, 1 fleet replenishment ship and a naval-manned Antarctic supply ship, the latter 2 with helicopter facilities. There are additionally some 6 service craft. Forces are based at Simonstown and Durban and 6 reserve units are situated in major centres.

Navy personnel in 1998 totalled 8,000.

Air Force. There is 1 fighter-bomber squadron with 30 Mirage F1-AZ ground attack aircraft and another with Atlas Cheetahs including some equipped for reconnaissance; and 1 coastal patrol squadron with C-47s. Transport squadrons have 7 C-130B Hercules, more than 20 C-47s, 10 Caravan 1s, 4 Boeing 707s and 3 twin-jet HS.125s. 3 helicopter squadrons have 60 Alouette IIIs and 48 Oryx. PC-7s are used for primary training, followed by advanced training on Impalas and Atlas Cheetahs, weapons training on Impalas, and multiengine crew training on C-47s. Total strength (1998) was about 11,000 with 234 combat aircraft and at least 14 armed helicopters.

INTERNATIONAL RELATIONS

Membership. South Africa is a member of the UN, the Commonwealth (except during 1961–94), SADC and the OAU.

ECONOMY

Policy. A Reconstruction and Development Programme (RDP) was instituted under a government minister in 1994 (since 1996 the minister of finance) to run until 1999. Its policy aims are to meet basic needs, develop human resources, build the economy and democratize the state and society, and include as targets: Redistributing 30% of agricultural land; raising the annual number of houses built from 50,000 to 0·3m.; providing safe drinking water for 12m. persons; providing sanitation for 21m.; creating 0·3m. non-agricultural jobs; reversing privatization 'contrary to the public interest'; introducing anti-trust legislation; 'de-racializing' business ownership; improving industrial relations. In 1996 a decision was taken to integrate the RDP Fund into the budgets of the various delivery departments.

Budget. Total revenue and expenditure of the central government's State Revenue Account in R1m.:

	1994–95	1995–96	1996–97	1997–98
Revenue	111,950	127,269	144,857	161,976
Expenditure	140,231	157,360	173,659	186,747

In December 1997 the Minister of Finance released a 3-year budget policy statement, which sets out the following spending and revenue targets (in Rbn.):

	1998–99	1999–2000	2000–01
Revenue	178·1	195·7	216·2
Expenditure	202·1	218·5	241·5

The main sources of State Revenue Fund, 1997–98, were: Income tax, R93,604m.; sales tax/VAT, R38,880m.; excise duties, R7,031m.; customs duties, R6,965m.; fuel levy, R10,795m. Consolidated main expenditure of government: education, R40,270m.; defence, R10,716m.; health, R20,223m.; social security; R18,433m.; housing, R4,162m.; economic services, R18,885m.; interest on public debt, R38,549m.

From Sept. 1991 VAT at 10% replaced the 13% general sales tax. From 7 April 1993 the rate at which VAT is levied was increased from 10% to 14%. Corporate tax was reduced from 50% to 48% as from April 1991. In the March 1993 Budget the company tax rate was lowered from 48% to 40% of taxable income, but an additional tax of 15% on distributed profits was introduced.

Public debt on 31 March 1997, R309,507m., of which R11,523m. was foreign debt; internal debt, R294,332m. Growth in GDP in 1996 was 3%, and inflation in 1997 8%.

Currency. The unit of currency is the *rand* (ZAR) of 100 *cents*. There are notes of R10, R20, R50, R100 and R200 and coins of 1c, 2c, 5c, 10c, 20c, 50c, R1, R2 and R5. Gold and foreign exchange reserves totalled R26,540m. on 30 Nov. 1997. A single free-floating exchange rate replaced the former 2-tier system on 13 March 1995.

Banking and Finance. The central bank and bank of issue is the South African Reserve Bank (established 1920), which functions independently. Its *Governor* is Dr Chris Stals. Total deposits, 30 Nov. 1997, R8,094m.; assets, R45,756m.

At 31 Oct. 1997 there were 43 registered banks, 5 mutual banks and 9 branches of foreign banks, collectively having total deposits of R416,373m. and total assets of R544,079m. There were 59 foreign banks with representative offices as at 31 Oct. 1997. Post Office Savings Bank deposits (31 Dec. 1993), R1,191m.

The Banks Act, 1990 (Act No. 94 of 1990) governs the operations and prudential requirements of banks. As at 31 Oct. 1997 the minimum capital adequacy requirement was 8%.

There is a stock exchange at Johannesburg (JSE). Foreign nationals have been eligible for membership since March 1996.

Weights and Measures. The metric system is in force.

ENERGY AND NATURAL RESOURCES

Electricity. There were (1996) 23 coal-fired power stations, 1 nuclear, 1 bagasse, 10 hydro-electric, 3 pumped storage and 3 gas turbine in service. Production available for consumption (1996) was 187,837m. MWh.

Oil and Gas. In 1994 reserves were sufficient to yield 30,000 bbls. a day of refined petroleum products until 2001 from gas produced at sea and converted on land. In 1995, 8,900,000 metric tonnes of oil were produced. 72,000 metric tonnes of natural gas and 348,362 tonnes of condensate were brought ashore in 1995.

Water. South Africa's average annual rainfall of about 470 mm is well below the world average. The unevenly distributed rainfall and high evaporation rate greatly affects the reliability and variability of river flow. Only about 62% or 33,000m. cu. metres of the mean annual run-off can be exploited economically. In addition about 5,400m. cu. metres may be obtainable from underground sources. Government activities are governed by the Water Act, 1956, which is due to be replaced by a new Water Act during 1998. It is administered by the Department of Water Affairs and Forestry which manages water quantity and quality as well as the demand for the resource. A Water Research Commission was established in 1971 to co-ordinate and promote water research. Water availability is distributed poorly in relation to regions of economic growth and major inter-basin water transfer schemes are therefore a feature of the South African infrastructure. The latest such scheme under construction is the Lesotho Highlands Water Project which will divert the Orange River headwaters within Lesotho through tunnels into the Vaal River System which serves an area where about 60% of the industrial production of the country is generated. Lesotho is to receive royalties in exchange.

Minerals. Value of the main mineral production sales (in R1,000):

	1993	1994	1995	1996
Asbestos	142,695	140,238	119,711	100,418
Chrome ore	355,769	400,056	606,826	811,221
Coal	9,713,960	10,352,607	12,817,789	14,909,980
Copper	1,035,360	1,253,874	1,673,145	1,488,737
Gold	23,239,318	24,953,110	23,333,195	26,482,352
Iron ore	1,278,879	1,400,258	1,657,887	1,691,683
Lime and limestone	536,122	604,767	693,440	692,484
Manganese ore	549,040	644,921	692,094	783,874
Silver	67,923	78,127	68,640	83,013
Nickel	457,700	547,662	851,519	983,480
Platinum-group metals	5,188,809	5,809,613	6,572,506	7,637,913

Total value of all minerals sold: 1995, R56,535m; 1996: R65,109m.

Mineral production (tonnes) 1996: Coal, 206·4m.; iron ore, 30·8m.; manganese, 3·2m.; chrome ore, 4·9m.; asbestos, 56,900; copper, 152,062; limestone, 19·2m.; gold, 497; silver, 169; nickel, 33,861; platinum-group metals, 188; diamonds, 9,946,750 carats.

South Africa is a major producer of gold. Reserves were estimated at 19,000 tonnes in 1996. The value of gold production was R26·5bn. In 1996 the number of persons engaged in the mining industry was 552,896 of which 240,334 were involved in underground gold mining operations.

Agriculture. The redistribution of 30% of land, expropriated since 1913, is envisaged by the Reconstruction and Development Programme. By 1994 1·2m. Black farmers were farming 17m. ha and 55,000 Whites with 1·1m. Black labourers were farming 102m. ha. Dispossessed landowners are entitled to restitution from the state, though the rights of present landowners must be respected and compensation paid.

Much of the land suitable for mechanized farming has unreliable rainfall. Of the total area natural pasture occupies 69% (58·2m. ha) and planted pasture 2% (2m. ha). Annual crops and orchards are cultivated on 9·9m. ha of dry land and 1·2m. ha under irrigation. There were some 66,000 commercial farming units in 1996.

In 1996, agriculture, forestry and fisheries contributed 4·8% of GDP.

Production (1996, in 1,000 tonnes): Maize, 10,168; sorghum, 536; wheat, 2,712; groundnuts, 145; sunflower seed, 784; sugar cane, 20,951; oranges, 889; potatoes, 1,563; other vegetables, 1,924; grapes, 113; apples, 608.

Livestock, in 1,000 (1996): 13,389 cattle, 28,934 sheep, 6,674 goats, 1,603 pigs.

The 1996 production of red meat was 715,000 tonnes, poultry meat, 804,000 tonnes, wool, 70,000 tonnes, eggs, 290,000 tonnes, milk, 2·7m. tonnes.

Cotton-growing is undertaken by some farmers, the plant being found a better drought resistant than either tobacco or maize. Viticulture and fruit-growing are important, and were valued at R5,106m. for 1996.

In 1996 the gross value of agricultural production was R39,190m. (field crops, R14,457m.; livestock products, R15,935m.; horticultural products, R8,797m.).

Forestry. The commercial forest plantations occupy about 1·49m. ha and there are about 136,000 ha of indigenous high forests. On 31 March 1996 there were 790,042 ha of pines, 583,456 ha of eucalypts, 104,575 ha of wattles and 8,850 ha of other hardwoods.

Production, 1995-96, of sawn timber, 1,158m. cu. metres (value R904m.); paper and board products, 2,372m. tonnes (R9·5bn.).

Fisheries. In 1995 sea fisheries landed 525,177m. tonnes of fish, shell-fish, seaweed and guano. Total output, wholesale value, 1995, R1,730m. The fishing fleet consisted of 3,974 vessels in 1995.

INDUSTRY. Net value of sales of the principal groups of industries (in R1m.) in 1996: food and food products, 51,306; beverages, 16,248; vehicles and vehicle parts, 34,158; basic iron and steel products, 22,279; basic precious and non-ferrous metal products, 10,842; petroleum products, 18,555; chemicals and products, 34,862; non-electrical machinery, 18,337; electrical machinery, 9,600; fabricated metal products except machinery, 19,689; printing and publishing, 9,430; wood and wood products, 5,265; clothing, 7,384; paper and products, 16,180; textiles, 9,064; plastic products, 8,883. Total net value including other groups, R331,858m. Manufacturing industry contributed R114,916m. (23·7%) of GDP of R484,057m. in 1996.

Labour. In Oct. 1995 the population of economically active age (15–64 years) numbered (in 1,000; females in parentheses) 26,444 (13,678), of whom economically active, 14,356 (6,259). Unemployed, 4,202 (2,380), a rate of 29·3% (38%) comprising Blacks, 3,665 (2,073); Coloureds, 347 (195); Whites, 135 (82); Asians, 57 (29). Unemployed in 1993, 3,586 (1,903).

Industrial employment (except mining) at Dec. 1995: Manufacturing employed 1,396,804 workers; construction, 336,939; trade and accommodation services, 751,629. In 1995, 582,766 persons were employed in mining, including 367,152 in gold mining. Average monthly earnings (excluding agriculture and mining) of employees, 1995, R3,159. The Employment Standards Act, 1997, shortened the working week to 40 hours.

The Labour Relations Act, 1996, aims to move industrial relations from an adversarial approach towards co-operation. It encourages the establishment of workplace forums and imposes collective bargaining in manufacturing industries. The Act set up the *Commission for Conciliation and Arbitration*.

Trade Unions. In 1994 there were 213 registered and 65 unregistered trade unions. Total membership of all trade unions (registered and unregistered) represented about

23·7% of the economically active population. There were 9 trade union federations, but most unions were not affiliated to these. The Congress of South African Trade Unions (COSATU; *General Secretary*, Sam Shilowa) has formed links with the ANC. It had 1·3m. members in 1994.

FOREIGN ECONOMIC RELATIONS. International sanctions on trade with South Africa were lifted by 1993.

Commerce. South Africa, Botswana, Lesotho, Namibia and Swaziland are members of a customs union and the foreign trade statistics shown below represent the combined imports and exports of these countries. The total value of the imports and exports was as follows (in R1m.):

	Imports		Exports
1994	79,471	1994	90,021
1995	98,513	1995	101,509
1996	115,591	1996	122,294

The main exports (in R1m.) in 1993 were: Natural cultured pearls, precious and semi-precious stones, precious metals, coins and imitation jewellery, 10,138; base metals and articles thereof, 9,905; mineral products, 8,444; chemical and allied products, 3,378; machinery and mechanical appliances, electrical equipment and parts, sound recorders and reproducers, and parts, 2,811; vehicles, aircraft and equipment, 2,701; vegetable products, 2,437; pulp of wood etc., paper and paperboard and articles thereof, 1,937; textiles and articles thereof, 1,812.

Tourism. In 1995, 4,684,064 tourists visited South Africa, of whom 3,452,164 were from African countries and 721,878 from Europe (252,437 from the UK and 172,502 from Germany).

COMMUNICATIONS. In 1990 Transnet, a public company comprising railways, harbours, pipelines and road transport, was set up, with the government as sole shareholder, as a first step to possible privatization.

Roads. In 1995 there were 360,522 km of national and provincial rural roads (61,679 km surfaced). In 1996, private firms and local authorities transported 474,409 passengers; Transnet carried 1·8m. tonnes of freight and private firms, 407,905 tonnes. Motor vehicles in operation (1993) included 3,813,904 passenger cars, 1,345,610 commercial vehicles, 228,318 minibuses, 22,884 buses and 273,244 motorcycles.

Railways. In 1995 there were 20,005 km of 1,065 mm gauge (9,087 km electrified) and 314 km of 762 mm gauge. In 1995, railways carried 6m. long-distance passengers and 175m. tonnes of freight. In 1990 the South African Rail Commuter Corporation was set up to run commuter trains in major cities; it carried 413m. passengers in 1994–95.

Civil Aviation. Civil aviation is controlled by the Ministry of Transport. Airports and air traffic and navigation services were commercialized in 1993. The Airports Company controls the major airports. There are international airports at Cape Town, Durban and Johannesburg.

South African Airways (SAA), Comair, Sun Air and SA Express operate scheduled international air services within Africa and to Europe, Latin America and the Middle and Far East. The Alliance airline was founded in Dec. 1994 as a joint venture between SAA and the governments and national carriers of Tanzania and Uganda. 13 independent operators provide internal flights which link up with SAA's, Comair's and SA Express's internal network. During 1992 SAA carried 4,686,422 passengers (843,981 on internal flights) and 55,377 tonnes of freight and mail. In 1995 SAA's fleet comprised 4 A300B2-200s, 2 A300B4-200s, 1 A300F4-200, 7 A320-200s, 12 B-737-200 Advs, 1 B-737-400 Adv (F), 5 B-747-200Bs, 1 B-747-200B Combi, 2 B-747-300s, 4 B-747-400s, 2 B-747SPs and 1 B-767-200ER. Services were also provided by Aero Zambia, Aeroflot, Aerolíneas Argentinas, Air Afrique, Air Austral, Air Botswana, Air France, Air Gabon, Air India, Air Madagascar, Air Malawi, Air Mauritius, Air Namibia, Air Seychelles, Air Tanzania, Air Zimbabwe, Airlink, Alitalia, American Airlines, Austrian Airlines, Balkan, British Airways, Cameroon

Airlines, Care Airlines, Cathay Pacific, China Airlines, Commercial Airways, Egyptair, El Al, Emirates, Ethiopian Airlines, Ghana Airways, Gulf Air, Kenya Airways, LAM, Lesotho Airways, LTU, Lufthansa, Malaysia Airlines, Metavia Airlines, Northwest Airlines, Olympic Airways, Qantas, Royal Air Maroc, Royal Swazi Airways, Sabena, Singapore Airlines, Sudan Airways, Swissair, TAAG, TAP, Uganda Airlines and Varig.

In Oct. 1994 there were 375 licensed aerodromes, of which 212 were public and 74 private, and 180 approved helistops. 6,182 civil aircraft were registered in Dec. 1995.

Shipping. In 1995 sea-going shipping totalled 0·28m. GRT, including oil tankers, 2,203 GRT and container ships, 0·2m. GRT. Ports are owned and managed by Portnet, a division of Transnet. The main ports are Durban, Cape Town, Saldanha and Richards Bay. Smaller ports are Mossel Bay, Port Elizabeth and East London. During 1995 the main ports handled 129·5m. tonnes of cargo. In the year ending March 1996 13,422 vessels (8,433 ocean-going) totalling 528,567,287 GRT put into South African ports.

Telecommunications. In 1991 the former Department of Posts and Telecommunications was divided into 2 independent public companies, the South African Post Office and Telkom SA Ltd. Telkom remained a wholly state-owned enterprise until May 1997 when a 30% equity stake was sold to the consortium of SBC Communications International Inc and Telekom Malaysia Berhad. The Telecommunications Act of 1996 awarded to Telkom 3 telecommunications licences, officially issued in May 1997. These were to provide public switched telecommunications services for an exclusivity period of 5–6 years; to provide value added network services; and to use radio spectrum.

In 1997 there were 2,459 post offices and postal agencies, with plans to increase the network to 2,761. In 1994 there were 7,300 telex subscribers. Line capacity of automatic telephone exchanges (1993), 4,406,795; there were (1993) 5,206,235 telephones and 25,600 users of data services. In March 1997 there were 2,444 automatic exchanges, of which 1,993 were digital, and 4,258,639 main telephone services in operation.

Broadcasting is supervised by the Independent Broadcasting Authority, set up in 1993 to establish a system free from political control. The South African Broadcasting Corporation broadcast 23 radio services in 16 languages and 4 TV services in 7 languages (colour by PAL). An external radio service broadcasts in 7 languages. There were (1995) 13·1m. radio receivers and 4·5m. TV sets. An independent TV company, M-Net, was permitted to broadcast news from 1 Jan. 1991.

Cinemas (1990). There were approximately 1,200.

Press (1995). There were 17 daily newspapers with a total circulation of 1,300,000.

SOCIAL INSTITUTIONS

Justice. The common law of the republic is the Roman–Dutch law—that is, the uncodified law of Holland as it was at the date of the cession of the Cape in 1806. The law of England as such is not recognized as authoritative, though by statute the principles of English law relating to evidence and to mercantile matters, e.g., companies, patents, trademarks, insolvency and the like, have been introduced. In shipping and insurance, English law is followed in the former Cape Province, and it has also largely influenced civil and criminal procedure throughout the republic. In all other matters, family relations, property, succession, contract, etc., Roman–Dutch law rules, English decisions being valued only so far as they agree therewith.

The Supreme Court of South Africa is constituted as follows: (i) The Supreme Court of Appeal consists of a Chief Justice, a Deputy Chief Justice and a number of judges as the President may stipulate. It is the highest court of appeal, except in constitutional matters, and its decisions are binding on all courts. Except for contempt of court in *faciae curiae*, it has no original jurisdiction, but is purely a court of appeal. (ii) The High Courts may decide any constitutional matter, except a matter that only the Constitutional Court may decide, or a matter which is assigned to another court of a status similar to a High Court by an Act of Parliament. The High Courts are divided into Provincial and Local Divisions. (iii) Provincial Divisions. The Judge President of a provincial division may divide the area under his jurisdiction into circuit districts. In each such district there shall be held at least twice in every year and at such times and places determined by the Judge President, a court which shall be presided over by a judge of the division in which that district is situated. Such a court is known as the circuit local division for the district in question and is deemed to be a local division. (iv) Local Divisions. The judges hold office till they attain the age of 70 years. A judge is expected to be available to perform service for an aggregate of 3 months a year until the age of 75. No judge can be removed from office except by the President after the National Assembly (at least two-thirds support from its members) has called for such judge to be removed on the grounds of incapacity, incompetence or gross misconduct.

The 9 provinces are further divided into 435 magisterial districts, each with a magistrate's court having a prescribed civil and criminal jurisdiction. There are (1998) 1,566 magistrates appointed. From this court there is an appeal to the provincial divisions of the High Court, and thence to the Supreme Court of Appeal. Magistrates' convictions carrying sentences above a prescribed limit are subject to automatic review by a judge. In addition, several regional divisions consisting of a number of districts have been constituted. Convictions of such courts are not subject to automatic review by a judge, but to appeal in the normal way.

All criminal and civil cases are dealt with by judges (in the Supreme Courts) and magistrates (in the lower courts). Judges and magistrates are entitled to take judicial cognizance of customary (indigenous) laws and must, where relevant, apply them. A limited civil and criminal jurisdiction is conferred upon the Black chief or headman over his own tribe.

In 1997 there were 114 small claims courts, which have been introduced in a number of areas since 1985. These courts (where Commissioners preside) have civil jurisdiction only, limited by the quantum of damages and the nature of the claim.

The death penalty was abolished in June 1995. No executions had taken place since 1989.

Religion. 1991 census results (excluding the former TBVC countries) as regards religious denominations: *Christian churches:* Nederduits Gereformeerde Kerk, 3,212,693; Roman Catholics, 2,343,944; Methodists, 1,813,365; Zion Christian Church, 1,517,021; other Black independent churches, 5,366,925; Anglicans, 836,015; Lutherans, 773,631; Presbyterians, 402,198; Apostolic Faith Mission of Southern Africa, 402,621; other Apostolic churches, 423,505; United Congregational Church of Southern Africa, 383,622; Nederduitsch Hervormde Kerk, 266,754; Baptists, 249,028; Full Gospel Church, 201,909; Church of England, 162,429; Gereformeerde Kerk, 159,826; Assemblies of God, 152,218; New Apostolic Church, 144,727; Church of the Province of South Africa, 137,437; Seventh Day Adventists, 84,112; Pentecostal Protestants, 70,344; Swiss Church, 42,610; Church of England in South Africa, 39,836; Afrikaanse Protestantse Kerk, 32,175; Salvation Army, 32,629; Greek Orthodox, 26,673; Mormons, 7,844; Pentecostal Church, 22,185; other Christian churches, 1,274,518.

In 1992 the Anglican Church of Southern Africa voted by 79% of votes cast for the ordination of women.

Non-Christian religions: Hindus, 389,573; Moslems, 338,142; Jews, 67,654; Buddhists, 2,391; Confucians, 1,498; other non-Christian religions, 24,212.

Education. Until April 1994 the provision of education was assigned to various state departments responsible for executing education policy, which was determined by the Minister of National Education. These state departments were largely racially-based, in accordance with the tricameral system then in effect.

The 1994 Transitional Constitution introduced a new education system. Education up to tertiary level falls within the legislative authority of the provinces, though the national parliament may legislate in this field to ensure nationwide uniform standardization and effective implementation.

In 1994 the Council of Education Ministers was set up to oversee the operation of the new system. It comprises the national Minister and Deputy Minister of Education and the members of the provincial executive councils responsible for education. The Council meets once a month.

It is intended that the first 10 years of schooling should be free and compulsory, but for economic reasons only the first year's primary schooling was free in 1995.

There is a policy to change syllabuses to remove bias, factual incorrectness and insensitivity without replacing textbooks. In 1996 over 25% of adults were illiterate.

Pre-primary Education. In 1995 there were 286,663 children and 10,525 teachers in 3,060 schools.

Primary and Secondary Education. In 1995 there were 8,060,506 children and 213,890 teachers in 20,428 primary schools; 3,571,395 pupils and 128,784 teachers in secondary schools.

Higher Education. In 1994 a Commission on Higher Education was appointed to investigate this sector in the light of the new goals and policies.

In 1995, there were 16 universities, 1 Christian university and 1 medical university, with 617,897 students and 27,099 academic staff. There are also 2 open (distance) universities, and 30 institutes of higher education (12 in agriculture, 4 in nursing and 14 technikons).

All the universities are open to all population groups but each has a different cultural ethos and the medium of instruction is English and/or Afrikaans. Technikons provide education at an advanced tertiary level for a variety of technical, commercial and general courses of study. They have the right to confer degrees. Technical colleges are mainly responsible for the training of apprentices and the education, on a part-time basis, of persons not subject to compulsory school attendance.

In 1993 there were 93,044 students and 3,735 teachers in technical colleges, 59,918 students and 4,865 teachers in teacher training colleges and 137,168 students and 2,415 teachers in technikons.

Adult literacy rate in 1995 was 81·8%. Public expenditure on education (1995) was R32,293m. (6·8% of GNP).

Health. In 1994 there were 26,452 medical practitioners of whom 7,167 had specialist qualifications, 4,029 dentists, 331 dental specialists, 9,622 pharmacists and 158,538 nurses and midwives. In 1995 there were 834 hospitals with about 150,000 beds, of which 18% were provided by private medical care.

Treatment in the public health service covers 75–80% of the population and is free of charge for the indigent, children under 6 years and pregnant mothers. Other patients are charged on a sliding scale based on their means. 60% of private health care is funded by medical insurance schemes and the remainder by privately paying patients. The free medical treatment scheme amounts to about R500m.

Welfare. Under the Social Assistance Act, 1992, grants are made to the aged, war veterans, blind and disabled, as well as maintenance grants to single mothers with inadequate income, and foster child grants. Assistance in the form of social relief is given to individuals and families unable to meet their primary needs.

The social welfare service is a partnership between the private and the public sectors. Services are delivered by private welfare organizations which are subsidized by the state.

In 1993 there were 1,742 registered private welfare organizations, partially funded by the state for services rendered. All are registered under the National Welfare Act, 1978.

The changing political situation necessitated the development of a new welfare dispensation to cope with the demands of the 'new' South Africa. Welfare services are divided into service fields, namely, family and child care, care of the aged, care of the disabled, drug dependent care, care of offenders and social security.

The Child Care Act, 1983 (as amended in 1991), is designed to protect children against neglect, abuse, ill-treatment and exploitation. The Act provides for preventive child care services, foster care and also for various children's allowances and financial assistance to children's homes and creches. The Primary School Nutrition Scheme was set up in 1994 to alleviate hunger which affects school attendance and concentration. It is administered jointly by the Department of Health and the Department of Education.

Policy regarding aging has moved away from care of the aged to age management. A national Discussion Group on Aging was instituted in 1994 to advise the Department of Welfare on legislation, policy, standards and criteria on financing. The consumers of services are involved in the design of affordable, accessible and equitable age management.

The National Strategy against the Abuse of Alcohol and other Drugs directs research into drug abuse. The Drug Advisory Board advises the Minister of Welfare and Population Development and brings together the voluntary and government agencies working on drug abuse.

The Committee for Marriage and Family Life of the South African Welfare Council was commissioned by the government to promote the quality of family life.

Excessive population growth and widespread illegal immigration and a low rate of economic development are seen as two facets of the same problem. The Chief Directorate Population Development is located in the Department of Welfare to ensure that population factors and objectives (accommodating to increasing population size, influencing demographic processes—especially high fertility) are integrated in overall socio-economic development policy. These are embodied in the government's Reconstruction and Development Programme (RDP).

DIPLOMATIC REPRESENTATIVES

Of South Africa in Great Britain (South Africa Hse., Trafalgar Sq., London, WC2N 5DP)
High Commissioner: Cheryll Carolus.

Of Great Britain in South Africa (255 Hill St., Arcadia, Pretoria, 0002)
High Commissioner: Maeve G. Fort, CMG.

Of South Africa in the USA (3051 Massachusetts Ave., NW, Washington, D.C., 20008)
Ambassador: Franklin Sonn.

Of the USA in South Africa (877 Pretorius St., Pretoria)
Ambassador: James Joseph.

Of South Africa to the United Nations
Ambassador: Khiphusizi Jele.

Of South Africa to the European Union
Ambassador: Elias Links.

Further Reading

Beinart, W., *Twentieth Century South Africa.* OUP, 1994
Brewer, J., (ed.) *Restructuring South Africa.* London, 1994
Davenport, T. R. H., *South Africa: a Modern History.* 4th ed. CUP, 1991
Davies, G. V., *South Africa.* [Bibliography]. 2nd ed. Oxford and Santa Barbara (CA), 1994
Fine, B and Rustomjee Z., *The Political Economy of South Africa*, 1997
Hough, M. and Du Plessis, A., (eds.) *Selected Documents and Commentaries on Negotiations and Constitutional Development in the RSA, 1989–1994.* Pretoria Univ., 1994
Johnson, R. W. and Schlemmer, L. (eds.). *Launching Democracy in South Africa: the First Open Election, 1994.* Yale Univ. Press, 1996
Mandela, N., *Long Walk to Freedom: the Autobiography of Nelson Mandela.* London, 1994
Meredith, M., *South Africa's New Era: the 1994 Election.* London, 1994
Mostert, N., *Frontiers: the Epic of South Africa's Creation and the Tragedy of the Xhosa People.* London, 1992
Nattrass, N. and Ardington, E. (eds.), *The Political Economy of South Africa.* Cape Town and OUP, 1990
Oxford History of South Africa. OUP, 1969
Thompson, L., *A History of South Africa.* 2nd ed. Yale Univ. Press, 1996
Waldmeir, P., *Anatomy of a Miracle: the end of apartheid and the birth of the new South Africa*, London, 1997
Who's Who in South African Politics. 5th ed. London, 1995

National statistical office: Central Statistical Service, Private Bag X44, Pretoria 0001.
Website: http://www.css.gov.za/

SOUTH AFRICAN PROVINCES

In 1994 the former provinces of the Cape of Good Hope, Natal, the Orange Free State and the Transvaal, together with the former 'homelands' or 'TBVC countries' of Transkei, Bophuthatswana, Venda and Ciskei, were replaced by 9 new provinces. Transkei and Ciskei were integrated into Eastern Cape, Venda into Northern Province and Bophuthatswana into Free State, Mpumalanga and North-West.

The administrative powers of the provincial governments in relation to the central government are set out in the 1999 Constitution after a revision of the original text demanded by the Constitutional Court in 1996.

EASTERN CAPE

Territory and Population. The area is 169,600 sq. km and the population was estimated at 6,481,300 in 1995 (3·51m. females; 5·65m. Blacks; 0·44m. Coloured; 0·37m. Whites; 16,300 Asians). At the 1991 Census, 82·6% spoke Xhosa as their home language, 9·6% Afrikaans, 4·2% English and 2·1% Sotho.

Constitution and Government. Eastern Cape comprises 77 administrative districts (including Umzimkulu district, an enclave within KwaZulu-Natal). The provincial capital is Bisho. There is a 56-seat provincial legislature; at the provincial elections held 27–29 April 1994, 48 seats were won by the ANC (with 84·6% of votes cast), 6 by the NP (with 9·9%), 1 by the DP (with 2·1%) and 1 by the PAC (with 2·0%).

In Jan. 1998 the Executive Council comprised:
Premier: Raymond Mhlaba (ANC).
Agriculture and Land Affairs: Ezra Sigwela (ANC). *Public Service and Administration:* Mandisa Marasha (ANC). *Economic Affairs, Environment and Tourism:* Smuts Ngonyama (ANC). *Finance and Provincial Expenditure:* Shepherd Mayatula (ANC). *Health and Welfare:* Dr Trudie Thomas (ANC). *Education, Culture and Sport:* Ziziwe Balindlela (ANC). *Public Works:* Thobile Mhlahlo (ANC). *Housing and Local Government:* Maxwell Mamase (ANC). *Transport:* Dr Tertius Delport (NP). *Safety and Security:* Denis Neer.

Agriculture. In 1988 (excluding the former Ciskei and Transkei now within the province) there were 6,588 farms with 105,585 agricultural workers; gross farming income amounted to R908·1m.

Labour. In 1995 the economically active population numbered 1,739,000, of whom 721,000 were unemployed. Of those employed in 1991, 15·5% were in agriculture, 0·3% in mining, 17·3% in manufacturing, 15·8% in trade and 33·7% in services.

Education. In 1993 there were 16,336 pupils in pre-primary schools, 4,289 pupils in special schools, 1,602,255 pupils in primary schools and 694,688 in secondary schools, with altogether 56,462 teachers; there were also 574 lecturers and 7,630 students in technical colleges, and 1,175 lecturers and 14,373 students in teachers' training establishments.

Roads. Motor vehicles registered (1991, excluding Ciskei and Transkei) totalled 341,759, including 197,151 passenger cars and 71,985 commercial vehicles.

Health. In 1992 there were 2,043 medical practitioners, 21,416 nurses, 586 hospitals and clinics and 29,806 hospital beds.

FREE STATE

Territory and Population. The area is 129,480 sq. km and the population was estimated at 2,782,500 in 1995 (1·31m. females; 2·33m. Blacks; 0·37m. Whites; 73,000 Coloureds; 3,200 Asians). At the 1991 Census, 57·4% of the population spoke Sotho as their home language, 14·7% Afrikaans, 9·4% Xhosa, 6·4% Tswana, 5·2% Zulu, 1·5% English and 1·1% Pedi.

Free State comprises 52 administrative districts. The provincial capital is Bloemfontein.

Constitution and Government. There is a 30-seat provincial legislature; at the provincial elections held 27–29 April 1994, 24 seats were won by the ANC (with 77·5% of the 1,339,251 votes cast), 4 by the NP (with 12·7%) and 2 by the FF (with 6·1%).

In Jan. 1998 the government comprised:
Premier: Patrick Lekota (ANC).
Finance, Expenditure and Economic Affairs: T. Saki Belot (ANC). *Education:* M. Dukoana (ANC). *Safety and Security:* Dr D. A. Kganare (ANC). *Public Works:* Gregory Nthatisi (ANC). *Health:* Senorita Nthlabathi (ANC). *Agriculture:* Cas Human (ANC). *Environmental Affairs and Tourism:* T. Makgoe (ANC). *Public Transport:* E. Magashule (ANC). *Local Government and Housing:* B. Kotsoane (ANC). *Social Services, Sport, Art and Culture:* M. Motsumi (ANC).

Agriculture. In 1988 (excluding the TBVC countries now within the province) there were 10,926 farms with 200,559 agricultural workers; gross farming income amounted to R2,473·6m.

Labour. In 1995 the economically active population numbered 1,050,000, of whom 274,000 were unemployed. Of those employed in 1991, 17·2% were in agriculture, 27·5% in mining, 7·0% in manufacturing, 10·5% in trade and 27·2% in services.

Education. In 1993 there were 19,392 pupils in pre-primary schools, 3,414 pupils in special schools, 457,060 pupils in primary schools and 279,153 in secondary schools, with altogether 23,338 teachers; there were also 215 lecturers and 3,549 students in technical colleges, and 447 lecturers and 4,091 students in teachers' training establishments.

Roads. Motor vehicles registered (1991, excluding Bophuthatswana) totalled 444,023 including 188,497 passenger cars and 93,648 commercial vehicles.

Health. In 1992 there were 1,303 medical practitioners, 10,723 nurses, 453 hospitals and clinics and 11,075 hospital beds.

GAUTENG

Territory and Population. The area is 18,810 sq. km and the population was estimated at 7,048,300 in 1995 (3·27m. females; 4·44m. Blacks; 2·15m. Whites; 0·28m. Coloureds; 0·17m. Asians). At the 1991 Census, 20·5% spoke Afrikaans as their home language, 18·4% Zulu, 16·1% English, 11·2% Sotho, 8·8% Pedi, 7·2% Tswana, 6·2% Xhosa, 3·8% Tsonga, 1·4% Ndebele, 1·3% Swazi and 1·1% Venda.

The province of Gauteng, at first called Pretoria-Witwatersrand-Vereeniging (PWV), comprises 23 administrative districts. The provincial capital is Johannesburg.

Constitution and Government. There is an 86-seat provincial legislature; at the provincial elections held 27–29 April 1994, 50 seats were won by the ANC (with 58·4% of the 4,143,901 votes cast), 21 by the NP (with 24·2%), 5 by the FF (6·2%), 5 by the DP (5·4%), 3 by the IFP (3·7%), and 1 each by the PAC (1·5%) and ACDP (0·6%).

In Jan. 1998 the government comprised:
Premier: Tokyo Sexwale (ANC).
Economic Affairs and Finance: Jabu Moleketi (ANC). *Health:* Amos Masondo (ANC). *Education:* Mary Metcalfe (ANC). *Welfare and Population Development:* Ignatius Jacobs (ANC). *Housing and Land Affairs:* Daniel Mofokeng (ANC). *Development Planning and Local Government:* Sicelo Shiceka (ANC). *Public Transport and Roads:* Paul Mashatile (ANC). *Safety and Security:* Jesse Duarte (ANC). *Conservation and Environment:* Nomvula Mokonyane (ANC). *Sport, Recreation and Culture:* Peter Skosana (ANC).

Agriculture. In 1988 there were 2,960 farms with 49,759 agricultural workers; gross farming income amounted to R890·9m.

Labour. In 1995 the economically active population numbered 3,584,000, of whom 750,000 were unemployed. Of those employed in 1991, only 2·4% were in agriculture, with 8·6% in mining, 19·5% in manufacturing, 16·7% in trade and 30·9% in services.

Education. In 1993 there were 45,522 pupils in pre-primary schools, 15,296 pupils in special schools, 903,157 pupils in primary schools and 692,783 in secondary schools, with altogether 59,804 teachers; there were also 1,196 lecturers and 21,639 students in technical colleges, and 1,094 lecturers and 12,361 students in teachers' training establishments.

Roads. Motor vehicles registered (1991) totalled 2,328,273 including 1,479,537 passenger cars and 404,468 commercial vehicles.

Health. In 1992 there were 8,720 medical practitioners, 42,339 nurses, 1,167 hospitals and clinics and 43,548 hospital beds.

KWAZULU-NATAL

Territory and Population. The area is 92,180 sq. km and the population was estimated at 8,713,100 in 1995 (4·55m. females; 7·21m. Blacks; 0·8m. Asians; 0·6m. Whites; 0·12m. Coloureds). At the 1991 Census, 79·3% spoke Zulu as their home language, 16·0% English, 1·9% Afrikaans and 1·2% Xhosa.

Constitution and Government. KwaZulu-Natal comprises 66 administrative districts. The provincial capital is Pietermaritzburg, chosen by referendum in 1995. There is an 81-seat provincial legislature; at the provincial elections held on 27–29 April 1994, 41 seats were won by the IFP (with 52·2% of votes cast), 26 by the ANC (with 33·4%), 9 by the NP (with 11·6%), 2 by the DP (with 2·2%) and 1 each by the PAC (0·8%), the African Christian Democratic Party (0·7%) and Minority Front (1·4%).

In Jan. 1998 the government comprised:
Premier: Frank Mdlalose (Inkatha).
Finance and Agriculture and Auxiliary Affairs, Racing, Wagering, Gambling and Casinos: Dr B. Ngubane (Inkatha). *Housing and Local Government:* Peter Miller (Inkatha). *Economic Affairs, Tourism, Trade and Industry:* Jacob Zuma (ANC). *Traditional and Environmental Affairs:* Nyanga Ngubane (Inkatha). *Health:* Dr Zweli Mkhize (ANC). *Transport:* J. S'bu Ndebele (ANC). *Welfare and Pensions:* Prince Gideon Zulu (Inkatha). *Education and Culture:* Dr Vincent Zulu (Inkatha). *Public Works:* Celani Mtetwa (Inkatha). *Safety and Security:* Dr F. Mdlalose.

Local Government: There are 2 tiers of local authority: 7 regional councils and 13 town or rural councils. Elections were held on 26 June 1996 (postponed for a second time from 1 Nov. 1995 and 29 May 1996 because of civil violence). Electors voted first for directly elected ward candidates and second for a party, seats being allotted by proportional representation. Turn-out was 44%. Inkatha won 44·4% of votes cast; ANC, 33%; NP, 12·7%; Democratic Party, 3%; ind, 6%. ANC won control of all town councils.

Agriculture. In 1988 there were 6,305 farms with 211,471 agricultural workers; gross farming income amounted to R2,078·8m.

Labour. In 1995 the economically active population numbered 2,634,000, of whom 274,000 were unemployed. Of those employed in 1991, 13·3% were in agriculture, 1·9% in mining, 20·4% in manufacturing, 16·7% in trade and 30·0% in services.

Education. In 1993 there were 38,127 pupils in pre-primary schools, 2,465 pupils in special schools, 1,481,712 pupils in primary schools and 818,976 in secondary schools, with altogether 63,921 teachers; there were also 717 lecturers and 9,188 students in technical colleges, and 1,062 lecturers and 12,147 students in teachers' training establishments.

Since 1995 education has been provided by a unified KwaZulu-Natal Education Department (KZNED).

Roads. Motor vehicles registered (1991) totalled 964,917, including 550,380 passenger cars and 200,317 commercial vehicles.

Health. In 1992 there were 4,576 medical practitioners, 36,921 nurses, 782 hospitals and clinics and 48,843 hospital beds.

MPUMALANGA

Territory and Population. The area is 78,370 sq. km and the population was estimated at 3,007,100 in 1995 (1·47m. females; 2·69m. Blacks; 0·3m. Whites; 15,100 Coloureds; 11,900 Asians). At the 1991 Census, 30·2% spoke Swazi as their home language, 24·2% Zulu, 11·3% Ndebele, 10·2% Pedi, 9·3% Afrikaans, 3·8% Tsonga, 2·6% Tswana, 2·0% English, 1·9% Sotho and 1·7% Xhosa.

Mpumalanga comprises 28 administrative districts. The provincial capital is Nelspruit.

Constitution and Government. There is a 30-seat provincial legislature; at the provincial elections held 27–29 April 1994, 25 seats were won by the ANC (with 81·5% of votes cast), 3 by the NP (with 9·1%) and 2 by the FF (with 5·7%).

In Jan. 1998 the government comprised:
Premier: Matthew Phosa (ANC).
Economic Affairs: Jacob Mabena (ANC). *Finance:* Jacques Modipane (ANC). *Local Government:* January Che Masilela (ANC). *Environmental Affairs:* David Mkhwanazi (ANC). *Education:* David Mabuza (ANC). *Works, Roads and Transport:* Ntimane Mathebula (ANC). *Safety and Security:* Jabulane Mabona (ANC). *Housing:* Craig Padayachee (ANC). *Agriculture:* Dr Lucas Nel (NP). *Health, Welfare and Gender Affairs:* Candith Mashego (ANC). *Youth Affairs:* Steven Mbuyisa (ANC). *Strategic Planning and Regional Development:* Joseph Mbazima (ANC).

Local Government: Local elections were held in Oct. 1996.

Agriculture. In 1988 (excluding that part of the former Bophuthatswana now within the province) there were 6,386 farms with 182,645 agricultural workers; gross farming income amounted to R2,186m.

Labour. In 1995 the economically active population numbered 973,000, of whom 325,000 were unemployed. Of those employed in 1991, 26·6% were in agriculture, 14·1% in mining, 10·1% in manufacturing, 11·2% in trade and 22·0% in services.

Education. In 1993 there were 6,731 pupils in pre-primary schools, 2,006 pupils in special schools, 471,079 pupils in primary schools and 285,345 in secondary schools, with altogether 21,952 teachers; there were also 250 lecturers and 3,884 students in technical colleges, and 302 lecturers and 3,628 students in teachers' training establishments.

Roads. Motor vehicles registered (mid 1991, excluding Bophuthatswana) totalled 381,346 including 158,587 passenger cars and 100,546 commercial vehicles; new vehicles registrations in the year to mid 1992 totalled 15,307 including 6,893 passenger cars and 4,184 commercial vehicles.

Health. In 1992 there were 825 medical practitioners and 7,738 nurses; 391 hospitals and clinics had 6,501 hospital beds; there were 149,842 admissions and 701,137 outpatients.

NORTHERN CAPE

Territory and Population. The area is 361,800 sq. km. The population was estimated at 742,000 in 1995 (0·37m. females; 0·4m. Coloureds; 0·22m. Blacks; 0·12m. Whites; 1,900 Asians). At the 1991 Census, 66·0% spoke Afrikaans as their home language, 19·0% Tswana, 6·2% Xhosa and 2·6% English.

Northern Cape comprises 26 administrative districts. The provincial capital is Kimberley.

Constitution and Government. There is a 30-seat provincial legislature; at the provincial elections held 27–29 April 1994, 15 seats were won by the ANC (with 50·0% of votes cast), 12 by the NP (with 40·7%), 2 by the FF (with 6·0%) and 1 by the DP (1·9%). An ANC-NP coalition government was formed.

In Jan. 1998 the government comprised:
Premier: Manne Dipico (ANC).
Finance, Economic Affairs, and Tourism: Goolam Akharwaray (ANC). *Education, Art and Culture:* Tina Joemat (ANC). *Health, Welfare and Environment Affairs:* Dr Modise Matlaopane (ANC). *Local Government and Housing:* Ouneas Dikgetsi (ANC). *Safety, Security and Public Works:* Eunice Komane (ANC). *Nature Conservation, Agriculture and Land Reform:* T. Makweya (ANC). *Sport, Recreation, Science, Technology and Transport:* Jozef Henning (FF).

Agriculture. In 1988 there were 6,857 farms with 80,900 agricultural workers; gross farming income amounted to R688·5m.

Labour. In 1995 the economically active population numbered 285,000, of whom 77,000 were unemployed. Of those employed in 1991, 26·2% were in agriculture, 12·9% in mining, 3·9% in manufacturing, 11·1% in trade and 30·4% in services.

Education. In 1993 there were 1,666 pupils in pre-primary schools, 1,801 pupils in special schools, 118,851 pupils in primary schools and 69,470 in secondary schools, with altogether 7,677 teachers; there were also 103 lecturers and 1,599 students in technical colleges, and 83 lecturers and 763 students in teachers' training establishments.

Roads. Motor vehicles registered (1991) totalled 143,315, including 63,504 passenger cars and 44,042 commercial vehicles.

Health. In 1992 there were 287 medical practitioners, 3,302 nurses, 295 hospitals and clinics and 4,064 hospital beds.

NORTHERN PROVINCE

Territory and Population. The area is 123,280 sq. km and the population was estimated at 5,397,200 in 1995 (2·9m. females; 5·24m. Blacks; 0·15m. Whites; 6,900 Coloureds; 4,600 Asians). At the 1991 Census (including the former Venda), 56·7% spoke Pedi as their home language, 22·7% Tsonga, 11·8% Venda, 2·6% Afrikaans and 1·6% Ndebele.

Northern Province comprises 32 administrative districts. The provincial capital is Pietersburg.

Constitution and Government. There is a 40-seat provincial legislature; at the provincial elections held 27–29 April 1994, 38 seats were won by the ANC (with 92·3% of votes cast) and 1 each by the NP (3·3%) and the FF (2·2%).

In Jan. 1998 the government comprised:
Premier: Ngoako Ramathlodi (ANC).
Trade, Industry and Tourism: Thaba Mufamadi (ANC). *Education, Art, Culture and Sport:* Dr P. Aaron Motsoaledi (ANC). *Agriculture, Land and Environmental Affairs:* Tiny Burgers (ANC). *Local Government and Traditional Affairs:* John Dombo (ANC). *Housing and Water Affairs:* Maris-Stella Sexwale-Mabitjie (ANC). *Public Works:* Dikeledi Magadzi (ANC). *Safety and Security:* Seth Nthai (ANC).

Finance and Expenditure: C. Edgar Mushwana (ANC). *Public Transport:* Johan Kriek (FF). *Health and Welfare:* Dr M. Joe Phaahla (ANC).

Agriculture. In 1988 (excluding the former Venda now within the province) there were 5,455 farms with 127,497 agricultural workers; gross farming income amounted to R936·6m.

Labour. In 1995 the economically active population numbered 1,119,000, of whom 459,000 were unemployed. Of those employed in 1991, 25·4% were in agriculture, 9·2% in mining, 6·3% in manufacturing, 13·4% in trade and 32·9% in services.

Education. In 1993 there were 72,805 pupils in pre-primary schools, 1,185 pupils in special schools, 1,043,566 pupils in primary schools and 757,058 in secondary schools, with altogether 53,026 teachers; there were also 387 lecturers and 3,123 students in technical colleges, and 1,532 lecturers and 20,085 students in teachers' training establishments.

Roads. Motor vehicles registered (1991, excluding Venda) totalled 240,801, including 95,627 passenger cars and 81,237 commercial vehicles.

Health. In 1992 there were 796 medical practitioners, 15,014 nurses, 849 hospitals and clinics and 23,122 hospital beds.

NORTH-WEST

Territory and Population. The area is 116,190 sq. km and the population was estimated at 3,351,800 in 1995 (1·62m. females; 3m. Blacks; 0·27m. Whites; 60,500 Coloureds; 10,600 Asians). At the 1991 Census (including the former Bophuthatswana), 59·0% spoke Tswana as their home language, 8·8% Afrikaans, 6·3% Xhosa, 5·4% Tsonga, 5·2% Pedi, 5·0% Sotho, 2·7% Zulu, 2·6% Ndebele, 1·0% English and 1·0% Swazi.

Constitution and Government. North-West Province comprises 32 administrative districts. The provincial capital is Mmabatho. There is a 30-seat provincial legislature; at the provincial elections held 27–29 April 1994, 26 seats were won by the ANC (with 83·5% of the 1,568,574 votes cast), 3 by the NP (with 8·9%) and 1 by the FF (with 4·6%).

In Jan. 1998 the government comprised:
Premier: Popo Molefe (ANC).
Education, Training, Arts and Culture: Mamokoena Gaoretelelwe (ANC). *Health, Social Welfare and Public Media:* Dr Molefi Paul Sefularo (ANC). *Local Government, Housing and Development:* Darkey Ephraim Africa (ANC). *Finance and Economic Affairs:* Martin Kuscus (ANC). *Public Works and Roads:* Zacharia Pitso Tolo (ANC). *Transport and Aviation:* Frans Vilakazi (ANC). *Agriculture:* Johannes Oabetswe Tselapedi (ANC). *Safety and Security:* Satish Roopa (ANC). *Tourism and Environmental Affairs:* E. Molewa (ANC).

Agriculture. In 1988 (excluding the TBVC countries now within the province) there were 8,203 farms with 152,181 agricultural workers; gross farming income amounted to R1,326·3m.

Labour. In 1995 the economically active population numbered 1,147,000, of whom 376,000 were unemployed. Of those employed in 1991, 24·8% were in agriculture, 30·7% in mining, 4·3% in manufacturing, 9·4% in trade and 22·5% in services.

Education. In 1993 there were 22,261 pupils in pre-primary schools, 2,708 pupils in special schools, 400,436 pupils in primary schools and 233,436 in secondary schools, with altogether 21,750 teachers; there were also 110 lecturers and 1,684 students in technical colleges, and 274 lecturers and 3,275 students in teachers' training establishments.

Roads. Motor vehicles registered (1991, excluding Bophuthatswana) totalled 319,805 including 140,802 passenger cars and 71,237 commercial vehicles.

Health. In 1992 there were 780 medical practitioners, 9,393 nurses, 457 hospitals and clinics and 15,409 hospital beds.

WESTERN CAPE

Territory and Population. The area is 129,370 sq. km. Population, 1996, 4,055,000 (3·5m. urban; Coloureds and Asians, 2·23m.; Whites, 935,000; Blacks, 0·89m.). At the 1991 Census, 62·2% spoke Afrikaans as their home language, 20·0% English and 15·3% Xhosa.

There are 41 administrative districts. The capital is Cape Town.

Constitution and Government. There is a 42-seat provincial legislature; at the provincial elections held 27–29 April 1994, 23 seats were won by the NP (with 54·2% of votes cast), 14 by the ANC (with 33·6%), 3 by the DP (with 6·8%), and 1 each by the FF (2·1%) and African Christian Democratic Party (1·2%).

In Jan. 1998 the government comprised:
Premier: Hernus Kriel (NP).
Police Services, Leader of the House: Gerald Morkel (NP). *Finance and Environment Affairs:* Kobus Meiring (NP). *Economic Affairs and Reconstruction and Development Programme:* Chris Nissen (ANC). *Agriculture, Planning and Tourism:* Lampie Fick (NP). *Roads, Transport and Public Works:* Leonard Ramatlakane (ANC). *Local Government and Development Management:* Peter Marais (NP). *Education and Cultural Affairs:* Martha Olckers (NP). *Health and Social Services:* Ebrahim Rasool (ANC). *Sport and Recreation:* Lerumo Kalako (ANC).

Local Government: Elections for some areas were held on 29 May 1996 (postponed from 1 Nov. 1995 while boundaries were finalized). The NP gained control of all 3 district councils comprising 11 regional councils.

Agriculture. In 1996 there were 8,747 farms with 288,438 agricultural workers; gross farming income amounted to R6,760·5m.

Labour. In 1996 the economically active age group numbered 2,755,000. Persons employed by branch, 1996 (in 1,000): Manufacturing, 316; commerce and catering, 237; agriculture, 158; construction, 117; transport and communications, 105; finance and business, 98; electricity and water, 11; others, 388. There were 0·3m. unemployed in Dec. 1996.

Education. In 1996 there were 886 pupils in pre-primary schools, 13,627 pupils in special schools, 517,057 pupils in primary schools, 74,408 in intermediate schools, 255,042 in secondary schools and 22,800 in combined schools, with altogether 32,272 teachers; there were also 794 lecturers and 14,637 students in technical colleges, and 410 lecturers and 6,790 students in teachers' training establishments.

Roads. Motor vehicles registered (1996) totalled 1,102,226, including 679,977 passenger cars, 238,087 light commercial vehicles, 35,478 heavy commercial vehicles and 28,153 motorcycles.

Health. In 1996 there were 1,822 medical practitioners, 13,864 nurses, 47 hospitals, 191 clinics and 13,992 hospital beds.

SPAIN

Reino de España

(Kingdom of Spain)

Capital: Madrid
Population: 40·46m.
GDP per head: (PPP$)14,324
HDI/world rank: 0·934/11

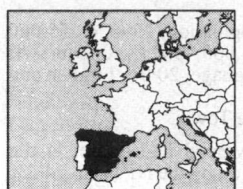

KEY HISTORICAL EVENTS. The modern Spanish state was founded with the marriage in 1469 of the heirs of the crowns of Castile and Aragón, respectively Isabel I and Fernando V. Under their joint reign Spain recovered Granada, the last Islamic territory in the Iberian peninsula, and sponsored the modern discovery of America, both events in 1492. This dynasty ended in 1700 and subsequently the French Bourbon dynasty was enthroned, with Felipe V as its first king; the present monarch, Juan Carlos I, installed in 1975, is his direct descendant.

Queen Isabel II, who came to the throne in 1833, was deposed and exiled in 1868 by a liberal revolution. A provisional government, headed by the Duke de la Torre, established universal male suffrage and convened a constituent election for Jan. 1869. The Cortes (Parliament) approved a new constitution, and the deputies chose as the new king Amadeo I, of the then reigning Italian dynasty of Savoy. He reigned as a scrupulous democrat from 2 Jan. 1871, but unable to adapt to Spanish politics, abdicated on 11 Feb. 1873. The Cortes immediately proclaimed a republic.

The first brief republican experience saw great instability. On 29 Dec. 1874, in Sagunto, Gen. Martínez Campos led a *coup* and restored the Bourbon monarchy, with Alfonso XII as king, the son of the exiled Queen Isabel II. A general election took place early in 1876 and the new Cortes approved a constitution which was effective until 1923. This period, known as the Restoration, saw the reimposition of a restricted suffrage (the universal one was not re-established until 1890), and was dominated by two parties, Conservative and Liberal, led respectively by A. Cánovas del Castillo and P. M. Sagasta, both of whom served as prime minister several times in the last quarter of the 19th century.

Alfonso XII died in 1885. His wife María Cristina of Hapsburg was regent till their son, Alfonso XIII, reached his majority in 1902.

During the period of the Restoration, Spain still had a very backward economy and very low standards of living. At the same time Spain was embroiled in external conflicts, with wars in northern Morocco and in the remaining colonies of Cuba and the Philippines. The US intervention led to the cession of Philippines, Puerto Rico and Guam, and also of Cuba which formally became independent in 1901.

Spain was neutral in the First World War, leading to a boom in industry and trade. A new industrial working class was then emerging, amongst a climate of industrial unrest and with a growing opposition to conscription for the war in the north of Morocco.

In Sept. 1923 Gen. Primo de Rivera led a *coup* and abolished the 1876 constitution, closed down the Cortes and governed by decree until his resignation in Jan. 1930. During his dictatorship the war in the Spanish Protectorate in Morocco came to an end.

An interim period followed until the municipal elections of 12 April 1931, which were won by a republican-socialist coalition in Madrid, provincial capitals and other urban areas. Two days later Alfonso XIII exiled himself and the republic was proclaimed a second time. In June a new Cortes was elected; it drafted a new constitution, which was in force by Dec. 1931. Complete religious freedom and an agrarian reform were the significant landmarks of this period. An election in 1932, for the first time with female suffrage, established a very conservative coalition government, which resulted in serious rioting in Oct. 1934. An election in Feb. 1936 gave power to the Popular Front, a coalition of all left parties, including the then tiny Communist party.

On 18 July 1936 the colonial army in northern Morocco, led by Gen. Francisco Franco, and some other military units rebelled against the government. The rebellion was crushed in a few days in Madrid, Barcelona, Valencia and almost all industrial and mining areas. But the rural regions were easily controlled by the rebels who received substantial help in men, tanks and aircraft from Germany, Italy and Portugal. The government, however, suffered from the 'non-intervention' policy declared by the democracies, notably Britain and France. The International Brigades, a volunteer force, and conditional aid from the USSR were the only significant foreign support received by the Spanish republic. Franco's forces finally overcame all resistance and the war ended on 1 April 1939. Gen. Franco was chief of state till his death on 20 Nov. 1975. His brutal régime was modelled on those of the Axis countries. Nevertheless, Franco's Spain did not take part in the Second World War. The 15 years following the Civil War saw extremely depressed economic conditions.

A nominal monarchy existed from 1947, but with a vacant throne until 1969 when the francoist state accepted the future succession in favour of Juan Carlos de Borbón, grandson of Alfonso XIII. Franco recognized the independence of Morocco in 1956 and ceded the small Spanish protectorate to the Moroccan Government. Spain also withdrew from Equatorial Guinea in 1968 but continued to occupy Western Sahara until 1976.

On 22 Nov. 1975, following Gen. Franco's death, Juan Carlos was proclaimed king. A gradual return to democracy began. A referendum held in Dec. 1976 endorsed some key reforms making possible a free election on 15 June 1977. The elected bicameral Cortes drafted a new constitution which came into force on 29 Dec. 1978.

TERRITORY AND POPULATION. Spain is bounded in the north by the Bay of Biscay, France and Andorra, east and south by the Mediterranean and the Straits of Gibraltar, south-west by the Atlantic and west by Portugal and the Atlantic. Continental Spain has an area of 492,592 sq. km, and including the Balearic and Canary Islands and the towns of Ceuta and Melilla on the northern coast of Morocco, 504,750 sq. km (194,884 sq. miles). Population (last census, 1991), 38,872,268 (19,835,822 female); estimate (1995), 40,460,055; projection (2025), 37·6m.

The growth of the population has been as follows:

Census year	Population	Rate of annual increase	Census year	Population	Rate of annual increase
1860	15,655,467	0·34	1950	27,976,755	0·81
1910	19,927,150	0·72	1960	30,903,137	0·88
1920	21,303,162	0·69	1970	33,823,918	0·94
1930	23,563,867	1·06	1981	37,746,260	1·15
1940	25,877,971	0·98	1991	38,872,268	0·29

In 1996 the number of foreigners legally registered was 526,014 (largest foreign communities: Moroccan, 78,045; British, 66,620).

Vital statistics for calendar years:

	Marriages	Births	Deaths
1993	201,463	385,786	339,661
1994	199,731	370,148	338,242
1995[1]	196,945	359,870	342,736

[1] Provisional.

Number of couples who have filed for divorce since it was legalized in 1981, 474,704; divorces, 342,982. Suicide rates (per 100,000 population), 1990–95: 7·7 (males, 11·6; females, 3·9).

Area and population of the autonomous communities and provinces, in 1995:

Autonomous community/ Province	Area (sq. km)	Population	Per sq. km	Autonomous community/ Province	Area (sq. km)	Population	Per sq. km
Andalusia	*87,268*	*7,314,644*	*83*	Málaga	7,276	1,224,959	168
Almería	8,774	493,126	56	Sevilla	14,001	1,719,446	122
Cádiz	7,385	1,127,622	152	*Aragón*	*47,669*	*1,205,663*	*25*
Córdoba	13,718	782,221	57	Huesca	15,671	210,276	13
Granada	12,531	841,829	67	Teruel	14,804	143,055	9
Huelva	10,085	458,674	45	Zaragoza	17,194	852,332	49
Jaén	13,498	666,767	49	*Asturias*	*10,565*	*1,117,370*	*105*

Autonomous community/ Province	Area (sq. km)	Population	Per sq. km	Autonomous community/ Province	Area (sq. km)	Population	Per sq. km
Baleares	5,014	787,984	157	Zamora	10,559	214,273	20
Basque				Catalonia	31,930	6,226,869	195
Country	7,261	2,130,783	293	Barcelona	7,773	4,748,236	610
Álava	3,047	282,944	92	Gerona	5,886	541,995	92
Guipúzcoa	1,997	684,113	342	Lérida	12,028	360,407	29
Vizcaya	2,217	1,163,726	524	Tarragona	6,283	576,231	91
Canary Islands	7,273	1,631,498	224	Extremadura	41,602	1,100,538	26
Palmas, Las	4,065	844,140	207	Badajoz	21,657	675,592	31
Santa Cruz				Cáceres	19,945	424,946	21
de Tenerife	3,208	787,358	245	Galicia	29,434	2,825,020	95
Cantabria	5,289	541,885	102	Coruña, La	7,876	1,136,283	144
Castilla-La				Lugo	9,803	386,405	39
Mancha	79,226	1,730,717	21	Orense	7,278	364,521	50
Albacete	14,858	361,327	24	Pontevedra	4,477	937,811	209
Ciudad Real	19,749	490,573	24	Madrid	7,995	5,181,659	648
Cuenca	17,061	207,499	12	Murcia	11,317	1,109,977	98
Guadalajara	12,190	155,884	12	Navarra	10,421	536,192	51
Toledo	15,368	515,434	33	Rioja, La	5,034	268,206	53
Castilla y León	94,147	2,584,407	27	Valencian			
Ávila	8,048	176,791	21	Community	23,305	4,028,774	172
Burgos	14,269	360,677	24	Alicante	5,863	1,363,785	232
León	15,468	532,706	34	Castellón	6,679	464,670	69
Palencia	8,029	186,035	23	Valencia	10,763	2,200,319	204
Salamanca	12,336	365,293	29	Ceuta[1]	18	73,142	4,063
Segovia	6,949	149,653	21	Melilla[1]	14	64,727	4,623
Soria	10,287	94,396	9				
Valladolid	8,202	504,583	61	Total	504,750	40,460,055	80

[1] Ceuta and Melilla gained limited autonomous status in 1994.

The capitals of the autonomous communities are: *Andalusia*: Seville; *Aragón*: Zaragoza (Saragossa); *Asturias*: Oviedo; *Baleares*: Palma de Mallorca; *Basque Country*: Vitoria; *Canary Islands*, dual and alternative capital, Las Palmas and Santa Cruz de Tenerife; *Cantabria*: Santander; *Castilla-La Mancha*: Toledo; *Castilla y León*: Valladolid; *Catalonia*: Barcelona; *Extremadura*: Mérida; *Galicia*: Santiago de Compostela; *Madrid*: Madrid; *Murcia*: Murcia (but regional parliament in Cartagena); *Navarra*: Pamplona; *La Rioja*: Logroño; *Valencian Community*: Valencia.

The capitals of the provinces are the towns from which they take the name, except in the cases of Álava (capital, Vitoria), Asturias (Oviedo), Baleares (Palma de Mallorca), Cantabria (Santander), Guipúzcoa (San Sebastián), La Rioja (Logroño), Navarra (Pamplona) and Vizcaya (Bilbao).

The islands which form the Balearics include Majorca, Minorca, Ibiza and Formentera. Those which form the Canary Archipelago are divided into 2 provinces, under the name of their respective capitals: Santa Cruz de Tenerife and Las Palmas de Gran Canaria. The province of Santa Cruz de Tenerife is constituted by the islands of Tenerife, La Palma, Gomera and Hierro; that of Las Palmas by Gran Canaria, Lanzarote and Fuerteventura, with the small barren islands of Alegranza, Roque del Este, Roque del Oeste, Graciosa, Montaña Clara and Lobos.

Places under Spanish sovereignty in Morocco (Alhucemas, Ceuta, Chafarinas, Melilla and Peñón de Vélez) constitute the 2 provinces of Ceuta and Melilla.

Populations of principal towns in 1995:

Town	Population	Town	Population	Town	Population
Albacete	143,779	Badajoz	132,154	Cartagena	180,553
Alcalá de Henares	166,925	Badalona	217,983	Castellón de	
Alcobendas	85,466	Baracaldo	102,561	la Plana	139,889
Alcorcón	143,532	Barcelona	1,614,571	Córdoba	318,030
Algeciras	104,216	Bilbao	370,997	Cornellá de	
Alicante	276,526	Burgos	166,732	Llobregat	83,287
Almería	169,509	Cáceres	81,037	Coruña, La	254,822
Avilés	88,450	Cádiz	154,511	Coslada	79,084

Town	Population	Madrid	3,029,734	Town	Population
Elche	192,424	Town	Population	San Sebastián	178,470
Ferrol, El	85,587	Málaga	532,425	Santa Coloma de	
Fuenlabrada	160,573	Marbella	87,679	Gramanet	129,751
Getafe	144,662	Mataró	102,137	Santa Cruz de	
Gijón	270,867	Móstoles	199,411	Tenerife	204,948
Granada	272,738	Murcia	344,904	Santander	194,837
Guecho	83,936	Orense	110,796	Santiago de	
Hermanas, Dos	84,948	Oviedo	202,421	Compostela	94,057
Hospitalet	262,501	Palencia	79,867	Sevilla	719,588
Huelva	145,712	Palma de Mallorca	323,138	Tarragona	114,931
Jaén	113,141	Palmas, Las	373,772	Tarrasa	162,327
Jerez de la Frontera	191,394	Pamplona	181,776	Telde	84,799
Laguna, La	127,743	Reus	90,221	Torrejón de Ardoz	88,224
Leganés	178,321	Sabadell	188,386	Valencia	763,299
León	147,780	Salamanca	167,316	Valladolid	334,820
Lérida	114,367	San Baudilio del		Vigo	290,582
Logroño	125,456	Llobregat	79,737	Vitoria	215,049
Lugo	88,253	San Fernando	88,212	Zaragoza	607,899

Languages. The Constitution states that 'Castilian is the Spanish official language of the State', but also that 'All other Spanish languages will also be official in the corresponding Autonomous Communities'. At the last census (1991) Catalan (an official EU language since 1990) was spoken in Catalonia by 68% of people, Baleares (66·9%), Valencian Community (51%, where it is frequently called Valencian), and in Aragón, a narrow strip close to the Catalonian and Valencian Community boundaries. Galician, a language very close to Portuguese, was spoken by a majority of people in Galicia (91%); Basque by a significant and increasing minority in the Basque Country (26·3%), and by a small minority in north-west Navarra (12%). It is estimated that one third of all Spaniards speaks one of the other 3 official languages as well as standard Castilian. In bilingual communities, both Castilian and the regional language are taught in schools and universities.

In the Basque region terrorist activity by the separatist organisation ETA has brought a reaction from the local population in the form of a strong peace movement. In 1994 it was believed that 10 ETA units were operational in Spain.

CLIMATE. Most of Spain has a form of Mediterranean climate with mild, moist winters and hot, dry summers, but the northern coastal region has a moist, equable climate, with rainfall well-distributed throughout the year, mild winters and warm summers, and less sunshine than the rest of Spain. The south, in particular Andalusia, is dry and prone to drought. At the Earth Summit in New York in 1997, the President of the Spanish Government, José María Aznar, highlighted the problem of desertification in Spain and the need to combat it.

Madrid. Jan. 41°F (5°C), July 77°F (25°C). Annual rainfall 16·8" (419 mm). *Barcelona.* Jan. 46°F (8°C), July 74°F (23·5°C). Annual rainfall 21" (525 mm). *Cartagena.* Jan. 51°F (10·5°C), July 75°F (24°C). Annual rainfall 14·9" (373 mm). *La Coruña.* Jan. 51°F (10·5°C), July 66°F (19°C). Annual rainfall 32" (800 mm). *Sevilla.* Jan. 51°F (10·5°C), July 85°F (29·5°C). Annual rainfall 19·5" (486 mm). *Palma de Mallorca.* Jan. 51°F (11°C), July 77°F (25°C). Annual rainfall 13·6" (347 mm). *Santa Cruz de Tenerife.* Jan. 64°F (17·9°C), July 76°F (24·4°C). Annual rainfall 7·72" (196 mm).

ROYAL HOUSE. The reigning king is Juan Carlos I, born 5 Jan. 1938. The eldest son of Don Juan, Conde de Barcelona, Juan Carlos was given precedence over his father as pretender to the Spanish throne in an agreement in 1954 between Don Juan and General Franco. Don Juan, who resigned his claims to the throne in May 1977, died on 1 April 1993. King (then Prince) Juan Carlos married, in 1962, Princess Sophia of Greece, daughter of the late King Paul of the Hellenes and Queen Frederika. *Offspring:* Elena, born 20 Dec. 1963, married 18 March 1995 Jaime de Marichalar; Cristina, born 13 June 1965, married 4 Oct. 1997 Iñaki Urdangarín; Felipe, Prince of Asturias, Heir to the throne, born 30 Jan. 1968.

The King receives an allowance, part of which is taxable, approved by parliament each year. In 1997 it was 990m. pesetas. There is no formal court; the (private) *Diputación de la Grandeza* represents the interests of the aristocracy.

CONSTITUTION AND GOVERNMENT. Following the death of General Franco in 1975 and the transition to a democracy, the first democratic elections were held on 15 June 1977. A new Constitution was approved by referendum on 6 Dec. 1978, and came into force 29 Dec. 1978. It established a parliamentary monarchy, with King Juan Carlos I as head of state. Legislative power is vested in the *Cortes Generales*, a bicameral parliament composed of the Congress of Deputies (lower house) and the Senate (upper house).

The *Congress of Deputies* has not less than 300 nor more than 400 members (350 in the general election of 1996) elected in a proportional system under which electors choose between party lists of candidates in multi-member constituencies.

The *Senate* has 257 members of whom 208 are elected by a majority system: the 47 mainland provinces elect 4 senators each, regardless of population; the island provinces 5 (Baleares, Las Palmas) or 6 (Santa Cruz de Tenerife); and Ceuta and Melilla, 2 senators each. To these are added 49 senators elected by the parliaments of the autonomous communities as regional representatives. Deputies and senators are elected by universal secret suffrage for 4-year terms. The Prime Minister is elected by the Congress of Deputies.

The *Constitutional Court* is empowered to solve conflicts between the State and the Autonomous Communities; to determine if legislation passed by the Cortes is contrary to the Constitution; and to protect the constitutional rights of individuals violated by any authority. Its 12 members are appointed by the monarch: 4 on the proposal of the Congress of Deputies; 4 on the proposal of the Senate; 2 on the proposal of the General Council of the Judicial Power (*see under* JUSTICE, *below*); and 2 on the proposal of the Cabinet. It has a 9-year term, with a third of the membership being renewed every 3 years.

The last general election took place on 3 March 1996 (the next is due by March 2000). 67 parties presented candidates. The electorate was 24,985,343; turn-out was 78·06%. In the *Congress of Deputies* the Popular Party (PP) won 156 seats with 38·2% of votes cast; the Spanish Workers' Socialist Party (PSOE), 141 with 37·4%; the Communist-led United Left Coalition (IU), 21 with 10·5%; Convergence and Union (CiU; Catalan nationalists), 16 with 4·6%; Basque Nationalist Party (PNV), 5 with 1·2%; Canarian Coalition (CC), 4 with 0·8%; Galician Nationalist Bloc (BNG), 2 with 0·8% (first time in Parliament); the Basque separatist Herri Batasuna Party (HB), 2 with 0·7%; the Catalan separatist Esquerra Republicana de Catalunya (ERC), 1 with 0·6%; the non-radical Basque separatist Eusko Alkartasuna Party (EA), 1 with 0·4%; Valencian Union (UV), 1 with 0·3%. In the *Senate*, the Popular Party won 112 seats; PSOE, 81; CiU, 8; PNV, 4; CC, 1; others, 1 each.

A government was formed in May 1996. José María Aznar, leader of the democratic right-wing Popular Party, was appointed President of the *Council of Ministers* at the head of a minority PP government supported by 3 regionalist parties, from Catalonia, the Basque Country and Canary Islands, of which the most decisive is the Catalan nationalist coalition, the CiU. In March 1998, the government comprised:

President: José María Aznar López (b. 1953; PP; elected 3 March 1996; sworn in 5 May 1996); *Deputy Vice-President and Minister of the Prime Minister's Office:* Francisco Álvarez Cascos (PP). *Deputy Vice-President and Minister of Economy and Finance:* Rodrigo Rato Figaredo (PP). *Foreign Affairs:* Abel Matutes Juan (PP). *Justice:* Margarita Mariscal de Gante y Mirón (ind). *Defence:* Eduardo Serra i Rexach (ind). *Interior:* Jaime Mayor Oreja (PP). *Development:* Rafael Arias-Salgado y Montalvo (PP). *Education and Culture:* Esperanza Aguirre y Gil de Biedma (PP). *Labour and Social Affairs:* Javier Arenas Bocanegra (PP). *Industry, Energy and Tourism:* Josep Piqué i Camps (ind). *Agriculture, Fisheries and Food:* Loyola de Palacio del Valle-Lersundi (PP). *Public Administration:* Mariano Rajoy Brey (PP). *Health and Consumer Affairs:* José Manuel Romay Beccaría (PP). *Environment:* Isabel Tocino Biscarolasaga (PP). The *Speaker* (and President) of the Congress of

Deputies is Federico Trillo (PP); the *Speaker* (and President) of the Senate is José Ignacio Barrero (PP).

The IU (United Left Coalition) adopted 6 resolutions in Sept. 1997 which effectively provoked the break-up of the coalition and distancing from it of its former regionalist elements, among them the Catalan Left.

National anthem: 'Marcha Real' ('Royal March'); no words, tune anonymous.

European Parliament. Spain has 64 representatives. At the June 1994 elections turn-out was 59·1%. The PP won 28 seats with 40·2% of votes cast (political affiliation in European Parliament: European People's Party); the PSOE, 22 with 30·6% (European Socialist Party); the IU, 9 with 13·4% (European United Left); the CiU, 3 with 4·6% (European People's Party; European Liberal Democratic and Reformist Group); the Nationalist Coalition, 2 with 2·8% (European People's Party).

Regional Government. The Constitution of 1978 establishes a semi-federal system of regional administration, with the Autonomous Community *(Comunidad Autónoma)* as its basic element. There are 17 autonomous communities, each of them having a Parliament elected by universal vote, and a regional government; all possess exclusive legislative and executive power in many matters, as listed in the national Constitution and in their own fundamental law *(estatuto de autonomía)*. The 17 communities comprise 50 provinces (established by the administrative division of 1833): 7 communities (Asturias, Baleares, Cantabria, La Rioja, Madrid, Murcia and Navarre) are composed of 1 province only; the other 10 are formed by 2 or more.

In Sept. 1994 Ceuta and Melilla gained limited autonomous status, with legislative assemblies replacing their municipal councils. In 1997, 10 Communities (Aragón, Asturias, Baleares, Cantabria, Castilla-La Mancha, Castilla y León, Extremadura, Madrid, Murcia, La Rioja) gained authority (not previously held) over matters such as health and education, under new statutes (Art 143 of the Constitution); and an all-party initiative to re-examine the constitutional status of the Basque Country and neighbouring part-Basque province of Navarre was mooted. This was following a year during which the government consolidated a tough approach to Basque separatist terrorism after national outrage in July over ETA's assassination of a young local councillor.

Date of last elections and party composition of the autonomous communities: *Andalusia* (March 1996), PSOE 52, PP 40, IU, 13, Andalusian Party 4. *Aragón* (May 1995), PP 27, PSOE 19, Aragonese Regionalist Party 14, IU 5, others 2. *Asturias* (May 1995), PP 21, PSOE 17, IU 6, others 1. *Baleares* (May 1995), PP 30, PSOE 16, nationalists 6, IU 3, others 4. *Basque Country* (Oct. 1994), PNV 22, PSOE-Euskadiko Ezquerra 12, HB 11, PP 11, EA 8, United Left-Ezker Batua 6, Alavese Unity 5. *Canary Islands* (May 1995), PP 18, PSOE 16, CC 22, others 4 *Cantabria* (May 1995), PP 13, PSOE 10, regionalists 6, IU 3, others 7. *Castilla-La Mancha* (May 1995), PSOE 24, PP 22, IU 1. *Castilla y León* (May 1995), PP 50, PSOE 27, IU 5, others 2. *Catalonia* (Nov. 1995), CiU 60, PSOE 34, PP 17, ERC 13, Iniciativa per Catalunya 11. *Extremadura* (May 1995), PSOE 31, PP 27, IU 6, others 1. *Galicia* (Oct. 1993), PP 43, PSOE 19, BNG 13 (elections were held in Oct. 1997). *La Rioja* (May 1995), PP 17, PSOE 12, regionalists 2, IU 2. *Madrid* (May 1995), PP 54, PSOE 32, IU 17. *Murcia* (May 1995), PP 26, PSOE 15, IU 4. *Navarra* (May 1995), PP 17, PSOE 11, regionalists 10, HB 5, EA 2, IU 5. *Valencian Community* (May 1995), PP 42, PSOE 32, UV 5, IU 10.

Local Government. The Provincial Council *(Diputación Provincial)* is the administrative organ of the province, except in the 7 autonomous communities composed of only one province, where there are only the regional legislative and executive powers. The provincial council is indirectly elected, except in the 3 Basque provinces where they are elected by universal suffrage every 4 years. Each of the 7 main islands of the Canaries has a directly elected corporation, the *Cabildo Insular,* to rule its special interests; in the main islands of the Balearics there is an elected *Consell Insular*.

The provinces are constituted by the association of municipalities (8,095 in 1997). Municipalities are autonomous in their own sphere. At their head stands the Municipal Council *(Ayuntamiento),* members of which are elected in a universal ballot every 4 years, and they, in turn, elect one amongst them as Mayor *(Alcalde)*. In 1997 6,462 municipalities had fewer than 3,000 inhabitants (3,713 less than 500). Resource-poor municipalities may form associations *(Mancomunidades)* to share services. Elections were held in May 1995 for 65,732 municipal councillors. The electorate was 32,019,932. Turn-out was 69·79%. The Popular Party won 35·2% of votes cast (25·1% in 1991), the PSOE 30·8% (38·5%), the IU coalition 11·6% (8·5%).

DEFENCE. Conscription is for 9 months. Civilian service may be offered as an alternative. Recruits to the national police are exempt from conscription. Since 1989 women have been accepted in all sections of the armed forces. In 1996 the government began the phased abolition of conscription (starting with males born in 1984).

Army. The Army is divided into 8 Regional Operation Commands (including 2 overseas) and consists of 1 mechanized division, 2 armoured cavalry, 1 mountain, 3 light infantry, 1 airborne, 1 artillery, 1 engineer and 1 air-portable brigade; 3 island garrisons, 3 special operations battalions and the Spanish Legion. A Rapid Reaction Force is formed from the Spanish Legion and the airborne and air-portable brigades. There is also an Army Aviation brigade. Equipment includes 210 AMX-30, 164 M-48A5E and 294 M-60 main battle tanks. The Aviation Brigade consists of 170 helicopters (40 attack).

Strength (1997) 128,500 (including 81,500 conscripts). Of these 2,500 are stationed on the Balearic Islands, 6,500 on the Canary Islands and 10,000 in Ceuta and Melilla.

Guardia Civil. The paramilitary *Guardia Civil* numbers 75,000 (2,200 conscripts).

Navy. The principal ship of the Navy is the 17,000-tonne *Príncipe de Asturias*, a light vertical/short take-off and landing aircraft carrier. Her air group comprises 8 AV-8S Matador, 8 Sea King anti-submarine helicopters, 2 Sea King early warning helicopters and about 4 AB-212 light helicopters. There are also 8 French-designed submarines (4 Daphne class, 4 Agosta class), 6 US-design Santa María guided missile frigates with Standard SM-1 surface-to-air missiles, 5 other guided missile frigates, and 6 smaller frigates, 5 offshore patrol vessels, 10 coastal and 16 inshore patrol craft, 4 ocean minesweepers, 8 coastal minesweepers, 2 amphibious troop transports, 2 tank landing ships and 13 landing craft. Major auxiliaries include 3 tankers, 2 transports, 5 ocean tugs, 1 training ship, 4 water carriers and 6 survey ships. There are about 80 minor auxiliaries and service craft.

The Naval Air Service operates 20 AV-8S Matador and EAV-8B Harrier-II attack aircraft, 34 S-70B Seahawk, Sea King, SH 60B, AB-212 and Hughes 500 anti-submarine helicopters, 3 radar early warning Sea Kings and a few additional training and utility aircraft. The Air Force operates 7 Orion maritime patrol aircraft on anti-submarine tasks.

There are 8,000 marines, who provide 1 amphibious regiment and garrison regiments at the main bases. Main naval bases are at Ferrol, Rota, Cádiz, Cartagena, Palma de Mallorca, Mahón and Las Palmas (Canary Islands).

In 1997 personnel totalled 39,000 (13,500 conscripts) including the marines and 1,000 naval air arm.

Air Force. The Air Force is organized as an independent service, dating from 1939. It is administered through 4 operational commands. These are geographically oriented following a reorganization in 1991 and comprise Central Air Command, Straits Air Command, Eastern Air Command and Air Command of the Canaries.

The Tactical Air Command has 2 fighter-bomber squadrons of Spanish-built Northrop SF-5s and 1 aero-naval co-operation squadron with P-3 Orion anti-submarine aircraft. Air Combat Command has 1 squadron of RF-4C Phantom IIs, 4 squadrons of F-18 Hornets and 3 squadrons of Mirage F-1s. 2 Boeing 707 and 5 KC-130H tankers support the fighter squadrons. 3 wings of Air Transport Command operate C-130 Hercules, CN-235s and Spanish-built CASA Aviocars. Air Command of the Canaries has 3 squadrons, equipped with Aviocar transports, Mirage F1 fighter-bombers, F27 Maritime aircraft and Super Puma helicopters for search and rescue. Other equipment includes 3 Boeing 707s, 8 Falcons and helicopters for VIP transport; and aircraft for photographic, firefighting, target towing and research duties. Air-sea rescue units have Aviocars and Super Puma helicopters.

American-built F33 Bonanza and Chilean-built Pillan piston-engined aircraft are used for basic training, after which pupil pilots progress to CASA C-101 jet aircraft. Two-seat versions of operational types are used as advanced trainers. Other training types include Hughes 300 and S-76 helicopters.

Strength (1997) 30,000 (13,000 conscripts).

INTERNATIONAL RELATIONS

Membership. Spain is a member of the UN, the Council of Europe, NATO, WEU, the EU, OSCE and OECD, and is a signatory to the Schengen Accord (*see* EUROPEAN UNION *under* MAJOR POLICY AREAS, *above*).

ECONOMY

Performance. Spain's current account on its balance of payments came out of deficit in 1995 for the first time since the mid-1980s. The balance showed a surplus of 586,500m. pesetas for the first 9 months of 1997; forecast 1997 (in US$): 1,400m. Real GDP growth was 2·1% in 1996 (2·8% in 1995) and was officially estimated at 3% for 1997. Total GDP (estimate 1997, in US$): 604,400m. Government debt (1996, % of GDP): 69·5%. Foreign debt (1995, in US$): 277,500m.

Spain and EMU. With inflation low, interest rates down (cut to 4% in 1997) and its budget deficit under control, in Jan. 1998 Spain looked on course to meet EU (Maastricht) criteria for first-wave entrants to EMU.

Budget. A Convergence Plan covering 1997-2000 envisages an annual GDP growth of 3.2%, a reduction of public debt to 1.6% of GDP, the limitation of inflation to below 2.5%, and the creation of 1m. jobs by deregulating and increasing the flexibility of the economy and redistributing taxes. Government expenditure (1996, % of GDP): 43·1% (1997 forecast: 41·6%).

Revenue and expenditure in 1m. pesetas:

	1995	1996	1997	1998
Revenue	19,402,252	18,448,253	16,209,545	17,351,000
Expenditure	19,402,252	19,448,253	23,882,592	24,111,000

The budget for 1998 was made up as follows (in 1m. pesetas):

Revenue		Expenditure	
Direct taxes	7,950,000	Staff costs	3,071,000
Indirect taxes	6,901,000	Current goods	
Levies and various revenues	355,000	and services	316,000
Current transfers	742,000	Financial costs	3,190,000
Income on assets	979,000	Current transfers	10,369,000
Sale on real investments	23,000	Real investment	873,000
Capital transfers	293,000	Capital transfers	911,000
Financial assets	109,000	Financial investments	1,048,000

VAT is normally 16%, with a rate of 7% on certain services (catering and hospitality), and 4% on basic foodstuffs.

Currency. The unit of currency is the peseta (notionally divided into 100 *céntimos* though they have not been in use since 1984). Bank-notes of 10,000, 5,000, 2,000 and 1,000 pesetas, and coins of 1, 5, 10, 25, 50, 100, 200 and 500 pesetas are in circulation. On 30 Nov. 1997 the circulation of bank-notes was 8,240,600m. pesetas; of coins, 350,000m. pesetas. Currency and gold reserves were US$72,000m. in 1997; reserves at 30 Nov. 1997 (in 1,000m. pesetas): gold 338; IMF 241; SDRs 67; foreign exchange 7,328; ecus 1,811; others 30. Inflation in 1997 was 2% (3·2% in Dec. 1996).

Banking and Finance. The central bank is the Bank of Spain (*Governor*: Luis Ángel Rojo) which gained autonomy under an ordinance of 1994. Its governor is appointed for a 6-year term. The Banking Corporation of Spain, *Argentaria*, groups together the shares of all state-owned banks, and competes in the financial market with private banks. In 1993 the government sold 49·9% of the capital of Argentaria; the remainder in 2 flotations ending on 13 Feb. 1998.

In terms of assets held in Nov. 1997 (in 1m. pesetas), the main banks were: Grupo Santander, 12,277,367; Banco Bilbao Vizcaya, 13,077,448; Banco Central Hispano, 10,444,037; Banco Popular, 2,433,008; Banesto, 5,305,252; Argentaria (no consolidated balance). On 31 Oct. 1997 Spanish banks deposits (in 1,000m. pesetas) amounted to 17,721 (private banks, 10,178; government banks, 7,543); foreign banks, 1,667; savings banks, 24,525; rural (farmers) savings banks, 3,235.

There are stock exchanges in Madrid, Barcelona, Bilbao and Valencia. The flotation in 1997 of public-sector holdings brought some 2m. new domestic investors into the Spanish equity market; privatization receipts in 1997 were expected to total 1,600,000m. pesetas.

Weights and Measures. The metric system was introduced in 1859.

ENERGY AND NATURAL RESOURCES

Electricity. Nuclear and hydroelectric power stations provided just over half of Spain's electricity in 1990. Electric power stations had a total installed capacity of 45·2m. kW in 1991; nuclear power stations (9 in 1997) had a net capacity of 7·3m. kW. The government announced in 1991 that no new nuclear power stations would commence operating before 2000. The total electricity output in 1996 amounted to 175,604m. kWh, of which 41,619m. was hydroelectric, 56,204m. nuclear, and 77,781m. other (carbon, natural gas, petroleum).

In Feb. 1997 the government disposed of a 25% stake in Endesa, the country's main electricity generator and distributor, reducing its shareholding in the group to 41%; full privatization is expected by 1999 or earlier. The Electrical Protocol drawn up between the government and electricity utilities to meet EU requirements is to be completed over a 10-year period, and will largely dismantle the highly regulated, interventionist structure which preceded it. This should provide for a more open market; construction of new generators will be liberalized and prices are expected to fall in real terms by 25-30% over 5 years. Industry analysts forecast a market which will favour hydro- and gas-powered generators.

Oil. Spain is heavily dependent on imported oil; Mexico is its largest supplier. Crude oil production (1996), 554,000 tonnes.

Gas. The government sold its remaining stake in the oil, gas and chemicals group Repsol in 1997. Natural gas production (1996) totalled 596m. cu. metres. Efforts are being made to increase consumption; on 1 Nov. 1996 Spain opened the Algerian gas link (Maghreb-Europe Pipeline), which is expected to supply 6,200m. cu. metres by 2000.

Minerals. Spain has a relatively wide range of minerals; the mining sector accounted for 1% of GDP in 1994. Coal production (1995), 13m. tonnes; other principal minerals (1992, in 1,000 tonnes): anthracite, 6,177; lignite, 18,689; iron, 1,334; pyrites, 406; copper, 9; lead, 30; zinc, 205; fluorspar, 97; potassium salts, 594; (1992, in tonnes) uranium, 862; tin, 7. The Huelva copper smelter capacity expanded by 20% from 150,000 tonnes to 180,000 tonnes in 1995. Also in 1995, a large mercury deposit was found in southern Spain which could raise mercury levels to within a quarter of proven world reserves. A modern gold mine in Asturias (opened Oct. 1996) is expected to produce about 1,000 troy ounces a year.

Agriculture. Agriculture contributed 4·8% of GDP in 1994 and employed about 10·1% of the workforce. Crop production accounted for 62·2% of total agricultural production in 1990; animal production for 37·8%.

19,354,700 ha were under cultivation in 1995, including 4,372,600 ha under irrigation and 6,434,000 ha under pasture. There were (1992) 766,267 tractors, 280,989 motor ploughs and 47,795 harvesters in use.

Principal	Area (in 1,000 ha)				Yield (in 1,000 tonnes)			
crops	1993	1994	1995	1996	1993	1994	1995	1996
Wheat	2,025	1,994	2,093	2,022	4,989	4,311	2,957	6,169
Barley	3,499	3,602	3,573	3,529	9,532	7,596	5,194	10,636
Oats	326	346	364	410	400	402	216	653
Rye	170	155	159	170	300	220	173	295
Rice	50	63	54	106	315	394	327	761
Maize	284	342	346	454	1,673	2,266	2,539	3,834
Potatoes	213	207	211	208	3,922	4,074	4,195	4,174
Sugar-beet	181	175	173	160	8,226	8,004	7,612	7,686
Sunflower	2,264	1,349	1,005	1,158	1,214	984	574	1,137

Spain has more land dedicated to the grape than any other country in the world and is ranked third among wine producers (behind Italy and France). Wine exports have increased in value by nearly 600% from 1991-97. Total export receipts in 1996 totalled some £600m. A large part of Spain's output goes to Italy for bottling. In 1992, 1,333,000 ha were under vines. Production of wine (1996), 32,720,000 hectolitres; of grapes, 3.3m. tonnes.

The area under onions in 1996 was 28,200 ha, yielding 1,018,100 tonnes; of tomatoes, 58,400 ha, 3,224,800 tonnes (21% of EU production).

In fruit, Spain contributes a fifth of EU total harvest, and more than half of all citrus fruits. Fruit production (1996, in tonnes; ha, 1992): Oranges and mandarins, 3·5m. (201,282 ha); lemons, 433,100 (45,022 ha); apples, 893,600; peaches, 892,300.

Production of olive oil (1996), 670,000 tonnes. EU policy to reform the complex aid system for olive-oil (based on hand-outs per tree rather than oil production) is strongly opposed in all 5 EU olive oil-producing countries, nowhere more than Spain which, in Andalusia, has the world's largest producing zone. In 1997 Spain's olive growers marched on Madrid in protest over the reforms, which have provoked fear of plantation neglect and loss of employment.

Other important products are esparto, flax, tobacco, hemp and pulse; raw cotton production (1995): 88,000 tonnes.

Livestock (1995): Cattle, 5·51m.; sheep, 21·32m.; goats, 2·60m.; pigs, 18·16m.; laying hens, 45·72m.; horses, 0·24m; asses and mules (1992), 0·25m. Livestock density per 100 ha is among the lowest in the EU. Livestock products (1995 in 1,000 tonnes): Pork, 2,174; beef, 508·49; mutton, 227·12; poultry meat, 924·31; goat, 14·93; rabbit, 110·88. Milk (1993), 6·7m. tonnes; eggs (1991), 888·3m. dozen; honey (1991), 24,000 tonnes.

Forestry. Spain is among the most wooded countries in the EU (around 26m. ha, 50·7% of its total area) and together with France and Germany, it has the largest areas of forest also (8·2m. ha in 1990). Wood production (1992), 10,378,000 cu. metres; other forest products (in tonnes): Resins, 1,771; cork, 72,090; esparto, 792. Total value of forest products (1992)· 127,815m. pesetas.

Fisheries. Spain is the second largest fishing country in the EU after Denmark. Its annual catch is around 1·4m. tonnes and accounts for a fifth of the EU's annual catch. Fishing vessels had a total tonnage of 524,602 tonnes in 1995 (596,441 GRT in 1994); fleets have been gradually reduced from 20,558 boats in 1991 to 18,091 in 1996. Total catch (1993), 1,443,581 tonnes. Fish-farming output (1991), 222,427 tonnes, of which 200,922 were molluscs and shellfish, 21,505 fish; Spain supplies around half of total EU mussel production.

INDUSTRY. The industrial sector represented 28·1% of GNP in 1995. In 1996-97 industrial production was up by 3·3% on the previous 12 months, and industry accounted for 22·9% of the labour force (29·7% in 1994).

Principal textile production (1993, in 1,000 tonnes): Yarn, 227; cotton cloth, 64; synthetic and artificial fabrics, 62; knitwear, 23. Industrial products (1993, in tonnes): Sulphuric acid, 1,161,000; nitrogenous fertilizers, 642,000; plastics, 2·7m.; pulp and paper, 6·06m.; cement (1995), 24·47m.; crude oil refined (1995, in the 9 oil refineries), 55·2m. tonnes; steel production (1996), 12·3m.

The number of vehicles manufactured in 1995 was 2,333,785 of which 1,958,789 were passenger cars and 374,998 commercial. In 1996 1·39m. refrigerators and freezers, 2·6m. cookers, hotplates and microwaves, and 1·53m. washing machines, dishwashers and clothes driers were manufactured; the number of TV sets (1993), 3·8m. There are also important toy and shoe industries.

Labour. The economically active population numbered 16·03m. in 1996. Of these, 12·52m. were employed: 1·05m. in agriculture and fishing, 2·5m. in industry, 1·2m. in construction and 7·73m. in trade, transport and other public and personal services. Post-Franco legislation brought radical changes to the labour market, including the legalization in 1984 of fixed-term contracts. A third of Spain's wage earners were on temporary contracts by 1998. The monthly minimum wage for adults (1998) was 68,040 pesetas; the average monthly wage for workers in industry and services was 190,500 pesetas (1,331 pesetas an hour); average hourly earnings increased by 4% in 1997. The retirement age is 65 years.

In terms of unemployment, Spain has the highest rate among developed countries. 22·7% of the active population was unemployed at the end of 1997. On 17 Sept. 1997, the Council of Ministers passed the Multi-Year Employment Plan which co-ordinates the actions of 9 ministries with the aim of creating 1m. jobs to bring unemployment down to 17% by the year 2000. The scheme represents a 20% increase in budget spending for job creation.

Trade Unions. The Constitution guarantees the establishment and activities of trade unions provided they have a democratic structure. The most important trade unions are *Unión General de Trabajadores* (UGT) and *Comisiones Obreras* (CO). In Jan. 1997 the UGT and CO and employers' associations signed an agreement to be in force until 2000 providing for compulsory mediation before strike action; in April, employers' associations and trade unions reached an agreement covering 1997-2000 to combat job insecurity and reform collective bargaining. A National Employment Committee was subsequently set up to oversee the workings of the agreement.

FOREIGN ECONOMIC RELATIONS. In the first quarter of 1997 exports were up by 15%, imports by 8%. The economy recorded a foreign trade surplus of 302,000m. pesetas and a 32% reduction in the trade deficit (1997 forecast in US$: 16,000m.).

Total foreign investments (Jan-July 1997), 535,202,000m. pesetas, representing a 16% increase on 1996: 21% to EU countries; and 61% to Latin America (forged mainly by Tisa, the international arm of Telefonica, which operates 10m. lines and services 1m. cable TV and cellular phone subscribers in the region, with assets of US$ 5,000m.).

Commerce. Foreign trade of Spain (including Baleares, Canaries, Ceuta, Melilla, in 1m. pesetas):

	1993	1994	1995	1996
Imports	10,482,688	12,348,734	14,318,133	11,290,380
Exports	7,982,704	9,796,340	11,423,085	9,253,281

Merchandise imports (1997 forecast in US$): 126,100m.; exports, 110,100m.

Breakdown of imports in 1996 (in 1m. pesetas): Semi-finished products, 2,440,658 (21·6%); capital goods, 2,765,974 (24·5%); vehicles and other transport equipment, 1,648,229 (14·6%); consumer manufactures, 283,549 (2·5%); food products, 1,409,992 (12·5%); energy products, 1,034,706 (9·2%); raw materials, 542,249 (4·6%); durable consumer goods, 1,148,525 (10·2%); other goods, 34,498 (0·3%).

Breakdown of exports in 1996 (in 1m. pesetas): Vehicles and other transport equipment, 2,134,154 (23·1%); semi-finished products, 2,048,939 (22·1%); capital goods, 1,843,791 (19·9%); food products, 1,416,740 (15·3%); consumer manufactures, 1,083,544 (11·7%); raw materials, 204,392 (2·2%); energy products, 230,700 (2·5%); durable consumer goods, 219,680 (2·4%); other goods, 71,342 (0·8%).

Distribution of trade (in 1m. pesetas) by origin and destination:

	Imports		Exports	
	1995	1996	1995	1996
EU	9,362,806	7,410,808	8,264,560	6,674,299
France	2,454,944	2,019,464	2,345,844	1,926,507
Germany	2,189,575	1,653,814	1,760,143	1,344,502

	Imports		Exports	
	1995	1996	1995	1996
Italy	1,310,004	1,078,200	1,045,250	818,109
UK	1,120,096	897,271	915,922	772,864
Netherlands	619,751	433,494	420,386	326,771
Belgium–Luxembourg	492,853	388,777	350,753	278,625
Portugal	421,658	329,891	951,129	792,512
USA	919,164	749,027	472,214	384,317
Japan	472,716	323,759	157,060	114,885
Latin America	558,963	431,169	522,523	430,742
Mexico	124,699	97,093	69,555	47,663
Brazil	141,483	114,736	107,411	83,842
Switzerland	212,175	143,842	127,927	105,725
Eastern Europe	370,940	269,393	196,064	194,502
Nigeria	141,979	137,337	9,989	15,316
Libya	148,740	102,156	21,133	17,661
Saudi Arabia	160,483	117,176	60,005	43,492
Iran	94,700	87,909	20,933	26,052
Algeria	121,705	103,427	126,833	63,948

Tourism. Spain is the recipient of 8% of world tourism, second only to the USA in the number of visitors it receives. In 1997 tourism accounted for 10·4% of GDP with net receipts up by 15% at 2,535,000m. pesetas (an expected revenue of £15,000m.). In 1996, 62m. tourists visited Spain (41·4m. staying overnight). Hotel beds (1996), 914,338.

COMMUNICATIONS

Roads. In 1995 the total length of highways and roads was 162,184 km. The main network in 1995 comprised 7,736 km of motorways and four-lane highways (2,011 km of toll motorways), and 22,536 km of first-class roads. Travel by road accounted for 90·6% of internal passenger traffic in 1995; and for 77·24% of freight. Number of cars (1994), 13,733,800; lorries and vans, 2,825,700; buses, 47,100; motorcycles, 1,287,900. In 1996 3,998 persons were killed in road accidents.

Railways. The total length of the state railways in 1995 was 13,060 km, mostly broad (1,668-mm) gauge (6,736 km electrified). State railways are run by the National Spanish Railway Network (RENFE). There is a high-speed standard-gauge (1,435 mm) railway from Madrid to Seville. In 1995 freight carried was 26m. tonnes (4·2% of total freight) and 464·8m. passengers (5·9% of internal passenger traffic). There are metros in Madrid (112 km), Barcelona (72 km) and Bilbao (26 km), and a light railway in Valencia.

Civil Aviation. There are international airports at Madrid (Barajas), Barcelona (Prat del Llobregat), Alicante, Almería, Bilbao, Gerona, Gran Canaria, Ibiza, Lanzarote, Málaga, Palma de Mallorca, Santiago de Compostela, Seville, Tenerife (Los Rodeos and Reina Sofia), Valladolid, Valencia and Zaragoza. There are 43 airports open to civil traffic. A small airport in Seo de Urgel operates in Andorra. The national carrier is Iberia Airlines (99·8% state-owned but scheduled for privatization in 1999). There are 3 other regular carriers: Air España, Aviaco and Viva Air; and one regional airline in Catalonia, Air Nostrum. Services are also provided by about 65 foreign airlines.

Aircraft movements in 1996, 1,027,920: 449,943 internal and 577,977 international. In 1996, 79,945,244 passengers (32·64m. internal and 47·3m. international) and 451,663 tonnes of freight were carried.

Shipping. The merchant navy in 1995 had 1,101 vessels with a gross tonnage of 637,000; shipyards launched 219,673 GRT in 1996. In 1994, 107,595 ships entered Spanish ports; 7·08m. passengers disembarked and 7·24m. embarked; total cargo discharged and loaded, 248m. tonnes.

Telecommunications. There were 11,693 post offices in 1993. Receipts (1994) totalled 137,626m. pesetas; expenses, 201,581m. pesetas.

In 1997 Telefonica was operating some 16m. lines; there were 411,930 mobile telephones in use in 1994. The government disposed of its remaining 21% stake in Telefonica in Feb. 1997, bringing 1·4m. shareholders into the company's equity base. A second operator, Rétévision, is expected to account for 10% of the domestic market, which is scheduled to be wholly deregulated by the end of 1998. The cellular phone business was deregulated in 1995; the market is shared by Telefonica and Airtel.

Radio Nacional de España broadcasts 5 programmes on medium-waves and FM, as well as many regional programmes; it has one commercial programme. The most successful domestic network is that of an independent, Cadena SER (*Sociedad Española de Radiodifusión*); *Cadena de Ondas Populares Españolas* (COPE) is owned by the Roman Catholic church. Two independent radio networks cover the whole of Spain. They are *Antena 3* and *Radio 80* (taken over by SER in 1992). *Radio Exterior* broadcasts abroad, and *Antena 3* has been broadcasting to 400,000 subscribers in Miami since Sept. 1997.

Televisión Española broadcasts 2 channels (TVE1 and TVE2) and has an international channel also. There are 3 nationwide commercial TV networks: *Antena 3, Tele 5* and the pay-TV channel *Canal Plus*, which had 1·4m. subscribers in 1997. There were in 1994 the following regional TV networks: *TV3* (1983) and *Canal 33* (1989), both broadcasting in Catalan; *ETB1* (1983) and *ETB2* (1987), both Basque, the first one broadcasting in Basque; *Televisión de Galicia* (1985), in Galician; *TM3* (1989), in Castilian, for the area of Madrid; *Canal 9* (1989), mostly in Valencian (Catalan); and *Tele-Sur* (1989), in Castilian, for Andalusia. There are 2 digital TV channels, Vía Digital and Canal Satelite Digital, both launched in 1997. Colour transmissions are carried by PAL.

Number of receivers: radios, 12m. (1992); TV sets, 42·7 per 100 population (1994).

Cinemas. There were (1996) 1,934 cinemas with an audience of 47·17m. In Nov. 1997 the Madrid School of Cinema was established. It has an annual budget of 225m. pesetas from the Community of Madrid, and is backed by the Spanish Academy and Ministry of Education and Culture.

Press. In 1996 there were about 90 daily newspapers with a total daily circulation of 3·93m. copies (valued at 262·3m. pesetas). 8 publishing groups controlled around 80% of the daily press, with another 100 or so independents accounting for the other 20%. Prisa, the biggest conglomerate, had a daily readership of 541,691 in 1996 (13·7% of the sector). The main titles are: *El Pais, ABC, El Mundo* and *Marca*.

In 1995, 51,934 book titles were published, including some 7,000 translations. 41,301 titles were in Castilian, 5,793 in Catalan, 968 in Basque and 1,148 in Galician.

Internet. In 1997 it was estimated that 2·5% of the population was on-line, compared with around 10% in France and Germany.

SOCIAL INSTITUTIONS

Justice. Justice is administered by Tribunals and Courts, which jointly form the Judicial Power. Judges and magistrates cannot be removed, suspended or transferred except as set forth by law. The Constitution of 1978 established the *General Council of the Judicial Power*, consisting of a President and 20 magistrates, judges, attorneys and lawyers, governing the Judicial Power in full independence from the state's legislative and executive organs. Its members are appointed by the *Cortes Generales*. Its President is that of the Supreme Court (*Tribunal Supremo*), who is appointed by the monarch on the proposal of the General Council of the Judicial.

The Judicature is composed of the Supreme Court; 17 Higher Courts of Justice, 1 for each autonomous community; 52 Provincial High Courts; Courts of First Instance; Courts of Judicial Proceedings, not passing sentences; and Penal Courts, passing sentences.

The Supreme Court consists of a President, and various judges distributed among 7 chambers: 1 for civil matters, 3 for administrative purposes, 1 for criminal trials, 1 for social matters and 1 for military cases. The Supreme Court has disciplinary faculties; is court of appeal in all criminal trials; for administrative purposes decides in first and second instance disputes arising between private individuals and the State; and in social matters makes final decisions.

A new penal code came into force in May 1996, replacing the code of 1848. It provides for a maximum of 30 years imprisonment in specified exceptional cases, with a normal maximum of 20 years. Sanctions with a rehabilitative intent include fines adjusted to means, community service and week-end imprisonment. The death penalty was abolished by the 1978 Constitution. The prison population in 1996 was 43,033 (39,051 men, 3,982 women); 901,696 criminal offences were reported in 1994.

A juvenile criminal law of 1995 lays emphasis on rehabilitation. It raised the age of responsibility from 12 to 14 years. Criminal conduct on the part of children under 14 is a matter for legal protection and custody. 14- and 15-year-olds are classified as 'minors'; 16- and 17-year-olds as 'young persons'; and the legal majority for criminal offences is set at 18 years. Persons up to the age of 21 may, at the courts' discretion, be dealt with as juveniles.

A jury system commenced operating in Nov. 1995 in criminal cases (first trials in May 1996). Juries consist of 9 members. In Sept. 1997 at the opening ceremony of the Judicial Year, presided over by the king, the President of the General Council of the Judicial Power called for a general agreement from Parliament and the government on legal reform for solving the problems in the administration of justice, namely its slowness and esoteric nature.

The *Audiencia Nacional* deals with terrorism, monetary offences and drug-trafficking where more than 1 province is involved. Its president is appointed by the General Council of the Judicial Power.

There is an Ombudsman (*Defensor del Pueblo*), who in 1994 received 18,594 complaints.

Religion. There is no official religion. Roman Catholicism is the religion of the majority. There are 11 metropolitan sees and 52 suffragan sees, the chief being Toledo, where the Primate resides. The archdioceses of Madrid-Alcalá and Barcelona depend directly from the Vatican. There are about 0·25m. other Christians, including several Protestant denominations, Jehovah's Witnesseses (about 60,000) and Mormons, and 0·45m. Moslems, including Spanish Moslems in Morocco. The first synagogue since the expulsion of the Jews in 1492 was opened in Madrid on 2 Oct. 1959. The number of people of Judaist faith is estimated at about 15,000.

Education. In 1991 the General Regulation of the Educational System Act came into force. This Act gradually extends the school-leaving age to 16 years and determines the following levels of education: Infants (3–5 years of age), primary (6–11), secondary (12–15) and baccalaureate or vocational and technical (16–17). Primary and secondary levels of education are now compulsory and free. Religious instruction is optional.

In Sept. 1997 a joint declaration with trade unions, parents' and schools' associations was signed in support of a new finance law guaranteeing that spending on education will reach 6% of GDP within 5 years, thus protecting it from changes in the political sphere.

A new compulsory secondary education programme has replaced the Basic General Education programme which was in force since 1970. In addition, university entrance exams underwent reform in 1997, resulting in greater emphasis now being placed on the teaching of Humanities at secondary level.

In 1997–98 pre-primary education (under 6 years) was undertaken by 2,522 schools, with 1,123,003 pupils; primary or basic education (6 to 14 years): 13,037 schools, with 2,607,602 pupils. There were 215,584 teachers in pre-primary and primary schools. Secondary education (14–17 years), including high schools and technical schools, was conducted at 5,449 schools, with 3,492,726 pupils and 150,220 teachers.

In 1997–98 there were 60 universities: 40 public state universities, 3 polytechnic universities, 13 private universities (including 3 Catholic), and 4 Open universities. In 1997–98 there were 1,571,300 students at state universities; 64,423 at private universities.

Health. In 1995 there were 162,089 doctors (3·8 per 1,000 inhabitants), 13,242 dentists, 40,323 pharmacists and 167,957 nurses (including 6,105 midwives). Number of hospitals (1992), 801, with 161,537 beds.

Welfare. The social security budget was 12,134,637m. pesetas in 1997. The budget for 1998 was: for pensions, 8,356,100m. pesetas; health, 3,822,000m.; social benefits and incapacity, 1,554,000m.; unemployment, 1,495,400m. The minimum monthly pension in 1996 was 53,435 pesetas.

In 1997 the system of contributions to the social security and employment scheme was: For pensions, sickness, invalidity, maternity and children, a contribution of 28·3% of the basic wage (23·6% paid by the employer, 4·7% by the employee); for unemployment benefit, a contribution of 7·8% (6·2% paid by the employer, 1·6% by the employee). There are also minor contributions for a Fund of Guaranteed Salaries, working accidents and professional sicknesses, and for vocational training.

DIPLOMATIC REPRESENTATIVES

Of Spain in Great Britain (24 Belgrave Sq., London SW1X 8QA)
Ambassador: Alberto Aza Arias.

Of Great Britain in Spain (Calle de Fernando el Santo, 16, 28010 Madrid)
Ambassador: A. D. Brighty, CMG, CVO.

Of Spain in the USA (2700 15th St., NW, Washington, D.C., 20009)
Ambassador: Antonio Oyarzabal.

Of the USA in Spain (Serrano 75, 28006 Madrid)
Acting Ambassador: Lawrence Rossin.

Of Spain to the United Nations
Ambassador: Inocencio F. Arias.

Of Spain to NATO
Ambassador: Javier Conde de Saro.

Further Reading

Conversi, D., *The Basques, The Catalans and Spain.* Hurst, 1997
Donaghy, P. J. and Newton, M. T., *Spain: a Guide to Political and Economic Institutions.* CUP, 1987
Heywood, P., *The Government and Politics of Spain.* London, 1995
Hooper, J., *The New Spaniards.* 2nd ed. [of *The Spaniards*] London, 1995
Péréz-Díaz, V. M., *The Return of Civil Society: the Emergence of Democratic Spain.* Harvard Univ. Press, 1993
Powell, C., *Juan Carlos of Spain: Self-Made Monarch.* London and New York, 1996
Preston, P., *The Triumph of Democracy in Spain.* London and New York, 1986
Shields, G. J., *Spain.* [Bibliography] 2nd ed. Oxford and Santa Barbara (CA), 1994
Shubert, A., *A Social History of Modern Spain.* London, 1990

National library: Biblioteca Nacional, Madrid.
National statistical office: Instituto Nacional de Estadística (INE), Paseo de la Castellana, 183, Madrid.
Website: http://www.ine.es.

SRI LANKA

Sri Lanka Prajathanthrika
Samajavadi Janarajaya

(Democratic Socialist
Republic of Sri Lanka)

Capital: Colombo
Population: 18·7m.
GDP per head: (PPP$) 3,277
GNP: US$11·6bn.
HDI/world rank: 0·711/91

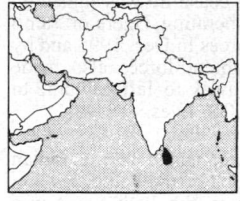

KEY HISTORICAL EVENTS. In the 18th century the central kingdom, Kandy, was the only surviving independent state on the island of Ceylon. The Dutch, who had obtained their first coastal possessions in 1636, had driven out the preceding Portuguese interests and become the dominant power in most of the island. The Dutch attacked Kandy but were unable to hold it. The interior terrain was mountainous and thickly forested and the king of Kandy's forces were well-trained to make use of it as guerrillas.

The king attracted British attention by asking for help against the Dutch. In 1796 the British East India Company sent a naval force to Ceylon (as the British then called it). The Dutch surrendered their possessions, which left the British in control of the maritime areas surrounding Kandy. These areas were at first attached to the Madras Presidency of India, whence the naval force had come, but in 1802 they were constituted a separate colony under the Crown.

Once the British began to develop their new territory they came to see Kandy as a threat. An attack in 1803 failed, but by 1815 the chiefs of Kandy were discontented with their king who was of alien (south Indian) stock and a despot. The chiefs approached the British, who invaded Kandy with their help. The king was deposed and the British crown succeeded him as sovereign.

The Kandyan Convention of 1815 annexed Kandy to British Ceylon while recognizing most of the traditional rights of the chiefs. However, in 1817, dissatisfied with the terms, the chiefs rebelled. The rebellion was suppressed and the rights established by the Convention were abolished.

Ceylon was then united for the first time since the 12th century. The British (like the preceding Dutch and Portuguese) built up a plantation economy. Coffee was dominant until an outbreak of *Hoemilia vastatrix* fungus destroyed the plants in 1870. Spices, cocoa and rice all followed but tea became the main cash crop after successful experiments in the 1880s.

Foreign rule served to subdue the traditional hostility between northern Tamils and southern Sinhalese, providing as it did a new frame of reference to an alien culture. The Ceylon National Congress, formed in 1919, contained both Sinhalese and Ceylon Tamil groups. (The Indian Tamils brought in as a labour force for the tea estates were a separate community.) Tamil national feeling, however, was expressed over the issue of the use of Tamil languages in schools.

On 4 Feb. 1948 the Ceylon Independence Act took effect, and Ceylon became a Dominion of the Commonwealth. UK defence forces were to be allowed to remain as mutually agreeable, although it was later decided that all UK bases should be transferred or withdrawn by 1962.

In 1956 Solomon Bandaranaike became prime minister at the head of the People's United Front, advocating neutral foreign policy and the promotion of Sinhalese national culture at home. In Sept. 1959 he was murdered; his widow Sirimavo Bandaranaike succeeded him in July 1960 at the head of an increasingly socialist government. Agreements were made with India (in 1964 and 1974) for the repatriation of Indian nationals. In May 1972 Ceylon became a republic and adopted the name Sri Lanka.

In July 1977 Mrs Bandaranaike's government fell, mainly because of economic failures and the repression of non-Sinhalese elements. The United National Party (dominant until 1956) returned to power and in 1978 a new constitution provided a presidential system with the United National Party leader Junius Jayawardene as the first executive president. Economic problems were approached through large-scale investment of foreign capital.

The problem of communal unrest remained unsolved and Tamil separatists were active. In 1983 the Tamil United Liberation Front members of parliament were asked to renounce their objective for a separate Tamil state. They refused and withdrew from parliament. Militant Tamils then began armed action which developed into civil war.

A state of emergency ended on 11 Jan. 1989, but violence continued. President Ranasinghe Premadasa was assassinated on 1 May 1993. A ceasefire was signed on 3 Jan. 1995, but fighting broke out again in April. The 'Liberation Tigers of Tamil Eelam' stronghold of Jaffna was captured by government forces in Dec. 1995 and by mid-1997 was firmly under government control. Government forces also made progress in opening a supply route along the northern highway to Jaffna, home to 0·5m. Tamils. The 14-year ethnic war has claimed up to 50,000 lives.

TERRITORY AND POPULATION. Sri Lanka is an island in the Indian Ocean, south of the Indian peninsula from which it is separated by the Palk Strait. On 28 June 1974 the frontier between India and Sri Lanka in the Palk Strait was redefined, giving to Sri Lanka the island of Kachchativu.

Area (in sq. km.), and census population on 17 March 1981:

Provinces	Area	Population	Provinces	Area	Population
Western	3,708·61	3,919,807	North-Central	10,723·59	849,492
Central	5,583·50	2,009,248	Uva	8,487·91	914,522
Southern	5,559·15	1,882,661	Sabaragamuwa	4,901·55	1,482,031
Northern	8,882·11	1,109,404			
Eastern	9,951·26	975,251	Total	65,609·86	14,846,750
North-Western	7,812·18	1,704,334			

Population (in 1,000) according to ethnic group and nationality at the 1981 census: 10,980 Sinhalese, 1,887 Sri Lanka Tamils, 1,047 Sri Lanka Moors, 39 Burghers, 47 Malays, 819 Indian Tamils, 28 others. Non-nationals of Sri Lanka totalled 635,150. Population, 1997 (estimate), 18,721,178 (9,437,515 females); density, 285 per sq. km. Ethnic mix, 74% Sinhalese, 18% Tamil. By 1997, approximately 0·3m. Tamils had left the country since the mid-1980s, one-third as refugees to India and two-thirds to seek political asylum in the West.

Vital statistics, 1997: Birth rate (per 1,000 population), 18·6; death rate, 5·9; infant mortality rate (per 1,000 live births), 16·5; life expectancy, 72·4 years.

The urban population was 21·5% of the total in 1981. The principal towns and their population according to the census of 1981 are: Colombo (the capital), 587,647; Dehiwela-Mt. Lavinia, 173,529; Moratuwa, 134,826; Jaffna, 118,224; Kotte, 101,039; Kandy, 97,872; Galle, 76,863; Negombo, 60,762; Trincomalee, 44,313; Batticaloa, 42,963; Matara, 38,843; Ratnapura, 37,497; Anuradhapura, 35,981; Badulla, 33,068; Kalutara, 31,503. Population of the Greater Colombo area, 1980, about 1m.

Sinhala and Tamil are the official languages; English is in use.

CLIMATE. Sri Lanka, which has an equatorial climate, is affected by the North-east Monsoon (Dec. to Feb.), the South-west Monsoon (May to July) and 2 inter-monsoons (March to April and Aug. to Nov.). Rainfall is heaviest in the south-west highlands while the north-west and south-east are relatively dry. Colombo. Jan. 79·9°F (26·6°C), July 81·7°F (27·6°C). Annual rainfall 95·4" (2,424 mm). Trincomalee. Jan. 78·8°F (26°C), July 86·2°F (30·1°C). Annual rainfall 62·2" (1,580 mm). Kandy. Jan. 73·9°F (23·3°C), July 76·1°F (24·5°C). Annual rainfall 72·4" (1,840 mm). Nuwara Eliya. Jan. 58·5°F (14·7°C), July 60·3°F (15·7°C). Annual rainfall 75" (1,905 mm).

CONSTITUTION AND GOVERNMENT. A new constitution for the Democratic Socialist Republic of Sri Lanka was promulgated in Sept. 1978. An amended constitution allowing for more devolved powers to the regions was under consideration in 1998.

The Executive *President* is directly elected for a 6-year term renewable once.
Parliament consists of one chamber, composed of 225 members (196 elected and 29 from the National List). Election is by proportional representation by universal suffrage at 18 years. The term of Parliament is 6 years. The Prime Minister and other Ministers, who must be members of Parliament, are appointed by the President.

Presidential elections were held on 9 Nov. 1994. The incumbent Prime Minister, Chandrika Kumaratunga, was elected against 1 opponent by 62·28% of votes cast.

Parliamentary elections were held on 16 Aug. 1994. 1,449 candidates in 13 parties and 26 independent groups stood for office. The People's Alliance (a coalition of 9 parties) gained 105 seats, the United National Party 94, the Tamil party (EPDP) 9, the Sri Lanka Moslem Congress 7, the Tamil United Liberation Front 5 and the Democratic People's Liberation Front 3.

In March 1998 the government comprised:

President, Minister of Finance and of Defence: Chandrika Kumaratunga (b. 1945; Sri Lanka Freedom Party; sworn in 12 Nov. 1994).

Prime Minister: Sirimavo Bandaranaike (b. 1916).

Agriculture and Lands: D. M. Jayaratna. *Buddha Sasana and Cultural and Religious Affairs:* Lakshman Jayakody. *Co-operative Development:* D. P. Wickremasinghe. *Education and Higher Education:* Richard Pathirana. *Ethnic Affairs, Justice and Constitutional Affairs and National Integration:* Gamini L. Peiris. *Fisheries and Aquatic Resources Development:* Mahinda Rajapakse. *Foreign Affairs:* Lakshman Kadirgamar. *Health and Indigenous Medicine:* Nimal Siripala de Silva. *Housing and Urban Development:* Indika Gunawardena. *Industrial Development:* Clement V. Gooneratne. *Internal and External Commerce and Food:* Kingsley Wickramaratne. *Irrigation and Power:* Gen. Anuruddha Ratwatte. *Labour:* John Seneviratne. *Livestock Development and Estate Infrastructure:* Sauvmiamoothy Thondaman. *Plantation Industries and Public Administration and Home Affairs:* Ratnasiri Wickramanayake. *Posts and Telecommunications and Media:* Mangala Samaraweera. *Rehabilitation (Eastern Province) and Shipping Ports:* Mohamed H. M. Ashraff. *Science and Technology:* Bernard Soysa. *Tourism and Civil Aviation:* Dharmasiri Senanayake. *Transport and Highways:* A. H. M. Fowzie. *Youth Affairs and Sports:* D. S. Dissanayaka.

National anthem: 'Sri Lanka Matha, Apa Sri Lanka' ('Mother Sri Lanka, thee Sri Lanka'); words and tune by A. Samarakone. There is a Tamil version, 'Sri Lanka thaaya, nam Sri Lanka'; words anonymous.

Local Government. Sri Lanka is divided into 25 districts, administered by government agents. There are 12 municipal councils, 39 urban councils and 257 pradeshiya sabas. There are 9 provincial councils, consisting of a governor, appointed by the President, a Chief Minister, a Board of Ministers and members elected for 5-year terms. Elections were held on 23 March 1997 for 238 local authorities. Some 18,000 candidates representing 12 parties stood.

DEFENCE

Army. The Army consists of 3 divisional and 4 task force headquarters, 1 independent special forces', 23 infantry, 1 mechanized infantry and 1 air mobile brigade and 3 armoured reconnaissance, 4 field artillery and 1 armoured regiment. Equipment includes 25 T-54/-55 main battle tanks. Strength (1997), 95,000. Paramilitary forces consist of the Ministry of Defence Police (80,000, including 1,000 women and a 3,000-strong anti-guerrilla force), the Home Guard (15,200) and the National Guard (some 15,000).

Navy. The naval force comprises 1 locally-built coastal patrol craft, 38 inshore patrol craft of varying types as well as about 30 small fast patrol boats and service craft. There are 2 mechanized landing craft of 270 tonnes full load. The main naval base is at Trincomalee. Personnel in 1997 numbered 12,000, with a reserve of about 1,100.

Air Force. Air Force bases are at Anuradhapura, Katunayake, Ratmalana, Vavuniya and China Bay, Trincomalee. Equipment of 10 squadrons and wings comprises

4 F-7 and 8 Kfir fighters, 10 SF.260 and 2 Cessna 150 trainers, 1 Pucara light strike aircraft, 2 HS748, 8 Chinese-built Y-12s, 5 An-32, 1 Chinese-built Y-8 (An-12), 1 Super King Air, 5 Cessna Skymasters, 1 Cessna 421 and 12 Bell 212, 4 Bell 412, 10 Mi-17, 3 Mi-24 and 6 JetRanger helicopters for internal security operations. Total strength (1997) about 10,000 with 42 combat aircraft and 26 armed helicopters.

INTERNATIONAL RELATIONS

Membership. Sri Lanka is a member of the UN, the Commonwealth, and the Colombo Plan.

ECONOMY

Policy. The 1993–97 plan aimed at a 6·4% annual growth rate. Investment allocated was mainly for completion of projects in priority areas such as power, irrigation, road rehabilitation, water supply and telecommunications. Total public investment was about Rs 325,000m. GDP growth in 1997 was estimated at 5·6%. Forecast for 1998, 5·4%.

Budget. Revenue and expenditure of central government in Rs 1m. for financial years ending 31 Dec.:

| | | Expenditure | | |
Year	Revenue	Current	Capital	Total
1992	85,870	89,638	24,948	114,586
1993	98,495	100,951	33,777	134,728
1994	110,038	127,085	30,391	157,476
1995	136,257	154,159	41,721	195,880
1996[1]	146,279	170,629	40,034	210,663

[1] Estimate.

The principal sources of revenue in 1992 were (in Rs 1m.): General sales and tax, 24,379; import levies, 21,391; export duties, 594; selective sales taxes, 14,550; property transfer taxes, 2,672; taxes on personal and corporate income, 11,561.

The principal items of recurrent expenditure in 1993 (in Rs 1m.): Finance, 32,365; defence, 15,441; public administration, 19,358; education, 5,994; agriculture, 564; health, 3,080. Capital expenditure on finance, 29,606; Mahaweli development, 5,219; power and energy, 5,955; transport and highways, 6,624.

Currency. The unit of currency is the *Sri Lankan rupee* (LKR) of 100 *cents*. There are coins of 1, 2, 5, 10, 25 and 50 cents and Rs 1, 2 and 5, and notes of Rs 5, 10, 20, 50, 100, 500 and 1,000. The total circulation was Rs 43,081m. on 31 Dec. 1994. Inflation was 10% in 1997.

Banking and Finance. The Central Bank of Sri Lanka is the bank of issue (*Governor* A. S. Jawardena). Two state-owned commercial banks, the Bank of Ceylon and the People's Bank, account for about 70% of bank lending. There are also 21 private banks (17 foreign). Total assets of commercial banks at 31 Dec. 1994, Rs 286,933m.

Sri Lanka National Savings Bank at 31 Dec. 1994 had a balance to depositors' credit of Rs 53,278·1m. There are 5 main long-term credit institutions.

There is a stock exchange in Colombo.

Weights and Measures. The metric system has been established.

ENERGY AND NATURAL RESOURCES

Electricity. Installed capacity (1994), 1,409,000 kW. Energy produced, 4,364m. kWh; the main source was hydro-electric (2,900m. kWh).

Water. The Mahaweli Ganga scheme irrigates 90,113 ha of new land and (1992) 100,653 ha of land already cultivated.

Minerals. Gems are among the chief minerals mined and exported. Graphite is also important; production in 1994 was 5,000 tonnes. Production of ilmenite, 1994, 60,400 tonnes. Some rutile is also produced (2,741 tonnes in 1992). Salt extraction is the oldest industry. The method is solar evaporation of sea-water. Production, 1992, 115,665 tonnes.

Agriculture. Agriculture accounted for 21% of GDP in 1994. About 2·5m. ha are under cultivation. Agriculture engages 47·5% of the labour force. Main crops in 1994: Paddy (2,684,000 tonnes from 929,621 ha), rubber (104,200 tonnes in 1993), tea (231,871 tonnes in 1993) and coconuts (2,628m. nuts). Tea plantations are being returned to the private sector after nationalization in 1975.

Livestock in 1994 (estimate): 1,705,800 cattle, 798,400 buffaloes, 93,800 swine, 589,600 goats, 20,200 sheep, 8,851,800 poultry (1992).

Agricultural output grew by 4% in 1997.

Forestry. In 1995, 94m. cu. metres of roundwood were cut.

Fisheries. Production of coastal, off-shore and deep-sea fisheries in 1995 was 235,829 tonnes. In 1992 there were 27,435 fishing craft, of which 15,637 were not motorized.

INDUSTRY. The main industries are the processing of rubber, tea, coconuts and other agricultural commodities, tobacco, textiles, clothing and leather goods, chemicals, plastics, cement, and petroleum refining. Industrial production grew by 7% in 1997.

Labour. In 1994 the labour force was 6·2m.: Agriculture 42%, services 40% and industry 18%.

Trade Unions. In 1994 there were 1,304 registered trade unions.

FOREIGN ECONOMIC RELATIONS. Foreign debt in 1997 was 54·4% of GDP. Foreign exchange reserves were US$2,100m.

Commerce. The values of total imports and exports (imports excluding bullion, specie and postal articles; exports, including re-exports and ship's stores) for calendar years (in Rs 1,000):

	1990	1991	1992	1993	1994
Imports	105,559,159	127,830,821	149,780,179	181,484,194	221,567,615
Exports	76,623,713	82,224,847	107,508,538	137,286,485	157,790,557

In 1997, total imports were US$5,748m. and exports US$4,522m. Principal exports in 1994 (in Rs 1m.): Tea, 20,964; rubber, 3,582; copra, coconut oil and desiccated coconut, 2,696; textiles and garments (1992), 52,588; precious stones, 12,159.

In 1996 the main export markets were the USA (34·1%), the UK (9·5%), Japan (6·2%), Germany (5·8%) and Belgium-Luxembourg (5·3%). The main import suppliers were India (11·2%), Japan (9·9%), Hong Kong (7%), South Korea (7%) and Singapore (7%).

Tourism. 407,511 tourists visited the country in 1994.

COMMUNICATIONS

Roads. There were (1994) 25,952 km of motorable roads, of which 11,077 km were blacktopped, first-class nationally-maintained roads. Number of motor vehicles, 31 Dec. 1995, 1,218,800, comprising 022m. passenger cars, 53,900 buses and coaches, 195,000 lorries and vans, 93,900 tractors and 656,000 motor cycles and mopeds.

Railways. In 1995 there were 1,459 km of railway (1,676 mm gauge). In 1995, 88m. passengers and 1·3m. tonnes of freight were carried.

Civil Aviation. There is an international airport at Colombo (Katunayake). The national carrier is Air Lanka, which operated 2 A320-200s, 3A340-300s and 3 other aircraft in 1995, and flew to 30 destinations in 20 countries. Services are also provided by Aeroflot, Air Maldives, AOM, Balkan, British Airways, Cathay Pacific, Condor, Emirates, Gulf Air, Indian Airlines, KLM, Kuwait Airways, LTU, Malaysia Airlines, Middle East Airlines, Northwest Airlines, Oman Air, Pakistan Airlines, Qatar Airways, Royal Jordanian, Saudia, Singapore Airlines and Thai Airways. In 1994, 1,067,000 passengers were carried on scheduled services.

Shipping. In 1996, the merchant marine comprised 26 ships (1,000 GRT or over) totalling 220,660 GRT, including 2 oil tankers. Colombo is a modern container port; Trincomalee and Galle are natural harbours. In 1994, 3,568 merchant vessels totalling 55m. GRT entered the ports: 9,588,000 tonnes of goods were unloaded and 5,892,000 tonnes loaded.

Telecommunications. In 1994 there were 557 post offices, 3,375 sub-post offices and 173 agency post offices. In 1989 there were 1,583 telex lines and in 1994, 181,000 telephones. Direct dialling was available to 85 countries in 1992. Broadcasting is provided by the Sri Lanka Broadcasting Corporation. In 1995 there were 3·7m. radio and 915,000 TV sets (colour by PAL).

Cinemas. In 1995 there were 259 cinemas and 27·2m. admissions.

Press. In 1995 there were 9 daily newspapers with a combined circulation of 0·45m. and 43 weekly newspapers, in Sinhalese, Tamil and English.

SOCIAL INSTITUTIONS

Justice. The systems of law which obtain are Roman-Dutch, English, Tesawalamai, Islamic and Kandyan.

Kandyan law applies in matters relating to inheritance, matrimonial rights and donations; Tesawalamai law applies in Jaffna as above and in sales of land. Islamic law is applied to all Moslems in respect of succession, donations, marriage, divorce and maintenance. These customary and religious laws have been modified by local enactments.

The courts of original jurisdiction are the High Court, Provincial Courts, District Courts, Magistrates' Courts and Primary Courts. District Courts have unlimited civil jurisdiction. The Magistrates' Courts exercise criminal jurisdiction. The Primary Courts exercise civil jurisdiction in petty disputes and criminal jurisdiction in respect of certain offences.

The Constitution of 1978 provided for the establishment of two superior courts, the Supreme Court and the Court of Appeal.

The Supreme Court is the highest and final superior court of record and exercises jurisdiction in respect of constitutional matters, jurisdiction for the protection of fundamental rights, final appellate jurisdiction in election petitions and jurisdiction in respect of any breach of the privileges of Parliament. The Court of Appeal has appellate jurisdiction to correct all errors in fact or law committed by any court, tribunal or institution.

Police. The strength of the police service in 1994 was 30,236.

Religion. In 1994 the population was 73% Buddhist, 15% Hinduist, 7% Moslem and 5% Christian.

Education. Education is free and is compulsory from age 5 to 14 years. Literacy rate, 1995, 90·2% (male, 90·4%; female, 86·2%).

In 1995 there were 9,657 primary schools with 70,537 teachers for 1·9m. pupils. There were 2·3m. secondary pupils with 103,572 teachers and 63,660 students in higher education with 2,636 staff.

There are 9 universities, 1 open (distance) university and 1 Buddhist and Pali university.

Health. In 1993 there were 426 hospitals, including 84 maternity homes, and 350 central dispensaries. The hospitals had 48,948 beds. There were 3,713 Department of Health doctors. Total state budget expenditure on health, 1993, Rs 7,160m.

Social Welfare. The activities of the Department of Social Services include: Payment of Public Assistance, monthly allowance, financial assistance to needy tuberculosis, leprosy and cancer patients and their dependants; relief of those affected by widespread distress, such as floods, drought, cyclone; custodial care and welfare services to the elderly and infirm; vocational training, aids and appliances for the physically and mentally handicapped; custodial care, vocational training and rehabilitation for socially handicapped persons; community-based rehabilitation of treated drug addicts; registration of and financial assistance to voluntary organizations which engage in social welfare activities.

The government's Poverty Alleviation ('Janasaviya') Programme targets 0·35m. of the neediest families, who received a monthly Rs 1,458 (in 1992) in return for 20 days' community service. Total budget was Rs 4,900m. in 1992.

DIPLOMATIC REPRESENTATIVES

Of Sri Lanka in Great Britain (13 Hyde Park Gdns., London, W2 2LU)
High Commissioner: Sarath Kusum Wickremesinghe.

Of Great Britain in Sri Lanka (190 Galle Rd., Kollupitiya, Colombo 3)
High Commissioner: David Tatham, CMG.

Of Sri Lanka in the USA (2148 Wyoming Ave., NW, Washington, D.C., 20008)
Ambassador: Warnasena Rasaputram.

Of the USA in Sri Lanka (210 Galle Rd., Kollupitiya, Colombo 3)
Ambassador: A. Peter Burleigh.

Of Sri Lanka to the United Nations
Ambassador: Herman de Silva.

Of Sri Lanka to the European Union
Ambassador: Christopher Casie Chetty.

Further Reading

De Silva, C. R. *Sri Lanka: a History.* Delhi, 1991
Johnson, B. L. C. and Scrivenor, M le M., *Sri Lanka. Land, People and Economy.* London, 1981
Manogaran, C., *Ethnic Conflict and Reconciliation in Sri Lanka.* Univ. Hawaii Press, 1987
Manor, J., *Sri Lanka: In Change and Crisis.* London, 1984
McGowan, W., *Only Man is Vile: the Tragedy of Sri Lanka.* New York, 1992
Moore, M., *The State and Peasant Politics in Sri Lanka.* CUP, 1985
Samaraweera, V., *Sri Lanka.* [Bibliography] Oxford and Santa Barbara, 1987
Schwarz, W., *The Tamils of Sri Lanka.* London, 1983
Tambiah, S. J., *Sri Lanka: Ethnic Fratricide and the Dismantling of Democracy.* London, 1986
Wilson, A. J., *The Break-Up of Sri Lanka: The Sinhalese-Tamil Conflict.* London, 1988

National statistical office: Department of Census and Statistics, POB 563, Colombo 7.

SUDAN

Jamhuryat es-Sudan

(Republic of Sudan)

Capital: Khartoum
Population: 32·6m.
GDP per head: (PPP$) 1,084
HDI/world rank: 0·333/158

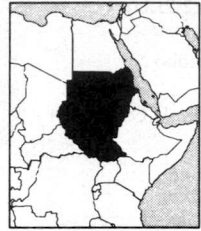

KEY HISTORICAL EVENTS. In 1821 the area that is now Sudan was conquered by the Egyptians. In 1881 Muhammad Ahmad, proclaiming himself the Mahdi, led an uprising and gained control until, in 1899, an Anglo–Egyptian army defeated the Mahdi and established an Anglo–Egyptian condominium.

On 19 Dec. 1955 the Sudanese parliament passed unanimously a declaration that a fully independent state should be established forthwith, and that a Council of State should assume the duties of head of state. The UK and Egypt gave their assent on 31 Dec. 1955 and on 1 Jan. 1956 Sudan was proclaimed a sovereign independent republic.

In 1958 there was a coup that established a military government until the end of 1964 when a civilian government was re-established. On 8 July 1965 the Constituent Assembly elected Ismail al Azhari as President of the Supreme Council, but the government was faced with constant difficulties from the southern provinces which considered themselves dominated by the north. Rebellions began in 1965.

On 23 April 1969 the prime minister, Muhammad Ahmed Mahgoub resigned; and on 25 May the government was taken over by a 10-man Revolutionary Council under Col. Jaafar al Nemery. The Council was dissolved in 1972, and a new constitution was introduced in 1973. Legislative power was placed with a National Assembly, an elected body; and some measure of self-government was granted to the southern provinces. However, discontent in these latter provinces continued, and in addition Nemery met considerable opposition in his attempts to make Sudan a formal Islamic state. On 6 April 1985 he was deposed in a military coup led by Gen. Abel-Rahman Swar al-Dahab, who established a Military Council to which the Cabinet was responsible prior to the promised re-establishment of civilian rule. Elections were held, although they were suspended in parts of the southern provinces, in April 1986.

On 30 June 1989 Brig.-Gen. (later Lieut.-Gen.) Omar Hassan Ahmad al-Bashir overthrew the civilian government in a military coup.

The rebel Sudan People's Liberation Army (SPLA), consisting of non-Moslem southerners, maintains guerrilla activities in the south while the National Democratic Alliance (NDA), northern Moslems opposed to the ruling National Islamic Front, and non-Moslem southerners of the SPLA fight on in the north. Fighting also erupted in Jan. 1997 along the border with Ethiopia. On 9 July 1997 at a meeting attended by representatives of Djibouti, Eritrea, Ethiopia, Kenya and Uganda the Sudanese government accepted a 'Declaration of Principles' as a framework for negotiations to end the civil war, including the separation of state and religion and self-determination for the south of Sudan.

After 14 years Sudan's civil war has killed some 1·3m. people and reduced the south to a level barely above subsistence.

TERRITORY AND POPULATION. Sudan is bounded in the north by Egypt, north-east by the Red Sea, east by Eritrea and Ethiopia, south by Kenya, Uganda and the Democratic Republic of the Congo, west by the Central African Republic and Chad, and north-west by Libya. Its area is 967,500 sq. miles (2,505,813 sq. km). Population (1983 census), 20,564,364; estimate (1997), 32,594,000.

Vital statistics rates, 1997 estimates (per 1,000 population). Births, 40·6; deaths, 11·2. Infant mortality (per 1,000 live births), 74·3. Expectation of life in 1997 was 55·5 years (54·6 for males and 56·5 for females). Growth rate, 3·06% per annum.

In Feb. 1994 the former 9 regions were subdivided to form 26 federal states as follows:

SUDAN 1307

Former region	New states
Khartoum	Khartoum
Bahr al-Ghazal	Western Bahr al-Ghazal; Northern Bahr al-Ghazal; Warab
Central	Gezira; White Nile; Sinnar; Blue Nile
Darfur	Northern Darfur; Southern Darfur; Western Darfur
Eastern	Red Sea; Gedaref; Kassala
Equatoria	Eastern Equatoria; Western Equatoria; Bahr al-Jabal
Kurdufan	Northern Kurdufan; Southern Kurdufan; Western Kurdufan
Northern	Nile; Northern State
Upper Nile	Upper Nile; Unity State; Jonglei; Buheyrat

The chief cities (census, 1983) are the capital, Khartoum (476,218), its suburbs Omdurman (526,287) and Khartoum North (341,146), Port Sudan (206,727), Wadi Medani (141,065), al-Obeid (140,024), Kassala (98,751 in 1973), Atbara (73,009), al-Qadarif (66,465 in 1973), Kosti (65,257 in 1973) and Juba (56,737 in 1973).

The northern and central thirds of the country are populated by Arab and Nubian peoples, while the southern third is inhabited by Nilotic and Bantu peoples; Arabic, the official language, is spoken by 60% of inhabitants.

CLIMATE. Lying wholly within the tropics, the country has a continental climate and only the Red Sea coast experiences maritime influences. Temperatures are generally high throughout the year, with May and June the hottest months. Winters are virtually cloudless and night temperatures are consequently cool. Summer is the rainy season inland, with amounts increasing from north to south, but the northern areas are virtually a desert region. On the Red Sea coast, most rain falls in winter. Khartoum. Jan. 74°F (23·3°C), July 89°F (31·7°C). Annual rainfall 6" (157 mm). Juba. Jan. 83°F (28·3°C), July 78°F (25·6°C). Annual rainfall 39" (968 mm). Port Sudan. Jan. 74°F (23·3°C), July 94°F (34·4°C). Annual rainfall 4" (94 mm). Wadi Halfa. Jan. 60°F (15·6°C), July 90°F (32·2°C). Annual rainfall 0·1" (2·5 mm).

CONSTITUTION AND GOVERNMENT. The constitution was suspended after the 1989 coup and a 12-member Revolutionary Council has ruled. A 300-member Provisional National Assembly was appointed in Feb. 1992 as a transitional legislature pending elections. These were held on 6–17 March 1996. The National assembly now has 400 members, 275 of whom are directly elected by popular vote and 125 indirectly. Presidential elections were also held in March 1996. President al-Bashir was re-elected by 75% of votes cast.

In March 1998 the government comprised:
President and Minister of Defence: Lieut.-Gen. Omar Hassan Ahmad al-Bashir (appointed Oct. 1993, elected March 1996).
First Vice-President: Maj. Gen. Zubir Mohammed Saleh. *Second Vice-President:* George Kongor Arop. *Minister of the Interior:* Brig. Bakri Hassan Salih. *Presidential Affairs:* Brig. Abd al-Rahim Mohammed Hussain. *Federal Relations:* Dr Ali al-Hajj Mohammed. *Cabinet Affairs:* Brig. Salah Eddin Karrar. *Foreign Affairs:* Ali Uthman Mohammed Taha. *Defence:* Gen. Hassan Abdel-Rahman. *Justice and Attorney General:* Abdel-Basit Sabdarat. *Culture and Information:* Brig. al-Tayeb Ibrahim Mohammed Khair. *Agriculture and Forests:* Nafi Ali Nafi. *Irrigation:* Dr Yacoub Abu Shura Musa. *Energy and Mining:* Awad Ahmed al-Jaz. *Industry:* Badr Eddin Suleiman. *Social Planning:* Mohammed Osman Khalifa. *Higher Education and Scientific Research:* Ahmed Omer Ibrahim. *Tourism and Environment:* Mohammed Tahir Eilla. *Commerce:* Osman al-Haj Ibrahim. *Education:* Kabosho Kuku. *Aviation:* Maj. Gen. (rtd) Al Tigania Adam Tahir. *Transport:* Maj. Gen. (rtd) Albino Akol Akol. *Roads and Communications:* Maj. Gen. (rtd) al-Hadj Bushra. *Public Services:* Angelo Beda. *Health:* Ihsan al-Ghabshawi. *Animal Resources:* Musa Mek Kur. *Finance and National Economy:* Dr Abdel-Wahab Osman. *National Assembly Affairs:* Abul Gazim Mohammed Ibrahim. *Survey and Architectural Development:* Col. Gatlouk Deng.

National anthem: 'Nahnu Djundullah' ('We are God's army'); words by A. M. Salih, tune by A. Murjan.

Regional and Local Government. In Feb. 1994 a federal system of 26 states was set up, each under a governor, a deputy governor and a cabinet of ministers. The states are subdivided into 66 provinces and 218 districts.

DEFENCE. There is conscription for 3 years.

Army. The Army is organized in 1 armoured, 1 engineer, 1 airborne and 6 infantry divisions, 1 mechanized infantry, 24 infantry, 10 artillery, 1 reconnaissance and 12 air defence artillery brigades and 3 artillery regiments. Equipment includes 250 T-54/T-55, 20 M-60A3 and 10 Ch Type-59 main battle tanks. Strength (1997) 75,000 (20,000 conscripts). There is a paramilitary People's Defence Force of about 15,000.

Navy. The Navy operates in the Red Sea and also on the River Nile. It comprises 2 inshore patrol craft, 4 riverine patrol craft, 7 ex-Yugoslav landing craft and some armed boats. The flotilla suffers from lack of maintenance and spares. Personnel in 1997 were believed to number 1,700.

Air Force. 2 combat squadrons are equipped with 12 F-7 (Chinese-built MiG-21s) fighters, 8 F-6 (Chinese-built MiG-19) fighter-bombers. There is 1 transport squadron with 3 C-130H Hercules, 6 Aviocars, 2 Y-8 and 2 DHC-5D Buffalo turbo-prop transports; 2 helicopter squadrons have 6 AB.212s, 9 Romanian-built Pumas, 5 Mi-8s; there are 3 F-7B conversion trainers. Personnel totalled (1996) about 3,000, with 20 combat aircraft. Effectiveness is reduced by economic problems and insurgency.

INTERNATIONAL RELATIONS

Membership. Sudan is a member of the UN, OAU, the Arab League and is an ACP state of the EU.

ECONOMY

Policy. Subsidies on consumer staples including sugar and fuel were abolished in Oct. 1991.

Performance. Real GDP growth was 4·7% in 1996.

Budget. In 1995 revenues were estimated to be US$382m. and expenditures US$1,006m. including capital expenditures of US$91m.

Currency. The monetary unit was the *Sudanese pound* (SDP) of 100 *piastres* and 1,000 *milliemes*. This was replaced in May 1992 by the *dinar* at a rate of 1 dinar = £S10. There are notes of 5, 10, 25 and 50 dinars. Sudanese pounds remain legal tender. Inflation was 118% in March 1997 (150% in 1996). Foreign exchange reserves were US$163·3m. at the end of 1995.

Banking and Finance. The Bank of Sudan opened in Feb. 1960 with an authorized capital of £S1·5m. as the central bank and bank of issue. Banks were nationalized in 1970 but in 1974 foreign banks were allowed to open branches. The application of Islamic law from 1 Jan. 1991 put an end to the charging of interest in official banking transactions, and 7 banks are run on Islamic principles. Mergers of 7 local banks in 1993 resulted in the formation of the Khartoum Bank, the Industrial Development Bank and the Savings Bank. In 1994 there were 27 commercial and private banks.

A stock exchange opened in 1995.

Weights and Measures. The metric system is in use.

ENERGY AND NATURAL RESOURCES

Electricity. Installed capacity was 500 MW in 1991. Production (1994) 1,300m. kWh.

Oil. Main production figures for 1994 were: Distillate fuel oils, 327,000 tonnes; residual fuel oils, 316,000 tonnes; motor spirit (petrol), 95,000 tonnes; jet fuels, 90,000 tonnes.

Minerals. Mineral deposits include graphite, sulphur, chromium, iron, manganese, copper, zinc, fluorspar, natron, gypsum and anhydrite, magnesite, asbestos, talc, halite, kaolin, white mica, coal, diatomite (kieselguhr), limestone and dolomite, pumice, lead, wollastonite, black sands and vermiculite pyrites. Chromite and gold are mined.

Agriculture. 80% of the population depends on agriculture. Land tenure is based on customary rights; land is ultimately owned by the government.

Production (1995 estimates) in 1,000 tonnes: Sugar-cane, 4,800; sorghum, 2,600; millet, 650; groundnuts, 630; wheat, 520; seed cotton, 400; cottonseed, 260; sesame seed, 195; tomatoes, 165.

One of the largest sugar complexes in the world was opened at Kenana in March 1981. It is capable of processing 330,000 tonnes a year. Production in 1992 was 513,000 tonnes.

Livestock (1995 estimates): Cattle, 22m.; sheep, 23m.; goats, 16·5m.; poultry, 37m.

Forestry. In 1994, 2·4m. cu. metres of roundwood were cut.

Fisheries. In 1994 the total catch was 45,000 tonnes.

INDUSTRY. About 17% of GDP came from industry in 1992, and 9% specifically from manufacturing.

Labour. The total workforce in 1996 was estimated to be 11m. Also in 1996 there was a monthly minimum wage of 15,000 dinars.

FOREIGN ECONOMIC RELATIONS. Foreign debt was US$20,000m. in March 1997.

Commerce. Imports and exports in 1996 (1995 in brackets) totalled respectively an estimated US$1,344m. (US$1,219m.) and US$600m. (US$556m.).

The main exports are cotton, sesame, gum arabic, sorghum, livestock, gold and sugar. Main imports are petroleum products, machinery and equipment, foodstuffs, manufactured goods, medicines and chemicals. Principal trading partners are Egypt, Saudi Arabia, the European Union, Japan and the USA.

Tourism. There were an estimated 18,000 visitors in 1993.

COMMUNICATIONS

Roads. In 1995 there were 11,610 km of roads, of which 4,203 km were paved, and 45,000 km of tracks. There were an estimated 211,000 cars and 26,000 commercial vehicles in 1993.

Railways. The total length of the railways is 5,516 km, of which 4,800 km is of 1,067 mm gauge and 716 km of 1,610 mm gauge. In 1994 the railways carried 0·6m. passengers and 1·9m. tonnes of freight.

Civil Aviation. There is an international airport at Khartoum. Sudan Airways, the government-owned national carrier operating domestic and international services, had 1 A300B4-600, 2 A310-300s, 1 A320-200, 3 B-707-320Cs, 2 B-737-200C Advs and 5 other aircraft in 1995.

Shipping. Supplementing the railways are regular river steamer services of the Sudan Railways. Port Sudan is the major seaport; another port at Suakin was opened in 1991. Traffic on the River Nile has ceased owing to the civil war. Sea-going shipping totalled 72,752 GRT in 1995, including oil tankers, 1,222 GRT.

Telecommunications. Number of telephones in 1993 was 66,000 (70% in Greater Khartoum). Broadcasting is controlled by the Sudan National Broadcasting Corporation and Sudan Television (Colour by PAL). There are also 2 regional TV stations, in the centre and in the north of the country. In 1995 there were some 7·2m. radio and 2·2m. TV sets.

Press. In 1995 there were 5 daily newspapers with a combined circulation of 650,000.

SOCIAL INSTITUTIONS

Justice. The judiciary is a separate and independent department of state directly and solely responsible to the President of the Republic. The general administrative supervision and control of the judiciary is vested in the High Judicial Council.

Civil Justice is administered by the courts constituted under the Civil Justice Ordinance, namely the High Court of Justice—consisting of the Court of Appeal and Judges of the High Court, sitting as courts of original jurisdiction—and Province Courts—consisting of the Courts of Province and District Judges. The law administered is 'justice, equity and good conscience' in all cases where there is no special enactment. Procedure is governed by the Civil Justice Ordinance.

Justice for the Moslem population has always been administered by the Islamic law courts, which form the Sharia Divisions of the Court of Appeal, High Courts and Kadis Courts; President of the Sharia Division is the Grand Kadi. In Dec. 1990 the government announced that Sharia would be applied in the non-Moslem southern parts of the country as well.

Criminal Justice is administered by the courts constituted under the Code of Criminal Procedure, namely major courts, minor courts and magistrates' courts. Serious crimes are tried by major courts, which are composed of a President and 2 members and have the power to pass the death sentence. Major Courts are, as a rule, presided over by a Judge of the High Court appointed to a Provincial Circuit or a Province Judge. There is a right of appeal to the Chief Justice against any decision or order of a Major Court, and all its findings and sentences are subject to confirmation by him.

Lesser crimes are tried by Minor Courts consisting of 3 Magistrates and presided over by a Second Class Magistrate, and by Magistrates' Courts.

Religion. Islam is the state religion. In 1992 there were 21·9m. Sunni Moslems, concentrated in the north, and 2·4m. Christians and some 5m. traditionalist animists in the south.

Education In 1995 there were 10,636 pre-primary schools with 11,992 teachers for 537,395 pupils and 12,187 primary schools with 83,306 teachers for 3·02m. pupils. In 1992 there were 718,298 secondary level pupils with 30,642 teachers. In 1996 there were 17 universities, 2 Islamic universities, 1 university of science and technology and an institute of advanced banking. There were also 14 colleges or other institutions of higher education. Adult literacy rate, 1994, 46·1% (male, 57·7%; female, 34·6%).

Health. In 1981 the Ministry of Health maintained 158 hospitals (with 17,205 beds), 887 dispensaries, 1,619 dressing stations and 220 health centres. There were 2,122 doctors and 12,871 nurses.

DIPLOMATIC REPRESENTATIVES

Of Sudan in Great Britain (3 Cleveland Row, London, SW1A 1DD)
Ambassador: Omer Yousif Bireedo.

Of Great Britain in Sudan (off Sharia Al Baladia, Khartoum East)
Ambassador: Alan F. Goulty.

Of Sudan in the USA (2210 Massachusetts Ave., NW, Washington, D.C., 20008)
Ambassador: Mahdi Ibrahim Mohamed.

Of the USA in Sudan (Sharia Ali Abdul Latif POB 699, Khartoum)
Ambassador: Timothy M. Carney.

Of Sudan to the United Nations
Ambassador: Elfatih Erwa.

Of Sudan to the European Union
Ambassador: Vacant.

Further Reading

Craig, G. M. (ed.) *Agriculture of the Sudan*. OUP, 1991
Daly, M. W., *Sudan*. [Bibliography] Oxford and Santa Barbara (CA), 1983
Gurdon, C., *Sudan in Transition: A Political Risk Analysis*. London, 1986
Halasa, A., *et al. The Return to Democracy in Sudan*. Geneva, 1986
Holt, P. M., *A Modern History of the Sudan*. New York, 3rd ed. 1979
Khalid, M., *The Government They Deserve: the Role of the Elite in Sudan's Political Evolution*. London, 1990
Woodward, P., *Sudan, 1898-1989: the Unstable State*. London, 1991

SURINAME

Republic of Suriname

Capital: Paramaribo
Population: 417,000
GNP: US$0·4bn.
HDI/world rank: 0·943/66

KEY HISTORICAL EVENTS. The first Europeans to reach the area were the Spanish in 1499, but it was the British who established a colony in 1650. At the peace of Breda (1667) between Great Britain and the United Netherlands, the area known as Suriname was assigned to the Netherlands in exchange for the colony of New Netherland in North America. This was confirmed by the treaty of Westminster of Feb. 1674. Suriname was twice in British possession during the Napoleonic Wars in 1799-1802 (when it was restored to the Batavian Republic at the peace of Amiens) and 1804-16, when it was returned to the Netherlands.

On 25 Nov. 1975, Suriname gained full independence and was admitted to the UN on 4 Dec. 1975. On 25 Feb. 1980 the government was ousted in a *coup*, and a National Military Council (NMC) established. A further *coup* on 13 Aug. replaced several members of the NMC and the State President. Other attempted *coups* took place in 1981 and 1982, with the NMC retaining control. In Oct. 1987 a new constitution was approved by referendum and following elections in Nov. Suriname returned to democracy in Jan. 1988 but on 24 Dec. 1990 a further military coup deposed the government. Ronald Venetiaan was elected President in Sept. 1991.

The government and rebel guerrilla groups reached a peace agreement in Aug. 1992 and after the elections of May 1996 Jules Wijdenbosch, a candidate of the National Democratic Party, was elected President.

TERRITORY AND POPULATION. Suriname is located on the northern coast of South America between 2-6 degrees North latitude and 54-59 degrees West longitude. It is bounded in the north by the Atlantic Ocean, east by French Guiana, west by Guyana, and south by Brazil. Area, 163,820 sq. km. Census population (1995), 407,000. Estimate, Jan. 1997, 417,000. The capital, Paramaribo, has (1995 estimate) 288,000 inhabitants.

Suriname is divided into 10 districts (with chief town): Brokopondo (Brokopondo), Commewijne (Nieuw Amsterdam), Coronie (Totness), Marowijne (Albina), Nickerie (Nieuw Nickerie), Para (Onverwacht), Paramaribo (Paramaribo), Saramacca (Groningen), Sipalwini (local authority in Paramaribo), Wanica (Lelydorp).

Major ethnic groups in percentages of the population in 1991: Creole, 35%; Indian, 33%; Javanese, 16%; Bushnegroes (Blacks),10%; Amerindian, 3%.

The official language is Dutch. English is widely spoken next to Hindi, Javanese and Chinese as inter-group communication. A vernacular, called 'Sranan' or 'Surinamese', is used as a lingua franca. In 1976 it was decided that Spanish would become the nation's principal working language.

CLIMATE. The climate is equatorial, with uniformly high temperatures and rainfall. There is no recognized dry season. Paramaribo. Jan. 21°C, July 32·4°C. Average rainfall 182·3 mm.

CONSTITUTION AND GOVERNMENT. Parliament is a 51-member *National Assembly*. The head of state is the *President*, elected for a 5-year term by a two-thirds majority by the National Assembly, or, failing that, by an electoral college, the United People's Conference (UPC) enlarged by the inclusion of regional and local councillors, by a simple majority.

The parliamentary elections on 23 May 1996 led to a coalition government headed by the National Democratic Party, which in March 1998 comprised:

President: Jules Wijdenbosch (NDP; elected by the UPC 5 Sept. 1996, sworn in 14 Sept. 1996).
Vice-President: Pretaapnarain Radhakisun.
Foreign Affairs: Errol Snijders. *Defence:* Ramon Dwarka-Panday. *Finance:* Tjan Gobardhan. *Justice and Police:* Paul Sjak Shie. *Public Works:* Rudolf Vishnudath Mangal. *Regional Affairs:* Yvonne Raveles-Resida. *Transport, Communication and Tourism:* Dick De Bie. *Public Health:* Theo Vishnudath. *Social Affairs:* Soewarto Moestadja. *Labour:* M. A. Faried Pierkhan. *Natural Resources:* Errol Alibuks. *Education:* Kries Mahadewsing. *Planning and International Co-operation:* Waldi Nain. *Agriculture, Animal Husbandry and Fisheries:* Saimin Redjosentono. *Home Affairs:* Sonny Kertowidjojo. *Trade and Industry:* Robby Dragman.

National anthem: 'God zij met ons Suriname' ('God be with our Suriname'); words by C. A. Hoekstra, tune by J. C. de Puy. There is a Sranan version, 'Opo kondreman oen opo'; words by H. de Ziel.

DEFENCE

Army. The armed forces consist of 1 infantry and 1 military police battalion and 1 mechanized cavalry squadron with a total strength of about 1,800 in 1997. Officers' ranks were abolished in Feb. 1986.

Navy. The flotilla comprises 5 inshore patrol craft, as well as 3 river patrol boats, all built in the Netherlands. In 1997 personnel totalled 240.

Air Force. Personnel: 160.

INTERNATIONAL RELATIONS

Membership. Suriname is a member of the UN, OAS, CARICOM and is an ACP state of the EU.

ECONOMY

Budget. 1995 revenue was (in 1m. Sf) 68,918, made up of direct taxes, 32,660·5; indirect taxes, 23,515·4; bauxite levy and other revenues, 9,255·6; aid, 3,486·5. Total expenditure was 62,697·3, made up of wages and salaries, 17,312·2; materials, 31,324·3; transfers, 12,909; interest, 69·4; development expenditure, 1,082·5.

Currency. The unit of currency is the *Suriname guilder* (SRG; written as Sf[lorin]) of 100 *cents.* There are coins of 1, 5, 10 and 25 cents and 1 and 2·5 Sf, and notes of 5, 10, 25, 100, 250, 500, 1,000 and 2,000 Sf. In June 1995, foreign exchange reserves totalled 12,459·7m. Sf; gold reserves were 9,099·7m. Sf.

Banking and Finance. The Central Bank of Suriname is a bankers' bank and also the bank of issue. There are 3 commercial banks; the Suriname People's Credit Bank operates under the auspices of the Government. There is a post office savings bank, a mortgage bank, an investment bank, a long-term investments agency, a National Development Bank and an Agrarian Bank.

Weights and Measures. The metric system is in force.

ENERGY AND NATURAL RESOURCES

Electricity. Production (1994) 1,332m. kWh.

Oil. Crude oil production (1992) 0·2m. tonnes.

Minerals. Bauxite is the most important mineral. Production (1995), 3,596,000 tonnes.

Agriculture. Agriculture is restricted to the alluvial coastal zone; cultivated area in 1992, 87,120 ha. The staple food crop is rice. Production (1995, in 1,000 tonnes): Paddy, 216; rice (white), 84·8; oranges, 14·3; grapefruit, 0·9; other citrus fruit, 2·3; bananas, 18·2; plantains, 47·5; vegetables, 35·7; coconuts, 10·4; cassava, 9·9; rootcrops, 11·2.

Livestock (1994, in 1,000): Cattle, 98·8; sheep and goats, 15·7; pigs, 20·2; poultry, 2·4 (millions).

Forestry. Forests cover 14·9m. ha. Production in 1995 was 108,783,000 cu. metres of roundwood and 31·8m. cu. metres of sawn logs.

Fisheries. The fish catch in 1994 amounted to 8,506 tonnes.

INDUSTRY. There are aluminium smelting, food-processing and wood-using industries. Production, 1994: Cement, 24,665 tons[1]; palm oil, 1,051,000 litres[1]; beer, 3,456,000 litres; alumina, 1,498,000 tonnes; aluminium, 26,700 tonnes; cigarettes, 443m.; shoes, 98,990 pairs[1]; plywood, 6,864 cu. metres.

[1] Estimate.

FOREIGN ECONOMIC RELATIONS

Commerce. In 1994 (provisional) imports totalled 59,609·5m. Sf and exports, 60,181·7m. Sf. Principal imports, 1994 (in 1m. Sf): Raw materials and semi-manufactured goods, 22,819; investment goods, 15,135·3; fuels and lubricants, 8,119·9; foodstuffs, 2,982·3; cars and motorcycles, 2,093·4; textiles, 437·7. Principal exports, 1994 (in 1m. Sf): Alumina, 42,358·2; aluminium, 5,278·2; shrimps, 5,257·4; rice, 3,402·3; bananas and plantains, 1,274·3; wood and wood products, 261·4.

In 1994 (provisional) exports, including re-exports, (in 1m. Sf) were mainly to Norway (17,523·2), Netherlands (13,581·9), USA (10,707·2), Japan (4,182·8) and Brazil (3,776·9); imports were mainly from the USA (28,268), Netherlands (10,603), Trinidad and Tobago (6,186·2), UK (2,705·3), Japan (1,678·3), Netherlands Antilles (805·6), and Brazil (723·6).

Tourism. In 1996 there were 19,130 tourist arrivals by air.

COMMUNICATIONS

Roads. There are 1,335 km of main roads. In 1996 there were 46,408 passenger cars, 16,738 goods vehicles, 2,517 buses, 833 motor cycles and 26,735 mopeds.

Railways. There are 2 single-track railways.

Civil Aviation. There is an international airport at Paramaribo (Johan Adolf Pengel). The national carrier is Suriname Airways, which had 3 aircraft in 1995. Services are also maintained by Air Aruba, Air France, Cruzeiro Gamair and KLM. In 1995 there were 83,671 passenger arrivals and 87,117 departures.

Shipping. The Royal Netherlands Steamship Co. operates services to the Netherlands, the USA and regionally. The Suriname Navigation Co. maintains services from Paramaribo to Georgetown, Cayenne and the Caribbean area.

Telecommunications. In 1995 there were 53,158 telephones. The government controls the partly commercial Stichting Radio Omroep Suriname and Radio Suriname Internationaal, and Surinaamse Televisie Stichting. In 1991 there were 0·25m. radio and 40,000 TV sets (colour by NTSC). There are 13 broadcasting and 3 television stations.

Press There are 2 daily newspapers.

SOCIAL INSTITUTIONS

Justice. Members of the court of justice are nominated by the President. There are 3 cantonal courts.

Religion. At the 1980 census the main religious bodies were: Hindus, 97,170; Roman Catholics, 80,922; Moslems, 69,638; Moravian Brethren, 55,625; Reformed, 6,265; Lutheran, 2,695; Jehovah's Witnesses, 1,626; Seventh Day Adventists, 1,061; others, 24,627.

Education. In 1993–94 there were 304 primary schools with 3,603 teachers and 63,674 pupils. 104 secondary schools had 2,124 teachers and 30,160 pupils. In 1995–96 the university had 1,335 students and 155 academic staff. There is a teacher training college with (1991–92) 1,478 students.

Health. There were (1995) 1,805 general hospital beds and 227 physicians.

DIPLOMATIC REPRESENTATIVES

Of Suriname in Great Britain
Ambassador: Evert Azimullah (resides in The Hague).

Of Great Britain in Suriname
Ambassador: D. J. Johnson (resides in Guyana).

Of Suriname in the USA (4301 Connecticut Ave., NW, Washington, D.C., 20008)
Ambassador: Willem A. Udenhout.

Of the USA in Suriname (Dr Sophie Redmondstraat 129, Paramaribo)
Ambassador: Roger Gamble.

Of Suriname to the United Nations
Ambassador: Subhas Chandra Mungra.

Of Suriname to the European Union
Ambassador: Ewald Leeflang.

Further Reading

Dew, F. M., *Trouble in Surinume, 1975–1993.* New York, 1995
Hoefte, R. A. L., *Suriname:* [Bibliography]. Oxford and Santa Barbara (CA), 1990

National statistical office: Algemeen Bureau voor de Statistiek, POB244, Paramaribo.

SWAZILAND

Umbuso weSwatini—
Kingdom of Swaziland

Capital: Mbabane
Population: 966,000
GDP per head: (PPP$) 2,821
GNP: US$1·0bn.
HDI/world rank: 0·582/114

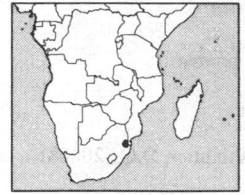

KEY HISTORICAL EVENTS. The Swazi migrated into the country to which they have given their name in the last half of the 18th century. They settled first in what is now southern Swaziland, but moved northwards under their chief, Sobhuza – known also to the Swazi as Somhlolo. Sobhuza died in 1838 and was succeeded by Mswati. The further order of succession has been Mbandzeni and Bhunu, whose son, Sobhuza II, was installed as King of the Swazi nation in 1921 after a long minority.

The independence of the Swazis was guaranteed in the conventions of 1881 and 1884 between the British Government and the Government of the South African Republic. In 1890, soon after the death of Mbandzeni, a provisional government was established representative of the Swazis, the British and the South African Republic Governments. In 1894 the South African Republic was given powers of protection and administration. In 1902, after the conclusion of the Boer War, a special commissioner took charge, and under an order-in-council in 1903 the Governor of the Transvaal administered the territory, through the special commissioner. Swaziland became independent on 6 Sept. 1968.

On 25 April 1967 the British Government gave the country internal self-government, changing the country's status to that of a protected state. The Ngwenyama, Sobhuza II, was recognized as King of Swaziland and head of state. King Sobhuza died on 21 Aug. 1982. On 25 April 1986, King Mswati III was installed as King of Swaziland. Despite a secret pact with the Republic of South Africa concluded in 1982 and providing for joint operations against guerrillas fighting apartheid, the South Africans launched an armed raid into Swaziland in Aug. 1986 aimed at the (South African) African National Congress. There is conflict within the Swazi government over the role of the royal family and relations with the Republic of South Africa.

TERRITORY AND POPULATION. Swaziland is bounded on the north, west and south by South Africa, and on the east by Mozambique. The area is 6,705 sq. miles (17,400 sq. km). Population (census 1986), 681,059. 1993 estimate, 850,628 (453,008 females). Estimate, 1997, 966,000. Vital statistics (1996): life expectancy, 58·3; birth rate, 35·4; death rate, 9·8. A census was held in 1996. Main urban areas with 1986 census populations: Mbabane, the administrative capital (38,290); Manzini (18,084); Big Bend (9,676); Mhlume (6,509); Havelock Mine (4,850); Nhlangano (4,107). The legislative capital is Lobamba.

The population is 84% Swazi and 10% Zulu. The official languages are Swazi and English.

CLIMATE. A temperate climate with two seasons. Nov. to March is the wet season, when temperatures range from mild to hot, with frequent thunderstorms. The cool, dry season from May to Sept. is characterized by clear, bright sunny days. Mbabane. Jan. 68°F (20°C), July 54°F (12·2°C). Annual rainfall 56" (1,402 mm).

ROYAL HOUSE. The reigning King is **Mswati III** (b. 1968; crowned 25 April 1986), who succeeded his father, King Sobhuza II (reigned 1921–82). The King rules in conjunction with the Queen Mother (his mother, or a senior wife).

CONSTITUTION AND GOVERNMENT. There is a *House of Assembly* of 65 members, 55 of whom are elected each from 1 constituency (*inkhundla*), and 10 appointed by the King, and a *House of Senators* of 30 members, 10 of whom are elected by the House of Assembly and 20 appointed by the King. Elections are held in 2 rounds, the second being a run-off between the 5 candidates who come first in each constituency.

There is also a traditional *Swazi National Council* headed by the King and Queen Mother at which all Swazi men are entitled to be heard.

At the elections of 26 Sept. and 11 Oct. 1993 the electorate was 283,693. There were 2,094 candidates.

In March 1998, the Cabinet was composed as follows:

Prime Minister: Sibusiso Barnabas Dlamini.
Deputy Prime Minister: Dr Sishayi Nxumalo. *Foreign Affairs and Trade:* Auther Khoza. *Enterprise and Employment:* Rev. Absalom Dlamini. *Agriculture:* Chief Dambuza Lukhele. *Public Works and Transport:* Dumisani Masango. *Education:* Solomon Dlamini. *Health:* Phetsile Dlamini. *Justice:* Chief Maweni Simelane. *Home Affairs:* Prince Guduza Dlamini. *Natural Resources, Land Utilization and Energy:* Majahenkhaba Dlamini. *Tourism and Communications:* Musa Nkambule. *Public Service and Information:* Muntu Mswane. *Economic Planning and Development:* Albert Shabangu. *Finance:* Thembu Masuku. *Housing and Township Development:* John Carmichael.

National anthem. 'Nkulunkulu mnikati wetibusiso temaSwati' ('O Lord our God bestower of blessings upon the Swazi'); words by A. E. Simelane, tune by D. K. Rycroft.

Local Government. The country is divided into the 4 regions of Shiselweni, Lubombo, Manzini and Hhohho. They are administered by Regional Administrators.

DEFENCE

Army Air Wing. There are 2 Israeli-built Arava light twin-turboprop transports with underwing weapon attachments for light attack duties.

INTERNATIONAL RELATIONS

Membership. Swaziland is a member of the UN, OAU, SADC, the Commonwealth and is an ACP state of the EU.

ECONOMY

Budget. Revenue and expenditure (in 1m. emalangeni) for financial years ending 31 March:

	1991–92	1992–93	1993–94	1994–95
Revenue	816·1	890·3	1,089·4	1,200·1
Expenditure	794·9	932·6	1,209·3	1,397·3

Currency. The unit of currency is the *lilangeni* (plural *emalangeni*) (SZL) of 100 cents but Swaziland remains in the Common (formerly Rand) Monetary Area and the South African rand is legal tender. There are coins of 1, 2, 5, 10, 20, 50 and 100 cents and notes of 2, 5, 10, 20 and 50 emalangeni. In 1990 48·2m. emalangeni were in circulation.

Banking and Finance. The central bank and bank of issue is the Central Bank of Swaziland, established in 1974. There were 24 commercial banks in 1992. Foreign banks include Barclays, Standard Chartered, Stanbic and First National. The Swaziland Development and Savings Bank concentrates on agricultural and housing loans. Total assets of the above were 1·05m. emalangeni in 1992. The Swaziland Building Society had assets of 84·6m. emalangeni in 1990–91.

In 1990 Swaziland Stock Brokers was established to trade in stocks and shares for institutional and private clients.

ENERGY AND NATURAL RESOURCES

Electricity. Production (1993), 366m. kWh.

Minerals. Output (in tonnes) in 1995: Coal, 171,666; asbestos, 28,591; quarry stone,

117,175 cu. metres. Diamond production was worth 15·2m. emalangeni in 1990 (20m. in 1989).

Agriculture. In 1993–94 the cultivated area was 178,121 ha and the grazing area 1,452,116 ha. Production (1993–94, in tonnes): Sugar-cane, 3,647,244; citrus, 88,263; pineapples, 19,700; tobacco, 394; seed cotton, 6,294; maize, 85,748; sorghum, 1,830; tomatoes, 242.

Livestock (1994): Cattle, 626,400; goats, 495,200; sheep, 27,000; poultry, 0·9m.

Forestry. The commercial forest area was 96,300 ha in 1993–94. Wood pulp output was 170,846 tonnes in 1993.

INDUSTRY. Most industries are based on processing agricultural products and timber. Footwear and textiles are also manufactured, and some engineering products.

Labour. The formal labour force numbered 88,290 in 1994; 15,892 Swazis worked in gold mines in South Africa.

Trade Unions. In 1992 there were 18 unions grouped in the Swaziland Federation of Trade Unions.

FOREIGN ECONOMIC RELATIONS. Swaziland has a customs union with South Africa and receives a *pro rata* share of the dues collected.

Commerce. In 1994 exports (in E1,000) were 2,831·8; imports, 2,935·9. Exports in 1991 included sugar, 411,572; unbleached wood pulp, 189,130; canned fruits, 67,273; asbestos, 13,762. Diamond and coal are also significant export earners (in 1990, E12·7m. and E12m. respectively). The major export market is South Africa. Imports in 1994 included machinery and transport equipment, 836,213; minerals, fuels and lubricants, 314,756; manufactured items, 719,116; food and live animals, 515,903.

Tourism. There were 287,023 visitors in 1993.

COMMUNICATIONS

Roads. Total length of roads (1995), 2,886 km, of which 828 km were tarred.

Railways. In 1997 the system comprised 301 km of route, and carried 4,129,000 tonnes of freight in 1995–96.

Civil Aviation. There is an international airport at Manzini (Matsapha). The national carrier, Royal Swazi National Airways is 50% state-owned, and had 2 aircraft (F28 and F100) in 1997. Services are also provided by Air Zimbabwe, Commercial Airways and LAM.

Telecommunications. There were (1987) 71 post offices, 2 telegraph stations and 29 postal agencies. In 1995 there were 35,131 telephones, 20,611 exchange connections and 155 telex exchange connections. The Broadcasting Corporation and Swaziland Television Authority are government-owned. Swaziland Broadcasting Services run on a semi-commercial basis. In 1992 there were some 60,000 radio and 12,500 television receivers (colour by PAL).

Cinemas. There were 5 cinemas in 1980 with a total seating capacity of 1,625.

Press. In 1995 there were 2 daily newspapers, both in English.

SOCIAL INSTITUTIONS

Justice. The constitutional courts practice Roman-Dutch law. The judiciary is headed by the Chief Justice. There is a High Court and various Magistrates and Courts. A Court of Appeal with a President and 3 Judges deals with appeals from the High Court. There are 16 courts of first instance. There are also traditional Swazi National Courts.

Religion. There are about 0·12m. Christians and about 30,000 of other faiths.

Education. There are 446 pre-schools with 19,000 children and 526 primary schools with 170,000 children and 5,347 teachers. The teacher/pupil ratio has decreased from 40/1 in the 1970s to 33/1. About half the children of secondary school age attend school. There are also private schools. In 1995 there were 69,009 children in secondary and high school classes.

The University of Swaziland, at Matsapha, had 2,132 students in 1994–95. There are 3 teacher training colleges (total enrolment in 1994–95, 857) and 8 vocational institutions (1,150 students and 147 teachers in 1991). There is also an institute of management.

Rural education centres offer formal education for children and adult education geared towards vocational training. The adult literacy rate is 75·2%.

Health. In 1996 there were 7 hospitals and 36 clinics.

DIPLOMATIC REPRESENTATIVES

Of Swaziland in Great Britain (20 Buckingham Gate, London SW1E 6LB)
High Commissioner: Rev. Percy Mngomezulu.

Of Great Britain in Swaziland (Allister Miller St., Mbabane)
High Commissioner: John Doble, OBE.

Of Swaziland in the USA (3400 International Dr., NW, Washington, D.C., 20008)
Ambassador: Mary M. Khanya.

Of the USA in Swaziland (PO Box 199, Mbabane)
Ambassador: Alan McKee.

Of Swaziland to the United Nations
Ambassador: Mathendele Dlamini.

Of Swaziland to the European Union
Ambassador: Thambayena Annastasia Diamini.

Further Reading

Booth, A., *Swaziland: Tradition and Change in a Southern African Kingdom.* Aldershot and Boulder (CO), 1984
Funnell, D. C., *Under the Shadow of Apartheid: Agrarian Transformation in Swaziland.* Avebury, 1991
Grotpeter, J. J., *Historical Dictionary of Swaziland.* Metuchen, 1975
Matsebula, J. S. M., *A History of Swaziland.* 3rd ed. London, 1992
Nyeko, B., *Swaziland.* [Bibliography] 2nd ed. Oxford and Santa Barbara (CA), 1994

National statistical office: Central Statistical Office, POB 456, Mbabane

SWEDEN

Konungariket Sverige

(Kingdom of Sweden)

Capital: Stockholm
Population: 8·87m.
GDP per head: (PPP$) 18,540
HDI/world rank: 0·936/10

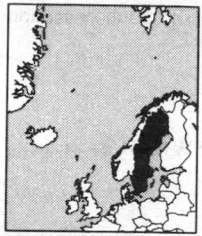

KEY HISTORICAL EVENTS. Sweden was organized as an independent unified state in the 10th century when the Swedes in the north of the country and the Goths in the south were united by Olof. Finland was acquired in the 13th century. In the 14th century Sweden was joined with Norway and Denmark in the Kalmar Union; however, under Gustav I, Sweden regained her independence in 1523.

Sweden became a constitutional monarchy in 1809, in which year she also ceded Finland to Russia. Norway was united with Sweden in 1815, but became independent in 1905. Sweden remained neutral during the two world wars of 1914-18 and 1939-45.

From 1932 to 1976, Sweden was governed by the Social Democratic Party which set the model for welfare reform combined with rapid economic growth. But high taxation brought a reaction in the 1970s when the Centre Party (representing chiefly small farmers and traders) and the Conservatives staged a comeback which brought them to power in coalition with the Liberal Party in 1976. However, in 1981 the Social Democrat leader, Olaf Palme, became prime minister with support from the Communist Party. On 28 Feb. 1986 Palme was assassinated in Stockholm by unknown assailants; Ingvar Carlsson succeeded him as prime minister.

In 1991, a Conservative-led coalition took over the government at a time of recession. Austerity measures helped in the revival of the Social Democrats who returned to power in 1994 but with a commitment to economic stringency.

TERRITORY AND POPULATION. Sweden is bounded in the west and north-west by Norway, east by Finland and the Gulf of Bothnia, south-east by the Baltic Sea and south-west by the Kattegat. The area is 449,964 sq. km. At the 1990 census the population was 8,587,353. Estimate, July 1997, 8,865,051. About 80–85% of the population live in the densely populated areas.

Area, population and population density of the counties (*län*).

	Land area (in sq. km)	Population (1990 census)	Population 31 Dec 1996	Density per sq. km 31 Dec. 1996
Stockholm	6,490	1,640,389	1,744,330	269
Uppsala	6,989	268,503	289,153	41
Södermanland	6,062	255,546	257,153	42
Östergötland	10,562	402,849	415,659	39
Jönköping	9,944	308,294	311,765	31
Kronoberg	8,458	177,880	179,655	21
Kalmar	11,171	241,149	241,896	22
Gotland	3,140	57,132	57,971	18
Blekinge	2,941	150,615	151,972	52
Skåne	11,027	1,068,587	1,114,368	101
Kristianstad	1,250	289,251	294,709	48
Malmöhus	4,938	778,939	817,022	165
Halland	5,454	254,568	270,060	50
Göteborg and Bohus	5,141	739,863	775,638	151
Älvsborg	11,395	441,031	448,074	39
Skaraborg	7,937	276,698	278,263	35
Värmland	17,586	283,148	282,147	16
Örebro	8,517	272,474	275,855	32
Västmanland	6,302	258,544	259,987	41
Kopparberg	28,193	288,919	288,171	10

	Land area (in sq. km)	Population (1990 census)	Population 31 Dec 1996	Density per sq. km 31 Dec. 1996
Gävleborg	18,192	289,346	286,789	16
Västernorrrland	21,678	261,099	256,587	12
Jämtland	49,443	135,724	134,561	3
Västerbotten	55,401	251,846	259,895	5
Norrbotten	98,911	263,546	264,320	3

There are some 17,000 Sami (Lapps). A parliament, the *Sameting*, was instituted for these in 1993.

On 31 Dec. 1996 aliens in Sweden numbered 433,174. Of these, 121,069 were from Nordic countries; 157,392 from Northern Europe; 24,862 from Africa; 12,371 from North America; 18,826 from South America; 94,474 from Asian countries; 2,410 from USSR; 1,695 from Oceania and 75 Country unknown.

Vital statistics for calendar years:

	Total living births	To mothers single, divorced or widowed	Stillborn	Marriages	Divorces	Deaths exclusive of still-born
1994	112,257	57,927	348	34,203	22,740	91,844
1995	103,422	54,769	350	33,642	22,885	93,955
1996	95,297	51,348	330	33,484	21,612	94,133

Expectation of life in 1997 (estimate): Males, 76·42 years; females, 81·89.

Immigration: 1995, 45,887; 1996, 39,895. Emigration: 1995, 33,984; 1996, 33,884.

Population of the 50 largest communities, 31 Dec. 1996:

Stockholm	718,462	Södertälje	82,589	Sollentuna	55,476
Göteborg	454,016	Karlstad	79,464	Falun	55,005
Malmö	248,007	Huddinge	78,873	Solna	54,644
Uppsala	184,507	Skellefteå	74,684	Mölndal	54,492
Linköping	131,898	Kristianstad	73,726	Trollhättan	52,338
Västerås	124,084	Växjö	73,089	Varberg	52,134
Norrköping	123,531	Luleå	71,238	Norrtälje	50,767
Örebro	120,774	Nacka	71,213	Hässleholm	49,681
Jönköping	115,636	Botkyrka	70,700	Skövde	49,643
Helsingborg	114,866	Haninge	66,100	Uddevalla	49,167
Umeå	102,487	Kungsbacka	61,477	Nyköping	48,730
Lund	97,208	Karlskrona	60,388	Borlänge	48,457
Borås	96,246	Östersund	59,497	Motala	42,754
Sundsvall	94,440	Täby	59,445	Piteå	40,859
Gävle	90,678	Järfälla	58,772	Västervik	39,256
Eskilstuna	88,688	Gotland	57,971	Falkenberg	39,010
Halmstad	83,549	Örnsköldsvik	57,742		

Source: Statistics Sweden

The official language is Swedish.

CLIMATE. The north has severe winters, with snow lying for 4–7 months. Summers are fine but cool, with long daylight hours. Further south, winters are less cold, summers are warm and rainfall well-distributed throughout the year, with a slight summer maximum. Stockholm. Jan. 3·2°C, July 18·4°C. Annual rainfall 385 mm.

ROYAL FAMILY. The reigning King is **Carl XVI Gustaf**, b. 30 April 1946, succeeded on the death of his grandfather Gustaf VI Adolf, 15 Sept. 1973, married 19 June 1976 to *Silvia* Renate Sommerlath, b. 23 Dec. 1943 (Queen of Sweden). *Daughter* and *Heir Apparent:* Crown Princess Victoria Ingrid Alice Désirée, Duchess of Västergötland, b. 14 July 1977; *son:* Prince Carl Philip Edmund Bertil, Duke of Värmland, b. 13 May 1979; *daughter:* Princess Madeleine Thérèse Amelie Josephine, Duchess of Hälsingland and Gästrikland, b. 10 June 1982.

Sisters of the King. Princess Margaretha, b. 31 Oct. 1934, married 30 June 1964 to John Ambler; Princess Birgitta (Princess of Sweden), b. 19 Jan. 1937, married 25

May 1961 (civil marriage) and 30 May 1961 (religious ceremony) to Johann Georg, Prince of Hohenzollern; Princess Désirée, b. 2 June 1938, married 5 June 1964 to Baron Niclas Silfverschiöld; Princess Christina, b. 3 Aug. 1943, married 15 June 1974 to Tord Magnuson.

Uncles of the King. Count Sigvard Bernadotte of Wisborg, b. on 7 June 1907; Count Carl Johan, Bernadotte of Wisborg, b. on 31 Oct. 1916.

Aunt of the King. Princess Ingrid (Princess of Sweden, Dowager Queen of Denmark), b. 28 March 1910, married 24 May 1935 to Frederik, Crown Prince of Denmark (King Frederik IX), died 14 Jan. 1972.

CONSTITUTION AND GOVERNMENT. Under the 1975 Constitution Sweden is a representative and parliamentary democracy. The King is Head of State, but does not participate in government. Parliament is the single-chamber *Riksdag* of 349 members elected for a period of 4 years in direct, general elections.

The manner of election to the *Riksdag* is proportional. The country is divided into 29 constituencies. In these constituencies 310 members are elected. The remaining 39 seats constitute a nation-wide pool intended to give absolute proportionality to parties that receive at least 4% of the votes. A party receiving less than 4% of the votes in the country is, however, entitled to participate in the distribution of seats in a constituency, if it has obtained at least 12% of the votes cast there.

At the elections of 18 Sept. 1994 turn-out was 86%. The Social Democratic Party (SDP) won 162 seats with 45·3% of votes cast (138 with 37·6% in 1991), the Moderate Party 80 with 22·4% (80 with 21·9%), the Centre Party 27 with 7·7% (31 with 8·5%), the Liberal Party 26 with 7·2% (33 with 9·1%), the Left Party (ex-Communists) 22 with 6·2% (16 with 4·5%), the Green Party 18 with 5% and the Christian Democratic Party 14 with 4·1% (26 with 7·1%).

A minority Social Democratic government was formed in Oct. 1994, which in March 1998 comprised:

Prime Minister: Göran Persson (b.1949).

Minister for Social Security: Maj-Inger Klingvall. *Justice:* Laila Freivalds. *Foreign Affairs:* Lena Hjelm-Wallén. *International Development Co-operation:* Pierre Schori. *Defence:* Björn von Sydow. *Health and Social Affairs:* Margot Wallström. *Transport and Communications:* Inez Uusmann. *Finance:* Erik Åsbrink. *Education and Science:* Carl Tham. *Schools and Adult Education:* Ylva Johansson. *Agriculture, Food and Fisheries:* Annika Åhnberg. *Labour:* Margareta Winberg. *Taxation:* Thomas Östros. *Industry and Trade:* Anders Sundström. *Equality Affairs:* Ulrica Messing. *Culture:* Marita Ulvskog. *Environment:* Anna Lindh. *Interior:* Jörgen Andersson. *Trade:* Leif Pagrotsky. *Integration and Consumers Protection:* Lars Enqvist. *Prime Minister's Office:* Thage G. Peterson.

The *Speaker* is Birgitta Dahl.

National Anthem: 'Du gamla, du fria, du fjällhöga nord' ('Thou ancient, thou free, thou mountainous north'); words by R. Dybeck; folk-tune.

Local Government. The country is divided into 24 counties (*län*) subdivided into 288 municipalities, each with an elected council. The Government appoints a Governor to each county who is chair of a 14-member board elected by the county council.

Gotland consists of only one municipality. The municipalities of Göteborg and Malmö do not belong to county councils. The parishes, 2,544 in 1996, are the local units of the Swedish Lutheran Church and have the same status as municipalities. The publicly-elected parochial church council is the supreme decision-making body in larger parishes. Small parishes have the parish meeting, a form of direct democracy.

Regional and local elections took place simultaneously with the parliamentary elections on 18 Sept. 1994.

DEFENCE. A Supreme Commander is, under the Government, in command of the three services. He is assisted by the Swedish Armed Forces HQ.

There is conscription for males of 7–15 months. Refresher training (3–34 days) is obligatory.

Army. The peace-time Army consists for training purposes of 38 armoured, cavalry, infantry, artillery and other units. On mobilization to a war footing the Field Army comprises 3 divisional HQs, 4 infantry, 3 Arctic, 1 mechanized Arctic, 2 armoured and 3 mechanized brigades and 7 artillery regiments. There are also Territorial Defence units. Equipment includes 150 Centurion, 240 Strv-103B and 160 Strv-121 main battle tanks. The Army Aviation Corps comprises 2 battalions operating 19 JetRanger helicopters for observation, 20 armed BO 105 helicopters, 16 AB.204B and 5 AB.412 transport helicopters, plus 25 Hughes 300C helicopters for training and observation duties. Army strength, 1997, 43,100 (33,900 conscripts and active reservists).

Navy. Naval forces are divided between 2 branches: Navy, and Coastal Artillery. There are 4 Naval Command Areas, covering southern, eastern, western and northern coasts.

The Coastal Artillery have 2 main tasks: Fixed coastal defence and mobile coastal defence. The fixed coastal defence is organized in Coast Artillery Brigades consisting of artillery up to 120 mm calibre and land-sea missiles. The mobile element consists of 3 Mobile Coastal Artillery Battalions, 1 Heavy Coastal Missile Battery and 6 Amphibious Battalions. The Coastal Artillery operates 8 coastal and 12 small patrol craft and some 140 small amphibious craft.

The Naval Air Arm comprises 14 Boeing Vertol Kawasaki KV 107 helicopters and 10 AB-206 Jet-Ranger helicopters, and 1 Aviocar for anti-submarine warfare and electronic surveillance.

The personnel of the Navy in 1997 totalled 8,800 (4,200 conscripts) of whom 2,300 serve in Coastal Defence.

A separate civil Coast Guard, 600 strong, operates some 70 inshore cutters, patrol boats and service craft and 4 aircraft.

Air Force. There are 3 air commands. After mobilization to a war footing the Air Force consists of 9 fighter, 3 medium attack/reconnaissance, 4 central transport and 4 regional transport squadrons, 6 helicopter units, 16 air-base and 6 combat command control and air surveillance battalions. Combat aircraft include the first Ja 39 Gripens, JA 37 and AJS 37 Viggens, J 35 Drakens, SK 60 trainers and 17 search-and-rescue helicopters.

Strength (1997) 10,000 (3,150 conscripts), with 314 combat aircraft and 105 SK 60s with capability for light attack.

INTERNATIONAL RELATIONS

Membership. Sweden is a member of the UN, EU and the NATO Partnership for Peace, and is a signatory to the Schengen Accord, which abolishes border controls between Austria, Belgium, Denmark, Finland, France, Germany, Greece, Iceland, Italy, Luxembourg, the Netherlands, Norway, Portugal, Spain and Sweden.

ECONOMY

Performance. Real GDP growth was 1·6% in 1996.

Budget. Revenue and expenditure of the total budget (Current and Capital) for financial years ending 30 June (in 1m. kr.):

	Revenue	Expenditure		Revenue	Expenditure
1992–93	377,743	565,548	1994–95	423,183	579,421
1993–94	376,925	554,023	1995–96	787,570	985,852

Revenue and expenditure for 1998 (1,000 kr.):

Revenue		Compensation for municipalities and	
Taxes on income	34,100	county councils	20,966
Tax on income—legal entities	58,964	Income from government activities	39,704
Other revenue	5,765	Income from sale of assets	15,001
Social security fees	208,777	Loans repaid	2,690
Estate tax	24,240	Computed revenue	5,337
Other taxes on property	10,865	Contributions etc. from the EU	11,249
VAT	154,884		
Excise duties	83,430	Total revenue	675,972

Expenditure

The Swedish political system	3,977	Culture, the media, religious organizations and leisure	7,335
Economy and fiscal administration	2,063	Planning, housing supply and construction	22,826
Tax administration and collection	5,662	Regional balance and development	3,605
Justice	21,034	General environment and conservation	1,178
Foreign policy administration and international co-operation	2,811	Energy	1,583
Total defence	41,244	Communications	24,101
International development assistance	11,343	Agriculture and forestry, fisheries etc.	13,726
Immigrants and refugees	3,864	Business sector	2,698
Health care, medical care, social services	22,500	General grants to municipalities	93,049
Financial security in the event of illness and disability	37,192	Interest on Central Government Debt. etc.	109,125
Financial security in old age	62,701	Contribution to the European Community	19,646
Financial security for families and children	35,814		
Financial security in the event of unemployment	42,723	Total areas of expenditure	687,815
The labour market and working life	47,542		
Study support	21,334	Take-up of funds previously allocated	5,000
Education and university research	27,051		
		Total Expenditure	692,815

In 1995-96 the national debt amounted to 1,373,616m. kr. VAT is 25% (reduced rate, 12%).

In 1996 the state debt amounted to 1,411,632m kr.

Currency. The unit of currency is the *krona* (SEK), of 100 *öre*. There are coins of 50 öre and 1, 5 and 10 kronor, and notes of 20, 50, 100, 500 and 1,000 kronor. Inflation was 0·8% in 1996.

Banking and Finance. The central bank and bank of issue is the *Sveriges Riksbank*, whose *Governor* is appointed for 5 years by 8 trustees, 7 of whom are appointed by Parliament. The *Governor* is Urban Backström. On 31 Dec. 1995 its note circulation amounted to 73,064m. kr.; its gold and foreign-exchange reserves totalled 171,320m. kr. On 31 Dec. 1996 there were 37 commercial. Their total deposits amounted to 771,476m. kr.; advances to the public amounted to 724,278m. kr. On 31 Dec. 1996 there were 87 savings banks.

There is a stock exchange in Stockholm.

Weights and Measures. The metric system is obligatory.

ENERGY AND NATURAL RESOURCES

Electricity. Sweden is rich in hydro-power resources. Electricity net production in 1995 was 143,316m. kWh. In 1994, 16,594 MW were produced in hydro-electric plants, 10,408 MW in nuclear plants and 8,814 MW in thermal plants. A referendum of 1980 called for the phasing out of nuclear power by 2010. In Feb. 1997 the government began denuclearization by designating one of the 10 reactors for decommissioning. The state corporation Vattenfall was given the responsibility of financing and overseeing the transition to the use of non-fossil fuel alternatives.

Minerals. Sweden is a leading producer of iron ore. There are also deposits of copper, lead, zinc and alum shale containing oil and uranium. Iron ore produced, 1994, 10,871,294 tonnes; copper ore, 297,999 tonnes.

Agriculture. In 1996 the total area of land given over to farms of 2ha or more was 8,134,160, of this 2,811,534 was arable land, 446,458 natural pasture, 4,077,481 forest and 798,689 other. Of the land used for arable farming, 2-5 ha holdings covered a total area of 55,858 ha; 5·1–10 holdings covered 132,551 ha; 10·1–20 ha, 278,256; 20·1–30 ha, 271,369; 30·1–50 ha, 490,386; 50·1–100 ha, 773,512 and holdings larger than 100 ha covered 809,602 ha.

		Area (1,000 ha)			Production (1,000 tonnes)	
Chief crops	1994	1995	1996	1994	1995	1996
Wheat	251·8	261·4	334·6	1,345	1,554	2,029·9
Rye	38·96	39·7	33·6	173	206	165·7
Barley	473·0	453·4	468·6	1,661	1,793	99·3
Oats	341·4	278·3	283·6	991	947	3,113·4
Potatoes	33·0	35·0	36·6	763	792	1,200·9
Sugarbeet	53·4	57·5	59·2	2,350	2,479	2,430
Tame hay	780·0	782·0	772·4	3,156	3,378	3,365·2
Oil seed	128·5	104·6	72·8	· · ·	· · ·	9·9

Milk production (in 1,000 tonnes) 1996 (1995): 3,304, (3,316). Butter production (in 1,000 tonnes): 57, (57) and cheese: 127, (129).

Livestock 1996: Cattle, 1,790,240; sheep and lambs, 469,035; pigs, 2,348,754; poultry, 7,897,240. There were 279,869 reindeer in Sami villages in 1994.

The harvest of moose during open season 1996: 91,079.

Forestry. Forests form one of the country's greatest natural assets. The growing stock consists of 45% Norway spruce, 39% Scots pine and 15% deciduous trees. In 1993 forests covered 22,739,000 ha. Municipal and state ownership accounts for 37% of the forests; companies own 13%, and the remaining half is in private hands, covering in 1996 22,518,000 ha of which 2,218,000 ha were publicly owned, 8,805,000 was owned by companies and 11,495,000 ha in private hands. In 1995, 59·9m. cu. metres (solid volume excluding bark) of wood were removed, including 31·1m. cu. metres of sawlogs and 24·1m. cu. metres of pulpwood. In 1996, 67·7m. cu. metres of wood was felled comprised of 30·8m. cu. metres sawlogs, 20·9m. cu. metres pulpwood and 3·8m. cu. metres other.

Fisheries. In 1996 the total catch of the sea fisheries was 361,693 tonnes.

INDUSTRY. Manufacturing is mainly based on metals and forest resources. Chemicals (especially petro-chemicals), building materials and decorative glass and china are also important.

Industry groups	No. of establishments 1995	Average no. of wage-earners 1995	Sales value of production (gross) in 1m. kr. 1995
Mines and quarries	162	5,461	10,441
Manufacturing industry	8,510	407,829	939,359
Food products, beverages and tobacco	853	43,203	103,131
Textiles and textile products, leather and leather products	281	88,842	10,359
Wood and wood products	709	24,062	43,706
Pulp, paper and paper products publishers and printers	1,169	55,214	146,409
Coke, refined petroleum products and nuclear fuel	17	1,228	21,826
Chemicals, chemical products and man-made fibres	315	14,112	67,672
Rubber and plastic products	376	15,009	21,664
Other non-metallic mineral products	356	11,518	16,408
Basic metals	170	24,935	80,736
Fabricated metal products, machinery and equipment	3,834	193,712	407,673
Other manufacturing industries	430	15,994	19,772

Source: Statistics Sweden

Labour. In 1996 there were 3,963,000 persons in the labour force, of whom 3,616,000 were employed: 794,000 in health and social work; 809,000 in manufacturing, mining, quarrying, electricity and water services; 762,000 in trade and communication; 433,000 in financial services and business activities; 315,000 in education, research and development; 300,000 (297,000) in personal services and cultural activities, and sanitation; 207,000 in public administration; 115,000 in agriculture, forestry and fishing.

Trade Unions. At 31 Dec. 1996 the Swedish Trade Union Confederation (LO) had 20 member unions with a total membership of 2,169,280; the Central Government Organization of Salaried Employees (TCO) had 25, with 1,302,147; the Swedish Confederation of Professional Associations (SACO) had 27, with 407,321; the Central Organization of Swedish Workers had 10,000 members.

In March 1997 employers' organizations and trade unions signed an agreement on the conduct of wage negotiations in 1998. The agreement involved 0·8m. workers, and provided for the establishment of an Industrial Committee to promote the development of industry.

FOREIGN ECONOMIC RELATIONS

Commerce. Imports and exports (in 1m. kr.):

	1992	1993	1994	1995	1996
Imports	290,929	334,257	399,152	460,578	446,508
Exports	326,031	388,290	471,602	567,836	566,480

Breakdown by Standard International Trade Classification (SITC, revision 3) categories (value in 1m. kr; 1996 figures are provisional):

	Imports		Exports	
	1995	1996	1995	1996
0. Food and live animals	26,232	26,866	11,182	12,004
1. Beverages and tobacco	2,897	3,940	1,553	1,777
2. Raw materials	17,795	14,070	43,905	35,754
3. Fuels and lubricants	28,522	38,203	11,923	15,161
4. Animal and vegetable oils	1,276	932	789	686
5. Chemicals	52,161	47,740	51,032	49,936
6. Manufactured materials	77,836	68,954	137,200	129,494
7. Machinery and transport equipment	189,899	184,985	260,609	271,294
8. Manufactured items	63,736	60,699	48,583	49,134
9. Other	224	119	1,059	1,240

Principal exports in 1996 (in tonnes): Paper and board, 4,494,688; lumber, sawn and planed, 10,962,00 sq. metres; power-generating non-electrical machinery, 13,390; chemical wood pulp, 2,744,532; newsprint, 1,958,019; mechanical handling equipment, 149,964; flat-rolled products of iron, 1,236,008; pumps and centrifuges, 61,265.

Imports and exports by countries (in 1m. kr.):

	Imports from		Exports to	
	1994	1996	1994	1996
Belgium	13,905	16,268	23,224	25,033
Denmark	27,032	33,422	32,621	34,783
Finland	25,104	25,183	22,547	28,865
France	22,278	25,014	24,125	26,313
Germany	73,607	83,818	62,777	66,284
Italy	15,339	14,312	17,833	18,304
Netherlands	16,279	33,483	24,941	31,331
Norway	24,341	34,828	38,358	47,910
Switzerland	7,643	8,420	9,120	10,083
UK	38,306	44,621	48,042	53,659
USA	34,167	25,880	37,624	46,982

Source: Statistics Sweden

Tourism. In 1996 (1995) foreign visitors stayed 3,930,464 (3,693,727) nights in hotels and 899,292 (1,014,027) in holiday villages and youth hostels.

COMMUNICATIONS

Roads. On 1 Jan. 1996 there were 0·21m. km of public roads comprising state administered roads, 97,908 km, municipal, 38,300 km, private roads with subsidies, 73,913 km, of which 74,642 km were surfaced. Motor vehicles on 31 Dec. 1995 included 3,631,000 passenger cars, 323,000 buses and lorries and 117,000 motor cycles.

Railways. Total length of railways at 31 Dec. 1996 was 10,939 km (7,469 km electrified). The state railway operator SJ carried 99m. passengers and 54m. tonnes of freight in 1996. Some lines are run under contract by private operators. There is a metro in Stockholm (108 km), and tram/light rail networks in Stockholm, Göteborg (81 km) and Norrköping.

Civil Aviation. There are international airports at Stockholm (Arlanda) and Göteborg (Landvetter). The main carrier is Scandinavian Airlines System (SAS), of which SAS Sverige AB is the Swedish partner (SAS Denmark and SAS Norge ASA being the other two). SAS has a joint paid-up capital of 10,588m. Sw. kr. Capitalization of ABA, 4,230m. Sw. kr., of which 50% is owned by the Government and 50% by private enterprises.

In 1996, the total distance flown was 104·6m. km; passenger-km, 8,553·6m.; goods, 266·7m. tonne-km. These figures represent the Swedish share of the SAS traffic (Swedish domestic and three-sevenths of international traffic). Services are also provided by Aeroflot, Air China, Air France, Air Malta, Alitalia, American Airlines, Austrian Airlines, Balkan, Braathens Safe, British Airways, Czech Airlines, Egyptair, Estonia Air, Finnair, Iberia, Icelandair, Kenya Airways, KLM, Lithuanian Airlines, LOT, Lufthansa, Maersk Air, Malév, Olympic Airways, Royal Air Maroc, Sabena, Sterling European, Swissair, TAP, Thai Airways and Turkish Airlines.

Shipping. There are major ports at Helsingborg, Malmö, Stockholm and Göteborg. The mercantile marine consisted on 31 Dec. 1996 of 450 vessels of 2·95m. gross tonnes. Vessels entered from and cleared for foreign countries, exclusive of passenger liners and ferries, with cargoes and in ballast, in 1995: With cargoes, 27,995 with a gross tonnage of 155·53m.; in ballast, 16,241 with a gross tonnage of 68·53m.

Telecommunications. There were 1,853 post offices at the end of 1995. In 1995 there were 6,830 telephone exchanges and 6,013,000 telephones. 2m. mobile telephones were in use in 1997.

3,368,000 combined radio and TV reception fees were paid in 1995. *Sveriges Radio AB* is a non-commercial semi-governmental corporation, transmitting 3 national programmes and regional programmes. It also broadcasts 2 TV programmes (colour by PAL). There are 3 commercial satellite channels (TV3, TV4 and Nordic), and a land-based commercial channel.

Cinemas (1996). There were 1,169 cinemas.

Press (1996). There were 168 daily newspapers with an average week-day net circulation of 4,284 ,000.

SOCIAL INSTITUTIONS

Justice. The administration of justice is independent. The Attorney-General (appointed by the Government) and 3 Ombudsmen exercise a check on judicial affairs administration. In 1995–96 the Ombudsmen received altogether 5,121 cases; of these, 125 were instituted on their own initiative.

There is a 3-tier hierarchy of courts: The Supreme Court; 6 intermediate courts of appeal and 97 district courts. Of the district courts 27 also serve as real estate courts and 6 as water rights courts.

District courts are courts of first instance and deal with both civil and criminal cases. Petty cases are tried by 1 judge. Civil and criminal cases are tried as a rule by 3 to 4 judges or in minor cases by 1 judge. Disputes of greater consequence relating to the Marriage Code or the Code relating to Parenthood and Guardianship are tried by a judge and a jury of 3–4 lay assessors. More serious criminal cases are tried by a judge and a jury of 5 members (lay assessors) in felony cases, and of 3 members in misdemeanour cases. The cases in courts of appeal are generally tried by 4 or 5 judges.

Those with low incomes can receive free legal aid out of public funds. In criminal cases a suspected person has the right to a defence counsel, paid out of public funds.

The Attorney-General and the Judicial Commissioner for the Judiciary and Civil Administration (Ombudsman) supervise the application in the public sector of acts of Parliament and regulations.

There were 76 penal and correctional institutions for offenders in 1996 with an average population of 6,000 inmates (including offenders in remand prison).

Religion. The national church is the Swedish Lutheran Church, due to be disestablished in 2000. It is headed by Archbishop Karl Gustaf Hammar (b. 1943) and has its metropolitan see at Uppsala. In 1996 there were 13 bishoprics and 2,544 parishes. The clergy are chiefly supported from the parishes and the proceeds of the church lands. Other denominations, in 1996: Pentecostal Movement, 91,939 members; The Mission Covenant Church of Sweden, 70,072; Salvation Army, 26,089; Orebo Missionary Society, 22,801; Swedish Evangelical Mission, 26,089; The Baptist Union of Sweden, 18,548; Swedish Alliance Missionary Society, 12, 846; Holiness Mission, 6,393. There were also 164,015 Roman Catholics (under a Bishop resident at Stockholm).

Education. In 1995–96 there were 640,797 pupils in primary education (grades 1–6 in compulsory comprehensive schools); secondary education at the lower stage (grades 7–9 in compulsory comprehensive schools) comprised 297,743 pupils. In secondary education at the higher stage (the integrated upper secondary school), there were 66,561 pupils in Oct. 1995 (excluding pupils in the fourth year of the technical course regarded as third-level education). The folk high schools, 'people's colleges', had 37,148 pupils in courses of more than 10 weeks in 1994–95.

In municipal adult education there were 155,971 students in 1995.

There are also special schools for pupils with visual and hearing handicaps (766 pupils in 1995) and for those who are mentally retarded (13,417 pupils).

In 1994–95 there were in integrated institutions for higher education 269,815 students enrolled for undergraduate studies. The number of students enrolled for post-graduate studies in 1995 was 16,079.

Source: Statistics Sweden

Health. In 1996 there were 23,000 doctors, 14,300 dentists, 73,600 nurses and midwives and 38,139 hospital beds. In 1994 the total cost of health care was 112,983m. kr., representing 7% of GDP.

Welfare. Social insurance benefits are granted mainly according to uniform statutory principles. All persons resident in Sweden are covered, regardless of citizenship. All schemes are compulsory, except for unemployment insurance. Benefits are usually income-related. Most social security schemes are at present undergoing extensive discussion and changes. Recent proposals include the introduction of a new pension scheme.

Type of scheme	Beneficiaries	Expenditure 1995 (in 1m. kr)
Sickness and parental insurance	All residents	53,352
Work injury insurance	All gainfully occupied persons	6,793
Unemployment insurance	Members of unemployment insurance societies	36,068
Basic and supplementary pensions (old-age, disability, survivors)	All resident or gainfully occupied persons (2,448,397)	182,894
Partial pensions	All gainfully occupied persons between 61 and 64 (38,000)	2,370
Child allowance	All children below 16 (1,770,000)	16,959

The total social insurance expenditure amounted to 309,000m. kr. in 1995, representing 19% of GDP.

DIPLOMATIC REPRESENTATIVES

Of Sweden in Great Britain (11 Montagu Pl., London, W1H 2AL)
Ambassador: Mats Bergquist, CMG.

Of Great Britain in Sweden (Skarpögatan 6-8, 115 93 Stockholm)
Ambassador: Roger Bone, CMG.

Of Sweden in the USA (600 New Hampshire Ave. NW, Washington, D.C., 20037)
Ambassador: Rolf Ekéus.

Of the USA in Sweden (Strandvägen 101, 115 89 Stockholm)
Ambassador: Lyndon L. Olson, Jr.

Of Sweden to the United Nations
Ambassador: Hans Dahlgren.

Further Reading

Statistics Sweden. *Statistik Årsbok/Statistical Yearbook of Sweden.—Historisk statistik för Sverige* (Historical Statistics of Sweden). 1955 ff.—*Allmän månadsstatistik* (Monthly Digest of Swedish Statistics).—*Statistiska meddelanden* (Statistical Reports). From 1963

Andersson, L., *A History of Sweden.* Stockholm, 1962
Grosskopf, G., *The Swedish Tax System.* Stockholm, 1986
Gustafsson, A., *Local Government in Sweden.* Stockholm, 1988
Hadenius, S., *Swedish Politics during the Twentieth Century.* Stockholm, 1988
Heclo, H. and Madsen, H., *Policy and Politics in Sweden: Principled Pragmatism.* Philadelphia, 1987
Henrekson, M., *An Economic Analysis of Swedish Government Expenditure.* Aldershot, 1992
Lindström, E., *The Swedish Parliamentary System.* Stockholm, 1983
Olsson, S. E., *Social Policy and Welfare State in Sweden.* Lund, 1990
Peterson, C.-G., *Local Self-Government and Democracy in Transition.* Stockholm, 1989
Petersson, O., *Swedish Government and Politics.* Stockholm, 1994
Sather, L. B. and Swanson, A., *Sweden.* [Bibliography] Oxford and Santa Barbara (CA), 1987
Scott, F. D., *Sweden: the Nation's History.* Univ. of Minnesota Press, 1983
Sveriges statskalender. Published by Vetenskapsakademien. Annual, from 1813

National library: Kungliga Biblioteket, Stockholm.
National statistical office: Statistics Sweden, S-11581 Stockholm.
Website: http://www.scb.se/

SWITZERLAND

Schweizerische
Eidtgenossenschaft—
Confédération Suisse—
Confederazione Svizzera[1]

Capital: Berne
Population: 7·06m.
GDP: (PPP$) 24,967
HDI/world rank: 0·930/16

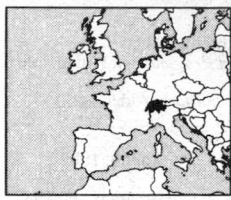

KEY HISTORICAL EVENTS. The history of Switzerland can be traced back to Aug. 1291 when the Uri, Schwyz and Unterwalden entered into a defensive league. In 1353 the league included 8 members and in 1515, 13. Various territories were acquired either by single cantons or by several in common, and in 1648 the league became formally independent of the Holy Roman Empire. No addition was made to the number of cantons until 1798, in which year, under the influence of France, the unified Helvetic Republic was formed. This failed to satisfy the Swiss, and in 1803 Napoleon, in the Act of Mediation, gave a new constitution, and out of the lands formerly allied or subject increased the number of cantons to 19. In 1815 the perpetual neutrality of Switzerland and the inviolability of her territory were guaranteed by Austria, France, Great Britain, Portugal, Prussia, Spain and Sweden, and the Federal Pact, which included 3 new cantons, was accepted by the Congress of Vienna. In 1848 a new constitution was passed. The 22 cantons set up a federal government (consisting of a federal parliament and a federal council) and a federal tribunal. This constitution, in turn, was on 29 May 1874 superseded by the present constitution, which also combines the federal principle with a national and local use of referendums. Though women constitute a third of the work-force, female franchise dates only from Feb. 1971. In a national referendum held in Sept. 1978, 69·9% voted in favour of the establishment of a new canton, Jura, which was established on 1 Jan. 1979.

Switzerland was neutral in both world wars. After the First World War, it joined the League of Nations, which was based in Geneva. But after the Second World War neutrality was thought to conflict with membership of the UN, though Switzerland participates in its agencies and since 1948 has been a contracting party to the Statute of the International Court of Justice.

TERRITORY AND POPULATION. Switzerland is bounded in the west and north-west by France, north by Germany, east by Austria and south by Italy. Area and population by canton (with date of establishment), according to the census held on 1 Dec. 1980 and estimates of 31 Dec. 1994 and 31 Dec. 1997:

Canton	Area (sq. km)	Census 1 Dec. 1980	(in 1,000) 31 Dec. 1994	Estimate (in 1,000) 31 Dec. 1997
Zurich (1351)	1,729	1,122,839	1,167·6	1,175·5
Berne (1553)	6,050	912,022	943·6	942·0
Lucerne (1332)	1,493	296,159	337·7	340·5
Uri (1291)	1,077	33,883	35·9	35·9
Schwyz (1291)	908	97,354	120·6	122·4
Obwalden (1291)	490	25,865	31·1	31·3
Nidwalden (1291)	276	28,617	36·0	36·5
Glarus (Glaris) (1352)	685	36,718	39·3	39·4
Zug (1352)	239	75,930	90·3	92·4
Fribourg (Freiburg) (1481)	1,671	185,246	222·1	224·6
Solothurn (Soleure) (1481)	791	218,102	237·1	239·3
Basel-Town (Bâle-V.) (1501)	37	203,915	197·7	195·8
Basel-Country (Bâle-C.) (1501)	428	219,822	251·4	252·3
Schaffhausen (Schaffhouse) (1501)	299	69,413	74·0	74·0
Appenzell-Outer Rhoden (1513)	243	47,611	54·4	54·1
Appenzell-Inner Rhoden (1513)	173	12,844	14·7	14·8

[1] The Latin 'Confoederatio Helvetica' is also in use.

Canton	Area (sq. km)	Census 1 Dec. 1980	(in 1,000) 31 Dec. 1994	Estimate (in 1,000) 31 Dec. 1997
St Gallen (St Gall) (1803)	2,026	391,995	440·7	442·4
Graubünden (Grisons) (1803)	7,105	164,641	184·3	185·1
Aargau (Argovie) (1803)	1,404	453,442	524·1	528·9
Thurgau (Thurgovie) (1803)	991	183,795	220·4	223·4
Ticino (Tessin) (1803)	2,812	265,899	302·4	305·2
Vaud (Waadt) (1803)	3,212	528,747	601·6	605·7
Valais (Wallis) (1815)	5,225	218,707	269·6	271·3
Neuchâtel (Neuenburg) (1815)	803	158,368	164·5	165·3
Geneva (1815)	282	349,040	391·1	395·5
Jura (1979)	836	64,986	69·0	69·2
Total	41,129	6,365,960	7,021·2	7,062·4

In 1994 there were 3,591,600 females and 1,331,600 resident foreign nationals.

German, French and Italian are the official languages; Romansch (spoken mostly in Graubünden), hitherto a national language, was upgraded to 'semi-official' in 1996. German is spoken by the majority of inhabitants in 19 of the 26 cantons, French in Fribourg, Vaud, Valais, Neuchâtel, Jura and Geneva, and Italian in Ticino. At the 1990 census 63·6% of the population gave German as their mother tongue, 19·2% French, 7·6% Italian, 0·6% Romansch and 8·9% other languages. 1997 statistics are 65% German, 18·4% French, 9·8% Italian, and 0·8% Romansch.

At the end of 1994 the 5 largest cities were Zurich (353,361); Basel (179,639); Geneva (174,363); Berne (134,129); Lausanne (123,266). At the end of 1990 the population figures of conurbations were: Zurich, 841,100; Geneva, 394,800; Basel, 360,400; Berne, 299,500; Lausanne, 263,600; other towns 1994, (and their conurbations 1992), Winterthur, 88,168 (109,800); St Gallen, 75,541 (127,400); Lucerne, 61,656 (161,000); Biel, 52,197 (83,000).

Vital statistics for calendar years:

	Live births	Marriages	Divorces	Deaths
1992	86,900	45,000	14,500	62,300
1993	83,762	43,257	15,053	62,512
1994	82,900	42,400	15,600	61,800
1995	82,203	40,820	15,703	63,387

Rates (1996, per 1,000 population): Birth, 8·3; death, 6·3: (1990, per 1,000 population): Marriage, 6·9; divorce, 2·0. Infant mortality, 1992 (per 1,000 live births), 6·4. Expectation of life, 1997 est.: Males, 75·59 years; females, 82·11. Over 1990–95 the suicide rate per 100,000 population was 22·7 (men, 34·3; women, 11·6).

CLIMATE. The climate is largely dictated by relief and altitude and includes continental and mountain types. Summers are generally warm, with quite considerable rainfall; winters are fine, with clear, cold air. Berne. Jan. 32°F (0°C), July, 65°F (18·5°C). Annual rainfall 39·4" (986 mm).

CONSTITUTION AND GOVERNMENT. The Constitution dates from 29 May 1879. Switzerland is a republic. The highest authority is vested in the electorate, *i.e.*, all Swiss citizens over 18. This electorate, besides electing its representatives to the Parliament has the voting power on amendments to, or on the revision of, the Constitution. It also takes decisions on laws and international treaties if requested by 50,000 voters or 8 cantons (facultative referendum), and it has the right of initiating constitutional amendments, the support required for such demands being 100,000 voters (popular initiative).

The Federal Government is supreme in matters of peace, war and treaties; it regulates the army, the railway, telecommunication systems, the coining of money, the issue and repayment of bank-notes and weights and measures. It also legislates on matters of copyright, bankruptcy, patents, sanitary policy in dangerous epidemics, and it may create and subsidize, besides the Polytechnic School at Zurich and at Lausanne, 2 federal universities and other educational institutions. There has also been entrusted to it the authority to decide concerning public works for the whole or great part of Switzerland, such as those relating to rivers, forests and the construction of national highways and railways. By referendum of 13 Nov. 1898 it is also the authority in the entire spheres of common law. In 1957 the Federation was empowered to legislate on atomic energy matters and in 1961 on the construction of pipelines of petroleum and gas.

The legislative authority is vested in a parliament of 2 chambers: the Council of States (*Ständerat/Conseil des États*) and the National Council (*Nationalrat/Conseil National*). The Council of States is composed of 46 members, chosen and paid by the 23 cantons of the Confederation, 2 for each canton. The mode of their election and the term of membership depend on the canton. 3 of the cantons are politically divided–Basel into Town and Country, Appenzell into Outer-Rhoden and Inner-Rhoden, and Unterwalden into Obwalden and Nidwalden. Each of these 'half-cantons' sends 1 member to the State Council.

The National Council has 200 members directly elected for 4 years, in proportion to the population of the cantons, with the proviso that each canton or half-canton is represented by at least 1 member. The members are paid from federal funds. The parliament sits for 16 three-day sessions annually.

The 200 members are distributed among the cantons as follows:

Zurich	35	Appenzell—Outer- and Inner-Rhoden	3
Berne	29	St Gallen (St Gall)	12
Lucerne	9	Graubünden (Grisons)	5
Uri	1	Aargau (Argovie)	14
Schwyz	3	Thurgau (Thurgovie)	6
Unterwalden–Upper and Lower	2	Ticino (Tessin)	8
Glarus (Glaris)	1	Vaud (Waadt)	17
Zug	2	Valais (Wallis)	7
Fribourg (Freiburg)	6	Neuchâtel (Neuenburg)	5
Solothurn (Soleure)	7	Geneva	11
Basel (Bâle)—town and country	13	Jura	2
Schaffhausen (Schaffhouse)	2		

A general election takes place by ballot every 4 years. Every citizen of the republic who has entered on his 18th year is entitled to a vote, and any voter, not a clergyman, may be elected a deputy. Laws passed by both chambers may be submitted to direct popular vote, when 50,000 citizens or 8 cantons demand it; the vote can be only 'Yes' or 'No'. This principle, called the *referendum*, is frequently acted on.

On 22 Oct. 1995 elections were held for both chambers of the federal parliament; turn-out was 42%. In the Council of States, the Radical Democratic Party (RDP) gained 17 seats (18 in 1991); the Christian Democratic Party (CDP), 16 (16); the Swiss Socialist Party (SSP), 5 (nil); the Swiss People's Party or Democratic Centre Union (SPPDCU), 5 (4); others, 3. In the National Council, SSP gained 54 seats (41 in 1991); RDP, 45 (44); CDP, 34 (35); SPPDCU, 29 (25); others, 38.

The chief executive authority is deputed to the *Bundesrat*, or Federal Council, consisting of 7 members, elected from 7 different cantons for 4 years by the *United Federal Assembly, i.e.*, joint sessions of both chambers. The members of this council must not hold any other office in the Confederation or cantons, nor engage in any calling or business. In the Federal Parliament legislation may be introduced either by a member, or by either chamber, or by the Federal Council (but not by the people). Every citizen who has a vote for the National Council is eligible to become a member of the executive.

The *President* of the Federal Council (called President of the Confederation) and the Vice-President are the first magistrates of the Confederation. Both are elected by the United Federal Assembly for 1 calendar year from among the Federal Councillors. and are not immediately re-eligible to the same offices. The Vice-President, however, may be, and usually is, elected to succeed the outgoing President.

President of the Confederation (1998): Flavio Cotti (CDP).

The 7 members of the Federal Council act as ministers, or chiefs of the 7 administrative departments of the republic. The city of Berne is the seat of the Federal Council and the central administrative authorities.

In March 1998 the Federal Council comprised:

Foreign Affairs: Flavio Cotti (CDP). *Interior:* Ruth Dreifuss (SSP). *Justice and Police:* Arnold Koller (CDP). *Military:* Adolf Ogi (SPPDCU). *Finance:* Kaspar Villiger (RDP). *Public Economy:* Jean-Pascal Delamuraz (RDP). *Transport, Communications and Energy:* Moritz Leuenberger (SSP).

National anthem: 'Trittst im Morgenrot daher'/'Sur nos monts quand le soleil'/'Quando il ciel' di porpora' ('Step into the rosy dawn'); German words by Leonard Widmer, French by C. Chatelanat, Italian by C. Valsangiacomo, tune by Alberik Zwyssig.

Cantonal and Local Government. Each of the 26 cantons and demi-cantons is sovereign, so far as its independence and legislative powers are not restricted by the federal constitution; all cantonal governments, though different in organization (membership varies from 5 to 11, and terms of office from 1 to 5 years), are based on the principle of sovereignty of the people.

In 21 cantons a body chosen by universal suffrage, usually called the *Great Council,* or *Canton Council,* exercises the functions of a parliament. In all the cantonal constitutions except those of the 5 cantons which have a *Landsgemeinde,* the referendum has a place. By this principle, where it is most fully developed, as in Zurich, all laws and concordats, or agreements with other cantons, and the chief matters of finance, as well as all revisions of the Constitution, must be submitted to the popular vote. In the 5 cantons of Appenzell, Glarus and Unterwalden the people exercise their powers direct in the *Landsgemeinde, i.e.,* the assembly in the open air of all citizens of full age. In all the cantons the *popular initiative* for constitutional affairs, as well as for legislation, has been introduced, except in Lucerne, where the *initiative* exists only for constitutional affairs. In most cantons there are districts (*Amtsbezirke*) consisting of a number of communes grouped together, each district having a Prefect (*Regierungsstatthalter*) representing the cantonal government. In the larger communes, for local affairs, there is an Assembly (legislative) and a Council (executive) with a president, mayor or syndic, and not less than 4 other members. In the smaller communes there is a council only, with its officials.

DEFENCE. There are fortifications in all entrances to the Alps and on the important passes crossing the Alps and the Jura. Large-scale destruction of bridges, tunnels and defiles are prepared for an emergency.

Army. There are about 3,400 regular soldiers, but some 360,000 conscripts undergo training annually in the following phases: At 20 years of age, 15 weeks recruit training; between 21 and 32, reservist refresher training (*Auszug*); between 33 and 42, 39 days training for the Militia (*Landwehr*). Proposals ('Army 95') implemented in 1995 envisaged a more flexible army to protect the population against military or natural catastrophes, combat terrorism and take part in international peacekeeping. The conscript sign-off age was reduced to 42 years, the number of conscripts reduced to 360,000, and the number of regular soldiers (including women) increased.

The Army is divided into 3 field corps each of 1 armoured and 2 infantry divisions and support groups, a corps with 3 mountain divisions, and independent redoubt-, fortress- and territorial-brigades.

The administration of the Swiss Army is partly in the hands of the Cantonal authorities, who can promote officers up to the rank of captain. But the Federal Government is concerned with all general questions and makes all the higher appointments.

In peace-time the Army has no general; in time of war the Federal Assembly in joint session of both Houses appoints a general.

Equipment includes about 370 Leopard, 186 Pz-68 and 186 Pz-68/88 main battle tanks.

Air Corps. The Air Corps is part of the Army. It has 3 flying regiments. The fighter squadrons are equipped with Swiss-built F-5E Tiger IIs (6 squadrons), Mirage IIIS supersonic interceptor/ground-attack (2 squadrons), Mirage IIIRS fighter/reconnaissance (3 squadrons), and Bloodhound surface-to-air missile batteries are operational.

Training aircraft are Pilatus PC-7 Turbo-Trainers and Hawks; there are also communications and transport aircraft and helicopters. Personnel (1996), 32,600 on mobilization, with 150 combat aircraft.

INTERNATIONAL RELATIONS

Membership. Switzerland is a member of OECD, EFTA, the Council of Europe and the NATO Partnership for Peace, and applied to join the EU on 26 May 1992. In referendums in 1986 the electorate voted against joining the UN, and in Dec. 1992 the European Economic Area.

ECONOMY

Performance. Total GDP was US$292,500m. in 1996, a decline of 0·7% on 1995.

Budget. Revenue and expenditure of the Confederation, in 1m. francs, for calendar years:

	1990	1991	1992	1993	1994	1995
Revenue	32,674	33,490	34,953	32,782	36,239	36,319
Expenditure	31,616	35,501	37,816	40,600	41,341	42,399

Main sources of revenue, 1995 (in 1m. francs): Direct federal taxes, 8,650; VAT, 7,700; corporation tax, 3,000; settlement taxes, 2,900; stamp duty, 1,850. Expenditure: Social security, 10,955; defence, 5,952; transport, 6,351; agriculture, 3,461; education and research, 3,233.

Currency. The unit of currency is the *Swiss franc* (CHF) of 100 *centimes* or *Rappen*. There are coins of 5, 10, 20 and 50 centimes and 1, 2 and 5 francs, and notes of 10, 20, 50, 100, 500 and 1,000 francs. Notes in circulation, 1991, 29,220m. francs. Foreign exchange reserves, Dec. 1996, US$36,800m.; gold reserves (1991), 11,900m. francs. Inflation was an annualized 0·8% in 1996.

Banking and Finance. The National Bank, with headquarters divided between Berne and Zurich, opened on 20 June 1907. It has the exclusive right to issue bank-notes. The *Chairman* is Hans Meyer (b. 1936).

On 31 Dec. 1995 there were 413 banks with total assets of 1,259,400m. Swiss francs. They included 25 cantonal banks (with 20·8% of total assets), 4 big banks (52·9%), 127 regional and saving banks (5·7%), 1 association (consisting of 1,229 member banks in 1992) of loan and *Raiffeisen* banks (4%), 155 foreign banks (8·9%), 17 private banks (0·6%) and 84 other banks (7·1%). In 1997 the 3 largest banks in order of capitalization were: Union Bank of Switzerland, Crédit Suisse, Swiss Bank Corporation. A planned merger was announced in Dec. 1997 between Union Bank of Switzerland and Swiss Bank Corporation.

Money laundering was made a criminal offence in Aug. 1990. Complete secrecy about clients' accounts remains intact, but anonymity was abolished in July 1991.

The stock exchange system has been reformed under federal legislation of 1990 on securities trading and capital market services. The 4 smaller exchanges have been closed and activity concentrated on the major exchanges of Zurich, Basel and Geneva, which have harmonized their operations with the introduction of the Swiss Electronic Exchange (EBS) in Dec. 1995. Zurich is a major international insurance centre.

Weights and Measures. The metric system is legal.

ENERGY AND NATURAL RESOURCES

Electricity. The Energy 2000 programme aims to stabilize consumption. The total production of energy amounted to 54,074m. kWh in 1990 of which 30,675m. kWh were hydro-electric, 22,298m. kWh nuclear and 1,101m. kWh thermal. In 1993 37·2% was nuclear-produced, but in Sept. 1990 54% of citizens voted for a 10-year moratorium on the construction of new nuclear plants.

Minerals. Salt is mined.

Agriculture. The country is self-sufficient in wheat and meat. Agriculture is protected by subsidies, price guarantees and import controls. Farmers are guaranteed an income equal to industrial workers. Agriculture occupied 6·5% of the total work-force and contributed 2·5% to GDP in 1990. The agricultural area, in 1990, totalled

1,071,346 ha, of which 312,372 ha were arable, 13,245 ha vineyards, 90,338 ha cultivated grassland and 638,904 ha natural grassland and pasture. In 1991 there were 108,296 farms (40% in mountain or hill regions), of which 23,493 were under 1 ha, 13,953 over 20 ha and 45,492 part-time.

Area harvested, 1988 (in 1,000 ha): Cereals, 186; coarse grains, 92; potatoes, 19; sugar-beet, 15. Production, 1988 (in 1,000 tonnes): Potatoes, 748; sugar-beet, 923; wheat, 553; barley, 299; maize, 237; tobacco, 1. Fruit production (in 1,000 tonnes) in 1988 was: Apples, 540; pears, 229; plums, 33; cherries, 35; nuts, 6.

Wine is produced in 18 of the cantons. In 1988 vineyards yielded 117 tonnes of wine.

Livestock, 1993: Cattle, 1,745,087 (including milch cows, 762,450); pigs, 1,691,781; horses, 54,527; sheep, 424,027; goats, 56,687.

Forestry. The forest area was 1,204,047 ha in 1993. Production (1993) 4,338 cu. metres of timber (73·1% coniferous and 26·9% broadleaved).

INDUSTRY. There were 347,500 firms in 1991, of which 84·9% employed fewer than 10 persons. The chief food producing industries, based on Swiss agriculture, are the manufacture of cheese, butter, sugar and meat.

Among the other industries, the manufacture of textiles, clothing and footwear, chemicals and pharmaceutical products, the production of machinery (including electrical machinery and scientific and optical instruments) and watch and clock making are the most important.

Labour. In 1994, the total working population was 3,776,000, of whom 145,000 were active in agriculture and forestry, 1,092,000 in manufacture and construction and 2,539,000 in services. 164,378 persons (44% female) were registered unemployed in Dec. 1994. In 1996 the unemployment rate had increased to 4·5%. The annual average for men was 4·4% and for women 5·1%. In Dec. 1997 it had further increased to 5%.

The foreign labour force with permit of temporary residence was 939,000 in Aug. 1995 (326,600 women). Of these 261,400 were Italian, 146,700 Yugoslav, 108,600 French, 103,400 Portuguese and 89,600 German.

Trade Unions. The Swiss Federation of Trade Unions had about 419,000 members in 1996.

FOREIGN ECONOMIC RELATIONS. Legislation of 1991 increased the possibilities of foreign ownership of domestic companies.

Commerce. Imports and exports, excluding gold (bullion and coins) and silver (coins), were (in 1m. Swiss francs):

	1990	1991	1992	1993	1994	1995	1996
Imports	96,610	95,032	92,330	89,830	92,608	94,483	96,664
Exports	88,260	87,947	92,142	93,289	95,827	96,236	98,589

Main import suppliers in 1996 (share of total trade): Germany, 31·4%; France, 11·6%; Italy, 10·7%; USA, 7·1%; UK, 6·4%. Main export markets: Germany, 22·7%; France, 9·3%; USA, 9·3%; Italy, 7·5%; UK, 6·3%.

Main imports in 1994 (in 1m. francs): Raw materials and semi-manufactures, 31,952; consumer goods, 35,263; producers' goods, 22,349. Exports: Machinery and apparatus, 26,123; chemicals, 23,492; precision instruments, clocks and watches and jewellery, 19,994; metals, 7,780; textiles, clothing and shoes, 4,292.

Tourism. Tourism is an important industry. In 1994, overnight stays by tourists totalled 74,788,000. There were 9·9m. foreign visitors in 1993, bringing receipts of 12,820m. francs. 9·56m. Swiss citizens travelled abroad in 1993.

COMMUNICATIONS

Roads. There were (1993) 71,045 km of main roads, including 1,530 km of national highways, 18,318 km of cantonal roads and 51,197 km of local roads. Motor vehicles in 1991 (in 1,000): Private cars, 3,066; lorries, 277; buses, 34; motor cycles, 323. Goods transport by road, 1992, was 10,374m. tonne-km. There were 83,379 road accidents in 1993, with 723 fatalities.

Railways. In 1993 the length of the general traffic railways was 5,029 km, and of special lines (funiculars etc.), 814 km. In 1995 the Federal Railway carried 253m. passengers and 47·3m. tonnes of freight. There are tram/light rail networks in Basel, Berne, Bex, Geneva, Lausanne, Neuchâtel and Zurich.

There are many other lines, the most important of which are the Berne–Lotschberg–Simplon (115 km) and Rhaetian (363 km) networks.

Civil Aviation. There are international airports at Berne (Belp), Basel (which also serves Mulhouse in France), Geneva and Zurich. Swissair is the national carrier. In 1995 it had 3 A310-200s, 5 A310-300s, 1 A320-200, 4 A321-100s, 2 B-747-300s, 3 B-747-300 Combis and 47 other aircraft. In 1991 Swissair carried 7·9m. passengers and 271,000 tonnes of freight. Services are also provided by 78 foreign airlines.

Shipping. In 1989 there were 1,208 km of navigable waterways. 13·3m. tonnes of freight were transported. A merchant marine was created in 1941, the place of registry of its vessels being Basel. In 1995 it consisted of 174 vessels with a total of 4·36m. DWT. GRT totalled 0·38m.

Telecommunications. In 1993 there were 4,266,000 primary telephones and (1994) 307,000 mobile telephones, and (1990) 23,953 fax and 24,300 telex machines.

Schweizerische Radio- und Fernsehgesellschaft/Société Suisse de Radiodiffusion et Télévision/Società Svizzera di Radiotelevisione is a non-profit-making company responsible for radio and television services. There are German, French and Italian radio and TV networks (colour by PAL). The German radio service has 3 programmes, local programmes and also broadcasts in Romansch; the French service ('Suisse Romande') has 3 programmes, as does the Italian. There is an external service, Swiss Radio International (Arabic, English, Spanish) and 4 city-based private stations. The UN and the Red Cross have radio stations. In 1994 there were 2,727,000 radio and 2,513,000 TV sets in use.

Cinemas. There were 406 screens in 1993.

Press. There were 96 daily newspapers in 1993 (76 German language, 16 French and 4 Italian) with a total circulation of 2,795,386. In 1996 daily newspaper sales averaged 365 per 1,000 population. 10,274 book titles were published in 1992 (10·9% in English).

SOCIAL INSTITUTIONS

Justice. The Federal Court, which sits at Lausanne, consists of 30 judges, 15 supplementary judges and 15 temporary supplementary judges, elected by the Federal Assembly for 6 years and eligible for re-election; the President and Vice-President serve for 2 years and cannot be re-elected. The Tribunal has original and final jurisdiction in suits between the Confederation and cantons; between cantons and cantons; between the Confederation or cantons and corporations or individuals; between parties who refer their case to it; in such suits as the constitution or legislation of cantons places within its authority; and in many classes of railway suits. It is a court of appeal against decisions of other federal authorities, and of cantonal authorities applying federal laws. The Tribunal comprises 2 courts of public law, 2 civil courts, a chamber of bankruptcy, a chamber of prosecution, a court of criminal appeal, a court of extraordinary appeal, a federal criminal court, and a criminal chamber for cases of treason (sits very rarely). The jurors who serve in the Assize Courts are elected by the people, and are paid a daily allowance.

A Federal Insurance Court sits in Lucerne, and comprises 9 judges and 9 supplementary judges elected for 6 years by the Federal Assembly.

A federal penal code replaced cantonal codes in 1942. It abolished capital punishment except for offences in war-time; this latter proviso was abolished in 1991.

There were 64,151 adult criminal convictions in 1992 (13·4% female; 44·4% foreign).

Religion. There is liberty of conscience and of creed. At the 1990 census 47·3% of the population were Protestant, 46·2% Roman Catholic and 7·4% without religion. In 1997 the proportions were: Roman Catholics, 48%; Protestants, 44%.

Education. Education is administered by the cantons and communes and is free and compulsory for 9 years. Compulsory education consists of 4 (Berne, Basel-Town, Jura Vaud), 5 (Aargau, Basel-Country, Neuchâtel) or 6 (other cantons except Ticino, which has 9) years of primary education and the balance in Stage I secondary education. This may be followed by 5 years of Stage II secondary education of general or vocational schools. Tertiary education is at universities, higher vocational schools and advanced vocational training institutes.

In 1995–96 there were 158,200 children in nursery schools. There were 777,100 pupils in compulsory education (452,800 at primary, 280,500 at lower secondary and 43,700 at special schools), 87,500 in Stage II general secondary education, 192,700 in Stage II vocational secondary education, and 148,000 students in higher education, including 88,200 at university.

There are 7 universities (date of foundation and students in 1989–90): Basel (1460, 6,763), Berne (1528, 9,511), Fribourg (1889, 5,814), Geneva (1559, 12,028), Lausanne (1537, 6,942), Neuchâtel (1866, 2,512), Zurich (1523, 20,690); and 5 institutions of equivalent status: Lucerne Theological Faculty (199), St Gallen PHS (171), St Gallen School of Economics and Social Science (3,952), Lausanne Federal Institute of Technology (3,495), Zurich Federal Institute of Technology (11,200).

Health. Medical facilities (number per 0·1m. population in 1992)· General hospitals, 605·7; psychiatric clinics, 162·7; old people's and nursing homes, 1,165·3; doctors in private practice, 160·2; dentists, 48·5; pharmacies, 22·5.

New cases of infectious diseases, 1992. Tuberculosis, 987; AIDS, 569; malaria, 261.

Welfare. The Federal Insurance Law against illness and accident, of 13 June 1911, entitles all citizens to insurance against illness; foreigners may be admitted to the benefits. Compulsory insurance against illness does not exist, but cantons and communities are entitled to declare insurance obligatory for certain classes or to establish public benefit (sick fund) associations, and to make employers responsible for the payment of the premiums of their employees.

Unemployment insurance is compulsory for all wage-earners. Insurance against accident is compulsory for all officials, employees and workmen of all the factories, trades, etc., which are under the federal liability law.

Old age and widows and widowers insurance has been compulsory since 1948. The following amounts (in 1m. francs) were paid in social security benefits:

	1993	1994	1995
Federal Old Age Pensions	23,047	23,363	24,503
Supplementary Benefits	1,541	1,567	1,575
Federal Disability Insurance	5,987	6,396	6,826
Loss of Earnings Insurance	831	810	621
Unemployment Insurance	5,986	5,921	5,240
Family Allowances	1,144	3,872	3,920

DIPLOMATIC REPRESENTATIVES

Of Switzerland in Great Britain (16–18 Montagu Pl., London, W1H 2BQ)
Ambassador: François Nordmann.

Of Great Britain in Switzerland (Thunstrasse 50, 3005 Bern)
Ambassador: C. Hulse, CMG., OBE.

Of Switzerland in the USA (2900 Cathedral Ave., NW, Washington, D.C., 20008)
Ambassador: Vacant.

Of the USA in Switzerland (Jubilaeumstrasse 93, 3005, Bern)
Ambassador: Madeleine Kunin.

Of the USA to the European Union
Ambassador: Alexis Lautenberg.

Further Reading

Office Fédéral de la Statistique. *Annuaire Statistique de la Suisse.*

Hilowitz, J. E., (ed.) *Switzerland in Perspective.* New York, 1991
Meier, H. K. and Meier, R. A., *Switzerland.* [bibliography] London and Santa Barbara (CA), 1990
New, M., *Switzerland Unwrapped: Exposing the Myths.* London, 1997
Wildblood, R., *What makes Switzerland tick?* London, 1988

National library: Bibliothèque Nationale Suisse, Hallwylstr. 15, 3003 Berne.
National statistical office: Office Fédéral de la Statistique, Schwarztorstr. 96, 3003 Berne.
SFSO Information Service e-mail: *information@bfs.admin.ch*
Website: http://www.admin.ch/bfs/

SYRIA

Jumhuriya al-Arabya as-Suriya

(Syrian Arab Republic)

Capital: Damascus
Population: 16·14m.
GDP per head: (PPP$) 5,397
HDI/world rank: 0·755/78

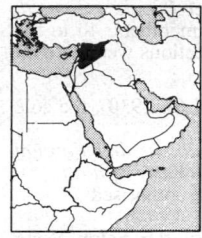

KEY HISTORICAL EVENTS. Syria was under Turkish control from the 12th century, and part of the Ottoman Empire from the 16th century until the First World War. Following the defeat of the Turks in that war, the League of Nations granted to France a mandate for Syria from 1920. On 27 Sept. 1941, Gen. Catroux, the Free French C.-in-C., in the name of the Allies, proclaimed the independence of Syria at Damascus. On 27 Dec. 1943 an agreement was signed between representatives of the French National Committee of Liberation and of Syria, by which most of the powers and capacities exercised hitherto by France under mandate were transferred as from 1 Jan. 1944 to the Syrian government. The evacuation of all foreign troops in April 1946 marked the complete independence of Syria, but the political situation was unsettled and military *coups* were staged in Dec. 1949 and in Feb. 1954.

Syria merged with Egypt to form the United Arab Republic from 2 Feb. 1958 until 29 Sept. 1961, when Syrian independence was resumed following a *coup* the previous day. Following the fifth *coup* of the decade, Lieut.-Gen. Hafez el Assad became prime minister on 13 Nov. 1970, and assumed the presidency on 22 Feb. 1971.

A new constitution, approved by plebiscite on 12 March 1973, confirmed the Arab Socialist Renaissance (Ba'ath) Party as the 'leading party in the state and society'.

TERRITORY AND POPULATION. Syria is bounded by the Mediterranean and Lebanon on the west, by Israel and Jordan on the south, by Iraq on the east and by Turkey on the north. The frontier between Syria and Turkey was settled by the Franco-Turkish agreement of 22 June 1929.The area is 185,180 sq. km (71,498 sq. miles). The census of 1994 gave a population of 13,782,000. Estimate (1997), 16,137,899 (50% urban); density, 74 per sq. km. Life expectancy was 66·4 years in 1992 (1997 estimate, 67·44; male, 66·21; female, 68·74). Population growth (1997) 3·3%.

Area and population (1996 estimate, in 1,000) of the 14 districts *(mohafaza)*:

	Sq. km	Population		Sq. km	Population
Damascus (City)	105	1,347	Idlib	6,097	1,270
Damascus (District)	18,032	1,237	Hasakah	23,334	1,013
Aleppo	18,500	3,694	Raqqah	19,616	592
Homs	42,223	1,471	Suwaydá	5,550	380
Hama	8,883	1,415	Dará	3,730	689
Lattakia	2,297	936	Tartous	1,892	730
Deir Ez-Zor	33,060	994	Qunaytirah	1,861	330

Principal towns (population, 1994 in 1,000): Damascus (the capital), 1,444; Aleppo, 1,542; Homs, 558; Lattakia, 303; Hama, 273; Al-Kamishli, 165; Raqqah, 138; Deir Ez-Zor, 133.

Vital statistics, 1997 estimate (rate per 1000 population): Birth, 38·7; death, 5·7; infant mortality (per 1000 live births), 38·8.

Arabic is the official language, spoken by 89% of the population, while 6% speak Kurdish (chiefly Hasakah governorate), 3% Armenian and 2% other languages.

CLIMATE. The climate is Mediterranean in type, with mild wet winters and dry, hot summers, though there are variations in temperatures and rainfall between the coastal regions and the interior, which even includes desert conditions. The more mountainous parts are subject to snowfall. Damascus. Jan. 38·1°F (3·4°C), July

77·4°F (25·2°C). Annual rainfall 8·8" (217 mm). Aleppo. Jan. 36·7°F (2·6°C), July 80·4°F (26·9°C). Annual rainfall 10·2" (258 mm). Homs. Jan. 38·7°F (3·7°C), July 82·4°F (28°C). Annual rainfall 3·4" (86·7 mm).

CONSTITUTION AND GOVERNMENT. A new Constitution was approved by plebiscite on 12 March 1973 and promulgated on 14 March. It confirmed the Arab Socialist Renaissance *(Ba'ath)* Party, in power since 1963, as the 'leading party in the State and society'. Legislative power is held by a 250-member *People's Council*, renewed every 4 years. 120 seats are allotted to Ba'ath Party members, 40 to the National Progressive Front and 90 independents are elected. Elections were held on 24–25 Aug. 1994.

At a referendum on 2 Dec. 1991 Lieut.-Gen. Hafez al-Assad (b. 1930), the sole candidate, was confirmed as *President* for a fourth 5-year term.

First Vice-President: Abd al-Halim ibn Said Khaddam *(Political and Foreign Affairs). Second Vice-President:* Mohammed Zuhayr Mashariqa *(Party Affairs).*

A government was formed in June 1992 which in March 1998 comprised:
Prime Minister: Mahmud Zubi.

Deputy Prime Ministers: Lt. Gen. Mustafa Talas *(Defence)*; Dr Salim Yasin *(Economic Affairs)*; Rashid Akhtarini *(Public Affairs). Minister of Education:* Ghassan Halabi. *Higher Education:* Saliha Sanqar. *Interior:* Mohammad Harbar. *Information:* Mohammad Salman. *Local Administration:* Yahya Abu Asali. *Supply and Internal Trade:* Nadim Akkash. *Transport:* Mufid Abd al-Karim. *Labour and Social Welfare:* Ali Khalil. *Economy and Foreign Trade:* Mohammad al-Imadi. *Culture and National Guidance:* Najah al-Attar. *Foreign Affairs:* Farouk al-Shara. *Tourism:* Danhu Dawud. *Health:* Iyad al-Shatti. *Irrigation:* Abd al-Rahman Madani. *Electricity:* Munib Saim al-Dahar. *Oil and Mineral Resources:* Muhammad Maher Hosni Jamal. *Construction:* Majid Izzu Ruhaybani. *Housing and Utilities:* Hussam al-Safadi. *Agriculture and Agrarian Reform:* Assad Mustafa. *Finance:* Khalid al-Mahayni. *Communications:* Radwan Martini. *Justice:* Hussein Hassun. *Industry:* Ahmad Nizam al-Din. *Religious Trusts:* Abdul-Raouf Ziada. *Presidential Affairs:* Wahib Fadil. The next elections are due to take place in 1998.

National anthem: 'Humata al Diyari al aykum salaam' ('Defenders of the Realm, on you be peace'); words by Khalil Mardam Bey, tune by M. S. and A. S. Flayfel.

Local Government. Syria is administratively divided into 14 districts *(mohafaza).* These are divided into 59 *mantika*, which are subdivided into 179 smaller administrative units *(nahia)*, each covering a number of villages.

DEFENCE. Military service is compulsory for a period of 30 months.

Army. The Army is organized into 6 armoured and 3 mechanized divisions, a Republican Guard division, 1 special forces division, 8 independent special forces regiments, 3 independent infantry brigades, 2 independent artillery, 3 surface-to-surface missile, 2 independent anti-tank and 1 coastal defence surface-to-surface missile brigade and 1 independent tank regiment. Equipment includes 2,100 T-54/-55, 1,000 T-62 and 1,500 T-72/-72M main battle tanks. Strength (1997) about 215,000 (including 250,000 conscripts).

Navy. The Navy includes 1 ex-Soviet 'Romeo'-class diesel submarine, 2 small frigates, 14 fast missile craft, 11 inshore patrol craft, 2 coastal and 5 inshore minesweepers, and 3 medium landing ships (all ex-Soviet). A small naval aviation branch of the Air Force operates 18 Soviet-built anti-submarine helicopters. Personnel in 1997 numbered 5,000. The main base is at Tartus.

Air Force. The Air Force, including Air Defence Command, had (1997) about 40,000 personnel, over 500 combat aircraft and 60 armed helicopters, including about 180 MiG-21, 80 MiG-23, 20 MiG-25 and 40 MiG-29 supersonic interceptors, 60 MiG-23, 60 Su-22 and 20 Su-24 fighter-bombers, as well as some MiG-25 reconnaissance aircraft. Training units have Spanish-built Flamingo and Pakistani-built Mushshak piston-engined primary trainers and Czechoslovakian L-29 Delfin and

L-39 jet basic trainers. There are also transport units with Il-76, An-12, An-24/26 and other types, and helicopter units with Soviet-built Mi-8/17s and Mi-24s and French-built Gazelles. 'Guideline', 'Goa', 'Gainful' and 'Gaskin' surface-to-air missiles are widely deployed in Syria by Air Defence Command, and 'Gammon' long-range surface-to-air missiles in Lebanon.

INTERNATIONAL RELATIONS. A Treaty of Brotherhood, Co-operation and Co-ordination with Lebanon of May 1991 provides for close relations in the fields of foreign policy, the economy, military affairs and security. By the treaty the Lebanese government's decisions are subject to review by 6 joint Syrian-Lebanese bodies.

Membership. Syria is a member of the UN and Arab League.

ECONOMY

Policy. The relaxation of state control and foreign exchange regulations in response to the 1980's recession has led to a consumer boom. Since 1991, the proportion of the economy in private hands has risen from 35% to 70%. But further reforms have stalled. Economic growth for 1997 is estimated at 3·4%.

Budget. The consolidated budget for the calendar year 1996 balanced at £Syr.188,050m.

Currency. The monetary unit is the *Syrian pound* (SYP) of 100 *piastres*. There are coins of 5, 10, 25, 50 and 100 piastres and £Syr.1, and notes of £Syr. 1, 5, 10, 25, 50, 100 and 500. Inflation was 12% in 1992.

Banking and Finance. The Central Bank is the bank of issue. Commercial banks were nationalized in 1963. The *Governor* of the Central Bank is Hisham Mutawalli.

Weights and Measures. The metric system is legal, though former weights and measures may still be in use: 1 *okiya* = 0·47 lb.; 6 *okiyas* = 1 *oke* = 2·82 lb.; 2 *okes* = 1 *rottol* = 5·64 lb.; 200 *okes* = 1 *kantar*.

ENERGY AND NATURAL RESOURCES

Electricity. Production (1995), 15,549m. kWh.

Oil. Estimated crude oil production (1995), 28m. tonnes. Reserves 1,521m. bbls.

Gas. Gas reserves (1982), 700,000m. cu. ft. Production (1985), 90 petajoules.

Water. In 1992 there were 5 main dams and 127 surface dams. Production of drinking water, 1995, 608·86m. cu. metres.

Minerals. Phosphate deposits have been discovered. Production, 1995, 1,598,000 tonnes; other minerals were salt, 111,000 tonnes and gypsum 336,000 tonnes. There are indications of lead, copper, antimony, nickel, chrome and other minerals widely distributed. Sodium chloride and bitumen deposits are being worked.

Agriculture. In 1994 agriculture accounted for 28·4% of GDP. The arable area in 1995 was 5,979,000 ha, there were 4,982,000 ha of crop-land and 8,287,000 ha of pasture. In 1995 there were 82,603 tractors.

Production of principal crops, 1995 (in 1,000 tonnes): Wheat, 4,184; barley, 1,705; maize, 199; seed cotton, 600; olives, 423; lentils, 148; millet, 5; sugar-beet, 1,406; potatoes, 471; tomatoes, 427; grapes, 384.

Production of animal products, 1995 (in tonnes): Milk, 1,414,000; butter, 14,007; cheese, 65,512; honey, 889; 2,136m. eggs.

Livestock (1995, in 1,000): Cattle, 775; horses, 27; mules, 17; asses, 200; sheep, 12,075; goats, 1,063; poultry, 18,746.

Forestry. In 1995 there were 493,000 ha of forest. The artificial forestry area was 22,576 ha, producing 16,076,000 woody plants, 2,773 tonnes of charcoal, 25,518 tonnes of firewood and 19,342 tonnes of industrial wood.

Fisheries. The total catch in 1995 was 11,639 tonnes.

INDUSTRY. Public sector industrial production in 1995 included (in tonnes): Cotton yarn, 40,417; cotton and mixed textiles, 16,597; mixed woollen yarn, 1,442; manufactured tobacco, 9,699; iron bars, 36,675; asbestos, 15,623; vegetable oil, 33,435; 77,001 electrical engines; 69,163 refrigerators; 80,010 water meters; woollen carpets, 538,000 sq. metres.

Trade Unions. In 1995 there were 199 trade unions with 460,967 members.

FOREIGN ECONOMIC RELATIONS. Legislation of 1991 permits foreign investors a 10-year tax exemption duty-free import of equipment and repatriation of profits. Foreign debt was US$16,400m. in 1990.

Commerce. Imports in 1995 totalled (in £Syr. 1m.) 52,856; exports, 44,562.

Main imports, 1995 (in £Syr. 1) included: Petroleum and products, 318,463; iron and steel bars and rods, 3,269,247; cane sugar, 1,014,390; yarn of continuous synthetic fibres, 1,627,972; alternating current motors and generators, 185,388; passenger transport motor vehicles, 374,583. Main exports included: Petroleum and products, 27,862,627; raw cotton, 2,390,774; printed woven cotton fabrics, 34,418; natural phosphate, 251,061.

In 1995 imports came mainly from Germany, Italy, USA, China, Turkey, Japan and Romania. Exports went mainly to Italy, France, Lebanon and Spain.

Tourism. In 1995, there were 2,252,787 visitors.

COMMUNICATIONS

Roads. In 1995 there were 27,769 km of asphalted roads, 9,327 km of paved non-asphalted road and 2,237 km of earth roads. In 1995 there were 486,776 motor vehicles, including 136,160 cars and taxis, 5,239 buses, 25,145 mini-buses, 58,717 goods vehicles and 89,038 motorcycles.

Railways. In 1995 the network totalled 2,423 km of 1,435 mm gauge (Syrian Railways) and 327 km of 1,050 mm gauge (Hedjaz-Syrian Railway). In 1995 Syrian Railways carried 2m. passengers and 4·3m. tonnes of freight.

Civil Aviation. The international airport is at Damascus. In 1995, 13,520 aircraft arrived at Damascus, Aleppo, Al-Kamishli, Lattakia and Deir Ez-Zor airports; 759,597 passengers arrived, 785,917 departed and 81,007 were in transit; 10,280 tonnes of freight was unloaded and 34,967 tonnes loaded. The national carrier is the state-owned Syrian Arab Airlines, which in 1995 had a fleet of 6 B-727-200 Advs, 2 B-747SPs, 7 ex-Soviet and 2 other aircraft. Services were also provided by Aeroflot, Air Algérie, Air France, Air Malta, Air Ukraine, Alitalia, Alyemda, Austrian Airlines, Balkan, British Airways, British Mediterranean Airways, Cyprus Airways, Czech Airlines, Egyptair, Emirates, Gulf Air, Iran Air, KLM, Kuwait Airways, Libyan Airlines, LOT, Lufthansa, Malév, Pakistan Airlines, Qatar Airways, Royal Jordanian, Saudia, Sudan Airways, Tarom, Tunis Air, Turkish Airlines and Yemenia.

Shipping. In 1995 the merchant marine totalled 0·45m. GRT.

Telecommunications. Number of telephones (1995), 984,196; of these, 358,642 were in Damascus and 179,725 in Aleppo. Mobile phones and the Internet are banned. Broadcasting is controlled by the government Syrian Broadcasting and Television Organization. There are 2 national radio programmes and an external service and 2 TV programmes (colour by SECAM and PAL). In 1993 there were 3·75m. radio and 950,000. TV sets.

Cinemas. In 1994 there were 49 cinemas with 25,111 seats.

Press. In 1995 there were 8 national daily newspapers with a combined circulation of 274,000.

SOCIAL INSTITUTIONS

Justice. Syrian law is based on both Islamic and French jurisprudence. There are 2 courts of first instance in each district, one for civil and 1 for criminal cases. There is also a Summary Court in each sub-district, under Justices of the Peace. There is a Court of Appeal in the capital of each governorate, with a Court of Cassation in Damascus. The death penalty is in force, and executions may be held in public.

Religion. In 1992 there were 11·61m. Moslems (namely Sunni with some Shi'ites and Ismailis). There are also Druzes and Alawites. Christians (1·15m. in 1992) include Greek Orthodox, Greek Catholics, Armenian Orthodox, Syrian Orthodox, Armenian Catholics, Protestants, Maronites, Syrian Catholics, Latins, Nestorians and Assyrians. There are also Jews and Yezides.

Education. In 1995 there were 1,037 kindergartens with 90,681 children; 10,420 primary schools with 113,384 teachers and 2,651,247 pupils; 2,526 intermediate and secondary schools with 50,779 teachers and 841,964 pupils. In 1995, 14 teachers' colleges had 766 teachers and 4,989 students; 292 schools for technical education had 10,105 teachers and 72,859 students. Adult literacy, 70·8% (male, 85·7%; female, 55·8%).

In 1995–96 there were 4 universities and 1 higher institution of political science, with 161,185 students and 4,806 academic staff.

Health. In 1995 there were 17,623 beds in 294 hospitals, and 795 health centres. In 1995 there were 15,391 doctors, 8,025 dentists, 5,919 pharmacists, 6,063 midwives and 23,151 nursing personnel.

DIPLOMATIC REPRESENTATIVES

Of Syria in Great Britain (8 Belgrave Sq., London SW1X 8PH)
Ambassador: Vacant.

Of Great Britain in Syria (11 Mohammad Kurd Ali St., Damascus POB 37)
Ambassador: Basil S. T. Eastwood, CMG.

Of Syria in the USA (2215 Wyoming Ave., NW, Washington, D.C., 20008)
Ambassador: Walid Moualem.

Of the USA in Syria (Abu Rumaneh, Al Mansur St. No. 2, Damascus)
Ambassador: Christopher W. S. Ross.

Of Syria to the United Nations
Ambassador: Mikhail Wahba.

Of Syria to the European Union
Ambassador: Vacant.

Further Reading

Choueiri, Y., *State and Society in Syria and Lebanon.* Exeter Univ. Press, 1994
Devlin, J. F., *Syria: Modern State in an Ancient Land.* Boulder, 1983
Maoz, M. and Yaniv, A., *Syria under Assad.* New York, 1986
Seale, P., *The Struggle for Syria.* London, 1986.—*Asad of Syria: the Struggle for the Middle East.* London, 1989
Seccombe, I. J., *Syria.* [Bibliography] Oxford and Santa Barbara (CA), 1987

National statistical office: Central Bureau of Statistics, Office of the Prime Minister, Damascus.

TAJIKISTAN

Jumkhurii Tojikiston

Capital: Dushanbe
Population: 5·95m.
GDP per head: (PPP$) 1,117
HDI/world rank: 0·580/115

KEY HISTORICAL EVENTS. The Tajik Soviet Socialist Republic was formed from those regions of Bokhara and Turkestan where the population consisted mainly of Tajiks. It was admitted as a constituent republic of the Soviet Union on 5 Dec. 1929. In Aug. 1990 the Tajik Supreme Soviet adopted a declaration of republican sovereignty, and in Dec. 1991 the republic became a member of the CIS.

After demonstrations and fighting the Communist government was replaced by a Revolutionary Coalition Council on 7 May 1992. Following further demonstrations President Nabiev was ousted on 7 Sept. Civil war broke out, and the government resigned on 10 Nov. On 30 Nov. it was announced that a CIS peacekeeping force would be sent to Tajikistan. A state of emergency was imposed in Jan. 1993.

On 23 Dec. 1996 a ceasefire was signed in the presence of the Russian prime minister between President Rakhmonov and insurgent leader Sayed Abdullo Nuri. A further agreement on 8 March 1997 provided for the disarmament of the insurgents and their eventual integration into the regular armed forces.

A peace agreement brokered by Iran and Russia was signed in Moscow on 27 June 1997. A Commission of National reconciliation was set up and it was stipulated that the opposition should have 30% of ministerial posts.

TERRITORY AND POPULATION. Tajikistan is bordered in the north and west by Uzbekistan and Kyrgyzstan; in the east by China and in the south by Afghanistan. Area, 143,100 sq. km (55,240 sq. miles). It includes 2 provinces (Khudzand and Khatlon) and 43 rural districts, 18 towns and 49 urban settlements, together with the Gorno-Badakhshan Autonomous Region. Of the 1989 census population of 5,092,603, 62·3% were Tajik, 23·5% Uzbek and 7·6% Russian. Population (1997 estimate), 5,945,903 (1,234,730 female); population growth, 1·18%. Vital statistics rates, 1997 estimate (per 1,000 population): Births, 27·93; deaths, 7·74; infant mortality (per 1,000 live births), 109·5. Life expectancy, 66·8 years.

The capital is Dushanbe (1991 population estimate, 592,000). Other large towns are Khudzand (formerly Leninabad), Kurgan-Tyube and Kulyab.

The official language is Tajik, written in Arabic script until 1930 and after 1992 (the Roman alphabet was used 1930–40; the Cyrillic, 1940–92).

CONSTITUTION AND GOVERNMENT. In Nov. 1994 a new Constitution was approved by a 90% favourable vote by the electorate which enhanced the President's powers. The head of state is the *President*, elected by universal suffrage. Parliament is the 181-member *Supreme Assembly*. At presidential elections on 6 Nov. 1994 the electorate was 2·6m.; turn-out was 90%. President Rakhmonov was re-elected by 58·3% of votes cast against 1 opponent.

At the elections of 26 Feb. 1995 for the Supreme Assembly the electorate was 2·6m.; turn-out was officially put at 84%. 40% of the seats were uncontested.

President: Emomali Rakhmonov (as Speaker elected by the former Supreme Soviet 19 Nov. 1992; re-elected 6 Nov. 1996).

In March 1998 the government comprised:
Prime Minister: Yakhyo Azimov.
First Deputy Prime Minister: Yuri Ponosov. *Deputy Ministers:* Ismat Eshmirzoev; Qadriddin Giyasov; Bozqul Dodkhodoeva; Jamoliddin Mansurov; Abdurakhman Azimov; Kholisjon Temurjanov. *Minister of Agriculture:* Moso Barotov. *Communications:* Nuriddin Mukhiddinov. *Culture, Press and Information:* Bobkhan Makhmadov. *Defence:* Maj.-Gen. Sherali Khairullaev. *Protection of the*

1344

Environment: Ismail Davlatov. *Finance:* Anvarsho Muzafarov. *Internal Affairs:* Khomiddin Sharipov. *Justice:* Shavkat Ismailov. *Economy and Foreign Economic Relations:* Tukhtaboj Gafarov. *Foreign Affairs:* Talbak Nasarov. *Transport:* Faridun Mukhitdinov. *Health:* Alamkhon Akhmedov. *Land Improvement and Water Resources:* Ismat Eshmirzoyev. *Social Security:* Abdusattar Dzhabarov. *Education:* Munira Inoyatova. *Labour and Employment:* Shukurjon Zukhurov. *Construction:* Odil Ochilov. *Grain Products:* Bekmurod Urokov. *Security:* Saidamir Zukhurov.

DEFENCE. In 1997 the Army had a strength of 7,000 and comprised 2 motor rifle (1 training) and 1 special forces brigade and 1 surface-to-air missile regiment. Equipment included 40 T-72 main battle tanks. There is a para-military Border Guard (mainly Russian) of 1,200. 25,000 Russian troops and some Air Force units are stationed in the country.

INTERNATIONAL RELATIONS

Membership. Tajikistan is a member of the UN and CIS.

ECONOMY

Budget. Income, 1993, 406,800m. roubles; expenditure 329,100m. roubles. Inflation for February 1997 was 3%; the reduction in inflation came about as a result of a US$22m. IMF loan in 1996 and maintenance of a tight monetary regime.

Currency. The unit of currency is the *Tajik rouble* (TJR) of 100 *tanga*, which replaced the Russian rouble on 10 May 1995 at 1 Tajik rouble = 100 Russian roubles.

Banking and Finance. The central bank and bank of issue is the National Bank (*Chair*, Murodali Alimordonov). In 1996, there were 8 commercial banks, 1 commercial savings bank and 1 state-owned bank for economic affairs.

ENERGY AND NATURAL RESOURCES

Electricity. Capacity in 1994 was 4·44m. kWh and output, 16bn. kWh.

Oil and Gas. In 1995 oil production (including gas concentrate) was 64,000 tonnes; natural gas, 50m. cu. metres.

Minerals. There are deposits of brown coal, lead, zinc and uranium. Coal production, 1993, 0·2m. tonnes. Aluminium production, 1996, 198,000 tonnes.

Agriculture. Area under cultivation in 1997 was 9·6m. ha, mainly in the hands of state and collective farms. Cotton, the major cash crop, accounts for around two-thirds of total production (315,000 tonnes in 1996/97). A variety of fruit is grown, and also sugar-cane. Jute, rice and millet are also grown. There are rich pasture lands. Livestock on 1 Jan. 1994. 1·3m. cattle, 2·9m. sheep and goats and 0·04m. pigs.

Output of main agricultural products (in 1,000 tonnes) in 1993: Grain, 254; potatoes, 147; vegetables, 485; fruit and berries, 148; meat, 69; milk, 432; and 154m. eggs.

Fisheries. 1995 catch, 3,900 tonnes.

INDUSTRY. Output, 1993 (in tonnes): Mineral fertilizer, 20,000; cement, 0·3m.; fabrics, 114m. cu. metres; footwear, 3·9m. pairs; 1,100 lathes; 18,000 refrigerators and freezers.

Labour. In 1993 the population of working age was 2·75m., of whom 1·86m. were employed, 55·3% in the state sector, 25·12% in the private sector and 18·4% in co-operatives. In Jan. 1994 there were 21,500 registered unemployed. Average monthly salaries in 1994 were 14,336 roubles. The monthly minimum wage was 14,400 roubles in 1995.

FOREIGN ECONOMIC RELATIONS

Commerce. In 1996 imports were estimated to be valued at US$657m. and exports at US$768m.

COMMUNICATIONS

Roads. In 1992 there were estimated to be 32,752 km of motor roads. (21,119 km hard surface). In 1993, 139·9m. passengers and 12·3m. tonnes of freight were carried.

Railways. Length of railways, 1990, 480 km. In 1993, 1·2m. passengers and 1·2m. tonnes of freight were carried.

Civil Aviation. There is an international airport at Dushanbe. The national carrier is Tajikistan Airlines, which operated 4 ex-Soviet aircraft in 1995. In 1993, 0·2m. passengers and 2,100 tonnes of freight were carried.

Telecommunications. Broadcasting is controlled by the State Teleradio Broadcasting Company. Tajik Radio broadcasts 3 national programmes, a Radio Moscow relay and a foreign service (Dari, Iranian).

Cinemas. In 1995 there were 159 cinemas with a seating capacity of 39,000 and an annual attendance of 400,000.

Press (1989). There were 74 newspapers, 63 in Tajik. Daily circulation of Tajik-language newspapers, 1,208,000; in all languages, 1,598,000.

SOCIAL INSTITUTIONS

Justice. In 1994, 14,279 crimes were reported, including 636 murders or attempted murders.

Religion. The Tajiks are predominantly Sunni Moslems (80%); Shi'a Moslems, 5%.

Education. In 1993–94 there were 3,179 primary and secondary schools with 1·3m. pupils, 13 higher educational institutions with 69,000 students and 43 technical colleges with 38,400 students. In Jan. 1992, 14% of eligible children were attending pre-school institutions.

There is 1 university, which had 7,220 students in 1994–95.

Health. In Jan. 1994 there were 374 hospitals with 60,000 beds, 13,000 doctors and 42,800 junior medical personnel.

Welfare. In Jan. 1994 there were 0·41m. age pensioners and 0·2m. other pensioners.

BADAKHSHAN AUTONOMOUS REPUBLIC

Comprising the Pamir massif along the borders of Afghanistan and China, the province was set up on 2 Jan. 1925, initially as the Special Pamir Province. Area, 63,700 sq. km (24,590 sq. miles). The population at the 1989 census was 161,000 (89·5% Tajik, 6·7% Kirghiz). Estimate, 1990, 164,300. Capital, Khorog (14,800). The inhabitants are predominantly Ismaili Moslems. Mining industries are developed (gold, rock-crystal, mica, coal, salt). Wheat, fruit and fodder crops are grown and cattle and sheep are bred in the western parts. In 1990 there were 74,200 cattle and 329,500 sheep and goats. Total area under cultivation, 18,400 ha. In 1990-91 there were 47,600 students at all levels of education. There were 140 doctors and 1,400 junior medical personnel in 1991.

DIPLOMATIC REPRESENTATIVES

Of Great Britain in Tajikistan
Ambassador: Alexander Bergne (resides in Uzbekistan).

Of the USA in Tajikistan (Oktyabrskaya Hotel, 105A Prospekt Rudaki, Dushanbe)
Ambassador: R. Grant Smith.

Of Tajikistan to the United Nations
Ambassador: Rashid Alimov.

TANZANIA

Jamhuri ya Muungano
wa Tanzania—United
Republic of Tanzania

Capital: Dodoma
Population: 29·5m.
GDP per head: (PPP$) 656
HDI/world rank: 0·357/149

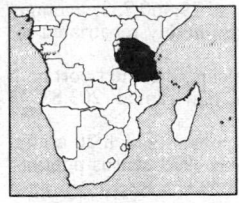

KEY HISTORICAL EVENTS. At the end of the 17th century the inhabitants of Zanzibar drove out the Portuguese with the assistance of the Arabs of Oman. Thereafter an Arab governor from Oman was sent to Zanzibar, but the government of the interior remained in the hands of a local ruler. In 1832 Seyyid Said bin Sultan, ruler of Oman, established his capital at Zanzibar. Arab merchants explored the mainland in search of slaves and ivory and soon the whole of that island and the island of Pemba together with a large strip of the east African mainland coast came under his effective rule. Seyyid Said died in 1856. Five years later his former African possessions were, under an arbitration award made by the British Governor-General of India, declared to be independent of Oman. In 1887 the Sultan of Zanzibar handed over the administration of his possessions to the north of Vanga on the African continent to the British East Africa Association. These territories eventually passed to the British government and are now part of Kenya. In 1888 a similar concession was granted to the German East Africa Association of the Sultan's mainland territories between the River Umba and Cape Delgado. In 1890 the German government bought these territories outright for 4m. marks. In 1892 the administration of the Benadir Ports (which had in 1889 been conceded to the British East Africa Association) was, with the consent of the Sultan, transferred to the Italian government in consideration of a quarterly payment of Rs 40,000. In 1886 the Sultan renounced in favour of Portugal all claims to the coast to the south of Cape Delgado.

German East Africa was conquered by the Allies in the first world war and subsequently divided between the Belgians, the Portuguese and the British. Ruanda and Urundi went to the Belgians, the Kionga triangle to Portugal, and Tanganyika to Britain. The country was administered as a League of Nations mandate until 1946, and then as a UN trusteeship territory until 9 Dec. 1961.

Tanganyika achieved responsible government in Sept. 1960 and full self-government on 1 May 1961. On 9 Dec. 1961 Tanganyika became a sovereign independent member state of the Commonwealth of Nations. The first prime minister, Dr Julius Nyerere, resigned in Jan. 1962; but on 9 Dec 1962 the country adopted a republican form of government (still within the British Commonwealth), and Dr Nyerere was elected as the first president.

On 24 June 1963 Zanzibar became an internal self-governing state, and on 9 Dec. 1963 she became independent from British rule. On 12 Jan. 1964 her sultanate was overthrown and the Sultan sent into exile by a revolt of the Afro-Shirazi Party leaders, who established the People's Republic of Zanzibar. Also in Jan. 1964 there was an attempted *coup* against Nyerere, who had to seek British military help to suppress it. On 26 April 1964 Tanganyika, Zanzibar and Pemba combined to form the United Republic of Tanzania.

Before independence the East Africa High Commission had been administering services of an inter-territorial nature for Kenya, Tanzania and Uganda and this continued after independence. The arrangement was changed to the East African Community in 1967. The Community practically ceased to function after 30 June 1977, chiefly because of the failure to agree a budget and the refusal of President Nyerere to negotiate with President Idi Amin of Uganda. In 1978 President Amin attacked Tanzania and the following year Tanzania invaded Uganda, overthrew the Amin régime and remained in occupation until 1981.

In 1991 a presidential commission recommended a multi-party political system. In 1993 regional parliaments for Zanzibar and mainland Tanzania (Tanganyika) were set up. The first multi-party elections were held in 1995.

TERRITORY AND POPULATION. Tanzania is bounded in the north-east by Kenya, north by Lake Victoria and Uganda, north-west by Rwanda and Burundi, west by Lake Tanganyika, south-west by Zambia and Malaŵi and south by Mozambique. Total area 945,037 sq. km (364,881 sq. miles) including the offshore islands of Zanzibar (1,660 sq. km) and Pemba (984 sq. km) and inland water surfaces (59,050 sq. km)). The total population was estimated in July 1997 as 29,460,753; average density, 31·5 per sq. km (1994). 0·5m. Hutu refugees were forcibly repatriated to Rwanda in Dec. 1996.

The chief towns (1988 census populations) are Dar es Salaam, the chief port and former capital (1,360,850), Mwanza (223,013), Dodoma, the new capital (203,833), Tanga (187,634), Zanzibar Town (157,634), Tabora and Mbeya.

The United Republic is divided into 25 administrative regions of which 20 are in mainland Tanzania, 3 in Zanzibar and 2 in Pemba. Areas and 1988 census populations of the regions:

Region	Sq. km	Population	Region	Sq. km	Population
Arusha	82,306	1,351,675	Pwani (Coast)	32,407	638,015
Dar es Salaam	1,393	1,360,850	Rukwa	68,635	694,974
Dodoma	41,311	1,237,819	Ruvuma	63,498	783,327
Iringa	56,864	1,208,914	Shinyanga	50,781	1,772,549
Kagera	28,388	1,326,183	Singida	49,341	791,814
Kigoma	37,037	854,817	Tabora	76,151	1,036,293
Kilimanjaro	13,309	1,108,699	Tanga	26,808	1,283,636
Lindi	66,046	646,550	*Zanzibar and Pemba*	*2,460*	*640,578*
Mara	19,566	970,942	Pemba North	574	137,399
Mbeya	60,350	1,476,199	Pemba South	332	127,640
Morogoro	70,799	1,222,737	Zanzibar North	470	97,028
Mtwara	16,707	889,494	Zanzibar South	854	70,184
Mwanza	19,592	1,878,271	Zanzibar West	230	208,327

The population growth rate was estimated in 1997 at 1·6%, with a birth rate of 41 births per 1,000 and a death rate of 19·8 deaths per 1,000. Life expectancy is 41·7 years (40·3 for men and 43·1 for women). 45% of the population is below 15 years old.

The official languages are English and Swahili (spoken as a mother tongue by only 8·8% of the population, but used as a lingua franca by 90%).

CLIMATE. The climate is very varied and is controlled very largely by altitude and distance from the sea. There are three climatic zones: the hot and humid coast, the drier central plateau with seasonal variations of temperature, and the semi-temperate mountains. Dodoma. Jan. 75°F (23·9°C), July 67°F (19·4°C). Annual rainfall 23" (572 mm). Dar es Salaam. Jan. 82°F (27·8°C), July 74°F (23·3°C). Annual rainfall 43" (1,064 mm).

CONSTITUTION AND GOVERNMENT. The *President* is head of state, chairman of the party and commander-in-chief of the armed forces. The second Vice-President is head of the executive in Zanzibar. The Prime Minister and first Vice-President is also the leader of government business in the National Assembly.

The *Bunge (National Assembly)* is composed of 232 Members of Parliament elected from the Constituencies, 5 delegates from the Zanzibar House of Representatives, the Attorney General, 42 co-opted members and 1 *ex-officio* member.

In Dec. 1979 a separate Constitution for Zanzibar was approved. Although at present under the same Constitution as Tanzania, Zanzibar has, in fact, been ruled by decree since 1964.

Presidential and parliamentary elections were held on 29 Oct. 1995, in many places postponed or extended because of administrative problems or faults. On 11 Nov. all opposition candidates withdrew from the presidential elections because of alleged irregularities. Benjamin Mkapa was elected President with 61·8% of votes cast. His party, Chama Cha Mapinduzi, gained 214 seats.

The Government in March 1998 consisted of:
President and Minister of Defence: Benjamin Mkapa (Chama Cha Mapinduzi; sworn in 30 Nov. 1995).
Vice-President: Dr Omar Ali Juma.
Prime Minister: Frederick Sumaye.
Minister of Home Affairs: Ali Ameir Mohammed. *Finance:* Daniel Yona. *Justice and Constitutional Affairs:* Bakari Mwapachu. *Defence:* Edgar Maokola Majogo. *Industries and Trade:* Dr Abdallah Omar Kigoda. *Communications and Transport:* William Kusila. *Agriculture and Co-operatives:* Paul Kimiti. *Health:* Aaron Chiduo. *Foreign Affairs and International Co-operation:* Jakaya Kikwete. *Education:* Juma Athumani Kapuya. *Energy and Mineral Resources:* Abdallah Kigoda. *Water and Livestock Development:* Pius Ng'wandu. *Tourism, Natural Resources and Environment:* Zakhia Meghji. *Lands, Housing and Urban Development:* Gideon Cheyo. *Science, Technology and Higher Education:* Jackson Makweta. *Works:* Anna Abdallah. *Labour and Youth Development:* Sebastian Rukiza Kinyondo. *Community Development, Women's Affairs and Children:* Mary Nagu.

National anthem: 'God Bless Africa/Mungu ibariki Afrika'; words collective, tune (same as that for Zambia and Zimbabwe) by M. E. Sontanga.

Regional and Local Government. There are regional parliaments for Zanzibar and mainland Tanzania (Tanganyika), and Zanzibar has a President, who is *ex officio* a Vice-President of Tanzania. Elections were held on 22 Oct. 1995. Salmin Amour (Chama Cha Mapinduzi) was elected *President* by 50·2% of votes cast against 1 opponent. Chama Cha Mapinduzi gained 26 seats; the Civic United Front, 24.

DEFENCE. Conscription is for 2 years, which may include civilian service.

Army. The Army consists of 5 infantry and 1 tank brigade and 2 artillery, 2 anti-aircraft, 2 mortar, 2 anti-tank and 1 engineer battalion. Equipment includes 30 Chinese Type-59 and 35 T-54 main battle tanks. Strength (1997), 30,000. There is also a Citizen's Militia of 80,000.

Navy. There are 4 ex-Chinese torpedo-armed hydrofoils and 12 inshore patrol craft of mixed Chinese and North Korean origins. 2 further British-built inshore patrol craft are based permanently in Zanzibar and 4 armed patrol boats on Lake Victoria Nyanza. Personnel in 1997 totalled about 1,000.

Air Force. The Tanzanian People's Defence Force Air Wing was built up initially with the help of Canada, but combat equipment has been acquired from China. Personnel totalled 3,600 in 1997 (including some 2,600 air defence troops), with about 10 F-7 (MiG-21) and 10 F-6 (MiG-19) combat aircraft, mostly in store; 4 Buffalo twin-engined short-take-off-and-land transports; 1 HS 748 turboprop transport; 2 Chinese-built Y-12 transports; 2 Cessna 404 liaison aircraft; 6 Agusta-Bell AB.205 transport helicopters, and 2 JetRanger helicopters.

INTERNATIONAL RELATIONS

Membership. Tanzania is a member of the UN, OAU, the Commonwealth, SADC and is an ACP state of the EU.

ECONOMY

Budget. The fiscal year ends 30 June. The 1992–93 budget balanced at Sh. 353,605m. Recurrent revenue was Sh. 215,617m.; foreign loans and grants, Sh. 140,988m. Recurrent expenditure was Sh. 251,543m.; capital expenditure, Sh. 102,062m.

Currency. The monetary unit is the *Tanzanian shilling* (TZS) of 100 *cents*. There are coins of 5, 10, 20, 50 cents and Sh. 1, 5, 10 and 20, and notes of Sh. 10, 20, 50, 100, 200, 500 and 1,000. Sh. 63,600m. were in circulation in 1991. Foreign exchange reserves were US$374·9m. in March 1993.

Banking and Finance. The central bank is the Bank of Tanzania (*Governor*, Idris Rashid).

On 6 Feb. 1967 all commercial banks with the exception of National Co-operative Banks were nationalized and their interests vested in the National Bank of Commerce on the mainland and the Peoples' Bank in Zanzibar. However, in 1993 private-sector commercial banks were allowed to open. In 1997 the National Commercial Bank, which controls 70% of the country's banking and has 172 branches, was split into a trade bank, a regional rural bank and a micro-finance bank.

A stock exchange opened in Dar es Salaam in 1996.

Weights and Measures. The metric system is in force.

ENERGY AND NATURAL RESOURCES

Electricity. Installed capacity was 440,000 kW in 1994. Production (1994) 1·91bn. kWh.

Minerals. Production in 1991 was recorded at: diamonds, 92,000 carats; gold, 3,018 kg; gemstones, 7,873 kg, but international funds injected to improve Tanzania's economy have resulted in notable increases, particularly in gold production. Large deposits of coal and tin exist but mining is on a small scale.

Agriculture. 90% of the workforce are engaged in agriculture, chiefly in subsistence farming. Agricultural produce accounts for 57% of GDP and 85% of exports. Production of main agricultural crops in 1992 (in 1,000 tonnes) was: Sisal, 35; seed cotton, 218; sugar-cane, 1,410; coffee, 56; tobacco, 17; maize, 2,226; millet, 263; sorghum, 587; wheat, 64; cashew nuts, 40; citrus, 34. Zanzibar is a major producer of cloves.

Livestock (1992): 13·2m. cattle, 3·7m. sheep, 9m. goats, 25m. chickens. Livestock products (1992): Honey, 15,500 tonnes.

Forestry. Forests cover 43m. ha. In 1994, 35m. cubic metres of roundwood were cut.

Fisheries. Catch (1995) 360,000 tonnes of which, inland waters, 345,000 tonnes.

INDUSTRY. Industry is limited, accounting for 17% of GDP, and is mainly textiles, petroleum and chemical products, food processing, tobacco, brewing and paper manufacturing.

FOREIGN ECONOMIC RELATIONS. Foreign debt was estimated at US$7·4bn. in 1994.

Commerce. Total trade (in US$1m.):

	1991	1993	1995
Imports	1,477	1,550	1,690
Exports	362	350	679

Principal exports, 1991 (in US$1m.): Coffee, 77·3; manufactures, 70·3; cotton, 63·3; minerals, 41·6; tea, 21·7; tobacco, 16·7; cashew nuts, 16·7; petroleum products, 7·3. Principal imports: Machinery, 254·2; transport equipment, 247·7; crude oil and products, 168·7; building materials, 110·7. Main export markets, 1992: Germany, 15·6%; UK, 11·3%; India, 11·5%; Netherlands, 6·7%; Belgium, 11·4%; Japan, 9·8%. Main import suppliers: UK, 9·8%; Japan, 7·7%; Italy, 4·8%; Oman, 2·7%; Germany, 8·0%.

Tourism. In 1991 there were 146,700 visitors spending 394,800 nights and bringing receipts of US$62·6m.

COMMUNICATIONS

Roads. In 1994 there were 88,000 km of classified roads, of which 3,700 km were tarred.

Railways. In 1977 the independent Tanzanian Railway Corporation was formed. The network totals 2,600 km (metre-gauge), excluding the joint Tanzanian Zambian (Tazara) railway's 969 km in Tanzania (1,067 mm gauge) operated by a separate administration. In 1994, the state railway carried 1·2m. passengers and 1·2m. tonnes of freight and the Tazara carried 1·8m. passengers and 0·6m. tonnes of freight.

Civil Aviation. There are 3 international airports (Dar es Salaam, Zanzibar and Kilimanjaro). Air Tanzania, the state-owned national carrier, had 2 B-737-200C Advs and 1 other aircraft in 1995, and provided domestic services and services to Mozambique, Zambia, Seychelles, Comoros, Rwanda, Burundi, Madagascar and (with Air Malawi) South Africa. Tanzania is a partner with Uganda and South African Airways in Alliance Airline. Services are also provided by Aeroflot, Air France, Air India, Air Malawi, Air Zimbabwe, Alyemda, British Airways, Egyptair, Ethiopian Airlines, Gulf Air, Kenya Airways, KLM, Lufthansa, Royal Swazi, SAA, Swissair and Uganda Airlines. 286,000 passengers were carried in 1991.

Shipping. In 1996, the merchant marine totalled 30,371 GRT, including oil tankers, 7,173 GRT. The main seaports are Dar es Salaam, Mtwara, Tanga and Zanzibar. There are also ports on the lakes. In 1991, 1,000,000 tonnes of freight were loaded and 2·9m. unloaded.

Telecommunications. In 1994 there were 88,000 telephones. The government-controlled Radio Tanzania and Sauti ya Tanzania Zanzibar are responsible for radio broadcasting on the mainland and on Zanzibar respectively. On the mainland there is a national service and a commercial programme in Swahili and an external service in English. There is television only on Zanzibar provided by the government-run Television Zanzibar (colour by PAL). There were about 8·3m. radio and 70,000 TV sets in 1995.

Cinema. (1995). There were 27 cinemas with a seating capacity of 10,000 and an annual attendance of 1·8m.

Press. (1995). There were 3 dailies (1 in English), with a combined circulation of 364,000.

SOCIAL INSTITUTIONS

Justice. The Judiciary is independent in both judicial and administrative matters and is composed of a 4-tier system of Courts: Primary Courts; District and Resident Magistrates' Courts; the High Court and the Court of Appeal. The Chief Justice is head of the Court of Appeal and the Judiciary Department. The Court's main registry is at Dar es Salaam; its jurisdiction includes Zanzibar. The Principal Judge is head of the High Court, also headquartered at Dar es Salaam, which has resident judges at 7 regional centres.

Religion. In 1992 there were 8·4m. Roman Catholics, Anglicans and Lutherans and 9m. Moslems. Moslems are concentrated in the coastal towns; Zanzibar is 99% Moslem. Some 23% follow traditional religions.

Education. In 1995 there were 10,927 primary schools with 105,280 teachers for 3·8m. pupils. At secondary level there were 212,763 pupils with 12,198 teachers and at university level there were 12,776 students with 1,650 staff.

Technical and vocational education is provided at several secondary and technical schools and at the Dar es Salaam Technical College. There are 42 teachers' colleges, including the college at Chang'ombe for secondary-school teachers.

There is 1 university, 1 university of agriculture and 1 open university. There are also 9 other institutions of higher education.

Adult literacy rate (1995): 67·8% (79·4% of men; 56·8% of women).

Health. In 1991 there were 1,112 doctors and dentists and 173 hospitals with 24,130 beds.

DIPLOMATIC REPRESENTATIVES

Of Tanzania in Great Britain (43 Hertford St., London, W1Y 8DB)
High Commissioner: Dr Abdul-Kader A. Shareef.

Of Great Britain in Tanzania (Hifadhi Hse., Samora Ave., Dar es Salaam)
High Commissioner: Alan E. Montgomery, CMG.

Of Tanzania in the USA (2139 R. St., NW, Washington, D.C., 20008)
Ambassador: Mustafa Salim Nyang'anyi.

Of the USA in Tanzania (36 Laibon Rd., Dar es Salaam)
Ambassador: J. Brady Anderson.

Of Tanzania to the United Nations
Ambassador: Daudi Ngelautwa Mwakawago.

Of Tanzania to the European Union
Ambassador: Ali Abeid Aman Karume.

Further Reading

Ayany, S. G., *A History of Zanzibar.* Nairobi, 1970
Coulson, A., *Tanzania: A Political Economy.* OUP, 1982
Darch, C., *Tanzania.* [Bibliography] 2nd ed. Oxford and Santa Barbara (CA), 1996
Hood, M., (ed.) *Tanzania and Nyerere.* London, 1988
Nyerere, J., *Freedom and Development.* New York, 1976
Resnick, I. N., *The Long Transition: Building Socialism in Tanzania.* New York and London, 1981
Yeager, R., *Tanzania: An African Experiment.* Aldershot, 1982

National statistical office: Bureau of Statistics, Dar es Salaam.

THAILAND

Prathet Thai

(Kingdom of Thailand)

Capital: Bangkok
Population: 59·45m.
GDP per head: (PPP$) 7,104
GNP: US$129·9bn.
HDI/world rank: 0·833/59

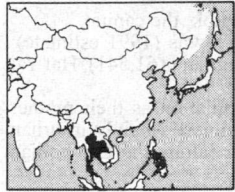

KEY HISTORICAL EVENTS. The Thais migrated to the present territory from Nan Chao in the Yunnan area of China in the 8th and 9th centuries. Thais today look back to the state of Sukhothai, a Buddhist kingdom which grew up in the central plain of Thailand in the 13th century, as their first historical state. A hundred years later Sukhothai was succeeded by the new kingdom of Ayutthaya, which served until the Burmese invasion of 1767. After some years of confusion Thailand's leading general, Chao Phraya Chakkri, assumed the throne in 1782, thus establishing the dynasty which still heads the Thai state.

Siam, as Thailand was called until 1939, remained an independent state ruled by an absolute monarchy until 24 June 1932. Discontented with the social, political and economic stagnation of the country, a group of rebels calling themselves the People's Party and headed by a young lawyer, Pridi Phanomyong, precipitated a bloodless *coup.* The rebels seized control of the army, imprisoned many royal officials and persuaded the king to accept the introduction of constitutional monarchy.

When, the following year, the king tried to dissolve the newly appointed General Assembly, the army moved to prevent him, thus becoming the dominant force behind the government, which they have remained ever since. Nationalism dominated political life through the 1930s. In 1939 Field Marshal Pibul Songgram became premier and embarked on a pro-Japanese irridentist policy that eventually brought Thailand into the second world war on Japan's side.

After 1945 political life was characterized by periods of military rule interspersed with short attempts at democratic, civilian government. Thus, three years of civilian rule from 1945 to 1948 were brought to an end when Songgram came back to power for a nine-year period. In 1957 power was seized from him by another army leader, Sarit Thanarat, who abolished the constitution and ruled without outside interference until his death in 1963, when he was replaced by the new Commander-in-Chief, Thano Kittikachon. Democratic government was reintroduced for a short time after 1963, when 100 students were killed in clashes with the army and again from 1969 to 1971 when another successful military *coup* was staged, aimed at checking the high crime rate and the growth of Communist insurgence A new, moderately democratic constitution was introduced in 1978.

On 23 Feb. 1991 a military junta seized power, deposing the prime minister. Following the appointment of Gen. Suchinda Kraprayoon as Prime Minister on 17 April 1992 there were massive anti-government demonstrations over several weeks in the course of which many demonstrators were killed. Gen. Suchinda resigned, and in May the legislative assembly voted that future prime ministers should be elected by its members rather than appointed by the military. A new government was elected on 13 Sept. led by Chuan Leekpai of the Democratic Party (DP). The 1995 election was fought against a background of political and financial corruption. The result was a coalition government which proved as ineffective as its predecessor in coming to grips with fundamental problems in the country. After the 1996 election a new constitution was drafted allowing for the separation of the executive, legislative and judicial branches of government.

TERRITORY AND POPULATION. Thailand is bounded in the west by Myanmar, north and east by Laos and south-east by Cambodia. In the south it becomes a peninsula bounded in the west by the Indian Ocean, south by Malaysia and east by the Gulf of Thailand. Area is 513,115 sq. km (198,114 sq. miles).

At the census taken in 1990 the total population was 54,548,530, of whom

1353

17,947,700 lived in the Central region, 19,037,300 in the North-East region, 6,964,000 in the South region, 10,583,300 in the North region. Estimated population, 1997: 59,450,818.

Vital statistics, 1992: Births, 964,557; deaths, 275,313. 1997 estimate of population growth rate: 1%, with 25% of the population below 15 years, 69% between 15 and 64 years and 6% aged 65 and over. Expectation of life (1997): 68·8 years (65·1 for men; 72·2 for women).

Thailand is divided into 4 regions, 76 provinces and Bangkok, the capital.

Population of Bangkok (1993 census), 5,572,712. Other towns (1991 estimate): Nonthaburi (264,201), Nakhon Ratchasima (202,503), Chiangmai (161,541), Hat Yai (142,351), Khon Kaen, (131,478), Nakhon Sawan (108,569).

Thai is the official language, spoken by 53% of the population as their mother tongue. 27% speak Lao (mainly in the north-east), 12% Chinese (mainly in urban areas), 3·7% Malay (mainly in the south) and 2·7% Khmer (along the Cambodian border).

CLIMATE. The climate is tropical, with high temperatures and humidity. Over most of the country, 3 seasons may be recognized. The rainy season is June to Oct., the cool season from Nov. to Feb. and the hot season is March to May. Rainfall is generally heaviest in the south and lightest in the north-east.

Bangkok. Jan. 78°F (25·6°C), July 83°F (28·3°C). Annual rainfall 56" (1,400 mm).

ROYAL HOUSE. The reigning King is **Bhumibol Adulyadej**, born 5 Dec. 1927. King Bhumibol married on 28 April 1950 Princess Sirikit, and was crowned 5 May 1950. Children: Princess Ubol Ratana (born 5 April 1951, married Aug. 1972 Peter Ladd Jensen), Crown Prince Vajiralongkorn (born 28 July 1952, married 3 Jan. 1977 Soamsawali Kitiyakra), Princess Maha Chakri Sirindhorn (born 2 April 1955), Princess Chulabhorn (born 4 July 1957, married 7 Jan. 1982 Virayudth Didyasarin).

CONSTITUTION AND GOVERNMENT. Parliament consists of a 270-member *Senate*, appointed by the King, and a 393-member *House of Representatives*, elected for 4-year terms by universal suffrage of citizens over 17 years. A constitutional amendment in 1995 restricted to two-thirds the proportion of the military in the House of Representatives. The *Prime Minister* is elected by the House of Representatives.

At the elections of 17 Nov. 1996, 11 parties fielded candidates. New Aspiration (NA) gained 125 seats; the Democratic Party, 123.

In March 1998 the government comprised:
Prime Minister and Minister of Defence: Chuan Leekpai (DP).
Deputy Prime Ministers: Bhichai Rattakul, Supachai Panitchpakdi (*Commerce*), Panja Kesornthong, Suwit Khunkitti; *Minister to the Prime Minister's Office:* Khunving Supatra Maskit. *Finance:* Tarrin Nimmanhaeminda. *Foreign Affairs:* Surin Pitsuwan. *Agriculture and Co-operatives:* Pongpol Adireksarn. *Transport and Communications:* Suthep Thaugsuban. *Interior:* Maj. Gen. Sanan Kajornprasart. *Justice:* Sutasn Ngenmune. *Labour and Social Welfare:* Trairong Suwankiri. *Science, Technology and Environment:* Yingpan Manasikarn. *Education:* Chumpol Silapa-archa. *Public Health:* Rakkeit Sugthana. *Industry:* Somsak Thepsutin. *University Affairs:* Cdr. Deja Sucarom.

National anthem: 'Prathet Thai ruam nua chat chua Thai' ('Thailand, cradle of Thais wherever they may be'); words by Luang Saranuprapan, tune by Phrachen Duriyang.

Local Government. Thailand is divided into 76 provinces *(changwads)*, each under the control of a *changwad* governor. The *changwads* are subdivided into 744 districts *(amphurs)* and 81 sub-districts *(king amphurs)*, 7,307 communes *(tambons)* and 65,277 villages *(moobans)*.

DEFENCE. Conscription is for 2 years.

Army. The Army is organized in 4 regions and includes 1 armoured, 1 cavalry, 2 mechanized infantry, 7 infantry (including the Royal Guard), 2 special forces and 1 artillery division; 19 engineer and 8 independent infantry battalions; 1 independent cavalry and 1 armoured air cavalry regiment and 3 reconnaissance companies. Equipment includes 150 M-48A5, 53 M-60A1 and about 50 Chinese Type-69 main battle tanks. There is also an Army Aviation force including more than 100 UH-1 and Bell 212 transport helicopters, and over 60 O-1 Bird Dog observation aircraft and about 20 fixed-wing transports as well as 4 AH-1 armed helicopters. Strength (1997) 150,000 (80,000 conscripts).

Navy. The Royal Thai Navy is, next to the Chinese, the most significant naval force in the South China Sea. The combatant fleet includes 2 ex-US Knox class, 5 missile-armed and 5 other frigates, 2 modern missile-armed 950-tonne corvettes and 3 anti-submarine corvettes, 6 German and Italian-built fast missile craft, 9 coastal and 40 inshore patrol craft, and about 40 riverine patrol boats. There is 1 mine counter-measures support vessel, 2 coastal minehunters and 2 coastal minesweepers. Amphibious capability is provided by 7 tank landing ships and 2 medium landing ships as well as 50 landing craft. Major auxiliaries are 1 small tanker, 3 surveying ships and 3 training ships. Minor auxiliaries and service craft number about 12. The new small Spanish-built vertical/short-take-off-and-land carrier *Chakrinareubet* entered service in 1997 and operates 8 ex-Spanish AV-8A Harrier aircraft and helicopters.

The Naval air element includes 3 P-3T Orion, 6 F-27 Maritime and 3 DO228 for maritime patrol, 4 F-27 Friendship transports, 9 Cessna T-337 armed light transports and 16 Bell anti-submarine and 14 utility and search-and-rescue helicopters. 18 A-7 Corsair II strike aircraft were delivered in 1997.

Naval personnel in 1997 totalled 73,000 including 22,000 marines and 1,700 Naval Air Arm. The main bases are at Bangkok, Sattahip, Songkla and Phang Nga, with the riverine forces based at Nakhon Phanom.

A separate coast guard force, the Royal Thai Marine Police, numbers 2,500 and operates 3 offshore, 3 coastal patrol, 32 riverine and inshore craft and numerous boats.

Air Force. The Royal Thai Air Force had a strength (1997) of 43,000 personnel and 210 combat aircraft, and is made up of a headquarters and Combat, Logistics Support, Training and Special Services Groups. Combat units comprise 2 squadrons of F-16s, 3 squadrons of F-5E/F interceptors, 4 squadrons with L-39 light strike aircraft, 1 with OV-10 Bronco light reconnaissance/attack aircraft, 2 with AU-23A Peacemakers and 1 with Nomads for security duties. 3 Aravas are used for electronic intelligence gathering and 3 Learjets for combat support. There are transport units equipped with a total of about 70 C-130H/H-30 Hercules, HS 748, C-47, G.??? and smaller aircraft, including Australian built Missionmasters; there are 30 UH-1H and 14 S-58T helicopters; training units with Airtrainer CT/4 primary trainers built in New Zealand, Italian-built SF.260MTs, and PC-9 and intermediate trainers.

INTERNATIONAL RELATIONS

Membership. Thailand is a member of the UN, ASEAN and the Colombo Plan.

ECONOMY

Policy. The financial crisis that spread across south-east Asia in 1997 hit Thailand with particular force. Over 50 finance companies suspended business, the Thai stock exchange lost 82% of its 1995 peak value and the baht devalued by 40% in the second half of 1997. An IMF rescue package of US$17·2bn. gained time to put reforms in place, including tighter budgetary control and the restructuring of the country's outmoded financial system. After a decade of economic growth averaging 8% a year, Thailand is projecting a modest 2·5% for 1997.

Performance. Real GDP growth was 7·8% in 1996 (8·6% in 1995).

Budget. The fiscal year starts in Oct. Total revenues and expenditures (in 1m. baht):

	1991	1992	1993	1994	1995	1996[1]
Revenue	462,623	495,780	558,302	653,217	761,802	851,179
Expenditure	348,471	419,975	494,774	578,331	647,808	739,603

[1] Provisional figures as at Sept.

Principle expenditure in 1996 (in 1m. baht) was on: defence (95,601), public order and safety (46,615), education (159,035), health (59,205) and social security and welfare (28,637).

Currency. The unit of currency is the *baht* (THB) of 100 *satang*. After being pegged to the US dollar, the baht was allowed to float in July 1997. There are coins of 25 and 50 satangs and 1, 2, 5 and 10 baht, and notes of 10, 20, 50, 100, 500 and 1,000 baht. In April 1991 the total amount of notes in circulation was 151,306m. baht. Foreign exchange reserves were US$30,000m. in 1994. Inflation was 5·5% in 1996.

Banking and Finance. The Bank of Thailand (founded in 1942) is the central bank and bank of issue, an independent body although its capital is government-owned. Its assets and liabilities in Dec. 1991 were 580,844·5m. baht. Its *Governor* is Rerngchai Marakanonda (b. 1942). In 1997 there were 21 domestic commercial banks, 14 foreign banks with branch licenses and 22 foreign banks with representative offices. Total credits of commercial banks, Dec. 1995, 4,144,000m. baht. Deposits, Dec. 1995, 3,141,500m. baht. There is a Government Savings Bank.

There is a stock exchange (SET) in Bangkok.

Weights and Measures. The metric system was made compulsory in 1923. Traditional units are also widely used.

ENERGY AND NATURAL RESOURCES

Electricity. Installed capacity, 1994, was 15·84m. kW. Output: 70·21bn. kWh. Privatization of the Electricity Generating Authority (EGAT) and the Petroleum Authority (PTT) is set to start in 1999.

Oil. Proven oil reserves in 1987 were less than 160m. bbls. Estimated production of crude oil (1993) 8,544 bbls.

Gas. Production of natural gas (1993) 343,581m. cu. ft. Estimated reserves, 1986, 12,922,000m. cu. ft.

Minerals. The mineral resources include cassiterite (tin ore), wolfram, scheelite, antimony, coal, copper, gold, iron, lead, manganese, molybdenum, rubies, sapphires, silver, zinc and zircons. Production, 1995 (in tonnes): Iron ore, 34,500; tin concentrates, 2,200; lead concentrates, 22,800; antimony ore, 500; zinc ore, 135,200; lignite, 18·4m.; gypsum, 8·5m.; tungsten concentrates, 100; fluorite ore, 24,100; marl, 563·7.

Agriculture. About 42% of land is given over to agricultural use, either for crops or pasture (1993 estimate). In 1996 agriculture produced an estimated 10·5% of GDP. The chief produce is rice, a staple of the national diet. Output of the major crops in 1995 was (in 1,000 tonnes): paddy (rice), 21,130; cassava (manioc/tapioca) (18,164); sugar cane, 50,597; maize, 3,965; bananas (1,700); rubber latex (1,721); pineapples (2,370); sorghum (228); dried beans (240); soybeans (528); groundnuts (150); watermelons (400); kenaf fibre (132); dried onions (250).

Livestock, 1995 (in 1,000): horses, 15; buffaloes, 4,807; cattle, 7,593; pigs, 4,507; sheep, 130; goats, 78; poultry and ducks, 101m.

Forestry. About 14·4m. ha was under forest in 1988. Teak and other hardwoods grow in the deciduous forests of the north; elsewhere tropical evergreen forests are found, with the timber yang the main crop (a source of yang oil). In 1994 3·8m. cubic metres of roundwood were cut.

Rubber production in 1993: 1·58m. tonnes.

Fisheries. In 1995 the catch of sea fish was 3,501,772 tonnes including marine prawns, shrimps and other shellfish.

INDUSTRY. In 1996 industry produced 30·5% and services 59% of GDP.

Production of manufactured goods in 1994 included: 29·9m. tonnes of cement, 5·2m. hectolitres of beer, 9,363 tonnes of tin plate (1993), 126,000 automobiles and 324,000 commercial vehicles, 2m. tonnes of synthetic fibre (non-cellolosic continuous filaments), 1·8m. tonnes of petroleum products, 4,168,000 tonnes of raw sugar and 100,000 tonnes of crude steel.

Labour. In 1996 the total labour force (aged 13 and over) was 34m., of whom 57% were in agriculture, 17% in industry, 11% in commerce and 15% in services industries (including government). The unemployment rate was 2·6%. A minimum wage is set by the National Wages Committee. It was 157 baht per day in Sept. 1996.

FOREIGN ECONOMIC RELATIONS. Foreign debt was US$61·6bn. in 1995.

Commerce. Tariffs on raw materials and semi-manufactures were reduced on 1 Jan. 1995. Total exports in 1996 was valued at US$57·3bn.; total imports at US$ 72·4bn.

Main exports by category in 1994, in US$m.: machinery and transport equipment (25,449·9), road vehicles and parts (excluding tyres, engines and electrical parts) (4,034·9), electrical apparatus (6,873·2), chemicals and chemical products (5,506·8), manufactures (10,313·4). Imports: machinery (15,039); manufactured articles (10,980); manufactures (5,506), food and live animals (9,291), seafood (4,181), clothing and accessories 4,531), office machinery (4,123) and other electrical machinery (4,913).

In 1993 exports (in 1m. baht) went mainly to USA (249,579), Japan (236,670), Singapore (199,019) and Hong Kong (72,656), imports were mainly from Japan (538,186), USA (210,066), Singapore (103,977), Germany (94,627), Taiwan (84,638) and Malaysia (80,746).

Tourism. In 1996, 7·19m. foreigners visited Thailand. Tourist revenue was estimated at 215,000m. baht.

COMMUNICATIONS

Roads. In 1993 there were 56,903 km of highways. Vehicles in use in 1996 comprised 1·56m. passenger cars, 2·83m. commercial vehicles and 10·7m motor cycles.

Railways. The State Railway totals 4,623 route km. In 1994 it carried 87m. passengers and 7·6m. tonnes of freight.

Civil Aviation. There are international airports at Bangkok, Chiangmai, Phuket, Hat Yai and U-tapao. The national carrier is Thai Airways International, 92·85% state-owned, which in 1995 operated 6 A300B4-100s, 4 A300B4-200s, 6 A300B4-600s, 10 A300B4-600Rs, 1 A300C4-200, 2 A310-200s, 6 A330-300s, 7 B-737-400s, 6 B-747-200Bs, 2 B-747-300s and 8 B-747-400s. Services were also provided by Aeroflot, Air China, Air France, Air India, Air Koryo, Air Lanka, Air Liberté, Air New Zealand, Alitalia, All Nippon, AOM, Asiana, Balkan, Biman Bangladesh, British Airways, Canadian Airlines, Cathay Pacific, China Airlines, China Eastern Airlines, China Southern Airlines, China Southwest Airlines, Condor, Czech Airlines, Delta, Dragonair, Druk-Air, Egyptair, El Al, Emirates, Ethiopian Airways, Eva, Finnair, Garuda Indonesia, Gulf Air, Indian Airlines, JAL, KLM, Korean Air, Kuwait Airways, Lao Aviation, Lauda Air, LOT, LTU, Lufthansa, Malaysia Airlines, Myanma Airways, Northwest Airlines, Olympic Airways, Pakistan Airlines, Philippine Airlines, Qantas, Royal Air Cambodge, Royal Brunei Airlines, Royal Jordanian, Royal Nepal Airlines, SAA, SAS, Saudia, Singapore Airlines, Swissair, Tarom, Turkish Airlines, United Airlines, Uzbekistan Airways, Varig, Vietnam Airlines and Yunnan Airlines.

Shipping. In 1996 Thailand had registered a total of 540 vessels with a total of 2·04 GRT, including 49 oil tankers, 154 cargo ships (10 refrigerated) and 15 liquefied gas tankers. In 1995, 2,524 vessels of 21·7m. NRT entered the port of Bangkok, where 17·9 tonnes of cargo were loaded.

Telecommunications. In 1994 there were 2,752,000 telephones.

The Radio and Television Executive Committee controls the administrative, legal, technical and programming aspects of broadcasting, and consists of representatives of various government bodies. All radio stations are operated by, or under the supervision of, government agencies. Radio Thailand broadcasts 3 national programmes, provincial programmes, an educational service and an external service (9 languages) and the Voice of Free Asia. Television of Thailand is the state service (colour by PAL). There are 3 commercial channels and an Army service. In 1995 there were 11m. radio and 11m. TV sets in use.

Cinemas. (1993). There were 600 cinemas with a seating capacity of 380,011.

Press. (1995). There are 35 daily newspapers, including 2 in English and 7 in Chinese, with a combined circulation of about 2·7m.

SOCIAL INSTITUTIONS

Justice. The judicial power is exercised in the name of the King, by *(a)* courts of first instance, *(b)* the court of appeal *(Uthorn)* and *(c)* the Supreme Court *(Dika)*. The King appoints, transfers and dismisses judges, who are independent in conducting trials and giving judgment in accordance with the law.

Courts of first instance are subdivided into 20 magistrates' courts *(Kwaeng)* with limited civil and minor criminal jurisdiction; 85 provincial courts *(Changwad)* with unlimited civil and criminal jurisdiction; the criminal and civil courts with exclusive jurisdiction in Bangkok; the central juvenile courts for persons under 18 years of age in Bangkok.

The court of appeal exercises appellate jurisdiction in civil and criminal cases from all courts of first instance. From it appeals lie to Dika Court on any point of law and, in certain cases, on questions of fact.

The Supreme Court is the supreme tribunal of the land. Besides its normal appellate jurisdiction in civil and criminal matters, it has semi-original jurisdiction over general election petitions. The decisions of Dika Court are final. Every person has the right to present a petition to the Government who will deal with all matters of grievance.

Religion. In 1993 there were 54·53m. Buddhists, 2·31m. Moslems, 0·29m. Christians and 0·69m. others.

Education. Education is compulsory for children for 9 years and free in local municipal schools. In 1996 there were 34,001 primary schools with 5·9m. pupils. There were 3·7m. secondary school pupils with (in 1994) 151,008 teachers. In higher education there were 1·2m. students (481,936 at university level). In 1996 there were 13 universities, 2 open (distance) universities, 4 institutes of technology and 1 institute of development administration in the public sector, and 9 universities and 1 institute of technology in the private sector.

Health. The Primary Health Care Programme had provided health services in 95% of villages in 1986. In 1990 there were 959 hospitals and 7,828 health centres. In 1990 there were 12,520 physicians, 2,285 dentists, 4,168 pharmacists, 77,186 nurses and 10,796 midwives.

DIPLOMATIC REPRESENTATIVES

Of Thailand in Great Britain (29–30 Queen's Gate, London, SW7 5JB)
Ambassador: Vidhya Rayananonda, KCVO.

Of Great Britain in Thailand (Wireless Rd., Bangkok 10330)
Ambassador: Sir James Hodge, KCVO, CMG.

Of Thailand in the USA (2300 Kalorama Rd., NW, Washington, D.C., 20008)
Ambassador: Nitya Pibulsonggram.

Of the USA in Thailand (120 Wireless Rd., Bangkok 10330)
Ambassador: William Itoh.

THAILAND 1359

Of Thailand to the United Nations
Ambassador: Asda Jayanama.

Of Thailand to the European Union
Ambassador: Somkiati Ariyapruchya.

Further Reading

National Statistical Office *Thailand Statistical Yearbook.*

Girling, J. I. S., *Thailand: Society and Politics.* Cornell Univ. Press, 1981
Krongkaew, M. (ed.) *Thailand's Industrialization and its Consequences.* London, 1995
Kulick, E. and Wilson, D., *Thailand's Turn: Profile of a New Dragon.* London and New York, 1993 (NY, 1994)
Watts, M., *Thailand* [Bibliography] Oxford and Santa Barbara (CA), 1986

National statistical office: National Statistical Office, Thanon Lan Luang, Bangkok 10100.

TOGO

République Togolaise

Capital: Lomé
Population: 4·7m.
GDP per head: (PPP$) 1,109
GNP: US$1·3bn.
HDI/world rank: 0·365/147

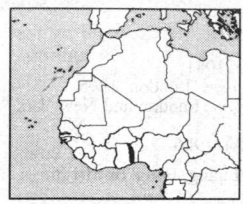

KEY HISTORICAL EVENTS. The Africans of Togo are of several tribes, including the Ewes of the south (also living in Ghana and Benin), and the Kabres, Dagombas, Tyokossis and others in the north. They had small pre-colonial states but were dominated by the powerful kingdoms of Ashanti to the west and Dahomey to the east. Europeans, beginning with the Portuguese who first visited the area in 1471-72, traded on the coast for centuries, especially in slaves, but the area between the Gold Coast forts and Whydah was for long relatively unimportant for them. In the 19th century, however, palm oil exports flourished at Anecho, Agoue and Porto Seguro, where British, French and German traders operated. Several prominent Togolese families of partly Brazilian or Portuguese origin, still important among the coastal African élite, arose at that time. Protestant and Catholic missions began working before the establishment of colonial rule. Despite the important rival influences of Britain and France in the area, it was Germany that established colonial rule on the coast in 1884.

German control was then extended inland but encountered strong resistance from the Kabres, Konkombas and other peoples, and only in 1912 was the colony fully subdued.

German Togo was overrun by the Allies in 1914. It was partitioned in 1919 into British and French Mandated Territories under the League of Nations. After the Second World War French Togo and British Togoland became Trust Territories under the United Nations. In British Togoland a referendum was held on 9 May 1956, in which a majority voted for union with Gold Coast, although most people in the south voted for union with French Togo. The whole territory was merged with what soon afterwards became independent Ghana, but many Togolese objected. In French Togo partial self-government was granted in 1956. On 27 April 1960 the country became independent and Sylvanus Olympio was elected president.

On 13 Jan. 1963 the President Olympio was murdered by soldiers. His successor, Nicolas Grunitzky, was deposed in a bloodless military coup in Jan. 1967 and on 14 April 1967 Gen. (then Col.) Gnassingbé Eyadéma assumed the Presidency. Following a general strike in June 1991 the government agreed to hold a National Conference, and this elected an interim Supreme Republican Council. A new constitution was approved in 1992.

TERRITORY AND POPULATION. Togo is bounded west by Ghana, north by Burkina Faso, east by Benin and south by the Gulf of Guinea. The area is 56,785 sq. km. The population of Togo in 1981 (census) was 2,700,982; 1997 (estimate) 4·7m., 25·7% urban. The capital is Lomé (population, 1990, 0·45m.), other towns being Sokodé (55,000), Kpalimé (31,000), Atakpamé (30,000), Tsévié (26,000), Bassar (19,000) and Aného (16,000).

Population growth in 1994 was 3% per annum; birth rate (per 1,000 population), 44·4; death rate, 15·1; life expectancy, 50·6 years.

Area, population and chief town of the 5 regions:

Region	Area in sq. km	Population (1981 census)	Population (1984 estimate)	Chief town
Des Savanes	8,602	326,826	358,700	Dapaong
De La Kara	11,630	432,626	444,200	Kara
Centrale	13,182	269,174	310,500	Sokodé
Des Plateaux	16,975	561,656	708,100	Atakpamé
Maritime	6,396	1,039,700	1,147,800	Lomé

There are 37 ethnic groups. The south is largely populated by Ewe-speaking peoples (forming 44% of the population) and related groups, while the north is

1360

mainly inhabited by Hamitic groups speaking Kabre (27%), Gurma (14%) and Tem (4%). The official language is French but Ewe and Kabre are also taught in schools.

CLIMATE. The tropical climate produces wet seasons from March to July and from Oct. to Nov. in the south. The north has one wet season, from April to July. The heaviest rainfall occurs in the mountains of the west, south-west and centre. Lomé. Jan. 81°F (27·2°C), July 76°F (24·4°C). Annual rainfall 35" (875 mm).

CONSTITUTION AND GOVERNMENT. A referendum on 27 Sept. 1992 approved a new constitution by 98·11% of votes cast. Under this the *President* and the *National Assembly* are directly elected for 5-year terms. The latter has 81 seats and is elected in 2 rounds on a first-past-the-post system.

At the presidential election of 25 Aug. 1993 turn-out was 39·5%. President Eyadéma was re-elected against 2 opponents by 96·49% of votes cast.

At the parliamentary elections in Feb. 1994 the electorate was 2m. 352 candidates stood. The Togolese People's Assembly (RPT, the former sole party) gained 38 seats, the Action Committee for Renewal 36 and the Togolese Union for Democracy (UTD) 7.

President: Gen. Gnassingbé Eyadéma (re-elected 25 Aug. 1993).

Kwassi Klutse (b. 1945) became *Prime Minister* on 20 Aug. 1996 and formed a new government, which in March 1998 comprised:

Minister of Agriculture, Animal Breeding and Fisheries: Kokou Dake Dominique Dogbe. *Communications and Civil Education:* Solitoki Esso. *Decentralization, Urban Development and Housing.* Koffivi Victor Ayassou. *Environment and Forest Resources:* Koffi Adade. *Foreign Affairs and Co-operation:* Koffi Panou. *Health:* Koffi Sama. *Interior and Security:* Gen. Seyi Memene. *Justice and Human Rights and Keeper of the Seals:* Stanislas Somolu Baba. *Labour and Civil Service:* Kissem Tchangai-Walla. *Mines, Equipment and Transport, Posts and Telecommunications:* Tchamdja Andjo. *National Defence:* Bitokotipou Yagninim. *National Education and Research:* Edo Kodjo Maurille Agbobli. *Planning and Territorial Development:* Kwassi Klutse. *Relations with the National Assembly:* Komi Dotse Amoudokpo. *State Companies and the Development of the Free Trade Zone:* Fayadowa Nukotchi. *Technical Education, Professional Training and Cottage Industry:* Comla Kadje. *Tourism and Leisure:* Tankpadja Lalle. *Women's Affairs and Social Welfare:* Kissem Tchagai-Walla. *Youth, Sports and Culture:* Kouami Agbogboli.

National anthem: 'Ecartons tout mauvais esprit qui gêne l'unité nationale' ('Let us sweep aside all ill feelings which foil the national unity'); words and tune collective.

Local Government: There are 5 regions, each under an inspector appointed by the President; they are divided into 31 *prefectures* and the capital Lomé, each administered by a district chief assisted by an elected district council.

DEFENCE. There is selective conscription for 2 years.

Army. The Army consists of 2 infantry, 1 Presidential Guard, 1 parachute commando and 1 support regiment. Equipment includes 2 T-54/-55 main battle tanks. Strength (1997) 6,500, with a further 750 in a paramilitary gendarmerie.

Navy. In 1996 the Naval wing of the armed forces operated 2 inshore patrol craft from the naval base at Lomé. Naval personnel number 150.

Air Force. An Air Force, established with French assistance, has 4 Brazilian-built EMB-326 Xavante (Aermacchi MB.326) armed jet trainers; 5 Alpha Jet advanced trainers, with strike capability, 1 turboprop Buffalo transport; 2 Beech King Air 200s and 1 Cessna 337 for liaison; 3 Epsilon armed trainers; 2 Lama helicopters. Personnel (1997), 250, with 9 combat aircraft.

INTERNATIONAL RELATIONS

Membership. Togo is a member of the UN, OAU and ECOWAS, and is an ACP state of the EU.

ECONOMY

Policy. After civil and economic turmoil in the early 1990s, a structural redevelopment programme, launched in 1994, increased annual growth rate to between 6% and 8%. Inflation dropped to below 5% in 1996. Private sector development is encouraged and there are plans to privatize some 20 state companies.

Budget. At the 1995 budget revenue was 97,100m. francs CFA; expenditure was 147,200m. francs CFA.

Currency. The unit of currency is the *franc* CFA with a parity rate of 100 francs CFA to 1 French franc. Gold reserves were US$3·3m. in 1992. Foreign exchange reserves were US$272·5m.; 28,000m. francs CFA were in circulation in 1993.

Banking and Finance. The bank of issue is the Central Bank of West African States (BCEAO). 7 commercial and 3 development banks are based in Lomé. Bank deposits totalled 168,700m. francs CFA in 1989.

Weights and Measures. The metric system is in use.

ENERGY AND NATURAL RESOURCES

Electricity. Installed capacity was 65,500 kWh in 1987 (35,500 kWh hydroelectric). Production (1988) 339·5m. kWh. There is a hydro-electric plant at Kpalimé.

Minerals. Output of phosphate rock (1992) 2,079,000 tonnes. Other minerals are limestone, iron ore (550m. tonnes) and marble.

Agriculture. Agriculture supports about 80% of the population and produces 30% of GDP. Most food production comes from individual holdings under 3 ha. Inland the country is hilly; dry plains alternate with arable land. There are considerable plantations of oil and cocoa palms, coffee, cacao, kola, cassava and cotton. Production, 1995 (in 1,000 tonnes): Cassava, 469; tomatoes, 9; yams, 375; maize, 296; sorghum, 109; millet, 82; seed cotton, 44; rice, 26; groundnuts, 32; coffee, 16.

Livestock (1995, in 1,000): Cattle, 248; sheep, 1,200; pigs, 850; goats, 1,900.

Forestry. In 1991 the wooded area was 1·6m. ha. Teak plantations covered 8,600 ha. Annual production for fuel, 1·3m. cu. metres.

Fisheries. Fishery is on a small scale. The annual catch averages 15,000 tonnes (65% marine).

INDUSTRY. Industry is small-scale. Cement and textiles are produced and food processed.

Labour. In 1990 the workforce was 1,396,000 (508,000 female, 54,000 aged 10–15). In 1994 the statutory minimum wage was 75·60 francs CFA per hour.

Trade Unions. With the abandonment of single-party politics the former monolithic Togo National Workers Confederation (CNTT) has split into several federations and independent trade unions.

FOREIGN ECONOMIC RELATIONS. A free trade zone was established in 1990. Foreign debt was US$1,356m. in 1992.

Commerce (in US$m.):

	1989	1990	1991
Imports	471·9	581·4	443·9
Exports	245·1	267·9	253·2

Chief trading partners are Côte d'Ivoire, Mauritania, The Netherlands, France, Germany and USA. Main import suppliers in 1992 were: France, 21·4%; China, 8·8%; Thailand, 7·3%; Netherlands, 5·8%; Côte d'Ivoire, 5·3%. Main export markets: Canada, 9·3%; Burkina Faso, 5·9%; France, 4·6%; India, 3·8%; Italy, 3·6%.

Tourism. There were 44,000 tourists in 1994; receipts were US$18m.

COMMUNICATIONS

Roads. There were, in 1990, 7,870 km of roads, of which 1,570 km were paved. In 1995 there were 74,662 passenger cars, 54,902 motorcycles and 32,514 commercial vehicles.

Railways. There are 4 metre-gauge railways connecting Lomé, with Aného (continuing to Cotonou in Benin), Kpalimé, Tabligbo and (via Atakpamé) Blitta; total length 525 km. In 1994 the railways carried 5·7 tonne-km and 0·6m. passengers.

Civil Aviation. The national carrier is Air Togo. Air services connect Tokoin airport, near Lomé, with Paris, Dakar, Abidjan, Douala, Accra, Lagos, Cotonou and Niamey and by internal services with Sokodé, Mango, Dapaong, Atakpamé and Niamtougou. 309,200 passengers and 3,796 tonnes of freight were handled in 1987.

Shipping. The merchant marine comprises 11 vessels of 77,989 DWT.

Telecommunications. There were (1994) 388 post offices and 21,000 telephones. Broadcasting is provided by the government-controlled Radiodiffusion-Télévision Togolaise. There were 0·8m. radio and 30,000 TV receivers (colour by SECAM) in 1994.

Press. There is 1 government-controlled daily newspaper (circulation 10,000).

SOCIAL INSTITUTIONS

Justice. The Supreme Court and two Appeal Courts are in Lomé, one for criminal cases and one for civil and commercial cases. Each receives appeal from a series of local tribunals.

Religion. In 1994, 18% of the population were Christian and 2% Moslem (chiefly in the north). Many follow traditional animist religions.

Education. Adult literacy was 50·4% in 1994. In 1986 there were 474,998 pupils and 10,209 teachers in 2,345 primary schools, 86,327 pupils in secondary schools, and 5,050 students and 198 teachers in technical schools and 374 students and 22 teachers at the teacher-training college. In 1990 about 50% of children of school age were attending school. The University of Benin at Lomé (founded in 1970) had 9,139 students and 134 academic staff in 1994–95.

Health. In 1988 there were 28 hospitals and 348 health centres with 5,275 beds and 278 doctors, 25 pharmacists, 348 midwives and 1,285 nursing staff.

DIPLOMATIC REPRESENTATIVES

The Embassy of Togo in Great Britain closed on 30 Sept. 1991.

Of Great Britain in Togo
Ambassador: Ian W. Mackley, CMG (resides in Ghana).

Of Togo in the USA (2208 Massachusetts Ave., NW, Washington, D.C., 20008)
Ambassador: Kossivo Osseyi.

Of the USA in Togo (Rue Pelletier Caventou, Lomé)
Ambassador: Johnny Young.

Of Togo to the United Nations
Ambassador: Roland Kpotsra.

Of Togo to the European Union
Ambassador: Elliott Latévi-Atcho Lawson.

Further Reading

Cornevin, R., *Histoire du Togo.* 3rd ed., Paris, 1969
Decalo, S., *Togo.* [Bibliography] Oxford and Santa Barbara (CA), 1995
Feuillet, C., *Le Togo en Général.* Paris, 1976

TONGA

Kingdom of Tonga

Capital: Nuku'alofa
Population: 107,335
GNP: US$170m.

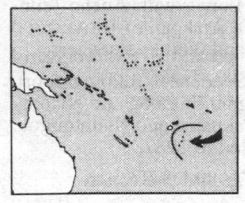

KEY HISTORICAL EVENTS. The Tongatapu group of islands in the south western Pacific Ocean was discovered by Tasman in 1643. The Kingdom of Tonga attained unity under Taufa'ahau Tupou (George I) who became ruler of his native Ha'apai in 1820, of Vava'u in 1833 and of Tongatapu in 1845. By 1860 the kingdom had become converted to Christianity (George himself having been baptized in 1831). In 1862 the king granted freedom to the people from arbitrary rule of minor chiefs and gave them the right to the allocation of land for their own needs. These institutional changes, together with the establishment of a parliament of chiefs, paved the way towards the democratic constitution under which the kingdom is now governed.

The kingdom continued up to 1899 as a neutral region in accordance with the Declaration of Berlin of 6 April 1886. By the Anglo-German Agreement of 14 Nov. 1899 subsequently accepted by the USA, the Tonga Islands were left under the Protectorate of Great Britain. A protectorate was proclaimed on 18 May 1900 and a British Agent and Consul appointed. The Protectorate was dissolved on June 4 1970 when Tonga, the only ancient kingdom surviving from the pre-European period in Polynesia, achieved complete independence within the Commonwealth.

TERRITORY AND POPULATION. The Kingdom consists of some 169 islands and islets with a total area of 289 sq. miles (748 sq. km; including inland waters), and lies between 15° and 23° 30' S. lat and 173° and 177° W. long, its western boundary being the eastern boundary of Fiji. The islands are split up into the following groups reading from north to south: The Niuas, Vava'u, Ha'apai, Tongatapu and 'Eua. The 3 main groups, both from historical and administrative significance, are Tongatapu in the south, Ha'apai in the centre and Vava'u in the north.

The capital is Nuku'alofa on Tongatapu, population (1986) 29,018.

There are 5 divisions comprising 23 districts:

Division	Sq. km	Census 1986	Capital
Niuas	72	2,368	Hihifo
Vava'u	119	15,175	Neiafu
Ha'apai	110	8,919	Pangai
Tongatapu	261	63,794	Nuku'alofa
'Eua	87	4,393	Ohonua

Census population (1996) 97,000. July 1997 estimate, 107,335.

CLIMATE. Generally a healthy climate, though Jan. to March is hot and humid, with temperatures of 90°F (32·2°C). Rainfall amounts are comparatively high, being greatest from Dec. to March. Nuku'alofa. Jan. 25·8°C, July 21·3°C. Annual rainfall 1,643 mm. Vava'u. Jan. 27·3°C, July 23·4°C. Annual rainfall 2,034 mm.

ROYAL HOUSE. The reigning King is **Taufa'ahau Tupou IV**, GCVO, GCMG, KBE, born 4 July 1918, succeeded on 16 Dec. 1965 on the death of his mother, Queen Salote Tupou III.

CONSTITUTION AND GOVERNMENT. The present Constitution is almost identical with that granted in 1875 by King George Tupou I. There is a Privy Council, Cabinet, Legislative Assembly and Judiciary. The 30-member *Legislative Assembly*, which meets annually, is composed of the King, 9 nobles elected by their peers, 9 elected representatives of the people and the Privy Councillors (numbering 11); the King appoints one of the 9 nobles to be the Speaker. The elections are held triennially.

Elections were held on 24–25 Jan. 1996 for the 9 elected seats. There were 61 candidates; 7 seats were gained by pro-democracy candidates.

In March 1998 the government comprised:

Prime Minister: The Hon. Baron Vaea.

Deputy Prime Minister and Minister of Education, Public Works and Civil Aviation: The Hon. Dr S. Langi Kavaliku. *Agriculture and Marine Affairs:* Prince Fatafehi Tu'ipelehake. *Labour, Commerce and Industry:* Giulio Masaso Paunga. *Foreign Affairs and Defence:* HRH The Crown Prince Tupouto'a. *Health:* Sione Tapa. *Attorney-General and Minister of Justice:* Tevita Tupou. *Police, Prisons and Fire Services:* The Hon. Clive Edwards. *Lands, Surveys and Natural Resources and Governor of Ha'apai:* S. Ma'afu Tupou. *Finance:* The Hon. Tutoatasi Fakafanua. *Without Portfolio:* The Hon. Ma'afu Tuku'i'aulahi. *Governor of Vava'u:* The Hon. Tu'i'afitu.

National anthem: "E 'Otua, Mafimafi, ko ho mau 'eiki Koe' ('Oh Almighty God above, thou art our Lord and sure defence'); words by Prince Uelingtoni Ngu Tupoumalohi, tune by K. G. Schmitt.

DEFENCE. A naval force some 125 strong in 1996 operates 3 inshore patrol craft, and 1 ex-Australian amphibious craft base at Tuliki, Nuku'alofa. An Air Force was created in 1996 and operates 3 Beech 18s for maritime patrol.

INTERNATIONAL RELATIONS

Membership. Tonga is a member of the Commonwealth, the Pacific Community and the South Pacific Forum, and is an ACP state of the EU.

ECONOMY

Budget. Recurrent revenue and expenditure in T$1,000:

	1990–91	1991–92	1992–93	1993-94
Revenue	47,442	46,229	52,287	54,766
Expenditure	47,438	51,984	49,928	52,230

Currency. The unit of currency is the *pa'anga* (TOP) of 100 *seniti.* There are notes of T$50, 20, 10, 5, 2 and 1 and coins of *seniti* 50, 20, 10, 5, 2 and 1.

Banking and Finance. The National Reserve Bank of Tonga was established in 1989 as a bank of issue and to manage foreign reserves. The Bank of Tonga and the Tonga Development Bank are both situated in Nuku'alofa with branches in the main islands.

ENERGY AND NATURAL RESOURCES

Electricity. Production (1994) 30m. kWh. Capacity (1995) 7,000 kWh.

Agriculture. Production (1992, in 1,000 tonnes): Coconuts, 25; fruit and vegetables, 28; copra, 2; cassava, 15.

Livestock (1992, in 1,000): Cattle, 10; horses, 12; pigs, 97; goats, 16.

FOREIGN ECONOMIC RELATIONS

Commerce. In 1991, imports were valued at T$76,817,269 while exports and re-exports were T$20,610,860 and T$854,263.

Main exports are coconut oil, vanilla beans, dessicated coconut and water melons.

Tourism. There were 100,000 visitors in 1996.

COMMUNICATIONS

Roads. In 1991 there were 7,364 motor vehicles and 415 km of paved roads.

Civil Aviation. There is an international airport at Fua'Amotu. The national carrier is the state-owned Royal Tongan Airlines, which operated 2 aircraft in 1995 and had services to Fiji and New Zealand. Services also provided by Air New Zealand, Air Pacific and Polynesian Airlines.

Shipping. In 1995, sea-going shipping totalled 12,307 GRT. 2 shipping lanes provide monthly services to American Samoa, Australia, Fiji, Kiribati, New Caledonia, New Zealand, Tuvalu and Samoa.

Telecommunications. Telephones numbered 6,000 in 1994. The operation of the International Telecommunication Services is undertaken by Cable and Wireless, under an agreement between the Company and the Government. The operation and development of the National Telecommunication Network and Services are the responsibilities of the Tonga Telecommunication Commission. The Tonga Broadcasting Commission is an independent statutory board which operates 2 programmes. There is also a religious service. There were about 66,000 radio sets in 1993. There are 2 television channels.

SOCIAL INSTITUTIONS

Justice. The judiciary is presided over by the Chief Justice. The enforcement of justice is the responsibility of the Attorney-General and the Minister of Police. In 1994 the UK ceased appointing Tongan judges and subsidizing their salaries.

Religion. The Tongans are Christian, 40,516 (1986), adherents of the Free Wesleyan Church.

Education. In 1993 there were 115 primary schools, with a total of 17,000 pupils. There were 7 government and 32 mission schools and 1 private school offering secondary education, with a total roll of 15,000. There is an extension centre of the University of the South Pacific at Nuku'alofa, a teacher training college and 3 technical institutes.

DIPLOMATIC REPRESENTATIVES

Of Tonga in Great Britain (36 Molyneux St., London, W1H 6AB)
High Commissioner: 'Akosita Fineanganofo.

Of Great Britain in Tonga (POB 56 Nuku'alofa)
High Commissioner: A. J. Morris.

Of Tonga in the USA
Ambassador: Vacant.

Of the USA in Tonga
Ambassador: Don Gevirtz (resident in Fiji).

Of Tonga to the European Union
Ambassador: 'Akosita Fineanganofo.

Further Reading

Campbell, I. C., *Island Kingdom: Tonga, Ancient and Modern.* Canterbury (NZ) Univ. Press, 1994

TRINIDAD AND TOBAGO

Republic of Trinidad and Tobago

Capital: Port-of-Spain
Population: 1·27m.
GDP per head: (PPP$) 9,124
GNP: US$4·8bn.
HDI/world rank: 0·880/40

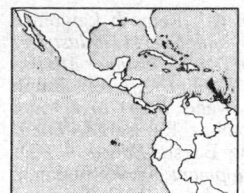

KEY HISTORICAL EVENTS. Trinidad and Tobago lie just off the coast of Venezuela in the Caribbean Sea. When Columbus visited Trinidad in 1498 the island was inhabited by Arawak Indians. Tobago was occupied by the Caribs. Trinidad remained a neglected Spanish possession for almost 300 years until it was surrendered to a British naval expedition in 1797. The main crop on the island was tobacco.

The British first attempted to settle Tobago in 1721 but the French captured the island in 1781 and transformed it into a sugar producing colony. In 1802 the British acquired Tobago and in 1899 it was administratively combined with Trinidad. When slavery was abolished in the late 1830s, the British subsidized immigration from India to replace plantation labourers. Sugar and cocoa declined towards the end of the 19th century. Oil and asphalt became the dominant sources of income.

On 31 Aug. 1962 Trinidad and Tobago became an independent member state of the Commonwealth. A Republican Constitution was adopted on 1 Aug. 1976.

During an attempted coup in July 1990 by a Moslem sect the prime minister was taken hostage and wounded.

TERRITORY AND POPULATION. The island of Trinidad is situated in the Caribbean Sea, about 12 km off the north-east coast of Venezuela; several islets, the largest being Chacachacare, Huevos, Monos and Gaspar Grande, lie in the Gulf of Paria which separates Trinidad from Venezuela. The smaller island of Tobago lies 30·7 km further to the north-east. Altogether, the islands cover 5,124 sq. km (1,978 sq. miles) of which Trinidad (including the islets) has 4,821 sq. km (1,861 sq. miles) and Tobago 303 sq. km (117 sq. miles). Population (census 1995) 1,259,972 (Trinidad, 1,208,625; Tobago, 51,347). Estimate, 1996, 1,272,500; density, 248 per sq. km. Capital, Port-of-Spain (1995 census, 45,284); other important towns, San Fernando (55,784), Arima (24,874) and Point Fortin (20,084). The main town on Tobago is Scarborough. Those of African descent are (1990 census) 39·6% of the population, Indians, 40·3%, mixed races, 18·4%, European, Chinese and others, 1·2%. English is spoken generally.

Growth rate, 1993, 0·73%; infant mortality, 15·3 per 1,000 live births; expectation of life, 72 years.

CLIMATE. A tropical climate cooled by the north-east trade winds. The dry season runs from Jan. to June, with a wet season for the rest of the year. Temperatures are uniformly high the year round. Port-of-Spain. Jan. 76·28°F (24·6°C), July 79·16°F (26·2°C). Annual rainfall 1,869·8 mm.

CONSTITUTION AND GOVERNMENT. The 1976 Constitution provides for a bicameral legislature of a *Senate* and a *House of Representatives*, who elect the *President*, who is head of state. The *Senate* consists of 31 members, 16 being appointed by the President on the advice of the Prime Minister, 6 on the advice of the Leader of the Opposition and 9 at the discretion of the President.

The *House of Representatives* consists of 36 (34 for Trinidad and 2 for Tobago) elected members and a Speaker elected from within or outside the House.

Executive power is vested in the Prime Minister, who is appointed by the President, and the Cabinet.

At the general election of 6 Nov. 1995 the People's National Movement (PNM) won 17 seats with 50% of votes cast, the United National Congress (UNC), 17 with

45% and the National Alliance for Reconstruction (NAR), 2 (the Tobago seats) with 5%. In 1995 the PNM became the official Opposition, while the UNC and NAR formed a coalition government. In 1997, two PNM members of Parliament declared themselves as independents.

President: His Excellency Arthur Napoleon Raymond Robinson.

In March 1998 the Cabinet comprised:
Prime Minister: Basdeo Panday (b.1933; UNC).
Finance and Tourism: Brian Kuei Tung. *Attorney General:* Ramesh Lawrence Maharaj. *Legal Affairs:* Kamla Persad-Bissessar. *Energy and Energy Industries:* Finbar Gangar. *Public Utilities:* Ganga Singh. *Trade, Industry and Consumer Affairs:* Mervyn Assam. *National Security:* Joseph Theodore. *Foreign Affairs:* Ralph Maharaj. *Public Administration and Information:* Mark Wade. *Sport and Youth Affairs:* Pamela Nicholson. *Social Development:* Manohar Ramsaran. *Local Government:* Dhanraj Singh. *Works and Transport:* Sadiq Baksh. *Education:* Dr Adesh Nanan. *Health:* Hamza Rafeek. *Planning and Development:* Trevor Sudama. *Labour and Co-operatives:* Harry Partap. *Community Development, Culture and Women's Affairs:* Dr Daphne Phillips. *Agriculture, Land and Marine Resources:* Dr Reeza Mohammed. *Housing and Settlements:* John Humphrey. *Tobago Affairs:* Dr Morgan Job. There are 2 Ministers in the Office of the Prime Minister: Dr Rupert Griffith and Dr Vincent Lasse, and 3 Parliamentary Secretaries: Chandesh Sharma (*Works and Transport*), Carol Cuffy-Dowlat *(Housing)*, Vimala Tota-Maharaj (*Agriculture, Lands and Marine Resources*)
The *Speaker* is Hector McClean.
Leader of the Opposition: Patrick Manning.

National anthem: 'Forged from the love of liberty'; words and music by P. Castagne.

Local Government. Trinidad is divided into 9 regional corporations, 2 city corporations, 3 borough corporations and Tobago, which has a 15-member elected House of Assembly with limited powers of self-government. Elections were held on 24 June 1996. The electorate was 816,809; turn-out was 43·95%. The PNM gained 43·95% of the votes cast, the UNC 49·92%, the NAR 5·81% and the independents 0·59%.

DEFENCE. The Defence Force has 2 infantry battalions and 1 support battalion. The small air element was disbanded in 1994. Security aircraft are operated by the police. Personnel in 1996 totalled 2,100.
The Coast Guard of 700 (1996) operates 8 inshore patrol craft, a number of boats and has 2 Cessna light aircraft for patrol duties.
The paramilitary police has 4,800 personnel.

INTERNATIONAL RELATIONS

Membership. Trinidad and Tobago is a member of the UN, the Commonwealth, OAS, CARICOM, Association of Caribbean States (ACS), and is an ACP state of the EU.

ECONOMY

Performance. Real GDP growth was 3·2% in 1996. The forecast for 1998 is 4·5%.

Budget. The fiscal year for the Budget is 1 Jan. to 31 Dec.
In 1996 total government revenue was TT$11,547m. and total expenditure was TT$11,010m. The budget envisaged total recurrent expenditure as TT$7,837m. and total capital expenditure as TT$2,269·1m.

Currency. The unit of currency is the *Trinidad and Tobago dollar* (TTD) of 100 cents. There are coins of 1, 5, 10, 25 and 50 cents, and banknotes of TT$1, 5, 10, 20 and 100. TT$3,539·2m. were in circulation in 1995. Net foreign exchange reserves were TT$611·4m. in Sept. 1996. Inflation was at an average of 3·5% by Oct. 1996.
In April 1994 the TT dollar was floated and managed by the Central Bank at

TT$6·06 to US$1·00. In Nov. 1997, the TT dollar depreciated to an all time low of TT$6·23 to US$1·00.

Banking and Finance. A Central Bank began operations in 1964 (*Governor*, Winston Dookeran). Its net reserves were US$507·4m. in December 1996. The present Governor is Ainsworth Harewood. There are 6 commercial banks. Government savings banks are established in 69 offices, with a head office in Port-of-Spain. The stock exchange in Port-of-Spain participates in the regional Caribbean exchange.

ENERGY AND NATURAL RESOURCES

Electricity. In 1996, 4,488m. kWh was generated.

Oil. Oil production is one of Trinidad's leading industries. Commercial production began in 1909; production of crude oil in 1996 was 47,171,100 bbls. Crude oil is also imported for refining. The 'Pitch Lake' is an important source of asphalt.

Natural Gas Liquids. In 1996 production was 4,459,700 bbls.

Agriculture. Sugar production in 1996 was 134,000 tonnes.

Livestock (1986 census): dairy cattle 25,331; (1992 in 1,000): sheep, 14; goats, 52; pigs, 50; poultry, 10m. Livestock products, 1995: Beef, 1,175 tonnes; pork, 1,585 tonnes; broilers, 15,532.

Fisheries. The catch in 1994 was 14,046 tonnes.

INDUSTRY. In 1995, 2,310,400 tonnes of iron and steel were produced. Other manufacturing includes ammonia and urea (production, 1991, 1,768,400 tonnes), methanol (1996, 1,317,400 tonnes), cement (1996, 617,000 tonnes), rum (1996, 4,499,000 proof gallons), beer (1996, 29,555,000 litres), cigarettes (1996, 812,000 kg), sugar (1996, 134,000 tonnes), fertilizer (1996, 2,674,200 tonnes).

Labour. The working population in 1996 was 538,000. The number of unemployed in 1996 was 85,600.

Trade Unions. About 30% of the labour force belong to unions, which are grouped under the National Trade Union Centre.

FOREIGN ECONOMIC RELATIONS. The Foreign Investment Act of 1990 permits foreign investors to acquire land and shares in local companies, and to form companies. External debt was TT$10,105·1m. in Dec. 1996.

Commerce. Exports in 1996 were TT$15,014m. of which TT$7,546m. was mineral fuels and products. Imports totalled TT$12,867m. of which TT$3,945m. was for machinery and transport equipment.

Tourism. There were 265,900 visitors in 1996. There were 48,145 cruise ship visitors in 1996.

COMMUNICATIONS

Roads. In 1996 there were 9,586 km of main and local roads. Motor vehicles registered in 1996 totalled 234,457.

Civil Aviation. There is an international airport at Port-of-Spain (Piarco). The national carrier is BWIA International Trinidad and Tobago Airways, which was privatized in March 1995 by the Acker group of companies. The airline operates 11 aircraft. Services are also provided by Air Canada, Air Caribbean, ALM, American Airlines, Avior (Venezuela), LIAT and Surinam Airways.

Shipping. Sea-going shipping totalled 17,037 GRT in 1995 and 11,703,768 tonnes of cargo were handled. A deep-water harbour at Scarborough (Tobago) was opened in 1991. The other main harbours are Point Lisas and Port-of-Spain.

Telecommunications. International and domestic communications are provided by Telecommunications Services of Trinidad and Tobago (TSTT) by means of a satellite earth station and various high quality radio circuits. The marine radio service is also maintained by TSTT. Number of post offices (1997), 75; postal agencies, 158; number of telephones (1997), 205,610. Radio programmes are overseen by the Telecommunications Authority. There are 14 commercial stations. There are 3 TV stations, as well as community and cable services.

Cinemas (1996). There were 19 cinemas and 1 drive-in cinema.

Press (Oct. 1996). There were 4 daily newspapers with a total daily circulation of 219,000, 4 Sunday newspapers with a total circulation of 224,000, 6 weekly and 1 bi-weekly newspaper.

SOCIAL INSTITUTIONS

Justice. The High Court consists of the Chief Justice and 11 puisne judges. In criminal cases a judge of the High Court sits with a jury of 12 in cases of treason and murder, and with 9 jurors in other cases. The Court of Appeal consists of the Chief Justice and 7 Justices of Appeal. In hearing appeals, the Court is comprised of three judges sitting together except when the appeal is from a Summary Court or from a decision of a High Court judge in chambers. In such cases two judges would comprise the Court. There is a limited right of appeal from it to the Privy Council. There are 3 High Courts and 12 magistrates' courts. There is an *Ombudsman*. The death penalty is authorized.

Religion. In 1997, 14·4% of the population were Anglicans (under the Bishop of Trinidad and Tobago), 32·2% Roman Catholics (under the Archbishop of Port-of-Spain), 24·3% Hindus and 6% Moslems.

Education. In 1995–96 there were 185,937 pupils enrolled in primary schools, 16,455 in government secondary schools, 19,602 in assisted secondary schools, 34,795 in junior secondary schools, 24,002 in senior comprehensive schools, 8,024 in composite schools and 4,135 in technical and vocational schools. The University of the West Indies campus in St Augustine (1995–96) had 5,348 students and 509 academic staff. 693 of the students were from other countries.

Health. In 1996 there were 957 physicians, 142 dentists, 514 pharmacists and 67 hospitals and nursing homes with 5,184 beds. There were 1,569 nurses and midwives and 1,428 nursing assistants in government institutions.

DIPLOMATIC REPRESENTATIVES

Of Trinidad and Tobago in Great Britain (42 Belgrave Sq., London, SW1X 8NT) *High Commissioner:* Sheelagh M. De Osuna.

Of Great Britain in Trinidad and Tobago (19 St Clair Ave., Port-of-Spain) *High Commissioner:* Gregory Faulkner.

Of Trinidad and Tobago in the USA (1708 Massachusetts Ave., NW, Washington, D.C., 20036) *Ambassador:* Michael Arneaud.

Of the USA in Trinidad and Tobago (15 Queen's Park West, Port-of-Spain) *Ambassador:* Edward Shumaker.

Of Trinidad and Tobago to the United Nations *Ambassador:* Vacant.

Of Trinidad and Tobago to the European Union *Ambassador:* Lingston Cumberbatch.

Further Reading

Chambers, F., *Trinidad and Tobago.* [Bibliography] Oxford and Santa Barbara, 1986
Cooper, St G. C. and Bacon, P. R. (eds.) *The Natural Resources of Trinidad and Tobago.* London, 1981
Central library: The Central Library of Trinidad and Tobago, Queen's Park East, Port-of-Spain.
National statistical office: Central Statistical Office, 2 Edward St., Port-of-Spain.

TUNISIA

Jumhuriya at-Tunisiya

(Republic of Tunisia)

Capital: Tunis
Population: 9·1m.
GNP: US$15·9bn.
HDI/world rank: 0·748/81

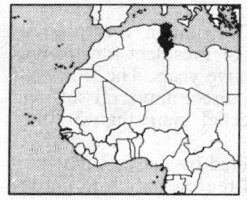

KEY HISTORICAL EVENTS. Settled by the Phoenicians, this area of the north African coast developed into the Carthaginian Empire and was later incorporated into the Roman Empire. It became a powerful state under the dynasty of the Berber Hafsids (1207-1574).

Tunisia was nominally a part of the Ottoman Empire from the end of the 17th century and descendants of the original Ottoman ruler remained Beys of Tunis until the modern state of Tunisia was established. A French protectorate since 1883, Tunisia saw considerable anti-French activity in the late 1930s including a general strike in 1938 led by the *Néo-Destour* party (renamed *Parti Socialiste Destourien* – PSD – in 1964) under Habib Bourguiba. Tunisia did, however, support the Allies in the Second World War and was the scene of heavy fighting.

France granted internal self-government in 1955 and Tunisia became fully independent on 20 March 1956. A constitutional assembly was established and Habib Bourguiba became prime minister. A republic was established in 1957, the Bey deposed and the monarchy was abolished; Bourguiba became president. In 1975 the constitution was changed so that Bourguiba could be made President-for-life.

Tunisia was a one-party (PSD) state until 1981. When elections were held on 2 Nov. 1986 all seats in the national assembly were won by *Front National*, an alliance of the PSD and the *Union générale des travailleurs tunisiens*. All other parties boycotted the elections.

Bourguiba was overthrown in a bloodless *coup* in 1987. His successor as president, Zine El Abidine Ben Ali, introduced democratic reforms but a long running struggle with Islamic fundamentalists has been marked by sporadic violence and the suspension of political rights.

TERRITORY AND POPULATION. Tunisia is bounded in the north and east by the Mediterranean Sea, west by Algeria and south by Libya. The area is 154,530 sq. km. The 1996 official estimate put the total population at 9,092,000. Vital statistics rates (1993): Birth, 24·4 per 1,000 population; death, 6·1. Expectation of life was 67·1 years in 1992. Growth rate, 1993, 1·9%.

The 1984 census populations of the 23 governorates:

	Area in sq. km	Population		Area in sq. km	Population
Aryanah	1,558	374,192	Qasrayn (Kassérine)	8,066	297,959
Bajah (Béja)	3,558	274,706	Qayrawan(Kairouan)	6,712	421,607
Banzart (Bizerta)	3,685	394,670	Qibili (Kebili)	22,084	95,371
Bin Arus	761	246,193	Safaqis (Sfax)	7,545	577,992
Jundubah (Jendouba)	3,102	359,429	Sidi Bu Zayd		
Kaf (Le Kef)	4,965	247,672	(Sidi Bouzid)	6,994	288,528
Madaniyin (Médénine)	8,588	295,889	Silyanah (Siliana)	4,631	222,038
Mahdiyah (Mahdia)	2,966	270,435	Susah (Sousse)	2,621	322,491
Munastir (Monastir)	1,019	278,478	Tatawin (Tataouine)	38,889	100,329
Nabul (Nabeul)	2,788	461,405	Tawzar (Tozeur)	4,719	67,943
Qabis (Gabès)	7,175	240,016	Tunis	346	774,364
Qafsah (Gafsa)	8,990	235,723	Zaghwan (Zaghouan)	2,768	118,743

Tunis, the capital, had (1994 census, in 1,000) 674·1 inhabitants: Sfax, 230·9; Aryanah, 152·7; Ettadhamen, 149·2; Sousse, 125; Kairouan, a holy city of the Moslems, 102·6; Gabès, 98·9; Bizerta, 98·9; Bardo, 72·7; Gafsa, 71·1.

The official language is Arabic but French is the main language in the media, commercial enterprise and government departments. Berber-speaking people form less than 1% of the population.

1371

CLIMATE. The climate ranges from warm temperate in the north, where winters are mild and wet and the summers hot and dry, to desert in the south. Tunis. Jan. 48°F (8·9°C), July 78°F (25·6°C). Annual rainfall 16" (400 mm). Bizerta. Jan. 52°F (11·1°C), July 77°F (25°C). Annual rainfall 25" (622 mm). Sfax. Jan. 52°F (11·1°C), July 78°F (25·6°C). Annual rainfall 8" (196 mm).

CONSTITUTION AND GOVERNMENT. The Constitution was promulgated on 1 June 1959 and reformed in 1988. The office of President-for-life was abolished and Presidential elections were to be held every five years. The *President* and the *National Assembly* are elected simultaneously by direct universal suffrage for a period of 5 years. The President cannot be re-elected more than 3 times consecutively.

The National Assembly has 163 seats, 144 directly elected by the first-past-the-post system and 19 distributed nationally by proportional representation to parties that fail to win seats under the first-pass-the-post system.

Presidential and parliamentary elections were held on 20 March 1994; turn-out was 93%. President Zine El Abidine Ben Ali, the sole candidate, was re-elected by 99·8% of votes cast. The Constitutional Democratic Assembly (CDA) won all 144 of the directly-elected National Assembly seats with 97·73% of votes cast. The next presidential parliamentary elections are due by March 1999. The Islamist opposition movement (al-Nahda) was crushed in 1991 and is no longer seen as a threat to the Western-leaning government.

President: Zine El Abidine Ben Ali (appointed 2 April 1989, re-elected 20 March 1994).

The Cabinet in March 1998 comprised:
Prime Minister: Hamed Karoui.
Minister, Head of the Presidential Cabinet: Mohamed Jegham. *Minister of Justice:* Abdullah Kallel. *Foreign Affairs:* Said Ben Mustapha. *Secretary General of the Government:* Ridha Grira. *Defence:* Habib Ben Yahia. *Interior:* Ali Chaouch. *International Co-operation and Foreign Investment:* Mohamed Ghannouchi. *Finance:* Mohamed Jeri. *Economic Development:* Taoufik Baccar. *Transport:* Hassine Chouk. *Equipment and Housing:* Slaheddine Belaid. *Tourism and Handicrafts:* Slaheddine Maaoui. *Social Affairs:* Chedli Neffati. *Education:* Ridha Ferchiou. *Higher Education and Scientific Research:* Daly Jazi. *Professional Training and Employment:* Moncer Rouissi. *Public Health:* Hedi Henni. *Youth and Children:* Raouf Najjar. *Culture:* Abdelbaki Hermassi. *Environment and Land Use Management:* Mohamed Mehdi Melika. *Agriculture:* Sadok Rabha. *State Property:* Mustapha Bouaziz. *Communications:* Ahmed Friaa. *Religious Affairs:* Ali Chebbi. *Industry:* Moncef Ben Abdallah. *Commerce:* Mondher Znaidi. *Family and Women's Affairs:* Neziha Zarrouk.

The *Speaker* is Habib Boulares.

National anthem: 'Humata al Hima' ('Defenders of the Homeland'); words by Mustapha al Rafi, tune by M. A. Wahab.

Local Government. The country is divided into 23 governorates, sub-divided into 199 districts and then into communes and imadas. On 21 May 1995 elections were held for the 3,774 seats on the 257 local councils. The CDA gained control of all councils.

DEFENCE. Selective conscription is 1 year.

Army. The Army consists of 3 mechanized, 1 Sahara and 1 special forces brigade; and 1 engineer regiment. Equipment includes 54 M-60A3 and 30 M-60A1 main battle tanks. Strength (1997) 27,000 (22,000 conscripts). There are also the paramilitary Police (13,000) and National Guard (10,000).

Navy. The Navy includes 3 French-built 380-tonne fast missile craft and 3 smaller craft with short range missiles. In 1996 naval personnel totalled 4,500. Forces are based at Bizerta, Sfax and Kelibia.

The Coast Guard operates 4 coastal and 19 inshore patrol craft.

Air Force. Equipment of the Air Force includes 1 squadron of Aermacchi M.B.326K/L; 1 squadron of L-59 jet light attack aircraft; 1 squadron of F-5E/F Tiger II fighters. Personnel (1996) about 3,500 (700 conscripts), with 44 combat aircraft.

INTERNATIONAL RELATIONS

Membership. Tunisia is a member of the UN, OAU, the Islamic Conference and the Arab League.

ECONOMY

Policy. The ninth 5-year development plan runs from 1997 to 2001. Growth is to reach 6% p.a.; inflation is to be held at 4·1%.

Currency. The unit of currency is the *Tunisian dinar* (TND) of 1,000 *millimes*. There are coins of 5, 10, 20, 50, 100 and 500 millimes and 1 dinar, and notes of 1, 5, 10 and 20 dinars. The currency was made convertible on 6 Jan. 1993. Foreign exchange reserves were 853·8m. dinars in 1993. Inflation was 3·7% in 1996.

Banking and Finance. The Central Bank of Tunisia is the bank of issue. In 1988 there were 9 development banks, 10 deposit banks and 9 off-shore banks.

There is a small stock exchange (16 companies trading in 1993).

Weights and Measures. The metric system is legal. Some traditional weights are still in use: 12 *sa* = 1 *wiba* = 1 bushel; 16 *wiba* = 1 *kfiz*; 1 *ounce* = 31·487 grammes.

ENERGY AND NATURAL RESOURCES

Electricity. Electrical energy generated was estimated at 6·5bn. kWh in 1995.

Oil and Gas. Crude oil production (1992) was 5·35m. tonnes. Gas production (1991) was 387m. cu. metres.

Water. In 1993 there were 20 large dams, 250 hillside dams and some 1,000 artificial lakes. In 1986, 257,000 ha were irrigated.

Minerals. Mineral production (in 1,000 tonnes) in 1995: Calcium phosphate, 6,302; iron ore, 225; lead ore (concentrated), 11·0; zinc ore (concentrated), 80·0; sea salt, 319.

Agriculture. There are 5 agricultural regions: The *north*, mountainous with large fertile valleys; the *north-east*, with the peninsula of Cap Bon, suited for the cultivation of oranges, lemons and tangerines; the *Sahel*, where olive trees abound; the *centre*, a region of high table lands and pastures, and the *desert* of the south, where dates are grown.

Some 23% of the population are employed in agriculture, which contributed 12·2% of GDP in 1989. Large estates predominate; smallholdings are tending to fragment, partly owing to inheritance laws. There were some 0·4m. farms in 1990 (0·32m. in 1960). Of the total area of 15,583,000 ha, about 9m. ha are productive, including 2m. under cereals, 3·6m. used as pasturage, 0·9m. forests and 1·3m. uncultivated. The main crops are cereals, citrus fruits, tomatoes, melons, olives, dates, grapes and olive oil. Production, 1995 (in 1,000 tonnes): Wheat, 530; barley, 80; olives, 630 (unofficial figure); dates, 84; almonds, 35; potatoes, 199 (unofficial figure); tomatoes, 452; peppers, 170; melons, including watermelons, 354; apples, 75; apricots, 24; citrus fruits, 271; pears, 42; peaches and nectarines, 59; plums 11; chickpeas, 27; sugar-beet, 246; tobacco, 6; wine, 237 (000 hl.); grapes, 108.

Livestock, 1995 (in 1,000): Horses, 56; asses, 231; mules, 81; cattle, 659; sheep, 7,110; goats, 1,417; camels, 231; pigs, 6. Livestock products, 1995 (in 1,000 tonnes): Meat, 141; milk, 565; eggs, 62·5.

Fisheries. In 1995 the catch amounted to 95,000 tonnes.

INDUSTRY. Production, 1996 (in 1,000 tonnes): phosphoric acid, 1,063; cement, 4,560; lime, 464. 2,010 cars, 450 lorries, 1,240 vans, 220 buses and coaches, 330 tractors.

Labour. Unemployment was 15·0% in 1996.

Trade Unions. The Union Générale des Travailleurs Tunisiens won 27 seats in the parliamentary elections (1 Nov. 1981). There are also the Union Tunisienne de l'Industrie, du Commerce et de l'Artisanat (UTICA, the employers' union) and the Union National des Agriculteurs (UNA, farmers' union).

FOREIGN ECONOMIC RELATIONS. In Feb. 1989 Tunisia signed a treaty of economic co-operation with the other countries of Maghreb: Algeria, Libya, Mauritania and Morocco. Foreign debt was US$9,200m. in 1993.

Commerce. The imports and exports for calendar years (US$1m.):

	1990	1991	1992	1993	1994
Imports	5,476	5,190	6,077	6,213	6,600
Exports	3,498	3,714	4,033	3,803	4,600

Main exports in 1991 (in 1,000 tonnes): Crude oil, 3,993; textiles, 90; olive oil, 158; phosphates, 808; fertilizers, 1,471; fruit, 48; leather and shoes, 5·7; fishery products, 13·6; machinery and electrical appliances, 13·1.

Main imports in 1991 (in 1,000 tonnes): Oil and by-products, 2,404; natural gas, 639; vegetable oil, 136; dairy products, 20; coffee, tea and spices, 21; cereals, 922; sugar, 168.

Exports and imports in 1991 by country (in 1m. dinars): France, 862·7, 1,247·5; Italy, 674·4, 835·6; Germany, 561·1, 682·4; Belgium, 213·5, 256·7.

Tunisia was the first country to sign a partnership agreement with the European Union. The agreement aims at creating a non-agricultural free trade zone by 2008.

Tourism. There were 3·88m. visitors in 1994. Revenues have doubled since 1987 from TND568m. to TND1·6bn., accounting for 10% of GDP.

COMMUNICATIONS

Roads. In 1993 there were 20,830 km of roads. Vehicles drive on the right.

Railways. In 1994 there were 2,152 km of railways (468 km of 1,435 mm gauge and 1,684 km of metre-gauge), of which 110 km were electrified. 28·3m. passengers and 11·8m. tonnes of freight were carried in 1994. There is a light rail network in Tunis (33 km).

Civil Aviation. The national carrier, Tunis Air, is 84·86% state-owned, and in 1995 had a fleet comprising 1 A300B4-100, 1 A300B4-200, 8 A320-200s, 1 B-727-200, 6 B-727-200 Advs, 3 B-737-200 Advs, 1 B-737-200C Adv and 4 B-737-500s. There are 6 international airports, the main one at Tunis-Carthage. In 1987, 4,429,000 passengers and 21,688 tonnes of freight were carried. Services are also provided by Aeroflot, Air Algérie, Air France, Air Inter, Air Liberté, Air Malta, Air Ukraine, Alitalia, Balkan, British Airways, Czech Airlines, Egyptair, Iberia, KLM, Libyan Airlines, Lufthansa, Middle East Airlines, Royal Air Maroc, Royal Jordanian, Saudia, Swissair, Syrian Airlines and Turkish Airlines.

Shipping. The main port is Tunis, and its outer port is Tunis-Goulette. These two ports and Sfax, Sousse and Bizerta are directly accessible to ocean-going vessels. The ports of La Skhirra and Gabès are used for the shipping of Algerian and Tunisian oil. In 1995, sea-going shipping totalled 0·18m. GRT, including oil tankers, 9,976 GRT.

Telecommunications. In 1994 there were 494,000 telephones. The government-controlled Radiodiffusion-Télévision Tunisienne provides a national radio programme, an international service; Radio Tunisie Internationale (French and Italian) and 2 regional programmes. There are Arabic and French TV networks (colour by SECAM). In 1994 there were 1,740,000 radio and 710,000 TV sets.

Cinemas There are 80 cinemas.

Press. In 1993 there were 20 daily and weekly newspapers (3 in French). Press freedom is severely limited.

SOCIAL INSTITUTIONS

Justice. There are 51 magistrates' courts, 13 courts of first instance, 3 courts of appeal (in Tunis, Sfax and Sousse) and the High Court in Tunis.

A Personal Status Code was promulgated on 13 Aug. 1956 and applied to Tunisians from 1 Jan. 1957. This raised the status of women, made divorce subject to a court decision, abolished polygamy and decreed a minimum marriage age.

Religion. The constitution recognizes Islam as the state religion. In 1992 there were 8·36m. Sunni Moslems. There are about 20,000 Roman Catholics, under the Prelate of Tunis.

Education. Adult literacy was 65% in 1993. All education is free from primary schools to university. Higher education includes 6 universities, 3 of them being specialized by faculty, teachers' training college, a school of law, 2 centres of economic studies, 2 schools of engineering, 2 medical schools, a faculty of agriculture, 2 institutes of business administration and 1 school of dentistry.

In 1994 there were 4,286 primary schools with 58,279 teachers and 1,472,844 pupils; 712 secondary schools with 27,785 teachers and 662,222 pupils.

Health. In 1987 there were 36 general hospitals (22 university and 14 regional), 20 specialized institutions, centres and university hospitals, and (1988) 92 district hospitals. In 1986 there were 15,814 beds.

Social Security. A system of social security was set up in 1950 (amended 1963, 1964 and 1970).

DIPLOMATIC REPRESENTATIVES

Of Tunisia in Great Britain (29 Prince's Gate, London, SW7 1QG)
Ambassador: Mohamed Ben Ahmed.

Of Great Britain in Tunisia (5 Place de la Victoire, Tunis)
Ambassador and Consul-General: Richard Edis CMG.

Of Tunisia in the USA (1515 Massachusetts Ave., NW, Washington, D.C., 20005)
Ambassador: Noureddine Mejdoub.

Of the USA in Tunisia (144 Ave. de la Liberté, Tunis)
Ambassador: Mary A. Casey.

Of Tunisia to the United Nations
Ambassador: Ali Hachani.

Of Tunisia to the European Union
Ambassador: Tahar Sioud.

Further Reading

Lawless R. I. *et al.*, *Tunisia.* [Bibliography] Oxford and Santa Barbara (CA), 1982
Salem, N., *Habib Bourguiba, Islam and the Creation of Tunisia.* London, 1984
National statistical office: Institut National de la Statistique, 27 Rue de Liban, Tunis.

TURKEY

Türkiye Çumhuriyeti

(Republic of Turkey)

Capital: Ankara
Population: 63·53m.
GDP per head: (PPP$) 5,193
GNP: US$149bn.
HDI/world rank: 0·772/74

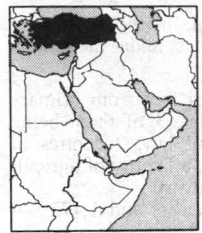

KEY HISTORICAL EVENTS. In the 13th century the kingdom of Othman I became the dominant power in Asia Minor (now the Asian part of Turkey). In 1453 the Turks captured Constantinople and destroyed the Eastern Roman Empire. Thereafter, the Ottoman Empire expanded to include an area from Morocco to Persia and westwards into the Balkans. From the 17th century, however, the Empire began to decline, its power weakening rapidly in the 19th century.

The Turkish War of Independence (1919-22), following the disintegration of the Ottoman Empire, was led and won by Mustafa Kemal (Atatürk) on behalf of the Grand National Assembly which first met in Ankara on 23 April 1920. On 20 Jan. 1921 the Grand National Assembly voted a constitution which declared that all sovereignty belonged to the people and vested all power, both executive and legislative, in the Grand National Assembly. The name 'Ottoman Empire' was later replaced by 'Turkey'. On 1 Nov. 1922 the Grand National Assembly abolished the office of Sultan and Turkey became a republic on 29 Oct. 1923.

Religious courts were abolished in 1924, Islam ceased to be the official state religion in 1928, women were given the franchise and western-style surnames were adopted in 1934.

On 27 May 1960 the Turkish Army, directed by a National Unity Committee under the leadership of Gen. Cemal Gürsel, overthrew the government of the Democratic Party. The Grand National Assembly was dissolved and party activities were suspended. Party activities were legally resumed on 12 Jan. 1961. A new constitution was approved in a referendum held on 9 July 1961 and general elections were held the same year.

On 12 Sept. 1980, the Turkish armed forces overthrew the Demirel Government (Justice Party). Parliament was dissolved and all activities of political parties were suspended. The Constituent Assembly was convened in Oct. 1981, and prepared a new constitution which was enforced after a national referendum on 7 Nov. 1982.

In the face of mounting Islamicization of government policy, the Supreme National Security Council convened on 28 Feb. 1997 and reaffirmed its commitment to the secularity of the state. On 6 March Prime Minister Neçmettin Erbakan, leader of the pro-Islamist Welfare Party, agreed to sign a list of measures to combat Moslem fundamentalism. In June he was forced to resign by a campaign led by the Army.

On 16 Jan.1998 a Constitutional Court ruling ordered the closure of the Welfare Party. In Feb. Mr Erbakan and 5 other party members were expelled from parliament and banned from political office for 5 years.

There are quarrels with Greece over the division of Cyprus, oil rights under the Aegean and ownership of uninhabited islands close to the Turkish coast.

TERRITORY AND POPULATION. Turkey is bounded in the west by the Aegean Sea and Greece, north by Bulgaria and the Black Sea, east by Georgia, Armenia and Iran, and south by Iraq, Syria and the Mediterranean. The area (including lakes) is 779,452 sq. km (300,947 sq. miles). At the 1990 census the population was 56,473,035. A census is scheduled for 2000. Population estimate (July 1997), 63,528,225; density, 81 per sq. km. Urban population (1990 census), 33,326,351 (59·01%); density, 73 per sq. km.

Vital statistics, 1994: Birth rate per 1,000 population, 21; death, 64. Marriages, 462,415; divorces, 28,041. Expectation of life, 68·2 years.

Some 12m. Kurds live in Turkey. Limited use of the Kurdish language (not in schools or publications) was sanctioned in Feb. 1991.

Area and population of the 73 provinces[1] at the 1990 census:

	Area in sq.km.	Population	Density per sq.km.
Adana	17,562	1,934,907	111
Adiyaman	7,423	513,131	70
Afyonkarahisar	14,295	739,223	52
Ağri	11,066	437,093	40
Aksaray	7,626	326,399	43
Amasya	5,452	357,191	66
Ankara	25,614	3,236,626	126
Antalya	20,815	1,132,211	55
Artvin	7,436	212,833	29
Aydin	7,870	824,816	105
Balikesir	14,456	973,314	68
Batman	4,694	344,669	74
Bayburt	3,652	107,330	30
Bilecik	4,321	175,526	40
Bingöl	8,319	250,966	30
Bitlis	8,010	330,115	41
Bolu	10,575	536,869	51
Burdur	7,167	254,899	36
Bursa	10,990	1,603,137	146
Çanakkale	9,950	432,263	44
Çankırı	8,659	279,129	33
Çorum	12,729	609,863	49
Denizli	11,874	750,882	64
Diyarbakir	4,908	1,094,996	73
Edirne	6,174	404,599	65
Elazığ	9,455	498,225	53
Erzincan	11,413	299,251	27
Erzurum	25,133	848,201	34
Eskişehir	13,477	641,057	48
Gaziantep	8,015	1,140,594	153
Giresun	6,965	499,087	75
Gümüşhane	6,748	169,375	25
Hakkâri	7,121	172,479	25
Hatay	5,570	1,109,754	204
İsparta	8,847	434,771	49
İçel	15,448	1,266,995	82
İstanbul	5,591	7,309,190	1,330
İzmir	12,263	2,694,770	220
Karaman	9,163	217,536	24
Kars	18,841	662,155	35
Kastamonu	12,982	423,611	33
Kayseri	16,537	943,484	57
Kırıkkale	4,365	349,396	84
Kırklareli	6,378	309,512	49
Kirşehir	6,501	256,862	40
Kocaeli	3,578	936,163	260
Konya	40,451	1,750,303	43
Kütahya	11,661	578,020	51
Malatya	11,752	702,055	57
Manisa	13,237	1,154,418	87
K. Maraş	14,680	892,952	61
Mardin	8,594	557,727	65
Muğla	12,504	562,809	45
Muş	8,413	376,543	45
Nevşehir	5,540	289,509	52
Niğde	7,831	305,861	39
Ordu	6,142	830,105	137
Rize	3,920	348,776	91
Sakarya	4,821	683,061	140
Samsun	9,739	1,158,400	120
Siirt	6,176	243,435	40
Sinop	5,657	265,153	48
Şırnak	7,172	262,006	40
Sivas	28,568	767,481	28

	Area in sq.km.	Population	Density per sq.km.
Tekirdağ	6,333	468,842	74
Tokat	9,869	719,251	73
Trabzon	4,498	795,849	180
Tunceli	7,954	133,143	17
Urfa	19,271	1,001,455	52
Uşak	5,389	290,283	54
Van	21,095	637,433	30
Yozgat	13,597	579,150	43
Zonguldak	8,560	1,073,560	126

[1] In 1995 there were 79 provinces.

Population of urban areas and towns of over 120,000 inhabitants in 1990:

	Urban area	Town		Urban area	Town
İstanbul	6,407,215	6,293,397	Erzurum	409,095	297,544
Ankara	3,022,236	2,541,899	Kahramanmaraş	395,872	237,456
İzmir	2,665,105	2,319,188	Zonguldak	381,824	124,862
Adana	1,429,677	972,318	Malatya	367,765	304,760
Bursa	1,030,737	775,388	Sivas	350,564	219,949
Konya	1,015,415	543,460	Trabzon	288,118	173,354
Gaziantep	759,893	573,968	Denizli	285,836	199,360
İçel	700,851	414,308	Elazığ	275,342	218,121
Kayseri	587,793	461,415	Kırıkkale	267,379	233,008
Diyarbakır	560,347	371,038	Sakarya	255,112	170,231
Manisa	556,787	158,426	Kütahya	232,632	135,432
Şanlıurfa	520,533	239,604	Van	217,442	126,010
Antalya	514,264	353,149	İsparta	204,311	113,693
Kocaeli	498,646	271,132	İskenderun	· · ·	175,998
Hatay	481,560	118,443	Tarsus	· · ·	168,654
Samsun	462,836	277,222	Batman	· · ·	131,812
Balıkesir	461,618	172,570	Osmaniye	· · ·	121,188
Eskişehir	455,478	415,831			

CLIMATE. Coastal regions have a Mediterranean climate, with mild, moist winters and hot, dry summers. The interior plateau has more extreme conditions, with low and irregular rainfall, cold and snowy winters and hot, almost rainless summers. Ankara. Jan. 32·5°F (0·3°C), July 73°F (23°C). Annual rainfall 14·7" (367 mm). Istanbul. Jan. 41°F (5°C), July 73°F (23°C). Annual rainfall 28·9" (723 mm). Izmir. Jan. 46°F (8°C), July 81°F (27°C). Annual rainfall 28" (700 mm).

CONSTITUTION AND GOVERNMENT. On 7 Nov. 1982 a referendum established that 98% of the electorate were in favour of new Constitution. The *President* is elected for 7-year terms. The Presidency is not an executive position, and the President may not be linked to a political party. There is a 550-member *Grand National Assembly*, elected by universal suffrage (at 18 years and over) for 5-year terms by proportional representation. There is a *Constitutional Court* consisting of 15 regular and 5 alternating members.

Elections were held in Dec. 1995. The electorate was 34,155,981; turn-out was 85·2%. The Welfare Party (pro-Islamist) gained 158 seats with 21·38% of votes cast (62 with 16·9% in 1991); the True Path Party, 135 with 19·18% (178 with 27%); the Motherland Party (MP), 132 with 19·65% (115 with 27%); the Democratic Left Party (DLP), 76 with 14·64% (7 with 10·8%); and the Republican Populist Party, 49 with 10·71%.

President: Suleyman Demirel (b. 1924; sworn in 16 May 1993).

In June 1997 a minority 3-party (MP/DLP/Democratic Turkey Party) coalition government was formed, comprising in March 1998:
   Prime Minister: Mesut Yilmaz (b. 1948; MP).
   Deputy Prime Minister: Bülent Ecevit. *Deputy Prime Minister and Minister of National Defence and Natural Resources:* Ismet Sezgin. *Agriculture:* Mustafa Tasar. *Culture:* Istemihan Talay. *Education:* Hikmet Ulugbay. *Energy:* Cumhur Ersümer. *Environment:* Imren Aykut. *Finance:* Zekeriya Temizel. *Foreign Affairs:* Ismail Cem. *Forestry:* Ersin Taranoğlu. *Health:* Halil Ibrahim Özsoy. *Industry and Trade:* Yalim

Erez. *Interior:* Murat Basesgioğlu. *Justice:* Oltan Sungurlu. *Labour and Social Security:* Nami Cagan. *Public Works and Housing:* Yasar Topçu. *Tourism:* Ibrahim Gürdal. *Transportation and Communications:* Necdet Menzir.

The *Speaker* is Wikmet Citin.

National anthem: 'Korkma! Sönmez bu şafaklarda yüzen al sancak' ('Be not afraid! Our flag will never fade'); words by Mehmed Akif Ersoy, tune by Zeki Güngör.

Local Government. The 79 provinces have elected councils, as do municipalities. Mayors (of metropolitan areas and municipalities) and village heads and councils of elders are also elected. At partial municipal elections on 4 June 1995 the TPP gained 22 of 36 seats with 39·6% of votes cast, the Republican Populist Party gained 20·36%, the Prosperity Party 17·4%.

DEFENCE. The *Supreme Council of National Security*, chaired by the Prime Minister and comprising military leaders and the ministers of defence and the economy, also functions as a *de facto* constitutional watchdog.

Conscription is 18 months.

Army. The Army consists of 1 mechanized divisional HQ, 1 mechanized and 1 infantry division, 9 infantry, 14 armoured, 17 mechanized and 4 commando brigades, 1 armoured, 1 Presidential Guard and 5 coastal defence regiments and 26 frontier defence battalions. Equipment includes 75 M-47, 2,876 M-48, 932 M-60 and 397 Leopard main battle tanks. Army Aviation has some 400 aircraft and helicopters. Strength (1997) 525,000 (462,000 conscripts). There is also a paramilitary gendarmerie cum national guard of 180,000.

Navy. Current strength includes 15 diesel submarines (8 reasonably modern, of German design and 7 very old ex-US built 1944–45), 5 ex-US destroyers (1943–46), 16 frigates of which 6 are modern German MEKO-type, 8 ex-US Knox class and 2 locally built in the 1970s. Light forces comprise 18 fast missile craft, 11 coastal and 21 inshore patrol craft. Mine warfare forces include 3 minelayers, 17 coastal and 4 inshore minesweepers. Amphibious lift is provided by 8 tank landing ships and about 60 landing craft. Major auxiliaries in service are 1 replenishment and 5 support tankers, 5 depot ships, 3 salvage/rescue ships, 2 survey ships and 1 training ship. Minor auxiliaries, coastal freighters and service craft number about 120. The main naval base is at Gölcük in the Gulf of İzmit. There are others at İskenderun, Eregli, Aksaz Karaağaç Mersin and İzmir. There are 3 naval shipyards: Gölcük, Taşkizak and İzmir.

The naval air component operates 10 S-2 mixed Air Force and Naval-manned Tracker anti-submarine aircraft and 20 helicopters for anti-submarine and patrol duties. There is a Marine Regiment some 3,000 strong with 18 artillery pieces.

Personnel in 1997 totalled 51,000 (34,500 conscripts) including marines.

The separate Coast Guard numbers about 2,000 and performs coastal police duties with a force of 40 inshore patrol vessels, 4 transports and numerous boats.

Air Force. The Air Force is organized as 2 tactical air forces, with headquarters at Eskisehir and Diyarbakir, each having a flight of UH-1H helicopters. Combat aircraft comprise F-5As in 3 squadrons; F-16A/Bs in 8 squadrons; F-4E and RF-4E Phantoms in 8 squadrons; plus Nike-Hercules surface-to-air missile batteries. The 4 transport squadrons are equipped with Transall C-160, C-130 Hercules, Citation, Gulfstream and CN-235 aircraft, and UH-1H helicopters. Training types include T-37 and T-38 advanced trainers, SF.260 basic and T-41 primary trainers. Personnel strength (1997), 63,000 (31,500 conscripts).

INTERNATIONAL RELATIONS

Membership. Turkey is a member of the UN, OECD, NATO and Council of Europe and an Associate Member of the WEU.

ECONOMY

Policy. Privatization is co-ordinated by the Public Participation Fund.

Budget. Budgets (in TL1,000m.):

	1993	1994	1995	1996
Revenue	349,248	741,557	1,380,356	2,683,175
Expenditure	416,381	795,331	1,524,762	3,546,114

Tax revenues were TL2,244,094,000m. in 1996.

Currency. The unit of currency is the *Turkish lira* (TRL) notionally of 100 *kuruş*. There are coins of TL500, 1,000, 2,500, 5,000, 10,000 and 25,000 and notes of TL20,000, 50,000, 100,000, 250,000 and 1m. In Sept. 1994 gold reserves were US$1,439m., and foreign exchange reserves, US$15,197m. Annualized inflation was 125% in 1994.

Banking and Finance. The Central Bank (Merkez Bankası; *Governor*, Gazi Erçel) is the bank of issue. In 1997 there were 57 commercial banks (7 state-owned, 29 private, 21 foreign), and 12 development and investment banks. The Central Bank's assets were TL1,486,927,500m. in 1995. The assets and liabilities of deposit money banks were TL3,673,689,800m.

There is a stock exchange in Istanbul (ISE).

Weights and Measures. The metric system is in use. The Gregorian calendar has been in exclusive use since 26 Dec. 1925.

ENERGY AND NATURAL RESOURCES

Electricity. In 1995 installed capacity was 20,951·8 MW (9,862·8 MW hydro-electric). Production was 81,858·6m. kWh.

Oil and Gas. Crude oil production (1995) was 3·5m. tonnes. Total refining capacity is 24m. tonnes a year. 198·63m. cu. metres of natural gas were produced in 1994.

Minerals. Turkey is rich in minerals, and is a major producer of chrome.
Production of principal minerals (in 1,000 tonnes) was:

	1991	1992	1993	1994
Coal	5,209	4,791	4,609	4,211
Lignite	50,769	54,458	51,359	55,038
Chrome	1,372	1,446	767	1,270
Copper concentrate	178	139	140	140
Bauxite	484	859	538	373
Iron	4,962	5,917	6,480	5,755
Boron	1,814	1,796	1,892	2,088
Salt	1,438	1,418	1,526	1,353

Agriculture. At the 1991 census of agriculture there were 4,091,530 households engaged in farming, of which 148,190 were engaged purely in animal farming. Holdings are increasingly fragmented by the custom of dividing land equally amongst sons. There are government price supports to cereal growers. The sown area in 1995 was 18,475,000 ha; 5,124,000 ha was fallow; vineyards, orchards and olive groves occupied 2,461,000 ha.

Production (in 1,000 tonnes) of principal crops:

	1991	1992	1993	1994	1995
Wheat	20,400	19,300	21,000	17,500	18,000
Barley	7,800	6,900	7,500	7,000	7,500
Maize	2,180	2,225	2,500	1,850	1,900
Rye	256	230	235	195	240
Tobacco	241	334	339	187	210
Oats	255	240	245	230	250
Rice	120	129	135	120	150

Other produce, 1995 (in 1,000 tonnes): Dry beans, 225; lentils, 665; chick peas, 730; cotton lint, 837; sugar-beet, 11,171; sunflower seeds, 900; cotton seed, 1,263; soya beans, 75; onions, 2,850; potatoes, 4,750; pears, 410; apples, 2,100; figs, 300; apricots, 281; grapes, 3,550; oranges, 846; tangerines, 453; lemons, 418; nuts, 715; tea, 103; olives, 515; olive oil (1992), 121.

Livestock, 1995 (in 1,000): Horses, 415; mules, 169; asses, 731; cattle, 11,789;

sheep, 33,791; goats, 9,111. Livestock products, 1995 (in 1,000 tonnes): Total meat, 415; milk, 10,602; greasy wool, 51; goat hair and mohair, 4,200 tonnes; 10,268,668 eggs; honey, 69.

Forestry. In 1995 total forest land was 20,199,000 ha. Produce (1,000 cu. metres) in 1995: Logs, 3,578; industrial wood, 936.

Fisheries. Catch (1995): Sea fish, 557,138 tonnes; crustaceans and molluscs, 25,472 tonnes; fresh water fish, 44,983 tonnes. Aquaculture production, 1995, 21,607 tonnes (mainly carp and trout). There were (1995) 1,063 sea fishing boats.

INDUSTRY. In 1990, 55 state enterprises accounted for about 30% of production. In 1993 there were 10,567 industrial enterprises. Production in 1995 (in 1,000 tonnes): Ammonia, 586; sulphuric acid, 630; PVC, 181; polyethylene, 300; ethylene, 411; fertilizers, 5,022; cotton yarn, 388; woollen yarn, 53; cotton textiles, 489·89m. metres; woollen textiles, 30·5m. metres; carpets, 16,215,974 sq. metres; paper, 515; cement, 33,153; pig-iron, 330; crude iron, 4,363; crude steel, 12,798; coke, 3,021; iron and steel bars, 1,426; sugar, 1,290; lorries, 19,172 units; motor cars, 222,145 units.

Labour. In Oct. 1995 the labour force was 22·9m. (6,956,000 females) of whom 21,378,000 (6,486,000) were employed: 10,226,000 were engaged in agriculture, forestry, hunting and fishing, 2,947,000 in manufacturing, 2·78m. in services and 2,612,000 in trade, restaurants and hotels. 1,522,000 were unemployed in Oct. 1995.

Trade Unions. There are 4 national confederations (including Türk-İş and Disk) and 6 federations. There are 35 unions affiliated to Türk-İş and 17 employers' federations affiliated to Disk, whose activities were banned on 12 Sept. 1980. In 1995, labour unions totalled 109 and employers' unions, 54. Some 2·2m. workers belonged to unions in 1990. Membership is forbidden to civil servants (including school-teachers). There were 120 strikes in 1995 with 4,838,241 working days lost, and 5 lockouts with 162,512 working days lost.

FOREIGN ECONOMIC RELATIONS. Total foreign debt in 1994 was US$73,779m. A customs union with the EU came into force on 1 Jan. 1996.

Commerce. Imports and exports (in US$1m.) for calendar years:

	1992	1993	1994	1995	1996
Imports	22,879	28,291	23,262	35,709	42,901
Exports	14,022	15,274	18,102	21,637	23,070

Chief exports (1996) in US$1m.: Wearing apparel, 5,714·6; iron and steel, 1,746·5; electrical machinery and apparatus, 1,317·7; fruits and nuts, 1,134·2. Chief imports: Nuclear reactor machinery, 8,286·5; electrical machinery and apparatus, 2,925·7; iron and steel, 2,685·2; road vehicles, 2,682·9.

The main export markets in 1996 (in US$1m.) were: Germany, 5,168·8; USA, 1,615·7; Russia, 1,494·5; Italy, 1,438·3; UK, 1,246·8; France, 1,040·6. Main import suppliers: Germany, 7,583·2; Italy, 4,245·1; USA, 3,287·8; France, 2,739·5; UK, 2,486·3; Russia, 1,900·5; Saudi Arabia, 1,706·2.

Tourism. The number of foreign visitors was 8,614,085 in 1996. Earnings from tourism in 1995, US$4,957m. 4,045,143 Turks travelled abroad in 1995. There were 0·6m. tourist beds in 1993.

COMMUNICATIONS

Roads. In 1995 there were 31,422 km of state highways (including 125 km of motor-way) and 28,577 km of provincial roads. In 1995 there were 3,058,511 cars, 719,164 lorries and pick-ups, 90,197 buses, 173,051 minibuses and 819,922 motorcycles. There were 279,663 road accidents in 1995, with 6,004 fatalities.

Railways. Total length of railway lines in 1995 was 8,549 km (1,435 mm gauge) of which 939 km were electrified; 104·6m. passengers and 15·3m. tonnes of freight were carried.

Civil Aviation. There are international airports at İstanbul (Atatürk), Muğla (Dalaman) and Ankara (Esenboga). The national carrier is Turkish Airlines, which is 98·2% state-owned, and in 1995 had a fleet of 7 A310-200s, 7 A310-300s, 3 A340-300s, 8 B-727-200 Advs, 28 B-737-400s, 2 B-737-500s and 8 other aircraft. In 1995 it flew 7,749,020 passengers (2,838,889 on international flights) and carried 737,052 tonnes (299,914) of freight. Services are also provided by Adria, Aeroflot, Air Algérie, Air France, Air Malta, Air Moldova, Air Ukraine, Albanian Airlines, Alitalia, AOM, Austrian Airlines, Azerbaijan Hava Yollary, Balkan, British Airways, Croatia Airlines, Cyprus Turkish Airlines, Czech Airlines, Delta, Donavia, Egyptair, El Al, Emirates, Finnair, Gulf Air, Hapag Lloyd, Iberia, Iran Air, Kazakhstan Airlines, KLM, Kuwait Airways, Kyrgyzstan Airlines, Latvian Airlines, Libyan Airlines, Lithuanian Airlines, LOT, LTU, Lufthansa, Malaysia Airlines, Malév, Middle East Airlines, Olympic Airways, Orbi, Pakistan Airlines, Palair Macedonian, Royal Air Maroc, Royal Jordanian, Sabena, SAS, Saudia, Singapore Airlines, Swissair, Syrian Airlines, Tarom, Thai Airways, Top Air, Tunis Air and Uzbekistan Airways.

Shipping. In 1995 there were 1,596 cargo ships totalling 5,151,025 GRT, 253 tankers totalling 1,058,727 GRT and 623 passenger ships totalling 206,744 GRT. The main ports are: İstanbul, İzmir, Samsun, Mersin, İskenderun and Trabzon.

Coastal shipping, 1995: 20,013 vessels handled; 291,768 passengers entered, and 307,577 cleared; 17·6m. tonnes of goods entered, 12·9m. cleared. International shipping: 22,655 vessels handled; 645,082 passengers entered, 603,702 cleared; 56·2m. tonnes of goods entered, 22·8m. cleared.

Telecommunications. In 1995 there were 31,222 post offices. In 1995 there were 13·33m. telephones.

Broadcasting is regulated by the 9-member Radio and Television Council. The government monopoly of broadcasting was abolished in 1994 and in 1997 there were 35 national, 109 regional and 990 local radio stations and 16 national, 15 regional and 304 local TV stations (colour by PAL). The Turkish Radio Television Corporation (TRT) broadcasts tourist radio programmes and a foreign service, Voice of Turkey. In 1995 there were 10m. radio and 11·5m. TV sets in use.

Press. In 1995 there were 400 daily newspapers with a combined circulation of 7m. and 1,321 non-daily newspapers with a combined circulation of 2m. 5,172 book titles were published in 1995.

SOCIAL INSTITUTIONS

Justice. The unified legal system consists of: (1) justices of the peace (single judges with limited but summary penal and civil jurisdiction); (2) courts of first instance (single judges, dealing with cases outside the jurisdiction of (3) and (4)); (3) central criminal courts (a president and 2 judges, dealing with cases where the crime is punishable by imprisonment over 5 years); (4) commercial courts (3 judges); (5) state security courts, to prosecute offences against the integrity of the state (a president and 4 judges, 2 of the latter being military).

The civil and military High Courts of Appeal sit at Ankara. The Council of State is the highest administrative tribunal; it consists of 5 chambers. Its 31 judges are nominated from among high-ranking personalities in politics, economy, law, the army, etc. The Military Administrative Court deals with the judicial control of administrative acts and deeds concerning military personnel. The Court of Jurisdictional Disputes is empowered to resolve disputes between civil, administrative and military courts. The Supreme Council of Judges and Public Prosecutors appoints judges and prosecutors to the profession and has disciplinary powers.

The Civil Code and the Code of Obligations have been adapted from the corresponding Swiss codes. The Penal Code is largely based upon the Italian Penal Code, and the Code of Civil Procedure closely resembles that of the Canton of Neuchâtel. The Commercial Code is based on the German.

Prison population (1994), 20,414 (480 females; 519 juveniles).

Religion. Islam ceased to be the official religion in 1928. The Constitution guarantees freedom of religion but forbids its political exploitation or any impairment of the secular character of the republic.

In 1992 there were 58·12m. Moslems, two-thirds Sunni and one-third Shi'ite (Alevis). The administration of the Sunni Moslem religious organizations is the responsibility of the Department of Religious Affairs. The Greek Orthodox, Gregorian Armenian, Armenian Apostolic and Roman Catholic Churches are represented in İstanbul, and there are small Uniate, Protestant and Jewish communities.

Education. Adult literacy was 80·3% (male 91·7%; female 72·4%) in 1998. Primary education from 6 to 14 is compulsory and co-educational and, in state schools, free. Religious instruction (Sunni Moslem) in state schools is now compulsory. In 1991 there were 5,197 religious secondary schools with 0·29m. pupils up to 14 years.

Statistics for 1994–95	Number	Teachers	Students
Pre-school institutions	5,169	9,098	148,088
Primary schools	48,429	233,073	6,466,648
Junior high schools	7,993	64,520	2,318,915
High schools	2,137	68,839	1,155,827
Vocational and technical junior high schools	904	351	356,071
Vocational and technical high schools	2,576	68,893	894,738
Higher education institutes	741	44,086	1,107,320

In 1994–95 there were 54 universities. In 1995, 29,399 students were studying abroad.

Health. In 1994 there were 38,268 general practitioners, 27,564 specialist doctors, 11,457 dentists, 18,366 pharmacists and 56,280 nurses. In 1995 there were 843 public hospitals and 156 health centres.

Social Security. In 1995, 1,001,216 beneficiaries received TL89,871,844m. from the Government Employees Retirement Fund; 2,337,755 beneficiaries received TL69,740,150m. from the Social Insurance Institution; and (1992) 664,621 beneficiaries received TL3,369,195m. from the Independent Insurance System.

Culture. In 1995 there were 14,846,993 visitors (7,875,029 foreign) to 163 museums and ruins maintained by museums.

In 1994-95 there were 60 theatre halls, where 389 shows were attended by 2,425,170 spectators, and 6 opera and ballet halls, where 52 shows (47 foreign) were attended by 236,077 spectators.

In 1995 there were 301 cinemas. Attendances totalled 9,399,794.

There were 1,806 libraries serving a readership of 22,478,681 in 1995.

DIPLOMATIC REPRESENTATIVES

Of Turkey in Great Britain (43 Belgrave Sq., London, SW1X 8PA)
Ambassador: Özdem Sanberk.

Of Great Britain in Turkey (Sehit Ersan Caddesi 46/A, Cankaya, Ankara)
Ambassador: David B. C. Logan, CMG.

Of Turkey in the USA (1606 23rd St., NW, Washington, D.C., 20008)
Ambassador: Nüzhet Kandemir.

Of the USA in Turkey (110 Atatürk Blvd., Ankara)
Ambassador: Vacant.

Of Turkey to the United Nations
Ambassador: Hüseyin Çelem.

Of Turkey to the European Union
Ambassador: Uluç Özülker.

Further Reading

State Institute of Statistics. *Türkiye İstatistik Yılliği/Statistical Yearbook of Turkey.—Diş Ticaret İstatistikleri/Foreign Trade Statistics* (Annual).—*Aylik İstatistik Bülten* (Monthly).

Ahmad, F., *The Making of Modern Turkey.* London, 1993

Birand, M. A., *Shirts of Steel: an Anatomy of the Turkish Armed Forces.* London, 1991
Güclü, M., *Turkey.* [Bibliography] Oxford and Santa Barbara (CA), 1981
Hale, W., *The Political and Economic Development of Modern Turkey.* London, 1981
Kedourie, S., *Turkey: Identity, Democracy, Politics.* London, 1996
Pettifer, J., *The Turkish Labyrinth: Atatürk and the new Islam.* London, 1997
Pope, N. and Pope, H., *Turkey Unveiled: Atatürk and After.* London 1997
Zürcher, E. J., *Turkey: a Modern History.* London and New York, 1993 (NY, 1994)

National statistical office: State Institute of Statistics Prime Ministry, Necatibey Caddesi no. 114, 06100 Ankara.
Website: http//:www.die.gov.tr

TURKMENISTAN

Turkmenostan Respublikasy

Capital: Ashgabat
Population: 4·2m.
GDP per head: (PPP$) 3,469
HDI/world rank: 0·723/85

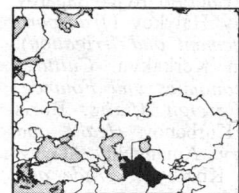

KEY HISTORICAL EVENTS. Descended from the Oghuz tribes who migrated to Central Asia in the 10th century, the Turkmen were conquered by the Russians in the 1860s. In 1866 Tashkent was occupied and in 1868 Samarkand and subsequently further territory was conquered and united with Russian Turkestan. In the 1870s Bokhara was subjugated, the emir, by an agreement of 1873, recognizing the suzerainty of Russia. In the same year Khiva became a vassal state to Russia. Until 1917 Russian Central Asia was divided politically into the Khanate of Khiva, the Emirate of Bokhara and the Governor-Generalship of Turkestan.

In the summer of 1919 the authority of the Soviet Government became definitely established in these regions. The Khan of Khiva was deposed in Feb. 1920 and a People's Soviet Republic was set up, the medieval name of Khorezm being revived. In Aug. 1920 the Emir of Bokhara suffered the same fate, and a similar regime was set up in Bokhara. The former Governor-Generalship of Turkestan was constituted an Autonomous Soviet Socialist Republic within the RSFSR on 11 April 1921.

In the autumn of 1924 the Soviets of the Turkestan, Bokhara and Khiva Republics decided to redistribute the territories of these republics on a nationality basis; at the same time Bokhara and Khiva became Socialist Republics. The redistribution was completed in May 1925 when the new states of Uzbekistan, Turkmenistan and Tadzhikistan were accepted into the USSR as Union Republics.

Following the break up of the Soviet Union, the Turkmen Supreme Soviet unanimously adopted a declaration of sovereignty in 1990. In Oct. 1991, following 94·1% support in a referendum, it adopted a declaration of independence. It became a member of the CIS in Dec. 1991.

TERRITORY AND POPULATION. Turkmenistan is bounded in the north by Kazakhstan, in the north and north-east by Uzbekistan, in the south-east by Afghanistan, in the south-west by Iran and in the west by the Caspian Sea. Area, 448,100 sq. km (186,400 sq. miles). In 1995 77% of the population were Turkmen, 9·2% Uzbek, 6·7% Russian, 2% Kazakh, and 5·1% other. The population was estimated at 4,229,249 in July 1997. Vital statistics rates (per 1,000 population), 1997: Births, 26·61; deaths, 8·65; population growth 1·61%; infant mortality (per 1,000 live births), 72·7. Life expectancy: 61·51.

There are 5 regions: Chardzhou, Mary, Ashgabat, Tashauz and Krasnovodsk, comprising 42 rural districts, 15 towns and 74 urban settlements. The capital is Ashgabat (formerly Ashkhabad; 1990 population, 411,000); other large towns are Chardzhou, Mary (Merv), Nebit-Dag and Krasnovodsk.

Languages spoken include Turkmen, 72%; Russian, 12%; Uzbek, 9%; other, 7%.

There is a dual citizenship agreement with Russia.

CONSTITUTION AND GOVERNMENT. A new constitution was adopted in 1992. It provides for an executive head of state, the *Turkmenbashi* (*Leader of Turkmens*). At the presidential elections of June 1992 the electorate was 1·86m. Saparmurad Niyazov was re-elected unopposed by 99·5% of votes cast. At a referendum on 16 Jan. 1994 99·99% of votes cast were in favour of prolonging President Niyazov's term of office to 2002.

Parliament is the 50-member *Majlis*. Parliamentary elections were held on 11 Dec. 1994. The only party standing was the Democratic Party (DP; former Communists). 1 candidate stood in each constituency, but to be elected had to receive 51% of the vote. Turn-out was said to be 99·8%.

In March 1998 the government comprised:
Head of State and Prime Minister: Saparmurad Niyazov (b. 1940; DP).

Deputy Chairmen, Cabinet of Ministers: Orazgeldy Aydogdyyev (*Culture*), Ilaman Shikhiyev (*Banking, Currency Exchange, Administration*), Mukhamed Abalakov (*Education, Health, Sciences*), Saparmurat Nuryyev (*Electrical Power, Machine-Building, Chemical Industry, Construction*), Batyr Sarjayev (*Energy*), Rejep Saparov (*Foreign Economic Relations, Light Industry*), Hudayguly Halykov (*Transport, Telecommunications*), Aleksandr Dadonov (*Water Management and Irrigation*). *Agriculture:* Ata Nobadov. *Communications:* Rovshen Kerkakvo. *Culture:* Orazgeldy Aydogdoiyev. *Defence:* Danatar Kopekov. *Economics and Finance:* Matkarim Rajapov. *Environment:* Pirdjan Kurbanov. *Foreign Affairs:* Boris Shikhmuradov. *Foreign and Economic Relations:* Toili Kurbanov. *Health and Medical Industry:* Gurganguly Berdimukhamedov. *Industry:* Amangeldy Atayev. *Internal Affairs:* Kurban Kasimov. *Justice:* Tagandurdy Khalliyev. *Trade and Resources:* Khalnazar Agakhanov. *Transport:* Penaguliy Rakhmanov.

National anthem. The anthem adopted after independence is no longer considered suitable, and a competition for a new text and tune was announced in 1996.

DEFENCE. Armed forces are under joint Russo-Turkmenistan control. In 1997 the Army was 16,000 strong and organized in 4 motor rifle divisions, 1 artillery and 1 engineer brigade and 1 multiple rocket launcher, 1 anti-tank and 3 engineer regiments. Equipment includes 570 T-72 main battle tanks. The Air Force, with 3,000 personnel, had 65 Su-17s and 2 air defence regiments of 48 MiG-23s and 24 MiG-25s. That part of the former Soviet Caspian Sea Flotilla (some 75%) not ceded to Azerbaijan and amounting to some 30 small warships has been relocated to Astrakhan, and operates under joint Russian, Kazakhstan and Turkmenistan command.

INTERNATIONAL RELATIONS

Membership. Turkmenistan is a member of the UN, CIS and the NATO Partnership for Peace.

ECONOMY

Policy. A privatization programme was launched on 1 June 1994. Enterprises with fewer than 100 employees are being sold to the employees or auctioned to citizens or foreign nationals. Large enterprises are to become joint stock companies, with the state retaining a controlling number of shares.

Performance. GNP in 1995 was US$11,900m.

Budget. Budgetary income in 1993 was 2,000m. manat; expenditure was 1,900m. manat.

Currency. The unit of currency is the *manat* (TMM) of 100 *tenesi*. There are notes of 1, 5, 10, 20, 50, 100, 500 and 1,000 manat. Foreign exchange reserves were US$300m. in 1993. The manat was devalued in 1994 to an official rate of US$1 = 230 manat.

Banking and Finance. The *governor* of the Central Bank is Khudayberdy Ozarov. In 1996 there were 9 commercial banks, the State Bank for Foreign Economic Affairs, the state savings bank and 1 foreign branch office (Iranian).

ENERGY AND NATURAL RESOURCES

Electricity. Output was 11,200m. kWh in 1995.

Oil and Gas. Turkmenistan possesses the world's fifth largest reserves of natural gas, and substantial oil resources. In 1997 gas reserves were estimated at 21,000,000m. cu. metres and oil reserves at 700m. tonnes. In 1993 crude oil production (including gas concentrate) was 5m. tonnes; natural gas (1995), 43,000m. cu. metres.

Turkmenistan is working hard to open up new gas export channels through Iran and Turkey to Europe at some time in the future.

Minerals. There are coal, sulphur, magnesium and salt.

Agriculture. Agriculture relies on irrigation. Maize, cotton, wool, silk and fruit are produced. Cotton production was 11·5m. tonnes in 1995.

Livestock on 1 Jan. 1994: Cattle, 1·1m.; pigs, 0·1m.; sheep and goats, 6·3m.

Forestry. 67,000 cu. metres of sawn timber were produced in 1989.

Fisheries. There are fisheries in the Caspian Sea. The total catch in 1995 was 15,000 tonnes.

INDUSTRY. Output, 1993 (in tonnes): Cement, 1·1m.; mineral fertilizer, 0·13m.; fabrics, 48·3m. sq. metres; footwear, 3·4m. pairs.

Labour. In 1993 the population of working age was 2·05m., of whom 1·6m. were employed, 53·8% in the state sector, 19·7% in the private sector and 25·9% in co-operatives. Average monthly wage in 1994 was 1,000 manat.

FOREIGN ECONOMIC RELATIONS

Commerce. Exports, 1995, US$2,000m.; imports, US$1,600m.

COMMUNICATIONS

Roads. Length of motor roads in Jan. 1990, 22,600 km (17,800 km hard surface). In 1993, 273·1m. passengers and 46·3m. tonnes of freight were carried.

Railways. Length of railways in 1995, 2,164 km of 1,520 mm gauge. A rail link to Iran was opened in May 1996, and there are plans to build a futher 2,000 km of rail network. In 1995, 5·5m. passengers and 22·2m. tonnes of freight were carried.

Civil Aviation. The national carrier is the state-owned Turkmenavia, which operated 3 B-737-300s, 1 B-757-200 and 32 ex-Soviet aircraft in 1995. Airlines carried 1·7m. passengers and 14,900 tonnes of freight in 1993.

Shipping. In 1995, sea-going shipping totalled 15,812 GRT, including oil tankers, 1,621 GRT. In 1993, 1·1m. tonnes of freight were carried by inland waterways.

Telecommunications. Turkmen Radio is government-controlled. It broadcasts 2 national and 1 regional programme, a Moscow Radio relay and a foreign service, Voice of Turkmen. There is 1 state-run TV station. In 1995 there were 330,000 radio receivers, and 735,000 televisions.

Press. In 1995 there were 130 newspapers and periodicals.

SOCIAL INSTITUTIONS

Justice. In 1994, 14,824 crimes were reported, including 308 murders and attempted murders.

Religion. Many of the population are Sunni Moslems.

Education. In 1993-94 there were 1,900 primary and secondary schools with 874,000 pupils, 11 higher educational institutions with 38,900 students, 41 technical colleges with 29,000 students, and 11 music and art schools.

In Jan. 1994, 0·2m. children (29·5% of those eligible) were attending pre-school institutions. In 1989 adult literacy was estimated at 98%.

Health. In Jan. 1994 there were 14,000 doctors, 43,000 junior medical personnel and 368 hospitals with 46,100 beds.

Welfare. In Jan. 1994 there were 0·3m. old age and 0·16m. other pensioners.

DIPLOMATIC REPRESENTATIVES

Of Turkmenistan in Great Britain (St George's Hse, 14-17 Wells St., W1P 3FP)
Ambassador: Murad Chariev.

Of Great Britain in Turkmenistan (Ak Atin Plaza Hotel, Ashgabat)
Ambassador: Neil Hook, MVO.

Of Turkmenistan in the USA (2207 Massachusetts Ave., NW, Washington, D.C. 20008)
Ambassador: Halil Ugar.

Of the USA in Turkmenistan (9 Puskin St., Ashgabat)
Ambassador: Michael W. Cotter.

Of Turkmenistan to the United Nations
Ambassador: Aksoltan Atayeva.

TUVALU

Capital: Fongafale
Population: 10,500

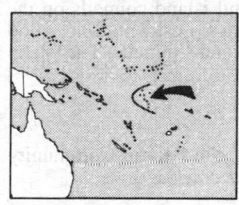

KEY HISTORICAL EVENTS. Formerly known as the Ellice Islands, Tuvalu is a group of nine islands in the western central Pacific. Traditions recorded by missionaries in the 19th century indicate Samoa or Tonga as the original home of Tuvalu's first Polynesian settlers. Tuvaluan language supports this and genealogical data suggests settlement dates back to 1325. A number of castaways and beachcombers settled and intermarried with the Tuvuluans during 1820–70, when whalers frequented the surrounding seas.

In 1892 when the British established the Gilbert Islands Protectorate, the Tuvalu islanders were encouraged to join. They became the Gilbert and Ellice Islands colony in 1916.

After the Japanese occupied the Gilbert Islands in 1942, US forces occupied the Ellice Islands and built air strips on 3 islands. Many Tuvaluans emigrated to Tarawa in the Gilberts after the Second World War for employment; rivalry between them and the Kiribatians set the stage for separation. On the recommendation of a commissioner, appointed by the British Government to consider requests that the island group be separated from the Gilbert islands, a referendum was held in 1974. There was a large majority in favour of separation and this took place in Oct. 1975. Independence was achieved on 1 Oct. 1978. Early in 1979 the US signed a treaty of friendship with Tuvalu and relinquished its claim to the four southern islands in return for access to its Second World War bases, and the right to veto any other nation's request to use any of Tuvalu's islands for military purposes.

TERRITORY AND POPULATION. Tuvalu lies between 5° 30' and 11° S. lat. and 176° and 180° E. long. and comprises Nanumea, Nanumanga, Niutao, Nui, Vaitupu, Nukufetau, Funafuti (administrative centre), Nukulaelae and Niulakita. Population (census 1991) 10,090, of whom 1,097 were working abroad, mainly in Nauru. Estimate, 1995, 10,500, of whom 1,000 were working abroad. Area approximately 9½ sq. miles (24 sq. km). The population is of a Polynesian race.

Vital statistics rates, 1996 (per 1,000 population): Births, 24; deaths, 9; infant mortality (per 1,000 live births), 28. Expectation of life: Males, 62; females, 65.

CLIMATE. A pleasant but monotonous climate with temperatures averaging 86°F (30°C), though trade winds from the east moderate conditions for much of the year. Rainfall ranges from 120" (3,000 mm) to over 160" (4,000 mm). Funafuti. Jan. 84°F (28·9°C), July 81°F (27·2°C). Annual rainfall 160" (4,003 mm). Although the islands are north of the recognized hurricane belt, they have been badly hit by hurricanes in the 1990s, raising fears for the long-term future of Tuvalu as the sea level continues to rise.

CONSTITUTION AND GOVERNMENT. The Constitution provides for a Prime Minister and 4 other Ministers to be elected from among the 12 elected members of the *House of Parliament.*

Governor-General: HE Tulaga Manuella.

In March 1998 the Cabinet comprised:
Prime Minister and Minister for Foreign Affairs: Bikenibeu Paeniu.

Deputy Prime Minister; Minister for Health and Human Resources Development; Tourism, Trade and Commerce: Ionatana Ionatana. *Natural Resources and Environment; Home Affairs and Rural Development:* Otinielu Tauteleimalae Tausi. *Finance and Economic Planning:* Alesana Kleis Seluka. *Works, Energy and Communications:* Vasa Founuku Vave. *Attorney-General:* Teleti Teo[1].

[1] Ex-officio member of the Cabinet and House of Parliament.

Speaker of the House: Dr Tomasi Puapua.

National anthem: 'Tuvalu mo te Atua' ('Tuvalu for the Almighty'); words and tune by A. Manoa.

Local Government. There is a town council on Funafuti and island councils on the 7 other atolls, each consisting of 6 elected members including a president. Since 1966 Members of Parliament have been *ex-officio* members of Island Councils. The island of Niulakita is administered as part of Niutao.

INTERNATIONAL RELATIONS

Membership. Tuvalu is a member of the Commonwealth, the Pacific Community and the South Pacific Forum, and is an ACP state of the EU.

ECONOMY

Budget. In 1994 the budget envisaged revenue of $A9·4m.

Currency. The unit of currency is the Australian *dollar* although Tuvaluan coins up to $A1 are in local circulation.

Banking and Finance. The Tuvalu National Bank was established at Funafuti in 1980 and is a joint venture between the Tuvalu Government and Wespac International.

ENERGY AND NATURAL RESOURCES

Electricity. Production (1992) 1·3m. kWh.

Agriculture. Coconut palms are the main crop. Production of coconuts (1991), 4,000 tonnes. Fruit and vegetables are grown for local consumption.

Fisheries. Sea fishing is excellent, particularly for tuna. Total catch (1993) 1,460 tonnes. A seamount was discovered in Tuvaluan waters in 1991 and is an excellent location for deep-sea fish. The sale of fishing licences to American and Japanese fleets provides a significant source of income.

FOREIGN ECONOMIC RELATIONS

Commerce. Commerce is dominated by co-operative societies, the Tuvalu Cooperative Wholesale Society being the main importer. Main sources of income are copra, stamps, handicrafts and remittances from Tuvaluans abroad.

Tourism. There were 639 visitor arrivals in 1995.

COMMUNICATIONS

Civil Aviation. Air Marshall operates a service between the Marshall Islands, Kiribati, Tuvalu and Fiji, Air Tungaru flies to Kiribati and Fiji Air to Fiji.

Shipping. Funafuti is the only port and a deep-water wharf was opened in 1980.

Telecommunications. The Tuvalu Broadcasting Service transmits daily and all islands have daily radio communication with Funafuti. There are about 4,000 radio receivers.

Press. The Government Broadcasting and Information Division produces *Tuvalu Echoes*, a fortnightly publication, and *Te Lama*, a monthly religious publication.

SOCIAL INSTITUTIONS

Justice. There is a High Court presided over by the Chief Justice of Fiji. A Court of Appeal is constituted if required. There are also 8 Island Courts with limited jurisdiction.

Religion. The majority of the population are Christians, mainly Protestant but with small groups of Roman Catholics, Seventh Day Adventists, Jehovah's Witnesses and Mormons. There are some Moslems and Baha'is.

Education. There are 12 primary and 2 secondary schools. There is a Maritime Training School at Funafuti, and the Fiji-based University of the South Pacific has an extension centre at Funafuti.

Health. In 1993 there was 1 central hospital situated at Funafuti. There was 1 doctor per 1,150 inhabitants.

DIPLOMATIC REPRESENTATIVES

Of Great Britain in Tuvalu
High Commissioner: Michael J. Peart, CMG, LVO (resides in Fiji).

Of Tuvalu in the USA
Ambassador: Vacant.

Of the USA in Tuvalu
Ambassador: Don Gevirtz (resides in Fiji).

UGANDA

Republic of Uganda

Capital: Kampala
Population: 15·24m.
GDP per head: (PPP$) 1,370
GNP: US$3·7bn.
HDI/world rank: 0·328/159

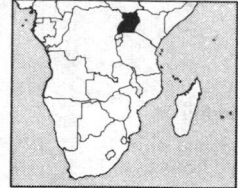

KEY HISTORICAL EVENTS. The Luo (a Nilotic-speaking people) invaded the territory of present-day Uganda in the late 15th and 16th centuries, and while assimilating with the existing Bantu-speaking inhabitants, also founded several strong centralized kingdoms. Buganda was the most prominent of these and prospered through the 19th century, assisting British forces in the conquest of its neighbours. Uganda became a British Protectorate in 1894, the province of Buganda being recognized as a native kingdom under its Kabaka.

In 1961, Uganda was granted internal self-government with federal status for Buganda.

Uganda became a fully independent member of the Commonwealth on 9 Oct. 1962 after nearly 70 years of British rule. Full sovereign status was granted by the Ugandan Independence Act 1962. The post of Governor-General was on 9 Oct. 1963 replaced by that of President as head of state, elected by the National Assembly for a five year term. Uganda became a republic on 8 Sept. 1967.

President Milton Obote set about returning land given to the Buganda by the British in 1900 to its original Bunyoro owners. He also abolished Buganda's federal status and autonomy in the country. A rebellion by Buganda was quelled, but in 1971 Obote was overthrown by troops under Gen. Idi Amin. Amin's rule was characterized by widespread repression and the expulsion of Asian residents in 1972.

In April 1979, a force of the Tanzanian Army and Ugandan exiles advanced into Uganda, taking Kampala on 11 April. Amin fled into exile. On 14 April, Dr. Yusuf Lule was sworn in as president and the country was administered, initially, by the Uganda National Liberation Front.

The former Attorney-General, Godfrey Lukonwa Binaisa QC, was appointed president by the National Consultative Council on 20 June 1979. Dr Lule subsequently left the country. Dr Binaisa was overthrown in May 1980 by the Military Commission, the military arm of the Uganda National Liberation Front.

In Dec. 1980, following elections, Dr Obote again became president, but on 27 July 1985 was overthrown, the constitution was suspended and the borders closed. Lieut. Gen. Tito Okello became head of state on 29 July, but on the following day the National Resistance Army (NRA) was not prepared to co-operate with the new régime.

After an abortive ceasefire between the NRA and government forces on 17 Dec. 1985 the NRA fought its way into Kampala and Yoweri Museveni was installed as President on 27 Jan. 1986.

There is insurgent activity near Gulu and Kitgun in Northern Uganda. Rebels belonging to a religious sect, the Lords Resistance Army, are covertly supported by Sudan.

TERRITORY AND POPULATION. Uganda is bounded on the north by Sudan, on the east by Kenya, on the south by Tanzania and Rwanda, and the west by the Democratic Republic of the Congo. Total area 241,038 sq. km, including 43,938 sq. km of water.

In 1996 the population was 15,240,000 (9·75m. females; 13·4% lived in urban areas), the largest towns being Kampala, the capital (874,241), Jinja (65,169), Mbale (53,634), Masaka (49,585), Gulu (38,297), Entebbe (41,638), Soroti (40,602) and Mbarara (40,383). Density, 84 per sq. km. Vital statistics rates per 1,000, 1994: Birth, 51·1; death, 22·3; infant mortality, 97 (1996); population growth, 0·35. Expectation of life for males in 1994 was 40·2 years and for females in 1990 was 52·7 years. By 1996, 0·45m. persons had died of AIDS, and 1·5m. were HIV-positive.

The country is administratively divided into 43 districts, which are grouped in 4 geographical regions (which do not have administrative status). Area and population in 1991:

Region/District	Area in sq. km.	Population in 1,000	Region/District	Area in sq. km.	Population in 1,000
Central Region	61,510	4,822·3	*Eastern Region*	39,953	4,110·3
Kalangala	5,716	16·4	Iganga	13,113	944·0
Kampala	238	773·5	Jinja	734	284·9
Kiboga	3,774	140·8	Kamuli	4,348	480·7
Luwero	9,198	449·2	Kapchorwa	1,738	116·3
Masaka	10,611	831·3	Kumi	2,861	237·0
Mpigi	6,222	915·4	Mbale	2,546	706·6
Mubende	6,536	497·5	Pallisa	1,919	356·0
Mukono	14,242	816·2	Soroti	10,060	430·9
Rakai	4,973	382·0	Tororo	2,634	554·0
Western Region	54,917	4,521·0	*Northern Region*	84,658	3,129·1
Bundibugyo	2,338	116·0	Apac	6,488	460·7
Bushenyi	5,396	734·8	Arua	7,830	624·6
Hoima	5,492	197·8	Gulu	11,735	338·7
Kabale	1,827	412·8	Kitgum	16,136	350·3
Kabalore	8,361	741·4	Kotido	13,208	190·7
Kasese	3,205	343·0	Lira	7,251	498·3
Kibaale	4,718	219·3	Moroto	14,113	171·5
Kisoro	662	184·9	Moyo	5,006	178·5
Masindi	9,326	253·5	Nebbi	2,891	315·9
Mbarara	10,839	929·6			
Rukungiri	2,753	388·0			

The official language is English, but Kiswahili is used as a lingua franca. About 70% of the population speak Bantu languages; Nilotic languages are spoken in the north and east.

CLIMATE. Although in equatorial latitudes, the climate is more tropical, because of its elevation, and is characterized by 2 distinct rainy seasons, March-May and Sept.-Nov. June-Aug. and Dec.-Feb. are comparatively dry. Temperatures vary little over the year. Kampala. Jan. 74°F (23·3°C), July 70°F (21·1°C). Annual rainfall 46·5" (1,180 mm). Entebbe. Jan. 72°F (22·2°C), July 69°F (20·6°C). Annual rainfall 63·9" (1,624 mm).

KABAKA. Having lapsed in 1966, the kabakaship was revived as a ceremonial office in 1993. Ronald Muwenda Mutebi (b. 13 April 1955) was crowned Mutebi II, 36th Kabaka, on 31 July 1993.

CONSTITUTION AND GOVERNMENT. The *President* is head of state and head of government and is elected for a 5-year term by adult suffrage. The national legislature was the 278-member National Resistance Council. This was replaced by a 278-member *Constituent Assembly* in March 1994, 214 of whose members were directly elected, 10 nominated by the President, 10 by the military and 39 (women) by women's associations. A new constitution was adopted on 8 Oct. 1995. The return of multi-party democracy is promised for the year 2000.

Presidential elections were held on 9 May 1996, for the first time by universal suffrage. Turn-out was 72·6%. President Museveni was re-elected by 74·2% of votes cast. He had two opponents.

Parliamentary elections were held on 27 June 1996. The electorate was 8·5m.

In March 1998 the government comprised:
President: Yoweri Museveni (b. 1945; sworn in 12 May 1996).
Vice-President, Minister of Agriculture, Animal Industry and Fisheries: Speciôsa Wandira Kazibwe.
Prime Minister: Kintu Musoke.
First Deputy Prime Minister and Minister of Foreign Affairs: Eriya Kategaya.
Second Deputy Prime Minister and Minister of Tourism, Wildlife and Antiquities: Brig. Moses Ali. *Third Deputy Prime Minister and Minister of Labour and Social*

Services: Paul Etyang. *Finance:* Joshua Mayanja Nkangi. *Trade and Industry:* Henry Muganwa Kajura. *Health:* Dr Crispus Kiyonga. *Works, Transport and Communications:* John Nasasira. *Information:* Dr Ruhakana Rugunda. *Natural Resources:* Gerald Ssendaula. *Education and Sports:* Amanya Mushega. *Local Government:* Jaberi Bidandi Ssali. *Interior:* Maj. Tom Butime. *Justice and Attorney General:* Bart Katureebe. *Gender and Community Development:* Janeti Mukwaya. *Lands, Housing and Urban Development:* Francis Ayume. *Public Services:* A. Nsibambi. *Planning and Economic Development:* Richard Kaijuka.

National anthem: 'Oh, Uganda, may God uphold thee'; words and tune by G. W. Kakoma.

Local Government. The 43 districts are divided into 150 counties, which are in turn divided into sub-counties which form the basic administrative units.

DEFENCE

Army. The Uganda Peoples Defence Forces had a strength of about 50,000 in 1997. Equipment includes 20 T-54/-55 main battle tanks. There is a Border Defence Unit about 600 strong.

Navy. A Marine unit of the police (400 strong in 1996) operates 8 small patrol craft.

Air Force. The Air Wing in 1997 had 5 SF-260 light strike aircraft, 9 Bell and Mi 1 transport helicopters, 4 communications helicopters and 5 AS-202 and 3 L-39 trainers.

INTERNATIONAL RELATIONS

Membership. Uganda is a member of UN, OAU, Islamic Conference Organization, the Commonwealth and is an ACP state of EU.

ECONOMY

Policy. A privatization programme was instituted in 1991 managed by the Public Enterprise Reform and Divestiture Secretariat. The state is to retain ownership of certain utilities, national parks and the development bank. About 100 enterprises were in state ownership, but most had been privatized by 1997.

Performance. Real GDP growth was 7% in 1996 (10% in 1995).

Budget. In 1994–95 revenue (excluding grants) was 522,390m. Uganda Sh. and expenditure (1991–92), 410,310m. Uganda Sh. Sources of revenue included (in 1m. Uganda Sh.): Tax, 213,609; export duties, 14,412; customs duties, 190,905. Expenditures (in 1991–92) included: Agriculture, animal industry and fisheries, 8,192; education, 38,009; health, 3,306; defence, 63,421.

Currency. The monetary unit is the *Uganda shilling* (UGS) notionally divided into 100 *cents*. In 1987 the currency was devalued by 77% and a new 'heavy' shilling was introduced worth 100 old shillings. There are notes of 50, 100, 200, 500, 1,000, 5,000 and 10,000 shillings. Annualized inflation in 1996 was 5%.

Banking and Finance. The Bank of Uganda (established 1966) is the central bank and bank of issue. The Uganda Credit and Savings Bank, established in 1950, was on 9 Oct. 1965 reconstituted as the Uganda Commercial Bank, with its capital fully owned by the Government. In 1992 it had 188 branches. In addition there are 4 foreign, 2 private and 2 development banks and 1 co-operative bank.

A stock exchange was scheduled to open in Kampala in 1996.

ENERGY AND NATURAL RESOURCES

Electricity. Installed capacity, 1992, was 168 MW, of which the Owen Falls hydro-electric scheme provided 162 MW. Production (1994) 1,016·8m. kWh.

Agriculture. The agricultural area includes 5·02m. ha of arable, 1·7m. ha of permanent crops and 1·8m. ha of pasture. Agriculture is one of the priority areas for increased production, with many projects funded both locally and externally. Production (1995) in 1,000 tonnes: Tobacco, 7; coffee, 200; cotton lint, 12; tea, 15; sugarcane, 1,450; plantains, 9,519; millet, 143; maize, 950; sorghum, 398; cassava, 2,625; dry beans, 387. Coffee is the mainstay of the economy.

Livestock (1995): Cattle, 5·2m.; sheep, 0·9m.; goats, 5·5m.; pigs, 1·3m.; poultry, 30m. Livestock products, 1995 (in 1,000 tonnes): Beef and veal, 90; pork, 51; poultry meat, 36; eggs, 18; honey, 250; milk, 455.

Forestry. Woodland covers 5·56m. ha and exploitable forests consist almost entirely of hardwoods. 16·68m. cu. metres of wood were cut in 1995.

Fisheries. Uganda possesses one of the largest fresh-water fisheries in the world. In 1996 fish production was 222,000 tonnes. Fish farming (especially carp and tilapia) is a growing industry.

INDUSTRY. Production (in 1,000 tonnes) in 1995: Cement, 88·5; soap, 55·7; sugar, 70·1; beer, 51·2m. litres.

Labour. The workforce was 8·13m. in 1990 (3·34m. female; 0·88m. between 10 and 15 years).

FOREIGN ECONOMIC RELATIONS. Foreign debt was US$3,300m. in 1996. Over 1981–96, foreign investment totalled US$850m.

Commerce. In 1995/6 imports were US$866·7m. and exports, US$548·9m.
Coffee, cotton, tea and tobacco are the principal exports.

Tourism. There were 175,000 visitors in 1995, of whom 20% were tourists.

COMMUNICATIONS

Roads. There are 7,582 km of all-weather roads, of which 1,934 km are two-lane bitumenized highways, and some 19,640 km of other roads, maintained by district governments. There were 35,000 passenger cars in 1996 and 50,000 commercial vehicles.

Railways. The Uganda Railways network totals 1,241 km (metre gauge). In 1996 railways carried 184,000 passengers and 877,000 tonnes of freight.

Civil Aviation. There is an international airport at Entebbe. The national carrier is the state-owned Uganda Airlines, which operated 1 B-737-200 Adv, and 1 other aircraft in 1995. Uganda and Tanzania are partners with South African Airways in Alliance Airline. Services are also provided by Air Burundi, Air Rwanda, Air Tanzania, Air France, British Airways, Egyptair, Ethiopian Airlines, Gulf Air, Inter Aviation, Kenya Airways, Royal Swazi, Sabena and Sudan Airways. Uganda Airlines carried 63,000 international passengers in 1994.

Telecommunications. There were 35,000 telephones in use in 1994. The government runs Radio Uganda, which has 10 stations and transmits 3 regional programmes, and Uganda Television with 9 stations and 1 programme. Colour is by PAL. There were about 0·5m. radio receivers and about 230,000 television sets in 1992. There are 3 private television operators.

Press. There were 2 daily newspapers in 1994 with a fluctuating circulation of 45,000–55,000, and 12 weekly, 1 bi-weekly and 5 monthly newspapers and magazines.

SOCIAL INSTITUTIONS

Justice. The Supreme Court of Uganda, presided over by the Chief Justice is the highest court. There is a Court of Appeal and a High Court below that. Subordinate courts, presided over by Chief Magistrates and Magistrates of the first, second and third grade, are established in all areas: Jurisdiction varies with the grade of Magistrate. Chief and first-grade Magistrates are professionally qualified; second- and third-grade Magistrates are trained to diploma level at the Law Development

Centre, Kampala. Chief Magistrates exercise supervision over and hear appeals from second- and third-grade courts and village courts.

Religion. In 1992 there were 8·53m. Roman Catholics, 4·5m. Anglicans and 1·13m. Moslems.

Education. In 1995 there were 2,636,400 pupils in 7,905 primary schools (of which 7,420 were Government-aided schools and 485 private schools); 255,158 students in 774 secondary schools; 13,174 students in 94 primary teacher training colleges; 13,360 students in 24 technical institutes and colleges; 22,703 students in 10 national teachers colleges; 1,628 students in 5 colleges of commerce; 504 students in the Uganda Polytechnic, Kyambogo; 800 students in the National College of Business Studies, Nakawa. In 1995–96 there was 1 university and 1 university of science and technology in the public sector, and 2 universities, 1 Christian, 1 Roman Catholic and 1 Islamic university in the private sector catering for 29,343 students. Adult literacy rate 61·1%.

Health. In 1988 there were 980 health centres (217 private), and in 1989 there were 81 hospitals and 20,136 hospital beds. The Ministry of Health has 16 schools for training nurses and other health staff, 105 health centres, 89 dispensaries with maternity units, 87 dispensaries, 35 maternity units, 371 sub-dispensaries, 14 leprosy centres and 169 aid posts. In 1984 there were about 700 doctors.

DIPLOMATIC REPRESENTATIVES

Of Uganda in Great Britain (Uganda Hse., 58/59 Trafalgar Sq., London, WC2N 5DX)
High Commissioner: George Kirya.

Of Great Britain in Uganda (10/12 Parliament Ave., Kampala)
High Commissioner: M. E. Cook.

Of Uganda in the USA (5909 16th St., NW, Washington, D.C., 20011)
Ambassador: Edith Ssempala.

Of the USA in Uganda (Parliament Ave., Kampala)
Ambassador: E. Michael Southwick.

Of Uganda to the United Nations
Ambassador: Matia Semakula Kiwanuka.

Of Uganda to the European Union
Ambassador: Kakima Ntambi.

Further Reading

Jørgensen, J. J., *Uganda: A Modern History.* London, 1981
Museveni, Y., *What is Africa's Problem?* London, 1993
Mutibwa, P., *Uganda since Independence: a Story of Unfulfilled Hopes.* London, 1992
Nyeko, B., *Uganda.* [Bibliography] 2nd ed. Oxford and Santa Barbara (CA), 1996
Museveni, Y., *The Mustard Seed.* London 1997.

National statistical office: Statistical Department, Ministry of Finance and Economic Planning, Kampala.

UKRAINE

Ukraina

Capital: Kiev
Population: 50·9m.
GDP per head: (PPP$) 2,718
HDI/world rank: 0·689/95

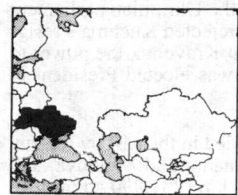

KEY HISTORICAL EVENTS. Kiev was the centre of the Rus principality in the 11th and 12th centuries and is still known as the Mother of Russian cities. In the 13th century the area was invaded by Tatar-Mongols, and the western Ukraine principality of Galicia was annexed by Poland in the 14th century. At about the same time, Kiev and the Ukrainian principality of Volhynia were conquered by Lithuania before being absorbed by Poland. Poland, however, could not subjugate the Ukrainian cossacks, who allied themselves with Russia. The lands east of the Dnepr River were ceded to Russia in 1667 (some parts of Ukraine had been annexed by Muscovy much earlier), and the remainder of Ukraine, except for Galicia (part of the Austrian Empire; 1772-1919), was incorporated into the Russian Empire after the second partition of Poland in 1793.

The Ukrainians under Austrian rule in Galicia and Bukovina and in the region of Hungary known as the Carpatho-Ukraine preserved their identity as a separate group and engendered a forceful nationalist movement. In 1917, following the Bolshevik revolution, the Ukrainians in Russia established an independent republic. Austrian Ukraine proclaimed itself a republic in 1918 and was federated with its Russian counterpart. The Allies ignored Ukrainian claims to Galicia, however, and in 1918 awarded that area to Poland. In 1919 the Russian Ukrainian republic, under the leader Simon Petlyura, declared war on Poland. In the same year Ukrainian Communists established a second government and declared the existence of the Ukrainian SSR. In 1920 the advance of the Russian Bolshevik armies caused the Petlyura government and Poland to become allies but they were unable to prevent the Soviet government from taking control of the country.

From 1922 to 1932, drastic efforts were made by the USSR to suppress Ukrainian nationalism. Ukraine suffered from the forced collectivization of agriculture and the expropriation of foodstuffs; the result was the famine of 1932-33 when more than 7m. people died.

Following the Soviet seizure of eastern Poland in Sept. 1939, Polish Galicia was incorporated into the Ukrainian SSR. When the Germans invaded Ukraine in 1941 hopes that an autonomous or independent Ukrainian republic would be set up under German protection were disappointed. Ukraine was retaken by the USSR in 1944. Parts of Bessarabia and northern Bukovina were added to Ukraine together with the Ruthenian region of Czechoslovakia. The Crimean region was joined to Ukraine in 1954.

On 5 Dec. 1991 the Supreme Soviet unanimously repudiated the 1922 Treaty of Union and declared Ukraine's independence. Ukraine was one of the founder member of the CIS in Dec. 1991.

After independence, political tension developed in Ukraine over several domestic and international issues. Crimea, which was part of Russia until 1954, became a source of contention between Moscow and Kiev. Shortly after Ukrainian indpendence in 1991, a Russian-led movement to secede from Ukraine was formed in Crimea, which succeeded in changing the status of the Crimean oblast to an autonomous republic. Crimea also issued a declaration of independence, which was rescinded in May 1992. In the same month, however, the Supreme Soviet of Russia declared the 1954 transfer of Crimea null and void. The Russian Supreme Soviet also laid claim to the Crimean port city of Sevastopol, the home port of the 350-ship Black Sea Fleet, despite an agreement to divide the fleet which was signed by President Kravchuk and Russian President Boris Yeltsin in Aug. 1992. Conflict between Ukraine and Russia also developed over possession and transfer of nuclear weapons, delivery of Russian fuel to Ukraine, the division of Soviet assets, and military and political integration within the CIS.

A second separatist movement developed in eastern Ukraine, where coal miners and other workers in eastern Ukraine went on strike in June 1993 to protest against the poor state of the economy. A political crisis developed within the government over the pace of economic reform in 1993. In May 1993, Prime Minister Leonid Kuchma threatened to resign if he was not granted additional powers. In response to the threat of resignation, President Kravchuk proposed that the Ukrainian parliament grant Kuchma additional executive powers. The parliament rejected Kuchma's resignation and most of Kravchuk's proposals, but they did grant Kravchuk the power to rule by decree on some economic issues. Leonid Kuchma was elected President in 1994.

TERRITORY AND POPULATION. Ukraine is bounded in the east by Russia, north by Belarus, west by Poland, Slovakia, Hungary, Romania and Moldova, and south by the Black Sea and Sea of Azov. Area, 603,700 sq. km (231,990 sq. miles). The 1995 census population was 51·7m. of whom 73% were Ukrainians, 22% Russians, 1% Jews and 4% other – Belarusians, Moldovans, Hungarians, Bulgarians, Poles and Crimean Tatars (most of the Tatars were forcibly transported to Central Asia in 1944 for anti-Soviet activities during the Second World War). Estimate, 1997, 50·9m. (68% urban).

Vital statistics rates (per 1,000 population), 1996 estimate: Births, 11·2; deaths, 15·2; growth, −0·4; infant mortality (per 1,000 live births), 22·5. Life expectancy, 1996 estimate: Males, 61·5 years, females, 72·3.

Ukraine is divided into 24 provinces and the Autonomous Republic of Crimea. Area and population of the provinces in 1991:

	Area (sq. km)	Population (in 1,000)		Area (sq. km)	Population (in 1,000)
Cherkasy	20,900	1,530·9	Lviv (Lvov)	21,800	2,764·4
Chernihiv	31,900	1,405·8	Mykolaïv	24,600	1,342·4
Chernivtsi	8,100	938·6	Odessa	33,300	2,635·3
Dnipropetrovsk	31,000	3,908·7	Poltava	28,800	1,756·9
Donetsk	26,500	5,346·7	Rivne (Rovno)	20,100	1,176·8
Ivano-Frankivsk	13,900	1,442·9	Sumy	23,800	1,430·2
Kharkov	31,400	3,194·8	Ternopil	13,800	1,175·1
Kherson	28,500	1,258·7	Vinnytsya	26,500	1,914·4
Khmelnytsky	20,600	1,520·6	Volyn	20,200	1,069·0
Kiev	28,900	4,589·8	Zakarpatska	12,800	1,265·9
Kirovohrad	24,600	1,245·3	Zaporizhya	27,200	2,099·6
Luhansk	26,700	2,871·1	Zhytomyr	29,900	1,510·7

The capital is Kiev (population 2·6m. in 1993). Other towns with 1991 populations over 0·2m. are:

	Population (in 1,000)		Population (in 1,000)		Population (in 1,000)
Kharkov	1,623	Vinnytsya	381	Dniprodzerzhynsk	284
Dnipropetrovsk	1,189	Sevastopol	366	Kirovohrad	278
Donetsk	1,121	Kherson	365	Chernivtsi	259
Odessa	1,101	Simferopol	353	Kremenchuk	241
Zaporizhzhya	897	Horlivka	337	Rivne (Rovno)	239
Lviv (Lvov)	802	Poltava	320	Ivano-Frankivsk	226
Kryvy Rih	724	Chernihiv	306	Ternopil	218
Mariupol	522	Cherkasy	302	Lutsk	210
Mykolaïv	512	Sumy	301	Bila Tserkva	204
Luhansk	504	Zhytomyr	298	Kramatorsk	201
Makiïvka	424				

The 1996 Constitution made Ukrainian the sole official language and abolished dual citizenship, previously available if there was a treaty with the other country (there was no such treaty with Russia). Anyone resident in Ukraine since 1991 may be naturalized.

CLIMATE. Temperate continental with a subtropical Mediterranean climate prevalent on the southern portions of the Crimean Peninsula. The average monthly temperature in winter ranges from 17·6°F to 35·6°F (−8°C to 2°C), while summer temperatures average 62·6°F to 77°F (17°C to 25°C). The Black Sea coast is subject to freezing and no Ukranian port is permanently ice-free. Precipitation generally decreases from north to south; it is greatest in the Carpathians where it exceeds more than 58·5" (1500 mm) per year, and least in the coastal lowlands of the Black Sea where it averages less than 11·7" (300 mm) per year.

CONSTITUTION AND GOVERNMENT. In a referendum on 1 Dec. 1991 90·3% of votes cast were in favour of independence. Turn-out was 83·7%.

A new Constitution was adopted on 28 June 1996. It defines Ukraine as a sovereign, democratic, unitary state governed by the rule of law and guaranteeing civil rights. The head of state is the *President*. Parliament is the 450-member unicameral *Supreme Council*, elected by universal suffrage for 4-year terms. For an election to be valid, turn-out in an electoral district must reach 50%. The Prime Minster is nominated by the President with the agreement of more than half the Supreme Council. There is an 18-member *Constitutional Court*, 6 members being appointed by the President, 6 by parliament and 6 by a panel of judges. Constitutional amendments may be initiated at the President's request to parliament, or by at least one third of parliamentary deputies. The Communist part was officially banned in the country in 1990, but was renamed the Socialist party of Ukraine and has retained political control. Hard-line Communists protested the ban, which was rescinded by the Supreme Council in May 1993. Several important democratic institutions have recently appeared in Ukraine, however, including a free press, a new constitution, and several popular opposition groups, such as Rukh and New Ukraine. Elections were held in 4 rounds in March, April, July and Nov. 1994 with run-offs in Aug. 1994. The electorate was 38,204,100. 5,833 candidates stood initially, of whom 3,633 were nominated by groups of voters, 1,557 by workers' collectives and 643 by political parties. The Communist Party gained 91 seats; Agrarian Party, 52; Centre Party, 37; Unity Party, 34; Inter-Regional Bloc for Reform, 34; Reform Party, 31; Statist Party, 30; Socialist Party, 30; Rukh, 27; ind, 34.

Presidential elections were held in 2 rounds on 26 June and 10 July 1994. At the first round, turn-out was 69%. President Leonid Kravchuk gained 37·8% of votes cast against 6 opponents. At the 2nd round, turn-out was 71·6%. Leonid Kuchma was elected against President Kravchuk by 51·5% of votes cast.

President: Leonid Kuchma (sworn in 19 July 1994).
In March 1998 the government comprised:
Prime Minister: Valeriy Pustovoitenko.
First Deputy Prime Minister: Anatoliy Holubchenko; *Deputy Prime Ministers,* Serhiy Tyhypko; Mykola Bilobloisyy; Valeriy Smoliy. *Minister of Foreign Affairs:* Hennadi Udovenko. *Defence:* Gen. Oleksandr Kuzmuk. *Foreign Economic Relations and Trade:* Serhi Osyka. *Minister of the Cabinet:* Anatoliy Tolstoukhov. *Interior:* Yuri Kravchenko. *Economy:* Viktor Suslov. *Culture:* Dmytro Ostapenko. *Forestry:* Valeri Samoplavsky. *Environmental Protection and Nuclear Safety:* Yuri Kostenko. *Statistics:* Hennadiy Osaulenko. *Finance:* Ihor Metyukiv. *Justice:* Suzanna Stanik. *Transport:* Valeriy Cherep. *Science and Technology:* Volodymyr Semynozhenko. *Emergency Situations:* Valeri Kalchenko. *Industrial Policy, Fuel and Energy:* Vasyl Hureyev. *Energy:* Oleksiy Sheberstov. *Education:* Mykhailo Zhurovsky. *Coal:* Stanislav Yanko. *Agriculture:* Yuriy Karasyk. *Press and Information:* Zinoviy Kulyk. *Fisheries:* Mykola Shvedenko. *Family and Youth Affairs:* Valentyna Dovzhenko. *Health:* Andriy Serdyuk. *Security Service:* Vlodymyr Radchenko.
Speaker: Oleksandr Moroz.

National anthem: 'Shche ne vmerla, Ukraïna' ('Thou hast not perished, Ukraine'); words by P. Chubynsky, tune by M. Verbytsky.

Local Government: The 24 provincial councils are subordinate to the President. Lower-level councils are subordinate to the provincial authorities. Elections were held on 4 March 1990.

DEFENCE. The 1996 Constitution bans the stationing of foreign troops on Ukrainian soil, but permits Russia to retain naval bases. Conscription is for 18 months. On 31 May 1997 the presidents of Ukraine and Russia signed a Treaty of Friendship and Co-operation which provided *inter alia* for the division of the former Soviet Black Sea Fleet and shore installations.

Army. In 1997 ground forces numbered about 187,800 organized as follows: Ministry of Defence troops comprised 1 training tank brigade, 1 training artillery division, 1 artillery, 1 anti-tank and 3 engineer brigades; Western Operations Command comprised 1 artillery division, 1 training tank division, 1 surface-to-surface missile brigade and 1 engineer regiment, and 3 corps (1 with 2 motor rifle divisions, 2 mechanized, 1 artillery and 1 engineer brigade, 1 multiple rocket launcher and 1 anti-tank regiment; 1 with 2 mechanized divisions, 1 mechanized and 1 artillery brigade, 1 reserve anti-tank and 1 reserve multiple rocket launcher regiment; and 1 with 1 tank division and 1 anti-tank regiment); Southern Operations Command comprised 2 mechanized, 1 air mobile and 1 artillery division, 1 surface-to-surface missile, 2 surface-to-air missile and 2 artillery brigades, and 3 corps (1 with 2 mechanized and 1 artillery brigade and 1 anti-tank, 1 multiple rocket launcher and 2 reserve artillery brigades; 1 with 1 reserve motor rifle and 1 mechanized division, and 1 multiple rocket launcher and 1 reserve anti-tank regiment; and 1 with 1 tank and 2 mechanized divisions, 1 artillery brigade and 1 anti-tank and 1 multiple rocket launcher regiment); 2 special forces units. Equipment includes 4,026 main battle tanks (182 T-55, 1 T-62, 2,216 T-64, 1,305 T-72 and 322 T-80), 636 medium-range launchers and 132 surface-to-surface missiles.

Navy. The former Soviet Black Sea Fleet continues to be the object of wrangling between Russia and Ukraine, and is financially and operationally paralyzed by the dispute. In 1996, the undisputed Ukrainian elements numbered 16,000, including 7,000 Naval Aviation and 4,000 in coastal defence, with fleet units based at Sevastopol and Odessa. The operational forces include 3 submarines, 2 Krivak-3 frigates, 2 smaller frigates and some 40 patrol craft and 6 amphibious units.

The aviation forces of the former Soviet Black Sea Fleet under Ukrainian command constitute about 40 bombers and about 40 anti-submarine and maritime reconnaissance aircraft. Main bomber types are Tu-26 'Backfire' and Tu-16 'Badger' armed principally with stand-off anti-ship missiles. There are also some 50 armed helicopters, most of seagoing types. The personnel of the Ukrainian Naval Aviation Force numbered (1996) about 7,000.

Air Force. Ukraine has taken over more than 2,000 ex-Soviet aircraft, nearly 1,500 of them combat equipment. It is limited to 1,090 combat aircraft and 330 armed helicopters under the Conventional Forces in Europe agreement and will have to dispose of some materiel. Equipment includes 190 MiG-29 and 60 Su-27 interceptors, several hundred MiG-23/27 and Su-17 fighter-bombers, 200 Su-24 strike aircraft, Tu-22M strategic bombers and 30 Il-76 tankers. Support equipment includes 200 Il-76 transports and 250 armed Mi-24 and 400 transport helicopters. Personnel (including Air Defence), 1996, 124,000.

INTERNATIONAL RELATIONS

Membership. Ukraine is a member of the UN, CIS, the Council of Europe, the Central European Initiative and the NATO Partnership for Peace.

ECONOMY

Policy. After considerable delay, the process of economic reform began in Ukraine. Prices on food, transportation and other services were deregulated in January 1993, although food prices remained low in comparison to prices in neighbouring countries. The government issued privatization certificates and set up the western city of Lviv as a model for future privatization. The country's leadership attempted to re-establish close economic ties with former Soviet republics, supporting economic cooperation between the member states of the CIS. In July 1993 Ukraine also agreed in principle to establish an economic and customs union with Russia and Belarus. In Feb. 1998 a 10-year economic agreement was signed between Ukraine and Russia.

Budget. 1993 budget (in 1,000m. karbovanets): Revenue, 49,621·8; expenditure, 57,248·8. Sources of revenue included: VAT, 17,206·5; profits tax, 14,473·6. Expenditure included: Welfare, 13,825·1; subsidies to state enterprises, 11,039·8; defence, 2,765·7; administration, 1,261·1.

Currency. The unit of currency is the *hryvna* of 100 *kopiykas*, which replaced karbovanets on 2 Sept. 1996 at 100,000 karbovanets = 1 hryvna. There are notes of 1, 5, 10,50, 100 and 200 hryvnas. Inflation was 38% in 1996.

Banking and Finance. A National Bank was founded in March 1991. It operates under government control, its Governor being appointed by the President with the approval of parliament. Its *governor* is Viktor Yushchenko. There were 219 banks in all in 1996.

There is a stock exchange in Kiev.

ENERGY AND NATURAL RESOURCES

Electricity. Power output was 202,900m. kWh in 1994. In 1997 there were 5 nuclear power stations producing 40% of output. A Soviet programme to greatly expand nuclear power generating capacity in the country was abandoned in the wake of the 1986 accident at Chernobyl.

Oil and Gas. In 1993 output of crude oil and gas concentrate was 4·2m. tonnes, and of natural gas 19,200m. cu. metres

Minerals. Ukraine's industrial economy, accounting for more than a quarter of total employment, is based largely on the republic's vast mineral resources. The Donetsk Basin contains huge reserves of coal and the nearby iron-ore reserves of Kryvy Rih are equally rich. Among Ukraine's other mineral resources are manganese, bauxite, titanium and salt. Coal accounts for roughly 30% of the country's energy production.

Agriculture. Ukraine has extremely fertile black-earth soils in the central and southern portions, totalling nearly two-thirds of the territory. The original vegetation of the area formed three broad belts that crossed the territory of Ukraine latitudinally. Mixed forest vegetation occupied the northern third of the country, forest-steppe the middle portion and steppe the southern third of the country. Now, however, much of the original vegetation has been cleared and replaced by cultivated crops. Ukraine is a major producer and exporter of a wide variety of agricultural products, including wheat and sugar beets. Other crops include potatoes, vegetables, fruit, sunflowers and flax. Livestock raising is also important. Agricultural production has suffered greatly since independence, however, and domestic food consumption has decreased. Crops include wheat, buckwheat, beet, sunflower, cotton, flax, tobacco, soya, hops, the rubber plant kok-sagyz, fruit and vegetables. The area under cultivation was 40·4m. ha in 1993.

State farm members may leave and receive a portion of land free; the land may be resold.

Output (in 1m. tonnes) in 1993: Grain, 45·6; sugar-beet, 33·6; potatoes, 20·9; vegetables, 5·8; fruit and berries, 2·9; meat, 2·9; milk, 18·1; 11,766m. eggs.

On 1 Jan. 1994 there were 21·6m. cattle, 15·3m. pigs, 6·9m. sheep and goats.

Forestry. In 1991, 7·8m. cu. metres of timber were produced.

INDUSTRY. In 1993 there were 9,100 industrial enterprises. Output, 1993, (in tonnes): Rolled ferrous metals, 24m.; mineral fertilizer, 2·5m.; synthetic fibre, 80,000; paper, 181,000; cement, 15,000; lathes, 25,800 units; motor cars, 140,000 units; tractors, 55,500 units; sugar, 3·8m.; milk products, 2·7m.; processed meats, 1·1m.; butter, 706,000; fabrics, 574m. sq. metres; footwear, 101m. pairs; TV sets, 1·9m.; refrigerators, 0·76m.

Labour. In 1993, 29·4m. persons were of working age, of whom 23·9m. were in paid employment (18·2m. in the state sector and 1·2m. in the private sector). In July 1994, 91,900 persons were registered as unemployed.

Trade Unions. There are 13 trade unions grouped in a Trades Union Federation (*Chair*, Oleksandr Stoyan).

FOREIGN ECONOMIC RELATIONS. In June 1994 total foreign debt was US$6,000m.

Commerce. Total foreign trade by year (in US$1m.):

	1994	1995
Imports	13,894	14,244
Exports	16,469	16,946

Main exports, 1995 (% share of trade): Ferrous metals and ferrous alloy products, 34·2%; machinery, 12%; transport equipment, 6·7%; fertilizer, 5·4%; mineral fuel, 4·5%; sugar, 4·3%. In 1997 Russia accounted for 47% of Ukraine's trade.

COMMUNICATIONS

Roads. In 1995 there were 163,300 km of hard-surfaced motor roads. In 1994 there were 4·3m. passenger cars

Railways. Total length was 22,504 km of 1,520 mm gauge in 1994, of which 8,512 km were electrified. In 1994 railways carried 736m. passengers and 473m. tonnes of freight. There are metros in Kiev and Kharkov.

Civil Aviation. There is an international airport at Kiev (Boryspol). The national carrier, Air Ukraine, operated 1 B-737-200 Adv and 94 ex-Soviet aircraft in 1995. Services are also provided by Aeroflot, Aerosweet, Air France, Austrian Airlines, Aviaprima-Sochi Airlines, Balkan, Czech Airlines, Delta, Egyptair, Estonian Air, Finnair, Iberia, JAT, KLM, LOT, Lufthansa, Malév, Northwest Airlines, Swissair, Tarom, Transaero and Turkish Airlines. In 1993, 1·7m. passengers and 0·2m. tonnes of freight were carried.

Shipping. In 1993, 8m. passengers and 25m. tonnes of freight were carried by inland waterways. In 1995 there were 649 ocean-going vessels, totalling 5·83m. DWT. 38 vessels (5·09% of total tonnage) were registered under foreign flags. GRT totalled 5·29m., including oil tankers, 84,276 GRT, and container ships, 139,187 GRT. The main seaports are Illichevsk, Pivdenny, Mariupol, Odessa, Reni, Kherson and Mykolaivsky. Odessa is the leading port, and takes 30m. tonnes of cargo annually.

Telecommunications. There were 35 telephones per 100 families in 1994. Broadcasting is administered by the government State Teleradio Company of the Ukraine. The state-controlled Ukrainian Radio broadcasts 3 national and various regional programmes, a shared relay with Radio Moscow, and a foreign service (Ukrainian, English, German and Romanian). There were 4 independent stations in 1993 and 41·7m. radio receivers. The state-controlled Ukrainian Television broadcasts on 2 channels (colour by SECAM). In 1993 there were 17·5m. television receivers

Press. At June 1996, 5,325 periodicals were registered, including 3,953 newspapers and 1,025 journals.

SOCIAL INSTITUTIONS

Justice. The death penalty is authorized. Over 1991–95, 642 death sentences were awarded and 442 carried out; there were 169 executions in 1996. 572,147 crimes were reported in 1994. A new civil code was voted into law in June 1997.

Religion. The majority faith is the Orthodox Church, which in 1996 was split into 3 factions: The Ukrainian Orthodox Church, which owes obedience to the Russian Orthodox Church in Moscow, and is headed by Volodymyr, Patriarch of Kiev and All Rus-Ukraine; the Autocephalous Ukrainian Orthodox Church, which served émigrés and dissidents during the Soviet era, headed by Patriarch Mstyslav; and the Kiev Patriarchate Ukrainian Orthodox Church, headed by Metropolitan Filaret, which was unified with the Autocephalous Church in the period 1991–92. Filaret was excommunicated by the Ukrainian Orthodox Church in Feb. 1997.

The hierarchy of the Uniate Church (*head*, Cardinal Myroslav Lubachivsky, b. 1914) was restored by the Pope's confirmation of 10 bishops in Jan. 1991.

Education. In 1994–95 the number of pupils in 22,300 primary and secondary schools was 7m.; 232 further education establishments had 888,500 students, and 754 technical colleges, 680,700 students; 47% of eligible children were attending preschool institutions.

In 1995–96 there were 7 universities and an international university of science and technology.

Adult literacy in 1995 was 99%.

Health. Doctors numbered 230,000 in Jan. 1994 and junior medical personnel, 600,000. There were 0·68m. beds in 3,900 hospitals.

Welfare. There were 10·9m. age pensioners in Jan. 1994 and 3·6m. other pensioners.

DIPLOMATIC REPRESENTATIVES

Of Ukraine in Great Britain (78 Kensington Park Rd., London W11 2PL)
Ambassador: Sergui Komissarenko.

Of Great Britain in Ukraine (9 Desyatinna, 252025 Kiev)
Ambassador: Roy Reeve.

Of Ukraine in the USA (L Street, NW, Washington DC 20036)
Ambassador: Yuri Shcherbak.

Of the USA in Ukraine (10 Yuria Kotsyubinskoho, 252053 Kiev 53)
Ambassador: William Miller.

Of Ukraine to the United Nations
Ambassador: Vlodymyr Y. Yel'chenko.

Of Ukraine to the European Union
Ambassador: Igor Mitiukov.

Further Reading

Encyclopedia of Ukraine, 5 vols. Toronto, 1984–93
Koropeckyj, I. S., *The Ukrainian Economy: Achievements, Problems, Challenges*. Harvard Univ. Press, 1993
Kuzio, T. and Wilson, A., *Ukraine: Perestroika to Independence*. London, 1994
Magocsi, P. R., *A History of Ukraine*. Toronto Univ. Press, 1997
Marples, D., *Ukraine under Perestroika: Ecology, Economics and the Workers' Revolt*. London, 1991
Motyl, A. J., *Dilemmas of Independence: Ukraine after Totalitarianism*. New York, 1993
Nahaylo, B., *Ukrainian Resurgence*. Farnborough, 1993
Solchanyk, R., (ed.) *Ukraine: from Chernobyl to Sovereignty*. London, 1991
Subtelny, O., *Ukraine: a History*. Toronto, 1989

CRIMEA

The Crimea is a peninsula extending southwards into the Black Sea with an area of 25,881 sq. km. Population (1991 estimate), 2,549,800 (Ethnic groups, Sept. 1993: Russians, 61·6%; Ukrainians, 23·6%; Tatars, 9·6%). The capital is Simferopol.

It was occupied by Tatars in 1239, conquered by Ottoman Turks in 1475 and retaken by Russia in 1783. In 1921 after the Communist revolution it became an autonomous republic, but was transformed into a province (*oblast*) of the Russian Federation in 1945 after the deportation of the Tatar population in 1944 for alleged collaboration with the German invaders in the Second World War. It was transferred to the Ukraine in 1954 and became an autonomous republic in 1991. About half the surviving Tatar population of 0·4m. had returned from exile by mid-1992.

At elections held in 2 rounds on 16 and 30 Jan. 1994 Yuri Meshkov was elected *President* for a 4-year term by 38·5% and 72% of votes cast against 5 opponents. The electorate was 1·8m. There is a 94-member local parliament. Parliamentary elections were held on 27 March 1994. The Russia Bloc gained 54 seats, Kurultai (Tatars) 14, ind 21.

On 2 Nov. 1995 parliament adopted a new constitution which defines the Crimea as 'an autonomous republic forming an integral part of Ukraine'. The status of 'autonomous republic' was confirmed by the 1996 Ukrainian Constitution, which provides for Crimea to have its own constitution as approved by its parliament. The Prime Minister is appointed by the Crimean parliament with the approval of the Ukrainian parliament.

The *Prime Minister* is Anatoliy Franchuk.

UNITED ARAB EMIRATES (UAE)

Imarat al-Arabiya al-Muttahida

Capital: Abu Dhabi
Population: 2·3m.
GDP per head: (PPP$) 16,000
HDI/world rank: 0·866/44

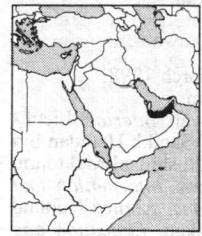

KEY HISTORICAL EVENTS. From Sha'am, 35 miles south-west of Ras Musam dam, for nearly 400 miles to Khor al Odeid at the south-eastern end of the peninsula of Qatar, the coast, formerly known as the Trucial Coast, of the Gulf (together with 50 miles of the coast of the Gulf of Oman) belongs to the rulers of the 7 Trucial States. In 1820 these rulers signed a treaty prescribing peace with the British Government. This treaty was followed by further agreements providing for the suppression of the slave trade and by a series of other engagements, of which the most important were the Perpetual Maritime Truce (May 1853) and the Exclusive Agreement (March 1892). Under the latter, the sheikhs, on behalf of themselves, their heirs and successors, undertook that they would on no account enter into any agreement or corres-pondence with any power other than the British Government, receive foreign agents, cede, sell or give for occupation any part of their territory save to the British Government.

British forces withdrew from the Gulf at the end of 1971 and the treaties whereby the UK had been responsible for the defence and foreign relations of the Trucial States were terminated, being replaced on 2 Dec. 1971 by a treaty of friendship between the UK and the United Arab Emirates. The United Arab Emirates (formed 2 Dec. 1971) consists of the former Trucial States: Abu Dhabi, Dubai, Sharjah, Ajman, Umm al Qaiwain, Ras al-Khaimah (joined in Feb. 1972) and Fujairah. The small state of Kalba was merged with Sharjah in 1952.

TERRITORY AND POPULATION. The Emirates are bounded in the north by the Persian (Arabian) Gulf, north-east by Oman, east by the Gulf of Oman and Oman, south and west by Saudi Arabia, and north-west by Qatar. Their area is approximately 32,300 sq. miles (83,657 sq. km), excluding over 100 offshore islands. The total population at census (1995, preliminary) was 2,377,453 (797,710 females). Estimate (1997) 2,262,309 (884,863 females). About one-tenth are nomads. Vital statistics, 1997: Birth rate (per 1,000 population), 18·46; death rate, 3; infant mortality rate (per 1,000 live births), 15·5; life expectancy, 74·6 years.

Populations of the 7 Emirates, 1995 census: Abu Dhabi, 928,360; Ajman, 118,812; Dubai, 674,101; Fujairah, 76,254; Ras al-Khaimah, 144,430; Sharjah, 400,339; Umm al Qaiwain, 35,157.

The chief cities are Abu Dhabi, the federal capital, Dubai, Sharjah and Ras al-Khaimah.

The official language is Arabic; English is widely spoken.

CLIMATE. The country experiences desert conditions, with rainfall both limited and erratic. The period May to Sept. is generally rainless. Dubai. Jan. 74°F (23·4°C), July 108°F (42·3°C). Annual rainfall 2·4" (60 mm). Sharjah. Jan. 64°F (17·8°C), July 91°F (32°C). Annual rainfall 4·2" (105 mm).

CONSTITUTION AND GOVERNMENT. The Emirates is a federation, headed by a *Supreme Council of Rulers* which is composed of the 7 rulers which elects from among its members a *President* and *Vice-President* for 5-year terms and appoints a *Council of Ministers*. The Council of Ministers drafts legislation and a federal budget; its proposals are submitted to a *Federal National Council* of 40 elected members which may propose amendments but has no executive power. There is a *National Consultative Council* made up of citizens.

1405

Members of the Supreme Council of Rulers:
President: HH Sheikh Zayed bin Sultan al-Nahyan, Ruler of Abu Dhabi (re-elected Oct. 1996).
Vice President, Prime Minister: HH Sheikh Maktoum bin Rashid al-Maktoum, Ruler of Dubai.
HH Dr Sheikh Sultan bin Mohammed al-Qassimi, Ruler of Sharjah.
HH Sheikh Saqr bin Mohammed al-Qassimi, Ruler of Ras al-Khaimah.
HH Sheikh Hamad bin Mohammed al-Sharqi, Ruler of Fujairah.
HH Sheikh Humaid bin Rashid al-Nuaimi, Ruler of Ajman.
HH Sheikh Rashid bin Ahmed al-Mualla, Ruler of Umm al Qaiwain.

The Council of Ministers appointed in March 1997 was in March 1998:
Prime Minister: HH Sheikh Maktoum bin Rashid al-Maktoum.
Deputy Prime Minister: HH Sheikh Sultan bin Zayed al-Nahyan. *Interior:* Lieut.-Gen. Dr Mohammed Saeed al-Badi. *Finance and Industry:* HH Sheikh Hamdan bin Rashid al-Maktoum. *Defence:* Gen. Sheikh Mohammed bin Rashid al-Maktoum. *Economy and Commerce:* Sheikh Fahim bin Sultan al-Qassimi. *Information and Culture:* Sheikh Abdullah bin Zayed al-Nahyan. *Communications:* Ahmed Humaid al-Tayer. *Public Works and Housing:* Rakad bin Salem al-Rakad. *Education and Youth:* Dr Abdul Aziz al-Sharhan. *Petroleum and Mineral Resources:* Obeid bin Saif al-Nassiri. *Electricity and Water:* Humaid bin Nasser al-Owais. *Labour and Social Affairs:* Mattar Humaid al-Tayer. *Planning:* HH Sheikh Humaid bin Ahmed al-Mualla. *Agriculture and Fisheries:* Saeed Mohammed al-Ragabani. *Justice, Islamic Affairs and Endowments:* Mohammed Mukhaira al-Dhahiri. *Foreign Affairs:* Rashid Abdullah al-Nuaimi. *Higher Education and Scientific Research:* Sheikh Nahyan bin Mubarak al-Nahyan. *Health:* Hamad Abdul Rahman al-Madfa.

National anthem: There are no words, tune by M. A. Wahab. A new anthem has been commissioned to celebrate 25 years of independence since 1971.

Local Government. Each Emirate has its own local institutions whose nature depends on size and population. Abu Dhabi has an Executive Council chaired by the Crown Prince.

DEFENCE

Army. The Army consists of 1 Royal Guard, 1 armoured, 1 mechanized infantry, 2 infantry and 1 artillery brigade. There are also 2 unintegrated infantry brigades in Dubai. Equipment includes 95 AMX-30 and 36 Lion OF-40 Mk 2 main battle tanks. The strength was (1997) 59,000.

Navy. The combined naval flotilla of the Emirates includes 1 leased ex-US guided missile frigate, 2 German-built missile corvettes, 8 German-built fast missile craft, 9 British-built inshore patrol craft, 3 tank landing craft, 2 transports, 1 maintenance ship and 3 service craft. Personnel in 1997 numbered 1,500. The main base is at Taweela (Sharjah), with minor bases in the other Emirates.
The Coast Guard flotilla comprises 40 inshore patrol craft and some 30 boats.

Air Force. Current equipment of the Abu Dhabi component of the service includes 21 Mirage 2000 and 23 Mirage 5 supersonic fighter-bombers, 8 Mirage 2000R and 3 Mirage 5R tactical reconnaissance aircraft, 5 Mirage 2000D and 3 Mirage 5D 2-seat trainers; 4 Hercules turboprop transports; 4 CASA C-212 Aviocar electronic countermeasures and intelligence aircraft; 30 Apache armed helicopters; about 50 Gazelle, Alouette III, Puma, Super Puma and Ecureuil transport and liaison helicopters; 23 PC-7 Turbo-Trainers and 40 Hawk light attack/trainers. Current equipment of the Dubai component comprises 3 Aermacchi MB 326K jet light attack aircraft, 5 SF.260TP turboprop trainers, and 2 MB 326L, 4 MB 339 and 8 Hawk jet trainers, 6 Bell 205A-1, 3 Bell 212, 8 Bell 214 and 6 JetRanger helicopters, as well as 2 L-100-30 Hercules transports and a variety of other types for VIP and transport use. Personnel (1997) 4,000 with 102 combat aircraft and 42 armed helicopters.

INTERNATIONAL RELATIONS

Membership. The UAE is a member of the UN, OPEC, the Gulf Co-operation Council and the Arab League.

ECONOMY

Performance. GDP was DH 164,000m. in 1996 (non-oil sector DH 114,000m.). Growth in 1996, 2·9%.

Budget. Revenue is principally derived from oil-concession payments. Revenue and grants and expenditure (in DH 1m.) for calendar years:

	1990	1991	1992	1993	1994
Revenue	1,971	1,626	4,110	2,975	3,294
Grants	12,927	12,997	12,511	12,273	12,689
Expenditure	14,442	15,248	15,571	15,571	15,693

Expenditure in 1994 (in DH 1m.) included: Defence, 5,827; education, 2,692; public order and safety, 2,021; health, 1,153; social security and welfare, 527.

Currency. The unit of currency is the *dirham* (AED) of 100 *fils*. There are notes of 5, 10, 50, 100 and 500 dirhams and coins of 1 and 5 dirhams and 1, 5, 10, 25 and 50 fils. Inflation was 3% in Sept. 1994.

Banking and Finance. The UAE Central Bank was established in 1980 (*Governor*, Sultan al-Suweidi). In 1994 there were 47 local and foreign banks with 349 branches and deposits of DH 13,200m. Foreign banks are restricted to 8 branches each.

ENERGY AND NATURAL RESOURCES

Electricity. Production (1994) 23,402m. kWh.

Oil. Oil and gas provided about 33·4% of GDP in 1994. Reserves of crude oil (1994) 98,100m. bbls. Production, 1995, 103m. tonnes.

Abu Dhabi. Proven reserves (1988) 31,000m. bbls. Estimated oil production is 85% of the UAE's total.

Dubai. In 1975 Dubai took control of foreign oil and gas operations and a Dubai producing group was set up to comprise the foreign interests. Estimated oil production, 1995, 0·3m. bbls a day.

Sharjah. Oil production, 1992, 1·92m. tonnes.

Ras al-Khaimah. Oil production (1990) 0·4m. tonnes.

Gas. Abu Dhabi has reserves of natural gas, nationalized in 1976. There is a gas liquefaction plant on Das Island. Gas proven reserves (1994) were 6,130,000m. cu. metres. Gas production, 1995, 1,113 petajoules.

Water. Production of drinking water by desalination of sea water (1994) was 117,000m. gallons.

Agriculture. The fertile Buraimi Oasis, known as Al Ain, is largely in Abu Dhabi territory. By 1994, 21,194 farms had been set up on land reclaimed from sand dunes. Owing to lack of water and good soil there are few natural opportunities for agriculture, but there is a programme of fostering agriculture by desalination of water, dam-building and tree-planting, and strawberries, flowers and dates are now cultivated for export. The total area under cultivation in 1994 was 72,370 ha. In 1990 there were 29,000 ha of arable land, 10,000 ha of crop-land and 0·2m. ha of pasture. Output, 1995 (in 1,000 tonnes): Dates, 240; tomatoes, 245; aubergines, 69; cucumbers and gherkins, 14; melons, 11; cereals, 7. Livestock products, 1995 (in 1,000 tonnes): Mutton and lamb, 31; poultry meat, 23; eggs, 12; goats' milk, 20.

Livestock (1995, in 1,000): Cattle, 65; camels, 155; sheep, 350; goats, 862.

Fisheries. In 1994 there were 4,000 fishing boats and (1992) 11,074 fishermen. Catch (1995) 105,554 tonnes.

INDUSTRY. In 1993 there were 904 industrial firms. Products include aluminium, cable, cement, chemicals, fertilizers (Abu Dhabi), rolled steel and plastics (Dubai, Sharjah) and tools and clothing (Dubai).

Labour. The labour force totalled 1,289,654 in 1995.

FOREIGN ECONOMIC RELATIONS. There are free trade zones at Jebel Ali (administered by Dubai), Sharjah and Fujairah. Foreign companies may set up wholly-owned subsidiaries. In 1994 there were 650 companies in the Jebel Ali zone.

Commerce. Imports in 1996 totalled US$22,300m.; exports US$31,300m., of which crude oil 66%. Oil and gas exports accounted for DH 44,480m. in 1994.

Main import suppliers, 1995: Japan (9%), USA (8%), UK (8%), Germany (7%) and South Korea (5%). Main export markets: Japan (38%), India (6%), South Korea (6%), Singapore (5%), Iran (4%) and Oman (4%).

Tourism. In 1994 there were 254 hotels which had 1,919,000 visitors.

COMMUNICATIONS

Roads. In 1996 there were 6,550 km of paved roads and in 1994, 447,000 vehicles.

Civil Aviation. There are international airports at Abu Dhabi, Al Ain, Dubai, Fujairah, Ras al-Khaimah and Sharjah. 7,946,000 passengers were handled in 1994. Gulf Air is owned equally by Abu Dhabi, Bahrain, Oman and Qatar. For details *see* BAHRAIN: Civil Aviation. Dubai set up its own airline, Emirates Air, in 1985. It now operates internationally; in 1995 its fleet comprised 6 A300B4-600Rs, 10 A310-300s and 1 B-727-200 Adv. Services are also provided by Aeroflot, Air Algérie, Air France, Air India, Air Lanka, Air Malta, Air Seychelles, Air Tanzania, Air Ukraine, Alitalia, Alyemda, American Airlines, Avia-Sochi Airlines, Azerbaijan Hava Yollary, Balkan, Biman Bangladesh, British Airways, Cathay Pacific, China Airlines, Condor, Cyprus Airways, Czech Airlines, Daallo, Egyptair, Ethiopian Airlines, Eva, Finnair, Garuda Indonesia, Indian Airlines, Iran Air, JAT, Kenya Airways, KLM, Kuwait Airways, Libyan Airlines, Lithuanian Airlines, LOT, LTU, Lufthansa, Malaysia Airlines, Mandarin, Middle East Airlines, Northwest Airlines, Olympic Airways, Oman Air, Pakistan Airlines, Philippine Airlines, Qatar Airways, Royal Air Maroc, Royal Brunei Airlines, Royal Jordanian, Royal Nepal Airlines, SAA, Saudia, Singapore Airlines, Sudan Airways, Swissair, Syrian Airlines, Tarom, Thai Airways, Tunis Air, Turkish Airlines, Uganda Airlines, United Airlines, Uzbekistan Airways, Vietnam Airlines, Virgin Atlantic, Yemenia and Zas.

Shipping. There are 15 commercial seaports, of which 5 major ports are on the Persian (Arabian) Gulf (Zayed in Abu Dhabi, Rashid and Jebel Ali in Dubai, Khalid in Sharjah and Saqr in Ras al-Khaimah) and 2 on the Gulf of Oman: Fujairah and Khor Fakkan. Rashid and Fujairah are important container terminals. 45m. tonnes of cargo were handled in 1994. In 1996, the merchant marine comprised 60 ships (1,000 GRT or over) totalling 1,128,495 GRT, including 22 oil tankers and 6 container ships.

Telecommunications. In 1993 there were 58 post offices, 128 postal agencies, 677,973 telephones, 536,606 fax machines and some 60,000 mobile telephones.

There are several government authorities providing broadcasting nationally (Voice of the United Arab Emirates, Capital Radio, which is partly commercial and United Arab Emirates Television Service) and regionally (UAE Radio and Television-Dubai, Ras al-Khaimah Broadcasting, Umm al Qaiwain Broadcasting, and Sharjah TV). In 1995 there were 0·1m. radio and 0·23m. TV sets (colour by PAL).

Press (1996). There were 9 daily newspapers (5 Arabic and 4 English) with a combined circulation of 0·3m.

SOCIAL INSTITUTIONS

Justice. The basic principles of the law are Islamic. Legislation seeks to promote the harmonious functioning of society's multi-national components while protecting the interests of the indigenous population. Each Emirate has its own penal code. A federal code takes precedence and ensures compatibility. There are federal courts with appellate powers which function under federal laws. Emirates have the option to merge their courts with the federal judiciary.

The death penalty for drug smuggling was introduced in April 1995.

Religion. Nearly all the inhabitants are Moslem of the Sunni, and a small minority of the Shi'ite, sects.

Education In 1996 there were 19,290 pre-primary pupils with 1,128 teachers, 152,741 primary pupils with 10,123 teachers and 121,736 secondary pupils with 9,832 teachers. In 1995 there were 11,576 students at the Emirates University and 2,324 students in 3 higher colleges of technology. Adult literacy was 84·6% in 1995.

Health. In 1996 there were 36 government hospitals with 4,344 beds. In 1994 there were 14 private hospitals, 128 government health centres, a herbal medicine centre, 752 private clinics, 4,095 doctors, 563 dentists and 8,506 nurses.

DIPLOMATIC REPRESENTATIVES

Of the UAE in Great Britain (30 Princes Gate, London, SW7 1PT)
Ambassador: Easa Saleh Al-Gurg, CBE.

Of Great Britain in the UAE (POB 248, Abu Dhabi)
Ambassador: A. D. Harris, CMG, LVO.

Of the UAE in the USA (3000 K St., NW, Washington, D.C., 20007)
Ambassador: Mohammed bin Hussein Al-Shaali.

Of the USA in the UAE (POB 4009, Abu Dhabi)
Ambassador: David C. Litt.

Of the UAE to the United Nations
Ambassador: Mohammed Jassim Samhan.

Of the UAE to the European Union
Ambassador: Salem Rached Salem Al-Agroobi.

Further Reading

Alkim, H. al.-, *The Foreign Policy of the UAE.* Saqi, 1989
Clements, F. A., *United Arab Emirates.* [Bibliography] Oxford and Santa Barbara (CA), 1983
Heard-Bey, F., *From Trucial States to United Arab Emirates.* London, 1982
Taryam, A. O., *The Establishment of the United Arab Emirates.* London, 1987

UNITED KINGDOM OF GREAT BRITAIN AND NORTHERN IRELAND

Capital: London
Population: 58·78m. (1996)
GDP per head: (PPP$) 18,620
HDI/world rank: 0·931/15

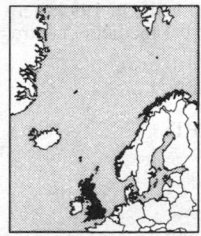

KEY HISTORICAL EVENTS. Great Britain became a political unit when England and Wales united with Scotland in a single parliament in 1707.

By 1790 British government was conducted by ministers responsible to Parliament, but The Church of England enjoyed extensive privileges while Non-conformists and Roman Catholics were penalized, the latter heavily because they were considered politically dangerous.

Ireland was governed by English law through a nominally independent parliament. The people, mainly Catholic, rebelled in 1798. The settlement proposed was legislative union and Catholic emancipation; the latter was delayed until 1828–29 (when Nonconformists also received full civic rights) but the union took effect in 1801, as the United Kingdom of Great Britain and Ireland.

In 1793 revolutionary France declared war, and was not finally defeated until 1815. The demands of war stimulated the new, steam-powered industries. After 1815 there was frequent unrest as an increasingly urban and industrial society found its interests poorly represented by a parliament composed chiefly of landowners.

The Reform Act of 1832 improved representation in Parliament, and further acts (1867, 1884, 1918 and 1928) led gradually to universal adult suffrage. Early industrial development produced great national wealth but its distribution was extremely uneven and the condition of the poor improved slowly. Legislation to improve working conditions, education and public health did not keep pace with the growth of industrial cities. The 1840s saw much immigration from Ireland (where there was famine) and from areas of political unrest in continental Europe; a second wave of immigration from the continent occurred after 1880, including Jewish refugees.

Abroad, there was war with Russia in the Crimea (1854–56); most wars, however, were fought to conquer or pacify colonies. The 19th century empire included India, Canada, Australasia, and vast territories in Africa and Eastern Asia. After 1870 the Suez Canal enabled Britain to control the empire more efficiently; she became a 40% shareholder in 1875 and the controlling power in Egypt in 1882.

The most serious imperial wars were the Boer Wars of 1881 and 1899–1902. British opinion was deeply divided, and the Liberal government elected in 1905 negotiated a Union of South Africa, by which South Africa enjoyed the same autonomy which had been agreed for Canada (1867), Australia (1901) and later New Zealand (1907). The 'dominion status' of these countries was clarified by the Statute of Westminster (1931).

Whereas early Victorian reforms were responses to obvious distress, governments after 1868 were more inclined towards preventive state action. The budget of 1910 was designed largely to finance a programme of welfare; its rejection in Parliament by the House of Lords led to the Parliament Act (1911) which ended the Lords' power to veto bills.

On 3 Aug. 1914 Germany invaded Belgium and Britain was obliged by treaty to retaliate by declaring war.

During the war with Germany a rebellion was staged in Ireland, born of the failure of successive attempts to agree a formula for Irish Home Rule. The issue was complicated by factional disagreement in southern Ireland and the wish of northern Ireland to remain in the United Kingdom. In 1920 after four years' conflict the

1410

Government of Ireland Act partitioned the country. The northern six counties remained British, a parliament was created and a Unionist government took office. The southern 26 counties moved by stages to complete independence as the Republic of Ireland.

After the First World War there followed a long period of economic decline and industrial difficulty. There was an unsuccessful General Strike in 1926. In 1931 an emergency coalition National Government was formed to deal with the impact of world depression.

The UK has no written constitution. Since the death of George IV in 1830 there had been steady progress to a fully constitutional monarchy, pragmatically developed, and though George V (1910–36) ruled actively he always adhered to this principle.

Germany revived as a military power in the 1930s, and invaded Poland on 1 Sept. 1939. Britain, bound once more by treaty, declared war.

The Second World War ended with German and Japanese defeat in 1945. It was a time of great social upheaval. In the 1945 election a Labour government was returned with a large majority and a socialist programme. Subsequent governments modified but generally accepted the changes then introduced. After 1979, however, Conservative governments reversed much of this legislation before Labour regained power in 1997.

Beginning with the independence and partition of India and Pakistan in 1947, a policy was adopted of rapid progress to independence of the colonies. The new concept was of a Commonwealth of freely-associated states, recognizing the British monarch as symbolic Commonwealth head (some states chose to retain the monarch as head of state).

In 1961 an application to join the European Economic Community was vetoed by France. A second application in 1973 was successful, and membership was endorsed by referendum in 1975.

GREAT BRITAIN

TERRITORY AND POPULATION. Area (in sq. km) and population (present on census night) at the census taken 21 April 1991:

Divisions	Area	Population
England	130,423	46,382,050
Wales	20,766	2,811,865
Scotland	77,167	4,962,152
	228,356	54,156,067

Population (present on census night) at the 4 previous decennial censuses:

Divisions	1951	1961	1971	1981
England[1]	41,159,213	43,460,525	46,018,371	46,226,100[2]
Wales	2,598,675	2,644,023	2,731,204	2,790,500[2]
Scotland	5,096,415	5,179,344	5,228,963	5,130,735
Great Britain	48,854,303	51,283,892	53,978,538	54,147,3002

[1] Areas now recognised as part of Gwent, Wales, formed the English county of Monmouthshire until 1974.   [2] The final counts for England and Wales are believed to be over-stated as a result of an error in processing. The preliminary counts presented here rounded to the nearest hundred are thought to be more accurate.

UK population estimate, 1996, 58,784,000 (29,930,000 females); density, 240 per sq. km. Vital statistics: Births, 1995, 732,000 (246,000 outside marriage); deaths, 642,000; marriages, 1994, 331,248; divorces, 167,748; abortions, 1993, 179,783; infant mortality (per 1,000 live births), 2,285. Life expectancy, 1995: Males, 73·9 years; females, 79·2. Over 1990–95, suicide rates per 100,000 population were 7·9 (men, 12·4; women, 3·6).

Birth rates (per 1,000 population), 1995, 12·5; death, 10·8.
Population (usually resident) at the census of 1991:

Divisions	Males	Females	Total
England	22,812,889	24,242,315	47,055,204
Wales	1,370,104	1,464,969	2,835,073
Scotland	2,391,961	2,606,606	4,998,567
Great Britain	26,574,954	28,313,890	54,888,844

In 1991 in Wales 508,098 persons were able to speak Welsh. In Scotland in 1991, 65,978 of the usually resident population could speak Gaelic (79,307 in 1981).

Private households at the 1991 census: England, 19,984,500; Wales, 1,201,700; Scotland, 2,164,081.

The age distribution in 1991 of the 'usually resident' population of England and Wales and Scotland was as follows (in 1,000):

Age-group		England and Wales	Scotland	Great Britain
Under	5	3,316	317	3,633
5 and under	10	3,123	318	3,440
10 ,,	15	2,988	312	3,299
15 ,,	20	3,205	332	3,547
20 ,,	25	3,731	375	4,106
25 ,,	35	7,594	768	8,361
35 ,,	45	6,970	695	7,665
45 ,,	55	5,793	578	6,372
55 ,,	65	5,126	537	5,663
65 ,,	70	2,491	247	2,737
70 ,,	75	2,014	193	2,208
75 ,,	85	2,776	259	3,035
85 and upwards		763	68	831

Population densities (persons per ha), 1991 census: Great Britain, 2·4; England, 3·6; Wales, 1·4; Scotland. 0·6.

England and Wales: The census population, (present on census night) of England and Wales 1801 to 1991:

Date of enumeration	Population	Pop. per sq. mile	Date of enumeration	Population	Pop. per sq. mile[1]
1801	8,892,536	152	1901	32,527,843	558
1811	10,164,256	174	1911	36,070,492	618
1821	12,000,236	206	1921	37,886,699	649
1831	13,896,797	238	1931	39,952,377	685
1841	15,914,148	273	1951	43,757,888	750
1851	17,927,609	307	1961	46,104,548	791
1861	20,066,224	344	1971	48,749,575	323
1871	22,712,266	389	1981	49,016,600	325
1881	25,974,439	445	1991	49,193,915	330
1891	29,002,525	497			

[1] Per sq. km from 1971.

Estimated population, 1996, 51,997,000 (26,445,000 females; 2,930,000 in Wales).

The birth places of the 1991 'usually resident' population were: England, 42,897,179; Wales, 2,747,790; Scotland, 5,221,038; Northern Ireland, 244,914; Ireland, 592,020; Commonwealth, 1,865,751; foreign countries, 1,287,821.

Ethnic Groups. The 1991 census was the first to include a question on ethnic status. Ethnic groups as enumerated:

	Total	Females	Total born in UK
White	51,873,794	26,807,415	49,703,681
Indian	840,225	417,364	352,448
Black Caribbean	499,964	260,480	268,318
Pakistani	476,555	230,983	240,552
Black African	212,362	105,562	77,315
Black Other	178,401	90,888	150,638
Bangladeshi	162,835	77,891	56,678

	Total	Females	Total born in UK
Chinese	156,938	79,269	44,635
Other Asian	197,534	103,929	43,265
Other	290,206	140,109	173,518

11 'Standard Regions' (also classified as 'level 1 regions' for EU purposes) are identified in the UK as economic planning regions. They have no administrative significance. They are: Northern Ireland, Scotland, Wales, and 8 regions of England. Estimated population of the regions (in 1,000), 1995, East Anglia, 2,123; East Midlands, 4,124; West Midlands, 5,306; North, 3,095; North West, 6,410; South East, 17,989 (including Greater London, 7,007); South West, 4,827; Yorkshire and Humberside, 5,029.

England is divided (apart from Greater London) into 35 counties and 50 unitary authorities with a single administrative tier, of which 36 are metropolitan boroughs and 27 unitary authorities established since 1995. The 35 counties are subdivided into 274 districts and the Isles of Scilly. Wales is divided into 22 unitary authorities (counties and county boroughs). Greater London comprises 32 boroughs and the City of London.

Area in sq. km of counties and usually resident population at the 1991 census:

	Area sq. km	Population		Area sq. km	Population
Metropolitan counties			*Non-metropolitan counties*—contd.		
ENGLAND			Isle of Wight (IOW)	380	124,577
Greater Manchester	1,286	2,499,441	Kent	3,735	1,508,873
Merseyside	655	1,403,642	Lancashire (Lancs)	3,070	1,383,998
South Yorkshire	1,559	1,262,630	Leicestershire (Leics)	2,551	867,521
Tyne and Wear	537	1,095,152	Lincolnshire (Lincs)	5,921	584,536
West Midlands	899	2,551,671	Norfolk	5,372	745,613
West Yorkshire	2,034	2,013,693	Northamptonshire		
			(Northants)	2,367	578,807
Non-metropolitan counties			Northumberland	5,026	304,694
ENGLAND			North Yorkshire		
Avon	1,332	932,674	(N. Yorks)	8,309	702,161
Bedfordshire (Beds)	1,236	524,105	Nottinghamshire		
Berkshire (Berks)	1,256	734,246	(Notts)	2,160	993,872
Buckinghamshire			Oxfordshire (Oxon)	2,583	547,584
(Bucks)	1,877	632,487	Shropshire (Salop)	3,488	406,387
Cambridgeshire			Somerset (Som)	3,452	460,368
(Camb)	3,400	645,125	Staffordshire (Staffs)	2,715	1,031,135
Cheshire	2,331	956,616	Suffolk	3,798	632,266
Cleveland	597	550,293	Surrey	1,677	1,018,003
Cornwall and Isles			Warwickshire	1,979	484,247
of Scilly	3,530	468,425	West Sussex	1,988	702,290
Cumbria	6,817	483,163	Wiltshire (Wilts)	3,476	564,471
Derbyshire	2,629	928,636			
Devon	6,703	1,009,950	WALES		
Dorset	2,653	645,166	Clwyd	2,430	408,090
Durham	2,429	593,430	Dyfed	5,766	343,543
East Sussex	1,794	690,447	Gwent	1,377	442,212
Essex	3,675	1,528,577	Gwynedd	3,863	235,452
Gloucestershire			Mid Glamorgan		
(Gloucs)	2,653	528,370	(M. Glam)	1,017	534,101
Hampshire (Hants)	3,779	1,541,547	Powys	5,072	117,647
Hereford and			South Glamorgan		
Worcester	3,923	676,747	(S. Glam)	416	392,780
Hertfordshire (Herts)	1,639	975,829	West Glamorgan		
Humberside (Humb)	3,508	858,040	(W. Glam)	820	361,428

Changes in the above administrative structure following the Local Government Act 1992 comprised the following as at 1 April 1997:

The Welsh counties, and the English counties of Avon, Cleveland, Humberside and the Isle of Wight had been abolished, and new unitary authorities had been established in England (Bath and North East Somerset, Bournemouth, Brighton and Hove, Bristol, Darlington, Derby, East Riding of Yorkshire, Hartlepool, Isle of Wight, Kingston-upon-Hull, Leicester, Luton, Middlesbrough, Milton Keynes, North East

Lincolnshire, North Lincolnshire, North Somerset, Poole, Portsmouth, Redcar and Cleveland, Rutland, South Gloucestershire, Southampton, Stockton-on-Tees, Stoke-on-Trent, Thamesdown and York) and Wales (*Counties:* Carmarthenshire, Ceredigion, Denbighshire, Flintshire, Gwynedd, Isle of Anglesey, Monmouthshire, Pembrokeshire, Powys; *County Boroughs:* Blaenau Gwent, Bridgend, Caerphilly, Cardiff, Conwy, Merthyr Tydfil, Neath Port Talbot, Newport, Rhondda Cynon Taff, Swansea, Torfaen, Vale of Glamorgan, Wrexham).

The following table shows the distribution of the urban and rural population of England and Wales (persons present) in 1951, 1961, 1971, and 1981.

	England and Wales	Population Urban districts[1]	Rural districts[1]	Percentage Urban	Rural
1951	43,757,888	35,335,721	8,422,167	80·8	19·2
1961	46,071,604	36,838,442	9,233,162	80·0	20·0
1971	48,755,000	38,151,000	10,598,000	78·2	21·5
1981	49,011,417	37,686,863	11,324,554	76·9	23·1

[1] As existing at each census.

Urban and rural areas were re-defined for the 1981 and 1991 censuses on a land use basis. In Scotland 'localities' correspond to urban areas. The 1981 census gave the usually resident population of England and Wales as 48,521,596, of which 43,599,431 were in urban areas; and of Scotland as 5,035,315, of which 4,486,140 were in localities.

Greater London Boroughs. Total area 1,580 sq. km. Usually resident total population at the 1991 census, 6,679,699 (inner London, 2,504,451). By borough:

Barking and Dagenham	143,681	Hammersmith and Fulham[1]	148,502	Lewisham[1]	230,983
Barnet	293,564	Haringey[1]	202,204	Merton	168,470
Bexley	215,615	Harrow	200,100	Newham[1]	212,170
Brent	243,025	Havering	229,492	Redbridge	226,218
Bromley	290,609	Hillingdon	231,602	Richmond upon Thames	160,732
Camden[1]	170,444	Hounslow	204,397	Southwark[1]	218,541
Croydon	313,510	Islington[1]	164,686	Sutton	168,880
Ealing	275,257	Kensington and Chelsea[1]	138,394	Tower Hamlets[1]	161,064
Enfield	257,417	Kingston upon Thames	132,996	Waltham Forest	212,033
Greenwich	207,650	Lambeth[1]	244,834	Wandsworth[1]	252,425
Hackney[1]	181,248			Westminster, City of[1]	174,718

[1] Inner London borough.

The City of London (677 acres) is administered by its Corporation which retains some independent powers. Resident population (1991 census) 4,142.

Scotland: Area 78,762 sq. km, including its islands, 186 in number, and inland water 1,580 sq. km.

Population (including military in the barracks and seamen on board vessels in the harbours) at the dates of each census:

Date of enumeration	Population	Pop. per sq. mile[1]	Date of enumeration	Population	Pop. per sq. mile
1811	1,805,864	60	1901	4,472,103	150
1821	2,091,521	70	1911	4,760,904	160
1831	2,364,386	79	1921	4,882,497	164
1841	2,620,184	88	1931	4,842,980	163
1851	2,888,742	97	1951	5,096,415	171
1861	3,062,294	100	1961	5,179,344	174
1871	3,360,018	113	1971	5,229,963	68
1881	3,735,573	125	1981	5,130,735	66
1891	4,025,647	135	1991	4,998,567	60

[1] Per sq. km from 1971.

The 1991 census population included 2,606,606 males. Until April 1996 Scotland was divided into 9 regions (subdivided into 53 districts) and 3 island authority areas. Area of regions and usually resident population figures of regions and districts at the 1991 census:

Regions (area sq. km) and Districts	Population	Regions (area sq. km) and Districts	Population
Borders (4,713)	103,881	Lothian (1,716)	726,010
Berwickshire	19,174	East Lothian	84,114
Ettrick and Lauderdale	34,038	Edinburgh City	418,914
Roxburgh	35,346	Midlothian	78,845
Tweeddale	15,323	West Lothian	144,137
Central (2,635)	267,492	Strathclyde (13,503)	2,248,706
Clackmannan	47,679	Argyll and Bute	65,140
Falkirk	140,980	Bearsden and Milngavie	40,612
Stirling	78,833	Clydebank	45,717
Dumfries and Galloway (6,396)	147,805	Clydesdale	57,588
Annandale and Eskdale	37,087	Cumbernauld and Kilsyth	62,412
Nithsdale	57,012	Cumnock and Doon Valley	42,594
Stewartry	23,629	Cunninghame	136,875
Wigtown	30,077	Dumbarton	77,173
		East Kilbride	82,777
Fife (1,312)	341,199	Eastwood	59,959
Dunfermline	127,258	Glasgow City	662,853
Kirkcaldy	147,053	Hamilton	105,202
North East Fife	66,888	Inverclyde	90,103
Grampian (8,698)	503,888	Kilmarnock and Loudoun	79,861
Aberdeen City	204,885	Kyle and Carrick	112,658
Banff and Buchan	85,303	Monklands	102,379
Gordon	76,642	Motherwell	142,632
Kincardine and Deeside	53,442	Renfrew	196,980
Moray	83,616	Strathkelvin	85,191
Highland (25,398)	204,004	Tayside (7,942)	383,848
Badenoch and Strathspey	11,008	Angus	94,480
Caithness	26,710	Dundee City	165,873
Inverness	62,186	Perth and Kinross	123,495
Lochaber	19,310		
Nairn	10,623	Island Authority Areas	
Ross and Cromarty	49,197	Orkney Islands (976)	19,612
Skye and Lochalsh	11,754	Shetland Islands (1,433)	22,522
Sutherland	13,216	Western Isles (2,898)	29,600

In April 1996, 29 new unitary authority areas came into being: Aberdeen City, Aberdeenshire, Angus, Argyll and Bute, Clackmannanshire, Dumfries and Galloway, Dundee City, East Ayrshire, East Dunbartonshire, East Lothian, East Renfrewshire, City of Edinburgh, Falkirk, Fife, Glasgow City, Highland, Inverclyde, Midlothian, Moray, North Ayrshire, North Lanarkshire, Perth and Kinross, Renfrewshire, Scottish Borders, South Ayrshire, South Lanarkshire, Stirling, West Dunbartonshire, West Lothian. The Island Authority Areas (Orkney, Shetland, Western Isles) remained as they were.

The birthplaces of the 1991 usually resident population were: Scotland, 4,454,065; England, 354,268; Wales, 4,710; Northern Ireland, 26,393; Ireland 22,773; Commonwealth, 59,134; foreign countries, 148,987.

Vital statistics. For England and Wales (in 1,000), 1995 (and 1994): Births, 648 (665); deaths, 273 (267); marriages, (291); divorces, 155 (158).

Vital statistics. For Scotland:

	Estimated resident population at 30 June[1]	Total births	Live births outside marriage	Deaths	Marriages	Divorces, annulments and dissolutions
1991	5,107,000	67,024	19,517	61,041	33,762	12,399
1992	5,111,200	65,789	19,950	60,937	35,057	12,479
1993	5,120,200	63,337	19,855	64,049	33,366	12,787
1994	5,132,400	61,656	19,224	59,328	31,480	13,133
1995	5,136,600	60,051	20,066	60,500	30,663	12,249
1996	5,128,000	59,308	21,361	60,671	30,242	11,123

[1] Includes merchant navy at home and forces stationed in Scotland.

Birth rate, 1996, per 1,000 population, 11·6; death rate, 11·8; marriage, 5·9; infant mortality per 1,000 live births, 6·2; sex ratio, 1,061 male births to 1,000 female.

Average age of marriage in 1996: Males, 29·1, females, 27·4. Expectation of life, 1996: Males, 72·0 years, females, 77·7.

British Citizenship. Under the British Nationality Act 1981 there are 3 main forms of citizenship: Citizenship for persons closely connected with the UK; British Dependent Territories citizenship; British Overseas citizenship. British citizenship is acquired automatically at birth by a child born in the UK if his or her mother or father is a British citizen or is settled in the UK. A child born abroad to a British citizen is a British citizen by descent. British citizenship may be acquired by registration for stateless persons, and for children not automatically acquiring such citizenship or born abroad to parents who are citizens by descent; and, for other adults, by naturalization. Requirements for the latter include 5 years' residence (3 years for applicants married to a British citizen). The Hong Kong (British Nationality) Order 1986 created the status of British National (Overseas) for citizens connected with Hong Kong before 1997, and the British Nationality (Hong Kong) Act 1990 made provision for up to 50,000 selected persons to register as British citizens.

In 1995, 40,500 persons were granted citizenship and a further 26,000 under the Hong Kong Act.

Emigration and Immigration. Immigration is mainly governed by the Immigration Act 1970 and Immigration Rules made under it. British and Commonwealth citizens with the right of abode before 1983 are not subject to immigration control, nor are citizens of European Economic Area countries. Other persons seeking to work or settle in the UK must obtain a visa or entry clearance.

Migration statistics are derived from the government's International Passenger Survey, and exclude the Republic of Ireland.

Immigrants (in 1,000) by sex and occupation:

	Total	Females	Professional	Manual/Clerical	Non-Employed
1992	216	99	62	44	27
1993	213	101	66	43	22
1994	253	126	82	56	25
Emigrants:					
1992	227	114	82	47	98
1993	216	103	70	45	101
1994	191	98	55	48	87

Percentages of immigrants in 1994 by place of origin: EU, 31%; Australia, Canada, New Zealand, South Africa, 16%; other Commonwealth countries, 21%; USA, 12%; Middle East, 4%; other countries, 16%. Emigrants by destination: EU, 29%; Australia, Canada, New Zealand, South Africa, 22%; other Commonwealth countries, 15%; USA, 13%; Middle East, 6%; other countries, 15%.

In 1995 (and 1994) there were 55,480 (55,110) acceptances for settlement in the UK, including from: European Economic Area, 220 (620); rest of Europe, 4,030; Pakistan, 6,310 (6,240); India, 4,860 (4,780); Bangladesh, 3,280 (3,050); Australia, 3,020; New Zealand, 1,390 (1,080); South Africa, 1,300 (1,260); Hong Kong, 1,310 (1,490); Japan, 1,870 (2,060).

Asylum. In 1995 there were 43,965 applications for asylum, amounting to some 55,000 persons with dependants (in 1984 there were 2,905 applications). While respecting its obligations to political refugees under the UN Convention and Protocol relating to the status of Refugees, the Government has powers under the Asylum and Immigration Act 1996 to weed out applicants seeking entry for non-political reasons and to designate certain countries as not giving risk of persecution. 6% of applicants were accepted in 1995.

Coleman, D. and Salt, J., *The British Population: Patterns, Trends and Processes.* OUP, 1992

CLIMATE. The climate is cool temperate oceanic, with mild conditions and rainfall evenly distributed over the year, though the weather is very changeable because of cyclonic influences. In general, temperatures are higher in the west and lower in the east in winter and rather the reverse in summer. Rainfall amounts are greatest in the west, where most of the high ground occurs.

London. Jan. 39°F (3·9°C), July 64°F (17·8°C). Annual rainfall 25" (635 mm).
Aberdeen. Jan. 38°F (3·3°C), July 57°F (13·9°C). Annual rainfall 32" (813 mm).
Belfast. Jan. 40°F (4·4°C), July 61°F (16·1°C). Annual rainfall 34·6" (879 mm).
Birmingham. Jan. 38°F (3·3°C), July 61°F (16·1°C). Annual rainfall 30" (749 mm).
Cardiff. Jan. 40°F (4·4°C), July 61°F (16·1°C). Annual rainfall 42·6" (1,065 mm).
Edinburgh. Jan. 38°F (3·3°C), July 58°F (14·5°C). Annual rainfall 27" (686 mm).
Glasgow. Jan. 39°F (3·9°C), July 59°F (15°C). Annual rainfall 38" (965 mm).
Manchester. Jan. 39°F (3·9°C), July 61°F (16·1°C). Annual rainfall 34·5" (876 mm).

THE ROYAL FAMILY. The reigning Queen, Head of the Commonwealth, is **Elizabeth II** Alexandra Mary, b. 21 April 1926, daughter of King George VI and Queen Elizabeth; married on 20 Nov. 1947 Lieut. Philip Mountbatten (formerly Prince Philip of Greece), created Duke of Edinburgh, Earl of Merioneth and Baron Greenwich on the same day and created Prince Philip, Duke of Edinburgh, 22 Feb. 1957; succeeded to the crown on the death of her father, on 6 Feb. 1952. Offspring: **Prince Charles Philip Arthur George, Prince of Wales** (Heir Apparent), b. 14 Nov. 1948, married Lady Diana Frances Spencer on 29 July 1981; after divorce, 28 Aug. 1996, **Diana, Princess of Wales.** She died in Paris in a road accident on 31 Aug. 1997. Offspring: *William* Arthur Philip Louis, b. 21 June 1982; *Henry* Charles Albert David, b. 15 Sept. 1984. **Princess Anne Elizabeth Alice Louise, the Princess Royal,** b. 15 Aug. 1950, married Mark Anthony Peter Phillips on 14 Nov. 1973; divorced, 1992; married Cdr Timothy Laurence on 12 Dec. 1992. Offspring of first marriage: *Peter* Mark Andrew, b. 15 Nov. 1977; *Zara* Anne Elizabeth, b. 15 May 1981. **Prince Andrew Albert Christian Edward, created Duke of York,** 23 July 1986, b. 19 Feb. 1960, married Sarah Margaret Ferguson on 23 July 1986; after divorce, 30 May 1996, **Sarah, Duchess of York.** Offspring: Princess *Beatrice* Mary, b. 8 Aug. 1988; Princess *Eugenie* Victoria Helena, b. 23 March 1990. **Prince Edward Antony Richard Louis,** b. 10 March 1964.

The Queen Mother: Queen *Elizabeth* Angela Marguerite, b. 4 Aug. 1900, daughter of the 14th Earl of Strathmore and Kinghorne; married the Duke of York, afterwards King George VI, on 26 April 1923.

Widow of the Uncle of the Queen: Princess *Alice* Christabel, Duchess of Gloucester, b. 25 Dec. 1901, married the late Duke of Gloucester 6 Nov. 1935.

Sister of the Queen: Princess *Margaret* Rose, Countess of Snowdon, b. 12 Aug. 1930; married Antony Armstrong-Jones (created Earl of Snowdon, 3 Oct. 1961) on 6 May 1960; divorced, 1978. Offspring: *David* Albert Charles (Viscount Linley), b. 3 Nov. 1961, married Serena Alleyne Stanhope on 8 Oct. 1993; Lady *Sarah* Frances Elizabeth Chatto, b. 1 May 1964, married Daniel Chatto on 14 July 1994. Offspring: *Samuel* David Benedict Chatto, b. 28 July 1996.

Cousins of the Queen: **Richard Alexander Walter George, Duke of Gloucester,** b. 26 Aug. 1944, married Birgitte van Deurs on 8 July 1972 (offspring: *Alexander* Patrick Gregers Richard, Earl of Ulster, b. 24 Oct. 1974; Lady *Davina* Elizabeth Alice Benedikte Windsor, b. 19 Nov. 1977; Lady *Rose* Victoria Birgitte Louise Windsor, b. 1 March 1980). **Edward George Nicholas Paul Patrick, Duke of Kent,** b. 9 Oct. 1935; married Katharine Worsley on 8 June 1961 (offspring: *George* Philip Nicholas, Earl of St Andrews, b. 26 June 1962, married Sylvania Tomaselli on 9 Jan. 1988 (offspring: *Edward* Edmund Maximilian George, Baron Downpatrick, b. 2 Dec. 1988; Lady *Marina* Charlotte Alexandra Katharine Windsor, b. 30 Sept. 1992); Lady *Helen* Marina Lucy Windsor, b. 28 April 1964, married 18 July 1992 Timothy Verner Taylor (offspring: *Columbus* George Donald Taylor, b. 6 Aug. 1994; *Cassius* Edward Taylor, b. 26 Dec. 1996); Lord *Nicholas* Charles Edward Jonathan Windsor, b. 25 July 1970). **Princess Alexandra Helen Elizabeth Olga Christabel, the Hon. Lady Ogilvy** b. 25 Dec. 1936; married 24 April 1963 Sir Angus Ogilvy (offspring: *James* Robert Bruce, b. 29 Feb. 1964, married 30 July 1988, Julia Rawlinson; Lady *Marina* Victoria Alexandra, Mrs Mowatt, b. 31 July 1966, married 2 Feb. 1990 Paul Mowatt (offspring: *Zenouska* May Mowatt, b. 26 May 1990; *Christian* Alexander Mowatt, b. 4 June 1993); separated, 11 April 1996. **Prince Michael George Charles Franklin,** b. 4 July 1942; married Baroness Marie-Christine von Reibnitz on 30 June 1978 (offspring: Lord *Frederick* Michael George David Louis Windsor, b. 6 April 1979; Lady *Gabriella* Marina Alexandra Ophelia Windsor, b. 23 April 1981).

The Queen's legal title rests on the statute of 12 and 13 Will. III, ch. 3, by which the succession to the Crown of Great Britain and Ireland was settled on the Princess Sophia of Hanover and the 'heirs of her body being Protestants'. By proclamation of 17 July 1917 the royal family became known as the House and Family of Windsor. On 8 Feb. 1960 the Queen issued a declaration varying her confirmatory declaration of 9 April 1952 to the effect that while the Queen and her children should continue to be known as the House of Windsor, her descendants, other than descendants entitled to the style of Royal Highness and the title of Prince or Princess, and female descendants who marry and their descendants should bear the name of Mountbatten-Windsor.

Lineage to the throne: 1. Prince of Wales. 2. Prince William of Wales. 3. Prince Henry of Wales. 4. Duke of York. 5. Princess Beatrice of York. 6. Princess Eugenie of York.

For the Royal Style and Titles of Queen Elizabeth *see* Commonwealth section. By letters patent of 30 Nov. 1917 the titles of Royal Highness and Prince or Princess are restricted to the Sovereign's children, the children of the Sovereign's sons and the eldest living son of the eldest son of the Prince of Wales.

Provision is made for the support of the royal household, after the surrender of hereditary revenues, by the settlement of the Civil List soon after the beginning of each reign. The Civil List Act of 1 Jan. 1972 provided for a decennial, and the Civil List (Increase of Financial Provision) Order 1975 for an annual review of the List, but in July 1990 it was again fixed for one decade.

The Civil List of 1991–2000 provided for an annuity of £7,900,000 to the Queen; £360,000 to Prince Philip; £640,500 to Queen Elizabeth (the Queen Mother); £230,500 to the Princess Royal; £220,000 to the Princess Margaret; £250,000 to the Duke of York; £100,000 to Prince Edward; £90,000 to Princess Alice. However, since April 1993 only the Queen, Prince Philip and the Queen Mother have received payments from the Civil List. The income of the Prince of Wales derives from the Duchy of Cornwall. The Civil List was exempted from taxation in 1910. The Queen has paid income tax on her private income since April 1993.

CONSTITUTION AND GOVERNMENT. The supreme legislative power is vested in Parliament, which consists of the Crown, the House of Lords and the House of Commons and dates in its present form from the middle of the 14th century. A Bill which is passed by both Houses and receives Royal Assent becomes an Act of Parliament and part of statute law.

Parliament is summoned, and a General Election is called, by the sovereign on the advice of the Prime Minister. A Parliament may last up to 5 years, normally divided into annual sessions. A session is ended by prorogation, and all Public Bills which have not been passed by both Houses then lapse. A Parliament ends by dissolution, either by will of the sovereign or by lapse of the 5-year period.

Under the Parliament Acts 1911 and 1949, all Money Bills (so certified by the Speaker of the House of Commons), if not passed by the Lords without amendment, may become law without their concurrence within 1 month of introduction in the Lords. Public Bills, other than Money Bills or a Bill extending the maximum duration of Parliament, if passed by the Commons in 2 successive sessions and rejected each time by the Lords, may become law without being passed by the Lords provided that 1 year has elapsed between Commons second reading in the first session and third reading in the second session, and that the Bill reaches the Lords at least 1 month before the end of the second session. In 1991 the War Crimes Act was passed in this way. This was the first time since 1949, because the Lords today respect the privileges of the elected House, especially as regards taxes and public spending, and act mainly as a revising chamber.

Peerages are created by the sovereign, with no limits on their number. There are 4 types of Lord: 1) *Lords Spiritual*, comprising 2 archbishops and 24 diocesan bishops of the Church of England, who leave the House when they retire; 2) *hereditary peers*—in August 1997 there were 752 peers who had succeeded to a peerage on the death of a relative and 10 who had themselves been granted a hereditary peerage; 3) *life peers*—there were 409 lords who had been given a peerage for their own lifetime only under the Life Peerages Act 1958; 4) *Lords of Appeal* (both active and retired)—there were 26 peers, granted a peerage for life under the Appellate Jurisdiction Act 1876, in order to enable them to hear appeal cases in the House of Lords. The full House thus consists of 1,223 lords, of whom 86 are women. The average attendance at each sitting of the House is approximately 380.

The House of Commons consists of members (of both sexes) representing constituencies determined by the Boundary Commissions. Persons under 21 years of age, Clergy of the Church of England and of the Scottish Episcopal Church, Ministers of the Church of Scotland, Roman Catholic clergymen, civil servants, members of the regular armed forces, policemen, most judicial officers and other office-holders named in the House of Commons (Disqualification) Act are disqualified from sitting in the House of Commons. No peer eligible to sit in the House of Lords can be elected to the House of Commons unless he has disclaimed his title, but Irish peers and holders of courtesy titles, who are not members of the House of Lords, are eligible.

The Representation of the People Act 1948, abolished the business premises and University franchises, and the only persons entitled to vote at Parliamentary elections are those registered as residents or as service voters. No person may vote in more than one constituency at a general election. Persons may apply on certain grounds to vote by post or by proxy. Elections are held on the first-past-the-post system, in which the candidate who receives the most votes is elected.

All persons over 18 years old and not subject to any legal incapacity to vote and who are either British subjects or citizens of Ireland are entitled to be included in the register of electors for the constituency containing the address at which they were residing on the qualifying date for the register and are entitled to vote at elections held during the period for which the register remains in force.

Members of the armed forces, Crown servants employed abroad, and the wives accompanying their husbands, are entitled, if otherwise qualified, to be registered as 'service voters' provided they make a 'service declaration'. To be effective for a particular register, the declaration must be made on or before the qualifying date for that register. In certain circumstances, British subjects living abroad may also vote.

The Parliamentary Constituencies Act 1986, as amended by the Boundary Commissions Act 1992, provided for the setting up of Boundary Commissions for England, Wales, Scotland and Northern Ireland. The Commissions' last reports were made in 1995, and thereafter reports are due at intervals of not less than 8 and not more than 12 years, and to submit reports from time to time with respect to the area comprised in any particular constituency or constituencies where some change appears necessary. Any changes giving effect to reports of the Commissions are to be made by Orders in Council laid before Parliament for approval by resolution of each the register in 1994 numbered 43,786,734, of whom 36,455,151 were in England, 2,222,091 in Wales, 3,947,157 in Scotland and 1,162,335 in Northern Ireland. The registered electorate for the United Kingdom was 44,203,694 in May 1997. In 1991 it was officially estimated that 7·1% of eligible voters failed to register on the electoral roll.

At the general election held in 1997, 659 members were returned, 529 from England, 72 from Scotland, 40 from Wales and 18 from Northern Ireland. Every constituency returns a single member.

In Aug. 1911 provision was first made for the payment of a salary of £400 per annum to members of the Commons, other than those already in receipt of salaries as officers of the House, as Ministers or as officers of Her Majesty's household. For current salaries *see below*. Members of the House of Lords are unsalaried but may recover expenses incurred in attending sittings of the House within maxima for each day's attendance of £33·50 for day subsistence, £75·50 for night subsistence and £32·50 for secretarial and research assistance and office expenses. Additionally, Members of the House who are disabled may recover the extra cost of attending the House incurred by reason of their disablement. In connection with attendance at the House and parliamentary duties within the UK Lords may also recover the cost of travelling to and from home.

The executive government is vested nominally in the Crown, but practically in a committee of Ministers, called the Cabinet, which is dependent on the support of a majority in the House of Commons. The head of the Cabinet is the *Prime Minister*, a position first constitutionally recognized in 1905. The Prime Minister's colleagues in the Cabinet are appointed on his recommendation.

Governments and Prime Ministers since the Second World War (Con = Conservative Party; Lab = Labour Party):

1945–51	Lab	Clement Attlee	1970–74	Con	Edward Heath
1951–55	Con	Winston Churchill	1974–76	Lab	Harold Wilson
1955–57	Con	Anthony Eden	1976–79	Lab	James Callaghan
1957–63	Con	Harold Macmillan	1979–90	Con	Margaret Thatcher
1963–64	Con	Alec Douglas-Home	1990–97	Con	John Major
1964–70	Lab	Harold Wilson	1997–	Lab	Tony Blair

At the general election of 1 May 1997 31,286,597 votes were cast, a turn-out of 71·5%. The Labour Party won 418 seats with 43·2% of votes cast (271 with 32% in 1992); the Conservative Party 165 with 30·7% (336 with 42·8%); the Liberal Democratic Party 46 with 17·2% (20 with 18·3%); independent 1 (none); 1 seat went to the Speaker. Regional parties (Scotland): the Scottish National Party gained 6 seats (3 in 1992); (Wales): Plaid Cymru 4 (4); (Northern Ireland): the Ulster Unionist Party 10 (9); the Democratic Unionist Party 2 (3); the Social and Democratic Labour Party 3 (4); Sinn Féin 2 (nil); the United Kingdom Unionist 1 (replaced the Ulster Popular Unionist Party, 1 seat in 1992).

Labour gained 146 seats and lost none; the Conservatives gained no seats and lost 178; the Liberal Democrats gained 30 seats and lost 2.

In March 1998 the Government consisted of the following ('Rt Hon.'—Right Honourable—signifies a member of the Privy Council):

(a) 22 MEMBERS OF THE CABINET

Prime Minister, First Lord of the Treasury and Minister for the Civil Service: Rt Hon. Tony Blair, MP, b. 1953.

First Secretary of State and Deputy Prime Minister and Secretary of State for the Environment, Transport and the Regions: Rt Hon. John Prescott, MP, b. 1938.

Chancellor of the Exchequer: Rt Hon. Gordon Brown, MP, b. 1951.

Secretary of State for Foreign and Commonwealth Affairs: Rt Hon. Robin Cook, MP, b. 1946.

Lord Chancellor: Rt Hon. Lord Irvine of Lairg, QC, b. 1940.

Secretary of State for the Home Department: Rt Hon. Jack Straw, MP, b. 1946.

Secretary of State for Education and Employment: Rt Hon. David Blunkett, MP, b. 1947.

President of the Board of Trade (Secretary of State for Trade and Industry): Rt Hon. Margaret Beckett, MP, b. 1943.

Minister of Agriculture, Fisheries and Food: Rt Hon. Jack Cunningham, MP, b. 1939.

Secretary of State for Scotland: Rt Hon. Donald Dewar, MP, b. 1937.

Secretary of State for Defence: Rt Hon. George Robertson, MP, b. 1946.

Secretary of State for Health: Rt Hon. Frank Dobson, MP, b. 1940.

Lord President of the Council, Leader of the House of Commons: Rt Hon. Ann Taylor, MP, b. 1947.

Secretary of State for National Heritage: Rt Hon. Chris Smith, MP, b. 1951.

Secretary of State for Social Security and Minister for Women: Rt Hon. Harriet Harman, MP, b. 1950.

Secretary of State for Northern Ireland: Rt Hon. Marjorie ('Mo') Mowlam MP, b. 1949.

Secretary of State for Wales: Rt Hon. Ron Davies, MP, b. 1946.

Secretary of State for International Development: Rt Hon. Clare Short, MP, b. 1946.

Lord Privy Seal and Leader of the House of Lords: Rt Hon. Lord Richard of Ammanford, QC, b. 1932.

Chancellor of the Duchy of Lancaster: Rt Hon. David Clark, MP, b. 1939.

Minister of Transport: Rt Hon. Gavin Strang, MP, b. 1943.

Chief Secretary to the Treasury: Rt Hon. Alistair Darling, MP, b. 1953.

(b) LAW OFFICERS

Attorney-General: Rt Hon. John Morris, QC, MP, b. 1931.

Lord Advocate: Andrew Hardie, QC, b. 1946.

Solicitor-General: Lord Falconer of Thoroton.

Solicitor-General for Scotland: Colin Boyd, QC.

(c) MINISTERS OF STATE (BY DEPARTMENT)

Ministry of Agriculture, Fisheries and Food: Jeff Rooker, MP, b. 1941.

Department of Culture, Media and Sport: Rt Hon. Tom Clarke, CBE, MP, b. 1941, *Minister for Film and Tourism.*

Ministry of Defence: Rt Hon. Dr John Gilbert, b. 1927, *Minister for Defence Procurement;* Dr John Reid, MP, b. 1947, *Minister for the Armed Forces.*

Department for Education and Employment: Rt Hon. Andrew Smith, MP, b. 1951, *Minister for Employment and Disability Rights;* Stephen Byers, MP, b. 1953, *Minister for School Standards;* Baroness Blackstone, b. 1942; *Minister for Education and Employment.*

Department of the Environment, Transport and the Regions: Rt Hon. Michael Meacher, MP, b. 1939, *Minister for the Environment;* Hilary Armstrong, MP, b. 1945, *Minister for Local Government and Housing;* Richard Caborn, MP, b. 1943, *Minister for Regions, Regeneration and Planning.*

Foreign and Commonwealth Affairs Office: Derek Fatchett, MP, b. 1945; Tony Lloyd, MP, b. 1950; Doug Henderson, MP, b. 1949, *Minister for Europe.*

Department of Health: Alan Milburn, MP, b. 1958; Baroness Jay of Paddington, b. 1939; Tessa Jowell, MP, b. 1947, *Minister for Public Health.*

Home Office: Alun Michael, MP, b. 1943; Joyce Quin, MP, b. 1944.

Northern Ireland Office: Adam Ingram, MP, b. 1947; Paul Murphy, MP, b. 1948.

Office of Public Service: Peter Mandelson, MP, b. 1953, *Minister without portfolio* (attends Cabinet meetings).

Scottish Office: Henry McLeish, MP, b. 1948, *Minister for Home Affairs and Devolution;* Brian Wilson, MP, b. 1948, *Minister for Education and Industry.*

Department of Social Security: Rt Hon. Frank Field, MP, b. 1942, *Minister for Welfare Reform.*

Department of Trade and Industry: Sir David Simon, b. 1939, *Minister for Trade and Competitiveness in Europe;* Lord Clinton-Davis, b. 1928, *Minister for Trade;* John Battle, MP, b. 1951, *Minister for Industry;* Ian McCartney, MP, b. 1951, *Minister for Competitiveness.*

Treasury: Dawn Primarolo, MP, b. 1954, *Financial Secretary;* Geoffrey Robinson, MP, b. 1938, *Paymaster-General;* Helen Liddell, MP, b. 1950, *Economic Secretary.*

(d) PARLIAMENTARY SECRETARIES (BY DEPARTMENT)

Ministry of Agriculture, Fisheries and Food: Elliott Morley, MP, b. 1952, *Minister for Fisheries and the Countryside;* Lord Donoghue, b. 1934, *Minister for Farming and Food Industry.*

Lord Chancellor's Department: Geoff Hoon, MP, b. 1953.

Office of Public Service: Peter Kilfoyle, MP, b. 1946.

Treasury: Rt Hon. Nick Brown, MP, b. 1950, *Chief Whip.*

There were also 28 Parliamentary Under-Secretaries of State.

Leader of the Opposition in the House of Commons: William Hague, b. 1961.

Leader of the Opposition in the House of Lords: Rt. Hon. Viscount Cranbourne.

The *Speaker* of the House of Commons is Betty Boothroyd (Labour), elected for a second term on 7 May 1997.

Salaries: Members of Parliament receive an annual parliamentary salary of £43,860. The salaries of Ministers who are MPs include this as a component (since 1997 no longer reduced) in addition to their ministerial salary. Total salaries received: Prime Minister, £143,860; Cabinet Ministers, £103,860 (Cabinet Ministers in the House of Lords, £77,963); Lord Chancellor, £142,508; Ministers of State, £74,985 (in the Lords £51,838); Parliamentary Under-Secretaries, £67,483 (in the Lords, £43,632); Chief Whip, £80,473; Leader of the Opposition, £98,860 (in the Lords, £43,632); Speaker, £103,860; Attorney-General, £107,616; Lord Advocate, £78,072; Solicitor-General, £78,072; Solicitor General in Scotland, £66,811. In addition to pay, MPs are entitled to Office Costs, Supplementary London, Additional Costs, Motor Mileage, Temporary Secretarial and Winding Up Allowances, reimbursement of costs due to recall during a recess and a Resettlement Grant. Ministers receive a severance payment of 3 month's salary.

In accordance with a formula linking salaries with senior civil service pay, salaries are to increase by 2% in April 1998. The Cabinet formed in May 1997 forwent salary increases announced under the previous government until April 1998.

The Privy Council: Before the development of the Cabinet System, the Privy Council was the chief source of executive power, but now its functions are largely formal. It advises the monarch to approve Orders in Council and on the issue of royal proclamations, and has some independent powers such as the supervision of the registration of the medical profession. It consists of all Cabinet members, the Archbishops of Canterbury and York, the Speaker of the House of Commons and senior British and Commonwealth statesmen. There are a number of advisory Privy Council committees. The *Judicial Committee* is the final court of appeal from courts of the UK dependencies, the Channel Islands and the Isle of Man, and some Commonwealth countries.

Boulton, C. J. (ed.), *Erskine May's Treatise on the Law Privileges, Proceedings and Usage of Parliament.* 21st ed. London, 1990
Bruce, A., *et al. The House of Lords: 1,000 Years of British Tradition.* London, 1994
Butler, D. and Butler, G., *British Political Facts, 1900–1994.* London, 1994
Dod's Parliamentary Companion. London [published after elections]
Drewry, G. (ed.), *The New Select Committees.* OUP, 1985
Griffith, J. A. G. and Ryle, M., *Parliament: Functions, Practices and Procedures.* London, 1990
Hanson, A. H. and Walles, M., *Governing Britain: a Guidebook to Political Institutions.* 5th ed. London, 1990
Harrison, B., *The Transformation of British Politics, 1860–1995.* OUP, 1996
Hennessy, P., *Whitehall.* London, 1989
King, A. (ed.), *The British Prime Minister.* Rev. ed. London, 1985
Norris, P., *Electoral Change in Britain since 1945.* Oxford, 1996
Parker, F. K., *Conduct of Parliamentary Elections.* London, 1983
Shell, D., *The House of Lords.* 2nd ed. Hemel Hempstead, 1992
Silk, E. P., *How Parliament Works.* London, 1987
The Times Guide to the House of Commons. London, [published after elections]
Waller, R., *The Almanac of British Politics.* 4th ed. London, 1991

National anthem: God Save the Queen (King) (words and tune anonymous; earliest known printed source, 1744).

European Parliament: The United Kingdom has 87 representatives. At the June 1994 elections turn-out was 36·4%. The Labour Party won 62 seats with 44·2% of votes cast (group in European Parliament: European Socialist Party); the Conservative Party, 18 with 27·8% (Popular European Party); the Liberal Democratic Party, 2 with 16·7% (Liberal, Democratic and Reformist Group); the Scottish National Party, 2 with 3·2% (European Radical Alliance). Voting for these parties was on the first-past-the-post system. Voting in Northern Ireland was by the single transferable vote system: the Democratic Ulster Unionist Party, the Social Democrat and Labour Party (European Socialist Party) and the Official Ulster Union Party (Popular European Party) gained 1 seat each.

Local Administration: This is carried out by 4 different types of bodies, namely: (i) local branches of some central ministries, such as the Departments of Health and Social Security; (ii) local sub-managements of nationalized industries; (iii) specialist authorities such as the National Rivers Authority; and (iv) the system of local government described below. The phrase 'local government' has come to mean that part of the local administration conducted by elected councils. There are separate systems for England, Wales and Scotland. For local government finance *see* Budget: *Local Taxation*, below.

The Local Government Act 1992 established a Local Government Commission, which completed its report in 1996 on whether the two-tier local government structure should be replaced by unitary authorities in some areas. Following its recommendations, 27 new unitary councils had been established by April 1997. The Commission is currently reviewing electoral arrangements.

Local Government: One of the main aspects of the Government's programme of constitutional reform is Scottish and Welsh devolution. In the referendum on Scottish devolution on 11 Sept. 1997, 1,775,045 votes (74·3%) were cast in favour of a Scottish parliament and 614,400 against (25·7%). The turn-out was 60·4%, so around 44·8% of the total electorate voted in favour. For the second question, on the Parliament's tax-raising powers, 1,512,889 votes were cast in favour (63·5%) and 870,263 against (36·5%). This represented 38·4% of the total electorate.

On 18 Sept. 1997 in Wales there were 559,419 votes cast in favour of a Welsh assembly (50·3%) and 552,698 against (49·7%). The turn-out was 51·3%.

Local authorities have statutory powers and claims on public funds. Relations with central government are maintained through the Department of the Environment in England, and through the Welsh and Scottish Offices. In England the Home Office and the Department of Education and Employment are also concerned with some local government functions. (These are performed by departments within the Welsh and Scottish Offices). Ministers have powers of intervention to protect individuals' rights and safeguard public health, and the Government has power to cap (i.e. limit) local authority budgets.

Local government is conducted by elected councils at different levels of administration. England, Wales and Scotland have different systems. In England, changes introduced by the Local Government Commission set up in 1992 included the introduction of single-tier unitary authorities alongside the previous two-tier county and district administrations. By 1997 there were (*two-tier*) 35 non-metropolitan county councils under which were 274 district councils and the Scilly Isles and (*single-tier*) 27 unitary authorities, 36 metropolitan district councils and 32 Greater London borough councils. In Wales, the Local Government (Wales) Act 1994 set up 22 unitary authorities (9 counties and 13 county boroughs), and in Scotland the Local Government (Scotland) Act 1994 set up 29 unitary authorities alongside the existing 3 Island Authority Areas. Greater London and the 6 metropolitan counties no longer have councils, the former county functions having devolved to the boroughs and districts, but some services (e.g. fire services) are administered by joint authorities nominated by the latter. In England there are also some 10,000 parishes, of which about 800 have elected councils. About 300 are former small boroughs or urban districts which became successor parishes. Parish councils manage local facilities and may act as agents for district council functions. In Wales, similar functions are discharged by 730 community councils. In Scotland there are about 1,000 community councils, but unlike their English and Welsh counterparts, they do not have statutory powers.

Resident citizens of the UK, Ireland, a Commonwealth country or an EU country may (at age 18) vote and (at age 21) stand for election. In England, councils are elected for 4 years, except that in the metropolitan and one-third of the other districts, one-third of councillors are elected in each of the 3 years that no county council election is held. Counties are divided into electoral divisions and districts into wards. In Wales, elections for the full councils are held every 4 years, and in Scotland every 3 years. The chair of the council is one of the councillors elected by the rest. In boroughs and cities his or her title is Mayor. Mayors of cities may have the title of Lord Mayor conferred on them. 51 towns in England and Wales and 4 in Scotland have the status of city. This status is granted by the personal command of the monarch and confers no special privileges or powers. In Scotland, the chair of city councils is deemed Lord Provost, and is elsewhere known as Convenor or Provost. In Wales, the chair is called Chairman in counties and Mayor in county boroughs. Any parish or community council can by simple resolution adopt the style 'town council' and the status of town for the parish or community. Basic and other allowances are payable to councillors (except Scottish community councillors).

Functions. Legislation in the 1980s initiated a trend for local authorities to arrange for the provision of services by, or in collaboration with, commercial or voluntary bodies rather than provide them directly. Savings in expenditure are encouraged by compulsory competitive tendering. In England, county councils are responsible for strategic planning, transport planning, non-trunk roads and regulation of traffic, personal social services, consumer protection, disposal of waste, the fire and library services and partially for education. District councils are responsible for environmental health, housing, local planning applications (in the first instance) and refuse collection. Unitary authorities combine the functions of both levels.

Finance. Revenue is derived from the Council Tax, which supports about one-fifth of current expenditure, the remainder being funded by central government grants and by the redistribution of revenue from the national non-domestic rate (property tax). Capital expenditure is financed by borrowing within government-set limits and sales of real estate.

Election Results. Elections for one third of the seats on the councils of the 32 London boroughs, 36 metropolitan districts and 118 non-metropolitan districts were held on 5 May 1994. The Labour Party gained control of 93 councils; the Liberal Democratic Party, 19; the Conservative Party, 15; ind, 5. There was no overall majority in 54 councils.

Elections were held outside the metropolitan areas ('the shires') on 4 May 1995. Labour made a net gain of 155 councils, the Liberal Democrats 45 and the Conservatives lost 51.

At the elections of 2 May 1996 for 32 metropolitan and 114 non-metropolitan and unitary councils, Labour took control of 84 councils and gained 431 seats, the Liberal Democrats took control of 23 councils and gained 142 seats, the Conservatives took control of 3 councils and lost 534 seats, and independents took control of 3 councils and lost 29 seats. In 33 councils no party gained an absolute majority.

On 6 April 1995 elections were held for the 29 newly-created unitary councils. 1,161 seats were contested. Labour won 614 seats with 47% of votes cast, and gained control of 20 of the councils; the Scottish National Party won 181 seats with 26% and gained 3 councils; the Liberal Democrats won 123 seats with 10%; the Conservative Party won 81 seats with 11%. Independents gained control of 3 councils, and 3 councils had no overall control.

County council elections and those for 19 further new unitary authorities took place on 1 May 1997. Elections for the 1,014 seats on the unitary authorities created shadow councils whose job was to prepare the area for transfer to the new status in April 1998. Councillors for these areas did not stand for election but will step down in April 1998 leaving those elected on 1 May 1997 in charge.

The next elections in Wales and Scotland are scheduled for 1999.

DEFENCE. The Defence Council was established on 1 April 1964 under the chairmanship of the Secretary of State for Defence, who is responsible to the Sovereign and Parliament for the defence of the realm. Vested in the Defence Council are the functions of commanding and administering the Armed Forces. The Secretary of State heads the Department of Defence. There are 3 subordinate Ministers; 2 Ministers of State and 1 Parliamentary Under-Secretary of State.

Defence Council membership comprises the Secretary of State, the 3 Ministers mentioned above, the Chief of the Defence Staff, the 3 single Service Chiefs of Staff, the Vice-Chief of Defence Staff, the Chief of Defence Procurement, the Chief Scientific Adviser, the Permanent Under-Secretary of State and the Second Permanent Under Secretary of State.

There are 3 Service Boards, each of which enjoys delegated powers for the administration of matters relating to the naval, military and air forces respectively.

Defence policy decision making is a collective Governmental responsibility. Important matters of policy are considered by the full Cabinet or, more frequently, by the Defence and Oversea Policy Committee under the chairmanship of the Prime Minister. Other members of this Committee include the Secretary of State for Defence, the Foreign and Commonwealth Secretary and the Home Secretary.

The Procurement Executive is responsible for procurement of equipment and supplies.

The ban on homosexuals serving in the armed forces was upheld by a House of Commons vote in May 1996.

Defence Budget: 1996–97, £21,425m. Estimates for 1997–98, £21,923m.; 1998–99, £22,624m.

Army. Control of the British Army is vested in the Defence Council and is exercised through the Army Board. The Secretary of State for Defence is Chairman of the Army Board. The other civilian members are the 3 subordinate Ministers and the Second Permanent Under Secretary of State.

The Military members of the Army Board are the Chief of the General Staff, the Adjutant General, the Quartermaster General, the Master General of the Ordnance, the C.-in-C. Land Command and the Assistant Chief of General Staff. The Chief of the General Staff is the professional head of his Service and the professional adviser to Ministers on the Army aspects of military matters. He is responsible for the fighting efficiency of his Service; for Army advice on the conduct of operations; and for the issuing of such single Service operational orders as may be appropriate resulting from defence policy decisions. He is also responsible for the Territorial Army. The Chief of the General Staff is a member of the Chiefs of Staff Committee which is chaired by the Chief of the Defence Staff, who is responsible to HM Government for professional advice on strategy and military operations and on the military implication of defence policy. The Adjutant-General is responsible for recruiting and selection of army manpower; for the administration and individual training of military personnel; for the discipline of the Army; for pay and allowances and pensions; for legal services; for the veterinary and remount services; for the Army Cadet Forces; for questions of Army welfare and education including school children overseas; and for resettlement and sports. The Quartermaster-General is responsible for logistic planning for the Army; for the storage, distribution, maintenance, repair and inspection of equipment, stores and ammunition; for development of stores; for supply, transport and accommodation; for the development, production and inspection of clothing; for military movements and transportation; for the Army postal, catering, salvage and fire services; and for questions connected with canteens, institutes and military labour. The Master General of the Ordnance is a member of both the Army Board and of the Procurement Executive Management Board. He is responsible to the Chief of Defence Procurement for the financial and technical management of the approved programme for the procurement of service equipment for the Armed Services, and to the Army Board for the co-ordination of the Army's total equipment programme.

The Field Army is run from Headquarters Land Command, based at Wilton. This consists of 2 operational divisions, 3 reserve divisions, 2 districts and United

Kingdom Support Command (Germany) (UKSC(G)). 1 (UK) Armoured Division, based in Germany, has 3 armoured brigades each consisting of 2 tank regiments, 2 armoured infantry battalions and supported by artillery, engineers, aviation, air defence and logistics units. 3 (UK) Division, based in the UK, consists of 2 mechanized and 1 airborne brigade, together with artillery, engineers, aviation, air defence and logistics units. Other forces assigned to NATO's Rapid Reaction Corps (ARRC) include 24 Airmobile Brigade, a reconnaissance Brigade, intelligence and Electronic Warfare units, signals regiments, a depth artillery brigade, air defence regiments, engineers and some general duty infantry battalions.

The Ministry of Defence retains direct control of units in Northern Ireland, although day to day military responsibility is given to the Chief of the General Staff. The Permanent Joint Headquarters, recently formed at Northwood, is resposible for overseas garrisons, which include the Falkland Islands, Cyprus and Brunei.

The established strength of the Regular Army in 1996 was 114,000 which includes soldiers under training and Gurkhas. In addition there were some 4,000 Royal Irish Home Service soldiers. The strengths of the Regular Reserves was 212,000.

The role of the Territorial Army (TA) is to act as a general Reserve for the Army by reinforcing it as required, with individuals, sub-units and other units, either in the UK or overseas; and by providing the framework and basis for regeneration and reconstruction to cater for unforeseen in times of national emergency. The TA also provides a nationwide link between the military and civil communities. Strength, 1996, 55,000. In addition, men who have completed service in the Regular Army normally have some liability to serve in the Regular Reserve. All members of the TA and Regular Reserve may be called out by a Queen's Order in time of emergency of imminent national danger and most of the TA and a large proportion of the Regular Reserve may be called out by a Queen's Order when warlike operations are in preparation or in progress. The Home Service Battalions of the Royal Irish Regiment are only liable for service in Northern Ireland.

Men, women and juniors enlist in the Army for up to 22 years' active service and reserve service up to 45 years of age. Soldiers enlist for a minimum of 3 years and can leave active service thereafter on one year's notice. Bonuses are paid to those who serve for certain periods and there are manning control points at which the Army may require soldiers to terminate their service, again on one year's notice. Those enlisting in certain technical trades must agree to serve for a minimum of 3 years. Recruits under the age of $17^1/_2$ on reaching the age of 18 are entitled either to confirm their original engagement or to reduce their period of service to 3 years.

Equipment includes 426 Challenger, 36 Challenger 2 and 79 Chieftain main battle tanks, 8 Scorpion light tanks, 1,225 armoured fighting vehicles, 524 artillery pieces, 63 multiple rocket launchers, 880 anti-tank guided weapons and 562 surface-to-air missiles.

Women serve throughout the Army in the same regiments and corps as men. There are only a few roles in which they are not employed such as the Infantry and Royal Armoured Corps.

Brereton, J. M., *The British Soldier*. London, 1985
The Oxford Illustrated History of the British Army. OUP, 1995
Strawson, J., *Gentlemen in Khaki: the British Army, 1890–1990*. London, 1985

Navy. Control of the Royal Navy is vested in the Defence Council and is exercised through the Admiralty Board, chaired by the Secretary of State for Defence. The other civilian members are the Ministers of State for the Armed Forces and Defence Procurement, the Parliamentary Under Secretary for Defence and the Second Permanent Under Secretary of State. The naval members are the Chief of Naval Staff (First Sea Lord) responsible for management, fighting efficiency, planning and operational advice; the combined Second Sea Lord and C.-in-C. Naval Home Command, responsible for the manning of the Fleet and all personnel aspects; the Controller of the Navy, responsible for procurement of ships, their weapons and equipment; the Chief of Fleet Support, responsible for logistic support, stores, fuels and transport, naval dockyards and the auxiliary services; the C.-in-C. Fleet, and the Assistant Chief of Naval Staff, responsible for co-ordinating advice on certain policy and operational matters. The Navy Board, an executive sub-committee of the Admiralty Board, is responsible for the professional management of the service.

In 1996, the changes in management structure, reductions in strength, base closures and rationalization initiated in 1994 began to approach completion. The Chief of Fleet Support and Controller of the Navy are now located in the Bristol area and their various support agencies rationalized. The naval bases at Rosyth and Portland closed in 1995. Although the dockyards at Rosyth and Devonport remain largely committed to naval refit work, both yards have now been sold to commercial operators.

The C.-in-C. Fleet, headquartered at Northwood, is responsible for the command of the fleet, while command of naval establishments in the UK is exercised by the C.-in-C. Naval Home Command from Portsmouth. Main naval bases are at Devonport, Portsmouth and Faslane, with a minor base overseas at Gibraltar.

The Royal Naval Reserve (RNR) and the Royal Marines Reserve (RMR) are volunteer forces which together in 1996 numbered 3,450. The RNR provides trained personnel in war to supplement regular forces. The main roles of the RMR are reinforcement and other specialist tasks with the UK-Netherlands Amphibious Force. In addition, men who have completed service in the Royal Navy and the Royal Marines have a commitment to serve in the Royal Fleet Reserve, currently 23,000 strong.

Royal Navy and Queen Alexandra's Royal Naval Nursing Service (QARNNS) ratings, both male and female, and Royal Marine ranks enlist on the 'Open Engagement' to complete 22 years active service with the option to leave at 18 months notice on completion of a minimum of 2 and a half years productive service. Those who leave before completing 22 years have a liability for up to 3 years service in the Royal Fleet Reserve.

The roles of the Royal Navy are first, to deploy the national strategic nuclear deterrent, second to provide maritime defence of the UK and its dependent territories, third to contribute to the maritime elements of NATO's force structure and fourth to meet national maritime objectives outside the NATO area. Personnel strength has reduced steadily over the past 5 years and is now stabilizing at about 47,500 (including Royal Marines) in 1997, with operational strength at 12 nuclear attack submarines, 2 aircraft carriers and about 35 destroyers and frigates.

The strategic deterrent is now borne principally by the new Trident submarines, of which the first 3 of 4, *Vanguard, Victorious* and *Vigilant*, each of 15,250 tonnes, and deploying 16 US-built Trident-2 D5 UGM-133A missiles with up to 96 British warheads per operational load, are now operational. The fourth ship, *Vengeance*, is scheduled to be operational in 1999. The last missile submarine of the Resolution class, *Renown*, deploying Polaris missiles, decommissioned in Aug. 1996.

The strength of the fleet's major units at the end of the respective years:

	1991	1992	1993	1994	1995	1996
Strategic Submarines	4	4	4	3	3	3
Nuclear Submarines	15	13	13	12	12	12
Diesel Submarines	6	4	4	nil	nil	nil
Aircraft Carriers	2[1]	2[1]	2[1]	2[1]	2[1]	2[1]
Destroyers	12	12	12	12	12	12
Frigates	33	30	25	24	23	23

[1] Following Government policy, of the 3 Carriers held, only 2 are kept in operational status.

The nuclear-powered submarine force numbers 12, of 2 classes, armed with torpedoes and Harpoon anti-ship missiles. There are 7 Trafalgar class, (5,300 tonnes) completed 1983–1991 and 5 Swiftsure (4,900 tonnes) completed 1973–79. The 4 diesel-electric submarines of the Upholder class were decommissioned in 1994 but remain serviceable awaiting a possible purchaser.

The principal surface ships are the Light vertical/short take-off and landing Aircraft Carriers of the Invincible class, (*Invincible, Illustrious* and *Ark Royal*), 20,900 tonnes, completed 1980–85, embarking an air group of 8 Sea Harrier vertical/short take-off and landing fighters, 9 anti-submarine Sea King and 3 radar early warning Sea King helicopters, armed with 1 twin Sea Dart surface-to-air missile system. 2 of these ships are maintained in the operational fleet, with the third (currently *Ark Royal*) either in refit or reserve.

The 12 destroyers are all Type 42 (completed 1976–85), armed with 1 twin Sea Dart surface-to-air missile system. Frigates comprise 10 Type 22 (completed 1979–89) and 13 Norfolk class (Type 23) completed 1989–96.

The lightly-armed patrol force comprises 1 ice patrol ship, 16 other offshore patrol vessels and 16 inshore patrol craft mostly employed in training. Mine counter-measures capability is provided by 13 offshore hunter/sweepers and 5 coastal mine-hunters. Amphibious lift for the Royal Marines is provided by 1 dock landing ship (with a second in reserve) and 5 tank landing ships (civil manned, and in peacetime employed on army freighting), supported by about 32 small amphibious craft. A new Helicopter Carrier, specifically designed for amphibious operations, HMS *Ocean*, 16,000 tonnes, has completed initial sea trials and is fitting out for entry into service in 1998.

Comprehensive support to the fleet is provided by 27 major auxiliaries including 5 replenishment and 4 support tankers, 2 multi-purpose fuel and ammunition ships, 3 ammunition and stores ships, 1 repair ship, 2 ocean tugs, 5 survey ships, 1 trials ship, 1 aviation training ship, 2 armament transports and the Royal Yacht. Second-line support is provided by about 200 harbour and coastal service craft and minor auxiliaries.

The Fleet Air Arm, 5,500 strong in 1996, has some 300 aircraft, in 19 operational, training and search-and-rescue squadrons, including 40 Sea Harrier vertical/short take-off and landing fighter aircraft, 70 Sea King and 76 Lynx anti-submarine helicopters, 10 Sea King airborne early warning helicopters and 36 Sea King (commando transports) and 70 miscellaneous support and training craft.

The Royal Marines corps, 6,750 strong in 1996, provides a commando brigade comprising 3 commando groups, each approximately 1,000 strong with artillery, air defence, engineering and logistic support, and three light utility helicopter squadrons. The Special Boat Squadron and specialist defence units complete the operational strength. Equipment includes 15 helicopters and 30 light assault craft.

The total number of male and female personnel (including Royal Marines) was (in 1,000) on 31 March: 1993, 59·4; 1994, 55·8; 1995, 50·9; 1996, 48·5 and 1997 (estimated), 47·5.

Jane's Fighting Ships. London, annual
The Oxford Illustrated History of the Royal Navy. OUP, 1996

Air Force. In May 1912 the Royal Flying Corps first came into existence with military and naval wings, of which the latter became the independent Royal Naval Air Service in July 1914. On 2 Jan. 1918 an Air Ministry was formed, and on 1 April 1918 the Royal Flying Corps and the Royal Naval Air Service were amalgamated, under the Air Ministry, as the Royal Air Force (RAF).

In 1937 the units based on aircraft carriers and naval shore stations again passed to the operational and administrative control of the Admiralty, as the Fleet Air Arm. In 1964 control of the RAF became a responsibility of the Ministry of Defence.

The RAF is administered by the Air Force Board, of which the Secretary of State for Defence is Chairman. The Minister of State for the Armed Forces is Vice-Chairman, and normally acts as Chairman on behalf of the Secretary of State. Other members of the Board are the Minister of State for Defence Procurement, the Under-Secretary of State for Defence, the Chief of the Air Staff, Air Member for Personnel, Air Member for Logistics, Air Officer Commanding-in-Chief Strike Command, Controller of Aircraft and the Second Permanent Under-Secretary of State.

The RAF is organized into 3 commands: Strike Command, Personnel and Training Command and Logistics Command.

Strike Command is responsible for all of the RAF's frontline forces, although day-to-day control of most operations is delegated to its 3 Groups. No 1 Group is respon-sible for strike/attack, offensive air support, support helicopters and reconnaissance. Tornado GR1s and Tornado GR1As are used in the strike, attack and reconnaissance roles, while Tornado GR1Bs are used primarily in the maritime attack role. Jaguars are used in the attack, reconnaissance and light anti-shipping roles. Battlefield support forces comprise Harrier GR7s, as well as Chinook, Puma and Wessex helicopters. No 1 Group also operates Canberra aircraft in the strategic photographic reconnaissance role. No 11/18 Group controls the air defence forces, Tornado F3 fighters and Boeing E-3D Airborne Early Warning aircraft, together with ground environment radars, associated communications systems and the Ballistic Missile Early Warning System at Fylingdales. Maritime air operations, together with the RAF's search and rescue flights, are also under the operational control of No 11/18 Group. A maritime patrol and anti-submarine warfare capability is provided by Nimrod aircraft, which also have a capability against surface ships. The search and rescue flights are equipped with Sea King helicopters. Additionally No 11/18 Group operates Nimrod Reconnaissance aircraft. No 38 Group is responsible for air-to-air refuelling and strategic air transport, which is carried out by VC10, Tristar and Hercules aircraft. No 38 Group also controls the aircraft of No 32 (The Royal) Squadron, comprising British Aerospace 146 and 125 aircraft and Wessex and Twin Squirrel helicopters. RAF forces in Germany, which are made up of Tornado GR1s, Harrier GR7s and Chinook and Puma helicopters, are under the day-to-day control of No 1 Group. The Military Air Traffic Operations organization also has the status of a Group.

The RAF Regiment, which is under the control of No 38 Group, has field squadrons in service with No 1 Group and short-range air defence squadrons armed with Rapier in service with No 1 Group and No 11/18 Group.

As well as the forces in Germany, the RAF has a flight of Tornado F3s, a flight of Hercules and a combined squadron comprising RAF Chinooks and Royal Navy Sea King helicopters based in the Falkland Islands, and a squadron of Wessex helicopters in Cyprus. In addition, Strike Command forces are deployed overseas in support of UN/WEU and Coalition operations.

Headquarters RAF Strike Command is based at RAF High Wycombe.

Personnel and Training Command was formed at RAF Innsworth on 1 April 1994.

2 agencies fall under the Command, the Training Group Defence Agency and the Personnel Management Agency (which formed on 1 Feb. 1997). The main RAF units within the Command are, for Ground Training: RAF Cosford, RAF Cranwell, RAF Halton and RAF Locking; for Flying Training: RAF Cranwell (where the Red Arrows are based), RAF Linton-on-Ouse, RAF Shawbury and RAF Valley. Initial Officer Training for commissioned candidates is undertaken at the RAF College, Cranwell. Further command and staff training for officers takes place at the Joint Service Command and Staff College, which was formed on 1 Jan. 1997 at Bracknell. Recruit training is undertaken at RAF Halton. A single, tri-Service Defence Helicopter Flying School was formed at RAF Shawbury on 1 April 1997.

Personnel and Training Command is equipped with the following aircraft types: Bulldog and Slingsby Firefly as primary trainers, Tucano as basic trainers for fast jet aircrew, Hawk as advanced fast jet trainers, Jetstreams for multi-engine pilot training, and Dominies for training navigators and other non-pilot aircrew. The Defence Helicopter Flying School uses Squirrel and Griffin helicopters.

Logistics Command was formed on 1 April 1994, with its headquarters at RAF Brampton and nearby RAF Wyton. The Command is responsible for providing the full range of logistics support activities to all RAF units worldwide and Joint Service support to Royal Navy and Army units for rationalized equipment ranges. It is responsible for: Support chain management, including the provisioning, storage, distribution and disposal of equipment; repair, overhaul, maintenance and modification programmes at 3rd and 4th line; provision and management of communications and information systems; RAF catering.

RAF personnel, 1 Jan. 1998, 56,064 (including 5,017 women). Since Dec. 1991 women have been eligible to fly combat aircraft. Total trained personnel, 1 Jan. 1998, 52,978.

McIntosh, M., *Managing British Defence*. London, 1990

INTERNATIONAL RELATIONS

Membership. The UK is a member of the UN, Commonwealth, the EU, OECD, the Council of Europe, the Pacific Community, WEU and NATO.

ECONOMY

Following the recession of 1990–92, the British economy has experienced continuous growth combined with low inflation; total output was in mid-1997 13% above the previous peak reached in 1990, although, within this overall figure, manufacturing output is only just under 5% higher.

The Treasury's Red Book, which sets out the government's tax and spending plans, says the aim of the 1998 Budget is to 'help turn the ambitions of many into achievements', by securing economic stability, rewarding work and encouraging enterprise. It includes details of the government's reforms to the tax and benefits system.

Spending. Government spending—excluding privatization proceeds—will be £326·5bn. in 1998–99. There are no privatization proceeds forecast for 1998–99. Spending plans over the medium term will be set after the Comprehensive Spending Review has been completed.

Tax changes. In total, the Budget increases annual tax receipts by £1·75bn., £2·25bn. and £2·75bn., between 1998–99 and 2000–01. Most of this extra revenue reflects the measures on company taxation and cars. Total receipts are projected to be £330bn. in 1998–99, rising to £344bn. in 1999–2000. Revenue in 1998–99 includes £126bn. from the Inland Revenue, net of tax credits, and £95·6bn. from Customs and Excise. VAT receipts are projected to rise from £51bn. to £53·3bn. in 1998–99. Taxes and social security contributions as a percentage of GDP will be 0·5 percentage points higher in 1998–99 over the previous year, at 37·7%. Total receipts will be 39·6% of GDP. Total net tax receipts are projected to have grown by 9·5% in 1997–98. Net tax receipts are projected to grow by 6% in 1998–99, reflecting real increases in fuel and tobacco duties.

Public Expenditure (in £1bn.)

	1996–97	1997–98
	Outturn	
Control Total	260·4	266·4
Welfare-to-Work	–	0·2
Local authority spending under the Capital Receipts Initiative	–	0·2
Cyclical social security	14·3	13·7
Central government debt interest	22·3	24·6
Accounting adjustments	11·4	10·1
General government expenditure	308·4	315·3
Privatization proceeds	-4·4	-2·0
Lottery-financed spending and interest and dividend receipts	5·1	6·2
General government expenditure	309·0	319·4

Note: Differences between totals and the sums of their component parts are due to rounding.

Projected Public Expenditure, Receitps and Borrowing Requirement (in £1bn.)

	1996–97	1997–98
General government expenditure	309·0	319·4
of which: Control Total	*260·4*	*266·4*
General government receipts	286·3	308·3
of which: income tax	*69·5*	*76·5*
corporation tax	*27·7*	*30·1*
VAT	*46·7*	*50·0*
fuel, alcohol and tobacco duties	*30·6*	*33·4*
social security contributions	*47·4*	*49·5*
Public sector borrowing requirement (PSBR)	22·7	10·9
PSBR[1] as percentage of GDP	3	1·75

[1] Excluding windfall tax and associated spending.

Government Receipts and Expenditure 1997–98

Sources of Revenue		Expenditure	
Income tax	23%	Social Security	32%
Social Security Contributions	16%	Health and Personal Social Services	17%
VAT	16%	Education	12%
Excise Duties	11%	Debt Interest	8%
Corporation Tax	9%	Defence	7%
Other Taxes and Royalties	8%	Housing, Heritage and the Environment	5%
Borrowing	6%	Law and Order	5%
Business Rates	5%	Industry, Agriculture and Employment	4%
Council Tax	3%	Transport	3%
Other Financing	4%	Other Expenditure	7%

Note: As a result of rounding and omission of minor items, percentages do not necessarily total 100.

General Government Receipts 1998–99 (in £1bn.)

Income tax	86·1
Social Security Contributions	53·7
VAT	53·3
Corporation Tax	30·0
Fuel Duties	21·5
Indirect Levies Including Alcohol and Tobacco	20·9
Council Tax and Other Levies	18·8
Business Rates	15·0
Other Inland Revenue Taxes Including Windfall Tax	11·8
Gross Trading Surpluses and Rent	11·5
Interest and Dividends	4·5
Other Receipts	4·9
Total Receipts[1] (excluding North Sea Revenues)	330·1

[1] Excluding £1·8bn. income tax credits.

The UK economy's momentum is unlikely to be maintained. A slowdown in real income growth is expected, employment growth is likely to slow and the exceptional growth in financial incomes seen in recent years is expected to weaken. Business investment is forecast to decelerate, although it is projected to rise as a share of GDP.

Growth. Depending on an improvement in labour market performance, GDP is forecast to grow 2–2·5% this year. The outlook for exports in the traded goods sector is problematic, with the effect of sterling's 25% appreciation compounded by financial developments in Asia. Consumer spending is forecast to grow 3·75–4% this year. Growth in 1999 is projected at 1·75–2·25%. The savings ratio is assumed to decline to 9% by 2000.

Inflation. In March 1998 the Treasury forecast slightly weaker inflationary pressures since its pre-Budget report in November 1997, reflecting slower growth in the early part of 1998 together with direct downwar pressure on traded goods prices. In March 1998 the Retail Price Index was forecast to be around 3% in the second quarter of the year, and 2·75% in the fourth quarter. But 'downstream' inflationary pressure could be stronger than expected if demand and wage pressures are higher than forecast.

Department Expenditure. Expenditure by department for year ended 31 March 1997 and the estimates for the year 1997–98 (in £1m.):

	Expenditure	
	1996–97	1997–98
Defence	22,130	21,810
Foreign Office	1,100	1,080
Overseas Development	2,340	2,220
Agriculture, Fisheries and Food	4,410	3,610
Trade and Industry	2,730	3,050
Transport	4,870	5,190
Local government	31,320	31,380
Environment	8,380	7,600

	Expenditure	
	1996–97	*1997–98*
Home Office	6,550	6,780
Legal departments	2,730	2,710
Education and Employment	14,810	13,950
National Heritage	1,020	920
Health	33,970	34,940
Social Security	76,920	79,740
Jobseekers' Allowance and Income Support	14,300	14,100
Scotland	15,590	14,330
Wales	6,820	6,900
Northern Ireland	8,190	8,220
Chancellor's departments	3,270	3,170
Cabinet Office	1,330	1,080
European Communities	1,400	2,250
Debt interest	22,200	24,800

Currency. The unit of currency is the *pound sterling* (£; GBP) of 100 *pence* (p.). (Before decimalization on 15 Feb. 1971 £1 = 20 shillings (*s*) of 12 pence (*d*). A gold standard was adopted in 1816, the sovereign or twenty-shilling piece weighing 7·98805 grammes 0·916²⁄₃ fine. Currency notes for £1 and 10*s*. were first issued by the Treasury in 1914, replacing the circulation of sovereigns. The issue of £1 and 10*s*. notes was taken over by the Bank of England in 1928. 10*s*. notes were withdrawn in 1970 and £1 notes (in England and Wales) in 1988. The UK is a member of the EU European Monetary System (EMS), but on 16 Sept. 1992 it suspended its membership of the Exchange Rate Mechanism (ERM), which it had entered on 8 Oct. 1990. Inflation was 2·9% in Dec. 1994 (1·9% in Dec. 1993).

Coinage. There are coins of 1, 2, 5, 10, 20 and 50p. and £1 and £2. A new, smaller 50p. coin was issued on 1 Sept. 1997 and a new, bi-colour £2 coin on 1 Nov. The old 50p was demonetized on 28 Feb. 1998.

There are in addition Britannia gold bullion coins with a face value of £100, £50, £20 and £10, and commemorative £5 crowns and £2 coins.

Coins in circulation at 31 Dec. 1996: £1, 1,095m.; 50p, 442m.; 20p, 1,630m.; 10p, 1,416m.; 5p, 2,999m.; 2p, 4,411m.; 1p, 7,239m.

Bank notes. The Bank of England issues notes in denominations of £5, £10, £20 and £50 for the amount of the fiduciary issue. Under the provisions of the Currency Act, 1983 the amount of the fiduciary issue is limited, but can be altered by direction of HM Treasury on the advice of the Bank of England. Since Feb. 1993 the limit has been £20,600m.

In Scotland the Bank of Scotland, Clydesdale Bank and the Royal Bank of Scotland have note-issuing powers. There is a £1 note in Scotland.

The total amount of Bank of England notes issued at 31 Dec. 1996 was £22,620m., of which £22,609m. represented notes with other banks and the public, and £11m. notes in the Banking Department of the Bank of England.

Banking and Finance. The Bank of England, Threadneedle Street, London, is the Government's banker and the 'banker's bank'. It has the sole right of note issue in England and Wales and manages the National Debt. It was founded by Royal Charter in 1694 and nationalized in 1946. The capital stock has, since 1 March 1946, been held by HM Treasury. The *Governor* (appointed for 5-year terms) is Eddie George (b. 1938; took office 1993).

The statutory Bank Return is published weekly. End-Dec. figures for the past 4 years are as follows (in £1m.):

	Notes in circulation	*Notes and coin in Banking Department*	*Public deposits (government)*	*Other deposits*[1]
1994	20,448	12	1,027	5,198
1995	21,720	3	1,281	5,281
1996	22,620	11	203	5,691

[1] Including Special Deposits.

Official reserves of gold and convertible currencies, SDR and reserve position in the IMF at the end of Dec. 1993 were US$42,926m. The value of paper-based credit transfers for 1993 was 432·2m. (volumes); of paperless credit transfers, 935·7m. (volumes); of direct debits, 1,046m. (volumes).

Major British Banking Groups' statistics at 31 Dec. 1996: Total deposits (sterling and currency), £627,874m.; sterling market loans, £116,361m.; market loans (sterling and currency), £182,330m.; advances (sterling and currency), £396,643m.; sterling investments, £50,430m.

In 1996 there were 520 overseas banks from 76 countries.

In May 1997 the power to set base interest rates was transferred from the Treasury to the Bank of England. The government continues to set the inflation target but the bank has responsibility for setting interest rates to meet the target. Base rates are now set by a 9-member Monetary Policy Committee at the Bank; members include the Governor. Membership of the Court (the governing body) was widened. Responsibility for supervising banks was transferred from the Bank to the Securities and Investments Board.

National Savings Bank. Statistics for 1995 and 1996 (provisional):

	Ordinary accounts		Investment accounts	
	1995	1996	1995	1996
Accounts opened at 31 Dec.	15,988,061 [1]	16,039,050 [1]	4,590,238	4,507,525
Amounts—	£1,000	£1,000	£1,000	£1,000
Received	623,558	647,040	1,257,287	1,508,928
Interest credited	39,332 [2]	32,976 [2]	523,689	499,566
Paid	678,105	688,491	1,783,643	1,846,771
Due to depositors at 31 Dec.	1,418,783	1,410,308	9,307,177	9,468,900
Average amount due to each depositor	£88·74	87·93	£2,027·60	£2,100·69

[1] Excluding non-computerized accounts, amounting to £101m. in 1995 and £102m. in 1996.
[2] The interest credited to depositors for the Ordinary account for 1996 was calculated on the same basis as 1995. The interest rate was lowered twice during the year; from 2·75% to 2·5%, payable to accounts with a minimum balance of £500, and from 1·75% to 1·5% on accounts with a minimum balance of less than £500. Interest is earned on each whole pound on deposit for complete calendar months.

The amount due to depositors on Ordinary Accounts on 1 Jan. 1998 was £1,416,556,595 and in Investment Accounts £9,220,546,660.

There are stock exchanges in Belfast, Birmingham, Glasgow and Manchester, which function mainly as representative offices for the London Stock Exchange (called International Stock Exchange until May 1991). In July 1991 the 91 shareholders voted unanimously for a new memorandum and articles of association which devolves power to a wider range of participants in the securities industry and replaces the Stock Exchange Council with a 14-member board.

Roberts, R. and Kynaston, D. (eds.) *The Bank of England: Money, Power and Influence, 1694–1994.* OUP, 1995

Weights and Measures. Conversion to the metric system, which replaced the imperial system, became obligatory on 1 Oct. 1995. The use of the pint for milk deliveries and bar sales, and use of miles and yards in road signs, is exempt indefinitely, and the use of the pound (weight) in selling greengrocery is exempt until 1999.

ENERGY AND NATURAL RESOURCES

Electricity. The Electricity Act of 1989 implemented the restructuring and transfer to the private sector of the electricity supply industry.

The Office of Electricity Regulation (Offer) was set up under the Act to protect consumer interests following privatization.

Generators. Under the provisions of the 1989 Electricity Act, National Power and PowerGen took over the fuel-fired and hydro-electric power stations, and were privatized in 1991. Nuclear Electric, responsible for operating the 12 nuclear power stations, and Scottish Nuclear were merged as a single holding company in 1996 with

2 new operating subsidiaries, Magnox Electric and British Energy. These were privatized in 1996. Under licence generating companies may also be involved in electricity supply.

A levy (Non-Fossil Fuel Obligation) is being imposed on generators until 1998 to fund the decommissioning of ageing nuclear plant and finance renewable energy sources, mainly wind generation, which in 1995 supplied 2% of demand.

Suppliers. The 12 Area Electricity Boards were replaced under the 1989 Electricity Act by 12 successor companies which were privatized in 1990. These are Eastern Electricity; East Midlands Electricity; London Electricity; Manweb; Midlands Electricity; Northern Electric; NORWEB; SEEBOARD; Southern Electric; SWALEC; South Western Electricity; Yorkshire Electricity. The companies are responsible for maintaining and operating their local distribution networks, and have a statutory duty to supply electricity to their tariff customers. Their main business, therefore, is in electricity supply. Some of the companies are involved in the retailing of electrical goods and electrical contracting. Some have diversified into other business activities.

The *Electricity Association* is the trade association of the UK electricity companies, providing a forum for members to discuss matters of common interest, a collective voice for the electricity industry when needed and specialist research and professional services.

The National Grid Company is responsible for operating the transmission system and for co-ordinating the operation of power stations connected to it. The company also operates the cross-Channel link with France and the interconnection with the Scottish power system.

In Scotland there are 3 main electricity companies. ScottishPower and Scottish Hydro-Electric are vertically-integrated companies carrying out generation, transmission, distribution and supply of electricity within their areas. Scottish Nuclear, responsible for operating the 2 Scottish nuclear power stations was merged with Nuclear Electric in 1996.

The electricity industry accounts for about 6% of total output production and 1·6% of GDP in the UK. Output capacity of all UK power stations as at the end of March 1997 was 73,261 MW. 42% of electricity generated was coal-fired, 28% nuclear, 21% gas, 4% oil, 3·3% combined heat and power schemes and 1·7% renewables (including hydro-electric). 298,878 GWh were supplied to 26·9m. customers in 1996, of which domestic users took 36%, industrial users 31% and commercial and other users 33%. The net electricity supplied in 1996 was 327,209 GWh.

Electricity Association. *Electricity Industry Review.* Annual
Surrey, J. (ed.) *The British Electricity Experience: Privatization – the Record, the Issues, the Lessons.* London, 1996

Oil and Gas. Production in 1,000 tonnes, in 1995 (and 1994): Throughput of crude and process oils, 92,743 (93,162); refinery use, 6,481 (6,356). Refinery output: Gases, 1,948 (1,737); naphtha, 2,711 (2,794); motor spirit, 27,264 (27,562); kerosene, 10,761 (10,664); diesel oil, 27,169 (27,127); fuel oil, 10,969 (11,378); lubricating oils, 1,261 (1,269); bitumen, 2,459 (2,569). Total output of refined products, 86,133 (86,644). Crude oil production, 130·3m. tonnes; 1994, 126·9m. tonnes. Estimated production, 1995, 2,672,000 bbls. a day.

Following the Gas Act of 1986, British Gas plc became the successor company to the British Gas Corporation. It conducts its operations under 3 business units: the UK gas business, exploration and production worldwide and Global Gas. The UK gas business has a headquarters and 12 regions. The Gas Act 1995 is extending competition to the domestic market progressively throughout Britain. Under the Act companies are licensed as Public Gas Transporters, who operate pipelines; Gas Shippers, who contract for gas to be transported through transporters' pipelines; and Gas Suppliers, who market gas. In 1997 there were 9 suppliers in addition to British Gas.

Gas reserves are some 590,000m. cu. metres. Production was 777,483,000 MW-hours in 1995, 35% of which was used by industrial or commercial consumers.

The Office of Gas Supply ('Ofgas') is the regulator charged with protecting gas consumers' interests.

Wind. In 1996 there were 31 wind farms with turbines for the generation of electricity.

Water. The Water Act of Sept. 1989 privatized the 10 water authorities in England and Wales: Anglian; North West; Northumbrian; Severn Trent; South West; Southern; Thames; Welsh; Wessex; Yorkshire. The Act also inaugurated the National Rivers Authority, with environmental and resource management responsibilities, and the 'regulator' Office of Water Services (Ofwat), charged with protecting consumer interests.

In Scotland water supply is the responsibility of the Regional and Island local authorities. 7 river purification boards are responsible for environmental management.

Minerals. Legislation to privatize the coal industry was introduced in 1994 and a new Coal Authority has taken over from British Coal. The Coal Authority is the owner of coal reserves; it licenses private coal-mining and deals with claims in former mining areas and disposes of unworked assets. In 1995 there were 15 British Coal collieries and 32 large deep mines in the private sector employing some 13,500 mineworkers. Total production from deep mines was 35·1m. tonnes in 1995 (31·9m. in 1994). 91 opencast sites were operating in 1996. Output, 1994, 16·8m. tonnes; 1995, 16·4m. tonnes. In 1995 inland coal consumption was 77m. tonnes, of which 78% was used by electricity generators, 11% by coke ovens and 3·7% by domestic consumers.

Output of non-fuel minerals in Great Britain, 1995 (in 1,000 tonnes): Limestone, 90,933; sandstone, 15,017; igneous rock, 49,641; clay and shale, 13,930; industrial sand, 4,344; chalk, 9,949; china clay, 3,076; sand and gravel, 89,656.

Steel and metals. There were 33 steel furnaces in 1997. Output in recent years (in 1m. tonnes):

	Steel production	Home consumption
1993	16·6	13·3
1994	17·3	14·5
1995	17·6	15·1
1996	18·0	14·9

Production of non-ferrous metals (in 1,000 tonnes) in 1994: Refined copper, 46·7; refined lead, 352·5; primary aluminium, 237·9; slab zinc, 101·3.

Agriculture. Land use in 1996: Agriculture, 77%; urban, 10%; forests, 10%; other, 3%. In 1995 (and 1994) agricultural land in the UK totalled (in 1,000 ha) 18,406 (18,503), comprising common grazing, 1,248 (1,246), and agricultural holdings, 17,158 (17,258). Land use of the latter: All grasses 6,696 (6,758); crops, 4,544 (4,469); rough grazing, 4,516 (4,551); bare fallow, 40 (44); other, 729 (708). Area sown to crops: Cereals, 3,180 (3,042); other arable crops, 1,003 (1,076); horticultural crops, 187 (189); fruit, 40 (45).

Farmers receiving financial support under the EU's Common Agricultural Policy are obliged to 'set-aside' land in order to control production. In 1995 such set-aside totalled 633,000 ha (728,000 ha in 1994).

The number of workers employed in agriculture in the UK was, in June 1995 (in 1,000), 243·4. Of these, 159·4 (12·9 females) were engaged full-time, 56·2 (24·3 females) part-time, and 84 (27·2 females) were seasonal or casual workers. In addition, there were in 1995 170,000 whole-time and 112,000 part-time farmers, partners, directors and 75,000 of their spouses engaged in farm work. There were some 234,900 farm holdings in 1995, about 66% owner-occupied. Average size of holdings, 72·4 ha.

Principal crops in the UK (1996 figures are provisional):

	Wheat	Barley	Oats	Potatoes	Sugar-beet	Oilseed rape
			Area (1,000 ha)			
1993	1,759	1,164	92	170	197	418
1994	1,811	1,106	109	164	195	496
1995	1,859	1,192	112	171	196	439
1996	1,976	1,267	96	177	199	429

	Wheat	Barley	Oats	Potatoes	Sugar-beet	Oilseed rape
			Total product (1,000 tonnes)			
1993	12,890	6,038	479	7,065	8,988	1,136
1994	13,314	5,945	597	6,531	8,720	1,253
1995	14,310	6,833	617	6,396	8,431	1,235
1996	16,041	7,765	594	7,020	9,555	1,453

Horticultural crops. 1995 output (in 1,000 tonnes): Cabbage, 438; carrots, 583; onions, 277; tomatoes, 113; apples, 246; soft fruit, 74.

Livestock in the UK as at June in each year (in 1,000):

	1991	1992	1993	1994	1995
Cattle	11,866	11,778	11,751	11,834	11,733
(dairy)	(2,770)	(2,682)	(2,667)	(2,175)	(2,602)
(beef)	(1,666)	(1,699)	(1,751)	(1,775)	(1,805)
Sheep	43,621	43,973	43,901	43,295	42,771
Pigs	7,596	7,608	7,756	7,797	7,534
Poultry	127,228	123,992	130,175	125,718	125,981

Livestock products, 1995: Milk, 13,950m. litres; hens' eggs, 9,504m.; poultry meat, 1·22m. tonnes; beef, 1m. tonnes; mutton, 0·4m. tonnes; pork, 0·81m. tonnes; bacon and ham, 0·2m. tonnes.

In March 1996 the Government acknowledged the possibility that bovine spongiform encephalopathy (BSE) might be transmitted to humans as a form of Creutzfeldt-Jakob disease via the food chain. Cases of BSE in cattle in the UK: 1988, 1,954; 1989, 6,955; 1990, 13,042; 1991, 22,939; 1992, 35,269; 1993, 37,020; 1994, 26,087; 1995, 15,600. British beef has been widely banned overseas. Government preventive measures include bans on sales of older meat and the use of meat in animal feed and fertilizer, and compensation schemes.

Forestry. On 31 March 1995 the area of productive woodland in Britain was 2,182,000 ha, of which the Forestry Commission managed 815,000 ha and the private sector 1,367,000 ha. The Forestry Commission employed 6,650 staff in 1995. In addition a further 10,400 were employed in private forestry with an estimated 11,215 engaged in the wood processing industry. In 1994–95 a total of 7·7m. cu. metres of timber was thinned and felled.

New planting (1994–95), 19,400 ha (2,900, Forestry Commission; 18,500, private woodlands).

Forestry Commission. *Forestry Facts and Figures.* Annual
James, N. D. G., *A History of English Forestry.* London, 1981

Fisheries. Quantity (in 1,000 tonnes) and value (in £1,000) of fish of British taking landed in Great Britain (excluding salmon and sea-trout):

Quantity	1991	1992	1993	1994	1995
Wet fish	477·7	505·6	536·2	576·5	601·0
Shell fish	84·6	108·0	102·5	111·1	124·6
	562·3	613·7	638·7	687·6	725·6
Value					
Wet fish	310,042	309,470	317,800	326,720	333,174
Shell fish	86,427	95,743	107,163	127,746	145,035
	396,469	405,213	423,963	454,466	478,209

In Dec. 1995 the fishing fleet comprised 9,174 registered vessels. Major fishing ports: (England) Fleetwood, Grimsby, Hull, Lowestoft, North Shields; (Wales) Milford Haven; (Scotland) Aberdeen, Mallaig, Lerwick, Peterhead.

Domestic Tourism. In 1996, 127m. residents made trips within the UK, passing 455m. nights in accommodation and spending £13,895m. Of these, 64·8m. were holiday-makers spending £9,365m.

INDUSTRY. In 1995 there were 156,310 manufacturing firms, of which 475 employed 1,000 or over persons, and 110,350, 9 or fewer. 1995 output (in 1,000 tonnes): Fertilizers, 2,656; cement, 11,805; man-made fibres, 195·3; woollen yarn, 63·7; cars, 1·5m.; bricks, 3,256m.; cotton, 80m. metres.

Engineering. Manufacturers' sales (in £1m.) for 1994 (and 1995): Motor vehicles, 16,344 (22,495); railway and tramway vehicles, (866); lifting and handling equipment, 2,213 (2,357); earth-moving equipment, 658 (1,000), agricultural tractors, 860; machine tools, 1,491 (1,763).

Electrical Goods. Manufacturers' sales (in £1m.) for 1994 (and 1995): Radio and electronic capital goods, 1,273; domestic electrical appliances, 1,739 (1,907); telephone and telegraph apparatus and equipment, 2,460 (3,012); lighting equipment, 1,059 (1,126).

Foodstuffs, etc. Manufacturers' sales (in £1m.) for 1994 (and 1995): Meat production and preservation, 3,719 (4,111); fish processing and preservation, 1,238 (1,274); cocoa, chocolate and sugar confectionery, 3,039 (3,127); tea and coffee, 1,696 (1,700); beer, 3,176 (3,161); tobacco products, 5,591 (5,859).

Textiles. Manufacturers' sales (in £1m.) in 1994 (and 1995): Preparation and spinning, 1,445 (1,368); weaving, 1,681 (1,344); carpets, 1,013 (1,096); men's clothes, 1,418 (1,511); women's clothes, 2,312 (3,644).

Wood products, furniture, pulp and paper. Manufacturers' sales (in £1m.) in 1994 (and 1995): Wood products except furniture, 3,584 (3,755); furniture of whatever construction, (6,047); paper and paper board, 3,789 (4,702); containers, 3,037 (3,419); stationery, 1,006 (1,081).

Chemicals. Manufacturers' sales, (in £1m.) in 1994 (and 1995): Dyes, 1,316 (1,430); inorganic chemicals, 1,335 (1,356); organic chemicals, 4,575 (4,839); fertilizers, 776 (934); primary plastics, 3,701 (4,212); synthetic rubber, 361 (427); pesticides, 1,459 (1,647); paints, etc., 2,412 (2,574); pharmaceuticals, 6,638 (6,701); soap, polish and detergents, 2,297 (2,307); rubber products, 2,849 (2,869).

Construction. Total value (in £1m.) of constructional work in Great Britain in 1994 (and 1995) was 49,439 (52,643), including new work, 25,086 (26,672), of which housing, 7,417 (7,135).

Labour. In June 1996 the UK workforce (*i.e.* all persons in employment plus the claimant unemployed) totalled (in 1,000) 27,969 (12,403 females), of whom 25,819 (11,884 females) were in employment, 22,216 (10,974 females) were employees, 3,282 (817 females) were self-employed and 221 (16 females) were in HM Forces. UK employees by form of employment in 1996 (in 1,000): Agriculture, forestry and fishing, 278; energy and water supply, 207; manufacturing industry, 4,015; construction, 825; wholesale trade, 960; retail trade, 2,276; hotels and restaurants, 1,289; transport and communications, 1,315; finance, 984; estate agency, 2,782; public administration, 1,391; education, 1,848; health and social work, 2,559. Registered unemployed in UK as at July (in 1,000; figures adjusted for seasonality and discontinuities): 1991, 2,294 (females, 554); 1992, 2,723 (634); 1993, 2,912 (674); 1994, 2,632; 1995, 2,311; 1996, 2,126. In Dec. 1996 the Government headline unemployment figure was 1,884,700. In Dec. 1992, 955,600 persons (165,200 females) had been unemployed for more than a year. In July 1996 there were 230,000 vacancies at Jobcentres.

Workers (in 1,000) involved in industrial stoppages (and working days lost): 1992, 148 (0·53m.); 1993, 385 (0·69m.); 1994, 107 (0·28m.); 1995, 174.

The Wages Councils set up in 1909 to establish minimum rates of pay (in 1992 of 2·5m. workers) were abolished in 1993. The Labour Government elected in May 1997 is committed to the introduction of a National Wage and has established a Low Pay Commission to advise on its implementation.

Trade Unions. In Jan. 1997 there were 75 unions affiliated to the Trades Union Congress (TUC) with a total membership of 6,799,619 (6,756,544 in 1996) (2·6m. of them women). The unions affiliated to the TUC in 1997 ranged in size from UNISON with 1·37m. members, to the Sheffield Wool Shear Workers' Union with 11 members. The 4 largest unions, however, account for more than half the total membership. In

1996, 61% of public sector employees and 21% of private sector employees were unionized. 46% of employees were in workplaces where trade unions were recognized for collective bargaining.

The TUC's executive body, the General Council, is elected at the annual Congress. Congress consists of representatives of all unions according to the size of the organization, and is the principal policy-making body.

The General Secretary (John Monks, b. 1945) is elected by the Congress but is not subject to annual re-election. The TUC draws up policies and promotes and publicizes them. It makes representations to government, employers and international bodies. The TUC also carries out research and campaigns and provides a range of services to unions including courses for union representatives.

The TUC is affiliated to the International Confederation of Free Trade Unions, the Trade Union Advisory Committee of OECD, the Commonwealth Trade Union Council and the European Trade Union Confederation. The TUC provides a service of trade union education. It provides members to serve, with representatives of employers, on the managing boards of such bodies as the Health and Safety Commission and the Advisory, Conciliation and Arbitration Service.

Clegg, H. A., *A History of British Trade Unions since 1889* [until 1951]. 3 vols. Oxford, 1994
Pelling, H., *A History of British Trade Unionism*. 5th ed. London, 1992.
Willman, P. *et al., Union Business: Trade Union Organization and Financial Reform in the Thatcher Years*. CUP, 1993

FOREIGN ECONOMIC RELATIONS

Commerce. Value of the imports and exports of merchandise, excluding bullion and specie (in £1,000):

	Total imports	Total exports		Total imports	Total exports
1990	126,165,755	103,910,969	1993	137,403,703	120,935,514
1991	118,871,355	104,818,449	1994	148,360,300	133,860,500
1992	125,843,872	108,289,964	1995	168,055,100	153,352,600

Until 1992 all overseas trade statistics were compiled from Customs declarations. With the inception of the Single Market on 1 Jan. 1993, however, the requirement for Customs declarations in intra-EU trade was removed; trade figures for EU countries since 1993 are compiled from VAT returns. The totals given in the table below include figures for 'Below Threshold Trade' (minimal) and a non-response estimate.

In 1996 the UK's trade with non-EU countries was: Imports, £84,647,464; exports, £72,302,591.

Provisional figures for trade by countries and groups of countries (in £1,000):

	Imports from		Exports to	
EU countries	1994	1995	1994	1995
EU	74,780,300	75,144,000	63,506,900	88,647,400
Austria	1,017,900	883,900	1,034,900	1,086,300
Belgium and Luxembourg	6,742,800	7,631,300	6,971,700	7,880,300
Denmark and Faroe Islands	2,024,400	2,075,200	1,685,000	1,996,100
Finland	2,253,300	2,345,200	1,297,300	1,630,900
France	14,343,000	15,498,400	12,779,100	14,442,200
Germany	20,862,400	24,899,600	16,389,100	19,224,100
Greece	331,900	403,900	871,700	990,200
Ireland	5,529,200	6,651,500	6,447,000	7,331,300
Italy	6,843,000	7,834,300	6,461,600	7,436,500
Netherlands	9,471,100	10,854,300	9,057,200	11,639,300
Portugal, Azores and Madeira	1,201,900	1,391,200	1,173,600	1,397,200
Spain	3,439,000	4,123,900	4,749,400	5,800,100
Sweden	4,159,900	4,286,400	3,348,000	3,894,800
Other foreign countries	1995	1996	1995	1996
Europe—				
EEA/EFTA	9,734,828	10,689,405	4,896,313	5,440,224
Albania	1,017	318	7,555	14,664
Andorra	8	3,394	13,043	19,096
Belarus	20,981	13,596	22,570	27,661
Bosnia-Hercegovina	240	635	4,084	16,644

Other foreign countries—contd.	Imports from 1995	1996	Exports to 1995	1996
Europe—contd.				
Bulgaria	118,550	116,018	104,224	87,260
Croatia	36,725	37,066	231,512	135,333
Czech Republic	321,497	372,796	567,923	714,613
Estonia	111,840	144,150	29,665	55,421
Hungary	371,571	423,294	295,859	347,111
Iceland	251,887	267,876	138,103	153,975
Latvia	170,411	307,121	40,058	78,986
Lithuania	173,228	184,542	49,435	83,539
Macedonia	5,323	9,282	18,079	17,955
Moldova	301	866	2,248	3,181
Norway	4,325,432	4,984,405	1,998,499	2,066,273
Poland	638,077	599,862	944,672	1,350,985
Romania	173,844	182,024	176,770	210,284
Russia	965,870	1,274,785	870,387	1,009,250
Slovakia	67,509	65,491	76,764	103,549
Slovenia	113,956	109,111	122,397	131,714
Switzerland and Liechtenstein	5,157,507	5,437,124	2,759,325	3,219,460
Turkey	794,890	932,876	1,157,777	1,565,938
Ukraine	22,941	23,875	111,106	141,896
Yugoslavia	560	13,855	9,970	32,518
Africa—				
Algeria	244,279	202,428	64,277	70,939
Angola	22,408	8,852	29,387	45,631
Burundi	3,670	2,712	3,339	2,439
Cameroon	31,328	42,682	25,234	33,745
Congo (Dem. Rep. of the)	11,350	14,754	15,671	17,092
Côte d'Ivoire	101,737	91,470	49,428	54,165
Egypt	246,619	281,502	383,541	431,424
Ethiopia	15,928	26,260	53,337	49,377
Liberia	544	11,707	8,456	6,095
Libya	131,787	150,380	227,369	248,818
Mali	225	681	24,074	24,335
Mauritania	14,579	13,982	6,026	14,150
Morocco	253,752	303,998	271,114	281,575
Mozambique	1,922	2,195	13,274	14,421
Rwanda	1,841	2,478	4,825	4,173
Senegal	8,485	13,350	32,217	34,882
Sudan	10,183	8,814	44,222	57,818
Tunisia	55,690	65,829	83,667	83,257
Asia and Oceania—				
Afghanistan	1,103	2,693	7,156	7,581
Bahrain	26,379	20,677	150,757	161,180
China	1,937,869	2,202,081	824,403	738,514
China (Taiwan)	1,726,761	2,088,483	961,933	941,241
Fiji	82,020	89,508	6,770	7,362
Indonesia	903,867	980,680	525,499	828,268
Iran	125,834	118,771	332,614	396,561
Iraq	164	105	5,044	10,927
Israel	692,156	831,845	1,108,455	1,265,773
Japan	9,613,810	8,994,299	3,782,955	4,263,666
Jordan	20,894	25,081	119,597	140,044
Korea (South)	1,561,755	2,038,376	1,153,116	1,303,560
Kuwait	151,377	179,865	550,870	579,097
Lebanon	14,198	12,200	175,132	173,766
Myanmar	9,283	13,732	15,244	21,421
Oman	74,232	86,993	447,922	415,750
Philippines	352,425	895,486	432,397	395,311
Qatar	14,950	10,502	146,289	191,848
Saudi Arabia	720,783	752,605	1,644,356	2,482,981
Syria	89,768	88,924	84,593	100,085
Thailand	1,039,849	1,187,872	836,622	974,064
United Arab Emirates	281,041	300,903	1,184,136	1,394,106

Other foreign countries—contd.	Imports from 1995	1996	Exports to 1995	1996
America—				
Argentina	252,265	285,487	233,682	331,631
Bolivia	14,732	39,142	17,042	11,270
Brazil	986,520	983,041	674,502	846,505
Chile	299,959	377,549	170,949	166,129
Colombia	174,109	211,476	145,244	177,767
Costa Rica	78,515	93,051	23,271	36,030
Cuba	8,184	19,378	19,160	24,504
Dominican Republic	24,343	25,725	27,946	27,322
Ecuador	20,390	29,150	52,825	41,430
El Salvador	3,419	5,724	22,737	18,900
Guatemala	14,898	19,635	31,103	27,878
Haiti	1,254	1,789	13,466	9,732
Honduras	18,130	13,772	15,537	12,203
Mexico	298,124	334,765	276,753	317,428
Nicaragua	8,265	3,433	7,334	5,924
Panama	2,553	11,186	67,975	66,942
Paraguay	3,468	15,802	66,430	55,019
Peru	122,645	130,434	57,500	62,876
Puerto Rico	81,961	104,799	466,196	307,035
Uruguay	62,379	78,357	56,833	66,251
USA	20,268,863	23,011,494	17,949,473	19,833,631
Venezuela	204,167	189,104	178,784	180,255
Total, foreign countries (including some not specified above)	58,285,098	64,828,167	47,456,375	53,928,167
Commonwealth countries				
In Europe—				
Cyprus	156,451	158,728	307,438	290,735
Gibraltar	10,598	4,225	79,579	87,110
Malta	79,790	94,910	284,346	242,572
In Africa—				
West Africa:				
Gambia	3,119	3,207	13,591	16,443
Ghana	163,812	190,386	240,081	299,791
Nigeria	181,038	293,749	431,509	432,972
Sierra Leone	4,774	5,709	26,319	32,624
Southern Africa:				
Botswana	23,647	48,269	25,837	23,444
Lesotho	399	60	1,324	1,864
Malawi	16,188	16,062	13,449	20,558
Namibia	26,635	25,280	5,983	6,892
South Africa	1,113,064	1,220,706	1,830,397	1,880,800
Swaziland	39,714	40,322	3,033	2,104
Zambia	19,460	17,726	49,819	51,544
Zimbabwe	149,344	136,516	87,696	103,819
East Africa:				
Kenya	162,198	191,262	244,347	241,132
Mauritius	345,149	344,161	71,018	73,417
Tanzania	27,480	28,983	87,412	81,851
Uganda	11,136	14,867	49,105	50,751
Maldives	8,879	7,549	3,850	5,895
Seychelles	9,827	9,249	19,217	16,975
St Helena	446	386	9,144	7,698
In Asia—				
Bangladesh	231,644	279,573	89,145	71,577
Hong Kong	3,538,821	4,072,935	2,656,583	2,923,391
India	1,435,481	1,610,996	1,682,709	1,706,606
Malaysia	1,487,884	2,380,115	1,189,582	1,160,025
Pakistan	363,068	390,923	340,382	344,507
Singapore	2,205,799	2,572,600	2,068,581	2,144,680
Sri Lanka	205,662	232,088	156,409	148,339
In Oceania—				
Australia	1,110,448	1,296,021	2,121,352	2,465,635
New Zealand	576,532	631,973	435,879	471,820

Other foreign countries—contd.	Imports from 1995	1996	Exports to 1995	1996
In Oceania—contd.				
Papua New Guinea	97,391	107,149	10,849	7,976
Western Samoa	16	12	567	1,264
In America—				
Bahamas	33,029	62,769	30,912	18,825
Barbados	25,639	65,524	101,144	35,538
Belize	47,010	47,863	14,261	10,192
Bermuda	3,085	7,150	17,316	19,032
Canada	2,379,624	2,484,044	1,811,964	1,974,524
Falkland Islands	4,721	5,568	15,665	19,932
Guyana	72,821	91,558	33,946	33,984
Jamaica	149,076	161,410	69,771	67,749
Trinidad and Tobago	43,600	53,139	103,434	83,792
Total, Commonwealth countries (including some not specified above)	16,858,880	19,819,297	17,248,820	18,374,424

Provisional figures for imports and exports classified by the sections of the 3rd revision of the Standard International Trade Classification (in £1,000):

	Imports from EU countries 1995	Imports (excluding EU countries) 1996	Exports to EU countries 1995	Exports (excluding EU countries) 1996
0. *Food and Live Animals*				
Live animals (excluding zoo animals, dogs and cats)	83,500	97,340	216,200	165,518
Meat and meat preparations	1,793,500	583,517	1,301,500	142,513
Dairy products and eggs	924,900	176,396	626,000	199,781
Fish and fish preparations	239,900	960,881	608,900	115,863
Cereals and cereal preparations	861,800	202,080	1,026,200	406,666
Fruit and vegetables	2,459,700	1,670,257	331,700	102,055
Sugar, sugar preparations, honey	234,400	645,584	207,500	214,831
Coffee, tea, cocoa, spices	604,500	697,419	357,600	302,291
Feeding stuff for animals	328,900	506,521	294,300	69,148
Miscellaneous food preparations	740,200	95,062	264,200	194,266
Total of Section 0	8,271,300	5,635,058	5,234,100	1,912,931
1. *Beverages and Tobacco*				
Beverages	1,634,100	520,511	1,222,700	1,836,769
Tobacco and tobacco manufactures	220,800	363,188	484,800	694,068
Total of Section 1	1,854,900	883,699	1,707,500	2,530,837
2. *Crude Materials, Inedible, except Fuels*				
Hides, skins and furskins, undressed	80,500	59,188	147,000	104,464
Oil seeds, oil nuts and oil kernels	101,600	307,277	17,100	17,524
Crude rubber (including synthetic and reclaimed)	134,700	217,473	227,100	77,676
Wood and cork	668,300	532,907	33,500	10,439
Pulp and waste paper	369,100	468,345	104,300	6,149
Textile fibres and their waste	313,500	402,975	336,800	289,079
Crude fertilizers and crude minerals (excluding fuels)	162,500	203,536	352,400	141,507
Metalliferous ores and metal scrap	345,300	1,282,756	458,600	309,988
Crude animal and vegetable materials, not elsewhere specified	496,800	235,110	97,600	56,242
Total of Section 2	2,672,200	3,709,567	1,774,000	1,013,067
3. *Mineral Fuels, Lubricants and Related Materials*				
Coal, coke and briquettes	50,600	651,158	49,800	22,740
Petroleum and petroleum products	822,100	4,651,089	5,454,400	3,446,757

	Imports from EU countries 1995	Imports (excluding EU countries) 1996	Exports to EU countries 1995	Exports (excluding EU countries) 1996
3. Mineral Fuels, Lubricants and Related Materials—contd.				
Gas, natural and manufactured	18,900	170,738	475,500	25,883
Electric current	408,400	nil	1,700	nil
Total of Section 3	1,299,900	5,472,985	5,963,300	3,495,380
4. Animal and Vegetable Oils and Fats				
Animal oils and fats	55,500	35,088	20,700	8,841
Vegetable fats and oils	227,500	189,630	95,600	31,856
Processed oils and fats	55,000	55,750	39,100	19,596
Total of Section 4	337,900	280,468	155,300	60,294
5. Chemicals				
Organic chemicals	3,473,200	1,450,181	3,208,700	2,148,610
Inorganic chemicals	623,700	600,133	751,700	473,568
Dyeing, tanning and colouring materials	650,400	319,292	894,100	719,521
Medicinal and pharmaceutical products	2,039,600	1,069,096	2,592,400	2,413,310
Essential oils and perfume; toilet and cleansing preparations	1,075,900	348,284	1,255,700	1,036,800
Fertilizers, manufactured	183,800	244,262	89,100	19,136
Primary plastics	2,593,300	532,167	1,435,900	574,851
Non-primary plastics	1,157,400	308,316	858,000	451,484
Other chemical products	1,237,400	564,269	1,399,900	1,565,969
Total of Section 5	13,034,600	5,425,999	12,485,600	9,403,248
6. Manufactured Goods Classified Chiefly by Material				
Leather and dressed furs	142,200	111,622	163,900	227,608
Rubber	938,900	529,326	1,019,900	349,915
Wood and cork (excluding furniture)	500,500	584,161	142,200	54,164
Paper, paperboard	4,193,900	1,034,375	1,491,300	873,710
Textile yarn, fabrics	2,890,300	2,143,986	2,185,500	1,235,130
Non-metallic mineral manufactures	1,683,900	3,102,625	2,508,100	2,527,466
Iron and steel	2,865,900	813,805	2,972,700	1,624,166
Non-ferrous metals	1,526,900	2,375,267	1,768,100	1,139,144
Manufactures of metal, not elsewhere specified	1,874,600	1,484,102	1,749,900	1,386,631
Total of Section 6	16,617,000	12,179,167	13,974,500	9,417,933
7. Machinery and Transport Equipment				
Power generating machinery	1,891,100	3,231,944	2,916,500	4,207,964
Machinery for particular industries	2,672,800	1,573,202	2,173,100	3,419,739
Metal working machinery	440,400	614,369	380,800	643,354
General industrial machinery	3,863,800	2,513,998	3,216,400	3,732,568
Office machinery	6,034,500	6,978,847	7,807,200	4,151,375
Telecommunications and sound recording apparatus	2,253,800	4,519,943	3,809,100	2,847,090
Electrical machinery	6,041,300	9,135,321	7,307,900	5,008,739
Road vehicles	15,006,200	3,190,552	7,936,900	4,972,129
Other transport equipment	1,194,300	2,658,092	1,590,100	3,975,015
Total of Section 7	39,398,300	34,416,267	37,138,000	32,957,974
8. Miscellaneous Manufactured Articles				
Prefabricated buildings, sanitary, plumbing, heating and lighting fixtures	351,200	160,791	200,900	201,426
Furniture	810,700	483,228	525,500	347,292

	Imports from EU countries 1995	Imports (ex-cluding EU countries) 1996	Exports to EU countries 1995	Exports (ex-cluding EU countries) 1996
8. *Miscellaneous Manufactured Articles*—contd.				
Travel goods, handbags and similar articles	105,100	411,488	71,600	53,895
Clothing	1,566,800	4,296,875	2,047,100	984,776
Footwear	827,800	814,714	289,100	251,188
Scientific instruments	1,321,000	2,180,726	1,912,500	2,531,590
Photographic apparatus, optical goods, clocks	852,000	1,478,285	1,033,600	930,118
Miscellaneous manufactured articles, not elsewhere specified	3,406,900	5,471,285	4,028,300	4,500,333
Total of Section 8	9,241,500	15,297,392	10,108,700	9,800,617
9. *Commodities and Transactions not Classified According to Kind*				
Total of Section 9	183,300	1,346,862	106,400	1,710,309
Total of all classes	92,911,100	84,647,464	88,647,400	72,302,591

Foreign Tourism. There were 26m. overseas visitors in 1997 spending £12,600m. 41·87m. UK residents journeyed abroad in 1995. The main countries of origin for foreign visitors in 1996 were: France (3·70m.), USA (3·08m.), Germany (2·98m.), Ireland (2·07m.) and Belgium (1·56m.).

COMMUNICATIONS

Roads. Responsibility for the construction and maintenance of trunk roads belongs to central government (in England, the Department of Transport, in Wales the Welsh Office and in Scotland the Scottish Office). Roads not classified as trunk roads are the responsibility of county or unitary councils.

In 1995 there were 366,999 km of public roads, classified as: Motorways, 3,189 km; trunk roads, 12,208 km; principal roads, 35,957 km; others, 315,744 km.

Motor vehicles for which licences were current at 31 Dec. 1995, numbered (in 1,000) 25,369, including 20,505 private cars, 594 mopeds, scooters and motor cycles, 82 public transport vehicles and 421 goods vehicles. New vehicle registrations in 1995, 2,307. Driving tests, 1995 (in 1,000): Applications, 1,631·4; tests held, 1,489; tests passed, 684·2. The driving test was extended in 1996 to include a written examination.

Road casualties in Great Britain, 1994, 315,189 including 3,650 killed; in 1995, 310,506 including 3,621 killed (the lowest figure since records began in 1926).

Inter- and intra-urban bus and coach journeys average 44,000m. passenger-km annually. Passenger journeys by public road transport, 1994–95, 5,050m., including 4,420m. by local bus services. For London buses *see* London Transport *under* RAILWAYS, *below*.

Railways. In 1994 the nationalized railway network was restructured to allow for privatization. Ownership of the track, stations and infrastructure was vested in a government-owned company, Railtrack, which was privatized in May 1996.

Passenger operations were reorganized into 25 train-operating companies, wholly-owned subsidiaries of the British Railways Board, and all had been transferred to the private sector by February 1997. These pay Railtrack for access to the rail network, and lease their rolling stock from 3 private sector companies. All freight operations have also now been privatized. Eurotunnel PLC holds a concession from the government to operate the Channel Tunnel (49·4 km), through which vehicle-carrying and Eurostar passenger trains are run in conjunction with French and Belgian railways. A new dedicated high speed line is planned to connect the Channel Tunnel to London

St Pancras. This line will be used by both international and domestic trains. Construction is due to begin in 1999 and the line should be completed in 2003.

In 1997 total route length was 16,666 km (5,176 km electrified). For the year 1996–97, passenger journeys totalled 884m. (32,200m. passenger km). 101m. tonnes of freight were lifted.

London Transport is responsible to the Secretary of State for the Environment, Transport and the Regions for the operations of the capital's metro, London Underground, and for the planning and procurement of bus services. In 1996, London Underground, its wholly-owned subsidiary, carried 2·7m. passengers a day to and from 267 stations (including 21 managed by Railtrack) on 12 lines. Some 5,000 buses run under contract to London Transport by independent companies carried 3·7m. passengers a day on some 700 routes.

The privately-franchised Docklands Light Railway is operated in east inner London.

There are metros in Glasgow and Newcastle, and light rail systems in Manchester and Sheffield.

Civil Aviation. Scheduled airports at Aberdeen, Birmingham, Bristol, Cardiff, Derby (East Midlands), Edinburgh, Glasgow, Leeds/Bradford, Liverpool, London (Gatwick), London (Heathrow), London (Luton), London (Stansted), London City, Manchester, Newcastle and Prestwick each handled more than 150,000 international passengers in 1996.

Following the Civil Aviation Act 1971, the Civil Aviation Authority (CAA) was established as an independent public body responsible for the economic and safety regulation of British civil aviation. A CAA wholly-owned subsidiary, National Air Traffic Services, operates air traffic control. Highlands and Islands Airports Ltd is owned by the Scottish Office and operates 8 airports.

Operating and traffic statistics of UK airlines on scheduled services during the calendar year 1995 (and 1994): Aircraft–km flown, 680m. (636m.); revenue passengers carried, 47·5m. (43·9m.); cargo (freight and mail) carried 643,181 (618,067) tonnes. Traffic between UK airports and places abroad in 1995 (and 1994) on all services included 968,493 (932,499) air transport aircraft movements.

There were 15,303 civil aircraft registered in the UK at 31 Dec. 1996.

British Airways is the largest UK airline. It operates long and short haul international services, as well as an extensive domestic network. In 1996 it operated 10 A320-100/200s, 22 B-737-200 Advs, 17 B-737-400s, 15 B-747-100s, 13 B-747-200Bs, 3 B-747-200B Combis, 34 B-747-400s, 44 B-757-200s, 11 B-767-300ERs, 13 B-767-300s, 14 BAe ATPs, 7 Concordes and 7 DC-10-30s. British Airways also have franchise agreements with other UK operators: British Regional Airways, Brymon Airways, City Flyer Express, GB Airways, Loganair and Maersk Air. Other airlines operating scheduled flights in 1996 (with numbers of aircraft): Air Belfast (3); Air UK (41); British Midland Airways (33); British World Airlines (19); Channel Express (14); Hunting Cargo (5); Jersey European Airways (16); Manx Airlines (27); Monarch Airlines (27); Virgin Atlantic Airways (15).

Shipping. The UK-owned merchant fleet (trading vessels over 100 GT) in June 1997 totalled 619 ships of 10·8m. DWT and 7·9m. GT. The UK-owned and registered fleet totalled 348 ships of 2·2m. DWT.

The average age of the UK-owned fleet was 16·7 years, while that of the world fleet was 13·8 years. Total gross international revenue in 1996 was £5,072m. The net contribution to the UK balance of payments was £905m.; there were import savings of £1,652m., giving a total contribution of £2,557m. The container and roll-on-roll-off (RoRo) shipping sectors are the leading revenue earners.

The principal ports are (with 1m. tonnes of cargo handled in 1996): London (52·9), Grimsby and Immingham (46·8), Forth (45·6), Tees and Hartlepool (44·6), Sullom Voe (38·2), Milford Haven (36·6), Southampton (34·2), Liverpool (30·9), Felixstowe (25·8), Medway (14·1), Dover (13·2), Port Talbot (13·2), Belfast (12·5), Orkneys (11·5) and Hull (9·7).

Inland Waterways. There are approximately 3,500 miles of navigable canals and river navigations in Great Britain. Of these, the publicly-owned British Waterways

(BW) is responsible for some 385 miles (620 km) of commercial waterways (maintained for freight traffic) and some 1,160 miles (1,868 km) of cruising waterways (maintained for pleasure cruising, fishing and amenity). BW is also responsible for a further 450 miles (732 km) of canals, some of which are not navigable. BW's external turnover for the year to 31 March 1997 was £46·8m. This comprised principally Freight Activities (£2·1m.), Leisure (£10·9m.), the Estate (£19·5m.) and Water Charges (£3·4m.). Additionally, British Waterways was in receipt of Department of the Environment grants of £51·8m.

River navigations and canals managed by other authorities include the Thames, Great Ouse and Nene, Norfolk Broads and Manchester Ship Canal.

Postal Services. The Post Office operates as a group of 4 distinct businesses: Royal Mail (letter delivery), Parcelforce (parcel delivery), Post Office Counters (retailing and agency services) and Subscription Services Ltd (television licensing). Every area of the country is served by regional offices for each of the businesses. Royal Mail collects and delivers 72m. letters a day to the 26m. UK addresses. Other services include electronic mail, guaranteed parcel deliveries (same-day and overnight to UK addresses) and swift deliveries to 140 other countries and territories. The British Postal Consultancy Service provides advice to administrations abroad.

In 1997 there were almost 20,000 post offices, 606 operated directly by the Post Office, the remainder (sub-post offices) on a franchise or agency basis; and 120,000 posting points. Staff numbered 193,000 in 1996–97. 17,296m. letters were posted in 1996–97.

The Post Office has a monopoly on the carriage of letters within the UK, but the government has suspended this subject to a minimum delivery charge of £1 and licensed mail transferred between document exchanges. Private services are permitted to handle door-to-door deliveries subject to a minimum fee of £1.

Telecommunications. In 1997 there were 148 licensed telecommunications operators: 125 cable operators, 19 national and regional public telecommunications operators and 4 mobile telephone (cellular) operators. Fixed-link telephone services are offered by BT, Mercury Communications, Kingston Communications (Hull), most of the cable operators and the public telecommunications operators. BT (then British Telecom) was established in 1981 to take over the management of telecommunications from the Post Office. In 1984 it was privatized as British Telecommunications plc, changing its trading name from British Telecom to BT in 1991.

In 1994 there were 7,327 digital or electronic analogue exchanges serving 84% of BT's customers' lines. The trunk network is completely digital. Almost 3m. km of optical fibre have been installed. In 1996 there were 20·5m. residential and 6·5m. business lines, 132,000 public payphones, 200,000 private rented payphones and 20,000 UK telex connections. BT handles a daily average of 103m. telephone calls a day and 22m. calls to emergency fire, police or ambulance service a year. In 1991 there were 0·9m. fax terminals. Electronic services include electronic mail ('email') and a complete corporate global messaging network. BT telephone, television and business services are carried by 15–20 satellites. In 1995 BT had some 20 offices worldwide and employed 137,561 persons.

In 1997 there were more than 7m. mobile telephone users.

Telecommunications services are regulated by OFTEL in the interests of consumers.

Broadcasting. Radio and television services are provided by the British Broadcasting Corporation (BBC), by licensees of the Radio Authority and the Independent Television Commission (ITC) and by the Welsh-language Sianel Pedwar Cymru (S4C, Channel 4 Wales). The BBC, constituted by Royal Charter until 31 Dec. 1996, has responsibility for providing domestic and external broadcast services, the former financed from the television licence revenue, the latter by Government grant. The domestic services include 2 national television services, 5 national radio network services and a network of local radio stations. Government proposals for the future of the BBC after 1996 were published in July 1994.

The ITC is responsible for licensing and regulating all non-BBC TV services (except S4C), including ITV (regional and breakfast-time licensees), Channel 4,

Channel 5, cable and satellite and additional services, such as teletext, carried on the spare capacity of TV signals. The Radio Authority is responsible for licensing and regulating independent national and local radio services. S4C is transmitted in Wales, and is funded by the government. It acts as both broadcaster and regulator.

The BBC's domestic radio services are available on Long Wave, FM and VHF; those of the Radio Authority on FM and VHF. Television services other than those only on cable and satellite are broadcast at UHF in 625-line definition and in colour (by PAL). The BBC World Service, which started life in 1932 as the Empire Service, broadcast in 42 languages to an audience estimated at 140m. in 1997. As the self-financed BBC Worldwide TV, the BBC is also involved in commercial joint ventures to provide international television services.

The broadcasting authorities, whose governing bodies are appointed (by HM the Queen in the case of the BBC and by the Secretary of State for National Heritage in the case of the ITC, the Radio Authority and S4C) as trustees for the public interest in broadcasting, are independent of government and are publicly accountable to Parliament for the discharge of their responsibilities. Their duties and powers are laid down in the BBC Royal Charter and the Broadcasting Act 1990.

All independent (non-BBC) radio and television services other than S4C are financed by the sale of broadcasting advertising time, commercial sponsorship, or, in some cable and satellite services, by subscription.

In 1981 the Broadcasting Complaints Commission was set up to consider and adjudicate upon complaints of unfair or unjust treatment in broadcast programmes or of unwarranted infringement of privacy in or in the making of programmes. These statutory functions have been continued in the Broadcasting Act of 1990. The Broadcasting Standards Council was set up in 1988 to act as a focus for public concern about the portrayal of violence and sex on television and radio. The Council's role is to monitor programmes, receive and examine complaints from the public, undertake and commission research, and to draw up a code of practice on the portrayal of sex and violence, and on matters of taste and decency. The Broadcasting Act 1990 requires the broadcasters to reflect the Council's code in their programme guidelines. It also empowers the Council to consider and adjudicate upon complaints and publish their findings.

The number of television receiving licences in force on 31 March 1996 was 21,105,000, including 20,505,000 for colour. There were 779,461 cable television subscribers in 1994.

Cinemas. In 1995 cinemas had 2,019 screens. By 2000 this will have increased to more than 2,200. Admissions were 130m. in 1996 (123m. in 1994, from a low point of 54m. in 1984). 127 full-length films were made in 1996.

Press. In 1996 there were 10 national dailies with a combined average circulation in June of 13,202,574, and 9 national Sunday newspapers (15,174,032). There were also about 100 morning, evening and Sunday regional newspapers and 2,000 weeklies (about 1,000 of these for free distribution). There were about 6,500 other commercial periodicals and 4,000 professional and business journals. In 1996, an average of 18·3m. newspapers were sold per day.

In Jan. 1991 the Press Complaints Commission replaced the former Press Council. It has 15 members and a chair (Lord Wakeham) including 7 editors. It is funded by the newspaper industry.

In 1996, 101,504 book titles were published, including 89,984 non-fiction. 95,064 titles were published in 1995.

SOCIAL INSTITUTIONS

Justice. *England and Wales.* The legal system of England and Wales, divided into civil and criminal courts has at the head of the superior courts, as the ultimate court of appeal, the House of Lords, which hears each year a number of appeals in civil matters, including a certain number from Scotland and Northern Ireland, as well as some appeals in criminal cases. In order that civil cases may go from the Court of Appeal to the House of Lords, it is necessary to obtain the leave of either the Court of Appeal or the House itself, although in certain cases an appeal may lie direct to the

House of Lords from the decision of the High Court. An appeal can be brought from a decision of the Court of Appeal or the Divisional Court of the Queen's Bench Division of the High Court in a criminal case provided that the Court is satisfied that a point of law 'of general public importance' is involved, and either the Court or the House of Lords is of the opinion that it is desirable in the public interest that a further appeal should be brought. As a judicial body, the House of Lords consists of the Lord Chancellor, the Lords of Appeal in Ordinary, commonly called Law Lords, and such other members of the House as hold or have held high judicial office. The final court of appeal for certain of the Commonwealth countries is the Judicial Committee of the Privy Council which, in addition to Privy Counsellors who are or have held high judicial office in the UK, includes others who are or have been Chief Justices or Judges of the Superior Courts of Commonwealth countries.

Civil Law. The main courts of original civil jurisdiction are the High Court and county courts.

The High Court has exclusive jurisdiction to deal with specialist classes of case e.g. Judicial Review. It has concurrent jurisdiction with county courts in cases involving contract and tort although it will only hear those cases where the issues are complex or important. The High Court also has appellate jurisdiction to hear appeals from lower tribunals.

The judges of the High Court are attached to one of its 3 divisions: Chancery, Queen's Bench and Family; each with its separate field of jurisdiction. The Heads of the 3 divisions are the Lord Chief Justice (Queen's Bench), the Vice-Chancellor (Chancery) and the President of the Family Division. In addition there are 95 High Court judges. For the hearing of cases at first instance, High Court judges sit singly. Appellate jurisdiction is usually exercised by Divisional Courts consisting of 2 (sometimes 3) judges, though in certain circumstances a judge sitting alone may hear the appeal. High Court business is dealt with in the Royal Courts of Justice and by over 130 District Registries outside London.

County courts can deal with all contract and tort cases and recovery of land actions, regardless of value. They have upper financial limits to deal with specialist classes of business such as equity and Admiralty cases. Certain county courts have been designated to deal with family, bankruptcy, patents and discrimination cases.

There are about 260 county courts located throughout the country each with its own district. A case may be heard by a Circuit Judge or by a District Judge, (the latter generally being restricted to cases valued at £5,000 or less). County courts have a small claims jurisdiction for actions for money worth £3,000 or less; this is an informal procedure where parties are encouraged to present cases without the need for legal representation.

The Restrictive Practices Court was set up in 1956 under the Restrictive Trade Practices Act and is responsible for deciding whether a restrictive trade agreement is in the public interest. It is presided over by a High Court judge, but laymen sit on the bench also. Another specialist court is the Employment Appeal Tribunal, with similar composition, which hears appeals in employment cases from lower tribunals.

The Court of Appeal (Civil Division) hears appeals in civil actions from the High Court and county courts and certain special courts such as the Restrictive Practice Court and Employment Appeal Tribunal. Its President is the Master of the Rolls, aided by up to 35 Lords Justices of Appeal setting in 6 or 7 divisions of 2 or 3 judges each.

Civil proceedings are instituted by the aggrieved person, but as they are a private matter, they are frequently settled by the parties through their lawyers before the matter comes to trial. In very limited classes of dispute (e.g. libel and slander), a party may request a jury to sit to decide questions of fact and the award of damages.

Criminal Law. At the base of the system of criminal courts in England and Wales are the magistrates' courts which deal with over 97% of criminal cases. In general, in exercising their summary jurisdiction, they have power to pass a sentence of up to six months imprisonment and to impose a fine of up to £5,000 on any one offence. They also deal with the preliminary hearing of cases triable at the Crown Court. In addition to dealing summarily with over 2·3m. cases, which include thefts, assaults, drug abuse, etc, they also have a limited civil and family jurisdiction.

Magistrates' courts normally sit with a bench of 3 lay justices. Although unpaid they are entitled to loss of earnings and travel and subsistence allowance. They undergo training after appointment and they are advised by a professional justices' clerk. In central London and in some provincial areas full-time stipendiary magistrates have been appointed. Generally they possess the same powers as the lay bench, but they sit alone. On 1 Jan. 1997 the total strength of the lay magistracy was 30,374 including 14,516 women. Justices are appointed on behalf of the Queen by the Lord Chancellor, except in Greater Manchester, Merseyside and Lancashire where they are appointed by the Chancellor of the Duchy of Lancaster.

Justices are selected and trained specially to sit in Youth and Family Proceedings Courts. Youth Courts deal with cases involving children and young persons up to the age of 18 charged with criminal offences (other than homicide and other grave offences). These courts normally sit with 3 justices, including at least one man or one woman, and are accommodated separately from other courts.

Family Proceedings Courts deal with matrimonial applications, Children Act matters, including care, residence and contact and adoption. These courts normally sit with three justices including at least one man and one woman.

Above the magistrates' courts is the Crown Court. This was set up by the Courts Act 1971 to replace quarter sessions and assizes. Unlike quarter sessions and assizes, which were individual courts, the Crown Court is a single court which is capable of sitting anywhere in England and Wales. It has power to deal with all trials on indictment and has inherited the jurisdiction of quarter sessions to hear appeals, proceedings on committal of persons from the magistrates' courts for sentence, and certain original proceedings on civil matters under individual statutes.

The jurisdiction of the Crown Court is exercisable by a High Court judge, a Circuit judge or a Recorder or Assistant Recorder (part-time judges) sitting alone, or, in specified circumstances, with justices of the peace. The Lord Chief Justice has given directions as to the types of case to be allocated to High Court judges (the more serious cases) and to Circuit judges or Recorders respectively.

Appeals from magistrates' courts go either to a Divisional Court of the High Court (when a point of law alone is involved) or to the Crown Court where there is a complete re-hearing on appeals against conviction and/or sentence. Appeals from the Crown Court in cases tried on indictment lie to the Court of Appeal (Criminal Division). Appeals on questions of law go by right, and appeals on other matters by leave. The Lord Chief Justice or a Lord Justice sits with judges of the High Court to constitute this court. Thereafter appeals in England and Wales can be made to the House of Lords.

There remains as a last resort the invocation of the royal prerogative exercised on the advice of the Home Secretary. In 1965 the death penalty was abolished for murder.

All contested criminal trials, except those which come before the magistrates' courts, are tried by a judge and a jury consisting of 12 members. The prosecution or defence may challenge any potential juror for cause. The jury decides whether the accused is guilty or not. The judge is responsible for summing up the facts and explaining the law; he sentences convicted offenders. If, after at least 2 hours and 10 minutes of deliberation, a jury is unable to reach a unanimous verdict it may, on the judge's direction, provided that in a full jury of 12 at least 10 of its members are agreed, bring in a majority verdict. The failure of a jury to agree on a unanimous verdict or to bring in a majority verdict may involve the retrial of the case before a new jury.

The Employment Appeal Tribunal. The Employment Appeal Tribunal which is a superior Court of Record with the like powers, rights, privileges and authority of the High Court, was set up in 1976 to hear appeals on questions of law against decisions of industrial tribunals and of the Certification Officer. The appeals are heard by a High Court Judge sitting with 2 members (in exceptional cases 4) appointed for their special knowledge or experience of industrial relations either on the employer or the trade union side, with always an equal number on each side. The great bulk of their work is concerned with the problems which can arise between employees and their employers.

Military Courts. Offences committed by persons subject to service law under the Army Act 1955, the Air Force Act 1955 or the Naval Discipline Act 1957 may be dealt with either summarily or by courts-martial.

The Personnel of the Law. All full-time judicial officers except the Lord Chancellor (who is a member of the Cabinet) are independent of Parliament and the Executive. They are appointed by the Crown on the advice of the Prime Minister or the Lord Chancellor, or by the Lord Chancellor, and hold office until retiring age. Under the Judicial Pensions and Retirement Act 1993 judges normally retire at age 70 years, though they may be called upon by the Lord Chancellor to serve till age 75. The legal profession is divided; barristers, who advise on legal problems and can conduct cases before all courts, usually act for the public only through solicitors, who deal directly with the legal business brought to them by the public and have rights to present cases before certain courts. Long-standing members of both professions are eligible for appointment to most judicial offices.

In 1994 the Lord Chancellor introduced developments to the procedures for making all judicial appointments below the level of the High Court. Suitably qualified practitioners are invited to apply for advertised vacancies, and shortlisted applicants are interviewed by a panel consisting of a judge, an official and a lay member. Panels make recommendations to the Lord Chancellor, who retains the right of final recommendation to the Sovereign or appointment, as appropriate. Most vacancies for full-time and part-time appointments below the level of High Court Bench are now filled under this procedure. The new arrangements are progressively being extended to the remaining tribunal and similar appointments for which the Lord Chancellor is responsible.

Legal Aid. Broadly there are 3 kinds of legal aid available in England and Wales. Firstly there is legal advice and assistance, otherwise known as the 'Green Form' scheme. This includes advice and assistance on almost any question of English law, both civil and criminal, but does not normally cover any form of representation before a court or tribunal. Qualification for 'Green Form' is dependent on the means of the applicant. As an extension of the scheme, however, assistance by way of representation is available for certain proceedings, chiefly civil, in magistrates' courts. Assistance by way of representation is also means-tested. In 1996–97 there were 1·5m. payments under the Legal Advice and Assistance Scheme. The net cost to the Legal Aid Fund of this part was £162·5m., of which £11·8m. was accounted for by assistance by way of representation. Legal advice and assistance also provides for duty solicitor schemes at magistrates' courts and police stations. Under the magistrates' courts scheme, initial advice, and representation where necessary, is available to unrepresented defendants at court from duty solicitors either in attendance at courts or on call. The scheme covers advice to a defendant in custody, making a bail application, representing a defendant in custody on a guilty plea, and certain other cases. The advice and assistance at police stations scheme enables any person who has been arrested and taken to a police station, or who is assisting the police with their enquiries, to receive advice and assistance, from either a duty solicitor or the person's own solicitor. The cost of these schemes, which are not subject to means test or contribution, is met from the Legal Aid Fund and in 1996–97 amounted to £103·8m. Secondly, under Part IV of the Legal Aid Act 1988, there is legal aid for civil court proceedings. Under regulations, aid is available to those of low or moderate means either free or subject to a contribution, depending on means. In 1996–97, 345,986 civil legal aid certificates were issued. The cost of legal aid is met from (*a*) contributions from assisted persons; (*b*) the operation of the statutory charge which gives the Legal Aid Board a first charge on money or property recovered or preserved for an assisted person; (*c*) costs recovered from opposing parties and (*d*) a grant from the Exchequer. The net cost of civil legal aid to the state (excluding administration costs of the scheme) in 1996–97 amounted to £670·6m. Thirdly under Part V of the Legal Aid Act 1988 a court dealing with criminal proceedings may order legal aid to be given if it considers it is desirable in the interests of justice and if it also considers that the defendant (or appellant) requires financial assistance in meeting the costs he or she may incur. The factors to be taken into account when determining whether it is in the interests of justice that criminal legal aid be granted are defined by statute to include cases where, for example, the defendant is likely to be deprived of his or her liberty, consideration of a substantial question of law may be involved, or the defendant may be unable to understand the proceedings or to state his or her case due to inadequate knowledge of English, mental illness or other mental or physical disability. Legal aid must be granted, subject to means, in the following circumstances: Where a person is committed for trial on a charge of murder, where the prosecutor appeals or applies for leave to appeal from the criminal division of the Court of Appeal or the Courts-Martial Appeal Court to the House of Lords, and in certain circumstances where the court is considering depriving a defendant of his liberty.

The costs of legal aid in criminal proceedings are paid by the central government, but courts have power to require legally aided persons to contribute towards the cost of legal aid given to them. The net cost of legal aid in criminal proceedings in 1996–97 was £539m. £313m. of this was for legal aid in the higher courts which is paid for out of the Lord Chancellor's vote, and £226m. for legal aid in the magistrates' courts which is paid from the Legal Aid Fund.

Police. In England and Wales outside London there are 41 police forces each maintained by a police authority typically comprising 9 local councillors, 3 magistrates and 5 independent members. In Scotland, the unitary councils are the police authorities. London is policed by the Metropolitan Police Service (responsible to the Home Secretary) and the City of London Police. In April 1995 the Home Office gave up central control of police manpower and authorized establishments of police no longer exist. Instead, chief constables recruit according to their budgets. The Home Office collates police strength in March and Sept. each year. The actual strength of the police service in England and Wales in Sept. 1997 was 126,798 (including 19,357 women). In addition there were 19,163 special constables (including 6,857 women). The estimated total revenue expenditure on the police service for 1996–97 was £6,700m.

SCOTLAND. The High Court of Justiciary is the supreme criminal court in Scotland and has jurisdiction in all cases of crime committed in any part of Scotland, unless expressly excluded by statute. It consists of the Lord Justice General, the Lord Justice Clerk and 24 other Judges, who are the same Judges who preside in the Court of Session, the Scottish Supreme Civil Court. One Judge is seconded to the Scottish Law Commission. The court is presided over by the Lord Justice General, whom failing, the Lord Justice Clerk, and exercises an appellate jurisdiction as well as being a court of first instance. The home of the High Court is Edinburgh, but the court visits other towns and cities in Scotland on circuit and indeed the busiest High Court sitting is in Glasgow. The court sits in Edinburgh both as a Court of Appeal (the *quorum* being 2 judges if the appeal is against sentence or other disposals and 3 in all other cases) and on circuit as a court of first instance. The decisions of the court are not subject to review by the House of Lords. One Judge sitting with a Jury of 15 persons can, and usually does, try cases, but 2 or more Judges (with a Jury) may do so in important or complex cases. The court has a privative jurisdiction over cases of treason, murder, rape, breach of duty by Magistrates and certain statutory offences under the Official Secrets Act 1911 and the Geneva Conventions Act 1957. It also tries the most serious crimes against person or property and those cases in which a sentence greater than imprisonment for 3 years is likely to be imposed. Moreover, the court has inherent power to try and to punish all acts which are plainly criminal though previously unknown to the law.

The appellate jurisdiction of the High Court of Justiciary extends to all cases tried on indictment, whether in the High Court or the Sheriff Court, and persons so convicted may appeal to the court against conviction or sentence or both except where the sentence is fixed by law. In such an appeal, a person may bring under review any alleged miscarriage of justice including an alleged miscarriage of justice based on the existence and significance of evidence not heard at the original proceedings provided there is reasonable explanation of why it was not heard and an alleged miscarriage of justice where the Jury returned a verdict which no reasonable Jury, properly directed, could have returned. It is also a court of review from courts of summary jurisdiction, and on the final termination of any summary prosecution the convicted person may appeal to the court by way of stated case on questions of law, but not on questions of fact, except in relation to a miscarriage of justice alleged by the person accused on the basis of the existence and significance of additional evidence not heard at the original proceedings provided that there is a reasonable explanation of why it was not heard. Before cases proceed to a full hearing, leave of appeal must first be granted. Grounds of appeal and any relevant reports are sifted by a Judge sitting alone in chambers, who will decide if there are arguable grounds of appeal. Should leave of appeal be refused, this decision may be appealed to the High Court within 14 days, when the matter will be reviewed by 3 Judges. The Lord Advocate is entitled to appeal to the High Court against any sentence passed on indictment on the ground that it is unduly lenient, or on a point of law. Both the prosecution and defence, at any time in solemn and summary proceedings, may appeal by way of Bill of Advocation in order to correct irregularities in the preliminary stages of a case. In summary proceedings the accused may appeal by Bill of Suspension where he desires to bring under review a warrant, conviction or judgement issued by an inferior Judge. In summary proceedings the accused can also appeal against sentence alone by way of Stated Case. In summary proceedings the Crown can appeal against a sentence on the grounds that it is unduly lenient. The court also hears appeals under the Courts-martial (Appeals) Act 1951.

The Sheriff Court has an inherent universal criminal jurisdiction (as well as an extensive civil one) limited in general to crimes and offences committed within a sheriffdom (a specifically defined region), which has, however, been curtailed by statute or practice under which the High Court of Justiciary has exclusive jurisdiction in relation to the crimes mentioned above. The Sheriff Court is presided over by a Sheriff Principal or a Sheriff, who when trying cases on indictment sits with a Jury of 15 people. His powers of awarding punishment involving imprisonment are restricted to a maximum of 3 years, but he may under certain statutory powers remit the prisoner to the High Court for sentence if this is felt to be insufficient. The Sheriff also exercises a wide summary criminal jurisdiction and when doing so sits without a Jury; and he has concurrent jurisdiction with every other court within his Sheriff Court district in regard to all offences competent for trial in summary courts. The great majority of offences which come before courts are of a more minor nature and as such are disposed of in the Sheriff Summary Courts or in the District Courts (*see* below). Where a case is to be tried on indictment either in the High Court of Justiciary or in the Sheriff Court, the Judge may, before the trial, hold a preliminary or first diet to decide questions of a preliminary nature, whether relating to the competency or relevancy of proceedings or otherwise. Any decision at a preliminary diet (other than a decision to adjourn the first or preliminary diet or discharge trial diet) can be the subject of an appeal to the High Court of Justiciary prior to the trial.

In cases to be tried on indictment in the Sheriff Court a first diet is mandatory before the trial diet to decide questions of a preliminary nature and to identify cases which are unlikely to go to trial on the date programmed. Likewise in summary proceedings, an intermediate diet is again mandatory before trial. In High Court cases such matters may be dealt with at a preliminary diet.

District Courts have jurisdiction in more minor offences occurring within a district which before recent local government reorganization corresponded to district council boundaries. These courts are presided over by Lay Magistrates, known as Justices, who have limited powers for fine and imprisonment. In Glasgow District there are also Stipendiary Magistrates, who are legally qualified, and who have the same sentencing powers as Sheriffs.

The Court of Session, presided over by the Lord President (the Lord Justice General in criminal cases), is divided into an inner-house comprising 2 divisions of 4 judges each with a mainly appellate function, and an outer-house comprising 18 single Judges sitting individually at first instance; it exercises the highest civil jurisdiction in Scotland, with the House of Lords as a Court of Appeal.

Police. Establishment levels in Scotland were abolished on 1 April 1996. The actual strength at 31 March 1997 was 12,752 men and 2,036 women. There were 1,876 special constables. The total police net expenditure in Scotland for 1995–96 was £615·3m.

CIVIL JUDICIAL STATISTICS

ENGLAND AND WALES	1995	1996
Appellate Courts		
Judicial Committee of the Privy Council	82	80
House of Lords	72	65
Court of Appeal	1,853	1,804
High Court of Justice (appeals and special cases from inferior courts)	4,674	4,891
Courts of First Instance (excluding Magistrates'		
Courts and Tribunals)		
High Court of Justice:		
Chancery Division	42,251	40,500
Queen's Bench Division	154,186	143,033
Official Referee's	1,804	1,564
County courts: Matrimonial suits	178,196	181,467
County courts: Other	2,472,637	2,363,017
Restrictive Practices Court	2	6

SCOTLAND	1995	1996
House of Lords (Appeals from Court of Session)	14	15
Court of Session—		
General Department	4,024	3,638
Petition Department	1,183	1,045
Sheriff's Courts—Ordinary Cause	46,096	45,660
Sheriff's Courts—Summary Cause	34,630	30,078
Small Claims	59,710	59,009

CRIMINAL STATISTICS

ENGLAND AND WALES

	Total number of offenders		Indictable offences	
	1995	1996	1995	1996
Aged 10 and over				
Proceeded against in magistrates' courts	1,836,307	1,919,494	463,521	464,677
Found guilty at magistrates' courts	1,284,218	1,368,942	234,068	233,854
Found guilty at the Crown Court	70,366	69,085	68,109	66,726
Cautioned	291,247	286,198	202,585	190,811
Aged 10 and under 18				
Proceeded against in magistrates' courts	110,029	119,937	71,252	74,813
Found guilty at magistrates' courts	65,142	71,184	39,572	40,991
Found guilty at the Crown Court	2,694	3,491	2,654	3,392
Cautioned	120,561	113,065	90,643	79,858

Source: Crime and Criminal Justice Unit, Home Office

CRIMINAL STATISTICS

SCOTLAND

	All Crimes and Offences		Crimes[1]	
	1994	1995	1994	1995
All persons and companies				
Cautioned	120,561	113,065	90,643	79,858
Proceeded against in all courts	178,292	176,420	62,432	61,859
Charge proved	158,119	156,707	51,265	51,073
Children (aged 8–15)				
Proceeded against in all courts	237	244	182	194

[1] Crimes are generally the more serious criminal acts and offences the less serious. 'Crimes' are not equivalent in coverage to 'indictable/triable either way offences'.

In 1996 the average prison population in England and Wales was 55,280; in Scotland it was 5,900.

Religion. The Anglican Communion has originated from the Church of England and parallels in its fellowship of autonomous churches the evolution of British influence beyond the seas from colonies to dominions and independent nations. The Archbishop of Canterbury presides as *primus inter pares* at the decennial meetings of the bishops of the Anglican Communion at the Lambeth Conference and at the biennial meetings of the Primates and the Anglican Consultative Council. The last Conference was held in Canterbury in 1988 and was attended by 518 bishops.

The Anglican Communion consists of 33 member Churches or Provinces. These are Australia, Brazil, Burma, Burundi, Rwanda and Zaïre, Canada, Central Africa, Ceylon, England, Indian Ocean, Ireland, Japan, Jerusalem and the Middle East, Kenya, Korea, Melanesia, Mexico, New Zealand, Nigeria, Papua New Guinea, the Philippines, Scotland, Southern Africa, Southern Cone of America, Sudan, Tanzania, Uganda, USA, Wales, West Africa, West Indies. There are also areas which come under the metro-political jurisdiction of the Archbishop of Canterbury. These are Bermuda, the Diocese in Europe, Falkland Islands, The Council of the Churches of East Asia, The Diocese of Hong Kong and Macao, Sabah, Kuching, Singapore, West Malaysia, The Lusitanian Church (Portugal) and The Spanish Reformed Episcopal Church.

England and Wales. The established Church of England, which baptizes about 25% of the children born in England (*i.e.* excluding Wales but including the Isle of Man and the Channel Islands), is Anglican. Civil disabilities on account of religion do not attach to any class of British subject. Under the Welsh Church Acts, 1914 and 1919, the Church in Wales and Monmouthshire was disestablished as from 1 April 1920, and Wales was formed into a separate Province.

The Queen is, under God, the supreme governor of the Church of England, with the right, regulated by statute, to nominate to the vacant archbishoprics and bishoprics. The Queen, on the advice of the First Lord of the Treasury, also appoints to such deaneries, prebendaries and canonries as are in the gift of the Crown, while a large number of livings and also some canonries are in the gift of the Lord Chancellor.

There are 2 archbishops (at the head of the 2 Provinces of Canterbury and York), and 42 diocesan bishops including the bishop of the diocese in Europe, which is part of the Province of Canterbury. Dr George Carey was enthroned as *Archbishop of Canterbury* in April 1991. Each archbishop has also his own particular diocese, wherein he exercises episcopal, as in his Province he exercises metropolitan, jurisdiction. In Dec. 1996 there were 68 suffragan and assistant bishops, 37 deans and provosts of cathedrals and 108 archdeacons. The *General Synod*, which replaced the Church Assembly in 1970 in England, consists of a House of Bishops, a House of Clergy and a House of Laity, and has power to frame legislation regarding Church matters. Each House has a veto over the others. The first two Houses consist of the members of the Convocations of Canterbury and York, each of which consists of the diocesan bishops and elected representatives of the suffragan bishops, 6 for Canterbury province and 3 for York (forming an Upper House), deans, provosts, and archdeacons, and a certain number of proctors elected as the representatives of the inferior clergy, together with, in the case of Canterbury Convocation, 4 representatives of the Universities of Oxford, Cambridge, London and the Southern Universities and in the case of York 2 representatives for the Universities of Durham and Newcastle and the other Northern Universities; 3 archdeacons to the Armed Forces, the Chaplain General of Prisons and 2 representatives of the Religious Communities (forming the Lower House). The House of Laity is elected by the lay members of the Deanery Synods but also includes 3 representatives of the Religious Communities and *ex-officio* Church Commissioners and Ecclesiastical Judges. Every Measure passed by the General Synod must be submitted to the Ecclesiastical Committee, consisting of 15 members of the House of Lords nominated by the Lord Chancellor and 15 members of the House of Commons nominated by the Speaker. This committee reports on each Measure to Parliament, and the Measure receives the Royal Assent and becomes law if each House of Parliament resolves that the Measure be presented to the Queen.

Parochial affairs are managed by annual parochial church meetings and parochial church councils. At 30 June 1996 there were 12,982 ecclesiastical parishes, inclusive of the Isle of Man and the Channel Islands. These parishes do not, in many cases, coincide with civil parishes. Although most parishes have their own churches, not every parish nowadays can have its own incumbent or minister.

In Dec. 1996 there were 5,735 beneficed clergy excluding dignitaries, 1,821 other clergy of incumbent status and 1,758 assistant curates working in the parishes.

Women have been admitted to Holy Orders (but not the Episcopate) as deacons since 1987 and as priests since 1994. On 11 Nov. 1992 the General Synod voted for the ordination of women to the priesthood (the Upper House, by 39 votes to 13; the Lower House, by 176 to 74; the House of Laity, by 169 to 82). The legislation received the Royal Assent on 5 Nov. 1993 and the Canon permitting women's ordination came into effect on 22 Feb. 1994. At 31 Dec. 1996 there were 859 full-time stipendiary women clergy, 816 of whom were in the parochial ministry. Over 2,000 non-stipendiary clergy hold a bishop's licence to officiate at services. In July 1995 the General Synod stated that 304 clergymen had left the Church of England because they disagreed with the ordination of women, and that perhaps 75% of these had joined the Roman Catholic Church.

Private persons possess the right of presentation to over 2,000 benefices; the patronage of the others belongs mainly to the Queen, the bishops and cathedrals, the Lord Chancellor, and the universities of Oxford and Cambridge. In addition to the 6,147 dignitaries and parochial incumbents, there were (1996) 124 cathedral, 3,202 parochial and 313 non-parochial clergy working within the diocesan framework. Although these figures account for the majority of active clergy in England, there are many others serving in parishes and institutions who cannot be quantified with any certainty. They include some 1,300 full-time hospital, Forces, prison, industrial and school and college chaplains.

Of the 40,397 buildings registered for the solemnization of marriages at 30 June 1994, (statistics from the Office of Population Censuses and Surveys) 16,538 belonged to the Established Church and the Church in Wales and 23,859 to other religious denominations (Methodist, 6,739; Roman Catholic, 3,331; Baptist, 3,109; United Reformed, 1,689; Congregational, 1,264; Calvinistic Methodist, 1,093; Jehovah's Witnesses, 786; Brethren, 744; Salvation Army, 737; Unitarians, 165; other Christian, 3,857; Sikhs, 129; Moslems, 90; other non-Christian, 126). Of the 306,756 marriages celebrated in 1991 (331,150 in 1990), 102,840 were in the Established Church and the Church in Wales, 52,583 in other denominations and 151,333 were civil marriages in Register Offices.

Roman Catholics in England and Wales were estimated at 4,404,056 in 1996. There are 22 dioceses in 5 provinces. There are 5 archbishops, 17 diocesan bishops and 10 auxiliary or assistant bishops. There are 5,732 priests in active ministry and 2,856 parish churches. There are 1,286 convents of female religious, who number 10,100.

Membership of other denominations in the UK in 1991 (and 1975):

Presbyterians, 1,291,672 (1·65m.); Methodists, 483,387 (0·61m.); Baptists, 241,842 (0·27m.); other Protestants, 123,677; independent churches, 408,999; Orthodox, 265,258 (0·2m.); Afro-Caribbean churches, 69,658; Mormons (1994), 163,800; Jehovah's Witnesses, 0·12m.; Spiritualists, 60,000; Moslems, 0·99m. (0·4m.); Sikhs, 0·39m. (0·12m.); Hindus, 0·14m. (0·1m.); Jews, 108,400 (0·11m.).

The Salvation Army is established in 94 countries. In 1991 in the UK and Ireland it had 1,792 ministers, 55,000 members and 837 churches.

There is a 400-member Board of Deputies of British Jews.

Scotland. The Church of Scotland, which was reformed in 1560, subsequently developed a presbyterian system of church government which was established in 1690 and has continued to the present day.

The supreme court is the General Assembly, which now consists of some 800 members, ministers and elders in equal numbers, together with members of the diaconate commissioned by presbyteries. It meets annually in May, under the presidency of a Moderator appointed by the Assembly. The Queen is normally represented by a Lord High Commissioner, but has occasionally attended in person. The royal presence in a special throne gallery in the hall but outside the Assembly symbolises the independence from state control of what is nevertheless recognised as the national Church in Scotland.

There are also 46 presbyteries in Scotland, roughly co-terminous with District Councils, together with 1 presbytery of England, 1 presbytery of Europe, and 1 presbytery of Jerusalem. At the base of this conciliar structure of Church courts are the kirk sessions, of which there were 1,603 on 31 Dec. 1996, with a total of 683,397 members.

The Episcopal Church of Scotland is a province of the Anglican Church and is one of the historic Scottish churches. It consists of 7 dioceses. As at 31 Dec. 1996 it had 316 churches and missions, 367 clergy and 53,599 members, of whom 32,833 were communicants.

There are in Scotland some small outstanding Presbyterian bodies and also Baptists, Congregationalists, Methodists and Unitarians.

The Roman Catholic Church which celebrated the centenary of the restoration of the Hierarchy in 1978, had in Scotland (1995) 1 cardinal archbishop, 1 archbishop, 6 bishops, 964 clergy, 461 parishes, and 730,835 adherents.

The proportion of marriages in Scotland according to the rites of the various Churches in 1995 was: Church of Scotland, 36·5%; Roman Catholic, 9·6%; Episcopal, 1·5%; others, 6%; civil, 46·4%.

Bradley, I., *Marching to the Promised Land: Has the Church a Future?*. London, 1992.
De La Noy, M., *The Church of England: a Portrait*. London, 1993.

Education (England and Wales). *The Publicly Maintained System of Education:* Compulsory schooling begins at the age of 5 and the minimum leaving age for all pupils is 16. No tuition fees are payable in any publicly maintained school (but it is open to parents, if they choose, to pay for their children to attend other schools). The post-school or tertiary stage, which is voluntary, includes universities, further education establishments and other higher education establishments (including those which provide courses for the training of teachers), as well as adult education centres and the youth service. Financial assistance (grants and loans) is generally available to students on higher education courses in the university and non-university sectors and to some students on other courses in further education.

National Curriculum. The Education Reform Act 1988 established a National Curriculum for gradual introduction into primary and secondary schools. It was revised in 1995. Statutory subjects at 5 to 11 years: English (and Welsh in Wales), mathematics, science (core subjects); design and technology, information technology, geography, history, physical education, art and music. At 11 to 14 years a foreign language is added. Statutory subjects at 14 to 16: English, mathematics, science, technology, a foreign language and physical education. Religious education and, at secondary level, sex education, are not prescribed in the curriculum but are requirements; parents may withdraw their children from these lessons. Careers education is also statutory at secondary level.

Nursery Education. Provision for children under 5 is made in either nursery schools or in nursery or infant classes in primary schools. In the public sector no fees are payable. In Jan. 1996 there were 547 public sector nursery and 5,581 primary schools with nursery classes in England; in addition, there were 1,531 independent schools with provision for children under 5. In 1996 there were 52,177 pupils under 5 attending nursery schools and 656,316 pupils under 5 in nursery and infant classes in primary schools. About 48% of all these children were attending part-time. In Wales there were 52 maintained nursery schools in 1995 and 52,360 pupils under 5 years provided for in nursery or infant classes in primary schools.

Primary Schools. These provide for pupils from the age of 5 up to the age of 11. In Jan. 1997 there were 18,186 primary schools in England of which 2,376 were infant schools providing for pupils up to the age of about 7, the remainder mainly taking pupils from age 5 through to 11. Nearly all primary schools take both boys and girls. 16% of primary schools had 100 full time pupils or less.

In Jan. 1996 there were 1,681 primary schools in Wales. In those primary schools (and some secondary schools) which are in the predominantly Welsh-speaking areas, the main language of instruction is Welsh. There are also 'Welsh', or, more accurately, bilingual schools in mainly English-speaking parts of Wales. Generally children transfer from primary to secondary schools at 11.

Middle Schools. A number of local education authorities operate a middle school system. These provide for pupils from the age of 8, 9 or 10 up to the age of 12, 13 or 14. In Jan. 1997 there were 590 middle schools in England deemed either primary or secondary according to the age range of the school concerned.

Secondary Schools. These usually provide for pupils from the age of 11 upwards. In Jan. 1997 there were 3,185 secondary schools in England and 228 in Wales. In England some local authorities have retained selection at age 11 for entry to grammar schools of which there were 158 in 1997. There were a small number of technical schools in 1997 which specialise in technical studies. There were 91 secondary modern schools in 1997 providing a general education up to the minimum school leaving age of 16, although exceptionally some pupils stay on beyond that age.

Almost all local education authorities operate a system of comprehensive schools to which pupils are admitted without reference to ability or aptitude. In Jan. 1997 there were 2,882 such schools in England with over 2·6m. pupils. With the development of comprehensive education various patterns of secondary schools have come into operation. Principally these are: 1. All through schools with pupils aged 11 to 18 or 11 to 16; pupils over 16 being able to transfer to an 11 to 18 school or a sixth form college providing for pupils aged 16 to 19. (There were 115 sixth form colleges in England in 1992). 2. Local education authorities operating a three-tier system involving middle schools where transfer to secondary school is at ages 12, 13 or 14. These correspond to 12 to 18, 13 to 18 and 14 to 18 comprehensive schools respectively; or 3. In areas where there are no middle schools a two-tier system of junior and senior comprehensive schools for pupils aged 11 to 18 with optional transfer to these schools at age 13 or 14.

The majority of secondary schools in Wales are classified as comprehensive. In 1996, 67 schools used Welsh as a teaching medium.

Grant Maintained Schools. Local education authority maintained secondary, middle and primary schools can apply for Grant Maintained (GM) status as self-governing state schools. Under GM status schools receive funding directly from the Funding Agency for Schools or, in Wales, from the Welsh Office. Their governing bodies are responsible for all aspects of school management, including the deployment of funds, employment of staff and provision of most of the educational support services for staff and pupils. The first GM primary schools were incorporated in 1991. By Sept. 1997 there were 1,196 GM schools in England (507 primary, 668 secondary and 21 special schools) and by Sept. 1997, 5 GM primary, 1 middle and 11 secondary schools in Wales.

Specialist Schools. 1. Technology Colleges, Language Colleges, Arts Colleges and Sports Colleges. A programme to help existing maintained secondary schools to specialize in a particular area of the curriculum, while continuing to cover the full National Curriculum. To be included in the programme, schools must raise sponsorship and then prepare development plans, in competition with other schools, to seek extra government funding. They must demonstrate how they will share their resources and expertise with local schools and the wider community. The first Technology Colleges operated from Sept. 1994. 2. City Technology Colleges. 15 independent all-ability secondary schools established in partnership between government and business sponsors, under the Education Reform Act 1988. They teach the full National Curriculum but give special emphasis to technology, science and mathematics. Government meets all recurrent costs. By Sept. 1997 some 258 schools had been designated in one or other of the categories of specialist school.

Assisted Places Scheme. It is no longer possible to get a place under the Assisted Places Scheme (APS). The Education (Schools) Act 1997 which came into force on 1 Sept. has the effect of preventing any further intakes to assisted places after the beginning of the 1997/98 academic year. The Government has a manifesto commitment to phase out the APS and use the resources saved to reduce class sizes for those children who are currently being educated in overcrowded infant classes.

Commitments to children holding assisted places at the start of the 1997/98 academic year will be honoured. Secondary school aged pupils will hold their assisted places until they complete their education at their current school—usually age 18. Primary aged children will normally hold their places until the end of their primary education—usually age 11.

Music and Ballet Scheme. The 'Aided Pupil Scheme' for boys and girls with outstanding talent in music or ballet helps parents with the fees and boarding costs at seven specialist private schools. This scheme provides a specialist provision not readily available in the maintained sector and will therefore continue to operate.

Special Education. Under the Education Act 1996 children have special educational needs if they have a learning difficulty which calls for special educational provision to be made for them. It has been estimated that, nationally, some 20% of the school population will have special educational needs at some time during their school career. In a minority of cases, perhaps just over 2% of children, the Local Education Authority will need to make a statutory assessment of special educational needs under the Education Act 1996, which may ultimately lead to a 'statement'. In England the total number of pupils with statements in 1997 was over 234,000 (14,521 in Wales in 1995). In England in 1997 there were 1,171 maintained special schools and 68 non-maintained special schools.

The Education Act 1996 and regulations made thereunder build upon the principles and practices first set out in the 1981 Education Act. They place duties and responsibilities on Local Education Authorities and schools, and all those who help them work with children with special educational needs. Maintained schools must use their best endeavours to make provision for such pupils. The Code of Practice on the Identification and Assessment of Special Educational Needs, which came into force on 1 Sept. 1994, gives practical guidance to these bodies as to how they fulfil their duties. Provision for all children with special educational needs will be made by the most appropriate agency, which in most cases will be the child's mainstream school. The Code of Practice recognizes that there is a continuum of needs and a continuum of provision, which may be made in a variety of different forms. However, even before reaching statutory school age, a child may have special educational needs requiring the intervention of the Local Education as well as the Health Authority.

Some pupils with statements remain in school after the age of 16. Local Education Authorities remain responsible for such pupils until they are 19. Others with statements leave school at 16, moving perhaps to a college within the further education sector, or to social services provision.

Ancillary Services. Local Education Authorities (LEAs) and the governing bodies of GM schools may provide registered pupils at schools maintained by them with meals, milk and other refreshment and make such charges as they think fit. However, they must charge the same price for the same quantity of the same item. It is for LEAs and GM schools to decide on the presentation and content of school meals. They must provide meals free of charge to pupils whose parents receive income support or income-based jobseekers' allowance, or to pupils who receive income support in their own right. Where LEAs or GM schools decide to provide milk, it must be free to these categories of pupils. The provision of free meals and milk must be made in the middle of the day.

Further Education (Non-University). There are 437 institutions in the further education sector in England providing FE programmes both academic and vocational, though mainly the latter. The colleges vary in size from those specializing in single areas to large institutions with courses from foundation to degree level, and offer lifelong learning opportunities mostly for people aged over 16. In 1996/97 some 4m. students enrolled, over three-quarters of whom were adults, and the majority study part-time. The majority of these courses were funded by the Further Education Funding Council (FEFC).

FE programmes were also provided in higher education institutions, local authority and voluntary adult education centres and other FE provider institutions. Some of these courses are also funded by the FEFC.

Education at institutions of further education is not free, but fees are generally low, and are not charged for students under the age of 19.

In Wales in Nov. 1996 there were 29 institutions in the further education sector and 191,385 students.

The Youth Service. The Youth Service forms part of the education system and is mainly concerned with the provision of personal and social education for young people to enable them to become responsible citizens. The Youth Service is chiefly provided by Local Education Authorities (the statutory sector) and a wide range of voluntary organizations. The priority age group for the service is usually regarded as 13-19 years old but this target age group extends to 11-25 year olds. A duty is laid upon Local Education Authorities by the provision of the (Consolidation) Education Act 1996 which has superseded earlier Education Acts, to secure adequate provision of further education which includes the Youth Service. Provision is usually in the form of a wide range of leisure-time activities or through 'detached' or outreach work aimed at young people at risk. The Department of Education and Employment awards grants to the headquarters of national voluntary youth organizations through its Grant Scheme. The current Scheme runs from 1996–97 until the end of 1998–99. Total funding will amount to £9·1m. over 3 years. Some 60 organizations are being funded to pursue approved programmes of work concerned with the social and personal education of young people, particularly those aged 13-19. The Scheme aims to widen access to the youth services especially for those who are disadvantaged, who have disabilities, who come from minority ethnic groups or inner city or rural areas and for girls and young women. It also places priority on work which aims to contribute to crime prevention and health education and encourage the involvement of volunteers.

Awards to Students. Local Education Authorities in England and Wales are currently responsible for making mandatory awards to eligible students enrolled on designated full-time or sandwich courses leading to a first degree or comparable qualification and on certain courses of initial teacher-training for existing students. These awards cover fees and maintenance but the maintenance grants are subject to the income of the student and his or her parents or spouse. For new students in 1998–99, awards to cover both fees (up to £1,000 a year) and maintenance will depend on income. In addition studentships may be available both from universities and other sources. The authorities may also give discretionary awards to students who are not eligible for mandatory awards including those taking non-degree level courses. In 1998–99 loans will form about three-quarters and grants about a quarter of the grant and loan package. Loans will not be available to help contribute towards tuition fees. Support for students through grants and loans rose in line with inflation, resulting in a 2·5% increase over the 1996–97 levels. In 1996–97 the Government provided further and higher education institutions with £27·7m. for Access Funds to help students with severe financial difficulties.

The Student Loans scheme was introduced by the Government in 1990 to supplement mandatory awards. Eligible students apply for loans to the Student Loans Company which is funded wholly by the Government. On leaving higher education former students begin to repay loans over a 5-year period when they reach an income threshold of 85% of average earnings. New students in 1998–99 will have new repayment arrangements once they have graduated and their income is at least £10,000 a year. They will begin to pay back their loans on an income contingent basis. In 1996–97 63% of students took out loans averaging £1,487.

In Scotland a broadly similar student support system is administered by the Student Awards Agency for Scotland. The Agency offers means-tested awards to eligible Scottish domiciled students undertaking courses of Higher Education. The arrangements described above for new students in 1998–99 will also apply to Scottish students. The Agency also administers the Postgraduate Students' Allowance Scheme and the Scottish Studentship Scheme (SSS) which offer means-tested awards to students studying at postgraduate and advanced postgraduate levels respectively. 75 new awards are offered each year under the SSS for study in the field of Arts and Humanities.

Awards known as state studentships are offered on a competitive basis by the British Academy and the Students Awards Agency for Scotland to candidates considered by the universities and other higher education institutions to be qualified for postgraduate studies in the humanities; similar awards, tenable at universities or other higher education institutions are offered by the Research Councils to students studying topics within the broad spectrum of agriculture and food; the biological sciences; man's natural environment; science and engineering and the social sciences at postgraduate level.

The 5 Research Councils made over 7,300 new awards in 1990–91 and there were more than 15,000 current awards in that academic year. In 1992–93 the British Academy gave 924 new awards and the Department 437 state bursaries, 204 library bursaries and 25 state studentships.

Career Development Loans (CDLs) were introduced by the Government in 1988 to provide wider opportunities for adults to acquire and improve vocational skills. The loans are aimed at those who would otherwise not have reasonable or adequate access to the funds required to train. Loans of between £300 and £8,000 can support up to 2 years of education or training, plus up to 1 year's practical work experience where it forms part of the course. Loans to pay for training are available through 4 high street banks. The Department of Education and Employment pays the interest on the loan for the period of the training and for 1 month afterwards. Borrowers registered unemployed and claiming benefit, i.e. Jobseekers' Allowance or National Insurance credits, may apply to the bank to defer repayments for up to a further 5 months. CDL Plus, launched in Sept. 1995, is piloting arrangements which allow the borrower to defer repayment of their loan for up to 18 months after completing their course if they are registered unemployed, employed and receiving certain benefits or need to extend their training. CDL Plus is available to residents of Somerset, Gwent, South Glamorgan, Mid Glamorgan and the former county of Avon.

By Oct. 1997 nearly £298m. had been advanced to over 95,000 applicants since the programme began.

Teachers. In order to teach in a maintained school or a non maintained special school in England or Wales, it is first necessary to achieve qualified teacher status. This is generally achieved by successfully completing an undergraduate or postgraduate course of initial teacher training.

Those who are recognized as qualified teachers in Scotland or Northern Ireland are also entitled to qualified teacher status. Teachers who are nationals of participating member states of the European Economic Area who are recognized as qualified in their own countries may also be entitled to qualified teacher status if they meet the requirements on the mutual recognition of qualifications.

Those who have trained overseas in a country outside of the European Economic Area or candidates over 24 who have successfully completed two or more years of higher education may be eligible to train on the job through what are known as 'employment-based' routes. These are the Graduate Teacher Programme (for graduates) and the Registered Teacher Programme (for those with two years of higher education).

In 1997–98 there were about 53,700 students on initial teacher training courses; this figure includes students on the Open University and school-centred courses.

On 1 Jan. 1997, 420,908 full-time equivalent teachers were employed by Local Education Authorities in maintained (including Grant-Maintained) nursery, primary and secondary schools in England and Wales.

Finance. Total current and capital expenditure on education in England from public funds is estimated at £28,111m. for 1994–95.

Education (Scotland). In Sept. 1997 there were 3,847 publicly funded (education authority, grant-aided and self-governing) schools in Scotland. All teachers employed in these schools require to be qualified; all figures on teaching relate to September 1996 and are full-time equivalents.

Nursery Education. There were 990 publicly funded nursery schools and classes in Scotland, with a total enrolment of 52,714 pupils in Sept. 1997.

Primary Education. In Sept. 1997 there were 2,298 publicly funded primary schools with 440,008 pupils. In Sept. 1996 there were 22,481 teachers.

Secondary Education. In Sept. 1997 there were 401 publicly funded secondary schools in Scotland with 314,076 pupils and 2,089 adults. All but 26 schools provided a full range of Scottish Certificate of Education courses and non-certificate courses. Pupils who start their secondary education in schools which do not cater for a full range of courses may be transferred at the end of their second or fourth year to schools where a full range of courses is provided. There were 24,265 full-time equivalent teachers in secondary schools in Sept. 1996.

Special Education. In Sept. 1997 there were 158 publicly funded special schools with 7,650 pupils.

Further Education. Under the Further and Higher Education (Scotland) Act 1992 funding of further education colleges was transferred to central government on 1 April 1993.

There are 43 incorporated colleges in Scotland as well as the education centres in Orkney and Shetland which are run by the education authorities but funded by direct payments from the Scottish Office Education and Industry Department. The colleges offer training in a wide range of vocational areas and co-operate with the Scottish Qualifications Authority and the Scottish Office Education and Industry Department in the development of new courses. Scottish Vocational Qualifications (SVQs) were introduced in 1989 and General SVQs were piloted in 1993. Both qualifications aim to improve the skills of the nation's workforce and increase the country's competitiveness. The colleges benefit from co-operation with industry, both by the involvement of Industry Lead Bodies and National Training Organizations in developing SVQs and by membership of the college boards of management.

In 1995–96 there were 285,557 students enrolled at the colleges (56,037 full-time and sandwich). The full-time equivalent staff number in the colleges was 6,799.

Independent Schools. Outside the state system of education there were in England 2,269 independent schools in Jan. 1997, ranging from large 'public' schools to small local ones. There were 550,000 pupils in these schools. In Wales (1994) 10,672 full-time pupils attended 64 independent schools. Independent schools are self-financing and self-resourcing, and receive no grant from central government. All independent schools in England (and Wales) are required to be registered by the Department for Education and Employment (and the Welsh Office) and are liable to the inspection by HM Inspectors from OFSTED. The term 'public schools' refers to independent schools in membership of the Headmasters' and Headmistresses' Conference, Governing Bodies Association or the Governing Bodies of Girls' Schools Association. Qualifications under which a school may be represented at the Headmasters' and Headmistresses' Conference include the measure of independence enjoyed by the governing body and the amount of advanced courses undertaken. Some of these schools are for boarders only, but the majority include non-resident 'day-pupils'. In Scotland there were 114 independent schools, with a total of 30,958 pupils in Sept. 1996. A small number of the Scottish independent schools are of the 'public school' type but they are not known as 'public schools' since in Scotland this term is used to denote education authority (*i.e.*, state) schools.

The earliest of the schools were founded by, and attached to, medieval churches. Many were founded as 'grammar' (classical) schools in the 16th century, receiving charters from the reigning sovereign. Reformed mainly in the middle of the 19th century, among the best-known are Eton College, founded in 1440 by Henry VI; Winchester College (1394) founded by William of Wykeham, Bishop of Winchester; Harrow School, founded in 1560 as a grammar school by John Lyon, a yeoman; and Charterhouse (1611). Among the earliest foundations are King's School, Canterbury, founded 600; King's School, Rochester (604) and St Peter's, York, (627).

Higher Education. The Further and Higher Education Act 1992 removed the polytechnics from local authority funding and gave them university title. The Act created the Higher Education Funding Council for England (HEFCE) and the Higher Education Funding Council for Wales (HEFCW). The Further and Higher Education (Scotland) Act 1992 established the Scottish Higher Education Funding Council (SHEFC). These are responsible for the funding of universities and other higher education institutions and prescribed courses of higher education in further education colleges. The higher education funding councils are non-departmental public bodies operating within a policy and funding context set by the government. Their task is to advise the Secretaries of State with responsibility for education on the funding needs of institutions and to distribute the funds that they make available for the provision of education and the undertaking of research.

Powers to award degrees and authority to adopt a university title are granted by the Privy Council.

Polytechnics created universities by the 1992 Act (P = Polytechnic): Anglia P became Anglia P Univ.; Birmingham P, Univ. of Central England in Birmingham; Bournemouth P, Bournemouth Univ.; Brighton P, Univ. of Brighton; Bristol P, Univ. of the West of England, Bristol; City of London P, London Guildhall Univ.; Coventry P, Coventry Univ.; Derby P, Univ. of Derby; Hatfield P, Univ. of Hertfordshire; Huddersfield P, Univ. of Huddersfield; Humberside P, Univ. of Humberside; Kingston P, Kingston Univ.; Leeds P, Leeds Metropolitan Univ.; Lancashire P, Univ. of Central Lancashire; Leicester P, De Montfort Univ.; Liverpool P, Liverpool John Moores Univ.; Manchester P, Manchester Metropolitan Univ.; Middlesex P, Middlesex Univ.; Newcastle P, Univ. of Northumbria at Newcastle; Nottingham P, Nottingham Trent Univ.; Oxford P, Oxford Brookes Univ.; P of Central London, Univ. of Westminster; P of East London, Univ. of East London; P of North London, Univ. of North London; P South West, Univ. of Plymouth; P of West London, Thames Valley Univ.; Portsmouth P, Univ. of Portsmouth; Sheffield City P, Sheffield Hallam Univ.; South Bank P, South Bank Univ.; Staffordshire P, Staffordshire Univ.; Sunderland P, Univ. of Sunderland; Teesside P, Univ. of Teesside; Thames P, Univ. of Greenwich; Wolverhampton P, Univ. of Wolverhampton.

In *England* in 1995–96 there were 137 institutions of higher education directly funded by the HEFCE, of which 70 were universities. The HEFCE allocates public funds for teaching and research to universities and colleges. It works in partnership with the higher education sector and advises the Government on higher education policy. In 1995–96 the HEFCE distributed £3,207m. in funding: £2,270m. for teaching, £636m. for research, £287m. of non-formula money and £14m. transitional funding. There were 1,137,000 students in funded institutions, including 727,000 full-time.

a) *Universities*

Name (Location)	No. of students (1994–95)	No. of academic staff (1994–95)
Anglia Polytechnic Univ. (Chelmsford)	12,006	517
Aston Univ. (Birmingham)	4,950	. . .
Univ. of Bath	7,031	377
Univ. of Birmingham	17,393	2,379
Bournemouth Univ. (Poole)	9,709	420
Univ. of Bradford	7,980	400
Univ. of Brighton	6,235	500
Univ. of Bristol	10,627	841
Brunel Univ. (Uxbridge)	7,374	267
Univ. of Cambridge	13,920	1,260
Univ. of Central England in Birmingham	6,000	650
Univ. of Central Lancashire (Preston)	16,990	516
City Univ. (London)	6,373	360
Coventry Univ.	8,345	550
Cranfield Univ. (Bedford)	2,090	. . .
De Montfort Univ. (Leicester)	26,000	600
Univ. of Derby	11,368	. . .
Univ. of Durham	5,600	435
Univ. of East Anglia (Norwich)	4,600	360
Univ. of East London (London)	10,000	500
Univ. of Essex (Colchester)	3,650	300
Univ. of Exeter	9,031	530
Univ. of Greenwich (London)	17,376	500
Univ. of Hertfordshire (Hatfield)	8,000	480
Univ. of Huddersfield	6,816[1]	. . .
Univ. of Hull	8,884	456
Univ. of Humberside (Hull)	12,580	362
Univ. of Keele	3,750	320
Univ. of Kent at Canterbury	5,981	403
Kingston Univ. (Kingston-upon-Thames)	6,868	430
Univ. of Lancaster	5,860	450
Univ. of Leeds	17,505	1,100
Leeds Metropolitan Univ.	16,800	1,260

Name (Location)	No. of students (1994–95)	No. of academic staff (1994–95)
Univ. of Leicester	9,357	603
Univ. of Liverpool	13,712	1,007
Liverpool John Moores Univ.	9,940[1]	· · ·
Univ. of London	59,427[1]	· · ·
London Guildhall Univ.	5,496[1]	· · ·
Loughborough Univ. of Technology	9,963	564
Luton Univ.	14,000	700
Univ. of Manchester	16,086	2,050
Univ. of Manchester Institute of Science and Technology	6,030	463
Manchester Metropolitan Univ.	29,891	900
Middlesex Univ. (London)	11,570	410
Univ. of Newcastle upon Tyne	12,870	1,852
Univ. of North London	8,500	525
Univ. of Northumbria at Newcastle	18,174	780
Univ. of Nottingham	12,960	1,062
Nottingham Trent Univ.	9,620	755
Univ. of Oxford	16,080	1,650
Oxford Brookes Univ.	11,000	590
Univ. of Plymouth	16,489	595
Univ. of Portsmouth	7,100	630
Univ. of Reading	9,700	760
Univ. of Salford	4,325	390
Univ. of Sheffield	13,288[1]	· · ·
Sheffield Hallam Univ.	18,645	927
Univ. of Southampton	9,238	740
South Bank Univ. (London)	19,674	545
Staffordshire Univ. (Stoke on Trent)	13,359	523
Univ. of Sunderland	4,380	400
Univ. of Surrey (Guildford)	5,301	376
Univ. of Sussex (Brighton)	8,905	520
Univ. of Teesside (Middlesbrough)	4,902[1]	· · ·
Thames Valley Univ. (London)	3,877[1]	· · ·
Univ. of Warwick (Coventry)	13,800	637
Univ. of Westminster (London)	19,246	395
Univ. of the West of England, Bristol	18,328	673
Univ. of Wolverhampton	21,384	453
Univ. of York	4,380	360

[1] 1993–94.

b) *Other Institutions*

Bath College of Higher Education[1]; Bishop Grosseteste College (Lincoln); Bolton Institute of Higher Education[1]; Bretton Hall (Wakefield); Buckinghamshire College of Higher Education (High Wycombe); Central School of Speech and Drama (London); Canterbury Christ Church College; Cheltenham and Gloucester College of Higher Education[1]; Chester College of Higher Education; College of Guidance Studies (Swanley); College of Ripon and York St. John (York); College of St. Mark and St. John (Plymouth); Dartington College of Arts (Totnes); Edge Hill College of Higher Education (Ormskirk); Falmouth School of Art and Design; Harper Adams Agricultural College (Newport); Homerton College (Cambridge); Institute of Advanced Nursing Education (London); Kent Institute of Art and Design (Maidstone); King Alfred's College, Winchester; La Sainte Union College of Higher Education (Southampton); Liverpool Institute of Higher Education; London Business School; The London Institute; Loughborough College of Art and Design; Nene College (Northampton); Newman College (Birmingham); North Riding College (Scarborough); Ravensbourne College of Design and Communication (Bromley); Roehampton Institute (London); Rose Bruford College of Speech and Drama (Sidcup); Royal Academy of Music (London); Royal College of Art (London); Royal College of Music (London); Royal Northern College of Music (Manchester); St. Martin's College (Lancaster); St. Mary's College (Twickenham); Salford College of Technology; Southampton Institute of Higher Education; Trinity and All Saints (Leeds); Trinity College of Music (London); Westhill College (Birmingham); West London Institute of Higher Education; Westminster College, Oxford; West Surrey

College of Art and Design (Farnham)[1]; West Sussex Institute of Higher Education (Chichester); Wimbledon School of Art; Winchester School of Art; Worcester College of Higher Education.

[1] May award degrees

In *Wales* in 1997 there were 13 institutions of higher education funded directly by the HEFCW, including the University of Glamorgan and the colleges of the University of Wales. In 1996–97 the Council allocated £230m. for teaching and research activities. There were 81,267 students in the higher education sector in Wales in 1996–97, excluding those registered with the Open University, including 60,397 full-time, 1,113 students on their year out and 20,097 part-time students, including those enrolled on higher education provision at further education colleges.

Name	Full-time students (1996–97, provisional)[1]	No. of academic staff (1995–96)[2]
Univ. of Glamorgan (Pontypridd)	8,595	573
Univ. of Wales, Aberystwyth	5,922	530
Univ. of Wales, Bangor	5,962	673
Univ. of Wales, Bangor	5,962	673
Univ. of Wales, Cardiff	12,850	1,396
Univ. of Wales, Lampeter	1,592	113
Univ. of Wales, Swansea	7,934	950
Univ. of Wales College of Medicine	2,132	687
Univ. of Wales Institute, Cardiff	5,066	321
Univ. of Wales College, Newport	2,653	243
North East Wales Institute of Higher Education (Wrexham)	2,466	187
Swansea Institute of Higher Education	2,661	209
Trinity College Carmarthen	1,567	108
Welsh College of Music and Drama	500	94

[1] Sandwich year out counted as 0·5 full-time
[2] Staff who meet the 25% full-time equivalent threshold

In *Scotland* in 1997 there were 21 institutions of higher education funded by the SHEFC, of which 5 were universities formed from former central institutions (*cf.* English polytechnics): Abertay Dundee Univ., Glasgow Caledonian Univ., Napier Univ. (Edinburgh), Univ. of Paisley, The Robert Gordon Univ. (Aberdeen); and 8 were already-existing universities:

a) *Universities*

Name (and Location)	Full-time and sandwich students (1996–97)	Full-time academic staff (1996–97)
Aberdeen Univ.	9,425	649
Abertay Dundee Univ.	3,698	247
Dundee Univ.	8,367	687
Edinburgh Univ.	15,880	1,232
Glasgow Univ.	15,270	1,339
Glasgow Caledonian Univ.	10,835	750
Heriot-Watt Univ. (Edinburgh)	4,550	331
Napier Univ. (Edinburgh)	8,437	618
Paisley Univ.	6,509	445
Robert Gordon Univ. (Aberdeen)	7,041	439
St Andrews Univ.	5,684	425
Stirling Univ.	6,466	402
Strathclyde Univ. (Glasgow)	14,980	913
Total	117,412	8,477

b) *Other Institutions*

Edinburgh College of Art, Glasgow School of Art, Moray House Institute of Education (Edinburgh), Northern College of Education (Aberdeen and Dundee), Queen Margaret College (Edinburgh), Royal Scottish Academy of Music and Drama (Glasgow), Scottish College of Textiles (Galashiels), St. Andrew's College of Education (Glasgow).

The Scottish Agricultural College (Perth) is funded by the Scottish Office Agriculture and Fisheries Department.

In 1996–97 there were 127,934 full-time and sandwich students at the institutions funded by SHEFC (67,095 female).

All the higher education institutions are independent and self-governing. In addition to funding through the higher education funding councils they receive tuition fees through local education authorities for students domiciled in England and Wales, and from the Students Awards Agency for Scotland for students domiciled in Scotland. Institutions which carry out research may also receive funding through the 5 Research Councils administered by the Office of Science and Technology.

The *Open University* received its Royal Charter on 1 June 1969 and is an independent, self-governing institution, awarding its own degrees at undergraduate and postgraduate level. It is financed by the Government through the HEFCE and by the receipt of students' fees. Tuition is by means of correspondence textbooks, audio and video cassettes, radio and television broadcasts and, for some courses, residential schools and access to a personal computer. There are also 311 local study centres where face-to-face tutorials may be offered. No formal qualifications are required for entry to undergraduate courses. Residents from most countries of Western Europe aged 18 or over may apply, though some courses are not available outside the UK. There are over 130 undergraduate courses; many are available on a one-off basis. In 1997 there were over 124,000 undergraduates, and over 27,000 postgraduate level students, The university has some 3,000 full-time staff working at its Milton Keynes headquarters and in 13 regional centres throughout the country. There are over 6,000 part-time associate lecturers.

One university is independent of the state system, the *University of Buckingham*, which opened in 1976 and received a Royal charter in 1983. It offers 2-year courses towards its own honours degrees, the academic year commencing in Jan. and consisting of four 10-week terms. There are 4 areas of study: Business; Humanities; Law; and Sciences. In 1997 there were 568 full-time and 39 part-time undergraduate students and 71 full-time and 11 part-time postgraduate students. There were 70 teachers (3 part-time).

All universities charge fees, but financial help is available to students from several sources (*see Awards to Students* above), and the majority of students receive some form of financial assistance.

The British Council. The British Council promotes cultural, educational and technical co-operation between Britain and other countries. Established in 1934 and incorporated by Royal Charter in 1940, it is Britain's principal agency for cultural relations overseas. An independent, non-political organization, it is represented in 109 countries, running a mix of offices, libraries, resource centres and English-teaching operations. Its headquarters are in London and Manchester with regional centres in Belfast, Cardiff and Edinburgh.

The British Council's total expenditure in 1996–97 was £433·9m. This was made up of government grants (£144·8m.), revenues from English language teaching and client-funded education services (£157m.) and development programmes, principally in education and training, which are managed on behalf of the British Government and other clients (£129m.).

The British Council seeks to maximize Britain's role in the world. It does this by extending the use and improving the teaching of English; promoting international partnerships in cultural, educational and scientific fields; demonstrating the achievements of British arts; extending Britain's contribution to overseas development; and promoting, in response to overseas demand, the use of British goods and services in education and training.

Chairman: Sir Martin Jacomb.
Director-General: Dr David Drewry.
Headquarters: 10 Spring Gdns., London, SW1A 2BN.

Donaldson, F., *The British Council: the First Fifty Years.* London, 1984.

Welfare. The National Insurance Act 1946 came into operation on 5 July 1948, repealing the existing schemes of health, pensions and unemployment insurance. This Act, along with later legislation, was consolidated as the National Insurance Act

1965. The scheme now operates under the Social Security Contributions and Benefits Act 1992 and the Social Security Administration Act 1992.

Since 1975, Class 1 contributions have been related to the employee's earnings and are collected with PAYE income tax, instead of by affixing stamps to a card. Class 2 and Class 3 contributions remain flat-rate, but, in addition to Class 2 contributions, those who are self-employed may be liable to pay Class 4 contributions, which for the year 1997–98 are at the rate of 6% on profits or gains between £7,010 and £24,180, which are assessable for income tax under Schedule D. The non-employed and others whose contribution record is not sufficient to give entitlement to benefits are able to pay a Class 3 contribution of £6·05 per week in 1997–98 voluntarily to qualify for a limited range of benefits. Class 2 weekly contributions for 1997–98 for men and women are £6·15. Class 1A contributions are paid by employers who provide employees with a car and fuel for their private use.

From 6 April 1978 the Social Security Pensions Act 1975 introduced earnings-related retirement, invalidity and widows' pensions. Members of occupational pension schemes may be contracted out of the earnings-related part of the state scheme relating to retirement and widows' benefits. Employee's national insurance contribution liability depends on whether he/she is in contracted-out or not contracted-out employment.

Full rate contributions for non-contracted-out employment in 1997–98:

Weekly Earnings (in £1)	Yearly earnings (in £1)	Employee pays	Employer pays
Nil–62	Nil–3,223	Nil	Nil
62–109	3,223–5,719	10%[1]	3%
110–154	5,720–8,059	10%[1]	5%
155 209	8,060–10,919	10%[1]	7%
210–464	10,920–24,180	10%[1]	10%
Over 465	Over 24,180	£41·54	10%

[1] Plus 2% of £62.

Where earnings exceed £62 per week the employee contributes 2% of earnings up to £62 and 10% thereafter.

For contracted-out employment the employees' contributions are as above but 8·2% on weekly earnings of £62–£465. The employer's rates are reduced by 3%.

From April 1996 employers who engage a trainee, or a person who has been unemployed for at least 2 years are eligible for a year's rebate of contributions.

Contributions together with interest on investments form the income of the *National Insurance Fund* from which benefits are paid. A Treasury grant was instituted in 1993. 23,749,000 persons (10,243,000 women) paid contributions in 1993–94, including 20,797,000 employees at standard rate.

Receipts, 1994–95 (in £1m.), 49,679·08, including: Contributions, 37,863·48; compensation from Consolidated Fund for recoveries, 541; investment income, 363·95. Disbursements, 49,679,084, including: Unemployment Benefit, 1,299·48; Sickness Benefit, 381·84; Invalidity Benefit, 7,705,134; Maternity Allowances, 27; Widow's Benefit, 1,022; Guardian's Allowances, 1; Retirement Pensions, 28,744·81; Pensioners' Lump Sums, 123·31; Personal Pensions, 1,956·62; transfers to Northern Ireland, 145; administration, 1,279·89; redundancy payments, 196·52. Total benefit expenditure, 1995–96, £88,787m.

Statutory Sick Pay (SSP). Employers are responsible for paying statutory sick pay (SSP) to their employees who are absent from work through illness or injury for up to 28 weeks in any 3-year period. Basically, all employees aged between 16 and 65 (60 for women) with earnings above the Lower Earnings Limit are covered by the scheme whenever they are sick for 4 or more days consecutively. The weekly rate is £54·55. For most employees SSP completely replaces their entitlement to state incapacity benefit which is not payable as long as any employer's responsibility for SSP remains.

Pregnant working women may be eligible to receive statutory maternity pay directly from their employer for a maximum of 18 weeks. There are 2 rates: Where a woman has been working for the same employer for at least 26 weeks, she is entitled to 90% of her average weekly earnings for the first 6 weeks and to the lower rate of £54·55 a week for the remaining 12 weeks. Employers are reimbursed by the state for 92% of the amount they pay.

Women who are not eligible for statutory maternity pay, those who are self-employed, have recently changed jobs or given up their job, may qualify for a weekly maternity allowance of £54·55 for employees and £47·35 for the self- or non-employed, which is payable for up to 18 weeks.

All pregnant employees have the right to take 14 weeks' maternity leave.

A payment of £100 from the Social Fund may be available if the mother or her partner are receiving income support, family credit or disability working allowance. It is also available if a woman adopts a baby.

Contributory benefits. Qualification for these depends upon fulfilment of the appropriate contribution conditions, except that persons who are incapable of work as the result of an industrial accident may receive incapacity benefit followed by invalidity benefit without having to satisfy the contributions conditions.

Jobseekers' Allowance. This replaced unemployment benefit on 7 Oct. 1996. Unemployed persons claiming the allowance must sign a 'Jobseekers' Agreement' setting out a plan of action to find work. The allowance is not payable to persons who left their job voluntarily or through misconduct. Claimants with sufficient National Insurance contributions are entitled to the allowance for 6 months regardless of their means; otherwise, recipients qualify through a means test and the allowance is fixed according to family circumstances at a rate corresponding to Income Support for an indefinite period. In 1995–96, there were some 30,000 recipients of Unemployment Benefit.

Incapacity benefit. This replaced the former sickness benefit and invalidity benefit on 13 April 1995. Entitlement begins when entitlement to SSP (if any) ends. There are 3 rates: A lower rate for the first 28 weeks; a higher rate between the 29th and 52nd week; and a long-term rate from the 53rd week of incapacity. It also comprises certain age additions and increases for adult and child dependants. A more objective medical test of incapacity for work was introduced for incapacity benefit as well as for other social security benefits paid on the basis of incapacity for work. This test applies after 28 weeks' incapacity for work and assesses ability to perform a range of work-related activities rather than the ability to perform a specific job. Benefit is taxable after 28 weeks. Some 1,881,000 claims were met in 1995–96.

Maternity Benefit. Women who do not qualify for statutory maternity pay may be entitled to maternity allowance if they satisfy a test of recent work and contributions paid. Maternity allowance can be paid for up to 18 weeks. Payment can start at the earliest 11 weeks before the expected week of confinement but the woman has some choice in deciding when to give up work and still retain title to the full 18 weeks. There were some 12,000 beneficiaries in 1995–96.

Widow's Benefits. From 11 April 1988 the three main widow's benefits are: Widow's payment, widowed mother's allowance, widow's pension.

A widow cannot get any widow's benefits based on her husband's National Insurance contributions (NIC) if: She had been divorced from the man who has died; or she was living with the man as if she were married to him, but without being legally married to him; or she is living with another man as if she is married to him; or she was in prison or held in legal custody. A widow can only get widow's benefits if her husband has paid enough NIC. *Widow's Payment* is a single tax-free payment of £1,000. A widow may be able to get this benefit if her husband has paid enough NIC and she was under 60 when her husband died; or her husband was not getting a State Retirement Pension when he died. *Widowed Mother's Allowance:* A widow may be able to get a widowed mother's allowance if her husband has paid enough NIC and she is receiving child benefit for one of her children, or her husband was receiving child benefit, or she is expecting her husband's baby, or if she was widowed before 11 April 1988 and has a young person under 19 living with her for whom she was receiving Child Benefit. A widow entitled to a widowed mother's allowance will get an amount based on her husband's NIC. She will also get benefit for her eldest dependent child and further higher benefit for each subsequent child and she may also get an additional pension based on her husband's earnings since 1978. Widowed mother's allowance is usually paid as long as the widow is getting child benefit. It is taxable. *Widow's Pension:* A widow may be able to get a widow's pension if her husband has paid enough NIC. She must be 45 or over (40 or over if widowed before 11 April 1988) when her husband died or when her widowed mother's allowance ends. A widow cannot get a widow's pension at the same time as a widowed mother's allowance. A widow who is entitled to a widow's pension will get an amount that depends on her age when her husband died or when her widowed mother's allowance ends. If she was 55 or over (50 or over if widowed before 11 April 1988) she will get the full rate of widow's pension. She may also get an additional pension based on her husband's earnings since 1978. If her late husband was a member of a contracted-out occupational scheme or a personal pension scheme that scheme is responsible for paying the whole or part of the additional pensions. Widow's pension is usually paid until the widow is entitled to state retirement pension, when she is 60 or older. Widow's pension is taxable. There were some 291,000 pensioners in 1995–96.

Retirement Pension. The state retirement ('old age') pension scheme has 2 components: A basic pension and an earnings-related pension (State Earnings Related Pension—SERPS). The amount of the first is subject to National Insurance contributions made; SERPS is 1·25% of average earnings between the lower weekly earnings limit for Class I contribution liability and the upper earnings limit for each year of such earnings, building up to 25% in 20 years. For individuals reaching pensionable age after 6 April 1999 changes in the way pensions are calculated will be phased in over 10 years to include a lifetime's earnings with an accrual rate of 20%. Pensions are payable to women at 60 years of age and men at 65, but the age differential will be progressively phased out starting in April 2010. Women born before 6 April 1950 will be unaffected; women born after 5 March 1955 will receive their pension at 65; pension age for women between these dates will move up gradually from 60 to 65. There are standard rates for single persons and for married couples, the latter being 159% of 2 single-person rates. Proportionately reduced pensions are payable where contribution records are deficient.

Employees in an occupational scheme may be contracted out of SERPS provided that the occupational scheme provides a pension not less than the 'guaranteed minimum pension'. Self-employed persons, and also employees, may substitute personal pension schemes for SERPS. An independent statutory body, the Occupational Pension Board, is responsible for supervising contracted-out schemes.

Self- and non-employed persons may contribute voluntarily for retirement pension.

Persons who defer claiming their pension during the 5 years following retirement age are paid an increased amount, as do men and women who had paid graduated contributions. Although no further graduated contributions have been paid after April 1975, pension already earned will be paid along with the basic pension in the normal way. In 1995–96 some 10,322,000 persons were receiving pensions. Since 1 Oct. 1989 the pension for which a person has qualified may be paid in full whether a person continues in work or not irrespective of the amount of earnings.

At the age of 80 a small age addition is payable. In addition non-contributory pensions are now payable, subject to residence conditions, to persons aged 80 and over who do not qualify for a retirement pension or qualify for one at a low rate. These pensions are financed by Exchequer funds.

Pensioners whose pension is insufficient to live on may qualify for Income Support.

Non-Contributory Benefits.

Child Benefit. Child benefit is a tax-free cash allowance for children normally paid to the mother. The weekly rates are highest for the eldest qualifying child and less for each other child. Child benefit is payable for children under 16, for 16 and 17 year olds registered for work or training and for those under 19 receiving full-time non-advanced education. Some 12,993,000 children in 7,125,000 families received benefit in 1995–96.

One Parent Benefit is a tax-free cash allowance for certain people bringing up children alone. It is payable for the first or only child in the family in addition to child benefit. There were some 1,067,000 beneficiaries in 1995–96.

Child Support Agency. The Agency, which started work in April 1993, is gradually replacing the court system for obtaining maintenance for children being brought up by single parents. The Agency is responsible for assessing, collecting and enforcing child maintenance payments and for tracing absent parents. Assessments are made using a formula which takes into account each parent's income and essential outgoings. Changes to the child support arrangements were introduced in Feb. 1994 to take account of concerns raised by members of the public and MPs. These are designed to reduce the amount of child maintenance that many absent parents are required to pay and to give some families more time to adjust to increased bills. Legislation of 1995 introduced the possibility of fixing maintenance alongside the formula-assessment method. Appeals on points of law may be made to the Child Support Commissioners. In 1994–95 the Agency took on 398,584 new cases and completed 568,149 assessments.

Family Credit. Family Credit is a tax-free benefit for working families with children. To be able to get Family Credit there must be at least one child under 16 in the family (or under 19 if in full-time education up to, and including, A level or equivalent standard). The claimant or partner (if there is one) must be working at least 16 hours a week to qualify. They may be employed or self-employed, a lone parent or a couple. The claim should be made by the woman in two-parent families. The amount of Family Credit payable depends on the income of the claimant and partner, how many children there are in the family and their ages. The same rates of benefit are paid for one-parent families as for two-parent families. There are adult rates as well as a rate for each child varying with age, payable if the family's income does not exceed a certain limit. The award is reduced by £0·70 for each extra £1 earned. Family Credit is not payable if the claimant (or claimant and partner together) have savings or capital of over £8,000. Benefit is reduced if savings or capital of more than £3,000 is held. Family Credit is paid at the same rate for 26 weeks. The amount of the award will usually stay the same even if earnings, or other circumstances, change during that period. There were some 658,000 recipients in 1995–96.

Earnings Top-up. This was introduced in Oct. 1996 on a pilot basis in 8 areas. Wages for workers with dependent children are topped up. There are different rates for couples and single persons.

Guardian's Allowance. A person responsible for an orphan child may be entitled to a guardian's allowance in addition to child benefit. Normally both the child's parents must be dead but when they never married or were divorced, or one is missing, or serving a long sentence of imprisonment, the allowance may be paid on the death of one parent only.

Attendance Allowance. This is a tax-free Social Security benefit for disabled people over 65 who need help with personal care. The rates are increased for the terminally ill. There were some 1,162,000 recipients in 1995–96.

Invalid Care Allowance. This is a taxable benefit which may be paid to those who forgo the opportunity of full-time work to care for a person who is receiving attendance allowance, constant attendance allowance or the highest or middle-core component of Disability Living Allowance. There is a weekly rate, with increases for dependants. There were some 339,000 recipients in 1995–96.

Disability Living Allowance. This is a non-taxable benefit available to people disabled before the age of 65 who need help with getting around or with personal care for at least 3 months. The mobility component has 2 weekly rates, the care component has 3. There were some 1,771,000 recipients in 1995–96.

Disability Working Allowance. This is a tax-free benefit for people with an illness or disability which puts them at a disadvantage in getting a job. It is income-related and is intended for people who are starting work or already working at least 16 hours a week. The allowance is not payable if assets exceed £16,000. About 8,000 people received the allowance in 1995–96.

Industrial Injuries Disablement and Death Benefits. The Industrial Injuries Act, which also came into operation on 5 July 1948, with its later amending Acts, was consolidated as the National Insurance (Industrial Injuries) Act, 1965. This legislation was incorporated in the Social Security Act, 1975. The scheme provides a system of insurance against 'personal injury by accident arising out of and in the course of employment' and against certain prescribed diseases and injuries due to the nature of the employment. It takes the place of the Workmen's Compensation Acts and covers persons who are employed earners under the Social Security Act. There are no contribution conditions for the payment of benefit. Three types of benefit are provided:

Disablement benefit. This is payable where, as the result of an industrial accident or prescribed disease, there is a loss of physical or mental faculty. The loss of faculty will be assessed as a percentage by comparison with a person of the same age and sex whose condition is normal. If the assessment is between 14–100% benefit will be paid as weekly pension; 14–19% are payable at the 20% rate. The rates vary from 20% disabled to 100% disablement. Assessments of less than 14% do not normally attract basic benefit except for certain progressive chest diseases. Pensions for persons under 18 are at a reduced rate. When injury benefit was abolished for industrial accidents occurring and prescribed diseases commencing on or after 6 April 1983, a common start date was introduced for the payment of disablement benefit 90 days (excluding Sundays) after the date of the relevant accident or onset of the disease. The following increases can be paid with disablement benefit: Constant attendance allowance – where the disability for which the claimant is receiving disablement benefit is assessed at 100% and is so severe that they need constant care and attention. There are 4 rates depending on the amount of attendance needed. Exceptionally severe disablement allowance – where the claimant is in receipt of constant attendance allowance at one of the two higher rates and the need for attendance is likely to be permanent.

Reduced earnings allowance (REA) is a separate benefit. Entitlement exists if the claimant has not retired and cannot go back to their normal job or do another job for the same pay because of the effects of the disability caused by an accident or disease which occurred on or before 30 Sept. 1990. It can be paid whether or not disablement benefit is paid, providing the disablement benefit assessment is 1% or more (*e.g.* where disablement is assessed at less than 14%) and on top of 100% disablement benefit. From 1 Oct. 1989, if a claimant is of pensionable age (60 for a woman, 65 for a man) they can continue to receive REA if they are in regular employment, or in some cases if they are receiving Sickness Benefit, Invalidity Benefit or Unemployment Benefit. It will not matter whether or not they receive State Retirement Pension. If they are not in regular employment then entitlement to REA will cease. In most cases it will be replaced by Retirement Allowance.

Death Benefit. This is payable to the widow of a person who died before 11 April 1988 as the result of an industrial accident or a prescribed disease. Deaths which occurred on or after 11 April 1988 – a widow is entitled to full widow's benefits even if her late husband did not satisfy the contribution condition, if he died as a result of an industrial accident or prescribed disease.

Allowances may be paid to people who are suffering from pneumoconiosis or byssinosis or certain other slowly developing diseases due to employment before 5 July 1948. They must not at any time have been entitled to benefit for the disabled under the Industrial Injuries provision of the Social Security Act or compensation under Workmen's Compensation Acts or received damages through the courts.

In certain cases supplementation allowances are payable to people who are getting or are entitled to compensation under the Workmen's Compensation Acts.

War Pensions. Pensions are payable for disablement or death as a result of service in the armed forces, Merchant Navy or Civil Defence during war, or to civilians injured by enemy action. The amount depends on the degree of disablement. Various supplements may apply. There were some 331,000 recipients in 1995–96.

Severe Disablement Allowance. A severe disablement allowance as well as an age-related addition may be payable to people under pensionable age who have been continuously incapable of work for at least 28 weeks but who do not qualify for incapacity benefit. Those over 20 who are unable to work and are 80% disabled but do not qualify for the National Insurance invalidity pension because they have not paid sufficient contributions may be entitled to severe disablement allowance. Additions for adult dependants and for children may also be paid. There were some 368,000 beneficiaries in 1995–96.

Housing Benefit. The housing benefit scheme assists persons who need help to pay their rent, using general assessment rules and benefit levels similar to those for the income support scheme. People whose net income is below certain specified levels qualify for housing benefit of up to 100% of their rent. The scheme sets a limit of £16,000 on the amount of capital a person may have and still remain entitled. Restrictions on the granting of benefit to persons under 25 were introduced in 1995. In 1995–96 some 2,918,000 claims for rent rebate and 1,870,000 for rent allowance were made.

Council Tax Benefit. The scheme offers help to those claiming income support and others with low incomes. Subject to rules broadly similar to those governing the provision of income support and housing benefit, people may receive rebates of up to 100% of their council tax. In 1995–96 some 5,735,000 households received such help. A person who is liable for the council tax may also claim benefit (called 'second adult rebate') for a second adult who is not liable to pay the council tax and who is living in the home on a non-commercial basis.

Income Support. Under the Social Security Act, 1986, benefit was payable to any persons aged 18 years or over not in full-time work who were without adequate resources. Since 7 Oct. 1996, Income Support has been payable only to persons not required to be available for work whose resources are below a certain level. These include single parents, pensioners, long-term sick or disabled persons and those caring for them who qualify for the invalid care allowance. Income Support is not payable if the claimant (or claimant and partner together) have savings or capital over £8,000. Benefit is reduced if savings or capital of more than £3,000 is held. A person who is excluded from benefit under the normal rules may receive payments to meet urgent need. Additional sums, known as premiums, are available. There were some 5,601,000 recipients in 1995–96 (under the 1986 Act).

The Social Fund. The Fund makes payments and loans to help recipients meet intermittent expenses. 'Regulated payments' comprise *Maternity Payments* (a payment of up to £100 for each baby expected, born or adopted, payable to persons receiving income support, income-based jobseekers' allowance, disability working allowance or family credit); *Funeral Payments* (a payment of reasonable funeral expenses up to £500 incurred by persons receiving income support, income-based jobseekers' allowance, housing benefit, Council Tax benefit, disability working allowance or family credit; recoverable from the estate of the deceased); *Cold Weather Payments* (a payment of £8·50 for any consecutive 7 days when the temperature is below freezing to persons receiving income support who are pensioners, disabled or have a child under 5). 'Discretionary Payments' comprise: *Community Care Grants* (payments to help persons receiving income support to move into the community or avoid institutional care); *Budgeting Loans* (interest-free loans to persons receiving income support for expenses difficult to budget for); *Crisis Loans* (interest-free loans to anyone without resources in an emergency where there is no other means of preventing serious risk to health or safety). Savings over £500 (£1,000 for persons aged 60 or over) are taken into account before payments are made.

Barr, N., *et al. The State of Welfare: the Welfare State in Britain since 1974.* Oxford, 1990
Hill, M., *The Welfare State in Britain: a Political History since 1945.* Aldershot, 1993
Timmins, N., *The Five Giants: a Biography of the Welfare State.* London, 1995

Health. The National Health Service (NHS) in England and Wales started on 5 July 1948 under the National Health Service Act, 1946. There is a separate Act for Scotland.

The NHS is a charge on the national income in the same way e.g. as the armed forces. Every person normally resident in the UK is entitled to use any complete part of the services, and no insurance qualification is necessary.

Since 1948 a weekly NHS contribution has been payable by employees and the self-employed. In 1957 this contribution was extended to employers. For convenience this contribution is collected with the National Insurance contribution and amounts to 1·05% of the latter for employees and 0·9% for employers. The NHS is funded 12·1% by these contributions, 82% by general taxation and 2·3% by charges for drugs and dental treatment and the rest from other receipts. Health authorities may raise funds from voluntary sources; hospitals may take private paying patients.

Organization. The National Health Service and Community Care Act, 1990, provided for a major restructuring of the NHS. From 1 April 1991, health authorities became the purchasers of health care, concentrating on their responsibilities to plan and obtain services for their local residents by the placement of health service contracts with the appropriate units. Day-to-day management tasks became the responsibility of hospitals and other units, with whom the contracts are placed, in their capacity as providers of care.

In April 1996 the Regional Health Authorities were replaced by 8 regional offices of the NHS Executive. The District Health Authorities and Family Health Service Authorities were replaced by comprehensive Health Authorities directly financed by central governments Hospital and Community Health Services funds. The budget for 1996–97 was £2,260m.

The key responsibility of Health Authorities is to ensure that the health needs of their local communities are met. They have the purchasing power to commission hospital and community health services for their residents. In doing so they have a duty to ensure that high standards are maintained and that they are securing the best possible value for money.

The Health Authorities manage the Family Doctor (or General Medical) Service and also organize the general dental, pharmaceutical and ophthalmic services for their areas. Any doctor may take part in the Family Doctor Service, and are paid for their NHS work; they may also take private fee-paying patients.

NHS Trusts are established as self-governing units within the NHS. Trusts are responsible for the ownership and management of the hospitals or other establishments or facilities vested in them, and for carrying out the individual functions set out in their establishment orders. In April 1996 there were 520 Trusts, representing most hospitals.

General practitioners (GPs) may apply for fundholding status, responsible for their own NHS budget for a specified range of goods and services. There are 2 types of fundholder: Standard fundholders for practices with at least 5,000 patients in England and 4,000 in Wales and Scotland, who purchase the full range of in- and out-patient services; and Community fundholders, for smaller practices of at least 3,000 patients, who purchase only community nursing services and diagnostic tests. In 1996 there were some 14,000 fundholding GPs in 3,300 practices, covering 47% of the population.

Services. The NHS broadly consists of hospital and specialist services, general medical, dental and ophthalmic services, pharmaceutical services, community health services and school health services. All these services are free of charge except for such things as prescriptions, spectacles, dental and optical examination, dentures and dental treatment, amenity beds in hospitals and for some of the community services, for which charges are made with certain exemptions.

The total cost of the NHS was estimated at £42,600m. for 1996–97.

In 1995 there were 26,702 GPs in England with an average of 1,887 patients each, 1,719 in Wales with 1,730 patients and 3,524 in Scotland with 1,506. There were 15,064 general dental practitioners in England, 817 in Wales and 1,764 in Scotland. In hospitals in Great Britain in 1995 there were 57,299 medical staff and 421,648 nurses and midwives (excluding agency staff). There were (1990) 338,630 average daily available hospital beds in the UK.

In the UK in 1995 there were 193 public and private hospices for the terminally ill with 2,982 beds.

Personal Social Services. Under the Local Authority Social Services Act, 1970, and in Scotland the Social Work (Scotland) Act, 1968, the welfare and social work services provided by local authorities were made the responsibility of a new local authority department—the Social Services Department in England and Wales, and Social Work Departments in Scotland headed by a Director of Social Work, responsibility in Scotland passing in 1975 to the local authorities. The social services thus administered include: the fostering, care and adoption of children, welfare services and social workers for people with learning difficulties and the mentally ill, the disabled and the aged, and accommodation for those needing residential care services. Legislation of 1996 permits local authorities to make cash payments as an alternative to community care. In Scotland the Social Work Departments' functions also include the supervision of persons on probation, of adult offenders and of persons released from penal institutions or subject to fine supervision orders.

Personal Social Services staff numbered 233,861 in 1995. The total cost of these services was estimated at £8,849m. for 1995–96. Expenditure is reviewed by the Social Services Inspectorate and the Audit Commission (in Scotland by the Social Work Services Inspectorate and the Accounts Commission).

DIPLOMATIC REPRESENTATIVES

Of the USA in Great Britain (Grosvenor Sq., London, W1A 1AE)
Ambassador: Philip Lader.

Of Great Britain in the USA (3100 Massachusetts Ave., NW, Washington, D.C., 20008)
Ambassador: Sir John Kerr, KCMG.

Of Great Britain to the United Nations
Ambassador: Sir John Weston, KCMG.

Great Britain's permanent representative to the European Union
Ambassador: Sir Stephen Wall, KCMG, LVO.

Further Reading

Government publications are published by HM Stationery Office (HMSO).
Office for National Statistics. *Annual Abstract of Statistics.* HMSO.—*Monthly Digest of Statistics.* HMSO.—*Social Trends.* HMSO.—*Regional Statistics.* HMSO
Central Office of Information. *Britain: An Official Handbook.* HMSO, annual.—*The Monarchy.* 1992
Directory of British Associations. Beckenham, annual
Cairncross, A., *The British Economy since 1945: Economic Policy and Performance, 1945–1995.* 2nd ed. London, 1995
Catterall, P., *British History, 1945–1987: an Annotated Bibliography.* Oxford, 1991
Gascoigne, B. (ed.) *Encyclopedia of Britain.* London, 1994
Harbury, C. D. and Lipsey, R. G., *Introduction to the UK Economy.* 4th ed. Oxford, 1993
Institute of Contemporary British History. *Contemporary Britain: an Annual Review.* Oxford, from 1990
Irwin, J. L., *Modern Britain: an Introduction.* 3rd ed. London, 1994
Marr, A., *Ruling Britannia: the Failure and Future of British Democracy.* London, 1995
Morgan, K.O., *The People's Peace: British History, 1945–89.* OUP, 1990
Oakland, J., *British Civilization: an Introduction.* 3rd ed. London, 1995
Oxford History of England. 16 vols. OUP, 1936–91
Palmer, A. and Palmer, V., *The Chronology of British History.* London, 1995
Penguin History of Britain. 9 vols. London, 1996–
Sked, A. and Cook, C., *Post-War Britain: a Political History.* 4th ed. London, 1993
Strong, R., *The Story of Britain.* London, 1996
Thompson, F. M. L. (ed.) *The Cambridge Social History of Britain, 1750–1950.* 3 vols. CUP, 1990
20th-Century Britain: an Encyclopedia, edited by F. M. Leventhal. New York, 1995

Other more specialized titles are listed under TERRITORY AND POPULATION; CONSTITUTION AND GOVERNMENT; DEFENCE; ELECTRICITY; FORESTRY; TRADE UNIONS; RELIGION; THE BRITISH COUNCIL; *and* WELFARE, *above.*

Website: http://www.ons.gov.uk

England

Day, A., *England.* [Bibliography]. Oxford and Santa Barbara (CA), 1993
Lloyd, T. O., *Empire, Welfare State, Europe: English History, 1906–1992.* 4th ed. OUP, 1993

Scotland

Scottish Office. *Scottish Economic Bulletin.* HMSO (quarterly).—*Scottish Abstract of Statistics.* HMSO (annual)
Brown, A. *et al., Politics and Society in Scotland.* London, 1996
Bruce, D., *The Mark of the Scots.* Birch Lane Press, 1997
Dennistoun, R. and Linklater, M. (eds.) *Anatomy of Scotland.* Edinburgh, 1992
Devine, T. M. and Finlay, R. J. (eds.) *Scotland in the 20th Century.* Edinburgh Univ. Press, 1996
Donaldson, G. (ed.) *The Edinburgh History of Scotland.* 4 vols. Edinburgh, 1965–75
Grant, E., *Scotland.* [Bibliography] Oxford and Santa Barbara (CA), 1982
Harvie, C., *Scotland and Nationalism: Scottish Society and Politics, 1707–1994.* 2nd ed. London, 1994
Hunter, J., *A Dance Called America.* Edinburgh, 1997
Lynch, M., *Scotland: a New History.* London, 1991
Macleod, J., *Highlanders: A History of the Gaels.* London, 1997
McCaffrey, J. F., *Scotland in the Nineteenth Century.* London, 1998

Wales

Digest of Welsh Statistics. HMSO (annual)
Davies, J., *History of Wales.* London, 1993
History of Wales. vols. 3, 4 (1415–1780). 2nd ed. OUP, 1993
Huws, G. and Roberts, H., *Wales* [Bibliography]. Oxford and Santa Barbara (CA), 1990
Jenkins, G. H., *The Foundations of Modern Wales 1642–1780.* Oxford, 1988
Jenkins, P.A., *A History of Modern Wales, 1536–1990.* Harlow, 1991
Jones, G. E., *Modern Wales: a Concise History.* 2nd ed. CUP, 1994
May, J. (ed.) *Reference Wales.* Wales Univ. Press, 1994

National Statistical Office: Office for National Statistics (ONS), 1 Drummond Gate, London SW1V 2QQ. ONS was formed from a merger of the former Central Statistical Office and the Office of Population Censuses and Surveys on 1 April 1996. *Director:* Dr Tim Holt.

NORTHERN IRELAND

KEY HISTORICAL EVENTS. Northern Ireland is part of the United Kingdom. The Government of Ireland Act 1920 granted Northern Ireland its own bicameral parliament (Stormont), and between 1921 and 1972 it had full responsibility for local affairs except for such matters as defence and the armed forces, foreign and trade policies, and taxation and customs. However, in the late 1960s a Civil Rights campaign and reactions to it escalated into serious rioting and sectarian violence involving the Irish Republican Army (IRA, an illegal organization aiming to unify Northern Ireland with the Republic of Ireland) and loyalist paramilitary organizations. The Northern Ireland government resigned and direct rule by the UK government began in 1972. The Northern Ireland parliament was abolished in 1973. The Northern Ireland Constitution Act 1973 provided for devolved government on a power-sharing basis, but this collapsed in May 1974.

Under the Northern Ireland Act 1974 the UK parliament approves all laws for Northern Ireland and the Northern Ireland departments are under the direction and control of a UK Cabinet Minister, the Secretary of State for Northern Ireland.

Attempts have been made by successive governments to find a means of restoring greater power to Northern Ireland's political representatives on a widely acceptable basis, including through a Constitutional Convention (1975–76), a Constitutional Conference (1979–80) and 78-member Northern Ireland Assembly elected by proportional representation in 1982. This was dissolved in 1986, partly in response to Unionist reaction to the Anglo-Irish Agreement signed by the governments of the UK and the Republic of Ireland on 15 Nov. 1985. The Agreement committed both the UK and the Irish governments to the principle that Northern Ireland should remain part of the UK for as long as that were the wish of the majority of population in Northern Ireland, that there was at present no wish for change, but if there were such a desire in the future, legislation would be introduced to give it effect. The Agreement established an Intergovernmental Conference of British and Irish ministers to monitor political, security, legal and other issues of concern to the nationalist community, and through which the Irish government could put forward views and proposals on specific matters affecting Northern Ireland affairs. There was to be no derogation from the sovereignty of the UK or Irish governments as a result of the Agreement.

Since 1990 the UK government has sought, through dialogue, to secure a political settlement encompassing all the relevant relationships—those within Northern Ireland, those within the island of Ireland and those between the UK and Irish governments. In 1991 and 1992 round table talks were held between the two governments and the Northern Ireland parties. Since then the search for a settlement has continued through bilateral discussions.

On 15 Dec. 1993 the Prime Ministers of the UK and the Republic of Ireland (John Major and Albert Reynolds) issued a joint declaration as a basis for all-party talks to achieve a political settlement, inviting Sinn Féin ('Ourselves Alone', pro-Republican nationalist party and the political wing of the IRA) to join the talks in an All-Ireland Forum 3 months after the cessation of terrorist violence. The declaration stated that both the UK and Irish governments affirmed that the status of Northern Ireland could only be changed with the consent of a greater number of its people; that the future of Ireland was to be decided by the people of the North and South alone; that the UK would give legislative effect to a united Ireland if a majority in the North so decided; and that the Irish government would abandon its constitutional claim to all the island of Ireland if there were a political settlement.

The IRA announced 'a complete cessation of military operations' on 31 Aug. 1994. On 13 Oct. 1994 the anti-IRA Combined Loyalist Military Command also announced a ceasefire 'dependent upon the continued cessation of all nationalist republican violence'.

Talks between UK government officials and Sinn Féin, and also with the political representatives of the loyalists, i.e. the Ulster Democratic Party and the Progressive Unionist Party, began in Dec. 1994 and continued at ministerial level in March and May 1995.

On 22 Feb. 1995 the British and Irish Prime Ministers (John Major and John Bruton) announced new joint UK-Irish proposals for a settlement in Northern Ireland contained in 2 documents: *A Framework for Accountable Government in Northern Ireland*, drawn up by the UK government, and *A New Framework for Agreement*, agreed by the UK and Irish governments.

The proposals envisaged: An elected single-chamber 90-member Northern Ireland assembly; a north-south body comprising members of this assembly and representatives of the Irish government and accountable to both. This body would have executive, harmonizing or consultative functions in matters designated by the UK and Irish parliaments, its decisions being reached by consensus; a standing inter-governmental conference to consider matters not transferred to the above proposed bodies; changes to the Irish constitution to withdraw the Republic's territorial claim to Northern Ireland if it were contrary to the will of a majority of its people; amendments to UK legislation to enable Northern Ireland's future status to be determined by a majority decision of its people; an undertaking by both governments to ensure the 'systematic and effective protection of common specified civil, political, social and cultural rights'.

On 28 Nov. 1995 the British and Irish Prime Ministers (John Major and John Bruton) agreed on a formula which would allow preliminary talks involving Northern Ireland's main political parties to start while a 3-member international body headed by former US Senator George Mitchell prepared a report on 'the arrangements necessary for the removal from the political equation' of paramilitary arms. The Mitchell commission report, published on 24 Jan. 1996, set out 6 principles to which all parties should adhere, including a commitment to renounce violence, verifiable disarmament of all paramilitaries and a pledge to adhere to any agreement reached through all-party negotiations. Concluding that the paramilitaries 'will not decommission any arms prior to all-party negotiations', the commission recommended that negotiations and decommissioning of weapons should proceed at the same time, and proposed a number of measures including an elective process. However, the British Prime Minister stated that, 'In the absence of prior decommissioning, there may well be another way forward', proposing elections to a temporary body which could be used as a forum for negotiations.

On 9 Feb. 1996 the IRA exploded a bomb in the Docklands area of London (the first of several incidents) and announced the end of their ceasefire.

Elections were held on 30 May to select delegates from among whom participants in negotiations may be drawn, constituting a 110-member forum to take part in talks with the British and Irish governments. Each of the 18 Northern Ireland constituencies returned 5 delegates. The 10 parties receiving the most votes received 2 extra delegates. Sinn Féin may participate in the forum, but not in the negotiations until the IRA restores its ceasefire. The Ulster Unionist Party won 30 seats with 24·2% of votes cast; the Social Democratic and Labour Party, 21 with 21·4%; the Democratic Unionist Party, 24 with 18·8%; Sinn Féin, 17 with 15·5%; the Alliance Party, 7 with 6·5%; the United Kingdom Unionist Party, 3 with 3·7%; the Progressive Unionist Party, 2 with 3·5%; the Ulster Democratic Party, 2 with 2·2%; the Northern Ireland Women's Coalition, 2 with 1%; Labour, 2 with 0·8%. The electorate was 1·1m.

Opening Plenary talks began under the chairmanship of Senator Mitchell on 12 June 1996, with Gen. John de Chastelain (Canada) and Harri Holkeri (Finland) as deputies. In the course of 1996 a Business Committee was set up and an agenda for the remainder of the Opening Plenary agreed by sufficient consensus.

A retaliatory bomb attack on a republican sympathizer on 22 Dec. 1996 marked the end of the observance of the ceasefire by paramilitary loyalist terrorists. However, the UK Secretary of State for Northern Ireland declared that the loyalist ceasefire remained intact, so when the Mitchell talks reconvened on 13 Jan. 1997 it was with the continued participation of the loyalist parties. At the beginning of 1997 discussion was focused on the decommissioning of arms, following which the talks were scheduled to divide into 3 sub-sections ('strands'): 1) New internal arrangements for Northern Ireland including some form of assembly; 2) Cross-border co-operation; 3) Relations between the UK and Irish governments.

The talks resumed again on 3 June 1997 under the newly-elected Labour Government in which Dr Marjorie ('Mo') Mowlam was appointed as Secretary of State for Northern Ireland. The Government stated its firm intention that substantive negotiations should begin in September 1997, with a view to reaching a conclusion by May 1998, when the final outcome would be put to the people of Ireland, North and South, for approval in concurrent referendums.

The new Government also announced that it was willing to organize meetings between its officials and Sinn Féin, to clarify Government policy. A restoration of the IRA ceasefire was declared from 20 July 1997; the Government indicated it would assess whether it was genuine over a period of some six weeks, and if satisfied it was so, would then invite Sinn Féin to the talks. The Secretary of State for Northern Ireland, Dr Marjorie Mowlam, MP, announced on 29 Aug. that she had decided to invite Sinn Féin to enter the talks. This decision was reached after careful consideration of all the circumstances following the IRA announcement.

The talks resumed on 9 Sept. when Sinn Féin affirmed their commitment to the six Mitchell principles of democracy and non violence.

On 24 Sept. there was a major breakthrough when the participants in the multiparty negotiations, meeting in plenary session, approved a procedural motion which concluded the business of the opening plenary session and launched the three strands of substantive political negotiations.

Under the chairmanship of George Mitchell, a marathon negotiating struggle on 9–10 April 1998 led to an agreemnt, albeit nearly 17 hours after the deadline.

What the negotiators from the 21 months of talks produced was a framework for sharing power designed to satisfy Protestant demands for a reaffirmation of their national identity as British, Catholic desires for a closer relationship with the predominanatly Catholis Republic of Ireland and Britain's wish to return to Norther Ireland the powers London assumed in 1972 when the local Stormont legislature was disbanded.

Under the agreement, there would be a new democratically elected legislature in

Belfast, a new ministerial council giving the governments of Northern Ireland and Ireland joint responsibilities in areas like tourism, transportation and the environment, and a new consultative council that twice a year would bring together minister from the British and Irish parliaments and the three assemblies being created in Northern Ireland and in Scotland and Wales.

The Irish government would move to eliminate its territorial clain on Northern Ireland from its constitution.

The critical issues of police and judicial-system reform, the release of parliamentary prisoners, and the dismantling of the vast underground arsenals of weaponry in the province would be submitted to new commissions for study and recommendations.

The settlement was to be put to referendums in both Northern Ireland and the Republic of Ireland on 22 May.

TERRITORY AND POPULATION. Area (revised by the Ordnance Survey Department) and population were as follows:

District	Population (usually resident) 1991 Census	Population present on 21 April 1991	Area in ha. (including inland water)
Antrim	44,516	44,322	57,793
Ards	64,764	64,026	38,067
Armagh	51,817	51,331	67,128
Ballymena	56,641	56,032	63,195
Ballymoney	24,198	23,984	41,855
Banbridge	33,482	33,102	44,556
Belfast	279,237	283,746	11,489
Carrickfergus	32,750	32,439	8,193
Castlereagh	60,799	60,649	8,500
Coleraine	50,438	51,062	48,555
Cookstown	31,082	30,808	62,171
Craigavon	74,986	74,494	37,925
Derry (Londonderry)	95,371	94,918	38,742
Down	58,008	57,511	64,953
Dungannon	45,428	45,322	78,323
Fermanagh	54,033	54,062	187,677
Larne	29,419	29,181	33,646
Limavady	29,57	29,201	58,635
Lisburn	99,458	99,162	44,638
Magherafelt	36,293	35,874	57,239
Moyle	14,789	14,617	49,440
Newry and Mourne	82,943	82,288	90,937
Newtownabbey	74,035	73,832	15,069
North Down	71,832	70,308	8,158
Omagh	45,809	45,343	112,990
Strabane	36,141	35,668	86,165
Northern Ireland	1,577,836	1,573,282	1,416,039

Chief town (population present on 21 April 1991): Belfast, 283,746.
Vital statistics for calendar years:

	Marriages	Divorces	Births	Deaths
1993	9,045	2,213	24,909	15,633
1994	8,683	2,303	24,289	15,114
1995	8,577	2,302	23,860	15,310

CONSTITUTION AND GOVERNMENT. Northern Ireland is part of the United Kingdom. The Government of Ireland Act 1920 granted Northern Ireland its own bicameral parliament (*Stormont*), and between 1921 and 1972 it had responsibility for internal affairs. Following rioting and sectarian violence involving the IRA and loyalist paramilitary organizations, the Northern Ireland government resigned and direct rule by the UK government began in 1972. The Northern Ireland parliament was abolished in 1973.

Under the Northern Ireland Act 1974 the UK parliament approves all laws for Northern Ireland and the Northern Ireland departments are under the direction and control of a UK Cabinet Minister, the Secretary of State for Northern Ireland.

Secretary of State for Northern Ireland: Rt Hon. Marjorie ('Mo') Mowlam, MP.

Local Government. Northern Ireland has a single-tier system of 26 district councils based on main centres of population. Elections were held on 19 May 1993 for the 582 council seats. The Ulster Unionist Party gained 201 seats with 34·5% of votes cast, the Social Democratic and Labour Party 127 with 21·8%, the Democratic Unionist Party 102 with 17·5%, Sinn Féin 51 with 8·8%, the Alliance 44 with 7·6%, the Conservative Party 6 with 1·8%, others 22. Independents gained 29 seats with 5%.

ECONOMY

Policy. The main Northern Ireland government department concerned with economic development is the Department of Economic Development (DED). The department and its agencies have responsibility for the promotion of inward investment and the development of larger home industry (Industrial Development Board, IDB); promotion of enterprise and small business (Local Enterprise Development Unit, LEDU); training and employment matters (Training and Employment Agency, T&EA); promotion of industrially-relevant research and development and technology transfer (Industrial Research and Technology Unit, IRTU); promotion and development of tourism (Northern Ireland Tourist Board, NITB); energy matters; mineral development; company regulation; consumer protection; health and safety at work; industrial relations; equality of opportunity in employment; and better regulation.

IDB's overall objective is to encourage the development of internationally competitive companies in the manufacturing and tradeable service sectors in Northern Ireland and to attract new inward investment, contributing to growth in durable employment. During 1996–97, IDB secured 35 investment projects by externally owned companies, promoting 1,641 new jobs and safeguarding a further 3,345 jobs. In addition, IDB assisted 56 projects by locally owned companies, promoting 1,364 new jobs and safeguarding a further 2,232 jobs.

The LEDU is the small business agency (for companies employing fewer than 50 people). It aims to strengthen the economy by encouraging enterprise and new business start-ups and by helping established small businesses achieve export-orientated, profitable growth. In 1996–97 LEDU assisted 1,545 new business start-ups. As a result, LEDU achieved 3,425 new jobs and a further 755 among existing businesses.

The T&EA is an Executive Agency within DED. It assists economic development and helps people find work through training and employment services delivered on the basis of equality of opportunity. It works closely with employers and business interests, and with the other economic development agencies in making training relevant to local needs. In 1996–97 T&EA placed 46,018 people into employment. At the end of 1996–97, 290 companies were receiving assistance to train and develop their management and workforce through the Company Development Programme. Jobskills, which commenced across Northern Ireland in April 1995, achieved its interim target for 1996–97 of 35% attainment of National Vocational Qualification (NVQ) at Level 2 or above and the Agency is confident that the 1997–98 target of 45% will be achieved.

The IRTU, an Executive Agency within DED, provides the focus for all aspects of industry-related technology and innovation policy, including grants for industrial research and development, information, advice, scientific testing and analysis services. In 1996–97, IRTU disbursed £13·1m. of Government funding to Research and Development projects; in addition, IRTU enabled companies to obtain support under EU programmes.

Currency. Banknotes are issued by Allied Irish Banks, Bank of Ireland, First Trust Bank, Northern Bank and Ulster Bank.

Public Finance. The Finance Department is responsible for control of the expenditure of Northern Ireland departments, liaison with HM Treasury and the Northern Ireland Office on financial matters, economic and social research and analysis, Citizens Charter Unit, the Valuation and Lands Agency, the Government Purchasing Service (Northern Ireland) and the Legal Services.

Income of the Northern Ireland Consolidated Fund (in £1,000 sterling):

	1994–95	1995–96	1996–97
Attributed share of UK taxes	4,052,593	3,903,450	3,960,600
Grant in Aid from UK Government	1,649,900	2,129,000	2,394,300
Regional and district rates	224,975	245,967	222,000
Other receipts	307,401	300,600	323,000
Total	6,234,870	6,579,018	6,899,900

The public debt at 31 March 1996 was as follows: Ulster Savings Certificates, £109,552,818; Ulster Development Bonds, £13,845; borrowing from UK Government, £1,627,376,855; borrowing from Northern Ireland Government Funds, £73,507,225; European Investment Bank Loan, £4,527,579.

The above amount of public debt is offset by equal assets in the form of loans from Government to public and local bodies and of cash balances.

ENERGY AND NATURAL RESOURCES

Electricity. There are 4 power stations with an installed capacity of some 2,200 MW.

Gas. An undersea pipeline from Scotland was completed in 1996 to bring natural gas to Northern Ireland for the first time. Ballylumford Power Station is now operating on natural gas and gas is currently being systematically made available to industrial, commercial and domestic consumers in the Greater Belfast and Larne areas.

Minerals. Output of minerals (in 1,000 tonnes), 1996: Basalt and igneous rock (other than granite), 6,974; sandstone, 4,941; limestone, 4,122; sand and gravel, 7,684; other minerals (rocksalt, fireclay, diatomite, granite, chalk, clay and shale), 1,392. There are lignite deposits of 1,000m. tonnes which have not yet been developed.

Agriculture. Provisional gross output in 1996:

	Quantity (1,000)	Value (£1m.)			Quantity (1,000)	Value (£1m.)
Finished cattle and calves	347	327·5	Other crops		. . .	2·1
Finished sheep and lambs	1,478	112·1	Fruit		40	7·4
Finished pigs	1,179	112·8	Vegetables	tonnes	41	9·3
Poultry (tonnes)	154	93·9	Mushrooms		24	29·4
Eggs: for human			Flowers		. . .	8·5
consumption (dozen)	77,355	44·6	Over thirty month			
Milk (litres)	1,444,000	343·1	scheme		159	82·4
Other livestock products	. . .	15·2	Calf processing aid			
Potatoes	185	15·3	scheme		32	2·7
Barley	82	15·9	Other items		. . .	14·0
Wheat tonnes	32	5·4	Total receipts			1,242·4
Oats	5	0·9	Value of changes in			
			stocks due to volume			−12·2
			Gross output			1,230·2

Area (in 1,000 ha) of crops at June census:

	1995	1996	1997[1]		1995	1996	1997[1]
Barley	32·7	33·5	35·6	Fruit	1·7	1·7	1·8
Wheat	6·4	6·7	6·7	Other crops	6·5	5·4	5·5
Oats	2·5	2·5	2·5	Grass	778·5	780·1	785·5
Potatoes	8·7	8·5	7·5	Rough grazing	173·6	171·6	166·6
Vegetables	1·4	1·4	1·3				

Livestock (in 1,000) at June census:

	1996	1997[1]		1996	1997[1]
Cattle	1,648·8	1,616·8	Pigs	549·1	599·3
Dairy	281·1	279	Sows	57·0	60·1
Beef	284·5	292·1	Poultry	14,829·9	14,536·0
Sheep	2,470·0	2,579·3	Laying hens	3,028·1	2,557·0
Ewes	1,235·3	1,274·5	Broilers	8,463·3	8,454·0

[1] Provisional.

INDUSTRY

Labour. The main sources of employment statistics are the Census of Employment, conducted every 2 years, and the Quarterly Employment Survey. In June 1997 there were 585,290 employees in employment, of whom 289,910 were males. Employment in manufacturing and construction amounted to 128,680, 22% of the total employees in employment. 19,740 of these jobs were in the food, drink and tobacco industries, 12,750 in the manufacture of wearing apparel, 10,640 in textiles, 24,240 in construction and 61,590 in other sectors of manufacturing.

Tourism. 1,436,000 visitors came to Northern Ireland in 1996, contributing £206m. to the economy. The Northern Ireland Tourist Board is responsible for encouraging tourism.

9 Areas of Outstanding Natural Beauty and 45 Statutory Nature Reserves have been declared, and there are many country and regional parks.

COMMUNICATIONS

Roads. Ulsterbus and Citybus subsidiaries of N.I. Transport Holding Company (NITHC) provide co-ordinated services with N.I. Railways (NIR) Ltd under the service brandname of Translink.

At 31 March 1997 there were 1,893 professional hauliers and 4,827 vehicles licensed to engage in road haulage.

The number of motor vehicles licensed at 31 Dec. 1996 was 639,286, comprising private light goods, 540,083; motor cycles, scooters and mopeds, 10,026; buses, 2,090; goods vehicles, 17,401; other vehicles, 6,930. In addition, there were 62,756 vehicles which were not subject to licence duty.

At 1 April 1993 the total mileage of roads was 15,060, graded for administrative purposes as follows: Motorway, 70 miles; Class I dual carriageway, 95 miles; Class I single carriageway, 1,287 miles; Class II, 1,770 miles; Class III, 2,935 miles; unclassified, 8,903 miles.

Railways. NIR, a subsidiary of NITHC, provide rail services within Northern Ireland and cross-border services to Dublin, jointly with Irish Rail. The number of track-km operated is 478·8. In 1996–97 railways carried 6·2m. passengers.

Civil Aviation. There are scheduled air services to 3 airports in Northern Ireland. Belfast International Airport is the main one of these. Scheduled services are provided by British Airways and its franchise partners British Regional Airlines & Maersk, British Midland, Jersey European Airways, Aer Lingus and Air UK. Belfast International is also Northern Ireland's holiday airport with holiday flights operated direct to European and transatlantic destinations by a wide range of local and UK tour operators. In the year to 31 March 1997, the airport handled 2·4m. passengers and 38,000 tonnes of freight and mail.

Belfast City Airport offers commuter services to 14 regional airports in Great Britain as well as services to London Gatwick and Luton, the Isle of Man, Channel Islands and Cork. A 'feeder' service operates between Belfast City and City of Derry Airports. In 1994 Belfast City Airport handled 1·35m. passengers. The City of Derry Airport is situated 14 km from Londonderry and provides services from the north-west of Ireland to 14 United Kingdom destinations (Aberdeen, Belfast, Birmingham, Blackpool, Bristol, Glasgow, Guernsey, Isle of Man, Jersey, Leeds/Bradford, Liverpool, London Gatwick, Manchester, Newcastle) and 4 European destinations (Amsterdam, Brussels, Frankfurt and Paris). In 1996 the City of Derry Airport handled 68,000 passengers. There are two other licensed airfields at St Angelo and Newtownards, the latter of which is used principally by flying clubs, private owners and air taxi businesses. St Angelo has commercial flights operated by Brymon Airways to Jersey and by Crossair to Zurich. It handled 3,500 passengers in 1996.

Shipping. There are passenger services from Belfast to Liverpool and Stranraer and from Larne to Cairnryan. Drive-on/drive-off cargo services operate from Belfast and Larne to other UK ports. Belfast, Londonderry and Warrenpoint offer conventional cargo services. A new port at Londonderry opened in 1993. A new car ferry service between Ballycastle and Campbeltown, in Scotland, commenced operations on 1 July 1997. It is hoped the season will be extended in future years.

SOCIAL INSTITUTIONS

Justice. The Lord Chancellor has responsibility for the administration of all courts through the Northern Ireland Court Service and for the appointment of judges and magistrates. The court structure has 3 tiers: The Supreme Court of Judicature of Northern Ireland (comprising the Court of Appeal, the High Court and the Crown Court), the County Courts and the Magistrates' Courts. There are 21 Petty Sessions districts which when grouped together for administration purposes form 7 County Court Divisions and 4 Crown Court Circuits.

The County Court has general civil jurisdiction subject to an upper monetary limit. Appeals from the Magistrates' Courts lie to the County Court, or to the Court of Appeal on a point of law, while appeals from the County Court lie to the High Court or, on a point of law, to the Court of Appeal.

Police. The police force consists of the Royal Ulster Constabulary, supported by the Royal Ulster Constabulary Reserve, a mainly part-time force.

Religion. According to the census of 1991 there were: Roman Catholics, 605,639; Presbyterians, 336,891; Church of Ireland, 279,280; Methodists, 59,517. Those belonging to other denominations numbered 122,448; to none, 59,234. 114,827 persons did not answer the voluntary question on religion.

Education. Public education, other than university education, is presently administered centrally by the *Department of Education for Northern Ireland* and locally by 5 Education and Library Boards. The Department is concerned with the whole range of education from nursery education through to higher education and continuing education; for sport and recreation; for youth services; for the arts and culture (including libraries) and for the development of community relations within and between schools.

Each *Education and Library Board* is the local education authority for its area. Boards were first appointed in 1973, the year of local government reorganization, and are normally reappointed every 4 years following the District Council elections. The membership of each Board consists of District councillors, representatives of transferors of schools, representatives of trustees of maintained schools and other persons who are interested in the service for which the Board is responsible. Boards have a duty, amongst other things, to ensure that there are sufficient schools of all kinds to meet the needs of their areas. The Boards are responsible for costs associated with capital works at controlled schools. Voluntary schools, including maintained and voluntary grammar schools, can receive grant-aid from the Department of Education toward capital works of up to 85%, or 100% if they have opted to change their management structures so that no single interest group has a majority of nominees. Most voluntary grammar schools can receive the same rate of grant on the purchase of equipment. The Boards award university and other scholarships; they provide school milk and meals; free books and transport for pupils; they enforce school attendance; provide a curriculum advisory and support service to all schools in their area; regulate the employment of children and young people; and secure the provision of youth and recreational facilities. They are also required to develop a comprehensive and efficient library service for their area. Board expenditure is funded at 100% by the Department of Education. Integrated schools receive 100% funding for recurrent costs from the Department of Education, and, where long-term viability has been established, for capital works.

The Education Reform (NI) Order 1989 made provision for the setting up of a *Council for Catholic Maintained Schools* with effect from April 1990. The Council has responsibility for all maintained schools under Roman Catholic Management which are under the auspices of the diocesan authorities and of religious orders. The main objective of the Council is to promote high standards of education in the schools for which it is responsible. Its functions include providing advice on matters relating to its schools, the employment of teaching staff and administration of appointment procedures, the promotion of effective management and the promotion and co-ordination of effective planning and rationalization of school provision in the Catholic Maintained sector. The membership of the Council consists of trustee representatives appointed by the Northern Roman Catholic Bishops, parents, teachers, and persons appointed by the Head of the Department of Education in consultation with the Bishops.

Integrated Schools. In recent years a small number of integrated schools have been established at primary and post-primary levels with the aim of providing education for Roman Catholic and Protestant children together. These schools began as independent schools and qualified for public funding (on the same basis as other non-state schools) when their longer-term viability had been adequately demonstrated. The Education Reform (NI) Order 1989 introduced new measures whereby new integrated schools may receive public funding right from the start. Grant Maintained Integrated schools are eligible for grants on capital works, including purchase of sites and buildings and equipment, at the rate of 100%. At Oct. 1997 there were 33 integrated schools with total enrolments of some 7,000 pupils, about 2% of all pupils.

Pre-school Education is provided in nursery schools and nursery or reception classes in primary schools. There were 91 nursery schools in 1996–97, with 5,496 pupils and 181 teachers. A further 3,026 nursery pupils and 2,544 reception pupils were situated in primary schools.

Primary Education is from 4 to 11 years. In 1996–97 there were 920 primary schools with 181,284 pupils and 9,383 teachers. There were also 25 preparatory departments of grammar schools with 3,354 pupils and 189 teachers.

Secondary Education is from 11 to 18 years. In 1996–97 there were 71 grammar schools with 61,997 pupils and 3,904 teachers and 167 secondary schools with 90,746 pupils and 6,631 teachers.

Further Education. There were 17 institutions of further education in 1996–97 with 2,144 full-time and 2,780 part-time teachers and an enrolment of 25,033 full-time, 28,519 part-time day and 31,550 evening students on vocational courses; and about 55,000 students on non-vocational (mostly evening) courses.

Special Education. The Education and Library Boards provide for children with special educational needs up to the age of 19. This provision may be made in ordinary classes in primary or secondary schools or in special units attached to those schools or in special schools. In 1996–97 there were 50 special schools with 4,858 pupils. This includes 3 hospital schools.

Universities. There are 2 universities: The Queen's University of Belfast (founded in 1849 as a college of the Queen's University of Ireland and reconstituted as a separate university in 1908) had 136 professors, 271 readers and senior lecturers, 341 lecturers, 16 other grades of academic staff and 13,228 full-time students in 1994–95 academic year. The University of Ulster, formed on 1 Oct. 1984, has campuses in Belfast, Coleraine, Jordanstown and Londonderry. In 1994–95 academic year the University had 107 professors, 245 readers and senior lecturers, 494 lecturers, 20 other grades of academic staff and 12,573 full-time students.

Teacher training takes place at both universities and at 2 colleges of education: Stranmillis, and St. Mary's, the latter mainly for the primary school sector, in respect of which 4-year (Hons) BEd courses and one-year Postgraduate Certificate in Education (PGCE) courses are available. The training of teachers for secondary schools is provided, in the main, in the education departments of the 2 universities, but 4-year (Hons) BEd courses are also available in the colleges for intending secondary teachers of religious education, business studies and craft, design and technology. Part-time PGCE courses (primary and secondary) are available through the Open University. There were a total of 1,988 students (1,530 women) in training at the 2 colleges and the 2 universities during 1996–97. The principal initial teacher-training courses are the Bachelor of Education (4-year honours), BA (Hons) with education (4-year) and the one year Certificate of Education for graduates.

Total expenditure by the Department of Education (1996–97) was £1,404m.

Health and Personal Social Services. The Department of Health and Social Services is responsible for the provision of integrated health and personal social services. 4 Health and Social Services Boards are responsible for assessing the requirements of their resident populations and for purchasing appropriate services. Since 1 April 1996 services have been delivered exclusively by HSS Trusts (similar to NHS Trusts in the rest of the UK) established under the Health and Personal Social Services (NI) Order 1991. A total of 20 HSS Trusts are fully operational. 8 HSS Trusts based on acute hospitals and the regional Northern Ireland Ambulance Service are identical in structure and management to NHS Trusts in Great Britain. Of the remaining 11, 6 provide community based health and personal social services and the other 5 provide both hospital and community based health and personal social services, reflecting the integrated nature of these services in Northern Ireland.

Social Security. Social security schemes are similar to those in Great Britain.

National Insurance. During the year ended 31 March 1997 the expenditure of the National Insurance Fund at £1,170m. exceeded contributions by £229·7m. The shortfall in income was made up by a Treasury Grant, investment income and a transfer from the Great Britain Fund.

Total benefit expenditure was £1,105·8m., excluding £2·9m. which was subsequently recovered from damages paid to recipients of National Insurance Fund Benefits.

Employers received £1·1m. reimbursement in respect of Statutory Sick Pay paid to their employees. £17·8m. was paid in Unemployment Benefit. Widows Benefit amounted to £35·6m. and Retirement Pensions to £708m. Incapacity Benefits totalled £331m. Maternity Allowance of £1·5m. was paid and employers were reimbursed £16·7m. in respect of Statutory Maternity Pay. £35·6m. was given to personal pension plan providers.

Child Benefit. During the year ended 31 March 1997, £238·4m. was paid.

Income Support. In 1996–97, £603·5m. was paid.

Family Credit. In 1996–97, £82·9m. was paid.

Further Reading

Arthur, P. and Jeffery, K., *Northern Ireland since 1968.* Oxford, 1988
Aughey, A. and Morrow, D. (eds.) *Northern Ireland Politics.* Harlow, 1996
Bow, P. and Gillespie, G., *Northern Ireland: a Chronology of the Troubles, 1968–1993.* Dublin, 1993
Cormack, R. J. and Osborne, R. D. (eds.) *Discrimination and Public Policy in Northern Ireland.* OUP, 1991
Cunningham, M. J., *British Government Policy in Northern Ireland, 1969–89.* Manchester Univ. Press, 1991
Hennessey, T., *History of Northern Ireland 1920–96.* London, 1998
Irvine, M., *Northern Ireland: Faith and Faction.* London, 1991
Kennedy–Pipe, C., *The Origins of the Present Troubles in Northern Ireland.* Harlow, 1997
Keogh, D. and Haltzel, M. (eds.) *Northern Ireland and the Politics of Reconciliation.* CUP, 1994
McGarry, J. and O'Leary, B., (eds.) *The Future of Northern Ireland.* Oxford, 1991.—*Explaining Northern Ireland: Broken Images.* Oxford, 1995
Roche, P. J. and Barton, B., (eds.) *The Northern Ireland Question: Myth and Reality.* London, 1991
Ruane, J. and Todd, J., *The Dynamics of Conflict in Northern Ireland: Power, Conflict and Emancipation.* CUP, 1997
Shannon, M. O., *Northern Ireland.* [Bibliography] Oxford and Santa Barbara (CA), 1991
Whyte, J., *Interpreting Northern Ireland.* Oxford Univ. Press, 1990

ISLE OF MAN

KEY HISTORICAL FACTS. The Isle of Man was first inhabited by the Celts and the island became attached to Norway in the 9th century. In 1266 it was ceded to Scotland, but it came under English control in 1406 when possession was granted to the Stanley family (the Earls of Derby) and was later purchased by the British.

The Isle of Man has been a British Crown Possession since 1828, with the British government responsible for its defence and foreign policy. Otherwise it has extensive right of self-government.

A special relationship exists between the Isle of Man and the European Union providing for free trade and adoption by the Isle of Man of the EU's external trade policies with third countries. The island remains free to levy its own system of taxes.

TERRITORY AND POPULATION. Area, 221 sq. miles (572 sq. km); resident population census April 1996, 71,714. The principal towns are Douglas (population, 23,487), Onchan (adjoining Douglas; 8,656), Ramsey (6,874), Peel (3,819), Castletown (2,958). The island is divided into 6 sheadings (Ayre, Garff, Glenfaba, Michael, Middle and Rushen) each subdivided into 3 parishes except Garff, which has 2.

Vital statistics, 1996: Births, 835; deaths, 945; marriages, 448.

CONSTITUTION AND GOVERNMENT. The Isle of Man is a Crown dependency administered in accordance with its own laws by the High Court of *Tynwald*, consisting of the President of Tynwald, elected by the Court, and the *Legislative Council*, composed of the Lord Bishop of Sodor and Man, the Attorney-General (who does not vote) and 8 members selected by the *House of Keys*; and the House of Keys, a representative assembly of 24 members chosen by adult suffrage. The Isle of Man is not bound by Acts of the UK Parliament unless specially mentioned in them or applied by Order in Council although the UK is responsible for conducting its foreign affairs. The Lieutenant Governor presided over Tynwald until 1990 when he was replaced by an elected President of Tynwald.

A Council of Ministers was instituted in 1990. This replaced the former Executive Council and consists of the Chief Minister (elected for a 5-year term) and the ministers of the 9 major departments of Government. Elections for the House of Keys were held on 21 Nov. 1996. 52 candidates stood, mostly independents. Turn-out was 62%.

Lieut.-Governor: Sir Timothy Daunt.
President: Sir Charles Kerruish (elected July 1990).
Chief Secretary: J. F. Kissack.

In Dec. 1997 the *Chief Minister* was Donald Gelling. *Finance Minister:* Richard Corkill.

ECONOMY

Budget. The Isle of Man levies its own taxes. Revenue is derived from customs duties, VAT and income tax. In the 1997–98 budget expenditure was estimated at £240·6m. to be balanced by income of £240·7m.

The standard rate of tax is 15% and there is a higher rate of 20%. The single person's allowance is £6,800 and the next £9,270 is taxed at the standard rate with the higher rate applying to the balance. The married couple's allowance is double the single person's allowance. There are no death or estate duties, gifts or inheritance taxes or capital gains taxes. Companies and trusts are liable at 20% on the whole of their taxable income. There is a duty of £600 on every company incorporated in the Isle of Man which trades and is controlled outside the island.

Currency. The Isle of Man Government issues its own notes and coin on a par with £ sterling. £50, £20, £10, £5, £1, and £5, £2, £1, 50p, 20p, 10p, 5p, 2p and 1p coins are issued. Various commemorative coins have been minted together with legal tender gold coins and a platinum bullion coin. Inflation was 2·7% in Sept. 1997.

Banking and Finance. Government regulation of the banking sector is exercised through the Financial Supervision Commission. The Commission was established in 1983 and is responsible for the licensing and supervision of banks, deposit-takers and certain financial intermediaries giving financial advice and receiving client monies for investment and management. As at March 1996 there were 61 licensed banking institutions, 63 investment businesses and 6 UK Building Societies with Isle of Man licences. As at June 1997 the deposit base was £17,650m. The Isle of Man has designated status under the UK Financial Services Act. A compensation fund to protect depositors was set up in Feb. 1991 under the Isle of Man Financial Supervision Commission. Financial business, including insurance, contributes some 37% of national income.

Agriculture. The area farmed is about 113,000 acres out of a total land area of around 0·14m. acres. About 64,000 acres is devoted to grass whilst a further 36,000 acres are accounted for by rough grazing. Barley accounts for most of the remaining land under cultivation and some barley is exported. There are approximately 0·16m. sheep, 32,000 cattle, 22,000 poultry and 6,000 pigs on farms. Agriculture contributes 2% of the Island's GNP.

Labour. The economically active population in 1996 was 34,811, of whom 5,695 were self-employed. Employment by sector: Professional, 18·1%; finance, 17·7%; building, 10%; manufacturing, 10·6%; distribution, 11%. 1,234 persons were unemployed at the April 1996 census.

External Economic Relations. A special relationship exists with the EU providing for free trade and the adoption of external trade policies with third countries.

Tourism. In 1995–96 tourism contributed around 6% of national income; there were 141,000 visitors during 1997.

COMMUNICATIONS

Roads. There are 500 miles of good roads. The International TT Motor Cycle Races and cycle races take place annually. Omnibus services operate to all parts of the island.

In March 1997 there were 53,367 licensed vehicles on the roads, of which 43,369 were private cars.

Railways. Several novel transport systems operate on the Island during the summer season, including 100-year-old horse-drawn trams, and the Manx Electric Railway, linking Douglas, Ramsey and Snaefell Mountain (2,036 ft). The Isle of Man Steam Railway also operates between Douglas and Port Erin.

Civil Aviation. Ronaldsway Airport handles scheduled services operated by Manx Airlines and Jersey European to and from London, Manchester, Belfast, Dublin, Glasgow, Liverpool, Blackpool, Birmingham, Leeds, Luton, Newcastle, Cardiff and Jersey. Emerald operate a service to Liverpool. Air taxi services also operate.

Shipping. Car ferries link the Island with Heysham throughout the year and Liverpool, Fleetwood, Dublin and Belfast during the summer. The Manx Marine Administration oversees the Marine Register on which were 208 vessels in 1997.

Telecommunications. Manx Radio is a commercial broadcaster operated by the Government from Douglas.

Press. In 1997 there were 4 weekly newspapers.

SOCIAL INSTITUTIONS

Justice. The judiciary is headed by the First Deemster. The police force numbered 213 all ranks in 1997.

Education. Education is compulsory between the ages of 5 and 16. In 1996 there were 6,087 pupils in the 33 primary schools and 4,683 pupils in the 5 secondary schools operated by the Department of Education. In addition, there was a private primary school (186 pupils) and a private secondary school (319 pupils). The Department also runs a college of further education and a special school.

Social Security. Numbers receiving certain benefits at July 1997: Retirement Pension, 15,079; Unemployment Benefit, 233; Sick and Disablement Benefit, 4,570; Child Benefit, 8,613; Supplementary Benefit, 4,154. Total benefit expenditure, 1997 estimate: £102m.

Further Reading

Additional information is available from: Economic Affairs Division, 2 Circular Rd, Douglas, Isle of Man IM1 1PQ.
Publications: *Isle of Man Key Facts 1996, Isle of Man Digest of Economic and Social Statistics 1996, Isle of Man Census Reports 1996, Isle of Man Passenger Survey Reports 1985–1996, Isle of Man National Income Estimates, Isle of Man General Index of Retail Prices* (Monthly), *Isle of Man Earnings Survey* (Annual).
Kinvig, R. H., *History of the Isle of Man.* Oxford, 1945.—*The Isle of Man: A Social, Cultural and Political History.* Liverpool Univ. Press, 1975
Robinson, V. and McCarroll, D., (eds.) *The Isle of Man: Celebrating a Sense of Place.* Liverpool Univ. Press, 1990
Solly, M., *Government and Law in the Isle of Man.* London, 1994
Stenning, E. H., *Portrait of the Isle of Man.* London, 1984

CHANNEL ISLANDS

KEY HISTORICAL FACTS. The Channel Islands consist of Jersey, Guernsey and the following dependencies of Guernsey: Alderney, Brechou, Great Sark, Little Sark, Herm, Jethou and Lihou, a total of 75 sq. miles (194 sq. km). They were an integral part of the Duchy of Normandy at the time of the Norman Conquest of England in 1066. Since then they have belonged to the British Crown and are not part of the UK. The islands have created their own form of self-government, with the British government at Westminster being responsible for defence and foreign policy. The Lieut.-Governors of Jersey and Guernsey, appointed by the Crown, are the personal representatives of the Sovereign as well as being the commanders of the armed forces. The legislature of Jersey is 'The States of Jersey', and that of Guernsey is 'The States of Deliberation'.

From 1940 to 1945 the islands were left undefended and were the only British territory to fall to the Germans.

CLIMATE. The climate is mild, with an average temperature for the year of 11·5°C. Average yearly rainfall totals: Jersey, 862·9 mm; Guernsey, 858·9 mm. The wettest months are in the winter. Highest temperatures recorded: Jersey, 34·8°C; Guernsey, 31·7°C. Maximum temperatures usually occur in July and Aug. (daily maximum 20·8°C in Jersey, slightly lower in Guernsey). Lowest temperatures recorded: Jersey, 10·3°C; Guernsey, −7·4°C Jan. and Feb. are the coldest months (mean temperature approximately 6°C).

CONSTITUTION. The Lieut.-Governors and Cs.-in-C. of Jersey and Guernsey are the personal representatives of the Sovereign, the Commanders of the Armed Forces of the Crown and the channel of communication between the Crown and the insular governments. They are appointed by the Crown and have a voice but no vote in the islands' legislatures. The Secretaries to the Lieut.-Governors are their staff officers.

The official languages are French and English, but English is now the main language.

EXTERNAL ECONOMIC RELATIONS. The Channel Islands are not members of the EU, but participate in ERM through their monetary union with the UK. Trade with the UK is classed as domestic.

COMMUNICATIONS

Civil Aviation. Scheduled air services are maintained by Aer Lingus, Air Corbière, Air UK, Aurigny Air Services, British Airways, British Midland, Crossair, Delta, Gill Aviation, Jersey European Airways, KLM, Loganair, Lufthansa and Manx Airlines.

Shipping. Passenger and cargo services between Jersey, Guernsey and England (Poole) are maintained by Condor Ltd hydrofoil; between Guernsey, Jersey and England and St Malo by the Commodore Shipping Co., Emeraude Ferries connect Jersey and Guernsey with St Malo; and between Guernsey, Alderney and England, and between Guernsey and Sark by local companies.

SOCIAL INSTITUTIONS

Justice. Justice is administered by the Royal Courts of Jersey and Guernsey, each of which consists of the Bailiff and 12 Jurats, the latter being elected by an electoral college. There is an appeal from the Royal Courts to the Courts of Appeal of Jersey and of Guernsey. A final appeal lies to the Privy Council in certain cases. A stipendiary magistrate in each, Jersey and Guernsey, deals with minor civil and criminal cases.

Church. Jersey and Guernsey each constitutes a deanery under the jurisdiction of the Bishop of Winchester. The rectories (12 in Jersey; 10 in Guernsey) are in the gift of the Crown. The Roman Catholic and various Nonconformist Churches are represented.

Further Reading

Coysh, V., *The Channel Islands: A New Study*. Newton Abbot, 1977
Lemprière, R., *History of the Channel Islands*. Rev. ed. London, 1980
Uttley, J., *The Story of the Channel Islands*. London, 1966

JERSEY

TERRITORY AND POPULATION. The area is 116·2 sq. km (44·9 sq. miles). Resident population (1991 census), 84,082 (43,220 females); density, 724 per sq. km. In 1996 there were 1,167 births (rate, 13·6 per 1,000 population) and 842 deaths (10·6). Infant mortality rate, 1995 (per 1,000 live births), 6·5. In 1996 there were 544 marriages and 285 divorces. Life expectancy, 1995: Males, 72 years; females, 79. The chief town is St Helier on the south coast. The official language is English (French until 1960).

CONSTITUTION AND GOVERNMENT. The island parliament is the *States of Jersey*. The States comprises the Bailiff, the Lieut.-Governor, the Dean of Jersey, the Attorney-General and the Solicitor-General, and 53 members elected by universal suffrage: 12 Senators (elected for 6 years, 6 retiring every third year), the Constables of the 12 parishes (every third year) and 29 Deputies (every third year). They all have the right to speak in the Assembly, but only the 53 elected members have the right to vote; the Bailiff has a casting vote. Except in specific instances, enactments passed by the States require the sanction of The Queen-in-Council. The Lieut.-Governor has the power of veto on certain forms of legislation.

Administration is carried out by Committees of the States.

Lieut.-Governor and C.-in-C. of Jersey: Gen. Sir Michael Wikes, KCB, CBE.
Secretary and ADC to the Lieut.-Governor: Lieut.-Colonel C. Woodrow, OBE, MC, QGM.
Bailiff of Jersey and President of the States: Sir Philip Bailhache.

ECONOMY

Performance. GNP was £1,650m. in 1994; GDP, £1,435m.

Budget (year ending 31 Dec. 1995). Revenue, £417·3m.; expenditure, £376·8m. Revenue expenditure was £376·8m. Income from taxation was £244·8m. The standard rate of income tax is 20p in the pound.

Parochial rates are payable by owners and occupiers.

Currency. The States issue bank-notes in denominations of £50, £20, £10, £5 and £1. Coinage from 1p to 50p is struck in the same denominations as the UK. £32·1m. were in circulation in 1991.

Banking and Finance. Financial services contributed 54% of GDP in 1994. In 1996 there were 77 banks from 16 countries. Bank deposits and balances due to parent companies, March 1996, totalled £90,443m. 30,232 companies were registered at the end of 1995.

AGRICULTURE AND FISHERIES. 54% of the island's land area was farmed commercially in 1995. 48% of cropland was sown to potatoes. In 1995 there were 455 commercial farms. Livestock, 1995: Cattle, 6,934 (milk cows, 4,281). There were 65 fishing vessels in 1995. The catch of fish in 1995 was 782 tonnes.

INDUSTRY. Principal activities: Tourism; total number of hotel and guesthouse bedrooms (1990), 23,069; expenditure of tourists (1990), £270m. Agriculture, total output (1988), £36·4m. and total exports, £30·7m. Light industry, mainly electrical goods, textiles and clothing. In 1991 47,547 persons were economically active (20,529 females). 367 persons were registered unemployed in June 1996.

Commerce. Since 1980 the Customs have ceased recording imports and exports. Principal imports: Machinery and transport equipment, manufactured goods, food, mineral fuels, and chemicals. Principal exports: Machinery and transport equipment, food, and manufactured goods.

Tourism. In 1994 tourism accounted for 25% of GDP. 798,000 leisure visitors came to the island in 1995, with a spend of £266m.

COMMUNICATIONS

Roads. In 1995 there were 50,796 private cars, 7,638 hire cars, 5,973 vans, 3,301 lorries, 811 buses and coaches and 5,177 motorcycles and scooters.

Civil Aviation. The Jersey airport is situated at St Peter. It covers approximately 375 acres. Number of aircraft movements excluding local flying (1990) 60,107; number of passengers: 1,890,714, cargo and mail, 8,792 tonnes.

Shipping (1990). All vessels arriving in Jersey from outside Jersey waters report at St Helier or Gorey on first arrival. There is a harbour of minor importance at St Aubin. Number of commercial vessels entering St Helier in 1990, 26,472; number of visiting yachts (1990), 12,097. Passengers arrived in 1990, 491,145.

Telecommunications. Postal, and overseas telephone and telegraph services, are maintained by the Postal Administration of Jersey. The local telephone service is maintained by the Insular Authority. In 1989 there were 43,880 telephones and 24 post offices.

JUSTICE. Justice is administered by the Royal Court, consisting of the Bailiff and 12 Jurats (magistrates). There is a final appeal in certain cases to the Sovereign in Council. There is also a Court of Appeal, consisting of the Bailiff and 2 judges. Minor civil and criminal cases are dealt with by a stipendiary magistrate.

EDUCATION. (1996). There were 5 States secondary schools and 1 high school, and 24 States primary schools; 6,906 pupils attended the primary schools, 4,924 the secondary schools. These figures include 8 private primary schools with 1,250 pupils and 8 private secondary schools with 843 pupils. There were 1,298 full-time students at the further education college.

HEALTH. Expenditure on public health in 1995 was £73·2m. In 1995 there were 5 hospitals with 651 beds. There were 95 doctors (general practitioners).

SOCIAL SECURITY. A contributory Health Insurance Scheme is administered by the Social Security Department. In 1994–95 income was £67·1m. Benefits paid totalled £71·2m. (long-term benefits, £53·2m.; sickness, £6·6m.; invalidity, £6·9m.). 2,672 families totalling 4,783 children were receiving family allowances as at Sept. 1995.

Further Reading

Balleine, G. R., *Biographical Dictionary of Jersey.* London, 1948.—*A History of the Island of Jersey.* Rev. ed. Chichester, 1981.—*The Bailiwick of Jersey.* 3rd ed. London, 1970
Bois, F. de L., *The Constitutional History of Jersey.* Jersey, 1970

States of Jersey Library: Halkett Place, St Helier.

GUERNSEY

TERRITORY AND POPULATION. The area is 63·4 sq. km. Census population (1996) 58,681. Births during 1996 were 670; deaths, 605 The town is St Peter Port.

CONSTITUTION. The States of Deliberation, the Parliament of Guernsey, is composed of the following members: The Bailiff, who is President *ex officio;* 12 Conseillers elected by popular franchise; H.M. Procureur and H.M. Comptroller (Law Officers of the Crown), who have a voice but no vote; 33 People's Deputies elected by popular franchise; 10 Douzaine Representatives elected by their Parochial Douzaines; 2 representatives of the States of Alderney.

Elections for People's Deputies were held on 20 April 1994.

The States of Election, an electoral college, elects the Jurats. It is composed of the following members: The Bailiff (President *ex officio*); the 12 Jurats or 'Jurés-Justiciers'; the 12 Conseillers; H.M. Procureur and H.M. Comptroller; the 33 People's Deputies and 34 Douzaine Representatives.

Since Jan. 1949 all legislative powers and functions (with minor exceptions) formerly exercised by the Royal Court have been vested in the States of Deliberation. Projets de Loi (Bills) require the sanction of The Queen-in-Council.

Lieut.-Governor and C.-in-C. of Guernsey and its Dependencies: Vice-Admiral Sir John Coward, KCB, DSO.

Secretary and Aide-de-Camp to the Lieut.-Governor: Capt. D. P. L. Hodgetts.

Bailiff of Guernsey and President of the States: Sir Graham Dorey.

Deputy Bailiff of Guernsey: de V. G. Carey.

BUDGET (year ended 31 Dec. 1996). Revenue, including Alderney, £182,016,695; expenditure, including Alderney, £166,817,571. The standard rate of income tax is 20p in the pound. States and parochial rates are very moderate. No super-tax or death duties are levied.

BANKING. There were 72 banks in 1996.

COMMERCE (1996). Principal imports: Petrol and oils, 169,443,000 litres. Principal exports: Tomatoes, £3·5m.; flowers and fern, £24·9m.; flowers by post, £3·9m.; vegetables, £2·1m.; plants, £7·8m. Manufacturing, £53m.; services £40m.

Tourism. There were 273,000 visitors in 1996, generating revenue of £176m. (£157m. in 1995).

COMMUNICATIONS

Civil Aviation. The airport is situated at La Villiaze. In 1995, passenger arrivals totalled 846,302.

Shipping. The principal port is St Peter Port. There is also a harbour at St Sampson's (mainly for commercial shipping). In 1996 passenger arrivals totalled 360,817. Ships registered at 31 Dec. 1996 numbered 2,025 and 314 fishing vessels. In 1996, 11,445 yachts visited Guernsey.

EDUCATION. There are 2 public schools, 1 grammar school and modern secondary and primary schools and a College of Further Education. The total number of school children was (1996) 8,723. Facilities are available for the study of art, domestic science and many other subjects of a technical nature.

HEALTH. Guernsey is not covered by the UK National Health Service. Public health is overseen by the States of Guernsey Insurance Authority and Board of Health. A private medical insurance scheme to provide specialist cover for all residents was implemented by the States on 1 Jan. 1996.

ALDERNEY. Population (1986 census, 2,130; 1994 estimate, 2,375). The island has an airport. The Constitution of the island (reformed 1987) provides for its own popularly elected President and States (12 members), and its own Court. Elections were held for the President and 4 members of the States in Dec. 1993. The town is St Anne's.

President of the States: Jon Kay-Mouat, OBE.
Clerk of the States: D. V. Jenkins.
Clerk of the Court: A. Johnson.

Alderney levies its taxes at Guernsey rates and passes the revenue to Guernsey, which charges for the services it provides.

SARK. Population (1986 estimate, 550). The Constitution is a mixture of feudal and popular government with its Chief Pleas (parliament), consisting of 40 tenants and 12 popularly elected deputies, presided over by the Seneschal. The head of the island is the Seigneur. Sark has no income tax. Motor vehicles, except tractors, are not allowed.

The Seigneur: J. M. Beaumont.
Seneschal: L. P. de Carteret.

Further Reading

Carteret, A. R. de, *The Story of Sark.* London, 1956
Coysh, V., *Alderney.* Newton Abbot, 1974
Hathaway, S., *Dame of Sark: An Autobiography.* London, 1961
Le Huray, C. P., *The Bailiwick of Guernsey.* London, 1952
Marr, L. J., *A History of Guernsey.* Chichester, 1982

BRITISH DEPENDENT TERRITORIES

After the retrocession of Hong Kong to China on 1 July 1997, 13 territories remained under British sovereignty as a legacy of the former Empire. 3 of these (British Antarctic Territory, British Indian Ocean Territory and South Georgia and the South Sandwich Islands) have no resident populations and are administered by a commissioner instead of a governor.

Gibraltar is an enclave in Spain; the remainder are islands in the Caribbean and South Atlantic. Gibraltar and the Falkland Islands are the subjects of territorial claims by Spain and Argentina respectively.

Governors of Dependent Territories are appointed by the Queen, and are responsible for external affairs, internal security and the public service. Territories have their own elected legislatures and ministers, but final responsibility for government belongs to the Foreign and Commonwealth Office in London. For the Caribbean Territories some aspects of administration are carried out by the Dependent Territories Regional Secretariat in Barbados. The citizenship status of residents is defined in the British Nationality Act 1981.

ANGUILLA

KEY HISTORICAL EVENTS. Anguilla was probably given its name by the Spaniards or the French because of its eel-like shape. It was inhabited by Arawaks for several centuries before the arrival of Europeans. Anguilla was colonized in 1650 by English settlers from neighbouring St Kitts. In 1688 the island was attacked by a party of Irishmen who then settled. Anguilla was subsequently administered as part of the Leeward Islands, and from 1825 became even more closely associated with St Kitts. In 1875 a petition sent to London requesting separate status and direct rule from Britain met with a negative response. Again in 1958 the islanders formally petitioned the Governor requesting a dissolution of the political and administrative association with St Kitts, but this too failed. From 1958 to 1962 Anguilla was part of the Federation of the West Indies.

Opposition to rule from St Kitts erupted on 30 May 1967 when St Kitts policemen were evicted from the island and Anguilla refused to recognize the authority of the State Government any longer. During 1968–69 the British Government maintained a 'Senior British Official' to advise the local Anguilla Council and devise some solution to the problem. In March 1969, following the ejection from the island of a high-ranking British civil servant, British security forces occupied Anguilla. A Commissioner was installed, and in 1969 Anguilla became *de facto* a separate dependency of Britain; a situation rendered *de jure* on 19 Dec. 1980 under the Anguilla Act 1980 when Anguilla formally separated from the state of St Kitts, Anguilla-Nevis. A new constitution came into effect in 1982 providing for a large measure of internal autonomy under the Crown.

TERRITORY AND POPULATION. Anguilla is the most northerly of the Leeward Islands, some 70 miles (112 km) to the north-west of St Kitts and 5 miles (8 km) to the north of St Martin/Sint Maarten. The territory also comprises the island of Sombrero and several other off-shore islets or cays. The total area of the territory is about 60 sq. miles (155 sq. km). Census population (1984) was 6,897. Population estimate, 1997, 10,663. The capital is The Valley.

CONSTITUTION AND GOVERNMENT. A set of amendments to the constitution came into effect in 1990, providing for a Deputy Governor, a Parliamentary Secretary and an Opposition Leader. The *House of Assembly* consists of a Speaker, Deputy Speaker, 7 directly elected members for 5-year terms, 2 nominated members and 2 *ex-officio* members: the Deputy Governor and the Attorney-General.

The Governor discharges his executive powers on the advice of an Executive Council comprising a Chief Minister, 3 Ministers and 2 *ex-officio* members: the Deputy Governor, Attorney-General and the Secretary to the Executive Council.

Elections were held in March 1994 for the House of Assembly. The Anguilla National Alliance gained 2 seats, the Anguilla National Party (ANP), 2, the Anguillan Democratic Party, 2 and ind, 1.

Governor: Alan Hoole, OBE.
Deputy-Governor: Robert Malcolm Harris.
Chief Minister and Minister of Lands, Tourism, Agriculture and Fisheries: Hubert Hughes (ANP).

ECONOMY

Budget. In 1997, current revenue is EC$52·7m. and expenditure, EC$50·2m. The main sources of revenue are custom duties, tourism and bank licence fees. There is little taxation. A 'Policy Plan' with the UK provided for £10·5m. of aid in 1994-97.

Currency. The *Eastern Caribbean dollar* (*see* ANTIGUA AND BARBUDA).

Banking and Finance. The East Caribbean Central Bank based in St Kitts-Nevis functions as a central bank. There is a small offshore banking sector. In 1996 there were 2 domestic and 2 foreign commercial banks.

ENERGY AND NATURAL RESOURCES

Electricity. Production (1996) 28·5m. kWh.

Agriculture. Because of low rainfall agriculture potential is limited. About 1,200 ha are cultivable. Main crops are pigeon peas, maize and sweet potatoes. Livestock consists of sheep, goats, cattle and poultry. The island relies on imports for food.

Fisheries. Fishing is a thriving industry (mainly lobster).

EXTERNAL ECONOMIC RELATIONS

Tourism. Tourism accounts for 50% of GDP. In 1996 there were 86,239 visitor arrivals (66% from the USA), bringing revenue of US$48m. in 1995.

COMMUNICATIONS

Roads. There are about 40 miles of tarred roads and 25 miles of secondary roads. In 1991 there were 2,450 passenger cars and 733 commercial vehicles.

Civil Aviation. Wallblake is the airport for The Valley. Anguilla is linked to neighbouring islands by services operated by Air Anguilla, LIAT, Tyden Air, WINAIR and American Eagle.

Shipping. The main seaports are Sandy Ground and Blowing Point, the latter serving passenger and cargo traffic to and from St Martin.

Telecommunications. There is a modern internal telephone service with (1992) 2,923 exchange lines; and international telegraph, telex, fax and internet services. There is 1 government (Radio Anguilla) and 2 other radio broadcasters. TV is privately owned; there are 2 channels and a cable system.

Press. In 1995 there were 1 daily, 2 weeklies and a quarterly periodical.

SOCIAL INSTITUTIONS

Justice. Based on UK common law as exercised by the Eastern Caribbean Supreme Court on St Lucia. Final appeal lies to the UK Privy Council.

Religion. There were in 1992 Anglicans, Roman Catholics, Methodists, Seventh Day Adventists, Church of God and Baptists.

Education. Adult literacy was 80% in 1995. Education is free and compulsory between the ages of 5 and 16 years. There are 6 government primary schools with (1996) 1,540 pupils and 1 comprehensive school with (1996) 1,060 pupils. Higher education is provided at regional universities and similar institutions.

Health. In 1996 there was 1 hospital with a total of 60 beds, 4 health centres and a government dental clinic. There were 5 government-employed and 3 private doctors.

Welfare. A social security system was instituted in 1982 to provide age and disability pensions and sickness and maternity benefits.

Further Reading

Petty, C. L., *Anguilla: Where there's a Will, there's a Way.* Anguilla, 1984.—*A Handbook History of Anguilla.* Anguilla, 1991.

BERMUDA

KEY HISTORICAL EVENTS. The islands were discovered by Juan Bermúdez, probably in 1503, but were uninhabited until British colonists were wrecked there in 1609. A plantation company was formed; in 1684 the Crown took over the government.

A referendum in Aug. 1995 rejected independence from the UK.

TERRITORY AND POPULATION. Bermuda consists of a group of 138 islands and islets (about 20 inhabited), situated in the western Atlantic (32° 18' N. lat., 64° 46' W. long.); the nearest point of the mainland, 940 km distant, is Cape Hatteras (North Carolina). The area is 20·59 sq. miles (53·3 sq. km). In June 1995 the USA surrendered its lease on land used since 1941 for naval and air force bases. At the 1991 census the population (excluding British military personnel) numbered 58,460. Estimate, 1996, 60,144.

Chief town, Hamilton; population, 1994, 1,100.

In 1996 there were 833 live births, 944 marriages and 444 deaths.

CLIMATE. A pleasantly warm and humid climate, with up to 60" (1,500 mm) of rain, spread evenly throughout the year. Hamilton. Jan. 63°F (17·2°C), July 79°F (26·1°C). Annual rainfall 58" (1,463 mm).

CONSTITUTION AND GOVERNMENT. At a referendum on 17 Aug. 1995, 16,369 votes were cast against the option of independence, and 5,714 were in favour. The electorate was 38,000; turn-out was 58%. Under the 1968 constitution the *Governor*, appointed by the Crown, is normally bound to accept the advice of the Cabinet in matters other than external affairs, defence, internal security and the police, for which he retains special responsibility. The legislature consists of a *Senate* of 11 members, 5 appointed by the Governor on the recommendation of the Premier, 3 by the Governor on the recommendation of the Opposition Leader and 3 by the Governor in his own discretion. The 40 members of the *House of Assembly* are elected, 2 from each of 20 constituencies by universal suffrage. A general election was held on 5 Oct. 1993; turn-out was 78%. The United Bermuda Party won 22 seats with 50% of votes cast, the Progressive Labour Party 18 with 46%.

Governor: John Thorold Masefield, CMG.
Premier: Pamela F. Gordon.

Local Government. The City of Hamilton and the Town of St. George's.

DEFENCE. The Bermuda Regiment numbered 684 in 1996.

ECONOMY

Performance. GNP per capita was US$29,900 in 1995/96.

Budget. The fiscal year ends on 31 March. The 1997–98 budget envisaged revenue of BD$488m. and current expenditure of BD$448m.
The estimated chief sources of revenue (in BD$1m.) in 1997–98: Customs duties, 144; payroll tax, 133; companies fees, 38; land tax, 24; passenger tax, 20; vehicle licences, 17.

Currency. The unit of currency is the *Bermuda dollar* (BMD) of 100 *cents* at parity with the US dollar. The Bermuda Monetary Authority issues notes in denominations of BD$100, 50, 20, 10, 5 and 2, and coins in values of BD$5, 1, 50c, 25c, 10c, 5c and 1c. Inflation averaged 2·5% in 1996.

Banking and Finance. Bermuda is an offshore financial centre with tax exemption facilities. In 1994, 8,224 international companies were registered. There are 3 commercial banks, with total assets of BD$8,475m. in 1995.
At the end of the first quarter of 1997 there were 8,703 exempted companies, 292 exempted partnership companies, 520 non-resident companies and 26 non-resident insurance companies on the Bermuda register. Bermuda is now the world's third largest insurance market after London and New York.

Weights and Measures. Metric, except that US and Imperial (British) measures are used in certain fields.

ENERGY AND NATURAL RESOURCES

Electricity. Production (1995) 467m. kWh.

Agriculture. The chief products are fresh vegetables, bananas and citrus fruit. In 1995, 839 acres were being used for production of vegetables, fruit and flowers as well as for pasture, forage and fallow. In 1996, 503 persons were employed in agriculture, fishing and quarrying.
In 1995 the total value of agricultural products was BD$5,989,000.

Fisheries. In 1996 there were 194 fishing vessels and 274 registered fishermen. Fishing is centred on reef-dwelling species such as groupers and lobsters.

INDUSTRY. At 31 Dec. 1996, 9,252 international companies were registered in Bermuda, with insurers the most important category.

Labour. The labour force numbered 34,633 in 1996. Unemployment was less than 1·5% of the working population.

Trade Unions. There are 9 trade unions with a total membership (1995) of 8,728.

EXTERNAL ECONOMIC RELATIONS. Foreign firms conducting business overseas only are not subject to a 60% Bermuda ownership requirement. In 1996, over 8,200 international companies had a physical presence in Bermuda.

Commerce. The visible adverse balance of trade is more than compensated for by invisible exports, including tourism and off-shore insurance business.

Merchandise imports and exports in BD$1m.:

	1992	1993	1994	1995	1996
Imports	483	519	551	551	569
Exports	84	35	51	57	. . .

Imports in 1996 from USA, BD$416·6m.; UK, BD$28·8m.; Canada, BD$25·3m.; Caribbean, BD$31·8m.

In 1992 the principal imports (in BD$1m.) were food, beverages and tobacco (106); machinery (68); chemicals (67); clothing (36); fuels (31); transport equipment (22). The bulk of exports comprise sales of fuel to aircraft and ships, and re-exports of pharmaceuticals.

Tourism. In 1996, 570,631 tourists visited Bermuda, including cruise ship passengers. Visitor expenditure in 1995 was BD$487m.

COMMUNICATIONS

Roads. There are 140 miles of public highway and 138 miles of private roads. There are approximately 21,100 private cars, 22,100 motorcycles, scooters and mopeds, 700 buses, taxis and limousines and 3,600 trucks and tank wagons.

Civil Aviation. The Bermuda International Airport is 19 km from Hamilton. Bermuda is served on a regularly scheduled basis by Air Canada, American Airlines, British Airways, Continental Airlines, Delta Airlines, Northwest Airlines and US Air.

Shipping. There are 3 ports, Hamilton, St George's and Dockyard. There is an open shipping registry. In 1995, ships registered totalled 4·49m. DWT, all foreign-owned.

Telecommunications. There were 15 post offices and 44,215 telephones in 1995. Radio and television broadcasting are commercial; there are 2 broadcasting companies which offer a choice of 5 AM and 3 FM radio stations and 3 TV channels. A cable TV service also offers some 40 channels. In 1992 there were 0·1m. radio and 30,000 TV receivers.

Press (1996). There is 1 daily newspaper with a circulation of about 17,000 and 2 weeklies with a total circulation of about 15,000.

SOCIAL INSTITUTIONS

Justice. There are 4 magistrates' courts, 3 Supreme Courts and a Court of Appeal. The police had a strength of about 500 men and women in 1996.

Religion. Many religions are represented but the larger number of worshippers are attracted to the Anglican, Roman Catholic, Seventh Day Adventist, African Methodist Episcopal, Methodist and Baptist faiths.

Education. Education is compulsory between the ages of 5 and 16, and government assistance is given by the payment of grants, and, where necessary, of school fees. In 1995–96 there were 6,362 pupils in state schools and 3,179 in independent schools. There were 515 full-time students attending the Bermuda College in 1995. A restructuring of secondary education has resulted in the construction of a new state-of-the-art secondary school, Cedarbridge Academy, which opened in September 1997.

Health. In 1996 there were 2 hospitals, 100 physicians and surgeons, 49 dentists and dental hygienists, 6 optometrists, 27 pharmacists, 8 dieticians and 553 nurses.

Further Reading

Government Statistical Department. *Bermuda Facts and Figures.* Annual.
Ministry of Finance. *Bermuda Digest of Statistics.* Annual.
Zuill, W. S., *The Story of Bermuda and Her People.* 2nd ed. London, 1992

National library: The Bermuda Library, Hamilton.
National statistical office: Government Statistical Department, Hamilton.

BRITISH ANTARCTIC TERRITORY

KEY HISTORICAL EVENTS. The British Antarctic Territory was established on 3 March 1962, as a consequence of the entry into force of the Antarctic Treaty, to separate those areas of the then Falkland Islands Dependencies which lay within the Treaty area from those which did not (i.e. South Georgia and the South Sandwich Islands).

TERRITORY AND POPULATION. The territory encompasses the lands and islands within the area south of 60°S latitude lying between 20°W and 80°W longitude (approximately due south of the Falkland Islands and the Dependencies). It covers an area of some 660,000 sq. miles, and its principal components are the South Orkney and South Shetland Islands, the Antarctic Peninsula (Palmer Land and Graham Land) the Filchner and Ronne Ice Shelves and Coats Land.

There is no indigenous or permanently resident population. There is however an itinerant population of scientists and logistics staff of about 300, manning a number of research stations.

Commissioner: Anthony J. Longrigg (non-resident).
Administrator: Dr. M. G. Richardson (non-resident).

BRITISH INDIAN OCEAN TERRITORY

KEY HISTORICAL EVENTS. This territory was established to meet UK and US defence requirements by an Order in Council on 8 Nov. 1965, consisting then of the Chagos Archipelago (formerly administered from Mauritius) and the islands of Aldabra, Desroches and Farquhar (all formerly administered from Seychelles). The latter islands became part of Seychelles when that country achieved independence on 29 June 1976.

TERRITORY AND POPULATION. The group, with a total land area of 23 sq. miles (60 sq. km) comprises 5 coral atolls (Diego Garcia, Peros Banhos, Salomon, Eagle and Egmont) of which the largest and southernmost, Diego Garcia, covers 17 sq. miles (44 sq. km) and lies 450 miles (724 km) south of the Maldives. A US Navy support facility has been established on Diego Garcia. There is no permanent population.

Commissioner: Bruce Dinwiddy (non-resident).
Administrator: Margaret Savill (non-resident).
Commissioner's Representative: Cdr S. Jackson.

BRITISH VIRGIN ISLANDS

KEY HISTORICAL EVENTS. Discovered by Columbus on his second voyage in 1493, British Virgin Islands were first settled by the Dutch in 1648 and taken over in 1666 by a group of English planters. In 1774 constitutional government was granted. The Islands became a Dependent Territory of the UK in 1967.

TERRITORY AND POPULATION. The Islands form the eastern extremity of the Greater Antilles and number 70, of which 16 are inhabited. The largest, with population (1991 census), are Tortola, 13,568, Virgin Gorda, 2,495, Anegada, 156 and Jost Van Dyke, 141. Other islands had a total population (estimate 1990) of 183; marine population (estimate 1989), 124. Total area 59 sq. miles (130 sq. km); total population (1991 census), 16,749; (1994 estimate, 17,896). The capital, Road Town, on the south-east of Tortola, is a port of entry; population (estimate, 1991), 6,330.

CLIMATE. A pleasantly healthy sub-tropical climate with summer temperatures lowered by sea breezes. Nights are cool and rainfall averages 50" (1,250 mm).

CONSTITUTION AND GOVERNMENT. The Constitution dates from 1967 as amended in 1977 and 1994. The Executive Council consists of the Governor, the Chief Minister, the Attorney-General *ex officio* and 3 ministers. The ministers are appointed by the Governor. The *Legislative Council* consists of the 4 ministers, 5 directly elected members from constituencies and 4 members from 'at large' seats covering the territory as a whole. The Speaker is elected from outside the Council. At the elections of Feb. 1995 the Virgin Islands Party gained 6 seats, the Independent People's Movement, 3, the United Party, 2, and the Concerned Citizens' Movement, 2.

Governor: David P. MacKilligin, CMG.
Chief Minister: Ralph T. O'Neal (Virgin Islands Party; sworn in 25 May 1995).

INTERNATIONAL RELATIONS

Membership. The Islands are an associate member of CARICOM and the Organization of Eastern Caribbean States.

ECONOMY

Performance. In 1994 GNP per capita was US$16,755.

Budget. In 1996 revenue (estimate) was US$100·6m.; expenditure, US$89·3m.

Currency. The unit of currency is the US dollar.

Banking and Finance. In 1996 there were 11 banks. As of 14 Dec. 1995 total deposits recorded amounted to US$1,875m. In 1996 there were 67 trust companies providing financial services other than banking. Financial services are the most important industry after tourism. 210,260 companies, almost all offshore, were registered at the end of 1996.

ENERGY AND NATURAL RESOURCES

Electricity. Production, 1994, 74·9m. kWh.

Agriculture. In 1994: Total land suitable for agriculture, 5,324 acres; crops, 1,767 acres and pastures, 3,557 acres. Agricultural production is limited, with the chief products being livestock (including poultry), fish, fruit and vegetables. Production, 1994, in tonnes: Fruits, 525; vegetables/root crop, 153; beef, 172; mutton, 29; pork, 39; and 1,535 cases of eggs.

Livestock (1994, in 1,000): Cattle, 3·5; pigs, 2·8; sheep, 5 and goats, 6.

INDUSTRY. The construction industry is a significant employer. There are a rum distillery, ice-making plants and cottage industries producing tourist items.

EXTERNAL ECONOMIC RELATIONS

Commerce. There is a very small export trade, almost entirely with the Virgin Islands of the USA. In 1993 imports were US$122·9m. and exports US$5·5m.

Tourism. Tourism is the most important industry and accounts for some 75% of economic activity. In 1995 there were 364,147 visitor arrivals, of whom 122,054 were cruise ship visitors and 23,712 day visitors. Total tourist expenditure for 1994 was US$197·7m.

COMMUNICATIONS

Roads. In 1994 there were 107 km of surfaced roads. In 1994 there were 6,265 registered vehicles on Tortola and 760 on Virgin Gorda.

Civil Aviation. Beef Island Airport, about 16 km from Road Town, is capable of receiving 80-seat short-take-off-and-landing jet aircraft. American Eagle and LIAT provide scheduled flights to Puerto Rico and the Eastern Caribbean.

Shipping. There are 2 deep water harbours: Port Purcell and Road Town. There are services to the Netherlands, UK, USA and other Caribbean islands.

Telecommunications. There were (1995) 9,282 telephones, 21 telex subscribers, 582 fax machine subscribers and an external telephone service links Tortola with Bermuda and the rest of the world. Radio ZBVI transmits 10,000 watts and British Virgin Islands Cable TV operates a cable system of 19 television channels and 8 pay-per-view channels.

Press. In 1994 there were 2 weekly newspapers and a periodical.

SOCIAL INSTITUTIONS

Justice. Law is based on UK common law. There are courts of first instance. The appeal court is in the UK.

Religion. There are Anglican, Methodist, Seventh-Day Adventist, Roman Catholic, Baptist, Pentecostal and other Christian churches in the Territory. There are also Jehovah's Witness and Hindu congregations.

Education. In 1995 adult literacy was 95%. Primary education is provided in 16 government schools, 3 with secondary divisions, and 16 private schools. Total number of pupils in primary and pre-primary schools (31 Dec. 1994) 2,855.

Secondary education to GCSE level and Caribbean Examination Council level is provided by the BVI High School and the secondary divisions of the schools on Virgin Gorda and Anegada. Total number of secondary level pupils (31 Dec. 1994) 1,363.

Government expenditure, 1995 (estimate), US$4·3m. In 1996 the total number of classroom teachers in all Government schools was 116. In 1986 a branch of the Hull University (England) School of Education was established.

Health. As of 31 Dec. 1995 there were 17 doctors, 67 nurses, 50 public hospital beds and 1 private hospital with 10 beds. Expenditure, 1994 (estimate) was US$5·3m.

Further Reading

Dookham, I., *A History of the British Virgin Islands.* Epping, 1975
Harrigan, N. and Varlack, P., *The Virgin Islands Story.* Road Town, 1975
Moll, V. P., *Virgin Islands.* [Bibliography] Oxford and Santa Barbara (CA), 1991
Pickering, V. W., *Early History of the British Virgin Islands.* London, 1983

CAYMAN ISLANDS

KEY HISTORICAL EVENTS. The islands were discovered by Columbus on 10 May 1503 and (with Jamaica) were recognized as British possessions by the Treaty of Madrid in 1670. Grand Cayman was settled in 1734 and the other islands in 1833. They were administered by Jamaica from 1863, but remained under British sovereignty when Jamaica became independent on 6 Aug. 1962.

TERRITORY AND POPULATION. The Islands consist of Grand Cayman, Little Cayman and Cayman Brac. Situated in the Caribbean Sea, about 200 miles north-west of Jamaica. Area, 100 sq. miles (260 sq. km). Census population of 1989, 25,355 (13,202 Caymanians by birth). Estimate, 1996, 35,000. The spoken language is English. The chief town is George Town, census (1989) 12,921. Vital statistics (1996): Births, 561; marriages, 300; deaths, 125.

The areas and populations of the islands are:

	Sq. km	Census 1979	Census 1989	Estimate 1996
Grand Cayman	197	15,000	23,881	33,584
Cayman Brac	36	1,607	1,441	1,300
Little Cayman	26	70	33	116

CLIMATE. The climate is tropical maritime, with a cool season from Nov. to March and temperatures some 10°F warmer for the remaining months. Rainfall averages 56" (1,400 mm) a year at George Town. Hurricanes may be experienced between July and Nov.

CONSTITUTION AND GOVERNMENT. The 1972 Constitution provides for a *Legislative Assembly* consisting of the Speaker, 3 official members, and 15 elected members. The *Executive Council* consists of the Governor (as Chairman), the 3 official members and 5 members elected by the elected members of the Legislative Assembly.

Governor: John W. Owen, MBE.

ECONOMY

Budget. Estimated revenue 1998, CI$248·2m.; expenditure, CI$204m. Public debt (Dec. 1994), CI$37m.; total reserves (Dec. 1997), CI$8·9m.

Currency. The unit of currency is the *Cayman Island dollar* (KYD) of 100 *cents*. There are coins of 1, 5, 10, 25 and 50 cents and CI$1, 2 and 5 and notes of CI$1, 5, 10, 25, 50 and 100.

Banking and Finance. A Monetary Authority was inaugurated in Jan. 1997. 576 commercial banks and trust companies held licences at Dec. 1996, which permit the holders to offer services to the public; 29 domestically. Financial services are the Islands' chief industry. 37,919 companies, almost all offshore, were registered at the end of 1996.

EXTERNAL ECONOMIC RELATIONS

Commerce. Exports, 1994 (f.o.b.), totalled CI$2m. Imports, (c.i.f.), CI$272·9m.

Tourism. Tourism is the chief industry after financial services, and there were (1994) 3,880 beds in hotels and 3,162 in apartments, guest houses and cottages. There were 940,578 visitors in 1994, including 341,491 by air.

COMMUNICATIONS

Roads. There were (1996) about 252 miles of motorable road, of which about 200 miles were surfaced with tarmac, and (1996) 19,164 motor vehicles.

Civil Aviation. There is an international airport at Grand Cayman. CAL provides a regular inter-island service. Cayman Airways operates a service to Cayman Brac and also flies to Miami, Orlando, Houston, Tampa, Honduras and Jamaica. American Airlines and Northwest Airlines provide services to Miami; US Air to Baltimore and North Carolina; American Airlines to Raleigh/Durham; Air Jamaica to Jamaica; and British Airways to Gatwick, London.

Shipping. Motor vessels ply regularly between the Cayman Islands, Jamaica, Costa Rica and Florida.

Telecommunications. There were 20,731 telephone lines in 1996 serving 29,500 stations and 2,900 cellular customers. There are 4 radio broadcasting stations in the Islands, with (1997) an estimated 20,000 receivers. There are 2 local commercial TV companies.

Press. The *Caymanian Compass* is published 5 days a week.

SOCIAL INSTITUTIONS

Justice. There is a Grand Court, sitting 6 times a year for criminal sessions at George Town under a Chief Justice and 2 puisne judges. There are 2 Magistrates presiding over the Summary Court.

Religion. There are Anglican, Roman Catholic, Presbyterian and other Christian communities represented in the islands.

Education. In 1996 there were 10 government primary schools with 1,739 pupils and 9 private schools. Post-primary education at the 3 government high schools was attended by 1,626 pupils. There is also a private institution for tertiary education; a government school for special educational needs; a government-operated community college offering technical, vocational and business studies and a 2-year programme in arts and sciences, as well as adult, educational and recreational courses; and a centre for training of handicapped persons.

Health. In 1996 there was a general hospital in George Town with 59 beds, a dental clinic, 4 district clinics and a hospital in Cayman Brac with specialist services (18 beds). There were 28 doctors in the government service and 26 in private practice.

Further Reading

Boultbee, P. G., *Cayman Islands.* [Bibliography]. Oxford and Santa Barbara (CA), 1996
Compendium of Statistics of the Cayman Islands, 1994. Cayman Islands Government Statistics Office, 1995
Cayman Islands Annual Report 1996. Cayman Islands Government Information Services, 1996

FALKLAND ISLANDS

KEY HISTORICAL EVENTS. France established a settlement in 1764 and Britain a second settlement in 1765. In 1770 Spain bought out the French and drove off the British. This action on the part of Spain brought that country and Britain to the verge of war. The Spanish restored the settlement to the British in 1771, but the settlement was withdrawn on economic grounds in 1774. In 1806 Spanish rule was overthrown in Argentina, and the Argentine claimed to succeed Spain in the French and British settlements in 1820. The British objected and reclaimed their settlement in 1832 as a Crown Colony.

On 2 April 1982 Argentine forces occupied the Falkland Islands. On 3 April the UN Security Council called, by 10 votes to 1, for Argentina's withdrawal. After a military campaign, but without a formal declaration of war, the UK regained possession on 14–15 June after Argentina surrendered.

In April 1990 Argentina's Congress declared the Falkland and other British-held South Atlantic islands part of the new Argentine province of Tierra del Fuego.

TERRITORY AND POPULATION. The Territory comprises numerous islands situated in the South Atlantic Ocean about 480 miles north-east of Cape Horn covering 4,700 sq. miles. The main East Falkland Island, 2,610 sq. miles; the West Falkland, 2,090 sq. miles, including the adjacent small islands. The population at the census of 1996 was 2,607. The only town is Stanley, in East Falkland, with a population of 1,636. The population is nearly all of British descent, with 1,267 born in the Islands (1996 census figures) and 885 in the UK. A British garrison of about 2,000 servicemen, stationed in East Falkland in 1991, is not included in the 1996 census figures, but the 483 civilians employed there are.

CLIMATE. A cool temperate climate, much affected by strong winds, particularly in spring. Stanley. Jan. 49°F (9·4°C), July 35°F (1·7°C). Annual rainfall 27" (681 mm).

CONSTITUTION AND GOVERNMENT. A new Constitution came into force on 3 Oct. 1985. This incorporated a chapter protecting fundamental human rights and in the preamble recalled the provisions on the right of self-determination contained in international covenants.

Executive power is vested in the Governor who must consult the Executive Council except on urgent or trivial matters. He must consult the Commander British Forces on matters relating to defence and internal security (except police).

There is a *Legislative Council* consisting of 8 elected members and 2 *ex officio* members, the Chief Executive and Financial Secretary. Only elected members have a vote. The Commander British Forces has a right to attend and take part in its proceedings but has no vote. The Attorney General also has a similar right to take part in proceedings with the consent of the person presiding. The Governor presides over sittings. He also presides over sittings of the Executive Council which consists of 3 elected members (elected by and from the elected members of Legislative Council) and the Chief Executive and Financial Secretary (*ex officio*). The Commander British Forces and Attorney General have a right to attend but may not vote.

British citizenship was withdrawn by the British Nationality Act 1981, but restored after the Argentine invasion of 1982.

Governor: Richard Ralph, CVO.
Chief Executive: Andrew Gurr.

DEFENCE. Since 1982 the Islands have been defended by a 2,000-strong garrison of British servicemen. In addition there is a local volunteer defence force.

ECONOMY

Policy. The Falkland Islands Development Corporation began operations in 1984. Projects assisted include a spinning mill dairy, hydroponic market garden, tourist lodges, agricultural supply co-operatives, and research into seabird populations and their diets.

Budget. Revenue and expenditure (in £ sterling) for fiscal years ending 30 June:

	1990–91	1991–92	1992–93	1993–94	1994–95	1995–96
Revenue	41,940,000	40,270,000	40,452,000	32,690,000	33,812,000	42,351,679
Expenditure	45,967,000	39,145,000	30,452,000	24,535,000	33,614,000	42,351,953

Currency. The unit of currency is the *Falkland Islands pound* (FKP) of 100 *pence*, at parity with £1 sterling.

Banking. The only bank is Standard Chartered Bank, which had assets of £31m. in 1997.

ENERGY AND NATURAL RESOURCES

Oil. The UK government authorized exploration for oil in Nov. 1991 in the 200-mile economic exclusion zone except where it overlapped Argentina's zone in the west. An Anglo-Argentine agreement of 27 Sept. 1995 establishes 2 legal frameworks for marine oil exploration areas without prejudice to either country's claim to sovereignty over the Falkland Islands. The first, close to the Islands, is to have licensing terms which give companies 22 years to explore and complete drilling. The second extends between the Islands and Argentina wherein licensing will be overseen by a joint Anglo-Argentine commission. Argentina may bid for licences in the first area, and draws revenue directly from the second.

Agriculture. The economy was formerly based solely on agriculture, principally sheep farming. Following a programme of sub-division, much of the land is divided into family size units. There were 100 farms in 1997, averaging 33,600 acres and 8,200 sheep. During 1991 the Falklands Islands Co. sold its agricultural holdings to the Falkland Island government. Less than 5% of the total land area is owned outside the islands. Wool is the principal product; output was 2,521 tonnes in 1991. In 1997 there were over 700,000 sheep.

Fisheries. Since the establishment of a 150-mile interim conservation and management zone around the Islands in 1986 and the consequent introduction, on 1 Feb. 1987, of a licensing regime for vessels fishing within the zone, income from the associated fishing activities is now the largest source of revenue. Licences raised £25m. in 1992. Some 0·2m. tonnes of illex squid are caught annually. In 1994 Argentina's quota was raised to 0·22m. tonnes; that of the Falkland Islands remained at 0·15m. tonnes. 79,803 tonnes were caught in the Falklands zone in 1996. 61,360 tonnes of Patagonian squid and 23,515 tonnes of blue whiting were also caught.

On 26 Dec. 1990 the Falklands outer conservation zone was introduced which extends beyond the 150 mile zone out to 200 miles from baselines. In Nov. 1992 commercial fishing in the outer zone was banned, the zone was reopened to fishing in 1994. A UK-Argentine South Atlantic Fisheries Commission was set up in 1990; it meets at least twice a year.

EXTERNAL ECONOMIC RELATIONS. 90% of trade is with the UK, the rest with Latin America, mainly Chile. In 1995 imports totalled £17m.; exports (mainly wool), £3·5m.

Tourism. There are about 200 tourists and 5,000 cruise ship visitors a year.

COMMUNICATIONS

Roads. There are 27 km of made-up roads in and around Stanley and another 54 km of all-weather road between Stanley and Mount Pleasant Airport. Other settlements outside Stanley are linked by tracks. There were about 1,100 private cars in 1996.

Civil Aviation. Air communication is currently via Ascension Island. An airport, completed in 1986, is sited at Mount Pleasant on East Falkland. RAF Tristar aircraft operate a twice-weekly service between the Falklands and the UK. Internal air links are provided by the government-operated air service, which carries passengers, mail, freight and medical patients between the settlements and Stanley on non-scheduled flights in Islander aircraft. A Chilean airline runs a weekly service to Punta Arenas.

Shipping. A charter vessel calls 4 or 5 times a year to/from the UK. Vessels of the Royal Fleet Auxiliary run regularly to South Georgia. Sea links with Chile and Uruguay began in 1989.

Telecommunications. Number of telephones (Sept. 1991) 1,180. International direct dialling is available, as are international telex and facsimile links. There is a government-operated radio and TV station at Stanley.

SOCIAL INSTITUTIONS

Justice. There is a Supreme Court, and a Court of Appeal sits in the UK; appeals may go from that court to the judicial committee of the Privy Council. Judges may only be removed for inability or misbehaviour on the advice of the judicial committee of the Privy Council. The senior resident judicial officer is the Senior Magistrate. There is an Attorney General and a Senior Crown Counsel.

Education. Education is compulsory between the ages of 5 and 15 years. In 1992 there were 350 children receiving education in the Islands. 60 of these were of primary school age living on isolated farms and receiving teacher visits and radio lessons. There is a primary school in Stanley, and a community school opened in 1992 with secondary study and sport facilities. Estimated recurrent expenditure on education and training from own funds in 1994–95 £2,041,440.

Health. The Government Medical Department is responsible for all medical services to civilians. Estimated expenditure (1994–95) £2,092,490. A new hospital and some sheltered accommodation was completed in March 1987. Services include all primary care for Stanley and the flying doctor service for outlying farm settlements.

Further Reading

Day, A., *The Falkland Islands*. [Bibliography]. Oxford and Santa Barbara (CA), 1995
Gough, B., *The Falkland Islands/Malvinas: the Contest for Empire in the South Atlantic.* London, 1992
Smith, W. S. (ed.) *Towards Resolution? The Falklands/Malvinas Dispute.* London, 1991

GIBRALTAR

KEY HISTORICAL EVENTS. The Rock of Gibraltar was settled by Moors in 711. In 1462 it was taken by the Spaniards, from Granada. It was captured by Admiral Sir George Rooke on 24 July 1704, and ceded to Great Britain by the Treaty of Utrecht, 1713. The cession was confirmed by the treaties of Paris (1763) and Versailles (1783).

On 10 Sept. 1967, in pursuance of a UN resolution on the decolonization of Gibraltar, a referendum was held to ascertain whether the people of Gibraltar wished to retain their link with the UK or pass under Spanish sovereignty. Out of an electorate of 12,762, 12,138 voted to retain the British connection.

The border was closed by Spain in 1969, opened to pedestrians in 1982 and fully opened in 1985.

In 1973 Gibraltar joined the European Community, as a dependent territory of the United Kingdom.

TERRITORY AND POPULATION. Area, $2^1/2$ sq. miles (6·5 sq. km) including port and harbour. Total population, (census, 1991), 28,074. Estimate (1996) 27,337 (of whom 20,608 were British Gibraltarian, 4,023 Other British and 2,706 Non-British). The population is mostly of Genoese, Portuguese and Maltese as well as Spanish descent.

Vital statistics (1996): Births, 436; marriages, 722; deaths, 218.

CLIMATE. The climate is warm temperate, with westerly winds in winter bringing rain. Summers are pleasantly warm and rainfall is low. Mean maximum temperatures: Jan. 16°C, July 28°C. Annual rainfall 722 mm.

CONSTITUTION AND GOVERNMENT. A new Constitution was introduced in 1969. The Legislative and City Councils were merged to produce an enlarged legislature known as the *Gibraltar House of Assembly*. Executive authority is exercised by the Governor, who is also Commander-in-Chief. The Governor, while retaining certain reserved powers, is normally required to act in accordance with the advice of the Gibraltar Council, which consists of 4 *ex-officio* members (the Deputy Governor, the Deputy Fortress Commander, the Attorney-General and the Financial and Development Secretary) together with 5 elected members of the House of Assembly appointed by the Governor after consultation with the Chief Minister. Matters of primarily domestic concern are devolved to elected Ministers, with Britain responsible for other matters, including external affairs, defence and internal security. There is a Council of Ministers presided over by the Chief Minister.

The House of Assembly consists of a Speaker appointed by the Governor, 15 elected and 2 *ex-officio* members (the Attorney-General and the Financial and Development Secretary). No more than 8 of the elected seats may go to the winning party at elections.

Gibraltarians have full UK citizenship.

A Mayor of Gibraltar is elected by the elected members of the Assembly.

At the elections of May 1996 the electorate was 18,437; turn-out was 88%. The Gibraltar Social Democratic Party (GSD) gained 8 seats with 52% of votes cast. The Gibraltar Socialist and Labour Party gained 7 with 43%.

Governor and C.-in-C.: Sir Richard Luce.
Chief Minister: Peter Caruana (b.1956; GSD).

DEFENCE. The Ministry of Defence presence consists of a tri-service garrison numbering approximately 900 uniformed personnel. Supporting the garrison are approximately 1,100 locally-employed civilian personnel. In addition to the defence of the Rock the garrison supports a NATO Headquarters, provides and operates communications and surveillance facilities, operates the airfield and provides berthing facilities for naval vessels in the harbour.

ECONOMY

Budget. Revenue and expenditure (in £1,000 sterling):

	1992–93	1993–94	1994–95	1995–96	1996–97
Revenue	72,735	73,443	69,808	70,688	72,017
Expenditure	77,915	74,697	73,215	73,255	73,304

Currency. The legal tender currency is UK sterling. Also legal tender are Government of Gibraltar Currency Notes and coins for the *Gibraltar pound* (GIP) of 100 *pence*, at parity with the UK £1 sterling. There are Gibraltar Government coins of 1, 2, 5, 10, 20 and 50 pence and Gib£1, 2 and 5, and notes of Gib£5, 10, 20 and 50. The amount in notes in circulation at 31 March 1996 was £10·99m.

Banking and Finance. In 1997 there were 25 banks and 3 building societies operating in Gibraltar. The annual rate of inflation was 2·1% in 1996.

INDUSTRY. There is a bottling plant and a floppy diskette manufacturer.

Labour. The total insured labour force at 31 Dec. 1995 was 11,698. 32·2% of the local labour force is employed by the UK departments and the Gibraltar Government. In the private sector the main sources of employment are the construction industry, wholesale and retail distribution, and banking, finance and insurance.

Trade Unions. In 1991 there were 8 registered trade unions.

EXTERNAL ECONOMIC RELATIONS. Gibraltar has a special status within the EU which exempts it from the latter's fiscal policy.

Commerce. Imports and exports (in £1,000 sterling):

	1991	1992	1993	1994	1995
Imports	278,866	327,536	370,884	420,192	379,919
Exports	70,102	92,971	161,400	175,643	172,599

Britain and the Commonwealth provide the bulk of imports, but fresh vegetables and fruit come mainly from the Netherlands and Spain. Foodstuffs accounted for 11% of total imports (about £39m.) in 1995; about 51% of non-fuel imports originated from the UK. Other sources include Japan, Spain and the Netherlands. Value of non-fuel imports, 1995, £276·2m. Exports are mainly re-exports of petroleum and petroleum products supplied to shipping. Gibraltar depends largely on tourism, offshore banking and other financial sector activity, the entrepôt trade and the provision of supplies to visiting ships. Exports of local produce are negligible.

Tourism. In 1996 more than 6m. tourists visited Gibraltar (including day-visitors).

COMMUNICATIONS

Roads. There are 33 miles of roads including 4·25 miles of pedestrian way.

Civil Aviation. There is an international airport, Gibraltar North Front. Scheduled flights are operated by GB Airways to London (Heathrow and Gatwick), Manchester, Tangiers, Marrakesh, Casablanca and Agadir, and by Monarch Airlines to London (Luton). 89,300 passengers arrived by air in 1995.

Shipping. A total of 4,222 merchant ships of 79·2m. GRT entered port during 1996, including 3,411 deep-sea ships of 78·2m. GRT. 5,042 calls were made by yachts of 191,613 GRT. 139 cruise liners called during 1996 involving 96,684 passengers.

Telecommunications. The telephone service is operated by Gibraltar Nynex Communications, a joint venture company between the Government of Gibraltar and Nynex Worldwide Systems from the United States of America. The number of telephone stations (1996) was 21,466. A new Digital System X Exchange became operational in 1990 with capacity for 25,800 lines in 1996. A Fibre Optic Network became operational in 1991. International direct dialling is available to over 150 countries via the Gibraltar Telecommunications Ltd (Gibtel) Earth Satellite Station and other international circuits. Gibtel began operating a mobile system in 1994. Radio Gibraltar broadcasts for 24 hours daily, in English and Spanish, and GBC Television operates for 24 hours daily in English. Number of TV licences as at 31 Dec. 1996, 7,014.

Press. There were (1997) 1 daily and 3 weeklies.

SOCIAL INSTITUTIONS

Justice. The judicial system is based on the English system. There is a Court of Appeal, a Supreme Court, presided over by the Chief Justice, a Court of First Instance and a Magistrates' Court.

Religion. The population are mostly Roman Catholic. In 1997 there were 7 Roman Catholic and 3 Anglican churches, 1 Presbyterian and 1 Methodist church and 4 synagogues, and a mosque is currently under construction. Annual subsidy to each communion, £500.

Education. Free compulsory education is provided between ages 5 and 15 years. The medium of instruction is English. The comprehensive system was introduced in Sept. 1972. There were (1996) 12 primary and 2 comprehensive schools. Primary schools are mixed and divided into first schools for children aged 4-8 years and middle schools for children aged 8-12 years. The comprehensives are single-sex. In addition, there is 1 Services primary school and 1 private primary school. A new purpose-built Special School for severely handicapped children aged 2-16 years was opened in 1977, and there are 4 Special Units for children with special educational needs (1 attached to a first school, 1 to a middle school and 1 at each secondary school), 3 nurseries for children aged 3-4 years and an occupational therapy centre for handicapped adults. Technical and vocational education and training is available at the Gibraltar College of Further Education managed by the Gibraltar Government. In Sept. 1996, there were 2,810 pupils at government primary schools, 200 at private and 294 at the Services school; 19 at the special school; 929 at the boys' comprehensive school and 878 at the girls' comprehensive. There were 165 full-time and 297 part-time students in the Gibraltar College of Further Education in Sept. 1996. Scholarships are made available for universities, teacher-training and other higher education in the UK. Government expenditure on education in the year ended 31 March 1996 was £11·5m.

Health. In 1994 there were 2 hospitals with 244 beds and 29 doctors. Total expenditure on medical and health services during year ended 31 March 1995 was £19,354,653.

Further Reading

Gibraltar Year Book. Gibraltar, (Annual)
Ellicott, D., *Our Gibraltar.* Gibraltar, 1975
Green, M. M., *A Gibraltar Bibliography.* London, 1980.—*Supplement.* London, 1982
Hills, G., *Rock of Contention: a History of Gibraltar.* London, 1974
Jackson, W. G. F., *The Rock of the Gibraltarians.* Farleigh Dickinson Univ. Press, 1987
Magauran, H. C., *Rock Siege: the Difficulties with Spain 1964–85.* Gibraltar, 1986
Morris, D. S. and Haigh, R. H., *Britain, Spain and Gibraltar, 1945–90: the Eternal Triangle.* London, 1992
Shields, G. J., *Gibraltar.* [Bibliography] Oxford and Santa Barbara (CA), 1988

MONTSERRAT

KEY HISTORICAL EVENTS. Montserrat was discovered by Columbus in 1493 and colonized by Britain in 1632 who brought Irish settlers to the island. Montserrat formed part of the federal colony of the Leeward Islands from 1871 until 1958, when it became a separate colony following the dissolution of the Federation.

On 18 July 1995 the Soufriere Hills volcano erupted for the first time in recorded history, which led to over half the inhabitants being evacuated to the north of the island and the relocation of the chief town, Plymouth. Another major eruption on 25 June 1997 caused a number of deaths and led to further evacuation. Many of the 4,000 or so residents who decided to stay are living in crowded emergency housing in the one area still considered to be safe.

TERRITORY AND POPULATION. Montserrat is situated in the Caribbean Sea 27 miles south-west of Antigua. The area is 39·5 sq. miles (102 sq. km). Population, 1991, 11,957. Estimate, Aug. 1997, 4,000. What was previously the chief town, Plymouth, is now deserted as a result of the continuing activity of the Soufriere Hills volcano. The safe area is in the north of the island.

CLIMATE. A tropical climate with an average annual rainfall of 60" (1,500 mm) the wettest months being Sept.–Dec., with a hurricane season June–Nov. Plymouth. Jan. 76°F (24·4°C), July 81°F (27·2°C).

CONSTITUTION AND GOVERNMENT. Montserrat is a British Dependent Territory. The Constitution dates from the 1989 Montserrat Constitutional Order. The head of state is Queen Elizabeth II, represented by a *Governor* who heads an Executive Council comprising also the Chief Minister, the Financial Secretary, the Attorney-General and 3 other ministers. The *Legislative Council* consists of 7 elected members, 2 civil service officials (the Attorney-General and Financial Secretary) and 2 nominated members; it sits for 5-year terms. Following elections to the Legislative Council on 11 Nov. 1996, a coalition government was formed comprising 2 members of the Movement for National Reconstruction, 1 member of the National Progressive Party and 1 independent.

Governor: Tony Abbott.
Chief Minister: David Brandt.

INTERNATIONAL RELATIONS

Membership. Montserrat is a member of CARICOM and the Organization of Eastern Caribbean States.

ECONOMY

Budget. In 1996 estimated expenditure was EC$39·7m.; revenue, EC$47·2m.

Currency. The *Eastern Caribbean dollar* (*see* ANTIGUA AND BARBUDA: Currency).

Banking and Finance. In 1996 there were 3 commercial and 21 offshore banks. Responsibility for overseeing offshore banking rests with the Governor.

ENERGY AND NATURAL RESOURCES

Electricity. Production (1995) 19·23m. kWh.

Agriculture. 3,700 ha are normally suitable for agriculture, with about half in use, but only 1,000 ha were available in 1996 because of the volcanic crisis. Potatoes, tomatoes, onions, mangoes and limes were produced in recent times. Meat production began in 1994 and the island soon became self-sufficient in chicken, mutton and beef.
Livestock (1995, in 1,000); Cattle, 4; pigs, 0·5; sheep, 5; goats, 7.

Fisheries. Catch (1995) 100 tonnes.

INDUSTRY. Manufacturing has in recent years contributed about 6% to GDP and accounted for 10% of employment, but has been responsible for about 80% of exports. It has been limited to rice milling and the production of light consumer goods such as electronic components, light fittings, plastic bags and leather goods.

FOREIGN ECONOMIC RELATIONS

Commerce. Imports in 1995 totalled US$80m.; exports, US$5m. The USA was the main trading partner. Chief exports were milled rice, electronic parts, lighting fittings, plastic bags and leather goods.

Tourism. Tourism has in recent years contributed about 30% of GDP; earnings in 1993 were EC$40m. There were 36,077 visitors including 11,636 cruise ship arrivals in 1994. However, since the volcanic eruptions the tourist industry has become practically non-existent.

COMMUNICATIONS

Roads. In 1995 there were 205 km of paved roads, 25 km of unsurfaced roads and 50 km of tracks. In 1995 there were 2,700 cars and 400 commercial vehicles registered.

Civil Aviation. At the W. H. Bramble airport LIAT used to provide services to Antigua with onward connections to the rest of the Eastern Caribbean, but it was closed in June 1997.

Shipping. Plymouth is the port of entry, but alternative anchorage is provided at Old Bay Road during the volcanic crisis.

Telecommunications. Number of telephones, 1995, 4,783. There is a government-owned radio station (ZJB) and 2 commercial stations (Radio Antilles and GEM Radio). There is a commercial cable TV company.

Press. In 1996 there was 1 weekly newspaper.

SOCIAL INSTITUTIONS

Justice. Law is based on UK common law as exercised by the Eastern Caribbean Supreme Court. Final appeal lies to the UK Privy Council. Law is administered by the West Indies Associated States Court, a Court of Summary Jurisdiction and Magistrate's Courts.

Religion. In 1997, 25% of the population were Anglican, 20% Methodist, 15% Pentecostal, 10% Roman Catholic and 10% Adventist.

Education. In 1996–97 there were 11 primary schools (only 4 open), a comprehensive secondary school with 3 campuses, and a technical college. Schools are run by the Government, the churches and the private sector. There is a medical school, the American University of the Caribbean.

Health. In 1996 there were 4 medical officers, 1 surgeon, 1 dentist and 1 hospital with 69 beds.

Further Reading

Fergus, H.A., *Montserrat: History of a Caribbean Colony.* London, 1994

PITCAIRN ISLAND

KEY HISTORICAL EVENTS. Pitcairn was discovered by Carteret in 1767, but remained uninhabited until 1790, when it was occupied by 9 mutineers of HMS *Bounty*, with 12 women and 6 men from Tahiti. Nothing was known of their existence until the island was visited in 1808.

TERRITORY AND POPULATION. Pitcairn Island (1·75 sq. miles; 4·6 sq. km) is situated in the Pacific Ocean, nearly equidistant from New Zealand and Panama (25° 04' S. lat., 130° 06' W. long.). Adamstown is the only settlement. The population in Dec. 1996 was 42. The uninhabited islands of Henderson (12 sq. miles), Ducie (1 1/2 sq. miles) and Oeno (2 sq. miles) were annexed in 1902. Henderson is a World Heritage Site.

CLIMATE. An equable climate, with average annual rainfall of 80" (2,000 mm), spread evenly throughout the year. Mean monthly temperatures range from 75°F (24°C) in Jan. to 66°F (19°C) in July.

CONSTITUTION. The Local Government Ordinance of 1964 constitutes a *Council* of 10 members, of whom 6 are elected, 3 are nominated (1 by the 6 elected members and 2 by the Governor) and the Island Secretary is an *ex-officio* member. The Island Magistrate, who is elected triennially, presides over the Council; other members hold office for only 1 year. Liaison between Governor and Council is through a Commissioner in the Auckland, New Zealand, office of the British Consulate-General.

Governor: R. J. Alston, CMG (UK High Commissioner in New Zealand).
Island Magistrate: Jay Warren (re-elected Dec. 1996).

BUDGET. For the year to 31 March 1997 revenue was $604,234 and expenditure $601,665.

CURRENCY. New Zealand currency is used.

ROADS. There were (1997) 6 km of roads. In 1997 there were 29 motor cycles.

JUSTICE. The Island Court consists of the Island Magistrate and 2 assessors.

EDUCATION. In Aug. 1997 there was 1 teacher and 8 pupils.

Further Reading

A Guide to Pitcairn. Pitcairn Island Administration, Auckland, revised ed. 1990
Ball, I., *Pitcairn: Children of the Bounty.* London, 1973
Murray, S., *Pitcairn Island: the First 200 Years.* La Canada (CA), 1992

ST HELENA

KEY HISTORICAL EVENTS. The island was uninhabited when discovered by the Portuguese in 1502. It was administered by the East India Company from 1659 and became a British colony in 1834.

Public demonstrations took place in April 1997 against government spending cuts and the Governor's imposition of his own, instead of the elected, head of social services.

TERRITORY AND POPULATION. St Helena, of volcanic origin, is 1,200 miles from the west coast of Africa. Area, 47 sq. miles (121·7 sq. km), with a cultivable area of 243 ha. Population (1997) 5,644. The capital and port is Jamestown, population (1992) 1,500.

CLIMATE. A mild climate, with little variation. Temperatures range from 75–85°F (24–29°C) in summer to 65–75°F (18–24°C) in winter. Rainfall varies between 13" (325 mm) and 37" (925 mm) according to altitude and situation.

GOVERNMENT. The *Legislative Council* consists of the Governor, 2 *ex-officio* members (the Government Secretary and the Treasurer) and 12 elected members. The Governor is assisted by an *Executive Council* consisting of the 2 *ex-officio* members and the chairs of the 6 Council Committees.

St Helenians do not have British citizenship.

Governor and C.-in-C.: D.L. Smallman, LVO.
Chief Secretary: J. G. Perrott.

FINANCE AND TRADE

Commerce. The economy is dependent on UK and EU aid of £8·5m. a year.

COMMUNICATIONS

Roads. There were (1988) 94 km of all-weather motor roads. There were 1,301 vehicles in 1987.

Shipping. There is a service from Cardiff (UK) 6 times a year, and links with South Africa and neighbouring islands.

Telecommunications. The Cable & Wireless Ltd cable connects St Helena with Cape Town and Ascension Island. St Helena Government Broadcasting Station, Radio St Helena, broadcasts daily and relays BBC programmes. Number of radio receivers (1993), 2,500. Television reception was introduced in 1996 from the BBC World Service, South African M-Net and a US Satellite channel.

SOCIAL INSTITUTIONS

Justice. Police force, 32; cases are dealt with by a police magistrate.

Religion. There are 10 Anglican churches, 4 Baptist chapels, 3 Salvation Army halls, 1 Seventh Day Adventist church and 1 Roman Catholic church.

Education. 3 pre-school playgroups, 7 primary and 1 comprehensive school controlled by the Government had 1,188 pupils in 1987. The Prince Andrew School (opened in 1989) offers vocational courses leading to British qualifications.

Health. There were 3 doctors, 1 dentist and 1 hospital in 1992.

Ascension is a small island of volcanic origin, of 34 sq. miles (88 sq. km), 700 miles north-west of St Helena. There are 120 ha providing fresh meat, vegetables and fruit. Population, 31 March 1993, was 1,117 (excluding military personnel).

The island is the resort of sea turtles, rabbits, the sooty tern or 'wideawake' and feral donkeys.

A cable station connects the island with St Helena, Sierra Leone, St Vincent, Rio de Janeiro and Buenos Aires. There is an airstrip (Miracle Mile) near the settlement of Georgetown; the Royal Air Force maintains an air link with the Falkland Islands.

Administrator: Roger Huxley.

Tristan da Cunha, is the largest of a small group of islands in the South Atlantic lying 1,320 miles (2,124 km) south-west of St Helena, of which they became dependencies on 12 Jan. 1938. Tristan da Cunha has an area of 98 sq. km and a population (1988) of 313, all living in the settlement of Edinburgh. Inaccessible Island (10 sq. km) lies 20 miles west and the 3 Nightingale Islands (2 sq. km) lie 20 miles south of Tristan da Cunha; they are uninhabited. Gough Island (90 sq. km) is 220 miles south of Tristan and has a meteorological station.

Tristan consists of a volcano rising to a height of 6,760 ft, with a circumference at its base of 21 miles. The volcano, believed to be extinct, erupted unexpectedly early in Oct. 1961. The whole population was evacuated without loss and settled temporarily in the UK; in 1963 they returned to Tristan. Potatoes remain the chief crop, cattle, sheep and pigs are now reared, and fish are plentiful.

Population in 1996, 292. The original inhabitants were shipwrecked sailors and soldiers who remained behind when the garrison from St Helena was withdrawn in 1817.

At the end of April 1942 Tristan da Cunha was commissioned as HMS *Atlantic Isle*, and became an important meteorological and radio station. In Jan. 1949 a South African company commenced crawfishing operations. An Administrator was appointed at the end of 1948 and a body of basic law brought into operation. The Island Council, which was set up in 1932, consists of a Chief Islander, 3 nominated and 8 elected members (including 1 woman) under the chairmanship of the Administrator.

Administrator: B. G. Dalley.

Further Reading

Crawford, A., *Tristan da Cunha and the Roaring Forties.* Edinburgh, 1982
Cross, A., *Saint Helena.* Newton Abbot, 1980
Day, A., *St. Helena, Ascension and Tristan da Cunha.* [Bibliography]. Oxford and Santa Barbara (CA), 1997

SOUTH GEORGIA AND THE SOUTH SANDWICH ISLANDS

KEY HISTORICAL EVENTS. The first landing and exploration was undertaken by Captain James Cook, who formally took possession in the name of George III on 17 Jan. 1775. British sealers arrived in 1788 and American sealers in 1791. Sealing reached its peak in 1800. A German team was the first to carry out scientific studies there in 1882–83. Whaling began in 1904 and ceased in 1966, and the civil administration was withdrawn. Argentine forces invaded South Georgia on 3 April 1982. A British naval task force recovered the Island on 25 April 1982.

TERRITORY AND POPULATION. South Georgia lies 800 miles south-east of the Falkland Islands and has an area of 1,450 sq. miles. The South Sandwich Islands are 470 miles south-east of South Georgia and have an area of 130 sq. miles. In 1993 crown sovereignty and jurisdiction were extended from 12 to 200 miles around the islands. There is no permanent population. There is a small military garrison. The British Antarctic Survey have a biological station on Bird Island. The South Sandwich Islands are uninhabited.

CLIMATE. The climate is wet and cold with strong winds and little seasonal variation. 15°C is occasionally reached on a windless day. Temperatures below −15°C at sea level are unusual.

CONSTITUTION AND GOVERNMENT. Under the new Constitution which came into force on 3 Oct. 1985 the Territories ceased to be dependencies of the Falkland Islands. Executive power is vested in a Commissioner who is the officer for the time being administering the Government of the Falkland Islands. The Commissioner is obliged to consult the officer for the time being commanding Her Majesty's British Forces in the South Atlantic on matters relating to defence and internal security (except police). The Commissioner whenever practicable consults the Executive Council of the Falkland Islands on the exercise of functions that in his opinion might affect the Falkland Islands. There is no Legislative Council. Laws are made by the Commissioner (Richard Ralph, CVO, resident in the Falkland Islands).

Economy. The total revenue of the Territories (estimate, 1988–89) £268,240, mainly from philatelic sales and investment income. Expenditure estimate £194,260.

Communications. There is occasional communication by sea with the Falkland Islands by means of research and ice patrol ships. Royal Fleet Auxiliary ships, which serve the garrison, run regularly to South Georgia. Mail is dropped from military aircraft.

Justice. There is a Supreme Court for the Territories and a Court of Appeal in the United Kingdom. Appeals may go from that court to the Judicial Committee of the Privy Council. There is no magistrate permanently in residence. The Officer Commanding the garrison is usually appointed a magistrate.

Further Reading
Headland, R. K., *The Island of South Georgia*. CUP, 1985

THE TURKS AND CAICOS ISLANDS

KEY HISTORICAL EVENTS. After a long period of rival French and Spanish claims the islands were eventually secured to the British Crown in 1766, and became a separate colony in 1973 after association at various times with the colonies of the Bahamas and Jamaica.

TERRITORY AND POPULATION. The Islands are situated between 21° and 22°N. lat. and 71° and 72°W. long., about 50 miles east of the Bahamas, of which they are geographically an extension. There are over 40 islands, covering an esti-mated area of 192 sq. miles (497 sq. km). Only 8 are inhabited: Grand Caicos, the largest, is 30 miles long by 2 to 3 miles broad; Grand Turk, the capital and main political and administrative centre, is 7 miles long by 1·25 broad. Population, 1990 census, 12,350; Grand Turk, 3,761; Providenciales, 5,586; South Caicos, 1,220; Middle Caicos, 275; North Caicos, 1,305; Salt Cay, 213. Estimate, 1995, 13,800.
  Vital statistics (1989): Births, 192; deaths, 58.

CLIMATE. An equable and healthy climate as a result of regular trade winds, though hurricanes are sometimes experienced. Grand Turk. Jan. 76°F (24·4°C), July 83°F (28·3°C). Annual rainfall 21".

CONSTITUTION AND GOVERNMENT. A new Constitution was intro-duced in 1988 and amended in 1992. The Executive Council comprises 2 official members: The Chief Secretary and the Attorney-General; a Chief Minister and 5 other ministers from among the elected members of the Legislative Council; and is presided over by the Governor. The Legislative Council consists of a Speaker, the 2 official members of the Executive Council, 13 elected members and 3 appointed members.
  At general elections held on 31 Jan. 1995 for the 13 elective seats on the Legislative Council, the People's Democratic Movement gained 8 seats; the People's National Party, 4; and ind, 1.

Governor: John P. Kelly, LVO, MBE.
Chief Minister: Derek Taylor.

INTERNATIONAL RELATIONS

Membership. The Islands are a member of CARICOM.

ECONOMY

Budget. 1993–94 recurrent revenue was US$27·3m. and expenditure, US$28·5m. Forecast for 1994–95: Revenue, US$31·2m.; expenditure, US$31m.

Currency. The US dollar is the official currency.

Banking and Finance. There are 4 commercial banks. Offshore finance is a major industry.

INDUSTRY

Labour. In 1989, out of a total population of 4,885 aged 14 or over, 4,043 were working, 573 unemployed and 269 economically inactive.

EXTERNAL ECONOMIC RELATIONS

Commerce. Exports, 1992–93, US$6·47m.; imports, US$39,835,000. The main export is dried, frozen and processed fish.

Tourism. Number of visitors, 1994, 70,946.

COMMUNICATIONS

Civil Aviation. The international airports are on Grand Turk and Providenciales. Turks and Caicos Airways had 2 aircraft in 1995. Services are also provided by American Airlines and Carnival Airlines. An internal air service provides regular daily flights between the inhabited islands.

Shipping. The main ports are at Grand Turk, Cockburn Harbour and Providenciales. There is a service to Miami.

Telecommunications. There are internal and international cable, telephone, telex, telegraph and fax services. The Government operates the semi-commercial Radio Turks and Caicos. There are also 2 commercial and 1 religious station. In 1995 there were about 6,000 radio sets. There is cable and satellite TV.

Press. There is 1 weekly and 1 bi-weekly newspaper.

SOCIAL INSTITUTIONS

Justice. Laws are a mixture of Statute and Common Law. There is a Magistrates Court and a Supreme Court. Appeals lie from the Supreme Court to the Court of Appeal which sits in Nassau, Bahamas. There is a further appeal in certain cases to the Privy Council in London.

Religion. There are Anglican, Methodist, Baptist and evangelists groups.

Education. Education is free between the ages of 5 and 14 in the 10 government primary schools; there are also 4 private primary schools. In March 1993 the average number of pupils in the 4 government secondary schools was 1,075.

Health. In 1995 there were 6 doctors, 1 dentist, 56 nurses and midwives and 36 hospital beds.

Further Reading

Boultbee, P. G., *Turks & Caicos Islands.* [Bibliography]. Oxford and Santa Barbara (CA), 1991

THE FUTURE AS PAST? AMERICAN INTERESTS AND WORLD ORDER

Professor Michael Cox

The lessons of history

Any evaluation of America's future role in world affairs has to begin with a brief examination of where the US has come from. Certainly, if we treat the present as history—and the future as the present projected forward in time—then understanding the past is not only useful, but actually critical in helping us explain the part the US is likely to play in the twenty-first century.

The first point to make is that those whose task it is to guide the last remaining superpower through the turbulent waters of world politics, do so in the sure knowledge that as an international player the US has performed extraordinarily well over the past fifty years. It defeated Japan, helped defeat Germany, went on to successfully contain the Soviet Union, and in the process helped construct a relatively stable world system. Critically, however, it managed to do all these things not because of its diplomatic skills or cultural superiority, but because of what one writer has termed its 'preponderance of power'. Not surprisingly, this has led modern American leaders to the not illogical conclusion that there is, in the end, no substitute for power and the US possessing as much of this essential commodity as possible. It was this, they reason, that helped it win the Cold War. And it will be this, they believe, that will help America maintain the peace in the future.

If the realist practice of power politics is likely to continue to shape the way in which the United States defines its role in the world, so too will a strong desire by US leaders to remain engaged in international affairs. Here again 'history' continues to cast its long shadow over contemporary discussions; and the lesson which decision-makers draw from their reading of the past is that when the US retreated into isolationism in the inter-war period there was chaos and instability, but when it became fully involved in world affairs—as it was finally impelled to in 1941 and again after 1947—the world could at least look forward to a better future. Moreover, in their view, there is no reason (even in the absence of a clear and present threat) for the US to turn its back on the world in the post-Cold War era. Indeed, according to Washington, it would be disastrous if it were to do so. America might be more selective in what it tries to do in the future. Disengagement however is not envisaged. It is simply not an option.

This brings us to the issue of American leadership. Much has been made about American indecision on key international issues such as Bosnia or Rwanda. Yet this should not blind us to the pivotal role the US has played over the past few years. It was, we should recall, the United States (and not her other European allies) that managed the problematic transition from German division to unification after 1989. It was America again that created, and then led, the coalition against Iraq between 1990 and 1991. And it was the US—and the US alone—that had the military capability, the diplomatic clout and the sense of political purpose to impose some sort of solution in ex-Yugoslavia. Thus whether it wants to or not, or others like it or not, America is 'bound to lead'. In effect, there is no substitute for the United States.

Finally, any understanding of America's future role must take account of what one writer has termed its 'mission' to promote democracy. Dismissed by some as mere rhetoric, it would nonetheless be foolish to underestimate the American desire to recast the international system in its own image: and to do this for more than just moral reasons. First, according to the new wisdom in Washington, democracies are preferable to any other form of government because they do not go to war with one another. Second, they tend to play by the rules of the international game. Finally, they have a vested interest in participating in those various multilateral bodies—such as the IMF and the European Union—upon which the US expects to build the stable world economic order of the future. Promoting democracy therefore is not merely an idealistic add-on, but an essential component of any programme aimed at advancing the American national interest in the twenty first-century.

But what is the American 'national interest', and how should it be defined? Remarkably, there has been very little discussion of this critical problem since the collapse of the communist alternative in the late 1980s. The reason for this however is not because American policy-makers cannot agree on the answer, but rather because the answer seems all too obvious. The end of the Cold War might have made American foreign policy less coherent. Americans as a people may no longer be prepared to pay any price or go anywhere to defend the cause for freedom. Yet in spite of this, there is still a good degree of consensus at the highest levels about the policies the US must pursue in order to advance its goals.

The US and the world economy

America's future role in the world begins with the death of two twentieth century myths: the myth of a separate 'Third World' functioning outside of the world economy and the myth of the communist economic alternative. The demise of the first, and the collapse of the second, have opened up the world in ways that would have once been thought inconceivable. This has created major opportunities for the United States. Some of these it has already realized. Some, it will no doubt seek to exploit in the years ahead; indeed, it is vital that it does so given its already huge stake in the international economy. With well over $700bn. invested abroad, and close to a trillion dollars of US goods and services being imported and exported around the world per annum, America has more than just an passing interest in maintaining a dynamic international economy. Indeed, through the 1990s, it has expended a good deal of energy in ensuring that the world economy remains buoyant. It has, for example, encouraged the creation of an economic zone bringing the United States, Canada and Mexico more closely together in the institutional shape of NAFTA. It has breathed new life into APEC (Asia Pacific Economic Cooperation). And it has strengthened the world trading system more generally by successfully negotiating the conclusion of the General Agreement and Tariffs and Trade (GATT)—a deal that promised to lead both to a vast expansion in international trade and the creation of thousands of new jobs in the United States.

In the end, of course, US policy-makers and politicians will not be rewarded for their prudent and careful management of the world economy, but rather for their success in advancing America's economic interests. In this respect, the much-criticized President Clinton has perhaps showed us the shape of things to come by recognizing that foreign policy is not to be judged by wars won abroad but prosperity sustained at home; and this will only be sustained over the longer term by competing successfully against one's rivals. Prediction may be a dangerous venture, but one can predict with some degree of certainty that all administrations will be assessed by their success in helping America compete with other nations. Moreover, if the record of the Clinton administration is anything to go by, it is not a competition the US intends to come second in. As a former US trade official put it, 'if you don't win, you lose'.

The US and military power

Though economics will dominate America's future international agenda, it would be wrong to ignore the centrality of military power in US calculations. Certainly, US military strategists do not do so. By the year 2000 they are planning to be spending well over $250bn. a year on security to ensure America's position of strength in the international system. Policy-makers are convinced that the US has to remain the number one power, with a capacity to deploy what a 1996 defence review called 'robust and flexible military forces'. These, it is felt, are vital if the United States is to deter potential enemies, provide the nation with a credible overseas presence, and make good on American promises to contribute to multilateral peace operations. However, military power is not just necessary for its own symbolic sake. It will also help ensure that the United States retains what one analyst has nicely characterized as the loudest 'voice in international affairs'. In the new world order, political influence will continue to grow out of the barrel of the gun.

But where precisely will new wars be fought? US policy-makers may disagree about specifics; nevertheless most are clear in their own minds that the threats of the future will not come in Europe nor, interestingly, from any upwardly mobile great power attempting to challenge US dominance, but rather from what they describe as 'backlash' or 'rogue' states like Iraq, Iran and North Korea. Whether or not the United States will be able to fight and win two wars simultaneously against such states (a scenario outlined in various defence plans) remains open to question. What is not open to doubt is the impressive array of weaponry at America's disposal. To all intents and purposes, the US is now the only serious military actor in the world with a capacity to intervene globally. For this reason, if no other, the twenty-first century might easily turn out to be more 'American' than the twentieth.

The US and nuclear proliferation

If the US is determined to remain the militarily hegemon of the future, it is equally keen to reduce the threat of nuclear war by preventing the proliferation of weapons of mass destruction. Some would even argue that this has become America's number one security problem, and is bound to remain so. It has undoubtedly played an important part in American foreign policy in the 1990s. It was, after all, fear of proliferation (amongst other things) which caused the US to go to war against Iraq. It was then worries about North Korea's nuclear potential that led the US to negotiate a much-criticized deal with Pyongyang three years later. And it has been concern about the spread of nuclear weapons which has impelled the US to engage so vigorously with the states of the former Soviet Union.

The question remains though, will the US be able to limit the spread of weapons of mass destruction over the longer term? There is neither an easy, nor even an optimistic answer to this. The desire by many less powerful countries to develop weapons denied to them by states like the US which already possess them, certainly points to further proliferation. In a world of increasingly porous borders, one must also doubt the ability of intelligence agencies to monitor the movement of dangerous fissile material. Indeed, such is the pessimism in certain American circles, that there are those who now feel that until the United States and the nuclear-have powers decide to abandon their own nuclear arsenals, then proliferation is virtually inevitable. Possibly so. Yet in the real world where great powers—or those who pretend to be great powers—still define their status in terms of being members of the nuclear club, there is little or no chance of this happening. Though persuaded of the virtues of non-proliferation for others, it is unlikely that countries like the US (or for that matter the UK, France or China) will ever be persuaded to denuclearize themselves. The future remains uncertain.

The US and NATO

A fourth issue that is bound to preoccupy US foreign policy-makers is how to manage, and sustain domestic support for, the eastward expansion of NATO. The American debate surrounding this particular proposal has thus far been noisy and acrimonious and shows no sign of abating. Opponents insist that expansion is not only unnecessary but more likely to provoke democratic Russia than reassure it. Supporters, on the other hand, argue that over time expansion will not only bring stability to the continent as a whole, but also accelerate the pace of European unification. Moreover, unless NATO does expand, then, according to Washington, the organization will become irrelevant, and in the end simply wither away. This, it is asserted, would be bad for the emerging states of Central Europe, bad for Europe as a whole, and bad for the United States which continues to regard NATO as the main source of its influence in European affairs.

Yet in spite of this plethora of apparently sound arguments in favour of NATO expansion, many in the United States remain highly sceptical. The costs involved and the impact of expansion upon the integrity of NATO have persuaded many ordinary Americans—and some rather extraordinary ones like the indefatigable George F. Kennan—that enlargement is simply not a very good idea. Policy-makers in the future therefore will face a most difficult task in selling what is now a policy *fait accompli* to an American public which sees no reason, and feels no strong desire to extend US guarantees to parts of Europe where the US seems to have few interests.

The US and China

Following US recognition in 1978, Washington warmly embraced the People's republic as a bulwark against Soviet power and the first communist state to experiment seriously with capitalism. The end of the Cold War, however, and the emergence of China as a more serious actor on the international stage, has soured what had been one of the more convenient alliances of modern times. The process began in 1989 with the repression at Tiananmen Square and has continued ever since with concerns about Chinese military power, China's various attempts to intimidate Taiwan and its appalling record on human rights. In effect, having encouraged the growth of China, the United States now finds itself in the situation of dealing with a nation that is becoming increasingly assertive. And there are some Americans who believe that sooner, rather than later, the US will have to confront Beijing.

The case for containment is a powerful one. Nonetheless, the official US position is, and will almost certainly remain, one of 'constructive engagement'. This it has been argued *ad nauseum* is the only way of managing China as it moves from isolation to closer association with the world. Moreover, according to Washington, it would be madness to leave China out in the cold. It possesses nuclear weapons. It is a central actor in the struggle against the weapons proliferation. Its economy is one of the most dynamic in the world. And in a potentially highly volatile region, it is a source of stability and order.

The US thus has a relatively clear perspective on China, and assumes (or at least hopes) that over time 'normal' rather than hostile relations between the two powers will gradually transform and tame China. Yet there is no doubting the problems which lay ahead, nor the extent of the challenge posed by modern China to US diplomacy. One might even argue that the greatest global test confronting US policymakers in the twenty-first century will be its successful management of a China that will not always say 'yes'—and might frequently say 'no'—to American demands.

The US and Russia

Finally, any assessment of the US role in world affairs has to speculate to some degree about its future relationship with post-communist Russia. Russia's large nuclear arsenal, its geographical position at the heart of Eurasia, and its still considerable international assets continue to make it an important power in its own right—one which America can hardly ignore. Many critics believe that America has probably devoted too much time to Russian affairs; and that in its rush to build what President Clinton hoped would one day become a 'strategic alliance with Russian reform', has tended to overlook the downside of Russia's triple transition from imperial power to normal nation, planning to market and totalitarianism to democracy. There is some truth to this. But critics of America's Russia policy (like those who would attack its stance on China) seem unable to propose any serious alternative. Furthermore, the alternatives they do propose only lead the US back to a state of conflict it is desperately trying to avoid. Certainly, having fought a long and costly Cold War against the old Soviet Union, America has no real desire to engage in another prolonged conflict with the new Russia.

The future

The transition in Russia raises a much larger question about the American role, and in particular about its 'grand strategy' towards those countries which have either made the leap into the brave new world of market economics, or are in the process of doing so. So far the movement from a world of hostile ideological camps to a more integrated world order has occurred relatively painlessly. Communism in Eastern Europe fell with little accompanying bloodshed. The USSR collapsed with remarkable ease. And the transition in China has been accomplished so far with minimal instability. There are several reasons for this quite smooth metamorphosis. One factor has been the US and its real, if at times, wavering commitment to building what President Bush in 1990 called a 'new world order'. Admittedly, the early and rather naïve expectation that the collapse of communism would usher in an age of perpetual peace has not been realized. Nor has history shown much sign of coming to an end. Yet the world is a much safer place today than it was during the Cold War. Europe has not become more unstable as some predicted it would. And relations between most states around the world are now in much better shape than they have been for decades. The United States cannot claim all the credit for this. Nonetheless, it is impossible to imagine our current state of affairs without the US.

There are those of course who claim to detect a fundamental shift in US resolve and anticipate (and fear) a less active American role in world affairs in the future. But this is a false reading of the situation. The end of the Cold War may have erased all 'strategic roadmaps' to use Charles Krauthammer's splendid phrase. But what it could not erase is the past and the lessons which policy-makers continue to derive from their reading of the past—one of which is that America cannot retreat into splendid isolation. Not because it seeks to dominate the world in any crude way, or because it has a higher moral duty to make the world a better place, but rather because it is not in its interest to do so. Talk of a homeward bound America is premature.

Professor Cox teaches in the Department of International Politics in Aberystwyth. His most recent study is US Foreign Policy after the Cold War: Superpower without a Mission? He is currently editor of the **Review of International Studies** *and an Associate Research Fellow at the Royal Institute of International Affairs, London.*

UNITED STATES OF AMERICA

Capital: Washington, DC
Population: 267·57m.
GNP per head: (PPP$) 26,397
HDI/world rank: 0·942/4

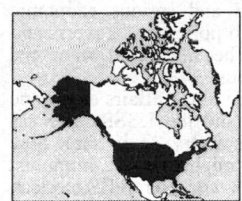

KEY HISTORICAL EVENTS. In 1775 white settlement in America was located in 13 British colonies on the east coast and in Spanish colonial territory in the south and south-west. The rest was Indian land, where former French claims to control had been given up in 1763. Spain succeeded to those claims in land west of the Mississippi and Britain in land east of it. Britain designated such land as Indian territory and forbade colonial expansion west of the Appalachians.

Britain's colonial subjects rebelled against her taxation and trading exploitation. The colonies declared their independence on 4 July 1776, provoking war with Britain which lasted until 1783 when Britain acknowledged the independent United States of America.

The Union extended south to the border of Florida (Spanish) and west to the Mississippi. A permanent constitution came into force in 1789, providing for a federal government. The rights of states to nullify federal laws if they contradicted state policies became a source of dispute, especially in relation to the slave-owning southern states which feared the Union preference for abolition.

In 1800 France bought back from Spain her title to 'Louisiana', the territory west of the Mississippi. In 1803 the USA bought it from France.

In 1812–14 the USA fought an inconclusive war with Britain on the grounds that Britain, operating from Canada, was encouraging Indian resistance; at sea, Britain was using her conduct of the Napoleonic War to harass American shipping.

Westward movement began almost with independence, increasing after the Homestead Act of 1832 and the removal of Indians to reservations during the 1830s.

The Spanish empire in the Americas had ended in 1821, and the north American territories had passed to Mexico, except for Florida which the USA acquired. In 1836 Texas broke away from Mexico, surviving as an independent republic until 1845 when the US, seeing strategic danger in its vulnerability, annexed it. This provoked war with Mexico which the US won in 1848, receiving the Mexican territories in the south-west including the present states of California, Arizona, Colorado, Utah, Nevada and New Mexico.

In the north-west, the Oregon Trail attracted thousands of migrants in the 1840s. In 1846 a long dispute with Britain was resolved, confirming the US title to the Oregon Territory. Westward migration was further stimulated by the California gold rush of 1848.

In the east and mid-west, tension over the question of slavery led to the secession of the southern states in 1860–61, and their formation as the Confederacy. Civil war broke out, ending in northern victory in 1865. Slavery was abolished and a period of radical reconstruction began for the South. Many reforms then implemented were cancelled after 1877, when the northern military presence was withdrawn and southern whites regained their political power, enforcing segregation and curtailing black civil and political rights.

During the late 19th century eastern and mid-western industrialization expanded rapidly. Growing cities attracted thousands of poor European immigrants, many of whom were escaping religious or political persecution as well as looking for work. This inward flow of labour continued into the 1930s and was matched by a flow of Asians to the west coast. A similar northward movement of Spanish-speakers from the Caribbean and Mexico, and of black workers from southern states, continues.

In the west there were Indian wars. The Apache and Navajo wars of the south-west lasted intermittently from 1861 until 1886. The Comanche fought for decades to protect their plains hunting grounds from settlement, as did the Cheyenne and Sioux. The latter's victory under Sitting Bull in 1876 only produced an increase in military action against them. Indian resistance ended after some 200 Sioux were shot at Wounded Knee in 1890.

In the Spanish-American war of 1898 the USA succeeded in replacing Spanish influence in the Caribbean with her own. She also replaced it in the Philippines, and acquired Guam in the western Pacific as a strategic base.

The USA entered the First World War in 1917, and afterwards reacted with an isolationist policy. In 1929 the stock market collapsed and serious economic depression lasted through the 1930s. The country turned to policies of government intervention in the economy; recovery began, but only became rapid when the Second World War necessitated a huge increase in production.

The war and subsequent victory led to active participation in the affairs of Europe and to a state of 'cold war' mistrust between the USA and the USSR. The US Marshall Plan financed the recovery of much of European industry. At the same time it appeared prudent to aid other nations where instability might admit Communist influence; this policy governed relations with Caribbean and Central American countries, and involved the USA in war against Communist forces in Korea (1950–53) and Vietnam (1961–73).

Following President Kennedy's assassination in 1963, US military involvement in Vietnam was intensified, but opposition at home led to withdrawal of forces in 1973.

In 1974 President Nixon was forced to resign amidst charges of corruption known collectively as Watergate. A revival of Republican fortunes came with the election of Ronald Reagan in the 1980 presidential race. In international affairs, Reagan was resolutely anti-Communist, raising fears of confrontation with the Soviet Union over his Strategic Defense Initiative, otherwise known as his 'Star Wars' system of defence. However, relations between the two super powers improved in the mid-eighties with successful negotiations on nuclear arms limitations. The collapse of the Soviet empire in 1990 extended US economic aid to Eastern Europe.

At home, the big social debate centred on civil rights—a movement that started in the 1960s with the campaign to end segregation in the southern states—feminism, environmental issues, urban crime and efforts to combat drug abuse.

In 1990 the invasion of Kuwait by Iraqi forces led to the Gulf War, 'Operation Desert Storm', the defeat of Iraq and renewed attempts to secure a Middle East peace settlement.

The Democrats regained control of the White House with the election of Bill Clinton, who mounted an economic recovery plan with a mix of reduced government spending and higher taxes.

In 1993 the US was involved in peacekeeping operations in the former Yugoslavia, and although there was reluctance to commit American troops, a US-brokered peace agreement led to American participation in a multinational supervisory force.

TERRITORY AND POPULATION. Population at each census from 1790 to 1990 (including Alaska and Hawaii from 1960). Figures do not include Puerto Rico, Guam, American Samoa or other Pacific islands, or the US population abroad. Residents of Indian reservations not included before 1890.

	White	Black	Other races	Total
1790	3,172,464	757,208	—	3,929,672
1800	4,306,446	1,002,037	—	5,308,483
1810	5,862,073	1,377,808	—	7,239,881
1820	7,866,797	1,771,562	—	9,638,359
1830	10,537,378	2,328,642	—	12,866,020
1840	14,195,805	2,873,648	—	17,069,453
1850	19,553,068	3,638,808	—	23,191,876
1860	26,922,537	4,441,830	78,954	31,443,321
1870	34,337,292	5,392,172	88,985	39,818,449
1880	43,402,970	6,580,793	172,020	50,155,783

	White	Black	Other races	Total
1890	55,101,258	7,488,676	357,780	62,947,714
1900	66,868,508	8,834,395	509,265	76,212,168
1910	81,812,405	9,828,667	587,459	92,228,531
1920	94,903,540	10,463,607	654,421	106,021,568
1930	110,395,753	11,891,842	915,065	123,202,660
1940	118,357,831	12,865,914	941,384	132,165,129
1950	135,149,629	15,044,937	1,131,232	151,325,798
1960	158,831,732	18,871,831	1,619,612	179,323,175
1970	177,748,975	22,580,289	2,882,662	203,211,926
1980	188,371,622	26,495,025	11,679,158	226,545,805
1990	199,686,070	29,986,060	19,037,743	248,709,873

Subsequent revised mid-year estimates have been:-

1991	210,979,000	31,107,000	10,020,000	252,106,000
1992	212,910,000	31,654,000	10,447,000	255,011,000
1993	214,760,000	32,168,000	10,867,000	257,795,000
1994	216,480,000	32,647,000	11,245,000	260,372,000
1995	218,149,000	33,095,000	11,646,000	262,890,000
1996	219,749,000	33,503,000	12,032,000	265,284,000
1997	221,242,000	33,924,000	12,409,000	267,575,000

Urban population (persons living in places with at least 2,500 inhabitants) at the 1990 census was 187,053,487 (75·2%); rural, 61,656,386. In 1980 the urban population was 73·7%; in 1970, 73·6%.

Sex distribution by race of the population at the 1990 census:

	Total population	White	Black	American Indian	Asian or Pacific	Other
Males:	121,239,418	97,475,880	14,170,151	967,186	3,558,038	5,068,163
Females:	127,470,455	102,210,190	15,815,909	992,048	3,715,624	4,736,684

Alongside these racial groups, and applicable to all of them, a category of 'Hispanic origin' comprised 22,354,059 persons (11,388,059 males; 10,966,000 females).

The 30–34 age group contained most people according to the 1990 census, with a total of 21,862,887 (10,985,954 females and 10,876,933 males), followed by 25–29, with 21,313,045 (10,617,109 females and 10,695,936 males).

The US population abroad at the time of the 1990 census was 925,845.

At the 1990 census there were 91,947,410 households. By 1996 this figure is estimated to have risen to 98,751,000.

Population (in 1,000) in July 1997 as estimated by the US Bureau of the Census (females in parentheses):

Total, 267,575 (136,570); White, 221,242 (112,374); Black, 33,924 (17,816); American Indian, Eskimo, Aleut, 2,322 (1,170); Asian and Pacific Islander, 10,086 (5,210); Hispanic origin, 29,240 (14,209). The July 1997 estimates included a figure of 60,000 people aged 100 or over, compared to 37,000 in 1990. Of the 60,000, an estimated 49,000 were female, and of the 37,000 in 1990, 29,000 were female.

The 1990 census showed that 31·8m. persons 5 years and over spoke a language other than English in the home, including Spanish by 17·3m.; French, 1·7m.; German, 1·5m.; Italian, 1·3m.; Chinese, 1·2m.

The following table includes population statistics, the year in which each of the original 13 states (Connecticut, Delaware, Georgia, Maryland, Massachusetts, New Hampshire, New Jersey, New York, North Carolina, Pennsylvania, Rhode Island, South Carolina, Virginia) ratified the constitution, and the year when each of the other states was admitted into the Union. Traditional abbreviations for the names of the states are shown in brackets with postal codes for use in addresses. The area of the USA is 3,717,796 sq. miles (9,629,091 sq. km), of which 3,536,278 sq. miles (9,158,960 sq. km) are land.

The USA is divided into 4 geographic regions comprised of 9 divisions. These are, with their 1990 census populations: Northeast (comprised of the New England and Middle Atlantic divisions), 50,809,229; Midwest (East North Central, West North Central), 59,668,632; South (South Atlantic, East South Central, West South Central), 85,445,930; West (Mountain, Pacific), 52,786,082.

Geographic divisions and states		Land area: sq. miles 1990	Census population 1 April 1990	Pop. per sq. mile, 1990
United States		3,536,278	248,709,873	70·3
New England		62,812	13,206,943	210·3
Maine (1820)	*(Me./ME)*	30,865	1,227,928	39·8
New Hampshire (1788)	*(N.H./NH)*	8,969	1,109,252	123·7
Vermont (1791)	*(Vt./VT)*	9,249	562,758	60·8
Massachusetts (1788)	*(Mass./MA)*	7,838	6,016,425	767·6
Rhode Island (1790)	*(R.I./RI)*	1,045	1,003,464	960·3
Connecticut (1788)	*(Conn./CT)*	4,845	3,287,116	678·4
Middle Atlantic		99,462	37,602,286	378·1
New York (1788)	*(N.Y./NY)*	47,224	17,990,455	381·0
New Jersey (1787)	*(N.J./NJ)*	7,419	7,730,188	1,042·0
Pennsylvania (1787)	*(Pa./PA)*	44,820	11,881,643	265·1
East North Central		243,539	42,008,942	172·5
Ohio (1803)	*(Oh./OH)*	40,953	10,847,115	264·9
Indiana (1816)	*(Ind./IN)*	35,870	5,544,159	154·6
Illinois (1818)	*(Ill./IL)*	55,593	11,430,602	205·6
Michigan (1837)	*(Mich./MI)*	56,809	9,295,297	163·6
Wisconsin (1848)	*(Wis./WI)*	54,314	4,891,769	90·1
West North Central		504,981	17,659,690	35·0
Minnesota (1858)	*(Minn./MN)*	79,617	4,375,099	55·0
Iowa (1846)	*(Ia./IA)*	55,875	2,776,755	49·7
Missouri (1821)	*(Mo./MO)*	68,898	5,117,073	74·3
North Dakota (1889)	*(N.D./ND)*	68,994	638,800	9·3
South Dakota (1889)	*(S.D./SD)*	75,896	696,004	9·2
Nebraska (1867)	*(Nebr./NE)*	76,878	1,578,385	20·5
Kansas (1861)	*(Kans./KS)*	81,823	2,477,574	30·3
South Atlantic		266,160	43,566,853	163·2
Delaware (1787)	*(Del./DE)*	1,955	666,168	340·8
Maryland (1788)	*(Md./MD)*	9,775	4,781,468	489·2
Dist. of Columbia (1791)	*(D.C./DC)*	61	606,900	9,884·4
Virginia (1788)	*(Va./VA)*	39,598	6,187,358	156·3
West Virginia (1863)	*(W. Va./WV)*	24,087	1,793,477	74·5
North Carolina (1789)	*(N.C./NC)*	48,718	6,628,637	136·1
South Carolina (1788)	*(S.C./SC)*	30,111	3,486,703	115·8
Georgia (1788)	*(Ga./GA)*	57,919	6,478,216	111·9
Florida (1845)	*(Fla./FL)*	53,937	12,937,926	239·9
East South Central		178,616	15,176,284	85·0
Kentucky (1792)	*(Ky./KY)*	39,732	3,685,296	92·8
Tennessee (1796)	*(Tenn./TN)*	41,220	4,877,185	118·3
Alabama (1819)	*(Al./AL)*	50,750	4,040,587	79·6
Mississippi (1817)	*(Miss./MS)*	46,914	2,573,216	54·8
West South Central		426,234	26,702,793	62·6
Arkansas (1836)	*(Ark./AR)*	52,075	2,350,725	45·1
Louisiana (1812)	*(La./LA)*	43,566	4,219,973	96·9
Oklahoma (1907)	*(Okla./OK)*	68,679	3,145,585	45·8
Texas (1845)	*(Tex./TX)*	261,914	16,986,510	64·9
Mountain		856,121	13,658,776	16·0
Montana (1889)	*(Mont./MT)*	145,556	799,065	5·5
Idaho (1890)	*(Id./ID)*	82,751	1,006,749	12·2

Geographic divisions and states		Land area: sq. miles 1990	Census population 1 April 1990	Pop. per sq. mile, 1990
Wyoming (1890)	(Wyo./WY)	97,105	453,588	4·7
Colorado (1876)	(Colo./CO)	103,729	3,294,394	31·8
New Mexico (1912)	(N. Mex./NM)	121,365	1,515,069	12·5
Arizona (1912)	(Ariz./AZ)	113,642	3,665,228	32·3
Utah (1896)	(Ut./UT)	82,168	1,722,850	21·0
Nevada (1864)	(Nev./NV)	109,806	1,201,833	10·9
Pacific		895,354	39,127,306	43·7
Washington (1889)	(Wash./WA)	66,581	4,866,692	73·1
Oregon (1859)	(Oreg./OR)	96,003	2,842,321	29·6
California (1850)	(Calif./CA)	155,973	29,760,021	190·8
Alaska (1959)	(Ak./AK)	570,374	550,043	1·0
Hawaii (1960)	(Hi./HI)	6,423	1,108,229	172·5

Geographic divisions and states	Land area: sq. miles 1990	Census population 1 April 1990	Pop. per sq. mile, 1990
Outlying Territories, total	4,691	3,862,431	760
Puerto Rico (1898)	3,427	3,522,037	1,028
Virgin Islands (1917)	134	101,809	761
American Samoa (1900)	77	46,773	607
Guam (1898)	209	133,152	637
Northern Marianas (1947)	184	43,345	235
Palau (1947)	192	15,122	79
Midway Islands (1867)	3	13	5
Wake Island (1898)	3	7	3
Johnston Atoll (1858)	1	173	157

Palau became an independent country on 1 Oct. 1994.

The 1990 census showed 19,767,316 foreign-born persons, by continent of origin: Latin America, 8,407,831 (42·5%); North America, 8,124,251 (41·1%); Asia, 4,979,043 (25·2%); Europe, 4,016,678 (20·3%); Africa, 363,819 (1·8%); Pacific, 104,145 (0·5%). The 9 countries contributing the largest numbers who were foreign-born were Mexico, 4,298,014; Philippines, 912,674; Canada, 744,830; Cuba, 736,971; Germany, 711,929; UK, 640,145; Italy, 580,592; South Korea, 568,397; Vietnam, 543,262. By 1996 the total of foreign-born persons had increased to an estimated 24,557,000 (9·3% of the total population), of whom an estimated 6,679,000 were from Mexico.

Increase or decrease of native White, and foreign-born White, population from 1870 to 1990, by decades:

	Native White			Foreign-born White		
	Total	Increase	Per cent increase	Total	Increase or decrease (−)	Per cent. change
1870	28,095,665	5,269,881	23·1	5,493,712	1,396,959	34·1
1880	36,843,291	8,747,626	31·1	6,559,679	1,065,967	19·4
1890	45,979,391	9,018,732[1]	24·5	9,121,867	2,562,188	39·1
1900	56,595,379	10,615,988	23·1	10,213,817	1,091,950	12·0
1910	68,386,412	11,791,033	20·8	13,345,545	3,131,728	30·7
1920	81,108,161	12,721,749	18·6	13,712,754	367,209	2·8
1930	96,303,335	15,195,174	18·7	13,983,405	270,651	2·0
1940	106,795,732	10,492,397	10·9	11,419,138	−2,564,267	−18·3
1950	124,780,860	17,985,128	16·8	10,161,168	−1,257,970	−11·0
1960	149,543,638	24,762,778	19·8	9,293,992	−867,176	−8·5
1970	169,385,451	19,841,813	13·3	8,733,770	−560,222	−6·0
1980	179,711,066	10,325,615	6·0	9,323,946	590,176	6·7
1990	189,663,258	9,952,192	5·5	10,022,812	698,866	7·5

[1] Exclusive of population specially enumerated in 1890 in Indian Territory and on Indian reservations.

Population of cities with over 100,000 inhabitants at the census of 1990 and as estimated on 1 July 1996:

Cities	Census 1990	Estimate 1996
New York, NY	7,322,564	7,380,906
Los Angeles, CA	3,485,557	3,553,638
Chicago, IL	2,783,726	2,721,547
Houston, TX	1,637,859	1,744,058
Philadelphia, PA	1,585,577	1,478,002
San Diego, CA	1,110,623	1,171,121
Phoenix, AZ	984,310	1,159,014
San Antonio, TX	959,295	1,067,816
Dallas, TX	1,007,618	1,053,292
Detroit, MI	1,027,974	1,000,272
San Jose, CA	782,224	838,744
Indianapolis, IN	731,278	746,737
San Francisco, CA	723,959	735,315
Jacksonville, FL	635,230	679,792
Baltimore, MD	736,014	675,401
Columbus, OH	632,945	657,053
El Paso, TX	515,342	599,865
Memphis, TN	618,652	596,725
Milwaukee, WI	628,088	590,503
Boston, MA	574,283	558,394
Washington, DC	606,900	543,213
Austin, TX	472,020	541,278
Seattle, WA	516,259	524,704
Nashville-Davidson, TN	488,366	511,263
Cleveland, OH	505,616	498,246
Denver, CO	467,610	497,840
Portland, OR	463,634	480,824
Fort Worth, TX	447,619	479,716
New Orleans, LA	496,938	476,625
Oklahoma City, OK	444,724	469,852
Tucson, AZ	411,480	449,002
Charlotte, NC	419,539	441,297
Kansas City, MO	434,829	441,259
Virginia Beach, VA	393,089	430,385
Honolulu, HI	377,059	423,475
Long Beach, CA	429,321	421,904
Albuquerque, NM	384,915	419,681
Atlanta, GA	393,929	401,907
Fresno, CA	354,091	396,011
Tulsa, OK	367,302	378,491
Las Vegas, NV	258,204	376,906
Sacramento, CA	369,365	376,243
Oakland, CA	372,242	367,230
Miami, FL	358,648	365,127
Omaha, NE	342,862	364,253
Minneapolis, MN	368,383	358,785
St. Louis, MO	396,685	351,565
Pittsburgh, PA	369,879	350,363
Cincinnati, OH	364,114	345,816
Colorado Springs, CO	280,430	345,127
Mesa, AZ	289,199	344,764
Wichita, KS	304,017	320,395
Toledo, OH	332,943	317,606
Buffalo, NY	328,175	310,548
Santa Ana, CA	293,827	302,419
Arlington, TX	261,717	294,816
Anaheim, CA	266,406	288,945
Tampa, FL	280,015	285,206
Corpus Christi, TX	257,453	280,260
Newark, NJ	275,221	268,510
Louisville, KY	269,555	260,689
St. Paul, MN	272,235	259,606
Birmingham, AL	265,347	258,543
Riverside, CA	226,546	255,069

Cities	Census 1990	Estimate 1996
Aurora, CO	222,103	252,341
Anchorage, AK	226,338	250,505
Raleigh, NC	212,092	243,835
Lexington-Fayette, KY	225,366	239,942
St. Petersburg, FL	240,318	235,988
Norfolk, VA	261,250	233,430
Stockton, CA	210,943	232,660
Jersey City, NJ	228,517	229,039
Rochester, NY	230,356	221,594
Akron, OH	223,019	216,882
Baton Rouge, LA	219,531	215,882
Lincoln, NE	191,972	209,192
Bakersfield, CA	176,264	205,508
Hialeah, FL	188,008	204,684
Mobile, AL	196,263	202,581
Richmond, VA	202,798	198,267
Madison, WI	190,766	197,630
Montgomery, AL	190,350	196,363
Greensboro, NC	183,894	195,426
Lubbock, TX	186,206	193,565
Des Moines, IA	193,189	193,422
Jackson, MS	202,062	192,923
Chesapeake, VA	151,982	192,342
Plano, TX	127,885	192,280
Shreveport, LA	198,525	191,558
Huntington Beach, CA	181,519	190,751
Yonkers, NY	188,082	190,316
Garland, TX	180,635	190,055
Grand Rapids, MI	189,126	188,242
Fremont, CA	173,339	187,800
Spokane, WA	177,165	186,562
Fort Wayne, IN	191,839	184,783
Glendale, CA	180,038	184,321
San Bernardino, CA	170,036	183,474
Columbus, GA	178,683	182,828
Glendale, AZ	147,864	182,219
Tacoma, WA	176,664	179,114
Scottsdale, AZ	130,075	179,012
Modesto, CA	164,746	178,559
Irving, TX	155,037	176,993
Newport News, VA	171,439	176,122
Little Rock, AR	175,727	175,752
Arlington, VA	170,897	175,334
Orlando, FL	164,674	173,902
Dayton, OH	182,005	172,947
Salt Lake City, UT	159,928	172,575
Huntsville, AL	159,880	170,424
Amarillo, TX	157,571	169,588
Knoxville, TN	169,761	167,535
Worcester, MA	169,759	166,350
Laredo, TX	122,899	164,899
Tempe, AZ	141,993	162,701
Syracuse, NY	163,860	155,865
Reno, NV	133,850	155,499
Winston-Salem, NC	150,958	153,541
Boise City	126,685	152,737
Providence, RI	160,728	152,558
Chula Vista, CA	135,160	151,963
Fort Lauderdale, FL	149,238	151,805
Oxnard, CA	142,560	151,009
Chattanooga, TN	152,393	150,425
Paterson, NJ	140,891	150,270
Springfield, MA	156,983	149,948
Durham, NC	138,894	149,799

Cities	Census 1990	Estimate 1996	Cities	Census 1990	Estimate 1996
Garden Grove, CA	142,965	149,208	Thousand Oaks, CA	104,381	113,368
Oceanside, CA	128,090	145,941	Macon, GA	107,365	113,352
Ontario, CA	133,179	144,854	Sioux Falls, SD	100,836	113,223
Rockford, IL	141,787	143,531	Springfield, IL	105,417	112,921
Springfield, MO	140,494	143,407	Columbia, SC	110,734	112,773
Chandler, AZ	89,862	142,918	Peoria, IL	113,513	112,306
Kansas City, KS	151,521	142,654	Mesquite, TX	101,484	111,947
Moreno Valley, CA	118,779	140,932	Salinas, CA	108,777	111,757
Hampton, VA	133,811	138,757	Beaumont, TX	114,323	111,224
Warren, MI	144,864	138,078	Inglewood, CA	109,602	111,040
Bridgeport, CT	141,686	137,990	Gary, IN	116,646	110,975
Tallahassee, FL	124,773	136,812	Independence, MO	112,301	110,303
Savannah, GA	137,812	136,262	Elizabeth, NJ	110,002	110,149
Torrance, CA	133,107	136,183	Stamford, CT	108,056	110,056
Lakewood, CO	126,475	134,999	El Monte, CA	106,162	110,026
Flint, MI	140,925	134,881	Vallejo, CA	109,199	109,593
Pomona, CA	131,700	134,706	Grand Prairie, TX	99,606	109,231
Pasadena, CA	131,586	134,116	Ann Arbor, MI	109,608	108,758
Hartford, CT	139,739	133,086	Abilene, TX	106,707	108,476
Brownsville, TX	107,027	132,091	Waco, TX	103,590	108,412
Pasadena, TX	119,604	131,620	Naperville, IL	85,806	107,001
Overland Park, KS	111,790	131,053	Simi Valley, CA	100,218	106,974
Hollywood, FL	121,720	127,894	Palmdale, CA	70,262	106,540
Irvine, CA	110,330	127,873	Waterbury, CT	108,961	106,412
Lansing, MI	127,321	125,736	Coral Springs, FL	78,864	105,275
Sunnyvale, CA	117,324	125,156	Erie, PA	108,718	105,270
Santa Clarita, CA	120,050	125,153	Livonia, MI	100,850	103,099
New Haven, CT	130,474	124,655	Lafayette, LA	101,852	104,899
Eugene, OR	112,733	123,718	Fort Collins, CO	87,491	104,196
Evansville, IN	126,272	123,456	Fontana, CA	87,535	104,124
Salem, OR	107,793	122,566	Albany, NY	100,031	103,564
Henderson, NV	64,948	122,339	McAllen, TX	84,021	103,352
Santa Rosa, CA	113,261	121,879	Berkeley, CA	102,724	103,243
Hayward, CA	114,705	121,631	Allentown, PA	105,301	102,211
Fullerton, CA	114,144	120,188	South Bend, IN	105,511	102,100
Orange, CA	110,658	119,890	Green Bay, WI	96,466	102,076
Topeka, KS	119,883	119,658	West Covina, CA	96,226	101,526
Sterling Heights, MI	117,810	118,698	Portsmouth, VA	103,910	101,308
Alexandria, VA	111,182	117,586	Lowell, MA	103,439	100,973
Rancho Cucamonga,			Manchester, NH	99,332	100,967
CA	101,409	116,613	Costa Mesa, CA	96,357	100,938
Aurora, IL	99,672	116,405	Pembroke Pines, FL	65,566	100,662
Escondido, CA	108,648	116,184	Norwalk, CA	94,279	100,209
Lancaster, CA	97,300	115,675	Corona, CA	75,943	100,208
Concord, CA	111,308	114,850	Wichita Falls, TX	96,259	100,138
Cedar Rapids, IA	108,772	113,482	Clearwater, FL	98,669	100,132

Of all the American cities with more than 100,000 inhabitants, Phoenix saw the greatest increase in its population between 1990 and 1996, with an additional 174,704 people based on the above estimates, and Henderson the highest percentage increase, with an 88·4% rise. Philadelphia's population saw the greatest decline, dropping by 107,575 based on these estimates, and St Louis the highest percentage fall, with an 11·4% drop.

Vital Statistics: Figures include Alaska beginning with 1959 and Hawaii beginning with 1960.

	Live births	Deaths	Marriages	Divorces	Deaths under 1 year
1900	—	343,217	709,000	56,000	
1910	2,777,000	696,856	948,000	83,000	—
1920	2,950,000	1,118,070	1,274,476	170,505	170,911
1930	2,618,000	1,327,240	1,126,856	195,961	143,201
1940	2,559,000	1,417,269	1,595,879	264,000	110,984
1950	3,632,000	1,452,454	1,667,231	385,144	103,825

	Live births	Deaths	Marriages	Divorces	Deaths under 1 year
1900	—	343,217	709,000	56,000	—
1960	4,257,850	1,711,982	1,523,000	393,000	110,873
1970	3,731,386	1,921,031	2,158,802	708,000	74,667
1980	3,612,258	1,989,841	2,390,252	1,189,000	45,526
1990	4,148,000	2,155,000	2,448,000	1,182,000	38,351
1991	4,111,000	2,170,000	2,371,100	1,189,000	36,766
1992	4,065,000	2,176,000	2,362,000	1,215,000	34,628
1993	4,000,000	2,269,000	2,334,000	1,187,000	—
1994	3,953,000	2,279,000	2,362,000	1,191,000	—
1995	3,900,000	2,312,000	2,336,000	1,169,000	—
1996	3,850,000	2,349,000	—	—	—

Rates (per 1,000 population):

	Birth	Death	Marriage	Divorce
1991	16·3	8·6	9·4	4·7
1992	15·9	8·5	9·3	4·8
1993	15·5	8·8	9·0	4·6
1994	15·2	8·8	9·1	4·6
1995	14·8	8·8	9·0	4·5
1996	14·5	8·9	8·9	4·4

Rate of natural increase per 1,000 population: 7·7 in 1991; 5·6 in 1996.

Estimated number of births to unmarried women in 1994 was 1,290,000 (32·61% of all births, 25·4% of White births, 70·4% of Black births), compared to 666,000 in 1980.

The infant mortality rates, per 1,000 live births: 29·2 in 1950; 12·9 in 1980; 7·4 in 1996.

Expectation of life, 1970: Males, 67·1 years; females, 74·7 years; 1995: Males, 72·8 years; females, 79·7 years.

Numbers of deaths by principal causes, 1995 (and as a percentage of all deaths): Heart disease, 738,781 (32·0%); cancer, 537,969 (23·3%); stroke, 158,061 (6·8%); obstructive lung disease, 104,756 (4·5%); accidents, 89,703 (3·9%); pneumonia and influenza, 83,528 (3·6%); diabetes mellitus, 59,085 (2·6%); AIDS, 42,506 (1·8%); suicide, 30,893 (1·3%); liver disease, 24,848 (1·1%). There were 21,600 homicides in 1995.

Immigration: The Immigration and Nationality Act, as amended, provides for the numerical limitation of most immigration. The Immigration Act of 1990 established major revisions in the numerical limits and preference system regulating legal immigration. The numerical limits are imposed on visas issued and not admissions. The maximum number of visas allowed to be issued under the preference categories in 1996 was 451,819: 311,819 for family-sponsored immigrants and 140,000 for employment-based immigrants. Within the overall limitations the per-country limit for independent countries is set to 7% of the total family and employment limits, while dependent areas are limited to 2% of the total. The 1996 limit allowed no more than 31,627 preference visas for any independent country and 9,036 for any dependency. Immigrants not subject to any numerical limitation are spouses, children, and parents of US citizens who are 21 years of age or older; certain former US citizens; ministers of religion; certain long-term US government employees; refugees and asylum-seekers adjusting to immigrant status; and certain other groups of immigrants.

Immigration data for 1996 include 4,635 aliens who were admitted as permanent residents under the legalization programme created by the Immigrant Reform and Control Act of 1986. These aliens have resided in the USA since before 1982 or were agricultural workers on perishable crops and have qualified as temporary residents under the first phase of the legalization programme; in the fiscal year 1989, they began qualifying for permanent status.

Immigrant aliens admitted to the USA for permanent residence, by country or region of birth, for fiscal years:

Country or region of birth	Immigrants admitted 1991	1992	1995	1996
All countries	1,827,167	973,977	720,500	915,900
Europe	135,234	145,392	128,200	147,581
Germany	6,509	9,888	6,200	6,748
Greece	2,079	1,858	1,300	1,452
Italy	2,619	2,592	2,200	2,501
Poland	19,199	25,504	13,800	15,772
Portugal	4,524	2,748	2,600	2,984
Spain	1,849	1,631	1,300	1,659
UK	13,903	19,973	12,400	13,624
Yugoslavia	2,713	2,604	8,300	11,854
Other Europe	81,839	78,594	80,100	90,987
Asia	358,533	356,955	267,900	307,807
China and Taiwan	46,299	55,251	44,900	55,129
Hong Kong	10,427	10,452	7,200	7,834
India	45,064	36,755	34,700	44,859
Japan	5,049	11,028	4,800	6,011
Korea (North and South)	26,518	19,359	16,000	18,185
Philippines	63,596	61,022	51,000	55,876
Thailand	7,397	7,090	5,100	4,310
Other Asia	154,183	155,998	104,200	115,603
North America	1,210,981	384,047	231,500	340,540
Canada	13,504	15,205	12,900	15,825
Mexico	946,167	213,802	89,900	163,572
Cuba	10,349	11,791	17,900	26,466
Dominican Republic	41,405	41,969	38,500	39,604
Haiti	47,527	11,002	14,000	18,386
Jamaica	23,828	18,915	16,400	19,089
Trinidad and Tobago	8,407	7,008	5,400	7,344
Other Caribbean	8,623	6,728	4,100	5,912
Central America	111,093	57,558	31,800	44,289
Other North America	78	69	60	53
South America	79,934	55,308	45,700	61,769
Colombia	19,702	13,201	10,800	14,283
Ecuador	9,958	7,286	6,400	8,321
Other South America	50,274	34,821	28,500	39,165
Africa	36,179	27,086	42,500	52,889
Australia and New Zealand	2,471	3,205	2,478	2,750
Other countries	3,835	1,984	2,219	2,564

The total number of immigrants admitted from 1820 up to 30 Sept. 1996 was 63,140,227; this included 7,142,593 from Germany, and 5,427,298 from Italy.

Aliens coming to the USA for temporary periods of time are classified as non-immigrants. During fiscal year 1996, a total of 24,842,503 non-immigrants were admitted. This total includes multiple entries but excludes border crossers, crewmen and insular travellers. Tourists numbered 19,110,004, with 10,172,487 coming from the Caribbean, Germany, Japan, Mexico and the UK. There were 1,641,455 aliens expelled during fiscal year 1996. Of this number, 68,657 were removed with a formal order from an immigration judge and 1,572,798 were required to depart without orders of deportation.

During fiscal year 1996, 1,044,689 persons became US citizens through naturalization, including 890,949 naturalized under the general provisions of 5-year residence in the USA, 35,449 spouses and children of US citizens and 6,948 members of the US Armed Forces. The new citizens included 43,087 from China and Taiwan, 62,168 from Cuba, 4,617 from Italy, 24,270 from Jamaica, 24,693 from Korea, 217,418 from Mexico, 45,210 from the Philippines and 47,625 from Vietnam.

The refugee admissions ceiling for the fiscal year 1996 was fixed at 90,000, including 45,000 from Eastern Europe and the former Soviet Union and 29,000 from south-east Asia.

CLIMATE. For temperature and rainfall figures, *see* entries on individual states as indicated by regions, below, of mainland USA.

Pacific Coast. The climate varies with latitude, distance from the sea and the effect of relief, ranging from polar conditions in North Alaska through cool to warm temperate climates further south. The extreme south is temperate desert. Rainfall everywhere is moderate. *See* Alaska, California, Oregon, Washington.

Mountain States. Very varied, with relief exerting the main control; very cold in the north in winter, with considerable snowfall. In the south, much higher temperatures and aridity produce desert conditions. Rainfall everywhere is very variable as a result of rain-shadow influences. *See* Arizona, Colorado, Idaho, Montana, Nevada, New Mexico, Utah, Wyoming.

High Plains. A continental climate with a large annual range of temperature and moderate rainfall, mainly in summer, although unreliable. Dust storms are common in summer and blizzards in winter. *See* Nebraska, North Dakota, South Dakota.

Central Plains. A temperate continental climate, with hot summers and cold winters, except in the extreme south. Rainfall is plentiful and comes at all seasons, but there is a summer maximum in western parts. *See* Mississippi, Missouri, Oklahoma, Texas.

Mid-West. Continental, with hot summers and cold winters. Rainfall is moderate, with a summer maximum in most parts. *See* Indiana, Iowa, Kansas.

Great Lakes. Continental, resembling that of the Central Plains, with hot summers but very cold winters because of the freezing of the lakes. Rainfall is moderate with a slight summer maximum. *See* Illinois, Michigan, Minnesota, Ohio, Wisconsin.

Appalachian Mountains. The north is cool temperate with cold winters, the south warm temperate with milder winters. Precipitation is heavy, increasing to the south but evenly distributed over the year. *See* Kentucky, Pennsylvania, Tennessee, West Virginia.

Gulf Coast. Conditions vary from warm temperate to sub-tropical, with plentiful rainfall, decreasing towards the west but evenly distributed over the year. *See* Alabama, Arkansas, Florida, Louisiana.

Atlantic Coast. Temperate maritime climate but with great differences in temperature according to latitude. Rainfall is ample at all seasons; snowfall in the north can be heavy. *See* Delaware, District of Columbia, Georgia, Maryland, New Jersey, New York, North Carolina, South Carolina, Virginia.

New England. Cool temperate, with severe winters and warm summers. Precipitation is well distributed with a slight winter maximum. Snowfall is heavy in winter. *See* Connecticut, Maine, Massachusetts, New Hampshire, Rhode Island, Vermont. *See* also Hawaii and Outlying Territories.

CONSTITUTION AND GOVERNMENT. The form of government of the USA is based on the constitution of 17 Sept. 1787.

By the constitution the government of the nation is composed of three co-ordinate branches, the executive, the legislative and the judicial.

The Federal Government has authority in matters of general taxation, treaties and other dealings with foreign countries, foreign and inter-state commerce, bankruptcy, postal service, coinage, weights and measures, patents and copyright, the armed forces (including, to a certain extent, the militia), and crimes against the USA; it has sole legislative authority over the District of Columbia and the possessions of the USA.

The 5th article of the constitution provides that Congress may, on a two-thirds vote of both houses, propose amendments to the constitution, or, on the application of the legislatures of two-thirds of all the states, call a convention for proposing amendments, which in either case shall be valid as part of the constitution when ratified by the legislatures of three-fourths of the several states, or by conventions in three-fourths thereof, whichever mode of ratification may be proposed by Congress. Ten amendments (called collectively 'the Bill of Rights') to the constitution were added 15 Dec. 1791; two in 1795 and 1804; a 13th amendment, 6 Dec. 1865, abolishing slavery; a 14th in 1868, including the important 'due process' clause; a 15th, 3 Feb. 1870, establishing equal voting rights for white and coloured; a 16th, 3 Feb. 1913, authorizing the income tax; a 17th, 8 April 1913, providing for popular election of senators; an 18th, 16 Jan. 1919, prohibiting alcoholic liquors; a 19th, 18 Aug. 1920, establishing woman suffrage; a 20th, 23 Jan. 1933, advancing the date of the President's and Vice-President's inauguration and abolishing the 'lameduck' sessions of Congress; a 21st, 5 Dec. 1933, repealing the 18th amendment; a 22nd, 26 Feb. 1951, limiting a President's tenure of office to 2 terms, or to 2 terms plus 2 years in the case of a Vice-President who has succeeded to the office of a President; a 23rd, 30 March 1961, granting citizens of the District of Columbia the right to vote in national elections; a 24th, 4 Feb. 1964, banning the use of the poll-tax in federal elections; a 25th, 10 Feb. 1967, dealing with Presidential disability and succession; a 26th, 22 June 1970, establishing the right of citizens who are 18 years of age and older to vote; a 27th, 7 May 1992, providing that no law varying the compensation of Senators or Representatives shall take effect until an election has taken place.

National anthem: The Star-spangled Banner, 'Oh say, can you see by the dawn's early light'; words by F. S. Key, 1814, tune by J. S. Smith; formally adopted by Congress 3 March 1931.

National motto: 'In God we trust'; formally adopted by Congress 30 July 1956.

Presidency. The executive power is vested in a president, who holds office for 4 years, and is elected, together with a vice-president chosen for the same term, by electors from each state, equal to the whole number of senators and representatives to which the state may be entitled in the Congress. The President must be a natural-born citizen, resident in the country for 14 years, and at least 35 years old.

The presidential election is held every fourth (leap) year on the Tuesday after the first Monday in November. Technically, this is an election of presidential electors, not of a president directly; the electors thus chosen meet and give their votes (for the candidate to whom they are pledged, in some states by law, but in most states by custom and prudent politics) at their respective state capitals on the first Monday after the second Wednesday in December next following their election; and the votes of the electors of all the states are opened and counted in the presence of both Houses of Congress on the sixth day of January. The total electorate vote is one for each senator and representative. Electors may not be a member of Congress or hold federal office. If no candidate secures the minimum 270 college votes needed for outright victory, the 12th Amendment to the Constitution applies, and the House of Representatives chooses a president from among the first 3 finishers in the electoral college. (This last happened in 1824).

If the successful candidate for President dies before taking office the Vice-President-elect becomes President; if no candidate has a majority or if the successful candidate fails to qualify, then, by the 20th amendment, the Vice-President acts as President until a president qualifies. The duties of the Presidency, in absence of the President and Vice-President by reason of death, resignation, removal, inability or failure to qualify, devolve upon the Speaker of the House under legislation enacted on 18 July 1947. In case of absence of a Speaker for like reason, the presidential duties devolve upon the President *pro tem.* of the Senate and successively upon those members of the Cabinet in order of precedence, who have the constitutional qualifications for President.

The presidential term, by the 20th amendment to the constitution, begins at noon on 20 Jan. of the inaugural year. This amendment also instals the newly elected Congress in office on 3 Jan. instead of—as formerly—in the following December. The President's salary is $200,000 per year (taxable), with in addition $50,000 to assist in defraying expenses resulting from official duties. Also he may spend up to $100,000 non-taxable for travel and $20,000 for official entertainment. The office of Vice-President carries a salary of $171,500 and $10,000 allowance for expenses, all taxable. The Vice-President is *ex-officio* President of the Senate, and in the case of 'the removal of the President, or of his death, resignation, or inability to discharge the powers and duties of his office', he becomes the President for the remainder of the term.

President of the United States: William (Bill) Jefferson Blythe IV Clinton, of Arkansas, b. 1946. (Governor of Arkansas, 1979–81, 1983–92).

Vice President: Albert Gore, of Tennessee, b. 1948 (House of Representatives, 1977–85; Senate, 1985–).

At the Presidential election on 5 Nov. 1996 turn-out was 49% (55·9% in 1992). Bill Clinton (D.) received 45,590,703 votes (49%), Bob Dole (R.) 37,816,307 (41%) and Ross Perot (Reform Party) 7,866,284 (8%). Electoral college votes: Clinton, 379; Dole, 159; Perot, nil.

Voting percentages and electoral college votes by state:

a) Majority for Clinton

State	Clinton (%)	Dole (%)	Perot (%)	Electoral College (votes)
Arizona	47	44	8	8
Arkansas	53	37	8	6
California	51	38	7	54
Connecticut	52	36	10	8
Delaware	52	37	11	3
DC	85	9	2	3
Florida	48	42	9	25
Hawaii	58	38	8	4
Illinois	54	37	8	22
Iowa	50	40	8	7
Kentucky	46	45	9	8
Louisiana	52	40	7	9
Maine	52	31	14	4
Maryland	54	36	7	10
Massachusetts	62	28	9	12
Michigan	51	39	9	18
Minnesota	51	35	12	10
Missouri	48	41	10	11
Nevada	44	42	9	4
New Hampshire	50	40	10	4
New Jersey	53	36	9	15
New Mexico	49	41	6	5
New York	59	31	8	33
Ohio	47	41	11	21
Oregon	47	37	11	7
Pennsylvania	49	40	10	23
Rhode Island	60	27	11	4
Tennessee	48	46	6	11
Vermont	54	31	12	3
Washington	51	36	9	11
West Virginia	51	37	11	5
Wisconsin	49	39	10	11

b) Majority for Dole

	Dole	Clinton	Perot	
Alabama	50	43	6	9
Alaska	51	33	11	3
Colorado	46	45	7	8
Georgia	47	46	6	13
Idaho	52	34	13	4
Indiana	48	41	10	12
Kansas	54	36	9	6
Mississippi	49	44	6	7
Montana	44	41	14	3
Nebraska	53	35	11	5
North Carolina	49	44	7	14
North Dakota	47	40	12	3
Oklahoma	48	40	11	8
South Carolina	50	44	6	8
South Dakota	46	43	10	3
Texas	49	44	7	32
Utah	54	33	10	5
Virginia	47	45	7	13
Wyoming	50	37	12	3

PRESIDENTS OF THE USA

Name	From state	Term of service	Born	Died
George Washington	Virginia	1789–97	1732	1799
John Adams	Massachusetts	1797–1801	1735	1826
Thomas Jefferson	Virginia	1801–09	1743	1826
James Madison	Virginia	1809–17	1751	1836
James Monroe	Virginia	1817–25	1759	1831
John Quincy Adams	Massachusetts	1825–29	1767	1848
Andrew Jackson	Tennessee	1829–37	1767	1845
Martin Van Buren	New York	1837–41	1782	1862
William H. Harrison	Ohio	Mar.–Apr. 1841	1773	1841
John Tyler	Virginia	1841–45	1790	1862
James K. Polk	Tennessee	1845–49	1795	1849
Zachary Taylor	Louisiana	1849–July 1850	1784	1850
Millard Fillmore	New York	1850–53	1800	1874
Franklin Pierce	New Hampshire	1853–57	1804	1869
James Buchanan	Pennsylvania	1857–61	1791	1868
Abraham Lincoln	Illinois	1861–Apr. 1865	1809	1865
Andrew Johnson	Tennessee	1865–69	1808	1875
Ulysses S. Grant	Illinois	1869–77	1822	1885
Rutherford B. Hayes	Ohio	1877–81	1822	1893
James A. Garfield	Ohio	Mar.–Sept. 1881	1831	1881
Chester A. Arthur	New York	1881–85	1830	1886
Grover Cleveland	New York	1885–89	1837	1908
Benjamin Harrison	Indiana	1889–93	1833	1901
Grover Cleveland	New York	1893–97	1837	1908
William McKinley	Ohio	1897–Sept. 1901	1843	1901
Theodore Roosevelt	New York	1901–09	1858	1919
William H. Taft	Ohio	1909–13	1857	1930
Woodrow Wilson	New Jersey	1913–21	1856	1924
Warren Gamaliel Harding	Ohio	1921–Aug. 1923	1865	1923
Calvin Coolidge	Massachusetts	1923–29	1872	1933
Herbert C. Hoover	California	1929–33	1874	1964
Franklin D. Roosevelt	New York	1933–Apr. 1945	1882	1945
Harry S Truman	Missouri	1945–53	1884	1972
Dwight D. Eisenhower	New York	1953–61	1890	1969
John F. Kennedy	Massachusetts	1961–Nov. 1963	1917	1963
Lyndon B. Johnson	Texas	1963–69	1908	1973
Richard M. Nixon	California	1969–74	1913	1994
Gerald R. Ford	Michigan	1974–77	1913	—
James Earl Carter	Georgia	1977–81	1924	—
Ronald W. Reagan	California	1981–89	1911	—
George H. Bush	Texas	1989–93	1924	—
Bill (William J.) Clinton	Arkansas	1993–	1946	—

VICE-PRESIDENTS OF THE USA

Name	From state	Term of service	Born	Died
John Adams	Massachusetts	1789–97	1735	1826
Thomas Jefferson	Virginia	1797–1801	1743	1826
Aaron Burr	New York	1801–05	1756	1836
George Clinton	New York	1805–12[1]	1739	1812
Elbridge Gerry	Massachusetts	1813–14[1]	1744	1814
Daniel D. Tompkins	New York	1817–25	1774	1825
John C. Calhoun	South Carolina	1825–32[1]	1782	1850
Martin Van Buren	New York	1833–37	1782	1862
Richard M. Johnson	Kentucky	1837–41	1780	1850
John Tyler	Virginia	Mar.–Apr.1841[1]	1790	1862
George M. Dallas	Pennsylvania	1845–49	1792	1864
Millard Fillmore	New York	1849–50[1]	1800	1874

[1] Position vacant thereafter until commencement of the next presidential term.

William R. King	Alabama	Mar.–Apr. 1853[1]	1786	1853
John C. Breckinridge	Kentucky	1857–61	1821	1875
Hannibal Hamlin	Maine	1861–65	1809	1891
Andrew Johnson	Tennessee	Mar.–Apr. 1865[1]	1808	1875
Schuyler Colfax	Indiana	1869–73	1823	1885
Henry Wilson	Massachusetts	1873–75[1]	1812	1875
William A. Wheeler	New York	1877–81	1819	1887
Chester A. Arthur	New York	Mar.–Sept. 1881[1]	1830	1886
Thomas A. Hendricks	Indiana	Mar.–Nov. 1885[1]	1819	1885
Levi P. Morton	New York	1889–93	1824	1920
Adlai Stevenson	Illinois	1893–97	1835	1914
Garret A. Hobart	New Jersey	1897–99[1]	1844	1899
Theodore Roosevelt	New York	Mar.–Sept. 1901[1]	1858	1919
Charles W. Fairbanks	Indiana	1905–09	1855	1920
James S. Sherman	New York	1909–12[1]	1855	1912
Thomas R. Marshall	Indiana	1913–21	1854	1925
Calvin Coolidge	Massachusetts	1921–Aug. 1923[1]	1872	1933
Charles G. Dawes	Illinois	1925–29	1865	1951
Charles Curtis	Kansas	1929–33	1860	1935
John N. Garner	Texas	1933–41	1868	1967
Henry A. Wallace	Iowa	1941–45	1888	1965
Harry S Truman	Missouri	1945–Apr. 1945[1]	1884	1972
Alben W. Barkley	Kentucky	1949–53	1877	1956
Richard M. Nixon	California	1953–61	1913	1994
Lyndon B. Johnson	Texas	1961–Nov. 1963[1]	1908	1973
Hubert H. Humphrey	Minnesota	1965–69	1911	1978
Spiro T. Agnew	Maryland	1969–73	1918	1996
Gerald R. Ford	Michigan	973–74	1913	—
Nelson Rockefeller	New York	1974–77	1908	1979
Walter Mondale	Minnesota	1977–81	1928	—
George Bush	Texas	1981–89	1924	—
Danforth Quayle	Indiana	1989–93	1947	—
Albert Gore	Tennessee	1993–	1948	—

[1] Position vacant thereafter until commencement of the next presidential term.

Cabinet. The administrative business of the nation has been traditionally vested in several executive departments, the heads of which, unofficially and *ex officio*, formed the President's Cabinet. Beginning with the Interstate Commerce Commission in 1887, however, an increasing amount of executive business has been entrusted to some 60 so-called independent agencies, such as the Housing and Home Finance Agency, Tariff Commission, etc.

All heads of departments and of the 60 or more administrative agencies are appointed by the President, but must be confirmed by the Senate.

The Cabinet consisted of the following (March 1998):

1. *Secretary of State* (created 1789). Madeleine Albright, b. Czechoslovakia, 1938. Professor of International Affairs; Head, Center for National Policy; Legislative aide to Democrat Senator Muskie; member of National Security Council staff; 1993–96 US Permanent Representative to the UN.

2. *Secretary of the Treasury* (1789). Robert Rubin, b. New York, 1938. Economist, investment banker; head of the National Economic Council; Economic Adviser to the President.

3. *Secretary of Defense* (1947). William Cohen, b. Maine, 1940. Lawyer, author; local government, mayor; basketball Hall of Fame team; Congress, 1973–96; Republican Senator.

4. *Attorney-General* (Department of Justice, 1870). Janet Reno, b. Florida, 1938. Lawyer; State Attorney of Dade County (FL), 1978–92.

5. *Secretary of the Interior* (1849). Bruce Babbitt, b. California, 1938. Lawyer, Attorney-General of Arizona, 1975–78; Governor of Arizona, 1978–87.

6. *Secretary of Agriculture* (1889). Dan Glickman, b. Kansas, 1944. Lawyer; Congress, 1977–94; member of House Agriculture, Judiciary and Science, Space and Technology Committees, chair Select Committee on Intelligence, 1993–94.

7. *Secretary of Commerce* (1903). William Daley, b. Illinois, 1949. Lawyer, Chicago politician, President Clinton's campaign manager, 1992; negotiator of the North American Free Trade Agreement, 1993.

8. *Secretary of Labor* (1913). Alexis Herman, b. Alabama, 1948. Director, Women's Bureau, Department of Labor; deputy chair, Democratic National Convention Commission; deputy chair, Presidential Transition Office; Director, White House Office of Public Liaison.

9. *Secretary of Health and Human Services* (1953). Dr Donna Shalala b. Ohio, 1941. Political scientist, educator; US Housing Department, 1977–81; President of Hunter College (NY), Chancellor of the Univ. of Wisconsin, 1988–92.

10. *Secretary of Housing and Urban Development* (1966). Andrew Cuomo, b. Alabama, 1958. Lawyer, Assistant District Attorney, Manhattan; chair, New York Commission on Homeless; Assistant Secretary, County Planning, Department of Housing and Urban Development; Assistant Housing Secretary.

11. *Secretary of Transportation* (1967). Rodney Slater, b. Mississippi, 1955. Lawyer, Assistant Attorney-General, Arkansas; Arkansas state government; Federal Highways Administrator. President Clinton's deputy campaign manager.

12. *Secretary of Energy* (1977). Federico Pena, b. Texas, 1949. Lawyer; Mayor of Denver; Congress as Representative for Colorado; House Democratic Leader.

13. *Secretary of Education* (1979). Richard Riley, b. South Carolina, 1933. Lawyer; South Carolina state representative, 1963–66; state senator, 1966–76; Governor of South Carolina, 1979–87.

14. *Veterans' Affairs Administrator (acting)* (1989). Togo D. West, Jr, b. North Carolina, 1942. Lawyer; Special Assistant to the Secretary of Defense and the Deputy appointed General Counsel of the Department of Defense, 1980.

Each of the above Cabinet officers receives an annual salary of $148,400 and holds office during the pleasure of the President.

A number of administrators also have honorary Cabinet status.

Key White House Posts: White House Chief of Staff: Erskine Bowles; National Security Adviser: Samuel Berger; Director of the National Economic Council: Gene Sperling; Chair, Council of Economic Advisers: Janet Yellen.

Congress: The legislative power is vested by the Constitution in a Congress, consisting of a Senate and House of Representatives.

Electorate: By amendments of the constitution, disqualification of voters on the ground of race, colour or sex is forbidden. The electorate consists of all citizens over 18 years of age. Literacy tests have been banned since 1970. In 1972 durational residency requirements were held to violate the constitution. In 1973 US citizens abroad were enfranchised.

With limitations imposed by the constitution, it is the states which determine voter eligibility. In general states exclude from voting: Persons who have not established residency in the jurisdiction in which they wish to vote; persons who have been convicted of felonies whose civil rights have not been restored; persons declared mentally incompetent by a court.

Illiterate voters are entitled to receive assistance in marking their ballots. Minority-language voters in jurisdictions with statutorily prescribed minority concentrations are entitled to have elections conducted in the minority language as well as English. Disabled voters are entitled to accessible polling places. Voters absent on election days or unable to go to the polls are generally entitled under state law to vote by absentee ballot.

The Constitution guarantees citizens that their votes will be of equal value under the 'one person, one vote' rule.

Senate: The Senate consists of 2 members from each state, chosen by popular vote for 6 years, approximately one-third retiring or seeking re-election every 2 years. Senators must be no less than 30 years of age; must have been citizens of the USA for 9 years, and be residents in the states for which they are chosen. The Senate has complete freedom to initiate legislation, except revenue bills (which must originate in the House of Representatives); it may, however, amend or reject any legislation originating in the lower house. The Senate is also entrusted with the power of giving or withholding its 'advice and consent' to the ratification of all treaties initiated by the President with foreign Powers, a two-thirds majority of senators present being required for approval. (However, it has no control over 'international executive agreements' made by the President with foreign governments; such 'agreements' cover a wide range and are more numerous than formal treaties.) It also has the power of confirming or rejecting major appointments to office made by the President, but it has no direct control over the appointment by the President of 'personal representatives' or 'personal envoys' on missions abroad. Members of the Senate constitute a High Court of Impeachment, with power, by a two-thirds vote, to remove from office and disqualify any civil officer of the USA impeached by the House of Representatives, which has the sole power of impeachment.

The Senate has 17 Standing Committees to which all bills are referred for study, revision or rejection. The House of Representatives has 19 such committees. In both Houses each Standing Committee has a chairman and a majority representing the majority party of the whole House; each has numerous sub-committees. The jurisdictions of these Committees correspond largely to those of the appropriate executive departments and agencies. Both Houses also have a few select or special Committees with limited duration.

House of Representatives: The House of Representatives consists of 435 members elected every second year. The number of each state's representatives is determined by the decennial census, in the absence of specific Congressional legislation affecting the basis. In 1997 the states had the following numbers of representatives:

Alabama	7	Indiana	10	Nebraska	3	South Carolina	6
Alaska	1	Iowa	5	Nevada	2	South Dakota	1
Arizona	6	Kansas	4	New Hampshire	2	Tennessee	9
Arkansas	4	Kentucky	6	New Jersey	13	Texas	30
California	52	Louisiana	7	New Mexico	3	Utah	3
Colorado	6	Maine	2	New York	31	Vermont	1
Connecticut	6	Maryland	8	North Carolina	12	Virginia	11
Delaware	1	Massachusetts	10	North Dakota	1	Washington	9
Florida	23	Michigan	16	Ohio	19	West Virginia	3
Georgia	11	Minnesota	8	Oklahoma	6	Wisconsin	9
Hawaii	2	Mississippi	5	Oregon	5	Wyoming	1
Idaho	2	Missouri	9	Pennsylvania	21		
Illinois	20	Montana	1	Rhode Island	2		

The constitution requires congressional districts within each state to be substantially equal in population. Final decisions on congressional district boundaries are taken by the state legislatures and governors. By custom the representative lives in the district from which he is elected. Representatives must be not less than 25 years of age, citizens of the USA for 7 years and residents in the state from which they are chosen.

In addition, 5 delegates (1 each from the District of Columbia, American Samoa, Guam, the US Virgin Islands and Puerto Rico) are also members of Congress. They have a voice but no vote, except in committees. The delegate from Puerto Rico is the resident commissioner. Puerto Ricans vote at primaries, but not at national elections. Each of the two Houses of Congress is sole 'judge of the elections, returns and qualifications of its own members'; and each of the Houses may, with the concurrence of two-thirds, expel a member. The period usually termed 'a Congress' in legislative language continues for 2 years, terminating at noon on 3 Jan.

The salary of a senator is $133,600 per annum, with tax-free expense allowance and allowances for travelling expenses and for clerical hire. The salary of the Speaker of the House of Representatives is $171,500 per annum, with a taxable allowance. The salary of a Member of the House is $133,600 ($148,400 for the Majority Leader and Minority Leader).

No senator or representative can, during the time for which he is elected, be appointed to any *civil* office under authority of the USA which shall have been created or the emoluments of which shall have been increased during such time; and no person holding *any* office under the USA can be a member of either House during his continuance in office. No religious text may be required as a qualification to any office or public trust under the USA or in any state.

Following the elections of 5 Nov. 1996, the 105th Congress (1997–99) was constituted as follows: Senate, 55 Republicans, 45 Democrats; House of Representatives, 227 Republicans, 207 Democrats, 1 independent.

The *Speaker* of the House of Representatives is Newt Gingrich (R). The *Majority Leader* of the Senate is Trent Lott (R).

Indians: By an Act passed on 2 June 1924 full citizenship was granted to all Indians born in the USA, though those remaining in tribal units were still under special federal jurisdiction. The Indian Reorganization Act of 1934 gave the tribal Indians, at their own option, substantial opportunities of self-government and the establishment of self-controlled corporate enterprises empowered to borrow money and buy land, machinery and equipment; these corporations are controlled by democratically elected tribal councils. Recently a trend towards releasing Indians from federal supervision has resulted in legislation terminating supervision over specific tribes. In 1988 the federal government recognized that it had a special relationship with, and a trust responsibility for, federally-recognized Indian entities in continental USA and tribal entities in Alaska. In 1993 the Bureau of Indian Affairs listed 552 'Indian Entities Recognized and Eligible to Receive Services'. Indian lands (1991) amounted to 52,092,247 acres, of which 41,868,582 was tribally owned and 10,233,665 in trust allotments. Indian lands are held free of taxes. Total Indian population at the 1990 census was 1,959,000, of which Oklahoma, Arizona, California and New Mexico accounted for 832,466.

State and Local Government: The Union comprises 13 original states, 7 states which were admitted without having been previously organized as territories, and 30 states which had been territories—50 states in all. Each state has its own constitution (which the USA guarantees shall be republican in form), deriving its authority, not from Congress, but from the people of the state. Admission of states into the Union has been granted by special Acts of Congress, either (1) in the form of 'enabling Acts' providing for the drafting and ratification of a state constitution by the people, in which case the territory becomes a state as soon as the conditions are fulfilled, or (2) accepting a constitution already framed, and at once granting admission.

Each state is provided with a legislature of two Houses (except Nebraska, which since 1937 has had a single-chamber legislature), a governor and other executive officials, and a judicial system. Both Houses of the legislature are elective, but the senators (having larger electoral districts usually covering 2 or 3 counties compared with the single county or, in some states, the town, which sends 1 representative to the Lower House) are less numerous than the representatives, while in 38 states their terms are 4 years; in 12 states the term is 2 years. Of the 4-year senates, Illinois, Montana and New Jersey provide for two 4-year terms and one 2-year term in each decade. Terms of the lower houses are usually shorter; in 45 states, 2 years.

Members of both Houses are paid at the same rate, which varies from $200 a year in New Hampshire to $57,500 a year in New York. The trend is towards annual sessions of state legislatures; most meet annually now whereas in 1939 only 4 did.

The Governor has power to summon an extraordinary session, but not to dissolve or adjourn. The duties of the two Houses are similar, but in many states money bills must be introduced first in the Lower House. The Senate sits as a court for the trial of officials impeached by the other House, and often has power to confirm or reject appointments made by the Governor.

State legislatures are competent to deal with all matters not reserved for the federal government by the federal constitution nor specifically prohibited by the federal or state constitutions. Among their powers are the determination of the qualifications for the right of suffrage, and the control of all elections to public office, including elections of members of Congress and electors of President and Vice-

President; the criminal law, both in its enactment and in its execution, with unimportant exceptions, and the administration of prisons; the civil law, including all matters pertaining to the possession and transfer of, and succession to, property; marriage and divorce, and all other civil relations; the chartering and control of all manufacturing, trading, transportation and other corporations, subject only to the right of Congress to regulate commerce passing from one state to another; labour; education; charities; licensing; fisheries within state waters, and game laws (apart from the hunting of migratory birds, which is a federal concern under treaties with Canada and Mexico). Taxes on income were left to the states until 1913, when the 16th amendment authorized the imposition of federal taxes on income without regard to apportionment.

The Governor is elected by direct vote of the people over the whole state for a term of office ranging in the various states from 2 to 4 years, and with a salary ranging from $60,000 (Arkansas) to $130,000 (New York). His duty is to see to the faithful administration of the law, and he has command of the military forces of the state. He may recommend measures but does not present bills to the legislature. In some states he presents estimates. In all but one of the states (North Carolina) the Governor has a veto upon legislation, which may, however, be overridden by the two Houses, in some states by a simple majority, in others by a three-fifths or two-thirds majority. In some states the Governor, on his death or resignation, is succeeded by a Lieut.-Governor who was elected at the same time and has been presiding over the state Senate. In several states the Speaker of the Lower House succeeds the Governor.

The chief officials by whom the administration of state affairs is carried on (secretaries, treasurers, members of boards of commissioners, etc.) are usually chosen by the people at the general state elections for terms similar to those for which governors hold office.

At the 11 state gubernatorial elections on 5 Nov. 1996 (Delaware, Indiana, Missouri, Montana, New Hampshire, North Carolina, North Dakota, Utah, Vermont, Washington, West Virginia) the Republicans won 4 governorships and the Democrats 7, making a nationwide tally of 30 Republicans, 19 Democrats and 1 independent.

Local Government. The chief unit of local government is the county, of which there were (1997) 2,994 with definite functions; in addition, Rhode Island has 5 'counties' which have no functions; Alaska does not have counties but 25 divisions and, since Oct. 1960, there has been no active county government in Connecticut. Louisiana has 64 'parishes'. The counties maintain public order through the sheriff and his deputies, who may, in a crisis, be drawn temporarily from willing citizens; in many states the counties maintain the smaller local highways; other functions are the granting of licences and the apportionment and collection of taxes. In a few states they also manage the schools.

The unit of local government in New England is the rural township, governed directly by the voters, who assemble annually or more often if necessary, and legislate in local affairs, levy taxes, make appropriations and appoint and instruct the local officials. Townships are grouped to form counties. Where cities exist, the township government is superseded by the city government.

Local elections and 94 referendums were held on 5 Nov. 1996.

The **District of Columbia,** ceded by the State of Maryland for the purposes of government in 1791, is the seat of the US Government. It includes the city of Washington, and embraces a land area of 61 sq. miles. The Reorganization Plan No. 3 of 1967 instituted a Mayor Council form of government with appointed officers. In 1973 an elected Mayor and elected councillors were introduced; in 1974 they received power to legislate in local matters. Congress retains power to enact legislation and to veto or supersede the Council's acts. Since 1961 citizens have had the right to vote in national elections. On 23 Aug. 1978 the Senate approved a constitutional amendment giving the District full voting representation in Congress. This has still to be ratified.

The **Commonwealth of Puerto Rico, American Samoa, Guam and the Virgin Islands** each have a local legislature, whose acts may be modified or annulled by

Congress, though in practice this has seldom been done. Puerto Rico, since its attainment of commonwealth status on 25 July 1952, enjoys practically complete self-government, including the election of its governor and other officials. The conduct of foreign relations, however, is still a federal function and federal bureaux and agencies still operate in the island.

General supervision of territorial administration is exercised by the Office of Territories in the Department of Interior.

DEFENCE. The President is C.-in-C. of the Army, Navy and Air Force.

The National Security Act of 1947 provides for the unification of the Army, Navy and Air Forces under a single Secretary of Defense with cabinet rank. The President is also advised by a National Security Council and the Office of Civil and Defense Mobilization.

The major components of the Department of Defense are the Office of the Secretary of Defense and the Joint Chiefs of Staff, who provide immediate staff assistance and advice to the Secretary; the departments of the Army, Navy and Air Force, each separately organized under a civilian head (not of cabinet rank); and the unified and specified commands.

Army. *Secretary of the Army:* Togo D. West, Jr.

Central Administration. The Secretary of the Army is the head of the Department of the Army. Subject to the authority of the President as C.-in-C. and of the Secretary of Defense, he is responsible for all affairs of the Department.

The Secretary of the Army is assisted by the Under Secretary of the Army, 5 Assistant Secretaries of the Army (Civil Works, Financial Management, Installations, Logistics and Environment, Manpower and Reserve Affairs, Research, Development and Acquisition), General Counsel, Administrative Assistant, Director for Information Systems for Command, Control, Communications and Computers, Inspector General, Auditor General, Chief of Legislative Liaison, Chief of Public Affairs, Director for Small and Disadvantaged Business Utilization, Chairman of the Army Reserve Forces Policy Committee and the Army Staff headed by the Chief of Staff, US Army. The Office of the Under Secretary of the Army includes a Deputy Under Secretary (Operations Research).

The Chief of Staff, Army, in his role as a member of the Joint Chiefs of Staff, takes part in the planning and supervision of the operational forces under the command of the Commanders-in-Chief. The Vice Chief of Staff assists and advises the Chief of Staff.

The Army General Staff is the principal element of the Army Staff and includes the Offices of the Chief of Staff, Deputy Chief of Staff for Operations and Plans, Deputy Chief of Staff for Personnel, Deputy Chief of Staff for Logistics, and Deputy Chief of Staff for Intelligence. Other elements of the Army Staff are the offices of the Judge Advocate General, Surgeon General, Chief of Chaplains, Chief, Army Reserve, Chief, National Guard Bureau, and Chief of Engineers.

The Army consists of the Active Army, the Army National Guard of the US, the Army Reserve and civilian workforce; and all persons appointed to or enlisted into the Army without component; and all persons serving under call or conscription, including members of the National Guard of the States, etc., when in the service of the US. The strength of the Active Army was (1 Aug. 1996) 495,000 (including 67,100 women).

The US Army Forces Command, with headquarters at Fort McPherson, Georgia, commands the Third US Army; 4 continental US Armies, and all assigned Active Army and US Army Reserve troop units in the continental US, the Commonwealth of Puerto Rico, and the Virgin Islands of the USA. The headquarters of the continental US Armies are: First US Army, Fort George G. Meade, Maryland; Second US Army, Fort Gillem, Georgia; Fifth US Army, Fort Sam Houston, Texas; Sixth US Army, Presidio of San Francisco, California. The US Army Training and Doctrine Command, with headquarters at Fort Monroe, Virginia, co-ordinates and integrates the total combat development effort of the Army as well as developing, managing, establishing and verifying the training of individuals of the US Army and authorized foreign nationals. The US Army Health Services Command, with headquarters at Fort Sam Houston, Texas, provides health services in the continental US for the US Army and provides professional education and training for medical personnel of the US Army and authorized foreign national personnel. The US Army Materiel Command, with headquarters in Alexandria, Virginia, is responsible for US Army activities dealing with equipment development, procurement, delivery, supply and maintenance. The US Army Information Systems Communications Command, with headquarters at Fort Huachuca, Arizona, provides worldwide communication automation support to the Department of the Army and supports the Defense Communications Systems. The US Army Military District of Washington, with headquarters at Fort McNair, Washington, DC, provides support to the Department of the Army and the Department of Defense at the seat of Government. The US Army Space Command, with headquarters in Colorado Springs (CO), is the Army component to the US Space Command.

Approximately 32% of the Active Army is deployed outside the continental USA. Several divisions, which are located in the USA, keep equipment in Germany and can be flown there in 48–72 hours. Headquarters of US Seventh and Eighth Armies are in Europe and Korea respectively.

Operational Commands and Weapons. The larger commands are the theater army and corps. The typical theater army may consist of a variable number of corps composed of combat forces of armour, infantry, air defense artillery, aviation and field artillery units; combat support forces of aviation, engineer, intelligence and signal elements; and combat service support forces. A typical corps consists of a variable number and mixture of infantry, mechanized infantry, armoured, air assault, or airborne divisions; one or more separate infantry, mechanized infantry or armoured brigades; one or more armoured cavalry regiments; corps artillery (155-mm howitzer, 203-mm howitzer, multiple launch rocket system (MLRS); corps air defense brigade (*Hawk, Chaparral, Patriot* and *Avenger* battalions), corps aviation brigade and combat support and combat service support forces.

US Army Divisions have a common base (containing command, divisional artillery, air defense artillery, combat support and combat service support units) aviation brigade, and a varying mixture of combat manoeuvre battalions (usually 9 or 10 in number in 3 brigades) to make up airborne, infantry, armoured, mechanized infantry and air assault divisions. Divisions can in this way be 'tailored' to fit a variety of strategic or tactical situations. A mechanized infantry division, with about 17,300 soldiers, may have 5 mechanized infantry battalions and 4 armoured battalions; an armoured division, with about 17,300 soldiers, may have 4 mechanized infantry battalions and 5 armoured battalions; an airborne division, with 13,100 soldiers, may have 9 infantry (airborne) battalions. The air assault division is a highly specialized force capable of battlefield helicopter operations for infantry, field artillery, air defense artillery and necessary support forces.

The 10,800-man light infantry divisions consist of 9 infantry battalions and offer rapid strategic force projection. Light divisions can operate in all environments and are general purpose forces. Special operations forces consist of special forces, rangers, special operations aviation psychological operations, and civil affairs units. The units are designed, equipped, and trained for special missions.

Small arms include the M-9 (9mm pistol), the M-16 series rifle and the M-249 Squad Automatic Weapon both of which fire a 5·56-mm cartridge. The standard generalpurpose machine-gun is the M-60 (23 lb; 550 rounds of 7·62-mm per minute). Infantry weapons also include M-203 grenade launcher attachment for the M-16A1 rifle, which fire a 40-mm grenade up to 400 metres, the *TOW* and *Dragon* anti-tank missile systems, and the M-72 rocket, a light anti-tank weapon.

Combat vehicles of the US Army are the tank, armoured personnel carrier, infantry fighting vehicle, and the armoured command vehicle. The first-line tanks are the M1A1 Abrams tank with a 120mm main gun, and the M1 Abrams. The standard armoured infantry personnel carrier is the M2 Bradley Fighting Vehicle (BFV), which is replacing the older M113. Both carry a mechanized infantry squad, but the BFV mounts a 25-mm Bushmaster gun and *TOW* missile launchers. The M3 version of the BFV is being used as the ground scout vehicle in armoured cavalry regiments, armoured and mechanized infantry divisional cavalry squadrons and in scout platoons of armoured and mechanized infantry battalions.

The approved calibres of artillery are: Light, 105-mm howitzer; medium, 155-mm howitzer; heavy, 203-mm howitzer. The Multiple Launch Rocket System (MLRS) is a 227-mm rapid firerocket system used in a non-nuclear counterfire, reinforcing and deep fires roles. The 107-mm mortar, the 81-mm mortar and the 60-mm mortar are used by the combat manoeuvre elements. The 120-mm mortar will replace the 107-mm mortar. The *TOW* is the primary anti-tank weapon. Forward-area air-defence weapons, including the *Chaparral, Stinger* and *Avenger* 20-mm gun, provide the capability of low-altitude defence against high-performance aircraft.

The Army has three categories of missiles—surface-to-surface (field artillery) and surface-to-air (air defence artillery) and anti-tank. Surface-to-surface missiles are now limited to the Army Tactical Missile System (ATACMS; fielded) and the Tri-Service Stand-Off Attack Missile (TSSAM; EMD). ATACMS is a semi-ballistic missile capable of carrying a variety of warheads to ranges in excess of 150 km. Planned improvements include an extended range variant with a range of 300+ km. TSSAM is a joint Army, Air Force, Navy cruise missile program. TSSAM carries the Bat submunition (anti-tank) to distances in excess of 200 km. Planned improvements modify Bat submunition for targets other than armour. Surface-to-air missiles, for air defence, are: *Patriot*, guided, conventional warhead, operational; *Hawk*, homing type, low-to-mid-altitude, field operational (product improvements continue to improve the effectiveness of the system); *Chaparral*, infra-red homing, low-altitude, forward area, operational (improvements to the basic system are under development); *Stinger*, hand-held or mobile-launched, infra-red homing, low-altitude, forward area, operational. Anti-tank missiles are: *TOW*, tube launched, optically tracked, wire guided, anti-armour, forward area, operational; *Hellfire*, laser-guided, anti-armour, operational and *Dragon*, wire-guided, medium anti-armour, forward area, operational.

The Army employs rotary- and fixed-wing aircraft as organic elements of its ground formations where their use is required on a full-time basis and their immediate and constant availability is essential. The front line commander exploits the benefits of aviation technology to perform traditional land battle tasks in the third dimension. This concept of airmobility for ground formation utilizes aerial vehicles as a highly integrated team to perform all five functions of land combat: reconnaissance, command and control, logistics and that inseparable combination, firepower and manoeuvre.

The Army has some 7,000 aircraft, all but about 400 of them helicopters. The principal types are 1,000 UH-1 Iroquois Huey and 1,600 UH-60 Black Hawk utility helicopters, 1,000 OH-58 Kiowa observation helicopters, 600 AH-1 Cobra and 700 AH-64 Apache attack helicopters, and 450 CH-47 Chinook cargo helicopters.

Enlistment, Terms of Service. Since 1974 the Army has operated an 'all volunteer' system making it, in effect, an all-regular force both regular and reserve components. Terms of service may be 2, 3, 4, 5 or 6 years. Men and women who enlist incur an 8-year obligation and must serve in the reserve components any part of the period not served on active duty. Over 95% of recruits enlisting in the Army have a high school education and over 50% of the Army is married. Women serve in both combat support and combat service support units.

The National Guard is a reserve military component with both a state and a federal role. Enlistment is voluntary. The members are recruited by each state, but are equipped and paid by the federal government (except when performing state missions). Training is supervised by the active Army (FORSCOM), and unit organization parallels that for the active army; training facilities are made available by the USA and each state. As the organized militia of the several states, the District of Columbia, Puerto Rico and the Territories of the Virgin Islands and Guam, the Guard may be called into service for local emergencies by the chief executives in those jurisdictions; and may be called into federal service by the President to thwart invasion or rebellion or to enforce federal law. In its role as a reserve component of the Army, the Guard is subject to the order of the President in the event of national emergency. In 1996 it numbered 499,800 (Army, 387,100; Air Force, 112,700).

The Army Reserve is designed to supply qualified and experienced units and individuals in an emergency. US Army Forces Command is charged with the command, support and training supervision of US Army Reserve units. Members of units are assigned to the Ready Reserve, which is subject to call by the President in case of national emergency without declaration of war by Congress. The Standby Reserve and the Retired Reserve may be called only after declaration of war or national emergency by Congress. In 1996 the Army Reserve numbered 596,700 (114,000 women).

Navy. *Secretary of the Navy:* John Dalton.

The Department of the Navy is administered under the Defense Secretary by the Secretary of the Navy, assisted by the Under Secretary and 4 Assistant Secretaries (for Financial Management; Installation and Environment; Manpower and Reserve Affairs; and Research, Development and Acquisition). Other divisions of the Department of the Navy are those of: Legislative Affairs, Information and the Judge Advocate General of the Navy.

The professional head of the Navy is the Chief of Naval Operations, whose staff includes the Vice Chief, 4 Deputy Chiefs responsible for Manpower and Personnel; Plans, Policy and Operations; Logistics; and Resources, Warfare Requirements and Assessments. There are 3 major staff directorates for Intelligence; Training; and Space and electronic warfare and 5 specialist divisions.

The Operating Forces include the Atlantic Fleet, divided between the 2nd fleet (home waters) and 6th fleet (Mediterranean); the Pacific Fleet, similarly divided between the 3rd fleet (home waters) and the 7th fleet (West Pacific); and the 5th fleet (Indian Ocean), formally activated in 1995 and maintained by units from both Pacific and Atlantic. All fleets include associated Fleet Marine Forces. Other operational commands include the Military Sealift Command, U.S. Naval Forces Europe, the Mine Warfare Command and the Operational Test and Evaluation Force.

The authorized budget for the Department of the Navy (which includes funding both for the Navy and Marine Corps) for current and recent fiscal years: 1995, $78,200m.; 1996, $76,400m.; 1997, $79,370m.; 1998, $79,340m.

Personnel and fleet strength declined during the mid-1990s but are now stabilizing. The '600-ship battle force' planned in the late 1980s has reduced to such an extent that the eventual figure is likely to be about 335. In late 1997 it was 347. The Navy personnel total in 1997 was 388,760, including 52,178 women who are eligible to serve at sea in support ships.

The operational strength of the Navy at the end of the year indicated:

Category	1992	1993	1994	1995	1996	1997
Strategic Submarines	23	22	16	17	17	18
Nuclear Attack Submarines	87	86	85	78	76	67
Aircraft Carriers	12	13	12	13[1]	12[1]	11[1]
Amphibious Carriers	13	14	13	11	11	11
Cruisers	46	49	44	31	31	30
Destroyers	51	40	39	46	52	56
Frigates	90	67	59	46	45	31

[1] Includes the USS *John F. Kennedy* as 'operational and training reserve carrier' in the Naval Reserve Force.

Ships in inactive reserve are not included in the table; but those serving as Naval Reserve Force training ships are. Amphibious Carriers are those ships of the WASP, Tarawa, and Iwo Jima classes capable of operating AV-8 Harrier-type aircraft as well as helicopters.

Submarine Forces. A principal part of the US naval task is to deploy the seaborne strategic deterrent from nuclear-powered ballistic missile-carrying submarines (SSBN), of which there were, in 1997, 18, all of the Ohio class. The 18th and final ship of the class, USS *Louisiana*, was commissioned in August 1997. These ships, the first of which entered service in 1981, are of 19,000 tonnes submerged displacement, and capable of 25 knots. They are designed to deploy the Trident-2 D-5 missile, with a maximum range of 4,000 nautical miles, carrying about 8 warheads with substantially improved targeting accuracy over the Trident-1 C-4 missile, which is deployed in the first 8 ships of the class. The first submarine deployed the Trident-2 operationally in 1990. The first 8 ships may be retrofitted with the Trident-2 in due course. The last of the Franklin class first generation strategic missile submarines was withdrawn in 1995.

The listed total of 67 nuclear-powered attack submarines (SSN) includes the first of 3 new Sea Wolf class 57 of the Los Angeles class (7,040 tonnes) in 3 major batches: A basic design (23 ships) completed 1976–85, a small group of 8 ships additionally equipped with vertical-launch missile tubes for Tomahawk cruise missiles completed 1985–89, and the remaining 23 ships, the building of which was completed in 1996. These latter are known as 'Improved' Los Angeles, incorporating cruise missile tubes, a new command system, and several important additional technical modifications. There are also 9 Sturgeon class (5,040 tonnes) completed 1967–75, and 3 others.

Surface Forces. The surface fleet is headed by the force of large aircraft carriers, the first class of which entered service in the late 1950s carrying nuclear bombers as the naval contribution to the strategic deterrent. When this role passed to the ballistic missile submarine force, the carrier force was gradually reoriented to its current tasks, which relate more to limited and littoral warfare. The target of '15 deployable carriers' set in 1986 was officially amended to 14 as a result of budgetary pressure in 1989, and has now fallen to 12 of which 11 are in operational service and 1 is used for training and reserve forces.

There are 7 Nimitz and improved Nimitz class ships, of about 88,000 tonnes, completed between 1975 and 1995, nuclear-powered and capable of 33 knots. The USS *Enterprise,* completed in 1961, displacing 81,000 tonnes, was the prototype nuclear-powered carrier and is also capable of 33 knots. The 3 ships of the Kitty Hawk and John F. Kennedy classes are of about 82,500 tonnes were completed between 1961 and 1968, and represent the last oil-fuelled carriers built by the US Navy. The force is completed by the remaining ship of the Forrestal class, USS *Independence,* completed in 1959, of about 82,000 tonnes full load.

All carriers deploy an air group which comprises on average 2 squadrons each of 10 F-14 Tomcat fighters and 3 squadrons each of 12 F/A-18 Hornet fighter/ground attack aircraft. They also carry a squadron of 4 E-2C Hawkeye early warning aircraft, 4 KA-6 airborne tankers, 4 EA-6B Prowler electronic combat aircraft, 6 S-3B Viking anti-submarine aircraft and 6 SH-3D Sea King, or SH-60F Oceanhawk anti-sub marine helicopters. The squadron of 10 A-6E Intruder medium bombers was withdrawn from carrier air groups in 1995–96, being replaced by the third Hornet squadron.

The cruiser force has stabilized at 31 ships following the major reductions in 1994–95. The force comprises the 27 ships of the Ticonderoga class commissioned between 1983 and 1993, of 9,600 tonnes, capable of 30 knots, equipped with the highly-capable Aegis air-defence control system and armed with Standard SM-2ER surface-to-air missiles (SAM), 2 127 mm guns and 2 SH-60B Seahawk LAMPS-III helicopters. All but the first 5 ships are equipped with 2 x 61-cell vertical launch system for their missiles, which additionally allows them to launch Harpoon anti-ship missiles and Tomahawk sea-launched cruise missiles (SLCM). The 2 nuclear-powered vessels of the Virginia class and 2 similar California class, completed between 1973 and 1980, are of 11,400 tonnes and 10,700 tonnes respectively, capable of 31 knots and armed with 2 twin Standard SAM launchers, 8 Harpoon anti-surface ship missiles, ASROC anti-submarine missiles, and (Virginia class only) 8 Tomahawk SLCM. Neither class carries a helicopter.

In addition, there are 21 guided-missile destroyers including 17 of the new Arleigh Burke class currently building, and equipped with the Aegis air-defence system and 4 Kidd class, 31 anti-submarine destroyers of the Spruance class, 45 guided-missile frigates of the Oliver Hazard Perry class and 24 inshore patrol craft. Mine warfare ships include 2 former amphibious helicopter carriers of the Iwo Jima class converted as mine counter measures command and support ships, 14 new mine countermeasure vessels of the Avenger class and the first 8 of a new Osprey class coastal minehunter based on an Italian design.

Amphibious Warfare. Amphibious capability comprises 42 specialist ships. The 5 Wasp (LHD-1) class and the 5 ships of the Tarawa (LHA-1) class are in many respects similar to the vertical/short take off and landing aircraft carriers in other principal navies and are capable of sea control tasks. The Wasp class, completed from 1989 to 1995 and still building, are of 41,200 tonnes, capable of 23 knots, equipped with an air group of some 6-8 Harrier AV-8B aircraft, and up to 42 mixed helicopters, and accommodating 1,900 troops. The 5 ships of the Tarawa class are of 40,000 tonnes, were completed between 1976 and 1981, deploy a similar air group and carry 1,700 troops. The 1 remaining ship of the Iwo Jima class is also capable of operating vertical/short take-off and landing aircraft but does not normally do so. It is of 18,800 tonnes, is capable of 21 knots and normally carries 20 mixed helicopters and accommodates 1,740 troops. Additionally there are 2 amphibious command ships, 16 dock landing ships and 2 tank landing ships. There are 129 amphibious craft including 91 air-cushion landing craft (hovercraft) and 38 others, and several hundred minor personnel and vehicle transports. The total oceanic lift capability of the amphibious forces amounts to over 50,000 personnel, 1,000 main battle tank equivalents, and operating facilities for about 180 helicopters.

Underway Support. The Navy is provided with global, long-term sustainability through a force of some 43 underway replenishment ships, including 17 tankers, 8 multi-purpose fast replenishment ships, 8 stores ships and 10 ammunition ships. Second-line support is provided by 12 depot ships, 10 support tankers, 10 tugs and 2 hospital ships. Special purpose auxiliaries include 2 command ships, 18 ocean surveillance ships, 4 missile and space support ships, and 16 survey and oceanographic vessels. Of these major auxiliaries, about half are operated by the civilian-manned Military Sealift Command. In addition there are some hundreds of minor auxiliaries, and several thousand service craft.

Shipbuilding. Major warship building yards involved in the current building programme are located at Groton, Conn. (submarines), Newport News, Va. (submarines and aircraft carriers), Pascagoula, Miss. (amphibious ships), Bath, Me. (destroyers), New Orleans, La. (amphibious and auxiliary ships) and San Diego, Ca. (auxiliary ships).

Naval Aviation. The principal function of the naval aviation organization (72,500 strong in 1997) is to provide and train the 10 Air Wings maintained for service in the Aircraft Carriers. These usually consist of 70 fixed wing and 6 rotary wing aircraft. In addition, 1 reserve carrier air wing is available. The main carrier-borne combat aircraft on inventory are 330 F-14 fighters, 780 F/A-18 Hornet dual-purpose fighter/attack aircraft and 150 S-3A Viking anti-submarine aircraft. Supporting roles are performed by 120 EA-6B electronic warfare aircraft, 90 E-2C Hawkeye airborne early warning aircraft, 50 KA-6D tankers, 30 SH-3 Sea King and 80 SH-60F Oceanhawk helicopters for inner-zone anti-submarine defence. Helicopters held for embarkation in cruisers and below are of 2 types, the older SH-2F Seasprite aircraft of which there are some 30 and the SH-60B Seahawk of which there are 165. Although the A-6E Intruder attack aircraft has been withdrawn from carrier service, some 100 are retained in reserve. The principal tasks of the shore-based elements of US naval aviation are maritime reconnaissance and anti-submarine warfare, for which there are holdings of about 240 P-3C Orion aircraft. Additional tasks include electronic warfare (12 EP-3), electronic intelligence (16 ES-3) and mine countermeasures for which 50 MH- and RH-53 helicopters are held. Finally there are some 700 training aircraft of types not previously mentioned, and other aircraft for transport and other miscellaneous duties.

The Marine Corps. While administratively part of the Department of the Navy, the Corps ranks as a separate armed service, with the Commandant serving in his own right as a member of the Joint Chiefs of Staff, and responsible directly to the Secretary of the Navy. Its strength had stabilized at 174,000 by late 1997.

The role of the Marine Corps is to provide specially trained and equipped amphibious expeditionary forces. It is organized into 3 divisions each some 48,000 strong, subdivided into Marine Expeditionary Brigades (16,000) and Marine Expeditionary Units (some 5,000 strong). In peacetime, Marine Expeditionary Units are permanently deployed afloat in the Eastern Atlantic/Mediterranean and the West Pacific/Indian Ocean. The principal equipment of the Corps consists of 400 M-1A1

Abrams tanks, 600 LAV-25 armoured infantry fighting vehicles, 1,320 armoured personnel carriers and about 800 artillery pieces of calibres between 105 mm and 155 mm. Additional heavy equipment for US-based Marine forces units, beyond that which can be embarked in the amphibious shipping, is provided in 3 squadrons each of 13 large cargo ships prepositioned at Diego Garcia (Indian Ocean), the Pacific, and in the Mediterranean. In addition the Corps includes an autonomous aviation element numbering 34,000 in 1998 and equipped with some 400 combat aircraft and 515 helicopters. There are 280 F/A 18 Hornet, 180 AV-8B Harriers, 25 EA-6B electronic warfare aircraft, 75 KC-130 tankers, and a miscellany of other support and training aircraft. Helicopters include 240 CH-46E and 175 CH-53 transport, as well as 180 AH-1 Cobra attack helicopters of various types. Harriers and helicopters are nor-mally employed afloat in the amphibious aircraft carriers and other suitable ships. The Hornets and other fixed wing aircraft are normally based ashore, but may be embarked in other aircraft carriers, given the operational need.

The US Coast Guard operates under the Department of Transportation in time of peace and as a part of the Navy in time of war or when directed by the President. The act of establishment stated the Coast Guard 'shall be a military service and branch of the armed forces of the United States at all times'. It comprises 250 ships including cutters of destroyer, frigate, corvette and patrol vessel types, 2 large Polar class ice-breakers, and various auxiliaries and tenders, as well as over 1,400 rescue and utility craft. It also maintains 74 fixed-wing aircraft and 137 helicopters. The work-force, in 1996, was made up of over 34,000 active duty personnel augmented by 7,340 reserve and 35,638 auxiliary members.

The Coast Guard missions include maintenance of aids to navigation, boating safety, defence operations, environmental response (oil spills), ice operations, mari-time law enforcement, marine inspection, marine licensing, marine science, port safety and security, search and rescue and waterways management.

On an average Coast Guard day, the service saves 12 lives, conducts 142 Search and Rescue cases and 128 maritime law enforcement boardings, responds to 34 oil or hazardous chemical spills, seizes over $8m. in illegal contraband, interdicts 22 illegal immigrants and services 150 aids to navigation.

Air Force. *Secretary of the Air Force:* Dr Sheila E. Widnall.

The Department of the Air Force was activated within the Department of Defense on 18 Sept. 1947, under the terms of the National Security Act of 1947. It is administered by the Secretary of the Air Force, assisted by an Under Secretary, a Deputy for International Affairs and 4 Assistant Secretaries (Acquisition; Space; Manpower, Reserve Affairs, Installations and Environment; and Financial Management and Comptroller). The USAF, under the administration of the Department of the Air Force, is supervised by a Chief of Staff, who is a member of the Joint Chiefs of Staff. He is assisted by a Vice Chief of Staff, Assistant Vice Chief of Staff, 4 Deputy Chiefs of Staff (Personnel; Plans and Operations; Logistics; Communications and Information) and an Assistant Chief of Staff for Intelligence.

The USAF consists of active duty Air Force officers and enlisted personnel, civilian employees, the Air National Guard and the Air Force Reserve. The USAF has the mission to defend the USA through control and exploitation of air and space. For operational purposes the service is divided into 8 major commands, 37 field operating agencies and 3 direct-reporting units. Under these organizations there are 88 major and 89 minor facilities world-wide including National Guard and Reserve bases.

Major commands are organized on a functional basis in the USA and a geographic basis overseas. They accomplish designated phases of Air Force world-wide activities. They also organize, administer, equip and train their subordinate elements for the accomplishment of assigned missions. Major commands are generally assigned specific responsibilities based on functions. In descending order of command, elements of major commands include numbered air forces, wings, groups, squadrons and flights.

The bulk of the combat forces are grouped under the Air Combat Command, which controls strategic bombing, tactical strike, air defence and reconnaissance assets in the USA. The Air Mobility Command provides air lift, air refuelling, special air mission and aeromedical evacuation for US forces. The newest major command is the Air Education and Training Command which provides a wide variety of training from initial to advanced degree-granting education.

The other major commands are the Air Force Materiel Command, Air Force Special Operations Command, Air Force Space Command, Pacific Air Forces and United States Air Forces in Europe. The Pacific (PACAF) and European (USAFE) are responsible for offensive and defensive air operations in the Pacific and Asia, and Europe and the Mediterranean, respectively.

The field operating agencies are (AF = Air Force): the AF Audit Agency, AF Base Disposal Agency, AF Center for Environmental Excellence, AF Civil Engineering Support Agency, AF Civilian Personnel Management Center, AF Combat Operations Staff, AF Command, Control, Communications and Computer Agency, AF Cost Analysis Agency, AF Flight Standards Agency, AF Frequency Management Agency, AF Historical Research Agency, AF Inspection Agency, AF Intelligence Command, AF Intelligence Support Agency, AF Legal Services Agency, AF Logistics Management Agency, AF Management Engineering Agency, AF Medical Operations Agency, AF Medical Support Agency, AF Military Personnel Center, AF Morale, Welfare, Recreation and Services Agency, AF News Agency, AF Office of Special Investigations, AF Program Executive Office, AF Real Estate Agency, AF Review Boards Agency, AF Safety Agency, AF Security Police Agency, AF Studies and Analyses Agency, AF Technical Applications Center, Air Reserve Personnel Center, Air Weather Service, Center for Air Force History, Joint Services Survival, Evasion, Resistance and Escape Agency, and 7th Communications Group.

The direct-reporting units are: AF Academy, AF District of Washington and AF Operational Test and Evaluation Center.

Air Force aircraft are categorized as bombers, fighters, attack and observation aircraft, reconnaissance and special duty aircraft, transports and tankers, trainers and helicopters. The bombers are the B-1B Lancer, a supersonic inter-continental, nuclear and conventional aircraft; the B-2A, a subsonic, multi-role strategic bomber; and the B-52G/H Stratofortress, which has been the primary manned strategic bomber for over 35 years.

In the fighter category are the F-15 Eagle for air superiority tactical missions; the F-16 Fighting Falcon, a compact, multi-role fighter and attack aircraft; the F-117A, the world's first operational aircraft to exploit low-observable stealth technology; the A-10/OA-10 Thunderbolt II attack aircraft; and the AC-130H/U for counter-insurgency.

Under the reconnaissance and special duty heading are the U-2R/S for reconnaissance; the EC-130E/H Commando/Compass Call and the EF-111A Raven for electronic countermeasures; the E-3B/C Sentry, the E-4B and E-8 Joint Surveillance and Target Attack Radar System for command and control functions; the E-9A for telemetry relay; and the WC-130E/H for weather reconnaissance.

The primary transporters are the C-5A/B Galaxy for long-range heavy loads; the C-9A/C Nightingale for aeromedical evacuation; the C-17A Globemaster III for cargo and tactical air lift, the C-141B Starlifter for long-range troop and cargo; and the C-130 Hercules for theatre tactical air lift. The 2 refuelling aircraft types are the KC-135 Stratotanker and the KC-10A Extender.

Strategic missiles in the Air Force's inventory include the LGM-30G Minuteman, the LGM-118A Peacekeeper, the AGM-69A Short-Range Attack Missile and the AGM-86B/C Air-Launched Cruise Missile.

In 1996 the Air Force had approximately 390,000 military personnel. Approximately 60,000 Air Force members are women. Since 1991 women have been authorized to fly combat aircraft, but not until 1993 were they allowed to fly fighters.

INTERNATIONAL RELATIONS

Membership. The USA is a member of the UN, OAS, NATO, OECD, the Pacific Community and the Colombo Plan.

ECONOMY

Budget. The budget covers virtually all the programmes of federal government, including those financed through trust funds, such as for social security, Medicare and highway construction. Receipts of the Government include all income from its sovereign or compulsory powers; income from business-type or market-orientated activities of the Government is offset against outlays. The fiscal year ends on 30 Sept. (before 1977 on 30 June). Budget receipts and outlays (in $1m.):

Fiscal year ending in	Receipts	Outlays	Surplus (+) or deficit (−)
1950	39,443	42,562	−3,119
1960	92,492	92,191	+301
1970	192,807	195,649	−2,842
1980	517,112	590,947	−73,835
1990	1,031,969	1,253,163	−221,194
1995	1,351,830	1,515,729	−163,899
1996	1,452,763	1,560,212	−107,449
1997	1,578,977	1,601,594	−22,617
1998[1]	1,631,577	1,689,914	−58,337

[1] Estimates.

Budget and off-budget receipts, by source, for fiscal years (in $1m.):

Source	1996	1997	1998[1]
Individual income taxes	656,417	737,466	748,642
Corporation income taxes	171,824	182,294	192,582
Social insurance taxes and contributions	509,415	539,371	564,838
Excise taxes	54,015	56,926	55,341
Other	61,092	62,920	70,174
Total	1,452,763	1,578,977	1,631,577

[1] Estimates.

Budget and off-budget outlays, by function, for fiscal years (in $1m.):

Function	1996	1997	1998[1]
National defence	265,748	270,084	266,384
International affairs	13,496	15,423	14,578
General science, space and technology	16,709	18,510	16,488
Energy	2,836	1,583	2,276
Natural resources and environment	21,608	20,977	23,352
Agriculture	9,159	10,663	11,922
Commerce and housing credit	−10,472	−13,963	2,371
Transportation	39,565	39,725	40,188
Community and regional development	10,685	11,695	12,107
Education, training, employment and social services	52,001	51,509	56,510
Health	119,074	123,130	139,155
Medicare	174,225	189,970	199,453
Income security	225,989	230,359	244,180
Social Security	349,676	365,257	383,141
Veterans' benefits and services	36,981	39,313	41,316
Administration of justice	17,548	20,224	24,833
General government	11,914	12,750	13,176
Net interest	241,090	244,058	248,371
Allowances	−	−	−1,348
Undistributed offsetting receipts	−37,620	−49,973	−48,539
Total	1,560,212	1,601,594	1,689,914

[1] Estimates.

Budget and off-budget outlays, by agency, for fiscal years (in $1m.):

Agency	1996	1997	1998[1]
Legislative branch	2,272	2,361	2,794
The Judiciary	3,061	3,259	3,693
Executive Office of the President	202	219	233
Funds appropriated to the President	9,711	10,192	10,156
Agriculture	54,338	52,558	55,394
Commerce	3,703	3,780	4,110

Agency	1996	1997	1998[1]
Defence—Military	253,258	258,330	254,316
Defence—Civil	32,535	33,833	35,051
Education	29,734	30,013	32,030
Energy	16,204	14,470	14,703
Health and Human Services	319,802	339,493	370,123
Housing and Urban Development	25,240	27,833	32,473
Interior	6,718	6,724	7,599
Justice	11,950	14,291	17,941
Labor	32,496	30,461	33,938
State	4,955	5,237	5,395
Transportation	38,776	39,838	39,386
Treasury	365,336	379,381	392,634
Veterans Affairs	36,915	39,279	41,235
Environmental Protection Agency	6,046	6,167	6,701
General Services Administration	731	1,083	653
National Aeronautics and Space Administration	13,882	14,358	13,595
Office of Personnel Management	42,872	45,385	46,781
Small Business Administration	872	334	136
Social Security Administration	375,232	393,309	412,247
Other independent agencies	9,076	4,378	19,586
Allowances	–	–	–1,348
Undistributed offsetting receipts	–135,705	–154,972	–161,641
Total	1,560,212	1,601,594	1,689,914

[1] Estimates.

National Debt: Federal debt held by the public (in $1m.), and *per capita* debt (in $1) on 30 June to 1976 and on 30 Sept. since then:

	Public debt	Per capita		Public debt	Per capita
1920	24,299	228	1991	2,688,137	10,625
1930	16,185	132	1992	2,998,834	11,760
1940	42,772	325	1993	3,247,471	12,587
1950	219,023	1,438	1994	3,432,117	13,150
1960	236,840	1,311	1995	3,603,373	13,701
1970	283,198	1,381	1996	3,732,964	14,140
1980	709,838	3,117	1997	3,771,127	14,177
1990	2,410,722	9,643			

National Income. The Bureau of Economic Analysis of the Department of Commerce prepares detailed estimates on the national income and product. In Jan. 1996, the Bureau revised these accounts back to 1959 (eventually 1929), notably by introducing a new featured measure of real output and prices. The principal tables are published monthly in *Survey of Current Business;* the complete set of national income and product tables are published in the *Survey* normally each July, showing data for recent years. *The National Income and Product Accounts of the United States* (vol. 1, 1929–58; vol. 2, 1959–92) were published in 1997. The conceptual framework and statistical methods underlying the accounts are described in National Income and Product Account (NIPA) Methodology Papers 1–6. Subsequent limited changes are described in the July 1995, Sept. 1995, Oct. 1995, Aug. 1996 and Aug. 1997 *Surveys.*

	Gross Domestic Product (in $1,000m.)				
	1992	1993	1994	1995	1996
Gross Domestic Product	6,244·4	6,558·1	6,947·0	7,265·4	7,636·0
Personal consumption expenditures	4,219·8	4,459·2	4,717·0	4,957·7	5,207·6
Durable goods	488·5	530·2	579·5	608·5	634·5
Nondurable goods	1,321·8	1,370·7	1,428·4	1,475·8	1,534·7
Services	2,409·4	2,558·4	2,709·1	2,873·4	3,038·4
Gross private domestic investment	790·4	876·2	1,007·9	1,038·2	1,116·5
Fixed investment	783·4	855·7	946·6	1,008·1	1,090·7
Nonresidential	557·9	604·1	660·6	723·0	781·4
Structures	169·2	176·4	184·5	200·6	215·2
Producers' durable equipment	388·7	427·7	476·1	522·4	566·2
Residential	225·6	251·6	286·0	285·1	309·2

	Gross Domestic Product (in $1,000m.)				
	1992	*1993*	*1994*	*1995*	*1996*
Change in business inventories	7·0	20·5	61·2	30·1	25·9
Net exports of goods and services	−29·5	−60·7	−90·9	−86·0	−94·8
Exports	639·4	658·6	721·2	818·4	870·9
Goods	448·7	459·7	509·6	583·9	617·5
Services	190·7	198·9	211·6	234·6	253·3
Imports	669·0	719·3	812·1	904·5	965·7
Goods	544·9	592·8	676·8	757·5	809·0
Services	124·1	126·5	135·3	146·9	156·7
Government consumption expenditures and gross investment	1,263·8	1,283·4	1,313·0	1,355·5	1,406·7
Federal	528·0	518·3	510·2	509·6	520·0
National defense	375·8	360·7	349·2	344·6	352·8
Nondefense	152·2	157·7	161·0	165·0	167·3
State and local	735·8	765·0	802·8	846·0	886·7

Relation of Gross Domestic Product, Gross National Product, Net National Product, National Income, and Personal Income

(in $1,000m.)					
	1992	*1993*	*1994*	*1995*	*1996*
Gross domestic product	6,244·4	6,558·1	6,947·0	7,265·4	7,636·0
Plus: Receipts of factor income from the rest of the world	137·9	150·8	176·5	222·8	234·3
Less: Payments of factor income to the rest of the world	126·8	132·1	168·3	217·5	232·6
Equals: Gross national product	6,255·5	6,576·8	6,955·2	7,270·6	7,637·7
Less: Consumption of fixed capital	713·5	727·9	777·5	796·8	830·1
Private	585·4	594·5	638·6	653·0	682·7
Capital consumption allowances	575·4	599·1	647·3	669·1	709·9
Less: Capital consumption adjustment	−10·0	4·6	8·7	16·1	27·1
Government	128·2	133·4	138·8	143·8	147·4
General government	110·2	114·3	118·2	122·4	125·1
Government enterprises	18·0	19·1	20·6	21·4	22·3
Equals: Net national product	5,542·0	5,848·9	6,177·7	6,473·9	6,807·6
Less: Indirect business tax and nontax liability	505·6	532·5	568·5	582·8	604·8
Business transfer payments	28·4	28·2	30·5	32·2	33·6
Statistical discrepancy	44·8	52·6	14·6	−28·2	−59·9
Plus: Subsidies less current surplus of government enterprises	27·1	31·1	26·6	25·2	25·4
Equals: National income	4,990·4	5,266·8	5,590·7	5,912·3	6,254·5
Less: Corporate profits with inventory valuation and capital consumption adjustments	428·0	492·8	570·5	650·0	735·9
Net interest	414·3	402·5	412·3	425·1	425·1
Contributions for social insurance	571·4	596·0	630·5	659·1	692·0
Wage accruals less disbursements	−15·8	4·4	13·3	13·1	1·1
Plus: Personal interest income	667·2	651·0	668·1	718·9	735·7
Personal dividend income	159·4	185·3	204·8	251·9	291·2
Government transfer payments to persons	835·7	889·8	930·9	990·0	1,042·0
Business transfer payments to persons	22·5	22·1	23·7	25·0	26·0
Equals: Personal income	5,277·2	5,519·2	5,791·8	6,150·8	6,495·2
Addenda:					
Gross domestic income	6,199·7	6,505·5	6,932·4	7,293·6	7,695·9
Gross national income	6,210·7	6,524·2	6,940·6	7,298·9	7,697·6
Net domestic product	5,530·9	5,830·2	6,169·5	6,468·6	6,805·9

	National Income by Type of Income (in $1,000m.)				
	1992	*1993*	*1994*	*1995*	*1996*
National income	4,990·4	5,266·8	5,590·7	5,912·3	6,254·5
Compensation of employees	3,644·9	3,814·9	4,012·0	4,215·4	4,426·9
Wage and salary accruals	2,970·6	3,094·0	3,254·0	3,442·6	3,633·6
Government	567·8	584·3	602·2	623·0	642·6

National Income by Type of Income (in $1,000m.)

	1992	1993	1994	1995	1996
Other	2,402·9	2,509·7	2,651·8	2,819·6	2,991·0
Supplement to wages and salaries	674·3	720·8	758·0	772·9	793·3
Employer contributions for social insurance	323·0	335·7	353·0	366·0	385·7
Other labor income	351·3	385·1	405·0	406·8	407·6
Proprietors' income with inventory valuation and capital consumption adjustments	423·	450·8	471·6	489·0	520·3
Farm	37·1	32·4	36·9	23·4	37·2
Proprietors' income with inventory valuation adjustment	45·2	40·4	44·8	31·4	45·0
Capital consumption adjustment	−8·1	−8·0	−7·9	−7·9	−7·8
Nonfarm	386·7	418·4	434·7	465·5	483·1
Proprietors' income	363·1	392·7	415·0	438·8	455·3
Inventory valuation adjustment	−0·7	−1·1	−0·6	−0·5	−0·2
Capital consumption adjustment	24·3	26·8	20·4	27·2	28·0
Rental income of persons with capital consumption adjustment	79·4	105·7	124·4	132·8	146·3
Rental income of persons	127·5	148·5	172·0	179·8	193·3
Capital consumption adjustment	−48·1	−42·8	−47·6	−47·0	−47·0
Corporate profits with inventory valuation and capital consumption adjustments	428·0	492·8	570·5	650·0	735·9
Corporate profits with inventory valuation adjustment	398·9	456·9	519·1	598·4	674·1
Profits before tax	406·4	465·4	535·1	622·6	676·6
Profits tax liability	143·0	165·2	186·6	213·2	229·0
Profits after tax	263·4	300·2	348·5	409·4	447·6
Dividends	169·5	195·8	216·2	264·4	304·8
Undistributed profits	93·9	104·5	132·3	145·0	142·8
Inventory valuation adjustment	−7·5	−8·5	−16·1	−24·3	−2·5
Capital consumption adjustment	29·1	36·0	51·4	51·6	61·8
Net interest	414·3	402·5	412·3	425·1	425·1
Addenda:					
Corporate profits after tax with inventory valuation and capital consumption adjustments	285·0	327·6	383·8	436·7	506·9
Net cash flow with inventory valuation and capital consumption adjustments	491·9	520·3	579·9	601·3	654·3
Undistributed profits with inventory valuation and capital consumption adjustments	115·5	131·9	167·6	172·4	202·1
Consumption of fixed capital	376·4	388·4	412·3	428·9	452·3
Less: Inventory valuation adjustment	−7·5	−8·5	−16·1	−24·3	−2·5
Equals: Net cash flow	499·4	528·8	596·0	625·5	656·8

Real Gross Domestic Product (in 1,000m. chained [1992] dollars[1])

	1992	1993	1994	1995	1996
Gross domestic product	6,244·4	6,386·4	6,608·7	6,742·9	6,906·8
Personal consumption expenditures	4,219·8	4,339·5	4,473·2	4,577·8	4,690·7
Durable goods	488·5	524·1	562·0	579·8	611·4
Nondurable goods	1,321·8	1,348·8	1,390·5	1,421·9	1,442·0
Services	2,409·4	2,466·7	2,521·4	2,577·0	2,638·3
Gross private domestic investment	790·4	857·3	979·6	1,010·2	1,056·6
Fixed investment	783·4	836·4	921·1	975·9	1,042·1
Nonresidential	557·9	593·6	652·1	714·3	766·8
Structures	169·2	166·3	168·8	181·1	190·0
Producers' durable equipment	388·7	427·6	484·1	534·5	578·6
Residential	225·6	242·7	268·9	262·7	276·7
Change in business inventories	7·3	19·1	58·9	33·1	13·6
Net exports of goods and services	−29·5	−72·0	−105·7	−107·6	−113·6
Exports	639·4	658·2	712·0	775·4	825·9
Goods	448·7	464·5	511·5	565·9	608·8
Services	190·7	193·7	200·9	210·4	218·2
Imports	669·0	730·2	817·6	883·0	939·5

| | Real Gross Domestic Product (in 1,000m. chained [1992] dollars[1]) | | | | |
	1992	1993	1994	1995	1996
Goods	544·9	602·6	684·1	744·7	796·3
Services	124·1	127·7	133·8	138·8	143·8
Government consumption expenditures and gross investment	1,263·8	1,261·0	1,260·0	1,260·2	1,270·6
Federal	528·0	509·2	489·8	472·3	467·1
National defense	375·8	355·4	337·0	319·6	313·9
Nondefense	152·2	153·8	152·6	152·3	152·8
State and local	735·8	751·8	770·5	788·6	804·3
Residual	−0·3	2·2	−0·5	−0·6	−1·7

[1] In 1996 the chain-weighted method of estimating GDP replaced that of constant base-year prices. In chain-weighting the weights used to value different sectors of the economy are continually updated to reflect changes in relative prices.

Currency. The unit of currency is the *dollar* (USD) of 100 *cents*. Notes are issued by the 12 Federal Reserve Banks, which are denoted by a branch letter (A = Boston, MA; B = New York, NY; C = Philadelphia, PA; D = Cleveland, OH; E = Richmond, VA; F = Atlanta, GA; G = Chicago, IL; H = St Louis, MO; I = Minneapolis, MN; J = Kansas City, MO; K = Dallas, TX; L = San Francisco, CA). There are coins of 1, 5 ('nickels'), 10 ('dimes'), 25 ('quarters') and 50 ('halves') cents, and notes of $1, 2, 5, 10, 20, 50 and 100.

Banking and Finance. The Federal Reserve System, established under The Federal Reserve Act of 1913, comprises the Board of 7 Governors, the 12 regional Federal Reserve Banks with their 25 branches, and the Federal Open Market Committee. The 7 members of the Board of Governors are appointed by the President with the consent of the Senate. Each Governor is appointed to a full term of 14 years or an unexpired portion of a term, one term expiring every 2 years. The Board exercises broad supervisory authority over the operations of the 12 Federal Reserve Banks, including approval of their budgets and of the appointments of their presidents and first vice presidents; it designates 3 of the 9 directors of each Reserve Bank including the Chairman and Deputy Chairman. The *Chairman* of the Federal Reserve Board is appointed by the President for 4-year terms. The Chairman for 1996–2000 is Alan Greenspan. The Board has supervisory and regulatory responsibilities over banks that are members of the Federal Reserve System, bank holding companies, bank mergers, Edge Act and agreement corporations, foreign activities of member banks, international banking facilities in the USA, and activities of the US branches and agencies of foreign banks. Legislation of 1991 requires foreign banks to prove that they are subject to comprehensive consolidated supervision by a regulator at home, and have the Board's approval to establish branches, agencies and representative offices. The Board also assures the smooth functioning and continued development of the nation's vast payments system. Another area of the Board's responsibilities involves the implementation by regulation of major federal laws governing consumer credit.

The 12 members of the Federal Open Market Committee (FOMC) include the 7 members of the Board of Governors and 5 of the 12 Federal Reserve Bank presidents. The latter serve 1-year terms on the FOMC in rotation except for the President of the Federal Reserve Bank of New York, who is a permanent member. The FOMC has an essential role in the formulation of monetary policy. It influences credit market conditions, money and bank credit, by buying or selling US Government securities; and it also oversees System operations in foreign currencies for the purpose of helping to safeguard the value of the dollar in international exchange markets and facilitating co-operation and efficiency in the international monetary system. The Board of Governors also influences credit conditions through powers to set reserve requirements, to approve discount rates at Federal Reserve Banks, and to fix margin requirements on stock-market credit.

The Reserve Banks advance funds to depository institutions, issue Federal Reserve notes, the only form of currency apart from coins, act as fiscal agent for the Government, and afford nationwide cheque-clearing and fund transfer arrangements.

They may increase or reduce the country's supply of reserve funds by buying or selling Government securities and other obligations at the direction of the FOMC. The purchase and sale of securities in the open market is conducted by the Federal Reserve Bank of New York. Their capital stock is held by the member banks, but it carries no voting rights except in the election of directors.

From 1968, the Congress passed a number of consumer financial protection acts, the first of which was the Truth in Lending Act, for which it has directed the Board to write implementing regulations and assume partial enforcement responsibility. Others include the Equal Credit Opportunity Act, Home Mortgage Disclosure Act, Consumer Leasing Act, Fair Credit Billing Act, Truth in Savings Act and Electronic Fund Transfer Act. To manage these responsibilities the Board has established a Division of Consumer and Community Affairs. To assist it, the Board consults with a Consumer Advisory Council, established by the Congress in 1976 as a statutory part of the Federal Reserve System.

Another statutory body, the Federal Advisory Council, consists of 12 members (one from each district); it meets in Washington four times a year to advise the Board of Governors on economic and banking developments. Following the passage of the Monetary Control Act of 1980, the Board of Governors established the Thrift Institutions Advisory Council to provide information and views on the special needs and problems of thrift institutions. The group is comprised of representatives of mutual savings banks, savings and loan associations, and credit unions.

All depository institutions (commercial and savings banks, savings and loan associations, credit unions, US agencies and branches of foreign banks, and Edge Act and agreement corporations) must meet reserve requirements set by the Federal Reserve and hold the reserves in the form of vault cash or deposits at Federal Reserve Banks.

Banks which participate in the federal deposit insurance fund have their deposits insured against loss up to $100,000 for each account. The fund is administered by the Federal Deposit Insurance Corporation established in 1933; it obtains resources through annual assessments on participating banks. All members of the Federal Reserve System are required to insure their deposits through the Corporation, and non-member banks may apply and qualify for insurance.

The Federal Deposit Insurance Corporation Improvement Act of 1992 originated with bank reform initiatives. It imposed new capital rules on banks, new reporting requirements and a code of 'safety and soundness' standards. The main aim of the Act is to reduce risk through rigorous enforcement of capital requirements. Regulators are required to take action where banks fail to observe these standards.

In June 1997 the 10 major banks in terms of assets ($1,000m.) were: Chase Manhattan, 281; Citibank, 254; Bank of America, 224; Morgan Guaranty, 189; NationsBank, 159; Bankers Trust, 99; Wells Fargo, 92; First Union, 84; Keybank, 66; BankBoston; 57.

The key stock exchanges are the New York Stock Exchange (NYSE), the Nasdaq Stock Exchange (NASDAQ) and the American Stock Exchange (ASE). There are several other stock exchanges, in Philadelphia, Boston, San Francisco (Pacific Stock Exchange) and Chicago, although trading is very limited in them.

Weights and Measures. The US Customary System derives from the British Imperial System. It differs in respect of the *gallon* (= 0·83268 Imperial gallon); *bushel* (= 0·969 Imperial bushel); *hundredweight* (= 100 lbs); and the *short* or *net ton* (= 2,000 lbs).

ENERGY AND NATURAL RESOURCES

Electricity. In 1996, 21·9% of electricity was produced by 110 nuclear reactors. (The last one was built in 1989.) Utility net generation (1996) 3,077,442m. kWh.

Oil and Gas. Crude oil production (includes natural gas plant liquids and other liquids), 1994, 8,645,000 bbls. a day; 1995, 8,626,000 bbls. a day; 1996, 8,607,000 bbls. a day. Proven reserves were 22,017m. bbls. at 31 Dec. 1996. 1996 output was valued at $43,680m. Dry natural gas production, 1996, was 18,793,000m. cu. ft. with marketed production 19,750,793m. cu. ft., valued at $42,859m.

Coal. Demonstrated coal reserves were 496,000m. short tons at 1 Jan. 1995. 1996 output (in 1m. short tons): 1,063·9 including bituminous coal, 630·7; sub-bituminous coal, 340·3; lignite, 88·1; anthracite, 4·8. Output from opencast workings, 654·0; underground mines, 409·8. Value of total output, 1996, $19,480m.

Non-Fuel Minerals. The USA is wholly dependent upon imports for columbium, bauxite, mica sheet, manganese, strontium and graphite, and imports over 80% of its requirements of industrial diamonds, fluorspar, platinum, tantalum, tungsten, chromium and tin.

Total value of non-fuel minerals produced in 1995 was $38,500m. ($33,464m. in 1990). Details of some of the main minerals produced are given in the following tables.

Production of metals:

	Unit	Quantity		Value ($1m.)	
		1990	1995	1990	1995
Copper	1,000 tonnes	1,590	1,850	4,311	5,640
Gold	tonnes	294	320	3,650	3,990
Iron ore	1m. tonnes	57	61	1,741	1,710
Lead	1,000 tonnes	497	386	491	359
Magnesium metal	1,000 tonnes	139	142	433	476
Silver	tonnes	2,121	1,640	329	271
Zinc	1,000 tonnes	515	614	847	756
Total metals				*12,442*	*14,100*

Precious metals are mined mainly in Nevada, California, and Utah (gold) and Nevada, Arizona and Idaho (silver).

Production of non-metals:

	Unit	Quantity		Value ($1m.)	
		1990	1995	1990	1995
Barite	1,000 tonnes	430	543	16	17
Boron	1,000 tonnes	1,094	796	436	372
Bromine	1,000 tonnes	177	218	173	186
Cement	1m. short tons	78·9	77·3	3,908	5,227
Clays	1,000 tonnes	42,904	43,100	1,620	1,730
Diatomite	1,000 tonnes	631	687	138	171
Feldspar	1,000 tonnes	630	882	28	37
Garnet (industrial)	1,000 tonnes	47·0	53·0	7	10
Gypsum	1m. tonnes	16·4	17·0	100	121
Lime	1m. short tons	17·5	18·5	902	1,100
Phosphate rock	1m. tonnes	46·3	44	1,075	945
Pumice	1,000 tonnes	443	529	11	13
Salt	1m. tonnes	36·9	41·0	827	1,000
Sand and gravel	1m. tonnes	852	938	3,686	4,410
Sodium sulphate	1,000 tonnes	349	327	34	29
Stone (crushed)	1m. tonnes	1,109	1,260	5,591	6,750
Sulphur (all forms)	1,000 tonnes	3,676	3,070	335	207

Agriculture. Agriculture in the USA is characterized by its ability to adapt to widely varying conditions, and still produce an abundance and variety of agricultural products. From colonial times to about 1920 the major increases in farm production were brought about by adding to the number of farms and the amount of land under cultivation. During this period nearly 320m. acres of virgin forest were converted to crop land or pasture, and extensive areas of grass lands were ploughed. Improvident use of soil and water resources was evident in many areas.

During the next 20 years the number of farms reached a plateau of about 6·5m., and the acreage planted to crops held relatively stable around 330m. acres. The major source of increase in farm output arose from the substitution of power-driven machines for horses and mules. Greater emphasis was placed on development and improvement of land, and the need for conservation of basic agricultural resources was recognized. A successful conservation programme, highly co-ordinated and on a national scale—to prevent further erosion, to restore the native fertility of damaged land and to adjust land uses to production capabilities and needs—has been in operation since early in the 1930s.

Following the Second World War the uptrend in farm output has been greatly accelerated by increased production per acre and per farm animal. These increases are associated with a higher degree of mechanization; greater use of lime and fertilizer; improved varieties, including hybrid maize and grain sorghums; more effective control of insects and disease; improved strains of livestock and poultry; and wider use of good husbandry practices, such as nutritionally balanced feeds, use of superior sites and better housing. During this period land included in farms decreased slowly, crop land harvested declined somewhat more rapidly, but the number of farms declined sharply.

All land in farms totalled less than 500m. acres in 1870, rose to a peak of over 1,200m. acres in the 1950s and declined to 968m. acres in 1996, even with the addition of the new States of Alaska and Hawaii in 1960. The number of farms declined from 6·35m. in 1940 to 2·06m. in 1996, as the average size of farms doubled. The average size of farms in 1996 was 469 acres, but ranged from a few acres to many thousand acres. In 1992, 554,000 farms (595,000 in 1987) were less than 50 acres; 584,000 (645,000), 50–179 acres; 614,000 (678,000), 180–999 acres; and 173,000 (169,000) 1,000 acres or more.

Farms operated by owners in 1992 were 1,112,000; by part-owners, 597,000; by tenants, 217,000.

Value of land and buildings in 1996 was $859,711m.

At the 1990 census 66,964,000 persons (22·5% of the population) were rural, of whom 4,591,000 (under 2%) lived on farms. In 1994 there were 1,453,000 farm operators and managers and 1,992,000 persons in other agricultural and related occupations, of which 748,000 were farm workers.

Cash receipts from farm marketings and government payments (in $1,000m.):

	Crops	Livestock and livestock products	Government payments	Total
1993	87·5	90·2	13·4	191·1
1994	92·6	88·1	7·9	188·6
1995	98·9	86·8	7·3	193·0

Gross farm income (including government payments), in $1,000m., was 210·4 in 1995 compared to 198·2 in 1990, although net farm income was greater in 1990 (44·8 compared to 34·8 for 1995). Total area of farm land under irrigation in 1992 was 49,404,000 acres. Water consumption was 137,000m. gallons a day in 1990.

Acreage and specified values of farms (area in 1m. acres; value in $1m.):

	Farm area	Crop land used for crops	Value of land and buildings
1990	987	341	671,419
1991	982	337	. . .
1992	979	337	687,432
1993	976	330	682,039
1994	973	339	725,711
1995	972	332	807,017
1996	968	346	859,711

The areas and production of the principal crops for 3 years were:

	1994 Harvested 1m. acres	1994 Production 1m.	1994 Yield per acre	1995 Harvested 1m. acres	1995 Production 1m.	1995 Yield per acre	1996 Harvested 1m. acres	1996 Production 1m.	1996 Yield per acre
Corn for grain (bu.)	72·9	10,103	139	65·0	7,374	114	73·1	9,293	127
Soybeans (bu.)	60·9	2,517	41·4	61·6	2,177	35·3	63·4	2,382	37·6
Wheat (bu.)	61·8	2,321	37·6	60·9	2,183	35·8	62·9	2,282	36·3
Cotton (bales)[1]	13·3	19·7	708	16·0	17·9	536	12·9	19·0	707
Tobacco (lbs.)	0·7	1,583	2,359	0·7	1,269	1,913	0·7	1,565	2,133
Potatoes (cwt.)	1·4	467	339	1·4	444	323	1·4	497	349
Sorghum for grain (bu.)	8·9	649	72·8	8·3	460	55·6	11·9	803	67·5
Rice (cwt.)[1]	3·3	198	5,964	3·1	174	5,621	2·8	171	6,121

[1] Yield in lbs.

Fruit. Utilized production :

	1994	1995	1996
Apples (1m. lbs)	11,331	10,390	10,392
Oranges and tangerines (1m. boxes[1])	248	278	280
Grapes (1,000 tons)	5,869	5,913	5,529

[1] Average net weight per box 75–95 lbs.

Dairy produce. In 1996 production of milk was 154,331m. lbs.; cheese, 7,218m. lbs.; butter, 1,174m. lbs.; ice-cream, 879m. gallons; non-fat dry milk, 1,068m. lbs.; yoghurt, 1,588m. lbs.

Livestock. In 1997 livestock numbered (in 1m.): Cattle and calves (including milk cows), 101·2; sheep and lambs, 7·9; hogs and pigs, 56·2.

In 1996 there were 7,598m. broilers and 301m. turkeys. Eggs produced, 1996, 76,400m.

Value of production (in $1m.) was:

	1994	1995	1996
Cattle and calves	26,861	24,830	22,259
Hogs and pigs	9,962	9,829	11,997
Broilers	11,372	11,762	13,906
Turkeys	2,644	2,776	3,102
Eggs	3,780	3,880	4,757

Value of livestock (in $1m.), 1997: Cattle, 53,100; hogs and pigs, 5,300; sheep and lambs, 762.

Forestry. In 1992 the gross area of National forest was 231·5m. acres (93·7m. ha), within which 191·5m. acres (77·5m. ha) were Federally owned ('National forest system'). Timber cut in 1994 was 4,815m. board ft with a value of $797m. In 1992 total forest land was 732m. acres (298m. ha), of which 490m. acres was timberland (97m. acres federally owned or managed, 35m. acres state, county or municipality owned, 358m. acres private).

Fisheries. In 1995 the domestic catch was 9,904m. lbs, valued at $3,770m. (including 1,267m. lbs of shellfish valued at $1,820m.). Main species landed in terms of value ($1m.): Shrimp, 570; salmon, 521; crab, 512; Alaska pollock, 260; flounder, 150. Disposition of the domestic catch (1m. lbs): Fresh or frozen, 7,215; tinned, 769; cured, 90; reduced to meal or oil, 1,830.

Tennessee Valley Authority. Established by Act of Congress, 1933, the TVA is a multiple-purpose federal agency which carries out its duties in an area embracing some 41,000 sq. miles in the 7 Tennessee RiverValley states: Tennessee, Kentucky, Mississippi, Alabama, North Carolina, Georgia and Virginia. In addition, 76 counties outside the Valley are served by TVA power distributors. Its 3 directors are appointed by the President, with the consent of the Senate; headquarters are in Knoxville (TN). Under a policy announced in Dec. 1994 the TVA is subject to a debt ceiling of $30,000m. Total debt in 1994 was $26,000m.

The primary task of the TVA was the multipurpose development of the Tennessee River for flood control, navigation, and electric power production. In 1994 3 nuclear reactors were in operation.

The TVA has also contributed to controlling erosion on the land, introducing better fertilizers and new farming practices, eradicating malaria, demonstrating ways electricity could lighten the burdens in the home and increase production on the farm, and the creation of potential job-producing enterprises.

INDUSTRY. The following table presents industry statistics of manufactures as reported at various censuses from 1909 to 1987 and from the Annual Survey of Manufactures for years in which no census was taken.

The annual Surveys of Manufactures carry forward the key measures of manufacturing activity which are covered in detail by the Census of Manufactures. The large plants in the surveys account for approximately two-thirds of the total employment in operating manufacturing establishments in the USA.

	Number of establishments	Production workers (average for year)	Production workers' wages total ($1,000)	Value added by manufacture ($1,000)
1909	264,810	3,261,736	3,205,213	8,160,075
1919	270,231	9,464,916	9,664,009	23,841,624
1929	206,663	8,369,705	10,884,919	30,591,435
1933	139,325	5,787,611	4,940,146	14,007,540
1939	173,802	7,808,205	8,997,515	24,487,304
1950	260,000	11,778,803	34,600,025	89,749,765
1960	. . .	12,209,514	55,555,452	163,998,531
1970	. . .	13,528,000	91,609,000	300,227,600
1980	. . .	13,900,100	198,164,000	773,831,300
1982	358,061	12,400,600	204,787,200	824,117,700
1984	. . .	12,572,800	231,783,900	983,227,700
1986	. . .	11,800,000	237,000,000	1,035,000,000
1988	. . .	12,400,000	264,000,000	1,262,000,000
1989	. . .	12,300,000	269,000,000	1,308,000,000
1990	. . .	12,100,000	272,000,000	1,326,000,000
1991	. . .	11,500,000	266,000,000	1,314,000,000
1992	382,000	11,641,000	282,000,000	1,428,707,000
1993	. . .	11,700,000	290,000,000	1,483,000,000
1994	. . .	11,900,000	304,000,000	1,598,000,000
1995	. . .	12,300,000	317,000,000	1,709,000,000

The total number of employees in 1995 was 18·7m.

In 1995 the principal commodities produced (by value of shipments, in $1m.) were: Motor vehicles and equipment, 326,181; refined petroleum, 136,023; electronic components and accessories, 119,288; meat products, 100,260.

The leading industries in 1995 in terms of value added by manufacture (in $1m.) were: Motor vehicles and car bodies, 55,696; semiconductors and related devices, 51,272; motor vehicle parts, 43,084; pharmaceutical preparations, 41,186.

Iron and Steel: Output of the iron and steel industries (in 1m. net tons of 2,000 lb.), according to figures supplied by the American Iron and Steel Institute, was:

	Pig-iron (including ferro-alloys)	Raw steel	Steel by method of production[1]	
			Electric	Basic Oxygen
1993	53·1	97·9	38·5	59·3
1994	54·4	100·6	39·6	61·0
1995	56·1	104·9	42·4	62·5
1996	54·5	105·3	44·9	60·4

[1] The sum of these 2 items should equal the total in the preceding column; any difference is due to rounding.

The iron and steel industry in 1994 employed 92,587 wage-earners who worked an average of 42 hours per week and earned an average of $21·96 per hour: total employment costs were $6,744m. and total employment costs for 33,031 salaried employees were $2,466m.

Labour. The Bureau of Labor Statistics estimated that in 1997 the civilian labour force was 136,297,000 (67·1% of those 16 years and over), of whom 129,558,000 were employed and 6,739,000 (4·9%) were unemployed. Employment by industry in 1997:

Industry Group	Male	Female	Total	Percentage distribution
Employed (1,000 persons):	69,685	59,873	129,558	100·0
Agriculture, forestry and fisheries	2,662	875	3,538	2·7
Mining	543	92	634	0·5
Construction	7,518	784	8,302	6·4
Manufacturing:				
Durable goods	9,086	3,351	12,437	9·6
Non-durable (including not specified)	5,067	3,332	8,399	6·5
Transportation, communication and other public utilities	6,539	2,643	9,182	7·1
Wholesale and retail trade	14,118	12,659	26,777	20·7

Industry Group	Male	Female	Total	Percentage distribution
Finance, insurance and real estate	3,449	4,848	8,297	6·4
Services	17,517	28,738	46,254	35·7
Private households	84	837	921	0·7
Other services	17,433	27,900	45,333	35·0
Professional services	9,477	21,458	30,935	23·9
Public administration	3,186	2,552	5,738	4·4

A total of 37 strikes and lockouts of 1,000 workers or more occurred in 1996, involving 273,000 workers and 4·9m. idle days; the number of idle days was 0·02% of the year's total working time of all workers.

The Federal Mediation and Conciliation Service, the National Labor Relations Board, the National Mediation Board and the National Railroad Adjustment Board provide formal machinery for the settlement of labour disputes.

On 1 Sept. 1997 the federal hourly minimum wage was raised from $4·75 to $5·15 an hour, the first time it had been raised since 1991.

Labour relations are legally regulated by the National Labor Relations Act, amended by the Labor–Management Relations (Taft–Hartley) Act, 1947 as amended by the Labor–Management Reporting and Disclosure Act, 1959, again amended in 1974, and the Railway Labor Act of 1926, as amended in 1934 and 1936.

Trade Unions. The labour movement comprises 78 national and international labour organizations plus a large number of small independent local or single-firm labour organizations. The American Federation of Labor and the Congress of Industrial Organizations merged into one organization, the AFL–CIO, in 1955, with 13m. members in 1995. Its *President* is John Sweeney, elected 1995.

Unaffiliated or independent labour organizations, inter-state in scope, had an estimated total membership excluding all foreign members (1993) of about 3m.

Labour organizations represented 16·2% (18·2m.) of wage and salary workers in 1996; a newly-developing 'associative unionism' is not based on the workplace, but provides representation for employees which is portable throughout their work history; 14·5% (16·3m.) were actual members of unions. In 1996 38% of employees in the public sector, and 10% in the private sector, were members of unions. Strongholds of organized labour are, industry-wise, iron and steel, railways, coal mining and car building; region-wise, East coast cities and the mid-West industrial belt.

FOREIGN ECONOMIC RELATIONS. The North American Free Trade Agreement (NAFTA) between the USA, Canada and Mexico was signed on 7 Oct. 1992 and came into effect on 1 Jan. 1994. The UK has had 'most-favoured-nation' status since 1815. In 1994, foreign investment totalled $47,200m., the leading investor still being the United Kingdom.

Commerce. Total value of imports, exports and re-exports (in $1m.):

	Exports	Imports
1993	465,091	580,659
1994	512,626	663,256
1995	584,742	743,445
1996	624,767	791,364

Exports and imports (in $1m.), 1996:

	Exports	Imports
Agricultural commodities	59,311	32,565
Animal feeds	4,183	633
Bulbs	106	312
Cereal flour	1,170	1,213
Cocoa	111	962
Coffee	4	2,491
Corn	8,623	116
Cotton, raw and linters	2,740	300
Dairy products, eggs	713	717
Fur skins, raw	181	74
Grains, unmilled	800	212

	Exports	Imports
Hides and skins	1,515	133
Live animals	533	1,395
Meat and preparations	6,958	2,317
Oils/fats, animal	613	43
Oils/fats, vegetable	1,024	1,416
Plants	94	145
Rice	1,029	157
Seeds	355	200
Soybeans	7,447	31
Sugar	5	1,001
Tobacco, unmanufactured	1,390	1,053
Vegetables and fruit	7,313	7,514
Wheat	6,302	247
Other agricultural	6,102	9,863
Manufactured goods	483,874	659,867
ADP equipment, office machinery	39,666	66,499
Airplanes	18,962	3,943
Airplane parts	11,723	3,463
Aluminium	3,485	4,828
Artwork/antiques	887	2,791
Basketware, etc.	2,239	3,014
Chemicals – cosmetics	4,323	2,443
Chemicals – dyeing	2,716	2,165
Chemicals – fertilizers	3,070	1,400
Chemicals – inorganic	4,657	4,954
Chemicals – medicinal	7,160	7,076
Chemicals – organic	14,744	14,820
Chemicals – plastics	15,467	7,443
Chemicals – other	9,651	4,568
Clothing	7,285	41,559
Copper	1,553	2,953
Electrical machinery	56,637	75,525
Footwear	761	12,749
Furniture and parts	3,323	9,431
Gem diamonds	151	6,588
General industrial machinery	26,599	25,286
Glass	1,814	1,679
Glassware	680	1,413
Gold, nonmonetary	6,641	2,737
Iron and steel mill products	4,795	13,368
Lighting, plumbing	1,358	2,579
Metal manufactures	9,234	10,843
Metalworking machinery	5,241	6,789
Motorcycles, bicycles	1,009	2,150
Nickel	307	1,137
Optical goods	1,378	2,327
Paper and paperboard	9,837	11,637
Photographic equipment	3,743	5,271
Plastic articles	4,439	5,306
Platinum	248	1,716
Pottery	95	1,569
Power generating machinery	22,292	22,499
Printed materials	4,346	2,700
Records/magnetic media	6,555	4,078
Rubber articles	972	1,465
Rubber tyres and tubes	1,959	3,074
Scientific instruments	20,599	12,385
Ships, boats	1,064	1,029
Silver and bullion	638	569
Spacecraft	636	232
Specialized industrial machinery	25,659	18,509
Telecommunications equipment	19,838	34,167
Textile yarn, fabric	7,814	10,248
Toys/games/sporting goods	3,693	14,734
Travel goods	306	3,581
Vehicles/new cars – Canada	7,899	25,351

	Exports	Imports
Vehicles/new cars – Japan	2,327	20,134
Vehicles/new cars – other	6,021	21,574
Vehicles/trucks	5,991	11,355
Vehicles/chassis/bodies	516	499
Vehicles/parts	24,628	20,859
Watches/clocks/parts	277	2,805
Wood manufactures	1,685	4,037
Other manufactured goods	32,281	49,963
Mineral fuel	12,057	73,028
Coal	3,849	606
Crude oil	460	50,582
Petroleum preparations	3,948	13,858
Liquefied propane/butane	302	1,263
Natural gas	261	4,002
Electricity	69	402
Other mineral fuels	3,168	2,315
Selected commodities:		
Fish and preparations	2,930	6,657
Cork, wood, lumber	5,501	7,532
Pulp and waste paper	4,034	2,648
Metal ores, scrap	4,278	4,048
Crude fertilizers	1,526	1,176
Cigarettes	4,736	69
Alcoholic beverages, distilled	385	2,048
All other (including re-exports)	46,135	1,726

Imports and exports by selected countries for the calendar years 1995 and 1996 (in $1m.):

Country	General imports		Exports incl. re-exports	
	1995	1996	1995	1996
UK	26,898	28,892	28,857	30,916
France	17,209	18,630	14,245	14,428
Germany	36,844	38,943	22,394	23,474
Italy	16,348	18,222	8,862	8,785
Netherlands	6,405	6,617	16,558	16,615
Russia	4,030	3,561	2,823	3,340
Canada	145,349	156,506	127,226	133,668
Mexico	61,685	72,963	46,292	56,761
China	45,543	51,495	11,754	11,978
Japan	123,479	115,218	64,343	67,536
South Korea	24,184	22,667	25,380	26,583
Taiwan	28,972	29,911	19,290	18,413
Australia	3,323	3,855	10,789	11,992
Hong Kong	10,291	9,868	14,231	13,956
Singapore	18,561	20,340	15,333	16,686

Tourism. In 1995 the USA received 43,318,000 visitors, of whom 17,612,000 were classified as tourists. Visitors spent US$61,137m. (excluding transportation paid to US international carriers). Of the 43,318,000 visitors, 14,663,000 were from Canada and 8,083,000 from Mexico. Tourists came mainly from Europe (7·01m., of which UK 2·34m. and Germany 1·55m.), Japan (3·99m.), Mexico (0·89m.) and the Caribbean (0·83m.). Expenditure by US travellers in foreign countries for 1995 was US$45,855m. (excluding transportation paid to foreign flag international carriers).

COMMUNICATIONS

Roads. On 31 Dec. 1994 the total public road mileage (rural and urban), amounted to 3,906,000 miles, of which 3,566,000 miles were surfaced roads. The total mileage cited includes about 690,000 miles of rural roads under control of the states, about 2,229,000 miles of local rural roads, about 174,000 miles of federal park and forest roads, and 814,000 miles of urban roads. Expenditure on highway administration and maintenance amounted to $89,258m. in 1994.

Motor vehicles registered in 1994: 198,045,000, including 133,930,000 auto-mobiles, 670,000 buses, 56,718,000 trucks and 3,718,000 motorcycles. There were

177·43m. licensed drivers in 1995 (87·2m. females). There were 41,800 deaths in road accidents in 1995.

Railways. Freight service is provided by 12 major independent railroad companies and several hundred smaller operators. Long-distance passenger trains are run by the National Railroad Passenger Corporation (Amtrak), which is federally-assisted. Amtrak was set up in 1971 to maintain a basic network of long-distance passenger trains, and is responsible for almost all non-commuter services over some 38,000 route-km, of which it owns only 1,256 km (555 km electrified). Outside the major conurbations, there are almost no regular passenger services other than those of Amtrak, which carried 20·3m. passengers in 1995.

Civil Aviation. There are international airports at Anchorage, Atlanta (Hartsfield), Baltimore (Baltimore/Washington), Boston (Logan), Chicago (O'Hare), Cincinnati (Northern Kentucky), Cleveland (Hopkins), Dallas/Fort Worth, Denver (Stapleton), Detroit Metropolitan, Honolulu, Houston Intercontinental, Kansas City, MO, Las Vegas (McCarran), Los Angeles, Miami, Minneapolis/St Paul, New Orleans, New York (John F. Kennedy), New York (La Guardia), New York (Newark), Orlando, Philadelphia, Phoenix (Sky Harbor), Pittsburgh, Portland, St Louis (Lambert), Salt Lake City, San Diego (Lindbergh Field), San Francisco, Seattle-Tacoma, Tampa, Washington DC (Dulles) and Washington DC (National).

The leading airports in 1995 on the basis of aircraft departures completed were Dallas/Fort Worth International (382,000); Chicago, O'Hare (381,000); Atlanta, Hartsfield International (346,000). The leading domestic routes for 1995 were New York to/from Los Angeles (2,991,060 passengers), New York to/from Chicago (2,981,610) and Honolulu to/from Kahului, Maui (2,761,470).

US flag carriers in scheduled service had 547·4m. revenue passengers enplaned in 1995, with 540,400m. revenue passenger miles.

Shipping. On 1 Oct. 1997 the US merchant marine included 478 sea-going vessels of 1,000 gross tons or over, with an aggregate 16·8m. DWT. This includes 162 tankers of 9·7m. DWT.

On 1 Oct. 1994, US merchant ocean-going vessels were employed as follows: Active, 345 of 15·2m. DWT, of which 132 of 4·7m. DWT were foreign trade, 129 of 7·3m. DWT in domestic trade and 24 of 1·8m. DWT in foreign to foreign operations. Inactive vessels totalled 4·7m. DWT; 26 of 1·4m. DWT privately owned were laid up and 136 of 2·7m. DWT were Government-owned National Defense reserve fleet. Of the total vessels in the US fleet, 333 of 15·1m. DWT were privately owned.

US exports and imports carried on dry cargo and tanker vessels in 1994 totalled 899·1m. long tons, of which 35m. long tons were carried in US flag vessels. In 1993, 54,838 vessels entered, and 53,637 cleared, all US ports.

Telecommunications. The US Postal Service superseded the Post Office Department on 1 July 1971.

Postal business for the years ended 30 Sept. included the following items:

	1993	1994	1995	1996
Number of post offices	28,728	28,657	39,749	38,212
Operating revenue ($1,000)	47,418,000	49,252,000	54,293,000	56,402,000
Expenditures ($1,000)	46,322,000	48,455,000	50,730,200	53,112,500

Regional private companies formed from the American Telephone and Telegraph Co. after its dissolution in 1995 ('Baby Bells') operate the telephone, telegraph, telex and electronic transmission services system at the national and local levels. Total domestic access lines in 1994, 157m. In 1996 there were 32·5m. mobile telephone users.

Legislation on the media and telecommunications of 1996 coming into force on 31 March 1999 deregulates the market while preserving safeguards against over-concentration of individual ownership: a single company may not control a network reaching more than 35% of TV viewers, or produce a newspaper and a television service in the same market. Local companies are now permitted to operate long-distance telephone services and also cable TV services.

The licensing agency for broadcasting stations is the Federal Communications

Commission, an independent federal body composed of 5 Commissioners appointed by the President. Its regulatory activities comprise: Allocation of spectrum space; consideration of applications to operate individual stations; and regulation of their operations. In 1994 there were 10,022 commercial radio stations, 1,145 commercial TV stations, 367 non-commercial TV stations and 11,230 cable TV systems. Programming is targeted to appeal to a given segment of the population or audience taste. There are 5 national TV networks (3 commercial; colour by NTSC) with 46 national cable networks. All major cities have network affiliates and additional commercial stations.

Broadcasting to countries abroad is conducted by The Voice of America, which functions under a 7-member council nominated by the President and reviewed by Congress. In 1996 Voice of America had 126m. listeners.

In 1993 there were 520m. radio and 215m. TV receivers in use.

Cinemas. In Jan. 1994 there were 25,737 screens (25,105 in 1993), including 850 drive-ins. Attendance in 1993 was 1,244m. (1,173m. in 1992). 431 full-length films were made in 1993.

Press. In 1995 there were 1,533 daily papers with an average circulation of 58,200,000. These included 656 morning papers, 891 evening papers and 888 Sunday papers (circulation, 61,200,000). In 1996, 58·2m. newspapers were sold on average every day. 40,584 book titles were published in 1994.

SOCIAL INSTITUTIONS

Justice. Legal controversies may be decided in two systems of courts: The federal courts, with jurisdiction confined to certain matters enumerated in Article III of the Constitution, and the state courts, with jurisdiction in all other proceedings. The federal courts have jurisdiction exclusive of the state courts in criminal prosecutions for the violation of federal statutes, in civil cases involving the government, in bankruptcy cases and in admiralty proceedings, and have jurisdiction concurrent with the state courts over suits between parties from different states, and certain suits involving questions of federal law.

The highest court is the Supreme Court of the US, which reviews cases from the lower federal courts and certain cases originating in state courts involving questions of federal law. It is the final arbiter of all questions involving federal statutes and the Constitution; and it has the power to invalidate any federal or state law or executive action which it finds repugnant to the Constitution. This court, consisting of 9 justices appointed by the President who receive salaries of $164,100 a year (the Chief Justice, $171,500), meets from Oct. until June every year. For the term ended June 1996 it disposed of 6,692 cases, deciding 129 on their merits. In the remainder of cases it either summarily affirms lower court decisions or declines to review. A few suits, usually brought by state governments, originate in the Supreme Court, but issues of fact are mostly referred to a master.

The US courts of appeals number 13 (in 11 circuits composed of 3 or more states and 1 circuit for the District of Columbia and 1 Court of Appeals for the Federal Circuit); the 179 circuit judges receive salaries of $141,700 a year. Any party to a suit in a lower federal court usually has a right of appeal to one of these courts. In addition, there are direct appeals to these courts from many federal administrative agencies. In the year ending 30 June 1997, 53,742 appeals were filed in the courts of appeals, including 1,417 in the Federal Circuit.

The trial courts in the federal system are the US district courts, of which there are 89 in the 50 states, 1 in the District of Columbia and 1 each in the Commonwealth of Puerto Rico and the Territories of the Virgin Islands, Guam and the Northern Marianas. Each state has at least 1 US district court, and 3 states have 4 apiece. Each district court has from 1 to 28 judgeships. There are 649 US district judges ($133,600 a year), who received 265,151 civil cases and 68,307 criminal defendants from 1 July 1996 to 30 June 1997.

In addition to these courts of general jurisdiction, there are special federal courts of limited jurisdiction. The US Court of Federal Claims (16 judges at $133,600 a year) decides claims for money damages against the federal government in a wide variety of matters; the Court of International Trade (9 judges at $133,600) determines controversies concerning the classification and valuation of imported merchandise.

The judges of all these courts are appointed by the President with the approval of the Senate; to assure their independence, they hold office during good behaviour and cannot have their salaries reduced. This does not apply to judges in the Territories, who hold their offices for a term of 10 years or to judges of the US Court of Federal Claims. The judges may retire with full pay at the age of 70 years if they have served a period of 10 years, or at 65 if they have 15 years of service, but they are subject to call for such judicial duties as they are willing to undertake. 11 US judges up to 1997 have been involved in impeachment proceedings, of whom 7 were convicted and removed from office.

In 1997, of the 265,151 civil cases filed in the district courts, 167,807 arose under various federal statutes (such as labour, social security, tax, patent, securities, antitrust and civil rights laws); 52,710 involved personal injury or property damage claims; 38,858 dealt with contracts; and 5,761 were actions concerning real property.

Among the 69,052 criminal defendants (48,682 criminal cases) filed in 1997 in the district courts, 25,090 persons were charged with alleged infractions of drug laws; 11,832 persons were charged with miscellaneous general offences; 11,664 with embezzlement and fraud; 4,089 for larceny and theft; 7,016 were charged with immigration violations; 1,763 with robbery; and 1,663 with forgery and counterfeiting and fraud.

Persons convicted of federal crimes may be fined, released on probation under the supervision of the probation officers of the federal courts, confined in prison, or confined in prison with a period of supervised release to follow, also under the supervision of probation officers of the federal courts. Federal prisoners are confined in 87 institutions incorporating various security levels that are operated by the Bureau of Prisons. Prisoners confined in Federal and State Prisons at June 1995, numbered 1,104,074 (6·1% women).

The state courts have jurisdiction over all civil and criminal cases arising under state laws, but decisions of the state courts of last resort as to the validity of treaties or of laws of the USA, or on other questions arising under the Constitution, are subject to review by the Supreme Court of the US. The state court systems are generally similar to the federal system, to the extent that they generally have a number of trial courts and intermediate appellate courts, and a single court of last resort. The highest court in each state is usually called the Supreme Court or Court of Appeals with a Chief Justice and Associate Justices, usually elected but sometimes appointed by the Governor with the advice and consent of the State Senate or other advisory body; they usually hold office for a term of years, but in some instances for life or during good behaviour. The lowest tribunals are usually those of Justices of the Peace; many towns and cities have municipal and police courts, with power to commit for trial in criminal matters and to determine misdemeanours for violation of the municipal ordinances; they frequently try civil cases involving limited amounts of damages.

There were no executions from 1968 to 1976. The US Supreme Court had held the death penalty, as applied in general criminal statutes, to contravene the eighth and fourteenth amendments of the US constitution, as a cruel and unusual punishment when used so irregularly and rarely as to destroy its deterrent value. The death penalty was reinstated by the Supreme Court in 1976, but has not been authorized in Alaska, the District of Columbia, Hawaii, Iowa, Kansas, Maine, Massachusetts, Michigan, Minnesota, North Dakota, Rhode Island, Vermont, West Virginia and Wisconsin.

Religion. *The Yearbook of American and Canadian Churches,* published by the National Council of the Churches of Christ in the USA, New York, gave the following figures available from official statisticians of church bodies: The principal religious bodies (numerically or historically) or groups of religious bodies are shown below:

	No. of churches	Membership (in 1,000)
Protestant Churches		
Baptist bodies		
Southern Baptist Convention	40,039	15,663
National Baptist Convention, USA	33,000	8,200

Protestant Churches	No. of churches	Membership (in 1,000)
Baptist bodies—contd.		
National Baptist Convention of America, Inc.	2,500	3,500
American Baptist Churches in the USA	5,823	1,517
American Baptist Association	1,705	250
Conservative Baptist Association of America	1,084	200
Free Will Baptists	2,496	208
Baptist Missionary Association of America	1,355	231
Christian Church (Disciples of Christ)	4,036	930
Christian Churches and Churches of Christ	5,579	1,071
Church of the Nazarene	5,135	602
Churches of Christ	13,020	1,655
The Episcopal Church	7,415	2,537
Jehovah's Witnesses	10,541	966
Latter-Day Saints:		
Church of Jesus Christ of Latter-Day Saints (Mormon)	10,417	4,712
Reorganized Church of Jesus Christ of Latter-Day Saints	1,160	178
Lutheran bodies		
Evangelical Lutheran Church in America	10,955	5,190
The Lutheran Church-Missouri Synod	6,154	2,595
Wisconsin Evangelical Lutheran Synod	1,252	412
Mennonite churches:		
Mennonite Church	986	91
Old Order Amish	898	81
Methodist bodies:		
United Methodist Church	36,361	8,539
African Methodist Episcopal Church	8,000	3,500
African Methodist Episcopal Zion Church	3,098	1,231
Wesleyan Church (USA)	1,609	117
Pentecostal bodies:		
The Church of God in Christ	15,300	5,500
Assemblies of God	11,764	2,325
Church of God (Cleveland, Tenn.)	5,918	723
United Pentecostal Church International	3,730	550
Presbyterian bodies:		
Presbyterian Church (USA)	11,399	3,698
Presbyterian Church in America	1,263	258
Reformed Churches:		
Reformed Church in America	915	309
Christian Reformed Church in North America	737	211
The Salvation Army	1,222	443
United Church of Christ	6,264	1,555
Seventh-day Adventist Church	4,303	775
Roman Catholic Church	19,723	60,191
Orthodox Churches	1,750	5,302
Non-Christian Religions:		
Hindus	–	910,000
Baha'i	–	300
Islam[1]	–	5,100
Jews	2,876	4,300

[1] Figures include Canada.

Education. Elementary and secondary education is mainly a state responsibility. Each state and the District of Columbia has a system of free public schools, established by law, with courses covering 12 years plus kindergarten. There are 3 structural patterns in common use; the K8-4 plan, meaning kindergarten plus 8 elementary grades followed by 4 high school grades; the K6-3-3 plan, or kindergarten plus 6 elementary grades followed by a 3-year junior high school and a 3-year senior high school; and the K5-3-4 plan, kindergarten plus 5 elementary grades followed by a 3-year middle school and a 4-year high school. All plans lead to high-school graduation, usually at age 17 or 18. Vocational education is an integral part of secondary education. Some states also have 2-year colleges in which education is provided at a nominal cost. Each state has delegated a large degree of control of the educational programme to local school districts (numbering 14,883 in school year 1995–96), each with a board of education (usually 3 to 9 members) selected locally and serving mostly without pay. The school policies of the local school districts must be in accord with the laws and the regulations of their state Departments of Education. While regulations differ from one jurisdiction to another, in general it may be said that school attendance is compulsory from age 7 to 16.

'Charter schools' are legal entities outside the school boards administration. They retain the basics of public school education, but may offer unconventional curricula and hours of attendance. Founders may be parents, teachers, public bodies or commercial firms. Organization and conditions depend upon individual states' legislation. The first charter schools were set up in Minnesota in 1991.

The Census Bureau estimates that in Nov. 1979 only 1m. or 0·6% of the 170m. persons who were 14 years of age or older were unable to read and write; in 1930 the percentage was 4·8. In 1940 a new category was established—the 'functionally illiterate', meaning those who had completed fewer than 5 years of elementary schooling; for persons 25 years of age or over this percentage was 1·8 in March 1996 (for the Black population it was 2·3%); it was 0·9% for white and 0·4% for Blacks in the 25–29-year-old group. The Bureau reported that in March 1996 81·7% of all persons 25 years old and over had completed 4 years of high school or more, and that 23·6% had completed 4 or more years of college. In the age group 25 to 29, 87·3% had completed 4 years of high school or more, and 27·1% had completed 4 or more years of college.

In the autumn of 1995, 14,262,000 students (7,919,000 women) were enrolled in 3,706 colleges and universities; 2,169,000 were first-time students. About 34·3% of the population between the ages of 18 and 24 were enrolled in colleges and universities.

Public elementary and secondary school revenue is supplied from the county and other local sources (46·4% in 1994–95), state sources (46·8%) and federal sources (6·8%). In 1996–76 expenditure for public elementary and secondary education totalled about $313,500m., including $281000m. for current operating expenses, $25,500m. for capital outlay and $7,000m. for interest on school debt. The current expenditure per pupil in average daily attendance was about $6,560. The total cost per pupil, also including capital outlay and interest, amounted to about $7,370. Estimated total expenditures, for private elementary and secondary schools in 1996–97 were about $26,200m. In 1996–97 college and university spending totalled about $224,500m., of which about $142,600m. was spent by institutions under public control. The federal government contributed about 12% of total current-fund revenue; state governments, 23%; student tuition and fees, 28%; and all other sources, 37%.

Vocational education below college grade, including the training of teachers to conduct such education, has been federally aided since 1918. Federal support for vocational education in 1995–96 amounted to about $1,087m. Many public high schools offer vocational courses in addition to their usual academic programmes.

Summary of statistics of regular schools (public and private), teachers and pupils for 1995–96 (compiled by the US National Center for Education Statistics):

Schools by level	Number of schools[1]	Teachers (in 1,000)	Enrolment (in 1,000)
Elementary schools:			
Public	63,961	1,546	29,429
Private	23,543[2]	269	4,427
Secondary schools:			
Public	23,793	1,531	15,411
Private	10,555[2]	111	1,260
Higher education:			
Public	1,655	645	11,092
Private	2,051	270	3,169
Total	125,558	3,894	64,788

[1] Schools with both elementary and secondary grades are counted twice, once with the elementary and once with the secondary schools.   [2] Data for 1993–94.

Most of the private elementary and secondary schools are affiliated with religious denominations. In 1995–96 there were 7,022 Roman Catholic elementary schools with 1·88m. pupils and 118,800 teachers, and 1,228 secondary schools with 607,000 pupils and 48,000 teachers.

During the school year 1996–97 high-school graduates numbered about 2,564,000 (of whom about 2,298,000 were from public schools). Institutions of higher education conferred about 1,183,000 bachelor's degrees during the year 1996–97, 529,000 associate's degrees; 410,000 master's degrees; 44,000 doctorates; and 77,000 first professional degrees. In 1995–96 the federal government provided $6,164m. in grants and work-study programmes and $21,541m. in loans and other financial assistance to students.

During the academic year 1995–96, 458,000 foreign students were enrolled in American colleges and universities. The countries with the largest numbers of students in American colleges were: Japan, 46,300; China, 42,500; South Korea, 37,100; India, 30,600; Taiwan, 30,500; Canada, 23,000.

In 1995–96, 89,200 US students were enrolled at colleges and universities abroad. The country attracting the most students from the USA was the United Kingdom, with 20,100.

School enrolment, Oct. 1995, embraced 96·0% of the children who were 5 and 6 years old; 98·9% of the children aged 7–13 years; 98·9% of those aged 14–15, 93·6% of those aged 16–17 and 59·4% of those aged 18–19.

The US National Center for Education Statistics estimates the total enrolment in the autumn of 1997 at all of the country's elementary, secondary and higher educational institutions (public and private) at 66·3m. (65·4m. in the autumn of 1996).

The number of teachers in regular public and private elementary and secondary schools in the autumn of 1997 was expected to increase slightly to 3,071,000. The average annual salary of the public school teachers was $38,550 in 1996–97.

Health. Admission to the practice of medicine (for both doctors of medicine and doctors of osteopathic medicine) is controlled in each state by examining boards directly representing the profession and acting with authority conferred by state law. Although there are a number of variations, the usual time now required to complete training is 8 years beyond the secondary school with up to 3 or more years of additional graduate training. Certification as a specialist may require between 3 and 5 more years of graduate training plus experience in practice. In Jan. 1994 the estimated number of active physicians (MD and DO—in all forms of practice) in the USA, Puerto Rico and outlying US areas was 684,400.

Active dentists in Dec. 1994 numbered 190,000.

Number of hospitals listed by the American Hospital Association in 1995 was 6,291, with 1,080,601 beds and 33,282,124 admissions during the year; average daily census was 709,746. Of the total, 299 hospitals with 77,079 beds were operated by the federal government; 1,370 with 157,270 beds by state and local government; 3,029 with 609,729 beds by non-profit organizations (including church groups); 752 with 105,737 beds are investor-owned. The categories of non-federal hospitals are 5,220 short-term general and special hospitals with 874,286 beds; 112 non-federal long-term general and special hospitals with 18,765 beds; 657 psychiatric hospitals with 110,257 beds; 3 tuberculosis hospitals with 214 beds.

Personal health-care costs in 1994 totalled $832,500m., distributed as follows: Hospital care, $341,700m.; doctors, $182,700m.; nursing-home care, $74,200m.; drugs, $79,000m.; dentists, $40,000m.; medical durables, $13,200m.; home health care, $24,200m.; other personal health care, $20,900m.

Welfare. Social welfare legislation was chiefly the province of the various states until the adoption of the Social Security Act of 14 Aug. 1935. This as amended provides for a federal system of old-age, survivors and disability insurance; health insurance for the aged and disabled; supplemental security income for the aged, blind and disabled; federal state unemployment insurance; and federal grants to states for public assistance (medical assistance for the aged and aid to families with dependent children generally and for maternal and child-health and child-welfare services). Legislation of Aug. 1996 began the transfer of aid administration back to the states, and also restricts the provision of aid to a maximum period of 5 years, and abolishes benefits to immigrants (both legal and illegal) for the first 5 years of their residence in the USA. The Social Security Administration (formerly part of the Department of Health and Human Services but an independent agency since March 1995) has responsibility for the programmes—old-age, survivors and disability insurance and supplemental security income. The Administration for Children and Families (ACF), an agency of the Department of Health and Human Services, is responsible for federal programmes which promote the economic and social well-being of families, children, individuals and communities. ACF has federal responsibility for the following programmes: The Aid to Families with Dependent Children Program (providing cash assistance to family and children in the 50 states, the District of Columbia, Guam, Puerto Rico and the Virgin Islands); low income energy assistance; Head Start; child care; child protective services; and a community services block grant. The ACF also has federal responsibility for social service programmes for children, youth, native Americans and persons with developmental disabilities.

The Administration of Aging (AOA), an agency of the Department of Health and Human Services, serves older persons and their families with social, nutritional, education, and aging-related research and demonstration projects through the administration of the Older Americans Act. In addition, AOA is the focal point for aging policy within the Federal government. The Assistant Secretary for Aging is the primary advocate for the elderly in the USA. In 1995–96, $830m. was expended through a network of 57 State Units on Aging, 661 Area Agencies on Aging, 228 tribal organizations, 6,000 senior centres, and more than 27,000 service providers. More than 250m. meals were also provided through this programme.

The Health Care Financing Administration, an agency of the Health and Human Services Department, has federal responsibility for health insurance for the aged and disabled. Unemployment insurance is the responsibility of the Department of Labor.

In 1994 an average of 14·2m. persons (adults and children) were receiving payments under Aid to Families with Dependent Children (average monthly payment, $376 per family). Total payments under Aid to Families with Dependent Children were $22,800m. in 1994. The role of Child Support Enforcement is to ensure that children are supported by their parents. Money collected is for children who live with only one parent because of divorce, separation or out-of-wedlock birth. In 1993, nearly $9,000m. was collected on behalf of these children.

In 1994, federal appropriations for the social services block grant amounted to $2,800m. In addition, 1994 federal appropriations for child care totalled $893m. Included in this amount were $109m. for persons with developmental disabilities and $38·6m. for native Americans.

The Social Security Act provides for protection against the cost of medical care through Medicare, a two-part programme of health insurance for people age 65 and over, people of any age with permanent kidney failure, and for certain disabled people under age 65 who receive Social Security disability benefits. In 1995, payments totalling $116,400m. were made under the hospital portion of Medicare on behalf of 37m. people. During the same period, $65,000m. was paid under the voluntary medical insurance portion of Medicare on behalf of 36m. people.

In 1995, 141m. persons worked in employment covered by old-age, survivors and disability insurance.

In 1996 about 43·3m. beneficiaries were on the rolls, and the average benefit paid to a retired worker (not counting any benefits paid to his/her dependants) was about $724 per month. Full retirement benefits are now payable at age 65, with reduced benefits available as early as age 62. Beginning in 2000, the age for full retirement benefits will gradually increase until it reaches 67 in 2027.

In Dec. 1995, 6·5m. persons were receiving Supplementary Security Income payments, including 1·4m. persons aged 65 or over and over 5·1m. disabled or blind persons, including nearly 1m. children. Payments, including supplemental amounts from various states, totalled $27,600m. in 1995.

Other block grants awarded by the Administration for Children and Families included $385·5m. for community services block grant programmes for 1993–94, and $1,300m. for the low income home energy assistance programme (LIHEAP).

During 1989, the Public Health Services awarded a total of $554·3m. for maternal and child health services, $465·3m. as block grants to the States, $82·1m. for special projects of regional and national significance, and $6·9m. for genetic screening. Other block grants awarded by the Public Health Service in 1988 included $88m. for preventive health; $487m. for alcohol, drug abuse and mental health; $155m. for alcohol and drug abuse treatment and rehabilitation. In 1989, $414·8m. was awarded for community health centres; $45·6m. for migrant health centres; $20·6m. for efforts to reduce infant mortality; $3·2m. for black lung clinics; and $135·1m. for family planning.

DIPLOMATIC REPRESENTATIVES

Of the USA in Great Britain (Grosvenor Sq., London, W1A 1AE)
Ambassador: Philip Lader.

Of Great Britain in the USA (3100 Massachusetts Ave., Washington, DC 20008)
Ambassador: Sir John Kerr, KCMG.

Of the United States to the United Nations
Ambassador: Bill Richardson.

Of the United States to the European Union
Ambassador: Vernon Weaver.

Further Reading

OFFICIAL STATISTICAL INFORMATION

The Office of Management and Budget, Washington, DC 20503 is part of the Executive Office of the President; it is responsible for co-ordinating all the statistical work of the different Federal Government agencies. The Office does not collect or publish data itself. The main statistical agencies are as follows:

(1) Data User Services Division, Bureau of the Census, Department of Commerce, Washington, DC 20233. Responsible for decennial censuses of population and housing, quinquennial census of agriculture, manufactures and business; current statistics on population and the labour force, manufacturing activity and commodity production, trade and services, foreign trade, state and local government finances and operations. (*Statistical Abstract of the United States*, annual, and others).

(2) Bureau of Labor Statistics, Department of Labor, 441 G Street NW, Washington, DC 20212. (*Monthly Labor Review* and others).

(3) Information Division, Economic Research Service, Department of Agriculture, Washington, DC 20250. (*Agricultural Statistics*, annual, and others).

(4) National Center for Health Statistics, Department of Health and Human Services, 3700 East-West Highway, Hyattsville, MD 20782. (*Vital Statistics of the United States*, monthly and annual, and others).

(5) Bureau of Mines Office of Technical Information, Department of the Interior, Washington, DC 20241. (*Minerals Yearbook*, annual, and others).

(6) Office of Energy Information Services, Energy Information Administration, Department of Energy, Washington, DC 20461.

(7) Statistical Publications, Department of Commerce, Room 5062 Main Commerce, 14th St and Constitution Avenue NW, Washington, DC 20230; the Department's Bureau of Economic Analysis and its Office of Industry and Trade Information are the main collectors of data.

(8) Center for Education Statistics, Department of Education, 555 New Jersey Avenue NW, Washington, DC 20208.

(9) Public Correspondence Division, Office of the Assistant Secretary of Defense (Public Affairs P.C.), The Pentagon, Washington, DC 20301-1400.

(10) Bureau of Justice Statistics, Department of Justice, 633 Indiana Avenue NW, Washington, DC 20531.

(11) Public Inquiry, APA 200, Federal Aviation Administration, Department of Transportation, 800 Independence Avenue SW, Washington, DC 20591.

(12) Office of Public Affairs, Federal Highway Administration, Department of Transportation, 400 7th St. SW, Washington, DC 20590.

(13) Statistics Division, Internal Revenue Service, Department of the Treasury, 1201 E St. NW, Washington, DC 20224.

Statistics on the economy are also published by the Division of Research and Statistics, Federal Reserve Board, Washington, DC 20551; the Congressional Joint Committee on the Economy, Capitol; the Office of the Secretary, Department of the Treasury, 1500 Pennsylvania Avenue NW, Washington, DC 20220.

OTHER OFFICIAL PUBLICATIONS

Economic Report of the President. Annual. Bureau of the Census. *Statistical Abstract of the United States.* Annual. *Historical Statistics of the United States, Colonial Times to 1970.*
United States Government Manual. Washington. Annual.
The official publications of the USA are issued by the US Government Printing Office and are distributed by the Superintendent of Documents, who issued in 1940 a cumulative *Catalog of the Public Documents of the. . . Congress and of All the Departments of the Government of the United States.* This *Catalog* is kept up to date by *United States Government Publications, Monthly Catalog* with annual index and supplemented by *Price Lists.* Each *Price List* is devoted to a special subject or type of material.
Treaties and other International Acts of the United States of America (Edited by Hunter Miller), 8 vols. Washington, 1929–48. This edition stops in 1863. It may be supplemented by *Treaties, Conventions. . . Between the US and Other Powers, 1776–1937* (Edited by William M. Malloy and others). 4 vols. 1909–38. A new Treaty Series, *US Treaties and Other International Agreements* was started in 1950.
Writings on American History. Washington, annual from 1902 (except 1904–5 and 1941–47).

NON-OFFICIAL PUBLICATIONS

The Cambridge Economic History of the United States. vol. 1–. CUP, 1996–

Brogan, H., *The Longman History of the United States of America.* London, 1985
Fawcett, E. and Thomas, T., *America and the Americans.* London, 1983
Foner, E. and Garraty, J. A. (eds.) *The Reader's Companion to American History.* New York, 1992
Herstein, S. R. and Robbins, N., *United States of America.* [Bibliography] Oxford and Santa Barbara (CA), 1982
Lord, C. L. and E. H., *Historical Atlas of the US.* Rev. ed. New York, 1969
Jentleson, B. W. and Paterson, T. G. (eds.) *Encyclopedia of US Foreign Relations.* 4 vols. OUP, 1997
Merriam, L. A. and Oberly, J. (eds.) *United States History: an Annotated Bibliography.* Manchester Univ. Press, 1995
Morison, S. E. with Commager, H. S., *The Growth of the American Republic.* 2 vols. 5th ed. OUP, 1962–63
Norton, M. B., *People and Nation: the History of the United States.* 4th ed. 2 vols. New York, 1994
Pfucha, F. P., *Handbook for Research in American History: a Guide to Bibliographies and Other Reference Works.* 2nd ed. Nebraska Univ. Press, 1994
Who's Who in America. Annual

National library: The Library of Congress, Independence Ave. SE, Washington, DC 20540.
Librarian: James H. Billington.
National statistical office: Bureau of the Census, Washington, DC 20233.
Website: http://www.census.gov

STATES AND TERRITORIES

See also the section 'State and Local Government' under UNITED STATES. Constitution and Government.
Against the names of the Governors and the Secretaries of State, (D.) stands for Democrat and (R.) for Republican.
Figures for the revenues and expenditures of the various states are those of the Federal Bureau of the Census unless otherwise stated, which takes the original state figures and arranges them on a common pattern so that those of one state can be compared with those of any other.

Further Reading

Official publications of the various states and insular possessions are listed in the *Monthly Check-List of State Publications*, issued by the Library of Congress since 1910.
The Book of the States. Biennial. Council of State Governments, Lexington, 1953 ff.
State Government Finances. Annual. Dept. of Commerce, 1966 ff.
Bureau of the Census. *State and Metropolitan Area Data Book*. Irregular.—*County and City Data Book*. Irregular.

Hill, K. Q., *Democracy in the 50 States*. Nebraska Univ. Press, 1995

ALABAMA

KEY HISTORICAL EVENTS. The first European explorers were Spanish, including Hernando de Soto in 1540, but the first permanent European settlement was French, as part of French Louisiana after 1699. During the 17th and 18th centuries the British, Spanish and French all fought for control of the territory; it passed to Britain in 1763 and thence to the US in 1783, except for a Spanish enclave on Mobile Bay, which lasted until 1813. Alabama was organized as a Territory in 1817 and was admitted to the Union as a state on 14 Dec. 1819.

The economy was then based on cotton, grown in white-owned plantations by black slave labour imported since 1719. Alabama seceded from the Union at the beginning of the Civil War (1861) and joined the Confederate States of America; its capital Montgomery became the Confederate capital. After the defeat of the Confederacy the state was readmitted to the Union in 1878. Attempts made during the reconstruction period to find a role for the newly-freed black slaves who made up about 50% of the population—largely failed, and when whites regained political control in the 1870s a strict policy of segregation came into force.

At the same time Birmingham began to develop as an important centre of iron- and steel-making. Most of the state was still rural. In 1915 a boll-weevil epidemic attacked the cotton and forced diversification into other farm produce. More industries developed from the power schemes of the Tennessee Valley Authority in the 1930s.

The black population remained mainly rural, poor and without political power, until the 1960s when confrontations on the issue of civil rights produced reforms.

TERRITORY AND POPULATION. Alabama is bounded in the north by Tennessee, east by Georgia, south by Florida and the Gulf of Mexico and west by Mississippi. Land area, 50,750 sq. miles (131,443 sq. km). Census population, 1 April 1990, 4,040,587 (60·4% urban), an increase of 3·87% since 1980. Population estimate (1995), 4,252,982 (48·0% male). Births, 1995, 60,764 (14·7 per 1,000 population); deaths, 42,321 (10·3), infant deaths (under 1 year), 592 (9·8 per 1,000 live births); marriages, 42,234 (10·3); divorces, 25,813 (6·3).

Population in 5 census years was:

	White	Black	Indian	Asiatic	Total	Per sq. mile
1930	1,700,844	944,834	465	105	2,646,248	51·3
1960	2,283,609	980,271	1,726	915	3,266,521	64·0

	White	Black	All others	Total	Per sq. mile
1970	2,533,831	903,467	6,867	3,444,165	66·7
1980	2,872,621	996,335	24,932	3,893,888	74·9
1990	2,975,797	1,020,705	44,085	4,040,587	79·6

Of the total population in 1990, 47·9% were male, 60·4% were urban and 68·7% were 21 years or older.

The large cities (1994 estimate) were: Birmingham, 264,527 (metropolitan area, 872,834); Mobile, 204,490 (512,657); Montgomery (the capital), 195,471 (312,141); Huntsville, 170,984 (316,909); Tuscaloosa, 79,797 (156,422).

CLIMATE. Birmingham. Jan. 46°F (7·8°C), July 80°F (26·7°C). Annual rainfall 54" (1,346 mm). Mobile. Jan. 52°F (11·1°C), July 82°F (27·8°C). Annual rainfall 63"

(1,577 mm). Montgomery. Jan. 49°F (9·4°C), July 81°F (27·2°C). Annual rainfall 53"(1,321 mm). The growing season ranges from 190 days (north) to 270 days (south). Alabama belongs to the Gulf Coast climate zone (*see* UNITED STATES: Climate).

CONSTITUTION AND GOVERNMENT. The present constitution dates from 1901; it has had 615 amendments (as at November 1996). The legislature consists of a Senate of 35 members and a House of Representatives of 105 members, all elected for 4 years. The Governor and Lieut.-Governor are elected for 4 years.

The state is represented in Congress by 7 representatives. Applicants for registration must take an oath of allegiance to the United States and fill out a questionnaire to the satisfaction of the registrars. In the 1996 presidential election Dole polled 771,529 votes; Clinton, 662,165; Perot, 92,149.

Montgomery is the capital.

Governor: Forrest H. (Fob) James, Jr. (R.), 1995–99 ($87,643).
Lieut.-Governor: Don Siegelman (D.), ($3,780).
Secretary of State: Jim Bennett (D.) ($61,779).

BUDGET. The total net revenue for the fiscal year 1994 was $11,599m.; total net expenditure was $10,815m. ($3,969m. on education, $2,168m. on public welfare, $487m. on health, $884m. on highways).

The outstanding debt in 1994 amounted to $3,854m.

Per capita income (1995) was $18,781.

NATURAL RESOURCES

Minerals. Principal minerals, 1995 (in net 1,000 tons): Limestone, 30,484; coal, 24,640; sand and gravel, 10,039. Total mineral output (1986) was valued at $2,001m.; non-fuel minerals (1990) $562m.

Agriculture. The number of farms in 1995 was some 47,000, covering 10·2m. acres; the average farm had 217 acres and was valued at $1,262 per acre in 1995.

Cash receipts from farm marketings, 1996: Crops, $815,000,000; livestock and poultry products, $2,363,000,000; and total, $3,178,000,000. Principal sources: broilers, cattle and calves, eggs, hogs, dairy products, greenhouses and nurseries, peanuts, soybeans, cotton, and vegetables. In 1994 broilers accounted for the largest percentage of cash receipts from farm marketings; cattle and calves were second, eggs third, cotton fourth.

Forestry. Area of national forest lands, 1992, 659,000 acres. Area of commercial timberland, 1990, 21,931,600 acres, of which 1,161,700 acres were public forests and 20,769,900 acres private forests. In 1990, 23,075m. cu. ft of timber was inventorized. Harvest volumes in 1995, 294·12m. cu. ft softwood saw timber, 78·63m. cu. ft hardwood saw timber, 744·47m. cu. ft paper fibre and 11·74m. cu. ft poles. Total harvest, 1994, was $1,128·9m. cu. ft. The estimated delivered timber value of forest products in 1994 was $1,359m.

INDUSTRY. Alabama is both an industrial and service-oriented state. The chief industries are textiles and clothing, paper, food, lumber and wood products. In 1995 1,811,870 were employed in non-agricultural sectors of which 381,933 were in government; 379,503 in trade; 540,041 in services; 103,824 in transport and public utilities; 405,318 in manufacturing; 131,334 in construction.

TOURISM. In 1996 tourists spent approximately $4·7 billion in Alabama, representing an increase of 8% over 1995 spending.

COMMUNICATIONS

Roads. Paved roads of all classes in 1996 totalled 70,255 miles; total highways, 93,337 miles. Registered motor vehicles, 1996, 4,315,381.

Railways. At Sept. 1997 the railways had a length of 5,072 miles including side and yard tracks.

Civil Aviation. In 1997 the state had 98 public-use airports. Eight airports are for commercial service, three are relief airports for Birmingham and the rest, general aviation.

Shipping. There are 1,600 miles of navigable inland water and 50 miles of Gulf Coast. The only deep-water port is Mobile, with a large ocean-going trade; total tonnage (1996), 17·6m. tons. The Alabama State Docks also operates a system of 10 inland docks; there are several privately-run inland docks.

SOCIAL INSTITUTIONS

Justice. In 1996 there were 365 law enforcement agencies and 5 state agencies employing 9,660 sworn and 4,643 civilian people. There were 203,463 offences reported of which 21% were cleared by arrest. Total property value stolen was $185,871,146 of which 19% was recovered. In total, for past and present felony and misdemeanour crimes, there were 36,900 people arrested for Part I offences, 180,096 for Part II offences, 15,580 for drug violations, and 39,564 for alcohol violations. As of 30 Sept. 1996, there were 21,481 people in prison or community-based facilities of which 152 were on death row awaiting execution. There were also 34,051 people on probation and/or parole.

Following the reinstatement of the death penalty by the US Supreme Court in 1976, death sentences have been awarded since 1983.

In 41 counties the sale of alcoholic beverage is permitted, and in 26 counties it is prohibited; but it is permitted in 8 cities within those 26 counties. Draught beverages are permitted in 22 counties.

Religion. Membership in selected religious bodies (in 1993): Southern Baptist Convention (1,049,441), Black Baptist (estimated 315,331), United Methodist Church (264,968), African Methodist Episcopal Zion Church (134,305), Roman Catholic (137,834 adherents), Churches of Christ (91,660), Assemblies of God (38,442).

Education. In the school year 1995–96 the 1,333 public elementary and high schools required 43,796 teachers to teach 735,912 students enrolled in grades K–12. In 1995–96 there were 16 public senior institutions with 127,465 students and 4,887 faculty members. In 1994–95 the average salary of public school teachers was $31,144. As of autumn 1996–97 the 19 community colleges had 75,879 students and 4,004 faculty members; 2 public junior colleges had 3,731 students and 192 faculty members; 10 public technical colleges had 9,342 students and 566 faculty members.

Health. In 1996 there were 123 hospitals licensed by the State Board of Health, 7 exempt from licensure with a total of 20,663 beds. In 1992 there were 5,281 patients in hospitals for mental illness and 1,449 residents in facilities for the mentally retarded.

Welfare. In June 1997 Alabama paid supplements (to federal welfare payments) to 684 recipients of old-age assistance, receiving an average of $49·52 each; 772 permanently and totally disabled, $55·68; 19 blind, $48·79. Combined state–federal aid to dependent children was paid to 31,981 families, average $139·96 per family.

Further Reading

Alabama Official and Statistical Register. Montgomery. Quadrennial
Alabama County Data Book. Alabama Dept. of Economic and Community Affairs. Annual
Directory of Health Care Facilities. Alabama State Board of Health
Economic Abstract of Alabama. Center for Business and Economic Research, Univ. of Alabama, 1992
McCurley, R. L., Jr., ed., *The Legislative Process.* Alabama Law Institute, 3rd ed., 1984
Thigpen, R. A., *Alabama Government Manual.* Alabama Law Institute, 7th ed., 1986
Wiggins, S. W., (ed.) *From Civil War to Civil Rights, 1860–1960.* Univ. of Alabama Press, 1987

ALASKA

KEY HISTORICAL EVENTS. Discovered in 1741 by Vitus Bering, its first settlement, on Kodiak Island, was in 1784. The area known as Russian America with its capital (1806) at Sitk was ruled by a Russo-American fur company and vaguely claimed as a Russian colony. Alaska was purchased by the United States from Russia under the treaty of 30 March 1867 for $7·2m. Settlement was boosted by gold workers in the 1880s. In 1884 Alaska became a 'district' governed by the code of the state of Oregon. By Act of Congress approved 24 Aug. 1912 Alaska became an incorporated Territory; its first legislature in 1913 granted votes to women, 7 years in advance of the Constitutional Amendment.

During the Second World War the Federal Government acquired large areas for defence purposes and for the construction of the strategic Alaska Highway. In the 1950s oil was found. Alaska became the 49th state of the Union on 3 Jan. 1959.

In the 1970s new oilfields were discovered and the Trans-Alaska pipeline was opened in 1977. The state obtained most of its income from petroleum by 1985.

Questions of land-use predominate; there are large areas with valuable mineral resources, other large areas held for the native peoples and some still held by the Federal Government. The population increased by over 400% between 1940 and 1980.

TERRITORY AND POPULATION. Alaska is bounded north by the Beaufort Sea, west and south by the Pacific and east by Canada. The land area is 570,374 sq. miles (1,477,268 sq. km). Census population, 1 April 1990, was 550,043 (67·5% urban), including military personnel, an increase of 37·4% over 1980. Population estimate (1995), 603,617. Births, 1992, 11,714 (20 per 1,000 population); deaths, 2,317 (3·9); infant deaths, 99 (9·8 per 1,000 live births); marriages, 5,771 (9·8); divorces, 3,639 (6·2).

Population in 5 census years was:

	White	Black	All Others	Total	Per sq. mile
1950	92,808	. . .	35,835	128,643	0·23
1960	174,649	. . .	51,518	226,167	0·40
1970	236,767	8,911	54,704	300,382	0·53
1980	309,728	13,643	78,480	401,851	1·00
1990	415,492	22,451	112,100	550,043	1·00

Of the total population in 1990, 52·7% were male, 67·5% were urban and 68·7% were aged 18 years or over.

The largest city is in the borough of Anchorage, which had a 1990 census population of 226,338 and an estimated 1994 population of 254,000. Census populations of the other 13 boroughs, 1990: Aleutians East, 2,464; Bristol Bay, 1,410; Fairbanks North Star, 77,720; Haines, 2,117; Juneau, 26,751; Kenai Peninsula, 40,802; Ketchikan Gateway, 13,828; Kodiak Island, 13,309; Lake and Peninsula, 1,668; Matanuska-Susitna 39,683; North Slope, 5,979; Northwest Arctic, 6,113; Sitka, 8,588. Other Census Area populations, 1990: Aleutians West, 9,478; Bethel, 13,656; Dillingham, 4,012; Nome, 8,288; Prince of Wales-Outer Ketchikan, 6,278; Skagway-Yakutat-Angoon, 4,385; Southeast Fairbanks, 5,913; Valdez-Cordova, 9,952; Wade Hampton, 5,791; Wrangell-Petersburg, 7,042; Yukon-Koyukuk, 8,478. In 1995 there were 16 boroughs and 145 incorporated cities.

CLIMATE. Anchorage. Jan. 12°F (−11·1°C), July 57°F (13·9°C). Annual rainfall 15" (371 mm). Fairbanks. Jan. −11°F (−23·9°C), July 60°F (15·6°C). Annual rainfall 12" (300 mm). Sitka. Jan. 33°F (0·6°C), July 55°F (12·8°C). Annual rainfall 87" (2,175 mm). Alaska belongs to the Pacific Coast climate zone (*see* UNITED STATES: Climate).

CONSTITUTION AND GOVERNMENT. The state has the right to select 103·55m. acres of vacant and unappropriated public lands in order to establish 'a tax basis'; it can open these lands to prospectors for minerals, and the state is to derive the principal advantage in all gains resulting from the discovery of minerals. In addition, certain federally administered lands reserved for conservation of fisheries and wild life have been transferred to the state. Special provision is made for federal control of land for defence in areas of high strategic importance.

The constitution of Alaska was adopted by public vote, 24 April 1956. The state legislature consists of a Senate of 20 members (elected for 4 years) and a House of Representatives of 40 members (elected for 2 years). The state sends 1 representative to Congress. The franchise may be exercised by all citizens over 18.

The capital is Juneau.

In the 1996 presidential election Dole polled 101,234 votes; Clinton, 66,508; Perot, 21,536.

Governor: Tony Knowles (D.), 1995–98 ($81,648).
Lieut.-Governor: Fran Ulmer (D.) ($76,188).

ECONOMY

Budget. Total state government revenue for the year ended Dec. 1994 (Annual Financial Report figures) was $6,203m. Total expenditure was $5,752m.

In 1976 a Permanent Fund was set up for the deposit of at least 25% of all mineral-related revenue; total assets at 30 June 1994, $14,977m.

General obligation bonds, 30 June 1994, $178m.

Per capita income (1995) was $24,182.

NATURAL RESOURCES

Oil and Gas. Commercial production of crude petroleum began in 1959 and by 1961 had become the most important mineral by value. Production: 1991, 672m. bbls, value $2,572m.; 1992, 627m. bbls, value $2,624m.; 1994, 569m. bbls. Oil comes mainly from Prudhoe Bay, the Kuparuk River field and several Cook Inlet fields. Natural gas (liquid) production, 1991, 20·4m. bbls; 1992 production, 26·91m. bbls; 1994 production, 19·3m. bbls. Revenue to the state from petroleum in 1993 was $2,684·8m. (87% of general fund revenues). General fund unrestricted revenues, 1993: Severance taxes, 33%; oil and gas royalties, 25%; investment earnings, 2%; other oil and gas, 27%; non-petroleum, 13%.

Oil from the Prudhoe Bay Arctic field is now carried by the Trans-Alaska pipeline to Prince William Sound on the south coast, where a tanker terminal has been built at Valdez.

Minerals. Estimated value of production, 1994, in $1,000: Gold, 70,291; silver, 10,391; lead, 25,513; zinc, 296,103; industrial minerals (including sand, gravel and building stone), 68,009; platinum, 2·07; coal, 36,750; peat, 439·5. Total 1994 value, $507·5m.

Agriculture. In some parts of the state the climate during the brief spring and summer (about 100 days in major areas and 152 days in the south-eastern coastal area) is suitable for agricultural operations, thanks to the long hours of sunlight, but Alaska is a food-importing area. In 1994 about 0·93m. acres was farmland and there were 520 farms and ranches with annual sales of $1,000 or more; crops covered 28,940 acres. In 1991 the average farm had 1,768 acres. At 1 Jan. 1995 there were 9,900 cattle and calves and 1,700 sheep and lambs; at 1 Dec. 1994, 2,000 hogs and pigs and 2,000 poultry.

Total value of agricultural products in 1994: $27,766,000 of which $2,828,000 was from feed crops, $2,738,000 from vegetables (including potatoes), $6·1m. from live-stock and poultry, $2,465,000 from dairy products and $15,833,000 from greenhouse and nursery industries.

There were about 33,000 reindeer in western Alaska in 1994. Sales of reindeer meat and by-products in 1994 were valued at $1,366,000.

Forestry. Of the 129m. forested acres of Alaska, 24m. acres are classified as timber-land or commercial forest. The interior forest covers 115m. acres; more than 13m. acres are considered commercial forest, of which 3·4m. acres are in designated parks or wilderness and unavailable for harvest. The coastal rain forests provide the bulk of commercial timber volume; of their 13·6m. acres, 7·6m. acres support commercial stands, of which 1·9m. acres are in parks or wilderness and unavailable for harvest. In 1992, 590m. bd ft of timber were harvested from private land for a total value of $548·9m., and in 1993 9·38m. bd ft from state land for $342·6m.

Fisheries. The catch for 1993 was 2·7m. lbs of fish and shellfish having a value to fishermen of $905m. The most important species are salmon, crab, herring, halibut and pollock.

INDUSTRY. The largest manufacturing sectors are wood processing, seafood products and printing and publishing.

Labour. Total non-agricultural employment, 1995, 280,000. Employees by branch, 1995 (in 1,000): Government service, 69; trade, 58·1; services, 63·4; construction, 15·5; manufacturing, 26·2; mining including oil and gas, 9·9; transport, communication and utilities, 25·3; finance, insurance and property, 12·6.

TOURISM. About 1·05m. tourists visited the state in 1993.

COMMUNICATIONS

Roads. Alaska's highway and road system, 1994, totalled 14,325 miles. Registered motor vehicles, 1994, 631,465.

The Alaska Highway extends 1,523 miles from Dawson Creek, British Columbia, to Fairbanks, Alaska. It was built by the US Army in 1942, at a cost of $138m. The greater portion of it, because it lies in Canada, is maintained by Canada.

Railways. There is a railway of 111 miles from Skagway to the town of Whitehorse, the White Pass and Yukon route, in the Canadian Yukon region (this service operates seasonally). The government-owned Alaska Railroad runs from Seward to Fairbanks, a distance of 471 miles. This is a freight service with only occasional passenger use. A passenger service operates from Anchorage to Fairbanks via Denali National Park in the tourist season.

Civil Aviation. Commercial passengers by air from Alaska's largest international airports Anchorage and Fairbanks in fiscal year 1994 numbered 4,358,437 at Anchorage and 721,496 at Fairbanks. General aviation aircraft in the state per 1,000 population is about 10 times the US average.

Shipping. Regular shipping services to and from the US are furnished by 2 steamship and several barge lines operating out of Seattle and other Pacific coast ports. A Canadian company also furnishes a regular service from Vancouver, BC Anchorage is the main port.

A 1,435 nautical-mile ferry system for motor cars and passengers (the 'Alaska Marine Highway') operates from Bellingham, Washington and Prince Rupert (British Columbia) to Juneau, Haines (for access to the Alaska Highway) and Skagway. A second system extends throughout the south-central region of Alaska linking the Cook Inlet area with Kodiak Island and Prince William Sound.

SOCIAL INSTITUTIONS

Justice. There is no death penalty in Alaska. In Oct. 1994 there were 3,340 adults and 245 juveniles in state and federal institutions.

Religion. Many religions are represented, including the Russian Orthodox, Roman Catholic, Episcopalian, Presbyterian, Methodist and other denominations.

Education. Total expenditure on public schools in fiscal year 1994 was $896,307,252. In 1994 there were 7,195 teachers; average salary, fiscal year 1994, $46,263. In 1994 there were 121,396 pupils enrolled at public schools. The University of Alaska (founded in 1922) main campuses had (autumn 1993) 33,087 students. Other colleges had 2,718 students in autumn 1993.

Health. In 1993 there were 27 acute care hospitals with 1,892 beds, of which 7 were federal public health hospitals and 1 mental hospital. Many hospitals offer mental health services and most communities have mental health services and/or centres.

Welfare. Old-age assistance was established under the Federal Social Security Act; in 1993 aid to dependent children covered a monthly average of 11,300 households; payments, an average of $834 per month; aid to the disabled was given to a monthly average of 4,698 persons receiving on average $348 per month. An average of 3,666 aged per month received $351.

Further Reading

Statistical Information: Department of Commerce and Economic Development, Economic Analysis Section, POB 110804 Juneau 99811. Publishes *The Alaska Economy Performance Report.*

Alaska Industry–Occupation Outlook to 1995, Department of Labor, Juneau.
Annual Financial Report, Department of Administration, Juneau.
Falk, M., *Alaska.* [Bibliography]. Oxford and Santa Barbara (CA), 1995
Gardey, J., *Alaska: The Sophisticated Wilderness.* London, 1976
Hulley, Clarence C., *Alaska Past and Present.* Portland, Oregon, 1970
Hunt, W. R., *Alaska: a Bicentennial History.* New York, 1976
Naske, C.-M. and Slotnick, H. E., *Alaska: a History of the 49th State.* 2nd ed. Univ. of Oklahoma Press, 1995
Thomas, L., Jr., *Alaska and the Yukon.* New York, 1983
Tourville, M., *Alaska: a Bibliography, 1570–1970.* 1971

State library: POB 110571, Juneau, Alaska 99811-0571.

ARIZONA

KEY HISTORICAL EVENTS. Spaniards looking for sources of gold or silver entered Arizona in the 16th century, finding there nomadic tribes of Navajo and Apache. The first Spanish Catholic mission was founded in 1692 by Father Eusebio Kino, settlements were made in 1752 and a Spanish army headquarters was set up at Tucson in 1776. The area was governed by Mexico after the collapse of Spanish colonial power. Mexico ceded it to the USA after the Mexican-American war (1848). Arizona was then part of New Mexico; the Gadsden Purchase (of land south of the Gila River) was added to it in 1853. The whole was organized as the Arizona Territory on 24 Feb. 1863.

Years of war between Indian and immigrant populations began when troops were withdrawn to serve in the Civil War. The Navajo surrendered in 1865, but the Apache continued to fight a series of wars, under Geronimo and other leaders, until 1886. After the wars the area settled to Mexican-style ranching. Arizona was admitted to the Union as the 48th state in 1912.

In the 20th century, and especially after 1920, irrigated farming began to replace ranching as the main activity. Large areas, however, were retained as Indian reservations and other large areas by the Federal Government to protect the exceptional desert and mountain landscape. In recent years this landscape and the Indian traditions have been used to attract tourist income.

TERRITORY AND POPULATION. Arizona is bounded north by Utah, east by New Mexico, south by Mexico, west by California and Nevada. Area, 114,006 sq. miles (295,276 sq. km), including 364 sq. miles (943 sq. km) of inland water. Of the total area in 1992, 28% was Indian Reservation, 17% was in individual or corporate ownership, 19% was held by the US Bureau of Land Management, 15% by the US Forest Service, 13% by the State and 8% by others. Census population on 1 April 1990 was 3,665,228 (87·5% urban), an increase of 34·92% over 1980. Population estimate (1996), 4,462,300. In 1996: Births, 75,094; deaths, 36,579; infant deaths, 576; marriages, 39,611; dissolutions of marriages, 26,483.

Population in 5 census years:

	White	Black	Indian	Chinese	Japanese	Total	Per sq. mile
1910	171,468	2,009	29,201	1,305	371	204,354	1·8
1930	378,551	10,749	43,726	1,110	879	435,573	3·8

	White	Black	Indian	Chinese	Japanese	Total	Per sq. mile
1960	1,169,517	43,403	83,387	2,937	1,501	1,302,161	11·3
				All others			
1980	2,260,288	74,159	162,854	383,768		2,718,215	23·9
1990	2,963,186	110,524	203,527	387,991		3,665,228	32·3

Of the population in 1990, 1,810,691 (49·4%) were male, 3,206,973 (87·5%) were urban and 2,684,109 (73·2%) were aged 18 and over.

The 1996 estimated population of Phoenix was 1,180,740; Tucson, 449,635; Mesa, 343,710; Glendale, 186,697; Scottsdale, 178,525; Tempe, 156,000; Chandler, 141,735; Peoria, 78,310; Gilbert, 67,440; Yuma, 63,150.

CLIMATE. Phoenix. Jan. 53·6°F (12°C), July 93·5°F (34°C). Annual rainfall 7·66" (194 mm). Yuma. Jan. 56·5°F (13·6°C), July 93·7°F (34·3°C). Annual rainfall 3·17" (80 mm). Flagstaff. Jan. 38·3°F (3·5°C), July 82·7°F (27·8°C). Annual rainfall 15·72" (396 mm). Arizona belongs to the Mountain States climate zone (*see* UNITED STATES: Climate).

CONSTITUTION AND GOVERNMENT. The state constitution (1911, with 116 amendments) placed the government under direct control of the people through the initiative, referendum and the recall provisions. The state Senate consists of 30 members, and the House of Representatives of 60, all elected for 2 years. Arizona sends to Congress 6 representatives. In the 1996 presidential election Clinton polled 612,412 votes; Dole, 576,126; Perot, 104,712.

The state capital is Phoenix. The state is divided into 15 counties.

Governor: Jane Dee Hull (R.), 1997–99 ($75,000).
Secretary of State: Betsey Bayless (R.), 1997–99 ($54,000).

BUDGET. General fund total revenues, year ending 30 June 1996, were $4,663·5m.; general fund operating total was $4,378·5m. (including education, $2,526·9m.; public health and welfare, $1,032·5m.; protection and safety, $469·6m.). *Per capita* income (1996) was $21,525.

NATURAL RESOURCES

Minerals. The mining industry historically has been and continues to be a significant part of the economy. By value the most important mineral produced is copper. Production (1996) 1,356,000 tons. Most of the state's silver and gold are recovered from copper ore. Other minerals include sand and gravel, molybdenum, coal and gemstones. Total value of minerals mined in 1996 was $4,487m.

Agriculture. Arizona, despite its dry climate, is well suited for agriculture along the water-courses and where irrigation is practised on a large scale from great reservoirs constructed by the US as well as by the state government and private interests. Irrigated area, 1992, 956,454 acres. The wide pasture lands are favourable for the rearing of cattle and sheep, but numbers are either stationary or declining compared with 1920.

In 1996 Arizona contained 7,500 farms and ranches and the total farm and pastoral area was 35·4m. acres. In 1992 there were 1,344,091 acres of crop land. The average farm was estimated in 1996 at 4,720 acres. Farming is highly commercialized and mechanized and concentrated largely on cotton picked by machines operated by Indian, Mexican and migratory workers.

Area under cotton (1995): Upland cotton, 365,000 acres (793,000 bales harvested); American Pima cotton, 48,600 acres (72,200 bales harvested).

Cash income, 1995, from crops, $1,445,568,000; from livestock and products, $810,318,000. Most important cereals are wheat, corn and barley; most important crops include cotton, citrus fruit, lettuce, broccoli, grapes, cauliflower, melons, onions, potatoes and carrots. In 1995 there were 850,000 cattle, 135,000 sheep, 125,000 hogs, 52,000 goats and 330,000 chickens.

Forestry. The national forests in the state had an area (1997) of 11,250,000 acres.

INDUSTRY. In the first quarter of 1997 the state had an average of 4,903 manufacturing employers with an average of 202,812 employees earning total wages of $2,022,035,640 for the quarter.

TOURISM. In 1995, 27·2m. tourists visited Arizona; tourism-related jobs, direct and indirect (1995), 300,001; Total taxes attributed to tourism for 1995, $228,332,135.

COMMUNICATIONS

Roads. As of 31 Dec. 1996 there were 54,895 miles of public roads and streets and 3,476,893 motor vehicles were registered.

Civil Aviation. Registered landing facilities, 1997, numbered 294, of which 83 were for public use; 5,347 aircraft were registered.

SOCIAL INSTITUTIONS

Justice. A 'right-to-work' amendment to the constitution, adopted 5 Nov. 1946, makes illegal any concessions to trade-union demands for a 'closed shop'.

The Arizona state prison 30 June 1997 held 21,725 male and 1,555 female prisoners. Chain gangs were reintroduced into prisons in 1995. The death penalty is authorized; the last execution was on 25 June 1997.

Religion. The leading religious bodies are Roman Catholics and Mormons (Latter Day Saints); others include United Methodists, Presbyterians, Baptists, Lutherans, Episcopalians, Eastern Orthodox, Jews and Muslims.

Education. School attendance is compulsory between the ages of 6 and 16. In 1995–96 K-12 enrolment numbered 761,410 students. There are 227 school districts containing 964 elementary schools and 183 high schools. Charter schools first opened their doors in 1995. There are 46 charter schools providing parents and students with expanded educational choices. In 1995–96, the total funds appropriated by the state legislature for all education, including the Board of Regents and community colleges was $2,511,527,000. The state maintains 3 universities: The University of Arizona (Tucson) with an enrolment of 30,740 in autumn 1997; Arizona State University (3 campuses) with 43,105; Northern Arizona University (Flagstaff) with 17,183.

Health. In 1996 there were 87 hospitals; capacity 12,311 beds; 14,179 licensed physicians and 3,029 dentists, 67,217 registered nurses and 20,669 licensed practical nurses.

Social Security. Old-age assistance (maximum depending on the programme) is given to needy citizens 65 years of age or older through the federal supplemental security income (SSI) programme. In March 1997, SSI payments went to 13,534 aged (average $234·01 each), 61,486 disabled (average $388·41 each) and 993 blind people (average $375·85 each). In September 1997, 134,827 people (average $104·87 each) in 49,201 families (average $287·37 each) received Aid for Families with Dependent Children.

Further Reading

Statistical information: College of Business and Public Administration, Univ. of Arizona, Tucson 85721. Publishes *Arizona Statistical Abstract.*
Arizona Commission of Indian Affairs. *Resource Directory.* Phoenix, 1997
Arizona Department of Commerce. *Community Profiles.* Phoenix, 1997
Arizona Department of Health Services, Center for Health Statistics. *Arizona Health Status and Vital Statistics, 1995.* Phoenix, 1996
Arizona Historical Society. *Official Directory, Arizona Historical Museums and Related Support Organizations.* Tucson, 1997
Goff, J., *Arizona: an Illustrated History of Grand Canyon State.* Northridge (CA), 1988
Office of the Secretary of State. *Arizona Blue Book, 1995–96.* 1996
Public Sector Information, Inc. *1997–98 Arizona Yearbook: A Guide to Government in the Grand Canyon State.* Eugene (OR); 1997

Richards, J. M., *History of the Arizona State Legislature, 1912–1967.* Phoenix, 1990
Trimble, M., *Arizona: A Cavalcade of History.* Tucson, 1989

State Government Web Site: http://www.state.az.us
State Legislature Web Site: http://www.azleg.state.az.us
Department of Library, Archives and Public Records Web Site: http://www.dlapr.lib.az.us

ARKANSAS

KEY HISTORICAL EVENTS. In the 16th and 17th centuries, French and
Spanish explorers entered Arkansas, finding there tribes of Chaddo, Osage and
Quapaw. The first European settlement was French, at Arkansas Post in 1686, and the
area became part of French Louisiana. The US bought Arkansas from France as part
of the Louisiana Purchase in 1803, it was organized as a Territory in 1819 and entered
the Union on 15 June 1836 as the 25th state.

The eastern plains by the Mississippi were settled by white plantation-owners who
grew cotton with black slave labour. The rest of the state attracted a scattered population of small farmers. The plantations were the centre of political power. Arkansas
seceded from the Union in 1861 and joined the Confederate States of America. At
that time the slave population was about 25% of the total.

In 1868 the state was readmitted to the Union. Attempts to integrate the black
population into state life achieved little, and a policy of segregation was rigidly
adhered to until the 1950s.

In 1957 federal law ordered that segregation in a public high school must end. The
state governor ordered the state militia to prevent desegregation; there was rioting,
and federal troops were called to Little Rock, the capital, to restore order. School
segregation ended within the following 10 years.

The main industrial development followed the discovery of large reserves of
bauxite.

TERRITORY AND POPULATION. Arkansas is bounded north by Missouri,
east by Tennessee and Mississippi, south by Louisiana, south-west by Texas and west
by Oklahoma. Area, 53,187 sq. miles (137,754 sq. km), 1,109 sq. miles being inland
water. Census population on 1 April 1990 was 2,350,725 (53·5% urban), an increase
of 2·8% from that of 1980. Population estimate (1995), 2,484,000. Births, 1992, were
34,803; deaths, 24,941 (infant deaths, 363); marriages, 37,164; divorces 17,999.

Population in 5 census years was:

	White	Black	Indian	Asiatic	Total	Per sq. mile
1910	1,131,026	442,891	460	472	1,574,449	30·0
1930	1,375,315	478,463	408	296	1,854,482	35·2
1960	1,395,703	388,787	580	1,202	1,786,272	34·0
			All others			
1980	1,890,332	373,768	22,335		2,286,435	43·9
1990	1,944,744	373,912	32,069		2,350,725	45·1

Of the total population in 1990, 48·2% were male and 68·9% were 21 years of age
or older.

Little Rock (capital) had a population of 175,795 in 1990; Fort Smith, 72,798;
North Little Rock, 61,741; Pine Bluff, 57,140; Fayetteville, 42,099; Hot Springs,
32,462; Jonesboro, 46,535; West Memphis, 28,259. The population of the largest
standard metropolitan statistical areas: Little Rock–North Little Rock, 513,117;
Fayetteville, 113,409; Fort Smith (Arkansas portion), 142,083; Pine Bluff, 85,487;
Memphis (Arkansas portion), 49,939; Texarkana (Arkansas portion), 38,467.

CLIMATE. Little Rock. Jan. 39·9°F, July 84°F. Annual rainfall 52·83 inches.
Arkansas belongs to the Gulf Coast climate zone (*see* UNITED STATES: Climate).

GOVERNMENT. The General Assembly consists of a Senate of 35 members
elected for 4 years, partially renewed every 2 years, and a House of Representatives

of 100 members elected for 2 years. The sessions are biennial and usually limited to 60 days. The Governor and Lieut.-Governor are elected for 4 years. The state is represented in Congress by 4 representatives.

In the 1996 presidential election Clinton polled 465,362 votes; Dole, 320,323; Perot, 67,245.

The state is divided into 75 counties; the capital is Little Rock.

Governor: Mike Huckabee (R.), 1995–99 ($87,000).
Lieut.-Governor: Vacant. ($29,000).
Secretary of State: Sharon Priest (D.) ($37,500).

FINANCE

Budget. The state and local government revenue for the fiscal year 1994 was $6,870m. General expenditure was $5,642m., of which education took $2,217m.; highways, $599m.; and public welfare, $1,387m.

Outstanding debt at end of fiscal year 1994 was $1,812m.

Per capita income (1995) was $17,429.

Banking. In 1993–94 total bank deposits were $22,107·8m.

NATURAL RESOURCES

Minerals. In 1988 crude petroleum amounted to 13,455,729 bbls; natural gas, 146,894,144m. cu. ft. The U.S. Bureau of Mines estimated Arkansas' mineral value in 1992 at $287m. Mining employment totalled 3,600 in Oct. 1992. Crushed stone was the leading mineral commodity produced, in terms of value, followed by bromine.

Agriculture. In 1995, 44,000 farms had a total area of 15·0m. acres; average farm was 341 acres. In 1993, 8·2m. acres were harvested cropland. In 1990, 2,406,338 acres were irrigated.

In 1993, Arkansas ranked first in the production of broilers (1,050m. birds) and in the acreage and production of rice (40% of US total production) and third in turkeys (25m. birds). 1,081,000 bales of cotton were harvested in 1991; soybean production yielded 90·4m. bu. in 1990. Dairy farmers received $122·6m. for the sale of milk in 1990.

Livestock in Jan. 1989 included 1·75m. all cattle and calves, total value (1990), was $425·9m.

Forestry. The national forests had a total area of 3,495,232 acres in 1997.

INDUSTRY. In 1996 total employment averaged 1,234,000 (including 254,000 manufacturing, 247,000 wholesale and retail trade, 179,000 government). The Arkansas Department of Labor estimated that 196,700 factory production workers earned an average $370.77 per week (41·8 hours). In the manufacturing group, food and kindred products employed 52,400, electric and electronic equipment, 20,500 and lumber and wood products, 21,500. In Aug. 1994 estimated employment was 1,153,700, including 1,025,300 non-agricultural waged and salaried jobs.

COMMUNICATIONS

Roads. Total road mileage (1994) 77,216 miles. State-maintained highways (1993) total 16,234 miles; local county highways, 51,157 miles; city streets, 9,807 miles; federal roads, 1,760 miles; roads not publicly maintained, 5,484 miles. In 1993 there were 2,097,872 registered motor vehicles.

Railways. In 1991 there were in the state 3,169 miles of commercial railway. In 1994 rail service was provided by 4 Class I and 23 short-line railways.

Civil Aviation. In Oct. 1994, 7 air carriers and 2 commuter airlines served the state; there were 175 airports (96 public-use and 79 private).

Waterways. There are about 1,000 miles of navigable streams, including the Mississippi, Arkansas, Red, White and Ouachita Rivers. The Arkansas River/Kerr-

McClellan Channel flows diagonally eastward across the state and gives access to the sea *via* the Mississippi River.

SOCIAL INSTITUTIONS

Justice. State prisons in Oct. 1994 had 8,999 inmates. The death penalty is authorized. The last execution took place in 1994.

Religion. Main Protestant churches in 1990: Southern Baptist (617,524), United Methodist (197,402), Church of Christ (86,502), Assembly of God (55,438). Roman Catholics (1990), 72,952.

Education. In the school year 1992–93 public elementary and secondary schools had 440,682 enrolled pupils and 25,771 classroom teachers. Average salary of teachers in elementary schools was $25,771, junior high $27,492 and high $27,760.

An educational TV network provides a full 18-hour-day telecasting; it has 5 stations (1994).

Higher education is provided at 34 institutions: 9 state universities, 1 medical college, 12 private or church colleges, 12 community or 2-year branch colleges and 12 technical colleges. Total enrolment in institutions of higher education in the autumn of 1993 was 99,344.

In the autumn of 1993 there were 2 vocational-training schools and 9 technical institutes with 28,261 students.

Health. There were 99 licensed hospitals (13,329 beds) in 1994, and 273 nursing facilities (25,888 licensed beds), excluding private facilities.

Social Welfare. In Dec. 1993, 481,910 persons drew social security payments; 271,510 were retired workers; 53,240 were disabled workers; 68,920 were widows and widowers; 36,050 were spouses. Monthly payments were $251·5m., $159·6m. to retired workers and their dependants and $31·6m. to disabled workers.

Further Reading

Statistical information: Arkansas Institute for Economic Advancement, Univ. of Arkansas at Little Rock, Little Rock, 72204. Publishes *Arkansas State and County Economic Data.*
Agricultural Statistics for Arkansas. Arkansas Agricultural Statistics Service, Little Rock, 1993
Current Employment Developments. Dept. of Labor, Little Rock, 1994
Statistical Summary for the Public Schools of Arkansas. Dept. of Education, Little Rock, 1990-92

CALIFORNIA

KEY HISTORICAL EVENTS. There were many small Indian tribes, but no central power, when the area was discovered in 1542 by the Spanish navigator Juan Cabrillo. The Spaniards did not begin to establish missions until the 18th century, when the Franciscan friar Junipero Serra settled at San Diego in 1769. The missions became farming and ranching villages with large Indian populations. When the Spanish empire collapsed in 1821, the area was governed from newly-independent Mexico.

The first wagon-train of American settlers arrived from Missouri in 1841. In 1846, during the war between Mexico and the USA, Americans in California proclaimed it to be part of the USA. The territory was ceded by Mexico on 2 Feb. 1848 and became the 31st state of the Union on 9 Sept. 1850.

Gold was discovered in 1848–49 and there was an immediate influx of population. The state remained isolated, however, until the development of railways in the 1860s. From then on the population doubled on average every 20 years. The sunny climate attracted fruit-growers, market-gardeners and wine producers. In the early 20th century the bright light and cheap labour attracted film-makers to Hollywood, Los Angeles.

Southern California remained mainly agricultural with an Indian or Spanish-speaking labour force until after the Second World War. Now more than 90% of the population is urban, with the main manufacture being electronic equipment, much of it for the defence and aerospace industries.

TERRITORY AND POPULATION. Land area, 155,973 sq. miles (403,971 sq. km). Census population, 1 April 1990, 29,760,021 (92·6% urban), an increase of 25·7% over 1980. Population estimate (1996), 31,878,000. Births in 1995 569,000 (17·7 per 1,000 population); deaths, 224,000 (7 per 1,000 population); infant deaths (1990), 4,622 (7·5 per 1,000 live births); marriages (1990), 236,693; divorces (1990), 127,967.

Population in 5 census years was:

	White	Black	Japanese	Chinese	Total (incl. all others)	Per sq. mile
1910	2,259,672	21,645	41,356	36,248	2,377,549	15·0
1930	5,408,260	81,048	97,456	37,361	5,677,251	35·8
1960	14,455,230	883,861	157,317	95,600	15,717,204	99·0

	White	Black	Asian/other	Hispanic	Total	Per sq. mile
1980	15,763,992	1,783,810	1,575,769	4,544,331	23,667,902	149·1
1990	17,029,126	2,092,446	2,950,511	7,687,938	29,760,021	190·8

Of the 1990 population 50·1% were male, 92·6% were urban and 69% were 21 years old or older.

The largest cities with 1997 estimated population are:

Los Angeles	3,681,700	Modesto	179,800	Fullerton	122,800
San Diego	1,197,100	Chula Vista	156,100	Orange	122,300
San Jose	873,300	Oxnard	152,800	Escondido	119,900
San Francisco	778,100	Garden Grove	152,000	Inglewood	117,300
Long Beach	441,700	Oceanside	149,200	Rancho	
Fresno	406,900	Torrance	141,500	Cucamonga	116,000
Sacramento	388,700	Pomona	141,400	El Monte	115,100
Oakland	388,100	Ontario	141,100	Palmdale	114,900
Santa Ana	307,000	Pasadena	138,900	Thousand Oaks	112,800
Anaheim	295,500	Moreno Valley	132,600	Concord	111,800
Riverside	241,600	Santa Clarita	131,400	Vallejo	110,500
Stockton	236,500	Irvine	129,300	Berkeley	105,900
Bakersfield	214,600	Sunnyvale	129,300	Fontana	104,200
Glendale	195,600	Santa Rosa	127,700	Simi Valley	103,700
Fremont	192,200	Hayward	123,900	West Covina	103,400
Huntington Beach	188,500	Salinas	123,300	Corona	102,800
San Bernardino	180,300	Lancaster	123,200	Costa Mesa	102,600

Urbanized areas (1990 census): Los Angeles, 11,402,946; San Francisco–Oakland, 3,629,516; San Diego, 2,348,417; San Jose, 1,435,019; Sacramento, 1,097,005; Riverside–San Bernardino, 1,170,196; Oxnard–Ventura, 480,482; Fresno, 453,388.

CLIMATE. Los Angeles. Jan. 55°F (12·8°C), July 70°F (21·1°C). Annual rainfall 15" (381 mm). Sacramento. Jan. 45°F (7·2°C), July 74°F (23·3°C). Annual rainfall 19" (472 mm). San Diego. Jan. 55°F (12·8°C), July 69°F (20·6°C). Annual rainfall 10" (259 mm). San Francisco. Jan. 50°F (10°C), July 59°F (15°C). Annual rainfall 22" (561 mm). Death Valley. Jan. 52°F (11°C), July 100°F (38°C). Annual rainfall 1·6" (40 mm). California belongs to the Pacific Coast climate zone (*see* UNITED STATES: Climate).

CONSTITUTION AND GOVERNMENT. The present constitution became effective from 4 July 1879; it has had numerous amendments since 1962. The Senate is composed of 40 members elected for 4 years—half being elected each 2 years—and the Assembly, of 80 members, elected for 2 years. Two-year regular sessions convene in Dec. of each even numbered year. The Governor and Lieut. Governor are elected for 4 years.

California is represented in Congress by 52 representatives.

In the 1996 presidential election Clinton polled 4,639,935 votes; Dole, 3,412,563; Perot, 667,702.

The capital is Sacramento. The state is divided into 58 counties.

Governor: Pete Wilson (R.), 1995–99 ($120,000).
Lieut.-Governor: Gray Davis (D.) ($90,000).
Secretary of State: Bill Jones (R.) ($90,000).

ECONOMY

Budget. For the year ending 30 June 1996 total General Fund revenues and transfers were $46,296m.; total General Fund expenditures were $45,393m. in fiscal year 1996 ($23,322m. for education, $14,264m. for health and welfare).

The long-term state debt (general obligation bonds outstanding) was $17,950m. on 30 June 1997.

Per capita personal income (1995) was $24,073.

Banking and Finance. In 1988 there were more than 440 banks, of which 18 were foreign-owned, 11 out-of-state and 400 independent. Total loans, 31 Dec. 1996 (preliminary), $264,883m., of which real estate loans were $125,855m. All insured commercial banks had demand deposits of $83,587m. and time and savings deposits of $185,379m. Savings and loan associations had savings capital of $166,833m. at 31 Dec. 1996.

NATURAL RESOURCES

Minerals. Crude oil output was estimated at 283m. bbls in 1996. Output of natural gas was 239,816m. cu. ft; of natural gas liquids from wells, 71,369 bbls in 1996. Gold output was 26,000 kg (1996 preliminary); asbestos, boron minerals, diatomite, tungsten, sand and gravel, salt, magnesium compounds, clays, cement, copper, silver, gypsum, calcium chloride and iron ore are also produced. The value of non-fuel minerals produced was $2,399m. in 1996. Mining employed 29,600 in 1996.

Agriculture. In 1996 there were some 82,000 farms, comprising 30m. acres; average farm, 366 acres. Cash receipts, 1995, $22,895m. Cotton, almonds, grapes, lettuce, cattle and calves, milk and cream were the main sources of farm cash receipts.

Production of cotton lint, 1995, was 608,800 short tons; other field crops included (in 1m. short tons): Sugar-beet, 3; hay and alfalfa, 9; rice, 1·8; wheat, 1. Principal fruit, nut and vegetable crops 1995 (in 1,000 short tons): Wine, table and raisin grapes, 5,248; tomatoes, 11,120; lettuce, 2,734; almonds, 185. Citrus fruit crops, 1995, were (in 1,000 short tons): Oranges, 2,288; lemons, 779; grapefruit, 312.

On 1 Jan. 1997 the farm animals were: 1·3m. milk cows, 4·6m. all cattle, 0·48m. sheep and 0·24m. swine.

Forestry. There are about 16·6m. acres of productive forest land, from which about 2,900m. bd ft are harvested annually. Lumber production, 1996, 2,273m. bd ft.

Fisheries. The catch in 1996 was 459m. lb.; leading species in landings were squid, mackerel, sardine, tuna, urchin, sole, rockfish and crab.

INDUSTRY. The fastest-growing industries are electronics manufacturing, business services, motion pictures and engineering and management consulting. In 1996 the civilian labour force was 15·60m., of whom 14,470,000 were employed (1,853,000 in manufacturing).

Tourism. In 1996 there were 289m. tourists, 279m. from within the United States and 10m. from abroad.

COMMUNICATIONS

Roads. In 1996 California had 68,325 miles of roads inside cities and 102,182 miles outside. In 1996 there were about 17·7m. registered cars and about 5·9m. commercial vehicles.

Railways. In addition to Amtrak's long-distance trains, local and medium-distance passenger trains run in the San Francisco Bay area sponsored by the California Department of Transportation, and a network of commuter trains around Los Angeles opened in 1992. There are metro and light rail systems in San Francisco and Los Angeles, and light rail lines in Sacramento, San Diego and San Jose.

Civil Aviation. In 1986 there were 283 public airports and 739 private airstrips.

Shipping. The chief ports are San Francisco and Los Angeles.

SOCIAL INSTITUTIONS

Justice. A '3 strikes law', making 25-years-to-life sentences mandatory for third felony offences was adopted in 1994 after an initiative (i.e. referendum) was 72% in favour. However, the state's Supreme Court ruled in June 1996 that judges may disregard previous convictions in awarding sentences. In 1996 there were 32 adult prisons. State prisons, 1 Jan. 1996, had 126,079 male and 9,054 female inmates. In April 1996 there were some 10,500 juveniles in custody, and 1,655 adults serving '3 strikes' sentences. The death penalty has been authorized following its reinstatement by the US Supreme Court in 1976. Death sentences have been passed since 1980. The last execution was in 1993.

Religion. There is a strong Roman Catholic presence. There were 719,000 Mormons in 1994.

Education. Full-time attendance at school is compulsory for children from 6 to 18 years of age for a minimum of 175 days per annum. In autumn 1996 there were 6·2m. pupils enrolled in both public and private elementary and secondary schools. Total state expenditure on public education, 1995–96, was $23,999m.

Community Colleges had 1,407,335 students in autumn 1996.

California has two publicly supported higher education systems: The University of California (1868) and the California State University and Colleges. In autumn 1996, the University of California with campuses for resident instruction and research at Berkeley, Los Angeles, San Francisco and 6 other centres, had 166,718 students. California State University and Colleges with campuses at Sacramento, Long Beach, Los Angeles, San Francisco and 15 other cities had 336,803 students. In addition to the 28 publicly supported institutions for higher education there are 117 private colleges and universities which had a total estimated enrolment of 222,709 in the autumn of 1996.

Health. In 1996 there were 500 general acute care hospitals; capacity, 105,096 beds. On 30 June 1997 state hospitals for the mentally disabled had 4,263 patients.

Social Security. On 1 Jan. 1974 the federal government (Social Security Administration) assumed responsibility for the Supplemental Security Income/State Supplemental Program which replaced the State Old-Age Security. The SSI/SSP provides financial assistance for needy aged (65 years or older), blind or disabled persons. An individual recipient may own assets up to $2,000; a couple up to $3,000, subject to specific exclusions. In 1996–97 fiscal year an average of 1,084 cases per month were receiving an average of $214·48 in assistance in the general relief programme.

Further Reading

California Almanac. Pacific Data Resources, Santa Barbara
California Government and Politics. Hoeber, T. R., et al, (eds.) Sacramento, Annual
California Statistical Abstract. 38th ed. Dept. of Finance, Sacramento, 1997
Economic Report of the Governor. Dept. of Finance, Sacramento, Annual
Bean, W. and Rawls, J. J., *California: an Interpretive History.* 6th ed. New York, 1993
Gerston, L. N. and Christensen, T., *California Politics and Government: a Practical Approach.* 3rd ed. New York, 1995
Lavender, D. S., *California.* New York, 1976
State Library: The California State Library, Library-Courts Bldg, Sacramento 95814.

COLORADO

KEY HISTORICAL EVENTS. Spanish explorers claimed the area for Spain in 1706; it was then the territory of the Arapaho, Cheyenne, Ute and other Plains and Great Basin Indians. Eastern Colorado, the hot, dry plains, passed to France in 1802 and then to the USA as part of the Louisiana Purchase in 1803. The rest remained Spanish, becoming Mexican when Spanish power in the Americas ended. In 1848, after war between Mexico and the USA, Mexican Colorado was ceded to the US. A gold rush in 1859 brought a great influx of population, and in 1861 Colorado was organized as a Territory. The Territory officially supported the Union in the Civil War of 1861–65, but its settlers were divided and served on both sides.

Colorado became a state in 1876. Mining and ranching were the mainstays of the economy. In the 1920s the first large projects were undertaken to exploit the Colorado River. The Colorado River Compact was agreed in 1922, and the Boulder Dam (now Hoover Dam) was authorized in 1928. Since then irrigated agriculture has overtaken mining as an industry and is as important as ranching. In 1945 the Colorado-Big Thompson project diverted water by tunnel beneath the Rocky Mountains to irrigate 700,000 acres (284,000 ha) of northern Colorado. Now more than 80% of the population is urban, and most engaged in trade and service industries, especially tourism.

TERRITORY AND POPULATION. Colorado is bounded north by Wyoming, north-east by Nebraska, east by Kansas, south-east by Oklahoma, south by New Mexico and west by Utah. Land area, 103,729 sq. miles (268,658 sq. km).

Census population, 1 July 1995, was 3,746,607 (83·1% urban). Population estimate (1996), 3,821,500. Births, 1995, were 53,748 (14·5 per 1,000 population); deaths, 24,898 (6·6); infant deaths, 352 (6·5 per 1,000 live births); marriages, 34,296 (9·2); divorces, 18,844.

Population in 5 census years was:

	White	Black	Indian	Asiatic	Total	Per sq. mile
1910	783,415	11,453	1,482	2,674	799,024	7·7
1930	1,018,793	11,828	1,395	3,775	1,035,791	10·0
1950	1,296,653	20,177	1,567	5,870	1,325,089	12·7
			All others			
1980	2,571,498	101,703	216,763		2,889,964	27·9
1990	2,658,945	128,057	22,068	56,773	3,294,394	31·8

Of the total population in 1995, 1,858,346 were male, 1,888,272 were female. Large cities with 1995 census population: Denver City, 490,924; Colorado Springs, 315,590; Aurora, 221,332; Lakewood, 134,310; Pueblo, 100,700; Arvada, 95,934; Fort Collins, 98,411; Boulder, 91,386; Westminster, 84,887.

Main metropolitan areas (1995): Denver, 1,826,468; Colorado Springs, 462,711; Boulder, 255,156; Fort Collins, 215,774; Greeley, 147,524; Pueblo, 129,332; Front Range Urban Area, 3,037,013.

CLIMATE. Denver. Jan. 31°F (−0·6°C), July 73°F (22·8°C). Annual rainfall 14" (358 mm). Pueblo. Jan. 30°F (−1·1°C), July 83°F (28·3°C). Annual rainfall 12" (312 mm). Colorado belongs to the Mountain States climate zone (*see* UNITED STATES: Climate).

CONSTITUTION AND GOVERNMENT. The constitution adopted in 1876 is still in effect with (1989) 115 amendments. The General Assembly consists of a Senate of 35 members elected for 4 years, one-half retiring every 2 years, and of a House of Representatives of 65 members elected for 2 years. Sessions are annual, beginning 1951. Qualified as electors are all citizens, male and female (except convicted, incarcerated criminals), 18 years of age, who have resided in the state and the precinct for 32 days immediately preceding the election.

The state sends 6 representatives to Congress.

In the 1996 presidential election Dole polled 691,290 votes; Clinton, 670,854; Perot, 99,510.

The capital is Denver. There are 63 counties.

Governor: Roy Romer (D.), 1995–99 ($70,000).
Lieut.-Governor: Gail Schoettler (D.) ($48,500).
Secretary of State: Vicky Buckley (R.) ($48,500).

BUDGET. Total budget, 1996, $4,269m.. Expenditure on education, $2,173m.; health care, $695·7m.; human services, $365·5m; corrections $236·4m.

The state has no general obligation debt. The state revenue bond debt on 30 June 1991 was $2,659m.

Per capita personal income (1995) was $23,449.

NATURAL RESOURCES

Minerals. Colorado has a variety of mineral resources. Among the most important are crude oil and coal and gas. Coal (1995) 25·3m. short tons; crude oil (also 1995), 28·3m. barrels; natural gas (also 1995), 551·0 billion cu. ft. In 1996 there were 13,619 people employed in mining, including 7,782 in extracting oil and natural gas.

Agriculture. In 1996 farms numbered 24,500, with a total area of 32·6m. acres. 5,748,610 acres were harvested crop land; average farm, 1,327 acres. Average value of farmland and buildings per acre in 1996 was $558. Farm income, 1995, from crops $1,361m.; from livestock, $2,624m.

Production of principal crops in 1990: Corn for grain, 128·65m. bu.; wheat for grain, 84·95m. bu.; barley for grain, 12m. bu.; hay, 3,805,000 tons; dry beans, 4,275,000 cwt; oats and sorghum, 12·59m. bu.; sugar beets, 944,000 tons; potatoes, 24,032,000 cwt; vegetables, 10,683 tons; fruits, 39,000 tons.

In 1995 the number of farm animals was: 3,100,000 cattle, 83,000 milk cows, 580,000 swine. In 1991 there were 708,070 sheep.

Forestry. In 1997 there were 15m. acres of national forest.

INDUSTRY. In 1996, 1,847,591 were employed in non-agricultural sectors, of which 466,411 were in trade; 536,084 in services; 293,698 in government; 196,517 in manufacturing; 111,064 in construction; 115,345 in transportation; 13,619 in mining; 114,561 in finance and insurance. In manufacturing in 1996 the biggest employers were 30,919 in non-electrical machinery; 26,916 in printing and publishing; 25,863 in food products.

COMMUNICATIONS

Roads. In 1995 there were 84,447 miles of road. In 1995 there were 2,811,790 motor vehicle registrations.

Railways. In 1995 there were in the state 3,439 miles of railway.

Civil Aviation. There were (1990) 81 airports open to the public; 14 with commercial service, 53 public non-commercial (general aviation) and 14 private non-commercial.

SOCIAL INSTITUTIONS

Justice. In 1996 there were 11,742 in federal and state prisoners. The death penalty is authorized.

Religion. In 1984 the Roman Catholic Church had 550,300 members; the ten main Protestant denominations had 350,900 members; the Jewish community had 45,000 members. Buddhism is among other religions represented.

Education. In 1995 the public elementary and secondary schools had 656,279 pupils, 35,364 teachers; teachers' salaries averaged $35,364. Enrolments in 4-year state universities and colleges were: University of Colorado (Boulder), 24,440 students; University of Colorado (Denver), 10,538; University of Colorado (Colorado Springs), 5,871; Colorado State University (Fort Collins), 21,393; Colorado School of Mines (Golden), 3,083; University of Northern Colorado (Greeley), 10,488; University of Southern Colorado (Pueblo), 4,331; Western State College (Gunnison), 2,473; Adams State College (Alamosa), 2,419; Mesa College (Grand Junction), 4,721; Fort Lewis College (Durango), 4,363; Metropolitan State College (Denver), 16,351; University of Colorado Health Sciences Centre (Denver), 2,281. 1994 total enrolments: Private 4-year universities and colleges, 27,899; 2-year colleges, 65,882; all universities and colleges, 207,039.

Health. Community hospitals, 1995, numbered 69.

Social Security. In 1995, total beneficiaries, 495,320 and total payments, $3,694m.

Further Reading

Statistical information: Business Research Division, Univ. of Colorado, Boulder 80309. Publishes *Statistical Abstract of Colorado.*
Griffiths, M. and Rubright, L., *Colorado: a Geography.* Boulder, 1983
Sprague, M., *Colorado: A History.* New York, 1976

State Library: Colorado State Library, State Capitol, Denver, 80203.

CONNECTICUT

KEY HISTORICAL EVENTS. Formerly territory of Algonquian-speaking Indians, Connecticut was first colonized by Europeans during the 1630s, when English Puritans moved there from Massachusetts Bay. Settlements were founded in the Connecticut River Valley at Hartford, Saybrook, Wethersfield and Windsor in 1635. They formed an organized commonwealth in 1637. A further settlement was made at New Haven in 1638 and was united to the commonwealth under a royal charter in 1662. The charter confirmed the commonwealth constitution, drawn up by mutual agreement in 1639 and called the Fundamental Orders of Connecticut.

The area was agricultural and its population of largely English descent until the early 19th century. After the War of Independence Connecticut was one of the original 13 states of the Union. Its state constitution came into force in 1818 and survived with amendment until 1965 when a new one was adopted.

In the early 1800s a textile industry was established using local water power. By 1850 the state had more employment in industry than in agriculture, and immigration from the continent of Europe (and especially from southern and eastern Europe) grew rapidly throughout the 19th century. Some immigrants worked in whaling and iron-mining, both now extinct, but most sought industrial employment. Settlement was spread over a large number of relatively small cities, with no single dominant culture.

Yale University was founded at New Haven in 1701. The US Coastguard Academy was founded in 1876 at New London, a former whaling port.

TERRITORY AND POPULATION. Connecticut is bounded in the north by Massachusetts, east by Rhode Island, south by the Atlantic and west by New York. Land area, 4,844 sq. miles (12,547 sq. km).

Census population, 1 April 1990, 3,287,116 (79·1% urban), an increase of 5·78% since 1980. Population estimate (1994), 3,275,251. Births (1993) were 46,658 (14·1 per 1,000 population); deaths, 28,905 (8·9); infant deaths (1990), 398 (7·9 per 1,000 live births); marriages, 26,046 (15·8); divorces, 11,617 (7·1).

Population in 4 census years was:

	White	Black	Indian	Asian	Total	Per sq. mile
1910	1,098,897	15,174	152	533	1,114,756	231·3
1930	1,576,700	29,354	162	687	1,606,903	328·0
1980	2,799,420	217,433	4,533	18,970	3,107,576	634·3

	White	Black	Indian	Asian	Others	Total	Per sq. mile
1990	2,859,353	274,269	6,654	50,698	96,142	3,287,116	678·6

Of the total population in 1993, 242,572 persons (of any race) were of Hispanic origin, 1,589,000 persons were male. Those 18 years old or older numbered 2,497,836. There were 183 residents in 5 Indian Reservations.

The chief cities and towns are (1994 state estimates):

Bridgeport	141,686	Stamford	108,056	Bristol	60,640
Hartford	139,739	Norwalk	78,331	West Hartford	60,110
New Haven	130,474	New Britain	75,491	Meriden	59,479
Waterbury	108,961	Danbury	65,585	Greenwich	58,441

CLIMATE. New Haven: Jan. 25°F (−3·8°C), July 74°F (23·4°C). Annual rainfall 45" (1,143 mm). Connecticut belongs to the New England climate zone (*see* UNITED STATES: Climate).

CONSTITUTION AND GOVERNMENT. The 1818 Constitution was revised in 1955. On 30 Dec. 1965 a new constitution went into effect, having been framed by a constitutional convention in the summer of 1965 and approved by the voters in Dec. 1965.

The General Assembly consists of a Senate of 36 members and a House of Representatives of 151 members. Members of each House are elected for the term of 2 years. Legislative sessions are annual.

The state sends 6 representatives to Congress.

In the 1996 presidential election Clinton polled 712,603 votes; Dole, 481,047; Perot, 137,784. The state capital is Hartford. There are 8 counties.

Governor: John G. Rowland (R.), 1995–99 ($78,000).
Lieut.-Governor: M. Jodi Rell (R.) ($55,000).
Secretary of State: Miles S. Rapoport (D.) ($50,000).

BUDGET. For the year ending 30 June 1994 (state government figures) general revenues were $11,286m. (taxation, $6,788m., and federal aid, $2,628m.); general expenditures were $11,207m. (education, $2,664m., transport, $793m., public welfare, $2,980m.).

Per capita income, 1995, was $31,776.

NATURAL RESOURCES

Minerals. The state has some mineral resources: crushed stone, sand, gravel, clay, dimension stone, feldspar and quartz; total production in 1995 was valued at $81m.

Agriculture. In 1995 the state had 4,000 farms with annual sales of at least $1,000 having a total area of 358,743 acres; the average farm size was 100 acres, valued at $5,959 per acre. Farm income (1992): Crops, $183m. and livestock, $153m. Principal crops are grains, hay, tobacco, vegetables, maize, melons, fruit, nuts, berries and greenhouse and nursery products.

Livestock (1993): 77,000 all cattle (value $59·3m.), 10,900 sheep ($1·1m.), 6,000 swine ($630,000) and 4·6m. poultry ($11·5m.).

Forestry. The state has 144,464 acres of state forest land.

INDUSTRY. Total non-agricultural employment in Sept. 1997 was 1,629,100. The main employers are manufacturers (275,000 workers mainly in transport equipment, machinery, computer, electronic and electrical equipment and fabricated metals); retail trade (273,000 workers); services (504,700) and government (225,800). There were 79,300 unemployed.

COMMUNICATIONS

Roads. The total length of highways in 1994 was 20,384 miles, all surfaced. Motor vehicles registered in 1994 numbered 2,046,000.

Railways. In 1994 there were 570 miles (912 km) of railway route miles.

Civil Aviation. In 1995 there were 61 airports (20 commercial, 6 state-owned and 35 private), 63 heliports and 8 seaplane bases.

Telecommunications (1994). There were 75 broadcasting stations and 11 television stations.

Press. In 1994 there were 141 daily, Sunday, weekly and monthly newspapers.

SOCIAL INSTITUTIONS

Justice. In 1995 there were 14,246 inmates in 19 state correctional institutions and centres. There were 57,000 adults under state correctional supervision. The death penalty for murder has been authorized.

Religion. The leading religious denominations (1990) in the state are the Roman Catholic (1,374,000 members), United Churches of Christ (135,000), Protestant Episcopal (78,000), Jewish (115,000), Methodist (56,000), Black Baptist (64,000), Presbyterian and Greek Orthodox.

Education. Elementary instruction is free for all children between the ages of 4 and 16 years, and compulsory for all children between the ages of 7 and 16 years. In 1993 there were 978 public local schools, 3 academies, 17 state vocational-technical schools, 30 state or state-aided schools, 6 regional educational service centres and 334 non-public schools. In 1994 there were 507,825 pupils and 39,816 public elementary and secondary teachers. Expenditure of the state on public schools, 1994, $4,000m. Mean salary of teachers in public schools, 1993, $48,300.

Connecticut has 42 colleges, of which one state university, 4 state colleges, and 12 community-technical colleges are state funded. The University of Connecticut at Storrs, founded 1881, had 1,502 faculty and 23,649 students in 1994. Yale University, New Haven, founded in 1701, had 2,358 faculty and 10,916 students; Wesleyan University, Middletown, founded 1831, 261 faculty and 3,270 students; Trinity College, Hartford, founded 1823, 166 faculty and 2,146 students; Connecticut College, New London, founded 1915, 175 faculty and 1,919 students; The University of Hartford, founded 1877, 331 faculty and 7,241 students. The state colleges faculty was 1,087 and the number of students was 35,111. The technical colleges had 718 faculty and 45,542 students. There were 18 independent (4-year course) colleges with 4,219 faculty and 55,234 students; 6 independent (2-year course) colleges and 74 faculty and 1,790 students and 1 US Coastguard Academy with 43 faculty and 930 students.

Health. Hospitals listed by the American Hospital Association, 1993, numbered 62. The state operated 1 general hospital (252 beds), 7 hospitals for the mentally ill (891 patients), 1 training school for the mentally retarded, and 6 regional centres (5,705 clients in residential settings). There were 12,387 physicians and surgeons, 3,059 dentists and 49,864 registered nurses.

Social Security. Disbursements in 1992 amounted to $42m. in aid to the aged and disabled, (with an average payment per month of $664·82). In other areas of welfare, there was an average of 57,000 cases for aid to families with dependent children comprising 162,000 recipients.

Further Reading

State Register and Manual. Secretary of State. Hartford (CT). Annual
The Structure of Connecticut's State Government. Connecticut Public Expenditure Council. Hartford, 1973
Halliburton, W. J., *The People of Connecticut.* Norwalk, 1985
Van Dusen, Albert E., *Connecticut.* New York, 1961

State Library: Connecticut State Library, 231 Capitol Avenue, Hartford (CT), 06105; Tel. 860-566-4971.
State Book Store: Dept. of Environmental Protection, 79 Elm St., Hartford (CT), 06106; Tel. 860-424-3555.
Business Incentives: Connecticut Economic Resource Center, 805 Brook St., Rocky Hill (CT), 06067; Tel. 860-571-7136.
Connecticut Tourism: Dept. of Economic and Community Development, 865 Brook St., Rocky Hill (CT), 06067; Tel. 860-258-4355.

DELAWARE

KEY HISTORICAL EVENTS. Delaware was the territory of Algonquian-speaking Indians who were displaced by European settlement in the 17th century. The first settlers were Swedes who came in 1638 to build Fort Christina (now Wilmington), and colonize what they called New Sweden. Their colony was taken by the Dutch from New Amsterdam in 1655. In 1664 the British took the whole New Amsterdam colony, including Delaware, and called it New York.

In 1682 Delaware was granted to William Penn, who wanted access to the coast for his Pennsylvania colony. Union of the two colonies was unpopular, and Delaware gained its own government in 1704, although it continued to share a royal governor with Pennsylvania until the War of Independence. Delaware then became one of the 13 original states of the Union and the first to ratify the federal constitution (on 7 Dec. 1787).

The population was of Swedish, Finnish, British and Irish extraction. The land was low-lying and fertile, and the use of slave labour was legal. There was a significant number of black slaves, but Delaware was a border state during the Civil War (1861–65) and did not leave the Union.

The main 19th century immigrants were European Jews, Poles, Germans and Italians. The north became industrial and densely populated, becoming more so after the Second World War with the rise of the petrochemical industry. Industry in general profited from the opening of the Chesapeake and Delaware Canal in 1829; it was converted to a toll-free deep channel for ocean-going ships in 1919.

TERRITORY AND POPULATION. Delaware is bounded north by Pennsylvania, north-east by New Jersey, east by Delaware Bay, south and west by Maryland. Land area 1,982 sq. miles (5,133 sq. km). Census population, 1 April 1990 was 666,168 (73% urban), an increase of 12·1% since 1980. Population estimate, (1995), 717,041. Births in 1995, 10,260 (14·3 per 1,000 population); deaths, 6,281 (8·6); infant deaths, 79 (8·9 per 1,000 live births); marriages, 5,378 (7·4); divorces, 3,175 (4·8).

Population in 5 census years was:

	White	Black	Indian	Asiatic	Total	Per sq. mile
1910	171,102	31,181	5	34	202,322	103·0
1930	205,718	32,602	5	55	238,380	120·5
1960	384,327	60,688	597	410	446,292	224·0
			All others			
1980	488,002	96,157	10,179		594,338	290·8
1990	535,094	112,460	18,614		666,168	325·9

Of the total population in 1990, 48·5% were male and 70·4% were 21 years old or older.

The 1990 census figures show Wilmington with population of 71,529; Newark, 25,098; Dover, 27,630; Elsmere Town, 5,935; Milford City, 6,040; Seaford City, 5,089.

CLIMATE. Wilmington. Jan. 32°F (0°C), July 75°F (23·9°C). Annual rainfall 43" (1,076 mm). Delaware belongs to the Atlantic Coast climate zone (*see* UNITED STATES: Climate).

CONSTITUTION AND GOVERNMENT. The present constitution (the fourth) dates from 1897, and has had 51 amendments; it was not ratified by the electorate but promulgated by the Constitutional Convention. The General Assembly consists of a Senate of 21 members elected for 4 years and a House of Representatives of 41 members elected for 2 years.

The state sends 1 representative to Congress.

In the 1996 presidential election Clinton polled 140,209 votes; Dole, 98,906; Perot, 28,693.

The state capital is Dover. Delaware is divided into 3 counties.

Governor: Thomas R. Carper (D.), 1997–2001 ($107,000).
Lieut.-Governor: Ruth Ann Minner (D.), ($44,600).
Secretary of State: Edward J. Freel (D.) ($89,900).

FINANCE. For the year ending 30 June 1996 total revenue was $1,656·2m., of which federal grants were an estimated $420·0m. Total expenditure, 1996, was $1,650·9m.

On 30 June 1996 the total debt was $654·7m.

Per capita income (1996) was $27,724.

NATURAL RESOURCES

Minerals. The mineral resources of Delaware are not extensive, consisting chiefly of clay products, stone, sand and gravel and magnesium compounds.

Agriculture. Delaware is mainly an industrial state, with agriculture as its main industry. There were 0·57m. acres in 2,500 farms in 1996; 0·48m. acres of this is harvested annually. The average farm was valued (land and buildings) at $656,982 in 1996. The major product is broilers, accounting for $524m. in cash receipts, out of total farm cash receipts of $860m. in 1996.

The chief field crops are soybeans and corn for feed.

INDUSTRY. In 1996 manufacturing establishments employed 56,600 people; main manufactures were chemicals, transport equipment and food.

COMMUNICATIONS

Roads. The state in 1996 maintained 5,051·59 miles of roads and streets including 1,430·39 miles of federally-aided highways and 321·04 miles of roads in the National Highway System. There were also 662·72 miles of municipally maintained streets. Vehicles registered in year ended 31 Dec. 1996, 661,781.

Railways. In 1996 the state had 288·5 miles of active rail line, 23·2 miles of which is part of Amtrak's high speed Northeast corridor. In 1996 there were 1,058,067 passenger trips beginning or ending in Delaware (581,285 intercity (Amtrak) and 476,782 commuter). An important component of Delaware's freight infrastructure is the rail access to the Port of Wilmington.

Civil Aviation. In 1996 Delaware had 11 public use airports and one helistop, all of which were for general use.

SOCIAL INSTITUTIONS

Justice. State prisons, 30 Sept. 1996–30 Sept. 1997, had daily average of 4,997 inmates. The death penalty has been authorized; the last execution was in 1996.

Religion. Membership, 1979–80: Methodists, 60,489; Roman Catholics, 103,060; Episcopalians, 18,696; Lutherans, 10,000.

Education. The state has free public schools and compulsory school attendance. In Sept. 1996 the elementary and secondary public schools had 110,549 enrolled pupils and 6,593 classroom teachers. Another 24,712 children were enrolled in private and parochial schools. State appropriation for public schools (financial year 1996–97) was about $554m. Average salary of classroom teachers (financial year 1996–97), $41,436. The state supports the University of Delaware at Newark (1834) which had 918 full-time faculty members and 21,380 students in Sept. 1996, Delaware State University, Dover (1892), with 173 full-time faculty members and 3,328 students, and the 4 campuses of Delaware Technical and Community College (Wilmington, Stanton, Dover and Georgetown) with 282 full-time faculty members and 11,871 students.

Health. In 1996 there were 7 short-term general hospitals. During fiscal year 1996 the average daily census in state mental hospitals was 337.

Social Security. In 1974 the federal Supplemental Security Income (SSI) programme lessened state responsibility for the aged, blind and disabled. Total SSI payments in Delaware (1994 fiscal year), $33,852,316. Provisions are also made for the care of dependent children; in fiscal year 1994 there were 26,925 recipients in 10,073 families (average monthly payment per family, $300). The total state programme for the year ending 30 June 1994 was $36,292,952 for the care of dependent children.

Further Reading

Statistical information: Delaware Economic Development Office POB 1401, Dover 19903. Publishes *Delaware Data Book.*
State Manual, Containing Official List of Officers, Commissions and County Officers. Secretary of State, Dover. Annual
Hoffecker, C. E., *Delaware: a Bicentennial History.* New York, 1977
Smeal, L., *Delaware Historical and Biographical Index.* New York, 1984
Weslager, C. A., *Delaware Indians, a History.* Rutgers Univ. Press, 1972
Topical History of Delaware. Division of Historical and Cultural Affairs. Dover, 1977

DISTRICT OF COLUMBIA

KEY HISTORICAL EVENTS. The District of Columbia, organized in 1790, is the seat of the Government of the USA, for which the land was ceded by the states of Maryland and Virginia to the USA as a site for the national capital. It was established under Acts of Congress in 1790 and 1791. Congress first met in it in 1800 and federal authority over it became vested in 1801. In 1846 the land ceded by Virginia (about 33 sq. miles) was given back.

TERRITORY AND POPULATION. The District forms an enclave on the Potomac River, where the river forms the south-west boundary of Maryland. The land area of the District of Columbia is 61 sq. miles (159 sq. km).

Census population, 1 April 1990, was 606,900 (100% urban), a decrease of 4·82% from that of 1980. Metropolitan statistical area of Washington, DC–Md–Va. (1980), 3m. Density of population in the District, 1990, 9,884 per sq. mile. Population estimate (1995), 554,000. Births, 1993, in the District were 10,629 (18·4 per 1,000 population); deaths, 7,000 (11·6); infant deaths (1991), 183 (18·7 per 1,000 live births); marriages, 5,031 (8·6); divorces, 2,290 (3·9).

Population in 5 census years was:

	White	Black	Indian	Chinese and Japanese	Total	Per sq. mile
1910	236,128	94,446	68	427	331,069	5,517·8
1930	353,981	132,068	40	780	486,869	7,981·5
1960	345,263	411,737	587	3,532	763,956	12,523·9

	White	Black	All others		Total	Per sq. mile
1970	209,272	537,712	9,526		756,510	12,321·0
1980	171,768	448,906	17,659		638,333	10,184·0

CLIMATE. Washington. Jan. 34°F (1·1°C), July 77°F (25°C). Annual rainfall 43" (1,064 mm). The District of Columbia belongs to the Atlantic Coast climate zone (*see* UNITED STATES: Climate).

GOVERNMENT. Local government, from 1 July 1878 until Aug. 1967, was that of a municipal corporation administered by a board of 3 commissioners, of whom 2 were appointed from civil life by the President, and confirmed by the Senate, for a term of 3 years each. The other commissioner was detailed by the President from the Engineer Corps of the Army. The Commission form of government was abolished in 1967 and a new Mayor Council instituted with officers appointed by the President with the advice and consent of the Senate. On 24 Dec. 1973 the appointed officers were replaced by an elected Mayor and councillors, with full legislative powers in local matters as from 1974. Congress retains the right to legislate, to veto or supersede the Council's acts. The 23rd amendment to the federal constitution (1961) conferred the right to vote in national elections. The District has 2 delegates in Congress who may vote in committees but not on the House floor. In the 1996 presidential election Clinton polled 152,031 votes; Dole, 16,637; Perot, 3,479.

BUDGET. The District's revenues are derived from a tax on real and personal property, sales taxes, taxes on corporations and companies, licences for conducting various businesses and from federal payments.

The District of Columbia has no bonded debt not covered by its accumulated sinking fund.

INDUSTRY. The District's main industries are government service; services; wholesale and retail trade; finance, real estate, insurance, communications, transport and utilities.

TOURISM. About 17m. visitors stay in the District every year and spend about $1,000m.

COMMUNICATIONS

Roads. Within the District are 340 miles of bus routes. There are 1,102 miles of streets maintained by the District; of these, 673 miles are local streets, 262 miles are major arterial roads. In 1991, 246,390 motor vehicles were registered.

Railways. There is a metro in Washington extending to 130 km, and 2 commuter rail networks.

Civil Aviation. The District is served by 3 general airports; across the Potomac River in Arlington, Va., is National Airport, in Chantilly, Va., is Dulles International Airport and in Maryland is Baltimore–Washington International Airport.

SOCIAL INSTITUTIONS

Justice. The death penalty was declared unconstitutional in the District of Columbia on 14 Nov. 1973. In 1994 there were 10,943 prisoners in state correctional institutions.

The District's Court system is the Judicial Branch of the District of Columbia. It is the only completely unified court system in the United States, possibly because of the District's unique city-state jurisdiction. Until the District of Columbia Court Reform and Criminal Procedure Act of 1970, the judicial system was almost entirely in the hands of Federal Government. Since that time, the system has been similar in most respects to the autonomous systems of the states.

Religion. The largest churches are the Protestant and Roman Catholic Christian churches; there are also Jewish, Eastern Orthodox and Islamic congregations.

Education. In 1992 there were 80,092 pupils and 6,014 teachers in public secondary and elementary schools. State and local government expenditure on public schools, 1991, $721,495,000. Higher education is given through the Consortium of Universities of the Metropolitan Washington Area, which consists of six universities and three colleges: Georgetown University, founded in 1795 by the Jesuit Order; George Washington University, non-sectarian founded in 1821; Howard University, founded in 1867; Catholic University of America, founded in 1887; American University (Methodist) founded in 1893; University of DC, founded 1976; Gallaudet College, founded 1864; Trinity College, founded 1897. There are altogether 18 institutes of higher education.

Social Security. The District government provides primary health care for residents, mainly through its Department of Human Services. In 1994 there were 12 community hospitals with 4,000 beds. There were 78,000 beneficiaries of social security in 1994 including 54,000 retired workers and dependants, 16,000 survivors of deceased workers and 9,000 disabled workers and dependants. Total annual payments were $509m.

Further Reading

Statistical Information: The Metropolitan Washington Board of Trade publications.
Reports of the Commissioners of the District of Columbia. Annual. Washington
Bowling, K. R., *The Creation of Washington DC: the Idea and the Location of the American Capital.* Washington (DC), 1991

FLORIDA

KEY HISTORICAL EVENTS. There were French and Spanish settlements in Florida in the 16th century, of which the Spanish, at St Augustine in 1565, proved permanent. Florida was claimed by Spain until 1763 when it passed to Britain. Although regained by Spain in 1783, the British used it as a base for attacks on American forces during the war of 1812. Gen. Andrew Jackson in 1818 captured Pensacola for the USA. In 1819 a treaty was signed which ceded Florida to the USA with effect from 1821 and it became a Territory of the USA in 1822.

Florida had been the home of the Apalachee and Timucua Indians. After 1770 groups of Creek Indians began to arrive as refugees from the European-Indian wars. These 'Seminoles' or runaways attracted other refugees including slaves, the recapture of whom was the motive for the first Seminole War of 1817–18. A second war followed in 1835–42, when the Seminoles retreated to the Everglades swamps. After a third war in 1855–58 most Seminoles were forced or persuaded to move to reserves in Oklahoma.

Florida became a state in 1845. About half of the population were black slaves. At the outbreak of Civil War in 1861 the state seceded from the Union.

During the 20th century Florida continued to grow fruit and vegetables, but real-estate development (often for retirement) and the growth of tourism and the aerospace industry set it apart from other ex-plantation states.

TERRITORY AND POPULATION. Florida is a peninsula bounded west by the Gulf of Mexico, south by the Straits of Florida, east by the Atlantic, north by Georgia and north-west by Alabama. Land area, 53,937 sq. miles (139,697 sq. km). Census population, 1 April 1990, 12,937,926, an increase of 32·8% since 1980. Estimate (1995), 14,166,000. Births in 1995 were 192,537; deaths, 148,000; in 1994, infant deaths, 1,567; marriages, 142,895; divorces and other dissolutions, 81,628.

Population in 5 federal census years was:

	White	Black	All Others	Total	Per Sq. mile
1950	2,166,051	603,101	2,153	2,771,305	51·1
1960	4,063,881	880,168	7,493	4,952,788	91·5
1970	5,719,343	1,041,651	28,449	6,789,443	125·6
1980	8,319,448	1,342,478	84,398	9,746,324	180·1
1990	10,749,285	1,759,534	429,107	12,937,926	238·9

Of the population in 1990, 84·8% were urban, 48·4% male and 73·8% were 20 years of age or over.

The largest cities in the state, 1990 census (and 1994) are: Jacksonville, 672,971 (676,718); Miami, 358,548 (365,498); Tampa, 280,015 (285,153); St Petersburg, 238,629 (241,563); Hialeah, 188,004 (203,911); Orlando, 164,693 (170,307); Fort Lauderdale, 149,377 (149,491); Tallahassee, 124,773 (137,057); Hollywood, 121,697 (125,342); Clearwater, 98,784 (101,162); Gainesville, 84,770 (96,052); Coral Springs, 79,443 (93,439); Miami Beach, 92,639 (91,775); Pembroke Pines, 65,452 (87,948); Cape Coral, 74,991 (85,807); West Palm Beach, 67,764 (76,418); Plantation, 66,814 (75,484); Lakeland, 70,576 (74,626); Pompano Beach, 72,411 (73,950).

Population of the largest metropolitan areas (1994): Tampa-St Petersburg-Clearwater, 2,163,509; Miami, 1,990,445; Orlando, 1,359,001; Fort Lauderdale, 1,340,220.

CLIMATE. Jacksonville. Jan. 55°F (12·8°C), July 81°F (27·2°C). Annual rainfall 54" (1,353 mm). Key West. Jan. 70°F (21·1°C), July 83°F (28·3°C). Annual rainfall 39" (968 mm). Miami. Jan. 67°F (19·4°C), July 82°F (27·8°C). Annual rainfall 60" (1,516 mm). Tampa. Jan. 61°F (16·1°C), July 81°F (27·2°C). Annual rainfall 51" (1,285 mm). Florida belongs to the Gulf Coast climate zone (*see* UNITED STATES: Climate).

CONSTITUTION AND GOVERNMENT. The 1968 Legislature revised the constitution of 1885. The state legislature consists of a Senate of 40 members, elected for 4 years, and House of Representatives with 120 members elected for 2 years. Sessions are held annually, and are limited to 60 days.

The state sends 23 representatives to Congress.

In the 1996 presidential election Clinton polled 2,533,502 votes; Dole, 2,226,117; Perot, 482,237.

The state capital is Tallahassee. The state is divided into 67 counties.

Governor: Lawton Chiles (D.), 1995–99 ($104,817).
Lieut.-Governor: Kenneth 'Buddy' MacKay (D.), ($100,403).
Secretary of State: Sandra Mortham (R.), ($103,757).

FINANCE. There is no state income tax on individuals. For the fiscal year 1994 the state had a total revenue of $34,805m. and total expenditure of $32,284m. General revenue fund expenditure was $29,991m.

Net long-term debt, 30 June 1994, amounted to $13,634m.

Per capita personal income (1995) was $22,916.

NATURAL RESOURCES

Minerals. Chief mineral is phosphate rock, of which marketable production in 1992 was 36·2m. tonnes. This was approximately 75% of US and 25% of the world supply of phosphate in 1992.

Agriculture. In 1994 area under crops, 3,937,292 acres; pasture and ranges, 6,324,067 acres. In 1995 there were 39,000 farms; net income per farm averaged $57,941. Total value of all farm land and buildings (1994), $25,297·6m. There were 10·3m. acres in farms and ranches in 1994, including 853,742 (of which 667,521 were orange) acres in citrus groves. Total cash receipts from crops and livestock (1994), $5,977·97m., of which crops provided $4,786·34m. Major crop contributors were oranges, grapefruit, tomatoes, peppers, other winter vegetables, indoor and landscaping plants and sugar-cane. Poultry farms produced 132·7m. chickens and 2,538m. eggs in 1994. On 1 Jan. 1995 the state had 2·02m. cattle, including 176,000 milk cows (1994), and about 0·1m. swine.

Forestry. The national forests covered an area of 1·1m. acres in 1997. There were 16,548,922 acres of commercial forest and 33 state forests of 596,137 acres.

Fisheries. Florida has extensive fisheries for oysters, shrimp, red snapper, crabs, mackerel and mullet. Catch (1990), 180m. lb. valued at $203m.

INDUSTRY. In 1994 there were 15,831 manufacturers. They employed 483,754 persons. The printing and publishing, machinery and computer equipment, apparel and finished products, fabricated metal products, and lumber and wood products industries are important.

TOURISM. During 1994, 39·8m. tourists visited Florida. They spent $33,390m. making tourism one of the biggest industries in the state. There were (1993) 148 state parks, 33 state forests, 3 national parks, 8 national memorials, monuments, seashores and preserves and 3 national forests. The state parks were visited by 11,586,999 people in 1992–93.

COMMUNICATIONS

Roads. The state (1994) had 113,478 miles of highways, roads, and streets all of which were in the state and local system (65,084 miles being county roads); in 1992, 19,814·8 miles were federally-aided roads (1,444 miles interstate).

In 1994 there were 10,252,000 vehicle registrations.

Railways. In 1993 there were 2,988 miles of railway and 14 rail companies. There is a metro of 20 miles (33 km), a peoplemover and a commuter rail route in Miami.

Civil Aviation. In 1993 Florida had 133 public use airports (12 international) of which 20 have scheduled commercial service, and 28 seaplane bases.

SOCIAL INSTITUTIONS

Justice. The death penalty is authorized; there have been over 30 executions since 1979. State prisons, 1994, had 56,275 inmates. Chain gangs were introduced in 1995.

Religion. The main Christian churches are Roman Catholic, Baptist, Methodist, Presbyterian and Episcopalian. There were 0·1m. Mormons in 1995.

Education. Attendance at school is compulsory between 7 and 16.

In the 1994–95 school year the public elementary and secondary schools had 2,107,514 pupils enrolled in grades K–12. Total expenditure on public schools (1994) was $17,035m. The state maintains 28 community colleges, with a full-time equivalent enrolment of 192,698 in 1995.

There are 9 universities in the state system, with a total of 207,812 students in 1995: The University of Florida at Gainesville (founded 1853) with 39,417 students; the Florida State University (founded at Tallahassee in 1857) with 30,268; the University of South Florida at Tampa (founded 1960) with 36,146; Florida A. & M. University at Tallahassee (founded 1887) with 10,267; Florida Atlantic University (founded 1964) at Boca Raton with 18,240; the University of West Florida at Pensacola with 8,250; the University of Central Florida at Orlando with 26,555; the University of North Florida at Jacksonville with 10,463; Florida International University at Miami with 28,206.

Health. In 1994 there were 218 community hospitals with 51,400 beds.

Social Security. From 1974 aid to the aged, blind and disabled became a federal responsibility. The state continued to give aid to families with dependent children and general assistance. Monthly payments, 1991–92: Aid to 3,220 blind averaged $275·40; aid to 142,071 dependent children averaged $251·59; aid to 135,735 disabled averaged $260·17; aid to 82,161 aged averaged $194·04.

Further Reading

Statistical information: Bureau of Economic and Business Research, Univ. of Florida, Gainesville 32611. Publishes *Florida Statistical Abstract.*
Denslow, D. A. *et al., The Economy of Florida.* Florida Univ. Press, 1990
Fernald, E. A. (ed.) *Atlas of Florida.* Florida State Univ., 1981
Huckshorn, R. J. (ed.) *Government and Politics in Florida.* Florida Univ. Press, 1991
Morris, A., *The Florida Handbook.* Tallahassee. Biennial
Shermyen, A. H. (ed.), *1991 Florida Statistical Abstract.* Florida Univ. Press, 1991

State Library: Gray Building, Tallahassee.

GEORGIA

KEY HISTORICAL EVENTS. Originally the territory of Creek and Cherokee tribes, Georgia was first settled by Europeans in the 18th century. James Oglethorpe founded Savannah in 1733, intending it as a colony which offered a new start to debtors, convicts and the poor. Settlement was slow until 1783, when growth began in the cotton-growing areas west of Augusta. The Indian population was cleared off the rich cotton land and moved beyond the Mississippi. Georgia became one of the original 13 states of the Union.

A plantation economy developed rapidly, using slave labour. In 1861 Georgia seceded from the Union and became an important source of supplies for the

Confederate cause, although some northern areas never accepted secession and continued in sympathy with the Union during the Civil War. At the beginning of the war 56% of the population were white, descendants of British, Austrian and New England immigrants; the remaining 44% were black slaves.

The city of Atlanta, which grew as a railway junction, was destroyed during the war but revived to become the centre of southern states during the reconstruction period. Atlanta was confirmed as state capital in 1877. Also in Atlanta were developed successive movements for black freedom in social, economic and political life. The Southern Christian Leadership Conference, led by Martin Luther King (assassinated in 1968), was based in King's native city of Atlanta.

TERRITORY AND POPULATION. Georgia is bounded north by Tennessee and North Carolina, north-east by South Carolina, east by the Atlantic, south by Florida and west by Alabama. Land area, 58,910 sq. miles (152,577 sq. km). Census population, 1 April 1990, was 6,478,216 (63·2% urban), an increase of 18·56% since 1980. Population estimate (1996), 7,353,000. Births, 1995, were 112,246 (15·8 per 1,000 population); deaths, 58,433 (8·2); infant deaths, 1,058 (9·4 per 1,000 live births); marriages, 61,908 (8·7); divorces and annulments, 37,070 (5·2).

Population in 5 census years was:

	White	Black	Indian	Asiatic	Total	Per sq. mile
1910	1,431,802	1,176,987	95	237	2,609,121	44·4
1930	1,837,021	1,071,125	43	317	2,908,506	49·7
			All others			
1970	3,391,242	1,187,149	11,184		4,589,575	79·0
1980	3,948,007	1,465,457	50,801		5,464,265	92·7
1990	4,600,148	1,746,565	131,507		6,478,216	110·0

Of the 1990 population, 3,144,503 were male, 4,097,339 were urban and those 20 years of age and over numbered 4,534,963.

The largest cities are: Atlanta (capital), with population, 1994 estimate, of 396,000; Columbus, 186,000; Savannah, 141,000; Macon, 109,000.

CLIMATE. Atlanta. Jan. 43°F (6·1°C), July 78°F (25·6°C). Annual rainfall 49" (1,234 mm). Georgia belongs to the Atlantic Coast climate zone (see UNITED STATES: Climate).

CONSTITUTION AND GOVERNMENT. A new constitution was ratified in the general election of 2 Nov. 1976, proclaimed on 22 Dec. 1976 and became effective 1 Jan. 1977. The General Assembly consists of a Senate of 56 members and a House of Representatives of 180 members, both elected for 2 years. Legislative sessions are annual, beginning the 2nd Monday in Jan. and lasting for 40 days.

Georgia was the first state to extend the franchise to all citizens 18 years old and above.

The state sends 11 representatives to Congress.

At the 1996 presidential election Clinton polled 1,052,928 votes; Dole, 1,078,837; Perot, 146,039.

The state capital is Atlanta. Georgia is divided into 159 counties.

Governor: Zell Miller (D.), 1995–99 ($103,074).
Lieut.-Governor: Pierre Howard (D.) ($67,319).
Secretary of State: Lewis Massey (D.) ($82,786).

BUDGET. For the fiscal year ending 30 June 1997 revenue was $11,793m.; general expenditure was $11,793m.

Per capita personal income (1996), was $22,709.

NATURAL RESOURCES

Minerals. Georgia is the leading producer of kaolin. The state ranks first in production of crushed and dimensional granite, second in production of fuller's earth and marble (crushed and dimensional).

Agriculture. In 1996, 43,000 farms covered 11·8m. acres; average farm was of 274 acres. In 1995 the average value of farmland and buildings was $1,256 per acre. For 1995 cotton output was 1,941m. bales (of 480 lbs). Other major crops include tobacco, corn, wheat, soybeans, peanuts and pecans. Cash income, 1995, $5,381m.: from crops, $2,377m.; from livestock, $2,789m.

In 1996 farm animals included 1·56m. all cattle, 0·90m. swine and 1,070m. (1995) poultry.

Forestry. The forested area in 1996 was 23·6m. acres.

INDUSTRY. In 1996 the state's 10,598 manufacturing establishments had 583,314 workers; the main groups were textiles, apparel, food and transport equipment. Trade employed 887,466, services, 826,165, government, 558,753.

TOURISM. In 1996 tourists spent $14,775m. There are 44 state parks.

COMMUNICATIONS

Roads. In 1995 there were 112,160 miles of public roads, including 1,244 miles of interstate highways. In 1995 there were 6,543,926 motor vehicles registered.

Railways. In 1996 there were 4,962 miles of railways and a metro in Atlanta.

Civil Aviation. In 1997 there were 106 public airports, 9 with scheduled commercial service.

Shipping. There are deepwater ports at Savannah, the principal port, and Brunswick.

SOCIAL INSTITUTIONS

Justice. In 1996, state prisons had 35,139 inmates. The death penalty is authorized for capital offences.

Under a Local Option Act, the sale of alcoholic beverages is prohibited in some counties.

Religion. An estimated 57·6% of the population are church members. Of the total population, 45·6% are Protestant, 3·2% are Roman Catholic and 1·1% are Jewish.

Education. Since 1945 education has been compulsory; tuition is free for pupils between the ages of 6 and 18 years. In 1996 there were 1,799 public elementary and public secondary schools with 1·3m. pupils and 81,058 teachers. Teachers' salaries averaged $33,869 in 1996. Expenditure on public schools (1995–96), $7,781m. or $1,080 per capita and $4,589 per pupil.

The University of Georgia (Athens) was founded in 1785 and was the first chartered State University in the US (29,404 students in 1996–97). Other institutions of higher learning include Georgia Institute of Technology, Atlanta (12,985), Emory University, Atlanta (11,308), Georgia State University, Atlanta (23,410) and Georgia Sourheev University, Statesboro (14,312). The Atlanta University Center, devoted primarily to Black education, includes Clark Atlanta University (5,230) and Morris Brown College (2,169) co-educational, Morehouse (2,884), a liberal arts college for men, Interdenominational Theological Center (419), a co-educational theological school, and Spelman College (1,961), the first liberal arts college for Black women in the US. Atlanta University serves as the graduate school centre for the complex. Wesleyan College (445) near Macon is the oldest chartered women's college in the world.

Health. In 1995, general hospitals licensed by the Department of Human Resources numbered 158 with 24,756 beds.

Social Security. In Dec. 1995, 43,666 persons were receiving SSI old-age assistance and 126,662 receiving benefits for blind and disabled persons. In 1996, there were 132,625 families receiving aid to dependent children.

Further Reading

Statistical information: Selig Center for Economic Growth, Univ. of Georgia, Athens 30602.
Publishes *Georgia Statistical Abstract.*
Rowland, A. R., *A Bibliography of the Writings on Georgia History.* Hamden, Conn., 1978

State Library: Judicial Building, Capital Sq., Atlanta.

HAWAII

KEY HISTORICAL EVENTS. The islands of Hawaii were settled by
Polynesian immigrants, probably from the Marquesas Islands, about AD 400. A
second major immigration, from Tahiti, occurred around 800–900. In the late 18th
century all the islands of the group were united into one kingdom by Kamehameha I.
Western exploration began in 1778, and Christian missions were established after
1820. Europeans called Hawaii the Sandwich Islands. The main foreign states
interested were the USA, Britain and France. Because of the threat imposed by their
rivalry, Kamehameha III placed Hawaii under US protection in 1851. US sugar-
growing companies became dominant in the economy and in 1887 the USA obtained
a naval base at Pearl Harbour. A struggle developed between forces for and against
annexation by the USA. In 1893 the monarchy was overthrown. The republican
government agreed to be annexed to the USA in 1898, and Hawaii became a US
Territory in 1900.

The islands and the naval base were of great strategic importance during the
Second World War, when the Japanese attack on Pearl Harbour brought the USA into
the war.

Hawaii became the 50th state of the Union in 1959. The 19th century plantation
economy led to much immigration of workers, especially from China and Japan. At
the same time the Hawaiians fell victim to foreign diseases, and their laws, religions
and culture were gradually adapted to foreign models.

TERRITORY AND POPULATION. The Hawaiian Islands lie in the North
Pacific Ocean, between 18° 56' and 28° 25' N. lat. and 154° 49' and 178° 22' W. long.,
about 2,090 nautical miles south-west of San Francisco. There are 136 named islands
and islets in the group, of which 7 major and 8 minor islands are inhabited. Land area,
6,423 sq. miles (16,636 sq. km). Census population, 1 April 1990, 1,108,229 (51%
male, 89% urban), an increase of 14·84% since 1980; density was 172·5 per sq. mile.
Estimated population (1996), 1,183,723.

The principal islands are Hawaii, 4,028 sq. miles and population, 1990, 120,317;
Maui, 727 and 91,361; Oahu, 600 and 836,231; Kauai, 552 and 50,947; Molokai, 260
and 6,717; Lanai, 141 and 2,426; Niihau, 70 and 230; Kahoolawe, 45 (uninhabited).
The capital Honolulu, on the island of Oahu, had a population in 1980 of 365,048 and
Hilo on the island of Hawaii, 37,808 in 1990.

Figures for racial groups, 1980, were: 331,925 White, 239,734 Japanese, 132,075
Filipinos, 118,251 Hawaiian, 55,916 Chinese, 17,453 Korean, 17,687 Black, 51,650
all others. In 1989, 35% of the population (outside barracks and other institutions)
was of mixed race. Of the total, 92·3% were citizens of the USA.

Inter-marriage between the races is common. Of the 9,709 resident marriages in
1988, 42·9% were between partners of different race. Births, 1991, were 20,014 (17·5
per 1,000 population); deaths, 6,715 (5·9); infant deaths in 1992, 131 (6·5 per 1,000
live births); marriages, 17,669 (15·4); divorces and annulments, 5,134 (4·5).

CLIMATE. All the islands have a tropical climate, with an abrupt change in
conditions between windward and leeward sides, most marked in rainfall.
Temperatures vary little. Honolulu. Jan. 71°F (21·7°C), July 78°F (25·6°C). Annual
rainfall 31" (775 mm).

CONSTITUTION AND GOVERNMENT. The constitution took effect on 21
Aug. 1959. Amended 1968 and 1978. The Legislature consists of a Senate of 25
members elected for 4 years, and a House of Representatives of 51 members elected

for 2 years. The constitution provides for annual meetings of the legislature with 60-day regular sessions.

The state sends 2 representatives to Congress.

In the 1996 presidential election Clinton polled 205,012 votes; Dole, 113,943; Perot, 27,358.

The state capital is Honolulu. There are 5 counties.

Governor: Benjamin Cayetano (D.), 1994–98 ($94,780).
Lieut.-Governor: Mazie Hirono (D.) ($90,041).

BUDGET. Revenue is derived mainly from taxation of sales and gross receipts, real property, corporate and personal income, and inheritance taxes, licences, public land sales and leases. For the year ending 30 June 1990 state general fund receipts amounted to $3,841·8m. and federal grants, $610·4m. State expenditures were $3,546·7m. (education, $1,113·5m.; highways, $201·7m.; public welfare, $431·3m.).

Net long-term debt, 31 Dec. 1991, amounted to $4,202m.

Estimated *per capita* personal income (1995) was $24,738.

NATURAL RESOURCES

Minerals. Total value of non-fuel mineral production, 1991, $100m., mainly crushed ‹ stone ($48m.) and cement ($49m.).

Agriculture. Farming is highly commercialized, and highly mechanized. In 1991 there were about 5,000 farms with an acreage of 2m. Average number of acres per farm, 372. Sugar and pineapples are the staple crops. Farm income, 1991, from crop sales, was $489m., and from livestock and products $89m. The sugar crop was valued at $209·9m.; pineapples, $107·4m.; other crops, $168·2m. in 1988.

Forestry. In 1991 there were 1·7m. acres of forest and 0·7m. acres of timber land.

Fisheries. In fiscal year 1991 the commercial fish catch was 22m. lbs with a value of $53m. to primary producers. There were 4,043 fishermen.

INDUSTRY. In 1996 manufacturing establishments employed 17,000 production workers. Defence is the second-largest industry; US armed forces spent $1,892m. in Hawaii in 1988.

COMMERCE. In 1988 imports were $1,118m.; exports, $131m.

TOURISM. Tourism is outstanding in Hawaii's economy. Tourist arrivals numbered 1·1m. in 1967, and reached 6·1m. in 1988. Tourist expenditures, $380m. in 1967, contributed $10,900m. to the state's economy in 1989.

COMMUNICATIONS

Roads. In 1996 there were 4,133 miles of roads (2,293 miles rural). In 1995 there were 802,000 registered motor vehicles.

Civil Aviation. There were 7 commercial airports in 1990; passengers arriving from overseas in 1988 numbered 6·65m., and there were 9m. passengers between the islands.

Shipping. Several lines of steamers connect the islands with the mainland USA, Canada, Australia, the Philippines, China and Japan. In 1989, 2,024 overseas and 3,101 inter-island vessels entered the port of Honolulu.

Telecommunications. There were 530,022 telephone access lines at 31 Dec. 1988. In 1989, Hawaii had 47 commercial and 2 other radio stations, 17 commercial and 2 other TV stations.

SOCIAL INSTITUTIONS

Justice. There is no capital punishment in Hawaii. In 1995 there were 2,926 prisoners in federal and state prisons.

Religion. The residents are mainly Christians, though there are many Buddhists. A sample survey in 1979 showed that 31% were Roman Catholic, 34% Protestant, 12% Buddhist, 2·5% Latter Day Saints.

Education. Education is free, and compulsory for children between the ages of 6 and 18. The language in the schools is English. In 1988–89 there were 235 public schools and 141 private schools. In 1992, there were 174,249 pupils and 9,189 teachers in public elementary and secondary schools. In 1991 state and local government expenditure was $1,269m. In 1994, total college and university enrolment was 64,322. The University of Hawaii-Manoa, founded in 1907, had 18,477 day students in 1988; total attendance at all campuses of the University of Hawaii system, 42,767; 9,612 at private colleges.

Health. In 1993 there were 26 hospitals with 3,900 beds.

Social Security. In 1994: Total beneficiaries, 162,000; total annual payments, $1,169m.

Further Reading

Statistical information: Hawaii State Department of Business, POB 2359, Honolulu 96804. Publishes *The State of Hawaii Data Book.*
Legislative Reference Bureau. *Guide to Government in Hawaii.* 8th ed. Honolulu, 1989
Atlas of Hawaii. Rev. ed. Hawaii Univ. Press, 1983
Bell, R. J., *Last Among Equals: Hawaiian Statehood and American Politics.* Honolulu, 1984
Kuykendall, R. S. and Day, A. G., *Hawaii: a History.* Rev. ed. New Jersey, 1961
Morgan, J. R., *Hawaii.* Boulder, 1982
Morris, N. J. and Dean, L. *Hawai'i* [Bibliography]. Santa Barbara and Oxford, 1992

IDAHO

KEY HISTORICAL EVENTS. The original people of Idaho were Kutenai, Kalispel, Nez Percé and other tribes, living on the Pacific watershed of the northern Rocky Mountains. European exploration began in 1805, and after 1809 there were trading posts and small settlements. The area was disputed between Britain and the USA until 1846 when British claims were dropped. In 1860 gold and silver were found, and there was a rush of immigrant prospectors. The newly enlarged population needed organized government. An area including that which is now Montana was created a Territory in March 1863. Montana was separated from it in 1864. Population growth continued, stimulated by refugees from the Confederate states after the Civil War and by settlements of Mormons from Utah.

Fur-trapping and mining gave way to farming, especially of potatoes, wheat and sugar-beet, as the main economic activity. Idaho became a state in 1890, with its capital at Boise. The Territory capital, Idaho City, had been a gold-mining boom town whose population (about 40,000 at its height) declined to 1,000 by 1869.

During the 20th century the Indian population shrunk to nearly 1%. The Mormon community has grown to include much of south-eastern Idaho and more than half the church-going population of the state.

Industrial history has been influenced by the development of the Snake River of southern Idaho for hydro-electricity and irrigation, especially at the American Falls and reservoir. Processing food, minerals and timber have become important to the economy. The population, however, remains mainly sparse and rural.

TERRITORY AND POPULATION. Idaho is bounded north by Canada, east by the Rocky Mountains of Montana and Wyoming, south by Nevada and Utah, west by Oregon and Washington. Land area, 82,751 sq. miles (214,325 sq. km). Census population, 1 April 1990, 1,006,749 (57·4% urban), an increase of 6·65% since 1980. Population estimate (1995), 1,163,000. Births (1993), 17,440 (15·8 per 1,000 population); deaths, 7,000 (7·6). Marriages (1991), 14,352 (13·8); divorces, 6,619 (6·4); infant deaths (1992), 122 (7·0 per 1,000 live births).

Population in 5 census years was:

	White	Black	Indian	Asiatic	Total	Per sq. mile
1910	319,221	651	3,488	2,234	325,594	3·9
1930	438,840	668	3,638	1,886	445,032	5·4
1960	657,383	1,502	5,231	2,958	667,191	8·1
1980	901,641	2,716	10,521	5,948	943,935	11·3
1990	950,451	3,370	13,780	9,365	1,006,749	12·2

Of the total 1990 population, 500,956 were male, 578,214 were urban and those 20 years of age or older 665,889.

The largest cities are: Boise City, with 1990 census population of 125,738; Pocatello, 46,117; Idaho Falls, 43,929; Nampa, 28,365; Lewiston, 28,082; Twin Falls, 27,591; Coeur d'Alene, 24,563.

CLIMATE. Boise City. Jan. 29°F (−1·7°C), July 74°F (23·3°C). Annual rainfall 12" (303 mm). Idaho belongs to the Mountain States climate zone (*see* UNITED STATES: Climate).

CONSTITUTION AND GOVERNMENT. The constitution adopted in 1890 is still in force; it has had 105 amendments. The Legislature consists of a Senate of 35 members and a House of Representatives of 70 members, all the legislators being elected for 2 years. It meets annually.

The state sends 2 representatives to Congress.

In the 1996 presidential election Dole polled 256,406 votes, Clinton, 165,545; Perot, 62,506.

The state is divided into 44 counties. The capital is Boise City.

Governor: Phil Batt (R.), 1995–99 ($85,000).
Lieut.-Governor: C. L. 'Butch' Otter (R.) ($22,500).
Secretary of State: Pete T. Cenarrusa (R.) ($67,500).

BUDGET. For 1994 total revenues were $3,628m. and total expenditures $2,989m. *Per capita* personal income (1995) was $19,264.

NATURAL RESOURCES

Minerals. Principal non-fuel minerals are phosphate rock, silver, gold, and sand and gravel. Value of total mineral output, 1992, was $338·6m.

Agriculture. Agriculture is the leading industry, although a great part of the state is naturally arid. Extensive irrigation works have been carried out, bringing an estimated 4m. acres under irrigation, and there are over 50 soil conservation districts.

In 1995 there were 22,000 farms with a total area of 14m. acres; average value per acre (1995), $836. In 1995 average farm was 628 acres.

Farm income, 1991, from crops, $1,566m., and livestock, $1,099m. The most important crops are potatoes and wheat. Other crops are sugar-beet, alfalfa, barley, field peas and beans, onions and apples. In 1993 there were 1·68m. cattle, 230,000 sheep, 60,000 hogs and 1·22m. poultry.

Forestry. In 1997 a total of 21,598,522 acres was in forests.

INDUSTRY. In 1992 105,800 were employed in trade, 87,600 in government, 90,500 in services, 65,600 in manufacturing.

TOURISM. Money spent by travellers in 1991 was about $1,500m.

COMMUNICATIONS

Roads. In 1994 there were 59,897 miles of roads (56,435 miles rural) and 1,035,000 registered motor vehicles.

Railways. The state had (1991) 1,910 miles of railways (including 2 Amtrak routes).

Civil Aviation. There were 68 municipally owned airports in 1991.

Shipping. Water transport is provided from the Pacific to the port of Lewiston, by way of the Columbia and Snake rivers, a distance of 464 miles.

SOCIAL INSTITUTIONS

Justice. The death penalty may be imposed for first degree murder or aggravated kidnapping, but the judge must consider mitigating circumstances before imposing a sentence of death. The last execution was in 1994. The state prison system, Nov. 1994, had 2,964 inmates.

Religion. The leading religious denominations are the Church of Jesus Christ of Latter Day Saints (Mormon Church, 321,000 adherents in 1994), Roman Catholics, Methodists, Presbyterians, Episcopalians and Lutherans.

Education. In 1991–92, public elementary schools (grades K to 6) had 127,959 pupils and (1992–93) 6,234 teachers; secondary schools had 5,588 pupils and (1990–91) 5,138 classroom teachers.

Average salary, 1992–93, of elementary and secondary teachers, $27,011. The University of Idaho, founded at Moscow in 1889, in 1993 had 546 full-time instructional faculty, and a total enrolment of 11,543. There are 9 other institutions of higher education, 5 of them are public institutions. College and university enrolment in autumn 1994, 60,393.

Health. In 1994 there were 3,400 licensed beds in 41 community hospitals.

Social Welfare. Old-age assistance is granted to persons 65 years of age and older if they meet needs qualifications. 1994: Total beneficiaries, 174,000 with annual benefit payments of $1,252m.

Further Reading

Statistical information: Department of Commerce, 700 West State St., Boise 83720. Publishes *Idaho Facts.*

Schwantes, C. A. *In Mountain Shadows: a History of Idaho.* Nebraska Univ. Press, 1996

ILLINOIS

KEY HISTORICAL EVENTS. Territory of a group of Algonquian-speaking tribes, Illinois was explored first by the French in 1673. France claimed the area until 1763 when, after the French and Indian War, it was ceded to Britain along with all the French land east of the Mississippi. In 1783 Britain recognized the US' title to Illinois, which became part of the North West Territory of the USA in 1787, and of Indiana Territory in 1800. Illinois became a Territory in its own right in 1809, and a state in 1818,

Settlers from the eastern states moved on to the fertile farmland, immigration increasing greatly with the opening in 1825 of the Erie Canal from New York along which settlers could move west and their produce back east for sale. Chicago was incorporated as a city in 1837 and quickly became the transport, trading and distribution centre of the middle west. Once industrial growth had begun there, a further wave of immigration took place in the 1840s, mainly of European refugees looking for work. This movement continued with varying force until the 1920s, when it was largely replaced by immigration of black work-seekers from the southern states.

During the 20th century the population became largely urban and heavy industry was established along an intensive network of rail and waterway routes. Chicago recovered from a destructive fire in 1871 to become the hub of this network and at one time the second largest American city.

TERRITORY AND POPULATION. Illinois is bounded north by Wisconsin, north-east by Lake Michigan, east by Indiana, south-east by the Ohio River (forming the boundary with Kentucky),west by the Mississippi River (forming the boundary with Missouri and Iowa). Land area 55,646 sq. miles (144,123 sq. km). Census population, 1990, 11,430,602 (84·6% urban), an increase of 0·36% since 1980. Population estimate (1995), 11,830,000. Births were 190,788 (16·3 per 1,000 population); deaths, 107,000 (9·2); 1992, infant deaths under 1 year, 2,013 (10·4 per live births); 1990, marriages, 100,632; divorces and annulments, 45,977.

Population in 5 census years was:

	White	Black	Indian	All others	Total	Per sq. mile
1910	5,526,962	109,049	188	2,392	5,638,591	100·6
1930	7,295,267	328,972	469	5,946	7,630,654	136·4

	White	Black		All others	Total	Per sq. mile
1970	9,600,381	1,425,674		87,921	11,113,976	199·4
1980	9,233,327	1,675,398		517,793	11,426,518	203·0

	White	Black	American Indian, Eskimo or Aleut	Asian or Pacific Islander	Other	Total	Per sq. mile
1990	8,952,978	1,694,273	21,836	285,311	476,204	11,430,602	205·6

Of the total population in 1980, 5,537,737 were male, 9,518,039 persons were urban and 5,597,360 were 18 years of age or older.

The most populous cities with population (1992 estimate), are: Chicago, 2,768,483; Rockford, 141,679; Peoria, 113,983; Springfield, 106,429; Aurora, 105,929; Naperville, 91,928; Decatur, 84,273; Elgin, 81,108; Joliet, 78,917; Arlington Heights, 76,518.

Primary Metropolitan Statistical Area population, 1990 census: Chicago, 6,069,974; East St Louis, 588,995; Peoria, 339,172; Rockford, 283,719; Springfield, 189,550; Decatur, 117,206.

CLIMATE. Chicago. Jan. 25·2°F (–3·8°C), July 79·9°F (26·6°C) average mean. Average annual rainfall 39·8". Illinois belongs to the Great Lakes climate zone (*see* UNITED STATES: Climate).

CONSTITUTION AND GOVERNMENT. The present constitution became effective on 1 July 1971. The General Assembly consists of a House of Representatives of 118 members, elected for 2 years and a Senate of 59 members who are divided into 3 groups; in one, they are elected for terms of 4 years, 4 years, and 2 years; in the next, for terms of 4 years, 2 years, and 4 years; and in the last, for terms of 2 years, 4 years, and 4 years. Sessions are annual. The state is divided into legislative districts, in each of which 1 senator is chosen; each district is divided into 2 representative districts, in each of which 1 representative is chosen.

The state sends 20 representatives to Congress.

In the 1996 presidential election Clinton polled 2,341,744 votes; Dole, 1,587,021; Perot, 344,311.

The capital is Springfield. The state has 102 counties.

Governor: Jim Edgar (R.), 1995–99 ($119,439).
Lieut.-Governor: Bob Kustra (R). ($84,310).
Secretary of State: George H. Ryan (R.) ($105,387).

BUDGET. For the year ending 30 June 1994 total revenues were $26,610m. and total expenditures were $25,991m.

Debt administration, 30 June 1994 (in $1m.): Total general and special obligation debt, 6,699·9; total revenue bonds, 4,060·8; total long-term obligations, 1,382.

Per capita personal income (1995) was $24,763.

NATURAL RESOURCES

Minerals. Chief mineral product is coal; 32 operative mines had an output (1994) of 54,026,365 tons. Mineral production also included: Crude petroleum, fluorspar, tripoli, lime, sand, gravel and stone; total estimated value in 1994, $2,100m.

Agriculture. In 1995, 77,000 farms had an area of 28m. acres with the average farm having 365 acres. In 1993 the average value of farmland and buildings per acre was $1,500.

Cash receipts, 1994, from crops, $5,834,555,000; from livestock and livestock products, $2,247,894,000. Illinois is a large producer of maize and soybeans, the state's leading cash commodities. Output, 1994: Soybeans, 4,038,000 bu; wheat, 50m. bu; maize, 1,786m. bu. In Jan. 1993 there were 186,000 milk cows, 2m. cattle and calves; 105,000 sheep and lambs and 5·9m. swine. The wool clip was 639,000 lbs in 1994.

Forestry. The gross forest area in 1997 was 714,890 acres of which 264,018 acres was National Forest Land.

INDUSTRY. In 1993 there were 284,261 establishments with (March) 4,697,442 employees. The annual payroll was $127,236,398,000. Largest industry was services. Gross state product, 1994, $333,200m.

LABOUR. In 1994 there were 5,463,000 non-agricultural employees, of whom 953,000 were in manufacturing, 1,276,000 in trade, 1,513,000 in services, 783,000 in government, 394,000 in finance, insurance and real estate and 317,000 in transport, communications and utilities, 213,000 in construction and 15,000 in mining.

TOURISM. Tourism revenue in 1994 was $15,900m.

COMMUNICATIONS

Roads. At 31 Dec. 1994 there were 10,083·58 miles of state primary roads, 2,013·6 miles of state supplementary roads and 168·25 miles of toll roads and toll bridges. In 1994 there were 6,710,578 passenger cars, 1,223,193 pickup trucks, 237,326 recreational vehicles, buses and trucks and 197,295 motor cycles registered in the state, and 153,416 Interstate Registration Plan vehicles.

Railways. There were, in 1990, more than 7,000 miles of Class I railway. Chicago is served by Amtrak long-distance trains on several routes, and by a metro (CTA) system, and by 7 groups of commuter railways controlled by the Northeast Illinois Railroad Corporation (now called METRA).

Civil Aviation. There were (1994) 138 public airports, 654 restricted landing areas and 274 heliports.

Shipping. In 1996 the seaport of Chicago handled 6,493,068 tons of foreign cargo.

SOCIAL INSTITUTIONS

Justice. In June 1994 the inmate population in state prisons was 35,614. The death penalty is authorized, and executions began in 1990 following the US Supreme Courts reinstatement of capital punishment in 1976. The last execution took place in 1994.

A Civil Rights Act (1941), as amended, bans all forms of discrimination by places of public accommodation, including inns, restaurants, retail stores, railroads, aeroplanes, buses, etc., against persons on account of 'race, religion, colour, national ancestry or physical or mental handicap'; another section similarly mentions 'race or colour.'

The Fair Employment Practices Act of 1961, as amended, prohibits discrimination in employment based on race, colour, sex, religion, national origin or ancestry, by employers, employment agencies, labour organizations and others. These principles are embodied in the 1971 constitution.

The Illinois Human Rights Act (1979), prevents unlawful discrimination in employment, real property transactions, access to financial credit, and public accommodations, by authorizing the creation of a Department of Human Rights to enforce, and a Human Rights Commission to adjudicate, allegations of unlawful discrimination.

Religion. Among the larger religious denominations are: Roman Catholic (3·6m.), Jewish (268,000), Presbyterian Church, USA (0·2m.), Lutheran Church in America (0·2m.), Lutheran Church Missouri Synod (325,000), American Baptist (105,000), Disciples of Christ (75,000), and United Methodist (505,000), Southern Baptist (265,000), United Church of Christ (192,000), Assembly of God (63,000), Church of Nazarene (50,000).

Education. Education is free and compulsory for children between 7 and 16 years of age. In 1994–95 public school elementary enrolments were 1,365,876; secondary enrolments, 550,296; total public school teachers (including special education teachers), 112,991. Enrolment (1994–95) in non-public schools was 250,807 elementary and 68,603 secondary; total non-public school teachers (including special education teachers), 17,672. Public school teachers' salaries, 1993–94, averaged $39,473. Total enrolment in 184 institutions of higher education (autumn 1993) was 740,185.

Major colleges and universities (autumn 1994):

Founded	Name	Place	Control	Enrolment
1851	Northwestern University	Evanston	Independent	17,781
1857	Illinois State University	Normal	Public	19,595
1867	University of Illinois	Urbana/Champaign and Chicago	Public	63,585
1867	Chicago State University	Chicago	Public	10,108
1869	Southern Illinois University	Carbondale and Edwardsville	Public	34,100
1890	Loyola University	Chicago	Roman Catholic	13,806
1891	University of Chicago	Chicago	Independent	11,616
1895	Eastern Illinois University	Charleston	Public	11,301
1895	Northern Illinois University	DeKalb	Public	22,881
1897	Bradley University	Peoria	Independent	5,882
1899	Western Illinois University	Macomb	Public	12,599
1940	Illinois Institute of Technology	Chicago	Independent	7,157
1945	Roosevelt University	Chicago	Independent	6,695
1961	Northeastern Illinois University	Chicago	Public	10,228

Health. In 1994 there were 207 community hospitals with 43,200 beds. At June 1993, 21 institutions served 18,456 patients.

Social Security. In 1994, there were 1,437,837 total monthly recipients of public and State-administered Supplemental Security Income (SSI) was paid to 189,355 recipients (monthly average) in financial year 1993; approximate total payments $773·87m.; medical payments, $3,109·58m. In 1992, aid to families with dependent children was paid to 232,419 families, average monthly payment per family, $312·53; total payments, $1,581·7m.; medical payments, $709·9m.

Further Reading

Statistical information: Department of Commerce and Community Affairs, 620 Adams St., Springfield 62701. Publishes *Illinois State and Regional Economic Data Book.* Bureau of Economic and Business Research, Univ. of Illinois, 1206 South 6th St., Champaign 61820. Publishes *Illinois Statistical Abstract.*

Blue Book of the State of Illinois. Edited by Secretary of State. Springfield. Biennial

Angle, P. M. and Beyer, R. L., *A Handbook of Illinois History.* Illinois State Historical Society, Springfield, 1943

Clayton, J., *The Illinois Fact Book and Historical Almanac 1673–1968.* Southern Illinois Univ., 1970

Howard, R. P., *Illinois: A History of the Prairie State.* Grand Rapids, 1972.—*Mostly Good and Competent Men: Illinois Governors, 1818–1988.* Springfield, 1989

Pease, T. C., *The Story of Illinois.* 3rd ed. Chicago, 1965

The Illinois State Library: Springfield, IL 62756.

INDIANA

KEY HISTORICAL EVENTS. The area was inhabited by Algonquian-speaking tribes when the first European explorers (French) laid claim to it in the 17th century. They established some fortified trading posts but there was little settlement.

In 1763 the area passed to Britain, with other French-claimed territory east of the Mississippi. In 1783 Indiana became part of the North West Territory of the USA; it became a separate territory in 1800 and a state in 1816. Until 1811 there had been continuing conflict with the Indian inhabitants, who were then defeated at Tippecanoe.

Early farming settlement was by families of British and German descent, including Amish and Mennonite communities. Later industrial development offered an incentive for more immigration from Europe, and, later, from the southern states. In 1906 the town of Gary was laid out by the United States Steel Corporation and named after its chairman, Elbert H. Gary. The industry flourished on navigable water midway between supplies of iron ore and of coal. Trade and distribution in general benefited from Indiana Port on Lake Michigan, especially after the opening of the St Lawrence Seaway in 1959. The Ohio River was also exploited for carrying freight.

Indianapolis was laid out after 1821 and became the state capital in 1825. Natural gas was discovered in the neighbourhood in the late 19th century, and this stimulated the growth of a motor industry, celebrated with the Indianapolis 500 race, held annually since 1911.

TERRITORY AND POPULATION. Indiana is bounded west by Illinois, north by Michigan and Lake Michigan, east by Ohio and south by Kentucky across the Ohio River. Land area, 35,870 sq. miles (92,903 sq. km). Census population, 1 April 1990, was 5,544,159 (64·9% urban), an increase of 0·98% since 1980. Population estimate (1995), 5,803,471. In 1994 live births were 83,381 (14·5 per 1,000 population); deaths, 53,290 (9·3); infant deaths (under 1 year) in 1992, 795 (9·4 per 1,000 live births); marriages (1994), 50,282 (8·7).

Population in 5 census years was:

	White	Black	Indian	Asiatic	Total	Per sq. mile
1930	3,125,778	111,982	285	458	3,238,503	89·4
1960	4,388,554	269,275	948	2,447	4,662,498	128·9

	White	Black	All others	Total	Per sq. mile
1970	4,820,324	357,464	15,881	5,193,669	143·9
1980	5,004,394	414,785	71,045	5,490,224	152·8
1990	5,020,700	432,092	91,367	5,544,159	154·6

Of the total in 1990, 2,688,281 were male and 3,545,431 were 21 years of age or older.

The largest cities with census population, 1990, are: Indianapolis (capital), 741,952; Fort Wayne, 173,072; Evansville, 126,272; Gary, 116,646; South Bend, 105,511; Hammond, 84,236; Muncie, 71,035; Bloomington, 60,633; Anderson, 59,459; Terre Haute, 57,483.

CLIMATE. Indianapolis. Jan. 29°F (−1·7°C), July 76°F (24·4°C). Annual rainfall 41" (1,034 mm). Indiana belongs to the Mid-West climate zone (see UNITED STATES: Climate).

CONSTITUTION AND GOVERNMENT. The present constitution (the second) dates from 1851; it has had (as of Nov. 1983) 34 amendments. The General Assembly consists of a Senate of 50 members elected for 4 years, and a House of Representatives of 100 members elected for 2 years. It meets annually.

In the 1996 presidential election Dole polled 995,082 votes; Clinton, 874,668; Perot, 218,739.

The state sends 10 representatives to Congress.

The state capital is Indianapolis. The state is divided into 92 counties and 1,008 townships.

Governor: Frank O'Bannon (D.), 1997–2001 ($77,200).

BUDGET. In the fiscal year 1994 total revenues were $15,813,000,000; total expenditures were $15,048,000,000 ($5,449,388,000 for education, $3,910,612,000 for public welfare and $1,347,306,000 for highways). Revenue from Federal Government, 1995, $3,545,758,000.

Debt outstanding at end of fiscal year 1994 was $5,572m.

Per capita personal income (1995) was $21,273.

NATURAL RESOURCES

Minerals. The state produced 36,862,000 metric tons of crushed stone and 155.62m. metric tons of dimension stone in 1993; the output of coal was 36·3m. short tons in 1990. Value of non-fuel mineral production, 1991, $403·29m.

Agriculture. Indiana is largely agricultural, about 75% of its total area being in farms. In 1995, 63,000 farms had 16m. acres (average, 252 acres). Cash income, 1992, from crops, including nursery and greenhouse crops, $2,698,335,000; from livestock, poultry and their products, $1,934,755,000. Acreage harvested in 1992 was 11·83m., with a market value of $4,633m.

The chief crops (1992) were corn for grain or seed (805,637,216 bu.), corn for silage or green crop (1,944,771 tons), wheat for grain (25,048,728 bu.), oats for grain (2,603,270 bu.), soybeans for beans (195,049,717 bu.), hay (alfalfa, other tame small grain, wild, grass silage, etc.) (1,712,613 tons, dry).

The livestock on 1 Jan. 1992 included 1,113,473 all cattle, 144,532 milk cows, 72,386 sheep and lambs, 4,618,663 hogs and pigs, 22,256,785 chickens, 12,648,219 turkeys. In 1992 the wool clip yielded 440,768 lbs of wool from 65,775 sheep and lambs.

Forestry. In 1997 there were 644,000 acres of forest including Hoosier National Forest (192,000 acres).

INDUSTRY. In 1993, 9,440 manufacturing establishments employed 636,495 workers, earning $20,690,996,000. The steel industry is the largest in the country.

COMMUNICATIONS

Roads. In 1994 there were 92,476 miles of road (73,161 miles rural). In 1993 there were 4,953,250 registered motor vehicles.

Railways. In 1989 there were 3,796 miles of mainline railway and 861·5 miles of secondary track.

Civil Aviation. Of airports, 1990, 115 were for public use and 486 were for private use.

SOCIAL INSTITUTIONS

Justice. Following the US Supreme Court's reinstatement of the death penalty in 1976, death sentences have been awarded since 1980. The total state prison population in 1994 was 15,014.

The Civil Rights Act of 1885 forbids places of public accommodation to bar any persons on grounds not applicable to all citizens alike; no citizen may be disqualified for jury service 'on account of race or colour'. An Act of 1947 makes it an offence to spread religious or racial hatred.

A 1961 Act provided 'all . . . citizens equal opportunity for education, employment and access to public conveniences and accommodations' and created a Civil Rights Commission.

Religion. Religious denominations include Methodists, Roman Catholic, Disciples of Christ, Baptists, Lutheran, Presbyterian churches, Society of Friends.

Education. School attendance is compulsory from 7 to 16 years. In autumn 1993 public and parochial schools and nursery schools had 965,599 pupils and 55,107 teachers. Teachers' salaries averaged $36,516 (1994–95). Total expenditure for public schools, 1992–93, $4,797,946,000.

The principal institutions for higher education are (1989–90):

Founded	Institution	Control	Students (full-time)
1801	Vincennes University	State	10,139
1824	Indiana University, Bloomington	State	34,863
1837	De Pauw University, Greencastle	Methodist	2,415
1842	University of Notre Dame	R.C.	9,700
1850	Butler University, Indianapolis	Independent	4,187
1859	Valparaiso University, Valparaiso	Evangelical Lutheran Church	3,858
1870	Indiana State University, Terre Haute	State	12,005
1874	Purdue University, Lafayette	State	35,817
1898	Ball State University, Muncie	State	18,993
1902	University of Indianapolis, Indianapolis	Methodist	3,119
1963	Indiana Vocational Technical College, Indianapolis	State	5,117
1985	University of Southern Indiana	State	5,713

Health. There were 114 community hospitals with 19,900 beds in 1994. In 1993 there were 3,568 patients in state mental hospitals.

Social Security. In 1994, under the Federal SSI programme and federally administered State Supplementary programme, payments to 15,546 aged persons, 56,502 disabled adults and 18,305 disabled children totalled $27·97m.

Further Reading

Statistical information: Indiana Business Research Center, Indiana Univ., Indianapolis 46202. Publishes *Indiana Factbook.*
Gray, R. D. (ed.) *Indiana History: a Book of Readings.* Indiana Univ. Press, 1994
Martin, J. B., *Indiana: an Interpretation.* Indiana Univ. Press, 1992

State Library: Indiana State Library, 140 North Senate, Indianapolis 46204.

IOWA

KEY HISTORICAL EVENTS. Originally the territory of the Iowa Indians, the area was explored by the Frenchmen Marquette and Joliet in 1673. French trading posts were set up, but there was little other settlement. In 1803 the French sold their claim to Iowa to the USA as part of the Louisiana Purchase. The land was still occupied by Indians but, in the 1830s, the tribes sold their land to the US government and migrated to reservations. Iowa became a US Territory in 1838 and a state in 1846.

The state was settled by immigrants drawn mainly from neighbouring states to the east. Later there was more immigration from Protestant states of northern Europe. The land was extremely fertile and most immigrants came to farm. Not all the Indian population had accepted the cession and there were some violent confrontations, notably the murder of settlers at Spirit Lake in 1857.

The population is still mainly rural and farming predominates, especially livestock farming with its associated stockfeed crops. Most industry is based on agriculture, either as food-processing or agricultural engineering.

The capital, Des Moines, was founded in 1843 as a fort to protect Indian rights. It expanded rapidly with the growth of a local coal field after 1910.

TERRITORY AND POPULATION. Iowa is bounded east by the Mississippi River (forming the boundary with Wisconsin and Illinois), south by Missouri, west by the Missouri River (forming the boundary with Nebraska), north-west by the Big Sioux River (forming the boundary with South Dakota) and north by Minnesota. Land area, 55,875 sq. miles (144,716 sq. km). Census population, 1 April 1990, 2,776,755 (60·6% urban), a decrease of 4·7% since 1980. Population estimate (1996), 2,852,000. Births, 1996, 37,130; deaths, 28,800; infant deaths, 259; marriages, 22,711; dissolutions of marriages, 10,347.

Population in 6 census years was:

	White	Black	Indian	Asiatic	Total	Per sq. mile
1870	1,188,207	5,762	48	3	1,194,020	21·5
1930	2,452,677	17,380	660	222	2,470,939	44·1
1960	2,728,709	25,354	1,708	1,022	2,757,537	49·2
			All others			
1970	2,782,762	32,596	10,010		2,825,368	50·5
1980	2,839,225	41,700	32,882		2,913,808	51·7
1990	2,683,090	48,090	45,575		2,776,755	49·7

At the census of 1990, 1,344,802 were male, 1,683,065 were urban and 2,057,875 were 18 years of age or older.

The largest cities in the state, with their estimated population in 1996 are: Des Moines (capital), 193,422; Cedar Rapids, 113,482; Davenport, 97,010; Sioux City, 83,791; Waterloo, 65,022; Iowa City, 60,923; Dubuque, 57,312; Council Bluffs, 55,569; Ames, 47,698; West Des Moines, 40,380; Cedar Falls, 34,884; Bettendorf, 31,015; Mason City, 28,972; Clinton, 28,323; Urbandale, 26,902.

CLIMATE. Cedar Rapids. Jan. 23·7°F, July 72·6°F. Annual rainfall 34". Des Moines. Jan. 22·6°F, July 72·4°F. Annual rainfall 32·1". Iowa belongs to the Mid-West climate zone (*see* UNITED STATES: Climate).

CONSTITUTION AND GOVERNMENT. The constitution of 1857 still exists; it has had 45 amendments. The General Assembly comprises a Senate of 50 and a House of Representatives of 100 members, meeting annually for an unlimited session. Senators are elected for 4 years, half retiring every second year: Representatives for 2 years. The Governor and Lieut.-Governor are elected for 4 years. The state is represented in Congress by 5 representatives. Iowa is divided into 99 counties; the capital is Des Moines.

In the 1996 presidential election Clinton polled 615,499 votes; Dole, 488,776; Perot, 104,401.

Governor: Terry Branstad (R.), 1995–99 ($98,200).
Lieut.-Governor: Joy Corning (R.), ($68,740).
Secretary of State: Paul Pate (R.) ($78,050).

BUDGET. For fiscal year 1995–96 state tax revenue was $4,038·9m. General fund expenditures were $2,242·6m. for education, $807·1m. for health and human services, $284·9m. for justice and $172·6m. for administration, economic development, transportation and commerce.

On 30 June 1995 the net general long-term debt was $315m.
Per capita personal income (1996) was $22,306.

NATURAL RESOURCES

Minerals. Production in 1996: Crushed stone, 34·4m. tons; sand and gravel, 15·9m. tons; gypsum, 2,380,000 tonnes; cement, 2,690,000 tonnes; coal (1994), 33,173 short tons. The value of mineral products in 1996 was $486m.

Agriculture. Iowa is the wealthiest of the agricultural states, partly because nearly the whole area (92·8%) is arable and included in farms. Large-scale commercial farming has not developed; the average farm at 1 June 1996 was 339 acres.

Cash receipts from farm markets (1996) were $12,800,000,000; from livestock, $5,400,000,000, and from crops, $7,400,000,000. Production of corn was 1,200m.[1] bu., value $4,500m. and soybeans, 415·8m.[1] bu., value $2,800m. In 1997 livestock included swine, 12·2m.[1]; milk cows, 250,000; all cattle, 3·9m., and sheep and lambs, 285,000. The wool clip (1996 estimate) yielded 2m. lbs of wool.

[1] More than any other state.

LABOUR. In 1996 manufacturing establishments employed 250,000 people; trade, 344,500; services, 370,800.

COMMUNICATIONS

Roads. On 1 Jan. 1997 there were 112,999 miles of streets and highways. On 1 June 1997 there were 1·96m. licensed drivers. In 1997 there were 3,321,140 registered vehicles.

Railways. The state, as of 1 Jan. 1997, had 4,292 miles of track, 5 Class I, 3 Class II and 13 Class III railways.

Civil Aviation. Airports (1996), numbered 226, which consisted of 113 publicly-owned, 103 privately-owned and 10 commercial facilities. As of 31 Dec. 1995 there were 2,250 private aircraft registered.

SOCIAL INSTITUTIONS

Justice. There is now no capital punishment in Iowa. The 8 state prisons, 1997, had 6,796 inmates.

Religion. Chief religious bodies: Roman Catholic, (1997) 509,141 members; United Methodists, (1997) 202,745; Evangelical Lutheran in America, (1996) 266,371 baptised members; USA Presbyterians, (1996) 61,958; United Church of Christ, (1996) 41,584.

Education. School attendance is compulsory for 24 consecutive weeks annually during school age (7–16). In 1996–97, 505,587 pupils were attending primary and secondary schools; 44,302 pupils attending non-public schools; classroom teachers numbered 32,716 for public schools with average salary of $33,272. In 1995 the state spent an average $5,685 on each elementary and secondary school student. Leading institutions for higher education with autumn enrolment (1997) were:

Founded	Institution	Control	Professors	Full-time Students
1843	Clarke College, Dubuque	Independent	27	1,160
1846	Grinnell College, Grinnell	Independent	43	1,327
1847	University of Iowa, Iowa City	State	1,645	27,871
1851	Coe College, Cedar Rapids	Independent	28	1,318
1852	Wartburg College, Waverly	Evangelical Lutheran	27	1,528
1853	Cornell College, Mount Vernon	Independent	37	1,079
1858	Iowa State University, Ames	State	1,103	25,384
1876	Univ. of Northern Iowa, Cedar Falls	State	162	13,108
1881	Drake University, Des Moines	Independent	267	3,100
1894	Morningside College, Sioux City	Methodist	41	1,177

Health. In 1997 the state had 117 community hospitals (12,675 beds).

Social Security. Iowa has a Civil Rights Act (1939) which makes it a misdemeanour for any place of public accommodation to deprive any person of 'full and equal enjoyment' of the facilities it offers the public.

Supplemental Security Income (SSI) assistance is available for the aged (65 or older), the blind and the disabled. As of June 1997, 5,360 elderly persons were drawing an average of $163·36 per month, 841 blind persons $284·92 per month, and 34,321 disabled persons $315·40 per month. As of July 1997, aid to dependent children (ADC) was received by 27,244 cases representing 73,329 recipients.

Further Reading

Statistical Information: Iowa Department of Economic Development Research Bureau, 200 East Grand Ave., Des Moines 50309. Publishes *Statistical Profile of Iowa.*
Annual Survey of Manufactures. US Department of Commerce
Government Finance. US Department of Commerce
Official Register. Secretary of State. Des Moines. Biennial
Petersen, W. J., *Iowa History Reference Guide.* Iowa City, 1952
Smeal, L., *Iowa Historical and Biographical Index.* New York, 1984
Vexler, R. I., *Iowa Chronology and Factbook.* Oceana, 1978

State Library of Iowa: Des Moines 50319.

KANSAS

KEY HISTORICAL EVENTS. The area was explored from Mexico in the 16th century, when Spanish travellers found groups of Kansa, Wichita, Osage and Pawnee tribes. The French claimed Kansas in 1682 and they established a valuable fur trade with local tribes in the 18th century. In 1803 the area passed to the USA as part of the Louisiana Purchase and became a base for pioneering trails further west. After 1830 it was 'Indian Territory' and a number of tribes displaced from eastern states were settled there. In 1854 the Kansas Territory was created and opened for white settlement. The early settlers were farmers from Europe or New England, but the Territory's position brought it into contact with southern ideas also. Until 1861 there were frequent outbursts of violence over the issue of slavery. Slavery had been excluded from the future Territory by the Missouri Compromise of 1820, but the 1854 Kansas-Nebraska Act had affirmed the principle of 'popular sovereignty' to settle the issue, which was then fought out by opposing factions throughout 'Bleeding Kansas'.

Kansas finally entered the Union (as a non-slavery state) in 1861; the part of Colorado which had formed part of the Kansas Territory was then separated from it.

The economy developed through a combination of cattle-ranching and railways. Herds were driven to the railheads and shipped from vast stockyards, or slaughtered and processed in railhead meat-packing plants. Wheat and sorghum also became important once the plains could be ploughed on a large scale.

TERRITORY AND POPULATION. Kansas is bounded north by Nebraska, east by Missouri, with the Missouri River as boundary in the north-east, south by Oklahoma and west by Colorado. Land area, 81,823 (211,922 sq. km). Census population, 1 April 1990, 2,477,574 (69·1% urban), an increase of 4·84% since 1980. Population estimate (1996), 2,572,000. Vital statistics: 1994, births, 37,379 (14·6 per 1,000 population); deaths, 23,000 (9·1); 1992, infant deaths, 316 (8·6 per 1,000 live births); 1991, marriages, 22,074 (8·7); divorces 13,897 (5·5).

Population in 5 federal census years was:

	White	Black	Indian	Asiatic	Total	Per sq. mile
1870	346,377	17,108	914	—	364,399	4·5
1930	1,811,997	66,344	2,454	204	1,880,999	22·9
1960	2,078,666	91,445	5,069	2,271	2,178,611	26·3
			All others			
1970	2,122,068	106,977	17,533		2,249,071	27·5
1980	2,168,221	126,127	69,888		2,364,236	28·8

Of the total population in 1980, 1,156,941 were male, 1,575,899 were urban and those 20 years of age or older numbered 1,620,368.

Cities, with 1990 census population: Wichita, 304,011; Kansas City, 149,767; Topeka (capital), 119,883; Overland Park, 111,790; Lawrence, 65,608; Olathe, 63,352.

CLIMATE. Dodge City. Jan. 29°F (−1·7°C), July 78°F (25·6°C). Annual rainfall 21" (518 mm). Kansas City. Jan. 30°F (−1·1°C), July 79°F (26·1°C). Annual rainfall 38" (947 mm). Topeka. Jan. 28°F (−2·2°C), July 78°F (25·6°C). Annual rainfall 35" (875 mm). Wichita. Jan. 31°F (−0·6°C), July 81°F (27·2°C). Annual rainfall 31" (777 mm). Kansas belongs to the Mid-West climate zone (*see* UNITED STATES: Climate).

CONSTITUTION AND GOVERNMENT. The year 1861 saw the adoption of the present constitution; it has had 78 amendments. The Legislature includes a Senate of 40 members, elected for 4 years, and a House of Representatives of 125 members, elected for 2 years. Sessions are annual.

The state sends 4 representatives to Congress.

In the 1996 presidential election Dole polled 578,572 votes; Clinton, 384,439; Perot, 92,093.

The capital is Topeka. The state is divided into 105 counties.

Governor: Bill Graves (R.), 1995–99 ($80,340).
Lieut.-Governor: Sheila Frahm (D.) ($81,600).
Secretary of State: Ron Thornburgh (R.) ($62,412).

BUDGET. For 1994 general revenue was $6,463m. General expenditures were $6,092m.
Per capita personal income (1995) was $21,825.

NATURAL RESOURCES

Minerals. Important fuel minerals are coal, petroleum and natural gas. Non-fuel minerals, mainly cement, salt and crushed stone, were worth $366·5m. in 1990.

Agriculture. Kansas is pre-eminently agricultural, but sometimes suffers from lack of rainfall in the west. In 1996 there were some 66,000 farms with a total acreage of 48m. Average number of acres per farm was 724. Average value of farmland and buildings per acre, in 1996, was $553. Farm income, 1991, from livestock and products, $4,731. Chief crops: Wheat, sorghum, maize, hay. Wheat production was 472m. bu. in 1990. There is an extensive livestock industry, comprising, in 1990, 5·7m. cattle, 887,000 sheep, 1·45m. pigs and 1·4m. poultry.

FORESTRY. In 1997 Kansas had 108,000 acres of National Forest System Land.

INDUSTRY. Employment distribution (1996): Total non-farm workforce 1,228,000, of which 303,000 were in wholesale and retail; 301,000 in services; 235,000 in government; 196,000 in manufacturing; 70,000 in transport and utilities; 59,000 in finance, insurance and real estate; 57,000 in construction. The slaughtering industry, other food processing, aircraft, the manufacture of transport equipment and petroleum refining are also important.

COMMUNICATIONS

Roads. In 1995 there were 133,323 miles of roads (123,632 miles rural). In 1995 there were 2,085,000 registered motor vehicles.

Railways. There were 7,273 miles of railway in Jan. 1982.

Civil Aviation. There is an international airport at Wichita.

SOCIAL INSTITUTIONS

Justice. There were 6,373 prisoners in state institutions in 1994. The death penalty is authorized for capital murder, although as of Dec. 1994 no prisoner was under sentence of death.

Religion. The most numerous religious bodies are Roman Catholic, Methodists and Disciples of Christ.

Education. In 1994–95 there were 460,905 public elementary and secondary pupils enrolled and 30,588 teachers.
Kansas has 6 state-supported institutions of higher education: Kansas State University, Manhattan (1863); The University of Kansas, Lawrence, founded in 1865; Emporia State University, Emporia; Pittsburg State University, Pittsburg; Fort Hays State University, Hays and Wichita State University, Wichita. The state also supports a two-year technical school, Kansas Technical Institute, at Salina.
Education expenditure by state and local governments in 1994 was $2,733·7m.

Health. In 1995 Kansas had 132 community hospitals with 10,800 beds.

Social Security. In 1995, 434,000 people received social security benefit totalling $3,418m. Average monthly payment to retired workers was $739.

Further Reading

Statistical information: Institute for Public Policy and Business Research, Univ. of Kansas, 607 Blake Hall, Lawrence 66045. Publishes *Kansas Statistical Abstract.*
Annual Economic Report of the Governor. Topeka
Drury, J. W., *The Government of Kansas.* Lawrence, Univ. of Kansas, 1970
Zornow, W. F., *Kansas: A History of the Jayhawk State.* Norman, Okla., 1957

State Library: Kansas State Library, Topeka.

KENTUCKY

KEY HISTORICAL EVENTS. Lying west of the Appalachians and south of the Ohio River, the area was the meeting place and battle-ground for the eastern Iroquois and the southern Cherokees. Northern Shawnees also penetrated. The first successful white settlement took place in 1769 when Daniel Boone reached the Bluegrass plains from the eastern, trans-Appalachian, colonies. After 1783 immigration from the east was rapid, settlers travelling by river or crossing the mountains by the Cumberland Gap. The area was originally attached to Virginia but became a separate state in 1792.

Large plantations dependant on slave labour were established, as were small farms worked by white owners. The state became divided on the issue of slavery, although plantation interests (mainly producing tobacco) dominated state government. In the event the state did not secede in 1861, and the majority of citizens supported the Union. Public opinion swung round in support of the south during the difficulties of the reconstruction period.

The eastern mountains became an important coal-mining area, tobacco-growing continued and the Bluegrass plains produced livestock, including especially fine thoroughbred horses.

TERRITORY AND POPULATION. Kentucky is bounded in the north by the Ohio River (forming the boundary with Illinois, Indiana and Ohio), north-east by the Big Sandy River (forming the boundary with West Virginia), east by Virginia, south by Tennessee and west by the Mississippi River (forming the boundary with Missouri). Land area, 39,732 sq. miles (102,907 sq. km). Census population, 1990, 3,685,296 (51·8% urban), an increase of 0·7% since 1980. Population estimate (1996), 3,884,000. Births in 1995, 52,054 (13·5 per 1,000 population); deaths, 37,085 (8·8); infant deaths, 391 (7·5 per 1,000 live births); marriages, 45,698 (11·8); divorces, 21,479 (5·6).

Population in 5 census years was:

	White	Black	All others	Total	Per sq. mile
1930	2,388,364	226,040	185	2,614,589	65·1
1950	2,742,090	201,921	795	2,944,806	73·9
1960	2,820,083	215,949	2,124	3,038,156	76·2
1980	3,379,006	259,477	22,294	3,660,777	92·3
1990	3,391,832	262,907	30,557	3,685,296	92·8

Of the total population in 1990, 1,785,235 were male and 1,136,272 were 21 years old or older.

The principal cities with census population in 1990 are: Louisville, 269,555 (urbanized area, 654,870); Lexington-Fayette, 225,336; Owensboro, 53,577; Covington, 43,646; Bowling Green, 41,688; Hopkinsville, 29,818; Paducah, 27,256; Frankfort (capital), 25,535; Henderson, 25,945.

CLIMATE. Kentucky is in the Appalachian Mountains climatic zone (*see* UNITED STATES: Climate). It has a temperate climate. Temperatures are moderate during both winter and summer, precipitation is ample without a pronounced dry season, and winter snowfall amounts are variable. Lexington. Jan. 33°F (0·6°C), July 76°F (24·4°C). Annual rainfall 43" (1,079 mm). Louisville. Jan. 34°F (1·1°C), July 78°F (25·6°C). Annual rainfall 43" (1,079 mm).

CONSTITUTION AND GOVERNMENT. The constitution dates from 1891; there had been 3 preceding it. The 1891 constitution was promulgated by convention and provides that amendments be submitted to the electorate for ratification. The General Assembly consists of a Senate of 38 members elected for 4 years, one half retiring every 2 years, and a House of Representatives of 100 members elected for 2 years. It has biennial sessions. All citizens of 18 or over are qualified as electors. Registered voters, Oct. 1996, 2,490,674. In the 1996 presidential election Clinton polled 635,451 votes; Dole, 621,842; Perot, 120,243.

The state sends 6 representatives to Congress.

The capital is Frankfort. The state is divided into 120 counties.

Governor: Paul E. Patton (D.), 1995–99 ($90,912).
Lieut.-Governor: Steve D. Henry (D.) ($77,292).
Secretary of State: John Y. Brown III (D.) ($77,292).

BUDGET. For the fiscal year ending 30 June 1996 revenues received within the five major operating funds amounted to $10,808·2m. Included in this figure are $5,336·9m. General Fund revenues and $2,923·8m. Federal Fund revenues. Total expenditures amounted to $10,101·5m. including education, $2,778·4m.; human resources benefits payments, $2,303·9m.; and transport; $770·8m.

The general obligation bonded indebtedness on 30 June 1996 was nil.

Per capita personal income (1996) was $19,797.

NATURAL RESOURCES

Minerals. The principal mineral is coal: 152m. short tons were mined in 1996, value $3,644·5m. Output of petroleum, 3·6m. bbls (of 42 gallons); natural gas, 81,435m. cu. ft; stone, 60m. short tons, value $261m.; clay, 0·9m. tonnes, value $4m.; sand and gravel, 7·0m. short tons, value $24·5m. Total value of non-fuel mineral products in 1996 was $453·5m. Other minerals include fluorspar, ball clay, gemstones, dolomite, cement and lime.

Agriculture. In 1997, 88,000 farms had an area of 14m. acres. The average farm was 158 acres. In 1996 the average value of farmland and buildings per acre was $1,377.

Cash income, 1996, from crops, $1,831·3m., and from livestock, $1,718·9m. The chief crop is tobacco: Production, in 1996, 366·3m. lbs, ranking second to North Carolina in the USA. Other principal crops include corn, soybeans, wheat, hay, fruit and vegetables, sorghum grain and barley.

Stock-raising is important in Kentucky, which has long been famous for its horses. The livestock in 1997 included 150,000 milk cows, 2·5m. cattle and calves, 22,000 sheep, 0·7m. swine.

Forestry. State forest area, 1997, 264,000 acres.

INDUSTRY. In 1996 the state's approximately 4,500 manufacturing plants had 242,400 production workers; value added by manufacture in 1994 was $30,208·5m. The leading manufacturing industries (by employment) are transportation equipment, electronic equipment, apparel, and food products.

TOURISM. In 1996 tourist expenditure was $7,156m., producing over $715·6m. in tax revenues and generating 143,891 jobs. The state had (1996) 979 hotels and motels, 246 camping grounds and 50 state parks.

COMMUNICATIONS

Roads. In 1996 the state had about 73,000 miles of federal, state and local roads. There were almost 2·9m. motor vehicle registrations in 1996.

Railways. In 1996 there were 2,350 miles of railway.

Civil Aviation. There were (1996) 70 publicly-used airports and (1992) 2,294 registered aircraft.

Shipping. There is barge traffic on the 1,100 miles of navigable rivers. There are 6 public river ports.

SOCIAL INSTITUTIONS

Justice. There are 12 adult prisons within the Department of Corrections Adult Institutions and 3 privately-run adult institutions; average daily population (1996–97), 10,205 in prisons, 773 in jails awaiting incarceration, and 2,059 in local community centres. There were also 16,173 individuals on probation or parole.

The death penalty is authorized for murder and kidnap. As of Nov. 1997 there were 31 persons under sentence of death. The last execution was in 1997.

Religion. The chief religious denominations in 1990 were: Southern Baptists, with 770,425 members, Roman Catholic (365,270), United Methodists (182,302), Christian Churches and Church of Christ (90,520) and Christian (Disciples of Christ) (66,798).

Education. Attendance at school between the ages of 5 and 15 years (inclusive) is compulsory, the normal term being 175 days. In 1995–96, 22,177 teachers were employed in public elementary and 10,032 in secondary schools. In 1995–96 there were 437,183 pupils in public elementary and 201,492 in secondary schools. Public school classroom teachers' salaries (1995–96) averaged $32,935. The average total expenditure per pupil was $4,607.

There were also 4,143 teachers working in private elementary and secondary schools with some 63,000 students in 1995–96.

The state has 27 universities and senior colleges, 1 junior college and 14 community colleges, with a total (autumn 1995) of 175,255 students. Of these universities and colleges, 23 are state-supported, and the remainder are supported privately. The largest of the institutions of higher learning are (autumn 1995): University of Kentucky, with 24,378 students; University of Louisville, 21,218; Eastern Kentucky University, 15,727; Western Kentucky University, 14,721; Northern Kentucky University, 11,637; Morehead State University, 8,454; Murray State University, 8,166; Kentucky State University, 2,579. Five of the several privately endowed colleges of standing are Berea College, Berea; Centre College, Danville; Transylvania University, Lexington; Georgetown College, Georgetown; and Bellarmine College, Louisville.

Health. In 1997 the state had 127 licensed hospitals (18,735 beds). There were 423 licensed long-term care facilities (35,263 beds), 365 family care homes, 120 home health agencies and 1,841 miscellaneous health facilities.

Welfare. In the all state funded Supplementation programme, payments were made in Sept. 1997 to 5,437 persons, of whom 2,633 were aged, 54 blind and 2,750 disabled. The average State Supplementation payment was $244·07 to aged, $139·07 to blind and $236·44 to disabled.

In the Aid to Families with Dependent Children Program as of Sept. 1997, aid was given to 145,713 persons in 59,504 families. The average payment per person was $91·20, per family $228·33.

In addition to money payments, medical assistance, food stamps and social services are available.

Further Reading

Kentucky Deskbook of Economic Statistics. Cabinet for Economic Development, Frankfort
Lee, L. G., *A Brief History of Kentucky and its Counties.* Berea, 1981
Miller, P. M., *Kentucky Politics and Government: Do We Stand United?* Nebraska Univ. Press, 1994

LOUISIANA

KEY HISTORICAL EVENTS. Originally the Territory of Choctaw and Caddo tribes, the whole area was claimed for France in 1682. The French founded New Orleans in 1718 and it became the centre of a crown colony in 1731. During the wars which the European powers fought over their American interests, the French ceded the area west of the Mississippi (most of the present state) to Spain in 1762 and the eastern area, north of New Orleans, to Britain in 1763. The British section passed to the USA in 1783, but France bought back the rest from Spain in 1800, including New Orleans and the mouth of the Mississippi. The USA, fearing to be excluded from a strategically important and commercially promising shipping area, persuaded France to sell Louisiana again in 1803. The present states of Missouri, Arkansas, Iowa, North Dakota, South Dakota, Nebraska and Oklahoma were included in the purchase.

The area became the Territory of New Orleans in 1804 and was admitted to the Union as a state in 1812. The economy at first depended on cotton and sugar-cane plantations. The population was of French, Spanish and black descent, with a growing number of American settlers. Plantation interests succeeded in achieving secession in 1861, but New Orleans was occupied by the Union in 1862. Planters re-emerged in the late 19th century and imposed rigid segregation of the black population, denying them their new rights.

The state has become mainly urban industrial, with the Mississippi ports growing rapidly. There is petroleum and natural gas, and a strong tourist industry based on the French culture and Caribbean atmosphere of New Orleans.

TERRITORY AND POPULATION. Louisiana is bounded north by Arkansas, east by Mississippi, south by the Gulf of Mexico and west by Texas. Land area, 43,566 sq. miles (112,836 sq. km). Census population, 1 April 1990, 4,219,973 (68·1% urban), an increase of 0·38% since 1980. Population estimate (1996), 4,351,000. Births, 1994, 67,802; marriages, 40,405; deaths, 38,950; infant deaths, 715. Divorces, 1993, 15,042.

Population in 5 census years was:

	White	Black	Indian	Asiatic	Total	Per sq. mile
1930	1,322,712	776,326	1,536	1,019	2,101,593	46·5
1960	2,211,715	1,039,207	3,587	2,004	3,257,022	72·2
				All others		
1970	2,541,498	1,086,832		12,976	3,641,306	81·1
1980	2,911,243	1,237,263		55,466	4,205,900	93·5
1990	2,839,138	1,299,281		81,554	4,219,973	97·0

Of the 1990 total, 2,031,386 were male, 2,872,038 were urban; those 20 years of age or older numbered 2,852,363.

The largest cities with their 1990 census population are: New Orleans, 496,938; Baton Rouge, 219,531; Shreveport, 198,525; Lafayette, 94,440; Kenner, 72,033; Lake Charles, 70,580; Monroe, 54,909; Bossier City, 52,721.

CLIMATE. New Orleans. Jan. 54°F (12·2°C), July 83°F (28·3°C). Annual rainfall 58" (1,458 mm). Louisiana belongs to the Gulf Coast climate zone (*see* UNITED STATES: Climate).

CONSTITUTION AND GOVERNMENT. The present constitution dates from 1974. The Legislature consists of a Senate of 39 members and a House of Representatives of 105 members, both chosen for 4 years. Sessions are annual; a fiscal session is held in odd years.

The state sends 7 representatives to Congress.

In the 1996 presidential election Clinton polled 928,983 votes; Dole, 710,240; Perot, 122,981.

Louisiana is divided into 64 parishes (corresponding to the counties of other states). The capital is Baton Rouge.

Governor: Murphy J. Foster (R.), 1996–2000 ($95,000).
Lieut. Governor: Kathleen Blanco (D.), ($85,000).
Secretary of State: W. Fox McKeithen (R.), ($85,000).

BUDGET. For the year ending 30 June 1995 total revenues were $4,480,526,000;

total expenditures were $9,997,807,000 (education, $2,643,175,000; transport and development, $235,452,000; health and welfare, $4,733,069).

Per capita personal income (1995) was $18,827.

NATURAL RESOURCES

Minerals. Production in 1995 (estimate) of crude oil was 124·8m. bbls; production of natural gas, 1,535·88m. cu. ft. Principal non-fuel minerals are sulphur, salt and sand and gravel. Value of 1991 output, $352m.

Agriculture. The state is divided into two parts, the uplands and the alluvial and swamp regions of the coast. A delta occupies about one-third of the total area. Manufacturing is the leading industry, but agriculture is important. The number of farms in 1996 was some 27,000 covering 9m. acres; the average farm had 322 acres. Average value of farmland and buildings per acre in 1995 was $1,082. Principal crops, with 1995 production, are: Soyabeans, 23·6m. bu.; sugar-cane, 2,088·9m. lbs sugar and 62·6m. gallons molasses; rice, 27·6m. cwt; maize, 23·2m bu.; cotton, 641·6m. lbs lint and 1,023·4m. lbs seed; sweet potatoes, 7·2m. bu.; pecans, 11·7m. lbs; grain sorghum, 3·2m. cwt. Livestock in 1990: Cattle, 0·84m.; pigs, 50,000; sheep, 16,000; poultry, 2·1m.

Fisheries. The value of the 1995 catch of marine and freshwater fish was $306·7m.; of aquaculture, $155m.

Forestry. State forests, 1m. acres in 1997. Income from manufactured products exceeds $2,500m. annually. Production, 1995: Sawtimber, 1,450,560,376 board feet; pulpwood, 5,250,459 standard cords.

INDUSTRY. The manufacturing industries are chiefly those associated with petroleum, chemicals, lumber, food, paper. In 1995, 10·9% of the workforce were employed in manufacturing, 24·2% in trade and 37·9% in service industries.

TOURISM. Travellers spent an estimated $5,900m. in 1994. Tourism is the second most important industry for state income.

COMMUNICATIONS

Roads. In 1996 there were 60,021 miles of public roads (46,268 miles rural in 1991) and, in Oct. 1996, 5,800,961 registered motor vehicles.

Railways. In 1995 there were about 3,817 miles of main line track in the state. There is a tramway in New Orleans.

Civil Aviation. In 1995 there were 72 public airports.

Shipping. There are ports at New Orleans, Baton Rouge and Lake Charles. The Mississippi and other waterways provide 7,500 miles of navigable water.

SOCIAL INSTITUTIONS

Justice. There were 25,742 prisoners in state correctional institutions in Dec. 1995. The death penalty is authorized; the last execution was in 1996.

Religion. The Roman Catholic Church is the largest denomination in Louisiana. The leading Protestant Churches are Southern Baptist and Methodist.

Education. School attendance is compulsory between the ages of 7 and 15, both inclusive. In 1994–95 there were 1,556 public elementary and secondary schools with 774,046 registered students, and 47,241 teachers paid an average salary of $26,285 in 1993–94. There are 20 four-year and 5 two-year public colleges and universities and 12 non-public four-year institutions of higher learning. There are 45 state trade and vocational-technical schools. In 1991 there were 158,119 students in public, and 25,757 in private colleges and universities. Enrolment, 1995, in Louisiana State University, Baton Rouge was 23,780; University of Southwestern Louisiana, 15,840; University of New Orleans, 14,625; Southeastern Louisiana University,

13,447; Northeast Louisiana University, 10,956; Tulane University, 10,840; Southern University, Baton Rouge, 9,420; Northwestern State University, 8,505; McNeese State University, 8,135; Grambling State University, 7,325; Nicholls State University, 6,992; Loyola University, 5,634; Louisiana State University in Shreveport, 3,949; Southern University of New Orleans (1993), 4,456; Xavier University, 3,419; Dillard University, 1,566.

Health. In 1994 the state had 166 licensed hospitals with 23,280 beds.

Social Security. In Dec. 1993, assistance was being given to 408,000 retired workers and dependants, 0·16m. survivors and 121,000 disabled workers and dependants. Total annual payments, 1993, $4,500m.

Further Reading

Statistical information: Division of Business and Economic Research, Univ. of New Orleans, New Orleans 70148. Publishes *Statistical Abstract of Louisiana.*
Davis, E. A., *Louisiana, the Pelican State.* Louisiana State Univ. Press, 1975
Kniffen, F. B., *Louisiana, its Land and People.* Louisiana State Univ. Press, 1968
Wilds, J. *et al.* (eds.) *Louisiana Yesterday and Today: a Historical Guide to the State.* Louisiana State Univ. Press, 1996

State library: The State Library of Louisiana, Baton Rouge, Louisiana.

MAINE

KEY HISTORICAL EVENTS. Originally occupied by Algonquian-speaking tribes, the Territory was disputed between different groups of British settlers, and between the British and French, throughout the 17th and most of the 18th centuries. After 1652 it was governed as part of Massachusetts, and French claims finally failed in 1763. Most of the early settlers were English and Protestant Irish, with many Quebec French.

The Massachusetts settlers had gained control when the original colonist, Sir Ferdinando Gorges, supported the losing royalist side in the English civil war. Their control was questioned during the English-American war of 1812, when Maine residents claimed that the Massachusetts government did not protect them against British raids. Maine was separated from Massachusetts and entered the Union as a state in 1820.

Maine is a mountainous state and even the coastline is rugged, but the coastal belt is where most settlement has developed. In the 19th century there were manufacturing towns making use of cheap water-power, and the rocky shore supported a shell-fish industry. The latter still flourishes, together with intensive horticulture, producing potatoes and fruit. The other main economic development has been in exploiting the forests for timber, pulp and paper.

The capital is Augusta, a river trading post which was fortified against Indian attacks in 1754, incorporated as a town in 1797 and chosen as capital in 1832.

TERRITORY AND POPULATION. Maine is bounded west, north and east by Canada, south-east by the Atlantic, south and south-west by New Hampshire. Land area, 30,865 sq. miles (79,931 sq. km). Census population, 1 April 1990 1,127,928 (44·6% urban), an increase of 9·18% since 1980. Population estimate (1996), 1,243,000. Births, 1994, 14,441 (11·6 per 1,000 population); deaths, 12,000 (9·4); infant deaths, 1992, 109 (6·8 per 1,000 live births); marriages, 11,077 (8·8); divorces 5,816 (4·6).

Population for 5 census years was:

	White	Black	Indian	Asiatic	Total	Per sq. mile
1910	739,995	1,363	992	121	742,371	24·8
1930	795,185	1,096	1,012	130	797,423	25·7
1950	910,846	1,221	1,522	185	913,774	29·4

	White	Black	*All others*	Total	Per sq. mile
1970	985,276	2,800	3,972	992,048	31·0
1980	1,109,850	3,128	12,049	1,125,027	36·3

Of the total population in 1980, 48·5% were male, 40·7% were urban and 60·5% were 21 years or older.

The largest city in the state is Portland with a census population of 61,572 in 1980. Other cities (with population in 1980) are: Lewiston, 40,481; Bangor, 31,643; Auburn, 23,128; South Portland, 22,712; Augusta (capital), 21,819; Biddeford, 19,638; Waterville, 17,779.

CLIMATE. Average maximum temperatures range from 56·3°F in Waterville to 48·3°F in Caribou, but record high (since *c.* 1950) is 103°F. Average minimum ranges from 36·9°F in Rockland to 28·3°F in Greenville, but record low (also in Greenville) is –42°F. Average annual rainfall ranges from 48·85" in Machias to 36·09" in Houlton. Average annual snowfall ranges from 118·7" in Greenville to 59·7" in Rockland. Maine belongs to the New England climate zone (*see* UNITED STATES: Climate).

CONSTITUTION AND GOVERNMENT. The constitution of 1820 is still in force, but it has been amended 153 times. In 1951, 1965 and 1973 the Legislature approved recodifications of the constitution as arranged by the Chief Justice under special authority.

The Legislature consists of the Senate with 35 members and the House of Representatives with 151 members, both Houses being elected simultaneously for 2 years. Sessions are annual.

The state sends 2 representatives to Congress.

In the 1996 presidential election Clinton polled 326,217 votes; Dole, 190,711; Perot, 88,082.

The capital is Augusta. The state is divided into 16 counties.

Governor: Angus King (ind.), 1995–99 ($69,992).
Secretary of State: G. William Diamond (D.) ($60,000).

BUDGET. For the financial year 1994 general revenue was $3,534m. and expenditure was $3,450m.

Per capita personal income (1995) was $20,527.

NATURAL RESOURCES

Minerals. Minerals include sand and gravel, stone, lead, clay, copper, peat, silver and zinc. Mineral output, 1990, was valued at $56m.

Agriculture. In 1996, some 7,000 farms occupied 1m. acres; the average farm was 181 acres. Average value of farmland and buildings per acre in 1995 was $1,245. Farm income, 1991: Crops, $203m.; livestock and products, $215m. Principal crops are potatoes, apples, hay and blueberries. Livestock in 1986: Cattle, 135,000; pigs, 79,000; sheep, 17,000; poultry, 4·9m.

Forestry. There are some 17·5m. acres of commercial forest, mainly pine, spruce and fir. Wood products industries are of great economic importance.

Fisheries. In 1990 the commercial catch was valued at $129·9m.

INDUSTRY. Total non-agricultural workforce, 1996, 540,000. Services employed 150,000; wholesale and retail, 136,000; government, 93,000; manufacturing, 88,000; the main manufacture is paper at 47 plants, producing about 34% of manufacturing value added.

TOURISM. Earnings were $2,000m. in 1989.

COMMUNICATIONS

Roads. In 1995 there were 22,577 miles of roads (19,957 miles rural). There were 967,000 registered motor vehicles.

Railways. In 1984 there were 1,516 miles of mainline railway tracks.

Civil Aviation. There are international airports at Portland and Bangor.

SOCIAL INSTITUTIONS

Justice. In 1994 there were 1,534 prisoners in state correctional institutions. There is no capital punishment.

Religion. The largest religious bodies are: Roman Catholic (270,283 members), Baptists (36,808 members) and Congregationalists (40,750 members), and other Christian Churches (34,066 members).

Education. Education is free for pupils from 5 to 21 years of age, and compulsory from 7 to 17. In 1994–95 there were 212,322 pupils and 15,398 teachers in public elementary and secondary schools. Education expenditure by state and local government in 1994, $1,041m.

The state University of Maine, founded in 1865, has 7 locations; Bowdoin College, founded in 1794 at Brunswick; Bates College at Lewiston; Colby College at Waterville; Husson College, Bangor; Westbrook College at Westbrook; Unity College at Unity, and the University of New England (formerly St Francis College) at Biddeford.

Health. In 1995 there were 39 community hospitals with 4,000 beds.

Social Security. Supplemental Security Income (SSI) is administered by the Social Security Administration. It became effective on 1 Jan. 1974 and replaces former aid to the aged, blind and disabled, administered by the state with state and federal funds. SSI is supplemented by Medicaid for nursing home patients or hospital patients. Aid to families with dependent children is granted where one or both parents are disabled or absent and income is insufficient. There is a programme of assistance for catastrophic illness. Child welfare services include basic child protective services, enforcing child support, establishing paternity and finding missing parents, foster home placements, adoptions; services in divorce cases and licensing of foster homes, day care and residential treatment services, and public guardianship. There are also protective services for adults.

Further Reading

Statistical information: Maine Department of Economic and Community Development, State House Station 59, Augusta 04333. Publishes *Maine: a Statistical Summary.*
Maine Register, State Year-Book and Legislative Manual. Tower Publishing, Portland. Annual
Banks, R., *Maine Becomes A State.* Wesleyan U.P., 1970
Clark, C., *Maine.* New York, 1977
Palmer, K. T. *et al., Maine Politics and Government.* Univ. of Nebraska Press, 1993

MARYLAND

KEY HISTORICAL EVENTS. The first European visitors found groups of Algonquian-speaking tribes, often under attack by Iroquois from further north. The first white settlement was made by the Calvert family, British Roman Catholics, in 1634. The settlers received some legislative rights in 1638. In 1649 their assembly passed the Act of Toleration, granting freedom of worship to all Christians. A peace treaty was signed with the Iroquois in 1652, after which it was possible for farming settlements to expand north and west. The capital (formerly at St Mary's City) was moved to Annapolis in 1694. Baltimore, which became the state's main city, was founded in 1729.

The first industry was tobacco-growing, which was based on slave-worked plantations. There were also many immigrant British small farmers, tradesmen and indentured servants.

At the close of the War of independence the treaty of Paris was ratified in Annapolis. Maryland became a state of the Union in 1788. In 1791 the state ceded land for the new federal capital, Washington, and its economy has depended on the capital's proximity ever since. Baltimore also grew as a port and industrial city, attracting much European immigration in the 19th century. Although strong sympathy for the south was expressed, Maryland remained within the Union in the Civil War albeit under the imposition of martial law.

TERRITORY AND POPULATION. Maryland is bounded north by Pennsylvania, east by Delaware and the Atlantic, south by Virginia and West Virginia, with the Potomac River forming most of the boundary, and west by West Virginia. Chesapeake Bay almost cuts off the eastern end of the state from the rest. Land area, 9,775 sq. miles (25,316 sq. km). Census population, 1 April 1990, 4,781,468 (81·3% urban), an increase since 1980 of 564,535 or 13·4%. Population estimate (1996), 5,072,000. In 1994 births were 73,971 (14·8 per 1,000 population); deaths, 41,000 (8·2); infant deaths, 1988, 856 (11·2 per 1,000 live births); 1994 rate, 9·0 per 1,000 live births; marriages, 1991, 44,399 (9·2); divorces, also 1991, 16,576 (3·4).

Population for 4 federal censuses was:

	White	Black	Indian	Asiatic	Total	Per sq. mile
1920	1,204,737	244,479	32	400	1,449,661	145·8
1930	1,354,226	276,379	50	857	1,631,526	165·0
1960	2,573,919	518,410	1,538	5,700	3,100,689	314·0
			All others			
1990	3,393,964	1,189,899	197,605		4,781,468	489·3

Of the total population in 1990, 2,318,671 were male, 3,888,429 persons were urban and those 20 years old or older numbered 3,484,455.

The largest city in the state (containing 15·4% of the population) is Baltimore, with 736,014 in 1990 (and 786,741 in 1980); Baltimore metropolitan area, 2·4m.Maryland residents in the Washington, DC, metropolitan area total more than 1·8m. Other cities (1990) are Dundalk (65,800); Towson (49,445); Silver Spring (76,046); Columbia (75,883); Bethesda (62,936). Incorporated places, 1990: Rockville, 44,835; Bowie, 37,589; Hagerstown, 35,445; Frederick, 40,148; Annapolis, 33,187; Gaithersburg, 39,542; Cumberland, 23,706; College Park, 21,927; Loreenbelt, 21,096; Salisbury, 20,592; Cambridge, 11,514.

CLIMATE. Baltimore. Jan. 36°F (2·2°C), July 79°F (26·1°C). Annual rainfall 41" (1,026 mm). Maryland belongs to the Atlantic Coast climate zone (*see* UNITED STATES: Climate).

CONSTITUTION AND GOVERNMENT. The present constitution dates from 1867; it has had 125 amendments. The General Assembly consists of a Senate of 47, and a House of Delegates of 141 members, both elected for 4 years, as are the Governor and Lieut.-Governor. Voters are citizens who have the usual residential qualifications. At the 1996 presidential election Clinton polled 924,284 votes; Dole, 651,682; Perot, 219,525.

Maryland sends to Congress 8 representatives.

The state capital is Annapolis. The state is divided into 23 counties and Baltimore City.

Governor: Parris N. Glendening (D.), 1995–99 ($120,000).
Lieut.-Governor: Kathleen K. Townsend (D.) ($100,000).
Secretary of State: John Willis (D.) ($70,000).

BUDGET. For the fiscal year ending 1994 general revenues were $12,870,000,000. General expenditures, $11,800,000,000, including $3,758,706,000 for education, $2,750,883,000 for welfare; $1,028,389,000 for highways.

Total authorized long-term state debt, 30 June 1990 was $2,979·8m. (Issued and outstanding, $1,986·9m.; authorized but not issued, $992·9m.)

Per capita personal income (1995) was $25,927.

NATURAL RESOURCES

Minerals. Value of non-fuel mineral production, 1993, was $314m. Sand and gravel

(11·2m. metric tons) and stone (42·4m. metric tons) account for 75% of the total value. Coal is probably still the leading mineral commodity by value followed by, stone, sand and gravel and Portland cement. Output of coal was 3·26m. short tons, valued at about $84m. Natural gas is produced from 1 field in Garrett County; 27·7m. cu. ft in 1993. A second gas field in the same county is used for natural gas storage.

Agriculture. Agriculture is an important industry in the state. In 1996 there were approximately 14,000 farms with an area of 2m. acres. The average number of acres per farm was 153. The average value per acre in 1995 was $3,707. In 1992, 16,960 people were employed in agriculture.

Farm animals, Dec. 1997, were: Milk cows, 86,000; all cattle, 270,000; swine, 73,000 and sheep, 32,000. As of Jan. 1996, chickens (not broilers), 3·6m. The most important crops, 1997, were: Corn for grain, 37·4m. bu.; soybeans, 14·7m. bu.; tobacco, 12·0m. lbs, and hay, 474,000 tons.

Cash receipts, 1996: $1·56m.; from livestock and livestock products, $901m., and crops, $664m. Dairy products and broilers are important.

INDUSTRY. In 1996 manufactories had 174,000 employed. Total value added by manufacture (1992), $15,241·8m. Chief industries are food and kindred products ($2,431), instruments and related products ($2,163·5), chemicals and products ($1,879·3), printing and publishing ($1,865·1) and transportation equipment ($1,584·3).

Total non-agricultural employment, 1996: 2,206,000.

TOURISM. Tourism is one of the state's leading industries. In 1995 tourists spent over $5,667m.

COMMUNICATIONS

Roads. The total length of road in 1995 was 29,680 miles, of which 15,781 miles were rural. As of March 1995, an estimated 3·7m. automobiles were registered.

Railways. Railways, in 1990, had 1,068 miles of line. There are metro and light rail lines in Baltimore.

Civil Aviation. There were, 1992, 48 commercially licensed airports.

Shipping. In 1990 Baltimore was the ninth largest US seaport in value of trade, twelfth in tonnage handled.

SOCIAL INSTITUTIONS

Justice. Prisons had about 21,000 inmates in 1994; the total in 1992 equalled 401 per 100,000 population, a high rate, which may be explained by the fact that Maryland incarcerates domestic relations law violators in state prisons; state prisons also receive a considerable number of persons committed for misdemeanours by magistrates' courts of the counties as well as from Baltimore's court system.

The death penalty is authorized.

Maryland's prison system has conducted a work-release programme for selected prisoners since 1963. All institutions have academic and vocational training programmes.

Religion. Maryland was the first US state to give religious freedom to all who came within its borders. Present religious affiliations of the population are approximately: Protestant, 32%; Roman Catholic, 24%; Jewish, 10%; remaining 34% is non-related and other faiths.

Education. Education is compulsory from 6 to 16 years of age. In 1994–95 the public elementary schools (including kindergartens and secondary schools) had 780,807 pupils. In Sept. 1994 teachers in the elementary and secondary schools numbered 45,300. Teachers' average salary in 1990–91 was $38,312. Current expenditure by local school boards on education, 1989–90, was $3,827·8m., of which the state's contribution was $1,504·8m.

In 1991 there were 34 degree-granting 4-year institutions and 23 2-year colleges. The largest was the University of Maryland system, with 106,514 students (Sept. 1991), consisting of 11 campuses with the highest enrolment at College Park (34,623) and Towson State University (15,403).

Health. In 1995 there were 50 community hospitals with 12,600 beds.

The Maryland State Department of Health, organized in 1874, was in 1969 made part of the Department of Health and Mental Hygiene which performs its functions through its central office, 23 county health departments and the Baltimore City Health Department. For the financial year 1990 the department's budget was $1,985·8m., of which $1,327·5m. were general funds and $46·4m. special funds appropriated by the General Assembly. The balance of the budget, $611·9m., derives from federal funds.

During financial year 1991 Maryland's programme of medical care for indigent and medically indigent patients covered about 442,100 persons. The programme, which covers in-patient and out-patient hospital services, laboratory services, skilled nursing home care, physician services, pharmacy services, dental services and home health services, cost approximately $1,357m.

Social Security. Under the supervision of the Department of Human Resources, local social service departments administer public assistance for needy persons. In March 1990 families with dependent children received $29,217,254 (218,342 recipients, average actual monthly payment $133·81); general public assistance payments were $5,394,836 (25,443 recipients, average actual monthly payments $212·04).

Further Reading

Statistical Information: Maryland Department of Economic and Employment Development, 217 East Redwood St., Baltimore, 21202. Publishes *Maryland Statistical Abstract.*
DiLisio, J. E., *Maryland.* Boulder, 1982
Rollo, V. F., *Maryland's Constitution and Government.* Maryland Hist. Press, Rev. ed., 1982

State Library: Maryland State Library, Annapolis.

MASSACHUSETTS

KEY HISTORICAL EVENTS. The first European settlement was at Plymouth, when the *Mayflower* landed its company of English religious separatists in 1620. In 1626–30 more colonists arrived, the main body being a large company of English Puritans who founded a Puritan commonwealth. This commonwealth, of about 1,000 colonists led by John Winthrop, became the Massachusetts Bay Colony and was founded under a company charter. Following disagreement between the English government and the colony the charter was withdrawn in 1684, but in 1691 a new charter united a number of settlements under the name of Massachusetts Bay. The colony's government was rigidly theocratic.

Shipbuilding, iron-working and manufacturing were more important than farming from the beginning, the land being poor. The colony was Protestant and of English descent until the War of Independence. The former colony adopted its present constitution in 1780. In the struggle which ended in the separation of the American colonies from the mother country, Massachusetts took the foremost part, and on 6 Feb. 1788 became the 6th state to ratify the US constitution. The state acquired its present boundaries (having previously included Maine) in 1820.

During the 19th century industrialization and immigration from Europe both increased while Catholic Irish and Italian immigrants began to change the population's character. The main inland industry was textile manufacture, the main coastal occupation was whaling; both have now gone. Boston has remained the most important city of New England, attracting a large black population since 1950.

TERRITORY AND POPULATION. Massachusetts is bounded north by Vermont and New Hampshire, east by the Atlantic, south by Connecticut and Rhode

Island and west by New York. Land area, 7,838 sq. miles (20,300 sq. km). Population estimate (1996), 6,092,000. Vital statistics: 1994, births, 83,787 (13·9 per 1,000 population); deaths, 55,000 (9·1); infant deaths in 1992, 529 (6); marriages, 43,429 (7·3); divorces, 13,547 (2·3).

Population at 5 federal census years was:

	White	Black	Other	Total	Per sq. mile
1950	4,611,503	73,171	5,840	4,690,514	598·4
1960	5,023,144	111,842	13,592	5,148,578	656·8
1970	5,477,624	175,817	35,729	5,689,170	725·8
1980	5,362,836	221,279	152,922	5,737,037	732·0
1990	. . .	. . .	. . .	6,016,425	767·6

Of the total population in 1980, 47·6% were male, 83·8% were urban and 32% were 21 years old or older.

Population of the largest cities at the 1990 census: Boston, 574,283; Lowell, 103,439; Springfield, 156,983; Worcester, 169,759; New Bedford, 99,922; Cambridge, 95,802; Brockton, 92,788; Fall River, 92,703; Quincy, 84,985; Newton, 82,585; Lynn, 81,245.

CLIMATE. Boston. Jan. 28°F (−2·2°C), July 71°F (21·7°C). Annual rainfall 41" (1,036 mm). Massachusetts belongs to the New England climate zone (*see* UNITED STATES: Climate).

CONSTITUTION AND GOVERNMENT. The constitution dates from 1780 and has had 116 amendments. The legislative body, styled the General Court of the Commonwealth of Massachusetts, meets annually, and consists of the Senate with 40 members and the House of Representatives of 160 members, both elected for 2 years.

The state sends 10 representatives to Congress.

At the 1996 presidential election Clinton polled 1,532,917 votes; Dole, 693,866; Perot, 219,525.

The capital is Boston. The state has 14 counties.

Governor: William F. Weld (R.), 1995–99 ($75,000).
Lieut.-Governor: A. Paul Cellucci (R.) ($75,000).
Secretary of State: William F. Galvin (D.) ($75,000).

BUDGET. For the fiscal year 1994 the total general revenue was $20,346m.; total general expenditures, $20,428m. ($3,716·1m. for education, $1,485·1m. for highways and $5,865·0m. for public welfare).

Per capita personal income (1995) was $26,994.

NATURAL RESOURCES

Minerals. Total mineral output in 1990 was valued at $111·3m., of which most came from sand, gravel, crushed stone and lime.

Agriculture. In 1996 there were approximately 6,000 farms with an average area of 92 and a total area of 1m. acres. Average value per acre in 1995 was $5,398. Farm income: Crops, $337m.; livestock and products, $116m.

Principal crops include cranberries and greenhouse products.

Forestry. About 68% of the state is forest. State forests cover about 256,000 acres. Total forest land covers about 3m. acres. Commercially important hardwoods are sugar maple, northern red oak and white ash; softwoods are white pine and hemlock. 85m. board feet of timber were cut in 1989.

Fisheries. The 1990 catch totalled 328m. lbs and was valued at $303m.

INDUSTRY. In 1996 the total non-agricultural workforce was 3,036,000. Manufacturing establishments employed an average of 444,000 workers, service industries employed 1,063,000 and wholesale and retail 697,000.

COMMUNICATIONS

Roads. In 1995 there were 30,751 miles of public roads (10,904 miles rural). In 1995 there were 4,502,000 registered motor vehicles.

Railways. In 1984 there were 1,310 miles of mainline railway. There are metro, light rail, tramway and commuter networks in and around Boston.

Civil Aviation. There is an international airport at Boston.

Shipping. The state has 3 deep-water harbours, the largest of which is Boston. Other ports are Fall River and New Bedford.

SOCIAL INSTITUTIONS

Justice. In 1994 state correctional institutions held 11,282 prisoners. The death penalty is not authorized.

Religion. The principal religious bodies are the Roman Catholics, Jewish Congregations, Methodists, Episcopalians and Unitarians.

Education. School attendance is compulsory for ages 6–16. In 1994–95 there were 58,893 classroom teachers and 890,240 pupils.

Some leading higher education institutions are:

Year opened	Name and location of universities and colleges	Students 1988
1636	Harvard University, Cambridge[1]	16,871
1839	Framingham State College	4,303
1839	Westfield State College	6,053
1840	Bridgewater State College	6,539
1852	Tufts University, Medford[1,3]	6,297
1854	Salem State College	6,364
1861	Mass. Institute of Technology, Cambridge[1]	9,158
1863	University of Massachusetts, Amherst[1]	26,233
1863	Boston College (RC), Chestnut Hill[1]	12,858
1865	Worcester Polytechnic Institute, Worcester[1]	4,022
1869	Boston University, Boston[1]	22,373
1874	Worcester College	4,899
1894	Fitchburg State College	5,212
1894	University of Lowell[1]	10,445
1895	Southeastern Massachusetts University	5,031
1898	Northeastern University, Boston[1,4]	20,618
1899	Simmons College, Boston[2]	2,594
1905	Wentworth Institute of Technology	3,350
1906	Suffolk University	5,978
1917	Bentley College	5,611
1919	Western New England College	3,686
1919	Babson College	3,163
1947	Merrimack College	2,300
1948	Brandeis University, Waltham[1]	3,484
1964	University of Massachusetts, Boston	8,027

[1] Co-educational.   [2] For women only.
[3] Includes Jackson College for women.   [4] Includes Forsyth Dental Center School.

Health. In 1995 there were 96 community hospitals with 18,900 beds and 106,000 personnel.

Social Security. In 1990 the Department of Public Welfare paid $647m. in aid to families with dependent children (some 282,000 recipients received an average monthly payment of $510). Medicare enrolments were 0·87m. and total payments $3,152m.; Medicaid, 0·59m. recipients, total payments $2,730m. 0·73m. persons received retirement, 0·15m. survivors' and 91,000 disability benefits.

Further Reading

Hart, Albert B., (ed.) *Commonwealth History of Massachusetts, Colony, Province and State.* 5 vols., New York, 1966
Levitan, D. with Mariner, E. C., *Your Massachusetts Government.* Newton, Mass., 1984

MICHIGAN

KEY HISTORICAL EVENTS. The French were the first European settlers, establishing a fur trade with the local Algonquian Indians in the late 17th century. They founded Sault Ste Marie in 1668 and Detroit in 1701. In 1763 Michigan passed to Britain, along with other French territory east of the Mississippi, and from Britain it passed to the USA in 1783. Britain, however, kept a force at Detroit until 1796, and recaptured Detroit in 1812. Regular American settlement did not begin until later. The Territory of Michigan (1805) had its boundaries extended after 1818 and was admitted to the Union as a state (with its present boundaries) in 1837.

During the 19th century there was rapid industrial growth, especially in mining and metalworking. Many groups of immigrants from Poland, Italy, the Netherlands and Scandinavia came to settle as miners, farmers and industrial workers. The motor industry became dominant, especially in Detroit. Lake Michigan ports shipped bulk cargo, especially iron-ore and grain.

Detroit was the capital until 1847, when that function passed to Lansing. Detroit remained, however, an important centre of flour-milling and shipping and, after the First World War, of the motor industry.

TERRITORY AND POPULATION. Michigan is divided into two by Lake Michigan. The northern part is bounded south by the lake and by Wisconsin, west and north by Lake Superior, east by the North Channel of Lake Huron; between the two latter lakes the Canadian border runs through straits at Sault Ste Marie. The southern part is bounded in the west and north by Lake Michigan, east by Lake Huron, Ontario and Lake Erie, south by Ohio and Indiana. Area, 58,110 sq. miles (150,544 sq. km). Census population, 1 April 1990, 9,295,297 (70·5% urban), an increase of 0·4% since 1980. Population estimate (1996), 9,594,350. In 1995 births were 134,169; deaths, 83,405; infant deaths, 1,110 (8·3 per 1,000 live births); marriages, 71,042; divorces, 39,449.

Population of 5 federal census years was:

	White	Black	Indian	Asiatic	Total	Per sq. mile
1910	2,785,247	17,115	7,519	292	2,810,173	48·9
1930	4,663,507	69,453	7,080	2,285	4,842,325	84·9
1960	7,085,865	717,581	9,701	10,047	7,823,194	137·2
			All others			
1980	7,872,241	1,199,023	190,814		9,262,078	162·6
1990	7,756,086	1,291,706	247,505		9,295,297	160·0

Of the total population in 1990, 4,512,781 were male, 6,554,846 persons were urban and those 20 years old or older numbered 6,540,323. 201,596 were Hispanic.

Population of the chief cities (1994 estimates) was: Ann Arbor, 108,817; Detroit, 992,038; Flint, 138,164; Grand Rapids, 190,395; Lansing, 119,590; Livonia, 100,415; Sterling Heights, 119,505; Warren, 142,625.

CLIMATE. Detroit. Jan. 22·9°F (−5·1°C), July 72·3°F (22·4°C). Annual rainfall 32·6" (828 mm). Grand Rapids. Jan. 21·8°F (−5·7°C), July 71·6°F (22·0°C). Annual rainfall 36·0" (914 mm). Lansing. Jan. 20·9°F (−6·2°C), July 70·8°F (21·6°C). Annual rainfall 30·6" (777 mm). Michigan belongs to the Great Lakes climate zone (*see* UNITED STATES: Climate).

CONSTITUTION AND GOVERNMENT. The present constitution became effective on 1 Jan. 1964. The Senate consists of 38 members, elected for 4 years, and the House of Representatives of 110 members, elected for 2 years. Sessions are biennial.

The state sends 16 representatives to Congress.

At the 1996 presidential election Clinton polled 1,989,653 votes; Dole, 1,481,212; Perot, 336,670.

The capital is Lansing. The state is organized in 83 counties.

Governor: John Engler (R.), 1995–99 ($121,166).
Lieut.-Governor: Connie Binsfeld (R.) ($89,450).
Secretary of State: Candice Miller (R.) ($112,000).

BUDGET. For the financial year ending 30 Sept. 1996, the general revenue was $18,434m. (taxation, $10,224m.); general expenditures, $17,360m.
Per capita personal income (1996) was $24,945.

NATURAL RESOURCES

Minerals. Output of petroleum, 1992, 16m. bbls; natural gas, 1996, 252,600m. cu. ft. Non-fuel mineral output in 1995 was valued at $1,510m., mainly iron ore, cement, stone, sand and gravel.

Agriculture. The state, formerly agricultural, is now chiefly industrial. In 1996 it contained 53,000 farms with a total area of 10·6m. acres; the average farm was 200 acres. Average value per acre in 1995 was $1,329. Principal crops are maize, oats, wheat, sugar-beet, soybeans and hay. 6,900,000 acres were harvested in 1995; the total value of crop production was $2,496m. In 1996 there were 328,000 milk cows, 122,000 beef cows and 6·56m. chickens. Farm income, 1995: crops, $2,197m.; livestock and products, $1,324m.

Forestry. The forests in 1993 covered 19·3m. acres. About 18·6m. acres of this total is timberland acreage. Three-quarters of the timber volume is hardwoods, principally hard and soft maples, aspen, oak and birch. Christmas trees are another important forest crop. Sawtimber harvests in 1990 totalled 1 billion board feet.

INDUSTRY. Manufacturing is important; among principal products are motor vehicles and trucks, machinery, fabricated metals, primary metals, cement, chemicals, furniture, paper, foodstuffs, rubber, plastics and pharmaceuticals. Total non-agricultural labour force, 1996, 4,345,000, of which 966,900 were in manufacturing.

COMMUNICATIONS

Roads. In 1995 there were 118,731 miles of roads (9,602 miles of state highways, 88,890 miles of county roads and 20,239 miles of municipal roads). In 1996 there were 9,072,739 registered motor vehicles.

Railways. In 1995 there were 3,900 miles of railway.

Civil Aviation. There are international airports at Detroit, Flint, Grand Rapids, Kalamazoo, Port Huron, Saginaw and Sault Ste Marie.

SOCIAL INSTITUTIONS

Justice. A Civil Rights Commission was established, and its powers and duties were implemented by legislation in the extra session of 1963. Statutory enactments guaranteeing civil rights in specific areas date from 1885. The legislature has a unique one-person grand jury system. In 1995 there were 38,854 prisoners in state correctional institutions. Michigan has no capital punishment statute.

Religion. Roman Catholics make up the largest body; largest Protestant denominations, Lutherans, United Methodists, United Presbyterians, Episcopalians.

Education. Education is compulsory for children from 6 to 16 years of age. Education expenditure by state and local governments in 1995 was $10,123m. In 1995–96 there were 1,641,456 pupils and 83,179 teachers in public elementary and secondary schools.

In 1995 there were 109 institutes of higher education with, autumn 1994, 551,307 students.

Universities and students (autumn 1996):

Founded	Name	Students
1817	University of Michigan, Ann Arbor	36,525
	University of Michigan, Dearborn	8,242
	University of Michigan, Flint	6,444

Founded	Name	Students
1849	Eastern Michigan University	22,541
1855	Michigan State University	41,545
1884	Ferris State University	9,495
1885	Michigan Technological University	6,195
1868	Wayne State University	31,185
1892	Central Michigan University	24,249
1899	Northern Michigan University	7,971
1903	Western Michigan University	25,699
1946	Lake Superior State University	3,392
1957	Oakland University	13,953
1960	Grand Valley State College	14,662
1963	Saginaw Valley College	7,316

Health. In 1995 the state had 190 hospitals (33,932 beds) including 163 general hospitals (29,902 beds), 17 psychiatric hospitals and 5 rehabilitation hospitals.

In the fiscal year 1996 the Medicaid programme disbursed (with federal support) $5,180m. in medical assistance payments to 1,171,622 persons.

Social Welfare. Old-age assistance is provided for persons 65 years of age or older who have resided in Michigan for one year before application; assets must not exceed various limits. In 1974 federal Supplementary Security Income (SSI) replaced the adults' programme. A monthly average of 201,336 families received $427 per month during fiscal year 1995 through the Aid to Families with Dependent Children programme.

Further Reading

Michigan Manual. Dept of *Management and Budget.* Lansing. Biennial
Michigan Employment Security Commission. *Michigan Statistical Abstract, 1996.* Univ of Michigan Press
Bald, F. C., *Michigan in Four Centuries.* 2nd ed. New York, 1961
Browne, W. P. and Verburg, K., *Michigan Politics and Government: Facing Change in a Complex State.* Nebraska Univ. Press, 1995
Catton. B., *Michigan–a Bicentennial History.* Norton, New York, 1976
Lewis, F. E., *State and Local Government in Michigan.* 9th ed. Hillsdale, 1984
Dunbar, W. F. and May, G. S., *Michigan: A History of the Wolverine State.* 3rd ed. Grand Rapids, 1995
Sommers, L. (ed.), *Atlas of Michigan.* East Lansing, 1977

State Library Services: Library of Michigan, Lansing 48909.

MINNESOTA

KEY HISTORICAL EVENTS. Minnesota remained an Indian territory until the middle of the 19th century, the main groups being Chippewa and Sioux, many of whom are still there. In the 17th century there had been some French exploration, but no permanent settlement. After passing under the nominal control of France, Britain and Spain, the area became part of the Louisiana Purchase and so was sold to the USA in 1803.

Fort Snelling was founded in 1819. Early settlers came from other states, especially New England, to exploit the great forests. Lumbering gave way to homesteading, and the American settlers were joined by Germans, Scandinavians and Poles. Agriculture, mining and forest industries became the mainstays of the economy. Minneapolis, founded as a village in 1856, grew first as a lumber centre, processing the logs floated down the Minnesota River, and then as a centre of flourmilling and grain marketing. St Paul, its twin city across the river, became Territorial capital in 1849 and state capital in 1858. St Paul also stands at the head of navigation on the Mississippi, which rises in Minnesota.

The Territory (1849) included parts of North and South Dakota, but at its admission to the Union in 1858, the state of Minnesota had its present boundaries.

TERRITORY AND POPULATION. Minnesota is bounded north by Canada, east by Lake Superior and Wisconsin, with the Mississippi River forming the boundary in the south-east, south by Iowa, west by South and North Dakota, with the Red River forming the boundary in the north-west. Land area, 79,617 sq. miles (206,207 sq. km). Census population, 1 April 1990, 4,375,099 (69·9% urban), an increase of 7·31% since 1980. Population estimate (1996), 4,658,484. Births in 1995, 63,258 (13·7 per 1,000 population); deaths, 37,429 (8·1); infant deaths, 494 (7·4 per 1,000 live births); marriages, 32,878 (7·1); divorces, 15,486 (3·3).

Population in 5 census years was:

	White	Black	Indian	Asiatic	Total	Per sq. mile
1910	2,059,227	7,084	9,053	344	2,075,708	25·7
1930	2,542,599	9,445	11,077	832	2,563,953	32·0
			All others			
1970	3,736,038	34,868	34,163		3,805,069	47·6
1980	3,935,770	53,344	86,856		4,075,970	51·4
1990	4,130,395	94,944	149,760		4,375,099	55·0

Of the 1990 population, 2,145,183 were male; 3,056,474 were urban; those 21 years of age or older numbered 3,015,507.

The largest cities (with 1990 census population) are Minneapolis (368,383), St Paul (272,253), Bloomington (86,335) and Duluth (85,931).

CLIMATE. Duluth. Jan. 8°F (−13·3°C), July 63°F (17·2°C). Annual rainfall 29" (719 mm). Minneapolis-St. Paul. Jan. 12°F (−11·1°C), July 71°F (21·7°C). Annual rainfall 26" (656 mm). Minnesota belongs to the Great Lakes climate zone (*see* UNITED STATES: Climate).

CONSTITUTION AND GOVERNMENT. The original constitution dated from 1857; it was extensively amended and given a new structure in 1974. The Legislature consists of a Senate of 67 members, elected for 4 years, and a House of Representatives of 134 members, elected for 2 years. It meets for 120 days within each 2 years.

The state sends 8 representatives to Congress.

In the 1996 presidential election Clinton polled 1,911,553 votes; Dole 1,413,812; Perot, 319,095.

The capital is St Paul. There are 87 counties.

Governor: Arne Carlson (R.), 1995–99 ($114,506).
Lieut.-Governor: Joanne Benson (R.) ($62,980).
Secretary of State: Joan A. Growe (Democratic-Farmer-Labor) ($62,980).

BUDGET. For 1994 the general revenues were $27,050m. and general expenditure $25,862m., including education $8,740·8m., public welfare $6,858·5m., health 1,935·4m. and highways $1,715·2m.

Net long-term debt, 30 June 1991, was $3,941m.

Per capita personal income (1995) was $23,118.

NATURAL RESOURCES

Minerals. The iron ore and taconite industry is the most important in the USA. Production of usable iron ore in 1996 was 46m. tons, value $1,390m. Other important minerals are sand and gravel, crushed and dimension stone, clays and peat. Total value of mineral production, 1996, $1,800m.

Agriculture. In 1995 there were some 87,000 farms with a total area of 29·8m. acres; the average farm was of 343 acres. Average value of land and buildings per acre, (1995) $936. Farm income, 1994, from crops, $2,747m.; from livestock, $3,685m. Important products: Sugar-beets, spring wheat, processing sweet corn, oats, dry milk, cheese, mink, turkeys, wild rice, butter, eggs, flaxseed, milk cows, milk, corn, barley, swine, cattle for market, soybeans, honey, potatoes, rye, chickens, sunflower seed and dry edible beans. In 1996 there were 2·9m. cattle (0·6m. milk cows) and 4·9m. hogs and pigs. In 1995 the wool clip amounted to 1·15m. lb. of wool from 170,000 sheep.

Forestry. Forests of commercial timber cover 14·7m. acres, of which 55% is government-owned. The value of forest products in 1994 was $7,500m.: $2,250m. from primary processing, of which $1,687m. was from pulp and paper; and $3,100m. from secondary manufacturing. Logging, pulping, saw-mills and associated industries employed 57,200 in 1995.

INDUSTRY. In 1996 manufacturing establishments employed 429,000 workers; value added by manufacture in 1995 was $32,600m. Largest manufacturing industry is computers and non-electric machinery (74,000 employees); then food products and kindred products (55,000) and printing and publishing (also 55,000).

TOURISM. In 1995, travellers spent about $8,699m. The industry employed about 162,800.

COMMUNICATIONS

Roads. In 1990 there were 129,553 miles of roads (115,458 miles rural). In 1996 there were 3·7m. registered motor vehicles.

Railways. There are 3 Class I and 16 Class II and smaller railroads operating, with total mileage of 4,650.

Civil Aviation. In 1989 there were 138 airports for public use and 8 public seaplane bases.

SOCIAL INSTITUTIONS

Justice. In 1994 there were 4,575 prisoners in state correctional institutions. There is no death penalty.

Religion. The chief religious bodies are: Lutheran with 1,126,008 members in 1990; Roman Catholic, 1,110,071; Methodist, 142,771. Total membership of all denominations, 2,837,415.

Education. In 1992, there were 775,567 students and 44,200 teachers in public elementary and secondary schools. In 1988 there were 1,511 public schools, and 82,165 kindergarten, elementary, and secondary students enrolled in 572 private schools. The University of Minnesota, chartered in 1851 and opened in 1869, had a total enrolment in 1988 of 54,515 students on all campuses. The 18 public community colleges (2-year) had a total enrolment of 49,589. There are seven state universities (4-year) at Bemidji, Mankato, Marshall, Moorhead, St Cloud, Winona, Minneapolis and St Paul. Enrolment in all institutions of higher education, 1988, 251,304.

Health. In 1989 the state had 163 general acute hospitals with 19,229 beds. Patients resident in institutions under the Department of Human Services in Sept. 1997 included 977 people with mental illness, 231 people with mental retardation, 178 with chemical dependency and 232 in state nursing homes.

Social Security. Programmes of old age assistance, aid to the disabled, and aid to the blind are administered under the federal Supplemental Security Income (SSI) Programme. Minnesota has a supplementary programme, Minnesota Supplemental Aid (MSA) to cover individuals not eligible for SSI, to supplement SSI benefits for others whose income is below state standards, and to provide one-time payments for emergency needs such as major home repair, essential furniture or appliances, moving expenses, fuel, food and shelter.

Further Reading

Statistical Information: Department of Trade and Economic Development, 500 Metro Square, St Paul 55101. Publishes *Compare Minnesota: an Economic and Statistical Factbook.— Economic Report to the Governor.*
Legislative Manual. Secretary of State. St Paul. Biennial
Minnesota Agriculture Statistics. Dept. of Agric., St Paul. Annual

MISSISSIPPI

KEY HISTORICAL EVENTS. Mississippi was one of the territories claimed by France since the 17th century and ceded to Britain in 1763. The indigenous people were Choctaw and Natchez. French settlers at first traded amicably with them, but in the course of three wars (1716, 1723 and 1729) the French allied with the Choctaw to drive the Natchez out. During hostilities the Natchez massacred the settlers of Fort Rosalie, which the French had founded in 1716 and which was later renamed Natchez.

In 1783 the area passed to the USA except for Natchez which was under Spanish control until 1798. The USA then made it the capital of the Territory of Mississippi. The boundaries of the Territory were extended in 1804 and 1812. In 1817 it was separated in two, the western part becoming the state of Mississippi. (The eastern part became the state of Alabama in 1819.) The city of Jackson was laid out in 1822 as the new state capital.

A cotton plantation economy developed, based on black slave labour, and by 1860 the majority of the population was black. Mississippi joined the Confederacy during the Civil War. After defeat and reconstruction there was a return to rigid segregation and denial of black rights. This situation lasted until the 1960s. There was a black majority until the Second World war, when out-migration began to change the pattern. By 1990 about 35% of the population was black, and manufacture (especially clothing and textiles) had become the largest single employer of labour.

TERRITORY AND POPULATION. Mississippi is bounded north by Tennessee, east by Alabama, south by the Gulf of Mexico and Louisiana, west by the Mississippi River forming the boundary with Louisiana and Arkansas. Area, 47,689 sq. miles (123,515 sq. km), 457 sq. miles (1,184 sq. km) being inland water. Census population, 1 July 1990, 2,573,216 (47·1% urban), an increase of 2·09% since 1980. Population estimate (1996), 2,716,115. Births occurring in the state, 1996, were 40,197; deaths, 25,809; infant deaths, 378; marriages, 21,550; divorces, 14,263.

Population of 5 federal census years was:

	White	Black	Indian	Asiatic	Total	Per sq. mile
1910	786,111	1,009,487	1,253	263	1,797,114	38·8
1930	998,077	1,009,718	1,458	568	2,009,821	42·4
1950	1,188,632	986,494	2,502	1,286	2,178,914	46·1

			All others		
1980	1,615,190	887,206	18,242	2,520,638	53·0
1990	1,633,461	915,057	24,698	2,573,216	54·8

Of the population in 1990, 1,230,617 were male, 1,210,729 were urban and 1,729,749 were 20 years old or older.

The largest city (1994 estimate) is Jackson, 193,000. Others (1990 figures) are: Biloxi, 46,369; Greenville, 45,226; Hattiesburg, 41,882; Meridian, 41,036; Gulfport, 40,775; Tupelo, 30,685; Pascagoula, 25,899; Columbus, 23,799; Clinton, 21,847; Vicksburg, 20,908.

CLIMATE. Jackson. Jan. 47°F (8·3°C), July 82°F (27·8°C). Annual rainfall 49" (1,221 mm). Vicksburg. Jan. 48°F (8·9°C), July 81°F (27·2°C). Annual rainfall 52" (1,311 mm). Mississippi belongs to the Central Plains climate zone (*see* UNITED STATES: Climate).

CONSTITUTION AND GOVERNMENT. The present constitution was adopted in 1890 without ratification by the electorate; 103 amendments by 1990.

The Legislature consists of a Senate (52 members) and a House of Representatives (122 members), both elected for 4 years. The state is represented in Congress by 2 senators and 5 representatives. Electors are all citizens who have resided in the state 1 year, in the county 1 year, in the election district 6 months before the election and have been registered according to law. In the 1996 presidential election Dole polled 434,547 votes, Clinton, 385,005; Perot, 51,500.

The capital is Jackson; there are 82 counties.

Governor: Kirk Fordice (R.), 1996–2000 ($83,160).
Lieut.-Governor: Ronnie Musgrove (D.) ($40,800).
Secretary of State: Eric Clark (D.) ($59,400).

BUDGET. For the fiscal year ending 30 June 1997 the general revenues were $8,269,815,103 (taxation, $3,773,180,825; federal aid, $2,486,718,020; other state revenues, $2,009,916,527), and general expenditures were $8,250,918,555 ($2,253,739,303 for education, $697,476,369 for highways and $799,395,514 for public welfare).

On 30 June 1997 the total net long-term debt was $1,428,384,000.

Per capita personal income (1995) was $116,531.

NATURAL RESOURCES

Minerals. Petroleum and natural gas account for about 90% (by value) of mineral production. Output of petroleum, 1996, was 19,534,635 bbls and of natural gas 122,201,486m. cu. ft. There are 4 oil refineries. Taxable value of oil and gas products sold in fiscal year 1996 was $470,426,856.

Agriculture. Agriculture is the leading industry of the state because of the semi-tropical climate and a rich productive soil. In 1997 there were 82 soil and water con-servation districts representing 24,500 co-operators on 3·4m. acres. In 1997 farms numbered 43,000 with an area of 12·5m. acres. Average size of farm was 291 acres. This compares with an average farm size of 138 acres in 1960. Average value of farm per acre in 1996 was $917.

Cash income from all crops and livestock during 1996, including government pay-ments, was $3,647,984,000. Cash income from crops was $1,523,358,000 and from livestock and products, $1,934,279,000. The chief product is cotton, cash income (1996) $631,236,000 from 980,000 acres producing 1,876,000 bales of 480 lbs. Soybeans, rice, corn, hay, wheat, oats, sorghum, peanuts, pecans, sweet potatoes, peaches, other vegetables, nursery and forest products continue to contribute.

On 1 Jan. 1997 there were 1·34m. head of cattle and calves on Mississippi farms. In Jan. 1997 milk cows totalled 48,000, beef cows, 682,000; (1996) hogs and pigs, 245,000. Of cash income from livestock and products, 1996, $137,940,000 was credited to cattle and calves. Cash income from poultry and eggs, 1996, totalled $1,353,844,000; dairy products, $105,616,000; swine, $49,926,000.

Forestry. In 1996 income from forestry amounted to $1,190,000,000; output of logs, lumber, etc., was 1,870,000,000 bd ft; pulpwood, 8·7m. There are about 18·6m. acres of forest (62% of the state's area). National forest area, 1996, 1·1m. acres.

INDUSTRY. In 1996 the 3,724 manufacturing establishments employed 245,984 workers, earning $5,983,137,001. The average annual wage was $24,323.

TOURISM. Total receipts in 1997 amounted to $4,800m.; an estimated 5m. overnight tourists visited the state in 1997.

COMMUNICATIONS

Roads. The state as of 31 Dec. 1996 maintained 10,653 miles of highways, of which all miles were paved. In fiscal year 1997, 2,314,419 passenger vehicles and pick-ups were registered.

Railways. The state in 1997 had 2,841·46 main-line miles of railway.

Civil Aviation. There were 76 public airports in 1997, 69 of them general aviation airports.

SOCIAL INSTITUTIONS

Justice. The death penalty is authorized; the last execution took place in 1989. As of 31 Oct. 1997, the state prison system had 15,311 inmates.

Religion. Southern Baptists in Mississippi (1996), 695,269 members; United Methodists (1996) 187,686; Roman Catholics (1997), 108,896 in Biloxi and Jackson dioceses.

Education. Attendance at school is compulsory as laid down in the Education Reform Act of 1982. The public elementary and secondary schools in 1996–97 had 503,967 pupils and 29,245 classroom teachers.

In 1996–97, teachers' average salary was $27,662. The expenditure per pupil in average daily attendance, 1996–97, was $4,491.

There are 20 universities and senior colleges, of which 8 are state-supported. In 1996–97, the University of Mississippi, Oxford had 1,294 instructors and 10,993 students; Mississippi State University, Starkville, 1,253 instructors and 14,859 students; Mississippi University for Women, Columbus, 191 instructors and 3,277 students; University of Southern Mississippi, Hattiesburg, 742 instructors and 14,117 students; Jackson State University, Jackson, 424 instructors and 6,218 students; Delta State University, Cleveland, 291 instructors and 4,015 students; Alcorn State University, Lorman, 201 instructors and 3,073 students; Mississippi Valley State University, Itta Bena, 155 instructors and 2,199 students. State support for the universities (1996–97) was $256,254,037.

Junior colleges had (1996–97) 64,630 full-time equivalent students and 2,938 full-time instructors. The state appropriation for junior colleges, 1996–97, was $134,040,782.

Health. In 1996 the state had 102 acute general hospitals (11,615 beds) listed by the State Department of Health; 17 hospitals with facilities for care of the mentally ill had 638 licensed beds; in addition, 1 rehabilitation hospital had 265 beds.

Social Security. The Division of Medicaid paid (fiscal year 1997) $1,431,930,682 for medical services, including $202,628,326 for drugs, $299,874,793 for skilled nursing home care, and $381,601,992 for hospital services. There were 64,413 persons eligible for Aged Medicaid benefits at 30 June 1997 and 137,342 persons eligible for Disabled Medicaid benefits. In June 1997, 36,411 families with 72,619 dependEnt children received $4,588,061 in the Aid to Dependent Children programme. The average monthly payment was $126·94 per family or $47·80 per recipient.

Further Reading

Statistical information: College of Business and Industry, Mississippi State Univ., Mississippi State 39762. Publishes *Mississippi Statistical Abstract.*
Secretary of State. *Mississippi Official and Statistical Register.* Biennial
Bettersworth, J. K., *Mississippi: A History.* Rev. ed. Austin, Tex., 1964

Mississippi Library Commission: PO Box 10700 Jackson, MS. 39289–0700. *Executive Director:* John A. Pritchard

MISSOURI

KEY HISTORICAL EVENTS. Territory of several Indian groups, including the Missouri, the area was not settled by European immigrants until the 18th century. The French founded Ste Genevieve in 1735, partly as a lead-mining community. St Louis was founded as a fur-trading base in 1764. The area was nominally under Spanish rule from 1770 until 1800 when it passed back to France. In 1803 the USA bought it as part of the Louisiana Purchase.

St Louis was made the capital of the whole Louisiana Territory in 1805, and of a new Missouri Territory in 1812. In that year American immigration increased markedly. The Territory became a state in 1821, but there had been bitter disputes between slave-owning and anti-slavery factions, with the former succeeding in obtaining statehood without the prohibition of slavery required of all other new states north of latitude 36°30'; this was achieved by the Missouri Compromise of 1820. The Compromise was repealed in 1854 and declared unconstitutional in 1857. During the Civil War the state held to the Union side, although St Louis was placed under martial law.

With the development of steamboat traffic on the Missouri and Mississippi rivers, and the expansion of railways, the state became the transport hub of all western movement. Lead and other mining remained important, as did livestock farming. European settlers came from Germany, Britain and Ireland.

TERRITORY AND POPULATION. Missouri is bounded north by Iowa, east by the Mississippi River forming the boundary with Illinois and Kentucky, south by Arkansas, south-east by Tennessee, south-west by Oklahoma, west by Kansas and Nebraska, with the Missouri River forming the boundary in the north-west. Land area, 68,898 sq. miles (178,446 sq. km).

Census population, 22 April 1990, 5,117,073 (68·7% urban), an increase since 1980 of 4·1%. Population estimate (1996), 5,359,000. Births, 1994, were 73,279; deaths, 53,611; infant deaths, 597 (8·1 per 1,000 live births); marriages, 45,070 (8·5 per 1,000 population); divorces, 26,441 (5).

Population of 5 federal census years was:

	White	Black	Indian	Asiatic	Total	Per sq. mile
1930	3,403,876	223,840	578	1,073	3,629,367	52·4
1960	3,922,967	390,853	1,723	3,146	4,319,813	62·5

	White	Black	All others	Total	Per sq. mile
1970	4,177,495	480,172	19,732	4,677,399	67·0
1980	4,345,521	514,276	56,889	4,916,686	71·3
1990	4,486,228	548,208	82,637	5,117,073	74·3

Of the total population in 1990, 2,464,315 were male. In 1990, 3,515,882 persons were urban and those 18 years of age or older numbered 3,939,284.

The principal cities at the 1990 census are:

Kansas City	435,146	Columbia	69,101
St Louis	396,685	St Charles	54,555
Springfield	140,494	Florissant	51,206
Independence	112,301	Joplin	40,961
St Joseph	71,852	University City	40,087

Metropolitan areas, 1990: St Louis, 2,444,099; Kansas City, 1,566,280.

CLIMATE. Kansas City. Jan. 30°F (−1·1°C), July 79°F (26·1°C). Annual rainfall 38" (947 mm). St Louis. Jan. 32°F (0°C), July 79°F (26·1°C). Annual rainfall 40" (1,004 mm). Missouri belongs to the Central Plains climate zone (see UNITED STATES: Climate).

CONSTITUTION AND GOVERNMENT. A new constitution, the fourth, was adopted on 27 Feb. 1945; it has been revised 9 times with over 100 amendments. The General Assembly consists of a Senate of 34 members elected for 4 years (half for re-election every 2 years), and a House of Representatives of 163 members elected for 2 years. The Governor and Lieut.-Governor are elected for 4 years.

The state sends 9 representatives to Congress.

In the 1996 presidential election Clinton polled 1,024,679 votes; Dole, 889,684; Perot, 217,101.

Jefferson City is the state capital. The state is divided into 114 counties and the city of St Louis.

Governor: Mel Carnahan (D.), 1997–2001 ($94,563).
Lieut.-Governor: Roger Wilson (D.) ($57,145).
Secretary of State: Rebecca McDowell Cook (D.) ($75,854).

BUDGET. For the year 1994 the total revenues from all funds were $13,359m. (general revenue, $11,345m.). Total expenditure was $11,549m. (general expenditure $10,590m.) including: education $3,942,657,000; public welfare $2,665,909,000; highways $1,110,567,000.

Total outstanding debt, 1993, was $6,516m.
Per capita personal income (1995) was $21,627.

NATURAL RESOURCES

Minerals. The 3 leading mineral commodities are lead, portland cement and crushed stone. Value of production (1992) $897·2m.

Agriculture. In 1996 there were 104,000 farms in Missouri producing crops and livestock on 30m. acres; the average farm had 288 acres and in 1994 was valued at $762 per acre. Production of principal crops, 1994: Corn, 273·7m. bu.; soybeans, 173·3m. bu.; wheat, 49·5m. bu.; sorghum grain, 49·5m. bu.; oats, 1·77m. bu.; rice, 6·5m. cwt; cotton, 615,000 bales (of 480 lbs). Cash receipts from farming, 1994, $2,450m. to which livestock and products contributed $2,300m. and soybeans $95·54m.

Forestry. Forest land area, 1997, 3·06m. acres.

INDUSTRY. The largest employer in 1996 was manufacturing, with 414,000 employees. Other large industries are food and kindred products, electronic and other electronic equipment, apparel and other textile products, industrial machinery and equipment, leather products, chemicals, paper, primary metal industries and metal products, printing and publishing, stone, clay, glass, rubber and plastic products, instruments, lumber and wood products. Wholesale and retail trade employed 561,001 as of March 1992.

LABOUR. The State Board of Mediation has jurisdiction in labour disputes involving only public utilities. The Prevailing Wage Law (1959) provides that no less than the local hourly rate of wages for work of a similar character shall be paid to any workmen engaged in public works. The Industrial Commission has authority to inspect records and to institute actions for penalties described in the Act. There is a state programme for industrial safety in hand, under the Federal Occupational and Health Act. In 1994 the annual average number of employed was 2,564,000, and 131,000 were unemployed; the unemployment rate was 4·9%.

COMMUNICATIONS

Roads. In 1995 there were 122,616 miles of roads (106,306 miles rural) and 4,255,000 registered motor vehicles.

Railways. The state has 8 Class I railways; approximate total mileage, 6,645. There are 9 Class II and Class III railways (switching, terminal or short-line), total mileage 435, in 1993. There is a light rail line in St Louis.

Civil Aviation. In 1994 there were 114 public airports and 359 private airports.

Shipping. Two major barge lines (1993) operated on about 1,050 miles of navigable waterways including the Missouri and Mississippi Rivers. Boat shipping seasons: Missouri River, April–end Nov.; Mississippi River, all seasons.

Post and Broadcasting. There were 196 commercial radio stations and 29 TV stations in 1995.

Press. There were (1995) 46 daily and 260 weekly newspapers.

SOCIAL INSTITUTIONS

Justice. State prisons in 1994 had an average of 18,346 inmates including 886 females. The median age was 33·3 in 1994. The death penalty was reinstated in 1978. The last execution was in 1996. The Missouri Law Enforcement Assistance Council was created in 1969 for law reform. With reorganization of state government in 1974 the duties of the Council were delegated to the Department of Public Safety. The Dept. of Corrections was organised as a separate department of State by an Act of the Legislature in 1981.

Religion. Chief religious bodies (1990) are Catholic, with 802,434 members, Southern Baptists (789,183), United Methodists (255,111), Christian Churches (166,412), Lutheran (142,824), Presbyterian (45,341). Total membership, all denominations, about 2·3m. in 1990.

Education. School attendance is compulsory for children from 7 to 16 years for the full term. In the 1993–94 school year, public schools (kindergarten through grade 12) had 851,086 pupils. Total expenditure for public schools in 1993–94, $3,563,419,000. Salaries for teachers (kindergarten through grade 12), 1993–94, averaged $30,227. Institutions for higher education include the University of Missouri, founded in 1839 with campuses at Columbia, Rolla, St Louis and Kansas City, with 3,469 accredited teachers and 48,072 students in 1994–95. Washington University at St Louis, founded in 1857, is an independent co-ed university with 11,655 students in 1994–95. St Louis University (1818), is an independent Roman Catholic co-ed university with 10,365 students in 1994–95. Seventeen state colleges had 129,466 students in 1994–95. Private colleges had (1994–95) 34,548 students. Church-affiliated colleges (1994–95) had 41,420 students. Public junior colleges had 66,853 students. There are about 90 secondary and post-secondary institutions offering vocational courses, and about 294 private career schools. There were 265,186 students in higher education in autumn 1994.

Health. In 1995 there were 126 community hospitals with 21,900 beds.

Social Security. The number of actual recipients of medicaid for the last 5 months of 1994 averaged 346,873; eligible to receive medicaid, 559,331. The number of recipients of Aid to families with Dependent Children was 259,048 with an average monthly payment per family of $264·79.

Further Reading

Statistical information: Business and Public Administration Research Center, Univ. of Missouri, Columbia 65211. Publishes *Statistical Abstract for Missouri.*
Missouri Area Labor Trends, Department of Labor and Industrial Relations, monthly
Missouri Farm Facts, Department of Agriculture, annual
Report of the Public Schools of Missouri. State Board of Education, annual

MONTANA

KEY HISTORICAL EVENTS. Originally the territory of many groups of Indian hunters including the Sioux, Cheyenne and Chippewa, Montana was not settled by American colonists until the 19th century. The area passed to the USA with the Louisiana Purchase of 1803, but the area west of the Rockies was disputed with Britain until 1846. Trappers and fur-traders were the first immigrants, and the forti-fied trading post at Fort Benton (1846) became the first permanent settlement. Colonization increased when gold was found in 1862. Montana was created a separate Territory (out of Idaho and Dakota Territories) in 1864. In 1866 large-scale grazing of sheep and cattle was allowed, and this provoked violent confrontation with the indigenous people whose hunting lands were invaded. Indian wars led to the defeat of federal forces at Little Bighorn in 1876 and at Big Hole Basin in 1877, but the Indians could not continue the fight and they had been moved to reservations by 1880. Montana became a state in 1889.

Helena, the capital, was founded as a mining town in the 1860s. In the early 20th century there were many European immigrants who settled as farmers or in the mines, especially in copper-mining at Butte.

TERRITORY AND POPULATION. Montana is bounded north by Canada, east by North and South Dakota, south by Wyoming and west by Idaho and the Bitterroot Range of the Rocky Mountains. Land area, 145,556 sq. miles (336,991 sq. km). US Bureau of Indian Affairs (1990) administered 5,574,835 acres, of which 2,663,385 were allotted to tribes. Census population, 1 April 1990, 799,065 (52·5% urban), an increase of 2% since 1980. Population estimate (1996), 879,000. Births in 1994, 11,067 (12·9 per 1,000 population); deaths, 7,000 (8·6); infant deaths in 1991, 106 (9·1 per 1,000 live births); marriages, 7,175 (8·9); divorces, 4,385 (5·4).

Population in 5 census years was:

	White	Black	Indian	Asiatic	Total	Per sq. mile
1910	360,580	1,834	10,745	2,870	376,053	2·6
1930	519,898	1,256	14,798	1,239	537,606	3·7
1950	572,038	1,232	16,606	—	591,024	4·1
1980	740,148	1,786	37,270	2,503	786,690	5·3
1990	741,111	2,381	47,679	4,259	799,065	5·4

Of the total population in 1990, 395,769 were male, 419,826 persons were urban. Persons 18 years of age or older numbered 576,961. Median age, 33·8 years. Households, 306,163.

The largest cities, 1990 are Billings, 81,151; Great Falls, 55,097. Others: Missoula, 42,918; Butte-Silver Bow, 33,336; Helena (capital), 24,569; Bozeman, 22,660; Kalispell, 11,917; Anaconda-Deer Lodge County, 10,278; Havre, 10,201.

CLIMATE. Helena. Jan. 18°F (−7·8°C), July 69°F (20·6°C). Annual rainfall 13" (325 mm). Montana belongs to the Mountain States climate zone (*see* UNITED STATES: Climate).

CONSTITUTION AND GOVERNMENT. A new constitution came into force on 1 July 1973. The Senate consists of 50 senators, elected for 4 years, one half at each biennial election. The 100 members of the House of Representatives are elected for 2 years.

The state sends 1 representative to Congress.

In the 1996 presidential election Dole polled 178,957 votes; Clinton, 167,169; Perot, 55,017.

The capital is Helena. The state is divided into 56 counties.

Governor: Marc Racicot (R.), 1997–2001 ($59,310).
Lieut.-Governor: Dennis Rehberg (R.), ($43,242).
Secretary of State: Mike Cooney (D.), ($40,101).

BUDGET. Total state revenues for 1994 were $3,166,000,000 (general revenues $2,518,000,000); total expenditures were $2,778,000,000 (general expenditure $2,393,000,000), including: education $895,905,000; public welfare $416,541,000; highways $301,859,000; health $108,807,000.

Total net long-term debt on 30 June 1990 was $396m.

Per capita personal income (1995) was $18,482.

NATURAL RESOURCES

Minerals. 1990 nonfuel mineral production value was $568m. Copper was the leading commodity in terms of value, followed by gold, platinum-group metals, molybdenum and silver.

Agriculture. In 1996 there were 22,000 farms and ranches (50,564 in 1935) with an area of 60,000,000 acres (47,511,868 acres in 1935). Large-scale farming predominates; in 1996 the average size per farm was 2,714 acres, and in 1995 the average value per acre was $277. The farm population in 1991, was 67,546 (2·8% people per farm). Irrigated area harvested in 1986 was 1·6m. acres; non-irrigated, 7·8m. acres.

The chief crops (cash receipts, 1990) are wheat, amounting in 1986 to 138·5m. bu. ($435,788); barley, 85m. bu. ($125,436); oats, 4·1m. bu.; sugar-beet, hay ($81,996), potatoes, corn, dry beans and cherries. Farm income, 1991: crops, $746m.; livestock and products, $854m. In 1986 there were 24,000 milk cows, 2·4m. all cattle; 190,000 swine and 423,000 sheep. In 1990 the cash receipts for cattle and calves were $725,476; dairy products, $45,292; hogs and pigs, $42,150; sheep and lambs, $18,655.

Forestry. In 1997 there were 19,106,569 acres within 11 national forests.

INDUSTRY. In 1996 manufacturing had 24,000 production workers.

LABOUR. (1996) total non-agricultural workers, 359,000. Workers employed by major industry group, 1991; mining, 5,900 (average net weekly earnings, $592.18); construction, 7,700 ($499.56); manufacturing, 20,200 ($442.37); transport and public utilities, 20,000 ($468.43; trade industry, 76,500 ($388.90); finance/insurance/real estate, 13,270; services, 75,500 ($258.34); government, 71,400 (no income figures available). Average weekly earnings for all workers in private non-agricultural industries $295.45. During 1990, 56 mass layoff events involved 5,001 workers laid off from their jobs (separations), 50% more separations than in 1989.

COMMUNICATIONS

Roads. In 1995 there were a total of 69,537 miles of roads and 968,000 registered motor vehicles.

Railways. In Feb. 1992 there were 3,329 route miles of railway in the state.

Civil Aviation. In 1992 there were 122 publicly owned airports.

Telecommunications. In 1992 there were 51 radio stations, 18 TV stations and 10 cable systems.

Press. In 1992 there were 12 daily newspapers and 74 semi-weekly, weekly, or shopper-type papers.

SOCIAL INSTITUTIONS

Justice. At 31 Dec. 1994 there were 1,498 prison inmates. The death penalty is authorized, but there have been no executions since 1943.

Religion. The leading religious bodies are (1987): Roman Catholic with 162,000 members; Lutheran, 68,654; Methodist (Yellowstone Conference, including N. Wyoming, Montana, and Salmon, Idaho), 21,609 (church estimates).

Education. In 1994 public elementary and secondary schools had 164,295 pupils and 10,079 teachers. Expenditure on public school education by state and local governments in 1994 was $895·9m.

At Autumn 1994, college and university enrolment was 40,095. The Montana University system consists of the Montana State University, at Bozeman (autumn 1992 enrolment: 10,111 students), the University of Montana, at Missoula, founded in 1895 (10,788), the Montana College of Mineral Science and Technology, at Butte (1,881), Northern Montana College, at Havre (1,973), Eastern Montana College, at Billings (3,631) and Western Montana College, at Dillon (1,106).

Health. In 1995 there were 55 community hospitals with 4,200 beds.

Social Security. In 1994 there were 150,000 beneficiaries receiving $1,078 annual payments.

Further Reading

Statistical information. Census and Economic Information Center, Montana Department of Commerce, 1425 9th Ave., Helena 59620.

Lang, W, L. and Myers, R. C., *Montana, Our Land and People.* Pruett, 1979

Malone, M. P. and Roeder, R. B., *Montana, A History of Two Centuries.* Univ. of Washington Press, 1976

Spence, C. C., *Montana: a History.* New York, 1978

NEBRASKA

KEY HISTORICAL EVENTS. The Nebraska region was first reached by Europeans from Mexico under the Spanish general Coronado in 1541. It was ceded by France to Spain in 1763, retroceded to France in 1801, and sold by Napoleon to the USA as part of the Louisiana Purchase in 1803. During the 1840s the Platte River valley became an established trail for thousands of pioneers' wagons heading for Oregon and California. The need to serve and protect the trail led to the creation of

Nebraska as a Territory in 1854. In 1862 the Homestead Act opened the area for settlement, but colonization was not very rapid until the Union Pacific Railroad was completed in 1869. The largest city, Omaha, developed as the starting point of the Union Pacific and became one of the largest railway towns in the country.

Nebraska became a state in 1867, with approximately its present boundaries except that it later received small areas from the Dakotas. Many early settlers were from Europe, brought in by railway-company schemes, but from the late 1880s eastern Nebraska suffered catastrophic drought. Crop and stock farming recovered, but crop growing was only established in the west by means of irrigation.

TERRITORY AND POPULATION. Nebraska is bounded in the north by South Dakota, with the Missouri River forming the boundary in the north-east and the boundary with Iowa and Missouri to the east; south by Kansas, south-west by Colorado and west by Wyoming. Land area, 76,878 sq. miles (199,113 sq. km). Population estimate (1996), 1,652,000. Births, 1995, were 23,221 (14·4 per 1,000 population); deaths, 15,216 (9·5); marriages, 12,351 (7·7); divorces, 6,262 (3·9); infant deaths in 1992, 186 (7·9 per 1,000 live births).

Population in 5 census years was:

	White	Black	Indian	Asiatic	Total	Per sq. mile
1910	1,180,293	7,689	3,502	730	1,192,214	15·5
1920	1,279,219	13,242	2,888	1,023	1,296,372	16·9
1960	1,374,764	29,262	5,545	1,195	1,411,330	18·3

	White	Black	All others	Total	Per sq. mile
1980	1,490,381	48,390	31,054	1,569,825	20·5
1990	1,480,558	57,409	40,423	1,578,385	20·5

Of the total population in 1990, 796,439 were male, 66·1% were urban 1,102,135 were 20 years of age or older. The largest cities in the state are: Omaha, with a census population, 1990, of 335,795; Lincoln, 191,972; Grand Island, (1986 estimate) 39,100; North Platte, 22,490; Fremont, 23,780; Hastings, 22,990; Bellevue, 32,200; Kearney, 22,770; Norfolk, 20,260.

The Bureau of Indian Affairs in 1990 administered 64,932 acres, of which 21,742 acres were allotted to tribal control.

CLIMATE. Omaha. Jan. 22°F (−5·6°C), July 77°F (25°C). Annual rainfall 29" (721 mm). Nebraska belongs to the High Plains climate zone (see UNITED STATES: Climate).

CONSTITUTION AND GOVERNMENT. The present constitution was adopted in 1875; it has been amended 184 times. By an amendment of 1934 Nebraska has a single-chambered legislature (elected for 4 years) of 49 members elected on a non-party ballot and classed as senators—the only state in the USA to have one. It meets annually.

The state sends 3 representatives to Congress.

In the 1996 presidential election Dole polled 355,562 votes; Clinton, 231,863; Perot, 76,103.

The capital is Lincoln. The state has 93 counties.

Governor: Ben Nelson (R.), 1995–99 ($65,000).
Lieut.-Governor: Kim Robak (D.) ($47,000).
Secretary of State: Scott Moore (R.) ($52,000).

BUDGET. In the fiscal year ending 1996 total revenue was $4,998,908, including taxes, $2,369,462 and inter-governmental revenue, $1,189,563; and total expenditure was $4,489,725, including general expenditure of $4,320,072 of which inter-governmental expenditure was $1,175,780 and direct expenditure, $3,144,292. Expenditure by function included: Education, $1,513,604; public welfare, $975,644; highways, $573,918.

Per capita personal income (1996) was $22,917.

NATURAL RESOURCES

Minerals. Output of non-fuel minerals, 1995 (in 1,000 short tons) and value (in $1,000): Clays, 243 (1,025); sand and gravel for construction, 17,637 (55·2); stone, 7,275 (39·6). Other minerals include limestone, potash, pumice, slate and shale. Petroleum output, 1995: 15,934·3m. gallons; gas, 683m. cu. ft.

Agriculture. Nebraska is one of the most important agricultural states. In 1996 it contained approximately 55,000 farms, with a total area of 47m. acres. The average farm was 841 acres. In 1994, net farm income was $2,264·2m. In 1990, 8m. acres were irrigated, 70% receiving water from irrigation wells.

Cash income from crops (1994), $3,200m., and from livestock, some $5,400m. Principal crops were maize, sorghum for grain, soybeans and wheat. Livestock, 1990: Cattle, 6m.; pigs, 4·2m.; sheep, 0·16m.; chickens, 2·1m.; turkeys, 2·1m. Value: 1994, $656m.; Dairy products, 1994: $14·3m.

Forestry. There were 346,485 acres of national forest in 1997.

INDUSTRY. In 1995 there were 2,071 manufacturing establishments with 112,951 employees. The chief industry is meat-packing. Pork products were worth $878m. in 1991.

Total labour force, 1996, 912,900. 207,500 workers were employed in trade, 220,300 in services, 151,500 in government, 113,800 in manufacturing, 53,100 in finance, insurance and real estate, 49,400 in transport, communication and utilities and 37,900 in construction and mining. 27,000 were unemployed; the average unemployment rate was 2·9%.

TOURISM. In 1995 there were an estimated 16·1m. visits. Travellers and tourists spent over $2,000m.

COMMUNICATIONS

Roads. In 1995 there were 95,933 miles of roads (90,826 miles rural). In 1996 there were 1,703,434 registered motor vehicles.

Railways. In 1996 there were 4,000 miles of railway.

Civil Aviation. Airports (1996) numbered 384 which were publicly owned.

SOCIAL INSTITUTIONS

Justice. A 'Civil Rights Act' revised in 1969 provides that all people are entitled to a full and equal enjoyment of public facilities.

In 1994 there were 2,633 prisoners in state correctional institutions. The death penalty is authorized. The last execution was in 1996.

Religion. The Roman Catholics had 337,855 members in 1985; Protestant Churches, 737,361; Jews, 7,865 members. Total, all denominations, 1,083,081.

Education. School attendance is compulsory for children from 7 to 16 years of age. Public elementary and secondary schools, in 1993–94, had 284,459 enrolled pupils and 19,465 teachers. Total enrolment in institutions of higher education, autumn 1994, was 95,560 students in public and 19,872 in independent institutions.

Opened	Institution	Students 1997
	University of Nebraska (State)	46,565
1869	Lincoln	22,823
1908	Omaha	13,710
	Medical Center	2,618
	College of Technology, Agriculture, Curtis	277
1905	Kearney	7,133
1911	Chardon State College	2,939
1867	Peru State College	1,814
1910	Wayne State College	3,839

Opened	Institution	Students 1997
	Nebraska Community Colleges (Local government)	34,442
	Central Area	6,743
	Metropolitan Area	11,213
	Mid Plains Area	2,825
	Northeast Area	4,573
	Southeast Area	7,080
	Western Area	2,008
1966	Bellevue College (Private)	2,928
	Clarkson College (Private)	597
1923	College of St. Mary (Roman Catholic)	1,001
1894	Concordia Teachers' College, Seward (Lutheran)	1,214
1878	Creighton University, Omaha (Roman Catholic)	6,424
	Dana College (American Lutheran)	594
1872	Doane College, Crete (United Church of Christ)	1,809
	Grace College of the Bible (Private)	519
1882	Hastings College (Presbyterian)	1,059
1883	Midland Lutheran College, Fremont (Lutheran Church of America)	1,038
	Nebraska Christian College (Church of Christ)	152
	Nebraska Methodist College (Private)	223
1887	Nebraska Wesleyan University (Private)	1,719
	Platt Valley Bible College (Private)	75
1891	Union College, Lincoln (Seventh Day Adventist)	630
	York College[1] (Private)	497
	Nebraska Indian Community College	n/a

[1] Two-year college.

Health. In 1997 there were 106 community hospitals.

Social Security. In 1996 public welfare provided financial aid and/or services as follows: (total expenditure) aid to dependent children, 14,717 families/month, $55·2m. total expenditure; aged, blind and disabled, 6,059 persons/month, $6·0m., food stamps, 102,053 recipients/month, $77·9m.; medicaid, 120,012 recipients/month, $645·1m.

Further Reading

Statistical information: Department of Economic Development, Box 94666, Lincoln 68509.
Agricultural Atlas of Nebraska. Univ. of Nebraska Press, 1977
Climatic Atlas of Nebraska. Univ. of Nebraska Press, 1977
Economic Atlas of Nebraska. Univ. of Nebraska Press, 1977
Nebraska. A Guide to the Cornhusker State. Univ. of Nebraska Press, 1979
Nebraska Blue-Book. Legislative Council. Lincoln. Biennial
Olson, J. C., *History of Nebraska.* Univ. of Nebraska Press, 3rd ed. 1997

State Library: State Law Library, State House, Lincoln.

NEVADA

KEY HISTORICAL EVENTS. The area was part of Spanish America until 1821, when it became part of the newly-independent state of Mexico. Following a war between Mexico and the USA, Nevada was ceded to the USA as part of California in 1848. Settlement began in 1849, and the area was separated from California and joined with Utah Territory in 1850. In 1859 a rich deposit of silver was found in the Comstock Lode. Virginia City was founded as a mining town and immigration increased rapidly. Nevada Territory was formed in 1861. During the Civil War the Federal Government, allegedly in order to obtain the wealth of silver for the Union cause, agreed to admit Nevada to the Union as the 36th state. Areas of Arizona and Utah Territories were added to it in 1866–67.

The silver boom lasted until 1882, by which time cattle ranching had become equally important in the valleys where the climate is less arid. Carson City, the capital, developed in association with the nearby silver-mining industry. The largest cities, Las Vegas and Reno, grew most in the 20th century with the building of the Hoover dam, the introduction of legal gambling and of easily obtained divorce.

After 1950 much of the desert area was adopted by the Federal Government for weapons testing and other military purposes.

TERRITORY AND POPULATION. Nevada is bounded north by Oregon and Idaho, east by Utah, south-east by Arizona, with the Colorado River forming most of the boundary, south and west by California. Land area, 105,540 sq. miles (273,349 sq. km). The federal government in 1995 owned 56,854,307 acres, or 80·4% of the land area.

Census population on 1 April 1990, 1,201,833 (88·3% urban), an increase of 401,325 since 1980. Population estimate (1996), 1,638,015. Births, 1995, were 25,175; deaths, 1995, 11,680; marriages, 129,034; divorces, 12,553; infant deaths, 143; abortions, 6,942.

Population in 5 census years was:

	White	Black	Indian	All others	Total	Per sq. mile
1910	74,276	513	5,240	1,846	81,875	0·7
1930	84,515	516	4,871	1,156	91,058	0·8
1970	449,850	27,579	7,329	3,980	488,738	4·4
1980	700,360	50,999	13,308	35,841	800,508	7·2
1990	1,012,695	78,771	19,637	90,730	1,201,833	10·9

Of the total population in 1990, 611,880 were male, 1,061,312 were urban and 364,109 were under 21 years of age. Nevada's population rise has made it the fastest-growing state in the USA every year since 1986.

The largest cities (with 1995 estimated population) are: Las Vegas, 368,360; Reno, 150,620; Henderson, 115,380; North Las Vegas, 77,820; Sparks, 59,880; Carson City (the capital), 46,770.

CLIMATE. Las Vegas. Jan. 44°F (6·7°C), July 85°F (29·4°C). Annual rainfall 4·13" (105 mm). Reno. Jan. 32°F (0°C), July 69°F (20·6°C). Annual rainfall 7·53" (191 mm). Nevada belongs to the Mountain States climate zone (*see* UNITED STATES: Climate).

CONSTITUTION AND GOVERNMENT. The constitution adopted in 1864 is still in force, with 119 amendments by 1994. The Legislature meets biennially (and in special sessions) and consists of a Senate of 21 members elected for 2 years, half their number retiring every 2 years, and an Assembly of 42 members elected for 4 years. The Governor may be elected for 2 consecutive 4-year terms.

The state sends 2 representatives to Congress.

In the 1996 presidential election Clinton polled 231,863 votes; Dole, 198,775; Perot, 43,855.

The state capital is Carson City. There are 16 counties, 18 incorporated cities and 44 unincorporated communities and 1 city-county (the Capitol District of Carson City).

Governor: Bob Miller (D.), 1995–99 ($90,000).
Lieut.-Governor: Lonnie Hammargren (R.) ($20,000).
Secretary of State: Dean Heller (R.) ($62,500).

BUDGET. For the fiscal year ending 30 June 1997, forecast state general fund revenues were $1,293·2m.; budget appropriations were $1,319,136·7m. from the general fund. Education (56·5% of the total), followed by human services (24·3%), received the largest appropriations in 1994. State bonded indebtedness on 30 June 1994, was $423m. The state has no franchise tax, capital stock tax, special intangibles tax, stock transfer tax, admissions tax, gift tax, or income tax. Taxes on gambling and the state's 2% share of the sales tax represent nearly 76% of the general fund revenues.

Per capita personal income (1995) was $25,013.

NATURAL RESOURCES

Minerals. Value and production, 1995: Gold $2,599m., 6,765,000 troy oz; silver, $128m., 24·02 troy oz; sand and gravel, $126m., 88m. short tons (includes stone);

barite, $23m., 467,000 short tons. Petroleum produced, 1·3m. bbls. Other minerals are iron ore, mercury, lime, lithium, gemstones, lead, molybdenum, fluorspar, perlite, pumice, clays, talc, salt, tungsten, magnesite, diatomite, gypsum and zinc.

Agriculture. In 1996 there were an estimated 3,000 farms with a total area of 9m. acres. Farms averaged 3,520 acres. Average value per acre in 1995 was $289. Area under irrigation (1989) was 569,800 acres compared with 542,976 acres in 1959.

Total farm income, 1993, from crops, $345·1m., including from marketing crops and livestock, $186·2m. Cattle, hay, dairy products, potatoes and sheep are the principal commodities in order of cash receipts. Crop production (in 1,000 tons) and value (in $1,000) 1995: Hay, 1,505 ($142,275); potatoes, 139 ($23,302); alfalfa seed, 10·35m. lbs ($12,213); onions, 43·7 ($11,362); garlic, 12·7 ($4,447) and all grain crops, 1,170 ($4,361). In 1996 there were 0·5m. cattle and 87,500 sheep. In 1995, 680,000 lbs. of wool were produced with a total value of $734,000 and 425m. lbs. of milk, total receipts $50,400.

Forestry. The national forests covered an area of 6,275,313 acres in 1997.

INDUSTRY. The main industry is the service industry (44·1% of employment in 1995), especially tourism and legalized gambling. In 1994 there were 1,475 manufacturing establishments with 30,546 employees, and 3,937 construction firms with 49,894 employees.

Gaming industry gross revenue for 1995 was $7,369m. In 1994 there were 361 non-restricted licensed casinos and 2,468 licences in force.

LABOUR. In 1995, industries employed an annual average total of 789,200 workers. Main industries and employees, 1994: Service industries, 327,550 (including gaming and tourism, 193,508); retail trade, 116,692; government, 92,158; finance, insurance and real estate, 34,142; transport, communications and public utilities, 37,833; mining, 12,350; manufacturing, 33,575. There were 48,000 unemployed in 1994.

COMMUNICATIONS

Roads. State maintained road mileage totalled 5,485 in 1996; motor vehicle registrations in 1995 numbered 1,182,459.

Railways. In 1995 there were 1,275 miles of main-line railway. Nevada is served by the Southern Pacific, Union Pacific and Northern Nevada railways, and Amtrak passenger service for Las Vegas, Elko, Reno, Caliente, Lovelock, Stateline, Winnemucca and Sparks.

Civil Aviation. There were 98 civil airports and 24 heliports in Jan. 1996. During 1995 McCarran International Airport (Las Vegas) handled 28,027,239 passengers and Reno-Cannon International Airport handled 5,801,644 passengers.

Telecommunications. In Sept. 1995 there were 84 telephone exchanges, and 981,941 telephones in service (not including cellular).

SOCIAL INSTITUTIONS

Justice. Capital punishment was reintroduced in 1978, and executions began in 1979. In 1996 there were 7,599 persons in state and federal prisons.

Religion. Roman Catholics are the most numerous religious group, followed by members of the Church of Jesus Christ of Latter-day Saints (Mormons) and various Protestant churches.

Education. School attendance is compulsory for children from 7 to 17 years of age. Numbers of pupils in public schools, 1995–96: Pre-kindergarten, 1,631; kindergarten, 22,074; elementary, 131,074; secondary grades 7–9, 60,081; secondary grades 10–12, 48,965; special education, 731. Numbers of teachers in public schools, 1994–95: Elementary, 6,642; secondary, 4,605; special education, 17,434; occupational, 239. Numbers of pupils in private schools, 1995–96: Kindergartens, 1,875;

elementary, 5,922; secondary grades 7–9, 2,313; secondary grades 10–12, 1,376; multi-grades, 496.

The University of Nevada System comprises campuses at Las Vegas and Reno and 4 community colleges. In 1995–96 it had 36,794 students and in 1994–95, 1,710 academic staff.

Health. In 1995 the state had 24 hospitals and medical centres (3,516 beds). In Jan. 1996 there were 36 nursing units (3,676 beds). In 1994 there were 2,322 physicians and 618 dentists. In 1995 there were 9,851 registered nurses.

Social Security. In 1994 benefits were paid to 218,000 persons: 161,000 retired (aged 62 and over) workers (average payment $661 per month); 30,000 widows and widowers ($674); 28,000 disabled workers ($669).

Further Reading

Statistical information: Budget and Planning Division, Department of Administration, Capitol Complex, Carson City, Nevada, 89710. Publishes *Nevada Statistical Abstract* (Biennial).
Bushnell, E. and Driggs, D. W., *The Nevada Constitution: Origin and Growth.* 5th ed. Univ. of Nevada Press, 1980
Hulse, J. W., *The Nevada Adventure: a History.* 6th ed. Univ. of Nevada Press, 1990
Laxalt, R., *Nevada: a History.* New York, 1977
Mack, E. M. and Sawyer, B. W., *Here is Nevada: a History of the State.* Sparks, 1965
Paher, S. W., *Nevada: an Annotated Bibliography.* Carson City, 1980

State Library: Nevada State Library, Carson City.

NEW HAMPSHIRE

KEY HISTORICAL EVENTS. The area was part of a grant by the English crown made to John Mason and fellow-colonists, and was first settled in 1623. In 1629 an area between the Merrimack and Piscatagua rivers was called New Hampshire. More settlements followed, and in 1641 they were taken under the jurisdiction of the governor of Massachusetts. New Hampshire became a separate colony in 1679.

After the War of Independence New Hampshire became one of the 13 original states of the Union, drawing up its constitution in 1784 and revising it on accession to the Union in 1792.

The settlers were Protestants from Britain and Northern Ireland. They developed manufacturing industries, especially shoe-making, textiles and clothing, to which large numbers of French Canadians were attracted after the Civil War.

Portsmouth, originally a fishing settlement, was the colonial capital and is the only seaport. In 1808 the state capital was moved to Concord (having had no permanent home since 1775); Concord produced the Concord Coach which was widely used on the stagecoach routes of the West until at least 1900.

TERRITORY AND POPULATION. New Hampshire is bounded in the north by Canada, east by Maine and the Atlantic, south by Massachusetts and west by Vermont. Land area, 8,993 sq. miles (23,292 sq. km). Census population, 1 April 1990, 1,109,252 (51% urban), an increase of 20·49% since 1980. Estimated population (1996), 1,162,000. Births, 1994, were 15,106 (13·3 per 1,000 population); deaths, 9,000 (7·8); infant deaths, 92 (5·5 per 1,000 live births); marriages, 1995, were 9,863; divorces, 4,949.

Population at 5 federal censuses was:

	White	Black	Indian	Asiatic	Total	Per sq. mile
1910	429,906	564	34	68	430,572	47·7
1960	604,334	1,903	135	549	606,921	65·2
			All others			
1970	733,106	2,505	2,070		737,681	81·7
1980	910,099	3,990	6,521		920,610	101·9
1990	1,087,433	7,198	14,621		1,109,252	123·7

The largest city in the state is Manchester, with an estimated 1996 population of 102,675. The capital is Concord, with 37,850. Other cities are: Nashua, 82,785; Rochester, 28,726; Dover, 26,200; Keene, 22,872; Portsmouth, 22,830; Laconia, 17,053; Claremont, 13,980; Lebanon, 12,662; Berlin, 11,923; Somersworth, 11,623; Franklin, 8,394. There are also 221 towns.

CLIMATE. New Hampshire is in the New England climate zone (*see* UNITED STATES: Climate). Manchester. Jan. 22°F (−5·6°C), July 70°F (21·1°C). Annual rainfall 40" (1,003 mm).

CONSTITUTION AND GOVERNMENT. While the present constitution dates from 1784, it was extensively revised in 1792 when the state joined the Union. Since 1775 there have been 16 state conventions with 49 amendments adopted to amend the constitution.

The Legislature (called the General Court) consists of a Senate of 24 members, elected for 2 years, and a House of Representatives, of 400 members, elected for 2 years. It meets annually. The Governor and 5 administrative officers called 'Councillors' are also elected for 2 years.

The state sends 2 representatives to Congress.

In the 1996 presidential election Clinton polled 245,260 votes; Dole, 196,740; Perot, 48,140.

The capital is Concord. The state is divided into 10 counties.

Governor: Jeanne Shaheen (D.), 1997–99 ($86,235).
Secretary of State: William M. Gardner (D.) ($68,768).

BUDGET. New Hampshire has no general sales tax or state income tax but does have local property taxes. Other government revenues come from rooms and meals tax, business profits tax, motor vehicle licences, fuel taxes, fishing and hunting licences, state-controlled sales of alcoholic beverages, cigarette and tobacco taxes. The state government's total revenue for 1994 was $3,081m. (general revenue $2,649m.); total expenditure $3,179m. (general expenditure $2,797m.) including $535·2m. on education, $1,081·5m. on public welfare, $214·1m. on highways.

Per capita personal income (1995) was $25,715.

NATURAL RESOURCES

Minerals. Minerals are little worked; they consist mainly of sand and gravel, stone, and clay for building and highway construction. Value of non-fuel mineral production, 1992, $33·1m.

Agriculture. In 1996 there were some 2,000 farms covering nearly 500,000 acres; average farm was 179 acres. Average value per acre in 1995, $2,486. The market value in 1992 from agricultural products sold was $45·7m. from crops and $68·3m. from livestock and products.

The chief field crops are hay and vegetables; the chief fruit crop is apples. Livestock, 1992: Cattle, 48,419; pigs, 4,458; sheep, 8,052; poultry, 212,748.

Forestry. In 1997 there were 798, 397 acres of national forest.

Fisheries. The 1990 catch was worth $10m.

INDUSTRY. Principal manufactures: Electrical and electronic goods, machinery, and metal products.

Labour. In 1996, 560,000 persons were in employment (excluding agriculture), of whom 162,000 worked in services, 145,000 in retail and 105,000 in manufacturing.

COMMUNICATIONS

Roads. In 1995 there were 15,086 miles of roads (12,173 miles rural). There were 1,122,000 registered motor vehicles.

Railways. In 1993 the length of operating railway in the state was 540 miles.

Civil Aviation. In 1997 there were 26 public and 21 private airports.

Telecommunications. Across the state there were 49 radio and 6 TV stations in 1997.

Press. In 1993 there were 11 daily and 57 weekly newspapers.

SOCIAL INSTITUTIONS

Justice. The Department of Corrections held 2,180 persons on 1 July 1997. The death penalty is authorized, but there have been no executions since 1939.

Religion. The Roman Catholic Church is the largest single body. The largest Protestant churches are Congregational, Episcopal, Methodist and United Baptist Convention of N.H.

Education. School attendance is compulsory for children from 6 to 14 years of age during the whole school term, or to 16 if their district provides a high school. Employed illiterate minors between 16 and 21 years of age must attend evening or special classes, if provided by the district.

In 1995 the public elementary and secondary schools had 209,150 pupils and 12,300 teachers. Public school salaries, 1995, averaged $35,792. An average of $6,449 was spent on education per pupil.

Of the 4-year colleges, the University of New Hampshire (founded in 1866) had 12,000 students in 1992–93; New Hampshire College (1932), 5,300; Keene State College (1909), 4,900; Plymouth State College (1871), 4,228; Dartmouth College (1769), 5,180. Total enrolment, 1995–96, in the 30 institutions of higher education, was 64,406.

Health. In 1995 the state had 29 community hospitals with 3,400 beds.

Social Assistance. The Division of Human Services handles public assistance for (1) aged citizens 65 years or over, (2) needy aged aliens, (3) needy blind persons, (4) needy citizens between 18 and 64 years inclusive, who are permanently and totally disabled, (5) needy children under 18 years, (6) Medicaid and the medically needy not eligible for a monthly grant.

In 1995 the annual average number of welfare cases were: 65 years or over, 8,446; disabled, 8,305; families with dependEnt children, 12,798.

Further Reading

Delorme, D. (ed.) *New Hampshire Atlas and Gazetteer.* Freeport, 1983
Morison, E. E. and E. F., *New Hampshire.* New York, 1976
Squires, J. D., *The Granite State of the United States: A History of New Hampshire from 1623 to the present.* 4 vols. New York, 1956

NEW JERSEY

KEY HISTORICAL EVENTS. Originally the territory of Delaware Indians, the area was first settled by immigrant colonists in the early 17th century, when Dutch and Swedish traders established fortified posts on the Hudson and Delaware Rivers. The Dutch took control but lost it to the English in 1664. In 1676 the English divided the area in two; the eastern portion was assigned to Sir George Carteret and the western granted to Quaker settlers. This division lasted until 1702 when New Jersey was united as a colony of the Crown and placed under the jurisdiction of the governor of New York. It became a separate colony in 1738.

During the War of Independence crucial battles were fought at Trenton, Princeton and Monmouth. New Jersey became the 3rd state of the Union in 1787. Trenton, the state capital since 1790, began as a Quaker settlement and became an iron-working town. Industrial development grew rapidly, there and elsewhere in the state, after the opening of canals and railways in the 1830s. Princeton, also a Quaker settlement, became an important post on the New York road; the college of New Jersey (Princeton University) was transferred there from Newark in 1756.

The need for supplies in the Civil War stimulated industry and New Jersey became a manufacturing state. The growth beyond its borders of New York and Philadelphia, however, produced a pattern of commuting to employment in both centres. By 1980 about 60% of the state's population lived within 30 miles of New York.

TERRITORY AND POPULATION. New Jersey is bounded north by New York, east by the Atlantic with Long Island and New York City to the north-east, south by Delaware Bay and west by Pennsylvania. Land area, 7,419 sq. miles (19,210 sq. km). Census population, 1 April 1990, 7,730,188 (89·4% urban), an increase of 4·96% since 1980. Population density, 1990, 1,042·2 per sq. mile. Population estimate (1996), 7,988,000. Vital statistics, 1994 (per 1,000): Births, 117,501 (14·9); deaths, 72,000 (9·1); infant deaths in 1993, 989 (8·2); marriages, 55,296 (7·1); divorces in 1992, 25,405 (3·3).

Population at 5 federal censuses was:

	White	Black	Indian	Asiatic	Others	Total
1910	2,445,894	89,760	168	1,345	—	2,537,167
1930	3,829,663	208,828	213	2,630	—	4,041,334
1960	5,539,003	514,875	1,699	8,778	2,427	6,066,782
1980	6,127,467	925,066	8,394	103,848	200,048	7,364,823
1990	6,130,465	1,036,825	14,970	272,521	275,407	7,730,188

Of the population in 1990, 3,735,685 were male, 6,910,220 persons were urban, 5,718,136 were 20 years of age or older and 739,861 were Hispanic.

Census population of the larger cities and towns in 1990 was:

Newark	275,221	East Orange	73,552	Vineland	54,780
Jersey City	228,537	Clifton	71,742	Gloucester	53,797
Paterson	140,891	Cherry Hill	69,348	Union Township	50,024
Elizabeth	110,002	Middletown	68,183	Parsippany-	
Woodbridge	93,086	Brick	66,473	Troy Hills	48,478
Edison	88,680	Bayonne	61,444	North Bergen	48,414
Trenton (capital)	88,675	Irvington	61,018	Piscataway	47,089
Camden	87,492	Passaic	58,041	Wayne	47,025
Hamilton	86,553	Union City	58,012	Plainfield	46,567
Dover	76,371	Old Bridge	56,475	Bloomfield	45,061

Largest metropolitan areas (1990) were: Newark, 1,824,321; Bergen-Passaic, 1,278,440; Jersey City, 553,099; Trenton, 325,824.

CLIMATE. Jersey City. Jan. 31°F (−0·6°C), July 75°F (23·9°C). Annual rainfall 41" (1,025 mm). Trenton. Jan. 32°F (0°C), July 76°F (24·4°C). Annual rainfall 40" (1,003 mm). New Jersey belongs to the Atlantic Coast climate zone (*see* UNITED STATES: Climate).

CONSTITUTION AND GOVERNMENT. The present constitution, ratified by the registered voters on 4 Nov. 1947, has been amended 45 times. There is a 40-member Senate and an 80-member General Assembly. Assembly members serve 2 years, senators 4 years, except those elected at the election following each census, who serve for 2 years. Sessions are held throughout the year.

The state sends 13 representatives to Congress.

In the 1996 presidential election Clinton polled 1,588,811 votes; Dole, 1,067,274; Perot, 254,941.

The capital is Trenton. The state is divided into 21 counties, which are subdivided into 567 municipalities—cities, towns, boroughs, villages and townships.

Governor: Christine Todd Whitman (R.), 1994–98 ($85,000).
Secretary of State: Lonna R. Hooks ($100,225).

BUDGET. For the year ending 30 June 1995 (budget figures) total revenues were $22,638m., expenditures were $22,602m.

Outstanding general obligation bonded debt, 30 June 1995, was approximately $3,647m.

Per capita personal income (1996) was $31,053.

NATURAL RESOURCES

Minerals. In 1992 the chief minerals were stone (17·1m. short tons, value $126m.) and sand and gravel (17,934,000, $104,717,000); others are clays, peat and gem-stones. New Jersey is a leading producer of greensand marl, magnesium compounds and peat. Total value of non-fuel mineral products, 1992, was $240,439,000.

Agriculture. Livestock raising, market-gardening, fruit-growing, horticulture and forestry are pursued. In 1996 there were some 9,000 farms with a total acreage of 1m., averaging 91 acres. Average value per acre in 1995 was $8,052.

Market value (preliminary) of agricultural products sold, 1993: Crops, including nursery and greenhouse, $507,581,000; livestock, poultry and their products, $198·68m.

Leading crops are tomatoes (value, $18·9m., 1993), corn for grain ($15·1m.), peaches ($25·3m.), blueberries ($26·4m.), soybeans ($25·7m.), sweet corn ($15·9m.), peppers ($21·8m.), cranberries ($18·8m.). Livestock, 1993: 25,000 milk cows, 75,000 all cattle, 13,000 sheep and lambs and (Dec. 1992) 28,000 swine.

INDUSTRY. In 1993 the top 100 corporate employers employed 501,908, listed by New Jersey Business and Industry Association. The unemployment rate in Sept. 1994 was 6·7%.

In Sept. 1997 there were 3,717,800 employees on non-agricultural payrolls; 2,000 in mining, 128,000 in construction, 479,300 in manufacturing, 258,500 in transportation and public utilities, 873,700 in wholesale and retail trade, 1,170,600 in services, 568,600 in government.

COMMUNICATIONS

Roads. In 1994 there were about 2,297 miles of state and interstate highways. At 9 Sept. 1994 there were 6,789 miles of county highways, 25,057 miles of municipal roads and 941 miles of other road. In 1995 there were 5,906,000 motor vehicle registrations.

Railways. In Oct. 1994, the state had 1,321 route miles of railway. There is a metro link to New York (22 km), a light rail line (7 km), and extensive commuter railways around Newark.

Civil Aviation. There is an international airport at Newark.

SOCIAL INSTITUTIONS

Justice. State prisons in Aug. 1994 had 25,443 inmates. The death penalty is authorized.

Religion. In 1994 the Roman Catholic population of New Jersey was 3·25m., and there were 436,000 Jews. Among Protestant sects were United Methodists, 132,000; United Presbyterians (1993), 106,700; Episcopalians, 64,200; Lutherans, 82,200; American Baptists (1992), 66,000.

Education. Elementary instruction is compulsory for all from 6 to 16 years of age and free to all from 5 to 20 years of age. In 1993–94 public elementary schools had 830,628 and secondary schools had 320,982 enrolled pupils; public colleges in autumn 1993 had 278,306 students, including 139,915 in community colleges; independent colleges had 63,051. Average salary of 83,289 elementary and secondary classroom teachers in public schools 1993–94 was $45,880.

In autumn 1993: Rutgers, the State University (founded as Queen's College in 1766) had, 48,062 students; Princeton (founded in 1746) had 6,592; Fairleigh Dickinson (1941), had 10,751; Montclair State College, 13,214; Rowan College (formerly Glassboro State College), 9,368; Trenton State College, 7,063.

Health. In 1995 there were 92 community hospitals with 29,900 beds.

Social Security. In the calendar year 1993, total Old Age, Survivors and Disability Insurance benefits were $10,239,000. Average monthly Title II social security payment was $739·30.

Further Reading

Statistical information: New Jersey State Data Center, Department of Labor, CN 388, Trenton 08625. Publishes *New Jersey Statistical Factbook.*
Legislative District Data Book. Bureau of Government Research. Annual
Manual of the Legislature of New Jersey. Trenton. Annual
Boyd, J. P. (ed.) *Fundamentals and Constitutions of New Jersey, 1664–1954.* Princeton, 1964
Cunningham, J. T., *New Jersey: America's Main Road.* Rev. ed. New York, 1976
Kull, I. Stoddard (ed.) *New Jersey: a History.* New York, 1930

State Library: 185 W. State Street, Trenton, CN 520. N.J. 08625.

NEW MEXICO

KEY HISTORICAL EVENTS. The first European settlement was established in 1598. Until 1771 New Mexico was the Spanish kings' 'Kingdom of New Mexico'. In 1771 it was annexed to the northern province of New Spain. When New Spain won its independence in 1821, it took the name of Republic of Mexico and established New Mexico as its northernmost department. Ceded to the USA in 1848 after war between the USA and Mexico, the area was organized as a Territory in 1850, by which time its population was Spanish and Indian. There was frequent conflict, especially between new settlers and raiding parties of Navajo and Apaches. The Indian war lasted from 1861 until 1866, and from 1864–68 about 8,000 Navajo were imprisoned at Bosque Redondo.

The boundaries were altered several times when land was taken into Texas, Utah, Colorado and lastly (1863) Arizona. New Mexico became a state in 1912.

Settlement proceeded by means of irrigated crop-growing and Mexican-style ranching. During the Second World War the desert areas were brought into use as testing zones for atomic weapons. Mineral extraction also developed, especially after the discovery of uranium and petroleum.

TERRITORY AND POPULATION. New Mexico is bounded north by Colorado, north-east by Oklahoma, east by Texas, south by Texas and Mexico and west by Arizona. Land area, 121,365 sq. miles (314,334 sq. km). Public lands, administered by federal agencies (1975) amounted to 26·7m. acres or 34% of the total area. The Bureau of Indian Affairs held 7·3m. acres; the State of New Mexico held 9·4m. acres; 34·4m. acres were privately owned.

Census population, 1 April 1990, 1,515,069 (73% urban), an increase of 211,767 or 16·2% since 1980. Population estimate (1996), 1,713,407. Vital statistics, 1996 (provisional): Births, 27,173 (15·9 per 1,000 population); marriages, 16,026 (9·4); divorces, 10,945 (6·4); deaths, 12,325 (7·2); infant deaths, 160 (5·9 per 1,000 live births).

The population in 5 census years was:

	White	Black	Indian	Asian and Pacific Island	Other	Total	Per sq. mile
1910	304,594	1,628	20,573	506		327,301	2·7
1940	492,312	4,672	34,510	324		531,818	4·4
1960	875,763	17,063	56,255	1,942		951,023	7·8
1980	977,587	24,020	106,119	6,825	188,343	1,302,894	10·7
1990	1,146,028	30,210	134,355	14,124	190,352	1,515,069	12·5

Of the 1990 total, 745,253 were male, 1,068,328 were 18 years of age or older, 163,062 were 65 years of age or older.

Before 1930 New Mexico was largely a Spanish-speaking state, but since 1945 an influx of population from other states has reduced the percentage of persons of Spanish origin or descent to 38·2% (1990).

The largest cities are Albuquerque, with estimated population, 1996, 419,681; Las Cruces, 74,779; Santa Fé, 66,522; Roswell, 47,559; Rio Rancho, 46,565.

CLIMATE. Santa Fé. Jan. 26·4°F (−1·6°C), July 68·4°F (20°C). Annual rainfall 15·2" (386 mm). New Mexico belongs to the Mountain States climate zone (*see* UNITED STATES: Climate).

CONSTITUTION AND GOVERNMENT. The constitution of 1912 is still in force with 137 amendments. The state Legislature, which meets annually, consists of 42 members of the Senate, elected for 4 years, and 70 members of the House of Representatives, elected for 2 years.

The state sends 3 representatives to Congress.

In the 1996 presidential election Clinton polled 252,215 votes; Dole, 210,791; Perot, 30,978.

The state capital is Santa Fé. The state is divided into 33 counties.

Governor: Gary Johnson (R.), 1995–98 ($90,000).
Lieut.-Governor: Walter Bradley (R.) ($65,000).
Secretary of State: Stephanie Gonzales (D.) ($65,000).

BUDGET. For the year ending 30 June 1994 (US Census Bureau figures) the state's general revenues were $6,318m. ($3,060m. from taxation and $1,794m. from intergovernmental transfers); general expenditures, $6,222m. (education, $2,457m.; highways, $651m., and public welfare, $1,118m.).

Per capita personal income (1996) was $18,803.

NATURAL RESOURCES

Minerals. New Mexico is one of the largest energy producing states in the US. Production in 1995: Potash, 2,568,000 short tons; copper, 276,000 short tons; petroleum, 64,508,000 bbls (of 42 gallons); natural gas, 1,426,000m. cu. ft; coal, 26,813,000 short tons. The value of the total mineral output (1995) was $4,897m. An average of 15,900 persons were employed in the mining industry in 1995, 10,000 in oil and gas extraction.

Agriculture. New Mexico produces grains, vegetables, fruit, livestock, cotton and nuts. Dry farming and irrigation have proved profitable in periods of high prices. In 1992 there were 14,279 farms covering 46·8m. acres; average farm size, 3,281 acres. In 1995 average value of farmland and buildings per acre was $225.

Cash receipts, 1996, from crops, $512m., and from livestock products, $1,197m. Principal crops are wheat (4·0m. bu. from 0·11m. acres), hay (1·6m. tons from 0·35m. acres) and sorghum/grains (7·4m. bu. from 0·225m. acres). Farm animals in 1997 included 197,000 milk cows, 1·5m. all cattle, 235,000 sheep and 5,000 swine.

Forestry. There were 10m. acres of national forest in 1997.

INDUSTRY. Average monthly non-agricultural employment during 1996 was 694,000: 45,900 were employed in manufacturing, 171,100 in government. Value of manufactures shipments, 1992, $9,491·5m.; leading industries, food and kindred products, electrical and electronic equipment, petroleum and coal products.

COMMUNICATIONS

Roads. In 1995 there were 61,289 miles of roads and (1996) 1,683,243 registered motor vehicles.

Railways. In 1994 there were 1,868 miles of railway in operation.

Civil Aviation. There were 64 public-use airports in Nov. 1995.

SOCIAL INSTITUTIONS

Justice. The number of state prison inmates in Feb. 1997 was 4,701, and there was an average of 602 in state-operated juvenile centres in the fiscal year 1996. The death penalty is authorized.

Since 1949 the denial of employment by reason of race, colour, religion, national origin or ancestry has been forbidden. A law of 1955 prohibits discrimination in public places because of race or colour. An 'equal rights' amendment was added to the constitution in 1972.

Religion. There were (1990) approximately 883,000 Christian Church adherents (421,868 Roman Catholics in 1996).

Education. Elementary education is free, and compulsory between 6 and 17 years or high-school graduation age. In 1995–96 the 89 school districts had an enrolment of 348,543 students in elementary and secondary schools of which private, parochial and state supported schools had 31,112. In 1994–95 there were 18,500 FTE teachers receiving an average salary of $29,074. Total revenue for public elementary and secondary schools was $1,702m. (1994–95).

The state-supported 4-year institutes of higher education are (autumn 1996[1]):

	Students
University of New Mexico, Albuquerque	30,534
New Mexico State University, Las Cruces	22,313
Eastern New Mexico University, Portales	7,008
New Mexico Highlands University, Las Vegas	2,787
Western New Mexico University, Silver City	2,533
New Mexico Institute of Mining and Technology, Socorro	1,467

[1] Figures include branches outside main campus in cities listed.

Health. In 1995 there were 36 community hospitals with 3,700 beds. The state had 2,009 active non-federal physicians.

Social Security. In fiscal year 1997 a monthly average of 30,280 cases received $140·4m. from aid to families with dependEnt children funds and 79,610 cases received $181·6m. in food stamp funds. In 1995 a total of 44,755 persons in the state were receiving federally administered payment totalling $165·6m. Among these 9,844 were receiving aid for the aged ($21·7m.), 644 were receiving aid to the blind ($2·3m.) and 34,267 were receiving aid for the disabled ($141·5m.).

Further Reading

Bureau of Business and Economic Research, Univ. of New Mexico–*Census in New Mexico* (Continuing scrics. Vols. 1–5, 1992–). –*Economic Census: New Mexico* (Continuing series. Vol. 1, 1996). –*New Mexico Business*. Monthly; annual review in Jan.-Feb. issue
Beck, W., *New Mexico: a History of Four Centuries*. Univ. of Oklahoma Press, 1979
Etulain. R., *Contemporary New Mexico, 1940–1990*. Univ. of New Mexico Press, 1994
Garcia, C., Haine, P. and Rhodes, H., *State and Local Government in New Mexico*. Albuquerque, 1979
Jenkins, M. and Schroeder, A., *A Brief History of New Mexico*. Univ. of New Mexico Press, 1974
Muench, D. and Hillerman, T., *New Mexico*. Portland (OR), 1974
Williams, J. L., *New Mexico in Maps*. Univ. of New Mexico Press, 1986

NEW YORK STATE

KEY HISTORICAL EVENTS. The first European immigrants came in the 17th century, when there were two powerful Indian groups in rivalry: the Iroquois confederacy (Mohawk, Oneida, Onondaga, Cayuga and Seneca) and the Algonquian-speaking Mohegan and Munsee. The Dutch made settlements at Fort Orange (now Albany) in 1624 and at New Amsterdam in 1625, trading with the Indians for furs. In the 1660s there was conflict between the Dutch and the British in the Caribbean; as part of the concluding treaty the British in 1664 received Dutch possessions in the Americas, including New Amsterdam, which they renamed New York.

In 1763 the Treaty of Paris ended war between the British and the French in North

America (in which the Iroquois had allied themselves with the British). Settlers of British descent in New England then felt confident enough to expand westward into the area. The climate of northern New York being severe, most settled in the Hudson river valley. After the War of Independence New York became the 11th state of the Union (1778), having first declared itself independent of Britain in 1777.

The economy depended on manufacturing, shipping and other means of distributing goods, and trade. During the 19th century New York became the most important city in the USA. Its manufacturing industries, especially clothing, attracted thousands of European immigrants. Industrial development spread along the Hudson-Mohawk valley, which was made the route of the Erie Canal (1825) linking New York with Buffalo on Lake Erie and thus with the developing farmlands of the middle west.

TERRITORY AND POPULATION. New York is bounded west and north by Canada with Lake Erie, Lake Ontario and the St Lawrence River forming the boundary; east by Vermont, Massachusetts and Connecticut, south-east by the Atlantic, south by New Jersey and Pennsylvania. Land area, 47,224 sq. miles (122,310 sq. km). Census population, 1 April 1990, 17,990,455 (84·3% urban), an increase of 2·47% since 1980. Population estimate (1996), 18,185,000. Births in 1994 were 278,392 (15·3 per 1,000 population); deaths, 169,000 (9·3); infant deaths in 1989, 3,076 (10·6 per 1,000 live births); marriages in 1989, 162,782 (9·1); divorces, also 1989, 55,610 (3·1).

Population in 5 census years was:

	White	Black	Indian	Asiatic	Total	Per sq. mile
1910	8,966,845	134,191	6,046	6,532	9,113,614	191·2
1930	12,143,191	412,814	6,973	15,088	12,588,066	262·6
1960	15,287,071	1,417,511	16,491	51,678	16,782,304	350·2
			All others			
1980	13,961,106	2,401,842	1,194,340		17,557,288	367·0
1990	12,460,189	2,569,126	2,961,140		17,990,455	381·0

Of the 1990 population, 8,625,673 were male, 14,857,202 (1980) were urban; those 20 years of age or older numbered 13,186,381. Aliens registered in Jan. 1980 numbered 801,411.

The population of New York City, by boroughs, census of 1 April 1990 was: Manhattan, 1,487,536; Bronx, 1,203,789; Brooklyn, 2,291,664; Queens, 1,951,598; Staten Island, 378,977; total, 7,322,564. The New York metropolitan statistical area had, in 1990, 8,546,846.

Population of other large cities and incorporated places census, April 1990, was:

Buffalo	328,123	Troy	54,269	Auburn	31,258
Rochester	231,636	Binghampton	53,008	Waterdown	29,429
Yonkers	188,082	Hempstead	49,453	Poughkeepsie	28,844
Syracuse	163,860	White Plains	48,718	Lindenhurst	26,879
Albany (capital)	101,082	Rome	44,350	Newburgh	26,454
Utica	68,637	Freeport	39,894	Rockville Center	24,727
New Rochelle	67,265	N. Tonawanda	34,989	Garden City	21,686
Mount Vernon	67,153	Jamestown	34,681	Massapequa Park	18,044
Schenectady	65,566	Valleystream	33,946		
Niagara Falls	61,840	Elmira	33,724		

Other large urbanized areas, census 1990; Buffalo, 968,532; Rochester, 1,002,410; Albany–Schenectady–Troy, 874,304.

CLIMATE. Albany. Jan. 24°F (−4·4°C), July 73°F (22·8°C). Annual rainfall 34" (855 mm). Buffalo. Jan. 24°F (−4·4°C), July 70°F (21·1°C). Annual rainfall 36" (905 mm). New York. Jan. 30°F (−1·1°C), July 74°F (23·3°C). Annual rainfall 43" (1,087 mm). New York belongs to the Atlantic Coast climate zone (see UNITED STATES: Climate).

CONSTITUTION AND GOVERNMENT. The present constitution dates from 1894; a later constitutional convention, 1938, is now legally considered merely to have amended the 1894 constitution, which has now had 93 amendments. A proposed new constitution in 1967 was rejected by the electorate. The Senate consists of

60 members, and the Assembly of 150 members, both elected every 2 years. The state capital is Albany. For local government the state is divided into 62 counties, 5 of which constitute the city of New York. There were state parks and recreation areas covering 260,198 acres in 1990.

In the 1996 presidential election Clinton polled 3,513,191 votes; Dole, 1,861,198; Perot, 485,547.

Each of the state's 62 cities is incorporated by charter, under special legislation. The government of New York City is vested in the mayor (David Dinkins), elected for 4 years, and a city council, whose president and members are elected for 4 years. The council has a President and 51 members, each elected from a district wholly within the city. The mayor appoints all the heads of departments, except the comptroller, who is elected. Each of the 5 city boroughs (Manhattan, Bronx, Brooklyn, Queens and Staten Island) has a president, elected for 4 years. Each borough is also a county bearing the same name except Manhattan borough, which, as a county, is called New York, and Brooklyn, which is Kings County.

The state sends 31 representatives to Congress.

Governor: George E. Pataki (R.), 1995–99 ($130,000).
Lieut.-Governor: Elizabeth McCaughey (D.) ($110,000).
Secretary of State: Alexander F. Treadwell (D.) ($87,338).

BUDGET. The figures for 1994 were: total revenues $82,202m. (general revenues $66,587m.); total expenditure $76,872m. (general expenditures $64,802m.) including $17,270·6m. for education, $24,008·5m. for public welfare, $2,693·6m. for highways.

Per capita personal income was $28,858 in 1995.

NATURAL RESOURCES

Minerals. Production of principal minerals in 1988: Sand and gravel (28·7m. short tons), salt (4,614 short tons), oil (495,000 bbls), natural gas (25,447m. cu. ft). The state is a leading producer of titanium concentrate, talc, abrasive garnet, wollastonite and emery. Quarry products include trap rock, slate, marble, limestone and sandstone. Value of mineral output in 1990, $773m.

Agriculture. New York has large agricultural interests. In 1996 it had some 36,000 farms, with a total area of 8m. acres; average farm was 214 acres. Average value per acre in 1995 was $1,380.

Farm income, 1991, from crops $1,089m. and livestock, $1,766m. Dairying is an important type of farming. Field crops comprise maize, winter wheat, oats and hay. New York ranks second in US in the production of apples, and maple syrup. Other products are grapes, tart cherries, peaches, pears, plums, strawberries, raspberries, cabbages, onions, potatoes, maple sugar. Estimated farm animals, 1990, included 1,540,000 all cattle, 966,000 milk cows, 92,000 sheep and lambs, 124,000 swine and 5·1m. chickens.

INDUSTRY. The main employers (1996) are service industries (2,610,000), retail and wholesale (1,621,000) and manufacture (922,000). Leading industries were clothing, non-electrical machinery, printing and publishing, electrical equipment, instruments, food and allied products and fabricated metals.

COMMUNICATIONS

Roads. In 1995 there were 112,193 miles of roads (71,873 miles rural). The New York State Thruway extends 559 miles from New York City to Buffalo. The Northway, a 176-mile toll-free highway, is a connecting road from the Thruway at Albany to the Canadian border at Champlain, Quebec.

Motor vehicle registrations in 1991 were 9,771,437.

Railways. There were in 1981, 3,891 miles of Class I railways. New York City has NYCTA and PATH metro systems, and commuter railways run by Metro-North, New Jersey Transit and Long Island Rail Road.

Civil Aviation. There were 489 airports and landing areas in 1989.

Shipping. The canals of the state, combined in 1918 in what is called the Improved Canal System, have a length of 524 miles, of which the Erie or Barge canal has 340 miles. In 1981 the canals carried 807,925 tons of freight.

SOCIAL INSTITUTIONS

Justice. The State Human Rights Law was approved on 12 March 1945, effective on 1 July 1945. The State Division of Human Rights is charged with the responsibility of enforcing this law. The division may request and utilize the services of all governmental departments and agencies; adopt and promulgate suitable rules and regulations; test, investigate and pass judgment upon complaints alleging discrimination in employment, in places of public accommodation, resort or amusement, education, and in housing, land and commercial space; hold hearings, sub-poena witnesses and require the production for examination of papers relating to matters under investigation; grant compensatory damages and require repayment of profits in certain housing cases among other provisions; apply for court injunctions to prevent frustration of orders of the Commissioner.

In 1994, 66,750 prisoners were in state correctional institutions.

The death penalty is authorized.

In 1988 murders reported in New York were 2,239. Police strength (sworn officers) in 1988 was 61,204 (43,218 New York City).

Religion. The churches are Roman Catholic, with 6,367,576 members in 1981, Jewish congregations (about 2m. in 1981) and Protestant Episcopal (299,929 in 1980).

Education. Education is compulsory between the ages of 7 and 16. In 1994–95 the public elementary and secondary schools had 2,790,700 pupils and 193,000 teachers. Expenditure on education in 1994 was $17,270·6m. Teachers' salaries, 1989, averaged $43,300.

The state's educational system, including public and private schools and secondary institutions, universities, colleges, libraries, museums, etc., constitutes (by legislative act) the 'University of the State of New York', which is governed by a Board of Regents consisting of 15 members appointed by the Legislature. Within the framework of this 'University' was established in 1948 a 'State University' which controls 64 colleges and educational centres, 30 of which are locally operated community colleges. The 'State University' is governed by a board of 16 Trustees, appointed by the Governor with the consent and advice of the Senate.

Higher education in the state is conducted in 296 institutions (627,676 full-time and 375,690 part-time students in autumn 1989).

In autumn 1990 the institutions of higher education in the state included:

Founded	Name and place	Teachers	Students
1754	Columbia University, New York	2,305	18,242
1795	Union University, Schenectady and Albany	228	2,877
1824	Rensselaer Polytechnic Institute, Troy	375	6,692
1831	New York University, New York	2,386	32,813
1846	Colgate University, New York	255	2,710
1846	Fordham University, New York	703	13,158
1847	University of the City of New York, New York	9,065	200,700
1848	University of Rochester, Rochester	1,250	9,291
1854	Polytechnic Institute of New York	261	3,701
1856	St Lawrence University, Canton	189	2,091
1857	Cooper Union Institute of Technology, New York	108	1,036
1861	Vassar College, Poughkeepsie	235	2,453
1863	Manhattan College, New York	234	3,794
1865	Cornell University, Ithaca	1,779	17,171
1870	Syracuse University, Syracuse	990	21,900
1948	State University of New York	18,852	403,028

The Saratoga Performing Arts Centre (5,100 seats), a non-profit, tax-exempt organization, which opened in 1966, is the summer residence of the New York City

Ballet and the Philadelphia Orchestra—two groups which present special educational programmes for students and teachers.

Health. In 1995 the state had 230 community hospitals (73,900 beds). In 1986 mental health facilities had 21,836 patients and institutions for the mentally retarded had 10,581 patients.

Social Security. The federal Supplemental Security Income programme covered aid to the needy aged, blind and disabled from 1 Jan. 1975. In the state programme for 1980, $4,543m. was paid in Medicaid to 2,288,000 people; aid to dependent children in 1985 went to 1,109,610 recipients, average benefits $371 per family per month.

Further Reading

Statistical information: Nelson Rockefeller Institute of Government, 411 State St., Albany 12203. Publishes *New York State Statistical Yearbook.*
Governing the Empire State: an Insider's Guide. Albany, Rockefeller Institute, 1988
New York Red Book. Albany. Biennial.
Legislative Manual. Department of State. Biennial.
Managing Modern New York: the Carey Era. Albany, Rockefeller Institute, 1985
The Modern New York State Legislature: Redressing the Balance. Albany, Rockefeller Institute, 1991
Rockefeller in Retrospect: the Governor's New York Legacy. Albany, Rockefeller Institute, 1987
Connery, R. and G. B., *Governing New York State: The Rockefeller Years.* New York, 1974
Ellis, D. M., *History of New York State.* Cornell Univ. Press, 1967
Flick, A. (ed.) *History of the State of New York.* Columbia Univ. Press, 1933–37
Zimmerman, J. F., *The Government and Politics of New York.* New York Univ. Pres, 1981

State Library: The New York State Library, Albany 12230.

NORTH CAROLINA

KEY HISTORICAL EVENTS. The early inhabitants were Cherokees. European settlement was attempted in 1585–87, following an exploratory visit by Sir Walter Raleigh, but this failed. Settlers from Virginia came to the shores of Albemarle Sound after 1650, and in 1633 Charles II chartered a private colony of Carolina. In 1691 the north was put under a deputy governor who ruled from Charleston in the south. The colony was formally separated into North and South Carolina in 1712. In 1729 control was taken from the private proprietors and vested in the Crown, whereupon settlement grew, and the boundary between north and south was finally fixed (1735).

After the War of Independence North Carolina became one of the original 13 states of the Union. The city of Raleigh was laid out as the new capital. Having been a plantation colony North Carolina continued to develop as a plantation state, growing tobacco with black slave labour. It was also an important source of gold before the western gold-rushes of 1848.

In 1861 at the outset of the Civil War North Carolina seceded from the Union, but General Sherman occupied the capital unopposed. A military governor was admitted in 1862, and civilian government restored with readmission to the Union in 1868.

TERRITORY AND POPULATION. North Carolina is bounded north by Virginia, east by the Atlantic, south by South Carolina, south-west by Georgia and west by Tennessee. Land area, 48,718 sq. miles (126,180 sq. km). Census population, 1 April 1990, 6,628,637 (50·4% urban), an increase of 12·84% since 1980. Population estimate (1996), 7,323,000. Births, 1994, were 101,420 (14·3 per 1,000 population); deaths, 63,000 (8·9); marriages, 1991, 48,966 (7·3); divorces, 33,763 (5); infant deaths, 1992, 1,073 (10·4 per 1,000 live births).

Population in 5 census years was:

	White	Black	Indian	Asiatic	Total	Per sq. mile
1910	1,500,511	697,843	7,851	82	2,206,287	45·3
1930	2,234,958	918,647	16,579	92	3,170,276	64·5
1950	2,983,121	1,047,353	3,742	—	4,061,929	82·7

	White	Black	All others	Total	Per sq. mile
1970	3,901,767	1,126,478	53,814	5,082,059	104·1
1980	4,453,010	1,316,050	105,369	5,874,429	111·5

Of the total population in 1980, 2,852,012 were male, 2,818,794 were urban and 3,976,359 were 20 years old or older.

The principal cities (with census population in 1990) are: Charlotte, 395,934; Raleigh, 207,951; Greensboro, 183,521; Winston-Salem, 143,485; Durham, 136,611; Fayetteville, 75,695; High Point, 69,496; Asheville, 61,607; Wilmington, 55,530.

CLIMATE. Climate varies sharply with altitude; the warmest area is in the south-east near Southport and Wilmington; the coldest is Mount Mitchell (6,684 ft). Raleigh. Jan. 42°F (5·6°C), July 79°F (26·1°C). Annual rainfall 46" (1,158 mm). North Carolina belongs to the Atlantic Coast climate zone (*see* UNITED STATES: Climate).

CONSTITUTION AND GOVERNMENT. The present constitution dates from 1971 (previous constitution, 1776 and 1868/76); it has had 19 amendments. The General Assembly consists of a Senate of 50 members and a House of Representatives of 120 members; all are elected by districts for 2 years. It meets in odd-numbered years in Jan.

The Governor and Lieut.-Governor are elected for 4 years. The Governor may succeed himself but has no veto. There are 19 other executive heads of department, 8 elected by the people and 9 appointed by the Governor.

The state sends 12 representatives to Congress.

In the presidential election of 1996 Dole polled 1,211,655 votes; Clinton, 1,099,123; Perot, 164,512.

The capital is Raleigh. There are 100 counties.

Governor: James B. Hunt Jr (D.), 1997–2001 ($103,012).
Lieut.-Governor: Dennis Wicker (D.) ($90,915).
Secretary of State: Janice H. Faulkner (D.) ($90,915).

BUDGET. The figures for 1994 were: total revenues $21,051m. (general revenues $17,959m.); total expenditure $19,040m. (general expenditures $17,642m.) including $7,670·2m. for education, $3,603·2m. for public welfare, $1,713·5m. for highways.

On 30 June 1991 the net total long-term debt amounted to $3,490m.

Per capita personal income (1995) was $20,604.

NATURAL RESOURCES

Minerals. Mining production in 1990 was valued at $578·4m. Principal minerals were stone, sand and gravel, phosphate rock, feldspar, lithium minerals, olivine, kaolin and talc. North Carolina is a leading producer of bricks, making more than 1,000m. bricks a year.

Agriculture. In 1996 there were some 58,000 farms covering 9m. acres; average size of farms was 159 acres and average value per acre in 1995 was $1,749.

Farm income, 1991, from crops, $2,272m. and from livestock and products, $2,554m. Main crop production: flue-cured tobacco, maize, soybeans, peanuts, wheat, sweet potatoes and apples.

Livestock, 1990: Cattle, 0·9m.; pigs, 2·6m.; chickens, 19·6m.

Forestry. Commercial forest covered 18,891,000 acres in 1990. Main products are hardwood veneer and hardwood plywood, furniture woods, pulp, paper and lumber.

Fisheries. Commercial fish catch, 1990, had a value of approximately $71·5m. The catch is mainly of menhaden, crabmeat, bay scallops, flounder, croaker, shrimps, sea trout, spots and clams.

INDUSTRY. North Carolina's manufacturing establishments in 1996 had 847,000 workers. The leading industries by employment are textiles, clothing, furniture, electrical machinery and equipment, non-electrical machinery, and food processing. In 1985 investment in new and expanded industry was $2,758m. About 576,200 were employed in trade, 422,800 in government and 427,600 in services.

TOURISM. Total receipts of the travel industry, $6,400m. in 1990.

COMMUNICATIONS

Roads. In 1995 there were 96,809 miles of roads (74,660 miles rural). In 1995 there were 5,682,000 registered motor vehicles.

Railways. The state in 1986 contained 3,682 miles of railway operating in 91 of the 100 counties. There are 22 Class I, II and III rail companies.

Civil Aviation. In 1986 there were 82 public airports of which 14 are served by major airlines.

Shipping. There are 2 ocean ports, Wilmington and Morehead City.

SOCIAL INSTITUTIONS

Justice. Following the US Supreme Court's reinstatement of the death penalty in 1976, capital punishment has been authorized. There was an execution in 1986. In 1994 there were 23,639 prisoners in state correctional institutions.

Religion. Leading denominations are the Baptists (48·9% of church membership), Methodists (20·7%), Presbyterians (7·7%), Lutherans (3%) and Roman Catholics (2·7%). Total estimate of all denominations in 1983 was 2·6m.

Education. School attendance is compulsory between 6 and 16.

In 1985–86 there were 1,968 public elementary and secondary schools. In 1994–95 there were 1,146,639 pupils and 71,070 teachers. State and local government expenditure in 1994 was $7,670m.

In autumn 1985–86 state-supported colleges and universities included 58 community and technical colleges with 654,000 full and part time students. The 16 senior universities are all part of the University of North Carolina system, the largest campus being North Carolina State University and Raleigh, with 23,400 students. The university system was founded in 1789 at Chapel Hill and first opened in 1792. Its 1986 autumn enrolment was 130,000 students.

In addition to the state-supported institutions there were 7 private junior colleges with an enrolment of 2,585 and 31 private senior institutions with a total enrolment of 19,009. The total undergraduate enrolment in private institutions for 1985 was 21,594.

Health. In 1995 the state had 119 community hospitals with 22,700 beds.

Social Security. In 1995 there were 1,232,000 persons receiving $893·4m. in social security benefits. Of that number 819,000 were retired (receiving $682 a month); 206,000 were disabled ($651 a month); and there were 206,000 others.

Further Reading

Statistical information: Office of State Planning, 116 West Jones St., Raleigh 27603. Publishes *Statistical Abstract of North Carolina Counties.*
North Carolina Manual. Secretary of State. Raleigh. Biennial
Clay, J. W. *et al* (eds.), *North Carolina Atlas: Portrait of a Changing Southern State.* Univ. of North Carolina Press, 1975
Corbitt, D. L., *The Formation of the North Carolina Counties.* Raleigh, 1969
Fleer, J. D., *North Carolina: Government and Population.* Univ. of Nebraska Press, 1995
Lefler, H. T. and Newsome, A. R., *North Carolina: The History of a Southern State.* Univ. of North Carolina Press, 1973

NORTH DAKOTA

KEY HISTORICAL EVENTS. The original inhabitants were various groups of Plains Indians. French explorers and traders were active among them in the 18th century, often operating from French possessions in Canada. France claimed the area until 1803, when it passed to the USA as part of the Louisiana Purchase, except for the north-eastern part which was held by the British until 1818.

Trading with the Indians, mainly for furs, continued until the 1860s, with American traders succeeding the French. In 1861 the Dakota Territory (North and South) was established. In 1862 the Homestead Act was passed (allowing 160 acres of public land free to any family who had worked and lived on it for 5 years) and this greatly stimulated settlement. Farming settlers came on to the wheat lands in great numbers, many of them from Canada, Norway and Germany.

Bismarck, the capital, began as a crossing-point on the Missouri and was fortified in 1872 to protect workers building the Northern Pacific Railway. There followed a gold-rush nearby, and the town became a service centre for prospectors. In 1899 North and South Dakota were admitted to the Union as separate states, and Bismarck became the Northern capital. The largest city is Fargo which was also a railway town, named after William George Fargo the express-company founder.

The population grew rapidly until 1890 and steadily until 1930 by which time it was about one-third European in parentage. Between 1930 and 1970 there was a steady population drain, increasing whenever farming was affected by the extremes of the continental climate. The state is still mainly agricultural although oil was discovered in 1951.

TERRITORY AND POPULATION. North Dakota is bounded north by Canada, east by the Red River (forming a boundary with Minnesota), south by South Dakota and west by Montana. Land area, 68,994 sq. miles (178,695 sq. km). The Federal Bureau of Indian Affairs administered (1992) 841,295 acres, of which 214,006 acres were assigned to tribes. Census population, 1 April 1990, 638,800 (53·3% urban), a decrease of 2·13% since 1980. Population estimate (1996), 644,000. Births in 1994 were 8,585 (13·44 per 1,000 population); deaths, 5,887 (9·2); infant deaths, 62 (7·2 per 1,000 live births); marriages, 4,813 (7·5); divorces, 2,197 (3·4).

Population at 5 census years was:

	White	Black	Indian	Asiatic	Total	Per sq. mile
1910	569,855	617	6,486	98	577,056	8·2
1930	671,851	377	8,617	194	680,845	9·7
			All others			
1970	599,485	2,494	15,782		617,761	9·0
1980	625,557	2,568	24,692		652,717	9·5
1990	604,142	3,524	31,134		638,800	9·3

Of the total population in 1990, 318,201 were male, 340,490 were urban and 436,665 were 21 years old or older. Estimated outward migration, 1980–90, 110 per 1,000 population.

The largest cities are Fargo with population, census 1990, of 74,111; Grand Forks, 49,425; Bismarck (capital), 49,256, and Minot, 34,544.

CLIMATE. Bismarck. Jan. 8°F (−13·3°C), July 71°F (21·1°C). Annual rainfall 16" (402 mm). Fargo. Jan. 6°F (−14·4°C), July 71°F (21·1°C). Annual rainfall 20" (503 mm). North Dakota belongs to the High Plains climate zone (see UNITED STATES: Climate).

CONSTITUTION AND GOVERNMENT. The present constitution dates from 1889; it has had 95 amendments. The Legislative Assembly consists of a Senate of 53 members elected for 4 years, and a House of Representatives of 106 members elected for 4 years. The Governor and Lieut.-Governor are elected for 4 years.

The state sends 1 representative to Congress.

In the 1996 presidential election Dole polled 125,050 votes; Clinton, 106,905; Perot, 32,515.

The capital is Bismarck. The state has 53 organized counties.

Governor: Edward Schafer (R.), 1997–2001 ($71,005).
Lieut.-Governor: Rosemarie Myrdal (R.) ($57,338).
Secretary of State: Alvin A. Jaeger (R.) ($53,843).

FINANCE. For 1994 the total revenues were $2,289m. (general revenues $2,010m.). Total expenditure was $2,083m. (general expenditure $1,886m.), including: education, $722·4 million; public welfare, 365·4m.; highways, $236·3m.

Per capita personal income (1995) was $18,663.

NATURAL RESOURCES

Minerals. The mineral resources of North Dakota consist chiefly of oil which was discovered in 1951. Production of crude petroleum in 1990 was 35,895,278 bbls; of natural gas (1991), 54·8m. cu. ft. Output of lignite coal in 1991 was 26·3m. tons. Total value of mineral output, 1991, $1,016,622,000.

Agriculture. Agriculture is the chief pursuit of the population. In 1996 there were some 31,000 farms (61,963 in 1954) with an area of 40·3m. acres. In 1994 per farm net farm income was $26,838. In 1994 the average value of farmland and buildings per acre was $409.

Cash income, 1993, from crops, $2,264·1m. and from livestock, $770·8m. In 1993, North Dakota led in the production of barley, sunflowers, flaxseed, spring wheat, durum wheat and oats. Other important products are navy beans, all beans, pinto beans, all wheat, rye and honey.

The state has also an active livestock industry, chiefly cattle raising. Livestock, 1996: Cattle, 1·9m.; pigs, 0·28m.; sheep, 125,000; poultry, 270,000.

Forestry. Forest area, 1990, 0·46m. acres.

INDUSTRY. In Oct. 1996, 43,700 persons were employed in production and 272,900 in services.

COMMUNICATIONS

Roads. In 1995 there were 86,830 miles of highway, of which 85,010 were rural. Motor vehicle registrations in 1995 numbered 695,000.

Railways. In 1994 there were 4,143 miles of railway.

Civil Aviation. In 1994 there were 100 public airports and 350 private airports.

SOCIAL INSTITUTIONS

Justice. The state penitentiary had an average daily population of 677 inmates in June 1995. The Missouri River Correctional Center is a minimum custody institution. There is no death penalty.

Religion. Church membership totalled 484,628 in 1990. The leading religious denominations were: Combined Lutherans, 179,711 members; Roman Catholics, 173,432; Methodists, 23,850; Presbyterians, 11,960.

Education. School attendance is compulsory between the ages of 7 and 16, or until the 17th birthday if the eighth grade has not been completed. In 1995–96 the public elementary schools had 81,798 pupils; secondary schools, 36,755 pupils. State expenditure per pupil in elementary and secondary schools, 1994, $4,497. Teachers (4,208 in elementary and 2,208 in secondary schools in 1994) earned an average $25,506 in 1993–94 school year.

The University of North Dakota in Grand Forks, founded in 1883, had 11,499 students in autumn 1994; North Dakota State University in Fargo, 9,665 students. Total enrolment in the 11 public institutions of higher education, autumn 1995, 35,199; in the 2 private, 2,911.

Health. In 1994 the state had 46 general hospitals (3,571 beds), and 86 nursing facilities (7,125 beds).

Social Security. In 1992, 113,810 people received $736m. in SSI payments. Monthly average, 18,300 recipients.

Further Reading

Statistical information: Bureau of Business and Economic Research, Univ. of North Dakota, Grand Forks 58202. Publishes *Statistical Abstract of North Dakota.*
North Dakota Blue Book. Secretary of State. Bismarck
Glaab, C. L. et al, *The North Dakota Political Tradition.* Iowa State Univ. Press, 1981
Jelliff, T. B., *North Dakota: A Living Legacy.* Fargo, 1983
Robinson, E. B., *History of North Dakota.* Univ. of Nebraska Press, 1966

OHIO

KEY HISTORICAL EVENTS. The land was inhabited by Delaware, Miami, Shawnee and Wyandot Indians. It was explored by French and British traders in the 18th century and confirmed as part of British North America in 1763. After the War of Independence it became part of the Northwest Territory of the new United States. Former American soldiers of the war came in from New England in 1788 and made the first permanent white settlement at Marietta, at the confluence of the Ohio and Muskingum rivers. In 1803 Ohio was separated from the rest of the Territory and admitted to the Union as the 17th state.

During the early 19th century there was steady immigration from Europe, mainly of Germans, Swiss, Irish and Welsh. Industrial growth began from the processing of local farm, forest and mining products; it increased rapidly with the need to supply the Union armies in the Civil War of 1861–65.

As the industrial cities grew, so immigration began again, with many whites from eastern Europe and the Balkans and blacks from the southern states looking for work in Ohio.

Cleveland, which developed rapidly as a Lake Erie port after the opening of commercial waterways to the interior and the Atlantic coast (1825, 1830 and 1855), became an iron-and-steel town during the Civil War.

TERRITORY AND POPULATION. Ohio is bounded north by Michigan and Lake Erie, east by Pennsylvania, south-east and south by the Ohio River (forming a boundary with West Virginia and Kentucky) and west by Indiana. Land area, 40,952 sq. miles (106,067 sq. km). Census population, 1 April 1990, 10,847,115 (74·1% urban), an increase of 89,695 or 0·8% since 1980. Population estimate (1996), 11,173,000. In 1994 births numbered 155,944 (14·0 per 1,000 population); deaths, 103,000 (9·3); in 1993 infant deaths numbered 1,444 (9·1 per 1,000 live births); still-births, 1,204 (7·6 per 1,000 live births); marriages, 88,796 (8·2); divorces, 51,070 (4·7).

Population at 6 census years was:

	White	Black	Indian	Asiatic	Total	Per sq. mile
1910	4,654,897	111,452	127	645	4,767,121	117·0
1930	6,335,173	309,304	435	1,785	6,646,697	161·6
1960	8,909,698	786,097	1,910	8,692	9,706,397	236·9
			All others			
1970	9,646,997	970,477	34,543		10,652,017	260·0
1980	9,597,458	1,076,748	123,424		10,797,630	263·2
1990	9,521,756	1,154,826	170,533		10,847,115	264·5

Of the total population in 1990, 5,226,340 were male. Those 18 years old or older numbered 8,047,371 in 1990.

Census population of chief cities on 1 April 1990 was:

Columbus	632,910	Dayton	182,044	Springfield	70,487
Cleveland	505,616	Youngstown	95,753	Hamilton	61,368
Cincinnati	364,040	Parma	87,876	Kettering	60,569
Toledo	332,943	Canton	84,161	Lakewood	59,718
Akron	223,019	Lorain	71,245	Elyria	56,746

Euclid	54,875	Middletown	46,022	Upper Arlington	34,128
Cleveland Heights	54,052	Lima	45,549	Marion	34,075
Warren	50,793	Newark	44,389	East Cleveland	33,096
Mansfield	50,627	Lancaster	34,507	Garfield Heights	31,793
Cuyahoga Falls	48,950	North Olmsted	34,204	Zanesville	26,788
Mentor	47,358				

Urbanized areas, 1990 census: Cleveland, 1,831,122; Cincinnati, 1,452,645; Columbus (the capital), 1,377,419; Dayton, 951,270; Akron, 657,575; Toledo, 614,128; Youngstown-Warren, 492,619; Canton, 394,106.

CLIMATE. Cincinnati. Jan. 39·1°F, July 77·1°F). Annual rainfall 43·82". Cleveland. Jan. 35°F, July 72·4°F. Annual rainfall 43·9". Columbus. Jan. 36·6°F, July 73·9°F. Annual rainfall 43·76". Ohio belongs to the Great Lakes climate zone (*see* UNITED STATES: Climate).

CONSTITUTION AND GOVERNMENT. The question of a general revision of the constitution drafted by an elected convention is submitted to the people every 20 years. The constitution of 1851 had 142 amendments by 1994.

The Senate consists of 33 members and the House of Representatives of 99 members. The Senate is elected for 4 years, half each 2 years; the House is elected for 2 years; the Governor, Lieut.-Governor and Secretary of State for 4 years. Qualified as electors are (with necessary exceptions) all citizens 18 years of age who have the usual residential qualifications. Ohio sends 19 representatives to Congress.

In the 1996 presidential election Clinton polled 2,099,395 votes; Dole, 1,821,750; Perot, 470,461.

The capital (since 1816) is Columbus. Ohio is divided into 88 counties.

Governor: George Voinovich (R.), 1995–99 ($115,763).
Lieut.-Governor: Nancy Hollister (R.) ($59,861).
Secretary of State: Bob Taft (R.) ($85,517).

BUDGET. For 1997 general revenue fund income was $16,682,733,000 and expenditure $14,071,794,000.

The bonded debt in 1997 was $5,367,341.
Per capita personal income (1995) was $22,514.

NATURAL RESOURCES

Minerals. Ohio has extensive mineral resources, of which coal is the most important by value: Output (1996) 28,323,773 short tons. Other 1996 figures included: crude petroleum, 8,305,366 bbls; natural gas, 120,443,871 cu. ft. Production of other minerals (in short tons), 1996: Limestone and dolomite, 69,098,412; sand and gravel, 52,767,008; salt, 4,885,957.

Agriculture. Ohio is extensively devoted to agriculture. In 1996, about 72,000 farms covered 15·1m. acres; average farm value per acre, $1,800 in 1995. In 1995 the average size of farm was 205 acres.

Cash income 1996, from crop and livestock and products, $5,063·5m. The most important crops in 1996 were: Maize (305m. bu.), wheat (51·9m. bu.), oats (5·1m. bu.), soybeans (157m. bu.). In 1996 there were 1·8m. pigs, 1·54m. cattle and 153,000 sheep.

Forestry. State forest area, 1997, 180,905 acres. In 1997 there were 72 state parks covering 262,919 acres.

INDUSTRY. In 1995, 18,647 manufacturing establishments employed 1,098,660 persons out of a total workforce of 4,550,690. The largest industries were manufacturing of transport equipment, industrial machinery and equipment, and fabricated metal products.

COMMUNICATIONS

Roads. In 1995 there were 114,563 miles of roads and 9·81m. registered motor vehicles.

Railways. In 1994 there were 6,458 miles of track used by 4 Class I freight railways, 1 regional railway and several short line railways. Amtrak also serves parts of Ohio.

Civil Aviation. In 1994 there were 8 major passenger airports and 1 cargo airport. There were also 177 public use general aviation airports and 28 heliports. There were 13·4m. passenger emplanements in 1991.

SOCIAL INSTITUTIONS

Justice. On 30 June 1995 there were 39,799 inmates in adult correctional institutions. The death penalty is authorized; the last execution was in 1963.

Religion. Many religious faiths are represented, including (but not limited to) the Baptist, Jewish, Lutheran, Methodist, Moslem, Orthodox, Presbyterian and Roman Catholic.

Education. School attendance during full term is compulsory for children from 6 to 18 years of age. In 1994–95 public schools had 1,827,624 enrolled pupils and 103,929 full-time equivalent classroom teachers. Teachers' salaries (1994) averaged $36,968. Operating expenditure on elementary and secondary schools for 1994 was $4,429m., 31·3% of the state budget. Universities and colleges had a total enrolment (1995) of 307,008 students. State appropriation to state universities 1990–91, $1,711,034. Average annual charge (undergraduate) at 4-year institutions: $3,405 (state); $11,782 (private).

Main campuses, 1996:

Founded	Institutions	Enrolments
1804	Ohio University, Athens (State)	19,729
1809	Miami University, Oxford (State)	15,723
1819	University of Cincinnati (State)	22,795
1826	Case Western Reserve University, Cleveland	9,569
1850	University of Dayton (R.C.)	1,709
1870	University of Akron (State)	15,847
1870	Ohio State University, Columbus (State)	44,428
1872	University of Toledo (State)	17,029
1908	Youngstown University (State)	9,547
1910	Bowling Green State University (State)	15,147
1910	Kent State University (State)	16,243
1964	Cleveland State University (State)	10,905
1964	Wright State University (State)	10,958
1986	Shawnee State University, Portsmouth (State)	2,778

(Figures for Case Western Reserve University and University of Dayton are for 1994 enrolments)

Health. In 1997 the state had 210 hospitals listed by the American Hospital Association with 43,317 beds. State facilities for the severely mentally retarded had 12 developmental centres serving 1,431 residents.

Social Security. Public assistance is administered through 7 basic programmes (with number of recipients as at June 1996): Aid to dependent children (518,395), family emergency assistance (8,449), Medicaid, 1995 (807,523), food stamps (1,009,599) and foster care (18,590).

In the fiscal year 1994–95 Medicaid cost $5,417·2m. Aid to dependent children cost $856m. Food stamps cost $1,029·6m. General assistance cost $57m. Optional State Supplement is paid to aged, blind or disabled adults. Free social services are available to those eligible by income or circumstances.

Further Reading

Official Roster: Federal, State, County Officers and Department Information. Secretary of State, Columbus. Biennial

Rosebloom, E. H. and Weisenburger, F. P., *A History of Ohio.* Columbus, State Archive and Historical Society, 1953

Shkurti, W. J. and Bartle, J. (eds.) *Benchmark Ohio.* Ohio State Univ. Press, 1991

OKLAHOMA

KEY HISTORICAL EVENTS. Francisco Coronado led a Spanish expedition in 1541, claiming the land for Spain. There were several Indian groups, but no strong political unit. In 1714 Juchereau de Saint Denis made the first French contact. During the 18th century French fur-traders were active, and France and Spain struggled for control, a struggle which was resolved by the French withdrawal in 1763. France returned briefly in 1800–03, and the territory then passed to the USA as part of the Louisiana Purchase.

In 1828 the Federal Government set aside the area of the present state as Indian Territory, that is, a reservation and sanctuary for Indian tribes who had been driven off their lands elsewhere by white settlement. About 70 tribes came, among whom were Creeks, Choctaws and Cherokees from the south-eastern states, and Plains Indians.

In 1889 the government took back about 2·5m. acres of the Territory and opened it to white settlement. About 10,000 homesteaders gathered at the site of Oklahoma City on the Santa Fe Railway in the rush to stake their land claims. The settlers' area, and others subsequently opened to settlement, were organized as the Oklahoma Territory in 1890. In 1907 the Oklahoma and Indian Territories were combined and admitted to the Union as a state. Indian reservations were established within the state.

The economy first depended on ranching and farming, with packing stations on the railways. A mining industry grew in the 1870s attracting foreign immigration, mainly from Europe. In 1901 oil was found near Tulsa, and the industry grew rapidly.

TERRITORY AND POPULATION. Oklahoma is bounded north by Kansas, north-east by Missouri, east by Arkansas, south by Texas (the Red River forming part of the boundary) and, at the western extremity of the 'panhandle', by New Mexico and Colorado. Land area, 68,679 sq. miles (177,877 sq. km). Census population, 1 April 1990, 3,189,456 (67·7% urban), an increase of 5·42% since 1980. Population estimate (1996), 3,301,000. Births, 1994, 46,711 (14·8 per 1,000 population); deaths, 32,574 (10·3); marriages, 30,495 (9·7); divorces, 22,784 (7·2). Infant deaths, 1992, 450 (9·6 per 1,000 live births).

The population at 5 federal censuses was:

	White	Black	Indian	Other	Total	Per sq. mile
1930	2,130,778	172,198	92,725	339	2,396,040	34·6
1960	2,107,900	153,084	68,689	1,414	2,328,284	33·8
1970	2,280,362	171,892	97,179	10,030	2,559,253	37·2
1980	2,597,783	204,658	169,292	53,557	3,025,486	43·2
1990	2,583,512	233,801	252,420	119,723	3,189,456	44·5

In 1980, 1,476,719 were male, 2,035,082 were urban and those 20 years of age or older numbered 2,052,729. The US Bureau of Indian Affairs is responsible for 1,097,004 acres (1990), of which 96,839 acres were allotted to tribes.

The most important cities with population, 1990 are Oklahoma City (capital), 444,719; Tulsa, 367,302; Lawton, 80,561; Norman, 80,071; Broken Arrow, 58,043; Edmond, 52,315; Midwest City, 52,267; Enid, 45,309; Moore, 40,318; Muskogee, 37,708; Stillwater, 36,676; Bartlesville, 34,252.

CLIMATE. 1988: Oklahoma City. Jan. 34·2°F (1·2°C), July 81·6°F (27·5°C). Annual rainfall 31·94" (8,113 mm). Tulsa. Jan. 34·8°F (1·5°C), July 82·6°F (27·5°C). Annual rainfall 33·22" (8,438 mm). Oklahoma belongs to the Central Plains climate zone (*see* UNITED STATES: Climate).

CONSTITUTION AND GOVERNMENT. The constitution, dating from 1907, provides for amendment by initiative petition and legislative referendum; it has had 155 amendments (as of Jan. 1995).

The Legislature consists of a Senate of 48 members, who are elected for 4 years, and a House of Representatives elected for 2 years and consisting of 101 members. The Governor and Lieut.-Governor are elected for 4-year terms; the Governor can only be elected for two terms in succession. Electors are (with necessary exceptions) all citizens 18 years or older, with the usual qualifications.

The state sends 6 representatives to Congress.

In the 1996 presidential election Dole polled 582,310 votes; Clinton, 488,102; Perot, 130,788.

The capital is Oklahoma City. The state has 77 counties.

Governor: Frank Keating (R.), 1995–99 ($70,000).
Lieut.-Governor: Mary Fallin (R.) ($62,500).
Secretary of State: Tom J. Cole (R.) ($43,700).

BUDGET. Total revenue for the year ending 30 June 1994 was $7,851,967,335. Total expenditure, $7,424,444,072.

General obligation debt, 1994, was $414·82m.

Per capita personal income (1995) was $18,152.

NATURAL RESOURCES

Minerals. Production of mineral fuels, 1993: Petroleum, 97m. bbls of oil; natural gas, 2,020,000m. cu. ft.; coal, 1,796,000m. tons. At the end of 1993 there were 122,094 oil and gas wells in production. Value of leading non-fuel minerals produced in 1993 (in $1m.): Crushed stone, 111; cement, 59; sand and gravel, 27; iodine, 20; glass sand, 18; gypsum, 16. Other principal minerals are helium, clay and sand; other minerals include zinc, lead, granite, tripoli, bentonite, lime and volcanic ash. Total value of non-fuel mineral production, 1993, $282m.

Agriculture. In 1996 the state had some 72,000 farms and ranches with a total area of 34m. acres; average size was 472 acres; average value per acre was $494. Area harvested, 1992, 8,272,889 acres. Livestock, 1992: Cattle, 4,736,594; sheep and lambs, 103,732; hogs and pigs, 260,682.

Market value of agricultural products sold, 1992: Crops, $778·8m.; livestock, poultry and products, $2,783·8m. The major cash grain is winter wheat (value, 1990, $492m.). In 1992, 138,121,986 bu. of wheat for grain were harvested from 5,197,545 acres. Other crops include barley, oats, rye, grain, corn, soybeans, grain sorghum, cotton, peanuts and peaches. Value of cattle and calves produced, 1990, $3,080m.; catfish, $1m.; racehorses, $63m.

The Oklahoma Conservation Commission works with 91 conservation districts, universities, state and federal government agencies. The early work of the conservation districts, beginning in 1937, was limited to flood and erosion control: since 1970, they include urban areas also.

Irrigated production has increased in the Oklahoma 'panhandle'. The Ogalala aquifer is the primary source of irrigation water there and in western Oklahoma, a finite source because of its isolation from major sources of recharge. Declining groundwater levels necessitate the most effective irrigation practices.

Forestry. There are 7·5m. acres of forest, one half considered commercial. The forest products industry is concentrated in the 118 eastern counties. There are 3 forest regions: Ozark (oak, hickory); Ouachita highlands (pine, oak); Cross-Timbers (post oak, black jack oak). Southern pine is the chief commercial species, at almost 80% of saw-timber harvested annually. Replanting is essential.

INDUSTRY. In 1994 there were 3,858 industrial firms: Major commodities produced include transportation equipment (accounting for 15·3% of manufactured goods), petroleum and coal products (14·1%), non-electrical machinery (12·2%), food products (9·7%), electronic and electrical equipment (9·2%).

Labour. Total non-agricultural labour force, 1996, 1,354,000, including: manufacturing, 174,000; construction, 50,000.

TOURISM. There are 72 state parks and 10 museums and monuments. Tourists spend some $3,000m. annually.

COMMUNICATIONS

Roads. In 1995 there were 112,035 miles of roads and in 1991, 2,669,312 registered motor vehicles.

Railways. In 1995 Oklahoma had 3,867 miles of railway operated by 21 companies.

Civil Aviation. Airports, 1995, numbered 421, of which 127 were publicly owned. 5 cities were served by commercial airlines.

Shipping. The McClellan-Kerr Arkansas Navigation System provides access from east central Oklahoma to New Orleans through the Verdigris, Arkansas and Mississippi rivers. In 1991, 63m. tons were shipped inbound and outbound on the Oklahoma Segment. Commodities shipped, 1989 were mainly chemical fertilizer, farm produce, petroleum products, iron and steel, coal, sand and gravel.

Telecommunications. In 1995 there were 172 radio and 25 television broadcasting stations, and 16 cable-TV companies.

Press. In 1995 there were 49 daily and, in 1990, 190 weekly newspapers.

SOCIAL INSTITUTIONS

Justice. There were 16,631 prisoners in state correctional institutions in 1994. In 1990 there were 15 penal institutions, 8 community treatment centres and 7 probation and parole centres.

The death penalty was suspended in 1966 and re-imposed in 1976. The last execution was in 1995.

Religion. The chief religious bodies are: Baptists, 674,766 members; United Methodists, 248,635; Roman Catholics, 122,820; Churches of Christ, about 80,000; Assembly of God, 63,992; Disciples of Christ, 45,070; Presbyterian, 38,605; Lutheran, 33,664; Nazarene, 22,090; Episcopal, 21,500.

Education. In 1991 there were over 0·61m. pupils enrolled in grades Kindergarten–12. In 1994–95 there were 609,800 pupils and 39,290 teachers at public elementary and secondary school. The average teacher salary per annum was $28,928. In 1992 total expenditure on the 554 school districts was $2,146,698,604. There were 32,945 students enrolled in 1992.

Institutions of higher education include:

Founded	Name	Place	1994 Enrolment
1890	University of Oklahoma	Norman	21,373
1890	Oklahoma State University	Stillwater	18,290
1890	University of Central Oklahoma	Edmond	16,039
1894	The University of Tulsa	Tulsa	4,579
1897	Northeastern State University	Tahlequah	9,374
1897	Northwestern Oklahoma State University	Alva	1,870
1897	Southwestern Oklahoma State University	Weatherford	5,289
1908	Cameron University	Lawton	5,863
1909	East Central University	Ada	4,468
1909	Southeastern Oklahoma State University	Durant	4,104
1909	Rogers State College	Claremore	3,404
1950	Oklahoma Christian University of Science and Arts	Oklahoma City	1,505
1969	Rose State College	Midwest City	9,234
1970	Tulsa Junior College	Tulsa	21,055
1972	Oklahoma City Community College	Oklahoma City	11,185

Health. In 1995 there were 110 community hospitals with 11,500 beds.

Welfare. In 1990–91 the Oklahoma Department of Human Services provided for medical services, $828·33m.; assistance payments and services, $321·94m.; field services, $20,167,000; Oklahoma Medical Center, $183,099,000; children and youth services, $102·55m.; mentally retarded and developmental disability, $53,849,000; rehabilitation, $137,392,000; the ageing, $30,597,000; administration, $36,452,000;

management information, $16,432,000; construction and special projects, $9,708,000.

In 1988–89, payments and benefits were: Grants and energy, $184,399,170; medical payments, $685,839,185; food stamps and commodities, $181,185,160; payroll and rent, $353,472,861; day care, $18,918,539. In 1990 there were 401,000 military veterans.

Further Reading

Center for Economic and Management Research, Univ. of Oklahoma, 307 West Brooks St., Norman 73019. *Statistical Abstract of Oklahoma.*
Oklahoma Department of Libraries. *Oklahoma Almanac.* Biennial
Gibson, A. M., *The History of Oklahoma.* Rev. ed. Oklahoma Univ. Press, 1984
Morris, J. W. *et al., Historical Atlas of Oklahoma.* 3rd ed. Oklahoma Univ. Press, 1986
Strain, J. W., *Outline of Oklahoma Government.* Rev. ed. Central State Univ., 1983

State library: Oklahoma Department of Libraries, 200 Northeast 18th Street, Oklahoma City 73105.

OREGON

KEY HISTORICAL EVENTS. The area was divided between many Indian groups including the Chinook, Tillamook, Cayuse and Modoc. In the 18th century English and Spanish visitors tried to establish national claims, based on explorations of the 16th century. The USA also laid claim by right of discovery when an expedition entered the mouth of the Columbia River in 1792.

Oregon was disputed between Britain and the USA. An American fur company established a trading settlement at Astoria in 1811, which the British took in 1812. The Hudson Bay Company were the most active force in Oregon until the 1830s when American pioneers began to migrate westwards along the Oregon Trail. The dispute between Britain and the USA was resolved in 1846 with the boundary fixed at 49°N. lat. Oregon was organized as a Territory in 1848 but with wider boundaries; it became a state with its present boundaries in 1859.

Early settlers were mainly American. They came to farm in the Willamette Valley and to exploit the western forests. Portland developed as a port for ocean-going traffic, although it was 100 miles inland at the confluence of the Willamette and Columbia rivers. Industries followed when the railways came and the rivers were exploited for hydro-electricity. The capital of the Territory from 1851 was Salem, a mission for Indians on the Willamette river; it was confirmed as state capital in 1864. Salem became the processing centre for the farming and market-gardening Willamette Valley.

TERRITORY AND POPULATION. Oregon is bounded in the north by Washington, with the Columbia River forming most of the boundary, east by Idaho, with the Snake River forming most of the boundary, south by Nevada and California and west by the Pacific. Land area, 97,060 sq. miles (251,385 sq. km). The federal government owned (1994) 32,132,581 acres (51·73% of the state area). Census population, 1 April 1990, 2,842,321 (70·5% urban), an increase of 8% since 1980. Population estimate (1996), 3,204,000. In 1994 births numbered 41,837 (13·6 per 1,000 population); deaths, 27,000 (8·9); in 1992 infant deaths numbered 297 (7 per 1,000 live births); marriages, 24,866 (8·3), and divorces, 16,067 (5·4).

Population at 5 federal censuses was:

	White	Black	Indian	Asiatic	Total	Per sq. mile
1930	938,598	2,234	4,776	8,179	953,786	9·9
1960	1,732,037	18,133	8,026	9,120	1,768,687	18·4
1970	2,032,079	26,308	13,510	13,290	2,091,385	21·7
1980	2,490,610	37,060	27,314	34,775	2,633,105	27·3
1990	2,636,787	48,178	38,496	69,269	2,842,321	29·6

Of the total population in 1990, 1,397,073 were male. In 1980 1,788,354 persons were urban, and those 18 years and older numbered 1,910,048.

The US Bureau of Indian Affairs (area headquarters in Portland) administers (1994) 783,227·13 acres, of which 627,615·54 acres are held by the USA in trust for Indian tribes and 138,950·05 acres for individual Indians, and 16,661·54 acres of mineral tracts.

The largest towns, according to 1990 census figures, are: Portland, 437,319; Eugene, 112,669; Salem (the capital), 107,786; Gresham, 68,235; Beaverton, 55,310; Medford, 46,951; Corvallis, 44,757; Springfield, 44,683; Albany, 29,462. Metropolitan areas (1990): Portland, 577,571; Eugene-Springfield, 199,009; Salem, 162,887.

CLIMATE. Jan. 32°F (0°C), July 66°F (19°C). Annual rainfall 28" (710 mm). Oregon belongs to the Pacific coast climate zone (*see* UNITED STATES: Climate).

CONSTITUTION AND GOVERNMENT. The present constitution dates from 1859; some 250 items in it have been amended. The Legislative Assembly consists of a Senate of 30 members, elected for 4 years (half their number retiring every 2 years), and a House of 60 representatives, elected for 2 years. The Governor is elected for 4 years. The constitution reserves to the voters the rights of initiative and referendum and recall.

The state sends 5 representatives to Congress.

In the 1996 presidential election Clinton polled 325,225 votes; Dole, 255,452; Perot, 73,011.

The capital is Salem. There are 36 counties in the state.

Governor: John Kitzhaber (D.), 1995–99 ($80,000).
Secretary of State: Phil Keisling (D.) ($61,500).

BUDGET. Oregon has 2-year financial periods. The total budget for the biennium 1993–95 was $20,016·8m. (federal funds, $3,370m.; general funds, $6,400m.). Budget allocations 1993–95 were: Education, $6,170m.; economic and community development, $3,808m.; human resources, $4,362m.

In 1991 the outstanding debt was $6,451m.

Per capita personal income (1995) was $21,736.

NATURAL RESOURCES

Minerals. Mineral resources include gold, silver, nickel copper, lead, mercury, chromite, sand and gravel, stone, clays, lime, silica, diatomite, expansible shale, scoria, pumice and uranium. There is geothermal potential. Mineral production value (1993), $233·5m.

Agriculture. Oregon, which has an area of 61,557,184 acres, is divided by the Cascade Range into two distinct zones as to climate. West of the Cascade Range there is a good rainfall and almost every variety of crop common to the temperate zone is grown; east of the Range stock-raising and wheat-growing are the principal industries and irrigation is needed for row crops and fruits. In 1993 the monthly average employed in agriculture was 22,500.

There were, in 1996, 39,000 farms with an acreage of 18m.; average farm size was 455 acres; most are family-owned corporate farms. Average value per acre (1995), $844.

Cash receipts from crops in 1992 amounted to $1,657·05m. and from livestock and livestock products, $795·31m. of which cattle made most. Principal crops: Greenhouse and nursery products ($415·8m.), hay ($104·4m.), farmforest products, wheat, potatoes, grass seed (ryegrass and fescue), Christmas trees, pears, onions ($255·8m.).

Livestock, 1 Jan. 1993: Milk cows (1992), 0·1m.; cattle and calves, 1·4m.; sheep and lambs, 415,000; swine (1992), 75,000.

Forestry. About 28·2m. acres is forested, almost half of the state. Of this amount, 22·4m. is commercial forest land suitable for timber production; ownership is as follows (acres): US Forestry Service, 13·1m.; US Bureau of Land Management,

2·7m.; other federal, 165,000; State of Oregon, 907,000; other public (city, county), 123,000; private owners, 10·8m., of which the forest industry owns 5·8m., non-industrial private owners, 4·6m., Indians, 399,000. Oregon's commercial forest lands provided a 1992 harvest of 5,742m. bd ft of logs, as well as the benefits of recreation, water, grazing, wildlife and fish. Trees vary from the coastal forest of hemlock and spruce to the state's primary species, Douglas-fir, throughout much of western Oregon. In eastern Oregon, ponderosa pine, lodgepole pine and true firs are found. Here, forestry is often combined with livestock grazing to provide an economic operation. Along the Cascade summit and in the mountains of north-east Oregon, alpine species are found.

Total covered payroll in lumber and wood products industry in 1991 was $1,475m.

Fisheries. All food and shellfish landings in the calendar year 1992 amounted to a value of $74·4m. The most important are: Ground fish, shrimp, crab, tuna, salmon.

INDUSTRY. Forest products manufacturing is Oregon's leading industry, and in 1992 employed 64,000. The second most important industry is high technology. Gross State product, 1991, $50,618m. Manufacturing employed 208,831 in 1992; trade, 328,824; services, 295,006; government, 214,659.

TOURISM. In 1992, the total income from tourism was estimated to be $3,100m.

COMMUNICATIONS

Roads. There were 83,944 miles of highway in 1995, of which 73,789 miles were rural. Registered vehicles, also 1995, totalled 2,785,000.

Railways. The state had (1994) 21 railways with a total mileage of 2,572 (4,115 km). There is a light rail network in Portland.

Civil Aviation. In 1994 there were 1 public-use and 93 personal-use heliports; 248 personal-use and 101 public-use airports of which 34 were state-owned airports, and 2 sea-plane bases, 1 public-use and 1 personal-use.

Shipping. Portland is a major seaport for large ocean-going vessels and is 101 miles inland from the mouth of the Columbia River. In 1993 Portland handled 11·7m. short tons of cargo and other Columbia River ports 13·7m. short tons, the main commodities being grain, petroleum and wood products; the ports of Coos Bay and Newport handled 2·7m. short tons of cargo, chiefly logs, lumber and wood products.

Telecommunications. In 1996 there were 194 commercial radio stations and 37 educational radio stations. There were 24 commercial television stations and 26 educational television stations. There were also 24 cable companies.

Press. In 1996 there were 21 daily newspapers with a circulation of more than 676,000 and 111 non-daily newspapers.

SOCIAL INSTITUTIONS

Justice. There are 12 correctional institutions in Oregon. Total inmates, Sept. 1994, 6,669, including those in treatment in mental hospitals. The sterilization law, originally passed in 1917, was amended in 1967 and abolished in 1993. Some categories of euthanasia were legalized in Dec. 1994.

The death penalty is authorized.

Religion. The chief religious bodies are Catholic, Baptist, Lutheran, Methodists, Presbyterian and Mormon.

Education. School attendance is compulsory from 7 to 18 years of age if the twelfth year of school has not been completed; those between the ages of 16 and 18 years, if legally employed, may attend part-time or evening schools. Others may be excused under certain circumstances. In 1994–95 the public elementary and secondary schools had 521,000 students and 27,000 teachers. Total expenditure on elementary and secondary education (1993–94) was $2,492,796,476; teachers' average salary (1993–94), $37,589.

Leading state-supported institutions of higher education (1993–94) included:

	Students
University of Oregon, Eugene	16,680
Oregon Health Sciences University	1,396
Oregon State University, Corvallis	14,131
Portland State University, Portland	14,428
Western Oregon State College, Monmouth	3,871
Southern Oregon State College, Ashland	4,535
Eastern Oregon State College, La Grande	1,931
Oregon Institute of Technology, Klamath Falls	2,444

Total enrolment in state colleges and universities, in autumn 1994, 164,447. Largest of the privately endowed universities are Lewis and Clark College, Portland, with 3,132 students (1993–94); University of Portland, 2,700 students; Willamette University, Salem, 2,451 students; Reed College, Portland, 1,277 students; Linfield College, McMinnville, 2,354 students; Marylhurst College, 1,183 students and George Fox College, 1,557 students. In 1993–94 there were 314,926 students (full-time equivalent) in community colleges.

Health. In 1995 there were 73 licensed hospitals, 2 state hospitals for the mentally ill (798 beds), 1 for the mentally retarded (400) and 1 with both programmes (133). There were 64 community hospitals with 7,200 beds.

Social Security. The State Adult and Family Services Division provides cash payments, medical care, food stamps, day care and help in finding jobs. As of July 1994 there were an estimated 495,000 people on low incomes. Many of them were children in single-parent families, benefiting from the Aid to Families with Dependent Children Programme; 282,500 people were receiving food stamps; an estimated 376,000 were below the poverty level. There is also a Children's Services Division.

A system of unemployment benefit payments, financed by employers, with administrative allotments made through a federal agency, started in 1938.

Further Reading

Oregon Blue Book. Issued by the Secretary of State. Salem. Biennial

Carey, C. H., *General History of Oregon, prior to 1861.* 2 vol. (1 vol. reprint, 1971) Portland, 1935

Conway, F. D. L., *Timber in Oregon: History and Projected Trends.* Oregon State Univ., 1993

Corning, H. M. (ed.), *Dictionary of Oregon History.* Rev. ed. New York, 1989

Dicken, E. F. and S. N., *Oregon Divided: A Regional Geography.* Portland, 1982

Dodds, G. B., *Oregon: A Bicentennial History.* New York, 1977.—*American North-West: a History of Oregon and Washington.* Arlington Heights, (Ill.), 1986

Friedman, R., *The Other Side of Oregon.* Caldwell (ID), 1993

Highsmith, R. M. Jr. (ed.), *Atlas of the Pacific Northwest.* Rev. ed. Corvallis, 1985

McArthur, L. A., *Oregon Geographic Names.* 6th ed., rev. and enlarged. Portland, 1992

Orr, E. L. *et al., Geology of Oregon.* Dubuque (IA), 1992

Patton, Clyde P., *Atlas of Oregon.* Univ. Oregon Press, Eugene, 1976

Ronda, J. P., *Astoria and Empire.* Univ. of Nebraska Press, 1990

State Library: The Oregon State Library, Salem.

PENNSYLVANIA

KEY HISTORICAL EVENTS. Pennsylvania was occupied by 4 powerful tribes in the 17th century: Delaware, Susquehanna, Shawnee and Iroquois. The first white settlers were Swedish, arriving in 1643. The British became dominant in 1664, and in 1681 William Penn, an English Quaker, was given a charter to colonize the area as a sanctuary for his fellow Quakers. Penn's ideal was peaceful co-operation with the Indians and religious toleration within the colony. Several religious groups were attracted to Pennsylvania because of this policy, including Protestant sects from Germany and France. During the 18th century, co-operation with the Indians failed as the settlers pushed into more territory and the Indians resisted.

During the War of Independence the Declaration of Independence was signed in

Philadelphia, the main city. Pennsylvania became one of the original 13 states of the Union. In 1812 Harrisburg, which began as a trading post and ferry point on the Susquehanna river, was chosen as the state capital. The new state's southern boundary was the Mason and Dixon Line, which became the dividing line between free and slave states during the conflict leading to the Civil War. During the war crucial battles were fought in the state, including Gettysburg. Industrial growth was rapid after the war. Pittsburgh, founded as a British fort in 1761 during war with the French, had become an iron-making town by 1800 and grew rapidly when canal and railway links opened in the 1830s. The American Federation of Labor was founded in Pittsburgh in 1881, by which time the city was of national importance in producing coal, iron, steel and glass.

In the 20th century, industry attracted immigration from Italy and eastern Europe. In farming areas the early sect communities survive, notably Amish and Mennonites. (The Pennsylvania 'Dutch' are of German extraction.)

TERRITORY AND POPULATION. Pennsylvania is bounded north by New York, east by New Jersey, south by Delaware and Maryland, south-west by West Virginia, west by Ohio and north-west by Lake Erie. Land area, 44,820 sq. miles (116,083 sq. km). Census population, 1 April 1990 (68·9% urban), 11,881,643, an increase of 0·13% since 1980. Population estimate (1996), 12,056,000. Births, 1995, 150,848 (12·5 per 1,000 population); deaths, 126,524 (10·5); infant deaths, 1,164 (7·7 per 1,000 live births); marriages, 74,504 (6·2); divorces, 39,493 (3·3).

Population at 5 census years was:

	White	Black	Indian	All others	Total	Per sq. mile
1910	7,467,713	193,919	1,503	1,976	7,665,111	171·0
1930	9,196,007	431,257	523	3,563	9,631,350	213·8
1960	10,454,004	852,750	2,122	10,490	11,319,366	251·5

	White	Black	All others	Total	Per sq. mile
1980	10,652,320	1,046,810	164,765	11,863,895	264·3
1990	10,520,201	1,089,795	271,647	11,881,643	265·1

Of the total population in 1990, 47·9% were male, 68·9% were urban and 76·5% were 21 years of age or older.

The population of the larger cities and townships, 1996 estimate, was:

Philadelphia	1,478,002	Scranton	77,189	Harrisburg	50,886
Pittsburgh	350,363	Reading	75,723	Altoona	50,101
Erie	105,270	Bethlehem	71,153		
Allentown	102,211	Lancaster	53,597		

CLIMATE. Philadelphia. Jan. 32°F (0°C), July 77°F (25°C). Annual rainfall 40" (1,006 mm). Pittsburgh. Jan. 31°F (−0·6°C), July 74°F (23·3°C). Annual rainfall 37" (914 mm). Pennsylvania belongs to the Appalachian Mountains climate zone (*see* UNITED STATES: Climate).

CONSTITUTION AND GOVERNMENT. The present constitution dates from 1968. The General Assembly consists of a Senate of 50 members chosen for 4 years, one-half being elected biennially, and a House of Representatives of 203 members chosen for 2 years. The Governor and Lieut.-Governor are elected for 4 years. Every citizen 18 years of age, with the usual residential qualifications, may vote. Registered voters in May 1997, 6,943,973.

The state sends 21 representatives to Congress.

In the 1996 presidential election Clinton polled 2,206,241 votes; Dole, 1,793,568; Perot, 430,082.

The state capital is Harrisburg. The state is organized in counties (numbering 67), cities, boroughs, townships and school districts.

Governor: Tom Ridge (R.), 1995–99 ($105,000).
Lieut.-Governor: Mark Schweiker (R.), ($83,000).
Secretary of the Commonwealth: Yvette Kane (R.), ($72,000).

BUDGET. Total general fund revenues for fiscal year 1996–97 were $16,625m.; general fund expenditures, $16,416m. (including public welfare, $6,246m.).

In 1996, outstanding long-term debt was $4,827m.

Per capita personal income (1996) was $24,668.

NATURAL RESOURCES

Minerals. Pennsylvania is almost the sole producer of anthracite coal. Production, 1996: Anthracite coal, 11,573,504 tons, bituminous coal, 68,973,910 tons; crude petroleum (1992), 1·2m. bbls; natural gas (1992), 138,000m. cu. ft. Non-fuel mineral production was worth $844m. in 1991.

Agriculture. Agriculture, market-gardening, fruit-growing, horticulture and forestry are pursued within the state. In 1996 there were 50,000 farms with a total farm area of 7·7m. acres (4·5m. acres in crops in 1988). Average number of acres per farm in 1996 was 154 and average value per acre in 1996 was $2,505. Cash receipts, 1996, from crops, $1,277·9m., and from livestock and products, $2,864·6m.

In 1996, Pennsylvania ranked first in the production of mushrooms (355m. lbs, value $254·6m.). Other production figures include: corn for grain (127·3m. bu., value $337·4m.); sweet corn (1·1m. cwt) and tomatoes (660,000 cwt). Pennsylvania is also a major fruit producing state; in 1996 apples totalled 391m. lbs, peaches 75m. lbs and grapes, 79,000 tons. In 1996 milk production was 10,640m. lb.; eggs numbered 5,640m. and chicken production (except broilers), 26m.; other products included 340·6m. lb. of cheese.

On 1 Jan. 1997 there were on farms: 1·75m. cattle and calves, 94,000 sheep, and 950,000 swine.

Forestry. In 1997 state forest land totalled 2,100,000 acres; state park land, 280,916 acres; state game lands, 1,382,412 acres.

INDUSTRY. In Oct. 1997 manufacturing employed 935,000 workers; services, 1,719,400; trade, 1,244,000; government, 736,900. The total workforce was 5,460,000.

COMMUNICATIONS

Roads. Highways and roads in the state (federal, local and state combined) totalled (1996) 118,647 miles. Registered motor vehicles for 1997 numbered 9,570,491.

Railways. In 1997, 70 railways operated within the state with a line mileage of 5,379. There are metro, light rail and tramway networks in Philadelphia and Pittsburgh, and commuter networks around Philadelphia.

Civil Aviation. There were (1997) 141 public airports, 304 private and 7 public heliports, 344 airports for personal use (includes seaplane bases).

Shipping. Trade at the ports of Philadelphia (1996): Imports, 4,642,035 short tons of bulk cargo and 24,034,142 of general cargo; exports, 7,357,703 of bulk cargo and 3,526,091 of general cargo.

Telecommunications. Broadcasting stations in 1996 included 46 television stations and 450 radio stations.

Press. There were (1996) 89 daily and 339 weekly newspapers.

SOCIAL INSTITUTIONS

Justice. The death penalty is authorized. The last execution was in 1995. There were 34,135 prisoners in state correctional institutions as of 30 Nov. 1997.

Religion. In 1990 there were 6,961,000 Christians and, in 1992, 329,000 Jews.

Education. School attendance is compulsory for children 8–17 years of age. In 1996–97 there were 1,804,256 pupils and 105,072 teachers in public elementary and secondary schools. The public kindergartens and elementary schools had 990,353 pupils (Grades K–6) and 813,903 pupils (Grades 7–12). Non-public schools had

333,781 pupils (Grades K–6) and 81,673 pupils (Grades 7–12). Average salary, public school professional personnel was $48,516; classroom teachers $47,147. In fiscal year 1994–95 state and local government expenditure for elementary and secondary schools was $11,555m.

Leading senior academic institutions included:

Founded	Institutions	Faculty (Autumn 1989)	Students (Autumn 1996)
1740	University of Pennsylvania (non-sect.)	1,007	21,869
1787	University of Pittsburgh	1,326	31,656
1832	Lafayette College, Easton (Presbyterian)	159	2,184
1833	Haverford College	83	1,137
1842	Villanova University (R.C.)	534	10,189
1846	Bucknell University (Baptist)	226	3,573
1851	St Joseph's University, Philadelphia (R.C.)	164	6,963
1852	California University of Pennsylvania	317	5,636
1855	Pennsylvania State University	1,704	72,637
1855	Millersville University of Pennsylvania	333	7,474
1863	LaSalle University, Philadelphia (R.C.)	208	5,313
1864	Swarthmore College	151	1,437
1866	Lehigh University, Bethlehem (non-sect.)	393	6,238
1871	West Chester University of Pennsylvania	465	11,261
1875	Indiana University of Pennsylvania	660	13,680
1878	Duquesne University, Pittsburgh (R.C.)	280	9,362
1884	Temple University, Philadelphia	1,194	27,979
1885	Bryn Mawr College	136	1,886
1888	University of Scranton (R.C.)	231	4,905
1891	Drexel University, Philadelphia	448	9,595
1900	Carnegie-Mellon University, Pittsburgh	489	7,749

Health. In June 1996 the state had 233 acute care and specialty (including federal) hospitals, and 48,339 beds licensed and approved by the Department of Health.

Social Security. During the year ending 30 June 1997 the monthly average number of cases receiving public assistance was 567,698, including: Temporary Assistance for Needy Families (formerly Aid to Families with Dependent Children), 486,985; general assistance, 79,487; State Blind Pension, 1,226.

Payments for medical assistance (state and federal) in fiscal year 1996–97 included: outpatient care, $1,722m.; inpatient care, $1,162m.; capitation, $1,940m., and long-term care, $1,124m.

Further Reading

Statistical information: Pennsylvania State Data Center, 777 West Harrisburg Pike, Midelleton 17057. Publishes *Pennsylvania Statistical Abstract.*

Encyclopaedia of Pennsylvania, New York, 1984

Cochran, T. C., *Pennsylvania,* New York, 1978

Downey, D. B. and Bremer, F. (eds.) *Guide to the History of Pennsylvania.* London, 1994

Klein, P. S. and Hoogenboom, A., *A History of Pennsylvania.* New York, 1973

Majumdar, S. K. and Miller, E. W., *Pennsylvania Coal: Resources, Technology and Utilisation.* Pennsylvania Science, 1983

Weigley, R. F., (ed.) *Philadelphia: A 300-year History.* New York, 1984

Wilkinson, N. B., *Bibliography of Pennsylvania History.* Harrisburg, 1957

RHODE ISLAND

KEY HISTORICAL EVENTS. The earliest white settlement was founded by Roger Williams, an English Puritan who was expelled from Massachusetts because of his dissident religious views and his insistence on the land-rights of the Indians. At Providence he bought land from the Narragansetts and founded a colony there in 1636. A charter was granted in 1663. The colony was governed according to policies of toleration, which attracted Jewish and nonconformist settlers; later there was French Canadian settlement also.

Shipping and fishing developed strongly, especially at Newport and Providence;

these two cities were twin capitals until 1900, when the capital was fixed at Providence.

Significant actions took place in Rhode Island during the War of Independence. In 1790 the state accepted the federal constitution and was admitted to the Union.

Early farming development was most successful in dairying and poultry. Early industrialization was mainly in textiles, beginning in the 1790s, and flourishing on abundant water power. Textiles dominated until the industry began to decline after the First World War. British, Irish, Polish, Italian and Portuguese workers settled in the state, working in the mils or in the shipbuilding, shipping, fishing and naval ports. The crowding of a new population into cities led to the abolition of the property qualification for the franchise in 1888.

TERRITORY AND POPULATION. Rhode Island is bounded north and east by Massachusetts, south by the Atlantic and west by Connecticut. Land area, 1,045 sq. miles (2,707 sq. km). Census population, 1 April 1990, 1,003,464 (86% urban) a decrease of 5·95% since 1980. Population estimate (1996), 990,000.

Births, 1994, were 13,466 (13·5 per 1,000 population); deaths, 9,000 (9·4); infant deaths, 1992, were 110 (7·5 per 1,000 live births); marriages, 1991, were 7,496 (7·4); divorces, also 1991, were 3,314 (3·3).

Population of 5 census years was:

	White	Black	Indian	Asiatic	Total	Per sq. mile
1910	532,492	9,529	284	305	542,610	508·5
1930	677,026	9,913	318	240	687,497	649·3
1960	838,712	18,332	932	1,190	859,488	812·4
			All others			
1980	896,692	27,584	22,878		947,154	903·0
1990	917,375	38,861	4,071	18,325	1,003,164	960·3

Of the total population in 1990, 481,496 were male, 777,474 were 18 years of age or older and 45,752 were of Hispanic origin. 824,004 were urban in 1980.

The chief cities and their population (census, 1990) are Providence, 160,728; Warwick, 85,427; Cranston, 76,060; Pawtucket, 72,644; East Providence, 50,380.

CLIMATE. Providence. Jan. 28°F (−2·2°C), July 72°F (22·2°C). Annual rainfall 43" (1,079 mm). Rhode Island belongs to the New England climate zone (*see* UNITED STATES: Climate).

CONSTITUTION AND GOVERNMENT. The present constitution dates from 1843; it has had 42 amendments. The General Assembly consists of a Senate of 50 members and a House of Representatives of 100 members, both elected for 2 years. The Governor and Lieut.-Governor are now elected for 4 years. Every citizen, 18 years of age, who has resided in the state for 30 days, and is duly registered, is qualified to vote.

The state sends 2 representatives to Congress.

At the 1996 presidential election Clinton polled 220,592 votes; Dole, 198,325; Perot, 39,965.

The capital is Providence. The state has 5 counties but no county governments. There are 39 municipalities, each having its own form of local government.

Governor: Lincoln C. Almond (R.), 1995–99 ($69,900).
Lieut.-Governor: Vacant ($52,000).
Secretary of State: James R. Langerin (D.) ($52,000).

BUDGET. For the fiscal year 1997 total revenues are $3,561m. (taxation, $1,700m., and federal aid, $1,037·2m.); general expenditures are $3,527m. (education, $971m.; and human services, $1,384·9m.)

Total net long-term debt on 30 June 1991 was $11,640m.

Per capita personal income (1995) was $23,310.

NATURAL RESOURCES

Minerals. The small mineral output, mostly stone, sand and gravel, was valued (1990) at an estimated $12·7m.

Agriculture. Agriculture contributed $141m. to the general cash income in 1990. In 1991 there were 700 farms with an area of some 66,000 acres. The average size of farm was 94 acres. In 1995 the average value per acre was $6,947. In 1990 60% of production value was in nursery and turf products. Farm income 1991: Crops, $58m.; livestock and products, $13m.

Fisheries. In 1990 the catch was 13·2m. lb (mainly lobster and quahang) valued at $72·9m.

INDUSTRY. Manufacturing is the chief source of income and the largest employer. Total non-agricultural employment in 1996 was 442,000, of which 82,000 were manufacturing (99,500 in 1990). Average weekly earnings for production workers in 1989 was $359·99. Principal industries are jewellery and silverware, electrical machinery, electronics, plastics, metal products, instruments, chemicals and boatbuilding.

COMMUNICATIONS

Roads. In 1995 there were 5,893 miles of roads (1,321 miles rural). There were 699,000 registered motor vehicles.

Railways. Amtrak's New York-Boston route runs through the state, serving Providence.

Civil Aviation. In 1988 there were 6 state-owned airports. Theodore Francis Green airport at Warwick, near Providence, is served by 9 airlines, and handled over 2m. passengers and 37m. lb. of freight in 1995.

Shipping. Waterborne freight through the port of Providence (1988) totalled 10·6m. tons.

Telecommunications. There are 24 radio stations and 5 television stations; there are 8 cable television companies.

SOCIAL INSTITUTIONS

Justice. The state's correctional institutions, in 1994, had 2,919 prisoners.

The death penalty is illegal, except that it is mandatory in the case of murder committed by a prisoner serving a life sentence.

Religion. Chief religious bodies are (estimated figures Sept. 1988): Roman Catholic with 550,000 members; Protestant Episcopal (baptized persons), 50,000; Baptist, 22,500; Congregational, 12,000; Methodist, 10,000; Jewish, 24,000.

Education. In 1996 there were 149,802 pupils in public elementary and secondary schools. There were 219 public elementary schools with 85,691 pupils; about 24,941 pupils were enrolled in private and parochial schools. The 38 public senior and vocational high schools had 64,111 pupils. Teachers' salaries (1987) averaged $23,400. State and local government expenditure, for schools in 1991 totalled $1,212·7m. The total expenditure per pupil in 1995 was $6,634.

There are 11 institutions of higher learning (3 public and 8 private). The state maintains Rhode Island College, at Providence, with over 350 faculty members, and 8,900 students (2,594 part-time, 1,816 graduates), and the University of Rhode Island, at South Kingstown, with over 650 faculty members and 13,707 students (2,198 part-time, 3,176 graduates). Brown University, at Providence, founded in 1764, is now non-sectarian; in 1996 it had over 500 faculty members and 7,458 students (1,786 part-time or graduate). Providence College, at Providence, founded in 1917 by the Order of Preachers (Dominican), had (1996) 300 faculty members and 5,520 students (1,911 part-time or graduate). The largest of the other colleges are Bryant College, at Smithfield, with over 200 faculty members and 3,310 students

(1,100 part-time or graduate), and the Rhode Island School of Design, in Providence, with over 250 faculty members and 1,830 students (170 graduates) in 1996.

Health. In 1995 there were 11 community hospitals with 2,700 beds.

Social Security. In 1995, 190,000 people were receiving benefit totalling $1,478m. including 140,000 retired workers and dependants and 25,000 disabled workers and dependants.

Further Reading

Statistical information: Rhode Island Economic Development Corporation, 1 West Exchange Street, Providence, RI 02903. Publishes *Rhode Island Basic Economic Statistics.*
Rhode Island Manual. Prepared by the Secretary of State. Providence
Providence Journal Almanac: A Reference Book for Rhode Islanders. Providence. Annual
McLoughlin, W. G., *Rhode Island: a History.* Norton, 1978
Wright, M. I. and Sullivan, R. J., *Rhode Island Atlas.* Rhode Island Pubs., 1983

State Library: Rhode Island State Library, State House, Providence 02908.

SOUTH CAROLINA

KEY HISTORICAL EVENTS. Originally the territory of Yamasee Indians, the area attracted French and Spanish explorers in the 16th century. There were attempts at settlement on the coast, none of which lasted. Charles I of England made a land grant in 1629, but the first permanent white settlement began at Charles Town in 1670, moving to Charleston in 1680. This was a proprietorial colony including North Carolina until 1712; both passed to the Crown in 1729.

The coastlands developed as plantations worked by slave labour. In the hills there were small farming settlements and many trading posts, dealing with Indian suppliers.

After active campaigns during the War of Independence, South Carolina became one of the original states of the Union in 1778.

In 1793 the cotton gin was invented, enabling the speedy mechanical separation of seed and fibre. This made it possible to grow huge areas of cotton and meet the rapidly growing needs of new textile industries. Plantation farming spread widely, and South Carolina became hostile to the anti-slavery campaign which was strong in northern states. The state first attempted to secede from the Union in 1847, but was not supported by other southern states until 1860, when secession led to civil war.

At that time the population was about 730,000, of whom 413,000 were black. During the reconstruction periods there was some political power for black citizens, but control was back in white hands by 1876. The constitution was amended in 1895 to disenfranchise most black voters, and they remained with hardly any voice in government until the Civil Rights movement of the 1960s. Columbia became the capital in 1786.

TERRITORY AND POPULATION. South Carolina is bounded in the north by North Carolina, east and south-east by the Atlantic, south-west and west by Georgia. Land area, 30,111 sq. miles (77,988 sq. km). Census population, 1 April 1990, 3,486,703 (54·6% urban), an increase of 11·73% since 1980. Population estimate (1996), 3,699,000. Births, 1995, were 50,913 (13·6 per 1,000 population); deaths, 33,500 (9·0); marriages, 60,013 (16·4); divorces and annulments, 15,171 (4·1); infant deaths, 480 (9·4 per 1,000 live births).

The population in 5 census years was:

	White	Black	Indian	Asiatic	Total	Per sq. mile
1910	679,161	835,843	331	65	1,515,400	49·7
1930	944,049	793,681	959	76	1,738,765	56·8

			All others			
1970	1,794,432	789,040	3,588		2,587,060	83·2
1980	2,150,507	948,623	22,703		3,121,833	100·3
1990	2,406,974	1,039,884	39,845		3,486,703	115·8

Of the total population in 1990, 1,905,378 (54·6%) were urban and 2,159,970 (61·9%) were 25 years old or older. Median age, 32.

Population estimate of large towns in 1994 (with those of associated metropolitan areas): Columbia (capital), 104,101 (486,339); Charleston, 76,854 and North Charleston, 66,431 (522,276); Greenville, 59,808; Spartanburg, 45,721 (Greenville–Spartanburg, 572,953).

CLIMATE. Columbia. Jan. 44·7°F (7°C), Aug. 80·2°F (26·9°C). Annual rainfall 49·12" (1,247·6 mm). South Carolina belongs to the Atlantic Coast climate zone (*see* UNITED STATES: Climate).

CONSTITUTION AND GOVERNMENT. The present constitution dates from 1895, when it went into force without ratification by the electorate. The General Assembly consists of a Senate of 46 members, elected for 4 years, and a House of Representatives of 124 members, elected for 2 years. It meets annually. The Governor and Lieut.-Governor are elected for 4 years.

The state sends 6 representatives to Congress.

At the 1996 presidential election Dole polled 573,339 votes; Clinton 506,152; Perot, 64,377.

The capital is Columbia. There are 46 counties.

Governor: David Beasley (R.), 1995–99 ($101,959).
Lieut.-Governor: Robert L. Peeler (R.), ($44,737).
Secretary of State: Jim Miles (R.), ($88,434).

BUDGET. For the fiscal year ending 30 June 1996 general revenues were $4,345·9m.; general expenditures were $4,269·3m.

Per capita personal income (1995) was $18,788.

NATURAL RESOURCES

Minerals. Gold is found, though non-metallic minerals are of chief importance: Value of non-fuel mineral output in 1994 was $415m., chiefly from cement (Portland), stone and gold. Production of kaolin, vermiculite, scrap mica and fuller's earth is also important.

Agriculture. In 1996 there were 21,500 farms covering a farm area of 5m. acres. The average farm was of 233 acres. The average value of farmland and buildings per acre was $1,337 in 1995.

Farm income in 1995, $817·8m. for crops and $611m. for livestock and products. Chief crops are tobacco, soybeans, wheat, cotton, peanuts and corn. Production, 1995: Cotton, 376,000 bales; peanuts, 30·8m. lb.; soybeans, 12·7m. bu.; tobacco, 105m. lb.; corn, 24·1m. bu.; wheat, 8·7m. bu. Livestock on farms, 1996: 520,000 all cattle, 350,000 swine (1995).

Forestry. The forest industry is important; total forest land (1993), 12·6m. acres. National forests amounted to 609,000 acres in 1993.

INDUSTRY. A monthly average of 377,246 workers were employed in manufacturing and 331,350 in service in 1995. Major sectors are textiles (25%), apparel (8·6%), chemicals (10·2%), business service (26·8%) and health service (22·6%). Tourism is important.

COMMUNICATIONS

Roads. Total highway mileage in the combined highway system in Dec. 1995 was 41,503·14 miles. Motor vehicle registrations numbered 2,892,990 in 1995.

Railways. In 1994 the length of railway in the state was 2,306·76 miles.

Civil Aviation. In 1995 there were 1,496,680 general aviation aircraft operations in South Carolina, 11,438 taxi and commuter aircraft operations, 88,766 air carrier aircraft operations and 80,948 military aircraft operations.

Shipping. The state has 3 deep-water ports.

SOCIAL INSTITUTIONS

Justice. As of 30 June 1996 there were 18,736 prisoners in state correctional institutions. The death penalty is authorized. The last execution was in 1997.

Education. In 1995–96 there were 648,677 pupils and 39,429 teachers in public elementary and secondary schools. In 1995–96 the average teaching salary was $31,622.

For higher education the state operates the University of South Carolina (USC), founded at Columbia in 1801, with (autumn 1995), 20,637 enrolled students; USC Aiken, with 2,255 students; USC Coastal, with 3,656 students; USC Spartanburg, with 2,558 students; USC 2-year regional campuses, with 2,752 students; Clemson University, founded in 1889, with 14,847 students; The Citadel, at Charleston, with 3,053 students; Winthrop University, Rock Hill, with 4,293 students; Medical University of S. Carolina, at Charleston, with 2,317 students; S. Carolina State University, at Orangeburg, with 4,373 students, and Francis Marion University, at Florence, with 3,200 students; the College of Charleston has 8,520 students and Lander University, Greenwood, 2,182. There are 16 technical institutions (35,382).

There are also 380 private kindergartens, elementary and high schools with total enrolment (1995–96) of 46,487 pupils, and 23 private and denominational colleges and 4 junior colleges with (autumn 1995) enrolments of 26,906 and 1,182 students respectively.

Health. In 1996 the state had 464 non-federal health facilities with 35,714 beds licensed by the South Carolina Department of Health and Environmental Control. There were 6,462 physicians and 24,587 registered nurses in 1994.

Social Security. In 1995 there were 363,362 recipients of social security benefits. The annual payment in benefits was $2,968·7m. and the average monthly benefit was $658.

Further Reading

Statistical information: Budget and Control Board, R.C. Dennis Bldg., Columbia 29201. Publishes *South Carolina Statistical Abstract.*
South Carolina Legislative Manual. Columbia. Annual
Edgar, W. B., *South Carolina in the Modern Age.* Univ. of South Carolina Press, 1992
Graham, C. B. and Moore, W. V., *South Carolina Politics and Government.* Univ. of Nebraska Press, 1995
Jones, L., *South Carolina: A Synoptic History for Laymen.* Lexington, 1978
State Library. South Carolina State Library, Columbia.

SOUTH DAKOTA

KEY HISTORICAL EVENTS. The area was part of the hunting grounds of nomadic Dakota (Sioux) Indians. French explorers visited the site of Fort Pierre in 1742–43, and claimed the area for France. In 1763 the claim fell and, together with French claims to all land west of the Mississippi, passed to Spain. Spain held the Dakotas until defeated by France in the Napoleonic Wars, when France regained the area and sold it to the US as part of the Louisiana Purchase in 1803.

Fur-traders were active, but there was no settlement until Fort Randall was founded on the Missouri river in 1856. In 1861 North and South Dakota were organized as the Dakota Territory, and the Homestead Act of 1862 stimulated settlement, mainly in the south-east until there was a gold-rush in the Black Hills of the west in 1875–76. Colonization developed as farming communities in the east, miners and ranchers in the west. Livestock farming predominated, attracting European settlers from Scandinavia, Germany and Russia.

In 1899 the North and South were separated and admitted to the Union as states. The capital of South Dakota is Pierre, founded as a railhead in 1880, chosen as a temporary capital and confirmed as permanent capital in 1904. It faces Fort Pierre, the former centre of the fur trade, across the Missouri river. During the 20th century there have been important schemes to exploit the Missouri for power and irrigation.

TERRITORY AND POPULATION. South Dakota is bounded in the north by North Dakota, east by Minnesota, south-east by the Big Sioux River (forming the boundary with Iowa), south by Nebraska (with the Missouri River forming part of the boundary) and west by Wyoming and Montana. Land area, 75,898 sq. miles (196,576 sq. km). Area administered by the Bureau of Indian Affairs, 1985, covered 5m. acres (10% of the state), of which 2·6m. acres were held by tribes. The federal government, 1994, owned 2,698,000 acres.

Census population, 1 April 1990, 696,004 (50% urban), an increase of 2·4% since 1980. Population estimate (1996), 732,405. In 1996: Births, 10,469 (15·0 per 1,000 population); deaths, 6,793 (9·8); infant deaths, 60 (5·7 per 1,000 live births); marriages, 6,991 (10·0); divorces, 2,749 (3·9).

Population in 5 federal censuses was:

	White	Black	American Indian	Asiatic	Total	Per sq. mile
1910	563,771	817	19,137	163	583,888	7·6
1930	669,453	646	21,833	101	692,849	9·0
1960	653,098	1,114	25,794	336	680,514	8·9
			All others			
1980	638,955	2,144	49,079		690,178	9·0
				Asian/ other		
1990	637,515	3,258	50,575	4,656	696,004	9·2

Of the total population in 1990, 497,942 were 18 years of age and over and 5,252 were of Hispanic origin. A total of 342,498 were male and 347,903 were urban.

Population of the chief cities (census of 1990) was: Sioux Falls, 100,814; Rapid City, 54,523; Aberdeen, 24,927; Watertown, 17,592; Mitchell, 13,798; Brookings, 16,270; Pierre, 12,906; Yankton, 12,703; Huron, 12,448; Vermillion, 10,034; Spearfish, 6,996; Madison, 6,257; Sturgis, 5,330; Belle Fourche, 4,335; Hot Springs, 4,325.

CLIMATE. Rapid City. Jan. 25°F (−3·9°C), July 73°F (22·8°C). Annual rainfall 19" (474 mm). Sioux Falls. Jan. 14°F (−10°C), July 73°F (22·8°C). Annual rainfall 25" (625 mm). South Dakota belongs to the High Plains climate zone (see UNITED STATES: Climate).

CONSTITUTION AND GOVERNMENT. Voters are all citizens 18 years of age or older. The people reserve the right of the initiative and referendum. The Senate has 35 members, and the House of Representatives 70 members, all elected for 2 years; the Governor and Lieut.-Governor are elected for 4 years.

The state sends 1 representative to Congress.

In the 1996 presidential election Dole polled 150,508 votes; Clinton, 139,295; Perot, 31,248.

The capital is Pierre. The state is divided into 66 organized counties.

Governor: William J. Janklow, (R.), 1995–99 ($84,739, with housing provided).
Lieut.-Governor: Carole Hillard, (R.) ($61,532).
Secretary of State: Joyce Hazeltine, (R.) ($57,577).

BUDGET. For the fiscal year ending 30 June 1998 the estimated general fund revenues were $711,959,465 ($388,940,959 from Sales and Use Tax); estimated expenditure was $706,452,130 ($273,477,191 on state aid to education).

Per capita personal income (1996) was $20,895.

NATURAL RESOURCES

Minerals. In 1996 the mineral products included gold, 17·4 tonnes (fourth largest yield of all states); silver, 7 tonnes. Mineral products, 1996, were valued at $353,000,000, including gold and silver.

Agriculture. In 1996 there were 32,500 farms, average size 1,354 acres. Average value of farmland and buildings per acre in 1996 was $319. Farm income, 1993: Crops, $1,150,614,000; livestock and products, $2,586,195,000.

South Dakota is a major producer of rye (1·5m. bu. in 1996), sunflower oil (1,056·2m. lb.), flaxseed (126,000 bu.), and oats (21·6m. bu.). The other important crops are all wheat (139,270,000 bu.), sorghum for grain (7,975,000 bu.), corn for grain (370m. bu.) and soybeans (90,780,000 bu.). The farm livestock on 1 Jan. 1997 included 3·8m. cattle, 0·45m. sheep and lambs, and 1·13m. hogs (1 March 1997). In 1996, 23,280,000 lb. of honey were produced.

Forestry. National forest area, 1992, 2,013,000 acres.

INDUSTRY. In 1996, 1,044 manufacturing establishments had 47,750 employees. Industrial machinery and computer equipment had 160 establishments with 13,559 workers; food and kindred products had 115 establishments with 8,590 workers. Construction had 2,925 companies with 14,646 workers. Also significant were transportation, communications and public utilities (1,811 establishments employing 15,576 workers). Mining establishments were 83 and employed 2,270 workers.

COMMUNICATIONS

Roads. In 1996 there were 83,358 miles of roads. There were 706,984 registered cars and lorries, 133,677 trailers, 24,704 motorcycles and 6,979 snowmobiles.

Railways. In 1997 there were 1,855 miles of track of which 811 miles were state-owned.

Civil Aviation. In 1996 there were 73 general aviation airports, of which 9 were 'air carrier' airports with regular passenger services utilizing turbo-prop or jet aircraft.

SOCIAL INSTITUTIONS

Justice. On 30 Nov. 1997 there were 2,232 adults in state prisons. The death penalty is authorized.

Religion. The chief religious bodies are: Lutherans, Roman Catholics, Methodist, United Church of Christ, Presbyterian, Baptist and Episcopal.

Education. Elementary and secondary education are free from 6 to 21 years of age. Between the ages of 6 and 16, attendance is compulsory. In 1997 there were 133,723 PK-12 public school students and 16,792 PK-12 non-public students.

Teachers' salaries (1997) averaged $27,072. Total expenditure on public schools (1995–96), $588,200,564.

Higher education (autumn 1997): The School of Mines at Rapid City, established 1885, had 2,210 students; South Dakota State University at Brookings, 8,162; the University of South Dakota, founded at Vermillion in 1882, 6,535; Northern State University, Aberdeen, 2,464; Black Hills State University at Spearfish, 2,773; Dakota State University at Madison, 1,326. There were 7,436 students at 12 of the 13 private colleges including 2 of 3 Indian colleges in the spring of 1996.

Health. In 1997 there were 60 licensed hospitals (3,478 beds).

Social Security. In fiscal year 1996, under Supplemental Security Income, there were on average 10,731 disabled persons receiving $42,965,196 in benefits; 131 blind persons received $505,556 and 2,462 aged persons received $4,378,038. Aid to Families with Dependent Children distributed $21,582,846 to 6,056 cases (average) involving 16,461 recipients (average) and 11,971 children (average).

Further Reading

Statistical information: State Data Center, Univ. of South Dakota, Vermillion 57069.
Governor's Budget Report. South Dakota Bureau of Finance and Management. Annual
South Dakota Historical Collections. 1902–82

South Dakota Legislative Manual. Secretary of State, Pierre, S.D. Biennial
Berg, F. M., *South Dakota: Land of Shining Gold.* Hettinger, 1982
Karolevitz, R. F., *Challenge: the South Dakota Story.* Sioux Falls, 1975
Milton, John R., *South Dakota; a Bicentennial History.* New York, 1977
Schell, H. S., *History of South Dakota.* 3rd ed. Lincoln, Neb., 1975
Vexler, R. I., *South Dakota Chronology and Factbook.* New York, 1978

State Library: South Dakota State Library, 800 Governor's Drive, Pierre, S.D., 57501-2294.

TENNESSEE

KEY HISTORICAL EVENTS. Bordered on the west by the Mississippi, Tennessee was part of an area inhabited by Cherokee. French, Spanish and British explorers penetrated the area up the Mississippi and traded with the Cherokee in the late 16th and 17th centuries. French claims were abandoned in 1763, colonists from the British colonies of Virginia and Carolina then began to cross the Appalachians westwards, but there was no organized Territory until after the War of Independence. In 1784 there was a short-lived, independent state called Franklin. In 1790 the South West Territory (including Tennessee) was formed, and Tennessee entered the Union as a state in 1796.

The state was active in the war against Britain in 1812. After the American victory, colonization increased and pressure for land mounted. The Cherokee were forcibly removed during the 1830s and taken to Oklahoma, a journey on which many died.

Tennessee was a slave state and seceded from the Union in 1861, although eastern Tennessee was against secession. There were important battles at Shiloh, Chattanooga, Stone River and Nashville. In 1866 Tennessee was readmitted to the Union.

Nashville, the capital since 1843, Memphis, Knoxville, and Chattanooga all developed as river towns, Memphis becoming an important cotton and timber port. Growth was greatly accelerated by the creation of the Tennessee Valley Authority in the 1930s, producing power for a manufacturing economy. Industry increased to the extent that, by 1970, the normal southern pattern of emigration and population loss had been reversed.

TERRITORY AND POPULATION. Tennessee is bounded north by Kentucky and Virginia, east by North Carolina, south by Georgia, Alabama and Mississippi and west by the Mississippi River (forming the boundary with Arkansas and Missouri). Land area, 41,220 sq. miles (106,759 sq. km). Census population, 1 April 1990, 4,877,185 (60·9% urban), an increase of 6·2% since 1980. Population estimate (1993), 5,098,798. Vital statistics, 1996: Births, 73,710 (13·9 per 1,000 population); deaths, 51,367 (9·7); infant deaths, 626 (8·5 per 1,000 live births); marriages, 82,031 (30·8); divorces, 33,161 (12·5).

Population in 5 census years was:

	White	Black	Indian	Asiatic	Total	Per sq. mile
1910	1,711,432	473,088	216	53	2,184,789	52·4
1930	2,138,644	477,646	161	105	2,616,556	62·4
			All others			
1970	3,293,930	621,261	8,496		3,923,687	95·3
1980	3,835,452	725,942	29,726		4,591,120	111·6
1990	4,048,068	778,035	51,082		4,877,185	115·7

Of the population in 1990, 2,348,928 were male, 2,969,948 were urban and those 21 years of age or older numbered 3,421,633.

The cities, with population, 1996, are Memphis, 596,725; Nashville (capital), 511,263; Knoxville, 167,535; Chattanooga, 150,425; Clarksville, 94,879; Jackson, 50,406; Johnson City, 55,542; Murfreesboro, 53,996; Kingsport, 41,335; Oak Ridge, 27,742. Metropolitan Statistical Areas, 1996 (1992): Memphis, 1,048,684 (1,033,183); Nashville, 1,117,178 (1,023,315); Knoxville, 649,277 (610,482);

Chattanooga, 446,096 (430,848); Johnson City–Kingsport–Bristol, 458,229 (444,625); Clarksville, 186,368 (178,155); Jackson, 98,489 (80,230).

CLIMATE. Memphis. Jan. 41°F (5°C), July 82°F (27·8°C). Annual rainfall 49" (1,221 mm). Nashville. Jan. 39°F (3·9°C), July 79°F (26·1°C). Annual rainfall 48" (1,196 mm). Tennessee belongs to the Appalachian Mountains climate zone (*see* UNITED STATES: Climate).

CONSTITUTION AND GOVERNMENT. The state has operated under 3 constitutions, the last of which was adopted in 1870 and has been since amended 22 times (first in 1953). Voters at an election may authorize the calling of a convention limited to altering or abolishing one or more specified sections of the constitution. The General Assembly consists of a Senate of 33 members and a House of Representatives of 99 members, senators elected for 4 years and representatives for 2 years. Qualified as electors are all citizens (usual residential and age (18) qualifications). Tennessee sends 9 representatives to Congress.

In the 1996 presidential election Clinton polled 905,999 votes; Dole, 860,809; Perot, 105,577.

The capital is Nashville. The state is divided into 95 counties.

Governor: Don Sundquist (R.), 1995–99 ($85,000).
Lieut.-Governor: John Wilder (D.), ($49,500).
Secretary of State: Riley C. Darnell (D.), ($80,700).

BUDGET. For 1995–96 total revenue was $12,118m.; general expenditure, $11,276m.

Total net long-term debt on 30 June 1996 amounted to $912m.
Per capita personal income (1996) was $21,949.

NATURAL RESOURCES

Minerals. Non-fuel mineral production was worth $577m. in 1994.

Agriculture. In 1996, 80,000 farms covered 11·8m. acres. The average farm was of 148 acres, valued (land and buildings) at $225,088.

Farm income (1996) from crops was $1,374m.; from livestock, $998m. Main crops were cotton, tobacco and soybeans.

On 1 Jan. 1997 the domestic animals included 115,000 milk cows, 2·4m. all cattle, 13,500 sheep, 0·4m. swine.

Forestry. Forests occupy 13,258,000 acres. The forest industry and industries dependent on it employ about 0·04m. workers. Wood products are valued at over $500m. per year. National forest system land (1991) 626,000 acres.

INDUSTRY. The manufacturing industries include iron and steel working, but the most important products are chemicals, including synthetic fibres and allied products, electrical equipment and food. In 1995, manufacturing establishments employed 552,400 workers; value added by manufactures was $43,126m.

TOURISM. In 1994, 29·9m. out-of-state tourists spent $5,900m.

COMMUNICATIONS

Roads. In 1995 there were 85,599 miles of roads (65,793 miles rural). In 1994 there were 5,058,653 registered motor vehicles.

Railways. The state had (1995) 3,065 miles of track. There is a tramway in Memphis.

Civil Aviation. The state is served by 23 major and regional airlines. In 1997 Tennessee had 83 public airports; there were also 71 heliports and 2 military air bases.

SOCIAL INSTITUTIONS

Justice. The death penalty is authorized, but there has been no execution since 1960. Prison population, 30 June 1996, 13,817.

Religion. In 1990 there were 1,086,680 Southern Baptists, 320,724 United Methodists, 199,698 Black Baptists, 168,933 members of the Church of Christ, 137,203 Catholics and 18,377 members of the African Methodist Episcopal Zion.

Education. School attendance has been compulsory since 1925 and the employment of children under 16 years of age in workshops, factories or mines is illegal.

In 1995–96 there were 1,562 public schools with a net enrolment of 948,217 pupils; 49,627 teachers earned an average salary of $33,646. Total expenditure for operating schools was $4,266m. Tennessee has 49 accredited colleges and universities, 16 2-year colleges and 27 vocational schools. The universities include the University of Tennessee, Knoxville (founded 1794), with 25,337 students in 1996–97, Vanderbilt University, Nashville (1873) with 10,253, Tennessee State University (1912) with 8,643, the University of Tennessee at Chattanooga (1886) with 8,296, University of Memphis (1912) with 19,271 and Fisk University (1866) with 812.

Health. In 1994 the state had 127 hospitals with 26,018 beds. State facilities for the mentally retarded had 1,290 resident patients and mental hospitals had 1,003 in 1996.

Social Security. In 1995 Tennessee paid $6,672m. to retired workers and their survivors and to disabled workers. Total beneficiaries: 587,940 retired; 172,110 survivors; 166,060 disabled. 1·5m. people received $2,772m. in Medicaid. Supplemental Security Income ($648m.) was paid to 179,676. 294,733 people (1994) received aid to dependent children ($212m.).

Further Reading

Statistical information: Center for Business and Economic Research, Univ. of Tennessee, Knoxville 37996. Publishes *Tennessee Statistical Abstract*
Tennessee Blue Book. Secretary of State, Nashville
Corlew, R. E., *Tennessee: a Short History.* 2nd ed. Univ. of Tennessee, 1981
Davidson, D., *Tennessee: Vol. I, The Old River Frontier to Secession,* Univ. of Tennessee, 1979
Dykeman, W., *Tennessee.* Rev. ed., New York, 1984

State Library: State Library and Archives, Nashville.

TEXAS

KEY HISTORICAL EVENTS. A number of Indian tribes occupied the area before French and Spanish explorers arrived in the 16th century. In 1685 La Salle established a colony at Fort St Louis, but Texas was confirmed as Spanish in 1713. Spanish missions increased during the 18th century with San Antonio (1718) as their headquarters.

In 1820 a Virginian colonist, Moses Austin, obtained permission to begin a settlement in Texas. In 1821 the Spanish empire in the Americas came to an end, and Texas, together with Coahuila, formed a state of the newly independent Mexico. The Mexicans agreed to the Austin venture, and settlers of British and American descent came in.

The settlers became discontented with Mexican government and declared their independence in 1836. Warfare, including the siege of the Alamo fort, ended with the foundation of the independent Republic of Texas, which lasted until 1845. During this period the Texas Rangers were organized as a policing force and border patrol. Texas was annexed to the Union in Dec. 1845, as the Federal Government feared its vulnerability to Mexican occupation. This led to war between Mexico and the USA from 1845 to 1848. In 1861 Texas left the Union and joined the southern states in the Civil War, being readmitted in 1869. Ranching and cotton-growing were the main activities before the discovery of oil in 1901.

TERRITORY AND POPULATION. Texas is bounded north by Oklahoma, north-east by Arkansas, east by Louisiana, south-east by the Gulf of Mexico, south by Mexico and west by New Mexico. Land area, 261,914 sq. miles (678,358 sq. km). Census population, 1990, 16,986,510 (80·3% urban). Population estimate (1996), 19,128,000. Vital statistics for 1996: Births, 330,238 (17·4 per 1,000 population); deaths, 139,678 (7·4); infant deaths, 2,079 (6·3 per 1,000 live births); marriages, 178,659 (9·4); divorces, 95,185 (5·0).

Population for 5 census years was:

	White	Black	American Indian	Asian	Total	Per sq. mile
1910	3,204,848	690,049	702	943	3,896,542	14·8
1930	4,967,172	854,964	1,001	1,578	5,824,715	22·1
				All others		
1970	9,717,128	1,399,005		80,597	11,196,730	42·7
1980	11,197,663	1,710,250		1,320,470	14,228,383	54·2
				Asian/ other		
1990	12,774,762	2,021,632	65,877	2,124,239	16,986,510	64·9

Of the population in 1980, 6,998,301 were male, 11,327,159 persons were urban. Persons of Hispanic origin were also identified in the last 2 censuses, numbering 2,985,643 in 1980 and 4,339,905 in 1990.

The largest cities, with census population in 1993, are:

Houston	1,700,677	Garland	181,439	Mesquite	108,960
Dallas	1,036,309	Irving	166,523	Waco	107,191
San Antonio	991,861	Amarillo	163,569	Grand Prairie	103,913
El Paso	554,496	Plano	153,624	Wichita Falls	98,356
Austin (capital)	501,637	Laredo	140,688	Midland	95,003
Fort Worth	459,085	Pasadena	127,843	Odessa	92,257
Arlington	277,939	Beaumont	118,289	McAllen	91,184
Corpus Christi	266,958	Brownsville	117,326	Carrollton	90,934
Lubbock	193,194	Abilene	110,661	San Angelo	87,980

Metropolitan statistical areas, 1993: Houston, 3,544,601; Dallas, 2,731,503; Fort Worth-Arlington, 1,379,539; San Antonio, 1,387,618.

CLIMATE. Dallas. Jan. 45°F (7·2°C). July 84°F (28·9°C). Annual rainfall 38" (945 mm). El Paso. Jan. 44°F (6·7°C), July 81°F (27·2°C). Annual rainfall 9" (221 mm). Galveston. Jan. 54°F (12·2°C), July 84°F (28·9°C). Annual rainfall 46" (1,159 mm). Houston. Jan. 52°F (11·1°C), July 83°F (28·3°C). Annual rainfall 48" (1,200 mm). Texas belongs to the Central Plains climate zone (*see* UNITED STATES. Climate).

CONSTITUTION AND GOVERNMENT. The present constitution dates from 1876; it had been amended 364 times as of Nov. 1995. The Legislature consists of a Senate of 31 members elected for 4 years (half their number retire every 2 years), and a House of Representatives of 150 members elected for 2 years. It meets in odd-numbered years in January. The Governor and Lieut.-Governor are elected for 4 years.

The state sends 30 representatives to Congress.

In the 1996 presidential election Dole polled 2,736,167 votes; Clinton, 2,459,683.

The capital is Austin. The state has 254 counties.

Governor: George W. Bush (R.), 1995–99 ($99,122).

Lieut.-Governor: Bob Bullock (D.) ($7,200).

Secretary of State: Antonio Garza (D.) ($76,966).

BUDGET. In the fiscal year ending 31 Aug. 1996 general revenues were $40,488,397,436 ($19,762,504,350 from taxes, $11,657,682,320 federal aid, $3,841,355,969 from licences, fees and permits, $2,075,830,016 from interest and investment income and $3,151m. from other sources); total expenditures were $39,669,455,477.

Per capita personal income (1995) was $20,654.

NATURAL RESOURCES

Minerals. Production, 1994: Crude petroleum, 559·6m. bbls, natural gas 6,400m. cu. ft; other minerals include natural gasoline, butane and propane gases, helium, crude gypsum, granite and sandstone, salt and cement. Total value of non-fuel mineral products in 1993, $1,400m.

Agriculture. Texas is one of the most important agricultural states. In 1995 it had 205,000 farms covering 127m. acres; average farm was of 620 acres. In 1995, land and buildings were valued at $550 per acre. Large-scale commercial farms, highly mechanized, dominate in Texas; farms of 1,000 acres or more in number far exceed that of any other state. But small-scale farming persists.

Soil erosion is serious in some parts. For some 97,297,000 acres drastic curative treatment has been indicated and for 51,164,000 acres, preventive treatment.

Production: Corn, barley, beans, cotton, hay, oats, peanuts, rye, sorghum, soybeans, sunflowers, wheat, oranges, grapefruit, peaches, sweet potatoes.

Farm income, 1994, from crops was $2,300m.; from livestock, $8,200m.

The state has a very great livestock industry, leading in the number of all cattle (15·1m.) and sheep (1·7m.), both figures for 1995; it also had 0·4m. milk cows, and 0·58m. swine in 1994.

Forestry. There were (1993) 22,032,000 acres of forested land.

INDUSTRY. In 1994 manufacturing establishments employed 1,015,800 workers; trade employed 1,889,400; government, 1,438,200; services, 2,014,500; construction, 393,000; finance, insurance and real estate, 445,300; transport and public utilities, 466,100. Chemical industries along the Gulf Coast, such as the production of synthetic rubber and of primary magnesium (from sea-water), are increasingly important.

Texas has adopted (1993) a labour code which includes laws concerning protection of labourers, employer-employee relations, employment services and unemployment, and workers' compensation.

COMMUNICATIONS

Roads. In 1995 there were 296,186 miles of highways (including 4,474 miles of inter-state highways. In 1996 there were 15,274,000 registered motor vehicles.

Civil Aviation. In 1993 there were 307 public and 1,308 private airports.

Shipping. The port of Houston, connected by the Houston Ship Channel (50 miles long) with the Gulf of Mexico, is a large cotton market. Total cargo handled by all ports, 1990, 335,311,608 short tons.

SOCIAL INSTITUTIONS

Justice. In 1994 there were 75,698 men and women in state prisons. There have been more than 100 executions since 1982, the latest in 1998.

Religion. Religious bodies represented include Roman Catholics, Baptists, Methodists, Churches of Christ, Lutherans, Presbyterians and Episcopalians.

Education. School attendance is compulsory from 6 to 18 years of age.

In 1995–96 public elementary and secondary schools had over 3,740,260 students; there were 240,371 teachers whose salaries averaged $31,400. State and Federal support for public schools, 1994–95, $11,256m.

In 1994 there were 138 higher education institutions (35 public, 38 independent colleges and universities, 50 public community college districts and 15 others). The largest institutions with student enrolment, (1995–96), were:

Founded	Institutions	Control	Students
1845	Baylor University, Waco	Baptist	12,202
1852	St Mary's University, San Antonio	R.C.	4,202
1869	Trinity University, San Antonio	Presb.	2,482
1873	Texas Christian University, Fort Worth	Christian	7,050
1876	Texas A. and M. Univ., College Station	State	38,636

Founded	Institutions	Control	Students
1878	Prairie View Agr. and Mech. Coll., Prairie View	State	5,999
1879	Sam Houston State University	State	12,439
1883	University of Texas System (every campus)	State	136,597
1890	University of North Texas, Denton	State	25,122
1891	Hardin-Simmons University, Abilene	Baptist	2,373
1889	East Texas State University, Commerce	State	7,629
1899	South West Texas State University, San Marcos	State	20,929
1901	Texas Woman's University, Denton	State	9,827
1906	Abilene Christian University, Abilene	Church of Christ	4,436
1911	Southern Methodist University, Dallas	Methodist	8,986
1912	Rice University	Independent	4,099
1923	Lamar University, Beaumont	State	8,419
1923	Stephen F. Austin State University	State	11,781
1923	Texas Technical University, Lubbock	State	24,185
1925	Texas A&M University, Kingsville	State	6,061
1927	University of Houston, Houston	State	30,358
1947	Texas Southern University, Houston	State	9,458

Health. In 1995, the state had 498 hospitals (70,881 beds) listed by the American Hospital Association. In the fiscal year 1989, the average daily census of patients was: State hospitals, 3,629; state schools, 7,265 and state centres, 331.

Social Security. Aid is from state and federal sources. Number of Social Security beneficiaries in 1990: 2,193,000 who received an average of $583 (for retired workers), $579 (for disabled workers) and $538 (for widows/widowers) per month.

Further Reading

Texas Almanac. Dallas. Biennial
Cruz, G. R. and Irby, J. A. (eds.) *Texas Bibliography.* Austin, 1982
Fehrenbach, T. R., *Lone Star: A History of Texas and the Texans.* London, 1986
Jordan, T. G. and Bean, J. L., Jr., *Texas.* Boulder, 1983
Kingston, M. *Texas Almanac's Political History of Texas.* Austin, 1992
Kraemer, R. and Newell, C. *Essentials of Texas Politics.* 5th ed. Austin, 1992
MacCorkle, S. A. and Smith, D., *Texas Government.* 7th ed. New York, 1974
Marten, J., *Texas* [Bibliography]. Santa Barbara and Oxford, 1992

Legislative Reference Library: Box 12488, Capitol Station, Austin, Texas 78711-2488.

UTAH

KEY HISTORICAL EVENTS. Spanish Franciscan missionaries explored the area in 1776, finding Shoshoni Indians. Spain laid claim to Utah and designated it part of Spanish Mexico. As such it passed into the hands of the Mexican Republic when Mexico rebelled against Spain and gained independence in 1821.

In 1848, at the conclusion of war between the USA and Mexico, the USA received Utah along with other south-western territory. Settlers had already arrived in 1847 when the Mormons (the Church of Jesus Christ of Latter-day Saints) arrived, having been driven on by local hostility in Ohio, Missouri and Illinois. Led by Brigham Young, they entered the Great Salt Valley and colonized it. In 1849 they applied for statehood but were refused. In 1850 Utah and Nevada were joined as one Territory. The Mormon community continued to ask for statehood but this was only granted in 1896, after they had renounced polygamy and disbanded their People's Party.

Mining, especially of copper, and livestock farming were the base of the economy. Settlement had to adapt to desert conditions, and the main centres of population were in the narrow belt between the Wasatch Mountains and the Great Salt Lake. Salt Lake City, the capital, was founded in 1847 and laid out according to Joseph Smith's plan for the city of Zion. It was the centre of the Mormons' provisional 'State of Desert' and Territorial capital from 1856 until 1896, except briefly in 1858 when federal forces occupied it during conflict between territorial and Union governments.

TERRITORY AND POPULATION. Utah is bounded north by Idaho and Wyoming, east by Colorado, south by Arizona and west by Nevada. Land area, 82,168 sq. miles (212,816 sq. km). The Bureau of Indian Affairs in 1990 administered 2,317,604 acres, 2,284,766 acres of which were allotted to Indian tribes.

Census population, 1 April 1990, 1,722,850 (87% urban), an increase of 17·92% since 1980. Population estimate (1996), 2,000,000. Births in 1994 were 38,279 (20·1 per 1,000 population); deaths, 10,000 (5·5); infant deaths in 1992, 226 (6·1 per 1,000 live births); marriages, 18,788 (10·8); divorces, 8,407 (4·8).

Population at 5 federal censuses was:

	White	Black	Indian	Asiatic	Total	Per sq. mile
1910	366,583	1,144	3,123	2,501	373,851	4·5
1930	499,967	1,108	2,869	3,903	507,847	6·2
1960	873,828	4,148	6,961	5,207	890,627	10·8
1970	1,031,926	6,617	11,273	6,230	1,059,273	12·9
1980	1,382,550	9,225	19,256	15,076	1,461,037	17·7

Of the total in 1980, 724,501 were male, 1,232,908 persons were urban; 860,304 were 20 years of age or older.

The largest cities are Salt Lake City, with a population (census, 1990) of 159,936; West Valley City, 86,976; Provo, 86,835; Sandy City, 75,058; Orem, 67,561; Ogden, 63,905.

CLIMATE. Salt Lake City. Jan. 29°F (–1·7°C), July 77°F (25°C). Annual rainfall 16" (401 mm). Utah belongs to the Mountain States climate region (*see* UNITED STATES: Climate).

CONSTITUTION AND GOVERNMENT. Utah adopted its present constitution in 1896 (now with 61 amendments). The Legislature consists of a Senate (in part renewed every 2 years) of 29 members, elected for 4 years, and of a House of Representatives of 75 members elected for 2 years. It sits annually in Jan. The Governor is elected for 4 years. The constitution provides for the initiative and referendum.

The state sends 3 representatives to Congress.

The capital is Salt Lake City. There are 29 counties in the state.

In the 1996 presidential election Dole polled 359,394 votes; Clinton, 220,197; Perot, 66,100.

Governor: Mike Leavitt (R.), 1997–2001 ($77,250).
Lieut.-Governor: Olene S. Walker (R.) ($60,000).

BUDGET. For 1994 total revenue was $5,907m. (general revenue $4,809m.). Total expenditure was $5,251m. (general expenditures $4,689m.) including: $2,251·2m. on education, $367·1m. on highways, $819·4m. on public welfare.

Per capita personal income (1995) was $18,223.

NATURAL RESOURCES

Minerals. The principal minerals are: Copper, gold, magnesium, petroleum, lead, silver and zinc. The state also has natural gas, clays, tungsten, molybdenum, uranium and phosphate rock. The value of non-fuel mineral production in 1990 was $1·2m.

Agriculture. In 1996 Utah had some 13,300 farms covering 11m. acres. In 1985 about 2m. acres were crop land, and about 300,000 acres pasture and about 1m. acres had irrigation. In 1996 the average farm was of 821 acres and the average value per acre in 1995 was $606.

Of the total surface area, 9% is severely eroded and only 9·4% is free from erosion; the balance is moderately eroded.

Farm income, 1991, from crops, $167m. and from livestock, $555m. The principal crops are: Barley, wheat (spring and winter), oats, potatoes, hay (alfalfa, sweet clover and lespedeza), maize. Livestock, 1990: Cattle, 855,000; pigs, 34,000; Sheep 0·6m.; poultry, 3·8m.

Forestry. Area of national forests, 1991, was 9,128,000 acres, of which 8,014,000 acres were under forest service administration.

INDUSTRY. In 1996 manufacturing establishments had 129,000 workers. Leading manufactures by value added are primary metals, ordinances and transport, food, fabricated metals and machinery, petroleum products. Service industries employed 256,000; trade, 231,000; government, 167,000.

COMMUNICATIONS

Roads. In 1995 there were 41,044 miles of roads (34,817 miles rural). In 1995 there were 1,447,000 registered motor vehicles.

Railways. On 1 July 1974 the state had 1,734 miles of railways.

Civil Aviation. There is an international airport at Salt Lake City.

SOCIAL INSTITUTIONS

Justice. In 1994 there were 1,961 prisoners in state correctional institutions. The death penalty is authorized.

Religion. Latter-Day Saints (Mormons) numbered 1,458,000 in 1994. World membership was 9,025,000. The President of the Mormon Church is Howard Hunter (born 1908). The Roman Catholic church and most Protestant denominations are represented.

Education. School attendance is compulsory for children from 6 to 18 years of age. There are 40 school districts. Teachers' salaries, 1994–95, averaged $29,672. There were 471,557 pupils and 21,778 teachers in public elementary and secondary schools in the same year. In 1994 education expenditure by state and local government was $2,251·2m.

In 1994 there were 146,196 enrolled in colleges and universities. The University of Utah (1850) (24,770 students in 1985–86) is in Salt Lake City; the Utah State University (1890) (11,804) is in Logan. The Mormon Church maintains the Brigham Young University at Provo (1875) with 26,894 students. Other colleges include: Westminster College, Salt Lake City (1,302); Weber State College, Ogden (11,117); Southern Utah State College, Cedar City (2,587); College of Eastern Utah, Price (1,132); Snow College, Ephraim (1,328); Dixie College, St George (2,234).

Health. In 1995 the state had 42 community hospital facilities (4,200 beds).

Social Security. In 1994, 219,000 beneficiaries received $1,592m. annual benefit payments.

Further Reading

Statistical information: Bureau of Economic and Business Research, Univ. of Utah, 401 Kendall D. Garff Bldg., Salt Lake City 84112. Publishes *Statistical Abstract of Utah.*
Utah Foundation. *Statistical Review of Government in Utah.* Salt Lake City; 1991
Arrington, L., *Great Basin Kingdom: An Economic History of the Latter-Day Saints, 1830–1900.* Cambridge, Mass., 1958
Petersen, C. S., *Utah: a History.* New York, 1977

VERMONT

KEY HISTORICAL EVENTS. The original Indian hunting grounds of the Green Mountains and lakes was explored by the Frenchman Samuel de Champlain in 1609 who reached Lake Champlain on the north-west border. The first attempt at permanent settlement was also French, on Isle la Motte in 1666. In 1763 the British gained the area from the French by the Treaty of Paris. The Treaty, which also brought peace with the Indian allies of the French, opened the way for settlement, but in a mountain state transport was slow and difficult. Montpelier, the state capital from 1805, was chartered as a township site in 1781 to command the main pass through the Green Mountains.

During the War of Independence Vermont declared itself an independent state, to avoid being taken over by New Hampshire and New York. In 1791 it became the 14th state of the Union.

Most early settlers were New Englanders of British and Protestant descent. After 1812 a granite-quarrying industry grew around the town of Barre, attracting immigrant workers from Italy and Scandinavia. French Canadians also settled in Winooski. When textile and engineering industries developed in the 19th century these brought more European workers.

Vermont saw the only Civil War action north of Pennsylvania, when a Confederate raiding party attacked from Canada in 1864.

During the 20th century the textile and engineering industries have declined but paper and lumber industries flourish. Settlement is still mainly rural or in small towns, and farming is pastoral.

TERRITORY AND POPULATION. Vermont is bounded in the north by Canada, east by New Hampshire, south by Massachusetts and west by New York. Land area, 9,614 sq. miles (23,955 sq. km). Census population, 1 April 1990, 562,758 (32·2% urban), an increase of 10% since 1980. Population estimate (1996), 589,000. Births, 1995, were 6,783 (11·6 per 1,000 population); deaths, 4,949 (8·5); infant deaths, 41 (6·0 per 1,000 live births); marriages, 6,000 (10·3); divorces, 2,520 (436).

Population at 5 census years was:

	White	Black	Indian	Asiatic	Total	Per sq. mile
1910	354,298	1,621	26	11	355,956	39·0
1930	358,966	568	36	41	359,611	38·8
1960	389,092	519	57	172	389,881	42·0
1980	506,736	1,135	984	1,355	511,456	55·1
1990	555,088	1,951	1,696[1]	3,215[2]	562,758	60·8

[1] Includes Eskimo and Aleut.   [2] Includes Pacific Islander.

Of the population in 1990, 275,494 were male; 180,904 were urban; those 20 years of age or older numbered 400,019. The largest cities are Burlington, with a population (1996 estimate) of 39,004; Rutland, 17,605; Essex, 16,498 (1994 estimate); Colchester, 16,400.

CLIMATE. Burlington. Jan. 17°F (−8·3°C), July 70°F (21·1°C). Annual rainfall 33" (820 mm). Vermont belongs to the New England climate zone (*see* UNITED STATES: Climate).

CONSTITUTION AND GOVERNMENT. The constitution was adopted in 1793 and has since been amended. Amendments are proposed by two-thirds vote of the Senate every 4 years, and must be accepted by two sessions of the legislature; they are then submitted to popular vote. The state Legislature, consisting of a Senate of 30 members and a House of Representatives of 150 members (both elected for 2 years), meets in Jan. every year. The Governor and Lieut.-Governor are elected for 2 years. Electors are all citizens who possess certain residential qualifications and have taken the freeman's oath set forth in the constitution.

The state sends 1 representative to Congress.

In the 1996 presidential election Clinton polled 137,030 votes; Dole, 79,675; Perot, 30,491.

The capital is Montpelier (8,254 in 1990). There are 14 counties and 251 cities, towns and other administrative divisions.

Governor: Howard Dean (D.), 1995–97 ($80,724).
Lieut.-Governor: Douglas Racine (D.) ($33,654).
Secretary of State: Jim Milne (R.) ($50,794).

BUDGET. The total revenue for the year ending 30 June 1994 was $1,738·2m.; total disbursements, $1,665·8m.

Total net long-term bonded debt, 30 June 1996, was $489·1m.

Per capita personal income (1995) was $20,927.

NATURAL RESOURCES

Minerals. Stone, chiefly granite, marble and slate, is the leading mineral produced in Vermont, contributing about 60% of the total value of mineral products. Other products include asbestos, talc, sand and gravel. Total value of non-fuel mineral products, 1991, $60m.

Agriculture. Agriculture is the most important industry. In 1996 the state had some 6,000 farms covering 1m. acres; the average farm was of 225 acres in 1996 and in 1995 the average value per acre was $1,479. Farm income, 1995, from livestock and products, $380m.; from crops, $35m. The dairy farms produced about 2,538,000 lb. of milk in 1995. The chief agricultural crops are hay, apples and silage. In 1995 Vermont had 290,000 cattle and calves, 19,500 sheep and lambs, 2,800 hogs and pigs, and 134,000 chickens and turkeys.

Forestry. In 1994 the harvest was 251,159m. bd ft, of which 50,663m. bd ft was veneer logs, and 415,985 cords of pulpwood and boltwood.

The state is 76% forest, with 10% in public ownership. National forests area (1996), 350,000 acres. State-owned forests, parks, fish and game areas, 250,000 acres; municipally-owned, 38,500 acres.

INDUSTRY. In 1996 service industries employed 82,000; trade, 65,000; manufacturing, 46,000; government, 45,000; construction, 13,000.

COMMUNICATIONS

Roads. The state had 13,964 miles of roads in 1996, including 7,376 miles of gravel, graded and drained, or unimproved roads. Motor vehicle registrations, 1996, 724,846 (including motorcycles and mopeds).

Railways. There were, in 1988, 793 miles of railway, 291 of which was leased by the state to private operators.

Civil Aviation. There were 18 airports in 1990, of which 11 were state operated, 1 municipally owned and 6 private. Some are only open in summer.

SOCIAL INSTITUTIONS

Justice. As of midnight on 11 Sept. 1997, prisons and centres had 1,238 inmates. The death penalty is not authorized.

Religion. The principal denominations are Roman Catholic, United Church of Christ, United Methodist, Protestant Episcopal, Baptist and Unitarian–Universalist.

Education. School attendance during the full school term is compulsory for children from 7 to 16 years of age, unless they have completed the 10th grade or undergo approved home instruction. In 1994–95 the public elementary and secondary schools had 101,045 pupils and 7,410 teachers. Average teacher's salary was $36,681. State and local governments expenditure on public schools, 1994, $569·2m.

In autumn 1993 there were 36,528 students in higher education. The University of Vermont (1791) had 10,146 students in 1996–97; Norwich University (1834, founded as the American Literary, Scientific and Military Academy in 1819), had 2,619; St Michael's College (1904), 2,212; there are 5 state colleges.

Health. In 1995 the state had 14 community hospitals (1,800 beds).

Social Security. Old-age assistance (SSI) was being granted in 1993 to 3,654 (including aged, blind and disabled) persons, drawing an average of $320·42 per month; aid to dependent children was being granted to 26,986 persons, drawing an average of $194·25 per month; and aid to the permanently and totally disabled was being granted to 10,177 persons, drawing an average of $355·36.

Further Reading

Statistical information: Office of Policy Research and Coordination, Montpelier 05602
Legislative Directory. Secretary of State, Montpelier. Biennial
Vermont Annual Financial Report. Auditor of Accounts, Montpelier. Annual
Vermont Year-Book, formerly *Walton's Register.* Chester. Annual
Bassett T. (ed.) *Vermont: A Bibliography of its History,* Boston, 1981
Vermont Atlas and Gazetteer, Rev. ed., Freeport, 1983
Morrissey, C. T., *Vermont,* New York, 1981

State Library: Vermont Dept. of Libraries, Montpelier.

VIRGINIA

KEY HISTORICAL EVENTS. In 1607 a British colony was founded at Jamestown, on a peninsula in the James River, to grow tobacco. The area was marshy and unhealthy but the colony survived and in 1619 introduced a form of representative government. The tobacco plantations expanded and African slaves were imported. Jamestown was later abandoned, but tobacco-growing continued and spread through the eastern part of the territory.

In 1624 control of the colony passed from the Virginia Company of London to the Crown. Growth was rapid during the 17th and 18th centuries. The movement for American independence was strong in Virginia; George Washington and Thomas Jefferson were both Virginians, and crucial battles of the War of Independence were fought there.

When the Union was formed, Virginia became one of the original states, but with reservations regarding the constitution because of its attachment to slave-owning. In 1831 there was a slave rebellion. The tobacco plantations began to decline, and plantation owners turned to the breeding of slaves. While the eastern plantation lands seceded from the Union in 1861, the small farmers and miners of the western hills refused to secede and remained in the Union as West Virginia.

Richmond, the capital, became the capital of the Confederacy. Much of the Civil War's decisive conflict took place in Virginia, with considerable damage to the economy. After the war the position of the black population was little improved. Blacks remained without political or civil rights until the 1960s.

TERRITORY AND POPULATION. Virginia is bounded north-west by West Virginia, north-east by Maryland, east by the Atlantic, south by North Carolina and Tennessee and west by Kentucky. Land area, 39,598 sq. miles (102,558 sq. km). Census population, 1 April 1990, 6,187,358 (69·4% urban), an increase of 15·73% since 1980. Population estimate (1996), 6,675,000. In 1995 there were 91,286 births (13·9 per 1,000 population), 52,507 deaths (9), 712 infant deaths under 1 year (7·8 per 1,000 live births), 67,858 marriages (10·3) and 29,629 divorces (4·5).

Population for 5 federal census years was:

	White	Black	Indian	Asian/Other	Total	Per sq. mile
1910	1,389,809	671,096	539	168	2,061,612	51·2
1930	1,770,441	650,165	779	466	2,421,851	60·7
1960	3,142,443	816,258	2,155	4,725	3,966,949	99·3
			All others			
1980	4,230,000	1,008,311		108,517	5,346,818	134·7
1990	4,791,739	1,162,994	15,282	217,343	6,187,358	155·9

Of the total population in 1990, 49% were male, 69·4% were urban and 70·7% were 21 years of age or older.

The population (census of 1990) of the principal cities was: Virginia Beach, 393,069; Norfolk, 261,229; Richmond, 203,056; Newport News, 170,045; Chesapeake, 151,976; Hampton, 133,793; Alexandria, 111,183; Portsmouth, 103,907.

CLIMATE. Average temperatures in Jan. are 41°F in the Tidewater coastal area and 32°F in the Blue Ridge mountains; July averages, 78°F and 68°F respectively.

Precipitation averages 36" in the Shenandoah valley and 44" in the south. Snowfall is 5-10" in the Tidewater and 25-30" in the western mountains. Norfolk. Jan. 41°F (5°C), July 79°F (26·1°C). Annual rainfall 46" (1,145 mm). Virginia belongs to the Atlantic Coast climate zone (*see* UNITED STATES: Climate).

CONSTITUTION AND GOVERNMENT. The present constitution dates from 1971. The General Assembly consists of a Senate of 40 members, elected for 4 years, and a House of Delegates of 100 members, elected for 2 years. It sits annually in Jan. The Governor and Lieut.-Governor are elected for 4 years.

The state sends 11 representatives to Congress.

In the 1996 presidential election Dole polled 1,119,974 votes; Clinton, 1,070,990; Perot, 158,707.

The state capital is Richmond; the state contains 95 counties and 40 independent cities.

Governor: George F. Allen (R.), 1994–98 ($110,000).
Lieut.-Governor: Donald S. Beyer, Jr (D.), 1994–98 ($32,000).
Secretary of the Commonwealth: Elizabeth Beamer (R.) ($73,023).

BUDGET. General revenue for the year ending 30 June 1994 was $14,817m. (taxation, $8,037m., and federal aid, $2,926m.); general expenditures, $14,263·3m. ($5,564·9m. for education, $2,543·2m. for public welfare and $1,639·2m. for highways).

Total debt, 1994, was $7,912m.

Per capita personal income (1995) was $20,288.

NATURAL RESOURCES

Minerals. Coal is the most important mineral, with output (1994) of 37,129,301 short tons. Lead and zinc ores, stone, sand and gravel, lime and titanium ore are also produced. Total non-fuel mineral output was valued at $514m. in 1994.

Agriculture. In 1996 there were 48,000 farms with an area of 8·6m. acres; the average farm had 179 acres, and the average value per acre was $1,771 in 1995. Farm income, 1995, from field crops, $556·2m.; from greenhouse, nursery and tree produce, $138·63m.; from vegetables, $87·8m.; from fruits, $52·19m. and from livestock and livestock products, $1,393·18m. The chief crops are tobacco, soybeans, peanuts, winter wheat, maize, tomatoes, apples, potatoes and sweet potatoes. Livestock, 1 Jan. 1996: Cattle and calves, 1·8m.; milk cows, 128,000; sheep and lambs, 84,000; 1 Dec. 1995: Hogs and pigs, 0·38m.; 1995: Turkeys, 23·5m.; broilers, 260·1m.

Forestry. Forests covered 16,026,874 acres in 1992 (63·1% of the total land area).

INDUSTRY. The manufacture of cigars and cigarettes and of rayon and allied products and the building of ships lead in value of products. In 1996 manufacturing employed 399,000 people out of a total non-agricultural workforce of 3,130,000.

TOURISM. Domestic tourists spent about $9,076m. in 1993.

COMMUNICATIONS

Roads. In 1995 there were 67,155 miles of roads (52,848 miles rural in 1993). In 1994 there were 5,383,500 registered motor vehicles.

Railways. In 1992 there were 3,295 miles of Class I track including commuter services to Washington.

Civil Aviation. There are international airports at Norfolk, Dulles, Richmond and Newport News.

SOCIAL INSTITUTIONS

Justice. Prison population, June 1996, 25,242 in federal and state prisons. The death penalty is authorized. The last execution was in 1997.

Religion. The principal churches are the Baptist, Methodist, Protestant-Episcopal, Roman Catholic and Presbyterian.

Education. Elementary and secondary instruction is free, and for ages 6–17 attendance is compulsory.

In 1994–95 the 133 school districts had, in primary schools, 684,000 pupils and 43,000 teachers and in public high schools, 377,000 pupils and 28,000 teachers. Teachers' salaries averaged $32,700 (primary school) and $35,300 (high school). Total expenditure on education, 1994–95, was $6,435m.

In 1993–94 there were 87 higher education institutions (48 private) including:

Founded	Name and place of college	Staff 1994–95	Students 1994
1693	College of William and Mary, Williamsburg (State)	479	7,547
1749	Washington and Lee University, Lexington	166	1,990
1776	Hampden-Sydney College, Hampden-Sydney (Pres.)	84	970
1819	University of Virginia, Charlottesville (State)	987	21,421
1832	Randolph-Macon College, Ashland (Methodist)	79	1,093
1832	University of Richmond, Richmond (Baptist)	228	4,258
1838	Virginia Commonwealth University, Richmond	777	21,523
1839	Virginia Military Institute Lexington (State)	97	1,179
1865	Virginia Union University, Richmond	83	1,525
1868	Hampton University	303	5,769
1872	Virginia Polytechnic Institute and State University	1,466	25,842
1882	Virginia State University, Petersburg	168	4,007
1908	James Madison University, Harrisonburg	520	11,680
1910	Radford University (State)	394	9,105
1930	Old Dominion University, Norfolk	634	16,49
1956	George Mason University (State)	677	21,774

Health. In 1994 the state had 123 hospitals listed by the American Hospital Association.

Social Security. In 1993 there were 901,000 Social Security beneficiaries (average monthly grant $642); 118,000 Supplemental Security Income beneficiaries (average monthly grant $279); 779,000 Medicare beneficiaries (average monthly grant $259); 576,000 recipients of Medicaid; 195,000 recipients of aid to families with dependent children (average monthly payment per family $262); 11,399 persons receiving Black Lung benefits (average monthly payment $373), and 10,650 children enrolled in the Head Start programme. In 1994 there were 232,000 households (547,000 persons) participating in the federal Food Stamp programme and 601,000 students participating in the National School Lunch programme; a total of 210,116 persons received some form of state-sponsored public assistance.

Further Reading

Statistical information: Cooper Center for Public Service, Univ. of Virginia, 918 Emmet St. N., Suite 300, Charlottesville 22903-4832. Publishes *Virginia Statistical Abstract. – Population Estimates of Virginia Cities and Counties.*

Dabney, V., *Virginia, the New Dominion.* 1971

Gottmann, J., *Virginia in our Century.* Charlottesville, 1969

Morton, R. L., *Colonial Virginia.* 2 vols. Univ. Press of Virginia, 1960

Rouse, P. *Virginia: a Pictorial History.* New York, 1975

Rubin, L. D. Jr., *Virginia: a Bicentennial History.* Norris, 1977

State Library: Virginia State Library, Richmond 23219.

WASHINGTON

KEY HISTORICAL EVENTS. The strongest Indian tribes in the 18th century were Chinook, Nez Percé, Salish and Yakima. The area was designated by European colonizers as part of the Oregon Country. Between 1775 and 1800 it had been claimed by explorers for Spain, Britain and the USA; the dispute between the two latter nations was not settled until 1846.

The first small white settlements were Indian missions and fur-trading posts. In the 1840s American settlers began to push westwards along the Oregon Trail, making a speedy solution of the dispute with Britain necessary. When this was achieved the whole area was organized as the Oregon Territory in 1848, and Washington was made a separate Territory in 1853.

Apart from trapping and fishing, the important industry was logging, mainly to supply building timbers to the new settlements of California. After 1870 the westward extension of railways helped to stimulate settlement. Statehood was granted in 1889. The early population was composed mainly of Americans from neighbouring states to the east, and Canadians. Scandinavian immigrants followed. Seattle, the chief city, was laid out in 1853 as a saw-milling town and named after the Indian chief who had ceded the land and befriended the settlers. It grew as a port during the Alaskan and Yukon gold-rushes of the 1890s. The economy thrived on exploiting the Columbia River for hydro-electric power.

TERRITORY AND POPULATION. Washington is bounded north by Canada, east by Idaho, south by Oregon with the Columbia River forming most of the boundary, and west by the Pacific. Land area, 66,582 sq. miles (172,447 sq. km). Lands owned by the federal government, 1993, were 12·7m. acres or 29·8% of the total area. Census population, 1 April 1990, 4,866,663 (76·4% urban), an increase of 17·83% since 1980. Population estimate (1997), 5,606,800. Births, 1997, were 77,000; deaths, 41,500. Marriages, 1996, were 41,537 (7·5 per 1,000 population); divorces, 28,012 (5·1).

Population in 5 federal census years was:

	White	Black	Indian	Asian/Other	Total	Per sq. mile
1910	1,109,111	6,058	10,997	15,824	1,141,990	17·1
1930	1,521,661	6,840	11,253	23,642	1,563,396	23·3
1960	2,751,675	48,738	21,076	31,725	2,853,214	42·8
1980	3,779,170	105,574	60,804	186,608	4,132,156	62·1
1990	4,308,937	149,801	81,483	326,471	4,866,663	73·1

Of the total population in 1990, 2,413,747 were male; 3,387,546 were 20 years of age or older.

There are 27 Indian reservations. Indian reservations in 1990 covered 2,718,516 acres, of which 2,250,731 acres were tribal lands.

Leading cities are Seattle, with a population in 1990 (and 1997 estimate) of 516,259 (536,600); Spokane, 177,165 (188,300); Tacoma, 176,664 (185,600); Vancouver, 46,380 (127,900); Bellevue, 86,872 (104,800). Others: Everett, 84,130; Federal Way, 75,960; Yakima, 63,510; Lakewood, 62,240; Kent, 62,006; Bellingham, 61,240; Shoreline, 50,380; Kennewick, 49,090; Renton, 45,920; Kirkland, 43,720; Redmond, 42,230.

CLIMATE. Seattle. Jan. 40°F (4·4°C), July 63°F (17·2°C). Annual rainfall 34" (848 mm). Spokane. Jan. 27°F (−2·8°C), July 70°F (21·1°C). Annual rainfall 14" (350 mm). Washington belongs to the Pacific Coast climate zone (*see* UNITED STATES: Climate).

CONSTITUTION AND GOVERNMENT. The constitution, adopted in 1889, has had 63 amendments. The Legislature consists of a Senate of 49 members elected for 4 years, half their number retiring every 2 years, and a House of Representatives of 98 members, elected for 2 years. The Governor and Lieut.-Governor are elected for 4 years.

The state sends 9 representatives to Congress.

In the 1996 presidential election Clinton polled 899,645 votes; Dole, 639,743; Perot, 161,642.

The capital is Olympia. The state contains 39 counties.

Governor: Gary Locke (D.), 1997–2001 ($121,000).

BUDGET. For the 1995–97 biennium final All Budgeted funds expenditures were $33,060·4m. and final All Budgeted funds revenues were $35,522·4m.

Total General Obligation Bonded Indebtedness at the end of the 1995–97 biennium was $5,939·4m.
Per capita personal income (1996) was $25,187.

NATURAL RESOURCES

Minerals. Mining and quarrying are not as important as forestry, agriculture or manufacturing.

Agriculture. Agriculture is constantly growing in value because of more intensive and diversified farming and because of the 1m.-acre Columbia Basin Irrigation Project.

In 1997 there were 36,000 farms with an acreage of 15·7m.; the average farm was 436 acres. Average value of farmland and buildings per acre in 1996 was $1,117. Apples, milk, wheat, potatoes, and cattle and calves are the top five commodities. On 1 Jan. 1997 livestock included 266,000 milk cows, 294,000 beef cows, 50,000 sheep and lambs. Hogs and pigs as of 1 Dec. 1996 totalled 35,000 head.

Value of agricultural production in 1996 (in $1m.): Field crops, 2,046·3; fruit, 1,263·7; vegetables, 299·5; livestock, poultry and their products, 1,464·8.

Forestry. Forests cover 21,856,000 acres, of which 9m. acres are national forest. In 1995, timber harvested was an estimated 4,393m. bd ft. Acres planted or seeded, 1993, 163,442, not including natural re-seeding. Production of wood residues, 1992, included 2,671,000 tons of pulp and board.

Fisheries. Salmon and shellfish are important; total fish catch, 1995, was worth an estimated $170,597,000.

INDUSTRY. In 1996 manufacturing employed 344,100 workers, of whom 86,100 were in aerospace and 52,400 in the forest products industry. Principal manufactures: Aircraft, pulp and paper, lumber and plywood, aluminium, processed fruit and vegetables. In 1996 trade employed 590,900, service industries, 649,200 and government, 450,400.

COMMUNICATIONS

Roads. In 1996 there were 79,555 miles of roads and 5,383,000 registered motor vehicles.

Railways. In 1996 there were 3,090 route miles.

Civil Aviation. There are international airports at Seattle/Tacoma, Spokane and Boeing Field.

SOCIAL INSTITUTIONS

Justice. The adult inmates in state prisons on 30 June 1997 numbered 12,735. The death penalty is authorized. The last execution was in 1994.

Religion. Religious faiths represented include the Roman Catholic, United Methodist, Lutheran, Presbyterian and Episcopalian. There were 211,000 Latter Day Saints (Mormons) in 1995.

Education. Education is given free to all children between the ages of 5 and 21 years, and is compulsory for children from 8 to 15 years of age. In Oct. 1997 there were 990,389 pupils in elementary and secondary schools. In Oct. 1995 there were 46,883 classroom teachers, average salary, $39,900.

The University of Washington, founded 1861, at Seattle, had, autumn 1997, 36,355 students, and Washington State University at Pullman, founded 1890, for science and agriculture, had 20,020 students. Eastern Washington University had 7,537; Central Washington University, 8,438; The Evergreen State College, 4,084; Western Washington University, 11,476. All counts are state-funded enrolment students. Community colleges had (1996) a total of 172,643 state-funded and excess enrolment students.

Health. In fiscal year 1997 the 2 state hospitals for mental illness, the 1 mental health facility and the child study and treatment centre had, together, a daily average of 1,278 patients.

In 1997 there were 93 accredited acute hospitals (11,484 beds) and 4 psychiatric hospitals (215 beds). In Sept. 1997 there were 16,790 doctors, 4,860 dentists, 58,120 registered nurses and 5,855 pharmacists.

Social Security. Old-age assistance is provided for persons 65 years of age or older without adequate resources (and not in need of continuing home care) who are residents of the state. In July 1997 the following assistance was provided: 916 blind persons received a monthly average of $362·07; 13,305 aged, $302·06; 80,251 disabled, $377·99. Aid was also given to 156,995 children in 88,266 families, averaging $376·90 per family monthly.

Further Reading

Statistical information: State Office of Financial Management, POB 43113, Olympia 98504-3113. Publishes *Washington State Data Book*

Dodds, G.B., *American North-West: a History of Oregon and Washington.* Arlington (Ill), 1986

Swanson, T., *Political Life in Washington.* Pullman, 1985

WEST VIRGINIA

KEY HISTORICAL EVENTS. In 1861 the state of Virginia seceded from the Union over the issue of slave-owning. The 40 western counties of the state were composed of hilly country, settled by miners and small farmers who were not slave-owners. In 1862 these counties ratified an ordinance providing for the creation of a new sate. On 20 June 1863 West Virginia became the 35th state of the Union.

The capital, Charleston, was an 18th-century fortified post on the early westward migration routes across the Appalachians. In 1795 local brine wells were tapped and the city grew as a salt town. Coal, oil, natural gas and a variety of salt brines were all found in due course. Huntington, the next largest town, developed as a railway terminus serving the same industrial area, and also providing transport on the Ohio river.

Three-quarters of the state is forest and settlement has been concentrated in the mineral-bearing Kanawha valley, along the Ohio river and in the industrial Monongahela valley of the north. More than half of the population is still classified as rural. The traditional small firms and small hill-mines, however, support few, and the majority of rural dwellers commute to industrial employment.

TERRITORY AND POPULATION. West Virginia is bounded north by Pennsylvania and Maryland, east and south by Virginia, south-west by the Big Sandy River (forming the boundary with Kentucky) and west by the Ohio River (forming the boundary with Ohio). Total area, 24,232 sq. miles (62,761 sq. km). Census population, 1 April 1990, 1,793,477 (36·1% urban), a decrease of 8·01% since 1980. Population estimate (1996), 1,826,000. Births, 1995, 21,158 (11·6 per 1,000 population); deaths, 20,128 (11·0); infant deaths, 160 (7·6 per 1,000 live births); marriages, 11,472 (6·3); divorces, 9,219 (5·0).

Population in 5 federal census years was:

	White	Black	Indian	Asiatic	Total	Per sq. mile
1910	1,156,817	64,173	36	93	1,221,119	50·8
1940	1,614,191	114,893	18	103	1,729,205	71·8
1960	1,770,133	89,378	181	419	1,860,421	77·3
1970	1,673,480	67,342	751	1,463	1,744,237	71·8
1980	1,874,751	65,051	1,610	5,194	1,949,644	80·3

Of the total population in 1980, 945,408 were male, 705,319 were urban; those 20 years of age or older numbered 1,319,566.

The 1990 census population of the principal cities was: Huntington, 58,844; Charleston, 57,287. Others: Wheeling, 38,882; Parkersburg, 33,882; Morgantown, 25,879; Weirton, 22,124; Fairmont, 20,210; Clarksburg, 18,059.

CLIMATE. Charleston. Jan. 34°F (1·1°C), July 76°F (24·4°C). Annual rainfall 40" (1,010 mm). West Virginia belongs to the Appalachian Mountains climate zone (*see* UNITED STATES: Climate).

CONSTITUTION AND GOVERNMENT. The present constitution was adopted in 1872; it has had 62 amendments. The Legislature consists of the Senate of 34 members elected for a term of 4 years, one-half being elected biennially, and the House of Delegates of 100 members, elected biennially. The Governor is elected for 4 years and may serve 1 successive term.

The state sends 3 representatives to Congress.

In the 1996 presidential election Clinton polled 257,225 votes; Dole, 179,937; Perot, 53,146.

The state capital is Charleston. There are 55 counties.

Governor: Cecil Underwood (R.), 1997–2001 ($90,000).
Secretary of State: Ken Hechler (D.) ($65,000).

FINANCE. Total revenues for the year ending 30 June 1995 were $6,638m. ($2,312m. from taxes, $1,909m. from federal funds, $482m. from highway funds, $1,935m. from special revenues); general expenditures were $6,568m. (education, $2,147m.; highways, $597m.; health and welfare, $1,825m.).

Tax-supported debt for 1995 was $988m., non-tax-supported debt was $2,751m.

Estimated *per capita* personal income (1996) was $18,444.

NATURAL RESOURCES

Minerals. 38% of the state is underlain with mineable coal; 174m. short tons of coal were produced in 1996. Petroleum output (1995), 1·95m. bbls; natural gas production (1995), 184,900m. cu. ft. Salt, sand and gravel, sandstone and limestone are also produced. The total non-fuel mineral output in 1996 was 16m. tons.

Agriculture. In 1995 the state had 20,000 farms with an area of 3·7m. acres; average size of farm was 185 acres and valued at $696 per acre (1994). Livestock farming predominates.

Cash income, 1995, from crops was $74·3m.; from government payments, $5·2m., and from livestock and products, $312·1m. Main crops harvested, 1995: Hay (1·1m. tons); all corn (4m. bu.); tobacco (2,600,000 lb). Area of main crops, 1994: Hay, 0·55m. acres; corn, 0·01m. acres. Apples (165m. lb in 1995) and peaches (16·5m. lb. in 1995) are important fruit crops. Livestock on farms, 1994, included 0·5m. cattle, of which 20,000 were milk cows; sheep, 60,000; hogs, 30,000; chickens, 2m. excluding broilers. Production, 1995, included 391m. lb. broilers, 19·9m. doz. eggs; 90m. lb. turkeys.

Forestry. State forests, 1996, covered 73,736 acres; national forests, 1,032,000 acres; 79% of the state is woodland.

INDUSTRY. In 1996, 2,032 manufactories had 81,842 production workers. Leading manufactures are primary and fabricated metals, glass, chemicals, wood products, textiles and apparel, machinery, plastics, speciality chemicals, aerospace, electronics, medical and related technologies and industrial products recycling.

In Oct. 1997 non-agricultural employment was 710,600 of whom 164,000 were in trade, 134,000 in government and 199,000 in service industries.

COMMUNICATIONS

Roads. In 1996 there were 37,884 miles of roads (34,928 miles rural) and 1,500,000 registered motor vehicles.

Railways. In 1996 the state had 2,583 miles of railway.

Civil Aviation. There were 37 public airports in 1996.

Shipping. There are some 300 miles of navigable rivers.

Telecommunications. In 1996 there were 168 commercial and public radio stations. Television stations number 12 commercial and 3 public.

Press. In 1996 daily newspapers numbered 23, weekly and college newspapers 78.

SOCIAL INSTITUTIONS

Justice. The state court system consists of a Supreme Court, 31 circuit courts, and magistrate courts in each county. The Supreme Court of Appeals, exercising original and appellate jurisdiction, has 5 members elected by the people for 12-year terms. Each circuit court has from 1 to 7 judges (as determined by the Legislature on the basis of population and case-load) chosen by the voters within each circuit for 8-year terms.

There are 12 penal and correctional institutions which had, in Dec. 1997, 2,556 inmates. Capital punishment was abolished in 1965. The last execution was in 1959.

Religion. Chief denominations in 1996 were United Methodist (121,920 members), American Baptists (95,559) and Roman Catholics (103,678 in 1997).

Education. Public school education is free for all from 5 to 21 years of age, and school attendance is compulsory for all between the ages of 7 and 16 (school term, 200 days—180–185 days of actual teaching). The public schools are non-sectarian. In 1995–96 public elementary and secondary schools had 302,254 pupils and 23,674 classroom teachers. Average salary of teachers was $33,085. Total 1994–95 education expenditures, including higher education, $2,146,982,684.

Leading institutions of higher education in the autumn of 1996:

Founded		Full-time students
1837	Marshall University, Huntington	13,164
1837	West Liberty State College, West Liberty	2,412
1867	Fairmont State College, Fairmont	6,555
1868	West Virginia University, Morgantown	21,743
1872	Concord College, Athens	2,400
1872	Glenville State College, Glenville	2,179
1872	Shepherd College, Shepherdstown	3,845
1895	West Virginia State College, Institute	4,545
1895	West Virginia Institute of Technology, Montgomery	2,486
1895	Bluefield State College, Bluefield	2,602
1901	Potomac State College of West Virginia Univ., Keyser	1,108
1961	West Virginia Univ. at Parkersburg, Parkersburg	3,421
1972	West Virginia Graduate College, Institute	2,506
1976	School of Osteopathic Medicine, Lewisburg	261

In addition to the universities and state-supported schools, there are 2 community colleges (5,609 students in 1996), 10 denominational and private institutions of higher education (10,156 students in 1996) and 11 business colleges.

Health. In 1996 the state had 65 licensed hospitals and 69 licensed personal care homes, 106 skilled-nursing homes and 4 mental hospitals.

Social Security. The Department of Health Human Resources, originating in the 1930s as the Department of Public Assistance, is both state and federally financed. In 1996, day care was provided for 146,942 children; 6,092 payments totalling $1,018,818·50 were given as aid to families with dependEnt children (average award, $167·24 per month).

Further Reading

West Virginia Blue Book. Legislature, Charleston. Annual, since 1916
Statistical Handbook, 1996. West Virginia Research League, Charleston, 1996
West Virginia History. Archives and History. Charleston. Quarterly, from 1939. Annual, from 1985
Doherty, W. T., *West Virginia: Our Land, Our People.* Charleston, 1990
Forbes, H. M., *West Virginia History: a Bibliography and Guide to Research.* Morgantown, 1981
Rice, O. K., *West Virginia: A History.* 2nd ed. Univ. Press of Kentucky, Lexington, 1994
Williams, J. A., *West Virginia: a Bicentennial History.* New York, 1976

State Library: Archives and History, Division of Culture and History, Charleston.

WISCONSIN

KEY HISTORICAL EVENTS. The French were the first European explorers of the territory; Jean Nicolet landed at Green Bay in 1634, a mission was founded in 1671 and a permanent settlement at Green Bay followed. In 1763 French claims were surrendered to Britain. In 1783 Britain ceded them to the USA, which designated the Northwest Territory, of which Wisconsin was part. In 1836 a separate Territory of Wisconsin was organized, including the present Iowa, Minnesota and parts of the Dakotas.

Territorial organization was a great stimulus to settlement. In 1836 James Duane Dooty founded the town site of Madison and successfully pressed its claim to be the capital of the Territory even before it was inhabited. In 1848 Wisconsin became a state, with its present boundaries.

The city of Milwaukee was founded, on Lake Michigan, when Indian tribes gave up their claims to the land in 1831–33. It grew rapidly as a port and industrial town, attracting Germans in the 1840s, Poles and Italians 50 years later. The Lake Michigan shore was developed as an industrial area; the rest of the south proved suitable for dairy farming; the north, mainly forests and lakes, has remained sparsely settled except for tourist bases.

There is a Menominee Indian reservation in the north-east, where many of the 29,000 remaining Indians live. Since the Second World War there has been black immigration from the southern states to the industrial lake-shore cities.

TERRITORY AND POPULATION. Wisconsin is bounded north by Lake Superior and the Upper Peninsula of Michigan, east by Lake Michigan, south by Illinois, west by Iowa and Minnesota, with the Mississippi River forming most of the boundary. Area, 56,154 sq. miles (145,439 sq. km), including 1,439 sq. miles of inland water, but excluding any part of the Great Lakes. Census population, 1 April 1990, 4,891,769 (65·7% urban), an increase of 4% since 1980. Estimated population (1996), 5,142,999. Births in 1995 were 67,493 (13·2 per 1,000 population); deaths in 1996 were 45,107 (8·7); infant deaths, 492 (7·3 per 1,000 live births); marriages, 36,186 (7·0); divorces and annulments, 17,218 (3·3).

Population in 5 census years was:

	White	Black	All others	Total	Per sq. mile
1910	2,320,555	2,900	10,405	2,333,860	42·2
1930	2,916,255	10,739	12,012	2,939,006	53·7
1960	3,858,903	74,546	18,328	3,951,777	72·2
1980	4,443,035	182,592	80,015	4,705,642	86·4
1990	4,512,523	244,539	134,767	4,891,769	90·1

Of the total population in 1990, 49% were male, 65·7% were urban and 73·7% were 18 years old or older.

Population of the larger cities, 1990 census, was as follows:

Milwaukee	628,088	Waukesha	56,958	Fond du Lac	37,757
Madison	191,262	Eau Claire	56,856	Wausau	37,060
Green Bay	96,466	Oshkosh	55,006	Beloit	35,573
Racine	84,298	Janesville	52,133	Brookfield	35,184
Kenosha	80,352	La Crosse	51,003	Neenah	33,592
Appleton	65,695	Sheboygan	49,676	Greenfield	33,403
West Allis	63,221	Wauwatosa	49,366		

Population of larger metropolitan areas, 1990 census: Milwaukee, 1,432,149; Madison, 367,085; Appleton-Neenah, 315,121; Duluth–Superior (Minn.–Wis.), 239,971; Green Bay, 194,594; Racine, 175,034.

CLIMATE. Milwaukee. Jan. 19°F (–7·2°C), July 70°F (21·1°C). Annual rainfall 29" (727 mm). Wisconsin belongs to the Great Lakes climate zone (*see* UNITED STATES: Climate).

CONSTITUTION AND GOVERNMENT. The constitution, which dates from 1848, has 136 amendments. The legislative power is vested in a Senate of 33 members elected for 4 years, one-half elected alternately, and an Assembly of 99 members all elected simultaneously for 2 years. The Governor and Lieut.-Governor are elected for 4 years.

The state sends 9 representatives to Congress.

In the 1996 presidential election Clinton polled 1,058,059 votes; Dole, 832,458; Perot, 218,043.

The capital is Madison. The state has 72 counties.

Governor: Tommy G. Thompson (R.), 1995–99 ($101,861).
Lieut.-Governor: Scott McCallum (R.) ($54,795).
Secretary of State: Douglas La Follette (D.) ($49,719).

BUDGET. For the year ending 30 June 1997 (Wisconsin Bureau of Financial Operations figures) total revenue for all funds was $27,410,758,000 ($8,817,536,000 from taxation and $4,015,928,000 from federal aid). General expenditure from all funds was $20,076,406,000 ($6,759,147,000 for education, $5,689,028,000 for human resources).

Per capita personal income (1996) was $23,320.

NATURAL RESOURCES

Minerals. Construction sand and gravel, crushed stone, industrial or specialty sand, lime, copper, gold and silver are the chief mineral products. Mineral production in 1996 was valued at over $399m. This value included $100m. of copper, gold and silver from the Flambeau Mine in Rusk County, $105m. for construction sand and gravel, $106m. for crushed stone, $33m. for industrial or specialty sand and $33m. for lime. The value of all other minerals including crushed trap rock, silica stone, peat and gemstones was around $20m.

Agriculture. On 1 Jan. 1997 there were 79,000 farms (27,000 dairy farms) with a total acreage of 16·8m. acres and an average size of 213 acres, compared with 142,000 farms with a total acreage of 22·4m. acres and an average of 158 acres in 1959. In 1996 the average value per acre was $1,284. Cash receipts from products sold by Wisconsin farms in 1996, $6,059m.; $4,288m. from livestock and livestock products and $1,771m. from crops.

Dairy farming is important, with 1·41m. milk cows. Production of cheese accounted for 29% of the USA's total. Production of the principal field crops in 1996 included: Corn for grain, 333m. bu.; corn for silage, 11·2m. tons; oats, 17·4m. bu.; all hay, 6·1m. tons. Other crops of importance: 31·6m. cwt of potatoes, 5·1m. lbs of tobacco, 1·9m. bbls of cranberries, 71·5m. tons of carrots and the processing crops of 701,200 tons of sweet corn, 88,100 tons of green peas, 231,800 tons of snap beans, 24,100 tons of cucumbers for pickles, 6·1m. lbs of tart cherries, 51,500 tons of beets for canning, 63,000 tons of cabbage for kraut and 1·1m. cwt of cabbage for fresh market.

Wisconsin is also a major producer of mink pelts.

Forestry. Wisconsin has an estimated 16·0m. acres of forest land. Of 15·7m. acres of timberland (Oct. 1997) national forests covered 1·4m. acres; state forests, 0·7m.; county and municipal forests, 2·3m.; forest industry, 1·1m.; private land, 10·1m.

Growing stock (1996), 18,500m. cu. ft, of which 14,100m. cu. ft is hardwood and 4,400m. cu. ft, softwood. Main hardwoods are maple, oak, aspen and basswood; main softwoods are red pine, white pine, northern white cedar and balsam fir. The timber industry employs 99,000, has a payroll of $3,400m. and shipments valued at $19,700m. (1996).

INDUSTRY. Wisconsin has much heavy industry, particularly in the Milwaukee area. Three fifths of manufacturing employees work on durable goods. Industrial machinery is the major industrial group (17% of all manufacturing employment) followed by fabricated metals, food and kindred products, printing and publishing, paper and allied products, electrical equipment and transportation equipment. Manufacturing establishments in 1996 provided 23% of non-farm wage and salary workers, 29% of all earnings. The total number of establishments was 10,454 in

1994; the biggest concentration is in the south-east. In 1996 manufacturing employed 121,000 people out of a total non-agricultural workforce of 2,602,000.

TOURISM. The tourist-vacation industry ranks among the first three in economic importance. The Department of Tourism budgeted $11,749,500 to promote tourism in financial year 1997–98.

COMMUNICATIONS

Roads. The state had, on 1 Jan. 1997, 111,500 miles of highway. 77% of all roads in the state have a bituminous (or similar) surface. There are 11,813 miles of state trunk roads and 19,621 miles of county trunk roads.

On 1 July 1997 Wisconsin registered 4,339,088 motor vehicles.

Railways. On 31 Dec. 1996 the state had 5,403 track-miles of railway.

Civil Aviation. There were, in 1997, 95 publicly operated airports. 11 scheduled air carrier airports were served by 17 regional and national air carriers.

Shipping. Lake Superior and Lake Michigan ports handled 47·9m. tons of freight in 1994; 87% of it at Superior, one of the world's biggest grain ports, and much of the rest at Milwaukee and Green Bay.

SOCIAL INSTITUTIONS

Justice. The state's penal, reformatory and correctional system on 28 Nov. 1997 held 13,695 men and 762 women in 11 state-owned prisons, 17 community facilities and other institutions for adult offenders (including 630 males in Texas county jails); the probation and parole system was supervising 64,745 adults, and 1,474 males and 277 females were being supervised under intensive sanctions. Average daily population in the state's 5 juvenile institutions as of 28 Nov. 1997 was 833 males and 75 females. Wisconsin does not impose the death penalty.

Religion. Wisconsin church affiliation, as a percentage of the 1990 population, was estimated at 31·8% Catholic, 20·1% Lutheran, 3·2% Methodist, 9·5% other churches and 35·4% un-affiliated.

Education. All children between the ages of 6 and 18 are required to attend school full-time to the end of the school term in which they become 18 years of age. In 1996–97 the public school grades kindergarten–12 had 859,988 pupils and 53,087 (full-time equivalent) teachers. Private schools enrolled 138,658 students grades kindergarten–12. Public pre-schools enrolled 19,989 children, and private, 11,482. Public elementary teachers' salaries, 1995–96, averaged $38,043; secondary, $39,424.

In 1995–96 vocational, technical and adult schools had an enrolment of 431,405 and 4,351 (full-time and part-time) teachers and 2 Indian tribe community colleges enrolled 670 (autumn 1996). There is a school for the visually handicapped and a school for the deaf.

The University of Wisconsin, established in 1848, was joined by law in 1971 with the Wisconsin State Universities System to become the University of Wisconsin System with 13 degree granting campuses, 13 2-year campuses in the Center System, and the University Extension. The system had, in 1996–97, 6,743 full-time professors and instructors. In autumn 1996, 149,330 students enrolled (10,495 at Eau Claire, 5,530 at Green Bay, 9,046 at La Crosse, 39,826 at Madison, 21,877 at Milwaukee, 10,359 at Oshkosh, 4,533 at Parkside, 4,901 at Platteville, 5,359 at River Falls, 8,362 at Stevens Point, 7,140 at Stout, 2,659 at Superior, 10,398 at Whitewater and 8,845 at the Center System freshman-sophomore centres). UW-Extension enrolled 267,782 students in its continuing education programmes in 1995–96. There are also several independent institutions of higher education. These (with autumn 1996 enrolment) include 3 universities (15,874), 16 colleges (30,733), 4 technical and professional schools (4,913), and 5 theological seminaries (388).

The total expenditure, 1995–96, for all public education (except capital outlay and debt service) was $9,075m. ($1,779 per capita).

The state maintains an educational broadcasting and television service.

Health. In fiscal year 1996 the state had 123 general medical and surgical hospitals (13,967 beds), 13 psychiatric hospitals (789 beds), 2 treatment centres for alcohol and drug abuse (60 beds) and 1 physical rehabilitation hospitals (69 beds). There were 2 state mental hospitals (587 beds) and 3 US Veterans' Administration hospitals. Patients in state mental hospitals and institutions for the developmentally disabled averaged 1,795 in 1995. On 31 Dec. 1995 the state had 460 licensed nursing homes with 46,482 residents.

Social Security. On 1 Jan. 1974 the US Social Security administration assumed responsibility for financial aid (Supplemental Security Income) to persons 65 years old and over, blind persons and totally disabled persons, who satisfy requirements as to need. Recipients receive a federal payment plus a federally administered state supplementary payment, except for those who reside in a medical institution. In Dec. 1997, there were 108,328 SSI recipients in the state; payments (1998) were $578 for a single individual, $624 for an eligible individual with an ineligible spouse, and $873 for an eligible couple. A special payment level of $674 for an individual and $1,218 for a couple may be paid with special approval for SSI recipients who are developmentally disabled or chronically mentally ill, living in a non-medical living arrangement not his or her own home. All SSI recipients receive state medical assistance coverage.

Under the Aid to Families with Dependent Children (AFDC) programme, 18,122 households of 48,944 persons received aid in Nov. 1997. Under the W-2 (Wisconsin Works) programme, 23,328 additional households continued to receive AFDC benefits. The W-2 programme, which is replacing AFDC with work and job training requirements, will be fully implemented in 1999. Medicaid cost $2,454m. (state share was $865·3m.) in financial year 1996–97.

Further Reading

Dictionary of Wisconsin Biography. Wisconsin Historical Society, Madison, 1960
Wisconsin Blue Book. Wisconsin Legislative Reference Bureau, Madison. Biennial
Current, R. N., *Wisconsin, a History.* New York, 1977
Danziger, S. and Witte, J. F., *State Policy Choices: The Wisconsin Experience.* Univ. Wisconsin Press, 1988
Martin, J., *The Physical Geography of Wisconsin.* Univ. Wisconsin Press, 3rd ed., 1965
Nesbit, R. C., *Wisconsin, A History.* State Historical Society of Wisconsin, Madison, rev. ed., 1989
Robinson, A. H. and Culver, J. B., (eds.) *The Atlas of Wisconsin.* Univ. Wisconsin Press, 1974
Vogeler, I., *Wisconsin: A Geography.* Boulder, 1986
State Historical Society of Wisconsin: *The History of Wisconsin.* Vol. I [Alice E. Smith], Madison, 1973.—Vol. II [R. N. Current], Madison, 1976.—Vol. III [R. C. Nesbit], Madison, 1985. Vol. VI [W. F. Thompson], Madison, 1988.—Vol. V (P. W. Glad), Madison, 1990

State Information Agency: Legislative Reference Bureau, 100 N. Hamilton St., P.O. Box 2037, Madison, WI 53701-2037. *Acting Chief:* Peter J. Dykman.

WYOMING

KEY HISTORICAL EVENTS. The territory was inhabited by Plains Indians (Arapahoes, Sioux and Cheyenne) in the early 19th century. There was some trading between them and white Americans, but very little white settlement. In the 1840s the great western migration routes, the Oregon and the Overland Trails, ran through the territory, Wyoming offering mountain passes accessible to wagons. Once migration became a steady flow it was necessary to protect the route from Indian attack, and forts were built.

In 1867 coal was discovered. In 1868 Wyoming was organized as a separate Territory, and in 1869 the Sioux and Arapaho were confined to reservations. At the same time the route of the Union Pacific Railway was laid out, and working settlements and railway towns grew up in southern Wyoming. Settlement of the north was delayed until after the final defeat of hostile Indians in 1876.

The economy of the settlements at first depended on ranching. Cheyenne had been made Territorial capital in 1869, and also functioned as a railway town moving cattle. Casper, on the site of a fort on the Pony Express route, was also a railway town on the Chicago and North Western. Laramie started as a Union Pacific construction workers' shanty town in 1868. In 1890 oil was discovered at Casper, and Wyoming became a state in the same year.

During the 20th century mineral extraction became the leading industry, as natural gas, uranium, bentonite and trona were exploited as well as oil and coal.

TERRITORY AND POPULATION. Wyoming is bounded north by Montana, east by South Dakota and Nebraska, south by Colorado, south-west by Utah and west by Idaho. Land area, 97,105 sq. miles (251,501 sq. km). The Yellowstone National Park occupies about 2·22m. acres; the Grand Teton National Park has 307,000 acres. The federal government in 1986 owned 49,838 sq. miles (50·9% of the total area of the state). The Federal Bureau of Land Management administers 17,546,188 acres.

Census population, 1 April 1990, 453,588 (65% urban), a decrease of 3·66% since 1980. Population estimate (1996), 481,400. Births in 1995 were 6,261; deaths, 3,720; marriages, 5,037; divorces, 3,149; infant deaths, 48 (7·7 per 1,000 live births).

Population in 5 census years was:

	White	Black	American Indian	Asiatic	Total	Per sq. mile
1910	140,318	2,235	1,486	1,926	145,965	1·5
1930	221,241	1,250	1,845	1,229	225,565	2·3

	White	Black	All others	Total	Per sq. mile
1970	323,619	2,568	6,229	332,416	3·4
1980	446,488	3,364	19,705	469,557	4·8

	White	Black	American Indian	Asian/ Pacific Islands	Other	Total	Per sq. mile
1990	427,061	3,606	9,479	2,806	10,636	453,588	4·7

Of the total population in 1990, 227,007 were male and those over 18 years of age numbered 318,063.

The largest towns (with 1990 census population) are Cheyenne, 50,008; Casper, 46,742; Laramie, 26,687; Rock Springs, 19,050; Gillette, 17,635; Sheridan, 13,900; Green River, 12,711.

CLIMATE. Cheyenne. Jan. 25°F (–3·9°C), July 66°F (18·9°C). Annual rainfall 15" (376 mm). Yellowstone Park. Jan. 18°F (–7·8°C), July 61°F (16·1°C). Annual rainfall 18" (444 mm). Wyoming belongs to the Mountain States climate region (*see* UNITED STATES: Climate).

CONSTITUTION AND GOVERNMENT. The constitution, drafted in 1890, has since had 43 amendments. The Legislature consists of a Senate of 30 members elected for 4 years, 15, retiring every 2 years, and a House of Representatives of 60 members elected for 2 years. It sits annually in Jan. or Feb. The Governor is elected for 4 years.

The state sends 1 representative to Congress.

In the 1996 presidential election Dole polled 105,347 votes; Clinton, 77,807; Perot, 25,854.

The capital is Cheyenne. The state contains 23 counties.

Governor: Jim Geringer (R.), 1995–99 ($95,000).
Secretary of State: Diana J. Ohman (R.) ($77,000).

ECONOMY

Budget. In the fiscal year ending 30 June 1996 total receipts were $2,834,811,000; disbursements were $2,477,735,000.

Per capita personal income (1995) was $21,544.

Banking and Finance. In June 1997 there were 21 national and 37 state banks with a total of $6,789,441,000 deposits.

NATURAL RESOURCES

Minerals. Wyoming is largely an oil-producing state. In 1995 the output of oil was 75·6m. bbls; natural gas, 994,300m. cu. ft. In 1992 there were 620 mining establishments. 1995 production: Coal, 263·9m. short tons; trona, 18·1m. short tons; uranium, 1·3m. lbs; bentonite, 4·3m. short tons. Total value of non-fuel mineral production, 1996, $316·7m.

Agriculture. Wyoming is semi-arid, and agriculture is carried on by irrigation and dry farming. In 1996 there were 9,100 farms and ranches; total farm area in 1996 was 34·6m. acres; average size of farm in 1996 was 3,802 acres, and average value per acre in 1995 was $192. In 1995, 12,594 people were employed on farms.

Total value, 1996, of crops produced, $297m.; of livestock and products, $411m. Crop production in 1996 (1,000 bushels): Corn for grain, 6,150; wheat, 7,110; oats, 1,696; barley, 10,320; sugar-beet, 1,074 tons. Animals on farms in 1996 included 1·49m. cattle, 0·72m. sheep and 35,000 hogs and pigs. Total egg production in 1996 was 2·4m.

Forestry. In 1992 there were 9,704 acres of gross forest land.

Fisheries. In 1991 the production of fish hatchery was 522,388 lbs.

INDUSTRY. In 1995 there were 604 manufacturing establishments. In 1995 there were 620 mining establishments. A large portion of the manufacturing in the state is based on natural resources, mainly oil and farm products. Leading industries are food, wood products (except furniture) and machinery (except electrical). The Wyoming Industrial Development Corporation assists in the development of small industries by providing credit.

LABOUR. In June 1997 the mining industry employed 15,700 wage and salary workers; construction, 15,500; manufacturing, 10,900; transportation and public utilities, 13,900. The total civilian labour force in June 1997 was 262,643, of whom 255,077 were employed; non-agricultural wage and salary employment, 231,300. The unemployment rate was 4·3% in June 1997. Total wages paid in covered employment in 1990, $3,825m.

Trade Unions. There were 21,694 working members in trade unions (10·2% of total employment) in 1989 (the last year for which official data were collected).

TOURISM. There are over 7m. tourists annually, mainly outdoor enthusiasts. The state has large elk and pronghorn antelope herds, 10 fish hatcheries and numerous wild game. In 1995, 7,933,493 people visited the 6 national areas; 2,147,633 people visited state parks and historic sites. In 1990, 811,183 fishing, game and bird licences were sold. There were (1994) 9 operational ski areas.

COMMUNICATIONS

Roads. In 1995 there were 2,298 miles of urban roads and 32,911 miles of rural roads, the latter including (1990, in miles): Federal, 3,882; state, 6,226; county, 13,636. There were 590,750 motor vehicle registrations in 1994.

Railways. In 1995, 1,795 miles of Class I railway were operated.

Civil Aviation. There were 10 towns with commuter air services and 2 towns on jet routes in 1995.

Telecommunications. In 1995 there were 29 AM, 35 FM radio stations and 9 television stations.

Press. (1995) there were 9 daily newspapers.

SOCIAL INSTITUTIONS

Justice. In the third quarter of 1995 there were 1,190 prisoners in state adult correctional institutions. The death penalty is authorized.

Religion. Chief religious bodies in 1990 were the Roman Catholic (with 59,565 members), Mormon (45,793) and Protestant churches (110,375). There were 5,000 members of the Eastern Orthodox Church in 1972.

Education. In 1996–97 public elementary and secondary schools had 98,777 pupils and 6,690 teachers. In 1990–91 enrolment in the parochial elementary and secondary schools was about 3,500. The average expenditure per pupil for 1996–97 was $5,638. State and local government expenditure in 1991 was $839·2m.

The University of Wyoming, founded at Laramie in 1887, had in academic year 1996–97, 11,251 students. There were 7 community colleges in 1991–92 with 20,517 students.

Social Welfare. In 1995 fiscal year, $24·6m. was distributed in food stamps; $19·6m. in aid to families with dependent children; and $129m. in Medicaid. Total expenditure on public assistance and social services programmes, fiscal year 1992, $190·1m.

Health. In 1993 the state had 29 general hospitals with 1,998 beds, and 37 registered nursing homes with 2,899 beds.

Further Reading

Statistical information: Department of Administration and Information, 327 E. Emerson Bldg., Cheyenne 82002. Publishes *Wyoming Data Handbook*
Equality State Almanac. Wyoming Department of Administration and Information, Cheyenne, WY 82002
Wyoming Official Directory. Secretary of State. Cheyenne, annual
Wyoming Data Handbook. Dept. of Administration and Information. Division of Economic Analysis. Cheyenne, annual
Brown, R. H., *Wyoming: A Geography.* Boulder, 1980
Larsen, T. A., *History of Wyoming.* Rev. ed. Univ. of Nebraska, 1979
Treadway, T., *Wyoming.* New York, 1982

OUTLYING TERRITORIES

GUAM

KEY HISTORICAL EVENTS. Magellan is said to have discovered the island in 1521; it was ceded by Spain to the USA by the Treaty of Paris (10 Dec. 1898). The island was captured by the Japanese on 10 Dec. 1941, and retaken by American forces from 21 July 1944. Guam is of great strategic importance; substantial numbers of naval and air force personnel occupy about one-third of the usable land.

TERRITORY AND POPULATION. Guam is the largest and most southern island of the Marianas Archipelago, in 13° 26' N. lat., 144° 43' E. long. Total area, 209 sq. miles (541 sq. km). Agaña, the seat of government is about 8 miles from the anchorage in Apra Harbour. The census on 1 April 1990 showed a population of 133,152, an increase of 27,173 since 1980 (50,801 urban; 62,207 female); density, 637·1 per sq. mile; estimate, 1996, 156,974. In 1990 those of Guamanian ancestry numbered 63,504; density was 637 per sq. mile. Vital statistics, 1996: Birth rate, 24·2 per 1,000 population; death rate, 3·9 per 1,000 population; infant mortality rate, 15·7 per 1,000 live births. The Malay strain is predominant. The native language is Chamorro; English is the official language and is taught in all schools.

CLIMATE. Tropical maritime, with little difference in temperatures over the year. Rainfall is copious at all seasons, but is greatest from July to Oct. Agaña. Jan. 81°F (27·2°C), July 81°F (27·2°C). Annual rainfall 93" (2,325 mm).

CONSTITUTION AND GOVERNMENT. Guam's constitutional status is that of an 'unincorporated territory' of the USA. Entry of US citizens is unrestricted; foreign nationals are subject to normal regulations. In 1949–50 the President transferred the administration of the island from the Navy Department (who held it from 1899) to the Interior Department. The transfer conferred full citizenship on the Guamanians, who had previously been 'nationals' of the USA. There was a referendum on status, 30 Jan. 1982. 38% of eligible voters voted; 48·5% of those favoured Commonwealth status.

The Governor and his staff constitute the executive arm of the government. The legislature is a 21-member *Senate*; its powers are similar to those of an American state legislature. At the general election of Nov. 1991, the Democratic Party won 14 seats and the Republicans 7. Guam returns 1 non-voting delegate to the House of Representatives.

Governor: Carl Gutierrez (D.), 1995–99.
Lieut.-Governor: Madeleine Bordallo.

ECONOMY

Budget. Total revenue (1991) $525m.; expenditure $395m.

Banking. Banking law makes it possible for foreign banks to operate in Guam.

NATURAL RESOURCES

Water. Supplies are from springs, reservoirs and groundwater; 65% comes from water-bearing limestone in the north. The Navy and Air Force conserve water in reservoirs. The Water Resources Research Centre is at Guam University.

Agriculture. The major products of the island are sweet potatoes, cucumbers, water melons and beans. In 1982 there were 140 full-time and 1,904 part-time farmers. Livestock (1988) included 2,000 cattle, 14,000 pigs, and (1984) 36,430 poultry. Commercial productions (1983) amounted to 6·6m. lb. of fruit and vegetables ($3·4m.), 567,000 doz. eggs ($811,093). There is an agricultural experimental station at Inarajan.

Fisheries. Fresh fish caught in 1982, 319,300 lb. Offshore fishing produced 100,687 lb., including 6,080 lb. of shrimps.

INDUSTRY AND TRADE

Industry. Guam Economic Development Authority controls three industrial estates: Cabras Island (32 acres); Calvo estate at Tamuning (26 acres); Harmon estate (16 acres). Industries include textile manufacture, cement and petroleum distribution, warehousing, printing, plastics and ship-repair. Other main sources of income are construction and tourism.

Labour. In 1990 there were 90,990 persons of employable age, of whom 66,138 were in the workforce (54,186 civilian). 2,042 were unemployed.

Trade. Guam is the only American territory which has complete 'free trade'; excise duties are levied only upon imports of tobacco, liquid fuel and liquor. In 1984 imports were valued at $493m. and exports at $34m.

Tourism. Tourism is developing; there were 1,900 visitors in 1964 and 407,100 in 1986. Visitors' receipts were $550m. in 1990.

COMMUNICATIONS

Roads. There are 674 km of all-weather roads.

Civil Aviation. There is an international airport at Tamuning. 7 commercial airlines serve Guam.

Shipping. There is a port at Apra Harbor.

Telecommunications. Overseas telephone and radio dispatch facilities are available. In 1989 there were 26,317 telephones. There are 4 commercial stations, a commercial television station, a public broadcasting station and a cable television station with 24 channels. In 1993 there were 105,000 radio and 75,000 TV sets (colour by NTSC).

Press. There is 1 daily newspaper, a twice-weekly paper, and 4 weekly publications (all of which are of military or religious interest only).

SOCIAL INSTITUTIONS

Justice. The Organic Act established a District Court with jurisdiction in matters arising under both federal and territorial law; the judge is appointed by the President subject to Senate approval. There is also a Supreme Court and a Superior Court; all judges are locally appointed except the Federal District judge. Misdemeanours are under the jurisdiction of the police court. The Spanish law was superseded in 1933 by 5 civil codes based upon California law.

Religion. About 98% of the Guamanians are Roman Catholics; the other 2% are Baptists, Episcopalians, Bahais, Lutherans, Mormons, Presbyterians, Jehovah's Witnesses and members of the Church of Christ and Seventh Day Adventists.

Education. 8 years of primary education to the age of 16 are compulsory. There are Chamorro Studies courses and bi-lingual teaching programmes to integrate the Chamorro language and culture into elementary and secondary school courses. In 1988-89 there were 18,713 pupils in primary schools and 7,223 in secondary schools. There were 1,403 teachers in 1986. There is a University of Guam.

Social Welfare. There is a hospital, 8 nutrition centres, a school health programme and an extensive immunization programme. Emphasis is on disease prevention, health education and nutrition. In 1990 $83·2m. was paid in Federal direct payments for individuals, including $1·91m. Medicare, $1·91m. disability insurance and $11·37m. retirement insurance.

Further Reading

Report (Annual) of the Governor of Guam to the US Department of Interior
Guam Annual Economic Review. Economic Research Center, Agaña

Carano, P. and Sanchez, P. C., *Complete History of Guam.* Rutland, (VT), 1964
Rogers, R. F., *Destiny's Landfall: a History of Guam.* Hawaii Univ. Press, 1995
Wuerch, W. L. and Ballendorf, D. A., *Historical Dictionary of Guam and Micronesia.* Metuchen (NJ), 1995

COMMONWEALTH OF THE NORTHERN MARIANA ISLANDS

KEY HISTORICAL EVENTS. In 1889 Spain ceded Guam (largest and southernmost of the Marianas Islands) to the USA and sold the rest to Germany. Occupied by Japan in 1914, the islands were administered by Japan under a League of Nations mandate until occupied by US forces in August 1944. In 1947 they became part of the US-administered Trust Territory of the Pacific Islands. On 17 June 1975 the electorate adopted a covenant to establish a Commonwealth in association with the USA; this was approved by the US government in April 1976 and came into force on 1 Jan. 1978. In Nov. 1986 the islanders were granted US citizenship. The UN terminated the Trusteeship status on 22 Dec. 1990.

TERRITORY AND POPULATION. The Northern Marianas form a single chain of 16 mountainous islands extending north of Guam for about 560 km, with a total area of 5,050 sq. km (1,950 sq. miles) of which 464 sq. km are dry land and a population (1990 Census) of 43,345 (urban, 12,151; female, 20,543); density, 235·6 per sq. mile. 16,752 persons were born in the Islands. Population estimate (1996)

52,284. In 1996 the birth rate was 33 per 1,000 population and the death rate 4·6 per 1,000 population. Infant mortality was 38 per 1,000 live births.

The areas and populations of the islands are as follows:

Island(s)	Sq. km	1980 Census	1990 Census
Northern Group[1]	171	104	36
Saipan	122	14,585	38,896
Tinian (with Aguijan)	101[2]	899	2,118
Rota	83	1,274	2,295

[1] Pagan, Agrihan, Alamagan and 9 uninhabited islands.   [2] Including uninhabited Aguijan.

In 1980, 55% spoke Chamorro, 11% Woleaian and 13% Filipino languages, but English remains the official language. The largest town is Chalan Kanoa on Saipan.

CONSTITUTION AND GOVERNMENT. The Constitution was approved by a referendum on 6 March 1977 and came into force on 9 Jan. 1978. The legislature comprises a 9-member *Senate*, with 3 Senators elected from each of the main 3 islands for a term of 4 *years*, and an 18-member *House of Representatives*, elected for a term of 2 years. At the elections of Nov. 1991 the Republican Party won 8 seats and the Democratic Party 1 in the Senate; the Republicans won 10, the Democrats 6 and independents 2 in the House of Representatives.

The Commonwealth is administered by a Governor and Lieut.-Governor, elected for 4 years.

Governor: Froilan C. Tenorio (D.), 1994–98.
Lieut.-Governor: Jesus C. Borja.

LABOUR. In 1990 there were 7,476 workers from the indigenous population and 21,188 were foreign workers; 2,699 were unemployed.

COMMERCE. In 1991 imports totalled $392·4m.; exports were $263·4m.

TOURISM. In 1995 there were 676,161 visitors.

COMMUNICATIONS

Roads. There are about 381 km of roads.

Civil Aviation. Air Micronesia provides inter-island services. There are 5 airports in all.

Telecommunications. In 1989 there were 10,500 radio and 4,100 television receivers, 3 radio stations and a 15-channel cable TV station in Saipan. Telephones (1993), 13,618.

SOCIAL INSTITUTIONS

Religion. The population is predominantly Roman Catholic.

Education. In 1989 there were 18 primary schools with 4,882 pupils and 9 secondary schools with 2,075 pupils. The tertiary college on Saipan had 1,097 students.

Health. In 1986 there were 23 doctors, 4 dentists, 103 nursing personnel, 2 pharmacists and 2 midwives. In 1988 there was 1 hospital with 70 beds.

AMERICAN SAMOA

KEY HISTORICAL EVENTS. The Samoan Islands were first visited by Europeans in the 18th century; the first recorded visit was in 1722. On 14 July 1889 a treaty between the USA, Germany and Great Britain proclaimed the Samoan islands neutral territory, under a 4-power government consisting of the 3 treaty powers and the local native government. By the Tripartite Treaty of 7 Nov. 1899, ratified 19 Feb. 1900, Great Britain and Germany renounced in favour of the USA all rights over the islands of the Samoan group east of 171° long. west of Greenwich, the islands to the west of that meridian being assigned to Germany (now the independent state of Samoa). The islands of Tutuila and Aunu'u were ceded to the USA by their High Chiefs on 17 April 1900, and the islands of the Manu'a group on 16 July 1904. Congress accepted the islands under a Joint Resolution approved 20 Feb. 1929. Swain's Island, 210 miles north of the Samoan Islands, was annexed in 1925 and is administered as an integral part of American Samoa.

TERRITORY AND POPULATION. The islands (Tutuila, Aunu'u, Ta'u, Olosega, Ofu and Rose) are approximately 650 miles east-north-east of Fiji. The total area is 1,511 sq. km (583 sq. miles), of which 200 sq. km are dry land; population (1990 Census), 46,773, nearly all Polynesians or part-Polynesians, of whom 25,573 were born in American Samoa (urban, 15,599; female, 22,750); density, 607·4 per sq. mile; estimate (July 1996), 59,566. In 1996 the birth rate was 35·6 per 1,000 population and the death rate 4·0 per 1,000 population. Infant mortality was 18·8 per 1,000 live births. The island's 3 Districts are Eastern (population, 1980, 17,311), Western (13,227) and Manu'a (1,732). There is also Swain's Island, with an area of 1·9 sq. miles and 100 inhabitants (1994), which lies 210 miles to the north west. Rose Island (uninhabited) is 0·4 sq. mile in area. In 1990 some 85,000 American Samoans lived in the USA.

CLIMATE. A tropical maritime climate with a small annual range of temperature and plentiful rainfall. Pago Pago, Jan. 83°F (28·3°C), July 80°F (26·7°C). Annual rainfall 194" (4,850 mm).

CONSTITUTION AND GOVERNMENT. American Samoa is constitutionally an unorganized unincorporated territory of the US administered under the Department of the Interior. Its indigenous inhabitants are US nationals and are classified locally as citizens of American Samoa with certain privileges under local laws not granted to non-indigenous persons. Polynesian customs (not inconsistent with US laws) are respected.

Fagatogo is the seat of the Government.

The islands are organized in 15 counties grouped in 3 districts; these counties and districts correspond to the traditional political units. On 25 Feb. 1948 a bicameral legislature was established, at the request of the Samoans, to have advisory legislative functions. With the adoption of the Constitution of 22 April 1960, and the revised Constitution of 1967, the legislature was vested with limited law-making authority. The lower house, or House of Representatives, is composed of 20 members elected by universal adult suffrage and 1 non-voting member for Swain's Island. The upper house, or Senate, is comprised of 18 members elected, in the traditional Samoan manner, in meetings of the chiefs. The Governor and Lieut.-Governor have been popularly elected since 1978.

Governor: A. P. Lutati (D.).
Lieut.-Governor: Tauese P. Sunia.

ECONOMY

Policy. The first formal Economic Development and Planning Office completed its first year in 1971. Much has been done to promote economic expansion within the Territory and a large amount of outside investment interest has been stimulated.

The Office initiated the first Territorial Comprehensive Plan. This plan when completed will, with periodic updating, provide a guideline to territorial development for 20 years. The planning programme was made possible under a Housing and Urban Development '701' grant programme, and Economic Development Administration '302' planning programmes.

The focus will be on physical development and the problems of a rapidly increasing population with severely limited labour resources.

Budget. The chief sources of revenue are annual federal grants from the USA, and local revenues from taxes, and duties, and receipts from commercial operations (enterprise and special revenue funds), utilities, rents and leases and liquor sales. In 1990–91 revenues were $97m. ($43m. in local revenue and $54m. in grant revenue).

Banking. The American Samoa branch of the Bank of Hawaii and the American Samoa Bank offer all commercial banking services. The Development Bank of American Samoa, government-owned, is concerned primarily through loans and guarantees with the economic advancement of the Territory.

ENERGY AND NATURAL RESOURCES

Electricity. Per capita consumption in 1993 was 1,505 kWh. All the Manu'a islands have electricity.

Agriculture. Of the 48,640 acres of land area, 11,000 acres are suitable for tropical crops; most commercial farms are in the Tafuna plains and west Tutuila. Principal crops are taro, bread-fruit, yams, bananas and coconuts. Production (1988 in 1,000 tonnes): Taro, 4; bananas, 1; fruit, 1; coconuts, 5.

Livestock (1988): Pigs, 11,000; (1984) goats, 8,000; poultry, 45,000.

INDUSTRY AND TRADE

Industry. Fish canning is important, employing the second largest number of people (after government). Attempts are being made to provide a variety of light industries. Tuna fishing and local inshore fishing are both expanding. In 1990 there were 27,991 persons of employable age, of whom 14,400 were in the workforce. The unemployment rate in 1991 was 12%.

Commerce. In 1989 American Samoa exported goods valued at $306m. and imported goods valued at $360·3m. Chief exports are canned tuna, watches, pet foods and handicrafts. Chief imports are building materials, fuel oil, food, jewellery, machines and parts, alcoholic beverages and cigarettes.

COMMUNICATIONS

Roads. There are about 150 km of paved roads and 200 km of unpaved roads in all. Motor vehicles registered, 1983, 3,657.

Civil Aviation. South Pacific Island Airways and Polynesian Airlines operate daily services between American Samoa and Samoa. South Pacific Island Airways also operates between Pago Pago and Honolulu, and between Pago Pago and Tonga. The islands are also served by Air Nauru which operates between Pago Pago, Tahiti and Auckland, and Air Pacific (Fiji and westward). South Pacific and Manu'a Air Transport run local services. There are 3 airports.

Shipping. The harbour at Pago Pago, which nearly bisects the island of Tutuila, is the only good harbour for large vessels in Samoa. By sea, there is a twice-monthly service between Fiji, New Zealand and Australia and regular service between the USA, South Pacific ports, Honolulu and Japan.

Telecommunications. A commercial radiogram service is available to all parts of the world. Commercial phone and telex services are operated to all parts of the world. Number of telephones (1996), 8,399. In 1993 there were about 20,000 radio and 8,000 TV (colour by NTSC) sets in use.

SOCIAL INSTITUTIONS

Justice. Judicial power is vested firstly in a High Court. The trial division has original jurisdiction of all criminal and civil cases. The probate division has jurisdiction of estates, guardianships, trusts and other matters. The land and title division decides cases relating to disputes involving communal land and Matai title court rules on questions and controversy over family titles. The appellate division hears appeals from trial, land and title and probate divisions as well as having original jurisdiction in selected matters. The appellate court is the court of last resort. Two American judges sit with 5 Samoan judges permanently. In addition there are temporary judges or assessors who sit occasionally on cases involving Samoan customs. There is also a District Court with limited jurisdiction and there are 69 village courts.

Religion. In 1992 about 55% of the population belonged to the Congregational Church and 19% were Roman Catholics. Methodists and Mormons are also represented.

Education. Education is compulsory between the ages of 6 and 18. In 1988-89 there were 8,313 pupils in elementary and 2,935 in secondary schools. There were 674 teachers in 1986.

Welfare. In 1990 Federal direct payments to individuals totalled $14·62m., of which $2·41m. were disability, and $4·33m. were retirement, insurance.

Further Reading

Hughes, H. G. A., *Samoa: American Samoa, Western Samoa, Samoans Abroad* [Bibliography]. Oxford and Santa Barbara (CA), 1997

OTHER PACIFIC TERRITORIES

Johnston Atoll. Two small islands 1,150 km south-west of Hawaii, administered by the US Air Force. Area, under 1 sq. mile; population (1996) totalled 1,200 US military and civilian contractor personnel.

Midway Islands. Two small islands at the western end of the Hawaiian chain, administered by the US Navy. Area, 2 sq. miles; population (1995) was 453 US military personnel.

Wake Island. Three small islands 3,700 km west of Hawaii, administered by the US Air Force. Area, 3 sq. miles; population (1995) numbered 302 US military and contract personnel.

COMMONWEALTH OF PUERTO RICO

KEY HISTORICAL EVENTS. A Spanish dependency since the 16th century, Puerto Rico was ceded to the USA in 1898 after the Spanish defeat in the Spanish-American war. In 1917 US citizenship was conferred and in 1932 there was a name change from Porto Rico to Puerto Rico. In 1952 Puerto Rico was proclaimed a commonwealth with a representative government and a directly elected governor.

TERRITORY AND POPULATION. Puerto Rico is the most easterly of the Greater Antilles and lies between the Dominican Republic and the US Virgin Islands. The total area is 13,791 sq. km (5,325 sq. miles), of which 8,875 sq. km are dry land; population, according to the census of 1990, of 3,522,037 (1,816,395 females), an increase of 10·2% over 1980; density, 1,027·9 per sq. mile. Urban population (1990) 2,508,346 (71·2%). Population estimate (1996), 3·82m. Vital statistics (1996): Births, 64,000 (17·2 per 1,000 population); deaths, 29,000 (7·9); infant mortality rate, 12·4 per 1,000 live births.

A law of April 1991 making Spanish the sole official language (which replaced a law of 1902 establishing Spanish and English as joint official languages) was reversed in 1993.

Chief towns, 1996 estimates, are: San Juan, 433,705; Bayamón, 231,845; Ponce, 189,988; Carolina, 188,427; Caguas, 140,114; Guaynabo, 104,927; Mayaguez, 100,937; Arecibo, 100,755.

The Puerto Rican island of Vieques, 10 miles to the east, has an area of 51·7 sq. miles and 9,503 (1996) inhabitants. The island of Culebra, between Puerto Rico and St Thomas, has an area of 10 sq. miles and 1,632 (1996) inhabitants. It has a good harbour.

CONSTITUTION AND GOVERNMENT. Puerto Rico has representative government, the franchise being restricted to citizens 18 years of age or over, residence (1 year) and such additional qualifications as may be prescribed by the Legislature of Puerto Rico, but no property qualification may be imposed. Puerto Ricans do not vote in the US presidential elections, though individuals living on the mainland are free to do so subject to the local electoral laws. The executive power resides in a Governor, elected directly by the people every 4 years. Twenty-two heads of departments form the Governor's Council of Secretaries. The legislative functions are vested in a Senate, composed of 28 members and the House of Representatives, composed of 54 members. Both houses meet annually in Jan. Puerto Rico sends to Congress a Resident Commissioner to the USA, elected by the people for a term of 4 years, but he has no vote in Congress. Puerto Rican men are subject to conscription in US services.

A new constitution was drafted by a Puerto Rican Constituent Assembly and approved by the electorate at a referendum on 3 March 1952. It was then submitted to Congress, which struck out Section 20 of Article 11 covering the 'right to work' and the 'right to an adequate standard of living'; the remainder was passed and proclaimed by the Governor on 25 July 1952.

On 27 Nov. 1953 President Eisenhower sent a message to the General Assembly of the UN stating 'if at any time the Legislative Assembly of Puerto Rico adopts a resolution in favour of more complete or even absolute independence' he 'will immediately thereafter recommend to Congress that such independence be granted'.

At the election on 5 Nov. 1996 the New Progressive Party, headed by Dr Pedro Rosselló, polled 978,263 votes (49·6% of the total); the Popular Democratic Party, headed by Hector L. Acevedo, polled 862,166 votes (43·7% of the total); the Puerto Rican Independence Party, headed by David Noriega, polled 70,516 votes (3·6% of the total).

At a plebiscite on 14 Nov. 1993 on Puerto Rico's future status, 48·6% of votes cast were for Commonwealth (status quo), 46·3% for Statehood (51st State of the USA) and 4·4% for full independence.

Governor: Dr Pedro Rossello (New Progressive Party), 1997–2001 ($70,000).

ECONOMY

Budget. Total consolidated budget balance as of 30 June 1996: consolidated revenues total, $16,844·6m.; consolidated budget total, $16,385·2m.; balance, $459·4m. GNP, 1996, $30,253·7m. GDP, 1996, $45,504·8m. Per capita GNP, 1996, $8,119. Per capita GDP, 1996, $12,212.

Bonded indebtedness for the commonwealth and municipalities, 30 June 1996, was $4,968·7m.

The USA administers and finances the postal service and maintains air and naval bases. Net US federal government payments in Puerto Rico, including direct expenditures (mainly military), grants-in-aid and other payments to individuals and to business totalled: 1994, $5,998·3m.; 1995, $6,314·4m.; 1996, $6,976·7m.

Per capita personal income (1996) was $7,882.

Banking and Finance. Banks on 30 June 1996 had total deposits of $27,502·2m. Bank loans were $17,940·5m. This includes 15 commercial banks, 3 government banks and 1 trust company.

ENERGY AND NATURAL RESOURCES

Electricity. Production in 1995 was 18,143·6m. kWh.

Minerals. There is stone, and some production of cement (1·54m. tons in 1995).

Agriculture. Gross income in agriculture in 1996 was $662·6m., of which $387·2m. consisted of livestock products and $71·2m. traditional crops, including: coffee, 12·0m. kg; raw sugar, 96 degrees basis, 33,484 tons. Livestock (1996): Cattle, 370,546; pigs, 182,247; poultry, 12,433,834.

LABOUR. In 1996 the total labour force was 1,268,000, with 1,092,000 employed. 175,000 persons were unemployed.

COMMERCE. In 1997 imports amounted to $21,387·4m., of which $13,317·8m. came from the USA; exports were valued at $23,946·8m., of which $21,187·3m. went to the USA.

In 1997, main exports (in $1m.) were: Chemical products, 10,627·8; machinery (except electrical), 3,490·0; food, 3,386·4. Main imports were: Chemical products, 5,416·3; electrical machinery, 2,423·8; transportation equipment, 2,241·2.

Puerto Rico is not permitted to levy taxes on imports.

COMMUNICATIONS

Roads. The Department of Public Works had under maintenance at 31 Dec. 1994, 23,291 km of paved road. Motor vehicles registered, 30 June 1996, 2,163,787.

Railways. There are 96 km of railway, although no passenger service.

Shipping. In 1996, 9,931 US and foreign vessels of 81,961,309 gross tons entered and cleared Puerto Rico.

Telecommunications. In 1995 there were 118 radio and 21 television stations. There were (1996) 1,601,658 telephones.

Press. In 1995 there were 3 main newspapers: *El Nuevo Día* had a daily circulation of 227,661; *El Vocero,* 206,125; *San Juan Star,* 33,353.

SOCIAL INSTITUTIONS

Justice. The Commonwealth judiciary system is headed by a Supreme Court of 7 members, appointed by the Governor, and consists of a First Instance court and an Appellative Court, all appointed by the Governor. The First Instance court consists of a Superior Tribunal with 78 judges and a municipal Tribunal of 70 judges. The Appellative Court has 33 judges.

Religion. In 1996, about 75% of the population were Roman Catholic.

Education. Education was made compulsory in 1899. The percentage of literacy in 1990 was 89·4% of those 10 years of age or older. Total enrolment in public day schools, Aug. 1995, was 627,620 (first school month). All private schools had a total enrolment of 148,610 pupils in 1995. All instruction below senior high school standard is given in Spanish only.

The University of Puerto Rico, in Río Piedras, 7 miles from San Juan, had 62,340 students in 1996. Higher education is also available in the Inter-American University of Puerto Rico (39,319 students in 1996), the Pontifical Catholic University of Puerto Rico (11,786), the Sacred Heart University (5,001) and the Fundación Ana G. Méndez (16,983). Other private colleges and universities had 35,717 students.

Further Reading

Statistical Information: The Area of Economic Research and Social Planning of the Puerto Rico Planning Board publishes: *(a)* annual *Economic Report to the Governor; (b) External Trade Statistics* (annual report); *(c) Reports on national income and balance of payments; (d) SocioEconomic Statistics* (since 1940); *(e) Puerto Rico Monthly Economic Indicators.*
Annual Reports. Governor of Puerto Rico. Washington
Bloomfield, R. J., *Puerto Rico: the Search for a National Policy.* Boulder (Colo.), 1985
Carr, R., *Puerto Rico: a Colonial Experiment.* New York Univ. Press, 1984
Cevallos, E., *Puerto Rico.* [Bibliography], Oxford and Santa Barbara, 1985
Crampsey, R. A., *Puerto Rico.* Newton Abbot, 1973
Dietz, J. L., *Economic History of Puerto Rico: Institutional Change and Capital Development.* Princeton Univ. Press, 1987
Falk, P. S., (ed.) *The Political Status of Puerto Rico.* Lexington, Mass., 1986

Commonwealth Library: Univ. of Puerto Rico Library, Rio Piedras.

VIRGIN ISLANDS OF THE UNITED STATES

KEY HISTORICAL EVENTS. The Virgin Islands of the United States, formerly known as the Danish West Indies, were named and claimed for Spain by Columbus in 1493. They were later settled by Dutch and English planters, invaded by France in the mid-17th century and abandoned by the French c. 1700, by which time Danish influence had been established. St Croix was held by the Knights of Malta between two periods of French rule.

They were purchased by the United States from Denmark for $25m. in a treaty ratified by both nations and proclaimed 31 March 1917. Their value was wholly strategic, inasmuch as they commanded the Anegada Passage from the Atlantic Ocean to the Caribbean Sea and the approach to the Panama Canal. Although the inhabitants were made US citizens in 1927, the islands are, constitutionally, an 'unincorporated territory'.

TERRITORY AND POPULATION. The Virgin Islands group, lying about 40 miles due east of Puerto Rico, comprises the islands of St Thomas (31 sq. miles), St Croix (83 sq. miles), St John (20 sq. miles) and 65 small islets or cays, mostly uninhabited. The total area is 1,910 sq. km (738 sq. miles), of which 346 sq. km are dry land.

The population, according to the census of 1 April 1990, was 101,809, a decrease of 8,991 since 1985 (52,599 females); density, 760·9 per sq. mile; population estimate, 1996, 97,120. Vital statistics (1996): Birth rate, 17·6 per 1,000 population; death rate, 5·2; infant mortality rate, 12·5 per 1,000 live births.

Population (1990 census) of St Croix, 50,139; St Thomas, 48,166; St John, 3,504. About 45% (1990) were native-born, 29% from other Caribbean islands, 13% from mainland USA and 5% from Puerto Rico. St Croix has over 40% of Puerto Rican origin or extraction, Spanish speaking.

The capital and only city, Charlotte Amalie, on St Thomas, had a population (1990 census) of 12,331; there are two towns on St Croix. Christiansted (2,555) and Frederiksted (1,064).

CLIMATE. Average temperatures vary from 77°F to 82°F throughout the year; humidity is low. Average annual rainfall, about 45 inches. The islands lie in the hurricane belt; tropical storms with heavy rainfall can occur in late summer, but hurricanes rarely.

CONSTITUTION AND GOVERNMENT. The Organic Act of 22 July 1954 gives the US Department of the Interior full jurisdiction; some limited legislative powers are given to a single-chambered legislature, composed of 15 senators elected for 2 years representing the two legislative districts of St Croix and St Thomas-St John.

The Governor is elected by the residents. Since 1954 there have been four attempts to redraft the Constitution, to provide for greater autonomy. Each has been rejected by the electorate. The latest was defeated in a referendum in Nov. 1981, 50% of the electorate participating.

For administration, there are 14 executive departments, 13 of which are under commissioners and the other, the Department of Justice, under an Attorney-General. The US Department of the Interior appoints a Federal Comptroller of government revenue and expenditure.

The franchise is vested in residents who are citizens of the United States, 18 years of age or over. In 1986 there were 34,183 voters, of whom 26,377 participated in the local elections that year.

They do not participate in the US presidential election but they have a non-voting representative in Congress.

The capital is Charlotte Amalie, on St Thomas Island.

Governor: Roy Schneider (ind), 1995–99 ($62,400).
Lieut.-Governor: Kenneth E. Mapp.

Administrator St Croix: Richard Roebuck, Jr.
Administrator St John: William Lomax.
Administrator St Thomas: Harold Robinson.

ECONOMY

Budget. Under the 1954 Organic Act finances are provided partly from local revenues—customs, federal income tax, real and personal property tax, trade tax, excise tax, pilotage fees, etc.—and partly from Federal Matching Funds, being the excise taxes collected by the federal government on such Virgin Islands products transported to the mainland as are liable.

Per capita income, 1990, $8,717.

Budget for financial year 1990: revenues, $364·4m.; expenditures, $364·4m.

Currency and Banking. United States currency became legal tender on 1 July 1934. Banks are the Chase Manhattan Bank; the Bank of Nova Scotia; the First Federal Savings and Loan Association of Puerto Rico; Barclays Bank International; Citibank; First Pennsylvania Bank; Banco Popular de Puerto Rico, and the First Virgin Islands Federal Savings Bank.

ENERGY AND NATURAL RESOURCES

Electricity. The Virgin Islands Water and Power Authority provides electric power from generating plants on St Croix and St Thomas; St John is served by power cable and emergency generator. Per capita consumption (1993) was 9,172 kWh.

Water. There are 6 de-salinization plants with maximum daily capacity of 8·7m. gallons of fresh water. Rain-water remains the most reliable source. Every building must have a cistern to provide rain-water for drinking, even in areas served by mains (10 gallons capacity per sq. ft of roof for a single-storey house).

Agriculture. Land for fruit, vegetables and animal feed is available on St Croix, and there are tax incentives for development. Sugar has been terminated as a commercial crop and over 4,000 acres of prime land could be utilized for food crops.

Livestock (1988): Cattle, 11,000; goats, 4,000; pigs, 3,000; sheep, 3,000, poultry (1986), 18,345.

Fisheries. There is a fishermen's co-operative with a market at Christiansted. There is a shellfish-farming project at Rust-op-Twist, St Croix.

INDUSTRY AND TRADE

Industry. The main occupations on St Thomas are tourism and government service; on St Croix manufacturing is more important. Manufactures include rum (the most valuable product), watches, pharmaceuticals and fragrances. Industries in order of revenue: Tourism, refining oil, watch assembly, rum distilling, construction.

Labour. In 1990 the total labour force was 45,990, of whom 13,640 were employed in government, 8,450 in retail trades, 9,030 in hotels and other lodgings, 3,550 self-employed and unpaid family workers, 2,290 in transportation and public utilities, 2,420 in manufacturing, 4,140 in construction, 930 in banking, 2,090 in finance, insurance and real estate, 970 in wholesale trades, 920 in business services, 350 in legal services, and 2,330 in gift shops.

Commerce. Exports, calendar year 1990, totalled $2,820·7m. and imports $3,294·6m. The main import is crude petroleum, while the principal exports are petroleum products.

Tourism. Tourism accounts for 70% of GDP. 522,900 tourists stayed and 1,311,200 day visitors arrived in 1990 spending $700·9m.; 697,800 came by air and 1,136,800 on cruise ships, mainly to St Thomas.

COMMUNICATIONS

Roads. The Virgin Islands have (1996) 856 km of roads. In 1986 there were 48,800 motor vehicles registered.

Civil Aviation. There is a daily cargo and passenger service between St Thomas and St Croix. Alexander Hamilton Airport on St Croix can take all aircraft except Concorde. Cyril E. King Airport on St Thomas takes 727-class aircraft. There are air connections to mainland USA, other Caribbean islands, Latin America and Europe. In 1991 1,023,055 passengers were handled.

Shipping. The whole territory has free port status. There is an hourly boat service between St Thomas and St John.

Telecommunications. All three Virgin Islands have a dial telephone system. In 1990 there were about 60,000 telephones. Direct dialling to Puerto Rico and the mainland, and internationally, is now possible. Worldwide radio telegraph service is also available.

There are 8 radio stations and 1 public and 1 commercial TV station. In 1993 there were some 90,000 radio and 31,500 TV (colour by NTSC) receivers in use.

Press. In 1991 there were 2 dailies, 1 fortnightly paper and 1 magazine.

SOCIAL INSTITUTIONS

Religion. There are churches of the Protestant, Roman Catholic and Jewish faiths in St Thomas and St Croix and Protestant and Roman Catholic churches in St John.

Education. In 1988 there were 13,359 pupils and 873 teachers in elementary schools, and 10,661 pupils and 723 teachers in secondary schools; 33 non-public schools had 5,079 pupils. In autumn 1991 the University of the Virgin Islands had 924 full-time students, 1,538 part-time students and 254 graduate students. The College is part of the United States land-grant network of higher education.

Welfare. In 1990 Federal direct payments for individuals totalled $95·4m., including: Medicare, $4·98m.; supplemental medical insurance, $3·72m.; disability insurance, $5·69m.; retirement insurance, $31·6m.; Food Stamps, 18·4m.

Further Reading

Boyer, W. W., *America's Virgin Islands.* Durham, (NC), 1983
Dookhan, I., *A History of the Virgin Islands of the United States.* Caribbean Univ. Press, 1974
Moll, V. P., *Virgin Islands.* [Bibliography]. Oxford and Santa Barbara (CA), 1991

URUGUAY

República Oriental
del Uruguay

Capital: Montevideo
Population: 3·27m.
GDP per head: (PPP$) 6,752
GNP: US$14·7bn.
HDI/world rank: 0·883/37

KEY HISTORICAL EVENTS. Uruguay was the last colony settled by Spain in the Americas. Part of the Spanish viceroyalty of Rio de la Plata until revolu-tionaries expelled the Spanish in 1811, and subse-quently a province of Brazil, Uruguay declared its independence 25 Aug. 1825 which was recognized by the treaty between Argentina and Brazil signed at Rio de Janeiro on 27 Aug. 1828. The first consti-tution was adopted on 18 July 1830. In the 1830s two political parties, the *blancos* (conservatives) and the *colorados* (liberals), emerged and conflict between the parties in 1865-70 precipitated the War of the Triple Alliance. In 1903, peace and prosperity were restored under President José Battle y Ordónezo. Since 1904 Uruguay has been unique in her constitutional innovations, all designed to protect her from the emergence of a dictatorship. The favourite device of the group known as the 'Batllistas' (a *colorado* faction) which, until defeated at the 1958 elections, held a parliamentary majority for over 90 years, has been the collegiate system of government, in which the two largest political parties were represented.

The early part of the 20th century saw the development of a welfare state in Uraguay which encouraged fairly extensive immigration.

In 1919 a new constitution was adopted providing for a colegiado—plural execu-tive based on the Swiss pattern. However, the system was abolished in 1933 and replaced by presidential government, with quadrennial elections. From 1951 to 1966 a collective form of leadership again replaced the presidency. During the 1960s, following a series of strikes and riots, the Army became increasingly influential, repressive measures such as censorship of the press were adopted and presidential government was restored in 1967. The Tupamaro, Marxist urban guerrillas, sought violent revolution but were finally defeated by the Army in 1972. In 1984 the military permitted presidential elections, although several candidates were banned.

The return to civilian rule came on 12 Feb. 1985 when Gen. Alvarez resigned as president and was succeeded by Dr Julio Maria Sanguinetti, who established a government of National Unity and ordered the release of all political prisoners.

TERRITORY AND POPULATION. Uruguay is bounded on the north-east by Brazil, on the south-east by the Atlantic, on the south by the Río de la Plata and on the west by Argentina. The area is 176,215 sq. km (68,037 sq. miles). The following table shows the area and the population of the 19 departments at census 1985:

Departments	Sq. km	Census 1985	Capital	Census 1985
Artigas	11,928	68,400	Artigas	34,551
Canelones	4,536	359,700	Canelones	17,316
Cerro-Largo	13,648	78,000	Melo	42,329
Colonia	6,106	112,100	Colonia	19,077
Durazno	11,643	54,700	Durazno	27,602
Flores	5,144	24,400	Trinidad	18,271
Florida	10,417	65,400	Florida	28,560
Lavalleja	10,016	61,700	Minas	34,634
Maldonado	4,793	93,000	Maldonado	33,498
Montevideo	530	1,309,100	Montevideo	1,247,920
Paysandú	13,922	104,500	Paysandú	75,081
Río Negro	9,282	47,500	Fray Bentos	20,431
Rivera	9,370	88,400	Rivera	56,335
Rocha	10,551	68,500	Rocha	23,910
Salto	14,163	107,300	Salto	80,787

Departments	Sq. km	Census 1985	Capital	Census 1985
San José	4,992	91,900	San José	31,732
Soriano	9,008	77,500	Mercedes	37,110
Tacuarembó	15,438	82,600	Tacuarembó	40,470
Treinta y Tres	9,529	45,500	Treinta y Tres	30,956

Total population, census (1996) 3,137,668 and estimate 1997 was 3·27m. (89·3% urban). Population density, 1996, 18·8 per sq. km. In 1996, Montevideo (the capital) accounted for 44·5% of the total population.

Vital statistics rates (per 1,000 population), 1996: Birth, 17·57; death, 9·7; growth, 0·74; infant mortality (per 1,000 live births), 14·7. Life expectancy was 72·4 years in 1996. 16·5% of the population are over 60; 27% are under $17\frac{1}{2}$; 66·1% are between 15 and 60.

The official language is Spanish.

CLIMATE. A warm temperate climate, with mild winters and warm summers. The wettest months are March to June, but there is really no dry season. Montevideo. Jan. 72°F (22·2°C), July 50°F (10°C). Annual rainfall 38" (950 mm).

CONSTITUTION AND GOVERNMENT. Congress consists of a *Senate* of 30 members and a *Chamber of Deputies* of 99 members, both elected by proportional representation for 5-year terms. The electoral system provides that the successful presidential candidate be a member of the party which gains a parliamentary majority. Electors vote for deputies on a first-past-the-post system, and simultaneously vote for a presidential candidate of the same party. The winners of the second vote are credited with the number of votes obtained by their party in the parliamentary elections. Referendums may be called at the instigation of 10,000 signatories. A referendum was held on 8 Dec. 1996 to prohibit parties from presenting more than 1 candidate in presidential elections, and to provide for 2 rounds of voting if no candidate gained an absolute majority in the first round. 50·2% of votes cast were in favour.

Presidential, parliamentary and gubernatorial elections were held on 27 Nov. 1994. The electorate was 2·4m. Julio Sanguinetti was elected President with 31·36% of votes cast against 18 opponents.

President: Dr Julio Maria Sanguinetti (b. 1939; Colorado Party; sworn in 1 March 1995).

Vice President: Dr Hugo Batalla.

The government in March 1998 comprised:

Minister of the Interior: Hierro López. *Foreign Affairs.* Dr Didier Operti. *Finance:* Luís Mosca Sobrero. *Transport and Public Works:* Lucio Cáceres Behrens. *Health:* Dr José Raúl Bustos Alonso. *Labour and Social Security:* Dr Ana Lia Piñeyrua. *Agriculture, Livestock and Fisheries:* Sergio Chiesa. *Education and Culture:* Samuel Lichtensztejn. *Defence:* Dr Raúl Iturria Igarzabal. *Industry and Energy:* Dr Julio Herrera. *Tourism:* Benito Stern Prac. *Housing and Environment:* Juan A. Chiruchi Fuentes.

National anthem: 'Orientales, la patria o la tumba' ('Easterners, the fatherland or the tomb'); words by F. Acuña de Figueroa, tune by F. J. Deballi.

Local Government. The 19 departments are each administered by a governor, elected for 5-year terms simultaneously with the presidential and parliamentary elections.

DEFENCE

Army. The Army consists of volunteers who enlist for 1-2 years service. There are 4 military regions with divisional headquarters. The Army is organized in 5 infantry, 1 engineer, 1 artillery and 3 cavalry brigades and 3 artillery and 4 combat engineer battalions. Equipment includes 17 M-24, 29 M-3A1 and 22 M-41A1 light tanks. Strength (1997) 17,600.

Navy. The navy consists of 3 ex-French frigates, 3 fast inshore patrol craft, 7 other inshore patrol vessels and 4 ex-German inshore minesweepers. Auxiliaries comprise 1 freighting tanker, 1 sail training ship, 1 ex-German support ship, 1 salvage ship and 2 service vessels. There are 4 small landing craft.

A naval aviation service 300 strong operates 6 S-2 Tracker anti-submarine aircraft, 1 King Air for maritime reconnaissance, 6 training aircraft and 6 general purpose helicopters. Personnel in 1997 totalled 5,000 including 400 naval infantry. The main base is at Montevideo.

An integrated coastguard operates 8 inshore patrol craft.

Air Force. Organized with US aid, the Air Force had (1997) about 3,000 personnel and 20 combat aircraft, including 2 counter-insurgency squadrons with 5 IA 58 Pucara, 4 AT-33 armed jet trainers and 10 A-37B light strike aircraft, a reconnaissance and training squadron with 6 PC-7 Turbo-Trainers, 3 transport squadrons with 1 turboprop F.27 Friendship, 3 turbo-prop C-130s, 3 Brazilian-built EMB-110 Bandeirantes (1 equipped for photographic duties), 2 CASA C-212 Aviocars and 5 Queen Airs, a search and rescue squadron with Cessna U-17A aircraft and Bell helicopters, and a number of Cessna 182 light aircraft for liaison duties. Basic training types are the T-41 and T-34.

INTERNATIONAL RELATIONS

Membership. Uruguay is a member of the UN, OAS, Mercosur and LAIA.

ECONOMY

Policy. Uruguay's small economy benefits from a favourable climate for agriculture and substantial hydropower potential. Economic development has been restrained in recent years by high—though declining—inflation and extensive government regulation. The Sanguinetti government's conservative monetary and fiscal policies are aimed at continuing to reduce inflation, at 24·3% at year end 1996; other priorities include extensive reform of the social security system and increased investment in education. Uruguay recovered from recession in 1996—partly due to the recovery in Argentina—and ended the year with a nearly 5% rise in GDP. Uruguayan trade continued to expand and the potential for new markets continued to open through the negotiations of Mercosur (Southern Cone Common Market) with neighbouring countries and the EU.

Budget. Central government finance (millions of pesos):

	1991	1992	1993	1994	1995	1996
Revenue	3,673	6,695	10,030	15,095	21,141	28,845
Expenditure	2,590	6,661	9,039	13,968	15,657	19,628

Components of 1995 revenue: VAT, 44·9%; customs duties, 5·7%; fuel tax, 7·9%; income tax, 10%; capital gains tax, 5·7%. Expenditure included: Social welfare and salaries, 60·8%; interest on public debt, 7%; capital expenditure, 10·9%.

Standard rate of VAT is 23%.

Currency. The unit of currency is the *Uruguayan peso* (UYP), of 100 *centésimos*, which replaced the nuevo peso in March 1993 at 1 Uruguayan peso = 1,000 nuevos pesos. There are notes of 0·50, 1, 2, 5, 10, 20, 50, 100, 200, 500 and 1,000 pesos. In 1993 foreign exchange reserves were US$509m.; gold reserves were US$522m. Inflation was 52·9% in 1993.

Banking and Finance. The Central Bank was inaugurated on 16 May 1967. It is the bank of issue and supreme regulatory authority. In 1994 there were 22 commercial banks, 3 state-supported and 18 foreign-owned. Savings banks deposits were 1,993,029m. pesos in 1995.

The State Insurance Bank has a monopoly of new insurance business. There is a stock exchange in Montevideo.

Weights and Measures. The metric system is in use.

ENERGY AND NATURAL RESOURCES

Electricity. Power output in 1995 was 6,167m. kWh.

Agriculture. Uruguay is primarily a pastoral country. In 1995, 8·8% of GDP was produced by agriculture. Some 41m. acres are devoted to farming, of which 90% to livestock and 10% to crops. Some large *estancias* have been divided up into family farms; the average farm is about 250 acres. In 1991 agriculture accounted for 9·8% of GDP.

Livestock, 1993 (in 1,000): cattle, 10,093; sheep, 25,702; pigs, 223; goats, 15; horses, 475; chickens, 9m.

Livestock products, 1993 (in 1,000 tonnes): Beef and veal 317; cow's milk (1995), 1·3m; wool, 83.

Main crops (in 1,000 tonnes), 1995: Rice, 804; maize, 108; 1993: Barley, 140; oats, 35; sugar-beet, 40; wheat, 300; sugar-cane, 350; potatoes, 170. Wine is produced for domestic consumption (107,000 tonnes in 1993). The country has some 6m. fruit trees, principally peaches, oranges, tangerines and pears.

Forestry. The forest area is 26,000 ha, mainly eucalyptus and pine. 3m. ha have been designated as suitable for reafforestation which is proceeding at the rate of 45,000 ha a year. In 1995 4m. cubic metres of roundwood were cut.

Fisheries. In 1995, the total catch was 126,514 tonnes.

INDUSTRY. In 1995 services accounted for 20·9% of GDP and manufacturing and building, 22·4%. Industries include meat packing, oil refining, cement manufacture, foodstuffs, beverages, leather and textile manufacture, chemicals, light engineering and transport equipment. 1991 output (in 1,000 tonnes): Cement, 436; sugar, 86; motor cars, 11,794 units; lorries, 567 units; meat-packing, 1,132,000 head (1,408,000 head in 1990); petroleum, 1,587,000 cu. metres.

Labour. In 1996 the retirement age was raised from 55 to 60 for women; it remains 60 for men. In 1995 the workforce was 1·21m. In 1991 40·2% of the workforce was engaged in services, 21·8% in manufacturing, 16·7% in trade, 6·9% in building and 5·6% in transport and communications.

FOREIGN ECONOMIC RELATIONS. External debt was US$7,890m. in 1993.

Commerce. The foreign trade (officially stated in US dollars, with the figure for imports based on the clearance permits granted and that for exports on export licences utilized) was as follows (in US$1m.):

	1991	1992	1993	1994	1995	1996
Imports	1,636·5	2,045	2,324	2,786	2,867	3,300
Exports	1,604·7	1,702	1,645	1,913	2,106	2,400

Principal exports in 1995 (in US$1,000): Textiles, 421·3 (including washed wool, 25·8); meat, live animals and by-products, 561·8; agricultural produce, 304·1 (including rice, 163·0); leather, hides and manufactures, 250·7; footwear, 17·8.

Main export markets in 1994 (in US$1m.): Argentina, 382·3; Brazil, 492·5; USA and Canada, 130·6; Germany, 121·3. Main import suppliers: Brazil, 709·6; Argentina, 652·6; USA and Canada, 259·6; Italy, 134·8.

Tourism. There were 2m. tourists in 1996, mainly from Argentina.

COMMUNICATIONS

Roads. In 1995, it was estimated that there were about 50,900 km of roads including 12,000 km of motorways.

Railways. The total railway system open for traffic was (1992) 2,073 km of 1,435 mm gauge, which carried 1m. tonnes of freight in 1994. Passenger service, which had been abandoned in 1988, was resumed on a limited basis in 1993.

Civil Aviation. There is an international airport at Montevideo (Carrasco). The national carrier is Pluna, which in 1995 operated 1 B-707-320B, 3 B-737-200 Advs and 1 DC-10-30. It maintains routes to Argentina, Bolivia, Brazil and Paraguay. Services were also provided by Aeroflot, Aerolíneas Argentinas, Air France, Iberia, KLM, Ladeco, Lan-Chile, LAPSA, Lloyd Aéreo Boliviano, United Airlines and Varig. There are 60 airports (1996), 45 with paved runways and 15 with unpaved runways.

Shipping. In 1995, sea-going shipping totalled 150,296 GRT; including oil tankers, 93,297 GRT and container ships, 28,153 GRT. Navigable inland waterways total 1,270 km.

Telecommunications. The telephone system in Montevideo is controlled by the State; small companies operate in the interior. Telephones, 1994 (est.), numbered 582,000. There were (1995) 1·9m. radio and 0·75m. television receivers (colour by PAL). There are 4 TV networks (3 commercial) and about 100 radio stations.

Press (1995). There were 32 daily newspapers with a combined circulation of 750,000. There were also 30 provincial newspapers, many bi-weekly.

SOCIAL INSTITUTIONS

Justice. The Supreme Court is elected by Congress; it appoints all other judges. There are 4 courts of appeal, each with 3 judges. There are civil and criminal courts. Each department has its court, and there are 224 lower courts.

Religion. State and Church are separated, and there is complete religious liberty. In 1992 there were 1·83m. Roman Catholics.

Education. Primary education is obligatory; both primary and secondary education are free. In 1995 there were 1693 pre-primary schools with 2,707 teachers for 69,464 pupils; 2,424 primary schools with 16,991 teachers for 341,197 pupils and at secondary level 263,616 pupils.

There is 1 state university, 1 independent Roman Catholic university and 1 private institute of technology. In 1995 there were 71,379 students and 6,683 academic staff.

Health. Hospital beds, 1983, numbered (estimate) 23,400; physicians numbered (1984) 5,736.

Welfare. The welfare state dates from the beginning of the 1900s. In 1994 there were 0·5m. recipients of pensions and benefits. A private pension scheme inaugurated in 1996 had 315,000 members at 31 Dec. 1996. State spending on social security has been capped at 15% of GDP.

DIPLOMATIC REPRESENTATIVES

Of Uruguay in Great Britain (140 Brompton Rd., London, SW3 1HY)
Ambassador: Juan Enrique Fischer.

Of Great Britain in Uruguay (Calle Marco Bruto 1073, 11300 Montevideo)
Ambassador: Robert A. M. Hendrie.

Of Uruguay in the USA (2715 M. St., NW, Washington, D.C., 20007)
Ambassador: Dr Alvaro Diez de Medina.

Of the USA in Uruguay (Lauro Muller 1776, Montevideo)
Ambassador: Thomas J. Dodd.

Of Uruguay to the United Nations
Ambassador: Dr Jorge Pérez Otermín.

Of Uruguay to the European Union
Ambassador: Guillermo Valles Galmes.

Further Reading

Finch, H., *Uruguay:* [Bibliography]. Oxford and Santa Barbara (CA), 1989
González, L. E., *Political Structures and Democracy in Uruguay.* Univ. of Notre Dame Press, 1992
Sosnowski, S. (ed.) *Repression, Exile and Democracy: Uruguayan Culture.* Duke Univ. Press, 1993
Weinstein, M., *Uruguay: Democracy at the Crossroads.* Boulder (CO), 1988

National library: Biblioteca Nacional del Uruguay, Guayabo 1793, Montevideo.

UZBEKISTAN

Uzbekiston Respublikasy

Capital: Tashkent
Population: 23·5m.
GDP per head: (PPP$) 2,438
HDI/world rank: 0·662/100

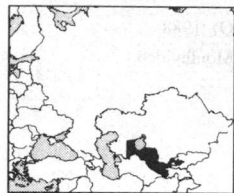

KEY HISTORICAL EVENTS. Descended from nomadic Mongol tribes who settled in Central Asia in the 13th century, the Uzbeks came under Russian control in the late 19th century.

In Oct. 1917 the Tashkent Soviet assumed authority, and in the following years established its power throughout Turkestan. The semi-independent Khanates of Khiva and Bokhara were first (1920) transformed into People's Republics, then (1923–24) into Soviet Socialist Republics and finally merged in the Uzbek SSR and other republics.

The Uzbek Soviet Socialist Republic was formed on 27 Oct. 1924 from lands formerly included in Turkestan. It included a large part of the Samarkand region, the southern part of the Syr Darya, Western Ferghana, the western plains of Bukhara, the Karakalpak ASSR and the Uzbek regions of Khorezm. In 1963 40,000 sq. km were transferred from Kazakhstan.

On 20 June 1990 the Supreme Soviet adopted a declaration of sovereignty, and in Aug. 1991, following an unsuccessful coup, declared independence as the 'Republic of Uzbekistan'. This was confirmed by referendum in Dec. In Dec. 1991 Uzbekistan became a member of the CIS.

TERRITORY AND POPULATION. Uzbekistan is bordered in the north by Kazakhstan, in the east by Kyrgyzstan and Tajikistan, in the south by Afghanistan and in the west by Turkmenistan. Area, 447,400 sq. km (172,741 sq. miles). At the 1989 census the population was 19,810,077 (71·4% Uzbek, 8·4% Russian, 4·7% Tajik, 4·1% Kazakh, 3·2% Tatar and 2·1% Karakalpak). The population in July 1997 was 23,467,724 (11,842,824 females). Vital statistics rates, 1997: Birth (per 1,000 population), 24; death, 7·6; infant mortality (per 1,000 live births), 70·5. Life expectancy, 1997, 64·3 years.

The country comprises the following regions: Andizhan, Bukhara, Dzhizak, Ferghana, Kashkadarya, Khorezm, Namangan, Navoi, Samarkand, Surkhan-Darya, Syr-Darya, Tashkent and the Karakalpak Autonomous Republic. The capital is Tashkent (2·1m. population in 1994); other large towns are Samarkand, Andizhan and Namangan. There are 124 towns, 97 urban settlements and 155 rural districts.

The Roman alphabet (in use 1929–40) was re-introduced in 1994 to be completely phased in by 2000. Arabic script was used prior to 1929 and Cyrillic, 1940–94.

CONSTITUTION AND GOVERNMENT. A new constitution was adopted on 8 Dec. 1992 which states that Uzbekistan is a pluralist democracy. Presidential elections were held on 29 Dec. 1991. Islam Karimov was elected against a single opponent with over 80% of the vote. A referendum on 26 March 1995 proposed the cancellation of elections due in 1997 and the extension of President Karimov's term of office to 2000. The electorate was 11m.; turn-out was reported to be 99·3%, with 99·62% of votes cast in favour.

Parliament is the 250-member *Oliy Majlis* (Supreme Assembly). Parliamentary elections were held in Dec. 1994 and Jan. 1995. The electorate was 11m. The People's Democratic Party (former Communists) won 69 seats, the Progress of the Fatherland won 14, and the remaining 167 seats were split between the Social Democratic Party (47) and a bloc of MPs elected from representative executive bodies.

President: Islam Karimov (b. 1938).
In March 1998 the government comprised:
Prime Minister: Utkur Sultanov.
First Deputy Prime Minister, Minister of Agriculture and Water Resources: Ismail

Jurabekov. *Deputy Prime Ministers:* Rustam Yunusov; Bakhtiar Hamidov (*Macro-Economics and Statistics*); Mirabror Usmanov; Alisher Azizkhojaev; Viktor Chzen; Dilbar Ghulomova; Kayim Hakkulov; Kamiljon Rakhimov. *Interior:* Zokirjon Almatov. *Foreign Economic Relations:* Elyor Ghaniev. *Finance:* Jamshed Saifiddinov. *Defence:* Maj.-Gen. Hikmatulla Tursunov. *Foreign Affairs:* Abdulaziz Komilov. *Justice:* Srojiddin Mirsafoev. *Power and Electrification:* Valeri Otaev. *Communications:* Abduvokhid Jurabaev. *Education:* Jura Yuldoshev. *Higher and Secondary Specialized Education:* Oqil Salimov. *Cultural Affairs:* Hairulla Juraev. *Health:* Shavkat Karimov. *Social Security:* Bakhodir Umurzakov. *Labour:* Oqiljon Obidov. *Housing and Municipal Economy:* Viktor Mikhailov. *Emergency Situations:* Rustam Akhmedov.

Local Government. Local authorities are headed by governors appointed by the President of the Republic and directly responsible to him. Local elections were held on 25 Dec. 1994.

DEFENCE. Conscription is for 18 months.

Army. The Army comprises 4 motor rifle, 1 airborne, 1 artillery and 1 special forces brigade and 2 tank and 3 artillery regiments. Equipment includes 179 T-62 main battle tanks. Personnel, 1997, 45,000. There are paramilitary forces totalling 16,000.

Air Force. Aviation units include a regiment of MiG-27 fighter-bombers and a regiment of An-12 transports, as well as some armed helicopters. Personnel, 1997, 4,000.

INTERNATIONAL RELATIONS. A major concern is a possible spillover of fighting from the troubles in Afghanistan.

Membership. Uzbekistan is a member of the UN, CIS and the NATO Partnership for Peace.

ECONOMY

Budget. The 1997 budget provided for revenue of 123,600m. som and expenditure of 150,400m. som.

Currency. A coupon for a new unit of currency, the *som* (UKS), was introduced alongside the rouble on 15 Nov. 1993. This was replaced by the *som* proper at 1 som = 1,000 coupons on 1 July 1994. Inflation was 40% in 1996 (270% in 1994). Exchange controls were abolished on 1 July 1995.

Banking and Finance. The Central Bank is the bank of issue (*Governor*, Dr Faizulla Mulladjanov). In 1996 there were 10 commercial banks, the National Bank for Foreign Economic Affairs (state owned), 3 specialized commercial banks and 1 co-operative bank. 2 foreign banks had representative offices.

ENERGY AND NATURAL RESOURCES

Electricity. Output was 45,150m. kWh in 1994.

Oil and Gas. Crude oil production (including gas concentrate) was 8m. tonnes in 1995; natural gas, 1,703 petajoules.

Minerals. 3·8m. tonnes of coal were produced in 1993. Some 70 tonnes of gold are produced annually. There are also large reserves of silver, uranium, copper, lead, zinc and tungsten; all uranium mined is exported.

Agriculture. Farming is intensive and based on irrigation. It is a major cotton-growing area. In 1993, 25·5m. ha were under cultivation, of which 428,500 ha were accounted for by private subsidiary agriculture and 149,900 ha by commercial agriculture, in 7,500 farms. By 1996, some 97% of the 715 state farms were co-operative, private or otherwise owned and in 1996 accounted for over 98% of agicultural production.

Cotton is the main crop, accounting for more than 40% of the value of total agricultural production. Fruit, vegetables and rice are also grown; sericulture and the production of astrakhan wool are important.

Livestock on 1 Jan. 1994: 5·3m. cattle, 10·2m. sheep and goats, and 0·4m. pigs.

Output of main agricultural products (in 1,000 tonnes) in 1993: Grain, 2,098; cotton, 4,234; potatoes, 463; vegetables, 2,941; fruit and berries, 486; meat, 452; milk, 3,566; and 1,663m. eggs.

Forestry. Afforestation over an area of 50,000 ha has been carried out. Output of sawn timber, 1989, 563,000 cu. metres.

Fisheries. The total catch in 1995 was 24,000 tonnes.

Environment. Irrigation of arid areas has caused the drying up of the Aral Sea.

INDUSTRY. Output, 1993 (in tonnes): Rolled ferrous metals, 0·6m.; cement, 5·3m.; mineral fertilizer, 1·3m.; chemical fibre, 22,600; paper, 13,100; fabrics, 632m. sq. metres; footwear, 39·6m. pairs; 11,500 tractors; 10,000 TV sets; 81,700 refrigerators and freezers; 10,300 washing machines.

Labour. In 1995 the labour force was 8·2m.: Agriculture and forestry, 44%; industry and construction, 20%; other, 36%. In Jan. 1994 there were 13,300 people officially registered as unemployed (0·2% of the labour force), of whom 7,600 were receiving benefits; in Dec. 1996, 0·3% were registered. Average monthly salaries in 1993 were 27,161 roubles. A minimum wage of 70,000 som-coupons a month was imposed on 1 June 1994.

FOREIGN ECONOMIC RELATIONS. In Jan. 1994 an agreement to create a single economic zone was signed with Kazakhstan and Kyrgyzstan. Foreign investors are entitled to a 2-year tax holiday and repatriation of hard currency. External debt was 17% of GDP in 1996.

Commerce. In 1996 imports were valued at US$3,200m. and exports at US$3,200m. Principal imports, 1996, were machinery (35% of the total), light industrial goods, food and raw materials; principal exports were cotton (38% of the total), textiles, machinery, chemicals, food and energy products.

Major trading partners, 1996, were Russia (16% of total trade), the USA (10%), Germany (9%) and the Republic of Korea (7%).

COMMUNICATIONS

Roads. Length of roads, 1995, was 80,000 km (hard surface, 69,760 km). In 1993, 2,347m. passengers and 217·2m. tonnes of freight were carried.

Railways. The total length of railway in 1993 was 3,483 km of 1,520 mm gauge (432 km electrified). In 1994, 22·4m. passengers and 40m. tonnes of freight were carried.

Civil Aviation. The national carrier is the state-owned Uzbekistan Airlines, which in 1996 operated 2 A310-300s, 2 Boeing 767s, 1 RJ-85 and 105 ex-Soviet aircraft, and flew services to Amsterdam, Athens, Bahrain, Beijing, Delhi, Frankfurt, Istanbul, Jeddah, Karachi, Kuala Lumpur, London, New York, Riga, Seoul and Tel Aviv. In 1993, 1·4m. passengers and 16,800 tonnes of freight were carried.

Inland Waterways. Total length in 1990 was 1,100 km.

Telecommunications. In 1995 there were 1,458,000 telephones. Broadcasting is under the aegis of the State Teleradio Broadcasting Company. The government-controlled Uzbek Radio transmits 2 national and several regional programmes, a Radio Moscow relay and a foreign service, Radio Tashkent (Uzbek, Arabic, English, Dari, Farsi, Hindi, Pushtu, Uighur). In 1995 there were 1·8m. radio and 4·3m. television receivers.

Cinemas. In 1993 there were 2,365 cinemas with a seating capacity of 609,300 and an annual attendance of 27·4m.

Press (1995). There were 3 daily newspapers with a combined circulation of 0·14m.

SOCIAL INSTITUTIONS

Justice. In 1994, 73,561 crimes were reported, including 1,219 murders and attempted murders.

Religion. The Uzbeks are predominantly Sunni Moslems.

Education. In 1995 there were 1·07m. pre-primary pupils with 96,100 teachers; 1·9m. primary pupils with 92,400 teachers, and 3·31m. secondary pupils with 340,200 teachers. There are (1998) 55 higher educational establishments with 272,300 students and 248 technical colleges with 240,100 students. There are universities and medical schools in Tashkent and Samarkand.

Health. In Jan. 1994 there were 77,700 doctors, 255,000 junior medical personnel and 1,361 hospitals with 208,000 beds.

Welfare. In Jan. 1994 there were 1,726,000 age pensioners and 1,007,000 other pensioners.

DIPLOMATIC REPRESENTATIVES

Of Uzbekistan in Great Britain (41 Holland Park, London, W11 2RP)
Ambassador: Fatih Gulyamovich Teshabaev.

Of Great Britain in Uzbekistan (Ul. Gogolya 67, Tashkent 700000)
Ambassador: Barbara L. Hay, MBE.

Of Uzbekistan in the USA (1746 Massachusetts Ave., NW, Washington, D.C., 20036)
Ambassador: Sodiq Safaev.

Of the USA in Uzbekistan (82 Chilanzarskaya, Tashkent)
Ambassador: Stanley T. Escudero.

Of Uzbekistan to the United Nations
Ambassador: Alisher Vohidov.

Of Uzbekistan to the European Union
Ambassador: Alisher Faizullaev.

Further Reading

Kangas, R. D., *Uzbekistan in the Twentieth Century: Political Development and the Evolution of Power.* New York, 1994

KARAKALPAK AUTONOMOUS REPUBLIC (KARAKALPAKSTAN)

Area, 164,900 sq. km (63,920 sq. miles); population (Jan. 1994), 1,343,000. Capital, Nukus (1989 census population, 174,000). The Karakalpaks came under Russian rule in the second half of the 19th century. On 11 May 1925 the territory was constituted within the then Kazakh Autonomous Republic (of the Russian Federation) as an Autonomous Region. On 20 March 1932 it became an Autonomous Republic within the Russian Federation, and on 5 Dec. 1936 it became part of the Uzbek SSR. At the 1989 census Karakalpaks were 32·1% of the population, Uzbeks, 32·8% and Kazakhs, 26·3%.

170 deputies were elected to its Supreme Soviet in Feb. 1990.

Its manufactures are in the field of light industry—bricks, leather goods, furniture, canning, wine. In Jan. 1990 cattle numbered 336,000 and sheep and goats, 518,100. There were 38 collective and 124 state farms in 1987. The total cultivated area in 1985 was 350,400 ha.

In 1990–91 there were 313,500 pupils at schools, 22,100 student at technical colleges, and 7,800 at Nukus University. There is a branch of the Uzbek Academy of Sciences.

There were 2,600 doctors and 12,800 hospital beds in 1987.

VANUATU

Ripablik blong Vanuatu—
Republic of Vanuatu

Capital: Vila
Population: 181,358
GDP per head: (PPP$) 2,276
GNP: US$0·2bn.
HDI/world rank: 0·547/124

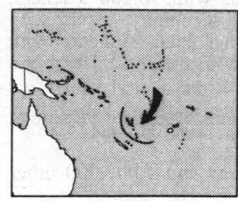

KEY HISTORICAL EVENTS. Vanuatu occupies the group of islands formerly known as the New Hebrides, in the south-western Pacific Ocean. Many of the northern islands have been inhabited by Melanesian peoples for at least 3,000 years. The islands which comprise the Republic of Vanuatu were first discovered in 1606 by the Portuguese. They were rediscovered by the French in 1768 and charted and named the New Hebrides by Captain Cook in 1774. Captain Bligh and his companions, cast adrift by the *Bounty* mutineers, sailed through part of the island group in 1789. Sandalwood merchants and European missionaries came to the islands in the mid 19th century and were then followed by cotton planters—mostly French and British—in 1868.

Complaints by missionaries regarding the activities of slave traders induced Britain to establish legislation to protect the islanders. Shortly thereafter British and French settlers began to arrive and French influence increased. In response to Australian calls to annexe the islands, Britain and France agreed on joint supervision, initially through an 1888 Joint Naval Commission and subsequently through a Condominium Government, established in 1906, which was superseded by an Anglo-French Protocol in 1914. Joint sovereignty was held over the indigenous Melanesia people, but each nation retained responsibility for its own nationals according to the protocol of 1914. The island group escaped Japanese invasion during the second world war and became an Allied base.

In 1972, the New Hebrides National Party, now known as the Vanuaaku Pati, was formed. The Vanuaaku Pati was instrumental in winning agreement from the condominium powers for independence and on 30 July 1980 New Hebrides became an independent nation under the name of Vanuatu, meaning 'Our Land Forever'.

TERRITORY AND POPULATION. Vanuatu comprises 80 islands, which lie roughly 500 miles west of Fiji and 250 miles north-east of New Caledonia. The estimated land area is 4,706 sq. miles (12,190 sq. km). The larger islands of the group are: (Espiritu) Santo, Malekula, Epi, Pentecost, Aoba, Maewo, Paama, Ambrym, Efate, Erromanga, Tanna and Aneityum. They also claim Matthew and Hunter islands. 67 islands were inhabited in 1990. Population at the census (1989), 142,944, and estimated population in 1997: 181,358. Vila (the capital) has a population of 31,800 (1996 estimate), and Luganville 10,000.

Vital statistics (1997): population growth rate: 2·12%, with a birth rate of 29·87 births per 1,00 and 8·63 deaths per 1,000. Life expectancy is 60·6 years (58·6 for men and 62·6 for women). 40% of the population is under 15 years of age, 57% between the ages of 15 and 64 and 3% 65 or over.

The national language is Bislama (spoken by 82% of the population): English and French are also official languages; about 50,000 speak French.

CLIMATE. The climate is tropical, but moderated by oceanic influences and by trade winds from May to Oct. High humidity occasionally occurs and cyclones are possible. Rainfall ranges from 90" (2,250 mm) in the south to 155" (3,875 mm) in the north. Vila. Jan. 80°F (26·7°C), July 72°F (22·2°C). Annual rainfall 84" (2,103 mm). A cyclone hit Vila in Feb. 1987.

CONSTITUTION AND GOVERNMENT. Legislative power resides in a 50-member unicameral Parliament elected for a term of 4 years. The President is elected for a 5-year term by an electoral college comprising Parliament and the presidents of the 11 regional councils. Executive power is vested in a Council of

Ministers, responsible to Parliament, and appointed and led by a Prime Minister who is elected from and by Parliament.

There is also a *Council of Chiefs*, comprising traditional tribal leaders, to advise on matters of custom. Parliamentary elections were held on 6 March 1998. The Party of Our Land (VP) gained 18 seats; the Union of Moderate Parties (UPM), 12; the National United Party (NUP), 11; others, 11.

President: Jean-Marie Leyé (b. 1932; UPM; elected 2 March 1994).

A VP-NUP coalition government was formed following the March 1998 election, consisting of:

Prime Minister, Minister of Foreign Affairs and Comprehensive Reform Programme: Donald Kalpokas (VP).

Deputy Prime Minister and Minister of Internal Affairs: Fr Walter Hadye Lini. *Education, Youth and Sports:* Joe Natuman. *Finance and Economic Develpment:* Sela Molisa. *Infrastructure and Public Utilities:* Stanley Reginald. *Lands, Geology and Mines:* Silas Hakwa. *Agriculture, Forestry and Fisheries:* John Morsen Willie. *Trade and Business Development:* James Bule. *Health:* John Robert Alick.

National anthem: 'Yumi yumi yumi i glat blong talem se, yumi, yumi yumi i man blong Vanuatu' ('We we we are glad to tell, we we we are the people of Vanuatu'); words and tune by F. Vincent.

DEFENCE. There is a paramilitary force with about 300 personnel. The Vanuatu Police maritime service operates 1 inshore patrol craft, and a former motor yacht, both lightly armed. Personnel numbered about 50 in 1996.

INTERNATIONAL RELATIONS

Membership. Vanuatu is a member of the UN, the Commonwealth, the Pacific Community and the South Pacific Forum, and is an ACP state of the EU.

ECONOMY

Budget. Total revenue totalled US$74·8m. and expenditure US$76·1m. in 1994.

Currency. The unit of currency is the *vatu* (VUV) with no minor unit. There are coins of 1, 2, 5, 10, 20, 50 and 100 vatu, and notes of 100, 500, 1,000 and 5,000 vatu.

Banking and Finance. The Reserve Bank blong Vanuatu is the central bank and bank of issue. The Finance Centre in Vila consists of 4 international banks and 6 trust companies. Commercial banks' assets at 31 Dec. 1988, 20,900m. vatu.

Weights and Measures. The metric system is in force.

ENERGY AND NATURAL RESOURCES

Electricity. Electrical capacity in 1995 was 11,000 kW, with production in 1994 of 30m. kWh.

Agriculture. About 65% of the labour force are employed in agriculture. The main commercial crops are copra, coconuts, cocoa and coffee. Production (1995, in tonnes): copra, 30,000; coconuts, 280,000 (estimated); cocoa, 2,000. 80% of the population are engaged in subsistence agriculture; yams, taro, cassava, sweet potatoes and bananas are grown for local consumption. A large number of cattle are reared on plantations, and a beef industry is developing.

Livestock (1995): cattle, 151,000; goats, 12,000; pigs, 60,000; horses, 3,000; poultry, 158,000.

Forestry. In 1990 there were 914,000 ha of forest and woodland. In 1994, 63,000 cubic metres of roundwood were cut.

Fisheries. The principal catch is tuna, mainly exported to the USA. The total catch in 1995 was 2,833 tonnes.

INDUSTRY. Industry in 1995 employed about 3% of the workforce, with 32% employed in services. Principal industries include copra processing, meat canning and fish freezing, a saw-mill, soft drinks factories and a print works. Building materials, furniture and aluminium were also produced, and in 1984 a cement plant opened.

Contributions to GDP in 1995 (in m. vatu) included: agriculture, forestry and fishing, 6,051; manufacturing, 1,386; electricity, gas and water, 462; construction, 1,721; wholesale and retail trade, restaurants and hotels, 8,611; transport, storage and communications, 2,247; finance and allied business services, 3,512; government services, 3,089.

FOREIGN ECONOMIC RELATIONS

Commerce. In 1995 imports were valued at US$93m. and exports at US$28m. Main import markets (1992): Australia (41%), France (15%), New Zealand (11%), Japan (9%) and Fiji (6%). Main export suppliers: EU (32%), Japan (29%), Australia (11%), New Caledonia (7%).

The main exports are copra, beef, timber, cocoa.

Tourism. In 1996 there were 46,123 visitors to Vanuatu.

COMMUNICATIONS

Roads. There are 1,050 km of roads, about 250 km paved, mostly on Efate Island and Espiritu Santo. There were 6,300 registered vehicles in 1993.

Civil Aviation. There is an international airport at Bauerfield Port Vila. The state-owned Air Vanuatu had 1 B-737-400 and 1 other aircraft in 1995. It provides services to Australia. Services are also provided by Air Calédonie, Air Pacific, Qantas and Solomon Airlines.

Shipping. Sea-going shipping totalled 2·57m. GRT in 1995, including oil tankers, 21,833 GRT, and container ships, 29,890 GRT. Several international shipping lines serve Vanuatu, linking the country with Australia, New Zealand, other Pacific territories, China (Hong Kong), Japan, North America and Europe. The chief ports are Vila and Santo. Small vessels provide frequent inter-island services.

Telecommunications. Services are provided by the Posts and Telecommunications and Radio Departments. There are automatic telephone exchanges at Vila and Santo; rural areas are served by a network of tele-radio stations. In 1994 there were 4,000 telephones.

External telephone, telegram and telex services are provided by VANITEL, through their satellite earth station at Vila. There are direct circuits to Nouméa, Sydney, Hong Kong and Paris and communications are available on a 24-hour basis to most countries. Air radio facilities are provided. Marine coast station facilities are available at Vila and Santo. The government-controlled Radio Vanuatu broadcasts in French, English and Bislama. In 1994 there were about 50,000 radio receivers and 2,000 televisions.

SOCIAL INSTITUTIONS

Justice. A study was begun in 1980 which could lead to unification of the judicial system.

Religion. Over 80% of the population are Christians, but animist beliefs are still prevalent.

Education. In 1994 there were 252 pre-primary schools and 272 primary schools with 852 teachers for 26,267 pupils. There were 4,184 secondary pupils in 1991. Tertiary education is provided at the Vanuatu Technical Institute and the Teachers College, while other technical and commercial training is through regional institutions in the Solomon Islands, Fiji and Papua New Guinea. The literacy rate (1979 estimates) is 53% (57% of men; 48% of women).

Health. In 1990 there were 5 hospitals with 364 beds, staffed by 20 doctors and 321 nurses.

DIPLOMATIC REPRESENTATIVES

Of Vanuatu in Great Britain
High Commissioner: Vacant.

Of Great Britain in Vanuatu (KPMG Hse., Rue Pasteur, Port Vila)
High Commissioner: Malcolm G. Hilson.

Of Vanuatu in the USA
Ambassador: Vacant.

Of the USA in Vanuatu
Ambassador: Richard W. Teare (resides in Papua New Guinea).

Of Vanuatu to the United Nations
Ambassador: Jean Ravou-Akii.

VATICAN CITY STATE

Stato della Città del Vaticano

KEY HISTORICAL EVENTS. For many centuries the Popes bore temporal sway over a territory stretching across mid-Italy from sea to sea and comprising some 17,000 sq. miles, with a population finally of over 3m. In 1859–60 and 1870 the Papal States were incorporated into the Italian Kingdom. The consequent dispute between Italy and successive Popes was only settled on 11 Feb. 1929 by three treaties between the Italian Government and the Vatican: a political treaty, which recognized the full and independent sovereignty of the Holy See in the city of the Vatican; a concordat, to regulate the condition of religion and of the Church in Italy; and a financial convention, in accordance with which the Holy See received 750m. lire in cash and 1,000m. lire in Italian 5% state bonds. This sum was to be a definitive settlement of all the financial claims of the Holy See against Italy in consequence of the loss of its temporal power in 1870. The treaty and concordat were ratified on 7 June 1929 and embodied in the Constitution of the Italian Republic of 1947. A revised Concordat between the Italian Republic and the Holy See was negotiated and signed in 1984, and came into force on 3 June 1985.

TERRITORY AND POPULATION. The area of the Vatican City is 44 ha (108·7 acres). It includes the Piazza di San Pietro (St Peter's Square), which is to remain normally open to the public and subject to the powers of the Italian police. It has its own railway station (for freight only), postal facilities, coins and radio. Twelve buildings in and outside Rome enjoy extra-territorial rights, including the Basilicas of St John Lateran, St Mary Major and St Paul without the Walls, the Pope's summer villa at Castel Gandolfo and a further Vatican radio station on Italian soil. *Radio Vaticana* broadcasts an extensive service in 34 languages from the transmitters in the Vatican City and in Italy.

The Vatican City has about 1,000 inhabitants.

CONSTITUTION. The Vatican City State is governed by a Commission appointed by the Pope. The reason for its existence is to provide an extra-territorial, independent base for the Holy See, the government of the Roman Catholic Church. The Pope exercises sovereignty and has absolute legislative, executive and judicial powers. The judicial power is delegated to a tribunal in the first instance, to the Sacred Roman Rota in appeal and to the Supreme Tribunal of the Signature in final appeal.

The Pope is elected by the College of Cardinals, meeting in secret conclave. The election is by scrutiny and requires a two-thirds majority.

Supreme Pontiff: **John Paul II** (Karol Wojtyła), born at Wadowice near Kraków, Poland, 18 May 1920. Archbishop of Kraków 1964–78, created Cardinal in 1967, elected Pope 16 Oct. 1978, inaugurated 22 Oct. 1978.

Pope John Paul II was the first non-Italian to be elected since Pope Adrian VI (a Dutchman) in 1522.

Secretary of State: Angelo Sodano.
Secretary for Relations with Other States: Jean-Louis Tauran.

ROMAN CATHOLIC CHURCH. The Roman Pontiff (in orders a Bishop, but in jurisdiction held to be by divine right the centre of all Catholic unity, and consequently Pastor and Teacher of all Christians) has for advisers and coadjutors the Sacred College of Cardinals, consisting in Nov. 1996 of 167 Cardinals appointed by him from senior ecclesiastics who are either the bishops of important Sees or the heads of departments at the Holy See. In addition to the College of Cardinals, the Pope has created a 'Synod of Bishops'. This consists of the Patriarchs and certain Metropolitans of the Catholic Church of Oriental Rite, of elected representatives of the national episcopal conferences and religious orders of the world, of the Cardinals in charge of the Roman Congregations and of other persons nominated by the Pope. The Synod meets as and when decided by the Pope. The last Synod (on the formation of priests) met in Oct. 1990.

The central administration of the Roman Catholic Church is carried on by a number of permanent committees called Sacred Congregations, each composed of a number of Cardinals and diocesan bishops (both appointed for 5-year periods), with Consultors and Officials. Besides the Secretariat of State and the Second Section of the Secretariat of State (Section for Relations with States) there are now 9 Sacred Congregations, viz.: Doctrine, Oriental Churches, Bishops, the Sacraments and Divine Worship, Clergy, Religious, Catholic Education, Evangelization of the Peoples and Causes of the Saints. Pontifical Councils have replaced some of the previously designated Secretariats and Prefectures and now represent the Laity, Christian Unity, the Family, Justice and Peace, Cor Unum, Migrants, Health Care Workers, Interpretation of Legislative Texts, Inter-Religious Dialogue, Culture, Preserving the Patrimony of Art and History, and a new Commission, for Latin America. There are also various Offices. The Pontifical Academy of Sciences was revived in 1936. The director of the Vatican Bank (Istituto per le Opere di Religione) is Giovanni Bodio.

DIPLOMATIC REPRESENTATIVES

In its diplomatic relations with foreign countries the Holy See is represented by the Secretariat of State and the Second Section (Relations with States) of the Council for Public Affairs of the Church. It maintains permanent observers to the UN.

Of the Holy See in Great Britain (54 Parkside, London, SW19 5NE)
Apostolic Nuncio: Archbishop Pablo Puente.

Of Great Britain at the Holy See (91 Via Condotti, I–00187, Rome).
Ambassador: Mark Pellew.

Of the Holy See in the USA (3339 Massachusetts Ave., NW, Washington, D.C., 20008).
Apostolic Nuncio: Agostino Cacciavillan.

Of the USA at the Holy See (Villino Pacelli, Via Aurelia 294, 00165, Rome).
Ambassador: Raymond L. Flynn.

Further Reading

Bull, G., *Inside the Vatican*. London, 1982
Cardinale, I., *The Holy See and the International Order.* Gerrards Cross, 1976
Mayer, F. *et al*, *The Vatican: Portrait of a State and a Community.* Dublin, 1980
Nichols, P., *The Pope's Divisions*. London, 1981
Reese, T., *Inside the Vatican*. Harvard Univ. Press, 1997
Walsh, M. J., *Vatican City State*. [Bibliography] Oxford and Santa Barbara (CA), 1983

VENEZUELA

República de Venezuela

Capital: Caracas
Population: 21·8m.
GDP per head: (PPP$) 8,120
GNP: US$59·0bn.
HDI/world rank: 0·861/47

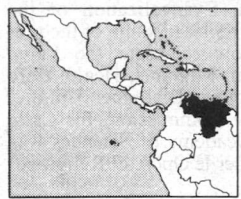

KEY HISTORICAL EVENTS. Columbus sighted Venezuela in 1498 and it was visited by Alonzo de Ojeda and Amerigo Vespucci in 1499 who named it Venezuela (Little Venice). It was part of the Spanish colony of New Granada until 1821 when it became independent, at first in union with Colombia and then as a separate independent republic from 1830.

Between 1830 and 1945 the country was governed mainly by dictators. In 1945 a three-day revolt against the reactionary government of Gen. Isaias Medina led to Romulo Betancourt assuming the presidency. Betancourt produced constitutional and economic reforms but he was replaced by Gen. Marcos Pérez Jiménez who seized power in 1952. Jiménez was himself overthrown by a military junta in a revolution in 1958, led by Adm. Wolfgang Larrazabal. Betancourt again became president.

In 1961 a new constitution was promulgated which provided for a presidential election every five years, a national congress, and state and municipal legislative assemblies.

Betancourt's progressive policies were continued by his successor, Dr Raúl Leoni. There was an abortive military uprising in 1966. In 1969 Dr Rafael Caldera Rodriguez became the first Christian Democratic president. In 1978 Dr Luis Herrera was chosen president but as his party, the *Partido Social-Christiano* (COPEI), failed to obtain an overall majority in congress he was forced to form alliances with smaller parties in order to make legislative progress.

Twenty political parties participated in the 1983 elections. Of 13 presidential candidates, Dr Jaime Lusinchi was elected with 57% of the votes. By now the economy was in crisis and social unrest was widespread. Corruption linked to drug trafficking led to further violence. In Feb. 1992 an attempt to overthrow the President by rebel troops was narrowly averted. There was another abortive coup in Nov. A state of emergency was declared. President Perez resisted demands for his resignation but he was later suspended from office. In Dec. 1993, Dr Rafael Caldera Rodriguez was returned to the presidency with 30·5% of the vote. Dr Caldera's election reflected disenchantment with the established political parties and concern over allegations of mismanagement and corruption. He took office in the early stages of a banking crisis which cost 15% of GDP to resolve. Fiscal tightening backed by the IMF brought rapid recovery.

TERRITORY AND POPULATION. Venezuela is bounded to the north by the Caribbean with a 2,813 km coastline, east by the Atlantic and Guyana, south by Brazil, south-west and west by Colombia. The area is 916,490 sq. km (353,857 sq. miles) including 72 islands in the Caribbean. Population (1990) census, 19,455,429 (84% urban). Estimate (1997) 21·8m.; density, 23·9 per sq. km. The official language is Spanish. English is taught as a mandatory second language in high schools.

Area, population and capitals of the 20 states and 4 federally-controlled areas:

State	Sq. km	Census 1990	Capital	Density; inhabitants per sq.km
Federal District	1,930	2,279,677	Caracas	1,181·18
Amazonas	175,750	94,59	Puerto Ayacucho	0·54
Anzoátegui	43,300	1,034,311	Barcelona	23·89
Apure	76,500	382,572	San Fernando	5·00
Aragua	7,014	1,334,099	Maracay	191·63
Barinas	35,200	519,197	Barinas	14·75

State	Sq. km	Census 1990	Capital	Density inhabitants per sq.km
Bolívar	238,000	1,142,210	Ciudad Bolívar	4·80
Carabobo	4,350	1,823,767	Valencia	419·26
Cojedes	14,800	227,741	San Carlos	15·39
Delta Amacuro	40,200	114,390	Tucupita	2·85
Falcón	24,800	699,232	Coro	28·19
Guárico	65,000	583,221	San Juan de los Morros	8·97
Lara	19,800	1,430,968	Barquisimeto	72·27
Mérida	11,300	680,503	Mérida	60·22
Miranda	7,950	2,303,302	Los Teques	289·72
Monagas	28,900	503,176	Maturín	19·23
Nueva Esparta	1,150	330,307	La Asunción	287·22
Portuguesa	15,200	720,865	Guanare	47·43
Sucre	11,800	781,756	Cumaná	66·25
Táchira	11,100	946,949	San Cristóbal	85·31
Trujillo	7,400	562,752	Trujillo	76·05
Zulia	63,100	2,820,250	Maracaibo	44·69

From 1981 to 1990 the population grew by 2·5% per annum. 84% of Venezuela's population lives in cities and towns with more than 2,500 inhabitants. 37·3% of all Venezuelans are under 15 years of age, 58·7% are between the ages of 15 and 64, and 4% are over the age of 65.

Caracas, Venezuela's largest city, is the political, financial, commercial, communications and cultural centre of the country. The population of metropolitan Caracas is approximately 3·1m. Maracaibo, the nation's second largest city, with an estimated population of 1·5m. is located near Venezuela's most important petroleum fields and richest agricultural areas.

CLIMATE. The climate ranges from warm temperate to tropical. Temperatures vary little throughout the year and rainfall is plentiful. The dry season is from Dec. to April. The hottest months are July and August. Caracas. Jan. 65°F (18·3°C), July 69°F (20·6°C). Annual rainfall 32" (833 mm). Ciudad Bolivar. Jan. 79°F (26·1°C), July 81°F (27·2°C). Annual rainfall 41" (1,016 mm). Maracaibo. Jan. 81°F (27·2°C), July 85°F (29·4°C). Annual rainfall 23" (577 mm).

CONSTITUTION AND GOVERNMENT. Venezuela is a federal republic, comprising 72 federal dependencies, 22 states, 2 federal territories and 1 federal district. Executive power is vested in the President. Re-elections can take place 10 years after the end of the first term. The ministers, who together constitute the Council of Ministers, are appointed by the President and head various executive departments. There are 17 ministries and 7 officials who also have the rank of Minister of State.

The Senate and Chamber of Deputies have similar legislative powers. For a bill to become law, it must be approved by a majority in both bodies. Differences between the 2 chambers are resolved through majority vote of the Congress, meeting in joint session. The constitution provides for procedures by which the President may reject bills passed by Congress, as well as provisions by which Congress may override such Presidential veto acts.

Main political organizations: the president's party, Convergencia Nacional (CN), which has 19 seats in the Chamber of Deputies and 5 in the Senate; Acción Democrática (AD); Comité de Organización Politica Electoral Independiente (Copei); Movimiento al Socialismo (MAS); La Causa R (LCR).

Presidential and Congressional elections were held on 5 Dec. 1993. Rafael Caldera was elected President against 3 opponents. Presidential elections are due in December 1998.

In March 1998 the government comprised:
President: Rafael Caldera Rodríguez (b. 1916; ind; sworn in 2 Feb. 1994).
Interior: Guillermo Andueza. *Foreign Affairs:* Miguel Angel Burelli. *Finance:* Freddy Rojas Parra. *Defence:* Tito Rincon-Bravo. *Transport and Communications:* Moisés Orozco Graterol. *Urban Development:* Julio Marti. *Energy and Mines:* Erwin

Arrieta Valera. *Industry and Commerce:* Hector Maldonado Lira. *Decentrtalization:* José Guillermo Andueza Acuña. *Environment and Natural Renewable Resources:* Rafael Martinez-Monro. *Health and Social Security:* José Felix Oletta. *Agriculture and Livestock:* Ramon Ramírez Lopez. *Education:* Antonio Luis Cárdenas. *The Family:* Carlos Altimari Gásperi. *Justice:* Hilarión Cardozo. *Presidential Secretariat:* Asdrúbal Aguíar. *Co-ordination and Planning:* Teodoro Petkoff. *Labour:* María Bernardoni de Govea. *Information:* Fernando Egaña. *Youth:* María de Pilar Iríbarren.

National anthem: 'Gloria al bravo pueblo' ('Glory to the brave people'); words by Vicente Salias, tune by Juan Landaeta.

Local Government. There are 22 states each with an elected assembly and governor. The states are divided into 156 districts and 613 municipalities. There is 1 federal territory with 7 departments, and a federal dependence with 2 departments and 2 parishes. Each district has a municipal council. The federal district and the 2 territories are administered by the President. Elections were held on 3 Dec. 1995 to elect 22 governors, 330 mayors and several thousand councillors. Turn-out was 40%. The Democratic Action Party gained 12 governorships.

DEFENCE. There is selective conscription for 30 months.

Army. The Army consists of 6 infantry divisions, 7 infantry brigades, 1 airborne, 1 Ranger, 1 armoured and 1 cavalry brigade and 1 aviation regiment. Equipment includes 70 AMX-30 main battle tanks. Army aviation comprises 24 helicopters and 14 aircraft. Strength (1997) 34,000 (27,000 conscripts).

A 22,000-strong volunteer National Guard is responsible for internal security.

Navy. The combatant fleet comprises 2 German-built submarines, 2 ex-US Knox Class and 6 Italian-built Lupo class frigates, 6 fast missile craft, 4 tank landing ships and 12 craft. Auxiliaries comprise 1 logistic support, 1 survey ship, 2 transports, and a sail training ship, as well as a few harbour service craft.

The Naval Air Arm, 1,000 strong, comprises 6 shore-based C-212 Aviocars and 8 S-2 Trackers for maritime reconnaissance and transport, 9 AB-212 ship-borne anti-submarine helicopters and 7 miscellaneous transport and liaison aircraft.

Personnel in 1997 totalled 15,000 (4,000 conscripts) including the 5,000-strong Marine Corps and 1,000 in Naval Aviation. Main bases are at Caracas, Puerto Cabello and Punto Fijo.

The Coastguard, 1,000 strong in 1997, organizationally separate but under Naval operational control, is responsible for control of the economic exclusion zone.

Air Force. The Air Force was 7,000 strong in 1997, and had 80 combat aircraft and 15 armed helicopters. There are 6 combat squadrons. Two are equipped with 16 F-16A and 5 F-16B Fighting Falcons. Two have 9 Canadair CF-5A fighter-bombers and 9 two-seat CF-5Ds, and one has 12 Mirage 50 single-seaters and 3 Mirage 50 trainers. 2 other operational squadrons have 15 OV-10 Bronco twin-turboprop counter-insurgency aircraft and there is 1 squadron of armed Tucano trainers. A helicopter force consists of more than 40 Super Pumas, Bell 212s, 214STs and 412s, UH-1B/D/H Iroquois and Alouette IIIs.

INTERNATIONAL RELATIONS

Membership. Venezuela is a member of the UN, OAS, LAIA, OPEC, WTO, GATT, FAO, G-77, Interpol, Intelsat, IADB, IAEA, IMO, SELA, PAHO, UNCTAD, UNESCO, UPU, WHO and the Andean Community.

ECONOMY

Policy. A stabilization programme of April 1996 introduced market-oriented reforms, liberalizing interest rates and sextupling petrol prices. An ambitious programme of privatization has stalled.

Performance. GDP declined 1% in 1996 but grew by 4% in the first semester of 1997.

Budget. The revenue and expenditure for 1994 were, in Bs 1m., as follows:

| Revenue | 1,635,864 |
| Expenditure | 1,627,732 |

Currency. The unit of currency is the *bolívar* (VEB) of 100 *céntimos*. There are notes of Bs 5, 10, 20, 50, 100, 500, 1,000 and 5,000, and coins of 5, 25 and 50 céntimos and Bs 1, 2 and 5. Foreign reserves were US$18,400m. in Sept. 1997. Exchange controls were abolished in April 1996. The bolívar was devalued by 41·4% in Dec. 1995. Inflation rate for 1997 was 42·0%. 1998 forecast: 25·0%.

Banking and Finance. A law of Dec. 1992 provided for greater autonomy for the Central Bank. Its governor is appointed by the President for 5-year terms. (*Governor*, Antonio Casas González). Since 1993 foreign banks have been allowed a controlling interest in domestic banks.

There is a stock exchange in Caracas.

ENERGY AND NATURAL RESOURCES

Electricity. Production (1994) 70·5m. kWh.

Oil and Gas. Proven resources of crude were 73 billion bbls. in 1996. The oil sector was nationalized in 1976, but private and foreign investment have again been permitted since 1992. Estimated crude oil production (1995) was 2,657,000 bbls. a day. Venezuela is the largest exporter of oil to the USA. Gas production (1994) 880 billion cu. feet. Oil provides about 40% of Venezuela's revenues.

Minerals. Output (in 1,000 tonnes) in 1995: iron ore, 23,424; coal 4,646; gold, 3,287 kg.

Agriculture. Coffee, cocoa, sugar-cane, maize, rice, wheat, tobacco, cotton, beans and sisal are grown. 50% of farmers are engaged in subsistence agriculture. There are government price supports and tax incentives.

Production (1995, in 1,000 tonnes): Rice, 643; cassava, 285; sugarcane, 6,900; bananas, 1,215; oranges, 440; potatoes, 215; tomatoes, 244.

Forestry. Forest covers a large portion of the country. Production 1994, 2,254,000 cu. metres.

Fisheries. Total catch (1994) was 424,000 tonnes.

INDUSTRY. Production (1994, tonnes): Steel, 3·14m.; aluminium, 617,000; cement, 4·56m.

Labour. The labour force in 1995 was 8,544,000, of whom 1m. worked in agriculture. Unemployment was 10·5% in 1997.

Trade Unions. The most powerful confederation of trade unions is the CTV (*Confederación de Trabajadores de Venezuela*, formed 1947).

FOREIGN ECONOMIC RELATIONS. The Group of Three free trade pact with Colombia and Mexico came into effect on 1 Jan. 1995. Foreign debt was estimated at US$35,100m. in 1992.

Commerce. In 1997 imports were valued at US$12·7 billion and exports at US$21·4 billion. Oil exports were valued at US$12·6bn. in 1991. The USA is Venezuela's principal trading partner, responsible for 42% of the country's imports and taking in 49% of exports.

Tourism. 596,676 tourists visited Venezuela in 1996.

COMMUNICATIONS

Roads. There are 62,000 km of road fit for traffic the year round; of these 24,000 km are paved.

Railways. Railways (336 km–1,435 mm gauge) carried 31·3m. passenger-km and 259,000 tonnes of freight in 1994.

There is a metro in Caracas.

Civil Aviation. There is an international airport at Caracas (Simon Bolívar). Services are provided by ALM, Aeroperú, Aerotour Dominicano, Air Aruba, Air France, Alitalia, American Airlines, Avianca, British Airways, BWIA, Compania Mexicana, Cubana, Iberia, KLM, LACSA, Lan-Chile, LIAT, Lloyd Aéreo Boliviano, Lufthansa, SAETA, Servivensa, TAP, United Airlines and Varig. Avensa, Servivensa, Aeropostal and Laser provide domestic services.

Shipping. Ocean-going shipping totalled 1·37m. GRT in 1995, including oil tankers, 0·69m. GRT, and container ships, 1,180 GRT. La Guaira, Maracaibo, Puerto Cabello, Puerto Ordaz and Guanta are the chief ports. The principal navigable rivers are the Orinoco and its tributaries the Apure and Arauca.

Telecommunications. There are 2 government and 4 cultural radio stations; the remainder are commercial. There are 4 government, 3 commercial and 3 other TV channels (colour by NTSC). In 1994 there were 9·5m. radio and 3·5m. TV receivers.

Press. There are 25 leading daily newspapers with a circulation of over 1·7m.

SOCIAL INSTITUTIONS

Justice. The Supreme Court, which operates in Divisions, each with 5 members, is elected by Congress for 5 years. The country is divided into 20 legal districts. The Federal Procurator-General is appointed for 5 years. There are lower federal courts. Each state has a Supreme Court with 3 members, a superior court, or superior tribunal, courts of first instance, district courts and municipal courts. In the territories there are civil and military judges of first instance, and also judges in the municipalities.

Religion. In 1992 there were 18·49m. Roman Catholics. There are 4 archbishops, 1 at Caracas, who is Primate of Venezuela, 2 at Mérida and 1 at Ciudad Bolívar. There are 19 bishops. Protestants number about 20,000.

Education. In 1994 there were 16,000 primary schools with 186,000 teachers and 4,200,000 pupils, 1,500 secondary schools with 34,000 teachers and 1,100,000 pupils.

In 1995–96 there were in the public sector 16 universities, 1 polytechnic university and 1 open (distance) university; and in the private sector, 12 universities, 2 Roman Catholic universities and 1 technological university.

Health. In 1996 there were 42,725 doctors and 52,394 beds in hospitals and dispensaries.

DIPLOMATIC REPRESENTATIVES

Of Venezuela in Great Britain (1 Cromwell Rd., London, SW7 2HW)
Ambassador: Roy Chaderton Matos.

Of Great Britain in Venezuela (Torre Las Mercedes, piso 3, Av. La Estancia, Chuao, Caracas 1060)
Ambassador: Richard D. Wilkinson.

Of Venezuela in the USA (1099 30th St., NW, Washington, D.C., 20007)
Ambassador: Pedro Luís Echeverría.

Of the USA in Venezuela (Calle Suapure, con calle F. Colinas de Valle Arriba, Caracas)
Ambassador: John Maisto.

Of Venezuela to the United Nations
Ambassador: Ramón Escóvar Salom.

Of Venezuela to the European Union
Ambassador: Luis Xavier Grisanti.

Further Reading

Dirección General de Estadística, Ministerio de Fomento, *Boletín Mensual de Estadística.—Anuario Estadístico de Venezuela.* Caracas, Annual

Ewell, J., *Venezuela: a Century of Change.* London, 1984

Hellinger, D.V., *Tarnished Democracy.* Boulder (CO), 1991

Naim, M., *Paper Tigers and Minotaurs: the Politics of Venezuela's Economic Reforms.* Washington (DC), 1993

VIETNAM

Công Hòa Xã Hôi Chu Nghĩa
Viêt Nam

(Socialist Republic of Vietnam)

Capital: Hanoi
Population: 76m.
GDP per head: (PPP$) 1,208
HDI/world rank: 0·557/121

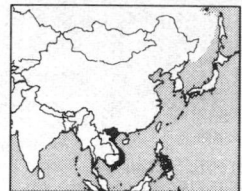

KEY HISTORICAL EVENTS. Vietnam was conquered by the Chinese in 111BC, and though it broke free of Chinese domination in 939AD, at many subsequent periods it was a nominal Chinese vassal.

By the end of the 15th century, the Vietnamese had conquered most of the Kingdom of Champa (now Vietnam's central area), and by the end of the 18th century had acquired Cochin-China (now its southern area). At the end of the 18th century, France helped to establish the Emperor Gia-Long (with whom Louis XVI had signed a treaty in 1787) as ruler of a unified Vietnam, known then as the Empire of Annam. French influence increased with a series of treaties between 1874 and 1884, the establishment of French protectorates over Tonkin and Annam, and the formation of the French colony of Cochin-China. By a Sino-French treaty of 1885, the Empire of Annam ceased to be a tributary to China. Cambodia had become a French protectorate in 1863, and in 1899 after the extension of French protection to Laos in 1893, the Indo Chinese Union was proclaimed.

In 1940, Vietnam was occupied by the Japanese. In 1941, a nationalist coalition of nationalist, revolutionary and Communist organizations, known as the Vietminh League, was founded by the Communists. On 9 March 1945, the Japanese interned the French authorities and proclaimed the independence of Indo-China. In Aug. 1945, they allowed the Vietminh movement to seize power, dethrone the Emperor of Annam and establish a republic known as Vietnam. On 6 March 1946, France recognized 'the Democratic Republic of Vietnam' as a 'Free State within the Indo-Chinese Federation'. On 19 Dec. Vietminh forces made a surprise attack on Hanoi, the signal for nearly eight years of hostilities. An agreement on the cessation of hostilities in Vietnam was reached on 20 July 1954 at the Geneva Conference. The French withdrew and by the Paris Agreement of 29 Dec. 1954, completed the transfer of sovereignty to Vietnam.

The conference divided Vietnam along the 17th parallel into Communist North Vietnam and non-Communist South Vietnam. From 1959, the North promoted insurgency in the south and from 1961, the USA came to the aid of the south and a full scale guerrilla war developed.

In 1963, the South Vietnamese president, Diem, was overthrown; Nguyen Van Thieu took power as chairman of a national leadership committee in 1965, becoming president in 1967.

In Paris on 27 Jan. 1973, an agreement was signed ending the war in Vietnam. After the US withdrawal in that year, however, hostilities continued between the North and the South until the latter's defeat in 1975. Between 150,000 and 200,000 South Vietnamese fled the country, including the former President Thieu.

After the collapse of Thieu's régime the provisional revolutionary government established an administration in Saigon. A general election was held on 25 April 1976 for a national assembly representing the whole country. Voting was by universal suffrage of all citizens of 18 or over, except former functionaries of South Vietnam undergoing 're-education'. The unification of North and South Vietnam into the Socialist Republic of Vietnam finally took place on 2 July 1976. Following the signing of a treaty of friendship with the USSR in 1978, relations with China correspondingly deteriorated. Vietnam invaded Cambodia in Dec. 1978 and China attacked Vietnam in consequence. Thailand's relations with Vietnam worsened considerably in view of Vietnam attacks on guerrilla bases along the Thai border. Many refugees escaped in small boats across the South China Sea.

In 1986, Vietnam implemented economic reforms, eliminating subsidies and gradually shifting to a multi-sectoral market economy under State regulation. On 11 July 1995, Vietnam and the USA officially normalized relations. On 28 July 1995, Vietnam became an official member of the Association of South East Asian Nations (ASEAN), and in the same month, signed a trade agreement with the European Union. At the present time, it has established diplomatic relations with more than 160 countries.

TERRITORY AND POPULATION. Vietnam is bounded in the west by Cambodia and Laos, north by China and east and south by the South China Sea. It has a total area of 331,690 sq. km and is divided into 60 provinces and a city under central government, grouped in 7 regions. Areas and populations (in 1,000):

Province/*Region*	*Sq. km*	*Census,* 1989	*Estimate,* 1992	*Capital*
Lai Chau	17,140	438	482	Lai Chau
Son La	14,210	682	754	Son La
Lao Cai	8,050		515	Lao Cai
Yen Bai	6,802		617	Yen Bai
Hoa Binh	4,612		699	Hoa Binh
Ha Giang	7,831	} 1,026	{ 506	Ha Giang
Tuyen Quang	7,801		614	Tuyen Quang
Cao Bang	8,445	566	614	Cao Bang
Lang Son	8,167	611	656	Lang Son
Bac Thai[1]	6,503	1,033	1,119	Thai Nguyen
Quang Ninh	5,939	814	874	Hai Duong
Vinh Phu[1]	4,836	1,806	2,164	Viet Tri
Ha Bac[1]	4,614	2,061	2,222	Bac Giang
North Mountain and Midland	102,949	11,909	11,823	
Hanoi	921	} 3,057	{ 2,106	Hanoi
Ha Tay	2,153		2,170	
Hai Phong	1,504	1,448	1,542	Hai Phong
Hai Hung[1]	2,552	2,440	2,612	Hai Duong
Thai Binh	1,524	1,632	1,738	Thai Binh
Nam Ha[1]	2,419	} 3,157	{ 2,531	Nam Ha
Ninh Binh	3,387		819	Ninh Binh
Red River Delta	12,457	11,734	13,518	
Thanh Hoa	11,168	2,991	3,233	Thanh Hoa
Nghe An	16,381	} 3,582	{ 2,623	Vinh
Ha Tinh	6,054		1,265	Ha Tinh
Quang Binh	7,983		{ 716	Dong Hoi
Quang Tri	4,592	} 1,995	{ 505	Dong Ha
Thua Thien (Hue)	5,009		945	Hue
Central North Region Coast	51,187	8,568	9,287	
Quang Nam (Da Nang)[1]	11,988	1,739	1,811	Da Nang
Quang Ngai	5,856	} 2,288	{ 1,120	Quang Ngai
Binh Dinh	6,076		1,137	Quy Nhon
Phu Yen	5,223	} 1,463	{ 689	Tuy Hoa
Khanh Hoa	5,258		897	Nha Trang
Ninh Thuan	3,430	} 1,170	{ 438	
Binh Thuan	7,992		830	Phan Thiet
Central Coast of North Region	45,823	6,660	7,193	
Kon Tum	9,934	} 873	{ 241	Kon Tum
Gia Lai	15,662		708	Play Cu
Dac Lat	19,800	974	1,126	Buon Me Thoat
Lam Dong	10,173	639	729	Da Lat
Central Highlands	55,569	2,486	2,805	
Song Be[1]	9,546	939	1,046	Thu Dau Mot
Tay Ninh	4,024	791	856	Ho Chi Minh City
Thanh Pho Ho Chi Minh	2,090	3,934	4,145	Ho Chi Minh City
Dong Nai	5,865		1,721	Bien Hoa
Ba Ria (Vung Tau)	1,957		637	Ba Ria
North Eastern South Region	23,481	7,807	8,406	
Long An	4,338	1,121	1,197	Tan An
Dong Thap	3,276	1,337	1,433	Cao Lamh

Province/Region	Sq. km	Census, 1989	Estimate, 1992	Capital
Tien Giang	2,339	1,484	1,591	My Tho
Ben Tre	2,246	1,214	1,285	Ben Tre
Tra Vinh	2,247	} 1,812	{ 924	Tra Vinh
Vinh Long	1,487		1,025	Vinh Long
An Giang	3,424	1,793	1,896	Long Xuyen
Can Tho	3,054	} 2,682	{ 1,739	Can Tho
Soc Trang	3,107		1,152	Soc Trang
Kien Giang	4,243	1,198	1,299	Rach Gia
Minh Hai[1]	7,689	1,562	1,681	Bac Lieu
Mekong River Delta	39,575	14,203	15,221	

[1] 8 provinces were split to produce 7 new provinces and a centrally-administered city (Da Nang) in 1997 as follows: Bac Thai became Bac Can and Thai Nguyen; Vinh Phu, Phu Tho and Vinh Phuc; Ha Bac, Bac Giang and Bac Ninh; Hai Hung, Hai Duong and Hung Yen; Nam Ha, Ha Nam and Nam Dinh; Quang Nam (Da Nang), Quang Nam Province and Da Nang City; Song Be,Binh Duong and Binh Phuoc; Minh Hai, Bac Lieu and Ca Mau.

At the 1989 census the population was 64,411,713 (20·1% urban); density, 195 per sq. km.

Estimated population (1992), 69,306,000 (33,555,000 females; 20·2% urban); (1998), approximately 76m. (51% women) consisting of 54 nationalities; density, 209·4 per sq. km. (Ho Chi Minh 4m.; Hanoi, 2m.).

Vital statistics rates (1994 per 1,000 population); Birth rate, 28·0; death rate, 7·4; growth rate (1992) 2·47%. Infant mortality was 36 per 1,000 live births in 1992. Expectation of life was 66 years in 1994. Sanctions are imposed on couples with more than two children.

Cities with over 0·2m. inhabitants at the 1989 census: Ho Chi Minh City (3,169,135), Hanoi (1,088,862), Hai Phong (456,049), Da Nang (370,670), Long Xuyen (217,171), Nha Trang (213,687), Hue (211,085), Can Tho (208,326).

87% of the population are Vietnamese (Kinh). There are also 53 minority groups thinly spread in the extensive mountainous regions. The largest minorities are: Tay, Khmer, Thai, Muong, Nung, Meo, Dao. The last remaining 'boat people' were repatriated from Hong Kong in 1997.

CLIMATE. The humid monsoon climate gives tropical conditions in the south, with a rainy season from May to Oct., and sub-tropical conditions in the north, though real winter conditions can affect the north when polar air blows south over Asia. In general, there is little variation in temperatures over the year. Hanoi. Jan. 62°F (16·7°C), July 84°F (28·9°C). Annual rainfall 72" (1,830 mm).

CONSTITUTION AND GOVERNMENT. The National Assembly unanimously approved a new constitution on 15 April 1992. Under this the Communist Party retains a monopoly of power and the responsibility for guiding the state according to the tenets of Marxism-Leninism and Ho Chi Minh, but with certain curbs on its administrative functions. The powers of the National Assembly are increased. The 450-member *National Assembly* is elected for 5-year terms. Candidates may be proposed by the Communist Party or the Fatherland Front (which groups various social organizations), or they may propose themselves as individual Independents. The Assembly convenes 3 times a year and appoints a prime minister and cabinet. It elects the *President*, the head of state. The latter heads a *State Council* which issues decrees when the National Assembly is not in session.

President (titular head of state): Tran Duc Luong.
Vice-President: Nguyen Thi Binh (b. 1927; elected Sept. 1992).

At the National Assembly elections of 19 July 1992 the electorate was 37·41m. There were 601 candidates (90% Communists).

The ultimate source of political power is the Communist Party of Vietnam, founded in 1930; it had 2·2m. members in 1996. Full members of its Politburo in Dec. 1997: Gen. Le Kha Phieu (b. 1932; *Secretary General*); Gen. Le Duc Anh; Vo Van Kiet; Nguyen Van An; Pham Van Tra; Tran Duc Luong; Nguyen Thi Xuan My; Truong Tan Sang; Le Xuan Tung; Le Minh Huong; Nguyen Tan Dung; Gen. Doan

Khue; Pham The Duyet; Nguyen Duc Binh; Nong Duc Manh; Phan Van Khai; Gen. Le Kha Phieu; Nguyen Manh Cam.

In March 1998 the government comprised:
Prime Minister: Phan Van Khai.
Deputy Prime Ministers: Nguyen Tan Dung, Nguyen Manh Cam, Nguyen Cong Tan, Ngo Xuan Loc, Pham Gia Khiem. *Foreign:* Nguyen Manh Cam. *Defence:* Pham Van Tra. *Interior:* Le Minh Huong. *Planning and Investment:* Tran Zuan Gia. *Justice:* Nguyen Dinh Loc. *Finance:* Nguyen Sinh Hung. *Trade:* Truong Dinh Tuyen. *Industry:* Dang Vu Chu. *Head, State Inspectoration Board:* Ta Huu Thanh. *Chairman of State Committee for Minorities and Mountainous Area:* Hoang Duc Nghi. *Population and Family Planning:* Tran Thi Trung Chien. *Acting Governor of the State Bank:* Do Que Luong. *Labour, War Invalids and Social Affairs:* Nguyen Thi Hang. *Construction:* Nguyen Manh Kiem. *Agriculture and Rural Development:* Le Huy Ngo. *Transport:* Le Ngoc Hoan. *Fisheries:* Ta Quang Ngoc. *Culture and Information:* Nguyen Khoa Diem. *Health:* Do Nguyen Phuong. *Education and Training:* Nguyen Minh Hien. *Child Care and Protection:* Tran Thi Thanh Thanh. *Chairman, State Committee for Gymnastics and Sport:* Ha Quang Du. *Government Personnel and Organization of Government Committee:* Do Quang Trung. *Science, Technology and the Environment:* Chu Tuan Nha. *Chairman, Government Office:* Lai Van Cu.

Speaker of the National Assembly: Nong Duc Manh.

National anthem: 'Doàn quân Việt Nam di chung lòng cúú quóc' ('Soldiers of Vietnam, we are advancing'); words and tune by Van Cao.

Local Government is administered by people's councils, which appoint executive committees. Local elections were held with the National Assembly elections in July 1992.

DEFENCE. Conscription of men and women is for 2 years, specialists 3 years. Since 1989 troops have been permitted to engage in economic activity.

Army. There are 8 military regions and 2 special areas. The Army consists of 14 corps headquarters, 50 infantry, 3 mechanized, 8 engineer and 10 to 16 economic construction divisions, 10 armoured, 10 field artillery and 20 independent engineer brigades and 15 independent infantry regiments. Special forces include an airborne brigade and a demolition engineer regiment. Equipment includes some 1,000 T-34/-54/-55, 200 T-62 and 100 Chinese Type-59 and M-48A3 main battle tanks. Strength, (1997), 0·5m. Paramilitary forces number 4·5m. and consist of the Peoples' Self-Defence Force (urban), a People's Militia (rural) and a rear force (reserves).

Navy. The fleet currently includes 5 ex-Soviet 'Petya' class frigates, 2 ex-US frigates (built 1943 and 1944), 2 ex-Soviet missile corvettes, 8 Soviet-built fast missile craft, 16 fast torpedo craft, 2 patrol hydrofoils, 21 inshore patrol craft, 6 coastal and 5 inshore minesweepers, 7 landing ships, and some 20 smaller amphibious craft.

In 1996 personnel were estimated to number 12,000 plus an additional Naval Infantry force of 30,000.

Air Force. In 1996 the Air Force had about 15,000 personnel and 196 combat aircraft and 33 armed helicopters. There are reported to be 3 squadrons of variable-geometry MiG-23s, 1 squadron of SU-27s, 3 squadrons of Su-22s, 12 squadrons of 150 MiG-21 interceptors; An-2, An-24 and An-26 transports; and a strong helicopter force with Ka-25, Mi-6, Mi-8/17 and Mi-24 helicopters. The 15,000 strong air defence force is organized in 14 divisions and deploys 66 surface-to-air missile sites.

INTERNATIONAL RELATIONS

Membership. Vietnam is a member of the UN and ASEAN.

ECONOMY

Policy. The sixth 5-year plan covers 1996–2000.

A reform programme (*Doi Moi*) injecting free enterprise principles and reducing central control has been implemented. The 'Draft Strategy for Socio-Economic Stabilization and Development to 2000' aims to double GDP through the 'socialist-oriented commodity economy, a market economy under state management' in which the state and collective sectors will play a 'predominant role'.

The 1992 constitution embodies the market-oriented reforms of recent years, recognizing citizens' right to engage in private business. A bankruptcy law was passed in Jan. 1994.

Budget. Revenue in 1991 (in 1,000m. dong), 8,210; expenditure, 9,230.

Currency. The unit of currency is the *dong* (VND). There are notes of 100, 1,000, 2,000, 5,000, 10,000, 20,000 and 50,000 dong. In March 1989 the dong was brought into line with free market rates. The direct use of foreign currency was made illegal in Oct. 1994. Foreign exchange reserves were US$830m. at the end of 1995. Currency in circulation, 1991, 5,340,000m. dong. Inflation was 15% in 1995. Gold reserves were 98,300 troy oz. in June 1991.

Banking and Finance. The central bank and bank of issue is the National Bank of Vietnam (founded in 1951; *Governor*, Cao Sy Kiem). There are 52 commercial banks (4 state run and 48 shareholding), 19 foreign branches and 4 joint ventures set up with foreign capital. Vietcombank is the foreign trade bank. 50 foreign banks had branches in 1998.

ENERGY AND NATURAL RESOURCES

Electricity. Total capacity of power generation in 1995 was 4,400 MW. In 1994, 12,473m. kWh. of electricity were produced (1995 estimated at 14,000m. kWh.). A hydro-electric power station with a capacity of 2m. kW. was opened at Hoa-Binh in 1994.

Oil and Gas. Estimated crude oil production in 1995, 7·7m. tonnes. Natural gas reserves estimated at 100bn. cu. metres.

Minerals. Vietnam is endowed with an abundance of mineral resources such as coal (3·5bn. tonnes), bauxite (3bn. tonnes), iron ore (700m. tonnes), copper (600,000 tonnes), tin (70,000 tonnes), chromate (10m. tonnes) and apatite (1bn. tonnes): Coal production was 4·8m. tonnes in 1992. There are also deposits of manganese, titanium, a little gold and marble. 1992 output (in 1,000 tonnes): Sand, 13,260; limestone, 667; salt, 542.

Agriculture. Accounts for nearly 30% of GDP and employs 70% of the workforce. Ownership of land is vested in the state, but since 1992 farmers may inherit and sell plots allocated on 20-year leases. The household is the basic production unit. Peasants may market their produce, or deal through the co-operatives.

Production in 1,000 tonnes in 1993: Coffee, 135; tea, 35; rubber, 76; coconut, 1,207; (1994) rice, 24,500. Other crops include sugar-cane and cotton. Total food output in 1995, 27·4m. tonnes.

Livestock, 1993 (in 1,000): Cattle, 3,320; pigs, 14,861; goats, 300; poultry, 113m.

Livestock products (1993): Eggs, 115,000 tonnes; meat, 1,126,000 tonnes.

37,627 tractors were in use in 1992.

Forestry. In 1995, forests covered 9·2m. ha (13·5m. ha in 1943). It is planned to reafforest 0·2m. ha annually. Timber exports were prohibited in 1992. Timber production was 4,846,000 cu. metres in 1991. 24,679,000 cu. metres were cut for fuel.

Fisheries. In 1992 there were 32 fishing vessels over 100 GRT with a total tonnage of 13,956 GRT. Total catch, 1990, 0·85m. tonnes, of which 0·24m. tonnes were freshwater fish. Fishery production in 1994 reached 1·1m. tonnes and is estimated to increase to 1·5m. tonnes in 1995.

INDUSTRY. The industrial sector generates about 30% (including construction) of GDP. 1992 production (in 1,000 tonnes): Crude steel, 175·2; cement, 3,727; fertilizers, 507; sulphuric acid, 8; dyestuffs, 4·3; glass and glassware, 32·3; textile fibre, 42·5; processed fish, 627·4; sugar, 304; tea, 20·1; (in units): Bricks, 3,675m.;

tiles, 410m.; machine tools, 2,316; hydraulic pumps, 500; threshing machines, 40,125; diesel motors, 3,300; ventilators, 257,000; batteries, 68m.; lamps, 9·6m.; woven fabrics, 450m. metres (1995); knitting fabric, 15,000 tonnes (1995); beer, 162·1m. litres; cigarettes, 1,524m. packets.

Labour. In 1995 the workforce was estimated at 40m. In 1991 (in 1,000) agriculture accounted for 22,276; forestry, 207; manufacturing, 3,394; building, 820; transport, 480; communications, 46; trade, 1,749; services, 296; research, 49; education, 804; culture, 46; health, social welfare and sport, 310; finance, 118; public administration, 240. In 1993, 32% of the workforce was female. In 1991, 58% of the workforce worked in co-operatives, 31% in the private sector and 11% in the state sector.

Trade Unions. There are 53 trade union associations.

FOREIGN ECONOMIC RELATIONS. In Feb. 1994 the USA lifted the trade embargo it had imposed in 1975. Foreign debt was US$19,600m. in 1994. The 1992 constitution regulates joint ventures with Western firms; full repatriation of profits and non-nationalization of investments are guaranteed. By May 1996 total foreign investment was US$19,925m., of which industry accounted for US$9,400m. services, US$6,700m.; oil and gas, was US$1,200m. and transport and communications, US$1,100m. 65% of Vietnam's trade is with Asian countries.

Commerce. Trade is conducted through the state import-export agencies. Value of exports in 1995, US$5·3bn.; imports, (1994) US$5bn. Earnings in 1995, from seafood exports reached US$580m. and from textiles, US$700m. Main export markets in 1992 (in US$1m.): Japan, 912·5; Singapore, 502·5; Hong Kong, 275·3; Germany, 237·7; France, 119·5. Main import suppliers: Singapore, 881; Hong Kong, 281; Japan, 192; South Korea, 185; France, 158; Taiwan, 120. Main exports are coal, farm produce, sea produce and livestock. Imports: Oil, steel, artificial fertilizers. Following the removal of rice cultivation from state control. Rice exports in 1992 were some 1·4m. tonnes, coal, 0·78m. tonnes (0·23m. in 1987), mainly to Japan and South Korea.

Tourism. There were 0·67m. foreign visitors in 1993 and 1·02m. in 1994.

COMMUNICATIONS

Roads. There are about 105,000 km of roads, of which 15% are hard-surfaced. In 1995 there were 0·31m. 4-wheeled vehicles and around 3m. motorcycles. 373·7m. passengers (1994) and 39·57m. tonnes of freight (1991) were transported.

Railways. Route length is 2,600 km of single-track line covering seven routes. Rail links with China were reopened in Feb. 1996. 20% of trains were steam-hauled in 1992. In 1995, 1·92m. passengers and 3·5m. tonnes of freight were carried.

Civil Aviation. There are international airports at Hanoi (Noi Bai) and Ho Chi Minh City (Tan Son Nhat) and 13 domestic airports. The national carrier is Vietnam Airlines, which operated 7 A320-200s, 1 B-767-200ER, 1 B-767-300ER, 23 ex-Soviet and 4 other aircraft in 1995. Services are also provided by Air France, British Airways, Cathay Pacific, Japan Airlines, KLM, Lufthansa and Qantas.

Shipping. In 1995, sea-going vessels totalled 1·21m. GRT, including oil tankers, 0·19m. GRT. The major ports are Hai Phong, which can handle ships of 10,000 tons, Ho Chi Minh City and Da Nang. There are regular services to Hong Kong, Singapore, Thailand, Cambodia and Japan. 0·7m. passengers and 4·88m. tonnes of freight were carried in 1991. There are some 19,500 km of navigable waterways.

Telecommunications. Vietnam Posts and Telecommunications and the military operate telephone systems with the assistance of foreign companies. In 1997, telephone provision was 10 phones per 1,000 population. In 1996 there were 3 mobile phone networks with some 35,000 subscribers. Broadcasting is controlled by the state Vietnam Radio and Television Committee. There are 2 national radio programmes from Hanoi and 1 from Ho Chi Minh City, 14 provincial programmes and an external service, the Voice of Vietnam (11 languages). There is a national and 2 provincial TV services. There were 6m. radio and 2·5m. TV sets in 1993 (colour by NTSC and SECAM).

Press. In 1994 there were some 350 newspaper and periodical titles. There are 2 national dailies, the Communist Party's *Nhan Dan* ('The People'), circulation, 0·2m., and the Army's *Quan Doi Nhan Dan*, 60,000. There are 3 major regional dailies with a combined circulation of 155,000. There were 10 titles in English, including 2 dailies in 1995. 3,043 book titles were published in 1991 totalling 62·4m. copies.

SOCIAL INSTITUTIONS

Justice. A new penal code came into force 1 Jan. 1986 'to complete the work of the 1980 Constitution'. Penalties (including death) are prescribed for opposition to the people's power, and for economic crimes. The judicial system comprises the Supreme People's Court, provincial courts and district courts. The president of the Supreme Court is responsible to the National Assembly, as is the Procurator-General, who heads the Supreme People's Office of Supervision and Control.

Religion. Taoism is the traditional religion but Buddhism is widespread. At a Conference for Buddhist Reunification in Nov. 1981, 9 sects adopted a charter for a new Buddhist church under the Council of Sangha. The Hoa Hao sect, associated with Buddhism, claimed 1·5m. adherents in 1976. Caodaism, a synthesis of Christianity, Buddhism and Confucianism founded in 1926, has some 2m. followers. In 1992, there were 38·2m. Buddhists and 6m. Roman Catholics (1997). There is an Archbishopric of Hanoi and 13 bishops. There were 2 seminaries in 1989. In 1983 the Government set up a Solidarity Committee of Catholic Patriots.

Education. Adult literacy rate is 93%. Primary education consists of a 10-year course divided into 3 levels of 4, 3 and 3 years respectively. In 1991–92 there were 16,076 primary schools with 11·8m. pupils and 389,000 teachers and 1,113 secondary and tertiary schools with 568,000 pupils and 35,100 teachers. In 1995–96 there were 7 universities, 2 open (distance) universities and 9 specialized universities (agriculture, 3; economics, 2; technology, 3; water resources, 1).

Health. In 1991 there were 1,550 hospitals with 118,100 beds, 10,710 medical centres with 73,500 beds and 115 sanatoria. There were 74,600 doctors, 68,300 nurses, 13,600 midwives and 12,400 pharmacists.

DIPLOMATIC REPRESENTATIVES

Of Vietnam in Great Britain (12–14 Victoria Rd., London, W8 5RD)
Ambassador: Huynh Ngoc An.

Of Great Britain in Vietnam (Central Building, 31 Hai Ba Trung, Hanoi)
Ambassador: David W. Fall.

Of Vietnam in the USA
Ambassador: Le Van Bang.

Of the USA in Vietnam (7 Lang Ha, Ba Dinh District, Hanoi)
Ambassador: Douglas Peterson.

Of Vietnam to the United Nations
Ambassador: Ngo Quang Xuan.

Of Vietnam to the European Union
Ambassador: Huynh Anh Dzung.

Further Reading

Trade and Tourism Information Centre with the General Statistical Office. *Economy and Trade of Vietnam* [various 5-year periods]
Beresford, M., *National Unification and Economic Development in Vietnam.* London, 1989
Dellinger, D., *Vietnam Revisited.* Boston (Mass.), 1986
Ho Chi Minh, *Selected Writings, 1920–1969.* Hanoi, 1977

Karnow, S., *Vietnam: a History.* 2nd ed. London, 1992
Morley, J. W. and Nishihara M., *Vietnam Joins the World.* Armonk (NY), 1997
Norlund, I. (ed.) *Vietnam in a Changing World.* London, 1994
Harvie C. and Tran Van Hoa V., *Reforms and Economic Growth.* London 1997
Post, K., *Revolution, Socialism and Nationalism in Vietnam.* vol. 1. Aldershot, 1989
Smith, R. B., *An International History of the Vietnam War.* London, 1983

National statistical office: General Statistical Office, Hanoi.

YEMEN

Jamhuriya al Yamaniya

(Republic of Yemen)

Capital: Sanaía
Commercial capital: Aden
Population: 15·8m.
GDP per head: (PPP$) 805
GNP: US$3·9bn.
HDI/world rank: 0·361/148

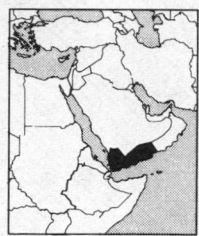

KEY HISTORICAL EVENTS. Following an agreement reached in Dec. 1989 on a constitution for a unified state, the (northern) Yemen Arab Republic and the (southern) People's Democratic Republic of Yemen were united as the Republic of Yemen on 22 May 1990.

In Aug. 1993 Vice-President Ali Salem Albidh withdrew to Aden and demanded the implementation of a reform programme as a condition of re-joining President Saleh in Sanaía. Albidh agreed to a modified reform programme at an agreement brokered by King Hussein of Jordan in Feb. 1994, but clashes between north and south escalated into full civil war at the beginning of May. Southern officials announced their secession from Yemen on 21 May 1994. Aden was captured by northern forces on 7 June 1994. The former vice-president and government went into exile.

TERRITORY AND POPULATION. Yemen is bounded in the north by Saudi Arabia, east by Oman, south by the Gulf of Aden and west by the Red Sea. The territory includes 112 islands including Kamaran (181 sq. km) and Perim (300 sq. km) in the Red Sea and Socotra (3,500 sq. km) in the Gulf of Aden. The islands of Greater and Lesser Hanish is claimed by both Yemen and Eritrea. On 15 Dec. 1995 Eritrean troops occupied it, and Yemen retaliated with aerial bombardments. A ceasefire was agreed at presidential level on 17 Dec. On 20 Dec. the UN resolved to send a good offices mission to the area. In an agreement of 21 May 1996 brokered by France, Yemen and Eritrea renounced the use of force to settle the dispute and agreed to submit it to arbitration. The area is 555,000 sq. km excluding the desert Empty Quarter (Rub Al-Khahi). A dispute with Saudi Arabia broke out in Dec. 1994 over some 1,500–2,000 km of undemarcated desert boundary. A memorandum of understanding signed on 26 Feb. 1995 reaffirmed the border agreement reached at Taif in 1934. An agreement of June 1995 completed the demarcation of the border with Oman.

The population was estimated at 15·8m. in 1995; density, 21 persons per sq. km. At the census of 1986 in the north and 1988 in the south the population was 9,664,939 (4,938,318 females; 1,793,861 urban). The birth rate in 1994 was 48·4; the death rate, 11·5. There were 1,168,199 citizens working abroad mainly in Saudi Arabia and the United Arab Emirates not included in the census total. Since 1990 Saudi Arabia has compulsorily repatriated almost all Yemeni workers. In 1988 there were 17 governorates:

	1986/88 census population		*1986/88 census population*
Sanaía (city)	427,502	Shabwah	192,324
Sanaía	1,237,016	Hajjah	720,000
Aden	326,919	Bayd	295,439
Taíiz	1,419,708	Hadhrama	537,095
Hodeida	1,052,086	Saíadah	323,124
Lahej	458,385	Mahwit	260,836
Ibb	1,254,128	Mahrah	44,225
Abyan	279,241	Marib	95,326
Dhamar	698,823	Jawf	42,762

The population of the capital, Sanaía, was estimated at 972,000 in 1995. The commercial capital is the port of Aden, with a population of (1995) 562,000. Other important towns are the port of Hodeida (population, 155,110), Mukalla (154,360), Taíiz (178,043), Ibb and Abyan.

CLIMATE. A desert climate, modified by relief. Sanaía. Jan. 57°F (13·9°C), July71°F (21·7°C). Aden, Jan. 75°F (24°C), July 90°F (32°C). Annual rainfall 20" (508 mm) in the north, but very low in coastal areas: 1·8" (46 mm).

CONSTITUTION AND GOVERNMENT. There is a 301-member *House of Representatives* which after the elections of April 1993 was composed of: General People's Congress (GPC), 123 seats; Islah, 62; Yemen Socialist Party, 56; ind, 47; others, 13.

On 28 Sept. 1994 the House of Representatives unanimously adopted a new constitution founded on Islamic law. This abolishes the former 5-member Presidential Council and installs a *President* elected by parliament for 5-year terms. Lieut.-Gen. Ali Abdullah Saleh was elected President on 1 Oct. 1994.

Parliamentary elections were held on 27 April 1997, in which the GPC gained 187 seats, the Independents 54, Islah 53, Baassists 3, and Nasserians 2. There were 21 women candidates, of whom 2 were elected.

President: Ali Abdullah Saleh (GPC; sworn in 2 Oct. 1994).
Vice-President: Abd Rabbah Mansour Hadi.

In March 1998 the government comprised:
Prime Minister: Faraj Saeed Bin Ghanem. *Deputy Prime Minister and Minister for Foreign Affairs:* Abdulkarim Al-Eryani. *Civil Service and Administrative Reform:* Mohamed Ahmed Al-Gonaid. *Planning and Development:* Abdulkader Bajammal. *Oil and Mineral Resources:* Mohamed Al-Khadem Al-Wajeeh. *Minister for Legal and Council of Ministers' Affairs:* Abdullah Ahmed Ghanem. *Justice:* Isamael Ahmed Al-Wazir. *Social Security and Social Affairs:* Mohamed Abdullah Al-Bitani. *Telecommunications:* Ahmed Mohamed Al-Anisi. *Local Administration:* Sadeq Amin Aburas. *Finance:* Alawi Salih Assalami. *Fisheries:* Ahmed Musaed Hussein. *Transport:* Brig. Abdulmalik Assyani. *Interior:* Col. Hussein Mohamed Arab. *Trade and Provisions:* Abdulrahman Mohamed Ali Othman. *Information:* Abdulrahman Al-Akawa'a. *Youth and Sports:* Abdulwahab Raweh. *Power and Water:* Ali Hamid Sharaf. *Agriculture and Water Resources:* Ahmed Salem Al-Gabali. *Industry:* Ahmed Mohamed Sofan. *Culture and Tourism:* Abdulmalek Mansour. *Construction, Housing and Urban Planning:* Abdullah Hussein Al-Dafee. *Defence:* Col. Mohamed Dhaifallah Mohamed. *Expatriates Abroad:* Abdullah Saleh Saba'a. *Labour and Vocational Training:* Mohamed Mohamed Attayeb. *Endowments and Guidance:* Judge Ahmed Mohamed Al-Shami. *Public Health:* Dr Abdullah Abdulwali Nasher. *Education:* Yahya Mohamed Abdullah Al-Shuaibi. *Minister of State for the Affairs of the Council of Ministers:* Ahmed Ali Al-Bushari.

The *Speaker* is Sheikh Abdullah Al-Ahmar (Islah).

National anthem: 'Raddidi Ayyatuha ad Dunya nashidi' ('Repeat, O World, my song'); words by A. Noman, tune by Ayub Tarish.

Local Government. The country is administratively divided into 27 governorates and the capital city.

DEFENCE. Conscription is for 3 years.

Army. The Army comprises 7 armoured, 18 infantry, 5 mechanized, 2 airborne commando, 5 militia, 4 artillery, 1 special forces and 1 surface-to-surface missile brigade. Equipment includes 250 T-34, 675 T-54/-55, 150 T-62 and 50 M-60A1 main battle tanks. Strength (1997) 37,000 (some 25,000 conscripts) with 39,500 reserves. There are paramilitary tribal levies numbering at least 20,000 and a Ministry of Security force of 50,000.

Navy. The Navy comprises 3 Chinese-built and 4 ex-Soviet fast missile craft, 8 inshore patrol craft, 3 inshore minesweepers, 2 tank landing ships and 2 craft. Forces are based at Aden and Hodeida, with other facilities at Mokha, Mukalla and Perim. Personnel in 1997 were estimated at 1,800.

Air Force. The unified Air Forces of the former Arab Republic and People's Democratic Republic are now under one command, although this unity was broken by the attempted secession of the south in 1994 which resulted in heavy fighting between the air forces of Sanaía and Aden. There are 80 interceptors (60 MiG-21s, 10 MiG-29s and 10 F-5Es), 20 MiG-23s and 20 Su-22s for strike duties, 15 Mi-24 gunship helicopters, 5 An-24 and 8 An-26 twin-turboprop transports, 15 other transports (including 2 C-130H Hercules) and about 40 Mi-8 and 12 other helicopters. Personnel (1997) about 3,500.

INTERNATIONAL RELATIONS

Membership. Yemen is a member of the UN and the Arab League.

ECONOMY

Policy. A 5-year plan is running from 1996 to 2000. It includes some privatization proposals.

Budget. Government revenue and expenditure (in 1,000,000 riyals):

	1991	1992	1993
Revenue			
Taxation	20,077	18,561	22,071
Taxes on income, profit etc	9,914	6,253	8,311
Excises	2,746	3,798	4,229
Import duties	6,031	6,646	7,535
Current	17,672	13,820	14,235
Property	15,489	12,296	12,891
Capital	233	530	468
Expenditure			
Defence	13,227	16,812	19,752
Education	8,461	10,537	13,491
Public services	4,644	7,445	7,619
Other	17,720	19,975	24,546

Budget revenues exclude grants from abroad: 300m. ryals in 1991 and 1,201m. ryals in 1993; budget expenditures exclude lending minus repayments: 1,335m. ryals in 1991, 1,491m. ryals in 1992 and 1,971m. ryals in 1993. The budget estimate for 1995 (in 1,000,000 ryals) was revenue, 87,000 and expenditure, 124,100. For 1996 it was revenue 155,886, expenditure 181,416. The government did not publish budget proposals for 1994.

Currency. The unit of currency is the *riyal* (YER) of 100 *fils.* There are notes of 1, 2, 5, 10, 20, 50 and 100 riyals. During the transitional period to north-south unification the northern *riyal* of 100 *fils* and the southern *dinar* of 1,000 *fils* coexisted. Inflation was an annualized 175% in 1995. There were 3 foreign exchange rates operating: an internal clearing rate, an official rate and a commercial rate. In 1996 the official rate was abolished.

Banking and Finance. Total assets of the Central Bank were 109,497m. riyals in 1992. There were 6,616m. riyals in savings deposits.

A stock exchange is scheduled to open at some stage in 1998.

ENERGY AND NATURAL RESOURCES

Electricity. Production (1994) 1,958m. kWh (estimate).

Oil and Gas. The first large-scale oilfield and pipeline was inaugurated in 1987. There are reserves of 2,000m. bbls on the former north-south border. Further major oil finds were announced in 1991. Crude oil production (1994): 16,005,000 metric tonnes. Gas reserves are some 7,000m. cu. metres.

Minerals. 107,000 tons of salt were produced in 1992. Reserves (estimate) 25m. tonnes. In 1992 647,000 cu. metres of stone and 77,898 tons of gypsum were extracted.

Agriculture. In 1992 the cultivable area was 1,630,972 ha, of which 1,040,254 ha were cultivated. In the south, agriculture is largely of a subsistence nature, sorghum, sesame and millet being the chief crops, and wheat and barley widely grown at the higher elevations. Cash crops include cotton. Fruit is plentiful in the north.

Owing to the meagre rainfall, cultivation is largely confined to fertile valleys and flood plains on silt. Irrigation schemes with permanent installations are in progress. Estimate production (1995, in 1,000 tonnes): Wheat, 170; seed cotton, 8; sesame seeds, 13; millet, 60; maize, 80; sorghum, 450; barley, 65; pulses, 70; potatoes, 200; tomatoes, 192; onions, 57; watermelons, 102; melons, 31; alfalfa, 149,087 (1992 figure); coffee, 9; dates, 21; grapes, 147; bananas, 74.

Estimated livestock in 1995 (in 1,000): Cattle, 1,130; camels, 173; sheep, 3,715; goats, 3,230; poultry, 22m. Estimated livestock produce, 1995 (in 1,000 tonnes): Meat,133; cows' milk, 155.

Fisheries. Fishing is a major industry. Total catch (1995) 103,964 tonnes.

INDUSTRY. In 1992 there were 211 industrial firms (142 private, 48 public, 13 mixed and 8 co-operative). 64 of these were producing foodstuffs, 50 chemicals and petroleum products, 27 textiles and leather goods and 27 metal goods. Output (in 1,000 tons), 1992: Edible oils, 102; flour, 247; cement, 820; cartons, 17; petrol, 947; fuel oil, 1,782; fuel gas, 160; jet fuel, 643; asphalt, 48.

Labour. In 1992 there were 30,381 industrial employees, of whom 13,139 were in the public sector. Unemployment was 36% at the end of 1993.

FOREIGN ECONOMIC RELATIONS. Foreign debt was US$7,800m. in 1992.

Commerce. Trade (in 1,000 riyals):

	1990	1991	1992
Exports	8,315,504	6,075,948	5,693,349
Imports	18,867,090	24,314,326	31,075,611

Main import suppliers, 1992 (in 1,000 riyals): USA, 2,858,220; UAE, 2,559,581; Saudi Arabia, 2,311,965; Japan, 2,172,044; UK, 1,713,618. Main export markets: USA, 1,396,053; Japan, 666,689; Germany, 470,723; Saudi Arabia, 268,769.

Cotton and fish are major exports, the largest imports being food and live animals. A large transhipment and entrepôt trade is centred on Aden, which was made a free trade zone in May 1991. Oil income (exports and concessions) was US$1,150m. in 1992.

Tourism. In 1994 40,000 tourists visited and spent US$41m.

COMMUNICATIONS

Roads. There were (1992) 7,264 km of roads, including 2,344 km paved. In 1995 there were 229,084 passenger cars, 2,835 buses and coaches, and 279,780 goods vehicles. In 1992 there were 9,267 road accidents with 1,290 fatalities.

Civil Aviation. There are international airports at Sanaía and Aden. 2 national carriers have merged into Yemen Airlines (Yemenia): The former southern state-owned Alyemda Yemen Airlines, which in 1995 operated 1 A310-300, 1 B-707-320C, 2 B-737-200C Advs and 2 other aircraft; and the former northern Yemenia Yemen Airways, 51% state-owned which had 1 A310-200, 3 B-727-200 Advs, 1 B-737-200 Adv and 2 other aircraft. Services are also provided by Aeroflot, Egyptair, Ethiopian Airlines, Gulf Air, KLM, Lufthansa, Qatar Airways, Royal Jordanian, Saudia, Sudan Airways and Syrian Airlines. 1·16m. passengers and 14·42m. tons of freight were handled in 1992.

Shipping. In 1995, sea-going shipping totalled 26,431 GRT, including oil tankers, 3,185 GRT. There are ports at Aden, Mokha, Hodeida, Mukalla and Nashtoon. 449,621 tons of cargo were discharged in 1992, and 7,697 tonnes of oil at the Ras Issa terminal.

Telecommunications. In 1992 there were 208 post offices. There were 173,000 telephones in 1994. Broadcasting is managed by the government-controlled Yemen

Radio and Television Corporation. Programmes are transmitted from Sanaía and Aden. In 1995 there were 650,000 radio and 420,000 TV receivers (colour by PAL and NTSC).

Cinemas. In 1992 there were 45 cinemas with 43,265 seats. Attendance was 8,319,805.

Press. In 1995 there were 3 daily (1 in English), 5 weekly and 4 monthly newspapers and 15 periodicals.

SOCIAL INSTITUTIONS

Justice. A civil code based on Islamic law was introduced in 1992.

Religion. In 1989 there were some 5·3m. Shi'ite and 5,925,000 Sunni Moslems.

Education. In 1994 there were 62 pre-primary schools with 680 teachers for 11,999 pupils. In 1992 there were 9,348 other schools with 2,214,292 pupils (553,685 girls) and 63,670 teachers. There are universities at Sanaía (founded 1974) and Aden (1975). The former had 3,520 students and 330 academic staff in 1994–95, the latter 4,800 and 470. The adult literacy rate is 41·1%.

Health. In 1992 there were 75 hospitals with 8,150 beds, 370 health centres with 1,777 beds, 912 primary health units and 2 maternity centres. There were 3,065 doctors, 163 dentists and 231 pharmacists with 1,137 pharmacies.

DIPLOMATIC REPRESENTATIVES

Of Yemen in Great Britain (57 Cromwell Rd., London, SW7 2ED)
Ambassador: Dr Hussein Abdullah Al-Amri.

Of Great Britain in Yemen (129 Haddah Rd., Sanaía)
Ambassador: V. J. Henderson.

Of Yemen in the USA (2600 Virginia Ave., NW, Washington, D.C., 20037)
Ambassador: Abdulwahab Al-Hajjiri.

Of the USA in Yemen (Dhahr Himyar Zone, Sheraton Hotel District, POB 22347, Sanaía)
Ambassador: David G. Newton.

Of Yemen to the United Nations
Ambassador: Abdalla Saleh Al-Ashtal.

Of Yemen to the European Union
Ambassador: Abdul Khaleq Al Aghbari.

Further Reading

Central Statistical Organization. *Statistical Year Book*
Auchterlonie, Paul, *Yemen.* [Bibliography] Oxford and Santa Barbara (CA), 1998
Bidwell, R., *The Two Yemens.* Boulder and London, 1983
El Mallakh, R., *The Economic Development of the Yemen Arab Republic.* London, 1986
Ismael, T. Y. and Ismael, J. S., *The People's Democratic Republic of Yemen.* London, 1986
Mackintosh-Smith, T., *Yemen—Travels in dictionary land.* London, 1997

National statistical office: Central Statistical Organization, Ministry of Planning and Development

YUGOSLAVIA

Savezna Republika Jugoslavija

(Federal Republic of Yugoslavia, comprising the republics of Serbia and Montenegro)

Capital: Belgrade
Population: 10·57m.
GDP per head: approx. US$1,600

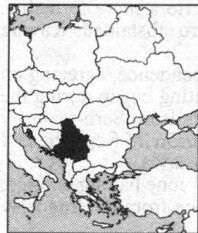

KEY HISTORICAL EVENTS. On 28 June 1914 Archduke Franz Ferdinand of Austria was assassinated in Bosnia by a young nationalist. Though Serbia complied with most of the terms of Austria's subsequent ultimatum, Austria declared war on 28 July, thus precipitating the First World War. In the winter of 1915–16 the Serbian army was forced to retreat to Corfu, where the government, under Prime Minister Pašić, was established. Montenegro capitulated in 1916 and its king fled. Exiles from Croatia and Slovenia had formed a Yugoslav Committee in 1914 whose aim was South Slav federation. This was not compatible with Pašič's goal of a centralized, Serb-run state, but the Committee and the government managed to contrive a joint 'Corfu Declaration' in July 1917 demanding a 'constitutional, democratic, parliamentary monarchy headed by the Karadjordevics'. This was accepted by the Allies as the basis for the new state. The Croats were forced by the pressure of events to join Serbia and Montenegro on 1 Dec. 1918. From 1918–29 the country was known as the Kingdom of the Serbs, Croats and Slovenes.

Boundary disputes with Italy and other neighbouring countries lasted into the 1920s. A constitution of 1921 established an assembly under King Alexander, but the trappings of parliamentarianism could not bridge the gulf between Serbs and Croats. The Croat peasant leader Radić was assassinated in 1928; his successor, Vlatko Maček, set up a separatist assembly in Zagreb. On 6 Jan. 1929 the king suspended the constitution and established a royal dictatorship, redrawing provincial boundaries without regard for ethnicity. In Oct. 1934 he was murdered by a Croat extremist while on an official visit to France.

During the 1930s Yugoslavia had become heavily dependent on the German economy. During the regency of Prince Paul, Prime Minister Stojadinović pursued a pro-fascist line. On 25 March 1941 Paul was induced to adhere to the Axis Tripartite Pact. On 27 March he was overthrown by military officers in favour of the boy king Peter. Germany invaded on 6 April. Within 10 days Yugoslavia surrendered; king and government fled to London. Two resistance movements came into being, a royalist group, under Draža Mihailović, and the communist-dominated partisans of Josip Broz, nicknamed Tito. The latter were imbued with revolutionary as well as liberationist aims. The movements often fought each other, and Mihailović collaborated to some extent with the Germans. Allied support was switched from him to Tito in 1944.

Tito succeeded in liberating Yugoslavia largely by his own efforts. The partisan Liberation Committee formed the nucleus of the post-war provisional government. A constituent assembly was elected in Nov. 1945 from a single list of People's Front candidates. A people's republic was proclaimed with a Soviet-type constitution. Tito embarked on a programme of enthusiastic Sovietization, but was too independent for Stalin, who sought to topple him by excommunicating Yugoslavia in 1948–49. However, Tito survived by the support of his people and a *rapprochement* with the west, and it was the Soviet Union under Khrushchev which had to extend the olive branch in 1956. As a spin-off from this schism Yugoslavia evolved its 'own road to socialism'. Collectivization of agriculture was abandoned; the principles of 'industrial self-management' were developed, and extended into the whole of the representative process; and Yugoslavia became a champion of international 'non-alignment'. A collective presidency came into being with the death of Tito in 1980.

Dissensions in Kosovo between Albanians and Serbs, and in parts of Croatia

1745

between Serbs and Croats, brought inter-ethnic tensions into prominence after 1988. With the election of new national assemblies in all 6 republics during 1990, several of the latter came increasingly into conflict with the federal government. At the end of 1990 both Croatia and Slovenia proclaimed their right to secede from federal Yugoslavia. In May 1991, following escalating Serb-Croat violence and demands for secession from predominantly Serb-inhabited areas of Croatia, the federal army was given powers to restrict the movement of unofficial armed groups. On 12 May the Krajina area held a self-styled referendum resulting, it was claimed, in an overwhelming vote for union with Serbia. Croatia rejected the poll.

On 15 May 1991 Croatia's representative in the federal presidency, Štipe Mesić, failed to secure the 5 votes needed to become president, hitherto a mere formality. Serbia, Kosovo and Vojvodina voted against and Montenegro abstained, leaving Yugoslavia without a head of state.

On 25 June Croatia and Slovenia made declarations of independence, agreeing on 30 June to an EU proposal to suspend them for 3 months. Fighting began during the summer in Croatia between Croatian forces and Serb irregulars from Serb-majority areas of Croatia. Federal forces had left Slovenia by July 1991. On 25 Sept. the UN Security Council imposed a mandatory arms embargo on Yugoslavia.

The 3-month moratorium agreed at the EU peace talks on 30 June having expired, both Slovenia and Croatia declared their complete independence from the Yugoslav federation on 8 Oct.

Trade sanctions on the whole of Yugoslavia were applied from 8 Nov., but restricted to Serbia after 2 weeks.

After 13 ceasefires had failed to be observed, a fourteenth was signed on 23 Nov. by the presidents of Croatia and Serbia and the federal defence minister, for the first time under UN auspices. Following a request on 26 Nov. from the federal government, a Security Council resolution of 27 Nov. proposed the deployment of a UN peace-keeping force if the ceasefire were kept. Fighting, however, continued.

On 15 Jan. 1992 the EU recognized Croatia and Slovenia as independent states. Bosnia-Hercegovina was recognized on 7 April 1992 and Macedonia on 8 April 1993. A UN delegation began monitoring the ceasefire on 17 Jan. and the UN Security Council on 21 Feb. voted unanimously to send a 14,000-strong peace-keeping force to Croatia and Yugoslavia.

On 27 April 1992 Serbia and Montenegro announced the formation of a federal republic of Yugoslavia constituted by themselves as the legal successor to the former Socialist Federal Republic of Yugoslavia (SFRY).

On 30 May, responding to further Serbian military activities in Bosnia and Croatia, the UN Security Council voted in favour of the imposition of sanctions.

In mid-1992 NATO countries began to commit air, sea and eventually land forces to enforce sanctions and protect humanitarian relief operations in Bosnia.

At a joint UN-EC peace conference on Yugoslavia held in London on 26–27 Aug. some 30 countries and all the former republics of Yugoslavia endorsed a plan to end the fighting in Croatia and Bosnia, install UN supervision of heavy weapons, recognize the borders of Bosnia-Hercegovina and return refugees. At a further conference at Geneva on 30 Sept. the Croatian and Yugoslav presidents agreed to make efforts to bring about a peaceful solution in Bosnia, but fighting continued.

On 22 Sept. the UN resolved (by 127 votes to 6 with 26 abstentions) that the self-proclaimed Federal Republic of Yugoslavia of Serbia and Montenegro could not automatically assume the seat of the former SFRY and excluded it from the General Assembly.

On 16 Nov. the UN Security Council voted for sanctions against Yugoslavia to be made more effective, and NATO agreed to lend naval support to their enforcement.

Further peace talks were held in Geneva in Jan. 1993, and transferred to the UN in Feb. On 22 Feb. the UN Security Council resolved to set up a war crimes tribunal for alleged violations of human rights in the former SFRY. A court was inaugurated at The Hague on 17 Nov. 1993. In 1995 the tribunal was merged into the International Penal Tribunal for Yugoslavia and Rwanda sitting at The Hague. The first sentence on a Yugoslav was delivered in Nov. 1996.

Following the Serbian President Milošević's announcement that Yugoslavia would no longer send supplies to Bosnian Serbs and would not accept international monitors on its borders, on 24 Sept. 1994 the UN Security Council lifted the non-trade sanctions against Yugoslavia affecting civil aviation, culture and sport. Following the Bosnian-Croatian-Yugoslav (Dayton) agreement all remaining UN sanctions were lifted in Nov. 1995.

Massive public anti-government demonstrations took place in Nov.–Dec. 1996 following the government's annulment of municipal election results where opposition candidates had been elected. An OSCE delegation investigated the disputed results and found that opposition candidates should have won in 22 municipalities. As demonstrations and protests from various quarters continued throughout Jan. 1997, Milošević conceded opposition victories in at first some, then finally on 7 Feb., all, the disputed municipalities.

In July 1997 Slobodan Milošević switched his power base to become president of federal Yugoslavia. Vojislav Seselj, leader of the ultra-nationalist Radical party defeated his Socialist rival in the run-off for the Serbian presidency. But since the turn-out fell short of the 50% required by the constitution there was a further election in Dec. in which the former Yugoslav foreign minister, Milan Milutinović finally succeeded Milošević. Meanwhile, in Montenegro, the pro-western Milo Djukanović succeeded a pro-Milošević president despite violent demonstrations which raised fears that Montenegro might break away from Serbia to create an independent state.

TERRITORY AND POPULATION. Yugoslavia is bounded in the north by Hungary, north-east by Romania, east by Bulgaria, south by Macedonia and Albania, and west by the Adriatic Sea, Bosnia-Hercegovina and Croatia. Area, 102,173 sq. km. Population (1991 census), 10,394,026 (5,236,906 females). Population density, 101·7 per sq. km. Estimate, 1996, 10,574,229.

Yugoslavia is a federation of 2 republics: Montenegro and Serbia, and 2 former autonomous provinces within Serbia: Kosovo and Metohija, and Vojvodina. The federal capital is Belgrade (Beograd); population estimate (1995), 1,601,373. Population (1991 census) of principal towns:

Belgrade	1,168,454	Subotica	100,386
Novi Sad	179,626	Zrenjanin	81,316
Niš	175,391	Pančevo	72,793
Kragujevac	147,305	Čačak	71,550
Podgorica	117,875	Smederevo	63,884

The 1991 census was not carried out in Kosovo and Metohija. 1991 estimated population: Priština, 155,499; Prizren 92,303; Peć, 68,163; Kosovska Mitrovica, 64,323.

Ethnic groups at the 1991 census: Serbs, 6,504,048; Albanians, 1,714,768; Montenegrins, 519,766; Hungarians, 344,147; Moslems, 336,025; Gypsies, 143,519; Croats, 111,650; Slovaks, 66,863; Macedonians, 47,118; Romanians, 42,364; Bulgarians, 26,922; Valachians, 17,810; Turks, 11,263. At the 1991 census, 361,452 nationals worked abroad.

Vital statistics, 1996 (provisional): Births, 136,757; deaths, 111,386; marriages, 57,035; divorces, 7,002. Rates (per 1,000 population): Births, 12·9; death, 10·5; marriage, 5·4; natural increase, 2·4; infant mortality, 14·3 (per 1,000 live births). Expectation of life in 1995: Males, 69·9; females, 74·7.

The official language is Serbian, the Eastern variant (Croatian is the Western) of Serbo-Croat, which was regarded as constituting one language in the Socialist Federal Republic of Yugoslavia. Serbian is written in the Cyrillic alphabet. There are also substantial Albanian and Hungarian-speaking minorities.

CLIMATE. Most parts have a central European type of climate, with cold winters and hot summers. Belgrade. Jan. 4·3°C, July 24·3°C. Annual rainfall 701 mm. Podgorica, Jan. 5·4°C, July 28·2°C. Annual rainfall 1,885 mm.

CONSTITUTION AND GOVERNMENT. The head of state is the *Federal President*, elected by both chambers of the federal parliament for a non-renewable 4-year term.

The federal parliament consists of 2 chambers: The *Chamber of the Republics* has 40 members, 20 each elected from the assemblies of Montenegro and Serbia. Its assent is necessary to all legislation. The *Chamber of Citizens* has 138 members, elected by universal suffrage.

At the elections to the Chamber of Citizens on 3 Nov. 1996 the Coalition of the left gained 64 seats; Zajedno ('Together'; opposition party), 22; the Democratic Party of Socialists of Montenegro, 20; the Radical Serb Party, 16. The other 16 seats were shared among 6 parties.

Federal President: Slobodan Miloševič.

In March 1998 the government comprised:

Prime Minister: Radoje Kontić.

Deputy Prime Ministers: Vojin Djukanović; Danko Djunić; Vladan Kutlesić; Zoran Lilić; Nikola Sainović. *Foreign Minister:* Zivadin Jovanović. *Interior:* Zoran Sokolović. *Defence:* Pavle Bulatović. *Domestic Trade:* Milorad Misković. *Foreign Trade:* Borislav Vuković. *Telecommunications:* Dojcilo Radojević. *Transport:* Dejan Drobnjaković. *Labour, Health and Social Affairs:* Miroslav Ivanišević. *Development, Science and Environment:* Jagos Zelenović. *Information:* Goran Matić. *Agriculture:* Nedeljko Sipovac. *Sport:* Zoran Bingulac. *Justice:* Zoran Knezević. *Finance:* Bozidar Gazivoda. *Economy:* Rade Filipović. *Government Secretary-General:* Ljubisa Popović.

The *Speaker* is Radoman Božović.

National anthem: 'Hej, Slaveni, jošte živi rečnaših dedova' ('O Slavs, our ancestors' words will live'); words by S. Tomašik, tune anonymous.

Local Government. Within the federal framework of republics Yugoslavia is administratively divided into 29 districts, 210 communes, 7,401 localities, 233 urban localities and 4,819 local communities.

DEFENCE. Military service for 12 to 15 months is compulsory.

Army. The Army comprises 8 tank, 7 motorized infantry, 6 mixed artillery, 1 surface-to-air missile, 1 anti-tank artillery, 2 mechanized, 1 airborne and 1 special forces brigades, 9 air defence and 2 task forces. Equipment includes 386T-54/-5 and 252 M-84 main battle tanks. Personnel (1997) were about 90,000 (37,000 conscripts).

Navy. The Navy comprises 4 small diesel submarines, 5 midget submarines, 2 Soviet and 2 locally built missile-armed frigates, 10 fast missile craft, 6 inshore patrol craft, 4 inshore minesweepers and 18 small landing craft. Auxiliaries include 3 transports and 1 headquarters ship.

The Air Force operates 4 Mi-14, 4 Ka-25 Hormone and 2 Ka-27 Helix anti-submarine helicopters. A Marine force of 900 is divided into 2 'brigades'.

Personnel in 1997 totalled 7,500 including Coastal Defence and Marines. The force is based at Kotor.

Air Force. There are 2 fighter divisions equipped primarily with Russian-built MiG-21s and MiG-29s and 2 ground-attack divisions of locally-built Jastreb and Orao jet attack aircraft. Transport units fly An-26 twin-engined aircraft, 4-turboprop An-12s, and a few other types in small numbers, notably Turbo-Porters and Yak-40s, Falcon 50s and Learjets for VIP duties. Training types are the nationally-designed UTVA-75 primary trainer, Galeb jet basic trainer and the Super Galeb jet advanced trainer. About 120 Gazelle, Agusta-Bell 205 and Mi-8 helicopters are in service. 'Guideline' and 'Goa' surface-to-air missiles have been supplied by the USSR. Personnel (1997) 16,700 (3,000 conscripts), with 155 combat aircraft and 71 armed helicopters.

INTERNATIONAL RELATIONS. Relations with Croatia were established in Jan. 1994 with the opening of mutual representative offices.

Membership. The former Yugoslavia (SFRY) was a member of the UN but its self-proclaimed successor state (Federal Republic of Yugoslavia) is excluded from the General Assembly and related bodies such as the IMF and World Bank.

ECONOMY

Budget. The federal budget for 1996 was set at 5,520,000,000 dinars; 71·6% of expenditure was on defence.

Currency. The unit of currency is the *dinar* (YUD) of 100 *para*. There are notes of 5, 10, 20, 50 and 100 dinars. On 24 Jan. 1994 a new convertible 'super-dinar' was introduced equivalent to 1,000m. previous dinars, at parity with, and pegged to, the Deutschmark, at 3·3 to the Deutschmark. This was devalued by 69·7% in Nov. 1995. In 1997 the unofficial rate of the dinar fell to 5·2 to the Deutschmark following a 50% increase in money supply. In Jan. 1998 foreign exchange reserves were estimated at less than US$200m., the equivalent of about 2 weeks of imports. A further official devaluation was anticipated. Inflation fell below 10% in 1997 but was expected to increase strongly in 1998. Foreign exchange reserves were 225,130m. dinars in 1992.

Banking and Finance. The National Bank is the bank of issue. The Governor of the National bank is Dusan Vlatković. There are also republican banks. A reform programme which started in Feb. 1989 has transformed banks into shareholding companies, empowers the National Bank to impose solvency ratios on financial institutions and strengthens its control of the money supply. The National Bank's reserves were below US$200m. in Jan. 1998.

There is a stock exchange at Belgrade.

Weights and Measures. The metric weights and measures have been in use since 1883. The Gregorian calendar was adopted in 1919.

ENERGY AND NATURAL RESOURCES

Electricity. Output in 1996, 38,093m. kWh, of which 23,420m. kWh were thermal and 14,673m. kWh hydro-electric.

Oil and Gas. Crude oil production (1996), 1,030,000 tonnes; natural gas, 671 cu. metres.

Minerals. Lignite production (1996), 37,828,000m. tonnes; coal, 38,429,000 tonnes; brown coal, 0·54m. tonnes; copper ore, 20,206,000 tonnes.

Agriculture. In 1996 there were 6,225,000 ha of agricultural land, of which 3,708,000 ha were arable (2,277,000 ha cereals; 386,000 ha industrial crops), 792,000 ha meadow and 1,335,000 ha pasture. 4·79m. ha of land were in private farms and 1,459,000 ha in agricultural organizations. The economically active agricultural population was 1,061,488 in 1991.

Crop production, 1996 (in 1,000 tonnes): Maize, 5,367; sugar beet, 2,418; wheat, 1,507; potatoes, 904; grapes, 487; plums, 619; soya beans, 153.

Livestock, 1996 (in 1,000): Cattle, 1,899; pigs, 4,216; sheep, 2,566; horses, 90; poultry, 25,712.

Livestock products, 1996: Meat, 583,000 tonnes; milk, 1,987,000 litres; wool, 3,881,000 tonnes; eggs, 1,783m. 209,686,000 litres of wine were produced in 1996.

Forestry. The forest area is 2,858,000 ha, of which 1,341,000 ha are in private hands. 3·50m. cu. metres of timber were cut in 1996.

Fisheries. In 1996 the landings of fish were (in tonnes): Salt-water, 383; freshwater, 7,078.

INDUSTRY. In Sept. 1997 there were 215,709 enterprises, including 140,455 private enterprises, 676 public enterprises, 203 co-operatives and 3,308 social enterprises.

Industrial output (in 1,000 tonnes) in 1996: Pig-iron, 535; crude steel, 679; steel castings, 21; tractors, 1,800 units; lorries, 826 units; passenger cars, 9,300 units; sugar, 382; TV sets, 24,000 units; refrigerators, 51,000 units; cement, 2,205; sulphuric acid, 231; artificial fertilizers, 701; plastics, 96.

Labour. In 1996 there were 2,079,000 workers in the social sector, including 852,000 in industry, 235,000 in trade, catering and tourism, 178,000 in education and culture, 142,000 in transport and communications, 91,000 in communities and organizations, 108,000 in agriculture, 78,000 in commercial services. In May 1996 in the private sector there were 370,079 self-employed and employed, including 60,986 in arts and crafts, 39,707 in catering and tourism, 25,157 in transport and communications, 131,385 in trade. Average monthly wage in Sept. 1997 was 844 dinars. Unemployment is officially 26% but may be as high as 40%.

FOREIGN ECONOMIC RELATIONS. In joint ventures the foreign partner may own up to 98% of the equity. 379 foreign-owned companies were operating in 1992. UN sanctions against Yugoslavia were lifted in Nov. 1995 following the Bosnian-Croatian-Yugoslav (Dayton) agreement on Bosnia.

Commerce. Foreign trade, in US$1m., for calendar year:

	1991	1992	1996
Imports	5,548	3,859	4,102
Exports	4,704	2,539	1,842

Exports, 1996 (in US$1m.): Manufactures and minerals (including machinery, 49; transport equipment, 57; electrical goods, 89; chemicals, 103; iron and steel, 85; textiles, 29; leather goods, 13; agricultural produce, 154; foodstuffs, 1,263. Imports: Transport equipment, 219; electrical goods, 348; machinery, 276; agricultural produce, 243; foodstuffs, 314; others, 442.

Main trading partners, 1996 (exports and imports in US$1m.): Germany, 146 and 524; Russia, 156 and 225; Italy, 181 and 435; USA, 33 and 119.

Tourism. In 1996 there were 162,000 foreign tourists plus 139,000 from other republics of the former Yugoslavia.

COMMUNICATIONS

Roads. In 1996 there were 49,620 km of roads comprising 6,123 km of main roads, 12,682 km of regional roads and 30,815 km of local roads. In 1990 there were 1,903,149 registered motor vehicles, including 1,405,455 private cars, 92,874 lorries and (1993) 13,133 buses. Passenger-km, 1996, 3·91m.; tonne-km of freight carried, 1·24m. There were 2,031 deaths in road accidents in 1991.

Railways. In 1996 there were 4,031 km of railway, of which 1,341 km were electrified in 1993. 24,120,000 passengers and 8,880,000 tonnes of freight were carried.

Civil Aviation. There are 5 airports, the chief ones at Belgrade and Podgorica. The national carrier is JAT (Jugoslovenski Aero Transport) which in 1995 operated 6 B-727-200 Advs, 5 B-737-300s and 16 other aircraft. In 1992, 876,000 passengers and 4,873 tonnes of freight were carried.

Shipping. In 1996 Yugoslavia possessed 1 sea-going passenger vessels and 22 cargo vessels totalling 390,347 GRT.
  Length of navigable waterways (1996), 1,419 km. In 1996 there were 601 cargo vessels and 4,591,000 tonnes of freight were transported.

Telecommunications. There were 1,648 post offices and 2,423,000 telephones in 1996. Alongside the state-run Serbian Radio and Television and Montenegrin Radio and Television there were 3 independent radio and TV networks in 1993. 2 independent radio stations were shut down by the government in Dec. 1996. The state-run Kosovar Radio and Kosovar Television broadcast a few hours a week in Albanian. In 1995 there were 108 broadcasting and 24 TV stations. There were 2,676,000 TV and 1,469,000 radio receivers in use in 1994.

Cinemas. In 1996 there were 156 cinemas. Cinema attendances were 4·09m. 10 full-length films were made in 1995.

Press. In 1996 there were 18 dailies with a circulation of 351,907,000; 602 other newspapers and 516 periodicals. 3,381 book titles (836 by foreign authors) were published in 1995 in a total of 16,669,000 copies.

SOCIAL INSTITUTIONS

Justice. In 1996 there were 2 supreme courts, 32 district courts and 153 communal courts, with 1,825 judges and 6,885 lay assessors. There were also 18 economic courts with 236 judges.

In 1995, 41,951 criminal sentences were passed.

Religion. Religious communities are separate from the State and are free to perform religious affairs. All religious communities recognized by law enjoy the same rights.

Serbia has been traditionally Orthodox. Moslems are found in the south as a result of the Turkish occupation. The Serbian Orthodox Church with its seat in Belgrade has 27 bishoprics within the boundaries of former Yugoslavia and 12 abroad (5 in the USA and Canada, 5 in Europe and 2 in Australia). The Serbian Orthodox Church numbers about 2,000 priests. Its *Patriarch* is Pavle (enthroned 22 May 1994).

The Serbian Orthodox Church is the official church in Montenegro, the Montenegrin church having been banned in 1922, but in Oct. 1993 a breakaway Montenegrin church was set up under its own patriarch.

Relations with the Vatican are regulated by a 'Protocol' of 1966.

The Moslem Religious Union has Superiorates in Podgorica and Priština.

The Jewish religion has 9 communities making up a common league of Jewish Communities with its seat in Belgrade.

Education. Compulsory primary education lasts 8 years, secondary 3–4 years. In 1996 there were 1,748 nursery schools with 182,125 pupils and 8,338 teachers. In 1995–96 there were 4,441 primary schools with 914,532 pupils and 51,728 teachers and 570 secondary schools with 352,346 pupils and 26,954 teachers. There were 53 institutions of tertiary education with 27,352 students and 1,701 teachers and 93 institutes of higher education with 131,689 full-time students and 10,544 academic staff.

Health. In 1994 there were 20,942 doctors, 4,060 dentists, 2,023 pharmacists and 57,116 hospital beds.

Social Security. In 1995 there were 1,283,530 pensioners, including 533,401 age, 443,551 disability and 306,578 survivors' pensioners. 13,609,409 working days were lost through sickness. In 1996 health expenditure totalled 11,029·4m. dinars; age, 4,388,421,000 dinars; and disability, 2,986·3m. dinars. In 1994, 207m. dinars were paid in child allowances.

DIPLOMATIC REPRESENTATIVES

Of Yugoslavia in Great Britain (5 Lexham Gdns., London, W8 5JJ)
Ambassador: Dr Miloš Radulović.

Of Great Britain in Yugoslavia (46 Generala Zdanova, 11000 Belgrade)
Ambassador: J. B. Donnelly.

Of Yugoslavia in the USA (2410 California St., NW, Washington, D.C., 20008)
Ambassador: Vacant.

Of the USA in Yugoslavia (Belgrade)
Ambassador: Vacant.

Of Yugoslavia to the United Nations
Ambassador: Vacant.

Of Yugoslavia to the European Union
Ambassador: Vacant.

Further Reading

Federal Statistical Office. *Statistical Yearbook of Yugoslavia.*

Bennett, C., *Yugoslavia's Bloody Collapse: Causes, Course and Consequences.* Farnborough, 1995

Bokovoy, M. K. et al (eds.) State-Society Relations in Yugoslavia 1945–1992. London, 1997

Cohen, L. J., *Broken Bonds: the Disintegration of Yugoslavia.* Boulder (CO), 1993

Djilas, A., *The Contested Country: Yugoslav Unity and Communist Revolution, 1919–1953.* Harvard Univ. Press, 1991

Dyker, D. and Vejvoda, I. (eds.) *Yugoslavia and After: a Study in Fragmentation, Despair and Rebirth.* Harlow, 1996

Friedman, F. (ed.) *Yugoslavia: a Comprehensive English-Language Bibliography.* London, 1993

Glenny, M., *The Fall of Yugoslavia.* London, 1992

Gow, J., *Triumph of the Lack of Will: International Diplomacy and the Yugoslav War.* London and Columbia University Press, 1997

Horton, J. J., *Yugoslavia.* [Bibliography] Oxford and Santa Barbara, 1978

Judah, T., *The Serbs: History, Myth and the Destruction of Yugoslavia.* Yale, 1997

Magaš, B., *The Destruction of Yugoslavia: Tracking the Break-up, 1980–92.* London, 1993

Singleton, F., *Twentieth Century Yugoslavia.* London, 1976.—*A Short History of the Yugoslav Peoples.* CUP, 1985

Tito, J. B., *The Essential Tito.* New York, 1970

Udovicki, J., and Ridgeway, J. (eds.), *Burn This House: The Making and Unmaking of Yugoslavia.* Duke, 1997

Woodward, S. L., *Balkan Tragedy: Chaos and Dissolution after the Cold War.* Brookings Institution (Washington), 1995

National statistical office: Federal Statistical Office, Kneza Miloša 20, Belgrade. *Director:* Milovan Živković.

Website: http://www.szs.sv.gov.yu/

REPUBLICS AND PROVINCES

In Dec. 1992 the new self-styled Federal Republic of Yugoslavia comprised the 2 republics of Montenegro and Serbia, and the 2 formerly autonomous provinces of Kosovo and Metohija, and Vojvodina within Serbia.

MONTENEGRO

KEY HISTORICAL EVENTS. Montenegro emerged as a separate entity on the break-up of the Serbian Empire in 1355. Owing to its mountainous terrain, it was never effectively subdued by Turkey. It was ruled by Bishop Princes until 1851, when a royal house was founded. The Treaty of Berlin (1828) recognized the independence of Montenegro and doubled the size of the territory. The remains of King Nicholas I, who was deposed in 1918, were returned to Montenegro for reburial in Oct. 1989.

TERRITORY AND POPULATION. Montenegro is a mountainous region which opens to the Adriatic in the south-west. It is bounded in the west by Croatia, north-west by Bosnia-Hercegovina, in the north-east by Serbia and in the south-east by Albania. The capital is Podgorica (population, 1996 estimate, 159,394). Its area is 13,812, sq. km. Population at the 1991 census was 615,035, of which the predominating ethnic groups were Montenegrins (380,467), Moslems (89,614), Serbs (57,453) and Albanians (40,415). Population density per sq. km, 44·5. Estimate, 1995, 635,012; density, 46 per sq. km.

Vital statistics:

	Live births	Marriages	Deaths	Growth rate per 1,000
1993	8,922	3,873	4,471	7·1
1994	8,887	3,753	4,660	6·7
1995	9,477	3,791	4,921	7·2
1996	9,193	3,869	5,029	6·5

CONSTITUTION AND GOVERNMENT. There is an 85-member single-chamber National Assembly.

A referendum was held on 29 Feb.–1 March 1992 to determine whether Montenegro should remain within a common state, Yugoslavia, as a sovereign republic. The electorate was 412,000, of whom 66% were in favour.

President: Milo Djukanović; sworn in on 15 Jan. 1998.

Prime Minister: Filip Vujanović.

ECONOMY

Agriculture. In 1997 the cultivated area was 187,000 ha. Yields (in 1,000 tonnes): Wheat, 7; maize, 14; potatoes, 57. Livestock (1,000 head): Cattle, 180; sheep, 439; pigs, 22. Timber cut in 1997: 232,000 cu. metres.

Industry. Production (1996): Electricity, 3,102m. kWh; lignite, 1,369,664 tonnes; bauxite, 323,000 tonnes; heavy semi-manufactures, 26,000 tonnes; cotton carded yarn, 146 tonnes.

SERBIA

KEY HISTORICAL EVENTS. The Serbs received Orthodox Christianity from the Byzantines in 891, but shook off the latter's suzerainty to form a prosperous state, firmly established under Stevan Nemanja (1167–96). A Serbian Patriarchate was established at Peć during the reign of Stevan Dušan (1331–55). Dušan planned the conquest of Constantinople, but he was forestalled by incursions of Turks. After he died many Serbian nobles accepted Turkish vassalage; the reduced Serbian state under Prince Lazar received the coup de grace at Kosovo on St Vitus day, 1389. Turkish preoccupations with a Mongol invasion and wars with Hungary, however, postponed the total incorporation of Serbia into the Ottoman Empire until 1459.

The Turks permitted the Orthodox church to practice, though the Patriarchate was abolished in 1776. The native aristocracy was eliminated and replaced by a system of ficfdoms held in return for military or civil service. Local self-government based on rural extended family units (*zadruga*) continued. In its heyday the Ottoman system probably bore no harder on the peasantry than the Christian feudalism it had replaced, but with the gradual decline of Ottoman power, corruption, oppression and reprisals led to economic deterioration and social unrest.

In 1804 murders carried out by mutinous Turkish infantry provoked a Serbian rising under Djordje Karadjordje. The Sultan's army disciplined the mutineers, but was then defeated by the intransigent Serbs. By the Treaty of Bucharest (1812), however, Russia agreed that Serbia, known as Servia until 1918, should remain Turkish. The Turks reoccupied Serbia with ferocious reprisals. A new rebellion broke out in 1815 under Miloš Obrenović which, this time with Russian support, won autonomy for Serbia within the Ottoman empire. Obrenović had Karadjordje murdered in 1817. In 1838 he was forced to grant a constitution establishing an appointed state council, and abdicated in 1839. In 1842 a coup overthrew the Obrenovićs and Alexander Karadjordjević was elected as ruler. He was deposed in 1858.

During the reign of the western-educated Michael Obrenović (1860 until his assassination in 1868) the foundations of a modern centralized and militarized state were laid, and the idea of a 'Great Serbia', first enunciated in Prime Minister Garašanin's *Draft Programme* of 1844, took root. Milan Obrenović, adopting the title of king, proclaimed formal independence in 1882. He suffered defeats against Turkey (1876) and Bulgaria (1885) and abdicated in 1889. Alexander Obrenović was assassinated in 1903, and replaced by Peter Karadjordjević, who brought in a period of stable constitutional rule.

In its foreign policy, Serbia's striving for an outlet to the sea was consistently thwarted by Austria. Annexing Bosnia in 1908, Austria forced the Serbs to withdraw from the Adriatic after the first Balkan war (1912).

TERRITORY AND POPULATION. Serbia is bounded in the north-west by Croatia, in the north by Hungary, in the north-east by Romania, in the east by Bulgaria, in the south by Macedonia and in the west by Albania, Montenegro and Bosnia-Hercegovina. It includes the 2 provinces (formerly autonomous) of Kosovo and Metohija in the south and Vojvodina in the north. With these Serbia's area is 88,361 sq. km; without, 55,968 sq. km. The capital is Belgrade (population estimate, 1995, 1,601,373). Population at the 1991 census was (with Kosovo and Vojvodina) 9,778,991, of which the predominating ethnic group was Serbs (6,446,595). Population density per sq. km, 110·7; (without Kosovo and Vojvodina), population estimate 5,808,906, of which the predominating ethnic group was Serbs (5,108,682).

Population density per sq. km, 103·8. 1996 estimate (with Kosovo and Vojvodina), 9,951,707; density, 112·6 per sq. km; (without) 5,799,810; density, 103·6 per sq. km.

Vital statistics *(without Kosovo and Vojvodina):*

	Live births	Marriages	Deaths	Growth rate per 1,000
1993	65,913	33,338	67,131	−0·2
1994	63,698	33,338	65,493	−0·3
1995	63,737	32,295	66,756	−0·5

In 1996 the live birth rate was 10·64 and the death rate 11·96, giving a growth rate of −1·32.

CONSTITUTION AND GOVERNMENT. In Sept. 1990 a new constitution was adopted by the National Assembly. It defines Serbia as a 'democratic' instead of a 'socialist' republic, lays down a framework for multi-party elections, and describes Serbia as 'united and sovereign on all its territory', thus stripping Kosovo and the Vojvodina of the attributes of autonomy granted by the 1974 federal constitution.

There is a 250-member single-chamber National Assembly. The *President* is elected by universal suffrage for not more than 2 5-year terms. At the elections on 20 Dec. 1992 Slobodan Milošević was re-elected *President* of Serbia with 56·32% of the votes cast against 34·05% for Milan Panić, the then prime minister. In July 1997 Milošović became President of Yugoslavia.

President: Milan Milutinović; sworn in on 29 Dec. 1997.
Prime Minister: Mirko Marjanović.

ECONOMY

Agriculture[1]. In 1997 the cultivated area was an estimated 2,614,000 ha. Yields in 1997 (in 1,000 tonnes): Wheat, 2,920; maize, 6,855; potatoes, 918; sugar-beet, 2,037; plums, 489; grapes, 397. Livestock estimates (in 1,000): Cattle, 402; sheep, 369; pigs, 74; poultry, 2,577. Timber cut in 1997: 1,614,000 cu. metres.

Industry[1]. (1996): Electricity, 34,991m. kWh.; lignite, 36,457,912 tonnes; steel, 574,468 tonnes; copper ore, 20,026,389 tonnes; lorries, 826 units; cars, 9,367 units; sulphuric acid, 230,514 tonnes; plastics, 107,573 tonnes; cement, 2·2m. tonnes; sugar, 382,040 tonnes; cotton fabrics, 22,209,000 sq. metres; woollen fabrics, 11,314,000 sq. metres.

[1] Excluding Kosovo and Vojvodina

KOSOVO AND METOHIJA

KEY HISTORICAL EVENTS. Kosovo has a large ethnic Albanian majority. Following Albanian-Serb conflicts the Kosovo and Serbian parliaments adopted constitutional amendments in March 1989 surrendering much of Kosovo's autonomy to Serbia. Renewed Albanian rioting broke out in 1990. The Prime Minister and 6 other ministers resigned in April 1990 over ethnic conflicts. In July 1990, 114 of the 130 Albanian members of the National Assembly voted for full republican status for Kosovo, but the Serbian National Assembly declared this vote invalid and unanimously voted to dissolve the Kosovo Assembly. Direct Serbian rule was imposed causing widespread violence. Western demands for negotiations in granting Kosovo some kind of special status were rejected. Ibrahim Rugova, the leader of the main Albanian party, the Democratic League of Kosovo (LDK), has declared himself 'president' but wants talks on independence. The official *President* is Hisen Kajdomci.

TERRITORY AND POPULATION. Area: 10,887 sq. km. The capital is Priština. The 1991 census was not taken. Population estimate of Kosovo and Metohija, 1991, 1,956,196 (1,596,072 Albanians, 194,190 Serbs); density, 179·7 per sq. km; 1996 estimate, 2,171,011 and density 197·7 per sq. km. Population estimate of Priština, 1995, 235,613.

Vital statistics:

	Live births	Marriages	Deaths	Growth rate per 1,000
1993	44,132	13,372	7,804	17·8
1994	43,450	11,959	7,667	17·2
1995	44,776	12,979	8,671	17·1
1996	45,343	12,309	8,142	17·3

ECONOMY

Agriculture. The cultivated area in 1997 was an estimated 398,000 ha. Yields in 1997 (in 1,000 tonnes): Wheat, 272; maize, 296; potatoes, 92; plums, 15; grapes, 69. Livestock (in 1,000): Cattle, 402; sheep, 369; pigs, 74; poultry, 2,577. Timber cut in 1997, 130,000 cu. metres.

Industry. Production (1996): Electricity, 4,352m. kWh; lignite, 7,314,363 tonnes; sulphuric acid, 40,528 tonnes; cement, 122,855 tonnes.

VOJVODINA

TERRITORY AND POPULATION. Area: 21,506 sq. km. The capital is Novi Sad. Population of Vojvodina at the 1991 census, 2,013,889 (1,143,723 Serbs, 339,491 Hungarians). Density, 93·6 per sq. km. Estimate, 1996, 1,980,886; density, 92·3 per sq. km. Population of Novi Sad, 1995, 266,329.

Vital statistics:

	Live births	Marriages	Deaths	Growth rate per 1,000
1993	22,018	11,462	27,990	−3·0
1994	21,595	11,048	27,518	−3·0
1995	22,499	11,260	27,177	−2·4
1996	20,483	11,112	28,832	−4·2

CONSTITUTION AND GOVERNMENT. The 1990 Serbian constitution deprived Vojvodina of its autonomy. Serbo-Croat was declared the only official language in 1991. In March 1993 the provincial assembly comprised 7 members of the Socialist Party of Serbia and 5 of the Serbian Radical Party. The *Prime Minister* was Boško Perošević.

ECONOMY

Agriculture. The cultivated area in 1997 was an estimated 1,649,000 ha. Yields (in 1,000 tonnes): Wheat, 1,423; maize, 3,847; potatoes, 255; sugar-beet, 1,805. Livestock estimates (in 1,000): Cattle, 231; sheep, 267; pigs, 1,691; poultry, 7,863. Timber cut in 1997: 548,000 cu. metres.

Industry. Production (1996): Electricity, 278m. kWh; crude petroleum, 1,018,655 tonnes; plastics, 91,979 tonnes; cement, 952,256 tonnes.

ZAMBIA

Republic of Zambia

Capital: Lusaka
Population: 9·35m.
GDP per head: (PPP$) 962
GNP: US$3·2bn.
HDI/world rank: 0·369/143

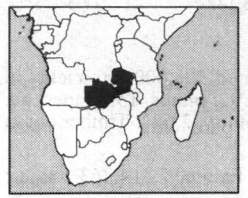

KEY HISTORICAL EVENTS. The early history of Zambia is obscure. The first expedition of real geographical value was Livingstone's missionary journey of 1851 during which he discovered the Victoria Falls.

The great majority of the present African population of the area is of Bantu origin, descended from invaders who swept over the country. There are more than 70 different tribes, the most important being the Bemba and the Bgoni in the north-east, and there are also about 30 different dialects in use. The chief invaders of the early 19th century were the Arabs from the north, the Ngoni Zulus fleeing from Shaka, and the Kololo, who fought their way from the south across the Zambezi and founded a kingdom with a high degree of social organization. One of the more successful of the invading tribes was the Lozi under Lewanika, who asked for and obtained the protection of the British government in 1891. In 1900 the chartered company acquired certain trading and mining rights over Lewanika's territory. These 2 territories were amalgamated in 1911 under the name of Northern Rhodesia, and in 1924 the Crown took over the administration of Northern Rhodesia from the British South Africa Company.

In 1953, following a referendum in Southern Rhodesia, the Federation of Rhodesia and Nyasaland, of which Northern Rhodesia was a component part, was created. Federation brought great economic benefits to Northern Rhodesia, but if was from the outset bitterly opposed by the African leaders there. Kenneth Kaunda led a sustained campaign against Federation, and after elections held under a new constitution of 1962, his United National Independence party gained wide success. In March 1963 Britain agreed in principle to Northern Rhodesia's right to secede from the Federation, which was duly dissolved at the end of the year. In Jan. 1964 full internal self-government was attained. On 24 Oct. Northern Rhodesia became an independent republic within the Commonwealth, changing its name to Zambia. Kaunda became its first president, and led the efforts to break the foreign hold on Zambia's mineral resources. He was ousted in the country's first multi-party elections in 1991.

A highly centralized one-party state was created which suffocated the emergent economy. Living standards fell sharply and the production of copper, Zambia's biggest foreign exchange earner, almost halved. In 1991 the Movement for Multiparty Democracy (MMD) was elected on a promise to transform the economy. Markets were liberalized and the budget deficit contained. Inflation fell from 46% in 1995 to around 20% in 1997. A Privatization Act was passed in 1992.

TERRITORY AND POPULATION. Zambia is bounded by the Democratic Republic of the Congo in the north, Tanzania in the north-east, Malaŵi in the east, Mozambique in the south-east and by Zimbabwe and Namibia in the south. The area is 290,586 sq. miles (752,614 sq. km). Population estimate (1997), 9·35m.; population density, 11·7 per sq. km.

The republic is divided into 9 provinces. Area, population and chief towns:

Province	Area (in sq. km)	Population (1991 census)	Chief Town
Central	94,395	697,000	Kabwe
Copperbelt	31,328	1,294,000	Ndola
Eastern	69,106	995,000	Chipata
Luapula	50,567	728,000	Mansa
Lusaka	21,898	1,327,000	Lusaka
Northern	147,826	972,000	Kasama
North-Western	125,827	415,000	Solwezi
Southern	85,283	944,000	Livingstone
Western	126,386	630,000	Mongu

Major towns (with estimated 1989 population in 1,000) are: Lusaka, 921; Kitwe, 495; Ndola, 467; Kabwe, 210; Mufulira, 206; Chingola, 201; Luanshya, 171; Livingstone, 102; Kalulushi, 100; Chililabombwe, 85.

The official language is English and the main ethnic groups are the Bemba (34%), Tonga (16%), Nyanja (14%) and Lozi (9%).

CLIMATE. The climate is tropical, but has three seasons. The cool, dry one is from May to Aug., a hot dry one follows until Nov., when the wet season commences. Frosts may occur in some areas in the cool season. Lusaka. Jan. 70°F (21·1°C), July 61°F (16·1°C). Annual rainfall 33" (836 mm). Livingstone. Jan. 75°F (23·9°C), July 61°F (16·1°C). Annual rainfall 27" (673 mm). Ndola. Jan. 70°F (21·1°C), July 59°F (15°C). Annual rainfall 52" (1,293 mm).

CONSTITUTION AND GOVERNMENT. In Aug. 1991 the National Assembly adopted a new constitution by 107 votes to 15 permitting multi-party elections for a new wholly-elected parliament of 150 members. Candidates for election as President must have both parents born in Zambia (this excludes ex-President Kaunda).

At the presidential and parliamentary elections on 18 Nov. 1996 the potential electorate was 6·4m., of whom only 60% registered. Turn-out was 40%. Frederick Chiluba was re-elected President by 70% of votes cast. The Movement for Multiparty Democracy (MMD) gained 129 seats.

A state of emergency was imposed in Oct. 1997 after a failed coup, but President Chiluba lifted the emergency in March 1998.

President: Frederick Chiluba (b. 1943; MMD; elected Oct. 1991, re-elected Nov. 1996).

Vice-President: Christon Tembo.

In March 1998 the government comprised:

Minister of Agriculture, Fisheries and Food Security: Edith Nawakwi. *Commerce, Trade and Industry:* Enock Kavindele. *Community Development and Social Welfare:* Dawson Lapunga. *Defence:* Chitalu Sampa. *Education:* Brig. Gen. Godfrey Miyanda. *Energy and Water Development:* Benjamin Mwila. *Environment:* Alfeyo Hambayi. *Finance:* Ronald Penza. *Foreign Affairs:* Sipakeli Walubita. *Health:* Katele Kalumba. *Home Affairs:* Dr Peter Machungwa. *Information and Broadcasting:* David Mpamba. *Labour and Social Security:* Newstead Zimba. *Lands:* Samuel Miyanda. *Legal Affairs:* Vincent Malambo. *Local Government and Housing:* Bennie Mwiinga. *Mines and Mineral Development:* Syamukayumbu Syamujaye. *Science and Technology:* Lawrence Shimba. *State:* Eric Silwamba. *Tourism.* Amusaa Mwanamwambwa. *Transport and Communications:* Anoshi Chipawa. *Works and Supply:* Suresh Desai. *Youth and Sport:* William Harrington. *Without Portfolio:* Michael Sata.

National anthem: 'Stand and Sing of Zambia, Proud and Free'; words collective, tune (same as that for Tanzania and Zimbabwe) by M. E. Sontanga.

Local Government. The 9 provinces (sub-divided into 61 districts) are administered by deputy ministers appointed by the President from elected or nominated members of parliament and with the Permanent Secretary as head of the civil service in each province. Elections are normally held every 3 years. Elections were held in Nov. 1992. Turn-out was 10%. The MMD won a majority of seats.

DEFENCE

Army. The Army consists of 1 armoured and 1 artillery regiment and 1 engineer and 9 infantry battalions. Equipment includes 10 T-54/-55 and 20 Chinese Type-59 main battle tanks. Strength (1997) 20,000. There are also 2 paramilitary police units totalling 1,400.

Air Force. In 1996 the Air Force had 23 Aermacchi M.B.326G armed jet basic trainers (of which 12 remain in service), 8 SIAI-Marchetti SF.260M piston-engined trainers and 16 Agusta-Bell 47G, 10 AB.205 and 2 AB.212 helicopters. 12 F-6

(MiG-19) jet fighter-bombers have been acquired from China, a squadron of 12 MiG-21 fighters, 3 Yak-40 light jet transports, 4 An-26 twin-turboprop transports and 6 Mi-8 helicopters from the Soviet Union. Serviceability of most types is reported to be low. Personnel (1996) 1,600.

INTERNATIONAL RELATIONS

Membership. Zambia is a member of the UN, the Commonwealth, SADC, OAU and is an ACP state of the EU.

ECONOMY

Policy. The privatization programme of 235 state-owned companies (157 had been sold by 1996, raising K38,734m.) has created one of the most liberal economies in Africa. More than 80% of the economy is now in private hands.

Performance. Real GDP growth was 6·4% in 1996 and 5·5% in 1997.

Budget. 1997 budget: Expenditure, 1,427,100m. kwacha; revenue, 1,489,100m. kwacha.

Currency. The unit of currency is the *kwacha* (ZMK) of 100 *ngwee*. There are coins of 50, 20, 10, 5, 2 and 1 ngwee and banknotes of K10,000, K500, K100, K50, K20, K10, K5 and K2. Foreign currency reserves were US$190m. in 1997. K5,749·9m. were in circulation in 1991. In Dec. 1992 the official and free market exchange rates were merged and the kwacha devalued 29%. Annualized inflation was 35% in 1996.

Banking and Finance. The central bank is the Bank of Zambia (*Governor,* Jacob Mwanza), which had deposits of K12,332m. in 1991 and assets of K33,393·4m. In 1996 20 banks were operating. Total assets of domestic and foreign commercial banks were K71,216·6m. in 1991. Assets of the Zambia National Building Society were K1,683·2m.

Banks and building societies are governed by the Banking and Financial Services Act 1994. The Bank of Zambia monitors and supervizes the operations of financial institutions.

There is a stock exchange at Lusaka.

ENERGY AND NATURAL RESOURCES

Electricity. Installed capacity, 1994, was 2·44m. kWh. Output in 1994 was 7·78bn. kWh.

Zambia is a net exporter of hydro-electric power and has huge potential for energy growth.

Minerals. Minerals produced (in 1,000 tonnes) in 1995: Copper, 307·8; cobalt, 2·93; silver, 7·88 tonnes; gold, 0·08 tonnes. Zambia is the world's fourth leading producer of copper and produces a fifth of the world's cobalt. It is well-endowed with gemstones, especially emeralds, amethysts, aquamarine, tourmaline and garnets. In 1990 the government freed the gemstones trade from restrictions.

Agriculture. 70% of the population is dependent on agriculture and 19·7% of GDP was provided by it and fishing in 1996. Principal agricultural products (1993, in 1,000 tonnes): Maize, 1,598; sugar-cane, 1,300; seed cotton, 58; tobacco, 7; ground-nuts, 42.

Livestock (1993, in 1,000): Cattle, 3,204; pigs, 293; sheep, 67; goats, 600 and 21m. poultry.

Forestry. Forests covered (1990) 28·8m. ha, about 39% of the total land area. Roundwood removals (1994) 14·7m. cu. metres (most of it for fuel).

Fisheries. Total catch (1995) 70,864 tonnes.

INDUSTRY. In 1996 manufacturing accounted for 25·5% of GDP.

Labour. In 1990 the workforce was 2,644,000 (767,000 female; 161,000 aged 10–15). In 1990 there were 111,630 employees in services, 56,810 in mining, 50,940 in manufacturing and 30,740 in catering. In 1989 there were 44 reported work stoppages with 58,434 workdays lost.

Trade Unions. There is a Zambia Congress of Trade Unions.

FOREIGN ECONOMIC RELATIONS. In 1995 foreign debt was some US$6,382m. Incentives contained in the 1993 Investment Act include tax holidays and exemptions, remittance of 75% of after-tax profits and guarantees against expropriation.

Commerce. In 1996 exports were valued at US$1,010m. and imports at US$890m.

In 1997, copper provided 80% of all exports (by value), cobalt 10%, zinc 2%. Since 1990 non-copper exports have increased in value from US$50m. to US$230m. Main export markets are South Africa, Japan, Saudi Arabia and Thailand; main import suppliers, South Africa and Japan.

Tourism. There were 48,589 international visitors in 1996. Revenue from international tourism was US$16·3m.

COMMUNICATIONS

Roads. There were (1996) 36,761 km of roads (6,476 km paved). In 1990 there were 9,473 road accidents with 888 fatalities.

Railways. In 1993 there were 1,273 km of the state-owned Zambia Railways Ltd. (ZRL) and 891 km of the Tanzania Zambia (Tazara) Railway, both on 1,067 mm gauge. ZRL carried 1·1m. passengers and 3·4m. tonnes of freight in 1993.

Civil Aviation. The national carrier, Zambia Airways, went into voluntary liquidation in 1995; some of its services have been taken over by Aero Zambia and Zambian Express. Lusaka is the principal international airport. Services are also provided by Aeroflot, Air Botswana, Air France, Air Malaŵi, Air Namibia, Air Tanzania, Air Zimbabwe, British Airways, Kenya Airways, Royal Swazi, SAA, TAAG and Uganda Airlines.

Telecommunications. In 1996 there were 123,338 telephones. In 1995 there were direct connections to 16 countries. Telecel (2) Ltd. has been licensed to run a cellular telecommunications service in addition to the Zambia Telecomms Company (ZAMTEL) since 1996. Internet services are provided by Zambia Communications Systems (ZAMNET), a private company of ZAMTEL. The telex network had 2,800 lines in 1995. The Zambia National Broadcasting Corporation is an independent statutory body which oversees 4 radio networks. There is also a religious radio station. In 1996 2 privately-owned radio stations also started operations. These were Radio Phoenix and Radio Ichengelo. In 1991 there were 1,660,360 radio and about 0·2m. TV receivers. Private broadcasting stations were licensed to operate in 1996. One such company was Multi Choice Kaleidoscope (2) Ltd. which commenced operations in Aug. 1995. By Oct. 1996 the number of subscribers was 6,617.

Press. There were (1996) 2 state-owned daily papers, *The Times of Zambia* and *Zambia Daily Mail*, and 3 weeklies. There were also 5 privately-owned newspapers in 1995.

SOCIAL INSTITUTIONS

Justice. The Judiciary consists of the Supreme Court, the High Court and 4 classes of magistrates' courts; all have civil and criminal jurisdiction.

The Supreme Court hears and determines appeals from the High Court. Its seat is at Lusaka. The High Court exercises the powers vested in the High Court in England, subject to the High Court ordinance of Zambia. Its sessions are held where occasion requires, mostly at Lusaka and Ndola. All criminal cases tried by subordinate courts are subject to revision by the High Court.

Religion. In 1993 the President declared Zambia to be a Christian nation, but freedom of worship is a constitutional right. In 1992 there were 5·98m. Christians.

Education. Schooling is for 9 years. In 1996 there were 1·67m. pupils in 3,907 primary schools; secondary schools, 255,000 in 246 schools.

There are 2 universities, 3 teachers' colleges and 1 Christian college. In 1995–96 there were 4,470 university students and 640 academic staff.

Health. In 1987 there were 42 state, 29 mission and 11 mining company hospitals with a total of 15,846 beds and 912 health centres with 7,081 beds. In 1984 there were 798 doctors.

DIPLOMATIC REPRESENTATIVES

Of Zambia in Great Britain (2 Palace Gate, London, W8 5NG)
High Commissioner: Prof. Moses Musonda.

Of Great Britain in Zambia (Independence Ave., Lusaka)
High Commissioner: Vacant.

Of Zambia in the USA (2419 Massachusetts Ave., NW, Washington, D.C., 20008)
Ambassador: Dunstan Weston Kamana.

Of the USA in Zambia (PO Box 31617, Lusaka)
Ambassador: Arlene Render.

Of Zambia to the United Nations
Ambassador: Peter Kasanda.

Of Zambia to the European Union
Ambassador: Isaiah Chabala.

Further Reading

Central Statistical Office. *Monthly Digest of Statistics.*

Bliss, A. M. and Rigg, J. A., *Zambia.* [Bibliography] Oxford and Santa Barbara (CA), 1984
Burdette, M. M., *Zambia: between Two Worlds.* Boulder (CO), 1988
Chiluba, F., *Democracy: the Challenge of Change.* Lusaka, 1995
De Waal, V., *The Politics of Reconciliation: Zambia's First Decade.* London, 1990
Roberts, A., *A History of Zambia.* London, 1977

National statistical office: Central Statistical Office, Lusaka

ZIMBABWE

Republic of Zimbabwe

Capital: Harare
Population: 11·54m.
GNP: US$5·4bn.
GDP per head: (PPP$) 2,196
HDI/world rank: 0·513/129

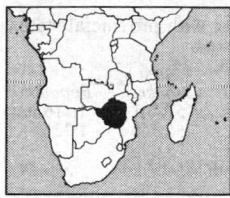

KEY HISTORICAL EVENTS. Shona-speaking people lived in Zimbabwe hundreds of years before the Europeans arrived. It was a major commercial centre in the 14th and 15th centuries, although the ruins of Great Zimbabwe date back to the 8th century. It became increasingly secondary of the Kingdom of Mwanamutapa which arose on the north. By backing rival kings, Portuguese traders managed to destroy Mwanamutapa by 1700. The Shona inhabitants were unable to repel the invasion of Ndebele people under Mzilikazi in 1870; the Ndebele had a very powerful state. However, it was not strong enough to defeat European settlers who forcibly aquired Shona lands in 1890 and turned to Ndebele territory in 1893. Revolts by both peoples several years later were also defeated.

The territory which now forms Zimbabwe was administered by the British South Africa Company from the beginning of European colonization in 1890 until 1923 when it was granted the status of a self-governing colony. In 1911 it had been divided into Southern and Northern Rhodesia (*see* Zambia).

In 1953 Southern and Northern Rhodesia were again united, along with Nyasaland to form the Federation of Rhodesia and Nyasaland. When this federation was dissolved on 31 Dec. 1963 Southern Rhodesia reverted to the status of a self-governing colony within the British Commonwealth.

Ian Smith, prime minister from April 1964, had discussions about independence on three occasions with two British prime ministers during 1964 and 1965. On 11 Nov. 1965 Smith and his government issued a unilateral declaration of independence (UDI). Thereupon the Governor dismissed Smith and his cabinet, and the British government reasserted its own formal responsibility for Rhodesia; but effective internal government was carried on by the Smith cabinet.

The UN Security Council on 20 Nov. called upon all member states to break off economic relations with Rhodesia. From 1-3 Dec. Harold Wilson, the British prime minister, and others met Smith on board H.M.S. *Tiger* and drafted a 'Working Document' on the procedure for progress towards legal independence. This statement was approved by the British cabinet, but rejected by the Smith government. As a result the Security Council voted for mandatory sanctions including oil. France and the USSR abstained. On 2 March 1970 the Smith government declared Rhodesia a republic and adopted a new constitution.

On 3 March 1978 Smith signed a constitutional agreement with the internationally-based black nationalist leaders. It decreed independence, as Zimbabwe, on 31 Dec. 1978. In Nov. 1978 the government considered it was impossible to meet the independence date. A draft constitution was published in Jan. 1979 and was accepted by the white electorate in a referendum. In April 1979 general elections were held for the 72 black seats in the 100-seat parliament. The United African National Council won 51 of the 72 seats and Bishop Abel Muzorewa became prime minister of Rhodesia-Zimbabwe on 1 June 1979.

At the Commonwealth Conference held in Lusaka in Aug. 1979 agreement was reached for a new constitutional conference to be held in London; elections took place in March 1980 resulting in a victory for the Zimbabwe African National Union (ZANU). Southern Rhodesia became the Republic of Zimbabwe, with Canaan Banana as president, and Robert Mugabe as prime minister. On 31 Dec. 1987, Robert Mugabe became the first executive president.

The state of emergency in force since 1965 was lifted in July 1990. In June 1991 the ZANU (PF) renounced Marxism.

TERRITORY AND POPULATION. Zimbabwe is bounded in the north by Zambia, east by Mozambique, south by South Africa and west by Botswana and the Caprivi Strip of Namibia. The area is 150,872 sq. miles (390,759 sq. km). The population was (1992 census) 10,401,767 (51·2% female). Estimate, 1995, 11,536,000 (50·4% female); density, 29·5 per sq. km.

Vital statistics (1990–95): Birth rate, 40·5 per 1,000; death rate, 11 per 1,000; infant mortality, 59 per 1,000 live births; growth rate, 2·96%. Life expectancy in 1994: Males, 54·4 years; females, 57·3.

There are 8 provinces and 2 cities, Harare and Bulawayo, with provincial status. Area and population (1992 census):

	Area (sq. km)	Population		Area (sq. km)	Population
Bulawayo	479	620,936	Mashonaland West	57,441	1,116,928
Harare	872	1,478,810	Masvingo	56,566	1,221,845
Manicaland	36,459	1,537,676	Matabeleland North	75,025	640,957
Mashonaland Central	28,374	857,318	Matabeleland South	54,172	591,747
Mashonaland East	32,230	1,033,336	Midlands	49,166	1,302,212

The chief cities (with 1992 census populations) were Harare, the capital (1,184,169), Bulawayo (620,936), Chitungwiza (274,035), Mutare (131,808) and Gweru (124,735). The main ethno-linguistic groups are the Shona (71%), Ndebele (16%) and Nyanja (3%).

The official language is English.

CLIMATE. Though situated in the tropics, conditions are remarkably temperate throughout the year because of altitude, and an inland position keeps humidity low. The warmest weather occurs in the three months before the main rainy season, which starts in Nov. and lasts till March. The cool season is from mid-May to mid-Aug. and, though days are mild and sunny, nights are chilly. Harare. Jan. 69°F (20·6°C), July 57°F (13·9°C). Annual rainfall 33" (828 mm). Bulawayo. Jan. 71°F(21·7°C), July 57°F (13·9°C). Annual rainfall 24" (594 mm). Victoria Falls. Jan. 78°F (25·6°C), July 61°F (16·1°C). Annual rainfall 28" (710 mm).

CONSTITUTION AND GOVERNMENT. The Constitution provides for a single-chamber 150-member Parliament (*House of Assembly*), universal suffrage for citizens over the age of 18, an *Executive President* (elected for a 6-year term of office by Parliament), an independent judiciary enjoying security of tenure and a Declaration of Rights, derogation from certain of the provisions being permitted, within specified limits, during a state of emergency. The House of Assembly is elected for 5 year terms: 120 members are elected by universal suffrage, 10 are chiefs elected by all the country's tribal chiefs, 12 are appointed by the President and 8 are provincial governors. The constitution can be amended by a two-thirds parliamentary majority.

Presidential elections were held on 17 March 1996. The electorate was 4·9m.; turn-out was 35%. President Mugabe was re-elected unopposed.

At the elections of 8–9 April 1995 turn-out was 54%. ZANU-PF gained 118 seats of the electable seats with 82% of votes cast (55 seats were uncontested), ZANU (Ndonga) 2 with 6·5%. Parliamentary party composition: ZANU-PF, 147 seats; ZANU (Ndonga), 2; an independent, 1.

Executive President: Robert G. Mugabe (b. 1924; sworn in on 30 Dec. 1987, re-elected April 1990; re-elected again March 1996).

Following the July 1997 reshuffle the council comprised in March 1998:

Vice-Presidents: Simon Muzenda, Dr Joshua Nkomo. *Minister of Foreign Affairs:* Dr Stanislaus Mudenge. *Justice, Legal and Parliamentary Affairs:* Emmerson Mnangagwa. *Defence:* Moven Mahachi. *Home Affairs:* Dumiso Dabengwa. *Lands and Agriculture:* Kumbirai Kangai. *Information, Posts and Telecommunications:* Chen Chimutengwende. *Public Service, Labour and Social Welfare:* Florence Chitauro. *Industry and Commerce:* Dr Nathan Shamuyarira. *Mines, Environment and Tourism:* Simon Moyo. *Transport and Energy:* Enos Chikowore. *Health and Child Welfare:* Dr Timothy Stamps. *Local Government and National Housing:* John

Nkomo. *Higher Education and Technology:* Dr Ignatius Chombo. *Education, Sport and Culture:* Gabriel Machinga. *National Security:* Dr Sidney Sekeramayi. *Finance:* Dr Herbert Murerwa. *Planning:* Dr Richard Hove. *National Affairs and Employment Creation:* Tenjiwe Lesaba. *Rural Resources and Water Development:* Joyce Mujuru. *President's Office:* Ceplas Msipa. *Without portfolio:* Dr Eddison Zvogbo, Joseph Msika.

National Anthem: 'Ngaikomborewe Nyika ye Zimbabwe' ('Blessed be the Land of Zimbabwe'); words by Dr Solomon M. Mutswairo; tune by Mr F. L. Changunclaga.

DEFENCE

Army. The Army consists of 1 air defence, 1 engineer, 1 armoured and 1 field artillery regiment, 22 infantry battalions and 1 tank squadron. Equipment includes 30 Chinese T-59 and 10 Chinese T-69 main battle tanks. Strength was (1997) 39,000, and there are a further 19,500 paramilitary police and a police support unit of 2,300.

Air Force. The Air Force (ZAF) has a strength of (1996) about 4,000 personnel and 58 combat aircraft. Headquarters ZAF and the main ZAF stations are in Harare; the second main base is at Gweru, with many secondary airfields throughout the country. Equipment includes 1 squadron of F-7 (MiG-21) interceptors, 1 squadron of Hunter fighter-bombers and 1 squadron of Hawk training and light attack aircraft, a transport squadron with 11 turbo-prop CASA Aviocars and 6 twin-engined Islanders; a squadron with 14 Reims/Cessna 337 Lynx attack aircraft; a squadron with 26 SIAI-Marchetti SF.260 trainers; a helicopter liaison/transport squadron with 20 Alouette IIIs; a helicopter casualty evacuation/transport squadron with 9 Bell 412s.

INTERNATIONAL RELATIONS

Membership. Zimbabwe is a member of UN, the Commonwealth, OAU and SADC and is an ACP state of the EU.

ECONOMY

Policy. The second phase of structural adjustment dubbed Zimbabwe Programme for Economic and Social Transformation (ZIMPREST) was to be launched in early 1998. Its goals are similar to those of the first phase (1991–95), promoting a market economy by economic stabilization, liberalization of trade, deregulation, reform of the public sector and social reform.

Performance. GDP is estimated to have grown by 5% in 1997. Agriculture contributes about 65% of GDP which was left in tatters in 1992 after a severe water shortage cut it by about 12%. In 1996, on the other hand, thanks to much more favourable weather conditions in the 1995/96 growing season, agricultural production jumped 45% and GDP rose 8·1%. Manufacturing industry is estimated to have grown by 7% in 1997, against a 2·1% rise in 1996.

Budget. Revenue and expenditure (in Z$1,000):

	1996–97	1997–98
Revenue	27,289	52,152
Expenditure	32,366	63,857

Since April 1995 corporate tax has been 35% and effective from January 1998 the top rate of income tax was to be 55% for $80,000.

Currency. The unit of currency is the *Zimbabwe dollar* (ZWD) divided into 100 *cents*. There are coins of 1, 5, 10, 20 and 50 cents and Z$1, and notes of Z$5, 10, 20, 50 and 100. Gold reserves were valued at US$150m. in 1996; foreign exchange reserves were US$800m. Z$1,226·8m. were in circulation in 1994. The currency was devalued 17% in Jan. 1994 and made fully convertible. 1996 inflation of 21% slowed in 1997.

Banking and Finance. The Reserve Bank of Zimbabwe is the central bank (established 1965; *Governor*, Dr Leonard Tsumba). It acts as banker to the Government and to the commercial banks, is the note-issuing authority and co-ordinates the application of the Government's monetary policy. The Zimbabwe Development Bank, established in 1983 as a development finance institution, is 51% Government-owned. In 1997 there were 7 commercial and 5 merchant banks. There are 5 registered finance houses, 3 of which are subsidiaries of commercial banks.

There is a stock exchange.

Weights and Measures. The metric system is in use but the US short ton is also used.

ENERGY AND NATURAL RESOURCES

Electricity. In 1997 Zimbabwe Electricity Supply Authority's (Zesa) five power stations supplied 7,323·3 GWh, and a further 3,171·5 GWh was imported via the Southern African Power Pool (SAPP). Electricity sales during the financial year 1996/96 increased by 3·6% and revenues grew by 28% from $2,222·7 million to $2,852·7 million.

Minerals. The total value of all minerals produced in 1995 was Z$5,249·3m. 1995 production: gold, 23·9 tonnes, value Z$2,395m.; nickel, value (1993) Z$369·1m.; asbestos, 0·70m. tonnes; coal, some 5m. tonnes.

Agriculture. Current Land distribution Pattern: i) 4,000 large scale communal farmers (mainly white) on 11·2m. hectares; ii) 1m. communal area families on 16·3m. hectares; iii) 10,000 small scale commercial farmers on 1·2m. hectares; iv) 60,000 resettlement families on 3·3m. hectares; v) state farming sector on 0·5m. hectares.

Replacing a constitutional provision that permitted the government to acquire land on a 'willing-seller willing-buyer' basis, legislation of March 1992 provides for its compulsory purchase at a fixed price for peasant resettlement. The possibility of compensation is not excluded. 60,000 peasants have been resettled on 3m. hectares of land purchased from white farmers. In 1990 some 4,000 farmers owned 12m. hectares while 0·75m. peasants occupied 15m. hectares of communal agricultural areas. In June 1996 the Supreme Court ruled that the Government's expropriation proposals were not unconstitutional. Land reform still remains a thorny political subject. In Nov. 1997 the Government designated 1,503 farms (nearly half the total area of big commercial farms) to be expropriated after the harvest of mid-1998. President Mugabe has said that he will not compensate white farmers, some of whom have been in the country for several generations, for land which is appropriated for settlement by black farmers. The British Government has told Zimbabwe that it will not assume responsibility for compensating the white farmers. In the past Britain has helped the Government to purchase farms for resettlement.

The staple food crop is maize. Tobacco is the most important cash crop. Production, 1993 in 1,000 tonnes: Maize, 2,562; tobacco, 205,000; sorghum, 90; barley, 24; millet, 95; soyabeans, 65; groundnuts, 64; fruit, 153; vegetables and melons, 140; seed cotton, 187; wheat, 300; tea, 14; coffee, 4; sugar-cane, 700. Zimbabwe is the world's second largest exporter of flue-cured tobacco. In 1996 more than 201m. kg of tobacco were sold at nearly 3m. kg up on the previous year, fetching Z$5·8bn. More than 150,000 people work in the tobacco industry. Tobacco is a highly commercial crop, worth nearly 60 times as much as the same acreage planted with soya or maize.

The commercially-owned beef cattle herd was 1·8m. in 1991 (3·2m. in 1975). Livestock (1993): Cattle, 4m.; pigs, 270,000; sheep, 530,000; goats, 2·5m. Milk production (1993): 400,000 tonnes.

Fisheries. Trout, prawns and bream are farmed to supplement supplies of fish caught in dams and lakes.

INDUSTRY. Metal products account for over 20% of industrial output. Important agro-industries include food processing, textiles, furniture and other wood products.

Trade Unions. There is a Zimbabwe Congress of Trade Unions.

FOREIGN ECONOMIC RELATIONS. Foreign debt was US$4,574m. in 1996. Since 1 Jan. 1995 foreign companies have been permitted to remit 100% of after-tax profits. The Customs Agreement with South Africa was extended in 1982.

Commerce. In 1995, exports totalled US$2,050m.; imports, US$1,850m.

Principal exports in 1993 (in US$1m.): Tobacco, 365; ferrochrome, 142; clothing and textiles, 122; nickel, 56; cotton lint, 26; steel, 16.

Main export markets, 1994 (% of total trade): UK, 12·9%; South Africa, 11·8%; Germany, 7·1%; USA, 6·3%; Japan, 5·7%. Main import suppliers: South Africa, 32·6%; UK, 10·3%; Germany, 5·9%; Japan, 5·7%; USA, 5·3%.

Recent estimates suggest a marked deterioration in balance of payments.

Tourism. In 1994, 1·1m. visitors visited Zimbabwe, bringing foreign exchange revenue of US$153m.

COMMUNICATIONS

Roads. The total length of roads is almost 86,000 km including surfaced, 12,900; gravel, 47,000; earth, 25,800. Number of motor vehicles, 1992: Passenger cars, 310,400; commercial vehicles, 30,200; motor cycles, 29,100; tractors, 7,200.

Railways. In 1995 the National Railways of Zimbabwe had 2,759 km (1,067 mm gauge) of route ways (313 km electrified). In 1995 the railways carried 12·2m. tonnes of freight and 1·9m. passengers.

Civil Aviation. There are 3 international airports: Harare, Bulawayo and Victoria Falls. Air Zimbabwe, the state-owned national carrier, operated 4 B-707-320Bs, 3 B-737-200 Advs, 2 B-767-200ERs and 3 other aircraft in 1995. The country is also served by British Airways, Kenya Airways, Ethiopian Airlines, Air Tanzania, Air Malawi, Zambian Airways, Balkan Bulgarian Airlines, Mozambique Airlines, South African Airways, Air Botswana, the Royal Swazi Airlines, TAP Air Portugal, Qantas, Lesotho Airways and Air India.

Shipping. Zimbabwe's outlets to the sea are Maputo and Beira in Mozambique, Dar-es-Salaam, Tanzania and the South African ports.

Telecommunications. At 3 Aug. 1995 there were 170 post offices, 47 postal telegraph agencies and 86 postal agencies. There were 251,344 telephones served by 96 exchanges; 2,102 telex connections, served by 2 telex exchanges. Zimbabwe Broadcasting Corporation is an statutory body broadcasting a general service in English, Shona, Ndebele, Nyanja, Tonga and Kalanga. There are 3 national semi-commercial services, Radio 1, 2 and 3, in English, Shona and Ndebele. Radio 4 transmits formal and informal educational programmes. Zimbabwe Television broadcasts on 2 channels (colour by PAL). In 1994 there were 297,000 television and 945,000 radio sets in use.

SOCIAL INSTITUTIONS

Justice. The general common law of Zimbabwe is the Roman Dutch law as it applied in the Colony of the Cape of Good Hope on 10 June 1891, as subsequently modified by statute. Provision is made by statute for the application of African customary law by all courts in appropriate cases.

The death penalty is authorized. The last execution took place in 1997.

The Supreme Court consists of the Chief Justice and at least 2 Supreme Court judges. It is the final court of appeal. It exercises appellate jurisdiction in appeals from the High Court and other courts and tribunals; its only original jurisdiction is that conferred on it by the Constitution to enforce the protective provisions of the Declaration of Rights. The Court's permanent seat is in Harare but it sits regularly in Bulawayo also.

The High Court is also headed by the Chief Justice, supported by the Judge President and an appropriate number of High Court judges. It has full original jurisdiction, in both Civil and Criminal cases, over all persons and all matters in Zimbabwe. The Judge President is in charge of the Court, subject to the directions of the Chief Justice. The Court has permanent seats in both Harare and Bulawayo and sittings are held three times a year in 3 other principal towns.

Regional courts, established in Harare and Bulawayo but also holding sittings in other centres, exercise a solely criminal jurisdiction that is intermediate between that of the High Court and the Magistrates' courts. Magistrates' courts, established in 20 centres throughout the country, and staffed by full-time professional magistrates, exercise both civil and criminal jurisdiction.

Primary courts consist of village courts and community courts. Village courts are presided over by officers selected for the purpose from the local population, sitting with two assessors. They deal with certain classes of civil cases only and have jurisdiction only where African customary law is applicable. Community courts are presided over by presiding officers in full-time public service who may be assisted by assessors. They have jurisdiction in all civil cases determinable by African customary law and also deal with appeals from village courts. They also have limited criminal jurisdiction in respect of petty offences. The death penalty is authorised.

Religion. Some of the population adhere to traditional animist religion. In 1989, 5·29m. persons were Christian: Anglicans, Roman Catholics, Methodists and Presbyterians.

Education. Education is compulsory. 'Manageable' school fees were introduced in 1991; primary education had hitherto been free to all. All instruction is given in English. There are also over 3,800 private primary schools and over 950 private secondary schools, all of which must be registered by the Ministry of Education. In 1996 there were 2,499,381 pupils at primary schools and 760,572 pupils at secondary schools. In 1992 69% of the population (aged 15 years and over) was classed as literate. In 1997 the literacy rate was 80·38%.

There are 10 teachers' training colleges, 8 of which are in association with the University of Zimbabwe. In addition, there are 4 special training centres for teacher trainees in the Zimbabwe Integrated National Teacher Education Course. In 1990 there were 17,873 students enrolled at teachers' training colleges, 1,003 students at agricultural colleges and 20,943 students at technical colleges. There are 4 universities and 10 technical colleges.

Health. In 1985 there were 162 hospitals, 1,062 static rural clinics and health centres and 32 mobile rural clinics operated by the Ministry of Health. All mission health institutions get 100% government grants-in-aid for recurrent expenditure.

Social Services. It is a statutory responsibility of the government in many areas to provide: Processing and administration of war pensions and old age pensions; protection of children; administration of remand, probation and correctional institutions; registration and supervision of welfare organisations.

DIPLOMATIC REPRESENTATIVES

Of Zimbabwe in Great Britain (Zimbabwe House, 429 Strand, London, WC2R 0SA)
High Commissioner: Dr Ngoni Chideya.

Of Great Britain in Zimbabwe (7th Floor Corner House, Samora Machel Ave, Harare, P.O. Box 4490)
High Commissioner: Martin Williams, CVO, OBE.

Of Zimbabwe in the USA (1608 New Hampshire Ave., NW, Washington, D.C., 20009)
Ambassador: Amos B. Muvengwa Midzi.

Of the USA in Zimbabwe (172 Herbert Chitepo Ave., Harare)
Ambassador: Johnny Carson.

Of Zimbabwe to the United Nations
Ambassador: Machivenyika Mapuranga.

Of Zimbabwe to the European Union
Ambassador: Simbarashe Mumbengegwi.

Further Reading

Central Statistical Office. *Monthly Digest of Statistics.*

Caute, D., *Under the Skin: the Death of White Rhodesia.* London, 1983

Cliffe, L. and Stoneman, C., *Zimbabwe: Politics, Economy and Society.* London, 1989

Hatchard, J., *Individual Freedoms and State Security in the African Context: the Case of Zimbabwe.* Ohio Univ. Press, 1993

Herbst, J., *State Politics in Zimbabwe.* Univ. of California, 1990

Keppel-Jones, A., *Rhodes and Rhodesia: the White Conquest of Zimbabwe, 1884–1902.* Univ. of Natal Press, 1983

Morris-Jones, W. H., (ed.) *From Rhodesia to Zimbabwe.* London, 1980

Potts, D., *Zimbabwe* [Bibliography]. 2nd ed. Oxford and Santa Barbara (CA), 1993

Schatzberg, M. G., *The Political Economy of Zimbabwe.* New York, 1984

Skålnes, T., *The Politics of Economic Reform in Zimbabwe: Continuity and Change in Development.* London, 1995

Stoneman, C., *Zimbabwe's Inheritance.* London, 1982.—*Zimbabwe: Politics, Economics and Society.* London, 1988

Verrier, A., *The Road to Zimbabwe, 1890–1980.* London, 1986

Weiss, R. *Zimbabwe and the New Elite.* London, 1994

Zimmerman, Z., *Zimbabwe's First Decade of Independence, 1980–1990: a Select and Annotated Bibliography.* Johannesburg, 1991

National statistical office: Central Statistical Office, POB 8063, Causeway, Harare.

CURRENCY RATES

As at 31 March 1998

European

Andorra—*Franc*
£1 = 10·16 US$1 = 6·10 DM1 = 3·32
—*Peseta*
£1 = 257·15 US$1 = 154·45 DM1 = 84·00

Austria—*Schilling*
£1 = 21·62 US$1 = 12·81 DM1 = 7·035

Belgium—*Franc*
£1 = 63·43 US$1 = 37·58 DM1 = 20·64

Denmark—*Krone*
£1 = 11·71 US$1 = 6·94 DM1 = 3·81

Finland—*Markka*
£1 = 9·33 US$1 = 5·53 DM1 = 3·03

France—*Franc*
£1 = 10·29 US$1 = 6·10 DM1 = 3·35

Germany—*Deutschmark*
£1 = 3·07 US$1 = 1·82

Greece—*Drachma*
£1 = 535·4 US$1 = 317·2 DM1 = 174·2

Ireland—*Punt*
£1 = 1·22 US$1 = 0·73 DM1 = 0·40

Italy—*Lira*
£1 = 3,021·6 US$1 = 1,814·8 DM1 = 987·0

Luxembourg—*Franc*
£1 = 63·67 US$1 = 37·58 DM1 = 20·80

Malta—*Maltese Lira*
£1 = 0·67 US$1 = 0·40 DM1 = 0·22

Netherlands—*Guilder*
£1 = 3·46 US$1 = 2·05 DM1 = 1·13

Norway—*Krone*
£1 = 12·67 US$1 = 7·51 DM1 = 4·12

Portugal—*Escudo*
£1 = 314·5 US$1 = 186·3 DM1 = 102·3

Spain—*Peseta*
£1 = 260·7 US$1 = 154·5 DM1 = 84·84

Sweden—*Krona*
£1 = 13·29 US$1 = 7·87 DM1 = 4·32

Switzerland—*Franc*

| £1 = 2·51 | US$1 = 1·49 | DM1 = 0·82 |

United Kingdom—*Pound*

| | US$1 = 0·59 | DM1 = 0·33 |

The Euro

On 1 Jan. 1999, the single European currency will be officially launched for Germany, France, Italy, Spain, The Netherlands, Finland, Austria, Luxembourg and Ireland. Initially the *euro* will be used for paper transactions only. National currencies will continue to exist as subdivisions of the *euro* until 2002. *Euro* notes and coins will come into circulation on 1 Jan. 2002. National currencies will be withdrawn on 1 July 2002. There will be notes worth 5, 10, 20, 50, 100, 200 and 500 *euros*. One hundredth of a *euro* will be a *cent*. There will be coins worth 1, 2, 5, 10, 20 and 50 *cents* and 1 and 2 *euros*.

Worldwide Currency Rates
as at 31 March 1998

Afghanistan—*Afghani*	US$1 = 4,750·00
Albania—*Lek*	US$1 = 158·75
Algeria—*Dinar*	US$1 = 58·99
Angola—*Kwanza*	US$1 = 257,128·00
Antigua & Barbuda—*Eastern Caribbean Dollar*	US$1 = 2·70
Argentina—*Peso*	US$1 = 0·99
Armenia—*Dram*	US$1 = 502·00
Australia—*Australian Dollar*	US$1 = 1·52
Azerbaijan—*Manat*	US$1 = 3,950·00
Bahamas—*Bahamian Dollar*	US$1 = 1·00
Bahrain—*Bahraini Dinar*	US$1 = 0·38
Bangladesh—*Taka*	US$1 = 46·30
Barbados—*Barbados Dollar*	US$1 = 2·01
Belarus—*Rouble*	US$1 = 57,000·00
Belize—*Belize Dollar*	US$1 = 2·00
Benin—*Franc*	US$1 = 610·10
Bhutan—*Ngultrum*	US$1 = 39·49
Bolivia—*Boliviano*	US$1 = 5·48
Bosnia-Hercegovina—*Dinar*	US$1 = N/A
Botswana—*Pula*	US$1 = 3·91
Brazil—*Real*	US$1 = 1·14
Brunei—*Brunei Dollar*	US$1 = 1·59
Bulgaria—*Lev*	US$1 = 1,811·60
Burkina Faso—*Franc*	US$1 = 610·10
Burundi—*Burundi Franc*	US$1 = 411·98
Cambodia—*Riel*	US$1 = 3,580·00
Cameroon—*Franc*	US$1 = 610·10
Canada—*Canadian Dollar*	US$1 = 1·42
Cape Verde—*Escudo*	US$1 = 97·95
Central African Republic—*Franc*	US$1 = 610·10
Chad—*Franc*	US$1 = 610·10
Chile—*Chilean Peso*	US$1 = 452·14
China—*Renminbi*	US$1 = 8·28
Colombia—*Colombian Peso*	US$1 = 1,365·95
Comoros—*Comorian Franc*	US$1 = 457·58
Congo (Republic of)—*Franc*	US$1 = 610·10
Congo (Democratic Republic of)—*New Zaire*	US$1 = 127,500·0
Costa Rica—*Costa Rican Colón*	US$1 = 249·84
Côte d'Ivoire—*Franc*	US$1 = 610·10
Croatia—*Kuna*	US$1 = 6·53
Cuba—*Cuban Peso*	US$1 = 23·00
Cyprus—*Cyprus Pound*	US$1 = 0·54
Czech Republic—*Koruna*	US$1 = 33·70

Djibouti—*Djibouti Franc*	US$1 = 177·72
Dominica—*East Caribbean Dollar*	US$1 = 2·70
Dominican Republic—*Peso Oro*	US$1 = 14·68
Ecuador—*Sucre*	US$1 = 4,896·00
Egypt—*Egyptian Pound*	US$1 = 3·42
El Salvador—*Colón*	US$1 = 8·76
Equatorial Guinea—*Franc*	US$1 = 610·10
Eritrea—*Birr*	US$1 = 6·78
Estonia—*Kroon*	US$1 = 14·56
Ethiopia—*Birr*	US$1 = 6·78
Fiji—*Fiji Dollar*	US$1 = 1·94
Gabon—*Franc*	US$1 = 610·10
The Gambia—*Dalasi*	US$1 = 10·60
Georgia—*Lari*	US$1 = 1·28 (Dec. 1996)
Ghana—*Cedi*	US$1 = 2,310·00
Grenada—*Eastern Caribbean Dollar*	US$1 = 2·70
Guatemala—*Quetzal*	US$1 = 6·27
Guinea—*Guinean Franc*	US$1 = 1,195·00
Guinea-Bissau—*Franc*	US$1 = 610·10
Guyana—*Guyanan Dollar*	US$1 = 144·30
Haiti—*Gourde*	US$1 = 17·38
Honduras—*Lempira*	US$1 = 13·31
Hungary—*Forint*	US$1 = 210·76
Iceland—*Króne*	US$1 = 72·23
India—*Rupee*	US$1 = 39·61
Indonesia—*Rupiah*	US$1 = 8,400·00
Iran—*Rial*	US$1 = 3,000·00
Iraq—*Iraqi Dinar*	US$1 = 1,200·00
Israel—*Shekel*	US$1 = 3·67
Jamaica—*Jamaican Dollar*	US$1 = 35·95
Japan—*Yen*	US$1 = 133·74
Jordan—*Jordanian Dinar*	US$1 = 0·71
Kazakhstan—*Tenge*	US$1 = 76·58
Kenya—*Kenya Shilling*	US$1 = 69·87
Kiribati—*Australian Dollar*	US$1 = 1·48
Korea (South)—*Won*	US$1 = 2·20
Korea (North)—*Won*	US$1 = 1,447·00
Kuwait—*Kuwaiti Dinar*	US$1 = 0·305
Kyrgyzstan—*Som*	US$1 = 14·6 (Jan. 1997)
Laos—*Kip*	US$1 = 2,009·00
Latvia—*Lats*	US$1 = 0·59
Lebanon—*Lebanese Pound*	US$1 = 1,527·90
Lesotho—*Maloti*	US$1 = 4·97
Liberia—*Dollar*	US$1 = 1·00
Libya—*Libyan Dinar*	US$1 = 0·39
Lithuania—*Litas*	US$1 = 4·00
Macedonia—*Denar*	US$1 = 56·55
Madagascar—*Malagasy Franc*	US$1 = 5,010·00
Malawi—*Kwacha*	US$1 = 25·20
Malaysia—*Ringgit*	US$1 = 3·70
Maldives—*Rufiyaa*	US$1 = 11·77
Mali—*Franc*	US$1 = 610·10
Mauritania—*Ouguiya*	US$1 = 175·10
Mauritius—*Mauritius Rupee*	US$1 = 23·47
Mexico—*Mexican Peso*	US$1 = 8·52
Moldova—*Leu*	US$1 = 4·72
Mongolia—*Tugrik*	US$1 = 813·18
Morocco—*Dirham*	US$1 = 9·79
Mozambique—*Metical*	US$1 = 11,523·00
Myanmar—*Kyat*	US$1 = 6·25
Namibia—*Namibia Dollar*	US$1 = 5·04

Nauru—*Australian Dollar*	US$1 = 1·48
Nepal—*Nepalese Rupee*	US$1 = 61·05
Nicaragua—*Córdoba*	US$1 = 10·26
Niger—*Franc*	US$1 = 610·10
Nigeria—*Naira*	US$1 = 85·50
Oman—*Omani Rial*	US$1 = 0·39
Pakistan—*Pakistan Rupee*	US$1 = 44·40
Panama—*Balboa*	US$1 = 1·00
Papua New Guinea—*Kina*	US$1 = 1·99
Paraguay—*Guarani*	US$1 = 2,550·00
Peru—*Nuevo Sol*	US$1 = 2·81
Philippines—*Piso*	US$1 = 37·73
Poland—*Zloty*	US$1 = 3·43
Qatar—*Qatari Riyal*	US$1 = 3·64
Romania—*Lei*	US$1 = 8,461·00
Russia—*Rouble*	US$1 = 6·13
Rwanda—*Rwanda Franc*	US$1 = 348·48
St Kitts and Nevis—*East Caribbean Dollar*	US$1 = 2·70
St Lucia—*East Caribbean Dollar*	US$1 = 2·70
St Vincent and The Grenadines—*East Caribbean Dollar*	US$1 = 2·70
Samoa—*Tala*	US$1 = 2·76
São Tomé e Príncipe—*Dobra*	US$1 = 2,390·00
Saudi Arabia—*Riyal*	US$1 = 3·75
Senegal—*Franc*	US$1 = 610·10
Seychelles—*Seychelles Rupee*	US$1 = 5·13
Sierra Leone—*Leone*	US$1 = 900·00
Singapore—*Singapore Dollar*	US$1 = 1·61
Slovakia—*Slovak Koruna*	US$1 = 35·05
Slovenia—*Tolar*	US$1 = 169·62
Solomon Isles—*Solomon Island Dollar*	US$1 = 4·78
Somalia—*Somali Shilling*	US$1 = 2,620·00
South Africa—*Rand*	US$1 = 5·05
Sri Lanka—*Sri Lankan Rupee*	US$1 = 62·28
Sudan—*Dinar*	US$1 = 161·29
Suriname—*Suriname Guilder*	US$1 = 401·00
Swaziland—*Lilangeni*	US$1 = 5·04
Syria—*Syrian Pound*	US$1 = 41·85
Tajikistan—*Tajik Rouble*	US$1 = 350·00 (Jan. 1997)
Tanzania—*Tanzanian Shilling*	US$1 = 653·69
Thailand—*Baht*	US$1 = 39·98
Togo—*Franc*	US$1 = 610·10
Tonga—*Pa'anga*	US$1 = 1·37
Trinidad & Tobago—*Trinidad & Tobago Dollar*	US$1 = 6·21
Tunisia—*Tunisian Dinar*	US$1 = 1·18
Turkey—*Turkish Lira*	US$1 = 247,900·00
Turkmenistan—*Manat*	US$1 = 4,070·00 (Jan. 1997)
Tuvalu—*Australian Dollar*	US$1 = 1·48
Uganda—*Uganda Shilling*	US$1 = 1,152·50
Ukraine—*Hryvna*	US$1 = 2·04
United Arab Emirates—*Dirham*	US$1 = 3·67
Uruguay—*Uruguayan Peso*	US$1 = 10·25
Uzbekistan—*Som*	US$1 = 51·1 (Jan. 1997)
Vanuatu—*Vatu*	US$1 = 123·80
Venezuela—*Bolívar*	US$1 = 526·50
Vietnam—*Dong*	US$1 = 12,981·00
Yemen—*Rial*	US$1 = 130·99
Yugoslavia—*Dinar*	US$1 = 6·05
Zambia—*Kwacha*	US$1 = 1,715·00
Zimbabwe—*Zimbabwe Dollar*	US$1 = 16·13

WEIGHTS AND MEASURES

On 1 Jan. 1960 following an agreement between the standards laboratories of Great Britain, Canada, Australia, New Zealand, South Africa and the USA, an international yard and an international pound (avoirdupois) came into existence. 1 yard = 91·44 centimetres; 1 lb. = 453·59237 grammes.

The abbreviation 'm.' signifies 'million(s)' and tonnes implies metric tons.

LENGTH		DRY MEASURE	
Centimetre	0·394 inch	Litre	0·91 quart
Metre	1·094 yards	Hectolitre	2·75 bushels
Kilometre	0·621 mile		
LIQUID MEASURE		**WEIGHT—AVOIRDUPOIS**	
Litre	1·75 pints	Gramme	15·42 grains
Hectolitre	22 gallons	Kilogramme	2·205 pounds
		Quintal (= 100 kg)	220·46 pounds
		Tonne (= 1,000 kg)	{ 0·984 long ton / 1·102 short tons }
SURFACE MEASURE		**WEIGHT—TROY**	
Square metre	10·76 sq. feet	Gramme	15·43 grains
Hectare	2·47 acres	Kilogramme	{ 32·15 ounces / 2·68 pounds }
Square kilometre	0·386 sq. mile		

BRITISH WEIGHTS AND MEASURES

LENGTH		DRY MEASURE	
1 foot	0·305 metre	1 ounce (= 437·2 grains)	28·350 grammes
1 yard	0·914 metre	1 lb. (= 7,000 grains)	453·6 grammes
1 mile (= 1,760 yds)	1·609 kilometres	1 cwt. (= 112 lb.)	50·802 kilogrammes
		1 long ton (= 2,240 lb.)	1·016 tonnes
		1 short ton (= 2,000 lb.)	0·907 tonne
SURFACE MEASURE		**LIQUID MEASURE**	
1 sq. foot	9·290 sq. decimetres	1 pint	0·568 litre
1 sq. yard	0·836 sq. metre	1 gallon	4·546 litres
1 acre	0·405 hectare	1 quarter	2·909 hectolitres
1 sq. mile	2·590 sq. kilometres		

CONVERSION OF UNITS

To convert from	To	Multiply by
acre	hectare	0·4047
barrel (oil)	cu. metre	0·159
bushel (imperial)	litre	36·37
bushel (US)	litre	35·24
carat	gramme	0·2
cu. foot	cu. metre	0·028317
cu. metre	cu. foot	35·315
foot	metre	0·3048
gigawatt-hour	kilowatt-hour	1,000,000
hectare	acre	2·471
hundredweight (long)	kilogramme	50·802
hundredweight (short)	kilogramme	45·359
inch	millimetre	25·4
kilogramme	pound	2·2046
kilometre	mile (statute)	0·62137
megawatt	kilowatt	1,000
metre	foot	3·2808
mile (nautical)	kilometre	1·852
mile (statute)	kilometre	1·6093
millimetre	inch	0·03937
ounce (troy)	gramme	31·103
pound	kilogramme	0·45359
register ton	cu. metre	2·832
sq. kilometre	sq. mile	0·3861
sq. mile	sq. kilometre	2·590
per sq. mile	per sq. kilometre	0·3861
ton (long)	tonne (metric)	1·016
ton (short)	tonne (metric)	0·9072
tonne	barrel (oil)	7·33

ABBREVIATIONS

ACP	African Caribbean Pacific
Adm.	Admiral
b.	born
bbls.	barrels
bd	board
bn.	billion (one thousand million)
Brig.	Brigadier
bu.	bushel
Cdr	Commander
CFA	Communauté Financière Africaine
CFP	Comptoirs Français du Pacifique
c.i.f.	cost, insurance, freight
C.-in-C.	Commander-in-Chief
CIS	Commonwealth of Independent States
cu.	cubic
CUP	Cambridge University Press
cwt	hundredweight
D.	Democratic Party
DWT	dead weight tonnes
ECOWAS	Economic Community of West African States
EEA	European Economic Area
EEZ	Exclusive Economic Zone
EMS	European Monetary System
EMU	European Monetary Union
ERM	Exchange Rate Mechanism
f.o.b.	free on board
ft	foot/feet
G8 Group	Canada, France, Germany, Italy, Japan, UK, USA, Russia
GDP	gross domestic product
Gen.	General
GNP	gross national product
GRT	gross registered tonnes
ha	hectare(s)
HDI	Human Development Index
ind	independent(s)
K	kindergarten
kg	kilogramme(s)
kl	kilolitre(s)
km	kilometre(s)
kW	kilowatt
kWh	kilowatt hours
lb(s)	pound(s) (weight)
Lieut.	Lieutenant

ABBREVIATIONS—*contd.*

m.	million
Maj.	Major
MW	megawatt
NRT	net registered tonnes
OUP	Oxford University Press
oz.	ounce(s)
PAYE	Pay-As-You-Earn
PPP	Purchasing Power Parity
R.	Republican Party
Rt Hon.	Right Honourable
SADC	Southern African Development Community
SDR	Special Drawing Rights
sq.	square
SSI	Supplemental Security Income
TAFE	technical and further education
TV	television
Univ.	University
VAT	value-added tax
vfd	value for duty

MARITIME LIMITS (IN MILES)

State	Territorial Sea	Jurisdiction over fisheries (measured from the baseline of the territorial sea)
Albania	12 (1976)	—
Algeria	12 (1963)	—
Angola	20 (1975)	200 (1975)
Antigua and Barbuda	12 (1982)	200 (1982)[1]
Argentina	12 (1991)	200 (1991)[1]
Australia	12 (1990)	200 (1979)
Bahamas	12 (1991)	200 (1977)
Bahrain	3	—
Bangladesh	12 (1974)	200 (1974)[1]
Barbados	12 (1977)	200 (1979)[1]
Belgium	12 (1987)	up to median line (1978)
Belize	12 (1992)	200 (1992)[1]
Benin	200 (1976)	—
Brazil	12 (1988)	200 (1988)
Brunei Darussalam	12 (1983)	200 (1983) (or median line)
Bulgaria	12 (1951)	200 (1987)[1]
Burma	12 (1988)	200 (1977)[1]
Cambodia	12 (1969)	200 (1979)[1]
Cameroon	50 (1974)	—
Canada	12 (1970)	200 (1977)
Cape Verde	12 (1977)	200 (1977)[1]
Chile	12 (1986)	200 (1986)[1]
China	12 (1958)	200 (1992)[1]
Colombia	12 (1978)	200 (1978)[1]
Comoros	12 (1976)	200 (1982)[1]
Congo (Democratic Republic of)	12 (1974)	200 (1992)
Congo (Republic of)	200 (1977)	
Costa Rica	12 (1982)	200 (1975)[1]
Côte d'Ivoire	12 (1977)	200 (1977)[1]
Cuba	12 (1977)	200 (1977)[1]
Cyprus	12 (1964)	—
Denmark (including Faroe Islands and Greenland)	3 (1966)	200 (1977)
Djibouti	12 (1979)	200 (1979)[1]
Dominica	12 (1981)	200 (1981)[1]
Dominican Republic	6 (1967)	200 (1977)[1]
Ecuador	200 (1966)	—
Egypt	12 (1958)	200 (1983)[1]
El Salvador	200 (1983)	
Equatorial Guinea	12 (1984)	200 (1984)[1]
Ethiopia	12 (1953)	—
Fiji	12 (1977)	200 (1981)[1]
Finland	4 (1956)	12 (1975) (or agreed boundary)
France	12 (1971)	200 (1977)[1] (except Mediterranean)
Gabon	12 (1986)	200 (1986)[1]
Gambia	12 (1969)	200 (1978)
Germany	3[2]	200 (1977)
Ghana	12 (1986)	200 (1986)[1]
Greece	6 (1936)	200 (1986)[1]
Grenada	12 (1978)[3]	200 (1978)[1]
Guatemala	12 (1976)	200 (1976)[1]

[1] Exclusive Economic Zone.
[2] In the Baltic Sea; off the former GDR, 12 miles; in the German Bight, at least 12 miles; area defined by coordinates.
[3] 10 miles for aviation purposes.

MARITIME LIMITS (IN MILES)—contd.

State	Territorial Sea	Jurisdiction over fisheries (measured from the baseline of the territorial sea)
Guinea	12 (1980)	200 (1980)[1]
Guinea-Bissau	12 (1978)	200 (1978)[1]
Guyana	12 (1977)	200 (1977)
Haiti	12 (1972)	200 (1977)[1]
Honduras	12 (1965)	200 (1951)[1]
Iceland	12 (1979)	200 (1979)[1]
India	12 (1967)	200 (1977)[1]
Indonesia	12 (1957)[2]	200 (1980)[1,6]
Iran	12 (1959)	[7]
Iraq	12 (1958)	—
Ireland	12 (1988)	200 (1977)
Israel	12 (1990)	—
Italy	12 (1974)	—
Jamaica	12 (1971)	—
Japan	12 (1977)	200 (1977)
Jordan	3 (1943)	—
Kenya	12 (1971)	200 (1979)[1]
Kiribati	12 (1983)	200 (1983)[1]
Korea (North)	12 (1967)	200 (1977)[1]
Korca (South)	12 (1978)	12
Kuwait	12 (1967)	—
Lebanon	12 (1983)	—
Liberia	200 (1976)	—
Libya	12 (1959)	—
Madagascar	12 (1985)	200 (1985)[1]
Malaysia	12 (1969)	200 (1984)[1]
Maldives	12 (1975)	(1976)[1,3]
Malta	12 (1978)	25 (1978)
Mauritania	12 (1988)	200 (1988)[1]
Mauritius	12 (1977)	200 (1977)[1]
Mexico	12 (1972)	200 (1976)[1]
Monaco	12 (1973)	(1985)[8]
Morocco	12 (1973)[4]	200 (1981)[1,4]
Mozambique	12 (1976)	200 (1976)[1]
Namibia	12 (1990)	200 (1990)
Nauru	12 (1971)	200 (1978)
Netherlands	12 (1985)	200 (1977)
New Zealand	12 (1977)	200 (1978)[1]
Nicaragua	200 (1979)[5]	200 (1979)[5]
Nigeria	30 (1971)	200 (1978)[1]
Norway	4 (1812)	200 (1977)[1]
Oman	12 (1977)	200 (1981)[1]
Pakistan	12 (1976)	200 (1976)[1]
Panama	200 (1967)	—
Papua New Guinea	12 (1977)	200 (1978) (offshore waters)
Peru	(1947)[5]	200 (1947)[5]

[1] Exclusive Economic Zone.
[2] The territorial sea of Indonesia is measured by straight lines surrounding the archipelago.
[3] Territorial limits and economic zone defined by geographical co-ordinates.
[4] Limits with opposite or adjacent states to be fixed by agreement, failing which median line principle to apply.
[5] Sovereignty and jurisdiction over the sea, its soil and subsoil up to 200 miles.
[6] 200 mile exclusive fisheries zone established 1985.
[7] Outer limits of the superjacent waters of the continental shelf. 50-mile fishing zone in the Sea of Oman (1973).
[8] Half way to Corsica.

MARITIME LIMITS (IN MILES)—*contd.*

State	Territorial Sea	Jurisdiction over fisheries (measured from the baseline of the territorial sea)
Philippines	[10]	200 (1978)[2]
Poland	12 (1978)	to be determined by international agreement (1978)
Portugal	12 (1977)	200 (1977)[2]
Qatar	12	[1]
Romania	12 (1956)	200 (1986)[2]
Russia[9]	12 (1982)	200 (1982)[2]
St Kitts and Nevis	12 (1984)	200 (1984)[2]
St Lucia	12 (1984)	200 (1984)[2]
St Vincent and the Grenadines	12 (1983)	200 (1983)[2]
Samoa	12 (1971)	200 (1980)[2]
São Tomé and Principe	12 (1978)	200 (1978)[2]
Saudi Arabia	12 (1958)	[6]
Senegal	12 (1985)	200 (1985)[2]
Seychelles	12 (1977)	200 (1977)[2]
Sierra Leone	200 (1971)	—
Singapore	3 (1878)	—
Solomon Islands	12 (1978)	200 (1986)
Somalia	200 (1972)	—
South Africa	12 (1977)	200 (1977)
Spain	12 (1977)	200 (1978)[2] (except Mediterranean)
Sri Lanka	12 (1977)	200 (1977)[2]
Sudan	12 (1987)	—
Suriname	12 (1978)	200 (1978)[2]
Sweden	12 (1980)	up to equidistance line with neighbouring states
Syria	35 (1981)	—
Tanzania	12 (1989)	200 (1989)[1]
Thailand	12 (1966)	200 (1980)[2]
Togo	30 (1977)	200 (1977)[2]
Tonga	12 (1978)[3]	200 (1978)
Trinidad and Tobago	12 (1969)	200 (1986)[2]
Tunisia	12 (1973)	[7]
Turkey		200 (1986)[1]
Tuvalu	12 (1984)	200 (1984)[2]
Ukraine[9]	12 (1982)	200 (1984)[2]
United Arab Emirates	3[4]	(1967)[5]
UK	12 (1987)	200 (1977)
USA	12 (1988)	200 (1983)[2]
Uruguay	200 (1969)	—
Vanuatu	12 (1978–82)	200 (1978–82)[2]
Venezuela	12 (1956)	200 (1978)[2]
Vietnam	12 (1977)	200 (1977)[2]
Yemen[8]	—	—
Yugoslavia	12 (1979)	—

[1] Limited by agreement by the outer limits of the superjacent waters of the continental shelf or by a median line (1974).

[2] Exclusive Economic Zone.

[3] 1978 legislation not yet in force.

[4] Sharjah, 12 miles.

[5] Limits to be defined by agreement, failing which median line to apply (1980).

[6] Outer limits of the superjacent waters of the continental shelf.

[7] 6 Aegean (1964), 12 Black Sea and Mediterranean.

[8] Situation under review following unification.

[9] Limits as determined for the former USSR.

[10] The territorial sea of the Philippines is determined by straight base-lines joining appropriate points of the outermost islands forming the Philippine archipelago in accordance with Treaties of 1898, 1900 and 1930 (1961).

The table above is reproduced from a survey prepared by the FAO.

Further Reading

Attard, D. J., *The Exclusive Economic Zone in International Law.* Oxford, 1987

Booth, K., *Law, Force and Diplomacy at Sea.* London, 1985

Buzan, B., *Seabed Politics.* New York, 1976

Churchill, R. R. and Lowe, A. V., *The Law of the Sea.* Manchester, 1988

Janis, M. W., *Sea Power and the Law of the Sea.* Lexington, 1977

Luard, E., *The Control of the Sea-Bed.* London, 1974

Moore, G., *Coastal State Requirements for Foreign Fishing. FAO Legislative Study No. 21.* 3rd revision, Rome, 1988

Sangar, C., *Ordering the Oceans: The Making of the Law of the Sea.* Univ. of Toronto Press, 1987

UN. *Law of the Sea: a Select Bibliography.* 1991

INDEX

PLACE AND INTERNATIONAL ORGANIZATIONS INDEX

Italicised page numbers refer to extended entries